The World Book Atlas

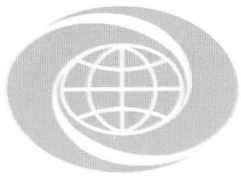

Published by World Book Encyclopedia, Inc.

A subsidiary of Field Enterprises Educational Corporation
Chicago Frankfurt London Paris Rome Sydney Tokyo Toronto

The World Book Atlas

Copyright © 1977 by Rand McNally & Company

Our Planet Earth section, pages 1A-74A inclusive,
Copyright © by Mitchell Beazley Publishers Limited 1973
as The Good Earth. Fully revised 1976

Printed in the United States of America

Library of Congress Card Number 76-57897
ISBN 0-7166-2026-X

Contents

Introduction

A map provides a unique way to communicate and store information about our world and its people. In effect, a map enables the reader to extend his view of the world from what he can see with his own eyes to whole cities, countries, continents—even the entire earth. A map is the most effective way to find answers to questions about location, size, direction, distance, and other geographic facts. An atlas also includes thematic maps as well as graphic and tabular information about our world. Thus, an atlas is an indispensable educational and reference tool for students, teachers, persons in business—anyone who needs or wants to know about our world.

The World Book Atlas opens with the exciting story of Our Planet Earth, told with fascinating illustrations and informative text. Next, a comprehensive section of World Thematic maps displays major geographic, economic, and social distributions. A special section of 62 maps of major cities is third. The main body of the Atlas is a section of Country and Regional maps. This includes reference maps of the countries and regions of the world along with thematic maps. The final map section—Ocean Floor Maps—provides the reader with a view of the world's ocean floors. Handy reference tables and indexes including geographic statistics, a glossary of foreign geographical terms, a separate index for the major city maps, and a pronouncing index for the reference maps complete the Atlas.

Each of the sections of the Atlas has a separate introduction. Appropriate legends for the maps in the major city and country and regional sections appear there. This helps the reader interpret and understand the material presented within each section.

CARTOGRAPHIC COMMUNICATION

The cartographer, or map maker, uses geographic information; his own knowledge of the world; and color, type, and other graphic elements to design a map for maximum communication. The map reader must then interpret the map. Consequently, the success of any map depends upon both the cartographer's skill and the map reader's own knowledge of the world and understanding of the functions and limitations of a map.

Maps can provide an almost infinite variety of information. They can show exact data, such as real numbers of people; generalized data, such as average income per capita country by country; or hypothetical data, such as predicted population densities for the year 2000. However, basically a map can show only (1) existence, (2) associative existence, and (3) spatially associated existence. *Existence* refers simply to the notation on a map that a point, such as a mountain peak, or an area, such as a country, exists. *Associative existence* implies adding an absolute or relative quantity to the identified point or area, such as the elevation of a mountain peak above sea level, or the terrain of a country. *Spatially associated existence* is information concerning relationships between points or areas, such as the distance and direction from one mountain peak to another or the countries that border each other.

It takes practice to learn to read and interpret maps effectively. However, map readers must understand the three major items on any map: (1) *scale,* (2) *projection,* and (3) the *information to be transmitted.*

Scale

A map can only show a reduced representation of the earth's surface or any part of it. Therefore, the reader has to answer the question: What is the relationship between the size of the map and the actual size of the portion of the earth it depicts? This proportional relationship is the *scale* of a map. To help the reader, most maps in this Atlas give the scale in three ways—as a ratio, in written form, and graphically.

As a *ratio,* the scale of a map is expressed as, for example, 1:4,000,000. This means one inch on the map represents four million inches on the earth. In *written form,* this ratio is expressed as: "one inch to sixty-four miles." This means one inch on the map represents sixty-four miles on the earth. *Graphically,* scale is shown with a bar scale, on which distance calculations may be made directly.

Projection

There is no way to represent the curved surface of the globe on the flat surface of a map without some distortion of distance, direction, shape, or area. Only a globe can show the earth without distortion. On large-scale maps that cover only a few square miles, this distortion is negligible. However, on maps that represent large areas, such as a large country, a continent, or the whole world, the distortion is considerable. Unless understood, distortion may result in serious misconceptions on the part of the reader.

A *map projection* is a way to transfer locations on the earth to locations on a map. The number of possible projections is unlimited and several hundred of them are used by cartographers. None avoids some distortion of the spatial relationships that only a globe can show truthfully. No single flat map can accurately show area, shape, angle, and scale. However, a cartographer can select a projection that will accurately depict a particular property, such as shape. It is also possible to compromise by limiting the distortion of one or more properties at the expense of the others.

Most of the maps used in this Atlas are drawn on projections that give equality of area, good land and ocean shapes, and parallels of latitude that are parallel. However, the maps do have distortions and the reader should make allowances for them. One of the best ways to understand the nature of a map's distortion is to compare the latitude and longitude grid lines of the flat map with the grid of the globe. To do this, the reader should understand the basic characteristics of a globe grid:

1. On a globe, all meridians of longitude are equal in length and meet at the poles.

2. All parallels of latitude are parallel.

3. The length, or circumference, of the parallels decreases from the equator to the poles. At 60° latitude, the circumference of the parallel is half the circumference of the equator.

4. Distances along the meridians between any two parallels are equal.

5. All parallels and meridians meet at right angles.

For example, the map on page 47 uses a projection that produces meridians and parallels that are straight lines which meet at right angles. But all the parallels are the same length, which is not true on a globe. This results in considerable exaggeration of areas in the higher latitudes, near the poles. For example, northern Canada looks much larger in proportion to the rest of the world than it really is. In the projection used on pages 4-5, parallels and meridians meet at oblique angles in higher latitudes, which distorts land shapes in such areas as Alaska and Greenland. Their areas, however, are accurately portrayed in relation to each other.

Some of the more commonly used projections and an indication of their properties are shown on pages viii and ix.

Information to be transmitted

Since all maps are reduced from the size of the earth itself, the information on them must be generalized. There is simply not sufficient space to show all the detail of the real world on a map. In addition to scale, three other factors affect the amount of generalization required for every map.

One factor is the graphic limitation (or limitations) under which the map is to be produced. For example, it is much easier to transmit information clearly when using several colors than when using only one color.

Another factor is the purpose of the map. The purpose of a reference map is to show a variety of locational characteristics and geographic information. The purpose of a thematic map is to transmit certain characteristics of, generally, one class of geographical information.

Thirdly, the reliability and precision of the data available to the cartographer also control both what should be communicated and what can be communicated.

Cartographic generalization consists of simplification, classification, symbolization, and induction.

Simplification is the omission of unnecessary detail which will clutter the map and hinder the flow of information to the reader. It must be accomplished in such a way that the reader can still recognize the information being transmitted. For example, identifying Cape Canaveral, Lake of the Woods, and Key West requires more detail than identifying the United States and Canada.

Classification is necessary in generalization in order to reduce the information to transmittable form. The number of different-width two-lane highways in the United States is probably quite large. But, by classifying all two-lane highways together and giving them one symbol, the cartographer can convey the intended information to the map reader. Likewise, very few cities have exactly the same population. So the cities are grouped into meaningful categories, using a distinct symbol for each category.

Symbolization. Cartographers use shape, size, color, and pattern to symbolize generalized information on maps. Data can be mapped in one of four ways of measurement: nominal, such as land and water; ordinal, such as major or minor ore deposits; interval, such as average temperatures; or ratio, such as people per square mile. For nominal data, the cartographer can use symbol shape, color, arrangement, or pattern orientation. For ordinal, interval, or ratios, symbol size, color value or intensity, or different patterns may be used. The choice of the method of symbolization usually depends on the way in which the original information is given.

Induction is the most difficult to describe of the four elements of generalization. Induction makes it possible for more information, yet less precise information, to be extracted from a map than is presented by the data used to create the map. For instance, a cartographer draws the lines on a rainfall map by connecting relatively few precise points where accurate information on rainfall is known. The user may choose to extract information at any point along a line even though no exact data for that point has been gathered. That is, the reader assumes that any point along a line connecting the known points of equal rainfall, has the same amount of rain as the known points. This is a form of generalization and may not accurately represent reality.

The described inherent general characteristics of maps have been carefully considered by cartographers in the design and preparation of The World Book Atlas. This introduction should serve as a guide for more effective use of the Atlas and make possible a better comprehension of the map as a unique means of graphic communication.

Acknowledgements

Maps on pages 1-227 are from Goode's World Atlas, edited by Edward B. Espenshade, Jr., Northwestern University, and Joel L. Morrison, University of Wisconsin.

Dr. Espenshade, Chairman of the Geography Department at Northwestern University since 1959, has served as President of the Association of American Geographers; Chairman of the Earth-Science Division of the National Academy of Sciences—National Research Council; and Chairman of the Commission on College Geography of the Association of American Geographers, which is sponsored by the National Science Foundation.

The Associate Editor, Dr. Morrison, is Associate Professor of Geography and Director of The Cartographic Laboratory of the University of Wisconsin at Madison. His specialties include cartographic communication and automation in map-making. A graduate of Miami University (Ohio), Dr. Morrison received his doctorate at the University of Wisconsin.

PROJECTIONS

A map projection is merely an orderly system of parallels and meridians on which a flat map can be drawn. There are hundreds of projections, but no one represents the earth's spherical surface without some distortion. The distortion is relatively small for most practical purposes when a small part of the sphere is projected. For larger areas, a sacrifice of some property is necessary.

Most projections are designed to preserve on the flat map some particular property of the sphere. By varying the systematic arrangement or spacing of the latitude and longitude lines, a projection may be made either equal-area or conformal. Although most projections are derived from mathematical formulas, some are easier to visualize if thought of as projected upon a plane, or upon a cone or cylinder which is then unrolled into a plane surface. Thus, many projections are classified as plane (azimuthal), conic, or cylindrical.

For a fuller discussion of map projections, see Preface. Figures with asterisks indicate projections used in this atlas.

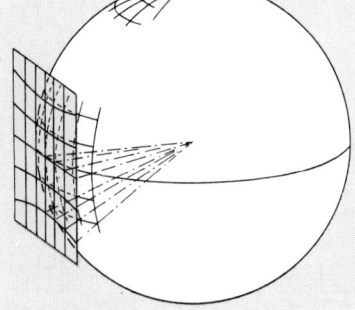

(A) GNOMONIC PROJECTION

A geometric or perspective projection on a tangent plane with the origin point at the center of the globe. Shapes and distances rapidly become increasingly distorted away from the center of the projection. Important in navigation, because all straight lines are great circles.

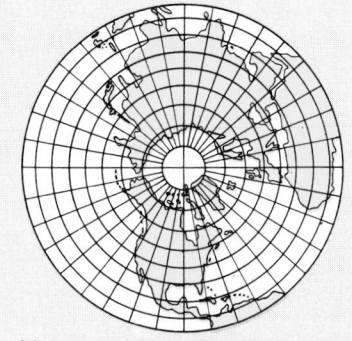

(B) LAMBERT EQUAL AREA PROJECTION*

A mathematically designed azimuthal equal-area projection. Excellent for continental areas. For larger areas away from the center, distortion of distances and shapes is appreciable.

FIGURE 1.—TYPICAL PLANE PROJECTIONS

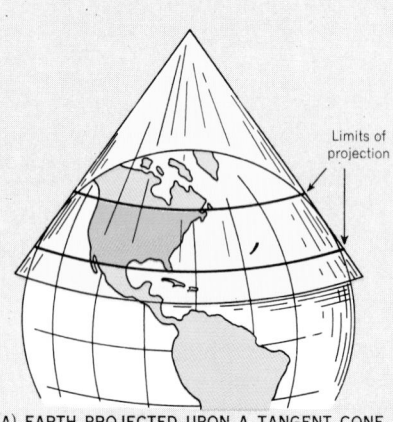

(A) EARTH PROJECTED UPON A TANGENT CONE

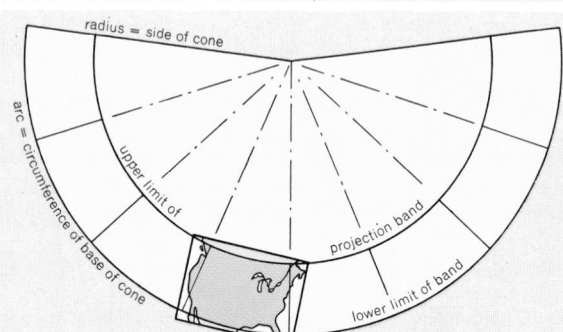

radius = side of cone

upper limit of

arc = circumference of base of cone

projection band

lower limit of band

(B) CONE CUT FROM BASE TO APEX

A perspective projection on a tangent cone with the origin point at the center of the globe. At the parallel of tangency, all elements of the map are

(C) CONE DEVELOPED INTO A PLANE SURFACE

true- angles,distances,shapes,areas.   Away from the tangent parallel, distances increase rapidly, giving bad distortion of shapes and areas.

FIGURE 2 – SIMPLE CONIC PROJECTIONS

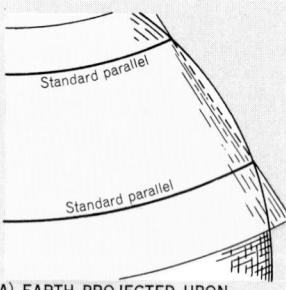

(A) EARTH PROJECTED UPON AN INTERSECTING CONE

This modification of the conic has two standard parallels, or lines of intersection. It is not an equal-area projection, the space being reduced in size between the standard parallels and

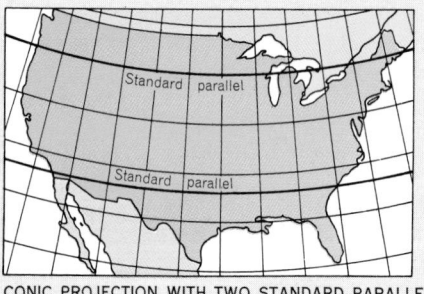

(B) CONIC PROJECTION WITH TWO STANDARD PARALLELS*

progressively enlarged beyond the standard parallels. Careful selection of the standard parallels provides, however, good representation for areas of limited latitudinal extent.

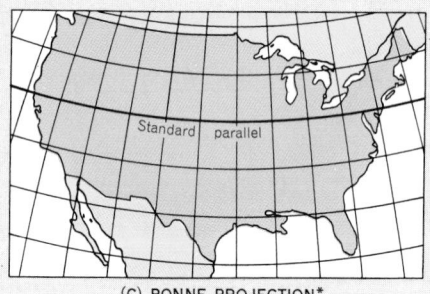

(C) BONNE PROJECTION*

An equal-area modification of the conic principle. Distances are true along all parallels and the central meridian; but away from it, increasing obliqueness of intersections and longitudinal distances, with their attendant distortion of shapes, limits the satisfactory area.

FIGURE 3.—MODIFIED CONIC PROJECTIONS

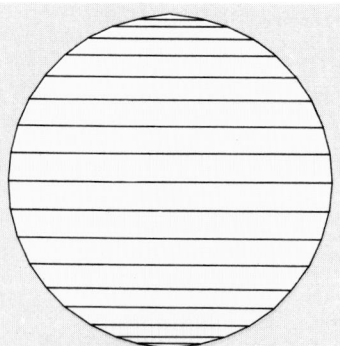

(A) EARTH CONSIDERED AS FORMED BY BASES OF CONES

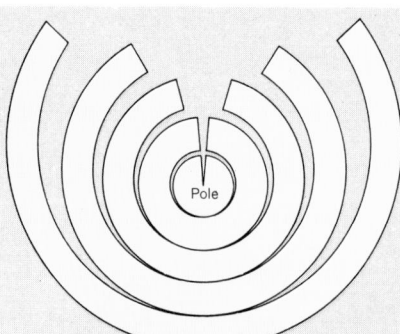

Pole

(B) DEVELOPMENT OF THE CONICAL BASES

This variation is not equal-area. Parallels are nonconcentric circles truly divided. Distances along the straight central meridian are also true, but along the curving meridians are increasingly exaggerated. Representation is good near the central meridian, but away from it there is marked distortion.

(C) POLYCONIC PROJECTION*

FIGURE 4.—POLYCONIC PROJECTION

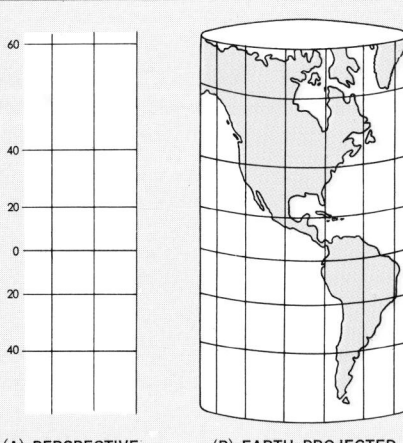

(A) PERSPECTIVE PROJECTION

A perspective projection on a tangent cylinder. Because of rapidly increasing distortion away from the line of tangency and the lack of any special advantage, it is rarely used.

(B) EARTH PROJECTED UPON A CYLINDER

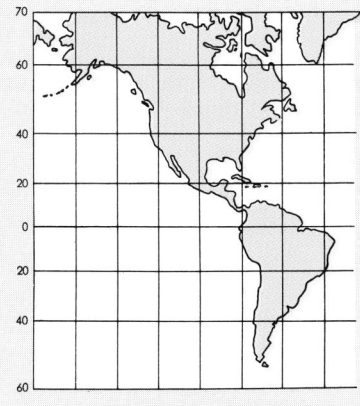

(C) MERCATOR CONFORMAL PROJECTION

Mercator's modification increases the latitudinal distances in the same proportion as longitudinal distances are increased. Thus, at any point shapes are true, but areas become increasingly exaggerated. Of value in navigation, because a line connecting any two points gives the true direction between them.

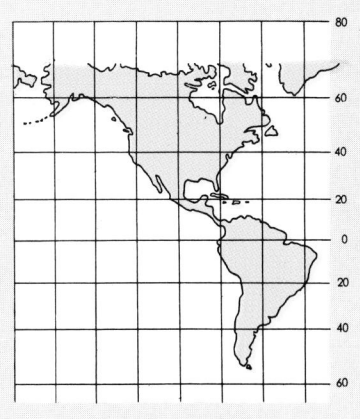

(D) MILLER PROJECTION*

This recent modification is neither conformal nor equal-area. Whereas shapes are less accurate than on the Mercator, the exaggeration of areas has been reduced somewhat.

FIGURE 5.—CYLINDRICAL PROJECTIONS

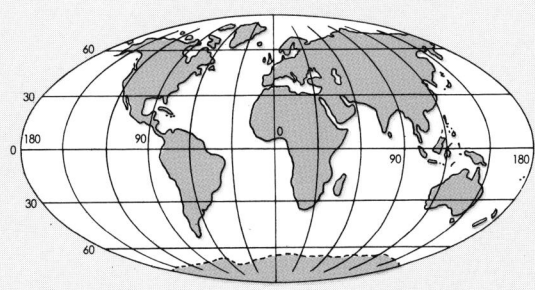

(A) MOLLWEIDE'S HOMOLOGRAPHIC PROJECTION

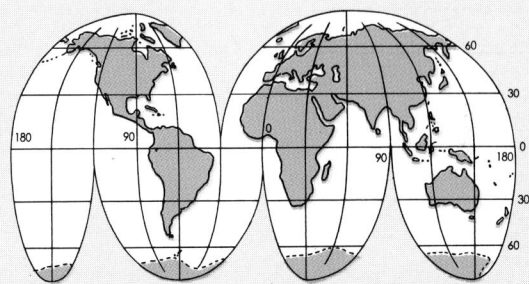

(B) GOODE'S INTERRUPTED HOMOLOGRAPHIC PROJECTION

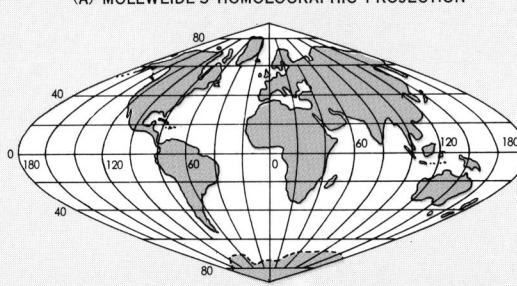

(C) SINUSOIDAL PROJECTION*

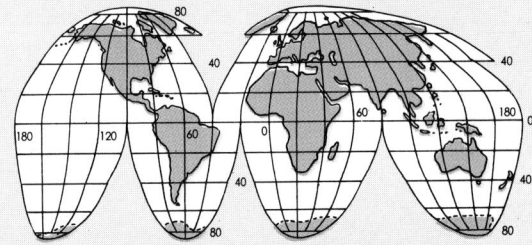

(D) GOODE'S INTERRUPTED HOMOLOSINE PROJECTION*

Although each of these projections is equal-area, differences in the spacing and arrangement of latitude and longitude lines result in differences in the distribution and relative degree of the shape and distance distortion within each grid. On the homolographic, there is no uniformity in scale. It is different on each parallel and each meridian. On the sinusoidal, only distances along all latitudes and the central meridian are true. The homolosine combines the homolographic, for areas poleward of 40°, with the sinusoidal. The principle of interruption permits each continent in turn the advantage of being in the center of the projection, resulting in better shapes.

FIGURE 6.—EQUAL AREA PROJECTIONS OF THE WORLD

A conformal projection in which a selected great circle of the globe is considered as the "equator" of the ordinary Mercator projection, with the cylinder tangent along the great circle. It is used chiefly for charts of great-circle air routes between distant cities.

FIGURE 7.—TRANSVERSE MERCATOR PROJECTION

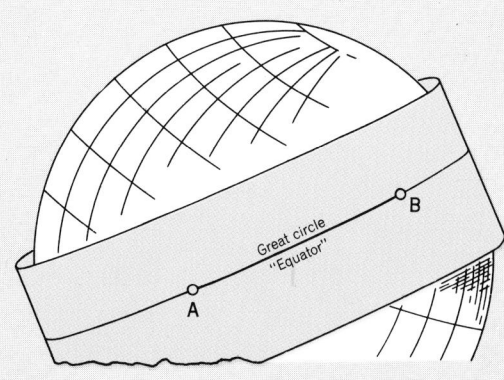

Our Planet Earth

Our home is the Earth, a small planet that revolves around the Sun. The Sun is a star, but only one of the hundred thousand million which exist in the local system of stars, or galaxy, of which we are a part. Our own galaxy, we now know, is just one of millions of other galaxies in the universe.

Scientists generally believe that the Earth was formed about 4.5 billion years ago. Since that time the planet's surface has been ceaselessly altered and its present physical features are the result of numerous processes that interact with each other, usually very slowly, but sometimes very violently. The land is eroded by the wind and rain, washed away by the rivers and seas, and reduced to sediment that builds up elsewhere. Other changes are created by more spectacular events, such as explosive volcanic eruptions and vast outpourings of molten lava. The records of these processes can be seen in the rocks themselves.

There are various theories about the exact origin of life on Earth. But one thing is certain, the planet upon which life came into being was very different from the world we know now. With agonizing slowness, through hundreds of millions of years, life gradually changed with the environment. The struggle to stay alive produced new plants and animals of millions of varieties, from tiny bugs to giant whales and from speck-like algae to towering trees. These formed a thin frosting of life over the surface of the planet. It was into this world that human beings eventually emerged.

Because of the vast size of the Earth, people long believed that its natural resources could never be exhausted. However, the dramatic growth in population and industrial and agricultural demands has made it obvious that our planet has limits, and in some instances these limits are being fast approached. Of course some new sources remain to be discovered and others will be replaced by man-made material, but we no longer can afford to waste our heritage.

The Sun is the controlling body of the solar system and is far more massive than all its planets combined. Even Jupiter, much the largest of the planets, has a diameter only about one-tenth that of the Sun. The solar system is divided into two main parts. The inner region includes four relatively small, solid planets: Mercury, Venus, the Earth and Mars. Beyond the orbit of Mars comes a wide gap in which move many thousands of small minor planets or asteroids, some of which are little more than rocks. Further out come the four giants: Jupiter, Saturn, Uranus and Neptune. Pluto, on the fringe of the system, is a curious little planet; it appears to be in a class of its own, but at present very little is known about it and even its size is a matter for conjecture. Maps of the solar system can be misleading in that they tend to give a false idea about distance. The outer planets are very widely separated. For example, Saturn is further away from Uranus than it is from the Earth.

The contrasting planets

The inner, or terrestrial, planets have some points in common, but a greater number of differences. Mercury, the planet closest to the Sun, has almost no atmosphere and that of Mars is very thin; but Venus, strikingly similar to the Earth in size and mass, has a dense atmosphere made up chiefly of carbon dioxide, and a surface temperature of over 400°C. The giant planets are entirely different. At least in their outer layers they are made up of gas, like a star; but, unlike a star, they have no light of their own and shine only by reflecting the light of their star, the Sun. Several of the planets have moons. The Earth has one (or it may be our partner in a binary system), Jupiter has 13, Saturn 10 (discounting its rings), Uranus five and Neptune two. Mars also has two satellites but these are less than 15 mi (24 km) in diameter and of a different type from the Earth's Moon. The Earth is unique in the solar system in having oceans on its surface and an atmosphere made up chiefly of nitrogen and oxygen. It is the only planet suited to life of terrestrial type. It is not now believed that highly evolved life can exist on any other planet in the Sun's family, though it is still possible that some primitive life forms may exist on Mars.

Observing the planets

Five of the planets, Mercury, Venus, Mars, Jupiter and Saturn, were known to the inhabitants of the Earth in very ancient times. They are starlike in aspect but easy to distinguish because, unlike the stars, they seem to wander slowly about the sky whereas the true stars appear to hold their position for century after century. The so-called proper motions of the stars are too slight to be noticed by the naked eye, but they can be measured by modern techniques. Mercury and Venus always appear to be in the same part of the sky as the Sun. Mercury is never prominent but Venus is dazzlingly bright, partly because its upper clouds are highly reflective and partly because it is close; it can come within 25,000,000 mi (40,000,000 km), only about 100 times as far as the Moon. Jupiter is generally very bright, as is Mars when it is well placed. Saturn is also conspicuous to the naked eye, but Uranus is only just visible and Neptune and Pluto are much fainter.

The Sun's active surface *right*

The structure of a star, such as the Sun, is immensely complex. The very concept of its surface is hard to define, and the size of the Sun depends on the wavelength of the light with which it is viewed. Using the 'hydrogen alpha' wavelength the bright surface of the Sun, known as the photosphere, appears as shown right, above. The surface, at about 5500 °C, is dotted with light and dark patches as a result of the violent upcurrents of hotter gas and cooler areas between them. Larger, darker regions are sunspots (right), temporary but very large disturbances.

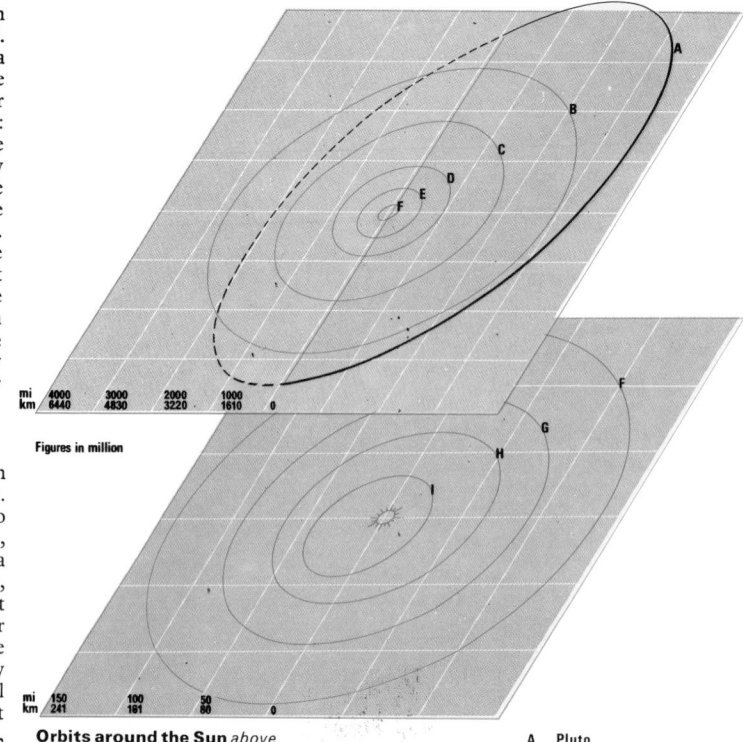

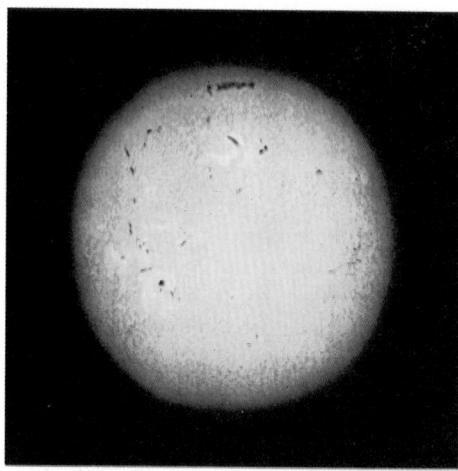

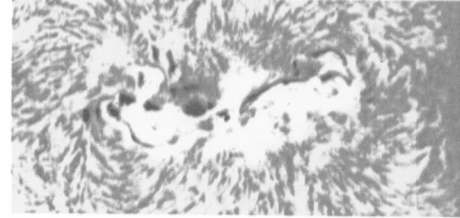

Orbits around the Sun *above*
The Sun's nine known planets, and the asteroids, describe heliocentric orbits in the same direction. But some planetary orbits are highly eccentric, while some asteroids are both eccentric and steeply inclined. The outermost planet, Pluto, passes within the orbit of Neptune, while one asteroid reaches almost to the radius of Saturn. Over 350 years ago Johannes Kepler showed that the planets do not move in perfect circles, and found that the line joining each planet to the Sun sweeps out a constant area in a given time. so that speed is greatest close to the Sun.

A	Pluto
B	Neptune
C	Uranus
D	Saturn
E	Jupiter
F	Mars
G	Earth
H	Venus
I	Mercury

mi 4000 3000 2000 1000 0
km 6440 4830 3220 1610 0

Figures in million

mi 150 100 50 0
km 241 181 80 0

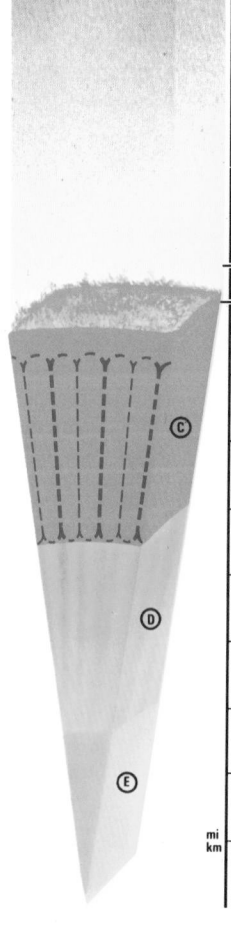

The Sun's structure *right*

The Sun is made up of highly dissimilar regions. This narrow sector includes the inner part of the corona (A) which, though very diffuse, has a temperature of some 1,000,000 °C. Into it leap solar prominences, 'flames' thousands of miles long which arch along the local magnetic field from the chromosphere (B), the outer layer of the Sun proper, which covers the visible photosphere with a layer of variable, highly mobile and rarefied gas about 6000 mi (10000 km) thick. Inside the Sun the outer layer (C) of gas is in constant movement and transfers heat from the interior. Inner region D is thought to transfer energy mainly by radiation. The innermost zone of all (E), the conditions of which can only be surmised but are thought to include a temperature of some 15,000,000 °C, sustains the energy of the Sun (and its planets) by continuous fusion of hydrogen into helium.

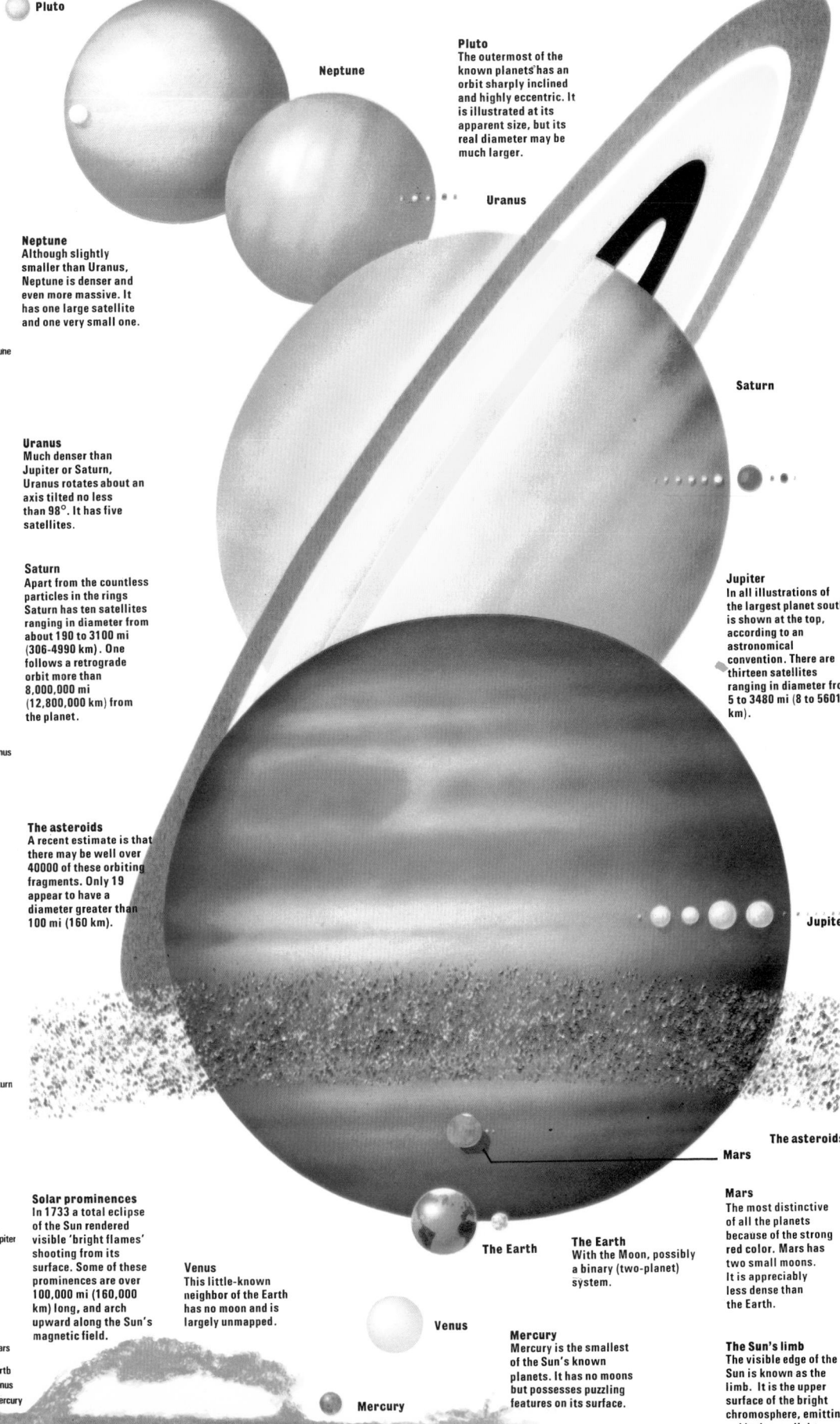

Pluto

Neptune

Pluto
The outermost of the known planets has an orbit sharply inclined and highly eccentric. It is illustrated at its apparent size, but its real diameter may be much larger.

Uranus

Neptune
Although slightly smaller than Uranus, Neptune is denser and even more massive. It has one large satellite and one very small one.

Saturn

Uranus
Much denser than Jupiter or Saturn, Uranus rotates about an axis tilted no less than 98°. It has five satellites.

Saturn
Apart from the countless particles in the rings Saturn has ten satellites ranging in diameter from about 190 to 3100 mi (306-4990 km). One follows a retrograde orbit more than 8,000,000 mi (12,800,000 km) from the planet.

Jupiter
In all illustrations of the largest planet south is shown at the top, according to an astronomical convention. There are thirteen satellites ranging in diameter from 5 to 3480 mi (8 to 5601 km).

The asteroids
A recent estimate is that there may be well over 40000 of these orbiting fragments. Only 19 appear to have a diameter greater than 100 mi (160 km).

Jupiter

The asteroids

Mars

Solar prominences
In 1733 a total eclipse of the Sun rendered visible 'bright flames' shooting from its surface. Some of these prominences are over 100,000 mi (160,000 km) long, and arch upward along the Sun's magnetic field.

Venus
This little-known neighbor of the Earth has no moon and is largely unmapped.

Venus

The Earth

The Earth
With the Moon, possibly a binary (two-planet) system.

Mars
The most distinctive of all the planets because of the strong red color. Mars has two small moons. It is appreciably less dense than the Earth.

Mercury
Mercury is the smallest of the Sun's known planets. It has no moons but possesses puzzling features on its surface.

Mercury

The Sun's limb
The visible edge of the Sun is known as the limb. It is the upper surface of the bright chromosphere, emitting red hydrogen light.

The solar system *left*
The Sun is the major body in the solar system. It lies 30000 light-years from the center of our galaxy and takes about 200 million years to complete one journey around it. There are nine planets and their satellites in the system, as well as comets and various minor bodies such as meteoroids. The diagram on the left shows the upper limb of the Sun (bottom) and the main constituent members of the solar system very greatly condensed into a smaller space. To indicate the amount of the radial compression, the limb of the Sun is drawn for a near-sphere of 5 ft (1.52 m) diameter. On this scale the Earth would be about 420 ft (127 m) away and the outermost planet Pluto, no less than 3 mi (4.9 km) distant.

Pluto, discovered in 1930, has a very eccentric orbit, with a radius varying between 2766 and 4566 million mi (4500 and 7400 million kilometers). Being so far from the Sun, it is extremely cold, and probably has no atmosphere.

Neptune, discovered in 1846, has a diameter of 30760 mi (49500 km) and is made up of gas, although little is known of its interior. It orbits the Sun once in 164¾ years. Seen through binoculars it is a small bluish disk.

Uranus, discovered in 1781, is apparently similar to Neptune, but less massive. Although faintly visible to the naked eye, even large telescopes show little detail upon its greenish surface

Saturn is the second largest planet, its equatorial diameter being 75100 mi (120,900 km). Visually it is unlike any other heavenly body, because of its equatorial system of rings made up of particles of various sizes. The planet itself is less dense than water and at least its outer layers are gaseous.

Jupiter, the largest planet, has an equatorial diameter of 88700 mi (142,700 km), but its rapid spin, once every 9¾ hours, makes it very flattened at the poles. It appears to have cloud belts, possibly of liquid ammonia, and various spots, of which the great red spot seems to be permanent.

The asteroids, a mass of apparent planetary material ranging in size from dust up to one lump about as large as the British Isles, orbit mainly between Mars and Jupiter, though some have eccentric orbits which approach the Earth.

Mars is about 4200 mi (6760 km) in diameter. It has a thin atmosphere, mainly of carbon dioxide, and its surface is pitted with Moon-like craters. It is not thought today that the planet contains any life.

The Earth/Moon system is today regarded as a double planet rather than a planet and satellite. The Moon has an average distance from Earth of 238,857 mi (384,403 km) and it is now known that it has never contained life.

Venus is almost the twin of the Earth in size and mass. It is too hot to contain life, and its very dense atmosphere is mainly carbon dioxide. It has a year of 224¾ Earth days, and it spins on its axis once every 243 Earth days.

Mercury, the innermost planet, is only about 3100 mi (5000 km) in diameter, and has lost almost all of its atmosphere. Like Venus it shows phases, but it is always close to the Sun when viewed from the Earth and cannot be seen clearly.

es in ions

6 mi | Pluto

93 mi | Neptune

783 mi | Uranus

886 mi | Saturn

483 mi | Jupiter

41·5 mi | Mars
93 mi | Earth
67 mi | Venus
36 mi | Mercury

4A Earth's Companion: The Moon

The Moon is our companion in space. Its mean distance from the Earth is less than a quarter of a million miles – it varies between 221,460 miles (356,410 km) and 252,700 miles (406,685 km) – and it was the first world other than our Earth to come within the range of man's space probes. At first mere masses, these then became instrument packages and finally spacecraft carrying men. With their aid our knowledge of the Moon has been vastly increased in the past decade. Astronauts Neil Armstrong and Edwin Aldrin made the first human journey to the lunar surface in July 1969, and the Moon has since been subjected to detailed and direct investigation.

The mean diameter of the Moon is 2158 miles (3473 km), and its mass is 1/81st as much as that of the Earth. Despite this wide difference the ratio is much less than that between other planets and their moons, and the Earth/Moon system is now widely regarded as a double planet rather than as a planet and satellite. The Moon's mean density is less than that of the Earth, and it may lack a comparable heavy core. Escape velocity from the lunar surface is only 1.5 mi/sec (2.4 km/sec), and this is so low that the Moon has lost any atmosphere it may once have had. To Earth life it is therefore an extremely hostile world. Analysis of lunar rock brought back to Earth laboratories and investigated by Soviet probes on the Moon has so far revealed no trace of any life. The Moon appears to have always been sterile.

Much of the surface of the Moon comprises large grey plains, mis-called 'maria'(seas), but most of it is extremely rough. There are great ranges of mountains, isolated peaks and countless craters which range from tiny pits up to vast enclosures more than 150 miles (240 km) in diameter. Many of the craters have central mountains or mountain-groups. Some of the larger craters show signs of having been produced by volcanic action, while others appear to have resulted from the impacts of meteorites.

The Moon rotates slowly, performing one complete turn on its axis every 27 days, 7 hours, 43 minutes. It always presents the same face to the Earth. But in October 1959 the Soviet probe *Lunik 3* photographed the hidden rear hemisphere and it has since been mapped in detail. It contains no large 'seas'. The appearance of the lunar surface depends strongly on the angle at which it is viewed and the direction of solar illumination. In the photograph on the right, taken from a height of about 70 miles (115 km) with the Earth having once more come into full view ahead, the lunar surface looks deceptively smooth; in fact, there is practically no level ground anywhere in the field of vision. The lunar horizon is always sharply defined, because there is no atmosphere to cause blurring or distortion. For the same reason, the sky seen from the Moon is always jet black.

Full Moon *below*
This striking photograph was taken by the *Apollo 11* astronauts in July 1969. It shows parts of both the Earth-turned and far hemispheres. The dark plain near the center is the Mare Crisium.

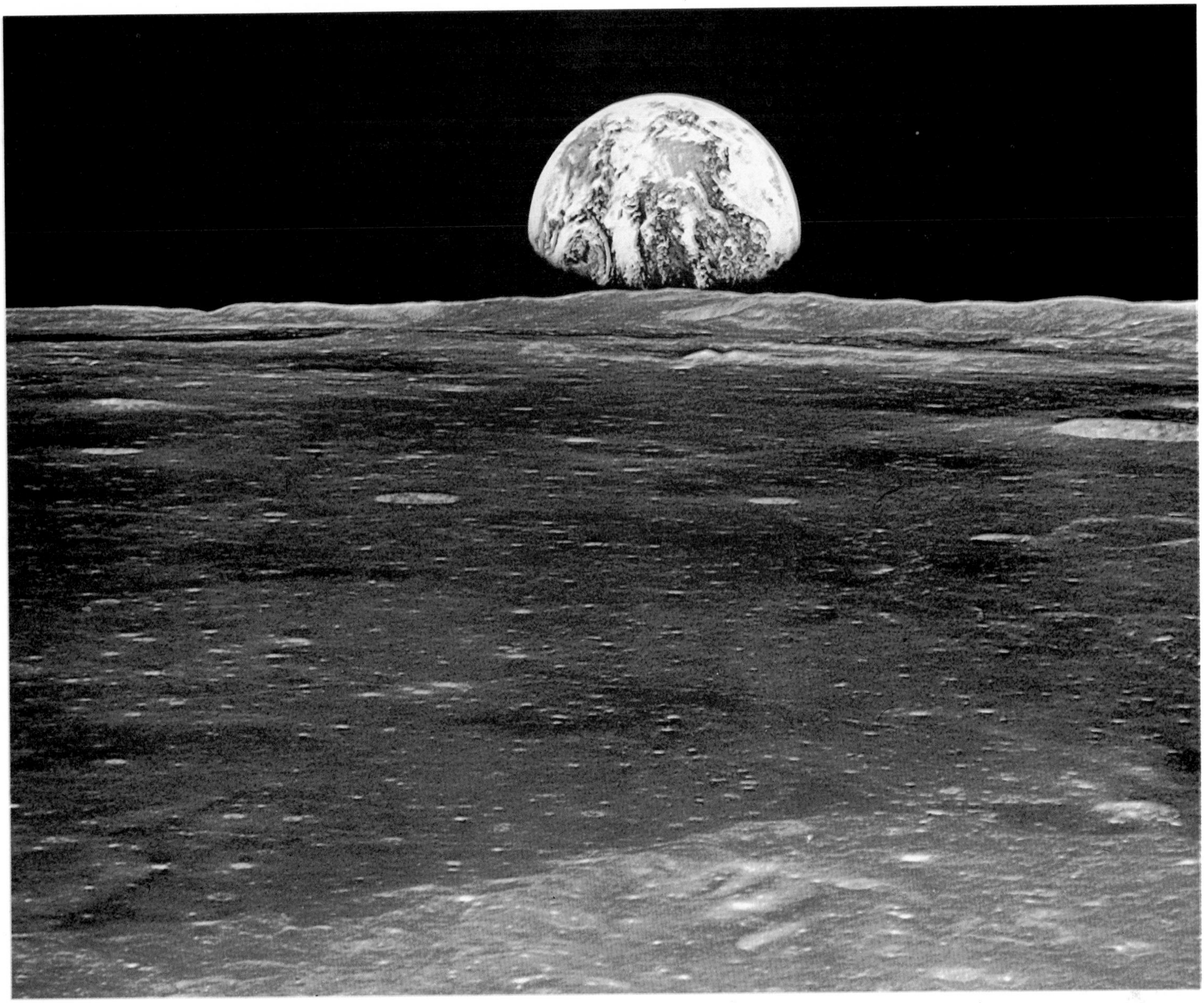

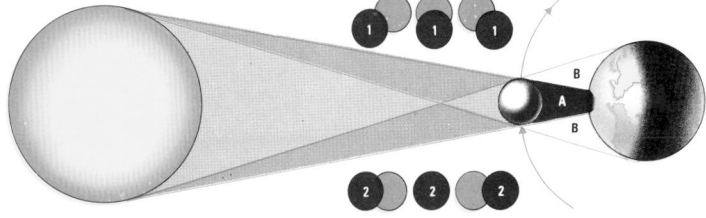

Earthrise *above*
This view of the Earth rising was visible to the crew of
Apollo 10 in May 1969 as they orbited the Moon 70 miles
(112 km) above the surface. They had just come round
from the Moon's rear hemisphere.

Eclipses

Once regarded as terrifying actions of angry gods,
eclipses are today merely useful. They provide a
different view of the Sun and Moon that opens up
fresh information. In a lunar eclipse the Earth passes
directly between the Sun and Moon; in a solar eclipse
the Moon passes between Sun and Earth. Both the
Earth and Moon constantly cast a shadow comprising
a dark inner cone surrounded by a region to which
part of the sunlight penetrates. A body passing
through the outer shadow experiences a *partial*
eclipse, while the inner cone causes a *total* eclipse in
which all direct sunlight is cut off.

A total solar eclipse is magnificent. The bright star
is blocked out by a black Moon, but around it the
Sun's atmosphere flashes into view. The pearly
corona of thin gas can be seen extending a million
miles from the Sun. Closer to the surface huge
'prominences' of red hydrogen leap into space and
curve back along the solar magnetic field. In a partial
solar eclipse these things cannot be seen, while in a
total eclipse caused by the Moon at its greatest
distance from Earth a ring of the Sun is left visible.
As the Moon's orbit is not in the same plane as the
Earth's, total solar eclipses occur very rarely, on
occasions when the tip of the Moon's dark shadow
crosses the Earth as a spot 169 miles (272 km) wide.

Eclipses *left and below*
When the Moon passes in
front of the Sun as in
sequence 1 its shadow B
causes a partial solar
eclipse (below, left, taken
21 November 1966).
But in the case of sequence
2, shadow cone A gives a
total eclipse (below, right,
15 February 1961).

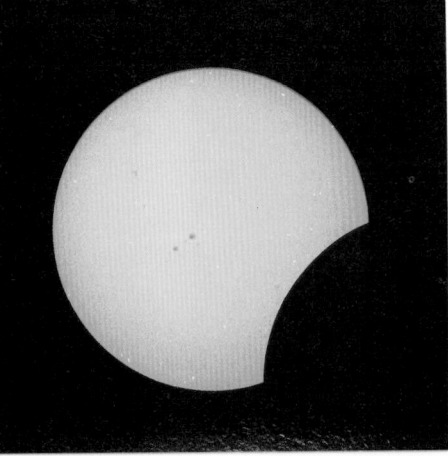

6A Life and Death of the Earth

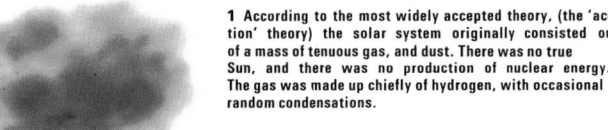

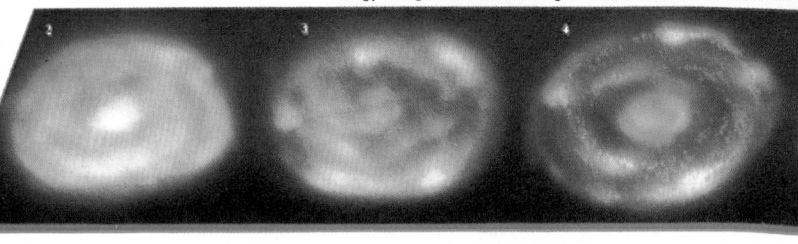

1 According to the most widely accepted theory, (the 'accretion' theory) the solar system originally consisted only of a mass of tenuous gas, and dust. There was no true Sun, and there was no production of nuclear energy. The gas was made up chiefly of hydrogen, with occasional random condensations.

2 Gravitational forces now cause the cloud to shrink and assume a more regular shape. Its density and mass near the center increase, but there are still no nuclear processes.

3 The gas cloud begins to assume the form of a regular disk. The infant Sun begins to shine - by the energy from gravitational shrinkage.

4 Material is thrown off from the Sun to join that already in the solar cloud, whose condensations have become more noticeable.

How did the Earth come into existence? This question has intrigued mankind for centuries, but it was not until the start of true science that plausible theories were advanced. Although some theories held sway for many years, they were eventually deposed by the discovery of some fatal flaw. Even today, it is impossible to be sure that the main problem has been solved, but at least some concrete facts exist as a guide. It is now reasonably certain that the age of the Earth is of the order of 4550-4700 million years. The other planets are presumably about the same age, since they were probably formed by the same process in the same epoch.

Several centuries ago Archbishop Ussher of Armagh maintained that the world had come into being at a definite moment in the year 4004 BC. This estimate was made on purely religious grounds, and it soon became clear that the Earth is much older. In 1796 the French astronomer Laplace put forward the famous Nebular Hypothesis, according to which the Sun and the planets were formed from a rotating cloud of gas which shrank under the influence of gravitation. As it shrank, the cloud shed gaseous rings, each of which condensed into a planet. This would mean that the outer planets were older than those closer to the Sun which itself would represent the remaining part of the gas cloud.

The Nebular Hypothesis was accepted for many years, but eventually serious mathematical weaknesses were found in it. Next came a number of tidal theories according to which the Earth and other planets were formed from a cigar-shaped tongue of matter torn from the Sun by the gravitational pull of a passing star. The first plausible theory of this kind came from the English astronomer Sir James Jeans, but this too was found to be mathematically untenable and the idea had to be given up.

Most modern theories assume that the planets were formed by accretion from a rotating solar cloud of gas and finely-dispersed dust. If the Sun were originally attended by such a cloud, this cloud would, over a sufficiently long period of time, become a flat disk.

If random concentration had become sufficiently massive, it would draw in extra material by virtue of its gravitational attraction, forming 'proto-planets'. When the Sun began to radiate strongly, part of the mass of each proto-planet would be driven off due to the high temperatures, leaving a solar system of the kind that exists today.

The fact that such an evolutionary sequence can be traced emphasizes that in talking about the origin of the Earth we are considering only a small part of a continuous story. What will become of the Earth in the far future? The Sun is radiating energy because of the nuclear process within it: hydrogen is being converted into helium causing mass to be lost with a resulting release of energy. However, when the supply of hydrogen begins to run low, the Sun must change radically. It will move towards a red giant stage swelling and engulfing the Earth. Fortunately, this will not happen for at least another 6000 million years, but eventually the Sun which sustains our planet will finally destroy it.

Alternative theories

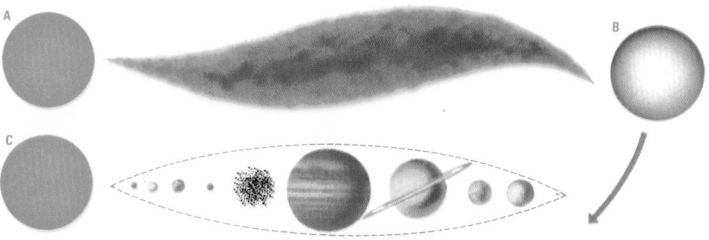

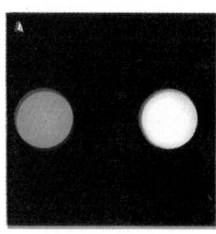

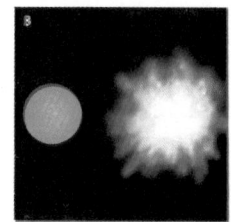

Contracting nebula *above* Laplace suggested that a contracting nebula might shed gas which then condensed.

Tidal theories *above* In 1917 Sir James Jeans postulated that Sun A was attracted to another star B which passed at close range. A cloud of matter was drawn off by their gravitational attraction. Star B moved on while the cloud condensed to form planets circling our Sun at C.

A violent beginning *above* One of the theories of how the solar system came to be formed assumes that the Sun once had a binary companion star. This exploded as a supernova (above) and was blown off as a white dwarf

16 As the 'fuel' runs out, the radiation pressure falls, and under internal gravity the Sun will collapse inwards changing in only 50000 years from a red giant into a super-dense white dwarf.

17 As a white dwarf, the Sun will continue to radiate feebly for an immense period. At last all radiation must cease, and the Sun will remain as a dead, dark globe - a black dwarf.

15 By now all the inner planets will have long since been destroyed. The Sun will become unstable, reaching the most violent stage of its career as a red giant, with a vast, relatively cool surface and an intensely hot, dense core.

14 When the center of the Sun has reached another critical temperature, the helium will begin to 'burn' giving the so-called 'helium flash'. After a temporary contraction the Sun will then swell out to a diameter 400 times that at present.

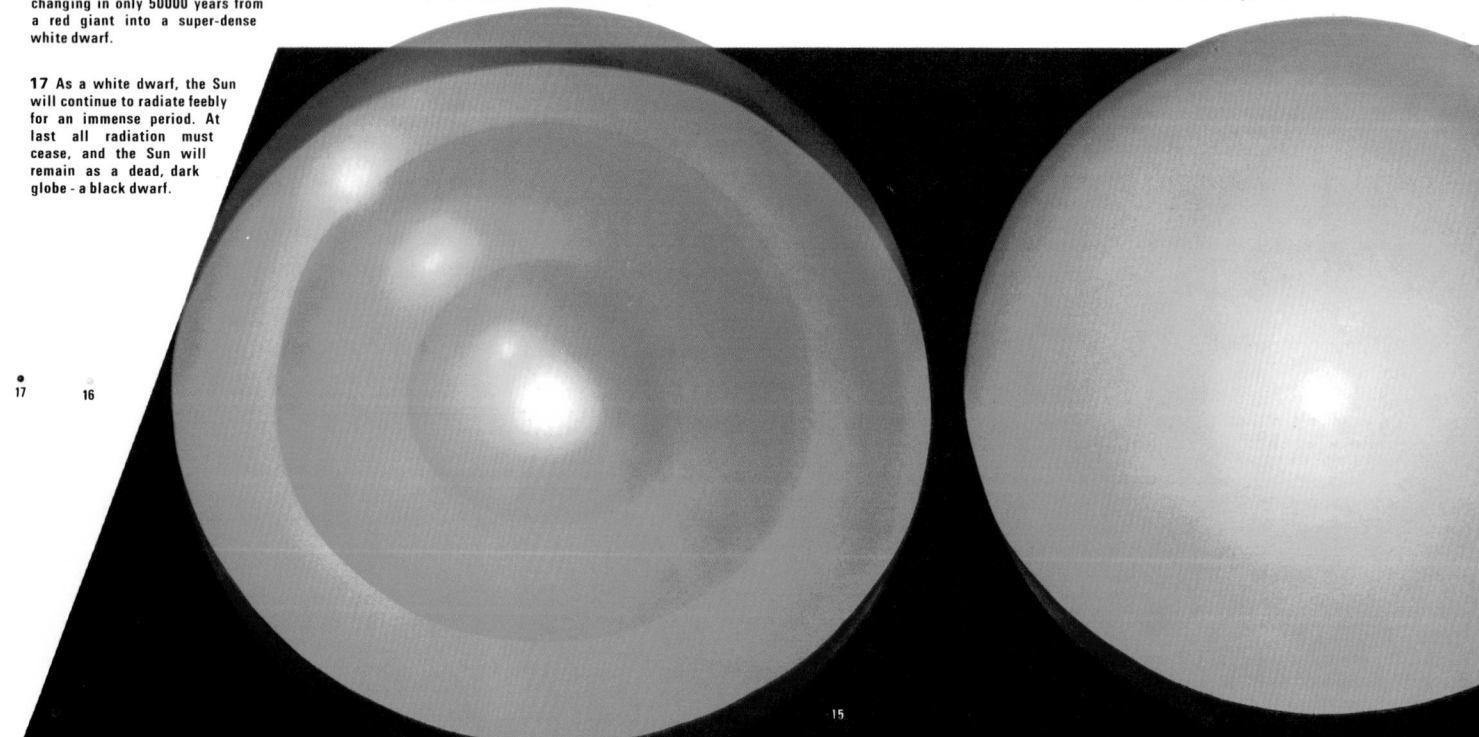

17   16

15

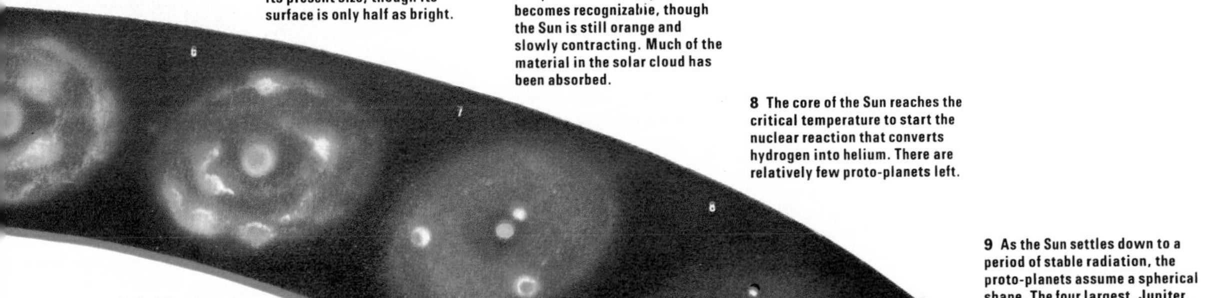

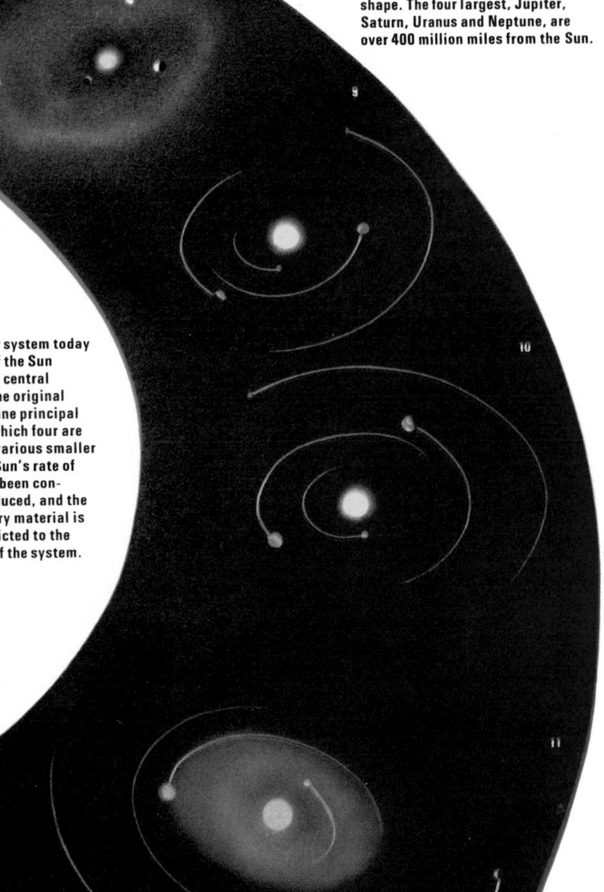

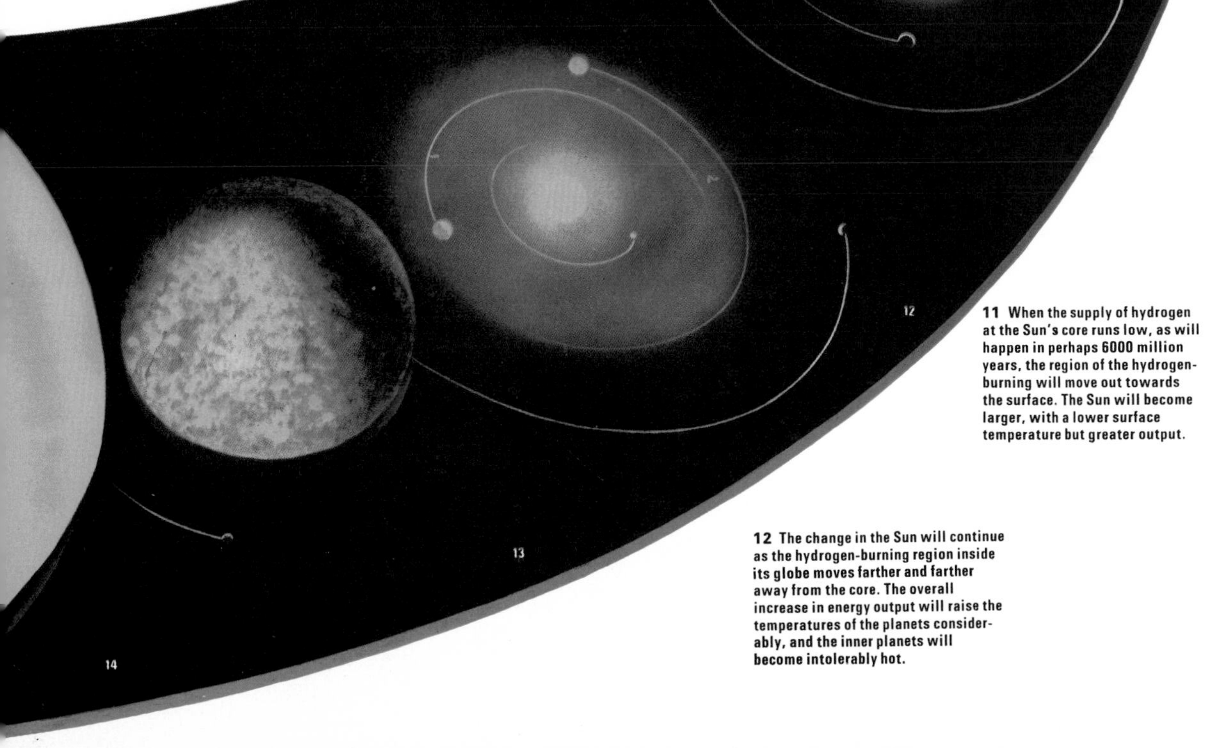

5 The Sun, still contracting, continues to radiate because of gravitational effects. More and more of the solar cloud collects into the condensations.

6 The Sun, surrounded by a system of regularly-shaped proto-planets, shrinks to about its present size, though its surface is only half as bright.

7 By now the solar system becomes recognizable, though the Sun is still orange and slowly contracting. Much of the material in the solar cloud has been absorbed.

8 The core of the Sun reaches the critical temperature to start the nuclear reaction that converts hydrogen into helium. There are relatively few proto-planets left.

9 As the Sun settles down to a period of stable radiation, the proto-planets assume a spherical shape. The four largest, Jupiter, Saturn, Uranus and Neptune, are over 400 million miles from the Sun.

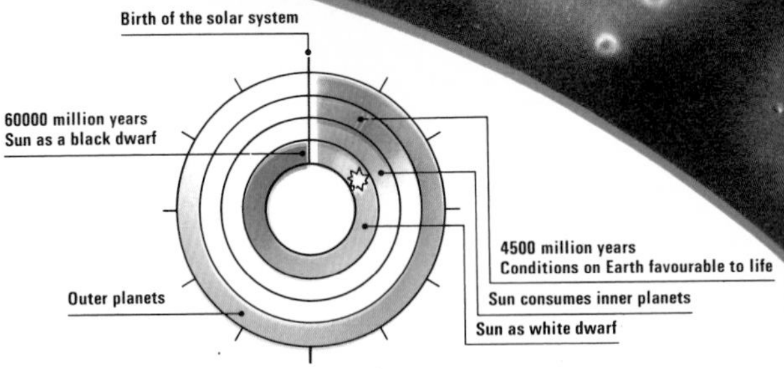

Birth of the solar system

60000 million years Sun as a black dwarf

Outer planets

4500 million years Conditions on Earth favourable to life

Sun consumes inner planets

Sun as white dwarf

Timescale of the solar system *above*
Taking the vertical 12 o'clock position as the time when the Sun and solar system were created (illustration 1 in the main sequence, above left) the present time appears at about the 1 o'clock position. By half-past two the Sun will flare up and consume its inner planets, thereafter dying a slow death.

10 The solar system today is made up of the Sun (which is the central remnant of the original cloud), the nine principal planets, of which four are giants, and various smaller bodies. The Sun's rate of rotation has been considerably reduced, and the interplanetary material is largely restricted to the main plane of the system.

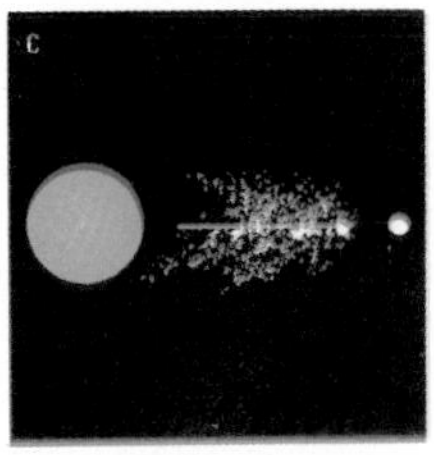

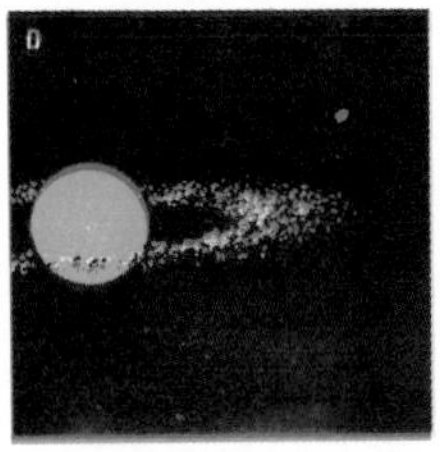

star (above). leaving behind a cloud of fragments. These then coalesced into the planets as we know

them today, having organized themselves into heliocentric orbits (above). Few subscribe to this theory now.

13 The expansion of the Sun will continue, with the hydrogen-burning region approaching the surface. After another 600 million years, the Sun will be fifty times its present diameter. It will have become a red giant, engulfing the inner planets, including Earth.

11 When the supply of hydrogen at the Sun's core runs low, as will happen in perhaps 6000 million years, the region of the hydrogen-burning will move out towards the surface. The Sun will become larger, with a lower surface temperature but greater output.

12 The change in the Sun will continue as the hydrogen-burning region inside its globe moves farther and farther away from the core. The overall increase in energy output will raise the temperatures of the planets considerably, and the inner planets will become intolerably hot.

The lifespan of the Earth

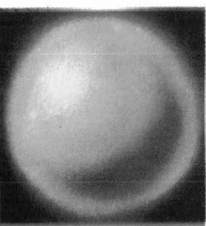

The Earth was produced from the solar cloud (1-6 on main diagram). It had no regular form, but, as more and more material was drawn in, it began to assume a spherical shape (7-8)

When it had reached its present size (9), the Earth had a dense atmosphere ; not the original hydrogen atmosphere but one produced by gas from the interior. Life had not started.

The Earth today (10), moving in a stable orbit, has an equable temperature and oxygen-rich atmosphere, so that it alone of all the planets in the solar system is suitable for life.

When the Sun nears the red giant stage (11-13), the Earth will be heated to an intolerable degree. The atmosphere will be driven off, the oceans will boil and life must come to an end.

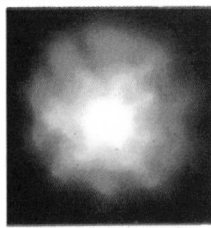

As the Sun reaches the peak of its violence (14-15) it will swell out until the Earth is engulfed. Its natural life is probably no more than 8000 million years : its end is certain

Man's most powerful nuclear weapons pale into insignificance beside the violence of an earthquake or the destructive and indiscriminate force of a volcano. These cataclysmic phenomena frequently occur along the same belts of instability in the Earth's crust and are often only different manifestations of the same fundamental processes. About 800 volcanoes are known to have been active in historical times, and many are extremely active today. All the mid-ocean ridges are volcanic in origin, and many underwater eruptions occur along these submarine mountain ranges. Spectacular volcanic eruptions sometimes break the ocean surface, such as during the formation in 1963 of the island of Surtsey, south of Iceland (photograph, right). Some islands, such as Iceland itself, are the products of continued outpourings of lava along the crest of the mid-ocean ridge.

Oceanic earthquakes caused by sudden sea-floor displacements may result in tsunamis or giant sea waves. About 80 per cent of the shallow earthquakes and almost all deep ones take place along the belt around the Pacific. Clear evidence of the large scale movements of the mantle are provided by the zones within which earthquake shocks are generated along some Pacific island arc systems. These zones plunge down from sea-floor level to depths as great as 400 miles (640 km) beneath the adjacent continents and mark the positions of downward flow of the mantle convection currents (page 11A). The corresponding upwelling regions lie along the mid-ocean ridges, where new basic volcanic material is continually being added to the ocean crust as outward movement takes place away from the ridges.

These sea-floor spreading movements act as 'conveyor belts' for the continents, and constitute the basic mechanism for the large displacements involved in continental drifting. Geological data confirm the former close fits of the margins of the reassembled continental jig-saw puzzle, and also corroborate the detailed paleomagnetic evidence visible in today's rocks of the movements of the continents relative to the geographic poles.

Geysers
Ground water and mud heated by volcanic activity can lie on the surface as puddles and hot springs, rendered colorful by dissolved minerals, or be pumped out in the form of geysers. The latter are connected to extensive underground reservoirs in which steam pressure builds up above the hot water. Intermittently the system discharges high into the air.

Fissure eruption
In this type of eruption freely flowing molten basaltic material exudes from apertures forced in the crust. The surface crack may be several miles in length and the more or less horizontal flow has on occasion covered more than 200 square miles (500 km²).

Hawaiian-type eruption
In this case large, shallow cones, often containing lakes of molten lava, generally release gas and vapor in a relatively passive way. But sometimes glowing lava is expelled as a fine spray which in a high wind can be drawn out into fine threads called Pelée's hair.

Emissions
Incandescent lava issues from the main cone or from side vents, while dense vapors pour from every crevice. Water vapor is the main gaseous component, but nitrogen and sulphur dioxide are also important.

Layering
Most volcanoes have a history extending back thousands or even millions of years. Over this time the main cone has built up in many stratified layers, sometimes of contrasting types of lava. Each fresh eruption produces at least one additional layer.

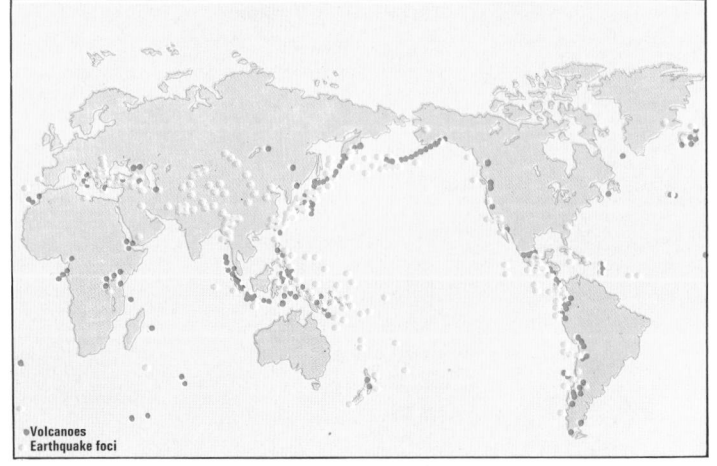

Underground water
Heated beyond normal boiling point, the pressurized water issues in a rush when pressure is relieved.

Magma chamber
Underlying every volcano is a volume of intensely hot fluid under high pressure.

Laccolith
Above the pipes and sills of the hot magma lies a giant lens-shaped intrusion of cold rock.

Metamorphic rock
The strata adjacent to the fiery magma are physically and chemically altered by the heat.

Where the Earth seems active *right*
Although we live on a white-hot globe with a thin cool crust, the fierce heat and energy of the interior is manifest only along fairly clearly defined belts. Around the Pacific, volcanoes and earthquakes are frequent. Another belt traverses the mountains from southeast Asia through the Middle East to the Mediterranean. Every site is an external expression of activity within the crust and upper mantle. The underlying cause is a slow flowing of the rocks of the mantle in response to changes in temperature and density.

• Volcanoes
• Earthquake foci

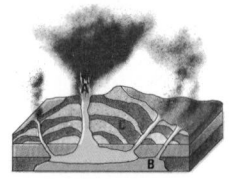

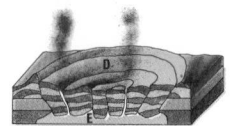

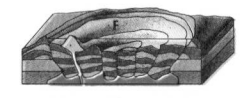

Types of eruption *above*
Volcanic cones differ in both shape and activity. The Strombolian (1) erupts every few minutes or hours; the Peléan form (2) gives a hot avalanche; the Vesuvian (3) is a fierce upward expulsion, while the Plinian (4) is the extreme form.

A caldera *left*
Expulsion of lava (A) from the magma chamber (B) may leave the central core (C) without support. A collapse results in a large, steep-sided caldera (D). The magma chamber may cool and solidify (E), and water may collect inside the caldera (F).

Earthquake *right*
Along lines of potential movement, such as fault planes, stresses may build up over many years until the breaking strength of some part of the rock is exceeded (A). A sudden break occurs and the two sides of the fault line move, generating shock-waves which travel outward in all directions from the focus at the point of rupture (B). The point on the surface directly above the focus is the epicenter (C). While the fault movement reaches its fullest extent, the shockwaves reach the surface (D). Far right the aftermath of an earthquake.

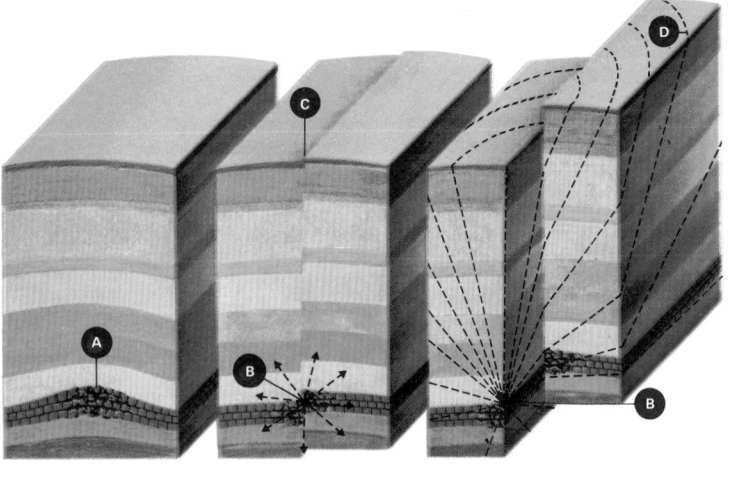

Destructive waves *right*
The Japanese, who have suffered severely from them, have given the name tsunami to the terrifying waves which follow earthquakes. Their character depends on the cause. In the case of a sudden rift and slump in the ocean bed (A) the wave at the surface is initially a trough, which travels away to both sides followed by a crest and subsequent smaller waves (B). A fault causing a sudden changed level of sea bed (C) can generate a tsunami that starts with a crest (D). Travelling at 400 miles (650 km) per hour or more the tsunami arrives at a beach as a series of waves up to 200 feet (60 m) high (E), the 'trough first' variety being heralded by a sudden withdrawal of the ocean from the shore. Warning stations ring the Pacific (far right) and the concentric rings show tsunami travel time from an earthquake site to Hawaii at the center.

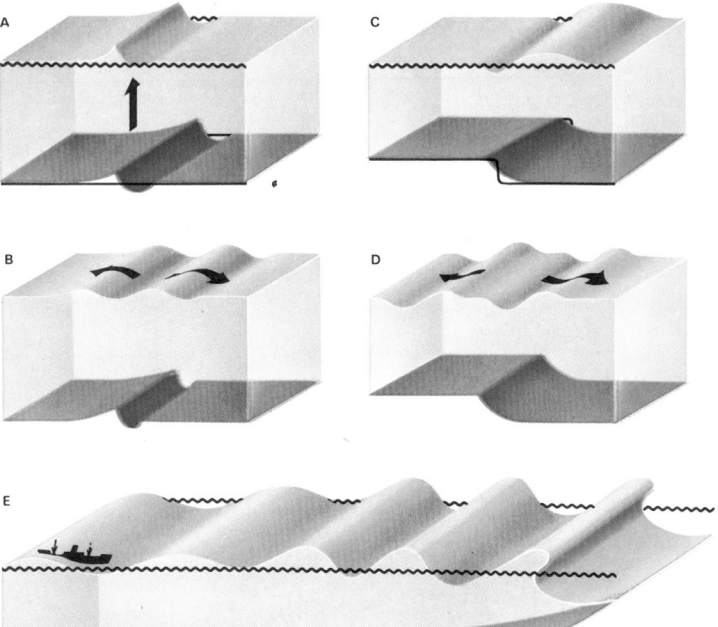

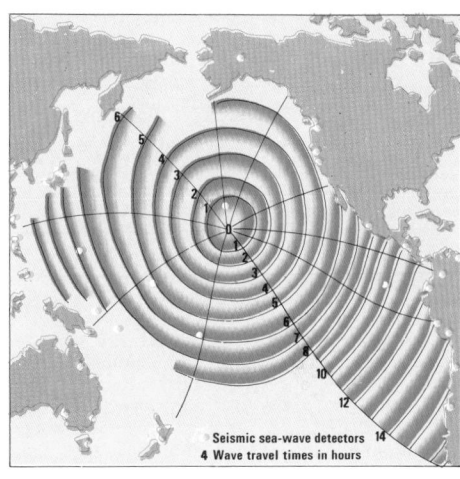

Tsunami warning *above*
Numerous seismographic warning stations around the earthquake belt of the Pacific Ocean maintain a continuous alert for earthquake shocks and for the tsunami waves that may follow it. Possible recipients of such waves plot a series of concentric rings, such as these centered on the Hawaiian Islands, which show the time in hours that would be taken for a tsunami to travel from any earthquake epicenter. Aircraft and satellites are increasingly helping to create a globally integrated life-saving system.

Seismic waves *right*
An earthquake caused by a sudden movement in the crust at the focus (A) sends out a pattern of shock waves radiating like ripples in a pond. These waves are of three kinds. Primary (P) waves (full lines) vibrate in the direction of propagation, and thus are a rapid succession of high and low pressures. Secondary (S) waves (broken lines), which travel only 60 per cent as fast, shake from side to side. Long waves (L) travel round the crust. In a belt around the world only waves of the L-type occur, giving rise to the concept of a shadow zone (B and shaded belt in inset at lower right). But intermittent records of P waves in this zone led seismologists to the belief that the Earth must have a very dense fluid core (D, lower drawing) capable of strongly refracting P waves like a lens. Seismic waves are almost man's only source of knowledge about the Earth's interior.

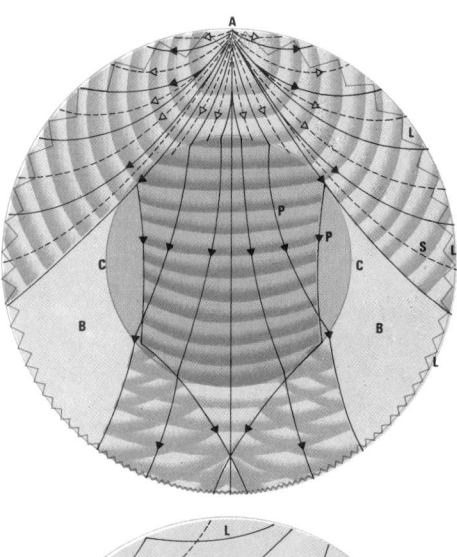

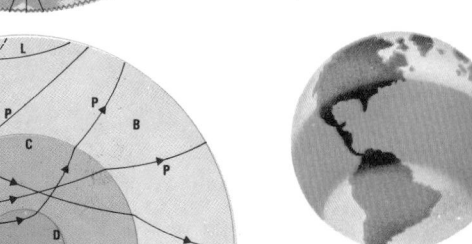

Seismology *right*
Seismic waves of all three types (P, S and L) are detected and recorded by seismographs. Usually these contain a sprung mass which, when an earthquake shock passes, stays still while the rest of the instrument moves. Some seismographs detect horizontal waves (A) while others detect vertical ones (B). The pen in the instrument leaves a distinctive trace (P-S-L). P (primary) waves are a succession of rarefactions and compressions, denoted by the packing of the dots; S (secondary) waves are a sideways shaking, shown here in plan view.

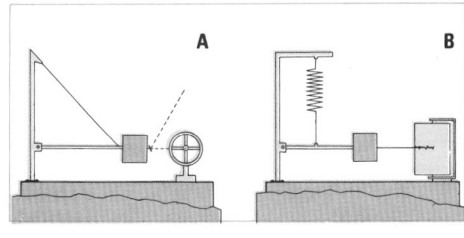

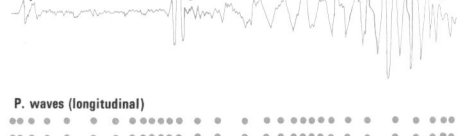

P. waves (longitudinal)

← Rarefaction → ← Compression →

Direction of travel

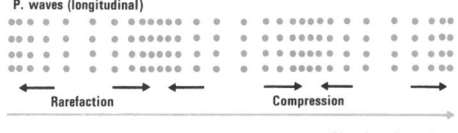

S. waves (transverse)

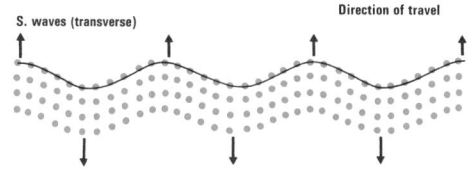

Anatomy of the Earth

A fundamental mystery that still confronts science even today is the detailed internal structure of the planet on which we live. Although Jules Verne's intrepid 'Professor Otto Lindenbrock was able to journey to the center of the Earth, this is one scientific fantasy that will never be achieved. The deepest boreholes and mines do little more than scratch the surface and so, deprived of direct observation, the geologist is forced to rely almost entirely on indirect evidence to construct his picture of the Earth's anatomy. In spite of these drawbacks, he can outline with some confidence the story of the planet's development from the time of its formation as a separate body in space some 4550 million years ago.

Since that time the Earth has been continuously evolving. The crust, mantle and inner core developed during its first 1000 million years, but there is only scant evidence of how they did so. Probably the original homogenous mass then partly or completely melted, whereupon gravitational attraction caused the densest material to form a part-liquid, part-solid central core overlaid by the less dense mantle. The extremely thin outermost layer of 'scum' began to form at an early stage and as long ago as 3500 million years parts of it had reached almost their present state. But most of the crust evolved in a complex way through long-term cyclic changes spanning immense periods of time. The evidence of today's rocks can be interpreted in different ways; for example, the core, mantle and crust could have separated out quickly at an early stage or gradually over a longer period.

Today's restless Earth

Many of the changes which have taken place in the Earth's structure and form have been very gradual. For example, although it may well be that our planet has been getting larger (as illustrated below), the rate of increase in radius has been no more rapid than 2½ inches (65 mm) per century. But this does not alter the fact that the Earth is very far from being a mere inert sphere of matter. Although it is not possible faithfully to portray it, almost the whole globe is at brilliant white heat. If the main drawing were true to life it would contain no color except for a thin band, about as thick as cardboard, around the outer crust in which the color would change from white through yellow and orange to red. With such high temperatures the interior of the Earth is able to flow under the influence of relatively small differences in density and stress. The result is to set up convection currents which are now believed to be the main driving force behind the formation of mountain ranges and the drifting apart of continents. But the fact remains that our knowledge of the interior of our planet is derived almost entirely from indirect evidence, such as the passage of earthquake shock waves through the mantle (page 13A). Direct exploration is confined to the surface and to boreholes which so far have never penetrated more than about five miles (8 km) into the crust. It is difficult to imagine how man could ever devise experiments that would greatly enhance and refine his knowledge of the Earth's interior. Indeed, he knows as much about the Moon and other much more distant heavenly bodies as he does about the Earth below a depth of a mere 20 miles (32 km).

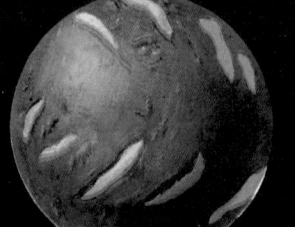

The crust (A)
This varies in thickness from 20 miles (32 km) in continental regions, where it is largely granitic, to 5 miles (8 km) under the oceans, where it is basaltic.

The upper mantle (B, C)
From the crust down to 375 miles (600 km), this layer is divided into upper and lower zones with differing P wave speeds (see page 39).

The lower mantle (D^1, D^2)
Made of peridotite, as is the upper mantle, this zone extends down to a depth of 1800 miles (2900 km). P wave speeds increase still further.

The outer core (E, F)
Largely iron and nickel, this molten zone reaches to 3200 miles (5120 km). Dynamo action of convection currents may cause the Earth's magnetic field.

Not a true sphere below
The Earth's shape is controlled by equilibrium between inward gravitational attraction and outward centrifugal force. This results in the average radius at the equator of 3963 miles (6378 km) slightly exceeding that at the poles of 3950 miles (6356 km).

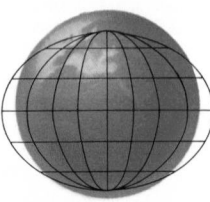

An expanding Earth?
During its history the Earth may have gradua'ly expanded. Some 4500 million years ago it may have been wholly covered with crust equal in area to today's continents. An intermediate stage with a radius of 2735 miles is suggested by the worn-down stumps of ancient mountain folds, while the symmetry of younger fold-mountains indicates that the radius when they were formed was approximately 3730 miles. If the shapes of the modern continents are preserved as nearly as possible they would fit a globe about 2600 miles in radius, which may be the size at which the crust was formed.

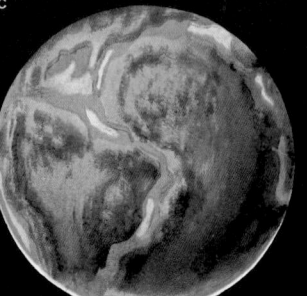

	A	B	C	D	E
Age Million years ago.	4500	3500	2800	600	present.
Size ratio	1.000	1.210	1.360	1.820	1.930
Radius in km.	3300	4000	4400	6000	6371

Temperature *left*
Temperature inside the Earth increases with depth, initially at a rate of 48°C per mile (30°C/km) so that 60 miles (100 km) down it is white hot. The rate of increase then falls, and the shaded area indicates how uncertain is man's knowledge of great depths.

Pressure *left*
This likewise increases with depth. Only 200 miles (320 km) down it reaches 100,000 atmospheres, 1200 times the pressure at the deepest point in the ocean. A change of state at the discontinuity between the mantle and core shows as a kink on the graph.

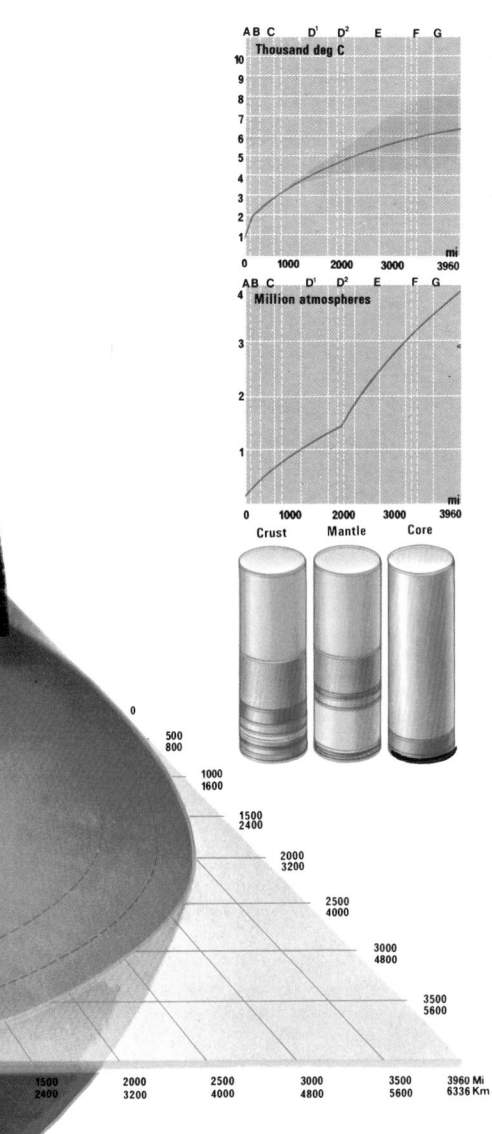

O₂ OXYGEN
Si SILICON
Al ALUMINUM
Fe IRON
Ni NICKEL
Co COBALT
Mg MAGNESIUM
Ca CALCIUM
Na SODIUM
K POTASSIUM

Chemical composition *above*
The crust is made of mainly light elements and has relatively low density. Towards the base of the crust the composition is probably richer in iron and magnesium. The mantle is composed of heavier elements and the core is probably of iron and nickel.

The inner core (G)
The pressure of 3½ million atmospheres (35000 kg/mm²) keeps this a solid ball of 800 miles (1300 km) radius. Its density varies from 14 to about 16.

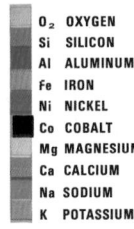

Density *left*
Virtually all man's knowledge of the interior of the Earth stems from measuring the transit of earthquake waves. The resulting data indicate sharp increases in density at the boundaries of both the outer core and the 'solid' inner core, with several intermediate zones.

Convection currents
The fundamental pattern of movement in the mantle (A) is modified by the Earth's rotation (B) and also by friction between adjacent cells as shown in the main figure, below, in which core (X) and mantle (Y) are shown but crust (Z) is removed.

X Core
Y Mantle
Z Crust

Convection theory
Geologists and geophysicists are not unanimous on the question of whether there are convection currents present in the Earth's mantle or not, nor on the part these could play in providing the driving mechanism for major movements of the continents. Slow movement of 'solid' rocks can occur over long periods of time when the temperature is high and only relatively small density differences would be required to trigger them. Another matter for debate is whether convection is confined to the upper mantle or is continuous throughout the whole. It is not certain whether changes of physical state at different levels would constitute barriers to mantle-wide convection. The convection cells above are highly schematic but could largely explain the formation of some of the major geosynclinal fold mountains in the crust over the past thousand million years. Large-scale convection current systems in the mantle could also be the driving force for sea floor spreading and the associated continental drift.

The watery Earth *below*
Almost three-quarters of the Earth is covered by water. Basically the continents are rafts of relatively light crust 'floating' on generally denser oceanic crust. They comprise not only the visible land but also the adjacent continental shelves covered by shallow water. Oceanic crust underlies the deep sea platforms and ocean trenches. The areas of the major lands and seas (below, left) do not take into account the continental shelves but are the gross areas reckoned in terms of the land and water distribution at mean sea level. Extra area due to terrain is not included.

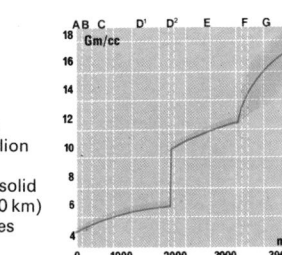

The watery Earth *right*
Key to numbered areas.

Oceans	Area (x 1000)	
	Sq mi	km²
1 Arctic	5541	14350
2 Pacific	63,800,000	165,200,000
3 Atlantic	31530	81660
4 Indian	28,356,000	73,441,700

Continents		
5 Americas	16,301,000	42,219,000
6 Europe (excluding USSR)	1903	4929
7 Asia (excluding USSR)	10661	27611
8 USSR	8649	22402
9 Africa	11,707,000	30,320,000
10 Oceania	3286	8510
11 Antarctica	5 100,000	13,209,000

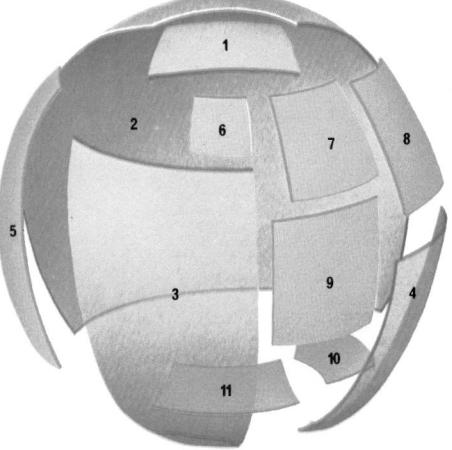

Measured against the time standards of everyday life, the major forces that shape the face of the Earth seem to act almost unbelievably slowly. But in geological terms the erosion of rock formations by river, marine or ice action is in fact rather rapid. Indeed in isolated locations, on coasts or below waterfalls, visible erosion can take place in a period of months or even days.

Over large regions of the Earth the rates of river erosion, expressed as the mass of material removed from each unit of land area in a given time, range between 34 and 6720 short tons per square mile per year (12–2354 metric tons /km^2/year). The main factor determining the rate at any place is the climate. The average rate of erosion for Eurasia, Africa, the Americas and Australia, a land area of some 50 million sq. mi. (130 million km^2), has been calculated to be about 392 short tons per sq. mi. per year (137 metric tons/km^2/year). This corresponds to a general lowering of the surface of the land by about 40 inches (one meter) every 22000 years. At this rate these continents would be worn down to sea level in less than 20 million years, which in geological terms is a fairly short span of time.

In practice, the surface of the land would be most unlikely to suffer such a fate. Although isolated areas could be worn away, worldwide erosion on this scale and at a steady rate would be balanced or prevented by a number of factors, one of which is the continuing large-scale uplift of the land in other regions. Nevertheless long-term estimates do emphasize the cumulative effects of the apparently slow processes of erosion. Even man's own structures wear away. Already the portland stone of St. Paul's cathedral in London has lost half an inch (13 mm) overall in 250 years, aided by the additional force of atmospheric pollution.

Where do all the products of this erosion go? By far the largest accumulations of sediments occur in river deltas, and at many periods in the geological past great thicknesses of such deposits have been laid down in extensive subsiding troughs called geosynclines. A rate of deposition of 1/250 inch (0.1 millimeter) per year is enough to lay down 12 miles (20 km) of strata in 200 million years.

The cycle of rock change

The agents of weathering
Gross break-up of the Earth's surface rocks is caused by earthquakes, the ceaseless cycle of diurnal and annual heating and cooling, and by the freezing of water trapped in fissures and crevices. The water of the seas, rivers and rain dissolves some rocks and in others leaches out particular minerals. Water is especially powerful as a weathering agent when it contains dissolved acidic chemicals. Today's main sources are plants and animals (1), but in the primeval world such chemicals were evolved mainly by volcanoes (2).

Erosion of the land
Only the material exposed at the surface of the Earth by volcanic action (2) or uplift (3) is subjected to erosion, but this material is constantly changing. Chemical erosion is an extension of the weathering process, converting the surface material into different and usually physically degraded substances. Physical erosion (4) is effected by running water and the wind (in both cases accelerated by the presence of an abrasive load) and by ice action and frost shattering.

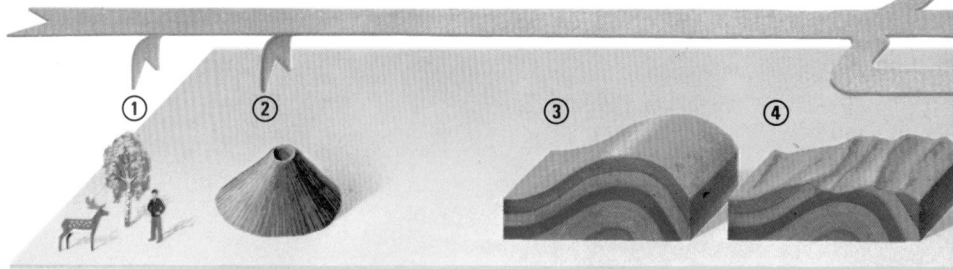

Extrusions
Most lavas are at a temperature of 900-1200°C. Acidic (granitic) lava is fairly viscous, but basic (basalt) lava flows relatively freely and when extruded from surface fissures or volcanoes can cover large areas (15). Lavas which have originated from partial melting of crustal rocks can also be erupted.

Basic magmas
Basic magma generated by partial melting in the mantle (14) may rise into and through the crust to be extruded from surface volcanoes. Basic magmas are the hottest, as well as the most freely flowing, and are often generated at very considerable depth. In their ascent they can intrude large areas of the crust and finally extrude through fissures in the surface.

Intrusions
Contact metamorphism is a form of baking and re-crystallization caused by the intrusion of hot magma into existing strata (13).

Granitic magmas
Partial melting deep in the crust generates new granitic magma—hot, rather viscous molten rock of an acidic nature which is able to migrate both upwards and laterally (12). This may then inject and mix with the surrounding rocks to form a migmatite complex.

Slow uplift
Strata can be slowly uplifted (11) until they once more appear at the surface; continued or violent uplift results in mountain-building. In either case, erosion begins afresh.

Deep metamorphism
If the strata are depressed far down, to depths up to about 25 miles (40 km), deep metamorphism at high pressures and high temperatures (10) results in complete re-crystallization. This gradually converts the original sediments into a complex of new rock types.

Erosion

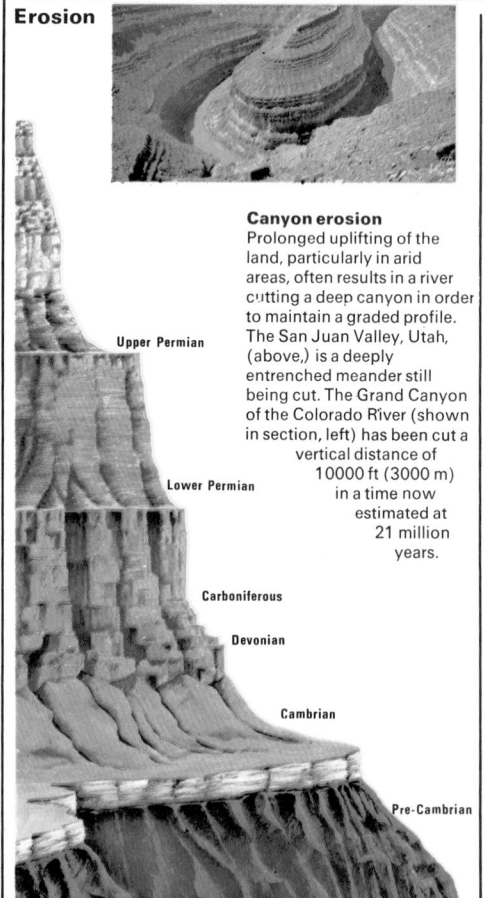

Canyon erosion
Prolonged uplifting of the land, particularly in arid areas, often results in a river cutting a deep canyon in order to maintain a graded profile. The San Juan Valley, Utah, (above,) is a deeply entrenched meander still being cut. The Grand Canyon of the Colorado River (shown in section, left) has been cut a vertical distance of 10000 ft (3000 m) in a time now estimated at 21 million years.

Upper Permian

Lower Permian

Carboniferous

Devonian

Cambrian

Pre-Cambrian

Wind erosion
Laden with grains of sand and other air-transportable debris, the wind exerts a powerful sculpturing effect. Rate of erosion varies with rock hardness, giving rise to odd effects (Mushroom Rock, Death Valley, California, left). Desert sand forms 'barchan' dunes (right), which slowly travel points-first.

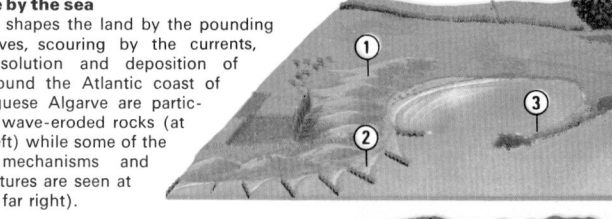

Sculpture by the sea
The ocean shapes the land by the pounding of the waves, scouring by the currents, chemical solution and deposition of debris. Around the Atlantic coast of the Portuguese Algarve are particularly fine wave-eroded rocks (at Piedade, left) while some of the principle mechanisms and coastal features are seen at right (key, far right).

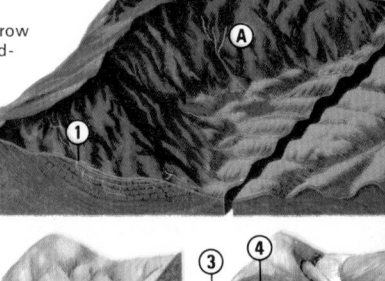

River development
The youthful river flows fast, eroding a narrow channel in an otherwise unchanged landscape. In maturity the channel is wider; flow is slower and some transported debris is deposited. The old river meanders across a broad flood plain (River Wye near Goodrich, left), some meanders becoming cut off as ox-bow lakes.

Glacial action
Briksdal Glacier, Norway (left), is a remnant of the Ice Ages, carving U-shaped valleys (2) in the pre-glacial rock (1). The bergschrund (3) forms close to the back wall, while other crevasses (4) form at gradient changes. Eroded rocks form a longitudinal moraine (5).

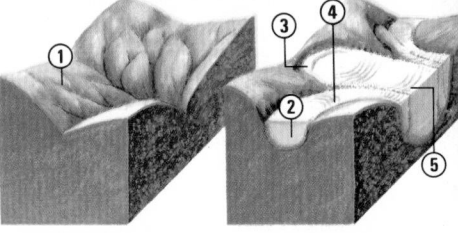

Transportation

As material is worn away from the surface rocks it is carried away by various processes. The most important transport system is flowing water (5), which can move sediments in suspension, in solution or carried along the beds of river channels. In open country, and especially over deserts, much solid debris is blown by the wind (6). Even slow-moving glaciers (7) perform a significant erosion and transport role by bearing heavy burdens of rock debris.

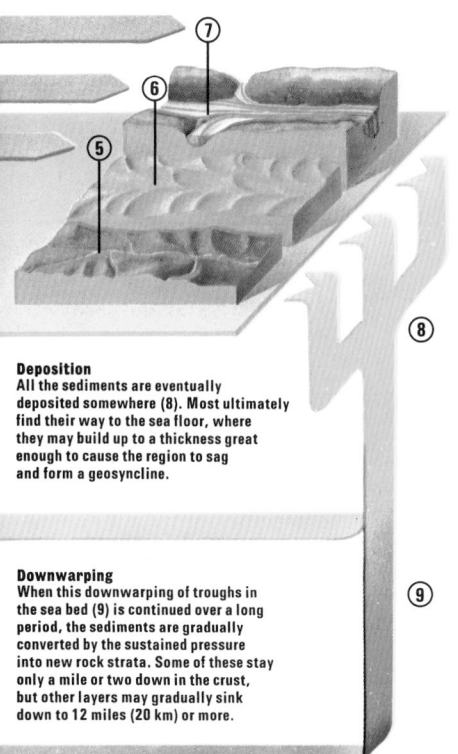

Deposition

All the sediments are eventually deposited somewhere (8). Most ultimately find their way to the sea floor, where they may build up to a thickness great enough to cause the region to sag and form a geosyncline.

Downwarping

When this downwarping of troughs in the sea bed (9) is continued over a long period, the sediments are gradually converted by the sustained pressure into new rock strata. Some of these stay only a mile or two down in the crust, but other layers may gradually sink down to 12 miles (20 km) or more.

250 million years ago

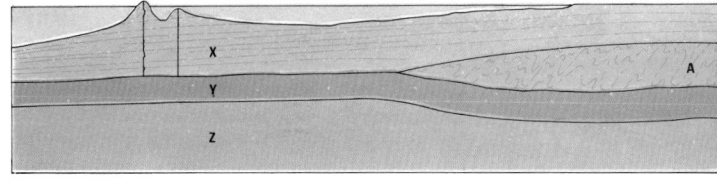

180 million years ago

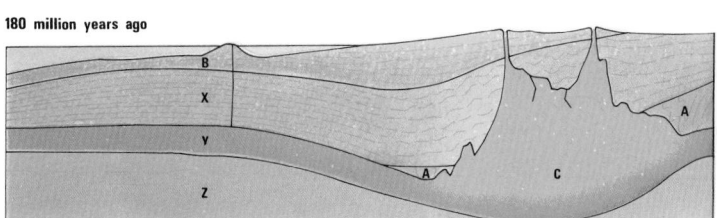

130 million years ago

Present day

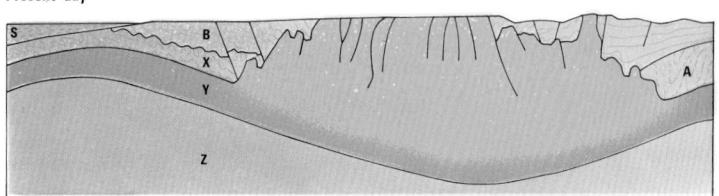

Late Paleozoic *left*
The formation of a geo-syncline begins with the laying down of heavy sediments. In the creation of the Sierra Nevada range sediments X were deposited by the primeval ocean on top of Precambrian rock A, basalt crust Y and peridotite mantle Z.

Jurassic *left*
Downwarping of the crust causes the deposition of Mesozoic sediments B and carries the lower basalt crust and sediments into the zone of the mantle's influence. The bottom of the bulge is gradually converted into hot, fluid magma C.

Cretaceous *left*
In this period the geosyn-clinal process is in a mature stage. The inner rocks reach their maximum downward penetration into the mantle and are metamorphosed by high temperature and pressure. The deep meta-morphism spreads (curved shading).

Present day *left*
Uplift and cooling opens the way to a new cycle of formation. The metamorphic rocks are exposed at the surface and subsequently eroded to yield today's complex landscape structure. Final withdrawal of the sea exposes marine sediments S.

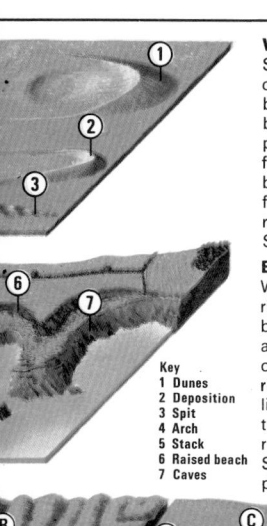

Wind-blown sand *left*
Sand deserts exhibit dunes of various forms. Unlike a barchan the parabolic blowout (1) travels with points trailing. In elongated form this becomes a para-bolic hairpin (2), and a third form is the longitudinal ridge (3), known in the Sahara as a seif dune.

Emerging coastline *right*
Where the shoreline is rising, the continental shelf becomes exposed. River silt accumulates and forms an offshore bar, pierced by the river flow. Eventually infill-ing forms a tidal salt marsh through which the braided river reaches a new shore. Spain (far right) and Italy provide good examples.

Key
1 Dunes
2 Deposition
3 Spit
4 Arch
5 Stack
6 Raised beach
7 Caves

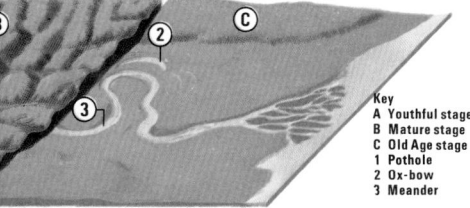

Key
A Youthful stage
B Mature stage
C Old Age stage
1 Pothole
2 Ox-bow
3 Meander

Glaciated landscape *left*
The landscape shows evidence of former ice coverage. Broken rock debris forms valley-floor moraines (6), the peaks are sharp and knife-edged (7), and hanging valleys (8) mark the entry of the glacier's tributaries. Terminal moraines (9) are a characteristic feature.

Key
A Initial stage
B Late youth
C Early maturity
1 Cut-off
2 Spit
3 4 Bars
5 Lagoon

Key
A Initial stage
B Bar development
C Emergence complete

Key
1 Esker
2 Recessional moraine
3 Drumlin
4 Lake
5 Terminal moraine
6 Outwash delta
7 Lake deposits
8 Kettle lake
9 Outwash plain
10 Kettle hole

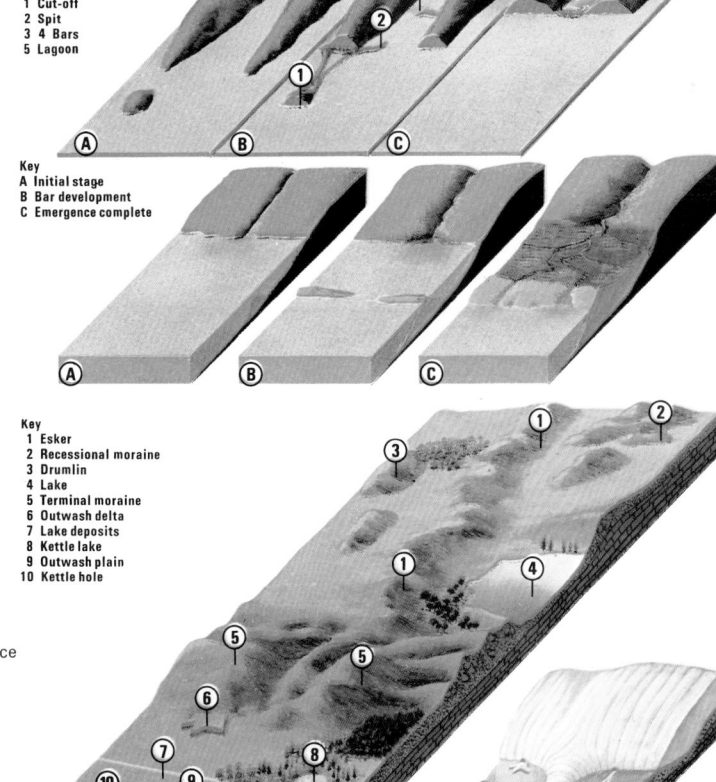

Subsiding coastline *left*
Most coastal regions under-going submergence are highly irregular. Drowned hills are eroded by the waves to form cliff headlands, or cut-offs; spits and bars cross the submerged valleys, enclose them and form lagoons. Finally all these features wear back to a new shoreline.

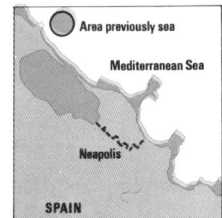

Area previously sea

Mediterranean Sea

Neapolis

SPAIN

Glaciated landforms *left*
Throughout a vast area of the temperate lands evidence of past glacial action is abundant. A geomorpholo-gist, studying the landscape shown in the larger illustration, would deduce the former glacial situation depicted in the inset. Weight and sculpture by the ice carved out characteristic depressions, some later filled with water. Sub-glacial streams left alluvial deposits in the form of eskers and an outwash fan or delta, while the limit of the glacier is suggested by rocks deposited as a terminal moraine. Kettle holes result from the melting of ice within moraine debris.

The Active Oceans

The surface of the oceans presents an infinite variety of contrasts ranging from glassy calm to terrifying storms with towering waves and wind-whipped wraiths of spray. But no part of the oceans is ever really still. Together the oceans comprise 300 million cubic miles (1250 million km³) of ever-active water. The whole mass ebbs and flows on a global scale with the tides. The surface is disturbed by winds into great patterns of waves which eventually break on the shores of the land. And the largest and most far-reaching movements of all are the ocean currents, some on or near the surface and others at great depths, which profoundly alter not only the oceans but also the weather.

Best known of all these currents is the Gulf Stream, which was discovered in late medieval times when early navigators found that their ships were consistently not in the place predicted by their calculations of course and estimated speed. Some 500 years ago it had become customary for Spanish captains voyaging to the New World to keep well south of the Gulf Stream on their outward journey and then use its swift four or five knot (8–9 km/hr) current to help them along on the return. The Gulf Stream brings mild weather to northwest Europe, and a corresponding role is played on the other side of the globe by the Kuroshio, a warm current which flows northeastward off Japan. Conversely, in the southeastern Pacific the Peru Current brings cold water from the sub-Antarctic region northward towards the equator. The surface flow is accompanied during most months of the year by an 'upwelling' of water rich in nutrients along the coast of Chile and Peru, and this, like many other cold currents elsewhere, supports great fisheries.

In coastal seas the water movements are often dominated by the currents that accompany the rise and fall of the tide. Because of the friction of the tides, the Moon is moving slowly further from the Earth.

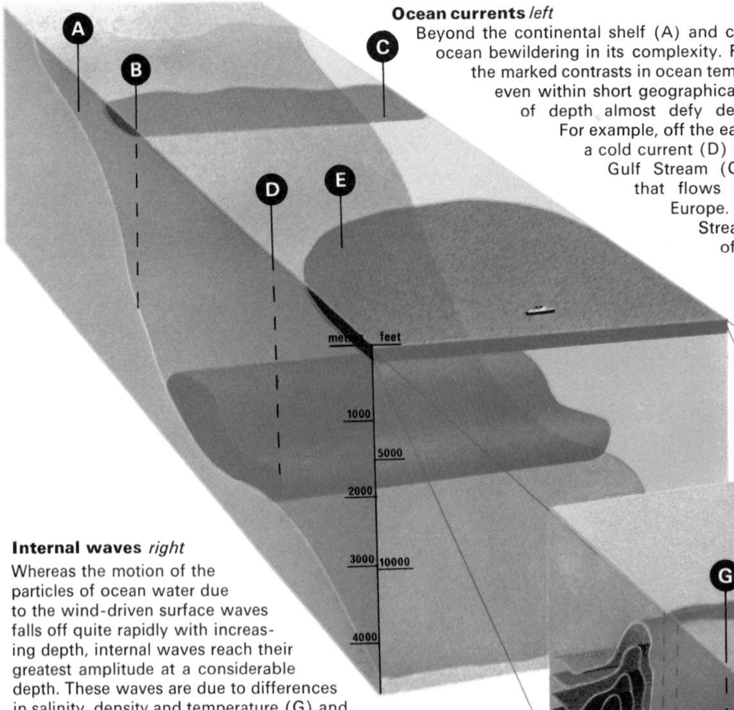

Wave generation *right*
Waves are generated on the surface by the wind. Once a slight undulation has been formed it will react on the air flow so that an eddying motion, with a reduced pressure, is produced on the lee side (A) of each crest. Combined with the wind pressure on the windward side (B), this causes the waves to grow in height. The wave travels forward in the direction of the wind, but the individual water particles (X) move in almost closed orbits (C).

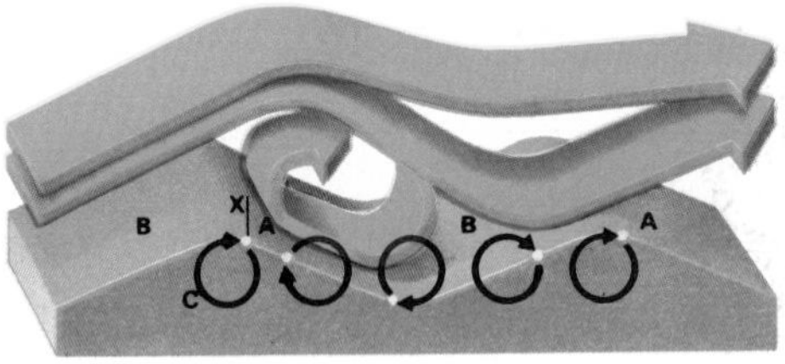

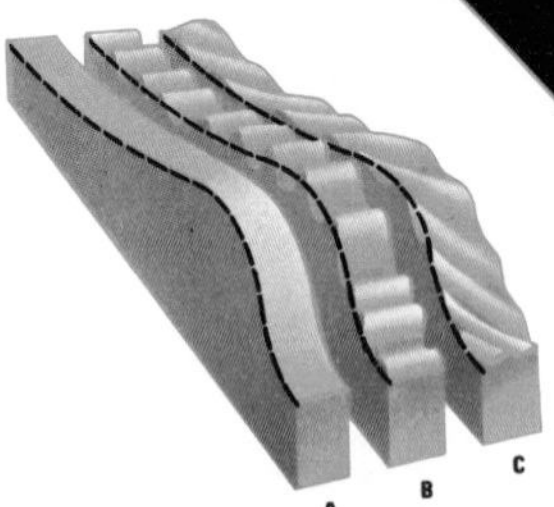

Internal motion *right*
On the surface of deep water these orbits are almost circular. Below the surface the radii of the orbits decrease with depth and become very small at a depth equal to half a wavelength. In shallow water the orbits are ellipses, becoming flatter towards the bottom.

Shore and rip currents *below*
In addition to its circular movement, each water particle slowly moves in the direction of propagation. When waves approach a coast water tends to pile up at the shoreline. This leads to a return flow seaward (X) which is concentrated in narrow, fast-flowing rip currents (Y). Beyond the breaker zone these spread out into a head and gradually disperse (Z).

Ocean currents *left*
Beyond the continental shelf (A) and continental slope (B) lies an ocean bewildering in its complexity. Far from being homogenous, the marked contrasts in ocean temperature, density and salinity even within short geographical distances or narrow ranges of depth almost defy description and measurement. For example, off the east coast of the United States a cold current (D) moves southward below the Gulf Stream (C), a warm surface current that flows northeast towards Western Europe. Near its source the Gulf Stream borders the western edge of the Sargasso Sea (E).

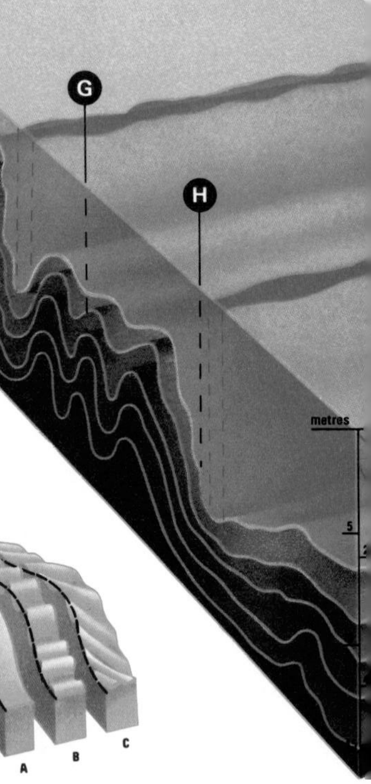

Internal waves *right*
Whereas the motion of the particles of ocean water due to the wind-driven surface waves falls off quite rapidly with increasing depth, internal waves reach their greatest amplitude at a considerable depth. These waves are due to differences in salinity, density and temperature (G) and are manifest in a motion similar to surface waves (H). They are most marked where there is a sharp transition — between, for example, warm water overlying cold, denser water. Their amplitude can exceed 100 feet (30 m) and their period can range from 30 minutes up to longer than the tidal period. Sometimes their presence is made evident by the appearance of banded slicks (J) on the surface of the sea lying directly over the troughs of the internal waves.

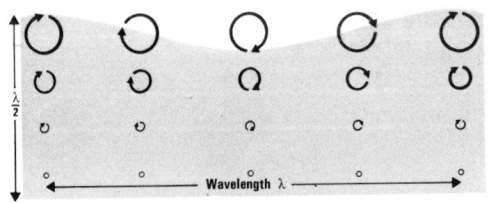

Waves and swell *above*
Ocean swell (A) is invariably present and travels hundreds of miles. On it the wind can superimpose small waves (B), which die out relatively rapidly. These smaller waves may be at any angle to the original swell (C).

Change of wave front *left, below*
When waves from the open sea pass into a region of shallow water where the depth is less than about half a wavelength their forward velocity is progressively reduced. One consequence of this is that the wave fronts are refracted so that they turn towards the shallower water, and the wave crests tend to line up parallel to the shore. In the diagram X-X is the original frontal axis of the waves coming in from the ocean. When the depth of water varies along a coast, waves tend to become focused on the shallower areas (Y) and to diverge from the deeper ones such as the head of a submarine valley or canyon (Z). For the same reason large waves can often be seen breaking on a headland while the breakers in an area of originally deeper water, leading to a bay, are relatively much smaller.

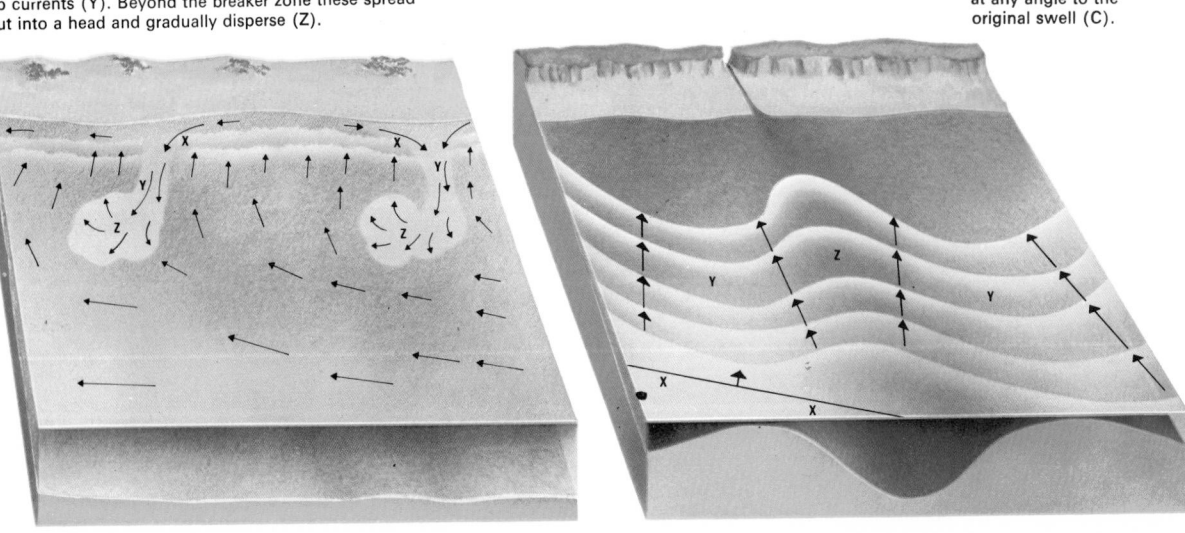

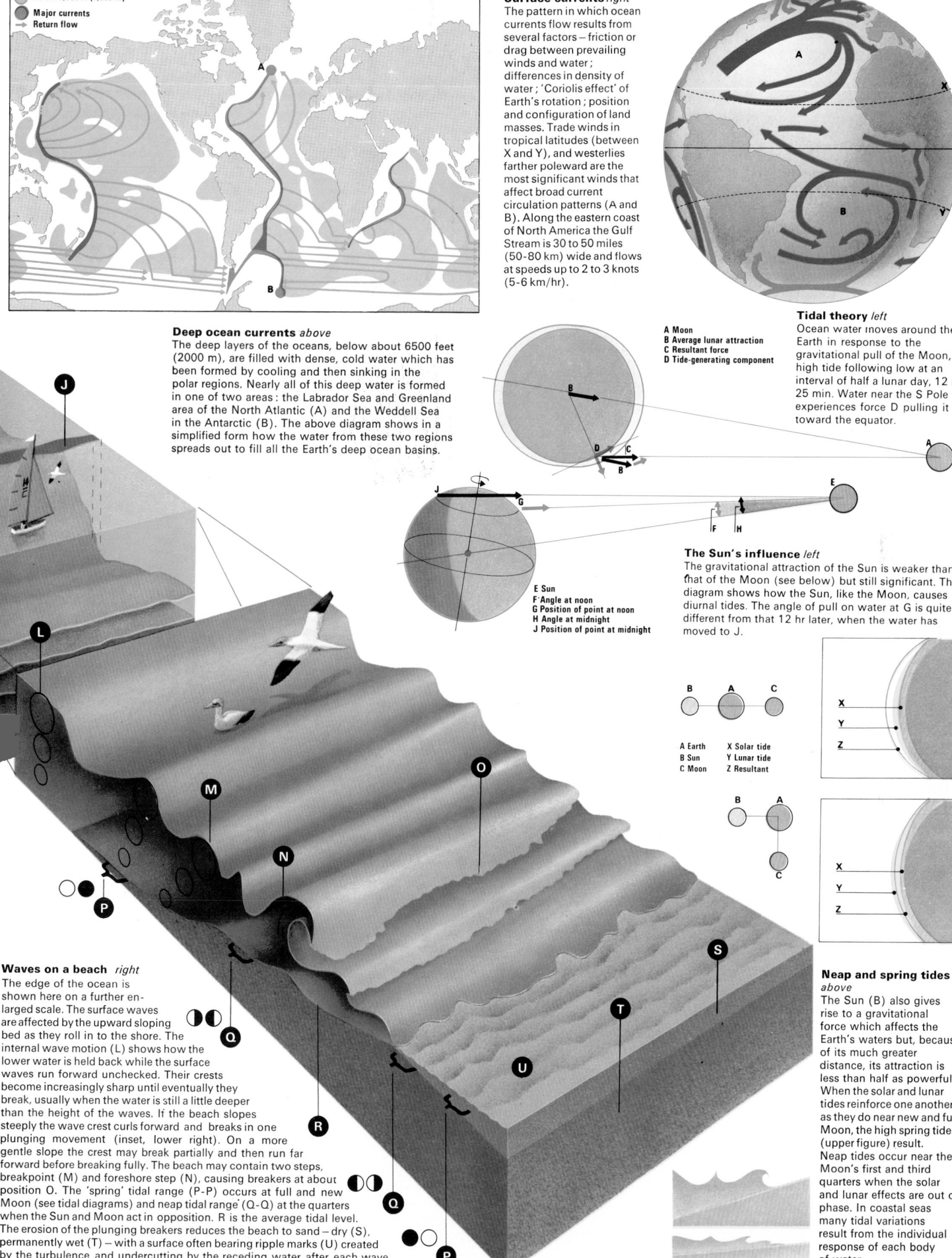

Surface currents *right*
The pattern in which ocean currents flow results from several factors – friction or drag between prevailing winds and water; differences in density of water; 'Coriolis effect' of Earth's rotation; position and configuration of land masses. Trade winds in tropical latitudes (between X and Y), and westerlies farther poleward are the most significant winds that affect broad current circulation patterns (A and B). Along the eastern coast of North America the Gulf Stream is 30 to 50 miles (50-80 km) wide and flows at speeds up to 2 to 3 knots (5-6 km/hr).

Deep ocean currents *above*
The deep layers of the oceans, below about 6500 feet (2000 m), are filled with dense, cold water which has been formed by cooling and then sinking in the polar regions. Nearly all of this deep water is formed in one of two areas: the Labrador Sea and Greenland area of the North Atlantic (A) and the Weddell Sea in the Antarctic (B). The above diagram shows in a simplified form how the water from these two regions spreads out to fill all the Earth's deep ocean basins.

A Moon
B Average lunar attraction
C Resultant force
D Tide-generating component

Tidal theory *left*
Ocean water moves around the Earth in response to the gravitational pull of the Moon, high tide following low at an interval of half a lunar day, 12 hr 25 min. Water near the S Pole experiences force D pulling it toward the equator.

E Sun
F Angle at noon
G Position of point at noon
H Angle at midnight
J Position of point at midnight

The Sun's influence *left*
The gravitational attraction of the Sun is weaker than that of the Moon (see below) but still significant. This diagram shows how the Sun, like the Moon, causes diurnal tides. The angle of pull on water at G is quite different from that 12 hr later, when the water has moved to J.

A Earth   X Solar tide
B Sun   Y Lunar tide
C Moon   Z Resultant

Waves on a beach *right*
The edge of the ocean is shown here on a further enlarged scale. The surface waves are affected by the upward sloping bed as they roll in to the shore. The internal wave motion (L) shows how the lower water is held back while the surface waves run forward unchecked. Their crests become increasingly sharp until eventually they break, usually when the water is still a little deeper than the height of the waves. If the beach slopes steeply the wave crest curls forward and breaks in one plunging movement (inset, lower right). On a more gentle slope the crest may break partially and then run far forward before breaking fully. The beach may contain two steps, breakpoint (M) and foreshore step (N), causing breakers at about position O. The 'spring' tidal range (P-P) occurs at full and new Moon (see tidal diagrams) and neap tidal range (Q-Q) at the quarters when the Sun and Moon act in opposition. R is the average tidal level. The erosion of the plunging breakers reduces the beach to sand – dry (S), permanently wet (T) – with a surface often bearing ripple marks (U) created by the turbulence and undercutting by the receding water after each wave.

Neap and spring tides *above*
The Sun (B) also gives rise to a gravitational force which affects the Earth's waters but, because of its much greater distance, its attraction is less than half as powerful. When the solar and lunar tides reinforce one another, as they do near new and full Moon, the high spring tides (upper figure) result. Neap tides occur near the Moon's first and third quarters when the solar and lunar effects are out of phase. In coastal seas many tidal variations result from the individual response of each body of water.

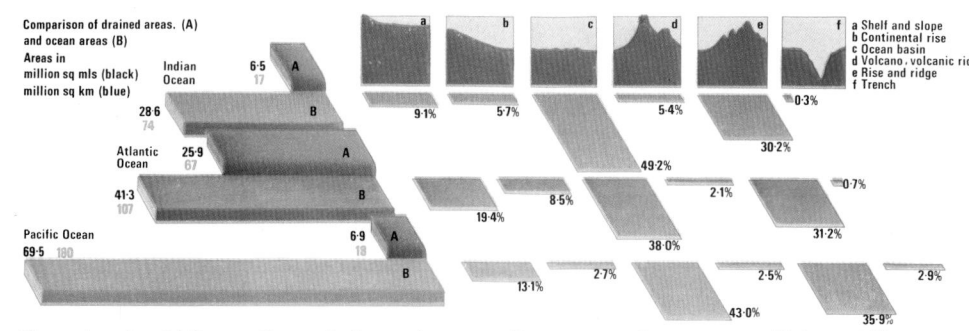

Comparison of drained areas. (A) and ocean areas (B)
Areas in million sq mls (black) million sq km (blue)

Indian Ocean	6·5 / 17	A
	28·6 / 74	B
Atlantic Ocean	25·9 / 67	A
	41·3 / 107	B
Pacific Ocean	6·9 / 18	A
69·5 / 180		B

a Shelf and slope
b Continental rise
c Ocean basin
d Volcano, volcanic ridge
e Rise and ridge
f Trench

a 9·1% / 19·4%
b 5·7% / 8·5%
c 5·4% / 49·2% / 38·0% / 43·0%
d 0·3% / 2·1% / 2·7% / 13·1%
e 30·2% / 2·5% / 2·5%
f 0·7% / 31·2% / 35·9% / 2·9%

The water planet *left*
From directly over Tahiti the Earth appears to be covered by water. The Pacific averages 2.5 miles (4 km) deep, with great mountains and trenches.

Ocean drainage *above*
The ratio between the areas of the oceans and the land they drain varies greatly. Many large rivers feed the Atlantic but few discharge into the Pacific.

Ocean proportions *above*
The major oceans show a similarity in the proportions of their submarine topography. By far the greatest areas contain deep plains with rises and ridges. More prominent features, the mid-ocean volcanic ridges and trenches, occupy much smaller areas. About one tenth of each ocean is continental shelf.

At present the sea covers about 71 per cent of the Earth's surface. But if the continents could be sliced away and put into the deep oceans to make a perfectly uniform sphere the sea would have an average depth of about 8000 feet (2500 m) over the whole planet. In the distant past the level of the sea has fluctuated violently. The main cause has been the comings and goings of the ice ages. Glaciers and ice-caps lock up enormous volumes of water and the advance and recession of ice has alternately covered the continental shelves with shallow seas and revealed them as dry land. If the Earth's present polar ice-caps and glaciers were to melt, the mean sea level would rise by about 200 feet (60 m), which would submerge half the world's population. Average depth of the sea is more than 12000 feet (3600 m), five times the average height of the land above sea level.

The deep oceans
Below the level of the continental shelf lies the deep ocean floor with great topographical contrasts ranging from abyssal plains at a depth of about 13000 feet (4 km) to towering submarine mountain ranges of the mid-ocean ridges which reach far up toward the surface. Great advances have recently been made in exploring the ocean floors which were previously unknown. Most of the ocean area is abyssal plain which extends over about 78 million square miles (200 million km²). But a more remarkable feature of the deep ocean is the almost continuous mid-ocean mountain range which sweeps 40000 miles (64000 km) around the globe and occasionally – as at Iceland – is seen above sea level in the form of isolated volcanic islands. The basic symmetry of the oceans is the central ridge flanked by abyssal plain sloping up to the continental shelves. On the deep floor sediments accumulate at a rate of 30–35 feet (10 m) per million years; they also build up more slowly at the central ridges. No ocean sediments have been found older than 150 million years, which suggests that the material which now makes up the floors of the deep oceans was formed comparatively recently. Exploration and detailed mapping of the ocean bed is still in its infancy.

Submarine landscape
Principal features of the bed of the oceans can be grouped into a much smaller space than they would actually occupy. Although each ocean differs in detail, all tend to conform to the general layout of a central volcanic ridge (which can break the surface in places), broad abyssal plains with occasional deep trenches and shallow slopes and shelves bordering the continents.

Submarine relief *below*
The bottom of the sea is very far from being flat. If the ocean waters were removed a new landscape would become visible, with immense relief features.

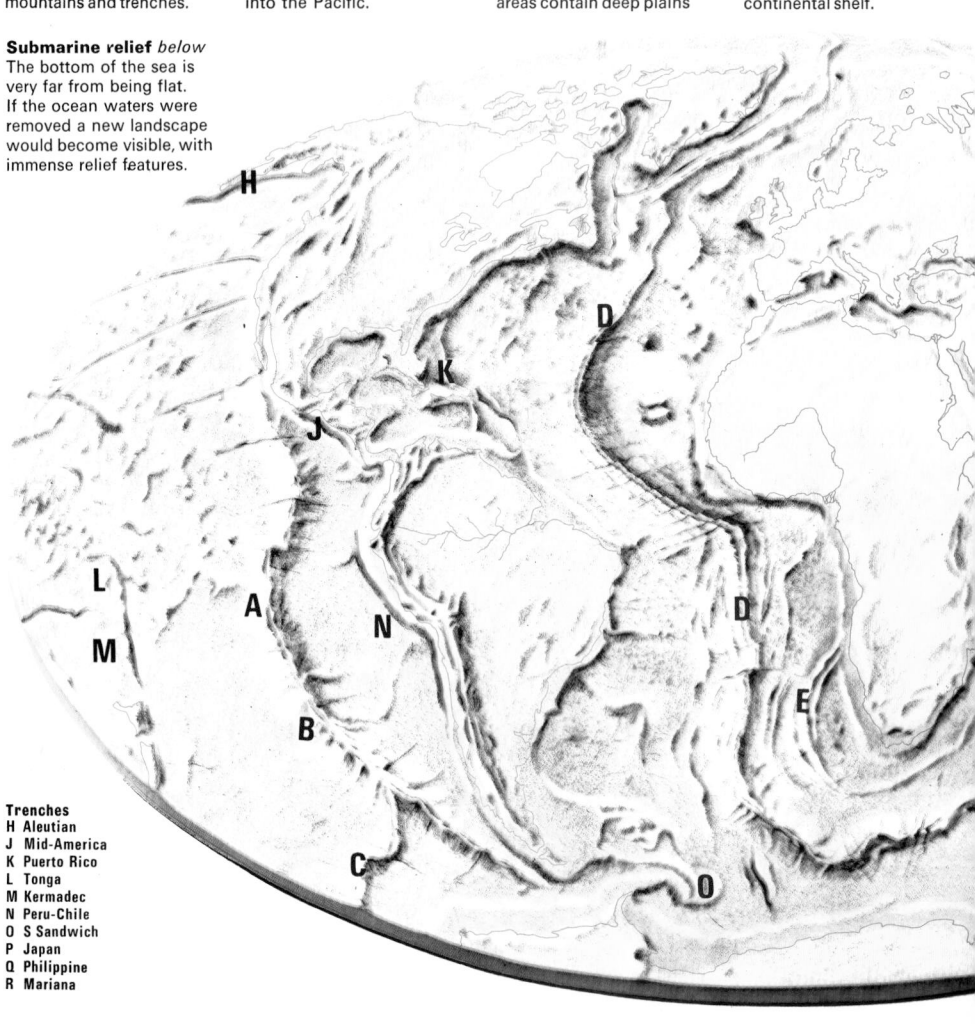

Trenches
H Aleutian
J Mid-America
K Puerto Rico
L Tonga
M Kermadec
N Peru-Chile
O S Sandwich
P Japan
Q Philippine
R Mariana

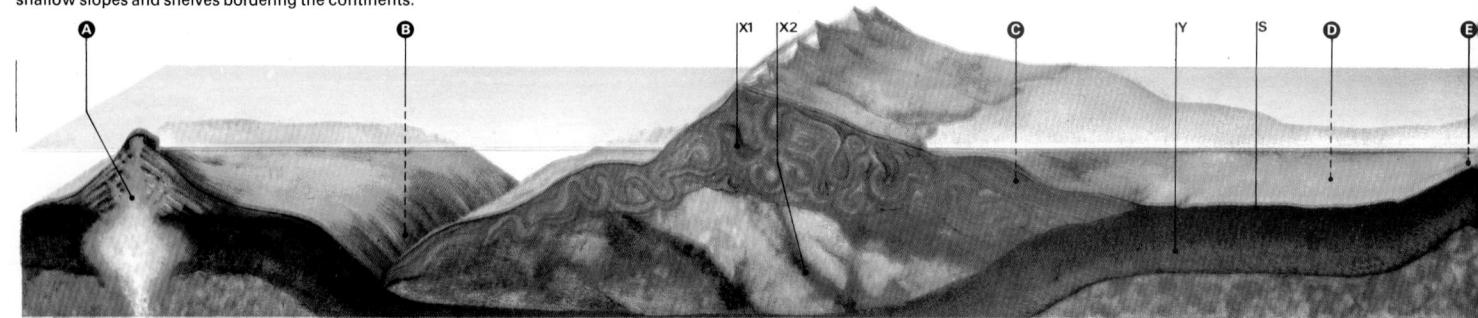

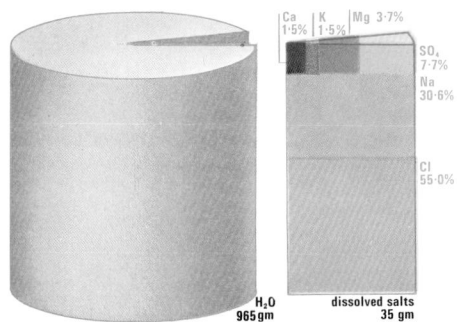

Composition of sea-water *above*
The water of the Earth's oceans is an exceedingly complex solution of many organic and inorganic salts, together with suspended solid matter. In a typical kilogram of sea-water there are 35 grams of chlorine, sodium, sulphates, magnesium, potassium and calcium.

Rises and Ridges
A E Pacific
B SE Pacific
C Pacific-Antarctic
D Mid-Atlantic
E Walvis
F Indian Ocean
G SE Indian

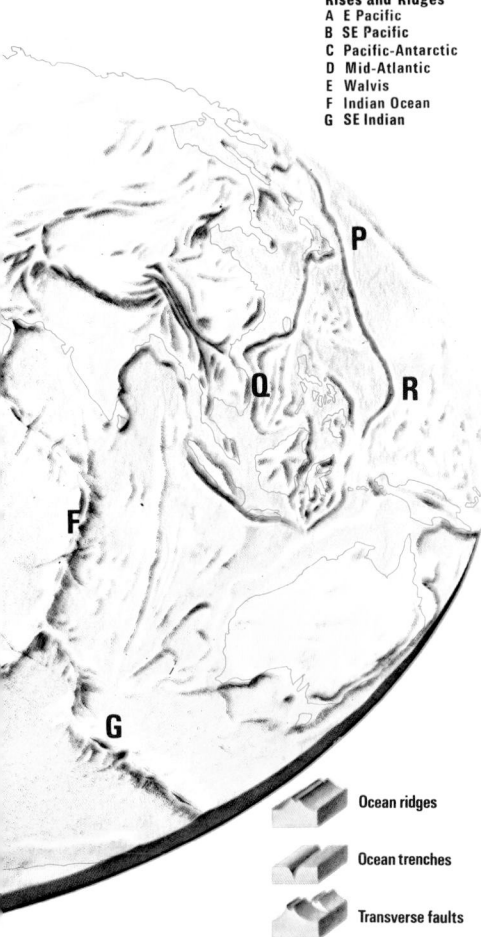

Ocean ridges

Ocean trenches

Transverse faults

A Volcano in mid-ocean ridge
B Deep oceanic trench
C Continental shelf
D Abyssal plain
E Mid-ocean ridge
F Guyots
G Oceanic islands
X1 Upper granitic crust and sediments
X2 Lower granitic crust
Y Basaltic crust
Z Mantle

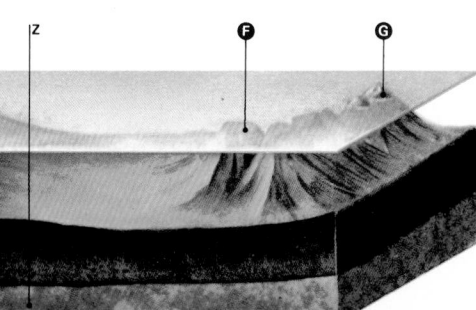

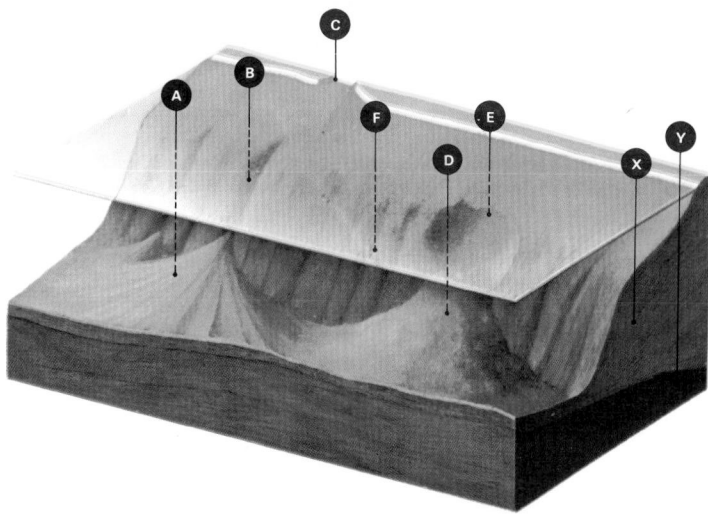

Continental shelf *left*
The submerged continental fringes lie at depths to about 450 feet (135 m) and have a total area of some 11 million square miles (28 million km²). The surface of the land is eroded and carried by rivers to form sedimentary deposits on the shelf. At its outer margin it slopes down to the abyssal plains of the deep ocean at about 2½ miles (4 km) below sea level.

A Scree fan
B Gully opposite river
C River delta
D Slump (turbidite) mass
E Scar left by (D)
F Continental slope
X Granite
Y Basalt

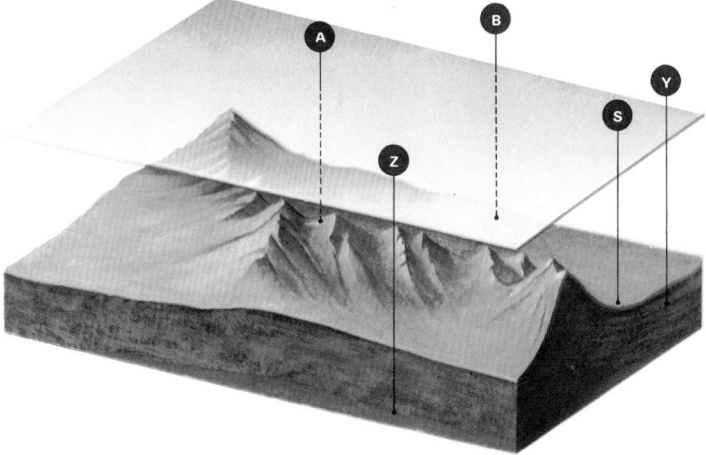

Mid-ocean ridge *left*
Well-marked ridges are found along the centers of the major oceans and form an extensive worldwide system. The central part of the ridge may have a double crest with an intervening deep trough forming a rift valley, or there may be several ridges. They are volcanic in nature and along them is generated new basaltic ocean crust. The volcanoes become progressively younger as the mid-ocean ridge is approached.

A Mid-ocean ridge
B Abyssal plain
S Ocean floor sediments
Y Basalt crust
Z Mantle

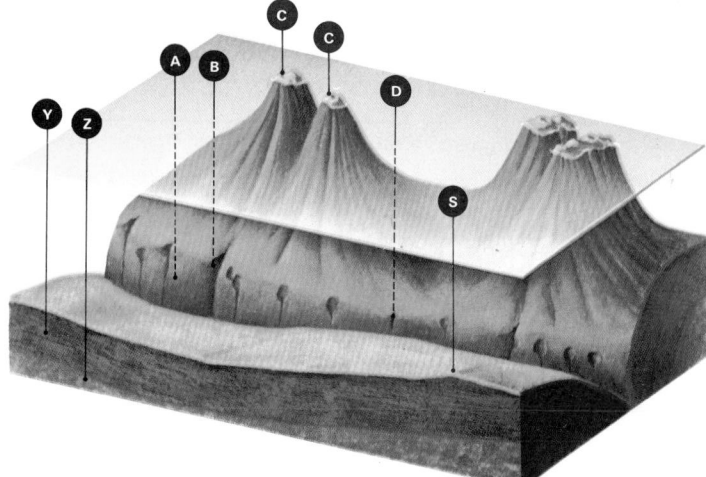

Oceanic trench *left*
These long and relatively narrow depressions are the deepest portions of the oceans, averaging over 30,000 feet (10 km) below sea level. Around the Pacific they lie close to the continental margins and in the western Pacific are often associated with chains of volcanic islands. Some trenches are slowly becoming narrower as the ocean floor plates on either side converge.

A Trench wall
B Canyon
C Island arc
D Trench
S Sediment
Y Basalt
Z Mantle

A sinking island *below*
A pre-requisite to the formation of a coral atoll is an island that is becoming submerged by the sea. Such islands are formed by the peaks of the volcanic mountains which are found on the flanks of the great mid-oceanic ridges.

Coral grows *below*
Millions of polyps, small marine animals, secrete a substance which forms the hard and often beautiful coral. The structure grows round the island in shallow water and extends above the sinking island to form an enclosed and shallow salt-water lagoon.

The mature atoll *below*
Continued submergence of the volcano results in the disappearance of the original island, but the upward growth of the coral continues unabated. The reef is then worn away by the sea and the coral debris fills in the central part of the lagoon.

A guyot *below*
Eventually the coral atoll itself begins to sink beneath the ocean surface. By this time the lagoon is likely to have become completely filled in by debris eroded from the reef, and the result is a submerged flat island, known as a guyot.

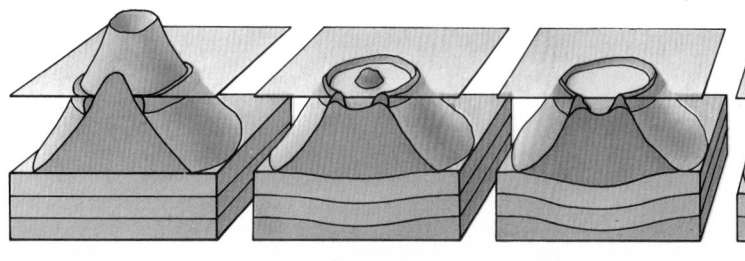

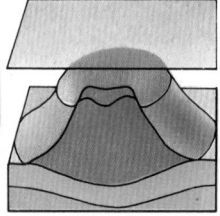

The Evolution of Land and Sea

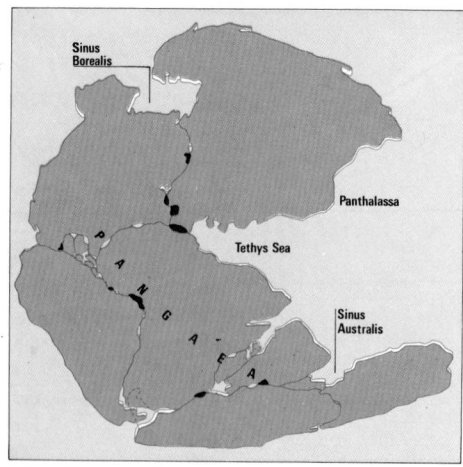

Pangaea *above*
About 200 million years ago there was only a single land mass on Earth, named Pangaea. The map shows how today's continents can be fitted together, with the aid of a computer, at the edge of the continental shelf at a depth of 1000 fathoms (6000 ft, 1830 m).

Although land and water first appeared on the Earth's surface several thousand million years before anyone could be there to watch, modern man has a very good idea of how it came about. The Earth's gravitational field caused the lighter, more volatile elements gradually to move outwards through the mantle and form a solid crust on the surface. By far the largest proportion of material newly added to the crust is basaltic volcanic rock derived from partial melting of the mantle beneath; in fact the oceanic crust which underlies the Earth's great water areas is made of almost nothing else. So the earliest crust to form was probably volcanic and of basaltic composition.

Air and water appear
The earliest records of the existence of an atmosphere of air and a hydrosphere of water are to be found in sediments laid down some 3300 million years ago from the residue of erosion of previously existing rocks. These sediments could not have been formed without atmospheric weathering, water transport and water deposition. The atmosphere was probably originally similar to the fumes which today issue from volcanoes and hot springs and which are about three-quarters water vapor. Once formed, the primitive atmosphere and oceans could erode the crust to produce vast layers of sediments of new chemical compositions. Gradually the oceans deepened and the land took on a more varied form. Convection in the mantle produced mountain ranges which in turn eroded to generate new sedimentary rocks. The ceaseless cycles of growth and decay had started, causing continually changing patterns of seas, mountains and plains. And in the past few years man has discovered how the continents and oceans have developed over the most recent 200 million years of geological time. The results of this research are to be seen in the maps on this page.

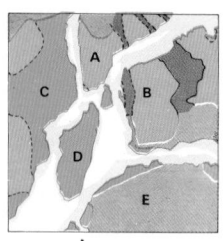

Another arrangement *left*
India (A) may have been separated by Australia (B) from East Antarctica (E) more than 200 million years ago on the evidence of today's geological deposition zones. Africa (C) and Madagascar (D) complete this convincing fit.

Migrant Australia *left*
By measuring the direction of magnetization of old Australian rocks it is possible to trace successive positions of that continent with respect to the Earth's magnetic pole. It appears to have moved across the world and back during the past 1000 million years.

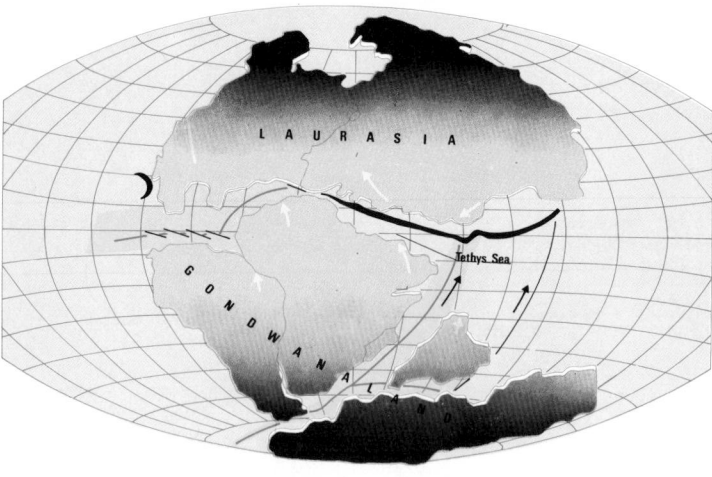

180 million years ago
At this time the original Pangaea land mass had just begun to break up. The continents first split along the lines of the North Atlantic and Indian Oceans. North America separated from Africa and so did India and Antarctica. The Tethys Sea, between Africa and Asia, closed somewhat, and the super continents of Laurasia to the north and Gondwanaland to the south became almost completely separated. In effect the Earth possessed three super landmasses, plus an India that had already begun to move strongly northward.

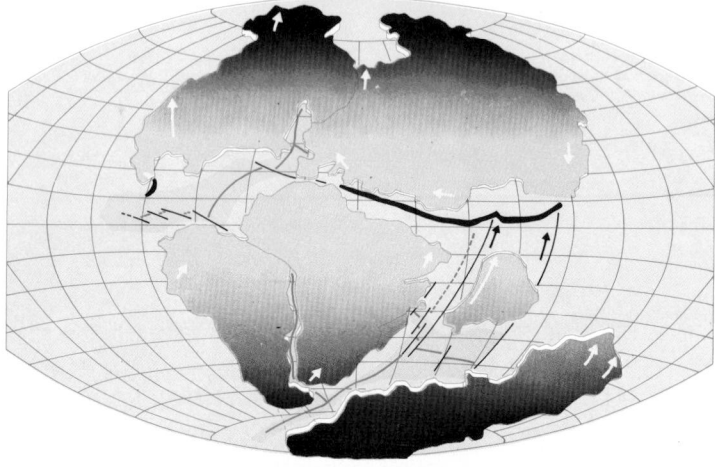

135 million years ago
After a further 45 million years of drifting, the world map had still not taken on a form that looks familiar today. But the two original splits, the North Atlantic and the Indian Ocean, have continued to open out. The North Atlantic is now about 600–650 miles (1000 km) wide. Rifting is extending towards the split which opened up the Labrador Sea and this will eventually separate Greenland from North America. India has firmly launched itself on its collision course with the southern coast of Asia, which is still 2000 miles (3200 km) away.

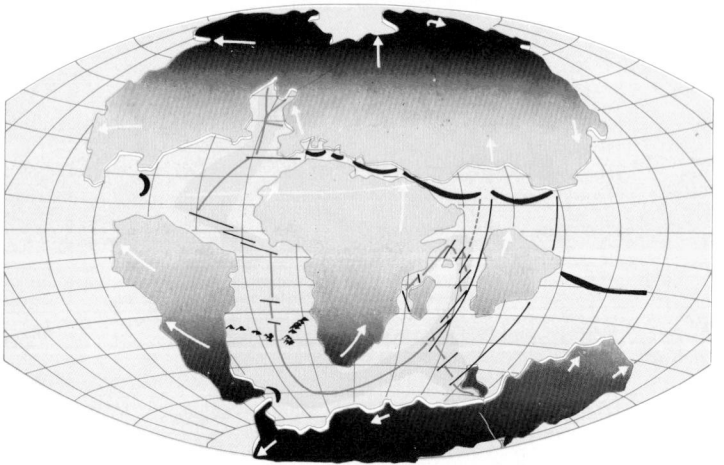

65 million years ago
Some 135 million years after the start of the drifting process the continents have begun to assume their present configuration. South America has at last separated from Africa and in Gondwanaland only Australia and Antarctica have yet to move apart. A continuation of the North Atlantic rifting will shortly bring about another big separation in Laurasia. Greenland will move apart from Europe and eventually North America will separate completely from the Eurasian landmass. The pink area (below) shows the extent of the crustal movements.

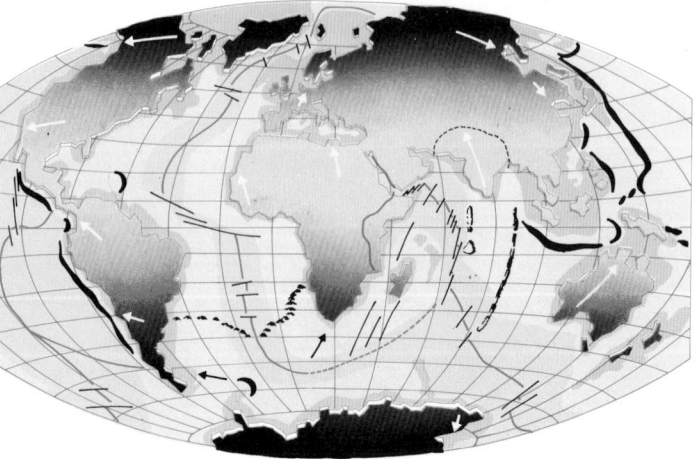

Today's positions
The Atlantic is now a wide ocean from Arctic to Antarctic, the Americas have joined and Australia has separated from Antarctica and moved far to the north. India has likewise moved northwards and its collision with Asia and continued movement has given rise to the extensive uplift of the Himalayas. All the continents which formerly made up the great land mass of Pangaea are now separated by wide oceans. Comparison of areas shows how much of India has been submerged by sliding underneath the crust of Asia (see facing page, far right).

Plate tectonics

This theory has revolutionized the way the Earth's crust – continents and oceans – is interpreted on a global scale. The crust is regarded as being made up of huge plates which converge or diverge along margins marked by earthquakes, volcanoes and other seismic activity. Major divergent margins are the mid-ocean ridges where molten lava forces its way upward and escapes. This causes vast regions of crust to move apart at a rate of an inch or two (some centimeters) per year. When sustained for up to 200 million years this means movements of thousands of miles or kilometers. The process can be seen in operation today in and around Iceland. Oceanic trenches are margins where the plates are moving together and the crust is consumed downward. The overall result is for the crustal plates to move as relatively rigid entities, carrying the continents along with them as if they were on a giant conveyor belt. Over further considerable periods of geologic time this will markedly change today's maps.

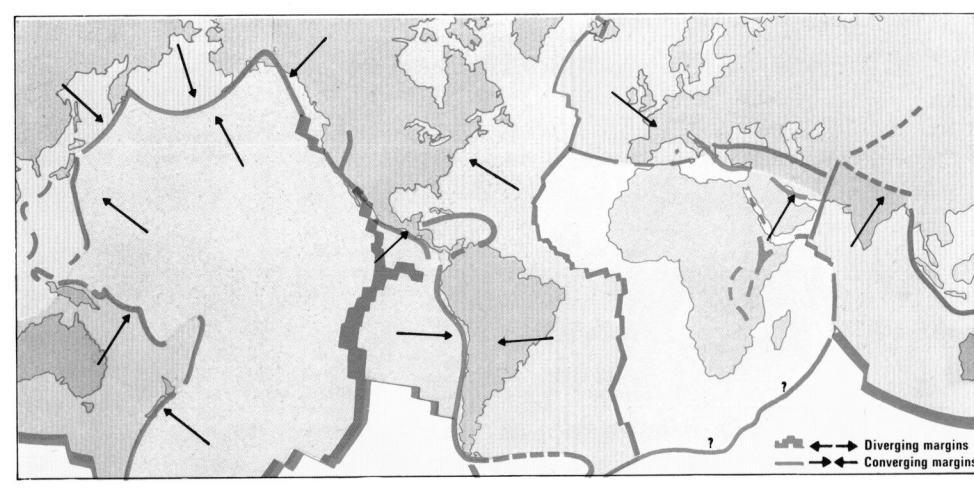

Diverging margins

Converging margins

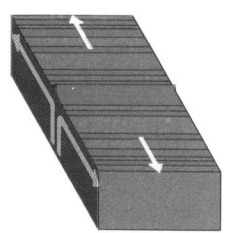

Sea-floor spreading *left*
Arrows show how the lava flows on the ocean bed spread out on each side of a mid-ocean ridge. Evidence for such movement is provided by the fact the rock is alternately magnetized in opposing directions (coloured stripes).

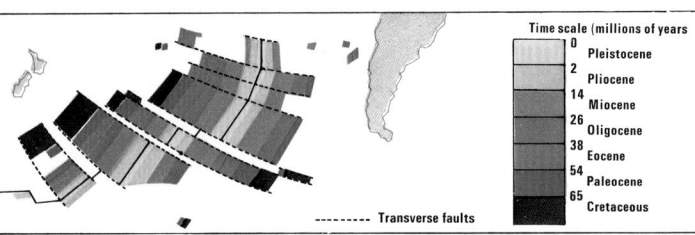

Time scale (millions of years)

0	
	Pleistocene
2	
	Pliocene
14	
	Miocene
26	
	Oligocene
38	
	Eocene
54	
	Paleocene
65	
	Cretaceous

-------- Transverse faults

Plate movements
above and left
The Earth's crust is a series of large plates 'floating' on the fluid mantle. At their edges the plates are either growing or disappearing. Magnetic measurements in the S. Pacific (left) show rock ages on each side of the mid-ocean ridges.

Plate movements in cross-section *above*
The basic mechanism of plate movements is illustrated above in simplified form with the vertical scale greatly exaggerated. This figure is explained in detail in both of the captions below.

Crustal divergence
above and right
The Earth's crust (1) behaves as a series of rigid plates which move on top of the fluid mantle (2). At their mating edges some of these plates are moving apart (3). This was the mechanism that separated North America (A) from Europe (B). The plates moved to the north and also away from each other under the influence of convection currents in the mantle (C). Between the land areas appeared an oceanic gap with a mid-ocean ridge (D) and lateral ridges (E). The movements continued for some 200 million years, fresh volcanoes being generated by igneous material escaping through the plate joint (F) to add to the lateral ridges which today cross the Atlantic (G). The volcanoes closest to the median line in mid-Atlantic are still young and active — whereas those nearer to the continents are old and extinct.

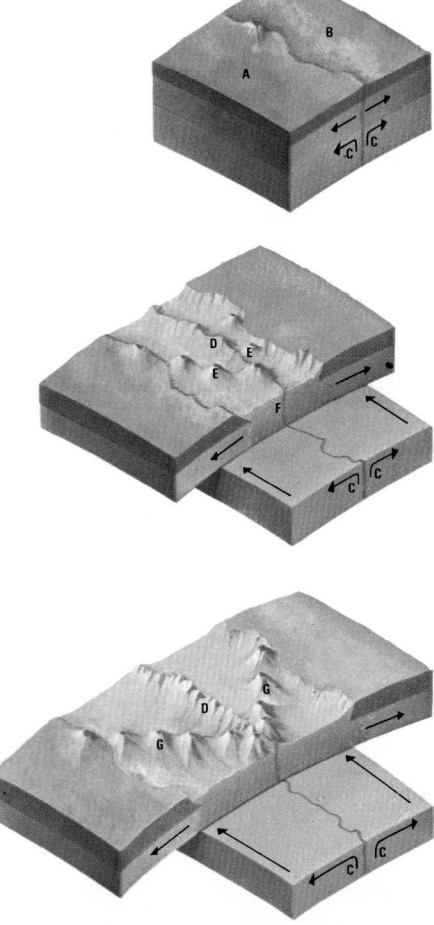

Crustal convergence
above and right
Diverging plate margins occur only in the centers of the major oceans (see map above) but plates are converging on both sea and land. Where an oceanic plate (4, above) is under-riding a continental plate (5) a deep ocean trench is the result (6). Such trenches extend around much of the Pacific; those around the northwest Pacific include the deepest on Earth where the sea bed is almost seven miles below the ocean surface. The continental margin is squeezed upward to form mountains such as the Andes or Rockies (7). If continental masses converge, such as India (A, right) and Asia (B), the convection in the mantle (C) pulls the plates together so hard that the upper crust crumples (D). Sedimentary deposits between the plates (E) are crushed and squeezed out upward (F), while the mantle on each side is turned downward, one side being forced under the other (G). Continued movement causes gross deformation at the point of collision. The static or slow-moving crust is crushed and tilted, and giant young mountains (the Himalayas, H) are thrust upward along the collision just behind the edge of the crumpled plate.

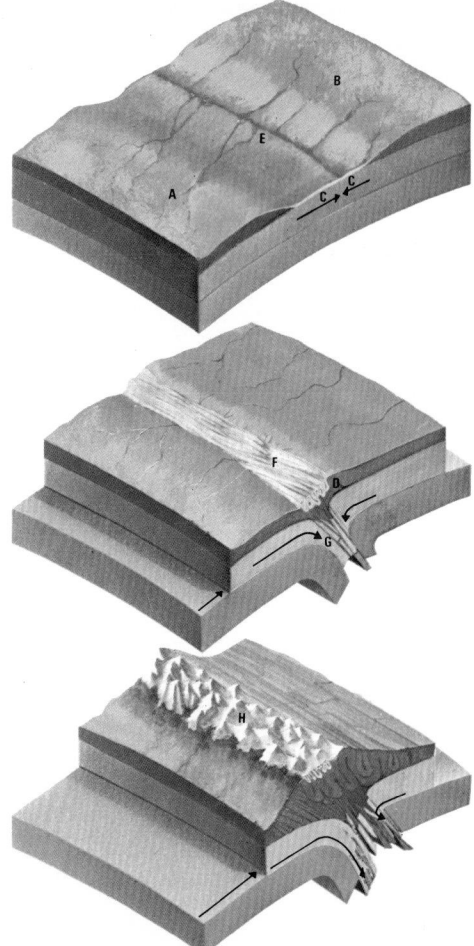

The Atmosphere

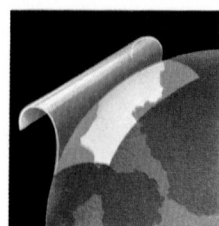

A thin coating *left*
The protective atmospheric shell around the Earth is proportionally no thicker than the skin of an apple. Gravity compresses the air so that half its mass lies within 3.5 miles (5.5 km) of the surface and all the weather within an average depth of 12 miles (20 km).

Space exploration has enabled man to stand back and take a fresh look at his Earth. Even though we, like all Earth life, have evolved to suit the Earth environment, we can see today as never before how miraculous that environment is. And by far the most important single factor in determining that environment is the atmosphere.

The Earth orbits round the Sun in a near-total vacuum. So rarefied is the interplanetary medium that it contains little heat energy, but the gas molecules that are present are vibrating so violently that their individual temperature is over 2000°C. And the surface of the Sun, at some 6000°C, would melt almost everything on the surface of the Earth, while the tenuous chromosphere around the Sun is as hot as 1,000,000°C. From the chromosphere, and from millions of other stars and heavenly objects, come radio waves. Various places in the universe, most of them far beyond the solar system, send us a penetrating kind of radiation known as cosmic rays. The Earth also receives gamma rays, X-rays and ultraviolet radiation, and from the asteroid belt in the solar system (see page 3A) comes a stream of solid material. Most of these are small micrometeorites, no more than flying specks, but the Earth also receives meteors and meteorites.

A meteorite is a substantial mass that strikes the Earth; fortunately, none has yet hit in a populous area. Apart from these extremely rare objects, every other influence from the environment that would be dangerous to life is filtered out by the atmosphere. Meteors burn up through friction as they plunge into the upper parts of the atmosphere. To avoid burning up in the same way, spacecraft designed to return to the Earth from lunar or interplanetary flight require a special re-entry shield.

Much of the ultraviolet radiation is arrested many miles above the Earth and creates ionized layers known as the ionosphere which man uses to reflect radio waves. Much of the infra-red (heat) radiation is likewise absorbed, lower down in the atmosphere, and most of the cosmic radiation is broken up by collisions far above the ground into such particles as 'mu-mesons'. Only a few cosmic rays, harmless radio waves and visible light penetrate the blanket of air to reach the planetary surface and its teeming life.

Credit for our vital atmosphere rests with the Earth's gravitational attraction, which both prevents the molecules and atoms in the atmosphere from escaping into space and also pulls them down tightly against the Earth. As a result nearly all the atmosphere's mass is concentrated in a very thin layer; three-quarters of it lies below 29000 feet (8840 m), the height of Mount Everest. The highest-flying aircraft, 19 miles (30 km) up, are above 99 per cent of the atmosphere. The total weight of the atmosphere is of the order of 5000 million million tons. In the lower parts are some 17 million million tons of water vapor.

The water vapor plays a great part in determining the weather on Earth, the only way in which the atmosphere consciously affects daily human life. All the weather is confined to the lower parts of the atmosphere below the tropopause. In this region, called the troposphere, temperature falls away sharply with increasing altitude. The Sun heats up the Earth's surface, water is evaporated from the surface of the oceans and an immensely complicated pattern of global and local weather systems is set up. Every part of the air in the troposphere is in motion. Sometimes the motion is so slow as to be barely perceptible, while on other occasions, or at the same time in other places, the air roars over the surface with terrifying force at speeds of 200 miles (320 km) per hour or more. It erodes the land, lashes the surface with rain and clogs cold regions with snow. Yet it is man's shield against dangers, an ocean of air without which we could not exist.

Characteristics of the atmosphere *right*

Basically the Earth's atmosphere consists of a layer of mixed gases covering the surface of the globe which, as a result of the Earth's gravitational attraction, increases in density as the surface is approached. But there is very much more to it than this. Temperature, composition and physical properties vary greatly through the depth of the atmosphere. The Earth's surface is assumed to lie along the bottom of the illustration, and the various major regions of the atmosphere—which imperceptibly merge into each other—are indicated by the numbers on the vertical scale on the facing page.

Exosphere (1)
This rarefied region is taken to start at a height of some 400 miles (650 km) and to merge above into the interplanetary medium. Atomic oxygen exists up to 600 mi (1000 km); from there up to about 1500 mi (2400 km) helium and hydrogen are approximately equally abundant, with hydrogen becoming dominant above 1500 mi. The highest auroras are found in this region. Traces of the exosphere extend out to at least 5000 mi (8000 km).

Ionosphere (2)
This contains electrically conducting layers capable of reflecting radio waves and thus of enabling radio signals to be received over great distances across the Earth. The major reflecting layers, designated D, E, F1 and F2, are at the approximate heights shown. Meteors burn up brightly at heights of around 100 mi (160 km). Charged particles coming in along the lines of force of the Earth's magnetic field produce aurorae in the ionosphere at high latitudes, some of them of the corona type with a series of radial rays; and the ionosphere's structure alters from day to night and according to the influence of the solar wind and incoming streams of other particles and radiation.

Stratosphere (3)
This lies above the tropopause which varies in altitude from about 10 mi (16 km) over the equator to just below 7 mi (11 km) in temperate latitudes. The lower stratosphere has a constant temperature of -56°C up to 19 mi (30 km); higher still the 'mesosphere' becomes warmer again. One of the vital properties of the stratosphere is its minute ozone content which shields the Earth life from some harmful short-wave radiations which, before the Earth's atmosphere had developed, penetrated to the surface.

Troposphere (4)
Within this relatively very shallow layer is concentrated about 80 per cent of the total mass of the atmosphere, as well as all the weather and all the Earth's life. The upper boundary of the troposphere is the tropopause, which is about 36000 ft (11000 m) above the surface in temperate latitudes; over the tropics it is higher, and therefore colder, while it is at a lower altitude over the poles. Air temperature falls uniformly with increasing height until the tropopause is reached; thereafter it remains constant in the stratosphere. Composition of the troposphere is essentially constant, apart from the vital factor of clouds and humidity.

Structure and features

Temperature   **Pressure**

	Temperature	Pressure
450mi / 720km		10^{-42}mb
400mi / 640km		10^{-37}mb
350mi / 560km		10^{-32}mb
300mi / 480km		10^{-27}mb
250mi / 400km	2227°C	10^{-22}mb
200mi / 320km		10^{-17}mb
	1487°C	
150mi / 240km	739°C	10^{-12}mb
100mi / 160km		
	-12°C	10^{-7}mb
50mi / 80km	-183°C / -63°C	10^{-2}mb
	2°C	
8mi / 11km	-38°C / -55°C / -63°C / -56°C / 15°C	10^{3}mb

Chemical composition
- Nitrogen
- Oxygen
- Argon
- Carbon dioxide
- Water vapour
- Ozone

Temperature
The mean temperature at the Earth's surface is about 15°C. As height is gained the temperature falls swiftly, to −56°C at the tropopause. It remains at this value to 19 miles (30 km), becomes warmer again, and then falls to a very low value around 60 miles (100 km). It rises once again in space.

Pressure
At sea level the pressure is some 1000 millibars, or about 14.7 pounds per square inch. The total force acting on the surface of an adult human body is thus of the order of 20 tons. But only 10 miles (16 km) above the Earth the pressure, and the atmospheric density, have both fallen by some 90 per cent.

Composition
Chemical composition of the atmosphere varies considerably with altitude. In the troposphere the mixture of nitrogen, oxygen and other gases is supplemented by water vapor, which exerts a profound influence on the weather. Ozone in the stratosphere shields life from harmful ultraviolet rays.

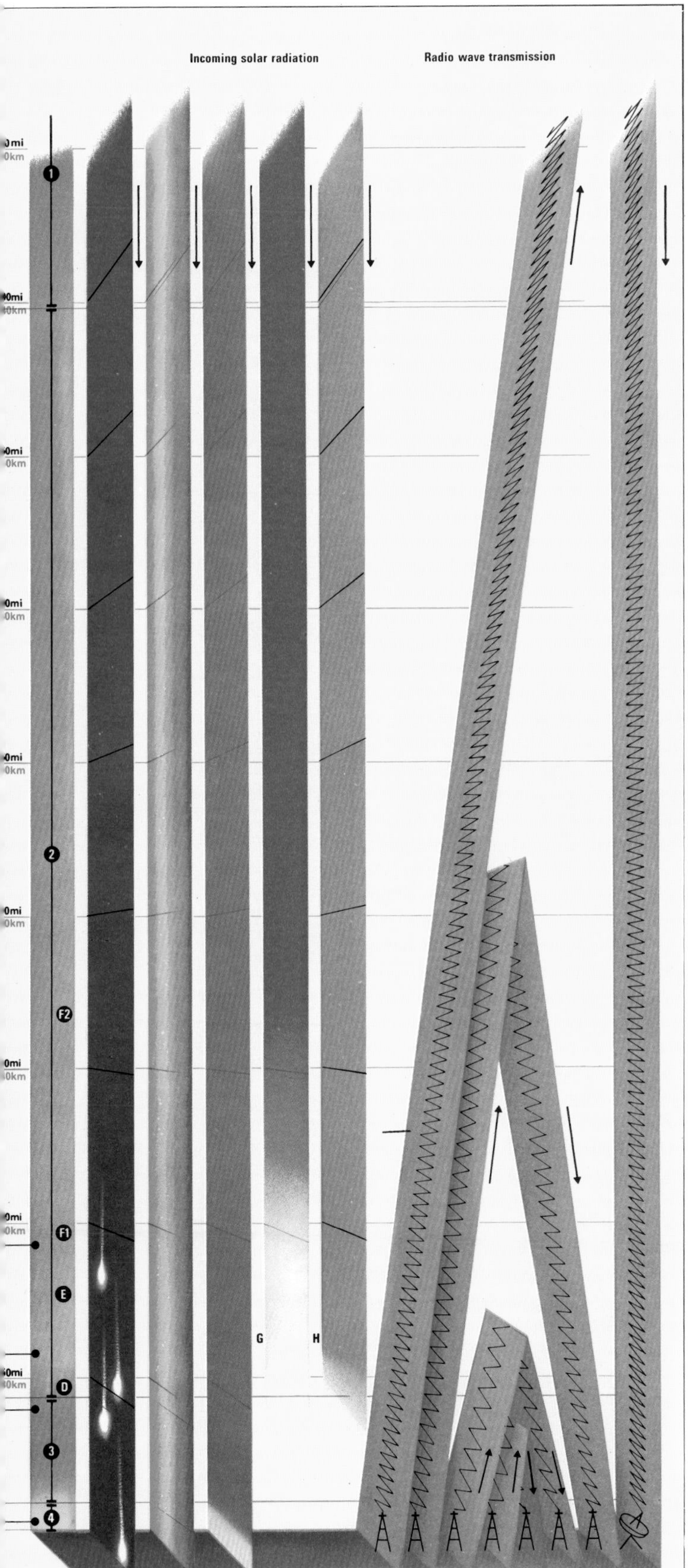

Incoming solar radiation   Radio wave transmission

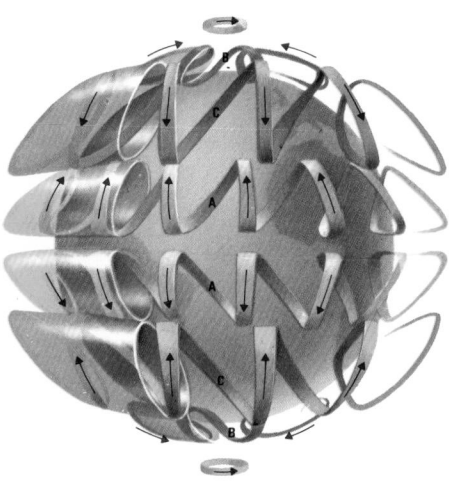

The circulation of the atmosphere *left*

The atmosphere maintains its equilibrium by transferring heat, moisture and momentum from low levels at low latitudes to high levels at high latitudes where the heat is radiated to space. This circulation appears to comprise three distinct 'cells' in each hemisphere. In the tropical (A) and polar (B) cells the circulations are thermally direct — warm air rises and cold air sinks — but the mid-latitude circulation, the Ferrel cell (C), is distorted by the polar front as shown in greater detail below.

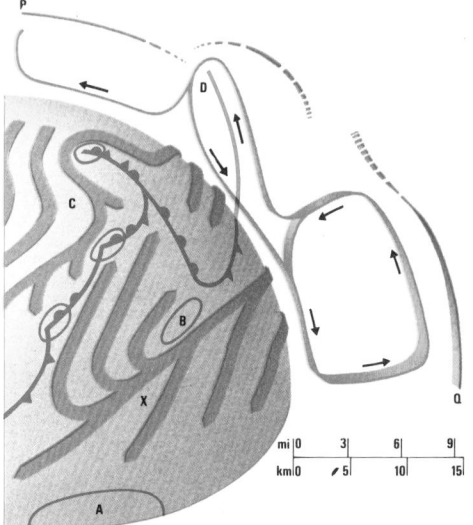

Warm front	A Area of low pressure	D Polar front
Cold front	B Area of high pressure	P Polar cell tropopause
	C Area of low pressure	Q Tropical tropopause

Frontal systems *left*

Although the figure above shows a true general picture, the actual circulation is more complicated. A portion of the Earth on a larger scale shows how frontal systems develop between the polar and tropical air masses. The tropopause, the demarcation between the troposphere in which temperature falls with height, and the strato-sphere above, is much higher in the tropics than in the polar cell. Between the cells the polar front causes constant successions of warm and cold fronts and changeable weather. Surface winds are shown, together with areas of low pressure and high pressure. The scale along the bottom, although exaggerated, indicates the greater height of the tropical tropopause compared with that in polar regions. Conventional symbols indicate warm and cold fronts.

A particle shield
The Earth is continuously bom-barded with solid particles from elsewhere in the solar system and possibly from more distant parts of the universe. Only the largest meteors (A) reach the surface. Small meteorites generally burn up through friction caused by passage through the thin air more than 40 miles (65 km) up.

A radiation shield
Most of the Sun's visible light (B) can penetrate the whole of the atmosphere right down to the Earth's surface, except where cloud intervenes. But only some of the infra-red radiation gets through (C); the rest (G) is cut off, along with the harmful ultraviolet radiation (H), by atmospheric gases.

Radio waves
Very-high-frequency radio waves (VHF) can penetrate the whole depth of the atmosphere (J), but short-wave transmissions are re-flected by the Appleton F2 layer (K). Medium (L) and long waves (M) are reflected at lower levels by the D, E or F1 layers. Yet radio waves from distant stellar sources can be received (N).

Precipitation *left*
This map shows the mean annual rain, hail and snow over the Earth.

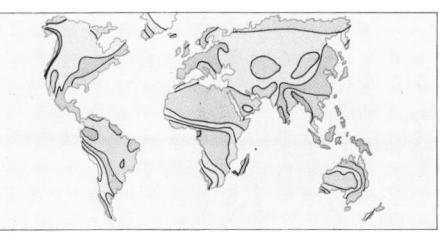

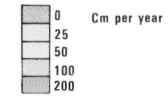

	Cm per year
0	
25	
50	
100	
200	

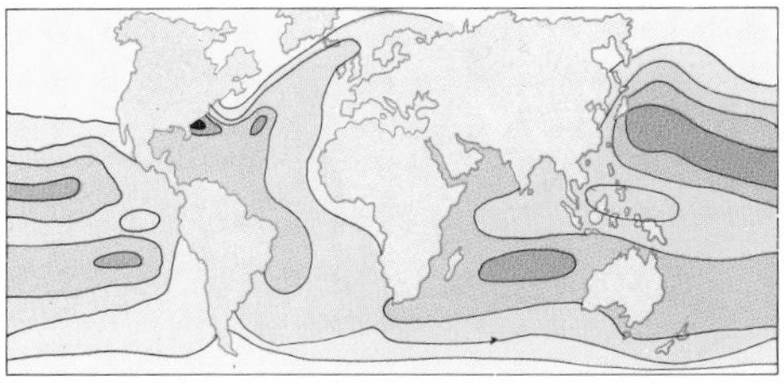

Evaporation *left*
Accurate estimates of evaporation can be made only over the oceans.

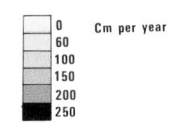

	Cm per year
0	
60	
100	
150	
200	
250	

Surface radiation *left*
Variations in heat output over the Earth's surface affect air and ocean circulations.

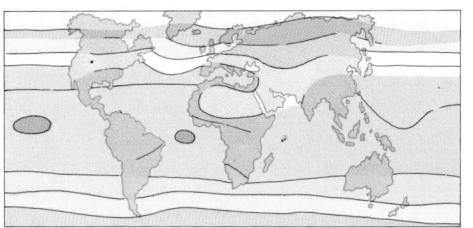

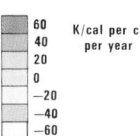

	K/cal per cm²
60	per year
40	
20	
0	
−20	
−40	
−60	

The Structure of Weather Systems

Until recently there were few scientists in the tropics or the polar regions, and the science of meteorology therefore evolved in the mid-latitudes. Likewise, the early concepts of meteorology were all based on observations of the mid-latitude atmosphere. Originally only two types of air mass were recognized: polar and tropical. Today a distinct equatorial air mass has been identified, as well as Arctic and Antarctic masses at latitudes even higher than the original polar ones. The concept of a 'front' between dissimilar air masses dates from as recently as 1919, and three years later the development of a cyclone – a large system of air rotating around an area of low pressure– was first described. Today satellite photographs have confirmed the validity of these early studies and enable the whole Earth's weather to be watched on daily computer processed photo-charts as it develops.

Why the weather varies

Anywhere in the Earth's mid-latitudes the climate is determined mainly by the frequency and intensity of the cyclones, with their frontal systems and contrasting air masses, which unceasingly alter the local temperature, wind velocity, air pressure and humidity. In turn, the frequency of the cyclonic visits is governed principally by the behavior of the long waves in the upper westerlies. When these waves change their shape and position the cyclonic depressions follow different paths. The major changes are seasonal, but significant variations also occur on a cycle of 5–6 weeks. It is still proving difficult to investigate the long wave variations. As a front passes, a fairly definite sequence of cloud, wind, humidity, temperature, precipitation and visibility can be seen. The most obvious change is the type of cloud, of which nine are shown opposite. Each cyclone contains numerous cloud types in its structure. Within these clouds several forms of precipitation can form; raindrops are the most common, but ice precipitation also forms, with snow in winter and hail in the summer when intense atmospheric instability produces towering cumulonimbus clouds topped by an 'anvil' of ice crystals.

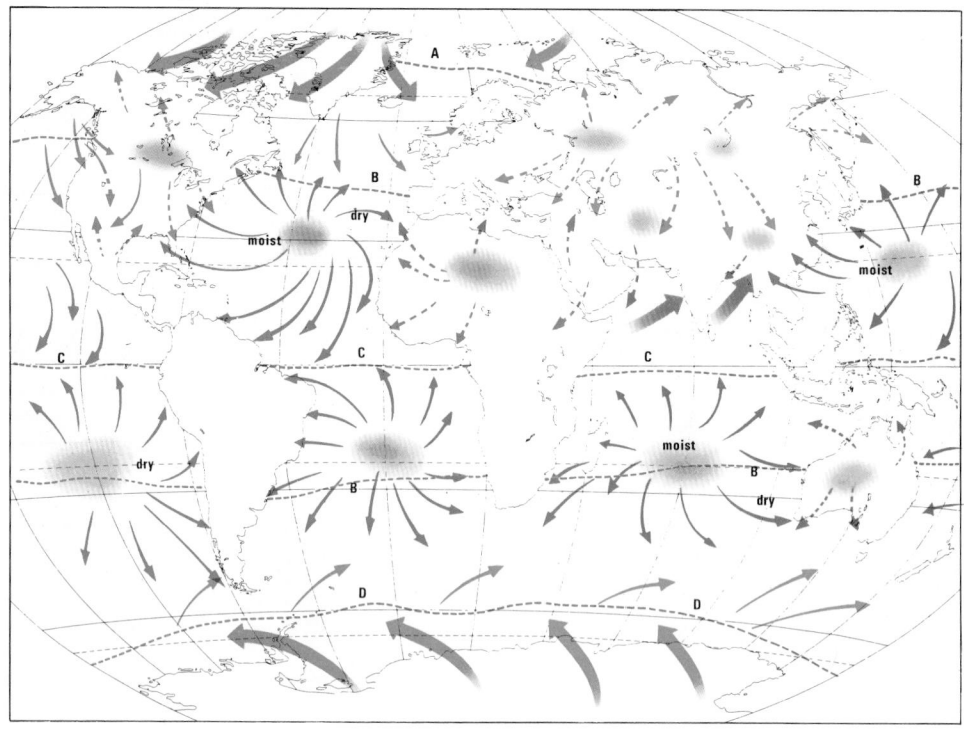

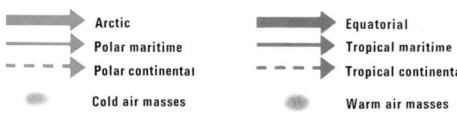

Air masses and convergences *above*

An air mass is an extensive portion of the atmosphere in which, at any given altitude, the moisture and temperature are almost uniform. Such a mass generally arises when the air rests for a time on a large area of land or water which has uniform surface conditions. There are some 20 source regions throughout the world. A second pre-requisite is large-scale subsidence and divergence over the source region. The boundary between air masses is a convergence or front. (A Arctic, B Polar, C Equatorial, D Antarctic.) The polar front is particularly important in governing much of the weather in mid-latitudes. The pattern depicted provides a raw framework for the world's weather. It is considerably modified by the air's vertical motion, by surface friction, land topography, the Earth's rotation and other factors.

→ Arctic	→ Equatorial
→ Polar maritime	→ Tropical maritime
--→ Polar continental	--→ Tropical continental
Cold air masses	Warm air masses

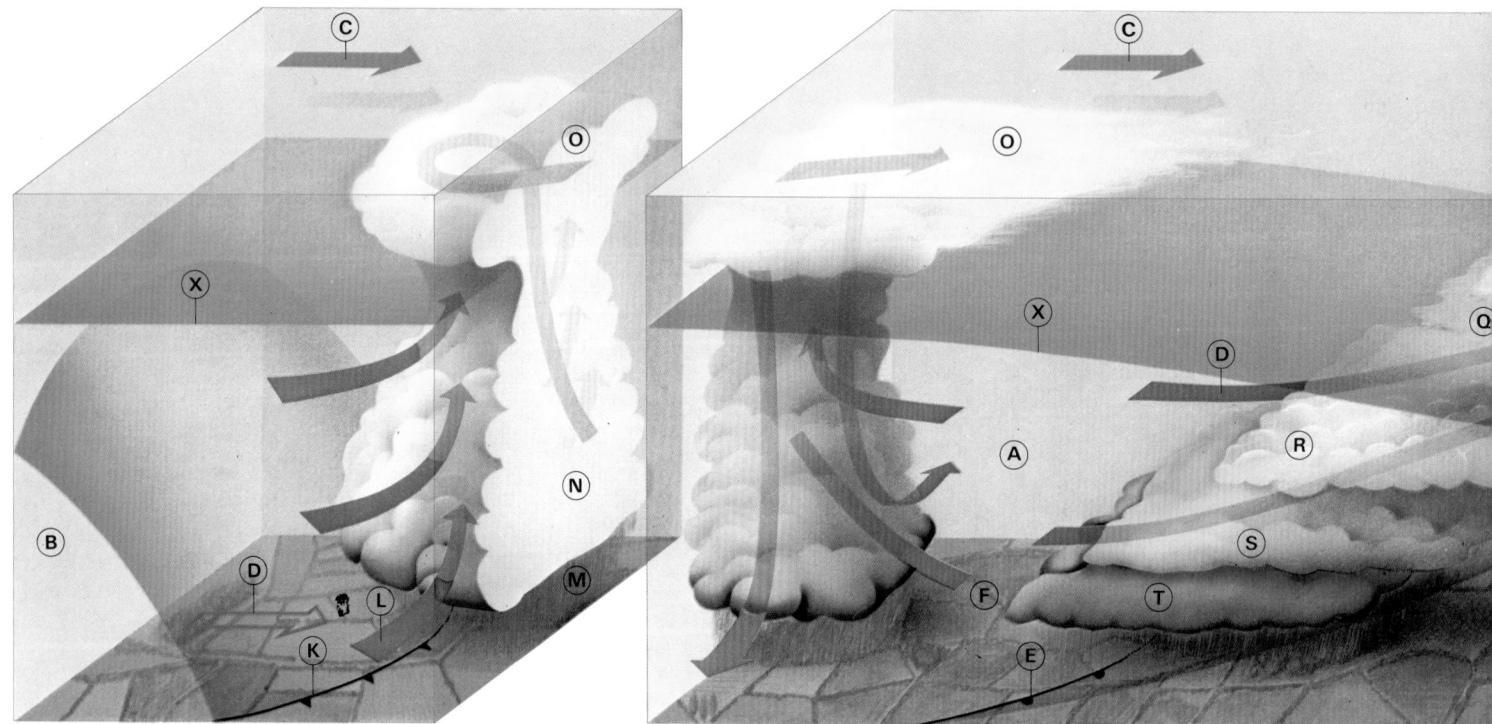

Anatomy of a depression

Seen in cross section, a mature mid-latitude cyclone forms a large system which always follows basically the same pattern. Essentially it comprises a wedge of warm air (A) riding over, and being undercut by; cold air masses (B). (Page 23A shows full development.) The entire cyclone is moving from left to right, and this is also the basic direction of the winds (C) and (D). To an observer on the ground the warm front (E) may take 12-24 hours to pass, followed by the warm sector (F) perhaps 180 miles (300 km) wide.

The cold front (K)

As this frontal zone, about one mile (1-2 km) wide, passes overhead the direction of the wind alters (L) and precipitation (M) pours from cumuliform clouds (N). If the air above the frontal surface is moving upwards then giant cumulonimbus (O) may grow, with heavy rain or hail. Cirrus clouds then form in air above the freezing level (X). Sometimes the front is weak with subsidence of air predominant on both sides of it. In this case there is little cloud development and near-zero surface precipitation.

The warm front (E)

The front is first heralded by cirrus clouds (P), followed by cirrostratus (Q), altocumulus (R), stratus (S) and finally nimbostratus (T). The descending layers are due partly to humidity distribution and partly to the warm air rising over the sloping frontal surface. Precipitation may be steady and last for hours. Alternatively some warm fronts have a predominantly subsident air motion, with the result that there is only a little thin cloud and negligible precipitation. Air temperature increases as the front passes.

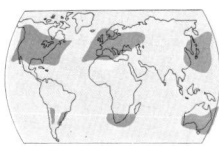

Development of a depression *right*

Most mid-latitude depressions (cyclones) develop on the polar front (map above). An initial disturbance along this front causes a fall in pressure and a confluence at the surface, deforming the front into a wave (1, right). The confluence and thermal structure accelerate the cyclonic spin into a fully developed depression (2). The depression comprises a warm sector bounded by a sharp cold front (A) and warm front (B). The fast-moving cold front overtakes the warm front and eventually the warm sector is lifted completely clear of the ground resulting in an occlusion (3). The continued overlapping of the two wedges of cold air eventually fills up the depression and causes it to weaken and disperse (4). By the time this occurs the warm sector has been lifted high in the atmosphere. In this way, depressions fulfil an essential role in transferring heat from low to high levels and from low to high latitudes.

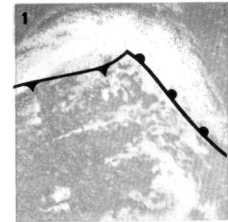

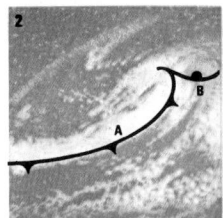

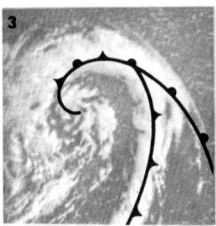

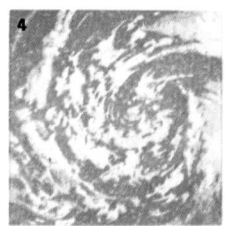

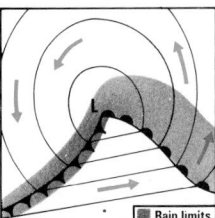

Plan view *left*

A developing cyclone will appear this way on the 'synoptic' weather chart. Lines of equal pressure (isobars) are nearly straight within the warm sector but curve sharply in the cold sector to enclose the low pressure focus of the system.

Examples of the three major cloud groups

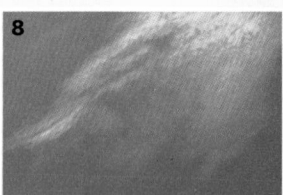

Low cloud *top*

Stratocumulus (1) is a grey or white layer of serried masses or rolls. Cumulus (2) is the familiar white cauliflower. It can develop into cumulonimbus (3), a large, threatening cloud, characterized by immense vertical development topped by an 'anvil' of ice crystals. These produce heavy rain or hail.

Medium cloud *left*

Nimbostratus (4) is a ragged grey layer producing drizzle or snow. Altocumulus (5) comprises rows of 'blobs' of ice and water forming a sheet at a height of 1.5-4.5 miles (2-7 km). Altostratus (6) occurs at similar heights but is a water/ice sheet either uniform, striated or fibrous in appearance.

High cloud *right*

Cirrus (7) is the highest cloud and appears as fine white ice filaments at 8–10 miles (13–16 km), often hair-like or silky. Cirro-cumulus (8) forms into thin white layers made up of very numerous icy globules or ripples. Cirrostratus (9) is a high-level veil of ice crystals often forming a halo round the Sun.

Four kinds of precipitation

Rain
Most rain results from the coalescence of microscopic droplets (1) which are condensed from vapor onto nuclei in the atmosphere. The repeated merging of small droplets eventually forms water droplets (2) which are too large to be kept up by the air currents. Rain drops may also form from melting of ice crystals in the atmosphere.

Glaze
In completely undisturbed air it is possible for water to remain liquid even at temperatures well below freezing point. So air above the freezing level (X) may contain large quantities of this 'supercooled water'. This can fall as rain and freeze on impact with objects, coating them with ice.

Dry snow
The origin of snow differs from that of rain in that the vapor droplets (1) settle on microscopic crystals of ice and freeze. The result is the growth of a white or translucent ice crystal having a basically hexagonal form (photomicrograph below). The crystals then agglomerate into flakes (2).

Hail
In cumulonimbus clouds raindrops (formed at 1,2) may encounter up-currents strong enough to lift them repeatedly back through a freezing level (X). On each pass (3) a fresh layer of ice is collected. The hailstone builds up like an onion until it is so heavy (4) that it falls to the ground.

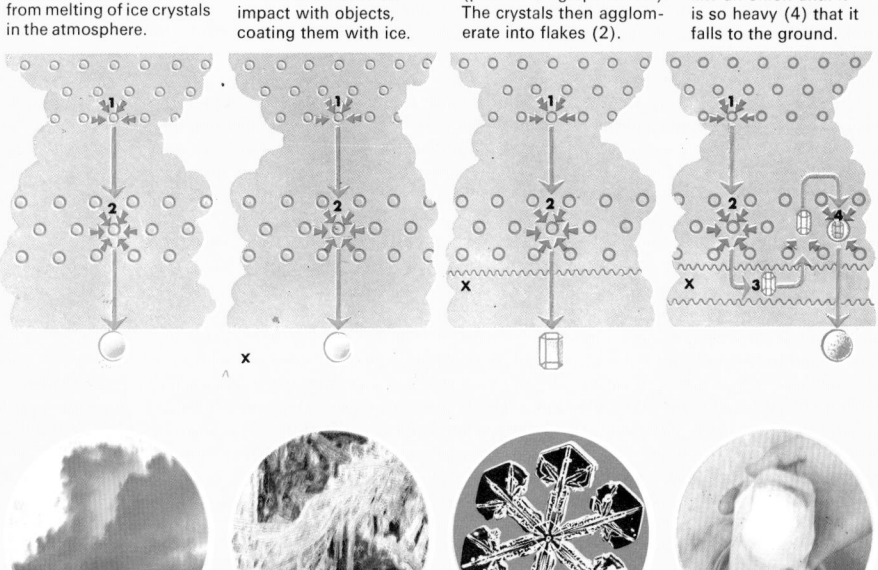

Tropical weather, between the Tropic of Cancer at 23½°N and the Tropic of Capricorn at 23½°S, differs fundamentally from that at higher latitudes. Overall there is a considerable surplus of heat, giving high mean temperatures; and the 'Coriolis force' due to the Earth's rotation, which deflects air currents to the right in the northern hemisphere and to the left in the southern, is almost non-existent. As a result, tropical weather hardly ever contains distinct air masses, fronts and cyclones. Instead the region is occupied mainly by the tradewinds, which are laden with moisture and potentially unstable. Thunderstorms are frequent, especially over land, and the pattern of land and sea leads to local anomalies, such as the monsoon of southeast Asia. This particular anomaly, too big to be called local, changes the prevailing wind over a vast area. It is superimposed on the apparently simple global circulation near the Equator.

Polar weather

At very high latitudes the atmosphere radiates heat to space. The Arctic is essentially an ocean surrounded by land, whereas the Antarctic is land surrounded by ocean. The land around the Arctic quickly takes up solar heat but the southern oceans transfer heat to deeper water to make the Antarctic the coldest region on Earth. Because the air is so intensely cold it can hold very little moisture, so the south polar region is a freezing desert with exceptionally clean air.

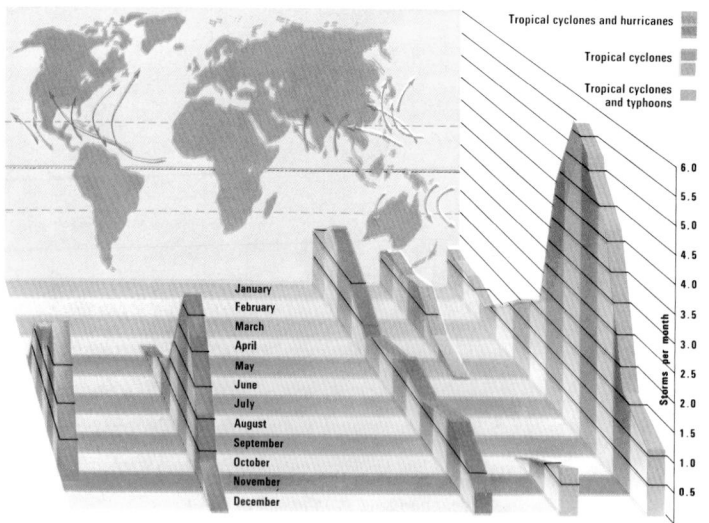
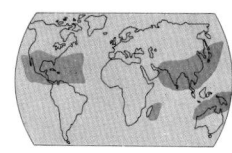

Tropical cyclones and hurricanes
Tropical cyclones
Tropical cyclones and typhoons

January
February
March
April
May
June
July
August
September
October
November
December

The afflicted areas *above*
Tropical cyclones build up over the warm oceans, and many of them—about half over the Caribbean and four-fifths over the western Pacific—develop into hurricanes. Precisely how a hurricane is triggered is still not fully known, but there is no doubt it is a thermodynamic engine on a giant scale which either misfires completely or runs with catastrophic effect.

Hurricanes *left*
These violent storms form over ocean warm enough (27°C) to maintain strong vertical circulation, except for the belt closest to the equator where lack of a Coriolis force prevents cyclonic spin from building up. Condensation of the moisture taken up from the ocean surface releases latent heat and thus provides energy to drive the storm. The daily energy can be equivalent to that released by several hundred H bombs. Despite their formidable power hurricanes are penetrated by specially equipped aircraft whose mission is both to provide early warning and to gather data enabling the storm's mechanism to be better understood.

Hurricane structure
A Spiral rainbands.
B High-altitude winds.
C Easterly tradewinds.

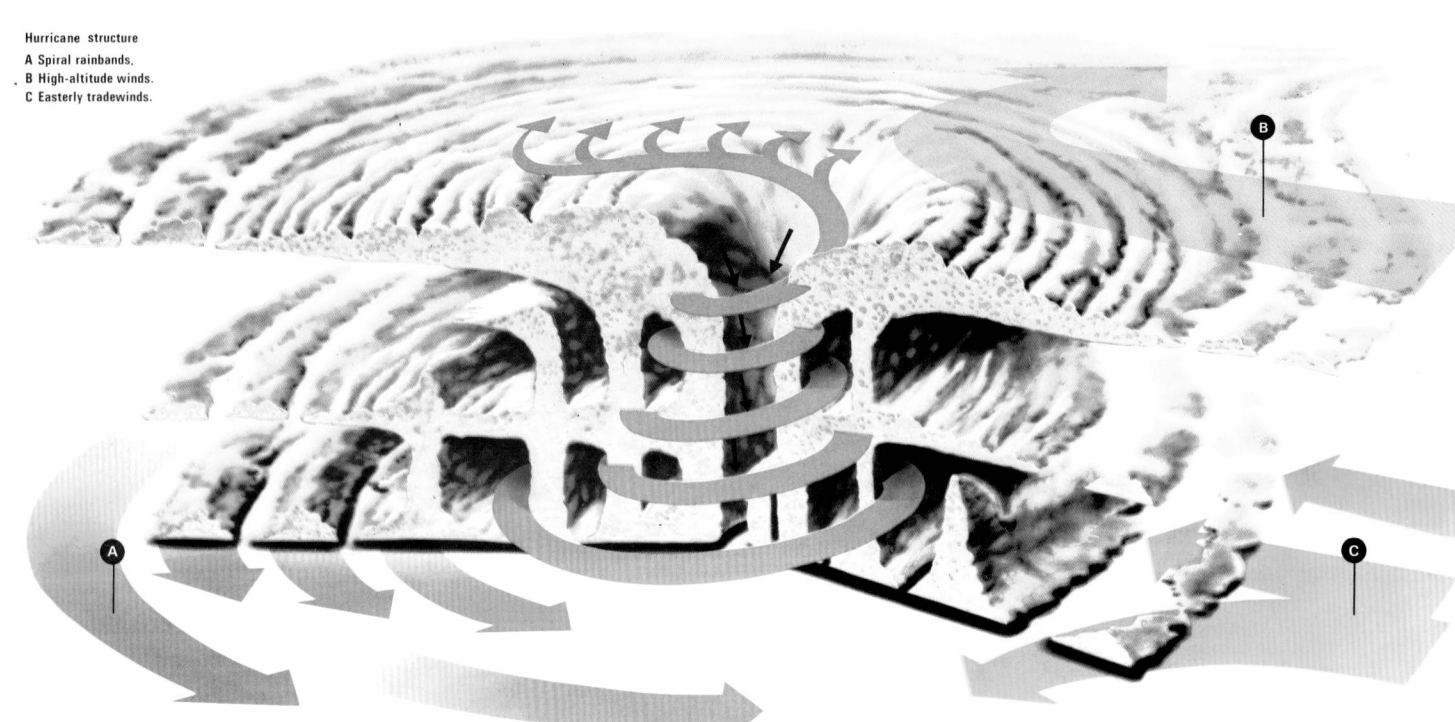

Structure of a hurricane *above*

A hurricane consists of a huge swirl of clouds rotating around a calm center known as the eye. This cyclonic circulation may be as much as 250 miles (400 km) in diameter, and it extends right through the troposphere which is about 9-12 miles (15-20 km) thick. The clouds, nearly all of the cumulonimbus type, are arranged in bands around the eye. The largest form the wall of the eye and it is here that precipitation is heaviest. The whole system is usually capped by streamers of cirrus. Wind speeds range from about 110 mph (180 kmh) at 20–25 miles (30–40 km) from the eye wall down to about 45 mph (72 kmh) at a distance of 90 miles (140 km). Warm, calm air in the eye is sucked downwards.

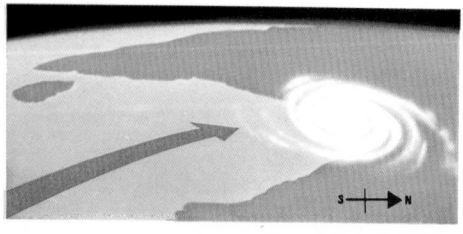

S ← → N

Nature's giant energy
left and above
A hurricane such as that which killed over half a million people in Bangladesh in November 1970 (left) dissipates thousands of millions of horsepower. The spiral structure is clearly visible from a satellite (above).

Hurricane development *below*

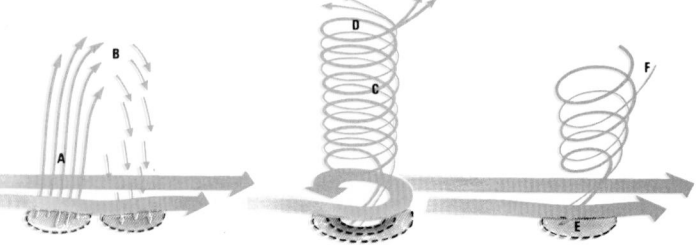

Birth of a storm.
Hurricanes usually have their origin in a low-pressure disturbance directing part of an easterly wind (A) to the north. The air rises to some 40,000 ft (12 km) where it releases heat and moisture (B) before descending.

The young hurricane
The Earth's rotation imparts a twist to the rising column which becomes a cylinder (C) spiralling round a relatively still core (D). Warm, moist air off the sea picks up speed and feeds energy at a very high rate to intensify the rising column.

Dying of starvation
The hurricane does not begin to die until it moves over colder water or over land (E). Then, cut off from its supply of energy, the speed of the spiralling winds falls away. The eye begins to fill with clouds, the hurricane expands (F) and dissipates.

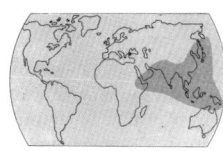

The monsoon *right*
In principle the processes which give rise to the monsoon are the same as those causing a sea breeze but on a vastly larger scale in space and time. In southeast Asia each May and June warm, moist air streams in from the south causing heavy rain and occasional violent storms. In winter the circulation is reversed and winds come mainly from high pressure over Siberia. In detail the monsoon is considerably modified by the Himalayas and the positions of the waves in the westerlies in the atmosphere's upper levels, but its mechanism is not fully known.

Duststorm *right*
In arid regions strong wind circulations can become filled with dust and extend over considerable areas. The storm typically arrives in the form of an advancing wall of dust possibly five miles (8 km) long and 1000 ft (300 m) high. The haboobs of the Sudan, a recurrent series of storms, are most frequent from May to September and can approach from almost any direction. They usually occur, after a few days of rising temperature and falling pressure, where the soil is very dry. Dust-devils, small local whirlwinds forming pillars of sand, can dot the land.

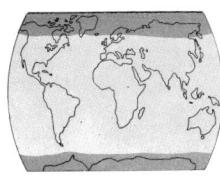

Nacreous cloud *right*
At high latitudes, when the Sun is below the horizon, these clouds sometimes come into view as fine filmy areas containing regions of bright spectral color. They look rather like a form of cirrus, but are far higher. Nacreous cloud in the Antarctic—such as that in the photograph, taken in Grahamland—has been measured at heights from 8.5 to 19 miles (13.5-30 km), and Scandinavian observations lie in the 20-30 km range. Despite their great altitude, nacreous clouds are undoubtedly formed as a result of air being lifted by passage across high mountains.

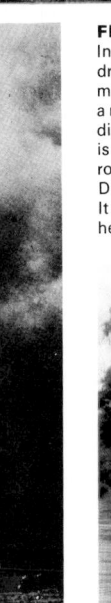

The monsoon seasons *below*
In summer an intense low-pressure area over northwest India overcomes the equatorial low pressure region. In winter an intense high over central Asia blows cold, dry air in the reverse direction.

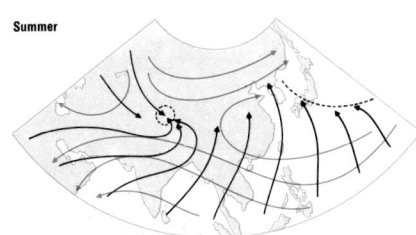

Summer

Winds near sea level → Winds at about 20,000 ft (6000 m) →

Winter

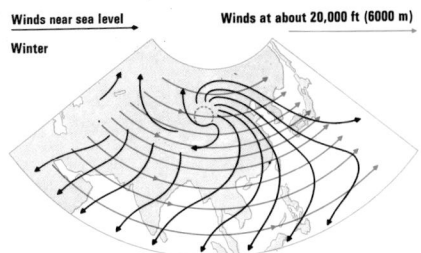

Flash flood *below*
In historic times floods have drowned millions. Even in a modern advanced country a major flood is a national disaster. The scene below is a flooded crossing on the road from Lake Grace to Dumbleyung, W Australia. It is a 'flash flood', caused by heavy rain and poor drainage.

After the hurricane *left*
Whereas a tornado can cause buildings to explode, as a result of the sudden violent difference in pressure between inside and outside, a hurricane just blows. But the wind can demolish sound houses, such as this residence in Biloxi, Mississippi.

Blown snow *above*
When the wind blows in polar regions it soon begins to lift dry powdery snow and ice granules from the surface. As the wind increases in strength this drifting snow forms a thicker layer, as at this British base in Antarctica. When the entrained material reaches eye level it is known as blown snow. Any further rise in wind velocity swiftly increases the concentration of particulate matter, causing the visibility rapidly to fall to zero. When this is the case the term blizzard is appropriate, as it also is when high winds are combined with a heavy snowfall.

The Record in the Rocks

All the past history of the Earth since the original formation of the crust is there to be discovered in the rocks existing today if only the appropriate techniques are used to find it. Sedimentary, igneous and metamorphic – the three basic types of rock – all have an enormous amount of information stored within them on such diverse aspects of the Earth's history as, for example, the variations of past climates in space and in time, the incidence of ice ages and the positions of former mountain ranges. The migrations of the ancient geo-magnetic poles at different periods of time can be discovered by studying some sedimentary and igneous rocks, while other types can yield their ages of formation or metamorphism – their changed character over long periods. The prevailing wind directions over certain regions, the direction of stream flow in river deltas that have long since vanished, or the ways in which the ice flowed in some past ice age are all there to be discovered. So are the past distributions of land and sea, areas of deposition, periods of uplift and the raising of great mountain chains (see pages 12–13A and 18-19A). Even lightning strikes millions of years old can be clearly seen.

The first task of the geologist is to make a map showing the positions and relative ages of the various rock types in a region. It is around this basic information incorporated into the geological map that all else is built, whether it is to be studies of the geological history and evolution of the region, or detailed investigations of the flora and fauna, or any of many other lines of research – such as the disentangling of various periods of deformation which have affected the region during which the rocks may have been folded or faulted (foot of this page) or eroded down to sea level. Two of the most important methods of dating, by which the age of rock is determined, are the study of fossils and the use of radiometric methods in which age is calculated by analyzing radioactive minerals having a known half-life (opposite page). Using a combination of 'correlation' techniques and either method of dating it is possible for a skilled geologist to compare the relative time sequences of geological events in any regions in the world.

A geological map *below*
A geological map records the outcrop pattern and the structural features of each region as they are today, corresponding with the final stage of the reconstruction—right.

How the story unfolds
right
The complex 3500 million year story of the rocks is very far from being superficially obvious. Even a skilled geologist can do no more than study the land as it is today, plot a geological map and then try to think backward over periods of millions of years in an endeavor to determine the sequences which produced the present terrain. On the right is depicted such a sequence, which might reasonably be arrived at after studying the map below, left. The history begins (A) with the landmass rising and the sea retreating, leaving behind 'off-lap' sediments. The landmass continues to rise and is folded by compressive forces, the fold tops then being eroded (B). Over a long period the landmass then subsides and tilts; the sea once more advances, laying down 'on-lap' sediments (C). Then a great upheaval causes the sea to retreat completely. The landmass is strongly uplifted and faulted, and the higher mass is at once attacked by erosion (D). Continued erosion gradually reduces the region to a more or less common level. Rivers, formed at stage C, carry eroded materials away and deposit them at lower levels (left side of E). Finally, the northeast part of the region is invaded by an extrusive mass of volcanic material. Of course, the processes of change would continue even now.

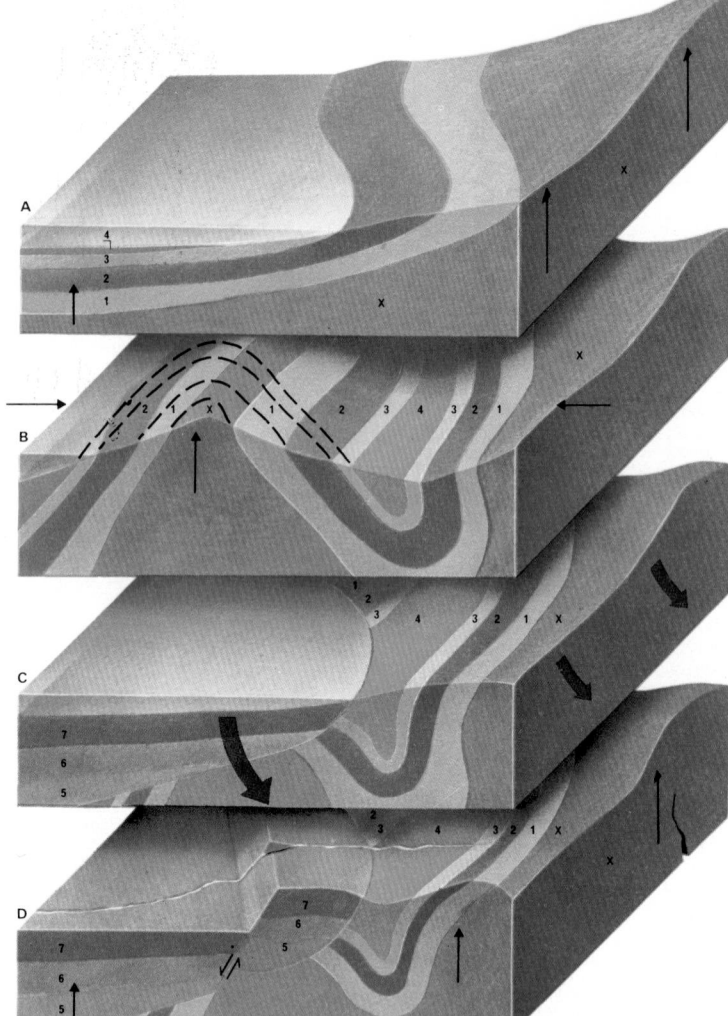

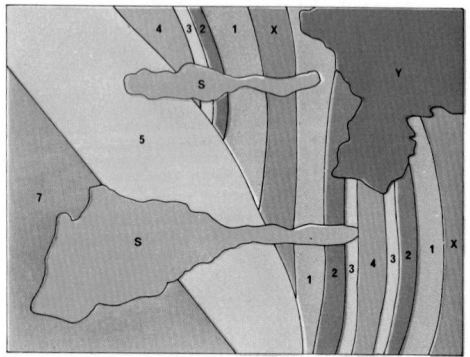

S	River sediments
Y	Volcanic extrusion
7	
6	Later sedimentary sequence
5	Period of erosion
4	
3	Early sedimentary sequence
2	
1	Period of erosion
X	Older basement rocks

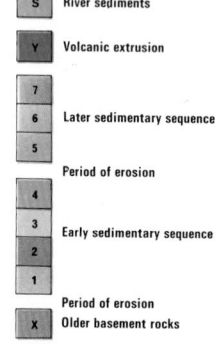

The language of geology
Plane of movement of a normal fault (1) displacing strata to right (downthrow side) relative to left (upthrow side).

Block of strata (2) dropped between two tensional faults forming a rift valley. Other strata are compressional.

Normal anticline (3) and syncline (4) with symmetrically dipping limbs on either side of the axial plane of the strata.

Positions of the axial planes (5, 6) passing through an asymmetrical anticline (5) and an asymmetrical syncline (6).

Compressional reversed fault (7). In this case the left side of the fault is over-riding basically horizontal strata on the right.

Monoclinal fold (8), with a relatively steep limb separating basically horizontal areas of strata at two levels.

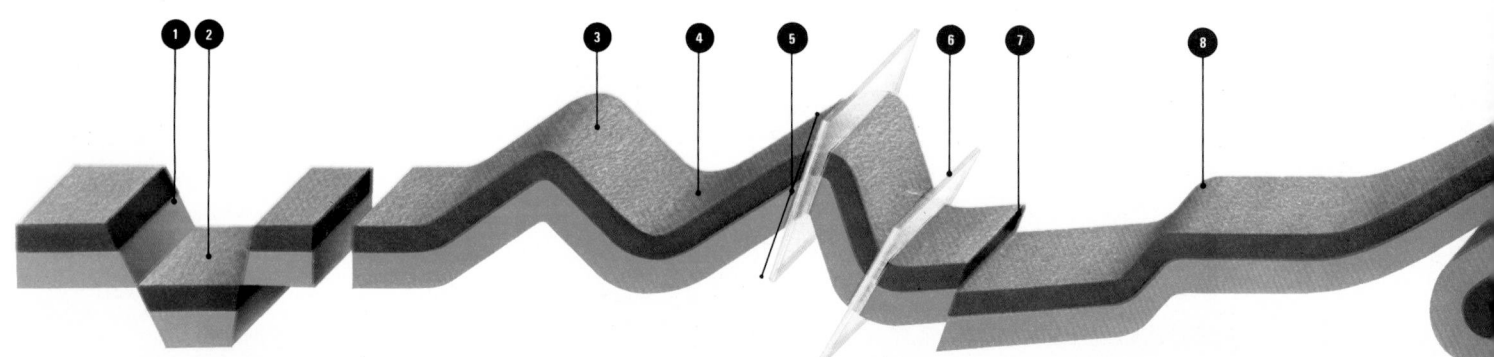

Geological dating

The relative dating of geological strata is found from the sequence in which the layers were deposited, the oldest being at the base of a local sequence and the youngest at the top. On this basis, together with correlations over wide areas based on the fossil evidence of the forms of life at different stages of the 'geological column', the main periods and sub-divisions can be worked out.

Prior to the Cambrian, the oldest epoch of the Paleozoic era (see scale at right), evidence of life is seldom found in the rocks. The extremely primitive earliest forms of life have generally not been preserved in the form of fossils, and so correlations by palaeontological methods cannot be applied to the Precambrian.

In recent years the progressive evolution of radio-metric dating has enabled geologists to assign actual dates to the relative sequences of strata. Since the formation of the Earth's crust various isotopes have been present in it which are radioactive, spon-taneously decaying over a precisely fixed period of time into a different element. For example a large number of geological dates have been based on the decay of potassium (K^{40}) to argon (A^{40}) and on that of rubidium (Rb^{87}) to strontium (Sr^{87}). The manner in which these valuable geological time-clocks decay over many millions of years is depicted below. No radioactive isotope is ever completely used up; millions of years later atoms are still present of both the original isotope and the end-product of its disintegration.

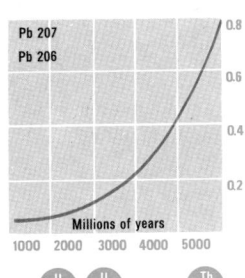

Half-life *left*
Radioactive materials decay according to a law. Each isotope has a characteristic half-life, the time required for the number of radioactive atoms to decay to half the original number. The half-life for each element is unalterable.

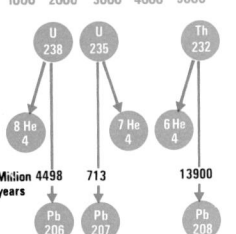

Degeneration
above and left
Some of the isotopes, shown above with their half-lives and end-products can be used for dating over the whole age of the Earth. For more recent dating, radio-carbon with a half-life of 5570 years is used (left).

1 Neutron
2 Nitrogen 14
3 Proton
4 Carbon 14
5 Nitrogen 14
6 β particle

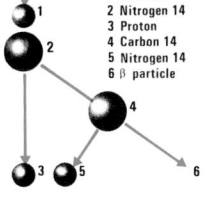

Overturned anticline (9) overlying an overturned syncline in a system distinguished by isoclinal (almost parallel) limbs.

Plane of thrusting (10) causes the overturned anticline (11) to ride over lower strata in form of a horizontally displaced 'nappe'.

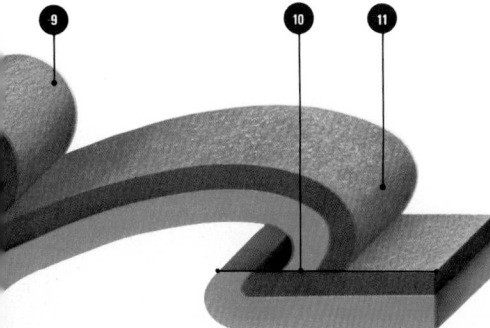

Million years — Major periods:
Cenozoic · Mesozoic · Palaeozoic · Upper Proterozoic · Lower Proterozoic · Archaean · Katarchaean · Oldest known crust · formation of the earth

500 · 1000 · 1500 · 2000 · 2500 · 3000 · 3500 · 4000 · 4500

Period scale / Million years:
65 · 100 · 136 · 190 · 200 · 225 · 280 · 300 · 345 · 395 · 400 · 430 · 500 · 570 · 600

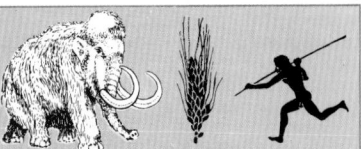

Quaternary
This most recent period of geological history leads up to the appearance of man and the present day. Changes of climate took place which brought on the great ice ages with glacial periods alternating with warmer sequences between them. And, of course, the period is still in progress.

Tertiary
A complex history of changes took place, each epoch of the Tertiary period from Paleocene to Pliocene showing a diverse sequence of volcanism and mountain-building in different regions. Shallow seas alternated with sub-tropical delta flats harboring the precursors of today's life.

Cretaceous
The Tethys Sea spread over large areas of the adjacent continents. Fossil evidence reveals a diverse flora and fauna. The South Atlantic reached a width of some 1900 miles (3000 km) and only Antarctica and Australia and the northern lands of the North Atlantic remained unseparated.

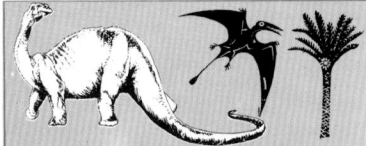

Jurassic
The North Atlantic had opened to a width of some 600 miles (1000 km). Sedimentary deposits formed marginal belt. around the continents which had separated, and deeper-water sediments were deposited in the Tethys Sea. Extensive eruption of basalts accompanied the rifting of the South Atlantic.

Triassic
This was the period in which the continental drift began. The progressive opening of the North Atlantic was accompanied by rift-valley faulting and large outpourings of basalt along the eastern seaboard of what is today North America. Gondwanaland in the south began to break up.

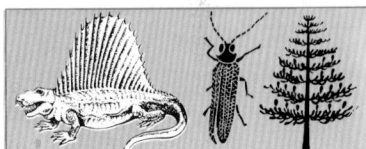

Permian
Many areas were characterized by arid or semi-arid climates, with frequent salt lakes giving rise to evaporite deposits and red desert sandstones. Much volcanic activity took place on a local scale. This was the last period in which Pangaea remained a single continental mass. New flora were abundant.

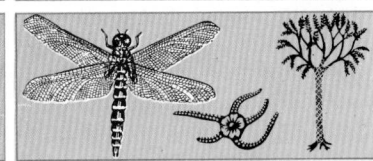

Carboniferous
Extensive forest and deltaic swamp conditions led to the eventual formation of coal basins in North America and Europe. Phases of folding and mountain formation occurred in many places. In Gondwanaland widespread glaciation occurred, with glaciers radiating from a great central ice-cap.

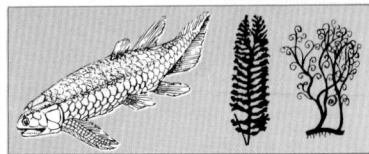

Devonian
Large areas of arid continental and sandstone deposits formed, partly as the products of erosion of the mountains formed previously. Intervening basins of shallow sea or lagoonal deposits occurred, with abundant fossil fish. Distinct faunal provinces have been recognized from this period.

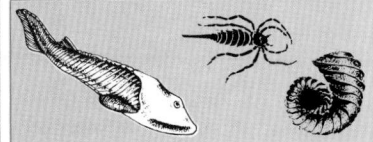

Silurian
In this period further widespread basins of thick sedimentary deposits were laid down. Many of these are characterized by the abundance of marine fossils, including corals. The Caledonian mountains were formed in Laurasia in which enormous volumes of granitic rocks were later emplaced.

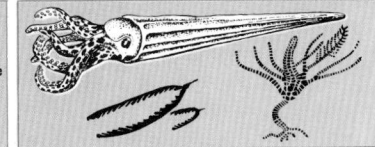

Ordovician
Graptolites and trilobites continued to be important forms of marine life. Thick marine sediments continued to be laid down, and there were extensive and widespread outbursts of volcanic activity. In some regions deformation and uplift of the rocks created major mountain ranges.

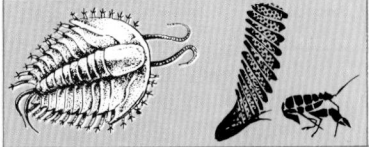

Cambrian
Rocks of this period contain the earliest fossilized remnants of more complex forms of life such as graptolites, brachiopods, trilobites and gastropods. In many regions the Cambrian period was characterized by the deposition of thick sequences of sedimentary rocks, usually on an eroded basement.

Precambrian
By far the longest period of geological time is included in the Precambrian. This encom-passes a complex history of sedimentation, mountain-building, volcanism, and granitic intrusions. Precambrian rocks form base-ments to many sedimentary deposits, and make up the nuclei of continents.

Digging for Man's History

In 1833 Charles Lyell courageously proposed that the fragments of bones of animals and men that persistently cropped up in deep geological strata could mean only one thing: that the Earth had been created long before the date of 4004 BC accepted by Christianity. Since then practically the whole of our knowledge of man's early development has come from systematic digging. At first a lone archaeologist could do the whole job, but today digging for early man involves a team of specialized archaeologists, geologists, technologists and laboratory workers. They hope to identify everything significant, study it in relation to its resting place, the history of the region and nearby finds, and also subject chosen items to detailed laboratory tests – such as accurate age determination by the potassium/argon method (p.27A). A major dig needs experts on rocks, on soils and on plant pollen.

Although there are remarkable instances of well-preserved human bodies being found (for example, in peat bogs) and of woolly mammoths whose flesh could be eaten after a million years in frozen Siberia, almost all archaeology rests on bones and on man's artifacts. Gradually, from small fragments of jaw, teeth, skull and other bones, it has been possible to piece together what appears to be a fairly complete history of human evolution. The artist can then cover a deduced skeleton with tissue, as has been done in these pages. But pigmentation of skin and degree of hairiness is still a matter for conjecture.

Among the significant factors studied in early man are his brain size, jaw structure, posture and locomotion. Today's great apes have a stooping, occasionally four-legged posture. So did ape-men from 20 million down to five million years ago; then, gradually, the hominid line learned to walk upright. Its members also learned to use tools, and to make them progressively better. Even later, true men began to leave behind evidence of their growing culture in their burials, their artifacts and their art. All these things can be studied in bone caves, such as the imaginary one illustrated on the right, and in excavation sites.

The cave in use
The cave is modeled after European examples of the Upper Paleolithic period of the order of 25000 years ago. It was at about this time that cave paintings appear to have become widespread. The river was then close to its present level, but the rock falls and piles of debris were still to come.

A bone cave *above and right*
From about 100,000 years ago caves provided many types of early men with a ready-made refuge. Probably most of these caves still exist. Although many are buried under later strata, and virtually all are greatly changed by subsequent developments, it is still possible with experience to read the message contained in them.

A burrow in the cave
Here a small animal has burrowed into the floor. It was deflected sideways by the hard flowstone until it could continue on down, throwing fossil bones up on to the floor above. Finally it died at the end of its burrow.

A buzzard's nest?
Just inside the lip of the cave mouth a bird of prey built its nest. Directly beneath it on the slope of the rock debris are scattered small rodent bones.

River level
In general, the lowest geological sediments are the oldest, but it is unwise to jump to this conclusion. In this hypothetical cave the earliest of all the deposits is a river terrace A above the cave on the hillside, indicating that the whole cave was originally submerged. At about this period insoluble limestone residue was settling on the cave floor at B. As the river cut its valley its level fell to C, leaving silt bed D. Continued deepening of the valley brought the river to its present level, leaving the cave dry and eroding the thick layer of silt at the mouth of the cave.

An obstructed mouth
Early man sheltered in the mouth of the cave and lit fires there for warmth and to cook food. The ashes of these fires gradually accumulated in three main layers, each denoting a long period of use. The 'contemporary' inset illustrates the third of these periods. Later the cave was abandoned by man and the mouth gradually became blocked by a pile of rock debris.

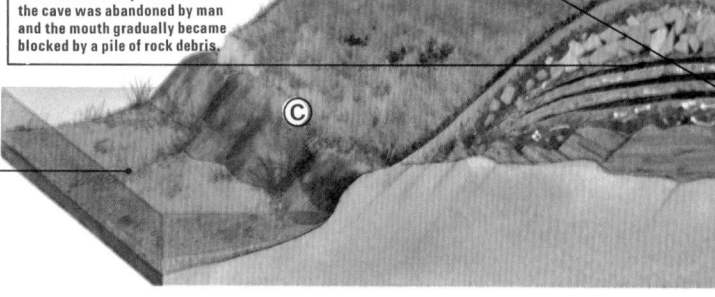

Mesolithic
About 10,000 years ago
About 20000 years ago the great ice sheets began slowly to recede, a process that is still continuing. As the climate grew warmer the Late Paleolithic people gave way to the Mesolithic (transitional) about the year 8000 BC. Milder conditions allowed man to exploit the rivers and seas, using fishing nets and even elaborate barricades and weirs made of woven saplings. The family had by now become a firm social unit, while people also explored the territory of their neighbors. For the first time there is evidence of large groups combining in habitation, hunting, art and making useful articles. Although farming of crops and animals had yet to come, the Mesolithic period saw a great enrichment of life and—probably—the development of a social conscience.

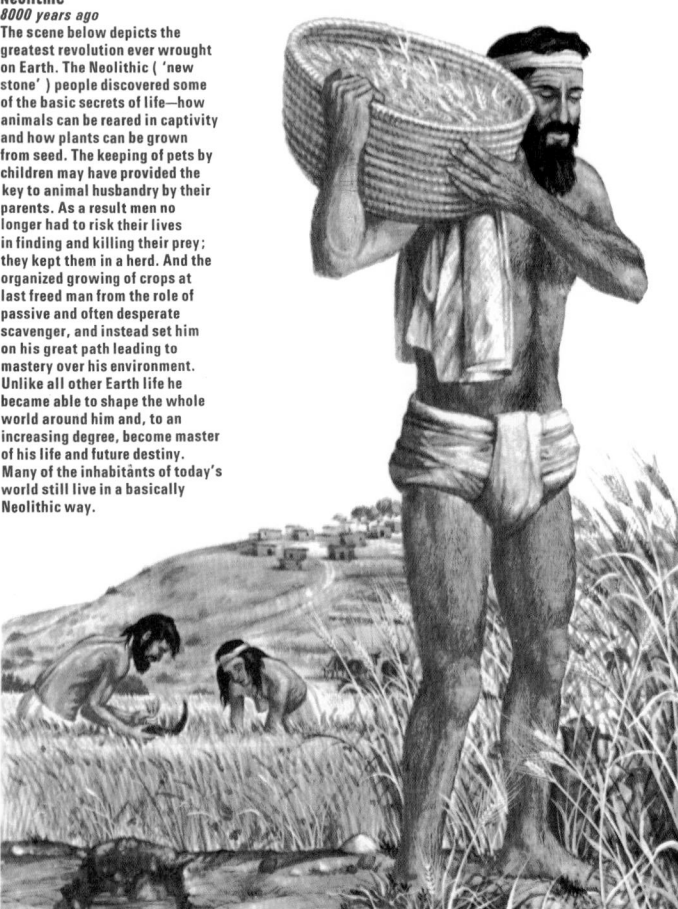

Neolithic
8000 years ago
The scene below depicts the greatest revolution ever wrought on Earth. The Neolithic ('new stone') people discovered some of the basic secrets of life—how animals can be reared in captivity and how plants can be grown from seed. The keeping of pets by children may have provided the key to animal husbandry by their parents. As a result men no longer had to risk their lives in finding and killing their prey; they kept them in a herd. And the organized growing of crops at last freed man from the role of passive and often desperate scavenger, and instead set him on his great path leading to mastery over his environment. Unlike all other Earth life he became able to shape the whole world around him and, to an increasing degree, become master of his life and future destiny. Many of the inhabitants of today's world still live in a basically Neolithic way.

Cave art
Many well preserved cave paintings are masterpieces. Most show animals being hunted by early man, and their power, color and dynamic energy can be startling. But they are often in difficult, inaccessible places, and appear to have been part of the hunter's semi-religious efforts to insure his success and safety in finding and then killing a powerful and dangerous opponent.

The bear cult
Another manifestation of early man's hunting superstitions is to be found in carefully prepared arrangements of cave bear skulls, leg bones and other fragments. Men could hardly have chosen a more dangerous opponent, and they could find meat much more easily; yet the cave bear cult is evident in many forms, such as this stone compartment filled with skulls.

Human burial
Early men buried their own kind in various ways. Some societies buried skulls only, arrayed with possessions or ornaments; others buried men but left female corpses on refuse heaps. This skeleton shows evidence of careful burial in a sleeping posture similar to that of the Grimaldi remains in the Grotte des Enfants, Monaco. Later the grave was overlain by rock debris, here removed.

Petrification
Even the interior of a structurally stable cave changes over a long period, and in this case a sudden gross alteration has resulted from a large fall of rock from the roof. Subsequent to this, slow seepage through the limestone roof of water containing dissolved minerals, especially calcium carbonate, caused gradual growth of pendulous stalactites and upright stalagmites.

Animal remains
The cave is littered to a depth of well over a foot (0.3 m) with the debris of the food and other refuse of carnivores. The great cone above the fall of rock is littered with the remains of animals which fell in through the hole above; and on top of the cone is a pile of bat dung.

A rock fall
A massive collapse of the cave roof left a pile of rock on the floor of the cave and a gaping open shaft above. New layers of flowstone accumulated, earth and rock debris built up above the growing cone reached the roof. Sediments then filled the shaft.

	LOWER PALEOLITHIC		MIDDLE PALEOLITHIC	UPPER PALEOLITHIC	MESOLITHIC
	Over 2 million yrs	500,000 yrs	100,000 yrs	40 000 yrs	10 000 yrs
	AUSTRALOPITHECUS	HOMO ERECTUS	H. SAPIENS	H. SAPIENS SAPIENS (MODERN MAN)	
Hunting and fishing methods	Food gathering (roots, berries, grubs, eggs). Hunting small game. Killing with stones and stabbing sticks.		Food gathering. Hunting large game. Use of fire hardened spears and stone clubs. Group hunting using ambush and stampede.	Food gathering, fowling and fishing. More specialized hunting of herd animals using traps and falls.	Food gathering, fowling and fishing with traps. Collection of shell fish. Beginnings of agriculture and domestication of animals.
Material culture	Oldowan pebble tools. 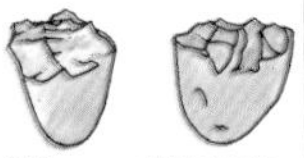 Oldowan pebble tools 500,000 yrs ago	Chopping tools and hand axes. Wooden spears. Use of fire (Pekin man). 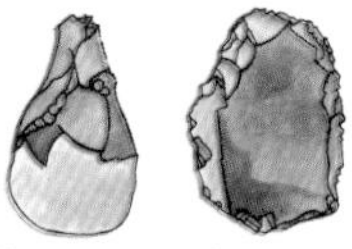 Hand axe Tortoise core tool	Development of varied stone tool kits (scrapers, burins points, blades). 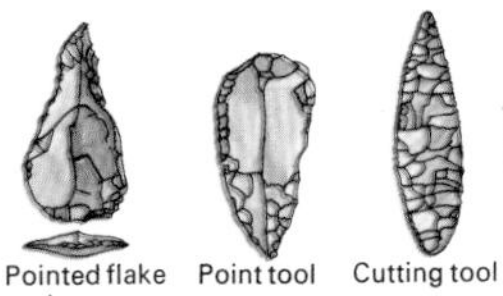 Pointed flake tool Point tool Cutting tool	Throwing spears with separate heads. Harpoons and fish-spears. Implements of bone, horn and ivory. 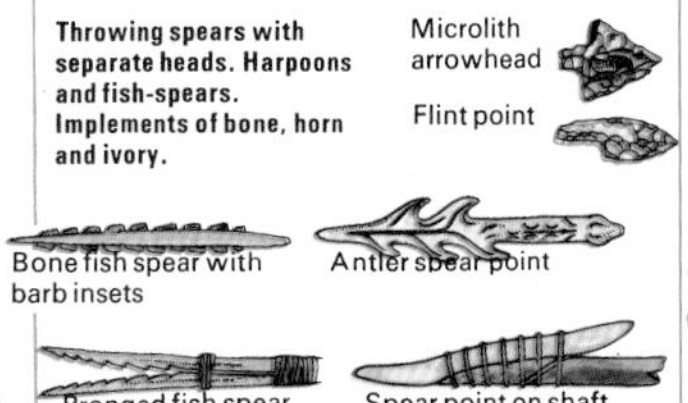 Bone fish spear with barb insets Antler spear point Pronged fish spear Spear point on shaft Microlith arrowhead Flint point	Use of bow and arrows. Transport by canoe, skis, and sledges. Development of basketry and pottery. 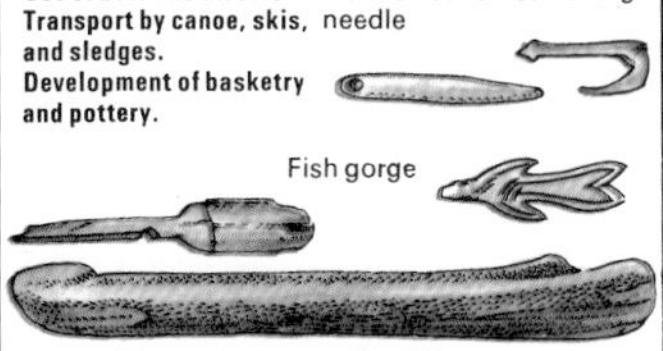 Fishhook and net making needle Fish gorge Dug-out canoe and paddle
Dwellings	Wind breaks, hunting hides and temporary shelters.	Use of caves, usually as temporary dwelling. Better shelters constructed.	Permanent cave dwellings and more sophisticated shelters.		Evidence of village communities, particularly in coastal areas.
Intellectual and religious activities		Possible existence of cannibalism. Skull : evidence of cannibalism. 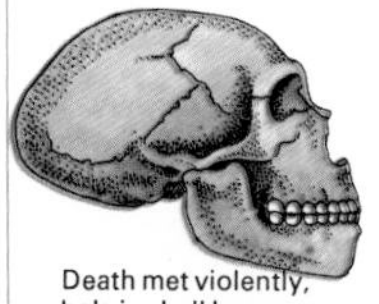 Death met violently, hole in skull base to extract brain.	Ritual burial (La Ferrassie). Possible cannibalism (Solo man). Growth of religious beliefs. 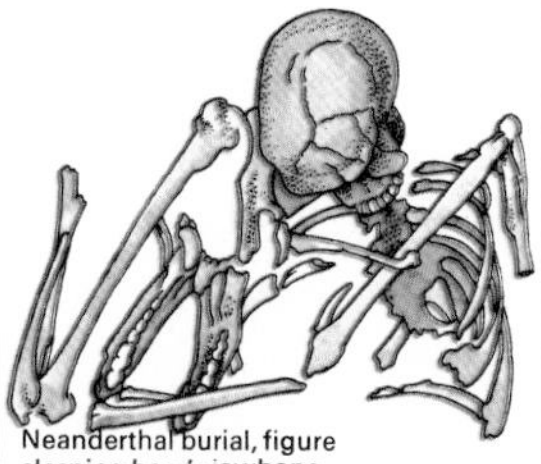 Neanderthal burial, figure clasping boar's jawbone.	Personal adornment and ritual mutilation. Development of cave painting and sculpture. 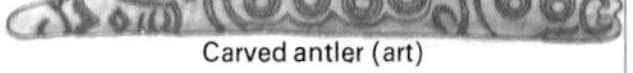 Carved antler (art)  Engraving of wounded aurochs (magic)	Carved ivory figurine (magic) 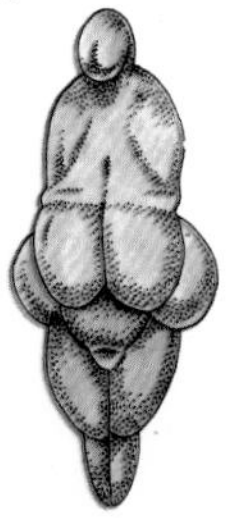  Necklace of carnivore canines (personal adornment)

One of the wonders of the Earth must be the subtle interplay between light and structure that transforms common minerals into precious jewels. In most cases man's hand can be detected in their creation, but even in the natural state many minerals have a range of color, shape, texture and form that makes them the treasures of the Earth.

By popular definition, anything that is mined is called a mineral and on this basis coal and oil are the most important minerals (pages 34–35A). However, geologists reserve the term for naturally occurring materials which have an unvarying chemical composition and crystalline structure. The basic structural elements are arranged in a rigid pattern within three-dimensional crystal matrices.

Each crystal grows from a nucleus by adding atoms layer by layer. A freely growing crystal assumes one of seven basic forms, depending on the relative angles of its faces and the distances between opposite parallel pairs. But in practice the shape of naturally occurring crystals is generally influenced by the space in which it is constrained to grow. Thus in nature crystals develop characteristic habits or over-all shapes. The faces may be all of the same size or unequal. They may occur in narrow layers or grow like a bunch of grapes.

Minerals can be identified by their structure, habit, hardness, density, and the ease with which they can be cleaved along particular planes. Hardness, for example, is normally measured against a scale of increasing hardness from talc to diamond, devised in 1822 by the German mineralogist, F. Mohs. Color is frequently the result of minute proportions of impurities. These often result in minerals of such startling beauty that they are coveted by man as gemstones. The brilliance of transparent gems is due to the way light is reflected inside the stone, and man has learned how to cut gems to enhance their optical properties. The stone is cut or ground to a precise external form with face angles arranged to insure the maximum brilliance based on the refractive index of the material. Rocks (below) are composed of different combinations of a limited number of minerals

Basic igneous rock
Dolerite, a basic igneous rock, is composed of laths of plagioclase (grey and black), pyroxene (yellow and orange) and oxides of iron and titanium (blackish regions).

Sedimentary rock *above*
Limestone is composed of finely crystalline calcite. It shows the fossilized remains of foraminifera.

Acid igneous rock *below*
Granite is a hard igneous rock made up of quartz, potassium feldspar and red-brown crystals of biotite.

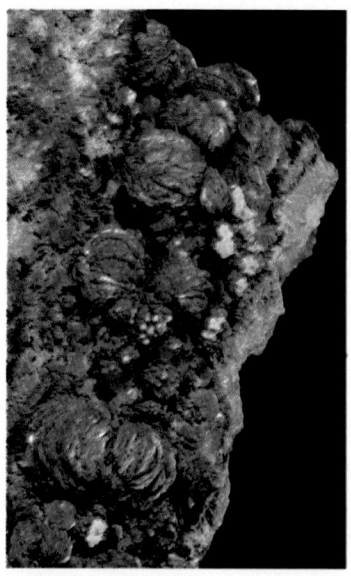

Azurite
Carbonate of copper, possibly the first metal used by man.

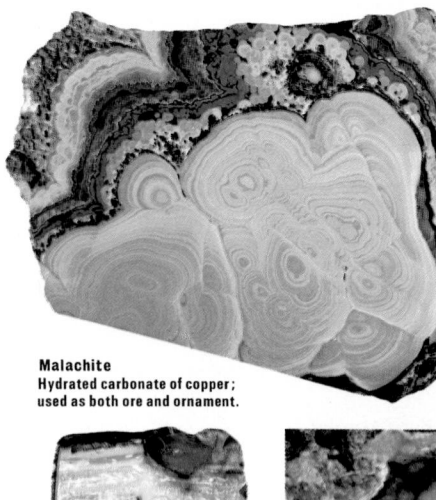

Malachite
Hydrated carbonate of copper; used as both ore and ornament.

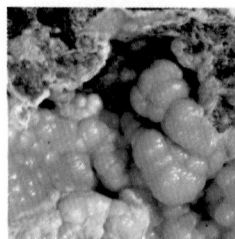

Hemimorphite
A zinc silicate, botryoidal crystal found with other zinc deposits.

Opal
Amorphous silicon dioxide with a variable content of water.

Cerussite
Very clearly defined crystals of lead carbonate.

Pyromorphite
A bed of fine hexagonal columns of lead chlorophosphate.

Crystal size
Although crystal shapes are governed by internal structure, individual sizes are controlled only by conditions of growth. For example, plates of mica—seen as minute biotite flakes in granite sections (lower left)—have reached 33ft (10m) by 14ft (4.3m) wide as in one 90-ton example discovered in Canada.

Quartz
Columnar crystals of silicon dioxide.

Sphene
Silicates are abundant; sphene is calcium titanium silicate.

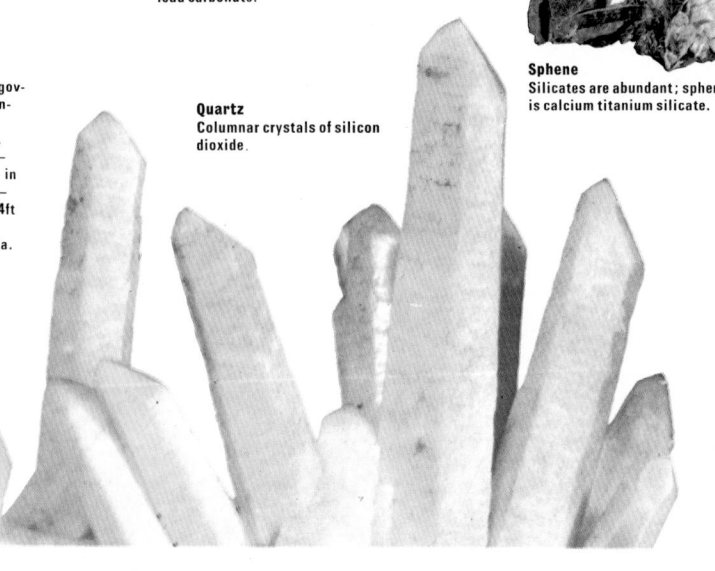

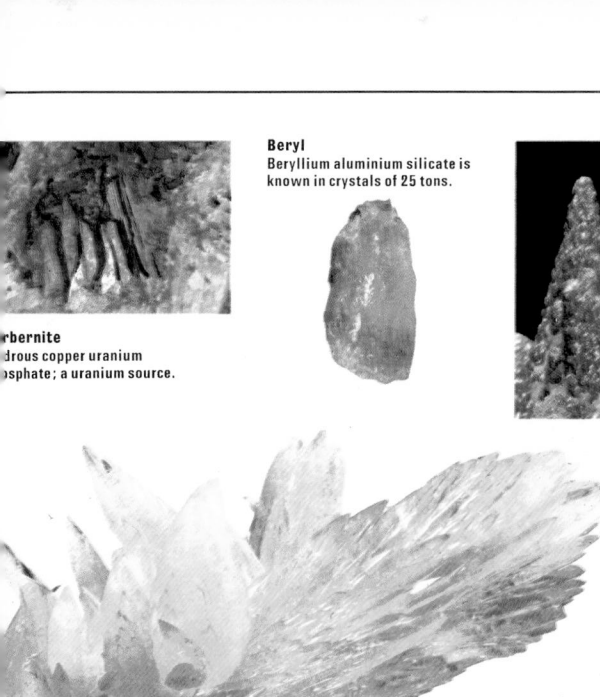

Beryl
Beryllium aluminium silicate is known in crystals of 25 tons.

rbernite
drous copper uranium
osphate; a uranium source.

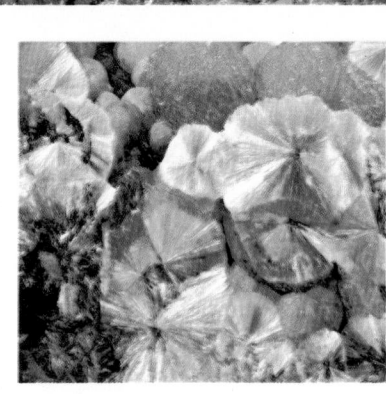

Pyrite on calcite
Crystals of iron disulphide, on calcium carbonate.

Wavelite
Crystals of hydrous basic aluminium phosphate.

Cassiterite
Tin was one of man's earliest metals; this is the dioxide ore.

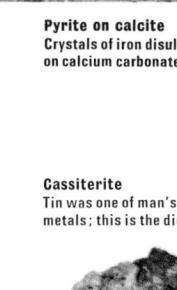

Calcite
Often occurs as stalactites and stalagmites.

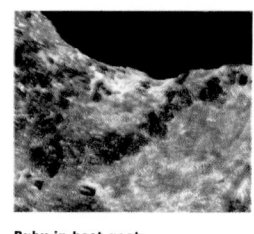

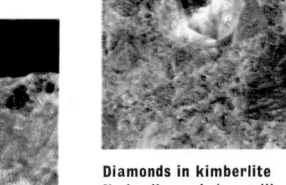

Ruby in host rock
The deep red variety of corundum (aluminium oxide).

Diamonds in kimberlite
Native diamonds (crystalline carbon) in their original rock.

Citrine
The yellowish variety of quartz (silicon dioxide).

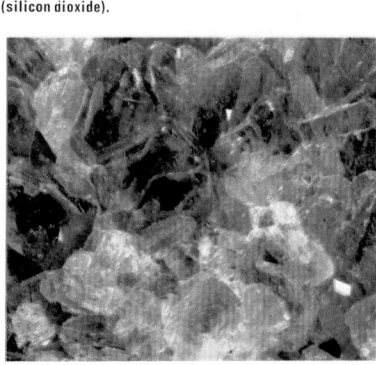

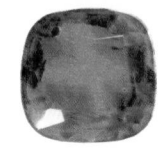

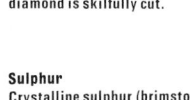

Polished diamond
For use as a gemstone the diamond is skilfully cut.

Polished ruby
Large rubies are among the most precious of all gemstones.

Sulphur
Crystalline sulphur (brimstone) occurs in nature.

ue John
alcium fluoride (fluorite), curs in various colorful forms.

Galena
Cubic crystals of lead sulphide, a major ore of lead.

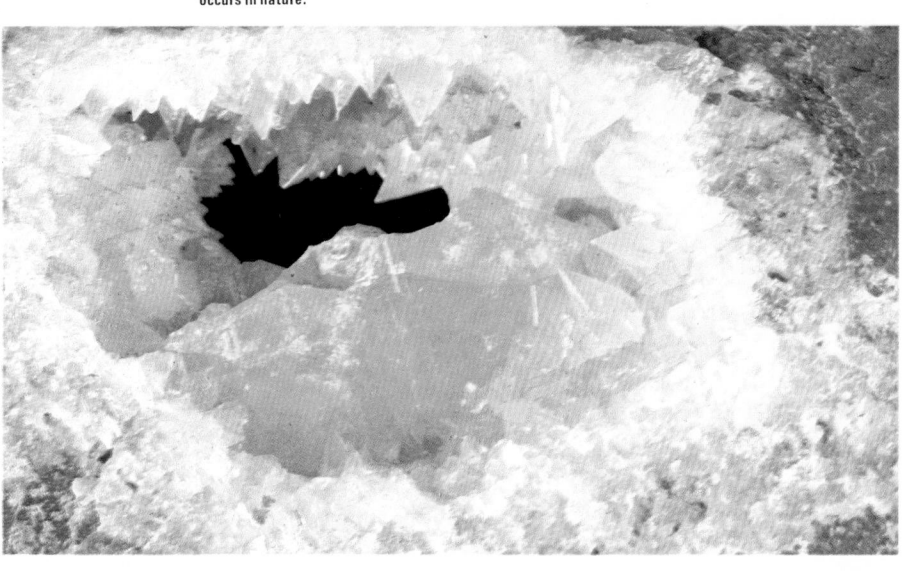

Minerals Under the Land

Of about 2000 minerals in the Earth's crust only 100 or so are of economic importance. These are distributed very irregularly, so that no country today can boast all the minerals it needs. As a result minerals are a source of great national wealth, exploitation and even of rivalry. And the strife is likely to intensify as man's demands grow, because the total of the Earth's minerals is limited.

Against this background of uneven distribution, economic warfare and sharply increasing demand, man's use of minerals constantly changes. Coal, in 1920 the most important mineral in the world on a tonnage basis, is today unable to compete in several of its former markets because of the high cost of transporting it, and its use is increasingly changing from that of a fuel to that of a raw material for plastics and chemicals. Nitrates for fertilizers and explosives sustained the economy of Chile until 1914, when Germany found a way to 'fix' nitrogen from the atmosphere. Aluminum, one the most abundant minerals, was costly and little used until a large-scale refining process was discovered which made use of cheap hydroelectricity.

Taking the broad view, the Earth's minerals are seen as a stern test of man's ability to make proper use of the resources available to him. Already some nations have amassed enormous stockpiles of what are today considered to be strategically important minerals. Nickel is one such metal, and the bulk of the world's supply comes from Canada. Another is manganese, and in this case the dominant supplier is the Soviet Union; but manganese is one of the many minerals which might be dredged from the sea bed.

Uneven distribution of minerals is paralleled by uneven consumption. Paradoxically, the industrialized countries which owed their original development to the presence of mineral resources, particularly iron and coal, now rely for their continued prosperity on developing nations. If the latter were to develop a similar demand for materials a mineral famine would ensue which would have repercussions throughout the world.

World output *right*
The most important commercial minerals and main producers. At the foot of each column is annual world output in millions of long tons. Precious mineral outputs (asterisked) are: gold 52 million fine troy ounces; silver 240 m.f.t.o.; platinum 3.4 m.f.t.o.; diamonds 30 million metric carats.

Key to mineral producers

1 Soviet Union	15 Zambia
2 USA	16 Australia
3 France	17 Spain
4 S Africa	18 Italy
5 Philippines	19 Malaysia
6 Congo (Kinshasa)	20 United Kingdom
7 Canada	21 Thailand
8 Morocco	22 Argentina
9 Brazil	23 Uganda
10 Chile	24 India
11 New Caledonia	25 Mexico
12 SW Africa	26 Peru
13 Finland	27 Congolese Rep.
14 China (People's Rep.)	28 Ghana

Ferro-alloy metals								Non-ferrous metals					Light metals	Nuclear fuels			Precious metals			
Iron ore	Chromite	Cobalt	Manganese	Molybdenum	Nickel	Vanadium	Tungsten	Copper	Lead	Mercury	Tin	Asbestos	Aluminum	Beryllium	Uranium	Thorium	Gold	Silver	Platinum	Diamonds	
661	4.7	0.019	18	0.11	0.5	0.01	0.04	5.3	2.9	0.01	0.21	3.47	7.7	0.003	0.024	0.0006	*	*	*	*	

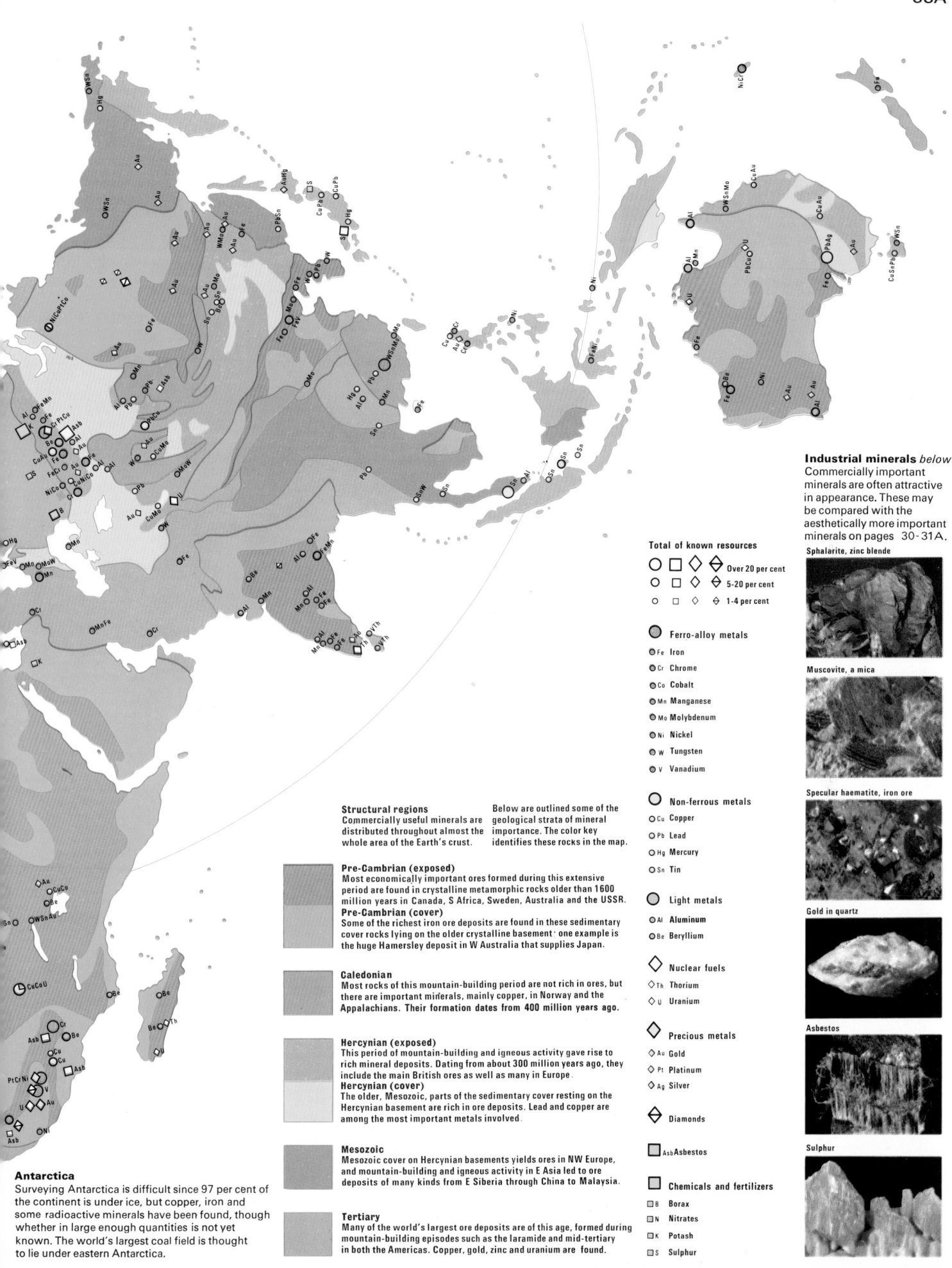

Industrial minerals *below*
Commercially important
minerals are often attractive
in appearance. These may
be compared with the
aesthetically more important
minerals on pages 30-31A.

Sphalarite, zinc blende

Muscovite, a mica

Specular haematite, iron ore

Gold in quartz

Asbestos

Sulphur

Total of known resources

○	□	◇	◈	Over 20 per cent
○	□	◇	◈	5-20 per cent
○	□	◇	◈	1-4 per cent

◉ **Ferro-alloy metals**

⊙ Fe Iron
⊙ Cr Chrome
⊙ Co Cobalt
⊙ Mn Manganese
⊙ Mo Molybdenum
⊙ Ni Nickel
⊙ W Tungsten
⊙ V Vanadium

◯ **Non-ferrous metals**

○ Cu Copper
○ Pb Lead
○ Hg Mercury
○ Sn Tin

◉ **Light metals**

◉ Al Aluminum
◉ Be Beryllium

◇ **Nuclear fuels**

◇ Th Thorium
◇ U Uranium

◇ **Precious metals**

◇ Au Gold
◇ Pt Platinum
◇ Ag Silver

◈ **Diamonds**

☐ Asb Asbestos

▣ **Chemicals and fertilizers**

☐ B Borax
☐ N Nitrates
☐ K Potash
☐ S Sulphur

Structural regions
Commercially useful minerals are
distributed throughout almost the
whole area of the Earth's crust.

Below are outlined some of the
geological strata of mineral
importance. The color key
identifies these rocks in the map.

Pre-Cambrian (exposed)
Most economically important ores formed during this extensive
period are found in crystalline metamorphic rocks older than 1600
million years in Canada, S Africa, Sweden, Australia and the USSR.
Pre-Cambrian (cover)
Some of the richest iron ore deposits are found in these sedimentary
cover rocks lying on the older crystalline basement: one example is
the huge Hamersley deposit in W Australia that supplies Japan.

Caledonian
Most rocks of this mountain-building period are not rich in ores, but
there are important minerals, mainly copper, in Norway and the
Appalachians. Their formation dates from 400 million years ago.

Hercynian (exposed)
This period of mountain-building and igneous activity gave rise to
rich mineral deposits. Dating from about 300 million years ago, they
include the main British ores as well as many in Europe.
Hercynian (cover)
The older, Mesozoic, parts of the sedimentary cover resting on the
Hercynian basement are rich in ore deposits. Lead and copper are
among the most important metals involved.

Mesozoic
Mesozoic cover on Hercynian basements yields ores in NW Europe,
and mountain-building and igneous activity in E Asia led to ore
deposits of many kinds from E Siberia through China to Malaysia.

Tertiary
Many of the world's largest ore deposits are of this age, formed during
mountain-building episodes such as the laramide and mid-tertiary
in both the Americas. Copper, gold, zinc and uranium are found.

Antarctica
Surveying Antarctica is difficult since 97 per cent of
the continent is under ice, but copper, iron and
some radioactive minerals have been found, though
whether in large enough quantities is not yet
known. The world's largest coal field is thought
to lie under eastern Antarctica.

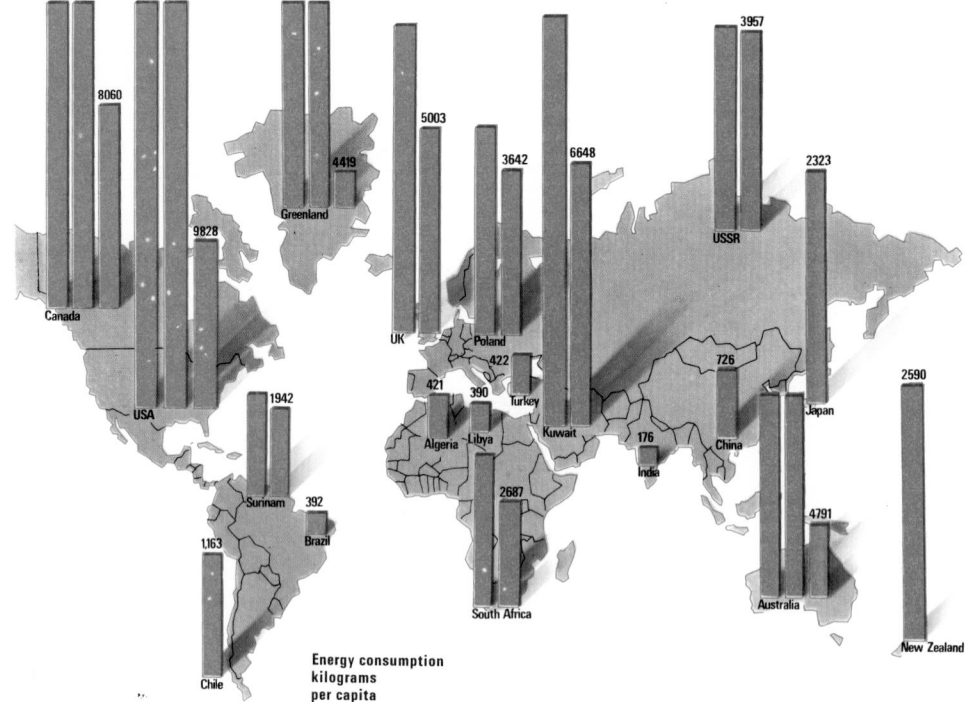

Energy consumption
kilograms
per capita

The concept of energy arose only very recently in the period of man's life on Earth, but already it dominates the whole quality of this life. Early man had no mechanical energy but that of his muscles. By about 2500 years ago he had learned to harness draft animals, such as the ox and horse, and to devise crude water wheels to harness part of the energy of the flow of water in a river. Soon afterwards he added sails to make the fickle wind propel his ships, and by 1000 years ago had started to dot his landscape with windmills. By this time he was adept at burning combustible materials, and during the past 500 years his energy has been increasingly based upon fire, first using wood, and subsequently coal, gas made from coal, petroleum, and natural gas.

All these energy sources, including animal muscle and the wind, are based on the energy radiated by the Sun. Although modern man has begun to use this energy directly in a few trivial installations in hot countries, almost all his energy is derived from solar heat locked up in fossil fuels. The known reserves of these fuels are tending to increase, as a result of prospecting, even faster than man is burning them up. But if no more were discovered most of man's world would come to a halt inside 20 years.

But there should be no energy gap. The promise of nuclear energy is such that, by using fast reactors that breed more fuel than they consume, energy should become one of the very few really plentiful and cheap commodities in man's world of the future. The challenges reside in extracting the fuels and using them effectively.

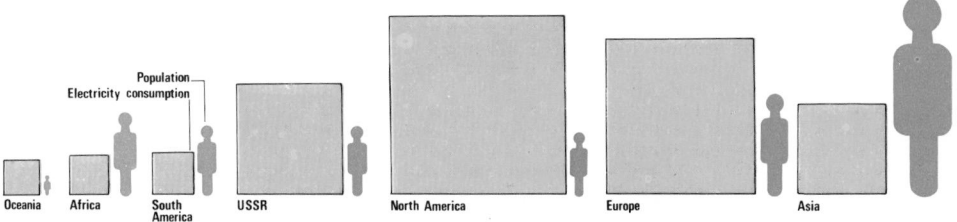

Power and people *above*
World consumption of energy is very uneven. One way of measuring it is to reduce all forms of energy to an equivalent weight of coal burned. The columns on the world map are proportional to the 'coal equivalent' of selected national consumptions expressed in kilograms per head. Electricity consumption is even more disproportionate, as witness the square areas and figure heights immediately above.

Fuels and energy *right*
The caloric value of a fuel is the quantity of heat generated by burning a unit mass. Figures are in British Thermal Units per pound. The surrounding curve shows the increase in the rate at which man is consuming energy; one joule (j) per second is equal to one watt.

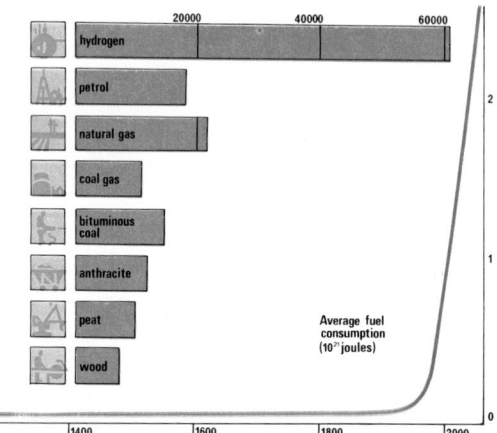

Average fuel
consumption
(10^{20} joules)

Sources of power *below*
For many centuries the only alternative sources of power to muscles were wood fires, waterwheels and windmills — and the latter had too slight an effect to be shown on the figure below. The left portion shows the way in which, since 1850, the United States has enjoyed successive new sources of energy. In 1920 the US economy was not untypical in being based on coal, but since then more energetic, cleaner and more efficiently used fuels have dominated the picture. In the future, nuclear power, shown in the right-hand figure, promises to make good shortages of fossil fuels.

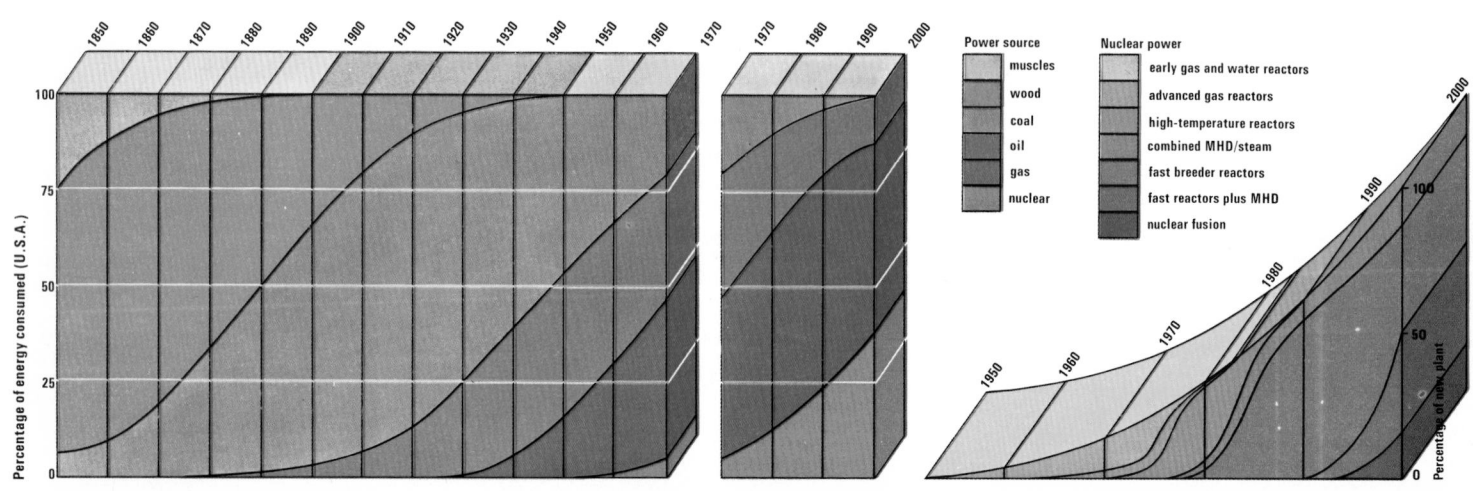

Power source
- muscles
- wood
- coal
- oil
- gas
- nuclear

Nuclear power
- early gas and water reactors
- advanced gas reactors
- high-temperature reactors
- combined MHD/steam
- fast breeder reactors
- fast reactors plus MHD
- nuclear fusion

Coal into electricity
To reduce costs modern coal-fired generating stations are sited on coalfields ; Lea Hall colliery feeds Rugeley power station (background).

Flare in the desert
Once oil has been struck, harmful gases are burned off in the atmosphere. Similar 'flares' are a prominent feature of petroleum refineries.

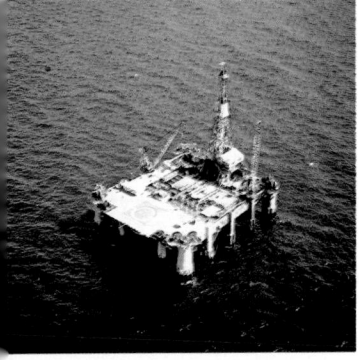

Drilling for gas
To reach natural gas trapped in submarine strata a drill rig is used to bore a hole at a location determined by the prospectors

Nuclear power station
Nearly all today's nuclear energy is used to generate electricity. One of the largest stations is Wylfa, Wales, rated at 1180 million watts.

Coal

For three centuries the most important of the fossil fuels, coal is the result of some 300 million years of subterranean decay of vegetation. Many thousands of generations of the Carboniferous trees have become compressed and hardened, first into peat, then into lignite, then into bituminous coal and finally into anthracite. Until this century coal was used inefficiently as a source of heat. Today it is becoming equally important as a raw material producing plastics, heavy chemicals, insecticides, perfumes, antiseptics, road surfaces and many other products. Great advances have been made in automating the mining of coal, but it remains a laborious task and is therefore becoming increasingly expensive. However, coal mining remains a worldwide industry that passes on to modern man the products of the solar energy captured by a younger Earth.

Petroleum

Like coal, oil is a mixture of fossil remains, but yields few clues as to its origin. Crude oil, from the locations shown on the map at right, is carried by tanker ships to refineries in the user countries. Here it is heated in pipe stills until the various constituent 'fractions' are boiled off. The result is a wide range of products from gasoline through kerosene and gas oil to heavy fuel oils, lubricants and vaseline, with a wide range of other by-products used in many thousands of chemicals and plastics materials. Petroleum fuels are replacing coal in heating and transport applications, partly owing to their easier handling and partly to reduce air pollution by sulphurous compounds. LPG, liquefied petroleum gas, is even cleaner burning and may become more important than gasoline and kerosene in road vehicles and aircraft over the next 25 years.

Gas

In 1807 a London street was lit by town gas, a mixture of hydrogen (about 50%), methane, carbon monoxide and dioxide and other gases, formed by cooking coal at high temperature in a retort. By 1950 this manufactured gas was an important fuel, but in many advanced countries its place is now being taken by natural gas, a primary fuel consisting mainly of methane piped straight from deposits sometimes conveniently sited from the user's point of view (right). Intensive prospecting is discovering natural gas faster than it is being used, and during the past 20 years natural gas has become man's largest single source of energy. In refrigerated form, as a compact liquid, it promises to become an attractive fuel for transport vehicles. A major benefit is that the exhaust from such a vehicle would contain less pollutants than from those using gasoline.

Nuclear energy

In 1956 Britain opened the world's first electricity generating station using the heat of nuclear fission. It was fuelled with rods of natural uranium, a heavy silvery metal containing a small proportion of atoms capable of spontaneous fission when struck by a free neutron. Fission releases further neutrons capable of sustaining a continuous chain reaction. Such a reaction generates heat which is used to provide steam for turbines. The prime advantage of nuclear power is that the fuel is used extremely slowly. Now the fast reactor, which uses raw 'fast' neutrons instead of ones artificially slowed down, has been developed. Not only can the fast reactor generate great energy from a small bulk but it creates fresh fuel faster than the original (plutonium) fuel is consumed. Fast reactors, using uranium from granite, could provide limitless cheap energy.

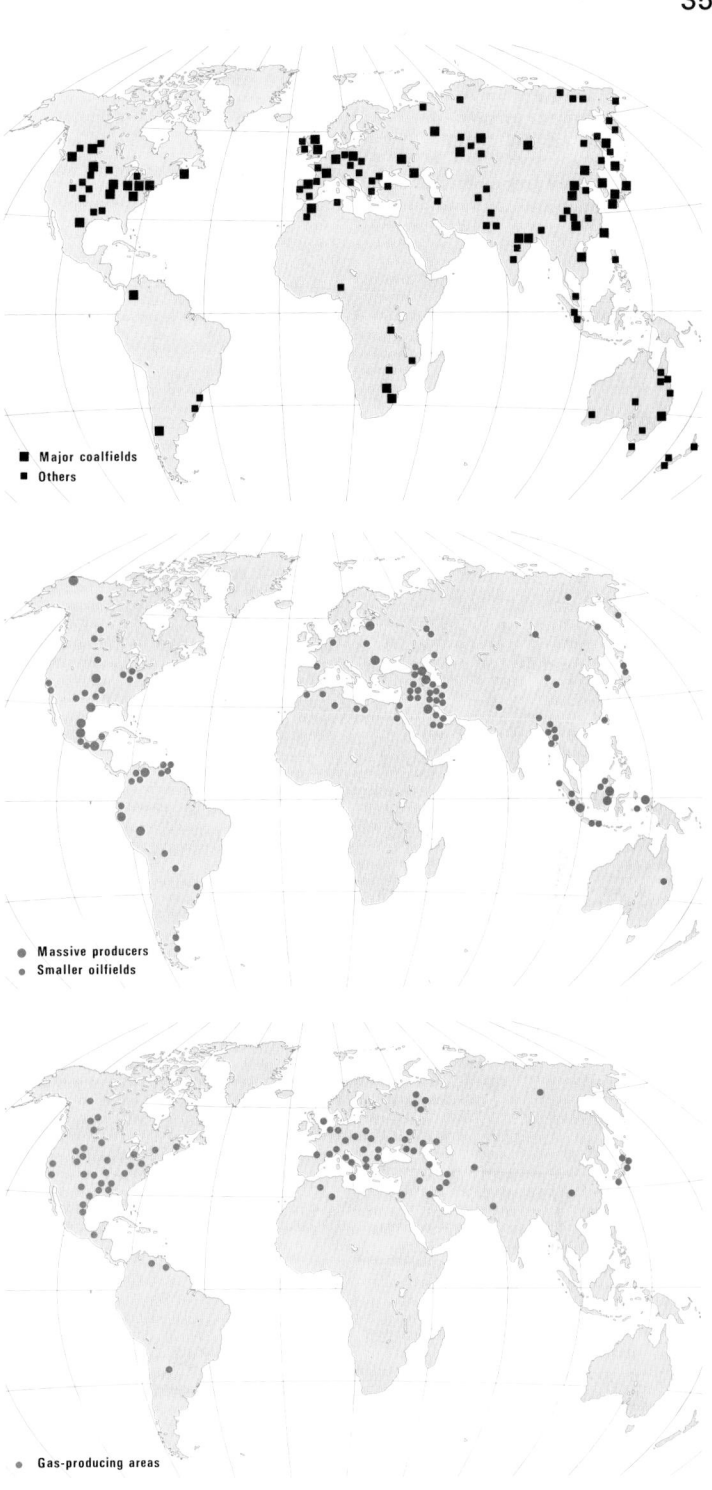

■ Major coalfields
■ Others

● Massive producers
• Smaller oilfields

● Gas-producing areas

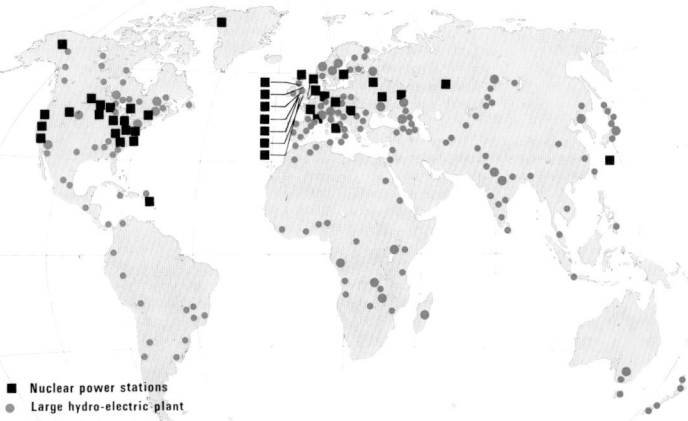

■ Nuclear power stations
● Large hydro-electric plant
• Smaller hydro schemes

Without water there would be no life as we know it on the Earth. Life began in the oceans and the life of the land, both plant and animal, still remains utterly dependent on water for its survival. The atmosphere plays a vital role in the terrestrial water system. Spurred by the energy of the Sun, the moist layer surrounding the globe forms a vast heat engine, operating at a rate of billions of horsepower. All the exposed water surface is constantly being converted into vapor. Eventually the air holding the vapor cools, and the vapor condenses as rain, hail or snow. Most of this precipitation falls into the sea, but nearly a quarter of it falls on the land. Altogether about two-thirds of it evaporates back into the air, or is transpired by plants; the rest runs off in rivers, or filters through the ground to the water table beneath.

Satisfying the collective thirst of man and his industry grows daily more difficult. Almost always the demand is for fresh water; but the proportion of the Earth's water in rivers and streams is less than one part in a million. If the Antarctic ice cap were to melt, it would feed all the rivers for 800 years. Although schemes have been suggested for towing giant fresh-water icebergs from Antarctica to the Californian coast, man is unlikely to make extensive use of the ice cap. Far more promising is the large supply of subterranean water. At the same time great strides are being made in desalination of sea water, using a variety of methods. Management of the Earth's water resources is seen ever more clearly as a technical challenge of the greatest magnitude.

Distribution of the world's water resources

- The atmosphere
- Lakes, rivers and streams
- Ground—water and soil
- Ice caps and glaciers
- Oceans, saline lakes and inland seas

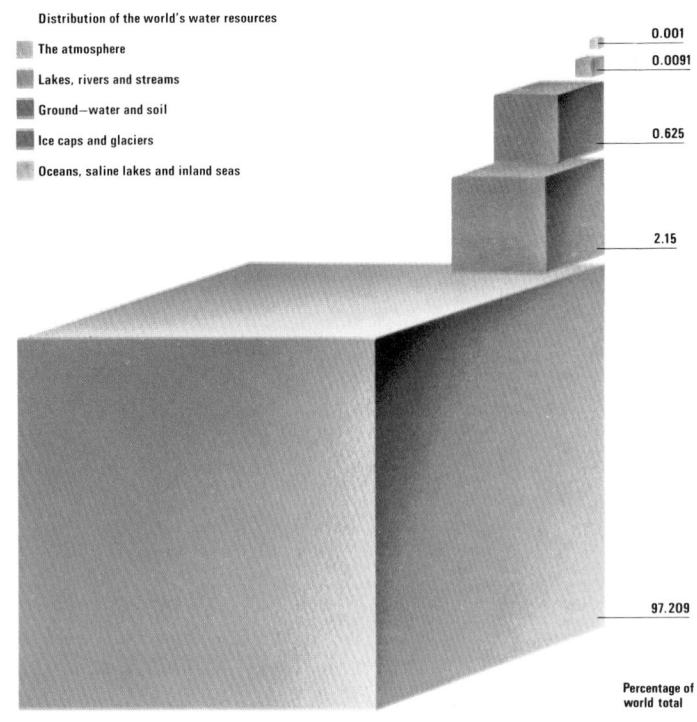

0.001
0.0091
0.625
2.15
97.209

Percentage of world total

Annual precipitation 100%

Forest and rough vegetation 16%

Farm crops and pasture 23%

Waste land 32%

Stream flow 29%

Irrigation 2·00%

Domestic 0·05%

Industry 0·05%

Consumed losses 2·10%

3·35%

1·35%

3·35%

3·30%

0·60%

0·55%

Return to sea 26·9%

The world's water *left*
The total volume of the Earth's water is about 326 million cubic miles (1400 million km³). Practically all of it is in the oceans, in a form rich in dissolved salts. Solar heating is constantly evaporating this mass, converting it ultimately into precipitation of fresh water which falls back to the surface. Run-off from the surface in rivers and streams is one of the forms of terrestrial water most visible to man, but it accounts for a negligible fraction of the total. Some 80 times as much water lies in salt lakes and inland seas, 90 times as much in fresh-water lakes, more than 6000 times as much in ground water beneath the land surface, and almost a quarter-million times as much in ice caps and glaciers. So far man has made little attempt to use these sources of fresh water. Instead he interrupts the hydrologic cycle in the easy places: the rivers and lakes, where, because of the small volumes and flows available, he causes significant pollution.

A valued resource *above*
Shiupur head, the head-waters of the Gang canal in Rajasthan province, India. This and other canal systems are gradually bringing to this arid province an assured supply of irrigation water from the Himalayas.

The hydrologic cycle *left*
This diagram is drawn for United States, but the basic features of the cycle are common to most of the Earth's land. Just over three-quarters of the rain snow and hail falls on the oceans. The usual measure for water in huge quantities is the acre-foot (one acre of water, one foot deep). Each year about 300 thousand million acre-feet of water falls on the oceans and 80 thousand million on the land. In the diagram all the figures are percentages. In the US, which is not unusual in its proportion of farmland, less than one-quarter of the water falling on the land falls directly on crops or pasture. A greater amount falls into rivers and streams, from which man takes varying small fractions for his own purposes. It can be seen that, even in the US, the total quantity of water withdrawn for use is only 7.3 per cent of the fraction of water falling on the land. Yet, to attain even this performance, Americans spend more than $10000 million each year on improving their water supplies.

Domestic use of water

In some countries the total consumption of water is less than one gallon per head, but in the United States more than 70 US gallons are consumed by each person daily, on average, in domestic use alone. The way this consumption is split up varies greatly, but these percentages, for 'an average home in Akron, Ohio' are typical for modern urban areas having piped water to flush toilets. Total domestic water consumption in the industrially advanced countries is usually between five and 30 per cent of the national total.

Flushing toilet 41%

Washing and bathing 37%

Kitchen use 6%

Drinking 5%

Laundry 4%

Household cleaning 3%

Garden 3%

Cleaning car 1%

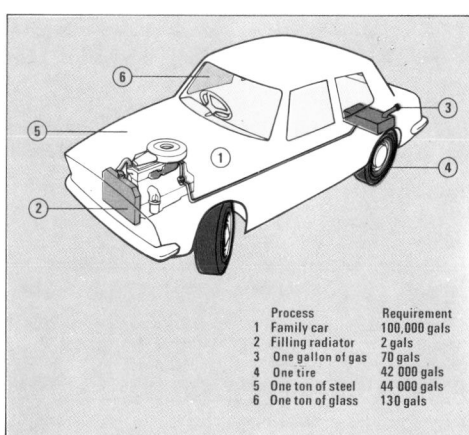
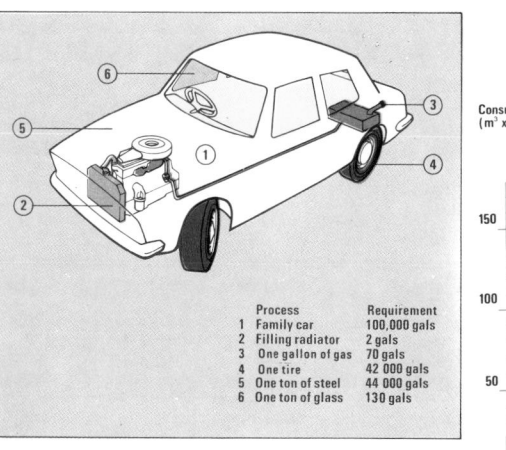

	Process	Requirement
1	Family car	100,000 gals
2	Filling radiator	2 gals
3	One gallon of gas	70 gals
4	One tire	42 000 gals
5	One ton of steel	44 000 gals
6	One ton of glass	130 gals

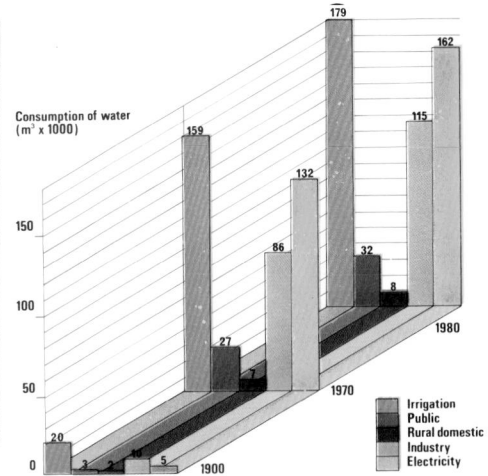

Consumption of water (m³ x 1000)

Irrigation
Public
Rural domestic
Industry
Electricity

1900 — 1970 — 1980

Rising demand *above*

Civilized man needs more water every year. Plotted graphically, the rising demand for water in the United States is startling; the rate of increase is about three times the rate of population growth. Rural domestic supplies are from wells; others are piped.

Irrigation *below*

Irrigation of land by man is at least 7000 years old, yet still in its infancy. The grey areas on the world map are virtually without irrigation. The last column of data shows the percentage of each continent irrigated. Only Japan and the UAR exceed 50 per cent.

Continent	Area : million acres (1 acre = 4047m²) Total	Cultivated (A)	Irrigated (B)	Ratio of B to A (x 100)
Africa	898	37	11.2	30
Asia	5062	1289	296.9	23
Australia	1900	38	3	8
Europe	288	122	5.8	5
N America	2809	485	49	10
S America	4620	187	13	7
U S S R	5540	568	23	4
Grand total	21117	2726	401.9	15

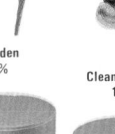
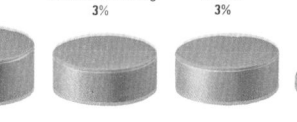

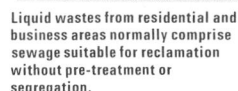
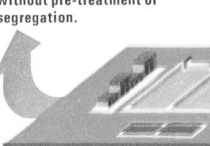
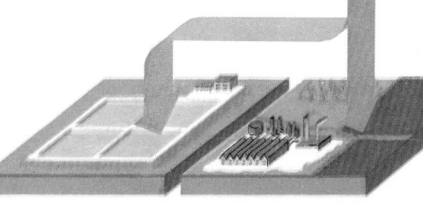

Most liquid wastes are generated by mixed human concentrations-including habitations, businesses and industry. Before reclamation, any wastes having excessive or toxic mineral content must be segregated from the main flow.

Oilfields on the land invariably generate large and varied liquid wastes, particularly including concentrated brines, which must be excluded from conventional reclamation processes.

Liquid wastes from residential and business areas normally comprise sewage suitable for reclamation without pre-treatment or segregation.

This water reclamation plant supplies water to the city (above) and to agriculture and industry (below, right). Sludge and grease are returned to the sewer (route, far right).

This water reclamation plant accepts mainly residential effluent. Water reclaimed is returned for re-use, while sludge and grease are returned to the sewer and piped to the main sewage treatment plant. A proportion of the output is supplied to spreading grounds at the coast (below) to replenish the ground water table.

Reclaimed waters may be used to maintain underground supplies by spreading them on percolation beds (above), where the water filters down to the storage basin.

Below, the main sewage treatment plant can operate by a variety of methods, including long-term open storage, aeration, mechanical filtration and softening.

Reclaiming used water

In almost every country the quality of the water pumped into domestic supplies is subject to precise controls, and the proportion of some substances may not exceed one or two parts per million. National water systems make maximum use of water reclaimed close to the point of consumption by plant which returns the heavy sludges and greases to the sewer for treatment at a large sewage works. This facilitates effluent quality control and also provides an emergency outlet for a temporarily overloaded or faulty reclamation plant. In the example here the main treatment plant discharges wastes into an ocean outfall (left), while the fresh water spreading grounds just inshore replenish the water table and thus prevent infiltration by the ocean water.

Desalination

Man's growing demand for fresh water cannot readily be met without an enormous increase in his capacity to desalinate salt water. A choice between several ways of doing this is invariably made on economic grounds. Nearly all the large installations in use are multi-stage flash evaporators in which some form of heat – if possible, heat otherwise wasted - is used to convert sea water to steam which is condensed by the incoming salt water. But in some circumstances more economic results can be obtained by freezing, reverse osmosis or other methods.

GROWTH OF DESALTING CAPACITY 1961 TO 1968

Year Ending	Municipal water use M gal per day	Industrial/other uses M gal per day	Total
1961	17.6	42.2	59.8
1962	20.9	45.5	66.4
1963	28.4	50.4	78.8
1964	32.5	53.5	86.0
1965	39.3	58.9	98.2
1966	52.6	101.6	154.2
1967	102.2	115.3	217.5
1968	121.4	125.8	247.2
Historical annual growth %	32	17	23
Projection to 1975	835	415	1250
Projected annual growth %	32	19	26

SIZE RANGES OF THE WORLD'S DESALTING PLANTS

Size range M gal per day	Number of Plants	Total capacity M gal per day
0.025—0.1	351	17.8
0.1—0.3	218	35.3
0.3—0.5	34	13.0
0.5—1.0	31	21.3
1.0—5.0	46	95.4
5.0—7.5	3	17.5
over 7.5	3	46.9
TOTAL	686	247.2

The Oceans' Mineral Resources

A submerged land almost equal to the area of the Moon is being urgently explored for its store of minerals. The continental shelf around the Earth's land has the proportions of a seventh continent; around Britain or Japan its area is several times larger than that of the land itself. The shelf is rich in minerals, some of which are accumulating faster than man can at present use them.

By far the most important resources of the shallow seas are the deposits of oil and gas locked in the strata below the bed. About 200 drilling rigs are constantly looking for new deposits, and already nearly 20 per cent of the world's supplies, worth annually $4800 million, are taken from under the sea. Geologists estimate that oil and gas resources under the oceans are at least as great as those under the land. Next to oil and gas the most important marine minerals are lowly sand and gravel. It is becoming increasingly difficult and costly to extract these from the land, and marine deposits are fast becoming of great commercial importance. Often their extraction is combined with land reclamation. The Dutch, for example, have devised several systems that help to create new land and, as at Europoort, deep-water channels.

Last in importance, but very high in speculative interest, come the heavy minerals. Some, such as gravels rich in ilmenite, rutile and zircon, have been concentrated by the sorting action of the waves. Others, including tin, gold and diamonds, have been derived from igneous deposits. But in most cases these minerals can still be obtained more cheaply on land, except in one or two freak instances where concentrated deposits can be easily reached.

Exploiting the shallow sea

One of the most important recent discoveries of oil and natural gas has occurred in the North Sea, on the very doorstep of industrial Western Europe. The North Sea gas is found mainly in layers of a porous sandstone deposited under desert conditions. Since both natural gas and oil are thought to have originated from the compressed remains of animals and plants that swarmed in the warm seas of the Carboniferous period, the gas could not have formed in the rocks where it is now found.

Immediately below the sandstone lie thick coal measures, and the gas appears to have risen from these into the porous sandstone until halted by a thick layer of salt and limestone. Where the limestone is broken and porous, the gas has risen into it and become trapped under salt domes. In the Gulf of Mexico these domes have themselves become a source of minerals. While drilling down to a promising dome an oil company came across the third largest sulphur deposit in the United States.

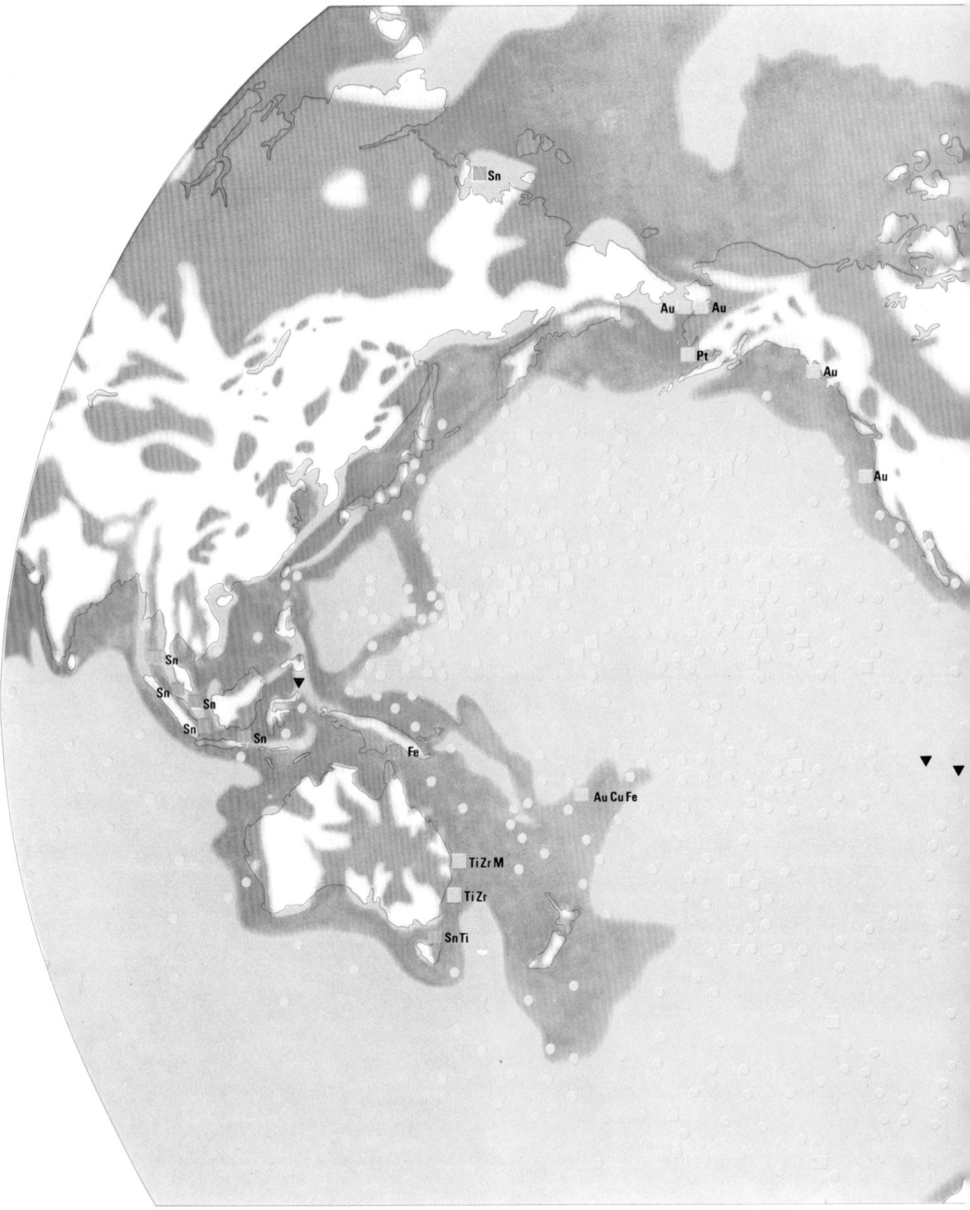

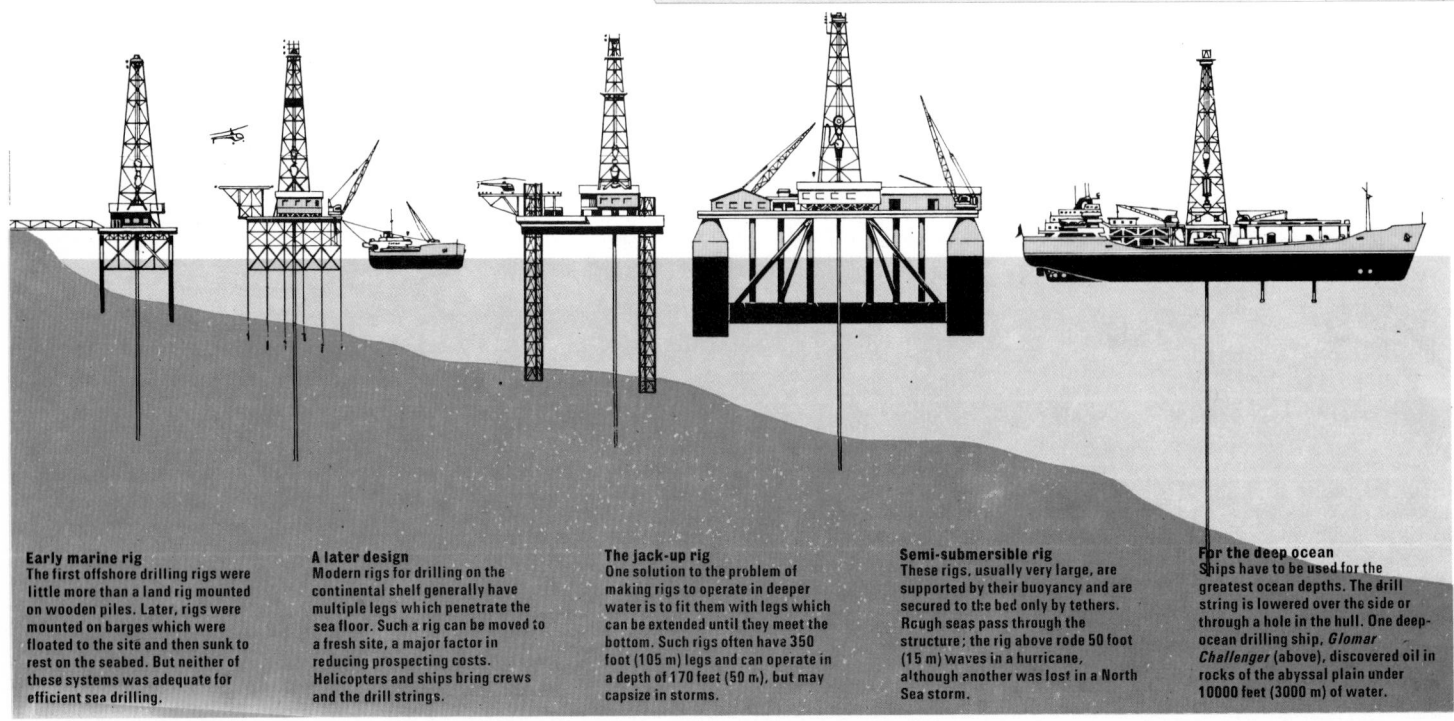

Early marine rig
The first offshore drilling rigs were little more than a land rig mounted on wooden piles. Later, rigs were mounted on barges which were floated to the site and then sunk to rest on the seabed. But neither of these systems was adequate for efficient sea drilling.

A later design
Modern rigs for drilling on the continental shelf generally have multiple legs which penetrate the sea floor. Such a rig can be moved to a fresh site, a major factor in reducing prospecting costs. Helicopters and ships bring crews and the drill strings.

The jack-up rig
One solution to the problem of making rigs to operate in deeper water is to fit them with legs which can be extended until they meet the bottom. Such rigs often have 350 foot (105 m) legs and can operate in a depth of 170 feet (50 m), but may capsize in storms.

Semi-submersible rig
These rigs, usually very large, are supported by their buoyancy and are secured to the bed only by tethers. Rough seas pass through the structure; the rig above rode 50 foot (15 m) waves in a hurricane, although another was lost in a North Sea storm.

For the deep ocean
Ships have to be used for the greatest ocean depths. The drill string is lowered over the side or through a hole in the hull. One deep-ocean drilling ship, *Glomar Challenger* (above), discovered oil in rocks of the abyssal plain under 10000 feet (3000 m) of water.

Undersea resources *left*

Deep ocean basins

Sedimentary basins locally favourable for petroleum

☐ Au: gold

▨ Sn: tin

▪ Fe: iron

☐ Ti: titanium

☐ D: diamonds

○ Mn sampled

☐ Mn photo 25+ per cent.

▽ Mn photo 25— per cent.

▼ Metal-bearing muds

The large map gives a broad general picture of the distribution of petroleum resources, shown as favorable sedimentary basins, and of major subsea mineral deposits, but does not attempt to indicate commercial value or even which regions are worth exploiting. These are multi-billion dollar questions which are taxing mining companies in many countries. The manganese oxide deposits are shown only where they have been sampled or photographed (with symbols to indicate whether the nodules cover more or less than one-quarter of the sea floor). The metal-bearing muds are a recent exciting discovery. Deep down in the Red Sea, off Indonesia and elsewhere, prospectors have discovered concentrated brines rich in valuable industrial metals.

Mining the oceans *below*

For 20 years industry has been tantalized by the prospect of literally sucking or sweeping valuable minerals off the ocean floor. But the most widespread loose nodules (see photograph below) have a composition ill-matched to world demand (foot of page), and even the mining system sketched below, in which ships operate what is in effect a giant vacuum cleaner, has yet to be used on a commercial scale. The technical, economic and political problems associated with such ventures are immense : but the potential rewards are great enough to sustain interest.

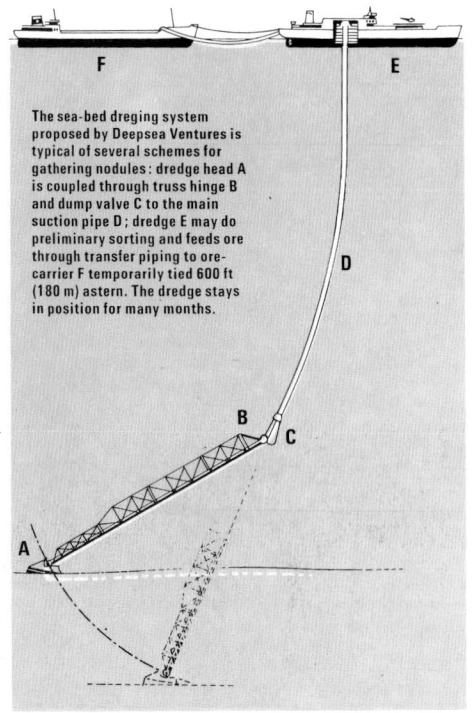

The sea-bed dreging system proposed by Deepsea Ventures is typical of several schemes for gathering nodules : dredge head A is coupled through truss hinge B and dump valve C to the main suction pipe D; dredge E may do preliminary sorting and feeds ore through transfer piping to ore-carrier F temporarily tied 600 ft (180 m) astern. The dredge stays in position for many months.

Manganese nodules

One of the most tempting concepts is to scoop minerals off the bed of the ocean. One of the few products which could thus be harvested is manganese, which is found in the form of potato-sized nodules scattered on the ocean floor. Unfortunately not only are there technical difficulties standing in the way of such an operation but production would be out of step with world needs. The undersea production of the world's needs of manganese, equivalent to more than 18.6 million tons of ore, would lead to a 453 per cent glut of cobalt. Similarly, if all the world demand for copper were met from the same source, the glut of cobalt would be no less than 11335 per cent (right).

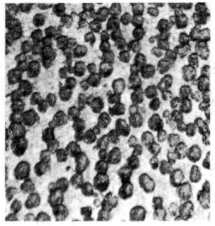

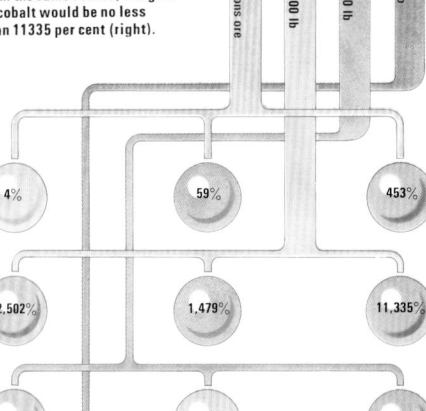

Manganese 18,650,000 tons ore	Copper 11,189,377,000 lb	Nickel 1,007,943,000 lb	Cobalt 32,890,000 lb
4%	59%		453%
2,502%	1,479%		11,335%
169%	8%		766%
22%	0.9%		13%

Undersea production

Man's commercial use of the ocean minerals is so far confined almost entirely to the continental shelves around the land.

▦ oil
▦ gas
△ tin
△ iron
⊙ salt
△ heavy minerals
▽ sulphur
▲ diamonds
☐ magnesium
⊙ fresh water
⊙ other minerals

▦ oil and gas exploration

The Oceans' Living Resources

Fish and shellfish were probably the first marine resources to be exploited by man. Many of his early settlements in coastal and estuarine areas bear witness to this with their ancient mounds of oyster and mussel shells. Even now, coastal fisheries remain a vital source of high quality protein for numerous primitive communities. And yet, in spite of this long history of coastal fishing, the commercial fisheries have been dominated by a mere handful of nations until recent times. Three-quarters of the world fish catch is still accounted for by only 14 countries.

The world fish catch is the only source of food that has managed to increase dramatically since the end of World War II. In the decade from 1958-68 alone, it rose from below 34 million tons to 64 million tons. Although the catch fell by two per cent in 1969, it is expected to continue to improve and may even top the 120 million ton mark by the mid-1980s.

The steady growth of the commercial fisheries since the war has relied on improvements in technology and boats, and the spread of these modern techniques from traditional northern fisheries to newer ones being developed in the southern oceans. Peru, for example, now has the world's largest single species fishery, catching some 10 million tons of anchoveta a year: in 1958 the catch was only 960,000 tons. However, the time is fast approaching when few fish stocks will remain unexploited.

Already many established fisheries are beginning to suffer from the effects of over-fishing with too many boats pursuing too few fish, leading to the capture of younger, smaller fish and a decline in the fish stocks and the fisheries that they support. Only the briefest respite may be needed for the fish to recover: a single female fish can lay thousands of eggs in a single season. Over-exploitation of the whales and turtles is a much more serious matter. Already several species of whale are on the verge of extinction and, with one young born to a female every two years, the prospects for their recovery are poor.

The living resources of the oceans must be conserved and managed if they are to continue to provide mankind with food. It is now clear that the world fish catch has a finite limit, possibly about 200 million tons. With adequate international agreement and controls, this limit might one day be approached. The productivity of the oceans could be increased further only by harvesting animals lower than fish in the marine food chain or by artificially fertilizing and farming the seas. Some of the first steps in this direction are now in progress. Perhaps in the future a new pattern of exploitation will emerge, with fleets harvesting the oceanic fish while other fish, shellfish and crustaceans such as lobster and prawn are farmed in the shallow coastal waters.

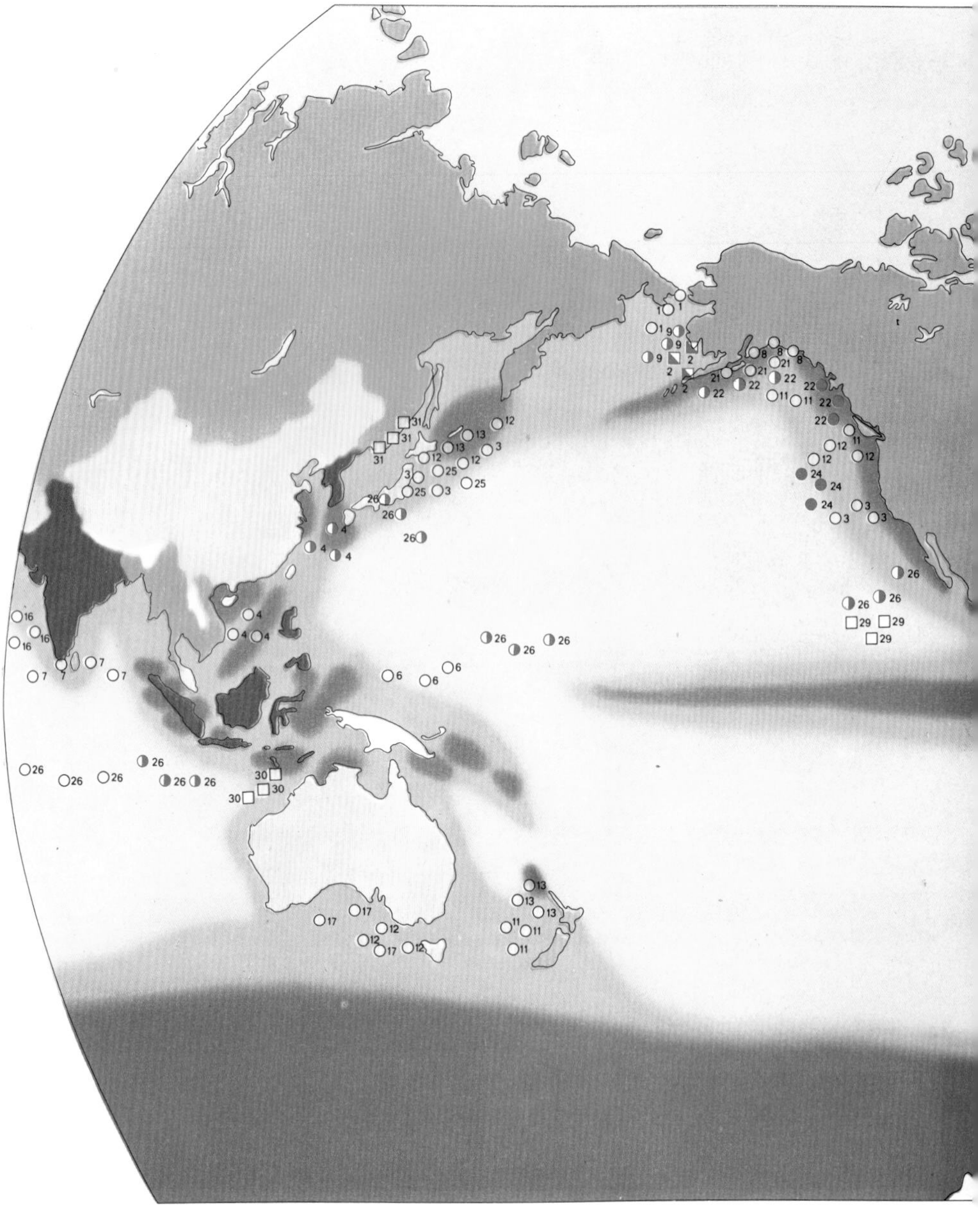

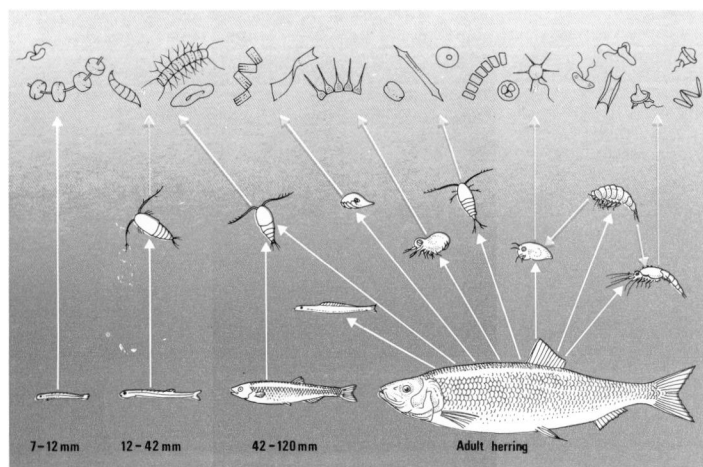

Marine food web *above*
The path leading to food fish such as the herring involves a succession of feeding and energy levels. The plants drifting in the plankton first convert the Sun's energy into a usable form through the process of photosynthesis (top band). The plants are then eaten by small planktonic animals (middle band). These in turn are eaten by the fish during its growth (bottom band). However, as the arrows indicate, the path from plant to fish is far from simple. At each point in the web, energy is exchanged and lost so that the adult fish receives less than a thousandth of the original energy captured in photosynthesis. This loss of energy has prompted suggestions for short-circuiting the process by harvesting members of the plankton itself – either the plants or the small crustaceans and other animals that feed on them.

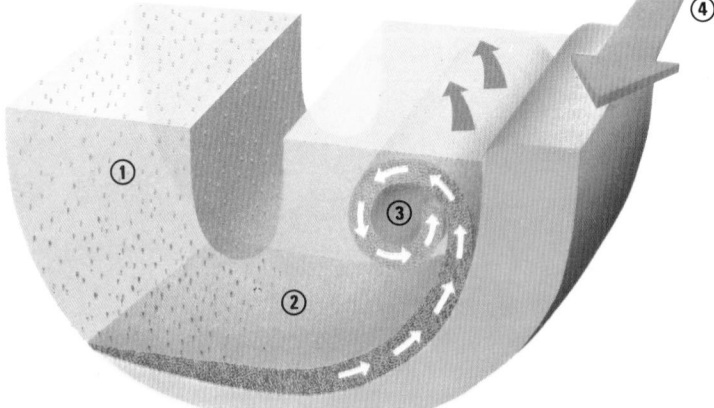

Upwelling *above*
Most of the world's great fisheries occur in regions of upwelling where nutrient-rich water rises to the surface and supports prolific marine life. Deep ocean waters accumulate the remains of dead and decaying organisms (1) that rain down from the surface. When this nutrient-rich water (2) rises to the surface (3) it contains all the minerals and salts necessary for plant growth in approximately the ratio best suited to stimulate maximum growth. The actual mechanism which causes the water to rise to the surface can vary, but a common source is the interaction between surface winds and ocean currents running along the edge of continents. The wind (4) causes the surface water to move away from the coast, enabling the deep water to swirl up to the surface where it renews the supplies of plant nutrients.

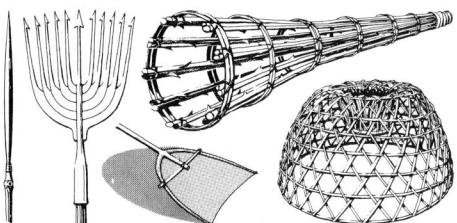

World fisheries *left*
With more nations claiming a share of the oceans' living resources few productive regions remain unexplored by fishing fleets. Already many fisheries show signs of over-exploitation and some coastal states are demanding exclusive rights to very large areas of sea, e.g. Iceland's demand for a 50 mile limit.

Biological productivity

Very favorable conditions for the growth of marine life

Moderately favorable conditions for the growth of marine life

Exploitation of fish stocks
- ● Over-exploited by 1949
- ◐ Over-exploited by 1968
- ○ Under-exploited

Exploitation of crustaceans
- ◨ Over-exploited by 1968
- ☐ Under-exploited

Key to numbers
1 Alaska pollack	17 Pilchard
2 Anchoveta	18 Plaice
3 Anchovy	19 Pamfret
4 Demersal fish	20 Red fish
5 Capelin	21 Rock fish
6 Carangidae	22 Salmon
7 Clupeidae	23 Sand eel
8 Cod	24 Sardine
9 Flat fish	25 Saury
10 Haddock	26 Tuna
11 Hake	27 King crab
12 Herring	28 Krill
13 Jack mackerel	29 Red crab
14 Mackerel	30 Shrimp
15 Menhaden	31 Squid
16 Pelagic	

Fishing limits
- Nations claiming a 3 mile exclusive zone
- Nations claiming a 6 mile exclusive zone
- Nations claiming a 12 mile exclusive zone
- Nations claiming more than 12 miles

Fishing gear
Primitive fisheries use a wide range of techniques (above) including spears, nets and basket traps.

Mainstays of the modern commercial fisheries (below) are the gill net (top), the seine net and the otter trawl (bottom).

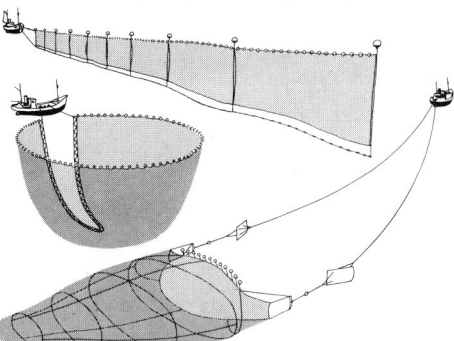

Anchoveta — 5 in, 13 cm / 2-3 oz, 85 g
Herring — 12 in, 30 cm / 8 oz, 227 g

Commercial fish
Although the oceans contain many thousands of different fish species, very few of these support large commercial fisheries. The anchoveta supplies the largest single species fishery in the world with an annual catch of about 10 million tons. This is slightly greater than the total catch of the other species illustrated here.

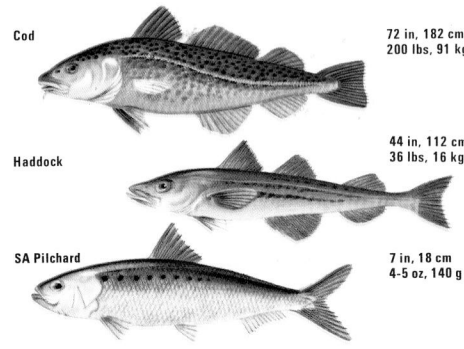
Cod — 72 in, 182 cm / 200 lbs, 91 kg
Haddock — 44 in, 112 cm / 36 lbs, 16 kg
SA Pilchard — 7 in, 18 cm / 4-5 oz, 140 g

The first marine farms, *right*
An early use of marine stockades was to keep alive fish caught at sea until they were needed for eating (A). An advance on this is to catch young fish and then fatten them in fertile coastal waters (B). But marine farming really begins with the production of 'seed fish' which can be reared until they are large enough to survive at sea (C). Such a scheme was proposed in the early 1900s as a means of increasing the productivity of the North Sea fisheries. The proposal was rejected, although marine fish hatcheries existed at the time. These hatcheries, however, were unable to feed their young fish once the yolk sacs had become exhausted. Success became possible with the discovery that brine shrimps, hatched in large numbers, could be used as fish food and that antibiotics would prevent marine bacteria from coating the eggs and killing or weakening the fish embryos inside. The point has now been reached at which fish farming is possible, although fish reared in this way are still too expensive to compete with those caught at sea. In one scheme, eggs collected from adult fish kept in ponds are hatched and the young fed on diatoms and brine shrimps until large enough to be put into marine enclosures (D).

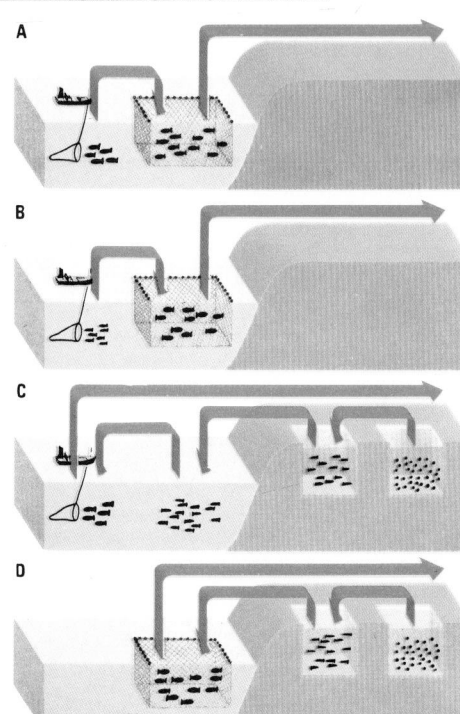

Enriching the sea *right, below*
Some marine farms in the future will exploit the store of nutrients that lie in the cold, deep ocean water. The value of this marine 'fertilizer' is clearly seen in areas where deep water rises to the surface. One project to create an artificial upwelling was started in the Virgin Islands in 1970. When completed it could include both a marine farm and provide fresh water supplies. In this system the cold nutrient-rich water (1) would be raised to the surface by a pump (2) driven by the warm, humid, prevailing winds (3). The cold water would then pass through a condenser (4) where it would be used to cool the wind and release its store of fresh water (5). Finally, the water, now warmed to the temperature of the surface waters, would be used to promote the growth of marine plants and animals such as shellfish, prawn and valuable food fish within net enclosures in the lagoon (6). Deep ocean water may also be used to combat thermal pollution, particularly in tropical areas where marine organisms live close to their upper temperature limit. The cold water would cool down the warm effluent discharged from power stations as well as provide valuable nutrients for marine aquiculture.

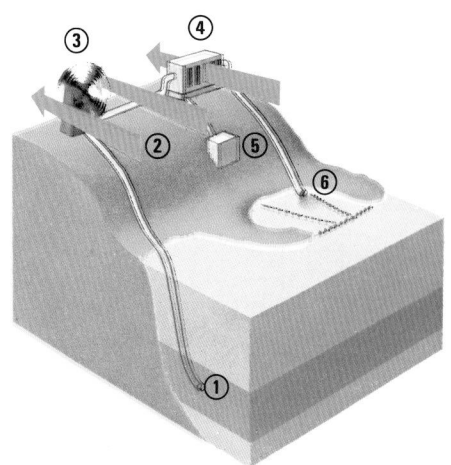

Combine harvester discharging wheat into trailer

Agriculture has always been a cornerstone of human civilization. Until man was able to give up the life of a nomadic hunter he could not be called civilized, and it was the settled life based on the land which enabled progress toward modern society to begin. Today agriculture is the occupation of more people than all other industries, but the pattern of their work varies greatly. In poor or developing lands as many as 90 per cent of the population live directly off the land, whereas in the most industrialized countries the proportion can be as low as three per cent.

The underlying purpose of farming is to convert the energy of sunlight into a form in which it can be assimilated by humans. Initially this can be done only by photosynthesis in green plants, and here the efficiency of the conversion process – expressed in terms of assimilable food energy obtained from a given amount of sunlight – varies from about two per cent down to less than one part in 1000. Further stages involve the consumption of plants by livestock to provide meat and other food for man, or the direct consumption of fruit, vegetables and cereals by man himself. Each additional step in this food chain involves large losses in energy, lowering the overall 'efficiency' of the process.

For many years research has led to improved methods of producing crops, by developing new plant strains with a higher edible yield or greater resistance to disease, by increasing both the area of land under cultivation and the nutritional value of the soil, by devising swifter and surer techniques of cultivation and by reducing the labor effort needed. Improved methods are especially needed in regions of poor farming. The 'Green Revolution' of SE Asia has already shown how yields can be increased dramatically, although at a greater cost in terms of agricultural chemicals and water supplies. Another promising way of increasing food supplies is to extract protein from plants such as soybean and even grass, and to convert them into forms that have the texture and taste of meat. For the more distant future there are prospects of growing single-cell protein and other revolutionary foods which in theory could at least double the Earth's ability to produce food.

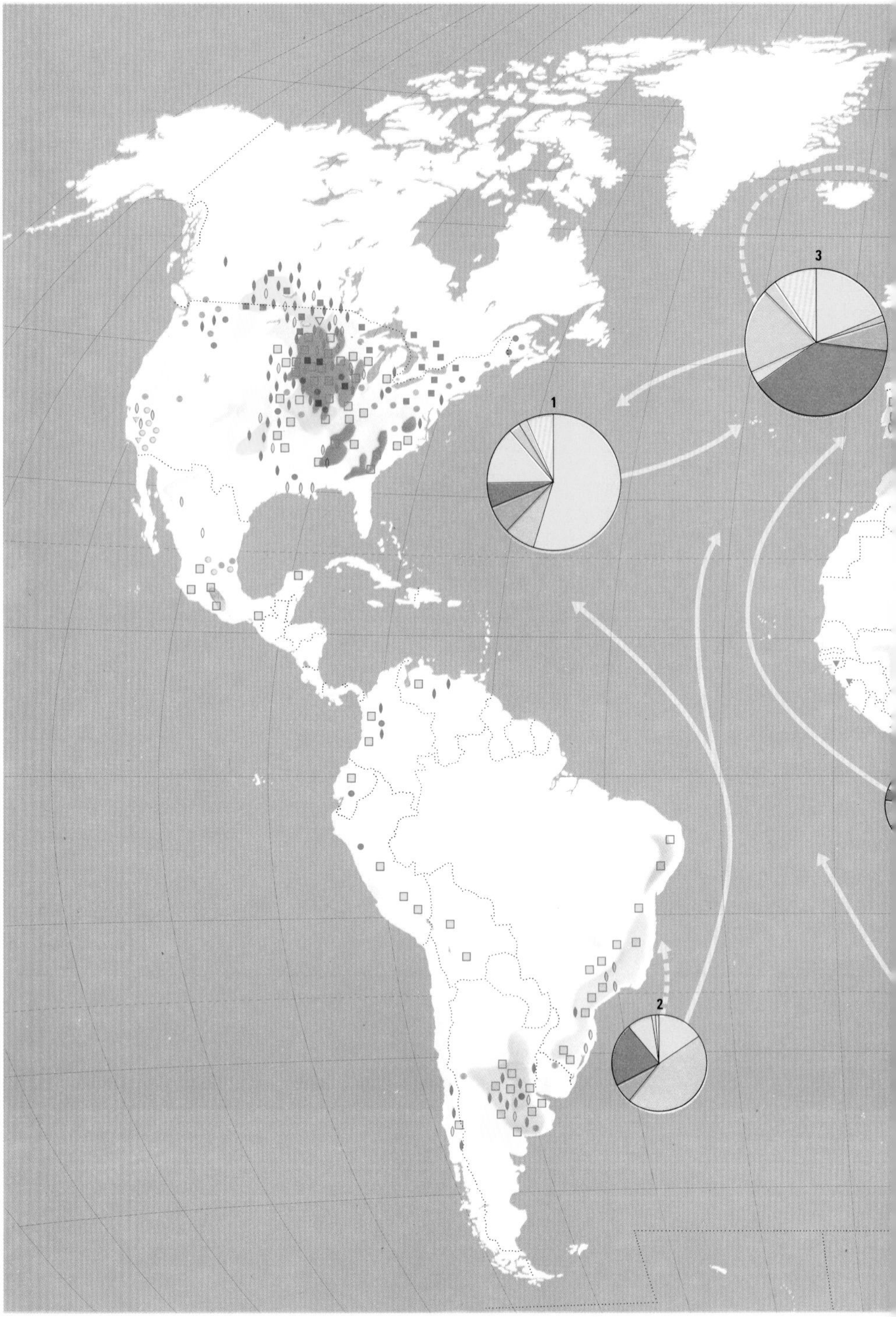

World crop production and trade *right above*
In the large map, symbols and shading indicate the pattern of distribution of a selection of the most important crops used for human food The distribution shown is that of growing area. This is often far removed from the plant's original center, and today the world crop pattern is being subjected to dramatic changes. For example, enormous increases have taken place in Italy's yield of maize (corn) and the United States' production of rice. Pie diagrams are used to show world crop trade, the pie area giving output and the color segments the products (key, far right).

Some important crops *right*
Eight of the world's chief human food crops are described individually at right. The figure below the name is the aggregate world production expressed in metric tons (1 m. ton is 0.984 British ton and 1.12 US tons). The pie diagrams in the form of segmented drums show the percentage of the world total raised by the three largest producing countries (in each case China is the People's Republic). The sketches illustrate the mature plant and its fruit, a form often unfamiliar to consumers. Similar panels on the next two pages deal with livestock, fish and oils.

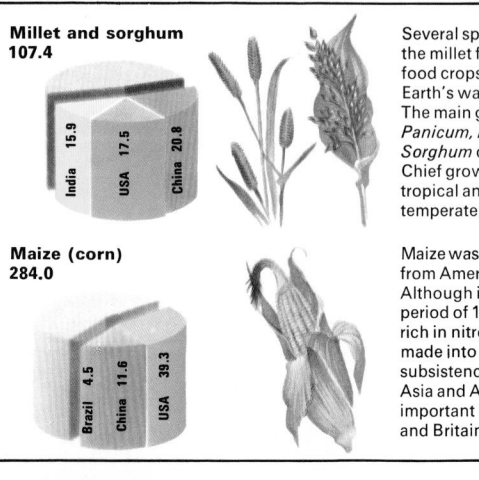

Millet and sorghum
107.4

India 15.9 | USA 17.5 | China 20.8

Maize (corn)
284.0

Brazil 4.5 | China 11.6 | USA 39.3

Several species of plant of the millet family form staple food crops throughout the Earth's warmer countries. The main genuses are *Panicum, Pennisetum,* and *Sorghum* or African millet. Chief growing regions are tropical and warm temperate Asia and Africa.

Maize was originally brought from America by Columbus. Although it needs a growing period of 140 days in a soil rich in nitrogen, it can be made into bread and is the subsistence diet of much of Asia and Africa and is important in North America and Britain.

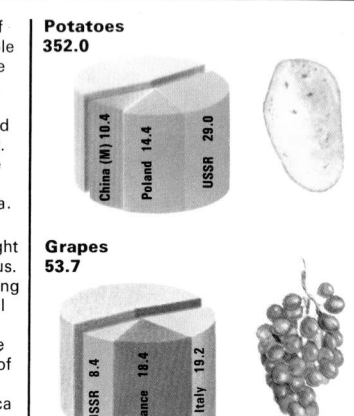

Potatoes
352.0

China (M) 10.4 | Poland 14.4 | USSR 29.0

Grapes
53.7

USSR 8.4 | France 18.4 | Italy 19.2

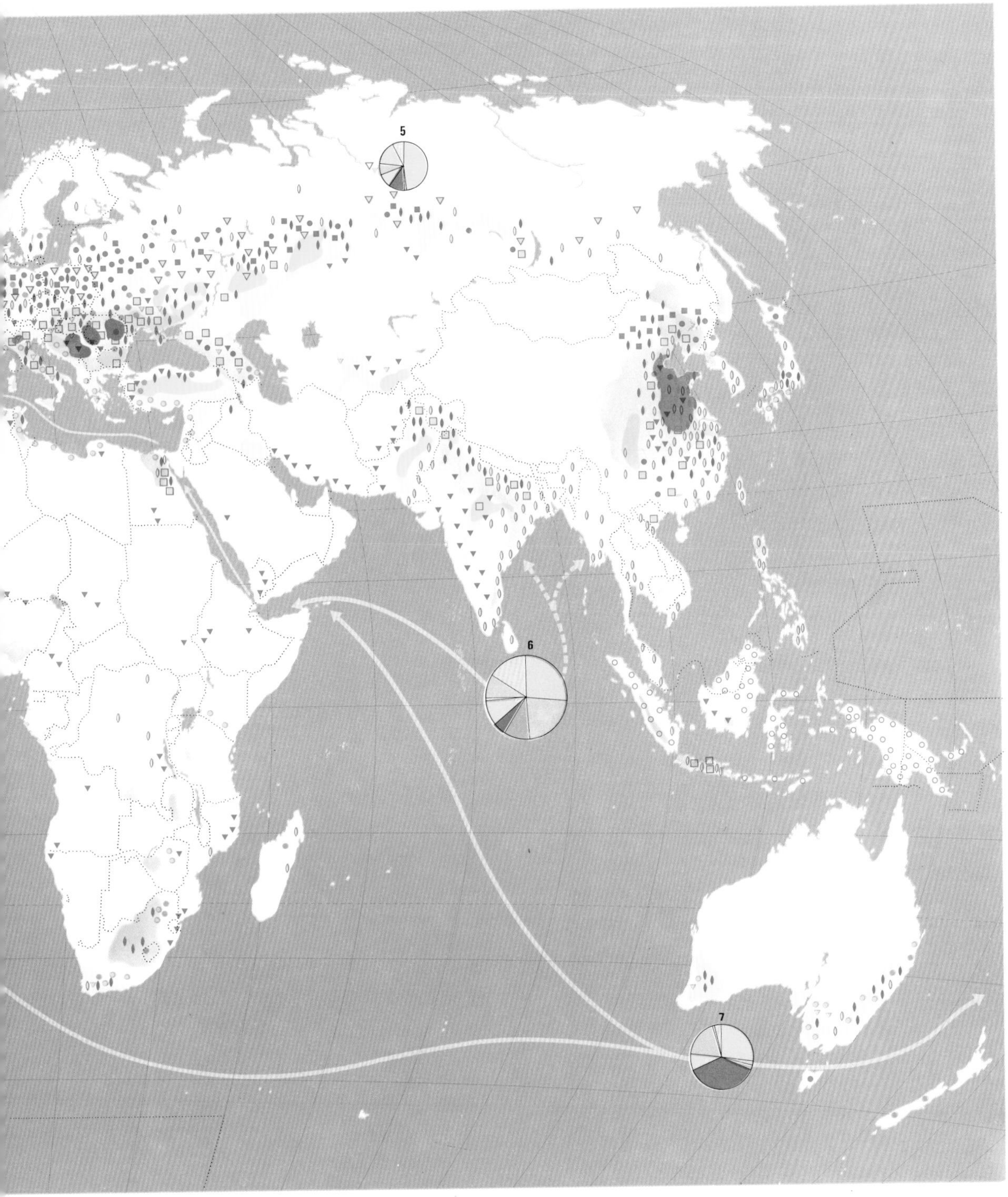

Cereals, predominantly wheat

Cereals, predominantly maize

Shading is proportional
to intensity of cultivation.

- ⸱ Wheat
- ⸱ Barley
- ▽ Rye
- □ Corn (maize)
- ○ Sago
- ■ Sorghum
- ▼ Millet
- ◊ Rice
- ● Potatoes
- ● Apples
- ◖ Citrus fruit
- ▽ Grapes

The circular 'pie diagrams'
depict world trade in selected
agricultural products in 1968:
1 N and Central America;
2 S America 3 Europe 4 Africa;
5 Soviet Union 6 Asia
7 Oceania Products considered
are cereals, beverages, meat
and meat products, fish and fish
products, dairy products, fruit
and vegetables, vegetable oils
and sugar.

- Cereals
- Beverages
- Fruit
- Meat and meat products
- Sugar
- Dairy products
- Vegetable oils
- Fish and fish products

Total trade US$ million

5000

2500

1250

Native to South America,
the potato was introduced
by Spanish explorers to an
intrigued Europe about
1572. Although it needs a
long, cool growing season,
and a high nutrient level. it
yields more food per area of
land than cereals. It is a
source of alcohol.

The vine thrives in warm,
temperate areas, although
the quality of its rootstock
is critical to its nutrient
demand and its resistance
to disease and drought.
About 80 per cent of the
world crop is made into
wine, but large quantities
are dried for raisins.

Rice
284.2

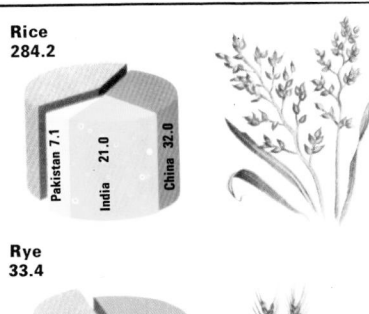

Pakistan 7.1 · India 21.0 · China 32.0

Rye
33.4

W Germany 9.5 · Poland 25.5 · USSR 42.2

Grown in Asia for at least
5000 years, rice was
introduced into Europe by
the Arabs. Irrigation or a
very heavy rainfall is
essential for growing rice,
with the fields being flooded
for most of the season. The
main source of vitamins, the
husk, is removed in milling.

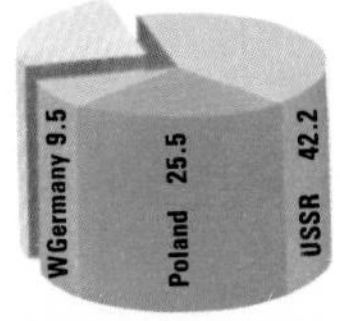

Gradually giving way to
other cereals, rye is
important where soils are
sandy and acid and the
winters long and harsh.
From Britain deep into
Siberia it remains a staple
foodstuff used for animal
feeds, for various forms of
bread and for whisky.

Wheat
332.5

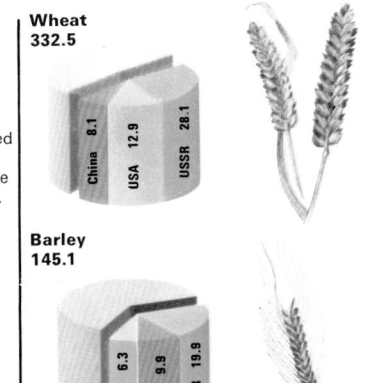

China 8.1 · USA 12.9 · USSR 28.1

Barley
145.1

USA 6.3 · China 9.9 · USSR 19.9

Wheat is the most basic
human food of the
temperate zone. It flourishes
in well-drained, fertile
conditions, but can rapidly
exhaust the soil. New breeds
have been genetically
tailored to improve yield
and resistance to disease

Barley has a very short
growing season and so can
be produced further north
and at a higher altitude than
any other cereal. It needs
good drainage and non-
acid soil. More than half the
world crop is eaten by
livestock, and 12 per cent
goes into making beer.

Unloading frozen lamb carcasses.

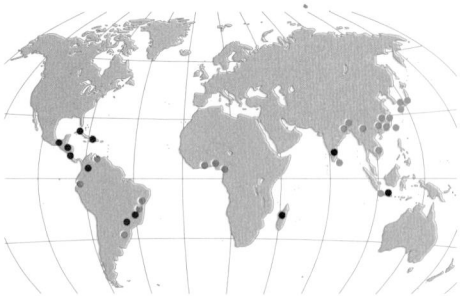

Beverages
Coffee, cocoa and tea are grown in the tropics for export to economically advanced countries where their chief role is to add flavor rather than to provide nutrition. Tea is the cheapest at present.

- Coffee
- Cocoa
- Tea

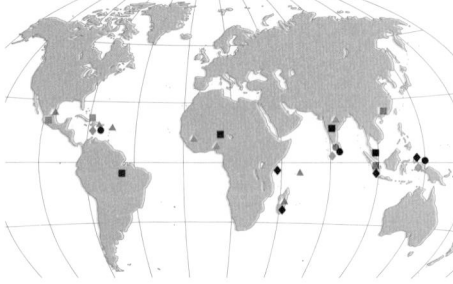

Spices
Invariably these are pungent, aromatic vegetable products. They have been important European imports since pre-Roman times, and a major source today is Indonesia. Spices are extracted from buds, bark and pods.

- Pimento
- Ginger
- Nutmeg
- Mace
- Pepper
- Cloves
- Cinnamon
- Cassia
- Vanilla

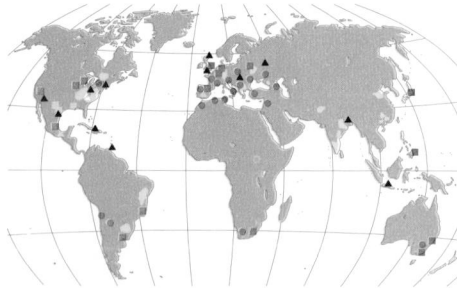

Alcohol and tobacco
Originally native to South America, tobacco was brought to Europe by the Spanish 400 years ago. Today, it is grown all over the world in various climates and soils. The US is the biggest producer.

- Beer
- Wine
- Spirits
- Tobacco

Beef cattle
Beef 29.7

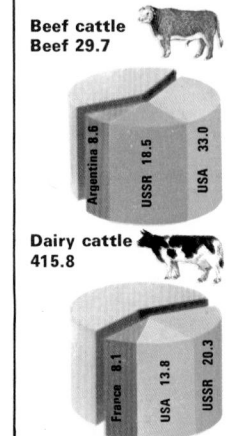

Argentina 8.6 | USSR 18.5 | USA 33.0

The two principal types of domestic cattle, the European and the tropical Zebu or humped type, are found all over the world in every type of climate. There is an urgent need in the developing countries for better breeding, disease control and management.

Dairy cattle
415.8

France 8.1 | USA 13.8 | USSR 20.3

Specialized dairy farming takes place mainly near densely populated urban areas with a high standard of living, though there is an increasing trend towards combined milk/meat herds. Various forms of processing, such as canning and freezing, extend product life.

Sheep
Mutton 4.5

India 8.2 | Australia 15.0 | USSR 22.3

Sheep are kept mainly for meat and wool, although in southern Europe they may be milked and in the tropics the hides are the most important product. Sheep do not lend themselves readily to 'factory farming' and are raised on marginal land only.

Pigs
Pork 24.5

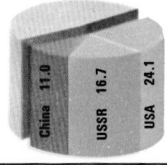

China 11.0 | USSR 16.7 | USA 24.1

Because they are often kept indoors, the distribution of pigs depends more on food supply than on the climate. They are often found on mixed farms where they are fed on by-products such as skim milk. Their breeding cycle is complete in about six months.

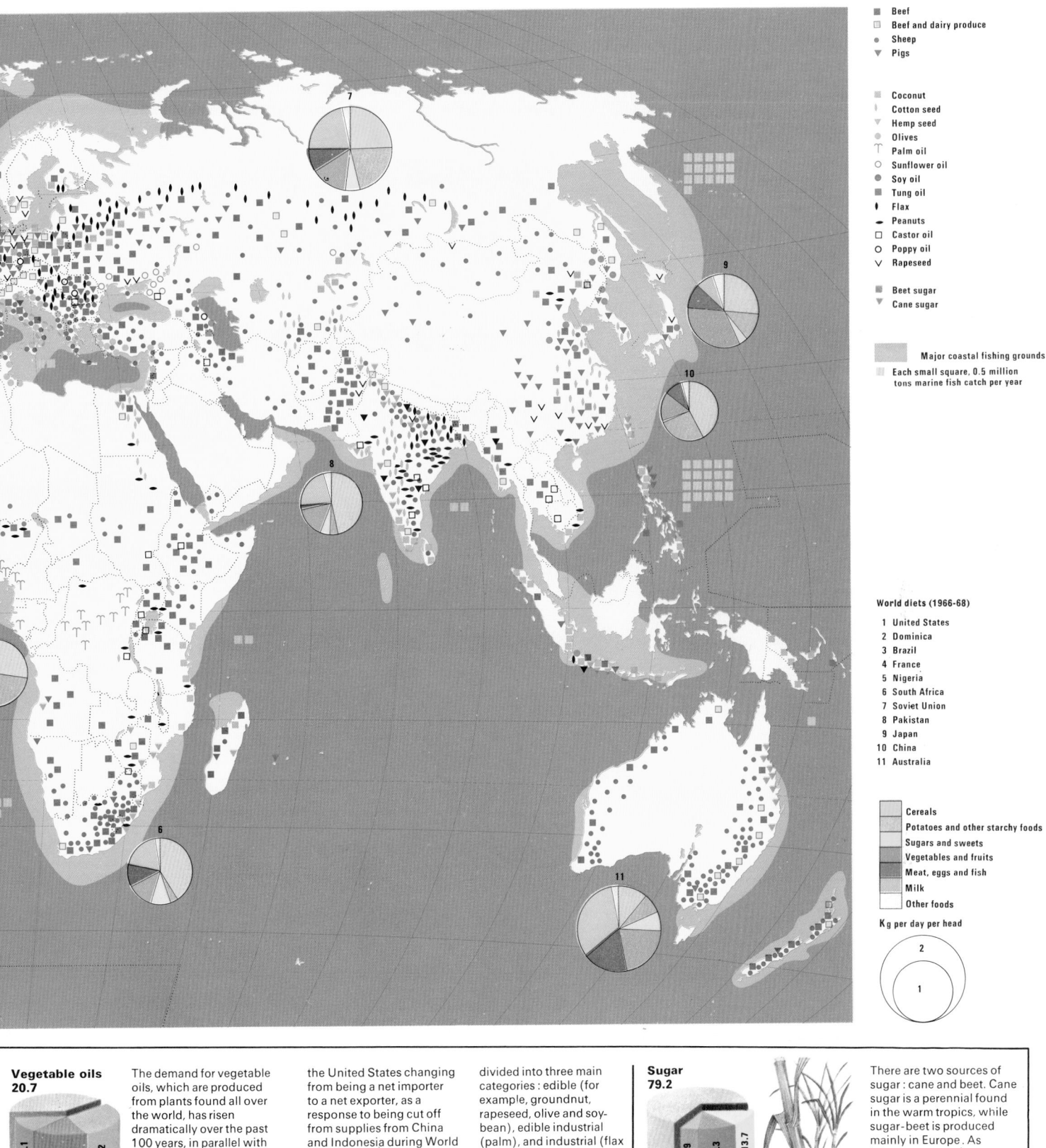

Beef
Beef and dairy produce
Sheep
Pigs

Coconut
Cotton seed
Hemp seed
Olives
Palm oil
Sunflower oil
Soy oil
Tung oil
Flax
Peanuts
Castor oil
Poppy oil
Rapeseed

Beet sugar
Cane sugar

Major coastal fishing grounds
Each small square, 0.5 million
tons marine fish catch per year

World diets (1966-68)

1 United States
2 Dominica
3 Brazil
4 France
5 Nigeria
6 South Africa
7 Soviet Union
8 Pakistan
9 Japan
10 China
11 Australia

Cereals
Potatoes and other starchy foods
Sugars and sweets
Vegetables and fruits
Meat, eggs and fish
Milk
Other foods

Kg per day per head

2

1

**Vegetable oils
20.7**

Groundnut   Soya bean   Olive   Flax   Sesame

Russia 14.1   China 17.4   USA 29.2

Cotton   Castor   Not to scale   Palm nut   Sunflower

The demand for vegetable oils, which are produced from plants found all over the world, has risen dramatically over the past 100 years, in parallel with the rise in prosperity and the discovery of new uses. The pattern of production has also altered markedly, with the United States changing from being a net importer to a net exporter, as a response to being cut off from supplies from China and Indonesia during World War 2. Vegetable oils are used in the manufacture of such products as margarine, soap and paint. They can be divided into three main categories: edible (for example, groundnut, rapeseed, olive and soy-bean), edible industrial (palm), and industrial (flax and castor). The oil is produced by crushing the seeds, and the residue often makes good cattle feed.

**Sugar
79.2**

Cuba 5.9   USSR 12.3   India 13.7

**Fish
64.0**

China 11.8   Japan 13.5   Peru 16.4

There are two sources of sugar: cane and beet. Cane sugar is a perennial found in the warm tropics, while sugar-beet is produced mainly in Europe. As it is more expensive to produce than cane its production is often protected by tariffs.

Fish are a valuable source of protein. As they putrify so easily and thus are subject to distribution problems, an increasing amount of the world catch is converted into meal for use in animal feeds. Most fish are caught near the coasts over the continental shelves.

Earth's Diverse Environments

To survive, animals must be adapted to their environment. They must be able to resist cold if they live in polar regions, drought if they live in deserts. They must find food, escape from predators and reproduce. Their offspring must mature and reproduce in turn. Adaptations of anatomy, physiology and behavior have evolved, so that today animals are found in all the Earth's diverse environments.

Ecologists divide the Earth into natural zones or 'biomes', each with its own highly adapted and integrated animal and plant communities. Inside each broad climatic zone animals have become adapted to various local environments or habitats. In tropical forests, for example, there are several layers of vegetation from the ground up to the tallest trees, and different animals with contrasting ways of life live in different layers. One species eats leaves and another eats berries, and so they avoid competition. Indeed the animals and plants of a community are interdependent. Herbivores eat plants, and carnivores eat herbivores. Food chains and the whole balance of a natural community can be altered by destroying one part of it. Thus, insecticides kill insects but also poison other animals in the area and the predators which prey on them.

Today's animals and plants are those whose ancestors survived immense changes. Continents drifted apart and moved together, seas rose and fell, mountains erupted and were levelled by erosion, glaciers advanced and retreated. Life evolved. Some animals became extinct; others adapted to the changes and spread to new areas. Sometimes they met impassable oceans, mountains and deserts. Groups of animals then became isolated and continued to evolve independently. Marsupials, mammals with pouches, were isolated in Australia before placental mammals, whose young are nourished for a long time in the mother's uterus, evolved in Europe and Asia. Placental mammals then supplanted marsupials everywhere but in Australia. Scientists divide the world into six zoogeographical realms each containing animals not found elsewhere. Some animals mix in transitional zones such as the Sahara Desert and the Himalayas.

Environmental factors

Climate is determined by the Sun's radiation on the Earth's atmosphere, oceans and continents. It varies with the time of day and season. Winds generated by the solar heating carry moisture inland, and heat away from the tropics. Ocean currents affect the prevailing temperature over large regions. Solar radiation, winds and ocean currents, together with latitude, altitude and the form of the land, combine to produce each local climate.

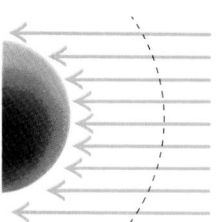

Solar heating *left*
The tropics are hotter than the poles because the Sun's rays pass almost vertically through a shallower depth of atmosphere and so are less attenuated. The Sun's vertical rays shift seasonally between the Tropics of Cancer and Capricorn, altering the length of daylight.

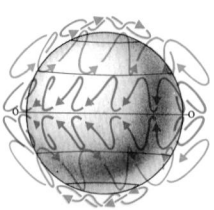

Wind and weather *left*
Hot air at the equator rises and moves north and south to higher latitudes. It subsides, producing trade winds, deflected by the rotation of the Earth, back again to the tropics. Westerly winds blow from the sub-tropics highs poleward toward the sub-polar lows.

Oceans *left*
Surface currents created by prevailing winds and variations in the density of the water are deflected by landmasses and the Coriolis effect' of rotation. Onshore winds across ocean currents are a major climatic control.

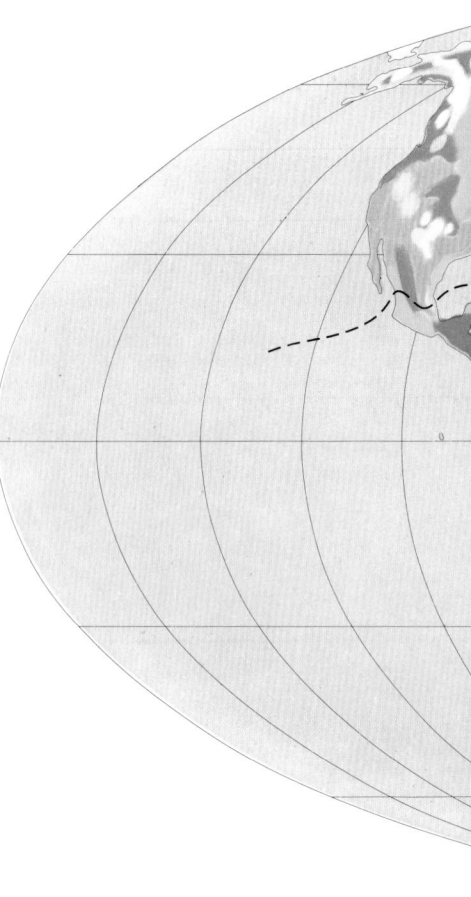

The zoogeographical classification of environments

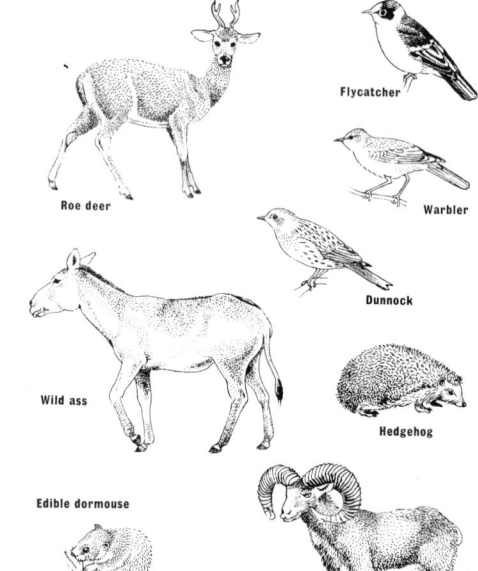
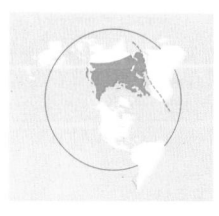

Flycatcher
Roe deer
Warbler
Dunnock
Wild ass
Hedgehog
Edible dormouse
Wild Sheep

Beaver
Pronghorn
Mocking bird
Skunk
Turkey
Bison
Rattlesnake

Tiger salamander
Orangutan
Tree shrew
Gibbon
Fairy bluebird
Tiger
Peacock
Indian elephant

Palearctic (A)
This zoogeographical realm, the extent of which is shown on the map at right, is often grouped with the Nearctic to form the so-called Holarctic region. Roe deer, hedgehogs, dormice and the Asian wild ass are all unique here. Ancestors of modern horses crossed into it from North America during an ice age when the continents were bridged with ice.

Nearctic (B)
Covering the whole of North America from Greenland to the high plateau of Mexico, this realm contains beavers, elk and caribou. The prairie buffalo, which were slaughtered in their millions by 19th century man, have been saved from total extinction. And the American wild turkey has now been very successfully domesticated.

Oriental (C)
Comprising the southern part of Asia, Indonesia and the Philippines, this realm is largely isolated from the Palearctic realm to the north by the great folded barrier of the Himalayas, thrown up when the Indian subcontinent collided with Asia. Indigenous animals include tree shrews, tarsiers, gibbons, orangutans and the Indian elephant.

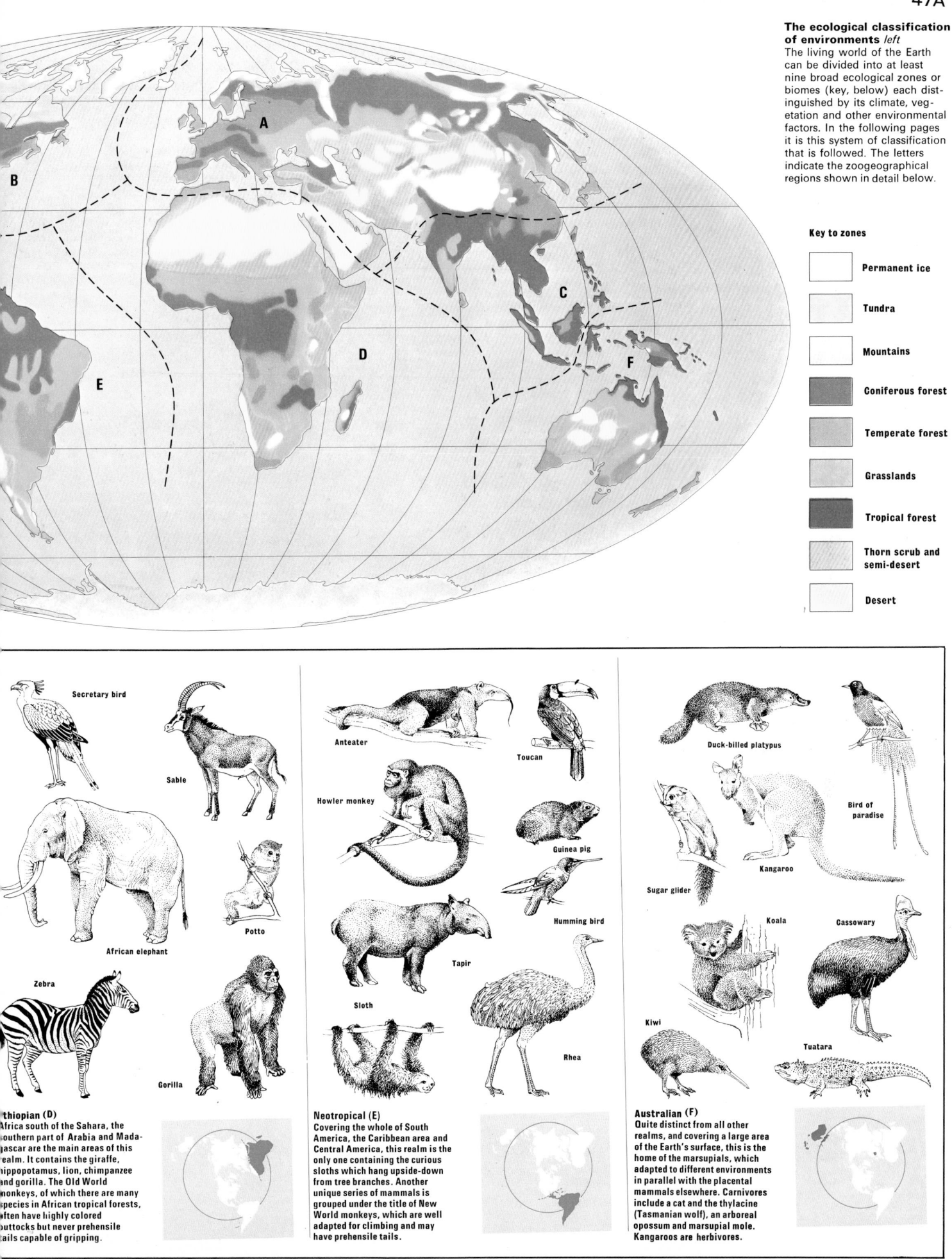

The ecological classification of environments *left*
The living world of the Earth can be divided into at least nine broad ecological zones or biomes (key, below) each distinguished by its climate, vegetation and other environmental factors. In the following pages it is this system of classification that is followed. The letters indicate the zoogeographical regions shown in detail below.

Key to zones

- Permanent ice
- Tundra
- Mountains
- Coniferous forest
- Temperate forest
- Grasslands
- Tropical forest
- Thorn scrub and semi-desert
- Desert

Ethiopian (D)
Africa south of the Sahara, the southern part of Arabia and Madagascar are the main areas of this realm. It contains the giraffe, hippopotamus, lion, chimpanzee and gorilla. The Old World monkeys, of which there are many species in African tropical forests, often have highly colored buttocks but never prehensile tails capable of gripping.

Neotropical (E)
Covering the whole of South America, the Caribbean area and Central America, this realm is the only one containing the curious sloths which hang upside-down from tree branches. Another unique series of mammals is grouped under the title of New World monkeys, which are well adapted for climbing and may have prehensile tails.

Australian (F)
Quite distinct from all other realms, and covering a large area of the Earth's surface, this is the home of the marsupials, which adapted to different environments in parallel with the placental mammals elsewhere. Carnivores include a cat and the thylacine (Tasmanian wolf), an arboreal opossum and marsupial mole. Kangaroos are herbivores.

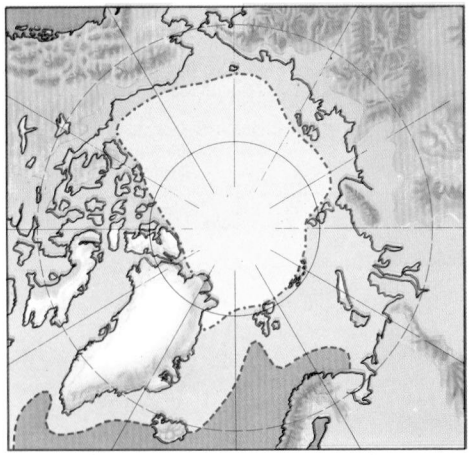

.—.—. Pack ice limit   - - - - Drifting ice limit

The Arctic ice cap is the opposite of Antarctica in much more than mere location. It is principally an area of permanently frozen sea ice, although it also includes part of Greenland. It has an indigenous human population, despite the average annual temperature of −24°F on the Greenland ice cap, who have managed to adapt themselves to a ferocious environment by copying the animals around them. Just as the seals and polar bears shelter under the snow, bearing their cubs in dens, the Eskimos developed the igloo built from blocks of wind-packed snow. These ice homes are windproof and the temperature inside can rise to 59°F.

Fur and feathers are good heat insulators because each hair or feather is surrounded by air, which conducts heat poorly and thus lessens the amount of body heat escaping. Polar animals have very thick fur. Eskimos wear two layers of skins, one fur side in and the other fur side out. But fur is less efficient if it is wet, so seals and walruses have a thick layer of fatty blubber under the skin. Fat, like air, is a poor heat conductor. Circulation can be restricted so that some animals maintain two body temperatures: one normally warm-blooded inside the body and one as cold as the environment in the feet, flippers and nostrils, which must be free of fur or blubber to function. Extremities from which heat is easily lost, such as ears, are small in polar bears and absent in seals. Heat lost through radiation is proportional to the body's surface. Relative to its volume, a large animal has less surface area than a small one. So a large animal will lose heat more slowly. Polar bears, for instance, are bigger than bears in more temperate regions.

Few eskimos are still hunters of seals, walruses and whales. There has been mass slaughter of seals for their skins, and the population has rapidly declined. Life in the Arctic is changing. Uranium, titanium and other minerals have been discovered. In Alaska oil is bringing prosperity and industrialization. Much of the energy devoted to opening up these great 'lands of tomorrow' has been triggered by military needs. Now the main spur is becoming an economic one.

Polar bears
Bigger animals have less surface area for each unit of body weight than small animals, and thus lose heat less rapidly. Polar bears are among the largest bears. The adult male (top right) can be 11 feet (3.4 m) long, compared with the 9-10 ft (2.7-3 m) of the brown grizzly (center right) and 4-4.5 ft (1.2-1.4 m) of the sun bear (bottom right). Most polar bears winter in a den roughly eight feet (2.4 m) long, but two-room dens have been found.

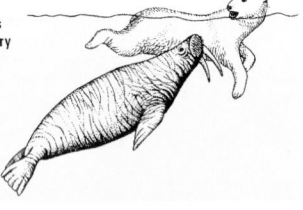

Vulnerable *right*
On land the polar bear is supreme, even on slippery ice. But if a bear is forced to enter deep water it becomes much more vulnerable and can be harried even by young seals. A big bull walrus, illustrated, can kill it swiftly.

Walrus bulls *below*
Weighing up to 3000 pounds. the 12 foot (3.7 m) bull walrus uses its tusks for digging out shellfish, breaking air-holes in the ice and fighting. One-third of its weight is blubber, in a 2½ inch (63.5 mm) thick layer under the skin (right).

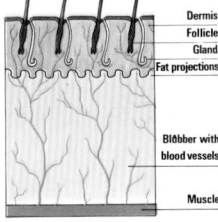

Dermis
Follicle
Gland
Fat projections

Blubber with blood vessels

Muscle

Pack ice *above*
Open pack ice, stretching as far as the eye can see, reflects the pink rays of the low Sun. Such ice is seldom more than one year old and usually gets crushed or melted in a shorter time. Unlike the dangerous bergs, it is no hazard to navigation.

Seal and tern *below*
The shores of the Irish Sea are among the wide areas of rocky coast on both sides of the North Atlantic inhabited by the grey seal (female illustrated : the male is larger) and sandwich tern (once common at Sandwich in Kent).

Arctic tern *below*
Distinguished from other terns by its vivid beak and feet, the Arctic tern migrates down the coasts of Europe and Africa to the Antarctic before returning to the Arctic to nest. The round trip (left) can be a remarkable 22000 miles (35000 km).

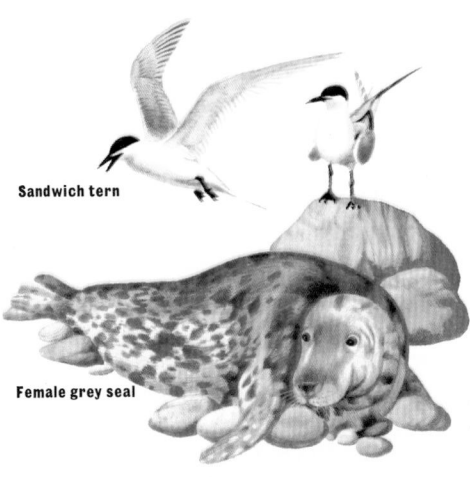

Sandwich tern

Female grey seal

Antarctic

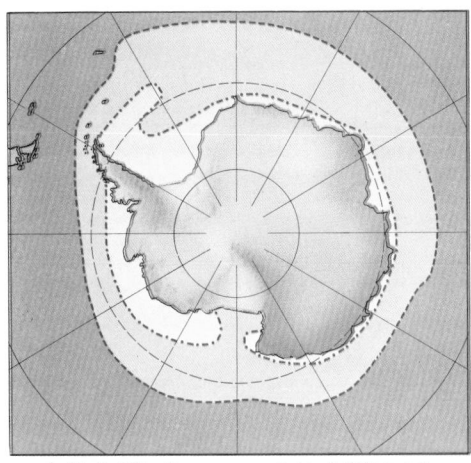

In complete contrast to the North Polar region, the Antarctic is a frozen continent encircled by ocean. Mountains surround low-lying land covered with ice so thick that it forms a high plateau. It is the coldest region on Earth. Throughout almost all of Antarctica no monthly average temperature exceeds 0°C, and the average annual temperature at the South Pole is –60°C. Blizzards blow when a shallow layer of colder air over the ice-sheet flows downslope, and the snow is packed into a hard pavement.

Around the continental edges, icebergs up to 1000 feet (300 m) thick break off the ice caps or valley glaciers and fall into the sea. The ice, formed of compacted and recrystallized snow, is only slightly less dense than sea-water, so icebergs float low in the ocean with five-sixths to eight-ninths of their bulk below the surface. The Antarctic icebergs are tabular, with flat tops and cliff-like sides; Arctic bergs from the Greenland ice cap are peaked and rarely break off in the sizes common in Antarctica, where the floating ice islands can be as much as ten miles (16 km) long.

Until 450 million years ago the Earth had no ice caps. In the Antarctic, ice formed in the center of the continent and moved out towards the sea. Cooling at the North Pole probably occurred later.

In summer, when the ice breaks up and the amount of daylight increases, there is a rapid growth of tiny floating plants called phytoplankton. These plants provide 'grazing' for the zooplankton, small animals of which the shrimp-like krill are the most numerous, which in turn are eaten by the larger animals, among them seals and whalebone whales. One of these whales, the blue whale, is the largest animal ever to inhabit the Earth. A variety of birds live in the Antarctic, including penguins and the skuas which prey on them, snow petrels and albatrosses. These warm-blooded animals all have to keep their body temperature well above that of the environment. Many birds avoid the polar winter by migrating to temperate lands. But emperor penguins stay, and in an Antarctic blizzard colonies of them huddle tightly together to reduce the exposed surface area of their bodies.

18in, 45cm

Adélie penguins *above*
They make devoted parents and may, as shown here, produce two chicks at different times in one season.

Emperor penguin *right*
Easily the largest penguin, the emperor (about 4 ft, 120 cm) breeds on Antarctic sea ice and coasts (see below).

Seals *left and below*
Seals abound in the Antarctic. The crab-eater (left) bears the scars of an encounter with a killer whale. The Weddell seal (below left) is guarding its three-week pup. South Georgia elephant seals (below) are wallowing among tussock grass.

Fjord *above*
A scene of rare beauty north of Marguerite Bay in the Antarctic Peninsula (Grahamland). Here the rock of the continent is visible, with a glacier at the right and brash ice at the left floating on water ruffled only by the gentle passage of the ship.

Incubating *above*
The male emperor hatches the eggs, which rest on the feet beneath a warm brood flap of fatty skin.

Macaroni *left*
There are several species of crested penguins. Tallest is the macaroni, here seated on its nest. (18 in, 45 cm)

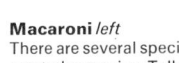

Great skua *right*
Skuas are scavengers. They steal food and eggs, kill young chicks and prey on weak adults.

Lichen *below*
The red lichen on this rock could be 1000 years old. Its slow metabolism survives the cold.

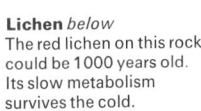

The cold lands *above*
In the northern hemisphere there are vast areas of land at latitudes higher than 60°. The warmer parts of these regions are colonized by immense numbers of conifers (facing page) which extend right across the Earth's widest land mass. Where the climate is too severe for trees, the forest gives way to tundra.

Permanent residents of the tundra
Life is hard in the Arctic tundra, but a great variety of animal life is adapted to it. Grass and other plant food grows for no more than two out of each 12 months, but many animals live off it all the year round and even eat the roots while the surface is covered with snow. Carnivores depend to a great degree on the population of lemmings (below) which reaches a peak about every third year. In spring the land becomes ablaze with flowers, and birds abound.

Lemmings
These small rodents are about five inches (125 mm) long. They have short tails, and ears hidden by thick fur. Every three or four years a population explosion triggers a mass migration in which thousands of lemmings die.

Surrounding the Arctic Ocean are the Arctic tundra and, further south, the coniferous forest. There is no land at such high latitude (60°-70°) in the southern hemisphere. Seasonal changes are extreme. The Sun may shine continuously in summer and not at all in mid-winter. Winter cold and summer heat are greatest in the continental interiors, where it is also drier than around the coasts. Interaction between polar and tropical air masses causes storms.

In the treeless tundra the average temperature of the warmest month is below 10°C (50°F). The land is forested where the average for at least one month is above that temperature. In some places the tundra and forest are divided by a distinct tree-line; in other regions the true coniferous forest is preceded by grasses, sedges and lichens. The soils are affected by 'permafrost' and are almost permanently frozen. In summer the surface becomes waterlogged and often flooded, but the seasonal thaw reaches a depth of only 4-24 inches (100-600 mm). Soil water under the plants melts, and a thick mud forms which may

flow downslope making bulging terraces. Because of recent glaciation there are many lakes and swamps, called muskeg in Canada.

Lemmings feed on the vegetation of the tundra. In winter they dig for roots in an underground network of tunnels where it is about 10°C (18°F) warmer than on the surface. If their population increases so much that there is competition for space, masses of lemmings move into the forest and cross streams, lakes and rivers as they go. Many drown.

Herds of American caribou and closely related European reindeer migrate up to several hundred miles from their summer pasture on the tundra to find winter food on the forest fringes. Nomadic Lapps follow the reindeer and use them for transport, food and clothing. They milk them and make cheese. In contrast, the caribou have never been domesticated: the Indians of northern Canada were hunters. Their skill as trappers was exploited by the European fur trade. And in the Siberian tundra every resource is being vigorously exploited; a new land is opening up.

Winter and summer
above and left
In winter the cold lands are dull and seemingly barren, although at the edges of the tundra stunted conifers are dotted among the lakes. But in summer the plant life flourishes. Reindeer graze among flowers from Norway to the Pacific.

Seasonal plumage
Many of the Arctic birds and animals change their appearance to blend into the contrasting summer and winter backgrounds. For example, the rock ptarmigan is mottled brown in July (left) but white in winter until May (below). Both hunted animals, such as

the Arctic hare, and their predators change their color. The Arctic fox, which preys on the rock ptarmigan, is white or very pale in winter (above) but changes into a summer coat which is usually brown but in the so-called "blue-foxes" is deep blue-grey (right).

Arctic color *below*
Tundra is not always dull. In the Alaskan September plant life is in full bloom.

Early blooms *above*
The Pasque flower is in evidence throughout Alaska as early as May.

The Coniferous Forests

Except for the Siberian larch, which sheds its needles in winter, the trees of the coniferous forest are ever-green. Spruce, fir, pine and hemlock (associated near water with mountain ash, poplar, balsam, willow and birch) are widespread through Eurasia and North America. The similarity between the distribution of plants and animals is the result of frequent freezing of the Bering Strait which allowed migration between the continents.

The forest animals depend on the trees for food. Beavers eat bark, and squirrels and birds eat buds and seeds. In summer, when there is more food, multitudes of birds migrate to the forest to nest.

The cold forests are of enormous extent. Lumbering is a major industry, and the numerous rivers are used to transport the logs to the sawmills. Great volumes of softwoods are consumed every year, mainly in the building industry and for papermaking. Minerals are now being mined in the cold lands. Iron ore is mined in Labrador and Quebec, and Alaska's gold, copper, iron, oil and gas are being exploited.

The beaver's handiwork
Throughout northern America, and in northern Europe and Asia, the beaver gnaws through trees to secure the soft inner bark from the upper branches. It stores these in a still pool formed by damming a river, and nearby constructs a remarkable lodge with as many as eight underwater entrances.

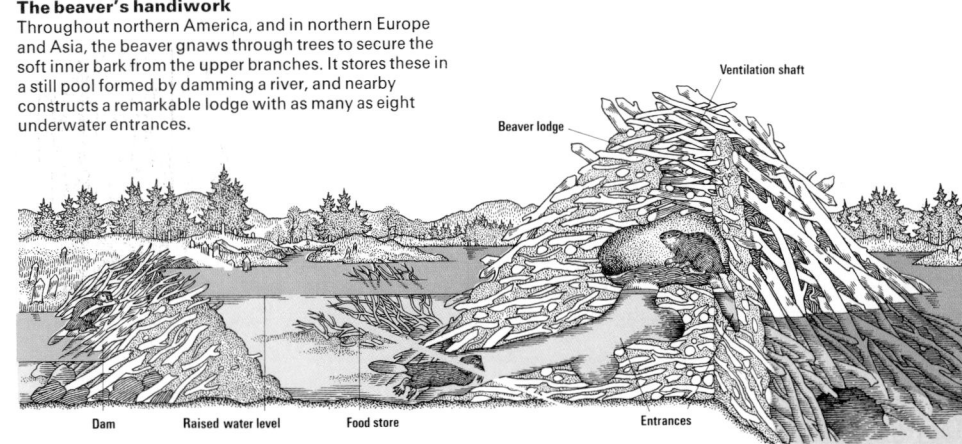

Ventilation shaft

Beaver lodge

Dam   Raised water level   Food store   Entrances

Tree types *above*
Temperate broad-leaved trees could not survive the northern winter. Most cold forest trees are conifers, with needle-like leaves. From the left : scots pine ; larch, which sheds its leaves ; Norway spruce ; Douglas fir.

Burrowers *right and below*
The woodchuck (right) is one of the cold forest dwellers that hibernates. Its winter metabolism falls almost to a standstill ; then it awakens in March and is busy until fall. The European polecat (below) sometimes kills marmots and uses their burrows.

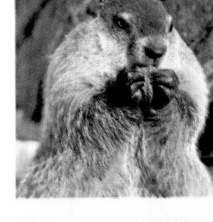

Grizzlies *above*
Although a carnivore, the giant brown bear often digs for roots, as here.

Ground squirrel *below*
The striped ground squirrel does not climb trees but eats roots, leaves and insects.

Contrasting diets
above and right
Despite its formidable appearance the moose lives on small plants, berries and tree shoots. Only the male has antlers. But the lynx (right) is a carnivore, whose population follows that of its principal prey, the hare.

South of the coniferous forest is extensive deciduous woodland of oak, beech and chestnut which flourishes wherever there is an annual rainfall of 30-60 inches (750-1500mm) distributed throughout the year. Woodland once covered large areas of the northern hemisphere, but most has now been cleared for agriculture. There are different mid-latitude climates on the east and west sides of continents: east coast climates are continental, with hot summers and cold winters, while winds blowing off the ocean bring rain to the more equable west coasts.

In winter the deciduous trees shed their broad leaves which would be vulnerable to frost. The leaves slowly rot to a rich humus, and in boggy places peat forms. Nutrients circulate by water draining through the soil and then being drawn up by evaporation and transpiration through the leaves.

Tree types

In North America and Asia the oak, beech, hickory and maple dominate; in Europe the oak, ash, lime and chestnut, with beech in cool moist areas. On damp ground near rivers willow, alder, ash and elm are found. Conifers grow faster so that they often supplant deciduous trees in managed forests. They form the natural forest on the west coast of North America, where some of the largest trees are found.

Near the tropics are the broadleaf evergreen forests. In Japan and the southeast of the United States there are evergreen oaks, laurel and magnolia, with palms, bays and ferns in the swamps of the Mississippi delta. The warm wet forest of New Zealand's South Island contains conifers, podocarp and evergreen beeches, with tree ferns, palms and bamboos. In a Mediterranean type of climate the summers are hot and dry. Cork oaks have hard, leathery leaves covered with a thick cuticle to minimize water loss. The Mediterranean forest is now only a narrow coastal belt. Tree felling and frequent summer fires have left scrub known as the maquis. The chaparral of California and Mexico is similar.

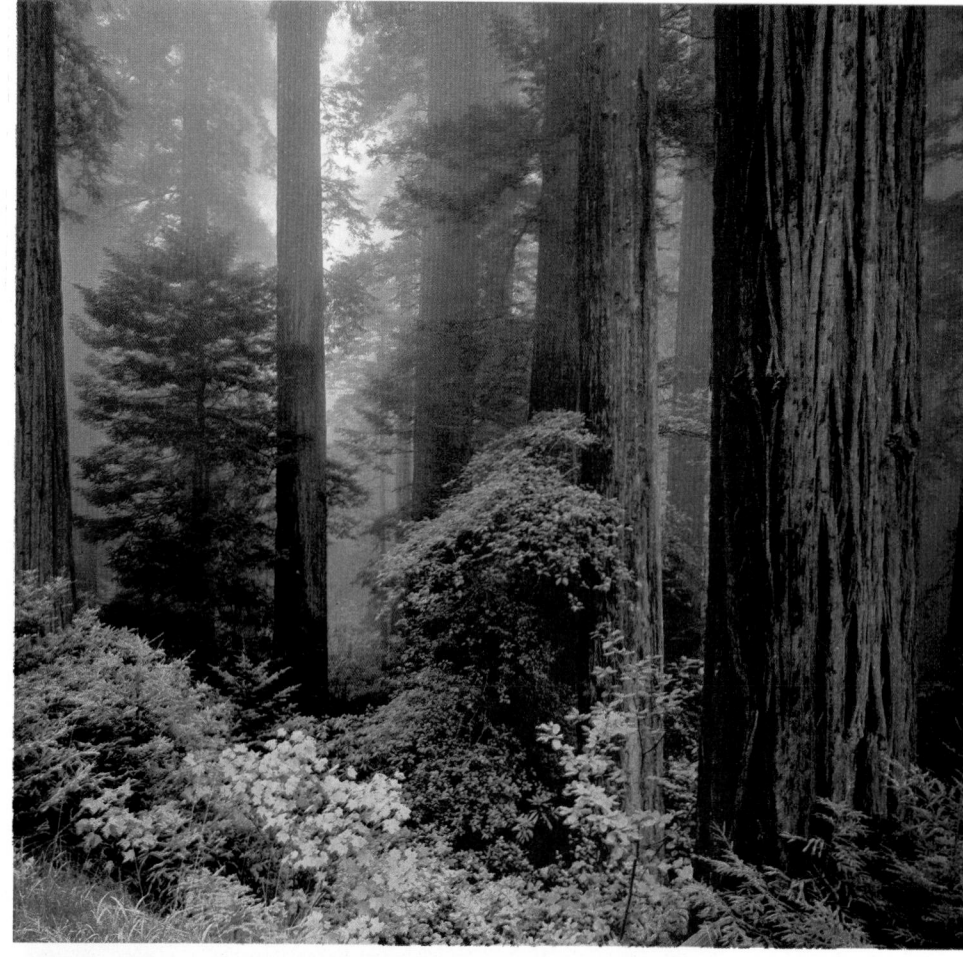

Redwoods *above*
Along the west coast of the United States is a foggy coastal belt where the redwood forests flourish. The giant redwoods and sequoias may be several thousand years old and up to 400 feet (120 m) high. They are among the Earth's oldest living things.

Beechwoods *left*
Typical of the cool northern deciduous forest, Burnham Beeches, near London, generates millions of beech leaves each year. Littering the ground, they decompose into a rich humus which overlies the soil and supports plant life, worms and a variety of insects.

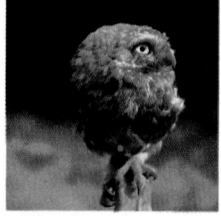

Little owl *above*
Predator of woodland animals, its forward-facing eyes give good binocular vision for judging distance in dim light.

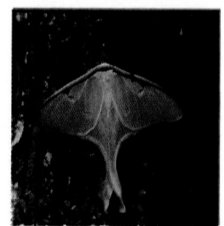

Luna moth *above*
Found in American deciduous forest, the moth prefers a diet of rhododendrons. India has a tropical variety.

Forest birds
The crossbill (left) can pry open tough pine cones; the pheasant (below,) of which there are 49 species, is concealed on the ground by its camouflage.

Animal variety
above and left
Woodland inhabitants of the New England states are the box turtle and wood frog (above). The Yugoslavian four-lined snake (left) has the slender body and angled scales common to snakes which need to obtain purchase on bark.

The ecology of an oak

Oaks of various sub-species are among the most important trees in the northern deciduous forests, and they play a major role in local wildlife. Oaks have a history dating back over 50 million years, and 7000 years ago covered vast tracts of temperate land. Throughout recorded history man has prized the oak for its hard, durable wood, which has been favored above all others for making houses, ships, furniture and other artifacts. The oak population has thus dwindled, and in modern managed forests the faster-growing conifers are preferred. But each remaining oak is a microcosm of nature. The autumn leaf-fall returns valuable nutrients to the soil, providing a source of humus. In the spring up to a quarter of a million new leaves grow, providing an area for photosynthesis as great as 10000 sq ft (930 m²). Small streamers of flowers are pollinated by wind-borne pollen, leading in midsummer to the crop of acorns which are stored by grey squirrels, badgers and many other animals for the coming winter. As many as 200 species of insect can feed on one tree. Largest is the leaf-eating stag beetle, and the most prominent the gall wasp whose marble gall houses the larva. The damage insects inflict often results in the tree producing a second crop of midsummer leaves. The serotine bat and tawny owl are the main nocturnal predators of the oak forest. The former takes winged insects in flight, while small rodents form the staple diet of the owl.

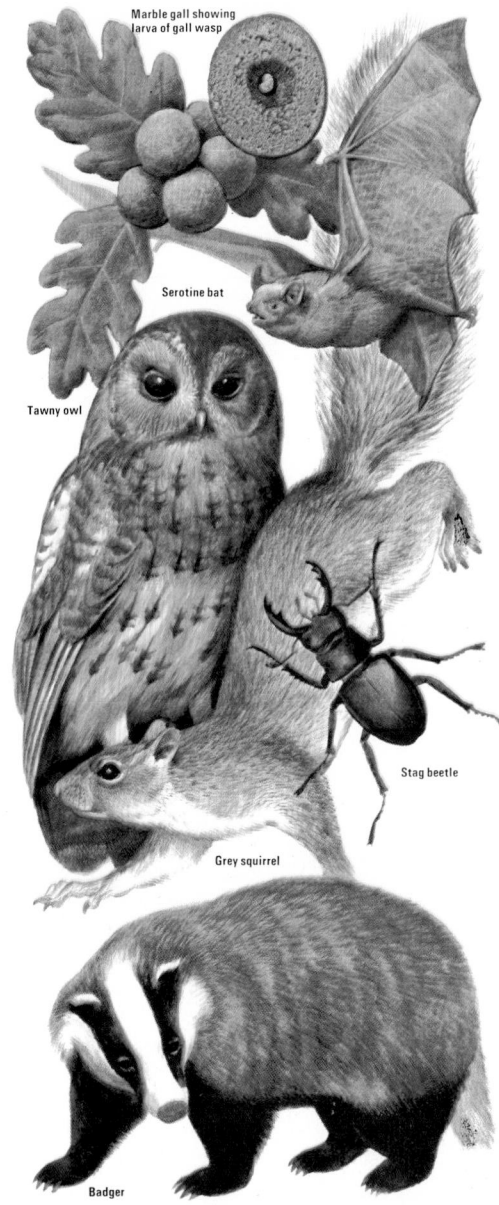

Marble gall showing larva of gall wasp

Serotine bat

Tawny owl

Stag beetle

Grey squirrel

Badger

The mature oak right

The extensive buttressed roots of an old oak can provide the portal through which a fox (1) tunnels to its lair. Low on the trunk a beefsteak fungus (2) may grow, providing fruiting bodies upon which feed many kinds of animals and insects. The trunk often decays locally (3), providing a home for both bats and owls. The fallow deer (female, 4) and jay (5) collect acorns, while in the branches a clump of mistletoe (6) grows, nurtured by the tree on which it is a parasite.

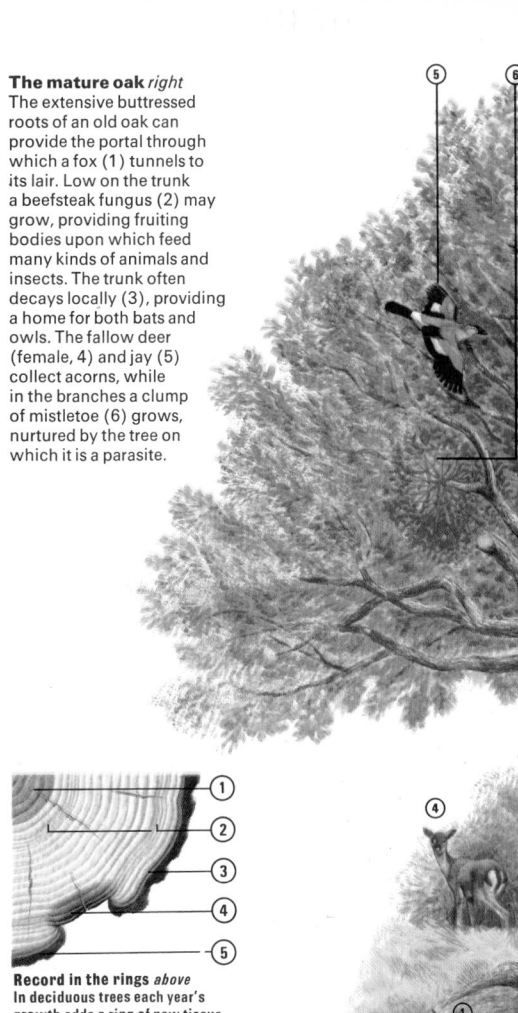

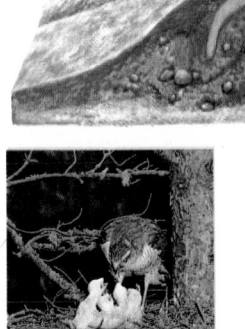

Record in the rings *above*
In deciduous trees each year's growth adds a ring of new tissue to the trunk, as shown by this section segment from an oak with an age of 24 years. Within the first five years is the dark heartwood (1). Between years 7-10 growth was slowed (2), possibly by drought or the crowding of other trees. Growth was also slow in years 19-22, and in the 21st year part of the tree was burned, leaving a scar (4) which gradually heals with further growth. Present growth takes place in the cambium (3) just inside the bark (5).

 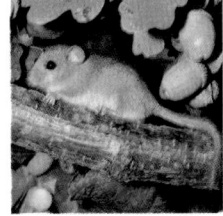 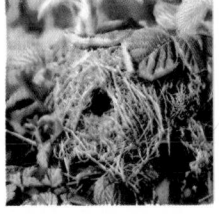

Paper wasp
The queen starts the football-like nest, which is made of chewed wood and has a paper-like consistency. Her subjects enlarge it.

Mole
Moles live in burrows excavated underground by their strong front claw-feet. Emerging into the open, their eyes see poorly.

Dormouse
Most of the forest rodents store food for the winter, but the dormouse hibernates, at a reduced body temperature.

Dormouse nest
Although the dormouse lives deep in the undergrowth, it is very agile, and builds a spherical nest above ground level.

Sparrowhawk
Like many birds of prey the sparrowhawk makes a substantial nest of twigs and forest debris high in a tree, where its young are safe.

Blue tit
A favorite choice of home for the blue tit is a hole in a tree. Inside the cavity it constructs a nest of moss and soft debris.

Common oak
Widespread and important to commerce and forest life, the oak grows slowly and is yielding to other species.

Silver birch
Mature at 50, the silver-barked birch is found in all temperate forest and extends far into the tundra.

Beech
Big and densely packed, the beech is very beneficial. Essentially a forest tree, it prefers drained chalky soil.

Ash
Although it exhausts soil, the ash produces tough wood. Its multi-leaflet leaves are one foot (0.25 m) long.

Sweet chestnut
Originally from Asia Minor, the sweet chestnut fruit is a preferred food of many forest animals.

Sycamore
One of the maple family, the sycamore prefers exposed positions where its seeds can travel on the wind.

Alder
The inconspicuous alder prefers marshy ground and river banks. Although not a conifer, it bears cone fruit.

The Tropical Forests

The hot, humid conditions in equatorial rainforests which encourage a profusion of life, change very little over the year, daily variations being greater than seasonal ones. The average temperature is about 27°C, while the rainfall, which is as high as 80-160 inches (2000-4000 mm) a year, falls regularly in heavy thunderstorms.

Tropical forests are the highest, densest and most varied on Earth, in spite of having infertile soil. This is because nutrients are contained in the plants which grow, flower and fruit throughout the year. As leaves and fruits fall to the ground and decay, the minerals are rapidly taken up again by the roots of the growing shrubs and trees. The crowns of the tall, broad-leaved trees form a canopy of foliage. Underneath, it is shady and the tree trunks are smooth and unbranched, while lianas and creepers thrust upwards to the light.

Forest animals find a variety of habitats in the different layers. Monkeys, apes, sloths, lizards and frogs are adapted to climbing or swinging through trees. Multitudes of birds feed on nectar, insects or fruit. Many animals browse on the forest floor, and a vast number of animal and plant species co-exist.

Lianas *below*
Long rope-like stems loop from tree to tree, ever climbing toward the light that pierces the canopy.

Deep rainforest *right*
The hot, humid atmosphere of tropical rainforest encourages most luxuriant plant growth.

Butterflies
right and below
There are more butterflies and moths in the rainforest than in all the rest of the Earth; typical species are the Ulysses butterfly (right), *Precis almana* (below right) and Rajah Brooke's bird-wing *Trogonoptera brookiana* (below).

Flowers *right and below*
Tropical blooms are famed for their size and beauty. The very small seasonal variation in climate means plants can germinate, grow and flower without interruption throughout the year. Right, blossoms of Royal Poinciana; below, Strelitzia, native to Africa.

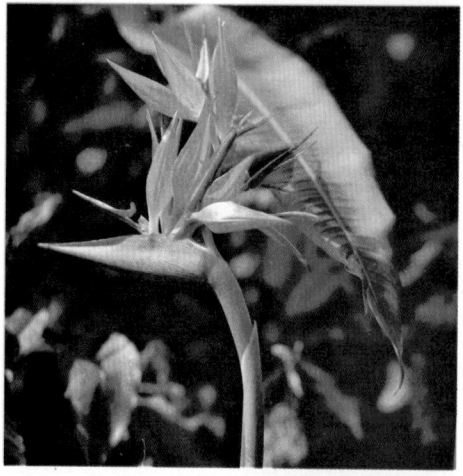

Hovering jewel *right*
Hummingbirds, such as Pucheran's emerald variety illustrated here, are found only in the Americas. Their wings, which beat about 100 times a second and allow them to hover while drinking nectar, are covered with iridescent feathers of brilliant hues.

Contrasting predators
right and below
Tropical forests are the home of the largest spiders and largest snakes. But, whereas the monkey spider of Trinidad (right) kills its prey by a venomous bite, the 30 foot (10 m) royal python (below) crushes and suffocates its victim.

Forest amphibians
above and right
As large as a man, the iguana (above) has feet with long digits provided with hard scales and curved claws adapted to tree-climbing. Another climber is the African grey tree frog (right) whose nest of foam overhangs the water.

Spinetail swift
White rumped swift
Indian crested swift
Harpy eagle

The emergents
Some trees break through the canopy formed by the main tree population. Many of these emergent trees reach to 150 ft (46 m), although all tree heights are reduced with increasing altitude or distance from the equator. Life at this topmost level is almost wholly insects and birds. The swifts, which fly above the forest at over 100 mph (160 kmh), catch insects on the wing. The harpy eagle preys on animals in the upper branches.

100 feet
30 m

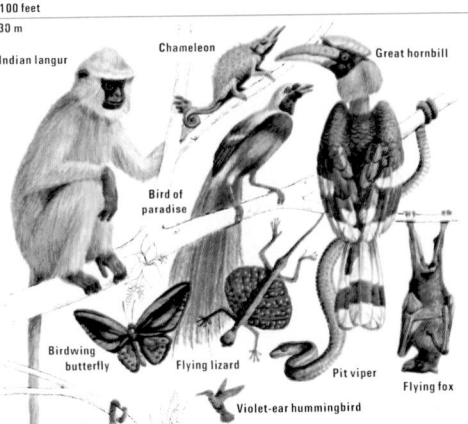

Indian langur, Chameleon, Great hornbill, Bird of paradise, Birdwing butterfly, Flying lizard, Pit viper, Flying fox

The canopy
This is one of the major life zones of the tropical forest, and it exerts a powerful effect on all the lower levels. Most of the forest trees grow to 100-120 ft (30-37 m) and form an almost continuous layer of leafy vegetation at this height, cutting off direct sunlight from below and markedly altering the climate inside' the forest to a shady coolness. Most of the trees of tropical forests have straight stems which do not branch until quite close to the canopy; emergent tree (1) passes straight through without branching. Many tropical trees are cauliflorous—they produce flowers which grow directly out of the trunks and branches and frequently dot the canopy with color (2). Inside the forest is a tangle of creepers and climbers which tend to bind the branches of the canopy into a tight mass. The fauna of the canopy is adapted to specialized feeding from particular flowers, fruit or other food. Winged insects and animals range readily through the whole stratum. Many of the birds (for example, the great hornbill and toucan) have long bills with which they can reach food through the mat of vegetation. The non-flying animals are invariably adapted to running along branches, swinging from one branch to another and even leaping 50 ft (15 m) or more.

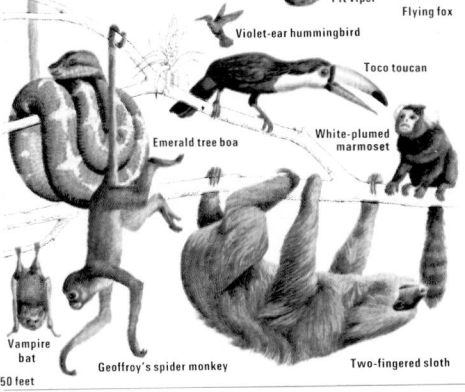

Violet-ear hummingbird, Toco toucan, Emerald tree boa, White-plumed marmoset, Vampire bat, Geoffroy's spider monkey, Two-fingered sloth

50 feet
15 m

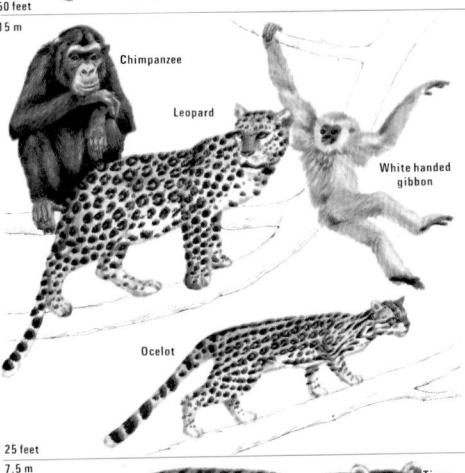

Chimpanzee, Leopard, White handed gibbon, Ocelot

The middle layer
There may be no sharp division between this layer and the canopy, but in general the middle is made up of smaller trees whose crowns do not form a continuous mat. In this layer are found nest epiphytes (3), non-parasitic plants growing in sunlight on trees where they seed in cracks in the bark. Some store water while others absorb it through hanging roots (4). Cauliflorous growths (5) hang from some trees, while many trunks are covered in vines and lianas (6). The trees are sturdy enough to bear heavy animals. Whereas many inhabitants of the canopy seldom if ever come down to ground level, a considerable proportion of the middle-level animals spend part of their life on the forest floor.

25 feet
7.5 m

Mandrill, Tiger, Bay duiker, Red jungle fowl, Giant armadillo, Jaguar, Red rumped agouti

The lower levels
The bottom strata of the humid tropical forest can be divided into a shrub layer below 15 ft (4.5 m), a herb layer below 3 ft (1 m) and a fungus layer on the surface. The fallen tree (7) may have died from strangulation by parasitic vegetation. At the right air roots (8) pick up moisture, while a trunk (9) is almost hidden by two types of epiphyte. Fungi (10) cover the ground near a massive buttressed tree root (11), while in the rear is a stilt root (12) of a kind common in swamp forest. The ground here is covered in sparse vegetation (13) typical of the shady floor. The features illustrated are typical of hot rain forest throughout the tropics, but the elephant (14) is Indian.

Flat or rolling grasslands lie between the forests and deserts in the dry interiors of all the continents, in the transitional zones where dry and moist climates merge into each other. There are two major types of grassland, the temperate which is hot in summer and cold in winter and the tropical which has a fairly uniform high temperature all the year round. The Russian steppe, North American prairie, South American pampas, South African veld and Australian downland are examples of temperate grassland, while more than one third of Africa is covered by tropical savanna.

The height of the grass is dependent upon the annual rainfall. There are few trees on these wide plains to break the wind or provide shelter. In spring or summer there is a short rainy season when the grasses and shrubs flourish and there is rich grazing; then the long dry season comes and growth halts as a severe drought develops. The grasslands may result from frequent fires during this period, which kill the trees and shrubs leaving grass-roots unharmed.

Animal life
Throughout most of the tropical grasslands the climate is semi-arid, the soil poor, yet their meager grazing supports a rich and varied assortment of animals. In most grassland regions the fauna has been used by man with care for the future, but in the biggest savanna of all, that of Africa, man has done little but misuse and destroy the grassland animals. To a considerable degree this has been the result of emphasis by both Africans and white ranchers, on domestic cattle. Such beasts graze only on certain species of grass, and have been bred principally for the temperate regions of Europe. In contrast, the natural fauna makes full use of the whole spectrum of vegetation, grazing selectively at different levels and in different places. As a result there is no deterioration of the environment despite the large numbers of animals supported by each area of land. Moreover, the wild animals need not be fed or sheltered, nor inoculated against the sleeping sickness carried by the tsetse fly which ravages cattle. Now that game can be seen to have a distinct commercial value the grassland animals, particularly easily domesticated species such as the eland, are at last being more generally preserved so that controlled game-cropping can provide an additional source of high quality protein.

The dust bowls
Man has often interfered in the grassland environment sometimes with disastrous consequences. The American grassland soil is rich and farmers have turned the wetter tall-grass prairie into the corn belt and the short-grass prairie into the wheat belt. Further west is the cattle country. But in years of drought crops fail and the valuable topsoil, lacking the protective cover of grass, blows away in great dust clouds, leaving behind large areas of barren land.

 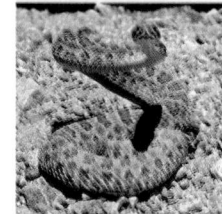

Venomous snakes *left*
Grasslands in every continent harbor dangerous snakes. The Egyptian cobra (far left) is the largest cobra in Africa. The prairie rattlesnake (near left) is the most common venomous snake in the United States and causes many deaths each year.

African savanna *above*
The Serengeti plains of Tanzania are among the most beautiful areas of big game country in the world. Here animals of a great range of species graze on fine grassland amongst the kopjes — rocky outcrops which are characteristic of central Africa.

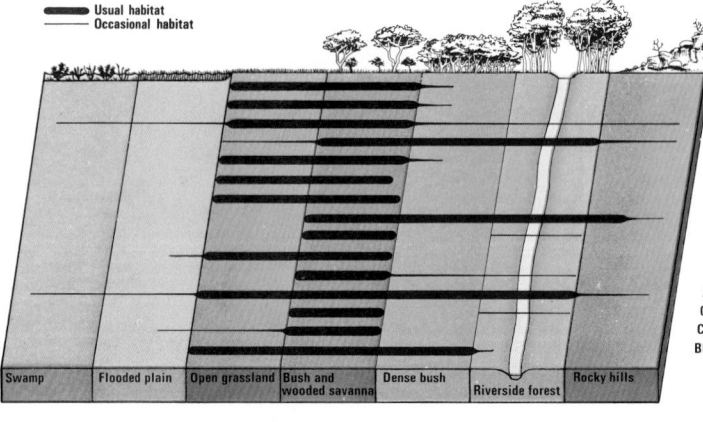

Lion
Spotted hyena
Griffon vulture
Anubis (olive) baboon
Grant's zebra
Brindled gnu (wildebeest)
White rhinoceros
Impala
Giraffe
Cape eland
Kirk's long-snouted dik-dik
African elephant
Gerenuk
Cape buffalo
Black rhinoceros

Usual habitat
Occasional habitat

Swamp | Flooded plain | Open grassland | Bush and wooded savanna | Dense bush | Riverside forest | Rocky hills

Ecological co-existence *above*
The African savanna supports a very large and varied animal population. Most of the animals are herbivores which have each adapted to a particular habitat and a particular section of the available food. These sections are divided geographically, as shown here, and also into different feeding levels above the ground.

Lion   Spotted hyena   Griffon vulture   Anubis baboon   Grant's zebra   Brindled gnu (wildebeest)   White rhino

Buffalo *above*
African buffalo at Manyara, Tanzania. Buffalo live in herds of up to 100 or more males and females of all ages, with a firm hierarchy among the males. They use their horns and horn-bosses in pushing contests that help to decide their ranks.

Impala *below*
African grassland has 72 species of antelope, weighing from a few pounds to 1800 lb (800 kg).

Tick bird *left*
The yellow-billed oxpecker rides on the backs of rhinos and other large animals and eats ticks and flies living in or on the hide. Sometimes the birds swoop off their perch to take large insects which have been disturbed by the animal.

Leopard *right*
Stealthy and athletic, the leopard is found through most of Africa and southern Asia. It often rests in trees, and this fine specimen has pulled its prey, a reedbuck, onto a high branch.

Giraffes *left*
Tallest of all land animals, the giraffe eats acacia leaves and other greenery high above the ground (see large illustration below). Here a group gallops past zebras across a bare patch of ground.

7ft, 213cm

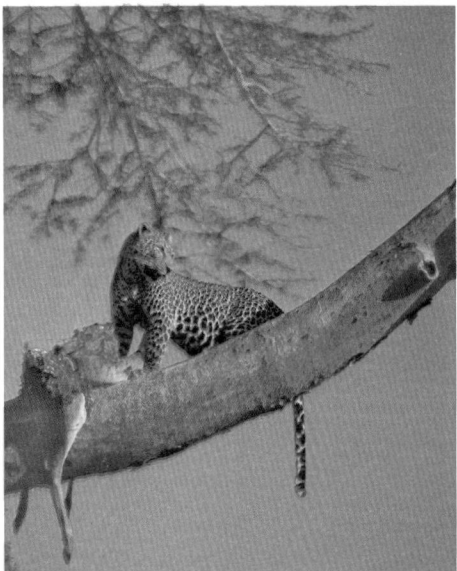

Griffon vulture *left*
Vultures soar at high altitudes on their large wings while searching to the horizon for carrion.

Jackrabbit *above*
Big ears are not only for keen hearing : they help radiate heat and control body temperature.

Ostrich *below*
The tall ostrich can see for miles across the African plains and run swiftly from danger.

8ft, 240cm

Feeding habits
The great grasslands of Africa, and to a lesser degree those of other continents, teem with wild life of remarkable variety. In this wide open environment conceal-ment is difficult and the majority of animals survive by having good long-distance vision and by being fleet of foot. Some of the smaller plant eaters escape their preda-tors by burrowing. The key to the co-existence of the herbivores is that they tend to feed at different levels. The elephant can reach up to 15 feet (4·5 m) above the ground to tear at broad-leafed trees, while the giraffe can feed on its favored acacias at even higher levels. The rhino, buffalo, gerenuk and eland eat not only low shrubs and trees but also grass. Only the gnus, zebras and some rhinos com-pete for the same areas, but these areas are so large that there is little fear of over-grazing. The baboon delves for roots and what-ever it can find, while the carni-vores include the carrion-eating hyenas and vultures and the pre-datory lion, cheetah and leopard. Left to themselves, the wild animals of the savanna do little harm to their habitat, but the growing herds of domesticated cattle and goats pose a threat. Whereas the native fauna leaves living shoots which can sprout into a fresh plant, the cattle and goats eat the whole of the grass and tree shoots so that the vegetation is soon eradicated. Over-grazing and poor range management are encouraged by the fact that some African tribes still regard cattle as symbols of wealth. The value of the indigen-ous savanna animals has been forcefully demonstrated in parts of South Africa and Rhodesia where ranges run down by domestic cattle have been restored by grazing 10 to 12 varieties of antelope in their place.

Impala   Giraffe   Cape eland   Kirk's dik-dik   African elephant   Gerenuk   Cape buffalo   Black rhinoceros

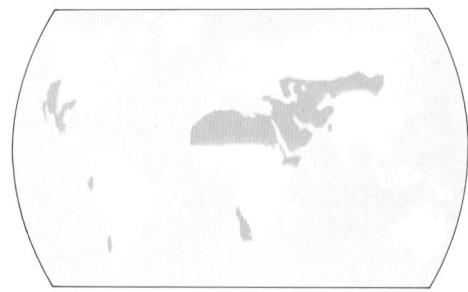

The desert is a harsh, arid and inhospitable environment of great variety where the average rainfall for a year is less than five inches (125 mm) and in some years there is none at all. The cloudless sky allows the Earth's surface to heat up to 40°C (104°F) by day and cool near to freezing at night. Relative humidity is low. On the basis of temperature arid lands are divided into low-latitude hot deserts and mid-latitude deserts. The latter, in central Asia and the Great Basin of the United States, are bitterly cold in winter. In the coastal deserts of Peru and Chile the cold offshore current flowing northward from the Antarctic Ocean cools the moist air producing a swirling sea fog.

Landscapes are rocky, and weathered to strange shapes by the winds and sudden rains (pp. 12-13A). Sand dunes shifted and shaped by the wind are common in Saudi Arabia and the Sahara. The dunes are almost sterile, but most deserts have some sparse plant cover. Stems and leaves are hard, to prevent loss of water and protect the plant from sand erosion. Succulent cacti and euphorbias store water in fleshy stems or leaves, and have widespread shallow roots to absorb the dew. Sahara oases were probably cultivated 7000 years ago, producing grain, olives, wine, figs and dates. The Egyptians channelled the waters of the flooding Nile to irrigate the land, and today the Imperial Valley of the Californian desert and the Arizona desert near Phoenix are highly productive agricultural land.

Water in the desert
Most of the world's deserts are neither billowing sand dunes (such as that on the opposite page) nor totally devoid of water. But in all deserts water, especially fresh water, is a precious commodity. In the great stony deserts brief rains allow stunted vegetation to provide a basis for animal life. The neighborhood of Monument Valley, Utah (above) is surprisingly full of life which has adapted to arid conditions. Some life is also found in the Sahara, where sudden torrential rains cause flash flood erosion (south of Ouargla, left) leaving smooth ridges and deep gullies Sometimes

the water table is at the surface. The water may be brackish and undrinkable, as in Cyrenaica west of the Siwa Oasis (below), but the true oasis contains fresh water at which a camel can drink copiously (right). Even the meager dew is stored by plants – nothing is wasted.

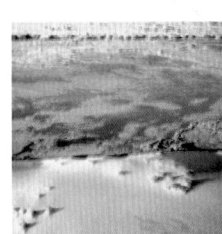

Desert plants *right*
Deserts test the ability of plants to adapt to a near absence of water. Plants survive by throwing out large catchment areas for dew at night, minimizing water loss by evaporation during the day, growing deep roots to find water far below the surface, storing what water they find, and in extreme cases by lying dormant during dry years and springing to life as soon as it rains.

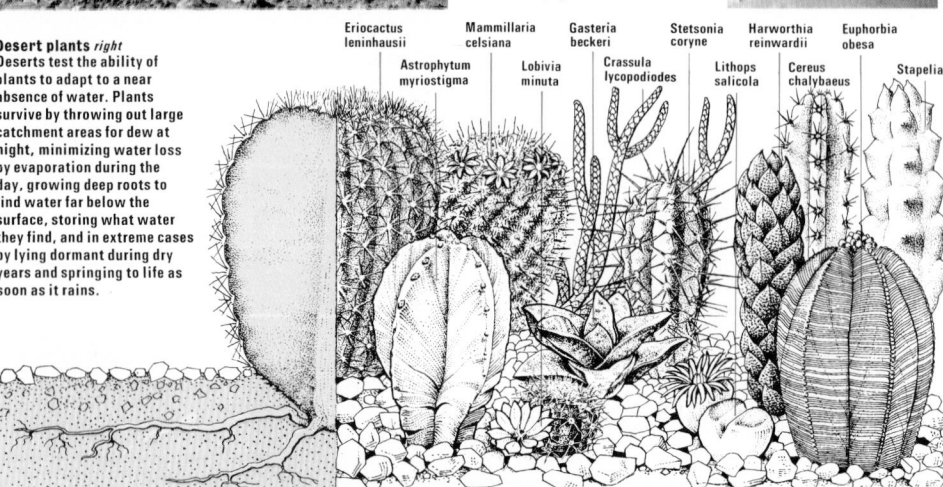

Eriocactus leninhausii
Mammillaria celsiana
Astrophytum myriostigma
Lobivia minuta
Gasteria beckeri
Crassula lycopodiodes
Stetsonia coryne
Lithops salicola
Harworthia reinwardii
Cereus chalybaeus
Euphorbia obesa
Stapelia

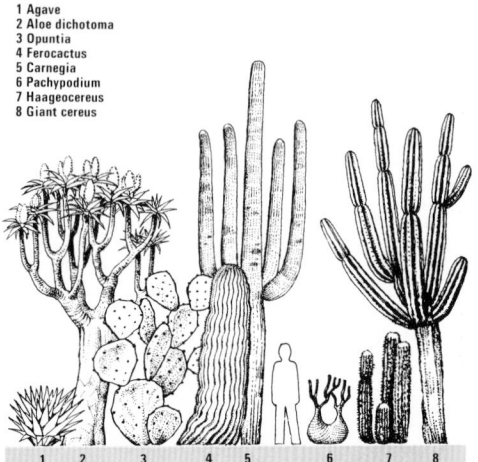

1 Agave
2 Aloe dichotoma
3 Opuntia
4 Ferocactus
5 Carnegia
6 Pachypodium
7 Haageocereus
8 Giant cereus

Desert animals

Many animals are so well adapted to retain water that they survive on the moisture in their food. Some, such as the armadillo lizard, scorpions, insects and spiders, have hard, impenetrable skins to reduce water loss. The urine of camels and gazelles is very concentrated to minimize excretion of water. Arabian camels can lose 30 per cent of their body weight (which would be lethal for a man) without distress, and then regain it by drinking up to 27 gallons (120 liters) at a time. This does not dilute their blood dangerously. A camel does not sweat until its body temperature reaches 40°C, and it loses heat easily during the cold night because it stores its fat in the hump and not as a layer under the skin. Its fur insulates against the heat, as do the loose clothes of the people. Snakes hide in crevices, and sand-swimming lizards burrow to avoid extreme temperatures. Jerboas and kangaroo rats hop along, and some lizards run on their hind legs to keep their bellies off the ground. As soon as it rains, swarms of dormant life surge into activity.

Ant lions *right and below*
Some types of ant lion catch their prey — mainly ants — by digging a smooth conical pit and waiting at the bottom; others bury themselves in the sand with only eyes and jaws protruding. The larval stage (right) precedes the winged adult (below).

8in, 21cm

Desert Burrowers

White-footed mouse · Burrow taken over by horned lizard · Horned lizard · American badger · Pocket mouse · Kit fox · Kangaroo rat in nest · Food store · Green-collared lizard · Kangaroo rat

Sand desert *above*
Only one-seventh of the Sahara looks like this Hollywood-style vista of giant dunes in Algeria.

Dung beetles *left*
These female scarabs are rolling a pellet of animal dung into a ball containing an egg.

Painted lady *above*
N African desert thistles provide nectar for their migration through Europe as far as Iceland.

Gila monster *right*
This venomous N American lizard tracks its prey with the aid of a sensor in its mouth (right, lower).

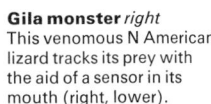

20in, 51cm

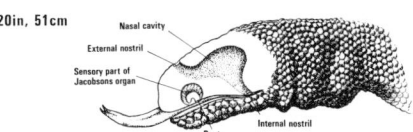

Nasal cavity · External nostril · Sensory part of Jacobsons organ · Internal nostril · Duct

Scorpion and snake
When scorpions mate, the male deposits a patch of sperm on the ground and then contrives to maneuver a female over it in what looks like a square dance (above, left). The dangerous rattlesnake (above) senses the heat radiated by its prey using organs on its face.

Plants and predator
The leopard tortoise (left) enjoys a meal of cactus, a plant which stores water and minimizes evaporation (Ferocactus of Arizona, right). Other desert blooms include Echinopsis rhodatricia and Chamacerus silvestri (far right, upper and lower).

The mountain environment varies enormously with height and the direction of the prevailing wind. Temperature falls about 2°C (3.4°F) for each 1000 feet (300 m) increase in altitude. Barometric pressure also falls until lack of oxygen makes any human exertion cause shortness of breath. Before people adjust to the conditions they often suffer from mountain sickness —headache, weakness and nausea.

Sun temperature may be 28°C (83°F) hotter than in the shade or at night, and the slope of a mountain facing the equator is warmer than the other sides. Mountains force rain-bearing winds to rise, so that they cool and have to release moisture. Clouds form, and rain falls on the windward slope; on the opposite slope the descending winds are drying.

High-altitude life

Altitude has the same effect on vegetation as latitude. At about 5000 feet (1500 m) tropical rainforest changes to montane forest resembling a temperate rainforest. At twice this height the broad-leaved trees disappear but there are conifers and shrubs such as laurel. Above the treeline, where the average monthly temperature never exceeds 10°C, is alpine tundra or heath. The snowline at the equator is at about 15000 feet (4500 m). In Peru irrigated sugar and cacao cover the lower slopes, and above the timberline corn grows at 11000 feet, wheat at 12000, barley at 13000 and potatoes up to 14000 feet. The Incas had terraced the Andes and had an efficient agricultural system by 1000 AD.

The mountain life zone which is unique is that above the treeline. The animal communities are isolated, since mountains act as a barrier to migration. Most plants and insects on mountain tops can withstand freezing. Some animals burrow or shelter under rocks where temperature variations are smaller. Ibexes, yaks, deer and sheep all have thick coats but move down the mountain-side in winter. Mountain animals have enlarged hearts and lungs and extra oxygen-carrying red blood corpuscles to make the most of the thin air. The vicuna, for example, has nearly three times the number of red corpuscles per cubic millimeter of blood as man.

Near Murren *above right*
The environment on a high mountain is essentially polar, even in a tropical country. Above the timberline ice and snow replace animals and plants, and the conditions are further modified by intense solar radiation and low atmospheric pressure.

Lichens *above and right*
Lichens comprise a fungus and an alga in close association. The alga govern the color (page 49A for red lichen). The metabolism of lichens is exceedingly slow; barely alive, they can subsist on mountain rock in harsh conditions for hundreds of years.

Altitude and latitude *right*
At extreme latitudes – for example, in the Antarctic – the climate is so severe at sea level that no very pronounced change takes place even as one climbs a mountain, although the mountain's presence can strongly modify the local weather. In contrast, mountains near the equator rise from hot, steamy forests into freezing, arid peaks, with almost every kind of Earth environment in between. To most kinds of terrestrial life large mountains offers fewer contrasts; much of mountains are barriers. As altitude increases, plants and animals become adapted to the environment and then peter out entirely.

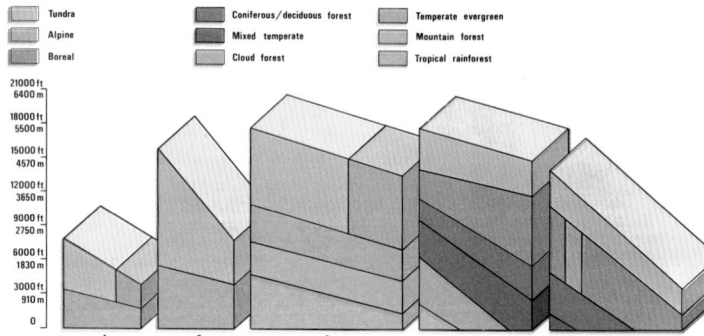

Tundra	Coniferous / deciduous forest	Temperate evergreen
Alpine	Mixed temperate	Mountain forest
Boreal	Cloud forest	Tropical rainforest

21000 ft / 6400 m
18000 ft / 5500 m
15000 ft / 4570 m
12000 ft / 3650 m
9000 ft / 2750 m
6000 ft / 1830 m
3000 ft / 910 m
0

1   2   3   4   5

Mountain zones *above*
At high latitudes a mountain offers fewer contrasts; much of New Zealand (1) has cool, humid cloud forest, topped by alpine heath and tundra. In SE Australia, SE Africa and S Brazil (2) the cloud forest extends to a greater altitude, with only tundra above. The high tropical Andes (3) afford contrasts surpassed only by the mountainous regions of the eastern Himalayas and SE Asia (4), where six distinct regions overlie one another, with very local regions of tropical mountain forest. Mountains of Europe (5) lie in regions where there are already great contrasts in climate at sea level. Boreal is a north-facing mountain region.

Tortoise *above*
The margined tortoise is native to mountainous regions in Greece and the Balkans.

Plants *left*
Purple gentian and (upper) auricula are typical of mountain dwarf perennials; some can resist freezing.

Butterflies
Mountains are often rich in insects. The six-spot burnet (mating, left) is common. Some Apollo butterflies (below) are found above 17000 feet (5200 m) in the Himalayas. Erebia (right) is carrying an orange mite, a parasite which can survive freezing. Mountain insects rely for much of their food on pollen, seeds and even insects swept up in the frequent updraft of winds from the warm lowlands.

4in, 8cm

African birds of prey
Small mountain rodents make a tasty meal for the jackal buzzard (left), a bird with exceedingly acute vision. The black eagle (with three-week chick, right) lives on rats and lizards but can tackle animals as large as the 7 lb (3.2 kg) rock hyrax. It nests in July.

Rodents
Whereas the alpine marmot (below) hibernates in winter, the pika of Tibet (in group, below right) stores its supplies. The chinchilla and cavy both come from South America. Above 10000 ft (3000 m) rodents outnumber all other animals.

Salamander *right*
This Pyrenean salamander is climbing out of a cool mountain stream, but the true alpine salamander has had to become adapted to an arid habitat. Much darker than the lowland varieties, it does not lay its eggs in water but bears its young alive. It remains amphibious.

American cougar *left*
Also known as the puma or mountain lion, the cougar hunts by day above the timberline. When it makes a large kill it is able to store the carcass for weeks at sub-zero temperature. Most of these beasts range over a fixed area, although some wander down to lower levels.

Yak *right*
Domesticated in its native Tibet, the shaggy yak is still found in local wild herds in central Asia. It is a hardy animal, adapted to eating snow in the absence of water, and moss and lichens when no better vegetation is available. It is found up to 20000 ft (6000 m).

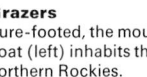

Grazers
Sure-footed, the mountain goat (left) inhabits the northern Rockies. The chamoix (above) is scattered through mountain regions of southern Europe, while ibexes (right) are a very widespread family. Specialized sheep also graze at high altitudes.

The Lakes and the Rivers

Freshwater environments range from puddles to lakes which cover thousands of square miles, from small streams to rivers that stretch hundreds of miles from mountain source to the ocean. Together, they provide a diversity of habitats that supports a wide range of plant and animal life.

In rivers the type and variety of life is controlled by the depth and speed of water. Fast mountain streams have few plants and the fish are either fast swimmers or shelter among stones. The slower, wider lowland rivers are rich in vegetation and many of the fish have mouths adapted to sucking food from the rich silt of the river bed. In the brackish waters of the estuary few freshwater animals can survive because of the increasing salinity. But migratory fish, such as eels and Atlantic salmon, adapt to fresh and salt water at different stages of their life cycles.

In standing water the surface is often much warmer than the depths. This produces layers which are so distinct that separate habitats are created. The deeper waters may be completely devoid of oxygen because they do not mix with the well-aerated surface layers. Lakes go through three stages of development: oligotrophic with barren sides and clear water; eutrophic when the lake has begun to silt up and is rich in life; and, finally, dystrophic with decayed organic matter developing into swamp or peat bog. This natural process of eutrophication normally takes thousands of years, but man can, by his indiscriminate pollution and over-enrichment of some lakes condense this process dangerously into a few decades.

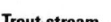

Near its source a river is cold, clear and well oxygenated, and flows swiftly.

In the middle reaches the river runs deep, but is still clear and fast-flowing.

A mature river is broad and sluggish; it may be clouded and polluted.

Fish of the river *below*
In the swift-flowing upper reaches only the powerful swimming fish can survive, although small fish nestle near the bottom. The water is well oxygenated, and remains so into the less tumultuous middle reaches. The sluggish lowland river contains deep-bodied fish.

Trout stream

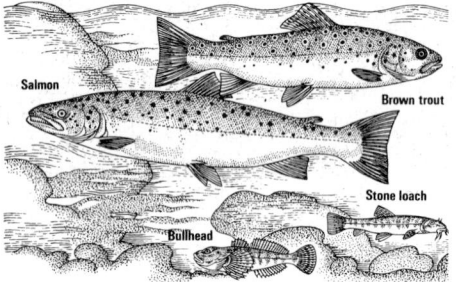

Salmon
Brown trout
Stone loach
Bullhead

Minnow reach

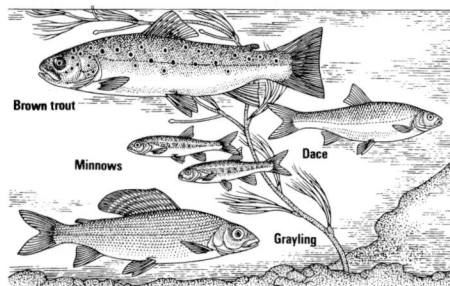

Brown trout
Minnows
Dace
Grayling

Lowland river

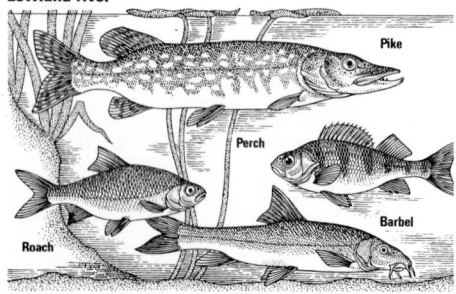

Pike
Perch
Barbel
Roach

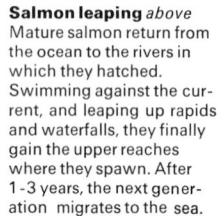

Salmon leaping *above*
Mature salmon return from the ocean to the rivers in which they hatched. Swimming against the current, and leaping up rapids and waterfalls, they finally gain the upper reaches where they spawn. After 1-3 years, the next generation migrates to the sea.

Kingfisher *above*
These colorful birds are by far the most numerous of the many species that take fish while on the wing. Plunging across the surface in a shallow dive, they seize in their long beaks prey they had spotted while on the branch of a tree. Average size 7 in (18 cm).

Teeming with life *left*
Most lakes begin life in the oligotrophic stage, barren of life and with clear, bright waters. After a time the water is colonized, and gradually a community rich in plant and animal species occupies the freshwater habitat. Such a lake is eutrophic.

A swamp *left*

The Indian name of Lake Okeefenokee, Georgia, means 'land of trembling earth'. Measuring some 30 miles by 40 (48 by 64 km), it is a region of perfect mirror-like reflections and teeming wild life.

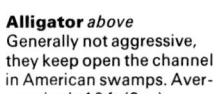

Swamp butterfly *above*

There are many sub-species of swallowtail; this is the eastern tiger swallowtail from the marshes of Georgia. Average size 4 in (10 cm).

Tree frog *above*

Devouring flies and gnats by the million, green tree frogs breed in the warm swamp waters. Average size is 2½in (6 cm).

Lubber grasshopper *left*

Bigger even than the majority of desert locusts, it makes a tasty meal for birds and young alligators.

Alligator *above*

Generally not aggressive, they keep open the channels in American swamps. Average size is 10 ft (3 m).

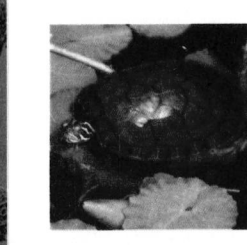

Terrapin *above*

The Suwannee river terrapin is sometimes found in the Gulf of Mexico. Average size is 7 in (18 cm).

Swamp turtle *above*

The soft-shelled turtles have a leathery skin without an outer covering of horny plates. Size 14 in (36 cm).

The pond environment *left*

1 Common frog (male, ×0.5)
2 Starwort (×0.5)
3 Water crowfoot (×0.25)
4 Aplecta hypnorum (×2)
5 Wandering snail (×0.75)
6 Keeled ramshorn snail (×0.5)
7 Curled pondweed (×0.25)
8 Bithynia (×1)
9 Ramshorn snail (×0.3)
10 Water lily root (×0.25)
11 Great pond snail (×0.8)

Pond life *below*

The essential characteristic of pond life is adaptation to a freshwater environment without a flowing current. As in almost every other habitat on Earth the life is divided into distinct zones —atmosphere, surface film, middle depths and bed—although many species cross from one zone to another. The newt, for example,

is active everywhere from the bed of a pond to dry land. Throughout the ecology of freshwater life all food is manufactured by green plants. First-order animals, such as zooplankton and many fish and insects, feed directly on the plants; everything else feeds on predators lower in the food chain or web. The water itself is very far from being a pure compound of

hydrogen and oxygen. It contains dissolved oxygen and nitrogen salts and much organic material. The life of the pond establishes ecological cycles which constantly balance inputs and outputs between water, air, and life. For example, the supply of nitrates washed in from the land is augmented by the decomposition of dead organisms in the water itself

Near the surface

12 Pond skater (×0.5)
13 Whirligig beetle (×0.25)
14 Water boatman (×1)
15 Non-biting midge (×5)
16 Mosquito pupa (×5)
17 Dragonfly (male, ×0.65)
18 China-marks moth (×0.75)
19 Mayfly (female, ×0.2)

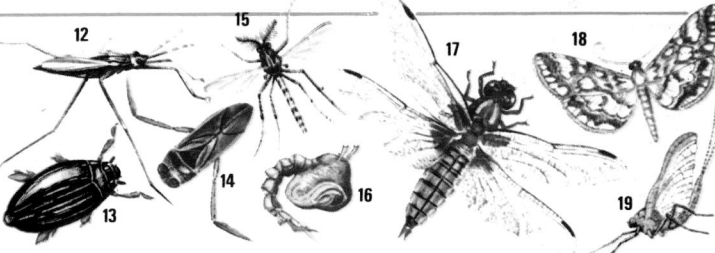

Middle depths

20 Water flea (Daphnia, ×2.5)
21 Smooth newt (male, ×0.5)
22 Cyclops (typical of species, ×8)
23 Flagellate (×650)
24 Great diving beetle (male, ×1)
25 Hydra (×4)
26 Stickleback (male, ×0.5)
27 Common frog tadpole (×1.5)
28 Flagellate (Euglena, ×180)
29 Water mite (×5)

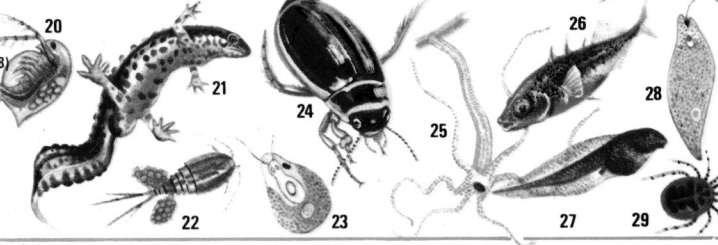

The bottom

30 Caddis-fly larva in case
31 Chaetonotus (×150)
32 Horny-orb shell (×1)
33 Tubifex worms (×0.2)
34 Midge larva (×3.5)
35 Pond sponge (×0.2)
36 Leech (Helobdella sp., ×4)
37 Water hog-louse (×2.5)
38 Flatworm (×2)

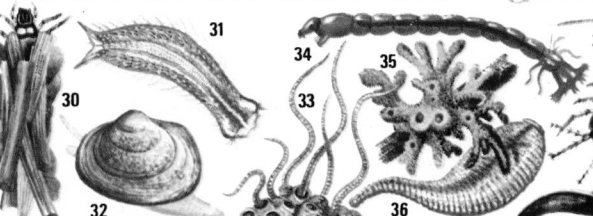

The oceans are a continuous mass of 5000 million million tons of water; but variations in light, pressure, salinity, temperature, currents, waves, and tides interact to create numerous regions each with its own typical forms of life.

Plants are the basis of ocean food chains, just as they are on land. Since all plants need sunlight they are found only in the upper layer of the sea. Myriads of tiny marine plants called phytoplankton are eaten by the small floating zooplankton and by tiny fish, which in turn support a succession of predators. Deep-water animals are adapted to great pressure and to darkness. Most are predators but some of them are scavengers which depend on a rain of food debris from above.

Some ocean islands are coral, built by millions of polyps resembling sea anemones which produce a hard stony skeleton (p. 17A). But most are thrust up by volcanic eruptions. They are completely isolated and were never joined to a continent. Such islands are usually wet and windswept.

Island plant and animal communities evolved from the few original forms which crossed the ocean and colonized. Island colonization is difficult, and is seldom accomplished by land mammals apart from bats, nor even by amphibians. Land and freshwater animals may have evolved from sea-dwelling ancestors. Once a species has colonized an island it interbreeds, because of its isolation, and adapts to its new conditions and competitors. Often new endemic species evolve.

The first colonizers are usually sea birds. They bring nutrients, so seeds and the spores of mosses, lichens and ferns carried by the wind can take root. The wind also brings insects, spiders and bats, and occasionally land birds in storms, but such birds rarely establish themselves. Reptiles and some land animals may cross the sea on driftwood rafts. Many island reptiles, perhaps because of the lack of mammals, have become unusually large. Examples include such creatures as the Komodo dragon and the giant tortoises of the Galapagos.

The ocean layers

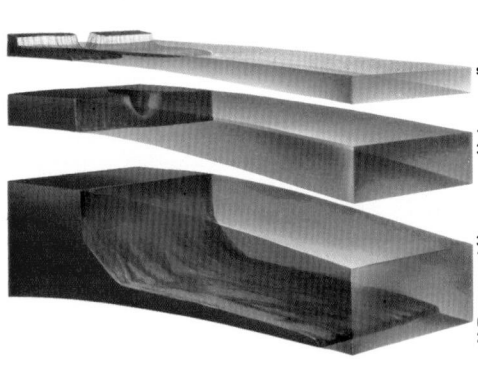

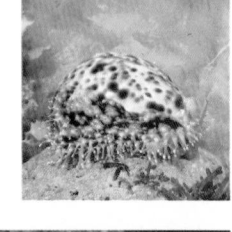

Phytoplankton *above*
All marine life depends ultimately on microscopic plant plankton, which is mostly single-celled. (x 20)

Tiger cowrie *right*
Cowries are tropical marine snails. This spotted example is feeding, with its mantle extended below.

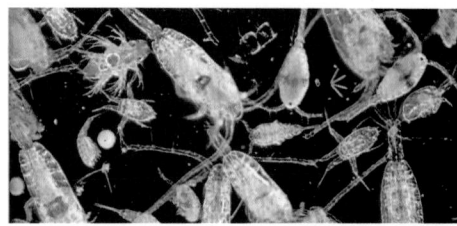

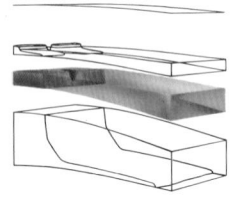

Zooplankton *above*
These microscopic animals feed on the phytoplankton and on each other. In turn they support fish. (x 8)

Leopard coral *right*
The derivation of the name of this hard coral is obvious. Each 'spot' is an individual in the colony.

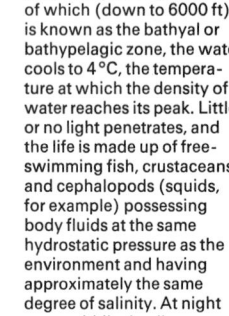

Air and surface life
The seabirds (right) are typical of a range of species, some of them exceptionally large birds, which navigate unerringly over thousands of miles of ocean. Most have wide wingspans and use favourable airflow over the waves to soar apparently without effort. Sunlight penetrates the warm upper layers of the ocean to provide energy for photosynthesis, permitting the prolific growth of the phytoplankton (plant life). This is the starting point for the whole complex web of marine life which leads ultimately to large predatory fish such as the tuna and marlin, and to human foods.

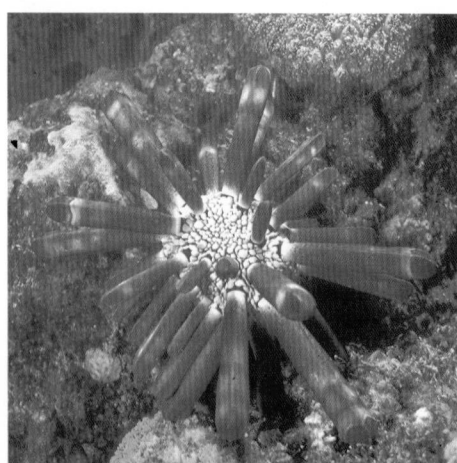

Soft coral *above*
Photographed in Mauritius, a bluish coral has almost finished reproducing by splitting into two.

Sea urchin *below*
This 'slate pencil' variety from Mozambique coral reefs contrasts with spiny types. Size 10 in (25 cm).

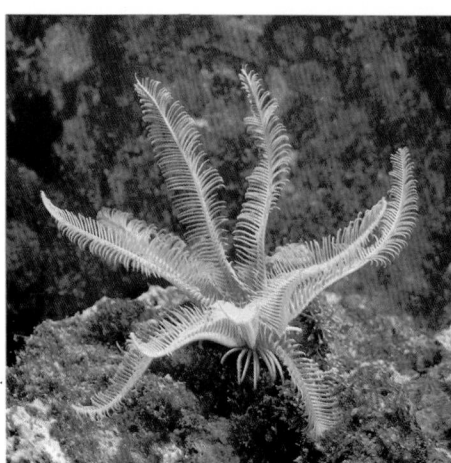

Sea slug *above*
Many of these marine relatives of land slugs are colorful. This one from the Indian Ocean is 4 in (10 cm).

Feather star *below*
Another of the starfish and sea urchin group from Mozambique, this has four inch (10 cm) arms.

Near the surface
above and right
Seabirds generally keep below 1000 ft (300 m) but can be found much higher. The upper layer of ocean is taken to extend down to 3300 ft (1000 m). Water temperature is about 10 °C and sunlight may reach to 650 ft (200 m).

Middle dwellers
In this range of depths, most of which (down to 6000 ft) is known as the bathyal or bathypelagic zone, the water cools to 4 °C, the temperature at which the density of water reaches its peak. Little or no light penetrates, and the life is made up of free-swimming fish, crustaceans and cephalopods (squids, for example) possessing body fluids at the same hydrostatic pressure as the environment and having approximately the same degree of salinity. At night some middle dwellers migrate to the surface to feed on other animals which in turn congregate to 'graze' on the plankton.

Middle depths
above and right
The horizontal 'slice' of ocean water in which live the middle-depth species illustrated opposite is taken to extend from 3300 down to 10000 ft (1000-3000 m). Here the temperature falls from 10 °C down to below 4 °C at the lower level.

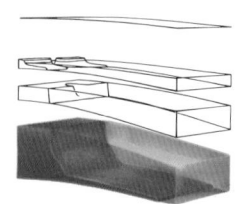

Bottom dwellers
Below 3000 meters the life comprises a range of animals, most of them very small, adapted to living in near-freezing water at extremely high pressures. The only light in this region comes from the curious luminescent organs common to many deep-sea creatures. Although the deep waters contain abundant salts and nutrient minerals, these are useless without the energy of sunlight. Every abyssal organism is therefore either a scavenger, depending for its supply of food on a rain of debris from above, or a predator. Yet the abyssal zone supports a surprising variety of life.

The abyss
above and right
The bottom layer of the ocean is here taken to extend down to about 20000 ft (6000 m). Temperature is always below 4 °C, hydrostatic pressure is enormous and the environment is perpetually devoid of sunlight.

Great Shearwater
span 8½ in 0.2 m

Wandering albatross
span 11 ft 3.35 m

Red-billed tropic bird
span 1 ft 0.3 m

Magnificent frigate bird
span 8 ft 2.45 m

Portuguese man o' war
11 in 0.28 m
(tentacles 100 ft 30 m)

Flying fish
9 in 0.23 m

Marlin
10 ft 3 m

Ocean sunfish
10 ft 3 m

Anchovies
6 in 0.15 m

Basking shark
40 ft 12 m

Dolphin fish
4 ft 1.2 m

Squid
1 ft 0.3 m

Bluefin tuna
7 ft 2 m

Ocean bonito
2 ft 0.6 m

Mackerel shark
12 ft 3.6 m

Lantern fish
3 in 0.075 m

Diretmus argentus
2 in 0.05 m

Photostomias guerni
7 in 0.18 m

Giant squid
55 ft 17 m

Hatchet fish
1 in 0.025 m

Oarfish
20 ft 6 m

Ghost shark
4 ft 1.2 m

Chiasmodus niger
3 in 0.075 m

Gulper eel
4 ft 6 in 1.4 m

Angler fish
3 in 0.075 m

Deep sea swimming cucumber
4 in 0.1 m

Prawn
4 in 0.1 m

Viper fish
1 ft 0.3 m

Angler fish
2 in 0.05 m

Pelican eel
10 in 0.25 m

Tripod fish
10 in 0.25 m

Abyssal octopus
4 in 0.1 m

Deep sea jellyfish
3 in 0.075 m

Rat tail
18 in 0.45 m

Abyssal sea cucumber
¼ in 0.02 m

Brotulid
6 in 0.15 m

Sea snail
9 in 0.23 m

Brittle star 3 in 0.075 m

The story of man's use of the land is one of increasing diversity and complexity. Preagricultural man developed perhaps six land uses; hunting, trapping, fishing, gathering wild fruits, fashioning tools and sheltering in caves. Modern man has developed several thousand forms, and frequently concentrates hundreds within a single square mile. For most of them he has created distinctive environments; one can tell at a glance whether the land is being used to grow carrots, make cement, repair ships, treat sewage, sell antiques, mine coal or educate children.

Although every place is unique in the ways its land uses intermingle, we can nevertheless recognize five major land-use patterns. Each has sprung into prominence at some major crossroads in human history. The first of the five is wildscape, which man uses so lightly and so rarely that nature is still in chief control. Some of it is still almost wholly natural, as in the remote parts of the Antarctic icecap. Other areas have been quite profoundly changed, as on the Pennine moorlands where generations of sheep have nibbled away tree seedlings and prevented the regeneration of forest, or where polluted air is now preventing the growth of sphagnum moss. But these areas are still wildscape. Man uses their resources but he leaves nature to replenish them.

The rural landscape evolves

Farmscape dates from man's first great technical advance, the Neolithic agricultural revolution of about 8000 years ago. For the first time he began to alter the landscape and live with the results instead of moving on; he ploughed and harvested, enclosed fields and diverted water for irrigation. During subsequent millennia this more controlled form of land-use spread over enormous areas of every continent, with a cumulative stream of diversifications as man applied his ingenuity to it in different environments. The rural landscape was now distinctively divided into the wild and the cultivated.

Townscape also existed from an early date, but had to await man's second great technical advance before it could develop at all extensively. Not until the twin agrarian and industrial revolutions of the 18th century did agriculture develop sufficiently to support a vastly greater population than its own labor force, or industry develop sufficiently to be able to employ a vast non-agricultural population. Once this possibility was established as a world trend, townscape began to develop rapidly.

Conflicts in land use

There are now three 'scapes' of increasing artificiality and complexity, respectively dominated by nature, the individual farmer and the public authority. So different are these three 'scapes' that problems tend to arise where they confront and interact with each other. Unfortunately such fringes of conflict have been intensified as side effects of two otherwise beneficial transport revolutions.

The first, or long-distance, transport revolution began with the steamship and the train in the 19th century. It opened up competition in foodstuffs on a global scale: the benefit was cheaper food from more favored areas, and the cost was the decline of less-favored areas. Some farmscape reverted to wildscape, resolving the problem. Elsewhere, the land remained good enough to reclaim in times of booming prices but too poor to be profitable in times of recession. The result in such areas is recurrent farm poverty.

The long-distance transport revolution also had a similar effect upon less competitive mining areas which tended to become derelict as a result, forming rurban (rural-urban) fringe. The main growth of rurban fringe, however, was stimulated by the second, or personal, transport revolution, in which the car gave city workers the opportunity to live in the country and commute daily to a neighboring city. The result was an unprecedented intermingling of urban areas and farmland, and an unprecedented degree of conflict between the two. Farmland became fragmented and subjected to many kinds of urban pressures so that much of it became uneconomic to farm. The urban area, on the other hand, experienced many difficulties in service facilities, because its sprawling layout multiplied distances and costs. Thus both marginal fringe and rurban fringe have become areas of patchy, conflicting landuses.

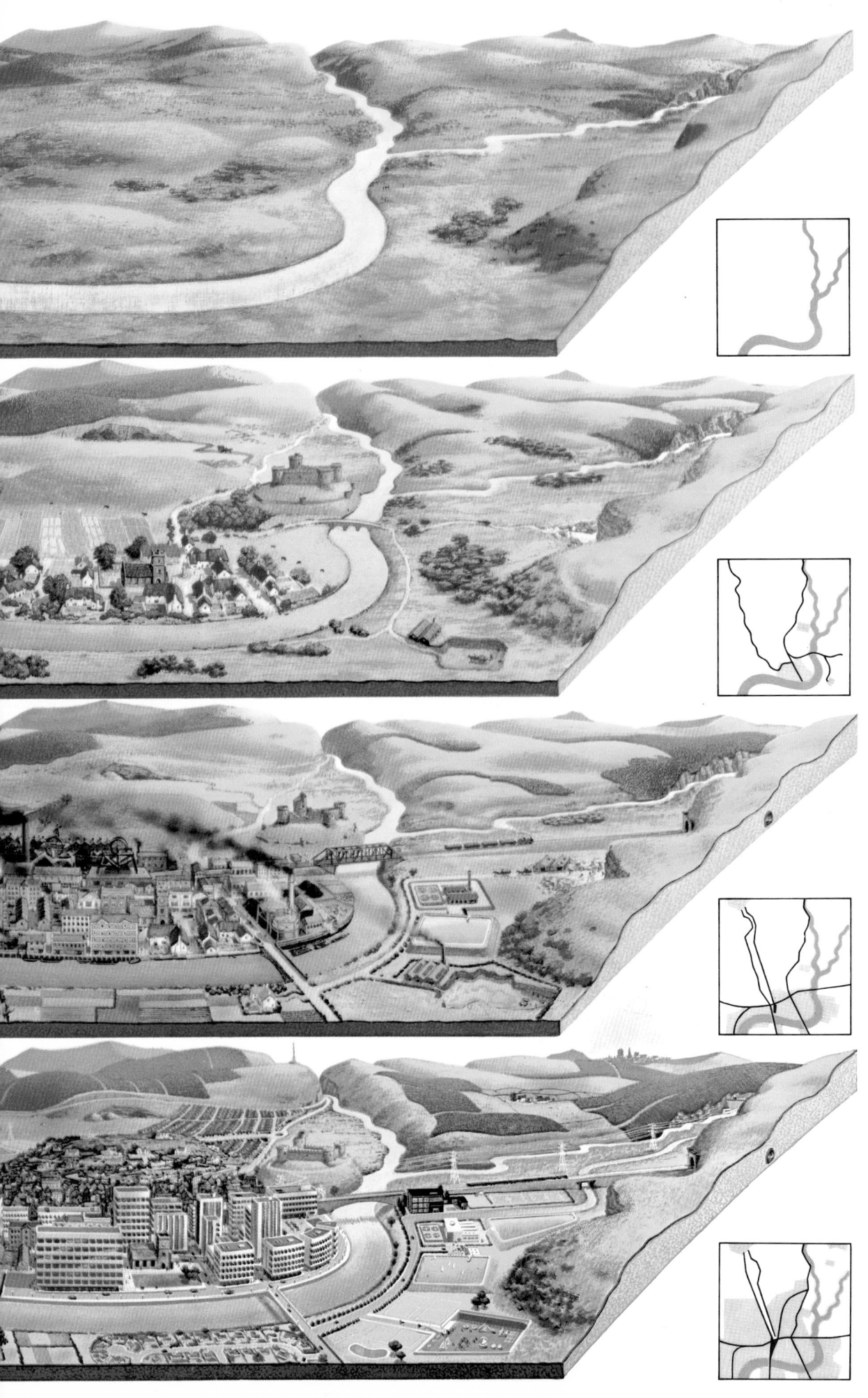

Prehistoric landscape

The natural prehistoric landscape consisted of a series of wildscape ecosystems wherein all forms of life interacted in a stable balance of nature. The land falls from distant hills to a coastal plain where the river widens into a broad estuary. Woodlands partially cover the plains, thinning into scrub on the hills. Stone age man used this wildscape in diffuse and restricted ways. He roamed the forest and heath hunting game but, apart from a cave shelter or toolmaking floor, rarely set aside land for a particular use. He exerted no perceptible influence upon the landscape apart from the fact that grazing animals gradually retarded the regeneration of the forest and led to a more open vegetation. But the presence of flat land, water, coal, stone and good access were ideal for later man.

Medieval

After he had developed agriculture man was able to use the land in more ways. It is possible by this time to detect at least a dozen types of stable land use. This was basically an age of slowly developing farmscape, when wildscape was reclaimed for food production and most settlement was designed to serve agricultural communities. Villagers are cultivating open strip fields in rotation for winter corn, spring corn and fallowing, surrounded by common grazing lands. The improved standard of shelter is reflected in clearance of forest to obtain timber, and the land is quarried for clay (near left), stone (left) and iron ore (back-ground). With such burdens man has improved his transport methods. And the river is now becoming polluted.

19th Century

The industrial revolution was a marked change in man's use of land. Coal was deep-mined as a source of unprecedented power which led to the concentration of crafts in large factories. Gasworks, flour mills and textile mills were basic industries, in turn leading to an industrial townscape. Different types of land use can be measured by the score. Building stone and brick-making continue to flourish, but imports have replaced the old ironworkings. Agriculture plays its part by more efficient production from larger fields to support the growing population. Greatly improved communications are evident. But there is marked pollution of both the river and the atmosphere, and filter beds and clean-water reservoirs are necessary.

Modern

Land uses are now so differentiated as to be countless. Many hundreds of new uses are service functions, ranging from financial institutions to children's playgrounds (the former brick pit) and hairdressers. Dwellings abound in great variety, many of them made of new materials by new methods Electricity has wrought a revolution that extends to virtually every human construction, and the urgent demand for better transport has led to a complete transformation of the scene on this ground alone. A more subtle effect of better transport is that uneconomic local farming has given way to imported food, and much of the land is being reforested. Perhaps most important of all is the fact that man has become concerned about his environment.

Abuse of the Earth

Pollution is harmful waste. All living creatures produce waste, often with marked effects on the environment. Pine leaves blanket out the flowers which would otherwise grow on the forest floor; the droppings of seabirds can cover nesting islands meters deep in guano. Plants as well as road vehicles give off carbon dioxide; volcanoes as well as power stations emit sulphur dioxide.

What turns man's waste into pollution? First, we produce too much waste: only man lives in such vast communities that his excreta de-oxygenates whole rivers. Secondly, the unwanted by-products of man's industrial metabolism change so rapidly that the environment has little hope of accommodating it. African grassland has evolved over millions of years to accept piles of elephant dung, with many species of animals specially adapted to living inside dungheaps and helping to decompose them. But the ecosystem is often unable to cope with our latest pollutants: few bacteria are able to digest plastics. Thirdly, man's waste is often extremely persistent: DDT may remain unchanged for decades, passing from one animal to another, poisoning and weakening them all.

Pollution may harm man directly: smoke causes bronchitis, and fouled drinking water can spread typhoid. Pollution may harm us indirectly, reducing the capacity of the land, rivers and seas to supply us with food. But perhaps the most insidious effects are the least obvious. Small doses of separate pollutants, each harmless by itself, may together weaken wild populations of animals so that they cannot recover from natural disasters. Acute pollution kills tens of thousands of animals; chronic pollution gradually reduces the quality of the entire human environment.

Pollution is wasteful. Too often modern technology painstakingly extracts a metal from the crust, uses it once and then discards it. For example, once unwanted chromium or mercury is released into the seas it will be diluted many millions of times and is unlikely ever to be recoverable except at prohibitive expense. If man is not to face raw material famines in the foreseeable future, he must learn to recycle everything from air and water to the rarer elements.

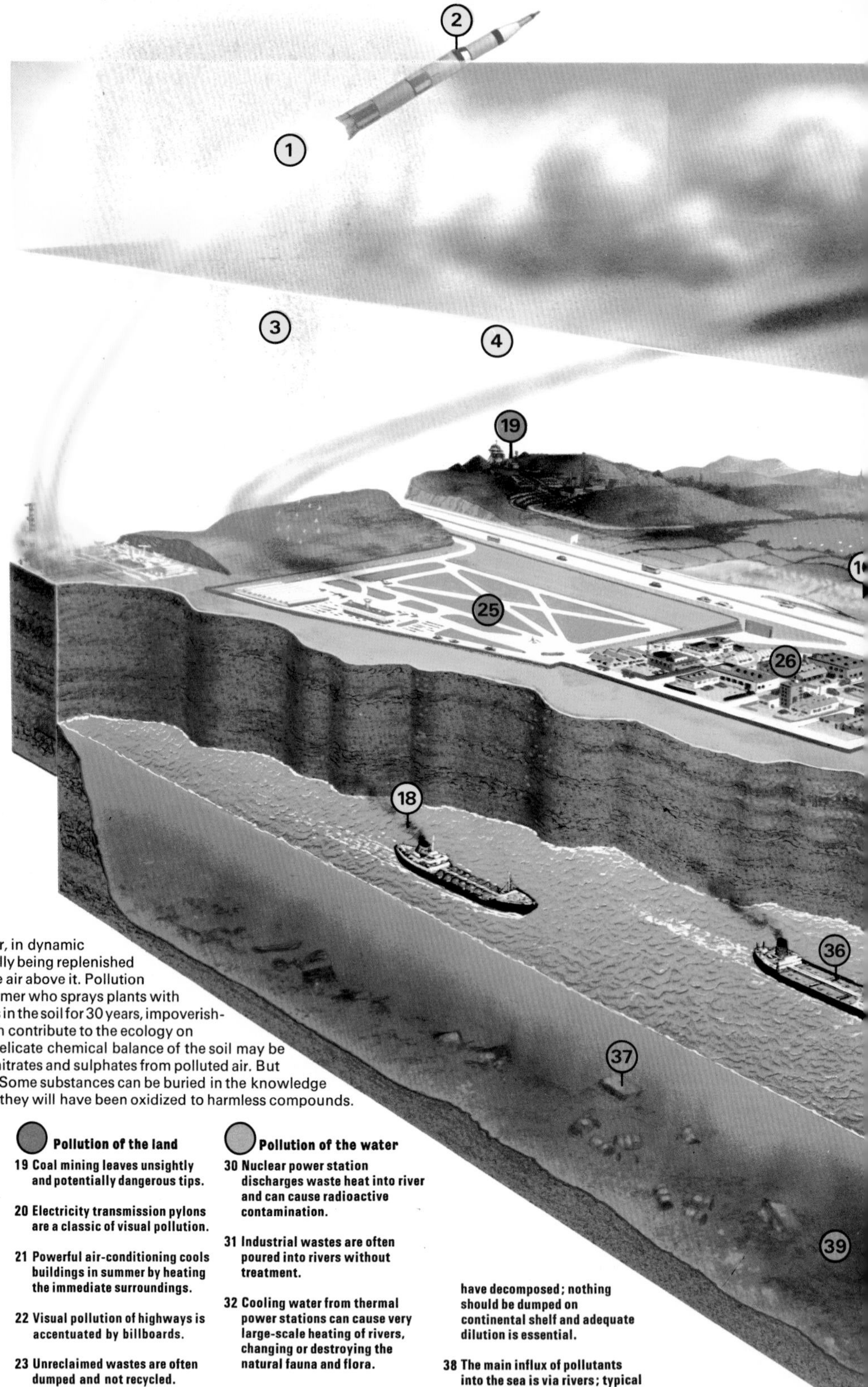

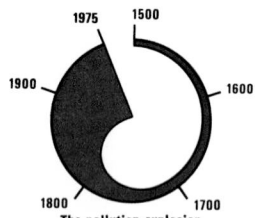

1975 1500
1900 1600
1800 1700
The pollution explosion

Pollution of the land
The soil is a living organic layer, in dynamic equilibrium with, and continually being replenished by, the rocks beneath it and the air above it. Pollution affects it in many ways. The farmer who sprays plants with insecticides may leave residues in the soil for 30 years, impoverishing the micro-organisms which contribute to the ecology on which his crops depend. The delicate chemical balance of the soil may be disrupted by rain loaded with nitrates and sulphates from polluted air. But the land is also a de-pollutant. Some substances can be buried in the knowledge that before they can re-appear they will have been oxidized to harmless compounds.

Pollution of the air
1 Rocket exhaust contains a variety of combustion products.

2 Space launchings leave jettisoned propellants and other debris orbiting above the atmosphere.

3 Nuclear weapon testing can leave fall-out on a global scale.

4 Increased air traffic creates noise pollution over wide areas.

5 Jet efflux contains kerosene combustion products, unburned fuel and particles of soot.

6 Nuclear weapons can cause radioactive contamination; together with chemical and biological devices they could eradicate all life on Earth.

7 Jet aircraft cause intense local noise, and supersonic aircraft create a shock-wave boom.

8 Large-scale aerial transport of pollutants distributes particles and gaseous matter.

9 Carbon dioxide build-up and 'greenhouse effect' traps solar heat within the atmosphere.

10 Pesticide spraying can cause widespread contamination, and organochlorine residues (such as DDT) can build up in animals and disrupt natural food chains.

11 Nuclear power station is potential source of escaping radioactive or liquid coolant.

12 Thermal (coal or oil fired) power station causes thermal and chemical pollution from exhaust stacks.

13 Power station cooling towers transfer waste heat to the air.

14 Sulphur dioxide from high roof-level chimneys falls into 'canyon streets' causing irritation to eyes and lungs.

15 Refinery waste gases burned in the air cause heavy pollution unless the flame is extremely hot.

16 Road vehicle exhausts and crankcase gases contain lead, unburned hydrocarbons, carbon monoxide and oxides of nitrogen, and can cause widespread pollution; action of sunlight on nitrogen oxides causes smog.

17 Most domestic fuels are very inefficiently burned, causing smoke and chemical pollution.

18 Steam boilers or diesel smoke can cause persistent trails of gaseous and particulate matter.

Pollution of the land
19 Coal mining leaves unsightly and potentially dangerous tips.

20 Electricity transmission pylons are a classic of visual pollution.

21 Powerful air-conditioning cools buildings in summer by heating the immediate surroundings.

22 Visual pollution of highways is accentuated by billboards.

23 Unreclaimed wastes are often dumped and not recycled.

24 Quarrying leaves unsightly scars.

25 Growth of air traffic is reflected in increasing size and number of airports which occupy otherwise valuable land.

26 Even modern industrial estates invariably cause chemical and thermal pollution, and pose waste-disposal problems.

27 Large motorways, especially intersections, occupy large areas of land.

28 Caravan and chalet sites may cause severe local chemical, as well as visual, pollution.

29 Modern litter includes high proportion of non-biodegradable plastics materials.

Pollution of the water
30 Nuclear power station discharges waste heat into river and can cause radioactive contamination.

31 Industrial wastes are often poured into rivers without treatment.

32 Cooling water from thermal power stations can cause very large-scale heating of rivers, changing or destroying the natural fauna and flora.

33 Refinery and other chemical plants generate waste heat and liquid refuse which may be discharged directly into the river.

34 Oil storage installation can cause intermittent pollution.

35 When it reaches the sea the river is heavily polluted by nitrates and phosphates from fertilizers and treated sewage, as well as by heavy toxic metals.

36 Tanker too close inshore risks severe beach pollution from accidental release of cargo.

37 Radioactive and corrosive wastes often dumped without enough knowledge of local conditions to insure that the containers will not leak before contents have decomposed; nothing should be dumped on continental shelf and adequate dilution is essential.

38 The main influx of pollutants into the sea is via rivers; typical categories include agricultural and industrial chemicals, waste heat, treated and untreated sewage and solid matter.

39 Excess nutrients from untreated sewage, agricultural chemicals and nuclear wastes can lead to 'blooms' of toxic marine plankton or, through their oxidation and decay, to severely reduced oxygen levels in the water.

40 Sewage sludge dumped at sea contains persistent chemicals such as PCB (polychlorinated biophenyl) compounds, toxic heavy metals and nutrients.

41 Large oil slicks are released by tanker accidents or deliberate washing at sea, and by oil-rig blow-outs.

42 Sediments stirred by mineral exploitation, dumped from ships or carried by rivers may form thick layers on the ocean floor which suffocate the organisms living there.

43 Clouds of particulate matter, both organic and inorganic wastes, reduce the penetration of sunlight and sharply curtail marine productivity.

44 Oil rigs suffer explosive blow-outs, a serious problem off the California coast.

45 In some waters wrecks, many of them uncharted, pose hazards to shipping which may lead to further pollution.

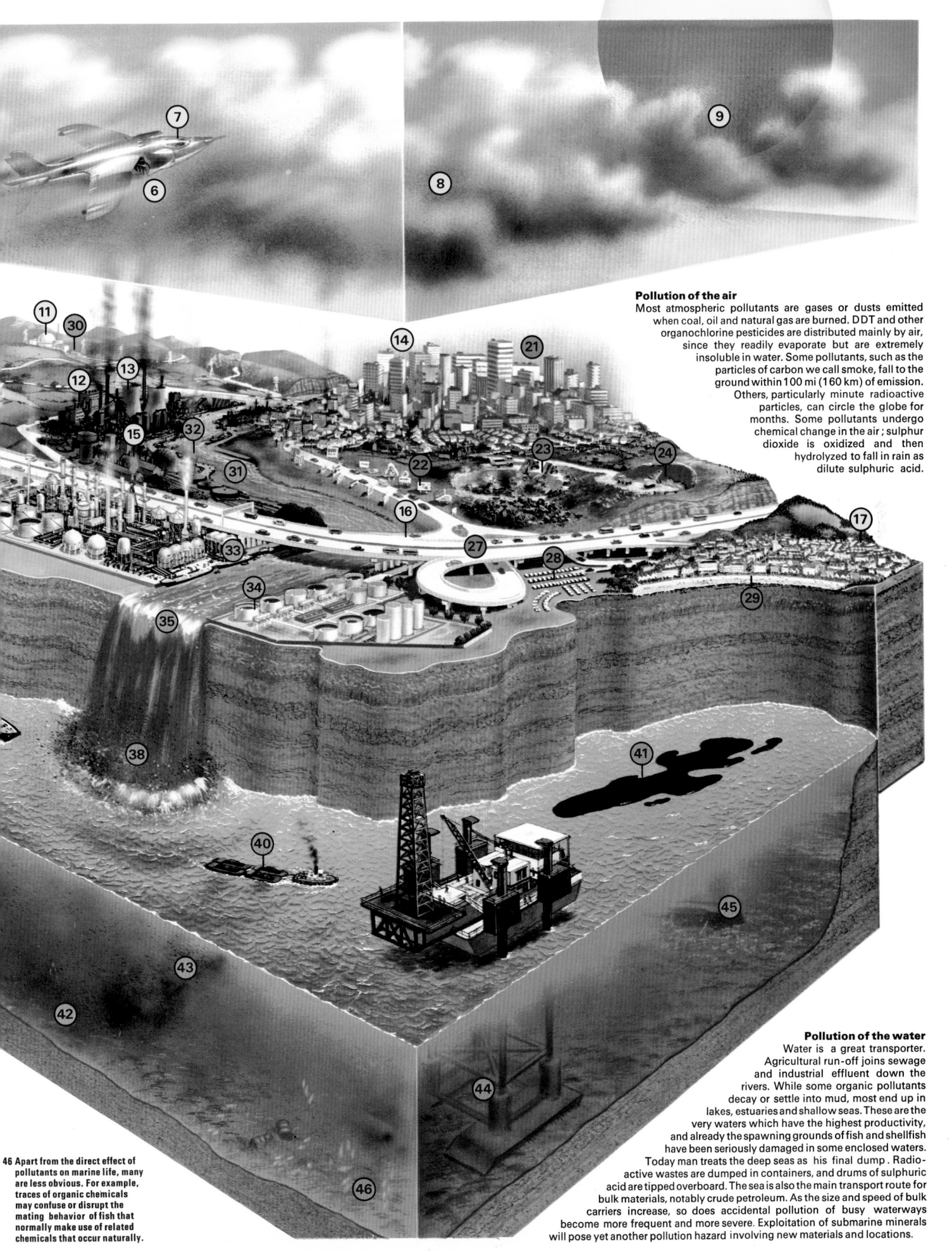

Pollution of the air

Most atmospheric pollutants are gases or dusts emitted when coal, oil and natural gas are burned. DDT and other organochlorine pesticides are distributed mainly by air, since they readily evaporate but are extremely insoluble in water. Some pollutants, such as the particles of carbon we call smoke, fall to the ground within 100 mi (160 km) of emission. Others, particularly minute radioactive particles, can circle the globe for months. Some pollutants undergo chemical change in the air; sulphur dioxide is oxidized and then hydrolyzed to fall in rain as dilute sulphuric acid.

Pollution of the water

Water is a great transporter. Agricultural run-off joins sewage and industrial effluent down the rivers. While some organic pollutants decay or settle into mud, most end up in lakes, estuaries and shallow seas. These are the very waters which have the highest productivity, and already the spawning grounds of fish and shellfish have been seriously damaged in some enclosed waters. Today man treats the deep seas as his final dump. Radioactive wastes are dumped in containers, and drums of sulphuric acid are tipped overboard. The sea is also the main transport route for bulk materials, notably crude petroleum. As the size and speed of bulk carriers increase, so does accidental pollution of busy waterways become more frequent and more severe. Exploitation of submarine minerals will pose yet another pollution hazard involving new materials and locations.

46 Apart from the direct effect of pollutants on marine life, many are less obvious. For example, traces of organic chemicals may confuse or disrupt the mating behavior of fish that normally make use of related chemicals that occur naturally.

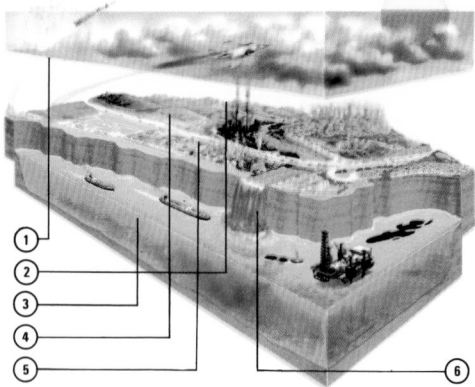

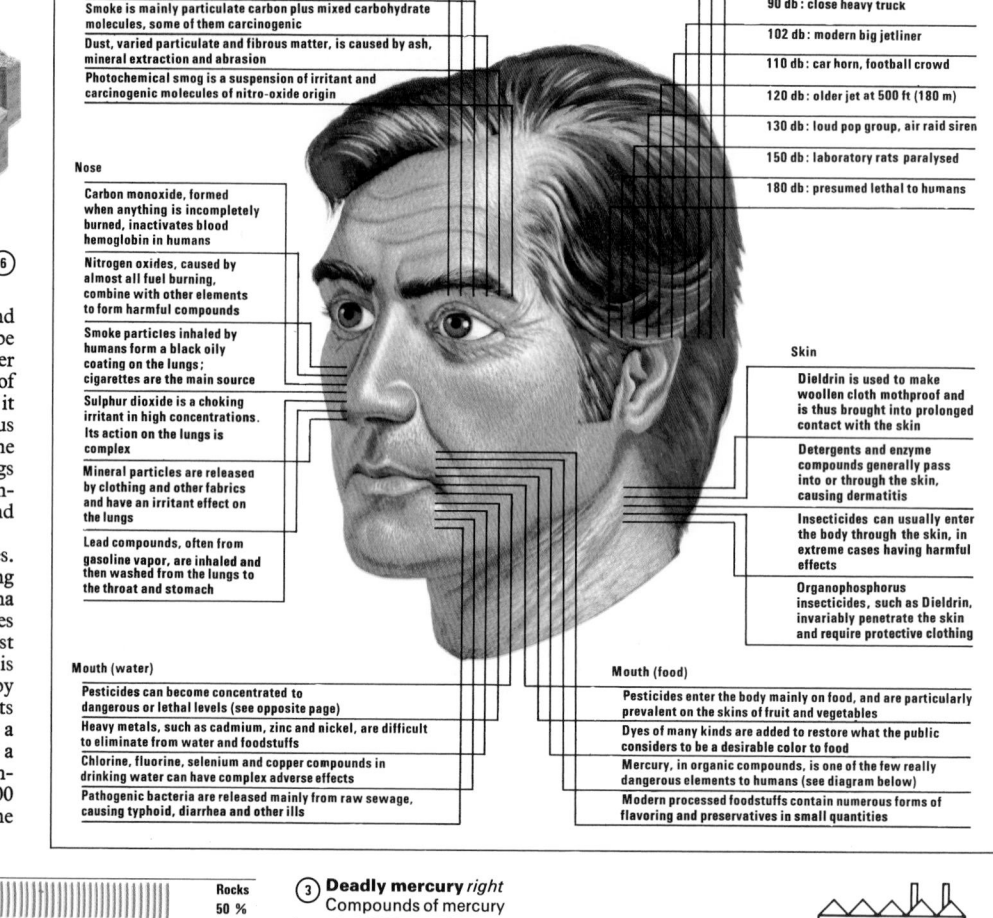

Pollution and health

Eyes

Ozone from various industrial processes is extremely toxic and irritates the eyes

Sulphur dioxide is generated by burning all sulphurous fuels: coal, oil and gas

Smoke is mainly particulate carbon plus mixed carbohydrate molecules, some of them carcinogenic

Dust, varied particulate and fibrous matter, is caused by ash, mineral extraction and abrasion

Photochemical smog is a suspension of irritant and carcinogenic molecules of nitro-oxide origin

Nose

Carbon monoxide, formed when anything is incompletely burned, inactivates blood hemoglobin in humans

Nitrogen oxides, caused by almost all fuel burning, combine with other elements to form harmful compounds

Smoke particles inhaled by humans form a black oily coating on the lungs; cigarettes are the main source

Sulphur dioxide is a choking irritant in high concentrations. Its action on the lungs is complex

Mineral particles are released by clothing and other fabrics and have an irritant effect on the lungs

Lead compounds, often from gasoline vapor, are inhaled and then washed from the lungs to the throat and stomach

Ears

30 decibels: watch ticking

60 db: normal conversation

90 db: close heavy truck

102 db: modern big jetliner

110 db: car horn, football crowd

120 db: older jet at 500 ft (180 m)

130 db: loud pop group, air raid siren

150 db: laboratory rats paralysed

180 db: presumed lethal to humans

Skin

Dieldrin is used to make woollen cloth mothproof and is thus brought into prolonged contact with the skin

Detergents and enzyme compounds generally pass into or through the skin, causing dermatitis

Insecticides can usually enter the body through the skin, in extreme cases having harmful effects

Organophosphorus insecticides, such as Dieldrin, invariably penetrate the skin and require protective clothing

Mouth (water)

Pesticides can become concentrated to dangerous or lethal levels (see opposite page)

Heavy metals, such as cadmium, zinc and nickel, are difficult to eliminate from water and foodstuffs

Chlorine, fluorine, selenium and copper compounds in drinking water can have complex adverse effects

Pathogenic bacteria are released mainly from raw sewage, causing typhoid, diarrhea and other ills

Mouth (food)

Pesticides enter the body mainly on food, and are particularly prevalent on the skins of fruit and vegetables

Dyes of many kinds are added to restore what the public considers to be a desirable color to food

Mercury, in organic compounds, is one of the few really dangerous elements to humans (see diagram below)

Modern processed foodstuffs contain numerous forms of flavoring and preservatives in small quantities

Pollution often travels along strange pathways, and these must be unravelled if the menace is to be controlled and its effects predicted. It is unwise ever to assume the obvious. DDT was found in the soil of apple orchards in Kent months after spraying, and it was also detected in local rivers. The obvious conclusion was that it was leaching down through the soil into the groundwater. But analysis of the springs and wells showed no DDT at all. In fact the insecticide was leaving the surface by evaporation and falling again as rain.

Pollution can be distributed over vast distances. The insecticide BHC is carried by the prevailing westerly winds from the Soviet Union across China and N America and to Europe. Water likewise carries contaminants down rivers to oceans. But the most important pathway is the food chain. A pollutant is released into the air, soil or sea. It is absorbed by plants. These are eaten by a herbivore, which in its turn is eaten by a carnivore which is itself eaten by a predator. The chain may have many links or only a few, but at every stage the pollutant is more concentrated. If a hawk eats 100 birds which each ate 100 insects it may die from pollution 10000 times the strength met by the insect.

(1) **Radiation** *right*
No pollutant has been so continuously monitored as nuclear radiation. But it is not a problem created solely by modern man. In the modern world nearly all the radioactivity issues from the rocks, and, as far as humans are concerned, from the body.

Rocks	50 %
Cosmic	25 %
Body	$23\frac{1}{4}$ %
Tests	$1\frac{1}{2}$ %
Waste	$\frac{1}{4}$ %

(2) **Radiation and life** *right*
Living cells concentrate radiation. In an above-ground nuclear-weapon test all heavy radioactive particles drop within hours in a narrow region downwind of the explosion. Their residence time in the atmosphere varies from four weeks in the troposphere to ten years in the mesosphere. One such product, strontium 90, is taken up from the soil by plants. Eaten by cattle and released in their milk, it ends up in human bone where it is only slowly liquidated. As it decays it can destroy the marrow which produces red blood cells, in extreme cases causing death through pentaemia. Radiation pollution can also arise from power reactors or nuclear waste. Plankton can concentrate radioactivity a thousandfold. Fish eat plankton, and on migration can disperse the radiation far from its source. In the 1950s this mechanism caused radiation sickness in Japanese fishermen hundreds of miles from US test sites in the Pacific.

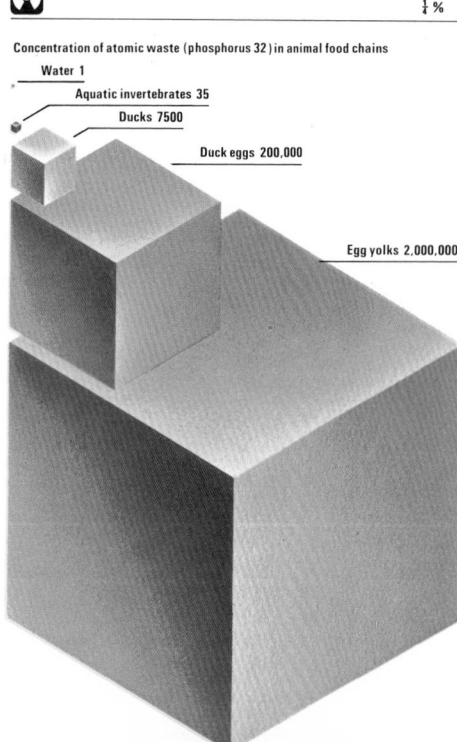

Concentration of atomic waste (phosphorus 32) in animal food chains

Water 1

Aquatic invertebrates 35

Ducks 7500

Duck eggs 200,000

Egg yolks 2,000,000

(3) **Deadly mercury** *right*
Compounds of mercury have for 1000 years been known to be highly toxic. An industrial plant often discharges such compounds, but it was thought these rested at the sea bed. Man has now learned that bacteria can convert inorganic mercury compounds to deadly methyl mercury, which can then be successively concentrated in marine food chains. Shellfish are particularly good concentrators of methyl mercury. When eaten by humans they cause severe disabling of the central nervous system, and in extreme cases cause death (below).

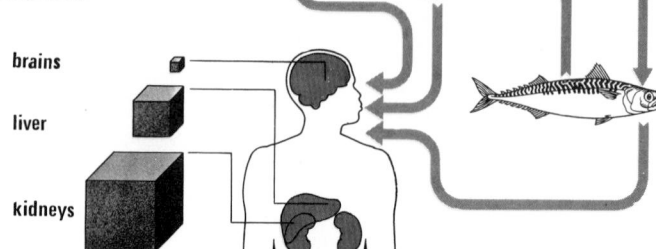

brains

liver

kidneys

Minimata tragedy *right*
In 1953 people living in this Japanese city became ill. Ultimately over 120 were afflicted, and 43 (black) died. The cause was methyl mercury concentrated in seafoods. Some acetaldehyde plants still emit methyl mercury.

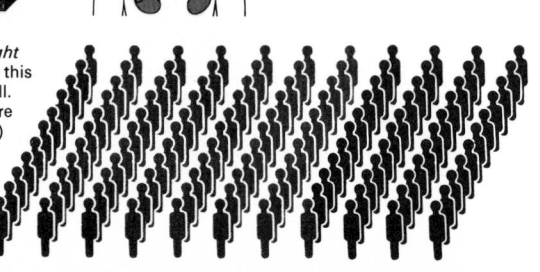

4 The DDT menace *right*
Introduced during World War 2, DDT appeared to be ideal. It would kill lice on soldiers weeks after the treatment of their clothes. Houses sprayed against malaria remained lethal to mosquitoes long after the health teams had departed. But the persistence brought its own problems. DDT and other organochlorine pesticides, such as BHC, Dieldrin, Endosulfan and Heptachlor, are only slightly broken down by animal metabolism. An insect receiving a non-lethal dose of DDT retains it in its body and passes it on up the food chain. Animals at the head of the chain often build up large residues in their fatty tissues. Under stress these residues can be released and fatally damage the liver, kidney and brain. DDT can evaporate from soil, travelling round the globe, before being adsorbed on to dust and falling as rain. The organochlorines soon penetrate every corner of an ecosystem.

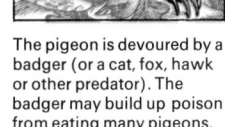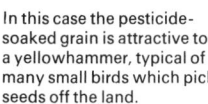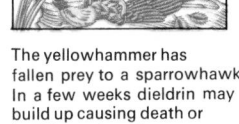

DIELDRIN

Seed that has been 'dressed' is eaten by a wood pigeon. The bird finds the seeds palatable, and may eat dozens to hundreds in a day.

The pigeon is devoured by a badger (or a cat, fox, hawk or other predator). The badger may build up poison from eating many pigeons.

In this case the pesticide-soaked grain is attractive to a yellowhammer, typical of many small birds which pick seeds off the land.

The yellowhammer has fallen prey to a sparrowhawk. In a few weeks dieldrin may build up causing death or inability to breed.

DDT

Sap-sucking insects, such as aphids, feed on sprayed wheat and build up a DDT concentration not sufficiently high to kill them.

A predator ladybird climbs wheat grain devouring aphids in large numbers. It soon builds up a very large residue of DDT in its body.

On a nettle at the edge of the field the ladybird is in turn eaten by a whitethroat, spotted flycatcher or other insect-eating bird.

Finally the bird suffering from severe DDT toxicity, is devoured by a hawk. In many countries birds of prey have almost vanished.

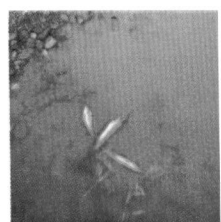

6 Misuse of a river by overloading *above and left*
In moderation, man can safely pour his effluents into the rivers. A farmhouse beside a river (above) causes a little local pollution which is soon oxidized; the fish population does not suffer. A village causes no lasting pollution but merely a depression of the dissolved oxygen in the water for a mile or two downstream. But a large city pours out so much effluent that the river is completely de-oxygenated. All the fish and plants are killed and the river becomes foul in an irreversible way (left). Whereas a river may be capable of processing pollutants from 50000 people, pollutants from 100000 may destroy the ecological cycle.

5 The PCB problem
PCBs (polychlorinated biphenyls) are persistent and can be scattered in smoke from burning or washed down a drain adsorbed on dust particles. Virtually all these molecules end up in the sea in the form of non-biodegradable particles which can be intensely concentrated as they move within the marine food chain. Their lethal effect was first driven home when the population of Irish sea birds, especially guillemots, crashed in 1969. Almost all the corpses were found to have liver and kidney lesions characteristic of PCB poisoning. Fat, healthy birds can carry a large PCB load safely, but the Irish birds were starving and had drawn on their fatty reserves, where the PCB was stored. Passing into the circulation, the chemical accumulated in the birds' organs in lethal amounts.

PCB uses *left*
Polychlorinated biphenyls have numerous uses in modern industry. They serve as plasticizers in paints, as fillers in plastics and in electrical capacitors.

Guillemots *right*
These sea birds live on fish and thus form the end link in a marine food chain.

Thin guillemot *below*
When a guillemot with 3400 ppb of PCB in its body becomes emaciated it draws on its reserves of fat. The chemical becomes concentrated in its organs, reaching a lethal level of 60000 ppb.

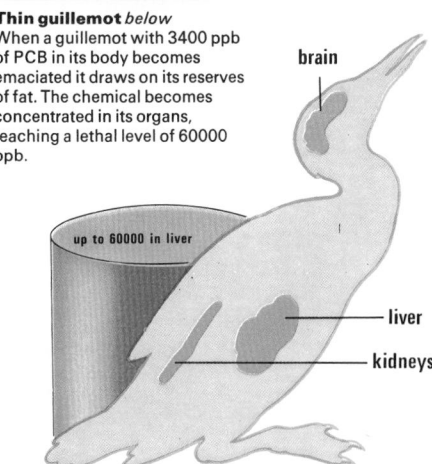

brain
up to 60000 in liver
liver
kidneys

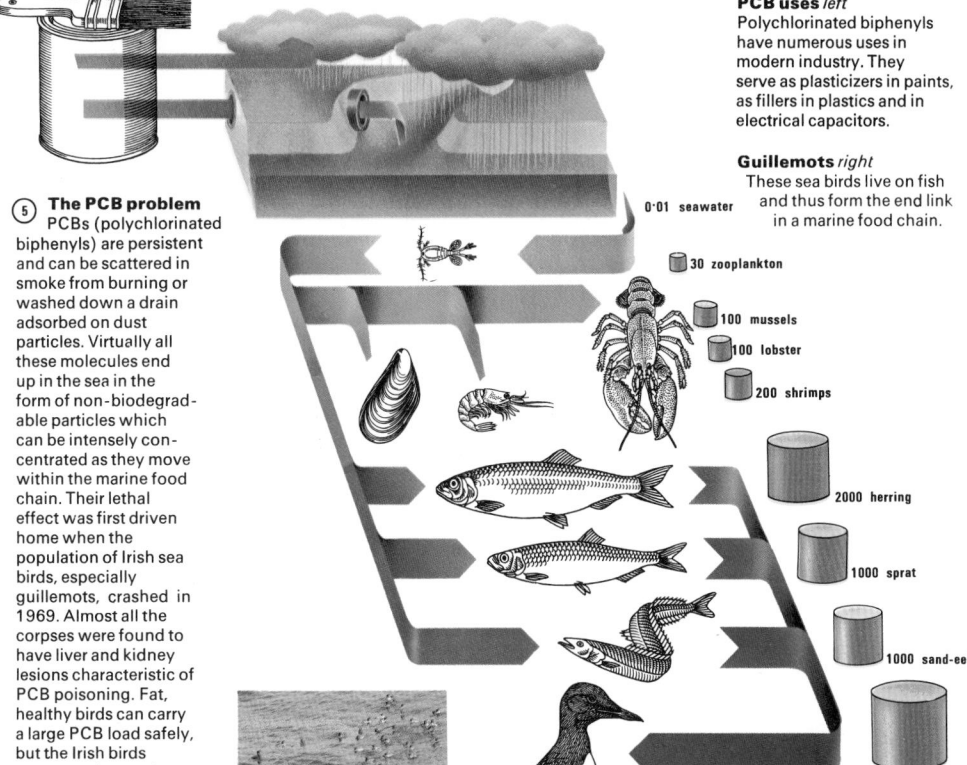

0·01 seawater
30 zooplankton
100 mussels
100 lobster
200 shrimps
2000 herring
1000 sprat
1000 sand-eel
3400 guillemot

Fat guillemot *left*
Healthy guillemots (feeding at sea, far left) can have 3400 parts per billion (ppb) of PCBs in the body but only 400 in the liver.

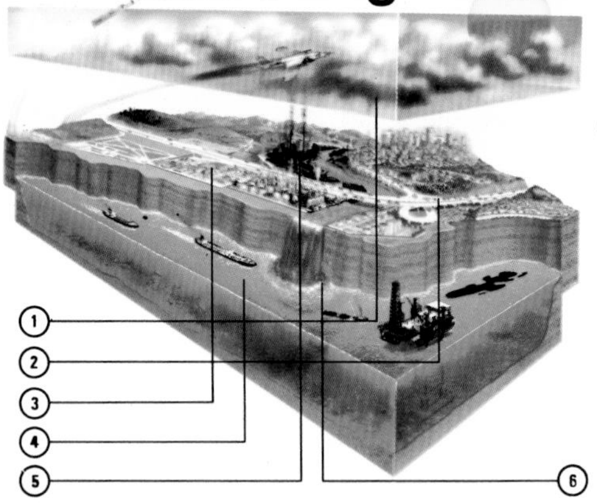

Pollution is a global problem. It affects the land, the sea and the atmosphere in an inter-related way that is incredibly complex and often very subtle. At least in the industrially developed countries man has learned that he must do better than merely bury his unwanted materials in the ground, pour them into the rivers or burn them to pollute the air. But learning the best ways of disposing of them – or, preferably, of storing them until they can be used again – is a difficult, long-term process; and time is not on man's side.

Once pollutants are dispersed, controlling them becomes extremely costly or even impossible. The answer is to prevent their release, wherever possible, into the arterial pathways of water and air. The growing awareness of this is reflected in the legislation of many countries. It is seen in the Clean Air Act of Great Britain, the German convention banning harmful detergents, the tight California restrictions on car exhaust gases, and so on. But this is only the start of the movement to clean-up the environment and conserve its resources.

Much of the action against pollution has been piecemeal in nature, often in response to particular disasters. Now comes the promise, in no small part due to the public mood, for more widespread action against pollutants that are already known to be harmful to the environment and man. For example, public health authorities in most countries are alive to the hazard of mercury contamination in fish and other foods. At the international level, the convention on oil pollution is being strengthened and the permissible levels of radioactive discharges reviewed. At the same time, industry is slowly becoming persuaded that waste should be regarded as a valued resource which is often capable of being recycled over and over again instead of discarded.

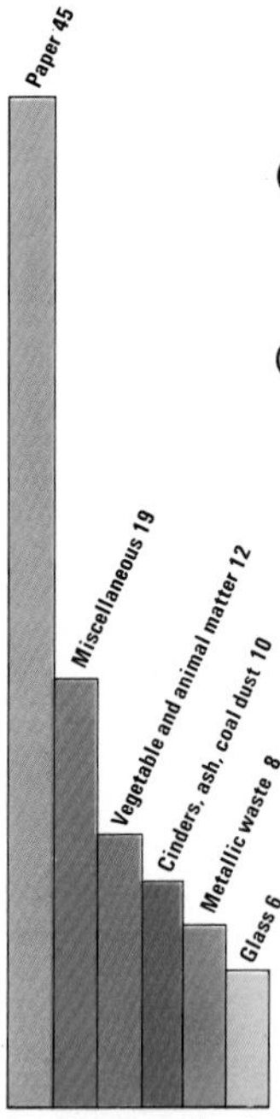

Percentage composition of domestic waste in U S A

Paper 45
Miscellaneous 19
Vegetable and animal matter 12
Cinders, ash, coal dust 10
Metallic waste 8
Glass 6

(2) Domestic waste
Man's garbage has never ceased to grow in volume and to change in character. In the past much of it, such as wood, cloth and paper, was biodegradable – exposure to micro-organisms and the weather slowly rotted them away. Even iron slowly oxidized. But today's refuse contains increasing amounts of materials which do not decay. These new materials demand new or improved methods of disposal, which with the growing recognition of the problem are now being adopted in many places.

Recyclable	1 Ferrous metals
	2 Non-ferrous metals
	3 Rubber
	4 Glass
	5 Paper and cardboard
	6 Cloth
Compostable	1 Vegetable matter
	2 Animal matter
	3 Cloth
Buried	1 Mineral dust
	2 Brick, stone
Incinerated	1 Plastics
	2 Polythene
	3 Polystyrene
	4 Linoleum

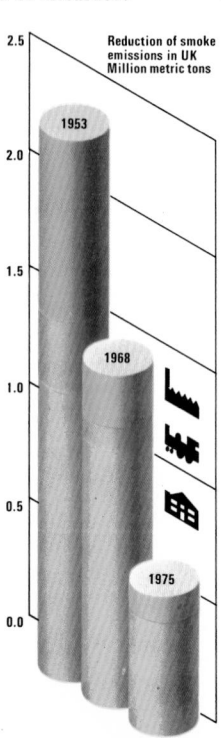

(1) Air pollution in cities
Smoke is one of the commonest, most dangerous and most visible of all air pollutants. It is the direct cause of bronchitis and other respiratory diseases. But many nations are cleaning their urban atmosphere by introducing smokeless zones. Since 1956 winter sunshine in British city centers has increased by over 50 per cent. Smoke from railways (violet segment, right) has dwindled as steam traction has been superseded. Industrial smoke has likewise been reduced, although iron oxide dust from steelworks (above) remains a problem as do domestic coal fires.

Reduction of smoke emissions in UK Million metric tons

1953
1968
1975

The menace of the car *below*
Dramatic reductions in air pollution will result as soon as simple alterations are universally adopted. One of the worst sources, the crankcase breather (1) is not opened to the air but piped through a vacuum-sensing valve (2) back to the intake. Fuel-tank vapor (3) is filtered and similarly dealt with. The exhaust is made oxygen-rich with extra fresh air (4) to burn up all but a few combustion products; the residue is oxidized to harmless compounds by passage through a high temperature furnace (5) in the presence of a chemical catalyst which promotes the desired reactions.

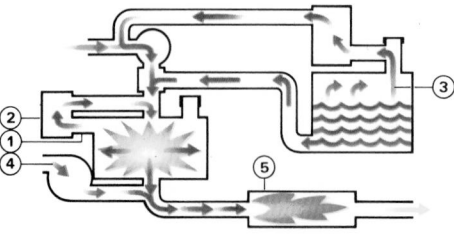

(3) Saving the eagle *right*
In the early 1960s ecologists became sure that organo-chlorine insecticides (DDT and Dieldrin, for example) were the cause of the sudden drop in breeding success of many predatory birds. But the charge could not be proved, and in most countries the use of these pesticides continued. One bird affected was the golden eagle. Scottish highland sheep were dipped in Dieldrin to kill ticks. The chemical became dissolved in the mutton fat, and this eagle lives largely on sheep carrion. In one area the proportion of eagle eyries producing young fell from 72 to 29 per cent, following the introduction of Dieldrin sheep dips in 1960. Scotland's 300 pairs of eagles seemed doomed. But in 1966 Britain banned Dieldrin sheep-dips. By the early 1970s more than enough young survived to maintain the eagle population.

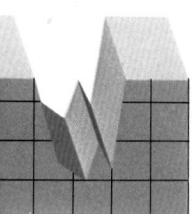

1960 1963 1966 1969
Golden eagle: percentage breeding successes

④ Oil pollution

Every year millions of tons of oil enter the oceans either directly through spills, accidents and deliberate discharge or indirectly via air and water from the land. Hardly any part of the ocean remains free from contamination. Some oil pollution is the disturbing result of industrial society's dependence on an oil-based technology. Equally, there is no doubt that much oil pollution is unnecessary and can be controlled or prevented. One of the earliest attempts to do this occurred in 1926 when the United States tried to obtan international agreement to limit the discharge of oil. This and later attempts by the United Kingdom failed and it was not until 1958 that the International Convention for the Prevention of Pollution of the Sea by Oil came into force – four years after it was agreed. Even then, the Convention did not ban completely the release of oil into the sea. This must be the ultimate goal. However, even if this is achieved, the problem will persist – oil pollution from sources on land is more than double that occurring directly at sea. One of the chief offenders are gasoline and diesel engines. The crankcases of such engines contribute at least 2.8 million metric tons of oil to the sea every year. A serious waste of a vital resource, steps are at last being taken in some countries to curb it.

The Torrey Canyon disaster

In 1967 the sea had its first major case of oil pollution when the Torrey Canyon ran aground off the Cornish coast (above left). Within a few days the first oil began to sweep onto the beaches. To disperse it, large quantities of detergent were sprayed both from boats (above) and on the shore, turning the sea creamy white with a froth of oily emulsion (center left). Unfortunately the use of these detergents probably caused more damage to marine life than did the oil – except for the early kill of seabirds (bottom left). The oil also drifted across to France coating the shore with congealed oil (right).

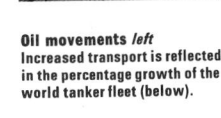

Oil movements *left*

Increased transport is reflected in the percentage growth of the world tanker fleet (below).

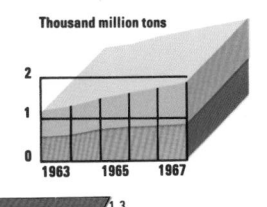

Thousand million tons

Oil tankers' new load-on-top system *below*

Before the introduction of this system, ballast water and tank washings, along with a hundred or so tons of oil which had originally stuck to the internal steelwork, were discharged into the sea before taking on a new cargo. In the load-on-top system, one cargo compartment (A) is used as a 'slop tank'. Water in a ballast tank (B) is run off until only oil and oily water remains (C). The residue together with washings from the tanks are collected in the slop tank (D). Here the mixture is finally separated before running clean water off (E). The load goes on top of the remaining oil.

Major oil routes

Oil entering the oceans — Million metric tons

- Industrial machine waste — 1.3
- Motor vehicle waste — 1.8
- Refineries — 0.3
- Accidental spillage — 0.2
- Offshore drilling — 0.1
- Tanker operations — 0.53
- Other ships — 0.5

Sources of oil pollution *left*

Although the spectacular incidents such as tanker collisions and drilling rig accidents receive most publicity, they release little oil compared with motor vehicles and industrial machines.

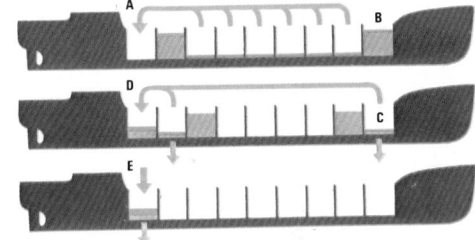

⑤ Thermal pollution *above and below*

Man throws away a great deal of unwanted heat into rivers. This is done on the largest scale by electricity generating stations whose condensers cycle cooling water in vast quantities. In Britain the hot effluent is spread as a thin film on an otherwise cool river, causing visible steam (above, River Trent) but minimal disturbance to river life. The problem is accentuated by the spread of very large nuclear stations (in the US, below), which for safety reasons have so far generally been sited miles from urban areas on rivers which previously were quite unpolluted. In Britian all such stations are on the sea shore or wide estuaries.

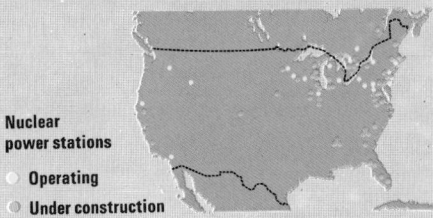

Nuclear power stations

○ Operating

○ Under construction

⑥ Lake pollution

Lakes pass through a sequence of physical and chemical states from youth to maturity (p66A). Man's sewage and industrial effluents accelerate the intake of nutrient salts — such as the phosphates and nitrates shown in the bar chart above the map — which feed the natural population of algae. Combined with sunny weather the result can be an algal 'bloom'. Billions of algae use up the water's dissolved oxygen, killing fish and other life. The aerobic (oxygen-breathing) bacteria needed to degrade sewage and other organic matter are replaced by anaerobic forms which decompose the refuse not to carbon dioxide and water but to foul gases and black slimes. Eventually the bloom is replaced by an algal 'crash' and the countless bodies, often visible as a colored tide, evolve toxic decomposition products which, concentrated in food chains, can prove lethal to sea birds and even humans. The answer is better water treatment plants, possibly combined with new forms of fertilizers, detergents and other products of modern civilization which contain smaller quantities of nutrient salts.

Main pollutants: percentages

| Phosphate | 20 | 43 | 37 |
| Nitrate | 9 | 17 | 74 |

☐ Lakeshore sewage
☐ Sewage from tributaries
■ Natural inflow from rivers

Ludwigshafen
Überlingen
Friedrichshafen
Radolfzell
Konstanz
Lindau
Steckborn
Kreuzlingen
Romanshorn
Bregenz
Rorschach

1
2
3
4
5
6
7

Numbers indicate increasing pollution

Reviving a dying lake *above*

One of the largest European freshwater lakes, Lake Constance (Bodensee), is a prime example of how the increasing load of industrial and domestic effluent causes serious pollution. The aim now is to install treatment plant at source rather than use the lake as a liquid refuse dump.

World Thematic Maps

This section contains more than 60 thematic maps that present world patterns and distributions in visual form. Together with accompanying graphs, these maps communicate basic information on mineral resources, agricultural products, trade, transportation, and other selected aspects of the natural and human environment.

The thematic map uses symbols to communicate information. Generally, each map tells about only one class of geographical information, such as climate or population. This "theme" of a thematic map is placed over a map that gives basic geographic information, such as coastlines, country boundaries, rivers, and oceans. A thematic map's primary purpose is to give the reader a general idea of the subject. For example, the map on page 37 shows the distribution of cattle by the use of dot symbols. From this, the reader can learn that cattle are distributed much more uniformly throughout the United States than in China. The reader can also see that America has more cattle than China. But there is no way to tell the exact number in each country.

This is true of most thematic maps. They are not intended to provide exact statistical information. A reader who wants precise statistics should consult the bar graphs that appear with the thematic maps in this Atlas or other sources, such as encyclopedias or almanacs.

Thematic maps use point, line, and area symbols, singly and in combination. These can show both *qualitative differences* (differences in kind) and *quantitative differences* (differences in amount). For example, the Natural Vegetation map (page 16) uses color and pattern symbols to show the kind of vegetation that grows naturally in various parts of the world. This is qualitative information. Quantitative information is shown on the Annual Precipitation map (page 14). By means of lines that connect points of equal rainfall, the reader can tell, in general, how much rain an area receives in a year. Color is used to show the area between the lines. Thus, the thematic maps communicate general information far better than could volumes of words and tables.

One of the most important uses of the thematic maps section, is to show comparisons and relationships. For example, a reader can compare the relationship of population density (page 20) with agriculture (page 28) and manufacturing and commerce (page 26).

The maps and graphs in this section also give an idea of the relative importance of countries in the distributions mapped. The maps are based on recent statistics gathered by the United Nations and various governmental and nongovernmental sources. However, no single year affords a realistic base for production, trade, and certain economic and demographic statistics; averages of data for three or four years are used.

2

POLITICAL

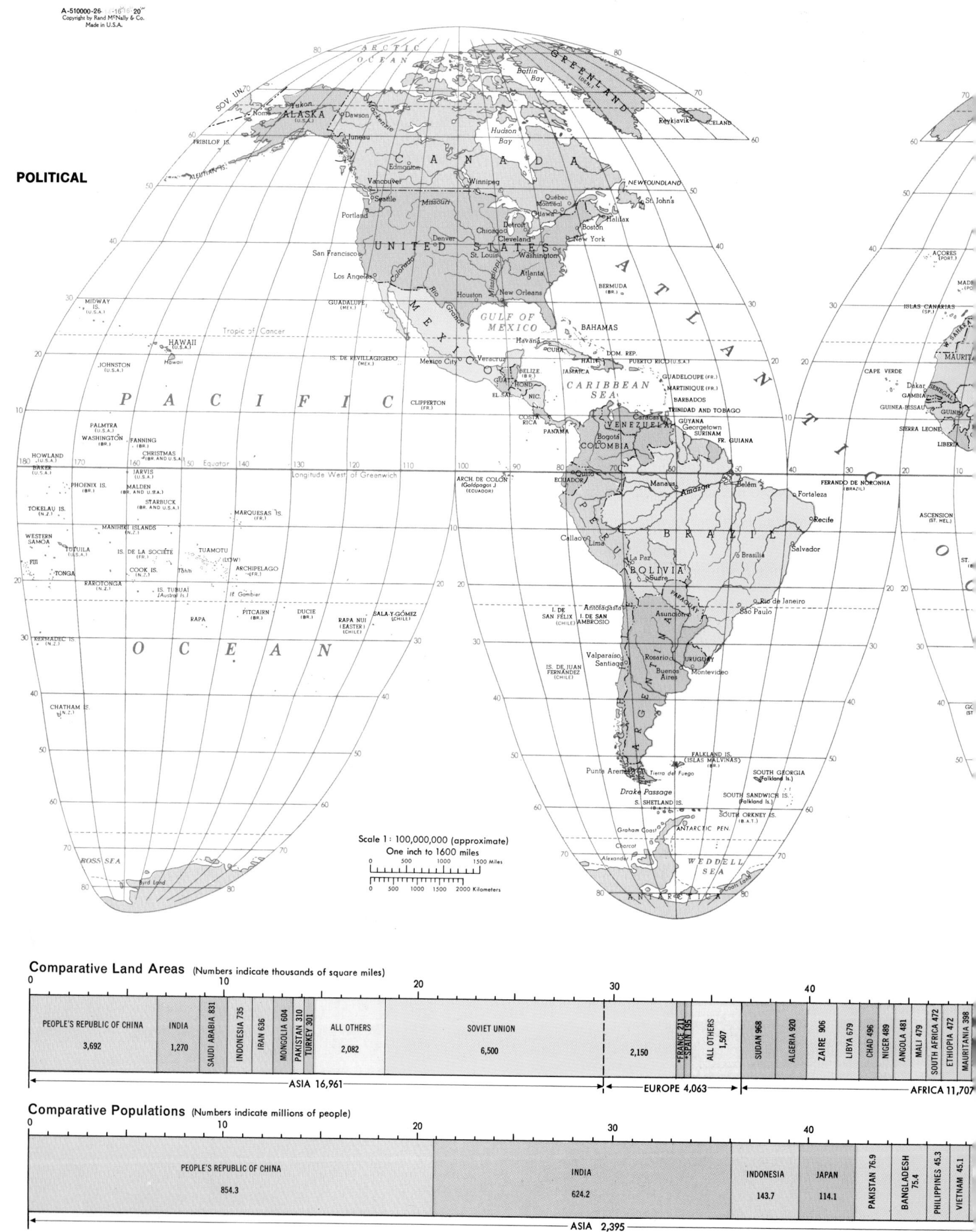

Scale 1 : 100,000,000 (approximate)
One inch to 1600 miles

0   500   1000   1500 Miles

0   500   1000   1500   2000 Kilometers

Comparative Land Areas (Numbers indicate thousands of square miles)

0	10	20	30	40

PEOPLE'S REPUBLIC OF CHINA 3,692 | INDIA 1,270 | SAUDI ARABIA 831 | INDONESIA 735 | IRAN 636 | MONGOLIA 604 | PAKISTAN 310 | TURKEY 301 | ALL OTHERS 2,082 | SOVIET UNION 6,500 | 2,150 | FRANCE 211 | SPAIN 195 | ALL OTHERS 1,507 | SUDAN 968 | ALGERIA 920 | ZAIRE 906 | LIBYA 679 | CHAD 496 | NIGER 489 | ANGOLA 481 | MALI 479 | SOUTH AFRICA 472 | ETHIOPIA 472 | MAURITANIA 398

←————————— ASIA 16,961 —————————→ ←— EUROPE 4,063 —→ ←———— AFRICA 11,707

Comparative Populations (Numbers indicate millions of people)

0	10	20	30	40

PEOPLE'S REPUBLIC OF CHINA 854.3 | INDIA 624.2 | INDONESIA 143.7 | JAPAN 114.1 | PAKISTAN 76.9 | BANGLADESH 75.4 | PHILIPPINES 45.3 | VIETNAM 45.1

←————————————————— ASIA 2,395 —————————————————→

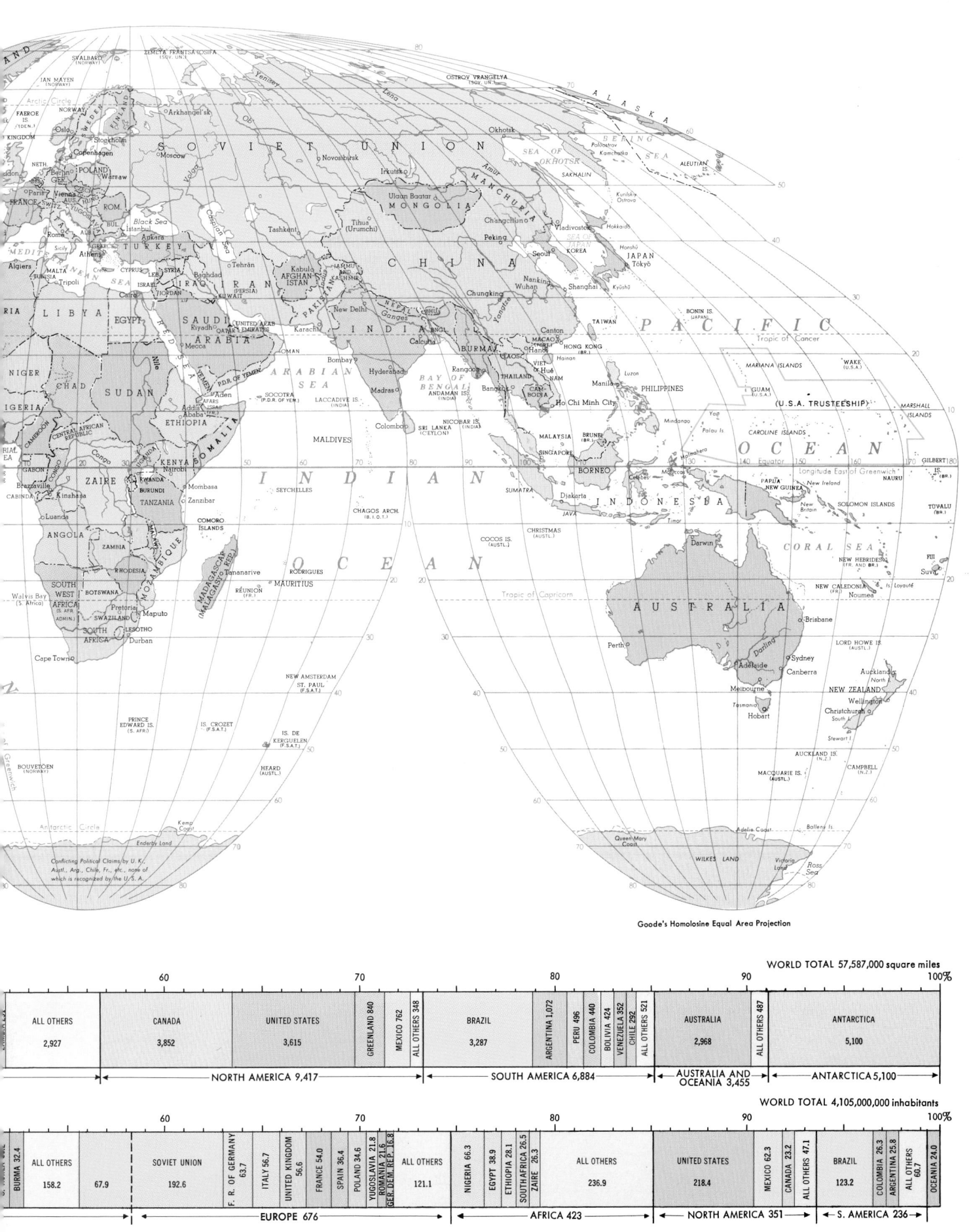

Goode's Homolosine Equal Area Projection

WORLD TOTAL 57,587,000 square miles

	60		70			80						90		100%

| ALL OTHERS 2,927 | CANADA 3,852 | UNITED STATES 3,615 | GREENLAND 840 | MEXICO 762 | ALL OTHERS 348 | BRAZIL 3,287 | ARGENTINA 1,072 | PERU 496 | COLOMBIA 440 | VENEZUELA 352 | BOLIVIA 424 | CHILE 292 | ALL OTHERS 521 | AUSTRALIA 2,968 | ALL OTHERS 487 | ANTARCTICA 5,100 |

NORTH AMERICA 9,417 — SOUTH AMERICA 6,884 — AUSTRALIA AND OCEANIA 3,455 — ANTARCTICA 5,100

WORLD TOTAL 4,105,000,000 inhabitants

	60			70			80				90			100%

| BURMA 32.4 | ALL OTHERS 158.2 | 67.9 | SOVIET UNION 192.6 | F. R. OF GERMANY 63.7 | ITALY 56.7 | UNITED KINGDOM 56.6 | FRANCE 54.0 | SPAIN 36.4 | POLAND 34.6 | YUGOSLAVIA 21.8 | ROMANIA 21.6 | GER. DEM. REP. 16.8 | ALL OTHERS 121.1 | NIGERIA 66.3 | EGYPT 38.9 | ETHIOPIA 28.1 | SOUTH AFRICA 26.5 | ZAIRE 26.3 | ALL OTHERS 236.9 | UNITED STATES 218.4 | MEXICO 62.3 | CANADA 23.2 | ALL OTHERS 47.1 | BRAZIL 123.2 | COLOMBIA 26.3 | ARGENTINA 25.8 | ALL OTHERS 60.7 | OCEANIA 24.0 |

EUROPE 676 — AFRICA 423 — NORTH AMERICA 351 — S. AMERICA 236

4

PHYSICAL

Scale 1:100,000,000 (approximate)
One inch to 1600 miles

0   500   1000   1500 Miles

0 500 1000 1500 2000 Kilometers

Meters	Feet
3 050	10 000
1 525	5 000
610	2 000
305	1 000
0	SEA L. 0
	BELOW SEA LEVEL
152.5	500
3 050	10 000
6 100	20 000

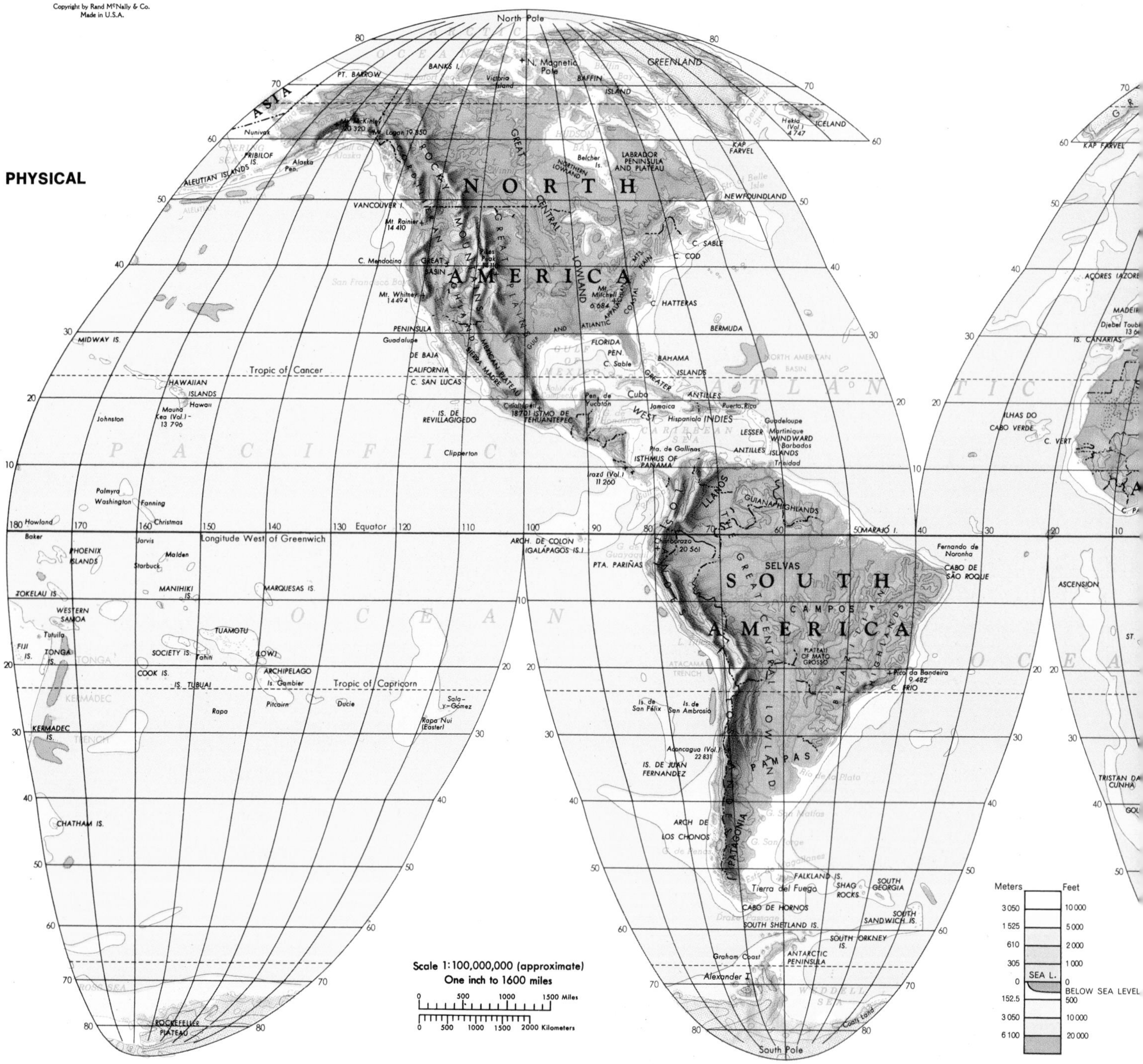

Land Elevations in Profile

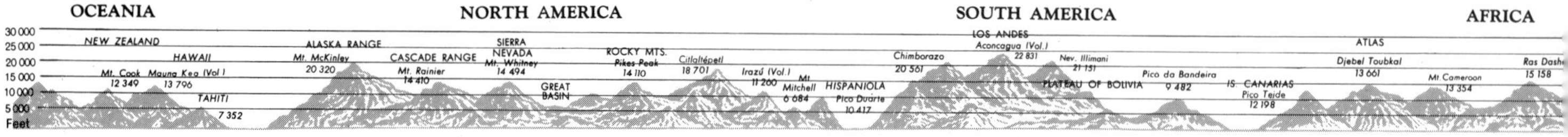

OCEANIA   NORTH AMERICA   SOUTH AMERICA   AFRICA

30 000
25 000
20 000
15 000
10 000
5 000
Feet

NEW ZEALAND

HAWAII

ALASKA RANGE   CASCADE RANGE   SIERRA NEVADA   ROCKY MTS.

LOS ANDES

ATLAS

Mt. Cook 12 349   Mauna Kea (Vol.) 13 796   TAHITI 7 352

Mt. McKinley 20 320   Mt. Rainier 14 410   Mt. Whitney 14 494   Pikes Peak 14 110   Citlaltépetl 18 701   GREAT BASIN   Irazú (Vol.) 11 200   Mt. Mitchell 6 084   HISPANIOLA   Pico Duarte 10 417

Chimborazo 20 561   Aconcagua (Vol.) 22 831   Nev. Illimani 21 151   PLATEAU OF BOLIVIA   Pico da Bandeira 9 482

Djebel Toubkal 13 661   IS. CANARIAS   Pico Teide 12 198   Mt Cameroon 13 354   Ras Dashen 15 158

Ocean Depths in Profile

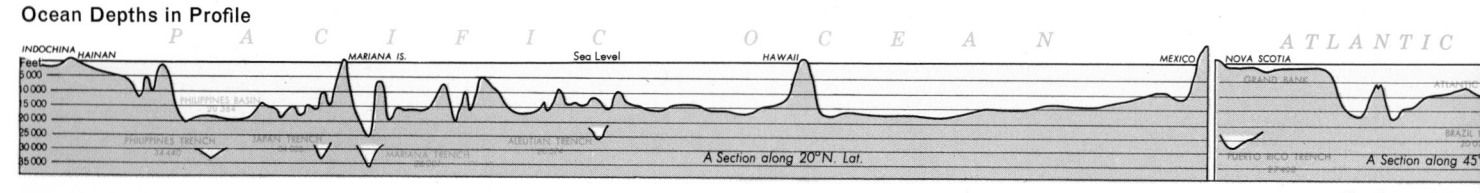

PACIFIC OCEAN   ATLANTIC

INDOCHINA   HAINAN   MARIANA IS.   Sea Level   HAWAII   MEXICO   NOVA SCOTIA   GRAND BANK   BRAZIL

Feet
5 000
10 000
15 000
20 000
25 000
35 000

PHILIPPINES BASIN   PHILIPPINES TRENCH   JAPAN TRENCH   MARIANA TRENCH   ALEUTIAN TRENCH

A Section along 20° N. Lat.   PUERTO RICO TRENCH   A Section along 45°

Elevations and depres

For Glossary of Foreign Geographical Terms see page 245

Goode's Homolosine Equal Area Projection

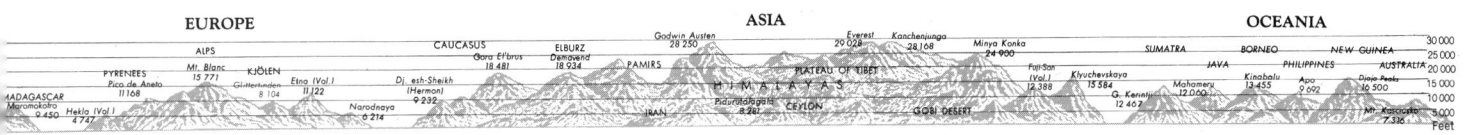

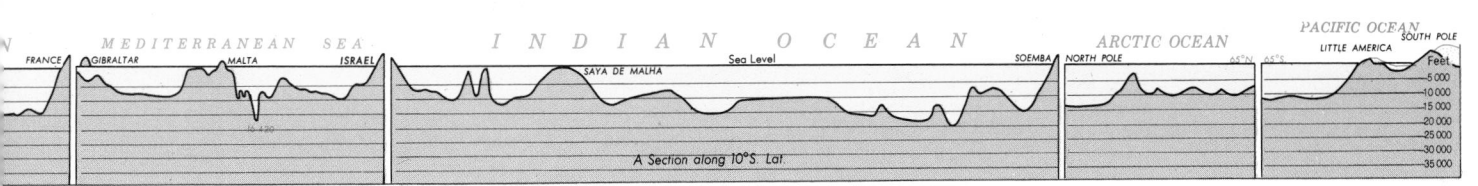

A Section along 10°S. Lat.

in feet

6

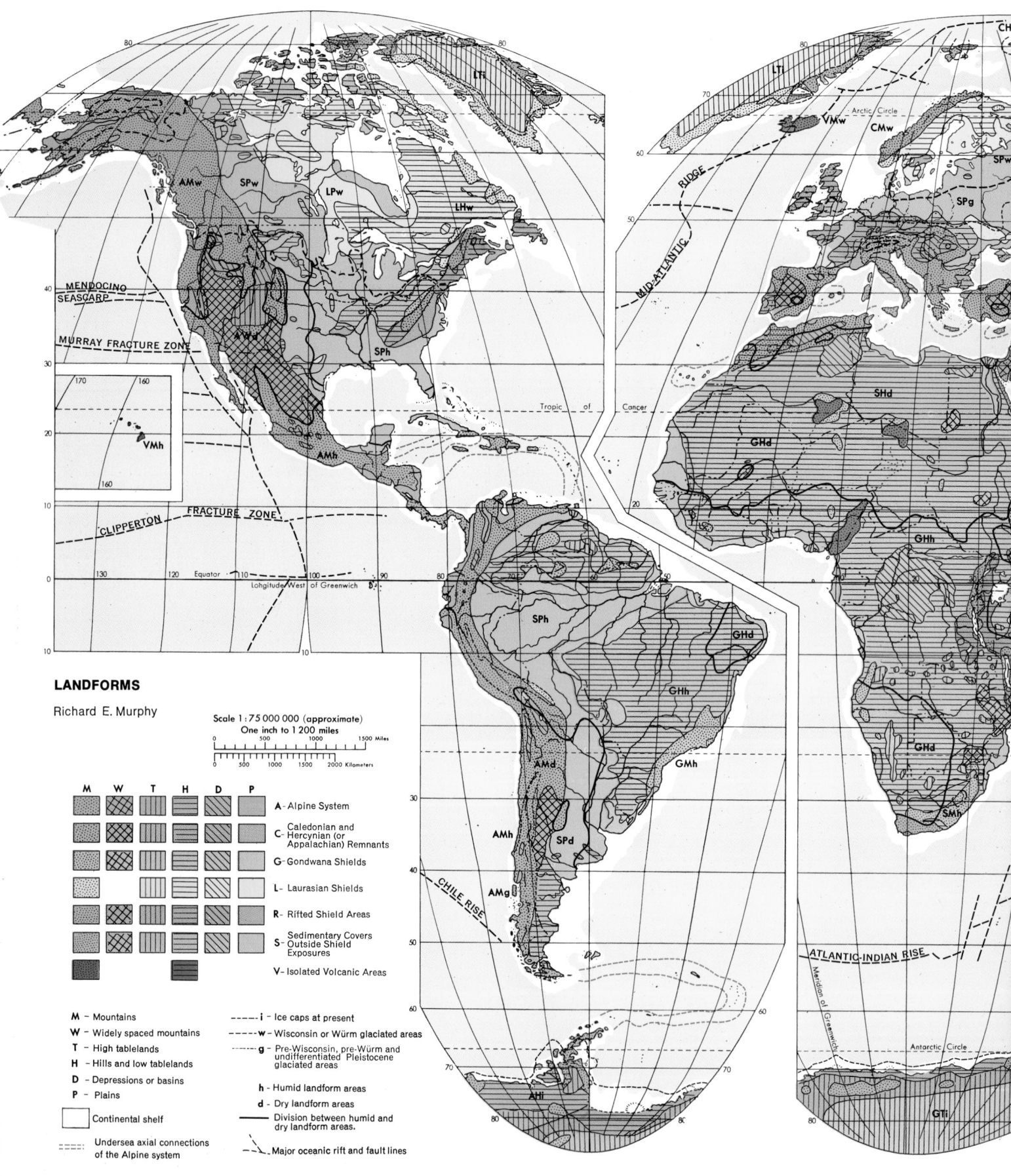

LANDFORMS

Richard E. Murphy

Scale 1:75 000 000 (approximate)
One inch to 1 200 miles

```
0    500    1000    1500 Miles
0  500  1000  1500  2000 Kilometers
```

	M	W	T	H	D	P	
							A- Alpine System
							C- Caledonian and Hercynian (or Appalachian) Remnants
							G- Gondwana Shields
							L- Laurasian Shields
							R- Rifted Shield Areas
							S- Sedimentary Covers Outside Shield Exposures
							V- Isolated Volcanic Areas

M – Mountains
W – Widely spaced mountains
T – High tablelands
H – Hills and low tablelands
D – Depressions or basins
P – Plains

☐ Continental shelf

⋯⋯ Undersea axial connections of the Alpine system

----- **i** - Ice caps at present
-·-·- **w** - Wisconsin or Würm glaciated areas
········· **g** - Pre-Wisconsin, pre-Würm and undifferentiated Pleistocene glaciated areas
—— **h** - Humid landform areas
d - Dry landform areas
—— Division between humid and dry landform areas.
-··-··- Major oceanic rift and fault lines

SPg

SHh

AMg

SPh

SPd

ADd

AMh

SHd

OWEN FRACTURE ZONE

GHh

CARLSBURG RIDGE

Longitude East of Greenwich

Tropic of Cancer

Equator

Tropic of Capricorn

INDIAN RIDGE

MID-INDIAN RIDGE

Mh

AMh

GHd

SPd

CHh

AMh

AMg

AUSTRALIAN-ANTARCTIC RISE

GTi

Goode's Homolosine Equal Area Projection (Condensed)

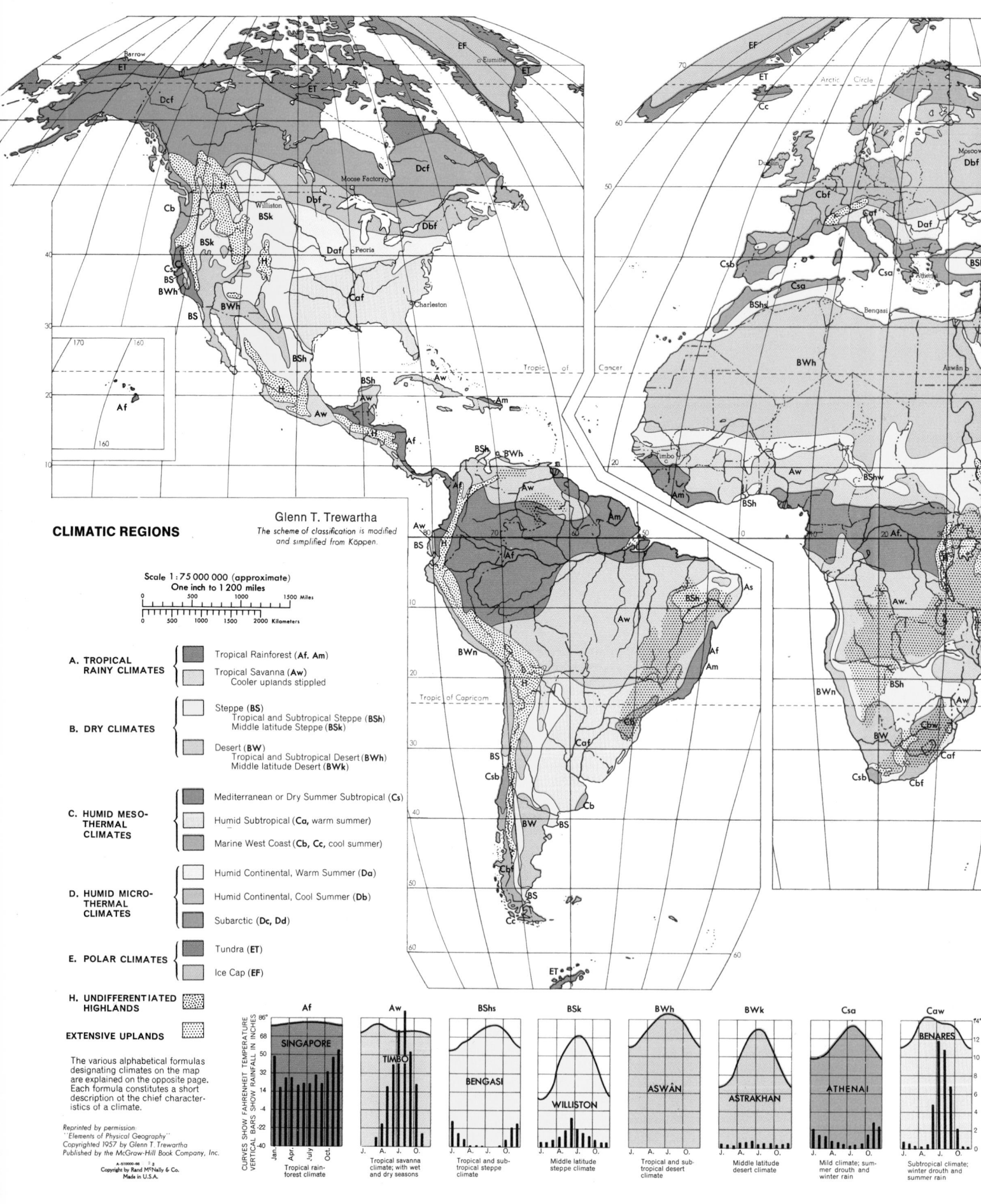

CLIMATIC REGIONS

Glenn T. Trewartha

The scheme of classification is modified and simplified from Köppen.

Scale 1:75 000 000 (approximate)
One inch to 1 200 miles

A. TROPICAL RAINY CLIMATES
- Tropical Rainforest (**Af. Am**)
- Tropical Savanna (**Aw**)
  Cooler uplands stippled

B. DRY CLIMATES
- Steppe (**BS**)
  Tropical and Subtropical Steppe (**BSh**)
  Middle latitude Steppe (**BSk**)
- Desert (**BW**)
  Tropical and Subtropical Desert (**BWh**)
  Middle latitude Desert (**BWk**)

C. HUMID MESO-THERMAL CLIMATES
- Mediterranean or Dry Summer Subtropical (**Cs**)
- Humid Subtropical (**Ca**, warm summer)
- Marine West Coast (**Cb, Cc**, cool summer)

D. HUMID MICRO-THERMAL CLIMATES
- Humid Continental, Warm Summer (**Da**)
- Humid Continental, Cool Summer (**Db**)
- Subarctic (**Dc, Dd**)

E. POLAR CLIMATES
- Tundra (**ET**)
- Ice Cap (**EF**)

H. UNDIFFERENTIATED HIGHLANDS

EXTENSIVE UPLANDS

The various alphabetical formulas designating climates on the map are explained on the opposite page. Each formula constitutes a short description of the chief characteristics of a climate.

Reprinted by permission.
"Elements of Physical Geography"
Copyrighted 1957 by Glenn T. Trewartha
Published by the McGraw-Hill Book Company, Inc.

Copyright by Rand McNally & Co.
Made in U.S.A.

CURVES SHOW FAHRENHEIT TEMPERATURE
VERTICAL BARS SHOW RAINFALL IN INCHES

Af	Aw	BShs	BSk	BWh	BWk	Csa	Caw
SINGAPORE	TIMBO	BENGASI	WILLISTON	ASWÂN	ASTRAKHAN	ATHENAI	BENARES
Tropical rainforest climate	Tropical savanna climate; with wet and dry seasons	Tropical and subtropical steppe climate	Middle latitude steppe climate	Tropical and subtropical desert climate	Middle latitude desert climate	Mild climate; summer drouth and winter rain	Subtropical climate; winter drouth and summer rain

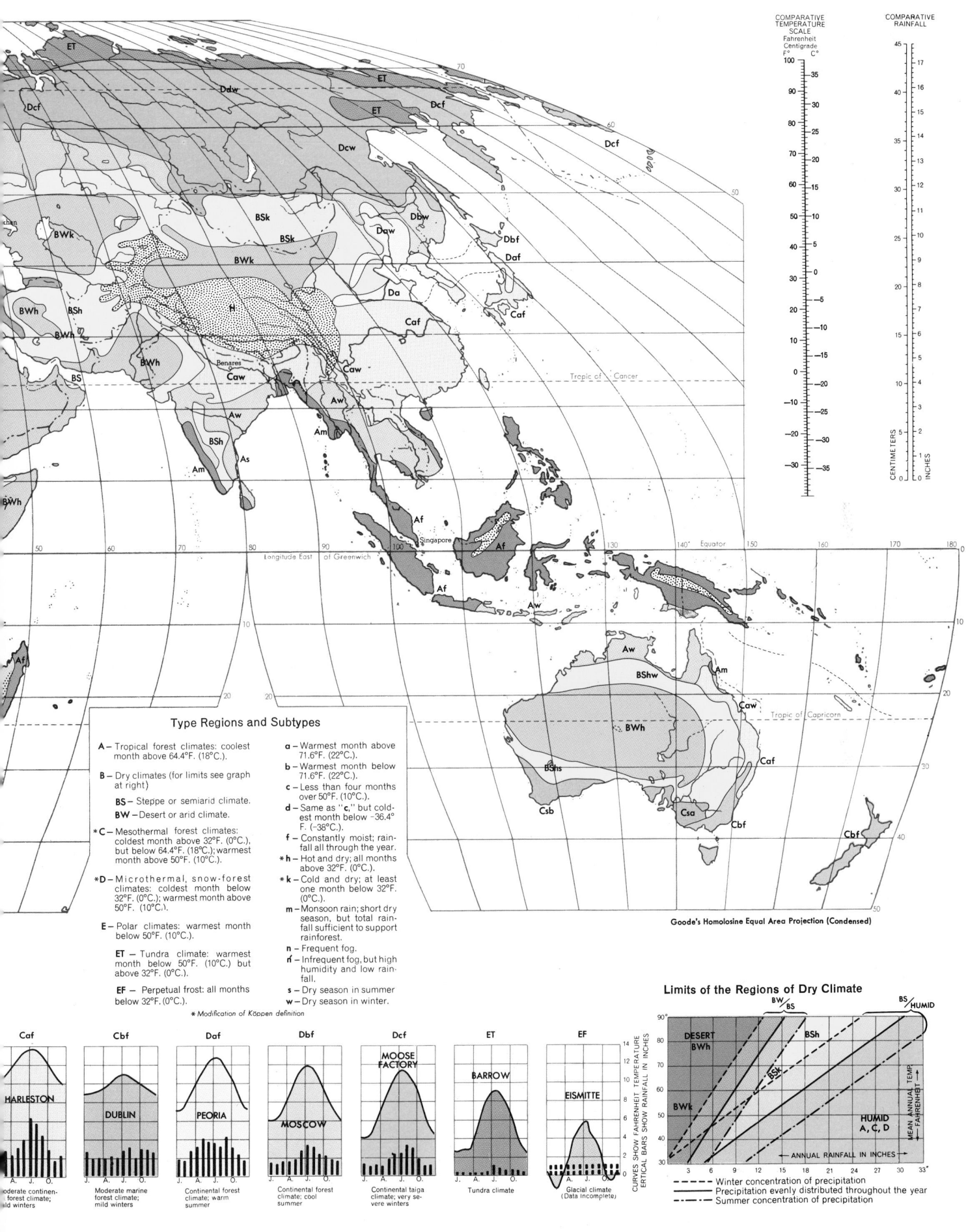

COMPARATIVE
TEMPERATURE
SCALE
Fahrenheit
Centigrade

COMPARATIVE
RAINFALL

CENTIMETERS   INCHES

Type Regions and Subtypes

A – Tropical forest climates: coolest month above 64.4°F. (18°C.).

B – Dry climates (for limits see graph at right)

   BS – Steppe or semiarid climate.

   BW – Desert or arid climate.

*****C** – Mesothermal forest climates: coldest month above 32°F. (0°C.), but below 64.4°F. (18°C.); warmest month above 50°F. (10°C.).

*****D** – Microthermal, snow-forest climates: coldest month below 32°F. (0°C.); warmest month above 50°F. (10°C.).

E – Polar climates: warmest month below 50°F. (10°C.).

   ET – Tundra climate: warmest month below 50°F. (10°C.) but above 32°F. (0°C.).

   EF – Perpetual frost: all months below 32°F. (0°C.).

a – Warmest month above 71.6°F. (22°C.).

b – Warmest month below 71.6°F. (22°C.).

c – Less than four months over 50°F. (10°C.).

d – Same as "c," but coldest month below –36.4° F. (–38°C.).

f – Constantly moist; rainfall all through the year.

*****h** – Hot and dry; all months above 32°F. (0°C.).

*****k** – Cold and dry; at least one month below 32°F. (0°C.).

m – Monsoon rain; short dry season, but total rainfall sufficient to support rainforest.

n – Frequent fog.

n′ – Infrequent fog, but high humidity and low rainfall.

s – Dry season in summer.

w – Dry season in winter.

* Modification of Köppen definition

Goode's Homolosine Equal Area Projection (Condensed)

Limits of the Regions of Dry Climate

BW / BS   BS / HUMID

90°
DESERT
BWh
80
BSh
70
BWk
60
BSk
50
HUMID
A, C, D
40
30

CURVES SHOW FAHRENHEIT TEMPERATURE
VERTICAL BARS SHOW RAINFALL IN INCHES

MEAN ANNUAL TEMP. FAHRENHEIT →

ANNUAL RAINFALL IN INCHES →

3   6   9   12   15   18   21   24   27   30   33"

- - - - Winter concentration of precipitation
———— Precipitation evenly distributed throughout the year
–·–·– Summer concentration of precipitation

Caf
HARLESTON
Moderate continental forest climate; mild winters

Cbf
DUBLIN
Moderate marine forest climate; mild winters

Daf
PEORIA
Continental forest climate; warm summer

Dbf
MOSCOW
Continental forest climate; cool summer

Dcf
MOOSE FACTORY
Continental taiga climate; very severe winters

ET
BARROW
Tundra climate

EF
EISMITTE
Glacial climate (Data incomplete)

14
12
10
8
6
4
2

FAHRENHEIT TEMPERATURE
RAINFALL IN INCHES

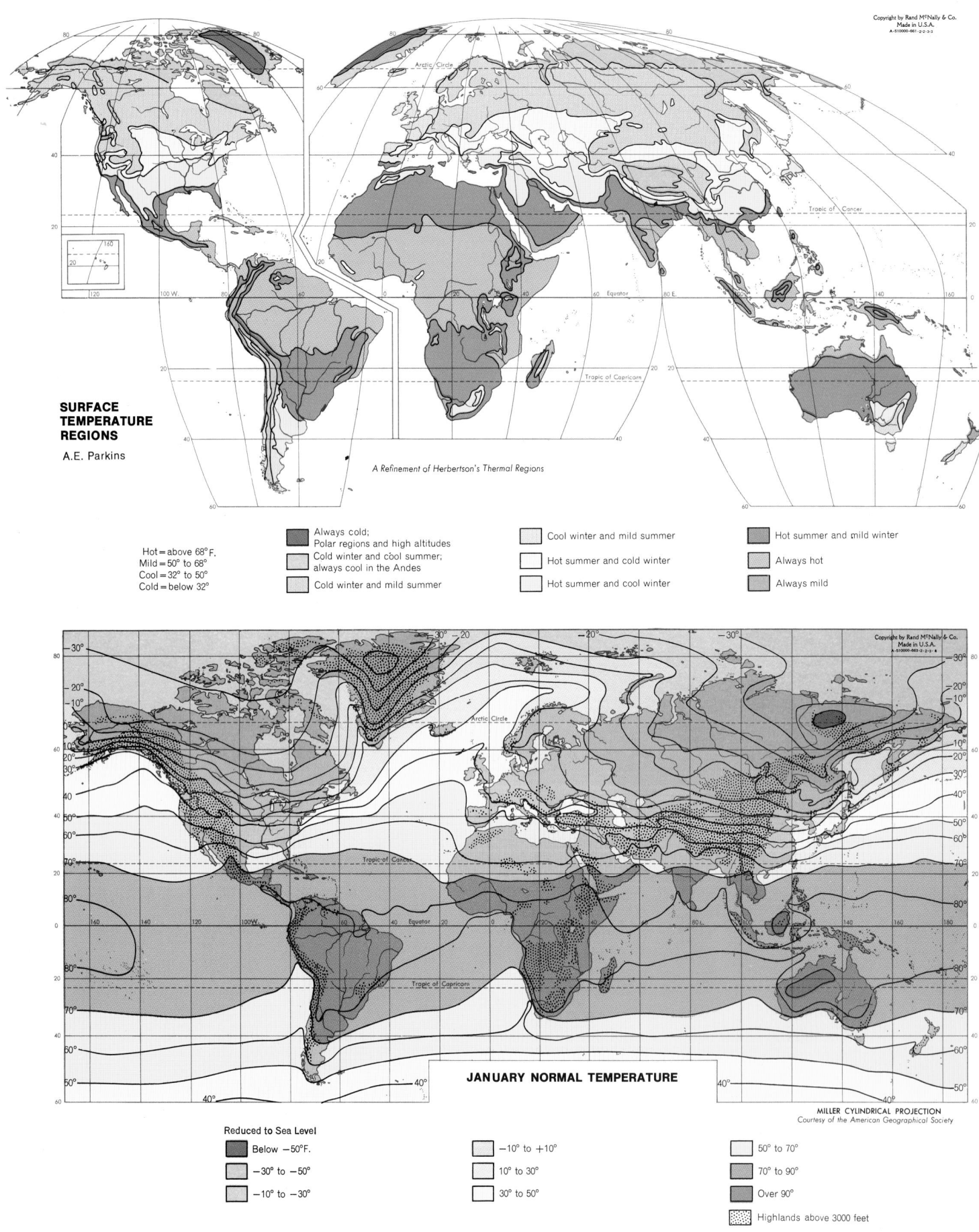

**SURFACE
TEMPERATURE
REGIONS**

A.E. Parkins

A Refinement of Herbertson's Thermal Regions

Hot = above 68° F.
Mild = 50° to 68°
Cool = 32° to 50°
Cold = below 32°

Always cold;
Polar regions and high altitudes

Cold winter and cool summer;
always cool in the Andes

Cold winter and mild summer

Cool winter and mild summer

Hot summer and cold winter

Hot summer and cool winter

Hot summer and mild winter

Always hot

Always mild

JANUARY NORMAL TEMPERATURE

MILLER CYLINDRICAL PROJECTION
Courtesy of the American Geographical Society

Reduced to Sea Level

Below −50°F.

−30° to −50°

−10° to −30°

−10° to +10°

10° to 30°

30° to 50°

50° to 70°

70° to 90°

Over 90°

Highlands above 3000 feet

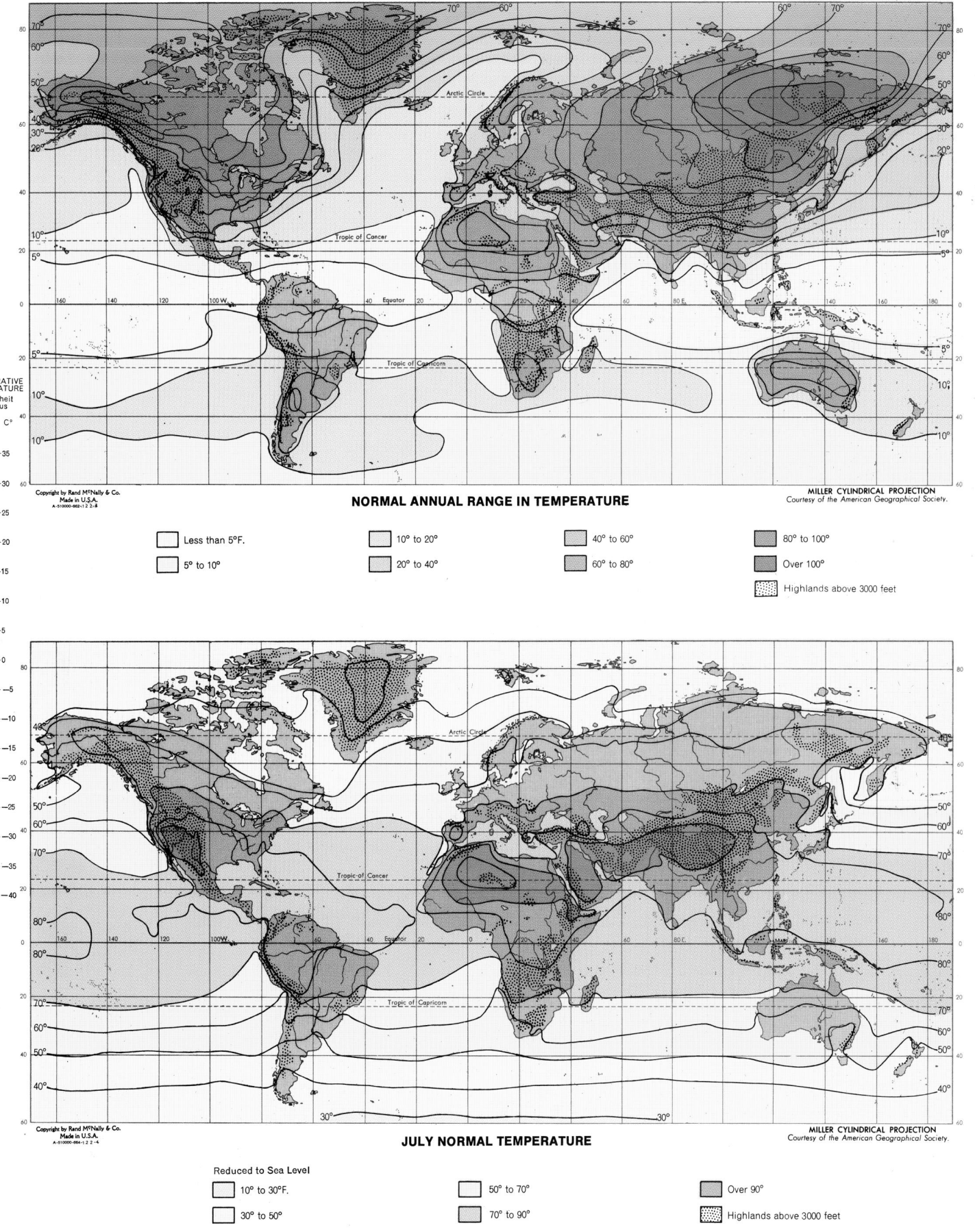

RELATIVE
ERATURE
nheit
cius
C°

— 35
— 30
— 25
— 20
— 15
— 10
— 5
— 0

Copyright by Rand McNally & Co.
Made in U.S.A.
A-510000-062-1 2 2-8

NORMAL ANNUAL RANGE IN TEMPERATURE

MILLER CYLINDRICAL PROJECTION
Courtesy of the American Geographical Society.

	Less than 5°F.		10° to 20°		40° to 60°		80° to 100°
	5° to 10°		20° to 40°		60° to 80°		Over 100°
							Highlands above 3000 feet

Copyright by Rand McNally & Co.
Made in U.S.A.
A-510000-064-1 2 2-4

JULY NORMAL TEMPERATURE

MILLER CYLINDRICAL PROJECTION
Courtesy of the American Geographical Society.

Reduced to Sea Level

	10° to 30°F.		50° to 70°		Over 90°
	30° to 50°		70° to 90°		Highlands above 3000 feet

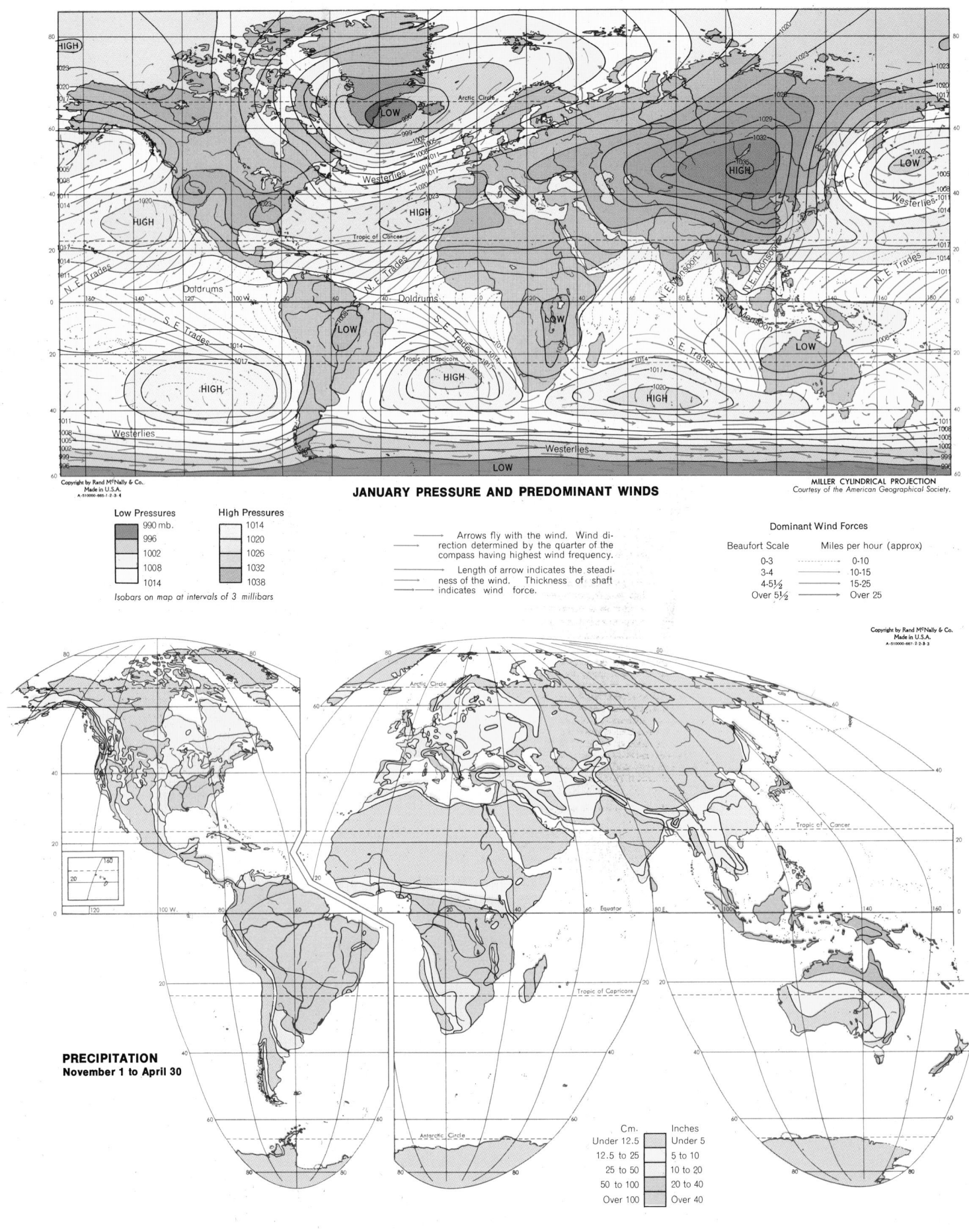

JANUARY PRESSURE AND PREDOMINANT WINDS

MILLER CYLINDRICAL PROJECTION
Courtesy of the American Geographical Society.

Copyright by Rand McNally & Co.,
Made in U.S.A.
A-510000-665-1-2-3- **4**

Low Pressures		High Pressures	
	990 mb.		1014
	996		1020
	1002		1026
	1008		1032
	1014		1038

Isobars on map at intervals of 3 millibars

→ Arrows fly with the wind. Wind direction determined by the quarter of the compass having highest wind frequency.

→ Length of arrow indicates the steadiness of the wind. Thickness of shaft indicates wind force.

Dominant Wind Forces

Beaufort Scale	Miles per hour (approx)
0-3	0-10
3-4	10-15
4-5½	15-25
Over 5½	Over 25

Copyright by Rand McNally & Co.
Made in U.S.A.
A-510000-687-2.2-3-3

PRECIPITATION
November 1 to April 30

Cm.		Inches
Under 12.5		Under 5
12.5 to 25		5 to 10
25 to 50		10 to 20
50 to 100		20 to 40
Over 100		Over 40

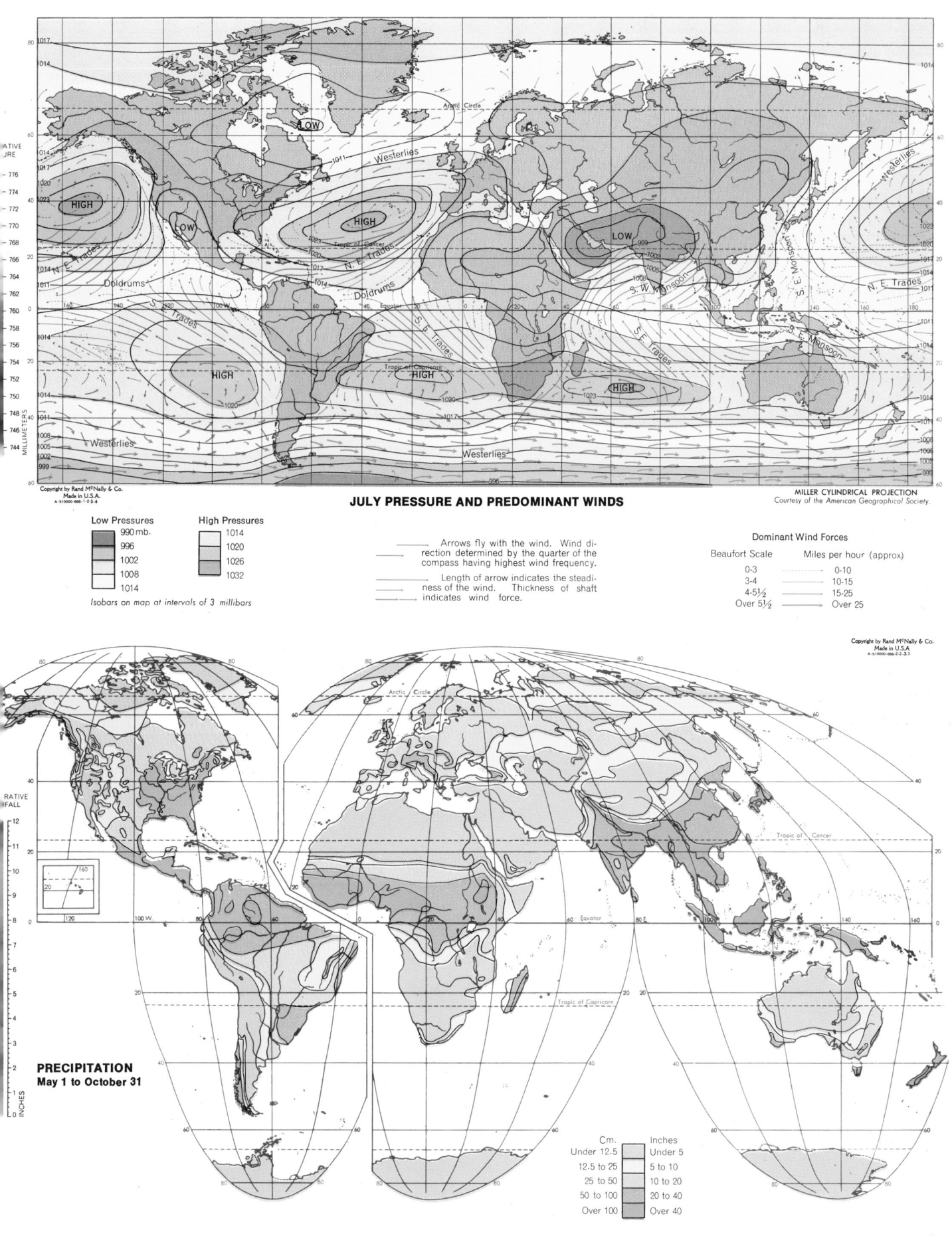

JULY PRESSURE AND PREDOMINANT WINDS

MILLER CYLINDRICAL PROJECTION
Courtesy of the American Geographical Society.

Copyright by Rand McNally & Co.
Made in U.S.A.
A-510000-666-1-2-3-4

Low Pressures
990 mb.
996
1002
1008
1014

High Pressures
1014
1020
1026
1032

Isobars on map at intervals of 3 millibars

Arrows fly with the wind. Wind direction determined by the quarter of the compass having highest wind frequency.

Length of arrow indicates the steadiness of the wind. Thickness of shaft indicates wind force.

Dominant Wind Forces

Beaufort Scale	Miles per hour (approx)
0-3	0-10
3-4	10-15
4-5½	15-25
Over 5½	Over 25

Copyright by Rand McNally & Co.
Made in U.S.A
A-510000-666-2-2-3-3

PRECIPITATION
May 1 to October 31

Cm.	Inches
Under 12.5	Under 5
12.5 to 25	5 to 10
25 to 50	10 to 20
50 to 100	20 to 40
Over 100	Over 40

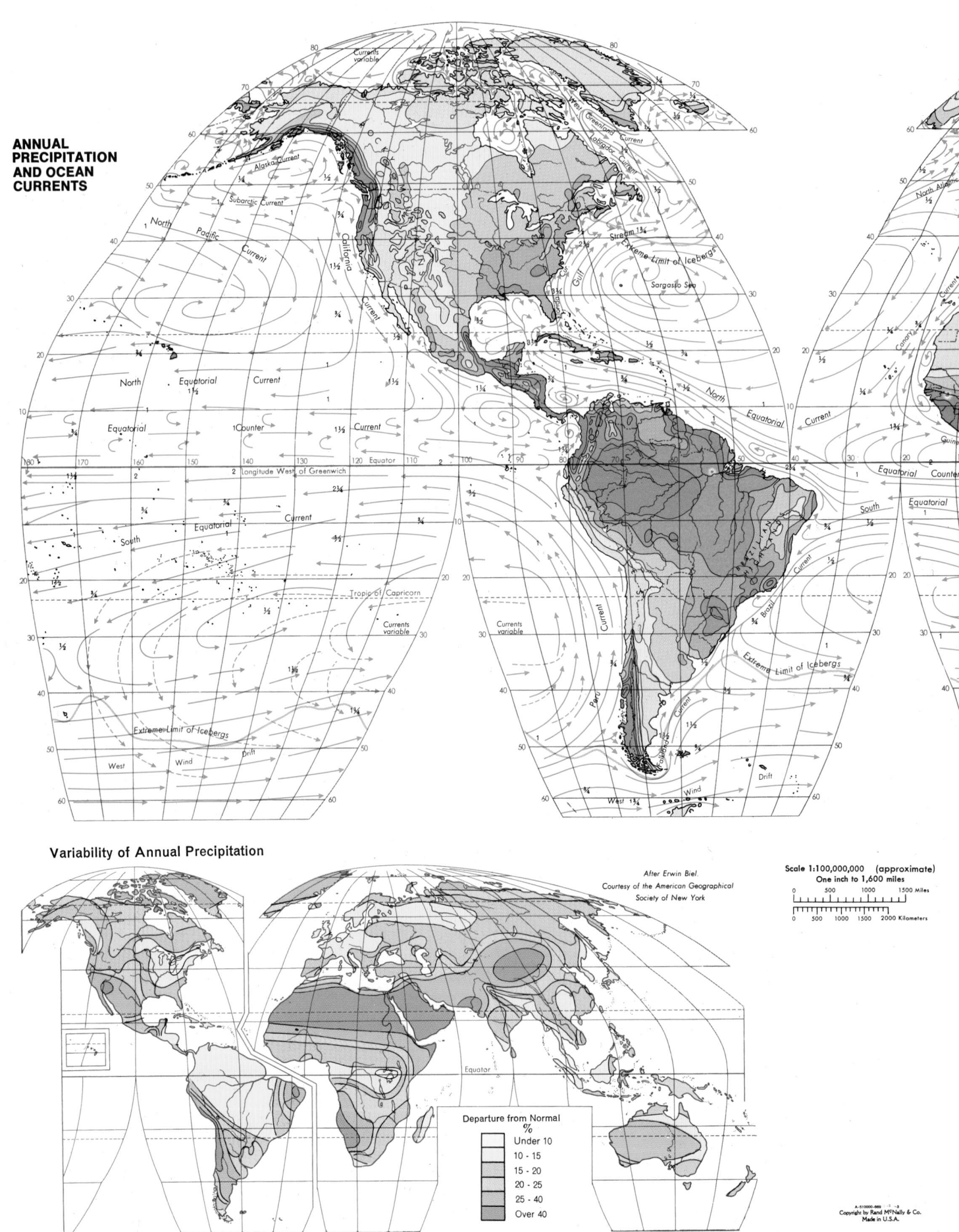

ANNUAL PRECIPITATION AND OCEAN CURRENTS

Variability of Annual Precipitation

After Erwin Biel.
Courtesy of the American Geographical
Society of New York

Scale 1:100,000,000 (approximate)
One inch to 1,600 miles

| 0 | 500 | 1000 | 1500 Miles |

| 0 | 500 | 1000 | 1500 | 2000 Kilometers |

Departure from Normal %
- Under 10
- 10 - 15
- 15 - 20
- 20 - 25
- 25 - 40
- Over 40

A-510000-869
Copyright by Rand M?Nally & Co.
Made in U.S.A.

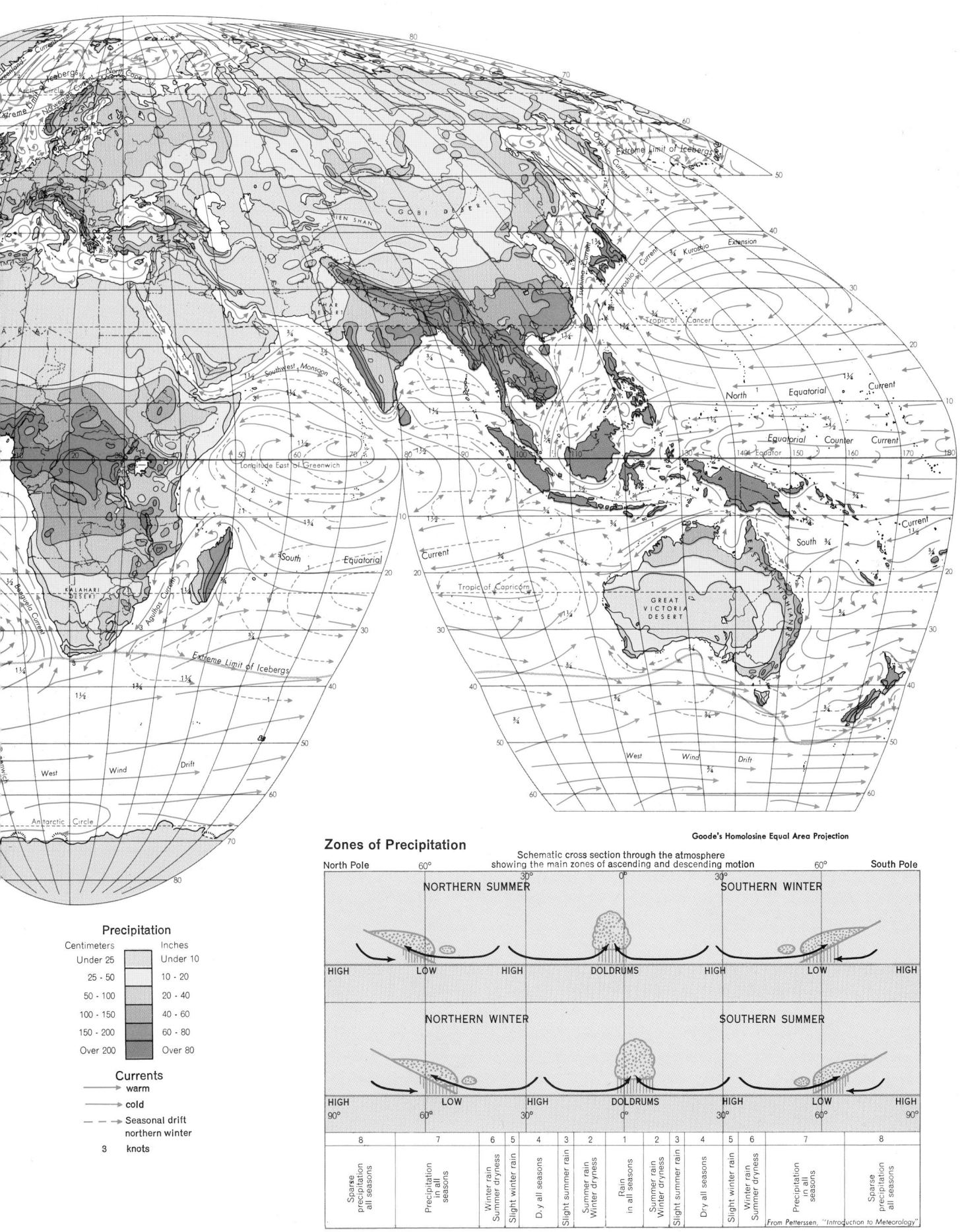

Goode's Homolosine Equal Area Projection

Zones of Precipitation

North Pole   60°   Schematic cross section through the atmosphere   60°   South Pole
                         showing the main zones of ascending and descending motion

30°   0°   30°

NORTHERN SUMMER   SOUTHERN WINTER

HIGH   LOW   HIGH   DOLDRUMS   HIGH   LOW   HIGH

NORTHERN WINTER   SOUTHERN SUMMER

HIGH   LOW   HIGH   DOLDRUMS   HIGH   LOW   HIGH
90°   60°   30°   0°   30°   60°   90°

From Petterssen, "Introduction to Meteorology"

8	7	6	5	4	3	2	1	2	3	4	5	6	7	8
Sparse precipitation all seasons	Precipitation in all seasons	Winter rain Summer dryness	Slight winter rain	Dry all seasons	Slight summer rain	Summer rain Winter dryness	Rain in all seasons	Summer rain Winter dryness	Slight summer rain	Dry all seasons	Slight winter rain	Winter rain Summer dryness	Precipitation in all seasons	Sparse precipitation all seasons

Precipitation

Centimeters	Inches
Under 25	Under 10
25 - 50	10 - 20
50 - 100	20 - 40
100 - 150	40 - 60
150 - 200	60 - 80
Over 200	Over 80

Currents

→ warm
→ cold
- - → Seasonal drift northern winter

3   knots

16

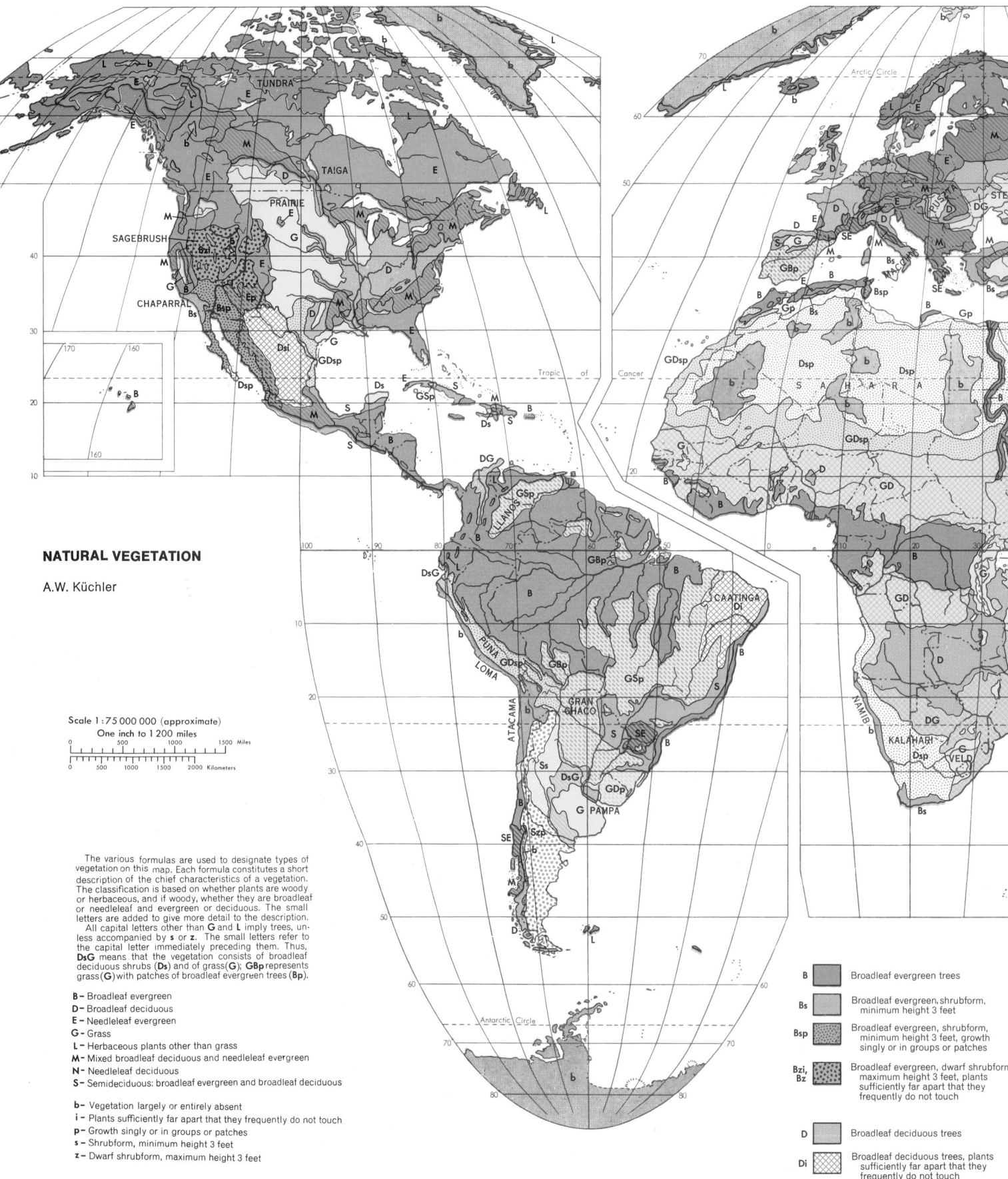

NATURAL VEGETATION

A.W. Küchler

Scale 1:75 000 000 (approximate)
One inch to 1 200 miles

0   500   1000   1500 Miles

0   500   1000   1500   2000 Kilometers

The various formulas are used to designate types of
vegetation on this map. Each formula constitutes a short
description of the chief characteristics of a vegetation.
The classification is based on whether plants are woody
or herbaceous, and if woody, whether they are broadleaf
or needleleaf and evergreen or deciduous. The small
letters are added to give more detail to the description.
All capital letters other than **G** and **L** imply trees, unless accompanied by **s** or **z**. The small letters refer to
the capital letter immediately preceding them. Thus,
DsG means that the vegetation consists of broadleaf
deciduous shrubs (**Ds**) and of grass(**G**); **GBp** represents
grass(**G**) with patches of broadleaf evergreen trees (**Bp**).

B – Broadleaf evergreen
D – Broadleaf deciduous
E – Needleleaf evergreen
G – Grass
L – Herbaceous plants other than grass
M – Mixed broadleaf deciduous and needleleaf evergreen
N – Needleleaf deciduous
S – Semideciduous: broadleaf evergreen and broadleaf deciduous

b – Vegetation largely or entirely absent
i – Plants sufficiently far apart that they frequently do not touch
p – Growth singly or in groups or patches
s – Shrubform, minimum height 3 feet
z – Dwarf shrubform, maximum height 3 feet

B	Broadleaf evergreen trees
Bs	Broadleaf evergreen, shrubform, minimum height 3 feet
Bsp	Broadleaf evergreen, shrubform, minimum height 3 feet, growth singly or in groups or patches
Bzi, Bz	Broadleaf evergreen, dwarf shrubform, maximum height 3 feet, plants sufficiently far apart that they frequently do not touch
D	Broadleaf deciduous trees
Di	Broadleaf deciduous trees, plants sufficiently far apart that they frequently do not touch

A-510000-86
Copyright by Rand McNally & Co.
Made in U.S.A.

Goode's Homolosine
Equal Area Projection
(Condensed)

	Broadleaf deciduous, shrubform, minimum height 3 feet	
	Broadleaf deciduous, shrubform, minimum height 3 feet, plants sufficiently far apart that they frequently do not touch	
	Broadleaf deciduous, shrubform, minimum height 3 feet, growth singly or in groups or patches	
	Broadleaf deciduous, dwarf shrubform, maximum height 3 feet, growth singly or in groups or patches	
	Broadleaf deciduous, shrubform, minimum height 3 feet Grass and other herbaceous plants	
	Broadleaf deciduous trees Grass and other herbaceous plants	
	Broadleaf deciduous trees Broadleaf evergreen, shrubform, minimum height 3 feet	

E	Needleleaf evergreen trees	
Ep	Needleleaf evergreen trees, growth singly or in groups or patches	
G	Grass and other herbaceous plants	
Gp	Grass and other herbaceous plants, growth singly or in groups or patches	
GBp	Grass and other herbaceous plants Broadleaf evergreen trees, growth singly or in groups or patches	
GD	Grass and other herbaceous plants Broadleaf deciduous trees	
GDp	Grass and other herbaceous plants Broadleaf deciduous trees, growth singly or in groups or patches	

GDsp	Grass and other herbaceous plants Broadleaf deciduous, shrubform, minimum height 3 feet, growth singly or in groups or patches	
GSp	Grass and other herbaceous plants Semideciduous: broadleaf evergreen and broadleaf deciduous trees, growth singly or in groups or patches	
L	Herbaceous plants other than grass	
M	Mixed: broadleaf deciduous and needleleaf evergreen trees	
N	Needleleaf deciduous trees	
ND	Needleleaf deciduous trees Broadleaf deciduous trees	

S	Semideciduous: broadleaf evergreen and broadleaf deciduous trees	
Ss	Semideciduous: broadleaf evergreen and broadleaf deciduous, shrubform, minimum height 3 feet	
SsG	Semideciduous: broadleaf evergreen and broadleaf deciduous, shrubform, minimum height 3 feet Grass and other herbaceous plants	
Szp	Semideciduous: broadleaf evergreen and broadleaf deciduous, dwarf shrubform, maximum height 3 feet, growth singly or in groups or patches	
SE	Semideciduous: broadleaf evergreen and broadleaf deciduous trees Needleleaf evergreen trees	
b	Vegetation largely or entirely absent	

18

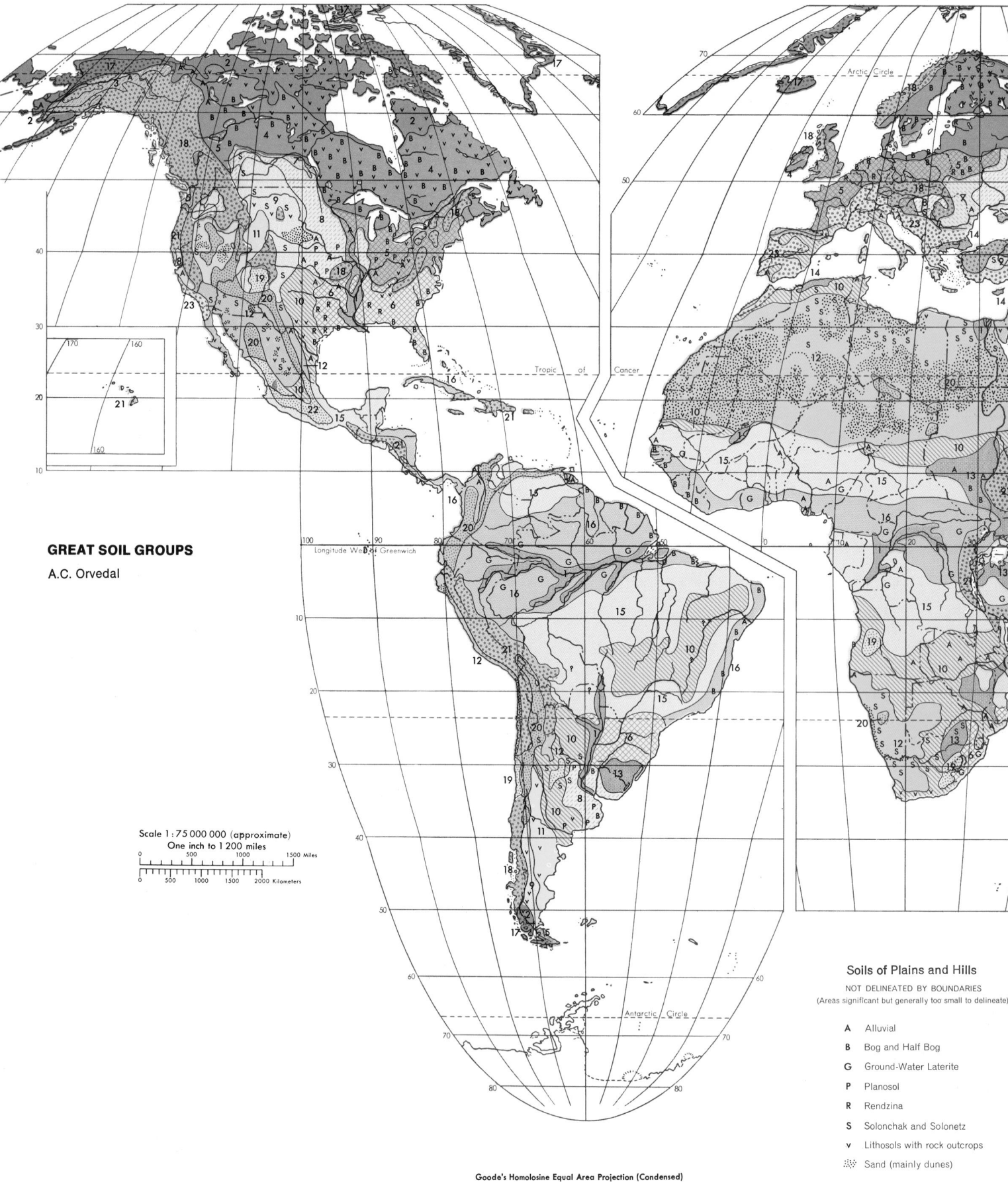

GREAT SOIL GROUPS

A.C. Orvedal

Scale 1 : 75 000 000 (approximate)
One inch to 1 200 miles

0   500   1000   1500 Miles

0   500   1000   1500   2000 Kilometers

Goode's Homolosine Equal Area Projection (Condensed)

A-510000-781-2-2-2-3
Copyright by Rand McNally & Co.
Made in U.S.A.

Soils of Plains and Hills

NOT DELINEATED BY BOUNDARIES
(Areas significant but generally too small to delineate)

A   Alluvial
B   Bog and Half Bog
G   Ground-Water Laterite
P   Planosol
R   Rendzina
S   Solonchak and Solonetz
v   Lithosols with rock outcrops
    Sand (mainly dunes)

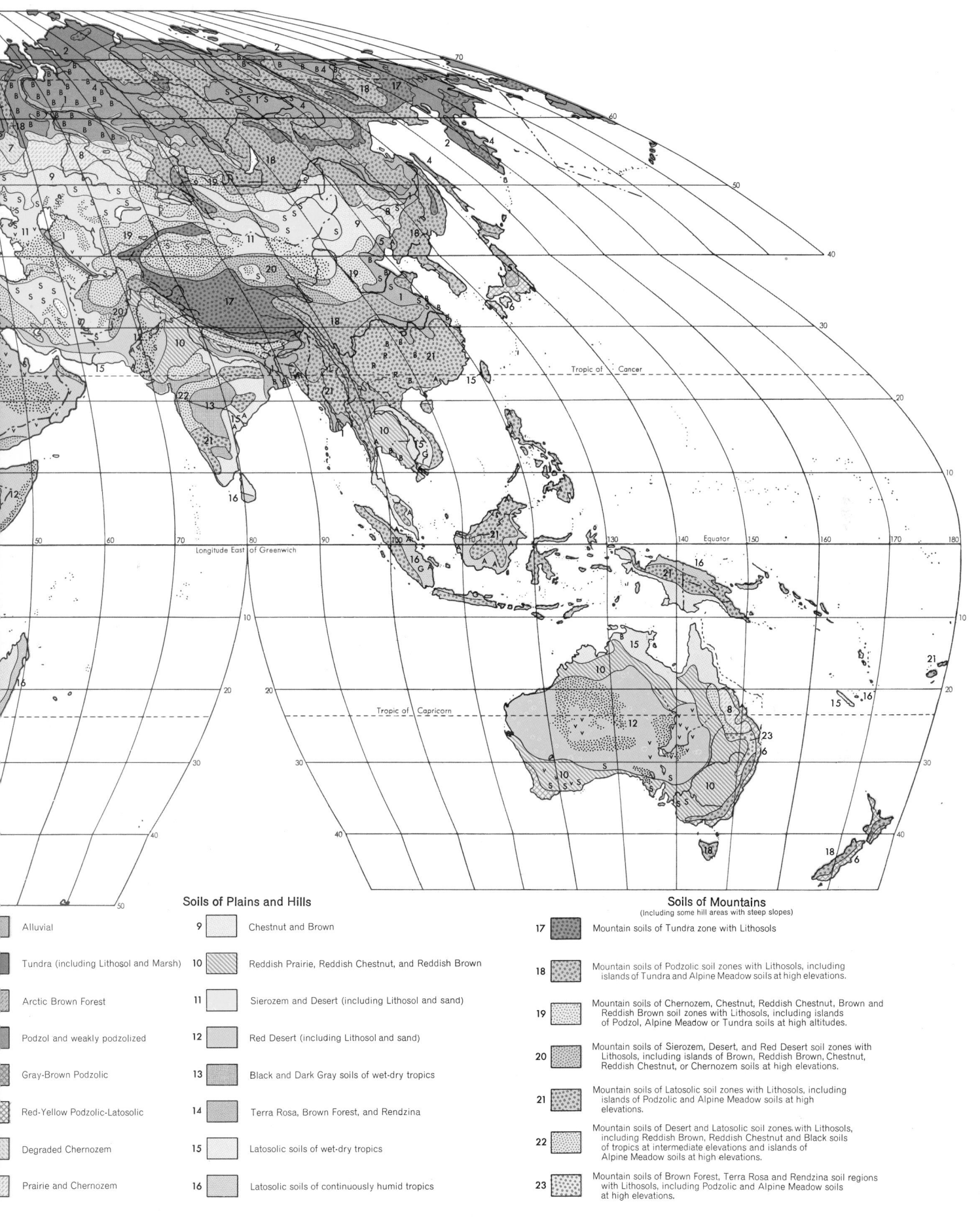

Soils of Plains and Hills

	Alluvial	**9**	Chestnut and Brown
	Tundra (including Lithosol and Marsh)	**10**	Reddish Prairie, Reddish Chestnut, and Reddish Brown
	Arctic Brown Forest	**11**	Sierozem and Desert (including Lithosol and sand)
	Podzol and weakly podzolized	**12**	Red Desert (including Lithosol and sand)
	Gray-Brown Podzolic	**13**	Black and Dark Gray soils of wet-dry tropics
	Red-Yellow Podzolic-Latosolic	**14**	Terra Rosa, Brown Forest, and Rendzina
	Degraded Chernozem	**15**	Latosolic soils of wet-dry tropics
	Prairie and Chernozem	**16**	Latosolic soils of continuously humid tropics

Soils of Mountains
(Including some hill areas with steep slopes)

17 Mountain soils of Tundra zone with Lithosols

18 Mountain soils of Podzolic soil zones with Lithosols, including islands of Tundra and Alpine Meadow soils at high elevations.

19 Mountain soils of Chernozem, Chestnut, Reddish Chestnut, Brown and Reddish Brown soil zones with Lithosols, including islands of Podzol, Alpine Meadow or Tundra soils at high altitudes.

20 Mountain soils of Sierozem, Desert, and Red Desert soil zones with Lithosols, including islands of Brown, Reddish Brown, Chestnut, Reddish Chestnut, or Chernozem soils at high elevations.

21 Mountain soils of Latosolic soil zones with Lithosols, including islands of Podzolic and Alpine Meadow soils at high elevations.

22 Mountain soils of Desert and Latosolic soil zones with Lithosols, including Reddish Brown, Reddish Chestnut and Black soils of tropics at intermediate elevations and islands of Alpine Meadow soils at high elevations.

23 Mountain soils of Brown Forest, Terra Rosa and Rendzina soil regions with Lithosols, including Podzolic and Alpine Meadow soils at high elevations.

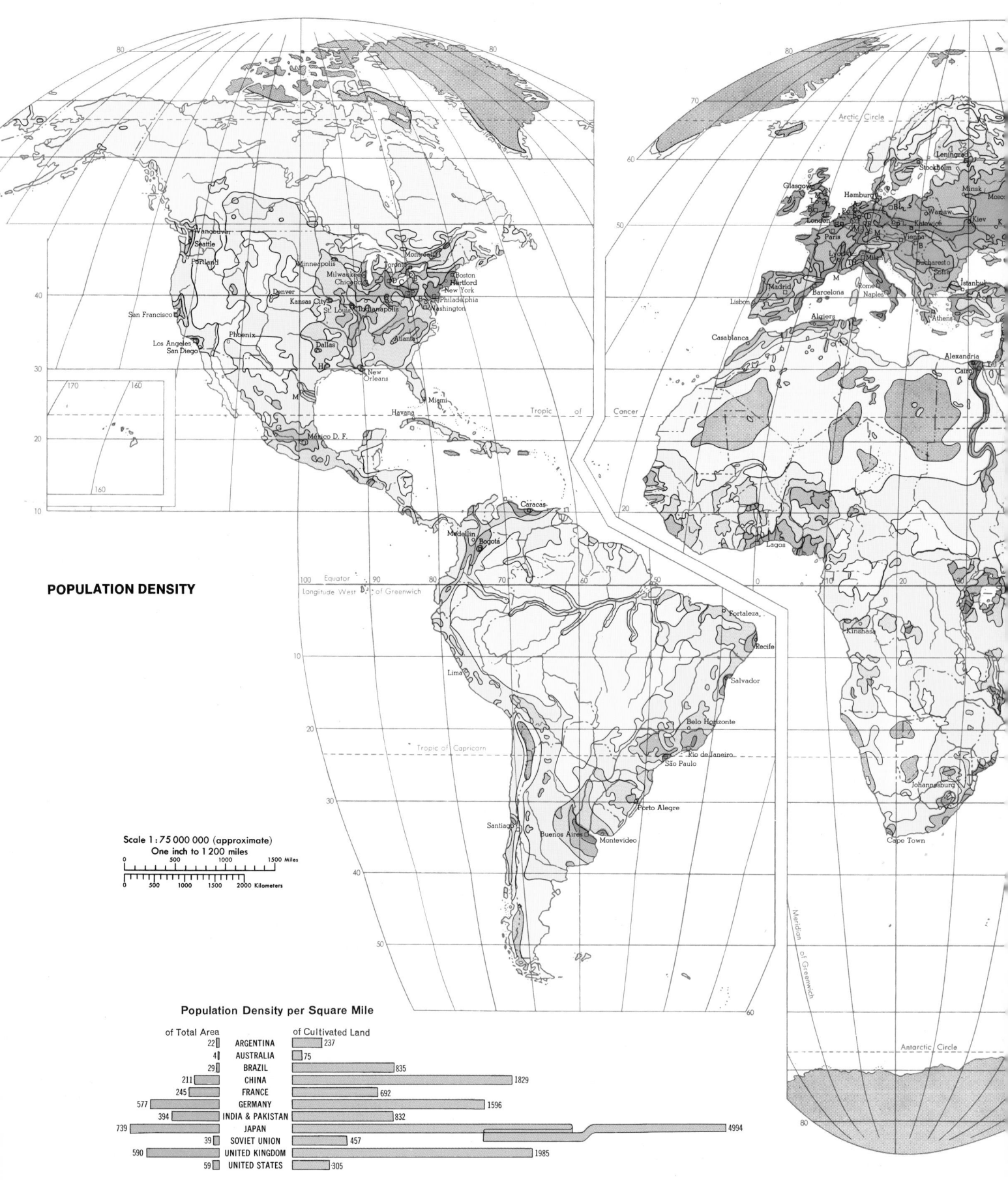

POPULATION DENSITY

Scale 1 : 75 000 000 (approximate)
One inch to 1 200 miles

0   500   1000   1500 Miles

0   500   1000   1500   2000 Kilometers

Population Density per Square Mile

of Total Area		of Cultivated Land	
22	ARGENTINA	237	
4	AUSTRALIA	75	
29	BRAZIL	835	
211	CHINA	1829	
245	FRANCE	692	
577	GERMANY	1596	
394	INDIA & PAKISTAN	832	
739	JAPAN	4994	
39	SOVIET UNION	457	
590	UNITED KINGDOM	1985	
59	UNITED STATES	305	

Goode's Homolosine Equal Area Projection (Condensed)

Per Sq. Km.	Per Sq. Mile
Uninhabited	Uninhabited
Under 1	Under 2
1-10	2-25
10-25	25-60
25-50	60-125
50-100	125-250
Over 100	Over 250

□ Metropolitan areas over 2,000,000 population
○ Metropolitan areas 1,000,000 to 2,000,000 population

*Not all cities are named and some
are identified by initial letter only.*

Rural/Urban Population Ratios

Rural		Urban
26%	ARGENTINA	74%
15	AUSTRALIA	85
44	BRAZIL	56
26	CANADA	74
87	CHINA	13
30	FRANCE	70
80	INDIA	20
28	JAPAN	72
44	SOVIET UNION	56
63	TURKEY	37
22	UNITED KINGDOM	78
26	UNITED STATES	74

A-510000-16- 4-2-5-
Copyright by Rand McNally & Co.
Made in U.S.A.

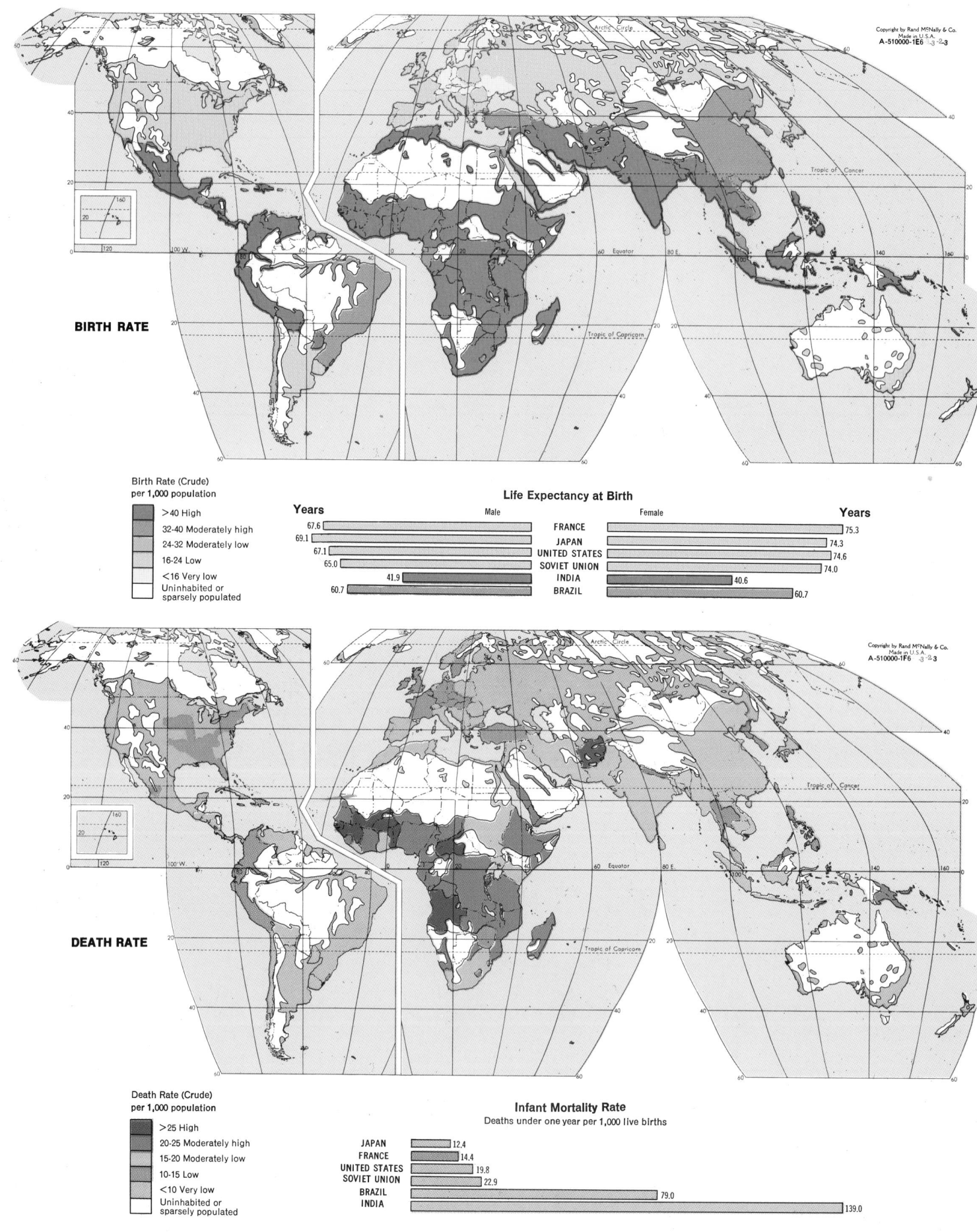

Copyright by Rand McNally & Co.
Made in U.S.A.
A-510000-1E6 -3-2-3

BIRTH RATE

**Birth Rate (Crude)
per 1,000 population**

	>40 High
	32-40 Moderately high
	24-32 Moderately low
	16-24 Low
	<16 Very low
	Uninhabited or sparsely populated

Life Expectancy at Birth

Years	Male		Female	Years
67.6		FRANCE		75.3
69.1		JAPAN		74.3
67.1		UNITED STATES		74.6
65.0		SOVIET UNION		74.0
41.9		INDIA	40.6	
60.7		BRAZIL	60.7	

Copyright by Rand McNally & Co.
Made in U.S.A.
A-510000-1F6 -3-2-3

DEATH RATE

**Death Rate (Crude)
per 1,000 population**

	>25 High
	20-25 Moderately high
	15-20 Moderately low
	10-15 Low
	<10 Very low
	Uninhabited or sparsely populated

Infant Mortality Rate
Deaths under one year per 1,000 live births

JAPAN	12.4
FRANCE	14.4
UNITED STATES	19.8
SOVIET UNION	22.9
BRAZIL	79.0
INDIA	139.0

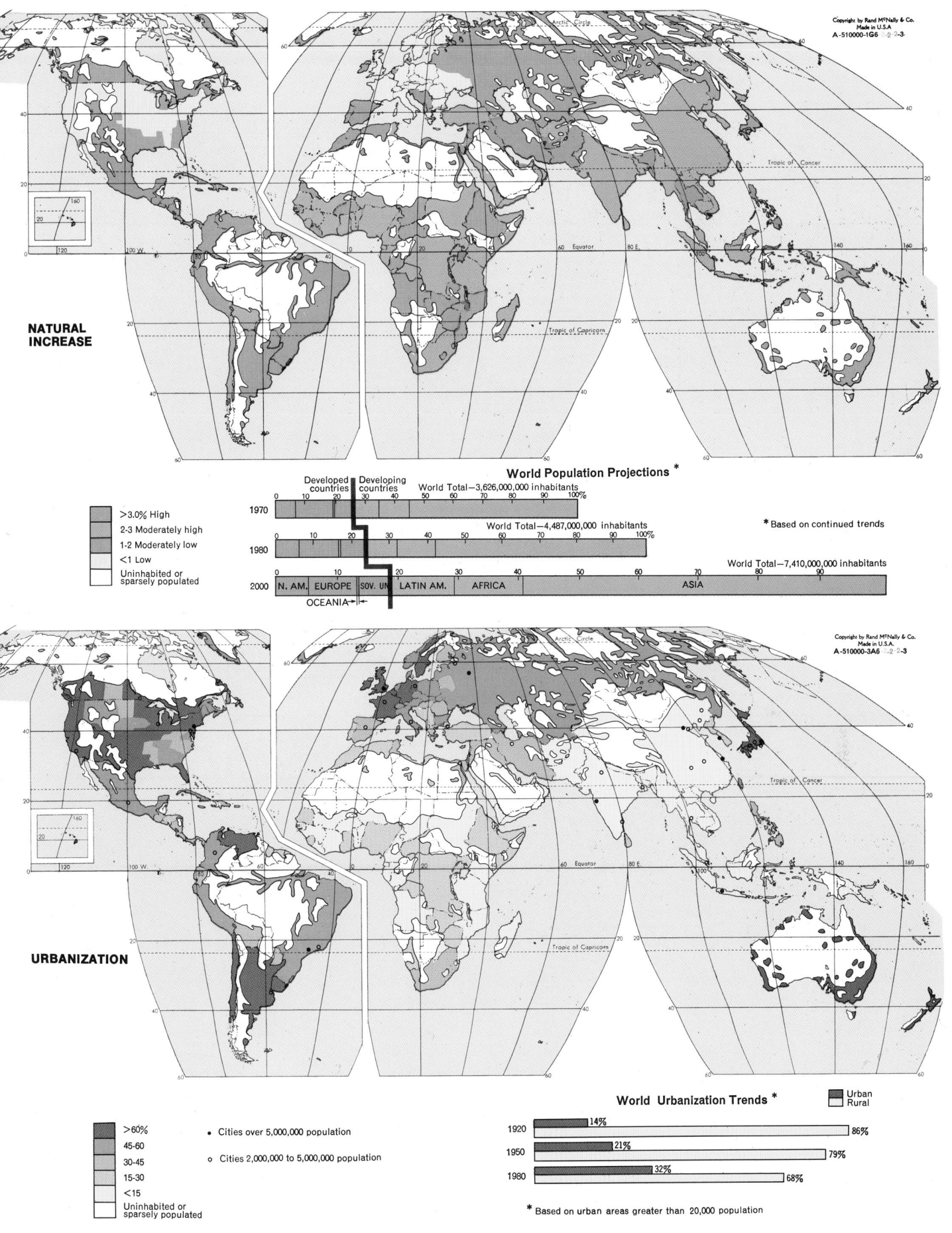

NATURAL INCREASE

>3.0% High
2-3 Moderately high
1-2 Moderately low
<1 Low
Uninhabited or
sparsely populated

Copyright by Rand McNally & Co.
Made in U.S.A
A-510000-1G6

World Population Projections *

Developed countries   Developing countries

World Total—3,626,000,000 inhabitants

1970   0 10 20 30 40 50 60 70 80 90 100%

World Total—4,487,000,000 inhabitants

1980   0 10 20 30 40 50 60 70 80 90 100%

World Total—7,410,000,000 inhabitants

2000   0 10 20 30 40 50 60 70 80 90

N. AM. EUROPE SOV. UN LATIN AM. AFRICA ASIA

OCEANIA →

* Based on continued trends

URBANIZATION

>60%
45-60
30-45
15-30
<15
Uninhabited or
sparsely populated

• Cities over 5,000,000 population
○ Cities 2,000,000 to 5,000,000 population

Copyright by Rand McNally & Co.
Made in U.S.A
A-510000-3A6

World Urbanization Trends *

Urban
Rural

1920   14%   86%
1950   21%   79%
1980   32%   68%

* Based on urban areas greater than 20,000 population

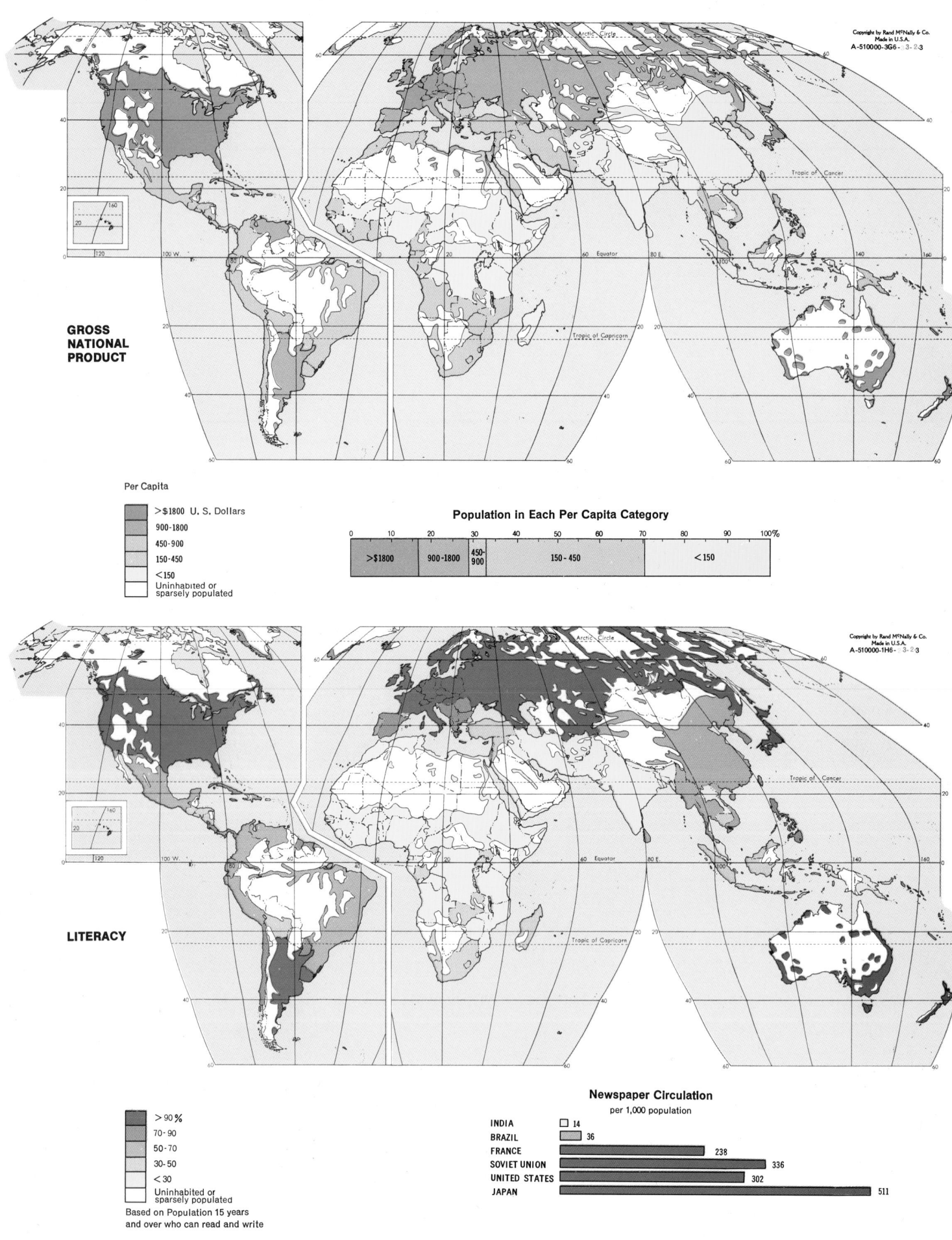

**GROSS
NATIONAL
PRODUCT**

Per Capita

>$1800 U. S. Dollars
900-1800
450-900
150-450
<150
Uninhabited or
sparsely populated

Population in Each Per Capita Category

0	10	20	30	40	50	60	70	80	90	100%

>$1800   900-1800   450-900   150 - 450   <150

LITERACY

>90 %
70- 90
50-70
30-50
<30
Uninhabited or
sparsely populated

Based on Population 15 years
and over who can read and write

Newspaper Circulation
per 1,000 population

INDIA	14
BRAZIL	36
FRANCE	238
SOVIET UNION	336
UNITED STATES	302
JAPAN	511

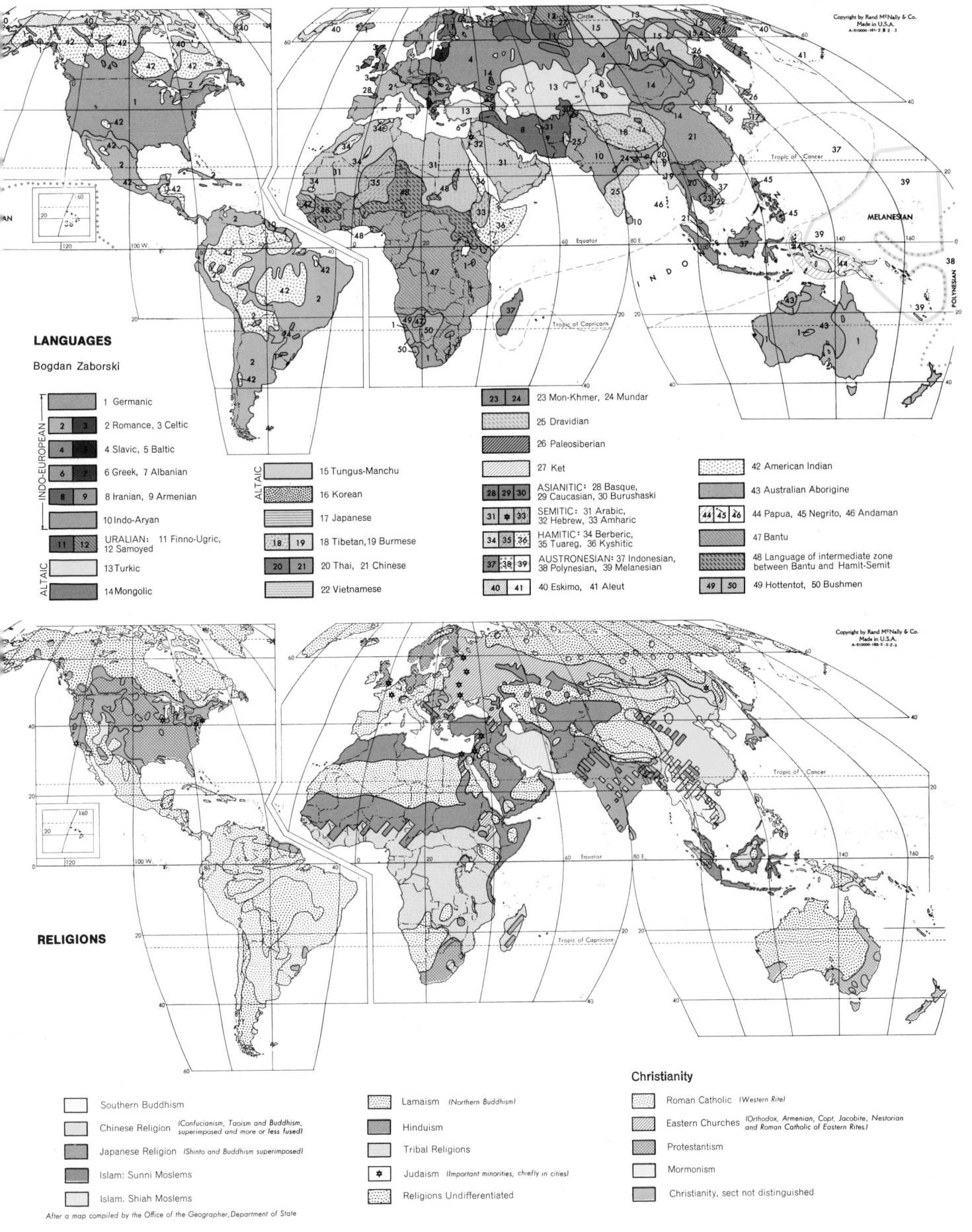

LANGUAGES

Bogdan Zaborski

INDO-EUROPEAN
1 Germanic
2 Romance, 3 Celtic
4 Slavic, 5 Baltic
6 Greek, 7 Albanian
8 Iranian, 9 Armenian
10 Indo-Aryan

URALIAN: 11 Finno-Ugric, 12 Samoyed

ALTAIC
13 Turkic
14 Mongolic
15 Tungus-Manchu
16 Korean
17 Japanese
18 Tibetan, 19 Burmese
20 Thai, 21 Chinese
22 Vietnamese

23 Mon-Khmer, 24 Mundar
25 Dravidian
26 Paleosiberian
27 Ket
ASIANITIC: 28 Basque, 29 Caucasian, 30 Burushaski
SEMITIC: 31 Arabic, 32 Hebrew, 33 Amharic
HAMITIC: 34 Berberic, 35 Tuareg, 36 Kyshitic
AUSTRONESIAN: 37 Indonesian, 38 Polynesian, 39 Melanesian
40 Eskimo, 41 Aleut

42 American Indian
43 Australian Aborigine
44 Papua, 45 Negrito, 46 Andaman
47 Bantu
48 Language of intermediate zone between Bantu and Hamit-Semit
49 Hottentot, 50 Bushmen

RELIGIONS

Southern Buddhism
Chinese Religion (Confucianism, Taoism and Buddhism, superimposed and more or less fused)
Japanese Religion (Shinto and Buddhism superimposed)
Islam: Sunni Moslems
Islam. Shiah Moslems

Lamaism (Northern Buddhism)
Hinduism
Tribal Religions
Judaism (Important minorities, chiefly in cities)
Religions Undifferentiated

Christianity
Roman Catholic (Western Rite)
Eastern Churches (Orthodox, Armenian, Copt, Jacobite, Nestorian and Roman Catholic of Eastern Rites.)
Protestantism
Mormonism
Christianity, sect not distinguished

After a map compiled by the Office of the Geographer, Department of State

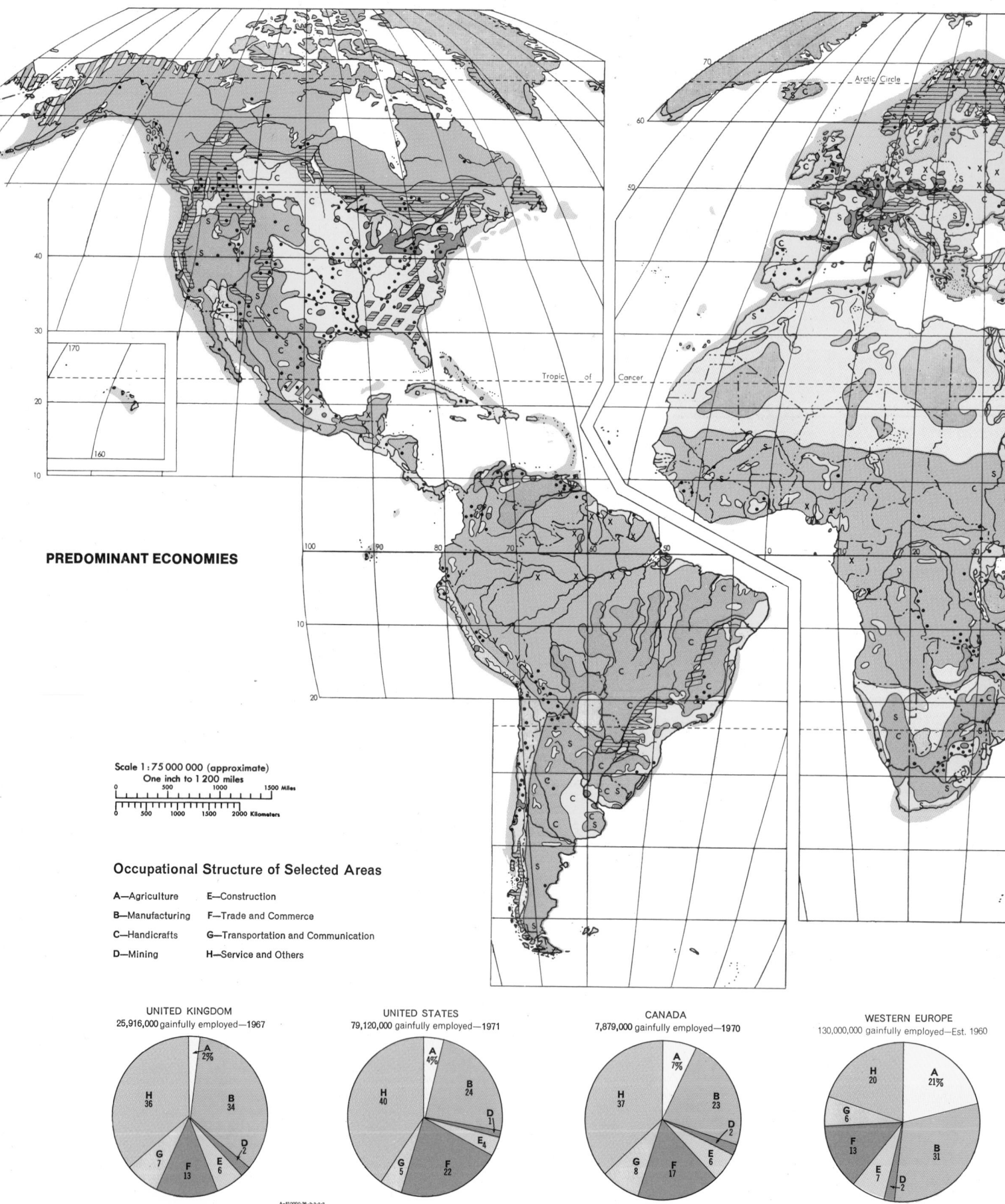

PREDOMINANT ECONOMIES

Scale 1 : 75 000 000 (approximate)
One inch to 1 200 miles

0   500   1000   1500 Miles

0   500   1000   1500   2000 Kilometers

Occupational Structure of Selected Areas

A—Agriculture   **E**—Construction

B—Manufacturing   **F**—Trade and Commerce

C—Handicrafts   **G**—Transportation and Communication

D—Mining   **H**—Service and Others

UNITED KINGDOM
25,916,000 gainfully employed—1967

A 2%, B 34, D 2, E 6, F 13, G 7, H 36

UNITED STATES
79,120,000 gainfully employed—1971

A 4%, B 24, D 1, E 4, F 22, G 5, H 40

CANADA
7,879,000 gainfully employed—1970

A 7%, B 23, D 2, E 6, F 17, G 8, H 37

WESTERN EUROPE
130,000,000 gainfully employed—Est. 1960

A 21%, B 31, D 2, E 7, F 13, G 6, H 20

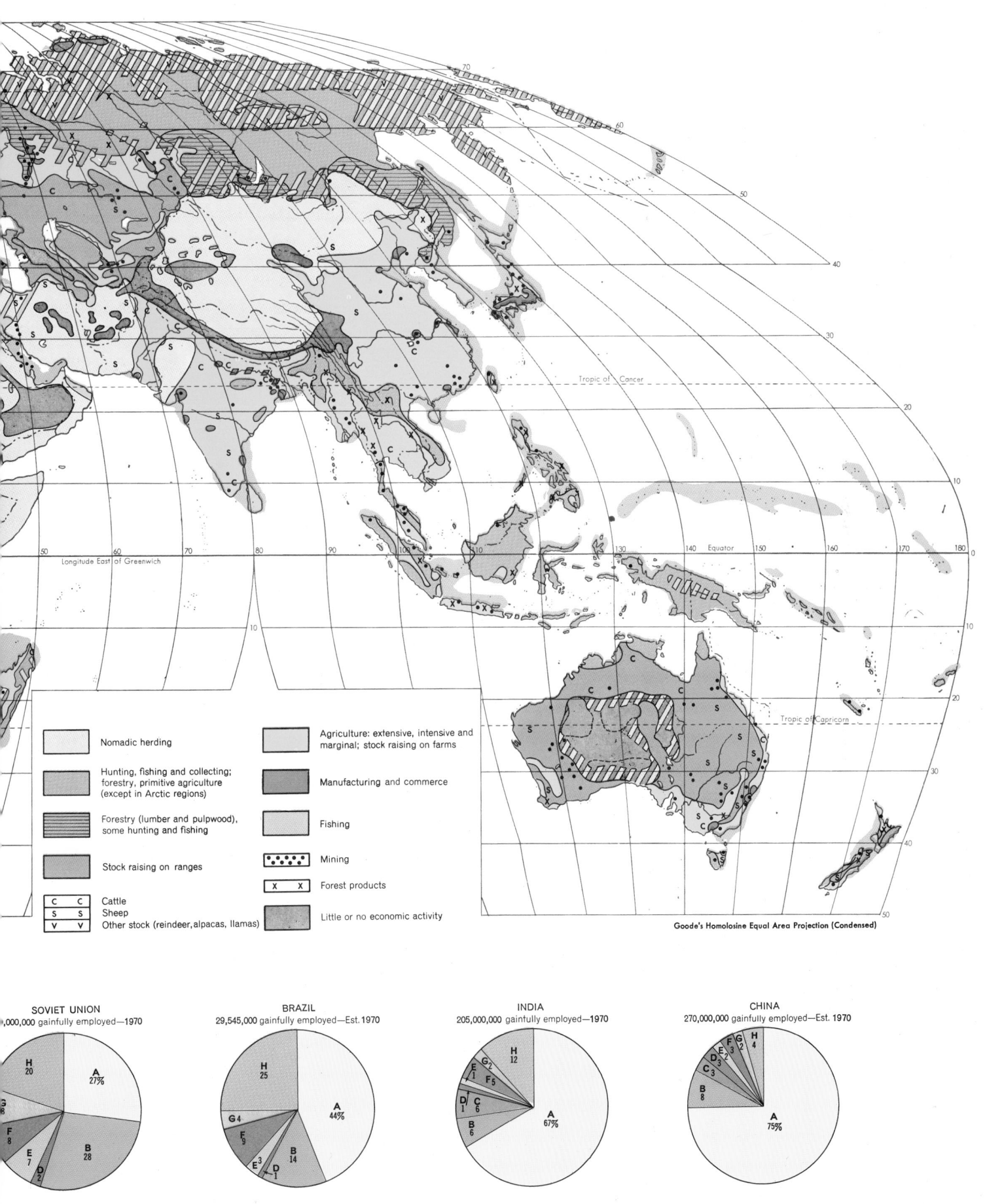

Nomadic herding

Hunting, fishing and collecting; forestry, primitive agriculture (except in Arctic regions)

Forestry (lumber and pulpwood), some hunting and fishing

Stock raising on ranges

C C   Cattle
S S   Sheep
V V   Other stock (reindeer, alpacas, llamas)

Agriculture: extensive, intensive and marginal; stock raising on farms

Manufacturing and commerce

Fishing

Mining

X   X   Forest products

Little or no economic activity

Longitude East of Greenwich

Tropic of Cancer

Equator

Tropic of Capricorn

Goode's Homolosine Equal Area Projection (Condensed)

SOVIET UNION
,000,000 gainfully employed—1970

H 20   A 27%   B 28   E 7   D 2   F 8

BRAZIL
29,545,000 gainfully employed—Est. 1970

H 25   A 44%   G 4   F 9   E 3   D 1   B 14

INDIA
205,000,000 gainfully employed—1970

H 12   A 67%   G 2   F 5   E 1   D 1   C 6   B 6

CHINA
270,000,000 gainfully employed—Est. 1970

H 4   G 2   F 3   E 2   D 3   C 3   B 8   A 75%

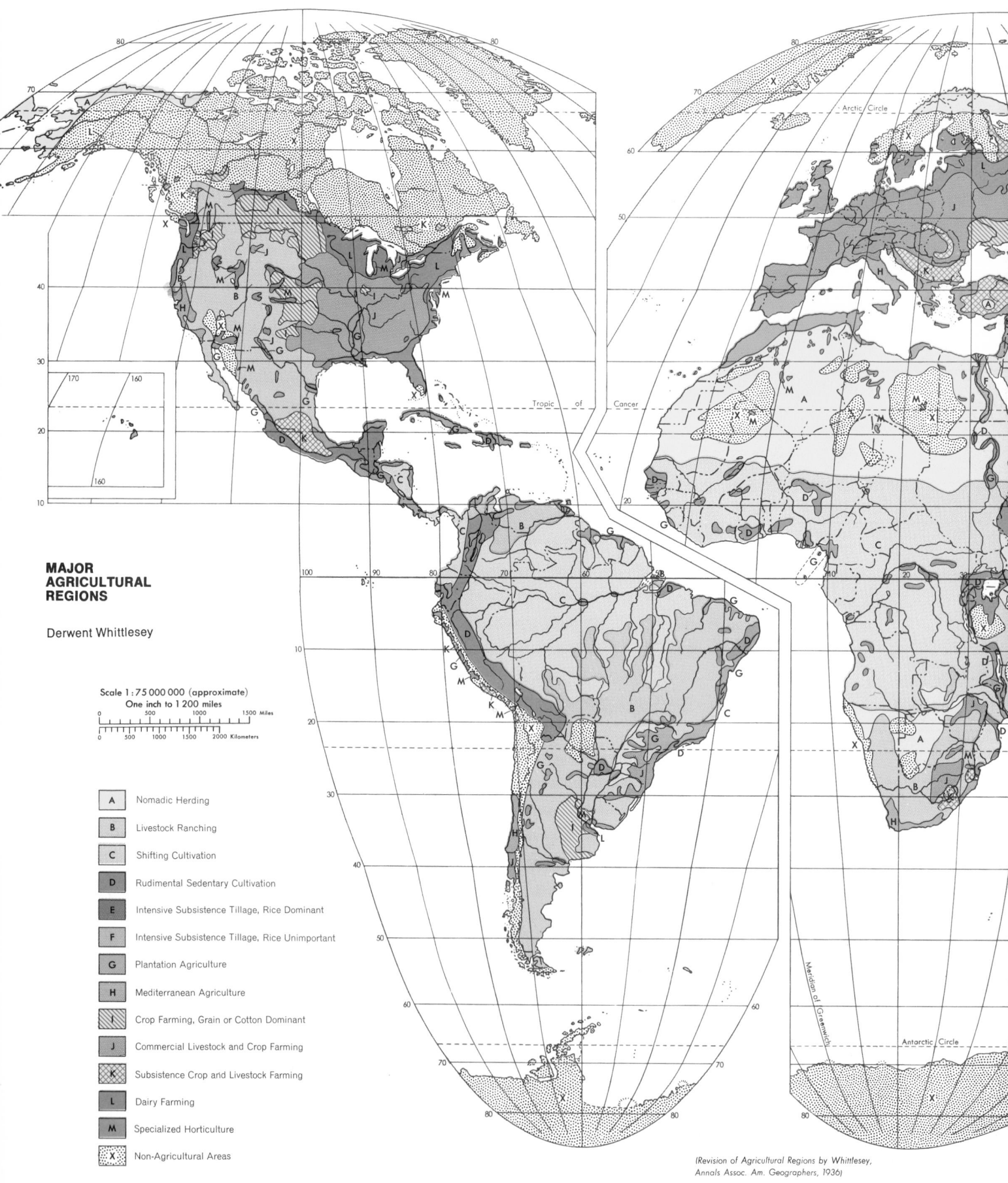

**MAJOR
AGRICULTURAL
REGIONS**

Derwent Whittlesey

Scale 1:75 000 000 (approximate)
One inch to 1 200 miles

| 0 | 500 | 1000 | 1500 Miles |

| 0 | 500 | 1000 | 1500 | 2000 Kilometers |

A	Nomadic Herding
B	Livestock Ranching
C	Shifting Cultivation
D	Rudimental Sedentary Cultivation
E	Intensive Subsistence Tillage, Rice Dominant
F	Intensive Subsistence Tillage, Rice Unimportant
G	Plantation Agriculture
H	Mediterranean Agriculture
I	Crop Farming, Grain or Cotton Dominant
J	Commercial Livestock and Crop Farming
K	Subsistence Crop and Livestock Farming
L	Dairy Farming
M	Specialized Horticulture
X	Non-Agricultural Areas

(Revision of Agricultural Regions by Whittlesey,
Annals Assoc. Am. Geographers, 1936)

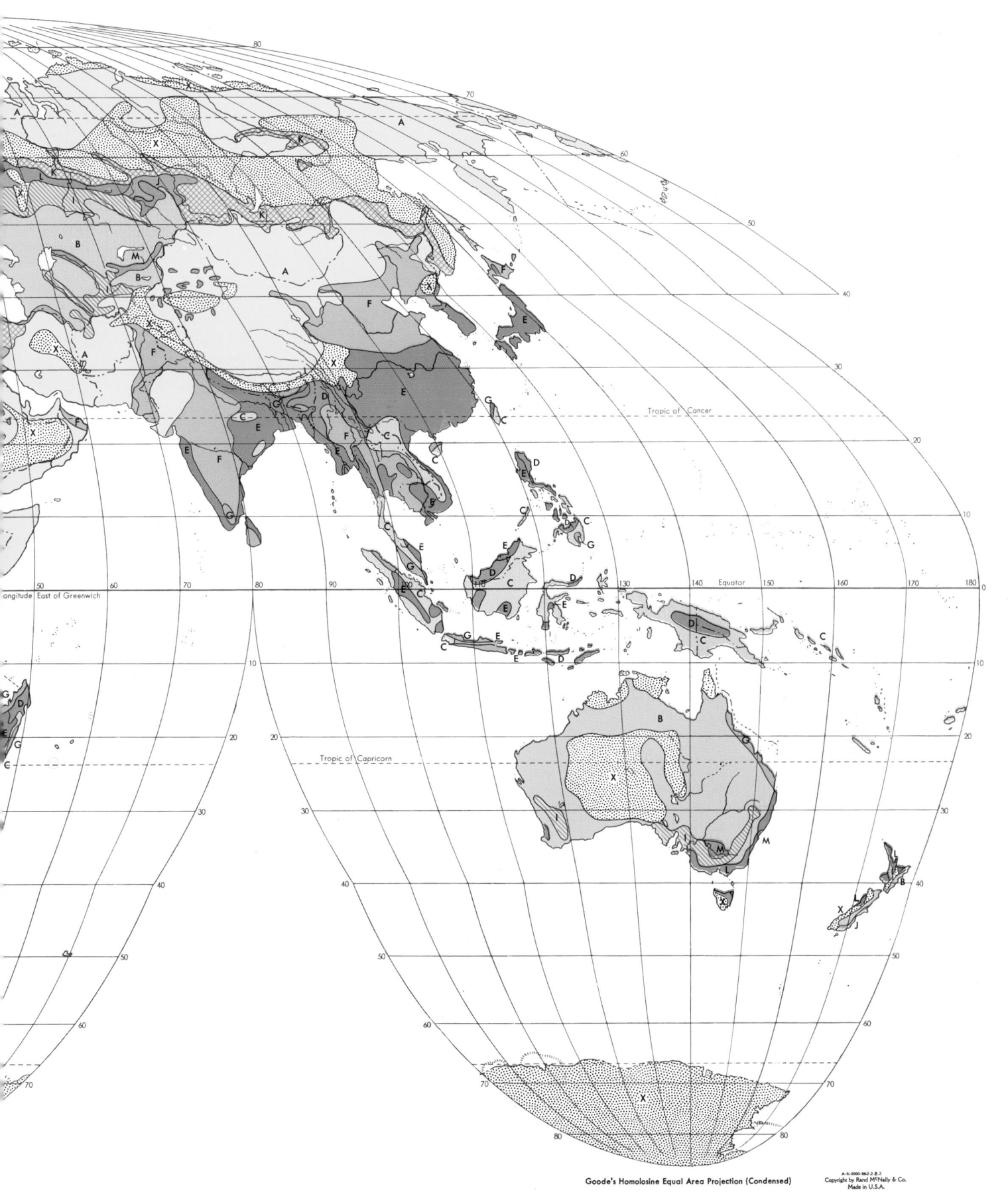

Goode's Homolosine Equal Area Projection (Condensed)

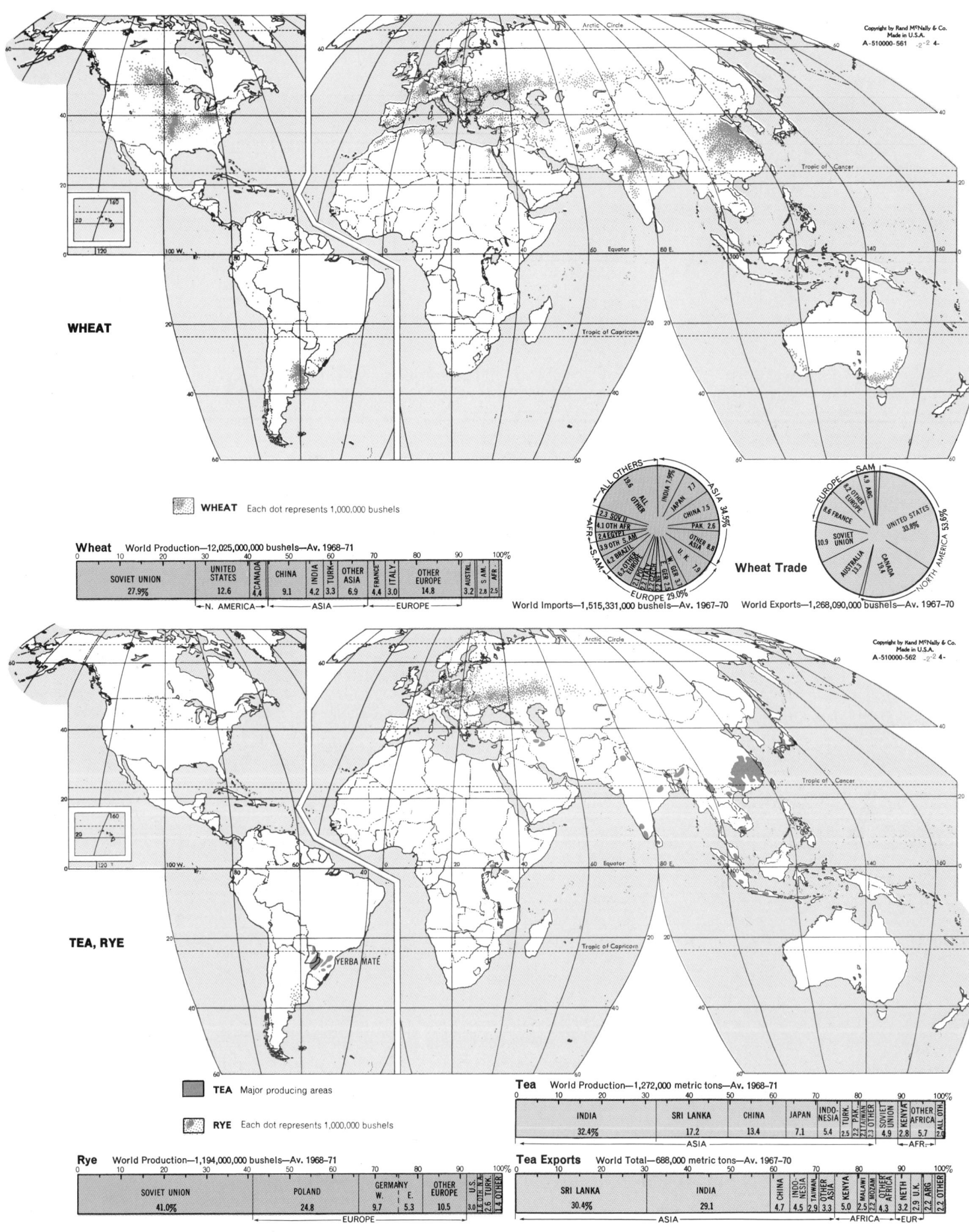

WHEAT

WHEAT Each dot represents 1,000,000 bushels

Wheat World Production—12,025,000,000 bushels—Av. 1968–71

0	10	20	30	40	50	60	70	80	90	100%

| SOVIET UNION 27.9% | UNITED STATES 12.6 | CANADA 4.4 | CHINA 9.1 | INDIA 4.2 | TURK. 3.3 | OTHER ASIA 6.9 | FRANCE 4.4 | ITALY 3.0 | OTHER EUROPE 14.8 | AUSTRL. 3.2 | S. AM. 2.8 | AFR. 2.5 |

← N. AMERICA →   ← ASIA →   ← EUROPE →

Wheat Trade

Pie chart: ALL OTHERS 18.6 / ALL OTHER / 2.3 SOV.U / 4.1 OTH AFR / 2.4 EGYPT / 3.9 OTH S. AM / 4.2 BRAZIL / 6.2 OTHER EUROPE / E. GER. / W. GER. 7.5 / U.K. 7.5 / OTHER ASIA 8.8 / PAK. 2.6 / CHINA 7.5 / JAPAN 7.7 / INDIA 7.9% / ASIA 34.5% / EUROPE 29.0%
World Imports—1,515,331,000 bushels—Av. 1967–70

Pie chart: S. AM. 4.9 ARG / EUROPE / 8.2 OTHER EUROPE / 8.6 FRANCE / SOVIET UNION 10.9 / AUSTRALIA 13.3 / CANADA 19.4 / UNITED STATES 33.8% / NORTH AMERICA 53.6%
World Exports—1,268,090,000 bushels—Av. 1967–70

TEA, RYE

YERBA MATÉ

TEA Major producing areas

RYE Each dot represents 1,000,000 bushels

Tea World Production—1,272,000 metric tons—Av. 1968–71

0	10	20	30	40	50	60	70	80	90	100%

| INDIA 32.4% | SRI LANKA 17.2 | CHINA 13.4 | JAPAN 7.1 | INDO-NESIA 5.4 | TURK. 2.5 | PAK. 2.2 | OTHER ASIA 2.3 | SOVIET UNION 4.9 | KENYA 2.8 | OTHER AFRICA 5.7 | ALL OTH. 2.0 |

← ASIA →   ← AFR. →

Rye World Production—1,194,000,000 bushels—Av. 1968–71

0	10	20	30	40	50	60	70	80	90	100%

| SOVIET UNION 41.0% | POLAND 24.8 | GERMANY W. 9.7 E. 5.3 | OTHER EUROPE 10.5 | U.S. 3.0 | OTH. N. AM. 1.6 | TURK. 2.6 | OTHER 1.4 |

← EUROPE →

Tea Exports World Total—688,000 metric tons—Av. 1967–70

0	10	20	30	40	50	60	70	80	90	100%

| SRI LANKA 30.4% | INDIA 29.1 | CHINA 4.7 | INDO-NESIA 4.5 | TAIWAN 2.9 | OTHER ASIA 3.3 | KENYA 5.0 | MALAWI 2.2 | MOZAM. 2.2 | OTHER AFRICA 3.2 | NETH. 2.9 | U.K. 2.2 | ARG. 2.2 | OTHER 2.2 |

← ASIA →   ← AFRICA →   ← EUR. →

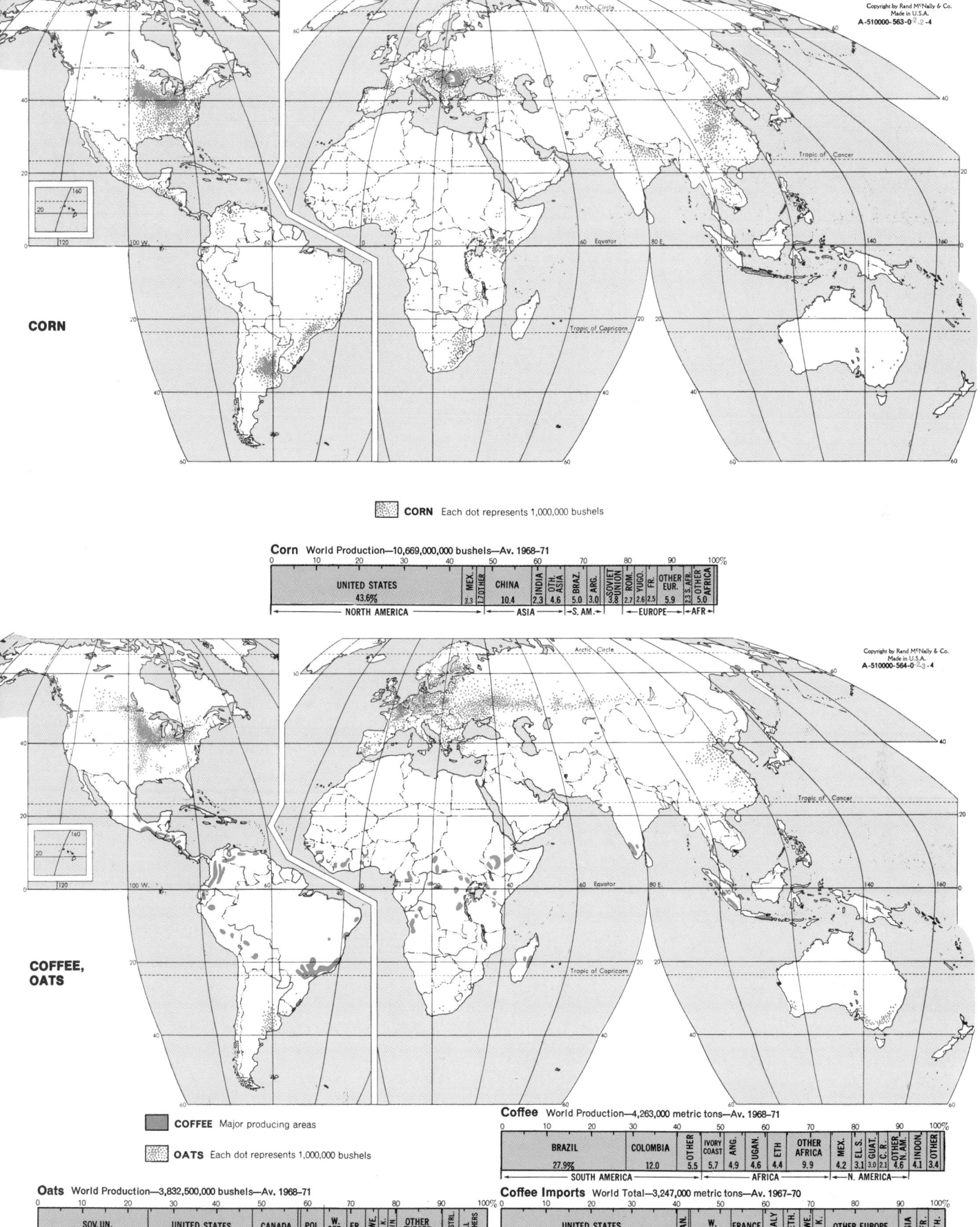

CORN

CORN Each dot represents 1,000,000 bushels

Corn World Production—10,669,000,000 bushels—Av. 1968–71

0	10	20	30	40	50	60	70	80	90	100%

| UNITED STATES 43.6% | MEX. 3.3 | OTHER 1.7 | CHINA 10.4 | INDIA 2.3 | OTH. ASIA 4.6 | BRAZ. 5.0 | ARG. 3.0 | SOVIET UNION 3.8 | ROM. 2.7 | YUGO. 2.6 | FR. 2.5 | OTHER EUR. 9.3 | S. AFR. 2.3 | OTHER AFRICA 5.0 |

← NORTH AMERICA → ← ASIA → ←S. AM.→ ← EUROPE → ←AFR→

COFFEE, OATS

COFFEE Major producing areas

OATS Each dot represents 1,000,000 bushels

Oats World Production—3,832,500,000 bushels—Av. 1968–71

0	10	20	30	40	50	60	70	80	90	100%

| SOV. UN. 24.2% | UNITED STATES 23.9 | CANADA 10.2 | POL. 5.3 | W. GER. 5.1 | FR. 4.2 | SWE. 2.8 | U.K. 2.3 | FIN. 2.2 | OTHER EUROPE 10.0 | AUSTRL. 2.7 | ALL OTHERS 6.9 |

← NORTH AMERICA → ← EUROPE →

Coffee World Production—4,263,000 metric tons—Av. 1968–71

0	10	20	30	40	50	60	70	80	90	100%

| BRAZIL 27.9% | COLOMBIA 12.0 | OTHER 5.5 | IVORY COAST 5.7 | ANG. 4.9 | UGAN. 4.6 | ETH. 4.4 | OTHER AFRICA 9.9 | MEX. 4.2 | EL S. 3.1 | GUAT. 3.0 | C.R. 2.1 | OTHER N. AM. 4.6 | INDON. 4.1 | OTHER 3.4 |

← SOUTH AMERICA → ← AFRICA → ← N. AMERICA →

Coffee Imports World Total—3,247,000 metric tons—Av. 1967–70

0	10	20	30	40	50	60	70	80	90	100%

| UNITED STATES 40.1% | CAN. 2.5 | W. GER. 9.2 | FRANCE 7.2 | ITALY 4.8 | NETH. 3.3 | SWE. 3.2 | U.K. 2.8 | OTHER EUROPE 16.4 | ASIA 4.5 | AFR. 2.5 | OTH. 3.3 |

← NORTH AMERICA → ← EUROPE →

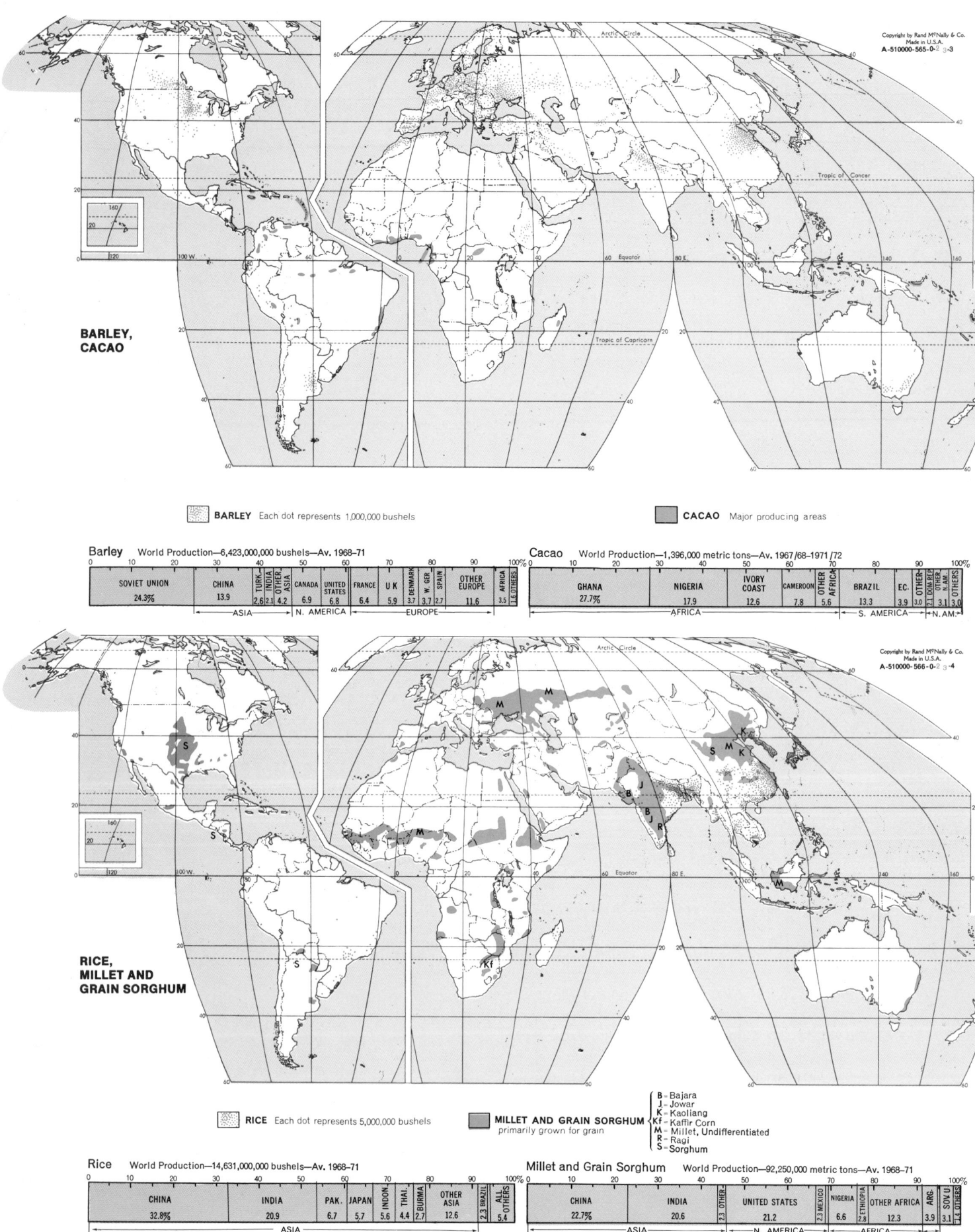

**BARLEY,
CACAO**

BARLEY Each dot represents 1,000,000 bushels

CACAO Major producing areas

Barley World Production—6,423,000,000 bushels—Av. 1968–71

0	10	20	30	40	50	60	70	80	90	100%

| SOVIET UNION 24.3% | CHINA 13.9 | TURK. 2.6 | INDIA 2.1 | OTHER ASIA 4.2 | CANADA 6.9 | UNITED STATES 6.8 | FRANCE 6.4 | U K 5.9 | DENMARK 3.7 | W. GER. 3.7 | SPAIN 2.7 | OTHER EUROPE 11.6 | AFRICA 3.5 | OTHERS 1.6 |

←————— ASIA —————→ ← N. AMERICA → ←———————— EUROPE ————————→

Cacao World Production—1,396,000 metric tons—Av. 1967/68–1971/72

0	10	20	30	40	50	60	70	80	90	100%

| GHANA 27.7% | NIGERIA 17.9 | IVORY COAST 12.6 | CAMEROON 7.8 | OTHER AFRICA 5.6 | BRAZIL 13.3 | EC. 3.9 | OTHER S. AM. 3.0 | DOM. REP. 2.1 | OTHER N. AM. 3.1 | OTHERS 3.0 |

←———————————————— AFRICA ————————————————→ ←——— S. AMERICA ———→ ←— N. AM.—→

**RICE,
MILLET AND
GRAIN SORGHUM**

RICE Each dot represents 5,000,000 bushels

MILLET AND GRAIN SORGHUM
primarily grown for grain

B – Bajara
J – Jowar
K – Kaoliang
Kf – Kaffir Corn
M – Millet, Undifferentiated
R – Ragi
S – Sorghum

Rice World Production—14,631,000,000 bushels—Av. 1968–71

0	10	20	30	40	50	60	70	80	90	100%

| CHINA 32.8% | INDIA 20.9 | PAK. 6.7 | JAPAN 5.7 | INDON. 5.6 | THAI. 4.4 | BURMA 2.7 | OTHER ASIA 12.6 | BRAZIL 2.3 | ALL OTHERS 5.4 |

←———————————————————— ASIA ————————————————————→

Millet and Grain Sorghum World Production—92,250,000 metric tons—Av. 1968–71

0	10	20	30	40	50	60	70	80	90	100%

| CHINA 22.7% | INDIA 20.6 | OTHER 2.3 | UNITED STATES 21.2 | MEXICO 2.3 | NIGERIA 6.6 | ETHIOPIA 2.8 | OTHER AFRICA 12.3 | ARG. 3.9 | SOV U. 3.1 | OTHERS 1.4 |

←——————————— ASIA ———————————→ ←— N. AMERICA —→ ←———— AFRICA ————→

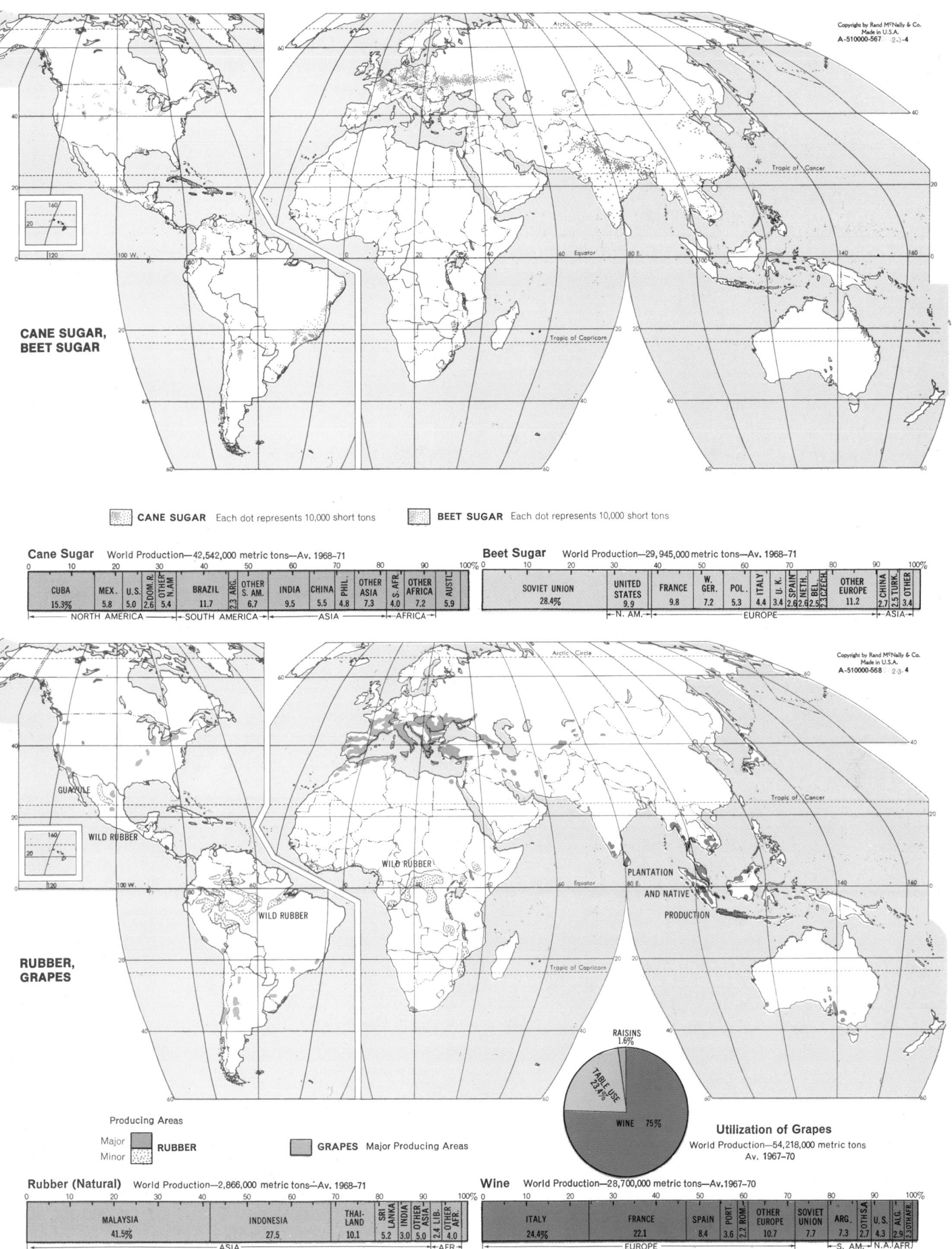

CANE SUGAR, BEET SUGAR

◼ **CANE SUGAR** Each dot represents 10,000 short tons ◼ **BEET SUGAR** Each dot represents 10,000 short tons

Cane Sugar World Production—42,542,000 metric tons—Av. 1968-71

CUBA 15.3%	MEX. 5.8	U.S. 5.0	DOM. R. 2.6	OTHER N.AM 5.4	BRAZIL 11.7	ARG. 2.3	OTHER S. AM. 6.7	INDIA 9.5	CHINA 5.5	PHIL. 4.8	OTHER ASIA 7.3	S. AFR. 4.0	OTHER AFRICA 7.2	AUSTL. 5.9	

NORTH AMERICA — SOUTH AMERICA — ASIA — AFRICA

Beet Sugar World Production—29,945,000 metric tons—Av. 1968-71

SOVIET UNION 28.4%	UNITED STATES 9.9	FRANCE 9.8	W. GER. 7.2	POL. 5.3	ITALY 4.4	U.K. 3.4	SPAIN 2.6	NETH. 2.6	BEL. 2.5	CZECH. 2.3	OTHER EUROPE 11.2	CHINA 2.5	TURK. 3.4	OTHER

N. AM. — EUROPE — ASIA

RUBBER, GRAPES

GUAYULE
WILD RUBBER
WILD RUBBER
WILD RUBBER
PLANTATION AND NATIVE PRODUCTION

Producing Areas

Major ◼ **RUBBER**
Minor

◼ **GRAPES** Major Producing Areas

RAISINS 1.6%
TABLE USE 23.4%
WINE 75%

Utilization of Grapes
World Production—54,218,000 metric tons
Av. 1967-70

Rubber (Natural) World Production—2,866,000 metric tons—Av. 1968-71

MALAYSIA 41.5%	INDONESIA 27.5	THAI-LAND 10.1	SRI LANKA 5.2	INDIA 3.0	OTHER ASIA 5.0	LIB. 2.4	OTHER AFR. 4.0

ASIA — AFR.

Wine World Production—28,700,000 metric tons—Av.1967-70

ITALY 24.4%	FRANCE 22.1	SPAIN 8.4	PORT. 3.6	ROM. 2.2	OTHER EUROPE 10.7	SOVIET UNION 7.7	ARG. 7.3	OTH. S.A. 2.7	U.S. 4.3	ALG. 2.9	OTHAFR.

EUROPE — S. AM. — N.A. AFR.

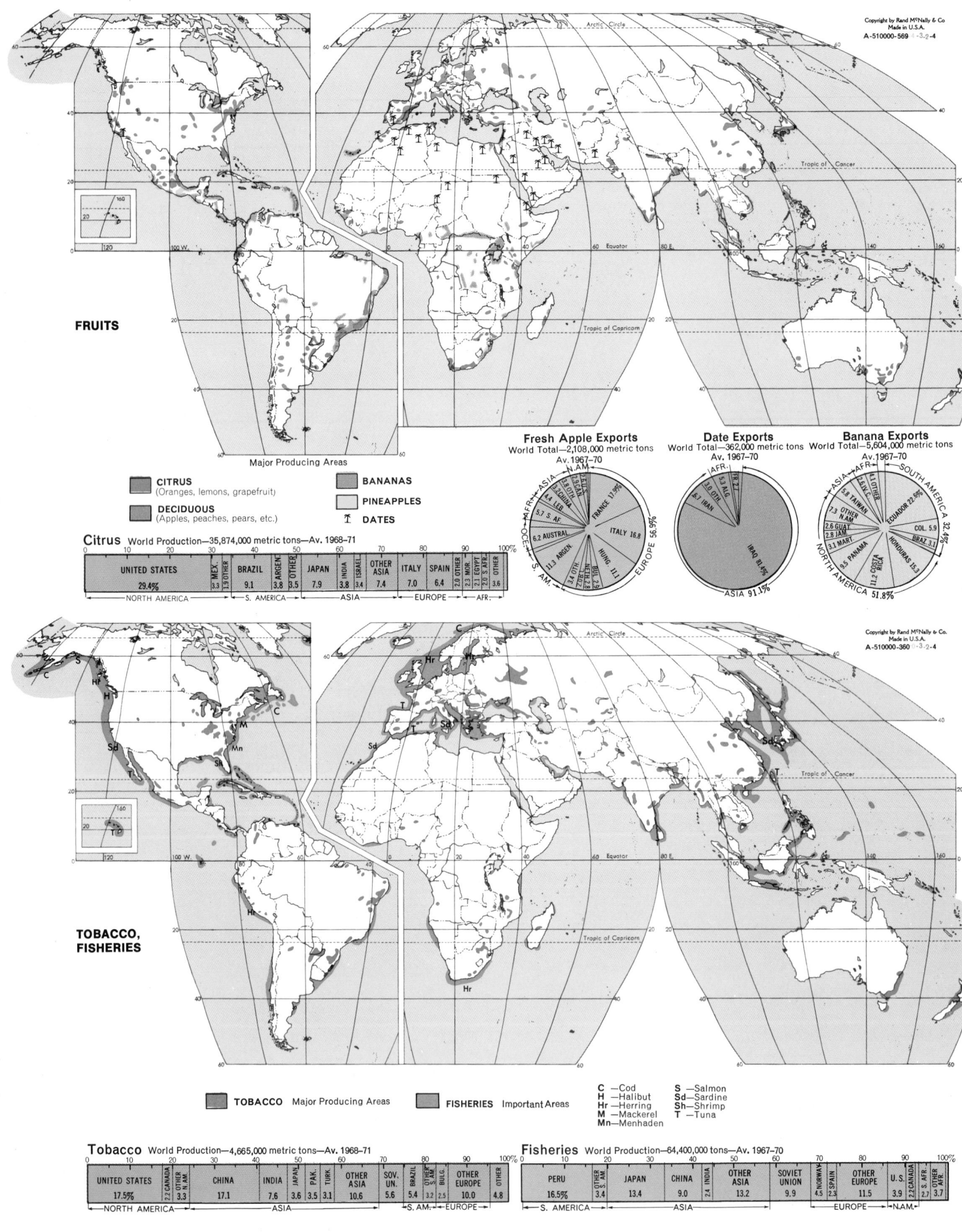

FRUITS

Major Producing Areas

CITRUS (Oranges, lemons, grapefruit)	BANANAS
DECIDUOUS (Apples, peaches, pears, etc.)	PINEAPPLES
	DATES

Citrus World Production—35,874,000 metric tons—Av. 1968–71

0	10	20	30	40	50	60	70	80	90	100%

| UNITED STATES 29.4% | MEX. 3.3 | OTHER 1.9 | BRAZIL 9.1 | ARGEN. 3.8 | OTHER 3.5 | JAPAN 7.9 | INDIA 3.8 | ISRAEL 3.4 | OTHER ASIA 7.4 | ITALY 7.0 | SPAIN 6.4 | MOR. 2.3 | EGYPT 2.1 | S.AFR. 2.0 | OTHER 3.6 |

NORTH AMERICA — S. AMERICA — ASIA — EUROPE — AFR.

Fresh Apple Exports
World Total—2,108,000 metric tons
Av. 1967–70

N.AM.
FRANCE 17.9%
ITALY 16.8
EUROPE 56.9%
HUNG. 11.1
BUL. 7.3
OTH. 7.7 NETH.
2.4 OTH.
11.3 ARGEN
6.2 AUSTRAL
S. AM.
5.7 S. AF.
4.4 LEB.
3.0 CHINA
2.3 OTH.
ASIA
AFR.

Date Exports
World Total—362,000 metric tons
Av. 1967–70

AFR.
3.0 OTH
5.3 ALG.
8.7 IRAN
IRAQ 83.6%
ASIA 91.1%

Banana Exports
World Total—5,604,000 metric tons
Av. 1967–70

ASIA AFR.
5.8 TAIWAN
7.3 OTHER N.AM.
2.6 GUAT.
2.8 JAM.
3.1 MART.
9.5 PANAMA
11.7 COSTA RICA
HONDURAS 15.3
NORTH AMERICA 51.8%
EQUADOR 22.8%
COL. 5.9
BRAZ. 3.1
SOUTH AMERICA 32.4%
6.1 OTHER

TOBACCO, FISHERIES

| TOBACCO Major Producing Areas | FISHERIES Important Areas |

C —Cod	S —Salmon
H —Halibut	Sd—Sardine
Hr —Herring	Sh—Shrimp
M —Mackerel	T —Tuna
Mn—Menhaden	

Tobacco World Production—4,665,000 metric tons—Av. 1968–71

0	10	20	30	40	50	60	70	80	90	100%

| UNITED STATES 17.5% | CANADA 2.2 | OTHER N.AM. 3.3 | CHINA 17.1 | INDIA 7.6 | JAPAN 3.6 | PAK. 3.5 | TURK. 3.1 | OTHER ASIA 10.6 | SOV. UN. 5.6 | BRAZIL 5.4 | OTHER S.AM. 3.2 | BULG. 2.5 | OTHER EUROPE 10.0 | OTHER 4.8 |

NORTH AMERICA — ASIA — S. AM. — EUROPE

Fisheries World Production—64,400,000 tons—Av. 1967–70

0	10	20	30	40	50	60	70	80	90	100%

| PERU 16.5% | OTHER S.AM. 3.4 | JAPAN 13.4 | CHINA 9.0 | INDIA 2.4 | OTHER ASIA 13.2 | SOVIET UNION 9.9 | NORWAY 4.5 | SPAIN 2.3 | OTHER EUROPE 11.5 | U.S. 3.9 | CANADA 2.2 | S. AFR. 2.7 | OTHER AFR. 3.7 |

S. AMERICA — ASIA — EUROPE — N.AM.

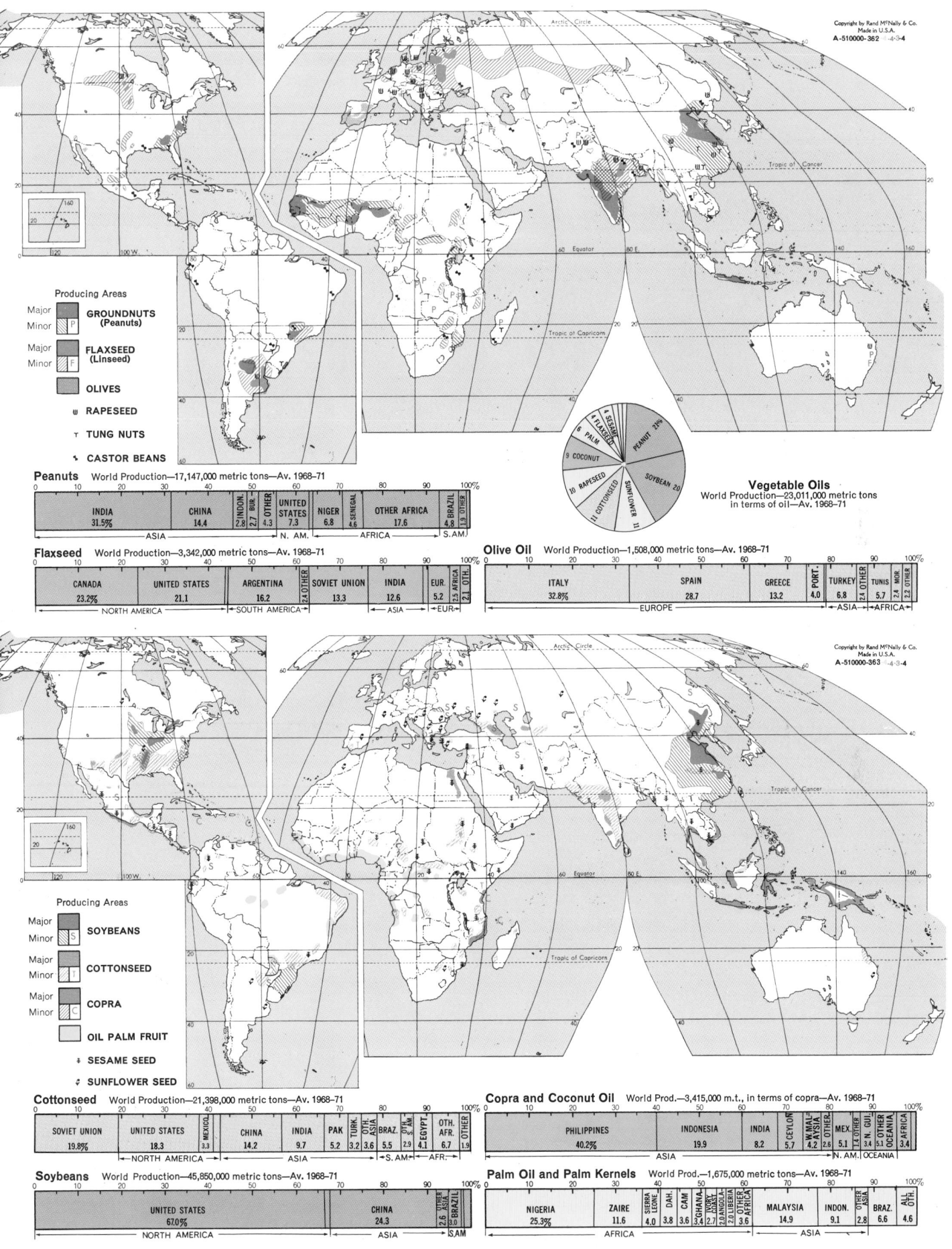

Copyright by Rand McNally & Co.
Made in U.S.A.
A-510000-362   4-3-4

Producing Areas

Major / Minor	**GROUNDNUTS** (Peanuts)	P
Major / Minor	**FLAXSEED** (Linseed)	F
	OLIVES	
	RAPESEED	ш
	TUNG NUTS	T
	CASTOR BEANS	

Vegetable Oils
World Production—23,011,000 metric tons
in terms of oil—Av. 1968–71

Pie chart: Peanut 21, Soybean 20, Sunflower 11, Cottonseed 11, Rapeseed 10, Coconut 9, Palm 6, Flaxseed 4, Sesame 4

Peanuts   World Production—17,147,000 metric tons—Av. 1968–71

INDIA 31.5%	CHINA 14.4	INDON. 2.8	BUR. 2.7	OTHER 4.3	UNITED STATES 7.3	NIGER 6.8	SENEGAL 4.6	OTHER AFRICA 17.6	BRAZIL 4.8	OTHER 1.9
ASIA					N. AM.	AFRICA			S. AM.	

Flaxseed   World Production—3,342,000 metric tons—Av. 1968–71

CANADA 23.2%	UNITED STATES 21.1	ARGENTINA 16.2	OTHER 2.4	SOVIET UNION 13.3	INDIA 12.6	EUR. 5.2	AFRICA 2.5	OTH. 2.1
NORTH AMERICA		SOUTH AMERICA		ASIA		EUR.		

Olive Oil   World Production—1,508,000 metric tons—Av. 1968–71

ITALY 32.8%	SPAIN 28.7	GREECE 13.2	PORT. 4.0	TURKEY 6.8	OTHER 2.4	TUNIS 5.1	MOR 2.4	OTHER 2.2
EUROPE				ASIA		AFRICA		

Copyright by Rand McNally & Co.
Made in U.S.A.
A-510000-363   4-3-4

Producing Areas

Major / Minor	**SOYBEANS**	S
Major / Minor	**COTTONSEED**	T
Major / Minor	**COPRA**	C
	OIL PALM FRUIT	
	SESAME SEED	≰
	SUNFLOWER SEED	✿

Cottonseed   World Production—21,398,000 metric tons—Av. 1968–71

SOVIET UNION 19.8%	UNITED STATES 18.3	MEXICO 3.3	CHINA 14.2	INDIA 9.7	PAK 5.2	TURK. 3.2	OTH. ASIA 3.6	BRAZ. 5.5	OTH. S. AM. 4.1	EGYPT 6.7	OTH. AFR. 1.9
	NORTH AMERICA		ASIA					S. AM.		AFR.	

Soybeans   World Production—45,850,000 metric tons—Av. 1968–71

UNITED STATES 67.0%	CHINA 24.3	OTHER ASIA 2.6	BRAZIL 3.0
NORTH AMERICA	ASIA		S.AM

Copra and Coconut Oil   World Prod.—3,415,000 m.t., in terms of copra—Av. 1968–71

PHILIPPINES 40.2%	INDONESIA 19.9	INDIA 8.2	CEYLON 5.7	W.MAL-AYSIA 4.2	OTHER 2.6	MEX. 5.1	N. GUI. 3.4	OTHER OCEANIA 5.1	AFRICA 3.4
ASIA						N. AM.	OCEANIA		

Palm Oil and Palm Kernels   World Prod.—1,675,000 metric tons—Av. 1968–71

NIGERIA 25.3%	ZAIRE 11.6	SIERRA LEONE 4.0	DAH. 3.8	CAM 3.6	GHANA 3.4	IVORY COAST 2.7	ANGOLA 2.0	LIBERIA 2.0	OTHER AFRICA 3.6	MALAYSIA 14.9	INDON. 9.1	OTHER ASIA 2.8	BRAZ. 6.6	ALL OTH. 4.6
AFRICA										ASIA				

Copyright by Rand McNally & Co.
Made in U.S.A.
A-510000-560

Producing Areas

Major		
Minor		**COTTON**

Major		
Minor		**HEMP**

ABACA (Manila Hemp)

Hemp (Fiber)
World Production—285,000 metric tons—Av. 1968–71

0	10	20	30	40	50	60	70	80	90	100%

SOVIET UNION 34.2%	INDIA 22.3	BNGL. 3.9	TURK. 3.0	S KOREA 2.4	OTH ASIA 2.7	ROMANIA 6.8	HUNG. 6.6	POLAND 5.9	YUGO 5.3	BUL. 3.0	OTH EUR 2.6

← ASIA → ← EUROPE →

Cotton (Ginned)
World Production—11,447,000 metric tons—Av. 1968–71

0	10	20	30	40	50	60	70	80	90	100%

UNITED STATES 19.8%	MEXICO 3.5	OTH N. AM. 1.7	SOVIET UNION 18.9	CHINA 16.4	INDIA 9.1	PAK. 4.8	TURK. 3.8	BRAZ. 5.4	OTH S. AM. 3.2	EGYPT 4.4	OTHER AFRICA 6.7	ALL OTH 1.7

← NORTH AMERICA → ← ASIA → ← S. AM. → ← AFR. →

Rayon
World Production—1,403,000 metric tons—Av. 1967–70

0	10	20	30	40	50	60	70	80	90	100%

UNITED STATES 24.5%	OTH N. AM. 3.1	SOVIET UNION 14.9	JAPAN 10.1	INDIA 3.7	OTH ASIA 2.1	U.K. 6.7	ITALY 6.4	GERMANY W. 5.2	E. 2.3	FR. 3.6	NETH. 2.5	OTHER EUROPE 9.9	BRAZ. 2.4	ALL O. S. AM. 1.6

← NORTH AMERICA → ← ASIA → ← EUROPE →

Copyright by Rand McNally & Co.
Made in U.S.A.
A-510000-364

Producing Areas

	SILK COCOONS
Major	**FLAX (Fiber)**
Minor	**JUTE**

SISAL   R **RAMIE**

KAPOK   P **PHORMIUM TENAX**

*Includes Kenaf in Thailand

Jute*
World Production—3,250,000 metric tons—Av. 1968–71

0	10	20	30	40	50	60	70	80	90	100%

BANGLADESH 34.9%	INDIA 34.4	CHINA 15.3	THAILAND 9.4	OTHER ASIA 3.6	ALL OTH 2.4

← ASIA →

Flax (Fiber)
World Production—644,000 metric tons—Av. 1968–71

0	10	20	30	40	50	60	70	80	90	100%

SOVIET UNION 69.7%	POLAND 8.7	FRANCE 7.5	CZECH 2.6	BELG. 2.3	OTH. EUR. 6.2	ALL OTHERS 3.0

← EUROPE →

Silk (Raw)
World Production—32,525 metric tons—Av. 1962–64

0	10	20	30	40	50	60	70	80	90	100%

JAPAN 58.9%	CHINA 21.5	INDIA 4.2	S. KOREA 2.1	SOVIET UNION 8.4	ITALY 2.0	OTHER 2.0

← ASIA →

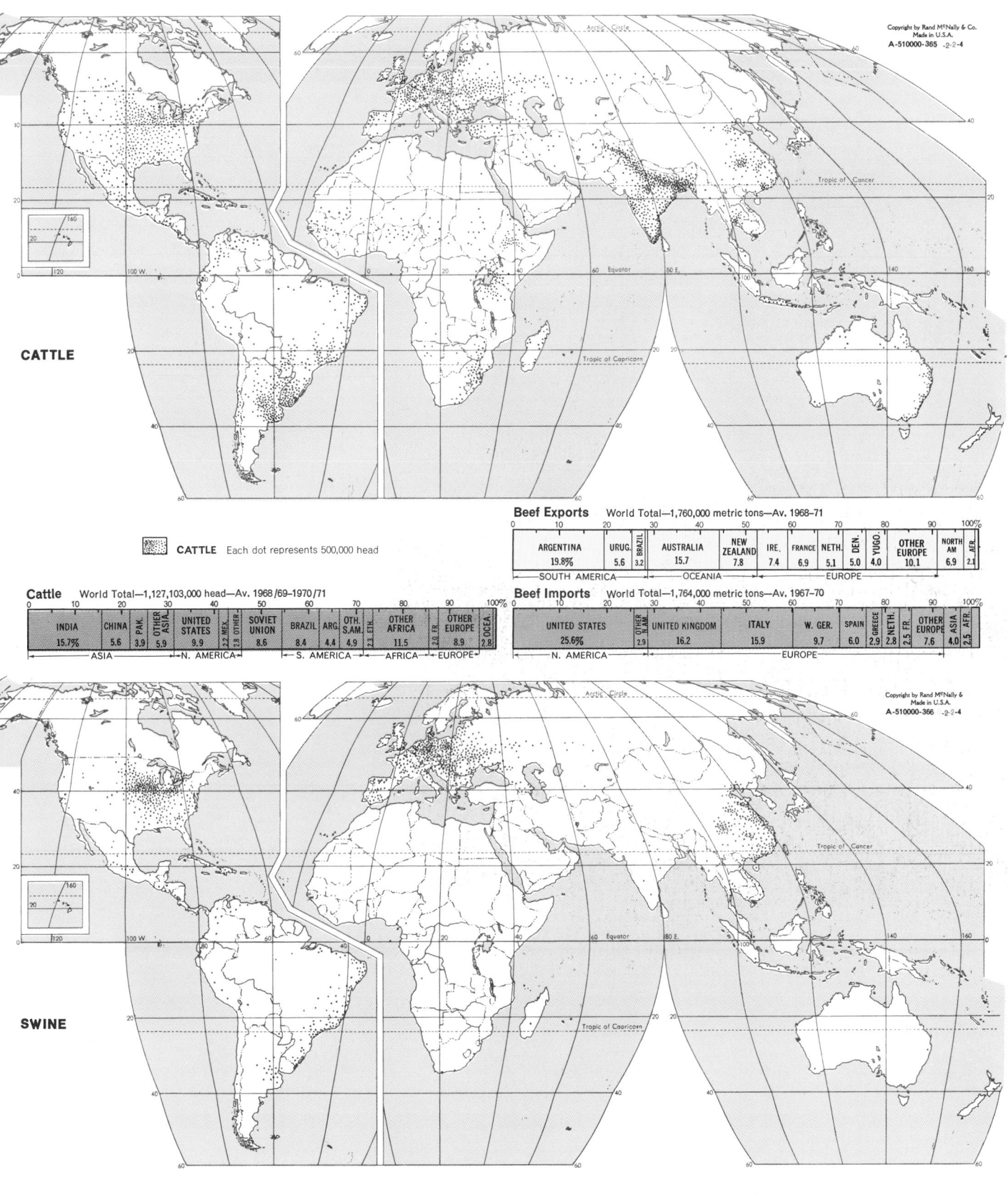

CATTLE

CATTLE Each dot represents 500,000 head

Cattle World Total—1,127,103,000 head—Av. 1968/69–1970/71

0	10	20	30	40	50	60	70	80	90	100%
INDIA 15.7%	CHINA 5.6	PAK. 3.9	OTHER ASIA 5.9	UNITED STATES 9.9	MEX. 2.2	OTHER 2.8	SOVIET UNION 8.6	BRAZIL 8.4	ARG. 4.4	OTH. S.AM. 4.9	ETH. 2.3	OTHER AFRICA 11.5	FR. 2.0	OTHER EUROPE 8.9	OCEA. 2.8

ASIA — N. AMERICA — S. AMERICA — AFRICA — EUROPE

Beef Exports World Total—1,760,000 metric tons—Av. 1968–71

0	10	20	30	40	50	60	70	80	90	100%
ARGENTINA 19.8%	URUG. 5.6	BRAZIL 3.2	AUSTRALIA 15.7	NEW ZEALAND 7.8	IRE. 7.4	FRANCE 6.9	NETH. 5.1	DEN. 5.0	YUGO. 4.0	OTHER EUROPE 10.1	NORTH AM. 6.9	AFR. 2.1

SOUTH AMERICA — OCEANIA — EUROPE

Beef Imports World Total—1,764,000 metric tons—Av. 1967–70

0	10	20	30	40	50	60	70	80	90	100%
UNITED STATES 25.6%	OTHER N.AM. 2.9	UNITED KINGDOM 16.2	ITALY 15.9	W. GER. 9.7	SPAIN 6.0	GREECE 2.9	NETH. 2.8	FR. 2.5	OTHER EUROPE 7.6	ASIA 4.0	AFR. 2.5

N. AMERICA — EUROPE

SWINE

SWINE Each dot represents 500,000 head

Swine World Total—637,955,000 head—Av. 1968–71

0	10	20	30	40	50	60	70	80	90	100%
CHINA 34.3%	OTHER ASIA 7.4	BRAZIL 10.3	OTH. S.A. 2.5	UNITED STATES 10.0	OTHER N.AM. 4.1	SOVIET UNION 9.1	W. GER. 3.1	POL. 2.2	OTHER EUROPE 15.3	ALL OTH. 1.7

ASIA — S.AM. — N.AM. — EUROPE

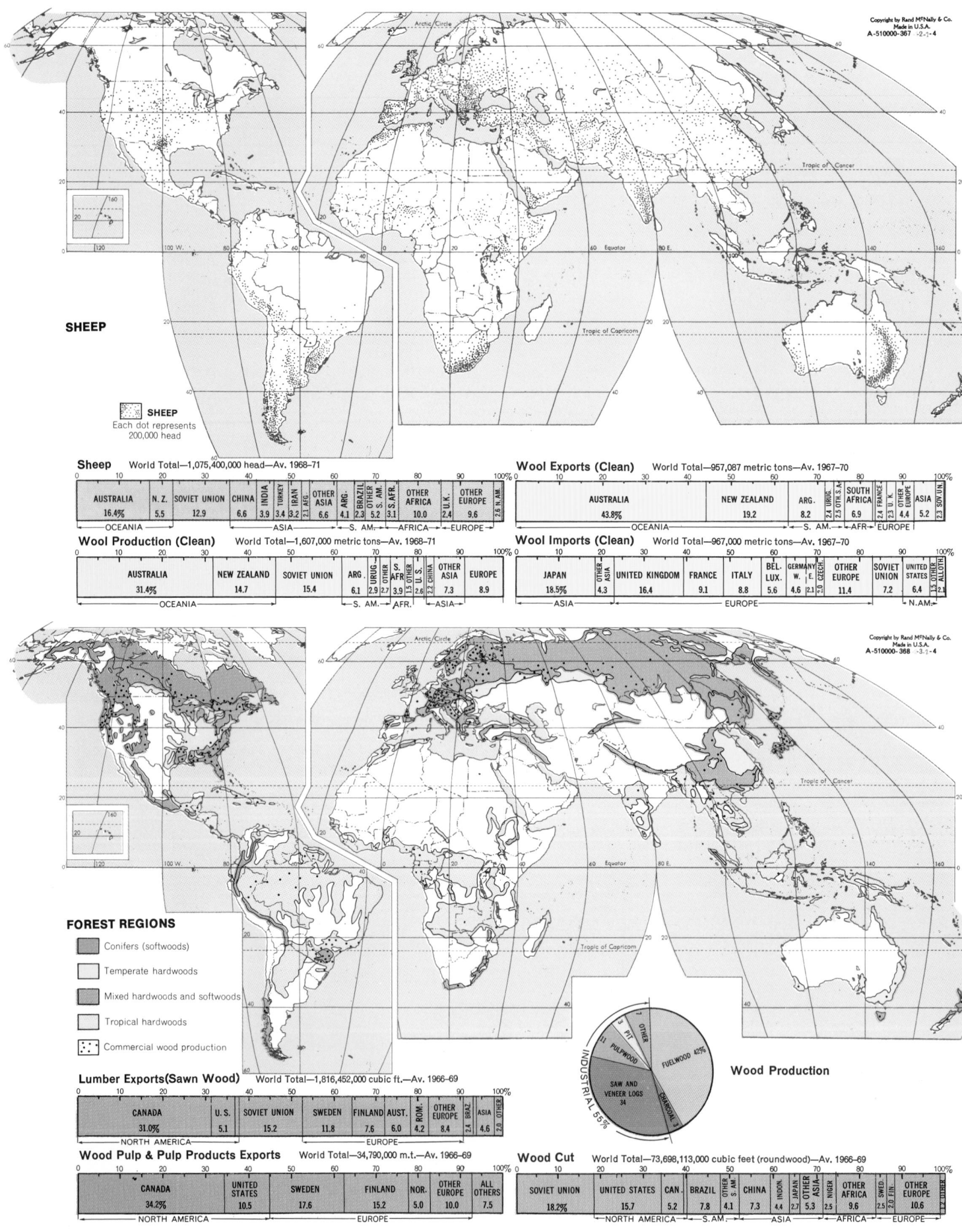

Copyright by Rand McNally & Co.
Made in U.S.A.
A-510000-367 -2-1-4

SHEEP

SHEEP
Each dot represents
200,000 head

Sheep
World Total—1,075,400,000 head—Av. 1968–71

0	10	20	30	40	50	60	70	80	90	100%

| AUSTRALIA 16.4% | N.Z. 5.5 | SOVIET UNION 12.9 | CHINA 6.6 | INDIA 3.9 | TURKEY 3.4 | IRAN 3.2 | ARG. 2.1 | OTHER ASIA 6.6 | ARG. 4.1 | BRAZIL 2.3 | OTHER S. AM. 5.2 | S. AFR. 3.1 | OTHER AFRICA 10.0 | U.K. 2.4 | OTHER EUROPE 9.6 | 2.6 N. AM. |

OCEANIA — ASIA — S. AM. — AFRICA — EUROPE

Wool Production (Clean)
World Total—1,607,000 metric tons—Av. 1968–71

| AUSTRALIA 31.4% | NEW ZEALAND 14.7 | SOVIET UNION 15.4 | ARG. 6.1 | URUG. 2.9 | OTHER 2.7 | S. AFR. 3.9 | OTHER 1.5 | U.S. 2.6 | CHINA 2.2 | OTHER ASIA 7.3 | EUROPE 8.9 |

OCEANIA — S. AM. — AFR. — ASIA — EUROPE

Wool Exports (Clean)
World Total—957,087 metric tons—Av. 1967–70

| AUSTRALIA 43.8% | NEW ZEALAND 19.2 | ARG. 8.2 | URUG. 2.4 | OTH. S.A. 2.5 | SOUTH AFRICA 6.9 | FRANCE 2.4 | U.K. 2.3 | OTHER EUROPE 4.4 | ASIA 5.2 | SOV. UN. 2.3 |

OCEANIA — S. AM. — AFR. — EUROPE

Wool Imports (Clean)
World Total—967,000 metric tons—Av. 1967–70

| JAPAN 18.5% | OTHER ASIA 4.3 | UNITED KINGDOM 16.4 | FRANCE 9.1 | ITALY 8.8 | BEL. LUX. 5.6 | GERMANY W. E. 4.6 | CZECH. 2.1 | OTHER EUROPE 11.4 | SOVIET UNION 7.2 | UNITED STATES 6.4 | OTHER 1.5 | ALL OTH. 2.1 |

ASIA — EUROPE — N. AM.

Copyright by Rand McNally & Co.
Made in U.S.A.
A-510000-368 -3-1-4

FOREST REGIONS

- Conifers (softwoods)
- Temperate hardwoods
- Mixed hardwoods and softwoods
- Tropical hardwoods
- Commercial wood production

Lumber Exports (Sawn Wood)
World Total—1,816,452,000 cubic ft.—Av. 1966–69

| CANADA 31.0% | U.S. 5.1 | SOVIET UNION 15.2 | SWEDEN 11.8 | FINLAND 7.6 | AUST. 6.0 | ROM. 4.2 | OTHER EUROPE 8.4 | BRAZ. 2.4 | ASIA 4.6 | OTHER 2.0 |

NORTH AMERICA — EUROPE

Wood Pulp & Pulp Products Exports
World Total—34,790,000 m.t.—Av. 1966–69

| CANADA 34.2% | UNITED STATES 10.5 | SWEDEN 17.6 | FINLAND 15.2 | NOR. 5.0 | OTHER EUROPE 10.0 | ALL OTHERS 7.5 |

NORTH AMERICA — EUROPE

Wood Production

(pie chart)
INDUSTRIAL 55%
FUELWOOD 42%
SAW AND VENEER LOGS 34
PULPWOOD 11
PIT 4
OTHER
CHARCOAL 3

Wood Cut
World Total—73,698,113,000 cubic feet (roundwood)—Av. 1966–69

| SOVIET UNION 18.2% | UNITED STATES 15.7 | CAN. 5.2 | BRAZIL 7.8 | OTHER S. AM. 4.1 | CHINA 7.3 | INDON. 4.4 | JAPAN 2.7 | OTHER ASIA 5.3 | NIGER 2.5 | OTHER AFRICA 9.6 | SWED. 2.5 | FIN. 2.0 | OTHER EUROPE 10.6 | OTHER 1.7 |

NORTH AMERICA — S. AM. — ASIA — AFRICA — EUROPE

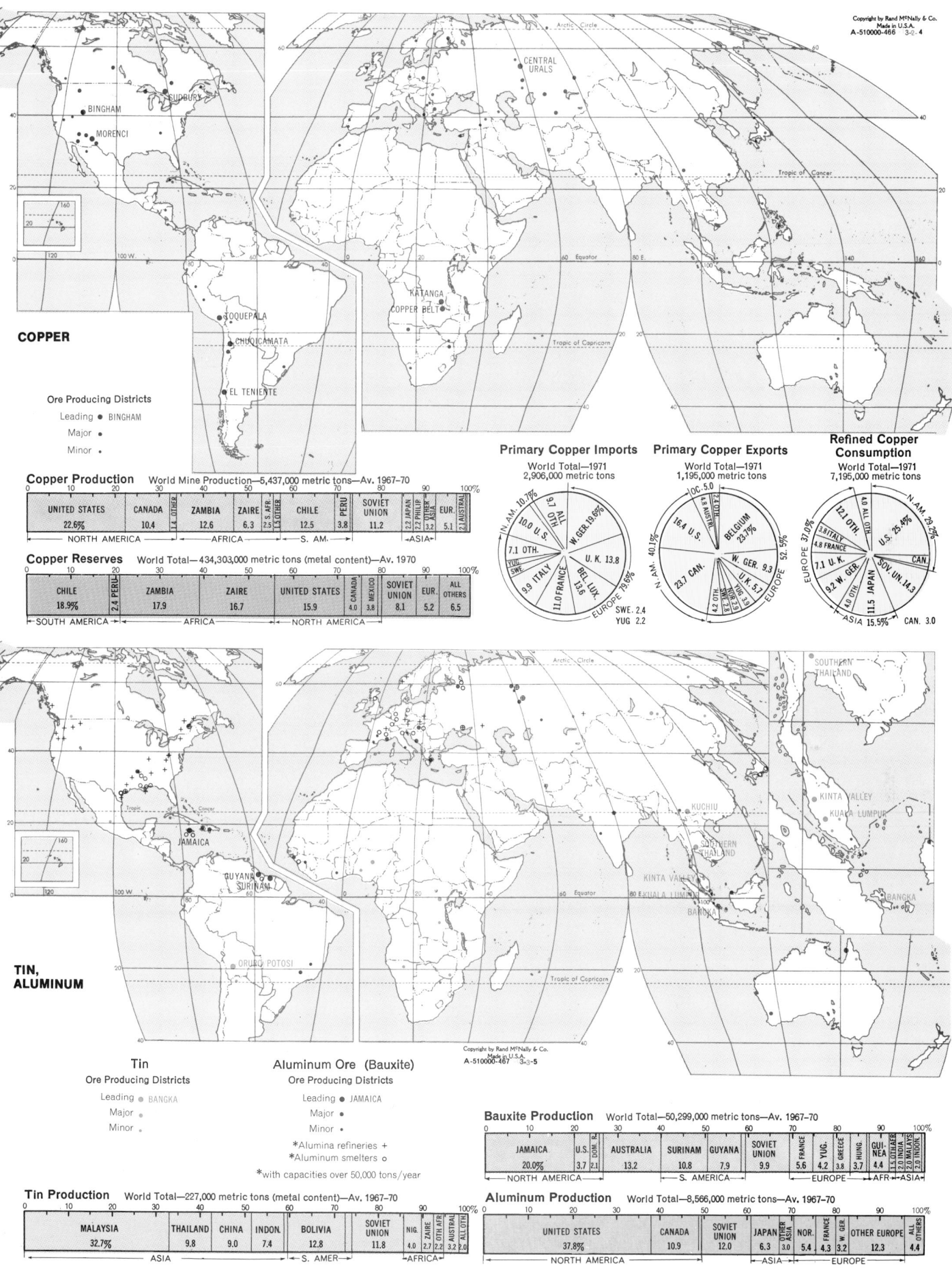

COPPER

Ore Producing Districts

Leading ● BINGHAM

Major ●

Minor ·

Copper Production   World Mine Production—5,437,000 metric tons—Av. 1967–70

UNITED STATES 22.6%	CANADA 10.4	1.4 OTHER	ZAMBIA 12.6	ZAIRE 6.3	2.5 S.AFR	1.3 S.OTHER	CHILE 12.5	PERU 3.8	SOVIET UNION 11.2	2.2 JAPAN	2.2 PHILIP	OTHER ASIA 3.2	EUR. 5.1	2.1 AUSTRAL

NORTH AMERICA — AFRICA — S. AM. — ASIA

Copper Reserves   World Total—434,303,000 metric tons (metal content)—Av. 1970

CHILE 18.9%	2.4 PERU	ZAMBIA 17.9	ZAIRE 16.7	UNITED STATES 15.9	CANADA 4.0	MEXICO 3.8	SOVIET UNION 8.1	EUR. 5.2	ALL OTHERS 6.5

SOUTH AMERICA — AFRICA — NORTH AMERICA

Primary Copper Imports
World Total—1971
2,906,000 metric tons
N. AM. 10.7%, 10.0 U.S., 7.1 OTH., YUG, SWE, 9.9 ITALY, 11.0 FRANCE, BEL. LUX. 13.6, U.K. 13.8, W. GER. 19.6%, ALL OTH 9.7, EUROPE 79.5%, SWE 2.4, YUG 2.2

Primary Copper Exports
World Total—1971
1,195,000 metric tons
OC. 5.0, 4.8 AUSTRAL, 2.0 OTH, 16.4 U.S., 23.7 CAN., N. AM. 40.1%, 4.2 OTH, YUG 2.9, U.K. 5.7, W. GER. 9.3, BELGIUM 23.7%, EUROPE 52.5%

Refined Copper Consumption
World Total—1971
7,195,000 metric tons
N. AM. 29.2%, 4.0 ALL OTH, 12.1 OTH, 3.8 ITALY, 4.8 FRANCE, 7.1 U.K., 9.2 W. GER., EUROPE 37.0%, U.S. 25.4%, CAN. 3.0, SOV. UN. 14.3, JAPAN 11.5, 4.0 OTH, ASIA 15.5%

TIN, ALUMINUM

Tin
Ore Producing Districts

Leading ● BANGKA

Major ●

Minor ·

Aluminum Ore (Bauxite)
Ore Producing Districts

Leading ● JAMAICA

Major ●

Minor ·

*Alumina refineries +

*Aluminum smelters o

*with capacities over 50,000 tons/year

Bauxite Production   World Total—50,299,000 metric tons—Av. 1967–70

JAMAICA 20.0%	U.S. 3.7	2.1 DOM. R.	AUSTRALIA 13.2	SURINAM 10.8	GUYANA 7.9	SOVIET UNION 9.9	FRANCE 5.6	YUG. 4.2	GREECE 3.8	HUNG. 3.7	GUINEA 4.4	1.5 OTH AFR	2.0 INDIA	2.0 MALAYS	2.0 INDON

NORTH AMERICA — S. AMERICA — EUROPE — AFR — ASIA

Tin Production   World Total—227,000 metric tons (metal content)—Av. 1967–70

MALAYSIA 32.7%	THAILAND 9.8	CHINA 9.0	INDON. 7.4	BOLIVIA 12.8	SOVIET UNION 11.8	NIG. 4.0	ZAIRE 2.7	OTH AFR 2.2	AUSTRAL 3.2	ALL OTH 2.0

ASIA — S. AMER — AFRICA

Aluminum Production   World Total—8,566,000 metric tons—Av. 1967–70

UNITED STATES 37.8%	CANADA 10.9	SOVIET UNION 12.0	JAPAN 6.3	OTHER ASIA 3.0	NOR. 5.4	FRANCE 4.3	W. GER. 3.2	OTHER EUROPE 12.3	ALL OTHERS 4.4

NORTH AMERICA — ASIA — EUROPE

40

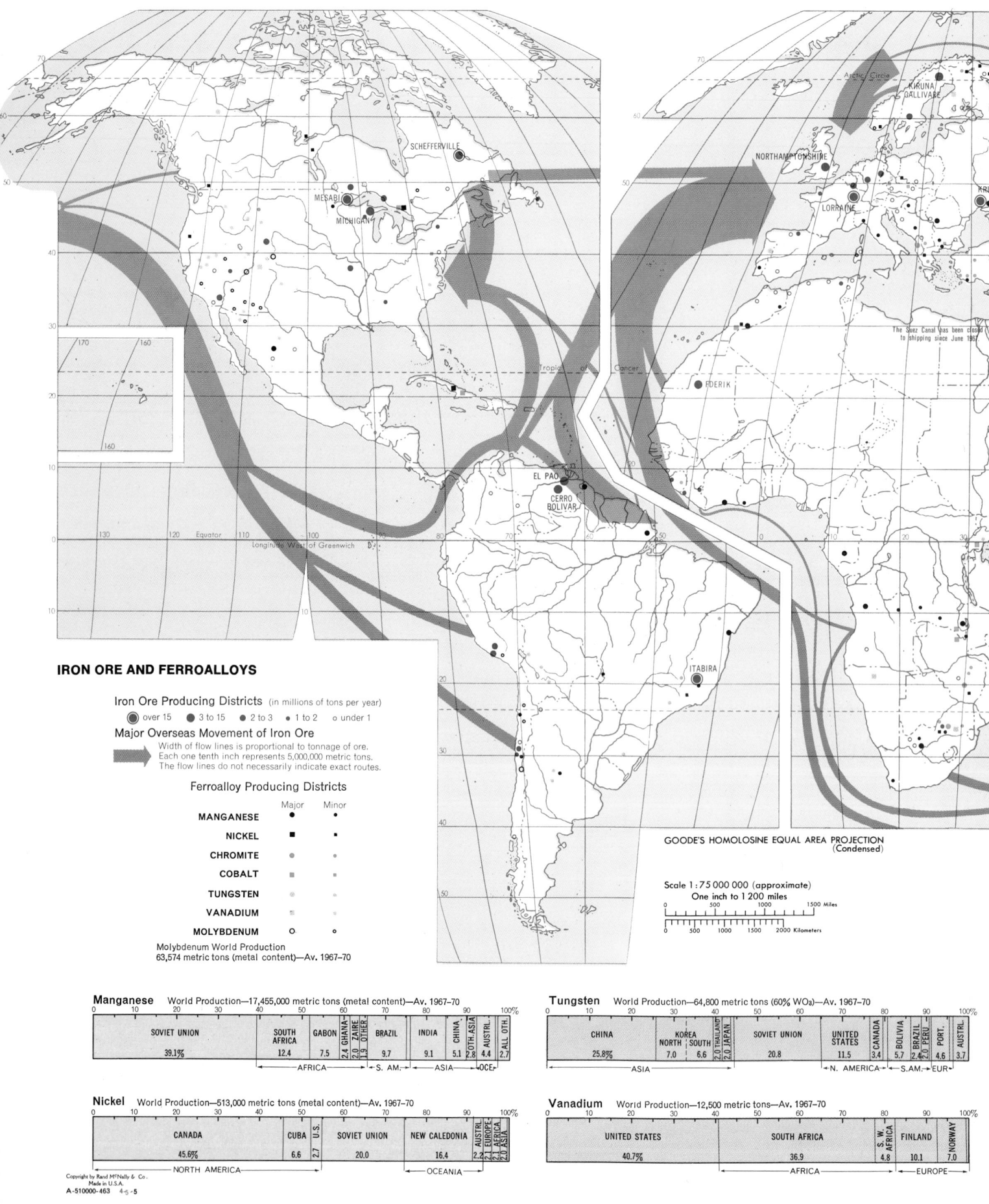

IRON ORE AND FERROALLOYS

Iron Ore Producing Districts (in millions of tons per year)
◉ over 15   ● 3 to 15   ● 2 to 3   ● 1 to 2   ○ under 1

Major Overseas Movement of Iron Ore

Width of flow lines is proportional to tonnage of ore.
Each one tenth inch represents 5,000,000 metric tons.
The flow lines do not necessarily indicate exact routes.

Ferroalloy Producing Districts

	Major	Minor
MANGANESE	●	•
NICKEL	■	▪
CHROMITE	●	•
COBALT	■	▪
TUNGSTEN	●	•
VANADIUM	■	▪
MOLYBDENUM	○	○

Molybdenum World Production
63,574 metric tons (metal content)—Av. 1967–70

GOODE'S HOMOLOSINE EQUAL AREA PROJECTION
(Condensed)

Scale 1:75 000 000 (approximate)
One inch to 1 200 miles

The Suez Canal has been closed
to shipping since June 1967

Manganese World Production—17,455,000 metric tons (metal content)—Av. 1967–70

SOVIET UNION	SOUTH AFRICA	GABON	GHANA	ZAIRE	OTHER	BRAZIL	INDIA	CHINA	OTH. ASIA	AUSTRL.	ALL OTH.
39.1%	12.4	7.5	2.4	2.0	1.9	9.7	9.1	5.1	2.8	4.4	2.7

AFRICA — S. AM. — ASIA — OCE.

Tungsten World Production—64,800 metric tons (60% WO₃)—Av. 1967–70

CHINA	KOREA NORTH	SOUTH	THAILAND	JAPAN	SOVIET UNION	UNITED STATES	CANADA	BOLIVIA	BRAZIL	PERU	PORT.	AUSTRL.
25.8%	7.0	6.6	2.0	2.0	20.8	11.5	3.4	5.7	2.0	2.0	4.6	3.7

ASIA — N. AMERICA — S.AM. — EUR.

Nickel World Production—513,000 metric tons (metal content)—Av. 1967–70

CANADA	CUBA	U.S.	SOVIET UNION	NEW CALEDONIA	AUSTRL.	EUROPE	AFRICA	ASIA
45.6%	6.6	2.7	20.0	16.4	2.2	2.1	2.0	

NORTH AMERICA — OCEANIA

Vanadium World Production—12,500 metric tons—Av. 1967–70

UNITED STATES	SOUTH AFRICA	S. W. AFRICA	FINLAND	NORWAY
40.7%	36.9	4.8	10.1	7.0

AFRICA — EUROPE

Copyright by Rand McNally & Co.
Made in U.S.A.
A-510000-463   4-5-5

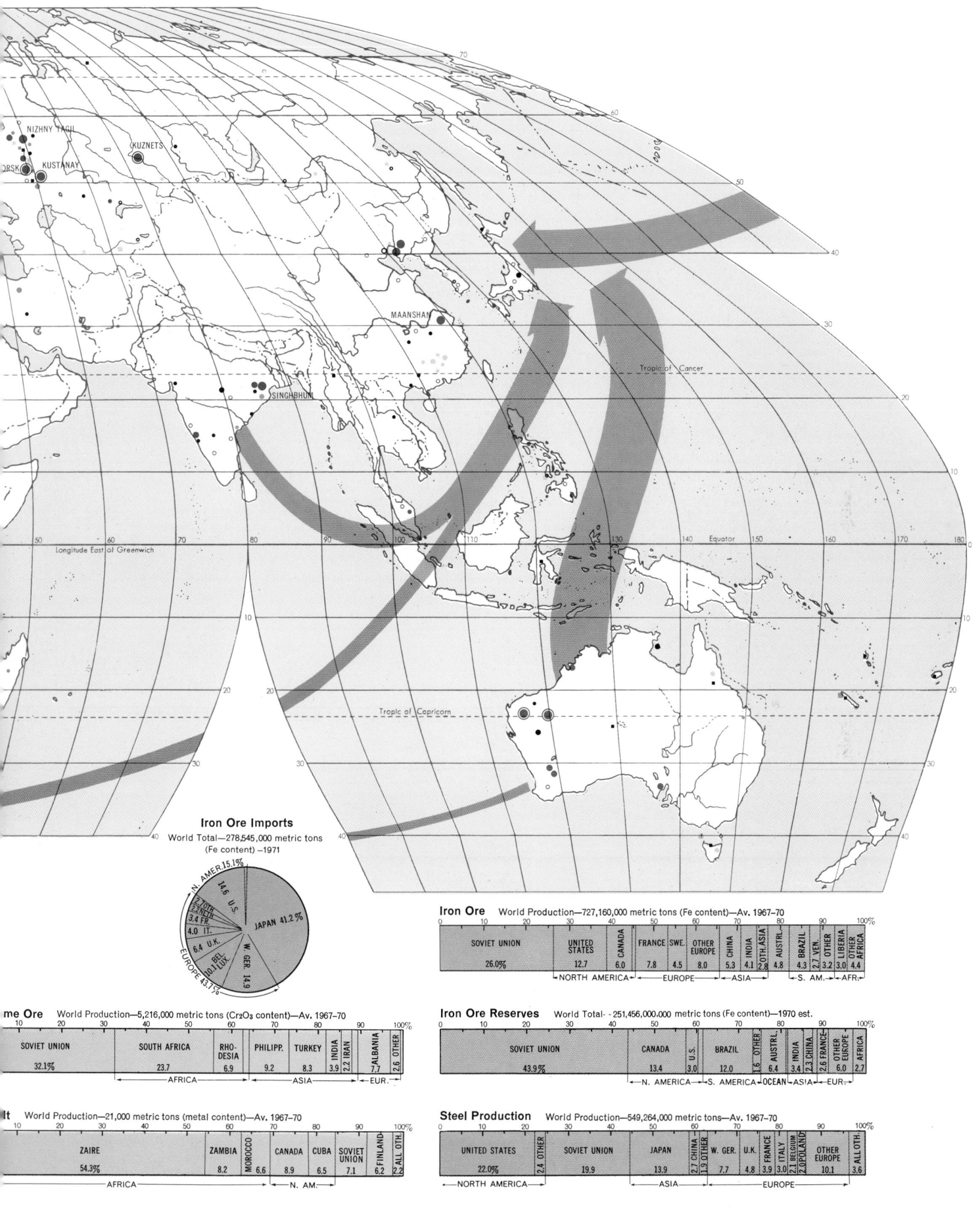

NIZHNY TAGIL

KUZNETS

ORSK KUSTANAY

MAANSHAN

SINGHBHUM

Tropic of Cancer

Equator

Longitude East of Greenwich

Tropic of Capricorn

Iron Ore Imports
World Total—278,545,000 metric tons
(Fe content) —1971

N. AMER.15.1%
14.6 U.S.
2.7 OTH.
5.2 NETH.
3.4 FR.
4.0 IT.
6.4 U.K.
10.1 LUX.
BEL.
EUROPE 43.7%
W. GER. 14.9
JAPAN 41.2%

Iron Ore
World Production—727,160,000 metric tons (Fe content)—Av. 1967-70

0	10	20	30	40	50	60	70	80	90						100%

SOVIET UNION	UNITED STATES	CANADA	FRANCE	SWE.	OTHER EUROPE	CHINA	INDIA	OTH.ASIA	AUSTRL.	BRAZIL	VEN.	OTHER	LIBERIA	OTHER AFRICA
26.0%	12.7	6.0	7.8	4.5	8.0	5.3	4.1	2.8	4.8	4.3	2.7	3.2	3.0	4.4

└NORTH AMERICA┘ └───EUROPE───┘ └────ASIA────┘ └S. AM.┘└AFR.┘

me Ore
World Production—5,216,000 metric tons (Cr₂O₃ content)—Av. 1967-70

10	20	30	40	50	60	70	80	90		100%

SOVIET UNION	SOUTH AFRICA	RHO-DESIA	PHILIPP.	TURKEY	INDIA	IRAN	ALBANIA	OTHER
32.1%	23.7	6.9	9.2	8.3	3.9	2.2	7.7	2.6

└───AFRICA───┘ └───ASIA───┘ └EUR.┘

Iron Ore Reserves
World Total- - 251,456,000,000 metric tons (Fe content)—1970 est.

0	10	20	30	40	50	60	70	80	90	100%

SOVIET UNION	CANADA	U.S.	BRAZIL	OTHER	AUSTRL.	INDIA	CHINA	FRANCE	OTHER EUROPE	AFRICA
43.9%	13.4	3.0	12.0	1.5	6.4	3.4	2.6		6.0	2.7

└N. AMERICA┘└S. AMERICA┘└OCEAN┘└ASIA┘└EUR.┘

lt
World Production—21,000 metric tons (metal content)—Av. 1967-70

10	20	30	40	50	60	70	80	90		100%

ZAIRE	ZAMBIA	MOROCCO	CANADA	CUBA	SOVIET UNION	FINLAND	ALL OTH.
54.3%	8.2	6.6	8.9	6.5	7.1	6.2	2.2

└───AFRICA───┘ └N. AM.┘

Steel Production
World Production—549,264,000 metric tons—Av. 1967-70

0	10	20	30	40	50	60	70	80	90	100%

UNITED STATES	OTHER	SOVIET UNION	JAPAN	CHINA	W. GER.	U.K.	FRANCE	ITALY	BELGIUM	POLAND	OTHER EUROPE	ALL OTH.
22.0%	2.4	19.9	13.9	2.7 1.9	7.7	4.8	3.9	3.0	2.1	2.0	10.1	3.6

└─NORTH AMERICA─┘ └────ASIA────┘ └───────EUROPE───────┘

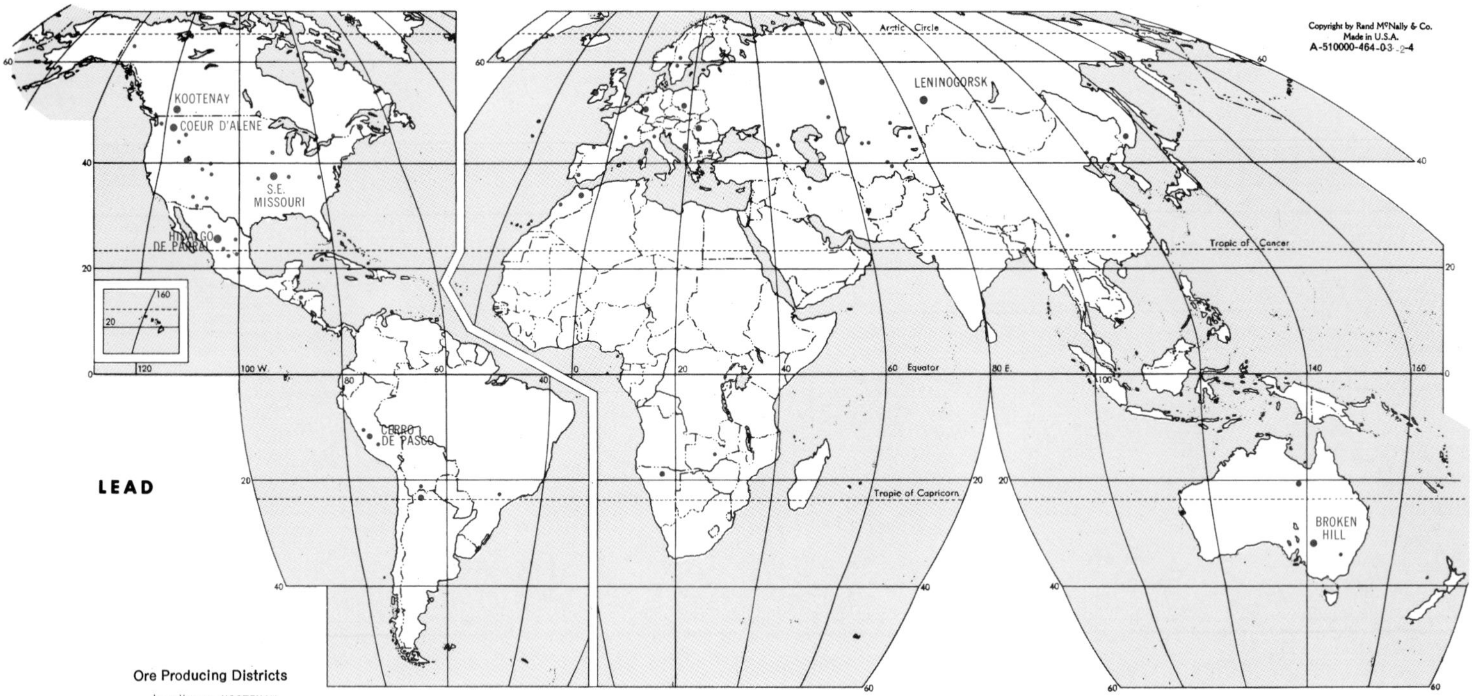

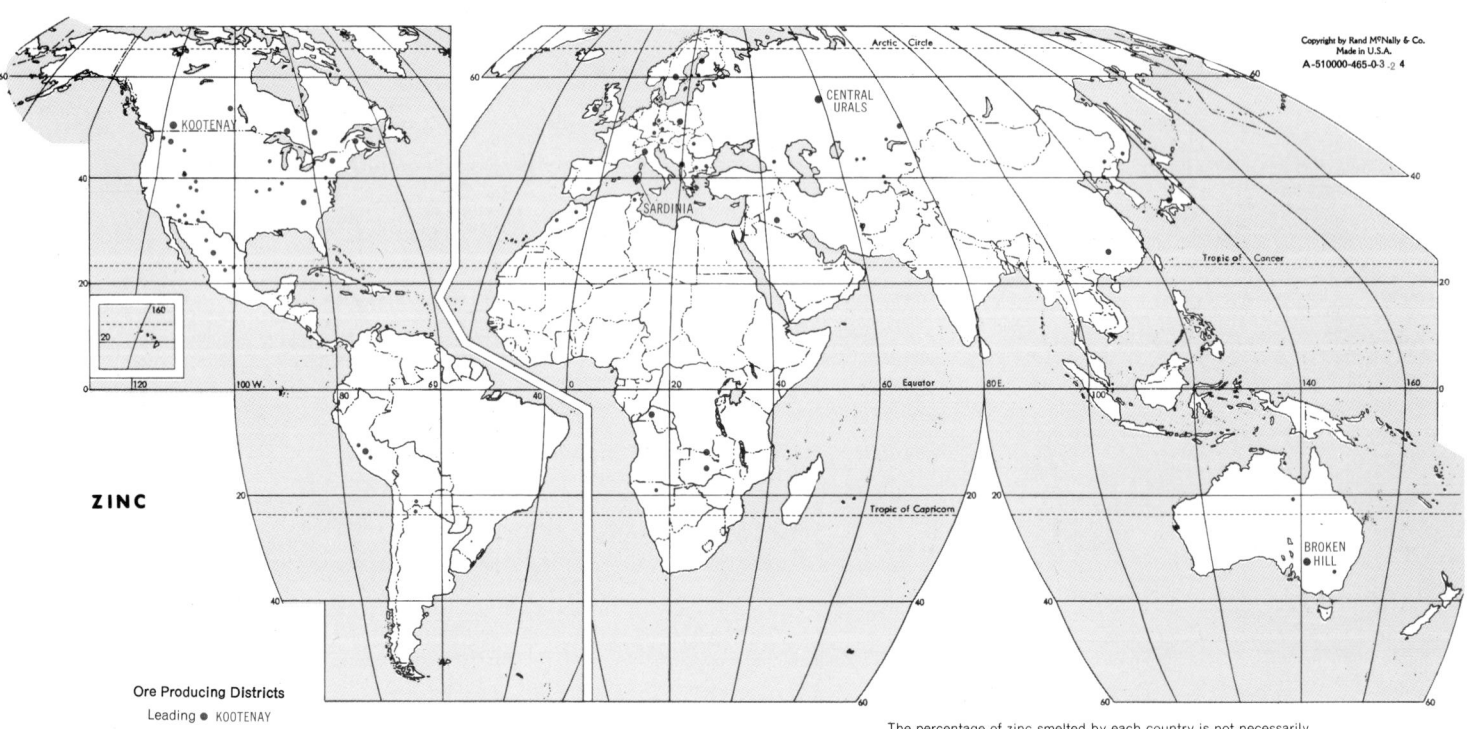

LEAD

Ore Producing Districts

Leading ● KOOTENAY

Major ●

Minor ·

The percentage of lead smelted by each country is not necessarily identical to its percentage of world lead ore production. Germany, an important smelter, imports over one half its lead ore, and Belgium imports nearly all of its lead ore. S. W. Africa and Morocco export most of their lead ore.

Lead Production World Mine Production—3,135,000 metric tons (metal content)—Av. 1967–70

0	10	20	30	40	50	60	70	80	90	100%

SOVIET UNION 13.5%	AUSTRALIA 13.3	UNITED STATES 12.8	CANADA 10.3	MEX. 5.6	PERU 5.0	YK 2.6	YUGO. 3.1	BULG. 3.1	SWE. 2.4	SPAIN 2.2	OTHER EUROPE 9.9	CHINA 3.1	N KOREA 2.7	JAPAN 2.0	OTHER 1.8	S.W.AFR 2.8	MOR. 2.2	OTHER 1.5

| NORTH AMERICA | S. AM | EUROPE | ASIA | AFR |

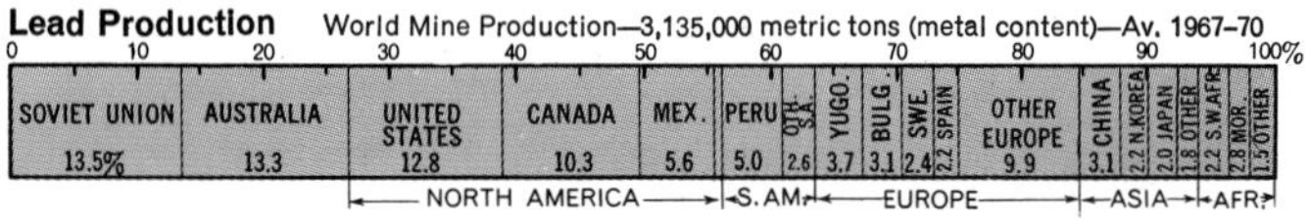

Lead Smelted World Production—3,100,000 metric tons—Av. 1967–70

0	10	20	30	40	50	60	70	80	90	100%

UNITED STATES 15.8%	CAN. 5.7	MEX. 5.2	SOVIET UNION 14.3	AUSTRALIA 10.3	JAPAN 5.7	CHINA 2.3	OTHER	W. GER. 4.0	FRANCE 3.6	YUGO 3.3	BELG. 3.1	BULG. 3.1	SPAIN 2.2	OTHER EUROPE 9.5	PERU 2.8	OTHER 1.7	S.W.AFR. 2.3	OTHER 2.0

| NORTH AMERICA | ASIA | EUROPE | S.A. | AFR. |

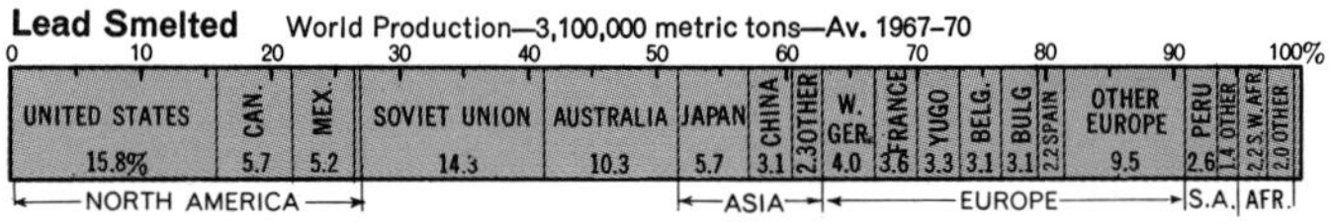

ZINC

Ore Producing Districts

Leading ● KOOTENAY

Major ●

Minor ·

The percentage of zinc smelted by each country is not necessarily identical to its percentage of world zinc ore production. Belgium smelts zinc from Australia and other countries but produces little zinc ore. On the other hand, Algeria, Morocco, S. W. Africa and Burma export zinc ore but smelt little or none.

Zinc Production World Mine Production—5,180,000 metric tons (metal content)—Av. 1967–70

0	10	20	30	40	50	60	70	80	90	100%

CANADA 22.9%	UNITED STATES 9.5	MEX. 4.8	SOVIET UNION 11.1	AUSTRL. 8.8	PERU 5.9	JAPAN 5.2	N. KOR. 2.4	OTHER ASIA 3.7	POL. 3.3	W.GER. 2.5	OTHER EUROPE 11.1	ZAIRE 2.0	OTH AFR 3.0

| NORTH AMERICA | S.AM | ASIA | EUROPE | AFR |

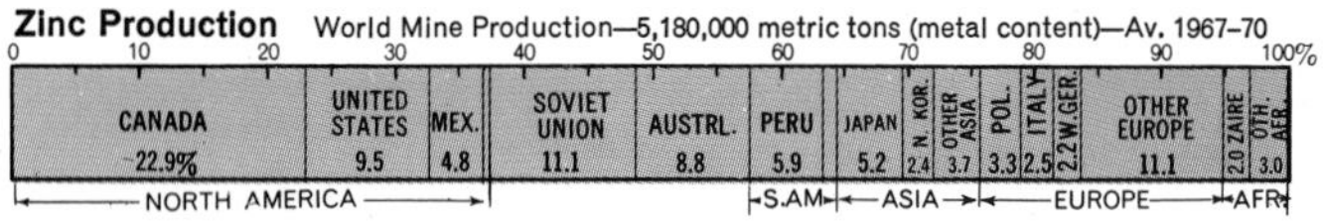

Zinc Smelted World Production—4,668,000 metric tons—Av. 1967–70

0	10	20	30	40	50	60	70	80	90	100%

UNITED STATES 18.9%	CANADA 8.6	JAPAN 13.5	OTHER ASIA 4.0	SOVIET UNION 12.5	BELG. 5.2	FR 4.7	POL. 4.4	U.K. 2.9	W.GER. 2.9	ITALY 2.5	OTHER EUROPE 8.6	AUSTRL. 4.9	AFR. 2.7	S.AM 2.0

| NORTH AMERICA | ASIA | EUROPE | |

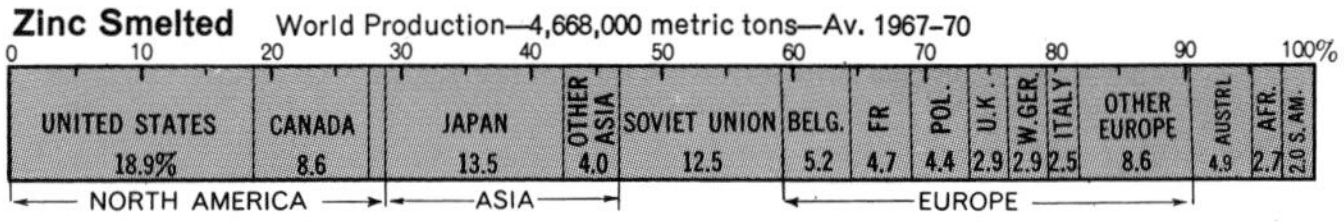

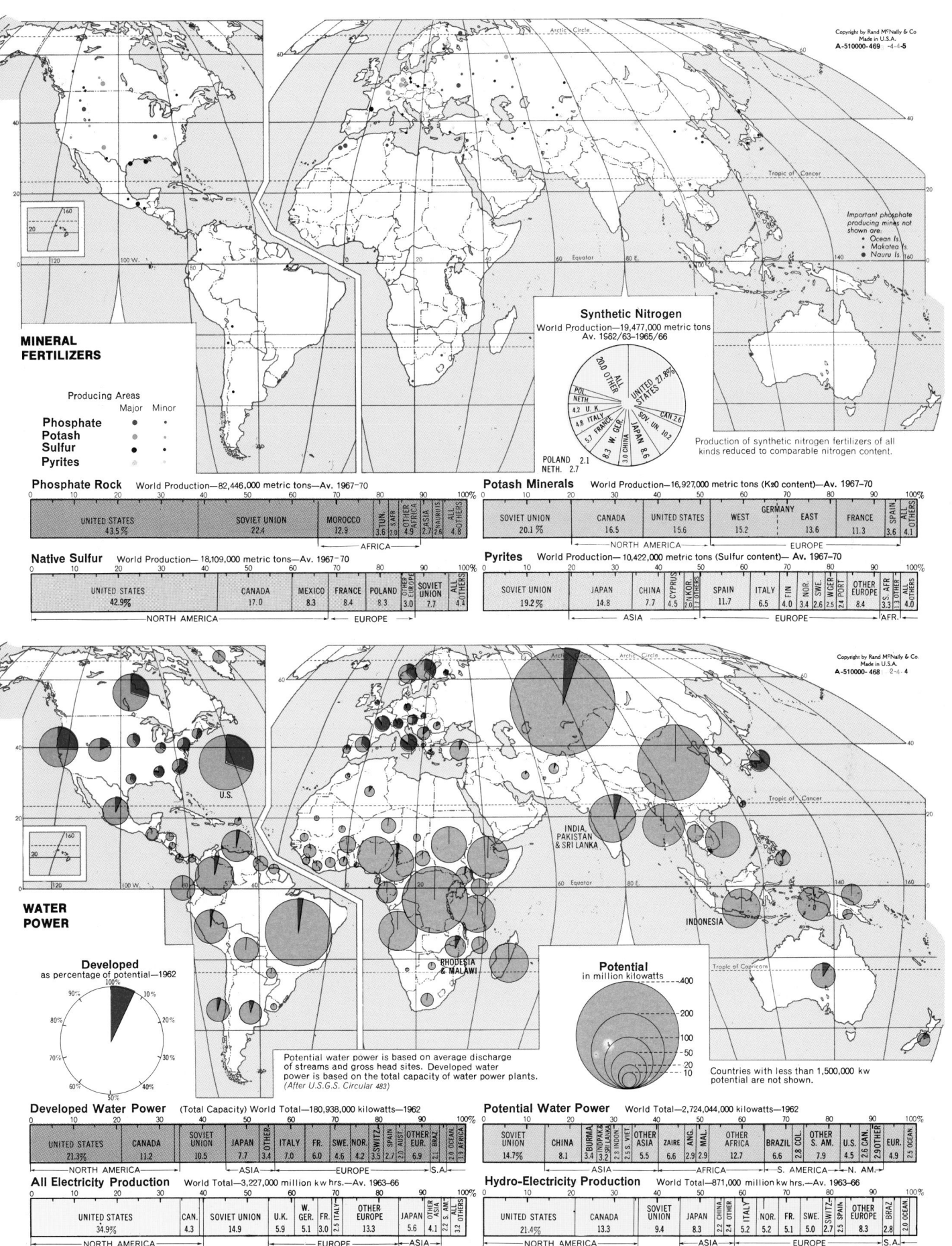

Important phosphate
producing mines not
shown are:
• Ocean Is.
• Makatea Is.
● Nauru Is.

MINERAL FERTILIZERS

Producing Areas

	Major	Minor
Phosphate	●	•
Potash	●	•
Sulfur	●	•
Pyrites	●	•

Synthetic Nitrogen
World Production—19,477,000 metric tons
Av. 1962/63–1965/66

ALL OTHER 20.0
UNITED STATES 27.8%
CAN. 2.6
SOV. UN. 10.2
JAPAN 8.6
POL. NETH. 4.2 U.K.
4.8 ITALY
5.7 FRANCE
W. GER. 8.3 CHINA 3.0
POLAND 2.1
NETH. 2.7

Production of synthetic nitrogen fertilizers of all
kinds reduced to comparable nitrogen content.

Phosphate Rock   World Production—82,446,000 metric tons—Av. 1967–70

0	10	20	30	40	50	60	70	80	90	100%
UNITED STATES 43.5%				SOVIET UNION 22.4			MOROCCO 12.9	TUN. 3.6	S.AFR. 2.0	OTHER AFRICA 4.9	ASIA 2.7	NAURU IS. 2.0	ALL OTHERS 4.8

— AFRICA —

Potash Minerals   World Production—16,927,000 metric tons (K₂O content)—Av. 1967–70

0	10	20	30	40	50	60	70	80	90	100%
SOVIET UNION 20.1%		CANADA 16.5		UNITED STATES 15.6		WEST GERMANY 15.2	EAST 13.6	FRANCE 11.3	SPAIN 3.6	ALL OTHERS 4.1

— NORTH AMERICA — — EUROPE —

Native Sulfur   World Production—18,109,000 metric tons—Av. 1967–70

0	10	20	30	40	50	60	70	80	90	100%
UNITED STATES 42.9%				CANADA 17.0		MEXICO 8.3	FRANCE 8.4	POLAND 8.3	OTHER EUROPE 3.0	SOVIET UNION 7.7	ALL OTHERS 4.4

— NORTH AMERICA — — EUROPE —

Pyrites   World Production—10,422,000 metric tons (Sulfur content)— Av. 1967–70

0	10	20	30	40	50	60	70	80	90	100%
SOVIET UNION 19.2%		JAPAN 14.8		CHINA 7.7	CYPRUS 4.5	N.KOR. 2.0	OTHERS	SPAIN 11.7	ITALY 6.5	FIN. 4.0	NOR. 3.4	SWE. 2.6	W.GER. 2.4	PORT.	OTHER EUROPE 8.4	S. AFR. 3.3	OTHER 1.3	ALL OTHERS 4.0

— ASIA — — EUROPE — AFR.

U.S.

INDIA,
PAKISTAN
& SRI LANKA

INDONESIA

WATER POWER

Developed
as percentage of potential—1962

100%
90% — 10%
80% — 20%
70% — 30%
60% — 40%
50%

RHODESIA
& MALAWI

Potential
in million kilowatts

— 400
— 200
— 100
— 50
— 20
— 10

Countries with less than 1,500,000 kw
potential are not shown.

Potential water power is based on average discharge
of streams and gross head sites. Developed water
power is based on the total capacity of water power plants.
(After U.S.G.S. Circular 483)

Developed Water Power   (Total Capacity) World Total—180,938,000 kilowatts—1962

0	10	20	30	40	50	60	70	80	90	100%
UNITED STATES 21.3%		CANADA 11.2	SOVIET UNION 10.5	JAPAN 7.7	OTHER	ITALY 7.0	FR. 6.0	SWE. 4.6	NOR. 4.2	SWITZ. 3.5	SPAIN 2.7	AUST. 2.1	OTHER EUR. 6.9	BRAZ.	S.A.	ALL AFRICA 1.3

— NORTH AMERICA — — ASIA — — EUROPE — S.A.

Potential Water Power   World Total—2,724,044,000 kilowatts—1962

0	10	20	30	40	50	60	70	80	90	100%
SOVIET UNION 14.7%		CHINA 8.1	BURMA 3.4	INDPAK. 3.2	S.LANKA	INDON.	2.5 VIET	OTHER ASIA 5.5	ZAIRE 6.6	ANG. 2.9	MAL. 2.9	OTHER AFRICA 12.7	BRAZIL 6.6	COL. 2.8	OTHER S. AM. 7.9	U.S. 4.5	CAN. 2.6	OTHER 2.9	EUR. 4.9	OCEAN. 2.5

— ASIA — — AFRICA — — S. AMERICA — N. AM.

All Electricity Production   World Total—3,227,000 million kw hrs.—Av. 1963–66

0	10	20	30	40	50	60	70	80	90	100%
UNITED STATES 34.9%			CAN. 4.3	SOVIET UNION 14.9	U.K. 5.9	W. GER. 5.1	ITALY 2.5	OTHER EUROPE 13.3	JAPAN 5.6	OTHER ASIA 4.1	ALL OTHERS 3.2

— NORTH AMERICA — — EUROPE — — ASIA —

Hydro-Electricity Production   World Total—871,000 million kw hrs.—Av. 1963–66

0	10	20	30	40	50	60	70	80	90	100%
UNITED STATES 21.4%		CANADA 13.3	SOVIET UNION 9.4	JAPAN 8.3	CHINA 2.2	ITALY 2.4	NOR. 5.2	FR. 5.1	SWE. 5.0	SWITZ. 2.5	SPAIN	OTHER EUROPE 8.3	BRAZ. 2.8	OCEAN. 2.0

— NORTH AMERICA — — ASIA — — EUROPE — S.A.

Arctic Circle

60

50

INTERIOR

APPALACHIAN

40

SILESIA

50

EAST TEXAS

GULF

30

The Suez Canal has been closed to all shipping since June 196

Tropic of Cancer

TAMPICO

20

MARACAIBO

MINERAL FUELS

100 90 80 70 60 20

10

Petroleum

▰ Major producing area

● Major field

○ Minor field

(Fields producing less than 200,000 barrels annually are not shown)

✛ Natural Gas Major field

⤸ Major Middle East and African pipe lines

Coal and Lignite

▰ Major bituminous coal deposit

≣ Minor bituminous coal deposit

▱ Lignite deposit

◣ Major anthracite deposit

‒ Minor anthracite deposit

Movement of Petroleum

➤ Width of flow lines is proportional to tonnage of oil. Each one tenth inch represents 60,000,000 metric tons. The flow lines do not necessarily indicate exact routes.

Scale 1:75 000 000 (approximate)
One inch to 1 200 miles

0 500 1000 1500 Miles

0 500 1000 1500 2000 Kilometers

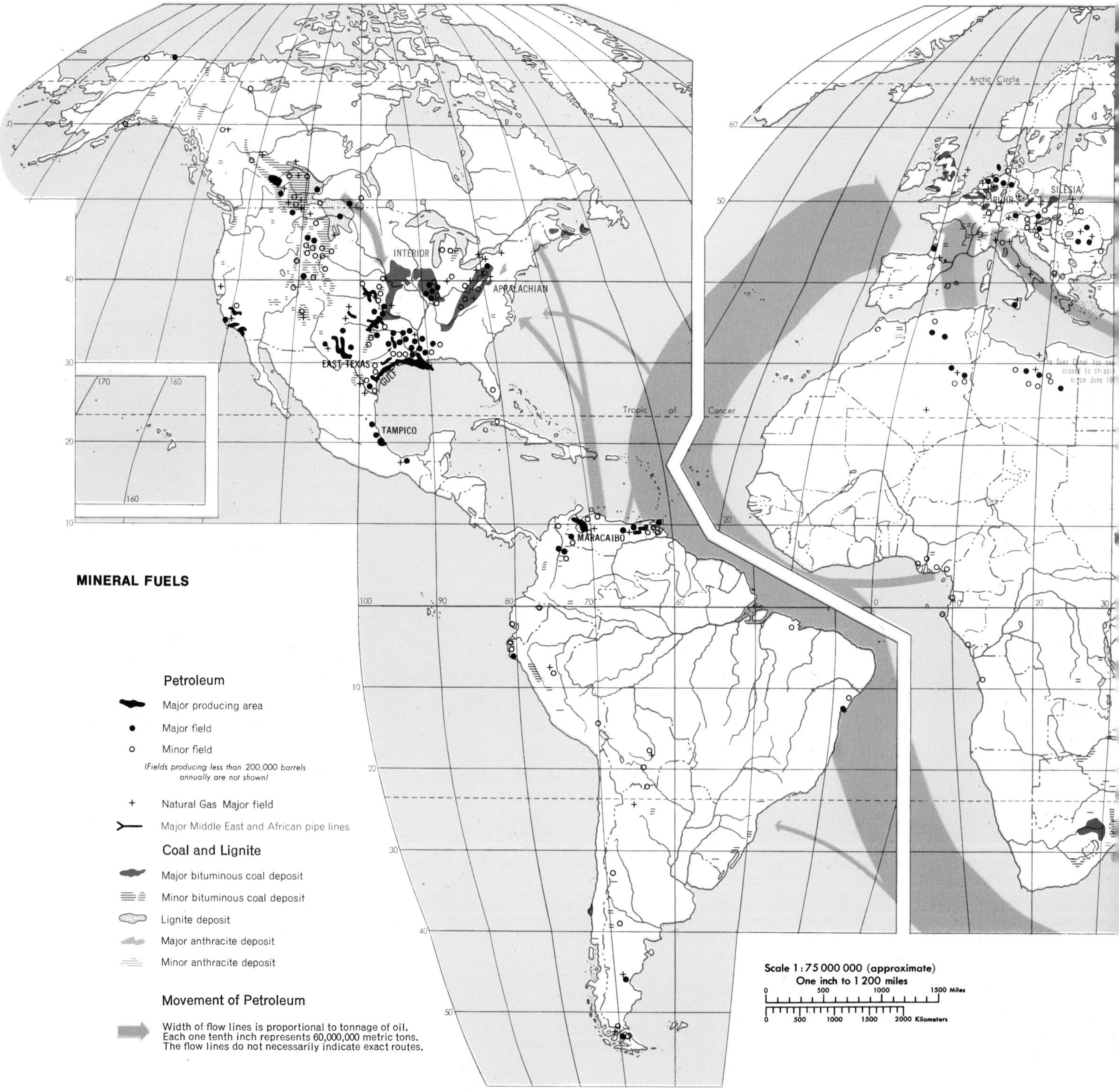

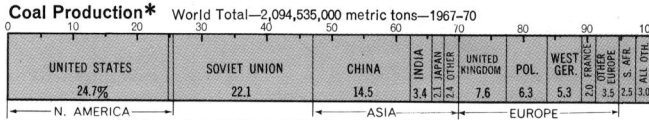

Coal Production* World Total—2,094,535,000 metric tons—1967-70

0	10	20	30	40	50	60	70	80	90	100%

| UNITED STATES 24.7% | SOVIET UNION 22.1 | CHINA 14.5 | INDIA 3.4 | JAPAN 2.1 | OTHER 2.4 | UNITED KINGDOM 7.6 | POL. 6.3 | WEST GER. 5.3 | FRANCE 2.0 | OTHER EUROPE | S. AFR. 3.5 | ALL OTH. 2.5 | 3.0 |

← N. AMERICA → ← ASIA → ← EUROPE →

*Bituminous and Anthracite Lignite World Total—749,975,000 metric tons, 19% of which was produced in the Soviet Union.

Coal Reserves* World Total—2,320,000,000,000 metric tons—1971

0	10	20	30	40	50	60	70	80	90	100%

| UNITED STATES 32.5% | OTHER 1.9 | SOVIET UNION 25.8 | CHINA 21.8 | OTHER 1.8 | GERMANY 6.2 | U.K. 3.7 | OTHER 3.1 | OTHERS 3.2 |

← NORTH AMERICA → ← ASIA → ← EUROPE →

**Including lignite and coke

Petroleum Production World Total—19,884,453,000 barrels—est. 1973

0	10	20	30	40	50	60	70	80	90	100

| UNITED STATES 17.0% | VEN. 6.1 | CANADA 3.3 | OTHER 3.2 | SOVIET UNION 15.0 | SAUDI ARABIA 13.3 | IRAN 10.7 | KUWAIT 5.8 | IRAQ 3.3 | ABU DH. 2.5 | INDONES 2.2 | OTHER ASIA 4.7 | LIBYA 4.2 | NIGERIA 2.0 | OTHERS |

← W. HEMISPHERE → ← ASIA → ← AFR. →

Proven Petroleum Reserves World Total—562,295,393,000 barrels—est. 1972

0	10	20	30	40	50	60	70	80	90	100

| U.S. 6.4% | VEN. 2.4 | OTHER 4.4 | SOVIET UNION 7.5 | SAUDI ARABIA 24.4 | KUWAIT 13.2 | IRAN 11.1 | IRAQ 5.9 | ABU DH. 3.2 | CHINA 2.2 | OTHER ASIA 5.1 | LIBYA 4.2 | NIGERIA 3.1 | ALL OTHER 2.1 |

← W. HEMIS. → ← ASIA → ← AFR. →

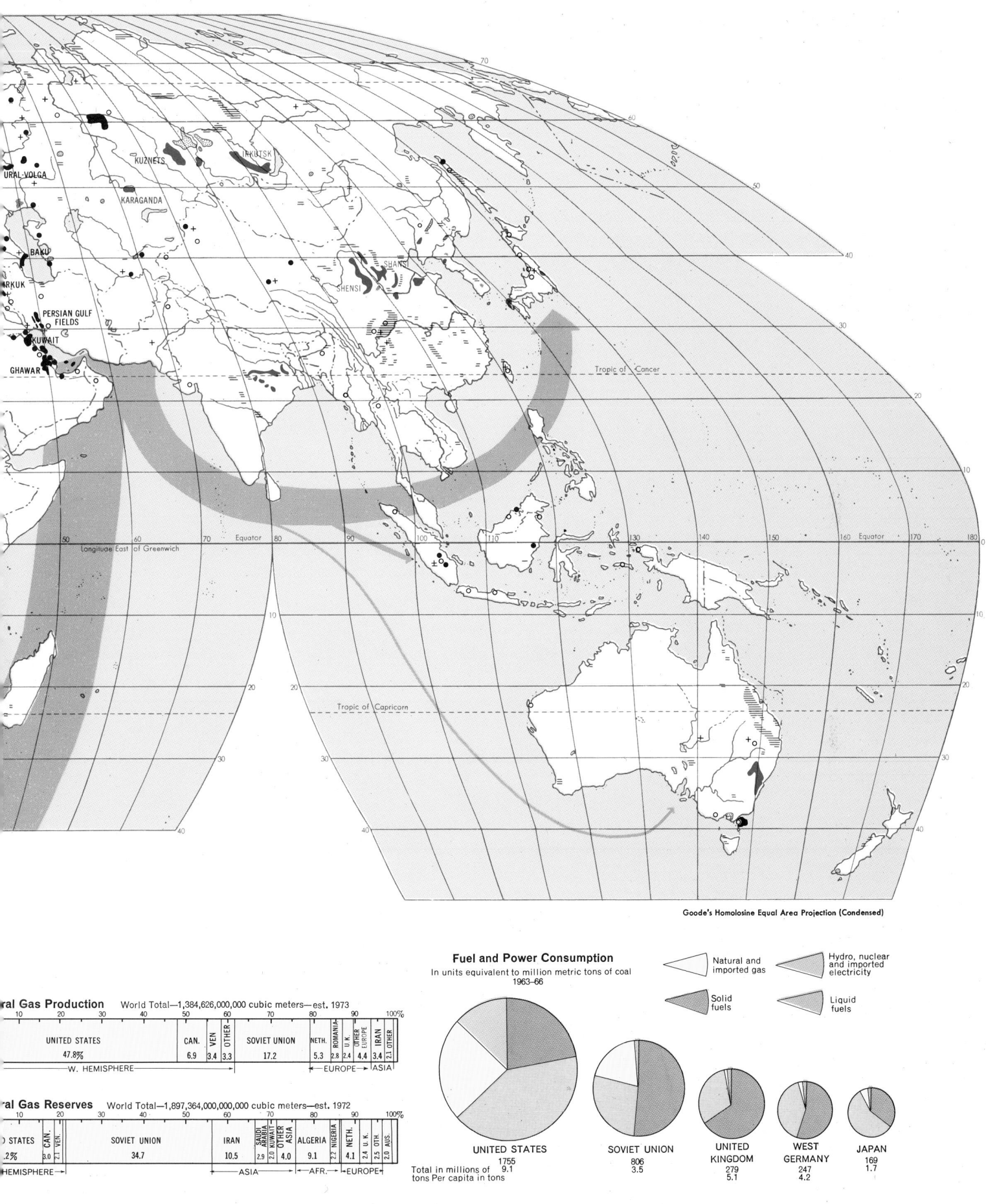

Goode's Homolosine Equal Area Projection (Condensed)

URAL-VOLGA
KUZNETS
KARAGANDA
IRKUTSK
BAKU
RKUK
PERSIAN GULF
FIELDS
KUWAIT
GHAWAR
SHENSI
SHANSI

Longitude East of Greenwich   Equator

Tropic of Cancer

Tropic of Capricorn

Equator

Fuel and Power Consumption
In units equivalent to million metric tons of coal
1963–66

Natural and imported gas

Hydro, nuclear and imported electricity

Solid fuels

Liquid fuels

UNITED STATES	SOVIET UNION	UNITED KINGDOM	WEST GERMANY	JAPAN
1755	806	279	247	169
9.1	3.5	5.1	4.2	1.7

Total in millions of tons   Per capita in tons

ral Gas Production
World Total—1,384,626,000,000 cubic meters—est. 1973

	10	20	30	40	50	60	70	80	90	100%

UNITED STATES 47.8%	CAN. 6.9	VEN 3.4	OTHER 3.3	SOVIET UNION 17.2	NETH. 5.3	ROMANIA 2.8	U.K. 2.4	OTHER EUROPE 4.4	IRAN 3.4	OTHER 2.1

|—————— W. HEMISPHERE ——————|————— EUROPE —————|— ASIA —|

ral Gas Reserves
World Total—1,897,364,000,000,000 cubic meters—est. 1972

	10	20	30	40	50	60	70	80	90	100%

STATES .2%	CAN. 3.0	VEN. 2.1	SOVIET UNION 34.7	IRAN 10.5	SAUDI ARABIA 2.9	KUWAIT 2.0	OTHER ASIA 4.0	ALGERIA 9.1	NIGERIA 2.2	NETH. 4.1	U.K. 2.4	OTH. 2.5	AUS. 2.0

| HEMISPHERE |———————— ASIA ————————|— AFR.—|— EUROPE —|

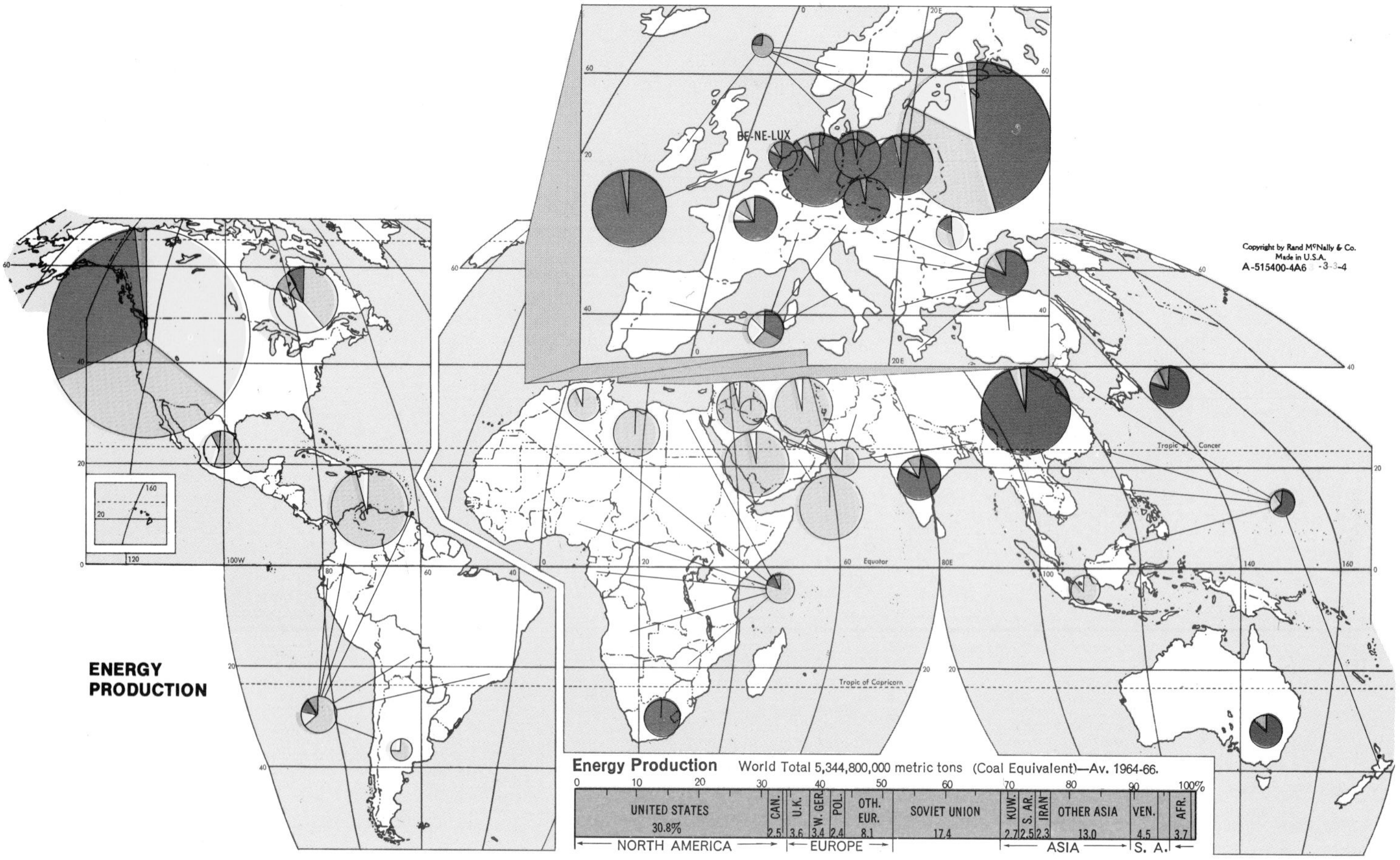

BE-NE-LUX

Copyright by Rand McNally & Co.
Made in U.S.A.
A-515400-4A6 -3--4

**ENERGY
PRODUCTION**

Tropic of Cancer

Equator

Tropic of Capricorn

Energy Production World Total 5,344,800,000 metric tons (Coal Equivalent)—Av. 1964-66.

0	10	20	30	40	50	60	70	80	90	100%

| UNITED STATES 30.8% | CAN. 2.5 | U.K. 3.6 | W. GER. 3.4 | POL. 2.4 | OTH. EUR. 8.1 | SOVIET UNION 17.4 | KUW. 2.7 | S. AR. 2.5 | IRAN 2.3 | OTHER ASIA 13.0 | VEN. 4.5 | AFR. 3.7 |

← NORTH AMERICA → ← EUROPE → ← ASIA → S. A.

Volume of Energy
in millions of metric tons
(Coal equivalent)

- 1,000
- 500
- 250
- 125
- 50
- 0-25

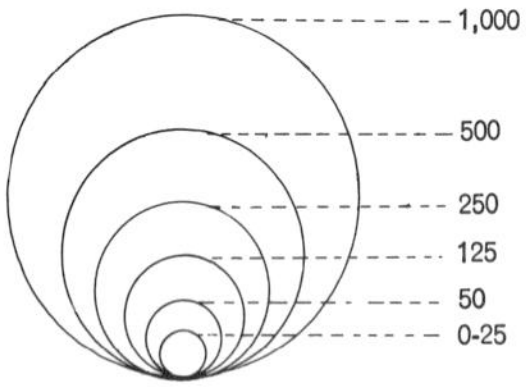

All countries with less than 0.5 million metric tons
(Coal Equivalent) are not shown.

Composition of Energy
(Data based on 3 year averages—1964-66.)

Solid fuels | Liquid fuels | Natural and imported gas | Hydro, nuclear & imported electricity | All other

Per Capita Consumption
(Kg. per capita—Av. 1964-66)

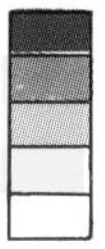

- 3,600-10,800 kg.*
- 1,200-3,600
- 400-1,200
- < 400
- Uninhabited or sparsely populated

* Netherland Antilles and Kuwait exceed this level.

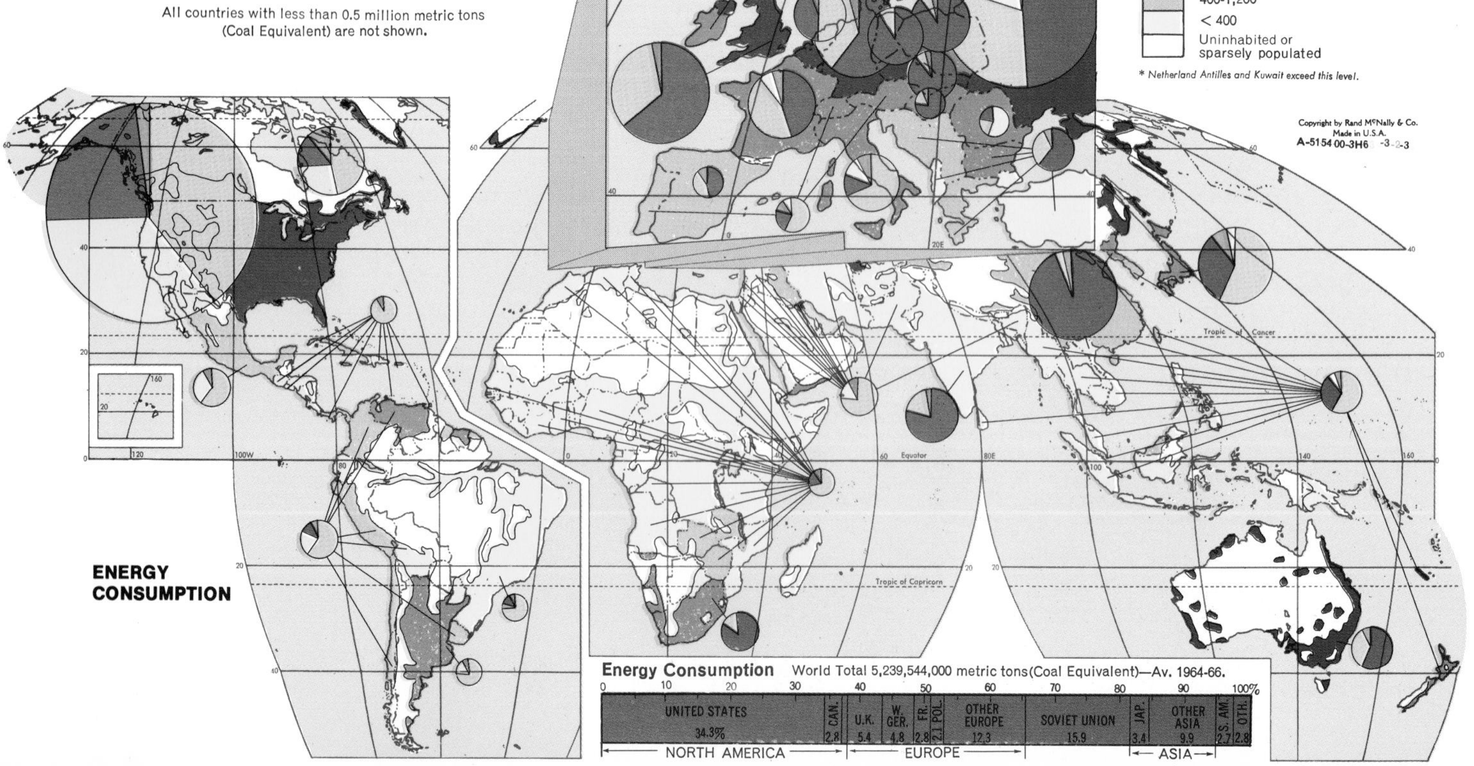

Copyright by Rand McNally & Co.
Made in U.S.A.
A-515400-3H6 -3--3

BE-NE-LUX

Tropic of Cancer

Equator

Tropic of Capricorn

**ENERGY
CONSUMPTION**

Energy Consumption World Total 5,239,544,000 metric tons (Coal Equivalent)—Av. 1964-66.

0	10	20	30	40	50	60	70	80	90	100%

| UNITED STATES 34.3% | CAN. 2.8 | U.K. 5.4 | W. GER. 4.8 | FR. 2.8 | POL. | OTHER EUROPE 12.3 | SOVIET UNION 15.9 | JAP. 3.4 | OTHER ASIA 9.9 | S. AM. 2.7 | OTH. 2.8 |

← NORTH AMERICA → ← EUROPE → ← ASIA →

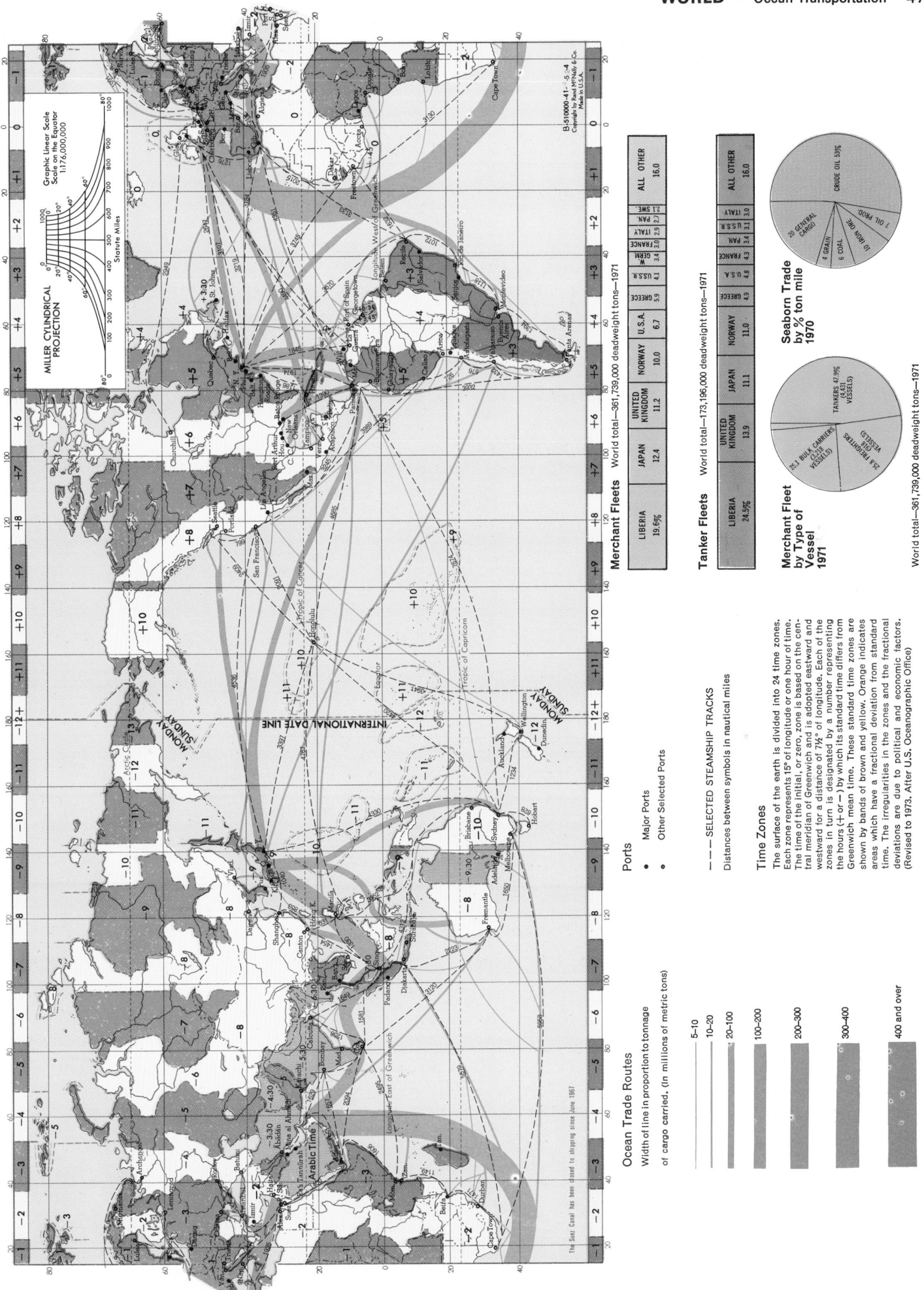

Merchant Fleets
World total—361,739,000 deadweight tons—1971

LIBERIA	JAPAN	UNITED KINGDOM	NORWAY	U.S.A.	GREECE	U.S.S.R.	W. GERM.	FRANCE	ITALY	PAN.	SWE.	ALL OTHER
19.6%	12.4	11.2	10.0	6.7	5.9	4.5	3.4	3.0	2.9	2.7	2.1	16.0

Tanker Fleets
World total—173,196,000 deadweight tons—1971

LIBERIA	UNITED KINGDOM	JAPAN	NORWAY	U.S.A.	GREECE	U.S.S.R.	FRANCE	PAN.	ITALY	ALL OTHER
24.5%	13.9	11.1	11.0	4.8	4.9	4.3	4.3	3.4	3.0	16.0

Seaborn Trade by % ton mile 1970

CRUDE OIL 53%
7 OIL PROD.
10 IRON ORE
6 COAL
4 GRAIN
20 GENERAL CARGO

Merchant Fleet by Type of Vessel 1971

TANKERS 47.9% (3,431 VESSELS)
25.1 BULK CARRIERS (4,021 VESSELS)
26.8 FREIGHTERS (8,921 VESSELS)

World total—361,739,000 deadweight tons—1971

Ports

● Major Ports
∘ Other Selected Ports

– – – SELECTED STEAMSHIP TRACKS

Distances between symbols in nautical miles

Time Zones

The surface of the earth is divided into 24 time zones. Each zone represents 15° of longitude or one hour of time. The time of the initial, or zero, zone is based on the central meridian of Greenwich and is adopted eastward and westward for a distance of 7½° of longitude. Each of the zones in turn is designated by a number representing the hours (+ or −) by which its standard time differs from Greenwich mean time. These standard time zones are shown by bands of brown and yellow. Orange indicates areas which have a fractional deviation from standard time. The irregularities in the zones and the fractional deviations are due to political and economic factors. (Revised to 1973. After U.S. Oceanographic Office)

Ocean Trade Routes

Width of line in proportion to tonnage

of cargo carried. (In millions of metric tons)

5–10
10–20
20–100
100–200
200–300
300–400
400 and over

MILLER CYLINDRICAL PROJECTION

Graphic Linear Scale
Scale on the Equator
1:176,000,000

Statute Miles

The Suez Canal has been closed to shipping since June 1967.

B.510000.41.−.5.−.4
Copyright by Rand McNally & Co.
Made in U.S.A.

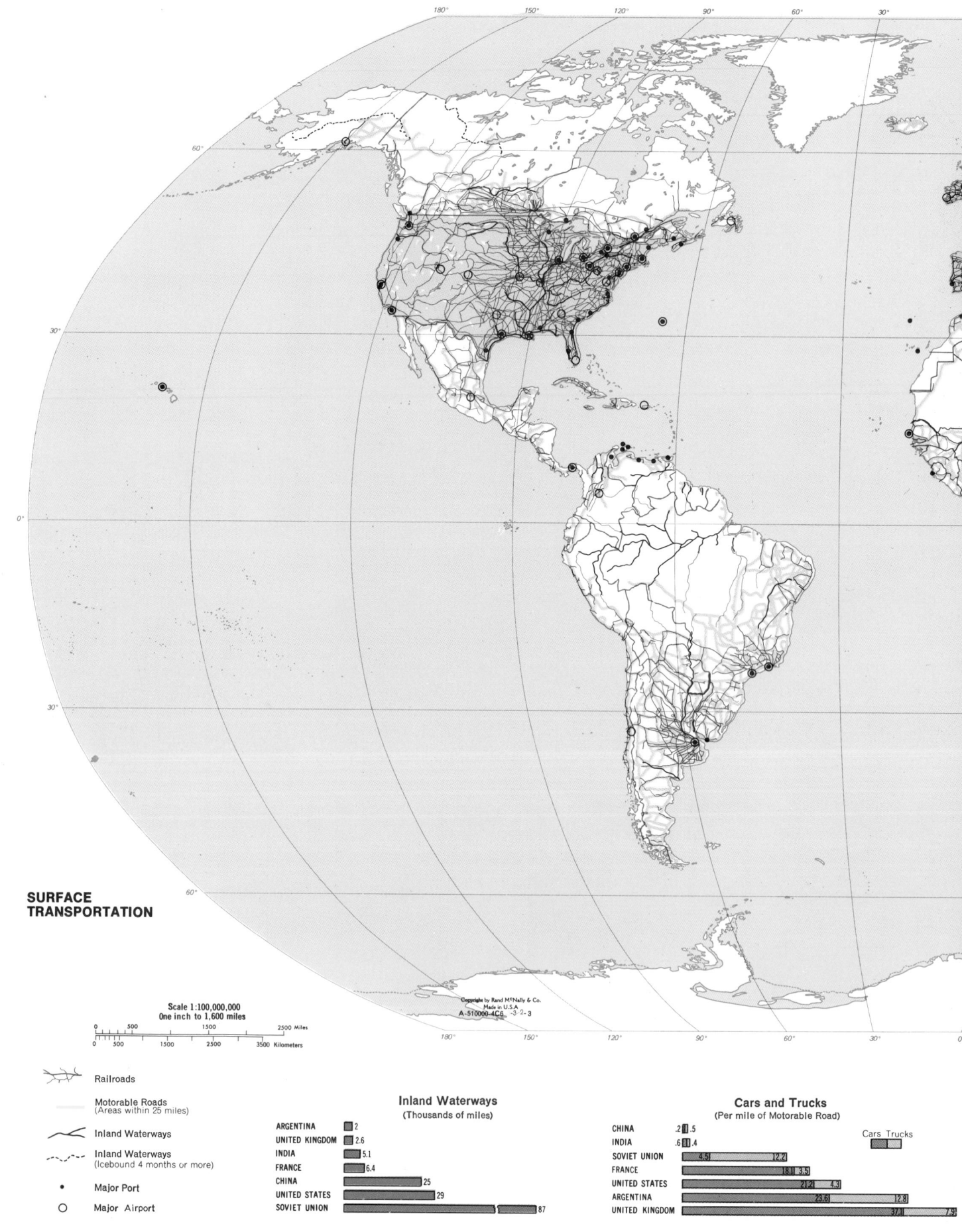

48

SURFACE TRANSPORTATION

Scale 1:100,000,000
One inch to 1,600 miles

0	500	1500	2500 Miles
0	500	1500	2500	3500 Kilometers

Copyright by Rand McNally & Co.
Made in U.S.A
A-510000-4C6 -3-2-3

Railroads

Motorable Roads
(Areas within 25 miles)

Inland Waterways

Inland Waterways
(Icebound 4 months or more)

• Major Port

○ Major Airport

Inland Waterways
(Thousands of miles)

ARGENTINA	2
UNITED KINGDOM	2.6
INDIA	5.1
FRANCE	6.4
CHINA	25
UNITED STATES	29
SOVIET UNION	87

Cars and Trucks
(Per mile of Motorable Road)

Cars Trucks

	Cars	Trucks
CHINA	.2	.5
INDIA	.6	1.4
SOVIET UNION	4.5	12.2
FRANCE	18.1	3.5
UNITED STATES	21.2	4.3
ARGENTINA	23.6	12.8
UNITED KINGDOM	37.11	7.9

Robinson Projection

Persons per passenger car

UNITED STATES	2.3
FRANCE	4.1
UNITED KINGDOM	4.7
ARGENTINA	15.6
SOVIET UNION	146.5
INDIA	902.8
CHINA	5,711.4

Railroads and Motorable Roads
(Miles per 100 square miles)

	Railroads	Motorable Roads (excluding city streets)
CHINA	1.6	3.2
ARGENTINA	2.6	3.6
SOVIET UNION	2.1	14.6
INDIA	3.2	48.4
UNITED STATES	5.9	100.3
FRANCE	14.2	230.9
UNITED KINGDOM	19.3	260.9

Inhabited Localities

The symbol represents the number of inhabitants within the locality

- · 0—10,000
- ○ 10,000—25,000
- ⊚ 25,000—100,000
- ⊡ 100,000—250,000
- ▣ 250,000—1,000,000
- ■ >1,000,000

The size of type indicates the relative economic and political importance of the locality

Écommoy	St.-Denis
Trouville	
Lisieux	PARIS

Hollywood   Section of a City,
Westminster   Neighborhood

Northland ■
Center   Major Shopping Center

 Urban Area (area of continuous industrial, commercial, and residential development)

 Major Industrial Area

Wooded Area

Political Boundaries

International (First-order political unit)
- ▬ ▬ ▬ Demarcated, Undemarcated, and Administrative
- ▬▬▬ Demarcation Line

Internal
- State, Province, etc. (Second-order political unit)
- County, Oblast, etc. (Third-order political unit)
- ----- Okrug, Kreis, etc. (Fourth-order political unit)
- -------- City or Municipality (may appear in combination with another boundary symbol)

Capitals of Political Units

BUDAPEST   Independent Nation

Recife   State, Province, etc.

White Plains   County, Oblast, etc.

Iserlohn   Okrug, Kreis, etc.

Transportation

Road

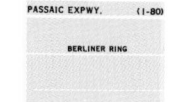 Primary

Secondary

Tertiary

Railway

 Primary

Secondary

Rapid Transit

Airport

 LONDON (HEATHROW) AIRPORT

Rail or Air Terminal

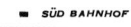 ■ SÜD BAHNHOF

Bridge

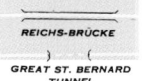 REICHS-BRÜCKE

Tunnel

GREAT ST. BERNARD TUNNEL

Houston Ship Channel   Shipping Channel

Canal du Midi   Navigable Canal

TO MALMÖ   Ferry

Hydrographic Features

Shoreline

Undefined or Fluctuating Shoreline

Amur   River, Stream

Intermittent Stream

Rapids, Falls

SALTO ANGEL   Navigable Canal

Canal du Midi

Irrigation or Drainage Canal

Los Angeles Aqueduct   Aqueduct

Pier, Breakwater

GREAT BARRIER REEF   Reef

L. Victoria   Lake, Reservoir

Intermittent Lake

The Everglades   Swamp

Miscellaneous Cultural Features

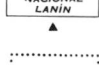 National or State Park or Monument

 Military Installation

 Cemetery

▲ SORBONNE   Point of Interest (Battlefield, museum, temple, university, etc.)

STEPHANSDOM   Church, Monastery

UXMAL   Ruins

▼ WINDSOR CASTLE   Castle

Lighthouse

ASWĀN DAM \   Dam

<>   Lock

Crib   Water Intake Crib

Quarry or Surface Mine

Subsurface Mine

Topographic Features

Mt. Kenya 5199 △   Elevation Above Sea Level

Elevations are given in meters

⋆ Rock

A N D E S Mountain Range, Plateau,
KUNLUNSHANMAI Valley, etc.

BAFFIN ISLAND   Island

POLUOSTROV KAMČATKA   Peninsula, Cape, Point, etc.
CABO DE HORNOS

Major Cities

This section consists of 62 maps of the world's most populous metropolitan areas. In order to make comparisons easier, all the metropolitan areas are shown at the same scale, 1:300,000. An index to the places shown on the maps in this section can be found on page 232. The names of many large settlements, towns, suburbs, and neighborhoods can be located in these large-scale maps. For the symbols used on the maps, see the legend on the facing page.

The world is becoming increasingly urbanized as people move from country areas to city areas. This makes the study of metropolitan areas more important than ever before. The maps in this section enable the reader to study and compare urban extent, major industrial areas, parks, public land, wooded areas, airports, shopping centers, streets, and railroads. A special effort has been made to portray the various metropolitan areas in a manner as standard and comparable as possible.

Notable differences occur in the way cities are laid out. In most of North America, cities developed from a rectangular pattern of streets, with well-defined residential, commercial, and industrial zones. Most European cities are different and more complex. They have irregular street patterns and less well-defined land-use zones. In Asia, Africa, and South America the form tends to be even more irregular and complex, partly due to widespread dispersion of craft and trade activities. Some cities have no identifiable city centers, and some cities have both old and modern city centers. High population densities produce more limited, compact urban places than in North America.

Major Cities

a

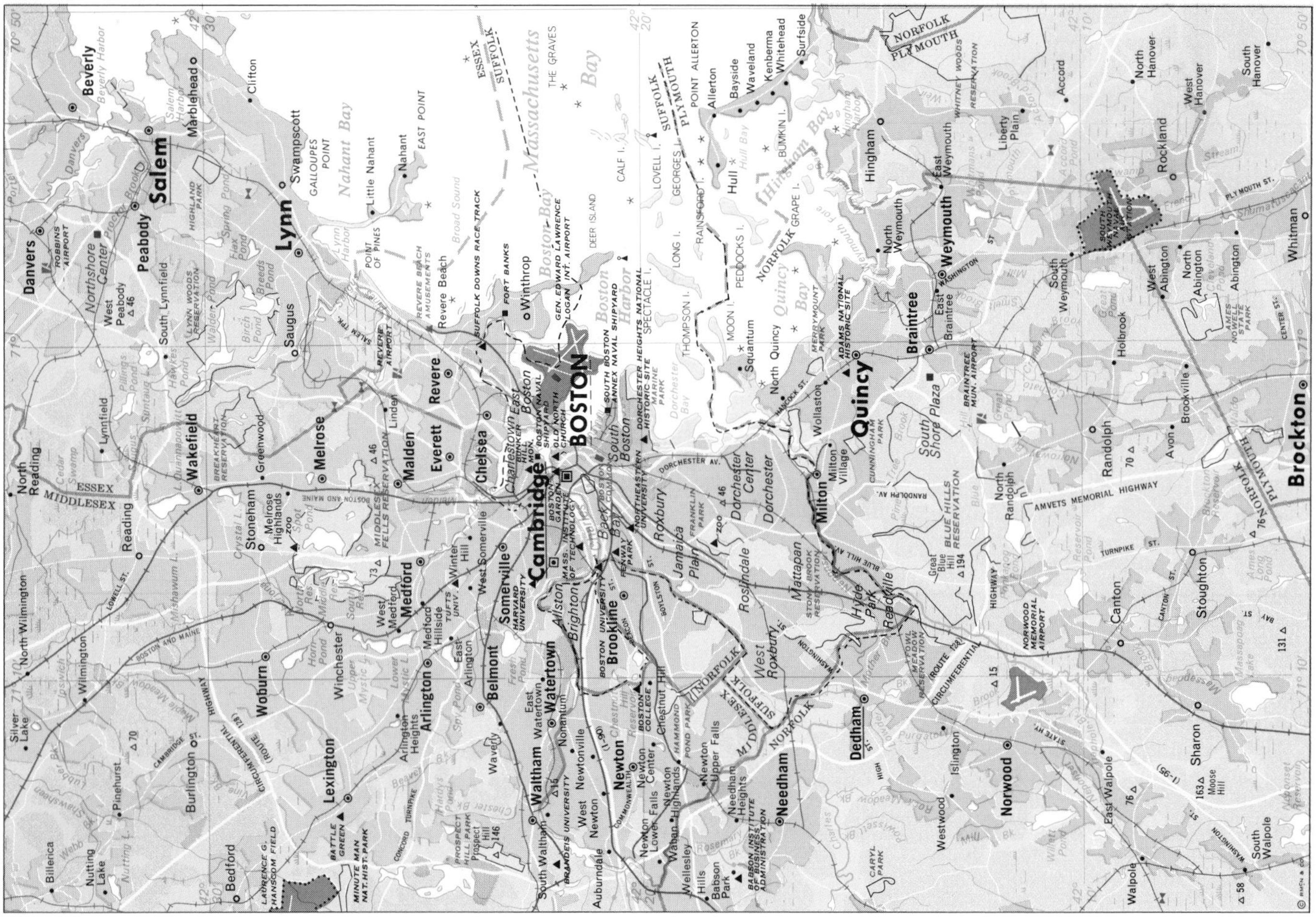

Boston area (Massachusetts):

Beverly, Marblehead, Clifton, Salem, Peabody, Danvers, Northshore Center, West Peabody, South Lynnfield, Lynnfield, Lynn, Swampscott, Nahant Bay, Little Nahant, East Point, Nahant, Broad Sound, Point of Pines, Revere Beach, Revere, Winthrop, Deer Island, The Graves, Massachusetts Bay, Essex, Suffolk, Norfolk, Plymouth, North Hanover, West Hanover, South Hanover, Accord, Rockland, North Cohasset, Cohasset, Scituate, Allerton, Hull, Nantasket Beach, Hingham Bay, Weymouth, East Weymouth, North Weymouth, Hingham, Liberty Plain, Bayside, Waveland, Whitehead, Kenberma, Surfside, North Reading, Reading, Wakefield, Stoneham, Melrose, Saugus, Malden, Everett, Chelsea, Charlestown, East Boston, Middlesex, Wilmington, North Wilmington, Woburn, Winchester, Medford, Winter Hill, Somerville, Cambridge, BOSTON, South Boston, Dorchester, Quincy, North Quincy, Wollaston, Squantum, Milton, Braintree, South Weymouth, West Abington, Abington, Holbrook, Randolph, Avon, Brockton, Burlington, Bedford, Lexington, Arlington, Belmont, Watertown, Brighton, Brookline, Newton, Roxbury, Jamaica Plain, Roslindale, West Roxbury, Mattapan, Hyde Park, Readville, Dedham, Needham, Wellesley, Auburndale, Waban, Westwood, Norwood, Islington, Canton, Stoughton, Sharon, East Walpole, Walpole, South Walpole, Billerica, Nutting, Webb, Silver Lake, Pinehurst

Nahant Bay, Massachusetts Bay, Boston Bay, Boston Harbor, Hingham Bay, Quincy Bay, Dorchester Bay

b

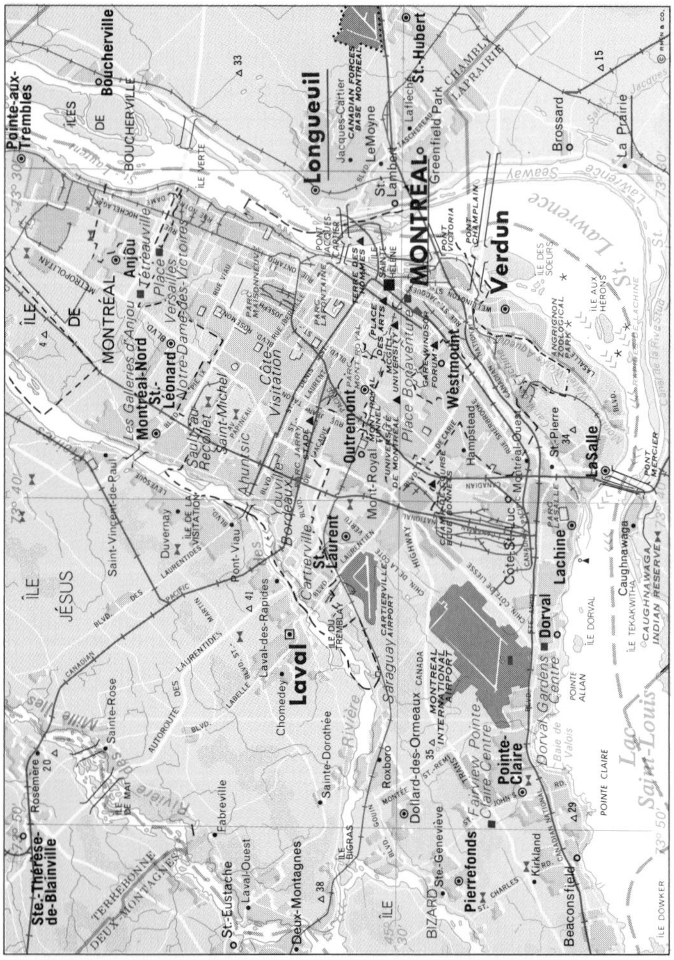

Montréal area:

Pointe-aux-Trembles, Boucherville, Longueuil, St-Hubert, Chambly, Laprairie, Brossard, La Prairie, LeMoyne, Greenfield Park, St-Lambert, ÎLE JÉSUS, Laval, Sainte-Rose, Chomedey, Duvernay, Laval-Ouest, Fabreville, Sainte-Dorothée, Saint-Vincent-de-Paul, Anjou, Montréal-Nord, Saint-Léonard, Saint-Michel, Outremont, MONTRÉAL, Westmount, Verdun, LaSalle, Lachine, Dorval, Pointe-Claire, Dollard-des-Ormeaux, Pierrefonds, Roxboro, Beaconsfield, Kirkland, Sainte-Geneviève, ÎLE BIZARD, Ste-Thérèse-de-Blainville, St-Eustache, Deux-Montagnes, Terrebonne, Rosemère, Montréal International Airport, Dorval Gardens, Caughnawaga Indian Reserve, St-Pierre, Hampstead, St-Laurent, Côte-St-Luc, St-Léonard, Lac St-Louis, Rivière des Prairies

St. Lawrence Seaway

c

Toronto area:

Scarborough, Scarborough Bluffs, Morningside, Markham, Woburn, Agincourt, Wexford, Maryvale, East York, TORONTO, North York, York, Mount Dennis, Weston, New Toronto, Mimico, Etobicoke, Mississauga, Malton, Vaughan, Thornhill, Thistletown, Rexdale, Islington, Long Branch, Elder Mills, Concord, Steeles Corners, Willowdale, Lansing, Don Mills, Leaside, Forest Hill, Downsview, Fairview Mall, Don Valley, Newton Brook, Silver Hills, Cedar Brae, Ontario Science Centre, Toronto Island Airport, Centre Island, Gibraltar Point, Toronto International Airport, Burnhamthorpe, Pine Grove, Edgeley

LAKE ONTARIO

Copyright by Rand McNally & Co.
Made in U.S.A.
A-520087-76 -1 -1

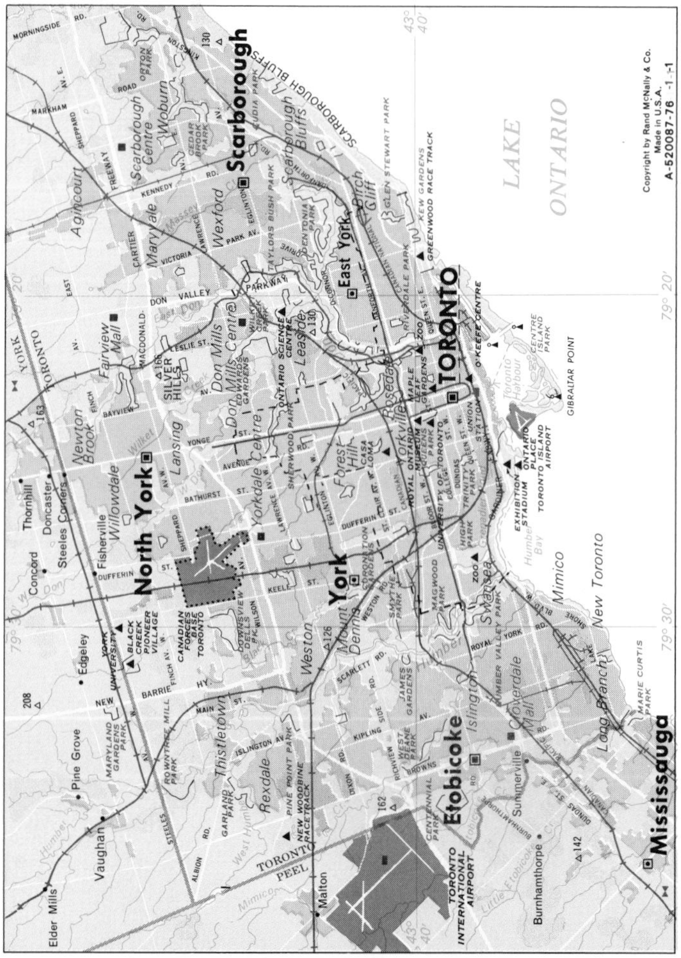

Scale 1:300,000; one inch to 4.7 miles.

10 Miles
10 Kilometers

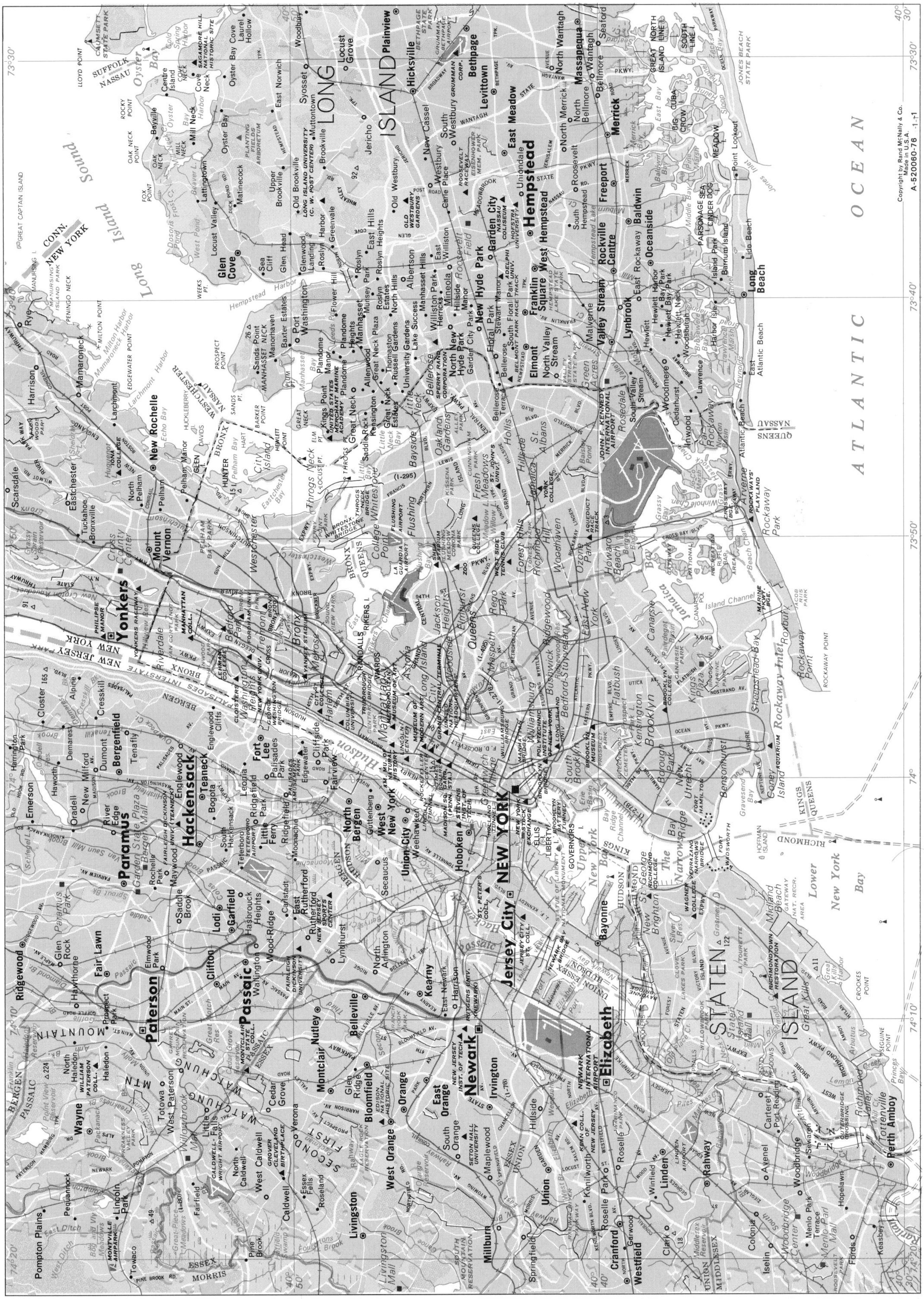

Scale 1:300,000; one inch to 4.7 miles.

ATLANTIC OCEAN

LONG ISLAND

Long Island Sound

CONN.
NEW YORK

STATEN ISLAND

NEW YORK

Jersey City

Newark

Elizabeth

Yonkers

Paterson

Passaic

Paramus

Hackensack

Hempstead

Glen Cove

a

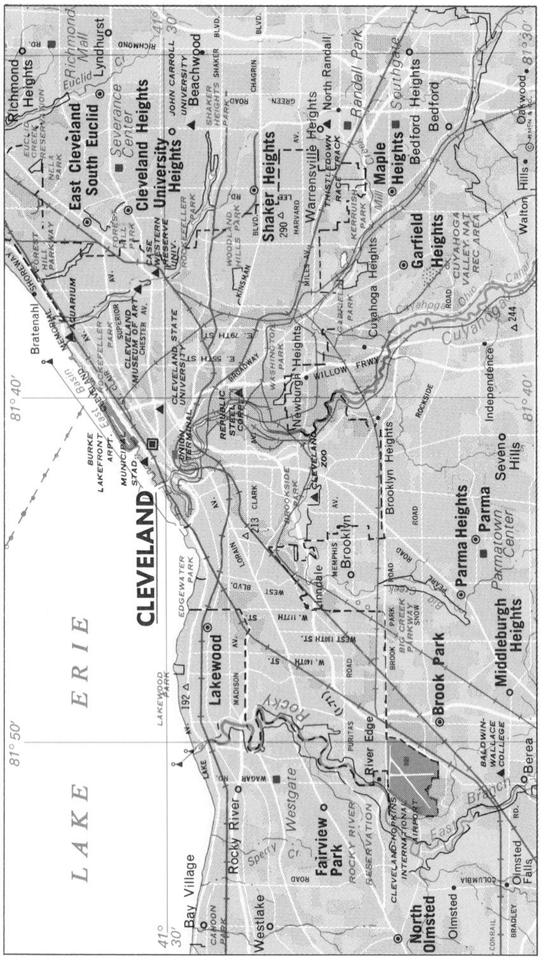

b

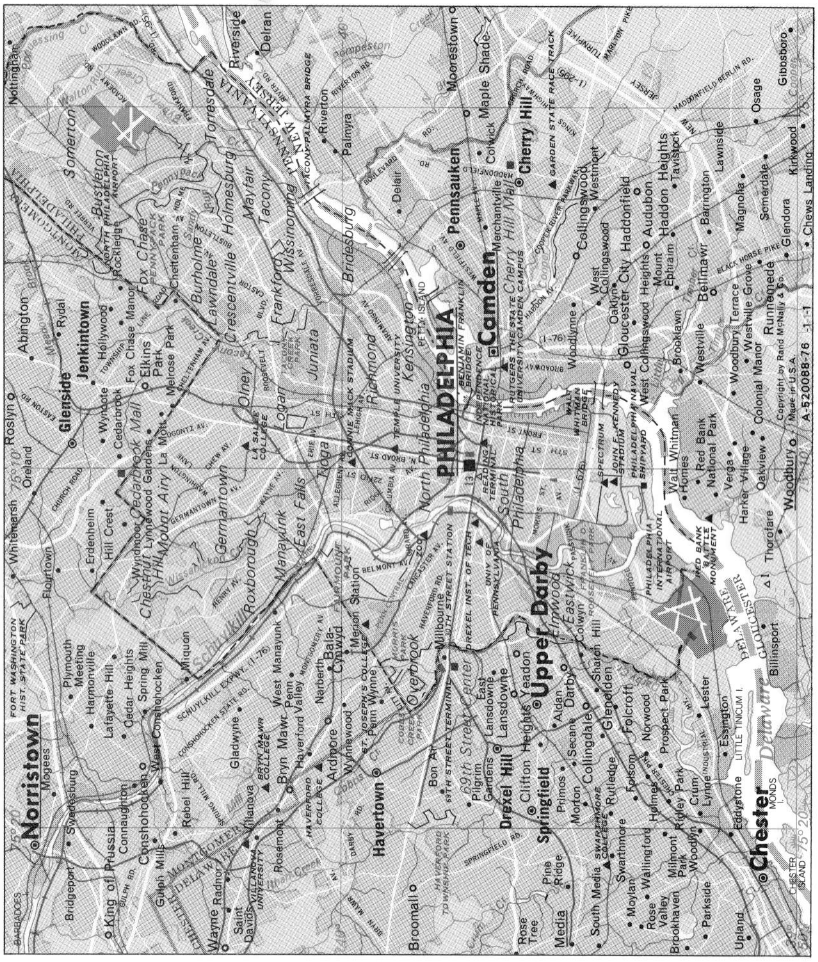

c

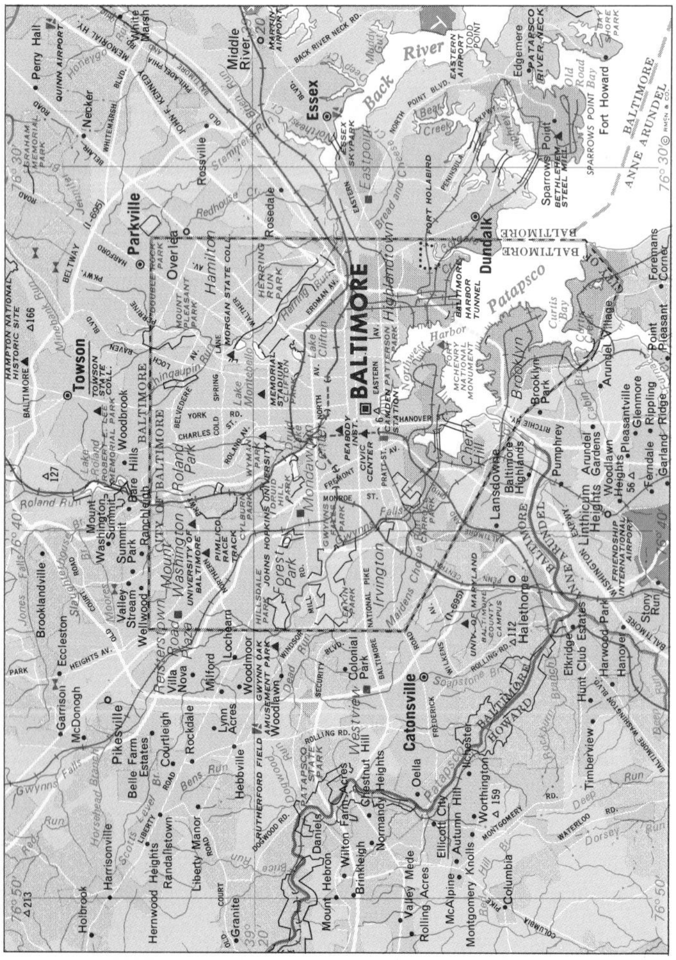

d

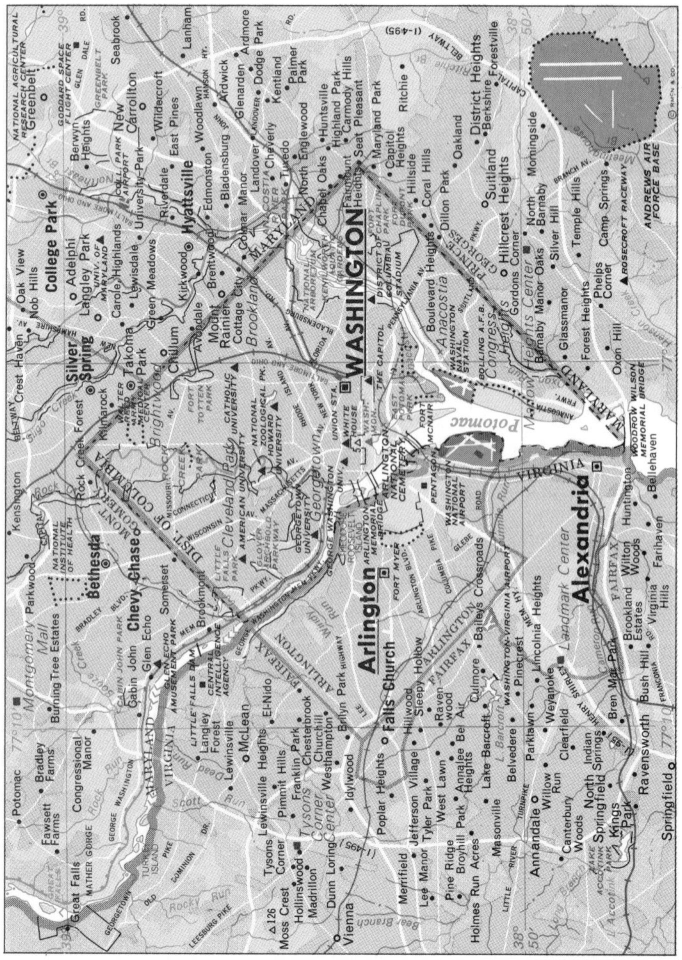

Scale 1:300,000; one inch to 4.7 miles.

0   5   10 Miles

0   5   10 Kilometers

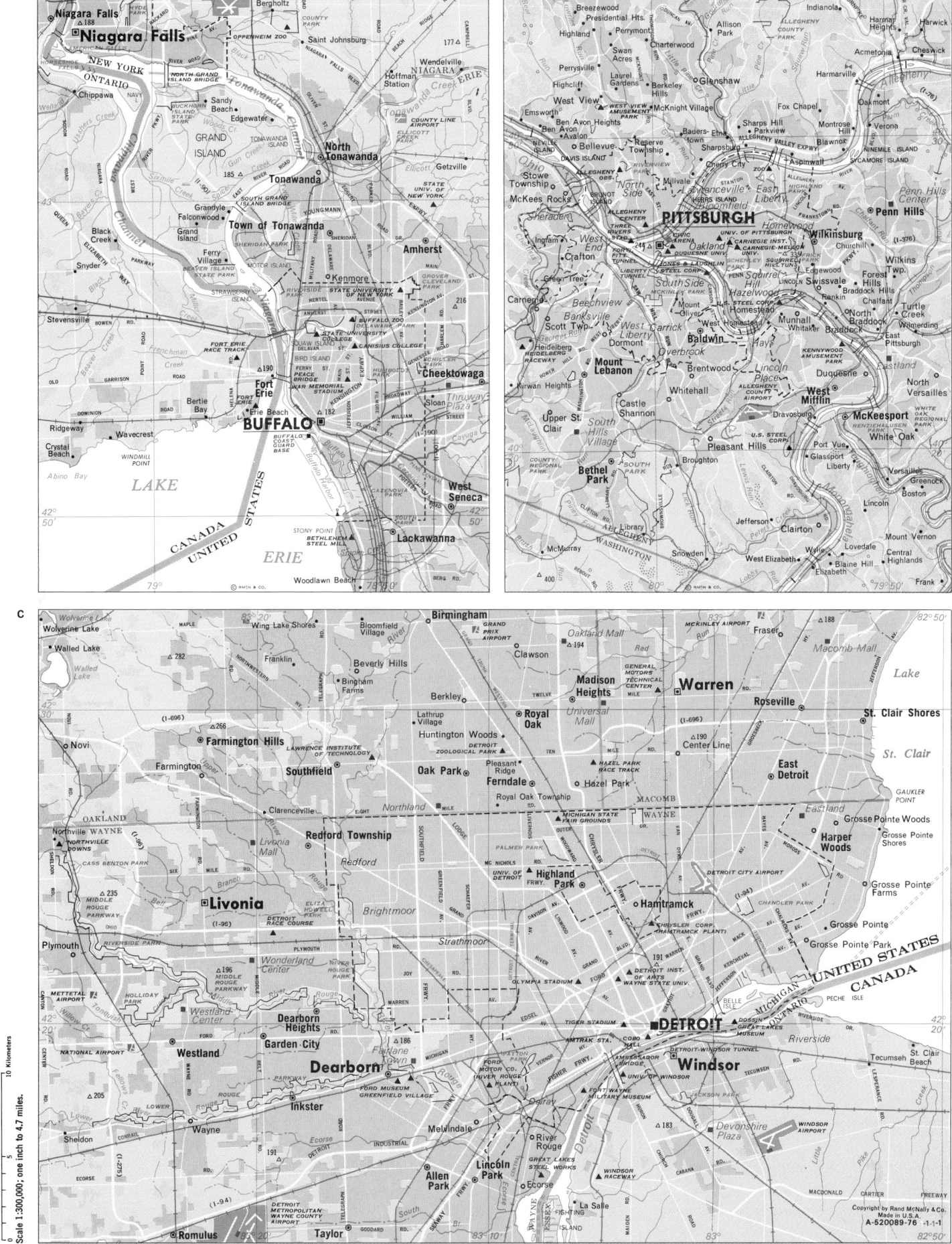

Scale 1:300,000; one inch to 4.7 miles.

Copyright by Rand McNally & Co.
Made in U.S.A.
A-520089-76

a

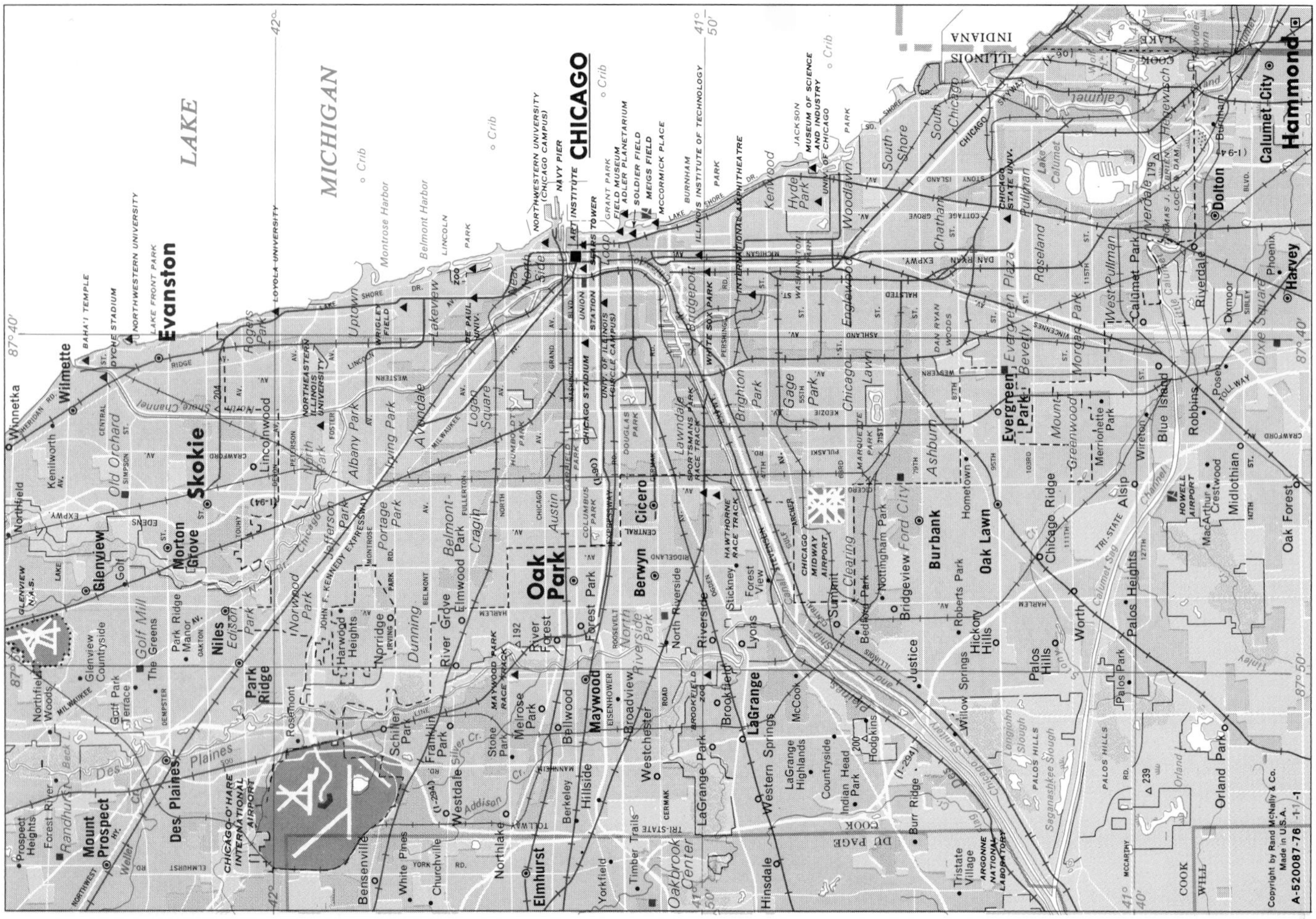

LAKE MICHIGAN

CHICAGO

Evanston

Wilmette

Winnetka

Skokie

Glenview

Morton Grove

Niles

Park Ridge

Des Plaines

Mount Prospect

Oak Park

Cicero

Berwyn

Maywood

LaGrange

Burbank

Oak Lawn

Elmhurst

Hinsdale

Evergreen Park

Calumet City

Hammond

Harvey

Phoenix

Dolton

Oak Forest

Chicago Ridge

Palos Heights

INDIANA

ILLINOIS

COOK

DU PAGE

Copyright by Rand McNally & Co.
A-520087-76-1-1

b

Briones Hills

Berkeley

OAKLAND

Alameda

Richmond

San Rafael

SAN FRANCISCO

South San Francisco

Daly City

San Bruno

Burlingame

San Mateo

San Carlos

Redwood City

Foster City

Belmont

Pacifica

San Leandro

Hayward

San Francisco Bay

PACIFIC OCEAN

Metropolitan Oakland International Airport

San Francisco International Airport

Golden Gate Bridge

Alcatraz Island

Angel Island

ALAMEDA

SAN MATEO

CONTRA COSTA

MARIN

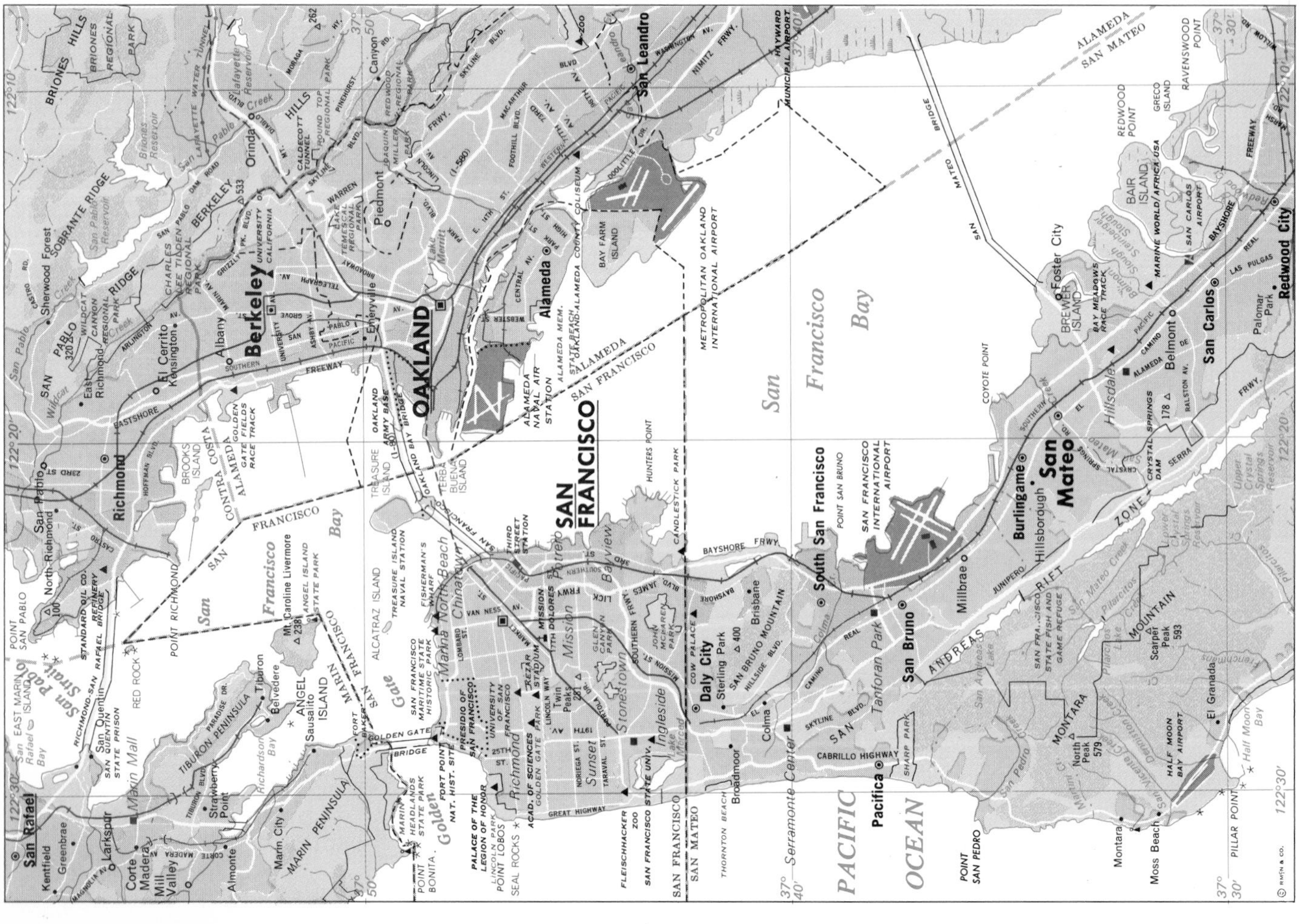

Scale 1:300,000; one inch to 4.7 miles.

10 Miles

10 Kilometers

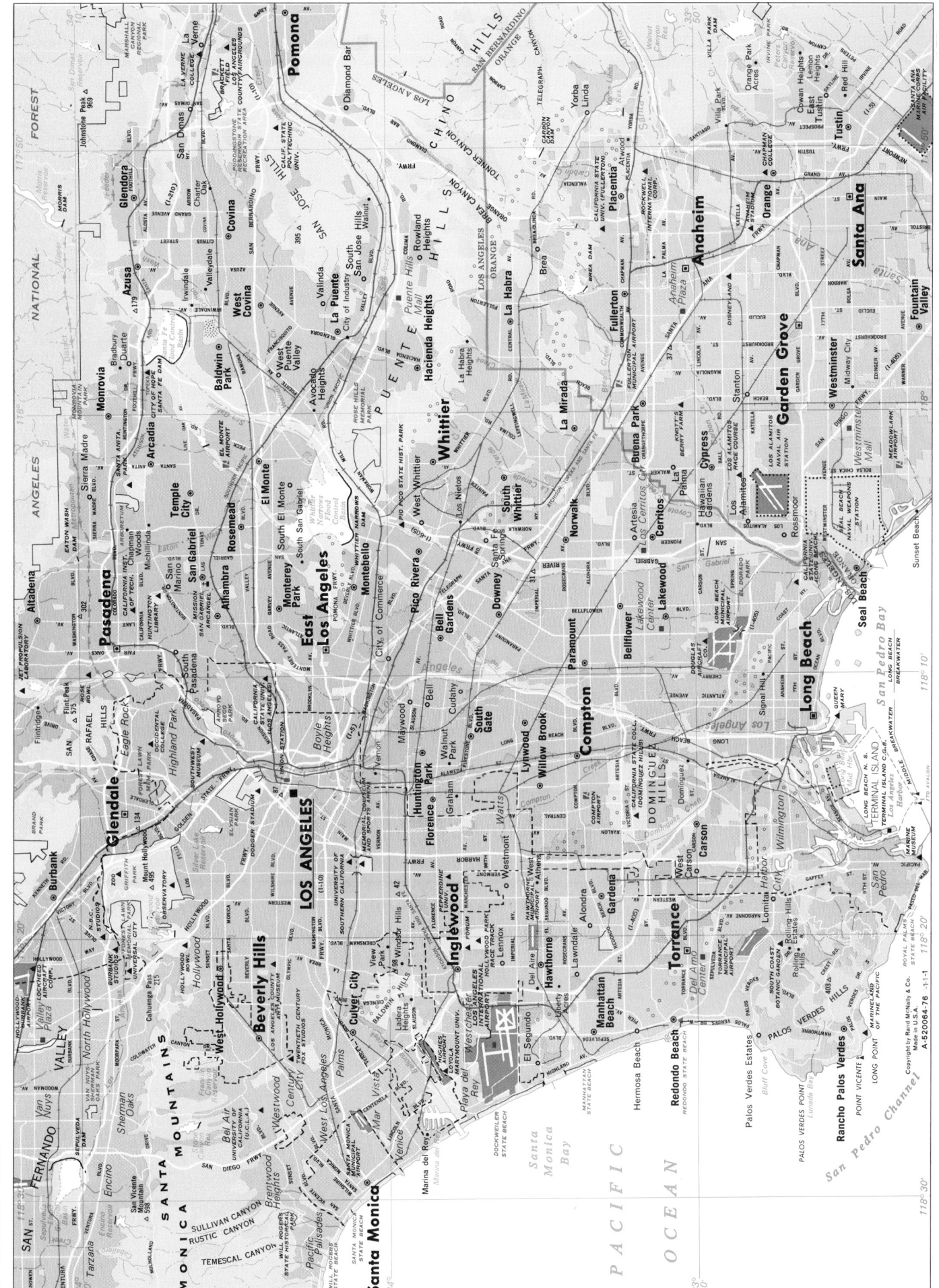

Scale 1:300,000; one inch to 4.7 miles.

Copyright by Rand McNally & Co.
Made in U.S.A.
A-520064-76 -1:1-1

a

b

c

d

BUENOS AIRES

RIO DE LA PLATA

San Fernando · San Isidro · Vicente López · General San Martín · Caseros (Tres de Febrero) · General Sarmiento (San Miguel) · Morón · Merlo · Moreno · San Justo · Avellaneda · Lanús · Lomas de Zamora · Quilmes · Berazategui

Scale 1:300,000; one inch to 4.7 miles.

0 5 10 Miles

0 5 10 Kilometers

A-540060-76 -1-1-1

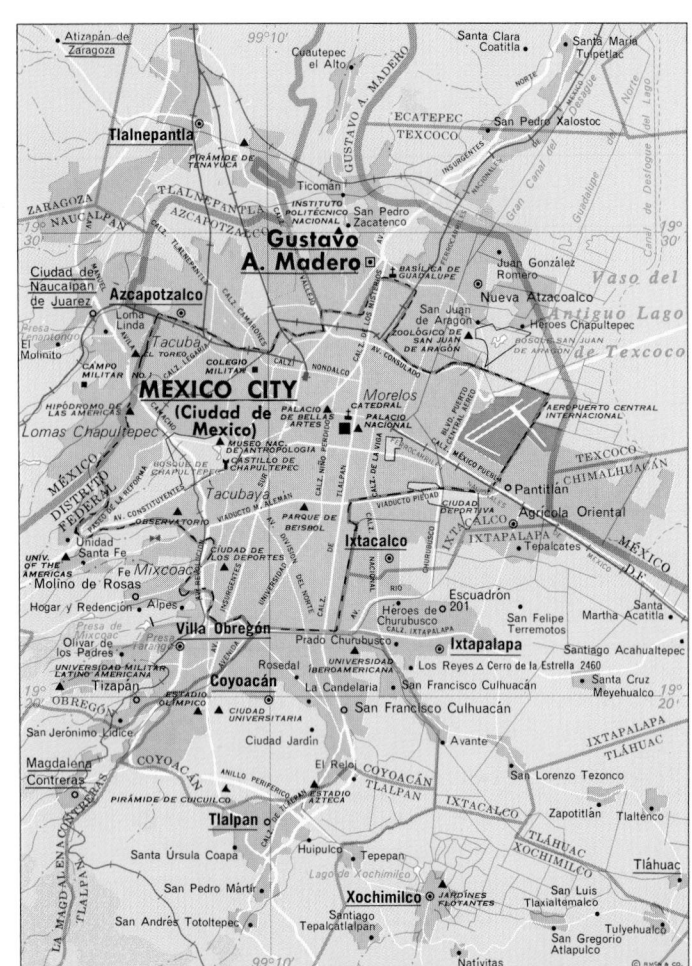

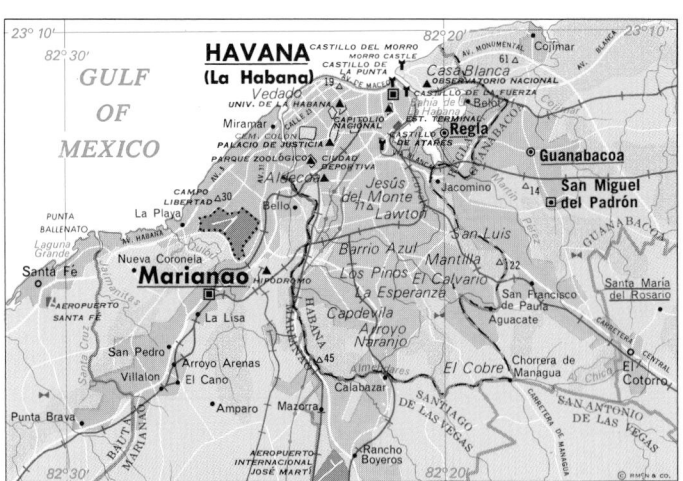

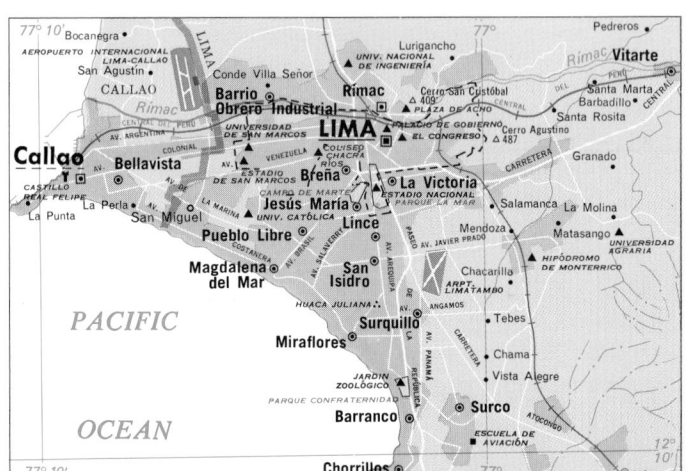

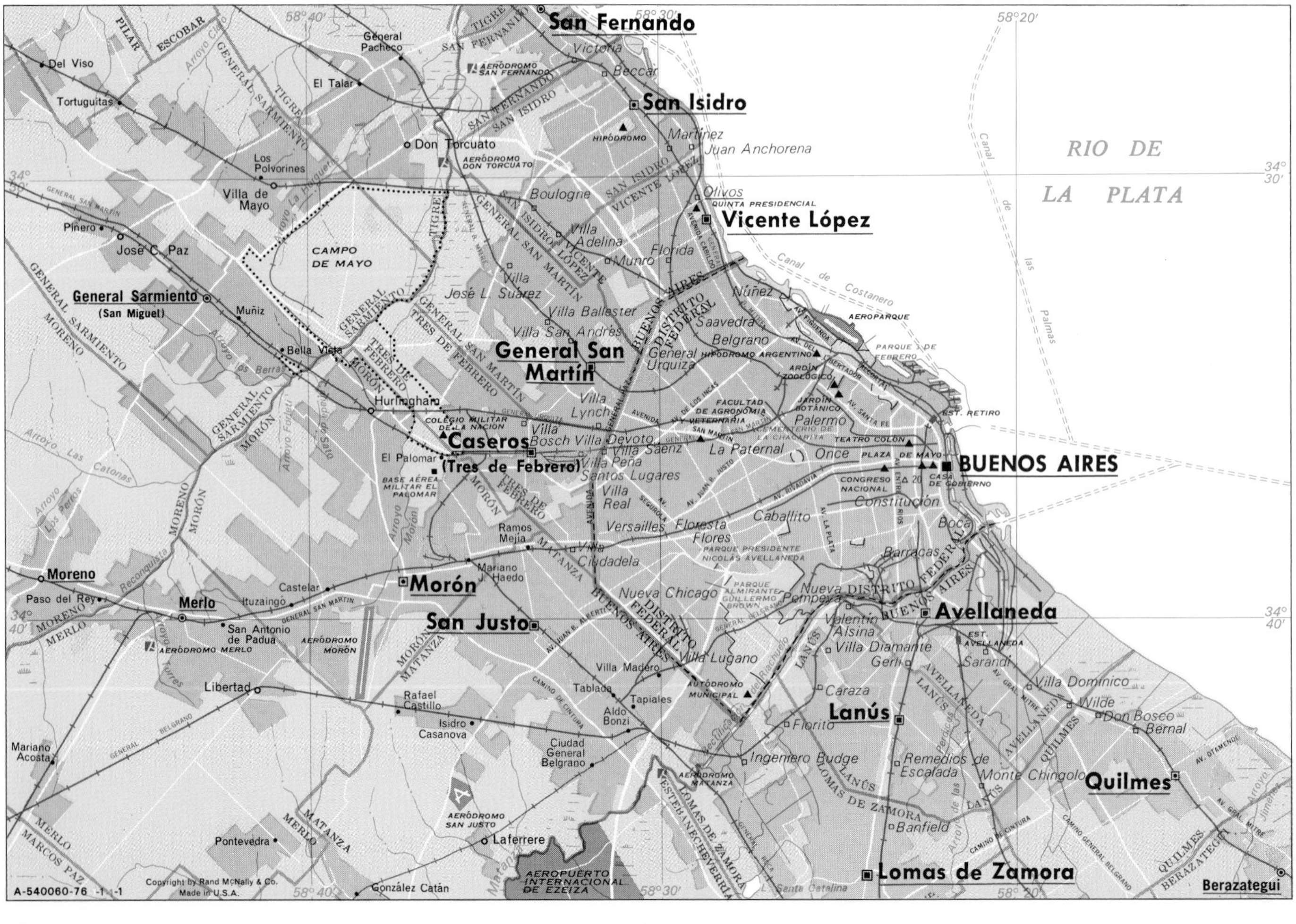

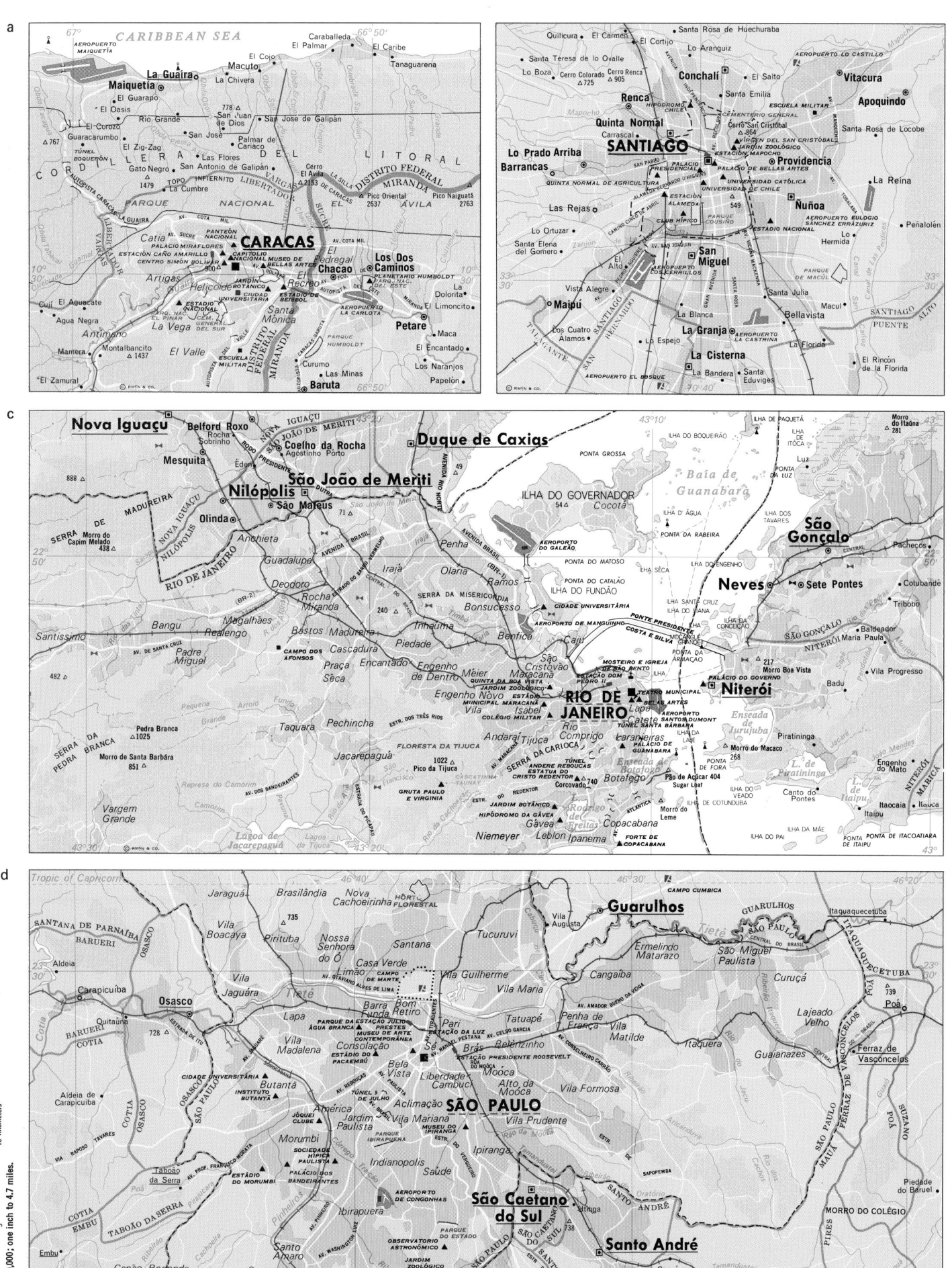

LONDON

Chelmsford

Basildon

Brentwood

Gravesend

Tilbury

Grays

Dartford

Sevenoaks

Chesthunt

Loughton

Chigwell

LONDON

Greenwich

Woolwich

City

Bromley

Croydon

Epsom

Saint Albans

Hemel Hempstead

Watford

Rickmansworth

Leatherhead

Weybridge

Staines

Chertsey

Woking

Slough

Windsor

Berkhamsted

EPPING FOREST

GREATER LONDON

HERTFORDSHIRE

ESSEX

KENT

SURREY

BUCKINGHAMSHIRE

BERKSHIRE

Scale 1:300,000; one inch to 4.7 miles

10 Miles

10 Kilometers

Great Bookham, Sy.

Copyright by Rand McNally & Co.

Made in U.S.A.

A-650052-76 -1-1

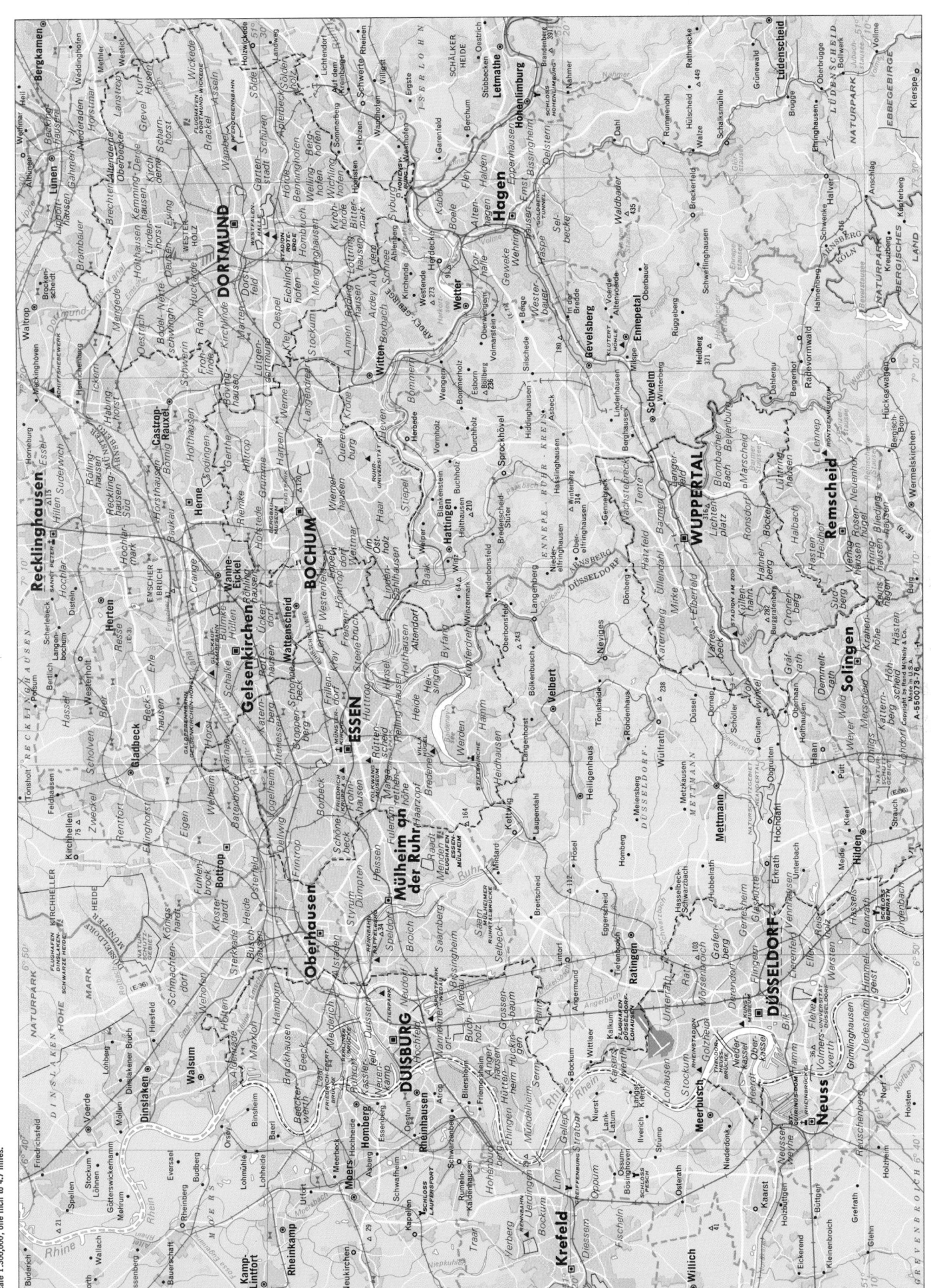
0 5 10 Miles
0 5 10 Kilometers
Scale 1:300,000; one inch to 4.7 miles.
Recklinghausen
DORTMUND
Gelsenkirchen
BOCHUM
ESSEN
Oberhausen
Mülheim an der Ruhr
DUISBURG
Krefeld
DÜSSELDORF
WUPPERTAL
Solingen
Remscheid
Hagen
Witten
Herne
Bottrop
Gladbeck
Moers
Neuss
Dinslaken
Walsum
Lünen
Bergkamen
Hattingen
Velbert
Ratingen
Mettmann
Hilden
Gevelsberg
Schwelm
Ennepetal
Wetter
Letmathe
Hohenlimburg
Lüdenscheid
Rhine
Copyright by Rand McNally & Co. Made in U.S.A.
A-550073-76

Scale 1:300,000; one inch to 4.7 miles.

Copyright by Rand McNally & Co. Made in U.S.A.

A-550078-76

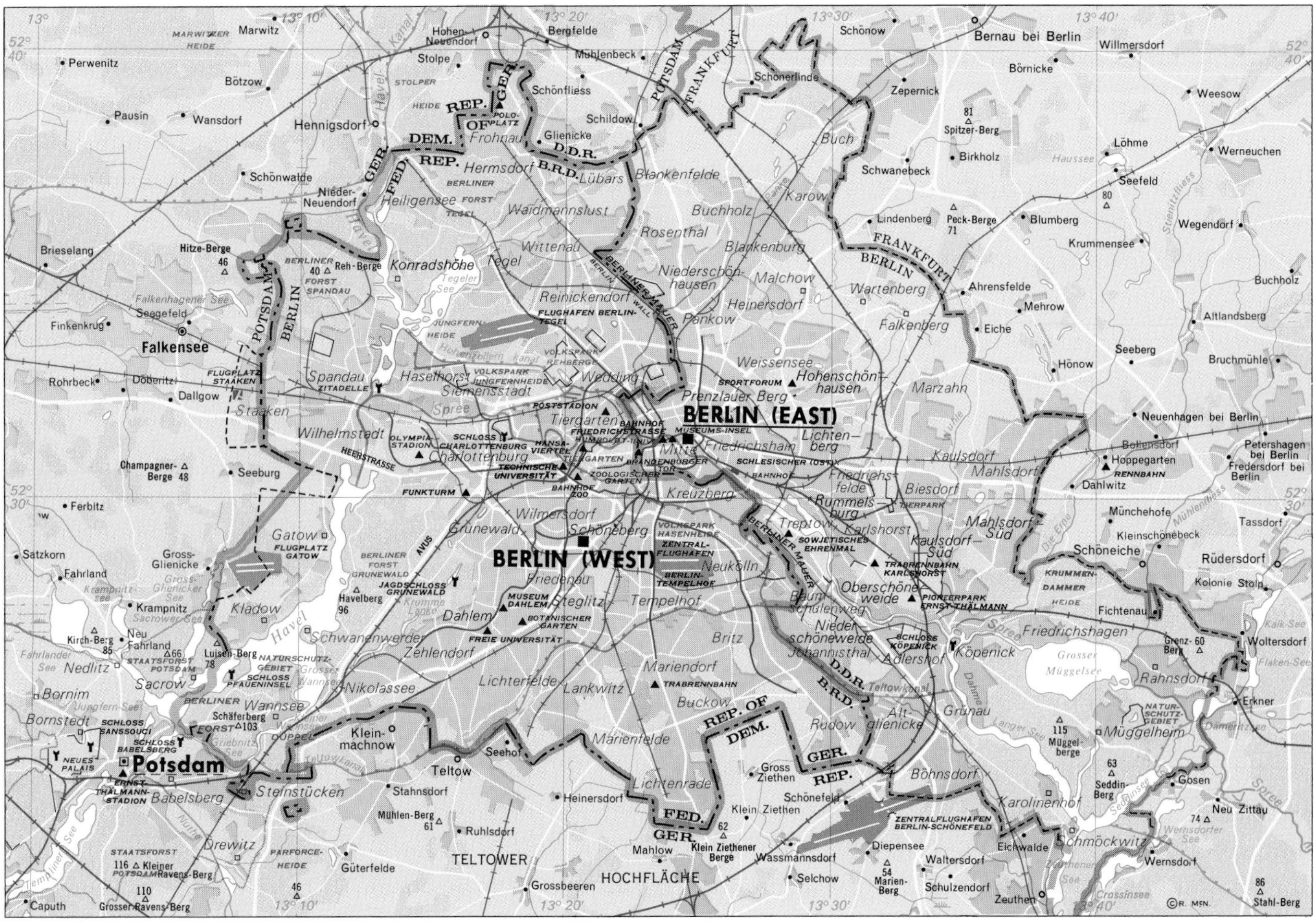

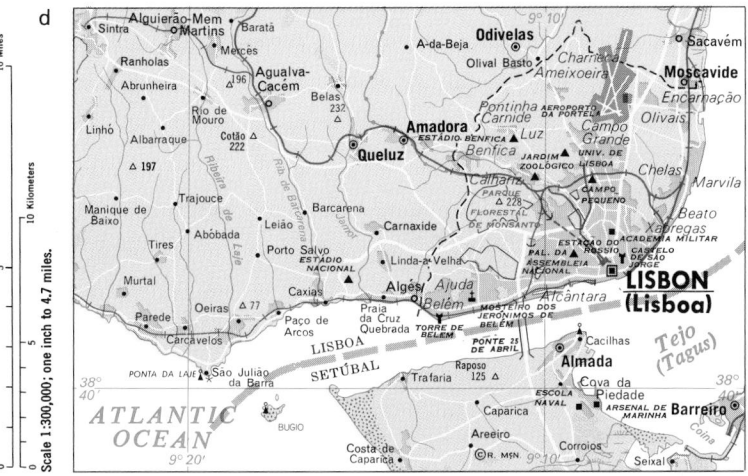

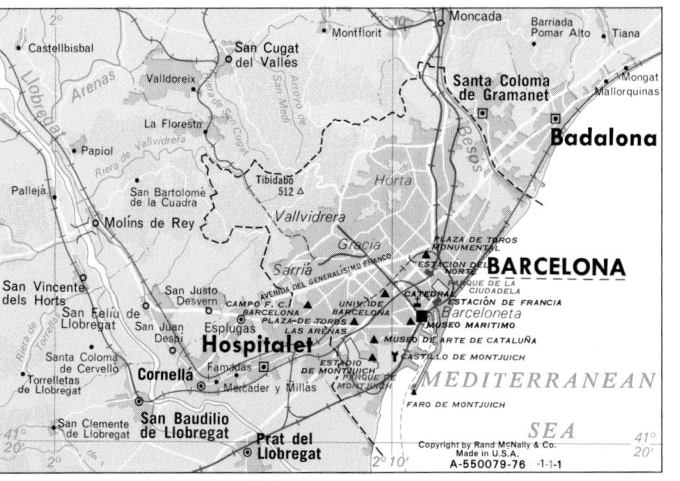

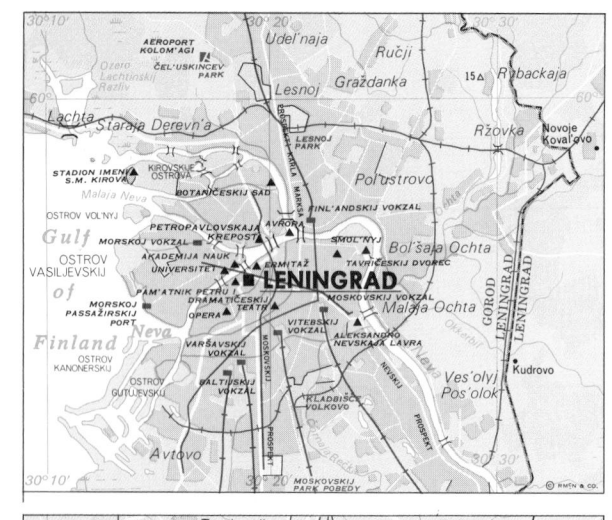

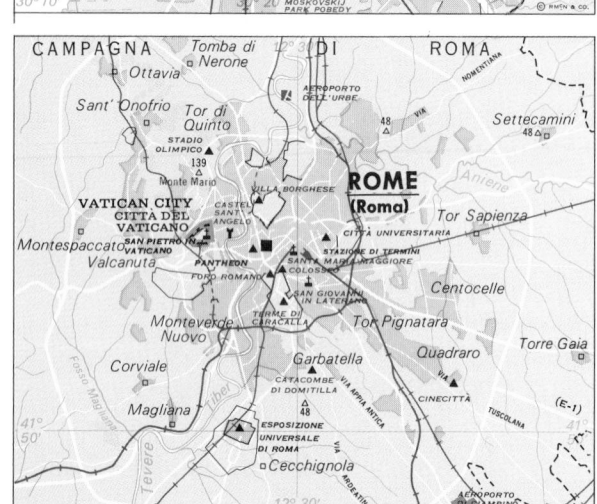

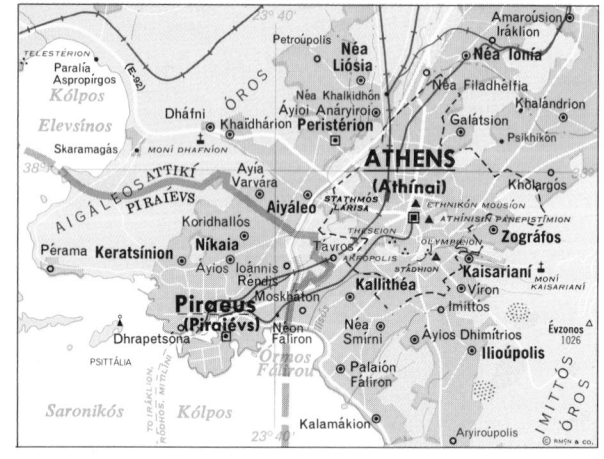

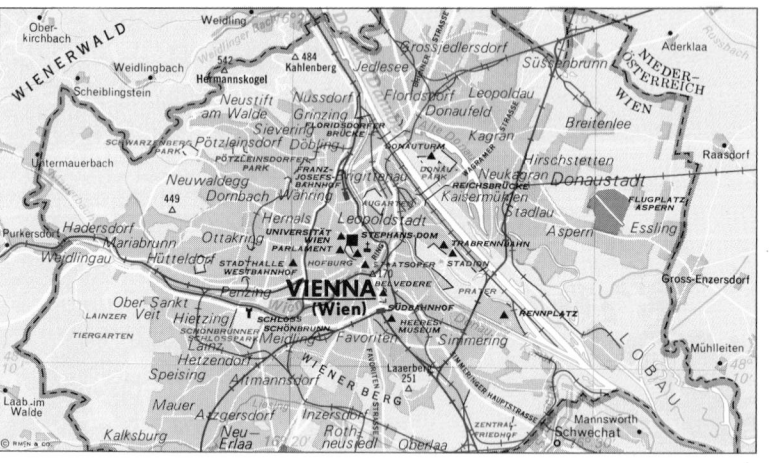

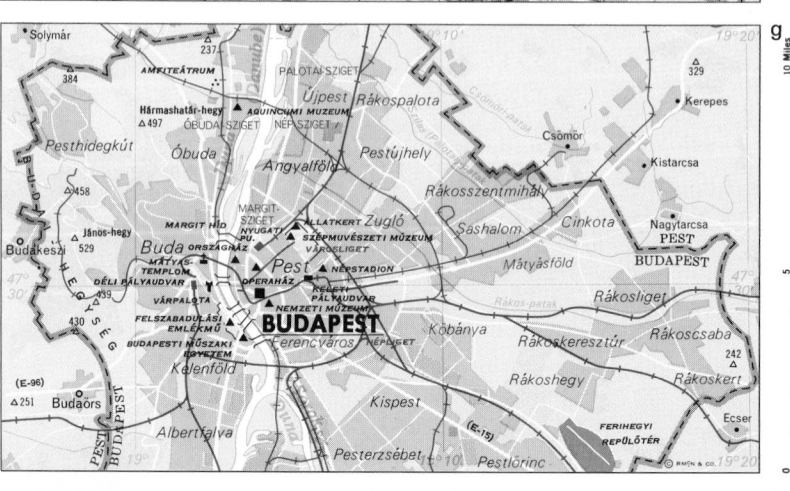

Scale 1:300,000; one inch to 4.7 miles.

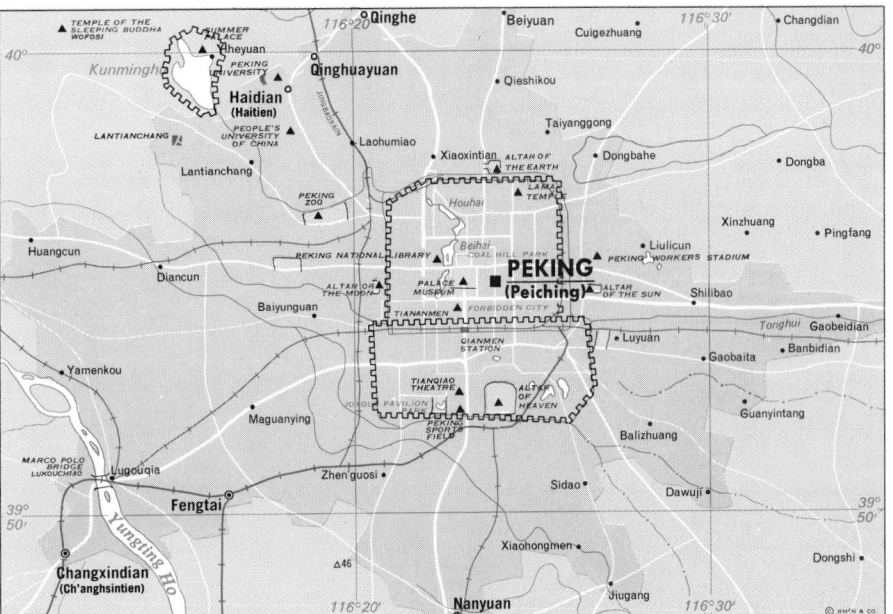

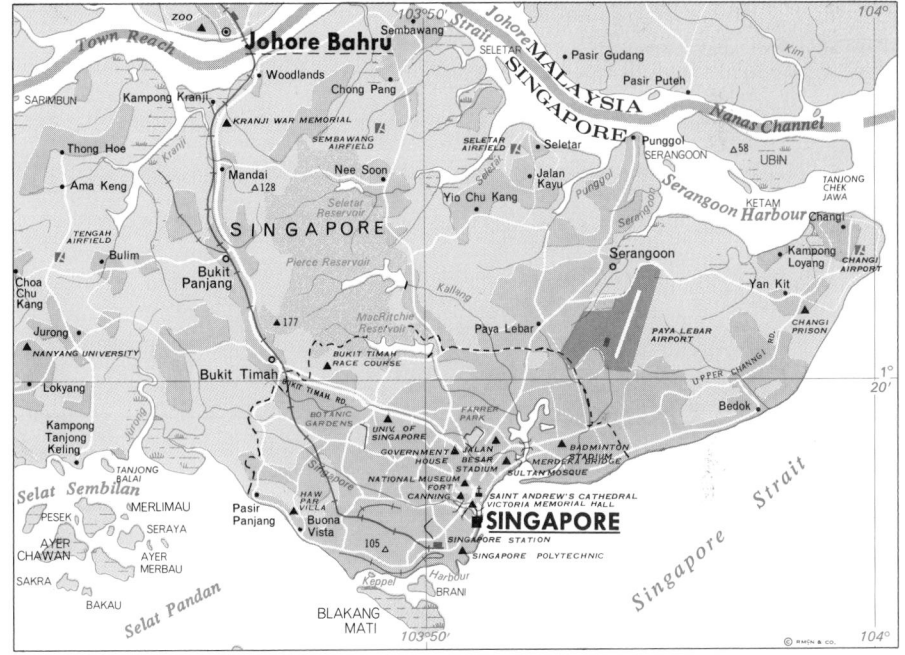

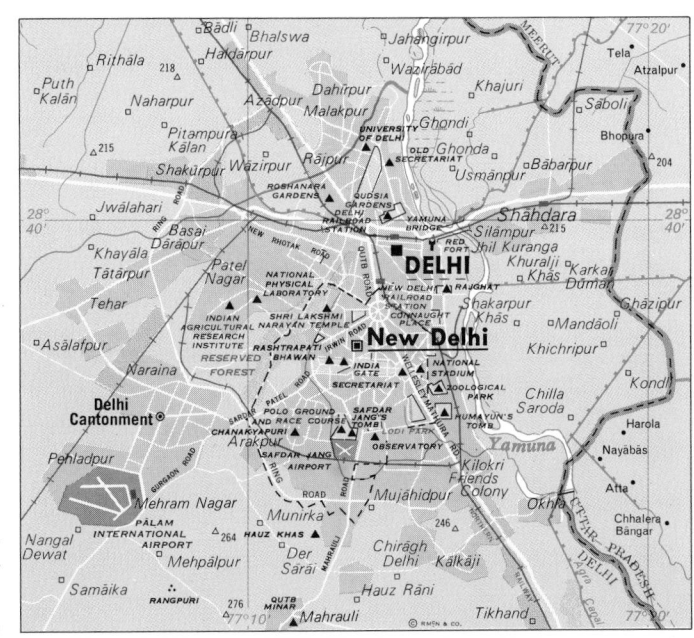

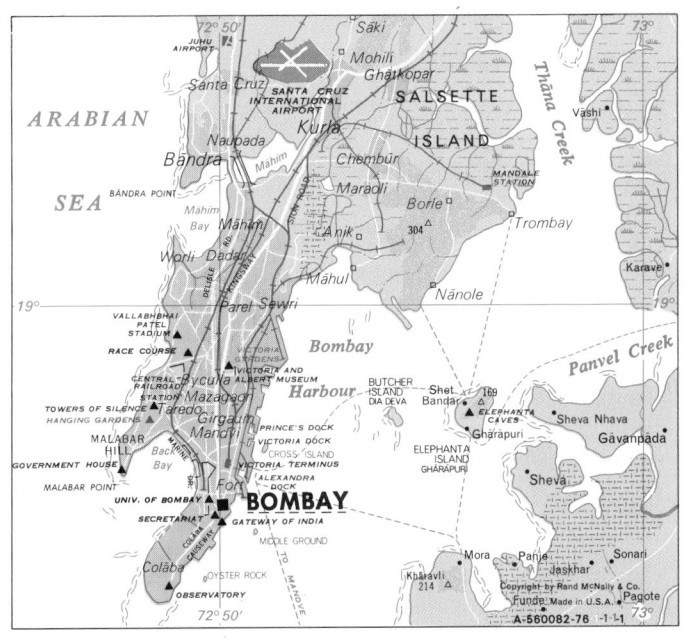

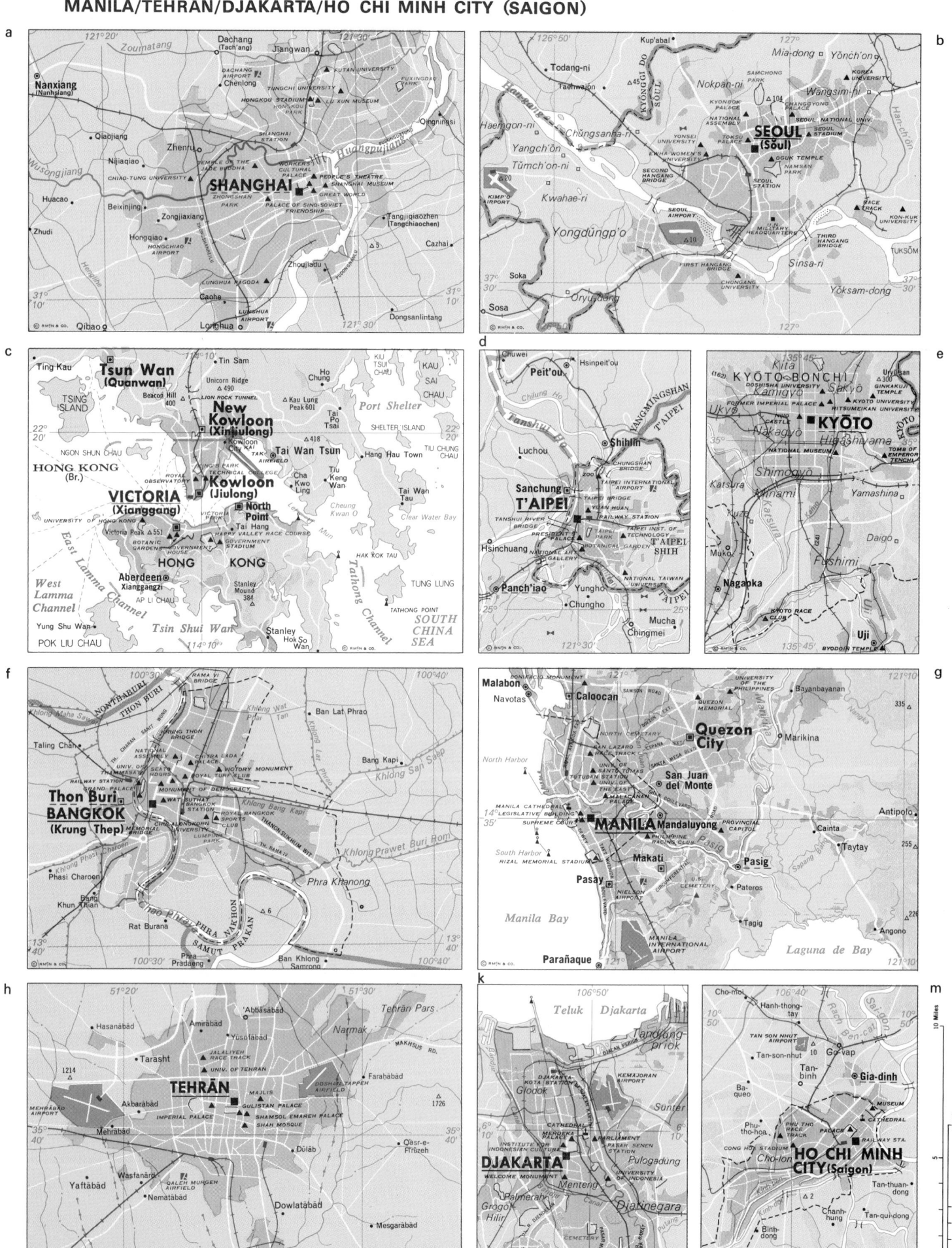
a
SHANGHAI
Nanxiang (Nanhsiang)
Dachang (Tach'ang)
Jiangwan
Chenlong
Qingningsi
Qiaojiang
Zhenru
Najiaqiao
Wusongjiang
Huangpujiang
Huacao
Beixinjing
Zongjiaxiang
Zhudi
Hongqiao
Hongqiao Airport
Tangjiqiaozhen (Tangchiaochen)
Cazhai
Zhoujiadu
Caohe
Longhua
Lunghua Airport
Qibao
Dongsanlintang
b
SEOUL (Sŏul)
Kup'abal
Mia-dong
Yŏnch'on
Todang-ni
Taehwajŏn
Nokpan-ni
Wangsim-ni
Haengon-ni
Chŭngsanha-ri
Yangch'ŏn
Tŭmch'on-ni
Kwahae-ri
Kimp'o Airport
Yongdŭngp'o
Seoul Airport
Sinsa-ri
Tuksŏm
Soka
Sosa
Oryu-dong
Yŏksam-dong
Han'gang
c
VICTORIA (Xianggang)
Tsun Wan (Quanwan)
Ting Kau
Tin Sam
Tsing Yi Island
New Kowloon (Xinjiulong)
Kowloon (Jiulong)
Tai Wan Tsun
Hang Hau Town
North Point
HONG KONG (Br.)
HONG KONG
Aberdeen
Xianggangzi
AP LI CHAU
Port Shelter
West Lamma Channel
East Lamma Channel
Tsin Shui Wan
Yung Shu Wan
POK LIU CHAU
Stanley
Tathong Channel
SOUTH CHINA SEA
TUNG LUNG
d
T'AIPEI
Chuwei
Hsinpeit'ou
Peit'ou
Shihlin
Luchou
Tanshui Ho
Sanchung
Hsinchuang
Panch'iao
Yungho
Chungho
Mucha
Chingmei
T'AIPEI SHIH
e
KYŌTO
KYŌTO-BONCHI
Kita
Kamigyō
Sakyō
Ukyō
Nakagyō
Higashiyama
Shimogyō
Minami
Katsura
Yamashina
Daigo
Fushimi
Mukō
Nagaoka
Uji
f
BANGKOK (Krung Thep)
Thon Buri
NONTHABURI
THON BURI
Ban Lat Phrao
Taling Chan
Bang Kapi
Khlong San Saep
Khlong Prawet Buri Rom
Phasi Charoen
Bang Khun Thian
Phra Khanong
Rat Burana
Chao Phraya
PHRA NAKHON
SAMUT PRAKAN
Phra Pradaeng
Ban Khlong Samrong
g
MANILA
Malabon
Navotas
Caloocan
Quezon City
Bayanbayanan
Marikina
North Harbor
San Juan del Monte
Mandaluyong
Antipolo
Cainta
Taytay
Pasig
Makati
Pasay
Pateros
Tagig
Manila Bay
Laguna de Bay
Angono
Parañaque
h
TEHRĀN
Hasanābād
'Abbāsābād
Tehrān Pārs
Amirābād
Yūsofābād
Narmak
Tarasht
Farahābād
Akbarābād
Mehrābād
Qasr-e-Firūzeh
Dūlāb
Wasfanārd
Yaftābād
Nematābād
Dowlatābād
Mesgarābād
Tepe Saif
Rey
k
DJAKARTA
Teluk Djakarta
Tandjungpriok
Glodok
Sunter
Pulogadung
Menteng
Djatinegara
Palmerah
Grogol
Hilir
Kebajoran
m
HO CHI MINH CITY (Saigon)
Cho-moi
Hanh-thong-tay
Tan-son-nhut
Go-vap
Tan-binh
Gia-dinh
Ba-queo
Phu-tho-hoa
Cho-lon
Tan-thuan-dong
Chanh-hung
Tan-qui-dong
Binh-dong
Scale 1:300,000; one inch to 4.7 miles.
Copyright by Rand McNally & Co. Made in U.S.A.
A-560081-76

a

SAYAMA-KYŪRYŌ · Kitano · Mizonuma · Toda · SAITAMA · TŌKYŌ · Kawaguchi · Mabashi △27

Tokorozawa · Niiza · Asaka · Takenotsuka · Nishiarai · Kanemachi · Kambari · MATSUDO RACE TRACK · Matsudo

· Tonogaya · Kiyose · Yamato · CAMP ASAKA (U.S.) · Kamikatsuka · Shimura · Inatsuke · Maeno · Gotanno · CHIBA

· Mizuho · YOKOTA AIR BASE (U.S.) · Nakato · Higashimurayama · Kurume · MUSASHINO-DAICHI · Katayama · CAMP ASAKA (U.S.) · Kitamachi · Higashiōizumi · Kita · Sumida · Adachi · Katsushika · Sugano · Ichikawa

· Murayama · YAMATO AIR STATION (U.S.) · Ogawa · Shimohoya · Nerima · CAMP NERIMA · Habashi · CAMP ICHIGAYA · Minamisenju · Ara · △25

· Hajima △106 · Yamato · Kodaira · Suzuki-shinden · Tanashi · Shimoshakuji · Egota · Ochiai · TŌKYŌ UNIV. OF EDUCATION · Hongō · Asakusa · Tōkagi · Edogawa · Tōkai

TACHIKAWA AIR BASE (U.S.) · Akishima · Jogawara △171 · Kokubunji · Musashino · Kichijōji · Shimoigusa · KAMIIGUSA STADIUM · Nakano · OCHANOMIZU WOMEN'S UNIV. · NATIONAL MUSEUM · WASEDA UNIV. · Taitō · Sumida · Kameido · Mizue · Hongyōroku

Tachikawa · HITOTSUBASHI UNIVERSITY · Koganei · INOKASHIRA PARK · TAMA CEMETERY · Asagaya · Suginami · HŌSEI UNIV. · Shinjuku · MEIJI UNIV. · Kanda · Nihonbashi · TŌKYŌ STATION · Kōtō · Ukita · Kasai

· Hino · Kunitachi · Yaho · FUCHŪ AIR STATION (U.S.) · CHŌFU ARPT. · Horinouchi · Takaido · SHIBUYA · MEIJI SHRINE · NATIONAL STADIUM · IMPERIAL PALACE · NATIONAL DIET · SUPREME COURT · Chūō · Fukagawa

Hachiōji · Manganji · Bubai · Kamiishihara · Shibasaki · Kamikitazawa · Akatsutsumi · KEIŌ UNIVERSITY · Minato · TOKYO TOWER · TŌKYŌ

· Toyoda · Fuchū · Chōfu · Inagi · Ikuta △121 · Noborito · Soshigaya · Setagaya · Sangenjaya · Meguro · Koyama · Magome · Ōi · Shinagawa · Tōkyō-kō

Shimoyugi · Higashinakano · Tama · Kaidori · KANAGAWA · Tamagawa · Yoga · Nakanobu · Ōta · Ōmori

△214 · Kamiyugi · Oyama · Nozuta · Kamiasao · TŌKYŪ · △92 · Eda · Maginu · Kizuki · Okusawa · Denenchōfu · Kamata △135 · Rokugō · TOKYO INTERNATIONAL AIRPORT

Seibeeshiden △131 · Kamioyamada · Kanai · TAMA-KYŪRYŌ · Kamoshida · Nakayama · Hiyoshi · Yakō · KAWASAKI STADIUM · Kawasaki

· Kamimizu · CAMP OCHINOBE (U.S.) · Hardmachidai · Onuma · Machida · Kanamori · Nagatsuta · Kawawa · Kōhoku · SŌJIJI TEMPLE · Tsurumi · Kawasaki-kō · Tōkyō-wan

· Shimomizo · Kamitsuruma · Nakayama · Tsunashima · Namamugi

Sagamihara · CAMP ZAMA (U.S.) · △75 · Kozukue · Tsurumi

· Sanda · Zama · Zama-iriya · Shimotsuruma · Yamato · Seya · Imajuku · Kanagawa · MITSUSAWA PARK RACE TRACK · Kawashima

· Kaneda · Ebina · Fukami · Futatsubashi · Putamatagawa · HODOGAYA BASEBALL GROUND · YOKOHAMA · Yokohama-kō

· Atsugi · ATSUGI N. ALS. (U.S.) · SAGAMIHARA-DAICHI · Ayase · Hodogaya · Nishi · YOKOHAMA PARK BASEBALL GROUND · Nakajima

139°30' · 139°40' · 139°50' · 35°40' · 35°30'

© RMSN & CO.

b

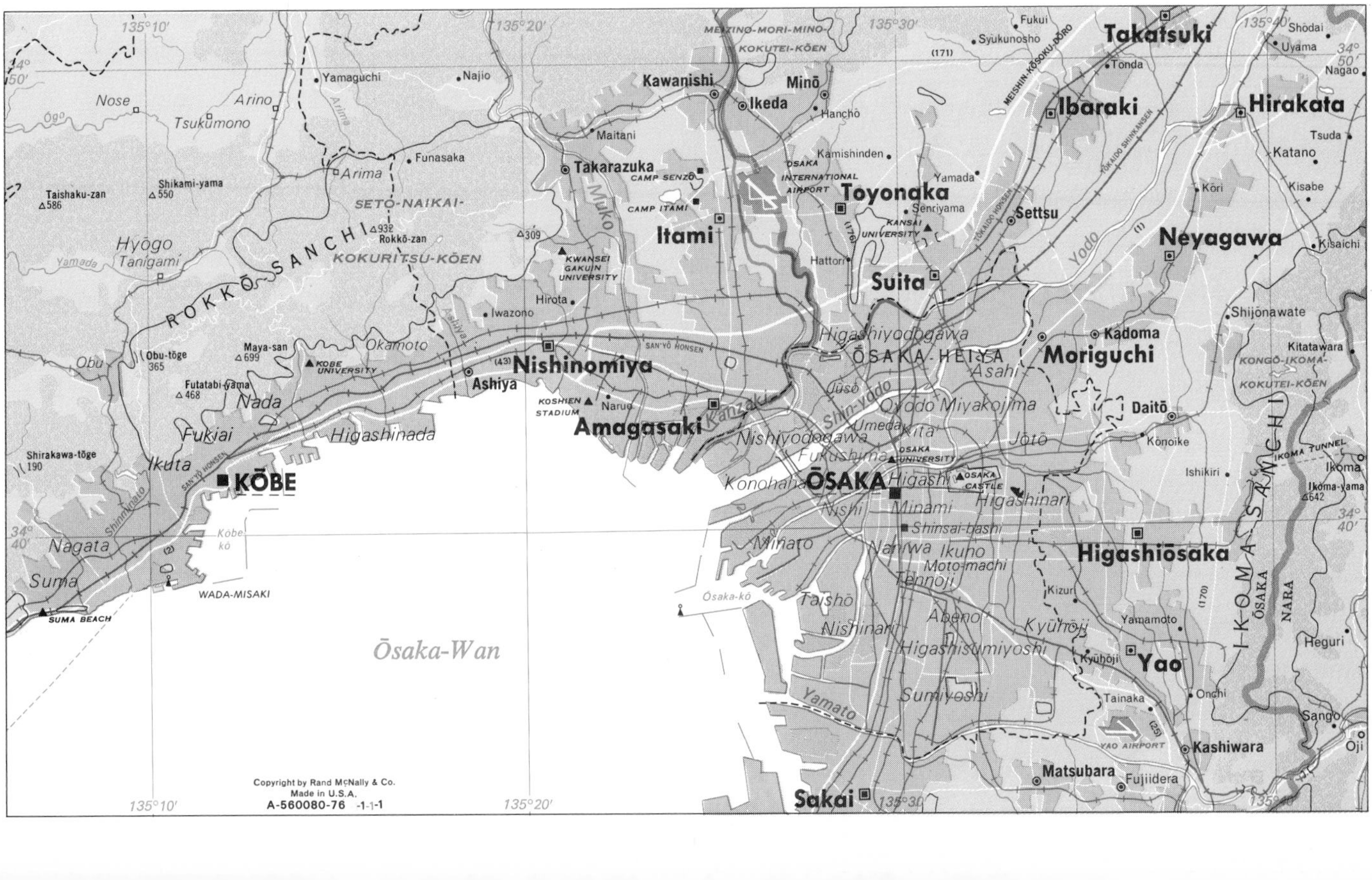

135°10' · 135°20' · MEIJINO-MORI-MINO-KOKUTEI-KŌEN · 135°30' · Fukui · Shōdai · 135°40' · 34°50'

· Yamaguchi · Najio · Kawanishi · Minō · (171) · Syukunosho · Tonda · Uyama · Nagao · Takatsuki

· Nose · Arino · Tsukumono · Maitani · Ikeda · Hancho · OSAKA INTERNATIONAL AIRPORT · Ibaraki · Tsuda · Katano · Hirakata

Taishaku-zan △586 · Shikami-yama △550 · Arima · Funasaka · SETO-NAIKAI- · Takarazuka · CAMP SENZO · Kamishinden · Yamada · KANSAI UNIVERSITY · Senriyama · Settsu · Kōri · Kisabe · Kisaichi

· Hyōgo · Tanigami · Rokkō-zan △932 · KOKURITSU-KŌEN · KWANSEI GAKUIN UNIVERSITY · Toyonaka · Neyagawa

ROKKŌ SANCHI · △309 · Itami · CAMP ITAMI · Hattori · Suita · Higashiyodogawa · ŌSAKA-HEIYA · Asahi · Moriguchi · Kadoma · Shijonawate

· Obu · Maya-san △699 · Okamoto · Hirota · Iwazono · Higashiyodogawa · KONGO-IKOMA KOKUTEI-KŌEN · Daitō · Kitatawara · Ishikiri · Ikoma

Taishaku-zan · KŌBE UNIVERSITY · Nishinomiya · Naruo · Jūsō · Miyakojima · Jōtō · Konoike · IKOMA TUNNEL · Ikoma-yama △642

Obu-tōge 365 · Futatabi-yama △468 · Ashiya · KOSHIEN STADIUM · Kita · Umeda · OSAKA UNIVERSITY · Higashi · Higashinari · Higashiōsaka · NARA

· Nada · Higashinada · Amagasaki · Nishiyodogawa · Fukushima · OSAKA CASTLE · Higashi · Higashinari

· Fukiai · Ikuta · Konohana · ŌSAKA · Higashi · Higashisumiyoshi · IKOMA SANCHI

Shirakawa-tōge 190 · KŌBE · Nishi · Minami · Shinsai-bashi · Ikuho · Yamamoto · Higashiōsaka

· Kōbe-kō · Naniwa · Moto-machi · Tennōji · Kizuri · Yao

· Nagata · Minato · Taishō · Abeno · Kyūhōji · Kyūhōji

· Suma · WADA-MISAKI · Nishinari · Higashisumiyoshi · Tainaka · Sango

SUMA BEACH · Ōsaka-kō · Ōsaka-Wan · Taishō · Sumiyoshi · Yamamoto · YAO AIRPORT · Kashiwara

· Yamato · Sakai · Matsubara · Fujiidera · Oji

135°10' · 135°20' · 135°30' · 135°40' · 34°40'

Copyright by Rand McNally & Co.
Made in U.S.A.
A-560080-76 -1-1-1

10 Miles · 10 Kilometers · Scale 1:300,000; one inch to 4.7 miles.

a

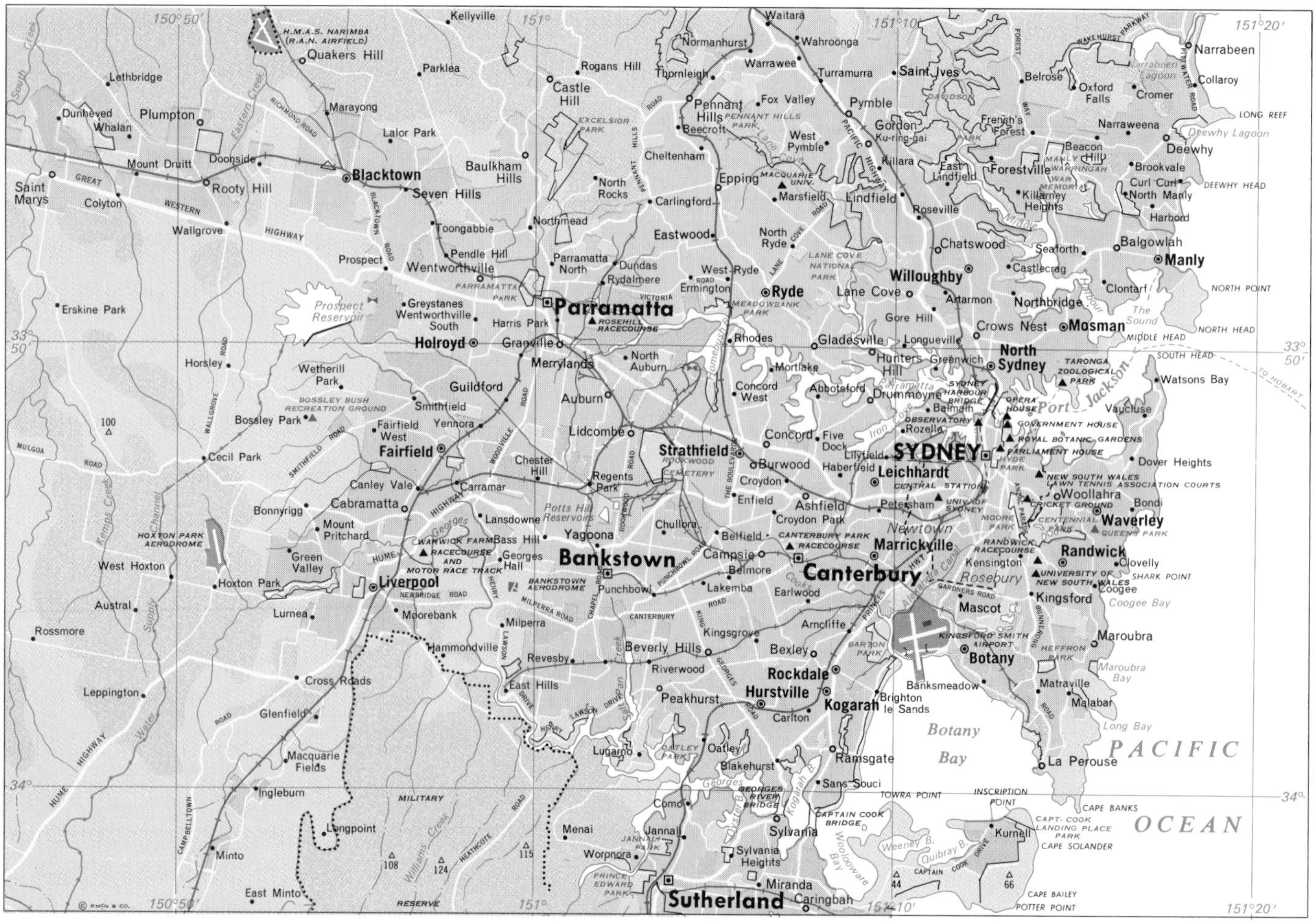

Sydney (map a)

PACIFIC OCEAN

Quakers Hill · Kellyville · Waitara · Normanhurst · Wahroonga · Narrabeen · Collaroy · Cromer
Lethbridge · Rogans Hill · Thornleigh · Warrawee · Turramurra · Saint Ives · Belrose · Oxford Falls
Dunheved · Whalan · Plumpton · Marayong · Parklea · Castle Hill · Pennant Hills · Fox Valley · Pymble · Gordon · French's Forest · Narraweena · Long Reef
Mount Druitt · Doonside · Rooty Hill · Seven Hills · Baulkham Hills · North Rocks · Cheltenham · Epping · West Pymble · Ku-ring-gai · Killara · Beacon Hill · Brookvale · Deewhy · Deewhy Head
Saint Marys · Colyton · Wallgrove · Prospect · Pendle Hill · Wentworthville · Northmead · Parramatta North · Dundas · Eastwood · Marsfield · Lindfield · East Lindfield · Forestville · Curl Curl · North Manly
Erskine Park · Greystanes · Wentworthville South · Harris Park · Ermington · West Ryde · North Ryde · Chatswood · Seaforth · Harbord
Horsley · Wetherill Park · Holroyd · Granville · Merrylands · Rhodes · Gladesville · Longueville · Crows Nest · Mosman · Clontarf · Manly · North Head
PARRAMATTA · Rosehill Racecourse · North Auburn · Concord West · Hunters Hill · Greenwich · North Bridge · Balgowlah
Bossley Park · Fairfield · Smithfield · Auburn · Lidcombe · Concord · Five Dock · Drummoyne · Belmain · North Sydney · Taronga Zoological Park · Watsons Bay
Cecil Park · Fairfield West · Yennora · Chester Hill · Regents Park · Burwood · Haberfield · Leichhardt · SYDNEY · Opera House · Vaucluse
Canley Vale · Carramar · Strathfield · Croydon · Enfield · Ashfield · Petersham · Univ of Sydney · Royal Botanic Gardens · Dover Heights
Bonnyrigg · Cabramatta · Lansdowne · Bass Hill · Chullora · Belfield · Croydon Park · Newtown · New South Wales Cricket Ground · Bondi
Green Valley · Mount Pritchard · Yagoona · Campsie · Marrickville · Randwick · University of New South Wales · Clovelly · Shark Point
West Hoxton · Liverpool · Bankstown · Punchbowl · Belmore · Lakemba · CANTERBURY · Randwick Racecourse · Kensington · Coogee · Coogee Bay
Austral · Moorebank · Milperra · Earlwood · Kingsgrove · Arncliffe · Mascot · Kingsford · Maroubra
Rossmore · Hammondville · Revesby · Beverly Hills · Bexley · Rockdale · Kogarah · Botany · Heffron Park · Matraville · Maroubra Bay
Leppington · Cross Roads · East Hills · Peakhurst · Hurstville · Carlton · Brighton le Sands · Malabar
Glenfield · Riverwood · Lugarno · Oatley · Blakehurst · Ramsgate · Sans Souci · Banksmeadow · Kingsford Smith Airport · Long Bay
Macquarie Fields · Ingleburn · Longpoint · Menai · Como · Jannali · Sylvania · Captain Cook Bridge · Towra Point · Botany Bay · La Perouse · PACIFIC OCEAN
Minto · Wornora · Sylvania Heights · Miranda · Caringbah · Cape Banks · Capt. Cook Landing Place Park · Cape Solander
East Minto · SUTHERLAND · Kurnell · Cape Bailey · Potter Point

b

Melbourne (map b)

Port Phillip Bay

Sydenham · BROADMEADOWS · Tullamarine · Thomastown · Campbellfield · Diamond Creek · Kangaroo Ground · Little Sugarloaf
Keilor · Tullamarine Airport · Jacana · Glenroy · Keon Park · Bundoora · Greensborough · Research · Mount Lofty
Saint Albans · Airport West · Oak Park · Hadfield · Reservoir · Watsonia · Mont Park · Montmorency · Eltham · Wonga Park · Clifford Park
Deer Park · Albion · West Essendon · Essendon · Pascoe Vale · Merlynston · Regent · East Preston · Macleod · Lower Plenty · Eltham · Warrandyte · Black Springs · Lilydale
Sunshine · Maidstone · Braybrook · Maribyrnong · Brunswick · COBURG · PRESTON · Thornbury · West Heidelberg · Heidelberg · Templestowe · South Warrandyte · Park Orchards · Black Springs Hill
Footscray · Kingsville · Yarraville · MELBOURNE · Fitzroy · NORTHCOTE · Ivanhoe · Doncaster · Doncaster East · Ringwood North · Mooroolbark · Croydon · Kilsyth · Montrose
Spotswood · South Melbourne · Richmond · KEW · HAWTHORN · North Balwyn · Box Hill · Mitcham · RINGWOOD · Mount Dandenong
Newport · Paisley · Port Melbourne · Prahran · CAMBERWELL · Balwyn · North Box Hill · Blackburn · NUNAWADING · Forest Hill · Bayswater North · The Basin
Altona North · Williamstown · Saint Kilda · Elwood · MALVERN · Burwood · Ashburton · Bennettswood · East Burwood · Vermont · Wantirna · Bayswater · Boronia · Olinda
Laverton · Altona · Brighton · CAULFIELD · Glenhuntly · Chadstone · Mount Waverley · Holmesglen · Glen Waverley · Wantirna South · One Tree Hill · Sassafras · FERNTREE GULLY
Seaholme · Galvin · Oakleigh · Bentleigh · Ormond · Notting Hill · Monash University · Wheelers Hill · Scoresby · Upper Ferntree Gully · Ferny Creek
Point Cook · Brighton · Moorabbin · Clayton · Mulgrave · Rowville · Lysterfield · Mount Morton · Belgrave
Sandringham · Hampton · Highett · South Oakleigh · Sandown Park Racecourse · Harrisfield · SPRINGVALE · Noble Park · Churchill National Park · Lysterfield Hills · Sugarloaf Hill
Black Rock · Cheltenham · Heatherton · Moorabbin Airport · Dingley · Springvale South · DANDENONG · Narre Warren North · Doveton
Beaumaris · Mentone · Braeside · Keysborough · Hallam · Harkaway · Mordialloc

Scale 1:300,000; one inch to 4.7 miles.

10 Miles · 10 Kilometers

a
b
c
d
CAIRO (Al-Qāhirah)
Al-Jīzah (Giza)
Imbābah
Shubrā al-Khaymah
Misr al-Jadīdah
Heliopolis
Old Cairo
GIZA PYRAMIDS
SPHINX
CAIRO INTERNATIONAL AIRPORT
CAIRO (ALMAZA) AIRPORT
BRAZZAVILLE
KINSHASA (Léopoldville)
CONGO
ZAIRE
ÎLE MBAMOU
LAGOS
Mushin
Ikeja
Agege
Shomolu
Lagos Lagoon
ATLANTIC OCEAN
IKEJA FEDERAL TERRITORY
JOHANNESBURG
Germiston
Boksburg
Benoni
Brakpan
Springs
Kempton Park
Alberton
Edenvale
Alexandra
Randburg
Roodepoort
Krugersdorp
Meadowlands
Soweto
W I T W A T E R S R A N D
KLIPRIVIERSBERG
Scale 1:300,000; one inch to 4.7 miles.
10 Miles
10 Kilometers
Copyright © by Rand McNally & Co. Made in U.S.A. A-580052-76 -1-1-1

Country and Regional Map Legend

Cultural Features

Political Boundaries

International (over water)
(Demarcated, Undemarcated, and Administrative)

Disputed de facto

Disputed de jure

Indefinite or Undefined

Secondary, State, Provincial, etc. (over water)

Parks, Indian Reservations

City Limits   Built-up Areas

Cities, Towns and Villages

PARIS — 1,000,000 and over (Metropolitan Area Population)

Ufa — 500,000 to 1,000,000 (Metropolitan Area Population)

Győr — 50,000 to 500,000

Agadir — 25,000 to 50,000

Moreno — 0 to 25,000

TŌKYŌ — National Capitals

Boise — Secondary Capitals

Note: On maps at 1:20,000,000 and smaller, and on maps at 1:1,000,000, the type size indicates the relative importance of cities, not the specific population classification shown above.

Transportation

Railroads

Railroads
On 1:1,000,000 scale maps

Railroad Ferries

Roads

Major
Other   On 1:1,000,000 scale maps

Major
Other   On 1:4,000,000 scale maps

On other scale maps

Caravan Routes

Airports

Other Cultural Features

Dams

Pipelines

Pyramids

Ruins

Land Features

Peaks, Spot Heights

Passes

Sand

Contours

Water Features

Lakes and Reservoirs

Fresh Water

Fresh Water: Intermittent

Salt Water

Salt Water: Intermittent

Other Water Features

Salt Basins, Flats

Swamps

Ice Caps and Glaciers

Rivers

Intermittent Rivers

Aqueducts and Canals

Ship Channels

Falls

Rapids

Springs

Water Depths

Fishing Banks

Sand Bars

Reefs

Country and Regional Maps

This section provides the reader with basic continental, regional, and country reference maps of the world's land areas. The maps are arranged by continents: North America, South America, Europe, Asia, Australia, and Africa. Each section begins with a series of basic thematic maps dealing with the environment, culture, and economy of each continent. Place names on the reference maps are listed in the unique pronouncing index, the last section of the Atlas. A complete legend on the facing page provides a key to the symbols on the reference maps in this section.

To aid the reader in making comparisons, uniform scales for comparable areas were used whenever possible. All continental maps are at the same scale, 1:40,000,000. In addition, most of the world is covered by a series of regional maps at scales of 1:16,000,000 and 1:12,000,000.

Maps at 1:10,000,000 provide even greater detail for parts of Europe, Africa, and Southeast Asia. The United States, parts of Canada, and much of Europe and the Soviet Union are mapped at 1:4,000,000. Seventy-six urbanized areas are shown at 1:1,000,-000. The separate major cities section on pages 52 to 69 contain larger-scale maps of selected urban areas.

The reference maps use different colors (layer tints) to show general elevation above and below sea level. A legend on each map provides a key to the colors used for elevation.

The maps also provide the reader with a three-dimensional impression of the way the land looks. This terrain representation, superimposed on the layer tints, provides a realistic and readily visualized impression of the surface.

This Atlas generally uses a *local name* policy for naming cities and towns and local land and water features. However, for a few major cities the Anglicized name is preferred and the local name given in parentheses, for instance, Moscow (Moskva), Vienna (Wien), Cologne (Köln). Names in Chinese, Japanese, and other nonalphabetic languages are transliterated into the Roman alphabet. In countries where more than one official language is used, the name is in the dominant local language. The generic parts of local names for land and water features are usually self-explanatory. A complete glossary of foreign geographical terms is given on page 245.

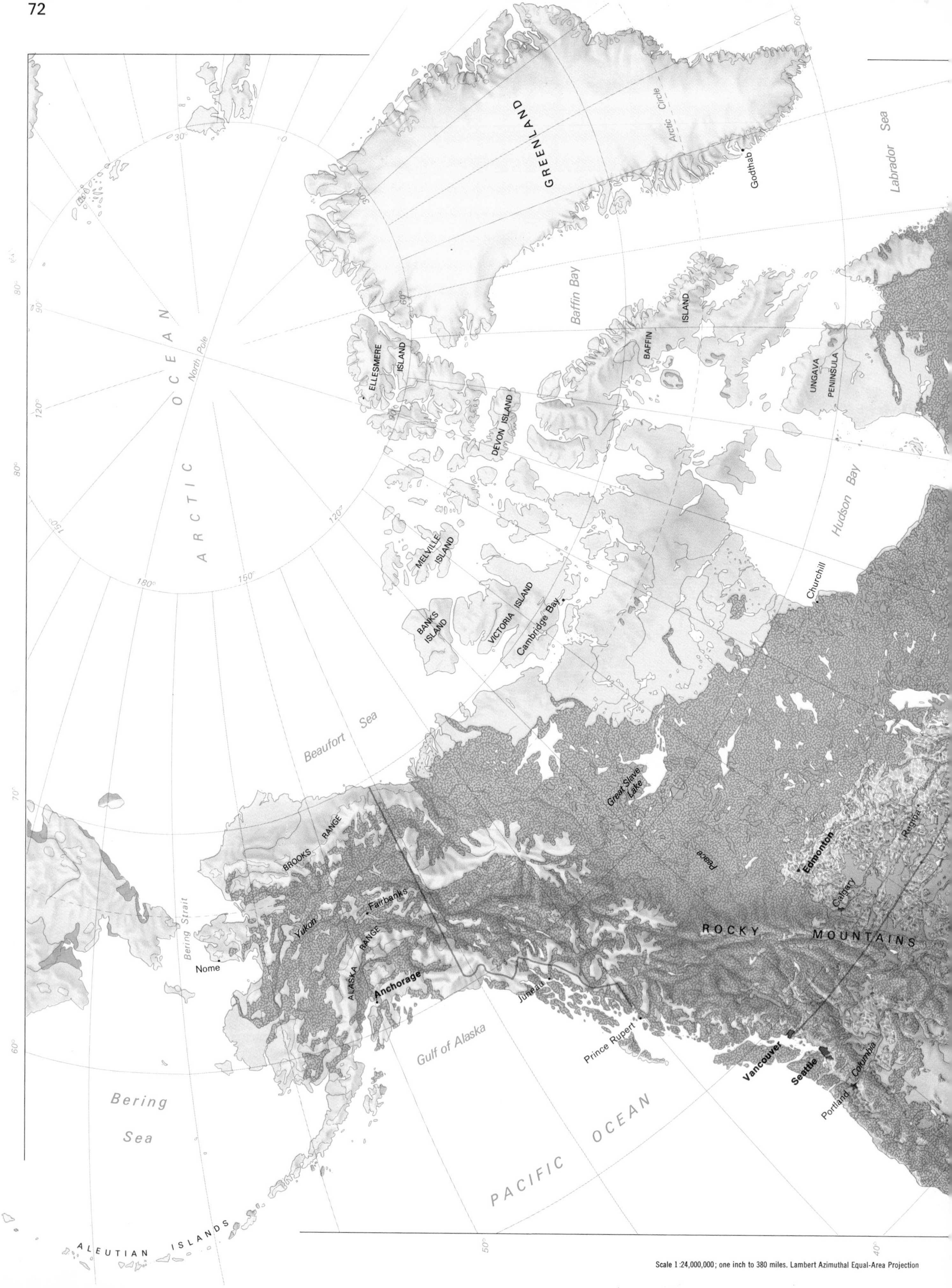

72

GREENLAND

Godthåb

Arctic Circle

Labrador Sea

Baffin Bay

ELLESMERE ISLAND

BAFFIN ISLAND

UNGAVA PENINSULA

DEVON ISLAND

Hudson Bay

MELVILLE ISLAND

Churchill

BANKS ISLAND

VICTORIA ISLAND

Cambridge Bay

A R C T I C   O C E A N

North Pole

Beaufort Sea

Great Slave Lake

Peace

Edmonton

Region

BROOKS RANGE

Yukon

Fairbanks

Calgary

Nome

ROCKY   MOUNTAINS

ALASKA RANGE

Anchorage

Juneau

Prince Rupert

Bering Strait

Vancouver

Seattle

Gulf of Alaska

Columbia

Portland

Bering Sea

P A C I F I C   O C E A N

ALEUTIAN   ISLANDS

Scale 1:24,000,000; one inch to 380 miles. Lambert Azimuthal Equal-Area Projection

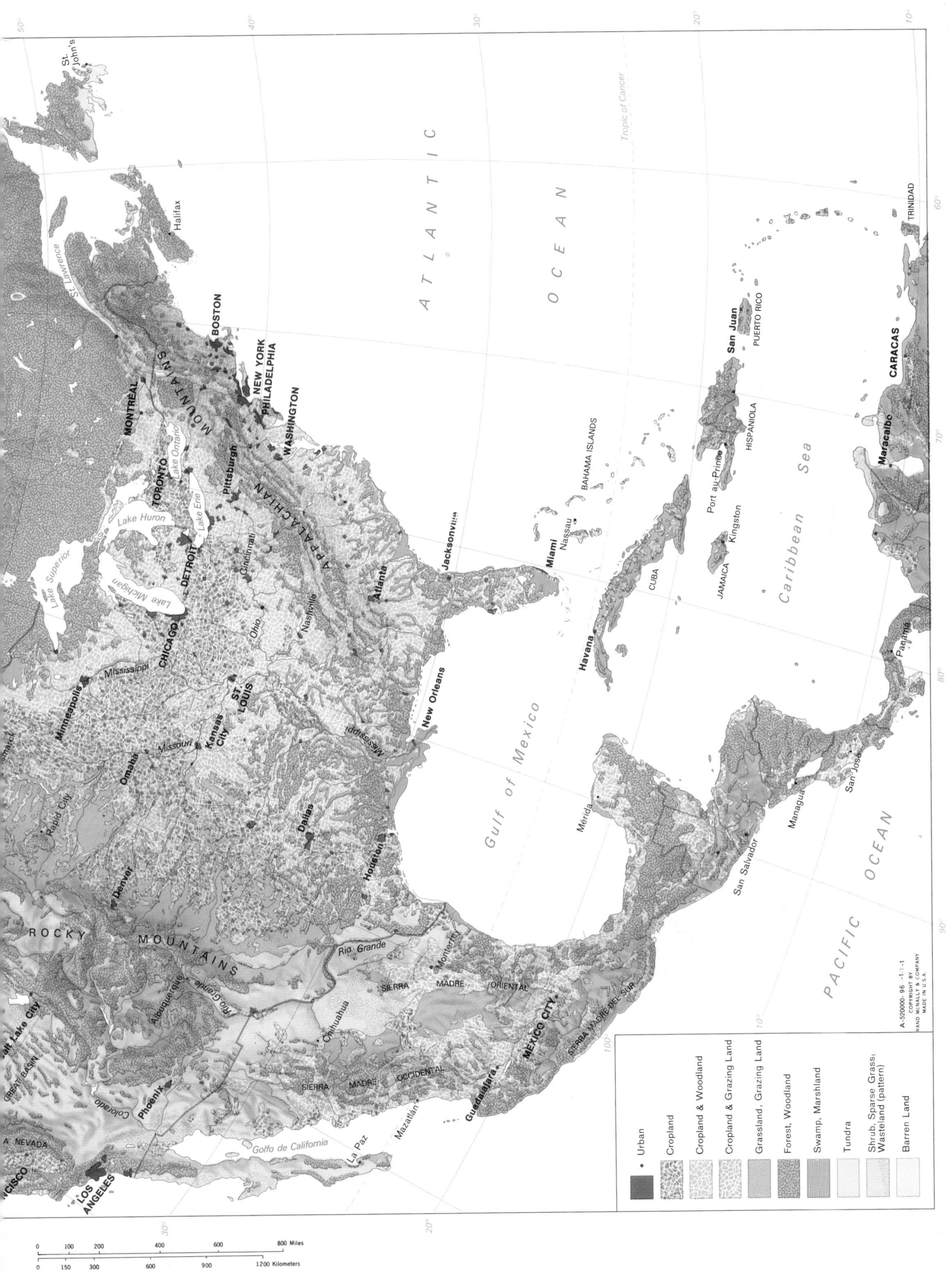

ATLANTIC OCEAN

St. Lawrence

St. John's

Halifax

MONTRÉAL
TORONTO
Lake Ontario
Lake Erie
BOSTON
NEW YORK
PHILADELPHIA
WASHINGTON
Pittsburgh
Lake Huron
Lake Superior
Lake Michigan
DETROIT
CHICAGO
Cincinnati
Ohio
Nashville
Atlanta
Jacksonville
Miami

APPALACHIAN MOUNTAINS

Minneapolis
Mississippi
ST. LOUIS
Kansas City
Missouri
Omaha
Rapid City
Dallas
Houston
New Orleans

Tropic of Cancer

BAHAMA ISLANDS
Nassau
Havana
CUBA
San Juan
PUERTO RICO
HISPANIOLA
Port au-Prince
Kingston
JAMAICA
CARACAS
Maracaibo
TRINIDAD

Caribbean Sea

Denver
ROCKY MOUNTAINS
Salt Lake City
GREAT BASIN
NEVADA
Colorado
Phoenix
Albuquerque
Rio Grande
Rio Grande
SIERRA MADRE ORIENTAL
Monterrey
Chihuahua
SIERRA MADRE OCCIDENTAL
MEXICO CITY
Guadalajara
SIERRA MADRE DEL SUR
Mazatlan
La Paz
Golfo de California

Gulf of Mexico

Mérida

San Salvador
Managua
San José
San Jose
Panama
Guatemala

PACIFIC OCEAN

SAN FRANCISCO
LOS ANGELES

A-500000-96 -1-.1.-1
COPYRIGHT BY
RAND McNALLY & COMPANY
MADE IN U.S.A.

Urban
Cropland
Cropland & Woodland
Cropland & Grazing Land
Grassland, Grazing Land
Forest, Woodland
Swamp, Marshland
Tundra
Shrub, Sparse Grass, Wasteland (pattern)
Barren Land

0 100 200 400 600 800 Miles
0 150 300 600 900 1200 Kilometers

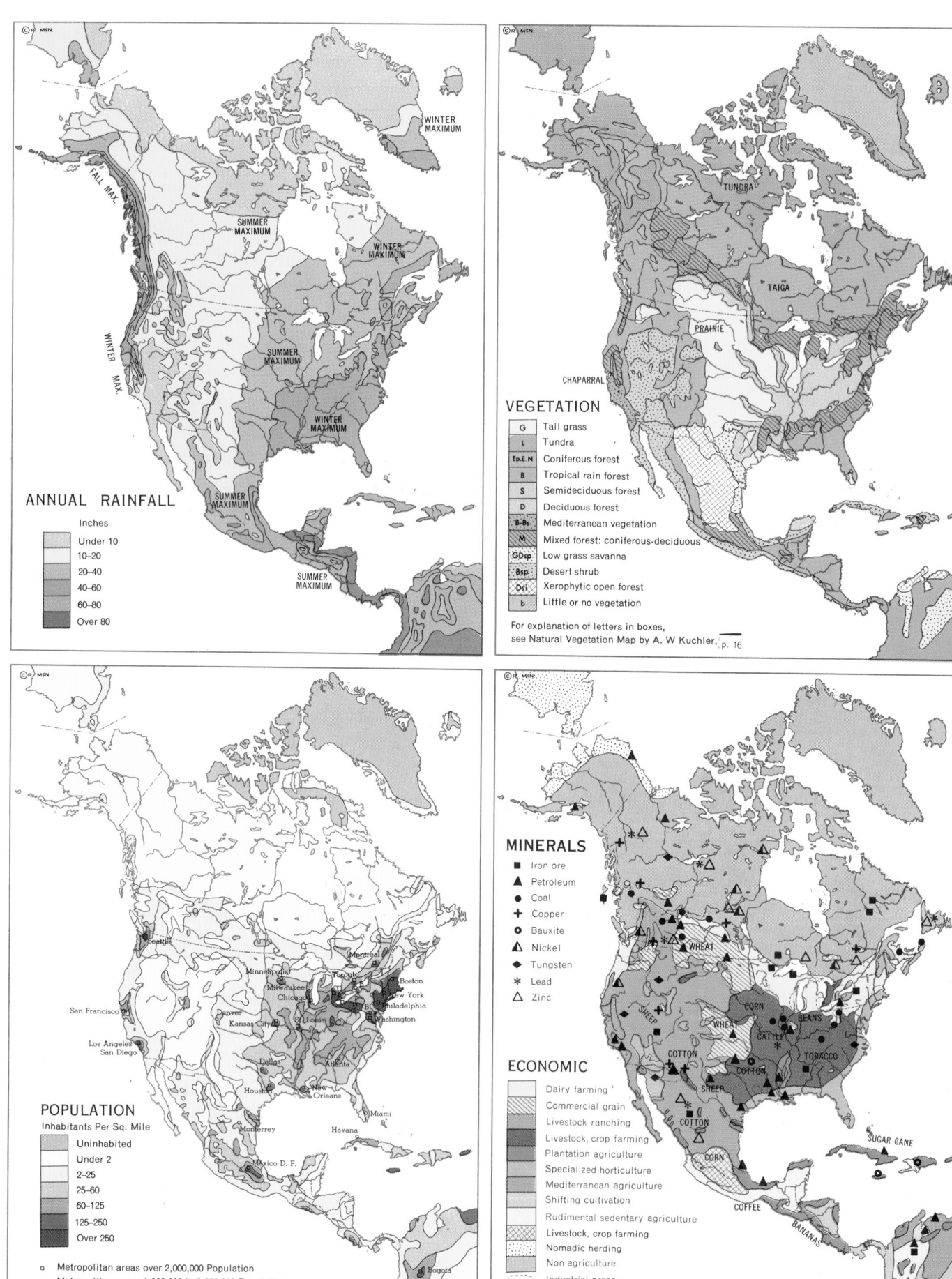

ANNUAL RAINFALL

Inches

- Under 10
- 10–20
- 20–40
- 40–60
- 60–80
- Over 80

WINTER MAXIMUM

FALL MAX.

WINTER MAX.

SUMMER MAXIMUM

WINTER MAXIMUM

SUMMER MAXIMUM

WINTER MAXIMUM

SUMMER MAXIMUM

SUMMER MAXIMUM

VEGETATION

G	Tall grass
L	Tundra
Ep.E.N	Coniferous forest
B	Tropical rain forest
S	Semideciduous forest
D	Deciduous forest
B-Bs	Mediterranean vegetation
M	Mixed forest: coniferous-deciduous
GDsp.	Low grass savanna
Bsp.	Desert shrub
Dsi	Xerophytic open forest
b	Little or no vegetation

For explanation of letters in boxes,
see Natural Vegetation Map by A. W Kuchler, p. 16

TUNDRA

TAIGA

PRAIRIE

CHAPARRAL

POPULATION

Inhabitants Per Sq. Mile

- Uninhabited
- Under 2
- 2–25
- 25–60
- 60–125
- 125–250
- Over 250

□ Metropolitan areas over 2,000,000 Population
○ Metropolitan areas 1,000,000 to 2,000,000 Population

Seattle
Montreal
Minneapolis
Milwaukee
Toronto
Boston
San Francisco
Chicago
New York
Philadelphia
Denver
St. Louis
Washington
Kansas City
Los Angeles
San Diego
Dallas
Atlanta
Houston
New Orleans
Miami
Monterrey
Havana
Mexico D. F.
Bogotá

MINERALS

- ■ Iron ore
- ▲ Petroleum
- ● Coal
- + Copper
- ○ Bauxite
- ▲ Nickel
- ◆ Tungsten
- ✳ Lead
- △ Zinc

ECONOMIC

	Dairy farming
	Commercial grain
	Livestock ranching
	Livestock, crop farming
	Plantation agriculture
	Specialized horticulture
	Mediterranean agriculture
	Shifting cultivation
	Rudimental sedentary agriculture
	Livestock, crop farming
	Nomadic herding
	Non agriculture
	Industrial areas

WHEAT
SHEEP
WHEAT
CORN
BEANS
CATTLE
COTTON
TOBACCO
COTTON
SHEEP
COTTON
CORN
COFFEE
SUGAR CANE
BANANAS

A-520000-16 - 1- -4

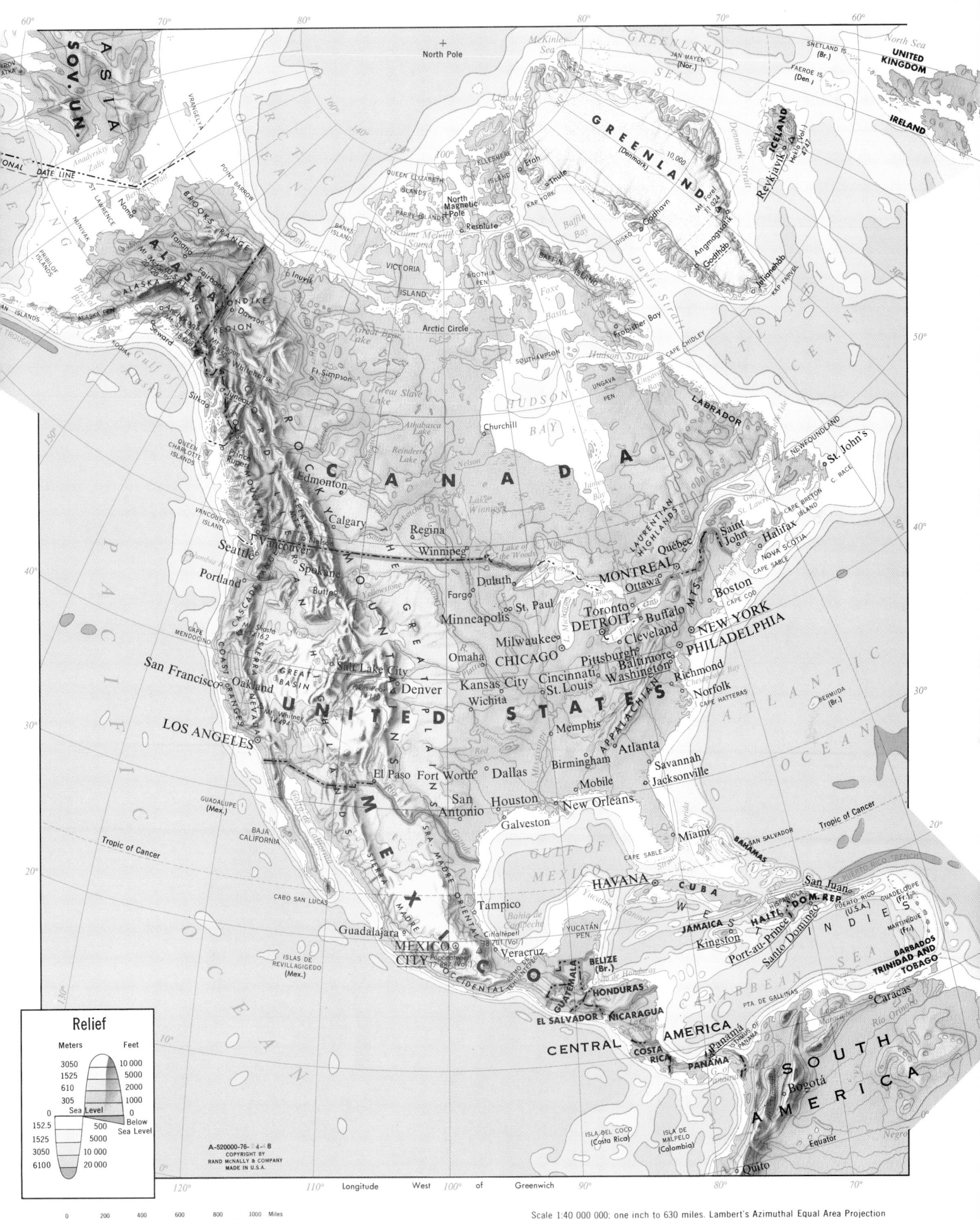

ASIA
SOV. UN.

UNITED KINGDOM

IRELAND

GREENLAND
(Denmark)

ICELAND
Reykjavik

North Pole

CANADA

ALASKA

BROOKS RANGE

Fairbanks

Anchorage

Whitehorse

Juneau

Edmonton

Calgary

Regina

Winnipeg

Vancouver

Seattle

Spokane

Portland

Butte

HUDSON
BAY

LABRADOR

NEWFOUNDLAND

St. John's

Duluth

Fargo

Minneapolis

St. Paul

Milwaukee

CHICAGO

Omaha

Salt Lake City

Denver

San Francisco

Oakland

LOS ANGELES

Kansas City

Wichita

St. Louis

Memphis

MONTREAL

Ottawa

Toronto

DETROIT

Cleveland

Buffalo

Québec

Saint John

Halifax

Boston

NEW YORK

PHILADELPHIA

Pittsburgh

Cincinnati

Baltimore

Washington

Richmond

Norfolk

Atlanta

Birmingham

Savannah

Jacksonville

Mobile

El Paso

Fort Worth

Dallas

San Antonio

Houston

New Orleans

Galveston

Miami

BAHAMAS

SAN SALVADOR

MEXICO

MEXICO CITY

Guadalajara

Tampico

Veracruz

HAVANA

CUBA

JAMAICA

Kingston

HAITI

DOM. REP.

Santo Domingo

San Juan

PUERTO RICO

BELIZE (Br.)

GUATEMALA

HONDURAS

EL SALVADOR

NICARAGUA

COSTA RICA

PANAMÁ

CENTRAL AMERICA

CARIBBEAN SEA

BARBADOS

TRINIDAD AND TOBAGO

Caracas

Bogotá

SOUTH AMERICA

Quito

PACIFIC OCEAN

ATLANTIC OCEAN

GULF OF MEXICO

Tropic of Cancer

Equator

Relief

Meters	Feet
3050	10 000
1525	5000
610	2000
305	1000
0 Sea Level	0
	Below Sea Level
152.5	500
1525	5000
3050	10 000
6100	20 000

A-520000-76-
COPYRIGHT BY
RAND MCNALLY & COMPANY
MADE IN U.S.A.

0 200 400 600 800 1000 Miles
0 400 800 1,200 1600 Kilometers

Scale 1:40 000 000; one inch to 630 miles. Lambert's Azimuthal Equal Area Projection
Elevations and depressions are given in feet

76

PACIFIC OCEAN

Vancouver

Seattle

Spokane

Portland

CASCADE RANGE

Columbia

Medford

Boise

Calgary

ROCKY MOUNTAINS

Regina

Billings

Bismarck

Rapid City

Missouri

Casper

Denver

Omah

Great Salt Lake

Salt Lake City

ROCKY

Reno

GREAT BASIN

SAN FRANCISCO

SIERRA NEVADA

Fresno

Las Vegas

Wichita

LOS ANGELES

Colorado

Albuquerque

MOUNTAINS

Amarillo

Oklaho City

San Diego

Phoenix

Red

El Paso

Odessa

PACIFIC OCÉAN

Hermosillo

Gulf of California

Rio Grande

San Antonio

SIERRA MADRE OCCIDENTAL

Chihuahua

SIERRA MADRE ORIENTAL

Torreon

Rio Grande

Monterrey

Lake Winnipeg

W

Moosonee

James Bay

Gulf of St. Lawrence

St. Lawrence

Halifax

Quebec

Thunder Bay

Lake Superior

Sudbury

MONTRÉAL

Bangor

Duluth

BOSTON

polis

Lake Huron

Lake Michigan

TORONTO

Lake Ontario

Buffalo

MOUNTAINS

Milwaukee

DETROIT

Lake Erie

NEW YORK

Mississippi

Cleveland

PHILADELPHIA

CHICAGO

Pittsburgh

WASHINGTON

Indianapolis

Cincinnati

APPALACHIAN

Missouri

Norfolk

ansas City

ST. LOUIS

Ohio

Roanoke

PLATEAU

Nashville

Charlotte

OZARK

Arkansas

Memphis

ATLANTIC OCEAN

Little Rock

Mississippi

Red

Atlanta

Charleston

Birmingham

Jacksonville

Tallahassee

ston

New Orleans

Tampa

Gulf of Mexico

Miami

Nassau

Legend

- Urban
- Cropland
- Cropland & Woodland
- Cropland & Grazing Land
- Grassland, Grazing Land
- Forest, Woodland
- Swamp, Marshland
- Shrub, Sparse Grass, Wasteland (pattern)
- Barren Land

Scale 1:12,000,000; one inch to 190 miles. Polyconic Projection

0 50 100 200 300 400 Miles

0 75 150 300 450 600 Kilometers

PHYSIOGRAPHIC DIVISIONS

1 Pacific Mountain System
2 Intermontane Plateaus
3 Rocky Mountain System
4 Interior Plains
5 Ozark-Ouachita Highlands
6 Gulf-Atlantic Plain
7 Appalachian Highlands
8 Laurentian Upland (Canadian Shield)
9 Hudson Bay Lowland

Scale 1: 12 000 000; One inch to 190 miles.   POLYCONIC PROJECTION

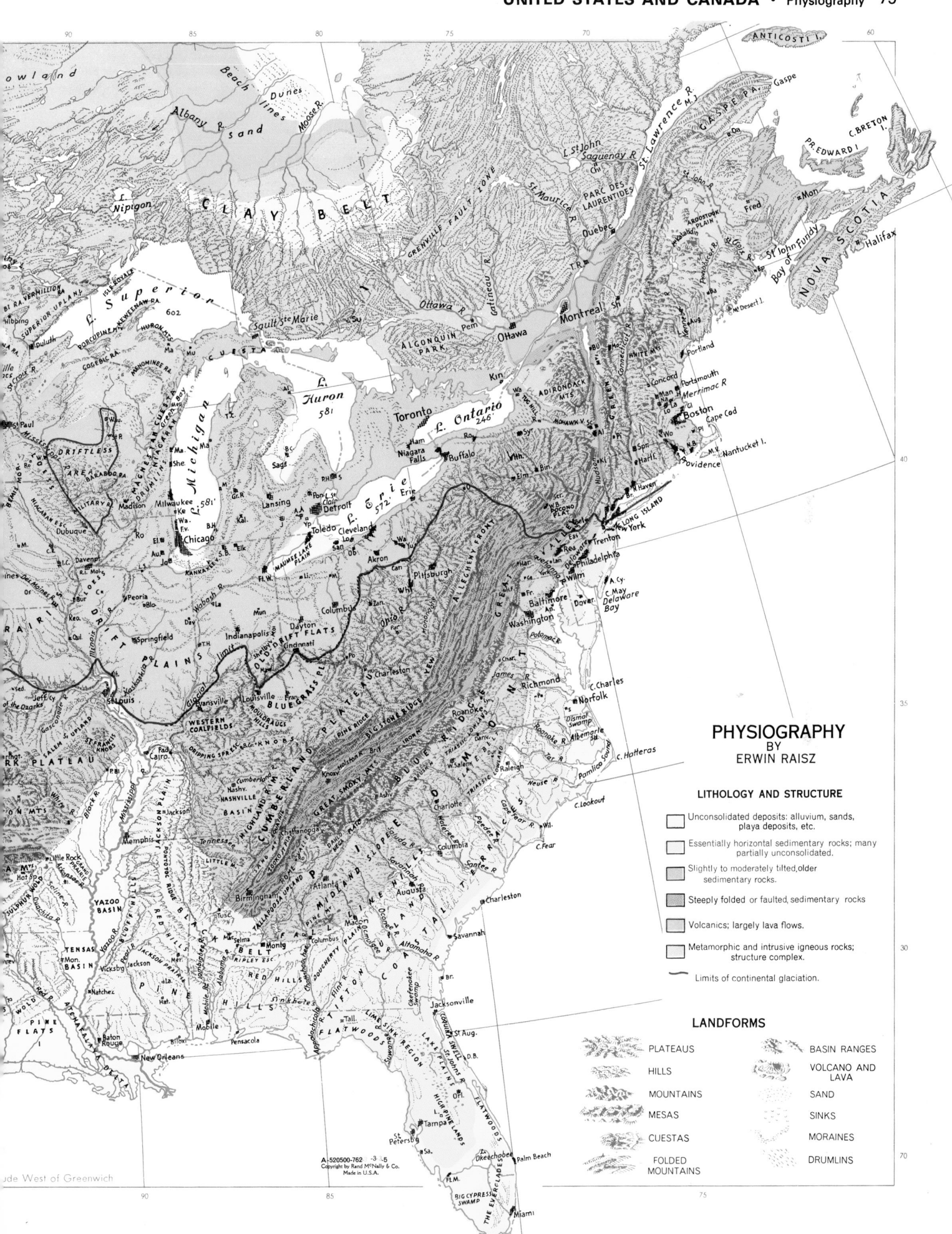

PHYSIOGRAPHY
BY
ERWIN RAISZ

LITHOLOGY AND STRUCTURE

Unconsolidated deposits: alluvium, sands,
playa deposits, etc.

Essentially horizontal sedimentary rocks; many
partially unconsolidated.

Slightly to moderately tilted, older
sedimentary rocks.

Steeply folded or faulted, sedimentary rocks

Volcanics; largely lava flows.

Metamorphic and intrusive igneous rocks;
structure complex.

Limits of continental glaciation.

LANDFORMS

PLATEAUS

HILLS

MOUNTAINS

MESAS

CUESTAS

FOLDED
MOUNTAINS

BASIN RANGES

VOLCANO AND
LAVA

SAND

SINKS

MORAINES

DRUMLINS

A-520500-762   -3   5
Copyright by Rand McNally & Co.
Made in U.S.A.

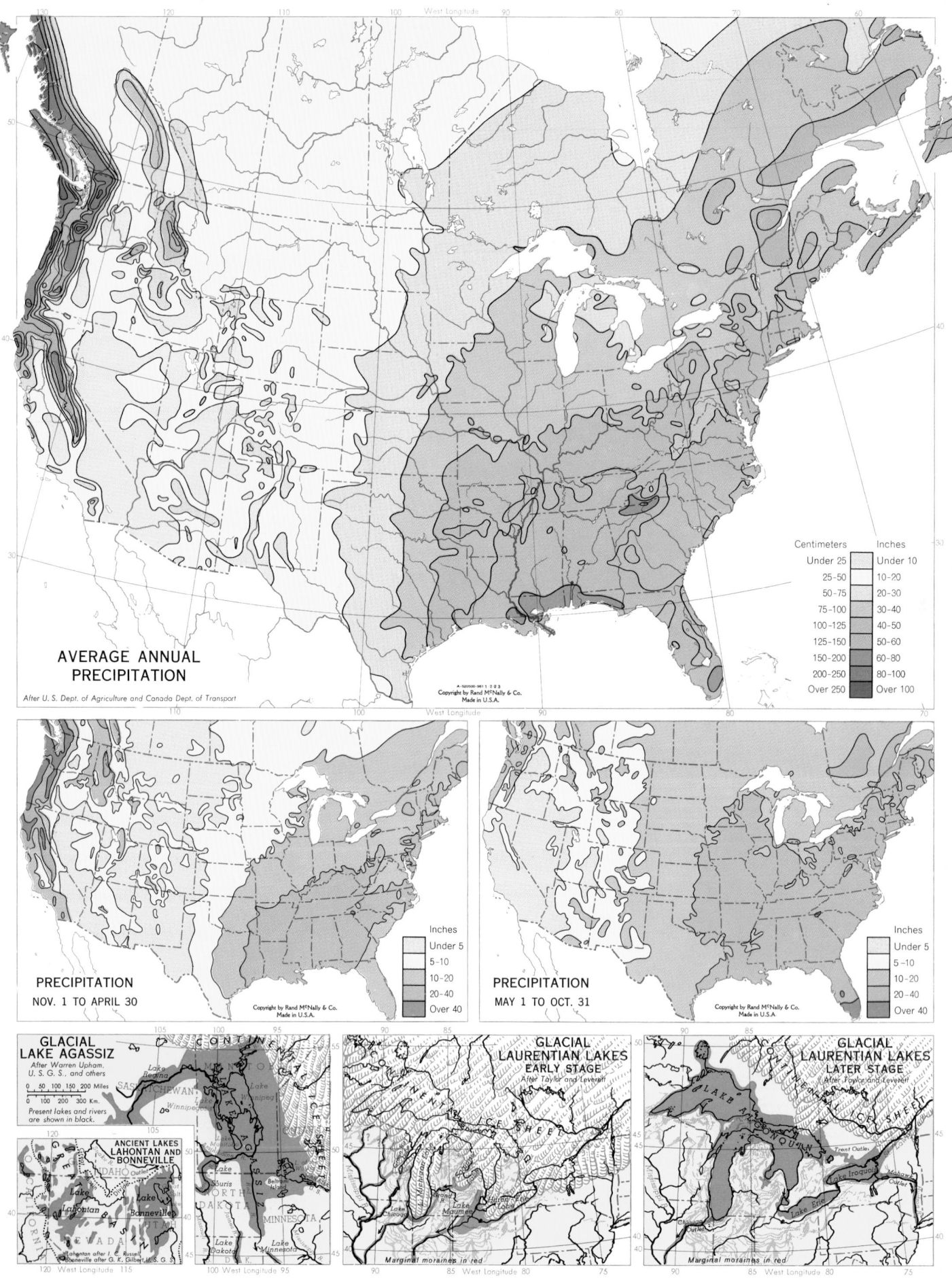

AVERAGE ANNUAL
PRECIPITATION

After U. S. Dept. of Agriculture and Canada Dept. of Transport

Copyright by Rand McNally & Co.
Made in U.S.A.

Centimeters	Inches
Under 25	Under 10
25–50	10–20
50–75	20–30
75–100	30–40
100–125	40–50
125–150	50–60
150–200	60–80
200–250	80–100
Over 250	Over 100

PRECIPITATION
NOV. 1 TO APRIL 30

Inches
Under 5
5–10
10–20
20–40
Over 40

Copyright by Rand McNally & Co.
Made in U.S.A.

PRECIPITATION
MAY 1 TO OCT. 31

Inches
Under 5
5–10
10–20
20–40
Over 40

Copyright by Rand McNally & Co.
Made in U.S.A.

GLACIAL
LAKE AGASSIZ
After Warren Upham,
U. S. G. S., and others

Present lakes and rivers
are shown in black.

ANCIENT LAKES
LAHONTAN AND
BONNEVILLE

GLACIAL
LAURENTIAN LAKES
EARLY STAGE
After Taylor and Leverett

Marginal moraines in red

GLACIAL
LAURENTIAN LAKES
LATER STAGE
After Taylor and Leverett

Marginal moraines in red

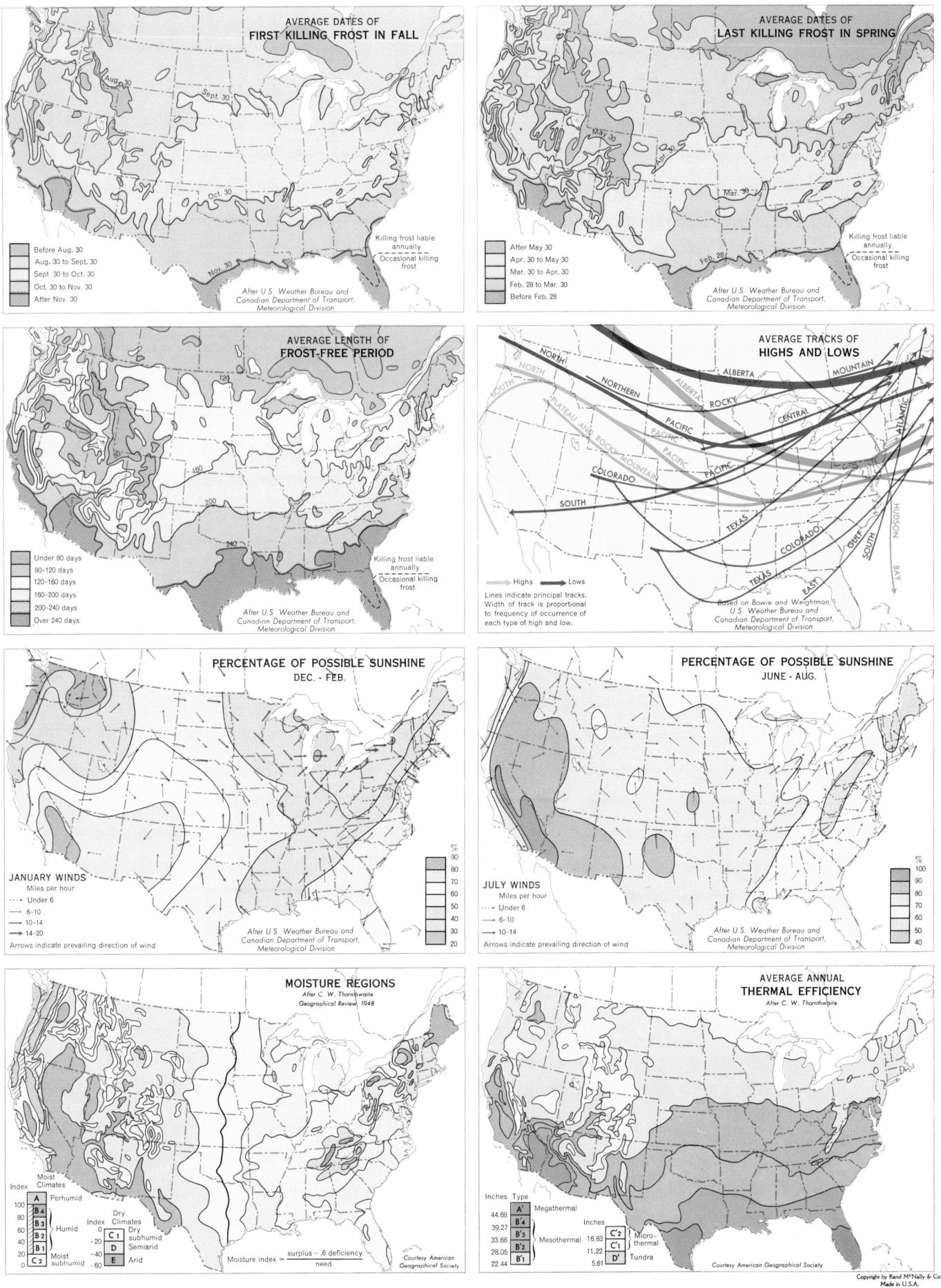

AVERAGE DATES OF FIRST KILLING FROST IN FALL

Aug. 30
Sept. 30
Oct. 30
Nov. 30

Before Aug. 30
Aug. 30 to Sept. 30
Sept. 30 to Oct. 30
Oct. 30 to Nov. 30
After Nov. 30

Killing frost liable annually
Occasional killing frost

After U.S. Weather Bureau and Canadian Department of Transport, Meteorological Division

AVERAGE DATES OF LAST KILLING FROST IN SPRING

May 30
Apr. 30
Mar. 30
Feb. 28

After May 30
Apr. 30 to May 30
Mar. 30 to Apr. 30
Feb. 28 to Mar. 30
Before Feb. 28

Killing frost liable annually
Occasional killing frost

After U.S. Weather Bureau and Canadian Department of Transport, Meteorological Division

AVERAGE LENGTH OF FROST-FREE PERIOD

120
80
160
200
240

Under 80 days
80-120 days
120-160 days
160-200 days
200-240 days
Over 240 days

Killing frost liable annually
Occasional killing frost

After U.S. Weather Bureau and Canadian Department of Transport, Meteorological Division

AVERAGE TRACKS OF HIGHS AND LOWS

NORTH
NORTH
SOUTH
NORTHERN
PLATEAU AND ROCKY MOUNTAIN
PACIFIC
PACIFIC
PACIFIC
PACIFIC
COLORADO
SOUTH
ALBERTA
ALBERTA
ROCKY
MOUNTAIN
CENTRAL
ATLANTIC
HUDSON BAY
TEXAS
COLORADO
SOUTH
GULF
EAST
TEXAS

→ Highs   → Lows

Lines indicate principal tracks. Width of track is proportional to frequency of occurrence of each type of high and low.

Based on Bowie and Weightman, U.S. Weather Bureau and Canadian Department of Transport, Meteorological Division

PERCENTAGE OF POSSIBLE SUNSHINE DEC. - FEB.

JANUARY WINDS
Miles per hour
Under 6
6-10
10-14
14-20
Arrows indicate prevailing direction of wind

%
90
80
70
60
50
40
30
20

After U.S. Weather Bureau and Canadian Department of Transport, Meteorological Division

PERCENTAGE OF POSSIBLE SUNSHINE JUNE - AUG.

JULY WINDS
Miles per hour
Under 6
6-10
10-14
Arrows indicate prevailing direction of wind

%
100
90
80
70
60
50
40

After U.S. Weather Bureau and Canadian Department of Transport, Meteorological Division

MOISTURE REGIONS
After C. W. Thornthwaite
Geographical Review, 1948

Moist Climates

Index		
100	A	Perhumid
80	B4	
60	B3	Humid
40	B2	
20	B1	
0	C2	Moist subhumid

Dry Climates

Index		
0	C1	Dry subhumid
-20	D	Semiarid
-40	E	Arid
-60		

Moisture index = $\dfrac{\text{surplus} - .6\ \text{deficiency}}{\text{need}}$

Courtesy American Geographical Society

AVERAGE ANNUAL THERMAL EFFICIENCY
After C. W. Thornthwaite

Inches	Type	
44.88	A'	Megathermal
39.27	B'4	
33.66	B'3	Mesothermal
28.05	B'2	
22.44	B'1	

Inches		
16.83	C'2	Microthermal
11.22	C'1	
5.61	D'	Tundra

Courtesy American Geographical Society

82

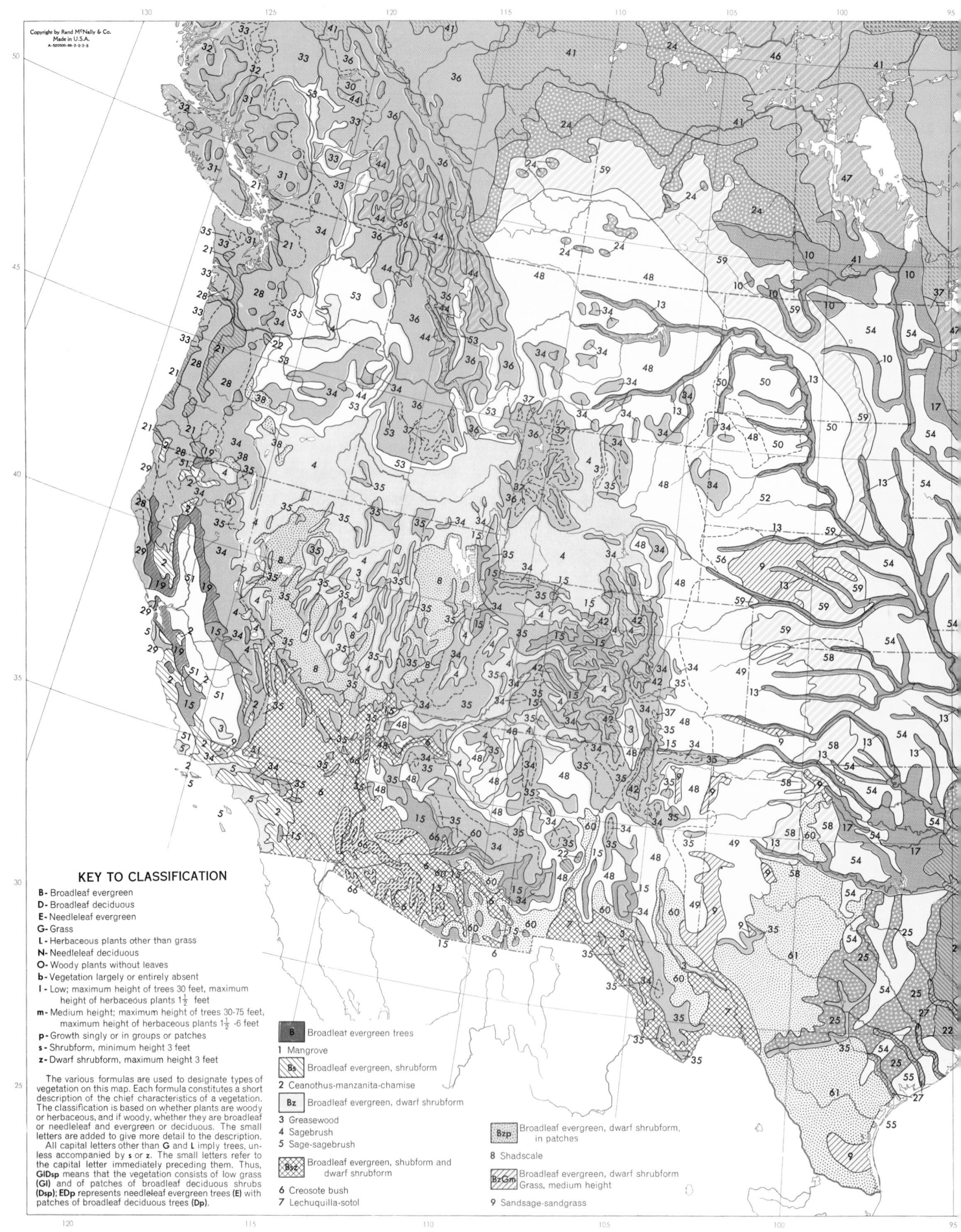

KEY TO CLASSIFICATION

B- Broadleaf evergreen
D- Broadleaf deciduous
E- Needleleaf evergreen
G- Grass
L- Herbaceous plants other than grass
N- Needleleaf deciduous
O- Woody plants without leaves
b- Vegetation largely or entirely absent
l - Low; maximum height of trees 30 feet, maximum height of herbaceous plants 1½ feet
m- Medium height; maximum height of trees 30-75 feet, maximum height of herbaceous plants 1½ -6 feet
p- Growth singly or in groups or patches
s- Shrubform, minimum height 3 feet
z- Dwarf shrubform, maximum height 3 feet

The various formulas are used to designate types of vegetation on this map. Each formula constitutes a short description of the chief characteristics of a vegetation. The classification is based on whether plants are woody or herbaceous, and if woody, whether they are broadleaf or needleleaf and evergreen or deciduous. The small letters are added to give more detail to the description.
All capital letters other than **G** and **L** imply trees, unless accompanied by **s** or **z**. The small letters refer to the capital letter immediately preceding them. Thus, **GlDsp** means that the vegetation consists of low grass (**Gl**) and of patches of broadleaf deciduous shrubs (**Dsp**); **EDp** represents needleleaf evergreen trees (**E**) with patches of broadleaf deciduous trees (**Dp**).

B Broadleaf evergreen trees
1 Mangrove
Bs Broadleaf evergreen, shrubform
2 Ceanothus-manzanita-chamise
Bz Broadleaf evergreen, dwarf shrubform
3 Greasewood
4 Sagebrush
5 Sage-sagebrush
Bsz Broadleaf evergreen, shubform and dwarf shrubform
6 Creosote bush
7 Lechuquilla-sotol

Bzp Broadleaf evergreen, dwarf shrubform, in patches
8 Shadscale
BzGm Broadleaf evergreen, dwarf shrubform Grass, medium height
9 Sandsage-sandgrass

0 25 50 75 100   200   300   400   500 Miles

0 50 100   200   400   600   800 Kilometers

Scale 1:14 000 000; One inch to 22

NATURAL VEGETATION

BY A. W. KÜCHLER

Based on "A Physiognomic Classification of Vegetation"
Annals of the Assoc. of American Geographers, Vol. 39, September, 1949

D Broadleaf deciduous trees

10 Aspen-oak
11 Beech-maple
12 Beech-tulip tree-maple-basswood
13 Cottonwood-willow
14 Maple-basswood
15 Oak
16 Oak-ash-maple
17 Oak-hickory
18 Oak-tulip tree

DB Broadleaf deciduous trees
Broadleaf evergreen trees

19 Oak-madrone

DE Broadleaf deciduous trees
Needleleaf evergreen trees

20 Maple-yellow birch-hemlock-pine
21 Oak-Douglas fir
22 Oak-pine
23 Maple-beech-hemlock

D/Gmp Broadleaf deciduous trees
Grass, medium height, in patches

24 Aspen-needle grass-wheat grass
25 Oak-hickory-bluestem

DN Broadleaf deciduous trees
Needleleaf deciduous trees

26 Bay trees-bald cypress
27 Tupelo-gum-bald cypress

E Needleleaf evergreen trees

28 Douglas fir
29 Douglas fir-redwood
30 Hemlock-arbor vitae
31 Hemlock-arbor vitae-Douglas fir
32 Hemlock-arbor vitae-fir
33 Hemlock-spruce
34 Pine
35 Pine-juniper
36 Pine-spruce
37 Spruce-fir

Esp Needleleaf evergreen, shrubform, in patches

38 Juniper

EDp Needleleaf evergreen trees
Broadleaf deciduous trees, in patches

39 Douglas fir-pine-aspen
40 Pine-spruce-birch
41 Spruce-aspen
42 Spruce-fir-aspen
43 Spruce-poplar-birch

EN Needleleaf evergreen trees
Needleleaf deciduous trees

44 Hemlock-arbor vitae-Douglas fir-larch
45 Pine-bald cypress
46 Pine-spruce-larch
47 Spruce-larch

Gl Grass, low

48 Grama grass
49 Grama grass-buffalo grass
50 Grama grass-needle grass
51 Needle grass-blue grass
52 Wheat grass
53 Wheat grass-blue grass

Gm Grass, medium height

54 Bluestem
55 Broom grass-water grass
56 Marsh grass
57 Saw grass

Gml Grass, medium and low height

58 Bluestem-bunch grass
59 Needle grass-wheat grass

Gl/Dsp Grass, low
Broadleaf deciduous, shrubform, in patches

60 Bunch grass-oak

Gm/Dsp Grass, medium height
Broadleaf deciduous, shrubform, in patches

61 Mesquite grass-mesquite

L Herbaceous plants other than grass

62 Lichens, etc.

LEp Herbaceous plants other than grass
Needleleaf evergreen trees, in patches

63 Lichens-spruce

LEp/Np Herbaceous plants other than grass
Needleleaf evergreen trees, in patches
Needleleaf deciduous trees, in patches

64 Lichens-spruce-larch

N Needleleaf deciduous trees

65 Bald cypress

Op Woody plants without leaves, in patches

66 Palo verde-cacti-ocotillo

b Vegetation largely or entirely absent

tude West of Greenwich

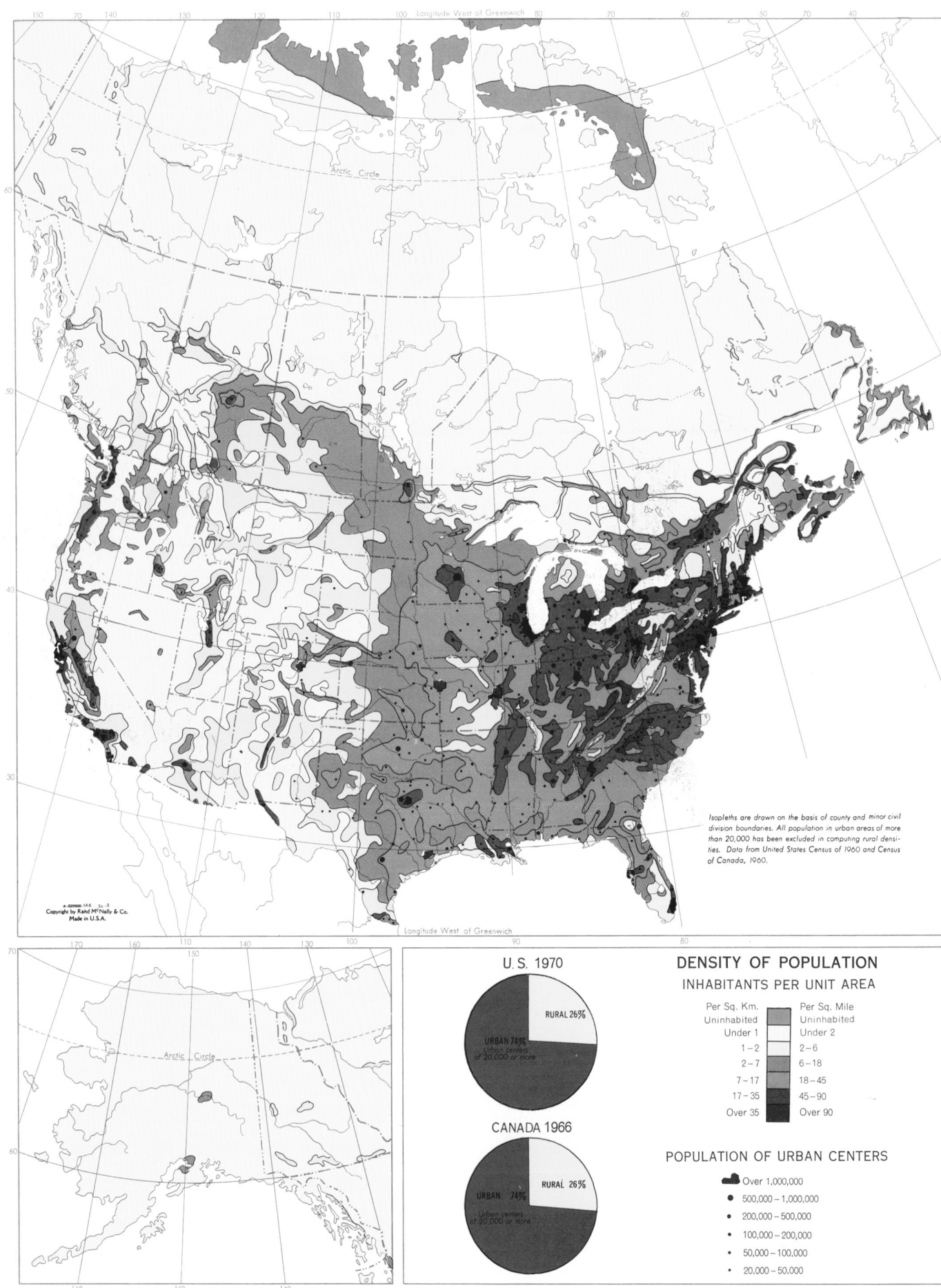

Isopleths are drawn on the basis of county and minor civil division boundaries. All population in urban areas of more than 20,000 has been excluded in computing rural densities. Data from United States Census of 1960 and Census of Canada, 1960.

A-520500-1A-6 3a -3
Copyright by Rand McNally & Co.
Made in U.S.A.

U.S. 1970

RURAL 26%

URBAN 74%
Urban centers
of 20,000 or more

CANADA 1966

RURAL 26%

URBAN 74%
Urban centers
of 20,000 or more

DENSITY OF POPULATION
INHABITANTS PER UNIT AREA

Per Sq. Km.	Per Sq. Mile
Uninhabited	Uninhabited
Under 1	Under 2
1 – 2	2 – 6
2 – 7	6 – 18
7 – 17	18 – 45
17 – 35	45 – 90
Over 35	Over 90

POPULATION OF URBAN CENTERS

Over 1,000,000

500,000 – 1,000,000

200,000 – 500,000

100,000 – 200,000

50,000 – 100,000

20,000 – 50,000

Scale 1: 32 000 000; One inch to 500 miles.   LAMBERT CONFORMAL CONIC PROJECTION

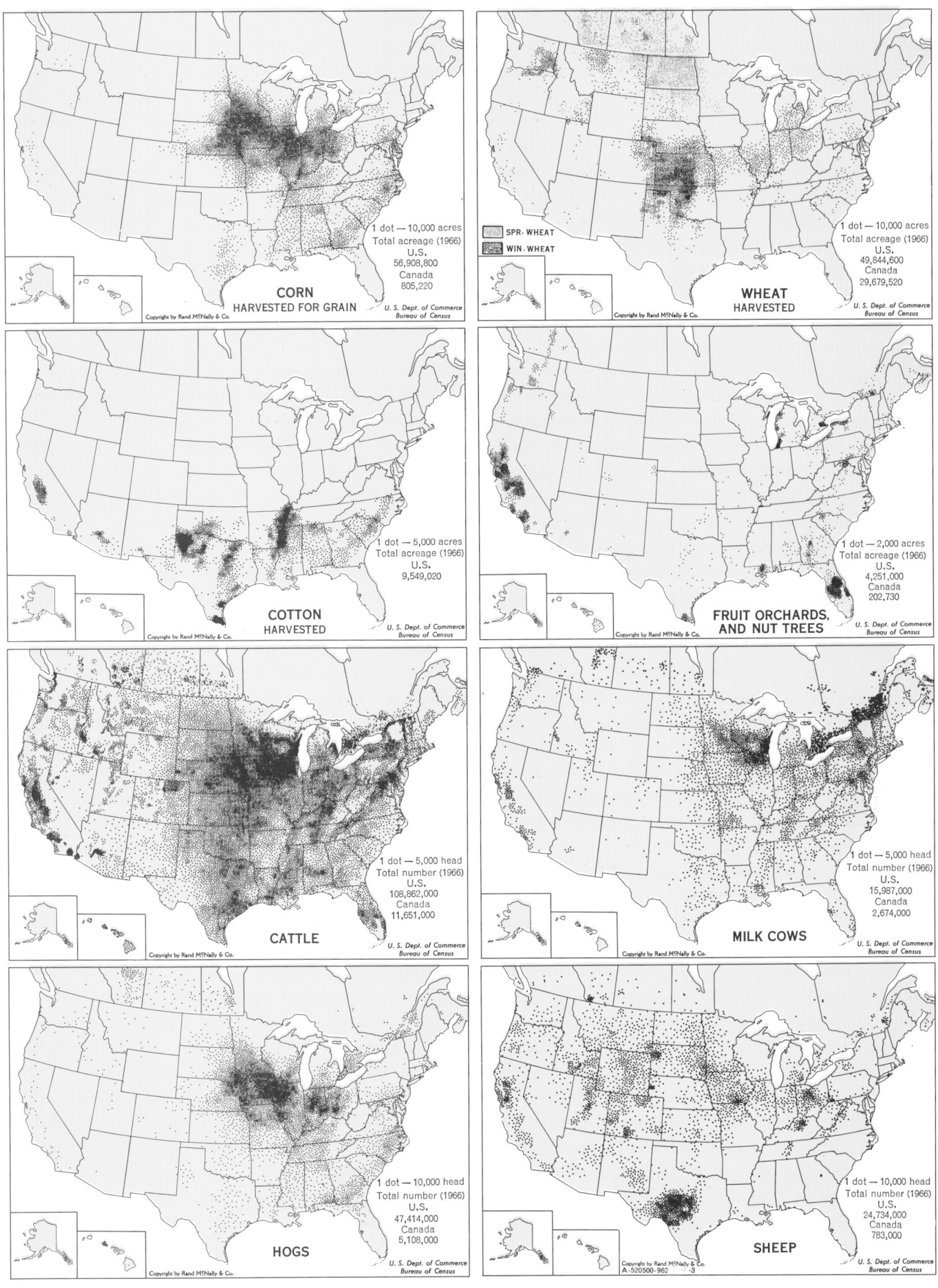

CORN
HARVESTED FOR GRAIN

1 dot — 10,000 acres
Total acreage (1966)
U.S.
56,908,800
Canada
805,220

U. S. Dept. of Commerce
Bureau of Census

Copyright by Rand McNally & Co.

SPR· WHEAT
WIN· WHEAT

WHEAT
HARVESTED

1 dot — 10,000 acres
Total acreage (1966)
U.S.
49,844,600
Canada
29,679,520

U. S. Dept. of Commerce
Bureau of Census

Copyright by Rand McNally & Co.

COTTON
HARVESTED

1 dot — 5,000 acres
Total acreage (1966)
U.S.
9,549,020

U. S. Dept. of Commerce
Bureau of Census

Copyright by Rand McNally & Co.

FRUIT ORCHARDS,
AND NUT TREES

1 dot — 2,000 acres
Total acreage (1966)
U.S.
4,251,000
Canada
202,730

U. S. Dept. of Commerce
Bureau of Census

Copyright by Rand McNally & Co.

CATTLE

1 dot — 5,000 head
Total number (1966)
U.S.
108,862,000
Canada
11,651,000

U. S. Dept. of Commerce
Bureau of Census

Copyright by Rand McNally & Co.

MILK COWS

1 dot — 5,000 head
Total number (1966)
U.S.
15,987,000
Canada
2,674,000

U. S. Dept. of Commerce
Bureau of Census

Copyright by Rand McNally & Co.

HOGS

1 dot — 10,000 head
Total number (1966)
U.S.
47,414,000
Canada
5,108,000

U. S. Dept. of Commerce
Bureau of Census

Copyright by Rand McNally & Co.

SHEEP

1 dot — 10,000 head
Total number (1966)
U.S.
24,734,000
Canada
783,000

U. S. Dept. of Commerce
Bureau of Census

Copyright by Rand McNally & Co.
A-520500-962   -3

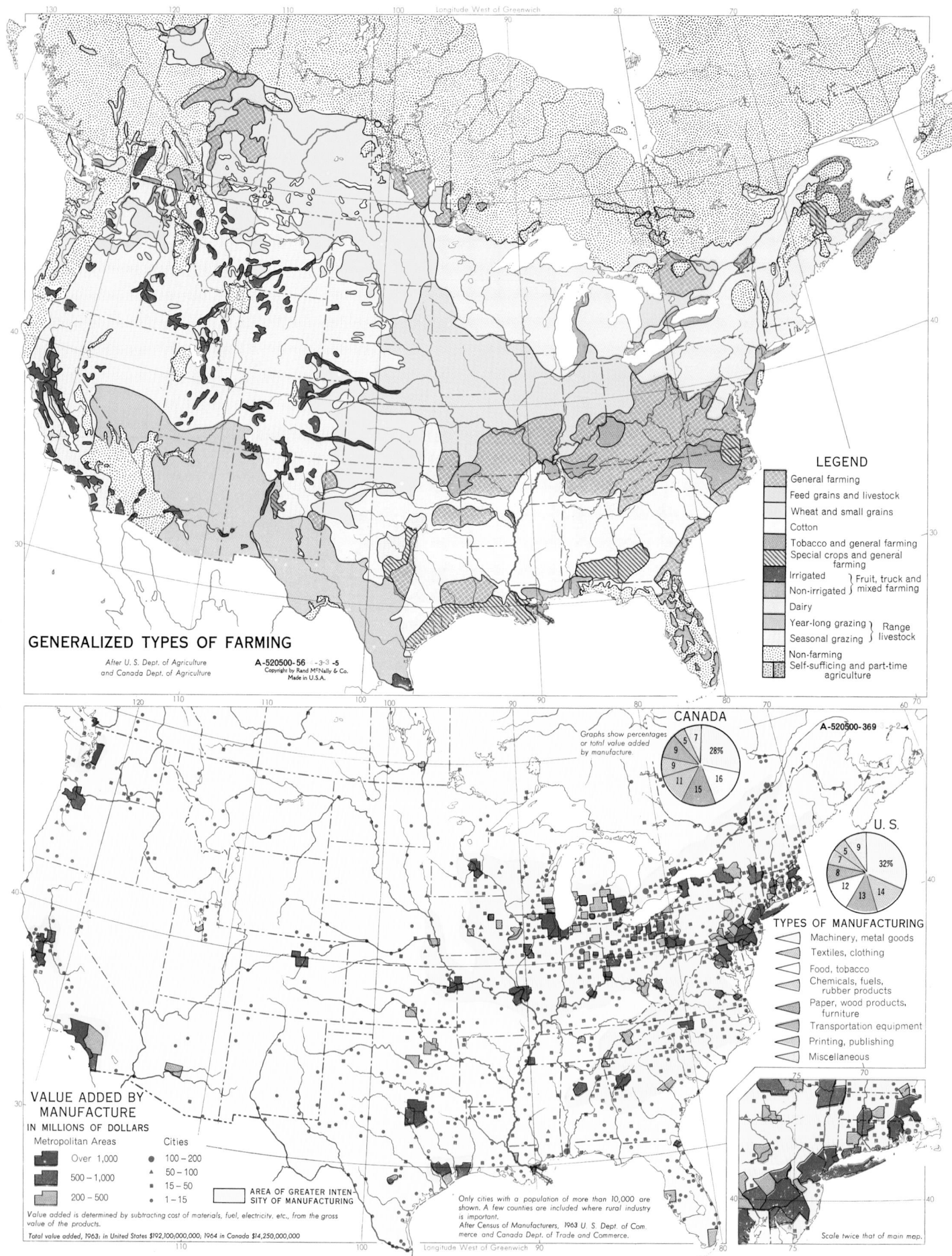

GENERALIZED TYPES OF FARMING

After U.S. Dept. of Agriculture
and Canada Dept. of Agriculture

A-520500-56 -3-3 -5
Copyright by Rand McNally & Co.
Made in U.S.A.

LEGEND

- General farming
- Feed grains and livestock
- Wheat and small grains
- Cotton
- Tobacco and general farming
- Special crops and general farming
- Irrigated } Fruit, truck and
- Non-irrigated } mixed farming
- Dairy
- Year-long grazing } Range
- Seasonal grazing } livestock
- Non-farming
- Self-sufficing and part-time agriculture

CANADA

Graphs show percentages or total value added by manufacture.

A-520500-369 -2-4

28%
7
5
9
9
11
16
15

U.S.

32%
9
5
7
8
14
12
13

TYPES OF MANUFACTURING

- Machinery, metal goods
- Textiles, clothing
- Food, tobacco
- Chemicals, fuels, rubber products
- Paper, wood products, furniture
- Transportation equipment
- Printing, publishing
- Miscellaneous

VALUE ADDED BY MANUFACTURE

IN MILLIONS OF DOLLARS

Metropolitan Areas

- Over 1,000
- 500 – 1,000
- 200 – 500

Cities

- 100 – 200
- 50 – 100
- 15 – 50
- 1 – 15

AREA OF GREATER INTENSITY OF MANUFACTURING

Value added is determined by subtracting cost of materials, fuel, electricity, etc., from the gross value of the products.

Total value added, 1963; in United States $192,100,000,000; 1964 in Canada $14,250,000,000

Only cities with a population of more than 10,000 are shown. A few counties are included where rural industry is important.
After Census of Manufacturers, 1963 U. S. Dept. of Commerce and Canada Dept. of Trade and Commerce.

Scale twice that of main map.

Scale 1: 28 000 000; One inch to 440 miles.   LAMBERT CONFORMAL CONIC PROJECTION

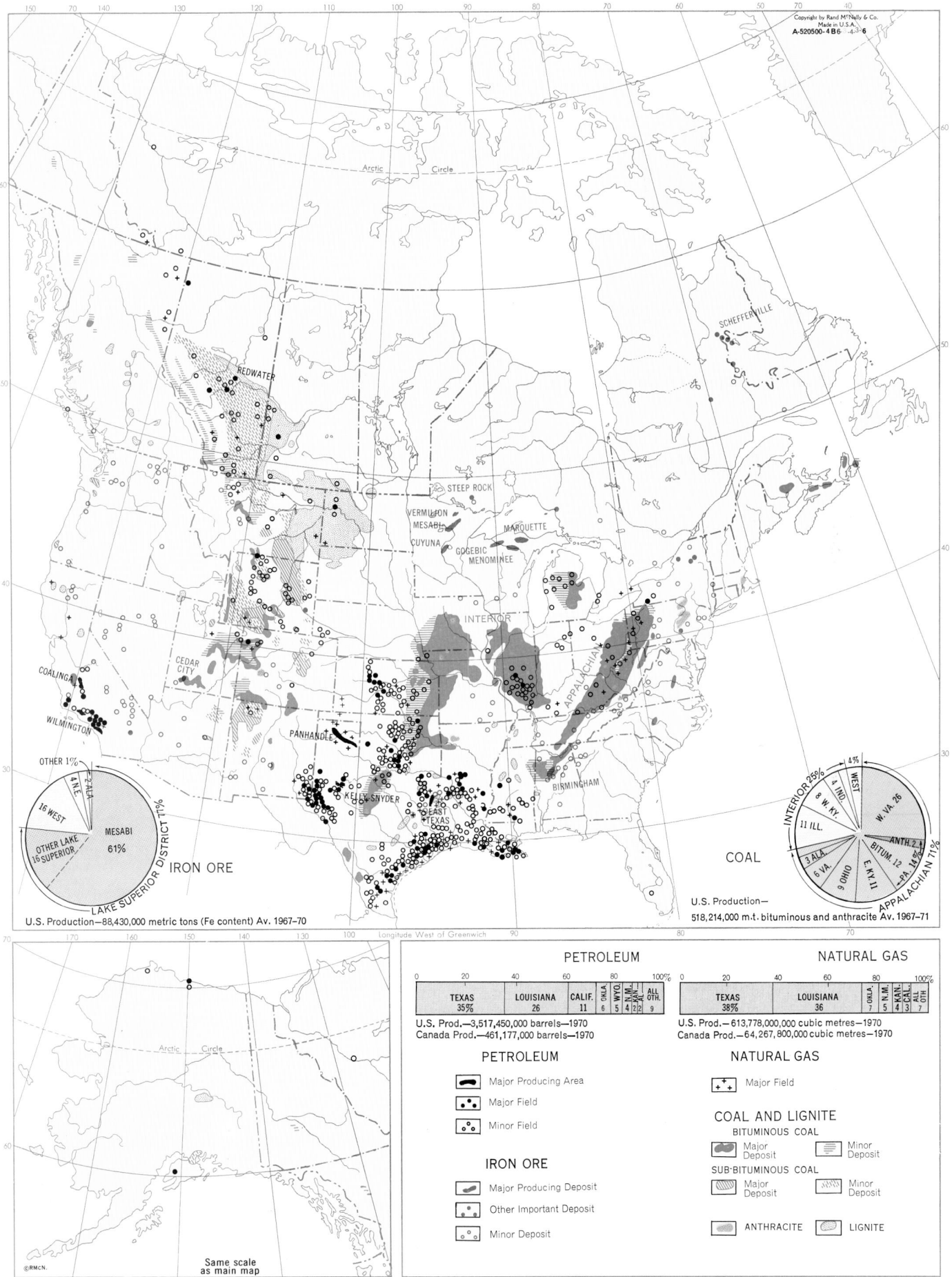

Copyright by Rand McNally & Co.
Made in U.S.A.
A-520500-4B6-4-6

Arctic Circle

REDWATER

SCHEFFERVILLE

STEEP ROCK
VERMILION
MESABI
CUYUNA
GOGEBIC
MENOMINEE
MARQUETTE

COALINGA
WILMINGTON
CEDAR CITY

INTERIOR

APPALACHIA

PANHANDLE

KELLY-SNYDER
EAST TEXAS

BIRMINGHAM

IRON ORE

OTHER 1%
4 N.E.
2 ALA.
16 WEST
MESABI 61%
OTHER LAKE SUPERIOR 16
LAKE SUPERIOR DISTRICT 77%

U.S. Production—88,430,000 metric tons (Fe content) Av. 1967-70

COAL

INTERIOR 25%
4 IND.
8 W. KY.
11 ILL.
3 ALA.
6 VA.
9 OHIO
E. KY. 11
W. VA. 26
ANTH. 2
BITUM. 12
PA. 14%
WEST 4%
APPALACHIAN 71%

U.S. Production—
518,214,000 m.t. bituminous and anthracite Av. 1967-71

Longitude West of Greenwich

Arctic Circle

@RMCN.

Same scale as main map

PETROLEUM

0	20	40	60	80	100%
TEXAS 35%	LOUISIANA 26	CALIF. 11	OKLA. 6	WYO. 5	N.M. 4	KAN. 2	LA. 2	ALL OTH. 9

U.S. Prod.—3,517,450,000 barrels—1970
Canada Prod.—461,177,000 barrels—1970

NATURAL GAS

0	20	40	60	80	100%
TEXAS 38%	LOUISIANA 36	OKLA. 7	N.M. 5	KAN. 4	CAL. 3	ALL OTH. 7

U.S. Prod.—613,778,000,000 cubic metres—1970
Canada Prod.—64,267,800,000 cubic metres—1970

PETROLEUM

- Major Producing Area
- Major Field
- Minor Field

IRON ORE

- Major Producing Deposit
- Other Important Deposit
- Minor Deposit

NATURAL GAS

+ Major Field

COAL AND LIGNITE

BITUMINOUS COAL
- Major Deposit
- Minor Deposit

SUB-BITUMINOUS COAL
- Major Deposit
- Minor Deposit

ANTHRACITE   LIGNITE

Scale 1: 32 000 000; One inch to 500 miles.   LAMBERT CONFORMAL CONIC PROJECTION

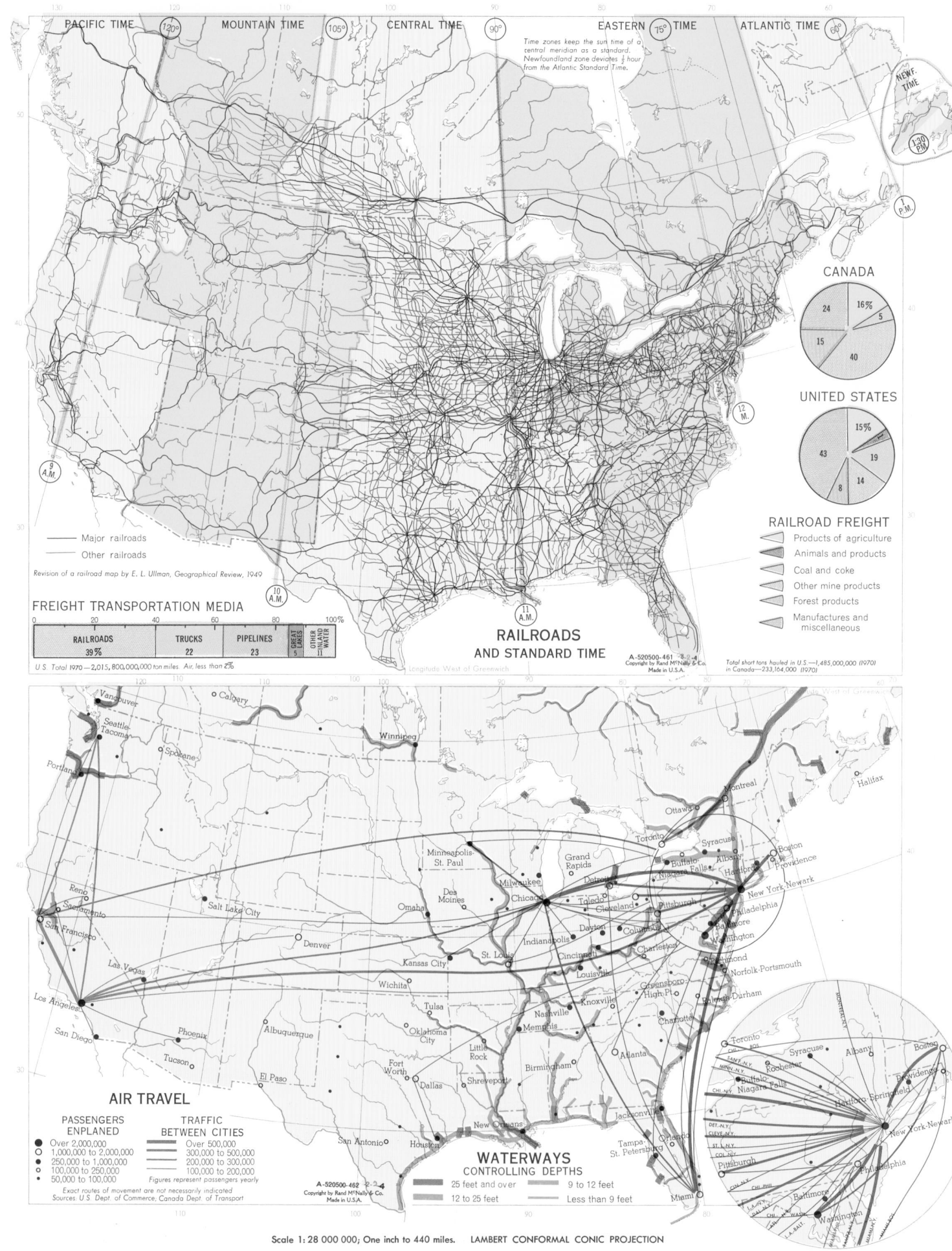

PACIFIC TIME | MOUNTAIN TIME | CENTRAL TIME | EASTERN TIME | ATLANTIC TIME

Time zones keep the sun time of a central meridian as a standard. Newfoundland zone deviates ½ hour from the Atlantic Standard Time.

NEWF. TIME

1:30 P.M.

CANADA

16%	5
24	
15	40

UNITED STATES

15%	
43	19
8	14

RAILROAD FREIGHT
- Products of agriculture
- Animals and products
- Coal and coke
- Other mine products
- Forest products
- Manufactures and miscellaneous

—— Major railroads
—— Other railroads

Revision of a railroad map by E. L. Ullman, Geographical Review, 1949

RAILROADS
AND STANDARD TIME

A-520500-461
Copyright by Rand McNally & Co.
Made in U.S.A.

Total short tons hauled in U.S.—1,485,000,000 (1970) in Canada—233,164,000 (1970)

FREIGHT TRANSPORTATION MEDIA

0   20   40   60   80   100%

| RAILROADS 39% | TRUCKS 22 | PIPELINES 23 | GREAT LAKES 5 | OTHER INLAND WATER 11 |

U.S. Total 1970—2,015,800,000,000 ton miles. Air, less than 2%

Longitude West of Greenwich

AIR TRAVEL

PASSENGERS ENPLANED
- ● Over 2,000,000
- ◉ 1,000,000 to 2,000,000
- ○ 250,000 to 1,000,000
- ○ 100,000 to 250,000
- • 50,000 to 100,000

TRAFFIC BETWEEN CITIES
- Over 500,000
- 300,000 to 500,000
- 200,000 to 300,000
- 100,000 to 200,000

Figures represent passengers yearly

Exact routes of movement are not necessarily indicated
Sources: U.S. Dept. of Commerce, Canada Dept. of Transport

A-520500-462
Copyright by Rand McNally & Co.
Made in U.S.A.

WATERWAYS
CONTROLLING DEPTHS
- 25 feet and over
- 12 to 25 feet
- 9 to 12 feet
- Less than 9 feet

Scale 1: 28 000 000; One inch to 440 miles.   LAMBERT CONFORMAL CONIC PROJECTION

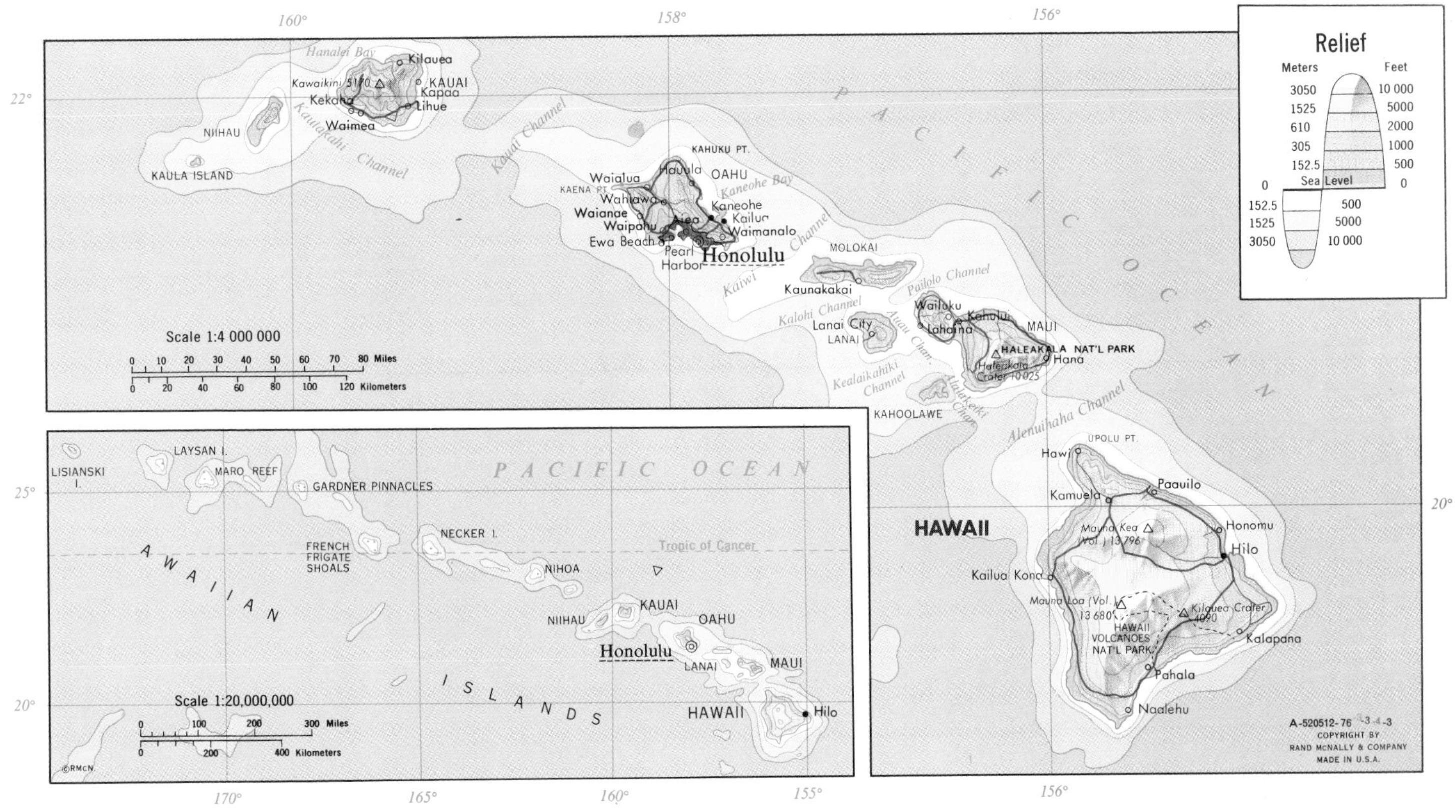

Relief

Meters		Feet
3050		10 000
1525		5000
610		2000
305		1000
152.5		500
0	Sea Level	0
152.5		500
1525		5000
3050		10 000

Scale 1:4 000 000

0 10 20 30 40 50 60 70 80 Miles

0 20 40 60 80 100 120 Kilometers

Hanalei Bay • Kilauea

Kawaikini 5170 △ KAUAI

Kekaha Kapaa

Waimea Lihue

NIIHAU

KAULA ISLAND

Kaulakahi Channel

Kauai Channel

KAHUKU PT.

Waialua Mauula OAHU *Kaneohe Bay*

KAENA PT. Wahiawa Kaneohe

Waianae Aiea Kailua

Waipahu Waimanalo

Ewa Beach **Honolulu**

Pearl Harbor

Kaiwi Channel

MOLOKAI

Kaunakakai

Kalohi Channel Lanai City *Auau Chan.* Wailuku Kahului

LANAI Lahaina MAUI

Kealaikahiki Channel △ HALEAKALA NAT'L PARK Hana

Haleakala Crater 10 025

KAHOOLAWE

Alenuihaha Channel

UPOLU PT.

Hawi Kamuela Paauilo

HAWAII

Mauna Kea △ Honomu

(Vol.) 13 796 Hilo

Kailua Kona

Mauna Loa (Vol.) △ Kilauea Crater

13 680 4090

HAWAII VOLCANOES NAT'L PARK Kalapana

Pahala

Naalehu

A-520512-76 -3-4-3

COPYRIGHT BY

RAND McNALLY & COMPANY

MADE IN U.S.A.

PACIFIC OCEAN

Tropic of Cancer

LISIANSKI I. LAYSAN I.

MARO REEF GARDNER PINNACLES

FRENCH FRIGATE SHOALS NECKER I.

NIHOA

H A W A I I A N KAUAI

NIIHAU OAHU

Honolulu LANAI MAUI

I S L A N D S HAWAII • Hilo

Scale 1:20,000,000

0 100 200 300 Miles

0 200 400 Kilometers

©RMcN.

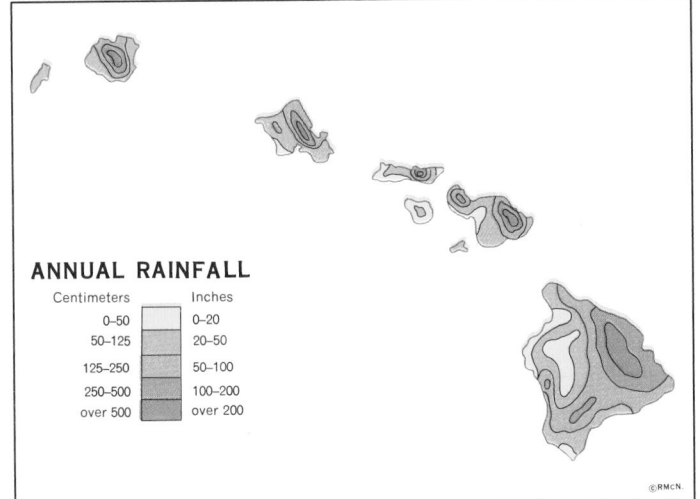

ANNUAL RAINFALL

Centimeters	Inches
0–50	0–20
50–125	20–50
125–250	50–100
250–500	100–200
over 500	over 200

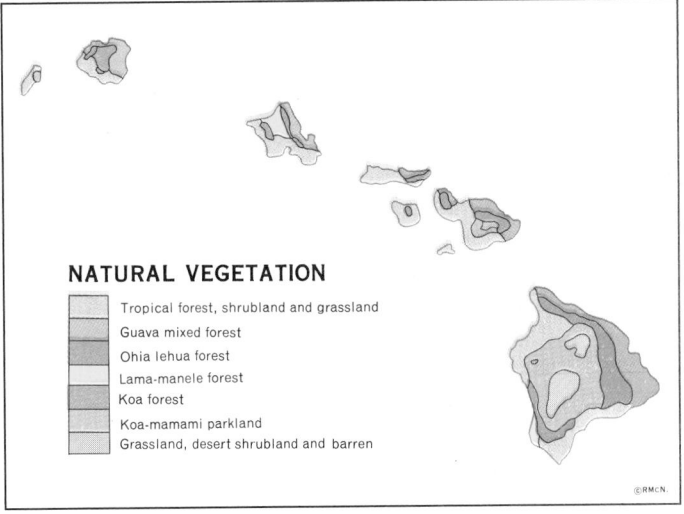

NATURAL VEGETATION

Tropical forest, shrubland and grassland

Guava mixed forest

Ohia lehua forest

Lama-manele forest

Koa forest

Koa-mamami parkland

Grassland, desert shrubland and barren

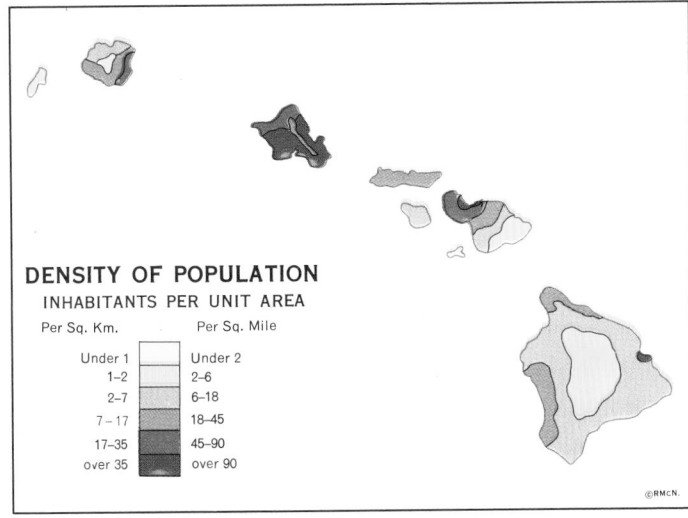

DENSITY OF POPULATION

INHABITANTS PER UNIT AREA

Per Sq. Km.	Per Sq. Mile
Under 1	Under 2
1–2	2–6
2–7	6–18
7–17	18–45
17–35	45–90
over 35	over 90

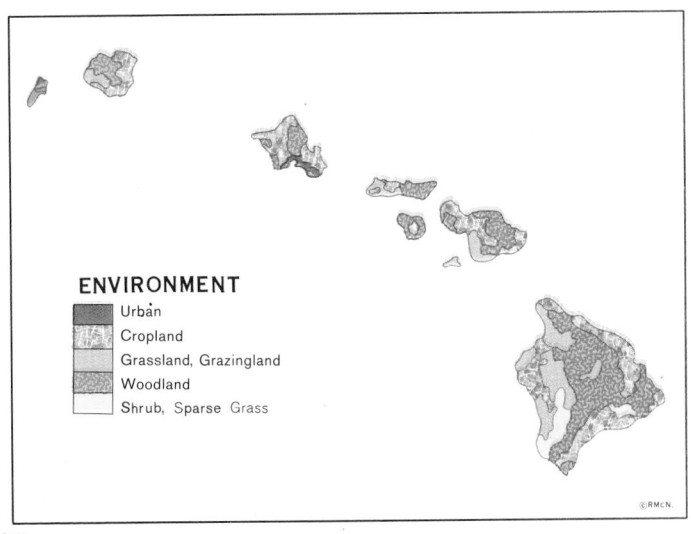

ENVIRONMENT

Urban

Cropland

Grassland, Grazingland

Woodland

Shrub, Sparse Grass

Cities, Towns, and Villages

0 to 25,000 ○

25,000 to 100,000 •

100,000 to 250,000 ⊙

250,000 to 1,000,000 ◎

1,000,000 and over ◉

Major urbanized area

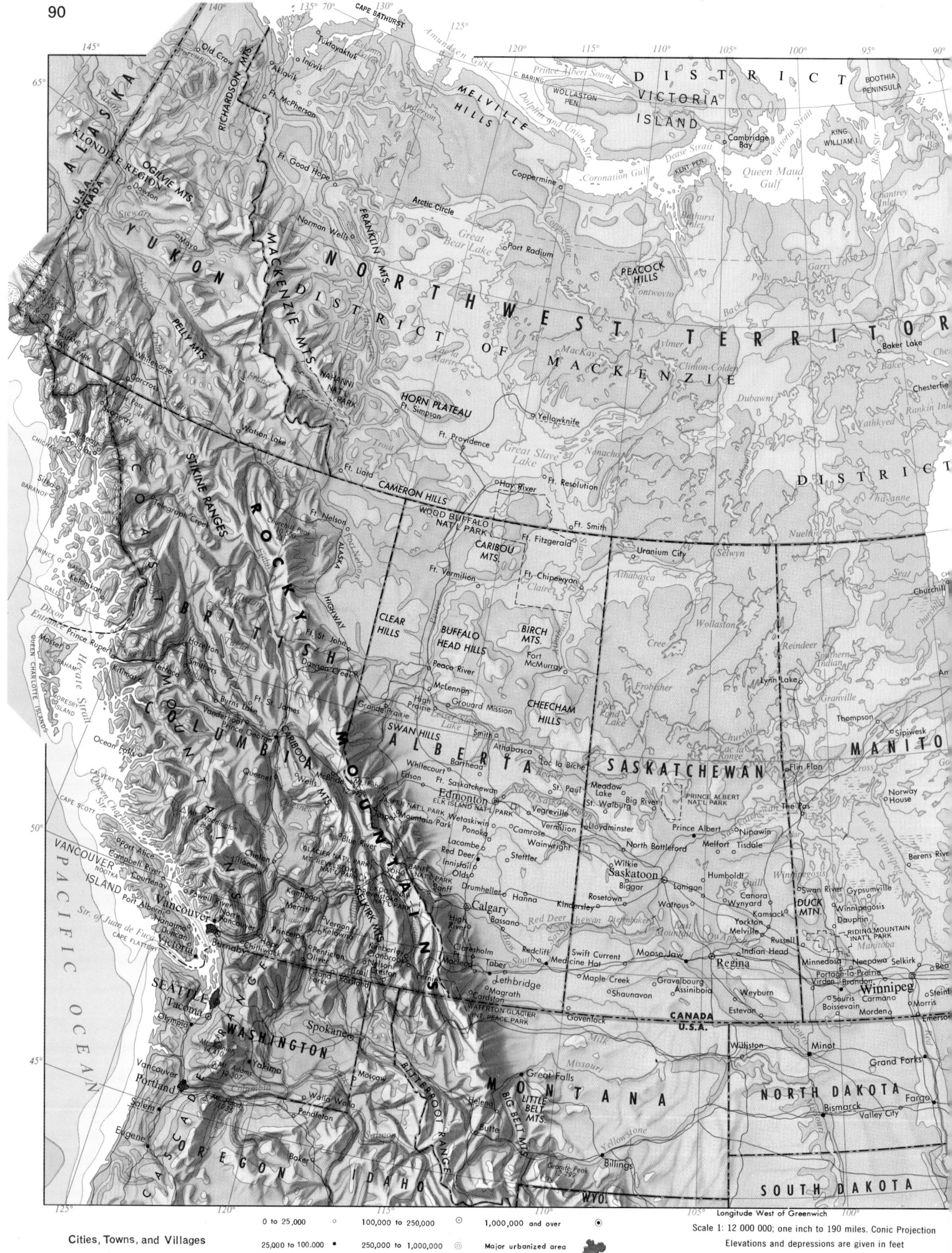

Cities, Towns, and Villages

0 to 25,000   100,000 to 250,000   1,000,000 and over

25,000 to 100,000   250,000 to 1,000,000   Major urbanized area

Longitude West of Greenwich

Scale 1: 12 000 000; one inch to 190 miles. Conic Projection

Elevations and depressions are given in feet

Longitude West of Greenwich

Same scale as main map

QUEBEC

CAPE BAULD

Gulf of
St. Lawrence

GROS MORNE
NAT'L PARK
Deer Lake
Corner Brook
Stephenville
C. ST. GEORGE

LONG RANGE MTS.

Botwood
Grand Falls
Windsor
Gander
TERRA NOVA
NAT'L PARK

Twillingate

Bonavista

NEWFOUNDLAND
St. George's
Trinity

CAPE RAY
Channel-Port-aux-Basques
CABOT STRAIT
CAPE NORTH
Grand Bank
Burin
CAPE BRETON ISLAND
ST PIERRE AND MIQUELON (FR.)

St. John's

Fortune Bay
Placentia Bay

ATLANTIC OCEAN

©RMcN

FRANKLIN

BAFFIN ISLAND
NAT'L PARK
Pangnirtung
CUMBERLAND
PEN.

MELVILLE PENINSULA

Foxe Basin

Arctic Circle

PRINCE CHARLES ISLAND

Cumberland Sound

C. MERCY

Frobisher Bay

HALL PEN.

Foxe Channel

FOXE PEN.

Lake Harbour
EVERETT MTS.

RESOLUTION

SOUTHAMPTON ISLAND
BELL PEN.

NOTTINGHAM ISLAND

SALISBURY
C. DE NOUVELLE-FRANCE

Hudson Strait

C. HOPES ADVANCE

AKPATOK

CAPE CHIDLEY

C. LOW

COATS

MANSEL

Ivugivik

TORNGAT MTS.

Hebron

KEEWATIN

Fr. Chimo

Nain

NEWFOUNDLAND

HUDSON

BAY

All islands within bays and straits lie within Northwest Territories.

PENINSULE D'UNGAVA

Payne

Ungava Bay

Hopedale

Makkovik

Hamilton Inlet

Cartwright

OTTAWA ISLANDS

Povungnituk

Rigolet

Battle Harbour

LONG RANGE MTS.

St. Anthony

BELCHER ISLANDS

Minto

Grand R. de la Baleine

Lac Bienville

MEALY MTS.

Goose Bay

LABRADOR

Churchill Falls

Little Mecatina

C. HENRIETTA MARIA

PTE. LOUIS-XIV

La Grande

Nichicun

Schefferville

Caniapiscau

QUEBEC

Natashquan

GROS MORNE NAT'L PARK

Corner Brook
Stephenville
St. George

Ft. Severn

James Bay

Ft. George

AKIMISKI

Eastmain

MTS. OTISH

Opinaca

Mistassini

Mingan
ILE D'ANTICOSTI

Sept-Iles

Clarke City

Ft. Albany

Winisk

Severn

Opinaca

R. aux Feuilles

Gulf of
St. Lawrence

ILES DE LA MADELEINE

Moosonee

Attawapiskat

Albany

Mattagami

Chibougamau

Betsiamites

C. Chat
CHIC-CHOCS
MTS.

Matane
GASPÉ PEN.

Gaspé

Chandler

New Carlisle

Caraquet

ST. George

ONTARIO

Trout Lake
St. Joseph

Lac Seul

Coral Rapids
Fraserdale

Dolbeau

Almo

Kenogami
Arvida

St. Félicien
Roberval
Chambord
Jonquière
Chicoutimi

La Malbaie

St. Paul

Rimouski

Rivière-du-Loup
Edmundston
Woodstock

CAMPBELLTON
Bathurst
Chatham
Newcastle

PRINCE EDWARD ISLAND

Summerside
Charlottetown

New Waterford
Glasgow
Sydney

NOVA SCOTIA

Halifax

ux Lookout

Armstrong Sta.
Nakina

Hearst

La Sarre
Rouyn
Amos
Sennetere

Parent

La Tuque

Quebec
Lévis

Victoriaville

Fredericton

Moncton

NEW BRUNSWICK

Richibucto

Truro

Dartmouth

Dryden

Geraldton
Longlac

Kapuskasing
Oba
Cochrane
Iroquois Falls
Timmins
Kirkland Lake

Malartic
Val-d'Or
Ville-Marie

Shawinigan
Trois-Rivières
Sorel
Drummondville

St. Hyacinthe
Granby

FUNDY NAT'L PARK

St. Andrews
St. Stephen

KOUCHIBOUGUAC NAT'L PARK

KENTVILLE
Kentville

Bridgewater
Liverpool

Nipigon

Cobalt
Témiscaming

Joliette

MONTREAL

Valleyfield

St. George

Digby

CAPE SABLE

Shelburne

Lake
of the Woods
Rainy

Marathon

PUKASKWA NAT'L PARK

Chapleau

Sudbury

Sturgeon Falls
Ottawa
North Bay

Pembroke
Renfrew

Hull

OTTAWA

Laval

Montpelier

Sherbrooke

MAINE

Portland

P. Augusta

Yarmouth

Thunder Bay

MICHIPICOTEN I.

Sault Ste. Marie
Thessalon
Blind River
Espanola

Huntsville
Parry Sound
Bancroft
Smiths Falls
Brockville
Kingston

Ogdensburg

Alexandria Bay

Cornwall

Concord

BOSTON

CAPE COD

ATLANTIC

OCEAN

Duluth
Superior

Marquette

Escanaba

MICHIGAN

Sault Ste. Marie

MANITOULIN

Georgian Bay

Wiarton
Owen Sound

Orillia
Midland
Barrie
Peterborough
Lindsay

Oshawa

Cobourg

NEW HAMPSHIRE
VERMONT

Albany

Providence

Stamford

MASS.

Hartford

R.I.

WISCONSIN

Green Bay

Kincardine

Port Huron

Owen Sound

Port Elgin

Barrie

Whitby

TORONTO

Hamilton
Catharines
BUFFALO

NEW YORK

Rochester

Niagara Falls

Lake Ontario

CONN.

Newport
N.J.

NEW YORK

St. Paul

Madison

MILWAUKEE

CHICAGO

Grand Rapids

Flint
Lansing

DETROIT

Leamington
Windsor
Chatham
Sarnia

Kitchener
London
St. Thomas

Lake Erie

PENNSYLVANIA

Scranton

OHIO

Toledo

NEAPOLIS

OTA

Relief		
Meters		**Feet**
3050		10 000
1525		5000
610		2000
305		1000
152.5		500
0	Sea Level	0
152.5		500
1525		5000
3050		10000

A-520200-76
COPYRIGHT BY
RAND McNALLY & COMPANY
MADE IN U.S.A.

0 25 50 75 100   200   300   400   500 Miles

0   100   200   400   600   800 Kilometers

PACIFIC

OCEAN

Relief

Meters		Feet
3050		10 000
1525		5000
610		2000
305		1000
152.5		500
0	Sea Level	0
152.5		500
1525		5000

A-520220-76- 4-4-5
COPYRIGHT BY
RAND McNALLY & COMPANY
MADE IN U.S.A.

Continued on pages 110–111

Longitude West of Greenwich

Scale 1:4 000 000; one inch to 64 miles. Conic Projection
Elevations and depressions are given in feet.

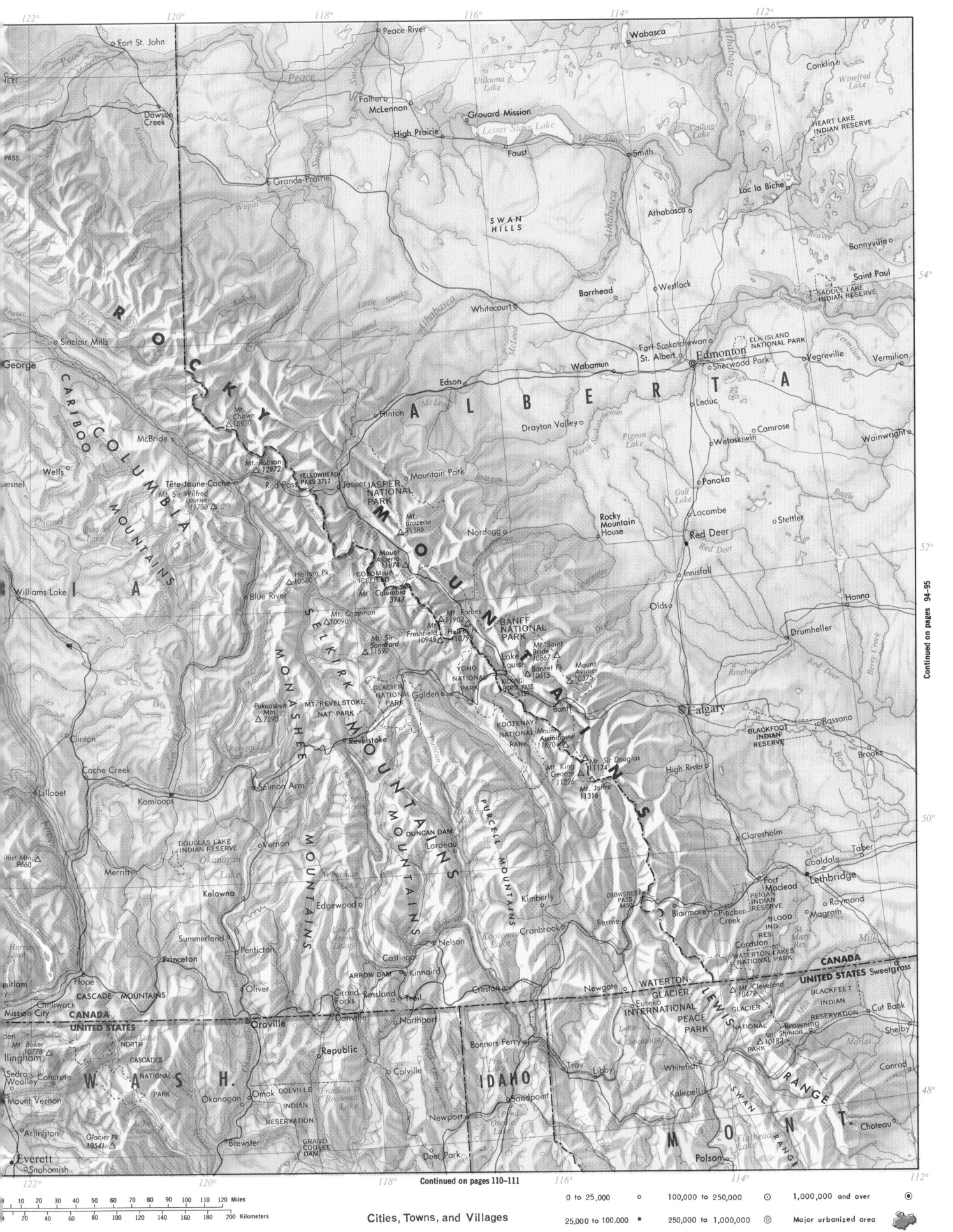

Continued on pages 94-95

Continued on pages 110-111

Cities, Towns, and Villages

0 to 25,000 ○	100,000 to 250,000 ◉	1,000,000 and over ◉
25,000 to 100,000 •	250,000 to 1,000,000 ◎	Major urbanized area

Miles
10 20 30 40 50 60 70 80 90 100 110 120 Miles
20 40 60 80 100 120 140 160 180 200 Kilometers

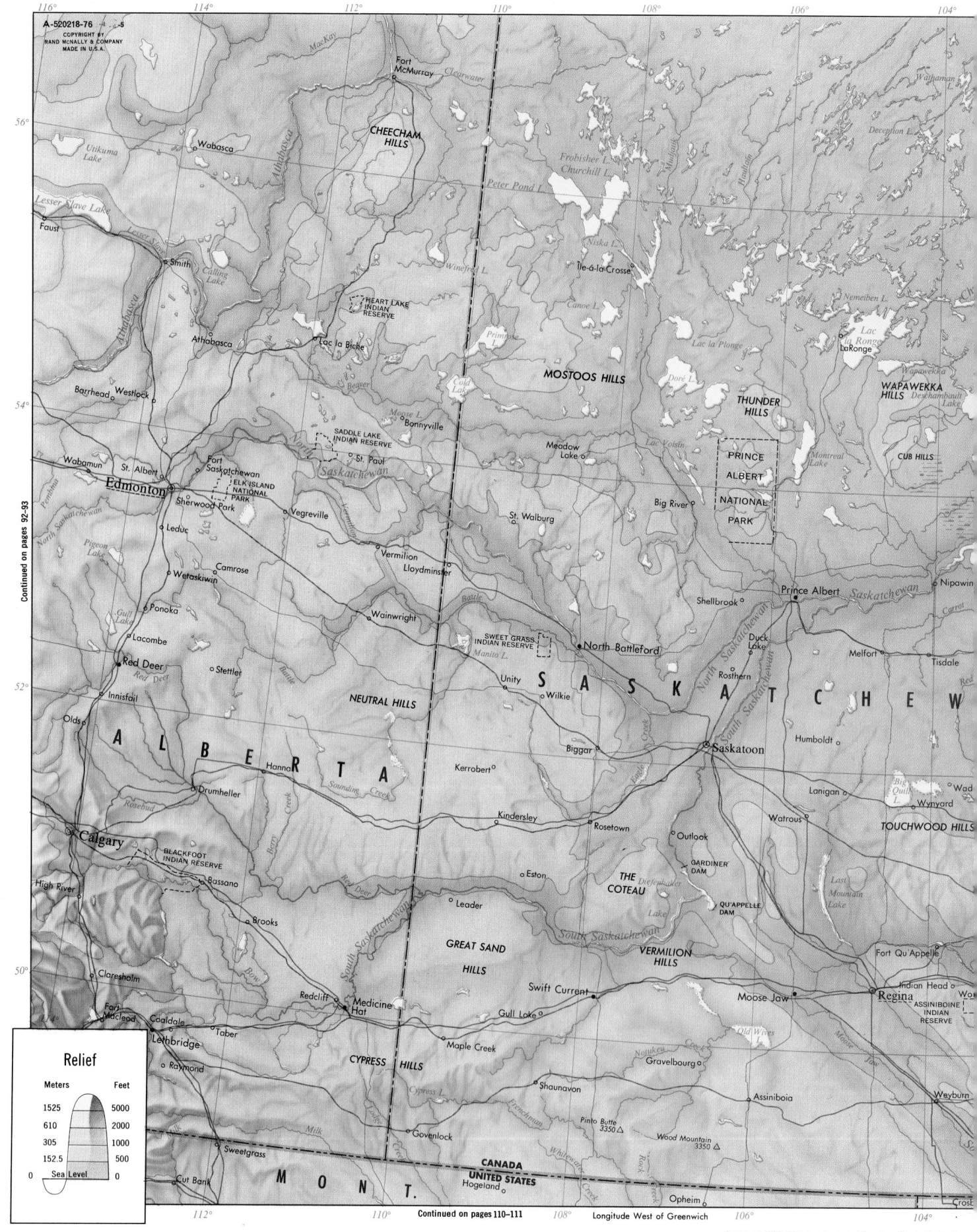

A-520218-76

COPYRIGHT BY
RAND McNALLY & COMPANY
MADE IN U.S.A.

116°   114°   112°   110°   108°   106°   104°

56°

CHEECHAM
HILLS

Fort
McMurray

Clearwater

MacKay

Utikuma
Lake

Wabasca

Frobisher L.
Churchill L.

Peter Pond L.

Waihaman L.

Devenion L.

Lesser Slave Lake

Faust

Athabasca

Winefred L.

Île-à-la-Crosse

Canoe L.

Nemeiben L.

Lac
la Ronge

LaRonge

Smith

Calling
Lake

HEART LAKE
INDIAN
RESERVE

Lac la Biche

Primose
L.

Doré L.

Lac la Plonge

Montreal
Lake

WAPAWEKKA
HILLS

Deschambault
Lake

54°

Barrhead   Westlock

Beaver

North

Saskatchewan

Moose L.

Bonnyville

SADDLE LAKE
INDIAN RESERVE

St. Paul

Cold
Lake

MOSTOOS HILLS

Meadow
Lake

Lac Volsin

THUNDER
HILLS

PRINCE

ALBERT

NATIONAL

PARK

Big River

CUB HILLS

Wabamun

St. Albert

Edmonton

Fort
Saskatchewan

ELK ISLAND
NATIONAL
PARK

Sherwood Park

Vegreville

St. Walburg

Pigeon
Lake

Leduc

Pembina

North Saskatchewan

Vermilion

Lloydminster

Shellbrook

Prince Albert

Saskatchewan

Nipawin

Wetaskiwin

Camrose

Duck
Lake

Melfort

Tisdale

Ponoka

Battle

Wainwright

North Battleford

Rosthern

Carrot

Gull
Lake

Lacombe

SWEET GRASS
INDIAN RESERVE

Manito L.

S A S K A T C H E W

Humboldt

Red Deer

Red Deer

Stettler

Battle

Unity

Wilkie

Big
Quill
L.

Wad

Innisfail

NEUTRAL HILLS

Biggar

Saskatoon

Lanigan

Wynyard

Olds

A L B E R T A

Hanna

Kerrobert

Sounding Creek

South Saskatchewan

Watrous

TOUCHWOOD HILLS

Drumheller

Rosebud

Berry Creek

Kindersley

Rosetown

Outlook

GARDINER
DAM

Last
Mountain
Lake

Calgary

BLACKFOOT
INDIAN RESERVE

Bassano

Eston

THE
COTEAU

Diefenbaker
Lake

QU'APPELLE
DAM

High River

Brooks

Leader

VERMILION
HILLS

Fort Qu'Appelle

Claresholm

Bow

Redcliff

South Saskatchewan

Swift Current

South Saskatchewan

Moose Jaw

Indian Head

Regina

Fort
Macleod

Medicine
Hat

GREAT SAND

HILLS

Gull Lake

Old Wives

ASSINIBOINE
INDIAN
RESERVE

Coaldale

Taber

Maple Creek

Gravelbourg

Wo

Lethbridge

CYPRESS HILLS

Shaunavon

Assiniboia

Weyburn

Raymond

Relief

Cypress L.

Frenchman

Pinto Butte
3350 △

Wood Mountain
3350 △

Sweetgrass

Milk

Govenlock

CANADA
UNITED STATES

Hogeland

Opheim

Cut Bank   M O N T.

Crost

Continued on pages 92-93

Continued on pages 110-111

Longitude West of Greenwich

112°   110°   108°   106°   104°

Relief

Meters	Feet
1525	5000
610	2000
305	1000
152.5	500
0 Sea Level	0

Scale 1:4 000 000; one inch to 64 miles. Conic Projection
Elevations and depressions are given in feet.

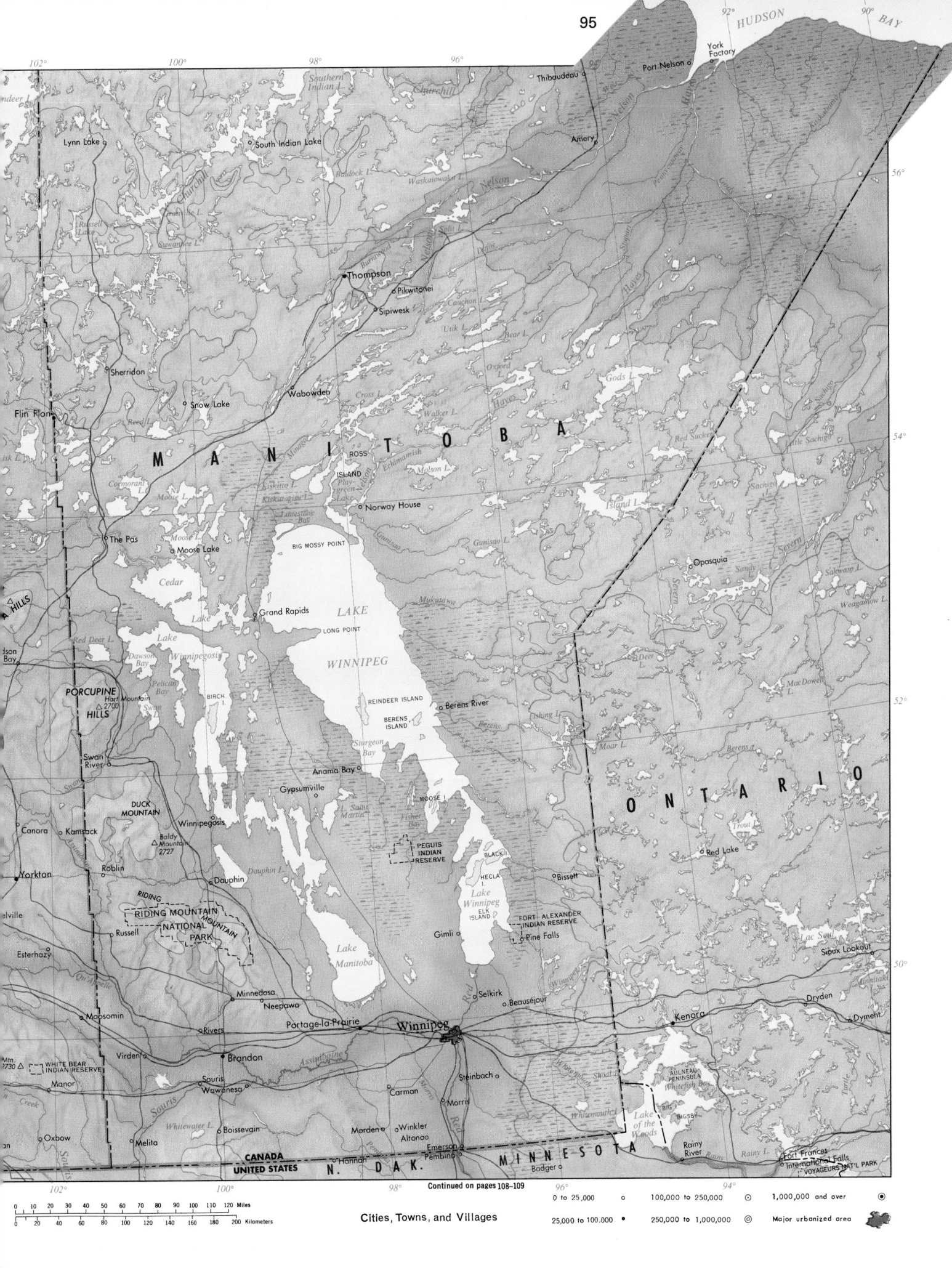

HUDSON   BAY

York
Factory
Port Nelson
Thibaudeau
Amery

56°

Lynn Lake
South Indian Lake
Baldock L.
Waskaiowaka L.

Southern
Indian L.
Churchill

Thompson
Pikwitonei
Sipiwesk

Russell
Lake
Suwannee L.

Sherridon

Flin Flon
Snow Lake
Wabowden

M A N I T O B A

Bear L.

Oxford L.

Gods L.

Red Sucker

54°

The Pas
Moose Lake
ROSS
ISLAND
Play-
green
Lake

Echimamish
Molson L.

Island L.

Sachigo

Norway House

Opasquia
Sandy

Cedar
Lake

Big Mossy Point

Grand Rapids
LAKE
LONG POINT

Guniso L.

Weagamow L.

Lake
Winnipegosis
Dawson
Bay
Pelican
Bay

WINNIPEG

MacDowell
L.

52°

PORCUPINE
Hart Mountain
△ 2700
HILLS

Swan
River

BIRCH

REINDEER ISLAND
BERENS
ISLAND

Berens River

Fishing L.

Berens R.

Moar L.

Berens R.

Red Lake

Lac Seul

Anama Bay

Gypsumville

Stargeon
Bay

MOOSE I.

Fisher
Bay

DUCK
MOUNTAIN

Canora
Kamsack

Baldy
Mountain
2727

Winnipegosis

L. Saint
Martin

PEGUIS
INDIAN
RESERVE

BLACK I.

Yorkton
Roblin
Dauphin
Dauphin L.

HECLA
I.
Lake
Winnipeg
ELK
ISLAND

Bissett

Sioux Lookout

Esterhazy
lville

RIDING
RIDING MOUNTAIN
NATIONAL
PARK

Russell

Lake
Manitoba

Gimli
FORT ALEXANDER
INDIAN RESERVE
Pine Falls

50°

Minnedosa
Neepawa

Selkirk
Beauséjour

Dryden
Dymeht

Moosomin
Rivers
Portage-la-Prairie
Winnipeg
Kenora

Mtn △
2730
WHITE BEAR
INDIAN RESERVE

Virden
Brandon

Assiniboine

Steinbach

AULNEAU
PENINSULA
Whitefish Bay

Souris
Wawanesa

Carman

Shoal L.

Manor

Morris

BIG
ISLAND
RIGSBY

Fort Frances

Oxbow
Melita

Whitewater L.
Boissevain

Morden
Winkler
Altonao

Lake
of the
Woods

Rainy
River
Rainy L.

Fort Frances
International Falls
VOYAGEURS NAT'L PARK

Creek

CANADA
UNITED STATES
Hannah
N. DAK.
Emerson
Pembina
Badger
MINNESOTA

102°   100°   98°   96°   94°

Continued on pages 108–109

0 10 20 30 40 50 60 70 80 90 100 110 120 Miles
0 20 40 60 80 100 120 140 160 180 200 Kilometers

Cities, Towns, and Villages

0 to 25,000 ○   100,000 to 250,000 ⊙   1,000,000 and over ◉

25,000 to 100,000 •   250,000 to 1,000,000 ◎   Major urbanized area

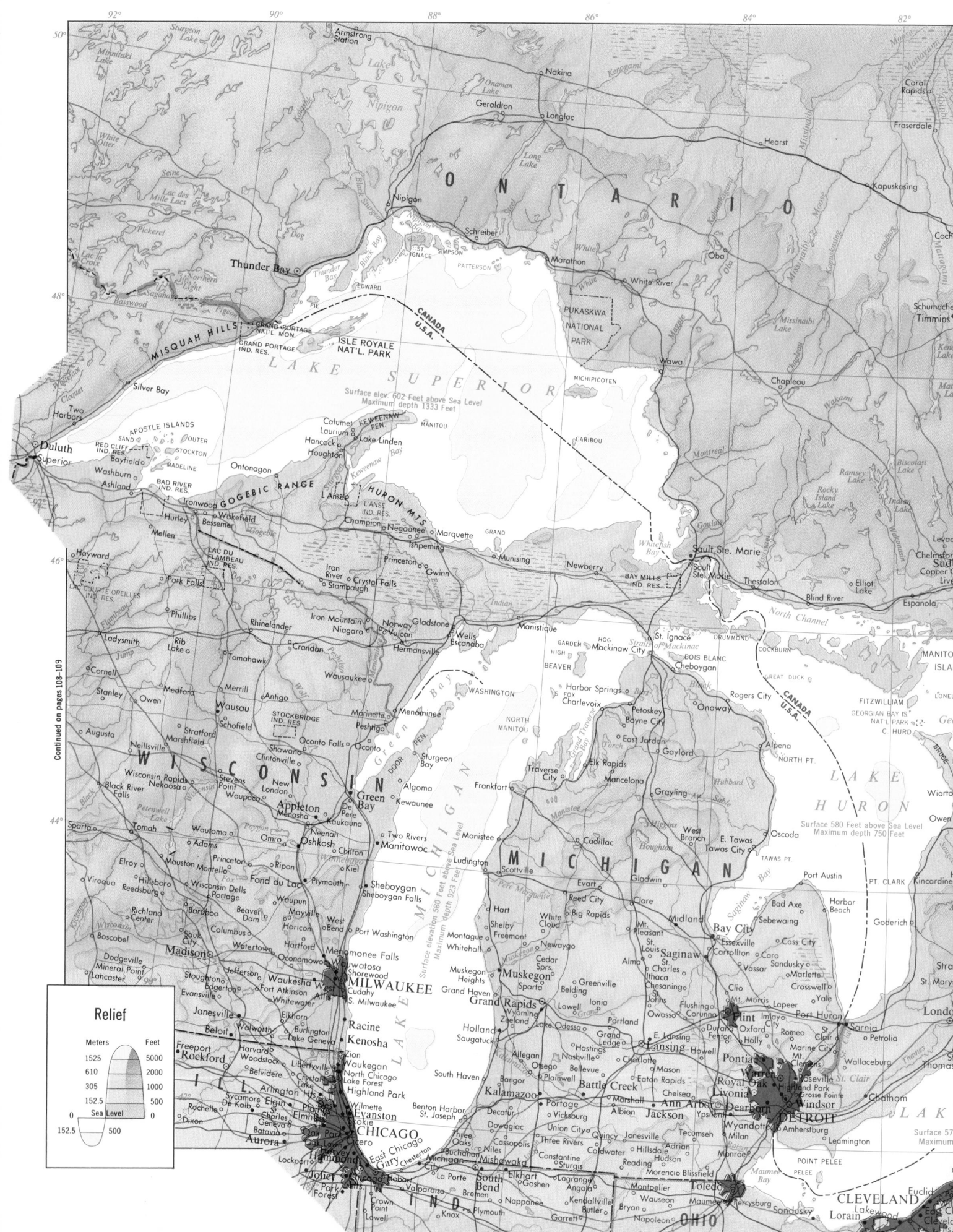

ONTARIO

Lake Nipigon

LAKE SUPERIOR

Surface elev. 602 Feet above Sea Level
Maximum depth 1333 Feet

Thunder Bay

MISQUAH HILLS

GRAND PORTAGE NAT'L. MON.
GRAND PORTAGE IND. RES.

ISLE ROYALE NAT'L. PARK

CANADA
U.S.A.

PUKASKWA NATIONAL PARK

Silver Bay

Duluth
Superior

APOSTLE ISLANDS
RED CLIFF IND. RES.
SAND OUTER
STOCKTON
BAYFIELD MADELINE

Washburn
Ashland
BAD RIVER IND. RES.

GOGEBIC RANGE

Ironwood Wakefield Bessemer

Hurley

KEWEENAW PEN.
Calumet
Laurium
Hancock
Houghton
Lake Linden

MANITOU

HURON MTS.

L'Anse
L'ANSE IND. RES.

Keweenaw Bay

Ontonagon

Michipicoten

Wawa

CARIBOU

Montreal

Whitefish Bay

Sault Ste. Marie

Mellen
LAC DU FLAMBEAU IND. RES.

Hayward

Champion
Negaunee
Ishpeming
Marquette

Iron River
Crystal Falls
Stambaugh

Princeton
Gwinn

GRAND

Munising
Newberry

BAY MILLS IND. RES.

Sault Ste. Marie

Thessalon

Blind River

North Channel

Espanola

MANITOULIN ISLAND

LAC COURTE OREILLES IND. RES.

Park Falls

Phillips

Ladysmith

Rhinelander
Tomahawk

Iron Mountain
Norway
Niagara
Vulcan

Gladstone

Hermansville

Manistique

Indian

GARDEN PEN.
HOG
HIGH
BEAVER

St. Ignace
Mackinaw City
Straits of Mackinac

DRUMMOND

COCKBURN

GREAT DUCK

MANITO ISLAND

Cornell
Stanley Owen

Merrill

Antigo

Crandon

STOCKBRIDGE IND. RES.

Wausaukee

Marinette
Menominee

Peshtigo

DOOR PEN.
Sturgeon Bay

Escanaba
Wells

WASHINGTON

FOX

Charlevoix
Petoskey
Boyne City

BOIS BLANC
Cheboygan

Onaway

Rogers City

CANADA
U.S.A.

FITZWILLIAM

GEORGIAN BAY IS. NAT'L. PARK
C. HURD

Harbor Springs

Augusta
Neillsville

WISCONSIN

Wisconsin Rapids
Nekoosa

Black River Falls

Sparta

Marshfield
Stratford
Schofield
Wausau

Clintonville
Shawano
New London
Waupaca

Oconto Falls
Oconto

Green Bay

Algoma
Kewaunee

NORTH MANITOU

Frankfort

Traverse City

Elk Rapids
Mancelona

East Jordan

Gaylord

Alpena
NORTH PT.

LAKE HURON

Surface 580 Feet above Sea Level
Maximum depth 750 Feet

Wisconsin Dells
Portage

Tomah
Adams

Wautoma
Omro

Princeton
Montello
Ripon

Waupun
Mayville
West Bend

Neenah
Oshkosh
Menasha

Appleton
Kaukauna
De Pere

Two Rivers
Manitowoc

Chilton
Kiel

Manistee

Ludington
Scottville

Cadillac

Houghton

Grayling

Higgins
Hubbard

West Branch
Oscoda

E. Tawas
Tawas City

TAWAS PT.

PT. CLARK
Kincardine

MICHIGAN

Viroqua
Hillsboro
Reedsburg

Richland Center

Elroy

Mauston
New Lisbon

Fond du Lac

Plymouth

Sheboygan
Sheboygan Falls

Hart
Shelby

White Cloud
Freemont
Newaygo

Reed City
Big Rapids

Evart

Clare

Gladwin

Mt. Pleasant

Midland

Bay City
Essexville

Bad Axe
Sebewaing

Harbor Beach

Goderich

Boscobel
Dodgeville
Mineral Point
Lancaster

Sauk City
Baraboo

Columbus

Beaver Dam
Horicon

Waupun

Port Washington

Montague
Whitehall

Muskegon Heights

St. Louis
Alma
Ithaca
St. Johns

Saginaw
Carrollton

Caro
Vassar

Sandusky
Marlette
Crosswell
Yale

Cass City

St. Marys

Madison
Stoughton
Edgerton

Jefferson
Fort Atkinson
Whitewater

Watertown
Hartford
Oconomowoc

Menomonee Falls
Wauwatosa
Shorewood

MILWAUKEE
Cudahy
S. Milwaukee

Muskegon
Sparta

Grand Haven

Grand Rapids
Wyoming
Zeeland

Greenville
Belding

Ionia

Lowell

Portland

Owosso
Corunna
Durand

Flushing

Flint

Lapeer
Mt. Morris
Clio

Romeo
Oxford

Imlay City

Marine City

Port Huron

Sarnia

Petrolia

Janesville
Beloit

Evansville
Elkhorn
Burlington

Walworth
Lake Geneva

Racine
Kenosha

Holland
Saugatuck

Allegan

Hastings
E. Lansing
Lansing
Howell

Grand Ledge

Nashville
Charlotte
Bellevue

Mason
Eaton Rapids

Holly
Fenton

Pontiac
Royal Oak
Livonia

Mt. Clemens
Roseville
Grosse Pointe

St. Clair

Wallaceburg

Freeport
Rockford

Harvard
Woodstock
Belvidere

Libertyville
Crystal Lake

Zion
Waukegan
North Chicago
Lake Forest
Highland Park

South Haven

Bangor

Kalamazoo

Portage
Vicksburg

Osego
Plainwell

Battle Creek

Marshall
Albion

Jackson

Ann Arbor
Ypsilanti

Dearborn

DETROIT

Windsor

Chatham

ILL.

Sycamore
De Kalb
Elgin
St. Charles
Geneva
Batavia

Rochelle
Dixon

Arlington Hts.
Elmhurst
Wilmette
Evanston
Oak Park
CHICAGO
Cicero

Benton Harbor
St. Joseph

Decatur
Dowagiac

Three Oaks

Niles
Buchanan
Michigan City

South Bend

Three Rivers
Constantine
Sturgis

Union City
Coldwater

Quincy
Hillsdale
Reading

Jonesville

Tecumseh

Adrian

Milan

Morenci
Blissfield

POINT PELEE
Leamington

Amherstburg

Wyandotte
Monroe

Aurora
Joliet
Lockport
Park Forest

Harvey
Hammond
East Chicago
Gary
Hobart
Crown Point
Lowell
Valparaiso
La Porte

Mishawaka
Elkhart
Goshen
Lagrange
Angola

Bremen
Nappanee
Kendallville
Butler

Bryan

Wauseon

Maumee
Bay

Toledo

CLEVELAND

Lorain

Sandusky

OHIO

Knox
Plymouth
Garrett

Napoleon

Montpelier

Mercysburg

IND.

LAKE MICHIGAN
Surface elevation 580 Feet above Sea Level
Maximum depth 923 Feet

GREEN BAY

Relief

Meters	Feet
1525	5000
610	2000
305	1000
152.5	500
0	Sea Level	0
152.5	500

Continued on pages 108-109

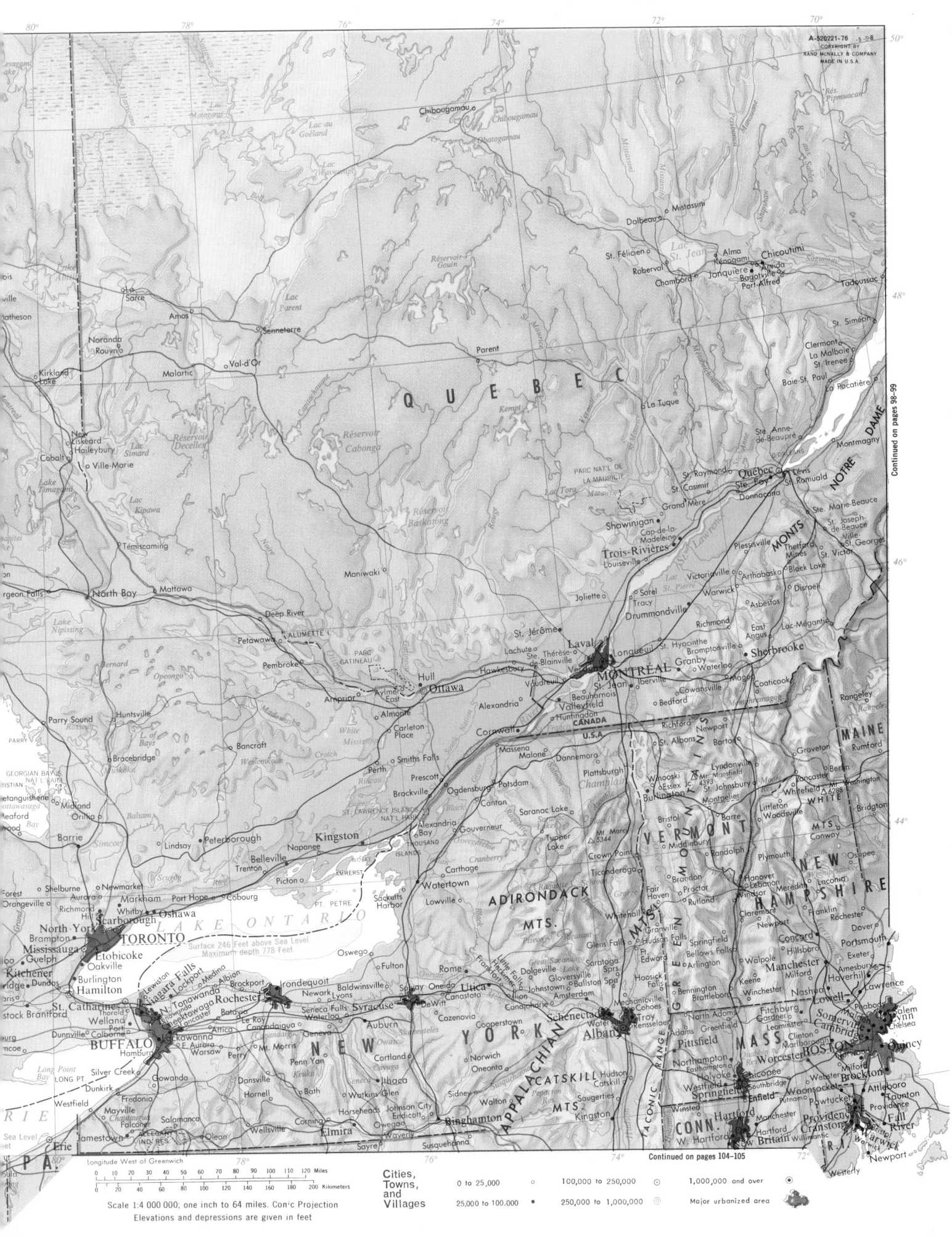

A-520221-76
COPYRIGHT BY
RAND McNALLY & COMPANY
MADE IN U.S.A.

Continued on pages 98-99

Q U E B E C

M O N T S   N O T R E   D A M E

MAINE

VERMONT

GREEN MTS.

NEW HAMPSHIRE

WHITE MTS.

ADIRONDACK MTS.

N E W   Y O R K

APPALACHIAN MTS.

CATSKILL MTS.

TACONIC RANGE

MASS.

CONN.

R.I.

LAKE ONTARIO
Surface 246 Feet above Sea Level
Maximum depth 778 Feet

TORONTO

BUFFALO

Niagara Falls

PA.

Longitude West of Greenwich

Continued on pages 104-105

Cities,
Towns,
and
Villages

| 0 to 25,000 | o | 100,000 to 250,000 | ⊙ | 1,000,000 and over | ◉ |
| 25,000 to 100,000 | • | 250,000 to 1,000,000 | ⊚ | Major urbanized area | |

Scale 1:4 000 000; one inch to 64 miles. Conic Projection
Elevations and depressions are given in feet

0 10 20 30 40 50 60 70 80 90 100 110 120 Miles
0 20 40 60 80 100 120 140 160 180 200 Kilometers

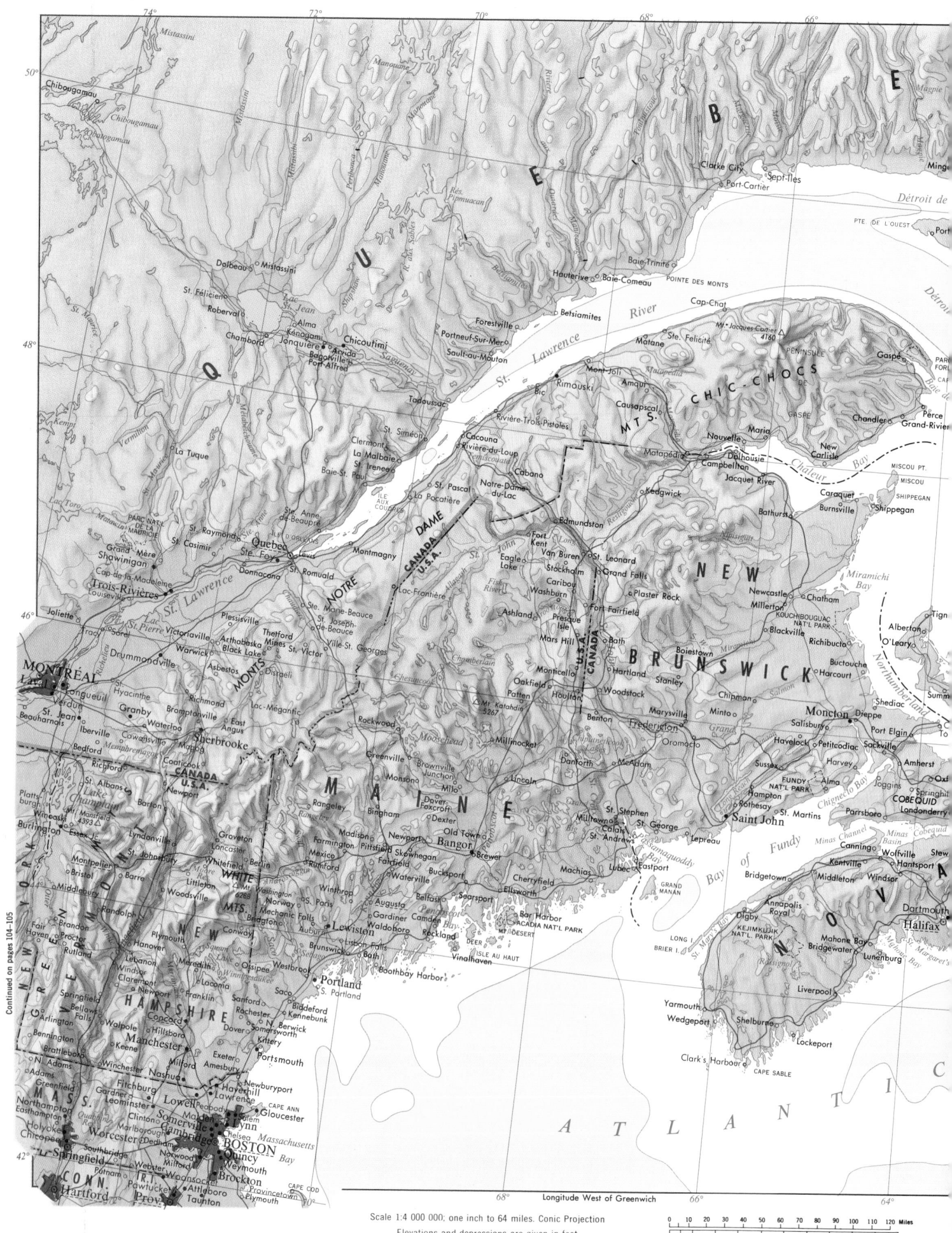

Continued on pages 104-105

Scale 1:4 000 000; one inch to 64 miles. Conic Projection
Elevations and depressions are given in feet.

Longitude West of Greenwich

0 10 20 30 40 50 60 70 80 90 100 110 120 Miles

0 20 40 60 80 100 120 140 160 180 200 Kilometers

Relief

Meters	Feet
1525	5000
610	2000
305	1000
152.5	500
0	Sea Level 0
152.5	500
1525	5000

LABRADOR (Newf.)

C. BAULD

St. Anthony

Hare Bay

Englee

GROAIS

BELL

Canada Bay

Blue Mtn. 2085'

Gros Pate 2115'

HORSE IS.

LABRADOR SEA

CAPE ST. JOHN

White Bay

Notre Dame Bay

NORTH TWILLINGATE

Twillingate

FOGO

Fogo

GROS-MORNE

Gros Morne 2,644'

NAT'L PARK

Mt. St. Gregory 2,251'

Springdale

Lewisporte

C. FREELS

Bonne Bay

Deer Lake

Sandy L.

Botwood

Wesleyville

Bay of Islands

Deer

Hodges Hill

Windsor

Glenwood

Gander

Bonavista Bay

Corner Brook

Humbermouth

Grand

Millertown

Grand Falls

Gander Lake

Glovertown

Bonavista

LONG PT.

Lewis Hills 2,672'

GLOVER I.

Buchans

Red Indian

TERRA NOVA NAT'L PARK

Trinity

Port au Port

Stephenville

Meelpaeg Lake

Crooked

Round Pond

Kepenkeck Lake

GRATES PT.

Bay de Verde

RANDOM I.

Heart's Content

C. ST. GEORGE

St. George's

Victoria Lake

Teddore Lake

Carbonear

Harbour Grace

Torbay

ST. LAWRENCE

St. George's Bay

Robinson

Granite Lake

Conception Bay

Bay Roberts

Brigus

St. John's

C. SPEAR

C. ANGUILLE

LONG RANGE MTS.

Burgeo

Belleoram

Belle Bay

MERASHEEN

Placentia

AVALON PEN.

C. RAY

Channel-Port-aux-Basques

La Poile Bay

Hermitage Bay

Harbour Breton

St. Mary's Bay

Ferryland

GULF OF ST. LAWRENCE

ÎLE D'ANTICOSTI (Que.)

PTE HEATH

St. Pierre

Natashquan

Wolf Bay

Mutton Bay

PETIT-MÉCATINA

STE. MARIE

GROS-MÉCATINA

Robertson

Cabot Strait

ST. PAUL

CAPE NORTH

Aspy Bay

BRION

GRINDSTONE ISLAND

ÎLES DE LA MADELEINE (Que.)

MARYSTOWN

Marystown

BRUNETTE

Grand Bank

BURIN

Burin

Fortune

St. Lawrence

Placentia Bay

MIQUELON

ST. PIERRE & MIQUELON (Fr.)

ST. PIERRE

CAPE BRETON HIGHLANDS NAT'L PARK

NCE EDWARD ISLAND

D ISLAND PARK

Mount Stewart

Souris

arlottetown

Montague

Georgetown

Murray Harbour

Inverness

L. Ainslie

Port Hood

St. Ann's Bay

Sydney Mines

N. Sydney

New Waterford

Dominion

Glace Bay

Sydney

SCATARI

P. Louisburg

CAPE BRETON ISLAND

Pictou

Antigonish

Trenton

ville

New Glasgow

llarton

St. Georges Bay

Havre Boucher

Port Hawkesbury

St. Peters

Bras d'Or Lake

Mulgrave

Arichat

MADAME

Guysborough

Canso

CAPE CANSO

Chedabucto Bay

OCEAN

SABLE (N.S.)

SCOTIA

[Boston area inset]

Scale 1:1 000 000

0   2   4   6   8   10 Miles

0   8   12   16 Kilometers

Derry

Hubbard

Amesbury

Merrimack

Merrimac

Newburyport

Newbury

W. Newbury

Merrimack R.

South Merrimack

Nashua

Salem

N.H.

MASS.

Haverhill

Groveland

Brookline

Pelham

Methuen

Georgetown

Rawley

Ipswich

Rockport

N.H.

MASS.

Hollis

Dracut

Lawrence

N. Andover

Hamilton

Essex

Townsend

Pepperell

Lowell

Andover

Middleton

Wenham

Gloucester

Fitchburg

Lunenburg

Groton

Chelmsford

Tewksbury

Wilmington

N. Reading

Danvers

Beverly

Manchester

Shirley

Ayer

Littleton

Billerica

Reading

Peabody

Salem

Leominster

Acton

Bedford

Burlington

Wakefield

Marblehead

Harvard

Concord

Lexington

Woburn

Melrose

Saugus

Swampscott

Lancaster

Stow

Maynard

Lincoln

Arlington

Medford

Malden

Everett

Lynn

Nahant

Sterling

Clinton

Hudson

Sudbury

Waltham

Somerville

Chelsea

MASSACHUSETTS BAY

Holden

W. Boylston

Marlborough

Weston

Cambridge

Brookline

BOSTON

Hull

Worcester

Northborough

Southborough

Shrewsbury

Framingham

Natick

Wellesley

Newton

Needham

Dedham

Milton

Quincy

Hingham

Cohasset

Westborough

Ashland

Westwood

Norwood

Braintree

Weymouth

Scituate

Grafton

Hopkinton

Holliston

Medfield

Canton

Randolph

Holbrook

Rockland

Hanover

Millbury

Upton

Milford

Millis

Norfolk

Stoughton

Avon

Abington

Whitman

Marshfield

Auburn

Northbridge

Bellingham

Walpole

Sharon

Pembroke

Sutton

Oxford

Whitinsville

Hopedale

Medway

Franklin

Wrentham

Foxboro

Brockton

Hanson

Webster

Uxbridge

Cities, Towns, and Villages

0 to 25,000   100,000 to 250,000   1,000,000 and over

25,000 to 100,000   250,000 to 1,000,000   Major urbanized area

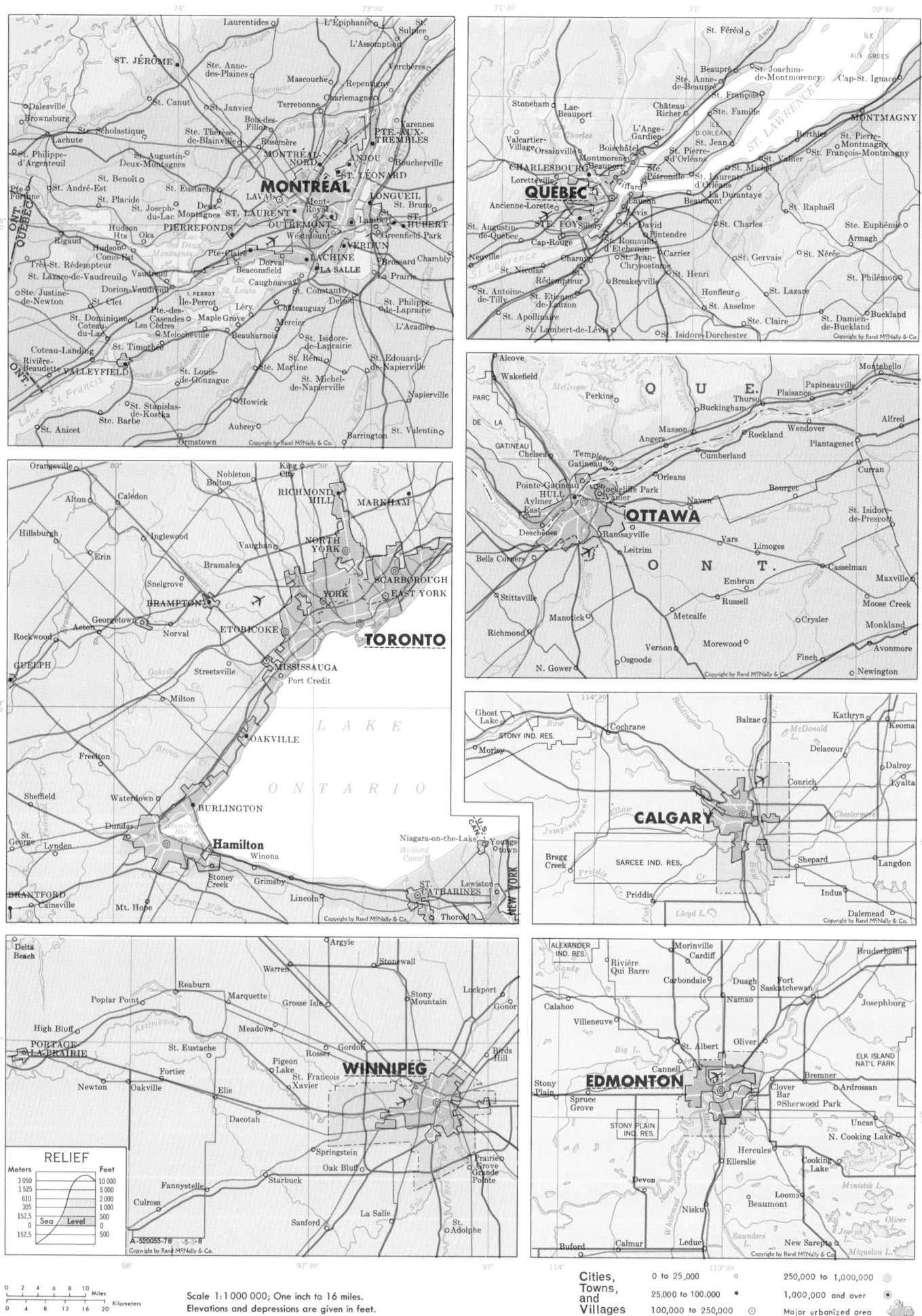

RELIEF

Meters		Feet
3 050		10 000
1 525		5 000
610		2 000
305		1 000
152.5		500
0	Sea Level	0
152.5		500

A-520055-76   -5 -5- 8
Copyright by Rand McNally & Co.

0 2 4   6   8 10 Miles
0 4 8 12 16 20 Kilometers

Scale 1:1 000 000; One inch to 16 miles.
Elevations and depressions are given in feet.

Cities, Towns, and Villages

0 to 25,000	250,000 to 1,000,000 ◎
25,000 to 100,000 •	1,000,000 and over ◉
100,000 to 250,000 ⊙	Major urbanized area

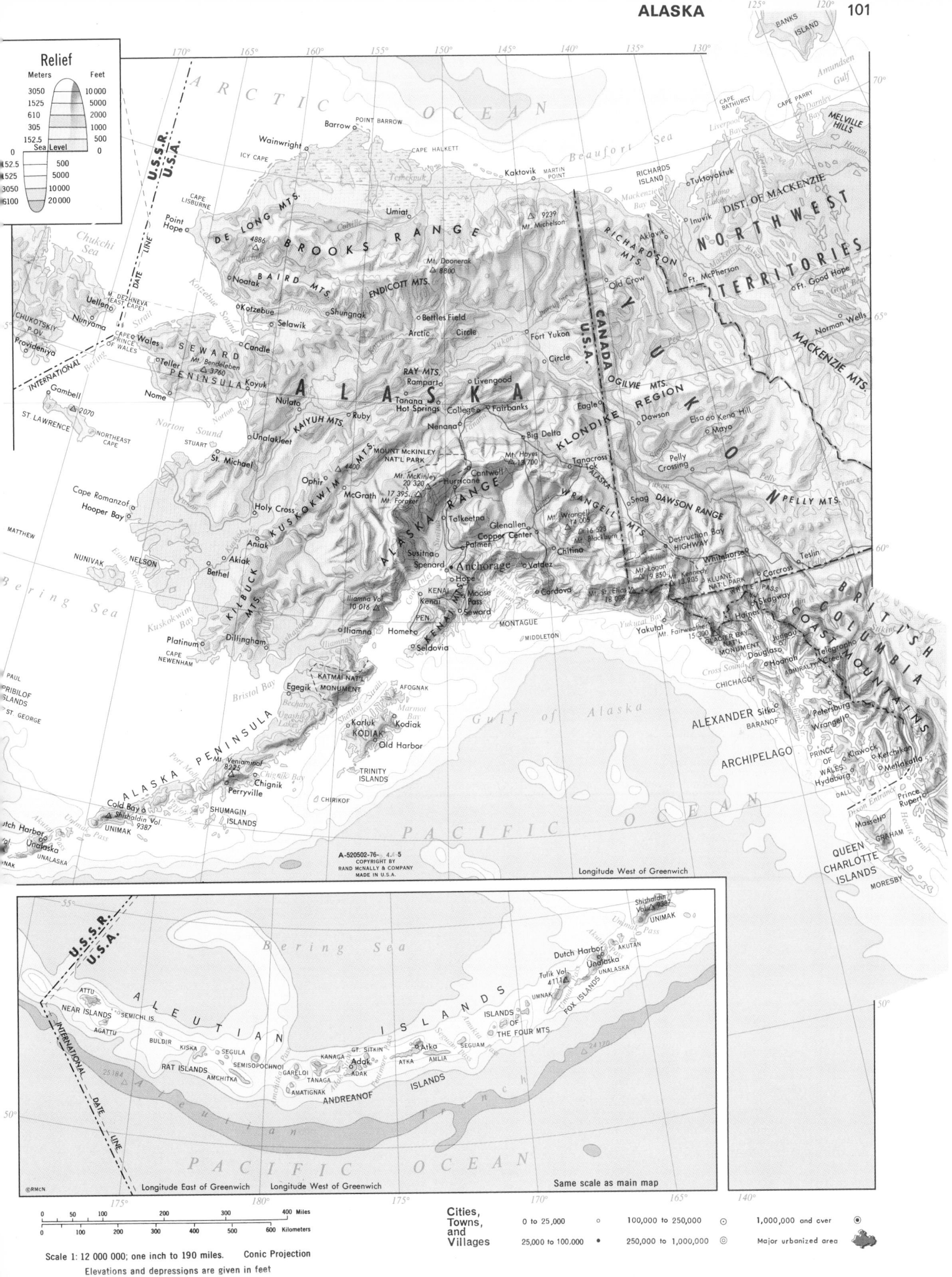

ARCTIC OCEAN

Beaufort Sea

BANKS ISLAND

Amundsen Gulf

CAPE BATHURST CAPE PARRY CAPE DARNLEY

MELVILLE HILLS

Point Barrow
Barrow
Wainwright
ICY CAPE
CAPE HALKETT
Kaktovik MARTIN POINT
Liverpool Bay

Tuktoyaktuk

DIST. OF MACKENZIE

NORTHWEST

TERRITORIES

Inuvik

CAPE LISBURNE

Point Hope

DE LONG MTS.
4886
BROOKS RANGE
BAIRD MTS.
Noatak 8800
ENDICOTT MTS.
Mt. Doonerak

Umiat

9239
Mt. Michelson

Aklavik

RICHARDS ISLAND

Ft. McPherson

Ft. Good Hope

Chukchi Sea

M. DEZHNEVA (EAST, CAPE)
Uelleto
Nunyama
CHUKOTSKIY P. OV.
Provideniya

CAPE PRINCE OF WALES
Wales
Teller Mt. Bendeleben 3760
SEWARD PENINSULA
Nome Koyuk

Kotzebue
Selawik
Shungnak
Candle

Bettles Field

Arctic Circle

RICHARDSON MTS.
Old Crow

Fort Yukon

Norman Wells

MACKENZIE MTS.

INTERNATIONAL

Gambell
ST. LAWRENCE 2070
NORTHEAST CAPE

Nulato
Ruby

RAY MTS.
Tanana Hot Springs
Ramparts Livengood

College Fairbanks
Nenana

Yukon

Circle

Eagle

CANADA
U.S.A.
KLONDIKE REGION
OGILVIE MTS.
Dawson

Elsa Keno Hill
Mayo

Pelly Crossing

NORMAN WELLS

St. Michael
Unalakleet
STUART

KAIYUH MTS.

ALASKA

Big Delta
Mt. Hayes 13,700

Tanacross Tok

Snag

PELLY MTS.

DAWSON RANGE

Norton Sound

MATTHEW

NUNIVAK

NELSON

Holy Cross
Ophir
McGrath

Cape Romanzof
Hooper Bay

Aniak
Bethel
Akiak

4400
MOUNT McKINLEY NAT'L PARK
Mt. McKinley 20,320
17,395
Mt. Foraker

KUSKOKWIM MTS.

ALASKA RANGE

Talkeetna
Susitna
Spenard
Anchorage
Hope

Hurricane
Cantwell

Glenallen
Copper Center
Palmer

Mt. Wrangell 14,005
WRANGELL MTS.
16,523
Mt. Blackburn
Chitina

Destruction Bay
HIGHWAY

Whitehorse
Mt. Logan 19,850
13,905
Mt. Kennedy

KLUANE NAT'L PARK

Teslin

YUKON

Bering Sea

Dillingham
Platinum
CAPE NEWENHAM

PAUL
PRIBILOF ISLANDS
ST. GEORGE

Kuskokwim Bay

Iliamna Vol 10,016
Iliamna

KILBUCK MTS.

KENAI
Kenai
Moose Pass
Seward
Homer
Seldovia

KENAI PEN.

Valdez
Cordova

MONTAGUE
MIDDLETON

Yakutat Bay
Yakutat
Mt. Fairweather 15,300

GLACIER BAY NAT'L MONUMENT

Mt. St. Elias 18,008

Haines
Skagway
Carcross

CHILKOOT PASS
WHITE PASS

Juneau
Douglas
Hoonah
ADMIRALTY I.

BRITISH COLUMBIA

COAST MOUNTAINS

Telegraph Creek

Egegik
KATMAI NAT'L MONUMENT
Becharof L.
Ugashik Lakes
Karluk
KODIAK
Kodiak
Old Harbor

AFOGNAK
Marmot Bay
Shelikof Strait

TRINITY ISLANDS

Gulf of Alaska

CHICHAGOF
Cross Sound

ALEXANDER
Sitka
BARANOF

Petersburg
Wrangell

ARCHIPELAGO

PRINCE OF WALES
Hydaburg

Klawock
Ketchikan
Metlakatla

DALL

Dixon Entrance

Masseto
GRAHAM

Prince Rupert

ALASKA PENINSULA
Mt. Veniaminof 8225
Chignik Chignik Bay
Perryville
SHUMAGIN ISLANDS
Cold Bay
Shishaldin Vol. 9387
UNIMAK

Dutch Harbor
Unalaska
UNALASKA

CHIRIKOF

PACIFIC OCEAN

QUEEN CHARLOTTE ISLANDS

MORESBY

A-520502-76-4 4 5
COPYRIGHT BY
RAND McNALLY & COMPANY
MADE IN U.S.A.

Longitude West of Greenwich

Relief

Meters	Feet
3050	10 000
1525	5000
610	2000
305	1000
152.5	500
0 Sea Level	0
152.5	500
1525	5000
3050	10 000
6100	20 000

U.S.S.R.
U.S.A.
DATE LINE

Inset map (bottom left):

U.S.S.R.
U.S.A.
INTERNATIONAL DATE LINE

Bering Sea

ATTU
NEAR ISLANDS
AGATTU
SEMICHI IS.

ALEUTIAN

BULDIR
KISKA SEGULA
RAT ISLANDS
AMCHITKA
SEMISOPOCHNOI
GARELOI
TANAGA
AMATIGNAK
KANAGA

ADAK
GT. SITKIN
ADAK
ANDREANOF

Atka
ATKA
AMLIA
SEGUAM

ISLANDS

ISLANDS

ISLANDS OF THE FOUR MTS.

AMUKTA
25,184

24,170

Aleutian Trench

Shishaldin Vol. 9387
UNIMAK
Dutch Harbor AKUTAN
Unalaska
Tulik Vol. 4111
UMNAK
FOX ISLANDS
UNALASKA

PACIFIC OCEAN

Longitude East of Greenwich Longitude West of Greenwich

Same scale as main map

0 50 100 200 300 400 Miles
0 100 200 300 400 500 600 Kilometers

Scale 1: 12 000 000; one inch to 190 miles. Conic Projection

Elevations and depressions are given in feet

Cities, Towns, and Villages

○ 0 to 25,000	⊙ 100,000 to 250,000	◉ 1,000,000 and over
● 25,000 to 100,000	◎ 250,000 to 1,000,000	Major urbanized area

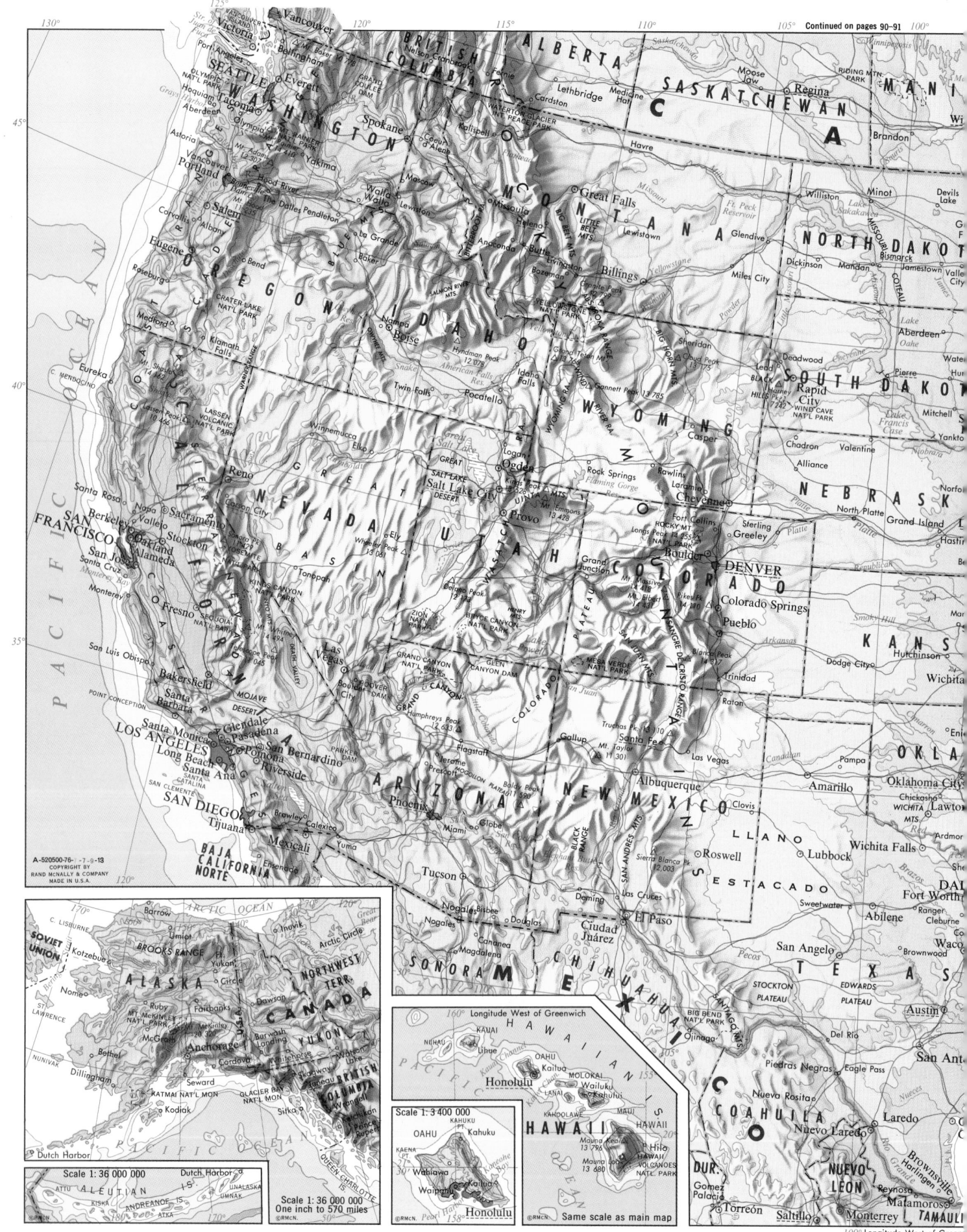

Continued on pages 90-91

Scale 1:12 000 000; one inch to 190 miles. Polyconic Project
Elevations and depressions are given in feet

A-520500-76-/-7-9-13
COPYRIGHT BY
RAND McNALLY & COMPANY
MADE IN U.S.A.

Scale 1:36 000 000

Scale 1:36 000 000
One inch to 570 miles

Scale 1:3 400 000

Same scale as main map

100° Longitude West of Green

Relief

Meters		Feet
3050		10 000
1525		5000
610		2000
305		1000
152.5		500
0	Sea Level	0
152.5		500 Below
1525		5 000 Sea Level
3050		10 000
6100		20 000

500 Miles

800 Kilometers

Continued on pages 108–109

Continued on pages 120–121

Longitude West of Greenwich

Scale 1:4 000 000; one inch to 64 miles. Conic Projection

Elevations and depressions are given in feet

Continued on pages 96-97

QUEBEC

MONTREAL

CANADA
U.S.A.

MAINE

ONTARIO

Peterborough

LAKE ONTARIO
Surface 246 Feet above Sea Level
maximum depth 778 Feet

TORONTO

ADIRONDACK
MTS.

VERMONT

NEW
HAMPSHIRE

Portland

Hamilton

BUFFALO

Niagara Falls

Rochester

Syracuse

Albany

Troy

BOSTON

NEW YORK

CATSKILL
MTS.

MASS.

Springfield

Hartford

CONN.

R.I.

Providence

New Haven

LONG ISLAND SOUND

PENNSYLVANIA

Elmira

Binghamton

Scranton

POCONO MTS.

Allentown

Reading

NEW YORK

Trenton

NEW
JERSEY

PITTSBURGH

Harrisburg

Lancaster

PHILADELPHIA

Camden

ATLANTIC

OCEAN

Atlantic City

BALTIMORE

MARYLAND

DEL.

WASHINGTON,
D.C.

VIRGINIA

BLUE RIDGE

SHENANDOAH
NAT'L PARK

GEO. WASHINGTON
BIRTHPLACE
NAT'L MON.

CAPE HENLOPEN

Richmond

Lynchburg

Newport News

Norfolk
Virginia Beach

Relief		
Meters		Feet
1525		5000
610		2000
305		1000
152.5		500
0	Sea Level	0
152.5		500
1525		5000
3050		10 000

0   20   40   60   80   100   120 Miles
0   20   40   60   80   100   120   140   160   180   200 Kilometers

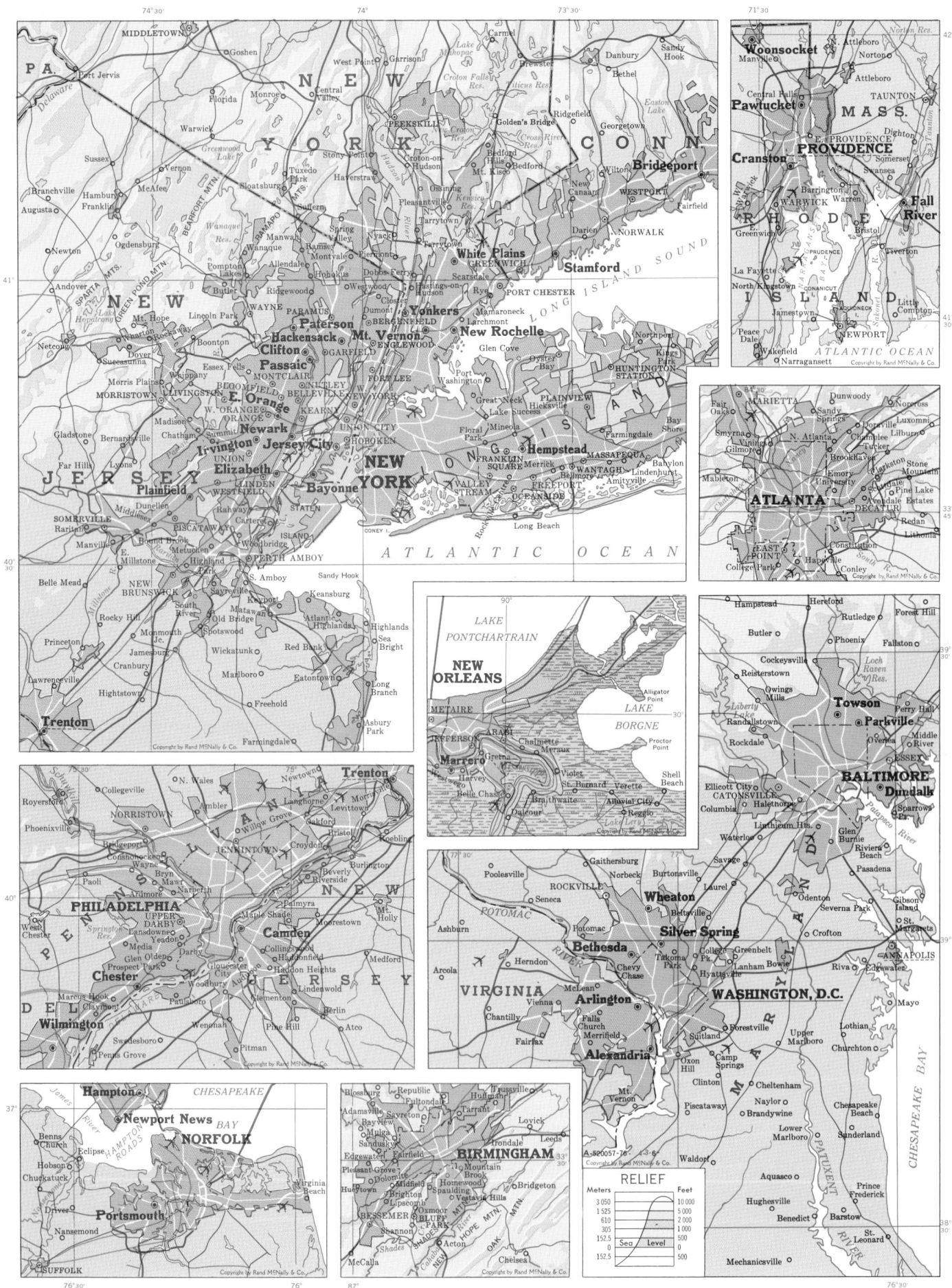

Scale 1:1 000 000; One inch to 16 miles.
Elevations and depressions are given in feet.

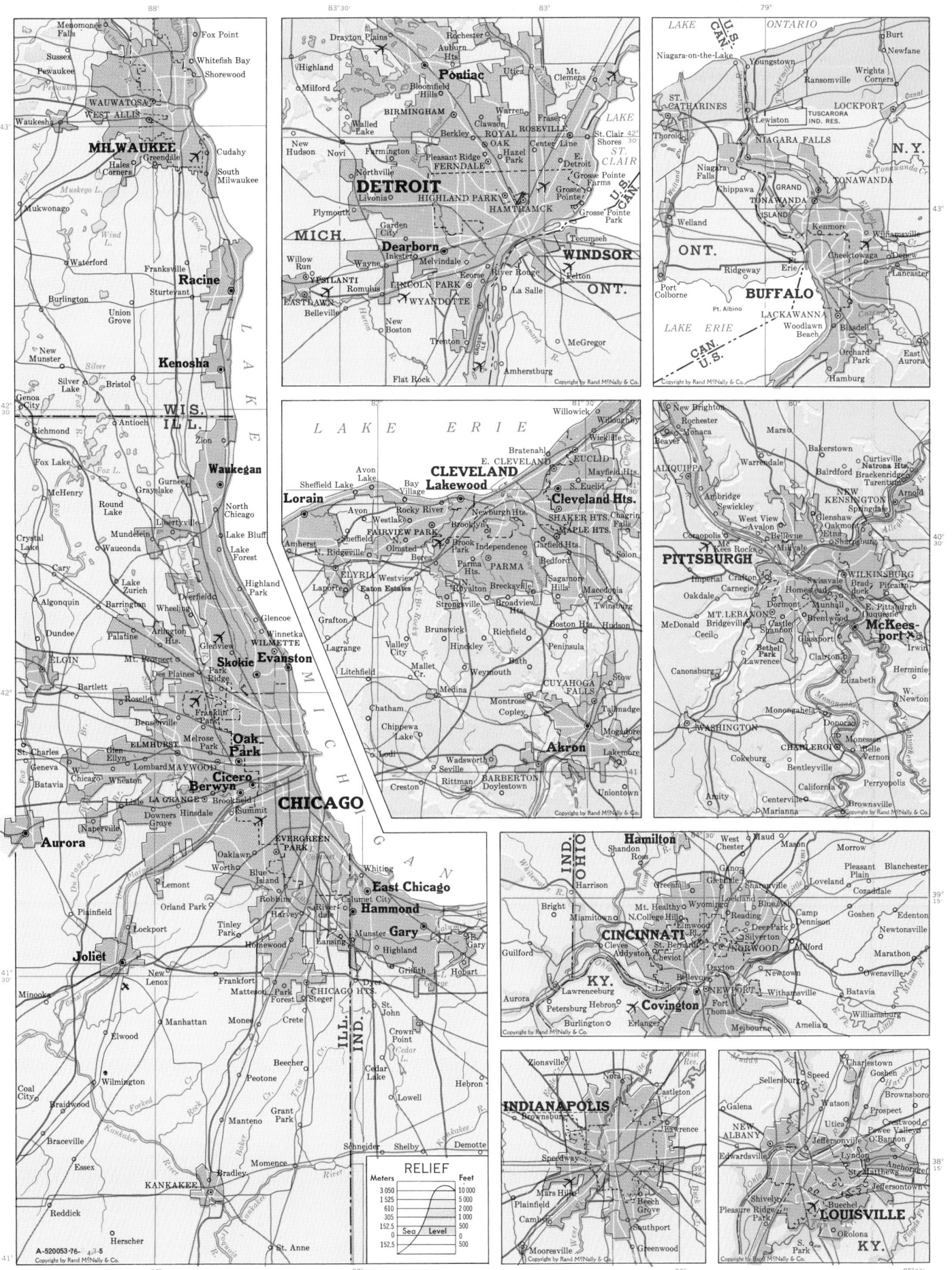

0 2 4 6 8 10 12 14 16 18 20 22 24 Miles
0 4 8 12 16 20 24 28 32 36 40 Kilometers

Scale 1:1 000 000; One inch to 16 miles.
Elevations and depressions are given in feet.

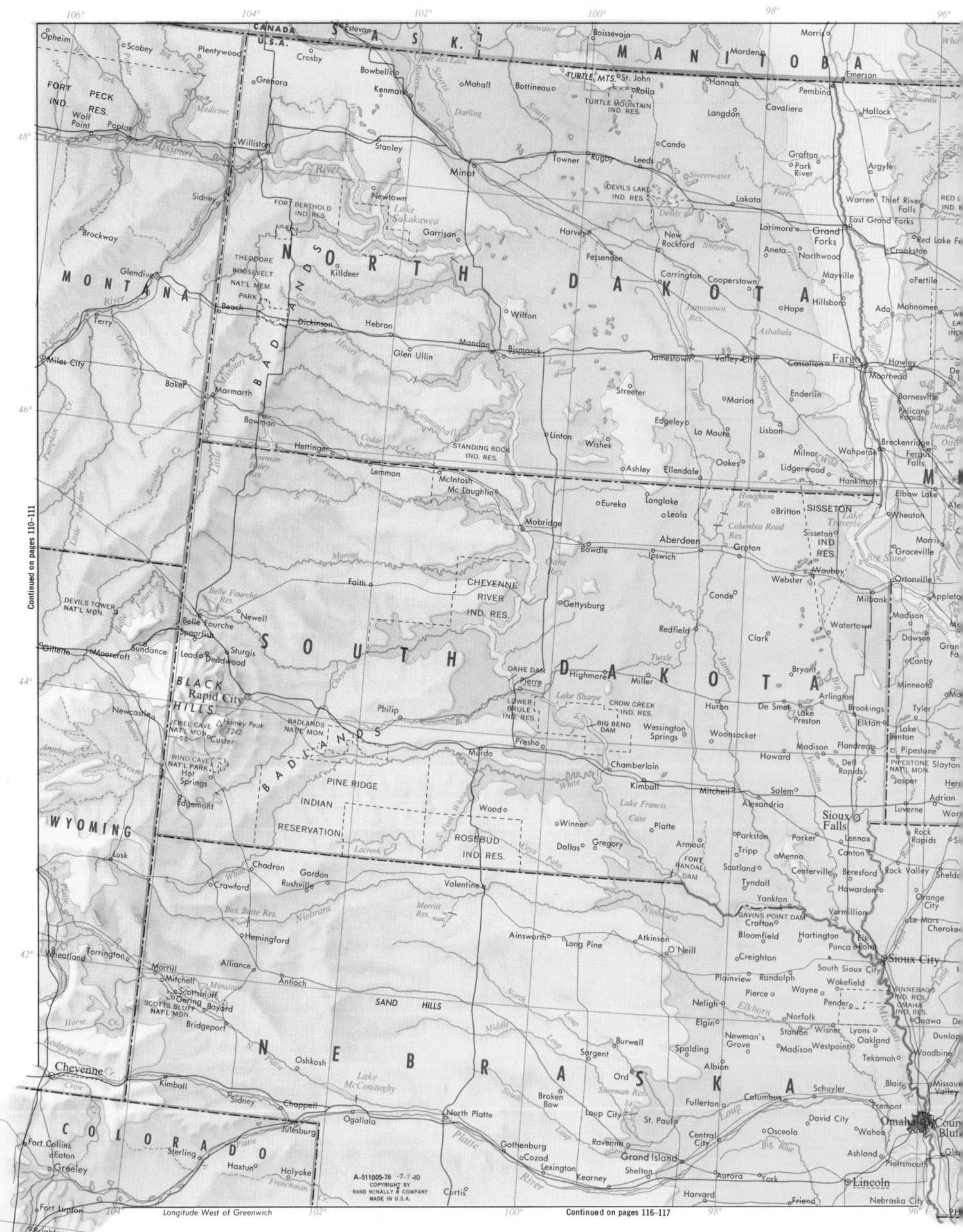

106° 104° 102° 100° 98° 96°

CANADA
U.S.A.

SASK. MANITOBA

Opheim Scobey Plentywood Estevan Whitewater Boissevain Morris

FORT
PECK
IND.
RES.

Grenora Crosby Bowbells Mohall Bottineau TURTLE MTS. St. John Rolla Hannah Cavalier Pembina Emerson

Wolf
Point Poplar

Kenmare TURTLE MOUNTAIN Langdon Grafton Argyle Hallock
IND. RES.

Williston Stanley Minot Towner Rugby Leeds Cando DEVILS LAKE Lakota Larimore Grand East Grand Forks Thief River
IND. RES. Forks Falls

48°

Sidney Newtown Garrison Harvey Fessenden New Carrington Cooperstown Northwood Mayville Fertile
Brockway Lake Rockford

FORT BERTHOLD Sakakawea Aneta
IND. RES.

NORTH D A K O T A Hope

MONTANA Killdeer Wilton Jamestown Valley City Casselton Fargo Hawley

Glendive THEODORE Hebron Mandan Bismarck Streeter Marion Enderlin Moorhead
ROOSEVELT Dickinson Glen Ullin
Beach NAT'L MEM. Jamestown Barnesville
PARK Edgeley La Moure Lisbon Pelican
Terry Rapids

46° Baker Bowman Hettinger Linton Wishek Ashley Ellendale Oakes Milnor Wahpeton Fergus
Miles City Marmarth STANDING ROCK Hankinson Falls
Lemmon IND. RES. Lidgerwood
Longlake Breckenridge

McIntosh Eureka Leola Elbow Lake
McLaughlin Houghton SISSETON

Faith Mobridge Bowdle Aberdeen Ipswich Groton Sisseton Graceville

SOUTH D A K O T A Oahe Gettysburg Conde Redfield Clark Watertown Madison
Res.

44° BLACK Rapid City Highmore Miller Huron De Smet Brookings Tyler

S. D A K O T A

ONTARIO

Lake of the Woods

Baudette
Fort Frances
International Falls
VOYAGEURS NAT'L PARK
QUETICO PROVINCIAL PARK
NETT LAKE IND. RES.
Thunder Bay
GRAND PORTAGE NAT'L MON.
GRAND PORTAGE IND. RES.
ISLE ROYALE NAT'L PARK
CANADA U.S.A.
Michipicoten Harbour
MICHIPICOTEN

VERMILION RANGE
Ely
LAKE SUPERIOR
Surface elev. 602 Feet above Sea Level
Maximum depth 1333 Feet
Copper Harbor
Sault Ste. Marie
Sault Ste. Marie

GREATER LEECH LAKE IND. RES.
Chisholm Buhl
Virginia Biwabik
Hibbing Eveleth Gilbert Aurora
Keewatin
Nashwauk
Coleraine
Grand Rapids
MESABI RANGE
Deer River
Hill City

KEWEENAW PEN.
Calumet
Laurium Lake Linden
Hancock Houghton
MANITOU

Two Harbors
Silver Bay
APOSTLE ISLANDS
OUTER
SAND STOCKTON
MADELINE
Bayfield
Ontonagon
HURON MTS.
L'Anse
VIEUX DESERT IND. RES.
Negaunee Ishpeming
Marquette
Munising
Newberry
Trout Lake
BAY MILLS IND. RES.

RED CLIFF IND. RES.
Washburno
BAD RIVER IND. RES.
Ashland
Bessemer
Hurley Ironwood
GOGEBIC RANGE
Wakefield
Champion
Gwinn
MICHIGAN

Proctor Duluth
Cloquet Superior
FOND DU LAC IND. RES.
Carlton
Mellen
Iron River
Stambaugh
Crystal Falls
MENOMINEE RANGE
Iron Mountain
Norway
Niagara
Gladstone
Escanaba
Manistique
GARDEN St. Ignace
Mackinaw City
BEAVER I. IND. RES.
Cheboygan

Aitkin
Brainerd
Sandstone
Pine City
LAC DU FLAMBEAU IND. RES.
Hayward LAC COURT OREILLE IND. RES.
Park Falls
Phillips
Rhinelander
Crandon
Wausaukee
HIGH BEAVER
Harbor Springs
Charlevoix
Petoskey
Boyne City

MILLE LACS IND. RES.
Mora
Spooner
Rice Lake
Ladysmith
ST. CROIX IND. RES.
Cumberland
Amery
Chetek
Bloomer
Medford
Merrill
Antigo
Tomahawk
Rib Lake
Shawano
Oconto Falls Oconto
Peshtigo
Menominee Marinette
DOOR PEN.
Sturgeon Bay
Algoma
Kewaunee
Two Rivers
E. Jordan
Elk Rapids
Mancelona
Traverse City
Frankfort
Jennings
Cadillac

St. Cloud
Princeton
Elk River
Cambridge
New Richmond
Chippewa Falls
Stanley Owen
Wausau
Schofield
Stratford
STOCKBRIDGE MUNSEE IND. RES.
De Pere Green Bay
Menasha Neenah Kaukauna
Appleton
Manitowoc
Reed City
Big Rapids
Hart Shelby
Fremont Newaygo

MINNEAPOLIS St. Paul
St. Louis Park
South St. Paul
Shakopee
PRAIRIE ISLAND IND. RES.
Hudson Menomonie
River Falls
Eau Claire
Augusta
Marshfield
Neillsville
Wisconsin Rapids
Stevens Point New London
Waupaca
Omro
Oshkosh Kiela
Chilton
Sheboygan
Sheboygan Falls
Muskegon Heights
Muskegon Grand Rapids
Greenville Belding

New Prague
Northfield
Red Wing
Lake City
Durand
Mondovi
Black River Falls
Wautoma
Berlin
Princeton
Montello
Fond du Lac
Plymouth
Port Washington
Whitehall
Grand Haven
Holland
Hastings
Allegan

Owatonna
Faribault
Waterville
Kenyon
Zumbrota
Alma
Arcadia
Galesville
Sparta
Tomah
New Lisbon
Mauston
Wisconsin Dells
Waupun
Beaver Dam
West Horicon Bend
Mayville
Cedarburg
Whitefish Bay
Shorewood
MILWAUKEE
Cudahy
South Milwaukee
South Haven
Otsego
Kalamazoo

Rochester
Winona
La Crosse
Westby
Hillsboro
Reedsburg
Baraboo
Portage
Columbus
Watertown
Hartford
Oconomowoc
Wauwatosa
West Allis
Racine
Kenosha
Benton Harbor
St. Joseph

Albert Lea
Austin
Caledonia
Viroqua
Richland Center
Sauk City
Madison
Jefferson
Waukesha
Fort Atkinson
Evansville Milton Elkhorn
Burlington
Lake Geneva Delavan
Walworth
Waukegan
North Chicago
Lake Forest
Highland Park
Winnetka Wilmette
Dowagiac
Three Rivers
Sturgis

Cresco
Decorah
Lansing
Boscobel
Dodgeville
Stoughton
Edgerton
Janesville
Beloit
Harvard
Zion
Libertyville
Fort Sheridan
Evanston

Northwood
Forest City
Osage
New Hampton
West Union
Fayette
EFFIGY MOUNDS NAT'L MON.
Mc Gregor
Prairie du Chien
Lancaster
Platteville
Shullsburg
Monroe
Dubuque
Galena
Freeport
Rockford
Belvidere
Woodstock
Elgin
St. Charles
Skokie
Oak Park Chicago
E. Chicago
Michigan City
Elkhart

Clear Lake Mason City
Charles City
Waterloo
Cedar Falls
Manchester
Dyersville
Monticello
Savanna
Oregon
Sycamore
De Kalb
Batavia
Geneva St. Charles
Aurora
Blue Island
Hammond Gary
Valparaiso
Crown Point
N. Judson

Eldora
Webster City
Reinbeck
La Porte City
Grundy Center
Anamosa
Maquoketa
Mt. Carroll
Rochelle
Rock Falls Dixon
Sterling
Joliet
Chicago Heights

Waverly
Oelwein
Cedar Rapids
Vinton
Marion
Bellevue
Clinton
Morrison
Hammond
Lowell
Kankakee
IND.

Marshalltown
Toledo
Tama
Belle Plaine
Marengo
De Witt
Tipton
Princeton
La Salle
Marseilles
Morris
Rensselaer

Des Moines
Newton
Colfax
Iowa City
Davenport
West Liberty
Rock Island
Moline
Geneseo
Springvalley
Oglesby
Ottawa
Streator
Dwight
Gilman
Fowler

Indianola
Pella
Oskaloosa
What Cheer
Washington
Sigourney
Wapello
Brighton
Aledo
Kewanee
Galva
Toluca
Minonk
Pontiac
Fairbury
Watseka

Knoxville
Albia
Fairfield
Mount Pleasant
Monmouth
Galesburg
Chillicothe
Minonk
Kentland

Chariton
Centerville
Bloomfield
Eldon
Burlington
Fort Madison
Abingdon
Farmington
Peoria

Corydon
Leon
Mystic
Seymour
Lamoni

WISCONSIN
ILLINOIS
IOWA
MINNESOTA

LAKE MICHIGAN
Surface elevation 580 Feet above Sea Level
Maximum depth 923 Feet

Continued on pages 104–105

Continued on pages 116–117

Relief
Meters		Feet
1525		5000
610		2000
305		1000
152.5		500
0	Sea Level	0
152.5		500

20 40 60 80 100 120 Miles
20 40 60 80 100 120 140 160 180 200 Kilometers

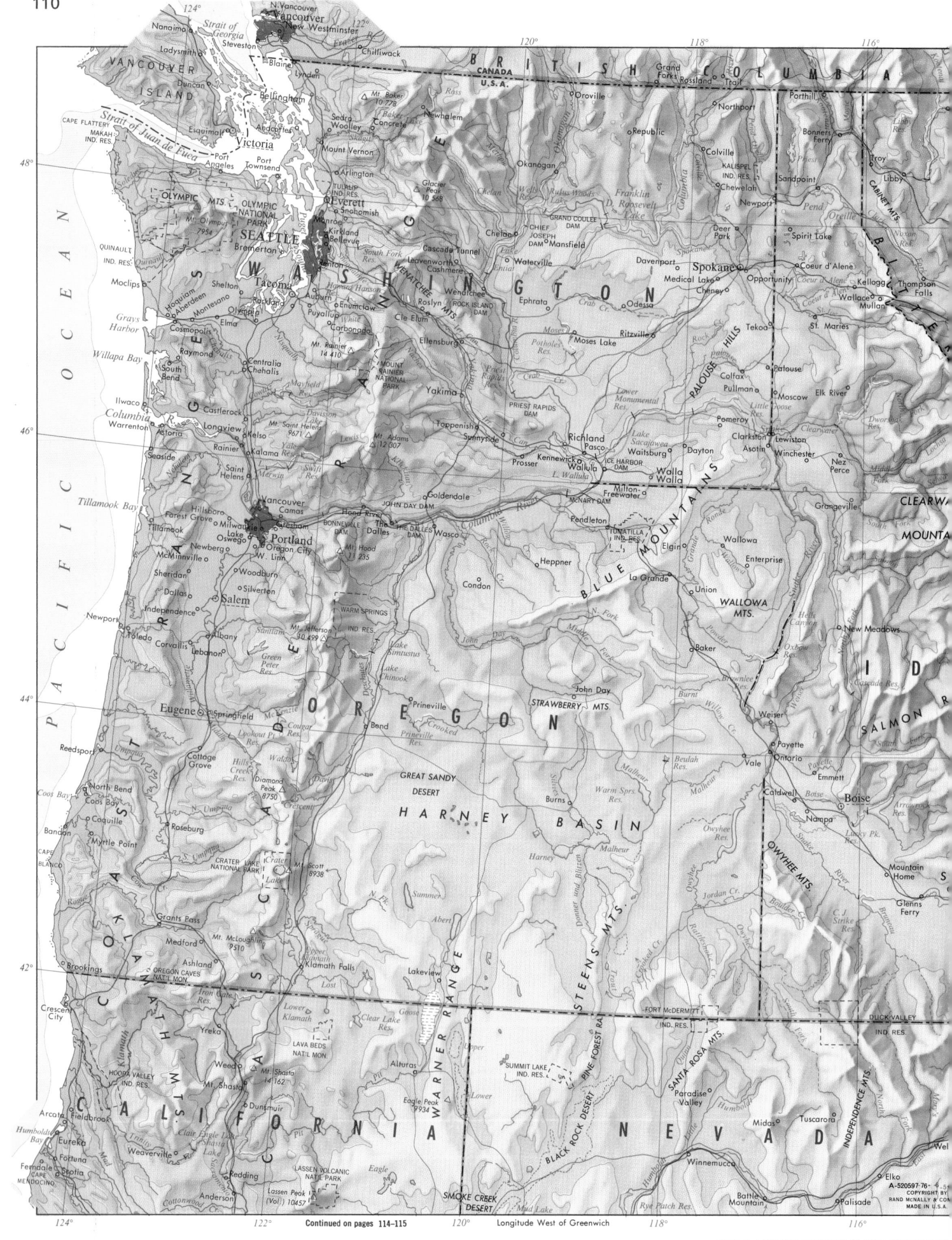

Continued on pages 114–115

Longitude West of Greenwich

Scale 1: 4,000 000; one inch to 64 miles. Conic Projecti
Elevations and depressions are given in feet

ALBERTA
SASKATCHEWAN
CANADA
U.S.A.

MONTANA

WYOMING

UTAH

N. DAK.

COLO.

IDAHO

Missouri River
Yellowstone River

ROCKY MOUNTAINS
SWAN RANGE
LEWIS RANGE
BIG BELT MTS.
LITTLE BELT MTS.
CRAZY MTS.
ABSAROKA RANGE
BEARTOOTH RANGE
PIONEER MTS.
BEAVERHEAD MTS.
LEMHI RANGE
LOST RIVER MTS.
BIG HORN MOUNTAINS
WIND RIVER RANGE
WYOMING RANGE
WASATCH RANGE
UINTA MTS.
FRONT RANGE
TOANA RANGE

WATERTON-GLACIER INTERNATIONAL PEACE PARK
BLACKFOOT IND. RES.
NATIONAL BISON RANGE
ROCKY BOYS IND. RES.
FORT PECK IND. RES.
Fort Peck Res.
CUSTER BATTLEFIELD NAT'L MON.
NORTHERN CHEYENNE IND. RES.
CROW IND. RES.
BIG HOLE NAT'L BATTLEFIELD
CRATERS OF THE MOON NAT'L MON.
FORT HALL IND. RES.
Blackfoot River Res.
WIND RIVER IND. RES.
DEVILS TOWER NAT'L MON.
YELLOWSTONE NATIONAL PARK
GRAND TETON NAT'L PARK
DINOSAUR NAT'L MON.
GREAT SALT LAKE DESERT
GREAT SALT LAKE
GREAT DIVIDE BASIN
RIVER PLAINS

Browning
Shelby
Cut Bank
Sunburst
Conrad
Valier
Choteau
Great Falls
Belt
Fort Benton
Winifred
Neihart
White Sulphur Spgs.
Lewistown
Winnett
Harlowton
Roundup
Helena
East Helena
Townsend
Bozeman
Livingston
Bigtimber
Columbus
Laurel
Billings
Hardin
Crow Agency
Lame Deer
Colstrip
Forsyth
Miles City
Terry
Glendive
Baker
Marmarth
Beach
Wibaux
Sidney
Williston
Wolf Point
Poplar
Glasgow
Ft. Peck
Malta
Harlem
Chinook
Havre
Hogeland
Morgan
Opheim
Scobey
Plentywood
Grenora
Medicine Lake
Brockway

Missoula
Lolo
Stevensville
Hamilton
Philipsburg
Deer Lodge
Anaconda
Walkerville
Butte
Three Forks
Twin Bridges
Dillon
Salmon
Mackay
Arco
Rexburg
Rigby
St. Anthony
Ashton
Idaho Falls
Shelley
Blackfoot
Pocatello
Soda Springs
Afton
Montpelier
Lava Hot Sprs.
American Falls
Rupert
Burley
Oakley
Malad
Preston
Richmond
Smithfield
Logan
Providence
Wallsville
Garland
Brigham
Huntsville
Ogden
Farmington
Bountiful
Murray
Midvale
Salt Lake City
Heber
Park City
Vernal
Wendover
Lucin
Tooele

Red Lodge
Cody
Powell
Lovell
Greybull
Basin
Worland
Thermopolis
Ten Sleep
Buffalo
Sheridan
Gillette
Moorcroft
Sundance
Gebo
Shoshoni
Riverton
Lander
Midwest
Powder River
Casper
Douglas
Orin
Glenrock
Rawlins
Wheatland
Hanna
Superior
Rock Springs
Green River
Granger
Kemmerer
Evanston

Ajax Mtn. 10 900
Borah Pk. 12 662
Hyndman Peak 12 078
Cloud Peak 13 175
Gannett Peak 13 785
Fremont Peak 13 730
Grand Teton Mt. 13 766
Electric Peak 11 155
Mt. Washburn 10 317
Granite Peak 12 799
Kings Peak 13 528
Wilson Peak 12 075
Meade Peak 9353
Hap Hawkins Lake
Hebgen Res.
Lima Res.
Madison Res.
American Falls Res.
Grays L.
Jackson Lake
Palisades Res.
Fontenelle Res.
Flaming Gorge Res.
Pathfinder Res.
Seminoe Res.
Alcova Res.
Glendo Res.
Wheatland Res.
Medicine Bow

Mammoth Hot Springs
7731 ft. above sea level
Gardiner

Surface elev. approx. 4200 ft. above sea level

Continued on pages 114-115
Continued on pages 108-109

Relief		
Meters		Feet
3050		10000
1525		5000
610		2000
305		1000
152.5		500
0	Sea Level	0
1525		500

20 40 60 80 100 120 Miles
20 40 60 80 100 120 140 160 180 200 Kilometers

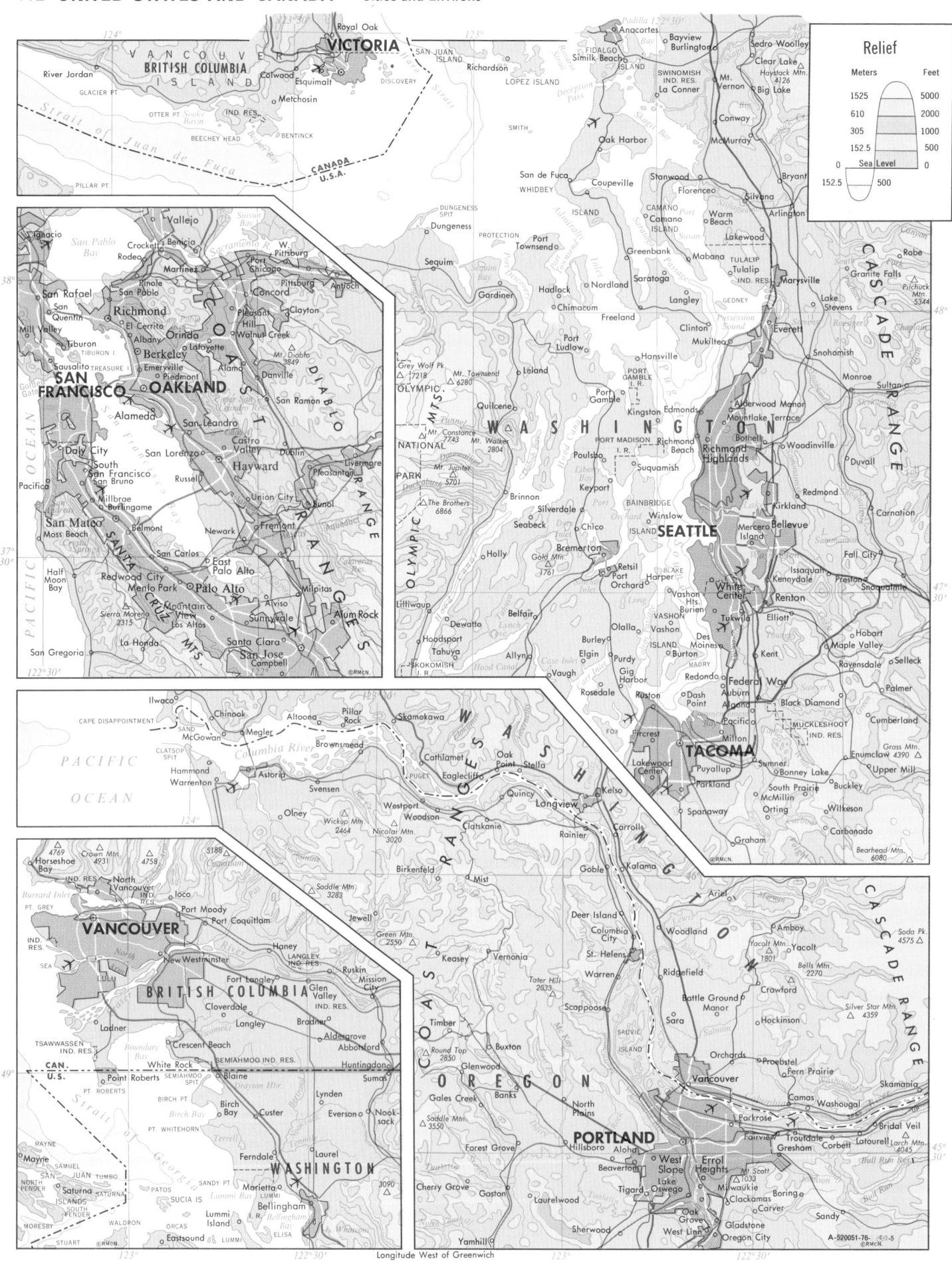

0 5 10 15 20 Miles
0 4 8 12 16 20 24 28 32 Kilometers

Scale 1:1 000 000; one inch to 16 miles.
Elevations and depressions are given in feet.

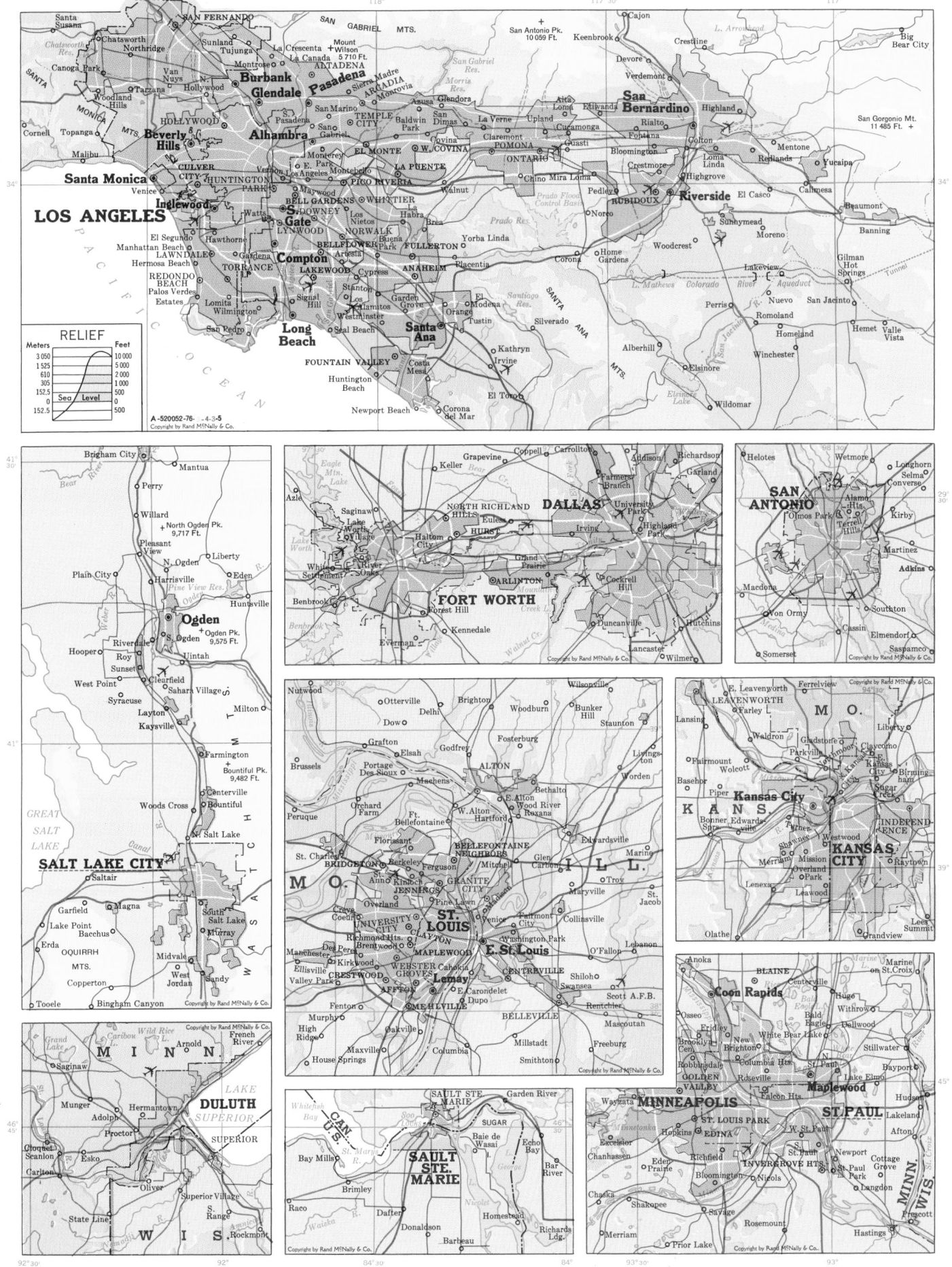

Scale 1:1 000 000; One inch to 16 miles.
Elevations and depressions are given in feet.

114

Relief

Meters		Feet
3050		10000
1525		5000
610		2000
305		1000
152.5		500
0	Sea Level	0
		Below
152.5		500
1525		5000
3050		10000

Continued on pages 110-111

NEVADA

CALIFORNIA

COAST RANGES

PACIFIC OCEAN

POINT ARENA
POINT REYES
MUIR WOODS NATL. MON.
POINT REYES

Anderson
Lassen Peak (Vol.) 10 457
LASSEN VOLCANIC NATL. PARK
Westwood
Red Bluff
Susanville
SMOKE CREEK DESERT
Mud
Battle Mountain
Palisade
Franklin

Willows
Honey Lake
Lovelock
Humboldt
RUBY MTS.
Ruby

Chico
PYRAMID LAKE
Winnemucca
Humboldt Sink
SPRING CO.
STILLWATER RA.
Humboldt Salt Marsh

Oroville
Downieville
INDIAN
RESERVATION
Sparks
Carson Sink

Gridley
Nevada City
Grass Valley
Truckee
Reno
Virginia City
Fallon
Austin
Eureka
Ruth
El

Colusa
Yuba City
Marysville
Auburn
Carson City
Yerington
WALKER RIVER IND. RES.

Ukiah
Lakeport
Lincoln
Roseville
Placerville
Lake Tahoe
Walker Lake
Hawthorne
TOYABE RANGE
Arc Dome 11 775
Duckwater Pk. 11 493

Cloverdale
Healdsburg
Woodland
Folsom City
Jackson
WASSUK RANGE

Sebastopol
Santa Rosa
Napa
Sacramento
San Andreas
Angels Camp
Sonora
Sonora Pk. 11 429
Coaldale
Tonopah

Petaluma
Vallejo
Benicia
Lodi
YOSEMITE
Dana Mtn. 13 055
Boundary Peak 13 145
Goldfield

San Rafael
Richmond
Berkeley
Pittsburg
Stockton
NATIONAL
Mt. Lyell 13 095
White Mt. Peak 14 246

SIERRA

San Francisco
Oakland
Alameda
Tracy
Oakdale
PARK
DEVILS POSTPILE N.M.
Bishop
Alamo

Daly City
Livermore
Modesto
Turlock
Bentona

San Mateo
Redwood City
Palo Alto
Santa Clara
Merced
Mariposa
Madera

San Jose
Los Gatos
KINGS CANYON NATL. PARK
INYO MTS.

Santa Cruz
Gilroy
Hollister
Fresno
Sanger
Reedley
Selma
Dinuba
Lone Pine
DEATH VALLEY 282 Ft below sea level
FRENCHMAN FLAT
Beatty

Watsonville
Salinas
Visalia
SEQUOIA
Mt. Whitney 14 494
Death Valley Jct.
SPRING MTS.

Monterey Bay
PINNACLES NATL. MON.
King City
Hanford
Exeter
NATL. PARK
Telescope Peak 11 045
DEATH VALLEY NATL. MON.

Pacific Grove
Monterey
Coalinga
Tulare
Owens
TULE RIVER IND. RES.
Trona
Inyokern
Las

Henderson
HOOVER D
Boulder C

Delano
Porterville
Searles
MOAPA IND. R

San Luis Obispo
Estero Bay
Atascadero
Paso Robles
Buena Vista Lake Reservoir
Bakersfield
MOJAVE
Soda
FORT I

Santa Maria
Lompoc
Taft
TEHACHAPI MTS.
Mojave
Barstow
Daggett
Goffs
Cadiz

POINT ARGUELLO
POINT CONCEPTION
Santa Barbara
Ventura
Oxnard
Santa Paula
MOJAVE DESERT

Santa Barbara Channel
SAN MIGUEL
SANTA CRUZ
SANTA ROSA
Burbank
Glendale
Pasadena
Monrovia
San Bernardino
JOSHUA TREE NATL. MON.
SAN BERNARDINO MTS.

LOS ANGELES
Alhambra
Pomona
Redlands
Palm Springs

Santa Monica
Huntington Park
Riverside
MORONGO IND. RES.

Inglewood
Compton
Orange
AGUA CALIENTE IND. RES.

SANTA BARBARA ISLANDS
Redondo Beach
San Pedro
Long Beach
Santa Ana
Newport Beach
Elsinore
SANTA ROSA IND. RES.
Colorado River

Huntington Beach
TORRES MARTINEZ IND. RES.
Salton Sea Bottom 235 Ft below sea level

SANTA BARBARA CHANNEL ISLANDS NAT'L. MON.
SANTA CATALINA
Avalon
Oceanside
Escondido
CAHUILLA IND. RES.
Calipatria
IMPERIAL VALLEY
Brawley
Holtville

SAN NICOLAS
Gulf of Santa Catalina
SANTA YSABEL IND. RES.
INAJA IND. RES.

SAN CLEMENTE
SAN DIEGO
Coronado
National City
Chula Vista
CUYAPAIPE IND. RES.
CAMP RES.
El Centro
Calexico
Mexicali

Tijuana
BAJA CALIFORNIA NORTE
Laguna Salada

Inset — San Diego

PACIFIC OCEAN
CALIFORNIA
Del Mar
La Jolla
Lakeside
Santee
El Cajon
La Mesa
Spring Valley
Lemon Grove
SAN DIEGO
CABRILLO NATL. MON.
National City
Chula Vista
Sweetwater Reservoir
Lower Otay Reservoir
Otay
Imperial Beach
Coronado
Tijuana
USA MEXICO
BAJA CALIFORNIA NORTE

Scale 1:1 000 000

| 0 | 5 | 10 Miles |
| 0 4 8 12 16 Kilometers | | |

A-520599-76 6 7-10
COPYRIGHT BY
RAND MCNALLY & COMPANY
MADE IN U.S.A.
©RMcN.

Longitude West of Greenwich

Scale 1:4 000 000; one inch to 64 miles. Conic Projection
Elevations and depressions are given in feet

| 0 | 20 | 40 | 60 | 80 | 100 | 120 Miles |
| 0 20 40 60 80 100 120 140 160 180 200 Kilometers | | | | | | |

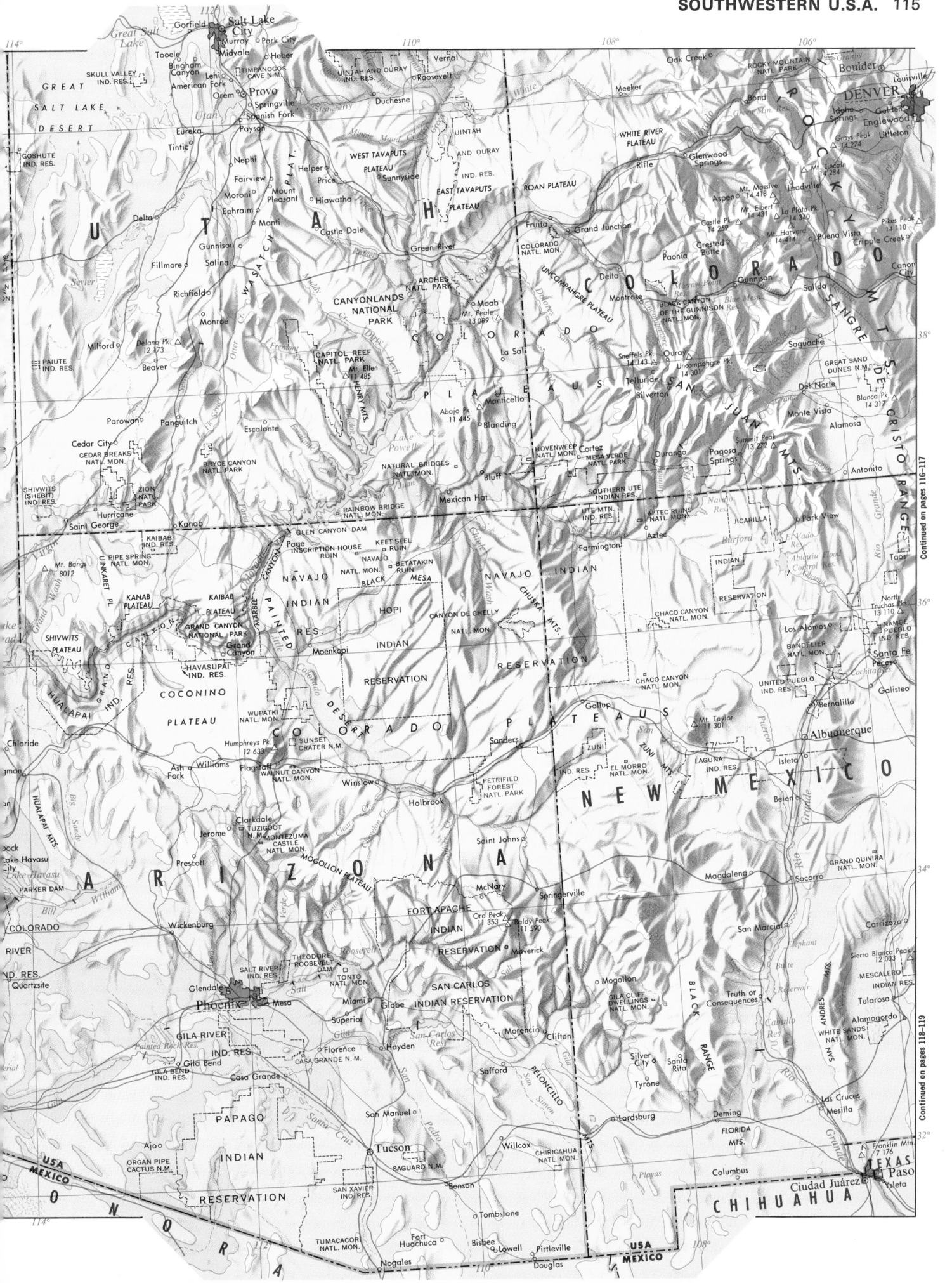

Continued on pages 116-117

Continued on pages 118-119

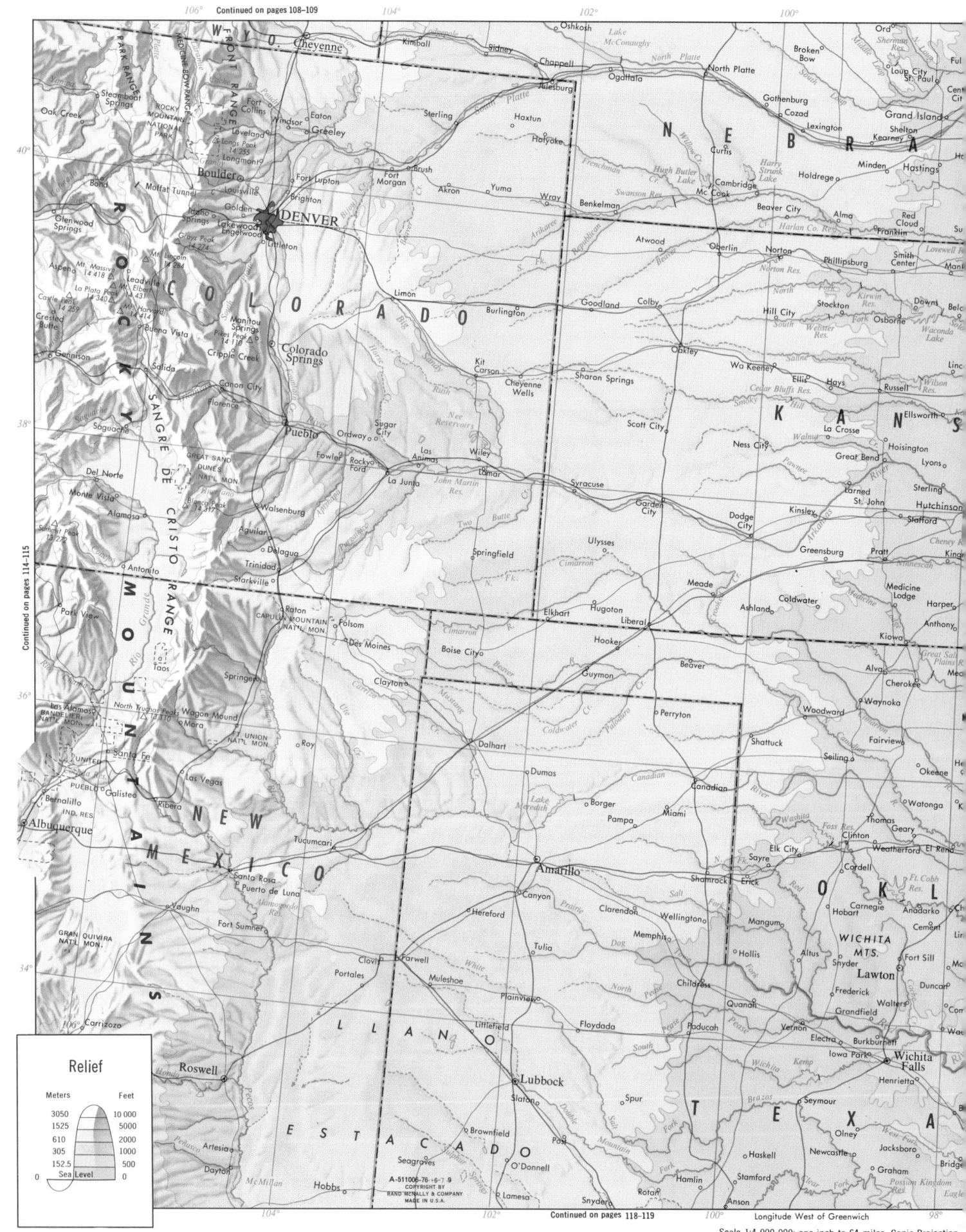

Continued on pages 108–109

106°   104°   102°   100°

WYO.
Cheyenne
Kimball
Oshkosh   Lake
McConaughy
Sidney
Chappell
North Platte
Ord   Sherman
Res.
Broken
Bow
Loup City   St. Paul
Ord   St.
City
North Platte
Loup   Middle Loup

FRONT RANGE
PARK RANGE
MEDICINE BOW RANGE
Steamboat
Springs
Fort
Collins
Windsor
Eaton
Greeley
Sterling
Julesburg
Ogallala
Gothenburg
Cozad
Lexington
Grand Island

Oak Creek
Loveland
Longmont
Longs Peak
14 255
Brush
Fort
Morgan
Akron
Yuma
Wray
Benkelman
Frenchman
Hugh Butler
Lake
Cambridge
Mc Cook
Harry
Strunk
Lake
Holdrege
Minden
Hastings

NEBRA

40°
Bond
Moffat Tunnel
Boulder
Louisville
Brighton
Fort Lupton
Haxtun
Holyoke
Swanson Res.
Beaver City
Alma
Red
Cloud
Franklin

Glenwood
Springs
Idaho
Springs
Golden
DENVER
Lakewood
Englewood
Littleton
Arikaree
Atwood
Oberlin
Norton
Phillipsburg
Smith
Center
Lovewell
Res.

Aspen
Mt. Massive
14 418
Leadville
Mt. Elbert
14 431
Grays Peak
14 274
Mt. Lincoln
14 284
Harlan Co. Res.

La Plata Peak
14 340
Mt. Harvard
14 414
Limon
Burlington
Goodland
Colby
Hill City
Stockton
Osborne
Downs

Castle Peak
14 259
Crested
Butte
Manitou
Springs
Pikes Peak
14 110
Colorado
Springs
Oakley
Wa Keeney
Ellis
Hays
Russell
Waconda
Lake

Gunnison
Buena Vista
Cripple Creek
Kit
Carson
Cheyenne
Wells
Sharon
Springs
Scott City
Ness City
La Crosse
Ellsworth

COLORADO

Salida
Canon City
Florence
Cedar Bluffs Res.
Smoky
Hill
Wilson
Res.

38°
Saguache
Del Norte
Monte Vista
Saguache
Pueblo
Ordway
Sugar
City
Nee
Reservoirs
Las
Animas
Wiley
Lamar
Syracuse
Garden
City
Kinsley
Larned
St. John
Hoisington
Great Bend
Lyons

KANS

Alamosa
GREAT SAND
DUNES
NAT'L MON.
Fowler
Rocky
Ford
La Junta
John Martin
Res.
Dodge
City
Sterling
Hutchinson
Stafford

Summit Peak
13 272
Blanca Peak
14 317
Walsenburg
Aguilar
Two   Butte
Springfield
Ulysses
Greensburg
Pratt
Minnescah

SANGRE DE CRISTO RANGE
Del Norte
Antonito
Trinidad
Delagua
Cimarron
N. Fk.
Meade
Medicine
Lodge
Harper
Anthony

Park View
Starkville
Raton
CAPULIN MOUNTAIN
NAT'L MON.
Folsom
Elkhart
Hugoton
Ashland
Coldwater

Taos
Des Moines
Boise City
Liberal
Kiowa
Great Salt
Plains

36°
North Truchas Peaks
13 110
Mora
Wagon Mound
Clayton
Hooker
Beaver
Guymon
Alva
Cherokee
Waynoka

Santa Fe
Las Vegas
Roy
Perryton
Woodward
Fairview

Los Alamos
BANDELIER
NAT'L MON.
Springer
Dalhart
Shattuck
Seiling
Okeene
Watonga

UNITED
PUEBLO
IND. RES.
Bernalillo
Galisteo
Ribera
Dumas
Borger
Canadian
Clinton
Thomas
Geary

Albuquerque
Tucumcari
Lake
Meredith
Pampa
Miami
Foss Res.
Weatherford
El Reno

NEW   MEXICO
Santa Rosa
Puerto de Luna
Canyon
Amarillo
Clarendon
Sayre
Erick
Cordell
Ft. Cobb
Res.

Vaughn
Fort Sumner
Hereford
Wellington
Memphis
Mangum
Hobart
Carnegie
Anadarko
Cement

GRAN QUIVIRA
NAT'L MON.
Tulia
Hollis
Altus
WICHITA
MTS.
Fort Sill
Lawton

34°
Carrizozo
Clovis
Farwell
Muleshoe
Plainview
Childress
Quanah
Frederick
Snyder
Walters
Duncan

Roswell
Portales
Littlefield
Floydada
Paducah
Vernon
Electra
Grandfield
Burkburnett
Iowa Park
Wichita
Falls

LLANO

Lubbock
Slaton
Spur
Seymour
Olney
Henrietta

ESTACADO
Brownfield
Seagraves
O'Donnell
Lamesa
Post
Rotan
Hamlin
Stamford
Anson
Haskell
Newcastle
Jacksboro
Graham
TEXA

Penasco
Artesia
Dayton
McMillan
Hobbs
Snyder

Longitude West of Greenwich

Scale 1:4 000 000; one inch to 64 miles. Conic Projection
Elevations and depressions are given in feet.

Relief

Meters		Feet
3050		10 000
1525		5000
610		2000
305		1000
152.5		500
0	Sea Level	0

Continued on pages 114–115

Continued on pages 108–109

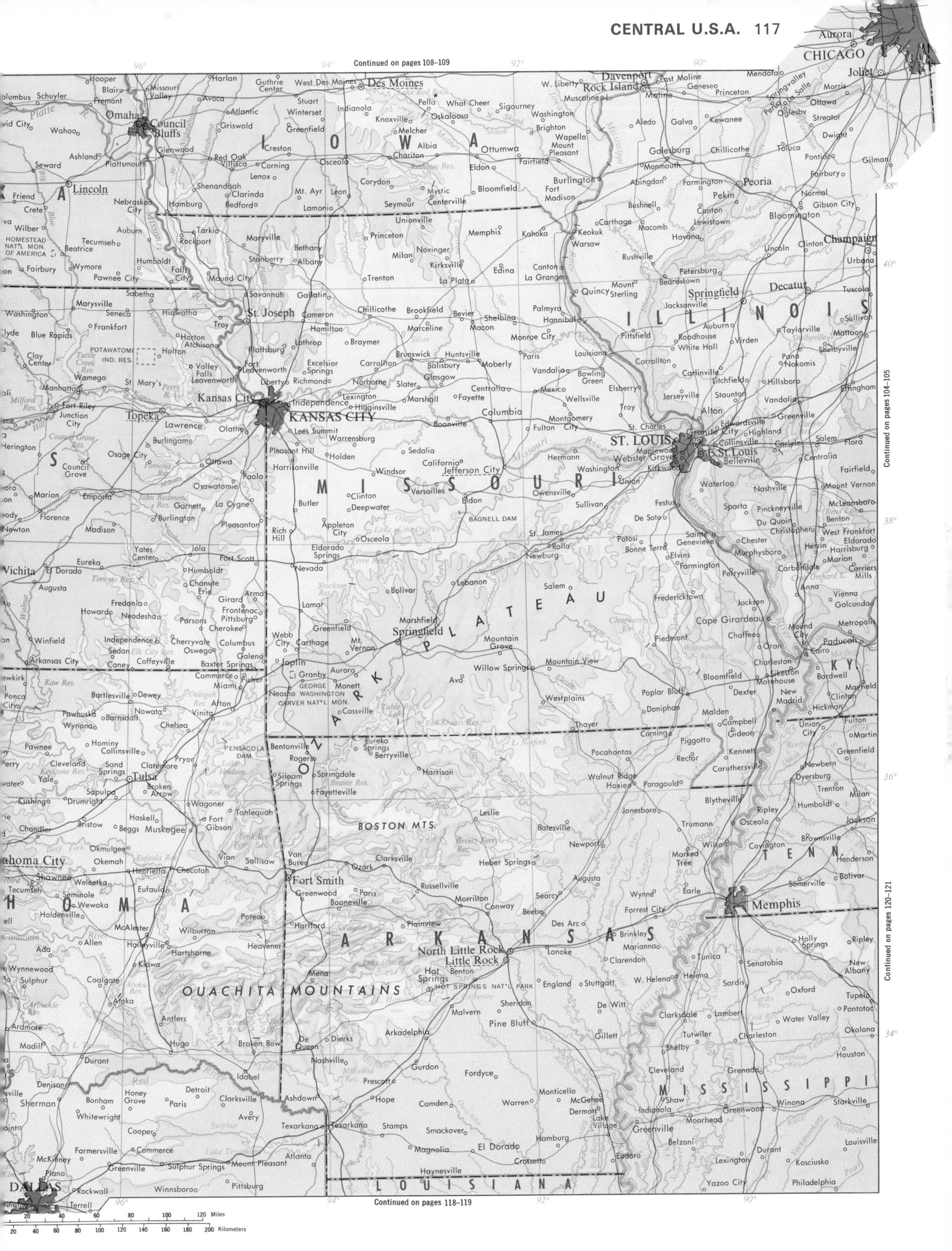

Continued on pages 104–105

Continued on pages 120–121

Continued on pages 118–119

CHICAGO

Aurora

Joliet

IOWA

Des Moines

Omaha

Council Bluffs

Lincoln

ILLINOIS

Peoria

Springfield

Decatur

Champaign

NEBRASKA

KANSAS

Topeka

Kansas City

KANSAS CITY

St. Joseph

MISSOURI

Jefferson City

St. Louis

E. St. Louis

Columbia

Springfield

OZARK PLATEAU

BOSTON MTS.

OUACHITA MOUNTAINS

OKLAHOMA

Tulsa

Fort Smith

ARKANSAS

North Little Rock
Little Rock

Hot Springs

HOT SPRINGS NAT'L PARK

Memphis

TENN.

KY.

MISSISSIPPI

LOUISIANA

DALLAS

Texarkana

GEORGE WASHINGTON CARVER NAT'L MON.

BAGNELL DAM

PENSACOLA DAM

HOMESTEAD NAT'L MON. OF AMERICA

POTAWATOMI IND. RES.

Lake of the Ozarks

Scale: 20 40 60 80 100 120 Miles
20 40 60 80 100 120 140 160 180 200 Kilometers

Continued on pages 116–117

106°   104°   102°   100°

32°

28°

26°

NEW MEXICO

White Sands Nat'l Mon.
Alamogordo
Alamo Pk. 7820
N. Franklin Mtn. 7176
El Paso
Ysleta
Ciudad Juárez
Fabens
Guadalupe

Penasco
Artesia
Dayton
McMillan
Carlsbad
Carlsbad Caverns Nat'l Park
Wind Mtn. 7278
Guadalupe Pk. 8751
Red Bluff Res.

Hobbs
Seagraves
Seminole

O'Donnell
Lamesa

Double Mountain Fork
Haskell   Newcastle   Graham
Rotan
Hamlin
Stamford
Anson
Albany   Ranger   Mineral Wells
Breckenridge
Hubbard Creek Res.   Strawn
Abilene
Baird   Cisco   Eastland   Desdemona
Gorman
De Leon   Dublin
Ste

Villa Ahumada
Sierra Blanca
Van Horn
Eagle Pk. 7495

Pecos
Toyah
Pecos
Wink
Odessa
Midland
Stanton
Big Spring

Snyder
Roscoe
Sweetwater
Colorado City
Merkel

Winters
Ballinger
Coleman
Santa Anna   Brownwood
Comanche

Brownwood

DAVIS MTS.
Baldy Peak 8382
Marfa
Alpine
Cathedral Mtn. 6560
Santiago Mts.
Chinati Pk. 7730

Toyah
Fort Stockton
STOCKTON PLATEAU
Big Canyon
Sanderson
Pecos

McCamey

Middle Concho
North Concho
San Angelo
Nasworthy

Eden
Sonora
Rocksprings

TEXAS
EDWARDS PLATEAU
Menard
Mason
Llano
Brady   San Saba
Buchanan
Llano
Junction
Kerrville
Fredericksburg

Goldthwaite
Lomet
San Saba

Chihuahua
Aldama
Coyame
Ojinaga
Presidio
Cuchillo Parado

BIG BEND NAT'L PARK
Emory Pk. 7835
SERRANÍAS DEL BURRO
U.S.A.
MEXICO

Del Rio
Villa Acuña
Jiménez

Camp Wood
Brackettville
Uvalde
Sabinal
Hondo
San Antonio
New Braunfels
Boerne

Floresville
Poteet
Pleasan

CHIHUAHUA
Meoqui
Naica
San Pedro
Concho
Toronto

Gigantes
Jaco

Muzquiz
San Juan de Sabinas

Piedras Negras
Fuente
Eagle Pass
Zaragoza
Morelos
Nava
Allende
Guerrero
Rosales

Crystal City
Carrizo Springs
Asherton
Cotulla
Encinal

Fowlerton
George West

Corpus

28°

Hidalgo del Parral
Jiménez
Santa Rosalía
Ciudad Camargo
Villa López
Valle de Allende
Santa Barbara
Villa Coronado
Escalon
Rosario
Villa Ocampo
Indé

SIERRA
Sierra Mojada
BOLSÓN
Laguna de la Leche
DE
MAPIMÍ
Rey
Palomas

COAHUILA
MADRE
ORIENTAL
Progreso
Nadadores
Abasolo
San Buenaventura
Sacramento
Nadadores
Cuatro Ciénegas
Monclova

Presa de D. Martin
Hidalgo
Dolores
Nuevo Laredo
Laredo

San Diego

Mirando City
Hebbronville
Zapata
Falcon Res.
Guerrero
Premont
Falfurrias

DURANGO
Rio de la Parida
Rio del Cerro Agudo
Santa Cruz
Mapimí
Sacramento
Gómez Palacio
Lerdo
Torreón
Matamoros
Viesca

MEXICO

Lampazos
Bustamante
Villaldama
Sabinas Hidalgo

NUEVO
Agualeguas
Cerralvo
Paredón
Salinas Victoria
García
General Zuazua
Los Herreras
Monterrey
Santa Catarina
Cadereyta Jiménez
China

INTER-AMERICAN HIGHWAY
Mier
Camargo
Riogrande
Mission
Reynosa
Presa de Azucar

26°

San Luis del Cordero
Rodeo
Nazas
Nazas
San Juan del Río
Laguna de Santiaguillo
Cuencame
Canatlán
Durango
San Bartolo
San Juan de Guadalupe
Santa Clara
Juan Aldama

Laguna de Mayran
Laguna de Viesca
Parras
Viesca

General Cepeda
Ramos Arizpe
Arteaga
Saltillo
Villa de Alfende
Montemorelos

Gomez Farias
Mazapil
Concepción del Oro
Galeana
Linares
Burgos

LEON
San Fernando
San Carlos
Villagrán
Cruillas

TAMAULI

ZACATECAS

Longitude West of Greenwich

Continued on pages 124–125

Relief

Meters		Feet
1525		5000
610		2000
305		1000
152.5		500
0	Sea Level	0
152.5		500
1525		5000
3050		10000

Scale 1:4 000 000; one inch to 64 miles. Conic Projecti
Elevations and depressions are given in feet

Continued on pages 116–117

Continued on pages 120 121

ARK.

MISSISSIPPI

LOUISIANA

Denton
McKinney
Farmersville
Garza-Little
Plano
Greenville
Sulphur Springs
Pittsburg
Atlanta
Vivian
Haynesville
Lake Providence
Yazoo City
Fort Worth
DALLAS
Rockwall
Lake Winnsboro
Jefferson
Bayou
Bodcau Res.
Homer
Arcadia
Monroe
Rayville
Delhi
Tallulah
Vicksburg
Jackson
Canton
Ross Barnette Res.
Forest
Arlington
Terrell
Wills Point
Mineola
Gilmer
Marshall
Caddo
Bossier City
Rustan
Minden
Shreveport
Eros
Winnsboro
Alto
Port Gibson
Hazlehurst
Pelahatchie
Waxahachie
Mabank
Longview
Kilgore
Carthage
Jonesboro
Winnfield
Crystal Springs
Kaufman
Ennis
Tyler
Henderson
Mansfield
Coushatta
Natchitoches
Catahoula
Jonesville
Ferriday
Natchez
Vidalia
Fayette
Brookhaven
Sumrall
Collins
Italy
Corsicana
Athens
Jacksonville
Timpson
Center
Toledo Bend Res.
Fisher
Colfax
Pineville
Marksville
Woodville
Gloster
McComb
Columbia
Hillsboro
Hubbard
Palestine
Elkhart
Rusk
Nacogdoches
San Augustine
Hemphill
Peason
Alexandria
Lecompte
McNary
Bunkie
Jackson
Kentwood
Magnolia
Franklinton
Tylertown
Lumberton
Poplarville
Clifton
Wortham
Teague
Oakwood
Ratcliff
Lufkin
Wiergate
Fullerton
Glenmora
Ville Platte
Amite
Picayune
Bogalusa
Waco
Mexia
Groesbeck
Buffalo
Crockett
Groveton
Jasper
Newton
De Ridder
Elizabeth
Oakdale
Melville
New Roads
Covington
McGregor
Marlin
Calvert
Madisonville
Trinity
Town Bluff Lake
Woodville
Merryville
Kinder
Opelousas
Baton Rouge
Madisonville
Bay St. Louis
Slidell
Moody
Temple
Cameron
Hearne
Huntsville
Kirbyville
Longville
De Quincy
Eunice
Plaquemine
White Castle
Maurepas
Lake Pontchartrain
Bartlett
Bryan
Willis
Conroe
Saratoga
Silsbee
Vinton
Lake Charles
Jennings
Crowley
Lafayette
St. Martinville
Donaldsonville
Kenner
Metairie
New Orleans
Gretna
Rockdale
Caldwell
Navasota
Cleveland
Sourlake
Orange
Ged
Lake Arthur
Rayne
New Iberia
Napoleonville
Taylor
Round Rock
Somerville
Brenham
Hempstead
Dayton
Liberty
Beaumont
Port Neches
Gueydan
Abbeville
Thibodaux
Houma
Port Sulphur
Elgin
Bastrop
Giddings
Bellville
Humble
HOUSTON
Baytown
Port Arthur
Sabine
Jeanerette
Franklin
Morgan City
Smithville
Lagrange
Sealy
Richmond
Galveston Bay
High Island
Bolivar Pen.
Patterson
Lovington
Caplen
Gonzales
Columbus
Eagle Lake
Alvin
Texas City
Port Bolivar
Galveston
West Cote Blanche Bay
East Cote Blanche Bay
Atchafalaya Bay
Columbia
Wharton
West Bay
Angleton
Freeport
Caillou Bay
Terrebonne Bay
Timbalier Bay
Barataria Bay
Yoakum
El Campo
Bay City
West Columbia
Victoria
Palacios
Goliad
Port Lavaca
Matagorda Bay
Cuero
Edna

ASan Antonio Bay
Refugio
MATAGORDA
Copano Bay
Sinton
Portland
Rockport
St. Joseph
Aransas Pass
Aransas Pass
MUSTANG
Corpus Christi Bay
Corpus Christi

GULF OF MEXICO

PADRE
ISLAND
Kingsville
Laguna Madre
Harlingen
San Benito
Brownsville
Matamoros

32°
30°
28°
26°

96°
94°
92°
90°

20 40 60 80 100 120 Miles
20 40 60 80 100 120 140 160 180 200 Kilometers

HOUSTON INSET

HOUSTON

Crosby
Sheldon
Highlands
Mont Belvieu
Wallisville
Hankamer
Turtle Bay
Anahuac
San Jacinto City
Galena Pk.
Channelview
Baytown
West University Place
Bellaire
Pasadena
La Porte
GALVESTON BAY
Missouri City
South Houston
Genoa
Seabrook
Smith Point
High Island
Pearland
Kemah
EAST BAY
Arcola
Friendswood
League City
BOLIVAR PENINSULA
Manvel
Dickinson
Sandy Point
Algoa
Alta Loma
La Marque
Texas City
Port Bolivar
Hitchcock
Galveston
GULF OF MEXICO
Liverpool
Danbury
Bastrop
WEST BAY
GALVESTON ISLAND
Angleton

29° 45'
29° 30'
29° 15'

95° 30'
95° 15'
95°
94° 45'
94° 30'
94°

Scale 1:1 000 000
0   5   10 Miles
0   4   8   12   16 Kilometers

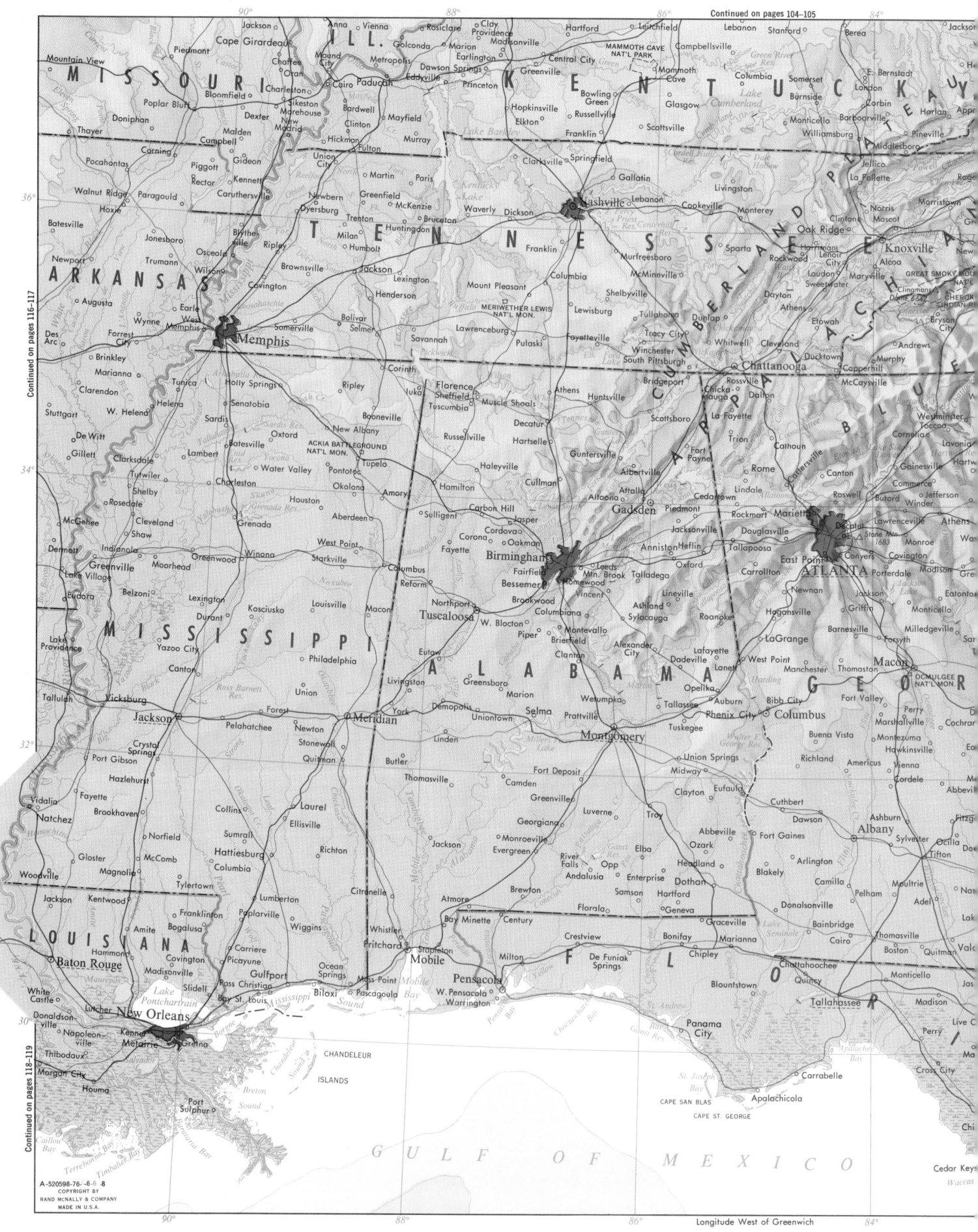

Continued on pages 104–105

Continued on pages 116–117

Continued on pages 118–119

A-520598-76- -6-6 -8
COPYRIGHT BY
RAND McNALLY & COMPANY
MADE IN U.S.A.

Scale 1:4 000 000; one inch to 64 miles. Conic Projection
Elevations and depressions are given in feet

Longitude West of Greenwich

Relief

Meters	Feet
1525	5000
610	2000
305	1000
152.5	500
0 Sea Level	0
152.5	500
1525	5000

Same scale as main map

W. VA.

Welch Filbert Princeton
Bluefield Radford Salem Vinton Bedford Lynchburg Richmond
Pulaski Christiansburg Roanoke Altavista Farmville Crewe Petersburg Hopewell Williamsburg Cape Charles
Saltville Wythville Marion Fries Galax Mount Airy Bassett Danville South Boston Victoria Blackstone Lawrenceville Franklin Newport News Hampton CAPE HENRY Virginia Beach
Bristol Abingdon Elizabethton North Wilkesboro Elkin Mayodan Spray Reidsville Oxford Chase City South Hill Emporia Suffolk Norfolk Portsmouth
Marion Madison Henderson Enfield Weldon Roanoke Rapids Elizabeth City Kitty Hawk
Grandfather Mt. Lenoir Winston-Salem Greensboro Burlington Graham Durham Wake Forest Louisburg Scotland Neck Tarboro Windsor Edenton Manteo

VIRGINIA

NORTH CAROLINA

Granite Falls Hickory Statesville Cooleemee Lexington High Point Chapel Hill Raleigh Rocky Mount Williamston Plymouth Belhaven New Holland
Morganton Newton Mooresville Salisbury Spencer Randleman Siler City Clayton Wilson Farmville Greenville Washington CAPE HATTERAS
Marion Lincolnton Concord Kannapolis Albemarle Asheboro Selma Smithfield Goldsboro Ayden Atlantic
Rutherfordton Cherryville Bessemer City Badin Troy Carthage Sanford Dunn Mount Olive Kinston New Bern Morehead City Beaufort
Forest City Shelby Kings Mt. Gastonia Norwood Southern Pines Erwin Warsaw CAPE LOOKOUT
Spartanburg Gaffney Blacksburg Charlotte Fort Mill Rockingham Fayetteville Clinton
Greer Clifton Clover Monroe Wadesboro Hamlet Raeford Laurinburg St. Pauls Burgaw
Greenville Woodruff York Rock Hill Lancaster Cheraw McColl Lumberton
Piedmont Lockhart Union Chester Bennettsville Dillon Chadbourn Whiteville Wilmington
Williamston Enoree Great Falls Winnsboro Hartsville Darlington Mullins CAPE FEAR
Laurens Honea Path Whitmire Newberry Camden Bishopville Florence Marion Conway Southport
Clinton Saluda Sumter Timmonsville Lake City Myrtle Beach

SOUTH CAROLINA

Greenwood W. Columbia Columbia Manning Kingstree Andrews
McCormick Batesburg Orangeburg Summerton Georgetown
Edgefield Graniteville Aiken Blackville Denmark Branchville Summerville
Langley Barnwell Bamberg St. George North Charleston Charleston Mount Pleasant
Augusta Allendale Fairfax Varnville Meggett FORT SUMTER NAT'L MON.
Waynesboro Louisville Millen Sylvania Estill Beaufort Edisto Island
Wadley Statesboro Metter Walterboro

GEORGIA

Lyons Claxton Glennville Savannah FORT PULASKI NAT'L MON.
Hazlehurst Baxley Jesup SEA ISLANDS
Blackshear Brunswick FORT FREDERICA NAT'L MON.
Okefenokee Waycross St. Marys Fernandina Beach Jacksonville Beach
Folkston St. Marys Jacksonville

ATLANTIC OCEAN

Chesapeake Bay
Cape Charles CAPE CHARLES
Raleigh Bay
Pamlico Sound
Albemarle Sound
Currituck Sound
Great Dismal Swamp
Onslow Bay
Long Bay
Waccamaw

FLORIDA

Jacksonville Jacksonville Beach
Starke Green Cove Springs CASTILLO DE SAN MARCOS NAT'L MON. St. Augustine
Gainesville Palatka FORT MATANZAS NAT'L MON.
Cedar Keys Ocala Crescent City Ormond Beach
Dunnellon De Land Daytona Beach New Smyrna Beach
Inverness Eustis Mount Dora Sanford ATLANTIC
Leesburg Winter Park OCEAN
Brooksville Apopka Titusville
Dade City Winter Garden Orlando Cocoa CAPE CANAVERAL
Tarpon Springs Kissimmee St. Cloud Cocoa Beach
Dunedin Plant City Lakeland Winter Haven
Clearwater Tampa Bartow Lake Wales
St. Petersburg Port Tampa Fort Meade Vero Beach
Palmetto Wauchula Avon Park Fort Pierce
Bradenton Sebring Okeechobee Stuart
Sarasota Arcadia SEMINOLE INDIAN RES. Lake Okeechobee Riviera Beach
Punta Gorda Pahokee W. Palm Beach Palm Beach
Clewiston Belle Glade Lake Worth
Fort Myers Chosen Delray Beach
SANIBEL I. SEMINOLE IND. RES. Pompano Beach
Naples SEMINOLE INDIAN RES. Fort Lauderdale
Everglades Dania
THE EVERGLADES Hollywood Miami Beach
CAPE ROMANO Hialeah MIAMI
TEN THOUSAND IS. Coral Gables Homestead
EVERGLADES NATIONAL PARK
CAPE SABLE Flamingo KEY LARGO

GULF OF MEXICO

ATLANTIC

FORT JEFFERSON N.M. DRY TORTUGAS MARQUESAS KEYS Key West Marathon FLORIDA KEYS

Jacksonville Jacksonville Beach
Green Cove Springs Starke CASTILLO DE SAN MARCOS NAT'L MON. St. Augustine
Palatka FORT MATANZAS NAT'L MON.
Crescent City Ormond Beach Daytona Beach New Smyrna Beach
Ocala De Land Dunnellon Leesburg Eustis

10 20 30 40 50 60 70 80 90 100 110 120 Miles
20 40 60 80 100 120 140 160 180 200 Kilometers

Scale 1:16 000 000; one inch to 250 miles. Polyconic Projecti
Elevations and depressions are given in feet

W. VIRGINIA
Richmond
VA

Roanoke
Norfolk

Raleigh
NORTH CAROLINA
Charlotte
Mt. Mitchell
6684

SOUTH CAROLINA
Columbia
Wilmington
CAPE FEAR

Augusta
Charleston
Savannah

Jacksonville
St. Augustine
Ocala

FLORIDA

Tampa

W. Palm Beach
MIAMI
CAPE SABLE
Key West
FLORIDA KEYS

HAVANA
Guanabacoa
Matanzas
Cárdenas
Santa Clara
Sancti Spíritus
Cienfuegos
Ciego de Ávila
Camagüey
Holguín
Guantánamo
Manzanillo
SIERRA MAESTRA
Santiago de Cuba

CUBA

Montego Bay
Mt. Denham
3236
Port Antonio
Spanish Town
JAMAICA
Kingston

GRAND CAYMAN
(Br.)

BERMUDA
(Br.)

ATLANTIC

OCEAN

NORTH AMERICAN
BASIN

GRAND BAHAMA
GREAT ABACO
Nassau
ELEUTHERA
CAT
ANDROS
San Salvador (Watling)
LONG
ACKLINS
CAICOS (Br.)
TURKS (Br.)
GT. INAGUA

GREATER
WEST
ANTILLES

Cap-Haïtien
Puerto Plata
Santiago de los Caballeros
Gonaïves
Sánchez
SAMANÁ
Pico Duarte
10,417
HAITI
DOMINICAN REPUBLIC
Port-au-Prince
Santo Domingo
ÎLE DE LA GONAVE
HISPANIOLA

▽ 27 498
PUERTO RICO TRENCH
Mayagüez
San Juan
Ponce
PUERTO RICO
(U.S.A.)
VIRGIN IS.
(ST. THOMAS)
Charlotte Amalie
SAINT CROIX
(U.S.A.)
ANGUILLA (Br.)
BARBUDA
(Br.)
ST. KITTS
(Br.)
NEVIS
(Br.)
ANTIGUA
(Br.)
MONTSERRAT
(Br.)
V. Soufrière
4869
Basse Terre
GUADELOUPE
(Fr.)
Pointe-à-Pitre
DOMINICA
(Br.)
Fort-de-France
MARTINIQUE (Fr.)
ST. LUCIA
(Br.)
ST. VINCENT
(Br.)
BARBADOS
Kingstown
Bridgetown
GRENADA

LESSER

ANTILLES

WINDWARD IS.

CARIBBEAN
SEA

AMERICA
CANAL ZONE
(U.S.A.)
Colón
Portobelo
Gulf of los Mosquitos
ISTHMUS
PANAMA
Panama
Gulf of Panama
Antón
David
Santiago
COIBA
PEN. DE AZUERO
Bluefields

ISLA DE MALPELO
(Colombia)

Buenaventura
Cali
Palmira

COLOMBIA
Medellín
Sonsón
Manizales
Pereira
Armenia
Ibagué
Girardot
BOGOTÁ
Villavicencio
Tunja
Bucaramanga
Barrancabermeja
Pamplona
Cúcuta
San Cristóbal
Ocaña
Mérida
Valera
Trujillo
Guanare
Barquisimeto
Valencia
Maracay
CARACAS
Puerto Cabello
La Guaira
Puerto la Cruz
Cumaná
Carúpano

Santa Marta
Barranquilla
Ciénaga
Cartagena
Soledad
PUNTA DE GALLINAS
PENÍNSULA DE GUAJIRA
Maracaibo
Cabimas
Lago de Maracaibo
Coro
San Felipe
ARUBA
(Neth.)
CURAÇAO
(Neth.)
BONAIRE
(Neth.)
SAN ROMAN
Willemstad
PEN. DE PARAGUANÁ
Golfo de Venezuela
ISLA LA TORTUGA
ISLA DE MARGARITA
TOBAGO
TRINIDAD AND TOBAGO
Port of Spain
TRINIDAD

VENEZUELA
Cerro icutú
7800
Calabozo
San Fernando de Apure
El Tigre
Ciudad Guayana
Ciudad Bolívar
Cerro Bolívar
Morawhanna
GUYANA
SERRA PACARAIMA
BRAZIL

Lorica
Sincelejo
Mompós
Magangué
Montería

Puerto de Nutrias
Río Apure
Río Meta
Arauca

San Fernando de Atabapo
Río Guaviare

Longitude West of Greenwich

Puerto Rico inset

ATLANTIC OCEAN
Arecibo
San Juan
Aguadilla
Bayamón
PTA. HIGÜERO
Utuado
CABEZAS DE SAN JUAN
ST. THOMAS
(U.S.A.)
TORTOLA
(Br.)
Fajardo
CULEBRA
Charlotte Amalie
ST. JOHN
(U.S.A.)
PUERTO RICO
(U.S.A.)
Mayagüez
Caguas
Coamo
Cayey
Vieques
VIEQUES
Humacao
CABO ROJO
Ponce
Salinas
Guayama
Christiansted
SAINT CROIX
(U.S.A.)
CARIBBEAN SEA

Scale 1:4 000 000
0 10 20 30 40 Miles
0 10 20 30 40 50 60 Kilometers
©RMcN.

St. Thomas inset

OUTER BRASS
LITTLE HANS LOLLICK
HANS LOLLICK
INNER BRASS
PICARA PT.
STORMY PT.
THATCH CAY
GRASS CAY
ST. THOMAS
Crown Mt. (U.S.A.)
1558
Charlotte Amalie
(St. Thomas)
Nadir
WATER
FLAMINGO PT.
St. Thomas Harbor
Scale 1:500 000
©RMcN.

Relief
Meters		Feet
3050		10 000
1525		5000
610		2000
305		1000
152.5		500
0	Sea Level	0
152.5		500
1525		5000
3050		10 000
6100		20 000

50 100 200 300 400 500 Miles
100 200 400 600 800 Kilometers

Continued on pages 118-119

Scale 1:4 000 000; one inch to 64 miles. Conic Projection
Elevations and depressions are given in feet

Longitude West of Greenwich

Relief

Meters		Feet
3050		10 000
1525		5000
610		2000
305		1000
152.5		500
0	Sea Level	0
152.5		500
1525		5000
3050		10 000

A-531695-76- 5 5 -9
COPYRIGHT BY
RAND McNALLY & COMPANY
MADE IN U.S.A.

MÉXICO

Morelos
Nicolás Romero
Cahuacán
Cuautitlán
Tecamac
Teotihuacán
Otumba
Acolman
Chiconautla
Tepexpan
Pyramids of Teotihuacán
HIDALGO
Apan
Calpulalpan
San Bartolo
Ixtlahuaca
Jiquipilco
Cerro La Catedral 13 000
Atizapán
Tlalnepantla
Tulpetlac
Tepetlaoxtoc
San Jerónimo
Texcoco
Coatlinchán
Nanacamilpa
TLAXCALA
Temoaya
Mimiapan
Mazatla
Atzcapotzalco
Naucalpan
Gustavo A. Madero
Lago de Texcoco (Dry Lake)
MEXICO CITY
Chimalpa
Huixquilucan
Cuajimalpa
Ixtacalco
Ixtapalapa
Chicoloapan
Toluca
Lerma
Villa Obregón Contreras
Coyoacán
Los Reyes
Río Frío
Ayotla
INTER-AMERICAN
Ixtapaluca
Texmelucan
PUEBLA
Capultitlán
Metepec
Mexicalcingo
Cerro Muneca 12 655
Tlálpan
Xochimilco
Tláhuac
Chalco
San Andrés
Topilejo
Almoloya
Coatepec
Cerro Ajusco 12 850
Ajusco
Oxtotepec
Tecómitl
Milpa Alta
Tlalmanalco
Tenango
Amecameca
Iztaccíhuatl 17 343
Nevado de Toluca 14 409
Tenango
DISTRITO FEDERAL
Tres Cumbres
Huitzilac
Tepoztlán
Ozumba
Tlalnepantla
Popocatépetl 17 883
MORELOS
Cuernavaca
Tlayacapan

Scale 1:1 000 000
0   5   10 Miles
0 4 8 12 16 Kilometers
©RMcN

GULF OF MEXICO

Tropic of Cancer

JEREZ

el Madero
pico
Cuauhtémoc
ico Alto

CABO ROJO
ARRECIFE BLANQUILLA
ISLA DE LOBOS
Tamiahua
coco
Álamo
ARRECIFE TANGUIJO
ARRECIFE TÚXPAN
Túxpan
huatlán
Poza Rica
Tecolutla
Gutiérrez Zamora
Furbero
Nautla
vutla
Coxquihui
Vega de Alatorre
Cuetzalan
del Progreso
Tlapacoyan
Misantla
Atempan
Jalacingo
Altotonga
Teziutlán
Naolinco
Las Vigas
PUNTA ZEMPOALA
Perote
Coatepec
Jalapa Enríquez
ibres
Nauchampatepetl 14 048
Teocelo
Antigua Veracruz

BAHÍA DE CAMPECHE

Lerma
Campeche
Sisal
Hunucma
YUCATÁN
Maxcanú
Halachó
Calkini
Dzitbalché
Hecelchakán

Seybaplaya
Champotón
Pustunich

Sabancuy
CAMPECHE
Chicbul
Mamantel

VLA
Huatusco
Coscomatepec
Citlaltépetl (Vol.) 18 701
Ciudad Serdán
Medellín
Veracruz
ARRECIFE CABEZA
Orizaba
Heroica
Nogales
Córdoba
Omealca
Cotaxtla
Tlalixcoyan
Alvarado
Maltrata
hidalgo
mpan
ISLA DEL CARMEN
Laguna de Términos
San Pedro
Ciudad del Carmen
PUNTA FONTERA
Frontera
Chivul
Arroyo Caribe
Tehuacan
Ajalpan
Gabriel
Chilac
Zoquitlán
Zinacatepec
Huatla
de Jiménez
Ojitlán (S. Lucas)
Tierra Blanca
Cosamaloápan
Chacaltianguis
San Martín (Vol.) 4000
PTA ZAPOTITLÁN
Santiago Tuxtla
San Andrés Tuxtla
Catemaco
Pajápan
Coatzacoalcos (Puerto México)
Paraíso
Allende
Comalcalco
TABASCO
Jalpa
Palizada
Chazumba
S. Miguel
Teotitlán del Camino (San Felipe)
Jalapa de Díaz
Tuxtepec
Tesecheacan
Soteapan
Jáltipan
Acayucan
Cosoleacaque
Minatitlán
Cárdenas
Cunduacán
Jonuta
Emiliano Zapata
MÉXICO
GUATEMALA
Tepelmeme
San Juan Evangelista
Sayula
Texistepec
Huimanguillo
San Carlos
Villahermosa
Balancán
Coixtlahuaca
Tejúpan (Santiago)
Cuicatlán
León
Playa Vicente
Tacotalpa
Teapa
Palenque
Tenosique
Nochixtlán (Asunción)
y San Pablo
laxiaco
Sta. María Asunción
Ixtlán de Juárez
Talea de Castro (San Miguel)
Villa Alta (San Ildefonso)
Jesús Carranza
Pueblo Viejo
Pichucalco
Chapultenango
Yajalón
Bachajón
Ocosingo
Continued on pages 126-127
Hidalgo Yalalag
Zempoaltépetl
ISTMO
Tecpatán
Pantepec
Simojovel
Jitotol
MESETA DE AGUA ESCONDIDA
Chalcatongo
San Mateo (Etlatongo)
Oaxaca de Juárez
Zaachila
Zimatlán de Álvarez
Tlacolula de Matamoros
Ocotlán de Morelos
DE
Zacatepec (Santiago)
Compainalá
Berriozabal
Tuxtla Gutiérrez 9400
Cancuc
Oxchuc
Bohom
Ciudad de las Casas
ta. Catarina
Sola de Vega (S. Miguel)
Táviche
Miahuatlán
Ejutla de Crespo
Mazatlán (San Juan)
Guichicovi (San Juan)
Ixtepec
Ixtaltepec (Asunción)
Zanatepec (Sto. Domingo)
TEHUANTEPEC
Cintalapa
Ocozocuautla
Chiapa de Corzo
Acala
Suchiapa
Teopisca
Amatenango
El SUR
Las Vacas
Jalapa del Marques
Unión Hidalgo
Las Cruces
Tapanatepec
8202
Villa Flores
Venustiano Carranza
Las Rosas
Socoltenango
Comitán
CHIAPAS
Loxicha (Sta. Catarina)
Pluma Hidalgo
Juchitán de Zaragoza
Ixhuatán (San Francisco)
Tehuantepec (Sto. Domingo)
Laguna Superior
Laguna Inferior
Mar Muerto
Arriaga
La Concordia
Trinitaria
SA. CUCHUMATANES
Pochutla (San Pedro)
Salina Cruz
Tonalá
La Concordia
GUATEMALA
Puerto Ángel
Golfo de Tehuantepec
CORD. DE CHIAPAS
Cuauhtémoc
Jacatenango
Pijijiapan
San Miguel
Mapastepec

SIERRA DE OAXACA

SIERRA MADRE

INTER-AMERICAN HY

20 40 60 80 100 120 Miles
20 40 60 80 100 120 140 160 180 200 Kilometers

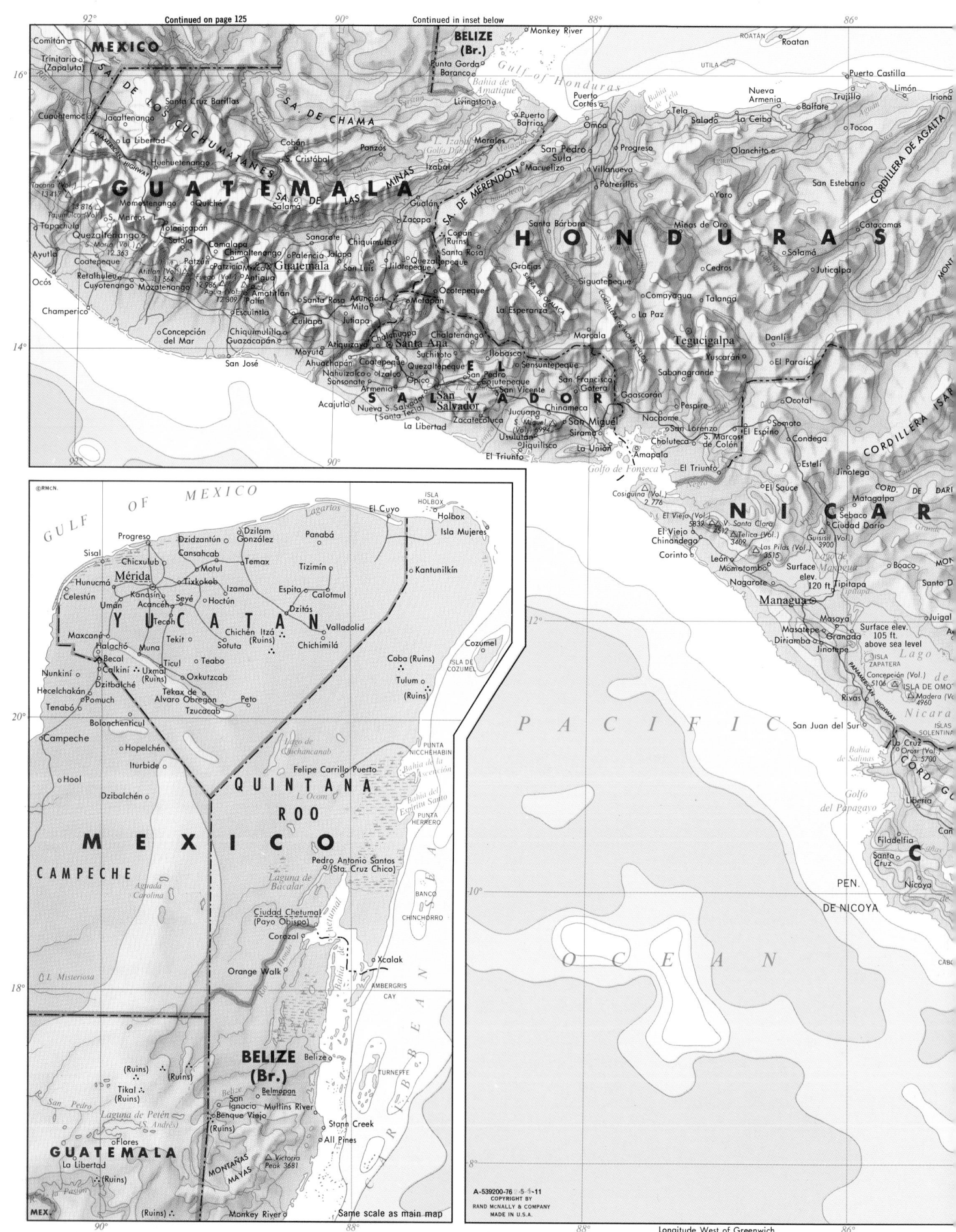

Scale 1:4 000 000; one inch to 64 miles. Sinusoidal Project

Elevations and depressions are given in feet

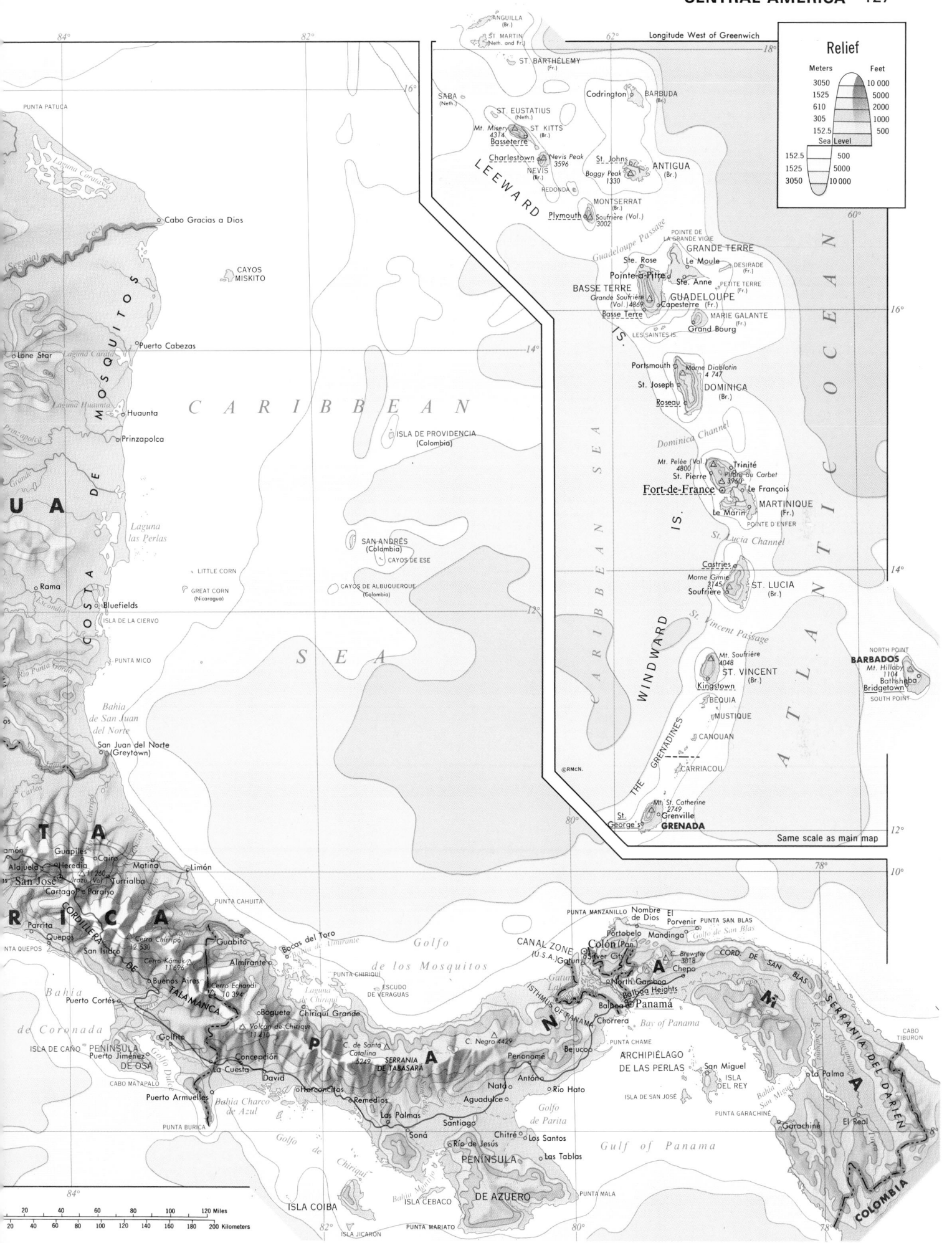

Longitude West of Greenwich

ANGUILLA
(Br.)
ST. MARTIN
(Neth. and Fr.)
ST. BARTHÉLEMY
(Fr.)
SABA
(Neth.)
Codrington
BARBUDA
(Br.)
ST. EUSTATIUS
(Neth.)
ST KITTS
(Br.)
Mt. Misery
4314
Basseterre
Charlestown
Nevis Peak
3596
St. Johns
ANTIGUA
(Br.)
NEVIS
(Br.)
Boggy Peak
1330
REDONDA

L E E W A R D

MONTSERRAT
(Br.)
Plymouth
Soufrière (Vol.)
3002

POINTE DE
LA GRANDE VIGIE
GRANDE TERRE
Ste. Rose
Le Moule
DÉSIRADE
(Fr.)
Pointe-à-Pitre
Ste. Anne
PETITE TERRE
(Fr.)
BASSE TERRE
Grande Soufrière
(Vol.) 4869
GUADELOUPE
Capesterre (Fr.)
Basse Terre
MARIE GALANTE
(Fr.)
Grand Bourg
LES SAINTES IS.

I S.

Portsmouth
Morne Diablotin
4 747
St. Joseph
DOMINICA
(Br.)
Roseau

Dominica Channel

Mt. Pelée (Vol.)
4800
Trinité
St. Pierre
Piton du Carbet
3960
Fort-de-France
Le François
MARTINIQUE
(Fr.)
Le Marin
POINTE D'ENFER

St. Lucia Channel

Castries
Morne Gimie
3145
ST. LUCIA
Soufrière
(Br.)

St. Vincent Passage

Mt. Soufrière
4048
ST. VINCENT
Kingstown
(Br.)
BEQUIA
MUSTIQUE
CANOUAN
CARRIACOU
®RMcN.
Mt. St. Catherine
2749
Grenville
St.
George's
GRENADA

Same scale as main map

W I N D W A R D

T H E G R E N A D I N E S

C A R I B B E A N   S E A   I S.

A T L A N T I C   O C E A N

NORTH POINT
BARBADOS
Mt. Hillaby
1104
Bathsheba
Bridgetown
SOUTH POINT

PUNTA PATUCA

Laguna Caratasca

Cabo Gracias a Dios

CAYOS
MISKITO

Segovia
(Coco)

Lone Star
Laguna Caratá
Puerto Cabezas

Prinzapolca
Huaunta
Laguna Huaunta

Prinzapolca

C A R I B B E A N

ISLA DE PROVIDENCIA
(Colombia)

SAN ANDRÉS
(Colombia)
CAYOS DE ESE

Rama
Laguna
las Perlas

LITTLE CORN
GREAT CORN
(Nicaragua)
CAYOS DE ALBUQUERQUE
(Colombia)

Bluefields
ISLA DE LA CIERVO

S E A

PUNTA MICO

Bahía
de San Juan
del Norte

San Juan del Norte
(Greytown)

U A

N I C A R A G U A

C O S T A

C O R D I L L E R A

Carlos

R I C A

Guápiles
Caño
Heredia
Matina
Limón

Alajuela
Irazú
Vol.
Turrialba
San José
Cartago
Paraíso

PUNTA CAHUITA

Parrita
Quepos

Cerro Chirripó
12 530

Guabito
Bocas del Toro
Bahía de Almirante

Golfo

NTA QUEPOS
San Isidro
Cerro Kámuk
11 696

D E

Almirante
PUNTA CHIRIQUÍ

de los Mosquitos

Buenos Aires

Bahía
de Coronada

Cerro Echandi
10 394
T A L A M A N C A

Puerto Cortés

ISLA DE CAÑO
PENÍNSULA
Puerto Jiménez
DE OSA

Golfito

Bóquete
Chiriquí Grande

Volcán de Chiriquí
11 410

ESCUDO
DE VERAGUAS

Laguna
de Chiriquí

CABO MATAPALO

Golfo
Dulce

Concepción
La Cuesta
David

P

C. de Santa
Catalina
5249

C. Negro 4429

Puerto Armuelles
Bahía Charco
de Azul

Horconcitos
Remedios

SERRANÍA
DE TABASARÁ

A

Las Palmas

PUNTA BURICA

Golfo
de

Soná
Santiago
Río de Jesús

Chiriquí

PENÍNSULA

ISLA COIBA

ISLA CEBACO
Bahía Montijo

DE AZUERO

ISLA JICARÓN

ISLA MARIATO

PUNTA MARIATO

Chitré
Los Santos
Las Tablas

PUNTA MALA

Nata
Antón
Río Hato
Aguadulce

Bejuco

Penonomé

Bahía de Parita

Gulf of Panama

PUNTA MANZANILLO
Nombre
de Dios
El
Porvenir
PUNTA SAN BLAS
Portobelo
Mandinga
Golfo de San Blas
CANAL ZONE
(U.S.A.)
Colón (Pan.)
Silver City
Gatun
Gatun
Lake
North Gamboa
C. Brewster
3018
CORD. DE SAN BLAS
Chepo
Balboa Heights
Balboa
Panamá
Chorrera
ISTHMUS OF PANAMA
Bay of Panama

A R C H I P I É L A G O
D E   L A S   P E R L A S

PUNTA CHAME

San Miguel
ISLA
DEL REY

ISLA DE SAN JOSÉ

PUNTA GARACHINE

P A N A M Á

S E R R A N Í A   D E L   D A R I E N

CABO
TIBURON

La Palma
Bahía
San Miguel

Garachiné
El Real

Tuira

COLOMBIA

GULF

OF

MEXICO

Tropic of Cancer

84°   82°   80°   78°

LITTLE BAHAMA BANK   GREAT SALE CAY

SETTLEMENT PT.   LITTLE ABACO

West End   Freeport   GRAND BAHAMA   Carrion Crow Harbor

PINDER POINT   GRAND BAHAMA

GREAT ABACO

The Marls

MORES   GORDA CAY

26°

FLORIDA   Delray Beach

Naples   SEMINOLE IND. RES.   THE EVERGLADES   Fort Lauderdale   Dania   GREAT ISAAC   NORTHWEST PROVIDENCE CHANNEL

CAPE ROMANO   Everglades   MIAMI   Miami Beach   LITTLE ISAAC   NORTH BIMINI   Barnett Harbor   SOUTH BIMINI   N. CAT CAY

TEN THOUSAND ISLANDS   EVERGLADES   Biscayne Bay   Dollar Harbor   GREAT STIRRUP CAY   GREAT HARBOUR CAY   BERRY   SOUTHWEST PT.

NATIONAL PARK   Homestead   KEY LARGO   RIDING ROCKS   ISLANDS   BONDS CAY   WHALE CAY

CAPE SABLE   Whitewater Bay   Florida Bay   ORANGE CAY   FRAZIERS HOG CAY   JOULTER'S CAYS

Nicolls Town   Nassau   PARADISE

SIMMS PT.   NEW PROVIDENCE

PINE IS.   Key West   FLORIDA KEYS   SHIP CHANNEL C   HIGHBORNE C

DRY TORTUGAS   MARQUESAS KEYS   Staniard Creek

24°   ANDROS   Straits of Florida   Santaren Channel

DOG ROCKS   CAY SAL   DAMAS CAYS

NORTH ELBOW CAYS   CAY SAL   BANK   Turner Sound

CAY SAL   HURRICANE FLATS   SNAP PT.   CURLY CUT CAYS

ANGUILLA CAYS   Nicholas Channel   TONGUE OF THE OCEAN   GREEN CAY

M E X I C O

Tropic of Cancer

HAVANA   Guanabacoa   Cayo Blancos   ARCHIPIELAGO DE SABANA   Old Bahama

Marianao   Regla   Bahía Matanzas   Bahía de Cárdenas   Bahía de Santa Clara   Old Bahama Channel

Bahía Honda   HABANA   Matanzas   Cárdenas   Corralillo   CAYO

Guanajay   San Antonio de los Baños   Güines   Jovellanos   Martí   Quemado de Güines   Sagua la Grande   FRAGOSO   CAYO SANTA MARÍA

Pan de Guajaibón   2532   Candelaria   Güira de Melena   Batabanó   Union de Reyes   Alacranes   Pedro Betancourt   Colón   Santo Domingo   Esperanza   Caibarién   CAYO COCO

Artemisa   Bejucal   MATANZAS   Navajas   Jagüey Grande   Aguada   Lajas   Cruces   Santa Clara   Remedios   Camajuaní   Zulueta   Yaguajay   Bahía Buena Vista   CAYO LOBOS

PINAR   Los Palacios   Ensenada de la Broa   Bolondrón   Roda   Palmira   Placetas   Morón   CAYO CRUZ

Mantua   SIERRA   Consolación del Sur   LOS PÓRGANOS   VUELTABAJO   PUNTA GORDA   PENÍNSULA DE ZAPATA   LAS VILLAS   Florida   Perros   TURIGUANO

Guane   DEL RÍO   San Juan   Pinar del Río   PUNTA GORDA   Cienfuegos   Pico San Juan   SIERRA DE   Sancti Spíritus   CAYO GUAJABA

Bahía de Guadiana   Martínez   GOLFO DE BATABANÓ   ISLAS DE MANGLES   CAYOS DE JUAN LUIS   Bahía Cochinos   Golfo de Cazones   TRINIDAD   CAMAGÜEY   CAYO SABINAL

PEN. DE GUANAHACABIBES   Ensenada de Cortés   CABO FRANCÉS   ARCHIPIELAGO DE LOS CANARREOS   CAYOS LAGUNA   Casilda   Trinidad   Sancti Spíritus   Ciego de Ávila   Nuevitas

CABO CORRIENTES   CAYOS DE SAN FELIPE   Nueva Gerona   CAYOS INGLES   BANCO JARDINES   Tunas de Zaza   Júcaro   Fomento   Camagüey   Santa Lucía

CAYOS DE LOS INDIOS   ISLA DE PINOS   Santa Fé   CAYO LARGO   BANCO XAGUA   CAYOS ANA MARÍA   Minas

PTA. FRANCES   la Siguanea   CAYO ROSARIO   CAYO CANTILES   Camagüey

CABO PEPE   CAYO DE DIOS   CAYOS CINCO BALAS   Victoria de las Tunas

CAYOS DE LAS DOCE LEGUAS   Santa Cruz del Sur   Guayabal   Puer

LABERINTO DE LAS DOCE LEGUAS   GOLFO DE   Manzan

Canal de Caballones   GUACANAYABO   Campechuela

20°   Niquero   SIERR

Pico Ojo del Toro   Pico de Turq

1748   CABO CRUZ

C A R I B B E A N

LITTLE CAYMAN   CAYMAN BRAC

CAYMAN   ISLANDS   (Br.)

Georgetown

GRAND CAYMAN

Montego Bay   Falmouth   St. Ann's Ba

Lucea   JAMAICA   Annotto

SOUTH NEGRIL PT.   Mt. Denham   3236   2726

Savanna la Mar   Bull Head   May Pen

Black River   GT. PEDRO BLUFF   PORTLAND PT.

18°

<table>
<tr><td colspan="2">Relief</td></tr>
<tr><td>Meters</td><td>Feet</td></tr>
<tr><td>3050</td><td>10 000</td></tr>
<tr><td>1525</td><td>5000</td></tr>
<tr><td>610</td><td>2000</td></tr>
<tr><td>305</td><td>1000</td></tr>
<tr><td>152.5</td><td>500</td></tr>
<tr><td>0 Sea Level</td><td>0</td></tr>
<tr><td>152.5</td><td>500</td></tr>
<tr><td>1525</td><td>5000</td></tr>
<tr><td>3050</td><td>10 000</td></tr>
<tr><td>6100</td><td>20 000</td></tr>
</table>

82°   80°   Longitude West of Greenwich   78°

Scale 1:4 000 000; one inch to 64 miles. Conic Proj

Elevations and depressions are given in feet.

Scale 1:1 000 000

HAVANA
(La Habana)

GULF OF MEXICO

Cojimar
Playa de Guanabo

Playa de Santa Fé
Guanabacoa
Regla
Campo Florido
San Francisco de Paula

Baracoa
Marianao
Cotorro
Cuatro Caminos

Arroya Arena
Calabazar

Bauta
Rancho Boyeros
Managua
San José de las Lajas
La Sabina

Caimito del Guayabal
Santiago de las Vegas
Bejucal

Ceiba del Agua
San Antonio de los Baños
Buenaventura
San Antonio de las Vegas

L. de Ariguanabo

△ 950

©rmcn.

Governor's Harbour
PALMETTO PT.
ELEUTHERA

A T L A N T I C

LITTLE SAN SALVADOR

Arthur's Town
NORTHEAST PT.
CAT

Old Bight

HAWKS NEST PT.
COLUMBUS PT.
SAN SALVADOR
(WATLING)
(Columbus, Oct. 12, 1492)
SOUTHWEST PT.

CONCEPTION

O C E A N

CAPE STA. MARIA
LEE STOCKING
Rolleville
RUM CAY

B
A
H
A
M
A
S

Tropic of Cancer

George Town
LITTLE EXUMA
HOG CAY
LONG

JUMENTO CAYS
Clarence Town
SAMANA OR ATWOOD CAY

WATER CAY
CAP VERDE
BIRD ROCK
CROOKED
NORTHEAST PT.

FLAMINGO CAY
FORTUNE
PLANA OR FLAT CAYS

JAMAICA CAY
DIANA BANK
FISH CAY
The Bight of Acklins

SEAL CAYS
SALINA PT.
ACKLINS

NURSE CAY
CASTLE
MAYAGUANA

RACCOON CAY
Abraham's Bay

GREAT RAGGED
MIRA POR VOS ISLETS

COLUMBUS BANK
CAY VERDE
Caicos Passage
PROVIDENCIALES
NORTH CAICOS
GRAND CAICOS
CAPE COMETE
EAST CAICOS

CAY STA. DOMINGO
WEST CAICOS
CAICOS IS. (Br.)
GRAND TURK
TURKS IS. (Br.)

HOGSTY REEF
CAICOS BANK
SOUTH CAICOS
Grand Turk

BROWN BANK
LITTLE INAGUA
WEST SAND SPIT
AMBERGRIS CAYS
SALT CAY

PALMETTO PT.
NORTHEAST PT.
SEAL CAYS
Turks I. Passage
Mouchoir Passage
MOUCHOIR BANK

Ocean Bight
The Lake
GREAT INAGUA
SILVER BANK

Man of War Bay
Matthew Town

CABO LUCRECIA
Banes
Slash Bay

Holguin
Antilla
Bahia de Nipe
Silver Bank Passage

Mayari
o Sagua de Tánamo
NAVIDAD BANK

ORIENTE
SA. DE NIPE
CUCHILLAS DE TOAR
Baracoa

Alto Songo
SA. DE PURIAL
PUNTA MAISÍ

Guantánamo
Bahia de Ovando

San Luis
Caney
Gran Piedra
ILE DE LA TORTUE
CABO ISABELA

Santiago de Cuba
Caimanera
Yateras
Canal de la Tortue
Port de Paix
Le Borgne
Cap-Haïtien
Monte Cristi
Puerto Plata

Naval Station (U.S.A.)
CAP ST. NICOLAS
Le Môle
Grande Rivière du Nord
Fort Liberté
CORDILLERA SEPTENTRIONAL
Pico Diego Ocampo
Gaspar Hernández
CABO FRANCÉS VIEJO

Bahia de Guantánamo
PTE. PLATEFORME
Guanaminthe
Dajabón
Santiago Rodriguez
Moca
Salcedo
San Francisco
Nagua

Gonaïves
Vallière
Santiago de los Caballeros
La Vega
Riva
Bahia Escocesa

A
Windward Passage
St. Michel-de-l'Atalaye
VEGA
Moda
Sánchez
CABO SAMANÁ

GOLFE DES GONAÏVES
Pic Bonhomme
Hinche
DOMINICAN
Jarabacoa
Cotuí
Bahia de Samaná
Samaná
CABO SAN RAFAEL

Jérémie
ILE GRANDE CAYEMITE
Pico Duarte
Cibao
CORDILLERA
San Juan
Yamasa
Hato Mayor
CORDILLERA ORIENTAL
Seibo

CAP DAME MARIE
POINT OUEST
ILE DE LA GONÂVE
Canal de Saint-Marc
Mirebalais
CENTRAL
Bánica
Bayaguana
Los Llanos
Higüey

Anse d'Hainault
CAP DES IROIS
HAITI
MASSIF DE LA HOTTE
Léogâne
Port-au-Prince
Pétionville
SIERRA DE NEIBA
Azua
San Cristóbal
La Romana

Tiburón
Coteaux
Miragoâne
Petit Goave
MASSIF DE LA SELLE
CUL DE SAC
Neiba
REPUBLIC
Santo Domingo
San Pedro de Macoris
CATALINA

Roche à Bateau
Aquín
Les Cayes
ILE À VACHE
Jacmel
Belle-Anse
SIERRA DE BAHORUCO
Enriquillo
Barahona
PTA. PALENQUE
SAONA

POINTE À GRAVOIS
H I S P A N I O L A
Oviedo
CABO FALSO
BEATA
CABO BEATA
ALTO VELO

130

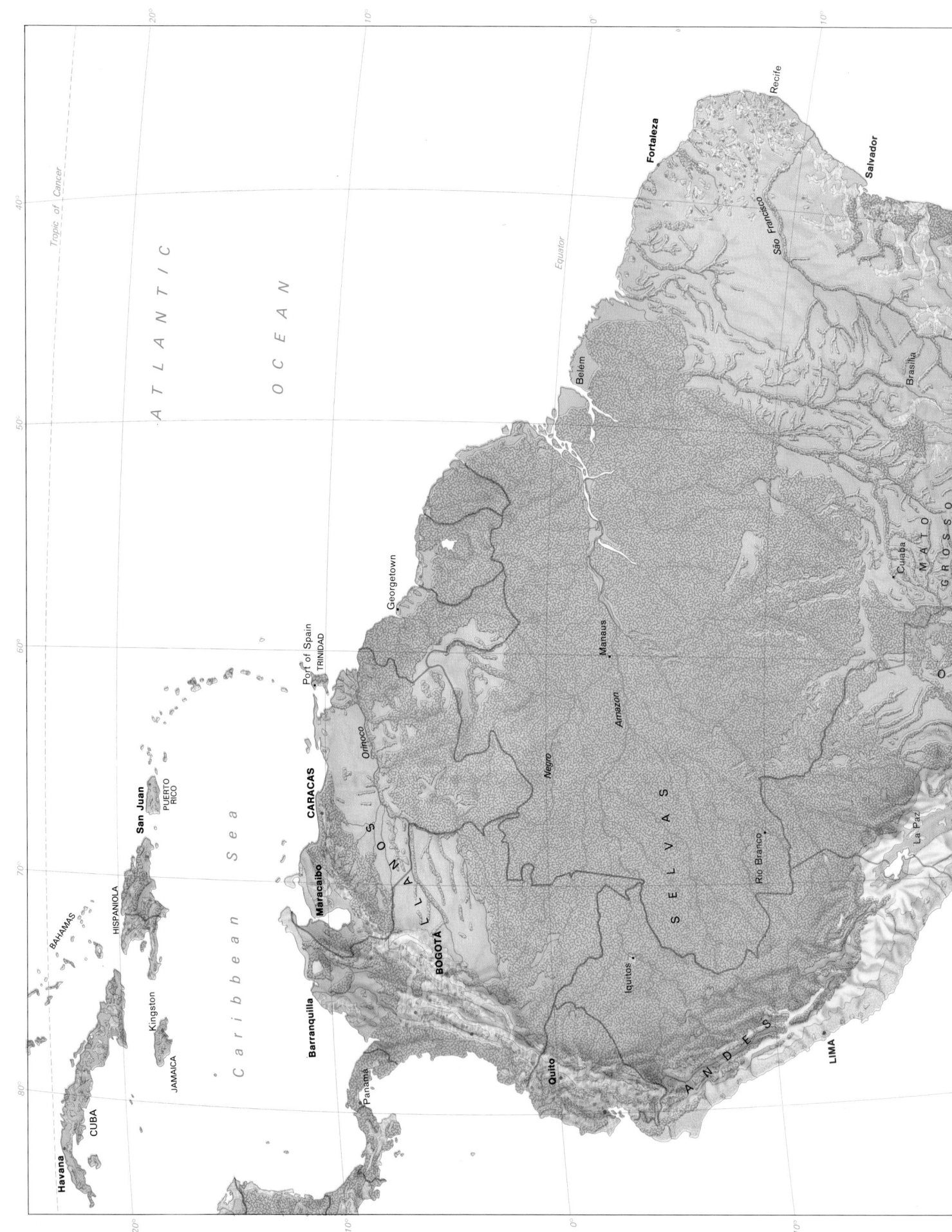

Tropic of Cancer

A T L A N T I C

O C E A N

Equator

Fortaleza

Recife

Salvador

São Francisco

Belém

Brasília

Cuiabá

M A T O

G R O S S O

Georgetown

Manaus

Port of Spain
TRINIDAD

Amazon

Orinoco

Negro

S E L V A S

San Juan

PUERTO
RICO

CARACAS

Rio Branco

La Paz

BAHAMAS

HISPANIOLA

Maracaibo

L L A N O S

Kingston

BOGOTÁ

Iquitos

JAMAICA

Barranquilla

Quito

A N D E S

LIMA

Havana

CUBA

Panama

Caribbean   Sea

Scale 1:24,000,000; one inch to 380 miles. Lambert Azimuthal Equal-Area Projection

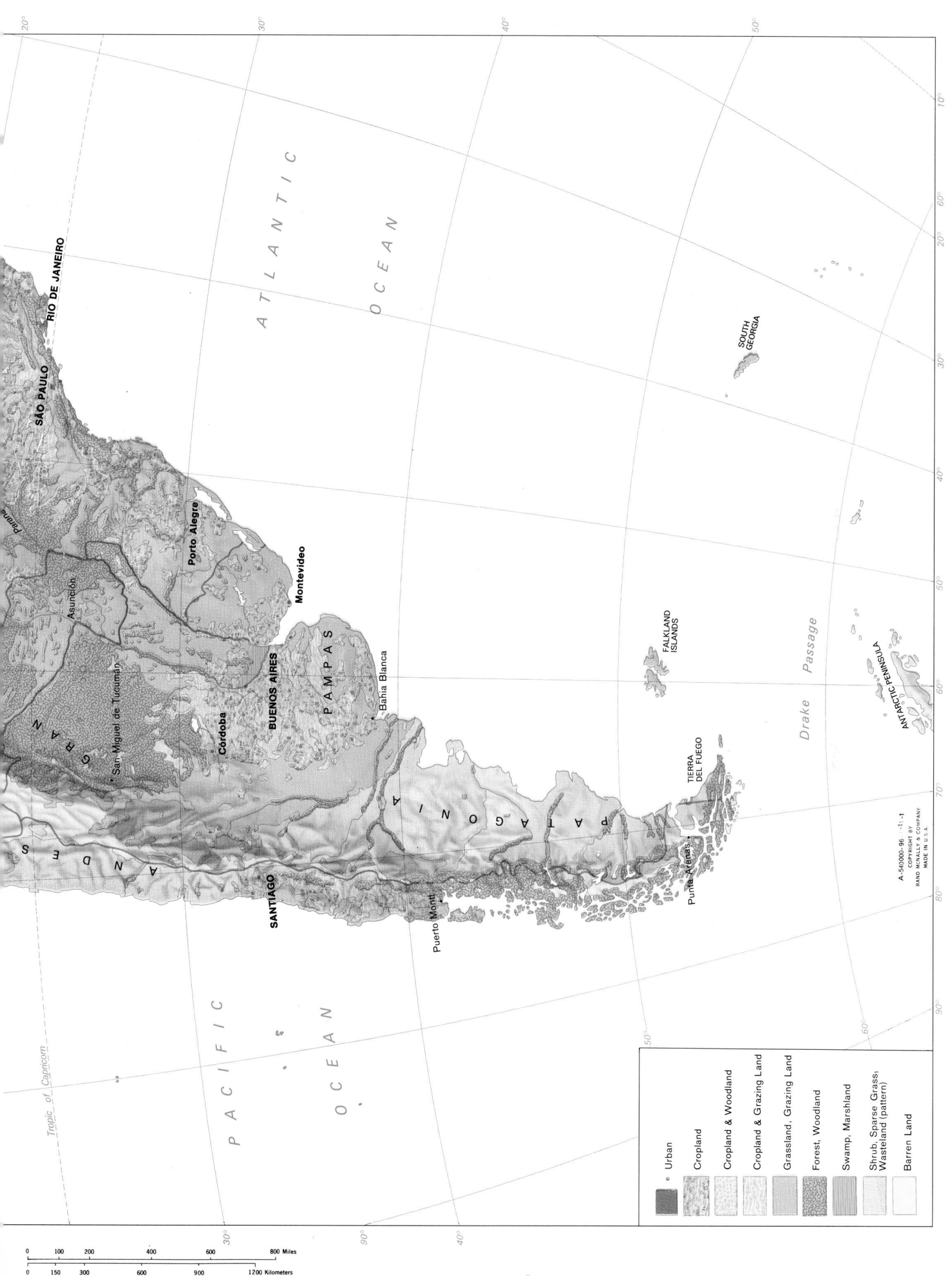

ATLANTIC

OCEAN

RIO DE JANEIRO

SÃO PAULO

SOUTH
GEORGIA

Porto Alegre

Montevideo

Asunción

FALKLAND
ISLANDS

PAMPAS

BUENOS AIRES

Bahía Blanca

Córdoba

San Miguel de Tucumán

Drake   Passage

ANTARCTIC PENINSULA

GRAN

PATAGONIA

TIERRA
DEL FUEGO

ANDES

Punta Arenas

SANTIAGO

Puerto Montt

A-540000-96 -11 -1
COPYRIGHT BY
RAND MCNALLY & COMPANY
MADE IN U.S.A.

PACIFIC

OCEAN

Tropic of Capricorn

Urban
Cropland
Cropland & Woodland
Cropland & Grazing Land
Grassland, Grazing Land
Forest, Woodland
Swamp, Marshland
Shrub, Sparse Grass;
Wasteland (pattern)
Barren Land

0	100	200	400	600	800 Miles

0	150	300	600	900	1200 Kilometers

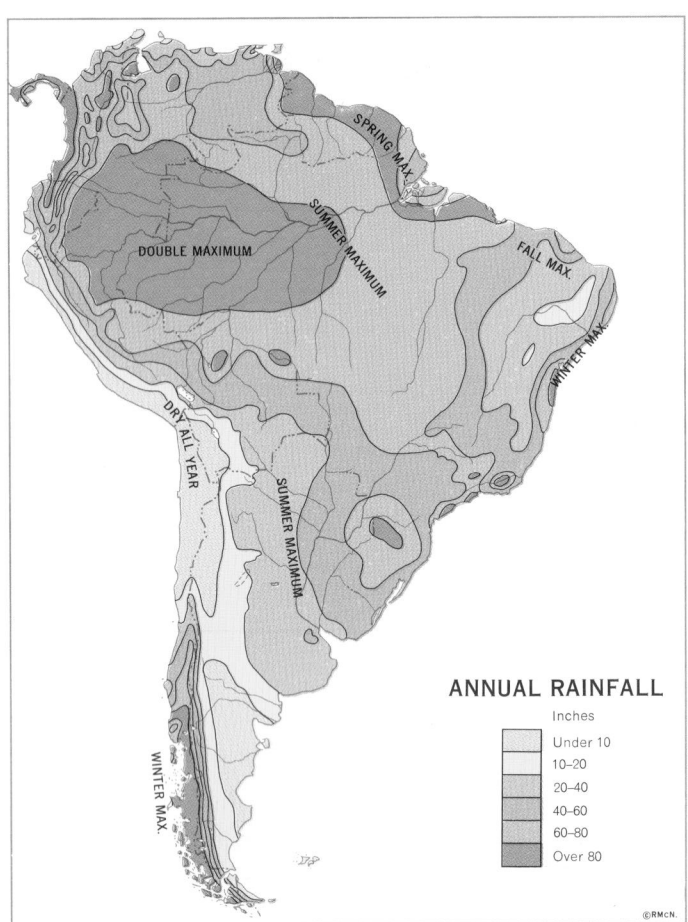

ANNUAL RAINFALL

DOUBLE MAXIMUM

SPRING MAX.

SUMMER MAXIMUM

FALL MAX.

WINTER MAX.

DRY ALL YEAR

SUMMER MAXIMUM

WINTER MAX.

Inches
- Under 10
- 10–20
- 20–40
- 40–60
- 60–80
- Over 80

©RMcN.

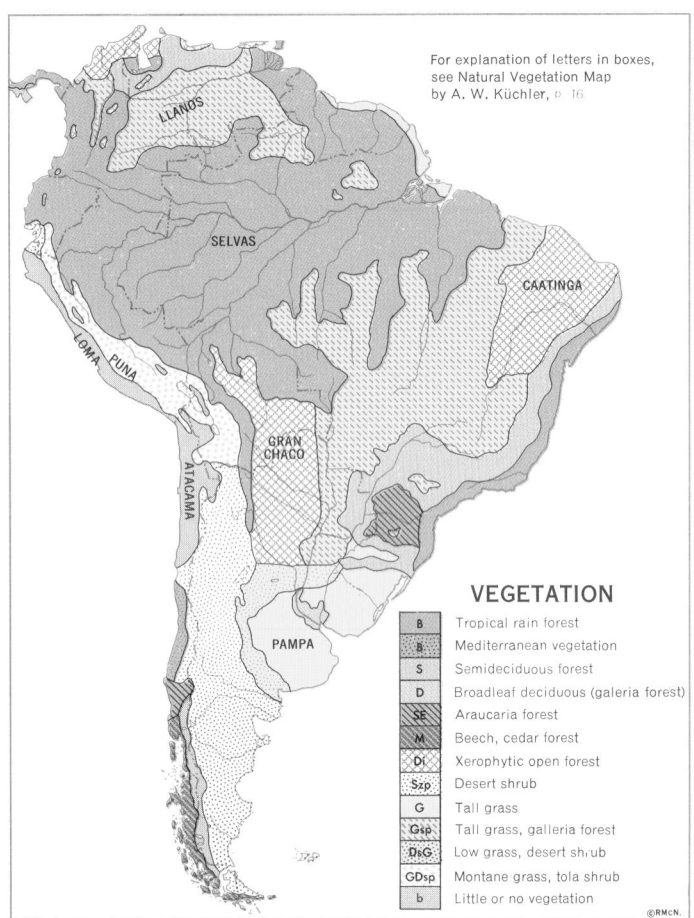

For explanation of letters in boxes, see Natural Vegetation Map by A. W. Küchler, p. 16

LLANOS

SELVAS

CAATINGA

LOMA

PUNA

ATACAMA

GRAN CHACO

PAMPA

VEGETATION

B	Tropical rain forest
B	Mediterranean vegetation
S	Semideciduous forest
D	Broadleaf deciduous (galeria forest)
SE	Araucaria forest
M	Beech, cedar forest
Di	Xerophytic open forest
Szp	Desert shrub
G	Tall grass
Gsp	Tall grass, galleria forest
DsG	Low grass, desert shrub
GDsp	Montane grass, tola shrub
b	Little or no vegetation

©RMcN.

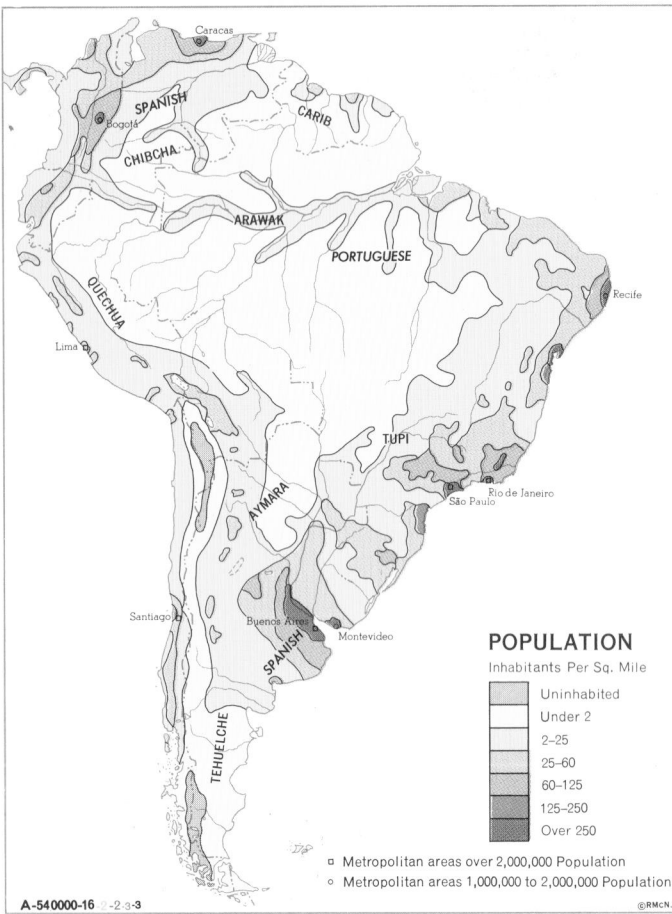

Caracas

SPANISH

CHIBCHA

Bogotá

CARIB

ARAWAK

QUECHUA

PORTUGUESE

Recife

Lima

TUPI

AYMARA

São Paulo

Rio de Janeiro

Santiago

Buenos Aires

SPANISH

Montevideo

TEHUELCHE

POPULATION

Inhabitants Per Sq. Mile
- Uninhabited
- Under 2
- 2–25
- 25–60
- 60–125
- 125–250
- Over 250

□ Metropolitan areas over 2,000,000 Population
○ Metropolitan areas 1,000,000 to 2,000,000 Population

A-540000-16 2-3-3   ©RMcN.

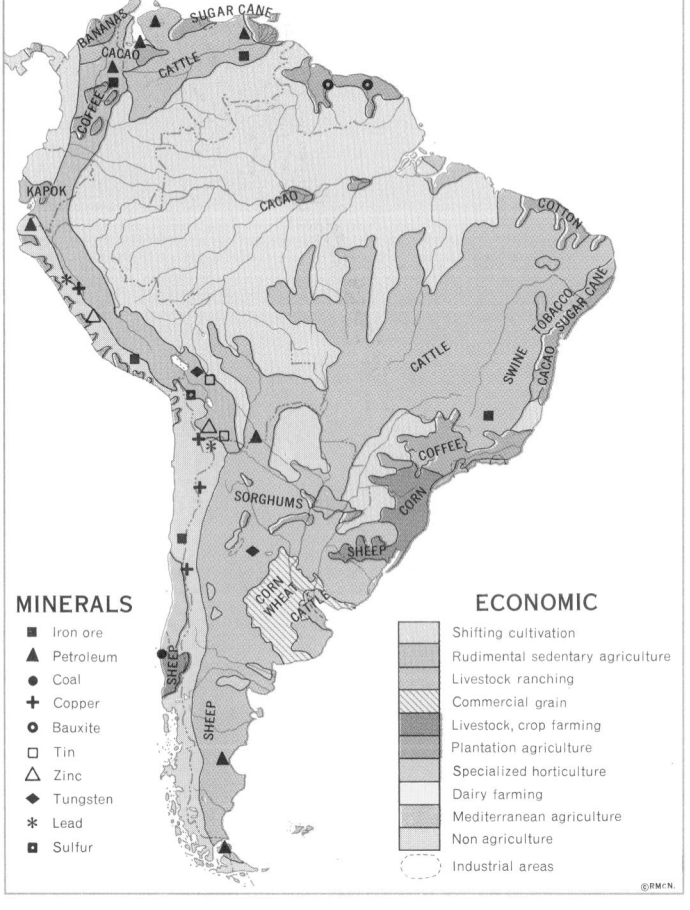

BANANAS

SUGAR CANE

CACAO

CATTLE

COFFEE

KAPOK

CACAO

COTTON

CACAO, SUGAR CANE

TOBACCO

CATTLE

SWINE

COFFEE

CORN

SORGHUMS

SHEEP

CORN WHEAT

CATTLE

SHEEP

SHEEP

MINERALS

- ■ Iron ore
- ▲ Petroleum
- ● Coal
- ✚ Copper
- ◉ Bauxite
- □ Tin
- △ Zinc
- ◆ Tungsten
- ✳ Lead
- ▣ Sulfur

ECONOMIC

- Shifting cultivation
- Rudimental sedentary agriculture
- Livestock ranching
- Commercial grain
- Livestock, crop farming
- Plantation agriculture
- Specialized horticulture
- Dairy farming
- Mediterranean agriculture
- Non agriculture
- Industrial areas

©RMcN.

Tropic of Cancer

HAVANA
CUBA
PEN. DE YUCATÁN
Bahía de Campeche
Golfo de Honduras
JAMAICA
HISPANIOLA
San Juan
PUERTO RICO (U.S.A.)
GUADELOUPE (Fr.)
MARTINIQUE (Fr.)
BARBADOS

CARIBBEAN SEA
WEST INDIES
NORTH AMERICAN BASIN

ATLANTIC OCEAN

CENTRAL AMERICA
Lago de Nicaragua
ISLA DEL COCO (Costa Rica)
ISLA DE MALPELO (Colombia)

Panamá
PUNTA DE GALLINAS
Barranquilla
Cartagena
Maracaibo
La Guaira
Valencia
CARACAS
TRINIDAD AND TOBAGO
Port of Spain
Mérida
Ciudad Bolívar
Golfo de Venezuela
Orinoco

VENEZUELA
Medellín
BOGOTÁ
COLOMBIA
Nevado del Tolima 17 110
Cerro Icutú 7800
Boa Vista do Rio Branco
GUYANA
Georgetown
Paramaribo
Cayenne
SURINAM
FR. GUIANA

GUIANA HIGHLANDS

ARCHIPIÉLAGO DE COLÓN (GALÁPAGOS ISLANDS) (Ec.)
Quito
ECUADOR
Cotopaxi 19 347
Chimborazo 20 561
Guayaquil
Golfo de Guayaquil
Iquitos
Leticia
Río Negro
Río Napo
Río Solimões (Amazonas)
Manaus (Manáos)
Río Amazonas
Equator
ILHA DE MARAJÓ
Belém (Pará)
São Luís (Maranhão)
ROCEDOS SÃO PEDRO E SÃO PAULO (Brazil)
ARQUIPÉLAGO FERNANDO DE NORONHA (Brazil)

Chiclayo
Trujillo
Nevs Huascarán 22 205
PERU
LIMA
Callao
Cuzco
Arequipa
Mollendo
Volcán Misti 19 098

La Paz
Nev Illimani
BOLIVIA
Sucre
Potosí

Río Branco
Pôrto Velho
Río Madeira
Purús
Juruá
Tapajós
Xingu
CHAPADA DE MATO GROSSO
Cuiabá

BRAZIL

Teresina
Fortaleza (Ceará)
CABO DE SÃO ROQUE
Natal
João Pessoa (Paraíba)
RECIFE (Pernambuco)
Maceió
Salvador (Bahia)

BRAZILIAN HIGHLANDS
SERRA DO PIAUÍ
Diamantina
Brasília
Belo Horizonte
Pico da Bandeira 9482
Vitória

Antofagasta
Salta
GRAN CHACO
PARAGUAY
Asunción
Corrientes
Tucumán
Iguaçú Falls
São Paulo
Santos
RIO DE JANEIRO
CABO FRIO

Tropic of Capricorn
ISLA DE SAN FÉLIX (Chile)
ISLA DE SAN AMBROSIO (Chile)
Cerro Azul Copiapó 19 847
Copiapó
Coquimbo
Valparaíso
SANTIAGO
ISLAS DE JUAN FERNÁNDEZ (Chile)
Cerro 22 881
Mendoza
Córdoba
Rosario
Santa Fe
Salto
URUGUAY
Río Grande
BUENOS AIRES
La Plata
MONTEVIDEO
PAMPAS
Florianópolis
Pôrto Alegre

CHILE
ANDES MTS
ARGENTINA
Concepción
Valdivia
Puerto Montt
ISLA DE CHILOÉ
ARCHIPIÉLAGO DE LOS CHONOS
Monte Valentín 3314
Bahía Blanca
Viedma
Golfo San Matías
Comodoro Rivadavia
Golfo San Jorge

WELLINGTON
HANOVER
Río Gallegos
Stanley
Estrecho de Magallanes
Punta Arenas
DESOLACIÓN
Mt. Sarmiento 8100
TIERRA DEL FUEGO
ISLA DE LOS ESTADOS
CABO DE HORNOS (CAPE HORN)
SOUTH GEORGIA (Falkland Is.)
SOUTH SANDWICH ISLANDS (Falkland Is.)
SOUTH ORKNEY IS. (B.A.T.)

Drake Passage
SOUTH SHETLAND ISLANDS (B.A.T.)
JOINVILLE
ANTARCTIC PENINSULA (B.A.T.)
JAMES ROSS
Antarctic Circle

PACIFIC OCEAN

ATLANTIC OCEAN

Longitude West of Greenwich

A-540000-76
COPYRIGHT BY
RAND McNALLY & COMPANY
MADE IN U.S.A.

Relief		
Meters		Feet
3050		10 000
1525		5000
610		2000
305		1000
0	Sea Level	0
152.5		500
1525		5000
3050		10 000
6100		20 000

0 200 400 600 800 1000 Miles
0 400 800 1200 1600 Kilometers

Scale 1:40 000 000; one inch to 630 miles. Lambert's Azimuthal, Equal Area Projection
Elevations and depressions are given in feet

NICARAGUA

EL SALVADOR

Managua
León
Bluefields
San Juan del Sur
San Juan del Norte (Greytown)

CARIBBEAN SEA

COSTA RICA
Limón
Irazú (Vol.)
11 260
San José
Puntarenas
Golfo de Nicoya

CANAL ZONE (U.S.A.)
Bocas del Toro
David
Golfo de los Mosquitos
Colón
Panamá
PANAMA
ISTHMUS OF PANAMA

Gulf of Panama

COIBA
PENINSULA DE AZUERO

PACIFIC OCEAN

PTA GALLINAS
PENÍNSULA DE GUAJIRA
Riohacha
Santa Marta
Barranquilla
Puerto Colombia
Sabanalarga
Cartagena
Calamar
El Carmen
Sincelejo
Plato
Lorica
Sincé
Cereté
Montería
Magangué
El Banco
Turbo

ARUBA (Neth.)
CURAÇAO (Neth.)
BONAIRE (Neth.)
ISLAS LOS ROQUES
Willemstad
Golfo de Venezuela
Coro
Cumarebo
Puerto Cabello
La Guaira
Maiquetía
ORCHILLA
ISLA DE MARGARITA
La Asunción
Cumaná

Maracaibo
Altagracia
Cabimas
Los Teques
CARACAS
Ocumare del Tuy
Puerto la Cruz
Barcelona

San Felipe
Barquisimeto
Valencia
La Victoria
Aragua de Barcelona
El Tigre

VENEZUELA

Fundación
Valledupar
Mompós
Ocaña
Cúcuta
Pamplona
Bucaramanga
Málaga
Arauca
Puerto Wilches
Barrancabermeja
Yarumal
Bello
Urrao
Antioquia
Puerto Berrío
Gil
Socorro
Alto Ritacuva 18 022
Cerro Icutú 7 800

MEDELLÍN
Quibdó
Aguadas
Sonsón
Honda
Chiquinquirá
Duitama
Sogamoso
Tunja
Miraflores
Orocué
San Fernando de Atabapo

Manizales
Pereira
Armenia
Ibagué
Girardot
Villavicencio

BOGOTÁ
Buenaventura
Cali
Palmira
Buga
Chaparral
Puerto Tejada
Espinal
Purificación
Salto de Tequendama

COLOMBIA
Maroa

Popayán
Bolívar
Neiva
Campoalegre
MESA DE YAMBÍ
Vaupés

Tumaco
Barbacoas
Pasto
Túquerres
Tulcán
Ipiales
Galeras (Vol.) 13997
Garzón
Pitalito
Florencia

Esmeraldas
Equator
Bahía de Caráquez
Manta
Chone
Portoviejo
Jipijapa
Quito
Otavalo
Ibarra
Cayambe
Latacunga
Cotopaxi 19 347
Archidona

ECUADOR
Ambato
Guaranda
Riobamba
Chimborazo 20 561
Babahoyo
Alausí

Guayaquil
Golfo de Guayaquil
Cuenca
Machala
Santa Rosa
Tumbes
Azogues
Sígsig
Loja

Iquitos
Caquetá
Putumayo
Içana
Uaupés

AMAZONAS
SELVA

São Paulo de Olivença

Talara
PTA PARIÑAS
Paita
Sullana
Chulucanas
Piura
Castilla

Leticia

Tefé
Fonte Boa

B

PTA AGUJA
LOBOS DE TIERRA
Lambayeque
Ferreñafe
Chiclayo
Puerto Eten
Pacasmayo
Chepén
Puerto Chicama

PONGO DE MANSERICHE
Jaén
Chachapoyas
Moyobamba
Lamas
Tarapoto

Marañón
Yurimaguas

Eirunepé
Lábrea

Chimbote
Trujillo
Salaverry
Cajamarca
Huamachuco

Nuevo Huscarán 22205
Tinga María
Huánuco
Nudo de Pasco 15118
Cerro de Pasco

Cruzeiro do Sul

ACRE
Pôrto Acre
Rio Branco
Villa Bella
Guajará Mirim

RONDÔNIA
MASSIÇO DE PÔRTO

CERROS DE CANCHYUAYA
GRAN PAJONAL
Puerto Bermúdez

Huacho
ISLAS CHINCHAS
Huaral
Callao
Chorrillos
LIMA
Huancayo
La Oroya
Huancavelica
Chincha Alta
Cañete
Ayacucho
Abancay
Cuzco
Machu Picchu
Sicuani
Ayaviri

PERU
CORDILLERA OCCIDENTAL
Tarma
Jauja
Catabamba

Rio Branco
Cobija
Riberalta
Rogoaguado
Puerto Maldonado
Reyes
Trinidad

Pisco
Ica
PTA CARRETAS
Palpa
Puquio
Coracora
Nudo de Coropuna 21696
Volcán Misti 19 098
Arequipa
Miraflores
Puno
Juliaca
Ayala
Lago Titicaca

Nev. Illampu 20873
Achacachi
La Paz
Guaqui
Viacha
Coroico
Cochabamba

BOLIVIA
ALTIPLANO
Oruro
Huanuni
Tarata
Punata
Valle Grande

Camaná
Mollendo
Ilo
Moquegua
Tacna
Arica

Nev. Sajama 21391
Lago de Poopó
Ucheza
Colquechaca

Pisagua
Iquique
Huanchaca
Uyuni
Salar de Uyuni
Pulacayo
San Lucas
Sucre
Lagunillas
Potosí
Monteagudo

ATACAMA TRENCH
Tocopilla
Calama
Chuquicamata
Ollagüe
PUNA DE ATACAMA
Villazón
CORD. DOMEYKO
Tupiza
Tarija

CHILE
Pedro de Valdivia
Mejillones
Antofagasta
Licancábur 19455
JUJUY
La Quiaca
ARGENTINA

Tropic of Capricorn

Inset map (lower left):

Pavarandocito
Alto de Tres Mortos 11 155
Ituango
Valdivia
Anorí
Segovia
Remedios

Dabeiba
Cañasgordas
Paramillo 12990
Yarumal
San Andrés
Amalfi

Alto Musinga 12 631
Antioquia
Santa Rosa
Cisneros
Yolombó
Maceo Jaramillo 9186
Sabanas Páramo 13 395
Sopetrán
Barbosa

ANTIOQUIA
Urrao
Anzá
Bello
San Roque
Puerto Berrío

Bebará
Itagüí
Rionegro
San Rafael
Nare

MEDELLÍN
Envigado
San Carlos

Neguá
Concordia
Caldas
La Ceja
San Luis

Quibdó
Andes
Aguadas
Sonsón

CHOCÓ
Cerro de los Paraíos 10 991
Fredonia
Pensilvania
Puerto Salgar

Certeguí
Cerro Caramanta 12 795
Salamina
La Dorada

Istmina
Riosucio
Manzanares
Fresno
Honda

RISARALDA
Tadó
Anserma
Neira
Mariquita
Villeta
Zipaquirá

Cerro Tamaná 13 780
Apía
CALDAS
Santa Rosa de Cabal
MANIZALES
Armero
Líbano
Facatativá
Guasca
Guachetá

El Cajón
Ansermanuevo
PEREIRA
Venadillo
Ambalema
La Mesa
Junín

Sipí
Cartago
Finlandia
Nevado del Ruiz 17716
Fontibón
La Calera

Cerro Torrá 12 721
Zarzal
Quimbaya
ARMENIA
IBAGUÉ
Nevado del Tolima 17110
Tocaima
Fusagasugá
Girardot
BOGOTÁ
Fómeque

Roldanillo
QUINDÍO
Cajamarca
Pico de Chili 16 894
Rovira
Pico de Mundonuevo 13123
Quetame
Villavicencio

Sevilla
Caicedonia
CUNDINAMARCA

Trujillo
Tuluá
VALLE
San Antonio
Rovira
Espinal
Guamo
Cerro el Nevado 14 961
Acacías

Darién
Buga
Guacarí
Ortega
Coyaima
Purificación
Prado
San Martín

CALI
Palmira
Pradera
Florida
Cerrito
Chaparral
Ataco
Natagaima
Dolores
Alpujarra
Colombia
Baraya
Villavieja
San Juan

Jamundí
Miranda
Corinto
Aipe

Puerto Tejada
TOLIMA
HUILA
Tello
Neiva
Palermo

Buenos Aires
Santander
Toribío
Nevado de Huila 18865
San Antonio

CORDILLERA OCCIDENTAL
CORDILLERA CENTRAL
CORDILLERA ORIENTAL
META

Scale 1:4 000 000
0 10 20 30 40 Miles
0 10 20 30 40 50 60 Kilometers

R. MON

A-549100-76 -7-7 12
COPYRIGHT BY
RAND McNALLY & COMPANY
MADE IN U.S.A.

Scale 1:16 000 000; one inch to 250 miles. Sinusoidal Projec.
Elevations and depressions are given in feet

TRINIDAD AND TOBAGO

of Spain

TOBAGO

TRINIDAD

Boca Grande

Morawhanna

Georgetown

Bartica Rosignol
Wismar New
Rockstone Amsterdam
Skeldon Nieuw
Nickerie Paranam
Totness
GUYANA
MERUME MTS.

SURINAM
Paramaribo
Moengo St. Laurent
Albina Sinnamary
Dr. H.W.J. Van ILE DU DIABLE (DEVIL'S I.)
GEBERGTE Cayenne
WILHELMINA CABO ORANGE
GEBERGTE FRENCH
GUIANA
TUMUC-HUMAC MTS. Saint-Georges
ACARAÍ MTS.

CARIBBEAN SEA

Tocuyo de la Costa
Chichiriviche
Puerto CAYO SOMBRERO
Cabello
Golfo Triste
Morón
El Cambur
Montalbán Guacara
Miranda
Valencia
San Joaquin
CARABOBO
Güigüe
COJEDES
Tinaquillo
Villa de Cura
San Juan
de los Morros
Parapara
GUARICO
Dos Caminos
Barbacoas

Maiquetía La Guaira
La Sabana
Carayaca
CARACAS
Petare
Los Teques
Santa Lucía
Santa Teresa
MIRANDA Caucagua
Cúa Ocumare
del Tuy
San Sebastián
GUARICO

ISLA LA TORTUGA

CABO CODERA

Río Chico
Laguna de
la Tacarigua
Boca de Uchire
El Guapo
Sabana de
de Macaira
San Antonio
de Tamanaco

Cumaná SUCRE

ISLA DE MARGARITA
Boca del Pozo 2302
PUNTA ARENAS
Punta de Piedras
NUEVA ESPARTA
ISLA CUBAGUA

PUNTA DE ARAYA
Manicuare

Puerto La Cruz
Guanta
Soublette
San José
de Gauribe
Valle de
Guanape
Onoto
Aragua de
Barcelona

Barcelona
Bergantín
Santa Inés

ANZOÁTEGUI

Scale 1:4 000 000

0 10 20 30 40 Miles
0 10 20 30 40 50 60 Kilometers

ATLANTIC OCEAN

Equator

PARÁ

Manaus
(Manáos)
Itacoatiara
ILHA
TUPINAMBARANAS
Maués
Borba
Parintins
Óbidos
Faro
Alenquer
Santarém
Itaituba
Brasília Legal
(Fordlândia)
Altamira
Tucuruí

Amapá
Macapá
ILHA CAVIANA
Mazagão
Breves
ILHA
DE
MARAJÓ
Belém (Pará)
Abaetetuba
Gurupá
Cametá
Marapanim
Bragança
Cururupu
Alcântara
Viana
São Luís
(Maranhão)

Tutóia
Camocim
Parnaíba
Acaraú
Sobral
Maranguape
FORTALEZA (Ceará)
Aracati
Areia Branca
Baturité
Macau
Ceará-Mirim

Ipu
Quixadá
Russas
Mossoró
Natal
Nova
Cruz

MARANHÃO
Teresina
Grajaú
Barra do Corda
Mirador
Loreto
Carolina
Balsas
Riachão

São João
do Araguaia
Araguatins
Tocantinópolis

A Z I L

Pedreiras
Caxias
Campo
Maior
Barras
Pedro II
Codó

PIAUÍ
Floriano
Picos
Oeiras
Amarante
Paulistana
Santa
Filomena
Parnaguá

CEARÁ
Iguatú
Icó
Crateús
Senador
Pompeu
Patos
Currais Novos
Campina
Grande
Juàzeiro
do Norte
Crato
Flores
RIO GRANDE
DO NORTE
Guarabira
João Pessoa
(Paraíba)
ARAÍBA
Nazaré da Mata
Olinda
RECIFE
(Pernambuco)

PLANALTO
DA BORBOREMA
PERNAMBUCO
Caruaru
Jaboatão

CABO DE SÃO ROQUE

ARQUIPÉLAGO
FERNANDO DE
NORONHA (Brazil)

ATOL
DAS ROCAS
(Brazil)

São Raimundo
Nonato
Juàzeiro
Petrolina
Cabrobó
Remanso
Sertânia
Garanhuns
Palmeira
dos Índios
Pôrto de Pedras
Maceió
ALAGOAS
Penedo

Propriá
SERGIPE
Aracaju
São
Cristóvão
Estância

Jeremoabo
Senhor do Bonfim
Itabaiana
Jacobina
Serrinha
Inhambupe
Alagoinhas
Catú
Santo Amaro
Cachoeira
Nazaré
SALVADOR (Bahia)

B A H I A
Morro do Chapéu
Feira de Santana
Lençóis
Mucugê
Caetité
Condeúba
Jequié
Vitória da
Conquista
Itabuna
Itabuna
Canavieiras
Belmonte
Pôrto Seguro
ARQUIPÉLAGO
DOS ABROLHOS
Caravelas
São Mateus

GOIÁS
Cavalcante
Pilar de
Goiás
Barreiras
Correntina
Carinhanha

CHAPADA DE MATO
GROSSO
Diamantino
MATO
GROSSO
Rosário Oeste
Mato Grosso
Cáceres
Barão de Melgaço
Cuiabá

Pirenópolis
Goiás
Anápolis
Luziânia
D.F.
Brasília
Formosa
São Francisco
Paracatú
Januária
Pirapora
Montes
Claros
Grão
Mogol

MINAS
GERAIS
Diamantina
Araçuaí
Teófilo
Otoni
Pedra Azul
Peçanha
Caravelas
São Mateus

Goiânia
Silvânia
Bela Vista de Goiás
Ipameri
Morrinhos
Rio
Verde

Catalão
Araguari
Patos
de Minas
Ituiutaba
Uberlândia
Uberaba
Araxá
Paracatú
Curvelo
Gov.
Valadares
Colatina

BELO
HORIZONTE
Sete
Lagoas
Pará
de Minas
Formiga
Divinópolis
Sta. Bárbara
Ponte
Nova
Aracruz
Vitória
ESPÍRITO SANTO
Guarapari
Cachoeiro de Itapemirim

Campo
Grande
Aquidauana
Nioaque
Três Lagoas
Presidente Epitácio
Bela
Vista
Pedro Juan
Caballero

São José
do Rio Prêto
Barretos
Franca
Ribeirão Prêto
Araraquara
São Carlos
Araçatuba
Tupã
Marília
Bauru
Botucatu
Assis
Piracicaba
Campinas
Jundiaí
Sorocaba
SÃO
PAULO
Mogí das Cruzes
SÃO
PAULO
Santos
São
Vicente

Passos
Alfenas
Poços
de Caldas
Barbacena
Juiz
de Fora
Petrópolis
Niterói
Nova Friburgo
RIO DE JANEIRO
RIO DE JANEIRO
Campos

Londrina
Jacarézinho
PARANÁ
Ponta Grossa
Curitiba
Guarapuava
Castro

PARAGUAY
Concepción
Belén
Pôrto Mendes
Guaíra

Tropic of Capricorn

Relief

Meters	Feet
3050	10 000
1525	5000
610	2000
305	1000
152.5	500
0 Sea Level	0
152.5	500
1525	5000
3050	10 000
6100	20 000

Continued on page 136

0 50 100 200 300 400 500 Miles
0 100 200 400 600 800 Kilometers

Continued on pages 134–135

BOLIVIA

PARAGUAY

GRAN CHACO

ARGENTINA

CHILE

URUGUAY

MONTEVIDEO

BUENOS AIRES

LA PAMPA

RÍO NEGRO

CHUBUT

SANTA CRUZ

TIERRA DEL FUEGO

PACIFIC OCEAN

ATLANTIC OCEAN

FALKLAND IS. (ISLAS MALVINAS) (Br.)
Stanley

CABO DE HORNOS (CAPE HORN)

BRASIL

MINAS GERAIS

SÃO PAULO

PARANÁ

SANTA CATARINA

RIO GRANDE DO SUL

PORTO ALEGRE

RÍO DE JANEIRO

BUENOS AIRES
Scale 1:1 000 000

RIO DE JANEIRO
SERRA DAS ARARAS
Scale 1:1 000 000

Relief

Meters		Feet
3050		10 000
1525		5000
610		2000
305		1000
152.5		500
0	Sea Level	0
152.5		500
1525	Below Sea Level	5000
3050		10 000
6100		20 000

Longitude West of Greenwich

A-549200-76- -9 -8
COPYRIGHT BY
RAND McNALLY & COMPANY
MADE IN U.S.A.

Scale 1:16 000 000; one inch to 250 miles. Sinusoidal Projection
Elevations and depressions are given in feet

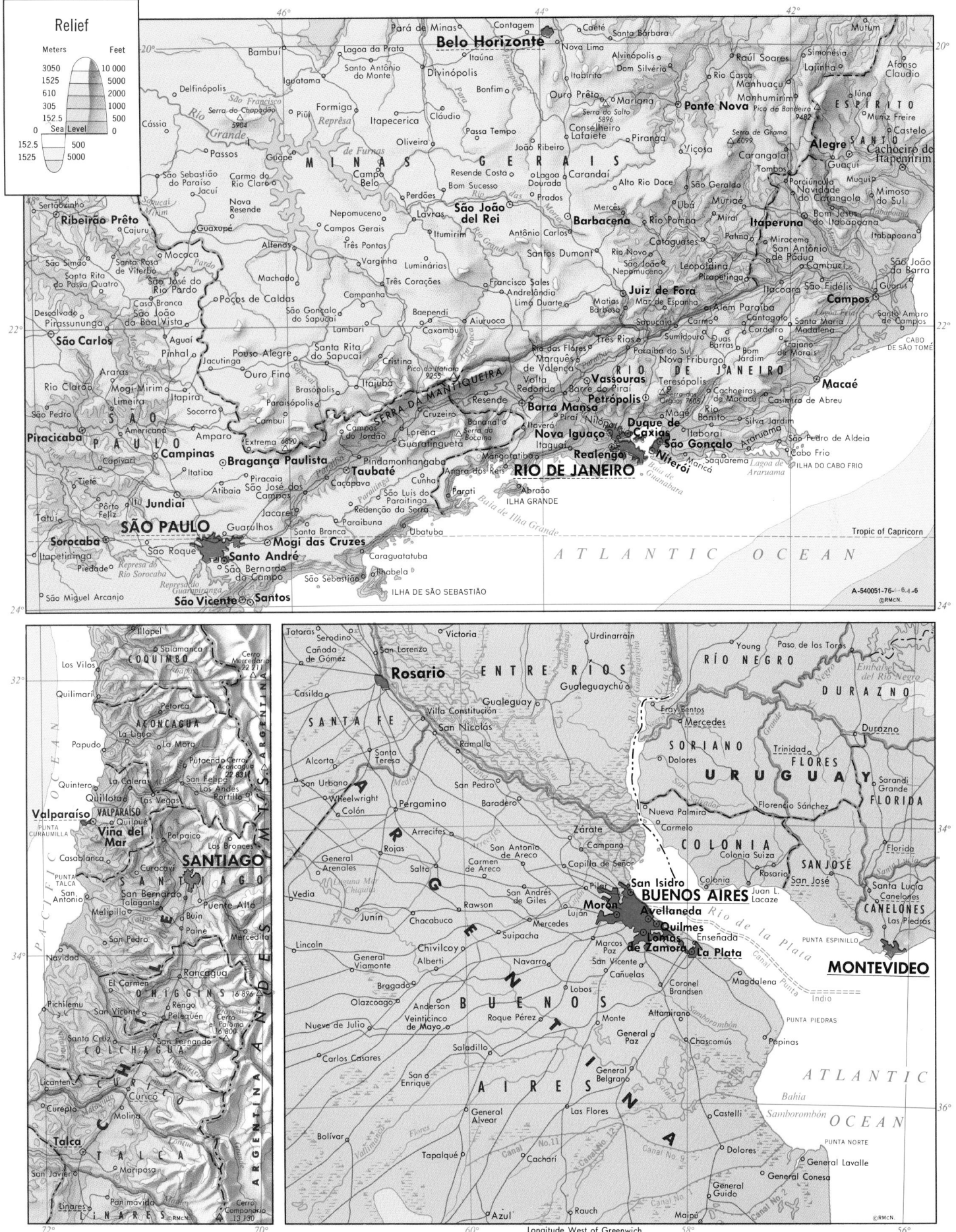

Relief

Meters	Feet
3050	10 000
1525	5000
610	2000
305	1000
152.5	500
0 Sea Level	
152.5	500
1525	5000

Pará de Minas Contagem Caeté Santa Bárbara Mutum
Bambuí Lagoa da Prata **Belo Horizonte** Nova Lima Alvinópolis Raúl Soares Simonésia Afonso Cláudio
Iguatama Itaúna Itabirito Dom Silvério Rio Casca Manhuaçu Lajinha Iúna
Delfinópolis Santo Antônio do Monte Divinópolis Bonfim Ouro Prêto Mariana Manhumirim ESPÍRITO Muniz Freire
Formiga Piuí Cláudio Passa Tempo Conselheiro Serra do Salto 5896 Pico da Bandeira 9482 Castelo
Serra do Chapadão 5904 Represa Itapecerica Lafaiete Piranga Serra de Grama 6099 **Alegre** Cachoeiro de Itapemirim
Cássia MINAS GERAIS de Furnas Resende Costa Carandaí Alto Rio Doce São Geraldo Viçosa Carangola Tombos Porciúncula Muqui
Passos Campo Belo Perdões Bom Sucesso Prados São Domingos do Carangola Mimoso do Sul
Sertãozinho São Sebastião do Paraíso Carmo do Rio Claro **São João del Rei** Mercês Ubá Mirai **Itaperuna** Bom Jesus do Itabapoana Itabapoana
Ribeirão Prêto Jacuí Nepomuceno Lavras Antônio Carlos Rio Pomba Cataguases Palma Miracema San Antônio de Pádua Cambuci **São João da Barra**
Cajuru Nova Resende Alfenas Itumirim Rio Novo Leopoldina Nepomuceno Pirapetinga Itacoara São Fidélis **Campos**
Mocóca Machado Campos Gerais Vargínha Três Pontas Luminárias Francisco Sales Lima Duarte **Juiz de Fora** Mar de Espanha Cantagalo Santa Maria Madalena
São Simão Santa Rosa de Viterbo Campanha Três Corações Andrelândia Matias Barbosa Além Paraíba Carmo Cordeiro Santo Amaro de Campos
São Carlos Santa Rita do Passa Quatro São José do Rio Pardo Poços de Caldas Santa Rita do Sapucaí Baependi Aiuruoca **Barbacena** Sumidouro Duas Barras CABO DE SÃO TOMÉ
Casa Branca São João da Boa Vista Pouso Alegre Lambari Caxambu Três Rios Paraíba do Sul Nova Friburgo Trajano de Morais
Descalvado Aguaí Ouro Fino Santa Rita do Sapucaí Cristina Pico da Itatiaia 9255 Rio das Flôres Paraíba do Sul Bom Jardim
Pirassununga Mogi-Mirim Pinhal Jacutinga Itajubá Marquês de Valença RIO DE JANEIRO Teresópolis Cachoeiras de Macacu Casimiro de Abreu
Rio Claro Limeira Itapira Brasópolis Resende **Vassouras** Volta Redonda **Petrópolis** **Macaé**
Piracicaba SÃO PAULO Socorro Paraisópolis Cruzeiro Itatiaia Barra do Piraí Cachoeiras de Macacu Silva Jardim
São Pedro Americana Amparo Cambuí SERRA DA MANTIQUEIRA Campos do Jordão Lorena Bananal **Barra Mansa** Piraí Nilópolis Mage Rio Bonito São Pedro de Aldeia
Campinas Extrema 6890 Guaratinguetá Serra da Bocaina **Nova Iguaçu** Itaguaí **Duque de Caxias** Itaboraí Araruama Cabo Frio
Capivari Itatiba Pindamonhangaba **Bragança Paulista** **Taubaté** Cunha Angra dos Reis **Realengo** **São Gonçalo** Maricá Saquarema Lagoa de Araruama ILHA DO CABO FRIO
Tietê Piracaia São José dos Campos Caçapava São Luís do Paraitinga **RIO DE JANEIRO** **Niterói** Baía de Guanabara
Jundiaí Atibaia Jacareí Redenção da Serra Parati Abraão ILHA GRANDE
Tatuí Pôrto Feliz Guarulhos Santa Branca Paraibuna Ubatuba Baía de Ilha Grande Tropic of Capricorn
Sorocaba **SÃO PAULO** Mogi das Cruzes Caraguatatuba ATLANTIC OCEAN
Itapetininga São Roque **Santo André** Ilhabela A-540051-76- 6.4-6
Piedade Represa do Rio Sorocaba São Bernardo do Campo São Sebastião ©RMCN
São Miguel Arcanjo Represa Guarapiranga **São Vicente** **Santos** ILHA DE SÃO SEBASTIÃO

Illapel Totoras Serodino Victoria Urdinarrain Young Paso de los Toros
COQUIMBO Salamanca Cañada de Gómez San Lorenzo RÍO NEGRO Embalse del Río Negro
Los Vilos Cerro Mercedario 22 211 **Rosario** ENTRE RÍOS Gualeguaychú DURAZNO
Quilimarí Petorca Casilda Gualeguay Fray Bentos **Durazno**
ACONCAGUA La Ligua Villa Constitución Mercedes Trinidad FLORES
Papudo La Mora SANTA FE San Nicolás Dolores SORIANO URUGUAY Sarandí Grande
Putaendo Cerro Aconcagua 22 831 Ramallo Nueva Palmira Florencio Sánchez FLORIDA
Quintero La Calera San Felipe Los Andes Alcorta San Pedro Carmelo COLONIA
Quillota Las Vegas Portillo 9' San Urbano Santa Teresa Zárate Colonia Suiza SAN JOSÉ **Florida**
Valparaíso VALPARAÍSO Wheelwright Pergamino Baradero Campana Colonia Rosario Santa Lucía
PUNTA CURAUMILLA Colón Arrecifes Capilla de Señor San José **Viña del Mar** Quilpué Rojas San Antonio de Areco Pilar Juan L. Lacaze CANELONES Las Piedras
PUNTA TALCA **SANTIAGO** Casablanca Vedia Salto Carmen de Areco **San Isidro** **BUENOS AIRES** Punta Espinillo
San Antonio Curacaví Junín Chacabuco San Andrés de Giles **Morón** **Avellaneda** Río de la Plata
Melipilla San Bernardo Talagante Puente Alto Lincoln Mercedes Luján **Quilmes** Enseñada PUNTA ESPINILLO
Navidad San Pedro Buin Paine Chivilcoy Alberti Navarro Marcos Paz **Lomas de Zamora** **La Plata** Canal Punta Indio
O'HIGGINS 16 896 Mercedita General Viamonte Suipacha San Vicente **MONTEVIDEO**
El Carmen Rengo Pelequén Cerro el Palomo 16 800 Olazcoaga General Alvear Cañuelas Magdalena
Pichilemu San Vicente Santa Cruz COLCHAGUA San Fernando Bragado Anderson Roque Pérez Lobos Coronel Brandsen Altamirano Papinas PUNTA PIEDRAS
Licantén CURICÓ Nueve de Julio Veinticinco de Mayo Monte General Paz Chascomús ATLANTIC OCEAN
Curepto Molina Carlos Casares Saladillo General Belgrano Bahía Samborombón
Talca TALCA Bolívar Tapalqué Las Flores Castelli PUNTA NORTE
San Javier Mariposa San Enrique General Alvear Dolores General Lavalle
Panimávida LINARES General Guido General Conesa
Linares Cerro Campanario 13 130 Azul Cachari Rauch Maipú
©RMCN Longitude West of Greenwich ©RMCN

0 10 20 30 40 50 60 70 80 90 100 110 120 Miles
0 20 40 60 80 100 120 140 160 180 200 Kilometers

Scale 1:4 000 000; one inch to 64 miles.
Elevations and depressions are given in feet.

Urban

Cropland

Cropland & Woodland

Cropland & Grazing Land

Grassland, Grazing Land

Forest, Woodland

Swamp, Marshland

Tundra

Shrub, Sparse Grass,
Wasteland (pattern)

Barren Land

• Oasis

ATLANTIC

OCEAN

North
Sea

Baltic Sea

Gulf of Bothnia

Reykjavik

Narvik

Trondheim

Bergen

Oslo

Göteborg

Stockholm

Helsinki

LENINGRAD

Tallinn

Copenhagen

Riga

Kaliningrad

Minsk

Glasgow

Belfast

MANCHESTER

Dublin

LONDON

Amsterdam

Hamburg

Elbe

BERLIN

Oder

Warsaw

Pripet

Essen

Leipzig

Kraków

L'vov

Antwerp

Frankfurt

Prague

CARPATHIANS

Brest

PARIS

Seine

Strasbourg

Rhine

Danube

VIENNA

Loire

Munich

Budapest

Tisza

Bay of Biscay

Zürich

Lyon

ALPS

MILAN

Zagreb

Sava

La Coruña

Bordeaux

Garonne

Rhône

Venice

Belgrade

Bucharest

Bilbao

PYRENEES

Genoa

Adriatic
Sea

Danube

Douro

Marseille

Sofia

MADRID

Ebro

Lisbon

BARCELONA

CORSICA

ROME

Tiranë

Sevilla

SARDINIA

Naples

Aegean
Sea

ISLAS BÁLEARES

Tyrrhenian Sea

Mediterranean

Tanger

Algiers

Palermo

Athens

Oran

ATLAS   MOUNTAINS

Tunis

SICILY

Casablanca

Sea

MALTA

CRETE

Longitude West of Greenwich   Longitude East of Greenwich

Scale 1: 16 000 000; one inch to 250 miles. Conic Projection

0   50   100   200   300   400   500 Miles

0   100   200   400   600   800 Kilometers

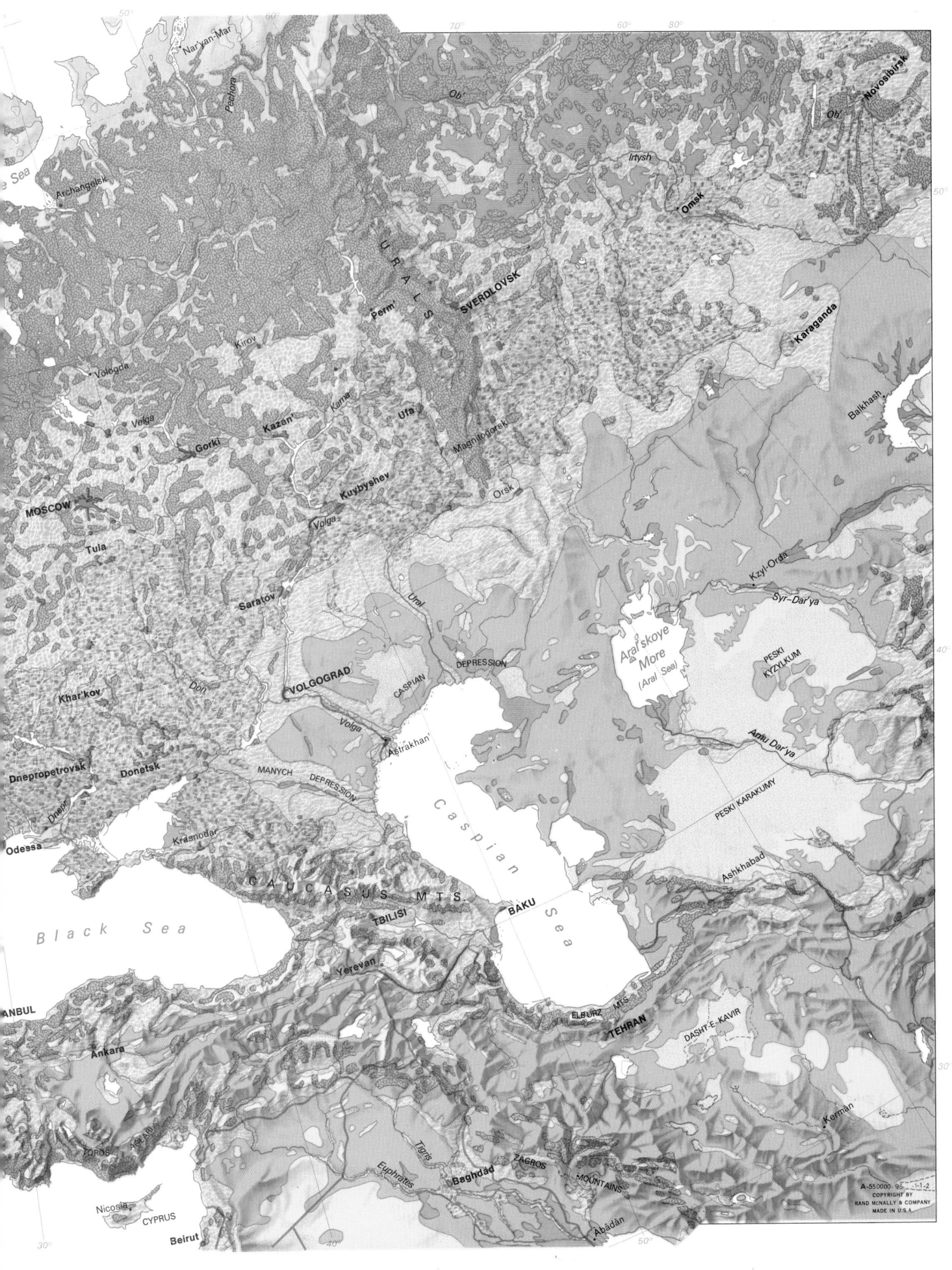

Nar'yan-Mar

Pechora

Archangelsk

Ob'

Novosibirsk

Irtysh

Omsk

URALS

Perm'

SVERDLOVSK

Karaganda

Kirov

Vologda

Volga

Kama

Kazan'

Gorki

Ufa

Balkhash

Magnitogorsk

MOSCOW

Kuybyshev

Orsk

Tula

Volga

Saratov

Ural

Kzyl-Orda

Syr-Dar'ya

DEPRESSION

*Aral'skoye
More
(Aral Sea)*

PESKI
KYZYLKUM

Khar'kov

Don

VOLGOGRAD

CASPIAN

Volga

Amu Dar'ya

Dnepropetrovsk

Donetsk

Dnepr

Astrakhan'

MANYCH   DEPRESSION

PESKI KARAKUMY

Odessa

Krasnodar

C a s p i a n

Ashkhabad

Black   Sea

CAUCASUS   MTS.

BAKU

S e a

TBILISI

Yerevan

ANBUL

ELBURZ   MTS.

Ankara

TEHRAN

DASHT-E KAVIR

TOROS

Kerman

Nicosia

CYPRUS

Tigris

ZAGROS

Euphrates

Baghdad

MOUNTAINS

Beirut

Ābādān

A-550000-95   1-1-2
COPYRIGHT BY
RAND MCNALLY & COMPANY
MADE IN U.S.A.

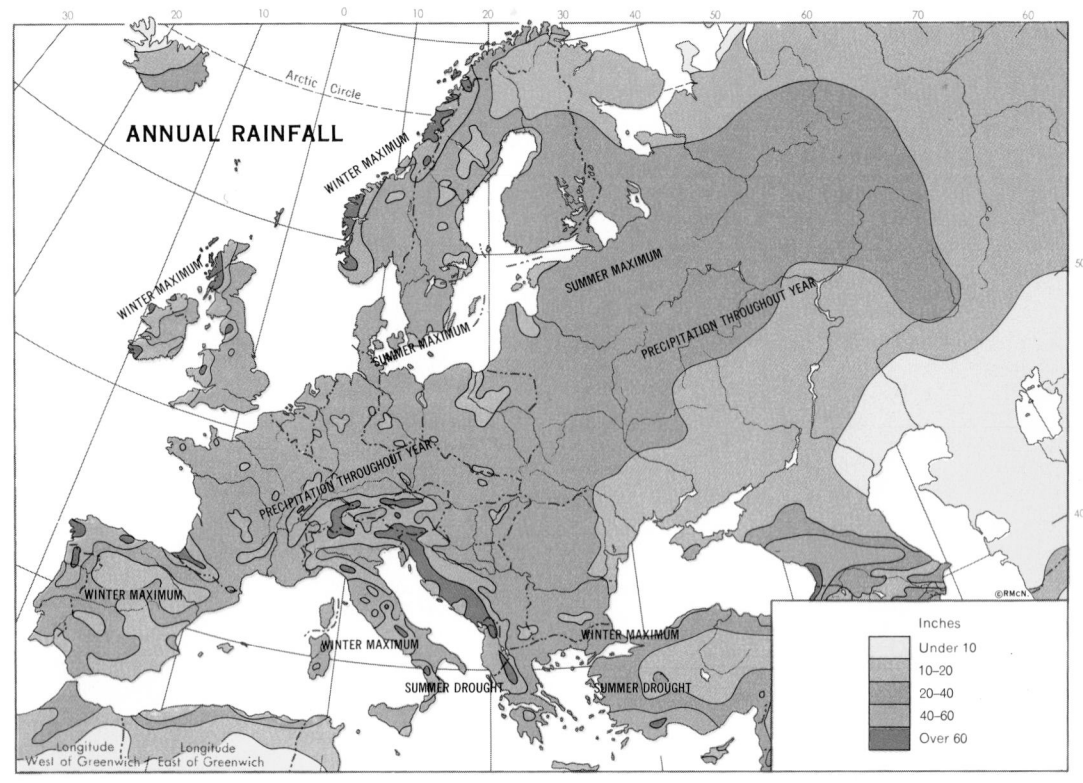

ANNUAL RAINFALL

Inches

	Under 10
	10–20
	20–40
	40–60
	Over 60

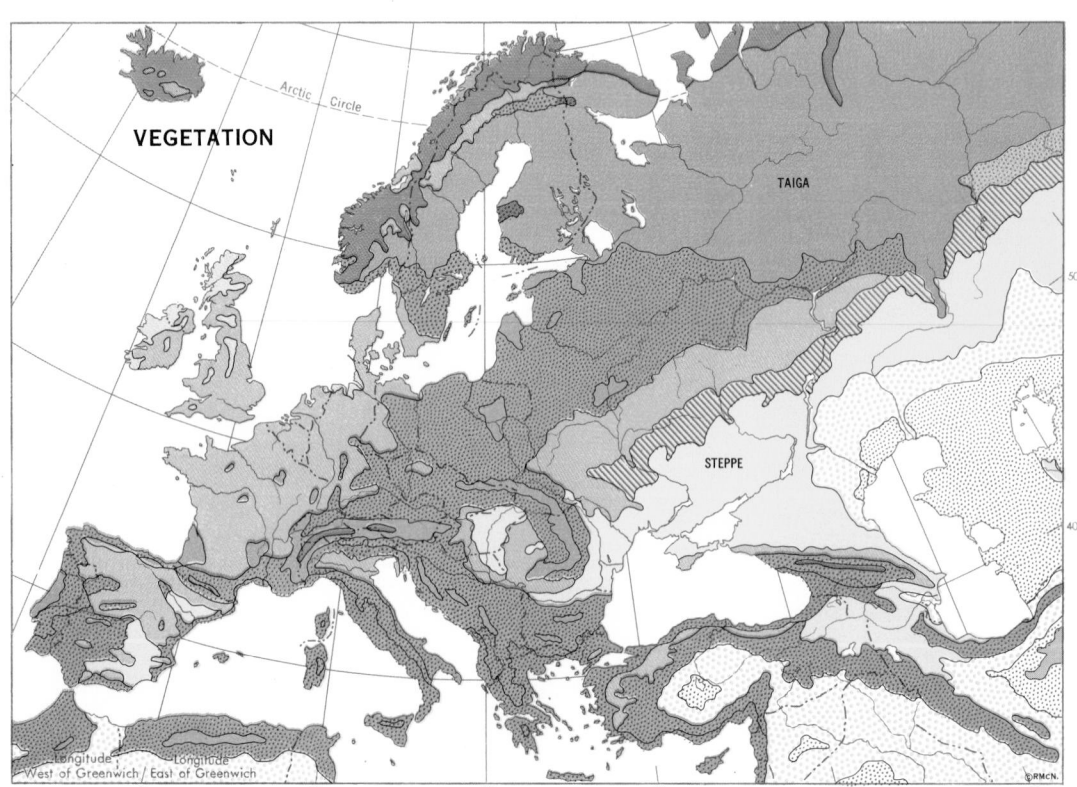

VEGETATION

TAIGA

STEPPE

VEGETATION

E	Coniferous forest
B, Bs	Mediterranean vegetation
M	Mixed forest: coniferous-deciduous
S	Semi-deciduous forest
D	Deciduous forest
DG	Wooded steppe
G	Grass (steppe)
Gp	Short grass
Dsp	Desert shrub
L	Heath and moor
L	Alpine vegetation, tundra
b	Little or no vegetation

For explanation of letters in boxes,
see Natural Vegetation Map
by A. W. Kuchler, p. 16

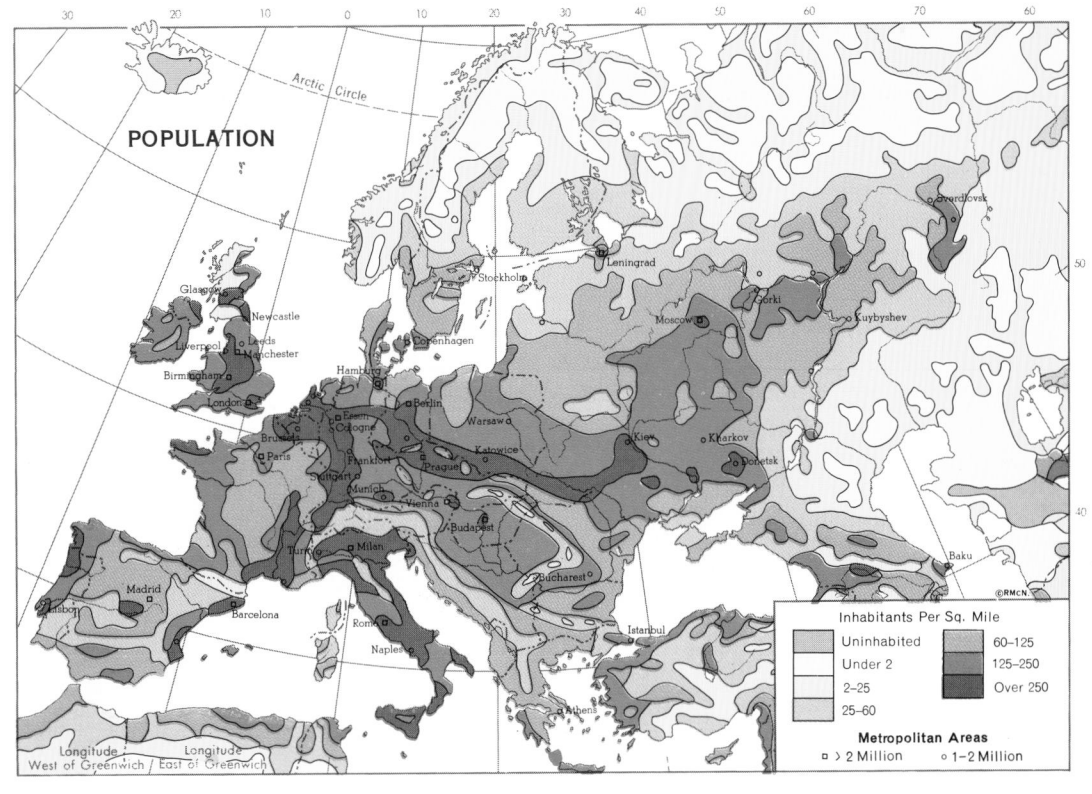

POPULATION

Glasgow
Newcastle
Liverpool
Leeds
Manchester
Birmingham
London
Hamburg
Copenhagen
Stockholm
Leningrad
Moscow
Gorki
Kuybyshev
Sverdlovsk
Brussels
Essen
Cologne
Berlin
Warsaw
Katowice
Kiev
Kharkov
Frankfurt
Paris
Stuttgart
Munich
Prague
Vienna
Donetsk
Turin
Milan
Budapest
Madrid
Barcelona
Rome
Bucharest
Baku
Lisbon
Naples
Istanbul
Athens

Arctic Circle

Longitude West of Greenwich / Longitude East of Greenwich

Inhabitants Per Sq. Mile

Uninhabited
Under 2
2–25
25–60
60–125
125–250
Over 250

Metropolitan Areas
▫ > 2 Million   ○ 1–2 Million

©RMcN.

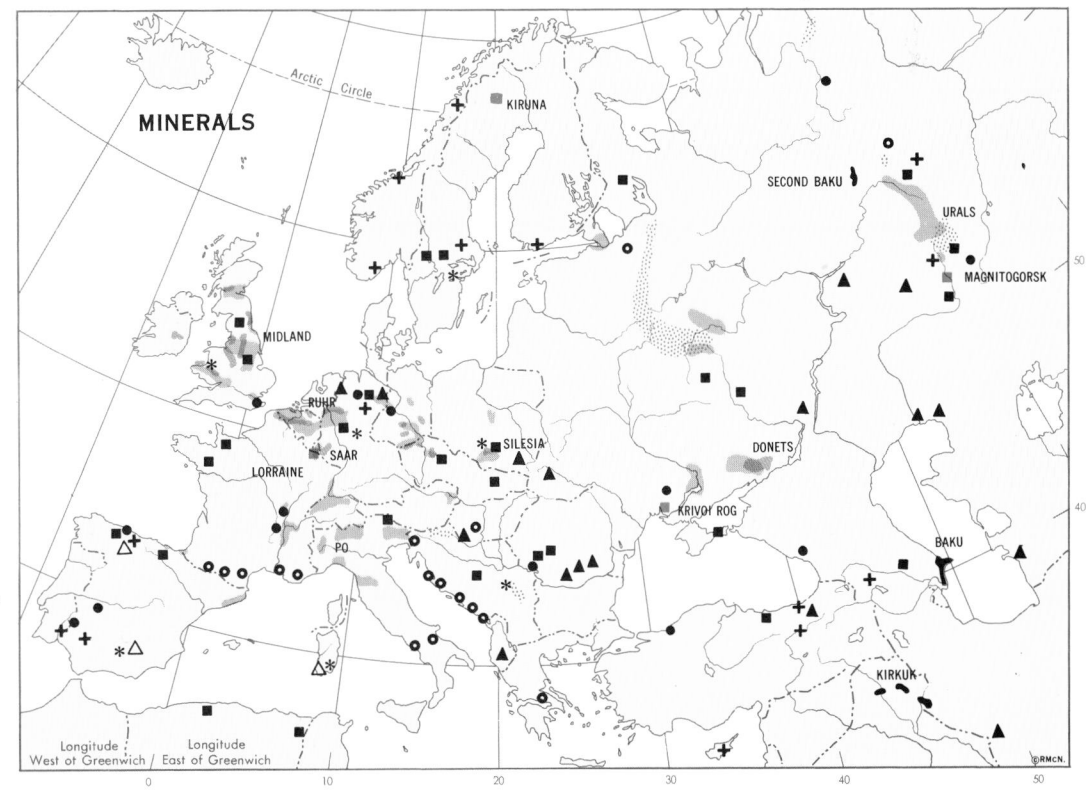

MINERALS

KIRUNA
SECOND BAKU
URALS
MAGNITOGORSK
MIDLAND
RUHR
SILESIA
SAAR
DONETS
LORRAINE
KRIVOI ROG
BAKU
PO
KIRKUK

Arctic Circle

Longitude West of Greenwich / Longitude East of Greenwich

©RMcN.

MINERALS

Industrial areas
Major coal deposits
● Major petroleum deposits
Lignite deposits
▲ Minor petroleum deposits
● Minor coal deposits
■ Major iron ore
■ Minor iron ore
✳ Lead
⊙ Bauxite
△ Zinc
✛ Copper

Longitude West of Greenwich 0° Longitude East of Greenwich

Scale 1:16 000 000; one inch to 250 miles. Conic Projection
Elevations and depressions are given in feet.

PHYSIOGRAPHIC PROVINCES
0 400
Miles
FENNO-SCANDIAN SHIELD
Lake Region
KARELIAN TROUGH
NORWAY UPLAND
SWED. LOWL'D
AREA OF LATEST GLACIATION
NORTH EUROPEAN GLACIATED PLAIN
SCOTTISH HIGHL.
HIBERNIAN UPL.
PENNINES
ENGLISH LL.
CORNISH-WELSH UPL.
ARMORICAN MASSIVE
PARIS BASIN
NETHERLANDS
CENTRAL GERMAN UPL.
BOHEMIAN MASSIVE
SWISS-BAVARIAN PLATEAU
POLESIEN SWAMPS
DNIEPER LL.
CENTRAL RUSSIAN RISE
OKA-DON LOWL.
DNIEPER PLAT.
DONETZ-AZOVIAN PLAT.
VOLYNO-PODOLIAN DISSECTED LL.
CARPATHIAN MTS.
HUNGARIAN BASIN
TRANSYLVAN. BASIN
WALLACHIAN PLAIN
AZOVIAN PLAIN
CRIM-CAUCASIAN MTS.
ALPS
PO VALLEY
CENTR. MASSIVE
AQUITANIAN PLAIN
CANTABRIAN MTS.
PYRENEES
EBRO LL.
SPANISH MESETA
ANDALUSIAN LL.
BETIC CORDILLERA
CORSARDINIAN HIGHL'DS
APENNINES
VOLCANIC LL.
DINARIC-GRECIAN MTS.
CENTRAL BALKAN RANGES
BALKAN RA.
RHODOPE MTS.
SICILIAN HIGHL'DS
PONTIAN UPLAND
ANATOLIAN PLATEAU
TAURUS MTS.
AEGEAN SLOPE
RIF ATLAS
MOROCCAN ATL. LL.
MIDDLE ATL.
HIGH ATLAS
TELL ATLAS
HIGH PLATEAU
SAHARAN-TUNISIAN ATLAS
Western Uplands (Mostly old rocks)
Great European Plain
Central Uplands
Alpine System
EUROPE DURING THE ICE AGE
GREENLAND
Floating Ice
THE GREAT ICE CAP (at its largest extent)
WEST SIBERIAN SEA
Probable interglacial and postglacial connections
ARAL-CASPIAN SEA
Loess tundra
Brush tundra
Loess
Conifers
Swamp
Steppe
Pontian Lake
Volcanoes
Altamira
Solutré
Moustier
Grimaldi
Tundra
Forest
Steppe
PHYSIOGRAPHY BY ERWIN RAISZ
LITHOLOGY AND STRUCTURE
Unconsolidated deposits: alluvium, sands, bottom lands.
Strongly folded and faulted rocks. The "Younger Series" in Norway.
Essentially horizontal sediments, also uplands and terraces in the plains.
Metamorphic and intrusive igneous rocks.
Moderately folded sedimentary rocks.
volcanics, lava flows, basalts, etc.
LANDFORMS
PLATEAUS
CUESTAS
SAND
HILLS
FOLDED MOUNTAINS
SINKS
MOUNTAINS
BASIN RANGES
MORAINES
MESAS
VOLCANO AND LAVA
DRUMLINS
TAIGA
TUNDRA
Many small lakes
Kanin Pen.
URAL MTS.
TIMAN HILLS
PECHORA BASIN
Pechora R.
Mezen R.
Archangel
Pinega R.
VYCHEGDA LOWLAND
Northern Dwina
PERM BASIN
Perm
Limit of Glaciation
Limit of Würm Glaciation
Kirov
VYATKA HILLS
Vyatka R.
Kama R.
BELAYA HILLS
VETLUGA LOWLAND
Kazan
Gorkiy
Rybinsk Res.
Volga R.
Moscow
MOSCOW PLATEAU
Oka
Tula
TULA HILLS
OKA-DON LOWLAND
VOLGA PLATEAU
BELEBEY HILLS
BASHKIR HILLS
Kuybyshev
Zhiguli Hills
OBSHCHY SYRT
Orenburg
MUGODZHAR HILLS
Penza
Tambov
Saratov
TRANSVOLGA PLAIN
Ural R.
CENTRAL RUSSIAN PLATEAU (Unglaciated)
Orel
Kursk
Voronezh
Kharkov
KALACH HILLS
DON PLATEAU
Black Earth Belt
Volgograd
CASPIAN DESERT
KALMUK STEPPE
Salt Domes
Astrakhan
DONETZ PLATEAU
Donetsk
AZOV PLATEAU
DNIEPER PLATEAU
Rostov
Manych Channel
MANYCH DEPRESSION
ERGENI PLAT.
NOGAY STEPPE
BUZACHI PEN.
MANGYSHLAK PEN.
CASPIAN SEA
PONTIAN PLAIN
Odessa
Azovian Sea
STAVROPOL PLATEAU
Kuban R.
Terek R.
Grozny
DAGESTAN
CRIMEAN PLAIN
Kerch Hills
Sevastopol
CRIMEAN MTS.
Elbrus
Kazbek
Sochi
Poti
Batumi
Tbilisi
SHIRAK PLAT.
SHAH DAGH
KURA BASIN
Baku
Apsheron Pen.
BLACK SEA
PONTIAN PLATEAU
Sinop
Kizil Irmak
KACKAR
Alagez
Sevan
Yerevan
Ararat
LAVA PLATEAU
QARA DAGH
TALYSH
Tabriz
Sahand
L. Van
KURDISH ALPS
GREAT TRENCH
ANKARA HILL
RED HILLS
MUNZUR
Murat R.
Ankara
HAYMANA HILLS
Kayseri
Erciyas
CENTRAL PLAIN
Tüz Gölü
SULTAN D.
KONYA PLAIN
TAURUS MTS.
ANTITAURUS
Cilician Gates
Diar.
Karaca Dağ Lava
MARDIN UPL.
Mosul
Erbil
Kirkuk
ZAGROS MTS.
Low Anticlines
HAMRIN
AL JAZIRA
ALEPPO RISE
Alep
Euphrates R.
TAURUS PLAT.
LYCIAN PLAT.
Antalia Plain
BUEYDA
PALMYRA RANGES
Homs
Baghdad
Tigris R.
LOWER WADIYAN
UPPER WADIYAN
HAJARA
CYPRUS
50 100 200 300 400 500 Miles
100 200 400 600 800 Kilometers

EUROPE LANGUAGES
BY
BOGDAN ZABORSKI

Scale 1:16,500,000; one inch to 260 miles Conic Projection

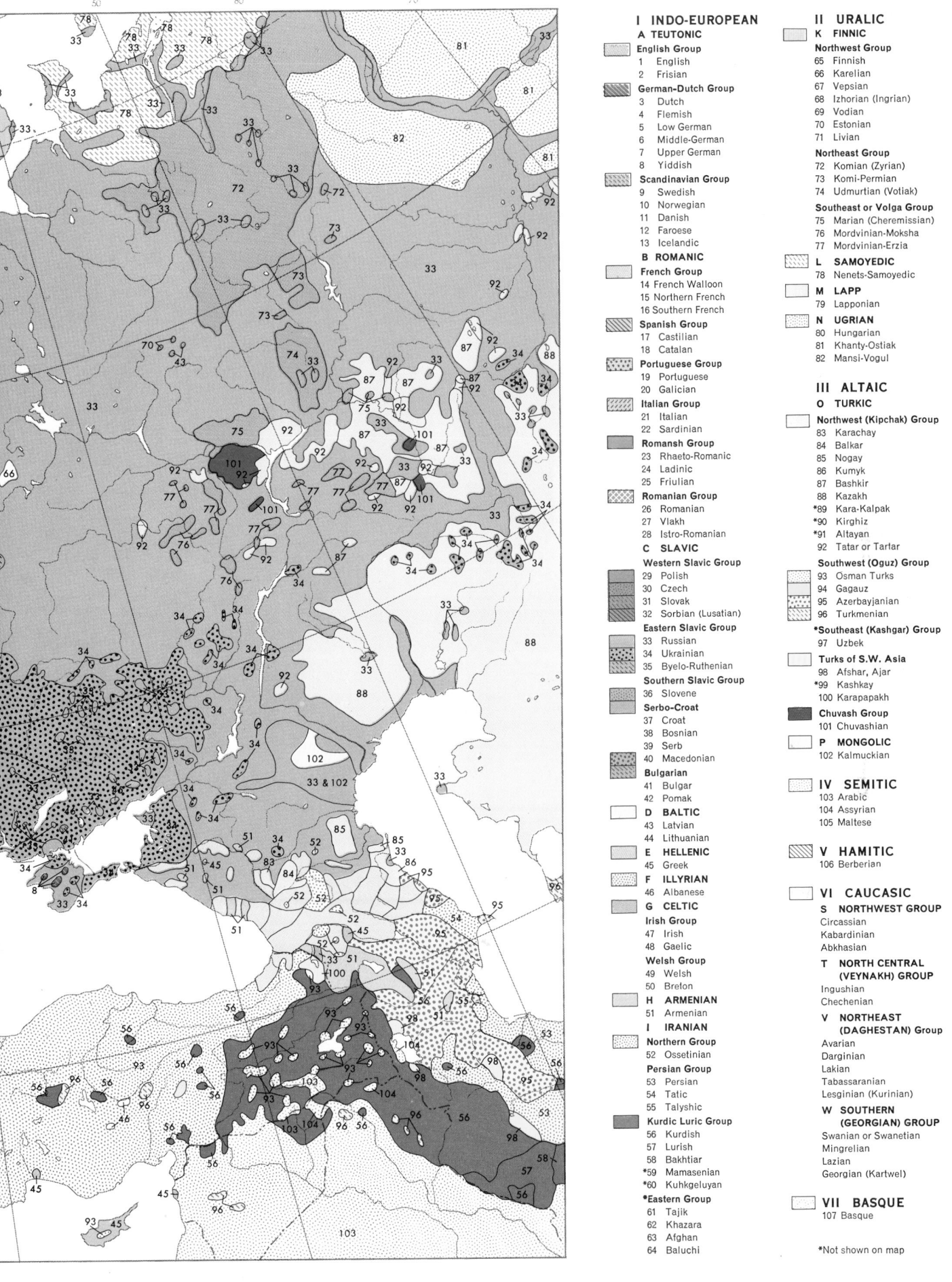

I INDO-EUROPEAN

A TEUTONIC

English Group
1 English
2 Frisian

German-Dutch Group
3 Dutch
4 Flemish
5 Low German
6 Middle-German
7 Upper German
8 Yiddish

Scandinavian Group
9 Swedish
10 Norwegian
11 Danish
12 Faroese
13 Icelandic

B ROMANIC

French Group
14 French Walloon
15 Northern French
16 Southern French

Spanish Group
17 Castilian
18 Catalan

Portuguese Group
19 Portuguese
20 Galician

Italian Group
21 Italian
22 Sardinian

Romansh Group
23 Rhaeto-Romanic
24 Ladinic
25 Friulian

Romanian Group
26 Romanian
27 Vlakh
28 Istro-Romanian

C SLAVIC

Western Slavic Group
29 Polish
30 Czech
31 Slovak
32 Sorbian (Lusatian)

Eastern Slavic Group
33 Russian
34 Ukrainian
35 Byelo-Ruthenian

Southern Slavic Group
36 Slovene

Serbo-Croat
37 Croat
38 Bosnian
39 Serb
40 Macedonian

Bulgarian
41 Bulgar
42 Pomak

D BALTIC
43 Latvian
44 Lithuanian

E HELLENIC
45 Greek

F ILLYRIAN
46 Albanese

G CELTIC

Irish Group
47 Irish
48 Gaelic

Welsh Group
49 Welsh
50 Breton

H ARMENIAN
51 Armenian

I IRANIAN

Northern Group
52 Ossetinian

Persian Group
53 Persian
54 Tatic
55 Talyshic

Kurdic Luric Group
56 Kurdish
57 Lurish
58 Bakhtiar
*59 Mamasenian
*60 Kuhgeluyan

Eastern Group
61 Tajik
62 Khazara
63 Afghan
64 Baluchi

II URALIC

K FINNIC

Northwest Group
65 Finnish
66 Karelian
67 Vepsian
68 Izhorian (Ingrian)
69 Vodian
70 Estonian
71 Livian

Northeast Group
72 Komian (Zyrian)
73 Komi-Permian
74 Udmurtian (Votiak)

Southeast or Volga Group
75 Marian (Cheremissian)
76 Mordvinian-Moksha
77 Mordvinian-Erzia

L SAMOYEDIC
78 Nenets-Samoyedic

M LAPP
79 Lapponian

N UGRIAN
80 Hungarian
81 Khanty-Ostiak
82 Mansi-Vogul

III ALTAIC

O TURKIC

Northwest (Kipchak) Group
83 Karachay
84 Balkar
85 Nogay
86 Kumyk
87 Bashkir
88 Kazakh
*89 Kara-Kalpak
*90 Kirghiz
*91 Altayan
92 Tatar or Tartar

Southwest (Oguz) Group
93 Osman Turks
94 Gagauz
95 Azerbayjanian
96 Turkmenian

Southeast (Kashgar) Group
97 Uzbek

Turks of S.W. Asia
98 Afshar, Ajar
*99 Kashkay
100 Karapapakh

Chuvash Group
101 Chuvashian

P MONGOLIC
102 Kalmuckian

IV SEMITIC
103 Arabic
104 Assyrian
105 Maltese

V HAMITIC
106 Berberian

VI CAUCASIC

S NORTHWEST GROUP
Circassian
Kabardinian
Abkhasian

T NORTH CENTRAL (VEYNAKH) GROUP
Ingushian
Chechenian

V NORTHEAST (DAGHESTAN) Group
Avarian
Darginian
Lakian
Tabassaranian
Lesginian (Kurinian)

W SOUTHERN (GEORGIAN) GROUP
Swanian or Swanetian
Mingrelian
Lazian
Georgian (Kartwel)

VII BASQUE
107 Basque

*Not shown on map

Relief

Meters		Feet
3050		10 000
1525		5000
610		2000
305		1000
152.5		500
0	Sea Level	0
152.5		500 Below
1525		5000 Sea Level
3050		10 000

Scale 1: 16 000 000; one inch to 250 miles. Conic Projection

Elevations and depressions are given in feet

Continued on pages 210–211

0	50	100	200	300	400	500 Miles
0	100	200	400	600		800 Kilometers

Longitude West of Greenwich   Longitude East of Greenwich

Continued on pages 172-173

Continued on pages 186-187

WHITE SEA

KOLGUYEV

P-OV KANIN

Nar'yan-Mar

△ Norodnaya 6214

Berezovo

Ob'

Surgut

NOVOSIBIRSK

Leninsk-Kuznetski Novokuznetsk

Barnaul Biysk

Mezen'

Arkhangelsk (Archangel)

Sev. Dvina

Syktyvkar

Serov

Tobol'sk

Irtysh

Taro

Omsk

Slavgorod

Novosibirsk

Onega

Solikamsk

Berezniki

Krasnoural'sk

Nizh. Tagil

Tyumen'

Ishim

Petropavlovsk

Barabinsk

Kuybyshev

Pavlodar

Semipalatinsk

Kotlas

Chusovoy Lys'va

Perm

Kamensk-Ural'skiy

Kurgan

Kokchetav

Onezhskoye Ozero (Onega)

Kirov

Krasnokamsk

Albest

Kustanay

Tselinograd (Akmolinsk)

Temir-Tau Karaganda

Karkaralinsk

Petrozavodsk

Votkinsk

Izhevsk

Sverdlovsk Chelyabinsk

Atbasar

Balkhash

Cherepovets Vologda

Rybinsk Kostroma

Yoshkar-Ola

Sarapul Kyshtym

Ufa Zlatoust Troitsk

Belorelsk

Novo-Kazalinsk Tyura-Tam

Ozero Balkhash +1112

Rybinskoye Vdkhr.

Ivanovo Kineshma

Cheboksary

Magnitogorsk

Orenburg

Orsk

Turgay

Baykonur

STEPPE

Chu

GORKI

Kazan'

Sterlitamak

Kirgiz

Aral'sk

Kzyl-Orda

Dzhambul

Vladimir Dzerzhinsk Kovrov

Ul'yanovsk

KUYBYSHEV

Syzran' Chapayevsk

K A Z A K H

Chelkar

Novo-Kazalinsk

TASHKENT

MOSCOW (Moskva)

Ryazan'

Penza

Saratov

Engel's

Ural'sk

Aktyubinsk

Irgiz

Chalkar Tengiz

Syr-Dar'ya

Chimkent

Serpukhov Kolomna

Novomoskovsk Morshansk

Vol'sk

Turkestan

Kaluga Tula

Tambov

Balashov Borisoglebsk

K A Z A K H

Ural

ARALSKOYE MORE (Aral Sea) +174

PESKI KYZYLKUM (DESERT)

Lenger

Bezhitsa Orël Michurinsk

Lipetsk

Kamyshin

Don

Turtkul

Bryansk Yelets

Voronezh

VOLGOGRAD

CASPIAN DEPRESSION

Nova-Kozalinsk

Chimbay

Urgench

PLATO UST'-URT

KHAR'KOV S.S.R.

Gur'yev

Astrakhan

Kungrad

Nukus

Tashauz

Khiva

Bukhara

Samarkand

Poltava

DNEPROPETROVSK

Voroshilovgrad

MANYCH DEPRESSION

Zerashan

Zaraf

U Z B E K

Amu

Dar'ya

Menchug Dneprodzerzhinsk

Makeyevka

Gorlovka Shakhty

Novocherkassk

Rostov-na-Donu

Volga

CASPIAN

Mangyshlak

Shevchenko

T U R K M E N S.S.R.

Chardzhou

Zaporozh'e

DONETSK

Taganrog

MANYCH DEPRESSION

Kura

PESKI KARAKUMY (DESERT)

Mary

rivoy Rog Nikopol Zhdanov

Berd'ansk

Stavropol'

Grozny

Makhachkala

Nikolayev Melitopol

AZOVSKOYE MORE (Sea of Azov)

Krasnodar

Pyatigorsk

Derbent

Zal Kara Bogaz-Gol

Kizyl-Arvat

KARA KUMY

Ashkhabad

Maimana

Odessa Kherson

Kerch

Armavir

Maykop

Gora Elbrus 18481

Kazbek 16558

Djaudzhikau

Surface —92 Ft. Below Sea Level

BAKU

Krasnovodsk

Nebit-Dag

Gorgan

AFGHAN-ISTAN

Simferopol'

KRYMSKY P-OV CRIMEA

Novorossiysk

CAUCASUS

MOUNTAINS

TRANSCAUCASIA

AZERBAYDZHAN S.S.R.

Atrek

Mashhad

Herat

Sevastopol' Yalta

Sochi

Sukhumi

Kutaisi

GEORGIAN S.S.R.

Kirovabad

BLACK SEA

Poti

TBILISI

Batumi

Leninakan Kars

Yerevan

ARMENIAN S.S.R.

Ararat 16946

Rasht

Babol

ELBURZ MTS. Damavand 18934

Gorgan

DASHT-E-KAVIR (DESERT)

NBUL but Bogazi (Bosporus)

Zonguldak

KUZEY ANADOLU DAGLARI

Samsun

Trabzon (Trebizond)

Erzurum

Tabriz

Kazvin

Tehran

Ankara (Angora)

Sinop

Sivas

KURDISTAN

ZAGROS

TEHRAN

KAVIR-E-LUT (DESERT)

isehir

T U R K E Y

ASIA MINOR

Kayseri

Diyarbakir

Nineveh (Ruins)

Hamadan

Kashan

I R A N (PERSIA)

Daryacheh Namak

Zahedan

Afyonkarahisar

Konya

Gaziantep

Al-Mawsil

Kirkuk

Esfahan

Yazd

Kerman

Antalya

TOROS DAGLARI

Adana

Mersin

Iskenderun

Aleppo

Euphrates

Shushtar

Persepolis (Ruins)

Nicosia

CYPRUS

Homs

Palmyra

Babylon (Ruins)

Baghdad

Basra

Khorramshahr

Abadan

Shiraz

A LEBANON Beirut

S Y R I A

I R A Q

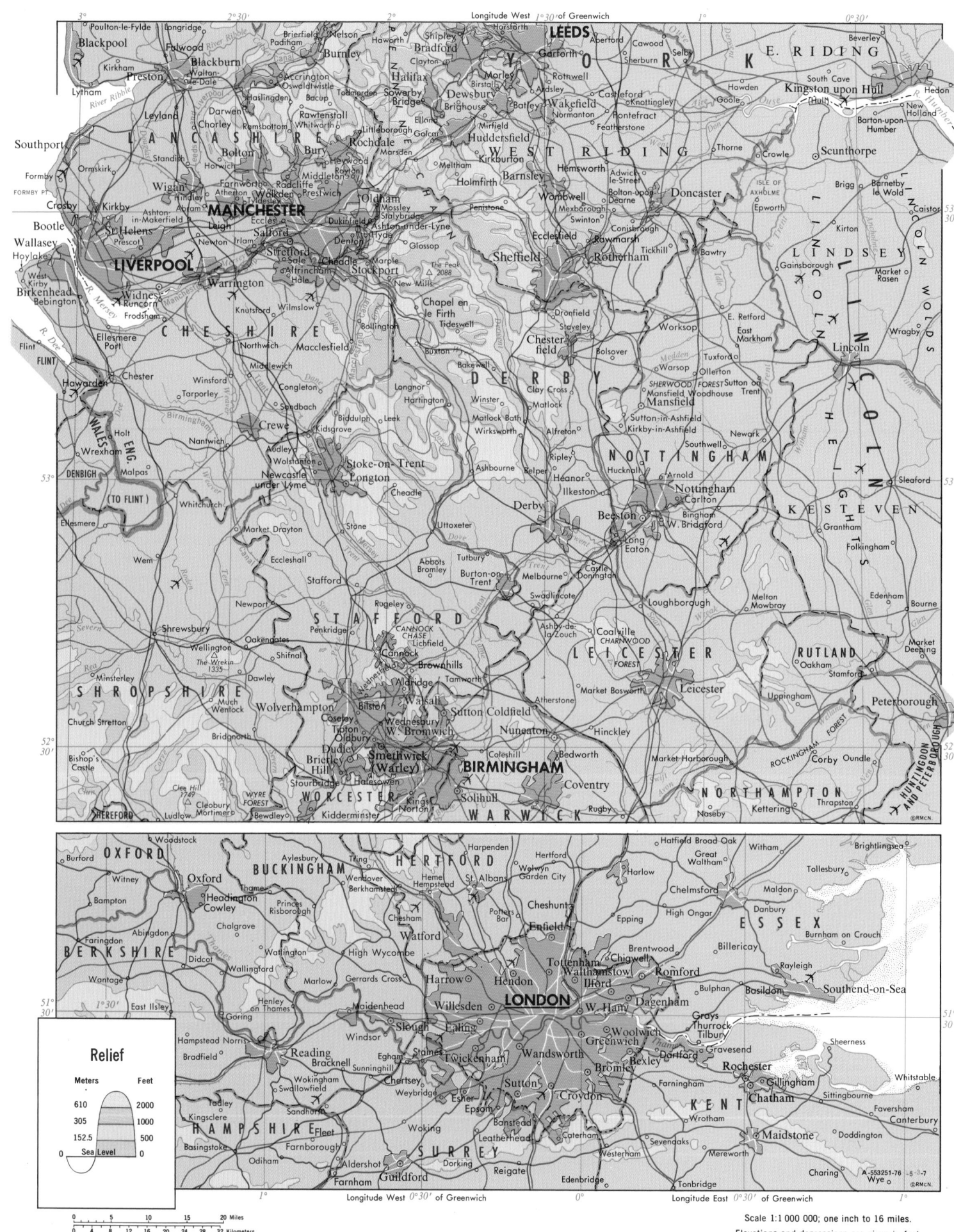

Relief

Meters	Feet
610	2000
305	1000
152.5	500
0 Sea Level	0

Scale 1:1 000 000; one inch to 16 miles.
Elevations and depressions are given in feet.

A-553251-76
®RMcN.

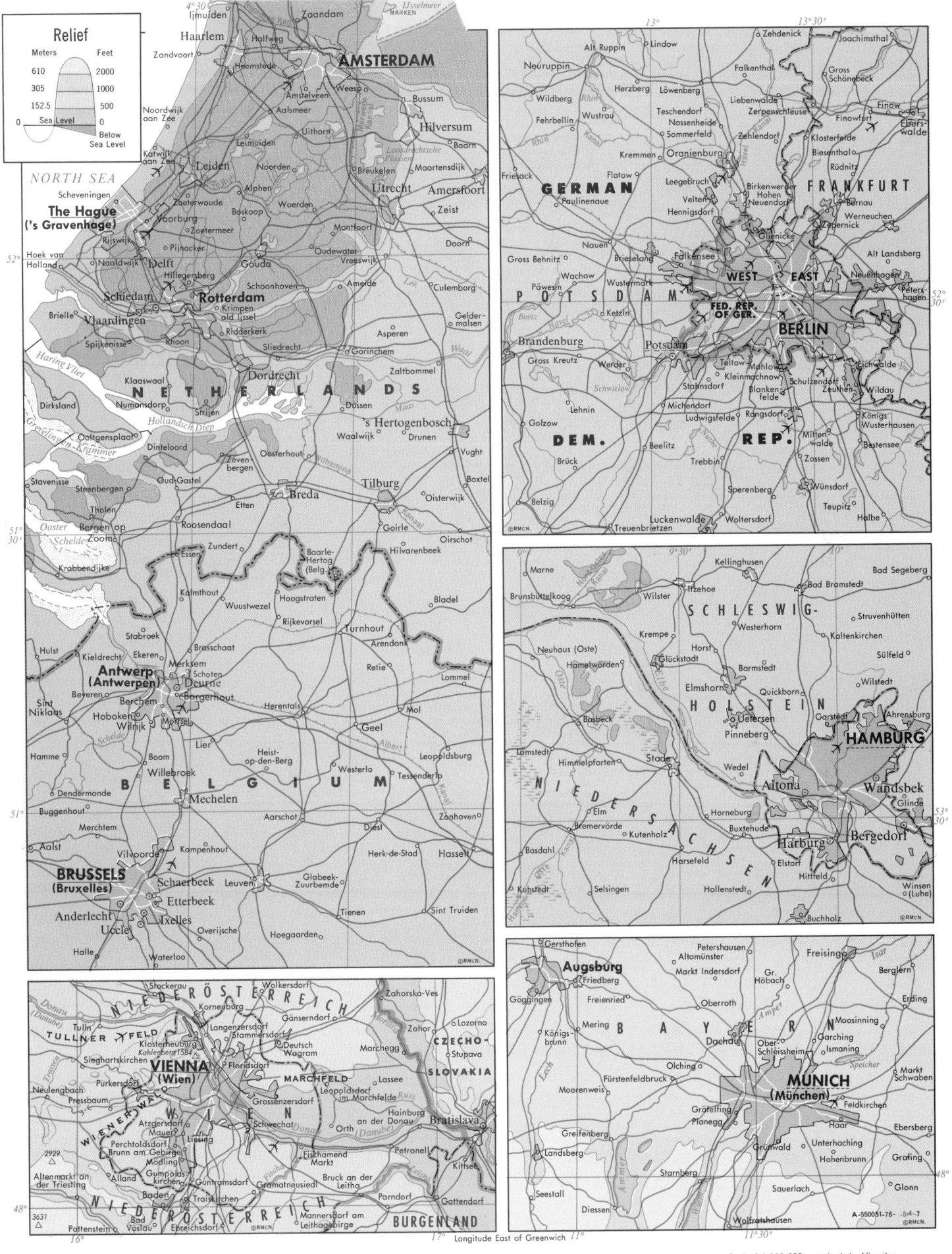

Relief

Meters	Feet
610	2000
305	1000
152.5	500
0 Sea Level	0 Sea Level
	Below Sea Level

NORTH SEA

Ijmuiden
MARKEN
Zaandam
Haarlem
Halfweg
Zandvoort
Heemstede
Zandvoort
Weesp
AMSTERDAM
Amstelveen
Aalsmeer
Bussum
Noordwijk aan Zee
Uithorn
Baarn
Hilversum
Leimuiden
Noorden
Maartensdijk
Katwijk aan Zee
Leiden
Alphen
Woerden
Utrecht
Amersfoort
Scheveningen
Zoeterwoude
Boskoop
Zeist
The Hague ('s Gravenhage)
Voorburg
Zoetermeer
Montfoort
Doorn
Rijswijk
Pijnacker
Gouda
Oudewater
Vreeswijk
Hoek van Holland
Naaldwijk
Delft
Hillegersberg
Schoonhoven
Culemborg
Ameide
Schiedam
Rotterdam
Krimpen aid IJssel
Ridderkerk
Geldermalsen
Vlaardingen
Brielle
Rhoon
Sliedrecht
Gorinchem
Asperen
Spijkenisse
Dordrecht
Zaltbommel
NETHERLANDS
Klaaswaal
Dussen
Maas
Dirksland
Numansdorp
Strijen
's Hertogenbosch
Ooltgensplaat
Drunen
Vught
Stavenisse
Oud Gastel
Zeven-bergen
Oosterhout
Steenbergen
Tilburg
Boxtel
Tholen
Breda
Oisterwijk
Bergen op Zoom
Etten
Goirle
Oirschot
Krabbendijke
Roosendaal
Zundert
Baarle-Hertog (Belg.)
Hilvarenbeek
Essen
Bladel
Kalmthout
Hoogstraten
Wuustwezel
Rijkevorsel
BELGIUM
Stabroek
Brasschaat
Turnhout
Arendonk
Kieldrecht
Ekeren
Merksem
Schoten
Retie
Lommel
Antwerp (Antwerpen)
Deurne
Borgerhout
Herentals
Mol
Beveren
Berchem
Geel
Sint Niklaas
Hoboken
Wilrijk
Mortsel
Lier
Heist-op-den-Berg
Leopoldsburg
Hamme
Boom
Westerlo
Tessenderlo
Dendermonde
Willebroek
Mechelen
Aarschot
Diest
Zonhoven
Buggenhout
Merchtem
Herk-de-Stad
Hasselt
Aalst
Vilvoorde
Kampenhout
BRUSSELS (Bruxelles)
Schaerbeek
Leuven
Glabeek-Zuurbemde
Anderlecht
Etterbeek
Sint Truiden
Uccle
Ixelles
Tienen
Halle
Overijsche
Hoegaarden
Waterloo

GERMAN
Alt Ruppin
Lindow
Zehdenick
Joachimsthal
Neuruppin
Falkenthal
Wildberg
Herzberg
Löwenberg
Gross Schönebeck
Fehrbellin
Wustrau
Teschendorf
Liebenwalde
Zerpenschleuse
Finow
Nassenheide
Sommerfeld
Zehlendorf
Klosterfelde
Finowfurt
Ebers-walde
Friesack
Flatow
Leegebruch
Birkenwerder
Rüdnitz
FRANKFURT
Kremmen
Oranienburg
Hohen Neuendorf
Bernau
Nauen
Gross Behnitz
Brieselang
Velten
Hennigsdorf
Werneuchen
Pawesin
Wachow
Wustermark
Glienicke
Zepernick
POTSDAM
WEST **EAST**
Alt Landsberg
Neuenhagen
Ketzin
FED. REP. OF GER.
Peters-hagen
Brandenburg
BERLIN
Gross Kreutz
Werder
Potsdam
Teltow
Mahlow
Eichwalde
Schwielow
Kleinmachnow
Stahnsdorf
Blankenfelde
Schulzendorf
Zeuthen
Wildau
Lehnin
Michendorf
DEM.
Golzow
Ludwigsfelde
Rangsdorf
Königs Wusterhausen
Brück
Beelitz
Mittenwalde
Bestensee
Belzig
Trebbin
Zossen
Sperenberg
Wünsdorf
Teupitz
Luckenwalde
Woltersdorf
Halbe
Treuenbrietzen
REP.

Kellinghusen
Bad Segeberg
Marne
Nord-Ostsee Kanal
Itzehoe
Bad Bramstedt
Brunsbüttelkoog
Wilster
SCHLESWIG-
Struvenhütten
Westerhorn
Kaltenkirchen
Krempe
Horst
Barmstedt
Sülfeld
Neuhaus (Oste)
Glückstadt
Wilstedt
Hamelwörden
Quickborn
Elmshorn
HOLSTEIN
Ahrensburg
Basbeck
Uetersen
Pinneberg
Garstedt
Lamstedt
Himmelpforten
Stade
HAMBURG
Wedel
Altona
Wandsbek
NIEDERSACHSEN
Elm
Horneburg
Glinde
Buxtehude
Harburg
Bergedorf
Bremervörde
Kutenholz
Basdahl
Harseteld
Elstorf
Hittfeld
Kühstedt
Selsingen
Hollenstedt
Buchholz
Winsen (Luhe)

Gersthofen
Petershausen
Freising
Augsburg
Friedberg
Altomünster
Markt Indersdorf
Berglern
Göggingen
Freienried
Oberroth
Gr. Höbach
Erding
Königs-brunn
Mering
BAYERN
Moosinning
Garching
Ismaning
Dachau
Olching
Ober-Schleissheim
Fürstenfeldbruck
Markt Schwaben
Moorenweis
MUNICH (München)
Haar
Feldkirchen
Greifenberg
Gräfelfing
Planegg
Unterhaching
Ebersberg
Landsberg
Grünwald
Hohenbrunn
Grafing
Starnberg
Seestall
Sauerlach
Glonn
Diessen
Wolfratshausen

NIEDERÖSTERREICH
Stockerau
Wolkersdorf
Zahorska-Ves
Donau (Danube)
Korneuburg
Gänserndorf
Tulln
Langenzersdorf
Stammersdorf
TULLNER FELD
Klosterneuburg
Deutsch Wagram
Zohor
Lozorno
Kahlenberg 1584
Floridsdorf
Marchegg
Stupava
CZECHO-
Sieghartskirchen
VIENNA (Wien)
Lassee
SLOVAKIA
Neulengbach
Purkersdorf
MARCHFELD
Pressbaum
Leopoldsdorf im Marchfelde
Russ
Bratislava
WIENERWALD
Grossenzersdorf
Hainburg an der Donau
Atzgersdorf
Schwechat
Orth (Danube)
Mauer
Liesing
Fischamend Markt
Petronell
Perchtoldsdorf
2929
Brunn am Gebirge
Kittsee
Mödling
Altmarkt an der Triesting
Alland
Gumpolds-kirchen
Guntramsdorf
Baden
Traiskirchen
3631
Fischa
Bruck an der Leitha
Gattendorf
NIEDERÖSTERREICH
Mannersdorf am Leithagebirge
Parndorf
BURGENLAND
Pattenstein
Bad Vöslau
Ebreichsdorf

Longitude East of Greenwich

Scale 1:1 000 000; one inch to 16 miles.
Elevations and depressions are given in feet.

0   5   10   15   20 Miles
0 4 8 12 16 20 24 28 32 Kilometers

A-550051-76- -5-4-7

Relief

Meters	Feet	
3050	10 000	
1525	5000	
610	2000	
305	1000	
152.5	500	
0	0	Below Sea Level

Sea Level 500 5000 10000
152.5 1525 3050

Scale 1: 10 000 000; one inch to 160 miles. Conic Project

Elevations and depressions are given in feet

Arctic Circle

ICELAND

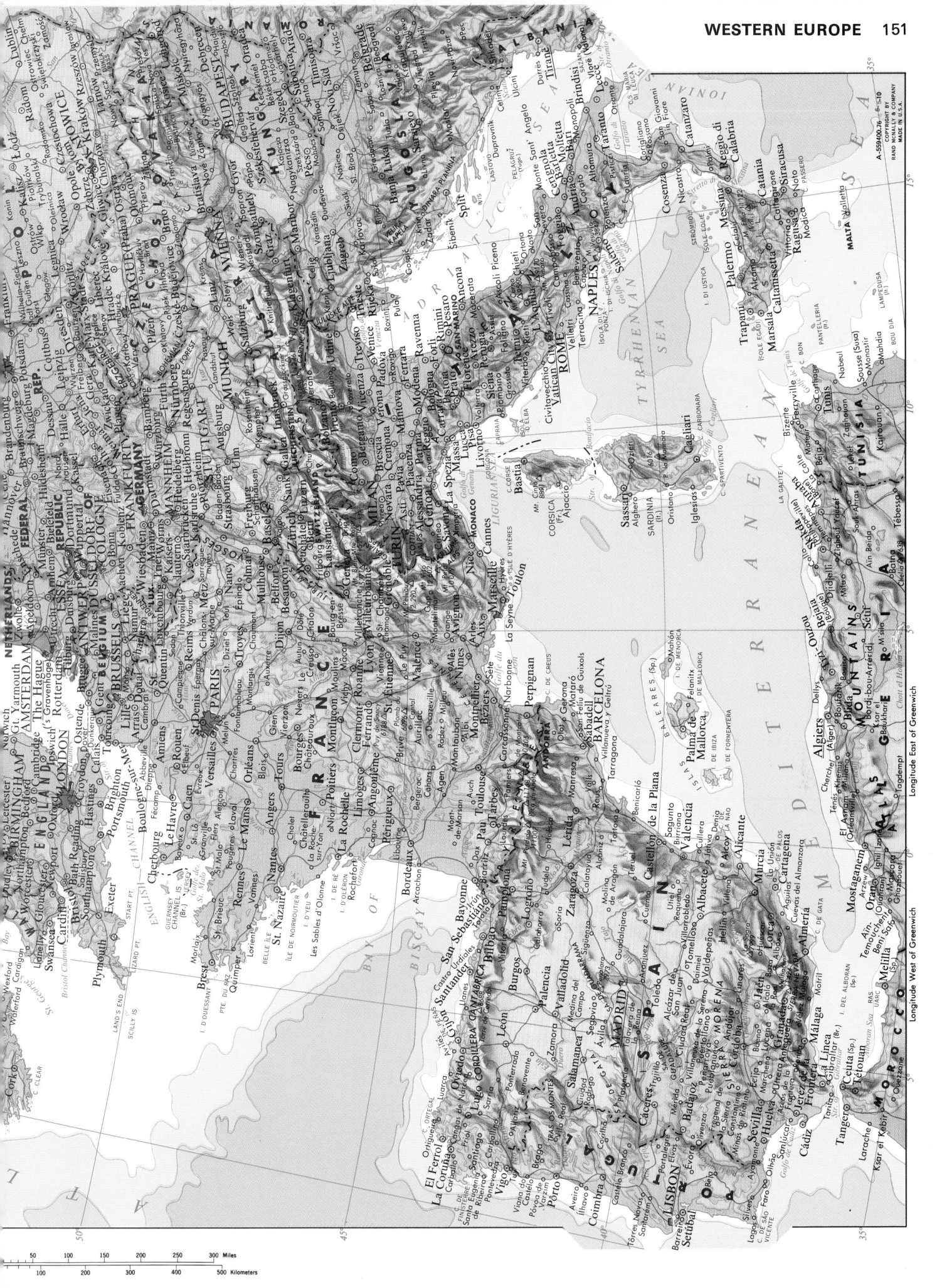
FRANCE
SPAIN
PORTUGAL
ITALY
SWITZERLAND
AUSTRIA
HUNGARY
YUGOSLAVIA
ALBANIA
CZECHOSLOVAKIA
BELGIUM
NETHERLANDS
FEDERAL REPUBLIC OF GERMANY
ENGLAND
ALGERIA
TUNISIA
MOROCCO
ATLAS MOUNTAINS
MEDITERRANEAN SEA
TYRRHENIAN SEA
ADRIATIC SEA
IONIAN SEA
LIGURIAN SEA
BAY OF BISCAY
ENGLISH CHANNEL
PARIS
MADRID
ROME
LISBON
LONDON
BRUSSELS
AMSTERDAM
VIENNA
BUDAPEST
PRAGUE
MUNICH
MILAN
TURIN
NAPLES
BARCELONA
Marseille
Algiers
CORSICA (Fr.)
SARDINIA (It.)
MALTA
Longitude West of Greenwich
Longitude East of Greenwich
0 50 100 150 200 250 300 Miles
0 100 200 300 400 500 Kilometers
A-559400-76 6 -10
COPYRIGHT BY RAND McNALLY & COMPANY MADE IN U.S.A.

ATLANTIC
OCEAN

BAY OF
BISCAY

GUERNSEY
CHANNEL IS.
(Br.) JERSEY
Golfe de
St. Malo

Cherbourg
Le Havre
Amiens
St.
Quentin
BEL.
Koblenz
FRANKFURT
PRAGUE
(Pra
Morlaix
Caen
Rouen
LUX.
Trier
Wiesbaden
Plauen
Brest
Flerso
Versailles
St. Denis
Reims
Verdun
Luxembourg
Worms
Darmstadt
Bamberg
Karlovy Vary
Plzeň
Quimper
St. Brieuc
Alençon
Chartres
PARIS
Châlons-sur-Marne
Metz
Thionville
Saarbrücken
Mannheim
Heidelberg
Würzburg
Nürnberg
BOHEMIAN
Lorient
Rennes
Fougères
Le Mans
Orléans
Montargis
Troyes
Toul
Nancy
Karlsruhe
Heilbronn
STUTTGART
Augsburg
Regensburg
Passau
BELLE ÎLE
Vannes
Laval
Angers
Tours
Blois
Bourges
Auxerre
Dijon
Mulhouse
Strasbourg
FED. REP. OF GER.
Ulm
MUNICH
Salzburg
ÎLE DE NOIRMOUTIER
Nantes
FRANCE
Poitiers
Châteauroux
Nevers
Besançon
Basel
Freiburg
Schaffhausen
Kempten
Rosenheim
Wels
I. D'YEU
La Roche-sur-Yon
Cholet
Vierzon
Moulins
Bourg-en-Bresse
Neuchâtel
Zürich
LIECHTENSTEIN
Innsbruck
Les Sables d'Olonne
Châtellerault
Vichy
Bern
Luzern
AUST
I. DE RÉ
La Rochelle
Limoges
Clermont-Ferrand
Roanne
Genève
Lausanne
SWITZERLAND
I. D'OLÉRON
Rochefort
Angoulême
St. Étienne
Lyon
Villeurbanne
MILAN
Rochefort
Cognac
Aurillac
Le Puy
Chambéry
TURIN

PORTUGAL
SPAIN
MADRID
LISBON

MOROCCO
ALGERIA
TUNISIA
TARABULU
(TRIPOLITANIA)

MEDITERRANEAN SEA
TYRRHENIAN SEA
LIGURIAN SEA

CORSICA (Fr.)
SARDINIA (It.)
SICILY

ROME
NAPLES
Palermo

HAMMADAH AL HAMRA

Relief

Meters	Feet
3050	10000
1525	5000
610	2000
305	1000
152.5	500
0 Sea Level	Sea Level 0
152.5	500
1525	5000
3050	10000

Below
Sea Level

A-558300-76
COPYRIGHT BY
RAND McNALLY & COMPANY
MADE IN U.S.A.

Scale 1: 10 000 000; one inch to 160 miles. Bonne's Proje
Elevations and depressions are given in feet

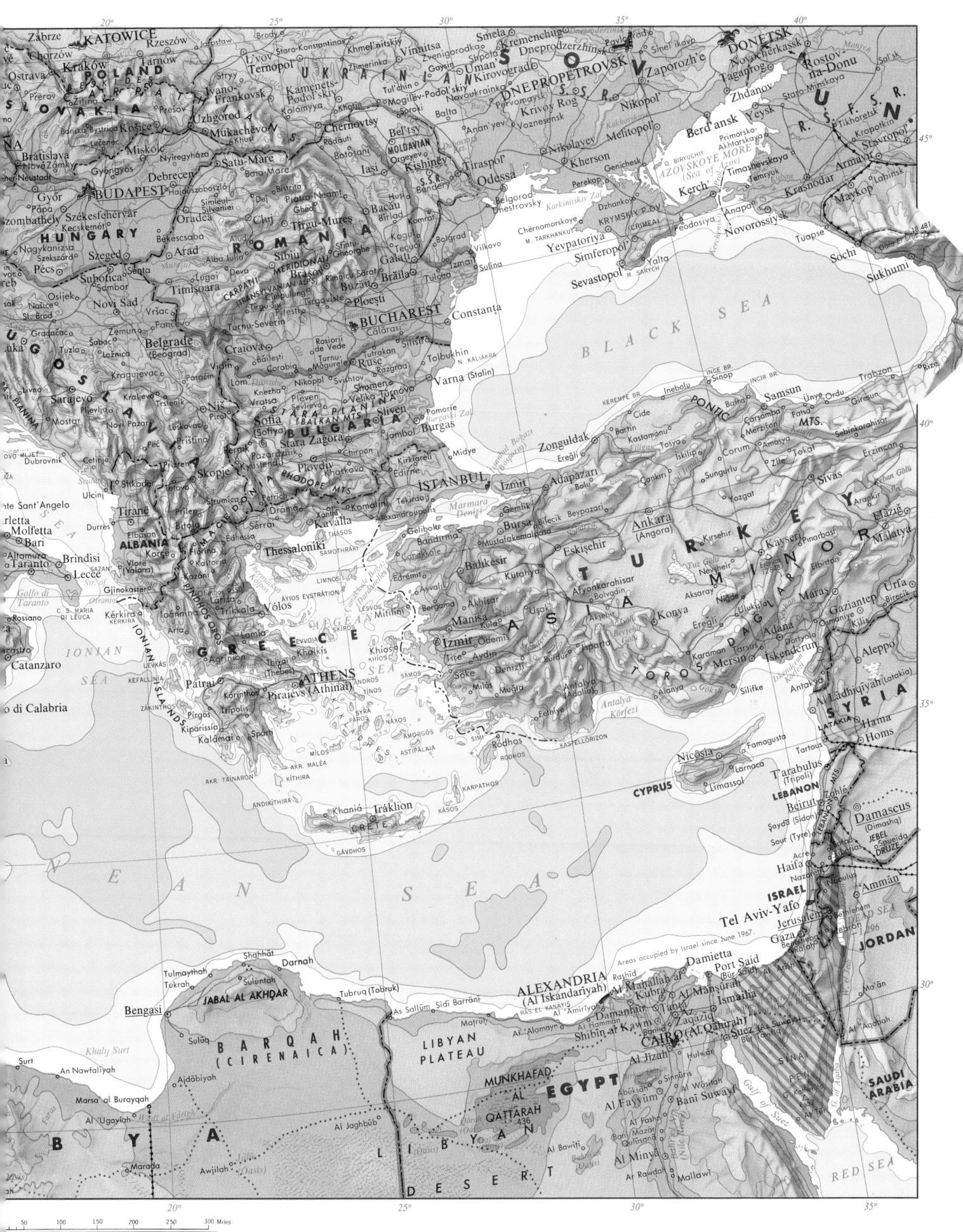

Map Labels

POLAND
SLOVAKIA
Katowice
Kraków
Rzeszów
Tarnów
Brody
L'vov
Jaroslaw
Staro-Konstantinov
Khmel'nitskiy
Vinnitsa
Smela
Kremenchug
Dneprodzerzhinsk
Pavlograd
DONETSK
Novocherkassk
Rostov-na-Donu
Ostrava
Přerov
Charzów
Zabrze
Żilina
Nové Zámky
Wiener-Neustadt
UKRAINIAN
Ternopol'
Zmerinka
Zvenigorodka
Uman'
Kirovograd
Dnepropetrovsk
Zaporozh'e
Taganrog
Sal'sk
R.S.F.S.R.

Bratislava
Banská Bystrica
Košice
Uzhgorod
Mukachevo
Khust
Ivano-Frankovsk
Kolomyya
Kamenets-Podol'skiy
Mogilëv-Podol'skiy
Gaysin
Balta
Novoukrainka
Pervomaysk
Krivoy Rog
Nikopol'
Sinel'nikovo
Zhdanov
Tikhoretsk
Armavir
Kropotkin
Stavropol'

Győr
Pápa
Szombathely
Zalaegerszeg
Nagykanizsa
Miskolc
Nyíregyháza
Satu-Mare
Baia-Mare
Dej
Bistrița
Rădăuți
Botoșani
Iași
Bel'tsy
MOLDAVIAN
Orgeyev
Kishinev
Tiraspol'
Bendery
S.S.R.
Soroki
Anan'yev
Voznesensk
Nikolayev
Kherson
Berdyansk
Primorsko-Akhtarskaya
Timashevskaya
Temryuk
Anapa
Novorossiysk
Krasnodar
Labinsk
Maykop

BUDAPEST
Hajdúszoboszló
Debrecen
Kecskemét
Szeged
Arad
Oradea
HUNGARY
Cluj
Tîrgu-Mureș
Sfîntu-Gheorghe
Kagul
Tecuci
Galați
Vilkovo
Sulina
Izmail
Odessa
Dnestrovskiy
Belgorod-Dnestrovskiy
Chërnomorskoye
M. Tarkhankut
Yevpatoriya
Simferopol'
KRYMSKIY P-OV (CRIMEA)
Dzhankoy
Genichesk
O. BIRYUCHIY
AZOVSKOYE MORE (Sea of Azov)
Kerch'
O. Dolgiy
Yeysk
Manych
El'brus

Pécs
Subotica
Sombor
Senta
Timișoara
Lugoj
Deva
ROMANIA
Alba Julia
Sibiu
Brașov
Cîmpulung
Pitești
Rîmnicu Sărat
Buzău
Brăila
Tulcea
Perekop
M. Kazantip
Feodosiya
Novorossiysk
Tuapse
Sochi
Sukhumi

Osijek
Sl. Brod
Novi Sad
Vršac
Pančevo
CARPAȚI MERIDIONALI
TRANSYLVANIAN ALPS
Tîrgu-Jiu
Târgoviște
Ploești
Rîmnicu Vîlcea
Fetești
Slobozia
Constanța
KARKINITSKIY ZAL.
Sevastopol'
M. Sarych
Yalta

YUGOSLAVIA
Zemun
Belgrade (Beograd)
Šabac
Loznica
Kragujevac
Craiova
Turnu-Severin
Băilești
Corabia
Turnu-Măgurele
Roșiori de Vede
Giurgiu
Tutrakan
Silistra
Călărași
BLACK SEA

Tuzla
Sarajevo
Valjevo
Čačak
Kraljevo
Trstenik
FRUŠKA GORA
Vidin
Lom
Kneža
Vratsa
Nikopol
Svishtov
Razgrad
Ruse
Shumen
Tolbukhin
N. KALIAKRA

Mostar
Pljevlja
Novi Pazar
Niš
Pirot
STARA PLANINA (BALKAN MTS.)
Sevlievo
Veliko Tŭrnovo
Sliven
Pomorie
Burgaski Zal.
Burgas

Dubrovnik
Cetinje
Peć
Priština
Sofia (Sofiya)
BULGARIA
Pazardzhik
Stara Zagora
Chirpan
Jambol

S. MARIJA DI LEUCA
Ulcinj
Skadar
Prizren
Skopje
RHODOPE MTS.
Plovdiv
Kŭrdzhali
Kirklareli
Edirne
Midye

Tirane
Durrës
Elbasan
Korçë
MACEDONIA
Petrich
Strumica
Drama
Xanthi
Komotini
Tekirdag
Marmara Denizi
ISTANBUL
Izmit
Adapazarı
Bolu
Çankırı
Sungurlu
Yozgat

ALBANIA
Vlorë (Valona)
SAZANI
Florina
Kastoria
Sérrai
Kavalla
THÁSOS
SAMOTHRÁKI
Gelibolu
Çanakkale
Bandırma
Bursa
Bilecik
Beypazarı
Ankara (Angora)
Kırşehir
Kayseri

Brindisi
Lecce
Gjirokastër
Ioánnina
Árta
PINDOS OROS
Trikkala
Lárisa
Vólos
LIMNOS
ÁYIOS EVSTRÁTIOS
Edremit
Ayvalık
Bergama
Akhisar
Manisa
Kütahya
Eskişehir
Afyonkarahisar
Bolvadin
Aksaray
Niğde
Ulukışla
Maraş

Altamura
Taranto
Rossano
C. S. MARIA DI LEUCA
Kérkira (KÉRKIRA)
IONIAN ISLANDS
LEVKÁS
KEFALLINÍA
ZÁKINTHOS
Agrínion
Thívai (Thebes)
Khalkís
EVVOIA
SKÍROS
Lamía
Mitilíni
LESVOS
Khíos
KHÍOS
Izmir
Ödemiş
Tire
Aydın
Uşak
Burdur
Isparta
Konya
Ereğli
Karaman
TOROS DAGLARI
Adana
Osmaniye
Kilis
Gaziantep
Birecik
Urfa

IONIAN SEA
Di Calabria
Pátrai
Korinthos
ATHENS
Piraiévs (Athínai)
SYRA
ÁNDROS
TÍNOS
SÁMOS
Söke
Milás
Muğla
Denizli
Antalya
Adalaiya
Antalya Körfezi
Alanya
Silifke
Mersin
İskenderun
Antakya
Aleppo
SYRIA

Catanzaro
Kateríni
Tríkala
Kalámai
Spárti
PÁROS
NÁXOS
AMORGÓS
ASTIPÁLAIA
SÍMI
Ródhos
RODHOS
KASTELLÓRIZON
Finike
Göksu
Al Ladhiqiyah (Latakia)
LATAKIA
Hama
Homs

Pírgos
Kiparissía
Trípolis
MÍLOS
AKR. MALÉA
KÍTHIRA
KÁRPATHOS
KÁSOS
Nicosia
Famagusta
Tartous
ŞAM JEBEL
Tarabulus (Tripoli)
LEBANON
Beirut
Damascus (Dimashq)

ANDIKÍTHIRA
Khaniá
Iráklion
CRETE
GÁVDHOS
Limassol
CYPRUS
Şaydā (Sidon)
Sour (Tyre)
LEBANON MTS.
JEBEL DRUZE
As Suwaydā'

MEDITERRANEAN SEA
AEGEAN SEA
AKR. TAÍNARON
Acre
Haifa
Nazareth
ISRAEL
Tel Aviv-Yafo
Jerusalem
Gaza
Amman
JORDAN
DEAD SEA

Areas occupied by Israel since June 1967

Tulmaytha
Shahhāt
Darnah
Sulūntah
Tūkrah
JABAL AL AKHDAR
Tubruq (Tobruk)
As Sallūm
Sīdī Barrāni
Marsá Matrūh
Rashid
Damietta
Port Said (Būr Sa'īd)
Al Manşūrah
Ismailia
Suez
Mā'in
Al 'Aqabah

Bengasi
Ajdābiyah
Sulūq
BARQAH (CIRENAICA)
LIBYAN PLATEAU
As Sallūm
Al 'Alamayn
Al Hammām
Abū Qīr
ALEXANDRIA (Al Iskandarīyah)
RAS EL KANAYIS
Al Ḩamām
Shibīn al Kawm
Damanhūr
Tanta
Zagāzīg
CAIRO (Al Qāhirah)
Ḩulwān
Al Jīzah
Būr Tawfīq
SINAI
SAUDI ARABIA

Surt
An Nawfaliyah
Marsá al Burayqah
LIBYA
Al Jaghbūb
MUNKHAFAD AL QATTĀRAH 436
EGYPT
Sīwah
Banī Suwayf
Gulf of Suez

Marada
Awjilah (Oasis)
LIBYAN DESERT
Al Baḩrīyah
Al Fayyūm
Al Fashn
Banī Mazār
Al Minyā
Mallawī
RED SEA
Gulf of Aqaba

BLACK SEA
PONTIC MTS.
Zonguldak
Ereğli
Kastamonu
Bartın
İnebolu
Sinop
Samsun
Ünye
Ordu
Giresun
Trabzon
Rize
KEREMPE BR.
INCE BR.
INCIR BR.
Cide
Tosya
İskilip
Çorum
Amasya
Merzifon
Sivas
Erzincan
Elazığ
Malatya
ASIA MINOR
TURKEY

Scale

50 100 150 200 250 300 Miles
100 200 300 400 500 Kilometers

154

Same scale as main map

ATLANTIC

HERMA NESS
UNST
YELL
SHETLAND
St. Magnus Bay
ISLANDS
(Br.)
Lerwick
MAINLAND
FOULA
SUMBURGH HD.

OCEAN

FAIR

WESTRAY
N. RONALDSAY
ROUSAY
SANDAY
STRONSAY
Kirkwall ORKNEY
MAINLAND
ISLANDS
HOY (Br.)
S. RONALDSAY
Pentland Firth
Thurso
DUNCANSBY HD.
SCOTLAND

©RMCN.

ATLANTIC

OCEAN

Relief

Meters	Feet
610	2000
305	1000
152.5	500
0	Sea Level	0
152.5	500	Below
1525	5000	Sea Level

A-559700-76 -6-5-10
COPYRIGHT BY
RAND McNALLY & COMPANY
MADE IN U.S.A.

HOY
N. RONALDSAY
Pentland Firth
DUNCANSBY HD.
CAPE WRATH
Thurso
Wick
Ben Hope
3040
BUTT OF LEWIS
FLANNAN IS.
LEWIS
Stornoway
HEBRIDES
ST. KILDA
HARRIS
NORTH
UIST
SOUTH
UIST
SKYE
INNER
Cullin Sd.
RHUM
The Hebrides
HEBRIDES
BARRA
ISLES
COLL
TIREE
MULL
Mallaig
Ben Alder
3383
Fort William
Ben Nevis
4406
Oban
COLONSAY
ISLAY

NORTHWEST HIGHLANDS
Ben More
Assynt 3273
Ben Dearg
3547
SCOTLAND
Garron
Shin
Ben Macdhui
4296
GRAMPIAN MTS.
Dornoch
Dornoch Firth
TARBAT NESS
Dingwall
Moray Firth
Nairn
Inverness
Elgin
Buckie
Banff
KINNAIRDS HD.
Fraserburgh
Peterhead
Ballater
Aberdeen
Stonehaven
Forfar
Montrose
Arbroath
Dundee
Perth
St. Andrews
FIFE NESS
Firth of Tay
Buchavoy
Kirkcaldy
Dunfermline
Firth of Forth
Dunbar
Stirling
Falkirk
Berwick
HOLY
FARNE IS.
Helensburgh
Dumbarton
EDINBURGH
Musselburgh
Greenock
Clydebank
Motherwell
GLASGOW
Paisley
Rothesay
Lanark
Peebles
Galashiels
Kilmarnock
Irvine
Ayr
Hawick
CHEVIOT HILLS
Firth of Lorne
Campbelltown
SOUTHERN UPLANDS
Dumfries
Tweed
Girvan
Stranraer
Luce Bay
Solway Firth
Carlisle
NEWCASTLE-ON-TYNE
Blyth
Tynemouth
South Shields
Sunderland
Gateshead
Durham
Hartlepool
Workington
Whitehaven
ST. BEES HD.
Stockton
Middlesbro
Darlington (Teessi
LAKE DISTRICT
Windermere
Northallerton
NORTH YORK MOORS
Kendal
Barrow
Lancaster
WALNEY

The Minch
The Little Minch
OUTER
Sea of
The Hebrides
Passage of Oronsay
Sound of Jura
Firth of Clyde
MALIN HD.
Lough Swilly
TORY
MT. ERRIGAL
ARAN
Carndonagh
Lough Foyle
RATHLIN
ANTRIM MTS.
Coleraine
Londonderry
SPERRIN MTS.
Strabane
NORTHERN
Omagh
ULSTER
Belfast
IRELAND
Lisburn
Newtownards
Enniskillen
Monaghan
Armagh
Lurgan
Belfast Lough
MOURNE MTS.
Strangford Lough
Dundrum Bay
North Channel
MULLET PEN.
Killala
Ballina
MTS. OF MAYO
Sligo
Cavan
Dundalk
Dundalk Bay
ISLE OF MAN (Br.)
Ramsey
Douglas
IRISH SEA
ACHILL
CLARE
Clew B.
Castlebar
Boyle
CONNACHT
Longford
Drogheda
Barrow
Westport
Claremorris
Lough Mask
Lough Corrib
Athlone
Lough Ree
Mullingar
Sheelin
MTS. OF CONNEMARA
Clifden
SLYNE HEAD
Galway
Ballinasloe
Grand Canal
Royal Canal
Dublin
(Baile Atha Cliath)
Dun Laoghaire
Bray
SKERRIES
Blackpool
Burnley
Halifax
Bradford
York
Blackburn
Preston
Rochdale
Wakefield
LEEDS
Southport
Bolton
Oldham
Doncaster
Wigan
Huddersfield
Bootle
St. Helens
Stockport
Sheffield
LIVERPOOL
MANCHESTER
Birkenhead
Chester
Crewe
Chesterfield
Lincoln
Galway Bay
ARAN IS.
IRELAND
(EIRE)
Tullamore
Kildare
Athy
Mt. Lugnaquilla
3039
WICKLOW MTS.
Cill Mantain
(Wicklow)
Arklow
Ennis
Lough Derg
Nenagh
Thurles
LEINSTER
Carlow
Kilkenny
Enniscorthy
New Ross
Wexford
R. Shannon
Limerick
Tipperary
MUNSTER
BEVERLEY E.
YORKSHIRE WOLDS
Morecambe Bay
Loop Head
Kilrush
GALTY MTS.
Clonmel
Carrick
CARNSORE PT.
Stoke-on-Trent
Nottingham
Stafford
Derby
Shrewsbury
Burton-on-Trent
Welshpool
BERWYN MTS.
Festiniog
Wolverhampton
Walsall
Leicester
Dudley
W. Bromwich
BIRMINGHAM
Coventry
Peter
BRANDON HILL
3127
Tralee
Killarney
Mallow
Fermoy
KNOCKMEALDOWN MTS.
Dungarvan
Waterford
Youghal
CAMBRIAN MTS.
Aberystwyth
Cardigan Bay
SOUTH SHROPSHIRE HILLS
Worcester
Warwick
Leamington
Stratford
Northamp
Bedford
GREAT BLASKET
DINGLE BAY
Dingle
MTS. OF KERRY
3414
Caragh
SHEHY MTS.
Killarney
Lee
Cork
Cobh
Cork Harbor
Youghal Bay
RADNOR FOREST
Hereford
Cheltenham
Gloucester
Bedford
Cardigan
BRECON BEACONS
Merthyr Tydfil
Abergavenny
COTSWOLD HILLS
Oxford
Aylesbury
Hertfo
St. Albans
VALENCIA
Bantry
Skibbereen
Kinsale Harbor
OLD HEAD OF KINSALE
Clonakilty Bay
C. CLEAR
Bantry Bay
ST. DAVID'S HD.
Carmarthen
St. BRIDES BAY
Milford Haven
Pembroke
Llanelly
Swansea
Neath
Aberdare
Rhondda
Newport
Cardiff
Swansea Bay
Bristol Channel
NYMPHE BANK
Llandudno
ANGLESEY
HOLY
Holyhead
Bangor
Conway
Denbigh
LLEYN PROMONTORY
Snowdon
3560
Carnarvon Bay
BARDSEY
Tremadoc Bay
Wrexham
Merthyr
High Wycombe
Windsor
Willesde
Newbury
Reading
LONDON
Croydon
Guil
ST. GEORGE'S CHANNEL
SALISBURY PLAIN
NORTH DOWNS
HAMPSHIRE DOWNS
Winchester
SOUTH DOWNS
Chichester
Tunbri
Wort
Aldershot
LUNDY
Ilfracombe
Barnstaple
EXMOOR
Weston-super-Mare
Bath
Bristol
Swindon
Salisbury
WESTERN DOWNS
HARTLAND PT.
BLACKDOWN HILLS
Taunton
Yeovil
Dorchester
HONITON HILLS
Exeter
Exmouth
Weymouth
Poole
Bournemouth
ISLE OF WIGHT
Cowes
Newport
Ryde
Southampton
Portsmouth
Wort
BODMIN MOOR
DARTMOOR
Launceston
Bodmin
Plymouth
Torquay
(Torbay)
Camborne
Truro
Penzance
LAND'S END
Falmouth
START PT.
LIZARD PT.
ST. ALBANS HD.
SCILLY IS.

ENGLISH

UNITE
U N I T E
K I N G D O
KINGDO

Longitude West of Greenwich

Scale 1: 4 000 000; one inch to 64 miles. Conic Proje
Elevations and depressions are given in feet

NORWAY

Egersund
Sogndal
Flekkefjord
Grimstad
Arendal
Kristiansand
Lillesand
Farsund
Mandal
LINDESNES

Skagen
SKAGEN
Göteborg
Kungälv
Mölndal
Alingsås
Ulricehamn
Borås

SWEDEN

Skagerrak

Hjørring
Frederikshavn
LÆSØ
Varberg
Bolmen

Brønderslev
Jammerbugt

Ålborg
Limfjorden
Anholt
Falkenberg
Oskarström

Thisted
Løgstør
Nykøbing
Hobro
Mariager
Mariager Fjord

Skive
Viborg
Randers
Grenå
Halmstad
Laholm

Skälderviken
Ängelholm

Struer
Holstebro
Silkeborg
Hillerød
Helsingborg

Nissum Fjord
JYLLAND
Århus
Skanderborg
Helsingør
Landskrona

Ringkøbing
Herning
Nykøbing S
SJÆLLAND
København (COPENHAGEN)
Lund

Ringkøbing Fjord
Horsens
SAMSØ
Roskilde
Malmö

DENMARK
Vejle
Kalundborg
Ringsted
Køge
Trelleborg

Varde
Fredericia
Bogense
Slagelse

Esbjerg
Kolding
Middelfart
Odense
Næstved

FANØ
Ribe
Assens
Nyborg
Korsør
Vordingborg
MØN

RØMØ
Haderslev
Fåborg
Svendborg
Rudkøbing
Nakskov
FALSTER
Nykøbing Fl.

NORTH
Åbenrå
Lille Bælt
LANGELAND
Maribo

SYLT
Tønder
Sønderborg
ALS
AERØ
LOLLAND

FØHR
Flensburg
FEHMARN

FRISIAN IS.
Schleswig
SCHLESWIG
Kiel Bay
BALTIC SEA

Husum
Eckernförde
Kiel
Rostock
Barth

Tønning
Rendsburg
Lübecker Bucht

HELGOLAND
Heide
Neumünster
HOLSTEIN
Neustadt
Wismar
Güstrow

Itzehoe
Bad Oldesloe
Lübeck
Ratzeburg
Teterow

Cuxhaven
Elmshorn
Schwerin
GERMAN
Parchim

Bremerhaven
Stade
HAMBURG
Bergedorf
Ludwigslust
MECKLENBURG
DEMOCRATIC

ISLANDS
NORDERNEY LANGEOOG
Norden
Wilhelmshaven
Lüneburg
LÜNEBURGER
Perleberg

JUIST
BÖRKUM
Emden
Leer
Bremen
HEIDE
Ülzen
Wittenberge
REPUBLIC

TERSCHELLING
FRISIAN
AMELAND
Delfzijl
Papenburg
Delmenhorst
Verden
Soltau
Salzwedel

VLIELAND
Leeuwarden
Groningen
Oldenburg
Delmenhorst
NIEDERSACHSEN
Stendal

TEXEL
Harlingen
Meppen
Lingen
Nienburg
Celle
Gardelegen
Tangermünde

Waddenzee
Emmen
Nordhorn
Minden
Hannover
Helmstedt
Schönebeck

Den Helder
Meppel
Rheine
Hameln
Braunschweig
Neuhaldensleben

IJsselmeer
Zwolle
Almelo
Osnabrück
Hildesheim
Goslar
Magdeburg

Alkmaar
NETHERLANDS
Hengelo
FED. REP. OF
Herford
Wolfenbüttel
Halberstadt
Bernberg

Zaandam
Deventer
Enschede
Bielefeld
GERMANY
Stassfurt
Quedlinburg
Blankenburg
Aschersleben

Haarlem
AMSTERDAM
Apeldoorn
Gronau
Münster
Gütersloh
Detmold
Einbeck
Northeim
Eisleben

Leiden
Utrecht
Rheden
Arnhem
Ahlen
Paderborn
Göttingen
Nordhausen
Halle
Merseburg

The Hague
('s Gravenhage)
Delft
Coesfeld
Hamm
Lippstadt
Soest
Heiligenstadt
Sangerhausen

Vlaardingen
Dordrecht
Nijmegen
Kleve
Wesel
Bocholt
Nordheim
Mühlhausen
Sondershausen

ROTTERDAM
Maas
Waal
Breda
's Hertogenbosch
Gelsenkirchen
Dortmund
THÜRINGEN

Bergen
op Zoom
Tilburg
Helmond
Duisburg
Oberhausen
Iserlohn
Kassel
Eschwege

Oosterschelde
Eindhoven
Weert
Mönchengladbach
Mülheim
ESSEN
Hagen
Lüdenscheid
Bad Hersfeld
Eisenach
Erfurt
Weimar

Vlissingen
Turnhout
Roermond
Solingen
Wuppertal
NORDRHEIN-WESTFALEN
Gotha
Jena

Zeebrugge
ANTWERP
Mechelen
DÜSSELDORF
Siegen
Marburg
Schmalkalden
Rudolstadt

Oostende
Brugge
Gent
Heerlen
Düren
COLOGNE (Köln)
Gummersbach
Giessen
Fulda
Zella-Mehlis
Ilmenau
Saalfeld

Dunkerque
Aalst
Leuven
Maastricht
Bonn
Siegburg
Meiningen
Suhl
Sonneberg

Calais
FLANDERS
Torhout
Roeselare
Anderlecht
Eupen
Ahrweiler
Neuwied
WESTERWALD
Hildburghausen
Neustadt b.C.
Coburg

St. Omer
Ieper
Kortrijk
BRUSSELS
Herstal
Verviers
Andernach
Bad Homburg
TAUNUS
Bad Kissingen
Kulmbach

Boulogne-
sur-Mer
Armentières
Lille
Roubaix
BELGIUM
Nivelles
Huy
Liège
Spa
Malmédy
Koblenz
FRANKFURT
AM MAIN
Schweinfurt

Étaples
Béthune
Douai
Mons
Namur
EIFEL
Mayen
HUNSRÜCK
Hofheim
Offenbach
Bayreuth
Bamberg

Hesdin
Arras
Denain
Valenciennes
Charleroi
Dinant
Boppard
Bad
Kreuznach
Wiesbaden
Hanau
Aschaffenburg
Würzburg
Forchheim
Erlangen

Crécy
Cambrai
Maubeuge
Givet
ARDENNES
Bastogne
Wittlich
Kirn
Bingen
Mainz
Bad
Darmstadt
Kitzingen

St. Valéry
Abbeville
Le Tréport
Fourmies
LUX.
Bad Homburg

Somme
FRANCE

Great Yarmouth
Lowestoft
Norwich
Thetford

Ipswich
Harwich

Southend-
on-Sea
R. Thames
Sheerness
Margate
North Foreland
Ramsgate
Canterbury
Maidstone
Dover
Folkestone

Strait of Dover

King's Lynn
Waveney

DOGGER
BANK
60–120 Ft.

NORTH SEA

10 20 30 40 50 60 70 80 90 100 110 120 Miles
20 40 60 80 100 120 140 160 180 200 Kilometers

NORWEGIAN SEA

SMÖLA
Kristiansund
AVERÖY
Molde
Ålesund
GURSKÖY
Hagefjord
TROLLHEIMEN
Veblungsnaes
Opdal
Snöhetta 7500 △

Trondheim (Nidaros)
Stjördalshalsen
Orkdal
Stören
Gula
Röros
Aursunden
Tynset
Faemund

Syltfjällen 5781 △
Helagsfjället 5892 △
Östersund
Ragunda
Storsjön
Sollefteå
Kramfors
HEMSÖ
Bräcke
Ånge
Torp
Stöde
Härnösand
Njurunda
Sundsvall
ALNÖ
Hässjö
Storsjö
Sveg
Ramsjö
Hassela
Sånfjället 4190 △ (NATIONAL PARK)
Töfsingdalens (NATIONAL PARK)
Stödjan 3924 △
Holmsjön
Hudiksvall
HORNSLANDET
△ 3891
Älvdalen
Morastrand
Ljusdal
Enånger
Orsa
Rättvik
Siljan
Leksand
Bollnäs
Söderhamn
Hamrånge
Ljungan

BREMANGERLAND
VÅGSÖY
Eid
Florö
Nordfjord
ATLÖY
INDRE SOLUND
YTRE SOLUND
RÅDÖY

JOSTEDALSBREEN
DOVRE FJELL
JOTUN FJELL
Galdhöpiggen 8097 △ △ Glittertinden 8104
Bövra
Ottarand

Leikanger
Sogndal
VIK
Lærdalsören
Lærdal
Flåm
Gudvangen
Evanger
Dale
Voss
Ulvik
Eidfjord
Hardanger Jöklen 6342

Lillehammer
Fagernes
Sör Aurdal
Ringsaker
Gjövik
Raufoss
Skreia
Röikenviken
Hamar
Mjösa
Elverum
Flisen
Limedsforsen
Torsby
Appelbo
Ludvika
Smedjebacken
Avesta
Krylbo
Falun
Borlänge
Säter
Hedemora
Kopparberg
Västanfors
Sala
Heby
Lena
Tierp

Äppelbo
Sunne
Charlottenberg
Arvika
Kil
Forshaga
Noro
Filipstad
Karlstad
Kristinehamn
Jannelund
Säffle
Åmål
Hallsberg
Örebro
Arboga
Köping
Lindesberg
Torshälla
Eskilstuna
Strängnäs
Mariefred
Södertälje
Malmköping
Trosa
Nynäshamn

Uppsala
Sigtuna
Enköping
Västerås
Sundbyberg

NORWAY

Göl
Hen
Kröderen
Rollag
Sigdal
Rjukan
Tinnosset
Notodden
Dalen
Saude
Haugesund
KOPERVIK
UTSIRA
KARMÖY
Skudeneshavn
Stavanger
Sandnes
Time
Egersund

RJUVEN-FJELL
HARDANGER FJELL
Odda
Jondal
Os
STORD
BÖMLO

Hönefoss
Sylling
Drammen
Svelvik
Holmsbu
Holmestrand
Horten
Tönsberg
Sandefjord
Larvik
Brevik
Porsgrunn
Skien
Tveitsund
Byglandsfjord
Risör
Tvedestrand
Grimstad
Lillesand
Kristiansand
Mandal
Farsund
Flekkefjord
Sogndal
LINDESNES

Oslo
Lilleström
Skulerud
Eidsberg
Strömstad
Grebbestad
Fjällbacka
Uddevalla
Lysekil
Marstrand
Kungälv
SKAGEN
Skagen
Göteborg
Mölndal
Kungsbacka
Borås
Mölnlycke
Alingsås
Börn
Ulricehamn
Jönköping
Nässjö
Eksjö
Vetlanda
Virserum
Huskvarna
Vimmerby
Gränna
Tranås
Mjölby
Ödeshög
Älvidaberg
Linköping
Norrköping
Söderköping
Nyköping
Kolmården
Gamleby
Västervik
Figeholm
Oskarshamn
Mönsterås
GOTLAND
Visby
Klintehamn
ÖLAND
Borgholm

Kongsvinger
Torsby
Eidsvoll
Kongsberg
Moss
Hölen
Drööbak
Sarpsborg
Fredrikstad
Halden
Skulerud

Mjösen
Töreboda
Mariestad
Lidköping
Vänersborg
Skara
Skövde
Tidaholm
Falköping
Vara
Trollhättan
Vänern
Hjo
Vadstena
Motala
Vättern
Skänninge

DENMARK

NORTH SEA
Hjörring
Frederikshavn
LÆSÖ
Saeby
Brönderslev
Ålborg
Norre Sundby
Nibe
ÖGsör
MORS
Nyköbing
Hobro
Mariager
Randers
Grenå
Ebeltoft
Århus
Skanderborg
Silkeborg
Herning
Ringköbing
Holstebro
Struer
Skive
Viborg
Lemvig
Thisted
Nyköbing Fl.
Limfjorden
Mariager Fjord
ANHOLT

Varberg
Falkenberg
Oskarström
Halmstad
Nyhem
Laholm
Markaryd
Båstad
Ängelholm
Klippan
Hässleholm
Helsingborg
Landskrona
Lund
Malmö
Trelleborg
Ystad
Skurup
Svedala
Skanör
SANDHAMMAREN
Simrishamn
Åhus
Kristianstad
Sölvesborg
Karlshamn
Ronneby
Karlskrona
Tingsryd
Almhult
Växjö
Alvesta
Värnamo
Ljungby
Nybro
Kalmar
Mörbylånga
Hanöbukten
BORNHOLM (Den.)
Allinge
Svaneke
Rönne
Aakirkeby
Neksö

Ringköbing Fjord
Skern
JYLLAND
Vejle
Horsens
Skanderborg
Varde
Esbjerg
FANÖ
NORTH FRISIAN ISLANDS
SYLT
FÖHR
Tönder
RÖMÖ
ALS
Sönderborg
Åbenrå
Haderslev
Kolding
Middelfart
FYN
Bogense
Assens
Fåborg
Svendborg
Odense
Nyborg
Korsör
Slagelse
Ringsted
SJÆLLAND
Holbæk
Kalundborg
Roskilde
COPENHAGEN (Köbenhavn)
Helsingör
Frederikssund
Hillerød
Köge Bugt
Köge
Vordingborg
Nakskov
LANGE LAND
RUDköbing
LOLLAND
Nyköbing
FALSTER
MÖN
Gedser
Nyköbing Fl.
AERÖ
LILLE BÆLT

Flensburg
SCHLESWIG
Schleswig
Husum
Eckernförde
Tönning
Heide
Rendsburg
Kiel
Neustadt
Neumünster
HOLSTEIN
FED. REP. OF GERMANY
Lübeck
Cuxhaven
Elbe
HELGOLAND
BLÅVANDS HUK
Ribe
HO

Fehmarn
Kiel Bay
RÜGEN
C. ARKONA
Bergen
Sassnitz
Stralsund
Greifswald
Barth
Warnemünde
Rostock
GERMAN DEMOCRATIC REPUBLIC
Wismar
Wolgast
Pomeranian Bay
Swinoujscie
Kamień Pomorski
POLAND
Kolobrzeg
Leba
Ustka
Wejherowo
Lebork
Dartowo
Stupsk
Gdynia
Longitude East of Greenwich

SKAGERRAK
KATTEGAT
BALTIC SEA
Öresund
Limfjorden
Nissum Fjord
Storå
Gudenå

Relief

Meters		Feet
1525		5000
610		2000
305		1000
152.5		500
0	Sea Level	0
152.5		500 Below Sea Level

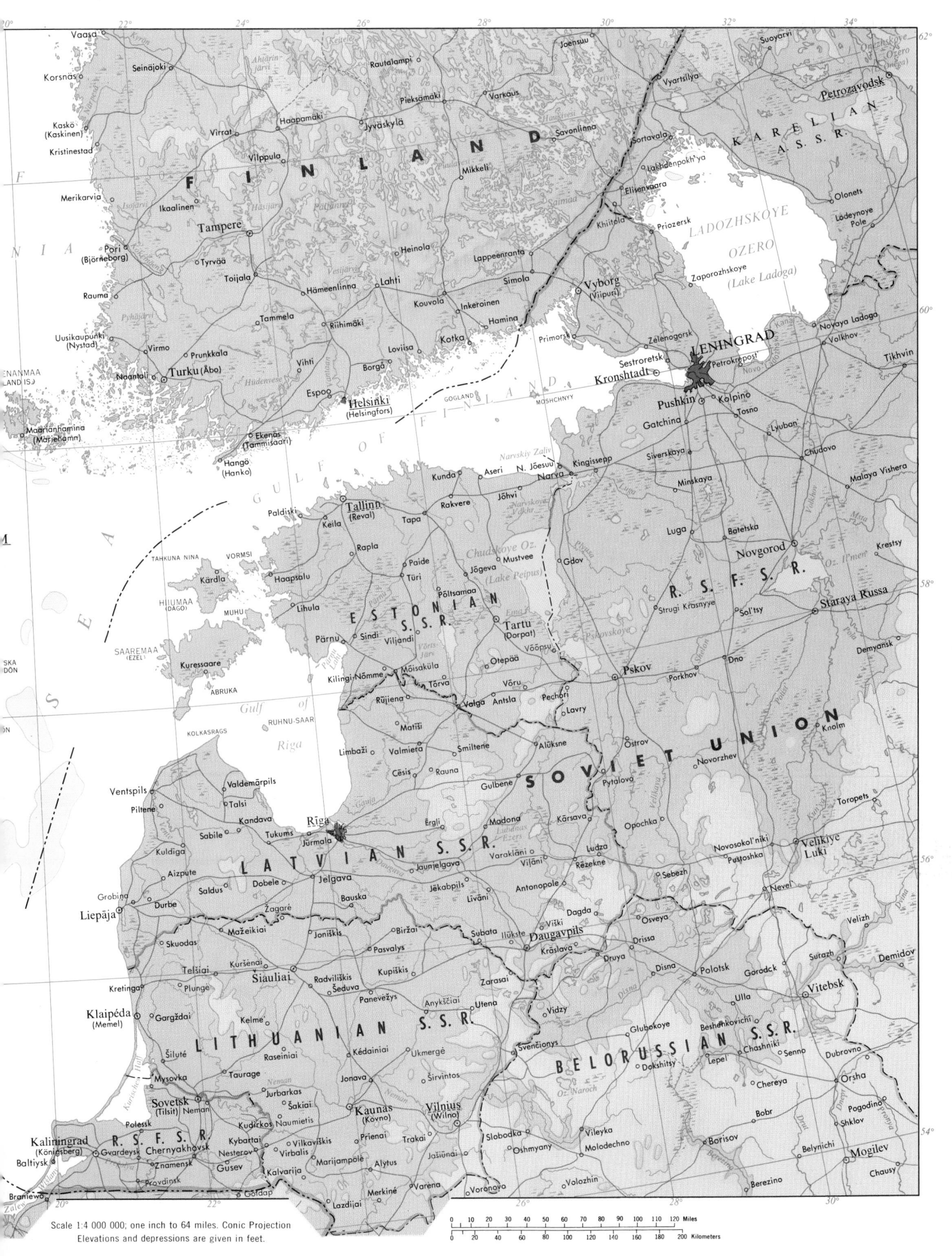

Vaasa
Seinäjoki
Korsnäs
Kaskö (Kaskinen)
Kristinestad
Merikarvia
Ikaalinen
Pori (Björneborg)
Tyrvää
Rauma
Toijala
Uusikaupunki (Nystad)
Virmo
Naantali
Turku (Åbo)
Espoo
ENANMAA LAND IS.)
Maarianhamina (Mariehamn)
Ekenäs (Tammisaari)
Hangö (Hanko)

Virrat
Vilppula
Tampere
Tammela
Hämeenlinna
Prunkkala
Riihimäki
Vihti
Borgå
Helsinki (Helsingfors)

Haapamäki
Jyväskylä
Heinola
Lahti
Kouvola
Loviisa
Hamina

FINLAND

Pieksämäki
Mikkeli
Lappeenranta
Simola
Inkeroinen
Kotka
Primorsk

Rautalampi
Varkaus
Savonlinna

Joensuu
Vyartsilya
Sortavala
Lakhdenpokh'ya
Elisenvaara
Khiitola
Priozersk
Zaporozhskoye

Petrozavodsk
KARELIAN A.S.S.R.
Olonets
Lödeynoye Pole

LADOZHSKOYE OZERO (Lake Ladoga)

Vyborg (Viipuri)
Zelenogorsk
Sestroretsk
Kronshtadt
Pushkin
Gatchina

LENINGRAD
Petrokrepost'
Kolpino
Tosno
Lyuban'

Novaya Ladoga
Volkhov
Tikhvin

GULF OF FINLAND
GGLAND
MOSHCHNYY

Narvskiy Zaliv
Kunda
Aseri
N. Jõesuu
Narva
Kingissepp
Siverskaya
Luga
Botetsk
Novgorod
Chudovo
Malaya Vishera

Tallinn (Reval)
Keila
Paldiski
Tapa
Rakvere
Jõhvi
Narvskoye Vdkhr.

TAHKUNA NINA
VORMSI
Rapla
Paide
Mustvee
Gdov
Strugi Krasnyye
Krestsy

Kärdla
HIIUMAA (DAGO)
MUHU
Haapsalu
Türi
Jõgeva
Chudskoye Oz. (Lake Peipus)
Lihula
Põltsamaa
ESTONIAN S.S.R.
Tartu (Dorpat)
Võõpsu
Pskov
Dno
Staraya Russa
Oz. Il'men'
Demyansk

SAAREMAA (EZEL)
Pärnu
Sindi
Viljandi
Võrts Järv
Otepää
Võru
Strugi Krasnyye
Pskovskoye
Sol'tsy

Kuressaare
Kilingi-Nõmme
Mõisaküla
Tõrva
Antsla
Pechori
Lavry
Ostrov
Novorzhev

ABRUKA
Gulf of Riga
RUHNU-SAAR
Matiši
Rūjiena
Valga
Smiltene
Alūksne
Pytalovo
Toropets

KOLKASRAGS
Limbaži
Valmiera
Cēsis
Rauna
Gulbene
SOVIET UNION
Knolm

Ventspils
Valdemārpils
Madona
Kārsava
Ostrov
Novosokol'niki
Velikiye Luki

Piltene
Talsi
Ērgli
Ludza
Opochka
Pustoshka
Nevel

Sabile
Kandava
Rīga
LATVIAN S.S.R.
Jaunjelgava
Varakļāni
Viļāni
Rēzekne
Sebezh

Kuldīga
Tukums
Jūrmala
Jelgava
Jēkabpils
Līvāni
Antonopole
Osveya

Aizpute
Dobele
Bauska
Subata
Višķi
Dagda
Drissa
Velizh

Grobiņa
Durbe
Saldus
Žagarē
Joniškis
Ilūkste
Daugavpils
Krāslava
Druya
Disna
Polotsk
Gorodok
Demidov

Liepāja
Mažeikiai
Pasvalys
Birżai
Zarasai
Kraslava
Ulla
Vitebsk

Skuodas
Telšiai
Kuršenai
Radviliškis
Kupiškis
Vidzy
Glubokoye
Beshenkovichi

Kretinga
Plungė
Šiauliai
Šeduva
Panevežys
Anykščiai
Utena
Svir'
Lepel
Chashniki
Senno
Dubrovno

Klaipėda (Memel)
Gargždai
Kelmė
Raseiniai
Kėdainiai
Ukmergė
Švenčionys
Glubokoye
Dokshitsy
Chereya
Orsha

LITHUANIAN S.S.R.
Šilutė
Tauragė
Jurbarkas
Jonava
Širvintos
Oz. Naroch
BELORUSSIAN S.S.R.
Bobr
Pogodino

Mysovka
Šakiai
Kaunas (Kovno)
Vilnius (Wilno)
Trakai
Slobodka
Oshmyany
Molodechno
Vileyka
Borisov
Shklov
Mogilev

Sovetsk (Tilsit) Neman
Kudirkos Naumiestis
Prienai
Jašiūnai
Smorgon'
Volozhin
Berezino
Chausy

Kaliningrad (Königsberg)
Gvardeysk
Chernyakhovsk
Znamensk
Gusev
Vilkaviškis
Nesterov
Virbalis
Marijampolė
Alytus
Kalvarija
Merkinė
Varėna
Voronovo

Baltiysk
R.S.F.S.R.
Polessk
Mamonovo
Lazdijai

Braniewo

Scale 1:4 000 000; one inch to 64 miles. Conic Projection
Elevations and depressions are given in feet.

0 10 20 30 40 50 60 70 80 90 100 110 120 Miles
0 20 40 60 80 100 120 140 160 180 200 Kilometers

NORTH SEA

DENMARK

BALTIC

NETHERLANDS

AMSTERDAM

FEDERAL REPUBLIC OF GERMANY

WEST GERMANY

GERMAN DEMOCRATIC REPUBLIC

EAST GERMANY

SCHLESWIG-HOLSTEIN

NIEDERSACHSEN

MECKLENBURG

BRANDENBURG

POMERANIA

WESTFALEN

NORDRHEIN

RHEINLAND-PFALZ

SAAR

HESSEN

THÜRINGEN

BAYERN (BAVARIA)

BADEN-WÜRTTEMBERG

FRANCE

ELSASS

LUXEMBOURG

BELGIUM

SWITZERLAND

LIECHTENSTEIN

VORARLBERG

OBERÖSTERNREICH

SALZBURG

TIROL

KÄRNTEN

STEIERMARK

ITALY

YUGOSLAVIA

CZECHOSLOVAKIA (ČESKÉ)

POLAND

BOHEMIA

 BOHMER WALD

ODENWALD

SCHWÄBISCHE ALB

HUNSRÜCK

EIFEL

WESTERWALD

ERZGEBIRGE

HARZ

LÜNEBURGER HEIDE

FRISIAN ISLANDS

Major cities and towns:
Flensburg, Schleswig, Husum, Heide, Kiel, Neumünster, Rendsburg, Eckernförde, Lübeck, Neustadt, Itzehoe, HAMBURG, Cuxhaven, Stade, Bremerhaven, Wilhelmshaven, Emden, Norden, Oldenburg, Delmenhorst, BREMEN, Bremen, Verden, Celle, Wolfsburg, Braunschweig, HANNOVER, Hildesheim, Hamelin, Bielefeld, Herford, Detmold, Gütersloh, Paderborn, Lippstadt, Hamm, DORTMUND, ESSEN, DÜSSELDORF, Gelsenkirchen, Bochum, Wuppertal, Solingen, Mönchengladbach, COLOGNE (Köln), Bonn, Aachen, Siegen, Kassel, Göttingen, Nordhausen, Halle, Leipzig, Merseburg, Weissenfels, Naumburg, Erfurt, Weimar, Jena, Gera, Gotha, Eisenach, Zwickau, Karl-Marx-Stadt, Plauen, Hof, Dresden, Görlitz, Zittau, Magdeburg, Dessau, Wittenberg, Potsdam, BERLIN (West) (East), Brandenburg, Schwerin, Rostock, Wismar, Stralsund, Greifswald, Neubrandenburg, Szczecin (Stettin), Cottbus, Frankfurt, Eisenhüttenstadt, Zielona Góra, Gorzów Wlkp., FRANKFURT AM MAIN, Wiesbaden, Mainz, Offenbach, Hanau, Darmstadt, Worms, MANNHEIM, Heidelberg, Ludwigshafen, Kaiserslautern, Saarbrücken, Trier, Koblenz, Giessen, Fulda, Schweinfurt, Würzburg, Bamberg, Bayreuth, Nürnberg, Fürth, Erlangen, Regensburg, Ingolstadt, Augsburg, MUNICH (München), STUTTGART, Pforzheim, Esslingen, Heilbronn, Karlsruhe, Baden-Baden, Tübingen, Reutlingen, Ulm, Neu Ulm, Freiburg, Ravensburg, Konstanz, Kempten, Rosenheim, Salzburg, Innsbruck, VIENNA (Wien), Linz, St. Pölten, Wiener Neustadt, Graz, Klagenfurt, Villach

Luxembourg, Metz, Nancy, Strasbourg, Colmar, Mulhouse, Basel, Zürich, Bern, Luzern, St. Gallen, Lausanne, Geneva (Genève)

PRAGUE (Praha), Plzeň, České Budějovice, Brno, Liberec, Hradec Králové, Pardubice

Scale 1:4 000 000; one inch to 64 miles. Conic Projection
Elevations and depressions are given in feet.

Continued on pages 160-161
Continued on pages 164-165

Longitude East of Greenwich

COPYRIGHT BY RAND MCNALLY & COMPANY
MADE IN U.S.A.

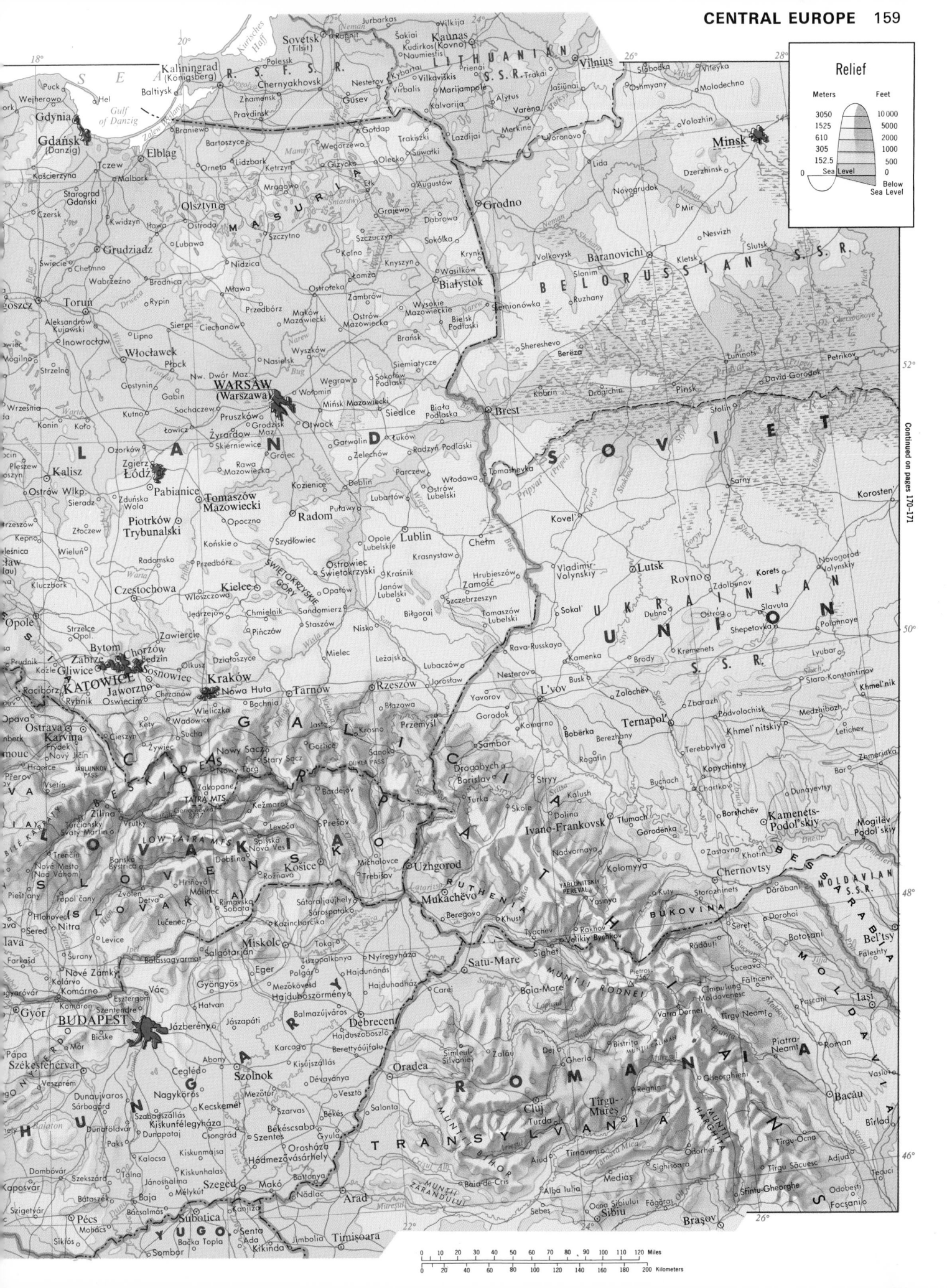

Continued on pages 170-171

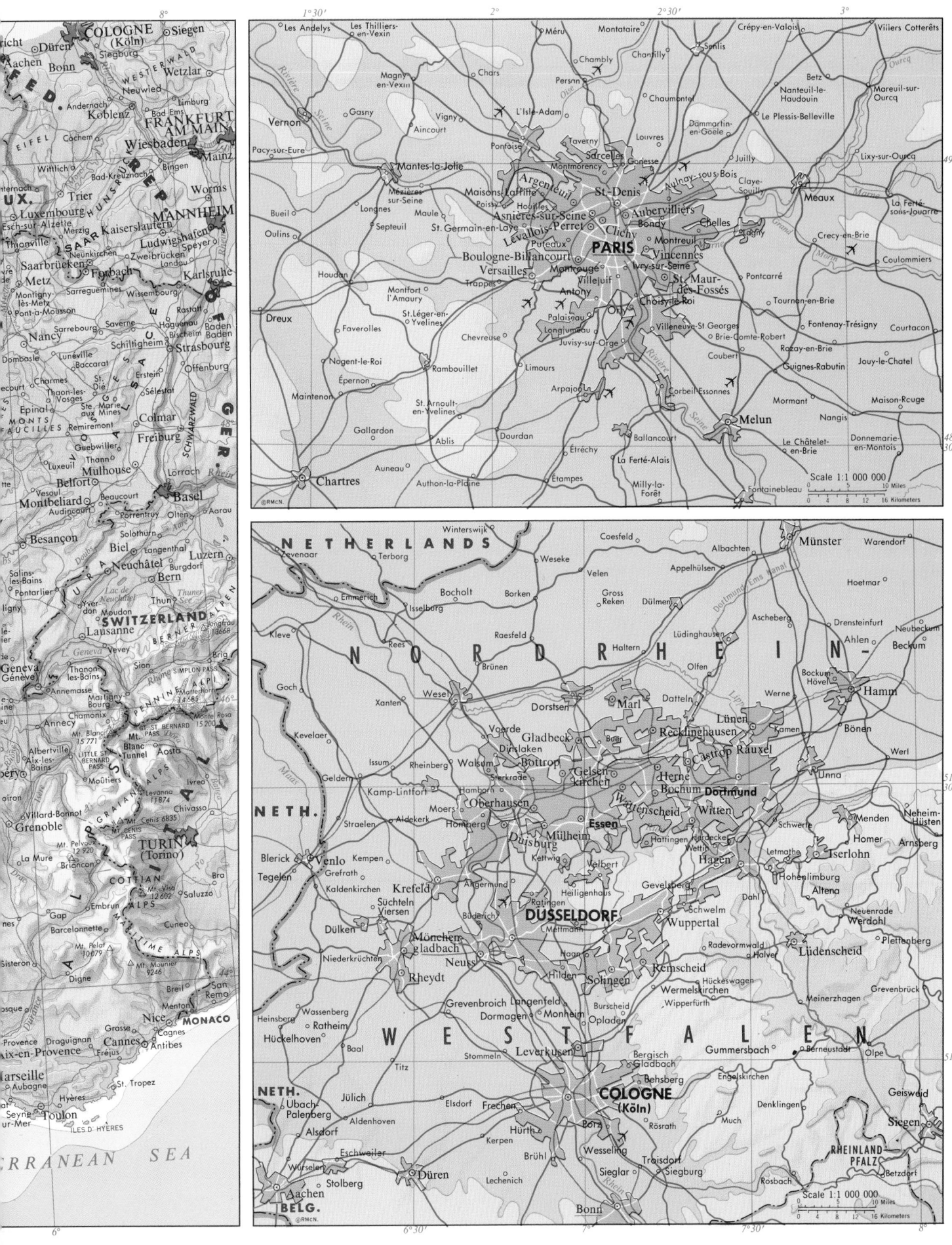
COLOGNE
(Köln)
Siegen
Düren
Aachen
Bonn
Siegburg
WESTERWALD
Wetzlar
Neuwied
Andernach
Koblenz
Bad Ems
Limburg
FRANKFURT AM MAIN
EIFEL
Cochem
Wiesbaden
Mainz
Wittlich
Bad-Kreuznach
Bingen
HUNSRÜCK
Trier
Worms
LUX.
Luxembourg
MANNHEIM
Esch-sur-Alzette
Merzig
Kaiserslautern
SAAR
Ludwigshafen
Speyer
Thionville
Neunkirchen
Zweibrücken
Saarbrücken
Landau
Metz
Forbach
Karlsruhe
Montigny-lès-Metz
Sarreguemines
Wissembourg
Pont-à-Mousson
Rastatt
Sarrebourg
Saverne
Haguenau
Baden Baden
Nancy
Bischheim
Schiltigheim
Strasbourg
Lunéville
Dombasle
Baccarat
Offenburg
Charmes
St. Dié
Erstein
Thaon-les-Vosges
Sélestat
Epinal
Ste. Marie aux Mines
MONTS FAUCILLES
Remiremont
Colmar
SCHWARZWALD
Freiburg
Guebwiller
Thann
Luxeuil
Mulhouse
Lörrach
Belfort
Vesoul
Basel
Montbeliard
Beaucourt
Audincourt
Porrentruy
Olten
Aarau
Besançon
Solothurn
Biel
Langenthal
Luzern
Neuchâtel
Burgdorf
Salins-les-Bains
Bern
Pontarlier
Thun
Yverdon
Moudon
SWITZERLAND
Jungfrau 13668
Lausanne
Vevey
Brig
Geneva
Genève
Sion
SIMPLON PASS
Thonon-les-Bains
Annemasse
Martigny
Bourg
Matterhorn 14685
PENNINE ALPS
Chamonix
Annecy
GT. ST. BERNARD PASS
Monte Rosa 15200
Mt. Blanc 15771
Mt. Blanc Tunnel
Albertville
Aosta
Aix-les-Bains
LITTLE ST. BERNARD PASS
Moûtiers
GRAIAN ALPS
Ivrea
Levanna 11874
Chivasso
Villard-Bonnot
Grenoble
Mt. Cenis 6835
MT. CENIS PASS
Mt. Pelvoux 12920
TURIN
(Torino)
La Mure
Briançon
COTTIAN ALPS
Mt. Viso 12602
Saluzzo
Embrun
Gap
Barcelonnette
Cuneo
Mt. Pelat 10079
MARITIME ALPS
Mt. Mounier 9246
Sisteron
Digne
Breil
San Remo
Menton
Nice
MONACO
Grasse
Cagnes
Draguignan
Cannes
Antibes
Aix-en-Provence
Fréjus
Marseille
Aubagne
St. Tropez
Hyères
Toulon
ILES D' HYÈRES
MEDITERRANEAN SEA
Les Andelys
Les Thilliers-en-Vexin
Méru
Montataire
Crépy-en-Valois
Viliers Cotterêts
Senlis
Chambly
Chantilly
Magny-en-Vexin
Chars
Persan
Betz
Nanteuil-le-Haudouin
Mareuil-sur-Ourcq
Chaumontel
Vernon
Gasny
Vigny
L'Isle-Adam
Le Plessis-Belleville
Aincourt
Dammartin-en-Goële
Louvres
Pacy-sur-Eure
Pontoise
Taverny
Sarcelles
Gonesse
Juilly
Lixy-sur-Ourcq
Mantes-la-Jolie
Montmorency
Argenteuil
Aulnay-sous-Bois
Claye-Souilly
Meaux
Mézières-sur-Seine
Maisons-Laffitte
St.-Denis
Poissy
Houilles
Aubervilliers
La Ferté-sous-Jouarre
Bueil
Longnes
Maule
Asnières-sur-Seine
Bondy
Chelles
Septeuil
St. Germain-en-Laye
Levallois-Perret
Clichy
Oulins
Lagny
Puteaux
Montreuil
Crecy-en-Brie
PARIS
Vincennes
Boulogne-Billancourt
Coulommiers
Houdan
Versailles
Montrouge
Ivry-sur-Seine
St. Maur-des-Fossés
Pontcarré
Trappes
Villejuif
Montfort l'Amaury
Antony
Tournan-en-Brie
Choisy-le-Roi
Dreux
St.Léger-en-Yvelines
Orly
Faverolles
Palaiseau
Villeneuve-St.Georges
Fontenay-Trésigny
Courtacon
Longjumeau
Chevreuse
Brie-Comte-Robert
Juvisy-sur-Orge
Rozay-en-Brie
Nogent-le-Roi
Coubert
Jouy-le-Chatel
Rambouillet
Limours
Guignes-Rabutin
Épernon
Maintenon
Arpajon
Corbeil-Essonnes
Mormant
Maison-Rouge
St. Arnoult-en-Yvelines
Nangis
Melun
Gallardon
Dourdan
Ballancourt
Le Châtelet-en-Brie
Donnemarie-en-Montois
Ablis
Étréchy
La Ferté-Alais
Auneau
Chartres
Étampes
Milly-la-Forêt
Authon-la-Plaine
Fontainebleau
Scale 1:1 000 000
©RMCN.
Winterswijk
Coesfeld
NETHERLANDS
Münster
Warendorf
Zevenaar
Terborg
Albachten
Weseke
Velen
Appelhülsen
Hoetmar
Emmerich
Bocholt
Borken
Gross Reken
Dülmen
Dortmund-Ems Kanal
Isselburg
Ascheberg
Drensteinfurt
Neubeckum
Raesfeld
Lüdinghausen
Kleve
Rees
Ahlen
Beckum
NORDRHEIN-WESTFALEN
Haltern
Brünen
Olfen
Bockum-Hövel
Hamm
Goch
Wesel
Werne
Xanten
Datteln
Dorstsen
Marl
Lünen
Kamen
Voerde
Gladbeck
Recklinghausen
Bönen
Kevelaer
Dinslaken
Castrop Rauxel
Werl
Issum
Rheinberg
Walsum
Bottrop
Gelsenkirchen
Sterkrade
Herne
Unna
Geldern
Hamborn
Bochum
Dortmund
Kamp-Lintfort
Oberhausen
Wattenscheid
Witten
Menden
NETH.
Moers
Neheim-Hüsten
Straelen
Aldekerk
Homberg
Essen
Schwerte
Homer
Mülheim
Hattingen
Herdecke
Arnsberg
Duisburg
Wetter
Blerick
Venlo
Kempen
Kettwig
Hagen
Letmathe
Iserlohn
Tegelen
Grefrath
Velbert
Hohenlimburg
Kaldenkirchen
Krefeld
Angermund
Gevelsberg
Altena
Ratingen
Heiligenhaus
Dahl
Süchteln
Schwelm
Neuenrade
Viersen
DÜSSELDORF
Werdohl
Büderich
Wuppertal
Dülken
Mettmann
Mönchengladbach
Radevormwald
Halver
Plettenberg
Lüdenscheid
Niederkrüchten
Neuss
Haan
Remscheid
Rheydt
Hilden
Solingen
Hückeswagen
Grevenbrück
Wermelskirchen
Grevenbroich
Langenfeld
Wipperfürth
Meinerzhagen
Burscheid
Wassenberg
Monheim
Heinsberg
Ratheim
Dormagen
Opladen
Hückelhoven
Gummersbach
Berneustadt
Olpe
Stommeln
Leverkusen
Baal
Bergisch Gladbach
Titz
Behsberg
Engelskirchen
Jülich
COLOGNE
(Köln)
Geisweid
Übach-Palenberg
Elsdorf
Frechen
Denklingen
Aldenhoven
Porz
Rösrath
Much
Siegen
Alsdorf
Hürth
Kerpen
RHEINLAND-PFALZ
Eschweiler
Wesseling
Troisdorf
Brühl
Würselen
Siegburg
Betzdorf
Stolberg
Düren
Sieglar
Lechenich
Rosbach
Aachen
Bonn
BELG.
Scale 1:1 000 000
©RMCN.
Miles
Kilometers

BAY OF BISCAY

ATLANTIC OCEAN

CABO ORTEGAL
Valdovino
El Ferrol
La Coruña
Puente Ceso
Carballo
CABO DE FINISTERRE
Muxia
Muros
Noya
Santa Eugenia de Ribeira
Pontevedra
Marín
Vigo
Redondela
Puenteareas
La Guardia
Caminha
Viana do Castelo
Esposende
Póvoa de Varzim
Vila do Conde
Matozinhos (Leixões)
Vila Nova de Gaia
PÔRTO (Oporto)
Peñafiel
Ovar
Estarreja
Aveiro
Ilhavo
CABO MONDEGO
Figueira da Foz
Coimbra
Cantanhede
Marinha Grande
Nazaré
FARILHÕES
BERLENGAS
CABO CARVOEIRO
Peniche
Tôrres Vedras
Sintra
CABO DA ROCA
Cascais
LISBON (Lisboa)
Barreiro
Setúbal
Ba. de Setúbal
CABO ESPICHEL
Grândola
Sines
Vila Nova de Milfontes
Odemira
CABO DE SÃO VICENTE
Lagos
Portimão

Vivero
Ribadeo
Luarca
Ortigueira
Mondoñedo
Villalba
Trasparga
Órdenes
Friol
Lugo
Becerreá
Cervantes
Arzúa
Santiago
La Estrada
Lalín
Chantada
Carballino
Orense
Allariz
Bande
Ginzo
Verín

CABO DE PEÑAS
Avilés
Gijón
Pravia
Oviedo
Grado
Siero
Pola de Allande
Mieres
Cangas de Narcea
Pola de Laviana
Villablino
SA. DE IISTREDO
La Robla
León
Astorga
Ponferrada
El Barco
SA. DEL EJE
Viana del Bollo
SA. DE QUEIJA
Vinhais
Bragança

Ribadesella
Llanes
Santander
Torrelavega
Reinosa
Boñar
Cistierna
Gradefes
Carrión de los Condes
Paredes de Nava
Benavente
SA. DE LA CULEBRA
Zamora
Toro

ASTURIAS
CORDILLERA CANTÁBRICA
Torre de Cerredo 8688
Cañangarita
Barruelo de Santullan

Santoña
Castro Urdiales
Pielagos
Portugalete
BILBAO

Laredo
Bermeo
Vergara
Eibar

San Sebastián
Le Boucau
Biarritz
St. Jean
Soustons

Irún
Tolosa
Roncesvalles
VASCONGADAS
Vitoria
Orduña
Miranda de Ebro
Briviesca
Haro
Logroño
Santo Domingo de la Calzada
Arnedo
SA. DE LA DEMANDA
SA. CEBOLLERA
Cervera del Río Alhama
Calahorra
Alfaro
Tudela
Tarazona
Soria
Moncayo 7605
La Almunia de Doña Godina
Pamplona
NAVARRA
Estella
Tafalla

Burgos
Lerma
Carrión de los Condes
Palencia
Medina de Rioseco
Villalpando
Aranda de Duero
Peñafiel
Valladolid
Osma
Almazán
Molina de Aragón

LEÓN
CASTILLA LA VIEJA

MADRID
Segovia
S. Ildefonso o la Granja
Peñalara 7973
SA. DE GUADARRAMA
Ávila
S. Lorenzo de El Escorial
Cebreros
Getafe
Aranjuez

Salamanca
Peñaranda de Bracamonte
Alba de Tormes
Béjar
SIERRA DE GREDOS
Arenas de S. Pedro
Candeleda
Talavera de la Reina
Navalmoral de la Mata
La Puebla de Montalbán
Toledo
MONTES DE TOLEDO
Madridejos

ESPAÑA
CASTILLA LA NUEVA

Sigüenza
Brihuega
Guadalajara
Molina de Aragón
MONTES UNIVERSALES
Huete
SA. DE CUENCA
Cuenca
Tarancón
Ocaña
Corral de Almaguer
Campillo de Altobuey
Quintanar
Villacañas
Quintanar de la Orden
Alarcón
San Clemente
Tarazona de la Mancha
La Roda
Albacete
Chinchilla

Guarda
SA. DA ESTRÊLA
Covilhã
Fundão
Castelo Branco
Idanha-a-Nova
Plasencia
Hervás
SA. DE GATA
Cáceres
SA. DE GUADALUPE
Trujillo
Logrosán
Zorita
Mérida
Don Benito
Villanueva de la Serena
Almadén

BEIRA
PORTUGAL
ESTREMADURA
ALENTEJO
ALGARVE

Viseu
Manguálde
Trancoso
Pinhel
Ciudad Rodrigo
Almeida
Mangualde

Leiria
Fátima
Tomar
Abrantes
Santarém
Alpiarça
Ponte de Sôr
Almeirim
Coruche
Montemor-o-Novo
Vendas Novas
Palmela
Alcácer do Sal
Ferreira do Alentejo
Beja
Aljustrel
Castro Verde
Ourique
Almodôvar
SA. DE MONCHIQUE
Silves
Loulé
Faro
Olhão
Tavira
Vila Real de Sto. Antonio
CABO DE SANTA MARIA

Badajoz
Olivenza
Elvas
Vila Viçosa
Évora
Estremoz
Arraiolos
Redondo
Reguengos de Monsaraz
Moura
Serpa
Mértola

ANDALUCÍA
SIERRA MORENA
SIERRA NEVADA
Mulhacén 11424
Córdoba
Sevilla
Jaén
Granada
Málaga
Huelva
Cádiz
Jerez de la Frontera
El Puerto de Sta. María
Algeciras
La Línea
Gibraltar (Br.)
Ceuta (Sp.)

Strait of Gibraltar
Alboran Sea
ISLA DEL ALBORÁN (Sp.)
MED

MOROCCO
Tanger (Tangier)
Tétouan
Arcila
Larache
Melilla (Sp.)

Scale 1:4 000 000, one inch to 64 miles. Conic Projection
Elevations and depressions are given in feet
Longitude West of Greenwich

Main map (France, Spain, Balearic Islands, Algeria)

FRANCE

Marsan, Condom, Lectoure, Gaillac, Albi, Grenade, Gimone, Gaillhac, Gers, Lavaur, Castres, Bédarieux, Lodève, Montpellier, Lunel, Miramas, Árles

Aire, Auch, Mureta, Toulouse, Villefranche, Lézignan, Montpellier, Hérault, Clermont, Frontignan, Mèze, Port-de-Bouc, Martigues

Pau, Tarbes, St. Gaudens, Pamiers, Carcassonne, Limoux, Sigean, Narbonne, Agde, Sète, Golfe du Lion

Lourdes, St. Girons, Foix, Tarascon, Quillan, Rivesaltes, Perpignan

Bagnères-de-Bigorre, Ax-les-Thermes, Prades, Céret, Port Vendres

Mt. Perdido 11,007, Pic de Montcalm, Carlitte, Prats-de-Mollo, CABO DE CREUS

MALADETTA, Pico de Aneto 11,168, ANDORRA, Andorra

Boltaña, SA. DE GUARA, SA. DE BOUMORT, La Pobla de Lillet, Ripoll, Olot, Golfo de Rosas

Huesca, Barbastro, Berga, Manlleu, Gerona, La Bisbal, Palafrugell

Monzón, Tamarite, Balaguer, Vich, Casa de la Selva, San Felíu de Guixols

Sariñena, Lérida, Tárrega, Granollers, Calella, Mataró

Fraga, Borjas Blancas, Igualada, Sabadell, Tarrasa, Manresa

Caspe, Maella, Mora, Montblanch, Valls, Villafranca del Panadés, BARCELONA, Badalona

Alcañiz, Reus, Villanueva y Geltrú

Morella, Roquetas, Tortosa, Tarragona

San Mateo, Amposta, Alcanar, CABO DE TORTOSA

Vinaroz, Benicarló

Villafamés, Alcalá de Chivert

Castellón de la Plana

BALEARIC SEA

COLUMBRETES

Villarreal, Burriana, Onda, Vall de Uxó, Sagunto

ISLAS BALEARES (BALEARIC ISLANDS)

ISLA DE MENORCA (MINORCA), Ciudadela, Mahón, Ba. de Alcudia, Pollensa, La Puebla, Sóller, Inca

Palma de Mallorca, Andraitx, Manacor, Felanitx, Lluchmayor, Santany, CAPE SALINAS

Ba. de Palma, ISLA DE MALLORCA (MAJORCA), CABRERA

Valencia, Catarroja, Golfo de Valencia

Liria, Sueca, Cullera

Játiva, Gandía, Oliva

ISLA DE IBIZA (IVIZA), San Antonio Abad, Sta. Eulalia del Río, Ibiza

Ontenente, Pego, Denia, Jávea, CABO DE LA NAO, ISLA DE FORMENTERA

Alcoy, Cocentaina, Villajoyosa

Jijona, Alicante, Elche

Segura, Torrevieja, Ba. de Alicante

Pacheco, Mar Menor, Unión, CABO DE PALOS, Cartagena

Dellys

Algiers (Alger), Boudouaou

CAP CAXINE, Douéra, L'Arba, Bouira

Cherchel, Boufarik, Sour el Ghozlane

Ténès, El Affroun, Médéa, Miliana, Blida

El Asnam (Orléansville), Carnot, Ksar el Boukhari, Sidi-Aïssa

Mostaganem, Arzew, Oued Rhiou, Aïne Oussera, Bouira-Sahary

P. FERRAT, Ighil Izane, ALGERIA, MONTS DES OUARSENIS

Oued Tlélat, Mohammadia, Mascara, Tagdempt, Ksar Chellala

Sebkha d'Oran, Mercier-Lacombe, Zahrez Chergui

MEDITERRANEAN SEA

GOLFE DU LION

Longitude East of Greenwich

Scale:
20 40 60 80 100 120 Miles
20 40 60 80 100 120 140 160 180 200 Kilometers

MADRID (inset) — Scale 1:1,000,000

SA. DEL HOYO 4606, S. Lorenzo de El Escorial, Colmenar Viejo, Fuente el Saz, Algete

El Escorial, Galapagar, Canal de Isabel II (Aqueduct), S. Sebastián de los Reyes, Alcobendas

Valdemorillo, Las Rozas de Madrid, El Pardo, Fuencarral, Barajas de Madrid, Tarnejón de Ardoz, Alcalá de Henares

Pozuelo de Alarcón, MADRID, Vicálvaro, S. Fernando de Henares

Brunete, Alcorcón, Vallecas, Loeches, Campo Real

Villaviciosa de Odón, Leganés, Móstoles, Getafe, Arganda, Valdilecha, Carabaña

Navalcarnero, Pinto, Tielmes

Parla, S. Martín de la Vega, Morata de Tajuña, Perales de Tajuña

Scale 1:1 000 000
0 5 10 Miles
0 4 8 12 16 Kilometers ©RMcN.

LISBON (inset) — Scale 1:1,000,000

Mafra, Cheleiros, Alhandra, Alverca, Samora Correia

São João das Lampas, Montelavar, Almargem, Loures, Tejo R.

Colares, Sintra, Odivelas, Sacavém, Alcochete

CABO DA ROCA, Belas, Barcarena, Olivais, LISBON (Lisboa)

Alcabideche, Estoril, Carnaxide, Oeiras, Rio Tejo, Almada, Montijo

Cascais, Ba. de Cascais, Caparica, Barreiro, Seixal, Altos Vedros, Pinhal Novo

ATLANTIC OCEAN

Coina, Palmela

Lagoa de Albufeira, Sesimbra, Setúbal

Ba. de Setúbal

Rio Sado

CABO ESPICHEL, Comporta

Scale 1:1 000 000
0 5 10 Miles
0 4 8 12 16 Kilometers ©RMcN.

NAPLES (inset) — Scale 1:1,000,000

Frattamaggiore, Acerra, Nola, Avellino

S. Antimo, Aragola, Pomigliano d'Arco, Monteforte Irpino

Marano di Napoli, Vesuvio 3710, Somma Vesuviana

NAPLES (Napoli), S. Giuseppe Vesuviano

Bacoli, Pozzuoli, Portici, Sarno, S. Severino

C. MISENO, Torre del Greco, Vesuvio 3842, Mercato

I. DI PROCIDA, Procida, Torre Annunziata, Nocera Inf., Cava de' Tirreni

Forio, Ischia, Golfo di Napoli, Pompeii Ruins, Angri, Gragnano, Salerno

2585, I. D'ISCHIA, Castellammare di Stabia

TYRRHENIAN SEA, Sorrento, 4734, Amalfi, Golfo di Salerno

PUNTA CAMPANELLA, I. DI CAPRI 1932, Capri

Scale 1:1 000 000
0 5 10 Miles
0 4 8 12 16 Kilometers ©RMcN.

ROME (inset) — Scale 1:1,000,000

Formello, Monterotondo, Sant'Angelo Romano

Cerveteri, Mentana, Guidonia, ROME (Roma), Tivoli

Ladispoli, Maccarese, VATICAN CITY, Colonna, Zagarolo

Fregene, Frascati, Marino, Colli Laziali 3235

Fiumicino, Ostia Antica, Albano Laziale, Genzano di Roma

Lido di Roma (Ostia Lido), Pomezia, Lanuvio, Velletri

TYRRHENIAN SEA, Aprilia, Cisterna di Latina

Borgo Montello, Nettuno, Anzio

Scale 1:1 000 000
0 5 10 Miles
0 4 8 12 16 Kilometers ©RMcN.

Continued on pages 158–159

Continued on pages 160–161

LIGURIAN SEA

TYRRHENIAN SEA

AEGEAN SEA

Same scale as main map

CRETE (Greece)

MEDITERRANEAN SEA

©RMCN

Scale 1:4 000 000; one inch to 64 miles. Conic Projection
Elevations and depressions are given in feet

Relief
Meters
Feet
3050
1525
610
305
152.5
0
Sea Level
152.5
1525
3050
10 000
5000
2000
1000
500
0
500
5000
10 000
ROMANIA
CARPATII MERIDIONALI
(TRANSYLVANIAN ALPS)
VALACHIA
BANAT
BUCHAREST
(București)
Brașov
Sibiu
Timișoara
Arad
Szeged
Subotica
Novi Sad
Belgrade
(Beograd)
Craiova
Ploești
Ruse (Russe)
Giurgiu
Varna
(Stalin)
Shumen
Pleven
Vidin
IRON GATE
Turnu-Severin
YUGOSLAVIA
SERBIA
BOSNIA
HERCEGOVINA
CRNA GORA
(MONTENEGRO)
Sarajevo
Kragujevac
Niš
Priština
Skopje
Titograd
ŠAR PLANINA
BULGARIA
STARA PLANINA
(BALKAN MTS.)
RHODOPE MTS.
Sofia (Sofiya)
Plovdiv
(Philippopolis)
Stara Zagora
Burgas
Kazanlŭk
Sliven
MACEDONIA
THRACE
ISTRANCA DAĞ
Edirne
(Adrianople)
Tekirdağ
(Rodosto)
TURKEY
Çanakkale
Çanakkale Boğazı
(Dardanelles)
(Troy Ruins)
ALBANIA
Tiranë
Shkodër
(Scutari)
Durrës
Vlorë
(Valona)
Korçë
Gjirokastër
GREECE
Thessaloníki
Kavála
Alexandroúpolis
(Dedeagats)
THÁSOS
SAMOTHRÁKI
ÁYION ÓROS
(MOUNT ATHOS)
Athos
6670
LÍMNOS
Thermaikos
Kólpos
AEGEAN SEA
THESSALIA
EPEIRUS
PINDHOS OROS
Ólimbos
9550
Lárisa
Vólos
Ioánnina
(Yannina)
Kérkira
KÉRKIRA
SPORÁDHES
SKÍROS
LÉSVOS
Mitilíni
KHÍOS
Khíos
PSARÁ
ÓROS ÓTHRIS
Lamía
Parnassós
8061
DELPHI RUINS
Khalkís
Thívai
(Thebes)
ATHENS (Athínai)
Piraiévs (Piraeus)
Korinthiakós
Kólpos
Pátrai
(Pátras)
KEFALLINÍA
Argostólion
ZÁKINTHOS
(ZANTE)
PELOPÓNNISOS
Kórinthos
(Corinth)
Tripolis
Spárti (Sparta)
Kalámai
Saronikós Kólpos
KIKLÁDHES
DHODHEKÁNISOS
(DODECANESE)
NÁXOS
PÁROS
MÍLOS
(MILO)
IKARÍA
AKR. MALÉA
Neápolis
IONIAN SEA
IONIAN ISLANDS
Strait of Otranto
Brindisi
Lecce
Otranto
C. D OTRANTO
C. S. MARIA DI LEUCA
Gallipoli
Longitude East of Greenwich
18°
20°
22°
24°
26°
28°
A-558396-76
COPYRIGHT BY
RAND McNALLY & COMPANY
MADE IN U.S.A.
0 10 20 30 40 50 60 70 80 90 100 110 120 Miles
0 20 40 60 80 100 120 140 160 180 200 Kilometers

Relief

Meters	Feet
1525	5000
610	2000
305	1000
152.5	500
0	Sea Level
152.5	500

Scale 1:4 000 000; one inch to 64 miles. Conic Project
Elevations and depressions are given in feet

U K R A I N I A N S. S. R.
U N I O N
MOLDAVIAN S.S.R.
BESSARABIA
ROMANIA
AZOVSKOYE MORE
(Sea of Azov)
BLACK SEA
KRYMSKIY (CRIMEA) P-OV
KRYMSKAYA
KURSK
VORONEZH
BELGOROD
SUMY
CHERNIGOV
KIEV
ZHITOMIR
KHMEL'NITSKIY
VINNITSA
CHERKASSY
POLTAVA
KHAR'KOV
VOROSHILOVGRAD
DONETSK
ROSTOV
KRASNODARSKIY
ZAPOROZH'YE
DNEPROPETROVSK
KIROVOGRAD
NIKOLAYEV
KHERSON
ODESSA
DONETS COAL BASIN
KIYEV (Kiev)
KHAR'KOV
DONETSK
Dnepropetrovsk
Zaporozh'ye
Odessa
Kishinev
Simferopol' (Akmechet)
Kerch'
Zhdanov
Rostov-na-Donu
Voronezh
Kursk
Belgorod
Chernigov
Zhitomir
Vinnitsa
Kirovograd
Nikolayev
Kherson
Poltava
Sumy
Krasnodar
Voroshilovgrad
Kremenchug
Krivoy Rog
Melitopol'
Berd'ansk
Taganrog
Yevpatoriya
Feodosiya (Kefe)
Novorossiysk
Galati
Brăila
Iaşi
Izmail
Tiraspol
Bendery
Uman'
Belaya Tserkov'
Berdichev
Kamenets-Podol'skiy
Proskurov
Longitude East of Greenwich
0 10 20 30 40 50 60 70 80 90 100 110 120 Miles
0 20 40 60 80 100 120 140 160 180 200 Kilometers
A-579900-76
COPYRIGHT BY RAND McNALLY & COMPANY MADE IN U.S.A.

Scale 1:20 000 000; one inch to 315 mile
Lambert's Azimuthal, Equal Area Project
Elevations and depressions are given in

Relief
Meters
Feet
3050
10 000
1525
5000
610
2000
305
1000
152.5
500
0
Sea Level
0
Below Sea Level
152.5
500
1525
5000
3050
10 000
OCEAN
LAPTEV SEA
EAST SIBERIAN SEA
SEVERNAYA ZEMLYA (NORTHERN LAND)
M. CHELYUSKIN
NOVOSIBIRSKIYE O-VA (NEW SIBERIAN ISLANDS)
KOTEL'NYY
FADDEYA
NOVAYA SIBIR
DE-LONGA
MALYY LYAKHOVSKIY
LYAKHOVSKIYE
VRANGELYA (WRANGEL)
M. SHELAGSKIY
AYON
MEDVEZH'I
CHUKOTSKIY P-OV
Anadyr'
Anadyrskiy Zaliv
CHUKOTSKOYE NAGOR'YE
KORYAKSKIY KHREBET
Arctic Circle
Ambarchik
Markovo
Penzhino
Nizhne-Kolymsk
Sredne-Kolymsk
Allaykha
M. SVYATOY NOS
M. BUOR-KHAYA
TAYMYR
P-OV
GORY BYRRANGA
Taymyr
Khatangskiy Zaliv
Nordvik
BOL'SHOY BEGICHEV
Khatanga
Ust'-Olenëk
Tiksi
Bulun
Kazach'ye
Yana
Abyy
Verkhoyansk
Zashiversk
Zyryanka
Kolyma
KHREBET CHERSKOGO
Gora Chen 10,177
KHREBET GYDAN (KOLYMSKIY)
Gizhiga
Tilichiki
M. OLYUTORSKIY
KARAGIN
M. TAYGONOS
Zaliv Shelekhova
Palana
Ust'-Kamchatsk
Klyuchevskaya (Vol.) 15,584
KAMCHATKA
P-OV
Petropavlovsk-Kamchatskiy
Verkhne-Kamchatsk
Ust'-Bol'sheretsk
Oymyakon
Magadan
Yamsk
M. ALEVINA
Okhotsk
SEA OF OKHOTSK
VERKHOYANSKIY KHREBET
Zhigansk
Olenëk
oril'sk
GORY PUTORANA
YAKUT A.S.S.R.
YAKUT AUTONOMOUS SOVIET SOCIALIST REPUBLIC
Aldan
Aldanskaya
Ust'-Maya
Yakutsk
Amga
Vilyuy
Vilyuysk
Lena
Suntar
Tura
Nizhnyaya Tunguska
Olekminsk
Tommot
Aldan
Nel'kan
DZHUGDZHUR KHREBET
Ayan
M. VELIZAVETY
SHANTAR
Udskaya Guba
Okha
SAKHALIN (Sov. Union)
Aleksandrovsk
Poronaysk
Uglegorsk
M. TERPENIYA
Yuzhno-Sakhalinsk
Korsakov
Kholmsk
Baykit
Podkamennaya Tunguska
Mukhtuya
Peleduy
Vitim
G. Golets Purpula 5377
PATOM PLATEAU
Bodaybo
Golets-Skalistyy 9186
Yartsevo
G. Polkan 3543
Yenisey
Kirensk
STANOVOY KHREBET
Tyndinskiy
Zeya
Chumikan
Nikolayevsk-na-Amure
Komsomol'sk-na-Amure
KHREBET BUREINSKIY
Sovetskaya Gavan'
Malmyzh
Ilimsk
Nizhne-Angarsk
BURYAT A.S.S.R.
BAYKAL'SKIY KHREBET
Oz. Baykal (Lake Baykal)
Barguzin
Surface elev. 1535 Ft. above sea level
Skovorodino
Svobodnyy
Belogorsk
Bureya
Ust'-Tyrma
Birobidzhan
Khabarovsk
KHREBET SIKHOTE ALIN
Amur
Tatar Strait
Krasnoyarsk
Kansk
Tayshet
Bratsk
Bratskoye Vdkhr.
Angara
Tulun
Balakhta
Nizhneudinsk
G. Piramida 10,801
Zhigalovo
Kachuga
Minusinsk
Abakan
KHREBET
Kutulik
Cheremkhovo
Angarsk
Irkutsk
Munku Sardyk 11,457
Kyren
SAYAN
Ulan-Ude
Chita
YABLONOVYY KHREBET
Sretensk
Nerchinsk
NERCHINSKIY KHREBET
Nerchinskiy Zavod
Blagoveshchensk
Aginskoye
Aksha
Borzya
Petrovsk-Zabaykal'skiy
Gorodok
Kyakhta
Kyzyl
TANNU-OLA
Ubsa Nuur
Khobsogol Dalai
Selenge Gol
Onon
Kerulen
LESSER KHINGAN RANGE
Nenchiang
Pok'o'u
Hailun
Ch'ich'ihaerh (Tsitsihar)
Suihua
P'oli
Sungari
HAERHPIN (Harbin)
Mutanchiang
Fuyü
Dalnerechensk
Spassk-Dal'niy
Ussuriysk
Artëm
Partizansk
Nakhodka
Olga
Vladivostok
Wakkanai
Soya Kaikyo
HOKKAIDO
Sapporo
Otaru
Esashi
GREATER KHINGAN RANGE
Wench'üan
Ulaan Baatar
Öndör Haan
Hara Usa
Jibhalanta
Urgalanta
HANGAYN NURUU (KHANGAI MTS.)
ALTAI MTS.
Tsast Bogdo Ula 13865
MONGOLIA
Sayr Usa
GOBI OR SHAMO (DESERT)
Hami
MANCHURIA
T'aonan
Chilin
Lupei
CH'ANGCH'UN
Shuangliao
Tunhua
Hunch'un
Najin
Chŏngjin
SEA OF JAPAN
HONSHU
JAPAN
FUSHUN
Ch'ihfeng
MUKDEN (Shenyang)
Weich'ang
Che'ngte
CHINA
P'yŏngyang
KOREA
Kaesŏng
SEOUL
Andong
Korea Bay
Changchiak'ou
PEKING (Peiching)
Fengchen
TIENTSIN (Tienching)
Lüshun
Lüta
Po Hai
SHANTUNG PANTAO
YELLOW SEA
Paoting
Taegu
PUSAN
Korea Strait
Kanazawa
KYOTO
Tottori
Matsue
KOBE
OSAKA
Okayama
Hiroshima
Kochi
A-570000-76 - 8-8-13
COPYRIGHT BY RAND McNALLY & COMPANY MADE IN U.S.A.
Longitude East of Greenwich
100°
110°
Miles
100
200
300
400
500
600
200
400
600
800
1000 Kilometers

170

Obskaya Guba

KARA SEA

KHREBET PAY-KHOY

PECHORA BASIN

DOMINI

UDMURT A.S.S.R.

SVERDLOVSK

BASHKIR A.S.S.R.

TATAR A.S.S.R.

CHUVASH A.S.S.R.

MARI A.S.S.R.

GORKI

Arctic Circle

WESTERN SIBERIAN LOWLAND

Krasnotur'insk

Nizhniy Tagil

Chelyabinsk

Magnitogorsk

Ufa

Kazan'

Syktyvkar

Kotlas

Kirov

R U S S I A N   S. F. S. R.

NOVAYA ZEMLYA

Kara Strait

VAYGACH

DOLGIY

BARENTS SEA

KOLGUYEV

P-OV KANIN

M. KANIN NOS

MORZHOVETS

Arkhangel'sk
(Archangel)

Onega

Vologda

Kostroma

MOSCOW
(Moskva)

Ryazan'

Vladimir

Murom

A R C T I C   O C E A N

Kirovsk

KOL'SKIY P-OV
(KOLA' PEN.)

Chavaniga

P-OV ONEZHSKIY

SOLOVETSKIY

Belomorsk

Petrozavodsk

KARELIAN A.S.S.R.

Onezhskoye Ozero
Lake Onega

LENINGRAD

RUSSIAN S.F.S.R.

NORWAY

NORD KAPP

MAGERØY

SØRØY

Murmansk

Monchegorsk

Kandalaksha

LAPLAND

Kirovsk

Ladozhskoye Ozero
Lake Ladoga

Vyborg

Kronshtadt
Pushkin

Novgorod

VALDAI HILLS

Smolensk

SWEDEN

NORWAY

FINLAND

Oulu

Helsinki

Tampere
Turku

GULF OF FINLAND

BALTIC SEA

ESTONIAN S.S.R.

Tallinn

Pskov

LATVIAN S.S.R.

Riga

LITHUANIAN S.S.R.

Vilnius
Kaunas

Klaipeda

Minsk

HIIUMAA (DAGÖ)

SAAREMAA (EZEL)

Relief

Meters	Feet
3050	10000
1525	5000
610	2000
305	1000
152.5	500
0	Sea Level
	Below Sea Level
152.5	500
1525	5000
3050	10000

0   50   100   150   200   250   300 Miles

0   100   200   300   400   500 Kilometers

Continued on pages 150–151

Scale 1:10 000 000; one inch to 160 miles. Conic Projection
Elevations and depressions are given in feet.

Continued on pages 152–153

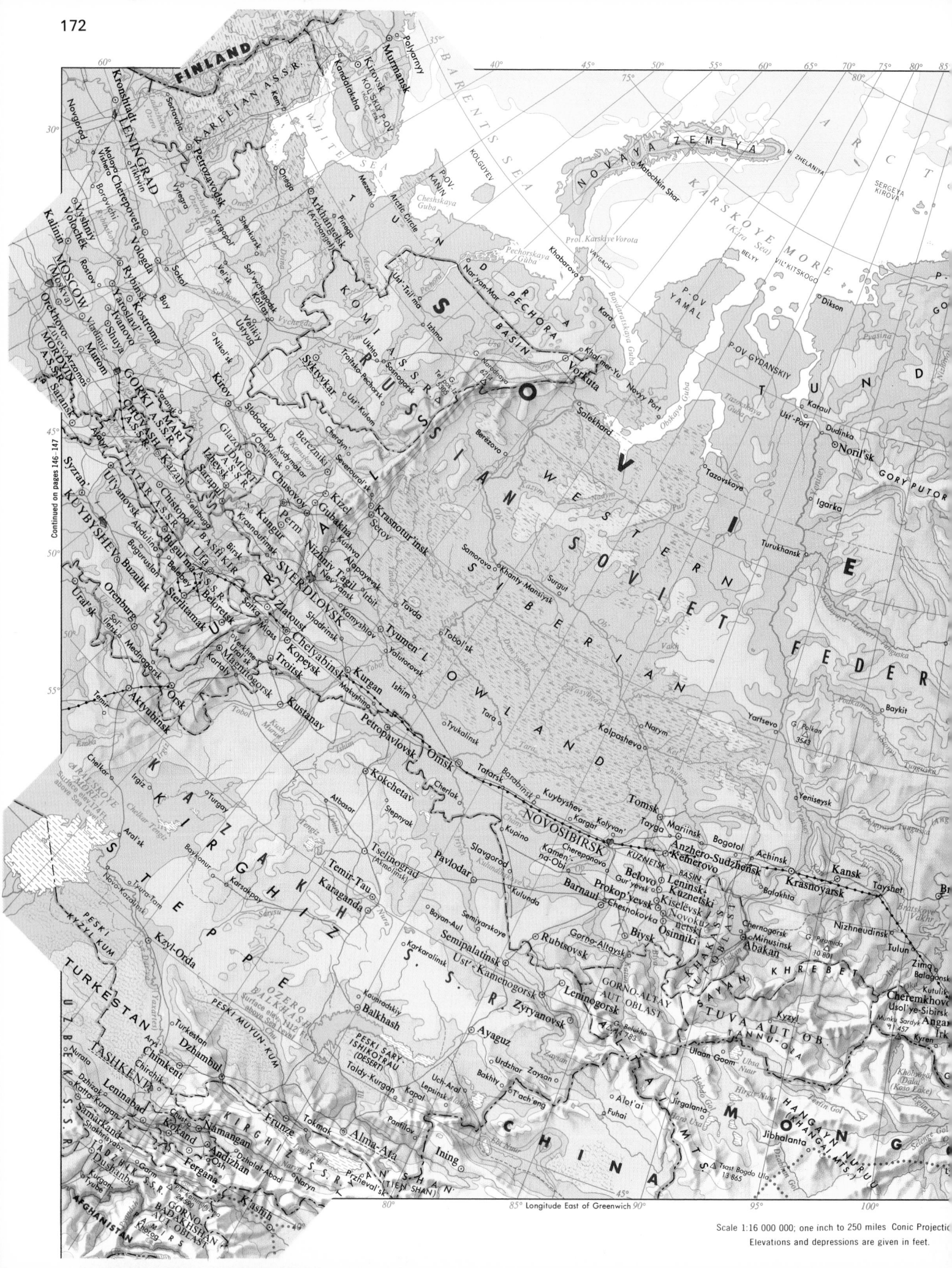

FINLAND

BARENTS SEA

NOVAYA ZEMLYA

KARELIAN A.S.S.R.

WHITE SEA

KARSKOYE MORE
(Kara Sea)

Murmansk
Polyarnyy
Kirovsk
Kandalaksha
Kem'
Kronshtadt
Petrozavodsk

KOLA P-OV

P-OV KANIN

KOMI A.S.S.R.

P-OV YAMAL

P-OV GYDANSKIY

LENINGRAD

Arkhangelsk
(Archangel)

Vorkuta
Salekhard
Dikson

MOSCOW
Moskva

GORKI
MARI A.S.S.R.

PECHORA BASIN

WESTERN SIBERIAN LOWLAND

Noril'sk

GORY PUTOR

CHUVASH A.S.S.R.

UDMURT A.S.S.R.

TATAR A.S.S.R.

Berëzovo

Turukhansk

Igarka

Dudinka

Ust'-Port

MORDVIN A.S.S.R.

KUYBYSHEV

BASHKIR A.S.S.R.

SVERDLOVSK

Perm'

Nizhniy Tagil

Khanty-Mansiysk

Surgut

Yeniseysk

S O V I E T   F E D E R

Orenburg

Ufa
Chelyabinsk
Magnitogorsk
Kopeysk
Troitsk

Kurgan
Tyumen'

Tobol'sk

Kolpashevo
Narym

Yartsevo

Baykit

Aktyubinsk
Orsk

Kustanay
Petropavlovsk
Omsk
Tatarsk

Tomsk

Kansk
Tayshet

K A Z A K H   S. S. R.

KIRGHIZ   STEPPE

OZERO BALKHASH

Kokchetav

NOVOSIBIRSK

KUZNETSK BASIN

Anzhero-Sudzhensk
Kemerovo
Achinsk

Krasnoyarsk
Nizhneudinsk
Tulun

Tselinograd
(Akmola)
Pavlodar

Barnaul
Prokop'yevsk
Kiselëvsk
Novokuznetsk

Abakan
Minusinsk

Cheremkhovo
Usol'ye-Sibirsk

Karaganda

Semipalatinsk
Ust'-Kamenogorsk

Biysk
Rubtsovsk

Zyryanovsk

GORNO-ALTAY
AUT OBLAST
Leninogorsk

TUVA AUT. OB.
TANNU-OLA

KHREBET

Kyzyl

Zima
Balagansk

Kzyl-Orda

Balkhash
Ayaguz

Zaysan

A L T A I   M T S.

M O N G O L

TURKESTAN

PESKI KYZYL KUM

PESKI MUYUN-KUM

Taldy-Kurgan

CHINA

HANGAYN (KHANGAI) NURU

TASHKENT

Chimkent
Dzhambul

Alma-Ata

TIEN SHAN

Frunze

KIRGHIZ S. S. R.

Namangan
Andizhan
Fergana

Dushanbe

AFGHANISTAN

Continued on pages 146-147

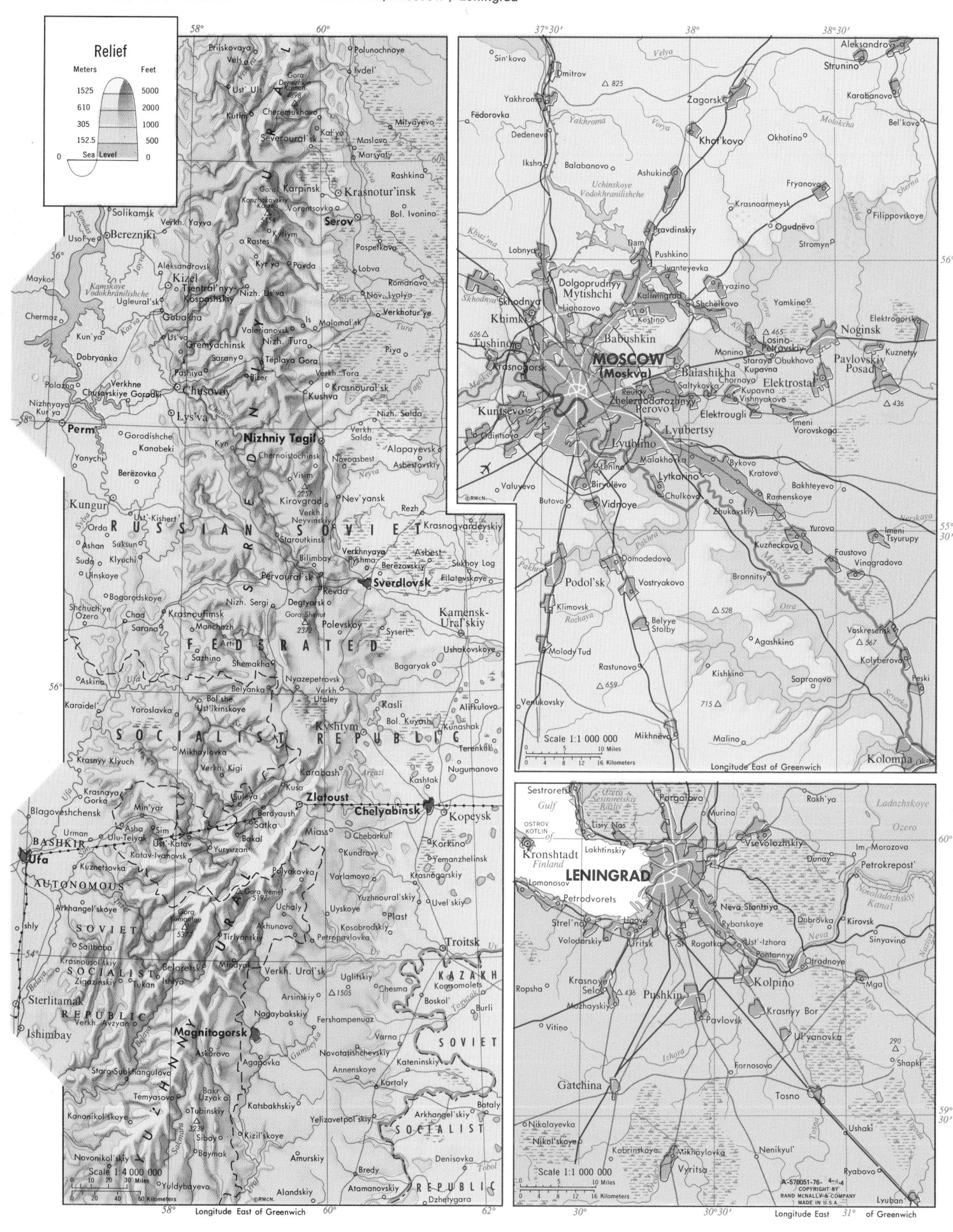
Relief
Meters
Feet
1525
5000
610
2000
305
1000
152.5
500
0
Sea Level
0
RUSSIAN SOVIET FEDERATED SOCIALIST REPUBLIC
BASHKIR AUTONOMOUS SOVIET SOCIALIST REPUBLIC
KAZAKH SOVIET SOCIALIST REPUBLIC
SREDNIY URAL
YUZHNNY URAL
Perm
Nizhniy Tagil
Sverdlovsk
Zlatoust
Chelyabinsk
Magnitogorsk
Ufa
Serov
Krasnotur'insk
Karpinsk
Solikamsk
Berezniki
Kizel
Gubakha
Chusovoy
Lys'va
Kungur
Pervoural'sk
Revda
Kamensk-Ural'skiy
Krasnoufimsk
Kyshtym
Miass
Kopeysk
Troitsk
Beloretsk
Sterlitamak
Ishimbay
Blagoveshchensk
Kamskoye Vodokhranilishche
Scale 1:4 000 000
Miles
Kilometers
Longitude East of Greenwich
MOSCOW (Moskva)
Dmitrov
Zagorsk
Aleksandrov
Strunino
Karabanovo
Yakhroma
Khot'kovo
Pravdinskiy
Pushkino
Ivanteyevka
Dolgoprudnyy
Mytishchi
Kaliningrad
Shchëlkovo
Fryazino
Skhodnya
Khimki
Tushino
Krasnogorsk
Babushkin
Balashikha
Noginsk
Elektrogorsk
Pavlovskiy Posad
Elektrostal'
Kuntsevo
Odintsovo
Reutov
Zheleznodorozhnyy
Perovo
Lyubertsy
Lyublino
Elektrougli
Lytkarino
Vidnoye
Biryulëvo
Ramenskoye
Zhukovskiy
Bronnitsy
Podol'sk
Domodedovo
Klimovsk
Voskresensk
Kolomna
Uchinskoye Vodokhranilishche
Moskva
Scale 1:1 000 000
10 Miles
16 Kilometers
Longitude East of Greenwich
LENINGRAD
Sestroretsk
Pargolovo
Vsevolozhskiy
Kronshtadt
OSTROV KOTLIN
Gulf of Finland
Lomonosov
Petrodvorets
Strel'na
Uritsk
Kolpino
Pushkin
Pavlovsk
Krasnoye Selo
Gatchina
Tosno
Petrokrepost'
Mga
Kirovsk
Otradnoye
Ul'yanovka
Lyuban'
Ladozhskoye Ozero
Neva
Scale 1:1 000 000
10 Miles
16 Kilometers
Longitude East of Greenwich
A-570051-76- 4-4
COPYRIGHT BY RAND McNALLY & COMPANY
MADE IN U.S.A.

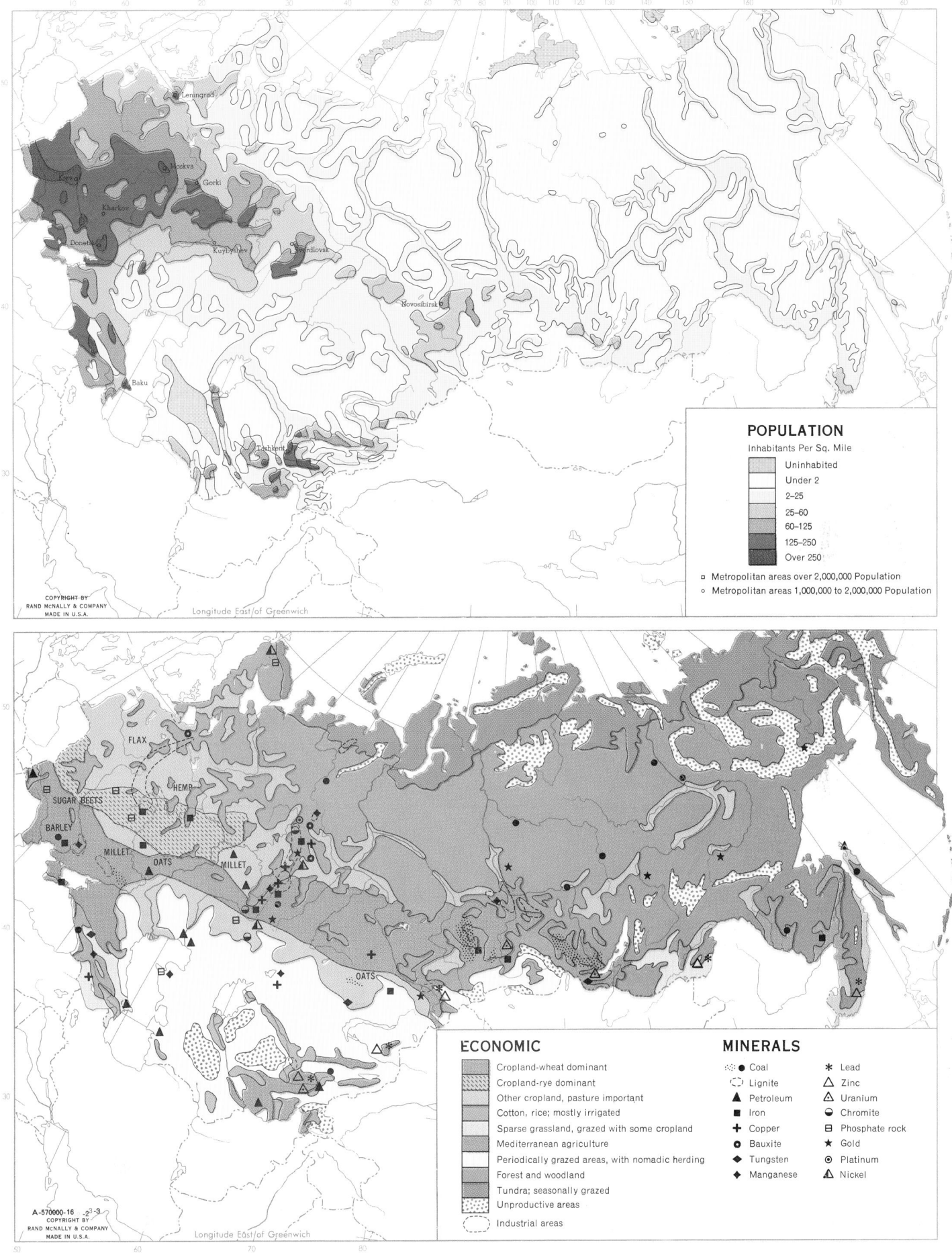

POPULATION

Inhabitants Per Sq. Mile

- Uninhabited
- Under 2
- 2–25
- 25–60
- 60–125
- 125–250
- Over 250

□ Metropolitan areas over 2,000,000 Population

○ Metropolitan areas 1,000,000 to 2,000,000 Population

COPYRIGHT BY
RAND McNALLY & COMPANY
MADE IN U.S.A.

Longitude East of Greenwich

ECONOMIC

- Cropland-wheat dominant
- Cropland-rye dominant
- Other cropland, pasture important
- Cotton, rice; mostly irrigated
- Sparse grassland, grazed with some cropland
- Mediterranean agriculture
- Periodically grazed areas, with nomadic herding
- Forest and woodland
- Tundra; seasonally grazed
- Unproductive areas
- Industrial areas

MINERALS

- ⦙● Coal
- ⦙ Lignite
- ▲ Petroleum
- ■ Iron
- ✚ Copper
- ◉ Bauxite
- ◆ Tungsten
- ◆ Manganese
- ✳ Lead
- △ Zinc
- △ Uranium
- ⬡ Chromite
- ⊟ Phosphate rock
- ★ Gold
- ⊙ Platinum
- ◬ Nickel

A-570000-16
COPYRIGHT BY
RAND McNALLY & COMPANY
MADE IN U.S.A.

Longitude East of Greenwich

176

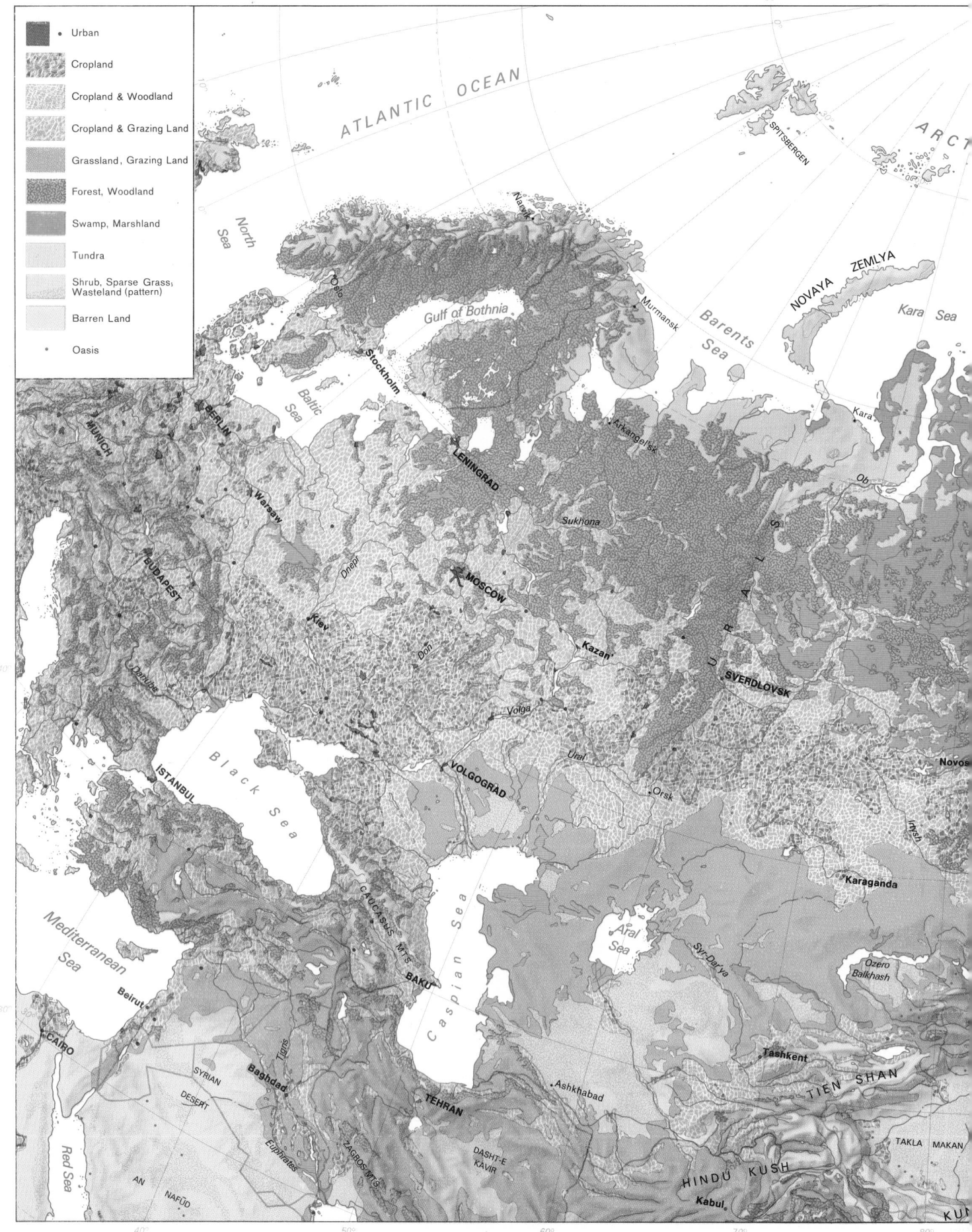

Legend:
- Urban
- Cropland
- Cropland & Woodland
- Cropland & Grazing Land
- Grassland, Grazing Land
- Forest, Woodland
- Swamp, Marshland
- Tundra
- Shrub, Sparse Grass; Wasteland (pattern)
- Barren Land
- Oasis

ATLANTIC OCEAN

ARCT

SPITSBERGEN

NOVAYA ZEMLYA

Kara Sea

North Sea

Oslo

Gulf of Bothnia

Barents Sea

Murmansk

Stockholm

Baltic Sea

Arkangel'sk

Kara

BERLIN

MUNICH

LENINGRAD

Ob

Warsaw

Sukhona

BUDAPEST

MOSCOW

Kiev

Dnepr

Kazan

U R A L S

Danube

Don

SVERDLOVSK

Volga

ISTANBUL

Black Sea

VOLGOGRAD

Ural

Novos

Orsk

Irtysh

Mediterranean Sea

CAUCASUS MTS.

Caspian Sea

Aral Sea

Karaganda

BAKU

Syr-Dar'ya

Ozero Balkhash

Beirut

CAIRO

SYRIAN DESERT

Baghdad

Tigris

TEHRAN

Ashkhabad

Tashkent

TIEN SHAN

Euphrates

ZAGROS MTS.

DASHT-E KAVIR

Red Sea

AN NAFŪD

HINDU KUSH

TAKLA MAKAN

Kabul

KUN

Scale 1:24,000,000; one inch to 380 miles. Lambert Azimuthal Equal-Area Projection

Anadyrskiy
Zaliv

East Siberian Sea

Bering Sea

Ambarchik

KHREBET GYDAN

Laptev Sea

OCEAN

Nordvik

Olenëk

Lena

GORY PUTORANA

Tura

Yakutsk

Lena

Krasnoyarsk

Lake Baikal

Irkutsk

Uhaan Baatar

ALTAI MTS

Tihua

GOBI (DESERT)

Hwang Ho

PEKING

Chengchou

Yangtze

SHANGHAI

Yellow Sea

East China Sea

Magadan

Tiliichiki

POLUOSTROV KAMCHATSKA

Petropavlovsk-Kamchatskiy

Sea of Okhotsk

SAKHALIN

Komsomol'sk-na-Amure

Amur

Argun

GREATER KHINGAN MTS.

Haerhpin

Vladivostok

MUKDEN

SEOUL

Sea of Japan

HOKKAIDŌ

Sapporo

HONSHŪ

TOKYO

KYŪSHŪ

PACIFIC OCEAN

NTAINS

0   100   200   400   600   800 Miles

0   150   300   600   900   1200 Kilometers

Mediterranean Sea
Red Sea
CAIRO
Beirut
SYRIAN DESERT
AN NAFŪD
Baghdad
Tigris
Euphrates
ZAGROS MTS.
CAUCASUS MTS.
BAKU
Caspian Sea
Aral Sea
Syr-Dar'ya
Karaganda
Ozero Balkhash
TEHRAN
Ashkhabad
Tashkent
TIEN SHAN
TAKLA MAKAN
DASHT-E KAVIR
HINDU KUSH
Kabul
KUN
Rawalpindi
Kermân
Mecca
Riyadh
Persian Gulf
DELHI
AR RUB' AL KHĀLĪ
Muscat
KARACHI
Nāgpur
DANAKIL
Aden
Gulf of Aden
Berbera
Arabian Sea
BOMBAY
WESTERN GHATS
EASTERN GHATS
MADRAS
Calicut
CEYLON
Colombo
INDIAN OCEAN

Urban
Cropland
Cropland & Woodland
Cropland & Grazing Land
Grassland, Grazing Land
Forest, Woodland
Swamp, Marshland
Tundra
Shrub, Sparse Grass, Wasteland (pattern)
Barren Land
Oasis

A-568600-96   -1- 4
COPYRIGHT BY
RAND McNALLY & COMPANY
MADE IN U.S.A.

Scale 1:24,000,000; one inch to 380 miles. Lambert Azimuthal Equal-Area Projection

ALTAI
MTS

Tihua

GOBI (DESERT)

Ulaan Baatar

GREATER KHINGAN MTS

Haerpin

MUKDEN

Vladivostok

HONSHŪ

Sea
of
Japan

TOKYO

SEOUL

KYŪSHŪ

PEKING

Hwang Ho

Yellow
Sea

PACIFIC

OCEAN

30°

140°

140°

Chengchou

SHANGHAI

East
China
Sea

WUHAN

CHUNGKING

Mekong

T'aipei

Tropic of Cancer

20°

INTAINS

TIBET

FORMOSA

MALAYAS

Brahmaputra

K'unming

CANTON

Philippine
Sea

130°

LCUTTA

nges

Mandalay

Salween

Hanoi

HAINAN TAO

MANILA

10°

Bay   of

Bengal

Rangoon

Mekong

Cebu

MINDANAO

South

China

BANGKOK

HO CHI MINH CITY

Sea

Celebes

Sea

Manado

Andaman

Sea

Kota Kinabalu

0°

Medan

Kuching

BORNEO

CELEBES

Equator

SINGAPORE

SUMATRA

Udjung Pandang

Java   Sea

90°

100°

DJAKARTA

JAVA

120°

10°

10°

0   100   200   400   600   800 Miles

0   150   300   600   900   1200 Kilometers

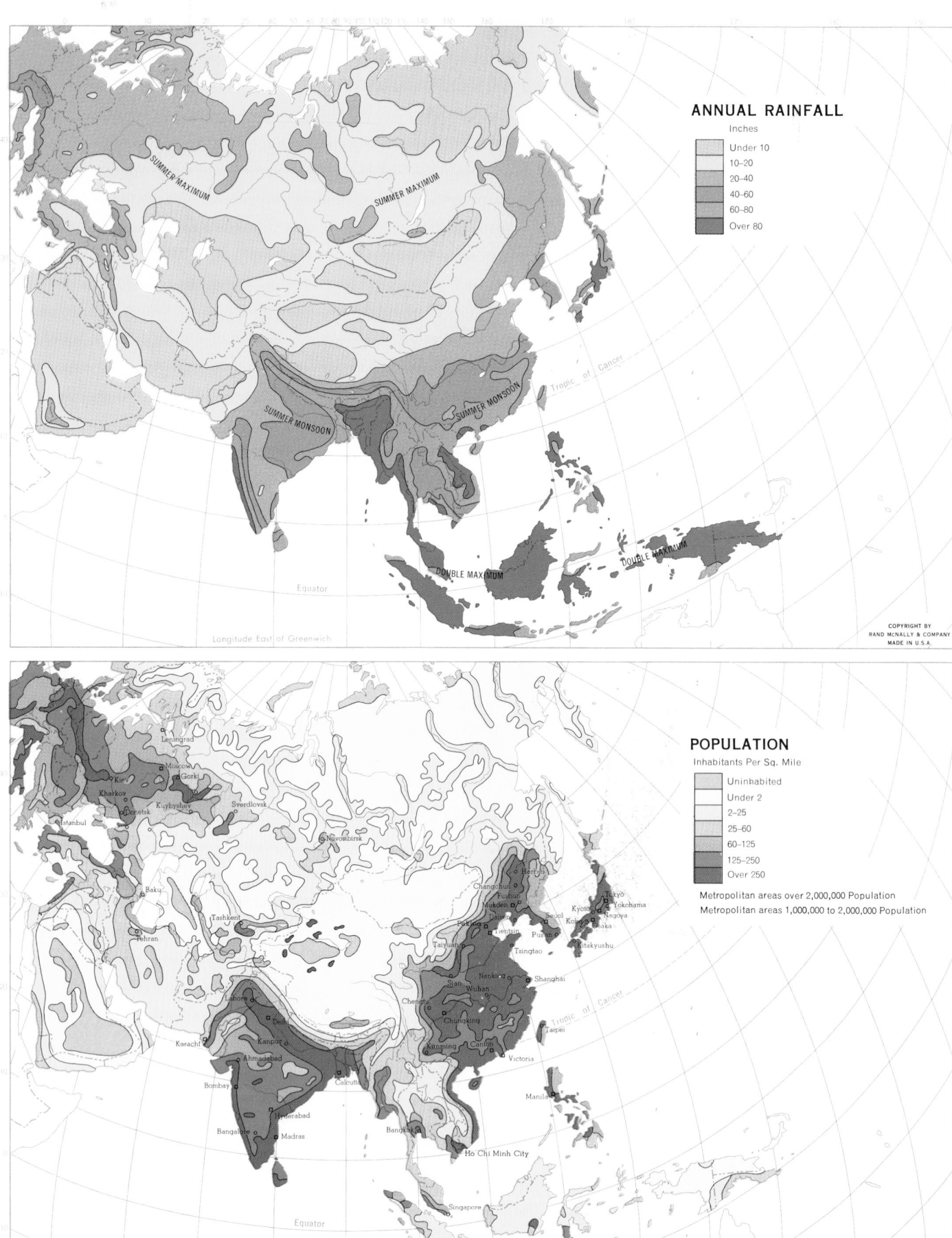

ANNUAL RAINFALL

Inches

- Under 10
- 10–20
- 20–40
- 40–60
- 60–80
- Over 80

SUMMER MAXIMUM

SUMMER MAXIMUM

SUMMER MONSOON

SUMMER MONSOON

DOUBLE MAXIMUM

DOUBLE MAXIMUM

Tropic of Cancer

Equator

Longitude East of Greenwich

POPULATION

Inhabitants Per Sq. Mile

- Uninhabited
- Under 2
- 2–25
- 25–60
- 60–125
- 125–250
- Over 250

Metropolitan areas over 2,000,000 Population

Metropolitan areas 1,000,000 to 2,000,000 Population

Leningrad
Moscow
Kiev
Gorki
Kharkov
Donetsk
Kuybyshev
Sverdlovsk
Istanbul
Novosibirsk
Baku
Tashkent
Tehran
Lahore
Delhi
Kanpur
Karachi
Ahmadabad
Bombay
Calcutta
Hyderabad
Bangalore
Madras

Harbin
Changchun
Fushun
Mukden
Dairen
Peking
Tientsin
Taiyuan
Tsingtao
Nanking
Sian
Wuhan
Shanghai
Chengtu
Chungking
Kunming
Canton
Taipei
Victoria

Tokyo
Yokohama
Kyoto
Nagoya
Seoul
Kobe
Osaka
Puran
Kitakyushu

Manila

Bangkok

Ho Chi Minh City

Singapore

Djakarta
Surabaja
Bandung

Tropic of Cancer

Equator

Longitude East of Greenwich

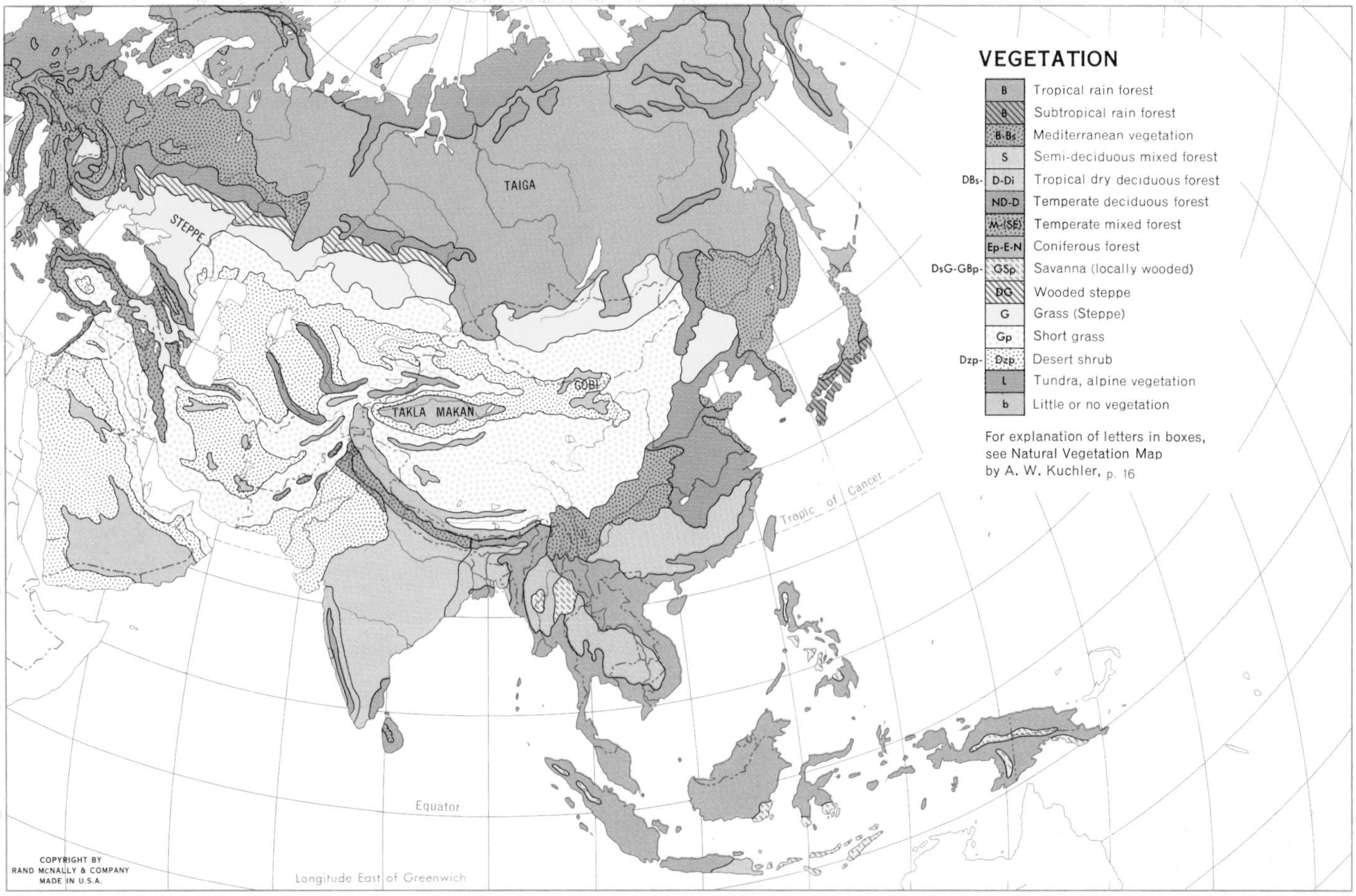

VEGETATION

	B	Tropical rain forest
	B	Subtropical rain forest
	B-Bs	Mediterranean vegetation
	S	Semi-deciduous mixed forest
DBs-	D-Di	Tropical dry deciduous forest
	ND-D	Temperate deciduous forest
	M-(SE)	Temperate mixed forest
	Ep-E-N	Coniferous forest
DsG-GBp-	GSp	Savanna (locally wooded)
	DG	Wooded steppe
	G	Grass (Steppe)
	Gp	Short grass
Dzp-	Dzp	Desert shrub
	L	Tundra, alpine vegetation
	b	Little or no vegetation

For explanation of letters in boxes,
see Natural Vegetation Map
by A. W. Kuchler, p. 16

TAIGA

STEPPE

GOBI

TAKLA MAKAN

Tropic of Cancer

Equator

Longitude East of Greenwich

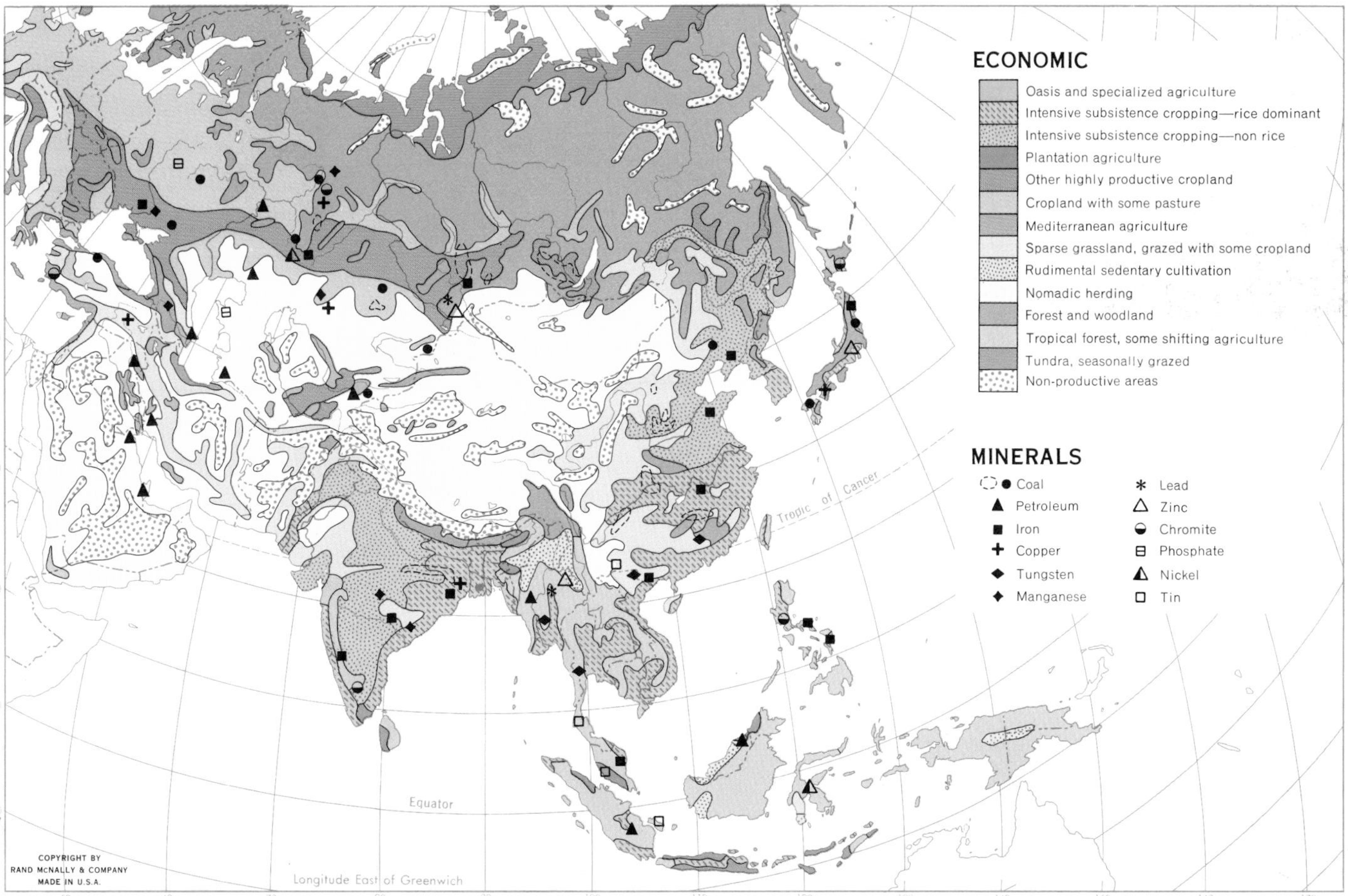

ECONOMIC

	Oasis and specialized agriculture
	Intensive subsistence cropping—rice dominant
	Intensive subsistence cropping—non rice
	Plantation agriculture
	Other highly productive cropland
	Cropland with some pasture
	Mediterranean agriculture
	Sparse grassland, grazed with some cropland
	Rudimental sedentary cultivation
	Nomadic herding
	Forest and woodland
	Tropical forest, some shifting agriculture
	Tundra, seasonally grazed
	Non-productive areas

MINERALS

⬭●	Coal	✳	Lead
▲	Petroleum	△	Zinc
■	Iron	◖	Chromite
✚	Copper	⊟	Phosphate
◆	Tungsten	▲	Nickel
◆	Manganese	▢	Tin

Tropic of Cancer

Equator

Longitude East of Greenwich

Continued on page 209

Scale 1:40 000 000; one inch to 630 miles. Lambert's Azimuthal, Equal Area Projection
Elevations and depressions are given in feet

NORTH AMERICA
Bering Str.
BERING SEA
ALEUTIAN ISLANDS (U.S.A.)
ALEUTIAN TRENCH
KOMANDORSKIYE OSTROVA (Sov. Union)
Petropavlovsk-Kamchatskiy
SEA OF OKHOTSK
Okhotsk
Yakutsk
SAKHALIN (Sov. Union)
KURIL ISLANDS (Sov. Union)
Komsomolsk
Sovetskaya Gavan
Blagoveshchensk
Khabarovsk
MANCHURIA
Vladivostok
HAERHPIN
CH'ANGCH'UN
MUKDEN
NORTH KOREA
P'yŏngyang
SEOUL
SOUTH KOREA
SEA OF JAPAN
JAPAN
Hakodate
Sendai
TOKYO
YOKOHAMA
KYOTO
KOBE
OSAKA
KITAKYUSHU
Nagasaki
Lüta (Dairen)
TSINGTAO
Tsinan
T'AIYÜAN
NANKING
SHANGHAI
EAST CHINA SEA
WUHAN
Fuchou
Amoy
Swatow
CANTON
HONG KONG
VICTORIA
Macau
T'AIPEI
TAIWAN (FORMOSA)
Tropic of Cancer
PHILIPPINE SEA
PACIFIC OCEAN
LUZON
PHILIPPINES
Quezon City
MANILA
MINDORO
PANAY
NEGROS
SAMAR
LEYTE
MINDANAO
PALAWAN
HAINAN TAO
Hue
HO CHI MINH CITY (Saigon)
SOUTH CHINA SEA
SULU SEA
CELEBES SEA
Kota Kinabalu
Sandakan
BRUNEI
MALAYSIA
Kuching
BORNEO
CELEBES
HALMAHERA
NEW GUINEA
Equator
East Longitude
West Longitude
120°
130°
Miles
Kilometers
CYPRUS
Lemesós
Lárnax
MEDITERRANEAN SEA
Longitude 35° East of Greenwich 36°
Ţarābulus (Tripoli)
Beirut (Bayrūt)
LEBANON
Şaydā (Sidon)
Şūr (Tyre)
Damascus (Dimashq)
SYRIA
Haifa (Ḥefa)
Nazareth
Irbid
Netanya
Tel Aviv-Yafo
Jerusalem
Ammān
Az Zarqā'
Ashdod
Ashqelon
Gaza (Ghazzah)
Khān Yūnus
Rafah
Be'er Sheva
ISRAEL
JORDAN
Areas occupied by Israel since June 1967
Port Said (Būr Sa'īd)
Ismailia (Al Ismā'īlīyah)
Suez (As Suways)
EGYPT
NEGEV
Eilat
Al 'Aqabah
Gulf of Suez
Gulf of Aqaba
SINAI PEN.
SAUDI ARABIA
Scale 1:4 000 000
Kuala Lumpur
PAHANG
SELANGOR
NEGERI SEMBILAN
Seremban
MELAKA
Melaka (Malacca)
MALAYSIA
JOHOR
MALAY PENINSULA
SOUTH CHINA SEA
STRAIT OF MALACCA
Johor Baharu
SINGAPORE
Singapore Strait
SUMATRA
RIAU
INDONESIA
KEPULAUAN RIAU
Longitude East of Greenwich
Cities, Towns, and Villages
0 to 25,000
25,000 to 100,000
100,000 to 250,000
250,000 to 1,000,000
1,000,000 and over
Major urbanized area

184

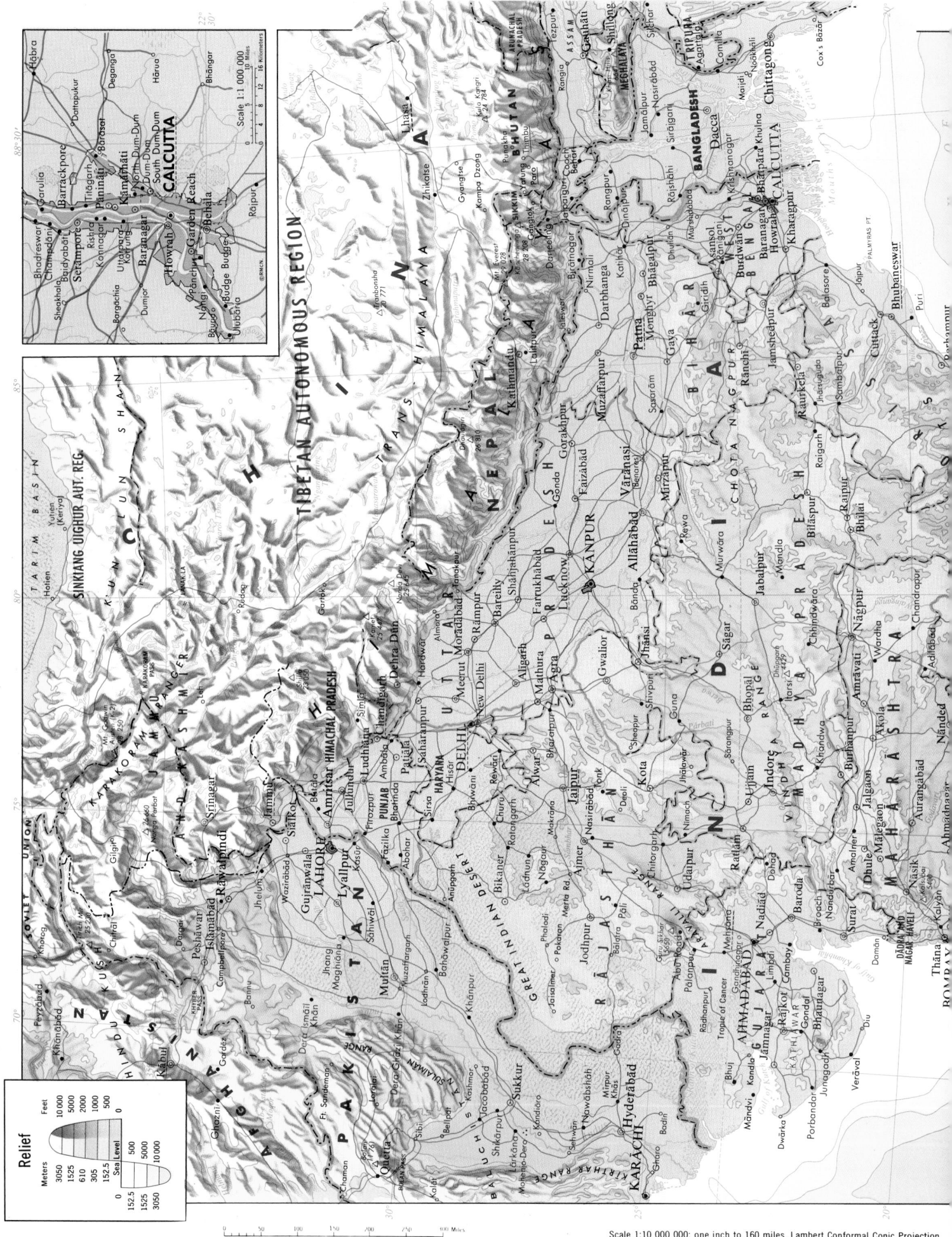

CALCUTTA
Scale 1:1 000 000
0 ... 10 Miles
0 ... 16 Kilometers

TIBETAN AUTONOMOUS REGION

SINKIANG UIGHUR AUT. REG.

TARIM BASIN

KUN LUN SHAN

C H I N A

Lhasa

Zhikatse

Gyangtse

Kampa Dzong

BHUTAN

Punakha   Tashigang
Thimbu
Paro

SIKKIM

Gangtok

Darjeeling

NEPAL

Kathmandu

Lalitpur

Mt. Everest
29 028

Kulo Kangri
△ 24 784

ARUNACHAL PRADESH

ASSAM

Shillong

MEGHALAYA

Gauhati

TRIPURA

Agartala

Comilla

Noākhāli

Chittagong

Cox's Bāzār

BANGLADESH

Dacca

WEST BENGAL

Khulna

Calcutta

Howrah

Kharagpur

PALMYRAS PT

Gyūbondrsha
△ 20 771

Namcha Barwa

Trans Himalaya

Jomolhari
△ 23 997

HIMALAYA

Dhaulagiri

Namcha
25 645
△

Kamet
25 447
△

Nanda Devi
25 645

TIBET

KASHMIR

KARAKORAM RANGE

HINDU KUSH

KARAKORAM PASS

Mt. Godwin
Austen K2
28 250

Trich Mir 25 230
△

SOVIET UNION

Khotog

Gilgit

Chitrāl

AFGHANISTAN

Khānābād

Feyzābād

Peshāwar

Campbellpore

Rāwalpindi

Islāmābād

Jammu

Siālkot

Wazīrābād

Gujrānwāla

Srīnagar

JAMMU AND KASHMIR

HIMACHAL PRADESH

Simla

Ambala

Chandīgarh

Dehra Dūn

Hardwār

Almora

UTTAR PRADESH

Bareilly

Morādābād

Rāmpur

Shāhjahānpur

Farrukhābād

Lucknow

KANPUR

Faizābād

Gonda

Gorakhpur

Allāhābad

Vārānasi

Mirzāpur

Rewa

BIHAR

Patna

Gaya

Muzaffarpur

Darbhanga

Monghyr

Bhāgalpur

Sāsarām

Giridih

Asansol

Rāniganj

Murshadābād

Rājshāhi

Burdwān

Baranagar

Naihāti

Sirājganj

Dinājpur

Rangpur

Jalpaiguri

Cooch
Behar

Kālimpur

Bogrā

Nirmali

Dhulian

PAKISTAN

LAHORE

Lyallpur

Amritsar

Jullundur

Ludhiāna

PUNJAB

Patiāla

Ambāla

Sahāranpur

Meerut

New Delhi

DELHI

Aligarh

Mathura

Agra

Gwalior

Jhānsi

MADHYA PRADESH

Sāgar

Jabalpur

Mandla

Chhindwāra

Nāgpur

Wardha

Amrāvati

Akola

Nānded

MAHĀRĀSHTRA

Aurangābād

Nāsik

Mālegaon

Jalgaon

Dhule

Amalner

Dhāggaon
△ 4429

VINDHYA RANGE

SATPURA RANGE

Bhopal

Sehore

Indore

Ujjain

Ratlām

Nimach

Chitorgarh

Udaipur

Dohad

Baroda

AHMADĀBAD

GUJARAT

Broach

Surat

Nandurbar

DĀDRA AND
NAGAR HAVELI

Dāmān

Thāna

BOMBAY

Kalyān
5549

RĀJASTHĀN

Jaipur

Ajmer

Nasīrābād

Tonk

Kota

Bundi

Jhālāwar

Shivpuri

Guna

Pārbati

Shājāpur

Sārangpur

Jhelum

Chenāb

Jhang Maghiāna

Montgomery

Multān

Muzaffargarh

Jhang

Lodhrān

Bahāwalpur

Fāzilka

Firozpur

Bhatinda

Sirsa

HARYĀNA

Hisār

Bhiwāni

Rohtak

Rewāri

Alwar

Bhāratpur

Dholpur

GREAT INDIAN DESERT

THAR DESERT

Bīkaner

Churu

Nāgaur

Lādnun

Ratangarh

Makrāna

Merta Rd.

Pokaran

Jaisalmer

Bālotra

Pāli

Jodhpur

Pholodi

ARĀVALLI RANGE

Guru Sikhar
△ 5650

Ābu Rd.

Pālanpur

Rādhanpur

Mehsāna

Nadiād

Limbdi

Gondal

Rājkot

KĀTHIĀWĀR

Jāmnagar

Mundra

Kandla

Bhāvnagar

Bhuj

Mārdvi

Verāval

Porbandar

Junāgadh

Dīu

Dwārka

Gulf of Kutch

Gulf of Khambhāt

Tropic of Cancer

BALUCHISTĀN

Quetta

Kalāt

Sibi

Bolān Pass

Fort Sandeman

Dera Ismāil Khān

Dera Ghāzi Khān

Bannu

Kohāt

KHYBER PASS

Kābul

Gardēz

Ghaznī

SULAIMAN RANGE

KIRTHAR RANGE

Jacobābād

Shikārpur

Sukkur

Lārkāna

Khairpur

Nawābshāh

Mīrpur Khās

Hyderābād

Badīn

Bādin

KARACHI

Indus

DELTA
OF THE
INDUS

S I N D

Relief
Feet | Meters
10 000 | 3050
5000 | 1525
2000 | 610
1000 | 305
500 | 152.5
Sea Level | 0
500 | 152.5
5000 | 1525
10 000 | 3050

0   50   100   150   200   250   400 Miles
0   100   200   300   400   500 Kilometers

Scale 1:10 000 000; one inch to 160 miles. Lambert Conformal Conic Projection
Elevations and depressions are given in feet

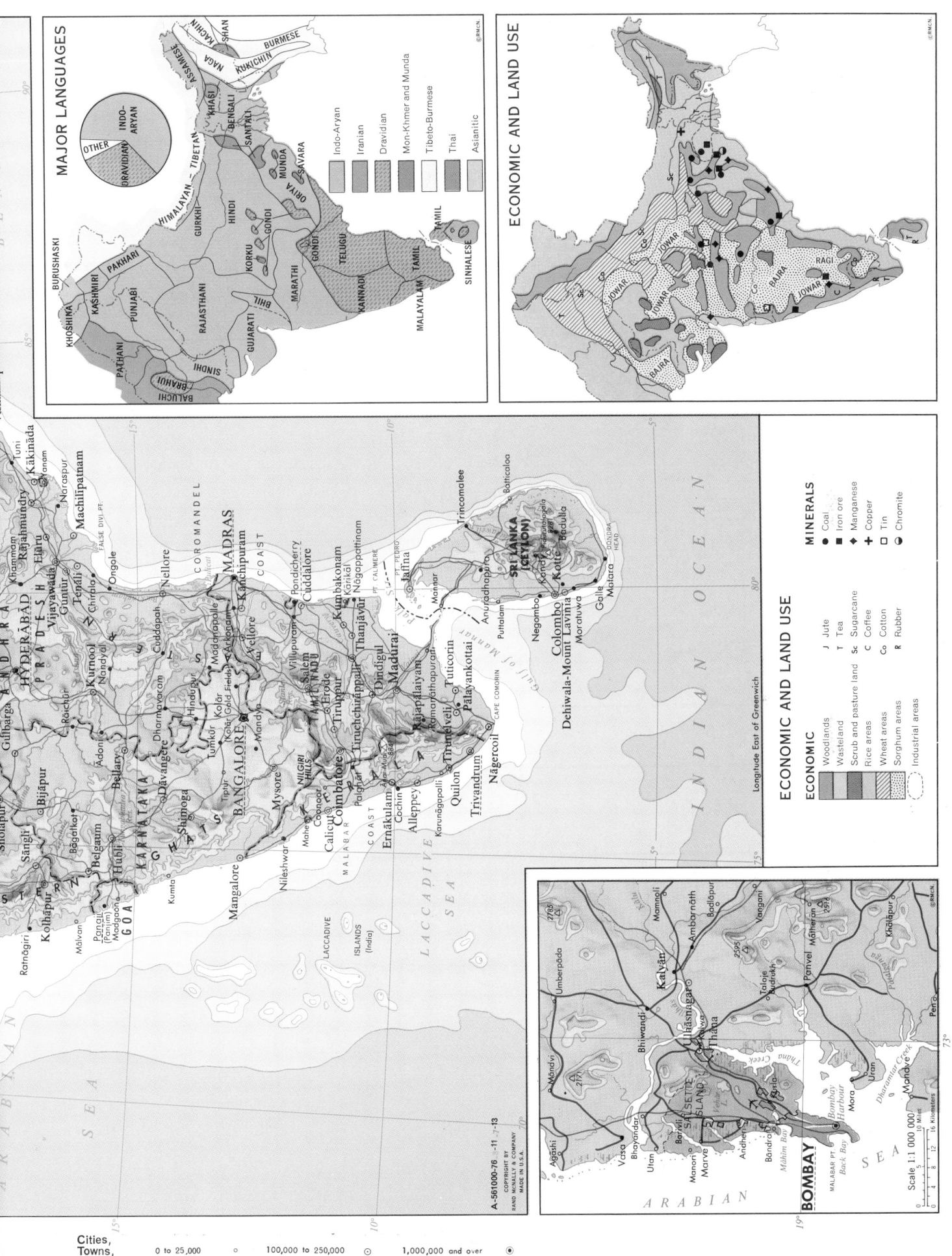

MAJOR LANGUAGES

BURMESE
SHAN
KACHIN
NAGA
KUKICHIN
ASSAMESE
KHASI
BENGALI
SANTALI
MUNDA
SAVARA
ORIYA
HINDI
GONDI
GONDI
TELUGU
TAMIL
HIMALAYAN — TIBETAN
GURKHI
PAKHARI
KASHMIRI
BURUSHASKI
KHOSHIMA
PUNJABI
RAJASTHANI
KORKU
MARATHI
KANNADI
MALAYALAM
TAMIL
SINHALESE
PATHANI
SINDHI
GUJARATI
BHIL
BALUCHI
BRAHUI

OTHER
INDO-ARYAN
DRAVIDIAN

Indo-Aryan
Iranian
Dravidian
Mon-Khmer and Munda
Tibeto-Burmese
Thai
Asianitic

BAY OF BENGAL

ECONOMIC AND LAND USE

JOWAR
JOWAR
JOWAR
BAJRA
RAGI
BAIRA
BAIRA

MINERALS

● Coal
■ Iron ore
♦ Manganese
✚ Copper
□ Tin
◐ Chromite

ECONOMIC AND LAND USE

ECONOMIC

Woodlands
Wasteland
Scrub and pasture land
Rice areas
Wheat areas
Sorghum areas
Industrial areas

J Jute
T Tea
Sc Sugarcane
C Coffee
Co Cotton
R Rubber

Longitude East of Greenwich

ANDHRA
PRADESH
HYDERABAD
MADRAS
COROMANDEL COAST
TAMIL NADU
KARNATAKA
BANGALORE
NILGIRI HILLS
GHATS
MALABAR COAST
GOA

Tuni
Kakinada
Rajahmundry
Machilipatnam
Khammam
Narasapur
Eluru
FALSE DIVI. PT.
Vijayawada
Guntur
Tenali
Chirala
Ongole
Kurnool
Nandyal
Nellore
Cuddapah
Pondicherry
Cuddalore
Kumbakonam
Karikal
Nagappattinam
PT. CALIMERE
PT. PEDRO
Jaffna
Raichur
Adoni
Bellary
Dharmavaram
Tumkur
Kolar
Kolar Gold Fields
Vellore
Arkonam
Madanapalle
Villupuram
Salem
Thanjavur
Tiruchchirappalli
Dindigul
Madurai
Karaikkudi
Tuticorin
Palayankottai
Tirunelveli
Nagercoil
CAPE COMORIN
Gulbarga
Bijapur
Raichur
Davangere
Hindupur
Tiptur
Mandya
Mysore
Erode
Tirupur
Coimbatore
Palghat
Coonoor
Mettur
Mahe
Calicut
Cochin
Ernakulam
Alleppey
Karunagappalli
Quilon
Trivandrum
Sholapur
Sangli
Bagalkot
Belgaum
Hubli
Shimoga
Nileshwar
Mangalore
Kumta
Ratnagiri
Malvan
Panaji (Panjim)
Madgaon

SRI LANKA (CEYLON)
Trincomalee
Batticaloa
Anuradhapura
Kandy
Badulla
DONDRA HEAD
Puttalam
Negombo
Colombo
Kotte
Dehiwala-Mount Lavinia
Moratuwa
Galle
Matara
Mannar

PALK STRAIT
GULF OF MANNAR
INDIAN OCEAN
LACCADIVE SEA
LACCADIVE ISLANDS (India)
ARABIAN SEA

A-561000-76 — 11-7-13
COPYRIGHT BY
RAND McNALLY & COMPANY
MADE IN U.S.A.

BOMBAY

Scale 1:1 000 000

SALSETTE ISLAND
THANA CREEK
Bombay Harbour
Back Bay
MALABAR PT.
Mahim Bay
ARABIAN SEA

Kalyan
Ulhasnagar
Thana
Bhiwandi
Ambarnath
Badlapur
Panvel
Uran
Mora
Bandra
Andheri
Borivli
Vasa
Bhayandar
Uttan
Manori
Marve
Agashi
Mandvi
Umberpada
Bhoyanpada

Cities, Towns, and Villages

0 to 25,000
25,000 to 100,000
100,000 to 250,000
250,000 to 1,000,000
1,000,000 and over
Major urbanized area

186

Continued on pages 210-211

BLACK SEA

İstanbul Boğazı (Bosporus)
Üsküdar
İSTANBUL
Zonguldak
Kastamonu
Sinop
Bursa
Eskişehir
Çankırı
Merzifon
Samsun
Bergama
İzmir
Kütahya
Ankara
Kırşehir
Çorum
Yozgat
Tokat
Giresun
Trabzon
CAUCASUS MTS.
Grozny
Fort Shevchenko
KAZAK
Ordzhonikidze
Shevchenko
Makhachkala
Aydın
Afyon
Sivas
Erzincan
Batumi
Poti
GEORGIAN S.S.R.
Kutaisi
Tbilisi
Leninakan
Kars
Kirovabad
Derbent
PLATO UST-URT
Chimbay
Nukus
Muğla
Isparta
TURKEY
Kayseri
Erzurum
ARMENIAN S.S.R.
Yerevan
Baku
Kungrad
TURKESTAN
Turtkul'
Khiva
Antalya
TOROS DAĞLARI
Maraş
Malatya
Elâzığ
KURDISTAN
Van
Tabriz
AZERBAYDZHAN S.S.R.
Kransovodsk
PESKI KARAKUMY (DESERT)
Ashkhabad
Chardzhou
Mersin
Adana
Diyarbakır
Siverek
Mardin
Cizre
Rawandiz
Rezā'īyeh
Ardabil
Nebit-Dag
Chikishlyar
KOPPEH DAGH
Bojnurd
Mary
Kushka
CYPRUS
Nicosia
İskenderun
Antakya
Aleppo
Urfa
Al Mawşil
Nineveh
Irbil
Miāneh
Bandar-e Pahlavī
Rasht
Gorgan
Shahrūd
Neyshābūr
Mashhad
MEDITERRANEAN SEA
Tarābulus (Tripoli)
LEBANON
Latakia (Al Lādhiqīyah)
Ḩamāh
Dayr az Zawr
Aş Sulaymānīyah
Zanjan
Qazvīn
Bābol
ELBURZ MTS.
Qolleh-ye Damāvand
Dāmghān
Bejestān
Ferdows
Qāyen
Herāt
AFG
Ḩimş
SYRIA
Palmyra (Ruins)
Abū Kamāl
Tikrīt
Kirkūk
Sanandaj
Hamadān
TEHRAN
Shāhrūd
Haifa
Şaydā (Sidon)
Beirut
Damascus (Dimashq)
Aş Şuwaydā'
Ar Ramādī
BAGHDAD
Karbalā
An Najaf
Babylon (Ruins)
Kangāvar
Borūjerd
Kermānshāh
Qom
Arāk
DASHT-E KAVIR DESERT
Rashīd
Damietta
Tel Aviv-Yafo
ISRAEL
Jerusalem
Gaza
Amman
JORDAN
Aţ Ţurayf
SYRIAN DESERT
IRAQ
Borūjerd
Dezfūl
Shūshtar
Masjed Soleymān
Eşfahān
Shahreżā
Yazd
Bāfq
PLATEAU OF IRAN
IRAN
Port Said
ALEXANDRIA (Al Iskandarīyah)
CAIRO (Al Qāhirah)
Suez (As Suways)
SINAI
Al 'Aqabah
Maʿān
An Nāşirīyah
Ahvāz
Bandar-e Shāhpūr
Khorramshahr
Shīrāz
Persepolis (Ruins)
Rafsanjān
Kermān
Farāh
EGYPT
GULF OF SUEZ
Jabal Katherīna
Areas occupied by Israel since June 1967
Al Jawf
Sakākah
Rafḩā
Al Başrah
Abādān
KUWAIT
Kuwait (Al Kuwayt)
Kāzerūn
Borāzjān
Būshehr
Daryācheh-ye Bakhtegān
Jahrom
Lār
Zāhedān
Khash
Rīgān
Bampūr
CHA
Rashīd
Bür Safājah
Al Quşayr
RAS BANAS
AN NAFŪD
Taymā'
Ḩāʾil
JABAL SHAMMAR
Al Qayşūmah
AL ḨASĀ
PERSIAN GULF
RAS AT TANNURAH
Al Qaţīf
BAHRAIN
Bandar-e Lengeh
Bandar ʿAbbās
QESHM I
STRAIT OF HORMUZ
Khaybar
SAUDI NAJD
Buraydah
ʿUnayzah
Sudair
Ash Shaqrā'
Ad Dammām
Az Zahrān (Dhahran)
Al Manāmah
QATAR
Ad Dawḩah
Ajman
OMAN
Dubayy
Jāsk
Chāh Bahār
Gwādar
Yanbu'
AL ḨIJĀZ
Al Madīnah (Medina)
Al Aflāj
Ad Dilam
Riyadh (Ar Riyāḑ)
AL DAHNĀ
AD DAHY
Al Hufūf
Abū Zaby
UNITED ARAB EMIRATES
Al Buraymī
Al Khābūrah
Maţraḩ
AL AKHDAR
JABAL
Jabal ash Shām
Muscat
Şūr
GULF OF OMAN
Juddah
Mecca (Makkah)
Aţ Ţāʾif
Al Khurmah
NAFŪD
Mubarraz
JABAL AL TUWAYQ
ARABIA
RAS AL HADD
RAS AL MADRAKAH
Al Qunfudhah
Jabal Ibrāhīm
Al Lidām
Wādī ad Dawāsir
AR RUBʿ AL KHĀLĪ
OMAN
AL MAŞĪRAH
Abha
Qalʿat Bīshah
RAS AL MADRAKAH
SUDAN
Būr Sūdān
Sawākin
Ţawkar
NAJRAN
Shibām
Tarīm
Say'ūn
KHŪRYĀN-MŪRYĀN (Oman)
Asmera
Kassalā
Kerēn (Massawa)
Akordat
JAZĀʾIR FARASĀN
Qizān
Abū ʿArīsh
Şaʿdah
P.D.R. OF YEMEN
Mirbāţ
Al Ḩawtah
HADRAMAWT
RAS FARTAK
DANAKIL
ETHIOPIA
DAHLAK ARCH.
KAMARĀN (P.D.R. of Yem.)
Ḩajr Shuqrā
San'ā
Al Ḩudaydah
YEMEN
Shihr
Al Mukallā
Sayḩūt
Dessē
Beylul
Al Mukhā (Mocha)
Madīnat ash Shaʿb
Aden
RAS ASIR
Bāb el Mandeb
Jabal Rafʿ
SUQUTRA (SOCOTRA) (P.D.R. of Yemen)
Hadībū
AFARS AND ISSAS
Djibouti
Zeila
Berbera
GULF OF ADEN
Las Khoreh
Alula
SOMALIA

A-569400-76- -10-9-17
COPYRIGHT BY
RAND McNALLY & COMPANY
MADE IN U.S.A.

Relief

Meters		Feet
3050		10 000
1525		5000
610		2000
305		1000
152.5		500
	Sea Level	0
0		Below Sea Level
152.5		500
1525		5000
3050		10 000

Scale 1:16 000 000; one inch to 250 miles. Polyconic Projection
Elevations and depressions are given in feet

Longitude East of Greenw

on pages 172–173

S.R.

Ozero Balkhash
-Orda
PESKI MUYUN-KUM

ION

Dzhambul
Chimkent
Arys

KIRGIZ S.S.R.
KIRGIZSKIY KHREBET
Frunze

SHKENT
Kokand
Namangan
Dzhalal-Abad
Andizhan
Osh
Leninabad
Fergana
Dzhizak

TABZHIK S.S.R.
Garm
Pik Kommunizma
Dushanbe
Kurgan-Tyube
Khorog

PAMIRS

Mazar-e Sharif
Feyzabad

HINDU KUSH
Gilgit
Chitral

Kabul
KHYBER PASS
Ghazni

PAKISTAN
Chaman
Loralai
Quetta
BOLAN PASS
Kalat

Shikarpur
Sukkur
Mohenjo-Daro (Ruins)

ACHI

AFGHANISTAN
Dargai
Jalalabad
MORGA RA.
KHYBER PASS

PAKISTAN
Charsadda
Peshawar

Scale 1:4 000 000

K'ashih (Kashgar)
Soch'e (Yarkand)
Hotien

TAKLA MAKAN

SINKIANG UIGHUR
AUT. REG.

Mt. Godwin
Austen (K2)
28 250
KARAKORAM PASS
PANAK LA

JAMMU AND KASHMIR

Islamabad
Srinagar
Rawalpindi
Jammu
Gartok
Rudog

AFGHANISTAN

PAKISTAN

IRAN

JAMMU AND KASHMIR
HIMACHAL PRADESH
PUNJAB
HARYANA
UTTAR PRADESH
RAJASTHAN

TIBET

CHINA

NEPAL
SIKKIM
BHUTAN
ARUNACHAL PRADESH
ASSAM
NAGALAND
MEGHALAYA
BANGLADESH
WEST BENGAL
MIZORAM
BURMA

BIHAR

GUJARAT
MADHYA PRADESH
ORISSA

MAHARASHTRA

ARABIAN SEA

BAY OF BENGAL

Tropic of Cancer

KARNATAKA
ANDHRA PRADESH

KERALA
TAMIL NADU

SRI LANKA
(CEYLON)

INDIA · POLITICAL

Scale 1:40 000 000

1-TRIPURA
2-MANIPUR
3-LAKSHADWEEP
4-DELHI
5-DADRA AND NAGAR HAVELI
6-PONDICHERRY
7-GOA, DAMAN, AND DIU

Continued on pages 188–189

Peshawar
Dera Ismail Khan
Jhelum
Sialkot
Gujranwala
Amritsar
LAHORE
Firozpur
Ludhiana
Simla
Jullundur
Chandigarh
Ambala
Patiala
Saharanpur
Bhatinda

HIMALAYA

TRANS-HIMALAYA

TIBETAN AUTONOMOUS REGION

Nam Tsho

Lhasa

Yamdrog Tsho
Gyangtse

Brahmaputra

Mt. Everest
29 028
Kanchenjunga
28 208

NEPAL
Kathmandu
Lalitpur
Darjeeling

SIKKIM
Gangtok
BHUTAN
Thimbu

ARUNACHAL PRADESH
Sadiya
Tinsukia
Silsagar
Jorhat

Sibsagar

ASSAM
NAGALAND
Kohima

Moggaung
Myitkyina

Bahawalpur
Multan

PUNJAB

HARYANA
Meerut
Moradabad
DELHI
New Delhi
Rampur
Bareilly

Bikaner
Alwar
Aligarh
Shahjahanpur

UTTAR PRADESH
Mathura
Bharatpur
Agra
Farrukhabad
KANPUR
Lucknow
Faizabad
Gorakhpur
Darbhanga

Rangpur

Gauhati
MEGHALAYA
Shillong
KHASI HILLS
Nasirabad
Silchar
Imphal
MANIPUR

Bhamo

DERA GHAZI KHAN

Ajmer
Jaipur
Gwalior
Jhansi
Banda
Sasaram
Gaya

RAJASTHAN
Jodhpur
Tonk
Sheopuri
Shivpuri
Kota

Allahabad
Varanasi
(Benares)
Mirzapur
Rewa

Patna
Monghyr
Bhagalpur

BIHAR
Giridih
Berhampore

Rajshahi
Siraiganj
BANGLADESH
Dacca
Comilla

Mandalay

BURMA

GUJARAT
Udaipur
AHMADABAD

Abu Road
Palanpur

Sagar
Murwara
Ranchi

Asansol
Burdwan

WEST BENGAL
Howrah
Bhatpara
CALCUTTA
Chittagong

Shwebo

Hyderabad

Great Indian Desert
ARAVALLI RANGE

INDIA

Bhuj
Rann of Kutch

Mandvi
GUJARAT
Rajkot
KATHIAWAR
Jamnagar
Bhaunagar
PENINSULA
Porbandar
Junagadh
Veraval
Diu
Gulf of Kutch
Gulf of Khambat

Indore
Baroda

MADHYA PRADESH
Ujjain
Bhopal
Jabalpur
Bilaspur
Raigarh

NINDHYA RA.

Surat
Daman

Dhule
Akola
Amravati
Nagpur
Raipur
Sambalpur

Jaipur
Cuttack
Bhubaneswar
Puri

ORISSA

Hoogly
Mouths of the Ganges

Khulna
Naokhali

Mouths of the Irrawaddy

Sittwe

Yenangyaung
Pyinmana

Magwe

ARAKAN YOMA

Kyaukpyu

Sandoway

PAGODA PT.

Nasik
Aurangabad
DECCAN
Chandrapur

BOMBAY
Ahmadnagar
MAHARASHTRA
Pune
Nizamabad
HYDERABAD
Warangal

Godavari

Vizianagaram

Vishakhapatnam

BAY OF BENGAL

Henzada
Bassein

Rangoon

PEGU

Sholapur
Gulbarga
Raichur
Vijayawada
Eluru
Machilipatnam

Kolhapur
Sangli
Bijapur
Guntur
Rajahmundry
Kakinada
Yanam

Krishna

HYDERABAD
ANDHRA PRADESH

EASTERN GHATS

COROMANDEL COAST

Belgaum
Hubli
Kurnool
Nellore

Panaji
(Panjim)
GOA

Bellary
Cuddapah

KARNATAKA

Mangalore

Kolar
Mysore
BANGALORE
Vellore

MADRAS
Kanchipuram
Pondicherry

WESTERN GHATS

LACCADIVE ISLANDS
(India)

Mahe
Calicut
Coimbatore
Tiruchchirappalli
Thanjavur
Madurai

Salem
Cuddalore
Kumbakonam
Nagappattinam

TAMIL NADU

KERALA

Ernakulam

Longitude East of Greenwich

Tiruchchirappalli
Thanjavur
Ernakulam
TAMIL NADU
Nagappattinam

KERALA
Alleppey
Quilon
Trivandrum
Madurai
Tuticorin
Tirunelveli

Jaffna

Mannar
Trincomalee

CAPE COMORIN
Gulf of Mannar
Puttalam
Anuradhapura

SRI LANKA
(CEYLON)
Colombo
Kandy

INDIAN OCEAN

Galle
DONDRA HEAD
Matara

Same scale as main map

Cities, Towns, and Villages

0 to 25,000
25,000 to 100,000
100,000 to 250,000
250,000 to 1,000,000
1,000,000 and over

Major urbanized area

500 Miles
800 Kilometers

Continued on pages 172–173

Scale 1:16 000 000; one inch to 250 miles. Polyconic Projection
Elevations and depressions are given in feet

SEA OF OKHOTSK

KURIL ISLANDS (Sov. Union) SIMUSHIR

URUP

ITURUP

KUNASHIR

Uglegorsk

SAKHALIN (Sov. Un.)

Dolinsk

Yuzhno-Sakhalinsk

Kholmsk ○ Korsakov

M ANIVA

Wakkanai

HOKKAIDŌ

Asahikawa ○ Kushiro

Otaru ○ Sapporo

Muroran

ERIMO SAKI

Esashi ○ Hakodate

Aomori ○ Kuji

Hirosaki ○ Morioka

Akita ○

Sakata ○ Ishinomaki

Yamagata ○ Sendai

SADO

Niigata ○

Nagaoka ○

NOTO HANTŌ

Toyama ○ Nagano ○ Utsunomiya

Kanazawa ○ Maebashi ○

OKI GUNTO TŌKYŌ

Fukui ○ Gifu ○ Chiba ○ YOKOHAMA

Tottori ○ KYŌTO ○ NAGOYA

Matsue ○ KŌBE ○ Nara

OSAKA

Okayama ○ Wakayama

Hiroshima ○ Kure

Shimonoseki ○ Takamatsu

KITAKYŪSHŪ Matsuyama SHIKOKU

Fukuoka ○ Kōchi

Sasebo ○ Kumamoto

Nagasaki ○ KYŪSHŪ

Kagoshima

HONSHŪ

IZU

SHICHITŌ

ŌSUMI GUNTŌ TANEGA

YAKU

TOKARA GUNTŌ

AMAMI GUNTŌ Kominato

TOKUNO

OKINAWA GUNTŌ

Okinawa

Naha

PACIFIC OCEAN

PHILIPPINE SEA

N I O N

KHREBET

Chita ○ Skovorodino

Nerchinsk ○ Moho ○ Komsomolsk-na-Amure

Chiuchichen

Aginskoye ○ Svobodnyy

Sretensk ○ Blagoveshchensk ○ Ussri Tyrma ○ Malmyzh

Nerchinski Zavod ○ Zavitinsk ○ Ust Tyrma ○ Sovetskaya Gavan

Aksha ○ Zavitinsk ○ Khabarovsk

Choybalsan ○ Manchouli (Lupin) ○ Hailaerh (Hailar) ○ Wuyün ○ Birobidzhan ○ Bikin

ör Haan ○ Chaybalsan ○ Nenchiang ○ K'oshan ○ Fuchin

Kerulen ○ Ch'ich'ihaerh (Tsitsihar) ○ Hailun ○ SIKHOTE ALIN

M A N C H U R I A ○ HEILUNGKIANG ○ Tungchiang

Angangch'i ○ Suihua ○ HAERHPIN (Harbin) ○ Spassk-Dal'niy

Wench'an ○ Hulan ○ Ol'ga

Sofun ○ Fuyü ○ Ningan ○ Vladimiro-Aleksandrovskoye

KIRIN ○ Chilin (Kirin) ○ Ussuriysk ○ Vladivostok

Lupei ○ CH'ANGCH'UN ○ Tunhua ○ Hunch'un

Shuangliao ○ Yenchi

CH'AHAERH ○ Ch'ihfeng ○ Tiehling ○ It'ung ○ Nalin ○ Musan

Tolun ○ FUSHUN ○ Tunghua ○ Chŏngjin

MUKDEN (Shenyang) ○ PAITOU

Changpei ○ Ch'engte (Jehol) ○ Ch'aoyang ○ Liaoyang ○ MUSU DAN

INNER MONGOLIAN AUT. REG. ○ Chinchou ○ Yingk'ou ○ Kanggye

Weich'ang ○ Hulutao ○ Uiju

Huhohaot'e ○ LIAONING ○ Antung ○ Hamhŭng

Fengchen ○ Changchiak'ou (Kalgan) ○ LIAOTUNG PANTAO ○ Sinŭiju ○ Wŏnsan

PEKING (Peiching) ○ Lüshun (Port Arthur) ○ Lüta (Dairen) ○ P'yŏngyang ○ NORTH KOREA

HOPEH ○ TIENTSIN (T'ienching) ○ Namp'o ○ Kaesŏng (Kaijo)

Paoting ○ Po Hai ○ SEOUL (Sŏul) ○ SOUTH

Chengting ○ Laichow ○ Yent'ai (Chefoo) ○ Inch'ŏn ○ SOUTH

'AIYÜAN ○ Huimin ○ Weihai ○ Andong ○ Andong

HANSI ○ Wan ○ Kyŏngju

Fenyang ○ Tsinan (Chinan) ○ SHANTUNG-PANTAO ○ Kunsan ○ Taegu

○ Poshan ○ Chiaohsien ○ TSINGTAO (Ch'ingtao) ○ Masan ○ PUSAN

Linfen ○ Weifang

Chingyang ○ Tzuyang ○ Mokp'o ○ TSU SHIMA

SHANTUNG ○ Lini

○ Chining ○ Lienyünchiang ○ KOREAN ARCHIPELAGO

○ Chian ○ CHEJU I (QUELPART)

Chengchou ○ K'aifeng ○ HONAN ○ KIANGSU ○ Huaiyin

Nanyang ○ Hsüchou

Fouyang ○ Huaiyin

HONAN ○ Pangfou

Hsinyang ○ NANKING (Nanching) ○ Chenchiang ○ Ch'angchou

Hofei ○ Soochow ○ SHANGHAI

TAPIEH-SHAN ○ ANHWEI ○ Wuhsi ○ SHANGHAI-SHIH

HUPEH ○ Anching ○ Wuhsing ○ Sungchiang

'ang ○ WUHAN ○ Chiahsing

Hanyang ○ EAST CHINA

angling ○ Shashih ○ Chiuchiang ○ Hangchou ○ CHOUSHAN ARCHIPELAGO

Yüehyang ○ Shaohsing ○ SEA

CHEKIANG ○ Ningpo

Ch'angsha ○ Nanch'ang ○ Ch'ühsien

HUNAN ○ KIANGSI ○ Linch'uan ○ Lishui ○ Wenchou

Hsiangt'an ○ Nancheng

Hengyang ○ Chian ○ Nanp'ing ○ Ningte ○ NANSEI SHOTŌ

in ○ Kanchou ○ Hsiap'u

MEILING PASS ○ Fuchou (Foochow) ○ Chilung

NAN ○ FUKIEN ○ T'AIPEI ○ IRIOMOTE JIMA

Shaokuan ○ Meihsien ○ Changchou ○ T'aichung ○ SAKISHIMA-GUNTŌ

Ch'aoan ○ Amoy (Hsiamen) ○ Hsinkao

KWANGTUNG ○ Swatow (Shant'ou) ○ TAIWAN (FORMOSA)

San Shui ○ Chiehyang ○ T'ainan

CANTON (Kuangchou) ○ Kaohsiung ○ Tropic of Cancer

Foshan ○ Chiehyang ○ BATAN IS

Kowloon ○ Hsinhui ○

Macau ○ VICTORIA ○ HONG KONG (Br.) ○ Bashi Channel

oming ○ anchiang (t. Bayard)

SOUTH CHINA SEA

HOU TAO ○ HAINAN TAO

Continued on pages 196–197

Longitude East of Greenwich

0 50 100 200 300 400 500 Miles

0 100 200 400 600 800 Kilometers

Relief

Meters		Feet
3050		10 000
1525		5000
610		2000
305		1000
152.5		500
0	Sea Level	0
		Below
152.5		500 Sea Level
1525		5000
3050		10 000
6100		20 000

A-569700-76 -9 -16
COPYRIGHT BY
RAND MCNALLY & COMPANY
MADE IN U.S.A.

Relief

Meters	Feet
1525	5000
610	2000
305	1000
152.5	500
0 Sea Level	0

Scale 1:4 000 000 one inch to 64 miles. Conic Projection
Elevations and depressions are given in feet

0 10 20 30 40 Miles
0 10 20 30 40 50 60 Kilometers

Longitude East of Greenwich

A-560796-76-· .64--6
COPYRIGHT BY
RAND McNALLY & COMPANY
MADE IN U.S.A.

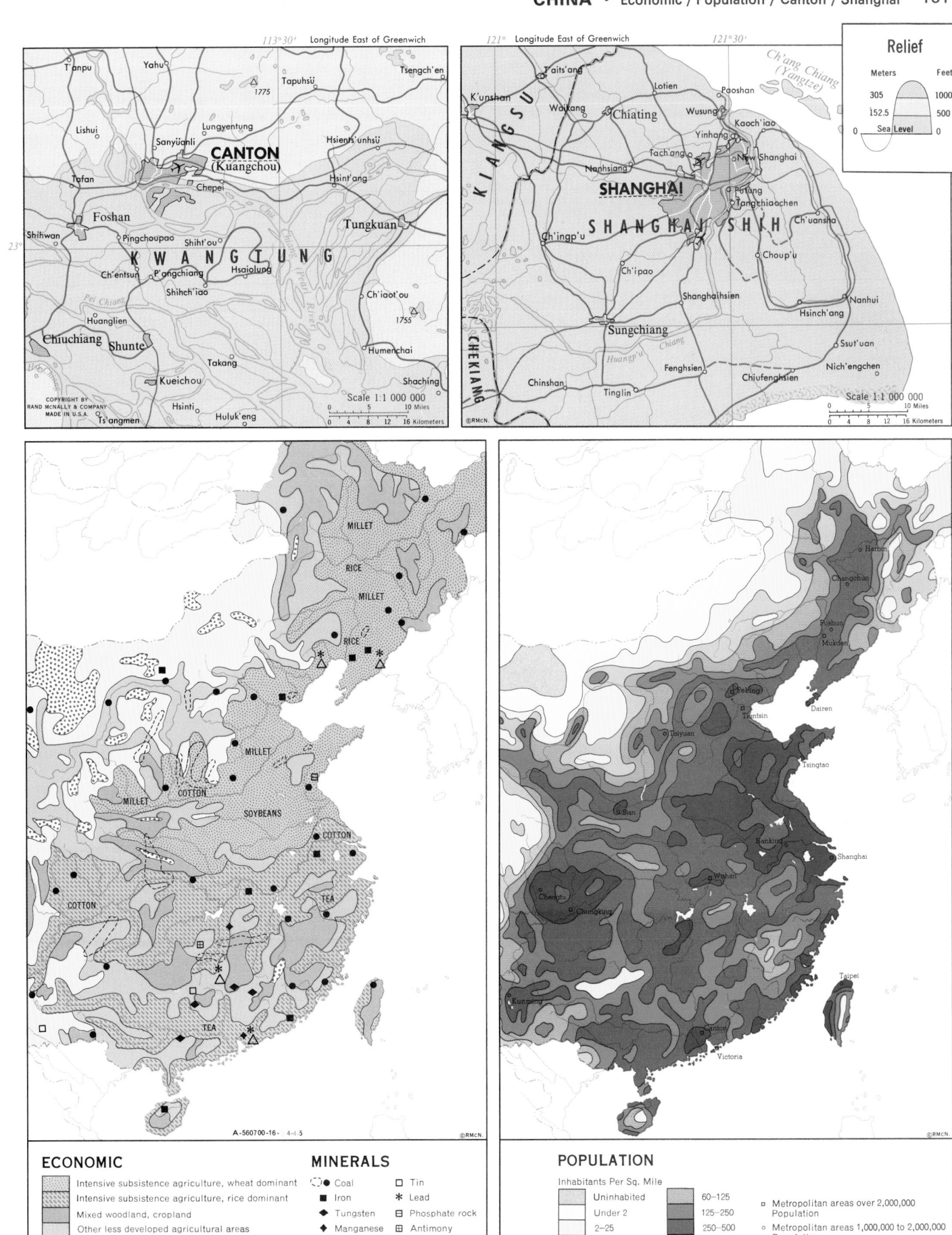

CANTON (Kuangchou)

T'anpu Yahu Tapuhsü Tsengch'en
Lishui Lungyentung Hsients'unhsü
Sanyüanli **CANTON (Kuangchou)** Hsint'ang
Tafan Chepei
Foshan Tungkuan
Shihwan Pingchoupao Shiht'ou **KWANGTUNG**
Ch'entsun P'ongchiang Hsaiolung
Chiuchiang Shunte Shihch'iao Ch'iaot'ou
Huanglien
Takang Humenchai
Kueichou Shaching
Hsinti
Ts'angmen Huluk'eng

Longitude East of Greenwich 113°30'
Scale 1:1 000 000
0 5 10 Miles
0 4 8 12 16 Kilometers

COPYRIGHT BY RAND McNALLY & COMPANY MADE IN U.S.A.

SHANGHAI

Longitude East of Greenwich 121° 121°30'
Ch'ang Chiang (Yangtze)

K'unshan T'aits'ang Lotien Paoshan
Waikang Chiating Wusung
Nanhsiang Yinhang Kaoch'iao
Tach'ang New Shanghai
SHANGHAI Ch'uansha
Ch'ingp'u **SHANGHAI SHIH** Putung Tangchiaochen
Ch'ipao Choup'u
KIANGSU
CHEKIANG Shanghaihsien Nanhui
Hsinch'ang
Sungchiang Ssut'uan
Chinshan Fenghsien Chiufenghsien Nich'engchen
Tinglin

Scale 1:1 000 000
0 5 10 Miles
0 4 8 12 16 Kilometers

Relief

Meters	Feet
305	1000
152.5	500
0	Sea Level	0

ECONOMIC

- Intensive subsistence agriculture, wheat dominant
- Intensive subsistence agriculture, rice dominant
- Mixed woodland, cropland
- Other less developed agricultural areas
- Nomadic herding
- Non-productive

MINERALS

- ● Coal
- ■ Iron
- ◆ Tungsten
- ◆ Manganese
- △ Zinc
- □ Tin
- ∗ Lead
- ⊟ Phosphate rock
- ⊞ Antimony

MILLET, RICE, MILLET, RICE, MILLET, COTTON, MILLET, SOYBEANS, COTTON, COTTON, TEA, TEA

A-560700-16- 4-4-5

POPULATION

Inhabitants Per Sq. Mile

- Uninhabited
- Under 2
- 2–25
- 25–60
- 60–125
- 125–250
- 250–500
- Over 500
- ▫ Metropolitan areas over 2,000,000 Population
- ○ Metropolitan areas 1,000,000 to 2,000,000 Population

Harbin, Changchun, Fushun, Mukden, Peiping, Tientsin, Dairen, Taiyuan, Tsingtao, Sian, Nanking, Shanghai, Wuhan, Chengtu, Chungking, Kunming, Canton, Taipei, Victoria

Continued on page 194

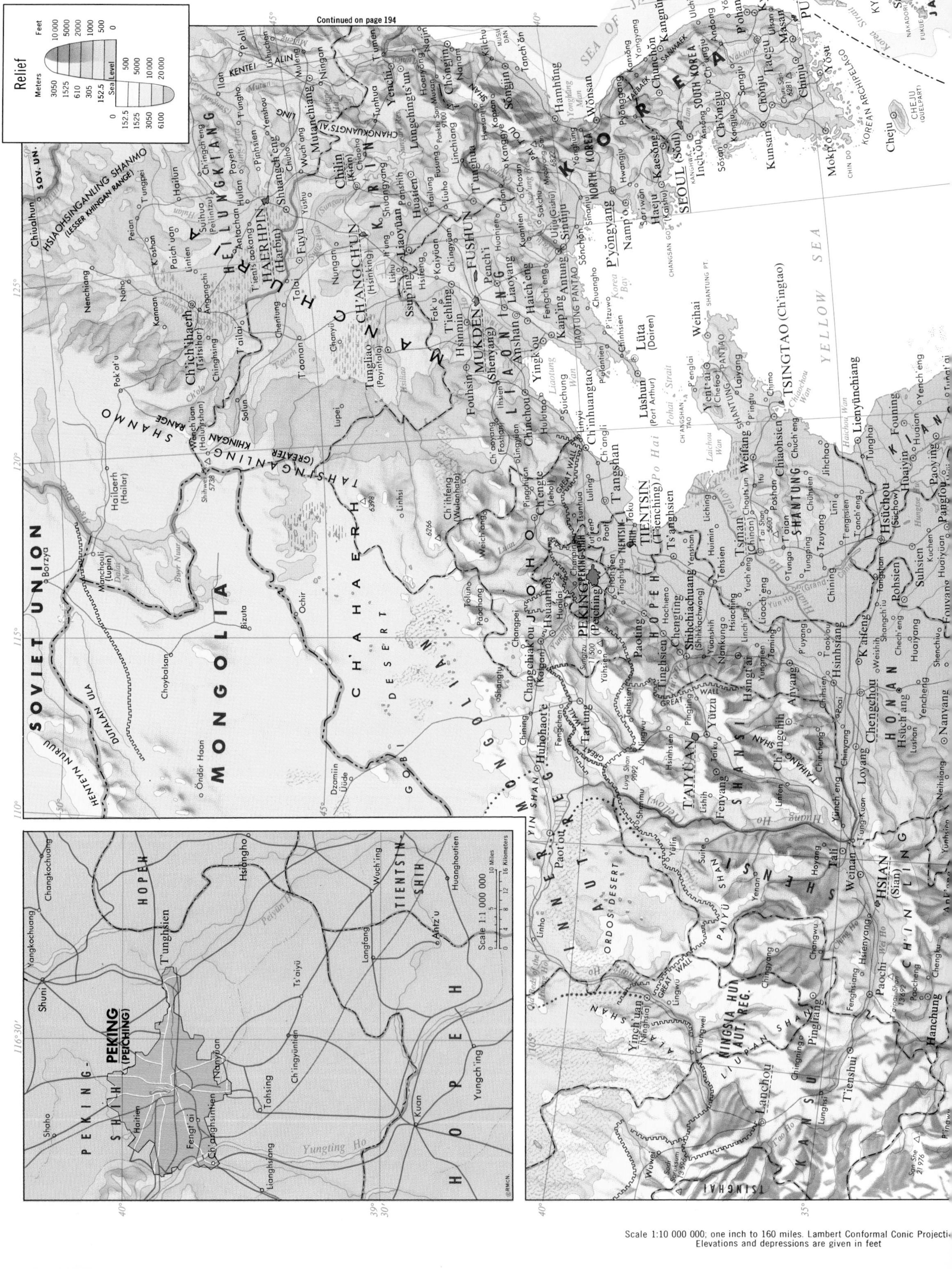

Relief

Feet
10 000
5000
2000
1000
500
0
Sea Level

Meters
3050
1525
610
305
152.5
0
152.5
1525
3050
6100

500
5000
10 000
20 000

SEA OF JAPAN

JAPAN
KYUSHU
TSU SHIMA
IKI
KOREA STRAIT
PUSAN

SOVIET UNION
SOV. UN.

HSIAOHSINGANLING SHANMO
(LESSER KHINGAN RANGE)

HEILUNGKIANG
HAERHPIN (Harbin)
Ch'ich'ihaerh (Tsitsihar)

KIRIN
Chilin (Kirin)
CHANGCHUN (Hsinking)

HENTEYN NURUU
DZHALAN ULA

MONGOLIA

SHAMO
KHINGAN RANGE
TAHSINGANLING (GREATER)

CH'AHAERH

GOBI DESERT

INNER MONGOLIA

ORDOS DESERT

FUSHUN
MUKDEN (Shenyang)
LIAONING
Anshan

NORTH KOREA
P'yŏngyang
Namp'o

SOUTH KOREA
SEOUL (Sŏul)
Inch'ŏn

YELLOW SEA

KOREA

PEKING (Peiching)
PEKING-SHIH

HOPEH
TIENTSIN (T'ienching)
T'angshan

GREAT WALL

Lüta (Dairen)
Lüshun (Port Arthur)

Po Hai

Weihai
TSINGTAO (Ch'ingtao)
SHANTUNG
Tsinan

PAN

SHANSI
T'AIYÜAN

SHENSI
HSIAN (Sian)
CHINLING

HONAN
Chengchou
Loyang

KANSU

KIANGSU

KINGSIA HUI AUT. REG.

TSINGHAI

Scale 1:10 000 000; one inch to 160 miles. Lambert Conformal Conic Projection
Elevations and depressions are given in feet

HOPEH
PEKING-SHIH
PEKING (PEICHING)
TIENTSIN SHIH
Tunghsien
Nanyüan
Fengt'ai
Yungting Ho

Scale 1:1 000 000
10 Miles
16 Kilometers

EAST CHINA SEA

NANSEI-SHOTO (RYUKYU ISLANDS)

SAKISHIMA-GUNTO

IRIOMOTE JIMA

JAPAN

Tropic of Cancer

PHILIPPINE SEA

YOG PT.

CATANDUANES

C. ENGAÑO

PALANAN PT.

CAPE SAN ILDEFONSO

Caramuan

Paracale 4500

Capalongo

Ragay

Daet

Nago

Tabaco

Polillo

LUZON

SIERRA MADRE

Cabanatuan

Dagupan

MANILA

Quezon City

Cavite

San Pablo

Batangas

Lipa

Lucena

MARINDUQUE

CHINA

SHANTUNG

SHANGHAI

CHOUSHAN ARCHIPELAGO

CHOUSHAN

Samwen Wan

Tungliu

Kuangte

Ch'ang

Kashing

Ch'üngte

Sungchiang

Wuhu

Kuangteh

Hsüancheng

Hangchow

Shaohsing

CHEKIANG

Chuchi Ningpo

Linhai

Chingtechen

Chinhwa

Yüyao

Wenling

Coching

Juian

Fuping Wan

Anking

Hukou

Poyang

Yüshan

Lishui

Wenchou

HAIT'AN TAO

Chilung (Kirin)

Ilan

Suao

Hualien

TAIWAN (FORMOSA)

BATAN ISLANDS

BABUYAN ISLANDS

Claveria

Aparri

Tuguegarao

Ilagan

Bontoc

Solano

Cervantes

Bangued

Vigan

San Fernando

Bauang

Baguio

Pozorrubio

Lingayen

Bolinao

CAPE BOLINAO

Iba

Subic

Mariveles

COCHINOS PT.

Olongapo

Manila Bay

TAIPEI

Hsinchu

Miaoli

T'aichung

Changhua

Chiai

Tainan

Kaohsiung

Pingtung

T'aitung

Hengch'un

Bashi Channel

Balintang Channel

Luzon Strait

FUKIEN

Fuchou (Foochow)

Chüanchou

P'ingt'an

Puch'eng

Nanp'ing

Putien

Tehua

Chüanchou

AMOY

QUEMOY (Chinmen)

Amoy (Hsiamen)

PESCADORES

Formosa Strait

SOUTH CHINA SEA

KIANGSI

Nanch'ang

Chingkiang

Chian

Kanchou

Swatow (Shant'ou)

Ch'aochou

Ch'aoyang

Haifeng

PRATAS (China)

CHELANG CHIAO

HUNAN

Ch'angsha

Hsiangt'an

Hengyang

Lingling

Ch'ench'ou

Shaokuan

CANTON (Kuangchou)

Foshan

KWANGTUNG

HONG KONG (Br.)

Kowloon

VICTORIA

Macau (Port.)

HSISHA CH'ÜNTAO (PARCEL IS.) (China)

KWEICHOW

Kueiyang

KWANGSI CHUANG AUT. REG.

Liuchou

Nanning

Wuchou (Tsangwu)

Yülin

Pehhai (Pakhoi)

Chanchiang (Ft. Bayard)

LEICHOU PANTAO

HAINAN TAO

Haik'ou

Wench'ang

Sanya

Yaihsien

YUNNAN

KUNMING (Yünnanfu)

RED BASIN

CHUNGKING (Chungk'ing)

SZECHWAN

VIETNAM

Hanoi

Haiphong

Nam Dinh

Ninh Binh

Hon Gay

Bac Ninh

Vinh

Thanh-Hoa

Dong Hoi

Hue

Da Nang (Tourane)

LAOS

ANNAMITIC CORDILLERA

THAILAND

CAMBODIA

Gulf of Tonkin

PHILIPPINES

Longitude East of Greenwich

A-560793-76 7-5-10

RAND McNALLY & COMPANY

COPYRIGHT

MADE IN U.S.A.

| 0 | 50 | 100 | 150 | 200 | 250 | 300 Miles |

| 0 | 100 | 200 | 300 | 400 | 500 Kilometers |

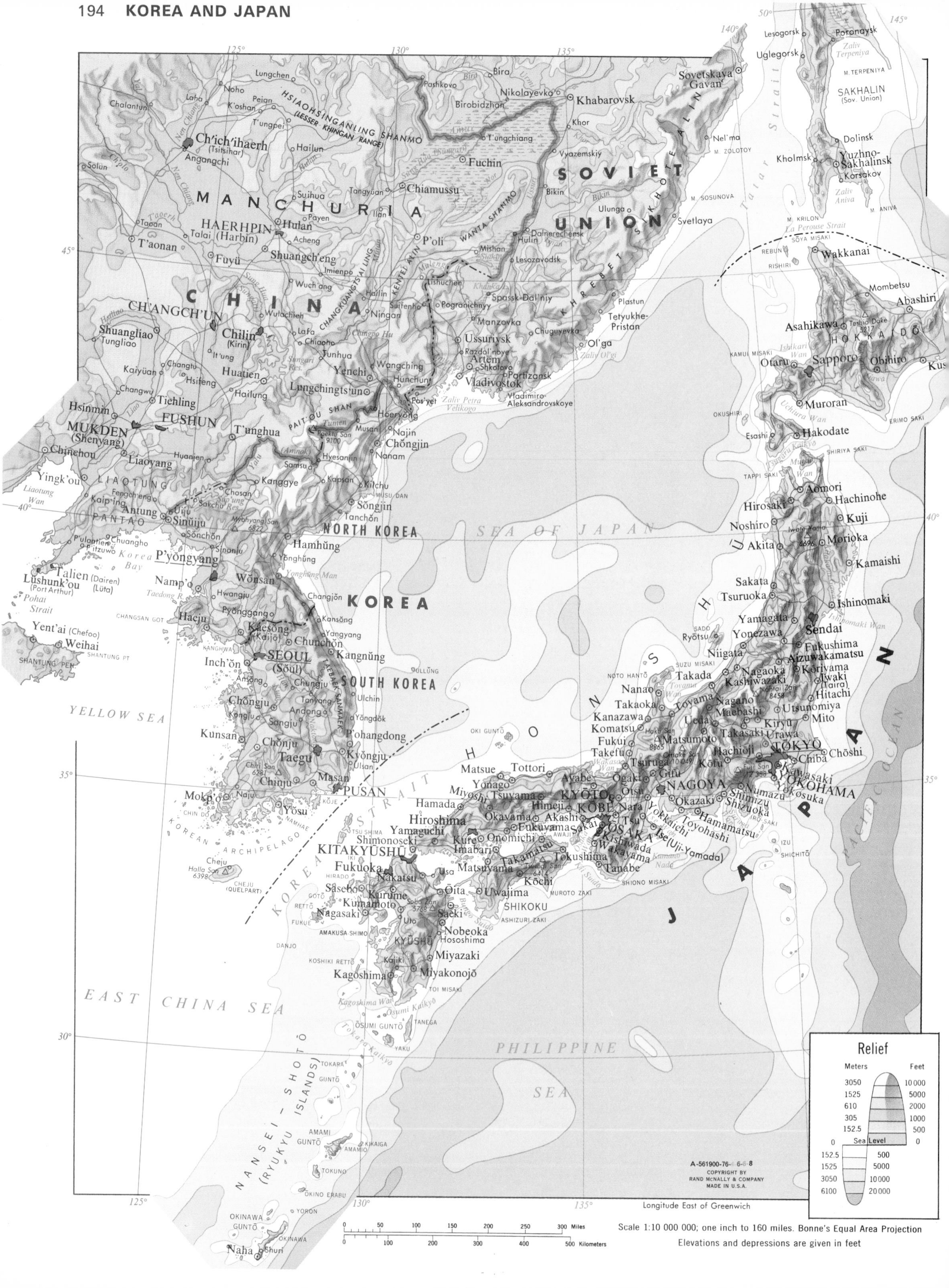

MANCHURIA

CHINA

SOVIET UNION

CH'ANGCH'UN

HAERHPIN (Harbin)

MUKDEN (Shenyang)

FUSHUN

LIAOTUNG

PANTAO

NORTH KOREA

KOREA

P'yŏngyang

Namp'o

SOUTH KOREA

SEOUL (Sŏul)

Inch'ŏn

Taegu

PUSAN

KITAKYŪSHŪ

Fukuoka

Nagasaki

KYŪSHŪ

Kagoshima

YELLOW SEA

EAST CHINA SEA

SEA OF JAPAN

KOREA STRAIT

HOKKAIDŌ

Sapporo

Hakodate

Aomori

HONSHU

Sendai

Niigata

TŌKYŌ

YOKOHAMA

KYŌTO

ŌSAKA

KŌBE

NAGOYA

Hiroshima

SHIKOKU

JAPAN

PACIFIC OCEAN

PHILIPPINE SEA

NANSEI-SHOTŌ (RYUKYU ISLANDS)

SAKHALIN (Sov. Union)

Yuzhno-Sakhalinsk

Khabarovsk

Vladivostok

OKINAWA GUNTŌ

Naha

Relief

Meters		Feet
3050		10 000
1525		5000
610		2000
305		1000
152.5		500
0	Sea Level	0
152.5		500
1525		5000
3050		10 000
6100		20 000

A-561900-76-   6-8-8
COPYRIGHT BY
RAND McNALLY & COMPANY
MADE IN U.S.A.

Longitude East of Greenwich

Scale 1:10 000 000; one inch to 160 miles. Bonne's Equal Area Projection

Elevations and depressions are given in feet

Miles: 0 50 100 150 200 250 300

Kilometers: 0 100 200 300 400 500

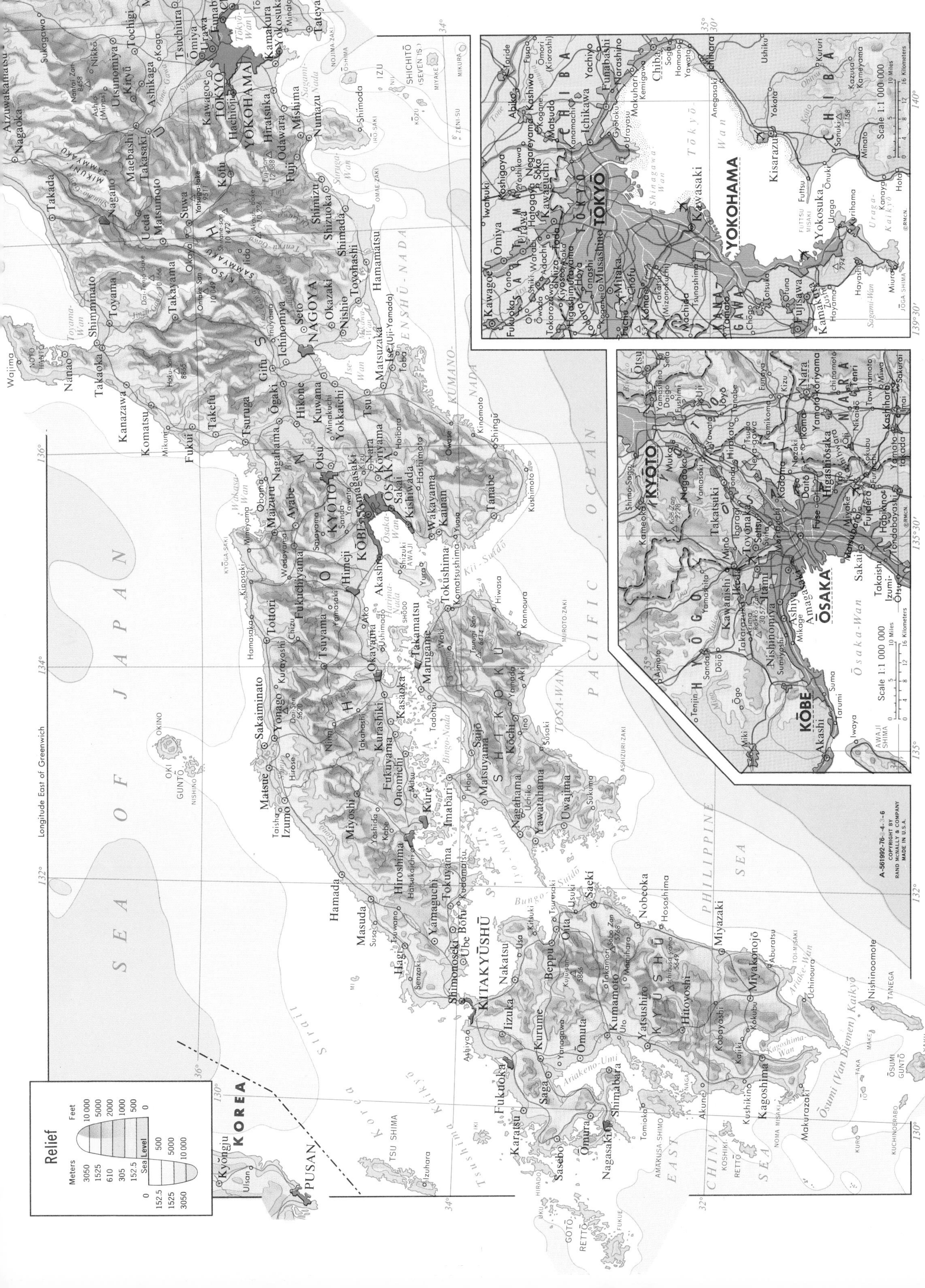

SOUTHERN JAPAN

Scale 1:4 000 000; one inch to 64 miles. Conic Projection
Elevations and depressions are given in feet.

Relief

Meters	Feet
3050	10 000
1525	5000
610	2000
305	1000
152.5	500
0	Sea Level
152.5	500
1525	5000
3050	10 000

TOKYO
YOKOHAMA
Scale 1:1 000 000

KYOTO
OSAKA
KOBE
Scale 1:1 000 000

A-561992-76-4--6
COPYRIGHT BY
RAND McNALLY & COMPANY
MADE IN U.S.A.

SEA OF JAPAN

PACIFIC OCEAN

PHILIPPINE SEA

EAST CHINA SEA

KOREA
PUSAN

TOKYO
YOKOHAMA
NAGOYA
KYOTO
OSAKA
KOBE
KITAKYŪSHŪ

HONSHŪ
SHIKOKU
KYŪSHŪ

Tōkyō Wan
Sagami Nada
Enshū-Nada
Kumano-Nada
Tosa-Wan
Bungo-Suidō
Kii-Suidō
Tsushima Kaikyō

INDONESIA AND THE PHILIPPINES

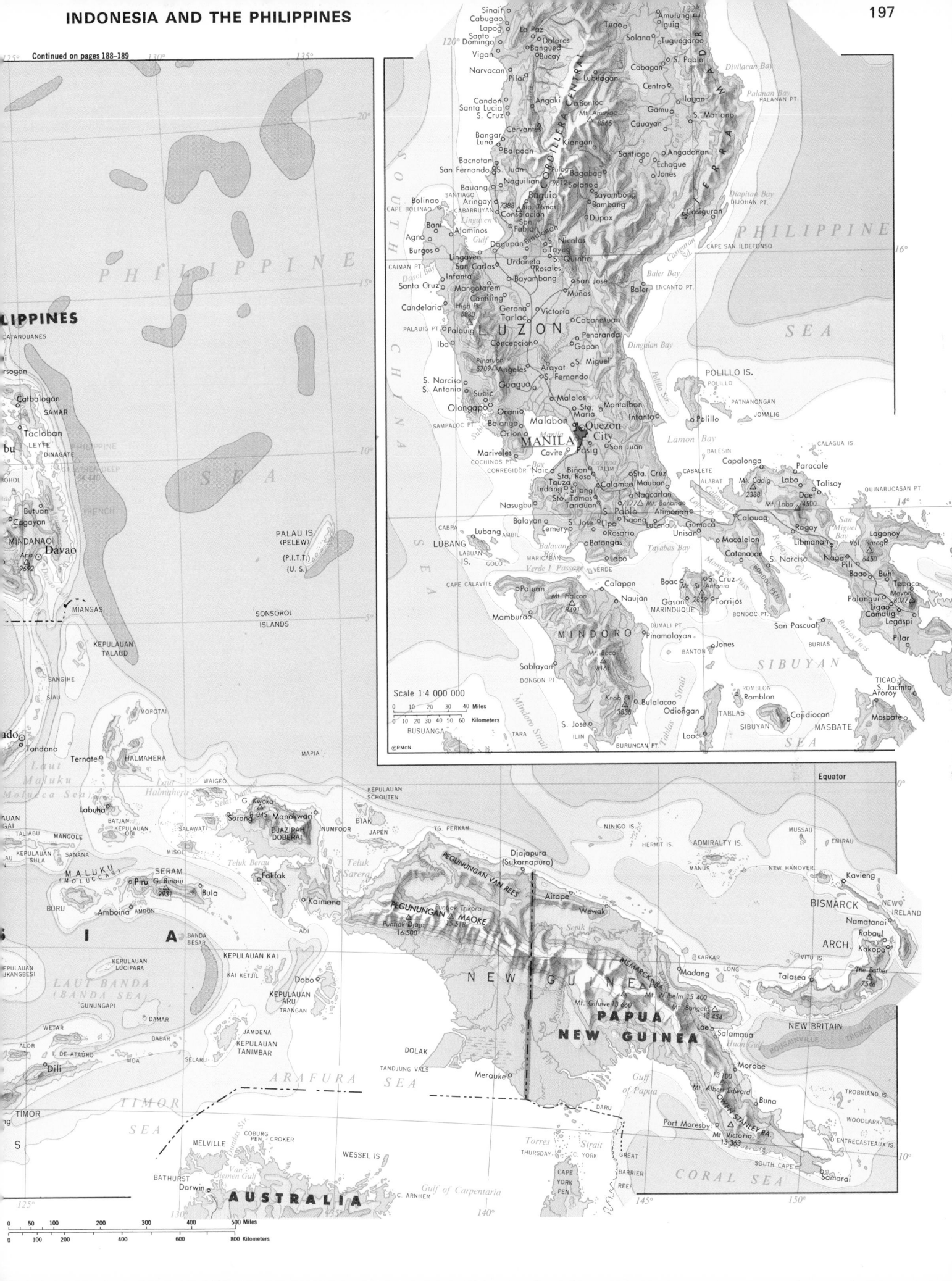

Continued on pages 188–189

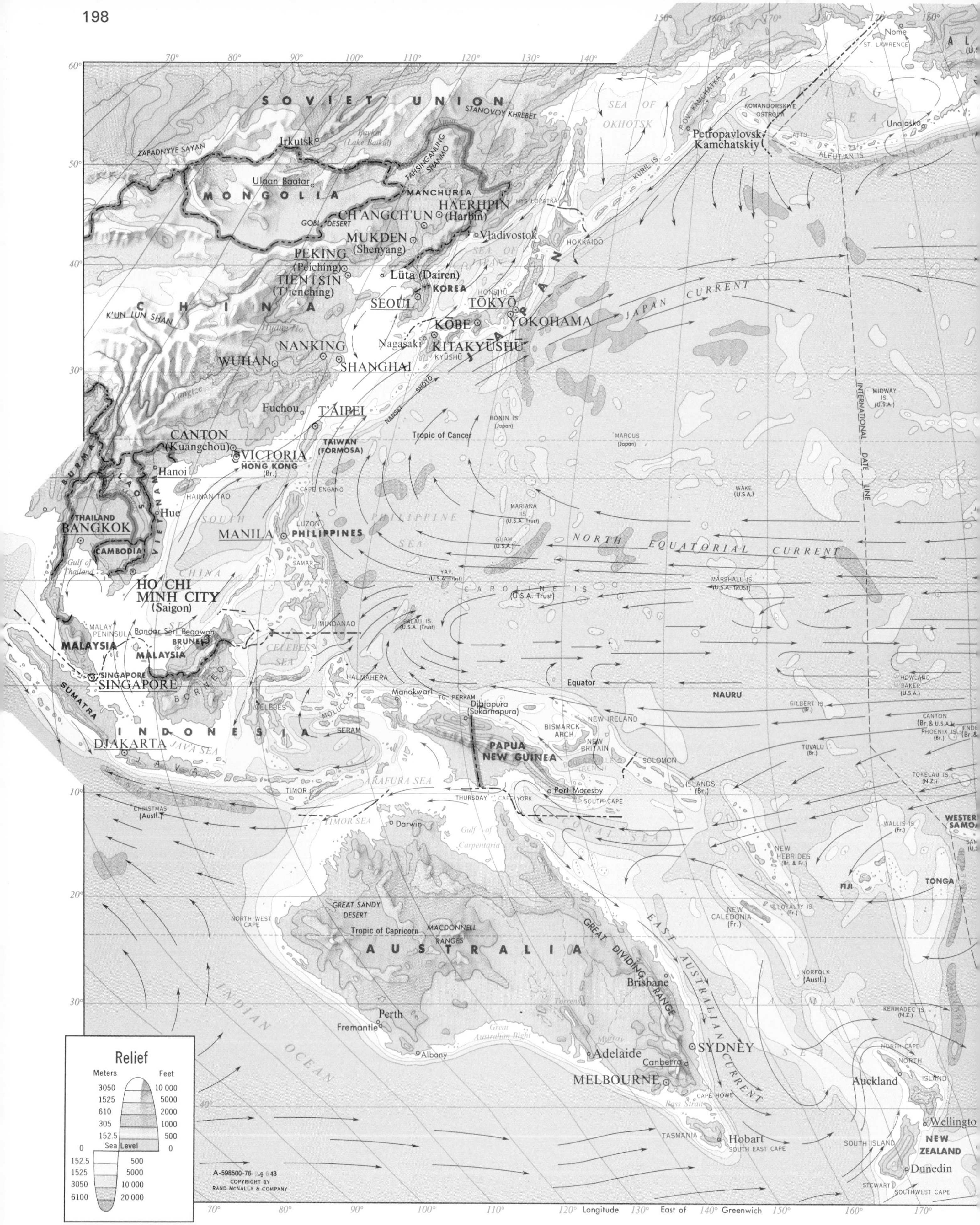

S O V I E T   U N I O N

ZAPADNYYE SAYAN
Irkutsk
Baykal
(Lake Baikal)
STANOVOY KHREBET
SEA OF
OKHOTSK
B E R I N G
Nome
ST. LAWRENCE
SEA
Unalaska
AL
(U.)

TAHSINGANLING
SHANMO
MYS LOPATKA
KOMANDORSKIYE
OSTROVA
Petropavlovsk-
Kamchatskiy
ATTU
ALEUTIAN IS.

Ulaan Baatar
MONGOLIA
GOBI DESERT
MANCHURIA
CH'ANGCH'UN
HAERHPIN
(Harbin)
Vladivostok
HOKKAIDO
KURIL IS.

MUKDEN
(Shenyang)
PEKING
(Peiching)
TIENTSIN
(T'ienching)
Lüta (Dairen)
KOREA
HONSHU
SEOUL
TŌKYŌ
KŌBE
YOKOHAMA
JAPAN CURRENT

C H I N A
K'UN LUN SHAN
Huang Ho
NANKING
Nagasaki
KITAKYUSHŪ
KYŪSHŪ
MIDWAY
IS.
(U.S.A.)

WUHAN
SHANGHAI
NANSEI SHOTO
Yangtze
Fuchou
T'AIPEI
TAIWAN
(FORMOSA)
BONIN IS.
(Japan)
MARCUS
(Japan)
INTERNATIONAL DATE LINE

CANTON
(Kuangchou)
VICTORIA
HONG KONG
(Br.)
Tropic of Cancer
WAKE
(U.S.A.)

Hanoi
HAINAN TAO
CAPE ENGANO
BURMA
Hue
LUZON
P H I L I P P I N E
S E A
MARIANA
IS.
(U.S.A. Trust)
GUAM
(U.S.A.)
N O R T H   E Q U A T O R I A L   C U R R E N T

THAILAND
BANGKOK
MANILA
PHILIPPINES
SAMAR
YAP.
(U.S.A. Trust)
MARSHALL IS.
(U.S.A. Trust)

CAMBODIA
SOUTH
CHINA
SEA
C A R O L I N E   I S.
(U.S.A. Trust)

HO CHI
MINH CITY
(Saigon)
MINDANAO
PALAU IS.
(U.S.A. Trust)

MALAY
PENINSULA
Bander Seri Begawan
BRUNEI
(Br.)
CELEBES
SEA
HALMAHERA

MALAYSIA
MALAYSIA
Equator
NAURU
HOWLAND
BAKER
(U.S.A.)

SINGAPORE
SINGAPORE
BORNEO
CELEBES
MOLUCCAS
Manokwari
TG. PERKAM
GILBERT IS.
(Br.)
CANTON
(Br. & U.S.A.)
PHOENIX IS. (Br. &

SUMATRA
SERAM
Djajapura
(Sukarnapura)
BISMARCK
ARCH.
NEW
IRELAND
TUVALU
(Br.)
TOKELAU
(N.Z.)

I N D O N E S I A
JAVA SEA
PAPUA
NEW GUINEA
NEW
BRITAIN
SOLOMON
WESTERN
SAMOA

DJAKARTA
J A V A
TIMOR
ARAFURA SEA
Port Moresby
SOUTH CAPE
ISLANDS
(Br.)
WALLIS IS.
(Fr.)

THURSDAY
CAPE YORK
C O R A L   S E A
NEW
HEBRIDES
(Br. & Fr.)

CHRISTMAS
(Austl.)
TIMOR SEA
Darwin
Gulf of
Carpentaria
FIJI
TONGA

NORTH WEST CAPE
GREAT SANDY
DESERT
Tropic of Capricorn
MACDONNELL
RANGES
GREAT DIVIDING RANGE
E A S T   A U S T R A L I A N   C U R R E N T
NEW
CALEDONIA
(Fr.)
LOYALTY IS.
(Fr.)

A U S T R A L I A
NORFOLK
(Austl.)

Perth
Brisbane
KERMADEC IS.
(N.Z.)

Fremantle
Great
Australian Bight
Murray
Adelaide
Canberra
SYDNEY
NORTH CAPE
NORTH
ISLAND

Albany
MELBOURNE
CAPE HOWE
Auckland

Relief
TASMANIA
Hobart
SOUTH EAST CAPE
SOUTH ISLAND
NEW
ZEALAND
Wellington

Meters	Feet
3050	10 000
1525	5000
610	2000
305	1000
152.5	500
0	Sea Level	0
152.5	500
1525	5000
3050	10 000
6100	20 000

Dunedin
STEWART
SOUTHWEST CAPE

A-598500-76-6 6.43
COPYRIGHT BY
RAND McNALLY & COMPANY

Longitude   East of   Greenwich

Warm ocean currents
Cold ocean currents

Scale 1:50 000 000; one inch to 800 miles. Goode's Homolosine Equal Area Projection
Elevations and depressions are given in feet

Scale 1:4 000 000

0   10   20   30   40 Miles
0 10 20 30 40 50 60 Kilometers

PACIFIC OCEAN

HAWAII (U.S.A.)

Hanalei Bay Kilauea
Kawaikini △ KAUAI
5170   Lihue
NIIHAU   Waimea

©RMCN.

Waialua OAHU KAHUKU PT.
KAENA PT. Kaneohe Bay
Waianae   Aiea Waimanalo
Waipahu Ewa Honolulu

MOLOKAI Halawa
Kaunakakai
Kalohi Channel LANAI Lahaina Pauwela
KAHOOLAWE   Wailuku Kahului MAUI
Keokea HALEAKALA NAT'L PARK
Halenalu Crater Hana

UPOLU PT.
Hawi
Paauilo
Waimea Laupahoehoe
Mauna Kea △ Honomu
(Vol.) 13,796 Hilo
Kailua Ohia
Mauna Loa △ 13,680 Kilauea Crater
(Vol.)   4090
Hookena HAWAII VOLCANOES
Pahala NAT'L PARK
Kalapana

Sitka
Prince Rupert
Vancouver
Victoria
SEATTLE
Portland
CANADIAN ROCKY MOUNTAINS
CASCADE RA.
Salt Lake City
SAN FRANCISCO COAST RANGES SIERRA NEVADA
LOS ANGELES
SAN DIEGO
CALIFORNIA CURRENT
CABO SAN LUCAS
Mazatlan
ISLAS DE REVILLAGIGEDO (Mex.)
MEXICO CITY Veracruz
Acapulco
ST. LOUIS
UNITED STATES
Missouri
Mississippi
Rio Grande
SIERRA MADRE OCCIDENTAL
MEXICO
New Orleans
Galveston
GULF OF MEXICO
Tampico

BELIZE (Br.)
GUAT. HOND.
Guatemala
EL SAL. NICARAGUA
Managua
COSTA RICA
Colón Panama Canal
PANAMA
CARIBBEAN SEA

lolulu
HAWAIIAN IS. (U.S.A.)
NORTH EQUATORIAL CURRENT

PALMYRA (U.S.A.)
FANNING (Br.)
CHRISTMAS (Br & USA)
EQUATORIAL COUNTER CURRENT

Buenaventura
COLOMBIA
Quito
ECUADOR
Guayaquil
ARCHIPELAGO DE COLON
(GALÁPAGOS IS.)
(Ecuador)

MALDEN (Br & USA)
SOUTH EQUATORIAL CURRENT

MANIHIKI IS. (N.Z.)
MARQUESAS IS. (Fr.)

SOCIETY IS. (Fr.)
TAHITI (Fr.)
TUAMOTU (LOW) ARCHIPELAGO (Fr.)
AITUTAKI COOK IS. (N.Z.)
RAROTONGA

LIMA
Callao
Arequipa
Mollendo
PERU CURRENT
ATACAMA TRENCH
Iquique
Antofagasta
PERU

PITCAIRN (Br.) DUCIE (Br.)

RAPA NUI (EASTER) (Chile)
SALA-Y-GÓMEZ (Chile)

ISLAS DE SAN FÉLIX (Chile)
ISLAS DE SAN AMBROSIO (Chile)
Coquimbo
Valparaíso
ISLAS DE JUAN FERNÁNDEZ (Chile)
SANTIAGO
Concepción
ANDES
CHILE
ARGENTINA
Valdivia
Bahía Blanca
Puerto Montt
CHILOE

WEST WIND DRIFT

170° 160° 150° Longitude 140° West of 130° Greenwich 120° 110° 100° 90° 80° 70° 60° 50°

0   500   1000   1500   2000 Miles
1000   2000   3000 Kilometers

Punta Arenas
Estrecho De Magallanes
CABO DE HORNOS

BORNEO

Palembang

SUMATRA

DJAKARTA

Surabaja

JAVA

SUMBA

Bandjarmasin

CELEBES

Udjung Pandang

Java Sea

SERAM

TIMOR

Arafura Sea

Dj

Darwin

Timor Sea

Gulf of Carpentaria

PEN

INDIAN OCEAN

KIMBERLEY PLATEAU

Broome

Fitzroy

Daly

Victoria

Mount Isa

GREAT SANDY DESERT

Alice Springs

GREA ARTESI BASI

GIBSON DESERT

SIMPSON DESERT

Tropic of Capricorn

Carnarvon

GREAT VICTORIA DESERT

Lake Eyre

Kalgoorlie

NULLARBOR PLAIN

Lake Gairdner

FLINDERS RANGES

Broken Hill

Murray

DARLING RA.

Perth

Great Australian Bight

Adelaide

INDIAN OCEAN

Urban

Cropland

Cropland & Woodland

Cropland & Grazing Land

Grassland, Grazing Land

Forest, Woodland

Swamp, Marshland

Shrub, Sparse Grass; Wasteland (pattern)

Barren Land

Scale 1:24,000,000; one inch to 380 miles. Lambert Azimuthal Equal-Area Projection

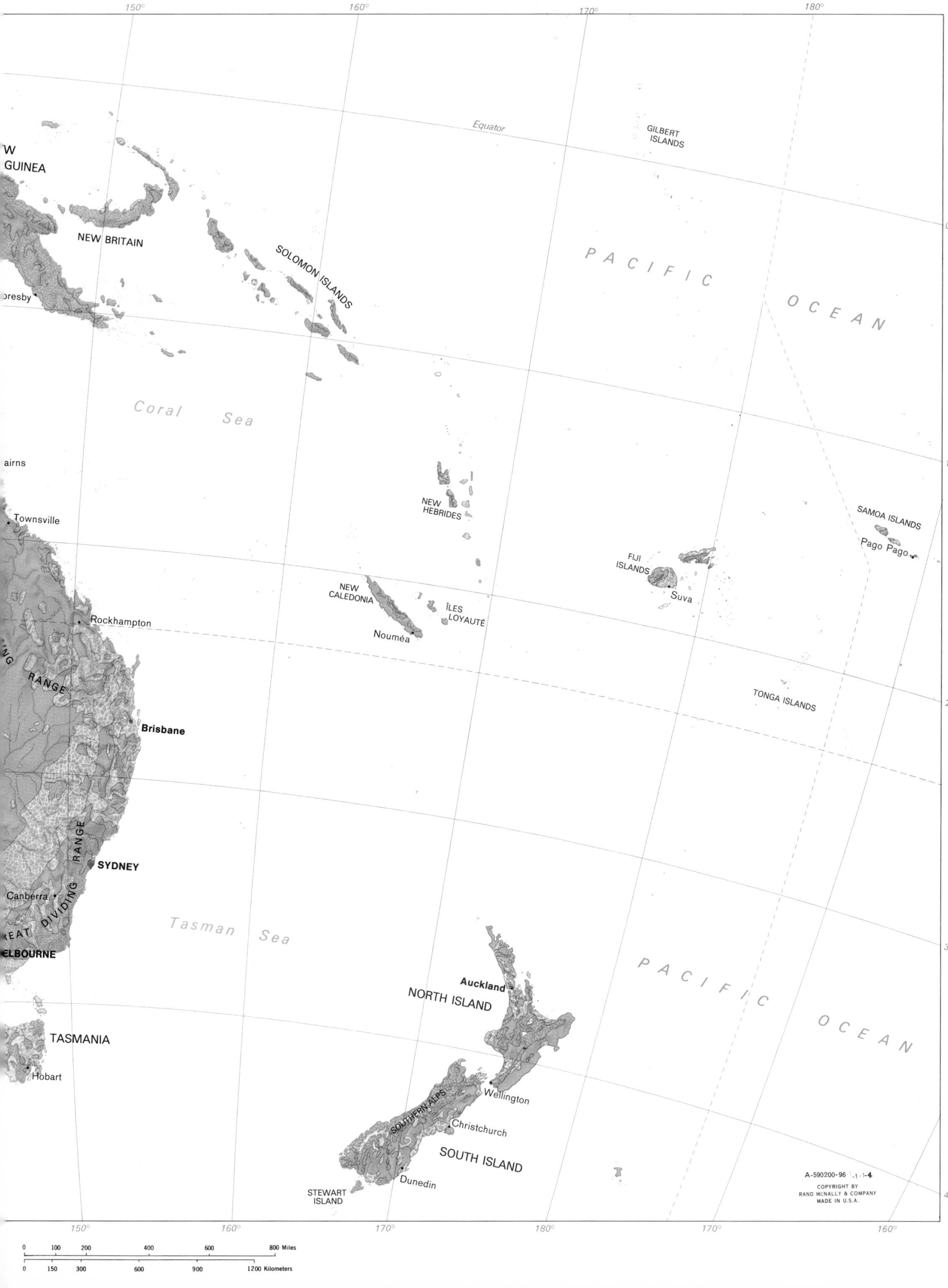

150° 160° 170° 180°

Equator

GILBERT
ISLANDS

NEW
GUINEA

NEW BRITAIN

SOLOMON ISLANDS

oresby •

PACIFIC

0°

OCEAN

Coral   Sea

10°

airns

• Townsville

NEW
HEBRIDES

SAMOA ISLANDS

Pago Pago

FIJI
ISLANDS

• Rockhampton

NEW
CALEDONIA

ÎLES
LOYAUTÉ

Suva

Nouméa •

RANGE

TONGA ISLANDS

20°

Brisbane

RANGE

DIVIDING

SYDNEY

Canberra •

Tasman   Sea

30°

EAT

PACIFIC

ELBOURNE

Auckland

NORTH ISLAND

• Hobart

TASMANIA

OCEAN

SOUTHERN ALPS

Wellington

Christchurch

SOUTH ISLAND

STEWART
ISLAND

• Dunedin

150° 160° 170° 180° 170° 160°

40°

0   100   200   400   600   800 Miles

0   150   300   600   900   1200 Kilometers

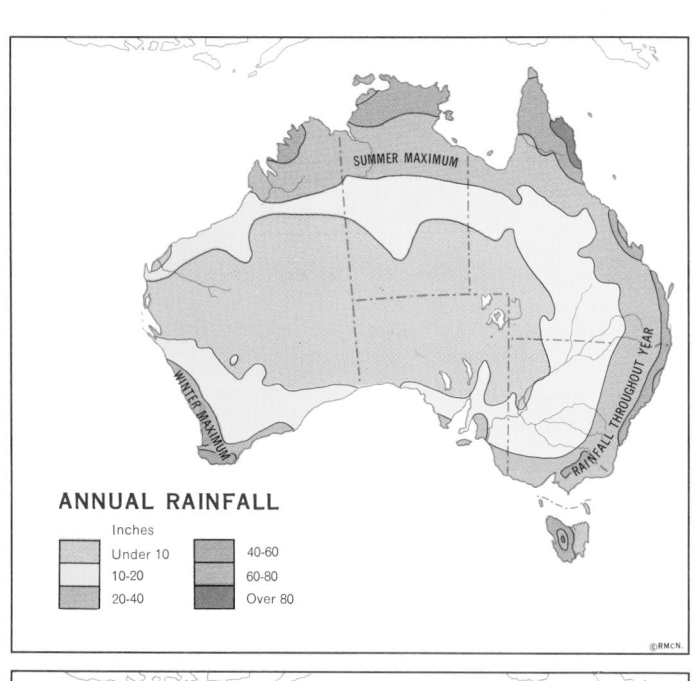

ANNUAL RAINFALL

Inches

Under 10	40-60
10-20	60-80
20-40	Over 80

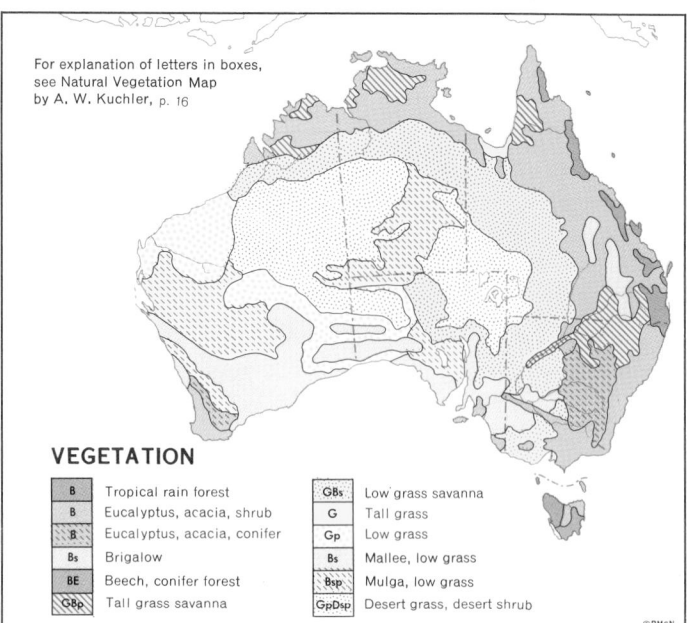

For explanation of letters in boxes, see Natural Vegetation Map by A. W. Kuchler, p. 16

VEGETATION

B	Tropical rain forest	GBs	Low grass savanna
B	Eucalyptus, acacia, shrub	G	Tall grass
B	Eucalyptus, acacia, conifer	Gp	Low grass
Bs	Brigalow	Bs	Mallee, low grass
BE	Beech, conifer forest	Bsp	Mulga, low grass
GBp	Tall grass savanna	GpDsp	Desert grass, desert shrub

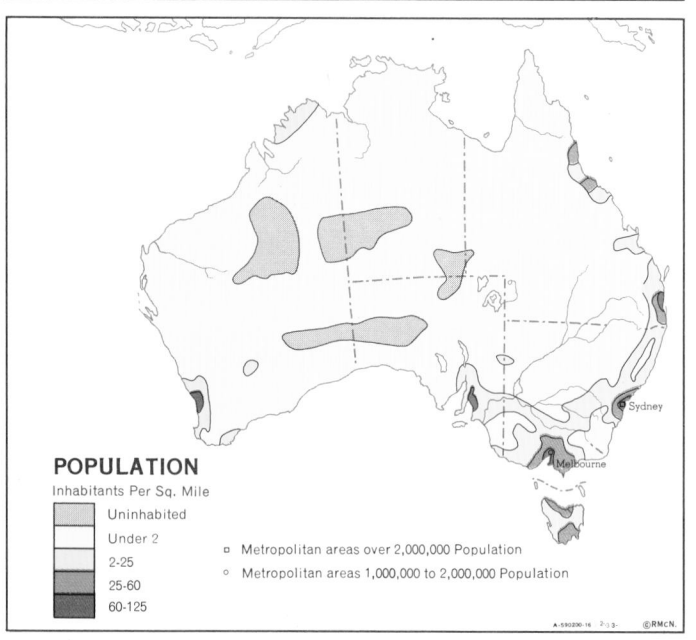

POPULATION

Inhabitants Per Sq. Mile

Uninhabited
Under 2
2-25
25-60
60-125

□ Metropolitan areas over 2,000,000 Population

○ Metropolitan areas 1,000,000 to 2,000,000 Population

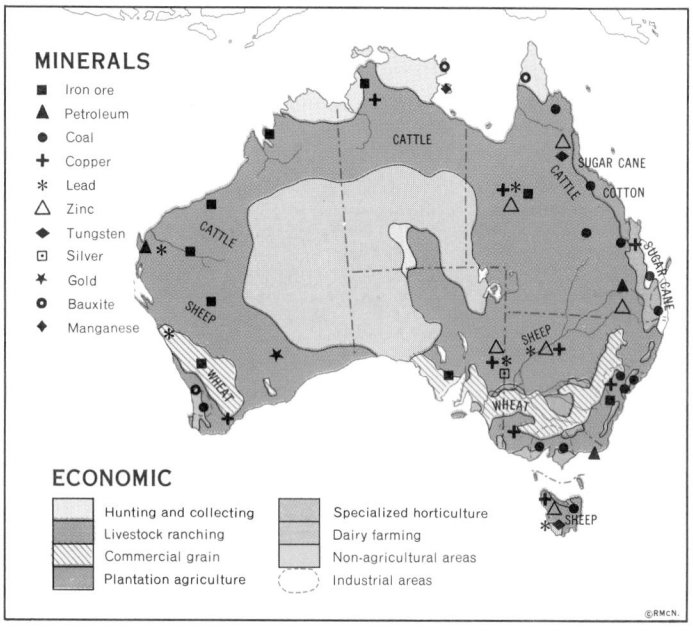

MINERALS

■ Iron ore
▲ Petroleum
● Coal
+ Copper
✳ Lead
△ Zinc
◆ Tungsten
⊡ Silver
✴ Gold
◎ Bauxite
◆ Manganese

ECONOMIC

	Hunting and collecting		Specialized horticulture
	Livestock ranching		Dairy farming
	Commercial grain		Non-agricultural areas
	Plantation agriculture		Industrial areas

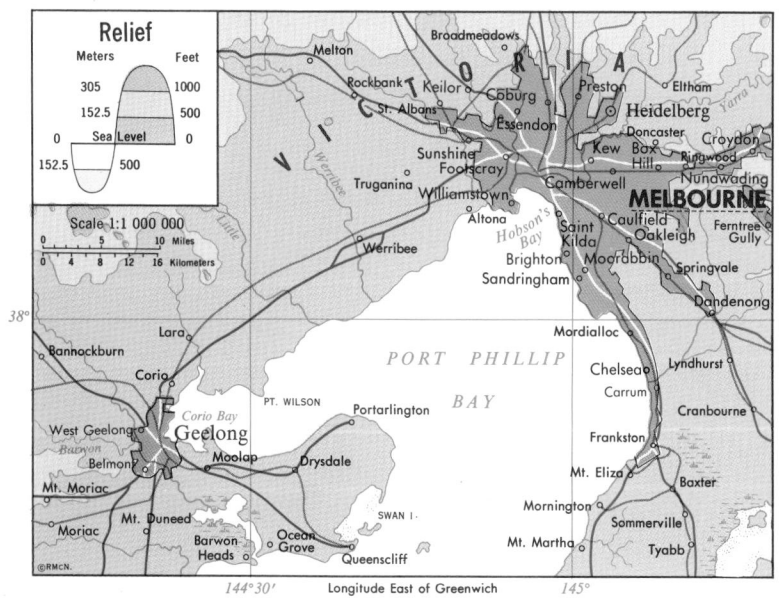

Relief

Meters	Feet
305	1000
152.5	500
Sea Level	0
152.5	500

Scale 1:1 000 000

0   5   10 Miles
0 4 8 12 16 Kilometers

38°

PORT PHILLIP BAY

144°30'   Longitude East of Greenwich   145°

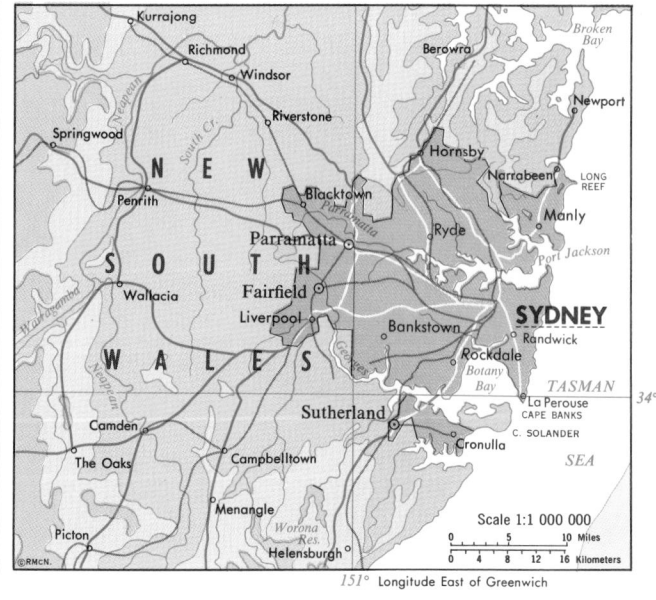

Scale 1:1 000 000

0   5   10 Miles
0 4 8 12 16 Kilometers

34°

151° Longitude East of Greenwich

Relief

Meters	Feet
1525	5000
610	2000
305	1000
152.5	500
0 Sea Level	0
2.5	500
25	5000
450	10 000

Sea Level

Below Sea Level

140° Longitude East of Greenwich

0   50   100   150   200 Miles

0   50   100   150   200   250   300 Kilometers

A-590298-76- -5-4.8
COPYRIGHT BY
RAND MCNALLY & COMPANY
MADE IN U.S.A.

Scale 1:8 000 000; one inch to 126 miles.
Lambert's Azimuthal, Equal Area Projection.
Elevations and depressions are given in feet.

204

I N D O N E S I A

Continued on pages 196–197

A R A F U R A   S E A

SELARU
TANDJUNG VALS

J A V A   10 932
G. Mohameti   225
12 060   Raung

Singaradja
Bali

Rindjani
Sumbawa
Besar   Raba

LOMBLEN PANTAR

Dili

ALOR

Singaradja

LOMBOK
SUMBAWA
FLORES

SAVU
SEA

Waingapu

TIMOR

C. VAN DIEMEN
CROKER

WESSEL IS.

SUMBA

SAWU
ROTI
Kupang

BATHURST
MELVILLE
Van Diemen
Gulf

Coburg Pen.

CAPE ARNHEM

SUNDA   ISLANDS

TIMOR   SEA

Clarence Str.
Darwin

Anson Bay

Blue Mud Bay

ARNHEM LAND

GULF

S U N D A

SUNDA   TRENCH

CAPE
LONDONDERRY
Joseph
Bonaparte Gulf

Pine Creek

Katherine

Groote
Eylandt

Limmen
Bight

CARPENT

I N D I A N

CAPE LEVEQUE

BUCCANEER

Sandu

ARCH.

King
Sound

Wyndham

Mt Hann
2800

KING
LEOPOLD
RANGES

Ord

Victoria River
Downs

Birdum

Daly Waters

Borroloola

SIR EDWARD PELLEW
GROUP

WELL

O C E A N

DAMPIER
LAND

Derby

Broome

GEIKIE
RANGE

Fitzroy
Crossing

Halls Creek

Newcastle Waters

Burketown

N O R T H E R N

Roebuck Bay

LaGrange

Fitzroy

Woods

Alexandria

BARKLY TABLELAND

Dc

EIGHTY MILE BEACH

Tanami

Tennant Creek

Camoowec

T E R R I T O R Y

Mount

LARREY POINT

Barrow Creek

DAMPIER
ARCH.   Port Hedland
RIPON

DeGrey

GREAT   SANDY   DESERT

Matka

MONTE BELLO IS.
BARROW

Roebourne

Marble Bar

Mt. Ziel
4955

RANGES

Arltunga

Q

NORTH WEST CAPE
Millstream
Onslow

Exmouth Gulf

HAMERSLEY RANGE

Nullagine

MACDONNELL

Alice Springs

JAMES RANGE

SIMPSON

POINT CLOATES

Mt. Bruce
4024

Jiggalong

Droppumpun

GIBSON   DESERT

Hooblut

Charlotte
Waters

DESERT

Tropic of Capricorn

W E S T E R N

Carnegie

Gilen

MUSGRAVE   RANGES
Mt. Woodroffe
4970

Birdsville

CAPE FARQUHAR

Carnarvon

Peak Hill

Nabberu

Wells

EVERARD RANGES

The Alberga

Oodnadatta

BERNIER IS.
DORRE IS.
Shark Bay

Gascoyne

Austin

Carnegie

DIRK HARTOG
STEEP POINT

Meekatharra

Nannine

Wiluna

Stuart
Range

William Creek

Marree

A U S T R A L I A

Cue

Sandstone

Ballard

Coopers

Ajana

Mount
Magnet

Laverton

Menzies

Cares

GREAT   VICTORIA   DESERT

SOUTH   AUSTRALIA

Farino

Northampton

HOUTMAN ROCKS

Geraldton

Mingenew
Dongara

Barlee
Moore

Kalgoorlie
Coolgardie
Boulder
Lefroy

Menzies

Rawlinna

Oldea Station

Hughes

Woomera

Pimba

FLINDERS RANGES

Pitharo
Milling
Mooral

Lake Brown
Southern Cross

Cowan
Dundas

Eucla

Penong

Ceduna

Whyalla

FLI
Port Aug

Perth
Fremantle

Northam
York

SWANLAND

Norseman
Salmon Gums

NULLARBOR   PLAIN

Eyre

Point Fowler

Port Pirie
Glads

DARLING RANGE

Narrogin

Ravensthorpe

Esperance

GREAT   AUSTRALIAN   BIGHT

EYRE
PENINSULA

Moonta

Port W

Collie

Hopetoun

ARCHIPELAGO
OF THE RECHERCHE

Wallaroo

Port Lincoln

KANGAROO

Geographe Bay
Bunbury
Busselton
Katanning

Spencer

CAPE NATURALISTE
Normalup
Albany

King George Sd.

Ga
A

CAPE LEEUWIN

N
King

PT. D'ENTRECASTEAUX
WEST CAPE HOWE

CAPE JA

Mt.

I N D I A N   O C E A N

Relief

Meters		Feet
3050		10 000
1525		5000
610		2000
305		1000
152.5		500
0	Sea Level	0
152.5		500 Below
1525		5000 Sea Level
3050		10 000
6100		20 000

A-590200-76-
COPYRIGHT BY
RAND McNALLY & COMPANY
MADE IN U.S.A.

Longitude   115°   East of Greenwich

Scale 1:16 000 000; one inch to 250 miles. Lambert's Azimuthal, Equal Area Projec
Elevations and depressions are given in feet

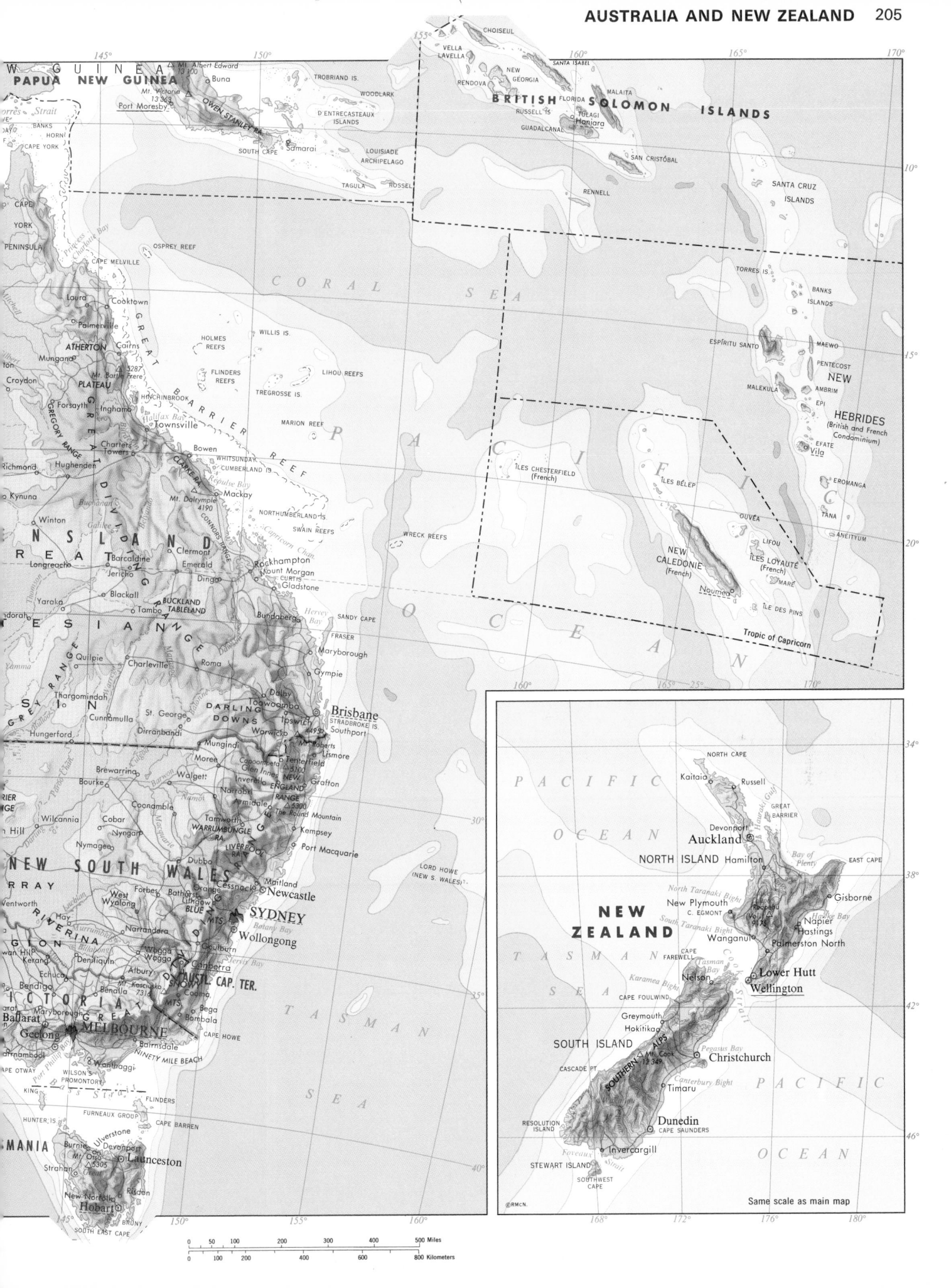

PAPUA NEW GUINEA

W GUINEA
Mt. Albert Edward 13,100
Buna
TROBRIAND IS.
Mt. Victoria 13,363
Port Moresby
OWEN STANLEY RA.
WOODLARK
Torres Strait
BANKS
HORN I.
CAPE YORK
D'ENTRECASTEAUX ISLANDS
SOUTH CAPE
Samarai
LOUISIADE ARCHIPELAGO
TAGULA
ROSSEL

CHOISEUL
VELLA LAVELLA
NEW GEORGIA
SANTA ISABEL
RENDOVA
RUSSELL IS.
FLORIDA
MALAITA
TULAGI
Honiara
GUADALCANAL
BRITISH SOLOMON ISLANDS
SAN CRISTÓBAL
RENNELL
SANTA CRUZ ISLANDS

CAPE YORK PENINSULA
CAPE MELVILLE
OSPREY REEF
Progress Chart
Chartout Bay

CORAL SEA

TORRES IS.
BANKS ISLANDS

ESPÍRITU SANTO
MAEWO
PENTECOST
NEW
MALEKULA
AMBRIM
EPI
HEBRIDES (British and French Condominium)
EFATE
Vila
EROMANGA
TANA
ANEITYUM

Loura
Cooktown
ATHERTON
Cairns
Mungana
PLATEAU
Croydon
Mt. Bartle Frere 5287
Forsayth
Inghamb
HINCHINBROOK I.
Townsville
Charters Towers
Hughenden
Bowen
Richmond
WHITSUNDAY IS.
CLARKE RA.
Mt. Dalrymple 4190
Mackay
CUMBERLAND IS.
Repulse Bay
HOLMES REEFS
WILLIS IS.
FLINDERS REEFS
LIHOU REEFS
TREGROSSE IS.
MARION REEF

PACIFIC

ÎLES CHESTERFIELD (French)
ÎLES BÉLEP
OUVÉA
LIFOU
ÎLES LOYAUTÉ (French)
NEW CALEDONIE (French)
MARÉ
Nouméa
ÎLE DES PINS

Winton
Barcaldine
Clermont
Emerald
Dingo
NORTHUMBERLAND IS.
CONNORS RANGE
SWAIN REEFS
Rockhampton
Mount Morgan
CURTIS I.
Gladstone
WRECK REEFS
Kynuna
Longreach
Jericho
Yaraka
Blackall
Tambo
BUCKLAND TABLELAND
Capricorn Chan.
Bundaberg
Hervey Bay
SANDY CAPE
Maryborough
FRASER I.
Tropic of Capricorn

GREAT DIVIDING RANGE

OCEAN

Quilpie
Charleville
Roma
Gympie
Thargomindah
Cunnamulla
St. George
Dirranbandi
DARLING DOWNS
Dalby
Toowoomba
Ipswich
Warwick
Brisbane
STRADBROKE IS.
Southport
Hungerford
Mungindi
Moree
Tenterfield
Lismore
NEW ENGLAND RANGE
Grafton
Brewarrina
Walgett
Narrabri
Glen Innes
Inverell
Bourke
Coonamble
Armidale
The Round Mountain 5300
Kempsey
Wilcannia
Cobar
Nyngan
Tamworth
WARRUMBUNGLE RA.
Port Macquarie
Broken Hill
Nymagee
LIVERPOOL RANGE
LORD HOWE (NEW S. WALES)
NEW SOUTH WALES
Dubbo
Maitland
Newcastle
Wentworth
Forbes
Bathurst
Orange
Lithgow
BLUE MTS.
Cessnock
SYDNEY
Hay
West Wyalong
Cowra
Botany Bay
Wollongong
RIVERINA
Narrandera
Goulburn
AUSTL. CAP. TER.
Canberra
Deniliquin
Wagga Wagga
Jervis Bay
Albury
SNOWY MTS.
Mt. Kosciusko 7316
Echuca
Benalla
Cooma
VICTORIA
Maryborough
Bega
Bendigo
GREAT DIVIDING RANGE
Bombala
Ballarat
MELBOURNE
Bairnsdale
CAPE HOWE
Geelong
NINETY MILE BEACH
Warrnambool
Wonthaggi
WILSON'S PROMONTORY
Port Phillip
CAPE OTWAY
KING I.
FLINDERS I.
FURNEAUX GROUP
CAPE BARREN
HUNTER IS.
CAPE BARREN
TASMANIA
Burnie
Ulverstone
Devonport
Mt. Ossa 5305
Launceston
Strahan
New Norfolk
Hobart
BRUNY I.
SOUTH EAST CAPE

TASMAN SEA

NEW ZEALAND

NORTH CAPE
Kaitaia
Russell
GREAT BARRIER
PACIFIC
OCEAN
Devonport
HAURAKI GULF
Auckland
NORTH ISLAND
Hamilton
Bay of Plenty
EAST CAPE
North Taranaki Bight
New Plymouth
C. EGMONT
Ruapehu 9175
Gisborne
South Taranaki Bight
Wanganui
Hawke Bay
Napier
Hastings
Palmerston North
CAPE FAREWELL
Karamea Bight
Tasman Bay
Nelson
COOK STRAIT
Lower Hutt
Wellington
CAPE FOULWIND
Greymouth
Hokitika
SOUTHERN ALPS
Mt. Cook 12,349
Pegasus Bay
Christchurch
CASCADE PT.
Canterbury Bight
Timaru
RESOLUTION ISLAND
Dunedin
CAPE SAUNDERS
Invercargill
Foveaux Strait
STEWART ISLAND
SOUTHWEST CAPE
SOUTH ISLAND

©RMCN

Same scale as main map

0 50 100   200   300   400   500 Miles
0   200   400   600   800 Kilometers

206

Scale 1:24,000,000; one inch to 380 miles. Lambert Azimuthal Equal-Area Projection

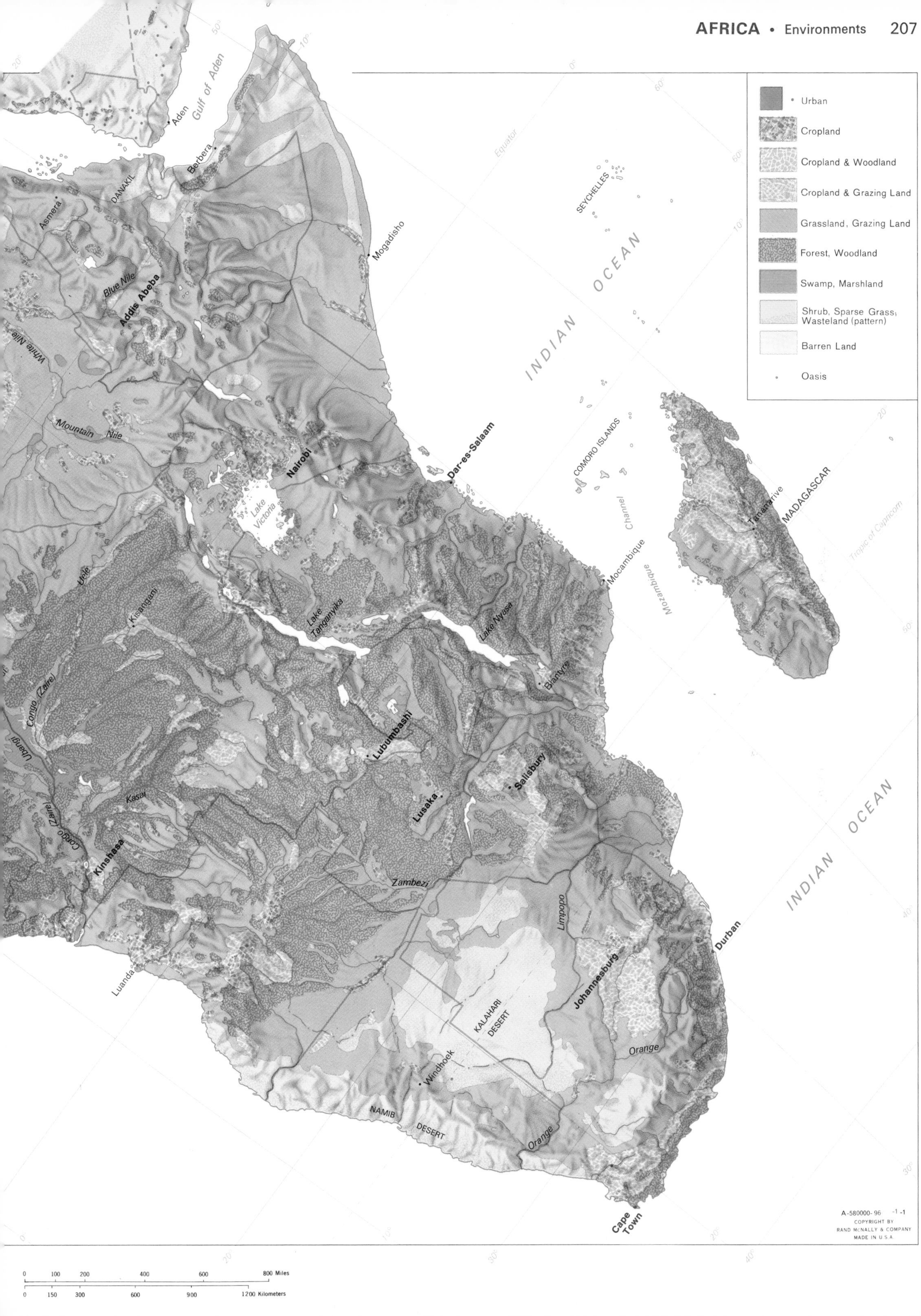
Urban
Cropland
Cropland & Woodland
Cropland & Grazing Land
Grassland, Grazing Land
Forest, Woodland
Swamp, Marshland
Shrub, Sparse Grass; Wasteland (pattern)
Barren Land
Oasis
Gulf of Aden
Aden
Berbera
DANAKIL
Asmera
Mogadisho
Blue Nile
Addis Abeba
White Nile
Mountain Nile
Equator
SEYCHELLES
INDIAN OCEAN
Nairobi
Dar-es-Salaam
Lake Victoria
COMORO ISLANDS
Mozambique Channel
Mocambique
MADAGASCAR
Tananarive
Tropic of Capricorn
Uele
Kisangani
Lake Tanganyika
Lake Nyasa
Blantyre
Congo (Zaire)
Ubangi
Lubumbashi
Salisbury
Lusaka
Kasai
Kinshasa
Zambezi
Limpopo
Durban
Johannesburg
Luanda
KALAHARI DESERT
Orange
Windhoek
NAMIB DESERT
Cape Town
A-580000-96 -1-1
COPYRIGHT BY RAND McNALLY & COMPANY
MADE IN U.S.A.
0 100 200 400 600 800 Miles
0 150 300 600 900 1200 Kilometers

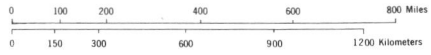

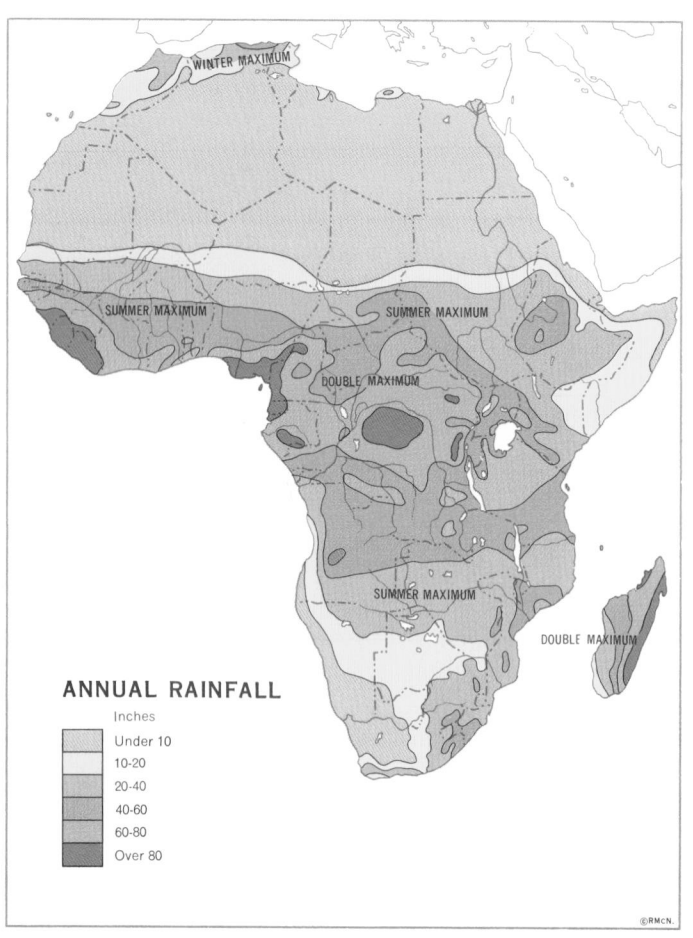

ANNUAL RAINFALL

Inches

	Under 10
	10-20
	20-40
	40-60
	60-80
	Over 80

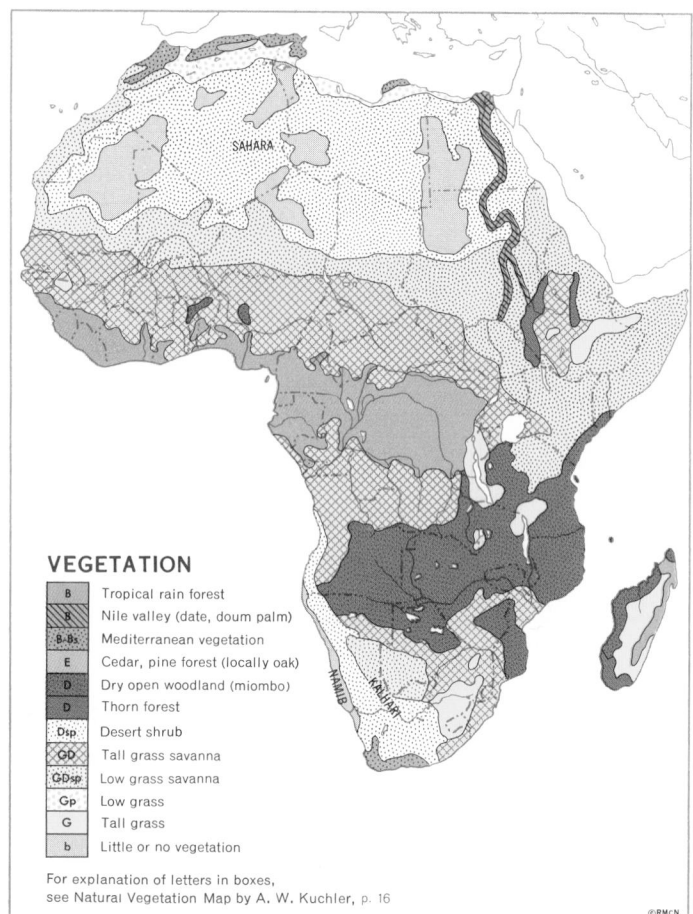

VEGETATION

B	Tropical rain forest
B	Nile valley (date, doum palm)
B-Bs	Mediterranean vegetation
E	Cedar, pine forest (locally oak)
D	Dry open woodland (miombo)
D	Thorn forest
Dsp	Desert shrub
GD	Tall grass savanna
GDsp	Low grass savanna
Gp	Low grass
G	Tall grass
b	Little or no vegetation

For explanation of letters in boxes,
see Natural Vegetation Map by A. W. Kuchler, p. 16

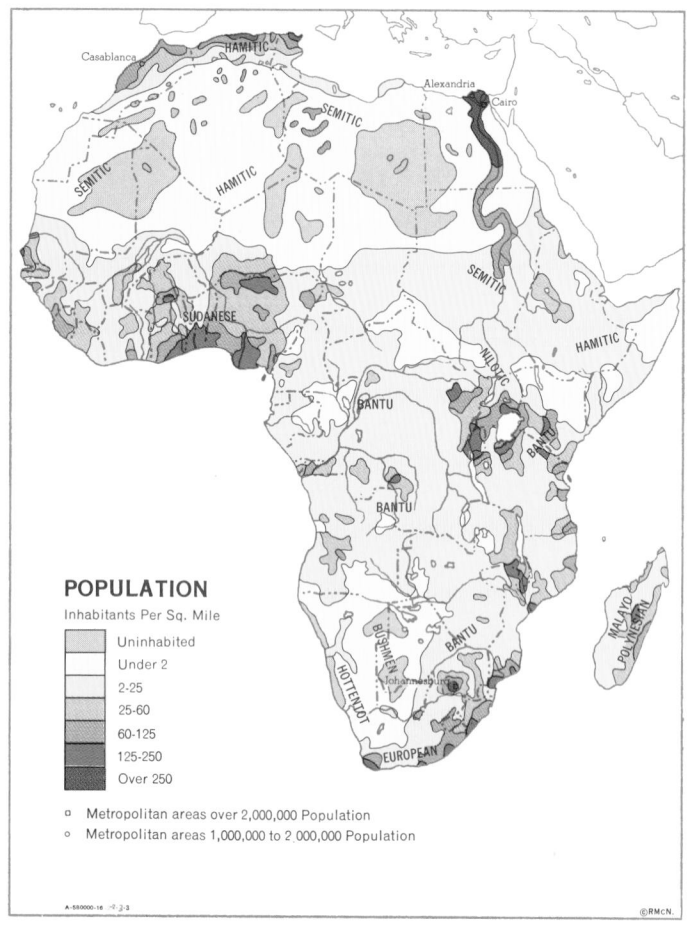

POPULATION

Inhabitants Per Sq. Mile

	Uninhabited
	Under 2
	2-25
	25-60
	60-125
	125-250
	Over 250

□   Metropolitan areas over 2,000,000 Population

○   Metropolitan areas 1,000,000 to 2,000,000 Population

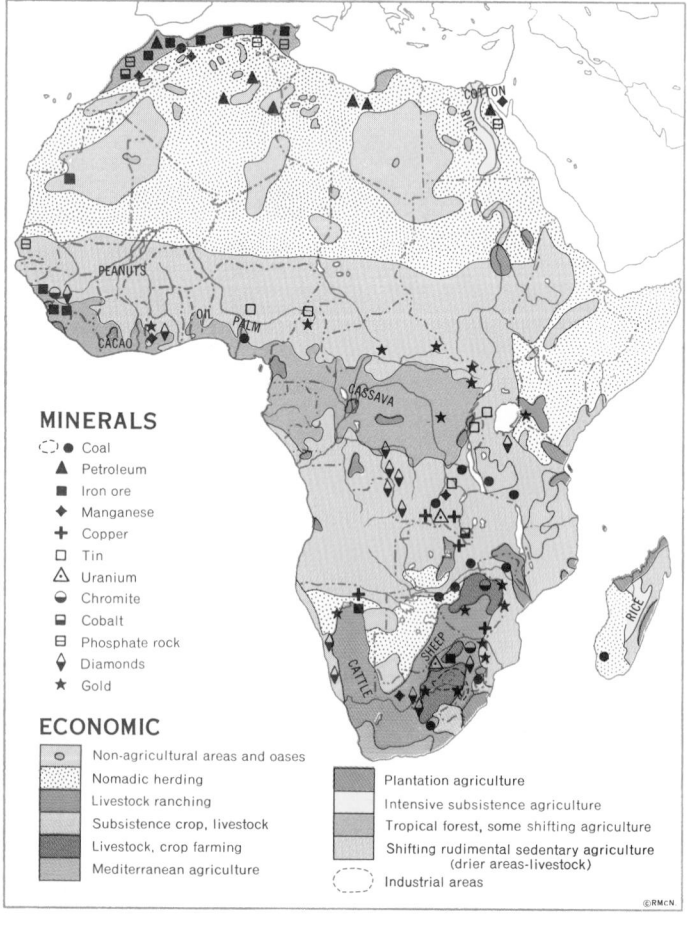

MINERALS

- ⊂⊃ ● Coal
- ▲ Petroleum
- ■ Iron ore
- ◆ Manganese
- + Copper
- □ Tin
- △ Uranium
- ◒ Chromite
- ▱ Cobalt
- ▤ Phosphate rock
- ◇ Diamonds
- ★ Gold

ECONOMIC

	Non-agricultural areas and oases
	Nomadic herding
	Livestock ranching
	Subsistence crop, livestock
	Livestock, crop farming
	Mediterranean agriculture

	Plantation agriculture
	Intensive subsistence agriculture
	Tropical forest, some shifting agriculture
	Shifting rudimental sedentary agriculture (drier areas-livestock)
	Industrial areas

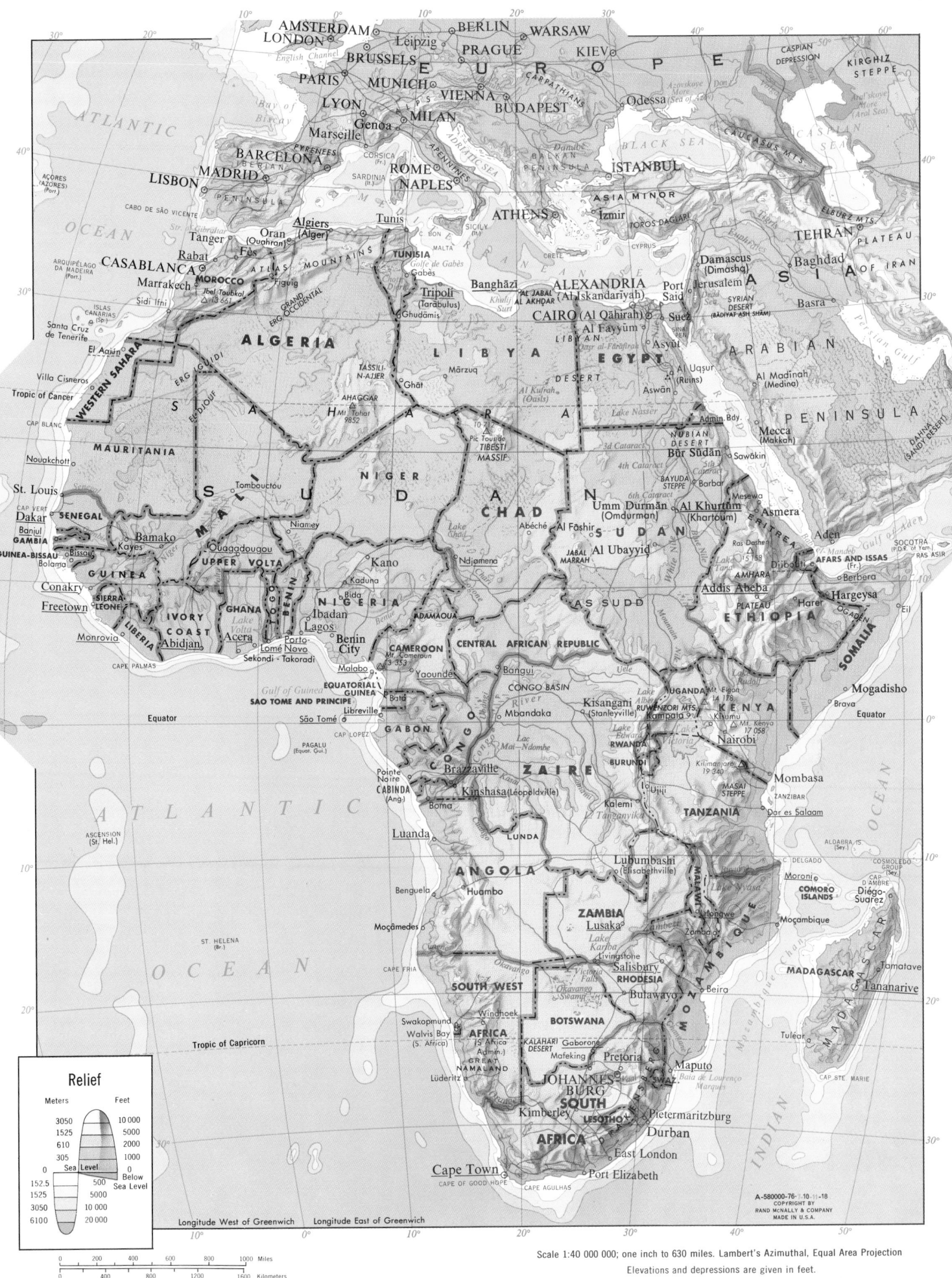

ATLANTIC OCEAN

English Channel

LONDON
AMSTERDAM
BRUSSELS
PARIS
LYON
Leipzig
BERLIN
WARSAW
PRAGUE
MUNICH
VIENNA
BUDAPEST
Odessa
KIEV
CASPIAN DEPRESSION
KIRGHIZ STEPPE

EUROPE

Bay of Biscay
BARCELONA
MADRID
LISBON
Marseille
Genoa
MILAN
ROME
NAPLES
CORSICA (Fr.)
SARDINIA (It.)
APENNINES
ADRIATIC SEA
BALKAN PENINSULA
İSTANBUL
BLACK SEA
CAUCASUS MTS.
CASPIAN SEA
Aral Sea (Aral'skoye More)

AÇORES (AZORES) (Port.)
CABO DE SÃO VICENTE
Str. of Gibraltar
SICILY (It.)
MALTA
ATHENS
İzmir
ASIA MINOR
CRETE
TOROS DAĞLARI
CYPRUS
ELBURZ MTS.
PLATEAU OF IRAN
TEHRAN

ARQUIPÉLAGO DA MADEIRA (Port.)
ISLAS CANARIAS (Sp.)
Santa Cruz de Tenerife
Tanger
Rabat
Fès
Oran (Ouahran)
Algiers (Alger)
Tunis
TUNISIA
Golfe de Gabès
Gabès
Banghāzī
AL JABAL AL AKHDAR
ALEXANDRIA (Al Iskandarīyah)
Port Said
Damascus (Dimashq)
Jerusalem
Baghdad
Basra
SYRIAN DESERT (BĀDIYAT ASH SHĀM)
Dead Sea
CAIRO (Al Qāhirah)
Suez
ARABIAN
El Aaiún
Sidi Ifni
MOROCCO
Marrakech
Jbel Toubkal 13 661
Figuig
ATLAS MOUNTAINS
ERG OCCIDENTAL
Tripoli (Ṭarābulus)
Ghudāmis
Khalīj Surt
LIBYAN DESERT
Al Fayyūm
Asyūt
Al Uqsur (Ruins)
Aswān
Al Madīnah (Medina)
Mecca (Makkah)
PENINSULA

WESTERN SAHARA
Villa Cisneros
Tropic of Cancer
CAP BLANC
Nouakchott
MAURITANIA
St. Louis
CAP VERT
Dakar
SENEGAL
Banjul
GAMBIA
GUINEA-BISSAU
Bissau
Bolama
Conakry
Freetown
SIERRA LEONE
LIBERIA
Monrovia
CAPE PALMAS
IVORY COAST
GUINEA
Kayes
Bamako
UPPER VOLTA
Ouagadougou
Tombouctou
Niamey
GHANA
Accra
Sekondi-Takoradi
Abidjan
TOGO
BENIN
Lomé
Porto Novo
Lagos
Benin City
Ibadan
Bida
Kaduna
Kano
NIGERIA
ADAMAOUA
ALGERIA
ERG GUIDI
EL DJOUF
TASSILI N-AJJER
AHAGGAR
Tamanrasset 9852
TIBESTI MASSIF
Pic Toussidé
Ghāt
Mārzuq
Al Kufrah (Oasis)
Qasr al-Farāfirah
Lake Nasser
NUBIAN DESERT
3d Cataract
4th Cataract
Admin. Bdy.
EGYPT
LIBYA
SAHARA
NIGER
MALI
SUDAN
Lake Chad
CHAD
Abéché
Al Fāshir
JABAL MARRAH
Ndjamena
N'Djaména
Umm Durmān (Omdurman)
Al Khurṭūm (Khartoum)
SUDAN
Al Ubayyid
5th Cataract
6th Cataract
Barbar
BAYUDA STEPPE
Būr Sūdān
Sawākin
Mesewa
Asmera
ERITREA
Aden (P.D.R. of Yem.)
SOCOTRA (P.D.R. of Yem.)
RAS ASIR
DAHNĀ (SANDY DESERT)
Al Madīnah (Medina)

ASIA

CAMEROON
Mt. Cameroun 13 353
Yaoundé
EQUATORIAL GUINEA
Malabo
Bata
SÃO TOMÉ AND PRÍNCIPE
Libreville
São Tomé
PAGALU (Equat. Gui.)
GABON
CAP LOPEZ
Pointe Noire
CABINDA (Ang.)
Boma
CENTRAL AFRICAN REPUBLIC
Bangui
CONGO BASIN
Mbandaka
Kisangani (Stanleyville)
CONGO River
Brazzaville
Kinshasa (Léopoldville)
ZAIRE
Lac Mai-Ndombe
Kasai
Kalemi
UGANDA
Kampala
RWANDA
BURUNDI
Lake Albert
Lake Edward
Lake Kivu
RUWENZORI MTS.
Mt. Elgon 14 178
L. Victoria
Kisumu
Mt. Kenya 17 058
Nairobi
KENYA
Lake Rudolf
Mogadishu
Brava
Equator
ASSUDD
JABAL MARRAH
Lake Tana
Ras Dashen 15 158
AMHARA
Addis Abeba
Harer
OGADEN
Hargeysa
Eil
ETHIOPIA
PLATEAU
Djibouti
AFARS AND ISSAS (Fr.)
Berbera
SOMALIA
Gulf of Aden
BĀB EL-MANDEB

Equator

ATLANTIC OCEAN
ASCENSION (St. Hel.)
ST. HELENA (Br.)

Luanda
Benguela
Moçâmedes
ANGOLA
Huambo
Lubumbashi (Elisabethville)
LUNDA
Lake Tanganyika
Lac Uvira
TANZANIA
Dar es Salaam
Zanzibar
Mombasa
Kilimanjaro 19 340
MASAI STEPPE
ZAMBIA
Lusaka
Lake Kariba
Livingstone
Lake Nyasa
MALAWI
Lilongwe
Zomba
Moçambique
CABO DELGADO
Moroni
COMORO ISLANDS
Diégo-Suarez
CAP D'AMBRE
ALDABRA IS. (Sey.)
COSMOLEDO GROUP (Sey.)

Tropic of Capricorn
SOUTH WEST AFRICA (S. Africa Admin.)
Swakopmund
Walvis Bay (S. Africa)
Windhoek
GREAT NAMALAND
KALAHARI DESERT
BOTSWANA
Gaborone
Mafeking
Pretoria
JOHANNESBURG
Kimberley
SOUTH AFRICA
Cape Town
CAPE OF GOOD HOPE
CAPE AGULHAS
Port Elizabeth
East London
Durban
Pietermaritzburg
LESOTHO
SWAZILAND
Maputo
Baía de Lourenço Marques
MOZAMBIQUE
Beira
RHODESIA
Salisbury
Bulawayo
Victoria Falls
Okavango Swamp
CAPE FRIA
Lüderitz
Cunene
Okavango
Zambezi
MADAGASCAR
Tamatave
Tananarive
Tuléar
CAP STE. MARIE
INDIAN OCEAN

Longitude West of Greenwich   Longitude East of Greenwich

Relief

Meters	Feet
3050	10 000
1525	5000
610	2000
305	1000
0 Sea Level	0 Sea Level
152.5	500 Below Sea Level
1525	5000
3050	10 000
6100	20 000

0 200 400 600 800 1000 Miles
0 400 800 1200 1600 Kilometers

Scale 1:40 000 000; one inch to 630 miles. Lambert's Azimuthal, Equal Area Projection
Elevations and depressions are given in feet.

A-580000-76-7.10-11-18
COPYRIGHT BY
RAND McNALLY & COMPANY
MADE IN U.S.A.

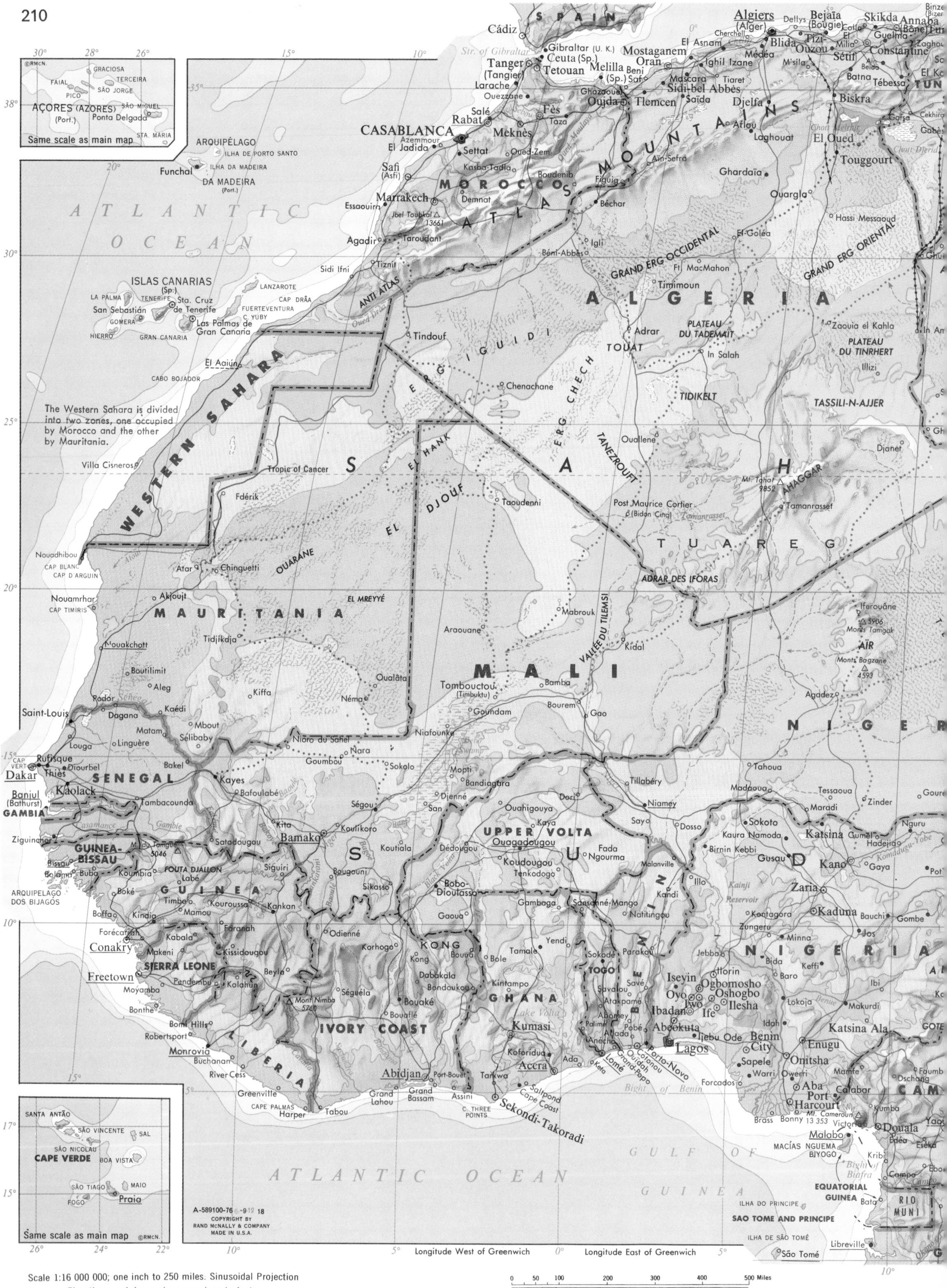

AÇORES (AZORES)
(Port.)
FAIAL
PICO
GRACIOSA
TERCEIRA
SÃO JORGE
SÃO MIGUEL
Ponta Delgada
STA. MARIA
Same scale as main map

ATLANTIC OCEAN

ARQUIPÉLAGO
ILHA DE PORTO SANTO
ILHA DA MADEIRA
DA MADEIRA
(Port.)
Funchal

SPAIN
Cádiz
Str. of Gibraltar
Gibraltar (U.K.)
Ceuta (Sp.)
Tanger
(Tangier)
Tetouan
(Tangier)
Larache
Melilla
(Sp.)
Beni Saf
Ouezzane
Salé
Rabat
Fès
Taza

Algiers
(Alger)
Deltys
Cherchell
El Asnam
Mostaganem
Oran
Ghazaouet
Sidi-bel Abbès
Tlemcen
Saïda
Oujda
Ighil Izane
Médéa
Blida
Tizi
Ouzou
Miliana
Bejaïa
(Bougie)
Skikda
Annaba
(Bône)
Guelma
Constantine
Sétif
M'sila
Batna
Tébessa
El K
TUN
Djelfa
Biskra
Aflou
Laghouat
El Oued
Touggourt
Gafsa
Chott Djerid

CASABLANCA
El Jadida
Azemmour
Settat
Oued-Zem
Kasba-Tadla
Meknès
MOROCCO
ATLAS MOUNTAINS
Boudenib
Aïn-Sefra
Figuig
Béchar
Ghardaïa
Ouargla
Hassi Messaoud
GRAND ERG OCCIDENTAL
GRAND ERG ORIENTAL
Safi
(Asfi)
Marrakech
Essaouira
Demnat
Jbel Toubkal
13661
Agadir
Taroudant
Béni-Abbès
Igli
El MacMahon
Timimoun
El-Goléa
Zaouia el Kahla
Ih Amn

Sidi Ifni
Tiznit
ANTI ATLAS
Oued Draa
CAP DRÂA
YUBY
WESTERN SAHARA
Tindouf
ERG IGUIDI
TOUAT
Adrar
PLATEAU
DU TADEMAIT
In Salah
PLATEAU
DU TINRHERT
Illizi
TIDIKELT
TASSILI-N-AJJER

ISLAS CANARIAS
(Sp.)
LA PALMA
LANZAROTE
Sta. Cruz
de Tenerife
TENERIFE
FUERTEVENTURA
San Sebastián
GOMERA
Las Palmas de
Gran Canaria
GRAN CANARIA
HIERRO

El Aaiún
CABO BOJADOR
ERG CHECH
Chenachane
Ouallene
Djanet

The Western Sahara is divided
into two zones, one occupied
by Morocco and the other
by Mauritania.

Villa Cisneros
Tropic of Cancer
S A H A R A
TANEZROUFT
EL HANK
Fdérik
EL DJOUF
Taoudenni
Post Maurice Cortier
(Bidon Cinq)
Mt. Tahat
9852
AHAGGAR
Tamanrasset
HAGGAR

Nouadhibou
CAP BLANC
CAP D'ARGUIN
Atar
Chinguetti
OUARANE
OUARÂNE
EL MREYYÉ
Araouane
Mabrouk
VALLÉE DU TILEMSI
ADRAR DES IFORAS
TUAREG
Iferouâne
5906
Monts Tamgak
AÏR
Monts Bagzane
4593

Nouamrhar
CAP TIMIRIS
Akjoujt
MAURITANIA
Nouakchott
Boutilimit
Tidjikdja
Rîdal
Kidal
Agadez

Rosso
Aleg
Kiffa
Néma
Oualâta
Tombouctou
(Timbuktu)
Bamba
M A L I
Gao
N I G E R

Saint-Louis
Dagana
Matam
Mbout
Sélibaby
Nioro du Sahel
Nara
Niafounké
Goundam
Bourem
Kayes
CAP VERT
Dakar
Thiès
Diourbel
SENEGAL
Bakel
Bafoulabé
Kita
Kayes
Goumbou
Sokolo
Mopti
Bandiagara
Tillabéry
Niamey
Tahoua
Madaoua
Tessaoua
Maradi
Zinder
Gouré
Nguru

Banjul
(Bathurst)
GAMBIA
Kaolack
Tambacounda
Kita
Koulikoro
Ségou
San
Djenné
Kaya
Dori
Sokoto
Kaura Namoda
Katsina
Gumel
Hadejia
Komddugu-Yobe

Ziguinchor
GUINEA-
BISSAU
Bissau
Bolama
Buba
FOUTA DJALLON
Mt. Tangue
5046
Labé
Siguiri
Bamako
S
Koutiala
Dédougou
UPPER VOLTA
Ouagadougou
Fada
N'gourma
Malanville
Kandi
Illo
Birnin Kebbi
Gusau
Kano
Gaya
Zaria
Kaduna

ARQUIPÉLAGO
DOS BIJAGÓS
GUINEA
Timbo
Boké
KourouBssa
Kankan
Sikasso
N
Bobo-
Dioulasso
Gambaga
Sansanné-Mango
Natitingou
Kontagora
Zungeru
Minna
Jos
Bauchi
Gombe

Boffa
Kindia
Mamou
Forécariah
Kabala
Makeni
SIERRA LEONE
Freetown
Moyamba
Bonthe
Kissidougou
Beyla
Kolahun
Pendembu
Mont Nimba
5748
Séguéla
Bouaflé
Kong
KONG
Dabakala
Bondoukou
Bouna
Bole
Kintampo
GHANA
Tamale
Yendi
Sokodé
Parakou
TOGO
Bida
Baro
Keffi
Ibi
NIGERIA
Minna
Jos
Jebba
Ilorin
Oyo
Iwo
Oshogbo
Ilesha
Ogbomosho
Lokoja
Idah
Makurdi
Katsina Ala
GOT

Conakry
Kalaba
Foranah
Odienné
Korhogo
Dabakala
IVORY COAST
Bouaké
Kumasi
Savalou
Atakpamé
Abomey
Ibadan
Ife
Abeokuta
Iseyin
Benin
City
Sapele
Warri
Onitsha
Enugu
Aba
Oweri
Owerri

Monrovia
Buchanan
River Cess
LIBERIA
Robertsport
Bomi Hills
CAPE PALMAS
Harper
Tabou
Greenville
Grand
Lahou
Grand
Bassam
Assini
Abidjan
Port-Bouet
Tarkwa
Accra
Cape Coast
Saltpond
Sekondi-Takoradi
C. THREE
POINTS
Lomé
Anecho
Aflao
Keta
Grand-Popo
Ouidah
Cotonou
Porto-Novo
Lagos
Ijebu Ode
Forcados
Port
Harcourt
Brass
Bonny
Calabar
Mamfe
Dschang
CAM
Mt. Cameroun
13 353
Victoria
Kumba
Douala
Kribi

GULF OF GUINEA
ATLANTIC OCEAN
BIGHT OF BENIN
Bight of Biafra
EQUATORIAL
GUINEA
MACÍAS NGUEMA
BIYOGO
Malabo
SAO TOME AND PRINCIPE
ILHA DO PRINCIPE
Bata
RIO
MUNI
ILHA DE SÃO TOMÉ
São Tomé
Libreville
Oyem

SANTA ANTÃO
SÃO VICENTE
SAL
SÃO NICOLAU
CAPE VERDE
BOA VISTA
SÃO TIAGO
MAIO
Praia
FOGO

Same scale as main map

A-589100-76-9-12 18
COPYRIGHT BY
RAND McNALLY & COMPANY
MADE IN U.S.A.

Longitude West of Greenwich
Longitude East of Greenwich

Scale 1:16 000 000; one inch to 250 miles. Sinusoidal Projection
Elevations and depressions are given in feet

0 50 100   200   300   400   500 Miles
0   100   200   400   600   800 Kilometers

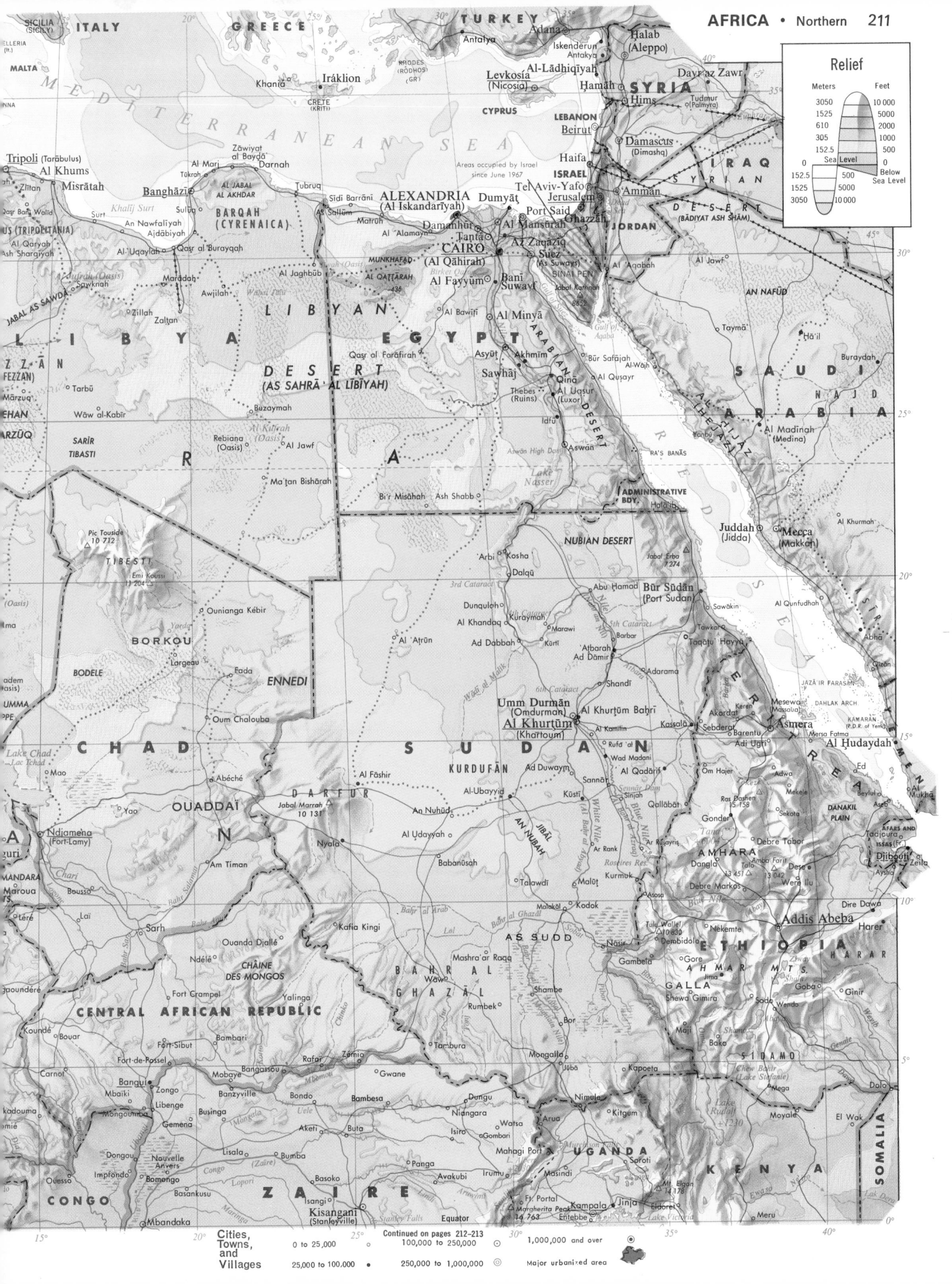

Relief

Meters		Feet
3050		10 000
1525		5000
610		2000
305		1000
152.5		500
0	Sea Level	0
152.5		Below
1525		500 Sea Level
3050		5000
		10 000

ITALY (SICILY)
SICILIA (SICILY)
PANTELLERIA (It.)
MALTA

GREECE
Khaniá
Iráklion
CRETE (KRITI)
RHODES (RÓDHOS) (GR.)

TURKEY
Antalya
Adana
Iskenderun
Antakya

Halab (Aleppo)
Dayr az Zawr
Al-Ládhiqíyah
Hamáh
Hims
SYRIA
Tudmur (Palmyra)
SYRIAN DESERT (BÁDIYAT ASH SHÁM)
IRAQ

LEBANON
Beirut
Damascus (Dimashq)
Levkosía (Nicosia)
CYPRUS

MEDITERRANEAN SEA

Haifa
Tel Aviv-Yafo
ISRAEL
Jerusalem
Amman
JORDAN

Areas occupied by Israel since June 1967

Tripoli (Tarábulus)
Al Khums
Zlitan
Misrátah
Qasr Bani Walid
Qaryah Ash Shargíyah
US (TRIPOLITANIA)

Záwiyat al Baydá
Darnah
Tukrah
Al Marj
Banghází
AL JABAL AL AKHDAR
BARQAH (CYRENAICA)
Tubruq
Sídí Barrání
As Sallúm
Matrúh
ALEXANDRIA (Al Iskandaríyah)
Dumyát
Al 'Alamayn
Damanhúr
Tanta
CAIRO (Al Qáhirah)
Az Zaqázíq
Port Said
Al Mansúrah
Ghazzah

Surt
Khalíj Surt
An Nawfalíyah
Ajdábiyah
Al Uqaylah
Qasr al Burayqah
MUNKHAFAD AL QATTÁRAH -436
Birket Qárún
Al Fayyúm
Bani Suwayf
Suez (As Suways)
Gulf of Suez
Al 'Aqabah
Gulf of Aqaba
SINAI PEN.
Jabal Katrínah 2637

JABAL AS SAWDÁ
(FEZZAN)
Maradah
Zillah
Zaltan
Awjilah
Al Jaghbúb
LIBYA
LIBYAN DESERT (AS SAHRÁ' AL LIBÍYAH)
Al Bawítí
Al Minyá
Qasr al Faráfirah
EGYPT
Asyút
Akhmím
Búr Safájah
AN NAFÚD
Taymá
Há'il
Buraydah
SAUDI
AL HIJAZ AL HEJAZ
NAJD

HAMADA
EHAN (FEZZAN)
Márzuq
Tarbú
Wáw al-Kabír
RZÚQ
SARÍR TIBASTI
Buzaymah
Rebiana (Oasis)
Al Kufrah (Oasis)
Al Jawf
Sawháj
Qiná
Thebes (Ruins)
Al Uqsur (Luxor)
Idfú
DESERT
Al Qusayr
ARABIAN
Yanbu
Al Madínah (Medina)

(Oasis)
UMMA
PPE
Ma'tan Bishárah
Aswán
Aswán High Dam
Lake Nasser
RA'S BANÁS

Pic Tousidé 10 712
TIBESTI
Emi Koussi 11 204
Ounianga Kébir
BORKOU
BODELE
Largeau
Fada
ENNEDI
Bi'r Misáhah
Ash Shabb
ADMINISTRATIVE BDY.
Halaíb
NUBIAN DESERT
Jabal Erba 7 274
Juddah (Jidda)
Mecca (Makkah)
Al Khurmah

Arbi
Kosha
Dalqú
3rd Cataract
Abu Hamad
Dunqulah
Al Khandaq
Kuraymah
Marawi
Búr Súdán (Port Sudan)
Sawákin
Al Qunfudhah
Abhá

Lake Chad Lac Tchad
Mao
CHAD
Oum Chalouba
Al 'Atrún
Ad Dabbah
Kúrtí
'Atbarah
Barbar
Taqátu Hayyá
JAZÁ IR FARASAN
KAMARAN (P.D.R. of Yemen)
Qizán
DAHLAK ARCH.

5th Cataract
Ad Dámir
Adarama
Keren
Mesewa (Massaua)

Abéché
Yao
OUADDAI
Jabal Marrah 10 131
DARFUR
An Nuhúd
Al Fáshir
Nyala
SUDAN
KURDUFÁN
Al-Ubayyid
Ad Duwaym
6th Cataract
Shandí
Umm Durmán (Omdurman)
Al Khurtúm Bahrí
Al Kámilin
Al Khurtúm (Khartoum)
Rufa' al
Wad Madani
Al Qadárif
Kassalá
Sebderat
Adi Ugri
Akordat
Asmera
Barentu
Merso Fatma
Al Hudaydah

Ndjamena (Fort-Lamy)
guri
MANDARA
Maroua
rs
Bousso
Léré
Laí
Sarh
Chari
Am Timan
Bahr Salamat
JIBÁL AN NUBAH
An Nuhúd
Al Udayyah
Babanúsah
Talawdí
Malút
Kústi
Sannár
Sinjah
Sennar Dam
Ar Rank
Ar Rusayris
Roseires Res.
Kurmuk
Asosa
AMHARA
Dangla
Gonder
Ras Dashen 15 158
Sekota
Mekele
Adwa
Amba Farit 13 451
Debre Tabor
Desé
Wera Ilu
DANAKIL PLAIN
AFARS AND ISSAS (Fr.)
Djibouti
Zeila
Aysha
Dire Dawa
Harer

Ndélé
CHÁINE DES MONGOS
Fort Crampel
Yalinga
Kafia Kingi
Lol
Bahr al Arab
AS SUDD
Malakál
Kodok
Násir
Gambela
Tule Wellel 10 830
Dembidolo
Gore
Nékemte
Addis Abeba
ETHIOPIA
HARAR
Harer

CENTRAL AFRICAN REPUBLIC
Koundé
Bouar
Fort-Sibut
Bambari
Rafaï
Zémia
Bangassou
Ouanda Djallé
Mashra'ar Raqq
Waw
BAHR AL GHAZÁL
Rumbek
Shambe
Bor
Tambura
Mongalla
Júba
Kapoeta
AHMAR MTS.
GALLA
Shewa Gimira
Maji
Bako
Sodo Wendo
Ginir
Goba
SIDAMO
Dolo
Chew Bahr (Lake Stefanie)
Mega
El Wak
SOMALIA

Carnot
Bangui
Mbaïki
Mongoumba
Zongo
Banzyville
Libenge
Gemena
Businga
Mobaye
Bondo
Bambesa
Dungu
Niangara
Gombari
Nimule
Kitgum
Soroti
Moyale
Lake Rudolf +1230
Mt. Elgon 14 178
Meru
KENYA

Ouesso
kadouma
mie
CONGO
Impfondo
Nouvelle Anvers
Dongou
Bomongo
Basankusu
Mbandaka
Lisala
Bumba
Basoko
Isangi
Kisangani (Stanleyville)
Stanley Falls
ZAIRE
Aketi
Buta
Isiro
Panga
Avakubi
Irumu
Watsa
Mahagi Port
Arua
Masindi
Ft. Portal
Margherita Peak 16 763
Kampala
Entebbe
Jinja
UGANDA
Eldoret
Lake Victoria
Equator

Continued on pages 212–213

Cities, Towns, and Villages

0 to 25,000	100,000 to 250,000
25,000 to 100,000	250,000 to 1,000,000
	1,000,000 and over
	Major urbanized area

Continued on pages 210-211

Scale 1:16 000 000; one inch to 250 miles. Sinusoidal Projection
Elevations and depressions are given in feet

CAPE TOWN
MOUILLE PT

Scale 1:1 000 000

0   5   10 Miles
0 4 8 12 16 Kilometers

©RMCN.

Johannesburg inset (Scale 1:1 000 000)

©RMCN.

Wolhuterskop · Jacksonstuin · Pretoria North · **Pretoria** · Cullinan

Kosmos · Harfsbeespoort · Swartspruit · Silverton · Rayton

Skeerpoort · Hennopsrivier · △4549 · Voortrekkerhoogte · Velhalla · 4426

Foothills · Olievenhoutpoort · △4602 · Lyttelton · Irene · Tierpoort

Tarlton · Halfway House · Kaaltontein · Bapsfontein · 26°

Krugersdorp · Moddersfontein · Kempton Park

Randfontein · **JOHANNESBURG** · Alexandra · Putfontein

Roodepoort · Discovery · 5557 · Edenvale · Primrose · Boksburg · Benoni

5725 · Florida · Maraisburg · Germiston · Brakpan

Orlando · Turffontein · Roseffenville · Alberton · Springs

Pimville · **WITWATERSRAND**

Scale 1:1 000 000
0   5   10 Miles
0 4 8 12 16 Kilometers

Main map — Madagascar, Mozambique, South Africa region

SOMALIA · Kismayo · Kenya 7 058 · Hall · robi · YA

Bur Gavo · Witu · Lamu · Takaungu · Mombasa

Vanga · PEMBA · Tanga · Pangani · ZANZIBAR · Zanzibar · Bagamoyo

Morogoro · Kisaki · Dar es Salaam · MAFIA · INDIAN

Utete · Kilwa Kivinje · Lindi · Mikindani · Masasi · CABO DELGADO

ALDABRA IS. (Sey.) · COSMOLEDO GROUP (Sey.) · 10°

Moçímboa da Praia · Ibo · Porto Amélia · Moroni · COMORO ISLANDS · ÎLES GLORIEUSES (Fr.) · CAP D'AMBRE

GRANDE COMORE · MOHÉLI · ANJOUAN · MAYOTTE (Fr.) · Diégo-Suarez

Lúrio · Memba · Nacala · Dzaoudzi · NOSSI BÉ · Vohémar

António Enes · ILHA ANGOCHE · CAP SAINT-ANDRÉ · Besalampy · Maromokotro △9450 · Maroantsetra · Baie d'Antongil · ÎLE SAINTE-MARIE

Moçambique · Majunga · Mandritsara · Fénérive

ÎLE JUAN DE NOVA (Fr.) · Maintirano · Tamatave

ÎLES BARREN · MADAGASCAR · Tananarive · Moramanga · Vatomandry

bane · ZAMBIQUE CHANNEL · Tsiribihina · Antsirabe · Mahanoro

Morondava · Ambositra · Mananjary

BASSAS DA INDIA (Fr.) · Fianarantsoa · Ihosy · Ivohibe

EUROPA (Fr.) · Morombe · Manakara

Tuléar · Farafangana · Betroka · Mahaly · Trafonomby △1477 · Fort-Dauphin

CAP STE. MARIE

Orange Free State / Lesotho / Natal / South Africa

Arlington · Dannhauser · Dundee · Mahlabatini

Paul Roux · Bethlehem · Glencoe · Nqutu

Senekal · Kestell · Harrismith · Wasbank · Babanango

ORANGE FREE STATE · ROYAL NATAL NAT'L PK. · Ladysmith · Pomeroy · Nkandla · Melmoth

Fouriesburg · Clarens · Colenso · Weenen · Greytown · Eshowe

Ficksburg · Butha Buthe · 10 822 Mt. aux Sources · Bergville · Winterton · Estcourt · Kranskop

Clocolan · Leribe · Cathedral Pk. 9856 · Mapumulo · Stanger

Pitseng · Cathkin Pk. 10 438 · Mooirivier · New Hanover · Dalton

Teyateyaneng · Mokhotlong · Mt. Gilboa △5803 · Wartburg · Howick

Machache 9464 · Thabana Ntlenyana 11 425 · Impendle · Nthoni △5851 · **Pietermaritzburg** · Verulam

Roma · LESOTHO · Bulwer · Richmond · Camper down · Pinetown

10 159 · Underberg · Creighton · Donnybrook · **Durban** · Isipingo

Mohale's Hoek · Orange · The Twins 8620 · Qacha's Nek · Swartberg 7619 · Franklin · Umzinto · Mid Illovo · 30°

Zastron · Matatiele · Cedarville · Umzimkulu · Umkomaas

Quthing · △9684 · 4426 △ Mt. Currie 7297 · Kokstad · Harding · Scottburgh

Herschel · Witberg △7853 · Rhodes · Ben Macdhui Fletcher 9846 · Mount · Mount Ayliff · Bizana · Park Rynie · Sezela

Lady Grey · Mount Frere · Flagstaff · Umtentweni · Port Shepstone · Uvongo Beach · Margate

Barkly East · Maclear · Qumbu · Tabankulu · Lusikisiki · Port Edward

Jamestown · Rossouw · 8430 · Ugie · Tsolo · Ngqeleni · Libode · Port St. Johns

Elliot · Umtata · RAME HEAD

Molteno · Dordrecht · Indwe · Cala · Engcobo · Mqanduli · Elliotdale · INDIAN

STORMBERG · Lady Frere · Tsomo · Idutywa · Willowvale

Stutterheim · Queenstown · Cofimvaba · Ncamakwe · Butterworth

Waverly · Tarkastad · Cradock · Whittlesea · Tylden · Carthcart · Kentani · CAPE OF GOOD HOPE · SOUTH AFRICA

BANKBERG 6606 · WINTERBERGE 7778 · Seymour · Frankfort · Komga · Kei Mouth · Morgan's Bay

Pearston · Bedford · Adelaide · Keiskammahoek · Stutterheim · Macleantown · 32°

Somerset East · Fort Beaufort · Fort Alice · King William's Town · Berlin · Breidbach · Gonubie · **East London**

Riebeek-Oos · Alicedale · Grahamstown · Peddie · Kidd's Beach

SUURBERGE · Kirkwood · Salem · Hamburg · OCEAN

Addo · Bathurst · Port Alfred (Kowie)

Uitenhage · Alexandria · SAINT CROIX ISLAND · BIRD ISLAND · 34°

Port Elizabeth · KAAP RECIFE

Scale 1:4 000 000
0 10 20 30 40 Miles
0 10 20 30 40 50 60 Kilometers

26° · 28° · 30° · Longitude East of Greenwich

40° · 45° · 50° · Equator · 28° · 28°30'

26° · INDIAN · OCEAN

Legend

Cities, Towns, and Villages

0 to 25,000	○	100,000 to 250,000	⊙	1,000,000 and over	◉
25,000 to 100,000	•	250,000 to 1,000,000	◎	Major urbanized area	

Relief

Meters		Feet
3050		10 000
1525		5000
610		2000
305		1000
152.5		500
0	Sea Level	0
152.5		500
1525		5000
3050		10 000

214

WESTERN
SAHARA

PUNTILLA
NEGRA
CABO
BARBAS
ADRAR SOTUF

Fdérik
Kediet Ijill

MAKTEÏR

OUARANE

EL DJOUF

S   A   H   A

Post Maur
Bidon
TANE
TAN

CAP BLANC
Nouadhibou

ÎLE TIDRA

Atar

MAURITANIA

ADÁFER EL ABIOD

EL MREYYE

AKLÉ 'ÂOUÂNA

AZAOUAD

Taoudenni

Timetrine
Monts

Bordj le P

CAP TIMIRIS
Nouamrhar

Akjoujt

Tidjikdja

AOUKÂR

Araouane

Aguelh

Anefis i-n-
Darane

M   A   L   I

Sebkha de
Ndrhamcha

Nouakchott

TRARZA

Rosso

Dagana
Saint-Louis
Louga

Aleg

Kiffa

Ayoun el Atrous

Néma

IRIGUI

Lac Faguibine

Tombouctou
(Timbuktu)

Lac Débo

Niger

Taoussa

Gao

Ansor

Kaédi
Matam

Linguère
Ranérou

Nioro du Sahel

Ballé

Léré

S

Lac Do

Hombori
Douentza

Macina

U

D

A

Thiès
CAP
VERT
Rufisque
Dakar
Diourbel
Touba

FERLO
SENEGAL

Naye
Kayes

Diéma

Didiéni

Goumbou

Kogoni

Mopti

Kona

Koro

Aribinda

Djibo

Dani

Kaolack
Sokone
CAPE
SAINT MARY
Banjul
(Bathurst)
GAMBIA

Tambacounda

Bafoulabé
Koulouguidi

PARC NATIONAL
DE LA BOUCLE
DU BAOULE

Banamba

Ségou

San

Djibasso

Tougan

Ouahigouya

Kaya

UPPER   VOLTA

Nyou

Ouagadougou

Dédougou

Koudougou

Toécé

Fada N

Kar

Bignona
Kolda
GUINEA-
BISSAU
Bissau

Medina Gonasse
PARC
NATIONAL
DU NIOKOLO
KOBA

Goumbati
1 368

Kita

Niger
Koulikoro

Bamako

Bla

Sido

Zangasso

Ouarkoye

Boromo

Houndé

Léo
Pô

Bolgatanga

Bawku
Dapang

PARC

Tenkodogo
Madjor

Sao
João

CAP ROXO
Ziguinchor

Kabot

ARQUIPÉLAGO
DOS
BIJAGÓS

Mansabá

Koundara

Satadougou

Massif Du
Tamgué 5 046

Danea

Labé

Casamance
Gâmbie

Tombadonkéa

Télimélé

Dinguiraye

Dabola

Siguiri

Badogo

Koualé

Sikasso

Bani

Banfora

Koualé

Koné

Tingréla

Niélé

Bobo Dioulasso

Lawra
Wa
Lokosse

Gushiago

Walewale

Niamtougou
Yendi

Etícoga

Bafing

Boffa

Fria

Kindia
Conakry

Mamou

Faranah

Kouroussa

Kankan

Odienné
Korhogo

Ferkéssédougou

Bouna

PARK
NATIONAL
DE BOUNA

Bole

White Volta

Tamale

Naftin

GUINEA

390 Loma
Mansa
Tingi

Kissidougou

Kérouané
Pic De Tio
4 934

Beyla

Boundiali

Niakaramandougou

Bondoukou

Wenchi

Kintampo

Forêt
Classée
Du Fazao
Diaboba
873

TO

SIERRA

Forécariah
Makeni

6 080
Sankanbiriwa

Touba

Séguéla

Katiola

Ouellé

Sunyani

Techiman

Mampong

Kwahu
Plateau

Agogo

Hohoe

Pal

Freetown
LEONE
Lonsai
Bo

Voinjama
Pendembu

Nzérékoré
Kenema

Nimba Mts.
MT. NIMBA
748 NAT PARK

Biankouma
Man
Danané

Mount
Kahoué
3 658

Bouaké

Bouaflé

Dimbokro

Abengourou

Bibiani

Obuasi

Kumasi

Dunkwa

Nkawkaw

Begoro

Koforidua
Nsawam

Anlog

Lom

Moyamba

Bonthe

SHERBRO ISLAND
TURNERS
PENINSULA

CAPE MOUNT
Robertsport
Breewerville
Monrovia

Gbarnga

Yomou
Sanniquellie

Gborna

Ganta

Duékoué

Daloa

Gagnoa

Divo

Agboville

Adzopé

Aboisso

Prestea

Tarkwa

Odo
Nyakrom

Winneba

Accra

Tema

Cape Coast

IVORY   COAST

GHANA

LIBERIA

Tchien

Duabo

Buchanan

Mont
Niénokoué
2 044

Guiglo

Sassandra

Greenville

Harper

CAPE
PALMAS

Tabou

Lagune
Tadio

Lagune
Ébrié

Abidjan

Grand-Bassam

Esiama

CAPE THREE
POINTS

Sekondi-Takoradi

GULF   OF

ATLANTIC   OCEAN

Relief

Meters	Feet	
3050	10 000	
1525	5000	
610	2000	
305	1000	
152.5	500	
0	Sea Level	0
152.5	500	
1525	5000	
3050	10 000	

Copyright by Rand McNally & Co.
Made in U.S.A.
A-589400-76   4

Scale 1:10,000,000; one inch to 160 miles. Lambert Azimuthal Equal Area Projection
Elevations and depressions are given in feet.

0   50   100   150   200   250   300 Miles
0   100   200   300   400   500 Kilometers

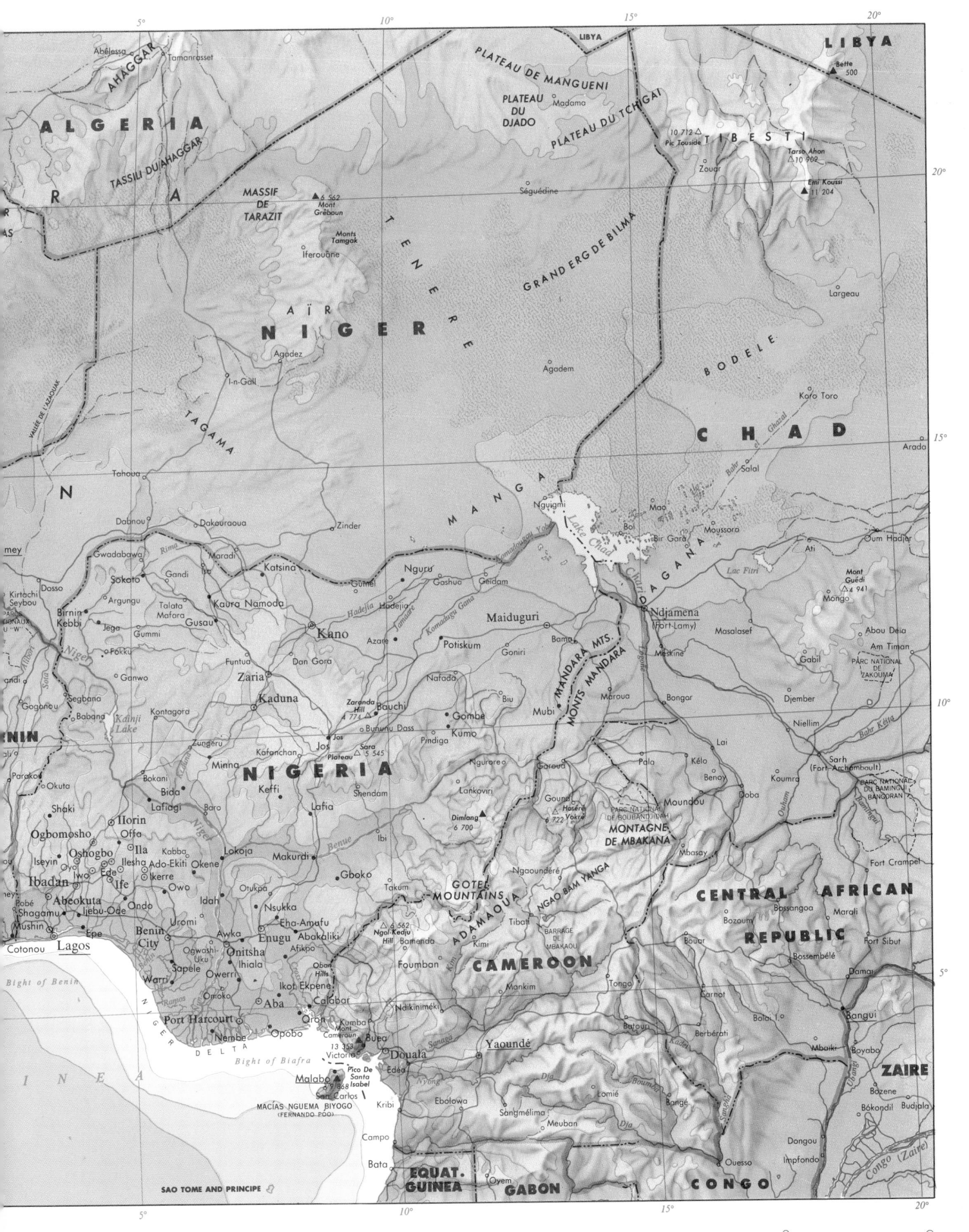

LIBYA

Bette
500 ▲

ALGERIA

AHAGGAR
Abélessa   Tamanrasset

TASSILI DU AHAGGAR

PLATEAU DE MANGUENI

PLATEAU DU DJADO

Madama

PLATEAU DU TCHIGAI

10 712 △
Pic Toussidé   TIBESTI

Tarso Ahon
△10 909

MASSIF DE TARAZIT   ▲6 562
Mont Grébour

Zouar

Emi Koussi
▲11 204

Monts Tamgak
Iférouâne

TENÉRÉ

Séguédine

20°

N I G E R

Agadez

GRAND ERG DE BILMA

Largeau

I-n-Gall

Agadem

B O D E L E

Koro Toro

TAGAMA

C H A D

15°

Tahoua

MANGA

N'guigmi

Bahr
Salal

Arada

Dabnou   Dakouraoua   Zinder

Gwadabawa
Sokoto   Gandi
Argungu   Talata   Maradi
Kirtachi Seybou   Mafara   Gusau
Birnin Kebbi   Jega   Gummi
Dosso   Katsina

Gumel   Nguru   Gashua   Geidam

Bir Gara   Mao   Moussora

Lake Chad
Bol

Ati   Oum Hadjer

Lac Fitri

Mont Guédi
△4 941
Mongo

Abou Deia

Am Timan

PARC NATIONAL DE ZAKOUMA

Kaura Namoda

Hadejia   Hadejia

Maiduguri

Ndjamena
(Fort-Lamy)

Masalaset

Gabil   Djember

Niellim

Kano   Azare

Fokku   Funtua   Dan Gora
Ganwo   Zaria

Potiskum   Goniri   Bama

Bongor

Gogonou   Babana   Kontagora
Segbana

Kaduna

Nafada

Biu

Mubi

MANDARA MTS.
MONTS MANDARA

Maroua

Lai

Bahr Kéita

Sarh
(Fort-Archambault)

Bende   Kainji Lake

Zaranda Hill
774   Bauchi
Bununu Dass
Jos
Plateau   Sara
5 545
Pindiga   Kumo
Gombe

Garoua

Pala   Kélo   Benoy   Koumra   Doba

PARC NATIONAL DU BAMINGUI BANGORAN

Zungeru

Minna   Keffi

N I G E R I A

Ngurore   Lankoviri

Goundi
Hosséré
6 722   Yokré

Moundou   Mbasay

Fort Crampel

Okuta   Bokani   Bida
Lafiagi   Baro   Lafia

Shendam   Ibi   Benue

Dimlang
6 700 ▲

PARC NATIONAL DE BOUBANDJIDAH

MONTAGNE DE MBAKANA

Parakou   Babana
Shaki   Ilorin   Offa   Kabba
Ogbomosho   Ila   Okene

Lokoja   Makurdi

Gboko   Takum   GOTEL MOUNTAINS

Ngaoundéré

Ngol-Kedju
Hill   Tibati

NGAO BAM YANGA

Bozoum   Marali

Oshogbo   Ede   Ilesha   Ado-Ekiti   Owo
Iseyin   Iwo   Ife   Ikerre
Ibadan   Idah

Otukpa

CENTRAL   AFRICAN

Bossangoa

Fort Sibut

Pobé   Abeokuta   Ondo   Nsukka
Shagamu   Ijebu-Ode   Uromi   Eha-Amafu
Mushin   Awka   Enugu   Abakaliki

ADAMAOUA

Kimi

Fouman

REPUBLIC

Bozoum   Bouar

Bossembélé   Damar

Cotonou   Lagos
Bight of Benin

Benin City   Ogwashi-Uku   Onitsha
Sapele   Ihiala   Afikpo
Warri   Owerri   Oban Hills
Omoko   Aba   Ikot Ekpene

Ngol Hill
6 562   Bamenda

Mankim   Tongo

C A M E R O O N

Carnot

Batouri   Berbérati

Bangui

NIGER DELTA
Port Harcourt   Oron
Nembe   Opobo   Kumba   Mont Cameroun
13 353   Buea   Victoria   Douala

Ndikinimeki

Yaoundé

Mbaïki   Boyabo

ZAIRE

Bozène

GUINEA   Malabo   Pico De Santa Isabel
9 868
San Carlos
MACIAS NGUEMA BIYOGO
(FERNANDO POO)

Kribi

Edéa   Nyong

Ebolowa

Lomié

Boumba

Bôkondil   Budjala

Campo

Sangmélima   Meuban

Dja

Dongou   Impfondo

Bata

SAO TOME AND PRINCIPE

EQUAT. GUINEA   GABON

Oyem

C O N G O

Ouesso

Congo (Zaïre)

5°   10°   15°   20°

CENTRAL AFRICAN REPUBLIC

NIGERIA
Opobo
Mont Cameroun 13 353
Douala
Buea
Edéa
Yaoundé
Doumé
Batouri
Berbérati
Bolai I.
Bangui
Kongba
Bangassou
Rafai
Fort de Passel
Boali
Mbaiki
Boyabo
Bosobolo
Mobaye
Yakoma
Bondo
Malabo
San Carlos
MACÍAS NGUEMA BIYOGO
(FERNANDO PÓO)
Ebolowa
Sangmélima
Lomié
Yokaduma
Bangé
Mongoumba
Gemena
Businga
Bodalang
Yandongi
Aketi
Bight of Biafra
Kribi
Meuban
Sauanké
Moloundou
Bozene
Budiala
Lisala
Bumba
Campo
EQUATORIAL
GUINEA
Bata
Oyem
Djoua
Ouesso
Dongou
Impfondo
Bomongo
Mange
Lifanga
Simba
Isangi
Kisanga (Stanleyville)
PRÍNCIPE
CABO SAN JUAN
Acalayong
MONTS DE CRISTAL
Mekambo
Lebango
Likouala
Loka
Lakofa
Boende
Tshuapa
Bakungu
SAO TOME AND
PRINCIPE
ISLA DE CORISCO
Kango
Booué
Owando
Mbandaka (Coquilhatville)
Kiri
Monkoto
Yayama
Ekoli
Litoi
São Tomé
SÃO TOMÉ
Libreville
GABON
CONGO
Lac Tumba
Bikoro
Inongo
ZAIRE
Ekanga
Port-Gentil
CAP LOPEZ
Bifoum
Ogooué
Lambaréné
Mount Iboundji 5 184
Koula-Moutou
St. François de Boundji
Gamboma
Lac Mai-Ndombe
Lokolama
Esambo
Omboué
Mouila
Franceville
Mbinda
Djambala
Fimi
Makaw
Dekese
Sankuru
Tiebo (Port-Francqui)
Domionga
Lusambo
Petit Loango
3 112
Monts De La Léketi
Mossendjo
Sibiti
Kindanba
Bandundu
Kwilu
Lukenie
Lomela
Tchibanga
Madingou
Brazzaville
Kinshasa (Léopoldville)
Masi-Manimba
Demba
Mbuji-M (Bakwang)
Mayumba
Madingo
Loubomo
Stanley Pool
Kasai
Kikwit
Charlesville
Bulunga
Kananga (Luluabourg)
Pointe-Noire
Chutes De Livingstone (Livingstone Falls)
Kisantu
Mbanza-Ngungu
Popokabaka
Kilembe
Tshikapa
Kanda-Kanda
CABINDA (Ang.)
Cabinda
Tshela
Kimvula
Kitenda
Kwenge
Kahemba
Portugália
Chicapa
PONTA DO PADRÃO
Boma
Matadi
Nóqui
São Salvador do Congo
Quimbele
Kibenga
Kapanga
Kam
Santo António do Zaire
SERRA DO CONGO
Damba
Caluango
Sambungo
ATLANTIC
Ambrizete
Mabaia
Carmona
Marimba
Quimbonge
KATANGA
Ambriz
Catoco
Kungowa
Luanda
Caxito
Duque de Bragança
Quela
Henrique de Carvalho
Malangal
Naso
PONTA DAS PALMEIRINHAS
Catete
Salazar
Dondo
Malanje
Nova Gaia
Cacolo
Teixeira de Sousa
Lucano
CABO DAS TRÊS PONTAS
PARQUE NACIONAL DE QUIÇAMA
Mussende
Saútar
ANGOLA
Luso
PARQUE NACIONAL DA CAMEIA
Calunda
Lum
Porto Amboim
Gabela
Cuvo
Cela
Calucinga
Coemba
Silva Porto
Curunga
Novo Redondo
KASHIJI PLAIN
Chitokoloki
OCEAN
Coyelo
SERRA CAMBONDA
Alto-Uama
Chitamba
Cangamba
LIUWA PLAIN
Lobito
Benguela
SERRA MOCO 8 596
Huambo (Nova Lisboa)
Chá Pungana
Mussuma
Ninda
Catumbela
SERRA DO CHILENGUE
Caconda
Serpa Pinto
Lunga
BAROTSE PLAIN
Mongu
CABO DE SANTA MARTA
SERRA DA NEVE
Caluquembe
Cacula
Caiundo
Mavinga
Nangweshi
São Nicolau
Mocâmedes
Sá da Bandeira
Falgares
Cassinga
Sá da Bandeira
PARQUE NACIONAL DO BIKUAR
Cangamba
SILOANA PLAINS
PONTA ALBINA
Porto Alexandre
Chianje
Cahama
Cuando
Catuala
Luiana
PONTA DA MARCA
Baía dos Tigres
Foz do Cunene
Oncocua
Cuamato
Melunga
Ruacana
Cuangar
Sambusu
CAPRIVI STRIP
BOTS.
S. W. AFRICA
CHOBE NAT'L
Kasinka

Relief
Meters / Feet
3050 / 10 000
1525 / 5000
610 / 2000
305 / 1000
152.5 / 500
Sea Level / 0
152.5 / 500
1525 / 5000
3050 / 10 000

Scale 1:10,000,000; one inch to 160 miles. Lambert Azimuthal Equal Area Projection
Elevations and depressions are given in feet.

0 50 100 150 200 250 300 Miles
0 100 200 300 400 500 Kilometers

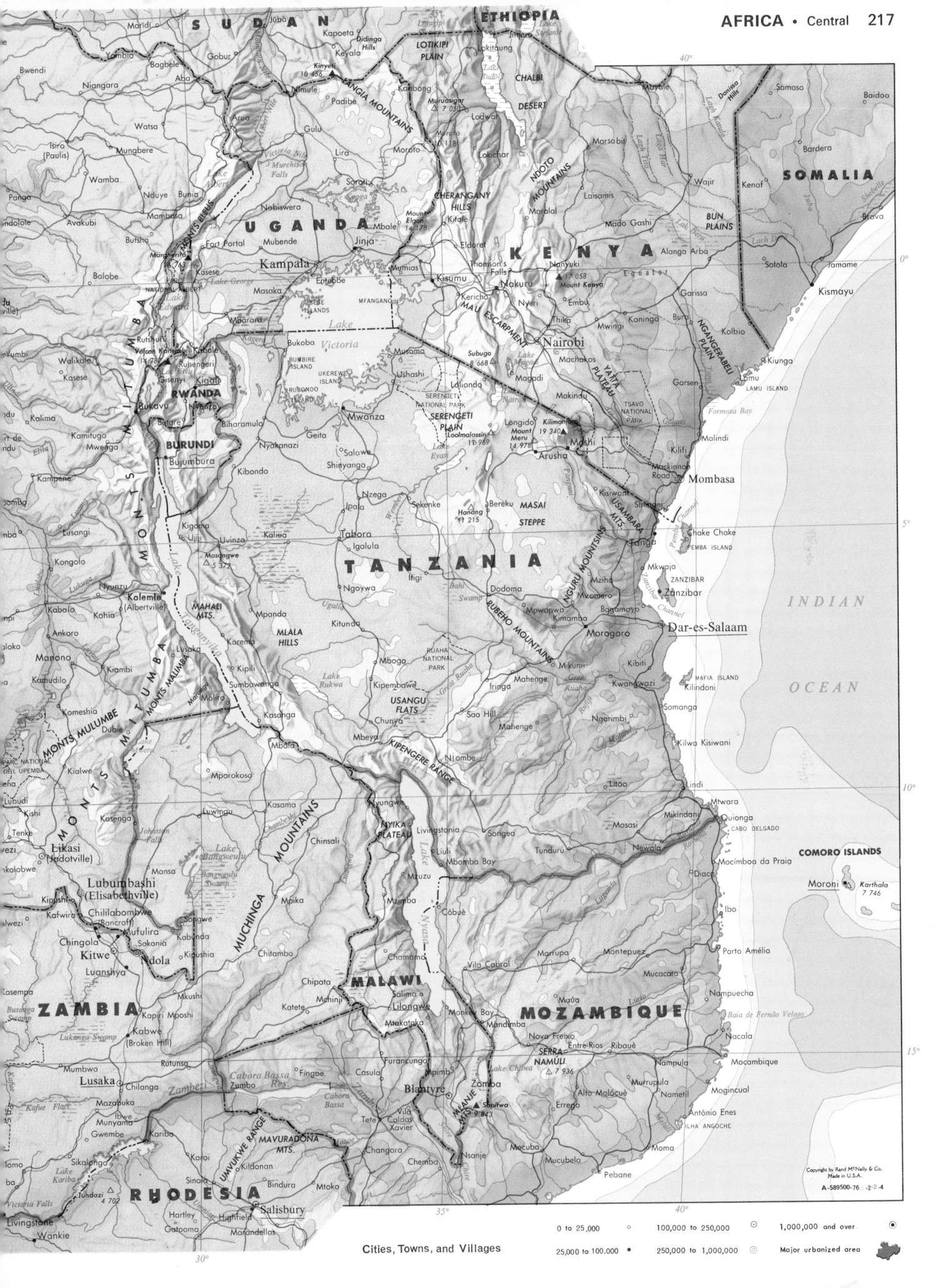

SUDAN
ETHIOPIA

Maridi
Yombio
Juba
Kapoeta
Didinga Hills
Jimma
Lake Stefanie

Bagbele
Gobur
Keyala
LOTIKIPI PLAIN
Lokitaung
Lake Rudolf
CHALBI DESERT

Bwendi
Niangara
Aba
Nimule
Padibe
Kinyeti 10 456
LANGIA MOUNTAINS
Kaabong
Lodwar
Maralal
Murasigar △ 7 050
Marsabit
Buraka
Danisa Hills
Samaso
Baidoa

Watsa
Mungbere
Arua
Gulu
Mereto 10 118
Lokichar
Lach Tror
Lach Dera
Bardera

Tsiro (Paulis)
Wamba
Mambasa
Bunia
Lira
Soroti
Lokichar
Mado Gashi
Wajir
Kenaf
SOMALIA

Panga
Nduye
Butsha
Nobiswera
CHERANGANY HILLS
Kitale
Eldoret
Laisamis
NDOTO MOUNTAINS
Alanga Arba
Sotola
Jamame
Bardera

ndolole
Avakubi
MONTS BLEUS
Fort Portal
Mubende
UGANDA
Mbale
Mount Elgon 14 178
Jinja
Mumias
Kisumu
Thomson's Falls
Nakuru
KENYA
Nanyuki 17 058
Mount Kenya
Garissa
Kismayu

Margherita 16 763
Kasese
Kampala
Entebbe
MAU ESCARPMENT
Kericho
Nyeri
Nairobi
Machakos
YATTA PLATEAU
Kiunga
LAMU ISLAND

NATIONAL ALBERT
Lake George
Masaka
MFANGANO
Subugo △ 8 668
Makindu
TSAVO NATIONAL PARK
Garsen
Formosa Bay
Lamu

Yumbi
Rutshuru
Kabale
SESE ISLANDS
Lake Victoria
Musama
Lolgorien
Lake Magadi
NGANGERABELI PLAIN

Walikale
Volcan Karisimbi 14 787
Ruhengeri
Gisenyi
Kigali
Nyanza
BUMBIRE ISLAND
UKEREWE ISLAND
Ushashi
SERENGETI NATIONAL PARK
Longido
Magadi
Malindi

Kasese
Bukavu
Butare
RWANDA
Bukoba
RUBONDO ISLAND
Mwanza
SERENGETI PLAIN
Loolmalasin 10 969
Mount Meru 14 978
Kilimanjaro 19 340 △
Moshi
Kilifi

ndu
Kalima
Kamituga
Mwenga
BURUNDI
Bujumbura
Biharamulo
Nyakanazi
Geita
Salawe
Lake Eyasi
Hanang △ 9 215
Bereku
Arusha
Kisiwani
Mackinnon Road
Mombasa

Kampene
MONTS MITUMBA
Kigoma Ujiji
Nzega
Shinyanga
Kibondo
MASAI STEPPE
USAMBARA MTS.
Tanga

omba
Lusangi
Kongolo
MONTS MITUMBA
Uvinza
Masangwe △ 5 372
Ipala
Sekenke
Dodoma
Mziha
Mwero
Mkwaja
PEMBA ISLAND
Chake Chake

nba
Kabalo
Kalemie (Albertville)
Kahia
Kaliua
Igalula
Tabora
Ngoywa
Itigi
Bahi Swamp
Ugalla
RUBEHO MOUNTAINS
Mpwapwa
Kimamba
NGURU MOUNTAINS
Mvomero
Bagamoyo
ZANZIBAR
Zanzibar

mpi
Ankoro
Nyunzu
MAHALI MTS.
Mpanda
Kitunda
TANZANIA
Morogoro
Dar-es-Salaam

aloko
Marono
Kambudilo
Kiambi
Karema
MLALA HILLS
Mbogo
RUAHA NATIONAL PARK
Iringa
Mahenge
Mkumi
Kibiti
INDIAN

Kahama
Komeshia
MONTS MALUMBA
Kipili
Sumbawanga
Lake Rukwa
Kipembawe
Sao Hill
Mahenge
Great Ruaha
Kwangwazi
MAFIA ISLAND
Kilindoni
OCEAN

Kialwe
MONTS MULUMBE
Dubie
Molira
Kasanga
USANGU FLATS
Chunya
Mbeya
Nlombe
KIPENGERE RANGE
Ngarimbi
Somanga

PARC NATIONAL DE L'UPEMBA
Likasi (Jadotville)
Johnston Falls
Kasama
Chinsali
Livingstonia
Songea
Kilwa Kisiwani

Lubudi
Kishi
Tenke
Kasenga
Luwingu
Chambeshi
NYIKA PLATEAU
MUCHINGA MOUNTAINS
Masasi
Litoo
Lindi
COMORO ISLANDS

ezi
Likasi
Kipushi
Mansa
Lake Bangweulu
Mbala
Mzuzu
Mbamba Bay
Liuli
Tunduru
Newala
Mikindani
Mtwara
Quionga
CABO DELGADO

nkolowe
Lubumbashi (Elisabethville)
Chililabombwe (Bancroft)
Songwe
Mpika
Bangweulu Swamp
Côbué
Mzimba
Diace
Mocímboa da Praia
Moroni
Karthala 7 746

lwezi
Kafwira
Mufulira
Sakania
Kabunda
Chitambo
Mzimba
Ibo
Porto Amélia

Chingola
Kitwe
Ndola
Kipushia
Chamama
Vila Cabral
Marrupa
Montepuez
Porto Amélia

Luanshya
Mkushi
Chitambo
Chipata
MALAWI
Salima
Mandimba
Maúa
Mucacata
Nampuecha

ZAMBIA
Kapiri Mposhi
Kabwe (Broken Hill)
Chilanga
Katete
Mchinji
Lilongwe
MOZAMBIQUE
Monkey Bay
Mtakataka
Mandimba
Baia de Fernão Veloso

asempa
Mumbwa
Lusaka
Lukanga Swamp
Rutunsa
Fingoe
Casula
Furancungo
Nova Freixo
Entre-Rios
Ribaué
Nampula
Mocambique
Nacala

Butaqa Swamp
Mazabuka
Ibwe Munyama
Cabora Bassa Res.
Zumbo
Cahora Bassa
Pimbi
Zomba
SERRA NAMÚLI △ 7 936
Alto Molócuè
Errego
Murrupula
Nametil
Mogincual
António Enes
ILHA ANGOCHE

Kafue Flat
Gwembe
Kariba
Tete
Vila Caldas Xavier
Blantyre
MLANJE MTS
Sapitwa △ 9 843
Mocuba
Moma

Sikalongo
Tuhdazi 4 702
UMVUKWE RANGE
MAVURADONA MTS.
Kildonan
Sinoia
Bindura
Mtoko
Changara
Chemba
Nsanje
Mucubela
Pebane

RHODESIA
Livingstone
Wankie
Lake Kariba
Karoi
Hartley
Highfield
Salisbury
Gatooma
Marandellas

Cities, Towns, and Villages

0 to 25,000   100,000 to 250,000   1,000,000 and over
25,000 to 100,000   250,000 to 1,000,000   Major urbanized area

Copyright by Rand McNally & Co.
Made in U.S.A.
A-589500-76 -2-2-4

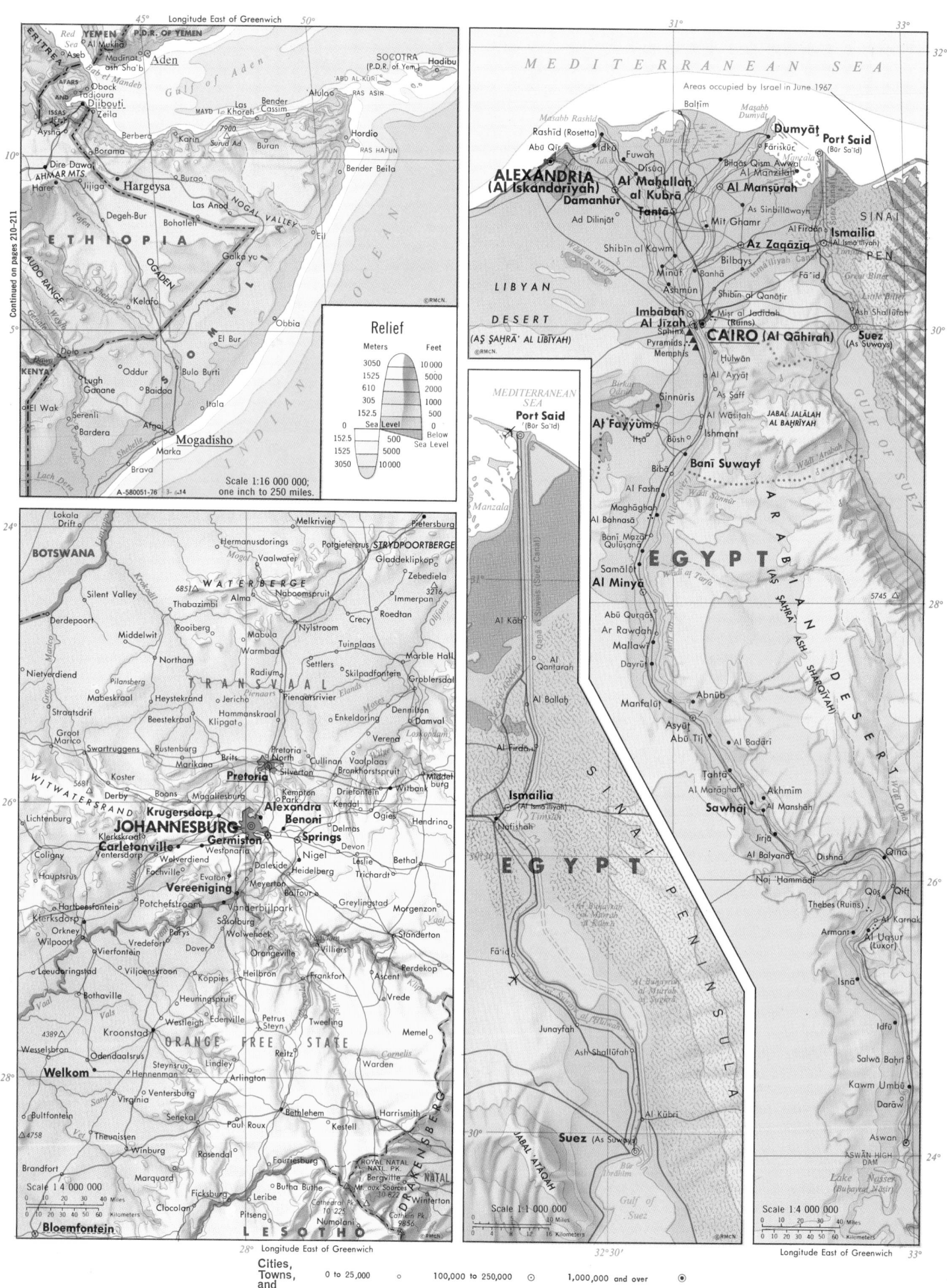

Cities, Towns, and Villages
0 to 25,000 ○
25,000 to 100,000 •
100,000 to 250,000 ⊙
250,000 to 1,000,000 ◎
1,000,000 and over ◉
Major urbanized area

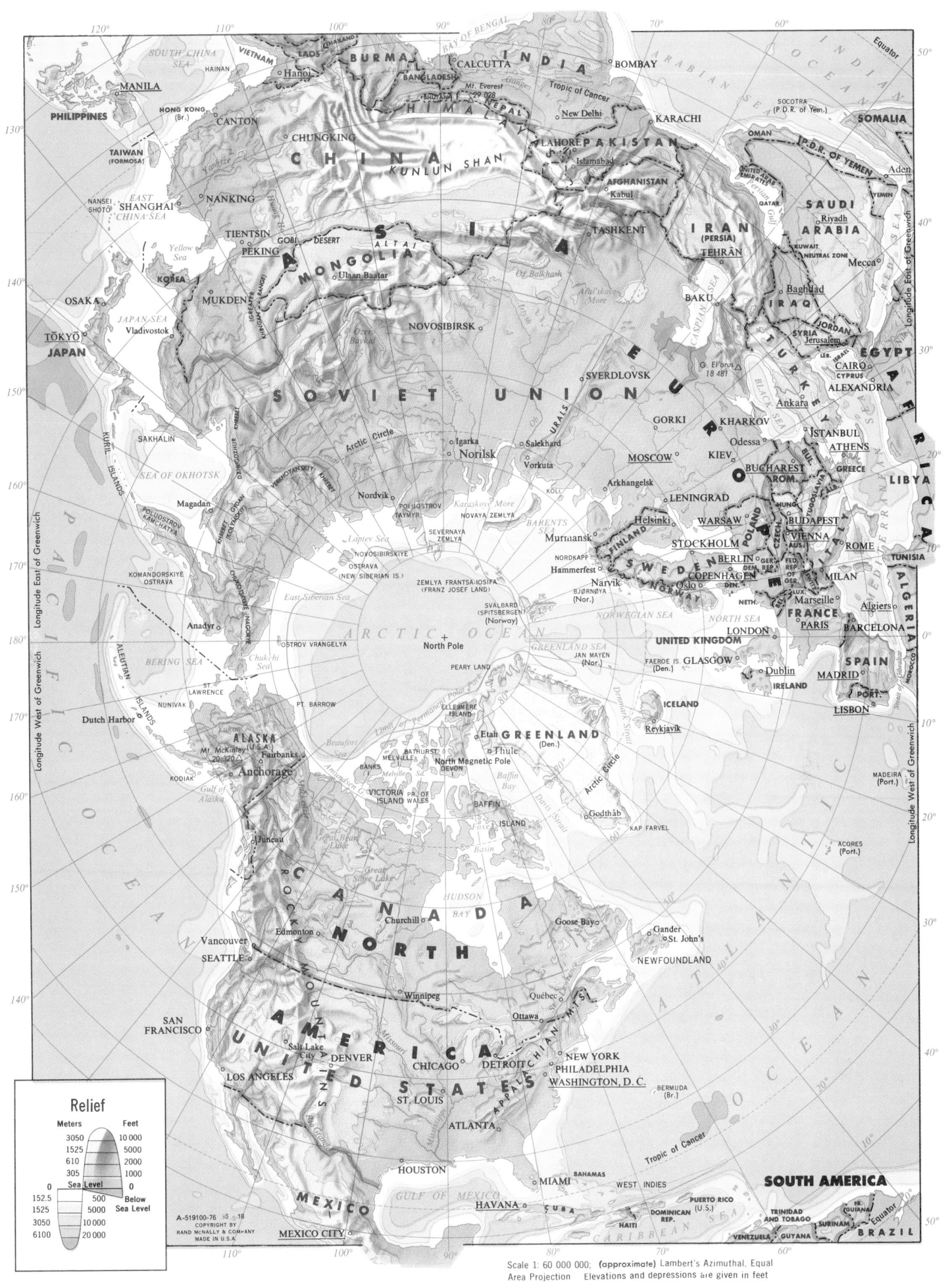

Relief

Meters	Feet
3050	10 000
1525	5000
610	2000
305	1000
0	Sea Level
	Below
152.5	500	Sea Level
1525	5000
3050	10 000
6100	20 000

A-519100-76 -5 -5 -18
COPYRIGHT BY
RAND McNALLY & COMPANY
MADE IN U.S.A.

Scale 1: 60 000 000; (approximate) Lambert's Azimuthal, Equal
Area Projection   Elevations and depressions are given in feet

Relief

Meters		Feet
3050		10 000
1525		5000
610		2000
305		1000
0	Sea Level	0
152.5	500	Below
1525	5000	Sea Level
3050	10 000	
6100	20 000	

A-594000-76 3-4-12
COPYRIGHT BY
RAND McNALLY & COMPANY
MADE IN U.S.A.

SOUTH AMERICA

PERU
La Paz
BOLIVIA
Sucre
BRAZIL
PARAGUAY
Asunción
Brasilia
SANTIAGO
Rosario
SÃO PAULO
CHILE
ARGENTINA
BUENOS AIRES
URUGUAY
MONTEVIDEO
Santos
RIO DE JANEIRO
ARCH. DE LOS CHONOS
Punta Arenas
Estr. de Magallanes
FALKLAND IS. (ISLAS MALVINAS) (Br.)
CABO DE HORNOS
Drake Passage

Tropic of Capricorn
SALA-Y-GÓMEZ (Chile)
I. DE SAN FÉLIX (Chile)
I. DE SAN AMBROSIO (Chile)
RAPA NUI (EASTER) (Chile)
IS. DE JUAN FERNÁNDEZ (Chile)

TUAMOTU (LOW) ARCHIPELAGO (Fr.)

PACIFIC OCEAN

ATLANTIC OCEAN

SOUTH SHETLAND ISLANDS (B.A.T.)
ADELAIDE
SOUTH ORKNEY IS. (B.A.T.)
SOUTH GEORGIA (Falkland Is.)
TRISTAN DA CUNHA (Br.)
SOUTH SANDWICH IS. (Falkland Is.)
GOUGH (Br.)

BELLINGSHAUSEN SEA
THURSTON I.
ALEXANDER
WEDDELL SEA
AMUNDSEN SEA
Mt. Rex 3 625
Mt. Siple 10 171
Mt. Ulmer 8 451
Mt. Hope 1 506
ELLSWORTH MTS.
RONNE ICE SHELF
EXECUTIVE COMMITTEE RANGE
Mt. Sidley 13 717
WHITMORE MTS.
BERKNER ISLAND
FILCHNER ICE SHELF
ROCKEFELLER PLATEAU
THIEL MTS.
PENSACOLA MTS.
COATS LAND
Little America
HORLICK MTS.
ROOSEVELT
QUEEN MAUD MTS.
MÜHLIG-HOFMANN MTS.
BOUVETØEN (BOUVET) (Nor.)
ROSS ICE SHELF
ROSS SEA
South Pole
10 000
SCOTT
QUEEN MAUD LAND
C. OF GOOD HOPE
Cape Town
Mt. Sabine 12 201
Mt. Erebus 12 280
McMurdo
Mt. Markham 14 272
Mt. Albert Markham 10 522
Mt. McClintock 11 457
SØR RONDANE MTS.
BELGICA MTS.
BALLENY IS.
VICTORIA LAND
ANTARCTICA
QUEEN FABIOLA MTS.
ENDERBY LAND
South Magnetic Pole
WILKES LAND
AMERICAN HIGHLAND
AMERY ICE SHELF
LAMBERT GLACIER
NAPIER MTS.
Antarctic Circle
PRINCE EDWARD IS. (S. Africa)
IS. CROZET (Fr.)
AFRICA
SOUTH AFRICA
LESOTHO
Pretoria
Durban
SWAZILAND
MOZAMBIQUE
SHACKLETON ICE SHELF
WEST ICE SHELF
DIBBLE ICEBERG TONGUE
HEARD (Austl.)
McDONALD (Austl.)
IS. DE KERGUELEN (Fr.)

Antarctic Circle
CHATHAM IS. (N.Z.)
NEW ZEALAND
BOUNTY IS. (N.Z.)
CAMPBELL (N.Z.)
SOUTH ISLAND
AUCKLAND IS. (N.Z.)
MACQUARIE (Austl.)

TASMAN SEA
Hobart
TASMANIA
MELBOURNE
Adelaide
AUSTRALIA
GREAT AUSTRALIAN BIGHT
C. LEEUWIN
Perth
GREAT VICTORIA DESERT
GREAT SANDY DESERT
NORTH WEST CAPE
TIMOR SEA
TIMOR
FLORES
INDONESIA

NEW AMSTERDAM (Fr.)
ST. PAUL (Fr.)
C. STE. MARIE
MADAGASCAR
COMORO ISLANDS
Tananarive
RÉUNION (Fr.)
MASCARENE IS.
MAURITIUS
C. D'AMBRE
AMIRANTE IS. (Sey.)
SEYCHELLES
Tropic of Capricorn

INDIAN OCEAN

Longitude West of Greenwich
Longitude East of Greenwich

ANTARCTICA IN PROFILE
SECTION ALONG LINE AB

15000	South Pole		15000
10000		Framnes Mts.	10000
5000	Horlick Mts.		5000
Feet (A)	Byrd Basin	Polar Basin	Sea Level	(B) Feet
5000			5000

Scale 1: 60 000 000; (approximate)
Lambert's Azimuthal, Equal Area Projection
Elevations and depressions are given in feet

Ocean Floor Maps

The maps in this section give an artist's view of what the land beneath the surface of the world's oceans looks like. In general, colors used are those which scientists believe may exist on the ocean floor. For continental shelves or shallow inland seas, grayish-green corresponds to sediments washed from the continental areas. Layers of mud, which scientists call *oozes,* cover the ocean bottom. In deeper parts of the oceans, the oozes consist largely of the skeletons of marine life. These appear in white. The fine mud from land is red. In the Atlantic Ocean, materials accumulate relatively rapidly and have a high iron content. These are shown in a brighter red than elsewhere. Slower accumulation in the Pacific and Indian Oceans results in more manganese, which results in darker colors. Undersea ridges are shown in black to suggest that they were formed relatively recently from molten rock. Around certain islands white is used to show coral reefs.

The ocean floor has towering mountain ranges, vast canyons, broad plains, and a variety of features that often exceed anything found on the continents. One of the most dramatic features of the ocean floor is the Mid-Atlantic Ridge, a chain of mountains that extends down the middle of the Atlantic Ocean. One distinct characteristic of this ridge, is a *trough,* or valley, that runs along the center of the ridge, in effect producing a double line of ridges.

Scientists believe that the ocean ridges mark lines where molten materials from the earth's interior rise to the ocean floor, to form gigantic plates that move slowly apart. This theory, called Continental Drift, suggests that the continents are moving away from each other, having been a single land mass in ancient times. The matching curves of the Atlantic Ocean shorelines of South America and Africa have long been cited as support for this theory.

Where the subsea plates meet certain continental areas or island chains, the ridges plunge downward to form deep trenches. Some of the deepest known trenches are found along the northern and western edges of the Pacific Ocean. These include the Mariana, Tonga, and Kuril trenches.

Deep trenches also parallel the western coasts of Central and South America, the northern coast of Puerto Rico and the Virgin Islands, and other coastal areas. Other identifiable ocean floor features include great submarine canyons that lead from the edges of the continents; seamounts that rise above the ocean floor to form islands; and the continental shelves, which appear to be underwater extensions of the continents.

Greenland
Iceland
Europe
Africa
North America
Svalbard
Barents Sea
Norwegian Sea
North Sea
Baltic Sea
British Isles
Black Sea
Aegean Sea
Mediterranean Sea
MEDITERRANEAN RIDGE
Baffin Bay
Baffin Island
Hudson Bay
Hudson Strait
Great Lakes
Gulf of Mexico
Caribbean Sea
Greater Antilles
LABRADOR BASIN
WEST EUROPEAN BASIN
IBERIAN ABYSSAL PLAIN
CANARY BASIN
CAPE VERDE BASIN
NORTH AMERICAN BASIN
SOHM ABYSSAL PLAIN
HATTERAS ABYSSAL PLAIN
NARES ABYSSAL PLAIN
GUIANA BASIN
MID-ATLANTIC RIDGE
REYKJANES RIDGE
AZORES PLATEAU
BERMUDA RISE
NEWFOUNDLAND BASIN
GRAND BANK
PUERTO RICO TRENCH
CAYMAN TRENCH
MIDDLE AMERICA TRENCH
SIERRA LEONE BASIN
Tropic of Cancer
Arctic Circle
Scale 1:44,000,000; one inch to 700 miles (approx.)
Modified Cylindrical Projection
▽ Depths in meters.

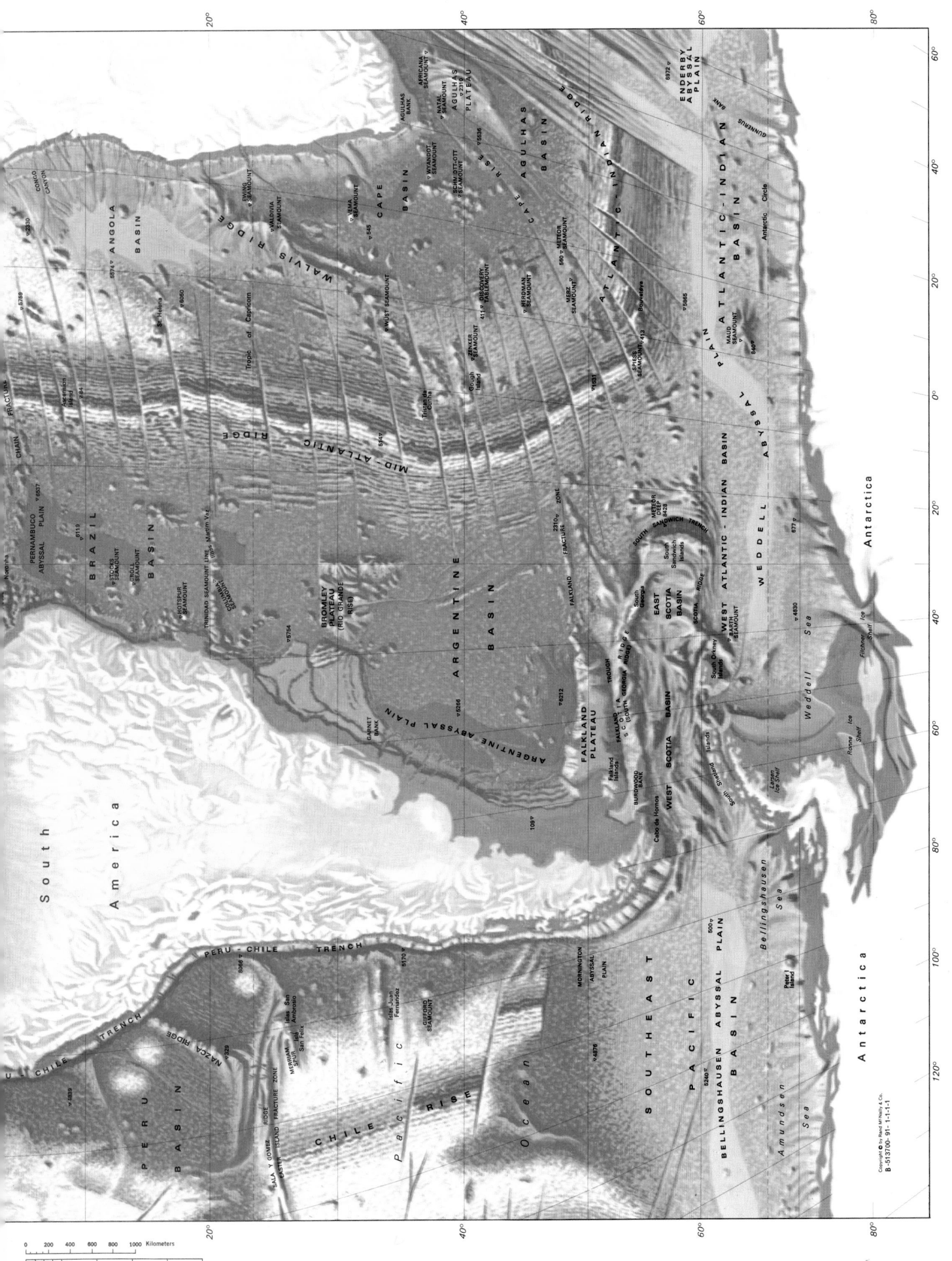
South America
Antarctica
PERU BASIN
NAZCA RIDGE
PERU-CHILE TRENCH
CHILE RISE
SALA Y GOMEZ RIDGE
EASTER ISLAND FRACTURE ZONE
MERRIAM SPUR
Islas San Ambrosio
Isla San Felix
Islas Juan Fernandez
GIFFORD SEAMOUNT
Pacific Ocean
MORNINGTON ABYSSAL PLAIN
SOUTHEAST PACIFIC BASIN
BELLINGSHAUSEN ABYSSAL PLAIN
BELLINGSHAUSEN BASIN
Bellingshausen Sea
Amundsen Sea
Peter I Island
PERNAMBUCO ABYSSAL PLAIN
CHAIN FRACTURE
Noronha
BRAZIL BASIN
STOCKS SEAMOUNT
GRÖLL SEAMOUNT
HOTSPUR SEAMOUNT
TRINIDAD SEAMOUNT LINE
Ilhas Martim Vaz
COLUMBIA SEAMOUNT
BROMLEY PLATEAU (RIO GRANDE RISE)
GARNET BANK
ARGENTINE ABYSSAL PLAIN
ARGENTINE BASIN
FALKLAND FRACTURE ZONE
FALKLAND PLATEAU
Falkland Islands
FALKLAND TROUGH
SCOTIA (SOUTH GEORGIA RIDGE) RIDGE
BURDWOOD BANK
Cabo de Hornos
WEST SCOTIA BASIN
EAST SCOTIA BASIN
SCOTIA RIDGE
South Georgia
SOUTH SANDWICH TRENCH
South Sandwich Islands
METEOR DEEP 8428
South Shetland Islands
South Orkney Islands
Larsen Ice Shelf
Weddell Sea
Ronne Ice Shelf
Filchner Ice Shelf
WEST ATLANTIC-INDIAN BASIN
BARTH SEAMOUNT
WEDDELL ABYSSAL PLAIN
MID-ATLANTIC RIDGE
Ascension Island
St. Helena
Tropic of Capricorn
Tristan da Cunha
Gough Island
ANGOLA BASIN
CONGO CANYON
WALVIS RIDGE
EWING SEAMOUNT
VALDIVIA SEAMOUNT
VEMA SEAMOUNT
WÜST SEAMOUNT
CAPE BASIN
AGULHAS BANK
AFRICANA SEAMOUNT
WYANDOT SEAMOUNT
NATAL SEAMOUNT
SCHMIDT-OTT SEAMOUNT
AGULHAS PLATEAU
ZENKER SEAMOUNT
DISCOVERY TABLEMOUNT
HERDMAN SEAMOUNT
CAPE RISE
AGULHAS BASIN
MERZ SEAMOUNT
METEOR SEAMOUNT
ATLANTIC-INDIAN RIDGE
SPIESS SEAMOUNT
Bouvetøya
ENDERBY ABYSSAL PLAIN
ATLANTIC-INDIAN BASIN
MAUD SEAMOUNT
GUNNERUS BANK
Antarctic Circle
0 200 400 600 800 1000 Kilometers
0 200 400 600 800 1000 Miles

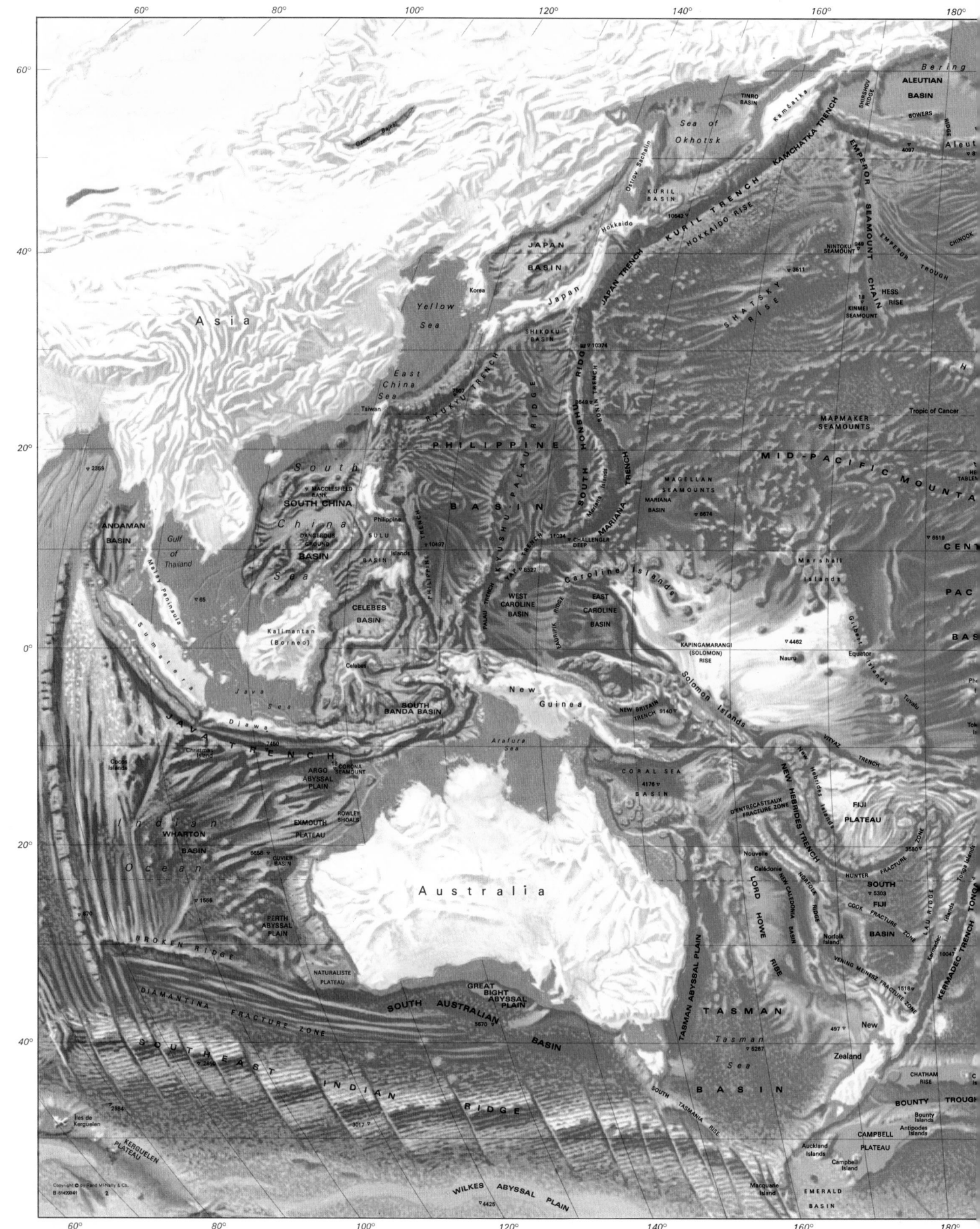

Scale 1:58 000 000; one inch to 900 miles (approx.)
Modified Cylindrical Projection   ▽ Depths in meters.

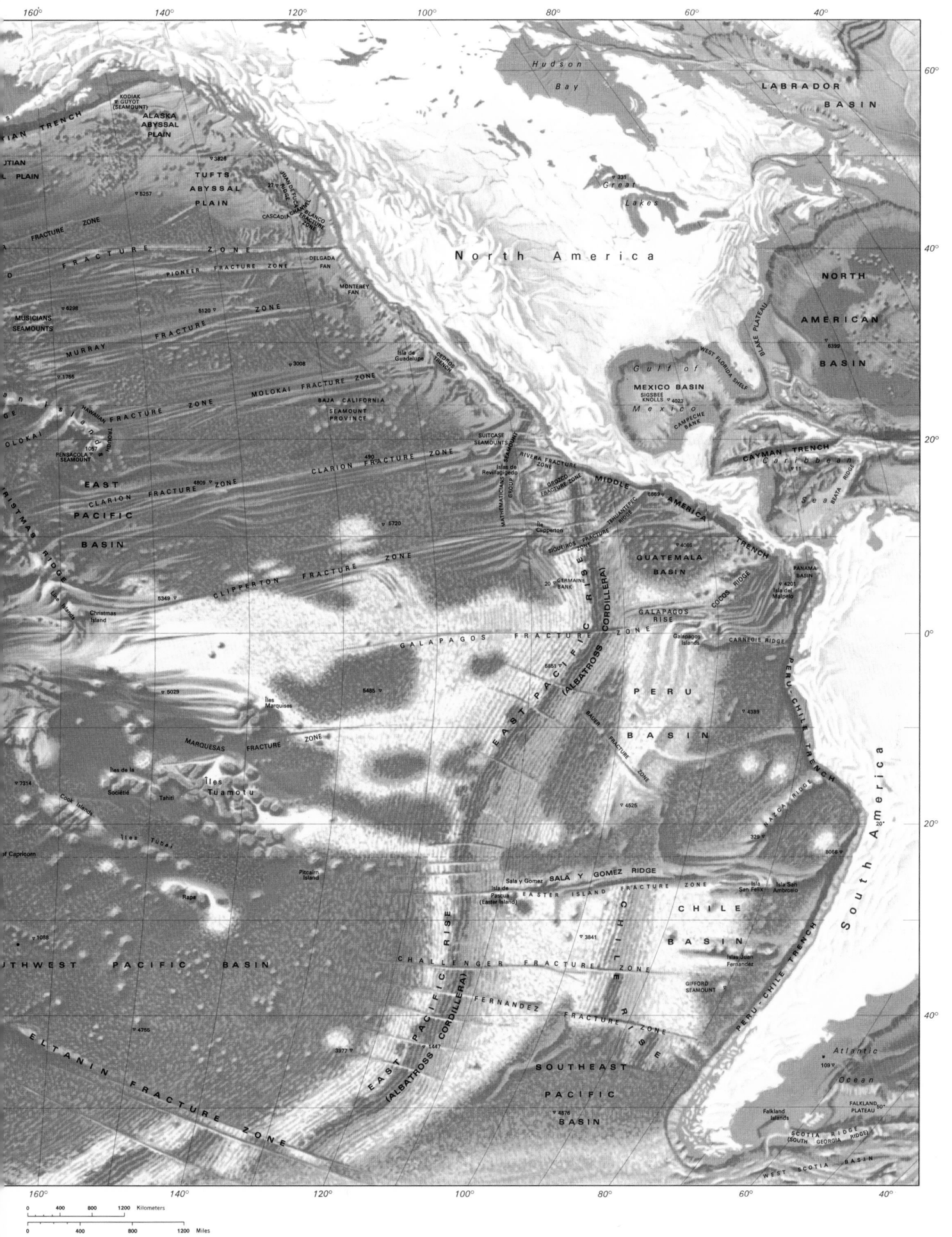

60°

Hudson
Bay

LABRADOR
BASIN

KODIAK
GUYOT
(SEAMOUNT)
ALASKA
ABYSSAL
PLAIN

▽3826

North America

NORTH

AMERICAN

BASIN

TUFTS
ABYSSAL
PLAIN

▽5257

331
Great
Lakes

40°

FRACTURE ZONE

▽6399

PIONEER FRACTURE ZONE

DELGADA
FAN

MONTEREY
FAN

MUSICIANS
SEAMOUNTS

▽6298

FRACTURE

5120 ▽

ZONE

MURRAY

BLAKE PLATEAU

Gulf of

WEST FLORIDA SHELF

MEXICO BASIN

▽1785

HAWAIIAN FRACTURE ZONE

▽3008

MOLOKAI FRACTURE ZONE

BAJA CALIFORNIA

Isla de
Guadalupe

CEDROS
TRENCH

SIGSBEE
KNOLLS ▽4023

Mexico

CAMPECHE
BANK

20°

OLOKAI

PENSACOLA
SEAMOUNT

1057

SEAMOUNT
PROVINCE

SUITCASE
SEAMOUNTS

RIVERA FRACTURE
ZONE

CAYMAN TRENCH

Caribbean

▽11

EAST

CLARION FRACTURE ZONE

4809 ▽

CLARION FRACTURE ZONE

Isla de
Revillagigedo

OROZCO
FRACTURE ZONE

TEHUANTEPEC
RIDGE

6869 ▽

MIDDLE

AMERICA

Seata

BEATA RIDGE

PACIFIC

490

Ile Clipperton

SIQUEIROS FRACTURE
ZONE

▽4085

GUATEMALA
BASIN

PANAMA
BASIN

Isla del
Malpelo

▽4201

BASIN

▽5720

20

GERMAINE
BANK

COCOS RIDGE

5349

CLIPPERTON FRACTURE ZONE

GALAPAGOS
RISE

Galapagos
Islands

CARNEGIE RIDGE

ISTMAS RIDGE

Line Islands

Christmas
Island

GALAPAGOS FRACTURE ZONE

5851 ▽

PERU

0°

EAST PACIFIC RISE

(ALBATROSS CORDILLERA)

BAUER
FRACTURE ZONE

BASIN

▽5029

Îles
Marquises

5485 ▽

▽4389

PERU-CHILE TRENCH

▽7314

Îles de la
Société

Tahiti

MARQUESAS FRACTURE ZONE

Îles Tuamotu

▽4525

20°

Îles Tubai

329 ▽

NAZCA RIDGE

8066 ▽

of Capricorn

Pitcairn
Island

Sala y Gomez

SALA Y GOMEZ RIDGE

Isla
San Felix
Isla San
Ambroaio

South America

Rapa

Isla de
Pascua
(Easter Island)

EASTER ISLAND FRACTURE ZONE

CHILE

▽1088

SOUTHWEST PACIFIC BASIN

EAST PACIFIC RISE

FERNANDEZ

▽3841

C
H
I
L
E

R
I
S
E

BASIN

Islas Juan
Fernandez

GIFFORD
SEAMOUNT

Atlantic

▽4755

CHALLENGER FRACTURE ZONE

FRACTURE

ZONE

Ocean

109 ▽

40°

ELTANIN FRACTURE ZONE

3977 ▽

▽1447

EAST PACIFIC RISE

(ALBATROSS CORDILLERA)

SOUTHEAST

PACIFIC

PERU-CHILE TRENCH

Falkland
Islands

FALKLAND
PLATEAU

▽4876

BASIN

SCOTIA RIDGE
(SOUTH GEORGIA RIDGE)

WEST SCOTIA BASIN

0   400   800   1200   Kilometers

0   400   800   1200   Miles

Asia

Persian Gulf

Arabian Sea

India

RED SEA RIFT

Gulf of Aden

Socotra

▽ 3854

INDUS CANYON

▽ 5143

INDUS FAN

▽ 3888

ARABIAN BASIN

INDIA ABYSSAL PLAIN

Bay of Bengal

▽ 2359

South China Sea

Taiwan

Philippine Islands

MACCLESFIELD BANK

GANGES CANYON

GANGES FAN

ANDAMAN BASIN

Andaman Islands

DANGEROUS GROUND

SULU BASIN

Laccadive Islands

CHAGOS-LACCADIVE PLATEAU

▽ 5870

Ceylon

Maldive Islands

Nicobar Islands

▽ 2095

NINETY EAST RIDGE

▽ 65

Malay Peninsula

Sumatra

Kalimantan (Borneo)

Africa

SOMALI ABYSSAL PLAIN

CHAIN RIDGE

▽ 545

CARLSBERG RIDGE

▽ 6115

▽ 1752

SOMALI BASIN

▽ 6340

Seychelles

▽ 3244

▽ 5243

COCOS BASIN

Equator

Chagos Archipelago

▽ 5405

MID-

INDIAN

BASIN

▽ 5935

Cocos Islands

CEYLON ABYSSAL PLAIN

NIKITIN (AFANASIY) SEAMOUNT 1549 ▽

MENTAWEI RIDGE

Djawa

Java Sea

JAVA TRENCH

▽ 7450

CHRISTMAS RISE

Christmas Island

ROO RISE

CORONA SEAMOUNT

18 ▽

ARGO ABYSSAL PLAIN

WHARTON BASIN

ROWLEY SHOALS

EXMOUTH PLATEAU

KARMA RISE

Aldabra Islands

Comoro Islands

COMORO RIDGE

Farquhar Group

Cerf

ALDABRA TRENCH

Cosmoly Island

Agalega Islands

SAYA DE MALHA BANK

▽ 1186

NAZARETH BANK

SEYCHELLES-MAURITIUS PLATEAU

VEMA TRENCH

▽ 6237

MASCARENE

PLATEAU

Tromelin

Cargados Carajos Shoals

MASCARENE

BASIN

▽ 6080

▽ 1708

WEST

AUSTRALIAN

BASIN

▽ 6668

CUVIER BASIN

Mozambique Channel

Madagascar

Rodriguez

RODRIGUEZ

FRACTURAL ZONE

▽ 6400

▽ 5347

Mauritius

Reunion

MID-INDIAN RIDGE

▽ 870

▽ 1555

PERTH ABYSSAL PLAIN

Australia

▽ 2067

BROKEN RIDGE

Basses da India

Ile Europe

MADAGASCAR

BASIN

NINETY EAST FRACTURE ZONE

DIAMANTINA FRACTURE ZONE

NATURALISTE PLATEAU

NATAL

BASIN

▽ 3640

MOZAMBIQUE RIDGE

MADAGASCAR RIDGE

▽ 945

SOUTHWEST INDIAN RIDGE

AMSTERDAM FRACTURE ZONE

ARGO FAULT

Ile Amsterdam

Ile St. Paul

SOUTHEAST

INDIAN

RIDGE

▽ 4472

▽ 5670

AGULHAS BANK

AFRICANA SEAMOUNT

AGULHAS PLATEAU

▽ 2310

AGULHAS BASIN

CROZET

BASIN

▽ 5440

Iles Crozet

CROZET RIDGE

▽ 2890

▽ 315

MOZAMBIQUE FRACTURE ZONE

PRINCE EDWARD FRACTURE ZONE

MALAGASY FRACTURE ZONE

Prince Edward Islands

▽ 2984

Iles de Kerguelen

KERGUELEN PLATEAU

ATLANTIC-INDIAN RIDGE

OB TABLEMOUNT

247 ▽

LENA TABLEMOUNT

Heard Island

BANZARE BANK

▽ 6088

SOUTH

WILKES ABYSSAL PLAIN

▽ 4426

WEDDELL ABYSSAL PLAIN

THIRTY EAST SPUR

▽ 6972

▽ 5124

SOUTH INDIAN

BASIN

ENDERBY ABYSSAL PLAIN

▽ 4974

GRIBB BANK

GAUSSBERG ABYSSAL PLAIN

Antarctic Circle

Copyright © by Rand McNally & Co.
B-5140091

Scale 1:46 000 000; one inch to 730 miles (approx.)
Modified Cylindrical Projection   ▽ Depths in meters.

0 200 400 600 800 1000 Kilometers

0 200 400 600 800 1000 Miles

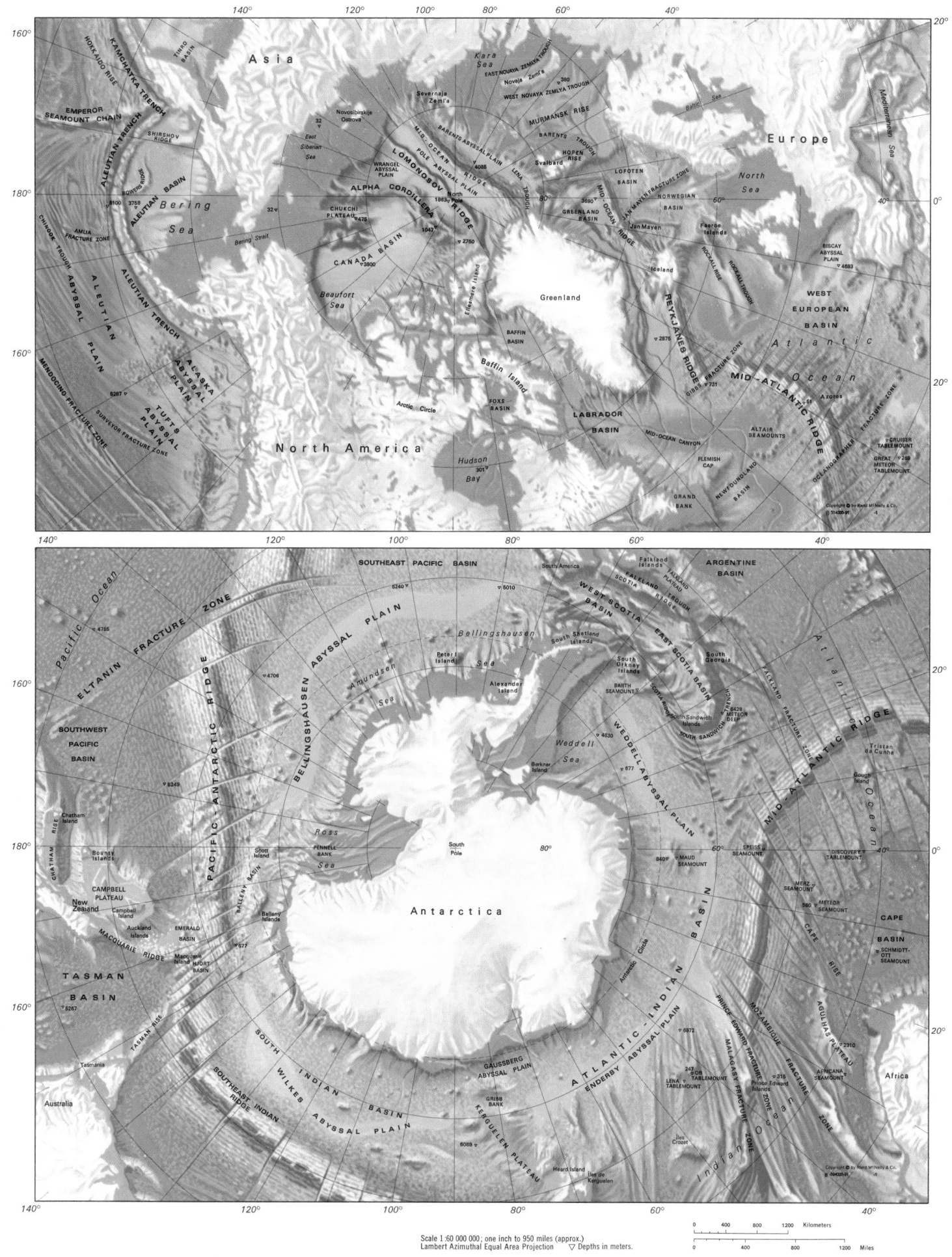

Scale 1:60 000 000; one inch to 950 miles (approx.)
Lambert Azimuthal Equal Area Projection   ▽ Depths in meters.

Index and World Facts

The following pages provide a vast store of factual information of geographical interest on the world, the continents, individual countries, and the 50 U.S. states.

Presented in tabular form, this information supplements the maps with data not readily available from the maps themselves. Here are answers to many of the questions raised by those who use the Atlas, particularly questions that ask "How large?" "How many?" and "Where?"

Two indexes are included, one for major cities, and a pronouncing index to the main body of reference maps. The pronouncing index also features latitude and longitude to make it easier for readers to locate places on the maps.

Other aids to the Atlas usage are populations, areas in both square miles and square kilometers, a glossary of foreign terms, and abbreviations.

Geographical Tables and Indexes

principal countries and regions of the world

Populations are given in thousands.

Political Division or Region	Area in sq. miles	Area in km²	Population
Afars & Issas (Fr.)	8,494	22,000	110
Afghanistan	250,000	647,497	20,036
Africa	11,707,000	30,320,000	423,000
Alabama (U.S.)	51,609	133,667	3,614
Alaska (U.S.)	586,412	1,518,800	352
Albania	11,100	28,748	2,662
Alberta (Can.)	225,285	661,185	1,701
Algeria	919,595	2,381,741	17,890
American Samoa (U.S.)	76	197	38
Andorra	175	453	27
Angola	481,354	1,246,700	6,340
Antarctica	5,100,000	13,209,000	....
Antigua (incl. Barbuda) (U.K.)	171	442	80
Argentina	1,072,163	2,776,889	25,776
Arizona (U.S.)	113,909	295,023	2,224
Arkansas (U.S.)	53,104	137,539	1,986
Asia	16,961,000	43,942,000	2,395,000
Australia (Comm.)	2,967,909	7,686,848	13,993
Austria	32,374	83,849	7,703
Azores (Port.)	905	2,344	291
Bahamas (Comm.)	5,380	13,935	228
Bahrain	240	622	244
Bangladesh (Comm.)	55,126	142,776	75,437
Barbados (Comm.)	166	431	251
Belgium	11,781	30,513	9,914
Belize (U.K.)	8,867	22,965	150
Benin	43,484	112,622	3,239
Bermuda (U.K.)	21	53	60
Bhutan	18,147	47,000	1,241
Bolivia	424,165	1,098,581	5,907
Botswana (Comm.)	231,805	600,372	747
Brazil	3,286,488	8,511,965	123,208
British Columbia (Can.)	366,255	948,596	2,362
Brunei (U.K.)	2,226	5,765	168
Bulgaria	42,823	110,912	8,793
Burma	261,790	678,033	32,375
Burundi	10,747	27,834	3,981
California (U.S.)	158,693	411,013	22,077
Cambodia	69,898	181,035	8,470
Cameroon	183,569	475,442	6,649
Canada (Comm.)	3,851,809	9,976,139	23,206
Canal Zone (U.S.)	553	1,432	46
Canary Is. (Sp.)	2,808	7,273	1,365
Cape Verde	1,557	4,033	305
Cayman Is. (U.K.)	100	259	11
Central African Rep.	240,535	622,984	1,880
Central America	201,976	523,115	19,971
Chad	495,755	1,284,000	4,187
Channel Is. (U.K.)	75	195	130
Chile	292,258	756,945	10,942
China (excl. Taiwan)	3,691,523	9,561,000	854,306
Colombia	439,737	1,138,914	26,326
Colorado (U.S.)	104,247	269,998	2,534
Comoro Is.	838	2,171	320
Congo	132,047	342,000	1,104
Connecticut (U.S.)	5,009	12,973	3,095
Cook Is. (N.Z.)	93	241	19
Costa Rica	19,575	50,700	2,115
Cuba	44,218	114,524	9,455
Cyprus (Comm.)	3,572	9,251	697
Czechoslovakia	49,371	127,869	14,931
Delaware (U.S.)	2,057	5,328	579
Denmark	16,629	43,069	5,167
Dist. of Columbia (U.S.)	68	176	756
Dominica (U.K.)	290	751	76
Dominican Republic	18,816	48,734	4,988
Ecuador	109,484	283,561	7,688
Egypt	386,662	1,001,449	38,859
El Salvador	8,260	21,393	4,349
England & Wales (U.K.)	58,355	151,139	49,878
Equatorial Guinea	10,830	28,051	316
Ethiopia	471,778	1,221,900	28,115
Europe	4,063,000	10,523,000	676,000
Faeroe Is. (Den.)	540	1,399	47
Falkland Is. (excl. Deps.) (U.K.)	4,618	11,961	2
Fiji (Comm.)	7,055	18,272	594
Finland	130,120	337,009	4,731
Florida (U.S.)	58,560	151,670	8,357
France	211,208	547,026	54,032
French Guiana (Fr.)	35,135	91,000	54
French Polynesia (Fr.)	1,544	4,000	137
Gabon	103,347	267,667	1,026
Gambia (Comm.)	4,361	11,295	543
Georgia (U.S.)	58,876	152,488	4,926
German Democratic Republic (East)	41,768	108,178	16,845
Germany, Fed. Rep. of (West)	95,934	248,468	63,721
Ghana (Comm.)	92,100	238,537	10,407
Gibraltar (U.K.)	2.3	6	33
Gilbert Is. (U.K.)	278	720	52
Greece	50,944	131,944	9,224
Greenland (Den.)	840,004	2,175,600	58
Grenada (Comm.)	133	344	95
Guadeloupe (Fr.)	687	1,779	363
Guam (U.S.)	212	549	103
Guatemala	42,042	108,889	6,187
Guinea	94,926	245,857	4,627
Guinea-Bissau	13,948	36,125	540
Guyana (Comm.)	83,000	214,969	814
Haiti	10,714	27,750	4,710
Hawaii (U.S.)	6,450	16,705	865
Honduras	43,277	112,088	3,070
Hong Kong (U.K.)	1,126	2,916	4,450
Hungary	35,919	93,030	10,494
Iceland	39,769	103,000	223
Idaho (U.S.)	83,557	216,412	735
Illinois (U.S.)	56,400	146,075	11,666
India (incl. part of Kashmir) (Comm.)	1,269,346	3,287,590	624,212
Indiana (U.S.)	36,291	93,993	5,311
Indonesia	741,035	1,919,270	143,732
Iowa (U.S.)	56,290	145,790	2,870
Iran	636,296	1,648,000	35,226
Iraq	167,925	434,924	11,857
Ireland	27,136	70,283	3,140
Isle of Man (U.K.)	227	588	66
Israel	7,992	20,700	3,686
Italy	116,314	301,253	56,666
Ivory Coast	124,504	322,463	5,123
Jamaica (Comm.)	4,232	10,962	2,131
Japan	145,711	377,389	114,091
Jordan	37,738	97,740	2,921
Kansas (U.S.)	82,264	213,063	2,267
Kentucky (U.S.)	40,395	104,623	3,396
Kenya (Comm.)	224,961	582,646	14,379
Korea, North	46,540	120,538	16,849
Korea, South	38,025	98,484	35,200
Kuwait	7,768	20,118	1,106
Laos	91,429	236,800	3,498
Lebanon	4,015	10,400	3,639
Lesotho (Comm.)	11,720	30,355	1,084
Liberia	43,000	11,369	1,860
Libya	679,362	1,759,540	2,661
Liechtenstein	61	157	22
Louisiana (U.S.)	48,523	125,674	3,791
Luxembourg	998	2,586	366
Macao (Port.)	6	16	279
Madagascar	226,658	587,041	7,737
Madeira Is. (Port.)	308	797	245
Maine (U.S.)	33,215	86,026	1,059
Malawi (Comm.)	45,747	118,484	5,309
Malaysia (Comm.)	127,316	329,749	12,550
Maldives	115	298	125
Mali	478,767	1,240,000	5,842
Malta (Comm.)	122	316	313
Manitoba (Can.)	251,000	650,087	1,006
Martinique (Fr.)	425	1,102	350
Maryland (U.S.)	10,577	27,394	4,098
Massachusetts (U.S.)	8,257	21,385	5,828
Mauritania	397,956	1,030,700	1,398
Mauritius (Comm.)	790	2,045	899
Mexico	761,605	1,972,547	62,314
Michigan (U.S.)	58,216	150,779	9,157
Midway Is. (U.S.)	2	5	2
Minnesota (U.S.)	84,068	217,735	3,926
Mississippi (U.S.)	47,716	123,584	2,227
Missouri (U.S.)	69,686	180,486	4,763
Monaco	0.58	1.49	28
Mongolia	604,250	1,565,000	1,524
Montana (U.S.)	147,138	381,086	748
Montserrat (U.K.)	38	98	12
Morocco	172,414	446,550	18,360
Mozambique	302,330	783,030	9,810
Nauru (Comm.)	8	21	7
Nebraska (U.S.)	77,227	200,017	1,546
Nepal	54,362	140,797	13,011
Netherlands	15,892	41,160	13,984
Neth. Antilles (Neth.)	383	993	251
Nevada (U.S.)	110,540	286,297	592
New Brunswick (Can.)	28,354	73,437	658
New Caledonia (incl. Deps.) (Fr.)	7,335	18,998	134
Newfoundland (Can.)	156,185	404,517	542
New Hampshire (U.S.)	9,304	24,097	818
New Hebrides (Fr.-U.K.)	5,700	14,763	96
New Jersey (U.S.)	7,836	20,295	7,725
New Mexico (U.S.)	121,666	315,113	1,147
New York (U.S.)	49,576	128,401	18,120
New Zealand (Comm.)	103,736	268,676	3,183
Nicaragua	50,193	130,000	2,280
Niger	489,191	1,267,000	4,714
Nigeria (Comm.)	356,669	923,768	66,310
Niue (N.Z.)	100	259	5
Norfolk I. (Austl.)	14	36	1
North America	9,417,000	24,390,000	351,000
North Carolina (U.S.)	52,586	136,197	5,277
North Dakota (U.S.)	70,665	183,021	635
Northern Ireland (U.K.)	5,452	14,120	1,578
Northwest Ters. (Can.)	1,304,903	3,379,683	38
Norway	125,182	324,219	4,073
Nova Scotia (Can.)	21,425	55,490	810
Ohio (U.S.)	41,222	106,764	10,759
Oklahoma (U.S.)	69,919	181,089	2,712
Oman	82,030	212,457	819
Ontario (Can.)	412,582	1,068,582	8,034
Oregon (U.S.)	96,981	251,180	2,288
Pac. Is. Tr. Ter. (U.S.)	717	1,857	95
Pakistan (incl. part of Kashmir) (Comm.)	310,404	803,943	76,892
Panama	29,209	75,650	1,774
Papua New Guinea (Comm.)	178,260	461,691	2,667
Paraguay	157,048	406,752	2,650
Pennsylvania (U.S.)	45,333	117,412	11,827
Peru	496,225	1,285,216	16,128
Philippines	115,831	300,000	45,267
Poland	120,725	312,677	34,578
Portugal	35,553	92,082	8,428
Prince Edward I. (Can.)	2,184	5,657	116
Puerto Rico (U.S.)	3,435	8,897	2,929
Qatar	4,247	11,000	96
Quebec (Can.)	594,860	1,540,680	6,113
Reunion (Fr.)	969	2,510	515
Rhode Island (U.S.)	1,214	3,144	927
Rhodesia	150,804	390,580	6,797
Romania	91,699	237,500	21,588
Rwanda	10,169	26,338	4,432
St. Helena (incl. Deps.) (U.K.)	162	419	6
St. Kitts-Nevis-Anguilla (U.K.)	138	357	66
St. Lucia (U.K.)	238	616	117
St. Pierre & Miquelon (Fr.)	93	242	6
St. Vincent (U.K.)	150	388	94
San Marino	24	61	19
Sao Tome & Principe	372	964	84
Saskatchewan (Can.)	251,700	651,900	908
Saudi Arabia	831,313	2,153,090	9,466
Scotland (U.K.)	30,415	78,775	5,199
Senegal	75,750	196,192	4,666
Seychelles (Comm.)	145	376	62
Sierra Leone (Comm.)	27,699	71,740	2,834
Singapore (Comm.)	224	581	2,337
Solomon Is. (U.K.)	10,983	28,446	203
Somalia	246,201	637,657	3,315
South Africa	471,445	1,221,037	26,495
South America	6,884,000	17,829,000	236,000
South Carolina (U.S.)	31,055	80,432	2,818
South Dakota (U.S.)	77,047	199,551	683
S. W. Africa (S. Afr.)	318,261	824,292	956
Soviet Union	8,649,500	22,402,000	259,151
Spain	194,885	504,750	36,429
Sri Lanka (Comm.)	25,332	65,610	14,285
Sudan	967,500	2,505,813	18,655
Surinam	63,037	163,265	490
Svalbard (Nor.)	23,958	62,050	....
Swaziland (Comm.)	6,704	17,363	548
Sweden	173,732	449,964	8,268
Switzerland	15,941	41,288	6,776
Syria	71,498	185,180	7,846
Taiwan (Natl. China)	13,885	35,961	16,769
Tanzania (Comm.)	364,900	945,087	15,980
Tennessee (U.S.)	42,244	109,411	4,188
Texas (U.S.)	267,338	692,402	12,237
Thailand	198,457	514,000	45,130
Togo	21,622	56,000	2,328
Tokelau Is. (N.Z.)	4	10	2
Tonga (Comm.)	270	699	100
Trinidad & Tobago (Comm.)	1,980	5,128	1,116
Tunisia	63,170	163,610	6,057
Turkey	301,382	780,576	41,946
Turks & Caicos Is. (U.K.)	166	430	6
Tuvalu (U.K.)	10	26	6
Uganda (Comm.)	91,134	236,036	12,309
United Arab Emirates	32,000	82,880	231
United Kingdom	94,222	244,034	56,555
United States	3,615,122	9,363,123	218,364
Upper Volta	105,869	274,200	6,234
Uruguay	68,536	177,508	3,138
Utah (U.S.)	84,916	219,931	1,206
Vatican City	0.17	0.44	1
Venezuela	352,145	912,050	12,612
Vermont (U.S.)	9,609	24,887	471
Vietnam	128,402	332,559	45,134
Virginia (U.S.)	40,817	105,716	4,965
Virgin Is. (U.S.-U.K.)	192	497	128
Wales (incl. Monmouthshire) (U.K.)	8,017	20,764	2,793
Washington (U.S.)	68,192	176,616	3,544
Western Sahara	102,703	266,000	139
Western Samoa (Comm.)	1,097	2,842	165
West Virginia (U.S.)	24,181	62,628	1,803
Wisconsin (U.S.)	56,154	145,438	4,607
World (approx.)	57,587,000	149,150,000	4,105,000
Wyoming (U.S.)	97,914	253,596	374
Yemen	75,290	195,000	6,820
Yemen, People's Dem. Rep. of	111,075	287,683	1,730
Yugoslavia	98,766	255,804	21,807
Yukon (Can.)	207,076	536,324	19
Zaire	905,568	2,345,409	26,315
Zambia (Comm.)	290,586	752,614	5,319

principal cities of the world

Each metropolitan area has been defined by Rand McNally & Company. A metropolitan area includes a central city, adjacent continuously built-up areas, and other communities if the bulk of their population is supported by commuters to the central city and its adjacent built-up areas.

Accra, Ghana (★738,498)....633,880
Addis Ababā, Ethiopia....1,011,565
Adelaide, Australia (★885,400)....14,700
Ahmadābād, India (★1,950,000)....1,585,544
Albany, New York (★745,000)....109,000
Aleppo (Halab), Syria....639,428
Alexandria (Al Iskandarīyah), Egypt (★2,250,000)....2,032,000
Algiers (Alger), Algeria (★1,800,000)....1,503,720
Alma-Ata, Soviet Union (★870,000)....837,000
'Ammān, Jordan....520,720
Amsterdam, Netherlands (★1,765,000)....757,958
Ankara (Angora), Turkey (★1,525,000)....1,461,300
Anshan, China....833,000
Antwerp (Antwerpen), Belgium (★1,060,000)....217,254
Asunción, Paraguay (★540,000)....392,753
Athens (Athínai), Greece (★2,540,241)....867,023
Atlanta, Georgia (★1,780,000)....455,000
Auckland, New Zealand (★765,000)....153,100

Baghdad, Iraq (★2,183,800)....1,300,000
Baku, Soviet Union (★1,465,000)....929,000
Baltimore, Maryland (★1,920,000)....847,000
Bandung, Indonesia (★1,250,000)....1,201,730
Bangalore, India (★1,750,000)....1,540,741
Bangkok (Krung Thep), Thailand (★3,125,000)....1,867,297
Barcelona, Spain (★3,365,000)....1,800,274
Beirut, Lebanon (★1,010,000)....474,870
Belfast, No. Ireland (★720,000)....414,600
Belgrade (Beograd), Yugoslavia (★1,150,000)....770,140
Belo Horizonte, Brazil (★1,550,000)....1,235,001
Berlin, East, Ger. Dem. Rep. (★Berlin)....1,094,147
Berlin, West, Fed. Rep. of Ger. (★3,860,000)....2,047,948
Bern, Switzerland (★288,100)....152,800
Birmingham, Alabama (★679,000)....281,000
Birmingham, England (★2,660,000)....1,086,500
Bogotá, Colombia (★2,925,000)....2,855,065
Bombay, India (★6,750,000)....5,970,575
Bonn, Fed. Rep. of Ger. (★510,000)....283,260
Boston, Massachusetts (★3,855,000)....601,000
Brasília, Brazil (★495,000)....272,002
Bremen, Fed. Rep. of Ger. (★820,000)....584,265
Brisbane, Australia (★940,800)....722,700
Bristol, England (★635,000)....418,600
Brussels (Bruxelles), Belgium (★2,020,000)....153,405
Bucharest (București), Romania (★1,735,000)....1,565,872
Budapest, Hungary (★2,485,000)....2,055,646
Buenos Aires, Argentina (★8,625,000)....2,972,453
Buffalo, New York (★1,572,000)....420,000

Cairo (Al Qāhirah), Egypt (★6,600,000)....4,961,000
Calcutta, India (★9,100,000)....3,148,746
Canberra, Australia (★206,095)....185,849
Canton (Kuangchou), China....1,867,000
Cape Town, South Africa (★1,125,000)....691,296
Caracas, Venezuela (★2,475,000)....1,658,500
Cardiff, Wales (★615,000)....284,700
Casablanca, Morocco (★1,575,000)....1,506,373
Ch'angch'un (Hsinking), China....988,000
Chelyabinsk, Soviet Union (★1,155,000)....969,000
Chengchou, China....785,000
Ch'engtu, China....1,135,000
Chicago, Illinois (★7,655,000)....3,115,000
Ch'ich'ihaerh (Tsitsihar), China....704,000
Chungking (Ch'ungch'ing) China....2,165,000
Cincinnati, Ohio (★1,422,000)....404,000
Cleveland, Ohio (★2,305,000)....660,000
Cologne (Köln), Fed. Rep. of Ger. (★1,700,000)....832,396
Colombo, Sri Lanka (★1,450,000)....607,000
Columbus, Ohio (★953,000)....582,000
Copenhagen (København), Denmark (★1,515,000)....562,405

Dacca, Bangladesh (★1,950,000)....1,310,976
Dallas, Texas (★2,470,000)....859,000
Damascus (Dimashq), Syria (★1,100,000)....836,668
Dayton, Ohio (★938,000)....219,000
Delhi, India (★4,500,000)....3,706,558
Denver, Colorado (★1,285,000)....506,000
Detroit, Michigan (★4,800,000)....1,355,000
Djakarta (Batavia), Indonesia (★4,650,000)....4,576,009
Dnepropetrovsk, Soviet Union (★1,365,000)....958,000
Donetsk (Stalino), Soviet Union (★1,975,000)....950,000

Dresden, Ger. Dem. Rep. (★640,000)....507,692
Dublin (Baile Atha Cliath), Ireland (★835,000)....567,866
Durban, South Africa (★1,040,000)....729,857
Düsseldorf, Fed. Rep. of Ger. (★1,135,000)....628,498

Edinburgh, Scotland (★660,000)....475,042
El Paso, Texas (★923,000)....370,000
Essen, Fed. Rep. of Ger. (★5,375,000)....674,000

Fortaleza, Brazil (★910,000)....859,135
Frankfurt am Main, Fed. Rep. of Ger. (★1,685,000)....663,422
Fuchou (Foochow), China....623,000
Fukuoka, Japan (★1,325,000)....940,833
Fushun, China....1,019,000

Geneva (Genève), Switzerland (★400,000)....159,200
Genoa (Genova), Italy (★875,000)....807,138
Glasgow, Scotland (★1,925,000)....905,032
Gorki (Gorkiy), Soviet Union (★1,775,000)....1,283,000
Guadalajara, Mexico (★1,800,000)....1,411,900
Guatemala, Guatemala (★945,000)....717,322

Haerhpin (Harbin), China....1,814,000
Hamburg, Fed. Rep. of Ger. (★2,300,000)....1,751,621
Hangchou, China....794,000
Hannover (Hanover), Fed. Rep. of Ger. (★845,000)....505,106
Hanoi, Vietnam (★643,576)....414,620
Hartford, Connecticut (★1,048,000)....146,500
Havana (La Habana), Cuba (★1,800,000)....1,755,400
Helsinki, Finland (★857,000)....510,205
Hiroshima, Japan (★1,175,000)....541,998
Ho Chi Minh City (Saigon), Vietnam (★2,750,000)....1,804,880
Honolulu, Hawaii (★685,000)....335,000
Houston, Texas (★2,140,000)....1,369,000
Hsian (Sian), China....1,368,000
Hsüchou (Süchow), China....710,000
Hyderābād, India (★2,000,000)....1,607,396

Ibadan, Nigeria....758,000
Indianapolis, Indiana (★1,010,000)....741,000
İstanbul, Turkey (★3,250,000)....2,376,300

Jacksonville, Florida (★595,000)....565,000
Jerusalem, Israel (★365,000)....344,200
Johannesburg, South Africa (★2,550,000)....654,682

Kābul, Afghanistan (★498,800)....318,094
Kānpur, India (★1,320,000)....1,154,388
Kansas City, Missouri (★1,239,000)....475,000
Kaohsiung, Taiwan (★1,115,000)....972,828
Karāchi, Pakistan (★3,498,634)....2,850,000
Kātmāndu, Nepal (★215,000)....150,402
Katowice, Poland (★2,150,000)....321,900
Kawasaki, Japan (★Tōkyō)....1,004,455
Kazan', Soviet Union (★985,500)....946,000
Khar'kov, Soviet Union (★1,625,000)....1,357,000
Khartoum, Sudan (★790,000)....333,921
Kiev, Soviet Union (★2,140,000)....1,947,000
Kingston, Jamaica....475,548
Kinshasa, Zaire....1,814,600
Kitakyūshū, Japan (★1,475,000)....1,052,133
Kōbe, Japan (★Ōsaka)....1,351,651
Kowloon, Hong Kong (★Victoria)....715,440
Kuala Lumpur, Malaysia (★750,000)....451,728
K'unming, China....900,000
Kuybyshev, Soviet Union (★1,375,000)....1,164,000
Kyōto, Japan (★Ōsaka)....1,438,714

Lagos, Nigeria (★1,250,000)....901,000
Lahore, Pakistan (★2,200,000)....2,050,000
La Paz, Bolivia....660,700
Leeds, England (★1,560,000)....748,300
Leipzig, Ger. Dem. Rep. (★725,000)....570,972
Leningrad, Soviet Union (★5,000,000)....3,850,000
Lille, France (★950,000)....190,546
Lima, Peru (★3,350,000)....340,339
Lisbon (Lisboa), Portugal (★1,800,000)....774,500
Liverpool, England (★1,595,000)....561,000
Łódź, Poland (★975,000)....787,000
London, England (★10,475,000)....7,167,600
Los Angeles, California (★8,960,000)....2,750,000
Louisville, Kentucky (★867,000)....333,000
Lucknow, India (★840,000)....749,239

Lüta (Dairen), China (1,590,000▲)....1,000,000
Luxembourg, Luxembourg (★100,000)....76,159
Lyon, France (★1,100,000)....527,800

Madras, India (★3,200,000)....2,469,449
Madrid, Spain (★3,785,000)....3,247,108
Managua, Nicaragua....398,514
Manchester, England (★2,865,000)....516,100
Manila, Philippines (★5,000,000)....1,435,500
Mannheim, Fed. Rep. of Ger. (★1,270,000)....325,386
Marseille, France (★1,015,000)....889,029
Mecca (Makkah), Saudi Arabia....270,000
Medellín, Colombia (★1,500,000)....1,100,082
Melbourne, Australia (★2,620,400)....74,400
Memphis, Tennessee (★846,000)....660,000
Mexico City, Mexico (★10,700,000)....7,768,000
Miami, Florida (★2,345,000)....345,000
Milan (Milano), Italy (★3,755,000)....1,732,451
Milwaukee, Wisconsin (★1,388,000)....685,000
Minneapolis, Minnesota (★1,930,000)....390,000
Minsk, Soviet Union (★1,165,000)....1,135,000
Monterrey, Mexico (★1,460,000)....973,000
Montevideo, Uruguay (★1,300,000)....1,202,757
Montréal, Canada (★2,743,208)....1,214,352
Moscow (Moskva), Soviet Union (★10,650,000)....7,469,000
Mukden (Shenyang), China....2,423,000
Munich (München), Fed. Rep. of Ger. (★1,895,000)....1,336,576

Nagoya, Japan (★3,500,000)....2,082,235
Nāgpur, India (★950,000)....866,076
Nanking (Nanching), China....1,455,000
Naples (Napoli), Italy (★1,995,000)....1,224,274
Newark, New Jersey (★New York)....352,000
Newcastle-on-Tyne, England (★1,330,000)....297,000
New Delhi, India (★Delhi)....301,801
New Orleans, Louisiana (★1,131,000)....569,000
New York, New York (★17,150,000)....7,605,000
Norfolk, Virginia (★768,000)....287,000
Novosibirsk, Soviet Union (★1,385,000)....1,265,000
Nürnberg (Nuremberg), Fed Rep. of Ger. (★855,000)....514,657

Odessa, Soviet Union (★1,050,000)....1,002,000
Oklahoma City, Oklahoma (★689,000)....378,000
Omaha, Nebraska (★558,000)....372,000
Omsk, Soviet Union....968,000
Osaka, Japan (★14,350,000)....2,802,065
Oslo, Norway (★720,000)....464,900
Ottawa, Canada (★602,510)....302,341

Palermo, Italy....661,235
Panamá, Panama (★500,000)....371,070
Paris, France (★9,150,000)....2,290,900
Peking (Peiching), China (7,570,000▲)....4,800,000
Perm', Soviet Union (★1,005,000)....939,000
Perth, Australia (★762,600)....92,700
Philadelphia, Pennsylvania (★5,280,000)....1,820,000
Phnom Penh, Cambodia....393,995
Phoenix, Arizona (★1,250,000)....705,000
Pittsburgh, Pennsylvania (★2,240,000)....472,000
Port-au-Prince, Haiti (★493,932)....458,675
Portland, Oregon (★1,077,000)....363,000
Pôrto (Oporto), Portugal (★890,000)....311,800
Pôrto Alegre, Brazil (★1,375,000)....885,564
Prague (Praha), Czechoslovakia (★1,240,000)....1,161,226
Pretoria, South Africa (★575,000)....543,950
Providence, Rhode Island (★898,000)....163,000
Pune, India (★1,175,000)....856,105
Pusan, Korea (South)....1,880,710
P'yŏngyang, Korea (North)....840,000

Québec, Canada (★480,502)....186,088
Quezon City, Philippines (★Manila)....896,200
Quito, Ecuador....597,133

Rabat, Morocco (★540,000)....367,620
Rangoon, Burma....1,854,000
Rawalpindi, Pakistan (★725,000)....375,000
Recife (Pernambuco), Brazil (★1,750,000)....1,060,752
Riga, Soviet Union (★870,000)....796,000
Rio de Janerio, Brazil (★7,000,000)....4,252,009

Riyadh, Saudi Arabia....450,000
Rochester, New York (★838,000)....282,000
Rome (Roma), Italy (★3,105,000)....2,856,309
Rosario, Argentina (★875,000)....750,455
Rostov-na-Donu, Soviet Union (★1,020,000)....888,000
Rotterdam, Netherlands (★1,095,000)....620,867

Sacramento, California (★748,000)....262,000
St. Louis, Missouri (★2,270,000)....538,000
St. Paul, Minnesota (★Minneapolis)....291,000
Salisbury, Rhodesia (★555,000)....105,000
Salt Lake City, Utah (★561,000)....172,000
Salvador, Brazil (★1,020,000)....1,007,744
San Antonio, Texas (★940,000)....758,000
San Bernardino, California (★609,000)....107,000
San Diego, California (★1,790,000)....765,000
San Francisco, California (★4,450,000)....675,000
San José, Costa Rica (★472,000)....218,700
San Juan, Puerto Rico (★1,185,000)....452,749
San Salvador, El Salvador (★600,000)....337,171
Santiago, Chile (★2,925,000)....517,473
Santo Domingo, Dominican Rep....673,470
São Paulo, Brazil (★8,050,000)....5,921,796
Sapporo, Japan (★1,200,000)....1,178,224
Saratov, Soviet Union (★1,045,000)....834,000
Seattle, Washington (★1,788,000)....490,000
Seoul, Korea (South) (★5,900,000)....5,536,377
Shanghai, China (10,820,000▲)....7,900,000
Sheffield, England (★725,000)....561,500
Singapore, Singapore (★2,225,000)....2,074,507
Sofia (Sofiya), Bulgaria (★1,035,480)....919,000
Soochow (Wuhsien) China....651,000
Stockholm, Sweden (★1,353,359)....671,226
Stuttgart, Fed. Rep. of Ger. (★1,655,000)....624,835
Surabaja, Indonesia (★1,650,000)....1,556,255
Sverdlovsk, Soviet Union (★1,350,000)....1,147,000
Sydney, Australia (★2,898,330)....55,770

Taegu, Korea (South)....1,082,750
T'aipei, Taiwan (★3,050,000)....2,003,604
T'aiyüan (Yangkü), China....1,053,000
Tangshan, China....812,000
Tashkent, Soviet Union (★1,780,000)....1,595,000
Tbilisi, Soviet Union (★1,155,000)....1,006,000
Tegucigalpa, Honduras....270,645
Tehrān, Iran (★4,400,000)....3,858,000
Tel Aviv-Yafo, Israel (★1,230,000)....357,600
The Hague ('s Gravenhage), Netherlands (★800,000)....482,879
Tientsin (T'ienching), China (4,280,000▲)....3,800,000
Tiranë, Albania....174,800
Tōkyō, Japan (★23,800,000)....8,678,642
Toronto, Canada (★2,628,043)....712,786
Tripoli (Tarābulus), Libya....264,000
Tsinan (Chinan), China....882,000
Tsingtao (Ch'ingtao), China....1,144,000
Tunis, Tunisia (★685,000)....468,997
Turin (Torino), Italy (★1,680,000)....1,202,846

Ufa, Soviet Union....895,000
Ulaan Baatar, Mongolia....267,400

Valencia, Spain (★970,000)....669,661
Vancouver, Canada (★1,082,352)....426,256
Venice (Venezia), Italy (★445,000)....365,431
Victoria, Hong Kong (★3,575,000)....521,612
Vienna (Wien), Austria (★1,940,000)....1,614,841
Vientiane, Laos....149,000
Volgograd (Stalingrad), Soviet Union (★1,160,000)....900,000

Warsaw (Warszawa), Poland (★1,875,000)....1,410,000
Washington, D.C. (★3,190,000)....715,000
Wellington, New Zealand (★353,000)....143,400
Winnipeg, Canada....548,573
Wuhan, China....2,226,000
Wuppertal, Fed. Rep. of Ger. (★920,000)....409,715

Yerevan, Soviet Union (★1,000,000)....899,000
Yokohama, Japan (★Tōkyō)....2,562,291

Zagreb, Yugoslavia....566,084
Zürich, Switzerland (★785,000)....396,300

★ Population of entire metropolitan area, including suburbs. Cities located in metropolitan areas of other cities have the latter designated thus: Newark (★New York).
▲ Population of entire municipality or district, including rural area.

This index includes the more important cities, towns and other localities that appear on the maps on pages 52–69. For a complete list of abbreviations, see page 246. If a page contains several maps, a lowercase letter identifies the particular map to which the entry is indexed.

A

Page	Name Region	Lat. °′	Long. °′
66h	'abbāsābād	35·44 N	51·25 E
60	Abbey Wood (Neigh.)	51·29 N	0·08 E
60	Abbots Langley	51·43 N	0·25 W
69a	'abd al-Shāhid	29·55 N	31·13 E
66c	Aberdeen (Xianggangzi)	22·15 N	114·09 E
54b	Abington	40·07 N	75·08 W
62c	Ablon-sur-Seine	48·43 N	2·25 E
63d	Abóbada	38·43 N	9·20 W
64b	Abramcevo	55·50 N	37·50 E
60	Abridge	51·39 N	0·07 E
63d	Abrunheira	38·46 N	9·21 W
69a	Abū an-Numrus	29·57 N	31·12 E
69a	Abū Şīr Pyramids (P. Int.)	29·54 N	31·12 E
52a	Accord	42·10 N	70·53 W
60	Acton (Neigh.)	51·30 N	0·16 W
67a	Adachi (Neigh.)	35·45 N	139·48 E
60	Addington	51·18 N	0·23 E
60	Addlestone	51·22 N	0·30 W
69a	Ad-Duqqī	30·04 N	31·15 E
54d	Adelphi	39·00 N	76·58 W
64e	Aderklaa	48·17 N	16·32 E
63a	Adlershof (Neigh.)	52·26 N	13·33 E
69d	Agege	6·37 N	3·20 E
52c	Agincourt (Neigh.)	43·48 N	79·17 W
59c	Agostinho Pôrto	22·47 S	43·23 W
58a	Agrícola Oriental	19·24 N	99·05 W
58b	Aguacate	22·59 N	81·49 W
63d	Agualva-Cacém	38·46 N	9·18 W
61	Ahlenberg	51·25 N	7·28 E
63a	Ahrensfelde	52·35 N	13·35 E
52b	Ahuntsic (Neigh.)	45·33 N	73·39 W
62b	Aigburth (Neigh.)	53·22 N	2·55 W
62b	Ainsworth	53·35 N	2·22 W
62b	Aintree	53·29 N	2·56 W
68b	Airport West	37·44 S	144·53 E
64d	Aiyáleo	37·59 N	23·41 E
63d	Ajuda (Neigh.)	38·43 N	9·12 W
66h	Akbarābād	35·41 N	51·21 E
67a	Akishima	35·41 N	139·22 E
64d	Akrópolis (P. Int.)	37·58 N	23·43 E
69d	Alaguntan	6·26 N	3·30 E
56b	Alameda	37·46 N	122·16 W
56b	Albany	37·53 N	122·18 W
56a	Albany Park (Neigh.)	41·58 N	87·43 W
69a	Al-Barājīl	30·04 N	31·09 E
64g	Albertfalva (Neigh.)	47·27 N	19·02 E
69b	Alberton	26·16 S	28·08 E
53	Albertson	40·46 N	73·39 W
69b	Albertville (Neigh.)	26·10 S	27·59 E
68b	Albion	37·47 S	144·49 E
63d	Alcântara (Neigh.)	38·42 N	9·10 W
59d	Aldeia	23·30 S	46·51 W
59d	Aldeia de Carapicuíba	23·35 S	46·48 W
60	Aldenham	51·40 N	0·21 W
61	Aldenrade (Neigh.)	51·31 N	6·44 E
69b	Alexandra	26·06 S	28·05 E
54d	Alexandria	38·48 N	77·03 W
62c	Alfortville	48·49 N	2·25 E
63d	Algés	38·42 N	9·13 W
63d	Alguierão-Mem Martins	38·48 N	9·20 W
57	Alhambra	34·06 N	118·08 W
69a	Al-Ḩawāmidīyah	29·54 N	31·15 E
65a	Alipore (Neigh.)	22·31 N	88·18 E
69a	Al-Jīzah (Giza)	30·01 N	31·13 E
69a	Al-Kunayyisah	29·59 N	31·11 E
55b	Allegheny (R.)	40·27 N	80·00 W
55c	Allen Park	42·15 N	83·13 W
52a	Allerton	42·18 N	70·53 W
62b	Allerton (Neigh.)	53·22 N	2·53 W
55b	Allison Park	40·34 N	79·57 W
69a	Al-Imām (Neigh.)	30·01 N	31·10 E
52a	Allston (Neigh.)	42·22 N	71·08 W
63d	Almada	38·41 N	9·09 W
69a	Al-Manāwāt	29·55 N	31·14 E
69a	Al-Marj (Neigh.)	30·09 N	31·20 E
57	Alondra	33·54 N	118·19 W
53	Alpine	40·56 N	73·56 W
56a	Alsip	41·40 N	87·44 W
57	Altadena	34·12 N	118·08 W
65b	Altar of Heaven (P. Int.)	39·53 N	116·25 E
65b	Altar of the Earth (P. Int.)	39·57 N	116·24 E
65b	Altar of the Moon (P. Int.)	39·55 N	116·20 E
65b	Altar of the Sun (P. Int.)	39·54 N	116·27 E
61	Altenderne Oberbecker (Neigh.)	51·35 N	7·33 E
61	Altenessen (Neigh.)	51·29 N	7·00 E
61	Altenhagen (Neigh.)	51·22 N	7·28 E
61	Altenvoerde	51·18 N	7·22 E
61	Altlünen	51·38 N	7·31 E
64e	Altmannsdorf (Neigh.)	48·10 N	16·20 E
59d	Alto da Moóca (Neigh.)	23·34 S	46·35 W
68b	Altona	37·52 S	144·50 E
68b	Altona B.	37·52 S	144·52 E
68b	Altona North	37·50 S	144·51 E
62b	Altrincham	53·24 N	2·21 W
62b	Alvanley	53·16 N	2·45 W
63d	Amadora	38·45 N	9·14 W
67b	Amagasaki	34·43 N	135·25 E
65c	Ama Keng	1·24 N	103·42 E
64d	Amaroúsion	38·03 N	23·49 E
63d	Ameixoeira (Neigh.)	38·47 N	9·10 W
60	Amersham	51·40 N	0·38 W
55a	Amherst	42·58 N	78·48 W
54d	Anacostia (Neigh.)	38·52 N	76·59 W
57	Anaheim	33·51 N	117·57 W
62c	Andrésy	48·59 N	2·04 E
54d	Andrews Air Force Base (P. Int.)	38·48 N	76·52 W
61	Angerhausen (Neigh.)	51·23 N	6·44 E
61	Angermund	51·20 N	6·47 E
66g	Angono	14·31 N	121·08 E
64g	Angyalföld (Neigh.)	47·33 N	19·05 E
65e	Anik (Neigh.)	19·02 N	72·53 E
52b	Anjou	45·36 N	73·33 W
54d	Annandale	38·50 N	77·12 W
69a	An-Narrānīyah	29·58 N	31·10 E
61	Annen (Neigh.)	51·27 N	7·22 E
62c	Annet-sur-Marne	48·56 N	2·43 E
61	Anschlag	51·10 N	7·29 E
58a	Antiguo Lago de Texcoco, Vaso del (L.)	19·30 N	99·00 W
59a	Antímano (Neigh.)	10·28 N	66·59 W
62c	Antony	48·45 N	2·18 E
69b	Antwerp	26·06 S	28·10 E
69d	Apese (Neigh.)	6·25 N	3·25 E
61	Aplerbeck (Neigh.)	51·29 N	7·33 E
59b	Apoquindo	33·24 S	70·32 W
67a	Ara (R.)	35·39 N	139·51 E
67a	Arakawa (Neigh.)	35·47 N	139·44 E
65d	Arakpur (Neigh.)	28·35 N	77·10 E
63b	Aravaca (Neigh.)	40·28 N	3·46 W
57	Arcadia	34·08 N	118·01 W
62c	Arc de Triomphe (P. Int.)	48·53 N	2·17 E
62c	Arcueil	48·48 N	2·20 E
61	Ardey (Neigh.)	51·26 N	7·23 E
54d	Ardmore, Md.	38·56 N	76·52 W
54b	Ardmore, Pa.	40·01 N	75·18 W
63d	Areeiro	38·39 N	9·12 W
62c	Argenteuil	48·57 N	2·15 E
67b	Arima (Neigh.)	34·48 N	135·15 E
67b	Arino (Neigh.)	34·50 N	135·14 E
52a	Arlington, Ma.	42·25 N	71·09 W
54d	Arlington, Va.	38·52 N	77·05 W
54d	Arlington National Cemetery (P. Int.)	38·53 N	77·04 W
62c	Arnouville-lès-Gonesse	49·00 N	2·25 E
58b	Arroyo Arenas	23·02 N	82·28 W
68a	Artarmon	33·49 S	151·11 E
57	Artesia	33·52 N	118·05 W
59a	Artigas (Neigh.)	10·30 N	66·56 W
54c	Arundel Gardens	39·13 N	76·37 W
54c	Arundel Village	39·13 N	76·36 W
67a	Asaka	35·48 N	139·36 E
65d	Asālafpur (Neigh.)	28·38 N	77·05 E
68a	Ashfield	33·53 S	151·08 E
60	Ashford	51·26 N	0·27 W
67b	Ashiya	34·43 N	135·17 E
62b	Ashley	53·21 N	2·20 W
60	Ashley Green	51·44 N	0·35 W
60	Ashtead	51·19 N	0·18 W
62b	Ashton-under-Lyne	53·29 N	2·06 W
62b	Ashton upon Mersey	53·26 N	2·19 W
62c	Asnières [-sur-Seine]	48·55 N	2·17 E
64e	Aspern (Neigh.)	48·13 N	16·29 E
55b	Aspinwall	40·30 N	79·55 W
61	Asseln (Neigh.)	51·32 N	7·35 E
62b	Astley Bridge	53·36 N	2·26 W
53	Astoria (Neigh.)	40·46 N	73·55 W
64d	Athens (Athínai	37·58 N	23·43 E
62c	Athis-Mons	48·43 N	2·24 E
58a	Atizapán de Zaragoza	19·33 N	99·15 W
53	Atlantic Beach	40·35 N	73·44 W
67a	Atsugi	35·27 N	139·22 E
65d	Atta	28·34 N	77·20 E
69a	Aṭ-Ṭālibīyah	30·00 N	31·11 E
65d	Atzalpur	28·43 N	77·21 E
64e	Atzgersdorf (Neigh.)	48·09 N	16·18 E
62c	Aubervilliers	48·55 N	2·23 E
68a	Auburn	33·51 S	151·02 E
52a	Auburndale	42·21 N	71·22 W
69b	Auckland Park (Neigh.)	26·11 S	28·00 E
62b	Audenshaw	53·28 N	2·08 W
54b	Audubon	40·07 N	75·27 W
61	Auf dem Kreinberge	51·27 N	7·36 E
61	Auf dem Schnee (Neigh.)	51·26 N	7·25 E
62b	Aughton	53·32 N	2·56 W
62b	Aughton Park	53·33 N	2·53 W
62c	Aulnay-sous-Bois	48·57 N	2·31 E
62c	Austerlitz (P. Int.)	48·50 N	2·22 E
56a	Austin (Neigh.)	41·54 N	87·45 W
68a	Austral	33·56 S	150·48 E
55b	Avalon	40·30 N	80·04 W
62b	Avanley	53·16 N	2·45 W
60	Aveley	51·30 N	0·16 E
58d	Avellaneda	34·40 S	58·20 W
53	Avenel	40·35 N	74·17 W
57	Avocado Heights	34·03 N	118·00 W
68b	Avondale Heights	37·46 S	144·51 E
66h	Awīn	35·48 N	51·24 E
69a	Awsīm	30·07 N	31·08 E
67a	Ayase	35·26 N	139·26 E
64d	Ayía Varvára	37·59 N	23·39 E
65d	Azādpur (Neigh.)	28·43 N	77·11 E
58a	Azcapotzalco	19·28 N	99·12 W
57	Azusa	34·08 N	117·55 W
69a	Az-Zamālik (Neigh.)	30·04 N	31·13 E

B

Page	Name Region	Lat. °′	Long. °′
61	Baak	51·25 N	7·10 E
65d	Bābarpur (Neigh.)	28·41 N	77·17 E
63a	Babelsberg (Neigh.)	52·24 N	13·05 E
52a	Babson Park	42·18 N	71·23 W
64b	Babuškin (Neigh.)	55·52 N	37·42 E
52a	Back Bay (Neigh.)	42·21 N	71·05 W
65e	Back B.	18·56 N	72·49 E
69c	Bacongo	4·18 S	15·16 E
63e	Badalona	41·27 N	2·15 E
60	Badger's Mount	51·20 N	0·09 E
65d	Bādli	28·45 N	77·09 E
61	Baerl	51·29 N	6·41 E
62c	Bagneux	48·48 N	2·18 E
62c	Bagnolet	48·52 N	2·25 E
69a	Bahtīm	30·08 N	31·17 E
65a	Baidyabāti	22·47 N	88·20 E
54d	Baileys Crossroads	38·51 N	77·08 W
65a	Bainchipota	22·52 N	88·16 E
65b	Baiyunguan	39·54 N	116·19 E
60	Baker Street	51·30 N	0·21 E
64f	Bakırköy (Neigh.)	40·59 N	28·52 E
54b	Bala-Cynwyd	40·00 N	75·14 W
53	Baldwin, NY.	40·39 N	73·37 W
55b	Baldwin, Pa.	40·23 N	79·58 W
57	Baldwin Park	34·06 N	117·58 W
68a	Balgowlah	33·48 S	151·16 E
65a	Bālihāti	22·44 N	88·19 E
65b	Balizhuang	39·52 N	116·28 E
65a	Ballabhpur	22·44 N	88·21 E
58b	Ballenato, Punta (C.)	23·06 N	82·30 W
65a	Ballygunge (Neigh.)	22·31 N	88·21 E
68a	Balmain	33·51 S	151·11 E
54c	Baltimore	39·17 N	76·37 W
54c	Baltimore Highlands	39·14 N	76·38 W
68b	Balwyn	37·49 S	145·05 E
65b	Banbidian	39·54 N	116·32 E
65a	Bāndel	22·56 N	88·22 E
66k	Bandir C.	6·11 S	106·49 E
65e	Bāndra (Neigh.)	19·03 N	72·49 E
66f	Bang Khun Thian	13·42 N	100·28 E
66f	Bangkok (Krung Thep)	13·45 N	100·31 E
59c	Bangu (Neigh.)	22·52 S	44·27 W
69a	Bani Majdūl	30·02 N	31·07 E
66f	Ban Khlong Samrong	13·39 N	100·36 E
68a	Banks, C.	34·00 S	151·15 E
68a	Banksmeadow	33·58 S	151·13 E
68a	Bankstown	33·55 S	151·02 E
66f	Ban Lat Phrao	13·47 N	100·36 E
65a	Banstala	22·32 N	88·25 E
60	Banstead	51·19 N	0·12 W
66m	Ba-queo	10·48 N	106·38 E
65a	Bara	22·46 N	88·17 E
69b	Baragwanath	26·16 S	27·59 E
63b	Barajas de Madrid (Neigh.)	40·28 N	3·35 E
65a	Baranagar	22·38 N	88·22 E
65a	Bārasat	22·51 N	88·22 E
63d	Barcarena	38·44 N	9·17 W
63e	Barcelona	41·23 N	2·11 E
63b	Barcelona (Neigh.)	40·22 N	3·34 E
54d	Barcroft, Lake (Res.)	38·51 N	77·09 W
54c	Bare Hills	39·23 N	76·40 W
65a	Bariti Bil (L.)	22·48 N	88·26 E
60	Barking (Neigh.)	51·33 N	0·06 E
60	Barkingside (Neigh.)	51·36 N	0·05 E
61	Barmen (Neigh.)	51·17 N	7·13 E
60	Barnes (Neigh.)	51·28 N	0·15 W
62b	Barnston	53·21 N	3·05 W
53	Barnum Island	40·36 N	73·39 W
58d	Barracas (Neigh.)	34·38 S	58·22 W
65a	Barrackpore	22·46 N	88·21 E
65a	Barrackpore Cantonment	22·46 N	88·22 E
59d	Barra Funda (Neigh.)	23·31 S	46·39 W
59b	Barrancas	33·27 S	70·46 W
58c	Barranco	12·09 S	77·02 W
63d	Barreiro	38·40 N	9·05 W
63e	Barriada Pomar Alto	41·29 N	2·14 E
54b	Barrington	39·52 N	75·04 W
58c	Barrio Obrero Industrial	12·04 S	77·04 W
59a	Baruta	10·26 N	66·53 W
65d	Basai Dārāpur (Neigh.)	28·40 N	77·08 E
69a	Bashtīl	30·05 N	31·11 E
60	Basildon	51·35 N	0·25 E
68a	Bass Hill	33·54 S	151·00 E
65a	Bāsudebpur	22·49 N	88·25 E
61	Batenbrock (Neigh.)	51·31 N	6·57 E
60	Battersea (Neigh.)	51·28 N	0·10 W
61	Bauernschaft	51·34 N	6·33 E
55b	Bauerstown	40·30 N	79·59 W
61	Baukau (Neigh.)	51·33 N	7·12 E
68a	Baulkham Hills	33·46 S	151·00 E
63a	Baumschulenweg (Neigh.)	52·28 N	13·29 E
60	Bayford	51·46 N	0·06 W
53	Bayonne	40·41 N	74·07 W
53	Bay Park	40·38 N	73·40 W
53	Bay Ridge (Neigh.)	40·37 N	74·02 W
52a	Bayside	42·18 N	70·53 W
53	Bayside (Neigh.)	40·46 N	73·46 W
68b	Bayswater	37·51 S	145·16 E
68b	Bayswater North	37·49 S	145·17 E
56b	Bayview (Neigh.)	37·44 N	122·23 W
54a	Bay Village	41·29 N	81·55 W
53	Bayville	40·54 N	73·33 W
54a	Beachwood	41·34 N	81·28 W
68a	Beacon Hill	33·45 S	151·15 E
66c	Beacon H.	22·21 N	114·09 E
52b	Beaconsfield	0·00	0·00
60	Bean	51·25 N	0·17 E
63d	Beato (Neigh.)	38·44 N	9·06 W
64f	Bebek (Neigh.)	41·04 N	29·02 E
62b	Bebington	53·23 N	3·01 W
58d	Beccar (Neigh.)	34·28 S	58·31 W
60	Beckenham (Neigh.)	51·24 N	0·02 W
60	Beddington (Neigh.)	51·22 N	0·08 W
52a	Bedford, Ma.	42·29 N	71·17 W
54a	Bedford, Oh.	41·23 N	81·32 W
54a	Bedford Heights	41·22 N	81·30 W
56a	Bedford Park	41·46 N	87·49 W
53	Bedford Park (Neigh.)	40·52 N	73·53 W
53	Bedford-Stuyvesant (Neigh.)	40·41 N	73·55 W
60	Bedmond	51·43 N	0·25 W
65c	Bedok	1·19 N	103·57 E
55b	Beechview (Neigh.)	40·25 N	80·02 W
61	Beeck (Neigh.)	51·29 N	6·44 E
61	Beeckerwerth (Neigh.)	51·29 N	6·41 E
65a	Behāla (South Suburban)	22·31 N	88·19 E
65b	Beiyuan	40·01 N	116·24 E
54d	Bel Air	38·52 N	77·10 W
57	Bel Air (Neigh.)	34·05 N	118·27 W
63d	Belas	38·47 N	9·16 W
59d	Bela Vista (Neigh.)	23·33 S	46·38 W
63d	Belém (Neigh.)	38·42 N	9·12 W
59d	Belènzinho (Neigh.)	23·32 S	46·35 W
59c	Belford Roxo	22·46 S	43·24 W
58d	Belgrano (Neigh.)	34·34 S	58·28 W
68b	Belgrave	37·55 S	145·21 E
57	Bell	33·58 N	118·11 W
58d	Bella Vista, Arg.	34·32 S	58·40 W
59b	Bellavista, Chile	33·31 S	70·37 W
58c	Bellavista, Peru	12·04 S	77·08 W
54c	Belle Farm Estates	39·23 N	76·45 W
54d	Bellehaven	38·47 N	77·04 W
53	Bellerose	40·44 N	73·43 W
53	Belleville	40·48 N	74·09 W
55b	Bellevue	40·30 N	80·03 W
57	Bellflower	33·53 N	118·07 W
57	Bell Gardens	33·58 N	118·09 W
54b	Bellmawr	39·51 N	75·06 W
53	Bellmore	40·40 N	73·32 W
58b	Bello	23·07 N	82·24 W
56a	Bellwood	41·53 N	87·52 W
56b	Belmont, Ca.	37·31 N	122·17 W
52a	Belmont, Ma.	42·24 N	71·10 W
68a	Belmore	33·55 S	151·05 E
58b	Belot	23·08 N	82·19 W
56b	Belvedere, Ca.	37·52 N	122·28 W
54d	Belvedere, Va.	38·50 N	77·10 W
60	Belvedere (Neigh.)	51·29 N	0·09 E
64e	Belvedere (P. Int.)	48·11 N	16·23 E
55b	Ben Avon	40·31 N	80·05 W
59c	Benfica (Neigh.), Braz.	22·53 S	43·15 W
63d	Benfica (Neigh.), Port.	38·45 N	9·12 W
68b	Bennettswood	37·51 S	145·07 E
61	Benninghofen (Neigh.)	51·29 N	7·31 E
69b	Benoni	26·12 S	28·18 E
69b	Benoni South	26·13 S	28·18 E
61	Benrath (Neigh.)	51·10 N	6·52 E
56a	Bensenville	41·57 N	87·57 W
53	Bensonhurst (Neigh.)	40·35 N	73·59 W
68b	Bentleigh	37·55 S	145·02 E

C

Page	Name Region	Lat. °′	Long. °′
52b	Dorval	45·27 N	73·44 W
68a	Dover Heights	33·53 S	151·17 E
68b	Doveton	38·00 S	145·14 E
66h	Dowlatābād	35·37 N	51·27 E
57	Downey	33·56 N	118·08 W
62c	Drancy	48·56 N	2·27 E
62c	Draveil	48·41 N	2·25 E
55b	Dravosburg	40·21 N	79·51 W
63a	Drewitz (Neigh.)	52·22 N	13·08 E
54b	Drexel Hill	39·57 N	75·19 W
62b	Droylsden	53·29 N	2·10 W
68a	Drummoyne	33·51 S	151·09 E
64b	Družba	55·53 N	37·45 E
57	Duarte	34·08 N	117·58 W
62c	Dugny	48·57 N	2·25 E
61	Duisburg	51·25 N	6·46 E
61	Duissern (Neigh.)	51·26 N	6·47 E
62b	Dukinfield	53·29 N	2·05 W
60	Dulwich (Neigh.)	51·26 N	0·05 W
65a	Dum-Dum	22·35 N	88·24 E
53	Dumont	40·56 N	74·00 W
61	Dümpten (Neigh.)	51·27 N	6·54 E
54c	Dundalk	39·15 N	76·31 W
68a	Dundas	33·48 S	151·02 E
62b	Dunham Town	53·23 N	2·24 W
68a	Dunheved	33·45 S	150·47 E
54d	Dunn Loring	38·53 N	77·14 W
60	Dunton Green	51·18 N	0·11 E
60	Dunton Wayletts	51·35 N	0·24 E
69b	Dunvegan	26·09 S	28·09 E
63c	Duomo (P. Int.)	45·27 N	9·11 E
59c	Duque de Caxias	22·47 S	43·18 W
55b	Duquesne	40·21 N	79·51 W
69b	Durban Roodepoort Deep Gold Mines (P. Int.)	26·10 S	27·51 E
61	Durchholz	51·23 N	7·17 E
61	Düssel	51·16 N	7·03 E
61	Düsseldorf	51·12 N	6·47 E
64b	Dzeržinskij	55·38 N	37·50 E

E

Page	Name Region	Lat. °′	Long. °′
57	Eagle Rock (Neigh.)	34·09 N	118·12 W
60	Ealing (Neigh.)	51·31 N	0·20 W
53	East (R.)	40·48 N	73·48 W
52a	East Arlington	42·25 N	71·08 W
60	East Barnet (Neigh.)	51·38 N	0·09 W
60	East Bedfont (Neigh.)	51·27 N	0·26 W
52a	East Braintree	42·13 N	70·58 W
68b	East Burwood	37·51 S	145·09 E
60	Eastbury	51·37 N	0·25 W
53	Eastchester	40·57 N	73·49 W
54a	East Cleveland	41·32 N	81·35 W
68b	East Coburg	37·45 S	144·59 E
60	Eastcote (Neigh.)	51·35 N	0·24 W
55c	East Detroit	42·28 N	82·56 W
69b	Eastern Native (Neigh.)	26·13 S	28·05 E
54b	East Falls (Neigh.)	40·01 N	75·11 W
62b	Eastham	53·19 N	2·58 W
60	East Ham (Neigh.)	51·32 N	0·03 E
68a	East Hills, Austl.	33·58 S	150·59 E
53	East Hills, NY.	40·47 N	73·38 W
66c	East Lamma Chan.	22·15 N	114·07 E
54b	East Lansdowne	39·56 N	75·16 W
55b	East Liberty (Neigh.)	40·27 N	79·55 W
68a	East Lindfield	33·46 S	151·11 E
57	East Los Angeles	34·01 N	118·09 W
60	East Malling	51·17 N	0·26 E
53	East Meadow	40·43 N	73·34 W
60	East Molesey	51·24 N	0·21 W
53	East Newark	40·45 N	74·10 W
53	East New York (Neigh.)	40·40 N	73·53 W
53	East Norwich	40·50 N	73·32 W
53	East Orange	40·46 N	74·13 W
55b	East Pittsburgh	40·24 N	79·48 W
56b	East Richmond	37·57 N	122·19 W
53	East Rockaway	40·39 N	73·40 W
60	East Tilbury	51·28 N	0·26 E
57	East Tustin	33·46 N	117·49 W
52a	East Walpole	42·10 N	71·13 W
52a	East Watertown	42·22 N	71·10 W
52a	East Weymouth	42·13 N	70·55 W
54b	Eastwick (Neigh.)	39·55 N	75·14 W
60	East Wickham (Neigh.)	51·28 N	0·07 E
68a	Eastwood	33·48 S	151·05 E
52c	East York	43·41 N	79·20 W
62c	Eaubonne	49·00 N	2·17 E
67a	Ebina	35·26 N	139·25 E
69d	Ebute-ikorodu	6·37 N	3·30 E
62b	Eccles	53·29 N	2·21 W
62b	Eccleston, Eng.	53·27 N	2·47 W
54c	Eccleston, Md.	39·24 N	76·44 W
55c	Ecorse	42·15 N	83·09 W
67a	Eda (Neigh.)	35·34 N	139·34 E
59c	Éden	22·48 S	43·24 W
69b	Edendale	26·09 S	28·09 E
69b	Edenvale	26·08 S	28·09 E
69b	Edenvale Location	26·08 S	28·11 E
62b	Edge Hill (Neigh.)	53·24 N	2·57 W
54c	Edgemere	39·14 N	76·27 W
53	Edgewater, NJ.	40·50 N	73·58 W
55a	Edgewater, NY.	43·03 N	78·55 W
60	Edgware (Neigh.)	51·37 N	0·17 W
62b	Edgworth	53·39 N	2·24 W
56a	Edison Park (Neigh.)	42·01 N	87·49 W

Page	Name Region	Lat. °′	Long. °′
54d	Edmonston	38·57 N	76·56 W
60	Edmonton (Neigh.)	51·37 N	0·04 W
67a	Edo (R.)	35·41 N	139·53 E
67a	Edogawa (Neigh.)	35·42 N	139·52 E
60	Egham	51·26 N	0·34 W
67a	Egota (Neigh.)	35·43 N	139·40 E
61	Ehingen (Neigh.)	51·22 N	6·42 E
61	Ehringhausen	51·11 N	7·33 E
61	Ehringhausen (Neigh.)	51·09 N	7·11 E
63a	Eiche	52·34 N	13·36 E
61	Eichlinghofen (Neigh.)	51·29 N	7·24 E
63a	Eichwalde	52·22 N	13·37 E
61	Eickerend	51·13 N	6·34 E
62c	Eiffel, Tour (P. Int.)	48·51 N	2·18 E
61	Eigen (Neigh.)	51·33 N	6·57 E
61	Eilpe (Neigh.)	51·21 N	7·29 E
65a	Eksāra	22·38 N	88·17 E
59a	El Aguacate	10·28 N	66·59 W
69b	Elandsfontein	26·10 S	28·12 E
61	Elberfeld (Neigh.)	51·16 N	7·08 E
58b	El Calvario (Neigh.)	23·05 N	82·20 W
63b	El Campamento (Neigh.)	40·24 N	3·46 W
59a	El Caribe	10·37 N	66·49 W
56b	El Cerrito	37·55 N	122·18 W
59a	El Cojo	10·37 N	66·53 W
59a	El Corozo	10·35 N	66·58 W
58b	El Cotorro	23·03 N	82·16 W
52c	Elder Mills	43·49 N	79·38 W
59a	El Encantado	10·27 N	66·47 W
65e	Elephanta I. (Ghārāpuri)	18·57 N	72·55 E
56b	El Granada	37·30 N	122·28 W
59a	El Guarapo	10·36 N	66·58 W
53	Elizabeth, NJ.	40·40 N	74·11 W
55b	Elizabeth, Pa.	40·16 N	79·53 W
54b	Elkins Park	40·05 N	75·08 W
54c	Elkridge	39·13 N	76·42 W
62b	Ellesmere Park	53·29 N	2·20 W
62b	Ellesmere Port	53·17 N	2·54 W
54c	Ellicott City	39·16 N	76·48 W
59a	El Limoncito	10·29 N	66·47 W
61	Ellinghorst (Neigh.)	51·34 N	6·57 E
56a	Elmhurst	41·53 N	87·56 W
53	Elmhurst (Neigh.)	40·44 N	73·53 W
58a	El Molinito	19·27 N	99·15 W
53	Elmont	40·42 N	73·42 W
54b	Elmwood (Neigh.)	39·56 N	75·14 W
56a	Elmwood Park	41·55 N	87·49 W
59a	El Palmar	10·38 N	66·52 W
59a	El Pedregal (Neigh.)	10·30 N	66·51 W
63b	El Plantío (Neigh.)	40·28 N	3·49 W
59a	El Recreo (Neigh.)	10·30 N	66·53 W
58a	El Reloj	19·18 N	99·08 W
59b	El Rincón de La Florida	33·33 S	70·34 W
69b	Elsburg	26·15 S	28·12 E
57	El Segundo	33·55 N	118·24 W
61	Elsey	51·22 N	7·34 E
60	Elstree	51·39 N	0·16 W
60	Eltham (Neigh.)	51·27 N	0·04 E
62b	Elton	53·16 N	2·49 W
58a	El Toreo (P. Int.)	19·27 N	99·13 W
59a	El Valle (Neigh.)	10·27 N	66·55 W
59a	El Zamural	10·27 N	67·00 W
59a	El Zig-Zag	10·33 N	66·58 W
59d	Embu	23·39 S	46·51 W
62c	Émerainville	48·49 N	2·37 E
53	Emerson	40·58 N	74·02 W
56b	Emeryville	37·50 N	122·17 W
69b	Emmarentia (Neigh.)	26·10 S	28·01 E
61	Emst (Neigh.)	51·21 N	7·30 E
55b	Emsworth	40·30 N	80·04 W
63d	Encarnação (Neigh.)	38·47 N	9·06 W
57	Encino (Neigh.)	34·09 N	118·30 W
68a	Enfield	33·53 S	151·06 E
59c	Engenho de Dentro (Neigh.)	22·54 S	43·18 W
59c	Engenho do Mato	22·52 S	43·01 W
59c	Engenho Nôvo (Neigh.)	22·55 S	43·17 W
62c	Enghien-les-Bains	48·58 N	2·19 E
60	Englefield Green	51·26 N	0·35 W
53	Englewood	40·54 N	73·59 W
56a	Englewood (Neigh.)	41·47 N	87·39 W
53	Englewood Cliffs	40·53 N	73·57 W
61	Ennepetal	51·18 N	7·22 E
62c	Épinay-sous-Sénart	48·42 N	2·31 E
62c	Épinay-sur-Seine	48·57 N	2·19 E
61	Eppendorf (Neigh.)	51·27 N	7·11 E
61	Eppenhausen (Neigh.)	51·21 N	7·31 E
68a	Epping, Austl.	33·46 S	151·05 E
60	Epping, Eng.	51·43 N	0·07 E
60	Epping Green, Eng.	51·44 N	0·05 E
60	Epping Upland	51·43 N	0·06 E
60	Epsom	51·20 N	0·16 W
64f	Erenköy (Neigh.)	40·58 N	29·04 E
61	Ergste	51·25 N	7·34 E
60	Erith (Neigh.)	51·29 N	0·10 E
61	Erkrath	51·13 N	6·55 E
61	Erle (Neigh.)	51·33 N	7·05 E
62c	Ermont	48·59 N	2·16 E
68a	Erskine Park	33·49 S	150·47 E
61	Esborn	51·23 N	7·20 E
58a	Escuadrón 201	19·22 N	99·06 W
60	Esher	51·23 N	0·22 W
63e	Esplugas	41·23 N	2·06 E
61	Essel (Neigh.)	51·37 N	7·15 E
61	Essen	51·28 N	7·01 E

Page	Name Region	Lat. °′	Long. °′
61	Essenberg	51·26 N	6·42 E
68b	Essendon	37·46 S	144·55 E
54c	Essex	39·18 N	76·29 W
53	Essex Fells	40·50 N	74·17 W
54b	Essington	39·52 N	75·18 W
64e	Essling (Neigh.)	48·13 N	16·32 E
58a	Estrella, Cerro de la (Mtn.)	19·21 N	99·05 W
55b	Etna	40·30 N	79·57 W
52c	Etobicoke	43·39 N	79·34 W
60	Eton	51·31 N	0·37 W
56a	Evanston	42·02 N	87·42 W
52a	Everett	42·24 N	71·03 W
56a	Evergreen Park	41·43 N	87·42 W
62b	Everton (Neigh.)	53·25 N	2·58 W
61	Eving (Neigh.)	51·33 N	7·29 E
60	Ewell	51·21 N	0·15 W
69d	Ewu	6·33 N	3·19 E
60	Eynsford	51·22 N	0·13 E
64f	Eyüp (Neigh.)	41·03 N	28·55 E
69a	Ezbekīyah (Neigh.)	30·03 N	31·15 E

F

Page	Name Region	Lat. °′	Long. °′
52b	Fabreville (Neigh.)	45·34 N	73·50 W
63a	Fahrland	52·28 N	13·01 E
62b	Failsworth	53·31 N	2·09 W
68a	Fairfield, Austl.	33·52 S	150·57 E
53	Fairfield, NJ.	40·53 N	74·17 W
68a	Fairfield West	33·52 S	150·55 E
54d	Fairhaven	38·47 N	77·05 W
53	Fair Lawn	40·56 N	74·07 W
54d	Fairlee	38·52 N	77·16 W
54d	Fairmount Heights	38·54 N	76·55 W
60	Fairseat	51·20 N	0·20 E
53	Fairview	40·49 N	74·00 W
54a	Fairview Park	41·27 N	81·51 W
63a	Falkensee	52·33 N	13·04 E
54d	Falls Church	38·53 N	77·11 W
63e	Famadas	41·21 N	2·05 E
66h	Farazād	35·47 N	51·21 E
55c	Farmington	42·28 N	83·22 W
55c	Farmington Hills	42·28 N	83·23 W
60	Farnborough (Neigh.)	51·21 N	0·04 E
60	Farningham	51·23 N	0·13 E
62b	Farnworth	53·33 N	2·24 W
53	Far Rockaway (Neigh.)	40·36 N	73·45 W
64e	Favoriten (Neigh.)	48·11 N	16·23 E
60	Fawkham Green	51·22 N	0·17 E
68b	Fawkner	37·43 S	144·58 E
54d	Fawsett Farms	38·59 N	77·14 W
65b	Fengtai	39·51 N	116·16 E
63a	Ferbitz	52·30 N	13·01 E
64g	Ferencváros (Neigh.)	47·28 N	19·06 E
54c	Ferndale, Md.	39·11 N	76·38 W
55c	Ferndale, Mi.	42·28 N	83·08 W
68b	Ferntree Gully	37·53 S	145·18 E
68b	Ferny Creek	37·53 S	145·21 E
59d	Ferraz de Vasconcelos	23·32 S	46·22 W
62c	Ferrières	48·49 N	2·42 E
55a	Ferry Village	43·58 N	78·57 W
60	Fetcham	51·17 N	0·22 W
63a	Fichtenau	52·27 N	13·42 E
60	Fiddlers Hamlet	51·41 N	0·08 E
64b	Fili (Neigh.)	55·45 N	37·31 E
69b	Finaalspan	26·17 S	28·15 E
60	Finchley (Neigh.)	51·36 N	0·10 W
63a	Finkenkrug	52·34 N	13·03 E
62b	Firgrove	53·37 N	2·08 W
61	Fischeln (Neigh.)	51·18 N	6·35 E
56b	Fisherman's Wharf (P. Int.)	37·48 N	122·25 W
52c	Fisherville	43·47 N	79·28 W
62b	Fishpool	53·35 N	2·17 W
68b	Fitzroy	37·48 S	144·59 E
68a	Five Dock	33·52 S	151·08 E
53	Flatbush (Neigh.)	40·39 N	73·56 W
60	Flaunden	51·42 N	0·32 W
61	Flehe (Neigh.)	51·12 N	6·47 E
61	Fley (Neigh.)	51·23 N	7·30 E
61	Flingern (Neigh.)	51·14 N	6·49 E
53	Floral Park	40·43 N	73·42 W
57	Florence	33·58 N	118·15 W
69b	Florentia	26·16 S	28·08 E
58d	Flores (Neigh.)	34·38 S	58·28 W
58d	Floresta (Neigh.)	34·38 S	58·29 W
69b	Florida	26·11 S	27·55 E
58a	Flotantes, Jardines (P. Int.)	19·16 N	99·06 W
54b	Flourtown	40·07 N	75·13 W
53	Flower Hill	40·49 N	73·41 W
53	Flushing (Neigh.)	40·45 N	73·49 W
54b	Folcroft	39·54 N	75·17 W
54b	Folsom	39·54 N	75·19 W
69b	Fontainebleau	26·07 S	27·59 E
62c	Fontenay-aux-Roses	48·47 N	2·17 E
62c	Fontenay-le-Fleury	48·49 N	2·03 E
62c	Fontenay-sous-Bois	48·51 N	2·29 E
68b	Footscray	37·48 S	144·54 E
59c	Fora, Ponta de (C.)	22·57 S	43·07 W
65b	Forbidden City (P. Int.)	39·55 N	116·23 E
53	Fordham University (P. Int.)	40·51 N	73·53 W
53	Fords	40·32 N	74·19 W
69b	Fordsburg (Neigh.)	26·13 S	28·02 E
60	Forest Gate (Neigh.)	51·33 N	0·02 E
54d	Forest Heights	38·49 N	77·00 W
68b	Forest Hill	37·50 S	145·11 E

Page	Name Region	Lat. °′	Long. °′
52c	Forest Hill (Neigh.)	43·42 N	79·24 W
55b	Forest Hills	40·26 N	79·52 W
53	Forest Hills (Neigh.)	40·42 N	73·51 W
56a	Forest Park	41·53 N	87·50 W
54c	Forest Park (Neigh.)	39·19 N	76·41 W
68a	Forestville, Austl.	33·46 S	151·13 E
54d	Forestville, Md.	38·50 N	76·52 W
62b	Formby	53·34 N	3·05 W
62b	Formby Pt.	53·33 N	3·06 W
65e	Fort (Neigh.)	18·56 N	72·50 E
55a	Fort Erie	42·54 N	78·56 W
54c	Fort Howard	39·12 N	76·27 W
53	Fort Lee	40·51 N	73·58 W
54c	Fort McHenry National Monument (P. Int.)	39·16 N	76·35 W
54d	Fort McNair (P. Int.)	38·52 N	77·04 W
55c	Fort Wayne Military Museum (P. Int.)	42·18 N	83·06 W
65a	Fort William (P. Int.)	22·33 N	88·20 E
56b	Foster City	37·34 N	122·16 W
62c	Fourqueux	48·53 N	2·04 E
55b	Fox Chapel	40·30 N	79·55 W
68a	Fox Valley	33·45 S	151·06 E
62c	Franconville	48·59 N	2·14 E
55b	Frank	40·16 N	79·48 W
62b	Frankby	53·22 N	3·08 W
54b	Frankford (Neigh.)	40·01 N	75·05 W
55c	Franklin	42·31 N	83·18 W
56a	Franklin Park, Il.	41·56 N	87·49 W
55b	Franklin Park, Pa.	40·35 N	80·06 W
54d	Franklin Park, Va.	38·55 N	77·09 W
69b	Franklin Roosevelt Park (Neigh.)	26·09 S	27·59 E
53	Franklin Square	40·43 N	73·40 W
55c	Fraser	42·32 N	82·57 W
63a	Fredersdorf bei Berlin	52·31 N	13·44 E
53	Freeport	40·39 N	73·35 W
61	Freisenbruch (Neigh.)	51·27 N	7·06 E
68a	French's Forest	33·45 S	151·14 E
62b	Freshfield	53·34 N	3·04 W
53	Fresh Meadows (Neigh.)	40·44 N	73·48 W
63a	Friedenau (Neigh.)	52·28 N	13·20 E
61	Friedrichsfeld	51·38 N	6·39 E
63a	Friedrichsfelde (Neigh.)	52·31 N	13·31 E
63a	Friedrichshagen (Neigh.)	52·27 N	13·38 E
63a	Friedrichshain (Neigh.)	52·31 N	13·27 E
61	Friemersheim	51·23 N	6·42 E
65d	Friends Colony (Neigh.)	28·34 N	77·16 E
54c	Friendship International Arpt.	39·11 N	76·40 W
60	Friern Barnet (Neigh.)	51·37 N	0·10 W
61	Frillendorf (Neigh.)	51·28 N	7·05 E
62b	Frodsham	53·18 N	2·44 W
63a	Frohnau (Neigh.)	52·38 N	13·18 E
61	Frohnhausen (Neigh.)	51·27 N	6·58 E
60	Fryerning	51·41 N	0·22 E
67a	Fuchū	35·40 N	139·29 E
63b	Fuencarral (Neigh.)	40·30 N	3·41 W
61	Fuhlenbrock (Neigh.)	51·32 N	6·54 E
67b	Fujiidera	34·34 N	135·36 E
67a	Fukagawa (Neigh.)	35·40 N	139·48 E
67b	Fukiai (Neigh.)	34·42 N	135·12 E
67b	Fukushima (Neigh.)	34·42 N	135·29 E
61	Fulerum (Neigh.)	51·26 N	6·57 E
57	Fullerton	33·52 N	117·55 W
60	Fulmer	51·33 N	0·34 W
67b	Funasaka	34·49 N	135·17 E
59c	Fundão, Ilha do (I.)	22·51 S	43·14 W
65e	Funde	18·54 N	72·58 E
67a	Futatsubashi	35·28 N	139·30 E
60	Fyfield	51·45 N	0·16 E

G

Page	Name Region	Lat. °′	Long. °′
62c	Gagny	48·53 N	2·32 E
61	Gahmen (Neigh.)	51·36 N	7·32 E
64f	Galata (Neigh.)	41·01 N	28·58 E
64f	Galata Köprüsü (P. Int.)	41·00 N	28·57 E
64d	Galátsion	38·01 N	23·45 E
68b	Galvin	37·51 S	144·49 E
65b	Gaobaita	39·53 N	116·30 E
65b	Gaobeidian	39·54 N	116·33 E
63c	Garbagnate Milanese	45·35 N	9·05 E
64c	Garbatella (Neigh.)	41·52 N	12·29 E
62c	Garches	48·51 N	2·11 E
57	Gardena	33·53 N	118·18 W
55c	Garden City, Mi.	42·20 N	83·20 W
53	Garden City, NY.	40·43 N	73·37 W
53	Garden City Park	40·44 N	73·40 W
57	Garden Grove	33·46 N	117·57 W
65a	Garden Reach	22·33 N	88·17 E
61	Garenfeld	51·24 N	7·31 E
53	Garfield	40·53 N	74·07 W
54a	Garfield Heights	41·26 N	81·37 W
62c	Garges-lès-Gonesse	48·58 N	2·25 E
54c	Garland	39·11 N	76·39 W
54c	Garrison	39·24 N	76·45 W
60	Garston	51·41 N	0·23 W
62b	Garston (Neigh.)	53·21 N	2·53 W
61	Gartenstadt (Neigh.)	51·30 N	7·26 E
65a	Garulia	22·49 N	88·22 E
53	Garwood	40·39 N	74·19 W
62b	Gateacre (Neigh.)	53·23 N	2·51 W

Page	Name Region	Lat. °′	Long. °′
65e	Gateway of India (P. Int.)	18·55 N	72·50 E
62b	Gatley	53·23 N	2·14 W
59a	Gato Negro	10·33 N	66·57 W
65e	Gāvanpāda	18·57 N	73·01 E
59c	Gávea (Neigh.)	22·58 S	43·14 W
62b	Gayton	53·19 N	3·06 W
62b	Gee Cross	53·26 N	2·04 W
61	Gellep-Stratum (Neigh.)	51·20 N	6·41 E
68b	Gellibrand, Pt.	37·52 S	144·54 E
61	Gelsenkirchen	51·31 N	7·07 E
58d	General Pacheco	34·28 S	58·40 W
58d	General San Martín	34·35 S	58·30 W
58d	General Sarmiento (San Miguel)	34·33 S	58·43 W
58d	General Urquiza (Neigh.)	34·34 S	58·29 W
61	Gennebreck	51·19 N	7·12 E
62c	Gennevilliers	48·56 N	2·18 E
62c	Gentilly	48·49 N	2·21 E
68a	Georges Hall	33·55 S	150·59 E
54d	Georgetown (Neigh.)	38·54 N	77·03 W
54d	Georgetown University (P. Int.)	38·54 N	77·04 W
69b	Gerdview	26·10 S	28·11 E
58d	Gerli (Neigh.)	34·41 S	58·23 W
54b	Germantown (Neigh.)	40·03 N	75·11 W
69b	Germiston	26·15 S	28·05 E
60	Gerrards Cross	51·35 N	0·34 W
63b	Getafe	40·18 N	3·43 W
55a	Getzville	43·01 N	78·46 W
61	Gevelsberg	51·19 N	7·20 E
61	Geweke (Neigh.)	51·22 N	7·25 E
65e	Ghārāpuri	18·54 N	72·56 E
65e	Ghātkopar (Neigh.)	19·05 N	72·54 E
65d	Ghāzipur (Neigh.)	28·38 N	77·19 E
65d	Ghonda (Neigh.)	28·41 N	77·16 E
65d	Ghondi (Neigh.)	28·42 N	77·16 E
65a	Ghushuri	22·37 N	88·22 E
66m	Gia-dinh	10·48 N	106·42 E
54b	Gibbsboro	39·50 N	74·58 W
52c	Gibraltar Pt.	43·36 N	79·23 W
60	Gidea Park (Neigh.)	51·35 N	0·12 E
62c	Gif-sur-Yvette	48·42 N	2·08 E
67a	Ginza (Neigh.)	35·40 N	139·47 E
65e	Girgaum (Neigh.)	18·57 N	72·48 E
69a	Giza Pyramids (P. Int.)	29·59 N	31·08 E
61	Gladbeck	51·34 N	6·59 E
68a	Gladesville	33·50 S	151·08 E
54b	Gladwyne	40·02 N	75·17 W
61	Glashütte (Neigh.)	51·13 N	6·52 E
54d	Glassmanor	38·49 N	76·59 W
55b	Glassport	40·19 N	79·54 W
61	Glehn	51·10 N	6·35 E
54d	Glenarden	38·56 N	76·52 W
53	Glen Cove	40·52 N	73·37 W
57	Glendale	34·10 N	118·17 W
57	Glendora, Ca.	34·08 N	117·52 W
54b	Glendora, NJ.	39·50 N	75·04 W
54d	Glen Echo	38·58 N	77·08 W
68a	Glenfield	33·58 S	150·54 E
53	Glen Head	40·50 N	73·37 W
68b	Glenhuntly	37·54 S	145·03 E
54c	Glenmore	39·11 N	76·36 W
54b	Glenolden	39·54 N	75·17 W
53	Glen Ridge	40·49 N	74·13 W
53	Glen Rock	40·58 N	74·08 W
68b	Glenroy	37·42 S	144·55 E
55b	Glenshaw	40·31 N	79·57 W
54b	Glenside	40·06 N	75·09 W
56a	Glenview	42·04 N	87·48 W
68b	Glen Waverley	37·53 S	145·10 E
53	Glenwood Landing	40·50 N	73·39 W
63a	Glienicke	52·37 N	13·19 E
54b	Gloucester City	39·54 N	75·07 W
60	Goff's Oak	51·43 N	0·05 W
65a	Golabāri	22·36 N	88·20 E
56b	Golden Gate (Str.)	37·49 N	122·29 W
60	Golders Green (Neigh.)	51·35 N	0·12 W
56a	Golf	42·03 N	87·48 W
56a	Golf Park Terrace	42·03 N	87·51 W
62c	Gonesse	48·59 N	2·27 E
58d	González Catán	34·46 S	58·39 W
68a	Gordon (Ku-ring-gai)	33·45 S	151·08 E
54d	Gordons Corner	38·50 N	76·57 W
68a	Gore Hill	33·49 S	151·11 E
62b	Gorton (Neigh.)	53·27 N	2·10 W
63a	Gosen	52·24 N	13·43 E
67a	Gotanno (Neigh.)	35·46 N	139·49 E
61	Götterswickerhamm	51·35 N	6·40 E
63a	Göttin	52·27 N	12·54 E
62c	Gournay-sur-Marne	48·52 N	2·34 E
62c	Goussainville	49·01 N	2·28 E
66m	Go-vap	10·49 N	106·42 E
59c	Governador, Ilha do (I.)	22·48 S	43·12 W
61	Grafenberg (Neigh.)	51·14 N	6·50 E
58a	Gran Canal del Desagüe (Can.)	19·29 N	99·05 W
55a	Grand Island	43·01 N	78·58 W
55a	Grand I.	43·02 N	78·58 W
55a	Grandyle	43·00 N	78·57 W
60	Grange Hill	51·37 N	0·05 E
54c	Granite	39·21 N	76·51 W
56a	Grant Park (P. Int.)	41·52 N	87·37 W
68a	Granville	33·50 S	151·01 E
62b	Grassendale (Neigh.)	53·21 N	2·54 W
60	Gravesend	51·27 N	0·24 E
60	Grays	51·29 N	0·20 E
62b	Greasby	53·23 N	3·07 W
62b	Great Altcar	53·33 N	3·01 W
60	Great Bookham	51·16 N	0·22 W
60	Great Burstead	51·36 N	0·25 E
62b	Great Crosby	53·29 N	3·01 W
54d	Great Falls	39·00 N	77·17 W
53	Great Kills (Neigh.)	40·33 N	74·10 W
53	Great Neck	40·47 N	73·44 W
60	Great Oxney Green	51·44 N	0·25 E
60	Great Parndon	51·45 N	0·05 E
62b	Great Sutton	53·17 N	2·56 W
60	Great Warley	51·35 N	0·17 E
63c	Greco (Neigh.)	45·30 N	9·13 E
54d	Greenbelt	39·01 N	76·53 W
56b	Greenbrae	37·57 N	122·31 W
52b	Greenfield Park	45·29 N	73·29 W
60	Greenhithe	51·27 N	0·17 E
54d	Green Meadows	38·58 N	76·57 W
62b	Greenmount	53·37 N	2·20 W
68b	Greensborough	37·42 S	145·06 E
69b	Greenside (Neigh.)	26·09 S	28·01 E
60	Greenstead	51·42 N	0·14 E
60	Green Street	51·40 N	0·16 W
60	Green Street Green (Neigh.)	51·21 N	0·04 E
53	Greenvale	40·49 N	73·38 W
68a	Green Valley	33·54 S	150·53 E
68a	Greenwich	33·50 S	151·11 E
60	Greenwich (Neigh.)	51·28 N	0·02 E
60	Greenwich Observatory (P. Int.)	51·28 N	0·00
53	Greenwich Village (Neigh.)	40·44 N	74·00 W
52a	Greenwood	42·29 N	71·04 W
61	Greiffenburg (P. Int.)	51·20 N	6·38 E
61	Grevel (Neigh.)	51·34 N	7·33 E
68a	Greystanes	0·00	0·00
61	Grimlinghausen (Neigh.)	51·10 N	6·44 E
64e	Grinzing (Neigh.)	48·15 N	16·21 E
63a	Grossbeeren	52·21 N	13·18 E
61	Grossenbaum (Neigh)	51·22 N	6·47 E
64e	Gross-Enzersdorf	48·12 N	16·33 E
55c	Grosse Pointe	42·24 N	82·55 W
55c	Grosse Pointe Farms	42·25 N	82·53 W
55c	Grosse Pointe Park	42·23 N	82·56 W
55c	Grosse Pointe Woods	42·27 N	82·55 W
64e	Grossjedlersdorf (Neigh.)	48·17 N	16·25 E
63a	Gross Ziethen	52·24 N	13·27 E
61	Gruiten	51·14 N	7·01 E
61	Grumme (Neigh.)	51·30 N	7·14 E
63a	Grünau (Neigh.)	52·25 N	13·34 E
61	Grünewald	51·13 N	7·37 E
63a	Grunewald (Neigh.)	52·30 N	13·17 E
58a	Guadalupe, Basílica de (P. Int.)	19·29 N	99·07 W
59d	Guaianazes (Neigh.)	23·33 S	46·25 W
59a	Guaire (R.)	10·25 N	66·46 W
58b	Guanabacoa	23·07 N	82·18 W
59c	Guanabara, Baía de (B.)	22·50 S	43·10 W
65b	Guanyintang	39·52 N	116·31 E
59a	Guaracarumbo	10·34 N	66·59 W
59d	Guarulhos	23·28 S	46·32 W
62c	Guermantes	48·51 N	2·42 E
68a	Guildford	33·51 S	150·59 E
54b	Gulph Mills	40·04 N	75·21 W
58a	Gustavo A. Madero	19·29 N	99·07 W
53	Guttenberg	40·48 N	74·01 W
62c	Guyancourt	48·46 N	2·04 E

H

Page	Name Region	Lat. °′	Long. °′
61	Haan	51·11 N	7·00 E
61	Haar (Neigh.)	51·26 N	7·13 E
68a	Haberfield	33·53 S	151·08 E
67a	Hachiōji	35·39 N	139·20 E
57	Hacienda Heights	33·58 N	117·58 W
53	Hackensack	40·53 N	74·03 W
60	Hacketts	51·45 N	0·05 W
60	Hackney (Neigh.)	51·33 N	0·03 W
54b	Haddonfield	39·54 N	75·02 W
54b	Haddon Heights	39·52 N	75·02 W
64e	Hadersdorf (Neigh.)	48·13 N	16·14 E
68b	Hadfield	37·42 S	144·56 E
66b	Haemgon-ni (Neigh.)	37·35 N	126·49 E
61	Hagen	51·22 N	7·28 E
61	Hahnenberg	51·12 N	7·24 E
65d	Haidārpur (Neigh.)	28·43 N	77·09 E
65b	Haidian	39·59 N	116·18 E
67a	Haijima	35·42 N	139·21 E
60	Hainault (Neigh.)	51·36 N	0·06 E
61	Halden (Neigh.)	51·23 N	7·31 E
62b	Hale, Eng.	53·23 N	2·21 W
62b	Halebarns	53·22 N	2·19 W
53	Haledon	40·56 N	74·11 W
54c	Halethorpe	39·15 N	76·41 W
62b	Halewood	53·22 N	2·49 W
64f	Haliç (B.)	41·02 N	28·58 E
68b	Hallam	38·01 S	145·06 E
60	Halstead	51·20 N	0·08 E
61	Halver	51·11 N	7·30 E
60	Ham (Neigh.)	51·26 N	0·19 W
69b	Hamberg	26·11 S	27·53 E
61	Hamborn (Neigh.)	51·29 N	6·46 E
61	Hamm (Neigh.), F.R.G.	51·12 N	6·44 E
60	Hammersmith (Neigh.)	51·30 N	0·14 W
56a	Hammond	41·36 N	87·30 W
68a	Hammondville	33·57 S	150·57 E
60	Hampstead (Neigh.)	51·33 N	0·11 W
60	Hampstead Heath (P. Int.)	51·34 N	0·10 W
68b	Hampton	37·56 S	145·00 E
60	Hampton (Neigh.)	51·25 N	0·22 W
54c	Hampton National Historic Site (P. Int.)	39·25 N	76·35 W
55c	Hamtramck	42·24 N	83·03 W
62b	Handforth	53·21 N	2·13 W
66b	Han-gang (R.)	37·36 N	126·47 E
66c	Hang Hau Town	22·19 N	114·16 E
66m	Hanh-thong-tay	10·50 N	106·40 E
54c	Hanover	39·11 N	76·42 W
60	Hanworth (Neigh.)	51·26 N	0·23 W
62b	Hapsford	53·16 N	2·48 W
67a	Haramachida	35·33 N	139·27 E
57	Harbor City (Neigh.)	33·48 N	118·17 W
68a	Harbord	33·45 S	151·26 E
53	Harbor Isle	40·36 N	73·40 W
60	Harefield (Neigh.)	51·36 N	0·29 W
60	Haringey (Neigh.)	51·35 N	0·07 W
54b	Harker Village	39·51 N	75·09 W
53	Harlem (Neigh.)	40·49 N	73·56 W
60	Harlesden (Neigh.)	51·32 N	0·15 W
60	Harlington (Neigh.)	51·29 N	0·26 W
55b	Harmar Heights	40·33 N	79·49 W
55b	Harmarville	40·32 N	79·51 W
65d	Harola	28·36 N	77·19 E
60	Harold Hill (Neigh.)	51·36 N	0·13 E
60	Harold Wood (Neigh.)	51·36 N	0·14 E
61	Harpen (Neigh.)	51·29 N	7·16 E
55c	Harper Woods	42·24 N	82·55 W
62b	Harpurhey (Neigh.)	53·31 N	2·13 W
53	Harrison, NJ.	40·45 N	74·10 W
53	Harrison, NY.	40·58 N	73·43 W
54c	Harrisonville	39·23 N	77·50 W
68a	Harris Park	33·49 S	151·01 E
60	Harrow (Neigh.)	51·35 N	0·21 W
60	Harrow on the Hill (Neigh.)	51·34 N	0·20 W
60	Hartley	51·23 N	0·19 E
60	Harvel	51·21 N	0·22 E
56a	Harvey	41·37 N	87·39 W
55b	Harwick	40·34 N	79·48 W
62b	Harwood, Eng.	53·35 N	2·23 W
54c	Harwood, Md.	38·52 N	76·37 W
56a	Harwood Heights	41·59 N	87·48 W
54c	Harwood Park	39·12 N	76·44 W
66h	Ḥasanābād	35·44 N	51·19 E
53	Hasbrouck Heights	40·52 N	74·04 W
62b	Haskayne	53·34 N	2·58 W
64f	Hasköy (Neigh.)	41·02 N	28·58 E
61	Hasselbeck-Schwarzbach	51·16 N	6·53 E
61	Hassels (Neigh.)	51·10 N	6·53 E
61	Hasslinghausen	51·20 N	7·17 E
61	Hästen (Neigh.), F.R.G.	51·09 N	7·06 E
61	Hasten (Neigh.), F.R.G.	51·12 N	7·09 E
60	Hastingwood	51·45 N	0·09 E
61	Hattingen	51·23 N	7·10 E
60	Hatton (Neigh.)	51·28 N	0·25 W
67b	Hattori	34·46 N	135·27 E
61	Hatzfeld (Neigh.)	51·17 N	7·11 E
62b	Haughton Green	53·27 N	2·06 W
65d	Hauz Rāni (Neigh.)	28·32 N	77·13 E
58b	Havana	23·08 N	82·22 W
63a	Havel-Kanal (Can.)	52·36 N	13·12 E
54b	Haverford	40·01 N	75·18 W
60	Havering (Neigh.)	51·34 N	0·14 E
60	Havering-atte-Bower (Neigh.)	51·37 N	0·11 E
60	Havering's Grove	51·38 N	0·23 E
54b	Havertown	39·59 N	75·18 W
57	Hawaiian Gardens	33·50 N	118·04 W
69a	Ḥawf, Jabal (Hills)	29·55 N	31·21 E
60	Hawley	51·25 N	0·14 E
53	Haworth	40·58 N	73·59 W
68b	Hawthorn	37·49 S	145·02 E
57	Hawthorne, Ca.	33·55 N	118·21 W
53	Hawthorne, NJ.	40·57 N	74·09 W
60	Hayes (Neigh.), Eng.	51·23 N	0·01 E
62b	Hazel Grove	53·23 N	2·08 W
60	Headley	51·17 N	0·16 W
62b	Heald Green	53·22 N	2·14 W
68b	Heathmont	37·49 S	145·15 E
62b	Heaton Moor	53·25 N	2·11 W
60	Heaverham	51·18 N	0·15 E
62b	Heaviley	53·24 N	2·09 W
54c	Hebbville	39·20 N	77·46 W
61	Heerdt (Neigh.)	51·13 N	6·43 E
61	Heide (Neigh.), F.R.G.	51·31 N	6·52 E
68b	Heidelberg, Austl.	37·45 S	145·04 E
55b	Heidelberg, Pa.	40·23 N	80·05 W
61	Heil	51·38 N	7·35 E
61	Heiligenhaus	51·19 N	6·59 E
63a	Heiligensee (Neigh.)	52·36 N	13·13 E
63a	Heinersdorf	52·23 N	13·20 E
63a	Heinersdorf (Neigh.)	52·34 N	13·27 E
61	Heisingen (Neigh.)	51·25 N	7·04 E
69a	Heliopolis, see Mişr al-Jadīdah (Neigh.)	30·06 N	31·20 E
69a	Heliopolis (P. Int.)	30·08 N	31·17 E
62b	Helsby	53·16 N	2·46 W
60	Hemel Hempstead	51·46 N	0·28 W
53	Hempstead	40·42 N	73·37 W
63a	Hennigsdorf	52·38 N	13·13 E
61	Herbede	51·25 N	7·16 E
61	Herdecke	51·24 N	7·26 E
64e	Hermannskogel (Mtn.)	48·16 N	16·18 E
57	Hermosa Beach	33·52 N	118·24 W
63a	Hermsdorf (Neigh.)	52·37 N	13·18 E
64e	Hernals (Neigh.)	48·13 N	16·20 E
61	Herne	51·32 N	7·13 E
54c	Hernwood Heights	39·22 N	77·50 W
58a	Héroes Chapultepec	19·28 N	99·04 W
58a	Héroes de Churubusco	19·22 N	99·06 W
60	Herongate	51·36 N	0·21 E
60	Heronsgate	51·38 N	0·31 W
60	Hersham	51·22 N	0·23 W
61	Herten	51·35 N	7·07 E
62b	Heswall	53·20 N	3·06 W
64e	Hetzendorf (Neigh.)	48·10 N	16·18 E
61	Heven (Neigh.)	51·26 N	7·17 E
53	Hewlett	40·38 N	73·42 W
53	Hewlett Harbor	40·38 N	73·41 W
60	Hextable	51·25 N	0·11 E
62b	Heywood	53·36 N	2·13 W
56a	Hickory Hills	41·43 N	87·49 W
53	Hicksville	40·46 N	73·32 W
61	Hiddinghausen	51·22 N	7·17 E
61	Hiesfeld	51·33 N	6·46 E
64e	Hietzing (Neigh.)	48·11 N	16·18 E
67b	Higashi (Neigh.)	34·41 N	135·31 E
67a	Higashimurayama	35·46 N	139·29 E
67b	Higashinada (Neigh.)	34·43 N	135·16 E
67a	Higashinakano	35·38 N	139·25 E
67b	Higashinari (Neigh.)	34·40 N	135·33 E
67a	Higashiōizumi (Neigh.)	35·45 N	139·36 E
67b	Higashiōsaka	34·39 N	135·35 E
67b	Higashisumiyoshi (Neigh.)	34·37 N	135·32 E
66e	Higashiyama (Neigh.)	34·52 N	135·48 E
67b	Higashiyodogawa (Neigh.)	34·44 N	135·29 E
60	Higham Upshire	51·26 N	0·28 E
60	High Beach	51·39 N	0·02 E
55b	Highcliff	40·32 N	80·03 W
62b	Higher Broughton (Neigh.)	53·30 N	2·15 W
55b	Highland	40·33 N	80·04 W
54d	Highland Park, Md.	38·54 N	76·54 W
55c	Highland Park, Mi.	42·24 N	83·06 W
69b	Highlands North (Neigh.)	26·09 S	28·05 E
60	High Laver	51·45 N	0·13 E
60	High Ongar	51·43 N	0·16 E
62b	Hightown	53·32 N	3·04 W
61	Hilden	51·10 N	6·56 E
69b	Hillbrow (Neigh.)	26·11 S	28·03 E
54b	Hill Crest	40·05 N	75·11 W
54d	Hillcrest Heights	38·52 N	76·57 W
61	Hillen (Neigh.)	51·37 N	7·13 E
60	Hillingdon (Neigh.)	51·32 N	0·27 W
54d	Hillside	38·52 N	76·55 W
53	Hillside (Neigh.)	40·42 N	73·47 W
54d	Hillwood	38·52 N	77·10 W
61	Hiltrop (Neigh.)	51·30 N	7·15 E
61	Himmelgeist (Neigh.)	51·10 N	6·49 E
52a	Hingham	42·14 N	70·53 W
52a	Hingham	42·17 N	70·55 W
67a	Hino	35·41 N	139·24 E
56a	Hinsdale	41·48 N	87·56 W
61	Hinsel (Neigh.)	51·26 N	7·05 E
67b	Hirota	34·45 N	135·21 E
64e	Hirschstetten (Neigh.)	48·14 N	16·29 E
60	Hither Green (Neigh.)	51·27 N	0·01 W
53	Hoboken	40·45 N	74·03 W
68b	Hobsons B.	37·51 S	144·56 E
61	Hochdahl	51·13 N	6·56 E
61	Hochheide	51·27 N	6·41 E
66m	Ho Chi Minh City (Saigon)	10·45 N	106·40 E
61	Hochlar (Neigh.)	51·36 N	7·10 E
61	Höchsten	51·27 N	7·29 E
56a	Hodgkins	41·46 N	87·51 W
64e	Hofburg (P. Int.)	48·12 N	16·22 E
58a	Hogar y Redención	19·22 N	99·13 W
61	Hohenlimburg	51·21 N	7·35 E
63a	Hohen-Neuendorf	52·40 N	13·16 E
63a	Hohenschönhausen (Neigh.)	52·33 N	13·30 E
61	Hohensyburg (P. Int.)	51·25 N	7·29 E
61	Höhscheid (Neigh.)	51·09 N	7·04 E
61	Hoisten	51·08 N	6·42 E
60	Holborn (Neigh.)	51·31 N	0·07 W
52a	Holbrook	42·09 N	71·01 W
62b	Hollins	53·34 N	2·17 W
53	Hollis (Neigh.)	40·43 N	73·46 W
57	Hollywood (Neigh.)	34·06 N	118·21 W
57	Hollywood Bowl (P. Int.)	34·07 N	118·20 W
54b	Holmes	39·54 N	75·19 W
54d	Holmes Run Acres	38·51 N	77·13 W
68a	Holroyd	33·50 S	150·58 E
61	Holten (Neigh.)	51·31 N	6·48 E
61	Holthausen (Neigh.)	51·34 N	7·26 E
61	Holzen	51·26 N	7·31 E
61	Holzheim	51·09 N	6·39 E
61	Holzwickede	51·30 N	7·36 E
61	Homberg, F.R.G.	51·28 N	6·43 E

Page	Name Region	Lat. °′	Long. °′
55b	Homestead	40·24 N	79·54 W
56a	Hometown	41·44 N	87·44 W
55b	Homewood (Neigh.)	40·27 N	79·54 W
61	Höntrop (Neigh.)	51·27 N	7·08 E
65a	Hooghly (R.)	22·33 N	88·15 E
65a	Hooghly-Chinsura	22·54 N	88·24 E
62b	Hooton	53·18 N	2·57 W
63a	Hoppegarten	52·31 N	13·40 E
61	Hörde (Neigh.)	51·29 N	7·30 E
67a	Horinouchi (Neigh.)	35·41 N	139·40 E
60	Hornchurch (Neigh.)	51·34 N	0·12 E
60	Horndon on the Hill	51·31 N	0·25 E
61	Horneburg	51·38 N	7·18 E
60	Horn Hill	51·37 N	0·32 W
68a	Hornsby	33·42 S	150·06 E
60	Hornsey (Neigh.)	51·35 N	0·07 W
60	Horsell	51·19 N	0·34 W
68a	Horsley	33·51 S	150·51 E
61	Horst (Neigh.)	51·32 N	7·02 E
61	Horsthausen (Neigh.)	51·33 N	7·13 E
61	Horstmar (Neigh.)	51·36 N	7·33 E
63b	Hortaleza (Neigh.)	40·28 N	3·39 W
60	Horton Kirby	51·23 N	0·15 E
61	Hösel	51·19 N	6·54 E
63e	Hospitalet	41·22 N	2·08 E
62b	Hough Green	53·23 N	2·47 W
62c	Houilles	48·56 N	2·11 E
60	Hounslow (Neigh.)	51·29 N	0·22 W
53	Howard Beach (Neigh.)	40·40 N	73·51 W
65a	Howrah	22·35 N	88·20 E
65a	Howrah Bridge (P. Int.)	22·35 N	88·21 E
68a	Hoxton Park	33·55 S	150·51 E
67a	Hōya	35·43 N	139·34 E
66d	Hsinchuang	25·02 N	121·26 E
65b	Huangcun	39·56 N	116·11 E
66a	Huangpujiang (R.)	31·18 N	121·33 E
61	Hubbelrath	51·16 N	6·55 E
61	Hückeswagen	51·08 N	7·20 E
53	Hudson (R.)	40·42 N	74·02 W
61	Hügel, Villa (P. Int.)	51·25 N	7·01 E
58a	Huipulco	19·17 N	99·09 W
61	Hülscheid	51·16 N	7·34 E
52c	Humber (R.)	43·38 N	79·28 W
59a	Humboldt, Planetario (P. Int.)	10·30 N	66·50 W
68a	Hunters Hill	33·50 S	151·09 E
54d	Huntington	38·48 N	77·15 W
57	Huntington Park	33·59 N	118·13 W
55c	Huntington Woods	42·29 N	83·10 W
62b	Hunt's Cross (Neigh.)	53·21 N	2·51 W
54d	Huntsville	38·55 N	76·54 W
58d	Hurlingham	34·36 S	58·38 W
68a	Hurstville	33·58 S	151·06 E
61	Husen (Neigh.)	51·33 N	7·36 E
64e	Hütteldorf (Neigh.)	48·12 N	16·16 E
61	Hüttenheim (Neigh.)	51·22 N	6·43 E
60	Hutton	51·38 N	0·22 E
61	Huttrop (Neigh.)	51·27 N	7·03 E
54d	Hyattsville	38·56 N	76·56 W
62b	Hyde	53·27 N	2·04 W
56a	Hyde Park (Neigh.)	41·48 N	87·36 W
67b	Hyōgo (Neigh.)	34·47 N	135·10 E
60	Hythe End	51·27 N	0·32 W

I

Page	Name Region	Lat. °′	Long. °′
67b	Ibaraki	34·49 N	135·34 E
58a	Iberoamericana, Universidad (P. Int.)	19·21 N	99·08 W
69d	Ibese	6·33 N	3·29 E
59d	Ibirapuera (Neigh.)	23·37 S	46·40 W
65a	Ichāpur	22·50 N	88·24 E
67a	Ichikawa	35·44 N	139·55 E
60	Ickenham (Neigh.)	51·34 N	0·27 W
61	Ickern (Neigh.)	51·36 N	7·21 E
69d	Iddo (Neigh.)	6·28 N	3·23 E
54d	Idylwood	38·54 N	77·12 W
69d	Iganmu (Neigh.)	6·29 N	3·22 E
69d	Igbobi	6·32 N	3·22 E
60	Ightham	51·17 N	0·17 E
67b	Ikeda	34·49 N	135·25 E
69d	Ikeja	6·36 N	3·21 E
67b	Ikoma	34·41 N	135·42 E
69d	Ikorodu	6·37 N	3·31 E
69d	Ikoyi (Neigh.)	6·27 N	3·26 E
69d	Ikoyi I.	6·27 N	3·26 E
67b	Ikuno (Neigh.)	34·39 N	135·33 E
67b	Ikuta (Neigh.)	34·42 N	135·11 E
54c	Ilchester	39·15 N	76·46 W
52b	Île-Cadieux	45·25 N	74·01 W
64d	Ilioúpolis	37·56 N	23·45 E
69b	Illovo	26·08 S	28·03 E
61	Ilverich	51·17 N	6·42 E
69a	Imbābah	30·04 N	31·13 E
67a	Inagi	35·38 N	139·30 E
67a	Inatsuke (Neigh.)	35·46 N	139·43 E
62b	Ince	53·17 N	2·49 W
62b	Ince Blundell	53·31 N	3·02 W
54a	Independence	41·23 N	81·39 W
54b	Independence National Historical Park (P. Int.)	39·57 N	75·09 W
61	In der Bredde	51·20 N	7·23 E
65d	India Gate (P. Int.)	28·37 N	77·18 E
56a	Indian Head Park	41·47 N	87·54 W
55b	Indianola	40·34 N	79·51 W
59d	Indianópolis (Neigh.)	23·36 S	46·38 W
54d	Indian Springs	38·49 N	77·10 W
66k	Indonesian Culture, Institute of (P. Int.)	6·09 N	106·49 E
69b	Industria (Neigh.)	26·12 S	27·59 E
60	Ingatestone	51·41 N	0·22 E
58d	Ingeniero Budge (Neigh.)	34·43 S	58·28 W
68a	Ingleburn	34·00 S	150·52 E
56b	Ingleside (Neigh.)	37·43 N	122·28 W
57	Inglewood	33·58 N	118·21 W
55b	Ingomar	40·35 N	80·05 W
55b	Ingram	40·26 N	80·04 W
60	Ingrave	51·36 N	0·21 E
55c	Inkster	42·17 N	83·17 W
53	Inwood	40·37 N	73·45 W
64e	Inzersdorf (Neigh.)	48·09 N	16·21 E
59c	Ipanema (Neigh.)	22·59 S	43·12 W
62b	Irby	53·21 N	3·07 W
62b	Irlam	53·28 N	2·25 W
68a	Iron Cove (B.)	33·52 S	151·10 E
56a	Irving Park (Neigh.)	41·57 N	87·43 W
54c	Irvington (Neigh.)	39·17 N	76·41 W
69b	Isando	26·09 S	28·12 E
53	Iselin	40·34 N	74·19 W
58d	Isidro Casanova	34·42 S	58·35 W
53	Island Park	40·36 N	73·40 W
60	Isleworth (Neigh.)	51·28 N	0·20 W
52c	Islington (Neigh.), Can.	43·39 N	79·32 W
60	Islington (Neigh.), Eng.	51·34 N	0·06 W
69a	Ismā'īlīyah (Neigh.)	30·03 N	31·14 E
62c	Issy-les-Moulineaux	48·49 N	2·17 E
64f	İstanbul	41·01 N	28·58 E
60	Istead Rise	51·24 N	0·22 E
59c	Itaipu	22·58 S	43·02 W
59c	Itaipu, Ponta de (C.)	22·59 S	43·03 W
67b	Itami	34·46 N	135·25 E
59d	Itaquaquecetuba	23·29 S	46·21 W
69d	Itire	6·31 N	3·21 E
58d	Ituzaingó	34·40 S	58·40 W
59d	Iupeba	23·41 S	46·22 W
68b	Ivanhoe	37·46 S	145·03 E
60	Iver	51·31 N	0·30 W
60	Iver Heath	51·32 N	0·31 W
62c	Ivry-sur-Seine	48·49 N	2·23 E
58a	Ixtacalco	19·23 N	99·07 W
58a	Ixtapalapa	19·21 N	99·06 W

J

Page	Name Region	Lat. °′	Long. °′
69b	Jabavu	26·15 S	27·53 E
59c	Jacarepaguá (Neigh.)	22·56 S	43·20 W
68a	Jackson, Port (B.)	33·50 S	151·16 E
53	Jackson Heights (Neigh.)	40·45 N	73·53 W
58b	Jacomino	23·06 N	82·20 W
66a	Jade Buddha, Temple of the (Yufosi) (P. Int.)	31·14 N	121·26 E
53	Jamaica (Neigh.)	40·42 N	73·47 W
53	Jamaica B.	40·36 N	73·51 W
69a	Jamālīyah (Neigh.)	30·03 N	31·16 E
69b	Jameson Raid Memorial (P. Int.)	26·11 S	27·49 E
59d	Jardim Paulista (Neigh.)	23·35 S	46·40 W
58a	Jardines del Pedregal de San Angel	19·18 N	99·13 W
64b	Jasenevo (Neigh.)	55·36 N	37·33 E
69a	Jazīrat Muḥammad	30·07 N	31·12 E
64e	Jedlesee (Neigh.)	48·16 N	16·23 E
55b	Jefferson	39·56 N	80·04 W
56a	Jefferson Park (Neigh.)	41·59 N	87·46 W
54b	Jenkintown	40·06 N	75·08 W
53	Jericho	40·48 N	73·32 W
53	Jersey City	40·44 N	74·02 W
52b	Jésus, Île (I.)	45·35 N	73·45 W
58b	Jesús del Monte (Neigh.)	23·06 N	82·22 W
58c	Jesús María	12·04 S	77·04 W
65a	Jhenkāri	22·46 N	88·18 E
65d	Jhil Kuranga (Neigh.)	28·40 N	77·17 E
66a	Jiangwan	31·18 N	121·29 E
65b	Jiugang	39·49 N	116·27 E
69b	Johannesburg	26·15 S	28·00 E
63a	Johannisthal (Neigh.)	52·26 N	13·30 E
54a	John Carroll University (P. Int.)	41·29 N	81·32 W
53	John F. Kennedy International Arpt.	40·38 N	73·47 W
54c	Johns Hopkins University (P. Int.)	39·20 N	76·37 W
65c	Johore Bahru	1·27 N	103·45 E
65c	Johore Str.	1·28 N	103·48 E
62c	Joinville-le-Pont	48·49 N	2·28 E
58d	José C. Paz	34·32 S	58·44 W
62c	Jouy-en-Josas	48·46 N	2·10 E
58d	Juan Anchorena (Neigh.)	34·29 S	58·30 W
58a	Juan González Romero	19·30 N	99·04 W
64b	Jugo-Zapad (Neigh.)	55·40 N	37·32 E
62c	Juilly	49·01 N	2·42 E
54b	Juniata (Neigh.)	40·01 N	75·07 W
65c	Jurong	1·21 N	103·42 E
56a	Justice	41·45 N	87·50 W
62c	Juvisy-sur-Orge	48·41 N	2·23 E
65d	Jwālahari (Neigh.)	28·40 N	77·06 E

K

Page	Name Region	Lat. °′	Long. °′
61	Kaarst	51·14 N	6·37 E
61	Kabel (Neigh.)	51·24 N	7·29 E
64f	Kadıköy (Neigh.)	40·59 N	29·01 E
67b	Kadoma	34·44 N	135·35 E
64e	Kagran (Neigh.)	48·15 N	16·27 E
67a	Kaidori	35·37 N	139·27 E
64d	Kaisarianí	37·58 N	23·47 E
64e	Kaisermühlen (Neigh.)	48·14 N	16·26 E
61	Kaiserswerth (Neigh.)	51·18 N	6·44 E
64d	Kalamákion	37·55 N	23·43 E
69c	Kalina (Neigh.)	4·18 S	15·16 E
65d	Kālkāji (Neigh.)	28·33 N	77·16 E
64e	Kalksburg (Neigh.)	48·08 N	16·15 E
61	Kalkum	51·18 N	6·46 E
64d	Kallithéa	37·57 N	23·42 E
65a	Kāmārhāti	22·40 N	88·22 E
67a	Kamata (Neigh.)	35·33 N	139·43 E
65a	Kāmdebpur	22·54 N	88·20 E
67a	Kameari (Neigh.)	35·46 N	139·51 E
67a	Kameido (Neigh.)	35·42 N	139·50 E
67a	Kamiakatsuka (Neigh.)	35·46 N	139·39 E
67a	Kamiasao	35·35 N	139·30 E
67a	Kamiishihara	35·39 N	139·32 E
67a	Kamikitazawa (Neigh.)	35·40 N	139·38 E
67a	Kamioyamada	35·35 N	139·24 E
67a	Kamitsuruma	35·31 N	139·25 E
67a	Kamoshida (Neigh.)	35·34 N	139·30 E
61	Kamp-Lintfort	51·30 N	6·31 E
65c	Kampong Kranji	1·26 N	103·46 E
65c	Kampong Loyang	1·22 N	103·58 E
65c	Kampong Tanjong Keling	1·18 N	103·42 E
67a	Kanai	35·35 N	139·28 E
67a	Kanamachi (Neigh.)	35·56 N	139·53 E
67a	Kanamori	35·32 N	139·28 E
68b	Kangaroo Ground	37·41 S	145·13 E
67b	Kanzaki (R.)	34·42 N	135·25 E
61	Kapellen	51·25 N	6·35 E
64b	Kapotn'a (Neigh.)	55·38 N	37·48 E
65e	Karave	19·01 N	73·01 E
65d	Karkar Dūmān (Neigh.)	28·39 N	77·18 E
61	Karnap	51·09 N	6·56 E
63a	Karolinenhof (Neigh.)	52·23 N	13·38 E
67a	Kasai (Neigh.)	35·39 N	139·53 E
67b	Kashiwara	34·35 N	135·37 E
61	Kasslerfeld (Neigh.)	51·26 N	6·45 E
67b	Katano	34·48 N	135·42 E
67a	Katayama (Neigh.)	35·46 N	139·34 E
61	Katernberg (Neigh.), F.R.G.	51·29 N	7·04 E
66e	Katsura (R.)	34·53 N	135·42 E
67a	Katsushika (Neigh.)	35·43 N	139·51 E
61	Katternberg (Neigh.)	51·09 N	7·02 E
63a	Kaulsdorf-Süd (Neigh.)	52·29 N	13·34 E
67a	Kawaguchi	35·48 N	139·43 E
67b	Kawanishi	34·49 N	135·24 E
67a	Kawasaki	35·32 N	139·43 E
67a	Kawashima (Neigh.)	35·28 N	139·35 E
53	Kearny	40·46 N	74·09 W
62b	Kearsley	53·32 N	2·23 W
66k	Kebondjeruk	6·12 S	106·46 E
68b	Keilor	37·43 S	144·50 E
64g	Kelenföld (Neigh.)	47·28 N	19·03 E
68a	Kellyville	33·43 S	150·57 E
60	Kelvedon Hatch	51·40 N	0·16 E
61	Kemminghausen (Neigh.)	51·34 N	7·29 E
69b	Kempton Park	26·06 S	28·14 E
60	Kemsing	51·18 N	0·14 E
52a	Kenberma	42·17 N	70·52 W
56a	Kenilworth, Il.	42·05 N	87·43 W
53	Kenilworth, NJ.	40·41 N	74·18 W
60	Kenley (Neigh.)	51·19 N	0·06 W
55a	Kenmore	42·58 N	78·53 W
68a	Kensington, Austl.	33·55 S	151·14 E
56b	Kensington, Ca.	37·54 N	122·16 W
54d	Kensington, Md.	39·02 N	77·03 W
53	Kensington (Neigh.), NY.	40·39 N	73·58 W
54b	Kensington (Neigh.), Pa.	39·58 N	75·08 W
69b	Kensington (Neigh.), S. Afr.	26·12 S	28·06 E
60	Kensington and Chelsea (Neigh.)	51·29 N	0·11 W
54d	Kentland	38·55 N	76·53 W
68b	Keon Park	37·42 S	145·01 E
64d	Keratsínion	37·58 N	23·37 E
61	Kettwig	51·22 N	6·56 E
68b	Kew, Austl.	37·49 S	145·02 E
69b	Kew, S. Afr.	26·08 S	28·06 E
60	Kew Gardens (P. Int.)	51·28 N	0·18 W
64d	Khaïdhárion	37·33 N	22·53 E
65d	Khajuri (Neigh.)	28·43 N	77·16 E
64d	Khalándrion	38·01 N	23·48 E
65a	Khardah	22·44 N	88·22 E
65d	Khayāla (Neigh.)	28·40 N	77·06 E
65d	Khichripur (Neigh.)	28·37 N	77·19 E
64d	Kholargós	38·00 N	23·48 E
65a	Khorel	22·42 N	88·19 E
69c	Kibouendé	4·19 S	15·11 E
67a	Kichijōji	35·42 N	139·35 E
65a	Kidderpore (Neigh.)	22·31 N	88·19 E
61	Kierspe	51·08 N	7·35 E
68a	Killara	33·46 S	151·09 E
68a	Killarney Heights	33·46 S	151·13 E
65d	Kilokri (Neigh.)	28·35 N	77·16 E
60	King George's Res.	51·39 N	0·01 W
54b	King of Prussia	40·05 N	75·23 W
60	Kingsbury (Neigh.)	51·35 N	0·17 W
60	Kingsdown	51·21 N	0·17 E
68a	Kingsford	33·56 S	151·14 E
68a	Kingsgrove	33·57 S	151·06 E
60	Kings Langley	51·43 N	0·28 W
54d	Kings Park	38·48 N	77·15 W
53	Kings Point	40·49 N	73·45 W
60	Kingston upon Thames (Neigh.)	51·25 N	0·19 W
69c	Kinshasa (Léopoldville)	4·18 S	15·18 E
69c	Kinshasa-Est (Neigh.)	4·18 S	15·18 E
69c	Kinshasa-Ouest (Neigh.)	4·20 S	15·15 E
69c	Kintamo, Rapides de	4·19 S	15·15 E
69c	Kintsana	4·19 S	15·10 E
61	Kirchderne (Neigh.)	51·33 N	7·30 E
61	Kirchende	51·25 N	7·26 E
61	Kirchhellen	51·36 N	6·55 E
61	Kirchhellen Heide (For.)	51·36 N	6·53 E
61	Kirchhörde (Neigh.)	51·27 N	7·27 E
61	Kirchlinde (Neigh.)	51·32 N	7·22 E
69a	Kirdāsah	30·02 N	31·07 E
62b	Kirkby	53·29 N	2·54 W
62b	Kirkdale (Neigh.)	53·26 N	2·59 W
52b	Kirkland	45·27 N	73·52 W
54d	Kirkwood	38·57 N	76·58 W
55b	Kirwan Heights	40·22 N	80·06 W
66h	Kishar Bāla	35·49 N	51·13 E
64f	Kısıklı (Neigh.)	41·01 N	29·03 E
67a	Kiso	35·34 N	139·26 E
64g	Kistarcsa	47·33 N	19·16 E
67a	Kita (Neigh.)	35·45 N	139·44 E
67a	Kitamachi (Neigh.)	35·46 N	139·39 E
69c	Kitamba (Neigh.)	4·19 S	15·14 E
67b	Kitatawara	34·44 N	135·42 E
67a	Kiyose	35·47 N	139·32 E
67a	Kizuki	35·34 N	139·40 E
67b	Kizuri	34·39 N	135·34 E
64e	Kledering (Neigh.)	48·08 N	16·26 E
61	Kleef	51·11 N	6·56 E
63a	Kleinbeeren	52·22 N	13·20 E
69b	Klein Elandsvlei	26·09 S	27·39 E
61	Kleinenbroich	51·12 N	6·35 E
63a	Kleinmachnow	52·24 N	13·15 E
63a	Klein Ziethen	52·23 N	13·27 E
61	Kley (Neigh.)	51·30 N	7·22 E
69b	Klip (R.)	26·16 S	27·49 E
69b	Klippoortje	26·17 S	28·14 E
69b	Kliptown	26·17 S	27·53 E
60	Knockholt	51·18 N	0·06 E
60	Knockholt Pound	51·19 N	0·08 E
69b	Knoppiesfontein	26·05 S	28·25 E
57	Knott's Berry Farm (P. Int.)	33·50 N	118·00 W
62b	Knotty Ash (Neigh.)	53·25 N	2·54 W
62b	Knowsley	53·27 N	2·51 W
62b	Knowsley Hall (P. Int.)	53·26 N	2·50 W
67b	Kōbe	34·41 N	135·10 E
67a	Kodaira	35·44 N	139·29 E
67a	Koganei	35·42 N	139·32 E
68a	Kogarah	33·58 S	151·08 E
67a	Kokubunji	35·42 N	139·29 E
64b	Kolomenskoje (Neigh.)	55·40 N	37·41 E
63a	Kolonie Stolp	52·28 N	13·46 E
67a	Komae	35·38 N	139·35 E
67a	Komagome (Neigh.)	35·44 N	139·45 E
65d	Kondli (Neigh.)	28·37 N	77·19 E
61	Königshardt (Neigh.)	51·33 N	6·51 E
65a	Konnagar	22·42 N	88·22 E
67b	Konohana (Neigh.)	34·41 N	135·16 E
67b	Kōnoike	34·42 N	135·37 E
68b	Kooyong	37·50 S	145·02 E
67b	Kōri	34·47 N	135·39 E
64d	Koridhallós	37·59 N	23·39 E
64b	Kosino	55·43 N	37·52 E
64b	Kosmosa, Monument (P. Int.)	55·49 N	37·38 E
67a	Kōtō (Neigh.)	35·41 N	139·48 E
66c	Kowloon (Jiulong)	22·18 N	114·10 E
66c	Kowloon City	22·19 N	114·11 E
67a	Kozukue (Neigh.)	35·30 N	139·36 E
61	Krahenhöhe (Neigh.)	51·10 N	7·06 E
63a	Krampnitz	52·28 N	13·04 E
64b	Krasnyj Stroitel' (Neigh.)	55·35 N	37·37 E
61	Kray (Neigh.)	51·28 N	7·05 E
61	Krefeld	51·20 N	6·34 E
64b	Kreml' (P. Int.)	55·45 N	37·37 E
61	Kreuzberg	51·09 N	7·27 E
63a	Kreuzberg (Neigh.)	52·30 N	13·23 E
65a	Krishnapur	22·36 N	88·26 E
69b	Krugersdorp	26·05 S	27·35 E
69b	Krugersdorp West	26·06 S	27·45 E
61	Krummenerl	51·05 N	7·45 E
63a	Krummensee	52·36 N	13·42 E
64b	Krylatskoje (Neigh.)	55·45 N	37·26 E
64f	Küçükbakkal	40·58 N	29·06 E
60	Kudbrooke (Neigh.)	51·28 N	0·03 E
61	Küllenhahn (Neigh.)	51·14 N	7·08 E
67a	Kunitachi	35·41 N	139·26 E
61	Kupferdreh (Neigh.)	51·23 N	7·05 E
61	Kurl (Neigh.)	51·35 N	7·35 E
65e	Kurla (Neigh.)	19·05 N	72·53 E
68a	Kurnell	34·01 S	151·13 E
64f	Kuruçeşme (Neigh.)	41·03 N	29·02 E

Page	Name Region	Lat. °′	Long. °′
63b	Prado, Museo del (P. Int.)	40·25 N	3·41 W
58a	Prado Churubusco	19·21 N	99·07 W
68b	Prahran	37·51 S	144·59 E
63d	Praia da Cruz Quebrada	38·42 N	9·14 W
63e	Prat del Llobregat	41·20 N	2·06 E
60	Pratt's Bottom (Neigh.)	51·20 N	0·07 E
62b	Prenton	53·22 N	3·03 W
63a	Prenzlauer Berg (Neigh.)	52·32 N	13·26 E
62b	Prescot	53·26 N	2·48 W
59d	Presidente Roosevelt, Estação (P. Int.)	23·33 S	46·36 W
56b	Presidio of San Francisco (P. Int.)	37·48 N	122·28 W
68b	Preston	37·45 S	145·01 E
62b	Prestwich	53·32 N	2·17 W
54b	Primos	39·55 N	75·18 W
69b	Primrose	26·12 S	28·10 E
68a	Prospect	33·48 S	150·56 E
56a	Prospect Heights	42·06 N	87·56 W
53	Prospect Park, NJ.	40·56 N	74·10 W
54b	Prospect Park, Pa.	39·53 N	75·19 W
69b	Protea	26·17 S	27·51 E
59b	Providencia	33·26 S	70·37 W
62b	Puddington	53·15 N	3·00 W
58c	Pueblo Libre	12·08 S	77·05 W
63b	Pueblo Nuevo (Neigh.)	40·26 N	3·39 W
56a	Pullman (Neigh.)	41·43 N	87·36 W
54c	Pumphrey	39·13 N	76·38 W
68a	Punchbowl	33·56 S	151·03 E
65c	Punggol	1·25 N	103·55 E
58b	Punta Brava	23·01 N	82·30 W
60	Purfleet	51·29 N	0·15 E
64e	Purkersdorf	48·12 N	16·11 E
60	Purley (Neigh.)	51·20 N	0·07 W
62c	Puteaux	48·53 N	2·14 E
69b	Putfontein	26·08 S	28·24 E
65d	Puth Kalān (Neigh.)	28·43 N	77·05 E
64b	Putilkovo	55·52 N	37·23 E
60	Putney (Neigh.)	51·28 N	0·13 W
61	Pütt	51·11 N	6·59 E
68a	Pymble	33·45 S	151·09 E
60	Pyrford	51·19 N	0·30 W

Q

Page	Name Region	Lat. °′	Long. °′
66h	Qaṣr-e Fīrūzeh	35·40 N	51·32 E
66a	Qibao	31·09 N	121·20 E
65b	Qieshikou	39·59 N	116·24 E
65b	Qinghe	40·01 N	116·20 E
65b	Qinghuayuan	40·00 N	116·19 E
64c	Quadraro (Neigh.)	41·51 N	12·33 E
68a	Quakers Hill	33·43 S	150·53 E
63d	Queluz	38·45 N	9·15 W
61	Querenburg (Neigh.)	51·27 N	7·16 E
66g	Quezon City	14·38 N	121·00 E
58d	Quilmes	34·43 S	58·15 W
52a	Quincy	42·15 N	71·01 W
52a	Quincy B.	42·17 N	70·58 W
59b	Quinta Normal	33·27 S	70·42 W
63c	Quinto Romano (Neigh.)	45·29 N	9·05 E
59d	Quitaúna	23·31 S	46·47 W

R

Page	Name Region	Lat. °′	Long. °′
61	Raadt (Neigh.)	51·24 N	6·56 E
64e	Raasdorf	48·15 N	16·34 E
62b	Raby	53·19 N	3·02 W
69b	Raceview	26·17 S	28·08 E
62b	Radcliffe	53·34 N	2·20 W
61	Radevormwald	51·12 N	7·21 E
60	Radlett	51·42 N	0·20 W
54b	Radnor	40·02 N	75·21 W
58d	Rafael Castillo	34·42 S	58·37 W
61	Rahm (Neigh.)	51·21 N	6·47 E
63a	Rahnsdorf (Neigh.)	52·26 N	13·42 E
53	Rahway	40·37 N	74·17 W
62b	Rainford	53·30 N	2·48 W
62b	Rainhill	53·26 N	2·46 W
62b	Rainhill Stoops	53·24 N	2·45 W
65d	Rājpur (Neigh.)	28·41 N	77·12 E
64g	Rákoscsaba (Neigh.)	47·29 N	19·17 E
64g	Rákoshegy (Neigh.)	47·28 N	19·14 E
64g	Rákoskeresztúr (Neigh.)	47·29 N	19·15 E
64g	Rákosliget (Neigh.)	47·30 N	19·16 E
64g	Rákospalota (Neigh.)	47·34 N	19·08 E
64g	Rákosszentmihály (Neigh.)	47·32 N	19·11 E
64b	Ramenka (Neigh.)	55·41 N	37·30 E
62b	Ramsbottom	53·40 N	2·19 W
60	Ramsden Heath	51·38 N	0·28 E
68a	Ramsgate	33·59 S	151·08 E
54c	Ranchleigh	39·22 N	76·40 W
57	Rancho Palos Verdes	33·45 N	118·24 W
54c	Randallstown	39·22 N	76·48 W
69b	Randburg	26·06 S	27·59 E
52a	Randolph	42·10 N	71·03 W
68a	Randwick	33·55 S	151·15 E
63d	Ranholas	38·47 N	9·22 W
55b	Rankin	40·25 N	79·53 W
61	Rath (Neigh.)	51·17 N	6·49 E
61	Rathmecke	51·15 N	7·38 E
61	Ratingen	51·18 N	6·51 E
69b	Ravenswood	26·11 S	28·15 E
54d	Ravensworth	38·48 N	77·13 W
54d	Ravenwood	38·52 N	77·09 W
52a	Reading	42·31 N	71·07 W
52a	Readville (Neigh.)	42·14 N	71·08 W
58c	Real Felipe, Castillo (P. Int.)	12·04 S	77·09 W
54b	Rebel Hill	40·04 N	75·20 W
61	Recklinghausen	51·36 N	7·13 E
61	Recklinghausen-Süd (Neigh.)	51·34 N	7·13 E
58d	Reconquista (R.)	34·27 S	58·36 W
54b	Red Bank	39·52 N	75·10 W
60	Redbridge (Neigh.)	51·34 N	0·05 E
62b	Reddish	53·26 N	2·09 W
55c	Redford (Neigh.)	42·25 N	83·16 W
55c	Redford Township	42·25 N	83·16 W
57	Red Hill	33·45 N	117·48 W
57	Redondo Beach	33·51 N	118·23 W
56b	Redwood City	37·29 N	122·13 W
68a	Regents Park	33·53 S	151·02 E
60	Regent's Park (P. Int.)	51·32 N	0·09 W
58b	Regla	23·08 N	82·20 W
53	Rego Park (Neigh.)	40·44 N	73·52 W
61	Reh	51·22 N	7·33 E
61	Reisholz (Neigh.)	51·11 N	6·52 E
58d	Remedios de Escalada (Neigh.)	34·43 S	58·23 W
61	Remscheid	51·11 N	7·11 E
59b	Renca	33·24 S	70·44 W
59b	Renca, Cerro (Mtn.)	33·23 S	70·43 W
57	Reseda (Neigh.)	34·12 N	118·31 W
68b	Reservoir	37·43 S	145·00 E
61	Resse (Neigh.)	51·34 N	7·07 E
63b	Retiro, Parque del (P. Int.)	40·25 N	3·41 W
61	Reusrath	51·06 N	6·57 E
64b	Reutov	55·46 N	37·52 E
52a	Revere	42·24 N	71·01 W
68a	Revesby	33·57 S	151·01 E
66h	Rey	35·35 N	51·25 E
61	Rheinberg	51·33 N	6·35 E
61	Rheinen	51·27 N	7·38 E
61	Rheinhausen	51·24 N	6·44 E
61	Rhein-Herne-Kanal (Can.)	51·27 N	6·47 E
61	Rheinkamp	51·30 N	6·37 E
61	Rhine (Rhein) (R.)	51·52 N	6·02 E
63c	Rho	45·32 N	9·02 E
68a	Rhodes, Austl.	33·50 S	151·05 E
62b	Rhodes, Eng.	53·33 N	2·14 W
62c	Rhodon	48·43 N	2·04 E
68b	Richmond, Austl.	37·49 S	145·00 E
56b	Richmond, Ca.	37·57 N	122·22 W
60	Richmond (Neigh.), Eng.	51·28 N	0·18 W
54b	Richmond (Neigh.), Pa.	39·59 N	75·06 W
54a	Richmond Heights	41·33 N	81·29 W
53	Richmond Hill (Neigh.)	40·42 N	73·49 W
53	Richmondtown Restoration (P. Int.)	40·34 N	74·09 W
53	Richmond Valley (Neigh.)	40·31 N	74·13 W
68b	Ricketts Pt.	38·00 S	145·02 E
60	Rickmansworth	51·39 N	0·29 W
60	Ridge	51·41 N	0·15 W
53	Ridgefield	40·50 N	74·00 W
53	Ridgefield Park	40·51 N	74·01 W
53	Ridgewood	40·59 N	74·07 W
53	Ridgewood (Neigh.)	40·42 N	73·53 W
54b	Ridley Park	39·53 N	75·19 W
61	Riemke (Neigh.)	51·30 N	7·13 E
69b	Rietvlei	26·18 S	28·03 E
58c	Rímac	12·02 S	77·03 W
58c	Rímac (R.)	12·02 S	77·09 W
58b	Rincón	22·57 N	82·25 W
68b	Ringwood	37·49 S	145·14 E
68b	Ringwood North	37·48 S	145·14 E
59c	Rio Comprido (Neigh.)	22·55 S	43·12 W
59c	Rio de Janeiro	22·54 S	43·15 W
63d	Rio de Mouro	38·46 N	9·20 W
59a	Rio Grande	10·35 N	66·57 W
60	Ripley	51·18 N	0·29 W
65a	Rishra	22·43 N	88·21 E
54d	Ritchie	38·52 N	76·52 W
65d	Rithāla (Neigh.)	28·43 N	77·06 E
54d	Riverdale	38·58 N	76·55 W
53	Riverdale (Neigh.)	40·54 N	73·54 W
53	River Edge	40·56 N	74·02 W
56a	River Forest	41·53 N	87·49 W
56a	River Grove	41·56 N	87·50 W
60	Riverhead	51·17 N	0·10 E
56a	Riverside, Il.	41·50 N	87·49 W
54b	Riverside, NJ.	40·02 N	74·58 W
56a	Robbins	41·39 N	87·42 W
69b	Robertsham (Neigh.)	26·15 S	28·00 E
69b	Robinson	26·09 S	27·43 E
59c	Rocha Miranda (Neigh.)	22·52 S	43·22 W
59c	Rocha Sobrinho	22·47 S	43·25 W
53	Rochelle Park	40·55 N	74·04 W
53	Rockaway Park (Neigh.)	40·35 N	73·50 W
53	Rockaway Point (Neigh.)	40·33 N	73·55 W
54d	Rock Creek Park (P. Int.)	38·58 N	77·03 W
68a	Rockdale, Austl.	33·57 S	151·08 E
54c	Rockdale, Md.	39·21 N	76·46 W
53	Rockefeller Center (P. Int.)	40·45 N	74·00 W
62b	Rock Ferry	53·22 N	3·00 W
52a	Rockland	42·08 N	70·55 W
54b	Rockledge	40·03 N	75·05 W
53	Rockville Centre	40·40 N	73·37 W
54a	Rocky (R.)	41·30 N	81·49 W
66c	Rocky Hbr.	22·20 N	114·19 E
54a	Rocky River	41·30 N	81·40 W
62c	Rocquencourt	48·50 N	2·07 E
60	Roehampton (Neigh.)	51·27 N	0·14 W
68a	Rogans Hill	33·44 S	151·01 E
56a	Rogers Park (Neigh.)	42·01 N	87·40 W
61	Rohdenhaus	51·18 N	7·01 E
61	Röhlinghausen (Neigh.)	51·36 N	7·14 E
63a	Rohrbeck	52·32 N	13·02 E
62c	Roissy	48·47 N	2·39 E
62c	Roissy-en-France	49·00 N	2·31 E
69b	Roksana	26·07 S	28·04 E
67a	Rokugō (Neigh.)	35·33 N	139·43 E
54c	Rolling Acres	39·17 N	76·52 W
61	Röllinghausen (Neigh.)	51·31 N	7·08 E
57	Rolling Hills	33·46 N	118·21 W
62c	Romainville	48·53 N	2·26 E
64c	Rome (Roma)	41·54 N	12·29 E
62b	Romiley	53·25 N	2·05 W
69b	Rondebult	26·18 S	28·14 E
61	Ronsdorf (Neigh.)	51·14 N	7·12 E
69b	Roodepoort-Maraisburg	26·10 S	27·52 E
53	Roosevelt	40·41 N	73·36 W
68a	Rooty Hill	33·46 S	150·50 E
68b	Rosanna	37·45 S	145·04 E
69b	Rosebank (Neigh.)	26·09 S	28·02 E
68a	Rosebury (Neigh.)	33·55 S	151·12 E
52c	Rosedale (Neigh.), Can.	43·41 N	79·22 W
53	Rosedale (Neigh.), NY.	40·39 N	73·45 W
56a	Roseland (Neigh.)	41·42 N	87·38 W
53	Roselle	40·40 N	74·16 W
57	Rosemead	34·04 N	118·03 W
52b	Rosemère	45·38 N	73·48 W
56a	Rosemont, Il.	41·59 N	87·52 W
54b	Rosemont, Pa.	40·01 N	75·19 W
69b	Roseneath	26·17 S	28·11 E
63a	Rosenthal (Neigh.)	52·36 N	13·23 E
54b	Rose Tree	39·56 N	75·23 W
68a	Roseville, Austl.	33·47 S	151·11 E
55c	Roseville, Mi.	42·30 N	82·56 W
53	Roslyn, NY.	40·48 N	73·39 W
54b	Roslyn, Pa.	40·07 N	75·08 W
53	Roslyn Estates	40·47 N	73·40 W
53	Roslyn Heights	40·47 N	73·39 W
62c	Rosny-sous-Bois	48·53 N	2·29 E
68a	Rossmore	33·57 S	150·46 E
54c	Rossville	39·20 N	76·29 W
62b	Rostherne	53·21 N	2·23 W
64e	Roth-neusiedl (Neigh.)	48·08 N	16·23 E
57	Rowland Heights	33·59 N	117·54 W
68b	Rowville	37·56 S	145·14 E
52b	Roxboro	45·31 N	73·48 W
54b	Roxborough (Neigh.)	40·02 N	75·13 W
53	Roxbury (Neigh.)	40·34 N	73·54 W
60	Royal Albert Hall (P. Int.)	51·30 N	0·11 W
60	Royal Naval College (P. Int.)	51·29 N	0·01 W
55c	Royal Oak	42·30 N	83·08 W
55c	Royal Oak Township	42·27 N	83·10 W
52c	Royal Ontario Museum (P. Int.)	43·40 N	79·24 W
62b	Royton	53·34 N	2·08 W
68a	Rozelle	33·52 S	151·10 E
63a	Rüdersdorf	52·29 N	13·47 E
59d	Rudge Ramos	23·41 S	46·34 W
61	Rüdinghausen (Neigh.)	51·27 N	7·25 E
63a	Rudow (Neigh.)	52·25 N	13·30 E
62c	Rueil-Malmaison	48·53 N	2·11 E
61	Rüggeberg	51·16 N	7·22 E
63a	Ruhlsdorf	52·23 N	13·16 E
61	Ruhr (R.)	51·27 N	6·44 E
61	Ruhrort (Neigh.)	51·26 N	6·45 E
60	Ruislip (Neigh.)	51·34 N	0·25 W
64b	Rum'ancevo	55·38 N	37·26 E
64f	Rumelihisarı (Neigh.)	41·05 N	29·03 E
61	Rumeln-Kaldenhausen	51·24 N	6·40 E
63a	Rummelsburg (Neigh.)	52·30 N	13·29 E
61	Rummenohl	51·17 N	7·32 E
62b	Runcorn	53·20 N	2·44 W
54b	Runnemede	39·51 N	75·04 W
60	Runnymede (P. Int.)	51·26 N	0·34 W
55b	Rural Ridge	40·35 N	79·50 W
62b	Rusholme (Neigh.)	53·27 N	2·12 W
53	Russell Gardens	40·47 N	73·43 W
69b	Rusville	26·10 S	28·18 E
53	Rutherford	40·49 N	74·07 W
54b	Rutledge	39·54 N	75·20 W
61	Rüttenscheid (Neigh.)	51·26 N	7·00 E
60	Ryarsh	51·19 N	0·24 E
54b	Rydal	40·06 N	75·06 W
68a	Rydalmere	33·49 S	151·02 E
68a	Ryde	33·49 S	151·06 E
53	Rye	40·59 N	73·41 W
69b	Rynfield	26·09 S	28·20 E

S

Page	Name Region	Lat. °′	Long. °′
61	Saarn (Neigh.)	51·24 N	6·53 E
61	Saarnberg (Neigh.)	51·25 N	6·53 E
64b	Saburovo (Neigh.)	55·38 N	37·42 E
63d	Sacavém	38·47 N	9·06 W
62c	Sacré-Cœur (P. Int.)	48·53 N	2·21 E
63a	Sacrow (Neigh.)	52·26 N	13·06 E
53	Saddle Brook	40·54 N	74·06 W
53	Saddle Rock	40·48 N	73·45 W
65d	Safdar Jang's Tomb (P. Int.)	28·36 N	77·13 E
67a	Sagamihara	35·32 N	139·23 E
66m	Saigon, see Ho Chi Minh City	10·45 N	106·40 E
68b	Saint Albans, Austl.	37·45 S	144·48 E
60	Saint Albans, Eng.	51·46 N	0·21 W
53	Saint Albans (Neigh.)	40·42 N	73·46 W
60	Saint Albans Cathedral (P. Int.)	51·45 N	0·20 W
69c	Saint Anne of the Congo (P. Int.)	4·16 S	15·17 E
62c	Saint-Brice-sous-Forêt	49·00 N	2·21 E
52c	Saint-Bruno	45·32 N	73·21 W
55c	Saint Clair Shores	42·30 N	82·54 W
62c	Saint-Cloud	48·51 N	2·13 E
62c	Saint-Cyr-l'Ecole	48·48 N	2·04 E
54b	Saint Davids	40·02 N	75·22 W
62c	Saint-Denis	48·56 N	2·22 E
52b	Sainte-Dorothée (Neigh.)	45·32 N	73·49 W
52b	Saint-Eustache	45·33 N	73·53 W
52b	Sainte-Geneviève	45·29 N	73·52 W
53	Saint George (Neigh.)	40·39 N	74·05 W
62c	Saint-Germain-en-Laye	48·54 N	2·05 E
62c	Saint-Gratien	48·58 N	2·17 E
52b	Sainte-Hélène, Île (I.)	45·31 N	73·32 W
62b	Saint Helens	53·28 N	2·44 W
52b	Saint-Hubert	45·30 N	73·25 W
68a	Saint Ives	33·44 S	151·10 E
55a	Saint Johnsburg	43·05 N	78·53 W
53	Saint John's University (P. Int.)	40·43 N	73·48 W
68b	Saint Kilda	37·52 S	144·59 E
52c	Saint-Lambert	45·30 N	73·30 W
52b	Saint Laurent	45·30 N	73·40 W
62c	Saint-Mandé	48·50 N	2·25 E
60	Saint Mary Cray (Neigh.)	51·23 N	0·07 E
60	Saint Marylebone (Neigh.)	51·31 N	0·10 W
68a	Saint Marys	33·47 S	150·47 E
62c	Saint-Maur-des-Fossés	48·48 N	2·30 E
62c	Saint-Maurice	48·49 N	2·25 E
62c	Saint-Mesmes	48·59 N	2·42 E
52b	Saint-Michel	45·35 N	73·35 W
62c	Saint-Nom-la-Bretèche	48·51 N	2·01 E
62c	Saint-Ouen	48·54 N	2·20 E
60	Saint Pancras (Neigh.)	51·32 N	0·07 W
60	Saint Paul's Cathedral (P. Int.)	51·31 N	0·06 W
60	Saint Paul's Cray (Neigh.)	51·24 N	0·07 E
52b	Saint-Pierre	45·27 N	73·39 W
62c	Saint-Prix	49·01 N	2·16 E
62c	Saint-Rémy-lès-Chevreuse	48·42 N	2·04 E
52b	Sainte-Rose (Neigh.)	45·36 N	73·47 W
52b	Sainte-Thérèse-de-Blainville	45·38 N	73·51 W
62c	Saint-Thibault-des-Vignes	48·52 N	2·41 E
52b	Saint-Vincent-de-Paul (Neigh.)	45·37 N	73·39 W
67b	Sakai	34·35 N	135·28 E
62b	Sale	53·26 N	2·19 W
52a	Salem	42·31 N	70·55 W
62b	Salford	53·28 N	2·18 W
65a	Salkhia	22·35 N	88·21 E
65d	Samāika (Neigh.)	28·32 N	77·05 E
58a	San Andrés Totoltepec	19·15 N	99·10 W
59a	San Antonio de Galipán	10·33 N	66·53 W
57	San Antonio Heights	34·10 N	117·40 W
63e	San Bartolomé de la Cuadra	41·26 N	2·02 E
63e	San Baudilio de Llobregat	41·21 N	2·03 E
56b	San Bruno	37·37 N	122·25 W
56b	San Carlos	37·31 N	122·16 W
66d	Sanchung	25·04 N	121·29 E
63e	San Clemente de Llobregat	41·20 N	2·00 E
63e	San Cugat del Vallés	41·28 N	2·05 E
60	Sanderstead (Neigh.)	51·20 N	0·05 W
57	San Dimas	34·06 N	117·49 W
68b	Sandringham	37·57 S	145·00 E
69b	Sandringham (Neigh.)	26·09 S	28·07 E
53	Sands Point	40·51 N	73·43 W
58a	San Felipe Terremotos	19·22 N	99·04 W
63e	San Feliu de Llobregat	41·23 N	2·03 E
58d	San Fernando	34·26 S	58·34 W
56b	San Francisco	37·48 N	122·24 W
56b	San Francisco B.	37·43 N	122·17 W
58a	San Francisco Culhuacán	19·20 N	99·06 W
58b	San Francisco de Paula	23·04 N	82·18 W

glossary of foreign geographical terms

Annam .... Annamese
Arab .... Arabic
Bantu .... Bantu
Bur .... Burmese
Camb .... Cambodian
Celt .... Celtic
Chn .... Chinese
Czech .... Czech
Dan .... Danish
Du .... Dutch
Fin .... Finnish
Fr .... French
Ger .... German
Gr .... Greek
Hung .... Hungarian
Ice .... Icelandic
India .... India
Indian .... American Indian
Indon .... Indonesian
It .... Italian
Jap .... Japanese
Kor .... Korean
Mal .... Malayan
Mong .... Mongolian
Nor .... Norwegian
Per .... Persian
Pol .... Polish
Port .... Portuguese
Rom .... Romanian
Rus .... Russian
Siam .... Siamese
So. Slav .... Southern Slavonic
Sp .... Spanish
Swe .... Swedish
Tib .... Tibetan
Tur .... Turkish
Yugo .... Yugoslav

å, *Nor., Swe* .... brook, river
aa, *Dan., Nor* .... brook
aas, *Dan., Nor* .... ridge
āb, *Per* .... water, river
abad, *India, Per* .... town, city
ada, *Tur* .... island
adrar, *Berber* .... mountain
air, *Indon* .... stream
akrotírion, *Gr* .... cape
älf, *Swe* .... river
alp, *Ger* .... mountain
altipiano, *It* .... plateau
alto, *Sp* .... height
archipel, *Fr* .... archipelago
archipiélago, *Sp* .... archipelago
arquipélago, *Port* .... archipelago
arroyo, *Sp* .... brook, stream
ås, *Nor., Swe* .... ridge
austral, *Sp* .... southern
baai, *Du* .... bay
bab, *Arab* .... gate, port
bach, *Ger* .... brook, stream
backe, *Swe* .... hill
bad, *Ger* .... bath, spa
bahía, *Sp* .... bay, gulf
bahr, *Arab* .... river, sea, lake
baia, *It* .... bay, gulf
baía, *Port* .... bay
baie, *Fr* .... bay, gulf
bajo, *Sp* .... depression
bak, *Indon* .... stream
bakke, *Dan., Nor* .... hill
balkan, *Tur* .... mountain range
bana, *Jap* .... point, cape
banco, *Sp* .... bank
bandar, *Mal., Per.* .... town, port, harbor
bang, *Siam* .... village
bassin, *Fr* .... basin
batang, *Indon., Mal* .... river
ben, *Celt* .... mountain, summit
bender, *Arab* .... harbor, port
bereg, *Rus* .... coast, shore
berg, *Du., Ger., Nor., Swe.* .... mountain, hill
bir, *Arab* .... well
birkat, *Arab* .... lake, pond, pool
bit, *Arab* .... house
bjaerg, *Dan., Nor* .... mountain
bocche, *It* .... mouth
boğazı, *Tur* .... strait
bois, *Fr* .... forest, wood
boloto, *Rus* .... marsh
bolsón, *Sp* . flat-floored desert valley
boreal, *Sp* .... northern
borg, *Dan., Nor., Swe* . castle, town
borgo, *It* .... town, suburb
bosch, *Du* .... forest, wood
bouche, *Fr* .... river mouth
bourg, *Fr* .... town, borough
bro, *Dan., Nor., Swe* .... bridge
brücke, *Ger* .... bridge
bucht, *Ger* .... bay, bight
bugt, *Dan., Nor., Swe* ... bay, gulf
bulu, *Indon* .... mountain
burg, *Du., Ger* .... castle, town
buri, *Siam* .... town
burun, burnu, *Tur* .... cape
by, *Dan., Nor., Swe* .... village
caatinga, *Port. (Brazil)* .... open brushland
cabezo, *Sp* .... summit
cabo, *Port., Sp* .... cape
campo, *It., Port., Sp* ... plain, field
campos, *Port. (Brazil)* .... plains
cañón, *Sp* .... canyon
cap, *Fr* .... cape
capo, *It* .... cape
casa, *It., Port., Sp* .... house
castello, *It., Port* .... castle, fort
castillo, *Sp* .... castle
càte, *Fr* .... hill
çay, *Tur* .... stream, river
cayo, *Sp* .... rock, shoal, islet
cerro, *Sp* .... mountain, hill
champ, *Fr* .... field
chang, *Chn* .... village, middle
château, *Fr* .... castle
chen, *Chn* .... market town
chiang, *Chn* .... river
chott, *Arab* .... salt lake
chou, *Chn* . capital of district; island
chu, *Tib* .... water, stream
cidade, *Port* .... town, city
cima, *Sp* .... summit, peak
città, *It* .... town, city
ciudad, *Sp* .... town, city
cochilha, *Port* .... ridge
col, *Fr* .... pass
colina, *Sp* .... hill
cordillera, *Sp* .... mountain chain
costa, *It., Port., Sp* .... coast
côte, *Fr* .... coast
cuchilla, *Sp* .... mountain ridge
dağ, *Tur* .... mountain(s)
dake, *Jap* .... peak, summit
dal, *Dan., Du., Nor., Swe* ... valley
dan, *Kor* .... point, cape
danau, *Indon* .... lake
dar, *Arab* ... house, abode, country
darya, *Per* .... river, sea
dasht, *Per* .... plain, desert
deniz, *Tur* .... sea
désert, *Fr* .... desert
deserto, *It* .... desert
desierto, *Sp* .... desert
détroit, *Fr* .... strait
dijk, *Du* .... dam, dike
djebel, *Arab* .... mountain
do, *Kor* .... island
dorf, *Ger* .... village
dorp, *Du* .... village
duin, *Du* .... dune
dzong, *Tib.* .... fort, administrative capital
eau, *Fr* .... water
ecuador, *Sp* .... equator
eiland, *Du* .... island
elv, *Dan., Nor* .... river, stream
embalse, *Sp* .... reservoir
erg, *Arab* .... dune, sandy desert
est, *Fr., It* .... east
estado, *Sp* .... state
este, *Port., Sp* .... east
estrecho, *Sp* .... strait
étang, *Fr* .... pond, lake
état, *Fr* .... state
eyjar, *Ice* .... islands
feld, *Ger* .... field, plain
festung, *Ger* .... fortress
fiume, *It* .... river
fjäll, *Swe* .... mountain
fjärd, *Swe* .... bay, inlet
fjeld, *Nor* .... mountain, hill
fjord, *Dan., Nor* .... fiord, inlet
fjördur, *Ice* .... fiord, inlet
fleuve, *Fr* .... river
flod, *Dan., Swe* .... river
flói, *Ice* .... bay, marshland
fluss, *Ger* .... river
foce, *It* .... river mouth
fontein, *Du* .... a spring
forêt, *Fr* .... forest
fors, *Swe* .... waterfall
forst, *Ger* .... forest
fos, *Dan., Nor* .... waterfall
fu, *Chn* .... town, residence
fuente, *Sp* .... spring, fountain
fuerte, *Sp* .... fort
furt, *Ger* .... ford
gang, *Kor* .... stream, river
gangri, *Tib* .... mountain
gat, *Dan., Nor* .... channel
gàve, *Fr* .... stream
gawa, *Jap* .... river
gebergte, *Du* .... mountain range
gebiet, *Ger* .... district, territory
gebirge, *Ger* .... mountains
ghat, *India* ... pass, mountain range
gobi, *Mong* .... desert
gol, *Mong* .... river
göl, gölü, *Tur* .... lake
golf, *Du., Ger* .... gulf, bay
golfe, *Fr* .... gulf, bay
golfo, *It., Port., Sp* .... gulf, bay
gomba, gompa, *Tib* .... monastery
gora, *Rus., So. Slav* .... mountain
góra, *Pol* .... mountain
gorod, *Rus* .... town
grad, *Rus., So. Slav* .... town
guba, *Rus* .... bay, gulf
gundung, *Indon* .... mountain
guntō, *Jap* .... archipelago
gunung, *Mal* .... mountain
haf, *Swe* .... sea, ocean
hafen, *Ger* .... port, harbor
haff, *Ger* .... gulf, inland sea
hai, *Chn* .... sea, lake
hama, *Jap* .... beach, shore
hamada, *Arab* .... rocky plateau
hamn, *Swe* .... harbor
hāmūn, *Per* .... swampy lake, plain
hantō, *Jap* .... peninsula
hassi, *Arab* .... well, spring
haus, *Ger* .... house
haut, *Fr* .... summit, top
hav, *Dan., Nor* .... sea, ocean
havn, *Dan., Nor* .... harbor, port
havre, *Fr* .... harbor, port
háza, *Hung* .... house, dwelling of
heim, *Ger* .... hamlet, home
hem, *Swe* .... hamlet, home
higashi, *Jap* .... east
hisar, *Tur* .... fortress
hissar, *Arab* .... fort
ho, *Chn* .... river
hoek, *Du* .... cape
hof, *Ger* .... court, farm house
höfn, *Ice* .... harbor
hoku, *Jap* .... north
holm, *Dan., Nor., Swe* .... island
hora, *Czech* .... mountain
horn, *Ger* .... peak
hoved, *Dan., Nor* .... cape
hsien, *Chn* .. district, district capital
hu, *Chn* .... lake
hügel, *Ger* .... hill
huk, *Dan., Swe* .... point
hus, *Dan., Nor., Swe* .... house
île, *Fr* .... island
ilha, *Port* .... island
indsö, *Dan., Nor* .... lake
insel, *Ger* .... island
insjö, *Swe* .... lake
irmak, irmagi, *Tur* .... river
isla, *Sp* .... island
isola, *It* .... island
istmo, *It., Sp* .... isthmus
järvi, jaur, *Fin* .... lake
jebel, *Arab* .... mountain
jima, *Jap* .... island
jökel, *Nor* .... glacier
joki, *Fin* .... river
jökull, *Ice* .... glacier
kaap, *Du* .... cape
kai, *Jap* .... bay, gulf, sea
kaikyō, *Jap* .... channel, strait
kalat, *Per* .... castle, fortress
kale, *Tur* .... fort
kali, *Mal* .... creek, river
kand, *Per* .... village
kang, *Chn* . mountain ridge; village
kap, *Dan., Ger* .... cape
kapp, *Nor., Swe* .... cape
kasr, *Arab* .... fort, castle
kawa, *Jap* .... river
kefr, *Arab* .... village
kei, *Jap* .... creek, river
ken, *Jap* .... prefecture
khor, *Arab* .... bay, inlet
khrebet, *Rus* .... mountain range
kiang, *Chn* .... large river
king, *Chn* .... capital city, town
kita, *Jap* .... north
ko, *Jap* .... lake
köbstad, *Dan* .... market-town
kol, *Mong* .... lake
kólpos, *Gr* .... gulf
kong, *Chn* .... river
kopf, *Ger* .... head, summit, peak
köpstad, *Swe* .... market-town
körfezi, *Tur* .... gulf
kosa, *Rus* .... spit
kou, *Chn* .... river mouth
köy, *Tur* .... village
kraal, *Du. (Africa)* ... native village
ksar, *Arab* .... fortified village
kuala, *Mal* .... bay, river mouth
kuh, *Per* .... mountain
kum, *Tur* .... sand
kuppe, *Ger* .... summit
küste, *Ger* .... coast
kyo, *Jap* .... town, capital
la, *Tib* .... mountain pass
labuan, *Mal* .... anchorage, port
lac, *Fr* .... lake
lago, *It., Port., Sp* .... lake
lagoa, *Port* .... lake, marsh
laguna, *It., Port., Sp* .... lagoon, lake
lahti, *Fin* .... bay, gulf
län, *Swe* .... county
landsby, *Dan., Nor* .... village
liehtao, *Chn* .... archipelago
liman, *Tur* .... bay, port
ling, *Chn* .... pass, ridge, mountain
llanos, *Sp* .... plains
loch, *Celt. (Scotland)* .... lake, bay
loma, *Sp* .... long, low hill
lough, *Celt. (Ireland)* .... lake, bay
machi, *Jap* .... town
man, *Kor* .... bay
mar, *Port., Sp* .... sea
mare, *It., Rom* .... sea
marisma, *Sp* .... marsh, swamp
mark, *Ger* .... boundary, limit
massif, *Fr* .... block of mountains
mato, *Port* .... forest, thicket
me, *Siam* .... river
meer, *Du., Ger* .... lake, sea
mer, *Fr* .... sea
mesa, *Sp* .... flat-topped mountain
meseta, *Sp* .... plateau
mina, *Port., Sp* .... mine
minami, *Jap* .... south
minato, *Jap* .... harbor, haven
misaki, *Jap* .... cape, headland
mont, *Fr* .... mount, mountain
montagna, *It* .... mountain
montagne, *Fr* .... mountain
montaña, *Sp* .... mountain
monte, *It., Port., Sp.* .... mount, mountain
more, *Rus., So. Slav* .... sea
morro, *Port., Sp* .... hill, bluff
mühle, *Ger* .... mill
mund, *Ger* .... mouth, opening
mündung, *Ger* .... river mouth
mura, *Jap* .... township
myit, *Bur* .... river
mys, *Rus* .... cape
nada, *Jap* .... sea
nadi, *India* .... river, creek
naes, *Dan., Nor* .... cape
nafud, *Arab* ... desert of sand dunes
nagar, *India* .... town, city
nahr, *Arab* .... river
nam, *Siam* .... river, water
nan, *Chn., Jap* .... south
näs, *Nor., Swe* .... cape
nez, *Fr* .... point, cape
nishi, nisi, *Jap* .... west
njarga, *Fin* .... peninsula
nong, *Siam* .... marsh
noord, *Du* .... north
nor, *Mong* .... lake
nord, *Dan., Fr., Ger., It., Nor., Swe* .... north
norte, *Port., Sp* .... north
nos, *Rus* .... cape
nyasa, *Bantu* .... lake
ö, *Dan., Nor., Swe* .... island
occidental, *Sp* .... western
ocna, *Rom* .... salt mine
odde, *Dan., Nor* .... point, cape
oedjoeng, *Mal* .... point, cape
oeste, *Port., Sp* .... west
oka, *Jap* .... hill
oost, *Du* .... east
oriental, *Sp* .... eastern
óros, *Gr* .... mountain
ost, *Ger., Swe* .... east
öster, *Dan., Nor., Swe* .... eastern
ostrov, *Rus* .... island
oued, *Arab* .... river, stream
ouest, *Fr* .... west
ozero, *Rus* .... lake
pää, *Fin* .... mountain
padang, *Mal* .... plain, field
pampas, *Sp. (Argentina)* .... grassy plains
pará, *Indian (Brazil)* .... river
pas, *Fr* .... channel, passage
paso, *Sp* ... mountain pass, passage
passo, *It., Port.* ... mountain pass, passage, strait
patam, *India* .... city, town
pei, *Chn* .... north
pélagos, *Gr* .... open sea
pegunungan, *Indon* .... mountains
peña, *Sp* .... rock
peresheyek, *Rus* .... isthmus
pertuis, *Fr* .... strait
peski, *Rus* .... desert
pic, *Fr* .... mountain peak
pico, *Port., Sp* .... mountain peak
piedra, *Sp* .... stone, rock
ping, *Chn* .... plain, flat
planalto, *Port* .... plateau
planina, *Yugo* .... mountains
playa, *Sp* .... shore, beach
pnom, *Camb* .... mountain
pointe, *Fr* .... point
polder, *Du., Ger* ... reclaimed marsh
polje, *So. Slav* .... plain, field
poluostrov, *Rus* .... peninsula
pont, *Fr* .... bridge
ponta, *Port* .... point, headland
ponte, *It., Port* .... bridge
pore, *India* .... city, town
porthmós, *Gr* .... strait
porto, *It., Port* .... port, harbor
potamós, *Gr* .... river
p'ov, *Rus* .... peninsula
prado, *Sp* .... field, meadow
presqu'île, *Fr* .... peninsula
proliv, *Rus* .... strait
pu, *Chn* .... commercial village
pueblo, *Sp* .... town, village
puerto, *Sp* .... port, harbor
pulau, *Mal* .... island
punkt, *Ger* .... point
punt, *Du* .... point
punta, *It., Sp* .... point
pur, *India* .... city, town
puy, *Fr* .... peak
qal'a, qal'at, *Arab* .... fort, village
qasr, *Arab* .... fort, castle
rann, *India* .... wasteland
ra's, *Arab* .... cape, head
reka, *Rus., So. Slav* .... river
reprêsa, *Port* .... reservoir
rettō, *Jap* .... island chain
ría, *Sp* .... estuary
ribeira, *Port* .... stream
riberão, *Port* .... river
rio, *It., Port* .... stream, river
río, *Sp* .... river
rivière, *Fr* .... river
roca, *Sp* .... rock
rt, *Yugo* .... cape
rūd, *Per* .... river
saari, *Fin* .... island
sable, *Fr* .... sand
sahara, *Arab* .... desert, plain
saki, *Jap* .... cape
sal, *Sp* .... salt
salar, *Sp* .... salt flat, salt lake
salto, *Sp* .... waterfall
san, *Jap., Kor* .... mountain, hill
sat, satul, *Rom* .... village
schloss, *Ger* .... castle
sebkha, *Arab* .... salt marsh
see, *Ger* .... lake, sea
şehir, *Tur* .... town, city
selat, *Indon* .... stream
selvas, *Port. (Brazil)* .... tropical rain forests
seno, *Sp* .... bay
serra, *Port* .... mountain chain
serranía, *Sp* .... mountain ridge
seto, *Jap* .... strait
severnaya, *Rus* .... northern
shahr, *Per* .... town, city
shan, *Chn* .... mountain, hill, island
shatt, *Arab* .... river
shi, *Jap* .... city
shima, *Jap* .... island
shōtō, *Jap* .... archipelago
si, *Chn* .... west, western
sierra, *Sp* .... mountain range
sjö, *Nor., Swe* .... lake, sea
sö, *Dan., Nor* .... lake, sea
söder, södra, *Swe* .... south
song, *Annam* .... river
sopka, *Rus* .... peak, volcano
source, *Fr* .... a spring
spitze, *Ger* .... summit, point
staat, *Ger* .... state
stad, *Dan., Du., Nor., Swe.* .... city, town
stadt, *Ger* .... city, town
stato, *It* .... state
step', *Rus* .... treeless plain, steppe
straat, *Du* .... strait
strand, *Dan., Du., Ger., Nor., Swe* .... shore, beach
stretto, *It* .... strait
strom, *Ger* .... river, stream
ström, *Dan., Nor., Swe* . stream, river
stroom, *Du* .... stream, river
su, suyu, *Tur* .... water, river
sud, *Fr., Sp* .... south
süd, *Ger* .... south
suidō, *Jap* .... channel
sul, *Port* .... south
sund, *Dan., Nor., Swe* .... sound
sungai, sungei, *Indon., Mal* ... river
sur, *Sp* .... south
syd, *Dan., Nor., Swe* .... south
tafelland, *Ger* .... plateau
take, *Jap* .... peak, summit
tal, *Ger* .... valley
tandjung, tanjong, *Mal* .... cape
tao, *Chn* .... island
târg, târgul, *Rom* .... market, town
tell, *Arab* .... hill
teluk, *Indon* .... bay, gulf
terra, *It* .... land
terre, *Fr* .... earth, land
thal, *Ger* .... valley
tierra, *Sp* .... earth, land
tō, *Jap* .... east; island
tonle, *Camb* .... river, lake
top, *Du* .... peak
torp, *Swe* .... hamlet, cottage
tsangpo, *Tib* .... river
tsi, *Chn* .... village, borough
tso, *Tib* .... lake
tsu, *Jap* .... harbor, port
tundra, *Rus* ... treeless arctic plains
tung, *Chn* .... east
tuz, *Tur* .... salt
udde, *Swe* .... cape
ufer, *Ger* .... shore, river bank
umi, *Jap* .... sea, gulf
ura, *Jap* .... bay, coast, creek
ust'ye, *Rus* .... river mouth
valle, *It., Port., Sp* .... valley
vallée, *Fr* .... valley
valli, *It* .... lake
vár, *Hung* .... fortress
város, *Hung* .... town
varoš, *So. Slav* .... town
veld, *Du* .... open plain, field
verkh, *Rus* .... top, summit
ves, *Czech* .... village
vest, *Dan., Nor., Swe* .... west
vik, *Swe* .... cove, bay
vila, *Port* .... town
villa, *Sp* .... town
villar, *Sp* .... village, hamlet
ville, *Fr* .... town, city
vostok, *Rus* .... east
wad, wādī, *Arab.* .... intermittent stream
wald, *Ger* .... forest, woodland
wan, *Chn., Jap* .... bay, gulf
weiler, *Ger* .... hamlet, village
westersch, *Du* .... western
wüste, *Ger* .... desert
yama, *Jap* .... mountain
yarimada, *Tur* .... peninsula
yug, *Rus* .... south
zaki, *Jap* .... cape
zaliv, *Rus* .... bay, gulf
zapad, *Rus* .... west
zee, *Du* .... sea
zemlya, *Rus* .... land
zuid, *Du* .... south

abbreviations of geographical names and terms

A. & I. ... Afars & Issas
Afg. ... Afghanistan
Afr. ... Africa
Ak. ... Alaska
Al. ... Alabama
Alb. ... Albania
Alg. ... Algeria
And. ... Andorra
Ang. ... Angola
Ant. ... Antarctica
Ar. ... Arkansas
Arch. ... Archipelago
Arc. O. ... Arctic Ocean
Arg. ... Argentina
A. S. S. R. ... Autonomous Soviet Socialist Republic
Atl. O. ... Atlantic Ocean
Aus. ... Austria
Austl. ... Australia
Aut. ... Autonomous
Az. ... Arizona

B. ... Bay, Bahia
Ba. ... Bahamas
Bngl. ... Bangladesh
Barb. ... Barbados
Bdy. ... Boundary
Bel. ... Belgium
Bg. ... Berg
Bhu. ... Bhutan
Bk. ... Bank
Bol. ... Bolivia
Bots. ... Botswana
Br. ... British
Braz. ... Brazil
Bru. ... Brunei
Bul. ... Bulgaria
Bur. ... Burma

C. ... Cerro, Cape
Ca. ... California
Cam. ... Cameroon
Camb. ... Cambodia
Can. ... Canal, Canada
Can. Is. ... Canary Is.
Cen. Afr. Rep. ... Central African Republic
Chan. ... Channel
Co. ... County, Colorado
Col. ... Colombia
Con. ... Congo
Comm. ... Commonwealth
C. R. ... Costa Rica
Cr. ... Creek
Ct. ... Connecticut
C. V. ... Cape Verde
C. Z. ... Canal Zone
Czech. ... Czechoslovakia

DC ... District of Columbia
De. ... Delaware
Den. ... Denmark
Dept. ... Department
Des. ... Desert
D. F. ... Distrito Federal
Dist. ... District
Div. ... Division
Dom. Rep. ... Dominican Republic

Ec. ... Ecuador
Eng. ... England
Equat. Gui. ... Equatorial Guinea
Eth. ... Ethiopia
Eur. ... Europe

Faer. ... Faeroe Is.
Falk. Is. ... Falkland Is.
Fd. ... Fjord
Fed. Rep. of Ger., F.R.G. ... Federal Republic of Germany
Fin. ... Finland
Fk. ... Fork
Fl. ... Florida
For. ... Forest
Fr. ... France
Fr. Gu. ... French Guiana
Ft. ... Fort

G. ... Gulf
Ga. ... Georgia
Gam. ... Gambia
Ger. Dem. Rep., G.D.R. ... German Democratic Republic
Gib. ... Gibraltar
Grc. ... Greece
Grnld. ... Greenland
Gt. ... Great
Gt. Brit. ... Great Britain
Guad. ... Guadeloupe
Guat. ... Guatemala
Gui. ... Guinea
Guy. ... Guyana

Hai. ... Haiti
Har., Hbr. ... Harbor, Harbour
Hd. ... Head
Hi. ... Hawaii
Hond. ... Honduras
Hts. ... Heights
Hung. ... Hungary

I. ... Island
Ia. ... Iowa
Ice. ... Iceland
Id. ... Idaho
Il. ... Illinois
In. ... Inset, Indiana
Ind. O. ... Indian Ocean
Indon. ... Indonesia
Ind. Res. ... Indian Reservation
Int., Intl. ... International
Ire. ... Ireland
Is. ... Islands
Isr. ... Israel
Isth. ... Isthmus
It. ... Italy

Jam. ... Jamaica
Jap. ... Japan
Jc. ... Junction

Ken. ... Kenya
Km. ... Kilometer, Kilometers
Kor. ... Korea
Ks. ... Kansas
Kuw. ... Kuwait
Ky. ... Kentucky

L. ... Lake, Loch, Lough
La. ... Louisiana
Lat. ... Latitude
Leb. ... Lebanon
Leso. ... Lesotho
Lib. ... Liberia
Liech. ... Liechtenstein
Long. ... Longitude
Lux. ... Luxembourg

M. ... Mile, Miles
Ma. ... Massachusetts
Mad. ... Madagascar
Mad. Is. ... Madeira Islands
Mala. ... Malaysia
Mand. ... Mandate
Mart. ... Martinique
Max. ... Maximum
Max. surf. elev. ... Maximum surface elevation
Md. ... Maryland
Me. ... Maine
Medit. ... Mediterranean
Mex. ... Mexico
Mi. ... Mile, Miles, Michigan
Mn. ... Minnesota
Mo. ... Missouri
Mong. ... Mongolia
Mor. ... Morocco
Moz. ... Mozambique
Ms. ... Mississippi
Mt. ... Mount, Montana
Mtn. ... Mountain
Mts. ... Mountains

N. A. ... North America
Natl. ... National
Natl. Mon. ... National Monument
Ne. ... Nebraska
NC ... North Carolina
N. Cal. ... New Caledonia
ND ... North Dakota
Neigh. ... Neighborhood
Nep. ... Nepal
Neth. ... Netherlands
New Hebr. ... New Hebrides
NH ... New Hampshire
Nic. ... Nicaragua
Nig. ... Nigeria
N. Ire. ... Northern Ireland
NJ ... New Jersey
NM ... New Mexico
Nor. ... Norway
Nv. ... Nevada
NY ... New York
N. Z. ... New Zealand

O. ... Ocean
Obs. ... Observatory
Oh. ... Ohio
Ok. ... Oklahoma
Om. ... Oman
Or. ... Oregon
O-va ... Ostrova

P. ... Pass
Pa. ... Pennsylvania
Pac. O. ... Pacific Ocean
Pak. ... Pakistan
Pan. ... Panama
Pap. N. Gui. ... Papua New Guinea
Par. ... Paraguay
Pass. ... Passage
P.D.R. of Yem. ... Yemen, People's Democratic Republic of
Pen. ... Peninsula
Phil. ... Philippines
P. Int. ... Point of Interest
Pk. ... Peak, Park
Plat. ... Plateau
Pln. ... Plain
Pol. ... Poland
Port. ... Portugal
P-Ov. ... Poluostrov
P. R. ... Puerto Rico
Prov. ... Province
Pt. ... Point
Pta. ... Punta
Pte. ... Pointe

R. ... River, Rio, Rivière
Ra. ... Range, Ranges
Reg. ... Region
Rep. ... Republic
Res. ... Reservation, Reservoir
Rf. ... Reef
Rh. ... Rhodesia
RI ... Rhode Island
Rom. ... Romania
R. R. ... Railroad
R. S. F. S. R. ... Russian Soviet Federated Socialist Republic
Rw. ... Rwanda
Ry. ... Railway
Rys. ... Railways

S. ... San, Santo, South
Sa. ... Serra, Sierra
S. A. ... South America
S. Afr. ... South Africa
Sal. ... El Salvador
Sau. Ar. ... Saudi Arabia
SC ... South Carolina
Scot. ... Scotland
SD ... South Dakota
Sd. ... Sound
S. L. ... Sierra Leone
Sol. Is. ... Solomon Is.
Som. ... Somalia
Sov. Un. ... Soviet Union
Sp. ... Spain
Spr., Sprs. ... Spring, Springs
S. S. R. ... Soviet Socialist Republic
St. ... Saint
Sta. ... Santa
Ste. ... Sainte
Str. ... Strait
Strm. ... Stream
Sud. ... Sudan
Sur. ... Surinam
S. W. Afr. ... South West Africa
Swaz. ... Swaziland
Swe. ... Sweden
Switz. ... Switzerland
Swp. ... Swamp
Syr. ... Syria

Tan. ... Tanzania
Tas. ... Tasmania
Ter. ... Territory
Thai. ... Thailand
Tn. ... Tennessee
Trin. ... Trinidad and Tobago
Tun. ... Tunisia
Tur. ... Turkey
Tx. ... Texas

U.A.E. ... United Arab Emirates
Ug. ... Uganda
U. K. ... United Kingdom of Gt. Brit. and N. Ire.
Ur. ... Uruguay
U. S., U. S. A. ... United States of America
Ut. ... Utah

Va. ... Virginia
Val. ... Valley
Ven. ... Venezuela
Viet. ... Vietnam
Vir. Is. ... Virgin Is.
Vol. ... Volcano
Vt. ... Vermont

Wa. ... Washington
Wi. ... Wisconsin
W. Sah. ... Western Sahara
W. Sam. ... Western Samoa
WV ... West Virginia
Wy. ... Wyoming

Yugo. ... Yugoslavia

pronunciation of geographical names

Key to the Sound Values of Letters and Symbols Used in the Index to Indicate Pronunciation

ă—ăt, căt, băttle
ă—*ă*ppeal, fin*ă*l
ā—rāte, elāte
å—inanimåte, senåte
ä—cälm, ärm
ȧ—ȧsk, bȧth
ȧ—m*ȧ*rine, sof*ȧ* (short neutral or indeterminate sound)
â—fâre, prepâre
ch—church, choose
dh—as th in other, either
ē—bē, ēve
ė—crėate, ėvent
ĕ—bĕt, ĕnd
ĕ—rec*ĕ*nt (short neutral or indeterminate sound)
ẽ—cratẽr, cindẽr
g—gō, gāme
gh—guttural g
ĭ—wĭll, bĭt
ĭ—short neutral or indeterminate sound
ī—rīde, bīte
ᴋ—guttural k as ch in German ich
ng—sing
ŋ—baŋk, liŋger
ɴ—indicates nasalized preceding vowel
ŏ—nŏd, ŏdd
ŏ—c*ŏ*mmit, c*ŏ*nnect
ō—ōld, bōld
ô—ôbey, hôtel
ô—ôrder, nôrth
oi—boil
ōō—fōōd, rōōt
ŏŏ—fŏŏt, wŏŏd
ou—thou, out
s—as in soft, so, sane
sh—dish, finish
th—thin, thick
ū—pūre, cūre
û—ûnite, ûsurp
û—ûrn, fûr
ŭ—stŭd, ŭp
ü—as in French tu or as "y" in study
ŭ—circ*ŭ*s, s*ŭ*bmit
zh—as z in azure
'—indeterminate vowel sound

In many cases the spelling of foreign geographic names does not even remotely indicate the pronunciation to an American, i. e., Słupsk in Poland is pronounced swŏŏpsk; Jujuy in Argentina is pronounced hōō-hwē'; La Spezia in Italy is lä-spĕ'zyä.

This condition is hardly surprising, however, when we consider that in our own language Worcester, Massachusetts, is pronounced wŏŏs'tẽr; Sioux City, Iowa, sōō sĭ'tĭ; Schuylkill Haven, Pennsylvania, skōōl'kĭl hā-vĕn; Poughkeepsie, New York, p*ŏ*-kĭp'sė.

The indication of pronunciation of geographic names presents several peculiar problems:

(1) Many foreign tongues use sounds that are not present in the English language and which an American cannot normally articulate. Thus, though the nearest English equivalent sound has been indicated, only approximate results are possible.

(2) There are several dialects in each foreign tongue which cause variation in the local pronunciation of names. This also occurs in identical names in the various divisions of a great language group, as the Slavic or the Latin.

(3) Within the United States there are marked differences in pronunciation, not only of local geographic names, but also of common words, indicating that the sound and tone values for letters as well as the placing of the emphasis vary considerably from one part of the country to another.

(4) A number of different letter and diacritical combinations could be used to indicate essentially the same or approximate pronunciations.

Some variation in pronunciation other than that indicated in this index may be encountered, but such a difference does not necessarily indicate that either is in error, and in many cases it is a matter of individual choice as to which is preferred. In fact, an exact indication of pronunciation of many foreign names using English letters and diacritical marks is extremely difficult and sometimes impossible.

a pronouncing index
of over 30,000 geographical names

This universal index includes in a single alphabetical list all important names that appear on the reference maps. Each place name is preceded by the page number of the map on which it appears. Place names are followed by the pronunciation of the name (see facing page for an explanation of the pronunciation system); the location; and the approximate geographic coordinates.

State locations are listed for all places in the United States. All other place name entries show only country locations. When a name is only shown on an inset map the name of the inset on which it appears is listed.

All minor political divisions are followed by a descriptive term (Dist., Reg., Prov., State, etc.) and by the country in which they are located.

The names of physical features and points of interest that are shown on the maps are listed in the index. Each entry is followed by a descriptive term (Bay, Hill, Mtn., Is., Plat., etc.) to indicate its nature.

The system of alphabetizing used in the index is standard. When more than one name with the same spelling is shown, including both political and physical names, the order of precedence is as follows: *first*, place names, *second*, political divisions, and *third*, physical features.

Local official names are used on the maps for nearly all cities and towns, with the exception of about fifty major world cities for which Anglicized conventional names have been preferred. For these exceptions the index gives a cross reference to the official local name.

Page	Name Pronunciation Region	Lat. °	Long. °
161	Aachen (ä′kĕn).F.R.G. (Ruhr In.)	50·46 N	6·07 E
156	Aakirkeby (ô-kǐr′kĕ-bü) .....Den.	55·04 N	15·00 E
158	Aalen (ä′lĕn) .F.R.G.	48·49 N	10·08 E
149	Aalsmeer..Neth. (Amsterdam In.)	52·16 N	4·44 E
149	Aalst....Bel. (Brussels In.)	50·58 N	4·00 E
158	Aarau (är′ou) Switz.	47·22 N	8·03 E
149	Aarschot....Bel. (Brussels In.)	50·59 N	4·51 E
215	Aba ....Nig.	5·06 N	7·21 E
217	Aba .....Zaïre	3·52 N	30·14 E
186	Ābādān (ä-bä-dän′) .....Iran	30·15 N	48·30 E
135	Abaetetuba (ä′bǎĕ-tĕ-tōō′bä) Braz.	1·44 S	48·45 W
115	Abajo Pk. (ä-bä′hô) ......Ut.	38·50 N	109·35 W
215	Abakaliki .....Nig.	6·21 N	8·06 E
172	Abakan (ŭ-bá-kän′)...Sov. Un.	53·43 N	91·28 E
172	Abakan (R.) ....Sov. Un.	53·00 N	91·06 E
134	Abancay (ä-bän-kä′ē) ......Peru	13·44 S	72·46 W
124	Abasolo (ä-bä-sō′lô)........Mex.	24·05 N	98·24 W
118	Abasolo........Mex.	27·13 N	101·25 W
	Abay (R.), see Blue Nile		
211	Abaya L. (ä-bä′yà)........Eth.	6·24 N	38·22 E
218	ʻAbbāsah, Turʻat al (Can.) Egypt (Suez In.)	30·45 N	32·15 E
120	Abbeville (ăb′ĕ-vǐl).......Al.	31·35 N	85·15 W
160	Abbeville (ăb-vēl′)........Fr.	50·08 N	1·49 E
120	Abbeville (ăb′ĕ-vǐl).......Ga.	31·53 N	83·23 W
119	Abbeville.......La.	29·59 N	92·07 W
121	Abbeville.......SC	34·09 N	82·25 W
164	Abbiategrasso (äb-byä′tä-gräs′sō) It.	45·23 N	8·52 E
148	Abbots Bromley (ăb′ŭts brŭm′lē) Eng.	52·49 N	1·52 W
112	Abbotsford (ăb′ŭts-fĕrd) Can. (Vancouver In.)	49·03 N	122·17 W
218	Abd Al Kuri (I.) (ăbd-ĕl-kōō′rē) P.D.R. of Yem. (Horn of Afr. In.)	12·12 N	51·00 E
170	Abdulino (äb-dōō-lē′nô)..Sov. Un.	53·40 N	53·45 E
211	Abéché (à-bē-shä′) ......Chad	13·48 N	20·39 E
214	Abengourou .....Ivory Coast	6·44 N	3·29 W
156	Åbenrå (ô′bĕn-rô) ......Den.	55·03 N	9·20 E
215	Abeokuta (ä-bå-ō-kōō′tä).....Nig.	7·10 N	3·26 E
	Abercorn, see Mbala		
154	Aberdare (ăb-ĕr-dâr′)......Wales	51·45 N	3·35 W
120	Aberdeen (ăb-ĕr-dēn′)......Ms.	33·49 N	88·33 W
154	Aberdeen......Scot.	57·10 N	2·05 W
108	Aberdeen......SD	45·28 N	98·29 W
110	Aberdeen......Wa.	47·00 N	123·48 W
148	Aberford (ăb′ĕr-fĕrd)......Eng.	53·49 N	1·21 W
154	Abergavenny (ăb′ĕr-gà-vĕn′ǐ) Wales	51·45 N	3·05 W
110	Abert L. (ä′bĕrt)......Or.	42·39 N	120·24 W
154	Aberystwyth (ǎ-bĕr-ĭst′wǐth) Wales	52·25 N	4·04 W
174	Abestovskiy (ä-bĕs′tôv-skǐ) Sov. Un. (Urals In.)	57·46 N	61·23 E
186	Abhā (ä-bä′)......Sau. Ar.	41·47 N	42·29 E
214	Abidjan (ä-bēd-zhän′).Ivory Coast	5·19 N	4·02 W
195	Abiko (ä-bē-kō)..Jap. (Tōkyō In.)	35·53 N	140·01 E
117	Abilene (ăb′ǐ-lēn)......Ks.	38·54 N	97·12 W
117	Abilene......Tx.	32·25 N	99·45 W
148	Abingdon...Eng. (London In.)	51·38 N	1·17 W
109	Abingdon (ăb′ǐng-dŭn)......Il.	40·48 N	90·21 W
121	Abingdon......Va.	36·42 N	81·57 W
99	Abington (ăb′ǐng-tǎn)..Ma. (In.)	42·07 N	70·57 W
115	Abiquiu Res......NM	36·26 N	106·42 W

Page	Name Pronunciation Region	Lat. °	Long. °
91	Abitibi (L.) (ăb-I-tĭb′I)......Can.	48·27 N	80·20 W
91	Abitibi (R.)......Can.	49·30 N	81·10 W
171	Abkhaz A.S.S.R........Sov. Un.	43·10 N	40·45 E
161	Ablis (à-blē′).....Fr. (Paris In.)	48·31 N	1·50 E
218	Abnūb (ăb-nōōb′). Egypt (Nile In.)	27·18 N	31·11 E
	Åbo, see Turku		
184	Abohar......India	30·12 N	74·13 E
214	Aboisso......Ivory Coast	5·28 N	3·12 W
215	Abomey (ăb-ô-mā′)......Benin	7·11 N	1·59 E
159	Abony (ô′bō-ny′).........Hung.	47·12 N	20·00 E
215	Abou Deï.........Chad	11·27 N	19·17 E
197	Abra (R.) (ä′brä)......Phil (In.)	17·16 N	120·38 E
137	Abraão (äbrä-oun′) Braz. (Rio de Janeiro In.)	23·10 S	44·10 W
129	Abraham's B.......Ba.	22·20 N	73·50 W
148	Abram (ā′brǎm)......Eng.	53·31 N	2·36 W
162	Abrantes (à-brän′tĕs)......Port.	39·28 N	8·13 W
135	Abrolhos, Arquipélago dos (Arch.) (ä-rô-gŏ-pě′lä-gŏ dŏs ä-brŏ′l-yŏs) Braz.	17·58 S	38·40 W
157	Abruka (I.) (ä-brŏō′ka)..Sov. Un.	58·09 N	22·30 E
164	Abruzzi E Molise (Reg.) (ä-brōōt′sē, mô′lĕ-zā)......It.	42·10 N	13·55 E
111	Absaroka Ra. (Mts.) (ăb-sà-rō-kǎ)......Wy.	44·50 N	109·47 W
184	Abu Road (à′bōō)......India	24·38 N	72·45 E
186	Abū Arīsh (ä-bōō á-rēsh′).Sau. Ar.	16·48 N	43·00 E
211	Abū Ḥamad (ä′bōō hä′-mĕd).Sud.	19·37 N	33·21 E
186	Abū Kamāl......Syr.	34·45 N	40·46 E
153	Abūksāh..........Egypt	29·29 N	30·40 E
134	Abunã (ä-bŏō-nä′).Bol.-Braz.	10·25 S	67·00 W
218	Abū Qīr (ä′bōō kēr′) Egypt (Nile In.)	31·18 N	30·06 E
218	Abū Qurqāṣ (ä′bōō kŏōr-käs′) Egypt (Nile In.)	27·57 N	30·51 E
183	Abu Qurūn, Ras (Mt.) Egypt (Palestine In.)	30·22 N	33·32 E
195	Aburatsu (ä′bōō-rät′sōō).....Jap.	31·33 N	131·20 E
218	Abū Tīj......Egypt (Nile In.)	27·03 N	31·19 E
186	Abū Ẓaby......U. A. E.	24·15 N	54·28 E
183	Abū Zanimah Egypt (Palestine In.)	29·03 N	33·08 E
	Abyad, Al-Baḥr al- (R.), see White Nile		
173	Abyy......Sov. Un.	68·24 N	134·00 E
134	Acacias (ä-kä′sēäs)....Col. (In.)	3·59 N	73·44 W
98	Acadia Natl. Park (à-kā′dǐ-á).Me.	44·19 N	68·01 W
126	Acajutla (ä-kä-hōōt′lä)......Sal.	13·37 N	89·50 W
125	Acala (ä-kä′lä)......Mex.	16·38 N	92·49 W
216	Acalayong......Equat. Gui.	1·05 N	9·40 E
124	Acámbaro (ä-käm′bä-rō)....Mex.	20·03 N	100·42 W
126	Acancéh (ä-kän-sĕ′)....Mex. (In.)	20·50 N	89·27 W
124	Acapetlahuaya (ä-kä-pĕt′lä-hwä′yä)......Mex.	18·24 N	100·04 W
124	Acaponeta (ä-kä-pô-nä′tä)...Mex.	22·31 N	105·25 W
124	Acaponeta (R.)......Mex.	22·47 N	105·23 W
124	Acapulco (ä-kä-pōōl′kō)......Mex.	16·49 N	99·57 W
135	Acaraí Mts.......Braz.	1·30 N	57·40 W
135	Acaraú (ä-kárhá-ōō′)......Braz.	2·55 S	40·04 W
134	Acarigua (äkä-rē′gwä)......Ven.	9·29 N	69·11 W
124	Acatlán de Osorio (ä-kät-län′dä ō-sō′rē-ō)..Mex.	18·11 N	98·04 W
125	Acatzingo de Hidalgo (ä-kät-zīn′gô dä ē-dhäl′gō).Mex.	18·58 N	97·47 W
125	Acayucan (ä-kä-yōō′kän)....Mex.	17·56 N	94·55 W
104	Accoville (äk′kô-vǐl)........WV	37·45 N	81·50 W

Page	Name Pronunciation Region	Lat. °	Long. °
214	Accra (ä′krà)......Ghana	5·33 N	0·13 W
148	Accrington (ăk′rǐng-tǎn)......Eng.	53·45 N	2·22 W
163	Acerra (ä-chĕ′r-rä) It. (Naples In.)	40·42 N	14·22 E
134	Achacachi (ä-chä-kä′chĕ).....Bol.	16·11 S	68·32 W
194	Acheng (ä′chĕng′)......China	45·32 N	126·59 E
154	Achill (ä-chǐl′)......Ire.	53·55 N	10·05 W
172	Achinsk (à-chēnsk′)......Sov. Un.	56·13 N	90·32 E
164	Acireale (ä-chē-rä-ä′lä)......It.	37·37 N	15·12 E
120	Ackia Battle Ground Natl. Mon. (ä-kyū′).Ms.	34·22 N	89·05 W
129	Acklins (I.) (ăk′lǐns)......Ba.	22·30 N	73·55 W
129	Acklins, The Bight of (B.)....Ba.	22·35 N	74·20 W
125	Acolman (ä-kôl-mä′n)..Mex. (In.)	19·38 N	98·56 W
137	Aconcagua (ä-kôn-kä′gwä) (Prov.) Chile (Santiago In.)	32·20 S	71·00 W
137	Aconcagua, Cerro (Mtn.) Arg. (Santiago In.)	32·38 S	70·00 W
137	Aconcagua (R.) Chile (Santiago In.)	32·43 S	70·53 W
210	Açores (Azores) (Is.) (à-zōrz′).Atl. O.	37·44 N	29·25 W
126	Acoyapa (ä-kô-yä′pä)......Nic.	11·54 N	85·11 W
164	Acqui (äk′kwē)......It.	44·41 N	8·22 E
134	Acre (State) (ä′krä)......Braz.	8·40 S	70·45 W
134	Acre (R.)......Braz.	10·33 S	68·34 W
106	Acton (äk′tŭn) Al. (Birmingham In.)	33·21 N	86·49 W
100	Acton...Can. (Toronto In.)	43·38 N	80·02 W
99	Acton......Ma. (In.)	42·29 N	71·26 W
124	Actopan (äk-tô-pän′)......Mex.	20·16 N	98·57 W
125	Actópan (R.) (äk-tô′pän)....Mex.	19·25 N	96·31 W
124	Acuitzio del Canje (ä-kwēt′zĕ-ō dĕl kän′hå).Mex.	19·28 N	101·21 W
129	Aguada, Baie de l' (B.) (ä-kōōl′).Hai.	19·55 N	72·20 W
108	Ada (ä′dǔ)......Mn.	47·17 N	96·32 W
104	Ada......Oh.	40·45 N	83·45 W
117	Ada......Ok.	34·45 N	96·43 W
165	Ada (ä′dä)......Yugo.	45·48 N	20·06 E
195	Adachi......Jap. (Tōkyō In.)	35·50 N	39·36 E
101	Adak (ä-däk′)......Ak.	56·50 N	176·48 W
101	Adak (I.)......Ak.	51·40 N	176·28 W
101	Adak Str.......Ak.	51·42 N	177·16 W
	Adalia, see Antalya		
215	Adamaoua (Mts.)......Cam.-Nig.	6·30 N	11·50 E
93	Adams (R.).......Can.	51·30 N	119·20 W
105	Adams (ǎd′ǎmz)......Ma.	42·35 N	73·10 W
109	Adams......Wi.	43·55 N	89·48 W
110	Adams, Mt.......Wa.	46·15 N	121·19 W
106	Adamsville (ǎd′ǎmz-vǐl) Al. (Birmingham In.)	33·36 N	86·57 W
106	Adamsville......Ga. (Atlanta In.)	33·45 N	84·31 W
171	Adana (ä′dä-nä)......Tur.	37·05 N	35·20 E
171	Adapazari (ä-dä-pä-zä′rē)...Tur.	40·45 N	30·20 E
211	Adarama (ä-dä-rä′mä)......Sud.	17·11 N	34·56 E
164	Adda (R.) (äd′dä)......It.	45·43 N	9·31 E
211	Ad Dabbah......Sud.	18·04 N	30·58 E
186	Ad Dahnā (Des.)....Sau. Ar.	26·05 N	47·15 E
211	Ad-Dāmir (ad-dä′mĕr)......Sud.	17·38 N	33·57 E
186	Ad Dammām......Sau. Ar.	26·27 N	49·59 E
183	Ad Damur...Leb. (Palestine In.)	33·44 N	35·27 E
186	Ad Dawhah......Qatar	25·02 N	51·28 E
186	Ad Dilam......Sau. Ar.	23·47 N	47·03 E
218	Ad Dilinjāt......Egypt (Nile In.)	30·48 N	30·32 E
211	Addis Abeba......Eth.	9·00 N	38·44 E

ng-sing; ŋ-baŋk; N-nasalized n; nŏd; cŏmmit; ōld; ôbey; ôrder; fōōd; fŏŏt; ou-out; s-soft; sh-dish; th-thin; pūre; ünite; ûrn; stŭd; circǎs; ü-as "y" in study; '-indeterminate vowel.

Page	Name	Pronunciation	Region	Lat. °'	Long. °'
113	Addison (ăd'ĭ-sŭn)				
		Tx. (Dallas, Fort Worth In.)		32·58 N	96·50 W
213	Addo (ădô)........S. Afr.	(Natal In.)		33·33 S	25·43 E
211	Ad Duwaym (dŏŏ-ām')	......Sud.		13·56 N	32·22 E
107	Addyston (ăd'ĕ-stŭn)				
		Oh. (Cincinnati In.)		39·09 N	84·42 W
120	Adel (ä-děl')	.........Ga.		31·08 N	83·55 W
203	Adelaide (ăd'ĕ-lād).........Austl.			34·46 S	139·08 E
213	Adelaide (ăd-ĕl'ād)				
		S. Afr. (Natal In.)		32·41 S	26·07 E
220	Adelaide I................Ant.			67·15 S	68·40 W
186	Aden (ä'dĕn)....P. D. R. of Yem.			12·48 N	45·00 E
186	Aden, G. of.............Asia			11·45 N	45·45 E
197	Adi (I.) (ä'dē)............Indon.			4·25 S	133·52 E
164	Adige, Fiume (R.)				
		(fyōō'mě ä'dĕ-jä).It.		46·38 N	10·43 E
152	Adige R. (ä'dĕ-jä).....Aus.-Switz.			46·34 N	10·51 E
184	Adilābād (ŭ-dĭl-ä-bäd')......India			19·47 N	78·30 E
185	Adini............India			15·42 N	77·18 E
105	Adirondack, Mts. (ăd-I-rŏn'dăk)				
		NY		43·45 N	74·40 W
211	Adi Ugri (ä-dē ōō'grē).......Eth.			14·54 N	38·52 E
159	Adjud (äd'zhŏŏd).......Rom.			46·05 N	27·12 E
113	Adkins....Tx. (San Antonio In.)			29·22 N	98·18 W
101	Admiralty (I.)............Ak.			57·50 N	133·50 W
112	Admiralty Inlet (ăd'mĭrăl-tĕ)				
		Wa. (Seattle In.)		48·10 N	122·45 W
197	Admiralty Is....Pap. N. Gui.			1·40 S	146·45 E
215	Ado-Ekiti...............Nig.			7·38 N	5·12 E
113	Adolph (ä'dolf).Mn. (Duluth In.)			46·47 N	92·17 W
160	Adour (R.) (á-dōōr').....Fr.			43·43 N	0·38 W
162	Adra (ä'drä)............Sp.			36·45 N	3·02 W
164	Adrano (ä-drä'nô)........It.			37·42 N	14·52 E
164	Adria (ä'drĕ-ä)..........It.			45·03 N	12·01 E
104	Adrian (ä'drĭ-ăn)........Mi.			41·55 N	84·00 W
108	Adrian...............Mn.			43·39 N	95·56 W
	Adrianople, see Edirne				
164	Adriatic Sea............Eur.			41·30 N	14·27 E
210	Adrir....................Alg.			27·53 N	0·15 W
136	Adrogué (ädrô-gā')				
		Arg. (Buenos Aires In.)		34·33 S	58·24 W
211	Adwa...................Eth.			14·02 N	38·58 E
148	Adwick-le-Street (ăd'wĭk-lĕ-strēt')				
		Eng.		53·35 N	1·11 W
173	Adycha (R.) (ä'dĭ-chä)....Sov. Un.			66·11 N	136·45 E
167	Adzhamka (ád-zhäm'ka)..Sov. Un.			48·33 N	32·28 E
214	Adzopé.............Ivory Coast			6·06 N	3·52 W
170	Adz'va (R.) (äd'vä).....Sov. Un.			66·10 N	59·20 E
153	Aegean Sea (ê-jē'ăn)....Asia-Eur.			39·04 N	24·56 E
136	Aerø (I.) (âr'ö)............Den.			54·52 N	10·22 E
209	Afars & Issas...........Afr.			11·35 N	48·08 E
113	Affton.......Mo. (St. Louis In.)			28·33 N	90·20 W
182	Afghanistan (ăf-găn-I-stăn') .. Asia			33·00 N	63·00 E
218	Afgoi (äf-gŏ'ĭ)				
		Som. (Horn of Afr. In.)		2·08 N	45·08 E
215	Afikpo................Nig.			5·53 N	7·56 E
210	Aflou (ä-flōō')...........Alg.			33·59 N	2·04 E
101	Afognak (I.) (ä-fŏg-nàk')....Ak.			58·28 N	151·35 W
163	Afragola (ä-frä'gō-lä)				
		It. (Naples In.)		40·40 N	14·19 E
209	Africa (ăf'rĭ-kà)..........Mn.				
113	Afton (ăf'tŭn)				
		(Minneapolis, St. Paul In.)		44·54 N	92·47 W
117	Afton..................Ok.			36·42 N	94·56 W
111	Afton..................Wy.			42·42 N	110·52 W
183	'Afula (ä-fŏŏ'lä)				
		Isr. (Palestine In.)		32·36 N	35·17 E
171	Afyonkarahisar				
		(ä-fê-ōn-kä-rà-hê-sär').Tur.		38·45 N	30·20 E
215	Agadem (ä'gá-děm).....Niger			16·50 N	13·17 E
215	Agadez (ä'gá-děs).......Niger			16·58 N	7·59 E
210	Agadir (ä-gá-dēr')........Mor.			30·30 N	9·37 W
126	Agalta, Cord. de (Mts.)				
		(kôr-dĕl-yĕ'ä-dĕ-ä-gä'l-tä)			
		Hond.		15·15 N	85·42 W
174	Agapovka (ä-gä-pŏv'kä)				
		Sov. Un. (Urals In.)		53·18 N	59·10 E
184	Agartala...............India			23·53 N	91·22 E
185	Agāshi................India (In.)			19·28 N	72·46 E
174	Agashkino (á-gäsh'kĭ-nô)				
		Sov. Un. (Moscow In.)		55·18 N	38·13 E
101	Agattu (I.) (ä'gä-tōō)......Ak.			52·14 N	173·40 E
167	Agayman (á-gä-ê-män')..Sov. Un.			46·39 N	34·20 E
214	Agboville.............Ivory Coast			5·56 N	4·13 W
171	Agdam (äg'däm).......Sov. Un.			40·00 N	47·00 E
160	Agde (ägd).............Fr.			43·19 N	3·30 E
160	Agen (á-zhän').........Fr.			44·13 N	0·31 E
173	Aginskoye (ä-hǐn'skô-yĕ).Sov. Un.			51·15 N	113·15 E
197	Agno (äg'nô)........Phil. (In.)			16·07 N	119·49 E
197	Agno (R.).........Phil. (In.)			16·10 N	120·28 E
164	Agnone (än-yō'nä).........It.			41·49 N	14·23 E
214	Agogo..................Ghana			6·47 N	1·04 W
184	Agra (ä'grä)............India			27·18 N	78·00 E
164	Agri (R.) (ä'grē)..........It.			40·15 N	16·21 E
165	Agrinion (ä-grē'nyôn).....Grc.			38·38 N	21·06 E
126	Agua (Vol.) (ä'gwä)......Guat.			14·28 N	90·43 W
124	Agua Blanca, Río (R.)				
		(rê'ô-ä-gwä-blä'n-kä).Mex.		21·46 N	102·54 W
124	Agua Brava, Laguna de (L.)				
		(lä-gŏŏ'nä-dĕ-ä'gwä-brä'vä).Mex.		22·04 N	105·40 W
114	Agua Caliente Ind. Res.				
		(ä'gwä kal-yĕn'tä).Ca.		33·50 N	116·24 W
128	Aguada (ä-gwä'dá)......Cuba			22·25 N	80·50 W
126	Aguada L........Mex. (In.)			18·46 N	89·40 W
134	Aguadas (ä-gwä'dàs)...Col. (In.)			5·37 N	75·27 W
123	Aguadilla (ä-gwä-dēl'yä)				
		P. R. (Puerto Rico In.)		18·27 N	67·10 W
127	Aguadulce (ä-gwä-dōōl'sä)...Pan.			8·15 N	80·33 W
125	Agua Escondida, Meseta de (Plat.)				
		(mě-sě'tä-dě-ä'gwä-ěs-kŏn-dē'dä)			
		Mex.		16·54 N	91·35 W
115	Agua Fria (R.) (ä'gûä frī'á)...Az.			33·43 N	112·22 W

Page	Name	Pronunciation	Region	Lat. °'	Long. °'
137	Aguai (ägwä-ē')				
		Braz. (Rio de Janeiro In.)		22·04 S	46·57 W
118	Agualeguas (ä-gwä-lä'gwäs)..Mex.			26·19 N	99·33 W
118	Aguanaval, R.				
		(ä-guä-nä-väl').Mex.		25·12 N	103·28 W
126	Aguán R. (ä-gwä'n).......Hond.			15·22 N	87·00 W
99	Aguanus (R.) (ä-gwä'nús)..Can.			50·45 N	62·03 W
124	Aguascalientes				
		(ä'gwäs-käl-yĕn'täs).Mex.		21·52 N	102·17 W
124	Aguascalientes (State)...Mex.			22·00 N	102·18 W
162	Agueda (ä-gwä'dá).......Port.			40·36 N	8·26 W
162	Agueda (R.) (ä-gĕ-dä)......Sp.			40·50 N	6·44 W
214	Aguelhok.............Mali			19·28 N	0·52 E
116	Aguilar (ä-gĕ-lär')........Co.			37·24 N	104·38 W
162	Aguilar................Sp.			37·32 N	4·39 W
162	Aguilas (ä-gĕ-läs)........Sp.			37·26 N	1·35 W
124	Aguililla (ä-gē-lēl-yä).....Mex.			18·44 N	102·44 W
124	Aguililla (R.)..........Mex.			18·30 N	102·48 W
134	Aguja, Pta. (Pt.)				
		(pŭn'tá à-gŏŏ' hä).Peru		6·00 S	81·15 W
212	Agulhas, C. (ä-gŏŏl'yäs)...S. Afr.			34·47 S	20·00 E
196	Agung, Gunung (Mtn.)				
		(ä-gŏŏng').Indon.		8·28 S	115·07 E
197	Agusan (R.) (ä-gŏŏ'sän)...Phil.			8·12 N	126·07 E
210	Ahaggar (Mts.) (á-há-gär')..Alg.			23·14 N	6·00 E
161	Ahlen (ä'lĕn)...F.R.G. (Ruhr In.)			51·45 N	7·52 E
184	Ahmadābād (ä-mĕd-ä-bäd')..India			23·04 N	72·38 E
184	Ahmadnagar (ä'mûd-nû-gŭr)				
		India		19·09 N	74·45 E
218	Ahmar Mts..............Eth.				
		(Horn of Afr. In.)		9·22 N	42·00 E
121	Ahoskie (ä-hŏs'kē)........NC			36·15 N	77·00 W
149	Ahrensburg (ä'rĕns-bŏŏrg)				
		F.R.G. (Hamburg In.)		53·40 N	10·14 E
158	Ahrweiler (är'vī-lĕr).....F.R.G.			50·34 N	7·05 E
157	Ähtärin-järvi (L.)........Fin.			62·46 N	24·25 E
124	Ahuacatlán (ä-wä-kät-län')..Mex.			21·05 N	104·28 W
126	Ahuachapan (ä-wä-chä-pän')..Sal.			13·57 N	89·53 W
124	Ahualulco (ä-wä-lŏŏl'kô)...Mex.			20·43 N	103·57 W
124	Ahuatempan (ä-wä-tĕm-pän)..Mex.			18·11 N	98·02 W
156	Åhus (ô'hŏŏs)...........Swe.			55·56 N	14·19 E
186	Ahvāz...............Iran			31·15 N	48·54 E
156	Ahvenanmaa (Åland Is.)				
		(ä'vĕ-nän-mô) (ô'länd) Fin.		60·36 N	19·55 E
199	Aiea (ä'vĕ-nän-mô)........Hi. (In.)			21·18 N	157·52 W
121	Aiken (ä'kĕn)...........SC			33·32 N	81·43 W
135	Aimorès, Serra dos (Mts.)				
		(sě'r-rä-dôs-ī-mō-rě's).Braz.		17·40 S	42·38 W
195	Aimoto (ä-ī-mō-tō)..Jap. (Ōsaka In.)			34·59 N	135·09 E
210	Aïn Beïda (ä'ĕn bä-dä')...Alg.			35·57 N	7·25 E
161	Aincourt (ăN-kōō'r).Fr. (Paris In.)			49·04 N	1·47 E
163	Aïne Oussera (ä ōō-sä-rä)...Alg.			35·25 N	2·50 E
210	Aïn Salah..............Alg.			27·13 N	2·22 E
108	Ainsworth (änz'wûrth).....Ne.			42·32 N	99·51 W
152	Aïn Taïba (ä'ĕn tä'ê-bä)...Alg.			30·20 N	5·30 E
151	Aïn-Temouchent				
		(ä'ĕntĕ-mōō-shan').Alg.		35·20 N	1·23 W
134	Aipe (ī'pĕ)..........Col. (In.)			3·13 N	75·15 W
215	Aïr (Mts.)..............Niger			18·00 N	8·30 E
160	Aire (âr)................Fr.			43·42 N	0·17 W
148	Aire (R.)..............Eng.			53·42 N	1·00 W
183	Airhitam, Selat (Str.)				
		Indon. (Singapore In.)		0·58 N	102·38 E
160	Aisne (R.) (ĕn)..........Fr.			49·28 N	3·32 E
197	Aitape (ä-ê-tä'pá).....Pap. N. Gui.			3·00 S	142·10 E
109	Aitkin (āt'kǐn)...........Mn.			46·32 N	93·43 W
165	Aitolikón (á-tō'lī-kôn)......Grc.			38·27 N	21·21 E
165	Aitos (ä-ē'tōs)..........Bul.			42·42 N	27·17 E
199	Aitutaki (I.) (ī-tōō-tä'kē).Cook Is.			19·00 S	162·00 W
159	Aiud (ä'ê-ŏŏd)...........Rom.			46·19 N	23·40 E
137	Aiuruoca (äě'ōō-rōŏô'-kä)				
		Braz. (Rio de Janeiro In.)		21·57 S	44·36 W
137	Aiuruoca (R.)				
		Braz. (Rio de Janeiro In.)		22·11 S	44·35 W
160	Aix-en-Provence (ĕks-prŏ-váNs)				
		Fr. (In.)		43·32 N	5·27 E
161	Aix-les-Bains (ĕks'-lä-baN')...Fr.			45·42 N	5·56 E
165	Aíyina (ä'ê-nä)..........Grc.			37·37 N	22·12 E
165	Aíyina (I.).............Grc.			37·43 N	23·35 E
165	Aíyion (ä'ê-tōs)..........Grc.			38·13 N	22·04 E
157	Aizpute (ä'ĕz-pōō-tê).....Sov. Un.			56·44 N	21·37 E
195	Aizuwakamatsu..........Jap.			37·27 N	139·51 E
164	Ajaccio (ä-yät'chō).......Fr.			41·55 N	8·42 E
125	Ajalpan (ä-häl'pän)......Mex.			18·21 N	97·14 W
204	Ajana (äj-än'ĕr)........Austl.			28·00 S	114·45 E
111	Ajax Mt. (ä'jăks).......Mt.			45·19 N	113·43 W
210	Ajdabiyah.............Libya			30·56 N	20·16 E
183	'Ajmah, Jabal al (Mts.)				
		Egypt (Palestine In.)		29·12 N	34·03 E
186	Ajman................U. A. E.			25·15 N	54·30 E
184	Ajmer (ŭj-mēr')........India			26·26 N	74·42 E
115	Ajo (ä'hō)..............Az.			32·20 N	112·55 W
124	Ajuchitlán del Progreso				
		(ä-hōō-chet-län).Mex.		18·11 N	100·32 W
125	Ajusco (ä-hōō's-kō)....Mex. (In.)			19·13 N	99·12 W
125	Ajusco, Cerro (sě'r-rō-ä-hōō's-kō)				
		Mex. (In.)		19·12 N	99·16 W
195	Akaishi-dake (Mtn.)				
		(ä-kī-shē dä'kä).Jap.		35·30 N	138·00 E
195	Akashi (ä-kä-shē).Jap. (Ōsaka In.)			34·38 N	134·59 E
216	Aketi (ä-kà-tê).........Zaire			2·44 N	23·46 E
171	Akhaltsikhe (äkä'l-tsi-kĕ)				
		Sov. Un.		41·40 N	42·50 E
211	Akhdar, Al Jabal al (Mts.)..Libya			32·00 N	22·00 E
165	Akhelóös (ä-kĕ'lô-ōs)......Grc.			38·45 N	21·26 E
171	Akhisar (äk-hǐs-sär')......Tur.			38·58 N	27·58 E
167	Akhtarskaya, Bukhta (B.)				
		Sov. Un.		45·54 N	38·22 E
165	Akhtopol (äk'tô-pôl)......Bul.			42·08 N	27·54 E
167	Akhtyrka (äk-tür'ká).....Sov. Un.			50·18 N	34·53 E
174	Akhunovo (ä-kû'nô-vô)				
		Sov. Un. (Urals In.)		54·13 N	59·36 E

Page	Name	Pronunciation	Region	Lat. °'	Long. °'
191	Aki (ä'kê)..............Jap.			33·31 N	133·51 E
101	Akiak (äk'yàk)...........Ak.			61·00 N	161·02 W
91	Akimiski (I.) (ä-kǐ-mǐ'skǐ)..Can.			52·54 N	80·22 W
194	Akita (ä'kē-tä)..........Jap.			39·40 N	140·12 E
214	Akjoujt................Mauritania			19·45 N	14·23 W
183	'Akko..Isr. (Palestine In.)			32·56 N	35·05 E
90	Aklavik (äk'lä-vīk)......Can.			68·28 N	135·26 W
214	'Aklé 'Âouâna (Dunes)				
		Mali-Mauritania		18·07 N	6·00 W
195	Ako (ä'kô)..............Jap.			34·44 N	134·22 E
184	Akola (ä-kô'lä)..........India			20·47 N	77·00 E
211	Akordat................Eth.			15·34 N	37·54 E
91	Akpatok (I.) (äk'pá-tŏk)...Can.			60·30 N	67·10 W
150	Akranes...............Ice.			64·18 N	21·40 W
165	Akrítas, Akr. (C.).........Grc.			37·45 N	23·53 E
116	Akron (äk'rŭn)...........Co.			40·09 N	103·14 W
107	Akron.......Oh. (Cleveland In.)			41·05 N	81·30 W
171	Aksaray (äk-sá-rī')......Tur.			38·30 N	34·05 E
171	Aksehir (äk'shä-hĕr).....Tur.			38·20 N	31·20 E
171	Aksehir (L.)............Tur.			38·30 N	31·30 E
173	Aksha (äk'shä).........Sov. Un.			50·28 N	113·00 E
188	Aksu, see Wensu				
	Aksu (äk'sōō').........China			40·34 N	77·15 E
171	Aktyubinsk (äk'tyōō-bĕnsk)				
		Sov. Un.		50·20 N	57·00 E
195	Akune (ä'kōō-nä).........Jap.			32·03 N	130·16 E
150	Akureyri (ä-kōō-rā'rē).....Ice.			65·39 N	18·01 W
101	Akutan (I.) (ä-kōō-tän')....Ak.			53·58 N	169·54 W
214	Akwatia...............Ghana			6·04 N	0·49 W
103	Alabama (State) (ăl-á-băm'á).U.S.			32·50 N	87·30 W
120	Alabama (R.)............Al.			31·20 N	87·39 W
197	Alabat (I.) (ä-lä-bät')...Phil. (In.)			14·14 N	122·05 E
197	Alaca (ä-lä-kä).......Phil. (In.)			17·56 N	121·39 E
171	Alacam (ä-lä-chäm').....Tur.			41·30 N	35·40 E
128	Alacranes (ä-lä-krä'näs)....Cuba			22·45 N	81·35 W
186	Alaflau (Des.).........Sau. Ar.			24·00 N	44·47 E
135	Alagôas (State) (ä-lä-gō'äzh).Braz.			9·50 S	36·33 W
135	Alagoinhas (ä-lä-gō-ēn'yäzh).Braz.			12·13 S	38·12 W
162	Alagón (ä-lä-gōn')........Sp.			41·46 N	1·07 W
162	Alagón (R.)............Sp.			39·53 N	6·42 W
124	Alahuatán (R.) (ä-lä-wä-tä'n).Mex.			18·30 N	100·00 W
127	Alajuela (ä-lä-hwa'lä)......C.R.			10·01 N	84·14 W
172	Alakol (L.).............Sov. Un.			45·45 N	81·13 E
199	Alalakeiki Chan. (ä-lä-lä-kä'kē)				
		Hi. (In.)		20·40 N	156·30 W
210	Al 'Alamayn.............Egypt			30·53 N	28·52 E
112	Alameda (ăl-á-mā'dá)				
		Ca. (San Francisco In.)		37·46 N	122·15 W
112	Alameda (R.)				
		Ca. (San Francisco In.)		37·36 N	122·02 W
197	Alaminos (ä-lä-mē'nôs)..Phil. (In.)			16·09 N	119·58 E
153	Al 'Amirīyah............Egypt			31·01 N	29·52 E
112	Alamo (ä'lá-mō)				
		Ca. (San Francisco In.)		37·51 N	122·02 W
125	Alamo (ä'lä-mō)........Mex.			21·07 N	99·35 W
114	Alamo (ä'lä-mō)........Nv.			37·22 N	115·10 W
118	Alamo, R. (ä'lä-mō)......Mex.			26·33 N	99·35 W
115	Alamogordo (ăl-á-mō-gŏr'dō).NM			32·55 N	106·00 W
113	Alamo Heights (ä'lá-mō)				
		Tx. (San Antonio In.)		29·28 N	98·27 W
118	Alamo Pk. (ä'lá-mō pēk)...NM			32·50 N	105·55 W
115	Alamosa (ăl-á-mō'sá)......Co.			37·25 N	105·50 W
174	Alandskiy (ä-länt'skǐ)				
		Sov. Un. (Urals In.)		52·14 N	59·48 E
217	Alanga Arba............Ken.			0·07 N	40·25 E
171	Alanya (ä-lä-ō'trä).......Tur.			36·40 N	32·10 E
213	Alaotra (L.) (ä-lä-ō'trä)....Mad.			17·15 S	48·17 E
174	Alapayevsk (ä-lä-pä'yĕfsk)				
		Sov. Un. (Urals In.)		57·50 N	61·35 E
183	Al 'Aqabah.Jordan (Palestine In.)			29·32 N	35·00 E
124	Alaquines (ä-lä-kē'nàs)....Mex.			22·07 N	99·35 W
183	Al 'Arīsh (a-rēsh')				
		Egypt (Palestine In.)		31·08 N	33·48 E
192	Ala Shan (Mts.) (ä'lä-shän').China			38·02 N	105·20 E
75	Alaska (State) (ä-lăs'ká)...U.S.			64·00 N	150·00 W
101	Alaska, G. of............Ak.			57·42 N	147·40 W
101	Alaska Hy..............Ak.			63·00 N	142·00 W
101	Alaska Pen.............Ak.			55·50 N	162·10 W
101	Alaska Ra..............Ak.			62·00 N	152·18 W
211	Al-'Aṭrūn..............Sud.			18·13 N	26·44 E
170	Alatyr' (ä'lä-tür).......Sov. Un.			54·55 N	46·30 E
134	Alausí (ä-lou-sē').........Ec.			2·15 S	78·45 W
218	Al 'Ayyāṭ (ä-ê-yät')				
		Egypt (Nile In.)		29·38 N	31·18 E
164	Alba (äl'bä)............It.			44·41 N	8·02 E
162	Albacete (äl-bä-thä'tä).....Sp.			39·00 N	1·49 W
161	Albachten (äl-bä'k-tĕn)				
		F.R.G. (Ruhr In.)		51·55 N	7·31 E
162	Alba de Tormes (äl-bá dä tôr'mäs)				
		Sp.		40·48 N	5·28 W
218	Al Bahnasā...Egypt (Nile In.)			28·35 N	30·30 E
159	Alba Iulia (äl-bä yōō'lyä)...Rom.			46·05 N	23·32 E
163	Albalate (äl-bä-lä'tä).......Sp.			41·07 N	0·34 W
218	Al Ballaḥ...Egypt (Suez In.)			30·46 N	32·20 E
218	Al Balyanā.....Egypt (Nile In.)			26·12 N	32·00 E
146	Albania (äl-bā'nǐ-á).......Eur.			41·45 N	20·00 E
163	Albano, Lago (L.)				
		It. (Rome In.)		41·45 N	12·44 E
163	Albano Laziale (äl-bä'nō				
		lät-zē-ä'lĕ).It. (Rome In.)		41·44 N	12·43 E
204	Albany (ôl'bá-nǐ)........Austl.			35·00 S	118·00 E
112	Albany...Ca. (San Francisco In.)			37·54 N	122·18 W
120	Albany.................Ga.			31·35 N	84·10 W
117	Albany.................Mo.			40·14 N	94·18 W
105	Albany.................NY			42·40 N	73·50 W
110	Albany.................Or.			44·38 N	123·06 W
113	Albany.................Tx.			32·43 N	99·17 W
91	Albany (R.)............Can.			51·45 N	83·30 W
186	Al Baṣrah...............Iraq			30·35 N	47·59 E
183	Al Batrūn (bä-trōōn')				
		Leb. (Palestine In.)		34·16 N	35·39 E

Page	Name Pronunciation Region	Lat. °′	Long. °′
211	Al Bawīṭi Egypt	28·19 N	29·00 E
197	Albay G. (äl-bä'ê) Phil (In.)	13·09 N	123·52 E
121	Albemarle (ăl'bê-märl) NC	35·24 N	80·36 W
121	Albemarle Sd. NC	36·00 N	76·17 W
164	Albenga (äl-bĕŋ'gä) It.	44·04 N	8·13 E
162	Alberche (R.) (äl-bĕr'chå) Sp.	40·08 N	4·19 W
204	Alberga, The (R.) (ăl-bûr'gȧ) Austl.	27·15 S	135·00 E
162	Albergaria a-Velha (äl-bĕr-gȧ-rē'ȧ-ä-väl'yȧ). Port.	40·47 N	8·31 W
113	Alberhill (ăl'bĕr-hĭl) Ca. (Los Angeles In.)	33·43 N	117·23 W
92	Alberni Can.	49·16 N	124·49 W
160	Albert (ál-bâr') Fr.	50·00 N	2·49 E
217	Albert (L.) (ăl'bĕrt) (ál-bâr') Afr.	1·50 N	30·40 E
217	Albert, Parc Natl. (Natl. Pk.) Zaire	0·05 N	29·30 E
90	Alberta (Prov.) (ăl-bûr'tȧ) Can.	54·33 N	117·10 W
93	Alberta, Mt. Can.	52·18 N	117·28 W
197	Albert Edward, Mt. (ăl'bĕrt ĕd'wẽrd). Pap. N. Gui.	8·25 S	147·25 E
137	Alberti (ál-bĕ'r-tē) Arg. (Buenos Aires In.)	35·01 S	60·16 W
149	Albert Kanal (Can.) Bel. (Brussels In.)	51·07 N	5·07 E
109	Albert Lea (ăl'bĕrt lē') Mn.	43·38 N	93·24 W
217	Albert Nile (R.) Ug.	3·25 N	31·35 E
98	Alberton (ăl'bĕr-tŭn) Can.	46·49 N	64·04 W
213	Alberton S. Afr. (Johannesburg & Pretoria In.)	26·16 S	28·08 E
120	Albertville (ăl'bĕrt-vĭl) Al.	34·15 N	86·10 W
161	Albertville (ál-bêr-vēl') Fr.	45·42 N	6·25 E
	Albertville, see Kalemi		
160	Albi (äl-bē') Fr.	43·54 N	2·07 E
109	Albia (ăl-bĭ-ȧ) Ia.	41·01 N	92·44 W
135	Albina (äl-bē'nä) Sur.	5·30 N	54·33 W
216	Albina, Ponta (Pt.) Ang.	15·51 S	11·44 E
107	Albino, Pt. (äl-bē'nō) Can. (Buffalo In.)	42·50 N	79·05 W
104	Albion (ăl'bĭ-ŭn) Mi.	42·15 N	84·50 W
108	Albion Nb.	41·42 N	99·00 W
105	Albion NY	43·15 N	78·10 W
162	Alboran, Isla del (I.) (ē's-lä-dĕl-äl-bō-rä'n). Sp.	35·58 N	3·02 W
162	Alboran Sea Afr.-Eur.	35·54 N	4·26 W
156	Ålborg (ôl'bôr) Den.	57·02 N	9·55 E
162	Albox (äl-bōk') Sp.	37·23 N	2·08 W
218	Al Buḥayrah al Murrah al Kubrā (Great Bitter) (Salt L.). Egypt (Suez In.)	30·24 N	32·27 E
218	Al Buḥayrah al Murrah aṣ Ṣughrā (Little Bitter) (Salt L.). Egypt (Suez In.)	30·10 N	32·36 E
115	Albuquerque (ăl-bû-kûr'kê) NM	35·05 N	106·40 W
127	Albuquerque, Cayus de (I.) (äl-bû-kûr'kê). Col.	12·12 N	81·24 W
186	Al Buraymī Om.	23·45 N	55·39 E
162	Alburquerque (äl-bōōr-kĕr'kä). Sp.	39·13 N	6·58 W
203	Albury (ôl'bĕr-ê) Austl.	36·00 S	147·00 E
163	Alcabideche (äl-kȧ-bē-dā'chå) Port. (Lisbon In.)	38·43 N	9·24 W
162	Alcacer do Sal (äl-kä'sĕr dŏŏ säl') Port.	38·24 N	8·33 W
163	Alcalá de Chivert (äl-kä-lä'dä chē-vĕrt'). Sp.	40·18 N	0·12 E
163	Alcalá de Henares (äl-kä-lä' dä ā-na'rās) Sp. (Madrid In.)	40·29 N	3·22 W
162	Alcalá de los Gazules (äl-kä-lä' dā lōs gä-thōō'lås). Sp.	36·29 N	5·44 W
162	Alcalá la Real (äl-kä-lä'lä rā-äl'). Sp.	37·27 N	3·57 W
164	Alcamo (äl'kȧ-mō) It.	37·58 N	13·03 E
163	Alcanadre (R.) (äl-kä-nä'drå). Sp.	41·41 N	0·18 W
163	Alcanar (äl-kä-när') Sp.	40·35 N	0·27 E
163	Alcañiz (äl-kän-yēth') Sp.	41·03 N	0·08 W
135	Alcântara (äl-kän'tȧ-rȧ) Braz.	2·17 S	44·29 W
162	Alcaraz (äl-kä-räth') Sp.	38·39 N	2·28 W
162	Alcaudete (äl-kou-dhā'tā) Sp.	37·38 N	4·05 W
162	Alcázar de San Juan (äl-kä'thär dā sän hwän'). Sp.	39·22 N	3·12 W
163	Alcira (ä-thē'rä) Sp.	39·09 N	0·26 W
120	Alcoa (ăl-kō'ȧ) Tn.	35·45 N	84·00 W
163	Alcobendas (äl-kō-bĕn'dås) Sp. (Madrid In.)	40·32 N	3·39 W
163	Alcochete (äl-kō-chā'ta) Port. (Lisbon In.)	38·45 N	8·58 W
163	Alcora (äl-kō'rä) Sp.	40·05 N	0·12 W
163	Alcorisa (äl-kō-rē'sä) Sp.	40·53 N	0·20 W
163	Alcorón (äl-kō-rō'n) Sp. (Madrid In.)	40·22 N	3·50 W
137	Alcorta (ál-kôr'tä) Arg. (Buenos Aires In.)	33·32 S	61·08 W
111	Alcova Res. (ăl-kō'vȧ) Wy.	42·31 N	106·33 W
100	Alcove (ăl-kōv'). Can. (Ottawa In.)	45·41 N	75·55 W
163	Alcoy (äl-koi') Sp.	38·42 N	0·30 W
163	Alcudia, Ba. de (B.) (bä-ē'ä-dĕ-äl-kōō-dhē'ä). Sp.	39·48 N	3·20 E
213	Aldabra Is. (äl-dä'brä) Afr.	9·16 S	46·17 E
124	Aldama (äl-dä'mä) Mex.	22·54 N	98·04 W
118	Aldama Mex.	28·50 N	105·54 W
173	Aldan Sov. Un.	58·46 N	125·19 E
173	Aldan (R.) Sov. Un.	63·30 N	132·14 E
173	Aldan Plat. Sov. Un.	57·42 N	130·28 E
173	Aldanskaya Sov. Un.	61·52 N	135·29 E
161	Aldekerk (äl'dĕ-kĕ'rk) F.R.G. (Ruhr In.)	51·26 N	6·26 E
161	Aldenhoven (äl'dĕn-hō'vĕn) F.R.G. (Ruhr In.)	50·54 N	6·18 E
112	Aldergrove (ôl'dĕr-grōv) Can. (Vancouver In.)	49·03 N	122·28 W
160	Alderney (I.) (ôl'dĕr-nĭ) Guernsey	49·43 N	2·11 W
148	Aldershot (ôl'dĕr-shŏt) Eng. (London In.)	51·14 N	0·46 W
104	Alderson (ôl-dĕr-sŭn) WV	37·40 N	80·40 W
112	Alderwood Manor (ôl'dĕr-wŏŏd măn'ŏr) Wa. (Seattle In.)	47·49 N	122·18 W
148	Aldridge-Brownhills Eng.	52·38 N	1·55 W
117	Aledo (ȧ-lē'dō) Il.	41·12 N	90·47 W
214	Aleg Mauritania	17·03 N	13·55 W
137	Alegre (ålĕ'grĕ) Braz. (Rio de Janeiro In.)	20·41 S	41·32 W
136	Alegre (R.) Braz. (Rio de Janeiro In.)	22·22 S	43·34 W
136	Alegrete (ä-lå-grā'tā) Braz.	29·46 S	55·44 W
174	Aleksandrov (ä-lyĕk-sän' drôf) Sov. Un. (Moscow In.)	56·24 N	38·45 E
174	Aleksandrovsk (ä-lyĕk-sän'drôfsk) Sov. Un. (Urals In.)	59·11 N	57·36 E
173	Aleksandrovsk Sov. Un.	51·02 N	142·21 E
159	Aleksandrow Kujawski (ä-lĕk-säh'drōōv kōō-yav'skē) Pol.	52·54 N	18·45 E
167	Alekseyevka (ä-lyĕk-sā-yĕf'kȧ) Sov. Un.	50·39 N	38·40 E
166	Aleksin (ä-lyĕk-sēn) Sov. Un.	54·31 N	37·07 E
165	Aleksinac (ȧ-lyĕk-sē-nȧk') Yugo.	43·33 N	21·42 E
137	Alem Paraíba (ä-lĕ'm-pȧ-räē'bȧ) Braz. (Rio de Janeiro In.)	21·54 S	42·40 W
160	Alençon (ȧ-läN-sôN') Fr.	48·26 N	0·08 E
135	Alenquer (ä-lĕŋ-kĕr') Braz.	1·58 S	54·44 W
162	Alenquer Port.	39·04 N	9·01 W
162	Alentjo (Reg.) (ä-lĕŋ-tä'zhōō) Port.	38·05 N	7·45 W
199	Alenuihaha Chan. (ä'lå-nōō-ê-hä'hä). Hi. (In.)	20·20 N	156·05 W
153	Aleppo (ȧ-lĕp-ō) Syr.	36·10 N	37·18 E
160	Alès (ä-lĕs') Fr.	44·07 N	4·06 E
164	Alessandria (ä-lĕs-sän'drê-ä) It.	44·53 N	8·35 E
	Alessio, see Lesh		
156	Ålesund (ô'lĕ-sōōn') Nor.	62·28 N	6·14 E
101	Aleutian Is. (ȧ-lu'shăn) Ak.	52·40 N	177·30 W
101	Aleutian Trench Ak.	50·40 N	177·10 E
173	Alevina, Mys (C.) Sov. Un.	58·49 N	151·44 E
101	Alexander Arch. (ăl-ĕg-zăn'dĕr) Ak.	57·05 N	138·10 W
120	Alexander City Al.	32·55 N	85·55 W
100	Alexander Ind. Res. Can. (Edmonton In.)	53·47 N	114·00 W
220	Alexander I Ant.	71·00 S	71·00 W
213	Alexandra (ál-ex-än'drȧ) S. Afr. (Johannesburg & Pretoria In.)	26·07 S	28·07 E
204	Alexandria (ăl-ĕg-zăn'drĭ-ȧ). Austl.	19·00 S	136·56 E
105	Alexandria Can.	45·50 N	74·35 W
104	Alexandria In.	40·20 N	85·20 W
119	Alexandria La.	31·18 N	92·28 W
108	Alexandria Mn.	45·53 N	95·23 W
165	Alexandria Rom.	43·55 N	25·21 E
213	Alexandria (ăl-ĕx-än-drĭ-ȧ) S. Afr. (Natal In.)	33·40 S	26·26 E
108	Alexandria SD	43·39 N	97·45 W
106	Alexandria (ăl-ĕg-zăn'drĭ-ȧ) Va. (Baltimore In.)	38·50 N	77·05 W
	Alexandria, see Al Iskandarīyah		
105	Alexandria Bay NY	44·20 N	75·55 W
165	Alexandroúpolis (Dedeagats) (ä-lĕk-sän-drōō'pō-lĭs) (de'dĕ-ä-gäts). Grc.	40·51 N	25·51 E
162	Alfaro (äl-färō) Sp.	42·08 N	1·43 W
211	Al-Fāshir (fä'shĕr) Sud.	13·38 N	25·21 E
218	Al Fashn Egypt (Nile In.)	28·47 N	30·53 E
211	Al Fayyūm Egypt	29·14 N	30·48 E
137	Alfenas (äl-fĕ'nås) Braz. (Rio de Janeiro In.)	21·26 S	45·55 W
165	Alfiós (R.) Grc.	37·33 N	21·50 E
218	Al Firdān (fer-dän') Egypt (Nile In.)	30·43 N	32·20 E
137	Alfonso Claudio (äl-fōn'sô-klou'dêō) Braz. (Rio de Janeiro In.)	20·05 S	41·05 W
100	Alfred (ăl'frĕd). Can. (Ottawa In.)	45·34 N	74·52 W
148	Alfreton (ăl'fēr-tŭn) Eng.	53·06 N	1·23 W
162	Algarve (Reg.) (äl-gär'vĕ) Port.	37·15 N	8·12 W
162	Algeciras (äl-hā-thē'räs) Sp.	36·08 N	5·25 W
210	Alger (Algiers) (äl-zhā') (ăl-jēr) Alg.	36·51 N	2·56 E
209	Algeria (ăl-gē'rĭ-ȧ) Afr.	34·58 N	4·00 E
163	Algete (äl-hā'tā). Sp. (Madrid In.)	40·36 N	3·30 W
164	Alghero (äl-gâ'rō) It.	40·32 N	8·22 E
	Algiers, see Alger		
119	Algoa (ăl-gō'ȧ) Tx. (In.)	29·24 N	95·11 W
213	Algoabaai (B.) (äl'gōȧ) S. Afr. (Natal In.)	33·51 S	24·50 E
112	Algoma Wa. (Seattle In.)	47·17 N	122·15 W
109	Algoma Wi.	44·38 N	87·29 W
109	Algona Ia.	43·04 N	94·11 W
104	Algonac (ăl'gō-năk) Mi.	42·35 N	82·30 W
107	Algonquin (ăl-gŏŋ'kwĭn) Il. (Chicago In.)	42·10 N	88·17 W
105	Algonquin Provincial Park Can.	45·50 N	78·20 W
162	Alhama (äl-hä'mä) Sp.	37·00 N	3·59 W
162	Alhama Sp.	27·50 N	1·24 W
113	Alhambra (ăl-hăm'brȧ) Ca. (Los Angeles In.)	34·05 N	118·08 W
153	Al Ḥammām Egypt	30·46 N	29·42 E
163	Alhandra (äl-yän'drȧ) Port. (Lisbon In.)	38·55 N	9·01 W
186	Al Hasā (Plain) Sau. Ar.	27·00 N	47·48 E
162	Alhaurín el Grande (ä-lou-rēn'ĕl-grä'n-dĕ). Sp.	36·40 N	4·40 W
186	Al Ḥijāz (Reg.) Sau. Ar.	23·45 N	39·08 E
183	Al Hirmil Leb. (Palestine In.)	34·23 N	36·22 E
163	Alhos Vedros (äl'yōs'vā'drōs) Port. (Lisbon In.)	38·39 N	9·02 W
162	Alhucemas, Baie d' (B.) Mor.	35·18 N	5·50 W
186	Al Ḥudaydah Yemen	14·43 N	43·03 E
186	Al Hufūf Sau. Ar.	25·15 N	49·43 E
165	Aliákmon (R.) (ál-ê-ák'mōn) Grc.	40·26 N	22·17 E
215	Alibori (R.) Dahomey	11·40 N	2·55 E
163	Alicante (ä-lê-kän'tā) Sp.	38·20 N	0·30 W
163	Alicante, Bahia de (B.) (bä-ē'ä-dĕ-ä-lê-kän'tā). Sp.	38·12 N	0·22 W
213	Alice (ăl-ĭs) S. Afr. (Natal In.)	32·47 S	26·51 E
118	Alice (ăl'ĭs) Tx.	27·45 N	98·04 W
92	Alice Arm Can.	55·29 N	129·29 W
213	Alicedale (ăl'ĭs-dāl) S. Afr. (Natal In.)	33·18 S	26·04 E
204	Alice Springs (ăl'ĭs) Austl.	23·38 S	133·56 E
164	Alicudi (I.) (ä-lē-kōō'dē) It.	38·34 N	14·21 E
174	Alifkulovo (ä-lĭf-kŭ'lô-vô) Sov. Un. (Urals In.)	55·57 N	62·06 E
184	Alīgarh (ä-lê-gŭr') India	27·58 N	78·08 E
156	Alingsås (å'lĭŋ-sôs) Swe.	57·57 N	12·30 E
107	Aliquippa (ăl-ĭ-kwĭp'ȧ) Pa. (Pittsburgh In.)	40·37 N	80·15 W
218	Al Iskandarīyah (Alexandria) Egypt (Nile In.)	31·12 N	29·58 E
	Al Ismā'ī-līyah, see Ismailia		
212	Aliwal North (ä-lê-wäl') S. Afr.	31.09 S	28·26 E
186	Al-Jabal Al-Akhḍar (Mts.) Om.	23·30 N	56·43 W
183	Al Jafr, Qa' (L.) Jordan (Palestine In.)	30·15 N	36·24 E
210	Al Jaghbūb Libya	29·46 N	24·32 E
210	Al Jawf Libya	24·14 N	23·15 E
186	Al Jawf Sau. Ar.	29·45 N	39·30 E
162	Aljezur (äl-zhā-zōōr') Port.	37·18 N	8·52 W
218	Al Jīzah Egypt (Nile In.)	30·01 N	31·12 E
210	Al Jufrah (Oasis) Libya	29·30 N	15·16 E
162	Aljustrel (äl-zhōō-strĕl') Port.	37·44 N	8·23 W
218	Al Kāb Egypt (Suez In.)	30·56 N	32·19 E
211	Al Kamilin (käm-lēn') Sud.	15·09 N	33·06 E
183	Al Karak (kĕ-räk') Jordan (Palestine In.)	31·11 N	35·42 E
218	Al Karnak (kär'nak) Egypt (Nile In.)	25·42 N	32·43 E
186	Al Khābūrah Om.	23·45 N	57·30 E
183	Al Khalīl (Hebron) Jordan (Palestine In.)	31·31 N	35·07 E
211	Al Khandaq (kän-däk') Sud.	18·38 N	30·29 E
210	Al Khums Libya	32·35 N	14·10 E
186	Al Khurmah Sau. Ar.	21·37 N	41·44 E
211	Al Khurṭūm (Khartoum) (kär-tōōm'). Sud.	15·34 N	32·36 E
211	Al-Khurṭūm Bahrī Sud.	15·43 N	32·41 E
183	Al Kiswah Syr. (Palestine In.)	33·31 N	36·13 E
155	Alkmaar (älk-mär') Neth.	52·39 N	4·42 E
218	Al Kūbrī (kōō'brê) Egypt (Suez In.)	30·01 N	32·35 E
210	Al Kufrah (Oasis) Libya	24·45 N	22·45 E
183	Al Kuntillah. Egypt (Palestine In.)	29·59 N	34·42 E
186	Al Kuwayt (Kuwait) (koō-wit) Kuw.	29·04 N	47·59 E
153	Al Lādhiqīyah (Latakia) Syr.	35·32 N	35·51 E
98	Allagash (R.) (ăl'ȧ-găsh) Me.	46·50 N	69·24 W
184	Allāhābād (ŭl-ŭ-hä-bäd') India	25·32 N	81·53 E
114	All American Can. (âl ȧ-mĕr'ĭ-kăn) Ca.	32·43 N	115·12 W
149	Alland Aus. (Vienna In.)	48·04 N	16·05 E
162	Allariz (äl-yä-rēth') Sp.	42·10 N	7·48 W
120	Allatoona (R.) (ăl'ȧ-tōōn'ȧ) Ga.	34·05 N	84·57 W
160	Allauch (ä-lĕ'ōō) Fr. (In.)	43·21 N	5·30 E
173	Allaykha (ä-lī'κȧ) Sov. Un.	70·32 N	148·53 E
96	Allegan (ăl'ē-găn) Mi.	42·30 N	85·55 W
105	Allegany Ind. Res. (ăl-ê-gā'nĭ) NY	42·05 N	78·55 W
105	Allegheny (R.) Pa.	41·10 N	79·20 W
105	Allegheny Front (Mts.) U. S.	38·12 N	80·03 W
103	Allegheny Mts. U. S.	37·35 N	81·55 W
104	Allegheny Plat. U. S.	39·00 N	81·15 W
105	Allegheny Res. Pa.	41·50 N	78·55 W
117	Allen (ăl'ĕn) Ok.	34·51 N	96·26 W
154	Allen, Lough (B.) (lŏk ăl'ĕn) Ire.	54·07 N	8·09 W
106	Allendale (ăl'ĕn-dāl) NJ (New York In.)	41·02 N	74·08 W
121	Allendale SC	33·00 N	81·19 W
125	Allende (äl-yĕn'dâ) Mex.	18·23 N	92·49 W
118	Allende Mex.	28·20 N	100·50 W
105	Allentown (ăl'en-toun) Pa.	40·35 N	75·30 W
185	Alleppey (ȧ-lĕp'ē) India	9·33 N	76·22 E
158	Aller R. (äl'ēr) F.R.G.	52·43 N	9·50 E
108	Alliance (ȧ-lī'ăns) Ne.	42·06 N	102·53 W
104	Alliance Oh.	40·55 N	81·10 W
186	Al Lidam Sau. Ar.	20·45 N	44·12 E
160	Allier (R.) (ȧ-lyā') Fr.	46·43 N	3·03 E
106	Alligator Pt. (al'ĭ-gā-tēr) La. (New Orleans In.)	30·57 N	89·41 W
156	Allinge (äl'ĭŋ-ĕ) Den.	55·16 N	14·48 E
126	All Pines (ôl pīnz) Belize (In.)	16·55 N	88·15 W
186	Al Luḥayyah Yemen	15·58 N	42·48 E
106	Alluvial City La. (New Orleans In.)	29·51 N	89·42 W
112	Allyn (ăl'ĭn) Wa. (Seattle In.)	47·23 N	122·51 W
98	Alma (ăl'mȧ) Can.	45·36 N	64·59 W
98	Alma Can.	48·29 N	71·42 W
121	Alma Ga.	31·33 N	82·31 W
104	Alma Mi.	43·25 N	84·40 W
116	Alma Ne.	40·08 N	99·21 W
218	Alma S. Afr. (Johannesburg & Pretoria In.)	24·30 S	28·05 E
109	Alma Wi.	44·21 N	91·57 W
172	Alma-Ata (ăl'mȧ ȧ'tȧ) Sov. Un.	43·19 N	77·08 E
183	Al Mabrak (R.) Sau. Ar. (Palestine In.)	29·16 N	35·12 E

ng-sing; ŋ-baŋk; N-nasalized n; nŏd; cŏmmit; ōld; ôbey; ôrder; fōōd; fŏŏt; ou-out; s-soft; sh-dish; th-thin; pūre; ûnite; ûrn; stŭd; circŭs; ü-as "y" in study; '-indeterminate vowel.

Page Name Pronunciation Region Lat. °' Long. °'
163 Almada (äl-mä'dä) Port. (Lisbon In.) 38·40 N 9·09 W
162 Almadén (äl-mȧ-dhän') Sp. 38·47 N 4·50 W
186 Al Madīnah (Medina) Sau. Ar. 24·26 N 39·42 E
183 Al Mafraq..Jordan (Palestine In.) 32·21 N 36·13 E
125 Almagre, Laguna (L.) (lä-gŏŏ'nä-äl-mä'grĕ) Mex. 22·48 N 97·45 W
162 Almagro (äl-mä'grō) Sp. 38·52 N 3·41 W
218 Al Maḩallah al Kubrā Egypt (Nile In.) 31·00 N 31·10 E
186 Al Manāmah Bahrain 26·01 N 50·33 E
114 Almanor (R.) (ăl-măn'ôr) Ca. 40·11 N 121·20 W
162 Almansa (äl-män'sä) Sp. 38·52 N 1·09 W
218 Al Manshāh Egypt (Nile In.) 26·31 N 31·46 E
162 Almansor (R.) (äl-män-sôr).. Port. 38·41 N 8·27 W
218 Al Manşūrah Egypt (Nile In.) 31·02 N 31·25 E
218 Al Manzilah (män'za-la) Egypt (Nile In.) 31·09 N 32·05 E
162 Almanzora (R.) (äl-män-thō'rä) Sp. 37·20 N 2·25 W
218 Al Marāghah Egypt (Nile In.) 26·41 N 31·35 E
163 Almargem (äl-mär-zhĕɴ) Port. (Lisbon In.) 38·51 N 9·16 W
211 Al-Marj Libya 32·44 N 21·08 E
186 Al Maşirah (I.) Om. 20·43 N 58·58 E
186 Al Mawsil Iraq 36·00 N 42·53 E
162 Almazán (äl-mä-thän') Sp. 41·30 N 2·33 W
183 Al Mazār...Jordan (Palestine In.) 31·04 N 35·41 E
183 Al Mazra'ah Jordan (Palestine In.) 31·17 N 35·33 E
162 Almeirim (äl-māī-rēɴ') Port. 39·13 N 8·31 W
155 Almelo (äl'mē-lō) Neth. 52·20 N 6·42 E
162 Almendralejo (äl-mān-drä-lā'hō) Sp. 38·43 N 6·24 W
162 Almería (äl-mā-rē'ä) Sp. 36·52 N 2·28 W
162 Almeria, Golfo de (G.) (gôl-fô-dĕ-äl-māī-rеɴ') Sp. 36·45 N 2·26 W
162 Almería (R.) Sp. 37·00 N 2·40 W
156 Älmhult (ĕlm'hŏŏlt) Swe. 56·35 N 14·08 E
162 Almina, Pta. (äl-mē'nä) Mor. 35·58 N 5·17 W
218 Al Minyā Egypt (Nile In.) 28·04 N 30·45 E
127 Almirante (äl-mē-rän'tā) Pan. 9·18 N 82·24 W
127 Almirante, Bahia de (B.) (bä-ē'ä-dĕ-äl-mē-rän'tā) Pan. 9·22 N 82·07 W
165 Almirós Grc. 39·13 N 22·47 E
162 Almodóvar (äl-mō-dhō'vär) Sp. 38·43 N 4·10 W
184 Almoi India 29·41 N 79·42 E
124 Almoloya (äl-mō-lō'yä) Mex. 19·32 N 99·44 W
125 Almoloya Mex. (In.) 19·11 N 99·28 W
105 Almonte (ăl-mŏn'tē) Can. 45·15 N 76·15 W
162 Almonte (äl-mōn'tā) Sp. 37·16 N 6·32 W
162 Almonte (R.) Sp. 39·35 N 5·50 W
184 Almora India 29·20 N 79·40 E
186 Al Mubarraz Sau. Ar. 22·31 N 46·27 E
183 Al Mudawwarah Jordan (Palestine In.) 29·20 N 36·01 E
186 Al Mukallā P. D. R. of Yem. 14·27 N 49·05 E
186 Al Mukhā Yemen 13·43 N 43·27 E
162 Almuñécar (äl-mōōn-yā'kär) Sp. 36·44 N 3·43 W
156 Alnö (I.) Swe. 62·20 N 17·39 E
112 Aloha (ä'lō-hā)..Or. (Portland In.) 45·29 N 122·52 W
197 Alor (I.) (ä'lôr) Indon. 8·07 S 125·00 E
162 Álora (ä'lō-rä) Sp. 36·49 N 4·42 W
183 Alor Gajah..Mala (Singapore In.) 2·23 N 102·13 E
196 Alor Setar (ä'lôr stär) Mala. 6·24 N 100·08 E
188 Alot'ai (ălŏt'ī) China 47·52 N 86·50 E
112 Alouette (R.) (ä-lōō-ĕt') Can. (Vancouver In.) 49·16 N 122·32 W
104 Alpena (ăl-pē'nȧ) Mi. 45·05 N 83·30 W
149 Alphen...Neth. (Amsterdam In.) 52·07 N 4·38 E
162 Alpiarca (ăl-pyär'sȧ) Port. 39·38 N 8·37 W
118 Alpine (ăl'pīn) Tx. 30·21 N 103·41 W
152 Alps (Mts.) (ălps) Eur. 46·18 N 8·42 E
134 Alpujarra (ȧl-pōō-ĸä'rȧ) Col. (In.) 3·23 N 74·56 W
162 Alpujarras (Mts.) (äl-pōō-här'räs) Sp. 36·55 N 3·25 W
211 Al Qadārif Sud. 14·03 N 35·11 E
218 Al Qāhirah (Cairo) Egypt (Nile In.) 30·00 N 31·17 E
218 Al Qanţarah Egypt (Suez In.) 30·51 N 32·20 E
211 Al Qaryah ash Shargiyah Libya 30·36 N 13·13 E
186 Al Qaţīf Sau. Ar. 26·30 N 50·00 E
186 Al Qayşūmah Sau. Ar. 28·15 N 46·20 E
183 Al Quarayyah Sau. Ar. (Palestine In.) 28·43 N 36·11 E
183 Al Qunaytirah.Syr. (Palestine In.) 33·09 N 35·49 E
186 Al Qunfudhah Sau. Ar. 14·48 N 41·20 E
183 Al Quşaymah Egypt (Palestine In.) 30·40 N 34·23 E
211 Al Quşayr Egypt 26·14 N 34·11 E
183 Al Qusayr...Egypt (Palestine In.) 34·32 N 36·33 E
156 Als (äls) Den. 55·06 N 9·40 E
161 Alsace (Reg.) (äl-sȧ's) Fr. 48·25 N 7·24 E
190 Al Shan (Mts.) (äī'shän) China 37·27 N 120·35 E
156 Alsterån (R.) Swe. 56·54 N 15·50 E
113 Altadena (ăl-tä-dē'nä) Ca. (Los Angeles In.) 34·12 N 118·08 W
136 Alta Gracia (äl'tä grä'sē-ä) Arg. 31·41 S 64·19 W
134 Altagracia Ven. 10·42 N 71·34 W
135 Altagracia de Orituco (ä'l-tȧ-grȧ'sēä-dĕ-ōrē-tōō'kô) Ven. (In.) 9·53 N 66·22 W
188 Altai Mts. (äl'tī') Asia 49·11 N 87·15 E
172 Altai Ter. Sov. Un. 53·39 N 78·52 E
113 Alta Loma (ăl'tȧ lō'mä) Ca. (Los Angeles In.) 34·07 N 117·35 W
119 Alta Loma (ăl'tȧ lō-mȧ)..Tx. (In.) 29·22 N 95·05 W
121 Altamaha (R.) (ôl-tȧ-mȧ-hô')..Ga. 31·50 N 82·00 W
135 Altamira (äl-tä-mē'rä) Braz. 3·13 S 52·14 W
125 Altamira Mex. 22·25 N 97·55 W
136 Altamirano (äl-tä-mē-rä'nō)..Arg. 35·26 S 58·12 W
164 Altamura (äl-tä-mōō'rä) It. 40·40 N 16·35 E
173 Altan Bulag Mong. 50·18 N 106·31 E
121 Altavista (äl-tä-vēs'tȧ) Va. 37·08 N 79·14 W
150 Alten (R.) (äl'tĕn) Nor. 69·40 N 24·09 E
158 Altenburg (äl-tĕn-bōōrgh) G.D.R. 50·59 N 12·27 E
149 Altenmarkt an der Triesting Aus. (Vienna In.) 48·02 N 16·00 E
162 Alter do Chão (äl-tĕr'dŏŏ shäɴ'ōɴ). Port. 39·13 N 7·38 W
124 Altiplanicie Mexicana (Plat.) (äl-tē-plä-nē'syĕ-mĕ-ĸē-kȧ-nä) Mex. 22·38 N 102·33 W
134 Altiplano (Plat.) (äl-tē-plȧ'nō) Bol. 18·38 S 68·20 W
149 Alt Landsberg (ält länts'bĕrgh) G.D.R. (Berlin In.) 52·34 N 13·44 E
119 Alto (ăl'tō) La. 32·21 N 91·52 W
134 Alto Marañón, Rio (R.) (rē'ō-ȧl'tô-mä-rän-yō'n). Peru 8·18 S 77·13 W
217 Alto Molócuè Moz. 15·38 S 37·42 E
149 Altomünster (äl'tō-mün'stĕr) F.R.G. (Munich In.) 48·24 N 11·16 E
100 Alton (ôl'tŭn)..Can. (Toronto In.) 43·52 N 80·05 W
113 Alton Il. (St. Louis In.) 38·53 N 90·11 W
202 Altona Austl. (Melbourne In.) 37·52 S 144·50 E
95 Altona Can. 49·06 N 97·33 W
149 Altona (äl'tō-nȧ) F.R.G. (Hamburg In.) 53·33 N 9·54 E
120 Altoona (ăl-tōō'nȧ) Al. 34·01 N 86·15 W
105 Altoona Pa. 40·25 N 78·25 W
112 Altoona Wa. (Portland In.) 46·16 N 123·39 W
137 Alto Rio Doce (äl'tô-rē'ô-dō'sĕ) Braz. (Rio de Janeiro In.) 21·02 S 43·23 W
129 Alto Songo (äl-fō-sôŋ'gō) Cuba 20·10 N 75·45 W
125 Altotonga (äl-tō-tôŋ'gä) Mex. 19·44 N 97·13 W
216 Alto-Uama Ang. 12·14 S 15·33 E
129 Alto Velo (I.) (äl-tô-vĕ'lō) Dom. Rep. 17·30 N 71·35 W
148 Altrincham (ôl'trĭng-ăm) Eng. 53·18 N 2·21 W
149 Alt Ruppin (ält rōō'pēn) G.D.R. (Berlin In.) 54·56 N 12·48 E
110 Alturas (ăl-tōō'rȧs) Ca. 41·29 N 120·33 W
116 Altus (ăl'tŭs) Ok. 34·38 N 99·20 W
211 Al-Ubayyiḑ Sud. 13·15 N 30·15 E
211 Al-Uḑayyah Sud. 12·06 N 28·16 E
211 Al-'Ugaylah Libya 30·15 N 19·07 E
166 Alūksne (ä'lŏŏks-nĕ) Sov. Un. 57·24 N 27·04 E
218 'Alula (ä-lōō'lä) Som. (Horn of Afr. In.) 11·53 N 50·40 E
105 Alumette I. (ȧ-lü-mĕt') Can. 45·50 N 77·00 W
112 Alum Rock Ca. (San Francisco In.) 37·23 N 121·50 W
218 Al Uqşur (Luxor). Egypt (Nile In.) 25·38 N 32·59 E
167 Alushta (ä'lshōō-tȧ) Sov. Un. 44·39 N 34·23 E
116 Alva (ăl'vȧ) Ok. 36·46 N 98·41 W
125 Alvarado (äl-vä-rä'dhō) Mex. 18·48 N 95·45 W
125 Alvarado, Luguna de (L.) (lä-gōō'nä-dĕ-äl-vä-rȧ'dô)..Mex. 18·44 N 96·45 W
156 Älvdalen (ĕlv'dä-lĕn) Swe. 61·14 N 14·04 E
163 Alverca (al-vĕr'kȧ) Port. (Lisbon In.) 38·53 N 9·02 W
156 Alvesta (äl-vĕs'tä) Swe. 56·55 N 14·29 E
119 Alvin (ăl'vĭn) Tx. (In.) 29·25 N 95·14 W
137 Alvinópolis (äl-vēnō'pō-lēs) Braz. (Rio de Janeiro In.) 20·07 S 43·03 W
112 Alviso (ăl-vī'sō) Ca. (San Francisco In.) 37·26 N 121·59 W
186 Al Wajh Sau. Ar. 26·15 N 36·32 E
184 Alwar (ŭl'wŭr) India 27·39 N 76·39 E
218 Al Wāsiţah Egypt (Nile In.) 29·21 N 31·15 E
157 Alytus (ä'lē-tŏŏs) Sov. Un. 54·25 N 24·05 E
156 Åmå (ô'môl) Swe. 59·05 N 12·40 E
124 Amacuzac (R.) (ä-mä-kōō-zȧk) Mex. 18·00 N 99·03 W
204 Amadeus, (L.) (ăm-ȧ-dē'ŭs). Austl. 24·30 S 131·25 E
91 Amadjuak (L.) (ä-mädj'wäk). Can. 64 50 N 69 20 W
195 Amagasaki (ä'mä-gä-sä'kē) Jap. (Ōsaka In.) 34·43 N 135·25 E
195 Amakusa-Shimo (I.) (ämä-kōō'sä shē-mō). Jap. 32·24 N 129·35 E
134 Amalfi (ä'mȧ'l-fē) Col. (In.) 6·55 N 75·04 W
163 Amalfi (ä-mä'l-fē). It. (Naples In.) 40·23 N 14·36 E
165 Amaliás (ȧ-mäl'yȧs) Grc. 37·48 N 21·23 E
184 Amalner India 21·07 N 75·06 E
135 Amambay, Cordillera de (Mts.) Braz. 20·06 S 57·08 W
194 Amami Guntō (Is.) (ä'mä'mē gŏŏn'tō'). Jap. 28·25 N 129·00 E
194 Amamio (I.) (ä-mä'mē-ō) Jap. 28·10 N 129·55 E
135 Amapá (ä-mä-pȧ') Braz. 2·14 N 50·48 W
135 Amapá (Ter.) Braz. 1·15 N 52·15 W
126 Amapala (ä-mä-pä'lä) Hond. 13·16 N 87·39 W
135 Amarante (ä-mä-rän'tā) Braz. 6·17 S 42·43 W
114 Amargosa (R.) (ȧ'mär-gō'sȧ)..Ca. 35·55 N 116·45 W
116 Amarillo (ăm-ȧ-rĭl'ō) Tx. 35·14 N 101·49 W
164 Amaro, Mt. (ä-mä'rō) It. 42·07 N 14·07 E
171 Amasya (ä-mä'sē-ȧ) Tur. 40·40 N 35·50 E
125 Amatenango (ä-mä-tā-naŋ'gō) Mex. 16·30 N 92·29 W
101 Amatignak (I.) (ä-mȧ'tē-näk)..Ak. 51·12 N 178·30 W
126 Amatique, Bahía de (B.) (bä-ē'ä-dĕ-ä-mä-tē'kä) Belize-Guat. 15·58 N 88·50 W
126 Amatitlán (ä-mä-tē-tlän')...Guat. 14·27 N 90·39 W
124 Amatlán de Cañas (ä-mät-län'dā kän-yäs). Mex. 20·50 N 104·22 W
134 Amazonas (State) (ä-mä-thō'näs). Braz. 4·15 S 64·30 W
135 Amazonas, Rio (R.) (rē'ō-ä-mä-thō'näs). Braz. 2·03 S 53·18 W
184 Ambāla (ŭm-bä'lŭ) India 30·31 N 76·48 E
134 Ambalema (äm-bä-lā'mä) Col. (In.) 4·47 N 74·45 W
173 Ambarchik (ŭm-bär'chĭk). Sov. Un. 69·39 N 162·18 E
185 Ambarnāth...India (Bombay In.) 19·12 N 73·10 E
134 Ambato (äm-bä'tō) Ec. 1·15 S 78·30 W
213 Ambatondrazaka Mad. 17·58 S 48·43 E
158 Amberg (äm'bĕrgh) F.R.G. 49·26 N 11·51 E
126 Ambergris Cay (I.) (ăm'bēr-grēs kāz). Belize 18·04 N 87·43 W
129 Ambergris Cays (Is.) Turks & Caicos Is. 21·20 N 71·40 W
161 Ambérieu (äɴ-bā-rē-u') Fr. 45·57 N 5·21 E
160 Ambert (äɴ-bĕr') Fr. 45·32 N 3·41 E
197 Ambil (I.) (äm'bēl)...Phil. (In.) 13·51 N 120·25 E
106 Ambler (ăm'blēr) Pa. (Philadelphia In.) 40·09 N 75·13 W
197 Amboina (ăm-boi'nȧ) Indon. 3·45 S 128·17 E
160 Amboise (äɴ-bwȧz') Fr. 47·25 N 0·56 E
197 Ambon (I.) Indon. 4·50 S 128·45 E
213 Ambositra (äɴ-bô-sē'trä) Mad. 20·31 S 47·28 E
104 Amboy (ăm'boi) Il. 41·41 N 89·15 W
112 Amboy Wa. (Portland In.) 45·55 N 122·27 W
213 Ambre, Cap d' (C.) Mad. 12·06 S 49·15 E
107 Ambridge (ăm'brĭdj) Pa. (Pittsburgh In.) 40·36 N 80·13 W
205 Ambrim (I.) New Heb. 16·28 S 158·17 E
216 Ambriz Ang. 7·50 S 13·06 E
216 Ambrizete Ang. 7·14 S 12·52 E
101 Amchitka P. (ăm-chĭt'kȧ) Ak. 51·30 N 179·36 W
124 Amealco (ä-mā-äl'kō) Mex. 20·12 N 100·08 W
124 Ameca (ä-mĕ'kä) Mex. 20·34 N 104·02 W
125 Amecameca (ä-mȧ-kȧ-mä'kä) Mex. (In.) 19·06 N 98·46 W
149 Ameide...Neth. (Amsterdam In.) 51·57 N 4·57 E
155 Ameland (I.) Neth. 53·29 N 5·54 E
107 Amelia (ȧ-mēl'yȧ) Oh. (Cincinnati In.) 39·01 N 84·12 W
114 American (R.) (ȧ-mĕr'ĭ-kăn)...Ca. 38·20 N 122·45 W
137 Americana (ä-mĕ-rē-kȧ'nȧ) Braz. (Rio de Janeiro In.) 22·46 S 47·19 W
111 American Falls (ȧ-mĕr-ĭ-kăn)..Id. 42·45 N 112·53 W
111 American Falls Res. Id. 42·56 N 113·18 W
115 American Fork Ut. 40·20 N 111·50 W
220 American Highland Ant. 72·00 S 79·00 E
120 Americus (ȧ-mĕr'ĭ-kŭs) Ga. 32·04 N 84·15 W
149 Amersfoort (ä'mērz-fōrt) Neth. (Amsterdam In.) 52·08 N 5·23 E
95 Amery (ā'mēr-ē) Can. 56·34 N 94·03 W
109 Amery Wi. 45·19 N 92·24 W
109 Ames (āmz) Ia. 42·00 N 93·36 W
99 Amesbury (āmz'bēr-ē)...Ma. (In.) 42·51 N 70·56 W
165 Ámfissa (ȧm-fĭ'sȧ) Grc. 38·32 N 22·26 E
173 Amga (ŭm-gä') Sov. Un. 61·08 N 132·09 E
173 Amga (R.) Sov. Un. 61·41 N 133·11 E
173 Amgun (R.) Sov. Un. 53·33 N 137·57 E
211 Amhara (Prov.) (äm-hä'rä)...Eth. 11·30 N 36·45 E
96 Amherst (ăm'hērst) Can. 45·49 N 64·14 W
107 Amherst Oh. (Cleveland In.) 41·24 N 82·13 W
97 Amherst (I.) Can. 44·08 N 76·45 W
160 Amiens (ä-myäɴ') Fr. 49·54 N 2·18 E
184 Amio Tsönag Tsho (L.) China 31·38 N 91·18 E
220 Amirante Is. Sey. 6·02 S 52·30 E
94 Amisk L. Can. 54·35 N 102·13 W
118 Amistad Res. Tx. 29·20 N 101·00 W
119 Amite (ȧ-mēt') La. 30·43 N 90·32 W
119 Amite R. La. 30·45 N 90·48 W
107 Amity (ăm'ĭ-tĭ) Pa. (In.) 40·02 N 80·11 W
106 Amityville (ăm'ĭ-tĭ-vĭl) NY (New York In.) 40·41 N 73·24 W
101 Amlia (I.) (ȧ'm-lēä) Ak. 52·00 N 173·28 W
183 'Ammān (äm'män) Jordan (Palestine In.) 31·57 N 35·57 E
149 Ammer L. (äm'mĕr) F.R.G. (Munich In.) 48·00 N 11·08 E
113 Amnicon R. (ăm'nē-kŏn) Wi. (Duluth In.) 46·35 N 91·56 W
Amnok (R.), see Yalu
165 Amorgós (I.) (ä-mŏr'gōs) Grc. 36·47 N 25·47 E
120 Amory (ām'ō-rē) Ms. 33·58 N 88·27 W
97 Amos (ā'mŭs) Can. 48·31 N 78·04 W
156 Åmot (Torpen) (ô'mōt) (tôr'pĕn) Nor. 61·08 N 11·17 E
Amoy, see Hsiamen
137 Amparo (äm-pȧ'-rô) Braz. (Rio de Janeiro In.) 22·43 S 46·44 W
149 Amper R. (äm'pĕr) F.R.G. (Munich In.) 48·18 N 11·32 E
163 Amposta (äm-pōs'tä) Sp. 40·42 N 0·34 E
96 Amqui Can. 48·28 N 67·28 W
184 Amrāvati India 20·58 N 77·47 E
184 Amritsar (ăm-rĭt'sŭr) India 31·43 N 74·52 E
149 Amstelveen Neth. (Amsterdam In.) 52·18 N 4·51 E
149 Amsterdam (äm-stēr-däm') Neth. (Amsterdam In.) 52·21 N 4·52 E
105 Amsterdam (ăm'stĕr-dăm) NY 42·55 N 74·10 W
220 Amsterdam (I.) Ind. O. 37·52 S 77·32 E
158 Amstetten (äm'stĕt-ĕn) Aus. 48·09 N 14·53 E
211 Am Timan (äm'tē-män') Chad 11·18 N 20·30 E
186 Amu Darya (R.) (ä-mōō-dä'rēä). Asia 40·40 N 62·00 E
101 Amukta P. (ä-mōōk'tȧ) Ak. 52·30 N 172·00 W
197 Amulung (ä'mōō'lōōng). Phil. (In.) 17·51 N 121·43 E
90 Amundsen G. (ä'mŭn-sĕn)...Can. 70·17 N 123·28 W
220 Amundsen Sea Ant. 72·00 S 110·00 W
156 Amungen (L.) Swe. 61·07 N 16·00 E
192 Amur R. (ä-mōōr') China and Sov. Un. 49·38 N 127·25 E
174 Amurskiy (ä-mûr'skĭ) Sov. Un. (Urals In.) 52·35 N 59·36 E
194 Amurskiy, Zaliv (B.) (zä'lĭf ä-mōōr'skĭ). Sov. Un. 43·20 N 131·40 E
124 Amusgos (San Pedro) (ä-mōō's-gōs) (sän-pĕ'drō). Mex. 16·39 N 98·09 W
197 Amuyao, Mt. (ä-mōō-yä'ō) Phil. (In.) 17·04 N 121·09 E

ăt; finăl; rāte; senāte; ärm; ȧsk; sofȧ; fâre; ch-choose; dh-as th in other; bē; ēvent; bĕt; recĕnt; cratēr; g-go; gh-guttural g; bĭt; ĭ-short neutral; rīde; ĸ-guttural k as ch in German ich;

PRONOUNCING INDEX Amvrakikos — 'Araba 251

Page	Name Pronunciation Region	Lat. °′	Long. °′
165	Amvrakikos Kólpos (G.) Grc.	39·00 N	21·00 E
183	Amyun Leb. (Palestine In.)	34·18 N	35·48 E
173	Anabar (R.) (ăn-à-bär') Sov. Un.	71·15 N	113·00 E
135	Anaco (ä-nà'kô) Ven. (In.)	9·29 N	64·27 W
111	Anaconda (ăn-à-kŏn'dà) Mt.	46·07 N	112·55 W
112	Anacortes (ăn-à-kôr'tĕz) Wa. (Seattle In.)	48·30 N	122·37 W
116	Anadarko (ăn-à-där'kō) Ok.	35·05 N	98·14 W
173	Anadyr (ŭ-nà-dĭr') Sov. Un.	64·47 N	177·01 E
173	Anadyr (R.) Sov. Un.	65·30 N	172·45 E
183	Anadyrskiy Zaliv (B.) Sov. Un.	64·10 N	178·00 W
113	Anaheim (ăn'à-hīm) Ca. (Los Angeles In.)	33·50 N	117·55 W
119	Anahuac (ä-nä'wäk) Tx. (In.)	29·46 N	94·41 W
185	Ānai Mudi (Mtn.) India	15·28 N	77·10 E
95	Anama Bay Can.	51·56 N	98·05 W
128	Ana María, Cayos (Is.) (kä'yōs-ä'nà mà-rē'à) Cuba	21·55 N	78·50 W
196	Anambas, Kepulauan (Is.) (ä-näm-bäs) Indon.	2·41 N	106·38 E
109	Anamosa (ăn-à-mō'sà) Ia.	42·06 N	91·18 W
167	Anan'yev (à-nä'nyĕf) Sov. Un.	47·43 N	29·59 E
167	Anapa (à-nä'pä) Sov. Un.	44·54 N	37·19 E
135	Anápolis (ä-nà'pō-lēs) Braz.	16·17 S	48·47 W
136	Añatuya (à-nyä-tōō'yà) Arg.	28·22 S	62·45 W
160	Ancenis (äN-sẽ-nē') Fr.	47·24 N	1·12 W
136	Anchieta (àn-chyĕ'tä) Braz. (Rio de Janeiro In.)	22·49 S	43·24 W
193	Anching (än'kĭng') China	30·32 N	117·00 E
101	Anchitka (I.) (än-chē't-kä) Ak.	51·25 N	178·10 E
190	Anch' iu (än'chē) China	36·26 N	119·12 E
148	Ancholme (R.) (ăn'chŭm) Eng.	53·28 N	0·27 W
101	Anchorage (ăŋ'kēr-āj) Ak.	61·12 N	149·48 W
107	Anchorage Ky. (Louisville In.)	38·16 N	85·32 W
100	Ancienne-Lorette (äN-syĕn' lō-rĕt') Can. (Quebec In.)	46·48 N	71·21 W
122	Ancon (ăŋ-kōn') C. Z. (In.)	8·55 N	79·32 W
164	Ancona (än-kō'nä) It.	43·37 N	13·32 E
136	Ancud (äŋ-kōōdh') Chile	41·52 S	73·45 W
136	Ancud, G. de (gôl-fô-dĕ-äŋ-kōōdh') Chile	41·15 S	73·00 W
136	Andalgalá (á'n-däl-gà-lá') Arg.	27·35 S	66·14 W
162	Andalucia (Reg.) (än-dä-lōō-sē'ä) Sp.	37·35 N	5·40 W
120	Andalusia (ăn-dà-lōō'zhĭà) Al.	31·19 N	86·19 W
196	Andaman Is. (ăn-dà-măn') Andaman & Nicobar Is.	11·38 N	92·17 E
196	Andaman Sea Asia	12·44 N	95·45 E
149	Anderlecht (än'dĕr-lĕkt) Bel. (Brussels In.)	50·49 N	4·16 E
158	Andernach (än'dĕr-näk) F.R.G.	50·25 N	7·23 E
137	Anderson (à'n-dĕr-sōn) Arg. (Buenos Aires In.)	35·15 S	60·15 W
110	Anderson (ăn'dĕr-sŭn) Ca.	40·28 N	122·19 W
104	Anderson In.	40·05 N	85·50 W
121	Anderson SC	34·30 N	82·40 W
90	Anderson (R.) Can.	68·32 N	125·12 W
133	Andes Mts.(ăn'dēz)(än'dās) S. A.	13·00 S	75·00 W
185	Andhei India (In.)	19·08 N	72·50 E
185	Andhra Pradesh (State) India	16·00 N	79·00 E
153	Andikíthira (I.) Grc.	35·50 N	23·20 E
172	Andizhan (än-dē-zhän') Sov. Un.	40·51 N	72·39 E
194	Andong (än'dŭng') Kor.	36·31 N	128·42 E
163	Andorra (än-dôr'rä) And.	42·38 N	1·30 E
151	Andorra Eur.	42·30 N	2·00 E
99	Andover (ăn'dô-vēr) Ma. (In.)	42·39 N	71·08 W
106	Andover NJ (New York In.)	40·59 N	74·45 W
150	Andöy (I.) (änd-ûē) Nor.	69·12 N	14·58 E
163	Andraitx (än-drà-ītsh') Sp.	39·34 N	2·25 E
101	Andreanof Is. (än-drâ-ä'nôf) Ak.	51·10 N	177·00 W
137	Andrelândia (än-drĕ-là'n-dyà) Braz. (Rio de Janeiro In.)	21·45 S	44·18 W
120	Andrew Johnson Natl. Mon. (ăn'drōō jŏn'sŭn) Tn.	36·15 N	82·55 W
120	Andrews (ăn'drōōz) NC	35·12 N	83·48 W
121	Andrews SC	33·25 N	79·32 W
167	Andreyevka (än-drâ-yĕf'kà) Sov. Un.	48·03 N	37·03 E
164	Andria (än'drē-ä) It.	41·17 N	15·55 E
165	Andros (än'dhrôs) Grc.	37·50 N	24·54 E
128	Andros I. (ăn'drŏs) Ba.	24·30 N	78·00 W
165	Andrós (I.) (än'drôs) Grc.	37·59 N	24·55 E
98	Androscoggin (R.) (ăn-drŭs-kŏg'ĭn) Me.	44·25 N	70·45 W
162	Andújar (än-dōō'här) Sp.	38·04 N	4·03 W
214	Anécho (à-nā'chō) Togo	6·14 N	1·36 E
214	Anefis i-n-Darane Mali	18·03 N	0·36 E
195	Anegasaki (ä'nâ-gä-sä'kē) Jap. (Tōkyō In.)	35·29 N	140·02 E
205	Aneityum (I.) (ä-nâ-ē'tē-ŭm) New Hebr.	20·15 S	169·49 E
108	Aneta (ă-nē'tà) ND	47·41 N	97·57 W
197	Angadanan (äŋ-gà-dä'nàn) Phil. (In.)	16·45 N	121·45 E
197	Angaki (än-gä'kē) Phil. (In.)	17·10 N	120·40 E
124	Angamacutiro (än'gä-mä-kōō-tē'rô) Mex.	20·08 N	101·44 W
192	Angangchi (än'gäng'kē') China	47·05 N	123·58 E
124	Angangueo (än-gäŋ'gwà-ô) Mex.	19·36 N	100·18 W
	Angara (R.), see Verkhnyaya Tunguska		
172	Angarsk Sov. Un.	52·48 N	104·15 E
156	Ånge (ông'ă) Swe.	62·31 N	15·39 E
135	Angel, Salto (Falls) (säl'tō-á'n-hĕl) Ven.	5·44 N	62·27 W
122	Angel De La Guarda (I.) (á'n-hĕl-dĕ-lä-gwä'r-dä) Mex.	29·30 N	113·00 W
197	Angeles (än'hâ-lās) Phil. (In.)	15·09 N	120·35 E
156	Ängelholm (ĕng'ĕl-hôlm) Swe.	56·14 N	12·50 E
119	Angelina R. (ăn-jē lē'nà) Tx.	31·30 N	94·53 W
114	Angels Camp (ān'jĕls kămp') Ca.	38·03 N	120·33 W
150	Angermanälven (R.) Swe.	64·02 N	17·15 E
161	Angermund (àn'ngĕr-mŭnd) F.R.G. (Ruhr In.)	51·20 N	6·47 E
158	Angermünde (äng'ĕr-mûn-dĕ) G.D.R.	53·02 N	14·00 E
100	Angers (äN-zhā') Can. (Ottawa In.)	41·31 N	75·29 W
160	Angers Fr.	47·29 N	0·36 W
196	Angkor (Ruins) (äng'kôr) Camb.	13·52 N	103·50 E
154	Anglesey (I.) (ăŋ'g'l-sē) Wales	52·28 N	4·35 W
119	Angleton (aŋ'g'l-tŭn) Tx. (In.)	29·10 N	95·25 W
75	Angmagssalik (àŋ-mà'sà-lĭk) Grnld.	65·40 N	37·40 W
217	Angoche, Ilha (I.) (ē'lä-ăn-gō'chå) Moz.	16·20 S	40·00 E
136	Angol (aŋ-gōl') Chile	37·47 S	72·43 W
104	Angola (ăŋ-gō'là) In.	41·35 N	85·00 W
209	Angola Afr.	14·15 S	16·00 E
	Angora, see Ankara		
160	Angoulême (äŋ'gōō-lâm') Fr.	45·40 N	0·09 E
137	Angra dos Reis (aŋ'grä dōs rā'ēs) Braz. (Rio de Janeiro In.)	23·01 S	44·17 W
163	Angri (ä'n-grē) It. (Naples In.)	40·30 N	14·35 E
128	Anguilla, Cays (Is.) (ăŋ-gwĭl'à) Ba.	23·30 N	79·35 W
127	Anguilla I. St. Kitts-Nevis-Anguilla (In.)	18·15 N	62·54 W
97	Anguille, C. (äŋ-gē'yĕ) Can.	47·55 N	59·25 W
156	Anholt (I). (än'hŏlt) Den.	56·43 N	11·34 E
188	Anhsi China	40·36 N	95·49 E
189	Anhwei (Anhui) (Prov.) China	31·30 N	117·15 E
101	Aniak (ä-nyà'k) Ak.	61·32 N	159·35 W
163	Aniene (ä-nyĕ'nĕ) It. (Rome In.)	41 34 N	12·49 E
115	Animas (R.) (ä'nē-màs) Co.	37·03 N	107·50 W
165	Anina (ä-nē'nä) Rom.	45·03 N	21·50 E
105	Anita (à-nē'à) Pa.	41·05 N	79·00 W
194	Aniva, Mys (Pt.) (mĭs à-nē'và) Sov. Un.	46·08 N	143·13 E
194	Aniva, Zaliv (B.) (zä'lĭf à-nē'và) Sov. Un.	46·28 N	143·30 E
100	Anjou Can. (Montreal In.)	45·37 N	73·33 W
213	Anjouan (I.) (äN-zhwäN) Comoro Is.	12·14 S	44·47 E
192	Ank'ang China	32·38 N	109·10 E
171	Ankara (Angora) (än'kà-rà) (ăn-gō'rà) Tur.	39·55 N	32·50 E
158	Anklam (än'kläm) G.D.R.	53·52 N	13·43 E
217	Ankoro (ăŋ-kō'rō) Zaire	6·45 S	26·57 E
190	Ankou (an'gōō ŭ) China	38·27 N	115·19 E
214	Anloga Ghana	5·47 N	0·50 E
193	Anlu (än'lōō') China	31·18 N	113·40 E
193	Anlung China	25·01 N	105·32 E
105	Ann, C. (ăn) Ma.	42·40 N	70·40 W
117	Anna (ăn'à) Il.	37·28 N	89·15 W
167	Anna (än'ä) Sov. Un.	51·31 N	40·27 E
210	Annaba (Bône) Alg.	36·57 N	7·39 E
158	Annaberg-Buchols (än'ä-bĕrgh) G.D.R.	50·35 N	13·02 E
186	An Nafūd (Des.) Sau. Ar.	28·30 N	40·30 E
186	An Najaf (än nä-jäf') Iraq	32·00 N	44·25 E
183	An Nakhl Egypt (Palestine In.)	29·55 N	33·45 E
196	Annamitic Cord. Mts. (ă-nà-mĭt'ĭk kôr-dĭl-yä'rà) Laos-Viet.	17·34 N	105·38 E
106	Annapolis (ă-năp'ô-lĭs) Md. (Baltimore In.)	39·00 N	76·25 W
98	Annapolis Royal Can.	44·45 N	65·31 W
104	Ann Arbor (ăn är'bēr) Mi.	42·15 N	83·45 W
186	An Nāṣirīyah Iraq	31·08 N	46·15 E
211	An Nawfalīyah) Libya	30·57 N	17·38 E
161	Annecy (àn'sē') Fr.	45·54 N	6·07 E
161	Annemasse (än'mäs') Fr.	46·09 N	6·13 E
174	Annenskoye (ä-nĕn'skô-yĕ) Sov. Un. (Urals In.)	53·09 N	60·25 E
92	Annette I. Ak.	55·13 N	131·30 W
99	Annieopsquotch Mts. Can.	48·37 N	57·17 W
120	Anniston (ăn'ĭs-tŭn) Al.	33·39 N	85·47 W
160	Annonay (à-nô-nĕ') Fr.	45·16 N	4·36 E
128	Annotto Bay (än-nō'tō) Jam.	18·15 N	76·45 W
211	An-Nudūh Sud.	12·39 N	28·18 E
113	Anoka (à-nō'kà) Mn (Minneapolis, St. Paul In.)	45·12 N	93·24 W
134	Anori (à-nō'rē) Col. (In.)	7·01 N	75·09 W
165	Áno Theológos Grc.	40·37 N	24·41 E
164	Áno Viánnos Grc. (In.)	35·52 N	25·26 E
193	Anp'u China	21·28 N	110·00 E
158	Ansbach (äns'bäk) F.R.G.	49·18 N	10·35 E
129	Anse à Veau (äNs' ä-vō') Hai.	18·30 N	73·25 W
129	Anse d' Hainault (äNs'dĕnō) Hai.	18·45 N	74·25 W
134	Anserma (á'n-sĕ'r-mä) Col. (In.)	5·13 N	75·47 W
134	Ansermanuevo (á'n-sĕ'r-mà-nwĕ'vō) Col. (In.)	4·47 N	75·59 W
192	Anshan China	41·00 N	123·00 E
193	Anshun (än-shōōn') China	26·12 N	105·50 E
118	Anson (ăn'sŭn) Tx.	32·45 N	99·52 W
204	Anson B. Austl.	13·10 S	34·25 E
194	Ansŏng (än'sŭng') Kor.	37·00 N	127·12 E
214	Ansongo Mali	15·40 N	0·30 E
105	Ansonia (ăn-sō'nĭ-à) Ct.	41·20 N	73·05 W
192	Antachan China	41·20 N	125·20 E
171	Antakya (än-täk'yä) Tur.	36·20 N	36·10 E
171	Antalya (Adalia) (än-tä'lē-ä) (ä-dä'lē-ä) Tur.	37·00 N	30·50 E
171	Antalya Kōrfezi (G.) Tur.	36·40 N	31·20 E
220	Antarctica	80·15 S	127·00 E
220	Antartic Pen. Ant.	70·00 S	65·00 W
111	Antelope Cr. (ăn'tē-lōp) Wy.	43·29 N	105·42 W
162	Antequera (än-tĕ-kĕ'rä) Sp.	37·01 N	4·34 W
116	Anthony (ăn'thô-nē) Ks.	37·08 N	98·01 W
210	Anti Atlas (Mts.) Mor.	28·45 N	9·30 W
161	Antibes (äN-tēb') Fr.	43·36 N	7·12 E
96	Anticosti, Ile (I.) (ăn-tĭ-kŏs'tē) Can.	49·30 N	63·00 W
109	Antigo (ăn'tĭ-gō) Wi.	45·09 N	89·11 W
99	Antigonish (ăn-tĭ-gô-nēsh') Can.	45·35 N	61·55 W
126	Antigua (än-tē'gwä) Guat.	14·32 N	90·43 W
123	Antigua N. A.	17·15 N	61·15 W
125	Antigua (R.) Mex.	19·16 N	96·36 W
125	Antigua Veracruz (än-tē'gwä vā-rä-krōōz') Mex.	19·18 N	96·17 W
129	Antilla (än-tē'lyä) Cuba	20·50 N	75·50 W
123	Antilles, Greater (Is.) N. A.	20·30 N	79·15 W
123	Antilles, Lesser (Is.) N. A.	12·15 N	65·00 W
112	Antioch (ăn'tĭ-ŏk) Ca. (San Francisco In.)	38·00 N	121·48 W
107	Antioch Il. (Chicago In.)	42·29 N	88·06 W
108	Antioch Ne.	42·05 N	102·36 W
134	Antioquia (än-tē-ō'kēä) Col. (In.)	6·34 N	75·49 W
134	Antioquia (Dept.) Col. (In.)	6·48 N	75·42 W
117	Antlers (ănt'lērz) Ok.	34·14 N	95·38 W
136	Antofagasta (än-tō-fä-gäs'tä) Chile	23·32 S	70·21 W
136	Antofalla, Salar de (Des.) (sà-lär'de àn'tō-fä'lä) Arg.	26·00 S	67·52 W
127	Antón (än-tōn') Pan.	8·24 N	80·15 W
213	Antongil, Baie d' (B.) (äN-tôN-zhēl') Mad.	16·15 S	50·15 E
137	Antonio Carlos (än-tō'nēōō-kà'r-lōs) Braz. (Rio de Janeiro In.)	21·19 S	43·45 W
217	António Enes (ăn-to'nyŏ ĕn'ēs) Moz.	16·14 S	39·58 E
116	Antonito (ăn-tô-nē'tō) Co.	37·04 N	106·01 W
166	Antonopole (än'tô-nô-pō lyĕ) Sov. Un.	56·19 N	27·11 E
154	Antrim Mts. (ăn'trĭm) N. Ire.	55·00 N	6·10 W
213	Antsirabe (änt-sē-rä'bā) Mad.	19·49 S	47·16 E
166	Antsla (änt'slà) Sov. Un.	57·49 N	26·29 E
136	Antuco (Vol.) (än-tōō'kō) Chile	37·30 S	72·30 W
192	Antung (än'tŏŏng') China	40·10 N	124·30 E
190	Antungwei (ändŏŏngwā) China	35·08 N	119·19 E
	Antwerp, see Antwerpen		
149	Antwerpen (Antwerp) (änt'wērpĕn) Bel. (Brussels In.)	51·13 N	4·24 E
192	Antz'u China (In.)	39·23 N	116·44 E
184	Anūpgarh (ŭ-nŏŏp'gŭr) India	29·22 N	73·20 E
185	Anuradhapura (ŭ-nōō'rä-dŭ-pōō'rŭ) Sri Lanka	8·24 N	80·25 E
190	Anyang (än'yäng) China	36·05 N	114·22 E
157	Anykščiai (aníksh-chä'ē) Sov. Un.	55·34 N	25·04 E
134	Anzá (àn-zà') Col. (In.)	6·19 N	75·51 W
172	Anzhero-Sudzhensk (än'zhâ-rô-sōōd'zhĕnsk) Sov. Un.	56·08 N	86·08 E
163	Anzio (änt'zē-ō) It. (Rome In.)	41·28 N	12·39 E
135	Anzoátegui (State) (àn-zôà'tĕ-gē) Ven. (In.)	9·38 N	64·45 W
194	Aomori (äô-mō'rē) Jap.	40·45 N	140·52 E
164	Aosta (ä-ôs'tä) It.	45·45 N	7·20 E
211	Aouk, Bahr (R.) (ä-ōōk') Chad	9·30 N	20·45 E
214	Aoukâr (Pln.) Mauritania	18·00 N	9·40 W
120	Apalachicola (ăp-à-lăch-ĭ-kō'là) Fl.	29·43 N	84·59 W
125	Apan (ä-pà'n) Mex. (In.)	19·43 N	98·27 W
124	Apango (ä-päŋ'gō) Mex.	17·41 N	99·22 W
134	Apaporis (R.) (ä-pä-pô'rĭs) Col.	0·48 N	72·32 W
196	Aparri (ä-pär'rē) Phil.	18·15 N	121·40 E
124	Apasco (ä-pà's-kō) Mex.	20·33 N	100·43 W
165	Apatin (ŏ'pŏ-tĭn) Yugo.	45·40 N	19·00 E
124	Apatzingán de la Constitución (ä-pät-zĭŋ-gän'dā lä cōn-stĭ-tōō-sē-ōn') Mex.	19·07 N	102·21 W
155	Apeldoorn (ä'pĕl-dōorn) Neth.	52·14 N	5·55 E
134	Apía (à-pē'à) Col. (In.)	5·07 N	75·58 W
124	Apipilulco (ä-pĭ-pĭ-lōōl'kō) Mex.	18·09 N	99·40 W
165	Apíranthos Grc.	37·07 N	25·32 E
116	Apishapa (R.) (ă-pĭ-shä'pà) Co.	37·40 N	104·08 W
124	Apizaco (ä-pē-zä'kō) Mex.	19·18 N	98·11 W
197	Apo (Mtn.) (ä'pō) Phil.	6·56 N	125·05 E
121	Apoka (ä-pŏp'kà) Fl. (In.)	28·37 N	81·30 W
121	Apoka (L.) Fl. (In.)	28·38 N	81·50 W
109	Apostle Is. (ă-pŏs'l) Wi.	97·03 N	90·55 W
120	Appalachia (ăpà-lăch'ĭ-à) Va.	36·54 N	82·49 W
103	Appalachian Mts. (ăp-à-lăch'ĭ-àn) U. S.	37·20 N	82·00 W
120	Appalachicola R. (ăpà-lăch'ĭ-cōlä) Fl.	30·11 N	85·00 W
156	Äppelbo (ĕp-ĕl-bōō) Swe.	60·30 N	14·02 E
161	Appelhülsen (ä'pĕl-hül'sĕn) F.R.G. (Ruhr In.)	51·55 N	7·26 E
164	Appennino (Mts.) (äp-pĕn-nē'nô) It.	43·48 N	11·06 E
158	Appenzell (äp'ĕn-tsĕl) Switz.	47·19 N	9·22 E
108	Appleton (ăp'l-tŭn) Mn.	45·10 N	96·01 W
109	Appleton Wi.	44·14 N	88·27 W
117	Appleton City Mo.	38·10 N	94·02 W
121	Appomattox (R.) (ăp-ô-măt'ŭks) Va.	37·22 N	78·09 W
163	Aprília (à-prē'lyà) It. (Rome In.)	41·36 N	12·40 E
171	Apsheronskiy, P-Ov. (Pen.) Sov. Un.	40·20 N	50·30 E
161	Apt (äpt) Fr.	43·54 N	5·19 E
	Apulia (Reg.), see Puglia		
134	Apure (R.) (ä-pōō'rä) Ven.	8·08 N	68·46 W
134	Apurimac (R.) (ä-pōō-rē-mäk') Peru	11·39 S	73·48 W
153	Aqaba, G. of (ä'kà-bà) Asia	28·30 N	34·40 E
183	Aqabah, Wādī al (R.) Egypt (Palestine In.)	29·48 N	34·05 E
106	Aquasco (á'gwă'scô) Md. (Baltimore In.)	38·35 N	76·44 W
135	Aquidauana (ä-kē-däwä'nä) Braz.	20·24 S	55·46 W
106	Aquidneck (à-kwĭd'nĭk) RI (Providence In.)	41·31 N	71·14 W
162	Aquilianos, Montes (Mts.) (mô'n-tĕs-ä-kē-lyä'nôs) Sp.	42·27 N	6·35 W
129	Aquin (ä-kăn') Hai.	18·20 N	73·25 W
195	Ara (R.) (ä-rä) Jap. (Tōkyō In.)	35·40 N	139·52 E
211	Arab, Bahr al- (R.) Sud.	9·46 N	26·52 E
218	'Araba, Wadi Egypt (Nile In.)	29·02 N	32·10 E

ng-sing; ŋ-baŋk; N-nasalized n; nŏd; cŏmmit; ōld; ŏbey; ôrder; fōōd; fŏŏt; ou-out; s-soft; sh-dish; th-thin; pūre; ūnite; ûrn; stŭd; circŭs; ü-as "y" in study; '-indeterminate vowel.

ăt; fìnăl; rāte; senâte; ärm; àsk; sofá; fâre; ch-choose; dh-as in other; bē; ĕvent; bĕt; recĕnt; cratēr; g-go; gh-guttural g; bĭt; ɨ-short neutral; rīde; ĸ-guttural k as ch in German ich:

PRONOUNCING INDEX

Aschaffenburg — Authon 253

Page	Name Pronunciation Region	Lat. °′	Long. °′
158	Aschaffenburg (ä-shäf'ĕn-bŏŏrgh) F.R.G.	49·58 N	9·12 E
161	Ascheberg (ä'shĕ-bĕrg) F.R.G. (Ruhr In.)	51·47 N	7·38 E
158	Aschersleben (äsh'ĕrs-lā-bĕn) G.D.R.	51·46 N	11·28 E
164	Ascoli Piceno (äs'kô-lēpê-chā'nō) It.	42·50 N	13·55 E
218	Aseb......Eth. (Horn of Afr. In.)	12·52 N	43·39 E
165	Asenovgrad................Bul.	42·00 N	24·49 E
166	Aseri (á'sĕ-rĭ)..........Sov. Un.	59·26 N	26·58 E
	Asfi, see Safi		
174	Asha (ä'shä).Sov. Un. (Urals In.)	55·01 N	57·17 E
108	Ashabula (L.) (ăsh'á-bū-lă)...ND	47·07 N	97·51 W
174	Ashan (ä'shän) Sov. Un. (Urals In.)	57·08 N	56·25 E
148	Ashbourne (ăsh'bŭrn).......Eng.	53·01 N	1·44 W
120	Ashburn (ăsh'bŭrn)..........Ga.	31·42 N	83·42 W
106	Ashburn......Va. (Baltimore In.)	39·02 N	77·30 W
204	Ashburton (R.) (ăsh'bûr-tŭn) Austl.	22·30 S	115·30 E
148	Ashby-de-la-Zouch (ăsh'bĭ-dê-lá zōōsh').Eng.	52·44 N	1·23 W
183	Ashdod........Isr. (Palestine In.)	31·46 N	34·39 E
117	Ashdown (ăsh'doun)..........Ar.	33·41 N	94·07 W
121	Asheboro (ăsh'bŭr-ô).........NC	35·41 N	79·50 W
118	Asherton (ăsh'ĕr-tŭn).........Tx.	28·26 N	99·45 W
121	Asheville (ăsh'vĭl)...........NC	35·35 N	82·35 W
115	Ash Fork....................Az.	35·13 N	112·29 W
195	Ashikaga (ä'shê-kä'gá).......Jap.	36·22 N	139·26 E
195	Ashiya (ä'shê-yä')...........Jap.	33·54 N	130·40 E
195	Ashiya..........Jap. (Ōsaka In.)	34·44 N	135·18 E
195	Ashizuri-Zaki (Pt.) (ä-shē-zōō-rē zä-kē).Jap.	32·43 N	133·04 E
147	Ashkhabad (ŭsh-kä-bät') Sov. Un.	39·45 N	58·13 E
120	Ashland (ăsh'lănd)...........Al.	33·15 N	85·50 W
116	Ashland.....................Ks.	37·11 N	99·46 W
104	Ashland.....................Ky.	38·25 N	82·40 W
98	Ashland.....................Me.	46·37 N	68·26 W
99	Ashland...............Ma. (In.)	42·16 N	71·28 W
108	Ashland.....................Nb.	41·02 N	96·23 W
104	Ashland.....................Oh.	40·50 N	82·15 W
110	Ashland.....................Or.	42·12 N	122·42 W
105	Ashland.....................Pa.	40·45 N	76·20 W
109	Ashland.....................Wi.	46·34 N	90·55 W
108	Ashley (ăsh'lê)..............ND	46·03 N	99·23 W
105	Ashley......................Pa.	41·15 N	75·55 W
196	Ashmore Rf. (ăsh'mōr).....Indon.	12·08 S	122·45 E
218	Ashmūn (ash-mōōn') Egypt (Nile In.)	30·19 N	30·57 E
183	Ashqelon (äsh'kĕ-lōn) Isr. (Palestine In.)	31·40 N	34·36 E
211	Ash Shabb (shĕb)..........Egypt	22·34 N	29·52 E
218	Ash Shallūfah (shäl'lōō-fá) Egypt (Suez In.)	30·09 N	32·33 E
186	Ash Shaqrā'............Sau. Ar.	25·10 N	45·08 E
183	Ash Shawbak Jordan (Palestine In.)	30·31 N	35·35 E
186	Ash Shiḥr........P.D.R. of Yem.	14·45 N	49·32 E
104	Ashtabula (ăsh-tá-bū'lá)......Oh.	41·55 N	80·50 W
111	Ashton (ăsh'tŭn).............Id.	44·04 N	111·28 W
148	Ashton-in-Makerfield (ăsh'tŭn-ĭn-māk'ēr-fēld).Eng.	53·29 N	2·39 W
148	Ashton-under-Lyne (ăsh'tŭn-ŭn-dēr-līn').Eng.	53·29 N	2·04 W
91	Ashuanipi (L.) (ăsh-wá-nĭp'ĭ) Can.	52·40 N	67·42 W
174	Ashukino (á-shōō'ki-nô) Sov. Un. (Moscow In.)	56·10 N	37·57 E
182	Asia (ā'zhá)		
147	Asia Minor (ā'zhá)..........Asia	38·18 N	31·18 E
124	Asientos (ä-sê-ĕn'tōs).......Mex.	22·13 N	102·05 W
164	Asinara, Golfo di (G.) (gōl'fō-dē-ä-sē-nä'rä)..It.	40·58 N	8·28 E
164	Asinara (I.) (ä-sē-nä'rä).......It.	41·02 N	8·22 E
186	Asīr (Reg.) (ä-sēr').......Sau. Ar.	19·30 N	21·27 E
218	Asir, Ras (C.) Som. (Horn of Afr. In.)	11·55 N	51·30 E
182	Askarovo (äs-kä-rô'vô) Sov. Un. (Urals In.)	53·21 N	58·32 E
156	Askersund (äs'kĕr-sōōnd)....Swe.	58·43 N	14·53 E
174	Askino (äs'kĭ-nô) Sov. Un. (Urals In.)	56·06 N	56·29 E
211	Asmera (äs-mä'rä)..........Eth.	15·17 N	38·56 E
161	Asnieres-sur-Seine (ä-nyâr'sür-sĕ'n).Fr. (Paris In.)	48·55 N	2·18 E
211	Asosa......................Eth.	10·13 N	34·28 E
110	Asotin (á-sō'tĭn).............Wa.	46·19 N	117·01 W
115	Aspen (ăs'pĕn)...............Co.	39·15 N	106·55 W
149	Asperen...Neth. (Amsterdam In.)	51·52 N	5·07 E
98	Aspy B. (ăs'pê).............Can.	46·55 N	60·25 W
218	Aş Şaff.........Egypt (Nile In.)	29·33 N	31·23 E
	Aş Şaḥrā' al Lībīyah, see Libyan Des.		
	Aş Şaḥrā' ash Sharqīyah, see Arabian Des.		
183	As Sallūm.................Egypt	31·34 N	25·09 E
183	As Salt.....Jordan (Palestine In.)	32·02 N	35·44 E
184	Assam (State) (ăs-săm').....India	26·00 N	91·00 E
156	Assens (äs'sĕns).............Den.	55·16 N	9·54 E
218	As Sinbillāwayn Egypt (Nile In.)	30·53 N	31·37 E
210	Assini (á-sê-nē')......Ivory Coast.	4·52 N	3·16 W
94	Assiniboia..................Can.	49·38 N	105·59 W
100	Assiniboine (R.) (ă-sĭn'ĭ-boin) Can. (Winnipeg In.)	49·45 N	98·50 W
93	Assiniboine, Mt.............Can.	50·52 N	115·39 W
135	Assis (ä-sē's)..............Braz.	22·39 S	50·21 W
164	Assisi.......................It.	43·04 N	12·37 E
211	As-Sudd (Reg.)..............Sud.	8·45 N	30·45 E
186	As Sulaymānīyah...........Iraq	35·47 N	45·23 E
186	As Suwaydā'................Syr.	32·41 N	36·41 E
218	As Suways (Suez) Egypt (Suez In.)	29·58 N	32·34 E
165	Astakós (äs'tä-kôs)..........Grc.	38·42 N	21·00 E
171	Astara................Sov. Un.	38·30 N	48·50 E
164	Asti (äs'tē)...................It.	44·54 N	8·12 E
188	Astin Tagh (Mts.).........China	36·58 N	85·09 E
153	Astipálaia (I.)..............Grc.	36·31 N	26·19 E
162	Astorga (äs-tôr'gä)...........Sp.	42·28 N	6·03 W
112	Astoria (ăs-tō'rĭ-á) Or. (Portland In.)	46·11 N	123·51 W
100	Astotin Cr. (äs-tō-tĕN') Can. (Edmonton In.)	53·43 N	113·00 W
171	Astrakhan' (äs-trá-kän').Sov. Un.	46·15 N	48·00 E
212	Astrida (äs-trē'dá)............Rw.	2·37 S	29·48 E
162	Asturias (Reg.) (äs-tōō'ryäs)..Sp.	43·21 N	6·00 W
136	Asunción (ä-sōōn-syōn')......Par.	25·25 S	57·30 W
	Asunción, see Ixtaltepec		
	Asunción, see Nochixtlán		
126	Asuncion Mita (ä-sōōn-syŏ'n-mē'tä)..Guat.	14·19 N	89·43 W
155	Åsunden (L.) (ô'sōōn-dĕn)....Swe.	57·46 N	13·16 E
218	Aswān (ä-swän')..Egypt (Nile In.)	24·05 N	32·57 E
218	Aswān High Dam Egypt (Nile In.)	23·58 N	32·53 E
218	Asyūţ (ä-syōōt') Egypt (Nile In.)	27·10 N	31·10 E
136	Atacama, Puna de (Reg.) (pōō'nä-dĕ-ätä-kå'mä).Chile	23·15 S	68·45 W
134	Atacama, Puna de (Plat.) (pōō'nä-dĕ-ä-tä-kå'mä).Bol.	21·35 S	66·58 W
133	Atacama, Desierto de (Des.) (dĕ-syĕ'r-tô-dĕ-ä-tä-kå'mä) Chile-Peru	23·50 S	69·00 W
136	Atacama, Salar de (L.) (sá-lär'dĕ-ätä-kå'mä).Chile	23·38 S	68·15 W
136	Atacama Trench.............S.A.	25·00 S	71·30 W
134	Ataco (ä-tá'kô)........Col. (In.)	3·36 N	75·22 W
214	Atacora, Chaîne de l' (Mts.) Dahomey	10·15 N	1·15 E
183	Atā 'itah, Jabal al (Mts.) Jordan (Palestine In.)	30·48 N	35·19 E
214	Atakpamé (ä'ták-pá-mā')...Togo	7·32 N	1·08 E
174	Atamanovskiy (ä-tä-mä'nôv-skĭ) Sov. Un. (Urals In.)	52·15 N	60·47 E
218	'Atāqah, Jabal (Mts.) Egypt (Suez In.)	29·59 N	32·20 E
210	Atar (ä-tär')..........Mauritania	20·45 N	13·16 W
114	Atascadero (ăt-ăs-ká-dâ'rō)...Ca.	35·29 N	120·40 W
118	Atascosa R. (ăt-ăs-kō'sá)......Tx.	28·50 N	98·17 W
211	Aţbarah (ät'bá-rä)..........Sud.	17·45 N	30·01 E
211	Atbara R...................Sud.	17·14 N	34·27 E
172	Atbasar (ät'bä-sär')......Sov. Un.	51·42 N	68·28 E
119	Atchafalaya B. (ăch-á-fá-lī'á)..La.	29·25 N	91·30 W
119	Atchafalaya R................La.	30·53 N	91·51 W
117	Atchison (ăch'ĭ-sŭn)...........Ks.	39·33 N	95·08 W
106	Atco (ăt'kō).NJ (Philadelphia In.)	39·46 N	74·53 W
125	Atempan (ä-tĕm-pá'n)......Mex.	19·49 N	97·25 W
124	Atenguillo (R.) (ä-tĕn-gē'l-yô) Mex.	20·18 N	104·35 W
90	Athabasca (ăth-á-băs'ká)....Can.	54·43 N	113·17 W
90	Athabasca (L.)..............Can.	59·04 N	109·10 W
93	Athabasca (R.)..............Can.	56·00 N	112·35 W
120	Athens (ăth'ĕnz)..............Al.	34·47 N	86·58 W
120	Athens.......................Ga.	33·55 N	83·24 W
104	Athens.......................Oh.	39·20 N	82·10 W
105	Athens.......................Pa.	42·00 N	76·30 W
120	Athens.......................Tn.	35·26 N	84·36 W
119	Athens.......................Tx.	32·13 N	95·51 W
	Athens, see Athinai		
148	Atherstone (ăth'ĕr-stŭn).....Eng.	52·34 N	1·33 W
148	Atherton (ăth'ĕr-tŭn).........Eng.	53·32 N	2·29 W
205	Atherton Plat. (ădh-ĕr-tŏn).Austl.	17·00 S	144·30 E
217	Athi (R.) (ä'tê)..............Ken.	2·43 S	38·30 E
165	Athinai (Athens) (ä-thē'nĕ)...Grc.	38·00 N	23·38 E
154	Athlone (ăth-lōn')............Ire.	53·24 N	7·30 W
165	Athos (Mtn.) (ăth'ŏs)........Grc.	40·10 N	24·15 E
183	Ath Thamad Egypt (Palestine In.)	29·41 N	34·17 E
154	Athy (á-thī)..................Ire.	52·59 N	7·08 W
215	Ati........................Chad	13·13 N	18·20 E
137	Atibaia (ä-tē-bá'yá) Braz. (Rio de Janeiro In.)	23·08 S	46·32 W
91	Atikonak (L.)...............Can.	52·34 N	63·49 W
204	Atimonan (ä-tê-mō'nän) Phil. (In.)	13·59 N	121·56 E
126	Atiquizaya (ä'tê-kê-zä'yä)...Sal.	14·00 N	89·42 W
126	Atitlan (Vol.) (ä-tê-tlän')...Guat.	14·35 N	91·11 W
126	Atitlan L. (ä-tê-tlän').......Guat.	14·38 N	91·23 W
125	Atizapán (ä'tê-zá-pän').Mex. (In.)	19·33 N	99·16 W
101	Atka (ăt'ká)..................Ak.	52·18 N	174·18 W
101	Atka (I.).....................Ak.	51·58 N	174·30 W
171	Atkarsk (át-kärsk')......Sov. Un.	51·50 N	45·00 E
108	Atkinson (ăt'kĭn-sŭn)..........Ne.	42·32 N	98·58 W
106	Atlanta (ăt-lăn'tá) Ga. (Atlanta In.)	33·45 N	84·23 W
117	Atlanta.......................Tx.	33·09 N	94·09 W
109	Atlantic (ăt-lăn'tĭk)...........Ia.	41·23 N	94·58 W
121	Atlantic......................NC	34·54 N	76·20 W
106	Atlantic Highlands NJ (New York In.)	40·25 N	74·04 W
105	Atlantic City.................NJ	39·20 N	74·30 W
6	Atlantic Ocean		
210	Atlas Mts. (ăt'lăs)......Alg.-Mor.	31·22 N	4·57 W
124	Atliaca (ät-lê-ä'kä).........Mex.	17·38 N	99·24 W
90	Atlin (L.) (ăt'lĭn)...........Can.	59·34 N	133·20 W
124	Atlixco (ät-lēz'kō)..........Mex.	18·52 N	98·27 W
156	Atlöy (I.) (ät-lûê)...........Nor.	61·24 N	4·46 E
120	Atmore (ăt'mōr)...............Al.	31·01 N	87·31 W
117	Atoka (á-tō'ká)...............Ok.	34·23 N	96·07 W
117	Atoka Res.....................Ok.	34·30 N	96·05 W
124	Atotonilco el Alto (ä'tô-tô-nēl'kō ĕl äl'tō).Mex.	20·35 N	102·32 W
124	Atotonilco el Grande (ä'tô-tô-nēl-kō ĕl grän'dā).Mex.	20·17 N	98·41 W
210	Atoui R. (á-tōō-ē') Mauritania-Sp. Sah.	21·00 N	15·32 W
124	Atoyac (ä-tô-yäk')...........Mex.	20·01 N	103·28 W
125	Atoyac (R.)..................Mex.	16·27 N	97·28 W
124	Atoyac (R.)..................Mex.	18·35 N	98·16 W
124	Atoyac de Alvarez (ä-tô-yäk'dā äl'vä-rāz).Mex.	17·13 N	100·29 W
125	Atoyatempan (ä-tō'yá-tĕm-pän') Mex.	18·47 N	97·54 W
186	Atrak (R.)...................Iran	37·45 N	56·30 E
156	Atran (R.)...................Swe.	57·02 N	12·43 E
135	Atrato, Rio (R.) (rē'ō-ä-trä'tō).Col.	7·00 N	77·12 W
134	Atrato (R.) (ä-trä'tō)...Col. (In.)	5·48 N	76·19 W
183	Aţ Ţafīlah (tä-fē'la) Jordan (Palestine In.)	30·50 N	35·36 E
186	Aţ Ţā'if................Sau. Ar.	21·03 N	41·00 E
120	Attalla (á-tăl'yá).............Al.	34·01 N	86·05 W
91	Attawapiskat (R.) (ăt'á-wá-pĭs'kăt).Can.	52·31 N	86·22 W
158	Atter See (L.) (Kammer)....Aus.	47·57 N	13·25 E
105	Attica (ăt'ĭ-ká)...............NY	42·55 N	78·15 W
106	Attleboro (ăt''l-bŭr-ô) Ma. (Providence In.)	41·56 N	71·15 W
154	Attow, Ben (Mtn.) (bĕn ăt'tô) Scot.	57·15 N	5·25 W
119	Attoyac Bay (ă-toi'yăk)......Tx.	31·45 N	94·23 W
101	Attu (I.) (ät-tōō')............Ak.	53·08 N	173·18 E
153	Aţ Ţūr.....................Egypt	28·09 N	33·47 E
186	Aţ Ţurayf..............Sau. Ar.	31·32 N	38·30 E
156	Åtvidaberg (ôt-vē'dá-bĕrgh)..Swe.	58·12 N	15·55 E
116	Atwood (ăt'wŏŏd).............Ks.	39·48 N	101·06 W
125	Atzcapotzalco (ät'zkä-pô-tzäl'kō) Mex. (In.)	19·29 N	99·11 W
149	Atzgersdorf.....Aus. (Vienna In.)	48·10 N	16·17 E
199	Auau Chan (ä'ŏŏ-ä'ŏŏ)...Hi. (In.)	20·55 N	156·50 W
161	Aubagne (ō-bän'y')...........Fr.	43·18 N	5·34 E
160	Aube (R.) (ōb)...............Fr.	48·42 N	3·49 E
160	Aubenas (ōb-nä').............Fr.	44·37 N	4·22 E
161	Aubervilliers (ō-bĕr-vē-yā') Fr. (Paris In.)	48·54 N	2·23 E
160	Aubin (ō-băN')...............Fr.	44·29 N	2·12 E
100	Aubrey (ô-brē') Can. (Montreal In.)	45·08 N	73·47 W
120	Auburn (ô'bŭrn)..............Al.	32·35 N	85·26 W
114	Auburn.......................Ca.	38·52 N	121·05 W
117	Auburn........................Il.	39·36 N	89·46 W
104	Auburn.......................In.	41·20 N	85·05 W
98	Auburn.......................Me.	44·04 N	70·24 W
99	Auburn...............Ma. (In.)	42·11 N	71·51 W
117	Auburn.......................Ne.	40·23 N	95·50 W
105	Auburn.......................NY	42·55 N	76·35 W
112	Auburn.........Wa. (Seattle In.)	47·18 N	122·14 W
107	Auburn Hts.....Mi. (Detroit In.)	42·37 N	83·13 W
160	Aubusson (ō-bü-sôN')..........Fr.	45·57 N	2·10 E
160	Auch (ōsh)....................Fr.	43·38 N	0·35 E
120	Aucilla (R.) (ô-sĭl'á).......Fl.-Ga.	30·15 N	83·55 W
205	Auckland (ôk'lănd)....N. Z. (In.)	36·53 S	174·45 E
220	Auckland Is.................N. Z.	50·30 S	166·30 E
160	Aude (R.) (ōd)................Fr.	42·55 N	2·08 E
160	Audierne (ō-dyĕrn')...........Fr.	48·02 N	4·31 W
161	Audincourt (ō-dăn-kōōr')......Fr.	47·30 N	6·49 E
148	Audley (ôd'lĭ)................Eng.	53·03 N	2·18 W
218	Audo Ra..Eth. (Horn of Afr. In.)	6·58 N	41·18 E
109	Audubon (ô'dōō-bŏn)..........Ia.	41·43 N	94·57 W
106	Audubon....NJ (Philadelphia In.)	39·54 N	75·04 W
158	Aue (ou'ĕ)................G.D.R.	50·35 N	12·44 E
203	Aughathella (ôr'gá'thĕ-lá)....Austl.	25·49 S	146·40 E
212	Aughrabiesvalle (Falls)....S. Afr.	28·30 S	20·00 E
149	Augsburg (ouks'bŏŏrgh) F.R.G. (Munich In.)	48·23 N	10·55 E
117	Augusta (ô-gŭs'tá)...........Ar.	35·16 N	91·21 W
121	Augusta......................Ga.	33·26 N	82·00 W
117	Augusta......................Ks.	37·41 N	96·58 W
104	Augusta......................Ky.	38·45 N	84·00 W
98	Augusta......................Me.	44·19 N	69·42 W
106	Augusta......NJ (New York In.)	41·07 N	74·44 W
109	Augusta......................Wi.	44·40 N	91·09 W
159	Augustow (ou-gŏŏs'tōōf)......Pol.	53·52 N	23·00 E
161	Aulnay-sous-Bois (ō-nĕ'sōō-bwä') Fr. (Paris In.)	48·56 N	2·30 E
160	Aulne (R.) (ōn)...............Fr.	48·08 N	3·53 W
161	Auneau (ō-nĕü)....Fr. (Paris In.)	48·28 N	1·45 E
212	Auob (R.) (ä'wŏb)......S. W. Afr.	25·00 S	19·00 E
183	Aur (I.)......Mala. (Singapore In.)	2·27 N	104·51 E
184	Aurangābād (ou-rŭŋ-gä-bäd') India	19·56 N	75·19 E
160	Auray (ō-rĕ')..................Fr.	47·42 N	3·00 W
160	Aurillac (ō-rē-yäk')...........Fr.	44·57 N	2·27 E
97	Aurora......................Can.	43·59 N	79·25 W
107	Aurora (ô-rō'rá)..Il. (Chicago In.)	41·45 N	88·18 W
107	Aurora.......In. (Cincinnati In.)	39·04 N	84·55 W
109	Aurora......................Mn.	47·31 N	92·17 W
117	Aurora......................Mo.	36·58 N	93·42 W
116	Aurora......................Ne.	40·54 N	98·01 W
156	Aursunden (L.) (äûr-sûndĕn).Nor.	62·42 N	11·10 E
104	Au Sable (R.) (ô-sā'b'l).......Mi.	44·40 N	84·25 W
105	Ausable (R.).................NY	44·25 N	73·50 W
	Aussig, see Ústí nad Labem		
109	Austin (ôs'tĭn)..............Mn.	43·40 N	92·58 W
114	Austin.......................Nv.	39·30 N	117·05 W
119	Austin.......................Tx.	30·15 N	97·42 W
204	Austin (L.)................Austl.	27·45 S	117·30 E
119	Austin Bay (ôs'tĭn bĭ-ōō').Tx. (In.)	29·17 N	95·21 W
204	Australia (ôs-trā'lĭ-á)		
203	Australian Alps (Mts.).....Austl.	37·10 S	147·55 E
203	Australian Capital Ter. (ôs-trā'lĭ-ăn).Austl.	35·30 S	148·40 E
146	Austria (ôs'trĭ-á).............Eur.	47·15 N	11·53 E
161	Authon-la-Plaine (ō-tôN-lä-plĕ'n) Fr. (Paris In.)	48·27 N	1·58 E

ng-sing; ŋ-baŋk; N-nasalized n; nŏd; cŏmmit; ōld; ôbey; ôrder; fōōd; fŏŏt; ou-out; s-soft; sh-dish; th-thin; pūre; ûnite; ûrn; stŭd; circŭs; ü-as "y" in study; '-indeterminate vowel.

Page	Name Pronunciation Region	Lat. °′	Long. °′
124	Autlán (ä-o͞ot-län′) . . . . Mex.	19·47 N	104·24 W
160	Autun (ō-tŭn′) . . . . Fr.	46·58 N	4·14 E
160	Auvergne (Mts.) (ō-vĕrn′y′) . . . Fr.	45·12 N	2·31 E
160	Auxerre (ō-sâr′) . . . . Fr.	47·48 N	3·32 E
100	Aux Grues, Ile (I.) (ō grü) Can. (Quebec In.)	47·05 N	70·32 W
117	Ava (ā′và) . . . . Mo.	36·56 N	92·40 W
217	Avakubi (ä-vä-ko͞o′bē) . . . . . . Zaire	1·20 N	27·34 E
160	Avallon (à-vá-lôN′) . . . . Fr.	47·30 N	3·58 E
107	Avalon (ăv′à-lŏn) Pa. (Pittsburgh In.)	40·31 N	80·05 W
114	Avalon . . . . Ca.	33·21 N	118·22 W
162	Aveiro (ä-vā′ro͝o) . . . . Port.	40·38 N	8·38 W
136	Avelar (ä′vĕ-lâ′r) Braz. (Rio de Janeiro In.)	22·20 S	43·25 W
136	Avellaneda (ä-vĕl-yä-nā′dhä) Arg. (Buenos Aires In.)	34·25 S	58·23 W
163	Avellino (ä-vĕl-lē′nō) It. (Naples In.)	40·40 N	14·46 E
156	Averöy (I.) (ävĕr-ûē) . . . . Nor.	63·40 N	7·16 E
164	Aversa (ä-vĕr′sä) . . . . It.	40·58 N	14·13 E
117	Avery (ā′vēr-ĭ) . . . . Tx.	33·34 N	94·46 W
156	Avesta (ä-vĕs′tä) . . . . Swe.	60·16 N	16·09 E
160	Aveyron (R.) (ä-vā-rôN) . . . . . . Fr.	44·07 N	1·45 E
164	Avezzano (ä-vāt-sä′nō) . . . . It.	42·03 N	13·27 E
164	Avigliano (ä-vēl-yä′nō) . . . . It.	40·45 N	15·44 E
160	Avignon (à-vē-nyôN′) . . . . Fr.	43·55 N	4·50 E
162	Avila (ä-vē-lä) . . . . Sp.	40·39 N	4·42 W
162	Avilés (ä-vē-lās′) . . . . Sp.	43·33 N	5·55 W
117	Avoca (à-vō′kà) . . . . Ia.	41·29 N	95·16 W
105	Avon (ā′vŏn) . . . . Ct.	41·40 N	72·50 W
99	Avon (ā′vŏn) . . . . Ma. (In.)	42·08 N	71·03 W
107	Avon . . . . Oh. (Cleveland In.)	41·27 N	82·02 W
154	Avon (R.) (ā′vŭn) . . . . Eng.	52·05 N	1·55 W
106	Avondale . . . . Ga. (Atlanta In.)	33·47 N	84·16 W
107	Avon Lake . . . . Oh. (Cleveland In.)	41·31 N	82·01 W
100	Avonmore (ā′vŏN-mōr) Can. (Ottawa In.)	45·11 N	74·58 W
121	Avon Park (ā′vŏn pärk′) . . Fl. (In.)	27·35 N	81·29 W
160	Avranches (à-vräNsh′) . . . . Fr.	48·43 N	1·34 W
195	Awaji (ä′wä-jē) . . . . Jap.	34·23 N	135·00 E
195	Awaji-Shima (I.) (ä′wä-jē shē-mä) Jap. (Ōsaka In.)	34·32 N	135·02 E
211	Awash R. (à-wäsh′) . . . . Eth.	9·19 N	40·30 E
154	Awe, Loch (L.) (lŏK ôr) . . . . . Scot.	56·22 N	5·04 W
211	Awjilah . . . . Libya	29·07 N	21·21 E
160	Ax-les-Thermes (äks′lā tĕrm′) . . Fr.	42·43 N	1·50 E
124	Axochiapan (äks-ō-chyä′pän). Mex.	18·29 N	98·49 W
160	Ay (à′ē) . . . . Fr.	49·05 N	3·58 E
170	Ay (R.) . . . . Sov. Un.	55·55 N	57·55 E
195	Ayabe (ä′yä-bĕ) . . . . Jap.	35·16 N	135·17 E
136	Ayacucho (ä-yä-ko͞o′chō) . . . . . Arg.	37·05 S	58·30 W
134	Ayacucho . . . . Peru	12·12 S	74·03 W
172	Ayaguz (ä-yà-go͞oz′) . . . . . Sov. Un.	48·00 N	80·12 E
162	Ayamonte (ä-yä-mô′n-tĕ) . . . . . Sp.	37·14 N	7·28 W
173	Ayan (à-yän′) . . . . Sov. Un.	56·26 N	138·18 E
134	Ayata (ä-yä′tä) . . . . Bol.	15·17 S	68·43 W
134	Ayaviri (ä-yä-vē′rē) . . . . Peru	14·46 S	70·38 W
167	Aydar (R.) (ī-där′) . . . . Sov. Un.	49·15 N	38·48 E
121	Ayden (ā′dĕn) . . . . NC	35·27 N	77·25 W
171	Aydin (āīy-dĕn) . . . . Tur.	37·40 N	27·40 E
99	Ayer (âr) . . . . Ma. (In.)	42·33 N	71·36 W
183	Ayer Hitam . Mala. (Singapore In.)	1·55 N	103·11 E
165	Ayiá (ā-yē′à) . . . . Grc.	39·42 N	22·47 E
165	Ayiassos . . . . Grc.	39·06 N	26·25 E
165	Áyion Óros (Mount Athos) (Reg.) Grc.	40·20 N	24·15 E
165	Áyios Evstrátion (I.) . . . . Grc.	39·30 N	24·58 E
148	Aylesbury (ălz′bĕr-ĭ) Eng. (London In.)	51·47 N	0·49 W
90	Aylmer (L.) (āl′mēr) . . . . Can.	64·27 N	108·22 W
93	Aylmer, Mt. . . . . Can.	51·19 N	115·26 W
100	Aylmer East (āl′mēr) Can. (Ottawa In.)	45·24 N	75·50 W
124	Ayo el Chico (ä′yō el chē′kō) . Mex.	20·31 N	102·21 W
173	Ayon (I.) (ī-ôn′) . . . . Sov. Un.	69·50 N	168·40 E
214	Ayorou . . . . Niger	14·44 N	0·55 E
125	Ayotla (ä-yōt′lä) . . . . Mex. (In.)	19·18 N	98·55 W
214	'Ayoûn el 'Atroûs . . . . . Mauritania	16·40 N	9·37 W
154	Ayr (âr) . . . . Scot.	55·27 N	4·40 W
154	Ayr (L.) . . . . Scot.	55·25 N	4·20 W
218	Aysha . . . . . Eth. (Horn of Afr. In.)	10·48 N	42·32 E
126	Ayutla (à-yo͞ot′lä) . . . . Guat.	14·44 N	92·11 W
124	Ayutla . . . . Mex.	16·50 N	99·16 W
124	Ayutla . . . . Mex.	20·09 N	104·20 W
196	Ayutthaya (à-yo͞ot′hē′ä) . . . . . Thai.	14·16 N	100·37 E
165	Ayvalik (āīy-wă-lĭk) . . . . Tur.	39·19 N	26·40 E
214	Azaouâd (Dunes) . . . . Mali	18·00 N	3·20 W
215	Azaouak, Vallée de l' (Val.) . . Mali	15·50 N	3·10 E
215	Azare . . . . Nig.	11·40 N	10·11 E
210	Azemmour (à-zē-mo͞or′) . . . . . Mor.	33·20 N	8·21 W
168	Azerbaydzhan (Azerbaijan) (S. S. R.) (ä′zēr-bä-ē-jän′) Sov. Un.	40·38 N	47·25 E
113	Azle (àz′lē) Tx. (Dallas, Fort Worth In.)	35·54 N	97·33 W
134	Azogues (ä-sō′gās) . . . . Ec.	2·47 S	78·45 W
	Azores (Is.), see Açores		
167	Azov (à-zôf′) (ä-zôf) . . . . Sov. Un.	47·07 N	39·19 E
	Azov, Sea of, see Azovskoye More		
167	Azovskoye More (Sea of Azov) (à-zôf′skô-yĕ mô′rĕ) . Sov. Un.	46·00 N	36·20 E
124	Azoyú (ä-zō-yo͞o′) . . . . Mex.	16·42 N	98·46 W
	Azraq, Al-Bahr al- (R.), see Blue Nile		
115	Aztec (ăz′tĕk) . . . . NM	36·40 N	108·00 W
115	Aztec Ruins Natl. Mon. . . . . . . NM	36·50 N	108·00 W
129	Azua (ä′swä) . . . . Dom. Rep.	18·30 N	70·45 W
162	Azuaga (ä-thwä′gä) . . . . Sp.	38·15 N	5·42 W
127	Azuero, Peninsula de (Pen.) (ä-swā′rō) . Pan.	7·30 N	80·34 W
118	Azucar, Presa de (Res.) (prĕ′sä-dĕ-ä-zo͞o′kär) . Mex.	26·06 N	98·44 W
136	Azufre, Cerro (Copiapó) (Vol.) (sĕr′rō ä-so͞o′frā) (kō-pê-äpō′) Chile	26·10 S	69·00 W
137	Azul (ä-so͞ol′) Arg. (Buenos Aires In.)	36·46 S	59·51 W
124	Azul, Sierra (Mts.) (sē-ĕ′r-rä-zo͞o′l) Mex.	23·20 N	98·28 W
134	Azul, Cordillera (Mts.) (kô′r-dē-lyĕ′rä-zo͞o′l) . Peru	7·15 S	75·30 W
113	Azusa (à-zo͞o′sà) Ca. (Los Angeles In.)	34·08 N	117·55 W
183	Az Zabdānī . . . . Syr. (Palestine In.)	33·45 N	36·06 E
186	Az Ẓahrān (Dhahran) (dä-rän′) Sau. Ar.	26·13 N	50·00 E
218	Az Zaqāzīq . . . . . . Egypt (Nile In.)	30·36 N	31·36 E
183	Az Zarqā′ . . Jordan (Palestine In.)	32·03 N	36·07 E
211	Az Zawiyah . . . . Libya	32·28 N	11·55 E

B

Page	Name Pronunciation Region	Lat. °′	Long. °′
161	Baal (bäl) . . . . . . F.R.G. (Ruhr In.)	51·02 N	6·17 E
197	Baao (bä′ō) . . . . Phil. (In.)	13·27 N	123·22 E
149	Baarle-Hertog . . Bel. (Brussels In.)	51·26 N	4·57 E
149	Baarn . . . . . Neth. (Amsterdam In.)	52·12 N	5·18 E
165	Babaeski (bä′bä-ĕs′kĭ) . . . . Tur.	41·25 N	27·05 E
134	Babahoyo (bä-bä-ō′yō) . . . . Ec.	1·56 S	79·24 W
215	Babana . . . . Nig.	10·36 N	3·50 E
218	Babanango . . . . . S. Afr. (Natal In.)	28·24 S	31·11 E
211	Babanūsah . . . . Sud.	11·30 N	27·55 E
197	Babar (I.) (bä′bàr) . . . . Indon.	7·50 S	129·15 E
186	Bābel . . . . Iran	36·30 N	52·48 E
218	Bab-el-Mandeb, Str. of (bäb′ĕl män-dĕb′) Afr.-Asia (Horn of Afr. In.)	13·17 N	42·49 E
118	Babia, Arroyo de la (är-rō′yō dā lä bä′bê-à) . Mex.	28·26 N	101·50 W
92	Babine (R.) . . . . Can.	55·10 N	127·00 W
92	Babine (L.) (băb′ēn) . . . . Can.	54·45 N	126·00 W
173	Babushkin (bä′bo͝osh-kĭn) Sov. Un.	51·47 N	106·08 W
174	Babushkin . Sov. Un. (Moscow In.)	55·52 N	37·42 E
196	Babuyan Is. (bä-bo͞o-yän′) . . . Phil.	4·30 N	122·38 E
165	Babyak (bäb′zhàk) . . . . Bul.	41·59 N	23·42 E
106	Babylon (băb′ĭ-lŏn) NY (New York In.)	40·42 N	73·19 W
186	Babylon (Ruins) . . . . Iraq	32·15 N	45·23 E
197	Bacacay (bä-kä-kī′) . . . . Phil. (In.)	13·17 N	123·48 E
126	Bacalar, Laguna de (L.) (lä-go͞o-nä-dĕ-bä-kä-lär′) Mex. (In.)	18·50 N	88·31 W
193	Bacarra (bä-kär′rä) . . . . Phil.	18·22 N	120·40 E
159	Bacău . . . . Rom.	46·34 N	27·00 E
161	Baccarat (bà-kà-rà′) . . . . Fr.	48·29 N	6·42 E
113	Bacchus (băk′ŭs) Ut. (Salt Lake City In.)	40·40 N	112·06 W
125	Bachajón (bä-chä-hōn′) . . . . . Mex.	17·08 N	92·18 W
90	Back (R.) . . . . Can.	65·30 N	104·15 W
165	Băcka Palanka (bäch′kä pälän-kä) Yugo.	45·14 N	19·24 E
165	Bačka Topola (bäch′kä tô′pô-lä′) Yugo.	45·48 N	19·38 E
185	Back Bay (băk) . . . . India (In.)	18·55 N	72·45 E
204	Backstairs Pass. (băk-stârs′) Austl.	35·50 S	138·15 E
193	Bac Ninh (bäk′nên″) . . . . Viet.	21·10 N	106·02 E
197	Bacnotan (bäk-nô-tän′) . Phil. (In.)	16·43 N	120·21 E
197	Baco, Mt. (bä′kô) . . . . . . Phil. (In.)	12·50 N	121·11 E
163	Bacoli (bä-kō-lē′) . . It. (Naples In.)	40·33 N	14·05 E
196	Bacolod (bä-kō′lôd) . . . . Phil.	10·42 N	123·03 E
197	Bacon (bä-kōn′) . . . . Phil. (In.)	13·02 N	124·04 E
159	Bácsalmás (bäch′ôl-mäs) . . . Hung.	46·07 N	19·18 E
148	Bacup (băk′ŭp) . . . . Eng.	53·42 N	2·12 W
108	Bad (R.) (băd) . . . . SD	44·04 N	100·58 W
162	Badajoz (bà-dhä-hōth′) . . . . Sp.	38·52 N	6·56 W
163	Badalona (bä-dhä-lō′nä) . . . . . . Sp.	41·27 N	2·15 E
186	Badanah . . . . Sau. Ar.	30·49 N	40·45 E
104	Bad Axe (băd′ ăks) . . . . Mi.	43·50 N	82·55 W
149	Bad Bramstedt (bät bräm′shtĕt) F.R.G. (Hamburg In.)	53·55 N	9·53 E
161	Bad Ems (bät ĕms) . . . . F.R.G.	50·20 N	7·45 E
149	Baden (bä′dĕn) . . Aus. (Vienna In.)	48·00 N	16·14 E
158	Baden . . . . Switz.	47·28 N	8·17 E
158	Baden-Baden (bä′dĕn-bä′dĕn) F.R.G.	48·46 N	8·11 E
158	Baden Württemberg (State) (bä′dĕn vür′tĕm-bĕrgh) . F.R.G.	48·38 N	9·00 E
158	Bad Freienwalde (bät frī′ĕn-văl′dĕ) . G.D.R.	52·47 N	14·00 E
158	Bad Hersfeld (bät hĕrsh′fĕlt) F.R.G.	50·53 N	9·43 E
155	Bad Homberg (bät hōm′bĕrgh) F.R.G.	50·14 N	8·35 E
121	Badin (bă′dĭn) . . . . NC	35·23 N	80·08 W
158	Bad Ischl (bät ĭsh″l) . . . . Aus.	47·46 N	13·37 E
158	Bad Kissingen (bät kĭs′ĭng-ĕn) F.R.G.	50·12 N	10·05 E
158	Bad Kreuznach (bät kroits′näk) F.R.G.	49·52 N	7·53 E
108	Badlands (Reg.) (băd′ lănds) . ND	46·43 N	103·22 W
108	Badlands (Reg.) . . . . SD	43·43 N	102·36 W
108	Badlands Natl. Mon. . . . . SD	43·56 N	102·37 W
185	Badlāpur . . . . India (In.)	19·12 N	73·12 E
214	Badogo . . . . Mali	11·02 N	8·13 W
158	Bad Oldeslow (bät ôl′dĕs-lōē) F.R.G.	53·48 N	10·21 E
158	Bad Reichenhall (bät rī′kĕn-häl) F.R.G.	47·43 N	12·53 E
109	Bad River Ind. Res. (băd) . . . . Wi.	46·41 N	90·36 W
149	Bad Segeburg (bät sĕ′gĕ-bo͝orgh) F.R.G. (Hamburg In.)	53·56 N	10·18 E
158	Bad Tölz (bät tûltz) . . . . F.R.G.	47·46 N	11·35 E
185	Badulla . . . . Sri Lanka	6·55 N	81·07 E
149	Bad Vöslau . . . . . Aus. (Vienna In.)	47·58 N	16·13 E
111	Badwater Cr. (băd′wô-tēr) . . . Wy.	43·13 N	107·55 W
162	Baena (bä-ā′nä) . . . . Sp.	37·38 N	4·20 W
137	Baependi (bä-â-pĕn′dĭ) Braz. (Rio de Janeiro In.)	21·57 S	44·51 W
75	Baffin B. (băf′ĭn) . . . . Can.	72·00 N	65·00 W
119	Baffin B. Tx.	27·11 N	97·35 W
75	Baffin I. . . . . Can.	67·20 N	71·00 W
214	Bafoulabé (bä-fo͞o-lä-bā′) . . . . Mali	13·48 N	10·50 W
186	Bāfq (bäfk) . . . . Iran	31·48 N	55·23 E
171	Bafra (bäf′rä) . . . . Tur.	41·30 N	35·50 E
197	Bagabag (bä-gä-bäg′) . . . Phil. (In.)	16·38 N	121·16 E
185	Bāgalkot . . . . India	16·14 N	75·40 E
217	Bagamoyo (bä-gä-mō′yō) . . . . Tan.	6·26 S	38·54 E
174	Bagaryak (bà-gàr-yäk′) Sov. Un. (Urals In.)	56·13 N	61·32 E
217	Bagbele . . . . Zaire	4·21 N	29·17 E
136	Bagé (bä-zhā′) . . . . Braz.	31·17 S	54·07 W
186	Baghdād (bàgh-däd′) (băg′dăd) Iraq	33·14 N	44·22 E
164	Bagheria (bä-gâ-rē′ä) . . . . It.	38·03 N	13·32 E
108	Bagley (băg′lê) . . . . Mn.	47·31 N	95·24 W
164	Bagnara (bän-yä′rä) . . . . It.	38·17 N	15·52 E
117	Bagnell Dam (băg′nĕl) . . . . Mo.	38·13 N	92·40 W
160	Bagnères-de-Bigorre (băn-yâr′dē-bê-gor′) . Fr.	43·40 N	0·70 E
160	Bagnères-de-Luchon (băn-yâr′ dē-lu chôN′) Fr.	42·46 N	0·36 E
160	Bagnols (bä-nyôl′) . . . . Fr.	44·09 N	4·37 E
210	Bagoé R. (bà-gō′â) . . . . Mali	12·22 N	6·34 W
97	Bagotville (bà-gô-vēl′) . . . . Can.	48·21 N	70·53 W
188	Bagrash Köl (L.) . . . . China	42·06 N	88·01 E
197	Baguio (bä-gê-ō′) . . . . . . Phil. (In.)	16·24 N	120·36 E
123	Bahamas (bà-hā′màs) . . . . . . N. A.	26·15 N	76·00 W
183	Bahua . . . . . . Mala. (Singapore In.)	2·48 N	102·25 E
184	Bahāwalpur (bŭ-hä′wŭl-po͞or) . Pak.	29·29 N	71·41 E
217	Bahi Swp . . . . Tan.	6·05 S	35·10 E
	Bahia, see Salvador		
135	Bahia (State) . . . . Braz.	11·05 S	43·00 W
122	Bahía, Islas de la (I.) (ē′s-lăs-dĕ-lä-bä-ē′ä) . Hond.	16·15 N	86·30 W
136	Bahia Blanca (bä-ē′ä bläŋ′kä) . Arg.	38·45 S	62·07 W
134	Bahía de Caraquez (bä-e′ä dā kä-rä′kĕz) . Ec.	0·45 S	80·29 W
135	Bahía Negra (bä-ē′ä nā′grä) . . Par.	20·11 S	58·05 W
136	Bahias, Cabo dos (C.) (kà′bô-dôs-bä-ē′äs) . Arg.	44·55 S	65·35 W
129	Bahoruco, Sierra de (Mts.) (sē-ĕ′r-rä-dĕ-bä-ō-ro͞o′kô) Dom. Rep.	18·10 N	71·25 W
186	Bahrain (bä-rān′) . . . . Asia	26·15 N	51·17 E
211	Bahr al Ghazāl (Prov.) (bär ĕl ghä-zäl′) . Sud.	7·56 N	27·15 E
153	Baḩrīyah (Oasis) (bà-hà-rē′yä) Egypt	28·34 N	29·01 E
183	Baḩrīyah, Jabal Jalālah al (Plat.) Egypt (Palestine In.)	29·15 N	32·20 E
159	Baia de Cris (bä′yä dā krēs′) Rom.	46·11 N	22·40 E
216	Baía dos Tigres . . . . Ang.	16·36 S	11·43 E
159	Baia-Mare (bä′yä-mä′rā) . . . . Rom.	47·40 N	23·35 E
196	Bai-Bung Mui (C.) . . . . Viet.	8·36 N	104·43 E
218	Baidoa . . . . Som. (Horn of Afr. In.)	3·19 N	44·20 E
184	Baidyabāti . . . . India (In.)	22·47 N	88·21 E
98	Baie-Comeau . . . . Can.	49·13 N	68·10 W
113	Baie de Wasai (bā dē wä-sä′ê) Mi. (Sault Ste. Marie In.)	46·27 N	84·15 W
97	Baie-St. Paul (bā′sânt-pôl′) . . Can.	47·27 N	70·30 W
98	Baie-Trinité . . . . Can.	49·24 N	67·19 W
	Baikal Mts., see Baykal'skiy Khrebet		
	Baikal, L., see Baykal, Ozero		
	Baile Atha Cliath, see Dublin		
162	Bailné (bä-ê-lān′) . . . . Sp.	38·05 N	3·48 W
165	Băileşti (bŭ-ĭ-lĕsh′tê) . . . . Rom.	44·01 N	23·21 E
120	Bainbridge (bān′brĭj) . . . . Ga.	30·52 N	84·35 W
112	Bainbridge I. . . . . Wa. (Seattle In.)	47·39 N	122·32 W
118	Baird (bârd) . . . . Tx.	32·22 N	99·28 W
107	Bairdford (bârd′fŏrd) Pa. (Pittsburgh In.)	40·37 N	79·53 W
101	Baird Mts. . . . . Ak.	67·35 N	160·10 W
203	Bairnsdale (bârnz′dāl) . . . . . . Austl.	37·50 S	147·39 E
160	Baïse (R.) (bä-ēz′) . . . . Fr.	43·52 N	0·23 E
159	Baja (bŏ′yŏ) . . . . Hung.	46·11 N	18·55 E
122	Baja California Norte (State) (bä-hä) . Mex.	30·15 N	117·25 W
122	Baja California Sur (State) . . Mex.	26·00 N	113·30 W
196	Bajak (I.) . . . . Indon.	2·08 N	97·15 E
174	Bakal (bä′kàl) . Sov. Un. (Urals In.)	54·57 N	58·50 E
111	Baker (bā′kēr) . . . . Mt.	46·21 N	104·12 W
110	Baker . . . . Or.	44·46 N	117·52 W
198	Baker (I.) . . . . Oceania	1·00 N	176·00 W
90	Baker (L.) . . . . Can.	63·51 N	96·10 W
110	Baker, Mt. . . . . Wa.	48·46 N	121·52 W
107	Baker Cr. . . . . Il. (Chicago In.)	41·13 N	87·47 W
114	Bakersfield (bā′kērz-fēld) . . . . . Ca.	35·23 N	119·00 W
107	Bakerstown (bā′kerz-toun) Pa. (Pittsburgh In.)	40·39 N	79·56 W
148	Bakewell (bāk′wĕl) . . . . Eng.	53·12 N	1·40 W

PRONOUNCING INDEX

Bakhchisaray — Barlee 255

Page	Name Pronunciation Region	Lat. °'	Long. °'
167	Bakhchisaray (bȧk'chē-sȧ-rī') Sov. Un.	44·46 N	33·54 E
167	Bakhmach (bȧk-mäch') . . Sov. Un.	51·09 N	32·47 E
186	Bakhtegan, Daryācheh-ye (L.) Iran	29·29 N	54·31 E
174	Bakhteyevo (bȧk-tyě'yě-vô) Sov. Un. (Moscow In.)	55·35 N	38·32 E
211	Bako (bä'kö) Eth.	5·47 N	36·39 E
159	Bakony-Erdo (Mts.) (bȯ-kōn'y') Hung.	46·57 N	17·30 E
214	Bakoye (R.) (bȧ-kô'ē) Mali	12·47 N	9·35 W
174	Bakr Uzyak (bȧkr ōōz'yȧk) Sov. Un. (Urals In.)	52·59 N	58·43 E
171	Baku (bȧ-kōō') Sov. Un.	40·28 N	49·45 E
	Bakwanga, see Mbuji-Mayi		
196	Balabac (I.) (bä'lä-bäk) Phil.	8·00 N	116·28 E
196	Balabac Str. Indon.-Phil.	7·23 N	116·30 E
183	Ba'labakk Leb. (Palestine In.)	34·00 N	36·13 E
196	Balabalagan, Kepulauan (Is.) (bä-lȧ-bä'lȧ-gän) Indon.	2·00 S	117·15 E
174	Balabanovo (bȧ-lȧ-bä'nô-vô) Sov. Un. (Moscow In.)	56·10 N	37·44 E
172	Balagansk (bä-lä-gänsk') Sov. Un.	53·58 N	103·09 E
163	Balaguer (bä-lä-gěr') Sp.	41·48 N	0·50 E
172	Balakhta (bȧ'lȧk-tȧ') Sov. Un.	55·22 N	91·43 E
167	Balakleya (bȧ'lȧ-klā'yȧ) Sov. Un.	49·28 N	36·51 E
171	Balakovo (bȧ'lȧ-kô'vô) Sov. Un.	52·00 N	47·40 E
125	Balancán (bä-läŋ-kän') Mex.	17·47 N	91·32 W
197	Balanga (bä-läŋ'gä) Phil. (In.)	14·41 N	120·31 E
197	Balaoan (bȧ-lou'än) Phil. (In.)	16·49 N	120·24 E
174	Balashikha (bȧ-lä'shĭ-kȧ) Sov. Un. (Moscow In.)	55·48 N	37·58 E
171	Balashov (bȧ'lȧ-shôf) Sov. Un.	51·30 N	43·00 E
184	Balasore (bä-lȧ-sōr') India	21·38 N	86·59 E
159	Balassagyarmat (bô'lôsh-shô-dyôr'môt) Hung.	48·04 N	19·19 E
159	Balaton L. (bô'lô-tôn) Hung.	46·47 N	17·55 E
197	Balayan (bä-lä-yän') Phil. (In.)	13·56 N	120·44 E
197	Balayan B. Phil. (In.)	13·46 N	120·46 E
122	Balboa (bäl-bô'ä) C. Z. (In.)	8·55 N	79·34 W
127	Balboa Heights C. Z.	8·59 N	79·33 W
122	Balboa Mt. C. Z. (In.)	9·05 N	79·44 W
136	Balcarce (bäl-kär'sä) Arg.	37·49 S	58·17 W
165	Balchik Bul.	43·24 N	28·13 E
113	Bald Eagle (bôld ē'g'l) Mn. (Minneapolis, St. Paul In.)	45·06 N	93·01 W
113	Bald Eagle L. Mn. (Minneapolis, St. Paul In.)	45·08 N	93·03 W
184	Baldin Pak.	24·47 N	69·51 E
95	Baldock L. Can.	56·33 N	97·57 W
113	Baldwin Park (bôld'wĭn) Ca. (Los Angeles In.)	34·05 N	117·58 W
105	Baldwinsville (bôld'wĭns-vĭl) . . NY	43·10 N	76·20 W
95	Baldy Mtn. Can.	51·28 N	100·44 W
115	Baldy Pk. (bôl'dē) Az.	33·55 N	109·35 W
118	Baldy Pk. (bôl'dē pēk) Tx.	30·38 N	104·11 W
163	Baleares, Islas (Balearic Is.) (ĕ's-läs bä-lĕ-ä'rĕs) Sp.	39·25 N	1·28 E
	Balearic Is., see Baleares, Islas		
163	Balearic Sea (băl-ē-ăr'ĭk) Eur.	39·40 N	1·05 E
91	Baleine, Grande Rivière de la (R.) Can.	54·45 N	74·20 W
197	Baler (bä-lär') Phil. (In.)	15·46 N	121·33 E
197	Baler B. Phil. (In.)	15·51 N	121·40 E
197	Balesin (I.) Phil. (In.)	14·28 N	122·10 E
173	Baley (bȧl-yā') Sov. Un.	51·29 N	116·12 E
126	Balfate (bäl-fä'tē) Hond.	15·48 N	86·24 W
218	Balfour (băl'fōōr) S. Afr. (Johannesburg & Pretoria In.)	26·41 S	28·37 E
196	Bali (I.) (bä'lē) Indon.	8·00 S	115·22 E
171	Balikesir (balĭk'ĭysĭr) Tur.	39·40 N	27·50 E
196	Balikpapan (bä'lēk-pä'pän) Indon.	1·13 N	116·52 E
196	Balintang Chan. (bā-lĭn-täng') Phil.	19·50 N	121·08 E
	Balkan Mts., see Stara Planina		
184	Balkh (bälk) Afg.	36·48 N	66·50 E
172	Balkhash (bȧl-käsh') Sov. Un.	46·58 N	75·00 E
172	Balkhash, Ozero (L.) Sov. Un.	45·58 N	72·15 E
167	Balki (bäl'kĭ) Sov. Un.	47·22 N	34·56 E
161	Ballancourt (bä-läN-kōōr') Fr. (Paris In.)	48·31 N	2·23 E
203	Ballarat (băl'ȧ-răt) Austl.	37·37 S	144·00 E
204	Ballard (I.) (băl'ȧrd) Austl.	29·15 S	120·45 E
154	Ballater (bäl'ȧ-tēr) Scot.	57·05 N	3·06 W
214	Ballé Mali.	15·20 N	8·35 W
220	Balleny Is. (băl'ĕ nē) Ant.	67·00 S	164·00 E
203	Ballina (băl-ĭ-nä') Austl.	28·50 S	153·35 E
154	Ballina Ire.	54·06 N	9·05 W
154	Ballinasloe (băl'ĭ-nȧ-slō') Ire.	53·20 N	8·09 W
118	Ballinger (băl'ĭn-jēr) Tx.	31·45 N	99·58 W
105	Ballston Spa (bôls'tŭn spä') . . NY	43·05 N	73·50 W
159	Balmazújváros (bŏl'mŏz-ōō'y'vä'rôsh) Hung.	47·35 N	21·23 E
217	Balobe Zaire	0·05 N	28·00 E
203	Balonne (R.) (băl-ōn') Austl.	27·00 S	149·10 E
184	Balotra India	25·56 N	72·12 E
203	Balranald (băl'-rȧn-ăld) Austl.	34·42 S	143·30 E
167	Balş (bälsh) Rom.	44·21 N	24·05 E
105	Balsam (L.) (bôl'sȧm) Can.	44·30 N	78·50 W
135	Balsas (bäl'säs) Braz.	7·09 S	46·04 W
122	Balsas (R.) Mex.	18·00 N	103·00 W
167	Balta (bäl'tȧ) Sov. Un.	47·57 N	29·38 E
150	Baltic Sea (bôl'tĭk) Eur.	55·20 N	16·50 E
218	Baltīm (bȧl-tēm') Egypt (Nile In.)	31·33 N	31·04 E
106	Baltimore (bôl'tĭ-môr) Md. (Baltimore In.)	39·20 N	76·38 W
157	Baltiysk (bäl-tēysk') Sov. Un.	54·40 N	19·55 E
187	Baluchistān (Reg.) (bȧ-lōō-chĭ-stän') Pak.	27·30 N	65·30 E
124	Balurte, Río del (rē'ō-dĕl-bä-lōō'r-tē) Mex.	23·09 N	105·42 W
93	Balzac (bôl'zăk) Can. (Calgary In.)	51·10 N	114·01 W
215	Bama Nig.	11·30 N	13·41 E
214	Bamako (bä-mä-kō') Mali	12·39 N	8·00 W
197	Bambang (bäm-bäng') . . Phil. (In.)	16·24 N	121·08 E
211	Bambari (bäm-bȧ-rē) Cen. Afr. Rep.	5·44 N	20·40 E
158	Bamberg (bäm'běrgh) F.R.G.	49·53 N	10·52 E
121	Bamberg (băm'bûrg) SC	33·17 N	81·04 W
137	Bambuí (bä'm-bōō-ē) Braz. (Rio de Janeiro In.)	20·01 S	45·59 W
215	Bamenda Cam.	5·56 N	10·10 E
215	Bamingui (R.) Cen. Afr. Rep.	7·35 N	19·45 E
215	Bamingui Bangoran, Parc Nat'l. du (Nat'l. Pk.) Cen. Afr. Rep.	8·05 N	19·35 E
148	Bampton (băm'tŭn) Eng. (London In.)	51·42 N	1·33 W
186	Bampūr (bŭm-pōōr') Iran	27·15 N	60·22 E
215	Bam Yanga, Ngao (Mts.) Cam.	8·20 N	14·40 E
197	Banahao, Mt. (bä-nä-hä'ô) Phil. (In.)	14·04 N	121·45 E
216	Banalia Zaire	1·33 N	25·20 E
214	Banamba Mali	13·33 N	7·27 W
137	Bananal (bä-nä-näl') Braz. (Rio de Janerio In.)	22·42 S	44·17 W
135	Bananal, Ilha do (I.) (ē'lä-dô-bä-nä-näl') Braz.	12·09 S	50·27 W
184	Banās (R.) (bän-äs') India	25·20 N	74·51 E
211	Banās, Ra's (C.) Egypt	23·48 N	36·39 E
165	Banat (Reg.) (bä-nät') Rom.-Yugo.	45·35 N	21·05 E
196	Ban Bangsaphan Thai.	11·19 N	99·27 E
105	Bancroft (băn'krôft) Can.	45·05 N	77·55 W
	Bancroft, see Chililabombwe		
184	Bānda (bän'dä) India	25·36 N	80·21 E
196	Banda Atjeh Indon.	5·10 N	95·10 E
203	Banda Banda, Mt. (băn'dȧ băn'dȧ) Austl.	31·09 S	152·15 E
197	Banda Besar (I.) Indon.	4·40 S	129·56 E
197	Banda Laut (Banda Sea) . . Indon.	6·05 S	127·28 E
214	Bandama Blanc (R.) (bän-dä'mä) Ivory Coast	6·15 N	5·00 W
186	Bandar 'Abbās (Hbr.) (bän-där' ȧb-bäs') Iran	27·04 N	56·22 E
186	Bandar-e Lengeh (Hbr.) Iran	26·44 N	54·47 E
186	Bandar-e Shāh Iran	37·05 N	54·08 E
186	Bandar-e-Shāhpūr (Hbr.) Iran	30·27 N	48·45 E
183	Bandar Maharani (bän-där' mä-hä-rä'nē) Mala. (Singapore In.)	2·02 N	102·34 E
196	Bandar Seri Begawan Bru.	5·00 N	114·59 E
137	Bandeira, Pico da (Pk.) (pē'kōō dā bän-dā'rä) Braz. (Rio de Janeiro In.)	20·27 S	41·47 W
115	Bandelier Natl. Mon. (băn-dē-lēr') NM	35·50 N	106·45 W
124	Banderas, Bahía de (B.) (bä-ē'ä dē bän-dě'räs) Mex.	20·38 N	103·25 W
171	Bandirma (bän-dĭr'mȧ) Tur.	40·25 N	27·50 E
196	Bandjarmasin (bän-jēr-mä'sēn) Indon.	3·18 S	114·32 E
162	Bando (bä'n-dô) Sp.	42·02 N	7·58 W
110	Bandon (băn'dŭn) Or.	43·06 N	124·25 W
185	Bāndra India (In.)	19·04 N	72·49 E
216	Bandundu Zaire	3·18 S	17·20 E
196	Bandung Indon.	7·00 S	107·22 E
129	Banes (bä'näs) Cuba	21·00 N	75·45 W
93	Banff (bănf) Can.	51·10 N	115·34 W
154	Banff Scot.	57·39 N	2·37 W
93	Banff Natl. Park Can.	51·38 N	116·22 W
136	Bánfield (bá'n-fyě'ld) Arg. (Buenos Aires In.)	34·30 S	58·24 W
214	Banfora Upper Volta	10·38 N	4·46 W
185	Bangalore (băŋ'gȧ'lôr) India	13·03 N	77·39 E
197	Bangar (bäŋ-gär') Phil. (In.)	16·54 N	120·24 E
211	Bangassou (bäN-gȧ-sōō') Cen. Afr. Rep.	4·47 N	22·49 E
215	Bangé Cam.	3·01 N	15·07 E
197	Bangeta, Mt. Pap. N. Gui.	6·20 S	147·00 E
197	Banggai, Kepulauan (Is.) (bäng-gī') Indon.	1·05 S	123·45 E
196	Banggi (I.) Mala.	7·12 N	117·10 E
211	Banghāzī (běn-gä'zē) Libya	32·08 N	20·06 E
196	Bangka (I.) (bäŋ'kȧ) Indon.	2·24 S	106·55 E
196	Bangkalan (bäng-kȧ-län') . . Indon.	6·07 S	112·50 E
	Bangkok, see Krung Thep		
187	Bangladesh Asia	24·15 N	90·00 E
98	Bangor (băn'gēr) Me.	44·47 N	68·47 W
104	Bangor Mi.	42·20 N	86·05 W
105	Bangor Pa.	40·55 N	75·10 W
154	Bangor (băŋ'ēr) (băŋ'ôr) Wales	53·13 N	4·05 W
115	Bangs, Mt. (băngs) Az.	36·45 N	113·50 W
197	Bangued (bän-gād') Phil. (In.)	17·36 N	120·38 E
215	Bangui (bäN-gē') Cen. Afr. Rep.	4·22 N	18·35 E
217	Bangweulu, L. (băng-wē-ōō'lōō) Zambia	10·55 S	30·10 E
217	Bangweulu Swp. Zambia	11·25 S	30·10 E
218	Banhā Egypt (Nile In.)	30·24 N	31·11 E
129	Bani (bä'-nē) Dom. Rep.	18·15 N	70·25 W
197	Bani (bä'nē) Phil. (In.)	16·11 N	119·51 E
214	Bani (R.) Mali	13·07 N	6·15 W
129	Bánica (bä'-nē-kä) Dom. Rep.	19·00 N	71·35 W
218	Banī Mazār Egypt (Nile In.)	28·29 N	30·48 E
218	Banī Suwayf Egypt (Nile In.)	29·05 N	31·06 E
164	Banja Luka (bän-yä-lōō'kȧ) Yugo.	44·45 N	17·11 E
214	Banjul (Bathurst) Gam.	13·28 N	16·39 W
196	Banjuwangi (bän-jōō-wäŋ'gē) Indon.	8·15 S	114·15 E
196	Ban Kantang (bän-kän'täng') Thai.	7·26 N	99·28 E
213	Bankberg (Mts.) (băŋk'bûrg) S. Afr. (Natal In.)	32·18 S	25·15 E
112	Banks (bănks) . . Or. (Portland In.)	45·37 N	123·07 W
205	Banks (Is.) Austl.	10·10 S	143·08 E
202	Banks, C. Austl. (Sydney In.)	34·01 S	151·17 E
92	Banks I. Can.	53·25 N	130·10 W
75	Banks I. Can.	73·00 N	123·00 W
205	Banks Is. New Hebr.	13·38 S	168·23 E
203	Banks Str. Austl.	40·45 S	148·00 E
196	Ban Kui Nua Thai.	12·04 N	99·50 E
154	Bann (R.) (băn) N. Ire.	54·50 N	6·29 W
113	Banning (băn'ĭng) Ca. (Los Angeles In.)	33·56 N	116·53 W
121	Bannister (R.) (băn'ĭs-tēr) Va.	36·45 N	79·17 W
202	Bannockburn Austl. (Melbourne In.)	38·03 S	144·11 E
184	Bannu Pak.	33·03 N	70·39 E
134	Baños (bä'-nyôs) Ec.	1·30 S	78·22 W
159	Banská Bystrica (bän'skä bē'strē-tzä) Czech.	48·46 N	19·10 E
165	Bansko (bän'skō) Bul.	41·51 N	23·33 E
148	Banstead (băn'stĕd) Eng. (In.)	51·18 N	0·09 W
197	Banton (bän-tōn') Phil. (In.)	12·54 N	121·55 E
154	Bantry (băn'trĭ) Ire.	51·39 N	9·30 W
154	Bantry B. Ire.	51·25 N	10·09 W
211	Banzyville (bäN-zē-vēl') Zaire	4·14 N	21·11 E
213	Bapsfontein (băps-fŏn-tān') S. Afr. (Johannesburg & Pretoria In.)	26·01 S	28·26 E
134	Baqueroncito (bä-kě-rô'n-sē-tô) Col. (In.)	3·18 N	74·40 W
167	Bar (bär) Sov. Un.	49·02 N	27·44 E
165	Bar Yugo.	42·05 N	19·09 E
172	Barabinsk (bȧ'rȧ-bĭnsk) . Sov. Un.	55·18 N	78·00 E
109	Baraboo (bâr'ȧ-bōō) Wi.	43·29 N	89·44 W
129	Baracoa (bä-rä-kō'ä) Cuba	20·20 N	74·25 W
129	Baracoa Cuba (In.)	23·03 N	82·34 W
137	Baradeo (bä-rä-dě'ô) Arg. (Buenos Aires In.)	33·50 S	59·30 W
129	Baradères, Baie des (B.) (bä-rä-dâr') . Hai.	18·35 N	73·35 W
129	Barahona (bä-rä-ô'nä) . Dom. Rep.	18·15 N	71·10 W
163	Barajas de Madrid (bä-rä'häs dā mä-drēdh') Sp. (Madrid In.)	40·28 N	3·35 W
184	Baranagar India (In.)	22·38 N	88·25 E
126	Baranco (bä-räŋ'kō) Belize	16·01 N	88·55 W
101	Baranof (I.) (bä-rä'nôf) Ak.	56·48 N	136·08 W
159	Baranovichi (bä'rä-nô-vē'chē) Sov. Un.	53·08 N	25·59 E
183	Baranpauh. Indon. (Singapore In.)	0·40 N	103·28 E
136	Barão de Juperanã (bä-rou'N-dě-zhōō-pe-rȧ'nȧ) Braz. (Rio de Janeiro In.)	22·21 S	43·41 W
135	Barão de Melgaço (bä-rouN-dě-měl-gä'sô) . Braz.	16·12 S	55·48 W
184	Bārāsat India (In.)	22·42 N	88·29 E
119	Barataria B. La.	29·13 N	89·90 W
134	Baraya (bä-rȧ'yä) Col. (In.)	3·10 N	75·04 W
137	Barbacena (bär-bä-sā'nȧ) Braz. (Rio de Janeiro In.)	21·15 S	43·46 W
134	Barbacoas (bär-bä-kō'äs) Col.	1·39 N	78·12 W
135	Barbacoas (bär-bä-kô'äs) Ven. (In.)	9·30 N	66·58 W
123	Barbados (bär-bā'dōz) N. A.	13·30 N	59·00 W
211	Barbar Sud.	18·11 N	34·00 E
163	Barbastro (bär-bäs'trō) Sp.	42·05 N	0·05 E
113	Barbeau (bȧr-bō') Mi. (Sault Ste. Marie In.)	46·17 N	84·16 W
107	Barberton (bär'bēr-tŭn) Oh. (Cleveland In.)	41·01 N	81·37 W
212	Barberton S. Afr.	25·48 S	31·04 E
160	Barbezieux (bärb'zyû') Fr.	45·30 N	0·11 W
120	Barboorville (bär'bēr-vĭl) Ky.	36·52 N	83·58 W
134	Barbosa (bär-bô'-sȧ) Col. (In.)	6·26 N	75·19 W
104	Barboursville (bär'bērs-vĭl) WV	38·20 N	82·20 W
123	Barbuda (I.) (bär-bōō'dȧ) Antigua	17·45 N	61·15 W
205	Barcaldine (bär'kôl-dīn) Austl.	28·30 S	145·43 E
163	Barcarena (bär-kä-rě'-nä) Port. (Lisbon In.)	38·29 N	9·17 W
162	Barcarrota (bär-kär-rō'tä) Sp.	38·31 N	6·50 W
164	Barcellona (bär-chěl-lō'nä) It.	38·07 N	15·15 E
163	Barcelona (bär-thâ-lō'nä) Sp.	41·25 N	2·08 E
135	Barcelona (bär-sȧ-lō'nä) . Ven. (In.)	10·09 N	64·41 W
161	Barcelonnette (bär-sē-lô-nět') . Fr.	44·24 N	6·42 E
134	Barcelos (bär-sě'lôs) Braz.	1·04 S	63·00 W
162	Barcélos (bär-thā'lōs) Port.	41·34 N	8·39 W
186	Bardar-e Pahlant Iran	37·16 N	49·15 E
183	Bardawīl, Sabkhat al (B.) Egypt (Palestine In.)	31·20 N	33·24 E
159	Bardejov (bär'dyě-yôf) Czech.	49·18 N	21·18 E
218	Bardera (bär-dā'rä) Som. (Horn of Afr. In.)	2·13 N	42·24 E
154	Bardsey (I.) (bärd'sē) Wales	52·45 N	4·50 W
104	Bardstown (bärds'toun) Ky.	37·50 N	85·30 W
120	Bardwell (bärd'wěl) Ky.	36·51 N	88·57 W
168	Barents Sea (bä'rěnts) . . Sov. Un.	72·14 N	37·28 E
211	Barentu (bä-rěn'tōō) Eth.	15·06 N	37·39 E
160	Barfleur, Pte. de (Pt.) (bȧr-flûr') . Fr.	49·43 N	1·17 W
184	Bargāchia India (In.)	22·39 N	88·07 E
173	Barguzin (bär'gōō-zĭn) . . Sov. Un.	53·44 N	109·28 E
98	Bar Harbor (bär här'bēr) Me.	44·22 N	68·13 W
164	Bari (bä'rē) It.	41·08 N	16·53 E
134	Barinas (bä-rē'näs) Ven.	8·36 N	70·14 W
96	Baring, C. (bâr'ĭng) Can.	70·07 N	119·48 W
196	Barisan, Pegunungan (Mts.) (bä-rē-sän') . Indon.	2·38 S	101·45 E
196	Barito (Strm.) (bä-rē'tō) . . Indon.	2·10 S	114·38 E
211	Barka (R.) Eth.	16·44 N	37·34 E
92	Barkley Sd. Can.	48·53 N	125·20 W
213	Barkly East (bärk'lē ēst) S. Afr. (Natal In.)	30·58 S	27·37 E
204	Barkly Tableland (Reg.) (bär'klē) Austl.	18·15 S	145·55 E
160	Bar-le-Duc (bär-lē-dük') Fr.	48·47 N	5·05 E
204	Barlee (L.) (bär-lē') Austl.	29·45 S	119·00 E

ng-sing; ŋ-baŋk; N-nasalized n; nŏd; cŏmmit; ōld; ôbey; ôrder; fōōd; fŏŏt; ou-out; s-soft; sh-dish; th-thin; pūre; ûnite; ûrn; stŭd; circŭs; ü-as "y" in study; '-indeterminate vowel.

256 Barletta — Beaver PRONOUNCING INDEX

Page Name Pronunciation Region Lat. °' Long. °'
164 Barletta (bär-lėt'tä)...........It. 41·19 N 16·20 E
149 Barmstedt (bärm'shtět) F.R.G. (Hamburg In.) 53·47 N 9·46 E
172 Barnaul (bär-nä-o͞ol')....Sov. Un. 53·18 N 83·23 E
105 Barnesboro (bärnz'bẽr-ô)......Pa. 40·45 N 78·50 W
120 Barnesville (bärnz'vĭl)........Ga. 33·03 N 84·10 W
108 Barnesville.................Mn. 46·38 N 96·25 W
104 Barnesville..................Oh. 39·55 N 81·10 W
105 Barnet (bär'nět)............Vt. 44·20 N 72·00 W
148 Barnetby (bär'nět-bĭ).......Eng. 53·34 N 0·26 W
128 Barnett Hbr.................Ba. 25·40 N 79·20 W
117 Barnsdall (bärnz'dôl).........Ok. 36·38 N 96·14 W
148 Barnsley (bärnz'lĭ)..........Eng. 53·33 N 1·29 W
154 Barnstaple (bärn'stā-p'l).....Eng. 51·06 N 4·05 W
121 Barnwell (bärn'wĕl)..........SC 33·14 N 81·23 W
215 Baro (bä'rô)................Nig. 8·37 N 6·25 E
184 Baroda (bä-rō'dä)..........India 22·21 N 73·12 E
211 Baro R....................Eth. 7·40 N 34·17 E
216 Barotse Pln.............Zambia 15·50 S 22·55 E
211 Barqah (Cyrenaica) (Prov.).Libya 31·09 N 21·45 E
134 Barquisimeto (bär-kē-sē-mä'tō) Ven. 10·04 N 69·16 W
135 Barra (bär'rä).............Braz. 11·04 S 43·11 W
203 Barraba.................Austl. 30·17 S 149·46 E
135 Barra do Corda (bär'rä do͞o cōr-dä) Braz. 5·33 S 45·13 W
154 Barra Is. (băr'ră)..........Scot. 57·00 N 7·30 W
137 Barra Mansa (bär'rä män'sä) Braz. (Rio de Janeiro In.) 22·35 S 44·09 W
134 Barrancabermeja (bär-rän'kä-bēr-mā'hä). Col. 7·06 N 73·49 W
134 Barranquilla (bär-rän-kēl'yä).Col. 10·57 N 75·00 W
135 Barras (bá'r-räs)..........Braz. 4·13 S 42·14 W
105 Barre (băr'ē)..............Vt. 44·15 N 72·30 W
137 Barre do Piraí (bar'rē-dô-pē'rä-ē') Braz. (Rio de Janeiro In.) 22·30 S 43·49 W
135 Barreiras (bär-rā'räs).......Braz. 12·13 S 44·59 W
163 Barreiro (bär-rĕ'ē-ro͞o) Port. (Lisbon In.) 38·39 N 9·05 W
203 Barren, C. (băr'ĕn)........Austl. 40·20 S 149·00 E
213 Barren, Îles (Is.)..........Mad. 18·18 S 43·57 E
120 Barren (R.)...............Ky. 37·00 N 86·20 W
135 Barretos (bär-rā'tōs).......Braz. 20·40 S 48·36 W
93 Barrhead (băr-hĕd) (băr'ĭd)..Can. 54·08 N 114·24 W
105 Barrie (băr'ĭ)..............Can. 44·25 N 79·45 W
101 Barrington (bă-rĕng-tŏn) Can. (Montreal In.) 45·07 N 73·35 W
107 Barrington......Il. (Chicago In.) 42·09 N 88·08 W
106 Barrington...RI (Providence In.) 41·44 N 71·16 W
203 Barrington Tops (Mtn.)....Austl. 32·00 S 151·25 E
113 Bar River (bär) Can. (Sault Ste. Marie In.) 46·27 N 84·02 W
109 Barron (băr'ŭn)............Wi. 45·24 N 91·51 W
101 Barrow (băr'ō)..............Ak. 71·20 N 156·00 W
154 Barrow.....................Eng. 54·10 N 3·15 W
204 Barrow (I.)................Austl. 21·05 S 11·30 E
204 Barrow Creek.............Austl. 21·23 S 133·55 E
101 Barrow Pt..................Ak. 71·20 N 156·00 W
154 Barrow R. (bă-rä)..........Ire. 52·35 N 7·05 W
162 Barruelo de Santullán (bär-ro͞o-ā-lō dā sän-to͞o-lyän') Sp. 42·55 N 4·19 W
113 Barry (băr'ĭ) Mo. (Kansas City In.) 39·14 N 94·36 W
114 Barstow (bär'stō)............Ca. 34·53 N 117·03 W
106 Barstow......Md. (Baltimore In.) 38·32 N 76·37 W
158 Barth (bärt)...........G.D.R. 54·20 N 12·43 E
117 Bartholomew Bay (bär-thŏl'ô-mū bī-o͞o').Ar. 33·53 N 91·45 W
98 Barthurst (băr-thŭrst')......Can. 47·38 N 65·40 W
135 Bartica (bär'tĭ-kå)..........Guy. 6·23 N 58·32 W
171 Bartin (bär'tĭn).............Tur. 41·35 N 32·12 E
205 Bartle Frere, Mt. (bärt''l frēr') Austl. 17·30 S 145·46 E
117 Bartlesville (bär'tlz-vil).......Ok. 36·44 N 95·58 W
107 Bartlett (bärt'lĕt).Il. (Chicago In.) 41·59 N 88·11 W
119 Bartlett....................Tx. 30·48 N 97·25 W
105 Barton (bär'tŭn)............Vt. 44·45 N 72·05 W
148 Barton-on-Humber (bär'tŭn-ŏn-hŭm'bẽr).Eng. 53·41 N 0·26 W
159 Bartoszyce (bär-tō-shĭ'tså)....Pol. 54·15 N 20·50 E
120 Bartow (bär'tō).........Fl. (In.) 27·51 N 81·50 W
167 Barvenkovo (bär'vĕn-kô'vô) Sov. Un. 48·55 N 36·59 E
203 Barwon (R.) (bär'wŭn).....Austl. 29·45 S 148·25 E
202 Barwon Heads Austl. (Melbourne In.) 38·17 S 144·59 E
158 Barycz R. (bä'rĭch).........Pol. 51·30 N 16·38 E
211 Basankusu (bä-sän-ko͞o'so͞o)..Zaire 1·14 N 19·45 E
149 Basbeck (bäs'bĕk) F.R.G. (Hamburg In.) 53·40 N 9·11 E
149 Basdahl (bäs'däl) F.R.G. (Hamburg In.) 53·27 N 9·00 E
113 Basehor (bās'hôr) Ks. (Kansas City In.) 39·08 N 94·55 W
158 Basel (bä'z'l)..............Switz. 47·32 N 7·35 E
213 Bashee (R.) (bă-shē') S. Afr. (Natal In.) 31·47 S 28·25 E
193 Bashi Chan (bäsh'ē)..........Phil. 21·20 N 120·22 E
170 Bashkir (A.S.S.R.) (bash-kēr') Sov. Un. 54·12 N 57·15 E
167 Bashtanka (bash-tän'kå).Sov. Un. 47·32 N 32·31 E
196 Basilan (I.)................Phil. 6·37 N 122·07 E
164 Basilicata (Reg.) (bä-zē-lē-kä'tä) It. 40·30 N 15·55 E
111 Basin (bā'sĭn)...............Wy. 44·22 N 108·02 W
148 Basingstoke (bā'zĭng-stōk) Eng. (London In.) 51·14 N 1·06 W
164 Baška (bäsh'ka)...........Yugo. 44·58 N 14·44 E
171 Baskale (bäsh-kä'lĕ).........Tur. 38·10 N 44·00 E
97 Baskatong Res..............Can. 46·50 N 75·50 W
171 Baskunchak (L.)........Sov. Un. 48·20 N 46·40 E
211 Basoko (bå-sō'kō)..........Zaire 0·52 N 23·50 E
93 Bassano (bäs-sän'ō).........Can. 50·47 N 112·28 W
164 Bassano.....................It. 45·46 N 11·44 E
214 Bassari....................Togo 9·15 N 0·47 E
213 Bassas da India (I.) (bäs'säs dä ēn'dē-å).Afr. 21·23 S 39·42 E
196 Bassein (bŭ-sēn')..........Bur. 16·46 N 94·47 E
121 Basset (băs'sĕt)............Va. 36·45 N 81·58 W
127 Basse Terre (bås' târ').Guad. (In.) 16·00 N 61·43 W
127 Basseterre St. Kitts-Nevis-Anguilla (In.) 17·20 N 62·42 W
127 Basse Terre I.........Guad. (In.) 16·10 N 62·14 W
104 Bass Is. (băs)..............Oh. 41·40 N 82·50 W
203 Bass Str.................Austl. 39·40 S 145·40 E
109 Basswood (L.) (băs'wo͝od) Can.-Mn. 48·10 N 91·36 W
156 Båstad (bô'stät)............Swe. 56·26 N 12·46 E
164 Bastia (bäs'tē-ä)...........Fr. 42·43 N 9·27 E
155 Bastogne (bäs-tôn'y')........Bel. 50·02 N 5·45 E
119 Bastrop (băs'trŭp)...........La. 32·47 N 91·55 W
119 Bastrop....................Tx. 30·08 N 97·18 W
119 Bastrop Bay............Tx. (In.) 29·07 N 95·22 W
216 Bata (bä'tä).........Equat. Gui. 1·51 N 9·45 E
128 Batabanó (bä-tä-bä-nō').....Cuba 22·45 N 82·20 W
128 Batabano, Golfo, de (G.) (gôl-fô-dē-bä-tä-bä'nô).Cuba 22·10 N 83·05 W
197 Batac................Phil. (In.) 17.56 N 120·29 E
184 Batāla...................India 31·54 N 75·18 E
174 Bataly (bå-tä'lĭ) Sov. Un. (Urals In.) 52·51 N 62·03 E
183 Batam I. (bä-täm') Indon. (Singapore In.) 1·03 N 104·00 E
197 Batan (bä-tän')........Phil. (In.) 13·20 N 124·00 E
193 Batan Is..................Phil. 20·58 N 122·20 E
193 Batangan, C...............Viet. 15·18 N 109·10 E
197 Batangas (bä-tän'gäs)..Phil. (In.) 13·45 N 121·04 E
159 Bataszék (bä'tå-sĕk).......Hung. 46·07 N 18·40 E
107 Batavia (bå-tā'vĭ-å) Il. (Chicago In.) 41·51 N 88·18 W
105 Batavia...................NY 43·00 N 78·15 W
107 Batavia.......Oh. (Cincinnati In.) 39·05 N 84·10 W
167 Bataysk (bå-tīsk')......Sov. Un. 47·08 N 39·44 E
121 Batesburg (bāts'bûrg).........SC 33·53 N 81·34 W
117 Batesville (bāts'vĭl)...........Ar. 35·46 N 91·39 W
104 Batesville..................In. 39·15 N 85·15 W
120 Batesville..................Ms. 34·17 N 89·55 W
166 Batetska (bå-tě'tskå)....Sov. Un. 58·36 N 30·21 E
98 Bath (bàth)................Can. 46·31 N 67·36 W
154 Bath......................Eng. 51·24 N 2·20 W
98 Bath......................Me. 43·54 N 69·50 W
105 Bath......................NY 42·25 N 77·20 W
107 Bath.........Oh. (Cleveland In.) 41·11 N 81·38 W
127 Bathsheba...........Barb. (In.) 13·13 N 60·30 W
205 Bathurst (băth'ŭrst).........Aust. 33·28 S 149·30 E
213 Bathurst (băt-hûrst) S. Afr. (Natal In.) 33·26 S 26·53 E
Bathurst, see Banjul
101 Bathurst, C. (băth'ŭrst).....Can. 70·33 N 127·55 W
204 Bathurst (I.)...............Austl. 11·19 S 130·13 E
90 Bathurst Inlet.............Can. 68·10 N 108·00 W
214 Batia.....................Benin 10·54 N 1·29 E
197 Batian (I.)...............Indon. 1·07 S 127·52 E
197 Batjan (I.) (bät-jän')......Indon. 1·07 S 127·52 E
186 Bātlaq-E Gāvkhūn (L.)........Iran 31·40 N 52·48 E
148 Batley (băt'lĭ)..............Eng. 53·43 N 1·37 W
210 Batna (bät'nä)..............Alg. 35·41 N 6·12 E
119 Baton Rouge (băt'ŭn ro͞ozh')..La. 30·28 N 91·10 W
215 Batouri..................Cam. 4·26 N 14·22 E
196 Battambang (bát-tám-bäng') Camb. 13·14 N 103·15 E
185 Batticaloa.............Sri Lanka 8·40 N 81·10 E
93 Battle (R.)................Can. 52·20 N 111·59 W
94 Battle (R.)................Can. 53·05 N 109·40 W
104 Battle Creek (băt''l krēk')....Mi. 42·20 N 85·15 W
112 Battle Ground (băt''l ground) Wa. (Portland In.) 45·47 N 122·32 W
91 Battle Harbour (băt''l här'bẽr) Can. 52·17 N 55·33 W
110 Battle Mountain............Nv. 40·40 N 116·56 W
159 Battonya (bät-tō'nyä)......Hung. 46·17 N 21·00 E
196 Batu Kepulauan (I.) (bä'to͞o) Indon. 0·10 S 99·55 E
171 Batumi (bŭ-to͞o'mē).....Sov. Un. 41·40 N 41·30 E
183 Batu Pahat..Mala. (Singapore In.) 1·51 N 102·56 E
183 Batupandjang Indon. (Singapore In.) 1·42 N 101·35 E
135 Baturité (bä-to͞o-rē-tā')......Braz. 4·16 S 38·47 W
197 Bauang (bä'wäng)......Phil. (In.) 16·31 N 120·19 E
215 Bauchi (bå-o͞o'chē)...........Nig. 10·19 N 9·50 E
212 Baudouinville (bō-dwăn-vēl') Zaire 7·12 S 29·39 E
99 Bauld, C..................Can. 51·38 N 55·25 W
184 Bāuria..............India (In.) 22·29 N 88·08 E
135 Bauru (bou-ro͞o')............Braz. 22·21 S 48·57 W
157 Bauska (bou'skå)........Sov. Un. 56·24 N 24·12 E
129 Bauta (bå'o͞o-tä)......Cuba (In.) 22·14 N 82·33 W
158 Bautzen (bout'sĕn).......G.D.R. 51·11 N 14·27 E
Bavaria (State), see Bayern
203 Baw Baw, Mt. (bå-bå).....Austl. 37·50 S 146·17 E
196 Bawean (I.) (bå'vē-än).....Indon. 5·50 S 112·40 E
148 Bawtry (bô'trĭ)..............Eng. 53·26 N 1·01 W
121 Baxley (băks'lĭ).............Ga. 31·47 N 82·22 W
202 Baxter (băks'tẽr) Austl. (Melbourne In.) 38·12 S 145·10 E
117 Baxter Springs (băks'tẽr springs') Ks. 37·01 N 94·44 W
129 Bayaguana (bä-yä-gwä'nä) Dom. Rep. 18·45 N 69·40 W
152 Bay al Kabīr Wadi (R.)....Libya 29·52 N 14·28 E
197 Bayambang (bä-yäm-bäng') Phil. (In.) 15·50 N 120·26 E
128 Bayamo (bä-yä'mō)........Cuba 20·25 N 76·35 W
123 Bayamón..P. R. (Puerto Rico In.) 18·27 N 66·13 W
172 Bayan-Aul (bä'yän-oul').Sov. Un. 50·43 N 75·37 E
108 Bayard (bā'ẽrd)............Ne. 41·45 N 103·20 W
105 Bayard....................WV 39·15 N 79·20 W
171 Bayburt (bä'ĭ-bo͝ort)........Tur. 40·15 N 40·10 E
104 Bay City (bā)..............Mi. 43·35 N 83·55 W
119 Bay City..................Tx. 28·59 N 95·58 W
188 Baydarag Gol (R.)........Mong. 46·09 N 98·52 E
170 Baydaratskaya Guba (B.) Sov. Un. 69·20 N 66·10 E
99 Bay de Verde.............Can. 48·05 N 52·54 W
158 Bayern (Bavaria) (State) (bī'ẽrn) (bå-vâ-rĭ-å).F.R.G. 49·00 N 11·16 E
160 Bayeux (bå-yû')............Fr. 49·19 N 0·41 W
109 Bayfield (bā'fēld)...........Wi. 46·48 N 90·51 W
173 Baykal, Ozero (Baikal, L.) (bī'käl') (bī'kôl).Sov. Un. 53·00 N 109·28 E
173 Baykals'kiy Khrebet (Baikal Mts.).Sov. Un. 53·30 N 102·00 E
172 Baykit (bī-kēt')........Sov. Un. 61·43 N 96·39 E
172 Baykonur (bī-kô-no͞or')..Sov. Un. 47·46 N 66·11 E
174 Baymak (båy'mäk) Sov. Un. (Urals In.) 52·35 N 58·21 E
113 Bay Mills (bā mĭlls) Mi. (Sault Ste. Marie In.) 46·27 N 84·36 W
109 Bay Mills Ind. Res...........Mi. 46·19 N 85·03 W
120 Bay Minette (bā'mĭn-ĕt').....Al. 30·52 N 87·44 W
197 Bayombong (bä-yôm-bŏng') Phil. (In.) 16·28 N 121·09 E
160 Bayonne (bå-yôn')...........Fr. 43·28 N 1·30 W
106 Bayonne (bā-yōn') NJ (New York In.) 40·40 N 74·07 W
119 Bayou Bodcau Res. (bī'yo͞o bŏd'kō).La. 32·49 N 93·22 W
113 Bayport (bā'pōrt) Mn. (Minneapolis, St. Paul In.) 45·02 N 92·46 W
165 Bayramic................Tur. 39·48 N 26·35 E
158 Bayreuth (bī-roit')........F.R.G. 49·56 N 11·35 E
99 Bay Roberts (bā rŏb'ẽrts)....Can. 47·36 N 53·16 W
Bayrūt, see Beirut
105 Bays, L. of (bās)...........Can. 45·15 N 79·00 W
120 Bay St. Louis (bā' sânt lo͞o'ĭs).Ms. 30·19 N 89·20 W
106 Bay Shore (bā' shôr) NY (New York In.) 40·44 N 73·15 W
183 Bayt Lahm (Bethlehem) (bĕth'lē-hĕm) Jordan (Palestine In.) 31·42 N 35·13 E
119 Baytown (bā'town).....Tx. (In.) 29·44 N 95·01 W
106 Bayview (bā'vū) Al. (Birmingham In.) 33·34 N 86·59 W
112 Bayview........Wa. (Seattle In.) 48·29 N 122·28 W
107 Bay Village (bā) Oh. (Cleveland In.) 41·29 N 81·56 W
162 Baza (bä'thä)...............Sp. 37·29 N 2·46 W
171 Bazar-Dyuzi, Gora (Mt.) (bä'zår-dyo͞oz'ē).Sov. Un. 41·20 N 47·40 E
212 Bazaruto, Ilha do (I.) (bä-zä-ro͞o'tō).Moz. 21·42 S 36·10 E
162 Baztán (bäth-tän')..........Sp. 43·12 N 1·30 W
108 Beach (bēch)................ND 46·55 N 104·00 W
155 Beachy Head (bēchē hĕd)....Eng. 50·40 N 0·25 E
105 Beacon (bē'kŭn).............NY 41·30 N 73·55 W
100 Beaconsfield (bē'kŭnz-fēld) Can. (Montreal In.) 45·26 N 73·51 W
106 Beafort Mtn. (bē'fōrt) NJ (New York In.) 41·08 N 74·23 W
118 Beals Cr. (bēls)..............Tx. 32·10 N 101·14 W
100 Bear Brook (R.) Can. (Ottawa In.) 45·24 N 75·15 W
111 Bear Creek (bâr krēk)........Mt. 45·11 N 109·07 W
120 Bear Cr. (bâr)...............Al. 34·27 N 88·00 W
113 Bear Cr. Tx. (Dallas, Fort Worth In.) 32·56 N 97·09 W
117 Beardstown (bērds'toun).......Il. 40·01 N 90·26 W
112 Bearhead Mtn. (bâr'hĕd) Wa. (Seattle In.) 47·01 N 121·49 W
95 Bear L....................Can. 55·08 N 96·00 W
111 Bear L..................Id.-Ut. 41·56 N 111·10 W
111 Bear R....................Id. 42·17 N 111·42 W
113 Bear R...Ut. (Salt Lake City In.) 41·28 N 112·10 W
162 Beas de Segura (bā'äs dā sā-go͞o'rä) Sp. 38·16 N 2·53 W
129 Beata (I.) (bĕ-ä'tä).....Dom. Rep. 17·40 N 71·40 W
129 Beata, Cabo (C.) (kå'bô-bĕ-ä'tä) Dom. Rep. 17·40 N 71·20 W
117 Beatrice (bē'å-trĭs)..........Ne. 40·16 N 96·45 W
114 Beatty (bēt'ē)..............Nv. 36·58 N 116·48 W
104 Beattyville (bēt'ē-vĭl)........Ky. 37·35 N 83·40 W
160 Beaucaire (bō-kâr')...........Fr. 43·49 N 4·37 E
161 Beaucourt (bō-ko͞or')........Fr. 47·30 N 6·54 E
121 Beaufort (bō'fērt)...........NC 34·43 N 76·40 W
121 Beaufort...................SC 32·25 N 80·40 W
101 Beaufort Sea...............Ak. 70·30 N 138·40 W
212 Beaufort West............S. Afr. 32·20 S 22·45 E
100 Beauharnois (bō-är-nwä') Can. (Montreal In.) 45·23 N 73·52 W
113 Beaumont (bō'mŏnt) Ca. (Los Angeles In.) 33·57 N 116·57 W
100 Beaumont...Can. (Edmonton In.) 53·22 N 113·18 W
100 Beaumont...Can. (Quebec In.) 46·50 N 71·01 W
119 Beaumont...................Tx. 30·05 N 94·06 W
160 Beaune (bōn)................Fr. 47·02 N 4·49 E
100 Beauport (bō-pôr') Can. (Quebec In.) 46·52 N 71·11 W
100 Beaupré (bō-prā') Can. (Quebec In.) 47·03 N 70·53 W
95 Beauséjour................Can. 50·04 N 96·33 W
160 Beauvais (bō-vĕ')............Fr. 49·25 N 2·05 E
116 Beaver (bē'vẽr).............Ok. 36·46 N 100·31 W
107 Beaver.......Pa. (Pittsburgh In.) 40·42 N 80·18 W
115 Beaver....................Ut. 38·15 N 112·40 W
104 Beaver (I.)................Mi. 45·40 N 85·30 W
94 Beaver (R.)................Can. 54·20 N 111·10 W
116 Beaver City................Nb. 40·08 N 99·52 W
116 Beaver Cr...................Co. 39·42 N 103·37 W

ăt; finăl; rāte; senāte; ärm; åsk; sofå; fâre; ch-choose; dh-as th in other; bē; ēvent; bĕt; recĕnt; cratẽr; g-go; gh-guttural g; bĭt; ĭ-short neutral; rīde; ĸ-guttural k as ch in German ich;

PRONOUNCING INDEX

Beaver — Berettyoujfalu 257

Page Name Pronunciation Region Lat. °' Long. °'

116 Beaver Cr. Ks. 39·44 N 101·05 W
108 Beaver Cr. Mt. 46·45 N 104·18 W
108 Beaver Cr. Wy. 43·46 N 104·25 W
109 Beaver Dam Wi. 43·29 N 88·50 W
111 Beaverhead Mts. (bē'vēr-hĕd). Mt. 44·33 N 112·59 W
111 Beaverhead R. Mt. 45·25 N 112·35 W
104 Beaver Ind. Res. Mi. 45·40 N 85·30 W
112 Beaverton (bē'vēr-tŭn) Or. (Portland In.) 45·29 N 122·49 W
134 Bebara' (bĕ-bä-rà') Col. (In.) 6·07 N 76·39 W
148 Bebington (bē'bĭng-tŭn) Eng. 53·20 N 2·59 W
125 Becal (bā-käl') Mex. 20·25 N 90·04 W
165 Bečej (bĕ'chā) Yugo. 45·36 N 20·03 E
162 Becerreá (bå-thā'rê-ä) Sp. 42·49 N 7·12 W
210 Béchar Alg. 31·39 N 2·14 W
101 Becharof (L.) (bĕk-à-rôf) Ak. 57·58 N 156·58 W
112 Becher B. (bēch'ēr) Can. (Seattle In.) 48·18 N 123·37 W
104 Beckley (bĕk'lĭ) WV 37·40 N 81·15 W
160 Bédarieux (bā-dà-ryû') Fr. 43·36 N 3·11 E
100 Beddington Cr. (bĕd'ĕng tŭn) Can. (Calgary In.) 51·14 N 114·13 W
105 Bedford (bĕd'fērd) Can. 45·10 N 73·00 W
154 Bedford Eng. 52·10 N 0·25 W
104 Bedford In. 38·50 N 86·30 W
109 Bedford Ia. 40·40 N 94·41 W
99 Bedford Ma. (In.) 42·30 N 71·17 W
106 Bedford NY (New York In.) 41·12 N 73·38 W
107 Bedford Oh. (Cleveland In.) 41·23 N 81·32 W
105 Bedford Pa. 40·05 N 78·20 W
213 Bedford S. Afr. (Natal In.) 32·43 S 26·19 E
121 Bedford Va. 37·19 N 79·27 W
106 Bedford Hill NY (New York In.) 41·14 N 73·41 W
148 Bedworth (bĕd'wērth) Eng. 52·29 N 1·28 W
159 Bedzin (bĕn-jēn') Pol. 50·19 N 19·10 E
117 Beebe (bē'bē) Ar. 35·04 N 91·54 W
107 Beecher (bē'chŭr). Il. (Chicago In.) 41·20 N 87·38 W
112 Beechey Hd. (bē'chĭ hĕd) Can. (Seattle In.) 48·19 N 123·40 W
107 Beech Grove (bēch grōv) In. (Indianapolis In.) 39·43 N 86·05 W
203 Beecroft Hd. (bē'krûft) Austl. 35·03 S 151·15 E
149 Beelitz (bĕ'lētz) G.D.R. (Berlin In.) 52·14 N 12·59 E
183 Be'er Sheva' (bēr-shĕ'bà) Isr. (Palestine In.) 31·15 N 34·48 E
183 Be'er Sheva' (R.) Isr. (Palestine In.) 31·23 N 34·30 E
218 Beestekraal S. Afr. (Johannesburg & Pretoria In.) 25·22 S 27·34 E
148 Beeston (bēs't'n) Eng. 52·55 N 1·11 W
149 Beetz R. (bĕtz) G.D.R. (Berlin In.) 52·28 N 12·37 E
119 Beeville (bē'vĭl) Tx. 28·24 N 97·44 W
203 Bega (bā'gȧ) Austl. 36·50 S 149·49 E
117 Beggs (bĕgz) Ok. 35·46 N 96·06 W
160 Bégles (bĕ'gl') Fr. 44·47 N 0·34 W
214 Begoro Ghana 6·23 N 0·23 W
184 Behāla India (Calcutta In.) 22·31 N 88·19 E
92 Behm Can. Ak. 55·41 N 131·35 W
212 Beira (bā'rȧ) Moz. 19·46 S 34·58 E
162 Beira (Reg.) (bĕ'y-rä) Port. 40·38 N 8·00 W
183 Beirut (Bayrūt) (bā-rōōt') Leb. (Palestine In.) 33·53 N 35·30 E
162 Beja (bā'zhä) Port. 38·03 N 7·53 W
151 Béja Tun. 36·52 N 9·20 E
210 Bejaïa (Bougie) Alg. 36·46 N 5·00 E
162 Béjar Sp. 40·25 N 5·43 W
186 Bejestān Iran 34·30 N 58·22 E
129 Bejucal (bā-hōō-käl') Cuba (In.) 22·08 N 82·23 W
127 Bejuco (bĕ-kōō'kô) Pan. 8·37 N 79·54 W
159 Békés (bā'kāsh) Hung. 46·45 N 21·08 E
159 Békéscsaba (bā'kāsh-chô'bô) Hung. 46·39 N 21·06 E
189 Beketova (bĕk'e-to'và) Sov. Un. 53·23 N 125·21 E
165 Bela Crkva (bĕ'lä tsĕrk'vä) Yugo. 44·53 N 21·25 E
162 Belalcázar (bāl-ål-kä'thär) Sp. 38·35 N 5·12 W
163 Belas (bĕ'-läs). Port. (Lisbon In.) 38·47 N 9·16 W
165 Bela-Slatina (byä'la slä'tēnä). Bul. 43·26 N 23·56 E
135 Bela Vista de Goia's Braz. 16·57 S 48·47 W
196 Belawan (bå-lä'wän) Indon. 3·43 N 98·43 E
170 Belaya (R.) (byĕ'lĭ-yà). Sov. Un. 52·45 N 61·15 E
167 Belaya Tserkov' (byĕ'lĭ-yà tsĕr'kôf). Sov. Un. 49·48 N 30·09 E
91 Belcher Is. (bĕl'chĕr) Can. 56·20 N 80·40 W
104 Belding (bĕl'dĭng) Mi. 43·05 N 85·25 W
170 Belebey (byĕ'lĕ-bå'ĭ) Sov. Un. 54·00 N 54·10 E
135 Belém (Pará) (bå-lĕN') (pä-rä') Braz. 1·18 S 48·27 W
115 Belen (bĕ-lån') NM 34·40 N 106·45 W
136 Belén (bā-lān') Par. 23·30 S 57·09 W
205 Bélep, Îsles N. Cal. 19·30 S 160·32 E
166 Belëv (byĕl'yĕf) Sov. Un. 53·49 N 36·06 E
112 Belfair (bĕl'far) Wa. (Seattle In.) 47·27 N 122·50 W
98 Belfast (bĕl'fàst) Me. 44·25 N 69·01 W
154 Belfast N. Ire. 54·36 N 5·45 W
154 Belfast, Lough (B.) (lŏK bĕl'fàst) Ire. 54·45 N 7·40 W
211 Bēlfodiyo Eth. 10·45 N 39·27 E
161 Belfort (bā-fôr') Fr. 47·40 N 7·50 E
185 Belgaum India 15·57 N 74·32 E
146 Belgium (bĕl'jĭ-ŭm) Eur. 51·00 N 2·52 E
167 Belgorod (byĕl'gŭ-rut) Sov. Un. 50·36 N 36·32 E
167 Belgorod (Oblast) Sov. Un. 50·40 N 36·42 E
167 Belgorod Dnestrovskiy (byĕl'gŭ-rŭd nyĕs-trôf'skē) Sov. Un. 46·09 N 30·19 E
Belgrade, see Beograd
121 Belhaven (bĕl'hā-vĕn) NC 35·33 N 76·37 W
105 Belington (bĕl'ĭng-tŭn) WV 39·00 N 79·55 W
165 Beli Timok (R.) (bĕ'lē tĕ'môk) Yugo. 43·35 N 22·13 E

196 Belitung (I.) Indon. 3·30 S 107·30 E
126 Belize (bĕ-lēz') Belize (In.) 17·31 N 88·10 W
122 Belize N.A. 17·00 N 88·40 W
126 Belize R. Belize (In.) 17·16 N 88·56 W
174 Bel'kovo (byĕl'kô-vô) Sov. Un. (Moscow In.) 56·15 N 38·49 E
173 Bel'kovskiy (I.) (byĕl-kôf'skĭ) Sov. Un. 75·52 N 133·00 E
99 Bell (I.) (bĕl) Can. 50·45 N 55·35 W
97 Bell (R.) Can. 49·25 N 77·15 W
92 Bella Bella Can. 52·10 N 128·07 W
92 Bella Coola Can. 52·22 N 126·46 W
104 Bellaire (bĕl-âr') Oh. 40·00 N 80·45 W
119 Bellaire Tx. (In.) 29·43 N 95·28 W
185 Bellary (bĕl-lä'rê) India 15·15 N 76·56 E
136 Bella Union (bĕ'l-yà-ōō-nyô'n). Ur. 30·18 S 57·26 W
136 Bella Vista (bā'lyà vēs'tà) Arg. 27·07 S 65·14 W
136 Bella Vista Arg. 28·35 S 58·53 W
136 Bella Vista Arg. (In.) 34·18 S 58·41 W
135 Bella Vista Braz. 22·16 S 56·14 W
129 Belle-Anse Hai 18·15 N 72·00 W
99 Belle B. (bĕl) Can. 47·35 N 55·15 W
106 Belle Chasse (bĕl shäs') La. (New Orleans In.) 29·52 N 90·00 W
104 Bellefontaine (bĕl-fŏn'tân) Oh. 40·25 N 83·50 W
113 Bellefontaine Neighbors Mo. (St. Louis In.) 38·46 N 90·13 W
108 Belle Fourche (bĕl' fōōrsh') SD 44·28 N 103·50 W
108 Belle Fourche (R.) Wy. 44·29 N 104·40 W
108 Belle Fourche Res. SD 44·51 N 103·44 W
161 Bellegarde-sur-Valserine (bĕl-gärd'sür-väl-sȧ-rēn'). Fr. 46·06 N 6·50 E
121 Belle Glade (bĕl glād) Fl. (In.) 26·39 N 80·37 W
160 Belle Ile (I.) (bĕlēl') Fr. 47·15 N 3·30 W
99 Belle Isle, Str. of Can. 51·35 N 56·30 W
106 Belle Mead (bĕl mēd) NJ (New York In.) 40·28 N 74·40 W
99 Belleoram Can. 47·31 N 55·25 W
109 Belle Plaine (bĕl plān') Ia. 41·52 N 92·19 W
107 Belle Vernon (bĕl vûr'nŭn) Pa. (Pittsburgh In.) 40·08 N 79·52 W
105 Belleville (bĕl'vĭl) Can. 44·15 N 77·25 W
113 Belleville Il. (St. Louis In.) 38·31 N 89·59 W
117 Belleville Ks. 39·49 N 97·37 W
107 Belleville Mi. (Detroit In.) 42·12 N 83·29 W
106 Belleville NJ (New York In.) 40·47 N 74·09 W
109 Bellevue (bĕl'vū) Ia. 42·14 N 90·26 W
107 Bellevue Ky. (Cincinnati In.) 39·06 N 84·29 W
104 Bellevue Mi. 42·30 N 85·00 W
104 Bellevue Oh. 41·15 N 82·45 W
107 Bellevue Pa. (Pittsburgh In.) 40·30 N 80·04 W
112 Bellevue Wa. (Seattle In.) 47·37 N 122·12 W
161 Belley (bĕ-lē') Fr. 45·46 N 5·41 E
113 Bellflower (bĕl-flou'ēr) Ca. (Los Angeles In.) 33·53 N 118·08 W
113 Bell Gardens. Ca. (Los Angeles In.) 33·59 N 118·11 W
99 Bellingham (bĕl'ĭng-hăm) Ma. (In.) 42·05 N 71·28 W
112 Bellingham. Wa. (Vancouver In.) 48·46 N 122·29 W
112 Bellingham B. Wa. (Vancouver In.) 48·44 N 122·34 W
220 Bellingshausen Sea (bĕl'ĭngz houz'n). Ant. 72·00 S 80·30 W
164 Bellinzona (bĕl-ĭn-tsō'nä) Switz. 46·10 N 9·09 E
99 Bell I Can. 50·44 N 55·35 W
106 Bellmore (bĕl-mōr) NY (New York In.) 40·40 N 73·31 W
134 Bello (bĕ'l-yô) Col. (In.) 6·20 N 75·33 W
105 Bellows Falls (bĕl'ōz fôls) Vt. 43·10 N 72·30 W
184 Bellpat Pak. 29·08 N 68·00 E
91 Bell Pen. Can. 63·50 N 81·16 W
100 Bells Corners. Can. (Ottawa In.) 45·20 N 75·49 W
112 Bells Mtn. (bĕls) Wa. (Portland In.) 45·50 N 122·21 W
164 Belluno (bĕl-lōō'nō) It. 46·08 N 12·14 E
136 Bell Ville (bĕl vēl') Arg. 32·33 S 62·36 W
212 Bellville S. Afr. (In.) 33·54 S 18·38 E
119 Bellville (bĕl'vĭl) Tx. 29·57 N 96·15 W
162 Bélmez (bĕl'mĕth) Sp. 38·17 N 5·17 W
109 Belmond (bĕl'mŏnd) Ia. 42·49 N 93·37 W
112 Belmont. Ca. (San Francisco In.) 37·34 N 122·18 W
135 Belmonte (bĕl-mōn'tà) Braz. 15·58 S 38·47 W
122 Belmopan Belize 17·15 N 88·47 W
133 Belogorsk Sov. Un. 51·09 N 128·32 E
137 Belo Horizonte (bĕ'lôre-sô'n-tĕ) Braz. (Rio de Janeiro In.) 19·54 S 43·56 W
116 Beloit (bê-loit') Ks. 39·26 N 98·06 W
109 Belcit Wi. 42·31 N 89·04 W
170 Belomorsk (byĕl-ô-môrsk') Sov. Un. 64·30 N 34·42 E
167 Belopol'ye (byĕ-lô-pôl'yĕ). Sov. Un. 51·10 N 34·19 E
174 Beloretsk (byĕ'lô-rĕtsk) Sov. Un. (Urals In.) 53·58 N 58·25 E
168 Belorussian (S. S. R.) Sov. Un. 53·30 N 25·33 E
167 Belosarayskaya, Kosa (C.) (kô-sä' byĕ'lô-sä-räy'skä'yä) Sov. Un. 46·43 N 37·18 E
172 Belovo (bvĕ'lŭ-vû) Sov. Un. 54·17 N 86·23 E
167 Belovodsk (byĕ-lŭ-vôdsk') Sov. Un. 49·12 N 39·36 E
170 Beloye (L.) Sov. Un. 60·10 N 38·05 E
170 Belozersk (byĕ-lŭ-zyôrsk'). Sov. Un. 60·00 N 38·00 E
148 Belper (bĕl'pēr) Eng. 53·01 N 1·28 W
111 Belt (bĕlt) Mt. 47·11 N 110·58 W
111 Belt Cr. Mt. 47·19 N 110·58 W
119 Belton (bĕl'tŭn) Tx. 31·04 N 97·27 W
119 Belton L. Tx. 31·15 N 97·35 W
106 Beltsville (belts-vĭl) Md. (Baltimore In.) 39·03 N 76·56 W
167 Bel'tsy (bĕl'tsē) Sov. Un. 47·47 N 27·57 E
172 Belukha, Gol'tsy (Mtn.). Sov. Un. 49·47 N 86·23 E
109 Belvidere (bĕl-vĕ-dēr') Il. 42·14 N 88·52 W
105 Belvidere Pa. 40·50 N 75·05 W

205 Belyando (R.) (bĕl-yän'dō). Austl. 22·09 S 146·48 E
174 Belyanka (byĕl'yán-kà) Sov. Un. (Urals In.) 56·04 N 59·16 E
166 Belynichi (byĕl-ĭ-nĭ'chĭ). Sov. Un. 54·02 N 29·42 E
166 Belyy (byĕ'lē) Sov. Un. 55·52 N 32·58 E
172 Belyy (I.) Sov. Un. 73·19 N 72·00 E
174 Belyye Stolby (byĕ'lĭ-ye stôl'bĭ) Sov. Un. (Moscow In.) 55·20 N 37·52 E
149 Belzig (bĕl'tsēg) G.D.R. (Berlin In.) 52·08 N 12·35 E
120 Belzoni (bĕl-zō'nê) Ms. 33·09 N 90·30 W
212 Bembe (bĕN'bĕ) Ang. 7·00 S 14·20 E
162 Bembezar (R.) (bĕm-bā-thär'). Sp. 38·00 N 5·18 W
109 Bemidji (bê-mĭj'ĭ) Mn. 47·28 N 94·54 W
212 Bena Dibele (bĕn'à dē-bĕ'lĕ). Zaire 4·00 S 22·49 E
203 Benalla (bĕn-ăl'à) Austl. 36·30 S 146·00 E
Benares, see Vārānasi
162 Benavente (bā-nä-vĕn'tä) Sp. 42·01 N 5·43 W
113 Benbrook (bĕn'brŏŏk) Tx. (Dallas, Fort Worth In.) 32·41 N 97·27 W
113 Benbrook Res. Tx. (Dallas, Fort Worth In.) 32·35 N 97·30 W
110 Bend (bĕnd) Or. 44·04 N 121·17 W
101 Bendeleben, Mt. (bĕn-dĕl-bĕn). Ak. 65·18 N 163·45 W
218 Bender Beila Som. (Horn of Afr. In.) 9·40 N 50·45 E
218 Bender Cassim Som. (Horn of Afr. In.) 11·19 N 49·10 E
167 Bendery (bĕn-dyĕ're) Sov. Un. 46·49 N 29·29 E
203 Bendigo (bĕn'dĭ-gō) Austl. 36·39 S 144·20 E
106 Benedict (bĕnĕ'dĭct) Md. (Baltimore In.) 38·31 N 76·41 W
158 Benešov (bĕn'ĕ-shôf) Czech. 49·48 N 14·40 E
164 Benevento (bā-nā-vĕn'tō) It. 41·08 N 14·46 E
182 Bengal, B. of (bĕn-gôl') Asia 17·30 N 87·00 E
216 Bengamisa Zaire 0·57 N 25·10 E
183 Bengkalis (bĕng-kä'lĭs) Indon. (Singapore In.) 1·29 N 102·06 E
196 Bengkulu Indon. 3·46 S 102·18 E
216 Benguela (bĕn-gĕl'ȧ) Ang. 12·35 S 13·25 E
212 Benguela (Reg.) Ang. 13·13 S 16·00 E
106 Ben Hill (bĕn hĭl). Ga. (Atlanta In.) 33·42 N 84·31 W
154 Ben Hope (Mtn.) (bĕn hōp). Scot. 58·25 N 4·25 W
134 Beni (R.) (bā'nê) Bol. 13·41 S 67·30 W
210 Beni-Abbès (bā'nê ä-bĕs') Alg. 30·11 N 2·13 W
163 Benicarló (bā-nē-kär-lō') Sp. 40·26 N 0·25 E
112 Benicia (bê-nĭsh'ĭ-ȧ) Ca. (San Francisco In.) 38·03 N 122·09 W
209 Benin Afr. 8·00 N 2·00 E
215 Benin (R.) (bĕn-ēn') Nig. 5·55 N 5·15 E
215 Benin City Nig. 6·19 N 5·41 E
210 Beni Saf (bā'nê säf') Alg. 35·23 N 1·20 W
216 Benito (R.) Equat. Gui. 1·35 N 10·45 E
116 Benkelman (bĕn-kĕl-măn) Ne. 40·05 N 101·35 W
164 Benkovac (bĕn'kō-văts) Yugo. 44·02 N 15·41 E
213 Ben Macdhui (Mtn.) (bĕn măk-dōō'ê) Leso-S. Afr. (Natal In.) 30·38 S 27·54 E
121 Bennettsville (bĕn'ĕts vĭl) SC 34·35 N 79·41 W
105 Bennington (bĕn'ĭng-tŭn) Vt. 42·55 N 73·15 W
106 Benns Church (bĕnz' chûrch') Va. (Norfolk In.) 36·47 N 76·35 W
213 Benoni (bĕ-nō'nī) S. Afr. (Johannesburg & Pretoria In.) 26·11 S 28·19 E
215 Benoy Chad 8·59 N 16·19 E
126 Benque Viejo (bĕn-kĕ bĭĕ'hō) Belize (In.) 17·07 N 89·07 W
107 Bensenville (bĕn'sĕn-vĭl) Il. (Chicago In.) 41·57 N 87·56 W
158 Bensheim (bĕns-hīm) F.R.G. 49·42 N 8·38 E
115 Benson (bĕn-sŭn) Az. 32·00 N 110·20 W
108 Benson Mn. 45·18 N 95·36 W
107 Bentleyville (bent'lē vĭl) Pa. (Pittsburgh In.) 40·07 N 80·01 W
117 Benton (bĕn'tŭn) Ar. 34·34 N 92·34 W
114 Benton Ca. 37·44 N 118·22 W
98 Benton Can. 45·59 N 67·36 W
148 Benton Eng. 53·27 N 2·07 W
104 Benton Il. 38·00 N 88·55 W
104 Benton Harbor (bĕn'tŭn här'bēr) Mi. 42·05 N 86·30 W
117 Bentonville (bĕn'tŭn-vĭl) Ar. 36·22 N 94·11 W
215 Benue (R.) (bā'nōō-å) Nig. 7·55 N 8·55 E
183 Benut (R.). Mala. (Singapore In.) 1·43 N 103·20 E
104 Benwood (bĕn-wŏŏd) WV 39·55 N 80·45 W
165 Beograd (Belgrade) (bĕ-ō'gräd) (bĕl'gräd). Yugo. 44·48 N 20·32 E
195 Beppu (bĕ'pōō) Jap. 33·16 N 131·30 E
127 Bequia I. (bĕk-ē'ä) N. A. (In.) 13·00 N 61·08 W
197 Beraoe, Teloek (B.) Indon. 2·22 S 131·40 E
165 Berat (bĕ-rät') Alb. 40·43 N 19·59 E
136 Berazategui (bĕ-rä-zä'tĕ-gē) Arg. (Buenos Aires In.) 34·31 S 58·12 W
218 Berbera (bûr'bûr-ȧ) Som. (Horn of Afr. In.) 10·25 N 45·05 E
215 Berbérati Cen. Afr. Rep. 4·16 N 15·47 E
160 Berck (bĕrk) Fr. 50·26 N 1·36 E
153 Berd'ansk Sov. Un. 46·45 N 36·47 E
167 Berdichev (bĕr-dē'chĕf) Sov. Un. 49·53 N 28·32 E
167 Berdyanskaya, Kosa (C.) (kô-sä' bĕr-dyän'skä-yä). Sov. Un. 46·38 N 36·42 E
174 Berdyaush (bĕr'dyȧûsh) Sov. Un. (Urals In.) 55·10 N 59·12 E
120 Berea (bê-rē'ȧ) Ky. 37·30 N 84·19 W
107 Berea Oh. (Cleveland In.) 41·22 N 81·51 W
159 Beregovo (bĕ'rĕ-gô-vô) Sov. Un. 48·13 N 22·40 E
217 Bereku Tan. 4·27 S 35·44 E
95 Berens (I.) (bĕr'ĕnz) Can. 52·18 N 96·30 W
95 Berens (R.) Can. 52·21 N 97·17 W
95 Berens River Can. 52·22 N 97·02 W
108 Beresford (bĕr'ĕs-fērd) SD 43·05 N 96·46 W
159 Berettyóújfalu (bĕ'rĕt-tyō-ōō'y'fô-lōō). Hung. 47·14 N 21·33 E

ng-sing; ŋ-baŋk; N-nasalized n; nŏd; cŏmmit; ōld; ôbey; ôrder; fōōd; fŏŏt; ou-out; s-soft; sh-dish; th-thin; pūre; ûnite; ûrn; stŭd; circŭs; ü-as "y" in study; '-indeterminate vowel.

Page	Name Pronunciation Region	Lat. °′	Long. °′
159	Berëza (bĕ-rā'zȧ) Sov. Un.	52·29 N	24·59 E
159	Berezhany (bĕr-yĕ'zhȧ-nĕ) Sov. Un.	49·25 N	24·58 E
166	Berezina (R.) (bĕr-yĕ'zē-nȧ) Sov. Un.	53·20 N	29·05 E
166	Berezino (bĕr-yä'zē-nô) Sov. Un.	53·51 N	28·54 E
167	Berezna (bĕr-yôz'nȧ) Sov. Un.	51·32 N	31·47 E
167	Bereznegovata Sov. Un.	47·19 N	32·58 E
174	Berezniki (bĕr-yôz'nyē-kē) Sov. Un. (Urals In.)	59·25 N	56·46 E
167	Berezovka (bĕr-yôz'ôf-kȧ) Sov. Un.	47·12 N	30·56 E
174	Berëzovka...Sov. Un. (Urals In.)	57·35 N	57·19 E
170	Berëzovo (bĭr-yô'zē-vû)..Sov. Un.	64·10 N	65·10 E
174	Berëzovskiy (bĕr-yô'zôf-skĭ) Sov. Un. (Urals In.)	56·54 N	60·47 E
163	Berga (bĕr'gä) Sp.	42·05 N	1·52 E
165	Bergama (bĕr'gä-mä) Tur.	39·08 N	27·09 E
164	Bergamo (bĕr'gä-mō) It.	45·43 N	9·41 E
135	Bergantín (bĕr-gän-tē'n).Ven. (In.)	10·04 N	64·23 W
149	Bergedorf (bĕr'gĕ-dôrf) F.R.G. (Hamburg In.)	53·29 N	10·12 E
158	Bergen (bĕr'gĕn) G.D.R.	54·26 N	13·26 E
156	Bergen Nor.	60·24 N	5·20 E
106	Bergenfield....NJ (New York In.)	40·55 N	73·59 W
149	Bergen op Zoom Neth. (Amsterdam In.)	51·29 N	3·16 E
160	Bergerac (bĕr-zhĕ-räk') Fr.	44·49 N	0·28 E
161	Bergisch Gladbach (bĕrg'ĭsh-glät'bäk) F.R.G. (Ruhr In.)	50·59 N	7·08 E
149	Berglern (bĕrgh'lĕrn) F.R.G. (Munich In.)	48·24 N	11·55 E
113	Bergs (bûrgs) Tx. (San Antonio In.)	29·19 N	98·26 W
213	Bergville (bĕrg'vĭl) S. Afr. (Natal In.)	28·46 S	29·22 E
184	Berhampur India	19·19 N	84·48 E
75	Bering Sea (bē'rĭng)....Asia-N. A.	58·00 N	175·00 W
101	Bering Str. Ak.	64·50 N	169·50 W
167	Berislav (byĕr'ĭ-släf) Sov. Un.	46·49 N	33·24 E
162	Berja (bĕr'hä) Sp.	36·50 N	2·56 W
112	Berkeley (bûrk'lĭ) Ca. (San Francisco In.)	37·52 N	122·17 W
113	Berkeley.....Mo. (St. Louis In.)	38·45 N	90·20 W
105	Berkeley Springs (bûrk'lĭ sprĭngz) WV	39·40 N	78·10 W
148	Berkhamsted (bĕrk'hăm'stĕd) Eng. (London In.)	51·44 N	0·34 W
107	Berkley (bûrk'lĭ).Mi. (Detroit In.)	42·30 N	83·10 W
165	Berkovitsa (bĕ-kō'vē-tsȧ) ....Bul.	43·14 N	23·08 E
93	Berland (R.) Can.	54·00 N	117·10 W
162	Berlengas (Is.) (bĕr-lĕn'gäzh).Port.	39·25 N	9·33 W
149	Berlin, East (bĕr-lēn') G.D.R. (Berlin In.)	52·31 N	13·28 E
149	Berlin, West...F.R.G. (Berlin In.)	52·31 N	13·20 E
105	Berlin (bûr-lĭn) NH	44·25 N	71·10 W
106	Berlin......NJ (Philadelphia In.)	39·47 N	74·56 W
213	Berlin (bĕr-lĭn).S. Afr. (Natal In.)	32·53 S	27·36 E
109	Berlin (bûr-lĭn') Wi.	43·58 N	88·58 W
162	Bermeja, Sierra (Mts.) (sē-ĕ'r-rä-bĕr-mĕ'hä).Sp.	36·35 N	5·03 W
136	Bermejo (R.) (bĕr-mā'hō)....Arg.	25·05 S	61·00 W
162	Bermeo (bĕr-mā'yō) Sp.	43·23 N	2·43 W
123	Bermuda (I.) N.A.	32·20 N	65·45 W
158	Bern (bĕrn) Switz.	46·55 N	7·25 E
136	Bernal (bĕr-näl') Arg. (Buenos Aires In.)	34·27 S	58·17 W
115	Bernalillo (bĕr-nä-lē'yō)......NM	35·20 N	106·30 W
105	Bernard (L.) (bĕr-närd')......Can.	45·45 N	79·25 W
106	Bernardsville (bûr nărds'vĭl) NJ (New York In.)	40·43 N	74·34 W
149	Bernau (bĕr'nou) G.D.R. (Berlin In.)	52·40 N	13·35 E
158	Bernburg (bĕrn'bŏŏrgh)...G.D.R.	51·48 N	11·43 E
158	Berndorf (bĕrn'dôrf) Aus.	47·57 N	16·05 E
104	Berne (bûrn) In.	40·40 N	84·55 W
158	Berner Alpen (Mts.) Switz.	46·29 N	7·30 E
161	Berneustadt (bĕr'noi'shtät) F.R.G. (Ruhr In.)	51·01 N	7·39 E
204	Bernier (I.) (bĕr-nēr') Austl.	24·58 S	113·15 E
158	Bernina Pizzo (Pk.) Switz.	46·23 N	9·58 E
216	Bero (R.) Ang.	15·10 S	12·20 E
158	Beroun (bā'rōn) Czech.	49·57 N	14·03 E
158	Berounka R. (bĕ-rōn'kȧ)...Czech.	49·53 N	13·40 E
202	Berowra......Austl. (Sydney In.)	33·36 S	151·10 E
160	Berre, Étang de (L.) (ā-tôN' dĕ bâr').Fr. (In.)	43·27 N	5·07 E
160	Berre-l' Étang (bâr'lā-tôN') Fr. (In.)	43·28 N	5·11 E
125	Berriozabal (bā'rēō-zä-bäl')..Mex.	16·47 N	93·16 W
152	Berryan (bĕr-ē-äN') Alg.	32·50 N	3·49 E
93	Berry Creek (R.) Can.	51·15 N	111·40 W
114	Berryessa (R.) (bĕ'rĭ ĕs'ȧ)....Ca.	38·35 N	122·33 W
128	Berry Is. Ba.	25·40 N	77·50 W
117	Berryville (bĕr'ē-vĭl) Ar.	36·21 N	93·34 W
167	Bershad' (byĕr'shät) Sov. Un.	48·22 N	29·31 E
98	Berthier (bĕr-tyā') Can.	46·04 N	73·14 W
100	Berthier.......Can. (Quebec In.)	46·56 N	70·44 W
112	Bertrand (R.) (bûr'trănd) Wa. (Vancouver In.)	48·58 N	122·31 W
105	Berwick (bûr'wĭk) Pa.	41·05 N	76·10 W
154	Berwick (bûr'ĭk) Scot.	55·45 N	2·01 W
107	Berwyn (bûr'wĭn).Il. (Chicago In.)	41·49 N	87·47 W
154	Berwyn Ra. Wales	52·45 N	3·41 W
213	Besalampy (bĕz-ȧ-lȧm-pē') Mad..	16·48 S	40·40 E
161	Besançon (bĕ-säN-sôn) Fr.	47·14 N	6·02 E
183	Besar, Gunong (Mt.) Mala. (Singapore In.)	2·31 N	103·09 E
166	Besed (R.) (byĕ'syĕt).Sov. Un.	52·58 N	31·36 E
166	Beshenkovichi (byĕ'shĕn-kōvē'chĭ).Sov. Un.	55·04 N	29·29 E
159	Beskides (Mts.) (bĕs'kēdz') Czech.-Pol.	49·23 N	19·00 E
160	Bessèges (bĕ-sĕzh') Fr.	44·20 N	4·07 E
106	Bessemer (bĕs'ĕ-mĕr) Al. (Birmingham In.)	33·24 N	86·58 W
109	Bessemer Mi.	46·29 N	90·04 W
121	Bessemer City NC	35·16 N	81·17 W
149	Bestensee (bĕs'tĕn-zā) G.D.R. (Berlin In.)	51·15 N	13·39 E
162	Betanzos (bĕ-tän'thōs) Sp.	43·18 N	8·14 W
115	Betatakin Ruin (bĕt-ȧ-täk'ĭn) . Az.	36·40 N	110·29 W
218	Bethal (bĕth'ăl).S. Afr. (Johannesburg & Pretoria In.)	26·27 S	29·28 E
113	Bethalto (bȧ-thăl'tō) Il. (St. Louis In.)	38·54 N	90·03 W
212	Bethanien S. W. Afr.	26·20 S	16·10 E
117	Bethany Mo.	40·15 N	94·04 W
101	Bethel (bĕth'ĕl) Ak.	60·50 N	161·50 W
106	Bethel........Ct. (New York In.)	41·22 N	73·24 W
105	Bethel Vt.	43·50 N	72·40 W
107	Bethel Park..Pa. (Pittsburgh In.)	40·19 N	80·02 W
106	Bethesda (bĕ-thĕs'dȧ) Md. (Baltimore In.)	39·00 N	77·10 W
105	Bethlehem (bĕth'lē-hĕm) Pa.	40·40 N	75·25 W
218	Bethlehem.S. Afr. (Johannesburg & Pretoria In.)	28·14 S	28·18 E
	Bethlehem, see Bayt Lahm		
160	Béthune (bā-tün') Fr.	50·32 N	2·37 E
213	Betroka (bĕ-trōk'ȧ) Mad.	23·13 S	46·17 E
183	Bet She'an.....Isr. (Palestine In.)	32·30 N	35·30 E
98	Betsiamites Can.	48·57 N	68·36 W
98	Betsiamites, (R.) Can.	49·11 N	69·20 W
213	Betsiboka (R.) (bĕt-sĭ-bō'kȧ).Mad.	16·47 S	46·45 E
101	Bettles Field (bĕt'tŭls) Ak.	66·58 N	151·48 W
184	Betwa (R.) (bĕt'wȧ) India	25·00 N	77·37 E
161	Betz (bĕ) Fr. (Paris In.)	49·09 N	2·58 E
161	Betzdorf (bĕtz'dôrf) F.R.G. (Ruhr In.)	50·47 N	7·53 E
149	Beveren.......Bel. (Brussels In.)	51·13 N	4·14 E
148	Beverly (bĕv'ĕr-lĭ) Eng.	53·50 N	0·25 W
99	Beverly.........Ma. (Boston In.)	42·34 N	70·53 W
106	Beverly.....NJ (Philadelphia In.)	40·03 N	74·56 W
113	Beverly Hills.Ca. (Los Angeles In.)	34·05 N	118·24 W
117	Bevier (bē-vēr') Mo.	39·44 N	92·36 W
148	Bewdley (būd'lĭ) Eng.	52·22 N	2·19 W
155	Bexhill (bĕks'hĭl) Eng.	50·49 N	0·25 E
148	Bexley (bĕks'ly) Eng. (London In.)	51·26 N	0·09 E
214	Beyla (bā'lȧ) Gui.	8·41 N	8·37 W
211	Beylul Eth.	13·15 N	42·21 E
171	Beypazari (bā-pȧ-zä'rĭ) Tur.	40·10 N	31·40 E
171	Beyşehir (bā-shĕ'h'r) Tur.	38·00 N	31·45 E
171	Beyşehir Gölü (L.) Tur.	38·00 N	31·30 E
167	Beysugskiy, Liman (B.) (lĭ-män' bĕy-sōōg'skĭ).Sov. Un.	46·07 N	38·35 E
166	Bezhetsk (byĕ-zhĕtsk')...Sov. Un.	57·46 N	36·40 E
166	Bezhitsa (byĕ-zhĭ'tsȧ)...Sov. Un.	53·19 N	34·18 E
160	Béziers (bā-zyā') Fr.	43·21 N	3·12 E
184	Bhadreswar India (In.)	22·49 N	88·22 E
184	Bhāgalpur (bä'gŭl-pŏŏr)....India	25·15 N	86·59 E
188	Bhamo (bŭ-mō') Bur.	24·00 N	96·15 E
184	Bhāngar India (In.)	22·30 N	88·36 E
184	Bharatpur (bĕrt'pŏŏr) India	27·21 N	77·33 E
184	Bhatinda (bŭ-tĭn-dȧ) India	30·19 N	74·56 E
184	Bhaunagar (bäv-nŭg'ŭr)....India	21·45 N	72·58 E
185	Bhayandar India (In.)	19·20 N	72·50 E
184	Bhilai India	21·14 N	81·23 E
184	Bhīma (R.) (bē'mȧ) India	17·44 N	75·00 E
185	Bhiwandi India (In.)	19·18 N	73·03 E
184	Bhiwāni India	28·53 N	76·08 E
184	Bhopāl (bō-päl) India	23·20 N	77·25 E
184	Bhorīla Pak.	24·48 N	70·11 E
184	Bhubaneswar (bōō-bû-năsh'vûr) India	20·21 N	85·53 E
184	Bhuj (bōōj) India	23·22 N	69·39 E
187	Bhutan (bōō-tän') Asia	27·15 N	90·30 E
216	Biafra, Bight of Afr.	4·05 N	7·10 E
197	Biak (I.) (bē'ăk) Indon.	1·00 S	136·00 E
159	Biała Podlaska (byä'wä pōd-läs'kä).Pol.	52·01 N	23·08 E
158	Białogard (byä-wō'gärd) Pol.	54·00 N	16·01 E
159	Białystok (byä-wĭs'tŏk) Pol.	53·08 N	23·12 E
214	Biankouma Ivory Coast	7·44 N	7·37 W
160	Biarritz (byä-rēts') Fr.	43·27 N	1·39 W
218	Bibā (bē'bȧ)....Egypt (Nile In.)	28·54 N	30·59 E
120	Bibb City (bĭb' sĭ'tē) Ga.	32·31 N	84·56 W
158	Biberach (bē'bĕräk) F.R.G.	48·06 N	9·49 E
214	Bibiani Ghana	6·28 N	2·20 W
98	Bic (bĭk) Can.	48·22 N	68·42 W
104	Bicknell (bĭk'nĕl) In.	38·45 N	87·20 W
159	Bicske (bĭsh'kē) Hung.	47·29 N	18·38 E
215	Bida (bē'dä) Nig.	9·05 N	6·01 E
98	Biddeford (bĭd'ē-fērd) Me.	43·29 N	70·29 W
148	Biddulph (bĭd'ŭlf) Eng.	53·07 N	2·10 W
	Bidon Cinq, see Post Maurice Cortier		
159	Biebrza R. (byĕb'zhȧ) Pol.	53·18 N	22·25 E
158	Biel (bēl) Switz.	47·09 N	7·12 E
158	Bielefeld (bē'lē-fĕlt).......F.R.G.	52·01 N	8·35 E
165	Bieljina (bē-yĕ'lyē-nä)......Yugo.	44·44 N	19·15 E
164	Biella (byĕl'lä) It.	45·34 N	8·05 E
159	Bielsk Podlaski (byĕlsk pŭd-lä'skĭ) Pol.	52·47 N	23·14 E
196	Bien Hoa Viet.	10·59 N	106·49 E
91	Bienville, Lac (L.) Can.	55·32 N	72·45 W
149	Biesenthal (bē'sĕn-täl) G.D.R. (Berlin In.)	52·46 N	13·38 E
164	Biferno (R.) (bē-fĕr'nō) It.	41·49 N	14·46 E
216	Bifoum Gabon	0·22 S	10·23 E
112	Big (L.) (bĭg)...Wa. (Seattle In.)	48·23 N	122·14 W
120	Big (R.) Ar.	35·55 N	90·10 W
165	Biğa (bē'ghȧ) Tur.	40·13 N	27·14 E
109	Big Bay de Noc (bĭg bā dē nok') Mi.	45·48 N	86·41 W
117	Big Bayou (bĭg' bī'yōō) Ar.	33·04 N	91·28 W
113	Big Bear City (bĭg bâr) Ca. (Los Angeles In.)	34·16 N	116·51 W
111	Big Belt Mts. (bĭg bĕlt) Mt.	46·53 N	111·43 W
108	Big Bend Dam (bĭg bĕnd) SD	44·11 N	99·33 W
118	Big Bend Natl. Park Tx.	29·15 N	103·15 W
120	Big Black (R.) (bĭg blăk) Ms.	32·05 N	90·49 W
117	Big Blue (R.) (bĭg blōō) Ne.	40·53 N	97·00 W
118	Big Canyon (bĭg kăn'yŭn) Tx.	30·27 N	102·19 W
121	Big Cypress Swp. (bĭg sī'prĕs) Fl. (In.)	26·02 N	81·20 W
101	Big Delta (bĭg dĕl'tȧ) Ak.	64·08 N	145·48 W
109	Big Fork (R.) (bĭg fôrk) Mn.	48·08 N	93·47 W
94	Biggar Can.	52·04 N	108·00 W
111	Big Hole (R.) (bĭg 'hōl) Mt.	45·53 N	113·15 W
111	Big Hole Natl. Battlefield (bĭg hōl băt''l-fēld).Mt.	45·44 N	113·35 W
111	Big Horn Mts. (bĭg hôrn)....Wy.	44·47 N	107·40 W
111	Bighorn R. Mt.	45·50 N	107·15 W
95	Big I. Can.	49·10 N	94·40 W
112	Big Lake (bĭg lăk) Wa. (Seattle In.)	48·24 N	122·14 W
100	Big L.......Can. (Edmonton In.)	53·35 N	113·47 W
95	Big Mossy Pt. Can.	53·45 N	97·50 W
104	Big Muddy (R.) Il.	37·50 N	89·00 W
111	Big Muddy Cr. (bĭg mŭd'ĭ)...Mt.	48·53 N	105·02 W
214	Bignona Senegal	12·49 N	16·14 W
94	Big Quill L. Can.	51·55 N	104·22 W
104	Big Rapids (bĭg răp'ĭdz) Mi.	43·40 N	85·30 W
94	Big River Can.	53·50 N	107·01 W
115	Big Sandy (R.) (bĭg sănd'ē)...Az.	34·59 N	113·36 W
104	Big Sandy (R.) Ky.-WV	38·15 N	82·35 W
116	Big Sandy Cr. Co.	39·08 N	103·36 W
111	Big Sandy Cr. Mt.	48·20 N	110·08 W
95	Bigsby I. Can.	49·04 N	94·35 W
108	Big Sioux (R.) (bĭg sōō) SD	44·34 N	97·00 W
118	Big Spring (bĭg sprĭng) Tx.	32·15 N	101·28 W
108	Big Stone (L.) (bĭg stōn) Mn.-SD	45·29 N	96·40 W
120	Big Stone Gap Va.	36·50 N	82·50 W
111	Bigtimber (bĭg'tĭm-bēr) Mt.	45·50 N	109·57 W
111	Big Wood R. (bĭg wŏŏd) Id.	43·02 N	114·30 W
164	Bihać (bē'hăch) Yugo.	44·48 N	15·52 E
184	Bihār (State) (bē-här') India	23·48 N	84·57 E
217	Biharamulo (bē-hä-rä-mōō'lō) Tan.	2·38 S	31·20 E
159	Bihor, Muntii (Mts.) (bē'hôr) Rom.	46·37 N	22·37 E
214	Bijagós, Arquipélago dos (Is.) (är-kē-pă'lä-gō dôs bē-zhä-gōs) Guinea-Bissau	11·20 N	17·10 W
185	Bijāpur India	16·53 N	75·42 E
165	Bijelo Polje (bē'yĕ-lō pō'lyĕ) Yugo.	43·02 N	19·48 E
116	Bijou Cr. (bē'zhōō) Co.	39·41 N	104·13 W
184	Bikaner (bĭ-kă'nûr) India	28·07 N	73·19 E
194	Bikin (bē-kēn') Sov. Un.	46·41 N	134·29 E
194	Bikin (R.) Sov. Un.	46·37 N	135·55 E
216	Bikoro (bē-kō'rō) Zaire	0.45 S	18·07 E
216	Bikuar, Parque Nacional do (Natl. Pk.).Ang.	15·07 S	14·40 E
184	Bilāspur (bē-läs'pŏŏr) India	22·08 N	82·12 E
197	Bilauktaung Ra. Thai.	14·27 N	98·53 E
162	Bilbao (bĭl-bä'ō) Sp.	43·12 N	2·48 W
218	Bilbays.........Egypt (Nile In.)	30·26 N	31·37 E
165	Bileća (bē'lĕ-chä) Yugo.	42·52 N	18·26 E
171	Bilecik (bē-lĕd-zhĕk') Tur.	40·10 N	29·58 E
159	Bilé Karpaty (Mts.) Czech.	48·53 N	17·35 E
159	Biłgoraj (bēw-gō'rī) Pol.	50·31 N	22·43 E
174	Bilimbay (bē'lĭm-bây) Sov. Un. (Urals In.)	56·59 N	59·53 E
203	Billabong (R.) (bĭl'ă-bŏng)..Austl.	35·15 S	145·20 E
99	Billerica (bĭl'rĭk-ȧ)......Ma. (In.)	42·33 N	71·46 W
148	Billericay.....Eng. (London In.)	51·38 N	0·25 E
111	Billings (bĭl'ĭngz) Mt.	45·47 N	108·29 W
115	Bill Williams (L.) (bĭl-wĭl'yumz) Az.	34·10 N	113·50 W
211	Bilma (bēl'mä) Niger	18·41 N	13·20 E
120	Biloxi (bĭ-lŏk'sĭ) Ms.	30·24 N	88·50 W
218	Bilqās Qism Awwal Egypt (Nile In.)	31·14 N	31·25 E
203	Bimberi Pk. (bĭm'bĕrĭ).....Austl.	35·45 S	148·50 E
197	Binaija, Gunung (Mtn.)....Indon.	3·07 S	129·25 E
197	Binalonan (bē-nä-lō'nän) Phil. (In.)	16·03 N	120·35 E
186	Binalud (Mtn.) Iran	36·32 N	58·34 E
197	Biñan (bē'nän)........Phil. (In.)	14·20 N	121·06 E
158	Bingen (bĭn'gĕn) F.R.G.	49·57 N	7·54 E
148	Bingham (bĭng'ăm) Eng.	52·57 N	0·57 W
98	Bingham Me.	45·03 N	69·51 W
113	Bingham Canyon Ut. (Salt Lake City In.)	40·33 N	112·09 W
105	Binghamton (bĭng'ăm-tŭn)....NY	42·05 N	75·55 W
195	Bingo-Nada (Sea) (bĭn'gō nä-dä) Jap.	34·06 N	133·14 E
196	Binh Dinh (bĭng'dĭng') Viet.	13·55 N	109·00 E
203	Binnaway (bĭn'ă-wā) Austl.	31·42 S	149·22 E
183	Bintan, Palau (I.) (bĭn'tän) Indon. (Singapore In.)	1·09 N	104·43 E
196	Bintulu (bēn'tōō-lōō) Mala.	3·07 N	113·06 E
210	Binzert (Bizerte) (bē-zĕrt')..Tun.	37·23 N	9·52 E
214	Bio Gorge (Val.) Ghana	8·30 N	2·05 W
194	Bira (bē'rȧ) Sov. Un.	49·00 N	133·18 E
194	Bira (R.) Sov. Un.	48·55 N	132·25 E
184	Biratnagar (bĭ-rät'nŭ-gŭr)...Nep.	26·35 N	87·18 E
112	Birch Bay (bûrch) Wa. (Vancouver In.)	48·55 N	122·45 W
112	Birch B.....Wa. (Vancouver In.)	48·55 N	122·52 W
95	Birch I. Can.	52·25 N	99·55 W
90	Birch Mts. Can.	57·36 N	113·10 W
112	Birch Pt.....Wa. (Vancouver In.)	48·57 N	122·50 W

Page	Name Pronunciation Region	Lat. °'	Long. °'
213	Bird I. (bẽrd)..S. Afr. (Natal In.)	33·51 s	26·21 E
129	Bird Rock (I.) (bûrd)........Ba.	22·50 N	74·20 W
100	Birds Hill (bûrds) Can. (Winnipeg In.)	49·58 N	97·00 W
203	Birdsville (bûrdz'vĭl).......Austl.	22·50 s	139·31 E
204	Birdum (bûrd'ŭm).........Austl.	15·45 s	133·25 E
171	Birecik (bē-rĕd-zhĕk')........Tur.	37·10 N	37·50 E
152	Bir er Ressof (bēr-ĕr-rĕ-sôf')..Alg.	32·19 N	7·58 E
215	Bir Gara................Chad	13·11 N	15·58 E
186	Bīrjand (bēr'jänd)..........Iran	33·07 N	59·16 E
112	Birkenfeld......Or. (Portland In.)	49·59 N	123·20 W
148	Birkenhead (bûr'kĕn-hĕd)....Eng.	53·23 N	3·02 W
149	Birkenwerder (bĕr'kĕn-vĕr-dĕr) G.D.R. (Berlin In.)	52·41 N	13·22 E
159	Bîrlad...................Rom.	46·15 N	27·43 E
106	Birmingham (bûr'mĭng-häm) Al. (Birmingham In.)	33·31 N	86·49 W
148	Birmingham...............Eng.	52·29 N	1·53 W
107	Birmingham.....Mi. (Detroit In.)	42·32 N	83·13 W
113	Birmingham Mo. (Kansas City In.)	39·10 N	94·22 W
148	Birmingham Can...........Eng.	53·07 N	2·40 W
211	Bi'r Misāhah.............Egypt	22·16 N	28·04 E
215	Birnin Kebbi..............Nig.	12·32 N	4·12 E
173	Birobidzhan (bē'rô-bê-jän') Sov. Un.	48·42 N	133·28 E
170	Birsk (bĭrsk)...........Sov. Un.	55·25 N	55·30 E
148	Birstall (bûr'stôl)...........Eng.	53·44 N	1·39 W
167	Biryuchiy (I.) (bĭr-yōō'chĭ) Sov. Un.	46·07 N	35·12 E
174	Biryulëvo (bĕr-yōōl'yô-vô) Sov. Un. (Moscow In.)	55·35 N	37·39 E
172	Biryusa (R.) (bĕr-yōō'sä).Sov. Un.	56·43 N	97·30 E
183	Bi'r Za'farānah Egypt (Palestine In.)	29·07 N	32·38 E
156	Biržai (bêr-zhä'ê)........Sov. Un.	56·11 N	24·45 E
115	Bisbee (bĭz'bē)..............Az.	31·30 N	109·55 W
151	Biscay, B. of (bĭs'kā')........Eur.	45·19 N	3·51 W
121	Biscayne B. (bĭs-kān')....Fl. (In.)	25·22 N	80·15 W
161	Bischeim (bĭsh'hīm)..........Fr.	48·40 N	7·48 E
96	Biscotasi L...............Can.	47·20 N	81·55 W
174	Biser (bē'sēr).Sov. Un. (Urals In.)	58·24 N	58·54 E
164	Biševo (Is.) (bē'shĕ-vō).....Yugo.	43·58 N	15·41 E
114	Bishop (bĭsh'ŭp).............Ca.	37·22 N	118·25 W
119	Bishop.....................Tx.	27·35 N	97·46 W
148	Bishop's Castle (bĭsh'ŏps käs'l) Eng.	52·29 N	2·57 W
121	Bishopville (bĭsh'ŭp-vĭl).......SC	34·11 N	80·13 W
210	Biskra (bēs'krà).............Alg.	34·52 N	5·39 E
108	Bismarck (bĭz'märk).........ND	46·48 N	100·46 W
197	Bismarck Arch......Pap. N. Gui.	3·15 s	150·45 E
197	Bismarck Ra........Pap. N. Gui.	5·15 s	144·15 E
214	Bissau (bê-sä'ōō)...Guinea-Bissau	11·51 N	15·35 W
95	Bissett....................Can.	51·01 N	95·45 W
119	Bistineau L. (bĭs-tĭ-nō').......La.	32·19 N	93·45 W
159	Bistrita (bĭs-trĭt-sà)........Rom.	47·09 N	24·29 E
159	Bistrita R.................Rom.	47·08 N	25·47 E
171	Bitlis (bĭt-lēs')..............Tur.	38·30 N	42·00 E
165	Bitola (Monastir) (bê'tô-lä) (mô'nä-stêr).Yugo.	41·02 N	21·22 E
164	Bitonto (bê-tôn'tō)...........It.	41·08 N	16·42 E
111	Bitter Cr. (bĭt'ēr)...........Wy.	41·36 N	108·29 W
158	Bitterfeld (bĭt'ēr-fĕlt).....G.D.R.	51·39 N	12·19 E
110	Bitterroot Ra. (bĭt'ēr-ōōt)....Mt.	47·15 N	115·13 W
111	Bitterroot R................Mt.	46·28 N	114·10 W
167	Bityug (R.) (bĭt'yŏŏg)...Sov. Un.	51·23 N	40·33 E
215	Biu........................Nig.	10·35 N	12·13 E
109	Biwabik (bê-wä'bĭk).........Mn.	47·32 N	92·24 W
195	Biwa-ko (L.) (bê-wä'kō) Jap. (Ōsaka In.)	35·03 N	135·51 E
172	Biya (R.) (bĭ'yà)........Sov. Un.	52·22 N	87·28 E
172	Biysk (bēsk)...........Sov. Un.	52·32 N	85·28 E
213	Bizana (bĭz-änä) S. Afr. (Natal In.)	30·51 s	29·54 E
	Bizerte, see Binzert		
192	Bizuta...................Mong.	46·28 N	115·10 E
164	Bjelovar (byĕ-lō'vär).......Yugo.	45·54 N	16·53 E
	Björneborg, see Pori		
156	Bjorne Fd. (byûr'nĕ fyôrd)...Nor.	60·11 N	5·26 E
214	Bla......................Mali	12·57 N	5·46 W
104	Black (L.) (blăk)............Mi.	45·25 N	84·15 W
105	Black (L.)..................NY	44·30 N	75·35 W
117	Black (R.)..................Ar.	35·47 N	91·22 W
96	Black (R.).................Can.	49·20 N	81·15 W
105	Black (R.)..................NY	43·45 N	75·20 W
121	Black (R.)..................SC	34·55 N	80·08 W
109	Black (R.)..................Wi.	44·07 N	90·56 W
205	Blackall (blăk'ŭl)..........Austl.	24·23 s	145·37 E
109	Black B. (blăk).............Can.	48·36 N	88·32 W
101	Blackburn (blăk'bûrn)........Ak.	63·20 N	159·45 W
148	Blackburn..................Eng.	53·45 N	2·28 W
101	Blackburn, Mt...............Ak.	61·50 N	143·12 W
115	Black Canyon of the Gunnison Natl. Mon. (blăk kăn'yŭn).Co.	38·35 N	107·45 W
112	Black Diamond (dī'mŭnd) Wa. (Seattle In.)	47·19 N	122·00 W
154	Blackdown Hills (blăk'doun).Eng.	50·58 N	3·19 W
109	Blackduck (blăk'dŭk).........Mn.	47·41 N	94·33 W
111	Blackfoot (blăk'fŏŏt)..........Id.	43·11 N	112·23 W
93	Blackfoot Ind. Res..........Can.	50·45 N	113·00 W
111	Blackfoot Ind. Res...........Mt.	48·49 N	112·53 W
111	Blackfoot R.................Mt.	46·53 N	113·33 W
111	Blackfoot River Res..........Id.	42·53 N	111·23 W
108	Black Hills.................SD	44·08 N	103·47 W
95	Black I....................Can.	51·10 N	96·30 W
98	Black Lake.................Can.	46·02 N	71·24 W
115	Black Mesa (blăk māsà).......Az.	36·33 N	110·40 W
100	Blackmud Cr. (blăk'mŭd) Can. (Edmonton In.)	53·28 N	113·34 W
148	Blackpool (blăk'pōōl)........Eng.	53·49 N	3·02 W
115	Black Ra...................NM	33·15 N	107·55 W
128	Black River (blăk').........Jam.	18·00 N	77·50 W
107	Black R.......Oh. (Cleveland In.)	41·26 N	82·08 W
193	Black R...................Viet.	20·56 N	104·30 E
109	Black River Falls............Wi.	44·18 N	90·51 W
110	Black Rock Des. (rŏk).......Nv.	40·55 N	119·00 W
121	Blacksburg (blăks'bûrg).......SC	35·09 N	81·30 W
147	Black Sea..............Eur.-Asia	43·01 N	32·16 E
121	Blackshear (blăk'shĭr)........Ga.	31·20 N	82·15 W
121	Blackstone (blăk'stŏn)........Va.	37·04 N	78·00 W
109	Black Sturgeon (R.) (stû'jŭn).Can.	49·12 N	88·41 W
202	Blacktown (blăk'toun) Austl. (Sydney In.)	33·47 s	150·55 E
98	Blackville (blăk'vĭl).........Can.	46·44 N	65·50 W
121	Blackville..................SC	33·21 N	81·19 W
214	Black Volta (Volta Noire) (R.) (vōl'tà).Afr.	8·55 N	2·30 W
120	Black Warrior (R.) (blăk wŏr'ĭ-ēr) Al.	32·37 N	87·42 W
120	Black Warrior (R.), Locust Fk..Al.	34·06 N	86·27 W
120	Black Warrior (R.), Mulberry Fk. Al.	34·06 N	86·32 W
154	Blackwater (blăk-wô'tēr).....Ire.	52·05 N	9·02 W
117	Blackwater (R.).............Mo.	38·53 N	93·22 W
121	Blackwater (R.).............Va.	37·07 N	77·10 W
117	Blackwell (blăk'wĕl).........Ok.	36·47 N	97·19 W
149	Bladel....Neth. (Amsterdam In.)	51·22 N	5·15 E
171	Blagodarnoye (blä'gô-där-nō'yĕ) Sov. Un.	45·00 N	43·30 E
165	Blagoevgrad (Gorna Dzhumaya) Bul.	42·01 N	23·06 E
173	Blagoveshchensk (blä'gŏ-vyĕsh'chĕnsk).Sov. Un.	50·16 N	127·47 E
174	Blagoveshchensk Sov. Un. (Urals In.)	55·03 N	56·00 E
113	Blaine (blān) Mn. (Minneapolis, St. Paul In.)	45·11 N	93·14 W
112	Blaine.......Wa. (Vancouver In.)	48·59 N	122·49 W
105	Blaine.....................WV	39·25 N	79·10 W
108	Blair (blâr).................Ne.	41·33 N	96·09 W
93	Blairmore..................Can.	49·38 N	114·25 W
105	Blairsville (blârs'vĭl)..........Pa.	40·30 N	79·40 W
112	Blake (I.) (blāk)..Wa. (Seattle In.)	47·37 N	122·28 W
120	Blakely (blāk'lê).............Ga.	31·22 N	84·55 W
210	Blanc, Cap (C.).......Mauritania	20·39 N	18·08 W
161	Blanc, Mt. (môn blän).....Fr.-It.	45·50 N	6·53 E
136	Blanca, Bahia (B.) (bä-ē'ä-blän'kä).Arg.	39·30 s	61·00 W
116	Blanca Pk. (blăŋ'kà).........Co.	37·36 N	105·22 W
203	Blanch, L. (blănch)........Austl.	29·20 s	139·12 E
100	Blanche, (R.)...Can. (Ottawa In.)	45·34 N	75·38 W
107	Blanchester (blăn'chĕs-tēr) Oh. (Cincinnati In.)	39·18 N	83·58 W
136	Blanco, C. (blăŋ'kō).........Arg.	47·08 s	65·47 W
126	Blanco, Cabo (C.) (kà'bô-blăŋ'kō) C. R.	9·29 N	85·15 W
110	Blanco, C. (blăn'kō).........Or.	42·53 N	124·38 W
125	Blanco (R.)................Mex.	18·42 N	96·03 W
124	Blanco (R.)................Mex.	24·05 N	99·21 W
128	Blancos, Cayo (I.) (kä'yō-blăŋ'kōs).Cuba	23·15 N	80·55 W
115	Blanding...................Ut.	37·40 N	109·31 W
155	Blankenburg (bläŋ'kĕn-bŏŏrgh) G.D.R	51·45 N	10·58 E
149	Blankenfelde (blän'kĕn-fĕl-dĕ) G.D.R. (Berlin In.)	52·20 N	13·24 E
124	Blanquilla, Arrecife (Reef) (är-rĕ-sē'fĕ-blän-kē'l-yä).Mex.	21·32 N	97·14 W
217	Blantyre (blăn-tīyr).......Malawi	15·47 s	35·00 E
107	Blasdell (blăz'dĕl) NY (Buffalo In.)	42·48 N	78·51 W
164	Blato (blä'tō)..............Yugo.	42·55 N	16·47 E
156	Blåvands Huk (Cape) (blô'văns-hōk).Den.	55·36 N	8·05 E
160	Blaye-et-Ste. Luce (blā'ā-sănt-lüs').Fr.	45·08 N	0·40 W
159	Błazowa (bwä-zhō'và)........Pol.	49·51 N	22·05 E
217	Bleus, Monts (Mts.)........Zaire	1·10 N	30·10 E
210	Blida......................Alg.	36·33 N	2·45 E
96	Blind River (blīnd)..........Can.	46·10 N	83·09 W
104	Blissfield (blĭs-fēld)..........Mi.	41·50 N	83·50 W
148	Blithe (R.) (blĭth)..........Eng.	52·22 N	1·49 W
214	Blitta.....................Togo	8·19 N	0·59 E
105	Block (I.) (blŏk).............RI	41·05 N	71·35 W
92	Bloedel....................Can.	50·07 N	125·23 W
218	Bloemfontein (blōōm'fŏn-tān) S. Afr. (Johannesburg & Pretoria In.)	29·09 s	26·16 E
160	Blois (blwä).................Fr.	47·36 N	1·21 E
93	Blood Ind. Res..............Can.	49·30 N	113·10 W
109	Bloomer (blōōm'ēr)...........Wi.	45·07 N	91·30 W
104	Bloomfield (blōōm'fēld) ......In.	39·00 N	86·55 W
109	Bloomfield..................Ia.	40·44 N	92·21 W
117	Bloomfield..................Mo.	36·54 N	89·55 W
108	Bloomfield..................Ne.	42·36 N	97·40 W
106	Bloomfield....NJ (New York In.)	40·48 N	74·12 W
107	Bloomfield Hills.Mi. (Detroit In.)	42·35 N	83·15 W
109	Blooming Prairie (blōōm'ĭng prā'rĭ).Mn.	43·52 N	93·04 W
113	Bloomington (blōōm'ĭng-tŭn) Ca. (Los Angeles In.)	34·04 N	117·24 W
104	Bloomington.................Il.	40·30 N	89·00 W
104	Bloomington.................In.	39·10 N	86·35 W
113	Bloomington Mn. (Minneapolis, St. Paul In.)	44·50 N	93·18 W
105	Bloomsburg (blōōmz'bûrg)....Pa.	41·00 N	76·25 W
106	Blossburg (blŏs'bûrg) Al. (Birmingham In.)	33·38 N	86·57 W
105	Blossburg..................Pa.	41·45 N	77·00 W
212	Bloubergstrand.......S. Afr. (In.)	33·48 s	18·28 E
120	Blountstown (blŭnts'tun)......Fl.	30·24 N	85·02 W
158	Bludenz (blōō-dĕnts').........Aus.	47·09 N	9·50 E
99	Blue, Mt...................Can.	50·28 N	57·11 W
107	Blue Ash (blōō ăsh) Oh. (Cincinnati In.)	39·14 N	84·23 W
109	Blue Earth (blōō ûrth).......Mn.	43·38 N	94·05 W
109	Blue Earth (R.).............Mn.	43·55 N	94·16 W
121	Bluefield (blōō'fēld)..........WV	37·15 N	81·11 W
127	Bluefields (blōō'fēldz)........Nic.	12·03 N	83·45 W
107	Blue Island......Il. (Chicago In.)	41·39 N	87·41 W
115	Blue Mesa Res...............Co.	38·25 N	107.00 W
203	Blue Mts..................Austl.	33·35 s	149·00 E
128	Blue Mts...................Jam.	18·05 N	76·35 W
110	Blue Mts....................Or.	45·15 N	118·50 W
204	Blue Mud B. (blōō mŭd)...Austl.	13·20 s	136·45 E
210	Blue Nile (Abay) (R.) (à-bä'ē).Eth.	9·45 N	37·23 E
211	Blue Nile (Al-Bahr al-Azraq) (R.) (bärĕlaz-räk').Sud.	12·50 N	34·10 E
117	Blue Rapids (blōō răp'ĭdz)....Ks.	39·40 N	96·41 W
103	Blue Ridge (Mts.) (blōō rĭj).U. S.	35·30 N	82·50 W
93	Blue River.................Can.	52·05 N	119·17 W
113	Blue R.....Mo. (Kansas City In.)	38·55 N	94·33 W
115	Bluff......................Ut.	37·18 N	109·34 W
106	Bluff Park..Al. (Birmingham In.)	33·24 N	86·52 W
104	Bluffton (blŭf-tŭn)...........In.	40·40 N	85·15 W
104	Bluffton...................Oh.	40·50 N	83·55 W
136	Blumenau (blōō'mĕn-ou)....Braz.	26·53 s	48·58 W
183	Blumut, Gunong (Mt.) Mala. (Singapore In.)	2·03 N	103·34 E
154	Blyth (blīth)...............Eng.	55·03 N	1·34 W
114	Blythe.....................Ca.	33·37 N	114·37 W
117	Blytheville (blīth'vĭl).........Ar.	35·55 N	89·51 W
214	Bo.......................S.L.	7·56 N	11·21 W
197	Boac................Phil. (In.)	13·26 N	121·50 E
126	Boaco (bô-ä'kō)..............Nic.	12·24 N	85·41 W
214	Boaka (R.).................Gui.	11·05 N	10·40 W
135	Boa Vista do Rio Branco (bō'ä vēsh'tà dōō rē'ōō brän'kōō).Braz.	2·46 N	60·45 W
210	Boa Vista I. (bō-ä-vēsh'tà) C. V. (In.)	16·01 N	23·52 W
159	Boberka (bō'bēr-kà).....Sov. Un.	49·36 N	24·18 E
214	Bobo Dioulasso (bô'bô-dyōō-làs-sō').Upper Volta	11·12 N	4·18 W
166	Bobr (bô'b'r)...........Sov. Un.	54·19 N	29·11 E
158	Bóbr (R.) (bŭ'br)............Pol.	51·44 N	15·13 E
167	Bobrinets (bô'brē-nyĭts).Sov. Un.	48·04 N	32·10 E
167	Bobrov (bŭb-rôf').......Sov. Un.	51·07 N	40·01 E
167	Bobrovitsa (bŭb-rô'vê-tsà) Sov. Un.	50·43 N	31·27 E
166	Bobruysk (bŏ-brōō'ĭsk)..Sov. Un.	53·07 N	29·13 E
135	Boca del Pozo (bô-kä-dĕl-pô'zō) Ven. (In.)	11·00 N	64·21 W
135	Boca de Uchire (bô-kä-dĕ-ōō-chē' rĕ).Ven. (In.)	10·09 N	65·27 W
137	Bocaina, Serra da (Mtn.) (sĕ'r-rä-dà-bô-kä'ē-nä) Braz. (Rio de Janeiro In.)	22·47 s	44·39 W
124	Bocas (bō'käs)..............Mex.	22·29 N	101·03 W
127	Bocas del Toro (bō'käs dĕl tō'rō) Pan.	9·24 N	82·15 W
159	Bochnia (bôĸ'nyä)...........Pol.	49·58 N	20·28 E
161	Bocholt (bō'ĸōlt) F.R.G. (Ruhr In.)	51·50 N	6·37 E
161	Bochum (bō'ĸōōm) F.R.G. (Ruhr In.)	51·29 N	7·13 E
161	Bockum-Hövel (bō'ĸōōm-hû'fĕl) F.R.G. (Ruhr In.)	51·41 N	7·45 E
216	Bodalangi.................Zaire	3·14 N	22·14 E
173	Bodaybo (bō-dī'bō)....Sov. Un.	57·12 N	114·46 E
215	Bodele (Depression) (bō-dà-lā') Chad	16·45 N	17·05 E
150	Boden.....................Swe.	65·51 N	21·29 E
158	Boden See (L.) (bō'dĕn zā) F.R.G.	47·48 N	9·22 E
154	Boderg (bō'dûrg).............Ire.	53·51 N	8·06 W
154	Bodmin (bŏd'mĭn)...........Eng.	50·29 N	4·45 W
154	Bodmin Moor (bŏd'mĭn mōōr) Eng.	50·36 N	4·43 W
150	Bodö (bôd'û)...............Nor.	67·13 N	14·19 E
171	Bodrum....................Tur.	37·10 N	27·07 E
216	Boende (bô-ĕn'dā)..........Zaire	0·13 s	20·52 E
118	Boerne (bō'ērn)..............Tx.	29·49 N	98·44 W
213	Boesmans (R.).S. Afr. (Natal In.)	33·29 s	26·09 E
119	Boeuf R. (bĕf)...............La.	32·23 N	91·57 W
214	Boffa (bôf'à)................Gui.	10·10 N	14·02 W
195	Bōfu (bō'fōō)................Jap.	34·03 N	131·35 E
119	Bogalusa (bō-gà-lōō'sà).......La.	30·48 N	89·52 W
203	Bogan (R.) (bō'gĕn)........Austl.	32·10 s	147·40 E
156	Bogense (bō'gĕn-sĕ).........Den.	55·34 N	10·09 E
127	Boggy Pk. (bŏg'ĭ-pēk) Antigua (In.)	17·03 N	61·50 W
167	Bogodukhov (bŏ-gŏ-dōō'ĸôf) Sov. Un.	50·10 N	35·31 E
203	Bogong, Mt...............Austl.	36·50 s	147·15 E
196	Bogor....................Indon.	6·45 s	106·45 E
166	Bogoroditsk (bŏ-gŏ'rô-dĭtsk) Sov. Un.	53·48 N	38·06 E
170	Bogorodsk.............Sov. Un.	56·02 N	43·40 E
174	Bogorodskoye (bŏ-gô-rôd'skô-yĕ) Sov. Un. (Urals In.)	56·43 N	56·53 E
134	Bogotá (bō-gō-tä')......Col. (In.)	4·38 N	74·06 W
134	Bogotá, Rio (R.) (rē'ō-bō-gō-tä') Col. (In.)	4·27 N	74·38 W
172	Bogotol (bŏ'gô-tŏl)......Sov. Un.	56·13 N	89·13 E
167	Bogoyavlenskoye (bŏ'gô-yäf'lĕn-skō'yĕ).Sov. Un.	48·46 N	33·19 E
171	Boguchar (bō'gōō-chär)..Sov. Un.	49·40 N	41·00 E
127	Boguete (bô-gĕ'tĕ)...........Pan.	8·54 N	82·29 W
167	Boguslav (bō'gōō-släf)...Sov. Un.	49·34 N	30·51 E
160	Bohain-en-Vermandois (bô-ăɴ-ŏɴ-vâr-măn-dwä').Fr.	49·58 N	3·22 E
	Bohemia (Prov.), see České		
158	Bohemian For. (bô-hē'mĭ-ăn) F.R.G.	49·35 N	12·27 E
197	Bohol (I.) (bô-hôl')..........Phil.	9·28 N	124·35 E
125	Bohom (bŏ-ô'm).............Mex.	16·47 N	92·42 W
218	Bohotleh (bô-hŏt'lĕ) Som. (Horn of Afr. In.)	8·15 N	46·20 E
98	Boiestown (boiz'toun).......Can.	46·27 N	66·25 W

ng-sing; ŋ-baŋk; ɴ-nasalized n; nŏd; cŏmmit; ōld; ôbey; ôrder; fōōd; fŏŏt; ou-out; s-soft; sh-dish; th-thin; pūre; ûnite; ûrn; stŭd; circŭs; ü-as "y" in study; '-indeterminate vowel.

Page	Name Pronunciation Region	Lat. °′	Long. °′
104	Bois Blanc (I.) (boi' blȧŋk)..Mi.	45·45 N	84·30 W
100	Boischâtel (bwä-shä-tĕl') Can. (Quebec In.)	46·54 N	71·08 W
100	Bois-des-Filion (bōō-ä'dĕ-fē-yôN') Can. (Montreal In.)	45·40 N	73·46 W
110	Boise (boi'zē) Id.	43·38 N	116·12 W
110	Boise (R.) Id.	43·43 N	116·30 W
116	Boise City Ok.	36·42 N	102·30 W
95	Boissevain (bois'vān) Can.	49·14 N	100·03 W
187	Boizabād Afg.	37·13 N	70·38 E
210	Bojador, Cabo (C.) (kȧ'bô-bō-hä-dōr') (bŏj-ȧ-dōr') W. Sah.	26·21 N	16·08 W
186	Bojnūrd Iran	37·29 N	57·13 E
215	Bokani Nig.	9·26 N	5·13 E
210	Boké (bō-kā') Gui.	10·58 N	14·15 W
156	Bokn Fd. (bôk''n fyôrd) Nor.	59·12 N	5·37 E
213	Boksburg (bŏks'bûrgh) S. Afr. (Johannesburg & Pretoria In.)	26·13 S	28·15 E
216	Bokungu Zaire	0·41 S	22·19 E
215	Bol Chad	13·28 N	14·43 E
215	Bolaï I Cen. Afr. Rep.	4·20 N	17·21 E
210	Bolama (bô-lä'mä) Guinea-Bissau	11·34 N	15·41 W
184	Bolan Mt. (bô-län') Pak.	30·13 N	67·09 E
124	Bolaños (bō-län'yôs) Mex.	21·40 N	103·48 W
124	Bolaños (R.) Mex.	21·26 N	103·54 W
184	Bolan P. Pak.	29·50 N	67·10 E
160	Bolbec (bôl-bĕk') Fr.	49·37 N	0·26 E
214	Bole (bō'lā) Ghana	9·02 N	2·29 W
158	Boleslawiec (bō-lĕ-slä'vyĕts) Pol.	51·15 N	15·35 E
214	Bolgatanga Ghana	10·46 N	0·52 W
167	Bolgrad (bŏl-grȧt) Sov. Un.	45·41 N	28·38 E
197	Bolinao (bō-lē-nä'ô) Phil. (In.)	16·24 N	119·53 E
197	Bolinao, C. Phil. (In.)	16·24 N	119·42 E
137	Bolívar (bô-lē'vär) Arg. (Buenos Aires In.)	36·15 S	61·05 W
134	Bolívar Col.	1·46 N	76·58 W
117	Bolivar (bŏl'ĭ-vȧr) Mo.	37·37 N	93·22 W
120	Bolivar Tn.	35·14 N	88·56 W
134	Bolívar (La Columna) (Mtn.) (bô-lē'vär) (lä-kô-lōō'm-nä) Ven.	8·44 N	70·54 W
119	Bolivar Pen. (bŏl'ĭ-vȧr) Tx. (In.)	29·25 N	94·40 W
133	Bolivia (bô-lĭv'ĭ-ȧ) S.A.	17·00 S	64·00 W
166	Bolkhov (bŏl-ĸôf') Sov. Un.	53·27 N	35·59 E
148	Bollin (R.) (bŏl'ĭn) Eng.	53·18 N	2·11 W
148	Bollington (bôl'ĭng-tŭn) Eng.	53·18 N	2·06 W
156	Bollnäs (bôl'nĕs) Swe.	61·22 N	16·20 E
156	Bolmen (L.) (bôl'mĕn) Swe.	56·58 N	13·25 E
212	Bolobo (bō'lô-bô) Zaire	2·14 S	16·18 E
164	Bologna (bô-lōn'yä) It.	44·30 N	11·18 E
166	Bologoye (bŏ-lō-gô'yĕ) Sov. Un.	57·52 N	34·02 E
126	Bolonchenticul (bô-lôn-chĕn-tē-kōō'l) Mex. (In.)	20·03 N	89·47 W
128	Bolondrón (bô-lôn-drōn') Cuba	22·45 N	81·25 W
164	Bolseno, Lago di (L.) (lä'gō-dē-bôl-sā'nô) It.	42·35 N	11·40 E
170	Bol'shaya Kinel' (R.) Sov. Un.	53·20 N	52·40 E
167	Bol'shaya Lepetikha (bŏl-shȧ'yȧ'lyĕ'pyĕ-tē'ĸȧ) Sov. Un.	47·11 N	33·58 E
167	Bol'shaya Viska (vĭs-kä') Sov. Un.	48·34 N	31·54 E
167	Bol'shaya Vradiyevka (vrȧ-dyĕ'f'kȧ) Sov. Un.	47·51 N	30·38 E
174	Bol'she Ust'ikinskoye (bŏl'she ŏŏs-tyĭ-kĕn'skô-yĕ) Sov. Un. (Urals In.)	55·58 N	58·18 E
173	Bolshoy Anyuy (R.) Sov. Un.	67·58 N	161·15 E
173	Bol'shoy Begichëv (I.) Sov. Un.	74·30 N	114·40 E
173	Bolshoy Chuva (R.) Sov. Un.	58·15 N	111·13 E
174	Bol'shoye Ivonino (ĭ-vô'nĭ-nô) Sov. Un. (Urals In.)	59·41 N	61·12 E
174	Bol'shoy Kuyash (bôl'-shôy kōō'yȧsh) Sov. Un. (Urals In.)	55·52 N	61·07 E
167	Bolshoy Tokmak (bŏl-shôy' tôk-mäk') Sov. Un.	47·17 N	35·48 E
118	Bolson de Mapimi (bôl-sŏ'n-dĕ-mä-pē'mē) Mex.	27·27 N	103·20 W
148	Bolsover (bōl'zō-vēr) Eng.	53·14 N	1·17 W
163	Boltana (bōl-tä'nä) Sp.	42·28 N	0·03 E
100	Bolton (bōl'tŭn) Can. (Toronto In.)	43·53 N	79·44 W
148	Bolton Eng.	53·35 N	2·26 W
148	Bolton-on-Dearne (bōl'tŭn-ŏn-dûrn) Eng.	53·31 N	1·19 W
171	Bolu (bō'lŏŏ) Tur.	40·45 N	31·45 E
166	Bolva (R.) (bŏl'vä) Sov. Un.	53·30 N	34·30 E
171	Bolvadin (bŏl-vä-dēn') Tur.	38·50 N	30·50 E
164	Bolzano (bôl-tsä'nō) It.	46·31 N	11·22 E
216	Boma (bō'mä) Zaire	5·51 S	13·03 E
203	Bombala (bŭm-bä'lȧ) Austl.	36·55 S	149·07 E
185	Bombay (bŏm-bā') India (In.)	18·58 N	72·50 E
185	Bombay Hbr. India (In.)	18·55 N	72·52 E
210	Bomi Hills Lib.	7·00 N	11·00 W
137	Bom Jardim (bôn zhär-dēN') Braz. (Rio de Janeiro In.)	22·10 S	42·25 W
137	Bom Jesus do Itabapoana (bôN-zhĕ-sōō's-dô-ē-tȧ'bä-pô-ȧ'nä) Braz. (Rio de Janeiro In.)	21·08 S	41·51 W
156	Bömlo (I.) (bûmlô) Nor.	59·47 N	4·57 E
216	Bomongo Zaire	1·22 N	18·21 E
137	Bom Sucesso (bôn-sōō-sĕ'sō) Braz. (Rio de Janeiro In.)	21·02 S	44·44 W
	Bomu, see Mbomou		
151	Bon, C. (bôN) Tun.	37·04 N	11·13 E
134	Bonaire (I.) (bô-nâr') Neth. Antilles	12·10 N	68·15 W
162	Boñar (bō-nyär') Sp.	42·53 N	5·18 W
99	Bonavista (bŏ-nȧ-vĭs'tȧ) Can.	48·39 N	53·07 W
99	Bonavista B. Can.	48·45 N	53·20 W
116	Bond (bŏnd) Co.	39·53 N	106·40 W
216	Bondo (bôn'dô) Zaire	3·49 N	23·40 E
197	Bondoc Pen. (bôn-dŏk') Phil. (In.)	13·24 N	122·30 E
214	Bondoukou (bŏn-dōō'kōō) Ivory Coast	8·02 N	2·48 W
128	Bonds Cay (I.) (bŏnds kē) Ba.	25·30 N	77·45 W
	Bône, see Annaba		
196	Bone, Teluk (L.) Indon.	4·09 S	121·00 E
196	Bone Rate, Kepulauan (I.) Indon.	6·52 S	121·45 E
136	Bonete, Cerro (Mt.) (bō'nĕtĕh çĕrrô) Arg.	27·50 S	68·35 W
137	Bonfim (bôN-fē'N) Braz. (Rio de Janeiro In.)	20·20 S	44·15 W
215	Bongor Chad	10·17 N	15·22 E
211	Bongos, Chaîne des (Mts.) Cen. Afr. Rep.	7·40 N	22·00 E
193	Bong Son Viet.	14·20 N	109·10 E
117	Bonham (bŏn'ȧm) Tx.	33·35 N	96·09 W
129	Bonhomme, Pic (Pk.) Hai.	19·10 N	72·20 W
164	Bonifacio (bō-nē-fä'chō) Fr.	41·23 N	9·10 E
164	Bonifacio, Str. of Eur.	41·14 N	9·02 E
120	Bonifay (bŏn-ĭ-fā') Fl.	30·46 N	85·40 W
198	Bonin Is. (bō'nĭn) Asia	26·30 N	141·00 E
161	Bonn (bŏn) F.R.G. (Ruhr In.)	50·44 N	7·06 E
99	Bonne B. (bŏn) Can.	49·33 N	57·55 W
110	Bonners Ferry (bon'erz fĕr'ĭ) Id.	48·41 N	116·19 W
113	Bonner Springs (bŏn'ēr sprĭngz) Ks. (Kansas City In.)	39·04 N	94·52 W
117	Bonne Terre (bŏn târ') Mo.	37·55 N	90·32 W
93	Bonnet Pk. (bŏn'ĭt) Can.	51·26 N	115·53 W
110	Bonneville Dam (bŏn'ē-vĭl) Or.-Wa.	45·37 N	121·57 W
99	Bonnie B. (bŏn'ē) Can.	49·38 N	58·15 W
210	Bonny (bŏn'ē) Nig.	4·29 N	7·13 E
112	Bonny Lake (bŏn'ē lăk) Wa. (Seattle In.)	47·11 N	122·11 W
93	Bonnyville (bŏn'ē-vĭl) Can.	54·16 N	110·44 W
164	Bonorva (bô-nôr'vä) It.	40·26 N	8·46 E
214	Bonoua Ivory Coast	5·16 N	3·36 W
196	Bonthain (bŏn-tīn') Indon.	5·30 S	119·52 E
214	Bonthe S. L.	7·32 N	12·30 W
197	Bontoc (bŏn-tŏk') Phil. (In.)	17·10 N	121·01 E
128	Booby Rocks (I.) (bōō'bĭ rŏks) Ba.	25·55 N	77·00 W
121	Booker T. Washington Natl. Mon. (bŏŏk'ēr tē wŏsh'ĭng-tŭn) Va.	37·07 N	79·45 W
149	Boom Bel. (Brussels In.)	51·05 N	4·22 E
109	Boone (bōōn) Ia.	42·04 N	93·51 W
117	Booneville (bōōn'vĭl) Ar.	35·09 N	93·54 W
104	Booneville Ky.	37·25 N	83·40 W
120	Booneville Ms.	34·37 N	88·35 W
218	Boons S. Afr. (Johannesburg & Pretoria In.)	25·59 S	27·15 E
106	Boonton (bōōn'tŭn) NJ (New York In.)	40·54 N	74·24 W
104	Boonville In.	38·00 N	87·15 W
117	Boonville Mo.	38·57 N	92·44 W
98	Boothbay Harbor (bōōth'bā här'bēr) Me.	43·51 N	69·39 W
91	Boothia, G. of (bōō'thĭ-ȧ) Can.	69·04 N	86·04 W
75	Boothia Pen. Can.	73·30 N	95·00 W
148	Bootle (bōōt'l) Eng.	53·29 N	3·02 W
216	Booué Gabon	0·06 S	11·56 E
158	Boppard (bôp'ärt) F.R.G.	50·14 N	7·35 E
211	Bor (bôr) Sud.	6·13 N	31·35 E
171	Bor (bōr) Tur.	37·50 N	34·40 E
111	Borah Pk. (bō'rä) Id.	44·12 N	113·47 W
218	Borama (bôr-á-mȧ) Som. (Horn of Afr. In.)	10·05 N	43·08 E
156	Borås (bōō'rōs) Swe.	57·43 N	12·55 E
186	Borāzjān (bō-räz-jän') Iran	29·13 N	51·13 E
135	Borba (bôr'bä) Braz.	4·23 S	59·31 W
135	Borborema, Planalto da (Plat.) (plä-nál'tô-dä-bôr-bō-rĕ'mä) Braz.	7·35 S	36·40 W
160	Bordeaux (bôr-dō') Fr.	44·50 N	0·37 W
105	Bordentown (bôr'dĕn-toun) NJ	40·05 N	74·40 W
151	Bordj-bou-Arréridj (bôrj-bōō-ȧ-rā-rēj') Alg.	36·03 N	4·48 E
157	Borgå (bôr'gō) Fin.	60·26 N	25·41 E
150	Borgarnes Ice.	64·31 N	21·40 W
116	Borger (bôr'gēr) Tx.	35·40 N	101·23 W
156	Borgholm (bôrg-hŏlm') Swe.	56·52 N	16·40 E
119	Borgne L. (bôrn'y') La.	30·03 N	89·36 W
164	Borgomanero (bôr'gō-mä-nâ'rō) It.	45·40 N	8·28 E
163	Borgo Montello (bô'r-zhō-môn-tĕ'lō) It. (Rome In.)	41·31 N	12·48 E
164	Borgo Val di Taro (bô'r-zhō-väl-dē-tȧ'rō) It.	44·29 N	9·44 E
112	Boring (bōrĭng) Or. (Portland In.)	45·26 N	122·22 W
159	Borislav (bō'rĭs-lôf) Sov. Un.	49·17 N	23·24 E
171	Borisoglebsk (bŏ-rē sô-glyĕpsk') Sov. Un.	51·20 N	42·00 E
166	Borisov (bŏ-rē'sôf) Sov. Un.	54·16 N	28·33 E
167	Borisovka (bŏ-rē-sôf'kȧ) Sov. Un.	50·38 N	36·00 E
167	Borispol' (bo-rĭs'pol) Sov. Un.	50·17 N	30·54 E
185	Borivli India (In.)	19·15 N	72·48 E
162	Borja (bôr'hä) Sp.	41·50 N	1·33 W
163	Borjas Blancas (bô'r-ĸäs-blä'n-käs) Sp.	41·29 N	0·53 E
161	Borken (bōr'kĕn) F.R.G. (Ruhr In.)	51·50 N	6·51 E
211	Borkou (Reg.) (bôr-kōō') Chad	18·11 N	18·28 E
158	Borkum I. (bōr'kōōm) F.R.G.	53·31 N	6·50 E
156	Borlänge (bôr-lĕŋ'gĕ) Swe.	60·30 N	15·24 E
196	Borneo (I.) (bôr'nē-ō) Asia	0·25 N	112·39 E
156	Bornholm (I.) (bôrn-hôlm) Den.	55·16 N	15·15 E
162	Bornos (bôr'nōs) Sp.	36·48 N	5·45 W
167	Borodayevka Sov. Un.	48·44 N	34·09 E
167	Boromlya (bŏ-rôm''l-yä) Sov. Un.	50·36 N	34·58 E
214	Boromo Upper Volta	11·45 N	2·56 W
165	Borovan (bŏ-rô-vän') Bul.	43·24 N	23·47 E
166	Borovichi (bŏ-rô-vē'chē) Sov. Un.	58·22 N	33·56 E
166	Borovsk (bô'rôvsk) Sov. Un.	55·13 N	36·26 E
135	Borracha, Isla la (I.) (ē's-lä-lä-bôr-rȧ'chä) Ven. (In.)	10·18 N	64·44 W
204	Borroloola (bŏr-rô-lōō'lȧ) Austl.	16·15 S	136·19 E
159	Borshchëv (bôrsh-chyôf') Sov. Un.	48·47 N	26·04 E
160	Bort-les-Orgues (bôr-lā-zôrg) Fr.	45·26 N	2·26 E
186	Borūjerd Iran	33·45 N	48·53 E
167	Borzna (bôrz'nȧ) Sov. Un.	51·15 N	32·26 E
173	Borzya (bôrz'yȧ) Sov. Un.	50·37 N	116·53 E
164	Bosa (bō'sä) It.	40·18 N	8·34 E
164	Bosanska Dubica (bō'sän-skä dōō'bĭt-sä) Yugo.	45·10 N	16·49 E
164	Bosanska Gradiška (bō'sän-skä grä-dĭsh'kä) Yugo.	45·08 N	17·15 E
164	Bosanski Novi (bō's sän-skĭ nō'vē) Yugo.	45·00 N	16·22 E
164	Bosanski Petrovac (bō'sän-skĭ pĕt'rō-väts) Yugo.	44·33 N	16·23 E
165	Bosanski Šamac (bō'sän-skĭ shä'mȧts) Yugo.	45·03 N	18·30 E
109	Boscobel (bŏs'kō-bĕl) Wi.	43·08 N	90·44 W
174	Boskol' (bȧs-kôl') Sov. Un. (Urals In.)	53·45 N	61·17 E
149	Boskoop Neth. (Amsterdam In.)	52·04 N	4·39 E
158	Boskovice (bŏs'kō-vē-tsĕ) Czech.	49·26 N	16·37 E
165	Bosna (R.) Yugo.	44·19 N	17·54 E
165	Bosnia (Reg.) (bŏs'nĭ-ȧ) Yugo.	44·17 N	16·58 E
216	Bosobolo Zaire	4·11 N	19·54 E
	Bosporous (Str.), see İstanbul Boğazı		
215	Bossangoa Cen. Afr. Rep.	6·29 N	17·27 E
215	Bossembélé Cen. Afr. Rep.	5·16 N	17·39 E
119	Bossier City (bŏsh'ēr) La.	32·31 N	93·42 W
120	Boston (bôs'tŭn) Ga.	30·47 N	83·47 W
99	Boston Ma. (In.)	42·15 N	71·07 W
107	Boston Heights Oh. (Cleveland In.)	41·15 N	81·30 W
117	Boston Mts. Ar.	35·46 N	93·32 W
202	Botany B. (bŏt'ȧ-nĭ) Austl. (Sydney In.)	33·58 S	151·11 E
165	Botevgrad Bul.	42·54 N	23·41 E
218	Bothaville (bō'tä-vĭl) S. Afr. (Johannesburg & Pretoria In.)	27·24 S	26·38 E
112	Bothell (bŏth'ĕl) Wa. (Seattle In.)	47·46 N	122·12 W
150	Bothnia, G. of (bŏth'nĭ-ȧ) Eur.	61·45 N	19·45 E
159	Botosani (bō-tō-shȧn'ĭ) Rom.	47·46 N	26·40 E
209	Botswana (bŏtswănă) Afr.	22·10 S	23·13 E
108	Bottineau (bŏt-ĭ-nō') ND	48·48 N	100·28 W
161	Bottrop (bōt'trōp) F.R.G. (Ruhr In.)	51·31 N	6·56 E
135	Botucatú (bô-tōō-kä-tōō') Braz.	22·50 S	48·23 W
99	Botwood (bŏt'wŏŏd) Can.	49·08 N	55·21 W
214	Bouaflé (bōō-á-flā') Ivory Coast	6·59 N	5·45 W
214	Bouaké (bōō-á-kā') Ivory Coast	7·41 N	5·02 W
215	Bouar (bōō-är) Cen. Afr. Rep.	5·57 N	15·36 E
215	Boubandjidah, Parc Natl. de (Natl. Pk.) Cam.	8·20 N	14·40 E
100	Boucherville (bōō-shȧ-vēl') Can. (Montreal In.)	45·37 N	73·27 W
214	Boucle du Baoulé, Parc Natl. de la (Natl. Pk.) Mali	13·50 N	9·15 W
210	Boudenib (bōō-dĕ-nĕb') Mor.	32·14 N	3·04 W
109	Boudette (bōō-dĕt) Mn.	48·42 N	94·34 W
151	Bou Dia, C. (bōō dē'ȧ)) Tun.	35·18 N	11·17 E
163	Boudouaou Alg.	36·44 N	1·27 E
163	Boufarik (bōō-fȧ-rēk') Alg.	36·35 N	2·55 E
198	Bougainville Trench (bōō-găN-vēl') Oceania	7·00 S	152·00 E
	Bougie, see Bejaïa		
210	Bougouni (bōō-gōō-nē') Mali	11·27 N	7·30 W
152	Bouira (boo-ē'rȧ) Alg.	36·25 N	3·55 E
163	Bouïra-Sahary (bwē-rȧ sȧ'ȧ-rē) Alg.	35·16 N	3·23 E
204	Boulder (bōl'dēr) Austl.	31·00 S	121·40 E
116	Boulder Co.	40·02 N	105·19 W
114	Boulder City Nv.	35·57 N	114·50 W
110	Boulder Cr. Id.	42·53 N	116·49 W
111	Boulder Pk. Id.	43·53 N	114·33 W
111	Boulder R. Mt.	46·10 N	112·07 W
161	Boulogne-Billancourt (bōō-lôn'y'-bē-yäN-kōōr') Fr. (Paris In.)	48·50 N	2·14 E
160	Boulogne-sur-Mer (bōō-lôn'y-sür-mâr') Fr.	50·44 N	1·37 E
215	Boumba (R.) Cam.	2·45 N	15·05 E
163	Bou-Mort, Sierra de (Mts.) (sē-ĕ'r-rä-dĕ-bô-ōō-mô'rt) Sp.	42·11 N	1·05 E
214	Bouna (bōō-nä') Ivory Coast	9·16 N	3·00 W
214	Bouna, Park Natl. de (Natl. Pk.) Ivory Coast	9·20 N	3·35 W
112	Boundary B. (boun'dȧ-rĭ) Can. (Vancouver In.)	49·03 N	122·59 W
114	Boundary Pk. Nv.	37·52 N	118·20 W
116	Bound Brook (bound brŏŏk) NJ (New York In.)	40·34 N	74·32 W
214	Boundiali Ivory Coast	9·31 N	6·29 W
113	Bountiful (boun'tĭ-fŏŏl) Ut. (Salt Lake City In.)	40·55 N	111·53 W
107	Bountiful Pk. (boun'tĭ-fŏŏl) Ut. (Salt Lake City In.)	40·58 N	111·49 W
220	Bounty Is. N. Z.	47·42 S	179·05 E
210	Bourem (bōō-rĕm') Mali	16·43 N	0·15 W
160	Bourg-en-Bresse (bōōr-gĕN-brĕs') Fr.	46·12 N	5·13 E
160	Bourges (bōōrzh) Fr.	47·06 N	2·22 E
100	Bourget (bōōr-zhĕ') Can. (Ottawa In.)	45·26 N	75·09 W
161	Bourgoin (bōōr-gwăN') Fr.	45·46 N	5·17 E
203	Bourke (bŭrk) Austl.	30·10 S	146·00 E
148	Bourne (bôrn) Eng.	52·46 N	0·22 W
154	Bournemouth (bôrn'mŭth) Eng.	50·44 N	1·55 W
152	Bou Saada (bōō-sä'dä) Alg.	35·13 N	4·17 E
211	Bousso (bōō-sô') Chad	10·33 N	16·45 E
210	Boutilimit (bōō-tē-lē-mē') Mauritania	17·30 N	14·54 W
	Bouvert (I.), see Bouvetöen		

ăt; finăl; rāte; senâte; ärm; ȧsk; sofȧ; fâre; ch-choose; dh-as th in other; bē; ēvent; bĕt; recĕnt; cratēr; g-go; gh-guttural g; bĭt; ĭ-short neutral; rīde; ĸ-guttural k as ch in German ich;

Page	Name Pronunciation	Region	Lat. °′	Long. °′
220	Bouvetöen (Bouvert) (I.)	Alt. O.	54·26 S	3·24 E
164	Bovino (bō-vē'nō)	It.	41·14 N	15·21 E
93	Bow (R.) (bō)	Can.	50·30 N	112·00 W
108	Bowbells (bō'bĕls)	ND	48·50 N	102·16 W
108	Bowdle (bōd''l)	SD	45·28 N	99·42 W
205	Bowen (bō'ĕn)	Austl.	20·02 S	148·14 E
106	Bowie (bōō'ī) (bō'ē)	Md. (Baltimore In.)	38·59 N	76·47 W
116	Bowie	Tx.	33·34 N	97·50 W
120	Bowling Green (bōlĭng grēn)	Ky.	37·00 N	86·26 W
117	Bowling Green	Mo.	39·19 N	91·09 W
104	Bowling Green	Oh.	41·25 N	83·40 W
108	Bowman (bō'măn)	ND	46·11 N	103·23 W
197	Bowokan, Pulau-Pulau (Is.)	Indon.	2·20 S	123·45 E
93	Bowron (R.) (bō'răn)	Can.	53·20 N	121·10 W
108	Boxelder Cr. (bŏks'ĕl-dēr)	Mt.	45·35 N	104·28 W
111	Boxelder Cr.	Mt.	47·17 N	108·37 W
149	Boxtel	Neth. (Amsterdam In.)	51·40 N	5·21 E
216	Boyabo	Zaire	3·43 N	18·46 E
100	Boyer (R.) (boi'ēr)	Can. (Quebec In.)	46·26 N	70·56 W
108	Boyer (R.)	Ia.	41·45 N	95·36 W
154	Boyle (boil)	Ire.	53·59 N	8·15 W
104	Boyne City	Mi.	45·15 N	85·05 W
154	Boyne R. (boin)	Ire.	53·40 N	6·40 W
165	Bozcaada (Tenedos) (bōz-cä'dä) (tĕ'nĕ-dōs)	Tur.	39·50 N	26·05 E
165	Bozcaada (I.)	Tur.	39·50 N	26·00 E
111	Bozeman (bōz'măn)	Mt.	45·41 N	111·00 W
216	Bozene	Zaire	2·56 N	19·12 E
215	Bozoum	Cen. Afr. Rep.	6·19 N	16·23 E
164	Bra (brä)	It.	44·41 N	7·52 E
164	Brač (I.) (bräch)	Yugo.	43·18 N	16·36 E
164	Bracciano, Lago di (L.) (lä'gō-dē-brä-chä'nō)	It.	42·05 N	12·00 E
105	Bracebridge (brās'brĭj)	Can.	45·05 N	79·20 W
107	Braceville (brās'vĭl)	Il. (Chicago In.)	41·13 N	88·16 W
156	Bräcke (brĕk'kĕ)	Swe.	62·44 N	15·28 E
107	Brackenridge (brăk'ĕn-rĭj)	Pa. (Pittsburgh In.)	40·37 N	79·44 W
118	Brackettville (brăk'ĕt-vĭl)	Tx.	29·19 N	100·24 W
135	Braço Maior (R.)	Braz.	11·00 S	51·00 W
135	Braço Menor (R.) (brä'zō-mĕ-nō'r)	Braz.	11·38 S	50·00 W
164	Brádano (R.) (brä-dä'nō)	It.	40·43 N	16·22 E
107	Braddock (brăd'ŭk)	Pa. (Pittsburgh In.)	40·24 N	79·52 W
121	Bradenton (brā'dĕn-tŭn)	Fl. (In.)	27·28 N	82·35 W
148	Bradfield (brăd-fēld)	Eng. (London In.)	51·25 N	1·08 W
148	Bradford (brăd'fērd)	Eng.	53·47 N	1·44 W
104	Bradford	Oh.	40·10 N	84·30 W
105	Bradford	Pa.	42·00 N	78·40 W
107	Bradley (brăd'lĭ)	Il. (Chicago In.)	41·09 N	87·52 W
112	Bradner (brăd'nēr)	Can. (Vancouver In.)	49·05 N	122·26 W
118	Brady (brā'dĭ)	Tx.	31·09 N	99·21 W
162	Braga (brä'gä)	Port.	41·20 N	8·25 W
137	Bragado (brä-gä'dō)	Arg. (Buenos Aires In.)	35·07 S	60·28 W
135	Bragança (brä-gän'sä)	Braz.	1·02 S	46·50 W
162	Bragança	Port.	41·48 N	6·46 W
137	Bragança Paulista (brä-gän'sä-pä'ōō-lē's-tà)	Braz. (Rio de Janeiro In.)	22·58 S	46·31 W
100	Bragg Creek (brăg)	Can. (Calgary In.)	50·57 N	114·35 W
187	Brahmaputra (R.) (brä'mȧ-pōō'trȧ)	India	26·45 N	92·45 E
187	Brahui (Reg.)	Pak.	28·32 N	66·15 E
107	Braidwood (brād'wŏŏd)	Il. (Chicago In.)	41·16 N	88·13 W
167	Brăila (brē'ēlà)	Rom.	45·15 N	27·58 E
109	Brainerd (brān'ērd)	Mn.	46·20 N	94·09 W
99	Braintree (brān'trē)	Ma. (In.)	42·14 N	71·00 W
106	Braithwaite (brīth'wīt)	La. (New Orleans In.)	29·52 N	89·57 W
213	Brakpan (brăk'păn)	S. Afr. (Johannesburg & Pretoria In.)	26·15 S	28·22 E
92	Bralorne (brā'lôrn)	Can.	50·47 N	122·49 W
100	Bramalea	Can. (Toronto In.)	43·44 N	75·38 W
100	Brampton (brămp'tŭn)	Can. (Toronto In.)	43·41 N	79·46 W
136	Branca, Pedra (Mtn.) (pĕ'drä-brà'n-kä)	Braz. (Rio de Janeiro In.)	22·55 S	43·28 W
106	Branchville (brănch'vĭl)	NJ (New York In.)	41·09 N	74·44 W
121	Branchville	SC	33·17 N	80·48 W
135	Branco (R.) (brāŋ'kō)	Braz.	2·21 N	60·38 W
212	Brandberg (Mtn.)	S. W. Afr.	21·15 S	14·15 E
149	Brandenburg (brän'dĕn-bŏŏrgh)	G.D.R. (Berlin In.)	52·25 N	12·33 E
158	Brandenburg (Reg.)	G.D.R.	52·12 N	13·31 E
218	Brandfort (brăn'd-fôrt)	S. Afr. (Johannesburg & Pretoria In.)	28·42 S	26·29 E
95	Brandon (brăn'dŭn)	Can.	49·50 N	99·57 W
105	Brandon	Vt.	43·45 N	73·05 W
154	Brandon Hill (brăn-dŏn)	Ire.	52·15 N	10·12 W
106	Brandywine (brăndĭ'wīn)	Md. (Baltimore In.)	38·42 N	76·51 W
105	Branford (brăn'fērd)	Ct.	41·15 N	72·50 W
159	Braniewo (brä-nyĕ'vō)	Pol.	54·23 N	19·50 E
218	Brankhorstspruit	S. Afr. (Johannesburg & Pretoria In.)	24·47 S	28·45 E
159	Brańsk (brän' sk)	Pol.	52·44 N	22·51 E
100	Brantford (brănt'fērd)	Can. (Toronto In.)	43·09 N	80·17 W
99	Bras d'Or L. (brä-dôr')	Can.	45·52 N	60·50 W
135	Brasília (brä-sē'lvä)	Braz.	15·49 S	47·39 W
135	Brasilia Legal (Fordlândia) (brä-sē'lyä-lĕ-gàl) (fô'rd-län-dyä)	Braz.	3·45 S	55·46 W
137	Brasópolis (brä-sô'pô-lēs)	Braz. (Rio de Janeiro In.)	22·30 S	45·36 W
165	Braşov (Oraşul-Stalin)	Rom.	45·39 N	25·35 E
210	Brass (brăs)	Nig.	4·28 N	6·28 E
100	Bras St. Michel (R.)	Can. (Quebec In.)	46·47 N	70·51 W
149	Brasschaat (bräs'kät)	Bel. (Brussels In.)	51·19 N	5·30 E
107	Bratenahl (bră'tĕn-ôl)	Oh. (Cleveland In.)	41·34 N	81·36 W
149	Bratislava (brä'tĭs-lä-vä)	Czech. (Vienna In.)	48·09 N	17·07 E
172	Bratsk (brätsk)	Sov. Un.	56·10 N	102·04 E
172	Bratskoye Vdkhr. (Res.)	Sov. Un.	56·10 N	102·05 E
167	Bratslav (brät'slàf)	Sov. Un.	48·48 N	28·59 E
105	Brattleboro (brăt''l-bŭr-ō)	Vt.	42·50 N	72·35 W
158	Braunau (brou'nou)	Aus.	48·15 N	13·05 E
158	Braunschweig (broun'shvīgh)	F.R.G.	52·16 N	10·32 E
218	Brava (brä'vä)	Som. (Horn of Afr. In.)	1·20 N	44·00 E
156	Bråviken (R.)	Swe.	58·40 N	16·40 E
	Bravo del Norte, Rio (R.), see Grande, Rio			
114	Brawley (brô'lĭ)	Ca.	32·59 N	115·32 W
154	Bray (brā)	Ire.	53·10 N	6·05 W
117	Braymer (brā'mēr)	Mo.	39·34 N	93·47 W
119	Brays Bay (brās'bī'yōō)	Tx. (In.)	29·41 N	95·33 W
93	Brazeau, Mt. (brä-zō')	Can.	52·33 N	117.21 W
93	Brazeau (R.)	Can.	52·55 N	116·10 W
104	Brazil (brȧ-zĭl')	In.	39·30 N	87·00 W
133	Brazil	S. A.	9·00 S	53·00 W
133	Brazilian Highlands (Mts.) (brȧ zĭl yȧn hī-lăndz)	Braz.	14·00 S	48·00 W
102	Brazos (R.) (brä'zōs)	U. S.	33·10 N	98·50 W
118	Brazos (R.), Clear Fk.	Tx.	32·56 N	99·14 W
116	Brazos (R.), Double Mountain Fk.	Tx.	33·23 N	101·21 W
116	Brazos (R.), Salt Fk. (sôlt fôrk)	Tx.	33·20 N	100·57 W
216	Brazzaville (brȧ-zȧ-vēl')	Con.	4·16 S	15·17 E
165	Brčko (bērch'kō)	Yugo.	44·54 N	18·46 E
159	Brda R. (bēr-dä')	Pol.	53·18 N	17·55 E
113	Brea (brē'ȧ)	Ca. (Los Angeles In.)	33·55 N	117·54 W
100	Breakeyville	Can. (Quebec In.)	46·40 N	71·13 W
108	Breckenridge (brĕk'ĕn-rĭj)	Mn.	46·17 N	96·35 W
118	Breckenridge	Tx.	32·46 N	98·53 W
107	Brecksville (brĕks'vĭl)	Oh. (Cleveland In.)	41·19 N	81·38 W
158	Břeclav (brzhĕl'làf)	Czech.	48·46 N	16·54 E
154	Brecon Beacons (brĕk'ŭn bē kŭns)	Wales	52·00 N	3·55 W
149	Breda (brā-dä')	Neth. (Amsterdam In.)	51·35 N	4·47 E
212	Bredasdorp (brā'das-dôrp)	S. Afr.	34·15 S	20·00 E
174	Bredy (brĕ'dĭ)	Sov. Un. (Urals In.)	52·25 N	60·23 E
158	Bregenz (brā'gĕnts)	Aus.	47·30 N	9·46 E
165	Bregovo (brĕ'gô-vô)	Bul.	44·07 N	22·45 E
213	Breidbach (brĕd'băk)	S. Afr. (Natal In.)	32·54 S	27·26 E
150	Breidha Fd. (brā'dĭ)	Ice.	65·15 N	22·50 W
161	Breil (brĕ'y')	Fr.	43·57 N	7·36 E
135	Brejo (brå'zhŏŏ)	Braz.	3·33 S	42·46 W
156	Bremangerland (I.) (brĕ-mängĕr-länd)	Nor.	61·51 N	4·25 E
158	Bremen (brā-mĕn)	F.R.G.	53·05 N	8·50 E
104	Bremen (brē'mĕn)	In.	41·25 N	86·05 W
158	Bremerhaven (brām-ĕr-hä'fĕn)	F.R.G.	53·33 N	8·38 E
112	Bremerton (brĕm'ēr-tŭn)	Wa. (Seattle In.)	47·34 N	122·38 W
149	Bremervörde (brĕ'mĕr-fûr-dĕ)	F.R.G. (Hamburg In.)	53·29 N	9·09 E
100	Bremner (brĕm'nēr)	Can. (Edmonton In.)	53·34 N	113·14 W
119	Bremond (brĕm'ŭnd)	Tx.	31·11 N	96·40 W
119	Brenham (brĕn'ăm)	Tx.	30·10 N	96·24 W
158	Brenner P. (brĕn'ēr)	Aus.-It.	47·00 N	11·30 E
148	Brentwood (brĕnt'wŏŏd)	Eng. (London In.)	51·37 N	0·18 E
105	Brentwood	Md.	39·00 N	76·55 W
113	Brentwood	Mo. (St. Louis In.)	38·37 N	90·21 W
107	Brentwood	Pa. (Pittsburgh In.)	40·22 N	79·59 W
164	Brescia (brā'shä)	It.	45·33 N	10·15 E
	Breslau, see Wrocław			
164	Bressanone (brĕs-sä-nō'nā)	It.	46·42 N	11·40 E
160	Bressuire (brĕ-swēr')	Fr.	46·49 N	0·14 W
160	Brest (brĕst)	Fr.	48·24 N	4·30 W
159	Brest	Sov. Un.	52·06 N	23·43 E
166	Brest (Oblast)	Sov. Un.	52·30 N	26·50 E
160	Bretagne, Monts de (Mts.) (mŏN-dĕ-brĕ-tän'yĕ)	Fr.	48·25 N	3·36 W
160	Breton, Pertvis (Str.) (pâr-twĕ'brĕ-tôN')	Fr.	46·18 N	1·43 W
120	Breton Sd. (brĕt'ŭn)	La.	29·38 N	89·15 W
149	Breukelen	Neth. (Amsterdam In.)	52·09 N	5·00 E
120	Brevard (brĕ-värd')	NC	35·14 N	82·45 W
135	Breves (brā'vĕzh)	Braz.	1·32 S	50·13 W
156	Brevik (brĕ'vēk)	Nor.	59·04 N	9·39 E
203	Brewarrina (brōō-ēr-rē'nȧ)	Austl.	29·54 S	146·50 E
98	Brewer (brōō'ēr)	Me.	44·46 N	68·46 W
214	Brewerville	Lib.	6·26 N	10·47 W
106	Brewster (brōō'stēr)	NY (New York In.)	41·23 N	73·38 W
117	Brewster, Cerro (Mt.) (sĕ'r-rô-brōō'stēr)	Pan.	9·19 N	79·15 W
120	Brewton (brōō'tŭn)	Al.	31·06 N	87·04 W
164	Brežice (brĕ'zhē-tsĕ)	Yugo.	45·55 N	15·37 E
165	Breznik (brĕs'nēk)	Bul.	42·44 N	22·55 E
161	Briancon (brē-äN-sôN')	Fr.	44·54 N	6·39 E
160	Briare (brē-är')	Fr.	47·40 N	2·46 E
112	Bridal Veil (brīd'ăl vāl)	Or. (Portland In.)	45·33 N	122·10 W
128	Bridge Pt. (brĭj)	Ba.	25·35 N	76·40 W
120	Bridgeport (brĭj'pôrt)	Al.	34·55 N	85·42 W
106	Bridgeport	Ct. (New York In.)	41·12 N	73·12 W
104	Bridgeport	Il.	38·40 N	87·45 W
108	Bridgeport	Ne.	41·40 N	103·06 W
104	Bridgeport	Oh.	40·00 N	80·45 W
106	Bridgeport	Pa. (Philadelphia In.)	40·06 N	75·21 W
116	Bridgeport	Tx.	33·13 N	97·46 W
106	Bridgeton (brĭj'tŭn)	Al. (Birmingham In.)	33·27 N	86·39 W
113	Bridgeton	Mo. (St. Louis In.)	38·45 N	90·23 W
105	Bridgeton	NJ	39·30 N	75·15 W
98	Bridgetown	Can.	44·51 N	65·18 W
117	Bridgetown (brĭj' toun)	Barb. (In.)	13·08 N	59·37 W
107	Bridgeville (brĭj'vĭl)	Pa. (Pittsburgh In.)	40·22 N	80·07 W
203	Bridgewater (brĭj'wô-tēr)	Austl.	42·50 S	147·28 E
98	Bridgewater	Can.	44·23 N	64·31 W
148	Bridgnorth (brĭj'nôrth)	Eng.	52·32 N	2·25 W
98	Bridgton (brĭj'tŭn)	Me.	44·04 N	70·45 W
154	Bridlington (brĭd'lĭng-tŭn)	Eng.	54·06 N	0·10 W
161	Brie-Comte-Robert (brē-kôNt-ĕ-rō-bâr')	Fr. (Paris In.)	48·42 N	2·37 E
149	Brielle	Neth. (Amsterdam In.)	51·54 N	4·08 E
98	Brier (I.) (brī'ēr)	Can.	44·16 N	66·24 W
120	Brierfield (brī'ēr-fēld)	Al.	33·01 N	86·55 W
148	Brierfield (brī'ēr fēld)	Eng.	53·49 N	2·14 W
148	Brierley Hill (brī'ēr-lē hĭl)	Eng.	52·28 N	2·07 W
149	Brieselang (brē'zĕ-läng)	G.D.R. (Berlin In.)	52·36 N	12·59 E
161	Briey (brē-ĕ')	Fr.	49·15 N	5·57 E
158	Brig (brēg)	Switz.	46·17 N	7·59 E
148	Brigg (brĭg)	Eng.	53·33 N	0·29 W
113	Brigham City (brĭg'ăm)	Ut. (Salt Lake City In.)	41·31 N	112·01 W
148	Brighouse (brĭg'hous)	Eng.	53·42 N	1·47 W
203	Bright (brīt)	Austl.	36·43 S	147·00 E
107	Bright (brīt)	In. (Cincinnati In.)	39·13 N	84·51 W
148	Brightlingsea (brī't-lĭng-sē)	Eng. (London In.)	51·50 N	1·00 E
106	Brighton (brīt'ŭn)	Al. (Birmingham In.)	33·27 N	86·56 W
116	Brighton	Co.	39·58 N	104·49 W
154	Brighton	Eng.	50·47 N	0·07 W
113	Brighton	Il. (St. Louis In.)	39·03 N	90·08 W
109	Brighton	Ia.	41·11 N	91·47 W
162	Brihuega (brē-wā'gä)	Sp.	40·32 N	2·52 W
113	Brimley (brĭm'lē)	Mi. (Sault Ste. Marie In.)	46·24 N	84·34 W
165	Brindisi (brēn'dē-zē)	It.	40·38 N	17·57 E
164	Brinje (brēn'yĕ)	Yugo.	45·00 N	15·08 E
117	Brinkley (brĭŋk'lĭ)	Ar.	34·52 N	91·12 W
112	Brinnon (brĭn'ŭn)	Wa. (Seattle In.)	47·41 N	122·54 W
99	Brion, Île de (I.) (brē-ôN')	Can.	47·47 N	61·29 W
160	Brioude (brē-ōōd')	Fr.	45·18 N	3·22 E
203	Brisbane (brĭz' bān)	Austl.	27·30 S	153·10 E
105	Bristol (brĭs'tŭl)	Ct.	41·40 N	72·55 W
154	Bristol	Eng.	51·29 N	2·39 W
106	Bristol	Pa. (Philadelphia In.)	40·06 N	74·51 W
106	Bristol	RI (Providence In.)	41·41 N	71·14 W
121	Bristol	Tn.	36·35 N	82·10 W
105	Bristol	Vt.	44·10 N	73·00 W
121	Bristol	Va.	36·36 N	82·12 W
107	Bristol	Wi. (Milwaukee In.)	42·32 N	88·04 W
101	Bristol B.	Ak.	58·08 N	158·54 W
154	Bristol Chan.	Eng.	51·20 N	3·47 E
117	Bristow (brĭs'tō)	Ok.	35·50 N	96·25 W
90	British Columbia (Prov.) (brĭt'ĭsh kŏl'ŭm-bĭ-ȧ)	Can.	56·00 N	124·53 W
205	British Solomon Islands (sŏ'lō-mŭn)	Oceania	8·50 S	157·52 E
218	Brits	S. Afr. (Johannesburg & Pretoria In.)	25·39 S	27·47 E
212	Britstown (brĭts'toun)	S. Afr.	30·30 S	23·40 E
109	Britt (brĭt)	Ia.	43·05 N	93·47 W
108	Britton (brĭt'ŭn)	SD	45·47 N	97·44 W
160	Brive-la-Gaillarde (brēv-lä-gī-yärd'ĕ)	Fr.	45·10 N	1·31 E
162	Briviesca (brē-vyās'kä)	Sp.	42·34 N	3·21 W
158	Brno (b'r'nō)	Czech.	49·18 N	16·37 E
128	Broa, Ensenada de la (B.) (ĕn-sĕ-nä'dä-dĕ-lä-brō'ȧ)	Cuba	22·30 N	82·00 W
184	Broach	India	21·47 N	72·58 E
120	Broad (R.) (brôd)	Ga.	34·15 N	83·14 W
121	Broad (R.)	NC	35·38 N	82·40 W
202	Broadmeadows (brôd'mĕd-ōz)	Austl. (Melbourne In.)	37·40 S	144·53 E
107	Broadview Heights (brôd'vū)	Oh. (Cleveland In.)	41·18 N	81·41 W
105	Brockport (brŏk'pōrt)	NY	43·15 N	77·55 W
99	Brockton (brŏk'tŭn)	Ma. (In.)	42·04 N	71·01 W
97	Brockville (brŏk'vĭl)	Can.	44·35 N	75·40 W
111	Brockway (brŏk'wā)	Mt.	47·24 N	105·41 W
159	Brodnica (brôd'nĭt-sȧ)	Pol.	53·16 N	19·26 E
159	Brody (brô'dĭ)	Sov. Un.	50·05 N	25·10 E
117	Broken Arrow (brō'kĕn ăr'ō)	Ok.	36·03 N	95·48 W
202	Broken B.	Austl. (Sydney In.)	33·34 S	151·20 E
108	Broken Bow (brō'kĕn bō)	Ne.	41·24 N	99·37 W
117	Broken Bow	Ok.	34·02 N	94·43 W
203	Broken Hill (brōk'ĕn)	Austl.	31·55 S	141·35 E
	Broken Hill, see Kabwe			
148	Bromley (brŭm'lĭ)	Eng. (London In.)	51·23 N	0·01 E
105	Bromptonville (brŭmp'tŭn-vĭl)	Can.	45·30 N	72·00 W
156	Brønderslev (brûn'dĕr-slĕv)	Den.	57·15 N	9·56 E
174	Bronnitsy (brô-nyĭ'tsĭ)	Sov. Un. (Moscow In.)	55·26 N	38·16 E

Page	Name Pronunciation Region	Lat. °'	Long. °'
104	Bronson (brŏn'sŭn)..........Mi.	41·55 N	85·15 W
100	Bronte Cr.....Can. (Toronto In.)	43·25 N	79·53 W
121	Brood (R.) (brōōd)..........SC	34·46 N	81·25 W
100	Brook, The (R.) Can. (Ottawa In.)	45·25 N	75·09 W
107	Brookfield (brŏŏk'fēld) Il. (Chicago In.)	41·49 N	87·51 W
117	Brookfield..........Mo.	39·45 N	93·04 W
106	Brookhaven (brŏŏk'hāv'n) Ga. (Atlanta In.)	33·52 N	84·21 W
120	Brookhaven..........Ms.	31·35 N	90·26 W
110	Brookings (brŏŏk'ĭngs)........Or.	42·04 N	124·16 W
108	Brookings..........SD	44·18 N	96·47 W
99	Brookline (brŏŏk'līn)....Ma. (In.)	42·20 N	71·08 W
99	Brookline..........NH (In.)	42·44 N	71·37 W
107	Brooklyn (brŏŏk'lĭn) Oh. (Cleveland In.)	41·26 N	81·44 W
113	Brooklyn Center Mn. (Minneapolis, St. Paul In.)	45·05 N	93·21 W
107	Brook Park (brŏŏk) Oh. (Cleveland In.)	41·24 N	81·50 W
93	Brooks..........Can.	50·35 N	111·53 W
101	Brooks Ra. (brŏŏks)........Ak.	68·20 N	159·00 W
121	Brooksville (brŏŏks'vĭl)...Fl. (In.)	28·32 N	82·28 W
104	Brookville (brŏŏk'vĭl)........In.	39·20 N	85·00 W
105	Brookville..........Pa.	41·10 N	79·00 W
120	Brookwood (brŏŏk'wŏŏd)......Al.	33·15 N	87·17 W
154	Broom (L.) (brōōm)........Scot.	57·59 N	5·32 W
204	Broome (brōōm)..........Austl.	18·00 S	122·15 E
100	Brossard.....Can. (Montreal In.)	45·26 N	73·28 W
128	Brothers (Is.) (brŭd'hērs).....Ba.	26·05 N	79·00 W
158	Broumov (brōō'môf).......Czech.	50·33 N	15·55 E
129	Brown Bk..........Ba.	21·30 N	74·35 W
116	Brownfield (broun'fēld).......Tx.	33·11 N	102·16 W
111	Browning (broun'ĭng)........Mt.	48·37 N	113·05 W
107	Brownsboro (brounz'bō-rō) Ky. (Louisville In.)	38·22 N	85·30 W
100	Brownsburg (brouns'bûrg) Can. (Montreal In.)	45·40 N	74·24 W
107	Brownsburg.In. (Indianapolis In.)	39·51 N	86·23 W
112	Brownsmead (brounz'-mēd) Or. (Portland In.)	46·13 N	123·33 W
104	Brownstown (brounz'toun)....In.	38·50 N	86·00 W
107	Brownsville (brounz'vĭl) Pa. (Pittsburgh In.)	40·01 N	79·53 W
120	Brownsville..........Tn.	35·35 N	89·15 W
113	Brownsville..........Tx.	25·55 N	97·30 W
98	Brownville Junction (broun'vĭl) Me.	45·20 N	69·04 W
118	Brownwood (broun'wŏŏd).....Tx.	31·44 N	98·58 W
118	Brownwood L..........Tx.	31·55 N	99·15 W
162	Brozas (brō'thäs)..........Sp.	39·37 N	6·44 W
204	Bruce, Mt. (brōōs).........Austl.	22·35 S	118·15 E
104	Bruce Pen..........Can.	44·50 N	81·20 W
120	Bruceton (brōōs'tŭn).........Tn.	36·02 N	88·14 W
158	Bruchsal (brŏŏk'zäl).......F.R.G.	49·08 N	8·34 E
158	Bruck (brŏŏk)..........Aus.	47·25 N	15·14 E
149	Brück (brük)..G.D.R. (Berlin In.)	52·12 N	12·45 E
149	Bruck an der Leitha Aus. (Vienna In.)	48·01 N	16·47 E
100	Bruderheim (brōō'dēr-hīm) Can. (Edmonton In.)	53·47 N	112·56 W
155	Brugge..........Bel.	51·13 N	3·05 E
161	Brühl (brül)....F.R.G. (Ruhr In.)	50·49 N	6·54 E
110	Bruneau R. (brōō-nō').........Id.	42·47 N	115·43 W
196	Brunei (brōō-nī')..........Asia	4·52 N	113·38 E
161	Brünen (brü'nĕn) F.R.G. (Ruhr In.)	51·43 N	6·41 E
163	Brunete (brōō-nā'tā) Sp. (Madrid In.)	40·24 N	4·00 W
99	Brunette (I.) (brōō-nĕt')......Can.	47·16 N	55·54 W
149	Brunn am Gebirge (brōōn'äm gĕ-bĭr'gĕ) Aus. (Vienna In.)	48·07 N	16·18 E
149	Brunsbüttelkoog (brōōns'büt-tĕl-kōg) F.R.G. (Hamburg In.)	53·58 N	9·10 E
121	Brunswick (brŭnz'wĭk).......Ga.	31·08 N	81·30 W
98	Brunswick..........Me.	43·54 N	69·57 W
105	Brunswick..........Md.	39·20 N	77·35 W
117	Brunswick..........Mo.	39·25 N	93·07 W
91	Brunswick....Oh. (Cleveland In.)	41·14 N	81·50 W
136	Brunswick, Pen. de.........Chile	53·25 S	71·15 W
205	Bruny (I.) (brōō'nē).......Austl.	43·30 S	147·50 E
116	Brush (brŭsh)..........Co.	40·14 N	103·40 W
136	Brusque (brōō's-kōōĕ).......Braz.	27·15 S	48·45 W
113	Brussels (brŭs'ĕls) Il. (St. Louis In.)	38·57 N	90·36 W
	Brussels, see Bruxelles		
149	Bruxelles (Brussels) (brü-sĕl') (brŭs'ĕls).Bel. (Brussels In.)	50·51 N	4·21 E
104	Bryan (brī'ăn)..........Oh.	41·25 N	84·30 W
113	Bryan..........Tx.	30·40 N	96·22 W
166	Bryansk (b'r-yänsk').....Sov. Un.	53·12 N	34·23 E
166	Bryansk (Oblast)........Sov. Un.	52·43 N	32·25 E
108	Bryant (brī'ănt)..........SD	44·35 N	97·29 W
112	Bryant.........Wa. (Seattle In.)	48·14 N	122·10 W
115	Bryce Canyon Natl. Park (brīs) Ut.	37·35 N	112·15 W
106	Bryn Mawr (brĭn mår') Pa. (Philadelphia In.)	40·02 N	75·20 W
120	Bryson City (brīs'ŭn)........NC	35·25 N	83·25 W
167	Bryukhovetskaya (b'ryŭk'ō-vyĕt-skä'yä).Sov. Un.	45·56 N	38·58 E
183	Buatan....Indon. (Singapore In.)	0·45 N	101·49 E
210	Buba (bōō'bȧ).....Guinea-Bissau	11·39 N	14·58 W
134	Bucaramanga (bōō-kä'rä-mäŋ'gä) Col.	7·12 N	73·14 W
197	Bucay (bōō-kī').......Phil. (In.)	17·32 N	120·42 E
204	Buccaneer Arch. (bŭk-ȧ-nēr') Austl.	16·05 S	122·00 E
159	Buchach (bŏŏ'chȧch)....Sov. Un.	49·04 N	25·25 E
214	Buchanan (bû-kăn'ăn).......Lib.	5·57 N	10·02 W
104	Buchanan..........Mi.	41·50 N	86·25 W
205	Buchanan (L.) (bû-kăn'nŏn).Austl.	21·45 S	21·02 E
118	Buchanan L. (bû-kăn'ăn).....Tx.	30·55 N	98·40 W
99	Buchans..........Can.	48·49 N	56·52 W
	Bucharest, see București		
149	Buchholtz (bōōk'hōltz) F.R.G. (Hamburg In.)	53·19 N	9·53 E
107	Buck Cr. (bŭk) In. (Indianapolis In.)	39·43 N	85·58 W
105	Buckhannon (bŭk-hăn'ăn)....WV	39·00 N	80·10 W
154	Buckhaven (bŭk-hā'v'n).....Scot.	56·10 N	3·10 W
154	Buckie (bŭk'ĭ)..........Scot.	57·40 N	2·50 W
101	Buckingham (bŭk'ĭng-ăm) Can. (Ottawa In.)	45·35 N	75·25 W
184	Buckingham (R.) (bŭk'ĭng-ăm) India	15·18 N	79·50 E
100	Buckland (bŭk'lănd) Can. (Quebec In.)	46·37 N	70·33 W
205	Buckland Tableland (Reg.)..Austl.	24·31 S	148·00 E
102	Buckley (buk'lē).Wa. (Seattle In.)	47·10 N	122·02 W
98	Bucksport (bŭks'pôrt)........Me.	44·35 N	68·47 W
98	Buctouche (bük-tōōsh')......Can.	46·28 N	64·43 W
165	București (Bucharest) (bōō-kōō-rĕsh'tĭ) (bōō-kȧ-rĕst').Rom.	44·23 N	26·10 E
104	Bucyrus (bû-sī'rŭs).........Oh.	40·50 N	82·55 W
159	Budapest (bōō'dȧ-pĕsht')...Hung.	47·30 N	19·05 E
161	Büderich (bü'dĕ-rēκ) F.R.G. (Ruhr In.)	51·15 N	6·41 E
184	Budge Budge.........India (In.)	22·28 N	88·08 E
216	Budjala..........Zaire	2·39 N	19·42 E
215	Buea..........Cam.	4·09 N	9·14 E
107	Buechel (bĕ-chûl') Ky. (Louisville In.)	38·12 N	85·38 W
161	Bueil (bwā').......Fr. (Paris In.)	48·55 N	1·27 E
113	Buena Park (bwā'nȧ pärk) Ca. (Los Angeles In.)	33·52 N	118·00 W
134	Buenaventura (bwā'nä-vĕn-tōō'rȧ) Col.	3·46 N	77·09 W
129	Buenaventura.........Cuba (In.)	22·08 N	82·22 W
134	Buenaventura, Bahia de (B.) (bä-ē'ä-dĕ-bwā'nä-vĕn-tōō'rȧ) Col.	3·45 N	79·23 W
116	Buena Vista (bū'nȧ vĭs'tȧ)....Co.	38·51 N	106·07 W
120	Buena Vista..........Ga.	32·15 N	84·30 W
105	Buena Vista..........Va.	37·45 N	79·20 W
128	Buena Vista, Bahía (B.) (bä-ē'ä-bwĕ-nä-vē's-tä).Cuba	22·30 N	79·10 W
114	Buena Vista Lake Res. (bū'nȧ vĭs'tȧ).Ca.	35·14 N	119·17 W
162	Buendia Res..........Sp.	40·30 N	2·45 W
136	Buenos Aires (bwā'nōs ī'rās)..Arg.	34·20 S	58·30 W
134	Buenos Aires........Col. (In.)	3·01 N	76·34 W
127	Buenos Aires.........C. R.	9·10 N	83·21 W
136	Buenos Aires (Prov.)........Arg.	36·15 S	61·45 W
136	Buenos Aires (L.)......Arg.-Chile	46·30 S	72·15 W
161	Buer (bür).....F.R.G. (Ruhr In.)	51·35 N	7·03 E
109	Buffalo (buf'ȧ lō)..........Mn.	45·10 N	93·50 W
107	Buffalo.........NY (Buffalo In.)	42·54 N	78·51 W
119	Buffalo..........Tx.	31·28 N	96·04 W
111	Buffalo..........Wy.	44·19 N	106·42 W
117	Buffalo (R.)..........Ar.	35·56 N	92·58 W
213	Buffalo (R.)....S. Afr. (Natal In.)	28·35 S	30·27 E
120	Buffalo (R.)..........Tn.	35·24 N	87·10 W
119	Buffalo Bay.........Tx. (In.)	29·46 N	95·32 W
109	Buffalo Cr..........Mn.	44·46 N	94·28 W
90	Buffalo Head Hills..........Can.	57·16 N	116·18 W
100	Buford (bū'fûrd) Can. (Edmonton In.)	53·15 N	113·55 W
120	Buford (bū'fērd)..........Ga.	34·05 N	84·00 W
115	Buford (L.)..........NM	36·37 N	107·12 W
167	Bug (R.) (bŏŏk)........Sov. Un.	48·12 N	30·13 E
134	Buga (bōō'gä).........Col. (In.)	3·54 N	76·17 W
149	Buggenhout....Bel. (Brussels In.)	51·01 N	4·10 E
121	Buggs Island L..........NC-Va.	36·30 N	78·38 W
164	Bugojno (bōō-gō ĭ nō)........Yugo.	44·03 N	17·28 E
159	Bug R. (bōōg)..........Pol.	52·29 N	21·20 E
170	Bugul'ma (bōō-gōōl'mȧ)..Sov. Un.	54·40 N	52·40 E
170	Buguruslan (bōō-gōō-rōōs-lȧn') Sov. Un.	53·30 N	52·32 E
197	Buhi (bōō'ē).........Phil. (In.)	13·26 N	123·31 E
110	Buhl (būl)..........Id.	42·36 N	114·45 W
109	Buhl..........Mn.	47·28 N	92·49 W
137	Buin (bōō-ēn').Chile (Santiago In.)	33·44 S	70·44 W
171	Buinaksk (bōō'ē-näksk)..Sov. Un.	42·40 N	47·20 E
162	Bujalance (bōō-hä-län'thā)....Sp.	37·54 N	4·22 W
217	Bujumbura..........Burundi	3·23 S	29·22 E
212	Bukama (bōō-kä'mä).......Zaire	9·08 S	26·00 E
217	Bukavu..........Zaire	2·30 S	28·52 E
147	Bukhara (bōō-kä'rä).....Sov. Un.	39·31 N	64·22 E
183	Bukitbatu..Indon. (Singapore In.)	1·25 N	101·58 E
196	Bukittinggi..........Indon.	0·25 S	100·28 E
217	Bukoba..........Tan.	1·20 S	31·49 E
159	Bukovina (Reg.) (bōō-kō'vĭ-nȧ) Sov. Un.	48·06 N	25·20 E
197	Bula (bōō'lä)..........Indon.	3·00 S	130·30 E
197	Bulalacao (bōō-lȧ-lȧ'kä-ō) Phil. (In.)	12·32 N	121·25 E
212	Bulawayo (bōō-lȧ-wä'yō).....Rh.	20·12 S	28·43 E
101	Buldir (I.) (bŭl dĭr).........Ak.	52·22 N	175·50 E
146	Bulgaria (bŏŏl-gā'rĭ-ă)......Eur.	42·12 N	24·13 E
92	Bulkley Ra. (bŭlk'lē).......Can.	54·30 N	127·30 W
162	Bullaque (R.) (bōō-lä'kȧ).....Sp.	39·15 N	4·13 W
162	Bullas (bōōl'yäs)..........Sp.	38·07 N	1·48 W
115	Bulldog Cr. (bŭl'dŏg')........Ut.	37·45 N	110·55 W
92	Bull Harbour (hăr'bēr).......Can.	50·45 N	127·55 W
128	Bull Head (Mtn.)..........Jam.	18·10 N	77·15 W
205	Bulloo (R.) (bŭ-lōō')........Austl.	25·23 S	143·30 E
112	Bull Run (R.) (bōōl) Or. (Portland In.)	45·26 N	122·11 W
112	Bull Run Res...Or. (Portland In.)	45·29 N	122·11 W
117	Bull Shoals Res. (bōōl shōlz) Ar.-Mo.	36·35 N	92·57 W
218	Bulo Burti (bōō'lō bōōr'tĭ) Som. (Horn of Afr. In.)	3·53 N	45·30 E
148	Bulphan (bōōl'făn) Eng. (London In.)	51·33 N	0·21 E
218	Bultfontein (bōōlt'fōn-tān') S. Afr. (Johannesburg & Pretoria In.)	28·18 S	26·10 E
173	Bulun (bōō-lōōn')..........Sov. Un.	70·48 N	127·27 E
216	Bulungu (bōō-lōōŋ'gōō).....Zaire	6·04 S	21·54 E
213	Bulwer (bōōl-wēr) S. Afr. (Natal In.)	29·49 S	29·48 E
216	Bumba (bōōm'bȧ)..........Zaire	2·11 N	22·28 E
217	Bumire I..........Tan.	1·40 S	32·05 E
197	Buna (bōō'nȧ).......Pap. N. Gui.	8·58 S	148·38 E
204	Bunbury (bŭn'bŭrĭ).......Austl.	33·25 S	115·45 E
203	Bundaberg (bŭn'dȧ-bûrg)...Austl.	24·45 S	152·18 E
195	Bungo-Suidō (Chan.) (bōōŋ'gō sōō-ē'dō).Jap.	33·26 N	131·54 E
217	Bunia..........Zaire	1·34 N	30·15 E
113	Bunker Hill (bŭnk'ēr hĭl) Il. (St. Louis In.)	39·03 N	89·57 W
119	Bunkie (bŭŋ'kĭ)..........La.	30·55 N	92·10 W
217	Bun Plns..........Ken.	0·55 N	40·35 E
215	Bununu Dass..........Nig.	10·00 N	9·31 E
173	Buor-Khaya, Guba (B.)..Sov. Un.	71·45 N	131·00 E
173	Buor Khaya, Mys (C.)..Sov. Un.	71·47 N	133·22 E
217	Bura..........Ken.	1·06 S	39·57 E
218	Buran (bûr'ăn) Som. (Horn of Afr. In.)	10·38 N	48·30 E
218	Burao....Som. (Horn of Afr. In.)	9·20 N	45·45 E
186	Buraydah..........Sau. Ar.	26·23 N	44·14 E
113	Burbank (bûr'bănk) Ca. (Los Angeles In.)	34·11 N	118·19 W
205	Burdekin (R.) (bûr'dē-kĭn).Austl.	19·22 S	145·07 E
171	Burdur (bōōr-dōōr')........Tur.	37·50 N	30·15 E
184	Burdwān (bōōrd-wän')......India	23·29 N	87·53 E
136	Burdwood, Banco (Bk.)..Atl. O.	54·00 S	60·45 W
173	Bureinskiy, Khrebet (Mts.) Sov. Un.	51·15 N	133·30 E
173	Bureya (bōōrā'ȧ)........Sov. Un.	49·55 N	130·00 E
173	Bureya (R.) (bōō-rā'yä)..Sov. Un.	51·00 N	130·14 E
148	Burford (bûr-fērd) Eng. (London In.)	51·46 N	1·38 W
165	Burgas (bōōr-gäs')..........Bul.	42·29 N	27·30 E
165	Burgaski Zaliv (G.).........Bul.	42·30 N	27·40 E
213	Bur Gavo..........Som.	1·14 S	41·47 E
121	Burgaw (bûr'gô)..........NC	34·31 N	77·56 W
158	Burgdorf (bōōrg'dôrf)......Switz.	47·04 N	7·37 E
149	Burgenland (State) Aus. (Vienna In.)	47·58 N	16·57 E
99	Burgeo..........Can.	47·36 N	57·34 W
105	Burgess..........Va.	37·53 N	76·21 W
118	Burgos (bōōr'gōs)..........Mex.	24·57 N	98·47 W
197	Burgos.........Phil. (In.)	16·03 N	119·52 E
162	Burgos (bōō'r-gōs)..........Sp.	42·20 N	3·44 E
156	Burgsvik (bōōrgs'vĭk).......Swe.	57·04 N	18·18 E
184	Burhānpur (bōōr'hän-pōōr).India	21·26 N	76·08 E
197	Burias I. (bōō'rē-äs)...Phil. (In.)	12·56 N	122·56 E
197	Burias Pass (bōō'rē-äs).Phil. (In.)	13 04 N	123·11 E
127	Burica, Punta (Pt.) (pōō'n-tä-bōō'rē-kä).Pan.	8·02 N	83·12 W
112	Burien (bū'rĭ-ĕn).Wa. (Seattle In.)	47·28 N	122·20 W
99	Burin (bûr'ĭn)..........Can.	47·02 N	55·10 W
99	Burin Pen..........Can.	47·00 N	55·40 W
116	Burkburnett (bûrk-bûr'nĕt)...Tx.	34·04 N	98·35 W
105	Burke (bûrk)..........Vt.	44·40 N	72·00 W
92	Burke Chan..........Can.	52·07 N	127·38 W
204	Burketown (bûrk'toun).....Austl.	17·50 S	139·30 E
111	Burley (bûr'lĭ)..........Id.	42·31 N	113·48 W
112	Burley.........Wa. (Seattle In.)	47·25 N	122·38 W
174	Burli.......Sov. Un. (Urals In.)	53·36 N	61·55 E
112	Burlingame (bûr'lĭn-gām) Ca. (San Francisco In.)	37·35 N	122·22 W
117	Burlingame..........Ks.	38·45 N	95·49 W
100	Burlington (bûr'lĭng-tŭn) Can. (Toronto In.)	43·19 N	79·48 W
116	Burlington..........Co.	39·17 N	102·26 W
109	Burlington..........Ia.	40·48 N	91·05 W
117	Burlington..........Ks.	38·10 N	95·46 W
107	Burlington...Ky. (Cincinnati In.)	39·01 N	84·44 W
99	Burlington.........Ma. (In.)	42·31 N	71·13 W
106	Burlington..NJ (Philadelphia In.)	40·04 N	74·52 W
121	Burlington..........NC	36·05 N	79·26 W
105	Burlington..........Vt.	44·30 N	73·15 W
112	Burlington.......Wa. (Seattle In.)	48·28 N	122·20 W
107	Burlington...Wi. (Milwaukee In.)	42·41 N	88·16 W
182	Burma (bûr'mȧ)..........Asia	21·00 N	95·15 E
92	Burnaby..........Can.	49·14 N	122·58 W
118	Burnet (bûrn'ĕt)..........Tx.	30·46 N	98·14 W
148	Burnham on Crouch (bûrn'ăm-ŏn-krouch) Eng. (London In.)	51·38 N	0·48 E
203	Burnie (bûr'nē)..........Austl.	41·15 S	146·05 E
148	Burnley (bûrn'lē)..........Eng.	53·47 N	2·19 W
110	Burns (bûrnz)..........Or.	43·35 N	119·05 W
120	Burnside (bûrn'sīd).........Ky.	36·57 N	84·33 W
92	Burns Lake (bûrnz lăk).......Can.	54·14 N	125·46 W
98	Burnsville (bûrnz'vĭl)........Can.	47·44 N	65·07 W
110	Burnt R. (bûrnt)..........Or.	44·26 N	117·53 W
95	Burntwood (R.)..........Can.	55·53 N	97·30 W
112	Burrard Inlet (bûr'ȧrd) Can. (Vancouver In.)	49·19 N	123·15 W
163	Burriana (bōōr-rē-ä'nä).......Sp.	39·53 N	0·05 W
171	Bursa (bōōr'sȧ)..........Tur.	40·10 N	28·10 E
211	Būr Safājah..........Egypt	26·57 N	33·56 E
218	Būr Sa'īd (Port Said) Egypt (Suez In.)	31·15 N	32·19
161	Burscheid (bōōr'shīd) F.R.G. (Ruhr In.)	51·05 N	7·07 E
211	Būr Sūdān (Port Sudan) (sōō-dān').Sud.	19·30 N	37·10 E
107	Burt (bûrt).....NY (Buffalo In.)	43·19 N	78·45 W
104	Burt (L.) (bûrt)..........Mi.	45·25 N	84·45 W

ăt; finăl; rāte; senâte; ärm; ȧsk; sofȧ; fâre; ch-choose; dh-as th in other; bē; ēvent; bĕt; recĕnt; cratẽr; g-go; gh-guttural g; bĭt; ĭ-short neutral; rīde; κ-guttural k as ch in German ich;

Page	Name Pronunciation Region	Lat. °′	Long. °′
112	Burton (bûr'tŭn). Wa. (Seattle In.)	47·24 N	122·28 W
148	Burton-on-Trent (bŭr'tŭn-ŏn-trĕnt). Eng.	52·48 N	1·37 W
120	Burton Res. ... Ga.	34·46 N	83·40 W
106	Burtonsville (bûrtŏns-vil) Md. (Baltimore In.)	39·07 N	76·57 W
197	Buru (I.) ... Indon.	3·30 S	126·30 E
218	Burullus L. ... Egypt (Nile In.)	31·20 N	30·58 E
197	Buruncan Pt. (bo͞o-ro͞on'kän) Phil. (In.)	12·11 N	121·23 E
209	Burundi ... Afr.	3·00 S	29·30 E
108	Burwell (bûr'wĕl) ... Ne.	41·46 N	99·08 W
148	Bury (bĕr'ĭ) ... Eng.	53·36 N	2·17 W
173	Buryat A.S.S.R. ... Sov. Un.	54·15 N	111·22 E
155	Bury St. Edmunds (bĕr'ĭ-sānt ĕd'mŭndz). Eng.	52·14 N	0·44 E
136	Burzaco (bo͞or-zà'kô) ... Arg. (In.)	34·35 S	58·23 W
217	Busanga Swp. ... Zambia	14·10 S	25·50 E
218	Būsh (bo͞osh) ... Egypt (Nile In.)	29·13 N	31·08 E
186	Būshehr ... Iran	28·48 N	50·53 E
212	Bushmanland (Reg.) (bo͝osh-măn lănd). S. Afr.	29·15 S	18·45 E
117	Bushnell (bo͝osh'nĕl) ... Il.	40·33 N	90·28 W
216	Businga (bo͞o-siŋ'gà) ... Zaire	3·20 N	20·53 E
216	Busira (R.) ... Zaire	0·05 S	19·20 E
159	Busk (bo͞o'sk) ... Sov. Un.	49·58 N	24·39 E
204	Busselton (bûs''l-tŭn) ... Austl.	33·40 S	115·30 E
149	Bussum ... Neth. (Amsterdam In.)	52·16 N	5·10 E
118	Bustamante (bo͞os-tà-män'tå). Mex.	26·34 N	100·30 W
164	Busto Arsizio (bo͞os'tō är-sēd'zē-ō). It	45·47 N	8·51 E
197	Busuanga (I.) (bo͞o-swäŋ'gä). Phil.	12·20 N	119·43 E
216	Buta (bo͞o'tà) ... Zaire	2·48 N	24·44 E
213	Butha Buthe (bo͞o-thà-bo͞o'thå) Leso. (Natal In.)	28·49 S	28·16 E
120	Butler (bŭt'lẽr) ... Al.	32·05 N	88·10 W
104	Butler ... In.	41·25 N	84·50 W
106	Butler ... Md. (Baltimore In.)	39·32 N	76·46 W
117	Butler ... Mo.	38·16 N	94·19 W
106	Butler ... NJ (New York In.)	41·00 N	74·20 W
105	Butler ... Pa.	40·50 N	79·55 W
174	Butovo (bo͝o-tô'vô) Sov. Un. (Moscow In.)	55·33 N	37·36 E
217	Butsha ... Zaire	0·57 N	29·13 E
120	Buttahatchie (R.) (bŭt-à-hăch'ė) Al.-Ms.	34·02 N	88·05 W
111	Butte (būt) ... Mt.	46·00 N	112·31 W
213	Butterworth (bŭ tẽr'wûrth) S. Afr. (Natal In.)	32·20 S	28·09 E
154	Butt of Lewis (C.) (bŭt ŏv lū'ĭs) Scot.	58·34 N	6·15 W
197	Butuan (bo͞o-to͞o'än) ... Phil.	8·40 N	125·33 E
196	Butung (I.) ... Indon.	5·00 S	122·55 E
167	Buturlinovka (bo͞o-to͞o'lė-nôf'ka) Sov. Un.	50·47 N	40·35 E
149	Buxtehude (bo͝oks-tĕ-ho͞o'dĕ) F.R.G. (Hamburg In.)	53·29 N	9·42 E
148	Buxton (bŭks't'n) ... Eng.	53·15 N	1·55 W
112	Buxton ... Or. (Portland In.)	45·41 N	123·11 W
170	Buy (bwē) ... Sov. Un.	58·30 N	41·48 E
192	Buyr Nuur (bo͞o'yĕr nôr) ... Mong	47·50 N	117·00 E
165	Buzău (bo͞o-zĕ'o͝o) ... Rom.	45·09 N	26·51 E
167	Buzâu (R.) ... Rom.	45·17 N	27·22 E
211	Buzaymah ... Libya	25·14 N	22·13 E
165	Buzîu (R.) ... Rom.	45·18 N	26·29 E
171	Buzuluk (bo͝o-zo͝o-lo͝ok') .. Sov. Un.	52·50 N	52·10 E
217	Bwendi ... Zaire	4·01 N	26·41 E
165	Byala ... Bul.	43·26 N	25·44 E
	Byblos, see Jubayl		
159	Bydgoszcz (bĭd'gôshch) ... Pol.	53·07 N	18·00 E
104	Byesville (bīz-vĭl) ... Oh.	39·55 N	81·35 W
156	Bygdin (bügh-dėn') ... Nor.	61·24 N	8·31 E
156	Byglandsfjord (bügh'länds-fyôr) Nor.	58·40 N	7·49 E
166	Bykhovo (bĭ-ĸô'vô) ... Sov. Un.	53·32 N	30·15 E
174	Bykovo (bĭ-kô'vô) Sov. Un. (Moscow In.)	55·38 N	38·05 E
172	Byrranga, Gory (Mts.) ... Sov. Un.	74·15 N	94·28 E
173	Bytantay (R.) (byän'täy). Sov. Un.	68·15 N	132·15 E
159	Bytom (bĭ'tŭm) ... Pol.	50·21 N	18·55 E
166	Bytosh' (bĭ-tôsh') ... Sov. Un.	53·48 N	34·06 E
159	Bytow (bĭ'tŭf) ... Pol.	54·10 N	17·30 E

C

Page	Name Pronunciation Region	Lat. °′	Long. °′
136	Caazapa' (kä-zä-pä') ... Par.	26·14 S	56·18 W
197	Cabagan (kä-bä-gän') ... Phil. (In.)	17·27 N	12·46 E
197	Cabalete (I.) (kä-bä-lā'tå) Phil. (In.)	14·19 N	122·00 E
128	Caballones, Canal de (Chan.) (kä-nä'l-dĕ-kä-bäl-yô'nĕs). Cuba	20·45 N	79·20 W
115	Caballo Res. (kä-bä-lyō') ... NM	33·00 N	107·20 W
162	Cabañaquinta (kä-bän-yä-kė'n-tä) Sp.	43·10 N	5·37 W
197	Cabanatuan (kä-bä-nä-twän') Phil. (In.)	15·30 N	120·56 E
98	Cabano (kä-bä-nō') ... Can.	47·41 N	68·54 W
203	Cabar (kă'bẽr) ... Austl.	31·28 S	145·50 E
197	Cabarruyan (I.) (kä-bä-ro͞o'yän) Phil. (In.)	16·21 N	120·10 E
135	Cabedelo (kä-bē-dā'lo͞o) ... Braz.	6·58 S	34·49 W
125	Cabeza, Arrecife (Reef) (är-rĕ-sē'fĕ-kä-bĕ-zä). Mex.	19·07 N	95·52 W
162	Cabeza del Buey (kà-bā'thä dĕl bwā'). Sp.	38·43 N	5·18 W
134	Cabimas (kä-bē'mäs) ... Ven.	10·21 N	71·27 W
209	Cabinda (kä-bĭn'dá) ... Ang.	5·10 S	10·00 E
216	Cabinda ... Ang.	5·33 S	12·12 E
110	Cabinet Mts. (kăb'ĭ-nĕt) ... Mt.	48·13 N	115·52 W
137	Cabo Frio (kä'bō-frē'ō) Braz. (Rio de Janeiro In.)	22·53 S	42·02 W
137	Cabo Frio, Ilha do (ē'lä-dô-kä'bô frē'ô). Braz. (Rio de Janeiro In.)	23·01 S	42·00 W
97	Cabonga Res. ... Can.	47·25 N	76·35 W
104	Cabot Hd. (kăb'ŭt) ... Can.	45·15 N	81·20 W
99	Cabot Str. (kăb'ŭt) ... Can.	47·35 N	60·00 W
162	Cabra (käb'rä) ... Sp.	37·28 N	4·29 W
197	Cabra (I.) ... Phil. (In.)	13·55 N	119·55 E
163	Cabrera (I.) (kä-brā'rä) ... Sp.	39·08 N	2·57 E
162	Cabriel (R.) (kä-brē-ĕl') ... Sp.	39·25 N	1·20 W
114	Cabrillo Natl. Mon. (kä-brēl'yō) Ca. (In.)	32·41 N	117·03 W
135	Cabrobó' (kä-brō-bô') ... Braz.	8·34 S	39·13 W
136	Cabuçu (R.) (kä-bo͞o'-so͞o) Braz. (Rio de Janeiro In.)	22·57 S	43·36 W
197	Cabugao (kä-bo͞o'gä-ō). Phil. (In.)	17·48 N	120·28 E
165	Čačak (chä'chåk) ... Yugo.	43·51 N	20·22 E
96	Cacaoui, Lac (L.) (kä-kä-wē'). Que.	50·54 N	66·58 W
137	Caçapava (kä'sä-pá'vä) Braz. (Rio de Janeiro In.)	23·05 S	45·52 W
135	Cáceres (kå'sĕ-rĕs) ... Braz.	16·11 S	57·32 W
162	Cáceres (ká'thâ-rās) ... Sp.	39·28 N	6·20 W
137	Cachapoal (R.) (kä-chä-pô-ä'l) Chile (Santiago In.)	34·23 S	70·19 W
137	Cacharí (kä-chä-rē') Arg. (Buenos Aires In.)	36·23 S	59·29 W
117	Cache (R.) (kăsh) ... Ar.	35·24 N	91·12 W
93	Cache Creek ... Can.	50·48 N	121·19 W
114	Cache Cr. (kăsh) ... Ca.	38·53 N	122·24 W
116	Cache la Poudre (R.) kåsh lå po͞od'r'). Co.	40·43 N	105·39 W
136	Cachi, Nevados de (Pk.) (nĕ-vá'dôs-dĕ-kä'chē). Arg.	25·05 S	66·40 W
136	Cachinal (kä-chē-näl') ... Chile	24·57 S	69·33 W
135	Cachoeira (kä-shô-ā'rä) ... Braz.	12·32 S	38·47 W
136	Cachoeira do Sul (kä-shô-ā'rä-dô-so͞o'l). Braz.	30·02 S	52·49 W
137	Cachoeiras de Macacu (kä-shô-ā'räs-dĕ-mä-kà'ko͞o) Braz. (Rio de Janeiro In.)	22·28 S	42·39 W
137	Cachoeiro de Itapemirim (kä-shô-ā'rô-dĕ-ē'tä-pĕmē-rē'ɴ) Braz. (Rio de Janeiro In.)	20·51 S	41·06 W
216	Cacólo ... Ang.	10·07 S	19·17 E
216	Caconda (kä-kōn'dä) ... Ang.	13·43 S	15·06 E
98	Cacouna ... Can.	47·54 N	69·31 W
216	Cacula ... Ang.	14·29 S	14·10 E
119	Caddo L. (kăd'ō) ... La.-Tx.	32·37 N	94·15 W
124	Cadereyta (kä-dâ-rā'tä) ... Mex.	20·42 N	99·47 W
118	Cadereyta Jimenez (kä-dä-rā'tä hē-mā'näz). Mex.	25·36 N	99·59 W
163	Cadi, Sierra de (Mts.) (sē-ĕ'r-rä-dĕ-kä'dē). Sp.	42·17 N	1·34 E
197	Cadig, Mt. (kä'dēg) ... Phil. (In.)	14·11 N	122·26 E
104	Cadillac (kăd'ĭ-lăk) ... Mi.	44·15 N	85·25 W
114	Cadiz (kā'dĭz) ... Ca.	34·33 N	115·30 W
104	Cadiz ... Oh.	40·15 N	81·00 W
162	Cádiz (kà'dēz) ... Sp.	36·34 N	6·20 W
162	Cádiz, Golfo de (G.) (gôl-fô-dĕ-kà'dēz). Sp.	36·50 N	7·00 W
160	Caen (kän) ... Fr.	49·13 N	0·22 W
137	Caeté (kä'ĕ-tĕ') Braz. (Rio de Janeiro In.)	19·53 S	43·41 W
135	Caetité (kä-å-tē-tā') ... Braz.	14·02 S	42·14 W
197	Cagayan (kä-gä-yän') ... Phil.	8·13 N	124·30 E
196	Cagayan (R.) ... Phil.	16·45 N	121·55 E
196	Cagayan Is. ... Phil.	9·40 N	120·30 E
196	Cagayan Sulu (I.) (kä-gä-yän so͞o'lo͞o). Phil.	7·00 N	118·30 E
164	Cagli (käl'yē) ... It.	43·33 N	12·38 E
164	Cagliari (käl'yä-rē) ... It.	39·16 N	9·08 E
164	Cagliari, Golfo di (G.) (gôl-fô-dē-käl'yä-rē). It.	39·08 N	9·12 E
161	Cagnes (kän'y') ... Fr.	43·40 N	7·14 E
135	Cagua (kä'-gwä) ... Ven. (In.)	10·12 N	67·27 W
123	Caguas (kä'gwäs) P. R. (Puerto Rico In.)	18·12 N	66·01 W
120	Cahaba (R.) (kå hä-bä) ... Al.	32·50 N	87·15 W
216	Cahama (kä-à'mä) ... Ang.	16·17 S	14·19 E
113	Cahokia (kȧ-hō'kĭ-ȧ) Il. (St. Louis In.)	38·34 N	90·11 W
217	Cahora-Bassa (Gorge) ... Moz.	15·40 S	32·50 E
160	Cahors (kå-ôr') ... Fr.	44·27 N	1·27 E
125	Cahuacán (kä-wä-kä'n). Mex. (In.)	19·38 N	99·25 W
127	Cahuita, Punta (Pt.) (po͞o'n-tä-kä-wē'tȧ). C. R.	9·47 N	82·41 W
135	Caiapó, Serra do (Mts.) (sĕ'r-rä-dô-kä-yä-pô'). Braz.	17·52 S	52·37 W
128	Caibarién (kī-bä-rē-ĕn') ... Cuba	22·35 N	79·30 W
134	Caicedonia (kī-sĕ-dô-nêä) Col. (In.)	4·21 N	75·48 W
129	Caicos Bk. (kī'kōs) ... Ba.	21·35 N	72·00 W
129	Caicos Is. ... Turks & Caicos Is.	21·45 N	71·50 W
129	Caicos Passage (Str.) ... Ba.	21·55 N	72·45 W
119	Caillou B. (kȧ-yo͞o') ... La.	29·07 N	91·00 W
129	Caimanera (kī-mä-nä'rä) ... Cuba	20·00 N	75·10 W
124	Caimanere, Laguna del (lä-go͞o'nä-dĕl-kä-ē-mä-nĕ-rĕ) Mex.	22·57 N	106·07 W
197	Caiman Pt. (kī'màn) ... Phil. (In.)	15·56 N	119·33 E
122	Caimito, (R.) (kä-ē-mē'tô) Pan. (In.)	8·50 N	79·45 W
129	Caimito del Guayabal (kä-ē-mė'tō-dĕl-gwä-yä-bä'l) Cuba (In.)	22·12 N	82·36 W
205	Cairns (kârnz) ... Austl.	17·02 S	145·49 E
127	Cairo (kī'-rô) ... C. R.	10·06 N	83·47 W
	Cairo, see Al Qāhirah		
120	Cairo (kā'rō) ... Ga.	30·48 N	84·12 W
117	Cairo ... Il.	36·59 N	89·11 W
148	Caistor (kâs'tẽr) ... Eng.	53·30 N	0·20 W
216	Caiundo ... Ang.	15·46 S	17·28 E
134	Cajamarca (kä-ĸä-mà'r-kä) Col. (In.)	4·25 N	75·25 W
134	Cajamarca (kä-hä-mär'kä) ... Peru	7·16 S	78·30 W
197	Cajidiocan (kä-hē-dyô'kän) ... Phil. (In.)	12·22 N	122·41 E
165	Čajniče (chī'nĭ-chĕ) ... Yugo.	43·32 N	19·04 E
113	Cajon (kà-hōn') Ca. (Los Angeles In.)	34·18 N	117·28 W
137	Cajuru (kà-zho͞o'-ro͞o) Braz. (Rio de Janeiro In.)	21·17 S	47·17 W
164	Čakovec (chà'kō-vĕts) ... Yugo.	46·23 N	16·27 E
213	Cala (cä-lȧ) ... S. Afr. (Natal In.)	31·33 S	27·41 E
215	Calabar (kăl-ȧ-bär') ... Nig.	4·57 N	8·19 E
129	Calabazar (kä-lä-bä-zä'r) Cuba (In.)	23·02 N	82·25 W
134	Calabozo (kä-lä-bō'zō) ... Ven.	8·48 N	67·27 W
164	Calabria (Reg.) (kä-lä'brė-ä) ... It.	39·26 N	16·23 E
165	Calafat (kà-là-fàt') ... Rom.	43·59 N	22·56 E
197	Calagua Is. (kä-läg'wä). Phil. (In.)	14·30 N	123·06 E
100	Calahoo (kă-là-ho͞o') Can. (Edmonton In.)	53·42 N	113·58 W
162	Calahorra (kä-lä-ôr'rä) ... Sp.	42·18 N	1·58 W
160	Calais (kà-lĕ') ... Fr.	50·56 N	1·51 E
98	Calais ... Me.	45·11 N	67·15 W
136	Calama (kä-lä'mä) ... Chile	22·17 S	68·58 W
134	Calamar (kä-lä-mär') ... Col.	10·24 N	75·00 W
134	Calamar ... Col.	1·55 N	72·33 W
197	Calamba (kä-läm'bä) ... Phil. (In.)	14·12 N	121·10 E
196	Calamian Group (Is.) (kä-lä-myän'). Phil.	12·14 N	118·38 E
162	Calañas (kä-län'yäs) ... Sp.	37·41 N	6·52 W
197	Calapan (kä-lä-pän') ... Phil. (In.)	13·25 N	121·11 E
153	Călărasi (kŭ-lŭ-ràsh'ĭ) ... Rom.	44·09 N	27·20 E
152	Calasparra (kä-lä-spär'rä) ... Sp.	38·13 N	1·40 W
162	Calatayud (kä-lä-tä-yo͞odh') ... Sp.	41·23 N	1·37 W
197	Calauag (kä-lä-wäg') ... Phil. (In.)	13·56 N	122·16 E
197	Calauag B. ... Phil. (In.)	14·07 N	122·10 E
112	Calaveras Res. (kăl-à-vẽr'ăs) Ca. (San Francisco In.)	37·29 N	121·47 W
197	Calavite, C. (kä-lä-vē'tā) Phil. (In.)	13·29 N	120·00 E
119	Calcasieu (R.) ... La.	30·22 N	93·08 W
119	Calcasieu L. (kăl'kà-shū) ... La.	29·58 N	93·08 W
184	Calcutta (kăl-kŭt'à) ... India (In.)	22·32 N	88·22 E
134	Caldas (kà'l-däs) ... Col. (In.)	6·06 N	75·38 W
134	Caldas (Dept.) ... Col. (In.)	5·20 N	75·38 W
162	Caldas de Rainha (käl'däs dä rīn'yă). Port.	39·25 N	9·08 W
148	Calder (R.) (kôl'dẽr) ... Eng.	53·39 N	1·30 W
136	Caldera (käl-dā'rä) ... Chile	27·02 S	70·53 W
148	Calder Can ... Eng.	53·48 N	2·25 W
110	Caldwell (kôld'wĕl) ... Id.	43·40 N	116·43 W
117	Caldwell ... Ks.	37·04 N	97·36 W
104	Caldwell ... Oh.	39·40 N	81·30 W
119	Caldwell ... Tx.	30·30 N	96·40 W
100	Caledon (kăl'ē-dŏn) Can. (Toronto In.)	43·52 N	79·59 W
109	Caledonia (kăl-ē-dō'nĭ-ȧ) ... Mn.	43·38 N	91·31 W
154	Caledonian Can. (kăl-ē-dō'nĭ-ȧn) Scot.	56·58 N	4·05 W
163	Calella (kä-lĕl'yä) ... Sp.	41·37 N	2·39 E
124	Calera Victor Rosales (kä-lā'rä-vē'k-tôr-rô-sà'lĕs). Mex.	22·57 N	102·42 W
114	Calexico (kȧ-lĕk'sĭ-kō) ... Ca.	32·41 N	115·30 W
100	Calgary (kăl'gȧ-rĭ) Can. (Calgary In.)	51·03 N	114·05 W
120	Calhoun (kăl-ho͞on') ... Ga.	34·30 N	84·56 W
134	Cali (kä'lē) ... Col. (In.)	3·26 N	76·30 W
181	Calicut (kăl'ĭ-kŭt) ... India	11·19 N	75·49 E
115	Caliente (käl-yĕn'tā) ... Nv.	37·38 N	114·30 W
117	California (kăl-ĭ-fôr'nĭ-ȧ) ... Mo.	38·38 N	92·38 W
107	California ... Pa. (Pittsburgh In.)	40·03 N	79·53 W
102	California (State) ... U.S.	38·10 N	121·20 W
122	California, Golfo de (G.) (gôl-fô-dĕ-kä-lē-fôr-nyä). Mex.	30·30 N	113·45 W
159	Căliman, Muntii (Mts.) ... Rom.	47·05 N	24·47 E
185	Calimere, Pt. ... India	15·25 N	80·05 E
113	Calimesa (kă-lĭ-mā'sà) Ca. (Los Angeles In.)	34·00 N	117·04 W
114	Calipatria (kăl-ĭ-pàt'rĭ-ȧ) ... Ca.	33·03 N	115·30 W
125	Calkini (käl-kē-nē') ... Mex.	20·21 N	90·06 W
203	Callabonna, L. (călă'bŏnȧ). Austl.	29·35 S	140·28 E
134	Callao (käl-yä'ô) ... Peru	12·02 S	77·07 W
93	Calling Lake (kôl'ĭng) ... Can.	55·15 N	113·12 W
93	Calmar (kăl'mär) Can. (Edmonton In.)	53·16 N	113·49 W
109	Calmar ... Ia.	43·12 N	91·54 W
124	Calnali (käl-nä-lē') ... Mex.	20·53 N	98·34 W
121	Calooshatchee (R.) (kȧ-loo-sȧ-hăch'ė). Fl. (In.)	26·45 N	81·41 W
126	Calotmul (kä-lôt-mo͞ol). Mex. (In.)	20·58 N	88·11 W
124	Calpulalpan (käl-po͞o-läl'pän) Mex.	19·35 N	98·33 W
164	Caltagirone (käl-tä-jē-rō'nå) ... It.	37·14 N	14·32 E
164	Caltanissetta (käl-tä-nē-sĕt'tä). It.	37·30 N	14·02 E
216	Caluango ... Ang.	8·21 S	19·40 E
216	Calucinga ... Ang.	11·18 S	16·12 E
109	Calumet (kă-lū-mĕt') ... Mi.	47·15 N	88·29 W
107	Calumet, L. ... Il. (Chicago In.)	41·43 N	87·36 W
107	Calumet City ... Il. (Chicago In.)	41·37 N	87·33 W
216	Calunda ... Ang.	12·06 S	23·23 E
216	Caluquembe ... Ang.	13·47 S	14·44 E
119	Calvert (kăl'vẽrt) ... Tx.	30·59 N	96·41 W

ng-sing; ŋ-baŋk; ɴ-nasalized n; nŏd; cŏmmit; ōld; ôbey; ôrder; fo͞od; fo͝ot; ou-out; s-soft; sh-dish; th-thin; pūre; ûnite; ûrn; stŭd; circŭs; ü-as "y" in study; '-indeterminate vowel.

ăt; final; rāte; senāte; ärm; ȧsk; sofa; fâre; ch-choose; dh-as th in other; bē; ēvent; bĕt; recĕnt; crātēr; g-go; gh-guttural g; bĭt; ĭ-short neutral; rīde; ᴋ-guttural k as ch in German ich;

PRONOUNCING INDEX Caramoan — Catalina 265

Page	Name Pronunciation Region	Lat. °′	Long. °′
197	Caramoan (kä-rä-mō'än) Phil. (In.)	13·46 N	123·52 E
137	Carandaí (kä-rän-dȧē') Braz. (Rio de Janeiro In.)	20·57 S	43·47 W
137	Carangola (kä-rȧn'gō'lä) Braz. (Rio de Janeiro In.)	20·46 S	42·02 W
165	Caransebes (kȧ-rȧn-sä'bĕsh). Rom.	45·24 N	22·13 E
98	Caraquet (kă-rȧ-kĕt') Can.	47·48 N	64·57 W
117	Carata, Laguna (L.) (lä-gōō'nä-kä-rä'tä). Nic.	13·59 N	83·41 W
117	Caratasca, Laguna (L.) (lä-gōō'nä-kä-rä-täs'kä). Hond.	15·20 N	83·45 W
162	Caravaca (kä-rä-vä'kä) Sp.	38·05 N	1·51 W
135	Caravelas (kȧ-rä-vĕl'äzh) Braz.	17·46 S	39·06 W
135	Carayaca (kȧ-rä-ïä'kä). Ven. (In.)	10·32 N	67·07 W
136	Caràzinho (kä-rȧ'zē-nyŏ) Braz.	28·22 S	52·33 W
162	Carballino (kär-bäl-yē'nō) Sp.	42·26 N	8·04 W
162	Carballo (kär-bäl'yō) Sp.	43·13 N	8·40 W
112	Carbon (R.) (kär'bŏn). Wa. (Seattle In.)	47·06 N	122·08 W
112	Carbonado (kȧr-bō-nä'dō) Wa. (Seattle In.)	47·05 N	122·03 W
164	Carbonara, C. (kär-bō-nä'rä) It.	39·08 N	9·33 E
101	Carbondale (kär'bŏn-dāl) Can. (Edmonton In.)	53·45 N	113·32 W
117	Carbondale Il.	37·42 N	89·12 W
105	Carbondale Pa.	41·35 N	75·30 W
99	Carbonear (kär-bō-nēr') Can.	47·45 N	53·14 W
120	Carbon Hill (kär'bŏn hĭl) Al.	33·53 N	87·34 W
163	Carcagente (kär-kä-hĕn'tā) Sp.	39·09 N	0·29 W
160	Carcans, Étang de (L.) (ā-taN-dĕ-kȧr-kȧn). Fr.	45·12 N	1·00 W
160	Carcassonne (kȧr-kȧ-sŏn') Fr.	43·12 N	2·23 E
90	Carcross (kär'krŏs) Can.	60·18 N	134·54 W
128	Cárdenas (kär'dȧ-näs) Cuba	23·00 N	81·10 W
125	Cárdenas (kȧ'r-dĕ-näs) Mex.	17·59 N	93·23 W
124	Cárdenas Mex.	22·01 N	99·38 W
129	Cardenas, Bahía de (B.) (bä-ē'ä-dĕ-kär'dȧ-näs). Cuba	23·10 N	81·10 W
100	Cardiff (kär'dĭf) Can. (Edmonton In.)	53·46 N	113·36 W
154	Cardiff Wales	51·30 N	3·18 W
154	Cardigan (kär'dĭ-găn) Wales	52·05 N	4·40 W
154	Cardigan B. Wales	52·35 N	4·40 W
93	Cardston (kärds'tŭn) Can.	49·12 N	113·18 W
159	Carei (kä-rē') Rom.	47·42 N	22·28 E
160	Carentan (kä-rôN-täN') Fr.	49·19 N	1·14 W
104	Carey (kā'rē) Oh.	40·55 N	83·25 W
204	Carey (I.) (kâr'ē) Austl.	29·20 S	123·35 E
160	Carhaix (kär-ĕ') Fr.	48·17 N	3·37 W
123	Caribbean Sea (kăr-ĭ-bē'ăn) N.A.-S.A.	14·30 N	75·30 W
93	Cariboo Mts. (kă'rĭ-bōō) Can.	53·00 N	121·00 W
98	Caribou Me.	46·51 N	68·01 W
96	Caribou (I.) Can.	47·22 N	85·42 W
113	Caribou L. Mn. (Duluth In.)	46·54 N	92·16 W
90	Caribou Mts. Can.	59·20 N	115·30 W
135	Carinhanha (kä-rĭ-nyän'yä). Braz.	14·14 S	43·44 W
164	Carini (kä-rē'nē) It.	38·09 N	13·10 E
	Carinthia (State), see Kärnten		
97	Carleton Place (kärl'tŭn) Can.	45·15 N	76·10 W
218	Carletonville S. Afr. (Johannesburg & Pretoria In.)	26·20 S	27·23 E
117	Carlinville (kär'lĭn-vĭl) Il.	39·16 N	89·52 W
154	Carlisle (kär-līl') Eng.	54·54 N	3·03 W
104	Carlisle Ky.	38·20 N	84·00 W
105	Carlisle Pa.	40·10 N	77·15 W
160	Carlitte, Pic (Pk.) (pēk' kar-lēt') Fr.	42·33 N	1·56 E
164	Carloforte (kär'lō-fôr-tȧ) It.	39·11 N	8·28 E
137	Carlos Casares (kär-lōs-kä-sä'rĕs) Arg. (Buenos Aires In.)	35·38 S	61·17 W
154	Carlow (kär'lō) Ire.	52·50 N	7·00 W
118	Carlsbad (kärlz'băd) NM	32·24 N	104·12 W
118	Carlsbad Caverns Nat'l Park NM	32·08 N	104·30 W
148	Carlton (kärl'tŭn) Eng.	52·58 N	1·05 W
113	Carlton Mn. (Duluth In.)	46·40 N	92·26 W
104	Carlton Center (kärl'tŭn sĕn'tēr) Mi.	42·45 N	85·20 W
117	Carlyle (kärlīl') Il.	38·37 N	89·23 W
164	Carmagnolo (kär-mä-nyô'lä) It.	44·52 N	7·48 E
95	Carman (kär'mȧn) Can.	49·32 N	98·00 W
154	Carmarthen (kär-mär'thĕn) Wales	51·50 N	4·20 W
154	Carmarthen B. (kär-mär'thĕn) Wales	51·33 N	4·50 W
160	Carmaux (kȧr-mō') Fr.	44·05 N	2·09 E
106	Carmel (kär'mĕl) NY (New York In.)	41·25 N	73·42 W
137	Carmelo (kär-mĕ'lo) Ur. (Buenos Aires In.)	33·59 S	58·15 W
124	Carmen, Isla del (I.) (ē's-lä-dĕl-kä'r-mĕn). Mex.	18·43 N	91·40 W
125	Carmen, Laguna del (L.) (lä-gōō'nä-dĕl-kä'r-mĕn). Mex.	18·15 N	93·26 W
137	Carmen de Areco (kär'mĕn' dā ä-rā'kō). Arg. (Buenos Aires In.)	34·21 S	59·50 W
136	Carmen de Patagones (kȧ'r-mĕn-dĕ-pä-tä-gô'nĕs). Arg.	41·00 S	63·00 W
104	Carmi (kär'mī) Il.	38·05 N	88·10 W
137	Carmo (kȧ'r-mô) Braz. (Rio de Janeiro In.)	21·57 S	42·06 W
137	Carmo do Rio Clara (kȧ'r-mô-dô-rē'ō-klä'rä) Braz. (Rio de Janeiro In.)	20·57 S	46·04 W
216	Carmona (kär-mo-nä) Ang	7·37 S	15·03 E
162	Carmona Sp.	37·28 N	5·38 W
204	Carnarvon (kär-när'vŭn) Austl.	24·45 S	113·45 E
212	Carnarvon S. Afr.	31·00 S	22·15 E
154	Carnarvon Wales	53·08 N	4·17 W
154	Carnarvon Bay Wales	53·09 N	4·56 W
112	Carnation (kär-nā'shŭn) Wa. (Seattle In.)	47·39 N	121·55 W
163	Carnaxide (kär-nä-shē'dĕ) Port. (Lisbon In.)	38·44 N	9·15 W
154	Carndonagh (kärn-dō-nä') Ire.	55·15 N	7·15 W
116	Carnegie (kär-nĕg'ĭ) Ok.	35·06 N	98·38 W
107	Carnegie Pa. (Pittsburgh In.)	40·24 N	80·06 W
105	Carneys Point (kär'nēs) NJ	39·45 N	75·25 W
158	Carnic Alps (Mts.) Aus.-It.	46·43 N	12·38 E
163	Carnot (kär nō') Alg.	36·15 N	1·40 E
215	Carnot Cen. Afr. Rep.	4·56 N	15·52 E
154	Carnsore Pt. (kärn'sôr) Ire.	52·10 N	6·16 W
104	Caro (kâ'rō) Mi.	43·30 N	83·25 W
135	Carolina (kä-rô-lē'nä) Braz.	7·26 S	47·16 W
212	Carolina (kăr-ô-lī'nȧ) S. Afr.	26·07 S	30·09 E
126	Carolina L. (kä-rō-lē'nä) Mex. (In.)	18·41 N	89·40 W
198	Caroline Is. (kăr'ô-līn) Pac. Is. Trust Ter.	9·30 N	143·00 E
134	Caroni (R.) (kä-rō'nē) Ven.	5·49 N	62·57 W
134	Carora (kä-rō'rä) Ven.	10·09 N	70·12 W
153	Carpathians Mts. (kär-pā'thĭ-ăn) Eur.	49·23 N	20·14 E
165	Carpatii Meridionali (Transylvanian Alps) (Mts.). Rom.	45·30 N	23·30 E
204	Carpentaria, G. of (kär-pĕn-târ'ĭȧ) Austl.	14·45 S	138·50 E
160	Carpentras (kär-pän-träs') Fr.	44·04 N	5·01 E
164	Carpi It.	44·48 N	10·54 E
120	Carabelle (kăr'ȧ-bĕl) Fl.	29·50 N	84·40 W
154	Carrantuohill (kă-răn-tōō'ĭl) Ire.	52·01 N	9·48 W
164	Carrara (kä-rä'rä) It.	44·05 N	10·05 E
134	Carretas, Punta (Pt.) (pōō'n-tä-kär-rĕ'tĕ'rȧs) Peru	14·15 S	76·25 W
127	Carriacou I. (kăr-ē-ȧ-kōō') Grenada (In.)	12·28 N	61·20 W
154	Carrick (kăr'ĭk) Ire.	52·20 N	7·35 W
100	Carrier (kăr'ĭ-ēr) Can. (Quebec In.)	46·43 N	71·05 W
120	Carriere (kȧ-rēr') Ms.	30·37 N	89·37 W
104	Carriers Mills (kăr'ĭ-ērs) Il.	37·40 N	88·40 W
108	Carrington (kăr'ĭng-tŭn) ND	47·26 N	99·06 W
112	Carr Inlet (kär ĭn'lĕt) Wa. (Seattle In.)	47·20 N	122·42 W
162	Carrion (kär-rē-ōn') Sp.	42·36 N	6·42 W
128	Carrion Crow Hbr. (kăr'ĭŭn krō) Ba.	26·35 N	77·55 W
162	Carrión de los Condes (kär-rē-ōn' dā lōs kōn'dās). Sp.	42·20 N	4·35 W
116	Carrizo Cr. (kär-rē'zō) NM	36·22 N	103·39 W
118	Carrizo Springs Tx.	28·32 N	99·51 W
115	Carrizozo (kär-rē-zō'zō) NM	33·40 N	105·55 W
109	Carroll (kăr'ŭl) Ia.	42·03 N	94·51 W
120	Carrollton (kăr-ŭl-tŭn) Ga.	33·35 N	84·05 W
117	Carrollton Il.	39·18 N	90·22 W
104	Carrollton Ky.	38·45 N	85·15 W
104	Carrollton Mi.	43·30 N	83·55 W
117	Carrollton Mo.	39·21 N	93·29 W
104	Carrollton Oh.	40·35 N	81·10 W
113	Carrollton Tx. (Dallas, Fort Worth In.)	32·58 N	96·53 W
112	Carrols (kăr'ŭlz) Wa. (Portland In.)	46·05 N	122·51 W
154	Carron (L.) (kȧ'rŭn) Scot.	57·25 N	5·25 W
94	Carrot (R.) Can.	53·12 N	103·50 W
160	Carry-le-Rouet (kä-rē'lĕ-rōō-ā') Fr. (In.)	43·20 N	5·10 E
171	Çarşamba (chär-shäm'bä) Tur.	41·05 N	36·40 E
114	Carson (R.) (kär'sŭn) Nv.	39·15 N	119·25 W
114	Carson City Nv.	39·10 N	119·45 W
114	Carson Sink Nv.	39·51 N	118·25 W
134	Cartagena (kär-tä-hā'nä) Col.	10·30 N	75·40 W
163	Cartagena (kär-tä-кē'nä) Sp.	37·46 N	1·00 W
134	Cartago (kär-tä'gō) Col. (In.)	4·44 N	75·54 W
127	Cartago C. R.	9·52 N	83·56 W
162	Cartaxo (kär-tä'shō) Port.	39·10 N	8·48 W
106	Carteret (kär'tē-rĕt) NJ (New York In.)	40·35 N	74·13 W
120	Cartersville (kär'tērs-vĭl) Ga.	34·09 N	84·47 W
117	Carthage (kär'thȧj) Il.	40·27 N	91·09 W
117	Carthage Mo.	37·10 N	94·18 W
105	Carthage NY	44·00 N	75·45 W
121	Carthage NC	35·22 N	79·25 W
119	Carthage Tx.	32·09 N	94·20 W
210	Carthage Tun.	37·04 N	10·18 E
213	Carthcart (cärth-cȧ't) S. Afr. (Natal In.)	32·18 S	27·11 E
91	Cartwright (kärt'rīt) Can.	53·36 N	57·00 W
135	Caruaru (kä-rōō-ȧ-rōō') Braz.	8·19 S	35·52 W
134	Carúpano (kä-rōō'pä-nō) Ven.	10·45 N	63·21 W
117	Caruthersville (kȧ-rŭdh'ērz-vĭl) Mo.	36·09 N	89·41 W
112	Carver (kärv'ēr). Or. (Portland In.)	45·24 N	122·30 W
162	Carvoeira, Cabo (C.) (kȧ'bō-kär-vô-ĕ'y-rä). Port.	39·22 N	9·24 W
107	Cary (kă'rē) Il. (Chicago In.)	42·13 N	88·14 W
137	Casablanca (kä-sä-bläŋ'kä) Chile (Santiago In.)	33·19 S	71·24 W
210	Casablanca Mor.	33·32 N	7·41 W
137	Casa Branca (kȧ'sä-brȧ'N-kä) Braz. (Rio de Janeiro In.)	21·47 S	47·04 W
115	Casa Grande (kä'sä grän'dā). Az.	32·50 N	111·45 W
115	Casa Grande Natl. Mon. Az.	33·00 N	111·33 W
164	Casale (kä-sä'lā) It.	45·08 N	8·26 E
164	Casalmaggiore (kä-säl-mäd-jō'rā). It.	45·00 N	10·24 E
214	Casamance (R.) (kä-sä-mäNs') Senegal	12·43 N	16·00 W
205	Cascade Pt. (kăs-kād'). N.Z. (In.)	43·59 S	168·23 E
102	Cascade Ra. U. S.	42·50 N	122·20 W
110	Cascade Tun. Wa.	47·41 N	120·53 W
163	Cascais (käs-kȧ-ēzh) Port. (Lisbon In.)	38·42 N	9·25 W
163	Cascais, Ba. de (B.) (bä-ē'ä-dĕ-käs-kī's) Port. (Lisbon In.)	38·41 N	9·24 W
112	Case Inlet (kās). Wa. (Seattle In.)	47·22 N	122·47 W
136	Caseros (kä-sä'rôs) Arg. (In.)	34·21 S	58·34 W
164	Caserta (kä-zĕr'tä) It.	41·04 N	14·21 E
104	Casey (kā'sĭ) Il.	39·20 N	88·00 W
110	Cashmere (kăsh'mĭr) Wa.	47·30 N	120·28 W
197	Casiguran (käs-sē-gōō'rän) Phil. (In.)	16·15 N	122·10 E
197	Casiguran Sd. Phil. (In.)	16·02 N	121·51 E
137	Casilda (kä-sē'l-dä) Arg. (Buenos Aires In.)	33·02 S	61·11 W
128	Casilda Cuba	21·50 N	80·00 W
137	Casimiro de Abreu (kä'sē-mē'ro-dĕ-ȧ-brĕ'ōō). Braz. (Rio de Janeiro In.)	22·30 S	42·11 W
203	Casino (kȧ-sē'nō) Austl.	28·35 S	153·10 E
134	Casiquiare (R.) (kä-sē-kyä'rā) Ven.	2·11 N	66·15 W
163	Caspe (käs'pȧ) Sp.	41·18 N	0·02 W
111	Casper (kăs'pēr) Wy.	42·51 N	106·18 W
170	Caspian Dep. (kăs'pĭ-ăn). Sov. Un.	47·40 N	51·40 E
168	Caspian Sea Asia	39·30 N	52·00 E
105	Cass (kăs) WV	38·25 N	79·55 W
109	Cass (L.) Mn.	47·23 N	94·28 W
163	Cassá de la Selva (käs-sä'dĕ-lä-sĕl-vä). Sp.	41·52 N	2·52 E
216	Cassai (R.) (kä-sä'ē) Ang.	7·30 S	21·45 E
104	Cas City (kăs) Mi.	43·35 N	83·10 W
100	Casselman (kăs''l-mȧn) Can. (Ottawa In.)	45·18 N	75·05 W
108	Casselton (kăs''l-tŭn) ND	46·53 N	97·14 W
137	Cássia (kȧ'syä) Braz. (Rio de Janeiro In.)	20·36 S	46·53 W
113	Cassin (kăs'ĭn) Tx. (San Antonio In.)	29·16 N	98·29 W
212	Cassinga (kä-sĭŋ'gȧ) Ang.	15·05 S	16·15 E
164	Cassino (käs-sē'nō) It.	41·30 N	13·50 E
109	Cass Lake (kăs) Mn.	47·23 N	94·37 W
104	Cassopolis (kăs-ŏ'pō-lĭs) Mi.	41·55 N	86·00 W
117	Cassville (kăs'vĭl) Mo.	36·41 N	93·52 W
162	Castanheira de Pêra (käs-tän-yā'rä-dĕ-pĕ'rä). Port.	40·00 N	8·07 W
160	Casteljaloux (käs-tĕl-zhä-lōō'). Fr.	44·20 N	0·04 E
163	Castellammare di Stabia (käs-tĕl-läm-mä'rā-dē-stä'byä) It. (Naples In.)	40·26 N	14·29 E
137	Castelli (kȧs-tĕ'zhē) Arg. (Buenos Aires In.)	36·07 S	57·48 W
163	Castellón de la Plana (käs-tĕl-yō'n-dĕ-lä-plä'nä). Sp.	39·59 N	0·05 W
160	Castelnaudary (kȧs'tĕl-nō-dȧ-rē') Fr.	43·20 N	1·57 E
137	Castelo (käs-tĕ'lô) Braz. (Rio de Janeiro In.)	21·37 S	41·13 W
162	Castelo Branco (käs-tā'lōō bräŋ'kōō). Port.	39·48 N	7·37 W
162	Castelo de Vide (käs-tā'lōō dĭ vē'dĭ). Port.	39·25 N	7·25 W
160	Castelsarrasin (kȧs'tĕl-sȧ-rȧ-zăN') Fr.	44·03 N	1·05 E
164	Castelvetrano (käs'tĕl-vē-trä'nō) It.	37·43 N	12·50 E
134	Castilla (kȧs-tē'l-yä) Peru	5·18 S	80·40 W
162	Castilla La Nueva (Reg.) (käs-tē'lyä lä nwā'vȧ). Sp.	39·15 N	3·55 W
162	Castilla La Vieja (Reg.) (käs-tēl'yä lä vyā'hä). Sp.	40·48 N	4·24 W
121	Castillo De San Marcos Natl. Mon. (käs-tē'lyā de-sän măr-kōs) Fl.	29·55 N	81·25 W
129	Castle (I.) (kȧs''l) Ba.	22·05 N	74·20 W
154	Castlebar (kȧs''l-bär) Ire.	53·55 N	9·15 W
115	Castle Dale (kȧs'l dāl) Ut.	39·15 N	111·00 W
148	Castle Donington (dŏn'ĭng-tŭn) Eng.	52·50 N	1·21 W
148	Castleford (kȧs''l-fērd) Eng.	53·43 N	1·21 W
93	Castlegar (kăs''l-gär) Can.	49·19 N	117·40 W
203	Castlemaine (käs''l-mān) Austl.	37·05 S	144·14 E
115	Castle Pk. Co.	39·00 N	106·50 W
110	Castlerock (kȧs''l-rŏk) Wa.	46·17 N	122·53 W
109	Castle Rock Res. Wi.	44·03 N	89·48 W
107	Castle Shannon (shăn'ŭn) Pa. (Pittsburgh In.)	40·22 N	80·02 W
107	Castleton (kȧs''l-tŏn) In. (Indianapolis In.)	39·54 N	86·03 W
100	Castor (R.) (kȧs'tôr) Can (Ottawa In.)	45·16 N	75·14 W
117	Castor (R.) Mo.	36·59 N	89·53 W
160	Castres (kȧs'tr') Fr.	43·36 N	2·13 E
127	Castries (kȧs-trē'). St. Lucia (In.)	14·01 N	61·00 W
136	Castro (käs'trōō) Braz.	24·56 S	50·00 W
136	Castro (käs'tro) Chile	42·27 S	73·48 W
162	Castro Daire (käs'trōō dīr'ĭ). Port.	40·56 N	7·57 W
162	Castro de Río (käs-trō-dĕ-rē'ō) Sp.	37·42 N	4·28 W
161	Castrop Rauxel (käs'trōp rou'ksĕl). F.R.G. (Ruhr In.)	51·33 N	7·19 E
162	Castro Urdiales (käs'trō ōōr-dyä'läs). Sp.	43·23 N	3·11 W
112	Castro Valley Ca. (San Francisco In.)	37·42 N	122·05 W
162	Castro Verde (käs-trō vĕr'dĕ). Port.	37·43 N	8·05 W
164	Castrovillari (käs'trō-vēl-lyä'rē) It.	39·48 N	16·11 E
162	Castuera (käs-tōō-ā'rä) Sp.	38·43 N	5·33 W
217	Casula Moz.	15·25 S	33·40 E
129	Cat (I.) Ba.	25·30 N	75·30 W
126	Catacamas (kä-tä-kä'mäs). Hond.	14·52 N	85·55 W
137	Cataguases (kä-tä-gwȧ'sĕs) Braz. (Rio de Janeiro In.)	21·23 S	42·42 W
119	Catahoula L. (kăt-ȧ-hōō'lȧ) La.	31·35 N	92·20 W
135	Catalão (kä-tä-louN') Braz.	18·09 S	47·42 W
129	Catalina (I.) (kä-tä-lē'nä) Dom. Rep.	18·20 N	69·00 W

ng-sing; ŋ-baŋk; N-nasalized n; nŏd; cŏmmit; ōld; ôbey; ôrder; fōōd; fŏŏt; ou-out; s-soft; sh-dish; th-thin; pūre; ûnite; ûrn; stŭd; circŭs; ü-as "y" in study; '-indeterminate vowel.

Page	Name Pronunciation Region	Lat. °'	Long. °'
163	Cataluma (Reg.) (kä-tä-lōō'mä) Sp.	41·23 N	0·50 E
136	Catamarca (Prov.) (kä-tä-mär'kä) Arg.	27·15 S	67·15 W
197	Catanduanes (I.) (kä-tän-dwä'nĕs) Phil.	13·55 N	125·00 E
135	Catanduva (kä-tån-dōō'vä) Braz.	21·12 S	48·47 W
164	Catania (kä-tä'nyä) It.	37·30 N	15·09 E
164	Catania, Golfo di (G.) (gôl-fô-dē-kå-tä'nyä). It.	37·24 N	15·28 E
197	Catanuan (kä-tä-nä'wän) Phil.	13·36 N	122·20 E
164	Catanzaro (kä-tän-dzä'rō) It.	38·53 N	16·34 E
163	Catarroja (kä-tär-rō'hä) Sp.	39·24 N	0·25 W
121	Catawba (L.) SC	35·02 N	81·21 W
121	Catawba (R.) (kå-tô'bå) NC	35·25 N	80·55 W
125	Catazajá, Laguna de (L.) (lä-gōō'nä-dĕ-kä-tä-zä-hä'). Mex.	17·45 N	92·03 W
197	Catbalogan (kät-bä-lō'gän) Phil.	11·45 N	124·52 E
125	Catemaco (kä-tā-mä'kō) Mex.	18·26 N	95·06 W
125	Catemaco, Lago (L.) (lä'gō-kä-tā-mä'kō). Mex.	18·23 N	95·04 W
148	Caterham (kā'tĕr-ŭm) Eng. (London In.)	51·16 N	0·04 W
216	Catete (kä-tĕ'tĕ) Ang.	9·06 S	13·43 E
118	Cathedral Mt. (kå-thē'drăl) Tx.	30·09 N	103·46 W
213	Cathedral Pk. (kå-thē'drăl) S. Afr. (Natal In.)	28·53 S	29·04 E
117	Catherine, L. (kă-thĕr-ĭn) Ar.	34·26 N	92·47 W
213	Cathkin Pk. (kăth'kĭn) S. Afr. (Natal In.)	29·08 S	29·22 E
112	Cathlamet (kăth-lăm'ĕt) Wa. (Portland In.)	46·12 N	123·53 W
104	Catlettsburg (kăt'lĕts-bûrg) Ky.	38·20 N	82·35 W
122	Catoche, C. (kä-tô'chĕ) Mex.	21·30 N	87·15 W
106	Catonsville (kā'tŭnz-vĭl) Md. (Baltimore In.)	39·16 N	76·45 W
124	Catorce (kä-tôr'så) Mex.	23·41 N	100·51 W
105	Catskill (kăts'kĭl) NY	42·15 N	73·50 W
105	Catskill Mts. NY	42·20 N	74·35 W
105	Cattaraugus Ind. Res. (kăt'tā-rå-gŭs). NY	42·30 N	79·05 W
135	Catu (kå-tōō) Braz.	12·26 S	38·12 W
216	Catuala Ang.	16·29 S	19·03 E
216	Catumbela (R.) (kä'tŏm-bĕl'å) Ang.	12·40 S	14·10 E
197	Cauayan (kou-ä'yän) Phil. (In.)	16·56 N	121·46 E
134	Cauca (R.) (kou'kä) Col.	7·30 N	75·26 W
135	Caucagua (käōō-kå'gwä). Ven. (In.)	10·17 N	66·22 W
171	Caucasus Mts. (kô'kå-sŭs). Sov. Un.	43·20 N	42·00 E
95	Cauchon L. (kô-shŏn') Can.	55·25 N	96·30 W
160	Cauderan (kō-dā-räN') Fr.	44·50 N	0·40 W
100	Caughnawaga Can. (Montreal In.)	45·24 N	73·41 W
164	Caulonia (kou-lō'nyä) It.	38·24 N	16·22 E
136	Cauquenes (kou-kā'nās) Chile	35·54 S	72·14 W
134	Caura (R.) (kou'rä) Ven.	6·48 N	64·40 W
98	Causapscal Can.	48·22 N	67·14 W
92	Caution, C. (kô'shŭn) Can.	51·10 N	127·47 W
129	Cauto (R.) (kou'tō) Cuba	18·35 N	76·20 W
184	Cauvery (R.) India	11·15 N	78·06 E
136	Cava (kå'vä) Braz. (In.)	22·41 S	43·26 W
163	Cava de' Tirreni (kä'vä-dĕ-tēr-rĕ'nē). It. (Naples In.)	40·27 N	14·43 E
162	Cavado (R.) (kä-vä'dō) Port.	41·43 N	8·08 W
135	Cavalcante (kä-väl-kän'tā) Braz.	13·45 S	47·33 W
108	Cavalier (kăv-å-lēr') ND	48·45 N	97·39 W
214	Cavally (R.) Ivory Coast-Lib.	6·30 N	8·20 W
154	Cavan (kăv'ăn) Ire.	54·01 N	7·00 W
164	Cavarzere (kä-vär'dzå-rā) It.	45·08 N	12·06 E
105	Cavendish (kăv'ĕn-dĭsh) Vt.	43·25 N	72·35 W
135	Caviana, Ilha (I.) (kä-vyä'nä) Braz.	0·45 N	49·33 W
197	Cavite (kä-vē'tā) Phil. (Manila In.)	14·30 N	120·54 E
148	Cawood (kā'wŏŏd) Eng.	53·49 N	1·07 W
137	Caxambu (kä-shå'm-bōō) Braz. (Rio de Janeiro In.)	22·00 S	44·45 W
135	Caxias (kä'shē-äzh) Braz.	4·48 S	43·16 W
136	Caxias do Sul (kä'shē-äzh-dô-sōō'l). Braz.	29·13 S	51·03 W
163	Caxine, Cap (C.) (kăp kăk'sēn) Alg.	36·47 N	2·52 E
216	Caxito (kä-shē'tŏŏ) Ang.	8·33 S	13·36 E
134	Cayambe (kå-īä'm-bĕ) Ec.	0·03 N	79·09 W
135	Cayenne (kā-ĕn') Fr. Gu.	4·56 N	52·18 W
124	Cayetano Rubio (kä-yĕ-tå-nô-rōō'byô). Mex.	20·37 N	100·21 W
123	Cayey...P. R. (Puerto Rico In.)	18·05 N	66·12 W
128	Cayman Brac (I.) (kī-män' bråk) Cayman Is.	19·45 N	79·50 W
128	Cayman Is. N. A.	19·30 N	80·30 W
128	Cay Sal Bk. (kē-săl) Ba.	23·55 N	80·20 W
105	Cayuga (L.) (kā-yōō'gå) NY	42·35 N	76·35 W
162	Cazalla de la Sierra (kä-thäl'yä-dĕ-lä-sē-ĕ'r-rä). Sp.	37·55 N	5·48 W
160	Cazaux, Étang de (L.) (ā-täN' dĕ kä-zō'). Fr.	44·32 N	0·59 W
105	Cazenovia (kăz-ē-nō'vĭ-å) NY	42·55 N	75·50 W
106	Cazenovia Cr...NY (Buffalo In.)	42·49 N	78·45 W
164	Čazma (chäz'mä) Yugo.	45·44 N	16·39 E
212	Cazombo (kä-zō'm-bō) Ang.	12·25 S	22·40 E
125	Cazones (R.) (kä-zō'nĕs) Mex.	20·37 N	97·28 W
128	Cazones, Ensenada de (B.) (ĕn-sĕ-nä-dä-dĕ-kä-zō'nås). Cuba	22·05 N	81·30 W
128	Cazones, Golfo de (G.) (gôl-fô-dĕ-kä-zō'nås). Cuba	23·55 N	81·15 W
162	Cazorla (kä-thôr'lå) Sp.	37·55 N	2·58 W
162	Cea (R.) (thā'ä) Sp.	42·18 N	5·10 W
	Ceará, see Fortaleza		
135	Ceará (State) (sā-å-rä') Braz.	5·13 S	39·43 W
135	Ceará-Mirim (sā-ä-rä'mē-rē'N) Braz.	6·00 S	35·13 W
127	Cebaco, Isla (I.) (ĕ's-lä-så-bä'kō) Pan.	7·27 N	81·08 W
115	Cebolla Cr. (sē-bōl'yä) Co.	38·15 N	107·10 W
162	Cebollera, Sierra (Mts.) (sē-ĕ'r-rä-sĕ-bôl-yĕ-rä). Sp.	42·03 N	2·53 W
162	Cebreros (sĕ-brĕ'rôs) Sp.	40·28 N	4·28 W
197	Cebu (sā-bōō') Phil.	10·22 N	123·49 E
106	Cecil (sē'sĭl)...Pa. (Pittsburgh In.)	40·20 N	80·10 W
109	Cedar (R.) Ia.	42·23 N	92·07 W
112	Cedar (R.)....Wa. (Portland In.)	45·56 N	122·32 W
109	Cedar (R.) West Fk. Ia.	42·49 N	93·10 W
119	Cedar Bay Tx. (In.)	29·54 N	94·58 W
115	Cedar Breaks Natl. Mon. Ut.	37·35 N	112·55 W
109	Cedarburg (sē'dēr bûrg) Wi.	43·23 N	88·00 W
115	Cedar City Ut.	37·40 N	113·10 W
108	Cedar Cr. ND	46·05 N	102·10 W
109	Cedar Falls Ia.	42·31 N	92·29 W
120	Cedar Keys Fl.	29·06 N	83·03 W
106	Cedar Lake....In. (Chicago In.)	41·22 N	87·27 W
106	Cedar L.....In. (Chicago In.)	41·23 N	87·25 W
109	Cedar Rapids Ia.	42·00 N	91·43 W
104	Cedar Springs Mi.	43·15 N	85·40 W
120	Cedartown (sē'dēr-toun) Ga.	34·00 N	85·15 W
213	Cedarville (cēdår'vĭl) S. Afr. (Natal In.)	30·23 S	29·04 E
124	Cedral (sā-dräl') Mex.	23·47 N	100·42 W
126	Cedros (sā'drōs) Hond.	14·36 N	87·07 W
122	Cedros (I.) Mex.	28·10 N	115·10 W
204	Ceduna (sē-dŏŏ'nå) Austl.	32·15 S	133·55 E
164	Cefalú (chā-fä-lōō') It.	38·01 N	14·01 E
162	Cega (R.) (thā'gä) Sp.	41·25 N	4·27 W
159	Cegléd (tsā'glād) Hung.	47·10 N	19·49 E
165	Ceglie (chĕ'lyĕ) It.	40·39 N	17·32 E
162	Cehegín (thā-å-hēn') Sp.	38·05 N	1·48 W
129	Ceiba del Agua (sā'bä-dĕl-å'gwä) Cuba (In.)	22·08 N	82·38 W
210	Cekhira Tun.	34·17 N	10·06 E
216	Cela (sĕ-lå) Ang.	11·25 S	15·07 E
124	Celaya (sā-lä'yä) Mex.	20·33 N	100·49 W
196	Celebes Sea Indon.	3·45 N	121·52 E
126	Celestún (sĕ-lĕs-tōō'n)..Mex. (In.)	20·57 N	90·18 W
104	Celina (sēlī'na) Oh.	40·30 N	84·35 W
164	Celje (tsĕl'yĕ) Yugo.	46·13 N	15·17 E
158	Celle (tsĕl'ē) F.R.G.	52·37 N	10·05 E
116	Cement (sē-mĕnt') Ok.	34·56 N	98·07 W
135	Ceniza, Pico (Mtn.) (pē'kô-sĕ-nē'zä). Ven. (In.)	10·24 N	67·26 W
160	Cenon (sĕ-nôN') Fr.	44·51 N	0·33 W
119	Center (sĕn'tĕr) Tx.	31·50 N	94·10 W
120	Centerhill Res. (sĕn'tĕr-hĭl) Tn.	36·02 N	86·00 W
107	Center Line (sĕn'tĕr lĭn) Mi. (Detroit In.)	42·29 N	83·01 W
109	Centerville (sĕn'tĕr-vĭl) Ia.	40·44 N	92·48 W
113	Centerville. Mn. (Minneapolis, St. Paul In.)	45·10 N	93·03 W
107	Centerville...Pa. (Pittsburgh In.)	40·02 N	79·58 W
108	Centerville SD	43·07 N	96·56 W
113	Centerville Ut. (Salt Lake City In.)	40·55 N	111·53 W
134	Central, Cordillera (Mts.) (kôr-dĕl-yĕ'rä-sĕn-trä'l). Bol.	19·18 S	65·29 W
134	Central, Cordillera (Mts.) Col. (In.)	3·58 N	75·55 W
129	Central, Cordillera (Cibao Mts.) (kôr-dēl-yā'rä sĕn'träl) (sē-bä'ō) Dom. Rep.	19·05 N	71·30 W
197	Central Cordillera (Mts.) (kôr-dēl-yĕ'rä-sĕn'träl) Phil. (In.)	17·05 N	120·55 E
209	Central African Republic Afr.	7·50 N	21·00 E
122	Central America (ä-mĕr'ĭ-kå) N. A.	10·45 N	87·15 W
120	Central City (sĕn'trăl) Ky.	37·15 N	87·09 W
108	Central City (sĕn'trăl sĭ'tĭ) Ne.	41·07 N	98·00 W
106	Central Falls (sĕn'trăl fôlz) RI (Providence In.)	41·54 N	71·23 W
104	Centralia (sĕn-trā'lĭ-å) Il.	38·35 N	89·05 W
117	Centralia Mo.	39·11 N	92·07 W
110	Centralia Wa.	46·42 N	122·58 W
171	Central Plat. Sov. Un.	55·00 N	33·30 E
106	Central Valley NY (New York In.)	41·19 N	74·07 W
113	Centreville (sĕn'tĕr-vĭl) Il. (St. Louis In.)	38·33 N	90·06 W
105	Centreville Md.	39·05 N	76·05 W
197	Centro (sĕ'n-trô) Phil .(In.)	17·16 N	121·48 E
120	Century (sĕn'tû-rĭ) Fl.	30·57 N	87·15 W
	Cephalonia (I.), see Kefallinéa		
160	Céret (sā-rĕ') Fr.	42·29 N	2·47 E
134	Cereté (sĕ-rĕ-tĕ') Col.	8·56 N	75·58 W
164	Cerignola (chā-rē-nyô'lä) It.	41·16 N	15·55 E
164	Cerknica (tsĕr'knē-tsä) Yugo.	45·48 N	14·21 E
118	Cerralvo (sĕr-räl'vō) Mex.	26·05 N	99·37 W
122	Cerralvo (I.) Mex.	24·00 N	109·59 W
134	Cerrito (sĕr-rē'-tô) Col. (In.)	3·41 N	76·17 W
124	Cerritos (sĕr-rē'tôs) Mex.	22·26 N	100·16 W
127	Cerro Chirripo (Mt.) (chē-rē'pō) C. R.	9·30 N	83·31 W
134	Cerro de Pasco (sĕr'rō dā päs'kō) Peru	10·45 S	76·14 W
118	Cerro Gordo, Arroyo de (är-rō-yô-dĕ-sĕ'r-rô-gôr-dŏ). Mex.	26·12 N	104·06 W
134	Certegui (sĕr-tĕ'gē) Col. (In.)	5·21 N	76·35 W
197	Cervantes (sĕr-vän'tās)..Phil (In.)	16·59 N	120·42 E
162	Cervantes (thĕr-vän'tās) Sp.	42·43 N	7·04 W
162	Cervera del Río Alhama (thĕr-vā'rä dĕl rē'ō-äl-ä'mä). Sp.	42·02 N	1·55 W
163	Cerveteri (chĕr-vĕ'tĕ-rē) It. (Rome In.)	42·00 N	12·06 E
164	Cesena (chĕ'sĕ-nä) It.	44·08 N	12·16 E
157	Cēsis (sā'sĭs) Sov. Un.	57·19 N	25·17 E
158	Česká Lípa (chĕs'kä lē'pa). Czech.	50·41 N	14·31 E
158	České (Bohemia) (Prov.) (chĕs'kā) (bō-hē'mĭ-å). Czech.	49·51 N	13·55 E
158	České Budějovice (chĕs'kā bōō'dyĕ-yō-vēt-sĕ). Czech.	49·00 N	14·30 E
158	Ceskomoravaska Vysočina (Mts.) Czech.	49·21 N	15·40 E
165	Cesme (chĕsh'mĕ) Tur.	38·20 N	26·20 E
203	Cessnock Austl.	32·58 S	151·15 E
214	Cestos (R.) Lib.	7·40 N	9·17 W
165	Cetinje (tsĕt'ĭn-yĕ) Yugo.	42·23 N	18·55 E
210	Ceuta (Sp.) (thā-ōō'tä) Afr.	36·04 N	5·36 W
160	Cévennes (Reg.) (sā-vĕn') Fr.	44·20 N	3·48 E
153	Ceyhan (R.) Tur.	37·19 N	36·06 E
	Ceylon, see Sri Lanka		
112	Chabot (L.) (sha'bŏt) Ca. (San Francisco In.)	37·44 N	122·06 W
137	Chacabuco (chä-kä-bōō'kō) Arg. (Buenos Aires In.)	34·37 S	60·27 W
125	Chacaltianguis (chä-käl-tē-äŋ'gwēs). Mex.	18·18 N	95·50 W
134	Chachapoyas (chä-chä-poi'yäs) Peru	6·16 S	77·48 W
136	Chaco (Prov.) (chä'kō) Arg.	26·00 S	60·45 W
115	Chaco Can. Natl. Mon. (chä'kô) NM	35·38 N	108·06 W
92	Chacon, C. (chăk'ŏn) Ak.	54·42 N	132·00 W
174	Chad (chäd). Sov. Un. (Urals In.)	56·33 N	57·11 E
209	Chad Afr.	17·48 N	19·00 E
215	Chad, L. Chad.	13·55 N	13·40 E
121	Chadbourn (chăd'bŭrn) NC	34·19 N	78·55 W
108	Chadron (chăd'rŭn) Ne.	42·50 N	103·10 W
162	Chafarinas (C.) Mor.	35·08 N	2·20 W
117	Chaffee (chăf'ē) Mo.	37·10 N	89·39 W
186	Chāgal Hills Afg.-Pak.	29·15 N	63·28 E
166	Chagodoshcha (R.) (chä-gō-dôsh-chä). Sov. Un.	59·08 N	35·13 E
127	Chagres R. (chä'grĕs) Pan.	9·18 N	79·22 W
107	Chagrin R. (shå'grĭn) Oh. (Cleveland In.)	41·34 N	81·24 W
107	Chagrin Falls (shå'grĭn fôls) Oh. (Cleveland In.)	41·26 N	81·23 W
192	Ch'ahaerh (Reg.) (chä'här). China	44·25 N	115·00 E
186	Chāh Bahār (chä'h' bă'hăr) Iran	25·18 N	60·45 E
217	Chake Chake Tan.	5·15 S	39·46 E
194	Chalantun (chä'län-tōōn') China	47·59 N	122·56 E
126	Chalatenango (chäl-ä-tĕ-näŋ'gō) Sal.	14·04 N	88·54 W
217	Chalbi Des. Ken.	3·40 N	36·50 E
125	Chalcatongo (chäl-kä-tôŋ'gō) Mex.	17·04 N	97·41 W
124	Chalchihuites (chäl-chē-wē'tås) Mex.	23·28 N	103·57 W
126	Chalchuapa (chäl-chwä'pä) Sal.	14·01 N	89·39 W
125	Chalco (chäl-kō) Mex. (In.)	19·15 N	98·54 W
98	Chaleur Bay (shå-lûr') Can.	48·07 N	64·50 W
148	Chalgrove (chăl'grôv) (Eng. (London In.)	51·38 N	1·05 W
193	Chaling (chä'lĭng) China	27·00 N	118·30 E
106	Chalmette (shăl-mĕt') La. (New Orleans In.)	29·57 N	89·57 W
160	Châlons-sur-Marne (shå-lôN'sür-märn). Fr.	48·57 N	4·23 E
160	Chalon-sur-Saône Fr.	46·47 N	4·54 E
136	Chaltel, Cerro (Mtn.) (sĕ'r-rô-chäl'tĕl). Arg.-Chile	48·10 S	73·18 W
115	Chama (R.) (chä'mä) NM	36·19 N	106·31 W
126	Chama, Sierra de (Mts.) (sē-ĕ'r-rä-dĕ-chä-mä). Guat.	15·48 N	90·20 W
160	Chamalières (shä-mä-lyår) Fr.	45·45 N	2·59 E
217	Chamama Malawi	12·55 S	33·43 E
184	Chaman (chŭm,-än') Pak.	30·58 N	66·21 E
184	Chambal (R.) (chŭm-bäl') India	26·05 N	76·37 E
108	Chamberlain (chām'bĕr-lĭn) SD	43·48 N	99·21 W
98	Chamberlain (L.) Me.	46·15 N	67·05 W
105	Chambersburg (chām'bĕrz-bûrg) Pa.	40·00 N	77·40 W
161	Chambéry (shäm-bā-rē') Fr.	45·35 N	5·54 E
217	Chambeshi (R.) Zambia	10·35 S	31·20 E
106	Chamblee (chăm-blē') Ga. (Atlanta In.)	33·35 N	84·18 W
100	Chambly (shäN-blē') Can. (Montreal In.)	45·27 N	73·17 W
161	Chambly Fr. (Paris In.)	49·11 N	2·14 E
91	Chambord Can.	48·22 N	72·01 W
127	Chame, Punta (Pt.) (pōō'n-tä-chä'må). Pan.	8·41 N	79·27 W
126	Chamelecón R. (chä-mĕ-lĕ-kô'n) Hond.	15·09 N	88·42 W
161	Chamonix (shå-mô-nē') Fr.	45·55 N	6·50 E
160	Champagne (Reg.) (shäm-pän'yĕ). Fr.	48·53 N	4·48 E
104	Champaign (shăm-pān') Il.	40·10 N	88·15 W
184	Champdāni India (In.)	22·48 N	88·21 E
126	Champerico (chăm-på-rĕ'kō) Guat.	14·18 N	91·55 W
109	Champion (chăm'pĭ-ŭn) Mi.	46·30 N	87·59 W
105	Champlain, L. (shăm-plān') NY-Vt.	44·45 N	73·20 W
161	Champlitte (shäN-plēt') Fr.	47·38 N	5·28 E
125	Champotón (chäm-pō-tōn') Mex.	19·21 N	90·43 W
125	Champotón (R.) Mex.	19·19 N	90·15 W
136	Chanaral (chän-yä-räl') Chile	26·20 S	70·46 W
162	Chanca (R.) . (chäŋ'kä) Sp.-Port.	38·15 N	7·22 W
193	Chanchiang (Fort Bayard). China	21·20 N	110·28 E
120	Chandeleur Is. (shăn-dē-lōōr'). La.	29·53 N	88·35 W
120	Chandeleur Sd. La.	29·47 N	89·08 W
184	Chandīgarh India	30·51 N	77·13 E
91	Chandler (chăn'dlĕr) Can.	48·21 N	64·41 W
117	Chandler Ok.	35·42 N	96·52 W
184	Chandrapur India	19·58 N	79·21 E
190	Chang (R.) (jäng) China	36·17 N	114·31 E
212	Changane (R.) Moz.	22·42 S	32·46 E
217	Changara Moz.	16·54 S	33·14 E
190	Ch'angch'ichuang (chäng'chē'zhōōäng). China	37·59 N	116·57 E
192	Ch'angchih China	35·58 N	112·58 E
190	Ch'angch'ing (chäng'chĭng). China	36·33 N	116·42 E

ăt; finăl; rāte; senåte; ärm; åsk; sofå; fâre; ch-choose; dh-as th in other; bē; ēvent; bĕt; recĕnt; cratĕr; g-go; gh-guttural g; bĭt; ĭ-short neutral; rīde; K-guttural k as ch in German ich;

PRONOUNCING INDEX

Changch'iu — Chernovtsy 267

Page	Name Pronunciation Region	Lat. °'	Long. °'
190	Changch'iu (zhängchĭû) China	36·50 N	117·29 E
190	Ch'angchou China	31·47 N	119·56 E
193	Changchou China	24·35 N	117·45 E
192	Ch'angch'un (Hsinking) (chäng'cho͞on') (hsĭn'kĭng) China	43·55 N	125·25 E
190	Ch'anghsing Tao (I.) (chängsĭng dou). China	39·38 N	121·10 E
192	Ch'anghsintien China (In.)	39·49 N	116·12 E
193	Changhua (chäng'hwä') Taiwan	24·02 N	120·32 E
190	Changhutien (jang'ho͞o'dĭan) China	32·07 N	114·44 E
190	Ch'angi (jäng'yē) China	36·51 N	119·23 E
194	Changjōn (chäng'jŭn') Kor.	38·38 N	128·02 E
192	Changkochuang China (In.)	40·09 N	116·56 E
192	Changkuangts'ai Ling (Mts.) China	43·50 N	127·55 E
190	Ch'angli (chäng'lē') China	39·46 N	119·10 E
192	Changpei (chäng'pē') China	41·12 N	114·50 E
194	Changsan Cot (I.) Kor.	38·06 N	124·50 E
193	Ch'angsha China	28·20 N	113·00 E
190	Ch'angshan Liehtao (Is.) (chäng'shän' lĭĕdou). China	39·08 N	122·26 E
190	Ch'angshan Tao (I.) (chäng'shän' dou). China	37·56 N	120·42 E
190	Ch'angshu (chäng'sho͞o') China	31·40 N	120·45 E
193	Ch'angte (chäng'tĕ') China	29·00 N	111·38 E
193	Changting China	25·50 N	116·18 E
188	Ch'angtu (chäng'to͞o') China	31·06 N	96·30 E
194	Changtu China	43·00 N	124·02 E
190	Ch'angtzu Tao (I.) (chäng'zho͞o dou). China	39·02 N	122·44 E
192	Changwu (chäng'wo͞o') China	35·12 N	107·45 E
194	Changwu China	42·21 N	123·00 E
188	Changyeh China	38·46 N	101·00 E
190	Ch'angyüan (chäng'yü-än'). China	35·10 N	114·41 E
113	Chanhassen (shăn'hăs-sĕn) Mn. (Minneapolis, St. Paul In.)	44·52 N	93·32 W
190	Chanhua (jän'ho͞oä) China	37·42 N	117·49 E
146	Channel Is. (chăn'ĕl) Eur.	49·15 N	3·30 W
91	Channel-Port-aux-Basques Can.	47·35 N	59·11 W
119	Channelview (chăn'elvū). Tx. (In.)	29·46 N	95·07 W
192	Chanping China	40·12 N	116·10 E
162	Chantada (chän-tä'dä) Sp.	42·38 N	7·36 W
196	Chanthaburi Thai.	12·37 N	102·04 E
161	Chantilly (shäɴ-tē-yē') Fr. (Paris In.)	49·12 N	2·30 E
106	Chantilly (shăn'tĭlē) Va. (Baltimore In.)	38·53 N	77·26 W
90	Chantrey Inlet (chăn-trē) Can.	67·49 N	94·30 W
117	Chanute (shȧ-no͞ot') Ks.	37·41 N	95·27 W
172	Chany (L.) (chä'nē) Sov. Un.	54·15 N	77·31 E
192	Chanyü China	44·30 N	122·30 E
193	Ch'aoan (chä'ō-än') China	23·48 N	117·10 E
190	Ch'aohsien (chou'sĭän) China	31·37 N	117·50 E
190	Chaohsien China	37·46 N	114·48 E
196	Chao Phraya, Mae Nam (R.) Thai.	16·13 N	99·33 E
190	Ch'aoshui (jĭouso͞oĭ) China	37·43 N	120·56 E
193	Chaot'ung (chä'ō-to͝ong) China	27·18 N	103·50 E
193	Ch'aoyang (chä'ō-yäng') China	23·18 N	116·32 E
192	Ch'aoyang (Foshan) China	41·32 N	120·20 E
190	Chaoyüan (chä'ō-yü-än') China	37·22 N	120·23 E
135	Chapada, Serra da (Mts.) (sĕ'r-rä-dä-shä-pä'dä). Braz.	14·57 S	54·34 W
137	Chapadão Serra do (Mtn.) (sĕ'r-rä-dô-shä-pä-dou'ɴ) Braz. (Rio de Janeiro In.)	20·31 S	46·20 W
124	Chapala, Lago de (L.) (lä'gô-dĕ-chä-pä'lä). Mex.	20·14 N	103·02 W
124	Chapalagana (R.) (chä-pä-lä-gȧ'nä). Mex.	22·11 N	104·09 W
134	Chaparral (chä-pär-rȧ'l). Col. (In.)	3·44 N	75·28 W
124	Chapata (chä-pá'tä) Mex.	20·18 N	103·10 W
171	Chapayevsk (châ-pī'ĕfsk). Sov. Un.	53·00 N	49·30 E
121	Chapel Hill (chăp''l hĭl) NC	35·55 N	79·05 W
112	Chaplain (L.) (chăp'lĭn) Wa. (Seattle In.)	47·58 N	121·50 W
91	Chapleau (chăp-lō') Can.	47·43 N	83·28 W
93	Chapman, Mt. (chăp'mȧn) Can.	51·50 N	118·20 W
212	Chapman's B. (chăp'mȧns bā) S. Afr. (In.)	34·06 S	18·17 E
108	Chappell (chă-pĕl') Ne.	41·06 N	102·29 W
125	Chapultenango (chä-po͞ol-tē-näŋ'gō). Mex.	17·19 N	93·08 W
216	Chá Pungana Ang.	13·44 S	18·39 E
124	Charcas (chär'käs) Mex.	23·09 N	101·09 W
127	Charco de Azul, Bahia (B.) (bä-ē'ä-chä'r-kô-dĕ-ä-zo͞o'l). Pan.	8·14 N	82·45 W
147	Chardzhou (chēr-jô'o͞o). Sov. Un.	38·52 N	63·37 E
160	Charente (R.) (shȧ-räɴt') Fr.	45·48 N	0·28 W
215	Chari (R.) (shä-rē') Chad	10·55 N	15·45 E
148	Charing (chă'rĭng) Eng. (London In.)	51·13 N	0·49 E
109	Chariton (chăr'ĭ-tŭn) Ia.	41·02 N	93·16 W
117	Chariton (R.) Mo.	40·24 N	92·38 W
100	Charlemagne (shärl-mäny') Can. (Montreal In.)	45·43 N	73·29 W
155	Charleroi (shȧr-lē-rwä') Bel.	50·25 N	4·35 E
107	Charleroi (shär'lē-roi) Pa. (Pittsburgh In.)	40·08 N	79·54 W
121	Charles, C. (chärlz) Va.	37·05 N	75·48 W
100	Charlesbourg (shȧrl-bo͞or') Can. (Quebec In.)	46·51 N	71·16 W
109	Charles City (chärlz) Ia.	43·03 N	92·40 W
104	Charleston (chärlz'tŭn) Il.	39·30 N	88·10 W
120	Charleston Ms.	34·00 N	90·02 W
117	Charleston Mo.	36·53 N	89·20 W
121	Charleston SC	32·47 N	79·56 W
104	Charleston WV	38·20 N	81·35 W
107	Charlestown (chärlz'toun) In. (Louisville In.)	38·46 N	85·39 W
127	Charlestown St. Kitts-Nevis-Anguilla (In.)	17·10 N	62·32 W
216	Charlesville Zaire	5·27 S	20·58 E
203	Charleville (chär'lē-vĭl) Austl.	26·16 S	146·28 E
160	Charleville Mézières (shärl-vēl') Fr.	49·48 N	4·41 E
104	Charlevoix (shär'lē-voi) Mi.	45·20 N	86·15 W
109	Charlevoix, L. Mi.	45·17 N	85·43 W
104	Charlotte (shär'lŏt) Mi.	42·35 N	84·50 W
121	Charlotte NC	35·15 N	80·50 W
123	Charlotte Amalie (St. Thomas) (shär-lŏt'ĕ ä-mä'lĭ-ȧ). Virgin Is. (U. S. A.) (St. Thomas In.)	18·21 N	64·54 W
92	Charlotte L. Can.	52·07 N	125·30 W
121	Charlotte Hbr. Fl. (In.)	26·47 N	81·58 W
156	Charlottenberg (shär-lŭt'ĕn-bĕrg) Swe.	59·53 N	12·17 E
105	Charlottesville (shär'lŏtz-vĭl). Va.	38·00 N	78·25 W
99	Charlottetown (shär'lŏt-toun) Can.	46·14 N	63·08 W
204	Charlotte Waters (shär'lŏt). Austl.	26·00 S	134·50 E
161	Charmes (shärm) Fr.	48·23 N	6·19 E
148	Charnwood Forest (chärn'wo͝od) Eng.	52·42 N	1·15 W
100	Charny (shär-nē') Can. (Quebec In.)	46·43 N	71·16 W
184	Charol Tsho (L.) China	34·00 N	81·47 E
161	Chars (shär) Fr. (Paris In.)	49·09 N	1·57 E
187	Chārsadda (chŭr-sä'dä) Pak. (Khyber Pass In.)	34·17 N	71·43 E
205	Charters Towers (chär'tērz). Austl.	20·03 S	146·20 E
161	Chartres (shärt'r'). Fr. (Paris In.)	48·26 N	1·29 E
137	Chascomús (chäs-kō-mo͞os') Arg. (Buenos Aires In.)	35·32 S	58·01 W
121	Chase City (chās) Va.	36·45 N	78·27 W
166	Chashniki (chäsh'nyē-kē). Sov. Un.	54·51 N	29·08 E
113	Chaska (chăs'kȧ) Mn. (Minneapolis, St. Paul In.)	44·48 N	93·36 W
160	Châteaubriant (shȧ-tō-brē-äɴ'). Fr.	47·43 N	1·23 W
160	Châteaudun (shä-tō-däɴ') Fr.	48·04 N	1·23 E
160	Château-Gontier (chȧ-tō'gôɴ tyā'). Fr.	47·48 N	0·43 W
100	Chateauguay (chȧ-tō-gā) Can. (Montreal In.)	45·22 N	73·45 W
100	Châteauguay (R.) Can. (Montreal In.)	45·13 N	73·51 W
160	Chateauneuf-les-Martigues (shä-tō-nûf'lā-mär-tēg'ĕ) Fr. (In.)	43·23 N	5·11 E
160	Château-Renault (shȧ-tō-rē-nō') Fr.	47·36 N	0·57 E
96	Château-Richer (shȧ-tō'rē-shā') Can. (Quebec In.)	47·00 N	71·01 W
160	Châteauroux (shȧ-tō-ro͞o') Fr.	46·47 N	1·39 E
160	Château-Thierry (shȧ-tō'tyĕr-rē') Fr.	49·03 N	3·22 E
160	Châtellerault (shä-tĕl-rō') Fr.	46·48 N	0·31 E
109	Chatfield (chăt'fēld) Mn.	43·50 N	92·10 W
90	Chatham (chăt'ȧm) Can.	42·25 N	82·10 W
98	Chatham Can.	47·02 N	65·28 W
148	Chatham (chăt'ăm) Eng. (London In.)	51·21 N	0·27 E
106	Chatham (chăt'ȧm) NJ (New York In.)	40·44 N	74·23 W
107	Chatham Oh. (Cleveland In.)	41·06 N	82·01 W
198	Chatham Is. N. Z.	44·00 S	178·00 W
92	Chatham Sd. Can.	54·32 N	130·35 W
101	Chatham Str. Ak.	57·00 N	134·40 W
113	Chatsworth (chătz'wûrth) Ca. (Los Angeles In.)	34·16 N	118·36 W
113	Chatsworth Res. Ca. (Los Angeles In.)	34·15 N	118·41 W
120	Chattahoochee (chăt-tȧ-ho͞o' chē) Fl.	30·42 N	84·47 W
120	Chattahoochee (R.) Al.-Ga.	31·17 N	85·10 W
120	Chattanooga (chăt-ȧ-no͞o'gȧ). Tn.	35·01 N	85·15 W
120	Chattooga (R.) (chȧ-to͞o'gȧ) Ga.-SC	34·47 N	83·13 W
97	Chaudière (R.) (shō-dyĕr') Can.	46·26 N	71·10 W
196	Chau Doc (shō-dôk') Camb.	10·49 N	104·57 E
160	Chaumont (shō-môɴ') Fr.	48·08 N	5·07 E
161	Chaumontel (shō-môɴ-tĕl') Fr. (Paris In.)	49·07 N	2·26 E
173	Chaunskaya Guba (B.). Sov. Un.	69·15 N	170·00 E
160	Chauny (shō-nē') Fr.	49·40 N	3·09 E
166	Chausy (chou'sĭ) Sov. Un.	53·57 N	30·58 E
105	Chautauqua (L.) (shȧ-tô'kwȧ). NY	42·10 N	79·25 W
170	Chavaniga Sov. Un.	66·02 N	37·50 E
162	Chaves (chä'vĕzh) Port.	41·44 N	7·30 W
124	Chavinda (chä-vē'n-dä) Mex.	20·01 N	102·27 W
125	Chazumba (chä-zo͞om'bä) Mex.	18·11 N	97·41 W
148	Cheadle (chē'd'l) Eng.	52·59 N	1·59 W
105	Cheat (R.) (chēt) WV	39·35 N	79·40 W
158	Cheb (kĕb) Czech.	50·05 N	12·23 E
174	Chebarkul (chĕ-bár-kûl') Sov. Un. (Urals In.)	54·59 N	60·22 E
170	Cheboksary (chyĕ-bôk-sä'rē) Sov. Un.	56·00 N	47·20 E
104	Cheboygan (shē-boi'gȧn) Mi.	45·40 N	84·30 W
210	Chech, Erg (Dune) Alg.	24·45 N	2·07 W
171	Chechen' (I.) (chyĕch'ĕn). Sov. Un.	44·00 N	48·10 E
190	Chech'eng (jĭŭcheng) China	34·05 N	115·19 E
	Chechiang (Prov.), see Chekiang		
117	Checotah (chē-kō'tȧ) Ok.	35·27 N	95·32 W
99	Chedabucto B. (chĕd-ȧ-bŭk-tō) Can.	45·23 N	61·10 W
196	Cheduba (I.) Bur.	18·45 N	93·01 E
94	Cheecham Hills (chē'hăm). Can.	56·20 N	111·10 W
107	Cheektowaga (chēk-tō-wä'gȧ) NY (Buffalo In.)	42·54 N	78·46 W
	Chefoo, see Yent'ai		
110	Chehalis (chē-hā'lĭs) Wa.	46·39 N	122·58 W
110	Chehalis R. Wa.	46·47 N	123·17 W
194	Cheju (chĕ'jo͞o') Kor.	33·29 N	126·40 E
194	Cheju (Quelpart) (I.) Kor.	33·20 N	126·25 E
166	Chekalin (chĕ-kä'lĭn) Sov. Un.	54·05 N	36·13 E
166	Chekao (jĭŭgou) China	31·47 N	117·44 E
189	Chekiang (Chechiang) (Prov.) China	29·30 N	120·00 E
216	Chela, Serra da (Mts.) (sĕr'rȧ dä shä'lȧ). Ang.	15·30 S	13·30 E
110	Chelan (chē-lăn') Wa.	47·51 N	119·59 W
193	Chelang Chiao (Pt.) China	22·38 N	116·00 E
110	Chelan R. Wa.	48·09 N	120·20 W
163	Cheleiros (shĕ-la'rōzh) Port. (Lisbon In.)	38·54 N	9·19 W
151	Chelic (Mt.) (shĕl-ĭk) Alg.	35·22 N	6·47 E
163	Chéliff, Oued (R.) (o͞o-ĕd shä-lĕf) Alg.	36·17 N	1·22 E
172	Chelkar (chyĕl'kär) Sov. Un.	47·52 N	59·41 E
171	Chelkar (L.) Sov. Un.	50·30 N	51·30 E
172	Chelkar Tengiz (L.) (chyĕl'kär tĕn'yēz). Sov. Un.	47·42 N	61·45 E
159	Chełm (kĕlm) Pol.	51·08 N	23·30 E
159	Chełmno (kĕlm'nō) Pol.	53·20 N	18·25 E
96	Chelmsford Can.	46·35 N	81·12 W
148	Chelmsford (chĕlm's-fērd) Eng. (London In.)	51·44 N	0·28 E
99	Chelmsford Ma. (In.)	42·36 N	71·21 W
106	Chelsea (chĕl'sē) Al. (Birmingham In.)	33·20 N	86·38 W
202	Chelsea Austl. (Melbourne In.)	38·05 S	145·08 E
100	Chelsea Can. (Ottawa In.)	45·30 N	75·46 W
99	Chelsea Ma. (In.)	42·23 N	71·02 W
104	Chelsea Mi.	42·20 N	84·00 W
117	Chelsea Ok.	36·32 N	95·23 W
154	Cheltenham (chĕlt'nȧm) Eng.	51·57 N	2·06 W
106	Cheltenham (chĕltēn-hăm) Md. (Baltimore In.)	38·45 N	76·50 W
163	Chelva (chĕl'vä) Sp.	39·43 N	1·00 W
174	Chelyabinsk (chĕl-yä-bēnsk') Sov. Un. (Urals In.)	55·10 N	61·25 E
173	Chelyuskin, Mys (C.) (chĕl-yo͞os'-kĭn). Sov. Un.	77·45 N	104·45 E
217	Chemba Moz.	17·08 S	34·52 E
160	Chemille (shē-mē-yā') Fr.	47·13 N	0·46 W
	Chemnitz, see Karl-Marx-Stadt		
105	Chemung (R.) (shē-mŭng) NY	42·20 N	77·25 W
173	Chĕn, Gora (Mtn.) Sov. Un.	65·13 N	142·12 E
184	Chenāb (R.) (chē-näb) Pak.	31·33 N	72·28 E
210	Chenachane (shē-nȧ-shän') Alg.	26·14 N	4·14 W
190	Chenchiang (jienjäng) China	32·13 N	119·24 E
110	Cheney (chē'nȧ) Wa.	47·29 N	117·34 W
190	Chengchou (jengjō) China	34·46 N	113·42 E
193	Ch'enghai China	23·22 N	116·40 E
193	Chengku China	33·05 N	107·25 E
192	Ch'engte (Jehol) (chĕng'tĕ') (rē-hŏl'). China	40·50 N	117·50 E
190	Chengting (chengding) China	38·10 N	114·35 E
193	Ch'engtu (chĕng'to͞o') China	30·30 N	104·10 E
190	Chengyang (chĕn'yäng') China	32·34 N	114·22 E
193	Ch'enshien China	25·40 N	113·00 E
191	Ch'entsun China (Canton In.)	22·58 N	113·14 E
192	Chentung China	45·28 N	123·42 E
193	Chenyüan (chĕn'yü-an') China	27·08 N	108·30 E
191	Chepei China (Canton In.)	23·07 N	113·23 E
134	Chepén (chĕ-pĕ'n) Peru	7·17 S	79·24 W
127	Chepo (chā'pō) Pan.	9·12 N	79·06 W
127	Chepo R. Pan.	9·10 N	78·36 W
160	Cher (R.) (shâr) Fr.	47·14 N	1·34 E
124	Cheran (chā-rän') Mex.	19·41 N	101·54 W
217	Cherangany Hills Ken.	1·25 N	35·20 E
121	Cheraw (chē'rô) SC	34·40 N	79·52 W
160	Cherbourg (shär-bo͞or') Fr.	49·39 N	1·43 W
210	Cherchell (shĕr-shĕl') Alg.	36·38 N	2·09 E
170	Cherdyn' (chĕr-dyēn') Sov. Un.	60·25 N	56·32 E
172	Cheremkhovo (chĕr'yĕm-kô-vō) Sov. Un.	52·58 N	103·18 E
174	Cherëmukhovo (chĕr-yĕ-mû-kô-vô). Sov. Un. (Urals In.)	60·20 N	60·00 E
211	Cheren (chĕr'ĕn) Eth.	15·46 N	38·28 E
172	Cherepanovo (chĕr'yĕ pä-nô'vô) Sov. Un.	54·13 N	83·18 E
166	Cherepovets (chĕr-yĕ-pô'vyĕtz) Sov. Un.	59·08 N	35·54 E
166	Chereya (chĕr-ā'yä) Sov. Un.	54·38 N	29·16 E
152	Chergui, Chott ech (L.) chĕr gē) Alg.	34·12 N	0·10 W
152	Chergui I. Tun.	34·48 N	11·41 E
166	Cherikov (chĕ'rē-kôf) Sov. Un.	53·34 N	31·22 E
167	Cherkassy (chĕr-kȧ'sĭ) Sov. Un.	49·26 N	32·03 E
167	Cherkassy (Oblast) Sov. Un.	48·58 N	30·55 E
172	Cherlak (chĭr-läk') Sov. Un.	54·04 N	74·28 E
174	Chermoz (chĕr-môz') Sov. Un. (Urals In.)	58·47 N	56·08 E
166	Chern' (chĕrn) Sov. Un.	53·28 N	36·49 E
167	Chërnaya Kalitva (R.) (chôr'nȧ yȧ kȧ-lēt'vȧ). Sov. Un.	50·15 N	39·16 E
167	Chernigov (chĕr-nē'gôf). Sov. Un.	51·28 N	31·18 E
167	Chernigov (Oblast) (chĕr-nē'gôf) Sov. Un.	51·23 N	31·15 E
167	Chernobay (chĕr-nō-bī'). Sov. Un.	49·41 N	32·24 E
167	Chernobyl' (chĕr-nō-bĭl') Sov. Un.	51·17 N	30·14 E
172	Chernogorsk (chĕr-nŏ-gôrsk') Sov. Un.	54·01 N	91·07 E
167	Chernogovka (chĕr-nô-gôf'kȧ) Sov. Un.	47·08 N	36·20 E
174	Chernoistochinsk (chĕr-nôy-stô'chĭnsk). Sov. Un. (Urals In.)	57·44 N	59·55 E
167	Chĕrnomorskoye (chĕr-nô-môr'skô-yĕ). Sov. Un.	45·29 N	32·43 E
159	Chernovtsy (Cernăuti) (chĭr-nôf'tsē) (chĕr-nou'tsĕ) Sov. Un.	48·18 N	25·56 E

268 Chernyakhovsk — Chipata PRONOUNCING INDEX

Page	Name Pronunciation Region	Lat. °′	Long. °′
157	Chernyakhovsk (chĕr-nyä′ĸôfsk).Sov. Un.	55·38 N	21·17 E
167	Chernyanka (chĕrn-yäŋ′kä) Sov. Un.	50·56 N	37·48 E
108	Cherokee (chĕr-ô-kē′).........Ia.	42·43 N	95·33 W
117	Cherokee...................Ks.	37·21 N	94·50 W
116	Cherokee...................Ok.	36·44 N	98·22 W
120	Cherokee (R.)...............Tn.	36·22 N	83·22 W
120	Cherokee Indian Res.........NC	35·33 N	83·12 W
128	Cherokee Sd.................Ba.	26·15 N	76·55 W
117	Cherokees, L. of the (chĕr-ô-kēz′).Ok.	36·32 N	95·14 W
98	Cherryfield (chĕr′ĭ-fēld)......Me.	44·37 N	67·56 W
112	Cherry Grove...Or. (Portland In.)	45·27 N	123·15 W
117	Cherryvale..................Ks.	37·16 N	95·33 W
121	Cherryville (chĕr′ĭ-vĭl)........NC	35·32 N	81·22 W
173	Cherskogo, Khrebet (Mts.) Sov. Un.	66·15 N	138·30 E
166	Cherven′ (chĕr′vyĕn)....Sov. Un.	53·43 N	28·26 E
166	Chervonoye (L.) (chĕr-vô′nô-yĕ) Sov. Un.	52·24 N	28·12 E
104	Chesaning (chĕs′ȧ-nĭng).......Mi.	43·10 N	84·10 W
106	Chesapeake (chĕs′ȧ-pēk) Va. (Norfolk In.)	36·48 N	76·16 W
105	Chesapeake B...............Md.	38·20 N	76·15 W
106	Chesapeake Beach Md. (Baltimore In.)	38·42 N	76·33 W
148	Chesham (chĕsh′ŭm) Eng. (London In.)	51·41 N	0·37 W
104	Cheshire (chĕsh′ĭr)...........Mi.	42·25 N	86·00 W
148	Cheshire (Co.)...............Eng.	53·16 N	2·30 W
170	Chëshskaya Guba (B.)...Sov. Un.	67·25 N	46·00 E
174	Chesma (chĕs′mȧ) Sov. Un. (Urals In.)	53·50 N	60·42 E
172	Chesnokovka (chĕs-nŏ-kôf′kȧ) Sov. Un.	53·28 N	83·41 E
148	Chester (chĕs′tẽr)...........Eng.	53·12 N	2·53 W
117	Chester......................Il.	37·54 N	89·48 W
106	Chester....Pa. (Philadelphia In.)	39·51 N	75·22 W
121	Chester.....................SC	34·42 N	81·11 W
121	Chester.....................Va.	37·20 N	77·24 W
104	Chester....................WV	40·35 N	80·30 W
148	Chesterfield (chĕs′tẽr-fēld)...Eng.	53·14 N	1·26 W
205	Chesterfield, Îsles.........N. Cal.	19·38 S	160·08 E
90	Chesterfield (Inlet)..........Can.	63·59 N	92·09 W
90	Chesterfield Inlet...........Can.	63·19 N	91·11 W
100	Chestermere L. (chĕs′tẽr-mẽr) Can. (Calgary In.)	51·03 N	113·45 W
104	Chesterton (chĕs′tẽr-tŭn)......In.	41·35 N	87·05 W
105	Chestertown (chĕs′tẽr-toun)..Md.	39·15 N	76·05 W
98	Chesuncook (chĕs′ŭn-kŏŏk)...Me.	46·03 N	69·40 W
109	Chetek (chĕ′tĕk).............Wi.	45·18 N	91·41 W
126	Chetumal, Bahía de (B.) (bä-ē-ä dĕ chĕt-ōō-mäl′) Belize (In.)	18·07 N	88·05 W
115	Chevelon Cr. (shĕv′ȧ-lŏn).....Az.	34·35 N	111·00 W
107	Cheviot (shĕv′ĭ-ŭt) Oh. (Cincinnati In.)	39·10 N	84·37 W
154	Cheviot Hills.........Scot.-Eng.	55·20 N	2·40 W
161	Chevreuse (shĕ-vrûz′) Fr. (Paris In.)	48·42 N	2·02 E
106	Chevy Chase (shĕvĭ chās) Md. (Baltimore In.)	38·58 N	77·06 W
211	Chew Bahir (Lake Stefanie) (stĕf-a-nē).Eth.	4·46 N	37·31 E
110	Chewelah (chē-wē′lä)........Wa.	48·17 N	117·42 W
190	Cheyang (R.) (Sĭyang).....China	33·42 N	119·40 E
108	Cheyenne (shī-ĕn′)..........Wy.	41·10 N	104·49 W
108	Cheyenne (R.)...............SD	44·20 N	102·15 W
108	Cheyenne River Ind. Res......SD	45·07 N	100·46 W
116	Cheyenne Wells..............Co.	38·46 N	102·21 W
184	Chhindwāra...............India	22·08 N	78·57 E
193	Chiachi...................China	19·10 N	110·28 E
193	Chiahsing.................China	30·45 N	120·50 E
193	Chiai (chī′ī′)............Taiwan	23·28 N	120·28 E
193	Chialing (R.)..............China	30·30 N	106·20 E
193	Chian.....................China	27·12 N	114·55 E
192	Chian.....................China	41·00 N	126·04 E
190	Chiangchanchi.............China	36·39 N	120·31 E
	Chiangshi (Prov.), see Kiangsi		
193	Chiangling.................China	30·30 N	112·10 E
188	Chiang Mai..................Thai.	18·38 N	98·44 E
196	Chiang Rai..................Thai.	19·53 N	99·48 E
	Chiangsu (Prov.), see Kiangsu		
190	Chiangyen (jĭäng′yĭn)......China	32·33 N	120·07 E
190	Chiangyin (jiäng′ĭn)........China	31·54 N	120·15 E
216	Chianje....................Ang.	15·45 S	13·48 E
190	Chiantochen (jĭäng′tô′jĕn) China	32·23 N	120·14 E
190	Chiaochou Wan (B.) (jĭou′zhēō wän).China	36·10 N	119·55 E
190	Chiaoho (jēou′hŭ).........China	38·03 N	116·18 E
192	Chiaoho....................China	43·40 N	127·20 E
190	Chiaohsien (jēou′sĭän)......China	36·18 N	120·01 E
191	Ch′iaot′ou....China (Canton In.)	22·55 N	113·39 E
190	Chiaow Shan (Mts.) (jēou shän) China	36·59 N	121·15 E
126	Chiapa, Rio de (R.) (rē-ô-dĕ-chē-ä′pä).Mex.	16·00 N	92·20 W
125	Chiapa de Corzo (chē-ä′pä dā kôr′zō).Mex.	16·44 N	93·01 W
122	Chiapas (State) (chē-ä′päs)..Mex.	17·10 N	93·00 W
125	Chiapas, Cordilla de (Mts.) (kôr-dēl-yĕ′rä-dĕ-chyä′räs).Mex.	15·55 N	93·15 W
164	Chiari (kyä′rē)..............It.	45·31 N	9·57 E
158	Chiasso....................Switz.	45·50 N	8·57 E
191	Chiating....China (Shanghai In.)	31·23 N	121·15 E
124	Chiautla (chyä-ōōt′lä).......Mex.	18·16 N	98·37 W
164	Chiavari (kyä-vä′rē)..........It.	44·18 N	9·21 E
193	Chiayü.....................China	33·00 N	114·00 E
195	Chiba (chē′bȧ)..Jap. (Tōkyō In.)	35·37 N	140·08 E
195	Chiba (Pref.)....Jap. (Tōkyō In.)	35·47 N	140·02 E
97	Chibougamau (chē-bōō′gä-mou) Can.	49·57 N	74·23 W
97	Chibougamau (L.)..........Can.	49·53 N	74·21 W
107	Chicago (shĭ-kô-gō) (chĭ-kȧ′gō) Il. (Chicago In.)	41·49 N	87·37 W
107	Chicago Heights (shĭ-kô′gō) (chĭ-kä′gō).Il. (Chicago In.)	41·30 N	87·38 W
216	Chicapa (R.) (chē-kä′pä)....Ang.	7·45 S	20·25 E
125	Chicbul (chēk-bōō′l)........Mex.	18·45 N	90·56 W
98	Chic-Chocs, Mts............Can.	48·38 N	66·37 W
101	Chichagof (I.) (chē-chä′gôf)...Ak.	57·50 N	137·00 W
126	Chichâncanab, Lago de (L.) (lä′gô-dĕ-chē-chän-kä-nä′b) Mex. (In.)	19·50 N	88·28 W
126	Chichen Itzá (Ruins) (chē-chĕ′n-ē-tsä′).Mex. (In.)	20·38 N	88·35 W
154	Chichester (chĭch′ĕs-tẽr).....Eng.	50·50 N	0·55 W
193	Chichiang..................China	29·05 N	106·40 E
190	Chichiashih (jĭ′jĭä′shē)......China	32·10 N	120·17 E
192	Ch′ich′ihaerh (Tsitsihar)...China	47·18 N	124·00 E
126	Chichimila (chē-chē-mē′lä) Mex. (In.)	20·36 N	88·14 W
135	Chichiriviche (chē-chē-rē-vē-chĕ) Ven. (In.)	10·56 N	68·17 W
120	Chickamauga (chĭk-ȧ-mô′gȧ)..Ga.	34·50 N	85·15 W
121	Chickamauga, (R.)...........Tn.	35·18 N	85·22 W
92	Chickamin (R.) (chĭk′ă-mĭn)..Ak.	55·50 N	131·00 W
120	Chickasawhay (R.) (chĭk-ȧ-sô′wā) Ms.	31·45 N	88·45 W
116	Chickasha (chĭk′ȧ-shā).......Ok.	35·04 N	97·56 W
162	Chiclana (chē-klä′nä).........Sp.	36·25 N	6·09 W
134	Chiclayo (chē-klä′yō)........Peru	6·46 S	79·50 W
114	Chico (chē′kō)...............Ca.	39·43 N	121·51 W
112	Chico..........Wa. (Seattle In.)	47·37 N	122·43 W
136	Chico (R.)...................Arg.	44·30 S	66·00 W
136	Chico (R.)...................Arg.	49·15 S	69·30 W
197	Chico (R.)............Phil. (In.)	17·33 N	121·24 E
217	Chicoa......................Moz.	15·37 S	32·24 E
125	Chicoloapan (chē-kō-lwä′pän) Mex. (In.)	19·24 N	98·54 W
125	Chiconautla (chē-kō-nä-ōō′tlȧ) Mex. (In.)	19·39 N	99·01 W
124	Chicontepec (chē-kōn′tĕ-pĕk′) Mex.	20·58 N	98·08 W
105	Chicopee (chĭk′ô-pē).........Ma.	42·10 N	72·35 W
96	Chicoutimi (shē-kōō′tē-mē′)..Can.	48·26 N	71·04 W
126	Chicxulub (chēk-sōō-lōō′b) Mex. (In.)	21·10 N	89·30 W
91	Chidley, C. (chĭd′lĭ).........Can.	60·32 N	63·56 W
110	Chief Joseph Dam............Wa.	48·00 N	119·39 W
120	Chiefland (chēf′lănd)..........Fl.	29·30 N	82·50 W
188	Ch′iehmo....................China	38·02 N	85·16 E
190	Chiehshou Hu (L.) (jĭeh′shō hōō) China	32·59 N	119·04 E
193	Chiehyang..................China	23·38 N	116·20 E
158	Chiem See (L.) (kēm zā)..F.R.G.	47·58 N	12·20 E
190	Chienchangying (jĭan′chang′yĭng) China	40·09 N	118·47 E
190	Chienkan (R.) (jĭan′gän)...China	39·35 N	117·34 E
193	Chienli....................China	29·50 N	112·52 E
193	Chienning..................China	26·50 N	116·55 E
193	Chienou.....................China	27·10 N	118·18 E
190	Ch′ienshanchen (chĭan′shän′jen) China	31·05 N	120·24 E
193	Chienshih..................China	30·40 N	109·45 E
193	Chienshui..................China	23·32 N	102·50 E
190	Ch′ienwei (chĭän′wā).......China	40·11 N	120·05 E
164	Chieri (kyâ′rē)...............It.	45·03 N	7·48 E
164	Chieti (kyĕ′tē)...............It.	42·22 N	14·22 E
167	Chigirin (chē-gē′rĕn).....Sov. Un.	49·02 N	32·39 E
124	Chignanuapan (chē′g-nä-nwä-pá′n) Mex.	19·49 N	98·02 W
104	Chignecto B. (shĭg-nĕk′tō)...Can.	45·33 N	64·50 W
101	Chignik (chĭg′nĭk)............Ak.	56·14 N	158·12 W
101	Chignik B....................Ak.	56·18 N	157·22 W
193	Chihchiang.................China	27·25 N	109·45 E
192	Ch′ihfeng (Wulanhata) (chĭ′fûng).China	42·18 N	118·52 E
190	Chihhochen (zhĭ′hŭ′jen)....China	32·32 N	117·57 E
190	Ch′ihsien (chĭ′hsyĕn′).......China	34·33 N	114·47 E
190	Chihsien....................China	35·25 N	114·03 E
190	Ch′ihsien....................China	35·36 N	114·13 E
190	Chihsien....................China	37·37 N	115·33 E
190	Chihsien....................China	40·03 N	117·25 E
118	Chihuahua (chē-wä′wä).......Mex.	28·37 N	106·06 W
122	Chihuahua (State)...........Mex.	29·00 N	107·30 W
212	Chicuane (chē-wä′nȧ).......Moz.	21·00 S	34·59 E
171	Chikishlyar (chē-kĕsh-lyär′) Sov. Un.	37·40 N	53·50 E
190	Ch′ik′ou (chē′kō)...........China	38·37 N	117·33 E
217	Chilanga...................Zambia	15·34 S	28·17 E
124	Chilapa (chē-lä′pä)..........Mex.	17·34 N	99·14 W
124	Chilchota (chēl-chō′tä)......Mex.	19·40 N	102·04 W
92	Chilcotin (R.) (chĭl-kō′tĭn)...Can.	52·20 N	124·15 W
116	Childress (chīld′rĕs)..........Tx.	34·26 N	100·11 W
133	Chile (chē′lā)...............S.A.	35·00 S	72·00 W
136	Chilecito (chē-lā-sē′tō).......Arg.	29·06 S	67·25 W
216	Chilengue, Serra do (Mts.)..Ang.	13·20 S	15·00 E
134	Chilí, Pico de (Pk.) (pē′kō-dĕ chē-lē′).Col. (In.)	4·14 N	75·38 W
122	Chilibre (chē-lē′brĕ)....Pan. (In.)	9·09 N	79·37 W
190	Ch′ili Hu (L.) (chē′lē hōō)..China	32·57 N	118·26 E
217	Chililabombwe (Bancroft) Zambia	12·18 S	27·43 E
192	Chilin (Kirin) (chĭl′ĭn′) (kĭr′ĭn) China	43·58 N	126·40 E
190	Chilip′ing (chē′lē′pĭng).....China	31·28 N	114·41 E
184	Chilka (L.).................India	19·26 N	85·42 E
92	Chilko (R.) (chĭl′kō)........Can.	52·00 N	124·15 W
92	Chilko L.....................Can.	51·20 N	124·05 W
136	Chillán (chēl-yän′).........Chile	36·44 S	72·06 W
104	Chillicothe (chĭl-ĭ-kŏth′ē)......Il.	41·55 N	89·30 W
117	Chillicothe..................Mo.	39·46 N	93·32 W
104	Chillicothe..................Oh.	39·20 N	83·00 W
93	Chilliwack (chĭl′ĭ-wăk).......Can.	49·10 N	121·57 W
136	Chiloé, Isla de (I.) (ē′s-lä-dĕ-chē-lō-ā′).Chile	43·00 S	76·30 W
124	Chilpancingo (chēl-pän-sēŋ′gō) Mex.	17·32 N	97·30 W
109	Chilton (chĭl′tŭn)............Wi.	44·00 N	88·12 W
193	Chilung (Kirin) (chĭ′lung).Taiwan	25·02 N	121·48 E
217	Chilwa, L...........Malawi-Moz.	14·45 S	35·45 E
112	Chimacum (chĭm′ä-kŭm) Wa. (Seattle In.)	48·01 N	122·47 W
125	Chimalpa (chē-mäl′pä).Mex. (In.)	19·26 N	99·22 W
126	Chimaltenango (chē-mäl-tā-näŋ′gō) Guat.	14·39 N	90·48 W
124	Chimaltitan (chēmäl-tē-tän′) Mex.	21·36 N	103·50 W
147	Chimbay (chĭm-bī′)......Sov. Un.	43·00 N	59·44 E
134	Chimborazo (Mtn.) (chēm-bô-rä′zō) Ec.	1·35 S	78·45 W
134	Chimbote (chēm-bō′tā)......Peru	9·02 S	78·33 W
172	Chimkent (chĭm-kĕnt)...Sov. Un.	42·17 N	69·42 E
190	Chimo (gē′mŭ)..........China	36·22 N	120·28 E
182	China (chī′nȧ)..............Asia	36·45 N	93·00 E
118	China (chē′nä)..............Mex.	25·43 N	99·13 W
126	Chinameca (chē-nä-mā′kä)....Sal.	13·31 N	88·18 W
	Chinan, see Tsinan		
126	Chinandega (chē-nän-dā′gä)..Nic.	12·38 N	87·08 W
118	Chinati Pk. (chĭ-nä′tē).......Tx.	29·56 N	104·29 W
187	Chinawin (R.)...............Bur.	23·30 N	94·30 E
134	Chincha Alta (chĭn′chä äl′tä) Peru	13·24 S	76·04 W
134	Chinchas, Islas (Is.) (ē′s-läs-chē′n-chäs).Peru	11·27 S	79·05 W
192	Chincheng..................China	35·30 N	112·50 E
190	Chinch′iao (jĭnchĭou).......China	31·46 N	116·46 E
203	Chinchilla (chĭn-chĭl′ȧ).....Austl.	26·44 S	150·36 E
162	Chinchilla (chēn-chē′lyä)......Sp.	38·54 N	1·43 W
126	Chinchorro, Banco (Bk.) (bä′n-kô-chĕn-chô′r-rŏ) Mex. (In.)	18·43 N	87·25 W
192	Chinchou...................China	41·00 N	121·00 E
190	Chinchou Wan (B.) (jĭn′zhō wän).China	39·07 N	121·17 E
212	Chinde (shēn′dĕ)............Moz.	17·39 S	36·34 E
194	Chin Do (I.)................Kor.	34·30 N	125·43 E
188	Chindwin R. (chĭn-dwĭn).....Bur.	23·30 N	94·34 E
190	Chinganchi (jĭng′än′jĭ).....China	34·30 N	116·55 E
190	Ch′ingcheng (chĭng′cheng)..China	37·12 N	117·43 E
192	Ch′ingch′eng.................China	46·50 N	127·30 E
193	Chingchiang (jĭng′jĭang)....China	28·00 N	115·30 E
190	Chingchiang.................China	32·02 N	120·15 E
190	Chingchih (jĭng′jē).........China	36·19 N	119·23 E
190	Ch′ingfeng (chingfeng).....China	35·52 N	115·05 E
188	Ch′ing Hai (Koko Nor) (L.) (kō′kō nor).China	37·26 N	98·30 E
190	Chinghai Wan (B.) (jĭng′hăĭ wän).China	36·47 N	122·10 E
192	Ching Ho (R.) (chĭng′hō′)...China	34·40 N	108·20 E
193	Chinghsien (jĭng′sĭan)......China	26·32 N	109·45 E
190	Chinghsien..................China	37·43 N	116·17 E
190	Ch′inghsien (chingsĭan).....China	38·37 N	116·48 E
192	Chinghsing..................China	47·00 N	123·00 E
190	Ching Hu (L.) (chĭng hōō)..China	39·00 N	115·45 E
190	Chingk′ouchen (chĭng′kō′jĕn) China	34·52 N	119·07 E
193	Chingliu....................China	26·15 N	116·50 E
192	Chingning..................China	35·28 N	105·50 E
217	Chingola (chĭng-gōlä).....Zambia	12·32 S	27·52 E
190	Ch′ingp′ing (chĭng′pĭng)....China	36·46 N	116·03 E
192	Chingpo Hu (L.)............China	44·10 N	129·00 E
191	Ch′ingp′u...China (Shanghai In.)	31·08 N	121·06 E
190	Ch′ingtao (Tsingtao) (tsĭng′dou) China	36·05 N	120·10 E
193	Chingtechen................China	29·18 N	117·18 E
212	Chinguar (chĭng-gär)........Ang.	12·35 S	16·15 E
210	Chinguetti (chĕŋ-gĕt′ē).Mauritania	20·34 N	12·34 W
190	Ch′ingyang (chĭng′yäng)....China	33·25 N	118·13 E
192	Chingyang..................China	36·02 N	107·42 E
193	Ch′ingyüang.................China	23·43 N	113·10 E
190	Ch′ingyun (chĭng′yōōn).....China	37·52 N	117·26 E
192	Ch′ingyütien...........China (In.)	39·41 N	116·31 E
190	Chinhsiang (jĭn′sĭäng)......China	35·03 N	116·20 E
190	Chinhsien (jĭn′sĭän)........China	37·08 N	121·43 E
193	Ch′inhsien..................China	22·00 N	108·35 E
193	Chinhua.....................China	29·10 N	119·42 E
190	Ch′inhuangtao (chĭnhōōäng′dou) China	39·57 N	119·34 E
190	Chining (jē′nĭng)...........China	35·26 N	116·34 E
192	Chining.....................China	41·00 N	113·10 E
194	Chinju (chĭn′jōō)...........Kor.	35·13 N	128·10 E
193	Chinkiang (chĭn′kyäng′).....China	32·05 N	119·25 E
211	Chinko (R.) (shĭn′kô) Cen. Afr. Rep.	6·37 N	24·31 E
93	Chin L. (chĭn)...............Can.	53·40 N	115·20 W
193	Chinmen....................China	24·42 N	118·05 E
	Chinmen, see Quemoy		
193	Chinmen (I.)................China	24·40 N	118·38 E
193	Chinmu Chiao (Pt.).........China	18·10 N	109·40 E
113	Chino (chē′nō) Ca. (Los Angeles In.)	34·01 N	117·42 W
160	Chinon (shē-nôɴ′)............Fr.	47·09 N	0·13 E
111	Chinook (shĭn-ōōk′)..........Mt.	48·35 N	109·15 W
112	Chinook (shĭn-ōōk′) Wa. (Portland In.)	46·17 N	123·57 W
217	Chinsali.....................Zambia	10·34 S	32·03 E
190	Chinshachen (jĭn′shä′jĕn)...China	32·08 N	121·06 E
191	Chinshan...China (Shanghai In.)	30·53 N	121·09 E
188	Chint′a.....................China	40·11 N	98·45 E
190	Chint′an (jĭn′tän)..........China	31·47 N	119·34 E
212	Chinteche (chĭn-tĕ′chĕ)....Malawi	11·48 S	34·14 E
192	Chinyang (chĭn′yäng′)......China	35·00 N	112·55 E
193	Chinyüh.....................China	28·40 N	120·08 E
164	Chioggia (kyôd′jä)............It.	45·12 N	12·17 E
191	Ch′ipao.....China (Shanghai In.)	31·06 N	121·16 E
217	Chipata....................Zambia	13·39 S	32·40 E

ăt; finăl; rāte; senâte; ärm; ȧsk; sofȧ; fâre; ch-choose; dh-as th in other; bē; êvent; bĕt; recĕnt; cratẽr; g-go; gh-guttural g; bĭt; ĭ-short neutral; rīde; ĸ-guttural k as ch in German ich;

PRONOUNCING INDEX

Chipera — Civitavecchia 269

Page	Name Pronunciation Region	Lat. °′	Long. °′
212	Chipera (zhē-pě'rä) . . . . Moz.	15·16 s	32·30 E
120	Chipley (chĭp'lĭ) . . . . Fl.	30·45 N	85·33 W
98	Chipman (chĭp'măn) . . . . Can.	46·11 N	65·53 W
120	Chipola (R.) (chĭ-pō'lȧ) . . . . Fl.	30·40 N	85·14 W
107	Chippawa (chĭp'ê-wä) Can. (Buffalo In.)	43·03 N	79·03 W
108	Chippewa (R.) (chĭp'ê-wä) . . . Mn.	45·07 N	95·41 W
109	Chippewa (R.) . . . . Wi.	45·07 N	91·19 W
109	Chippewa Falls . . . . Wi.	44·55 N	91·26 W
107	Chippewa Lake . Oh. (Cleveland In.)	41·04 N	81·54 W
98	Chiputneticook (L.) (chĭ-po͞ot-nĕt'ĭ-ko͝ok) . Can.	45·47 N	67·35 W
126	Chiquimula (chē-kê-mo͞o'lä) . Guat.	14·47 N	89·31 W
126	Chiquimulilla (chē-kē-mo͞o-lē'l-yä) Guat.	14·08 N	90·23 W
134	Chiquinquira (chê-kēŋ'kê-rä') . Col.	5·33 N	73·49 W
137	Chiquita, Laguna Mar (L.) (lä-go͞o'nä-mär-chê-kē'tä) Arg. (Buenos Aires In.)	34·25 s	61·10 W
185	Chirald . . . . India	15·52 N	80·22 E
172	Chirchik (chĭr-chĕk') . . . . . Sov. Un.	41·28 N	69·18 E
217	Chire (R.) . . . . Moz.	17·15 s	35·25 E
115	Chiricahua Natl. Mon. (chĭ-rä-cä'hwä) . Az.	32·02 N	109·18 W
101	Chirikof (I.) (chĭ'rĭ-kôf) . . . . . . Ak.	55·50 N	155·35 W
117	Chiriquí, Golfo de (G.) (gôl-fô-dĕ-chē-rê-kē') . Pan.	7·56 N	82·18 W
117	Chiriquí, Laguna de (L.) (lä-go͞o'nä-dĕ-chē-rê-kē') . Pan.	9·06 N	82·02 W
117	Chiriqui, Punta (Pt.) (po͞o'n-tä-chē-rê-kē') . Pan.	9·13 N	81·39 W
117	Chiriqui, Volcán de (Vol.) (vôl-kä'n-dĕ-chē-rē-kē') . Pan.	8·48 N	82·37 W
117	Chiriquí Grande (chē-rê-kē' grän'dā) . Pan.	8·57 N	82·08 W
194	Chiri San (Mt.) (chĭ'rĭ-sän') . Kor.	35·20 N	127·39 E
212	Chiromo . . . . Malawi	16·34 s	35·13 E
165	Chirpan . . . . Bul.	42·12 N	25·19 E
117	Chirripo, R. (chêr-rē'pō) . . . . C. R.	9·50 N	83·20 W
117	Chirripo Grande (Mt.) (chêr-rē'pō grän'dā) . C. R.	9·30 N	83·31 W
109	Chisholm (chĭz'ŭm) . . . . Mn.	47·28 N	92·53 W
170	Chistopol' (chĭs-tô'pôl-y') Sov. Un.	55·18 N	50·30 E
173	Chita (chê-tá') . . . . Sov. Un.	52·09 N	113·39 E
188	Ch'it'ai . . . . China	44·07 N	89·04 E
217	Chitambo . . . . Zambia	12·55 s	30·39 E
216	Chitembo . . . . Ang.	13·34 s	16·40 E
101	Chitina (chĭ-tē'ná) . . . . Ak.	61·28 N	144·35 W
216	Chitokoloki . . . . Zambia	13·50 s	23·13 E
184	Chitorgarh . . . . India	24·59 N	74·42 E
184	Chitrāl (chē-träl') . . . . Pak.	35·58 N	71·48 E
127	Chitré (chē'trā) . . . . Pan.	7·59 N	80·26 W
184	Chittagong (chĭt-á-gông') . . . . Bngl.	22·26 N	90·51 E
192	Chiualhun . . . . China	49·59 N	127·15 E
190	Chiuch'eng (jĭō'chĕng) . . . . . . China	37·14 N	116·03 E
188	Chiuch'ian . . . . China	39·46 N	98·26 E
193	Chiuchiang . . . . China	29·43 N	116·00 E
191	Chiuchiang . . . . China (Canton In.)	23·50 N	113·02 E
189	Chiuchichien . . . . China	52·23 N	121·04 E
191	Chiufenghsien China (Shanghai In.)	30·55 N	121·38 E
190	Ch'iuhsien (chĭō'sĭän) . . . . . . China	36·43 N	115·13 E
190	Chiuhsihsien (jĭo'sĕ'sĭän) . . . . China	32·20 N	114·42 E
190	Chiuhuang (R.) (jĭō'hooäng) China	33·48 N	119·30 E
216	Chiumbe (R.) (chê-o͝om'bå) . . Ang.	9·05 s	21·00 E
190	Chiunü Shan (Mts.) (jĭō'nü'shän) . China	35·47 N	117·23 E
164	Chivasso (kê-väs'sō) . . . . It.	45·13 N	7·52 E
137	Chivilcoy (chē-vêl-koi') Arg. (Buenos Aires In.)	34·51 s	60·03 W
126	Chixoy R. (chē-Koi') . . . . Guat.	15·40 N	90·35 W
193	Chiyang . . . . China	26·40 N	112·00 E
193	Ch'iyao Shan (Mtn.) . . . . China	30·00 N	108·50 E
195	Chizu (chê-zo͞o') . . . . Jap.	35·16 N	134·15 E
115	Chloride (klō'rīd) . . . . Az.	35·25 N	114·15 W
159	Chmielnik (Kmyĕl'nĕK) . . . . Pol.	50·36 N	20·46 E
137	Choapa (chô-á'pä) (R.) Chile (Santiago In.)	31·56 s	70·48 W
134	Chocó (chô-kô') (Dept.) . Col. (In.)	5·33 N	76·28 W
120	Choctawhatchee, B. (chôk-tô-hăch'ê) . Fl.	30·15 N	86·32 W
120	Choctawhatchee, R. . . . . Fl.-Ga.	30·37 N	85·56 W
158	Chodziez (Kōj'yĕsh) . . . . Pol.	52·59 N	16·55 E
136	Choele Choel (chô-ĕ'lĕ-chôĕ'l) . Arg.	39·14 s	66·46 W
195	Chōfu (chō'fo͞o') . Jap. (Tōkyō In.)	35·39 N	139·33 E
195	Chōgo (chō-gō) . . Jap. (Tōkyō In.)	35·25 N	139·28 E
190	Chohsien (jōoŭ'sĭän) . . . . China	39·30 N	115·59 E
205	Choiseul, (I.) (shwä-zûl') . . Sol. Is.	7·30 s	157·30 E
159	Chojnice (Kōĭ-nē-tsĕ) . . . . Pol.	53·41 N	17·34 E
160	Cholet (shô-lĕ') . . . . Fr.	47·06 N	0·54 W
192	Ch'olo (R.) . . . . China	47·20 N	121·40 E
124	Cholula (chō-lo͞o'lä) . . . . Mex.	19·04 N	98·19 W
126	Choluteca (chō-lo͞o-tā'kä) . . . Hond.	13·18 N	87·12 W
126	Choluteco R. . . . . Hond.	13·34 N	86·59 W
158	Chomutov (kō'mo͝o-tôf) . . . . Czech.	50·27 N	13·23 E
173	Chona (R.) (chō'nä) . . . . . Sov. Un.	60·45 N	109·15 E
134	Chone (chô'nĕ) . . . . Ec.	0·48 s	80·06 W
194	Chŏngjin (chŭng-jĭn') . . . . Kor.	41·48 N	129·46 E
194	Chŏngju (chŭng-jo͞o') . . . . Kor.	36·35 N	127·30 E
194	Chŏnju (chŭn-jo͞o') . . . . Kor.	35·48 N	127·08 E
148	Chorley (chôr'lĭ) . . . . Eng.	53·40 N	2·38 W
174	Chornaya . . Sov. Un. (Moscow In.)	55·45 N	38·04 E
134	Chorrillos (chôr-rē'l-yōs) . . . . . Peru	12·17 s	76·55 W
159	Chortkov (chôrt'kôf) . . . . Sov. Un.	49·01 N	25·48 E
159	Chorzów (kô-zho͝of') . . . . Pol.	50·17 N	19·00 E
194	Chosan (chō-sän') . . . . Kor.	40·44 N	125·48 E
121	Chosen (chō'z'n) . . . . Fl. (In.)	26·41 N	80·41 W
194	Chōshi (chō'shē) . . . . Jap.	35·40 N	140·55 E
158	Choszczno (chôsh'chnô) . . . . . . Pol.	53·10 N	15·25 E
184	Chota Nagpur (Reg.) . . . . India	28·20 N	81·40 E
111	Choteau (shō'tō) . . . . Mt.	47·51 N	112·10 W
151	Chott el Hodna (L.) . . . . Alg.	35·20 N	3·27 E
190	Chou (R.) (jēō) . . . . China	31·59 N	114·57 E
190	Chouchiak'ou (jēō'jĭä'kō) . . . China	33·39 N	114·40 E
191	Choup'u . . . China (Shanghai In.)	31·07 N	121·33 E
193	Choushan Arch. (Is.) (chou'shăn) China	30·00 N	123·00 E
190	Chouts'un (jēō'tso͞on) . . . . . . China	36·49 N	117·52 E
121	Chowan (R.) (chô-wăn') . . . . . . NC	36·13 N	76·46 W
203	Chowilla Res. . . . . Austl.	34·05 s	141·20 E
93	Chown, Mt. (choun) . . . . Can.	53·24 N	119·22 W
192	Choybalsan . . . . Mong.	47·50 N	114·15 E
205	Christchurch (krīst'chûrch) N. Z. (In.)	43·30 s	172·38 E
104	Christian (I.) (krĭs'chăn) . . . . . Can.	44·50 N	80·00 W
121	Christiansburg (krĭs'chănz-bûrg) Va.	37·08 N	80·25 W
123	Christiansted Vir. Is. (U. S. A.) (Puerto Rico In.)	17·45 N	64·44 W
196	Christmas (I.) . . . . Austl.	10·35 s	105·40 E
199	Christmas (I.) . . . . Oceania	2·20 N	157·40 W
117	Christopher (krĭs'tô-fẽr) . . . . Il.	37·58 N	89·04 W
158	Chrudim (Kro͞o'dyĕm) . . . . . . Czech.	49·57 N	15·46 E
159	Chrzanów (Kzhä'no͞of) . . . . Pol.	50·08 N	19·24 E
190	Ch'üanch'iao (chüän'jĭou) . . China	32·06 N	118·17 E
193	Ch'üanchow . . . . China	24·58 N	118·40 E
192	Chuangho . . . . China	39·40 N	123·00 E
193	Ch'üanhsien . . . . China	25·58 N	111·02 E
191	Ch'uansha . . . China (Shanghai In.)	31·12 N	121·41 E
136	Chubut (Prov.) (cho͞o-bo͞ot') . . Arg.	44·00 s	69·15 W
136	Chubut (cho͞o-bo͞ot') (R.) . . . . Arg.	43·05 s	69·00 W
190	Chuch'eng (cho͞o'chĕng') . . . . China	36·01 N	119·24 E
193	Chuchi . . . . China	29·58 N	120·10 E
191	Chu Chiang (Pearl R.) China (Canton In.)	23·04 N	113·28 E
190	Ch'üchou (chü'jēō) . . . . China	36·47 N	114·58 E
106	Chuckatuck (chŭck á-tŭck) Va. (Norfolk In.)	36·51 N	76·35 W
127	Chucunague, R. (cho͞o-ko͞o-nä'kå) Pan.	8·36 N	77·48 W
166	Chudovo (cho͝o'dô-vô) . . . Sov. Un.	59·03 N	31·56 S
166	Chudskoye Oz. (Peipus, L.) (cho͝ot'skô-yĕ) . Sov. Un.	58·43 N	26·45 E
190	Ch'üfou (chü'fo͞o) . . . . China	35·37 N	116·59 E
	Chuguchak, see T'ach'eng		
188	Chuguchak (Reg.) (cho͞o'go͞o-chäk') . China	46·09 N	83·58 E
167	Chuguyev (cho͞o'go͝o-yĕf) . Sov. Un.	49·52 N	36·40 E
194	Chuguyevka (cho͞o-go͞o'yĕf-kå) Sov. Un.	43·58 N	133·49 E
108	Chugwater Cr. (chŭg'wô-tẽr) . Wy.	41·43 N	104·54 W
192	Chuho . . . . China	45·18 N	127·52 E
193	Ch'ühsien . . . . China	28·58 N	118·58 E
190	Ch'ühsien (cho͞o'sĭän) . . . . . . China	32·19 N	118·19 E
190	Chühsien (jü'sĭän) . . . . China	35·35 N	118·50 E
188	Ch'uhsiung . . . . China	25·19 N	101·34 E
190	Chühua Tao (I.) (jü'ho͞oȧ dou) China	40·30 N	120·47 E
190	Chüjung (jü'ro͞ong) . . . . China	31·58 N	119·12 E
173	Chukot Natl. Okrug (Reg.) Sov. Un.	68·15 N	170·00 E
173	Chukotskiy (Chukot) P-Ov (Pen.) Sov. Un.	66·12 N	175·00 W
173	Chukotskoye Nagor'ye (Mts.) Sov. Un.	66·00 N	166·00 E
114	Chula Vista (cho͞o'lȧ vĭs'tȧ) Ca. (In.)	32·38 N	117·05 W
174	Chulkovo (cho͞ol-kô vô) Sov. Un. (Moscow In.)	55·33 N	38·04 E
134	Chulucanas (cho͞o-lo͞o-kä'näs) . Peru	5·13 s	80·13 W
172	Chulum (R.) . . . . Sov. Un.	57·52 N	84·45 E
190	Chüma (R.) (jü'mȧ) . . . . China	39·37 N	115·45 E
173	Chumikan (cho͞o-mē-kän') Sov. Un.	54·47 N	135·09 E
194	Chunchŏn (cho͞on-chŭn') . . . . . Kor.	37·51 N	127·46 E
190	Chungchia Shān (Mts.) (jo͞ong'jĭä shän) . China	32·42 N	118·19 E
193	Ch'ungch'ing (Chungking) (ch'ung'ch'ing) (cho͞ong'kĭng') China	29·38 N	107·30 E
193	Chunghsien . . . . China	30·20 N	108·00 E
190	Chunghsing (jo͞ong'sĭng) . . . . China	33·43 N	118·42 E
194	Chungju (chŭng'jo͞o') . . . . Kor.	37·00 N	128·19 E
	Chungking, see Ch'ungch'ing		
193	Ch'ungming Tao (I.) . . . . China	31·40 N	122·30 E
192	Chungwei (cho͞ong'wā) . . . . . . China	37·32 N	105·10 E
217	Chunya . . . . Tan.	8·32 s	33·25 E
172	Chunya (R.) (cho͞on'yä') Sov. Un.	61·45 N	101·28 E
136	Chuquicamata (cho͞o-kê-kä-mä'tä) Chile	22·08 s	68·57 W
158	Chur (ko͞or) . . . . Switz.	46·51 N	9·32 E
90	Churchill (chûrch'ĭl) . . . . Can.	58·48 N	94·10 W
90	Churchill, C. . . . . Can.	59·07 N	93·50 W
95	Churchill (R.) . . . . Can.	57·20 N	96·30 W
91	Churchill Falls . . . . Can.	53·35 N	64·27 W
94	Churchill L. . . . . Can.	55·55 N	108·20 W
90	Churchill Pk. . . . . Can.	58·10 N	125·14 W
148	Church Stretton (chûrch strĕt'ŭn) . Eng.	52·32 N	2·49 W
106	Churchton . . . Md. (Baltimore In.)	38·49 N	76·33 W
184	Churu . . . . India	28·22 N	75·00 E
124	Churumuco (cho͞o-ro͞o-mo͞o'kō) Mex.	18·39 N	101·40 W
193	Ch'ushien . . . . China	30·40 N	106·48 E
115	Chuska, Mts. (chŭs-kȧ) . Az.-NM	36·21 N	109·11 W
174	Chusovaya R. (cho͞o-sô-vä'yȧ) Sov. Un. (Urals In.)	58·08 N	58·35 E
174	Chusovoy (cho͞o-sô-vôy') Sov. Un. (Urals In.)	58·18 N	57·50 E
172	Chust (cho͞ost) . . . . Sov. Un.	41·05 N	71·28 E
190	Chut'angtien (jō'däng'dĭän) China	31·59 N	114·13 E
190	Ch'uti (chü'tē) . . . . China	37·07 N	117·17 E
170	Chuvash (A. S. S. R.) (cho͞o'våsh) Sov. Un.	55·45 N	46·00 E
118	Chuviscar R. (cho͞o-vês-kär') . Mex.	28·34 N	105·36 W
190	Ch'uwang (cho͞o'wäng) . . . . . China	36·08 N	114·53 E
196	Chu Yang Sin (Pk.) . . . . Viet.	12·22 N	108·20 E
190	Chüyen (jü'yĕ) . . . . China	35·24 N	116·05 E
	Cibao Mts., see Central, Cordillera		
118	Cibolo Cr. (sē'bô-lō) . . . . Tx.	29·28 N	98·13 W
107	Cicero (sĭs'ẽr-ō) . . Il. (Chicago In.)	41·50 N	87·46 W
171	Cide (jē'dĕ) . . . . Tur.	41·50 N	33·00 E
159	Ciechanów (tsyĕ-kä'no͞of) . . . . . Pol.	52·52 N	20·39 E
128	Ciego de Avila (syā'gō dā ä'vê-lä) Cuba	21·50 N	78·45 W
162	Ciempozuelos (thyĕm-pô-thwā'lōs) Sp.	40·09 N	3·36 W
134	Ciénaga (syā'nä-gä) . . . . Col.	11·01 N	74·15 W
128	Cienfuegos (syĕn-fwā'gōs) . . . Cuba	22·10 N	80·30 W
128	Cienfuegos, Bahía (B.) (bä-ē'ä-syĕn-fwā'gōs) . Cuba	22·00 N	80·35 W
127	Ciervo, Isla de la (I.) (ē's-lä-dĕ-lä-syĕ'r-vô) . Nic.	11·56 N	83·20 W
159	Cieszyn (tsyĕ'shĕn) . . . . Pol.	49·47 N	18·45 E
162	Cieza (thyā'thä) . . . . Sp.	38·13 N	1·25 W
124	Cihuatlán (sē-wä-tlä'n) . . . . . . Mex.	19·13 N	104·36 W
124	Cihuatlán (R.) . . . . Mex.	19·11 N	104·30 W
162	Cijara Res. . . . . Sp.	39·25 N	5·00 W
171	Cilician Gates (P.) . . . . Tur.	37·30 N	35·30 E
154	Cill Mantainn (Wicklow) (kĭl män'tán) (wĭk'lō) . Ire.	52·59 N	6·06 W
116	Cimarron (R.), North Fk. . . . . . Co.	37·13 N	102·30 W
116	Cimarron R. (sĭm-ȧ-rōn') . . . . . Ok.	36·26 N	98·47 W
165	Cîmpina . . . . Rom.	45·08 N	25·47 E
165	Cîmpulung . . . . Rom.	45·15 N	25·03 E
159	Cîmpulung Moldovenesc . . . . Rom.	47·31 N	25·36 E
163	Cinca (R.) (thēŋ'kä) . . . . Sp.	42·09 N	0·08 E
107	Cincinnati (sĭn-sĭ-nát'ĭ) Oh. (Cincinnati In.)	39·08 N	84·30 W
128	Cnco Balas, Cayos (Is.) (kä'yōs-thēŋ'kō bä'läs) . Cuba	21·05 N	79·25 W
125	Cintalapa (sên-tä-lä'pä) . . . . . Mex.	16·41 N	93·44 W
125	Cintalapa (R.) . . . . Mex.	16·46 N	93·36 W
164	Cinto, Mt. (chēn'tō) . . . . Fr.	42·24 N	8·54 E
101	Circle (sûr'k'l) . . . . Ak.	65·49 N	144·22 W
104	Circleville (sûr'k'lvĭl) . . . . Oh.	39·35 N	83·00 W
	Cirenaica (Prov.), see Barqah		
118	Cisco (sĭs'kō) . . . . Tx.	32·23 N	98·57 W
134	Cisneros (sês-nĕ'rôs) . . . . Col. (In.)	5·33 N	75·05 W
163	Cisterna di Latina (chēs-tĕ'r-nä-dē-lä-tē'nä) . (Rome In.)	41·36 N	12·53 E
162	Cistierna (thês-tyĕr'nä) . . . . Sp.	42·48 N	5·08 W
125	Citlaltépetl (Vol.) (sē-tlàl-tĕ'pĕtl) Mex.	19·04 N	97·14 W
120	Citronelle (cĭt-rô'nĕl) . . . . Al.	33·04 N	88·12 W
164	Cittadella (chēt-tä-dĕl'lä) . . . . . . It.	45·39 N	11·51 E
164	Città di Castello (chēt-tä'dē käs-tĕl'lō) . It.	43·27 N	12·17 E
124	Ciudad Altamirano (syo͞o-dä'd-äl-tä-mē-rä'nô) . Mex.	18·24 N	100·38 W
134	Ciudad Bolívar (syo͞o-dhädh' bô-lē'vär) . Ven.	8·07 N	63·41 W
118	Ciudad Camargo (Santa Rosalia) (syo͞o-dhädh' kä-mär'gō) (sän'tá rō-sä'lēá) . Mex.	27·42 N	105·10 W
126	Ciudad Chetumal (Payo Obispo) (syo͞o-dhädh' chĕt-o͞o-mäl) (pä'yō ō-bēs'pō) . Mex. (In.)	18·30 N	88·17 W
126	Ciudad Dario (syo͞o-dhädh'dä'rê-ō) . Nic.	12·44 N	86·08 W
125	Ciudad de las Casas (syo͞o-dä'd-dĕ-läs-kȧ'säs) . Mex.	16·44 N	92·39 W
125	Ciudad del Carmen (syo͞o-dä'd-dĕl-kȧ'r-mĕn) . Mex.	18·39 N	91·49 W
124	Ciudad del Maíz (syo͞o-dhädh'del mä-ēz') . Mex.	22·24 N	99·37 W
124	Ciudad de Valles (syo͞o-dhädh'dā vä'lyās) . Mex.	21·59 N	99·02 W
163	Ciudadela (thyo͞o-dhä-dhā'lä) . Sp.	40·00 N	3·52 E
124	Ciudad Fernández (syo͞o-dhädh'fĕr-nän'dĕz) . Mex.	21·56 N	100·03 W
124	Ciudad Garcia (syo͞o-dhädh'gär-sē'ä) . Mex.	22·39 N	103·02 W
134	Ciudad Guayana . . . . Ven.	8·30 N	62·45 W
124	Ciudad Guzmán (syo͞o-dhädh'go͞oz-män) . Mex.	19·40 N	103·29 W
124	Ciudad Hidalgo (syo͞o-dä'd-ē-dä'l-gô) . Mex.	19·41 N	100·35 W
118	Ciudad Juárez (syo͞o-dhädh hwä'rāz) . Mex.	31·44 N	106·28 W
125	Ciudad Madero (syo͞o-dä'd-mä-dĕ'rô) . Mex.	22·16 N	97·52 W
124	Ciudad Mante (syo͞o-dä'd-mán'tĕ) . Mex.	22·34 N	98·58 W
124	Ciudad Manuel Doblado (syo͞o-dä'd-män-wāl' dō-blä'dō) Mex.	20·43 N	101·57 W
122	Ciudad Obregon (syo͞o-dhädh-ô-brĕ-gô'n) . Mex.	27·40 N	109·58 W
162	Ciudad Real (thyo͞o-dhädh'rā-äl') . Sp.	38·59 N	3·55 W
162	Ciudad Rodrigo (thyo͞o-dhädh'rô-drē'gō) . Sp.	40·38 N	6·34 W
125	Ciudad Serdán (syo͞o-dä'd-sĕr-dá'n) . Mex.	18·58 N	97·26 W
124	Ciudad Victoria (syo͞o-dhädh'vêk-tō'rê-ä) . Mex.	23·43 N	99·09 W
164	Cividale del Friuli (chē-vê-dä'lā-dĕl-frē-o͞o'lē) . It.	46·06 N	13·24 E
164	Civitavecchia (chē'vê-tä-vĕk'kyä) It.	42·06 N	11·49 E

ng-sing; ŋ-baŋk; N-nasalized n; nŏd; cŏmmit; ōld; ôbey; ôrder; fo͞od; fo͝ot; ou-out; s-soft; sh-dish; th-thin; pūre; ûnite; ûrn; stŭd; circŭs; ü-as "y" in study; '-indeterminate vowel.

270 Clackamas — College Park PRONOUNCING INDEX

Page	Name Pronunciation Region	Lat. °′	Long. °′
112	Clackamas (klăc-kȧ'măs) Or. (Portland In.)	42·25 N	122·34 W
90	Claire (L.) (klâr) Can.	58·33 N	113·16 W
110	Clair Engle Lake Ca.	40·51 N	122·41 W
107	Clairton (klârtŭn) Pa. (Pittsburgh In.)	40·17 N	79·53 W
120	Clanton (klăn'tŭn) Al.	32·50 N	86·38 W
104	Clare (klâr) Mi.	43·50 N	84·45 W
154	Clare (I.) Ire.	53·46 N	10·00 W
113	Claremont (klâr'mŏnt) Ca. (Los Angeles In.)	34·06 N	117·43 W
105	Claremont (klâr'mŏnt) NH	43·20 N	72·20 W
104	Claremont WV	37·55 N	81·00 W
117	Claremore (klâr'mōr) Ok.	36·16 N	95·37 W
154	Claremorris (klâr-mŏr'ĭs) Ire.	53·46 N	9·05 W
92	Clarence Str. Ak.	55·25 N	132·00 W
204	Clarence Str. (klăr'ĕns) Austl.	12·15 S	130·05 E
129	Clarence Town Ba.	23·05 N	75·00 W
117	Clarendon (klâr'ĕn-dŭn) Ar.	34·42 N	91·17 W
116	Clarendon Tx.	34·55 N	100·52 W
213	Clarens (clâ-rĕns) S. Afr. (Natal In.)	28·34 S	28·26 E
94	Claresholm (klâr'ĕs-hōlm) Can.	50·02 N	113·35 W
109	Clarinda (klȧ-rĭn'dȧ) Ia.	40·42 N	95·00 W
135	Clarines (klä-rē'nĕs) Ven. (In.)	9·57 N	65·10 W
109	Clarion (klăr'ĭ-ŭn) Ia.	42·43 N	93·45 W
105	Clarion Pa.	41·10 N	79·25 W
108	Clark (klärk) SD	44·52 N	97·45 W
104	Clark, Pt. Can.	44·05 N	81·50 W
98	Clarke City Can.	50·12 N	66·38 W
115	Clarkdale (klärk-dāl) Az	34·45 N	112·05 W
205	Clarke Ra. Austl.	20·30 S	148·00 E
111	Clark Fork R. Mt.	47·50 N	115·35 W
121	Clark Hill Res. (klärk-hĭl) Ga.-SC	33·50 N	82·35 W
105	Clarksburg (klärkz'bûrg) WV	39·15 N	80·20 W
120	Clarksdale (klärks-dāl) Ms.	34·10 N	90·31 W
98	Clark's Harbour (klärks) Can.	43·26 N	65·38 W
106	Clarkston (klärks'tŭn) Ga. (Altanta In.)	33·49 N	84·15 W
110	Clarkston Wa.	46·24 N	117·01 W
117	Clarksville (klärks-vĭl) Ar.	35·28 N	93·26 W
120	Clarksville Tn.	36·30 N	87·23 W
117	Clarksville Tx.	33·37 N	95·02 W
112	Clatskanie Or. (Portland In.)	46·04 N	123·11 W
112	Clatskanie (R.) (klăt-skā'nē) Or. (Portland In.)	46·06 N	123·11 W
112	Clatsop Spit (klăt-sŏp) Or. (Portland In.)	46·13 N	124·04 W
137	Cláudio (klou'-dēō) Braz. (Rio de Janeiro In.)	20·26 S	44·44 W
193	Claveria (klä-vȧ-rē'ä) Phil.	18·38 N	121·08 E
107	Clawson (klô's'n) Mi. (Detroit In.)	42·32 N	83·09 W
121	Claxton (klăks'tŭn) Ga.	32·07 N	81·54 W
120	Clay (klā) Ky.	37·28 N	87·50 W
117	Clay Center (klā sĕn'tĕr) Ks.	39·23 N	97·08 W
104	Clay City (klā sĭ'tĭ) Ky.	37·50 N	83·55 W
113	Claycomo (kla-kō'mo) Mo. (Kansas City In.)	39·12 N	94·30 W
148	Clay Cross (klā krŏs) Eng.	53·10 N	1·25 W
161	Claye-Souilly (klĕ-sōō-yē') Fr. (Paris In.)	48·56 N	2·43 E
106	Claymont (klā-mŏnt) De. (Philadelphia In.)	39·48 N	75·28 W
120	Clayton (klā'tŭn) Al.	31·52 N	85·25 W
112	Clayton Ca. (San Francisco In.)	37·56 N	122·56 W
148	Clayton Eng.	53·47 N	1·49 W
113	Clayton Mo. (St. Louis In.)	38·39 N	90·20 W
116	Clayton NM	36·26 N	103·12 W
121	Clayton NC	35·40 N	78·27 W
114	Clear, (L.) Ca.	39·05 N	122·50 W
154	Clear, C. (klēr) Ire.	51·24 N	9·15 W
117	Clear Boggy Cr. (klēr bŏg'ĭ krēk) Ok.	34·21 N	96·22 W
115	Clear Cr. Az.	34·40 N	111·05 W
111	Clear Cr. Wy.	44·35 N	106·20 W
105	Clearfield (klēr-fēld) Pa.	41·00 N	78·25 W
113	Clearfield. Ut. (Salt Lake City In.)	41·07 N	112·01 W
90	Clear Hills Can.	57·11 N	119·20 W
109	Clear Lake Ia.	43·09 N	93·23 W
112	Clear Lake Wa. (Seattle In.)	48·27 N	122·14 W
110	Clear Lake Res. Ca.	41·53 N	121·00 W
119	Clear R. Tx. (In.)	29·34 N	95·13 W
121	Clearwater (klēr-wô'tēr) Fl. (In.)	27·43 N	82·45 W
110	Clearwater Mts. Id.	45·56 N	115·15 W
117	Clearwater Res. Mo.	37·20 N	91·04 W
93	Clearwater (R.) Can.	52·00 N	114·50 W
93	Clearwater (R.) Can.	52·00 N	120·10 W
94	Clearwater (R.) Can.	56·10 N	110·40 W
110	Clearwater R. Id.	46·27 N	116·33 W
110	Clearwater R., Middle Fork Id.	46·10 N	115·48 W
110	Clearwater R., North Fork Id.	46·34 N	116·08 W
110	Clearwater R., South Fork Id.	45·46 N	115·53 W
119	Cleburne (klē'bŭrn) Tx.	32·21 N	97·23 W
148	Clee Hill (klē) Eng.	52·24 N	2·37 W
110	Cle Elum (klē ĕl'ŭm) Wa.	47·12 N	120·55 W
106	Clementon (klē'mĕn-tŭn) NJ (Philadelphia In.)	39·49 N	75·00 W
148	Cleobury Mortimer (klē'ô-bĕr'ĭ môr'tĭ-mĕr) Eng.	52·22 N	2·29 W
205	Clermont (klēr'mŏnt) Austl.	23·02 S	147·46 E
98	Clermont Can.	47·45 N	70·20 W
160	Clermont-Ferrand (klĕr-mŏN'fĕr-răN') Fr.	45·47 N	3·03 E
160	Clermont l'Herault (klĕr-mŏN'lā-rō') Fr.	43·38 N	3·22 E
120	Cleveland (klēv'lănd) Ms.	33·45 N	90·42 W
107	Cleveland Oh. (Cleveland In.)	41·30 N	81·42 W
117	Cleveland Ok.	36·18 N	96·28 W
120	Cleveland Tn.	35·09 N	84·52 W
119	Cleveland Tx.	30·18 N	95·05 W
107	Cleveland Heights Oh. (Cleveland In.)	41·30 N	81·35 W
92	Cleveland Pen. Ak.	55·45 N	132·00 W
107	Cleves (klē'vĕs) Oh. (Cincinnati In.)	39·10 N	84·45 W
154	Clew (B.) (klōō) Ire.	53·47 N	9·45 W
121	Clewiston (klē'wĭs-tŭn) Fl. (In.)	26·44 N	80·55 W
161	Clichy (klē-shē') Fr. (Paris In.)	48·54 N	2·18 E
154	Clifden (klĭf'dĕn) Ire.	53·31 N	10·04 W
115	Clifton (klĭf'tŭn) Az.	33·05 N	109·20 W
106	Clifton NJ (New York In.)	40·35 N	74·09 W
121	Clifton SC	35·00 N	81·47 W
119	Clifton Tx.	31·45 N	97·31 W
105	Clifton Forge Va.	37·50 N	79·50 W
120	Clinch Res. (klĭnch) Tn.-Va.	36·30 N	83·19 W
120	Clingmans Dome (Mtn.) (klĭng'măns dōm) NC	35·37 N	83·26 W
93	Clinton (klĭn-'tŭn) Can.	51·05 N	121·35 W
104	Clinton Il.	40·10 N	88·55 W
104	Clinton In.	39·40 N	87·25 W
109	Clinton Ia.	41·50 N	90·13 W
121	Clinton Ky.	36·39 N	88·56 W
106	Clinton Md. (Baltimore In.)	38·46 N	76·54 W
99	Clinton Ma. (In.)	42·25 N	71·41 W
117	Clinton Mo.	38·23 N	93·46 W
121	Clinton NC	35·58 N	78·20 W
116	Clinton Ok.	35·31 N	98·56 W
121	Clinton SC	34·27 N	81·53 W
120	Clinton Tn.	36·05 N	84·08 W
112	Clinton Wa. (Seattle In.)	47·59 N	122·22 W
90	Clinton-Colden (L.) Can.	63·58 N	106·34 W
107	Clinton R. Mi. (Detroit In.)	42·36 N	83·00 W
109	Clintonville (klĭn'tŭn-vĭl) Wi.	44·37 N	88·46 W
104	Clio (klē'ō) Mi.	43·10 N	83·45 W
204	Cloates, Pt. (klōts) Austl.	22·47 S	113·45 E
218	Clocolan. S. Afr. (Johannesburg & Pretoria In.)	28·56 S	27·35 E
154	Clonakilty B. (klŏn-ȧ-kĭltē) Ire.	51·30 N	8·50 W
204	Cloncurry (klŏn-kŭr'ē) Austl.	20·58 S	140·42 E
154	Clonmel (klŏn-mĕl) Ire.	52·21 N	7·45 W
113	Cloquet(klô-kā'). Mn.(Duluth In.)	46·28 N	92·28 W
109	Cloquet (R.) Mn.	47·02 N	92·17 W
106	Closter (clŏs'tēr) NJ (New York In.)	40·58 N	73·57 W
111	Cloud Pk. (kloud) Wy.	44·23 N	107·11 W
121	Clover (klō'vēr) SC	35·08 N	81·08 W
100	Clover Bar (klō'vēr bär) Can. (Edmonton In.)	53·34 N	113·20 W
114	Cloverdale (klō'vēr-dāl) Ca.	38·47 N	123·03 W
112	Cloverdale. Can. (Vancouver In.)	49·06 N	122·44 W
104	Cloverport (klō'vēr pōrt) Ky.	37·50 N	86·35 W
116	Clovis (klō'vĭs) NM	34·24 N	103·11 W
159	Cluj (klōōzh) Rom.	46·46 N	23·34 E
148	Clun (R.) (klŭn) Eng.	52·25 N	2·56 W
160	Cluny (klü-nē') Fr.	46·27 N	4·40 E
205	Clutha (R.) (klōō'thȧ). N. Z. (In.)	45·26 S	169·15 E
117	Clyde Ks.	39·34 N	97·23 W
104	Clyde Oh.	41·15 N	83·00 W
154	Clyde (L.) Scot.	55·35 N	3·50 W
154	Clyde, Firth of (fûrth ŏv klīd) Scot.	55·28 N	5·01 W
154	Clydebank Scot.	55·56 N	4·20 W
162	Côa (R.) (kō'ä) Port.	40·28 N	6·55 W
125	Coacalco (kō-ä-kăl'kō). Mex. (In.)	19·37 N	99·06 W
114	Coachella, Can. (kō'chĕl-lȧ) Ca.	30·10 N	115·23 W
124	Coahuayana, Rio de (R.) (rē'ō-dĕ-kō-ä-wä-yä'nä). Mex.	19·00 N	103·33 W
124	Coahuayutla (kō-ä-wē'lȧ) Mex.	18·19 N	101·44 W
122	Coahuila (State) (kō-ä-wē'lȧ). Mex.	27·30 N	103·00 W
107	Coal City (kōl sĭ'tĭ) Il. (Chicago In.)	41·17 N	88·17 W
124	Coalcomán, Rio de (R.) (rē'ō-dĕ-kō-äl-kō-män'). Mex.	18·30 N	102·48 W
124	Coalcomán, Sierra de (Mts.) (syĕr'rä dā kō-äl-kō-män'). Mex.	18·30 N	102·45 W
124	Coalcomán de Matamoros (kō-äl-kō-män' dä mä-tä-mō'rōs) Mex.	18·46 N	103·10 W
94	Coaldale (kōl'dāl) Can.	49·43 N	112·37 W
114	Coaldale Nv.	38·02 N	117·57 W
117	Coalgate (kōl'gāt) Ok.	34·33 N	96·13 W
104	Coal Grove (kōl grōv) Oh.	38·20 N	82·40 W
114	Coalinga (kō-ȧ-lĭŋ'gȧ) Ca.	36·09 N	120·23 W
148	Coalville (kōl'vĭl) Eng.	52·43 N	1·21 W
123	Coamo (kō-ä'mō) P.R. (Puerto Rico In.)	18·05 N	66·21 W
134	Coari (kō-är'ē) Braz.	4·06 S	63·10 W
92	Coast Mts. (kōst) Can.	53·00 N	128·00 W
102	Coast Ranges, (Mts.) U. S.	41·28 N	123·30 W
124	Coatepec (kō-ä-tä-pĕk) Mex.	19·23 N	98·44 W
125	Coatepec Mex.	19·26 N	96·56 W
125	Coatepec Mex. (In.)	19·08 N	99·25 W
126	Coatepeque (kō-ä-tȧ-pā'kȧ). Guat.	14·40 N	91·52 W
126	Coatepeque Sal.	13·56 N	89·30 W
105	Coatesville (kōts'vĭl) Pa.	40·00 N	75·50 W
124	Coatetelco (kō-ä-tȧ-tĕl'kō). Mex.	18·43 N	99·47 W
105	Coaticook (kō'tĭ-kŏŏk) Can.	45·10 N	71·55 W
125	Coatlinchán (kô-ä-tlē'n-chä'n) Mex. (In.)	19·26 N	98·52 W
91	Coats (I.) (kōts) Can.	62·23 N	82·11 W
220	Coats Land (Reg.) Ant.	74·00 S	12·00 W
125	Coatzacoalcos (Puerto Mexico) (kō-ät'zä-kō-äl'kōs) (pwĕ'r-tō-mĕ'-kē-kō). Mex.	18·09 N	94·26 W
125	Coatzacoalcos (R.) Mex.	17·40 N	94·41 W
126	Coba (Ruins) (kô'bä). Mex. (In.)	20·23 N	87·23 W
91	Cobalt (kō'bôlt) Can.	47·21 N	79·40 W
126	Cobán (kō-bän') Guat.	15·28 N	90·19 W
203	Cobberas, Mt. (cŏ-bēr-ăs). Austl.	36·45 S	148·15 E
98	Cobequid Mts. Can.	45·35 N	64·10 W
154	Cobh (kôv) Ire.	51·52 N	8·09 W
134	Cobija (kô-bē'hä) Bol.	11·12 S	68·49 W
105	Cobourg (kō'bōōrg) Can.	43·55 N	78·05 W
128	Cobre (R.) (kō'brā) Jam.	18·05 N	77·00 W
217	Cóbuè Moz.	12·04 S	34·50 E
158	Coburg (kō'bōōrg) F.R.G.	50·16 N	10·57 E
163	Cocentaina (kō-thân-tä-ē'nȧ). Sp.	38·44 N	0·27 W
134	Cochabamba (kō-chä-bäm'bȧ). Bol.	17·28 S	65·43 W
161	Cochem (kō'κĕm) F.R.G.	50·10 N	7·06 E
185	Cochin (kō-chĭn') India	9·58 N	76·19 E
128	Cochinos, Bahia (B.) (bä-ē'ä-kô-chê'nōs). Cuba	22·05 N	81·10 W
129	Cochinos Bks. Ba.	22·20 N	76·15 W
197	Cochinos Pt. (kô-chē'-nōs) Phil. (In.)	14·25 N	120·15 E
115	Cochita Res. NM	35·45 N	106·10 W
120	Cochran (kŏk'răn) Ga.	32·23 N	83·23 W
91	Cochrane (kŏk'răn) Can.	49·01 N	81·06 W
93	Cochrane Can. (Calgary In.)	51·11 N	114·28 W
104	Cockburn (I.) (kŏk-bûrn) Can.	45·55 N	83·25 W
106	Cockeysville (kŏk'ĭz-vĭl) Md. (Baltimore In.)	39·30 N	76·40 W
113	Cockrell Hill (kŏk'rĕl) Tx. (Dallas, Fort Worth In.)	32·44 N	96·53 W
127	Coco (Segovia) (R.) (kô-kô) (sĕ-gô'vyä) Hond-Nic.	14·55 N	83·45 W
128	Coco, Cayo (I.) (kä'-yō-kô'kô) Cuba	22·30 N	78·30 W
134	Coco, Isla del (I.) (ê's-lä-dĕl-kô-kô) C. R.	5·33 N	87·02 W
121	Cocoa (kō'kō) Fl. (In.)	28·21 N	80·44 W
121	Cocoa Beach Fl. (In.)	28·20 N	80·35 W
122	Cocoli (kō-kô'lē) C. Z. (In.)	8·58 N	79·36 W
115	Coconino, Plat. (kō kō nē'nō). Az.	35·45 N	112·28 W
7	Cocos (Keeling) Is. (kō'kôs) (kē'lĭng). Oceania	11·50 S	90·50 E
122	Coco Solito (kô-kô-sŏ-lē'tŏ) C. Z. (In.)	9·21 N	79·53 W
98	Cocouna Can.	47·54 N	69·31 W
124	Cocula (kō-kōō'lä) Mex.	20·23 N	103·47 W
124	Cocula (R.) Mex.	18·17 N	99·11 W
134	Codajás (kō-dä-häzh') Braz.	3·44 S	62·09 W
135	Codera, Cabo (C.) (kȧ'bô-kō-dĕ'rä). Ven. (In.)	10·35 N	66·06 W
135	Codó (kō'dō) Braz.	4·21 S	43·52 W
164	Codogno (kō-dō'nyō) It.	45·08 N	9·43 E
127	Codrington (kŏd'rĭng-tŭn) Antigua (In.)	17·39 N	61·49 W
111	Cody (kō'dĭ) Wy.	44·31 N	109·02 W
216	Coemba Ang.	12·08 S	18·05 E
161	Coesfeld (kûs'fĕld) F.R.G. (Ruhr In.)	51·56 N	7·10 E
110	Coeur d' Alene (kûr dȧ-lān'). Id.	47·43 N	116·35 W
110	Coeur d' Alene L. Id.	47·32 N	116·39 W
110	Coeur d' Alene R. Id.	47·26 N	116·35 W
117	Coffeyville (kŏf'ĭ-vĭl) Ks.	37·01 N	95·38 W
203	Coff's Harbour Austl.	30·20 S	153·10 E
213	Cofimvaba (căfĭm'vä-bȧ) S. Afr. (Natal In.)	32·01 S	27·37 E
164	Coghinas (R.) (kō'gē-nȧs) It.	40·31 N	9·00 E
160	Cognac (kōn-yak') Fr.	45·41 N	0·22 W
99	Cohasset (kō-hăs'ĕt). Ma. (In.)	42·14 N	70·48 W
105	Cohoes (kô-hōz') NY	42·50 N	73·40 W
136	Coig (kô'ĕk) (R.) Arg.	51·15 S	71·00 W
185	Coimbatore (kō-ēm-bȧ-tôr'). India	11·03 N	76·56 E
162	Coimbra (kō-ēm'brä) Port.	40·14 N	8·23 W
162	Coín (kō-ēn') Sp.	36·40 N	4·45 W
163	Coina (kō-ē'nȧ). Port. (Lisbon In.)	38·35 N	9·03 W
163	Coina (R.) (kô'y-nä) Port. (Lisbon In.)	38·35 N	9·02 W
134	Coipasa, Salar de (Salt Flat) (sä-lä'r-dĕ-koi-pä'-sä). Chile	19·12 S	69·13 W
125	Coixtlahuaca (kō-ēks'tlä-wä'kä) Mex.	17·42 N	97·17 W
135	Cojedes (State) (kô-kĕ'dĕs) Ven. (In.)	9·50 N	68·21 W
129	Cojimar (kō-hē-mär'). Cuba (In.)	23·10 N	82·19 W
126	Cojutepeque (kô-hōō-tĕ-pā'kȧ) Sal.	13·45 N	88·50 W
109	Cokato (kô-kā'tō) Mn.	45·03 N	94·11 W
107	Cokeburg (kōk bûgh) Pa. (Pittsburgh In.)	40·06 N	80·03 W
203	Colac (kŏ'lăc) Austl.	38·25 S	143·40 E
163	Colares (kô-lä'rĕs) Port. (Lisbon In.)	38·47 N	9·27 W
135	Colatina (kô-lä-tē'nä) Braz.	19·33 S	40·42 W
116	Colby (kōl'bĭ) Ks.	39·23 N	101·04 W
137	Colchagua (Prov.) (kôl-chä'gwä) Chile (Santiago In.)	36·42 S	71·24 W
155	Colchester (kōl'chĕs-tēr) Eng.	51·52 N	0·50 E
94	Cold L. (kōld) Can.	54·33 N	110·05 W
116	Coldwater (kōld'wô-tēr) Ks.	37·14 N	99·21 W
104	Coldwater Mi.	41·55 N	85·00 W
120	Coldwater (R.) Ms.	34·25 N	90·12 W
116	Coldwater Cr. Tx.	36·10 N	101·45 W
118	Coleman (kōl'mȧn) Tx.	31·50 N	99·25 W
213	Colenso (kō-lĕnz'ō) S. Afr. (Natal In.)	28·48 S	29·49 E
109	Coleraine (kōl-rān') Mn.	47·16 N	93·29 W
154	Coleraine N. Ire.	55·08 N	6·40 W
148	Coleshill (kōlz'hĭl) Eng.	52·30 N	1·42 W
109	Colfax (kōl'făks) Ia.	41·40 N	93·13 W
119	Colfax La.	31·31 N	92·42 W
110	Colfax Wa.	46·53 N	117·21 W
136	Colhué Huapi (L.) (kôl-wä'ōōȧ'pē). Arg.	45·30 S	68·45 W
218	Coligny. S. Afr. (Johannesburg Pretoria In.)	26·20 S	26·18 E
124	Colima (kōlē'mä) Mex.	19·13 N	103·45 W
124	Colima (State) Mex.	19·10 N	104·00 W
124	Colima, Nevado de (nĕ-vä'dô-dĕ-kô-lē'mä) (Mtn.) Mex.	19·30 N	103·38 W
154	Coll (I.) (kōl) Scot.	56·42 N	6·23 W
101	College Ak.	64·43 N	147·50 W
106	College Park (kŏl'ĕj) Ga. (Atlanta In.)	33·39 N	84·27 W
106	College Park. Md. (Baltimore In.)	38·59 N	76·58 W

ăt; finăl; rāte; senâte; ärm; ȧsk; sofȧ; fâre; ch-choose; dh-as th in other; bē; ēvent; bĕt; recĕnt; cratēr; g-go; gh-guttural g; bĭt; ĭ-short neutral; rīde; κ-guttural k as ch in German ich;

PRONOUNCING INDEX

Collegeville — Corbie 271

Page	Name Pronunciation Region	Lat. °'	Long. °'
106	Collegeville (kŏl'ĕj-vĭl) Pa. (Philadelphia In.)	40·11 N	75·27 W
204	Collie (kŏl'ē) Austl.	33·20 S	116·20 E
204	Collier B. (kŏl-yĕr) Austl.	15·30 S	123·30 E
163	Colli Laziali (Mtn.) (kô'lē-lät-zyä'lē). It. (Rome In.)	41·46 N	12·45 E
106	Collingswood (kŏl'ĭngz-wŏŏd) NJ (Philadelphia In.)	39·54 N	75·04 W
104	Collingwood Can.	44·30 N	80·20 W
120	Collins (kŏl'ĭns) Ms.	31·40 N	89·34 W
113	Collinsville (kŏl'ĭnz-vĭl) Il. (St. Louis In.)	38·41 N	89·59 W
117	Collinsville Ok.	36·21 N	95·50 W
210	Collo (kôl'ō) Alg.	37·02 N	6·29 E
161	Colmar (kōl'mär) Fr.	48·40 N	7·22 E
162	Colmenar de Oreja (kôl-mä-när'dāōrā'hä). Sp.	40·06 N	3·25 W
163	Colmenar Viejo (kōl-mä-när'vyā'hō) Sp. (Madrid In.)	40·40 N	3·46 W
	Cologne, see Köln		
134	Colombia (kô-lôm'bê-ä). Col. (In.)	3·23 N	74·48 W
133	Colombia S. A.	3·30 N	72·30 W
185	Colombo (kô-lôm'bō)... Sri Lanka	6·58 N	79·52 E
137	Colón (kō-lōn') Arg. (Buenos Aires In.)	33·55 S	61·08 W
128	Colón (kô-lô'n) Cuba	22·45 N	80·55 W
124	Colón (kō-lōn') Mex.	20·46 N	100·02 W
120	Colón (kŏ-lô'n) Pan. (In.)	9·22 N	79·54 W
134	Colon, Arch. de (Galápagos Is.) (är-chê-pyĕ'l-ágô-dĕ-kō-lōn') (gä-lá'pägôs). Ec.	0·10 S	87·45 W
127	Colōn, Montañas de (Mts.) (môn-tä'n-yäs-dĕ-kō-lô'n) Hond.	14·58 N	84·39 W
137	Colonia (kō-lō'nê-ä) Ur. (Buenos Aires In.)	34·27 S	57·50 W
137	Colonia (Dept.) Ur. (Buenos Aires In.)	34·08 S	57·50 W
137	Colonia Suiza (kō-lō'nêä-sōōē'zä) Ur. (Buenos Aires In.)	34·17 S	57·15 W
163	Colonna (kô-lô'n-nä). It. (Rome In.)	41·50 N	12·48 E
165	Colonne, C. di (kô-lô'n-nĕ) It.	39·02 N	17·15 E
154	Colonsay (I.) (kŏl-ôn-sā') Scot.	56·08 N	6·08 W
136	Coloradas, Lomas (Hills) (lô'mäs-kō-lō-rä'däs). Arg.	43·30 S	68·00 W
102	Colorado (State) U. S.	39·30 N	106·55 W
118	Colorado City (kŏl-ō-rä'dō sĭ'tĭ) Tx.	32·24 N	100·50 W
136	Colorado, Rio (R.) Arg.	38·30 S	66·00 W
115	Colorado Natl. Mon. Co.	39·00 N	108·40 W
102	Colorado Plat. U. S.	36·20 N	109·25 W
119	Colorado R. Tx.	30·08 N	97·33 W
102	Colorado, R. U. S.	36·25 N	112·00 W
104	Colorado River Aqueducts Ca.	33·38 N	115·43 W
105	Colorado River Ind. Res. Az.	34·03 N	114·02 W
128	Colorados, Arch. de los (Is.) (är-chē-pyĕ-lä-gô-dĕ-lôs-kô-lô-rä'dôs) Cuba	22·25 N	84·25 W
116	Colorado Springs (kŏl-ō-rä'dō). Co.	38·49 N	104·48 W
125	Colotepec (R.) (kô-lô'tĕ-pĕk) Mex.	15·56 N	96·57 W
124	Colotlán' (kô-lô-tlän') Mex.	22·06 N	103·14 W
124	Colotlán (R.) Mex.	22·09 N	103·17 W
122	Colquechaca (kôl-kā-chä'kä).. Bol.	18·47 S	66·02 W
111	Colstrip (kōl'strĭp) Mt.	45·54 N	106·38 W
113	Colton (kōl'tŭn) Ca. (Los Angeles In.)	34·04 N	117·20 W
113	Columbia (kō-lŭm'bĭ-ȧ) Il. (St. Louis In.)	38·26 N	90·12 W
120	Columbia Ky.	37·06 N	85·15 W
106	Columbia Md. (Baltimore In.)	39·15 N	76·51 W
120	Columbia Ms.	31·15 N	89·49 W
117	Columbia Mo.	38·55 N	92·19 W
105	Columbia Pa.	40·00 N	76·25 W
121	Columbia SC	34·00 N	81·00 W
120	Columbia Tn.	35·36 N	87·02 W
93	Columbia, Mt. Can.	52·09 N	117·25 W
93	Columbia (R.) Can.	51·30 N	119·00 W
104	Columbia City In.	41·10 N	85·30 W
112	Columbia City. Or. (Portland In.)	45·53 N	112·49 W
113	Columbia Heights Mn. (Minneapolis, St. Paul In.)	45·03 N	93·15 W
93	Columbia Icefield Can.	52·08 N	117·26 W
93	Columbia Mts. Can.	51·30 N	118·30 W
120	Columbiana (kô-ŭm-bĭ-ă'nȧ).. Al.	33·10 N	86·35 W
90	Columbia R. U. S.-Can.	46·20 N	123·00 W
163	Columbretes (I.) (kô-lōōm-brĕ'tĕs). Sp.	39·54 N	0·54 E
120	Columbus (kô-lŭm'bŭs) Ga.	32·29 N	84·56 W
104	Columbus In.	39·15 N	85·55 W
117	Columbus Ks.	37·10 N	94·50 W
120	Columbus Ms.	33·30 N	88·25 W
111	Columbus Mt.	45·39 N	109·15 W
108	Columbus Ne.	41·25 N	97·25 W
115	Columbus NM	31·50 N	107·40 W
104	Columbus Oh.	40·00 N	83·00 W
119	Columbus Tx.	29·44 N	96·34 W
109	Columbus Wi.	43·20 N	89·01 W
119	Columbus Bk. (kô-lŭm'bŭs)... Ba.	22·05 N	75·30 W
104	Columbus Grove Oh.	40·55 N	84·00 W
119	Columbus Pt. Ba.	24·10 N	75·15 W
114	Colusa (kô-lū'sȧ) Ca.	39·12 N	122·01 W
110	Colville (kŏl'vĭl) Wa.	48·33 N	117·53 W
101	Colville (R.) Ak.	69·00 N	156·25 W
110	Colville R. Wa.	48·25 N	117·58 W
112	Colvos Pass. (kōl'vōs) Wa. (Seattle In.)	47·24 N	122·32 W
112	Colwood (kŏl'wŏŏd) Can. (Seattle In.)	48·26 N	123·30 W
164	Comacchio (kô-mäk'kyō) It.	44·42 N	12·12 E
124	Comala (kô-mä-lä') Mex.	19·22 N	103·47 W
126	Comalapa (kō-mä-lä'-pä) Guat.	14·43 N	90·56 W
125	Comalcalco (kō-mäl-käl'kō).. Mex.	18·16 N	93·13 W
116	Comanche (kô-măn'chê) Ok.	34·20 N	97·58 W
118	Comanche Tx.	31·54 N	98·37 W
118	Comanche Cr. Tx.	31·02 N	102·47 W
126	Comayagua (kō-mä-yä'gwä). Hond.	14·24 N	87·36 W
121	Combahee (R.) (kŏm-bȧ-hē').. SC	32·42 N	80·40 W
120	Comer (kŭm'ẽr) Ga.	34·02 N	83·07 W
129	Comete, C. (kô-mä'tâ) Turks & Caicos	21·45 N	71·25 W
184	Comilla (kô-mĭl'ä) Bngl.	23·33 N	91·17 E
164	Comino, C. (kô-mē'nō) It.	40·30 N	9·48 E
127	Comitán (kô-mē-tän') Mex.	16·16 N	92·09 W
112	Commencement Bay (kŏ-mĕns'mĕnt bā) Wa. (Seattle In.)	47·17 N	122·21 W
160	Commentry (kô-mäN-trē') Fr.	46·16 N	2·44 E
120	Commerce (kŏm'ẽrs) Ga.	34·10 N	83·27 W
117	Commerce Ok.	36·57 N	94·54 W
117	Commerce Tx.	33·15 N	95·52 W
164	Como (kō'mō) It.	45·48 N	9·03 E
164	Como, Lago di (L.) (lä'gō-dē-kō'mō). It.	46·00 N	9·30 E
136	Comodoro Rivadavia (kŏ'mô-dō'rô rē-vä-dä'vê-ä). Arg.	45·47 S	67·31 W
100	Como-Est... Can. (Montreal In.)	45·27 N	74·08 W
124	Comonfort (kô-mōn-fô'rt)... Mex.	20·43 N	100·47 W
185	Comorin C. (kŏ'mô-rĭn) In.	13·18 N	77·16 E
209	Comoro Is. Afr.	12·30 S	42·45 E
92	Comox (kō'mŏks) Can.	49·40 N	124·55 W
125	Compainalá (kôm-pä-ē-nä-lá') Mex.	17·05 N	93·11 W
137	Companario, Cerro (Mtn.) (sĕ'r-rô-kôm-pä-nä'ryô) Arg.-Chile (Santiago In.)	35·54 S	70·23 W
160	Compiègne (kôN-pyĕn'y') Fr..	49·25 N	2·49 E
163	Comporta (kôm-pôr'tȧ) Port. (Lisbon In.)	38·24 N	8·48 W
124	Compostela (kōm-pô-stā'lä).. Mex.	21·41 N	104·54 W
113	Compton (kŏmp'tŭn) Ca. (Los Angeles In.)	33·54 N	118·14 W
120	Cona (R.) (kô-nȧ) Ga.	34·40 N	84·51 W
214	Conakry (kô-nȧ-krē') Gui.	9·31 N	13·43 W
106	Conanicut (kŏn'ȧ-nĭ-kŭt) RI (Providence In.)	41·34 N	71·20 W
160	Concarneau (kôN-kär-nō') Fr.	47·54 N	3·52 W
135	Concepción (kôn-sĕp'syōn')... Bol.	15·47 S	61·08 W
136	Concepción Chile	36·51 S	72·59 W
127'	Concepción Pan.	8·31 N	82·38 W
136	Concepción Par.	23·29 S	57·18 W
197	Concepcion Phil. (In.)	15·19 N	120·40 E
122	Concepción (R.) Mex.	30·25 N	112·20 W
126	Concepción (Vol.) Nic.	11·36 N	85·43 W
126	Concepcion del Mar (kôn-sĕp-syōn' dĕl mär'). Guat	14·07 N	91·23 W
118	Concepcion del Oro (kôn-sĕp-syōn' dĕl ō'rō). Mex.	24·39 N	101·24 W
136	Concepción del Uruguay (kôn-sĕp-syô'n-dĕl-ōō-rōō-gwī'). Arg.	32·31 S	58·10 W
119	Conception (I.) Ba.	23·50 N	75·05 W
114	Conception, Pt. Ca.	34·27 N	120·28 W
99	Conception B. (kŏn-sĕp'shŭn). Can.	47·50 N	52·50 W
118	Concho R. (kŏn'chō) Tx.	31·34 N	100·02 W
118	Conchos R. (kōn'chōs) Mex.	25·03 N	99·00 W
118	Conchos R. Mex.	29·08 N	105·02 W
112	Concord (kŏŋ'kŏrd) Ca. (San Francisco In.)	37·58 N	122·02 W
99	Concord Ma. (Boston In.)	42·28 N	71·21 W
105	Concord NH	43·10 N	71·30 W
120	Concord NC	35·23 N	80·11 W
136	Concordia (kŏn-kôr'dĭ-ȧ) Arg.	31·18 S	57·59 W
134	Concordia Col. (In.)	6·04 N	75·54 W
117	Concordia Ks.	39·32 N	97·39 W
124	Concordia (kôn-kô'r-dyä) Mex.	23·17 N	106·06 W
110	Concrete (kŏn'krēt) Wa.	48·33 N	121·44 W
108	Conde (kŏn-dē') SD	45·10 N	98·06 W
126	Condega (kŏn-dĕ'gä) Nic.	13·20 N	86·27 W
160	Condem (kôN-dĕN) Fr.	43·58 N	0·22 E
160	Condé-sur-Noireau (kôN-dā'sür-nwä-rō'). Fr.	48·50 N	0·36 W
135	Condeúba (kōn-dā-ōō'bä) Braz.	14·47 S	41·44 W
110	Condon (kŏn'dŭn) Or.	45·14 N	120·10 W
120	Conecun (R.) (kō-nē'kŭ) Al.	31·05 N	86·52 W
164	Conegliano (kō-nâl-yä'nō) It.	45·59 N	12·17 E
115	Conejos (R.) (kō-nā'hōs) Co.	37·07 N	106·19 W
105	Conemaugh (kŏn'ê-mô) Pa.	40·25 N	78·50 W
116	Coney I. (kō'nĭ) NY (New York In.)	40·34 N	73·27 W
160	Confolens (kôN-fä-läN') Fr.	46·01 N	0·41 E
121	Congaree (R.) (kŏŋ-gá-rē') SC	33·53 N	80·55 W
148	Congleton (kŏŋ'g'l-tŭn) Eng.	53·10 N	2·13 W
209	Congo (kŏŋ'gō) Afr.	3·00 S	13·48 E
212	Congo (Reg.) Ang.	6·40 S	14·00 E
216	Congo (Zaire) (R.) Afr.	1·10 N	18·25 E
216	Congo, Serra do (Mts.) Ang.	6·25 S	13·50 E
	Congo, The, see Zaire		
209	Congo Basin Zaire	2·47 N	20·58 E
148	Conisbrough (kŏn'ĭs-bŭr-ō).. Eng.	53·29 N	1·13 W
97	Coniston Can.	46·29 N	80·51 W
93	Conklin (kŏŋk'lĭn) Can.	55·38 N	111·05 W
106	Conley (kŏn'lĭ). Ga. (Atlanta In.)	33·38 N	84·19 W
154	Conn, Lough (B.) (lŏk kŏn)... Ire.	53·56 N	9·25 W
154	Connacht (cŏn'ât) Ire.	53·50 N	8·45 W
102	Conneaut (kŏn-ê-ôt') Oh.	41·55 N	80·35 W
103	Connecticut (State) (kŏ-nĕt'ĭ-kŭt) U. S.	41·40 N	73·10 W
105	Connecticut R. U. S.	43·55 N	72·15 W
105	Connellsville (kŏn'nĕlz-vĭl)... Pa.	40·00 N	79·40 W
154	Connemara, Mts. (kŏn-nê-mȧ'rȧ) Ire.	53·30 N	9·54 W
104	Connersville (kŏn'ẽrz-vĭl) In.	39·35 N	85·10 W
205	Connors Ra. (kŏn'nŏrs) Austl.	22·15 S	149·00 E
111	Conrad (kŏn'răd) Mt.	48·11 N	111·56 W
100	Conrich (kŏn'rĭch) Can. (Calgary In.)	51·06 N	113·51 W
119	Conroe (kŏn'rō) Tx.	30·18 N	95·23 W
137	Conselheiro Lafaiete (kŏn-sĕ-lā'rô-lȧ-fā'ĕ-tĕ) Braz. (Rio de Janeiro In.)	20·40 S	43·46 W
106	Conshohocken (kŏn-shô-hŏk'ĕn) Pa. (Philadelphia In.)	40·04 N	75·18 W
128	Consolación (kōn-sô-lä-syōn') Cuba	22·30 N	83·55 W
197	Consolacion (kôn-sô-lä-syô'n) Phil. (In.)	16·20 N	120·21 E
196	Con Son (Is.) Viet.	8·30 N	106·28 E
112	Constance, Mt. (kŏn'stȧns) Wa. (Seattle In.)	47·46 N	123·08 W
153	Constanţa (kōn-stän'tsä) Rom.	44·12 N	28·36 E
162	Constantina (kŏn-stän-tē'nä).. Sp.	37·52 N	5·39 W
210	Constantine (kôN-stäN'tēn')... Alg.	36·28 N	6·38 E
104	Constantine (kŏn'stȧn-tēn)... Mi.	41·50 N	85·40 W
101	Constantine Harbor Ak.	51·22 N	179·20 E
136	Constitución (kōn'stĭ-tōō-syōn') Chile	35·24 S	72·25 W
106	Constitution (kŏn-stĭ-tū'shŭn) Ga. (Atlanta In.)	33·41 N	84·20 W
137	Contagem (kōn-tá'zhĕm) Braz. (Rio de Janerio In.)	19·54 S	44·05 W
124	Contepec (kōn-tĕ-pĕk') Mex.	20·04 N	100·07 W
125	Contreras (kôn-trĕ'räs). Mex. (In.)	19·18 N	99·14 W
100	Contwoyto (L.) Can.	65·42 N	110·50 W
113	Converse (kŏn'vẽrs) Tx. (San Antonio In.)	29·31 N	98·17 W
117	Conway (kŏn'wā) Ar.	35·06 N	92·27 W
105	Conway NH	44·00 N	71·10 W
121	Conway SC	33·49 N	79·01 W
112	Conway Wa. (Seattle In.)	48·20 N	122·20 W
120	Conyers (kŏn'yŏrz) Ga.	33·41 N	84·01 W
184	Cooch Behār (kōōch bê-här') India	26·25 N	89·34 E
92	Cook, C. (kŏŏk) Can.	50·08 N	127·55 W
205	Cook, Mt. N. Z. (In.)	43·27 S	170·13 E
120	Cookeville (kŏŏk'vĭl) Tn.	36·07 N	85·30 W
100	Cooking Lake (kŏŏk'ĭng) Can. (Edmonton In.)	53·10 N	113·08 W
101	Cooking L... Can. (Edmonton In.)	53·25 N	113·02 W
101	Cook Inlet Ak.	60·50 N	151·38 W
199	Cook Is. Oceania	19·20 S	158·00 W
205	Cook Str. N. Z. (In.)	40·37 S	174·15 E
205	Cooktown (kŏŏk'toun) Austl.	15·40 S	145·20 E
121	Cooleemee (kōō-lē'mē) NC	35·50 N	80·32 W
204	Coolgardie (kōōl-gär'dê)... Austl.	31·00 S	121·25 E
203	Cooma (kōō'mȧ) Austl.	36·22 S	149·10 E
203	Coonamble (kōō-năm'b'l)... Austl.	30·50 S	144·27 E
185	Coonoort India	10·22 N	76·15 E
113	Coon Rapids (kōōn). Mn. (Minneapolis, St. Paul In.)	45·09 N	93·17 W
117	Cooper (kōōp'ẽr) Tx.	33·23 N	95·40 W
101	Cooper Center (kōōp'ẽr sĕn'tẽr) Ak.	61·54 N	145·30 W
203	Coopers Cr. (kōō'pẽrz) Austl.	27·32 S	141·19 E
105	Cooperstown (kōōp'ẽrs-toun).. NY	42·45 N	74·55 W
108	Cooperstown ND	47·26 N	98·07 W
203	Coorong, The (L.) (kōō'rŏng) Austl.	36·07 S	139·45 E
120	Coosa (kōō'sȧ) Al.	32·43 N	86·25 W
120	Coosa (R.) Al.	34·00 N	86·00 W
120	Coosawattee (R.) (kōō-sȧ-wôt'ē) Ga.	34·37 N	84·45 W
110	Coos Bay (kōōs) Or.	43·21 N	124·12 W
110	Coos B. Or.	43·19 N	124·40 W
203	Cootamundra (kōōtȧ-mŭnd'rȧ) Austl.	34·25 S	148·00 E
136	Copacabana (kô'pä-kȧ-bä'nä) Braz. (Rio de Janeiro In.)	22·57 S	43·11 W
125	Copalita (R.) (kō-pä-lē'tä)... Mex.	15·55 N	96·06 W
126	Copán (Ruins) (kō-pän')... Hond.	14·50 N	89·10 W
119	Copano B. (kō-pän'ō) Tx.	28·08 N	97·25 W
	Copenhagen, see København		
136	Copiapó (kō-pyä-pō') Chile	27·16 S	70·28 W
107	Copley (kŏp'lē) Oh. (Cleveland In.)	41·06 N	81·38 W
164	Copparo (kôp-pä'rō) It.	44·53 N	11·50 E
113	Coppell (kŏp'pĕl) Tx. (Dallas, Fort Worth In.)	32·57 N	97·00 W
101	Copper (R.) (kŏp'ẽr) Ak.	62·38 N	145·00 W
96	Copper Cliff Can.	46·28 N	81·04 W
109	Copper Harbor Mi.	47·27 N	87·53 W
110	Copperhill (kŏp'ẽr hĭl) Tn.	35·00 N	84·22 W
90	Coppermine (kŏp'ẽr-mīn) Can.	67·46 N	115·19 W
92	Copper Mtn. Ak.	55·14 N	132·36 W
90	Copperinine (R.) Can.	66·48 N	114·59 W
113	Copperton (kŏp'ẽr-tŭn) Ut. (Salt Lake City In.)	40·34 N	112·06 W
	Coquilhatville, see Mbandaka		
110	Coquille (kô-kēl') Or.	43·11 N	124·11 W
136	Coquimbo (kō-kēm'bō) Chile	29·58 S	71·31 W
137	Coquimbo (Prov.) Chile (Santiago In.)	31·50 S	71·05 W
133	Coquitlam (L.) (kō-kwĭt-lȧm) Can. (Vancouver In.)	49·23 N	122·44 W
165	Corabia (kô-rä'bĭ-ȧ) Rom.	43·45 N	24·29 E
134	Coracora (kō'rä-kō'rä) Peru	15·12 S	73·42 W
121	Coral Gables Fl. (In.)	25·43 N	80·14 W
128	Coralillo (kô-rä-lē-yō) Cuba	23·00 N	80·40 W
100	Coral Rapids (kŏr'ăl) Can.	50·18 N	81·49 W
198	Coral Sea (kŏr'ăl) Oceania	13·30 S	150·00 E
109	Coralville Res. Ia.	41·45 N	91·50 W
203	Corangamite, L. (cŏr-ăŋg'ȧ-mĭt) Austl.	38·05 S	142·55 E
107	Coraopolis (kō-rä-ŏp'ô-lĭs) Pa. (Pittsburgh In.)	40·30 N	80·09 W
164	Corato (kô'rä-tô) It.	41·08 N	16·28 E
161	Corbeil-Essonnes (kôr-bā'yĕ-sŏn') Fr. (Paris In.)	48·31 N	2·29 E
112	Corbett (kôr'bĕt) Or. (Portland In.)	45·31 N	122·17 W
160	Corbie (kôr-bē') Fr.	49·55 N	2·27 E

272 Corbin — Croix PRONOUNCING INDEX

Page	Name Pronunciation Region	Lat. °'	Long. °'
120	Corbin (kôr'bĭn). Ky.	36·55 N	84·06 W
148	Corby (kôr'bĭ). Eng.	52·29 N	0·38 W
136	Corcovado (Mtn.) (kôr-kô-vä'dōō) Braz. (Rio de Janeiro In.)	22·57 S	43·13 W
136	Corcovado, Golfo (G.) (kôr-kô-vä'dhō). Chile	43·40 S	75·00 W
137	Cordeiro (kôr-dā'rō) Braz. (Rio de Janeiro In.)	22·03 S	42·22 W
120	Cordele (kôr-dēl'). Ga.	31·55 N	83·50 W
116	Cordell (kôr-děl'). Ok.	35·19 N	98·58 W
75	Cordilleran Highlands (Reg.) (kōr dĭl'lŭr ȧn). N. A.	55·00 N	125·00 W
136	Córdoba (kôr'dô-vä). Arg.	30·20 S	64·03 W
125	Córdoba (kô'r-dô-bä). Mex.	18·53 N	96·54 W
162	Córdoba (kô'r-dô-bä). Sp.	37·55 N	4·45 W
136	Córdoba (Prov.) (kôr'dô-vä). Arg.	32·00 S	64·00 W
136	Córdoba, Sa. de (Mts.). Arg.	31·15 S	64·30 W
120	Cordova (kôr'dô-vȧ). Al.	33·45 N	86·11 W
101	Cordova (kôr'dô-vä). Ak.	60·34 N	145·38 W
92	Cordova B. Ak.	54·55 N	132·35 W
162	Corella (kô-rěl-yä). Sp.	42·07 N	1·48 W
164	Corigliano (kō-rē-lyä'nō). It.	39·35 N	16·30 E
120	Corinth (kŏr'ĭnth). Ms.	34·55 N	88·30 W
	Corinth, see Kórinthos		
135	Corinto (kô-rē'n-tō). Braz.	18·20 S	44·16 W
134	Corinto. Col. (In.)	3·09 N	76·12 W
126	Corinto (kōr-ĭn'to). Nic.	12·30 N	87·12 W
202	Corio. Austl. (Melbourne In.)	38·05 S	144·22 E
202	Corio B. Austl. (Melbourne In.)	38·07 S	144·25 E
216	Corisco, Isal de (I.). Equat. Gui.	0·50 N	8·40 E
154	Cork (kôrk). Ire.	51·54 N	8·25 W
154	Cork Hbr. Ire.	51·44 N	8·15 W
164	Corleone (kôr-lå-ō'nā). It.	37·48 N	13·18 E
165	Corlu (chôr'lōō). Tur.	41·09 N	27·48 E
95	Cormorant L. Can.	54·13 N	100·47 W
120	Cornelia (kôr-nē'lyȧ). Ga.	34·31 N	83·30 W
218	Cornelis R. (kôr-nē lĭs). S. Afr. (Johannesburg & Pretoria In.)	27·48 S	29·15 E
113	Cornell (kôr-něl') Ca. (Los Angeles In.)	34·06 N	118·46 W
109	Cornell. Wi.	45·10 N	91·10 W
91	Corner Brook (kôr'nēr). Can.	48·57 N	57·57 W
203	Corner Inlet. Austl.	38·55 S	146·45 E
	Corneto, see Targuinia		
117	Corning (kôr'nĭng). Ar.	36·26 N	90·35 W
109	Corning. Ia.	40·58 N	94·40 W
105	Corning. NY	42·10 N	77·05 W
164	Corno, M. (Mtn.) (kôr'nō). It.	42·28 N	13·37 E
128	Cornwall. Ba.	25·55 N	77·15 W
105	Cornwall (kôrn'wôl). Can.	45·05 N	74·35 W
154	Cornwall Pen. (kôrn'wăl). Eng.	50·25 N	5·04 W
134	Coro (kō'rô). Ven.	11·22 N	69·43 W
134	Corocoro (kō-rô-kō'rô). Bol.	17·15 S	68·21 W
185	Coromandel Coast (kŏr-ô-man'dĕl) India	13·30 N	80·30 E
120	Corona (kô-rō'nȧ). Al.	33·42 N	87·28 W
113	Corona. Ca. (Los Angeles In.)	33·52 N	117·34 W
127	Coronada, Bahia de (B.) (bä-ē'ä-dě-kô-rô-nä'dō). C.R.	8·47 N	84·04 W
113	Corona del Mar (kô-rō'nȧ dĕl mär) Ca. (Los Angeles In.)	33·36 N	117·53 W
114	Coronado (kŏr-ô-nä'dō). Ca. (In.)	32·42 N	117·12 W
90	Coronation G. (kŏr-ô-nā'shŭn) Can.	68·07 N	112·50 W
136	Coronel (kō-rô-nĕl'). Chile	37·00 S	73·10 W
137	Coronel Brandsen (kô-rô-něl-brá'nd-sěn) Arg. (Buenos Aires In.)	35·09 S	58·15 W
136	Coronel Dorrego (kô-rô-něl-dôr-rě'gô). Arg.	38·43 S	61·16 W
136	Coronel Oviedo (kô-rô-něl-ô-vēě'dô). Par.	25·28 S	56·22 W
136	Coronel Pringles (kô-rô-něl-prēn'glěs). Arg.	37·54 S	61·22 W
136	Coronel Suárez (kô-rô-něl-swä'rās). Arg.	37·24 S	66·49 W
203	Corowa (cŏr-ôwȧ). Austl.	36·02 S	146·23 E
126	Corozal (cŏr-ŏth-äl'). Belize (In.)	18·25 N	88·23 W
119	Corpus Christi (kôr'pŭs krĭs'tē) Tx.	27·48 N	97·24 W
119	Corpus Christi B. Tx.	27·47 N	97·14 W
118	Corpus Christi L. Tx.	28·08 N	98·20 W
136	Corral (kô-räl'). Chile	39·57 S	73·15 W
162	Corral de Almaguer (kô-räl'dā äl-mä-gâr'). Sp.	39·45 N	3·10 W
197	Corregidor (I.) (kô-rā-hē-dōr') Phil. (In.)	14·21 N	120·25 E
135	Correntina (kô-rěn-tē-nȧ). Braz.	13·18 S	44·33 W
154	Corrib, Lough (B.) (lŏk kŏr'ĭb) Ire.	53·56 N	9·19 W
136	Corrientes (kō-ryěn'tās). Arg.	27·25 S	58·39 W
136	Corrientes (Prov.). Arg.	28·45 S	58·00 W
134	Corrientes, Cabo (C.) (kä'bô-kō-ryěn'tās). Col.	5·34 N	77·35 W
128	Corrientes, Cabo (C.) (kä'bô-kôr-rē-ěn'těs). Cuba	21·50 N	84·25 W
124	Corrientes, Cabo (C.). Mex.	20·25 N	105·41 W
128	Corrientes, Ensenada de (B.) (ěn-sě-nä-dä-dě-kō-ryěn'tās) Cuba	21·45 N	84·45 W
164	Corse, C. (kôrs). Fr.	42·59 N	9·19 E
164	Corsica (I.) (kô'r-sē-kä). Fr.	42·10 N	8·55 E
119	Corsicana (kôr-sĭ-kăn'ȧ). Tx.	32·06 N	96·28 W
124	Cortazar (kôr-tä-zär). Mex.	20·30 N	100·57 W
164	Corte (kôr'tā). Fr.	42·18 N	9·10 E
162	Cortegana (kôr-tå-gä'nä). Sp.	37·54 N	6·48 W
162	Cortes (kôr-tās'). Sp.	36·38 N	5·20 W
128	Cortés, Ensenada de (B.) (ěn-sě-nä-dä-dě-kôr-tās'). Cuba	22·05 N	83·45 W
115	Cortez. Co.	37·21 N	108·35 W
105	Cortland (kôrt'lănd). NY	42·35 N	76·10 W
164	Cortona (kôr-tō'nä). It.	43·16 N	12·00 E
214	Corubal (R.). Guinea-Bissau	11·43 N	14·40 W
162	Coruche (kô-rōō'she). Port.	38·58 N	8·34 W
171	Coruh (R.) (chō-rōōk'). Tur.	40·30 N	41·10 E
171	Corum (chô-rōōm'). Tur.	39·30 N	34·50 E
135	Corumbá (kō-rōōm-bä'). Braz.	19·01 S	57·28 W
104	Corunna (kô-rŭn'ȧ). Mi.	43·00 N	84·05 W
135	Coruripe (kô-rōō-rē'pĭ). Braz.	10·09 S	36·13 W
110	Corvallis (kŏr-văl'ĭs). Or.	44·34 N	123·17 W
148	Corve (R.) (kôr'vē). Eng.	52·28 N	2·43 W
105	Cory (kŏr'ĭ). Pa.	41·55 N	79·40 W
104	Corydon (kŏr'ĭ-dŭn). In.	38·10 N	86·05 W
109	Corydon. Ia.	40·45 N	93·20 W
104	Corydon. Ky.	37·45 N	87·40 W
125	Cosamaloápan (kô-sä-mä-lwä'pän) Mex.	18·21 N	95·48 W
125	Coscomatepec (kôs'kōmä-tě-pěk') Mex.	19·04 N	97·03 W
148	Coseley (kôs'lē). Eng.	52·33 N	2·10 W
164	Cosenza (kô-zěnt'sä). It.	39·18 N	16·15 E
104	Coshocton (kô-shŏk'tŭn). Oh.	40·15 N	81·55 W
104	Cosigüina (Vol.). Nic.	12·59 N	83·35 W
213	Cosmoledo Group (Is.) (kŏs-mô-lā'dō). Afr.	9·42 S	47·45 E
110	Cosmopolis (kŏz-mŏp'ô-lĭs). Wa.	46·58 N	123·47 W
160	Cosne-sur-Loire (kōn-sür-lwär') Fr.	47·25 N	2·57 E
125	Cosoleacaque (kō sō lā-ä-kä'kē) Mex.	18·01 N	94·38 W
113	Costa Mesa (kŏs'tȧ mā'sȧ) Ca. (Los Angeles In.)	33·39 N	118·54 W
123	Costa Rica (kŏs'tȧ rē'kȧ). N. A.	10·30 N	84·30 W
114	Cosumnes (R.) (kŏ-sŭm'nēz). Ca.	38·21 N	121·17 W
134	Cotabambas (kô-tä-bám'bäs). Peru	13·49 S	72·17 W
197	Cotabato (kō-tä-bä'tō). Phil.	7·06 N	124·13 E
125	Cotaxtla (kō-täs'tlä). Mex.	18·49 N	96·22 W
125	Cotaxtla (R.). Mex.	18·54 N	96·21 W
100	Coteau-du-Lac (cō-tō'dü-läk) Can. (Montreal In.)	45·17 N	74·11 W
100	Coteau-Landing Can. (Montreal In.)	45·15 N	74·13 W
129	Coteaux. Hai.	18·15 N	74·05 W
160	Côte d'Or (hill) (kōr-dŏr'). Fr.	47·02 N	4·35 E
124	Cotija de la Paz (kô-tē'-kä-dě-lä-pá'z). Mex.	19·46 N	102·43 W
215	Cotonou (kô-tô-nōō'). Dahomey	6·21 N	2·26 E
134	Cotopaxi (Mtn.) (kō-tô-păk'sē) Ec.	0·40 S	78·26 W
129	Cotorro (kô-tôr-rō). Cuba (In.)	23·03 N	82·17 W
154	Cotswold Hills (kŭtz'wōld). Eng.	51·35 N	2·16 W
113	Cottage Grove (kŏt'āj grōv) Mn. (Minneapolis, St. Paul In.)	44·50 N	92·52 W
110	Cottage Grove. Or.	43·48 N	123·04 W
158	Cottbus (kōtt'bōōs). G.D.R.	51·47 N	14·20 E
161	Cottian Alps (Mts.) (kŏ'tē-ŭn-ălps). Fr.-It.	44·46 N	7·02 E
108	Cottonwood (R.) (kŏt'ŭn-wŏŏd) Mn.	44·25 N	95·35 W
110	Cottonwood Cr. Ca.	40·24 N	122·50 W
129	Cotui (kô-tōō'-ē). Dom. Rep.	19·05 N	70·10 W
118	Cotulla (kō-tŭl'lȧ). Tx.	28·26 N	99·14 W
161	Coubert (kōō-bâr'). Fr. (Paris In.)	48·40 N	2·43 E
105	Coudersport (koŭ'dērz-port). Pa.	41·45 N	78·00 W
98	Coudres, Île aux (I.). Can.	47·17 N	70·12 W
60	Couéron (kōō-â-rôɴ'). Fr.	47·16 N	1·45 W
161	Coulommiers (kōō-lô-myā') Fr. (Paris In.)	48·49 N	3·05 E
136	Coulto, Serra do (Mts.) (sě'r-rä-dô-kô-ōō'tô) Braz. (Rio de Janeiro In.)	22·33 S	43·27 W
101	Council (koun'sĭl). Ak.	64·55 N	163·40 W
108	Council Bluffs (koun'sĭl blŭf). Ia.	41·16 N	95·53 W
117	Council Grove (koun'sĭl grōv). Ks.	38·39 N	96·30 W
112	Coupeville (kōōp'vĭl) Wa. (Seattle In.)	48·13 N	122·41 W
135	Courantyne (R.) (kôr'ăntīn) Guy.-Sur.	4·28 N	57·42 W
92	Courtenay (cōōrt-nā'). Can.	49·41 N	125·00 W
119	Coushatta (kou-shăt'ȧ). La.	32·02 N	93·21 W
160	Coutras (kōō-trá'). Fr.	45·02 N	0·07 W
216	Covelo. Ang.	12·06 S	13·55 E
148	Coventry (kŭv'ĕn-trĭ). Eng.	52·25 N	1·29 W
162	Covilhã (kô-vēl'yăɴ). Port.	40·18 N	7·29 W
113	Covina (kô-vē'nȧ) Ca. (Los Angeles In.)	34·06 N	117·54 W
120	Covington (kŭv'ĭng-tŭn). Ga.	33·36 N	83·50 W
104	Covington. In.	40·10 N	87·15 W
107	Covington. Ky. (Cincinnati In.)	39·05 N	84·31 W
113	Covington. La.	30·30 N	90·06 W
104	Covington. Oh.	40·10 N	84·20 W
117	Covington. Ok.	36·18 N	97·32 W
120	Covington. Tn.	35·33 N	89·40 W
105	Covington. Va.	37·50 N	80·00 W
203	Cowal, L. (kou'ăl). Austl.	33·30 S	147·10 E
204	Cowan, (L.) (kou'ăn). Austl.	32·00 S	122·30 E
98	Cowansville. Can.	45·13 N	72·47 W
110	Cow Cr. (kou). Or.	42·45 N	123·35 W
154	Cowes (kouz). Eng.	50·43 N	1·25 W
92	Cowichan L. Can.	48·54 N	124·20 W
110	Cowlitz R. (kou'lĭts). Wa.	46·30 N	122·45 W
203	Cowra (kou'rȧ). Austl.	33·50 S	148·33 E
135	Coxim (kō-shēɴ'). Braz.	18·32 S	54·43 W
125	Coxquihui (kōz-kē-wē'). Mex.	20·10 N	97·34 W
184	Coxs Bazar. Bngl.	21·32 N	92·00 E
134	Coyaima (kō-yaē'mä). Col. (In.)	3·48 N	75·11 W
118	Coyame (kō-yä'mä). Mex.	29·26 N	105·05 W
118	Coyanosa Draw (kō yá-nō'sä). Tx.	30·55 N	103·07 W
125	Coyoacàn (kō-yô-ä-kän') Mex. (In.)	19·21 N	99·10 W
112	Coyote (R.) (kī'ōt) Ca. (San Francisco In.)	37·27 N	121·57 W
124	Coyuca de Benítez (kō-yōō'kä dā bā-nē'tāz). Mex.	17·04 N	100·06 W
124	Coyuca de Catalán (kō-yōō'kä dā kä-tä-län'). Mex.	18·19 N	100·41 W
125	Coyutla (kō-yōō'tlä). Mex.	20·13 N	97·40 W
116	Cozad (kō'zăd). Ne.	40·53 N	99·59 W
107	Cozaddale (kō-zăd-dāl). Oh. (Cincinnati In.)	39·16 N	84·09 W
124	Cozoyoapan (kô-zō-yô-ä-pà'n) Mex.	16·45 N	98·17 W
126	Cozumel (kŏ-zōō-mě'l). Mex. (In.)	20·31 N	86·55 W
126	Cozumel, Isla de (I.) (ē's-lä-dě-kŏ-zōō-mě'l) Mex. (In.)	20·26 N	87·10 W
110	Crab Cr. (krăb). Wa.	46·47 N	119·43 W
110	Crab Cr. Wa.	47·21 N	119·09 W
213	Cradock (kră'dŭk) S. Afr. (Natal In.)	32·12 S	25·38 E
107	Crafton (krăf'tŭn) Pa. (Pittsburgh In.)	40·26 N	80·04 W
92	Craig (krāg). Ak.	55·29 N	133·09 W
111	Craig. Co.	40·32 N	107·31 W
165	Craiova (krä-yō'vȧ). Rom.	44·18 N	23·50 E
105	Cranberry (L.) (krăn'běr-ĭ). NY	44·10 N	74·50 W
202	Cranbourne Austl. (Melbourne In.)	38·07 S	145·16 E
93	Cranbrook (krăn'brŏŏk). Can.	49·31 N	115·46 W
106	Cranbury (krăn'bē-rĭ) NJ (New York In.)	40·19 N	74·31 W
109	Crandon (krăn'dŭn). Wi.	45·35 N	88·55 W
160	Cransac (kräɴ-zȧk'). Fr.	44·28 N	2·19 E
106	Cranston (krăns'tŭn) RI (Providence In.)	41·46 N	71·25 W
110	Crater L. (krā'tēr). Or.	43·00 N	122·08 W
110	Crater Lake Natl. Park. Or.	42·58 N	122·40 W
111	Craters of the Moon Natl. Park (krā'tēr). Id.	43·28 N	113·15 W
135	Crateús (krä-tå-ōōzh'). Braz.	5·09 S	40·35 W
135	Crato (krä'tōō). Braz.	7·19 S	39·13 W
108	Crawford (krô'fērd). Ne.	42·41 N	103·25 W
112	Crawford. Wa. (Portland In.)	45·49 N	122·24 W
104	Crawfordsville (krô'fērdz-vĭl). In.	40·00 N	86·55 W
111	Crazy Mts. (krā'zĭ). Mt.	46·11 N	110·25 W
111	Crazy Woman Cr. Wy.	44·08 N	106·40 W
160	Crécy (krā-sē'). Fr.	50·13 N	1·48 E
218	Crecy (krě-sē) S. Afr. (Johannesburg & Pretoria In.)	24·38 S	28·52 E
161	Crecy-en-Brie (krā-sē'-ěɴ-brē') Fr. (Paris In.)	48·52 N	2·55 E
100	Credit R. Can. (Toronto In.)	43·41 N	79·55 W
90	Cree (L.) (krē). Can.	57·35 N	107·52 W
108	Creighton (krā'tŭn). Ne.	42·27 N	97·54 W
213	Creighton (cre-tŏn) S. Afr. (Natal In.)	30·02 S	28·52 E
160	Creil (krě'y'). Fr.	49·18 N	2·28 E
164	Crema (krā'mä). It.	45·21 N	9·53 E
164	Cremona (krā-mō'nä). It.	45·09 N	10·02 E
164	Crépy-en-Valois (krā-pē'-ěɴ-vä-lwä'). Fr. (In.)	49·14 N	2·53 E
164	Cres (Tsrěs). Yugo.	44·58 N	14·21 E
164	Cres (I.). Yugo.	44·50 N	14·31 E
121	Crescent (R.) (krěs'ĕnt). Fl.	29·33 N	81·30 W
112	Crescent Beach Can. (Vancouver In.)	49·03 N	122·58 W
110	Crescent City (krěs'ĕnt). Ca.	41·46 N	124·13 W
121	Crescent City. Fl.	29·26 N	81·35 W
110	Cresent L. Or.	43·25 N	121·58 W
109	Cresco (krěs'kō). Ia.	43·23 N	92·07 W
115	Crested Butte (krěst'ěd būt). Co.	38·50 N	107·00 W
113	Crestline (krěst-līn) Ca. (Los Angeles In.)	34·15 N	117·17 W
104	Crestline. Oh.	40·50 N	82·40 W
113	Crestmore (krěst'môr) Ca. (Los Angeles In.)	34·02 N	117·23 W
93	Creston (krěs'tŭn). Can.	49·06 N	116·31 W
109	Creston. Ia.	41·04 N	94·22 W
107	Creston. Oh. (Cleveland In.)	40·59 N	81·54 W
120	Crestview (krěst'vū). Fl.	30·44 N	86·35 W
107	Crestwood (krěst'wŏŏd) Ky. (Louisville In.)	38·20 N	85·28 W
113	Crestwood. Mo. (St. Louis In.)	38·33 N	90·23 W
107	Crete (krēt). Il. (Chicago In.)	41·26 N	87·38 W
117	Crete. Ne.	40·38 N	96·56 W
164	Crete (I.). Grc. (In.)	35·15 N	24·30 E
163	Creus, Cabo de (C.) (kà'-bô-dě-krě-ōōs). Sp.	42·16 N	3·18 E
160	Creuse (R.) (krûz). Fr.	46·51 N	0·49 E
113	Creve Coeur (krēv kōōr) Mo. (St. Louis In.)	38·40 N	90·27 W
163	Crevillente (krâ-vē-lyěn'tâ). Sp.	38·12 N	0·48 W
148	Crewe (krōō). Eng.	53·06 N	2·27 W
121	Crewe. Va.	37·09 N	78·08 W
	Crimea P-Ov (Pen.), see Krymskiy		
158	Crimmitschau (krĭm'ĭt-shou) G.D.R.	50·49 N	12·22 E
116	Cripple Creek (krĭp''l). Co.	38·44 N	105·12 W
105	Crisfield (krĭs-fēld). Md.	38·00 N	78·50 W
216	Cristal, Monts de (Mts.). Gabon	0·50 N	10·30 E
137	Cristina (krēs-tē'-nä) Braz. (Rio de Janeiro In.)	22·13 S	45·15 W
134	Cristobal Colón, Pico (Pk.) (pē'kô-krēs-tô'bäl-kō-lôn'). Col.	11·00 N	74·00 W
159	Crisul Alb R. (krē'shōōl älb). Rom.	46·20 N	22·15 E
165	Črna (R.) (ts'r'nȧ). Yugo.	41·03 N	21·46 E
165	Črna Gora (Montenegro) (Reg.) (ts'r-nȧ-gō'rȧ) (mōn-tå-nā'grō) (mōn-tē-nē'grō). Yugo.	42·55 N	18·52 E
164	Črnomelj (ch'r'nō-māl'). Yugo.	45·35 N	15·11 E
	Croatia (Reg.), see Hrvatska		
112	Crockett (krŏk'ĕt) Ca. (San Francisco In.)	38·03 N	122·14 W
119	Crockett. Tx.	31·19 N	95·28 W
106	Crofton. Md. (Baltimore In.)	39·01 N	76·43 W
108	Crofton. Ne.	42·44 N	97·32 W
109	Croix, Lac la (L.) (krōō-ä' läk lä). Can.-Mn.	48·19 N	91·53 W

ăt; finăl; rāte; senâte; ärm; ȧsk; sofȧ; fâre; ch-choose; dh-as th in other; bē; ėvent; bět; recěnt; cratēr; g-go; gh-guttural g; bĭt; ĭ-short neutral; rīde; ĸ-guttural k as ch in German ich;

Page	Name Pronunciation Region	Lat. °'	Long. °'
204	Croker (krô'kȧ) Austl.	10·45 S	132·25 E
202	Cronulla (krō-nŭl'ȧ) Austl. (Sydney In.)	34·03 S	151·09 E
129	Crooked (I.) Ba.	22·45 N	74·10 W
99	Crooked (L.) Can.	48·25 N	56·05 W
92	Crooked (R.) Can.	54·30 N	122·55 W
117	Crooked Cr. (kro͝ok'ĕd) Il.	40·21 N	90·49 W
110	Crooked Cr. Or.	42·23 N	118·14 W
129	Crooked Island Passage (Str.) Ba.	22·40 N	74·50 W
110	Crooked R. Or.	44·07 N	120·30 W
108	Crookston (kro͝oks'tŭn) Mn.	47·44 N	96·35 W
104	Crooksville (kro͝oks'vĭl) Oh.	39·45 N	82·05 W
109	Crosby (krôz'bĭ) Mn.	46·29 N	93·58 W
108	Crosby ND	48·55 N	103·18 W
119	Crosby Tx. (In.)	29·55 N	95·04 W
100	Cross (L.) (krôs) Can.	54·40 N	98·47 W
105	Cross (L.) Can.	44·55 N	76·55 W
215	Cross (R.) Nig.	5·35 N	8·05 E
120	Cross City Fl.	29·55 N	83·25 W
117	Crossett (krôs'ĕt) Ar.	33·08 N	91·56 W
128	Cross Hbr. Ba.	25·55 N	77·15 W
95	Cross Lake Can.	54·37 N	97·47 W
95	Cross L. Can.	54·45 N	97·30 W
113	Cross L. La.	32·33 N	93·58 W
106	Cross River Res. (krôs) NY (New York In.)	41·14 N	73·34 W
101	Cross Sd. (krôs) Ak.	58·12 N	137·20 W
104	Crosswell (krŏz'wĕl) Mi.	43·15 N	82·35 W
97	Crotch (R.) Can.	45·02 N	76·55 W
165	Crotone (krō-tô'nĕ) It.	39·05 N	17·08 E
106	Croton Falls Res. (krōtŭn) NY (New York In.)	41·22 N	73·44 W
106	Croton-on-Hudson (krō'tŭn-ŏn hŭd'sŭn) . NY (New York In.)	41·12 N	73·53 W
109	Crow (L.) Can.	49·13 N	93·29 W
111	Crow Agency Mt.	45·36 N	107·27 W
116	Crow Cr. Co.	41·08 N	104·25 W
108	Crow Creek Ind. Res. SD	44·17 N	99·17 W
111	Crow Ind. Res. (krō) Mt.	45·26 N	108·12 W
109	Crow Lake Can.	49·12 N	93·57 W
148	Crowle (kroul) Eng.	53·36 N	0·49 W
119	Crowley (krou'lē) La.	30·13 N	92·22 W
123	Crown, Mt. Vir. Is. (U. S. A.) (St. Thomas In.)	18·22 N	64·58 W
112	Crown Mtn. (kroun) Can. (Vancouver In.)	49·24 N	123·05 W
107	Crown Point (kroun point') In. (Chicago In.)	41·25 N	87·22 W
105	Crown Point NY	44·00 N	73·25 W
93	Crowsnest Pass Can.	49·39 N	114·45 W
109	Crow Wing (R.) (krō) Mn.	44·50 N	94·01 W
109	Crow Wing (R.) Mn.	46·42 N	94·48 W
109	Crow Wing (R.), North Fork Mn.	45·16 N	94·28 W
109	Crow Wing (R.), South Fork Mn.	44·59 N	94·42 W
205	Croydon (kroi'dŭn) Austl.	18·15 S	142·15 E
202	Croydon Austl. (Melbourne In.)	37·48 S	145·17 E
148	Croydon Eng. (London In.)	51·22 N	0·06 W
106	Croydon Pa. (Philadelphia In.)	40·05 N	74·55 W
220	Crozet I. (krō-zĕ') Ind. O.	46·20 S	51·30 E
128	Cruces (kro͞o'sås) Cuba	22·20 N	80·20 W
118	Cruces, Arroyo de (är-rō'yō-dĕ-kro͞o'sĕs) Mex.	26·17 N	104·32 W
118	Cruillas (kro͞o-ēl'yäs) Mex.	24·45 N	98·31 W
128	Cruz, Cabo (C.) (kȧ'-bô-kro͞oz) Cuba	19·50 N	77·45 W
128	Cruz, Cayo (I.) (kä'yō-kro͞oz) Cuba	22·15 N	77·50 W
136	Cruz Alta (kro͞oz äl'tä) Braz.	28·41 S	54·02 W
136	Cruz del Eje (kro͞o's-dĕl-ĕ-kĕ) Arg.	30·46 S	64·45 W
137	Cruzeiro (kro͞o-zā'rō͞o) Braz. (Rio de Janeiro In.)	22·36 S	44·57 W
135	Cruzeiro do Sul (kro͞o-zā'rō͞o dō͞o so͞ol) . Braz.	7·34 S	72·40 W
100	Crysler Can. (Ottawa In.)	45·13 N	75·09 W
118	Crystal City (krĭs'tăl sĭ'tĭ) Tx.	28·40 N	99·90 W
109	Crystal Falls (krĭs'tăl fôls) Mi.	46·06 N	88·21 W
107	Crystal Lake (krĭs'tăl lāk) Il. (Chicago In.)	42·15 N	88·18 W
120	Crystal Springs (krĭs'tăl sprĭngz) Ms.	31·58 N	90·20 W
112	Crystal Sprs. Ca. (San Francisco In.)	37·31 N	122·26 W
159	Csongrád (chôn'gräd) Hung.	46·42 N	20·09 E
159	Csorna (chôr'nä) Hung.	47·39 N	17·11 E
135	Cúa (ko͞o'ä) Ven. (In.)	10·10 N	66·54 W
125	Cuajimalpa (kwä-hē-mäl'pä) Mex. (In.)	19·21 N	99·18 W
124	Cuale, Sierra del (Mts.) (sē-ĕ'r-rä-dĕl-kwȧ'lĕ) . Mex.	20·20 N	104·58 W
216	Cuamato (kwä-mä'tō) Ang.	17·05 S	15·09 E
216	Cuando (kwän'dō) Ang.	16·32 S	22·07 E
216	Cuando (R.) Ang.	16·50 S	22·40 E
216	Cuangar Ang.	17·36 S	18·39 E
216	Cuango (Kwango) (R.) (kwäŋ'gō) . Afr.	6·35 S	16·50 E
216	Cuanza (R.) (kwän'zä) Ang.	9·05 S	13·15 E
136	Cuarto Saladillo (R.) (kwär'tō-sä-lä-dē'l-yō) . Arg.	33·00 S	63·25 W
129	Cuatro Caminos (kwä'trō-kä-mē'nōs) . Cuba (In.)	23·01 N	82·13 W
118	Cuatro Ciénegas (kwä'trō syā'nā-gäs) . Mex.	26·59 N	102·03 W
126	Cuauhtemoc (kwä-o͞o-tē-mŏk') Mex.	15·43 N	91·57 W
124	Cuautepec (kwä-o͞o-tē-pĕk) . . Mex.	16·41 N	99·04 W
124	Cuautepec Mex.	20·01 N	98·19 W
125	Cuautitlán (kwä-o͞o-tēt-län') Mex. (In.)	19·40 N	99·12 W
124	Cuautla (kwä-o͞o'tlä) Mex.	18·47 N	98·57 W
162	Cuba (ko͞o'bä) Port.	38·10 N	7·55 W
123	Cuba (kū'bȧ) N. A.	22·00 N	79·00 W

Page	Name Pronunciation Region	Lat. °'	Long. °'
135	Cubagua, Isla (ē's-lä-ko͞o-bä'gwä) Ven. (In.)	10·48 N	64·10 W
216	Cubango (Okavango) (R.) (ko͞o-bäŋ'gō) . Ang.-S.W. Afr.	17·10 S	18·20 E
94	Cub Hills (kŭb) Can.	54·20 N	104·30 W
113	Cucamonga (ko͞o-kȧ-mŏŋ'gȧ) Ca. (Los Angeles In.)	34·05 N	117·35 W
212	Cuchi Ang.	14·40 S	16·50 E
118	Cuchillo Parado (ko͞o-chē'lyō pä-rä'dō) . Mex.	29·26 N	104·52 W
126	Cuchumatanes, Sierra de los (Mts.) Guat.	16·02 N	91·50 W
134	Cúcuta (ko͞o'ko͞o-tä) Col.	7·56 N	72·30 W
107	Cudahy (kŭd'ȧ-hī) Wi. (Milwaukee In.)	42·57 N	87·52 W
185	Cuddalore (kŭd ȧ-lōr') India	11·49 N	79·46 E
185	Cuddapah (kŭd'ȧ-pä) India	14·31 N	78·52 E
204	Cue (kū) Austl.	27·30 S	118·10 E
162	Cuellar (kwā'lyär') Sp.	41·24 N	4·15 W
134	Cuenca (kwĕn'kä) Ec.	2·52 S	78·54 W
162	Cuenca Sp.	40·05 N	2·07 W
162	Cuenca, Sierra de (Mts.) (sē-ĕ'r-rä-dĕ-kwĕ'n-kä) . Sp.	40·02 N	1·50 W
118	Cuencame (kwĕn-kä-mā') Mex.	24·52 N	103·42 W
124	Cuerámaro (kwā-rä'mä-rô) Mex.	20·39 N	101·44 W
125	Cuernavaca (kwĕr-nä-vä'kä) Mex. (In.)	18·55 N	99·15 W
119	Cuero (kwā'rō) Tx.	29·05 N	97·16 W
124	Cuetzalá del Progreso (kwĕt-zä-lä dĕl prō-grā'sō) . Mex.	18·07 N	99·51 W
125	Cuetzalan del Progreso (kwĕt-zä-län dĕl prō-grā'sō) . Mex.	20·02 N	97·33 W
162	Cuevas del Almanzora (kwĕ'väs-dĕl-äl-män-zô-rä) . . Sp.	37·19 N	1·54 W
164	Cuglieri (ko͞o-lyā'rē) It.	40·11 N	8·37 E
135	Cuiabá (ko͞o-yä-bä') Braz.	15·33 S	56·03 W
125	Cuicatlan (kwē-kä-tlän') Mex.	17·46 N	96·57 W
126	Cuilapa (ko͞o-ē-lä'pä) Guat.	14·16 N	90·20 W
154	Cuillin Sd. Scot.	57·09 N	6·20 W
216	Cuilo (R.) Ang.	9·15 S	19·30 E
216	Cuito (R.) (ko͞o-ē'tō) Ang.	14·15 S	19·00 E
124	Cuitzeo (kwēt'zā-ō) Mex.	19·57 N	101·11 W
124	Cuitzeo, Laguna de (L.) (lä-ō͞o'nä-dĕ-kwēt'zā-ō) . Mex.	19·58 N	101·05 W
129	Cul de Sac (Val.) (ko͞o'l-dĕ-sä'k) Dom. Rep.-Hai.	18·35 N	72·05 W
123	Culebra (I.) (ko͞o-lā'brä) P. R. (Puerto Rico In.)	18·19 N	65·32 W
149	Culemborg Neth. (Amsterdam In.)	51·57 N	5·14 E
205	Culgoa (R.) (kŭl-gō'ȧ) Austl.	29·21 S	147·00 E
122	Culiacán (ko͞o-lyä-kä'n) Mex.	24·45 N	107·30 W
196	Culion (ko͞o-lē-ōn') Phil.	11·43 N	119·58 E
162	Cúllar de Baza (ko͞o'l-yär-dĕ-bä'zä) . Sp.	37·36 N	2·35 W
163	Cullera (ko͞o-lyā'rä) Sp.	39·12 N	0·15 W
213	Cullinan (ko͝o'lĭ-năn) S. Afr. (Johannesburg & Pretoria In.)	25·41 S	28·32 E
120	Cullman (kŭl'măn) Ala.	34·10 N	86·50 W
105	Culpeper (kŭl'pĕp-ēr) Va.	38·30 N	77·55 W
100	Culross (kŭl'rôs) Can. (Winnipeg In.)	49·43 N	97·54 W
104	Culver (kŭl'vēr) In.	41·15 N	86·25 W
113	Culver City Ca. (Los Angeles In.)	34·00 N	118·23 W
135	Cumaná (ko͞o-mä-nä') . . Ven. (In.)	10·28 N	64·10 W
100	Cumberland (kŭm'bēr-lănd) Can. (Ottawa In.)	45·31 N	75·25 W
105	Cumberland Md.	39·40 N	78·40 W
112	Cumberland Wa. (Seattle In.)	47·17 N	121·55 W
109	Cumberland Wi.	45·31 N	92·01 W
103	Cumberland (R.) U. S.	36·30 N	87·40 W
120	Cumberland, L. Ky.	36·55 N	85·20 W
205	Cumberland Is. Austl.	20·29 S	149·46 E
91	Cumberland Pen. Can.	65·59 N	64·05 W
120	Cumberland Plat. Tn.	35·25 N	85·30 W
91	Cumberland Sd. Can.	65·27 N	65·44 W
134	Cundinamarca (Dept.) (ko͞on-dē-nä-mä'r-kȧ) . Col. (In.)	4·57 N	74·27 W
125	Cunduacán (ko͞on-do͞o-ȧ-kän') Mex.	18·04 N	93·23 W
216	Cunene (Kunene (R.) Ang.-S. W. Afr.	17·05 S	12·35 E
164	Cuneo (ko͞o'nā-ō) It.	44·24 N	7·31 E
137	Cunha (ko͞o'nyȧ) Braz. (Rio de Janeiro In.)	23·05 S	44·56 W
212	Cunjamba (ko͞on-kä'm-bä) . . . Ang.	15·45 S	20·15 E
203	Cunnamulla (kŭn-ȧ-mŭl-ȧ) . . Austl.	28·00 S	145·55 E
122	Cupula, Pico (Mtn.) (pē'kō-ko͞o'po͞o-lä) . Mex.	24·45 N	111·10 W
124	Cuquío (ko͞o-kē'ō) Mex.	20·55 N	103·03 W
134	Curaçao (ko͞o-rä-sä'ō) (I.) Neth. Antilles	12·12 N	68·58 W
136	Curacautín (kä-rä-käo͞o-tē'n) . Chile	38·25 S	71·53 W
137	Curacaví (ko͞o-rä-kä-vē') Chile (Santiago In.)	33·23 S	71·09 W
137	Curaumilla, Punta (Pt.) (ko͞o-rou-mē'lyä) . Chile (Santiago In.)	33·05 S	71·44 W
137	Curepto (ko͞o-rĕp-tō) Chile (Santiago In.)	35·06 S	72·02 W
137	Curicó (ko͞o-rē-kō') Chile (Santiago In.)	34·57 S	71·14 W
137	Curicó (Prov.) . Chile (Santiago In.)	34·55 S	71·15 W
136	Curitiba (ko͞o-rē-tē'bȧ) Braz.	25·20 S	49·15 W
128	Curly Cut Cays (Is.) Ba.	23·40 N	77·40 W
135	Currais Novos (ko͞or-rä'ēs nō-vōs) . Braz.	6·02 S	36·39 W
100	Curran (kŭ-räɴ') Can. (Ottawa In.)	45·30 N	74·59 W
128	Current (I.) (kŭ-rĕnt) Ba.	25·20 N	76·50 W
117	Current (R.) (kûr'ĕnt) Mo.	37·18 N	91·21 W
213	Currie, Mt. (cŭ-rē) S. Afr. (Natal In.)	30·28 S	29·23 E

Page	Name Pronunciation Region	Lat. °'	Long. °'
121	Currituck Sd. (kûr'ĭ-tŭk) NC	36·27 N	75·42 W
165	Curtea de Argeş (ko͞or'tē-ȧ dĕ ár'zhĕsh) . Rom.	45·09 N	24·40 E
116	Curtis (kûr'tĭs) Ne.	40·36 N	100·29 W
205	Curtis (I.) Austl.	23·38 S	151·43 E
107	Curtisville (kûr'tĭs-vĭl) Pa. (Pittsburgh In.)	40·38 N	79·50 W
135	Curuá (R.) (ko͞o-ro͞o-ä') Braz.	6·26 S	54·39 W
165	Ćurug (cho͞o'ro͝og) Yugo.	45·27 N	20·26 E
216	Curunga Ang.	12·51 S	21·12 E
134	Curupira, Serra (Mts.) (sĕr'rȧ ko͞o-ro͞o-pē'rȧ) Braz.-Ven.	1·00 N	65·30 W
135	Cururupu (ko͞o-ro͞o-ro͞o-po͞o') . Braz.	1·40 S	44·56 W
136	Curuzú Cuatiá (ko͞o-ro͞o-zo͞o' kwä-tē-ä') . Arg.	29·45 S	57·58 W
135	Curvelo (ko͝or-vĕl'o͞o) Braz.	18·47 S	44·14 W
117	Cushing (kŭsh'ĭng) Ok.	35·58 N	96·46 W
160	Cusset (kü-sĕ') Fr.	46·08 N	3·29 E
108	Custer (kŭs'tēr) SD	43·46 N	103·36 W
112	Custer Wa. (Vancouver In.)	48·55 N	122·39 W
123	Custer Battlefield Nat'l. Mon. (kŭs'tēr băt''l-fēld) . Mt.	45·44 N	107·15 W
111	Cut Bank (kŭt bănk) Mt.	48·38 N	112·19 W
120	Cuthbert (kŭth'bērt) Ga.	31·47 N	84·48 W
184	Cuttack (kŭ-tăk') India	20·38 N	85·53 E
124	Cutzamala (R.) (ko͞o-tzä-mä-lä') Mex.	18·57 N	100·41 W
124	Cutzamalá de Pinzón (ko͞o-tzä-mä-lä'dĕ-pēn-zō'n) . Mex.	18·28 N	100·36 W
216	Cuvo (R.) (ko͞o'vō) Ang.	10·55 S	14·00 E
158	Cuxhaven (ko͝oks' hä-fĕn) . . F.R.G.	53·51 N	8·43 E
107	Cuyahoga Falls Oh. (Cleveland In.)	41·08 N	81·29 W
107	Cuyahoga R. (kī-ȧ-hō'gȧ) Oh. (Cleveland In.)	41·22 N	81·38 W
114	Cuyapaire Ind. Res. (kū-yȧ-pâr) Ca.	32·46 N	116·20 W
196	Cuyo Is. (ko͞o'yō) Phil.	10·54 N	120·08 E
126	Cuyotenango (ko͞o-yō-tĕ-näŋ'gô) Guat.	14·30 N	91·35 W
135	Cuyuni (R.) (ko͞o-yo͞o'nē) Guy.-Ven.	6·40 N	60·44 W
124	Cuyutlán (ko͞o-yo͞o-tlän') . . . . Mex.	18·54 N	104·04 W
134	Cuzco Peru	13·36 S	71·52 W
104	Cynthiana (sĭn-thĭ-ăn'ȧ) Ky.	38·20 N	84·20 W
113	Cypress (sī'prĕs) Ca. (Los Angeles In.)	33·50 N	118·03 W
119	Cypress Cr. Tx.	32·49 N	94·35 W
94	Cypress Hills Can.	49·40 N	109·30 W
94	Cypress L. Can.	49·28 N	109·29 W
182	Cyprus (sī'prŭs) Asia	35·00 N	31·00 E
146	Czechoslovakia (chĕk'ō-slō-vä'kĭ-ȧ) . Eur.	49·28 N	16·00 E
159	Czersk (chĕrsk) Pol.	53·47 N	17·58 E
159	Częstochowa (chăɴ-stô κô'vȧ) . Pol.	50·49 N	19·10 E

D

Page	Name Pronunciation Region	Lat. °'	Long. °'
210	Dabakala (dä-bä-kä'lä) Ivory Coast	8·16 N	4·36 W
134	Dabeiba (dȧ-bā'bä) . . . . Col. (In.)	7·01 N	76·16 W
215	Dabnou Niger	14·09 N	5·22 E
112	Dabob B. (dā'bŏb) Wa. (Seattle In.)	47·50 N	122·50 W
214	Dabola Gui.	10·45 N	11·07 W
159	Dabrowa (dŏɴ-brō'vȧ) Pol.	53·37 N	23·18 E
184	Dacca (dä'kä) (dăk'ȧ) Bngl.	23·45 N	90·29 E
149	Dachau (dä'κou) F.R.G. (Munich In.)	48·16 N	11·26 E
100	Dacotah (dȧ-kō'tȧ) Can. (Winnipeg In.)	49·52 N	97·38 W
121	Dade City (dād) Fl. (In.)	28·22 N	82·09 W
120	Dadeville (dād'vĭl) Al.	32·48 N	85·44 W
184	Dādra & Nagar Haveli (Union Ter.) . India	20·00 N	73·00 E
197	Daet (Mtn.) (dä'ĕt) . . . . Phil. (In.)	14·07 N	122·59 E
95	Dafoe (R.) Can.	55·50 N	95·50 W
113	Dafter (dăf'tēr) Mi. (Sault Ste. Marie In.)	46·21 N	84·26 W
214	Dagana (dä-gä'nä) Senegal	16·31 N	15·30 W
215	Dagana (Reg.) Chad.	12·20 N	15·15 E
166	Dagda (däg'dȧ) Sov. Un.	56·04 N	27·30 E
148	Dagenham (dăg'ĕn-ăm) Eng. (London In.)	51·32 N	0·09 E
171	Dagestan (Reg.) (dä-gĕs-tän') Sov. Un.	43·40 N	46·10 E
114	Daggett (dăg'ĕt) Ca.	34·50 N	116·52 W
197	Dagupan (dä-go͞o'pän) . . Phil. (In.)	16·02 N	120·20 E
161	Dahl (däl) . . . . F.R.G. (Ruhr In.)	51·18 N	7·33 E
211	Dahlak Arch. (Is.) Eth.	15·45 N	40·30 E
	Dahomey, see Benin		
195	Daigo (dī-gō) . . . . Jap. (Ōsaka In.)	34·57 N	135·49 E
162	Daimiel Manzanares (dī-myĕl' män-zä-nä'rĕs) . Sp.	39·05 N	3·36 W
	Dairen, see Lüta		
112	Dairy (R.) (dâr'ĭ) Or. (Portland In.)	45·33 N	123·04 W
112	Dairy (R.) East Fk. Or. (Portland In.)	45·40 N	123·03 W
195	Dai-Sen (Mtn.) (dī'sĕn') . . . . . Jap.	35·22 N	133·35 E

ng-sing; ŋ-baŋk; ɴ-nasalized n; nŏd; cŏmmit; ōld; ôbey; ôrder; fo͞od; fo͝ot; ou-out; s-soft; sh-dish; th-thin; pūre; ûnite; ûrn; stŭd; circŭs; ü-as "y" in study; '-indeterminate vowel.

ăt; fĭnǎl; rāte; senäte; ärm; àsk; sofá; fâre; ch-choose; dh-as th in other; bē; ēvent; bět; recěnt; cratěr; g-go; gh-guttural g; bĭt; ɪ-short neutral; rīde; ĸ-guttural k as ch in German ich;

ng-sing; ŋ-baŋk; N-nasalized n; nŏd; cŏmmit; ōld; ŏbey; ôrder; fōōd; fŏŏt; ou-out; s-soft; sh-dish; th-thin; pūre; únite; ûrn; stŭd; circᵘs; ü-as "y" in study; '-indeterminate vowel.

PRONOUNCING INDEX

Dublin — East Syracuse 277

Page	Name Pronunciation Region	Lat. °′	Long. °′
120	Dublin....Ga.	32·33 N	82·55 W
154	Dublin (Baile Atha Cliath) (bŭ'lĕŏ'hŏclē'ŏh).Ire.	53·20 N	6·15 W
118	Dublin....Tx.	32·05 N	98·20 W
159	Dubno (dōō'b-nô)....Sov. Un.	50·24 N	25·44 E
105	Du Bois (dōō-bois')....Pa.	41·10 N	78·45 W
167	Dubossary (dōō-bŏ-sä'rĭ).Sov. Un.	47·16 N	29·11 E
171	Dubovka (dōō-bôf'kȧ)...Sov. Un.	49·00 N	44·50 E
174	Dubrovka (dōō-brôf'kȧ) Sov. Un. (Leningrad In.)	59·51 N	30·56 S
165	Dubrovnik (Ragusa) (dōō'brôv-nêk) (rä-gōō'sä) Yugo.	42·40 N	18·10 E
166	Dubrovno (dōō-brôf'nö)..Sov. Un.	54·39 N	30·54 E
109	Dubuque (dŏŏ-būk')....Ia.	42·30 N	90·43 W
115	Duchesne (dōō-shān')....Ut.	40·12 N	110·23 W
115	Duchesne (R.)....Ut.	40·20 N	110·50 W
204	Duchess (dŭch'ĕs)....Austl.	21·30 S	139·55 E
199	Ducie I. (dü-sē')....Oceania	25·30 S	126·20 W
120	Duck (R.)....Tn.	35·55 N	87·40 W
112	Duckabush (R.) (dŭk'ȧ-bŏŏsh) Wa. (Seattle In.)	47·41 N	123·09 W
94	Duck Lake....Can.	52·47 N	106·13 W
95	Duck Mtn....Can.	51·35 N	101·00 W
120	Ducktown (dŭk'toun)....Tn.	35·03 N	84·20 W
110	Duck Valley Ind. Res....Id.-Nv.	42·02 N	115·49 W
114	Duckwater Pk. (dŭk-wô-tẽr).Nv.	39·00 N	115·31 W
134	Duda (dōō'dä) (R.)....Col. (In.)	3·25 N	74·23 W
172	Dudinka (dōō-dĭn'kȧ)....Sov. Un.	69·15 N	85·42 E
148	Dudley (dŭd'lĭ)....Eng.	52·31 N	2·04 W
214	Duékoué....Ivory Coast	6·45 N	7·21 W
162	Duero (R.) (dwĕ'rō)....Sp.	41·30 N	5·10 W
104	Dugger (dŭg'ẽr)....In.	39·00 N	87·10 W
164	Dugi Otok (I.) (dōō'gē O'tôk) Yugo.	44·03 N	14·40 E
161	Duisburg (dōō'ĭs-bŏŏrgh) F.R.G. (Ruhr In.)	51·26 N	6·46 E
134	Duitama (dŏŏē-tä'mä)....Col.	5·48 N	73·09 W
92	Duke L (dōōk)....Ak.	54·56 N	131·20 W
166	Dukhovshchina (dōō-ĸôfsh'chēnȧ) Sov. Un.	55·13 N	32·26 E
148	Dukinfield (dŭk'ĭn-fēld)....Eng.	53·28 N	2·05 W
159	Dukla P. (dŏŏ'klä)....Pol.	49·25 N	21·44 E
127	Dulce, Golfo (G.) (gōl'fō dōōl'sä) C. R.	8·25 N	83·13 W
	Dulcigno, see Ulcinj		
161	Dülken (dül'kĕn) F.R.G. (Ruhr In.)	51·15 N	6·21 E
161	Dülmen (dül'mĕn) F.R.G. (Ruhr In.)	51·50 N	7·17 E
113	Duluth (dŏŏ-lōōth') Mn. (Duluth In.)	46·50 N	92·07 W
183	Dūmā....Syria (Palestine In.)	33·34 N	36·17 E
197	Dumaguete City (dōō-mä-gā'tā) Phil.	9·14 N	123·15 E
183	Dumai....Indon. (Singapore In.)	1·39 N	101·30 E
197	Dumali Pt. (dōō-mä'lē).Phil. (In.)	13·07 N	121·42 E
116	Dumas....Tx.	35·52 N	101·58 W
154	Dumbarton (dŭm'bȧr-tŭn)...Scot.	56·00 N	4·35 W
184	Dum-Dum....India (In.)	22·37 N	88·25 E
154	Dumfries (dŭm-frēs')....Scot.	54·05 N	3·40 W
184	Dumjor....India (In.)	22·37 N	88·14 E
106	Dumont (dōō'mŏnt) NJ (New York In.)	40·56 N	74·00 W
218	Dumyāţ....Egypt (Nile In.)	31·22 N	31·50 E
218	Dumyāţ, Maşabb (Chan.) Egypt (Nile In.)	31·36 N	31·45 E
159	Dunaföldvar (dŏŏ'nô-fûld'vär) Hung.	46·48 N	18·55 E
159	Dunajec R. (dōō-nä'yĕts)....Pol.	49·52 N	20·53 E
159	Dunapataj (doo'nô-pô-toi).Hung.	46·42 N	19·03 E
159	Duna R. (dōō'nä)....Hung.	46·07 N	18·45 E
159	Dunaujvaros....Hung.	46·57 N	18·55 E
174	Dunay (dōō'nī) Sov. Un. (Leningrad In.)	59·59 N	30·57 E
167	Dunayevtsy (dōō-nä'yĕf-tsĭ) Sov. Un.	48·52 N	26·51 E
154	Dunbar (dŭn'bär)....Scot.	56·00 N	2·25 W
94	Dunblane (dŭn-blān')....Can.	51·11 N	106·52 W
104	Dunbar....WV	38·20 N	81·45 W
92	Duncan (dŭŋ'kȧn)....Can.	48·47 N	123·42 W
116	Duncan....Ok.	34·29 N	97·56 W
93	Duncan Dam....Can.	50·15 N	116·55 W
93	Duncan (R.)....Can.	50·30 N	116·45 W
93	Duncan L....Can.	50·20 N	117·00 W
154	Duncansby Hd. (dŭn'kȧnz-bĭ).. Scot.	58·40 N	3·01 W
113	Duncanville (dŭn'kȧn-vĭl) Tx. (Dallas, Fort Worth In.)	32·39 N	96·55 W
154	Dundalk (dŭn'dôk)....Ire.	54·00 N	6·18 W
106	Dundalk....Md. (Baltimore In.)	39·16 N	76·31 W
154	Dundalk B. (dŭn'dôk)....Ire.	53·55 N	6·15 W
100	Dundas (dŭn-dăs') Can. (Toronto In.)	43·16 N	79·58 W
92	Dundas I....Can.	54·33 N	130·55 W
107	Dundee (dŭn-dē).Il. (Chicago In.)	42·06 N	88·17 W
154	Dundee....Scot.	56·30 N	2·55 W
213	Dundee....S. Afr. (Natal In.)	28·14 S	30·16 E
204	Dundras (L.) (dŭn-drȧs)...Austl.	32·15 S	132·00 E
204	Dundras Str. (dŭn'drȧs)....Austl.	10·35 S	131·15 E
154	Dundrum B. (dŭn-drŭm')....Ire.	54·13 N	5·47 W
121	Dunedin (dŭn-ē'dĭn)....Fl. (In.)	28·00 N	82·43 W
205	Dunedin....N. Z. (In.)	45·48 S	170·32 E
106	Dunellen (dŭn-ĕl'ĕn) NJ (New York In.)	40·36 N	74·28 W
154	Dunfermline (dŭn-fẽrm'lĭn)..Scot.	56·05 N	3·30 W
154	Dungarvin (dŭn-gȧr'vȧn)....Ire.	52·06 N	7·50 W
112	Dungeness (dŭnj-nĕs') Wa. (Seattle In.)	48·09 N	123·07 W
112	Dungeness (R.)..Wa. (Seattle In.)	48·03 N	123·10 W
112	Dungeness Spit..Wa. (Seattle In.)	48·11 N	123·03 W
160	Dunkerque (dŭɴ-kĕrk')....Fr.	51·02 N	2·37 E
104	Dunkirk (dŭn'kûrk)....In.	40·20 N	85·25 W
105	Dunkirk....NY	42·30 N	79·20 W
214	Dunkwa....Ghana	5·22 N	1·12 W
154	Dun Laoghaire (dŭn-lâ'rĕ)....Ire.	53·16 N	6·09 W
108	Dunlap (dŭn'lăp)....Ia.	41·53 N	95·33 W
120	Dunlap....Tn.	35·23 N	85·23 W
105	Dunmore (dŭn'mōr)....Pa.	41·25 N	75·30 W
121	Dunn (dŭn)....NC	35·18 N	78·37 W
121	Dunnellon (dŭn-ĕl'ŏn)....Fl.	29·02 N	82·28 W
105	Dunnville (dŭn'vĭl)....Can.	42·55 N	79·40 W
211	Dunqulah....Sud.	19·21 N	30·19 E
110	Dunsmuir (dŭnz'mūr)....Ca.	41·08 N	122·17 W
106	Dunwoody (dŭn-wŏŏd'ĭ) Ga. (Atlanta In.)	33·57 N	84·20 W
107	Du Page R. (dōō pāj) Il. (Chicago In.)	41·41 N	88·11 W
107	Du Page R., E. Br. Il. (Chicago In.)	41·49 N	88·05 W
107	Du Page R., W. Br. Il. (Chicago In.)	41·48 N	88·10 W
197	Dupax (dōō'päks)....Phil. (In.)	16·16 N	121·06 E
165	Dupnitsa (dŏŏp'nē-tsȧ)....Bul.	42·15 N	23·07 E
113	Dupo (dū'pō)...Il. (St. Louis In.)	38·31 N	90·12 W
216	Duque de Bragança (dōō'kȧ dȧ brä-gäɴ'sä).Ang.	9·06 S	15·57 E
136	Duque de Caxias (dōō'kĕ-dĕ-kȧ'shyȧs) Braz. (Rio de Janeiro In.)	22·46 S	43·18 W
107	Duquesne (dŏŏ-kān') Pa. (Pittsburgh In.)	40·22 N	79·51 W
117	Du Quoin (dŏŏ-kwoin')....Il.	38·01 N	89·14 W
141	Durance (R.) (dü-räɴs')....Fr.	43·46 N	5.52 E
104	Durand (dŭ-rănd')....Mi.	42·50 N	84·00 W
109	Durand....Wi.	44·37 N	91·58 W
115	Durango (dōō-răŋ'gō)....Co.	37·15 N	107·55 W
124	Durango (dōō-rä'n-gô)....Mex.	24·02 N	104·42 W
122	Durango (State)....Mex.	25·00 N	106·00 W
120	Durant (dŭ-rănt')....Ms.	33·05 N	89·50 W
117	Durant....Ok.	33·59 N	96·23 W
162	Duratón (R.) (dōō-rä-tōn')....Sp.	41·55 N	3·55 W
137	Durazno (dōō-räz'nō) Ur. (Buenos Aires In.)	33·21 S	56·31 W
137	Durazno (Dept.) Ur. (Buenos Aires In.)	33·00 S	56·35 W
213	Durban (dûr'bȧn) S. Afr. (Natal In.)	29·48 S	31·00 E
212	Durbanville (dûr-bȧn'vĭl) S. Afr. (In.)	33·50 S	18·39 E
157	Durbe (dŏŏr'bĕ)....Sov. Un.	56·36 N	21·24 E
164	Đurđevac (dūr'dyĕ-vȧts')...Yugo.	46·03 N	17·03 E
161	Düren (dü'rĕn).F.R.G. (Ruhr In.)	50·48 N	6·30 E
154	Durham (dûr'ăm)....Eng.	54·47 N	1·46 W
121	Durham....NC	36·00 N	78·55 W
203	Durham Downs....Austl.	27·30 S	141·55 E
165	Durrës (dŏŏr'ĕs)....Alb.	41·19 N	19·27 E
105	Duryea (dŏŏr-yā')....Pa.	41·20 N	75·50 W
187	Dushanbe....Sov. Un.	38·30 N	68·45 E
161	Düsseldorf (düs'ĕl-dôrf) F.R.G. (Ruhr In.)	51·14 N	6·47 E
149	Dussen...Neth. (Amsterdam In.)	51·43 N	4·58 E
192	Dutalan Ula (Mtn.)....Mong.	49·25 N	112·40 E
101	Dutch Harbor (dŭch här'bẽr)..Ak.	53·58 N	166·30 W
112	Duvall (dōō'vâl).Wa. (Seattle In.)	47·44 N	121·59 W
129	Duvergé (dōō-vĕr-hĕ').Dom. Rep.	18·20 N	71·20 W
112	Duwamish (R.) (dōō-wăm'ĭsh) Wa. (Seattle In.)	47·24 N	122·18 W
	Dvina, Western, R., see Zapadnaya Dvina		
170	Dvinskaya Guba (G.)...Sov. Un.	65·10 N	38·40 E
158	Dvŭr Králové nad Labem (dvōōr' krä'lô-vā).Czech.	50·28 N	15·43 E
184	Dwārka....India	22·18 N	68·59 E
104	Dwight (dwīt)....Il.	41·00 N	88·20 W
110	Dworshak Res....Id.	46·45 N	116·15 W
166	Dyat'kovo (dyät'kō-vō)..Sov. Un.	53·36 N	34·19 E
107	Dyer (dī'ẽr)....In. (Chicago In.)	41·30 N	87·31 W
120	Dyersburg (dī'ẽrz-bûrg)....Tn.	36·02 N	89·23 W
109	Dyersville (dī'ẽrz-vĭl)....Ia.	42·28 N	91·09 W
112	Dyes Inlet (dīz)..Wa. (Seattle In.)	47·37 N	122·45 W
95	Dyment (dī'mĕnt)....Can.	49·37 N	92·19 W
188	Dzabhan Gol (R.)....Mong.	48·19 N	94·08 E
192	Dzamiin Üüde....Mong.	44·38 N	111·32 E
213	Dzaoudzi (dzou'dzĭ) Comoro Is.	12·44 S	45·15 E
147	Dzaudzhikau (dzou-jĭ-kou') Sov. Un.	48·00 N	44·52 E
167	Dzerzhinsk (dzhĕr-zhĭnsk') Sov. Un.	48·24 N	37·58 E
166	Dzerzhinsk....Sov. Un.	53·41 N	27·14 E
170	Dzerzhinsk....Sov. Un.	56·20 N	43·50 E
172	Dzhalal-Abad (jȧ-läl'ȧ-bät') Sov. Un.	41·13 N	73·35 E
172	Dzhambul (dzhäm-bōōl').Sov. Un.	42·51 N	71·29 E
167	Dzhankoy (dzhän'koi)...Sov. Un.	45·43 N	34·22 E
174	Dzhetygara (dzhĕt'-gä'rȧ) Sov. Un. (Urals In.)	52·12 N	61·18 E
172	Dzhizak (dzhĕ'zăk)....Sov. Un.	40·13 N	67·58 E
173	Dzhugdzhur Khrebet (Mts.) (jŏŏg-jōōr').Sov. Un.	56·15 N	137·00 E
159	Działoszyce (jyä-wō-shē'tsĕ)..Pol.	50·21 N	20·22 E
126	Dzibalchén (zē-bäl-chĕ'n) Mex. (In.)	19·25 N	89·39 W
126	Dzidzantún (zēd-zän-tōō'n) Mex. (In.)	21·18 N	89·00 W
158	Dzierzoniów (dzyĕr-zhôn'yŭf).Pol.	50·44 N	16·38 E
126	Dzilam Gonzalez (zē-lä'm-gôn-zä'lĕz).Mex. (In.)	21·21 N	88·53 W
126	Dzitás (zē-tá's)....Mex. (In.)	20·47 N	88·32 W
126	Dzitbalché (dzēt-bäl-chā') Mex. (In.)	20·18 N	90·03 W
188	Dzungaria (Reg.) (dzōōŋ-gä'rĭ-ȧ).China	44·39 N	86·13 E

E

Page	Name Pronunciation Region	Lat. °′	Long. °′
101	Eagle (ē'g'l)....Ak.	64·42 N	141·20 W
104	Eagle....WV	38·10 N	81·20 W
115	Eagle (R.)....Co.	39·32 N	106·28 W
112	Eaglecliff (ē'g'l-klĭf) Wa. (Portland In.)	46·10 N	123·13 W
107	Eagle Cr....In. (Indianapolis In.)	39·54 N	86·17 W
109	Eagle Grove....Ia.	42·39 N	93·55 W
98	Eagle Lake....Me.	47·03 N	68·38 W
119	Eagle Lake....Tx.	29·37 N	96·20 W
110	Eagle L....Ca.	40·45 N	120·52 W
113	Eagle Mountain L. Tx. (Dallas, Fort Worth In.)	32·56 N	97·27 W
118	Eagle Pass....Tx.	28·49 N	100·30 W
110	Eagle Pk....Ca.	41·18 N	120·11 W
148	Ealing (ē'lĭng)..Eng. (London In.)	51·29 N	0·19 W
117	Earle (ûrl)....Ar.	35·14 N	90·28 W
120	Earlington (ûr'lĭng-tŭn)....Ky.	37·15 N	87·31 W
121	Easley (ēz'lĭ)....SC	34·48 N	82·37 W
122	East, Mt....C. Z. (In.)	9·09 N	79·16 W
113	East Alton (ôl'tŭn) Il. (St. Louis In.)	38·53 N	90·08 W
97	East Angus (ăŋ'gŭs)....Can.	45·35 N	71·40 W
107	East Aurora (ô-rō'rȧ) NY (Buffalo In.)	42·46 N	78·38 W
119	East B....Tx. (In.)	29·30 N	94·41 W
149	East Berlin (bĕr-lēn') G.D.R. (Berlin In.)	52·31 N	13·28 E
120	East Bernstadt (bûrn'stăt)....Ky.	37·09 N	84·08 W
155	Eastbourne (ēst'bôrn)....Eng.	50·48 N	0·16 E
129	East Caicos (I.) (kī'kōs) Turk & Caicos Is.	21·40 N	71·35 W
205	East Cape (C.)....N. Z. (In.)	37·37 S	178·33 E
	East Cape, see Dezhneva, Mys		
113	East Carondelet (kȧ-rŏn'dĕ-lĕt) Il. (St. Louis In.)	38·33 N	90·14 W
107	East Chicago (shĭ-kô'gō) In. (Chicago In.)	41·39 N	87·29 W
189	East China Sea....Asia	30·28 N	125·52 E
107	East Cleveland (klēv'lănd) Oh. (Cleveland In.)	41·33 N	81·35 W
119	East Cote Blanche B. (kōt blänsh').La.	29·30 N	92·07 W
109	East Des Moines (R.) (dē moin') Ia.	42·57 N	94·17 W
107	East Detroit (dē-troit') Mi. (Detroit In.)	42·28 N	82·57 W
	Easter (I.), see Rapa Nui		
158	Eastern Alps (Mts.).Aus.-Switz.	47·03 N	10·55 E
185	Eastern Ghāts (Mts.)....India	13·50 N	78·45 E
188	Eastern Turkestan (Reg.) (tōōr-kĕ-stän') (tûr-kĕ-stăn') China	38·23 N	80·41 E
107	East Gary (gā'rĭ).In. (Chicago In.)	41·34 N	87·15 W
108	East Grand Forks (grănd fôrks) Mn.	47·56 N	97·02 W
106	East Greenwich (grĭn'ĭj) RI (Providence In.)	41·40 N	71·27 W
105	Easthampton (ēst-hămp'tŭn)..Ma.	42·15 N	72·45 W
105	East Hartford (härt'fẽrd)....Ct.	41·45 N	72·35 W
111	East Helena (hĕ-lē'nȧ)....Mt.	46·31 N	111·50 W
148	East Ilsley (ĭl'slē) Eng. (London In.)	51·30 N	1·18 W
104	East Jordan (jôr'dȧn)....Mi.	45·05 N	85·05 W
113	East Kansas City (kăn'zȧs) Mo. (Kansas City In.)	39·09 N	94·30 W
118	Eastland (ēst'lănd)....Tx.	32·24 N	98·47 W
104	East Lansing (lăn'sĭng)....Mi.	42·45 N	84·30 W
107	Eastlawn....Mi. (Detroit In.)	42·15 N	83·35 W
113	East Leavenworth (lĕv'ĕn-wûrth) Mo. (Kansas City In.)	39·18 N	94·50 W
104	East Liverpool (lĭv'ẽr-pōōl)...Oh.	40·40 N	80·35 W
213	East London (lŭn'dŭn) S. Afr. (Natal In.)	33·02 S	27·54 E
113	East Los Angeles (lōs ăŋ'hȧ-lās) Ca. (Los Angeles In.)	34·01 N	118·09 W
91	Eastmain (R.) (ēst'mān)....Can.	52·12 N	73·19 W
120	Eastman (ēst'mȧn)....Ga.	32·10 N	83·11 W
106	East Millstone (mĭl'stōn) NJ (New York In.)	40·30 N	74·35 W
109	East Moline (mō-lēn')....Il.	41·31 N	90·28 W
115	East Nishnabotna (R.) (nĭsh-nȧ-bŏt'nȧ).Ia.	40·53 N	95·23 W
105	Easton (ēs'tŭn)....Md.	72·45 N	76·05 W
105	Easton....Pa.	40·45 N	75·15 W
106	Easton L....Ct. (New York In.)	41·18 N	73·17 W
106	East Orange (ŏr'ĕnj) NJ (New York In.)	40·46 N	74·12 W
112	East Palo Alto Ca. (San Francisco In.)	37·27 N	122·07 W
104	East Peoria (pē-ō'rĭ-ȧ)....Il.	40·40 N	89·30 W
107	East Pittsburgh (pĭts'bûrg) Pa. (Pittsburgh In.)	40·24 N	79·50 W
106	East Point....Ga. (Atlanta In.)	33·41 N	84·27 W
98	Eastport (ēst'pōrt)....Me.	44·53 N	67·01 W
106	East Providence (prŏv'ĭ-dĕns) RI (Providence In.)	41·49 N	71·22 W
148	East Retford (rĕt'fẽrd)....Eng.	53·19 N	0·56 W
148	East Riding (Co.) (rīd'ĭng)...Eng.	53·47 N	0·36 W
105	East Rochester (rŏch'ĕs-tẽr)..NY.	43·10 N	77·30 W
113	East St. Louis (sānt lōō'ĭs) (lōō-ĭ) Il. (St. Louis In.)	38·38 N	90·10 W
168	East Siberian Sea (sī-bĭr'y'n) Sov. Un.	73·00 N	153·28 E
112	Eastsound (ēst-sound) Wa. (Vancouver In.)	48·42 N	122·42 W
105	East Stroudsburg (stroudz'bûrg) Pa.	41·00 N	75·10 W
105	East Syracuse (sĭr'ȧ-kūs)....NY	43·05 N	76·00 W

278 East Tavaputs — El Paso PRONOUNCING INDEX

Page Name Pronunciation Region Lat. °' Long. °'

115 East Tavaputs Plat. (tă-vă'-pŭts) Ut. 39·25 N 109·45 W
104 East Tawas (tô'wăs) Mi. 44·15 N 83·30 W
114 East Walker (R.) (wôk'ēr) Nv. 38·36 N 119·02 W
100 East York Can. (Toronto In.) 43·41 N 79·20 W
107 Eaton (ē'tŭn) Co. 40·31 N 104·42 W
104 Eaton Oh. 39·45 N 84·40 W
107 Eaton Estates Oh. (Cleveland In.) 41·19 N 82·01 W
104 Eaton Rapids (răp'ĭdz) Mi. 42·30 N 84·40 W
120 Eatonton (ē'tŭn-tŭn) Ga. 33·20 N 83·24 W
106 Eatontown (ē'tŭn-toun) NJ (New York In.) 40·18 N 74·04 W
109 Eau Claire (ō klâr') Wi. 44·47 N 91·32 W
156 Ebeltoft (ĕ'bĕl-tŭft) Den. 56·11 N 10·39 E
105 Ebensburg Pa. 40·29 N 78·44 W
149 Ebersberg (ĕ'bĕrs-bĕrgh) F.R.G. (Munich In.) 48·05 N 11·58 E
158 Ebingen (ā'bĭng-ĕn) F.R.G. 48·13 N 9·04 E
188 Ebi Nuur (L.) (ā'bē) China 45·09 N 83·15 E
164 Eboli (ĕb'ô-lē) It. 40·38 N 15·04 E
215 Ebolowa Cam. 2·54 N 11·09 E
149 Ebreichsdorf Aus. (Vienna In.) 47·58 N 16·24 E
214 Ebrie, Lagune (Lagoon) Ivory Coast 5·20 N 4·50 W
163 Ebro, Río (R.) (rē'-ô-ā'brō) Sp. 41·30 N 0·35 W
148 Eccles (ĕk''lz) Eng. 53·29 N 2·20 W
104 Eccles WV 37·45 N 81·10 W
148 Eccleshall (ĕk''lz-hôl) Eng. 52·51 N 2·15 W
165 Eceabat (Maidos) Tur. 40·10 N 26·21 E
197 Echague (ā-chä'gwä) Phil. (In.) 16·43 N 121·40 E
127 Echandi, Cerro (Mt.) (sĕ'r-rô-ĕ-chä'nd) Pan. 9·05 N 82·51 W
95 Echimamish (R.) Can. 54·15 N 97·30 W
113 Echo Bay (ĕk'ō) Can. (Sault Ste. Marie In.) 46·29 N 84·04 W
95 Echoing (R.) (ĕk'ō-ĭng) Can. 55·15 N 91·30 W
161 Echternach (ĕk'tēr-näk) Lux. 49·48 N 6·25 E
203 Echuca (ē-chōō'kȧ) Austl. 36·10 S 144·47 E
162 Écija (ā'thē-hä) Sp. 37·20 N 5·07 W
158 Eckernförde F.R.G. 54·27 N 9·51 E
106 Eclipse (ē-klĭps') Va. (Norfolk In.) 36·55 N 76·29 W
107 Ecorse (ē-kôrs') Mi. (Detroit In.) 42·15 N 83·09 W
133 Ecuador (ĕk'wȧ-dôr) S. A. 0·00 N 78·30 W
211 Ed Eth. 13·57 N 41·37 E
120 Eddyville (ĕd'ĭ-vĭl) Ky. 37·03 N 88·03 W
215 Ede Nig. 7·44 N 4·27 E
215 Edéa (ĕ-dā'ä) Cam. 3·48 N 10·08 E
118 Eden Tx. 31·13 N 99·51 W
113 Eden Ut. (Salt Lake City In.) 41·18 N 111·49 W
154 Eden (R.) (ē'dĕn) Eng. 54·40 N 2·35 W
148 Edenbridge (ē'dĕn-brĭj) Eng. (London In.) 51·11 N 0·05 E
148 Edenham (ē'd'n-ăm) Eng. 52·46 N 0·25 W
113 Eden Prairie (prâr'ĭ) Mn. (Minneapolis, St. Paul In.) 44·51 N 93·29 W
121 Edenton (ē'dĕn-tŭn) NC 36·02 N 76·37 W
107 Edenton Oh. (Cincinnati In.) 39·14 N 84·02 W
213 Edenvale (ĕd'ĕn-vāl) S. Afr. (Johannesburg & Pretoria In.) 29·06 S 28·10 E
218 Edenville (ē'd'n-vĭl) S. Afr. (Johannesburg & Pretoria In.) 27·33 S 27·42 E
158 Eder R. (ā'dēr) F.R.G. 51·05 N 8·52 E
121 Edgefield (ĕj'fēld) SC 33·52 N 81·55 W
108 Edgeley (ĕj'lĭ) ND 46·24 N 98·43 W
108 Edgemont (ĕj'mŏnt) SD 43·19 N 103·50 W
109 Edgerton (ĕj'ēr-tŭn) Wi. 42·49 N 89·06 W
106 Edgewater (ĕj-wô-tēr) Al. (Birmingham In.) 33·31 N 86·52 W
106 Edgewater Md. (Baltimore In.) 38·58 N 76·35 W
93 Edgewood (ĕj'wŏŏd) Can. 49·47 N 118·08 W
165 Édhessa Grc. 40·48 N 22·04 E
113 Edina (ē-dī'nȧ) Mn. (Minneapolis, St. Paul In.) 44·55 N 93·20 W
117 Edina Mo. 40·10 N 92·11 W
104 Edinburg (ĕd''n-bûrg) In. 39·20 N 85·55 W
118 Edinburg Tx. 26·18 N 98·08 W
154 Edinburgh (ĕd''n-bŭr-ō) Scot. 55·57 N 3·10 W
165 Edirne (Adrianople) (ĕ-dĭr'nĕ) (ā-drĭ-ăn-ō'p'l) Tur. 41·41 N 26·35 E
121 Edisto, (R.) (ĕd'ĭs-tō) SC 33·10 N 80·50 W
121 Edisto (R.), North Fk. SC 33·42 N 81·24 W
121 Edisto (R.), South Fk. SC 33·43 N 81·35 W
121 Edisto Island SC 32·32 N 80·20 W
117 Edmond (ĕd'mŭnd) Ok. 35·39 N 97·29 W
112 Edmonds (ĕd'mŭndz) Wa. (Seattle In.) 47·49 N 122·23 W
100 Edmonton Can. (Edmonton In.) 53·33 N 113·28 W
98 Edmundston (ĕd'mŭn-stŭn) Can. 47·22 N 68·20 W
119 Edna (ĕd'nȧ) Tx. 28·59 N 96·39 W
165 Edremit (ĕd-rĕ-mēt') Tur. 39·35 N 27·00 E
165 Edremit Körfezi (G.) Tur. 39·28 N 26·35 E
93 Edson (ĕd'sŭn) Can. 53·35 N 116·26 W
96 Edward (I.) (ĕd'wērd) Can. 48·21 N 88·29 W
217 Edward (L.) Zaire 0·25 S 29·40 E
113 Edwardsville (ĕd'wērdz-vĭl) Il. (St. Louis In.) 38·49 N 89·58 W
107 Edwardsville In. (Louisville In.) 38·17 N 85·53 W
113 Edwardsville Ks. (Kansas City In.) 39·04 N 94·49 W
110 Eel R. (ēl) Ca. 40·39 N 124·15 W
104 Eel (R.) In. 40·50 N 85·55 W
205 Efate (I.) (ā-fä'tä) New Hebr. 18·02 S 168·29 E
109 Effigy Mounds Natl. Mon. (ĕf'ĭ-jŭ mounds) Ia. 43·04 N 91·15 W
104 Effingham (ĕf'ĭng-hăm) Il. 39·05 N 88·30 W
162 Ega (R.) (ā'gä) Sp. 42·40 N 2·20 W
164 Egadi, Isole (Is.) (ĕ'sō-lĕ-ĕ'gä-dē) It. 38·01 N 12·00 E
162 Egea de los Caballeros (ā-kā'ȧ dā lōs kä-bäl-yä'rôs) Sp. 42·07 N 1·05 W
101 Egegik (ĕg'ĕ-jĭt) Ak. 58·10 N 157·22 W
159 Eger (ĕ gĕr) Hung. 47·53 N 20·24 E
Eger (R.), see Ohře
156 Egersund (ĕ'ghĕr-sŏŏn') Nor. 58·29 N 6·01 E
105 Egg Harbor (ĕg här'bēr) NJ 39·30 N 74·35 W
148 Egham (ĕg'ăm) Eng. (London In.) 51·24 N 0·33 W
188 Egiin Gol (R.) (å-gēn') Mong. 49·41 N 100·40 E
205 Egmont, C. (ĕg'mŏnt) N. Z. (In.) 39·18 S 173·49 E
171 Egridir Gölü (L.) (ā-rĭ-dĭr') Tur. 38·10 N 30·00 E
160 Eguilles (ĕ-gwē') Fr. (In.) 43·34 N 5·21 E
209 Egypt (ē'jĭpt) Afr. 26·58 N 27·01 E
215 Eha-Amufu Nig. 6·40 N 7·46 E
162 Eibar (ā'ê-bär) Sp. 43·12 N 2·20 W
158 Eichstätt (ĭk'shtät) F.R.G. 48·54 N 11·14 E
149 Eichwalde (ĭĸ'väl-dĕ) G.D.R. (Berlin In.) 52·22 N 13·37 E
156 Eid (ĭdh) Nor. 61·54 N 6·01 E
156 Eidsberg (ĭdhs'bĕrgh) Nor. 59·32 N 11·16 E
156 Eidsvoll (ĭdhs'vôl) Nor. 60·19 N 11·15 E
158 Eifel (Plat.) (ī'fĕl) F.R.G. 50·08 N 6·30 E
204 Eighty Mile Beach Austl. 20·45 S 121·00 E
218 Eil Som. (Horn of Afr. In.) 7·53 N 49·45 E
158 Eilenburg (ī'lĕn-bŏŏrgh) G.D.R. 51·27 N 12·38 E
213 Eilliot S. Afr. (Natal In.) 31·19 S 27·52 E
158 Einbeck (īn'bĕk) F.R.G. 51·49 N 9·52 E
155 Eindhoven (īnd'hō-vĕn) Neth. 51·29 N 5·20 E
134 Eirunepé (ā-rōō-nĕ-pĕ') Braz. 6·37 S 69·58 W
158 Eisenach (ī'zĕn-äĸ) G.D.R. 50·58 N 10·18 E
158 Eisenhüttenstadt G.D.R. 52·08 N 14·40 E
158 Eisleben (īs'lā'bĕn) G.D.R. 51·31 N 11·33 E
156 Ejdfjord (ĕĭd'fyōr) Nor. 60·28 N 7·04 E
214 Ejura Ghana 7·23 N 1·22 W
125 Ejutla de Crespo (å-hōōt'lä dā krās'pō) Mex. 16·34 N 96·44 W
216 Ekanga Zaire 2·23 S 23·14 E
157 Ekenäs (Tammisaari) (ĕ'kĕ-nâs) (tàm'ĭ-sä'rĭ) Fin. 59·59 N 23·25 E
149 Ekeren Bel. (Brussels In.) 51·17 N 4·27 E
216 Ekoli Zaire 0·23 S 24·16 E
156 Eksjö (ĕk'shû) Swe. 57·41 N 14·55 E
210 El Aaiún W. Sah. 26·45 N 13·15 W
163 El Affroun (ĕl ȧf-froun') Alg 36·28 N 2·38 E
213 Elands (R.) S. Afr. (Natal In.) 31·48 S 26·09 E
218 Elands R. (ēlånds) S. Afr. (Johannesburg & Pretoria In.) 25·11 S 28·52 E
162 El Arahal (ĕl ä-rä-äl') Sp. 37·17 N 5·32 W
152 El Asnam (Orléansville) Alg. 36·14 N 1·32 E
183 Elat Isr. (Palestine In.) 29·34 N 34·57 E
171 Elâzig (ĕl-ä'zĕz) Tur. 38·40 N 39·00 E
120 Elba (ĕl'bȧ) Al. 31·25 N 86·01 W
164 Elba, Isola di (I.) (ē-sō lä-dē-ĕl'bȧ) It. 42·42 N 10·25 E
134 El Banco (ĕl băn'cō) Col. 8·58 N 74·01 W
162 El Barco (ĕl bär'kō) Sp. 42·26 N 6·58 W
165 Elbasan (ĕl-bä-sän') Alb. 41·08 N 20·05 E
152 El Bayadh Alg. 33·42 N 1·06 E
Elbe (R.), see Labe
158 Elbe R. (ĕl'bē) G.D.R. 53·47 N 9·20 E
115 Elbert, Mt. (ĕl'bērt) Co. 39·05 N 106·25 W
120 Elberton (ĕl'bēr-tŭn) Ga. 34·05 N 82·53 W
160 Elbeuf (ĕl-bûf') Fr. 49·16 N 0·59 E
171 Elbistan (ĕl-bē-stän') Tur. 38·20 N 37·10 E
159 Elblag (ĕl'blăŋg) Pol. 54·11 N 19·25 E
162 El Bonillo (ĕl bō-nēl'yō) Sp. 38·56 N 2·31 W
100 Elbow (R.) (ĕl'bō) Can. (Calgary In.) 51·03 N 114·24 W
128 Elbow Cay (I.) Ba. 26·25 N 77·55 W
108 Elbow Lake Mn. 46·00 N 95·59 W
171 El'brus, Gora (Mt.) (ĕl'brōōs') Sov. Un. 43·20 N 42·25 E
218 El Bur Som. (Horn of Afr. In.) 4·35 N 46·40 E
171 Elburz Mts. (ĕl'bōōrz') Iran 36·30 N 51·00 E
114 El Cajon Ca. (In.) 32·48 N 116·58 W
134 El Cajon (ĕl-kä-kô'n) Col. (In.) 4·50 N 76·35 W
135 El Cambur (käm-bōōr') Ven. (In.) 10·24 N 68·06 W
119 El Campo (kăm'pō) Tx. 29·13 N 96·17 W
137 El Carmen (kȧ'r-mĕn) Chile (Santiago In.) 34·14 S 71·23 W
134 El Carmen (kȧ'r-mĕn) Col. 9·54 N 75·12 W
113 El Casco (kăs'kō) Ca. (Los Angeles In.) 33·59 N 117·08 W
114 El Centro (sĕn'trō) Ca. 32·47 N 115·33 W
112 El Cerrito (sĕr-rē'tō) Ca. (San Francisco In.) 37·55 N 122·19 W
163 Elche (ĕl'chā) Sp. 38·15 N 0·42 W
126 El Cuyo Mex. (In.) 21·30 N 87·42 W
163 Elda (ĕl'dä) Sp. 38·28 N 0·44 W
158 Elde R. (ĕl'dē) G.D.R. 53·11 N 11·30 E
210 El Djouf (Des.) (ĕl djōōf) Mauritania 21·45 N 7·05 W
109 Eldon (ĕl-dŭn) Ia. 40·55 N 92·15 W
115 Eldon Mo. 38·21 N 92·36 W
109 Eldora (ĕl-dō'rȧ) Ia. 42·21 N 93·08 W
117 El Dorado (ĕl dō-rä'dō) Ar. 33·13 N 92·39 W
104 Eldorado Il. 37·50 N 88·30 W
117 El Dorado Ks. 37·49 N 96·51 W
117 Eldorado Springs (sprĭngz) Mo. 37·51 N 94·02 W
217 Eldoret (ĕl-dō-rĕt') Ken. 0·31 N 35·17 E
124 El Ebano (ā-bä'nō) Mex. 22·13 N 98·26 W
116 Electra (ē-lĕk'trȧ) Tx. 34·02 N 98·54 W
111 Electric Pk. (ē-lĕk'trĭk) Mt. 45·03 N 110·52 W
174 Elektrogorsk (ĕl-yĕk'trô-gôrsk) Sov. Un. (Moscow In.) 55·53 N 38·48 E
174 Elektrostal (ĕl-yĕk'trô-stál) Sov. Un. (Moscow In.) 55·47 N 38·27 E
174 Elektrougli Sov. Un. (Moscow In.) 55·43 N 38·13 E
115 Elephant Butte Res. (ĕl'ē-fănt būt) NM 33·25 N 107·10 W
163 El Escorial (ĕl-ĕs-kô-ryä'l) Sp. (Madrid In.) 40·38 N 4·08 W
126 El Espino (ĕl-ĕs-pē'nō) Nic. 13·26 N 86·48 W
129 Eleuthera (I.) (ē-lū'thēr-ȧ) Ba. 25·05 N 76·10 W
129 Eleuthera Pt. Ba. 24·35 N 76·05 W
117 Eleven Point (R.) (ē-lĕv'ĕn) Mo. 36·53 N 91·39 W
162 El Ferrol (fā-rōl') Sp. 43·30 N 8·12 W
107 Elgin (ĕl'jĭn) Il. (Chicago In.) 42·03 N 88·16 W
108 Elgin Ne. 41·58 N 98·04 W
110 Elgin Or. 45·34 N 117·58 W
154 Elgin Scot. 57·40 N 3·30 W
119 Elgin Tx. 30·21 N 97·22 W
112 Elgin Wa. (Seattle In.) 47·23 N 122·42 W
210 El Goléa (gô-lā-ä') Alg. 30·39 N 2·52 E
217 Elgon, Mt. (ĕl'gŏn) Ken. 1·00 N 34·25 E
124 El Grullo (grōōl-yō) Mex. 19·46 N 104·10 W
135 El Guapo (gwä'pō) Ven. (In.) 10·07 N 66·00 W
152 El Hamada (Plat.) (häm'ä-dä) Alg. 30·53 N 1·52 W
110 El Hank (Bluffs) Mauritania-Mali 23·44 N 6·45 W
135 El Hatillo (ä-tē'l-yō) Ven. (In.) 10·08 N 65·13 W
200 Elie (ē'lē) Can. (Winnipeg In.) 49·55 N 97·45 W
217 Elila (R.) (ĕ-lē'lȧ) Zaire 3·00 S 26·50 E
112 Elisa (I.) (ē-lī'sȧ) Wa. (Vancouver In.) 48·43 N 122·37 W
Élisabethville, see Lubumbashi
157 Elisenvaara (ā-lē'sĕn-vä'rȧ) Sov. Un. 61·25 N 29·46 E
119 Elizabeth (ē-lĭz'ȧ-bĕth) La. 30·50 N 92·47 W
106 Elizabeth NJ (New York In.) 40·40 N 74·13 W
107 Elizabeth Pa. (Pittsburgh In.) 40·16 N 79·53 W
121 Elizabeth City NC 36·15 N 76·15 W
121 Elizabethton (ē-lĭz-ȧ-bĕth'tŭn) Tn. 36·19 N 82·12 W
104 Elizabethtown (ē-lĭz'ȧ-bĕth-toun) Ky. 37·40 N 85·55 W
210 El Jadida Mor. 33·14 N 8·34 W
159 Ełk Pol. 53·53 N 22·23 E
93 Elk (R.) Can. 50·00 N 115·00 W
120 Elk (R.) Tn. 35·05 N 86·36 W
104 Elk (R.) WV 38·30 N 81·05 W
210 El Kairouan (kĕr-ōō-än) Tun. 35·46 N 10·04 E
116 Elk City (ĕlk) Ok. 35·23 N 99·23 W
104 Elkhart (ĕlk'härt) In. 41·40 N 86·00 W
116 Elkhart Ks. 37·00 N 101·54 W
119 Elkhart Tx. 31·38 N 95·35 W
109 Elkhorn (ĕlk'hôrn) Wi. 42·39 N 88·32 W
108 Elkhorn (R.) Ne. 42·06 N 97·46 W
121 Elkin (ĕl'kĭn) NC 36·15 N 80·50 W
105 Elkins (ĕl'kĭnz) WV 38·55 N 79·50 W
95 Elk I. Can. 50·45 N 96·32 W
93 Elk Island Natl. Park (ĕlk ī'lănd) Can. 53·37 N 112·45 W
110 Elko (ĕl'kō) Nv. 40·51 N 115·46 W
108 Elk Point SD 42·41 N 96·41 W
104 Elk Rapids (răp'ĭdz) Mi. 44·55 N 85·25 W
110 Elk River (rĭv'ēr) Id. 46·47 N 116·11 W
109 Elk River Mn. 45·17 N 93·33 W
120 Elkton (ĕlk'tŭn) Ky. 36·47 N 87·08 W
105 Elkton Md. 39·35 N 75·50 W
108 Elkton SD 44·15 N 96·28 W
148 Elland (el'ănd) Eng. 53·41 N 1·50 W
115 Ellen, Mt. (ĕl'ĕn) Ut. 38·05 N 110·50 W
108 Ellendale (ĕl'ĕn-dāl) ND 46·01 N 98·33 W
110 Ellensburg (ĕl'ĕnz-bûrg) Wa. 47·00 N 120·31 W
105 Ellenville (ĕl'ĕn-vĭl) NY 41·40 N 74·25 W
100 Ellerslie (ĕl'ērz-lē) Can. (Edmonton In.) 53·25 N 113·30 W
148 Ellesmere (ĕlz'mēr) Eng. 52·55 N 2·54 W
75 Ellesmere I. Can. 81·00 N 80·00 W
148 Ellesmere Port Eng. 53·17 N 2·54 W
Ellice Is., see Tuvalu
106 Ellicott City (ĕl'ĭ-kŏt sĭ'tē) Md. (Baltimore In.) 39·16 N 76·48 W
107 Ellicott Cr. NY (Buffalo In.) 43·00 N 78·46 W
213 Elliotdale (ĕl-ĭ-ŏt'dăl) S. Afr. (Natal In.) 31·58 S 28·42 E
96 Elliot Lake Can. 46·23 N 82·39 W
112 Elliot (el'ĭ-ŭt) Wa. (Seattle In.) 47·28 N 122·08 W
116 Ellis (ĕl'ĭs) Ks. 38·56 N 99·34 W
120 Ellisville (ĕl'ĭs-vĭl) Ms. 31·37 N 89·10 W
113 Ellisville Mo. (St. Louis In.) 38·35 N 90·35 W
116 Ellsworth (ĕlz'wûrth) Ks. 38·43 N 98·14 W
98 Ellsworth Me. 44·33 N 68·26 W
220 Ellsworth Highland Ant. 77·00 S 90·00 W
158 Ellwangen (ĕl'väŋ-gĕn) F.R.G. 48·47 N 10·08 E
149 Elm (ĕlm) F.R.G. (Hamburg In.) 53·31 N 9·13 E
108 Elm (R.) SD 45·47 N 98·28 W
104 Elm (R.) WV 38·30 N 81·05 W
110 Elma (ĕl'mȧ) Wa. 47·02 N 123·20 W
152 El Maadid Mor. 31·32 N 4·30 W
117 Elm Cr. Tx. 33·34 N 97·25 W
113 Elmendorf (ĕl'mĕn-dôrf) Tx. (San Antonio In.) 29·16 N 98·20 W
113 Elm Fork (ĕlm fôrk) Tx. (Dallas, Fort Worth In.) 32·55 N 96·56 W
107 Elmhurst (ĕlm'hûrst) Il. (Chicago In.) 41·54 N 87·56 W
210 El Milia (mē'ä) Alg. 36·30 N 6·16 E
105 Elmira (ĕl-mī'rȧ) NY 42·05 N 76·50 W
105 Elmira Heights NY 42·10 N 76·50 W
134 El Misti (Vol.) (mē's-tē) Peru 16·04 S 71·20 W
113 El Modena (mô-dē'nō) Ca. (Los Angeles In.) 33·47 N 117·48 W
113 El Monte (mŏn'tā) Ca. (Los Angeles In.) 34·04 N 118·02 W
115 El Morro Natl. Mon. NM 35·05 N 108·20 W
214 El Mreyyé (Des.) Mauritania 19·15 N 7·50 W
149 Elmshorn (ĕlms'hôrn) F.R.G. (Hamburg In.) 53·45 N 9·39 E
107 Elmwood Place (ĕlm'wŏŏd plās) Oh. (Cincinnati In.) 39·11 N 84·30 W
111 Elokomin (R.) (ē-lō'kō-mĭn) Wa. (Portland In.) 46·16 N 123·16 W
124 El Oro (ô-rō) Mex. 19·49 N 100·04 W
210 El Oued (wĕd') Alg. 33·23 N 6·49 E
134 El Pao (ĕl pä'ō) Ven. 8·08 N 62·37 W
126 El Paraíso (pä-rä-ē'sō) Hond. 13·55 N 86·35 W
163 El Pardo (pä'r-dô) Sp. (Madrid In.) 40·31 N 3·47 W
118 El Paso (pas'ō) Tx. 31·47 N 106·27 W

ăt; finăl; rāte; senâte; ärm; åsk; sofȧ; fâre; ch-choose; dh-as th in other; bē; êvent; bĕt; recĕnt; cratēr; g-go; gh-guttural g; bĭt; ĭ-short neutral; rīde; ĸ-guttural k as ch in German ich;

Page	Name	Pronunciation	Region	Lat. ° ′	Long. ° ′
135	El Pilar	(pē-lä′r)	Ven. (In.)	9.56 N	64.48 W
127	El Porvenir	(pôr-vä-nēr′)	Pan.	9.34 N	78.55 W
162	El Puerto de Sta. María	(pwĕr tō dä sän tä mä-rē′ä)	Sp.	36.36 N	6.18 W
127	El Real	(rā-äl)	Pan.	8.07 N	77.43 W
116	El Reno	(rē′nō)	Ok.	35.31 N	97.57 W
135	El Roboré	(rô-bō-rē′)	Bol.	18.23 S	59.43 W
109	Elroy	(ĕl′roi)	Wi.	43.44 N	90.17 W
101	Elsa		Can.	63.55 N	135.25 W
113	Elsah	(ĕl′zȧ)	Il. (St. Louis In.)	38.57 N	90.22 W
124	El Salto	(säl′tō)	Mex.	22.48 N	105.22 W
122	El Salvador		N. A.	14.00 N	89.30 W
126	El Sauce	(ĕl-sä′ōō-sĕ)	Nic.	13.00 N	86.40 W
117	Elsberry	(ĕlz′bĕr-ĭ)	Mo.	39.09 N	90.44 W
161	Elsdorf	(ĕls′dôrf)	F.R.G. (Ruhr In.)	50.56 N	6.35 E
113	El Segundo	(sĕgŭn′dō)	Ca. (Los Angeles In.)	33.55 N	118.24 W
113	Elsinore	(ĕl′sĭ-nôr)	Ca. (Los Angeles In.)	33.40 N	117.19 W
113	Elsinore L.		Ca. (Los Angeles In.)	33.38 N	117.21 W
149	Elstorf	(ĕls′tôrf)	F.R.G. (Hamburg In.)	53.25 N	9.48 E
202	Eltham	(ĕl′thăm)	Austl. (Melbourne In.)	37.43 S	145.08 E
134	El Tigre	(tē′grĕ)	Ven.	8.49 N	64.15 W
171	El'ton		Sov. Un.	49.10 N	47.00 E
113	El Toro	(tō′rō)	Ca. (Los Angeles In.)	33.37 N	117.42 W
126	El Triunfo	(ĕl-trē-ōō′n-fō)	Hond.	13.06 N	87.00 W
126	El Triunfo		Sal.	13.17 N	88.32 W
187	Elūru		India	16.44 N	80.09 E
162	El Vado Res.		NM	36.37 N	106.30 W
162	Elvas	(ĕl′väzh)	Port.	38.53 N	7.11 W
156	Elverum	(ĕl′vĕ-rŏŏm)	Nor.	60.53 N	11.33 E
126	El Viejo	(ĕl-vyĕ′kō)	Nic.	12.10 N	87.10 W
126	El Viejo (Vol.)		Nic.	12.44 N	87.03 W
117	Elvins	(ĕl′vĭnz)	Mo.	37.49 N	90.31 W
211	El Wak	(wäk′)	Ken.	3.00 N	41.00 E
107	Elwood	(ĕl′wŏŏd)	Il. (Chicago In.)	41.24 N	88.07 W
104	Elwood		In.	40.15 N	85.50 W
155	Ely	(ē′lĭ)	Eng.	52.25 N	0.17 E
109	Ely		Mn.	47.54 N	91.53 W
114	Ely		Nv.	39.16 N	114.53 W
107	Elyria	(ē-lĭr′ĭ-ȧ)	Oh. (Cleveland In.)	41.22 N	82.07 W
157	Ema (R.)	(ä′mȧ)	Sov. Un.	58.25 N	27.00 E
156	Emån (R.)		Swe.	57.15 N	15.46 E
171	Emba (R.)	(yĕm′bä)	Sov. Un.	46.50 N	54.10 E
134	Embalse Guri (L.)		Ven.	7.30 N	63.00 W
104	Embarrass (R.)	(ĕm-băr′ȧs)	Il.	39.15 N	88.05 W
100	Embrun	(ĕm′brŭn)	Can. (Ottawa In.)	45.16 N	75.17 W
161	Embrun	(äN-brŭN′)	Fr.	44.35 N	6.32 E
217	Embu		Ken.	0.32 S	37.27 E
158	Emden	(ĕm′dĕn)	F.R.G.	53.21 N	7.15 E
205	Emerald	(ĕm′ĕr-ȧld)	Austl.	28.34 S	148.00 E
95	Emerson	(ĕm′ĕr-sŭn)	Can.	49.00 N	97.12 W
112	Emeryville	(ĕm′ĕr-ĭ-vĭl)	Ca. (San Francisco In.)	37.50 N	122.17 W
215	Emi Koussi, (Mtn.)	(ä′mĕ kōō-sē′)	Chad	19.50 N	18.30 E
164	Emilia-Romagna (Reg.)	(ä-mēl′yä rô-mä′n-yä)	It.	44.35 N	10.48 E
125	Emiliano Zapata	(ä-mē-lyä′nô-zä-pä′tä)	Mex.	17.45 N	91.46 W
104	Eminence	(ĕm′-ĭ-nĕns)	Ky.	38.25 N	85.15 W
197	Emirau (I.)	(ä-mê-rä′ōō)	Pap. N. Gui.	1.40 S	150.28 E
155	Emmen	(ĕm′ĕn)	Neth.	52.47 N	6.55 E
161	Emmerich	(ĕm′ĕr-ĭk)	F.R.G. (Ruhr In.)	51.51 N	6.16 E
109	Emmetsburg	(ĕm′ĕts-bûrg)	Ia.	43.07 N	94.41 W
110	Emmett	(ĕm′ĕt)	Id.	43.53 N	116.30 W
111	Emmons Mt.	(ĕm′ŭnz)	Ut.	40.43 N	110.20 W
118	Emory Pk.	(ē′mŏ-rē pēk)	Tx.	29.13 N	103.20 W
164	Empoli	(ām′pō-lē)	It.	43.43 N	10.55 E
117	Emporia	(ĕm-pō′rĭ-ȧ)	Ks.	38.24 N	96.11 W
121	Emporia		Va.	37.40 N	77.34 W
105	Emporium	(ĕm-pō′rĭ-ŭm)	Pa.	41.30 N	78.15 W
158	Ems R.	(ĕms)	F.R.G.	52.52 N	7.16 E
158	Ems-Weser (Can.)	(vä′zĕr)	F.R.G.	52.23 N	8.11 E
158	Enånger	(ĕn-ôŋ′gĕr)	Swe.	61.36 N	16.55 E
122	Encantada, Cerro de la (Mtn.)	(sĕr′rō-dĕ-lä-ĕn-kän-tä′dä)	Mex.	31.58 N	115.15 W
197	Encanto Pt.	(ĕn-kän′tō)	Phil. (In.)	15.44 N	121.46 E
136	Encarnación	(ĕn-kär-nä-syōn′)	Par.	27.26 S	55.52 W
124	Encarnación de Diaz	(ĕn-kär-nä-syōn dä dē′az)	Mex.	21.34 N	102.15 W
118	Encinal	(ĕn′sĭ-nôl)	Tx.	28.02 N	99.22 W
134	Encontrados	(ĕn-kōn-trä′dōs)	Ven.	9.01 N	72.10 W
203	Encounter B.	(ĕn-koun′tĕr)	Austl.	35.50 S	138.45 E
92	Endako (R.)		Can.	54.05 N	125.30 W
183	Endau (R.)		Mala. (Singapore In.)	2.29 N	103.40 E
198	Enderbury (I.)	(ĕn′dĕr-bûrĭ)	Oceania	2.00 S	107.50 W
220	Enderby Land (Reg.)	(ĕn′dĕr bĭī)	Ant.	72.00 S	52.00 E
108	Enderlin	(ĕn′dĕr-lĭn)	ND	46.38 N	97.37 W
105	Endicott	(ĕn′dĭ-kŏt)	NY	42.05 N	76.00 W
101	Endicott Mts.		Ak.	67.30 N	153.45 W
165	Enez		Tur.	40.42 N	26.05 E
105	Enfield	(ĕn′fēld)	Ct.	41.55 N	72.35 W
148	Enfield		Eng. (London In.)	51.38 N	0.06 W
121	Enfield		NC	36.10 N	77.41 W
129	Engano, Cabo (C.)	(kä′-bŏ-ĕn-gä-nŏ)	Dom. Rep.	18.40 N	68.30 W
196	Engaño, C.	(ĕn-gä′nyō)	Phil.	18.40 N	122.45 E
213	Engcobo	(ĕŋ-cō-bŏ)	S. Afr. (Natal In.)	31.41 S	27.59 E
171	Engel's	(ĕn′gĕls)	Sov. Un.	51.20 N	45.40 E
161	Engelskirchen	(ĕn′gĕls-kēr′кĕn)	F.R.G. (Ruhr In.)	50.59 N	7.25 E
116	Engelwood	(ĕn′g'l-wŏŏd)	Co.	39.39 N	105.00 W
196	Enggano (I.)	(ĕng-gä′nō)	Indon.	5.22 S	102.18 E
117	England	(ĭn′glănd)	Ar.	34.33 N	91.58 W
154	England (Reg.)	(ĭŋ′glănd)	U. K.	51.35 N	1.40 W
99	Englee	(ĕn-glēē)	Can.	50.44 N	56.06 W
106	Englewood		NJ (New York In.)	40.54 N	73.59 W
104	Englewood	(ĭn′glĭsh)	In.	38.15 N	86.25 W
91	English (R.)		Can.	50.31 N	94.12 W
151	English Chan.		Eng.	49.45 N	3.06 W
163	Énguera	(än′gärä)	Sp.	38.58 N	0.42 W
116	Enid	(ē′nĭd)	Ok.	36.25 N	97.52 W
120	Enid Res.		Ms.	34.13 N	89.47 W
212	Enkeldoorn	(ĕn′k'l-dōōrn)	Rh.	19.59 S	30.58 E
218	Enkeldoring	(ĕn′k'l-dôr-ĭng)	S.Afr. (Johannesburg & Pretoria In.)	25.24 S	28.43 E
156	Enköping	(ĕn′kŭ-pĭng)	Swe.	59.39 N	17.05 E
211	Ennedi (Plat.)	(ĕn-nĕd′ē)	Chad.	16.45 N	22.45 E
154	Ennis	(ĕn′ĭs)	Ire.	52.54 N	9.05 W
119	Ennis		Tx.	32.20 N	96.38 W
154	Enniscorthy	(ĕn-ĭs-kôr′thĭ)	Ire.	52.33 N	6.27 W
154	Enniskillen	(ĕn-ĭs-kĭl′ĕn)	N. Ire.	54.20 N	7.25 W
158	Enns R.	(ĕns)	Aus.	47.37 N	14.35 E
121	Enoree	(ê-nō′rē)	SC	34.43 N	81.58 W
121	Enoree, (R.)		SC	34.35 N	81.55 W
129	Enriquillo	(ĕn-rê-kê′l-yō)	Dom. Rep.	17.55 N	71.15 W
129	Enriquillo, Lago (L.)	(lä′gô-ĕn-rê-kê′l-yô)	Dom. Rep.	18.35 N	71.35 W
155	Enschede	(ĕns′кȧ-dĕ)	Neth.	52.10 N	6.50 E
122	Ensenada	(ĕn-sĕ-nä′dä)	Mex.	32.00 N	116.30 W
137	Enseñada		Arg. (Buenos Aires In.)	34.50 S	57.55 W
193	Enshih		China	30.18 N	109.25 E
195	Enshū-Nada (Sea)	(ĕn′shōō nä-dä)	Jap.	34.25 N	137.14 E
217	Entebbe	(ĕn-tĕb′ĕ)	Ug.	0.04 N	32.28 E
120	Enterprise	(ĕn′tĕr-prīz)	Al.	31.20 N	85.50 W
110	Enterprise		Or.	45.25 N	117.16 W
110	Entiat, L.		Wa.	45.43 N	120.11 W
160	Entraygues	(ĕn-trĕg′)	Fr.	44.39 N	2.33 E
217	Entre-Rios	(ĕn-trä rē′ōs)	Moz.	14.57 S	37.20 E
136	Entre Ríos (Prov.)		Arg.	31.30 S	59.00 W
215	Enugu	(ĕn-ōō′gōō)	Nig.	6.27 N	7.27 E
112	Enumclaw	(ĕn′ŭm-klô)	Wa. (Seattle In.)	47.12 N	121.59 W
134	Envigado	(ĕn-vē-gä′dō)	Col. (In.)	6.10 N	75.34 W
164	Eolie, Isole (Is.)	(ĕ′sō-lĕ-ĕ-ô′lyĕ)	It.	38.43 N	14.43 E
215	Epe		Nig.	6.37 N	3.59 E
165	Epeirus (Reg.)		Grc.	39.35 N	20.45 E
160	Épernay	(ā-pĕr-nĕ′)	Fr.	49.02 N	3.54 E
161	Épernon	(ā-pĕr-nôN′)	Fr. (Paris In.)	48.36 N	1.41 E
115	Ephraim	(ē′frȧ-ĭm)	Ut.	39.20 N	111.40 W
110	Ephrata	(ê frā′tȧ)	Wa.	47.18 N	119.35 W
205	Epi	(ā′pē)	New Hebr.	16.59 S	168.29 E
162	Épila	(ā′pê-lä)	Sp.	41.38 N	1.15 W
161	Épinal	(ā-pē-näl′)	Fr.	48.11 N	6.27 E
183	Episkopi		Cyprus (Palestine In.)	34.38 N	32.55 E
148	Epping	(ĕp′ĭng)	Eng. (London In.)	51.41 N	0.06 E
216	Epupa Falls		Ang.	17.00 S	13.05 E
148	Epworth	(ĕp′wûrth)	Eng.	53.31 N	0.50 W
210	Equatorial Guinea		Afr.	2.00 N	7.15 E
160	Equeurdreville	(ā-kûr-dr′vĕl′)	Fr.	49.38 N	1.42 W
100	Eramosa (R.)	(ĕr-ȧ-mō′sȧ)	Can. (Toronto In.)	43.39 N	80.08 W
211	Erba, Jabal (Mtn.)	(ĕr′bä)	Sud.	20.53 N	36.45 E
153	Erciyas (Mtn.)		Tur.	38.30 N	35.36 E
113	Erda	(ēr′dä)	Ut. (Salt Lake City In.)	40.41 N	112.17 W
149	Erding	(ĕr′dĕng)	F.R.G. (Munich In.)	48.19 N	11.54 E
136	Erechim	(ĕ-rĕ-shē′N)	Braz.	27.43 S	52.11 W
171	Ereğli	(ĕ-rä′ĭ-le)	Tur.	37.40 N	34.00 E
171	Ereğli		Tur.	41.15 N	31.25 E
158	Erfurt	(ĕr′fŏŏrt)	G.D.R.	50.59 N	11.04 E
165	Ergene (R.)	(ĕr′gĕ-nĕ)	Tur.	41.17 N	26.50 E
162	Erges (R.)	(ĕr′-zhĕs)	Port.-Sp.	39.45 N	7.01 W
157	Ērgli		Sov. Un.	56.54 N	25.38 E
190	Erhlangtien	(ê′läng′diän)	China	31.33 N	114.07 E
162	Eria (R.)	(ā-rē′ä)	Sp.	42.10 N	6.08 W
116	Erick	(ĕr′ĭk)	Ok.	35.14 N	99.51 W
117	Erie	(ē′rĭ)	Ks.	37.35 N	95.17 W
105	Erie		Pa.	42.05 N	80.05 W
103	Erie, L.		U. S.-Can.	42.15 N	81.25 W
194	Erimo Saki (C.)	(ā′rē-mō sä-kē)	Jap.	41.53 N	143.20 E
101	Erin	(ē′rĭn)	Can. (Toronto In.)	43.46 N	80.04 W
211	Eritrea (Reg.)	(ā-rê-trā′ȧ)	Eth.	16.15 N	38.30 E
158	Erlangen	(ĕr′läng-ĕn)	F.R.G.	49.36 N	11.03 E
107	Erlanger	(ĕr′läng-ēr)	Ky. (Cincinnati In.)	39.01 N	84.36 W
185	Ernākulam		India	9.58 N	76.23 E
	Ermoúpolis, see Síros				
154	Erne, Upper Lough (L.)	(lŏk ûrn)	N. Ire.	54.20 N	7.24 W
154	Erne, Lough (L.)		N. Ire.	54.30 N	7.40 W
91	Ernest Sound	(ûr′nĭst)	Ak.	55.52 N	132.10 W
185	Erode		India	11.20 N	77.45 E
205	Eromanga (I.)		New Hebr.	18.58 S	169.18 E
119	Eros	(ē′rōs)	La.	32.23 N	92.22 W
217	Errego		Moz.	16.02 S	37.14 E
152	Er Ricani		Mor.	31.09 N	4.20 W
154	Errigal, Mt.	(ĕr-ĭ-gôl′)	Ire.	55.02 N	8.07 W
112	Errol Heights		Or. (Portland In.)	45.29 N	122.38 W
161	Erstein	(ĕr′shtīn)	Fr.	48.27 N	7.40 E
121	Erwin	(ûr′wĭn)	NC	35.16 N	78.40 W
121	Erwin		Tn.	36.07 N	82.25 W
158	Erzgebirge (Ore Mts.)	(ĕrts′gĕ-bē′gĕ)	G.D.R.	50.29 N	12.40 E
171	Erzincan	(ĕr-zĭn-jän′)	Tur.	39.50 N	39.30 E
171	Erzurum	(ĕrz′rŏŏm′)	Tur.	39.55 N	41.10 E
216	Esambo		Zaire	3.40 S	23.24 E
194	Esashi	(ĕs′ä-shē)	Jap.	41.50 N	140.10 E
156	Esbjerg	(ĕs′byĕrgh)	Den.	55.29 N	8.25 E
162	Escairón	(ĕs-kī-rō′n)	Sp.	42.34 N	7.40 W
115	Escalante	(ĕs-kȧ-lán′tĕ)	Ut.	37.50 N	111.40 W
115	Escalante (R.)		Ut.	37.40 N	111.20 W
118	Escalón		Mex.	26.45 N	104.20 W
120	Escambia	(ĕs-kăm′bĭ-ȧ)	Fl.	30.38 N	87.20 W
109	Escanaba	(ĕs-kȧ-nô′bȧ)	Mi.	45.44 N	87.05 W
109	Escanaba (R.)		Mi.	46.10 N	87.22 W
161	Esch-sur-Alzette		Lux.	49.32 N	6.21 E
158	Eschwege	(ĕsh′vĕgĕ)	F.R.G.	51.11 N	10.02 E
161	Eschweiler	(ĕsh′vī-lēr)	F.R.G. (Ruhr In.)	50.49 N	6.15 E
129	Escocesá, Bahia	(bä-ē′ä-ĕs-kō-sĕ′sä)	Dom. Rep.	19.25 N	69.40 W
114	Escondido	(ĕs-kōn-dē′dō)	Ca.	33.07 N	117.00 W
118	Escondido, Rio (R.)	(rē′ō-ĕs-kōn-dĕ′dō)	Nic.	28.30 N	100.45 W
127	Escondido R.		Nic.	12.04 N	84.09 W
127	Escudo de Veraguas I.	(ĕs-kōō′dä dä vĕ-rä′gwäs)	Pan.	9.07 N	81.25 W
124	Escuinapa	(ĕs-kwē-nä′pä)	Mex.	22.49 N	105.44 W
126	Escuintla	(ĕs-kwēn′tlä)	Guat.	14.16 N	90.47 W
125	Escuintla		Mex.	15.20 N	92.45 W
127	Ese, Cayos de (I.)		Col.	12.24 N	81.07 W
186	Esfahān		Iran	32.38 N	51.30 E
162	Esgueva (R.)	(ĕs-gē′vä)	Sp.	41.48 N	4.10 W
213	Eshowe	(ĕsh′ō-wĕ)	S. Afr. (Natal In.)	28.54 S	31.28 E
214	Esiama		Ghana	4.56 N	2.21 W
104	Eskdale	(ĕsk′dāl)	WV	38.05 N	81.25 W
150	Eskifjördhur	(ĕs′kĕ-fyûr′dōōr)	Ice.	65.04 N	14.01 W
156	Eskilstuna	(ä′shĕl-stü-na)	Swe.	59.23 N	16.28 E
90	Eskimo Lakes (L.)	(ĕs′kĭ-mō)	Can.	69.40 N	130.10 W
171	Eskişehir	(ĕs-kĕ-shĕ′h′r)	Tur.	39.40 N	30.20 E
113	Esko	(ĕs′kō)	Mn. (Duluth In.)	46.27 N	92.22 W
162	Esla (R.)	(ĕs-lä)	Sp.	41.50 N	5.48 W
156	Eslöv	(ĕs′lûv)	Swe.	55.50 N	13.17 E
134	Esmeraldas	(ĕs-mä-räl′däs)	Ec.	0.58 N	79.45 W
129	Espada, Punta (Pt.)	(pōō′n-tä-ĕs-pä′dä)	Dom. Rep.	18.30 N	68.30 W
96	Espanola	(ĕs-pȧ-nō′lȧ)	Can.	46.11 N	81.59 W
127	Esparta	(ĕs-pär′tä)	C. R.	9.59 N	84.40 W
204	Esperance	(ĕs′pĕ-răns)	Austl.	33.45 S	122.07 E
128	Esperanza	(ĕs-pĕ-rä′n-zä)	Cuba	22.30 N	80.10 W
163	Espichel, Cabo (C.)	(ĕs-pē-shĕl′)	Port. (Lisbon In.)	38.25 N	9.13 W
134	Espinal	(ĕs-pē-näl′)	Col. (In.)	4.10 N	74.53 W
135	Espinhaço, Serra do (Mts.)	(sĕ′r-rä-dä ĕs-pē-nä-sô)	Braz.	16.06 S	44.54 W
137	Espinillo, Punta (Pt.)	(pōō′n-tä-ĕs-pē-nē′l-yō)	Ur. (Buenos Aires In.)	34.49 S	56.27 W
135	Espírito Santo		Braz.	20.27 S	40.18 W
135	Espírito Santo (State)		Braz.	19.57 S	40.58 W
126	Espíritu Santo, Bahia del (B.)	(bä-ē′ä-dĕl-ĕs-pē′rē-tōō-sän′tô)	Mex. (In.)	19.25 N	87.28 W
205	Espiritu Santo (I.)	(ĕs-pē′rē-tōō sän′tō)	New Hebr.	15.45 N	166.50 E
126	Espita	(ĕs-pē′tä)	Mex. (In.)	20.57 N	88.22 W
157	Espoo		Fin.	60.13 N	24.41 E
162	Esposende	(ĕs-pō-zĕn′dĕ)	Port.	41.33 N	8.45 W
136	Esquel	(ĕs-kĕl′)	Arg.	42.47 S	71.22 W
112	Esquimalt	(ĕs-kwī′môlt)	Can. (Seattle In.)	48.26 N	123.24 W
210	Essaouira	(ĕs-sä-ōō′ē-rä)	Mor.	31.34 N	9.44 W
149	Essen		Bel. (Brussels In.)	51.28 N	4.27 E
161	Essen	(ĕs′sĕn)	F.R.G. (Ruhr In.)	51.26 N	6.59 E
135	Essequibo (R.)	(ĕs-ā-kē′bō)	Guy.	6.24 N	58.17 W
107	Essex		Il. (Chicago In.)	41.11 N	88.11 W
106	Essex		Md. (Baltimore In.)	39.19 N	76.29 W
99	Essex		Can.	42.38 N	70.47 W
105	Essex		Vt.	44.30 N	73.05 W
106	Essex Fells	(ĕs′ĕks fĕlz)	NJ (New York In.)	40.50 N	74.16 W
104	Essexville	(ĕs′ĕks-vĭl)	Mi.	43.35 N	83.50 W
158	Esslingen	(ĕs′slĕn-gĕn)	F.R.G.	48.45 N	9.19 E
102	Estacado, Llano (Plain)	(yä-nō ĕs-tá-cá-dō′)	U. S.	33.50 N	103.20 W
136	Estados, Isla de los		S. A.	55.05 S	63.00 W
135	Estância	(ĕs-tän′sĭ-ä)	Braz.	11.17 S	37.18 W
162	Estarreja	(ĕs-tär-rā′zhä)	Port.	40.44 N	8.39 W
210	Estcourt	(ĕst-coort)	S. Afr. (Natal In.)	29.04 S	29.53 E
164	Este	(ĕs′tā)	It.	45.13 N	11.40 E
126	Estelí	(ĕs-tā-lē′)	Nic.	13.10 N	86.23 W
162	Estella	(ĕs-tāl′yä)	Sp.	42.40 N	2.01 W
162	Estepa	(ĕs-tā′pä)	Sp.	37.18 N	4.54 W
162	Estepona	(ĕs-tä-pō′nä)	Sp.	36.26 N	5.08 W
95	Esterhazy	(ĕs′tĕr-hä-zē)	Can.	50.40 N	102.08 W
114	Esteros, B.	(ĕs-tä′rōs)	Ca.	35.22 N	121.04 W
94	Estevan	(ê-stē′vȧn)	Can.	49.07 N	103.05 W
92	Estevan Group (I.)		Can.	53.05 N	129.40 W
109	Estherville	(ĕs′tĕr-vĭl)	Ia.	43.24 N	94.49 W
121	Estill	(ĕs′tĭl)	SC	32.45 N	81.15 W
94	Eston		Can.	51.10 N	108.45 W
168	Estonian S. S. R.	(ĕs-tō′nĭ-ä)	Sov. Un.	59.10 N	25.00 E
163	Estoril	(ĕs-tô-rēl′)	Port. (Lisbon In.)	38.45 N	9.24 W
136	Estrêla (R.)	(ĕs-trē′lä)	Braz. (Rio de Janeiro In.)	22.39 S	43.16 W
162	Estrêla, Serra da (Mts.)	(sĕr′rä dä ĕs-trä′lȧ)	Port.	40.25 N	7.45 W
162	Estremadura	(ĕs-trä-mä-dōō′rȧ)	Port.	41.35 N	8.36 W
162	Estremoz	(ĕs-trä-mŏzh′)	Port.	38.50 N	7.35 W
135	Estrondo, Serra do (Mts.)	(sĕr′rá dōō ĕs-trôn′dōō)	Braz.	9.52 S	48.56 W

280 Esumba — Feldkirchen

PRONOUNCING INDEX

Page	Name Pronunciation Region	Lat. °′	Long. °′
216	Esumba, Île (I.)............Zaire	2·00 N	21·12 E
159	Esztergom (ĕs′tĕr-gōm).....Hung.	47·46 N	18·45 E
75	Etah (ē′tȧ)..............Grnld.	78·20 N	72·42 W
161	Étampes (ā-täɴp′)..Fr. (Paris In.)	48·26 N	2·09 E
160	Étaples (ā-täp′l′)............Fr.	50·32 N	1·38 E
100	Etchemin (R.) (ĕch′ĕ-mĭn) Can. (Quebec In.)	46·39 N	71·03 W
209	Ethiopa (ē-thē-ō′pē-ȧ)........Afr.	7·53 N	37·55 E
214	Eticoga...........Guinea-Bissau	11·09 N	16·08 W
113	Etiwanda (ĕ-tĭ-wän′dȧ) Ca. (Los Angeles In.)	34·07 N	117·31 W
	Etlatongo, see San Mateo		
107	Etna (ĕt′nȧ)..Pa. (Pittsburgh In.)	40·30 N	79·55 W
164	Etna, Mt. (Vol.)..............It.	37·48 N	15·00 E
100	Etobicoke.....Can. (Toronto In.)	43·39 N	79·34 W
100	Etobicoke Cr...Can. (Toronto In.)	43·44 N	79·48 W
101	Etolin Str. (ĕt ō lĭn)..........Ak.	60·35 S	165·40 W
212	Etoshapan (L.) (ētō′shä).S. W. Afr.	19·07 S	15·30 E
120	Etowah (ĕt′ô-wä)............Tn.	35·18 N	84·31 W
120	Etowah (R.)..................Ga.	34·23 N	84·19 W
161	Étréchy (ā-trā-shē′).Fr. (Paris In.)	48·29 N	2·12 E
149	Etten.....Neth. (Amsterdam In.)	51·34 N	4·38 E
149	Etterbeek (ĕt′ĕr-bāk) Bel. (Brussels In.)	50·51 N	4·24 E
124	Etzatlán (ĕt-zä-tlän′).......Mex.	20·44 N	104·04 W
204	Eucla (ū′klȧ)..............Austl.	31·45 S	128·50 E
107	Euclid (ū′klĭd).Oh. (Cleveland In.)	41·34 N	81·32 W
117	Eudora (u-dō′rȧ).............Ar.	33·07 N	91·16 W
120	Eufaula (û-fô′lȧ).............Al.	31·53 N	85·09 W
117	Eufaula.....................Ok.	35·16 N	95·35 W
117	Eufaula Res.................Ok.	35·00 N	94·45 W
110	Eugene (û-jēn′).............Or.	44·02 N	123·06 W
113	Euless (ū′lĕs) Tx. (Dallas, Fort Worth In.)	32·50 N	97·05 W
119	Eunice (ū′nĭs)...............La.	30·30 N	92·25 W
155	Eupen (oi′pĕn)..............Bel.	50·39 N	6·05 E
186	Euphrates (R.) (û-frā′tēz)....Asia	36·00 N	39·30 E
160	Eure (R.) (ûr)................Fr.	49·03 N	1·22 E
110	Eureka (û-rē′kȧ)............Ca.	40·45 N	124·10 W
117	Eureka......................Ks.	37·48 N	96·17 W
110	Eureka......................Mt.	48·53 N	115·07 W
114	Eureka......................Nv.	39·33 N	115·58 W
108	Eureka......................SD	45·46 N	99·38 W
115	Eureka......................Ut.	39·55 N	112·10 W
117	Eureka Springs..............Ar.	36·24 N	93·43 W
186	Eurgun (Mtn.)..............Iran	28·47 N	57·00 E
146	Europe (ū′rŭp)		
121	Eustis (ūs′tĭs)...............Fl.	28·50 N	81·41 W
120	Eutaw (ū-tȧ).................Al.	32·48 N	87·50 W
92	Eutsuk L. (ōōt′sŭk).........Can.	53·20 N	126·44 W
156	Evanger (ĕ-väŋ′gĕr).........Nor.	60·40 N	6·06 E
107	Evanston (ĕv′ăn-stŭn) Il. (Chicago In.)	42·03 N	87·41 W
111	Evanston...................Wy.	41·17 N	111·02 W
104	Evansville (ĕv′ănz-vĭl)........In.	38·00 N	87·30 W
109	Evansville..................Wi.	42·46 N	89·19 W
104	Evart (ĕv′ērt)...............Mi.	43·55 N	85·10 W
218	Evaton (ĕv′ȧ-tŏn).........S. Afr. (Johannesburg & Pretoria In.)	26·32 S	27·53 E
109	Eveleth (ĕv′ē-lĕth)..........Mn.	47·27 N	92·35 W
204	Everard (L.) (ĕv′ĕr-ȧrd)....Austl.	36·20 S	134·10 E
204	Everard Ra.................Austl.	27·15 S	132·00 E
184	Everest, Mt. (ĕv′ĕr-ĕst) Nep.-China	28·00 N	86·57 E
99	Everett (ĕv′ĕr-ĕt).......Ma. (In.)	42·24 N	71·03 W
112	Everett (ĕv′ĕr-ĕt) Wa. (Seattle In.)	47·59 N	122·11 W
91	Everett Mts.................Can.	62·34 N	68·00 W
121	Everglades (ĕv′ĕr-glādz)..Fl. (In.)	25·50 N	81·25 W
128	Everglades, The (Swp.)........Fl.	25·35 N	80·55 W
121	Everglades Natl. Park....Fl. (In.)	25·39 N	80·57 W
120	Evergreen (ĕv′ĕr-grēn)........Al.	31·25 N	87·56 W
107	Evergreen Park..Il. (Chicago In.)	41·44 N	87·42 W
113	Everman (ĕv′ēr-măn).. Tx. (Dallas, Fort Worth In.)	32·38 N	97·17 W
112	Everson (ĕv′ĕr-sŭn) Wa. (Vancouver In.)	48·55 N	122·21 W
162	Évora (ĕv′ô-rä).............Port.	38·35 N	7·54 W
160	Évreux (ā-vrû′)...............Fr.	49·02 N	1·11 E
165	Evrotas (R.) (ĕv-rō′täs)......Grc.	37·15 N	22·17 E
165	Evvoia (I.).................Grc.	38·38 N	23·45 E
89	Ewa Beach (ē′wä).............Hi.	21·17 N	158·03 E
211	Ewaso Ng'iro (R.)...........Ken.	0·59 N	37·47 E
113	Excelsior (ĕk-sel′sĭ-ŏr) Mn. (Minneapolis, St. Paul In.)	44·54 N	93·35 W
117	Excelsior Springs............Mo.	39·20 N	94·13 W
154	Exe (R.) (ĕks)..............Eng.	50·57 N	3·37 W
114	Exeter (ĕk′sē-tēr)...........Ca.	36·18 N	119·09 W
154	Exeter......................Eng.	50·45 N	3·33 W
105	Exeter......................NH	43·00 N	71·00 W
154	Exmoor (ĕks′mōōr)..........Eng.	51·10 N	3·55 W
154	Exmouth (ĕks′mŭth)..........Eng.	50·40 N	3·20 W
204	Exmouth, G.................Austl.	21·45 S	114·30 E
99	Exploits (R.) (ĕks-ploits′)....Can.	48·50 N	56·15 W
124	Extórrax (R.) (ĕx-tō′rȧx)....Mex.	21·04 N	99·39 W
137	Extrema (ĕsh-trĕ′mä) Braz. (Rio de Janeiro In.)	22·52 S	46·19 W
162	Extremadura (Reg.) (ĕks-trā-mä-doo′rä).Sp.	38·43 N	6·30 W
129	Exuma Sd. (ĕk-sōō′mä).......Ba.	24·20 N	76·20 W
217	Eyasi, L. (ȧ-yä′sē)..........Tan.	3·25 S	34·55 E
150	Eyja Fd.....................Ice.	66·21 N	18·20 W
150	Eyrarbakki..................Ice.	63·51 N	20·52 W
204	Eyre (âr)...................Austl.	32·15 S	126·20 E
203	Eyre (L.)...................Austl.	28·43 S	137·50 E
204	Eyre Pen....................Austl.	33·30 S	136·00 E
136	Ezeiza (ĕ-zä′zä) Arg. (Buenos Aires In.)	34·36 S	58·31 W
165	Ezine (ȧ′zĭ-nȧ)..............Tur.	39·47 N	26·18 E
	F		
118	Fabens (fā′bĕnz)............Tx.	31·30 N	106·07 W
156	Fåborg (fô′bôrg)...........Den.	55·06 N	10·19 E
164	Fabriano (fä-brē-ä′nō).........It.	43·20 N	12·55 E
134	Facatativá (fä-kä-tä-tē-vä′) Col. (In.)	4·49 N	74·09 W
211	Fada (fä′dä)................Chad	17·06 N	21·18 E
214	Fada Ngourma (fä′dä′′n gōōr′mä).Upper Volta	12·04 N	0·21 E
173	Faddeya (I.) (fȧd-yä′)...Sov. Un.	76·12 N	145·00 E
156	Faemund (L.) (fä′mōōn′)....Nor.	62·17 N	11·40 E
164	Faenza (fä-ĕnd′zä)...........It.	44·16 N	11·53 E
146	Faeroe Is. (fā′rō)...........Eur.	62·00 N	5·45 W
162	Fafe (fä′fä)................Port.	41·30 N	8·10 W
218	Fafen (R.).Eth. (Horn of Afr. In.)	8·15 N	42·40 E
165	Făgăras (fȧ-gä′räsh).........Rom.	45·50 N	24·55 E
156	Fagerness (fä′ghĕr-nĕs)......Nor.	61·00 N	9·10 E
136	Fagnano (L.) (fäk-nä′nô) Arg.-Chile	54·35 S	68·20 W
214	Faguibine, Lac (L.).........Mali	16·50 N	4·20 W
210	Faial I. (fä-yä′l)......Açores (In.)	38·40 N	29·19 W
218	Fā'id (fä-yēd′)...Egypt (Suez In.)	30·19 N	32·18 E
154	Fair I. (fâr ....Scot.	59·34 N	1·41 W
101	Fairbanks (fâr′bănks)........Ak.	64·50 N	147·48 W
104	Fairbury (fâr′bĕr-ĭ)...........Il.	40·45 N	88·25 W
117	Fairbury....................Ne.	40·09 N	97·11 W
100	Fairchild Cr. (fâr′chīld) Can. (Toronto In.)	43·18 N	80·10 W
109	Fairfax (fâr′făks)............Mn.	44·29 N	94·44 W
121	Fairfax.....................SC	32·29 N	81·13 W
106	Fairfax.......Va. (Baltimore In.)	38·51 N	77·20 W
106	Fairfield (fâr′fēld) Al. (Birmingham In.)	33·30 N	86·50 W
202	Fairfield......Austl. (Sydney In.)	33·52 S	150·57 E
106	Fairfield......Ct. (New York In.)	41·08 N	73·22 W
104	Fairfield.....................Il.	38·25 N	88·20 W
109	Fairfield.....................Ia.	41·00 N	91·59 W
98	Fairfield....................Me.	44·35 N	69·38 W
105	Fairhaven (fâr-hā′vĕn).......Ma.	41·35 N	70·55 W
105	Fair Haven..................Vt.	43·35 N	73·15 W
109	Fairmont (fâr′mŏnt).........Mn.	43·39 N	94·26 W
105	Fairmont....................WV	39·30 N	80·10 W
113	Fairmont City..Il. (St. Louis In.)	38·39 N	90·05 W
104	Fairmount...................In.	40·25 N	85·45 W
113	Fairmount..Ks. (Kansas City In.)	39·12 N	95·55 W
106	Fair Oaks (fâr ōks) Ga. (Atlanta In.)	33·56 N	84·33 W
105	Fairport (fâr′pōrt)...........NY	43·05 N	77·30 W
104	Fairport Harbor.............Oh.	41·45 N	81·15 W
116	Fairview (fâr′vū)............Ok.	36·16 N	98·28 W
112	Fairview.......Or. (Portland In.)	45·32 N	122·26 W
115	Fairview.....................Ut.	39·35 N	111·30 W
107	Fairview Park.Oh. (Cleveland In.)	41·27 N	81·52 W
101	Fairweather, Mt. (fâr-wĕdh′ĕr) Can.	59·12 N	137·22 W
108	Faith (fāth).................SD	45·02 N	120·02 W
184	Faizābād...................India	26·50 N	82·17 E
123	Fajardo...P. R. (Puerto Rico In.)	18·20 N	65·40 W
197	Fakfak.....................Indon.	2·56 S	132·25 E
192	Fak'u......................China	42·28 N	123·20 E
193	Falalise, C..................Viet.	19·20 N	106·18 E
135	Falcón (State) (fäl-kō′n).Ven. (In.)	11·00 N	68·28 W
105	Falconer (fô′k′n-ēr)..........NY	42·10 N	79·10 W
113	Falcon Heights (fô′k′n) Mn. (Minneapolis, St. Paul In.)	44·59 N	93·10 W
118	Falcon Res. (fôk′n)..........Tx.	26·47 N	99·03 W
214	Falemé R. (fȧ-lā-mā′).......Afr.	13·40 N	12·00 W
167	Faleshty (fä-lĕsh′tĭ).....Sov. Un.	47·33 N	27·46 E
118	Falfurrias (fäl′fōō-rē′ȧs)......Tx.	27·15 N	98·08 W
93	Falher (fäl′ĕr)..............Can.	55·44 N	117·12 W
156	Falkenberg (fäl′kĕn-bĕrgh)...Swe.	56·54 N	12·25 E
149	Falkensee (fäl′kĕn-zā) G.D.R. (Berlin In.)	52·34 N	13·05 E
149	Falkenthal (fäl′kĕn-täl) G.D.R. (Berlin In.)	52·54 N	13·18 E
154	Falkirk (fôl′kûrk)...........Scot.	55·59 N	3·55 W
136	Falkland Is. (fôk′lȧnd)......S. A.	50·45 S	61·00 W
156	Falköping (fäl′chûp-ĭng).....Swe.	58·09 N	13·30 E
112	Fall City........Wa. (Seattle In.)	47·34 N	121·53 W
107	Fall Cr. (fôl).In. (Indianapolis In.)	39·52 N	86·04 W
114	Fallon (făl′ŭn)..............Nv.	39·30 N	118·48 W
106	Fall River...Ma. (Providence In.)	41·42 N	71·07 W
106	Falls Church (fälz chûrch) Va. (Baltimore In.)	38·53 N	77·10 W
117	Falls City...................Ne.	40·04 N	95·37 W
106	Fallston (fâls′ton) Md. (Baltimore In.)	39·32 N	76·26 W
154	Falmouth (făl′mŭth)........Eng.	50·08 N	3·04 W
128	Falmouth...................Jam.	18·30 N	77·40 W
104	Falmouth...................Ky.	38·40 N	84·20 W
	False (B.), see Valsbaai		
183	False Divi Pt...............India	15·45 N	80·50 E
129	Falso, Cabo (C.) (kȧ′bô-fäl-sô) Dom. Rep.	17·45 N	71·55 W
156	Falster (I.) (fäls′tĕr)........Den.	54·48 N	11·58 E
159	Fălticeni (fŭl-tē-chān′y′).....Rom.	47·27 N	26·17 E
156	Falun (fä-lōōn′).............Swe.	60·38 N	15·35 E
153	Famagusta (fä-mä-gōōs′tä).Cyprus	35·08 N	33·59 E
136	Famatina, Sierra de (Mts.) (sē-ĕ′r-rä-dĕ-fä-mä-tē′-nä).Arg.	29·00 S	67·50 W
193	Fan Ching Shan (Mts.).....China	26·46 N	107·42 E
193	Fanghsien..................China	32·05 N	110·45 E
199	Fanning (I.) (făn′ĭng) Gilbert & Ellice Is.	4·20 N	159·00 W
100	Fannystelle (făn′ĭ-stĕl) Can. (Winnipeg In.)	49·45 N	97·46 W
164	Fano (fä′nō).................It.	43·49 N	13·01 E
156	Fanø (I.) (fän′û)...........Den.	55·24 N	8·10 E
213	Farafangana (fä-rä-fäŋ-gä′nä) Mad.	21·18 S	47·59 E
186	Farāh (fä-rä′)..............Afg.	32·15 N	62·13 E
124	Farallón, Punta (Pt.) (pōō′n-tä-fä-rä-lōn).Mex.	19·21 N	105·03 W
214	Faranah (fä-rä′nä)..........Gui.	10·02 N	10·44 W
211	Farasān, Jaza'ir (Is.)........Eth.	16·45 N	41·08 E
153	Faras R...................Libya	30·18 N	17·19 E
153	Faregh, Wadi al (R.) (wädē ĕl fä-rĕg′).Libya	30·10 N	19·34 E
205	Farewell, C. (fâr-wĕl′)..N. Z. (In.)	40·37 S	171·46 E
108	Fargo (fär′gō)...............ND	46·53 N	96·48 W
108	Far Hills (fär hĭlz) NJ (New York In.)	40·41 N	74·38 W
109	Faribault (fâ′rĭ-bō)..........Mn.	44·19 N	93·16 W
162	Farilhoes (Is.) (fä-rē-lyôɴzh′) Port.	39·28 N	9·32 W
148	Faringdon (fă′rĭng-dŏn) Eng. (London In.)	51·38 N	1·35 W
218	Fāriskūr (fä-rēs-kōōr′) Egypt (Nile In.)	31·19 N	31·46 E
211	Farit, Amba (Mt.)..........Eth.	10·51 N	37·52 E
159	Farkašd (fär′kăsht).........Czech.	48·00 N	17·43 E
113	Farley (fär′lē) Mo. (Kansas City In.)	39·16 N	94·49 W
113	Farmers Branch (fär′mērz brȧnch) Tx. (Dallas, Fort Worth In.)	32·56 N	96·53 W
104	Farmersburg (fär′mērz-bûrg)...In.	39·15 N	87·25 W
117	Farmersville (fär′mērz-vĭl)....Tx.	33·11 N	96·22 W
106	Farmingdale (färm′ĕng-dāl) NJ (New York In.)	40·11 N	74·10 W
106	Farmingdale..NY (New York In.)	40·44 N	73·26 W
99	Farmingham (färm-ĭng-hăm) Ma. (In.)	42·17 N	71·25 W
117	Farmington (färm-ĭng-tŭn).....Il.	40·42 N	90·01 W
98	Farmington..................Me.	44·40 N	70·10 W
107	Farmington.....Mi. (Detroit In.)	42·28 N	83·23 W
117	Farmington..................Mo.	37·46 N	90·26 W
115	Farmington..................NM	36·40 N	108·10 W
113	Farmington Ut. (Salt Lake City In.)	40·59 N	111·53 W
121	Farmville (färm-vĭl)..........NC	35·35 N	77·35 W
121	Farmville...................Va.	37·15 N	78·23 W
148	Farnborough (färn′bŭr-ô) Eng. (London In.)	51·15 N	0·45 W
154	Farne (I.) (färn)............Eng.	55·40 N	1·32 W
105	Farnham (fär′nȧm)..........Can.	45·15 N	72·55 W
148	Farningham (fär′nĭng-ŭm)...Eng.	51·22 N	0·14 E
148	Farnworth (färn′wŭrth)......Eng.	53·34 N	2·24 W
135	Faro (fä′rōō)................Braz.	2·05 S	56·32 W
162	Faro.......................Port.	37·01 N	7·57 W
157	Fåron (I.)..................Swe.	57·57 N	19·10 E
204	Farquhar, C. (fär′kwȧr)....Austl.	23·50 S	112·55 E
104	Farrell (făr′ĕl)...............Pa.	41·10 N	80·30 W
184	Farrukhābād (fŭ-rōōk-hä-bäd′) India	27·29 N	79·35 E
165	Fársala (Pharsalus)..........Grc.	39·18 N	22·25 E
156	Farsund (fär′sōōn)...........Nor.	58·05 N	6·47 E
136	Fartura, Serra da (Mts.) (sĕ′r-rä-dȧ-fär-tōō′rä).Braz.	26·40 S	53·15 W
75	Farvel, Kap (C.)...........Grnld.	60·00 N	44·00 W
116	Farwell (fär′wĕl)............Tx.	34·24 N	103·03 W
165	Fasano (fä-zä′nō)............It.	40·50 N	17·22 E
167	Fastov (fäs′tôf).........Sov. Un.	50·04 N	29·57 E
167	Fatëzh...................Sov. Un.	52·06 N	35·51 E
162	Fatima.....................Port.	39·36 N	9·36 E
171	Fatsa (fät′sä)...............Tur.	40·50 N	37·30 E
161	Faucilles, Monts (Mts.) (môɴ′ fō-sēl′).Fr.	48·07 N	6·13 E
150	Fauske.....................Nor.	67·15 N	15·24 E
93	Faust (foust)...............Can.	55·19 N	115·38 W
174	Faustovo..Sov. Un. (Moscow In.)	55·27 N	38·29 E
161	Faverolles (fä-vrôl′).Fr. (Paris In.)	48·42 N	1·34 E
148	Faversham (fă′vĕr-sh′m) Eng. (London In.)	51·19 N	0·54 E
150	Faxaflói (B.)................Ice.	64·33 N	22·40 W
120	Fayette (fȧ-yĕt′)..............Al.	33·40 N	87·54 W
109	Fayette......................Ia.	42·49 N	91·49 W
120	Fayette.....................Ms.	31·43 N	91·00 W
117	Fayette.....................Mo.	39·09 N	92·41 W
117	Fayetteville (fȧ-yĕt′vĭl).......Ar.	36·03 N	94·08 W
121	Fayetteville..................NC	35·02 N	78·54 W
120	Fayetteville..................Tn.	35·10 N	86·33 W
214	Fazao, Forêt Classée du (For.) Togo	8·50 N	0·40 E
184	Fazilka....................India	30·30 N	74·02 E
211	Fazzān (Fezzan) (Prov.) ... Libya	26·45 N	13·01 E
210	Fdérik................Mauritania	22·45 N	12·38 W
121	Fear, C. (fēr)................NC	33·52 N	77·48 W
114	Feather (R.) (fĕth′ēr)........Ca.	38·56 N	121·41 W
114	Feather, Middle Fk. of (R.)...Ca.	39·49 N	121·10 W
114	Feather, North Fk. of (R.)....Ca.	40·00 N	121·20 W
148	Featherstone (fĕdh′ēr stŭn)...Eng.	53·39 N	1·21 W
160	Fécamp (fā-käɴ′)............Fr.	49·45 N	0·20 E
135	Federal, Distrito (Dist.) (dēs-trē′tô-fĕ-dĕ-rä′l).Ven. (In.)	10·34 N	66·55 W
112	Federal Way....Wa. (Seattle In.)	47·20 N	122·20 W
174	Fëdorovka (fyô′dō-rôf-kȧ) Sov. Un. (Moscow In.)	56·15 N	37·14 E
158	Fehmarn I. (fā′märn)......F.R.G.	54·28 N	11·15 E
149	Fehrbellin (fĕr′bĕl-lēn) G.D.R. (Berlin In.)	52·49 N	12·46 E
137	Feia, Logoa (L.) (lô-gôȧ-fĕ′yä) Braz. (Rio de Janeiro In.)	21·54 S	41·45 W
190	Feich'eng (fā′chĕng)........China	36·18 N	116·45 E
190	Feihsien (fā′ē-hsyĕn′).......China	35·17 N	117·59 E
135	Feira de Santana (fĕ′ē-rä dā sänt-än′ä).Braz.	12·16 S	38·46 W
163	Felanitx (fā-lä-nēch′)..........Sp.	39·29 N	3·09 E
158	Feldkirch (fĕlt′kĭrk).........Aus.	47·15 N	9·36 E
149	Feldkirchen (fĕld′kĕr-ĸĕn) F.R.G. (Munich In.)	48·09 N	11·44 E

Page	Name Pronunciation Region	Lat. °'	Long. °'
126	Felipe Carrillo Puerto (fē-lē'pě-kär-rē'l-yô-pwě'r-tô) Mex. (In.)	19·36 N	88·04 W
164	Feltre (fěl'trā) It.	46·02 N	11·56 E
213	Fénérive (fē-nā-rēv') Mad.	17·30 S	49·31 E
192	Fengchen (fŭng'chěn') China	40·28 N	113·20 E
192	Fengch'eng (fŭng'chŭng') China	40·28 N	124·03 E
193	Fengchieh China	31·02 N	109·30 E
192	Fenghsiang China	34·25 N	107·20 E
191	Fenghsien (fŭng'hsyěn') China (Shanghai In.)	30·55 N	121·26 E
190	Fenghsien China	34·41 N	116·36 E
190	Fengjun (fěng'yěn) China	39·51 N	118·06 E
190	Fengming Tao (I.) (fěng'mĭng dou) China	39·19 N	121·15 E
192	Fengt'ai (fŭng'tī') China (In.)	39·51 N	116·19 E
193	Fengtu (fŭng'tōō') China	29·58 N	107·50 E
190	Fengyang (fŭng'yäng') China	32·55 N	117·32 E
101	Fenimore P. (fěn-ĭ-mōr) Ak.	51·40 N	175·38 W
104	Fenton (fěn-tŭn) Mi.	42·50 N	83·40 W
113	Fenton Mo. (St. Louis In.)	38·31 N	90·27 W
192	Fenyang China	37·20 N	111·48 E
167	Feodosiya (Kefe) (fě-ô-dō'sē'yá) (kyě'fě) Sov. Un.	45·02 N	35·21 E
186	Ferdows Iran	34·00 N	58·13 E
164	Ferentino (fā-rěn-tē'nō) It.	41·42 N	13·18 E
172	Fergana Sov. Un.	40·16 N	72·07 E
108	Fergus Falls (fûr'gŭs) Mn.	46·17 N	96·03 W
113	Ferguson (fûr-gŭ-sŭn) Mo. (St. Louis In.)	38·45 N	90·18 W
214	Ferkéssédougou Ivory Coast	9·36 N	5·12 W
164	Fermo (fěr'mō) It.	43·10 N	13·43 E
162	Fermoselle (fěr-mō-säl'yå) Sp.	41·20 N	6·23 W
154	Fermoy (fûr-moi') Ire.	52·05 N	8·06 W
121	Fernandina Beach (fûr-năn-dē'ná) Fl.	30·38 N	81·29 W
135	Fernando de Noronha, Arquipélago (Arch.) (är-kê-pě'lä-gô-fěr-nän-dō-dě-nô-rō'n-yä) Braz.	3·50 S	33·15 W
	Fernando Póo (Prov.), see Macías Nguema Biyogo		
162	Fernān-Núñez (fěr-nän'nōōn'yāth) Sp.	37·42 N	4·43 W
217	Fernâo Veloso, Baia de (B.) Moz.	14·20 S	40·55 E
110	Ferndale (fûrn'dāl) Ca.	40·34 N	124·18 W
107	Ferndale Mi. (Detroit In.)	42·27 N	83·08 W
112	Ferndale Wa. (Vancouver In.)	48·51 N	122·36 W
93	Fernie (fûr'nĭ) Can.	49·30 N	115·03 W
112	Fern Prairie (fûrn prâr'ĭ) Wa. (Portland In.)	45·38 N	122·25 W
202	Ferntree Gully Austl. (Melbourne In.)	37·53 S	145·18 E
164	Ferrara (fěr-rä'rä) It.	44·50 N	11·37 E
163	Ferrat, Cap (C.) (käp fěr-rät) Alg.	35·49 N	0·29 W
162	Ferreira do Alentejo (fěr-rě'ê-rä dōō ä-lěn-tā'zhōō) Port.	38·03 N	8·06 W
162	Ferreira do Zezere (fěr-rě'ê-rä dōō zā-zā'rě) Port.	39·49 N	8·17 W
113	Ferrelview (fěr'rěl-vū) Mo. (Kansas City In.)	39·18 N	94·40 W
134	Ferreñafe (fěr-rěn-yá'fě) Peru	6·38 S	79·48 W
119	Ferriday (fěr'ĭ-dā) La.	31·38 N	91·33 W
151	Ferryville (fěr-ē-vēl') Tun.	37·12 N	9·51 E
174	Fershampenuaz (fěr-shäm'pěn-wäz) Sov. Un. (Urals In.)	53·32 N	59·50 E
108	Fertile (fur'tĭl) Mn.	47·33 N	96·18 W
210	Fès (fěs) Mor.	34·08 N	5·00 W
108	Fessenden (fěs'ěn-děn) ND	47·39 N	99·40 W
154	Festiniog (fěs-tĭn-ĭ-ŏg) Wales	52·59 N	3·58 W
117	Festus (fěst'ŭs) Mo.	38·12 N	90·22 W
171	Fethiye (fět-hē'yě) Tur.	36·40 N	29·05 E
91	Feuilles, Rivière aux (R.) Can.	58·30 N	70·50 W
	Fezzan (Prov.), see Fazzān		
213	Fianarantsoa (fyá-nä'rán-tsō'á) Mad.	21·21 S	47·15 E
218	Ficksburg (fĭks'bûrg) S. Afr. (Johannesburg & Pretoria In.)	28·53 S	27·53 E
112	Fidalgo I. (fĭ-dăl'gō) Wa. (Seattle In.)	48·28 N	122·39 W
112	Fieldbrook (fēld'brŏŏk) Ca.	40·59 N	124·02 W
165	Fier (fyěr) Alb.	40·43 N	19·34 E
154	Fife Ness (C.) (fīf'nes') Scot.	56·15 N	2·19 W
211	Fifth Cataract Sud.	18·27 N	33·38 E
162	Figalo, Cap (C.) (kăp fē-gä-lō) Alg.	35·35 N	1·12 W
160	Figeac (fē-zhák') Fr.	44·37 N	2·02 E
156	Figeholm (fē-ghě-hōlm) Swe.	57·24 N	16·33 E
162	Figueira da Foz (fê-gwěy-rä-dá-fô'z) Port.	40·10 N	8·50 W
210	Figuig Mor.	32·20 N	1·30 W
198	Fiji (fē'jē) Oceania	18·50 S	175·00 E
126	Filadelfia (fĭl-á-děl'fĭ-á) C. R.	10·26 N	85·37 W
174	Filatovskoye (fĭ-lä'tŏf-skô-yě) Sov. Un. (Urals In.)	56·49 N	62·20 E
121	Filbert (fĭl'běrt) WV	37·18 N	81·29 W
220	Filchner Ice Shelf (fĭlk'něr) Ant.	80·00 S	35·00 W
165	Filiatrá Grc.	37·10 N	21·35 E
164	Filicudi (I.) (fē'le-kōō'dē) It.	38·34 N	14·39 E
153	Filiğas (R.) Tur.	41·10 N	32·53 E
174	Filippovskoye (fĭ-lĭ-pôf'skô-yě) Sov. Un. (Moscow In.)	56·06 N	38·38 E
156	Filipstad (fĭl'ĭps-städh) Swe.	59·44 N	14·09 E
115	Fillmore (fĭl'môr) Ut.	39·00 N	112·20 W
216	Fimi (R.) Zaire	2·43 S	17·50 E
100	Finch (fĭnch) Can. (Ottawa In.)	45·09 N	75·06 W
104	Findlay (fĭnd'lå) Oh.	41·05 N	83·40 W
217	Fingoè Moz.	15·12 S	31·50 E
162	Finisterre, Cabo de (C.) (ká'bô-dě-fĭn-ĭs-târ') Sp.	42·52 N	9·48 W
204	Finke (R.) (fĭŋ'kě) Austl.	25·25 S	134·30 E
146	Finland (fĭn'lănd) Eur.	62·45 N	26·13 E
157	Finland, G. of (fĭn'lănd) Eur.	59·35 N	23·35 E
134	Finlandia (fēn-lä'n-dēä) Col. (In.)	4·38 N	75·39 W
90	Finlay (R.) (fĭn'lå) Can.	57·45 N	125·30 W
149	Finow (fē'nōv) G.D.R. (Berlin In.)	52·50 N	13·44 E
149	Finowfurt (fē'nō-fōōrt) G.D.R. (Berlin In.)	52·50 N	13·41 E
158	Finsterwalde (fĭn'stēr-väl-dě) G.D.R.	51·38 N	13·42 E
171	Firat (R.) (fē-rät') Tur.	39·40 N	38·30 E
112	Fircrest (fûr'krěst) Wa. (Seattle In.)	47·14 N	122·31 W
164	Firenze (Florence) (fē-rěnt'sä) It.	43·47 N	11·15 E
164	Firenzuola (fē-rěnt-swô'lä) It.	44·08 N	11·21 E
184	Firozpur India	30·58 N	74·39 E
149	Fischa (R.) Aus. (Vienna In.)	48·04 N	16·33 E
149	Fischamend Markt Aus. (Vienna In.)	48·07 N	16·37 E
212	Fish (R.) (fĭsh) S. W. Afr.	27·30 S	17·45 E
129	Fish Cay (I.) Ba.	22·30 N	74·20 W
100	Fish Cr. (fĭsh) Can. (Calgary In.)	50·52 N	114·21 W
119	Fisher (fĭsh'ēr) La.	31·28 N	93·30 W
95	Fisher B. Can.	51·30 N	97·16 W
92	Fisher Chan. Can.	52·10 N	127·42 W
91	Fisher Str. Can.	62·43 N	84·28 W
95	Fishing L. (fĭsh'ĭng) Can.	52·07 N	95·25 W
99	Fitchburg (fĭch'bûrg) Ma. (In.)	42·35 N	71·48 W
215	Fitri, Lac (L.) Chad	12·50 N	17·28 E
120	Fitzgerald (fĭts-jěr'ăld) Ga.	31·42 N	83·17 W
92	Fitz Hugh Sd. (fĭts hū) Can.	51·40 N	127·57 W
204	Fitzroy (R.) (fĭts-roi') Austl.	18·00 S	124·05 E
205	Fitzroy (R.) Austl.	23·45 S	150·02 E
204	Fitzroy Crossing Austl.	18·08 S	126·00 E
104	Fitzwilliam (I.) (fĭts-wĭl'yŭm) Can.	45·30 N	81·45 W
	Fiume, see Rijeka		
163	Fiumicino (fyōō-mē-chē'nô) It. (Rome In.)	41·47 N	12·19 E
156	Fjällbacka (fyěl'bäk-å) Swe.	58·37 N	11·17 E
156	Flaam (flôm) Nor.	60·15 N	7·01 E
115	Flagstaff (flăg-stâf) Az.	35·15 N	111·40 W
213	Flagstaff (flăg'stâf) S. Afr. (Natal In.)	31·06 S	29·31 E
105	Flagstaff (L.) (flăg-stâf) Me.	45·05 N	70·30 W
149	Flalow (flä'lōv) G.D.R. (Berlin In.)	52·44 N	12·58 E
109	Flambeau (R.) (flăm-bō') Wi.	45·32 N	91·05 W
111	Flaming Gorge Res. Wy.	41·13 N	109·30 W
121	Flamingo (flá-mĭŋ'gô) Fl.	25·10 N	80·55 W
129	Flamingo Cay (I.) (flá-mĭŋ'gô) Ba.	22·50 N	75·50 W
123	Flamingo Pt. Vir. Is. (U. S. A.) (St. Thomas In.)	18·19 N	65·00 W
155	Flanders (Reg.) (flăn'dērz) Fr.	50·53 N	2·29 E
108	Flandreau (flăn'drō) SD	44·02 N	96·35 W
154	Flannan (Is.) (flăn'ăn) Scot.	58·13 N	8·14 W
93	Flathead (R.) Can.	49·30 N	114·30 W
111	Flathead L. (flăt'hěd) Mt.	47·57 N	114·20 W
111	Flathead R. Mt.	48·45 N	114·20 W
111	Flathead R., Middle Fork Mt.	48·30 N	113·47 W
111	Flathead R., South Fork Mt.	48·05 N	113·45 W
107	Flat Rock (flăt rŏk) Mi. (Detroit In.)	42·06 N	83·17 W
110	Flattery C. (flăt'ēr-ĭ) Wa.	48·22 N	125·10 W
111	Flat Willow Cr. (flăt wĭl'ō) Mt.	46·45 N	108·47 W
156	Flekkefjord (fläk'kē-fyôr) Nor.	58·19 N	6·38 E
104	Flemingsburg (flěm'ĭngz-bûrg) Ky.	38·25 N	83·45 W
158	Flensburg (flěns'bŏŏrgh) F.R.G.	54·48 N	9·27 E
160	Flers-del-l'Orne (flěr-dě-lôrn') Fr.	48·43 N	0·37 W
121	Fletcher NC	35·26 N	82·30 W
204	Flinders (Reg.) (flĭn'dērz) Austl.	32·15 S	138·45 E
203	Flinders (I.) Austl.	39·35 S	148·10 E
205	Flinders (R.) Austl.	18·48 S	141·07 E
205	Flinders Rfs. Austl.	17·30 S	149·02 E
104	Flin Flon (flĭn flŏn) Can.	54·46 N	101·53 W
148	Flint Wales	53·15 N	3·07 W
104	Flint Mi.	43·00 N	83·45 W
148	Flint (Co.) Wales	53·13 N	3·06 W
120	Flint (R.) (flĭnt) Ga.	31·25 N	84·15 W
156	Flisen (flē'sěn) Nor.	60·35 N	12·03 E
104	Flora (flô'rá) Il.	38·40 N	88·25 W
104	Flora In.	40·25 N	86·30 W
120	Florala (flŏr-ăl'á) Al.	31·01 N	86·19 W
106	Floral Park (flôr'ál pärk) NY (New York In.)	40·42 N	73·42 W
120	Florence (flŏr'ěns) Al.	34·46 N	87·40 W
115	Florence Az.	33·00 N	111·25 W
116	Florence Co.	38·23 N	105·08 W
117	Florence Ks.	38·14 N	96·56 W
121	Florence SC	34·10 N	79·45 W
112	Florence Wa. (Seattle In.)	48·13 N	122·21 W
	Florence, see Firenze		
134	Florencia (flō-rěn'sē-á) Col.	1·31 N	75·13 W
137	Florencio Sanchez (flō-rěn-sēō-sá'n-chěz) Ur. (Buenos Aires In.)	33·52 S	57·24 W
136	Florencio Varela (flō-rěn'sê-o vä-rā'lä) Arg. (Buenos Aires In.)	34·34 S	58·16 W
135	Flores (flō'rězh) Braz.	7·57 S	37·48 W
126	Flores Guat. (In.)	16·53 N	89·54 W
137	Flores (Dept.) Ur. (Buenos Aires In.)	33·33 S	57·00 W
196	Flores (I.) Indon.	8·14 S	121·08 E
137	Flores (R.) Arg. (Buenos Aires In.)	36·13 S	60·28 W
196	Flores Laut (Flores Sea) Indon.	7·09 N	120·30 E
118	Floresville (flō'rěs-vĭl) Tx.	29·10 N	98·08 W
135	Floriano (flō-rá-ä'nōō) Braz.	6·17 S	42·58 W
136	Florianópolis (flō-rē-ä-nō'pō-lēs) Braz.	27·30 S	48·30 W
134	Florida (flō-rē'dä) Col. (In.)	3·20 N	76·12 W
128	Florida Cuba	22·10 N	79·50 W
106	Florida (flŏr'ĭ-dá) NY (New York In.)	41·20 N	74·21 W
213	Florida S. Afr. (Johannesburg & Pretoria In.)	26·11 S	27·56 E
137	Florida (flô-rê-dhä) Ur. (Buenos Aires In.)	34·06 S	56·14 W
103	Florida (State) (flŏr'ĭ-dá) U.S.	30·30 N	84·40 W
137	Florida (Dept.) (flô-rě'dhä) Ur. (Buenos Aires In.)	33·48 S	56·15 W
205	Florida (I.) Sol. Is.	8·56 S	159·45 E
128	Florida, Strs. of N. A.	24·10 N	81·00 W
121	Florida B. (flŏr'ĭ-dá) Fl. (In.)	24·55 N	80·55 W
121	Florida Keys (Is.) Fl. (In.)	24·33 N	81·20 W
115	Florida Mts. NM	32·10 N	107·35 W
118	Florido, R. (flô-rē'dō) Mex.	27·21 N	104·48 W
149	Floridsdorf (flô'rĭds-dôrf) Aus. (Vienna In.)	48·16 N	16·25 E
165	Florina (flô-rē'nä) Grc.	40·48 N	21·24 E
113	Florissant (flŏr'ĭ-sănt) Mo. (St. Louis In.)	38·47 N	90·20 W
156	Florö (flô'ü) Nor.	61·36 N	5·01 E
108	Floyd (R.) (floid) Ia.	42·38 N	96·15 W
116	Floydada (floi-dā'dá) Tx.	33·59 N	101·19 W
107	Floyds Fk. (R.) (floi-dz) Ky. (Louisville In.)	38·08 N	85·30 W
164	Flumendosa, R. (flōō-měn-dô'sä) It.	39·45 N	9·18 E
104	Flushing (flûsh'ĭng) Mi.	43·05 N	83·50 W
197	Fly (R.) (flī) Pap. N. Gui.	8·00 S	141·45 E
165	Foča (fō'chä) Yugo.	43·29 N	18·48 E
218	Fochville (fŏk'vĭl) S. Afr. (Johannesburg & Pretoria In.)	26·29 S	27·29 E
159	Focsani (fôk-shä'nê) Rom.	45·41 N	27·17 E
164	Foggia (fôd'jä) It.	41·30 N	15·34 E
97	Fogo (fô'gō) Can.	49·43 N	54·17 W
97	Fogo I. Can.	49·40 N	54·13 W
210	Fogo I. C. V. (In.)	14·46 N	24·51 W
158	Fohnsdorf (fōns'dôrf) Aus.	47·13 N	14·40 E
158	Föhr I. (fûr) F.R.G.	54·47 N	8·30 E
160	Foix (fwä) Fr.	42·58 N	1·34 E
193	Fokang China	23·50 N	113·35 E
215	Fokku Nig.	11·40 N	4·31 E
216	Folgares Ang.	14·54 S	15·08 E
164	Foligno (fô-lēn'yō) It.	42·58 N	12·41 E
155	Folkeston Eng.	51·05 N	1·18 E
148	Folkingham (fō'kĭng-ăm) Eng.	52·53 N	0·24 W
121	Folkston Ga.	30·50 N	82·01 W
116	Folsom (fŏl'sŭm) NM	36·47 N	103·56 W
114	Folsom City Ca.	38·40 N	121·10 W
128	Fomento (fô-mě'n-tō) Cuba	21·35 N	78·20 W
134	Fómeque (fô'mě-kě) Col. (In.)	4·29 N	73·52 W
109	Fonda (fŏn'dá) Ia.	42·33 N	94·51 W
109	Fond du Lac (fŏn dū lăk') Wi.	43·47 N	88·29 W
109	Fond du Lac Ind. Res. Mn.	46·44 N	93·04 W
164	Fondi (fōn'dē) It.	41·23 N	13·25 E
162	Fonsagrada (fôn-sä-grä'dhä) Sp.	43·08 N	7·07 W
126	Fonseca, Golfo de (G.) (gôl-fô-dě-fôn-sā'kä) Hond.	13·09 N	87·55 W
161	Fontainebleau (fôN-těn-blō') Fr. (Paris In.)	48·24 N	2·42 E
113	Fontana (fŏn-tă'ná) Ca. (Los Angeles In.)	34·06 N	117·27 W
134	Fonte Boa (fōn'tå bō'ă) Braz.	2·32 S	66·05 W
160	Fontenay-le-Comte (fôNt-ně'lē-kôNt') Fr.	46·28 N	0·53 W
161	Fontenay-Trésigny (fôN-te-hā' tra-sēn-yē') Fr. (Paris In.)	48·43 N	2·53 E
111	Fontenelle Res. Wy.	42·05 N	110·05 W
125	Fontera, Punta (Pt.) (pōō'n-tä-fôn-tě'rä) Mex.	18·36 N	92·43 W
134	Fontibón (fōn-tē-bōn') Col. (In.)	4·42 N	74·09 W
	Foochow, see Fuchou		
213	Foothills (fōōt-hĭls) S. Afr. (Johannesburg & Pretoria In.)	25·55 S	27·36 E
101	Foraker, Mt. (fôr'á-kēr) Ak.	62·40 N	152·40 W
161	Forbach (fôr'bäk) Fr.	49·12 N	6·54 E
203	Forbes (fôrbz) Austl.	33·24 S	148·05 E
93	Forbes, Mt. Can.	51·52 N	116·56 W
158	Forchheim (fôrk'hīm) F.R.G.	49·43 N	11·05 E
	Fordlândia, see Brasília Legal		
117	Fordyce (fôr'dīs) Ar.	33·48 N	92·24 W
214	Forecariah (fōr-ká-rē'ä') Gui.	9·26 N	13·06 W
75	Forel, Mt. Grnld.	65·50 N	37·41 W
120	Forest (fŏr'ěst) Ms.	32·22 N	89·29 W
108	Forest (R.) ND	48·08 N	97·45 W
109	Forest City Ia.	43·14 N	93·40 W
121	Forest City NC	35·20 N	81·52 W
105	Forest City Pa.	41·35 N	75·30 W
112	Forest Grove (grōv) Or. (Portland In.)	45·31 N	123·07 W
106	Forest Hill Md. (Baltimore In.)	39·35 N	76·26 W
113	Forest Hill Tx. (Dallas, Fort Worth In.)	32·40 N	97·16 W
98	Forestville (fŏr'ěst-vĭl) Can.	48·45 N	69·06 W
106	Forestville Md. (Baltimore In.)	38·51 N	76·55 W
160	Forez, Mts. du (môN dü fô-rā') Fr.	44·55 N	3·43 E
154	Forfar (fôr'fár) Scot.	57·10 N	2·55 W
98	Forillon, Parc Natl. (Natl. Pk.) Can.	48·50 N	64·05 W
163	Forio (Mtn.) (fô'ryō) It. (Naples In.)	40·29 N	13·55 E
107	Forked Cr. (fôrk'd) Il. (Chicago In.)	41·16 N	88·01 W
116	Forked Deer (R.) Tn.	35·53 N	89·29 W
164	Forli (fôr-lē') It.	44·13 N	12·03 E
148	Formby (fôrm'bê) Eng.	53·34 N	3·04 W
148	Formby Pt. Eng.	53·33 N	3·06 W
163	Formello (fôr-mě'lō) It. (Rome In.)	42·04 N	12·25 E
163	Formentera, Isla de (I.) (ē's-lä-dě-fôr-měn-tä'rä) Sp.	38·43 N	1·25 E
137	Formiga (fôr-mē'gá) Braz. (Rio de Janeiro In.)	20·27 S	45·25 W

ng-sing; ŋ-baŋk; N-nasalized n; nŏd; cŏmmit; ōld; ôbey; ôrder; fōōd; fŏŏt; ou-out; s-soft; sh-dish; th-thin; pūre; ûnite; ûrn; stŭd; circŭs; ü-as "y" in study; '-indeterminate vowel.

282 Formigas — Fremont PRONOUNCING INDEX

Page	Name Pronunciation Region	Lat. °′	Long. °′
129	Formigas Bk. (fŏr-mē'gäs) N. A.	18·30 N	75·40 W
136	Formosa (fôr-mō'sä) Arg.	27·25 S	58·12 W
135	Formosa Braz.	15·32 S	47·10 W
136	Formosa (Prov.) Arg.	24·30 S	60·45 W
217	Formosa B. Ken.	2·45 S	40·30 E
	Formosa (I.), see Taiwan		
135	Formosa, Serra (Mts.) (sĕ'r-rä) Braz.	12·59 S	55·11 W
183	Formosa Str. (fŏr-mō'sȧ) Asia	24·30 N	120·00 E
174	Fornosovo (fôr-nô'sô vô) Sov. Un. (Leningrad In.)	59·35 N	30·34 E
117	Forrest City (fŏr'ĕst sĭ'tĭ) Ar.	35·00 N	90·46 W
205	Forsayth (fôr-sīth') Austl.	18·33 S	143·42 E
156	Forshaga (fôrs'hä'gä) Swe.	59·34 N	13·25 E
158	Forst (fôrst) G.D.R.	51·45 N	14·38 E
120	Forsyth (fôr-sīth') Ga.	33·02 N	83·56 W
111	Forsyth Mt.	46·15 N	106·41 W
91	Fort Albany (fôrt ôl'bȧ nĭ) Can.	52·20 N	81·20 W
95	Fort Alexander Ind. Res. Can.	50·27 N	96·15 W
135	Fortaleza (Ceará) (fôr'tä-lā'zȧ) (sā-ä-rä') Braz.	3·35 S	38·31 W
115	Fort Apache Ind. Res. (ȧ-păch'ē) Az.	34·02 N	110·27 W
109	Fort Atkinson (ăt'kĭn-sŭn) Wi.	42·55 N	88·46 W
	Fort Bayard, see Chanchiang		
213	Fort Beaufort (bō'fôrt) S. Afr. (Natal In.)	32·47 S	26·39 E
113	Fort Bellefontaine (bĕl-fŏn-tān') Mo. (St. Louis In.)	38·50 N	90·15 W
111	Fort Benton (bĕn'tŭn) Mt.	47·51 N	110·40 W
108	Fort Berthold Ind. Res. (bĕrth'ôld) ND	47·47 N	103·28 W
104	Fort Branch (brănch) In.	38·15 N	87·35 W
100	Fort Chipewyan Can.	58·46 N	111·15 W
116	Fort Cobb Res. Ok.	35·12 N	98·28 W
116	Fort Collins (kŏl'ĭns) Co.	40·36 N	105·04 W
215	Fort-Crampel (krȧm-pĕl') Cen. Afr. Rep.	6·59 N	19·11 E
213	Fort-Dauphin (dō-fǎN') Mad.	24·59 S	46·58 E
127	Fort-de-France (dē fräNs) Mart. (In.)	14·37 N	61·06 W
120	Fort Deposit (dē-pŏz'ĭt) Al.	31·58 N	86·35 W
211	Fort de Possel (dē pô-sĕl') Cen. Afr. Rep.	5·03 N	19·11 E
109	Fort Dodge (dŏj) Ia.	42·31 N	94·10 W
105	Fort Edward (wērd) NY	43·15 N	73·30 W
107	Fort Erie (ē'rĭ) Can. (Buffalo In.)	42·55 N	78·56 W
204	Fortescue (R.) (fôr'tĕs-kū) Austl.	21·25 S	116·50 E
98	Fort Fairfield (fâr'fēld) Me.	46·46 N	67·53 W
100	Fort Fitzgerald (fĭts-jĕr'ăld) Can.	59·48 N	111·50 W
95	Fort Frances (frǎn'sĕs) Can.	48·36 N	93·24 W
121	Fort Frederica Natl. Mon. (frĕd'ē-rĭ-kȧ) Ga.	31·12 N	85·25 W
120	Fort Gaines (gānz) Ga.	31·35 N	85·03 W
91	Fort George (jôrj) Can.	53·40 N	78·58 W
117	Fort Gibson (gĭb'sŭn) Ok.	35·50 N	95·13 W
102	Fort Good Hope (gŏŏd hōp) Can.	66·19 N	128·52 W
154	Forth, Firth of (fûrth ŏv fôrth) Scot.	56·04 N	3·03 W
211	Fort Hall (hôl) Ken.	0·47 S	37·13 E
111	Fort Hall Ind. Res. Id.	43·02 N	112·21 W
115	Fort Huachuca (wä-chōō'kä) Az.	31·30 N	110·25 W
100	Fortier (fôr'tyā') Can. (Winnipeg In.)	49·56 N	97·55 W
212	Fort Jameson (jām'sŭn) Zambia	13·35 S	32·43 E
121	Fort Jefferson Natl. Mon. (jĕf'ĕr-sŭn) Fl. (In.)	24·42 N	83·02 W
212	Fort Johnston Malawi	14·16 S	35·14 E
98	Fort Kent (kĕnt) Me.	47·14 N	68·37 W
112	Fort Langley (lăng'lĭ) Can. (Vancouver In.)	49·10 N	122·35 W
121	Fort Lauderdale (lô'dĕr-dāl) Fl. (In.)	26·07 N	80·09 W
106	Fort Lee NJ (New York In.)	40·50 N	73·58 W
90	Fort Liard Can.	60·16 N	123·34 W
129	Fort Liberté (lē-bĕr-tā') Hai.	19·40 N	71·50 W
120	Fort Louden (R.) (fôrt lou'dĕn) Tn.	35·52 N	84·10 W
116	Fort Lupton (lŭp'tŭn) Co.	40·04 N	104·45 W
110	Fort McDermitt Ind. Res. (mǎk dēr'mĭt) Or.	42·04 N	118·07 W
93	Fort Macleod (mȧ-Kloud') Can.	49·43 N	113·25 W
210	Fort MacMahon (mȧk mȧ-ôN') Alg.	29·55 N	1·49 E
94	Fort McMurray (mȧk-mŭr'ĭ) Can.	56·44 N	111·23 W
90	Fort McPherson (mȧk-fŭr's'n) Can.	67·37 N	134·59 W
109	Fort Madison (măd'ĭ-sŭn) Ia.	40·40 N	91·17 W
121	Fort Matanzas (mä-tän'zäs) Fl.	29·39 N	81·17 W
121	Fort Meade (mēd) Fl. (In.)	27·45 N	81·48 W
121	Fort Mill (mĭl) SC	35·03 N	80·57 W
152	Fort Miribel (mē-rē-bĕl') Alg.	28·50 N	2·51 E
114	Fort Mohave Ind. Res. (mô-hä'vȧ) Ca.	34·59 N	115·02 W
116	Fort Morgan (môr'gȧn) Co.	40·14 N	103·49 W
121	Fort Myers (mī'ĕrz) Fl. (In.)	26·36 N	81·45 W
152	Fort National (fô nȧ-syō-nȧl') Alg.	36·45 N	4·15 E
90	Fort Nelson (nĕl'sŭn) Can.	58·57 N	122·30 W
90	Fort Nelson (R.) (nĕl'sŭn) Can.	58·44 N	122·20 W
120	Fort Payne (pān) Al.	34·26 N	85·41 W
111	Fort Peck (pĕk) Mt.	47·58 N	106·30 W
108	Fort Peck Ind. Res. Mt.	48·22 N	105·40 W
111	Fort Peck Res. Mt.	47·52 N	106·59 W
121	Fort Pierce (pērs) Fl. (In.)	27·25 N	80·20 W
217	Fort Portal (pôr'tȧl) Ug.	0·40 N	30·16 E
90	Fort Providence (prŏv'ĭ-dĕns) Can.	61·27 N	117·59 W
121	Fort Pulaski Natl. Mon. (pu-lăs'kĭ) Ga.	31·59 N	80·56 W
94	Fort Qu'Appelle Can.	50·46 N	103·55 W
101	Fort Randall (răn'd'l) Ak.	55·12 N	162·38 W
102	Fort Randall Dam U. S.	42·48 N	98·35 W
90	Fort Resolution (rĕz'ô-lū'shŭn) Can.	61·08 N	113·42 W
117	Fort Riley (rī'lĭ) Ks.	39·05 N	96·46 W
92	Fort St. James (fôrt sānt jāmz) Can.	54·26 N	124·15 W
93	Fort St. John (sānt jŏn) Can.	56·15 N	120·51 W
184	Fort Sandeman (săn'da-mǎn) Pak.	31·28 N	69·29 E
100	Fort Saskatchewan (săs-kăt'chōō-ân) Can. (Edmonton In.)	53·43 N	113·13 W
117	Fort Scott (skŏt) Ks.	37·50 N	94·43 W
91	Fort Severn (sĕv'ĕrn) Can.	56·58 N	87·50 W
171	Fort Shevchenko (shĕv-chĕn'kô) Sov. Un.	44·30 N	50·18 E
215	Fort Sibut (fôr sē-bü') Cen. Afr. Rep.	5·44 N	19·05 E
116	Fort Sill (fôrt sĭl) Ok.	34·41 N	98·25 W
90	Fort Simpson (sĭmp'sŭn) Can.	61·52 N	121·48 W
117	Fort Smith (smĭth) Ar.	35·23 N	94·24 W
90	Fort Smith Can.	60·09 N	112·08 W
118	Fort Stockton (stŏk'tŭn) Tx.	30·54 N	102·51 W
116	Fort Sumner (sŭm'nĕr) NM	34·30 N	104·17 W
121	Fort Sumter Natl. Mon. (sŭm'tĕr) SC	32·43 N	79·54 W
107	Fort Thomas (tŏm'ȧs) Ky. (Cincinnati In.)	39·05 N	84·27 W
110	Fortuna (fŏr-tū'nȧ) Ca.	40·36 N	124·10 W
99	Fortune (fôr'tûn) Can.	47·04 N	55·51 W
129	Fortune (I.) Ba.	22·35 N	74·20 W
99	Fortune B. Can.	47·25 N	55·25 W
116	Fort Union Natl. Mon. (ūn'yŭn) NM	35·51 N	104·57 W
120	Fort Valley (văl'ĭ) Ga.	32·33 N	83·53 W
90	Fort Vermilion (vēr-mĭl'yŭn) Can.	58·23 N	115·50 W
212	Fort Victoria Rh.	20·07 S	30·47 E
104	Fortville (fôrt-vĭl) In.	40·00 N	85·50 W
104	Fort Wayne (wān) In.	41·00 N	85·10 W
154	Fort William (wĭl'yăm) Scot.	56·50 N	3·00 W
203	Fort William, Mt. (wĭ'ĭ-ăm) Austl.	24·45 S	151·15 E
113	Fort Worth (wûrth) Tx. (Dallas, Fort Worth In.)	32·45 N	97·20 W
101	Fort Yukon (yōō'kŏn) Ak.	66·30 N	145·00 W
114	Fort Yuma Ind. Res. (yōō'mä) Ca.	32·54 N	114·47 W
160	Fos, Golfe de (G.) (gôlf'dĕ-fōs') Fr. (In.)	43·22 N	4·55 E
191	Foshan China (Canton In.)	23·02 N	113·07 E
	Foshan, see Ch'aoyang		
164	Fossano (fôs-sä'nō) It.	44·34 N	7·42 E
113	Fossil Cr. (fŏs-ĭl) Tx. (Dallas, Fort Worth In.)	32·53 N	97·19 W
164	Fossombrone (fôs-sôm-brō'nā) It.	43·41 N	12·48 E
116	Foss Res. Ok.	35·38 N	99·11 W
108	Fosston (fôs'tŭn) Mn.	47·34 N	95·44 W
113	Fosterburg (fŏs'tĕr-bûrg) Il. (St. Louis In.)	38·58 N	90·04 W
104	Fostoria (fŏs-tō'rĭ-ȧ) Oh.	41·10 N	83·20 W
190	Fouch'eng (fōō'chĕng) China	37·53 N	116·08 E
160	Fougéres (fōō-zhâr') Fr.	48·23 N	1·14 W
192	Fouhsin China	42·05 N	121·40 E
154	Foula (I.) (fou'lȧ) Scot.	60·08 N	2·04 W
193	Fouling China	29·40 N	107·30 E
205	Foulwind, C. (foul'wĭnd) N. Z. (In.)	41·45 S	171·37 E
215	Foumban (fōōm-bän') Cam.	5·43 N	10·55 E
190	Founing (fōō'nĭng) China	33·55 N	119·54 E
116	Fountain Cr. (foun'tĭn) Co.	38·36 N	104·37 W
113	Fountain Valley Ca. (Los Angeles In.)	33·42 N	117·57 W
117	Fourche le Fave (R.) (fōōrsh lē fäv') Ar.	34·46 N	93·45 W
218	Fouriesburg (fōō'rēz-bûrg) S. Afr. (Johannesburg & Pretoria In.)	28·38 S	28·13 E
160	Fourmies (fōōr-mē') Fr.	50·01 N	4·01 E
101	Four Mts., Is. of the (fōr) Ak.	52·58 N	170·40 W
211	Fourth Cataract Sud.	18·52 N	32·07 E
210	Fouta Djallon (Mts.) (fōō'tä jä-lôN) Gui.	11·37 N	12·29 W
190	Fouts'un (fōō'tsōōn) China	36·38 N	117·26 E
190	Foutzuchi (fōō'tzĕ'jē) China	33·48 N	118·13 E
190	Fouyang (fōō'yäng) China	32·53 N	115·48 E
205	Foveaux Str. (fô-vō') N. Z. (In.)	46·30 S	167·43 E
116	Fowler (foul'ĕr) Co.	38·04 N	104·02 W
104	Fowler In.	40·35 N	87·20 W
204	Fowler, Pt. Austl.	32·05 S	132·30 E
118	Fowlerton (foul'ĕr-tŭn) Tx.	28·26 N	98·48 W
112	Fox (I.) (fŏks) Wa. (Seattle In.)	47·15 N	122·08 W
109	Fox (R.) Il.	41·35 N	88·43 W
109	Fox (R.) Wi.	44·18 N	88·23 W
99	Foxboro (fŏks'bŭrō) Ma. (In.)	42·04 N	71·15 W
90	Foxe Basin (fŏks) Can.	67·35 N	79·21 W
91	Foxe Chan. Can.	64·30 N	79·23 W
91	Foxe Pen. Can.	64·57 N	77·26 W
101	Fox Is. (fŏks) Ak.	53·04 N	167·30 W
107	Fox Lake (lāk) Il. (Chicago In.)	42·24 N	88·11 W
107	Fox L. Il. (Chicago In.)	42·24 N	88·07 W
107	Fox Point Wi. (Milwaukee In.)	43·10 N	87·54 W
154	Foyle, Lough (B.) (lŏk foil') Ire.	55·07 N	7·08 W
216	Foz do Cunene Ang.	17·16 S	11·50 E
163	Fraga (frä'gä) Sp.	41·31 N	0·20 E
128	Fragoso, Cayo (I.) (kä'yō-frä-gō'sô) Cuba	22·45 N	79·30 W
135	Franca (frä'n-kä) Braz.	20·28 S	47·20 W
165	Francavilla (frän-kä-vēl'lä) It.	40·32 N	17·37 E
146	France (frâns) Eur.	46·39 N	0·47 E
90	Frances (L.) (frăn'sĭs) Can.	61·27 N	128·28 W
128	Frances, Cabo (C.) (kä'bō-frän-sĕ's) Cuba	21·55 N	84·05 W
128	Frances, Punta (Pt.) (pōō'n-tä-frän-sĕ's) Cuba	21·45 N	83·10 W
129	Frances Viejo, Cabo (C.) (kȧ'bô-frän'sȧs vyā'hō) Dom. Rep.	19·40 N	69·35 W
216	Franceville (fräNs-vēl') Gabon.	1·38 S	13·35 E
108	Francis Case, L. (frăn'sĭs) SD	43·15 N	99·00 W
137	Francisco Sales (frän-sē's-kô-sȧ'lĕs) Braz. (Rio de Janeiro In.)	21·42 S	44·26 W
212	Francistown (frăn'sĭs-toun) Bots.	21·17 S	27·28 E
107	Frankfort (frăŋk'fŭrt) Il. (Chicago In.)	41·30 N	87·51 W
104	Frankfort In.	40·15 N	86·30 W
117	Frankfort Ks.	39·42 N	96·27 W
104	Frankfort Ky.	38·10 N	84·55 W
104	Frankfort Mi.	44·40 N	86·15 W
105	Frankfort NY	43·05 N	75·05 W
218	Frankfort S. Afr. (Johannesburg & Pretoria In.)	27·17 S	28·30 E
213	Frankfort (frănk'fŏrt) S. Afr. (Natal In.)	32·43 S	27·28 E
158	Frankfurt (fräŋk'fŏŏrt) G.D.R.	52·20 N	14·31 E
149	Frankfurt (Dist.) G.D.R. (Berlin In.)	52·42 N	13·37 E
158	Frankfurt am Main F.R.G.	50·07 N	8·40 E
104	Franklin (frănk'lĭn) In.	39·25 N	86·00 W
120	Franklin Ky.	36·42 N	86·34 W
119	Franklin La.	29·47 N	91·31 W
99	Franklin Ma. (In.)	42·05 N	71·24 W
116	Franklin Ne.	40·06 N	99·01 W
105	Franklin NH	43·25 N	71·40 W
106	Franklin NJ (New York In.)	41·08 N	74·35 W
104	Franklin Oh.	39·30 N	84·20 W
105	Franklin Pa.	41·25 N	79·50 W
120	Franklin Tn.	35·54 N	86·54 W
213	Franklin S. Afr. (Natal In.)	30·19 S	29·28 E
121	Franklin Va.	36·41 N	76·57 W
90	Franklin, Dist. of Can.	70·46 N	105·22 W
114	Franklin (L.) Nv.	40·23 N	115·10 W
110	Franklin D. Roosevelt L. Wa.	48·12 N	118·43 W
90	Franklin Mts. Can.	65·36 N	125·55 W
107	Franklin Park Il. (Chicago In.)	41·56 N	87·53 W
106	Franklin Square NY (New York In.)	40·43 N	73·40 W
119	Franklinton (frăŋk'lĭn-tŭn) La.	30·49 N	90·09 W
202	Frankston Austl. (Melbourne In.)	38·09 S	145·08 E
107	Franksville (frănkz'vĭl) Wi. (Milwaukee In.)	42·46 N	87·55 W
	Franz Josef Land (Is.), see Zemlya Frantsa Iosifa		
163	Frascati (fräs-kä'tē) It. (Rome In.)	41·49 N	12·45 E
107	Fraser (frā'zēr) Mi. (Detroit In.)	42·32 N	82·57 W
203	Fraser (Great Sandy) (I.) (frā'zēr) Austl.	25·12 S	153·00 E
92	Fraser (R.) Can.	52·20 N	122·35 W
154	Fraserburgh (frā'zēr-bûrg) Scot.	57·40 N	2·01 W
92	Fraser Plateau Can.	51·30 N	122·00 W
163	Frattamaggiore (frät-tä-mäg-zhyô'rē) It. (Naples In.)	40·41 N	14·16 E
137	Fray Bentos (frī bĕn'tōs) Ur. (Buenos Aires In.)	33·10 S	58·19 W
108	Frazee (frā-zē') Mn.	46·42 N	95·43 W
128	Fraziers Hog Cay (I.) Ba.	25·25 N	77·55 W
161	Frechen (frĕ'kĕn) F.R.G. (Ruhr In.)	50·54 N	6·49 E
156	Fredericia (frĕdh-ĕ-rē'tsē-ȧ) Den.	55·35 N	9·45 E
105	Frederick (frĕd'ēr-ĭk) Md.	39·25 N	77·25 W
116	Frederick Ok.	34·23 N	99·01 W
96	Frederick House (R.) Can.	49·05 N	81·20 W
118	Fredericksburg (frĕd'ēr-ĭkz-bûrg) Tx.	30·16 N	98·52 W
105	Fredericksburg Va.	38·20 N	77·30 W
117	Fredericktown (frĕd'ēr-ĭk-toun) Mo.	37·32 N	90·16 W
98	Fredericton (frĕd'ēr-ĭk-tŭn) Can.	45·48 N	66·39 W
156	Frederikshavn (frĕdh'ĕ-rĕks-houn) Den.	57·27 N	10·31 E
156	Frederikssund (frĕdh'ĕ-rĕks-sōōn) Den.	55·51 N	12·04 E
134	Fredonia (frē-dō'nyȧ) Col. (In.)	5·55 N	75·40 W
117	Fredonia (frē-dō'nĭ-ȧ) Ks.	36·31 N	95·50 W
105	Fredonia NY	42·25 N	79·20 W
156	Fredrikstad (frĕdh'rĕks-städ) Nor.	59·14 N	10·58 E
113	Freeburg (frē'bûrg) Il. (St. Louis In.)	38·26 N	89·59 W
106	Freehold (frē'hōld) NJ (New York In.)	40·15 N	74·16 W
106	Freeland (frē'lȧnd) Pa.	41·00 N	75·50 W
110	Freeland Wa. (Seattle In.)	48·01 N	122·32 W
99	Freels, C. (frēlz) Can.	46·37 N	53·45 W
100	Freelton (frēl'tŭn) Can. (Toronto In.)	43·24 N	80·02 W
128	Freeport Ba.	26·30 N	78·45 W
109	Freeport (frē'pōrt) Il.	42·19 N	89·30 W
106	Freeport NY (New York In.)	40·39 N	73·35 W
113	Freeport Tx.	28·56 N	95·21 W
214	Freetown (frē'toun) S. L.	8·30 N	13·15 W
162	Fregenal de la Sierra (frā-hȧ-näl' dā lä syĕr'rä) Sp.	38·09 N	6·40 W
163	Fregene (frĕ-zhĕ'-nĕ) It. (Rome In.)	41·52 N	12·12 E
158	Freiberg (frī'bĕrgh) G.D.R.	50·54 N	13·18 E
158	Freiburg G.D.R.	48·00 N	7·50 E
149	Freienried (frī'ĕn-rēd) F.R.G. (Munich In.)	48·20 N	11·08 E
136	Freirina (frā-ĭ-rē'nä) Chile	28·35 S	71·26 W
149	Freising (frī'zĭng) F.R.G. (Munich In.)	48·25 N	11·45 E
161	Fréjus (frā-zhüs') Fr.	43·28 N	6·46 E
204	Fremantle (frē'măn-t'l) Austl.	32·03 S	116·05 E
112	Fremont (frē-mŏnt') Ca. (San Francisco In.)	37·33 N	122·00 W
104	Fremont Mi.	43·25 N	85·55 W
108	Fremont Ne.	41·26 N	96·30 W
104	Fremont Oh.	41·20 N	83·05 W
115	Fremont (R.) Ut.	38·20 N	111·30 W
111	Fremont Pk. Wy.	43·05 N	109·35 W

PRONOUNCING INDEX French Broad — Garfield 283

Page	Name / Pronunciation / Region	Lat. °′	Long. °′
120	French Broad (R.) (frĕnch brôd) Tn.-NC	35·59 N	83·01 W
133	French Guiana (gē-ä'nä) S. A.	4·20 N	53·00 W
104	French Lick (frĕnch lĭk) In.	38·35 N	86·35 W
94	Frenchman (R.) Can.	49·25 N	108·30 W
111	Frenchman Cr. (frĕnch-măn) Mt.	48·51 N	107·20 W
116	Frenchman Cr. Ne.	40·24 N	101·50 W
114	Frenchman F. Nv.	36·55 N	116·11 W
113	French River Mn. (Duluth In.)	46·54 N	91·54 W
93	Freshfield, Mt. (frĕsh'fēld) Can.	51·44 N	116·57 W
124	Fresnillo (frås-nēl'yō) Mex.	23·10 N	102·52 W
114	Fresno (frĕz'nō) Ca.	36·43 N	119·47 W
134	Fresno (frĕs'-nō) Col. (In.)	5·10 N	75·01 W
114	Fresno (R.) (frĕz'nō) Ca.	37·00 N	120·24 W
114	Fresno Slough Ca.	36·39 N	120·12 W
158	Freudenstadt (froi'den-shtät) F.R.G.	48·28 N	8·26 E
203	Freycinet Pen. (frā-sē-nĕ') Austl.	42·13 S	148·56 E
115	Fria (R.) (frê-ä) Az.	34·03 N	112·12 W
212	Fria, C. (fria) S. W. Afr.	18·15 S	12·10 E
214	Fria Gui.	10·05 N	13·32 W
136	Frias (frē-äs) Arg.	28·43 S	65·03 W
158	Fribourg (frē-bōōr') Switz.	46·48 N	7·07 E
113	Fridley (frĭd'lĭ) Mn. (Minneapolis, St. Paul In.)	45·05 N	93·16 W
158	Frieburg (frī'bōōrgh) F.R.G.	47·59 N	7·50 E
149	Friedberg (frēd'bĕrgh) F.R.G. (Munich In.)	48·22 N	11·00 E
158	Friedland (frēt'länt) G.D.R.	53·39 N	13·34 E
158	Friedrichshafen (frē-drēks-häf'ĕn) F.R.G.	47·39 N	9·28 E
117	Friend (frĕnd) Ne.	40·40 N	97·16 W
119	Friendswood (frĕnds'-wŏŏd) Tx. (In.)	29·31 N	95·11 W
121	Fries (frēz) Va.	36·42 N	80·59 W
149	Friesack (frē'säk) G.D.R. (Berlin In.)	52·44 N	12·35 E
135	Frio, Cabo (C.) (kä'bō-frē'ō). Braz.	22·58 S	42·08 W
118	Frio R. Tx.	29·00 N	99·15 W
162	Friol (frê-ōl') Sp.	43·02 N	7·48 W
155	Frisian (Is.) (frē'zhăn) Neth.	53·30 N	5·20 E
164	Friuli-Venezia Giulia (Reg.) It.	46·20 N	13·20 E
94	Frobisher L. (frŏb'ĭsh-ēr) Can.	56·25 N	108·20 W
91	Frobisher Bay Can.	63·48 N	68·31 W
91	Frobisher B. Can.	62·49 N	66·41 W
148	Frodsham (frŏdz'ăm) Eng.	53·18 N	2·48 W
203	Frome, L. (frōōm) Austl.	30·40 S	140·13 E
117	Frontenac (frŏn'tē-năk) Ks.	37·27 N	94·41 W
125	Frontera (frôn-tā'rä) Mex.	18·34 N	92·38 W
160	Frontignan (frôN-tē-nyäN') Fr.	43·26 N	3·45 E
111	Front Ra. (frŭnt) Wy.	42·17 N	105·53 W
105	Front Royal (frŭnt) Va.	38·55 N	78·10 W
150	Fro Sea (frô) Nor.	63·49 N	9·12 E
164	Frosinone (frō-zē-nō'nå) It.	41·38 N	13·22 E
105	Frostburg (frôst'bûrg) Md.	39·40 N	78·55 W
115	Fruita (frōōt-à) Co.	39·10 N	108·45 W
172	Frunze (frōōn'zĕ) Sov. Un.	42·49 N	74·42 E
174	Fryanovo (f'ryä'nô-vô) Sov. Un. (Moscow In.)	56·08 N	38·28 E
174	Fryanzino (f'ryä'zĭ-nô) Sov. Un. (Moscow In.)	55·58 N	38·05 E
159	Frýdek (frē'dĕk) Czech.	49·43 N	18·22 E
158	Frydlant (frēd'länt) Czech.	50·56 N	15·05 E
	Fuchien (Prov.), see Fukien		
189	Fuchin (fōō'chĭn') China	47·13 N	132·11 E
193	Fuchou (Foochow) (fōō'chō) China	26·02 N	119·18 E
190	Fuchow (fōō'chō') China	39·46 N	121·44 E
195	Fuchu (fōō'chōō). Jap. (Tōkyō In.)	35·41 N	139·29 E
193	Fuch'un (R.) China	29·50 N	120·00 E
126	Fuego (Vol.) (fwā'gō) Guat.	14·29 N	90·52 W
163	Fuencarral (fuān-kär-räl') Sp. (Madrid In.)	40·29 N	3·42 W
162	Fuensalida (fwān-sä-lē'dä) Sp.	40·04 N	4·15 W
118	Fuente (fwĕ'n-tĕ) Mex.	28·39 N	100·34 W
162	Fuente de Cantos (fwĕn'tå dā kän'tōs). Sp.	38·15 N	6·18 W
163	Fuente el Saz (fwĕn'tå ĕl säth') Sp. (Madrid In.)	40·39 N	3·30 W
162	Fuente-Ovejuna (fwĕn'tå-ō-vå-hōō'nä). Sp.	38·15 N	5·30 W
162	Fuentesaúco (fwĕn-tå-sä-ōō'kō) Sp.	41·18 N	5·25 W
122	Fuerte, Rio del (R.) (rê'ō-dĕl-fōō-ĕ'r-tĕ). Mex.	26·15 N	108·50 W
135	Fuerte Olimpo (fwĕr'tå ō-lēm-pō) Par.	21·10 S	57·49 W
210	Fuerteventura I. (fwĕr'tå-vĕn-tōō'rä). Can. Is.	28·24 N	13·21 W
188	Fuhai China	47·01 N	87·07 E
190	Fuhsien (fōō'siän) China	39·36 N	121·59 E
195	Fuji (fōō'jê) Jap.	35·11 N	138·44 E
195	Fuji (R.) Jap.	35·20 N	138·23 E
195	Fujidera Jap. (Ōsaka In.)	34·34 N	135·37 E
195	Fuji-san (Mtn.) (fōō'jê sän). Jap.	35·23 N	138·44 E
195	Fujisawa (fōō'jê-sä'wa) Jap. (Tōkyō In.)	35·20 N	139·29 E
189	Fuckien (Fuchien) (Prov.). China	25·40 N	117·30 E
195	Fukuchiyama (fōō'kōō-chê-yä'mä). Jap.	35·18 N	135·07 E
195	Fukue (I.) (fōō-kōō'ä) Jap.	32·40 N	129·02 E
195	Fukui (fōō'kōō-ê) Jap.	36·05 N	136·14 E
195	Fukuoka (fōō'kōō-ō'kå) Jap.	33·35 N	130·23 E
195	Fukuoka Jap. (Tōkyō In.)	31·52 N	139·31 E
194	Fukushima (fōō'kōō-shē'mä). Jap.	37·45 N	140·29 E
195	Fukuyama (fōō'kōō-yä'mä) Jap.	34·31 N	133·21 E
187	Fūlādī, Kūh-e (Mtn.) Afg.	34·38 N	67·55 E
158	Fulda R. (fōōl'dä) F.R.G.	51·05 N	9·40 E
113	Fullerton (fōōl'ēr-tŭn) Ca. (Los Angeles In.)	33·53 N	117·56 W
119	Fullerton La.	31·00 N	93·00 W
108	Fullerton Ne.	41·21 N	97·59 W
120	Fulton (fŭl'tŭn) Ky.	36·30 N	88·53 W
117	Fulton Mo.	38·51 N	91·56 W
105	Fulton NY	43·20 N	76·25 W
106	Fultondale (fŭl'tŭn-dāl) Al. (Birmingham In.)	33·37 N	86·48 W
195	Funabashi (fōō'nà-bä'shē) Jap. (Tōkyō In.)	35·43 N	139·59 E
195	Funaya (fōō-nä'yä) Jap. (Osaka In.)	34·45 N	135·52 E
210	Funchal (fōōn-shäl') Mad. Is.	32·41 N	16·15 W
134	Fundación (fōōn-dä-syō'n) Col.	10·43 N	74·13 W
162	Fundão (fōōn-douN') Port.	40·08 N	7·32 W
96	Fundy, B. of (fŭn'dĭ) Can.	45·00 N	66·00 W
96	Fundy Natl. Park Can.	45·38 N	65·00 W
190	Funing (fōō'nĭng') China	39·55 N	119·16 E
193	Funing Wan (B.) (fōō'nĭng'). China	26·48 N	120·35 E
215	Funtua Nig.	11·31 N	7·17 E
217	Furancungo Moz.	14·55 S	33·35 E
125	Furbero (fōōr-bĕ'rô) Mex.	20·21 N	97·32 W
166	Furmanov (fûr-mä'nôf). Sov. Un.	57·14 N	41·11 E
136	Furnas, Represa de (Res.) Braz. (Rio dê Janeiro In.)	21·00 S	46·00 W
205	Furneaux Group (Is.) (fûr'nō) Austl.	40·15 S	146·27 E
158	Fürstenfeld (für'stĕn-fĕlt) Aus.	47·02 N	16·03 E
149	Fürstenfeldbruck (fur'stĕn-fĕld' brōōk) F.R.G. (Munich In.)	48·11 N	11·16 E
158	Fürstenwalde (für'stĕn-väl-dĕ) G.D.R.	52·21 N	14·04 E
158	Fürth (fürt) F.R.G.	49·28 N	11·03 E
195	Furuichi (fōō'rōō-ē'chê) Jap. (Ōsaka In.)	34·33 N	135·37 E
195	Fusa (fōō'sä) Jap. (Tōkyō In.)	35·52 N	140·08 E
134	Fusagasugá (fōō-sä-gä-sōō-gä') Col. (In.)	4·22 N	74·22 W
195	Fuse Jap. (Ōsaka In.)	34·40 N	135·43 E
	Fushih, see Yenan		
195	Fushimi (fōō'shē-mê) Jap. (Ōsaka In.)	34·57 N	135·47 E
192	Fushun (fōō'shōōn') China	41·50 N	124·00 E
192	Fusung China	42·12 N	127·12 E
195	Futtsu (fōō'tsōō') Jap. (Tōkyō In.)	35·19 N	139·49 E
195	Futtsu Misaki (C.) (fōōt'tsōō' mê-sä'kē). Jap. (Tōkyō In.)	35·19 N	139·46 E
218	Fuwah (fōō'wå). Egypt (Nile In.)	31·13 N	30·35 E
193	Fuyang China	30·10 N	119·58 E
192	Fuyü (fōō'yōō) China	45·20 N	125·00 E
156	Fyn (I.) (fü''n) Den.	55·24 N	10·33 E
154	Fyne (L.) (fīn) Scot.	56·14 N	5·10 W
156	Fyresdal Vand (L.) (fu'rĕs-däl vän). Nor.	59·04 N	7·55 E

G

Page	Name / Pronunciation / Region	Lat. °′	Long. °′
216	Gabela Ang.	10·48 S	14·20 E
212	Gaborone Bots.	24·28 S	25·59 E
210	Gabès (gä'bĕs) Tun.	33·51 N	10·04 E
210	Gabès, Golfe de (G.) Tun.	32·22 N	10·59 E
215	Gabil Chad	11·09 N	18·12 E
202	Gabin (gôN'bēn) Pol.	52·23 N	19·47 E
209	Gabon (gà-bôN') Afr.	0·30 S	10·45 E
119	Gabriel R. (gā'brĭ-ĕl) Tx.	30·38 N	97·15 W
165	Gabrovo (gäb'rô-vō) Bul.	42·52 N	25·19 E
134	Gachetá (gä-chä'tä) Col (In.)	4·50 N	73·36 W
165	Gacko (gäts'kô) Yugo.	43·10 N	18·34 E
120	Gadsden (gădz'dĕn) Al.	34·00 N	86·00 W
167	Gadyach (gäd-yäch') Sov. Un.	50·22 N	33·59 E
165	Gaesti (gä-yĕsh'tē) Rom.	44·43 N	25·21 E
164	Gaeta (gä-å'tä) It.	41·18 N	13·34 E
121	Gaffney (găf'nĭ) SC	35·04 N	81·47 W
210	Gafsa (gäf'sä) Tun.	34·16 N	8·37 E
166	Gagarin Sov. Un.	55·32 N	34·58 E
98	Gagetown (gāj'toun) Can.	45·47 N	66·09 W
214	Gagnoa Ivory Coast	6·08 N	5·56 W
197	Gagrary (I.) (gä-grä-rē). Phil. (In.)	13·23 N	123·58 E
164	Gaidhouronísi (I.) Grc. (Inset)	34·53 N	25·58 E
146	Gaillac-sur-Tarn (gà-yäk'sür-tärn'). Fr.	43·54 N	1·52 E
122	Gaillard Cut (gä-ēl-yä'rd) C. Z. (Panama Canal In.)	9·03 N	79·42 W
121	Gainesville (gānz'vĭl) Fl.	29·40 N	82·20 W
120	Gainesville Ga.	34·16 N	83·48 W
117	Gainesville Tx.	33·38 N	97·08 W
148	Gainsborough (gānz'bŭr-ō) Eng.	53·23 N	0·46 W
203	Gairdner, L. (gård'nēr) Austl.	32·20 S	136·30 E
106	Gaithersburg (gā'thērs'bûrg) Md. (Baltimore In.)	39·08 N	77·13 W
217	Galana (R.) Ken.	3·00 S	39·30 E
163	Galapagar (gä-lä-pä-gär') Sp. (Madrid In.)	40·36 N	4·00 W
	Galápagos Is., see Colon, Arch. de		
154	Galashiels (găl-à-shēlz) Scot.	55·40 N	2·57 W
167	Galati (gä-lätz'ĭ) Rom.	45·25 N	28·05 E
165	Galatina (gä-lä-tē'nä) It.	40·10 N	18·12 E
165	Galaxidhion Grc.	38·26 N	22·22 E
156	Galdhöpiggen Nor.	61·37 N	8·17 E
118	Galeana (gä-lå-ä'nä) Mex.	24·50 N	100·04 W
109	Galena (gà-lē'nà) Il.	42·26 N	90·27 W
107	Galena In. (Louisville In.)	38·21 N	85·55 W
117	Galena Ks.	37·06 N	94·39 W
119	Galena Pk. Tx. (In.)	29·44 N	95·14 W
122	Galera, Cerro (Mtn.) (sĕ'r-rō-gä-lĕ'rä). C. Z. (In.)	8·55 N	79·38 W
163	Galera (R.) (gä-lĕ'rä) It. (Rome In.)	41·58 N	12·21 E
134	Galeras (Vol.) (gä-lĕ'räs) Col.	0·57 N	77·27 W
112	Gales (R.) (gālz). Or. (Portland In.)	45·33 N	123·11 W
117	Galesburg (gālz'bûrg) Il.	40·56 N	90·21 W
109	Galesville (gālz'vĭl) Wi.	44·04 N	91·22 W
105	Galeton (gāl'tŭn) Pa.	41·45 N	77·40 W
165	Galibolu (Gallipoli) (gĕ-lĭb'ō-lōō) (gà-lĭp'ō-lē). Tur.	40·25 N	26·40 E
170	Galich (gål'ĭch) Sov. Un.	58·20 N	42·38 E
159	Galicia (Reg.) (gà-lĭsh'ĭ-à) Pol.-Sov. Un.	49·48 N	21·05 E
162	Galicia (Reg.) (gä-lē'thyä) Sp.	43·35 N	8·03 W
205	Galilee (L.) (găl'ĭ-lē) Austl.	22·23 S	145·09 E
183	Galilee, Sea of. Isr. (Palestine In.)	32·53 N	35·45 E
128	Galina Pt. (gä-lē'nä) Jam.	18·25 N	76·50 W
123	Galion (găl'ĭ-ŭn) Oh.	40·45 N	82·50 W
117	Galisteo (gä-lĭs-tā'ō) NM	35·20 N	106·00 W
151	Galite, I. La (gä-lēt) Alg.	37·36 N	8·03 E
218	Galka'yo. Som. (Horn of Afr. In.)	7·00 N	47·30 E
211	Galla (Prov.) (gäl'lä) Eth.	7·22 N	35·28 E
164	Gallarate (gäl-lä-rä'tā) It.	45·37 N	8·48 E
161	Gallardon (gä-lär-dôN') Fr. (Paris In.)	48·31 N	1·40 E
117	Gallatin (găl'à-tĭn) Mo.	39·55 N	93·58 W
120	Gallatin Tn.	36·23 N	86·28 W
111	Gallatin R. Mt.	45·12 N	111·10 W
185	Galle (gäl) Sri Lanka	6·13 N	80·10 E
163	Gállego (R.) (gäl-yā'gō) Sp.	42·27 N	0·37 W
134	Gallinas, Pta. de (Pt.) (gä-lyē'näs) Col.	12·10 N	72·10 W
165	Gallipoli (gäl-lē'pô-lē) It.	40·03 N	17·58 E
	Gallipoli, see Galibolu		
104	Gallipolis (găl-ĭ-pō-lēs) Oh.	38·50 N	82·10 W
150	Gällivare (yĕl-ĭ-vär'ĕ) Swe.	68·06 N	20·29 E
162	Gallo (R.) (gäl'yō) Sp.	40·43 N	1·42 W
117	Gallup (găl'ŭp) NM	35·30 N	108·45 W
211	Galnale Doria R. Eth.	5·35 N	40·26 E
104	Galt Can.	43·22 N	80·19 W
154	Galty Mts. Ire.	52·19 N	8·20 W
117	Galva (găl'vå) Il.	41·11 N	90·02 W
119	Galveston (găl'vĕs-tŭn). Tx. (In.)	29·18 N	94·48 W
119	Galveston B. Tx.	29·39 N	94·45 W
119	Galveston I. Tx. (In.)	29·12 N	94·53 W
154	Galway Ire.	53·16 N	9·05 W
154	Galway B. (gôl'wā) Ire.	53·10 N	9·47 W
214	Gambaga (gäm-bä'gä) Ghana	10·32 N	0·26 W
211	Gambela (găm-bā'lå) Eth.	8·15 N	34·33 E
210	Gambia (găm'bê-à) Afr.	13·38 N	19·38 W
214	Gambia (R.) (Gambie) Afr.	13·20 N	15·55 W
214	Gambie (R.) (Gambia) Afr.	13·20 N	15·55 W
216	Gamboma (gäm-bō'mä) Con.	1·53 S	15·51 E
156	Gamleby (gäm'lĕ-bü) Swe.	57·54 N	16·20 E
197	Gamu (gä-mōō') Phil. (In.)	17·05 N	121·50 E
184	Gandak (R.) India	26·37 N	84·22 E
99	Gander (găn'dĕr) Can.	48·57 N	54·34 W
99	Gander (R.) Can.	49·10 N	54·35 W
99	Gander L. Can.	48·55 N	55·40 W
184	Gandhinagar India	23·30 N	72·47 E
215	Gandi Nig.	12·55 N	5·49 E
163	Gandia (gän-dē'ä) Sp.	38·56 N	0·10 W
184	Ganges, Mouths of (găn'jēz). India	21·18 N	88·40 E
184	Ganges (R.) (găn'jēz) India	24·32 N	87·58 E
164	Gangi (gän'jē) It.	37·48 N	14·15 E
188	Gangtok India	27·15 N	88·30 E
111	Gannett Pk. (găn'ĕt) Wy.	43·10 N	109·38 W
107	Gano (gă'nô). Oh. (Cincinnati In.)	39·18 N	84·24 W
149	Gänserndorf Aus. (Vienna In.)	48·21 N	16·43 E
215	Ganwo Nig.	11·13 N	4·42 E
214	Gao (gä'ō) Mali	16·16 N	0·03 W
161	Gap (gåp) Fr.	44·34 N	6·08 E
197	Gapan (gä-pän) Phil. (In.)	15·18 N	120·56 E
127	Garachiné (gä-rä-chē'nå) Pan.	8·02 N	78·22 W
127	Garachiné, Punta (Pt.) (pōō'n-tä-gä-rä-chē'nå). Pan.	8·08 N	78·35 W
135	Garanhuns (gä-rän-yōōNsh'). Braz.	8·49 S	36·28 W
117	Garber (gär'bĕr) Ok.	36·28 N	97·35 W
149	Garching (gär'kĕng) F.R.G. (Munich In.)	48·15 N	11·39 E
118	Garcia (gär-sē'ä) Mex.	25·90 N	100·37 W
124	Garcia de la Cadena (dĕ-lä-kä-dĕ-nä). Mex.	21·14 N	103·26 W
164	Garda, Lago di (L.) (lä-gō-dē-gär'dä). It.	45·43 N	10·26 E
160	Gardanne (gàr-dän') Fr. (In.)	43·28 N	5·29 E
158	Gardelegen (gär-dē-lå'ghĕn) G.D.R.	52·32 N	11·22 E
104	Garden (I.) (gär'd'n) Mi.	45·50 N	85·50 W
113	Gardena (gär-dē'nå) Ca. (Los Angeles In.)	33·53 N	118·19 W
107	Garden City Mi. (Detroit In.)	42·20 N	83·21 W
116	Garden City Ks.	37·58 N	100·52 W
113	Garden Grove (gär'd'n grōv) Ca. (Los Angeles In.)	33·47 N	117·56 W
184	Garden Reach. India (Calcutta In.)	22·33 N	88·17 E
113	Garden River Can. (Sault Ste. Marie In.)	46·33 N	84·10 W
184	Gardēz Afg.	33·43 N	69·09 E
98	Gardiner (gärd'nēr) Me.	44·12 N	69·46 W
111	Gardiner Mt.	45·03 N	110·43 W
112	Gardiner Wa. (Seattle In.)	48·03 N	122·55 W
94	Gardiner Dam Can.	51·17 N	106·51 W
105	Gardner Ma.	42·35 N	72·00 W
92	Gardner, Can. Can.	53·28 N	128·15 W
101	Gareloi (I.) (gär-lōō-ä') Ak.	51·40 N	178·48 W
106	Garfield (gär'fēld) NJ (New York In.)	40·53 N	74·06 W
113	Garfield. Ut. (Salt Lake City In.)	40·45 N	112·10 W

ng-sing; ŋ-baŋk; N-nasalized n; nŏd; cŏmmit; ōld; ôbey; ôrder; fōōd; fŏŏt; ou-out; s-soft; sh-dish; th-thin; pūre; ûnite; ûrn; stŭd; circŭs; ü-as "y" in study; '-indeterminate vowel.

284 Garfield Heights — Giresun PRONOUNCING INDEX

Page	Name Pronunciation Region	Lat. °'	Long. °'
107	Garfield Heights Oh. (Cleveland In.)	41·25 N	81·36 W
165	Gargaliánoi (gár-gä-lyä'nē)...Grc.	37·07 N	21·50 E
157	Gargždai (gärgzh'dī).....Sov. Un.	55·43 N	20·09 E
92	Garibaldi, Mt. (gâr-ĭ-băl'dê)..Can.	49·51 N	123·01 W
136	Garin (gä-rē'n) Arg. (Buenos Aires In.)	34·10 S	58·44 W
217	Garissa.....Ken.	0·28 S	39·38 E
113	Garland (gär'lănd) Tx. (Dallas, Fort Worth In.)	32·55 N	96·39 W
111	Garland.....Ut.	41·45 N	112·10 W
172	Garm.....Sov. Un.	39·12 N	70·28 E
158	Garmisch-Partenkirchen (gär'mēsh pär'tĕn-kēr'kĕn)....F.R.G.	47·38 N	11·10 E
117	Garnett (gär'nĕt).....Ks.	38·16 N	95·15 W
160	Garonne Rivière (R.) (gá-rôn)..Fr.	44·43 N	0·25 W
215	Garoua (gär'wä).....Cam.	9·18 N	13·24 E
104	Garrett (găr'ĕt).....In.	41·20 N	85·10 W
106	Garrison (găr'ĭ-sŭn) NY (New York In.)	41·23 N	73·57 W
108	Garrison.....ND	47·38 N	101·24 W
162	Garrovillas (gä-rô-vēl'yäs).....Sp.	39·42 N	6·30 W
90	Garry (L.) (găr'ĭ).....Can.	66·16 N	99·23 W
217	Garsen.....Ken.	2·16 S	40·07 E
98	Garson.....Can.	46·34 N	80·52 W
149	Garstedt (gär'shtĕt) F.R.G. (Hamburg In.)	53·40 N	9·58 E
184	Gartok (gär-tŏk').....China	31·11 N	80·35 E
184	Garulia.....India (In.)	22·48 N	88·23 E
159	Garwolin (gär-vō'lēn).....Pol.	51·54 N	21·40 E
107	Gary (gā'rĭ)....In. (Chicago In.)	41·35 N	87·21 W
119	Garza-Little Elm Res.....Tx.	33·16 N	96·54 W
134	Garzón (gär-thōn').....Col.	2·13 N	75·44 W
197	Gasan (gä-sän').....Phil. (In.)	13·19 N	121·52 E
171	Gasan-Kuli.....Sov. Un.	37·25 N	53·55 E
104	Gas City (găs).....In.	40·30 N	85·40 W
160	Gascogne (Reg.) (gäs-kôn'yĕ).Fr.	43·45 N	1·49 W
117	Gasconade (R.) (găs-kô-nād') Mo.	37·46 N	92·15 W
204	Gascoyne (R.) (găs-koin')..Austl.	25·15 S	117·00 E
113	Gashland (găsh'-lănd) Mo. (Kansas City In.)	39·15 N	94·35 W
215	Gashua.....Nig.	12·54 N	11·00 E
161	Gasny (gäs-nē')....Fr. (Paris In.)	49·05 N	1·36 E
98	Gaspé.....Can.	48·50 N	64·29 W
98	Gaspé, Baie de (B.) (gas'pā) (gȧs-pā').Can.	48·35 N	63·45 W
98	Gaspé, Cape de (C.).....Can.	48·45 N	63·34 W
98	Gaspé, Péninsule de (Pen.)...Can.	48·23 N	65·42 W
129	Gasper Hernandez (gäs-pär' ĕr-nän'dāth).Dom. Rep.	19·40 N	70·15 W
104	Gassaway (găs'ȧ-wā).....WV	38·40 N	80·45 W
112	Gaston (găs'tŭn) Or. (Portland In.)	45·26 N	123·08 W
121	Gastonia (găs-tô'nĭ-ȧ).....NC	35·15 N	81·14 W
136	Gastre (gäs-trĕ).....Arg.	42·12 S	68·50 W
162	Gata, Cabo de (C.) (kȧ'bô-dĕ-gä'tä).Sp.	36·42 N	2·00 W
162	Gata, Sierra de (Mts.) (syĕr'rȧ dā gȧ'tä).Sp.	40·12 N	6·39 W
183	Gátes, Akrotírion (C.) Cyprus (Palestine In.)	34·30 N	33·15 E
174	Gatchina (gä-chē'nȧ) Sov. Un. (Leningrad In.)	59·33 N	30·08 E
154	Gateshead (gāts'hĕd).....Eng.	54·56 N	1·38 W
119	Gatesville (gāts'vĭl).....Mex.	31·26 N	97·34 W
100	Gatineau (gȧ'tē-nō) Can. (Ottawa In.)	45·29 N	75·38 W
100	Gatineau (R.)..Can. (Ottawa In.)	45·45 N	75·50 W
100	Gatineau, Parc de la (Natl. Pk.) Can. (Ottawa In.)	45·32 N	75·53 W
217	Gatooma (gȧ-tōō'mä).....Rh.	18·21 S	29·55 E
149	Gattendorf.....Aus. (Vienna In.)	48·01 N	17·00 E
122	Gatun (gä-tōōn').....C. Z. (In.)	9·16 N	79·25 W
122	Gatun, L.....Pan.-C. Z. (In.)	9·13 N	79·24 W
122	Gatun (R.).....Pan. (In.)	9·21 N	79·10 W
122	Gatun Locks.....C. Z. (In.)	9·16 N	79·27 W
184	Gauhāti.....India	26·09 N	91·51 E
157	Gauja (R.) (gȧ'ōō-yȧ)....Sov. Un.	57·10 N	24·30 E
197	Gauttier-Gebergte (Mts.) (gō-tyā') Indon.	2·30 S	138·45 E
164	Gávdhos (I.) (gäv'dôs)..Grc. (In.)	34·48 N	24·08 E
108	Gavins Point Dam (gă'-vĭns).Ne.	42·47 N	97·47 W
156	Gävle (yĕv'lĕ).....Swe.	60·40 N	17·07 E
156	Gavle-bukten (B.).....Swe.	60·45 N	17·30 E
166	Gavrilov Posad (gȧ'vrê-lôf'ka po-sȧt').Sov. Un.	56·34 N	40·09 E
166	Gavrilov-Yam (gȧ'vrê-lôf yäm') Sov. Un.	57·17 N	39·49 E
203	Gawler (gô'lēr).....Austl.	34·35 S	138·47 E
203	Gawler Ra.....Austl.	32·35 S	136·30 E
184	Gaya (gŭ'yä) (gī'ȧ).....India	24·53 N	85·00 E
210	Gaya (gä'yä).....Nig.	11·58 N	9·05 E
104	Gaylord (gā'lôrd).....Mi.	45·00 N	84·35 W
203	Gayndah (gān'dăh).....Austl.	25·43 S	151·33 E
167	Gaysin.....Sov. Un.	48·46 N	29·22 E
	Gaza, see Ghazzah		
171	Gaziantep (gä-zē-än'tĕp).....Tur.	37·10 N	37·30 E
214	Gbarnga.....Lib.	7·00 N	9·29 W
159	Gdańsk (Danzig) (g'dänsk) (dän'tsĕg).Pol.	54·20 N	18·40 E
166	Gdov (g'dôf').....Sov. Un.	58·44 N	27·51 E
159	Gdynia (g'dēn'yȧ).....Pol.	54·29 N	18·30 E
116	Geary (gē'rĭ).....Ok.	35·36 N	98·19 W
214	Géba (R.).....Guinea-Bissau	12·25 N	14·35 W
111	Gebo (gĕb'ō).....Wy.	43·49 N	108·13 W
119	Ged (gĕd).....La.	30·07 N	93·36 W
153	Gediz (R.).....Tur.	38·44 N	28·45 E
112	Gedney (I.) (gĕd-nē) Wa. (Seattle In.)	48·01 N	122·18 W
158	Gedser.....Den.	54·35 N	12·08 E
149	Geel.....Bel. (Brussels In.)	51·09 N	5·01 E
202	Geelong (jē-lông') Austl. (Melbourne In.)	38·06 S	144·13 E
197	Geelvink-baai (B.) (gäl'vĭnk) Indon.	2·20 S	135·30 E
215	Geidam.....Nig.	12·57 N	11·57 E
204	Geikie Ra. (gē'kē).....Austl.	17·35 S	125·32 E
158	Geislingen (gis'lĭng-ĕn).....F.R.G.	48·37 N	9·52 E
107	Geist Res. (gēst) In. (Indianapolis In.)	39·57 N	85·59 W
217	Geita.....Tan.	2·52 S	32·10 E
149	Geldermalsen Neth. (Amsterdam In.)	51·53 N	5·18 E
161	Geldern (gĕl'dĕrn) F.R.G. (Ruhr In.)	51·31 N	6·20 E
165	Gelibolu, Yarimada (Pen.) (gĕ-lĭb'ô-lōō).Tur.	40·23 N	25·10 E
167	Gel'myazov.....Sov. Un.	49·49 N	31·54 E
161	Gelsenkirchen (gĕl-zĕn-kĭrk-ĕn) F.R.G. (Ruhr In.)	51·31 N	7·05 E
183	Gemas (jĕm'ȧs) Mala. (Singapore In.)	2·35 N	102·37 E
216	Gemena.....Zaire	3·15 N	19·46 E
171	Gemlik (gĕm'lĭk).....Tur.	40·30 N	29·10 E
218	Genale (R.).....Eth.	5·00 N	41·15 E
137	General Alvear (gĕ-nĕ-räl'ál-vĕ-ȧ'r).Arg. (Buenos Aires In.)	36·04 S	60·02 W
137	General Arenales (ä-rĕ-nä'lĕs) Arg. (Buenos Aires In.)	34·19 S	61·16 W
137	General Belgrano (bĕl-grȧ'nô) Arg. (Buenos Aires In.)	35·45 S	58·32 W
118	General Cepeda (sĕ-pĕ'dä)...Mex.	25·24 N	101·29 W
137	General Conesa (kô-nĕ'sä) Arg. (Buenos Aires In.)	36·30 S	57·19 W
137	General Guido (gē'dô) Arg. (Buenos Aires In.)	36·41 S	57·48 W
137	General Lavalle (lȧ-vȧ'l-yĕ) Arg. (Buenos Aires In.)	36·25 S	56·55 W
136	General Madariaga (män-dȧ-rêȧ'gä).Arg.	36·59 S	57·14 W
137	General Paz (pȧ'z) Arg. (Buenos Aires In.)	35·30 S	58·20 W
124	General Pedro Antonio Santios (pĕ'drô-än-tô'nyô-sän-tyôs). Mex.	21·37 N	98·58 W
136	General Pico (pē'kô).....Arg.	36·46 S	63·44 W
136	General Roca (rô-kä).....Arg.	39·01 S	67·31 W
136	General San Martín (sän-mȧr-tē'n) Arg. (Buenos Aires In.)	34·19 S	58·32 W
137	General Viamonte (vēȧ'môn-tĕ) Arg. (Buenos Aires In.)	35·01 S	60·59 W
118	General Zuazua (zwä'zwä)..Mex.	25·54 N	100·07 W
105	Genesee (R.) (jĕn-ê-sē').....NY	42·25 N	78·10 W
104	Geneseo (jē-nĕs'eō).....Il.	41·28 N	90·11 W
120	Geneva (jê-nē'vȧ).....Al.	31·03 N	85·50 W
107	Geneva.....Il. (Chicago In.)	41·53 N	88·18 W
117	Geneva.....Ne.	40·32 N	97·37 W
105	Geneva.....NY	42·50 N	77·00 W
104	Geneva.....Oh.	41·45 N	80·55 W
	Geneva, see Génève		
158	Geneva, L.....Switz.	46·28 N	6·30 E
158	Génève (Geneva) (zhē-nĕv').Switz.	46·14 N	6·04 E
167	Genichesk (gânê-chyĕsk') Sov. Un.	46·11 N	34·47 E
162	Genil (R.) (hå-nēl').....Sp.	37·15 N	4·05 W
117	Genoa (jen'ô-ȧ).....Ne.	41·26 N	97·43 W
	Genoa, see Genova		
107	Genoa City..Wi. (Milwaukee In.)	42·31 N	88·19 W
164	Genova (Genoa) (jĕn'ō-vä).....It.	44·23 N	9·52 E
164	Genova, Golfo di (G.) (gôl-fô-dē-jĕn'ō-vä).It.	44·10 N	8·45 E
122	Genovesa (I.) (ĕ's-lä-gĕ-nō-vĕ-sä) Ec.	0·08 N	90·15 W
155	Gent.....Bel.	51·05 N	3·40 E
158	Genthin (gĕn-tēn').....G.D.R.	52·24 N	12·10 E
163	Genzano di Roma (gzhĕnt-zá'-nô-dē-rô'-mä) It. (Rome In.)	41·43 N	12·49 E
204	Geographe B. (jē-ô-grăf')...Austl.	33·00 S	114·00 E
204	Geographic Chan. (jēō'gră-fĭk) Austl.	24·15 S	112·50 E
171	Geokchay (gĕ-ôk'chī)....Sov. Un.	40·40 N	47·40 E
121	George (L.) (jôr-ĭj).....Fl.	29·10 N	81·50 W
105	George (L.) (jôrj).....NY	43·40 N	73·30 W
113	George L. (jôrg) Can.-U. S. (Sault Ste. Marie In.)	46·26 N	84·09 W
107	George, L.....In. (Chicago In.)	41·31 N	87·17 W
217	George, L.....Ug.	0·02 N	30·25 E
202	Georges (R.)..Austl. (Sydney In.)	33·57 S	151·00 E
129	George Town.....Ba.	23·30 N	75·50 W
135	Georgetown (jôrj'toun).....Guy.	7·45 N	58·04 W
99	Georgetown (jôr-ĭj-toun).....Can.	46·11 N	62·32 W
100	Georgetown (jôrg-toun) Can. (Toronto In.)	43·39 N	79·56 W
106	Georgetown..Ct. (New York In.)	41·15 N	73·25 W
105	Georgetown.....De.	38·40 N	75·20 W
128	Georgetown.....Cayman Is.	19·20 N	81·20 W
104	Georgetown.....Il.	40·00 N	87·40 W
104	Georgetown.....Ky.	38·10 N	84·35 W
105	Georgetown.....Md.	39·25 N	75·55 W
99	Georgetown (jôrg-toun)..Ma. (In.)	42·43 N	71·00 W
121	Georgetown (jôr-ĭj-toun).....S. C.	33·22 N	79·17 W
119	Georgetown (jôrg-toun).....Tx.	30·37 N	97·40 W
105	George Washington Birthplace Natl. Mon. (jôrj wŏsh'ĭng-tŭn) Va.	38·10 N	77·00 W
117	George Washington Carver Natl. Mon. (jôrg wăsh-ĭng-tŭn kär'vēr).Mo.	36·58 N	94·21 W
118	George West.....Tx.	28·20 N	98·07 W
103	Georgia (State) (jôr'jĭ-ă)....U. S.	32·40 N	83·50 W
92	Georgia, Str. of.....Can.	49·20 N	124·00 W
112	Georgia, Str. of Wa. (Vancouver In.)	48·56 N	123·06 W
168	Georgian (S. S. R.).....Sov. Un.	42·17 N	43·00 E
96	Georgian B.....Can.	45·15 N	80·50 W
96	Georgian Bay Is. Natl. Pk....Can.	45·20 N	81·40 W
120	Georgiana (jôr-jē-ăn'ȧ).....Al.	31·39 N	86·44 W
204	Georgina (R.) (jôr-jē'nȧ)...Austl.	22·00 S	138·15 E
171	Georgiyevsk (gyôr-gyĕfsk') Sov. Un.	44·05 N	43·30 E
158	Gera (gā'rä).....G.D.R.	50·52 N	12·06 E
136	Geral, Serra (Mts.) (sĕr'rȧ zhȧ-räl').Braz.	28·30 S	51·00 W
153	Geral de Goiás, Serra (Mts.) (zhȧ-räl'-dĕ-gô-yȧ's).Braz.	14·22 S	45·40 W
204	Geraldton (jĕr'ăld-tŭn).....Austl.	28·40 S	114·35 E
91	Geraldton.....Can.	49·43 N	87·00 W
162	Gérgal (gĕr'gäl).....Sp.	37·08 N	2·29 W
108	Gering (gē'rĭng).....Ne.	41·49 N	103·41 W
159	Gerlachovka Pk.....Czech.	49·12 N	20·05 E
146	German Democratic Republic Eur.	53·30 N	12·30 E
104	Germantown (jûr'măn-toun)..Oh.	39·35 N	84·25 W
146	Germany, Federal Republic of (jûr'mȧ-nĭ).Eur.	51·45 N	8·30 E
213	Germiston (jûr'mĭs-tŭn)...S. Afr. (Johannesburg & Pretoria In.)	26·19 S	28·11 E
197	Gerona (hā-rō'nä).....Phil. (In.)	15·36 N	120·36 E
162	Gerona (hĕ-rō'nä).....Sp.	41·55 N	2·48 E
148	Gerrards Cross (jĕr'ards krŏs) Eng. (London In.)	51·34 N	0·33 W
163	Gers (R.) (zhĕr).....Fr.	43·25 N	0·30 E
149	Gersthofen (gĕrst-hō'fĕn) F.R.G. (Munich In.)	48·26 N	10·54 E
163	Getafe (hā-tä'fâ).Sp. (Madrid In.)	40·19 N	3·44 W
105	Gettysburg (gĕt'ĭs-bûrg).....Pa.	39·50 N	77·15 W
108	Gettysburg.....SD	45·01 N	99·59 W
161	Gevelsberg (gĕ-fĕls'bĕrgh) F.R.G. (Ruhr In.)	51·18 N	7·20 E
184	Ghāghra (R.).....India	27·19 N	81·22 E
209	Ghana (gän'ä).....Afr.	8·00 N	2·00 W
212	Ghanzi (gän'zē).....Bots.	21·30 S	22·00 E
210	Ghardaïa (gär-dä'ē-ä).....Alg.	32·29 N	3·38 E
184	Gharo.....Pak.	24·50 N	68·35 E
210	Ghāt.....Libya	24·52 N	10·16 E
211	Ghazāl, Bahr al- (R.).....Sud.	9·11 N	29·37 E
215	Ghazal, Bahr el (R.) (bär ĕl ghä-zäl').Chad.	14·30 N	17·00 E
151	Ghazaouet.....Alg.	35·19 N	1·09 W
184	Ghaznī (gŭz'nê).....Afg.	33·43 N	68·18 E
183	Ghazzah (Gaza) Gaza Strip (Palestine In.)	31·30 N	34·29 E
159	Gheorghieni.....Rom.	46·48 N	25·30 E
159	Gherla (gĕr'lä).....Rom.	47·01 N	23·55 E
100	Ghost Lake....Can. (Calgary In.)	51·15 N	114·46 W
210	Ghudāmis.....Libya	30·07 N	9·26 E
164	Giannutri, I. di (jän-nōō'trē)...It.	42·15 N	11·06 E
129	Gibara (hē-bä'rä).....Cuba	21·05 N	76·10 W
212	Gibeon (gĭb'ê-ŭn).....S. W. Afr.	24·45 S	16·40 E
162	Gibraleón (hē-brä-lā-ōn').....Sp.	37·24 N	7·00 W
151	Gibraltar (hē-bräl-tä'r).....Eur.	36·08 N	5·22 W
162	Gibraltar, Bay of.....Sp.	35·04 N	5·10 W
162	Gibraltar, Str. of.....Afr.-Eur.	35·55 N	5·45 W
104	Gibson City (gĭb'sŭn).....Il.	40·25 N	88·20 W
204	Gibson Des.....Austl.	24·45 S	123·15 E
106	Gibson Island.Md. (Baltimore In.)	39·05 N	76·26 W
117	Gibson Res.....Ok.	36·07 N	95·08 W
119	Giddings (gĭd'ĭngz).....Tx.	30·11 N	96·55 W
117	Gideon (gĭd'ê-ŭn).....Mo.	36·27 N	89·56 W
160	Gien (zhē-ăN').....Fr.	47·43 N	2·37 E
158	Giessen (gēs'sĕn).....F.R.G.	50·35 N	8·40 E
100	Giffard (zhē-färd') Can. (Quebec In.)	46·51 N	71·12 W
195	Gifu (gē'fōō).....Jap.	35·25 N	136·45 E
112	Gig Harbor (gĭg).Wa. (Seattle In.)	47·20 N	122·36 W
164	Giglio, I. di (jēl'yō).....It.	42·23 N	10·55 E
162	Gigüela (R.) (hê-gā'lä).....Sp.	39·53 N	2·54 W
162	Gijón (hê-hōn').....Sp.	43·33 N	5·37 W
115	Gila (R.) (hē'lȧ).....Az.	32·41 N	113·50 W
115	Gila Bend.....Az.	32·59 N	112·41 W
115	Gila Bend Ind. Res.....Az.	33·02 N	112·48 W
115	Gila Cliff Dwellings Natl. Mon. NM	33·15 N	108·20 W
115	Gila River Ind. Res.....Az.	33·11 N	112·38 W
109	Gilbert (gĭl'bērt).....Mn.	47·27 N	92·29 W
205	Gilbert (R.) (gĭl-bĕrt).....Austl.	17·15 S	142·09 E
92	Gilbert, Mt.....Can.	50·51 N	124·20 W
198	Gilbert Is.....Oceania	1·30 S	173·00 E
213	Gilboa, Mt. (gĭl-bôȧ) S. Afr. (Natal In.)	29·13 S	30·17 E
92	Gilford I. (gĭl'fērd).....Can.	50·45 N	126·25 W
184	Gilgit (gĭl'gĭt).....Pak.	35·58 N	73·48 E
92	Gil I. (gĭl).....Can.	53·13 N	129·15 W
204	Gillen (I.) (jĭl'ĕn).....Austl.	26·15 S	125·15 E
117	Gillett (jĭ-lĕt').....Ar.	34·07 N	91·22 W
111	Gillette.....Wy.	44·17 N	105·30 W
148	Gillingham (gĭl'ĭng ăm) Eng. (London In.)	51·23 N	0·33 E
104	Gilman (gĭl'măn).....Il.	40·45 N	87·55 W
113	Gilman Hot Springs Ca. (Los Angeles In.)	33·49 N	116·57 W
119	Gilmer (gĭl'mēr).....Tx.	32·43 N	94·57 W
106	Gilmore (gĭl'môr).Ga. (Atlanta In.)	33·51 N	84·29 W
114	Gilroy (gĭl-roi').....Ca.	37·00 N	121·34 W
197	Giluwe, Mt.....Pap. N. Gui.	6·04 S	144·00 E
95	Gimli (gĭm'lē).....Can.	50·39 N	97·00 W
160	Gimone (R.) (zhē-mōn').....Fr.	43·26 N	0·36 E
211	Ginir.....Eth.	7·13 N	40·44 E
164	Ginosa (jē-nō'zä).....It.	40·35 N	16·48 E
162	Ginzo (hēn-thō').....Sp.	42·03 N	7·43 W
164	Gioia del Colle (jô'yä dĕl kôl'lā).It.	40·48 N	16·55 E
135	Gi-Paraná (R.) (zhē-pä-rä-ná') Braz.	9·33 S	61·35 W
117	Girard (jĭ-rärd').....Ks.	37·30 N	94·50 W
134	Girardot (hē-rär-dōt')...Col. (In.)	4·19 N	75·47 W
171	Giresun (ghĕr'ĕ-sōōn').....Tur.	40·55 N	38·20 E

ăt; finăl; rāte; senâte; ärm; ȧsk; sofȧ; fâre; ch-choose; dh-as th in other; bē; êvent; bĕt; recĕnt; cratēr; g-go; gh-guttural g; bĭt; ĭ-short neutral; rīde; ĸ-guttural k as ch in German ich;

Page	Name	Pronunciation	Region	Lat. ° ′	Long. ° ′
184	Giridih	(jē'rē-dē)	India	24.12 N	81.18 E
160	Gironde (Est.)	(zhē-rônd')	Fr.	45.31 N	1.00 W
154	Girvan	(gûr'vǎn)	Scot.	55.15 N	5.01 W
205	Gisborne	(gǐz'bûrn)	N. Z. (In.)	38.40 S	178.08 E
217	Gisenyi		Rw.	1.43 S	29.15 E
160	Gisors	(zhē-zôr')	Fr.	49.19 N	1.47 E
216	Gitambo		Zaire	4.21 S	24.45 E
212	Gitega		Burundi	3.39 S	30.05 E
165	Giurgui	(jōōr'jōō)	Rom.	43.53 N	25.58 E
160	Givet	(zhē-vě')	Fr.	50.80 N	4.47 E
165	Givors	(zhē-vôr')	Fr.	45.35 N	4.46 E
173	Gizhiga	(gē'zhǐ-gà)	Sov. Un.	61.59 N	160.46 E
159	Gizycko	(gǐ'zhǐ-ko)	Pol.	54.03 N	21.48 E
165	Gjinokastër		Alb.	40.04 N	20.10 E
156	Gjøvik	(gyû'věk)	Nor.	60.47 N	10.36 E
149	Glabeek-Zuurbemde		Bel. (Brussels In.)	50.52 N	4.59 E
99	Glace Bay	(glās bā)	N.S.	46.12 N	59.57 W
101	Glacier Bay Natl. Mon.	(glā'shēr)	Ak.	58.40 N	136.50 W
93	Glacier Natl. Park		Can.	51.45 N	117.35 W
110	Glacier Pk.		Wa.	48.07 N	121.10 W
112	Glacier Pt.		Can. (Seattle In.)	48.24 N	123.59 W
161	Gladbeck	(glåd'běk)	F.R.G. (Ruhr In.)	51.35 N	6.59 E
218	Gladdeklipkop		S. Afr. (Johannesburg & Pretoria In.)	24.17 S	29.36 E
203	Gladstone	(glåd'stōn)	Austl.	23.45 S	150.00 E
203	Gladstone		Austl.	33.15 S	138.20 E
102	Gladstone		Can.	50.15 N	98.50 W
109	Gladstone		Mi.	45.50 N	87.04 W
106	Gladstone		NJ (New York In.)	40.43 N	74.39 W
112	Gladstone		Or. (Portland In.)	45.23 N	122.36 W
104	Gladwin	(glåd'wǐn)	Mi.	44.00 N	84.25 W
104	Glamoč	(gläm'ŏch)	Yugo.	44.03 N	16.51 E
158	Glarus	(glä'rōōs)	Switz.	47.02 N	9.03 E
120	Glasgow	(glås'gō)	Ky.	37.00 N	85.55 W
117	Glasgow		Mo.	39.14 N	92.48 W
111	Glasgow		Mt.	48.12 N	106.39 W
154	Glasgow	(glås'gō)	Scot.	55.54 N	4.25 W
107	Glassport	(glås'pōrt)	Pa. (Pittsburgh In.)	40.19 N	79.53 W
158	Glauchau	(glou'кou)	G.D.R.	50.51 N	12.28 E
173	Glazov	(glä'zôf)	Sov. Un.	58.05 N	52.52 E
158	Glda R.	(g'l'dá)	Pol.	53.27 N	16.52 E
148	Glen	(glen)	Eng.	52.44 N	0.18 W
160	Glénans, Iles de (Is.)	(ēl-dě-glä-nän')	Fr.	47.43 N	4.42 W
106	Glen Burnie	(bûr'nè)	Md. (Baltimore In.)	39.10 N	76.38 W
115	Glen Canyon Dam	(glen kǎn'yǔn)	Az.	36.57 N	111.25 W
113	Glen Carbon	(kär'bǒn)	Il. (St. Louis In.)	38.45 N	89.59 W
107	Glencoe		Il. (Chicago In.)	42.08 N	87.45 W
109	Glencoe	(glěn'kō)	Mn.	44.44 N	94.07 W
213	Glencoe	(glěn-cō)	S. Afr. (Natal In.)	28.14 S	30.09 E
106	Glen Cove	(kōv)	NY (New York In.)	40.51 N	73.38 W
115	Glendale	(glěn'dāl)	Az.	33.30 N	112.15 W
113	Glendale		Ca. (Los Angeles In.)	34.09 N	118.15 W
107	Glendale		Oh. (Cincinnati In.)	31.16 N	84.22 W
111	Glendive	(glěn'dǐv)	Mt.	47.08 N	104.41 W
111	Glendo		Wy.	42.32 N	104.54 W
113	Glendora	(glěn-dō'rá)	Ca. (Los Angeles In.)	34.08 N	117.52 W
203	Glenelg (R.)		Austl.	37.20 S	141.30 E
107	Glen Ellyn	(glěn ěl'-lěn)	Il. (Chicago In.)	41.53 N	88.04 W
203	Glen Innes	(ǐn'ěs)	Austl.	29.45 S	152.02 E
119	Glenmora	(glěn-mō'rá)	La.	30.58 N	92.36 W
110	Glenns Ferry	(fěr'ǐ)	Id.	42.58 N	115.21 W
121	Glenville	(glěn'vǐl)	Ga.	31.55 N	81.56 W
106	Glen Olden	(ōl'd'n)	Pa. (Philadelphia In.)	39.54 N	75.17 W
111	Glenrock	(glěn'rǒk)	Wy.	42.50 N	105.53 W
105	Glens Falls	(glěnz fôlz)	NY	43.20 N	73.40 W
107	Glenshaw	(glěn'shô)	Pa. (Pittsburgh In.)	40.33 N	79.57 W
108	Glen Ullin	(glěn'ŭl'ǐn)	ND	46.47 N	101.49 W
112	Glen Valley		Can. (Vancouver In.)	49.09 N	122.30 W
107	Glenview	(glěn'vū)	Il. (Chicago In.)	42.04 N	87.48 W
108	Glenwood		Ia.	41.03 N	95.44 W
108	Glenwood		Mn.	45.39 N	95.23 W
115	Glenwood Springs		Co.	39.35 N	107.20 W
149	Glienicke	(glē'nē-kě)	G.D.R. (Berlin In.)	52.38 N	13.19 E
149	Glinde	(glēn'dě)	F.R.G. (Hamburg In.)	53.32 N	10.13 E
156	Glittertinden (Mtn.)		Nor.	61.39 N	8.12 E
159	Gliwice	(gwǐ-wǐt'sě)	Pol.	50.18 N	18.40 E
115	Globe	(glōb)	Az.	33.20 N	110.50 W
167	Globino	(glôb'ē-nô)	Sov. Un.	49.22 N	33.17 E
158	Głogow	(glō'goov)	Pol.	51.40 N	16.04 E
156	Glomma (R.)	(glômmä)	Nor.	61.22 N	11.02 E
156	Glommen (R.)	(glôm'ěn)	Nor.	60.03 N	11.15 E
149	Glonn	(glônn)	F.R.G. (Munich In.)	47.59 N	11.52 E
213	Glorieuses, Îles (Is.)		Afr.	11.28 S	47.50 E
148	Glossop	(glŏs'ŭp)	Eng.	53.26 N	1.57 W
154	Gloster	(glŏs'tēr)	Ms.	31.10 N	91.00 W
121	Gloucester	(glŏs'tēr)	Eng.	51.54 N	2.11 W
99	Gloucester		Ma. (In.)	42.37 N	70.40 W
106	Gloucester City		NJ (Philadelphia In.)	39.53 N	75.08 W
104	Glouster	(glou'stēr)	Oh.	39.35 N	82.05 W
99	Glover I.	(glŭv'ēr)	Can.	48.44 N	57.45 W
105	Gloversville	(glŭv'ērz-vǐl)	NY	43.05 N	74.20 W
99	Glovertown	(glŭv'ēr-toun)	Can.	48.41 N	54.02 W
166	Glubokoye	(glōō-bô-kō'yě)	Sov. Un.	55.08 N	27.44 E
149	Glückstadt	(glük-shtät)	F.R.G. (Hamburg In.)	53.47 N	9.25 E
167	Glukhov	(glōō'кôf')	Sov. Un.	51.42 N	33.52 E
167	Glushkovo	(glōōsh'kô-vō)	Sov. Un.	51.21 N	34.43 E
158	Gmünden	(g'mōōn'děn)	Aus.	47.57 N	13.47 E
159	Gniezno	(g'nyáz'nô)	Pol.	52.32 N	17.34 E
165	Gnjilane	(gnyě'lä-ně)	Yugo.	42.28 N	21.27 E
185	Goa (Ter.)	(gō'á)	India	15.45 N	74.00 E
126	Goascorán	(gō-äs'kô-rän)	Hond.	13.37 N	87.43 W
211	Goba	(gō'bä)	Eth.	7.17 N	39.58 E
212	Gobabis	(gō-bä'bǐs)	S. W. Afr.	22.25 S	18.50 E
188	Gobi or Shamo (Des.)	(gō'be)	Mong.	43.29 N	103.15 E
112	Goble	(gō'b'l)	Or. (Portland In.)	46.01 N	122.53 W
161	Goch	(gôк)	F.R.G. (Ruhr In.)	51.35 N	6.10 E
184	Godāvari (R.)	(gō-dä'vǔ-rē)	India	17.42 N	81.15 E
204	Goddards Soak (Swp.)	(gŏd'árdz)	Austl.	31.20 S	123.30 E
104	Goderich	(gŏd'rǐch)	Can.	43.45 N	81.45 W
113	Godfrey	(gŏd'frě)	Il. (St. Louis In.)	38.57 N	90.12 W
75	Godhavn	(gōdh'hȧvn)	Grnld.	69.15 N	53.30 W
95	Gods (R.)	(gŏdz)	Can.	55.17 N	93.35 W
95	Gods Lake		Can.	54.40 N	94.09 W
75	Godthåb	(gôt'hōōb)	Grnld.	64.10 N	51.32 W
189	Godwin Austen, Mt.	(gōd'wǐn ôs'těn)	Pak.	36.06 N	76.38 E
97	Goéland, Lac au (L.)		Can.	49.47 N	76.41 W
114	Goffs	(gŏfs)	Ca.	34.57 N	115.06 W
109	Gogebic (L.)	(gô-gē'bǐk)	Mi.	46.24 N	89.25 W
109	Gogebic Ra.		Mi.	46.37 N	89.48 W
149	Goggingen	(gŭg'gěn-gěn)	F.R.G. (Munich In.)	48.21 N	10.53 E
157	Gogland (I.)		Sov. Un.	60.04 N	26.55 E
215	Gogonou		Benin	10.50 N	2.50 E
124	Gogorrón	(gō-gô-rōn')	Mex.	21.51 N	100.54 W
135	Goiânia	(gō-vä'nyä)	Braz.	16.41 S	48.57 W
135	Goiás	(gō-vá's)	Braz.	15.57 S	50.10 W
135	Goiás (State)		Braz.	12.35 S	48.38 W
149	Goirle		Neth. (Amsterdam In.)	51.31 N	5.06 E
171	Göksu (R.)	(gûk'sōō')	Tur.	36.40 N	33.30 E
156	Göl	(gül)	Nor.	60.58 N	8.54 E
121	Golax	(gō'läks)	Va.	36.41 N	80.56 W
148	Golcar	(gōl'kär)	Eng.	53.38 N	1.52 W
117	Golconda	(gŏl-kǒn'dá)	Il.	37.21 N	88.32 W
159	Goldap	(gōl'dăp)	Pol.	54.17 N	22.17 E
93	Golden		Can.	51.18 N	116.58 W
116	Golden		Co.	39.44 N	105.15 W
110	Goldendale	(gōl'děn-dāl)	Wa.	45.49 N	120.48 W
112	Golden Gate (Str.)	(gōl'děn gāt)	Ca. (San Francisco In.)	37.48 N	122.32 W
92	Golden Hinde	(hǐnd)	Can.	49.40 N	125.45 W
106	Golden's Bridge		NY (New York In.)	41.17 N	73.41 W
113	Golden Valley. Mn.		(Minneapolis, St. Paul In.)	44.58 N	93.23 W
114	Goldfield	(gōld'fēld)	Nv.	37.42 N	117.15 W
122	Gold Hill (Mtn.)		C. Z. (In.)	9.03 N	79.08 W
112	Gold Mtn.	(gōld)	Wa. (Seattle In.)	47.33 N	122.48 W
121	Goldsboro	(gōldz-bûr'ô)	NC	35.23 N	77.59 W
118	Goldthwaite	(gōld'thwāt)	Tx.	31.27 N	98.34 W
158	Goleniów	(gô-lě-nyûf')	Pol.	53.33 N	14.51 E
173	Golets-Purpula, Gol'tsy (Mtn.)		Sov. Un.	59.08 N	115.22 E
127	Golfito	(gôl-fē'tō)	C. R.	8.40 N	83.12 W
	Golfo Dulce, see Izabal, L.				
119	Goliad	(gō-lǐ-ăd')	Tx.	28.40 N	97.12 W
197	Golo	(gō'lō)	Phil. (In.)	13.38 N	120.17 E
164	Golo (R.)		Fr.	42.28 N	9.18 E
167	Golovchino	(gō-lôf'chē-nō)	Sov. Un.	50.34 N	35.52 E
165	Golyamo Konare	(gō'lä-mō-kō'nä-rě)	Bul.	42.16 N	24.33 E
149	Golzow	(gōl'tsōv)	G.D.R. (Berlin In.)	52.17 N	12.36 E
217	Gombari	(gōōm-bä-rê)	Zaire	2.45 N	29.00 E
215	Gombe		Nig.	10.19 N	11.02 E
166	Gomel	(go'měl)	Sov. Un.	52.20 N	31.03 E
166	Gomel' (Oblast)		Sov. Un.	52.18 N	29.00 E
210	Gomera I.	(gō-mā'rä)	Can. Is.	28.00 N	18.01 W
118	Gomez Farías	(gō'mǎz fä-rē'ás)	Mex.	24.59 N	101.02 W
118	Gómez Palacio	(pä-lä'syō)	Mex.	25.35 N	103.30 W
129	Gonaïves	(gō-nà-ēv')	Hai.	19.25 N	72.45 W
129	Gonaïves, Golfe des (G.)	(gō-nà-ēv')	Hai.	19.20 N	73.20 W
129	Gonâve, Ile De La (I.)	(gō-nàv')	Hai.	18.50 N	73.30 W
184	Gonda		India	27.13 N	82.00 E
184	Gondal		India	22.02 N	70.47 E
211	Gonder		Eth.	12.39 N	37.30 E
161	Gonesse	(gō-něs')	Fr. (Paris In.)	48.59 N	2.28 E
215	Goniri		Nig.	11.30 N	12.13 E
195	Gonō (R.)	(gō'nō)	Jap.	35.00 N	132.25 E
100	Gonor	(gō'nôr)	Can. (Winnepeg In.)	50.04 N	96.57 W
213	Gonubie	(gōn'ōō-bē)	S. Afr. (Natal In.)	32.56 S	28.02 E
124	Gonzales	(gôn-zá'lěs)	Mex.	22.47 N	98.26 W
119	Gonzales	(gôn-zä'lěz)	Tx.	29.31 N	97.25 W
136	González Catán	(gôn-zä'lěz-kä-tä'n)	Arg. (Buenos Aires In.)	34.31 S	58.39 W
92	Good Hope Mtn.		Can.	51.09 N	124.10 W
212	Good Hope, C. of	(kāp ov gŏŏd hōp)	S. Afr. (In.)	34.21 S	18.29 E
110	Gooding	(gŏŏd'ǐng)	Id.	42.55 N	114.43 W
104	Goodland	(gŏŏd'lånd)	In.	40.50 N	87.17 W
116	Goodland		Ks.	39.19 N	101.43 W
212	Goodwood	(gŏŏd'wŏŏd)	S. Afr. (In.)	33.54 S	18.33 E
148	Goole	(gōōl)	Eng.	53.42 N	0.52 W
108	Goose (R.)		ND	47.40 N	97.41 W
91	Goose Bay		Can.	53.19 N	60.33 W
111	Gooseberry Cr.	(gōōs-běr'ǐ)	Wy.	44.04 N	108.35 W
111	Goose Cr.	(gōōs)	Id.	42.07 N	113.53 W
110	Goose L.	(gōōs)	Ca.	41.56 N	120.35 W
184	Gorakhpur	(gō'rŭk-poor)	India	26.45 N	82.39 E
128	Gorda, Punta (Pt.)	(pōō'n-tä-gôr-dä)	Cuba	22.25 N	82.10 W
128	Gorda Cay	(gôr'dä)	Ba.	26.05 N	77.30 W
100	Gordon	(gôr'dǔn)	Can. (Winnipeg In.)	50.00 N	97.20 W
108	Gordon		Ne.	42.47 N	102.14 W
211	Gore	(gō'rě)	Eth.	8.12 N	35.34 E
186	Gorgān		Iran	36.44 N	54.30 E
164	Gorgona (I.)	(gôr-gō'nä)	It.	43.27 N	9.55 E
171	Gori	(gō'rě)	Sov. Un.	42.00 N	44.08 E
149	Gorinchem	(gō'rǐn-кěm)	Neth. (Amsterdam In.)	51.50 N	4.59 E
148	Goring	(gôr'ǐng)	Eng. (London In.)	51.30 N	1.08 W
164	Gorizia	(gō-rē'tsē-yä)	It.	44.56 N	13.40 E
170	Gorki	(gôr'kē)	Sov. Un.	56.15 N	44.05 E
170	Gor'kovskoye		Sov. Un.	56.38 N	43.40 E
166	Gor'kovskoye Vdkhr. (Res.)	(gôr'kôf-skô-yě)	Sov. Un.	57.38 N	41.18 E
159	Gorlice	(gôr-lē'tsě)	Pol.	49.38 N	21.11 E
158	Görlitz	(gûr'lǐts)	G.D.R.	51.10 N	15.01 E
167	Gorlovka	(gôr'lôf-kä)	Sov. Un.	48.17 N	38.03 E
118	Gorman	(gôr'măn)	Tx.	32.13 N	98.40 W
165	Gorna-Oryakhovitsa		Bul.	43.08 N	25.40 E
165	Gornji Milanovac	(gôrn'yē-mē'la-nô-väts)	Yugo.	44.02 N	20.29 E
172	Gorno-Altay Aut. Oblast		Sov. Un.	51.00 N	86.00 E
172	Gorno-Altaysk	(gôr'nǔ'ŭl-tīsk')	Sov. Un.	52.28 N	82.45 E
159	Gorodënka	(gō-rô-děn'kä)	Sov. Un.	48.40 N	25.30 E
170	Gorodets (Res.)		Sov. Un.	57.00 N	43.55 E
174	Gorodishche	(gō-rô'dǐsh-chě)	Sov. Un. (Urals In.)	57.57 N	57.03 E
167	Gorodnya	(gō-rôd'nyä)	Sov. Un.	51.54 N	31.31 E
159	Gorodok	(gō-rô-dôk')	Sov. Un.	49.37 N	23.40 E
166	Gorodok		Sov. Un.	55.27 N	29.58 E
172	Gorodok		Sov. Un.	50.30 N	103.58 E
196	Gorontalo	(gō-rôn-tä'lo)	Indon.	0.40 N	123.04 E
159	Goryn' R.	(gō'rěn')	Sov. Un.	50.55 N	26.07 E
158	Gorzow Wielkopolski	(gō-zhōōv'vyěl-ko-pōl'skě)	Pol.	53.44 N	15.15 E
104	Goshen	(gō'shěn)	In.	41.35 N	85.50 W
107	Goshen		Ky. (Louisville In.)	38.24 N	85.34 W
106	Goshen		NY (New York In.)	41.24 N	74.19 W
107	Goshen		Oh. (Cincinnati In.)	39.14 N	84.09 W
115	Goshute Ind. Res.	(gō-shōōt')	Ut.	39.50 N	114.00 W
158	Goslar	(gôs'lär)	F.R.G.	51.55 N	10.25 E
135	Gospa (R.)	(gôs-pä)	Ven.	9.43 N	64.23 W
164	Gospić	(gôs'pēch)	Yugo.	44.31 N	15.03 E
165	Gostivar	(gos'tē-vär)	Yugo.	41.46 N	20.58 E
159	Gostynin	(gôs-tē'nǐn)	Pol.	52.24 N	19.30 E
156	Göta alv (R.)	(gûtä äěl'v)	Swe.	58.11 N	12.03 E
156	Göta Can.	(yû'tä)	Swe.	58.35 N	15.24 E
156	Göteborg	(yû'tě-bôrgh)	Swe.	57.39 N	11.56 E
215	Gotera	(gō-tā'rä)	Sal.	13.41 N	88.06 W
158	Gotha	(gō'tá)	G.D.R.	50.57 N	10.43 E
116	Gothenburg	(gôth'ěn-bûrg)	Ne.	40.57 N	100.08 W
156	Gotland (I.)		Swe.	57.35 N	17.35 E
195	Gotō-Rettō (Is.)	(gō'tō rět'tō)	Jap.	33.06 N	128.54 E
157	Gotska Sandön (I.)		Swe.	58.24 N	19.15 E
158	Göttingen	(gût'ǐng-ěn)	F.R.G.	51.32 N	9.57 E
149	Gouda	(gou'dä)	Neth. (Amsterdam In.)	52.00 N	4.42 E
220	Gough (I.)	(gôf)	Atl. O.	40.00 S	10.00 W
91	Gouin, Rés.		Can.	48.15 N	74.15 W
96	Goulais	(gōō-lā')	Can.	46.45 N	84.10 W
203	Goulburn	(gōōl'bûrn)	Austl.	34.47 S	149.40 E
214	Goumbati (Mtn.)		Senegal	13.08 N	12.06 W
214	Goumbou	(gōōm-bōō')	Mali	14.59 N	7.27 W
215	Gouna		Cam.	8.32 N	13.34 E
210	Goundam	(gōōn-dän')	Mali	16.29 N	3.37 W
210	Gouré	(gōō-rā')	Niger	13.53 N	10.44 E
105	Gouverneur	(gŭv-ēr-nōōr')	NY	44.20 N	75.25 W
94	Govenlock	(gô-wěn'dä)	Can.	49.15 N	109.48 W
136	Governador Ilhado (I.)	(gô-věr-nä-dō'r-ē-lá'dô)	Braz. (Rio de Janeiro In.)	22.48 S	43.13 W
136	Governador Portela	(pōr-tě'lä)	Braz. (Rio de Janeiro In.)	22.28 S	43.30 W
135	Governador Valadares	(vä-lä-dä'rěs)	Braz.	18.47 S	41.45 W
129	Governor's Harbour		Ba.	25.15 N	76.15 W
105	Gowanda	(gô-wǒn'dá)	NY	42.30 N	78.55 W
136	Goya	(gō'yä)	Arg.	29.06 S	59.12 W
148	Goyt (R.)	(goit)	Eng.	53.19 N	2.03 W
212	Graaff-Reinet	(gräf'rī'nět)	S. Afr.	32.10 S	24.40 E
164	Gracac	(grä'chäts)	Yugo.	44.16 N	15.50 E
165	Gračanico		Yugo.	44.42 N	18.19 E
120	Graceville	(grās'vǐl)	Fl.	30.57 N	85.30 W
108	Graceville		Mn.	45.33 N	96.25 W
126	Gracias	(grä'sē-äs)	Hond.	14.35 N	88.37 W
127	Gracias a Dios, Cabo (C.)	(kä'sē-äs-syäs-ä-dyō's)	Hond.	15.00 N	83.13 W
210	Graciosa I.	(grä-syō'sä)	Açores (In.)	39.07 N	27.30 W
165	Gradačac	(gra-dä'chats)	Yugo.	44.50 N	18.28 E
162	Gradelos	(grä-dě-lôs)	Sp.	42.38 N	5.15 W
167	Gradizhsk	(grä-dēzhsk')	Sov. Un.	49.12 N	33.06 E
162	Grado	(grä'dō)	Sp.	43.24 N	6.04 W
149	Gräfelfing	(grä'fěl-fēng)	F.R.G. (Munich In.)	48.07 N	11.27 E
149	Grafing	(grä'fěng)	F.R.G. (Munich In.)	48.03 N	11.58 E
203	Grafton	(graf'tǒn)	Austl.	29.38 S	153.05 E
113	Grafton		Il. (St. Louis In.)	38.58 N	90.26 W
99	Grafton		Ma. (In.)	42.13 N	71.41 W

286 Grafton — Greenwood PRONOUNCING INDEX

Page	Name Pronunciation Region	Lat. °′	Long. °′
108	Grafton . . . ND	48·24 N	97·25 W
107	Grafton . . . Oh. (Cleveland In.)	41·16 N	82·04 W
105	Grafton . . . WV	39·20 N	80·00 W
163	Gragnano (grän-yä'nō) It. (Naples In.)	40·27 N	14·32 E
121	Graham (grā'ăm) . . . NC	36·03 N	79·23 W
116	Graham . . . Tx.	33·07 N	98·34 W
112	Graham . . . Wa. (Seattle In.)	47·03 N	122·18 W
90	Graham (I.) . . . Can.	53·50 N	132·40 W
213	Grahamstown (grā'ăms'toun) S. Afr. (Natal In.)	33·19 S	26·33 E
161	Graian Alps (Mts.) (grā'yăn) Fr.-It.	45·17 N	6·52 E
135	Grajaú (grȧ-zhȧ-ōō') . . . Braz.	5·59 S	46·03 W
135	Grajaú (R.) . . . Braz.	4·24 S	46·04 W
159	Grajewo (grä-yā'vo) . . . Pol.	53·38 N	22·28 E
137	Grama, Serra de (Mtn.) (sĕ'r-rä-dĕ-grá'mȧ) Braz. (Rio de Janeiro In.)	23·42 S	42·28 W
165	Gramada (grä'mä-dä) . . . Bul.	43·46 N	22·41 E
149	Gramatneusiedl. Aus. (Vienna In.)	48·02 N	16·29 E
164	Grammichele (gräm-mē-kĕ'lā) . . It.	37·15 N	14·40 E
154	Grampian Mts. (grăm'pĭ-ăn) . Scot.	56·30 N	4·55 W
126	Granada (grä-nä'dhä) . . . Nic.	11·55 N	85·58 W
162	Granada (grä-nä'dä) . . . Sp.	37·13 N	3·37 W
136	Gran Bajo (Pln.) (grȧn'bä'kŏ) . Arg.	47·35 S	68·45 W
119	Granbury (grăn'bĕr-ĭ) . . . Tx.	32·26 N	97·45 W
105	Granby (grăn'bĭ) . . . Can.	45·30 N	72·40 W
117	Granby . . . Mo.	36·54 N	94·15 W
116	Granby (L.) . . . Co.	40·07 N	105·40 W
210	Gran Canaria I. (grän'kä-nä'rê-ä) . Can. Is.	27·39 N	15·39 W
136	Gran Chaco (Reg.) (grȧn'chȧ'kŏ) Arg.-Par.	25·30 S	62·15 W
109	Grand (I.) . . . Mi.	46·37 N	86·38 W
98	Grand (L.) . . . Can.	45·17 N	67·42 W
98	Grand (L.) . . . Can.	66·15 N	45·59 W
97	Grand (R.) . . . Can.	43·45 N	80·20 W
104	Grand (R.) . . . Mi.	42·58 N	85·13 W
117	Grand (R.) . . . Mo.	39·50 N	93·52 W
108	Grand (R.) . . . SD	45·40 N	101·55 W
108	Grand (R.), North Fork . . . SD	45·52 N	102·49 W
108	Grand (R.), South Fork . . . SD	45·38 N	102·56 W
128	Grand Bahama (I.) . . . Ba.	26·35 N	78·30 W
99	Grand Bank (grănd băngk) . . Can.	47·06 N	55·47 W
214	Grand Bassam (gräN bȧ-säN') Ivory Coast	5·12 N	3·44 W
127	Grand Bourg (gräN bōōr') Guad. (In.)	15·54 N	61·20 W
129	Grand Caicos (I.) (grănd kä-ē'kōs) Turks & Caicos Is.	21·45 N	71·50 W
154	Grand Canal . . . Ire.	53·21 N	7·15 W
	Grand Canal, see Yün Ho		
115	Grand Canyon (grănd kăn'yŭn) Az.	36·05 N	112·10 W
115	Grand Canyon . . . Az.	35·50 N	113·16 W
115	Grand Canyon Natl. Park . . . Az.	36·15 N	112·20 W
128	Grand Cayman (I.) (kă'măn) Cayman Is.	19·15 N	81·15 W
110	Grand Coulee Dam (kōō'lē) . . Wa.	47·58 N	119·28 W
137	Grande (R.) . . Chili (Santiago In.)	35·25 S	70·14 W
125	Grande (R.) . . . Mex.	17·37 N	96·41 W
137	Grande (R.) Ur. (Buenos Aires In.)	33·19 S	57·15 W
138	Grande, Boca (B.) (bä-ē'ä-grȧn'dĕ) . Arg.	50·45 S	68·00 W
135	Grande, Boca (Est.) (bŏ'kä-grä'n-dĕ) . Ven.	8·46 N	60·17 W
122	Grande, Ciri (R.) (sē'rē-grȧ'n'dĕ) . Pan. (In.)	8·55 N	80·04 W
138	Grande, Cuchilla (Mts.) (kōō-chē'l-yä) . Ur.	33·00 S	55·15 W
137	Grande, Ilha (I.) (grän'dĕ) Braz. (Rio de Janeiro In.)	23·11 S	44·14 W
134	Grande, Rio (R.) . . . Bol.	16·49 S	63·19 W
135	Grande, Rio (R.) . . . Braz.	19·48 S	49·54 W
102	Grande, Rio (R.) (Bravo del Norte, Rio) (grän'dā) . Mex.-U. S.	26·50 N	99·10 W
136	Grande, Salinas (F.) (sä-lē'näs) . Arg.	29·45 S	65·00 W
135	Grande, Salto (Falls) (säl-tô) . Braz.	16·18 S	39·38 W
129	Grande Cayemite, Ile (I.) . . . Hai.	18·45 N	73·45 W
213	Grande Comore (grä'n-dĕ-kô-mô-rĕ) . Comoro Is.	11·44 S	42·38 E
126	Grande de Otoro (grän'dȧ dā ô-tō'rō) . . . Hond.	14·42 N	88·21 W
100	Grande Pointe (grănd point') Can. (Winnipeg In.)	49·47 N	97·03 W
93	Grande Prairie (prâr'ĭ) . . . Can.	55·10 N	118·48 W
127	Grande R. (grän'dĕ) . . . Nic.	13·01 N	84·21 W
210	Grand Erg Occidental (Dunes) Alg.	29·37 N	6·04 E
129	Grande Rivière du Nord (rē-vyâr' dü nôr') . Hai.	19·35 N	72·10 W
110	Grande Ronde R. (rônd') . . . Or.	45·32 N	117·52 W
114	Gran Desierto (Des.) (grän-dĕ-syĕ'r-tô) . Mex.	32·14 N	114·28 W
127	Grande Soufriere Vol. (sōō-frē-âr') Guad. (In.)	16·06 N	61·42 W
127	Grande Terre I. (târ') . Guad. (In.)	16·28 N	61·13 W
127	Grande Vigie, Pointe de la (Pt.) (gränd vē-gē') . Grande Terre (In.)	16·32 N	61·25 W
99	Grand Falls (fôlz) . . . Can.	48·56 N	55·40 W
95	Grandfather, Mt. (grănd-fä-thēr) NC	36·07 N	81·48 W
116	Grandfield (grănd'fēld) . . . Ok.	34·13 N	98·39 W
93	Grand Forks (fôrks) . . . Can.	49·02 N	118·27 W
108	Grand Forks . . . ND	47·55 N	97·05 W
104	Grand Haven (hā'v'n) . . . Mi.	43·05 N	86·15 W
116	Grand Island (ī'lănd) . . . Ne.	40·56 N	98·20 W
107	Grand I. . . . NY (Buffalo In.)	43·03 N	78·58 W
115	Grand Junction (jŭngk'shŭn) . . Co.	39·05 N	108·35 W
99	Grand L. (lăk) . . . Can.	49·00 N	57·10 W
119	Grand L. . . . La.	29·57 N	91·25 W
113	Grand L. . . . Mn. (Duluth In.)	46·54 N	92·26 W
104	Grand Ledge (lĕj) . . . Mi.	42·45 N	84·50 W
160	Grand-Lieu, L. de (gräN'-lyû) . Fr.	46·00 N	1·45 W
98	Grand Manan (I.) (mȧ-năn) . . Can.	44·40 N	66·50 W
97	Grand Mère (gräN mâr') . . . Can.	46·36 N	72·43 W
161	Grand Morin (R.) (mô-răN') Fr. (Paris In.)	48·23 N	2·19 E
162	Grândola (grăN'dô-lȧ) . . . Port.	38·10 N	8·36 W
109	Grand Portage Ind. Res. (pōr'tĭj) Mn.	47·54 N	89·34 W
109	Grand Portage Nat'l. Mon. . . . Mi.	47·59 N	89·47 W
113	Grand Prairie (prĕ'rē) Tx. (Dallas, Fort Worth In.)	32·45 N	97·00 W
115	Grand Quivira Natl. Mon. (kē-vē'rȧ) . NM	34·10 N	106·05 W
95	Grand Rapids . . . Can.	53·08 N	99·20 W
104	Grand Rapids (răp'ĭdz) . . . Mi.	43·00 N	85·45 W
109	Grand Rapids . . . Mn.	47·16 N	93·33 W
95	Grand Rapids Forebay (Res.) . Can.	53·10 N	100·00 W
98	Grand-Riviere . . . Can.	48·26 N	64·30 W
111	Grand Teton Mt. . . . Wy.	43·46 N	110·50 W
111	Grand Teton Natl. Park (tē'tŏn) Wy.	43·54 N	110·15 W
104	Grand Traverse B. (trăv'ērs) . . . Mi.	45·00 N	85·30 W
129	Grand Turk (tûrk) Turks & Caicos Is.	21·30 N	71·10 W
119	Grand Turk (I.) . Turks & Caicos Is.	21·30 N	71·10 W
113	Grandview (grănd'vyōō) Mo. (Kansas City In.)	38·53 N	94·32 W
115	Grand Wash (R.) (wŏsh) . . . Az.	36·20 N	113·52 W
111	Granger (grān'jēr) . . . Wy.	41·37 N	109·58 W
110	Grangeville (grānj'vĭl) . . . Id.	45·56 N	116·08 W
113	Granite City (grăn'ĭt sĭt'ĭ) Il. (St. Louis In.)	38·42 N	90·09 W
108	Granite Falls (fôlz) . . . Mn.	44·46 N	95·34 W
121	Granite Falls . . . NC	35·49 N	81·25 W
112	Granite Falls . . . Wa. (Seattle In.)	48·05 N	121·59 W
99	Granite L. . . . Can.	48·01 N	57·00 W
92	Granite Mtn. . . . Ak.	55·30 N	132·35 W
111	Granite Pk. . . . Mt.	45·13 N	109·48 W
121	Graniteville (grăn'ĭt-vĭl) . . . SC	33·35 N	81·50 W
135	Granito (grä-nē'tō) . . . Braz.	7·39 S	39·34 W
162	Granja de Torrehermosa (grän'hä dā tôr'rā-ēr-mō'sä) . Sp.	38·21 N	5·38 W
156	Gränna (grĕn'ȧ) . . . Swe.	58·02 N	14·38 E
163	Granollérs (grä-nôl-yĕrs') . . . Sp.	41·36 N	2·19 E
134	Gran Pajonal (Marsh) (grä'n-pä-Kô-näl') . Peru	11·14 S	71·45 W
119	Gran Piedra (Mtn.) (grän-pyĕ'drä) . Cuba	20·00 N	75·40 W
148	Grantham (grăn'tăm) . . . Eng.	52·54 N	0·38 W
107	Grant Park (grănt pärk) Il. (Chicago In.)	41·14 N	87·39 W
110	Grants Pass (grȧnts pȧs) . . . Or.	42·26 N	123·20 W
160	Granville (gräN-vēl') . . . Fr.	48·52 N	1·35 W
105	Granville (grăn'vĭl) . . . NY	43·25 N	73·15 W
95	Granville (L.) . . . Can.	56·18 N	100·30 W
135	Grão Mogol (grouN' mōō-gôl') Braz.	16·34 S	42·35 W
113	Grapevine (grāp'vīn) Tx. (Dallas, Fort Worth In.)	32·56 N	97·05 W
156	Gräso (I.) . . . Swe.	60·30 N	18·35 E
105	Grass (R.) . . . NY	44·45 N	75·10 W
123	Grass Cay (I.) Vir. Is. (U.S.A.) (St. Thomas In.)	18·22 N	64·50 W
161	Grasse (gräs) . . . Fr.	43·39 N	6·57 E
112	Grass Mtn. (grȧs) Wa. (Seattle In.)	47·13 N	121·48 W
114	Grass Valley . . . Ca.	39·12 N	121·04 W
99	Grates Pt. (grāts) . . . Can.	48·09 N	52·57 W
160	Graulhet (grō-lĕ') . . . Fr.	43·46 N	1·58 E
94	Gravelbourg (grăv'ĕl-bôrg) . . . Can.	49·53 N	106·34 W
148	Gravesend (grāvz'ĕnd') Eng. (London In.)	51·26 N	0·22 E
164	Gravina (grä-vē'nä) . . . It.	40·48 N	16·27 E
129	Gravois, Pte. (grȧ-vwä') . . . Hai.	18·00 N	74·20 W
161	Gray (grā) . . . Fr.	47·26 N	5·35 E
104	Grayling (grā'lĭng) . . . Mi.	44·40 N	84·40 W
107	Grayslake (grāz'lāk) Il. (Chicago In.)	42·20 N	88·20 W
116	Grays Pk. (grāz) . . . Co.	39·29 N	105·52 W
167	Grayvoron (grá-ē'vô-rôn) . Sov. Un.	50·28 N	35·41 E
158	Graz (gräts) . . . Aus.	47·05 N	15·26 E
128	Great Abaco (I.) (ă'bä-kō) . . . Ba.	26·30 N	77·05 W
205	Great Artesian Basin (Reg.) (är-tēzh-ăn bā-sĭn) . Austl.	23·16 S	143·37 E
204	Great Australian Bight (ôs-trā'lĭ-ăn bīt) . Austl.	33·30 S	127·00 E
128	Great Bahama Bk. (bȧ-hā'mȧ) . Ba.	25·00 N	78·50 W
205	Great Barrier (I.) (băr'ĭ-ēr) N. Z. (In.)	37·00 S	175·31 E
205	Great Barrier Rf. (bȧ-rĭ-ēr rēf) Austl.	16·43 S	146·34 E
102	Great Basin (grāt bā's'n) . . . U. S.	40·08 N	117·10 W
90	Great Bear L. (bâr) . . . Can.	66·10 N	119·53 W
116	Great Bend (bĕnd) . . . Ks.	38·41 N	98·46 W
	Great Bitter, see Al Buḩayrah al Murrah al Kubrā		
154	Great Blasket (Is.) (blăs'kĕt) . Ire.	52·05 N	10·55 W
146	Great Britian (brĭt'n) . . . U. K.	56·53 N	0·02 W
127	Great Corn I. . . . Nic.	12·10 N	82·54 W
111	Great Divide Basin (dĭ-vīd' bā's'n) . Wy.	42·10 N	108·10 W
205	Great Dividing Ra. (dĭ-vī-dĭng rānj) . Austl.	35·16 S	146·38 E
96	Great Duck (I.) (dŭk) . . . Can.	45·40 N	83·22 W
	Greater Khingan Ra., see Tahsinganling Shanmo		
109	Greater Leech Ind. Res. (grāt'ēr lēch) . Mn.	47·39 N	94·27 W
129	Great Exuma (I.) (ĕk-sōō'mä) . Ba.	23·35 N	76·00 W
111	Great Falls (fôlz) . . . Mt.	47·30 N	111·15 W
121	Great Falls . . . SC	34·32 N	80·53 W
129	Great Guana Cay (I.) (gwä'nä) . Ba.	24·00 N	76·20 W
128	Great Harbor Cay (I.) (kē) . . . Ba.	25·45 N	77·50 W
129	Great Inagua (I.) (ê-nä'gwä) . . . Ba.	21·00 N	73·15 W
184	Great Indian Des. . . . India	27·35 N	71·37 E
128	Great Isaac (I.) (ī'zȧk) . . . Ba.	26·05 N	79·05 W
212	Great Karroo (Mts.) (grāt kȧ'rōō) S. Afr.	32·45 S	22·00 E
212	Great Namaland (Reg.) S. W. Afr.	25·45 S	16·15 E
106	Great Neck (nĕk) NY (New York In.)	40·48 N	73·44 W
196	Great Nicobar I. (nĭk-ô-bär') Andaman & Nicobar Is.	7·00 N	94·18 E
128	Great Pedro Bluff (Hd.) . . . Jam.	17·50 N	78·05 W
75	Great Plains, The (Reg.) (plāns) N. A.	45·00 N	104·00 W
129	Great Ragged (I.) . . . Ba.	22·10 N	75·45 W
217	Great Ruaha (R.) . . . Tan.	7·45 S	34·50 E
164	Great St. Bernard Pass (sānt bēr-närd') . Switz.-It.	45·53 N	7·15 E
128	Great Sale Cay (I.) (sāl kē) . . . Ba.	27·00 N	78·15 W
111	Great Salt L. (sôlt lāk) . . . Ut.	41·19 N	112·48 W
102	Great Sale Lake Des. . . . U. S.	41·00 N	113·30 W
116	Great Salt Plains Res. . . . Ok.	36·56 N	98·14 W
116	Great Sand Dunes Natl. Mon. . . Co.	37·56 N	105·25 W
94	Great Sand Hills (sănd) . . . Can.	50·35 N	109·05 W
	Great Sandy (I.), see Fraser		
204	Great Sandy Des. (săn'dē) . . Austl.	21·50 S	123·10 E
110	Great Sandy Des. (săn'dĭ) . . . Or.	43·43 N	120·44 W
101	Great Sitkin (I.) (sĭt-kĭn) . . . Ak.	52·18 N	176·22 W
90	Great Slave (L.) (slāv) . . . Can.	61·37 N	114·58 W
120	Great Smoky Mts. Natl. Park (smōk-ē) . NC-Tn.	35·43 N	83·20 W
128	Great Stirrup Cay (I.) (stĭr-ŭp) Ba.	25·50 N	77·55 W
204	Great Victoria Des. (vĭk-tō'rĭ-ȧ) Austl.	29·45 S	124·30 E
148	Great Waltham (wôl'thŭm) . . Eng.	51·47 N	0·27 E
155	Great Yarmouth (yär-mŭth) . Eng.	52·35 N	1·45 E
156	Grebbestad (grĕb-bĕ-städh) . . Swe.	58·42 N	11·15 E
215	Gréboun, Mont (Mtn.) . . . Niger	20·00 N	8·35 E
162	Gredos, Sierra de (Mts.) (syĕr'rä dā grā'dōs) . Sp.	40·13 N	5·30 W
146	Greece (grēs) . . . Eur.	39·00 N	21·30 E
116	Greeley (grē'lĭ) . . . Co.	40·25 N	104·41 W
120	Green (R.) (grēn) . . . Ky.	37·13 N	86·30 W
108	Green (R.) . . . ND	47·05 N	103·05 W
102	Green (R.) . . . U. S.	38·30 N	110·10 W
115	Green (R.) . . . Ut.	38·30 N	110·05 W
102	Green (R.) . . . Wa. (Seattle In.)	47·17 N	121·57 W
102	Greenbank (grēn'bănk) Wa. (Seattle In.)	48·06 N	122·35 W
119	Green Bay . . . Tx. (In.)	29·53 N	95·13 W
109	Green Bay . . . Wi.	44·30 N	88·04 W
103	Green B. . . . U. S.	44·55 N	87·40 W
106	Greenbelt (grēn'bĕlt) Md. (Baltimore In.)	38·59 N	76·53 W
104	Greencastle (grēn-kȧs''l) . . . In.	39·40 N	86·50 W
128	Green Cay (I.) . . . Ba.	24·05 N	77·10 W
121	Green Cove Springs (kōv) . . . Fl.	29·56 N	81·42 W
107	Greendale (grēn'dāl) Wi. (Milwaukee In.)	42·56 N	87·59 W
104	Greenfield (grēn'fēld) . . . In.	39·45 N	85·40 W
109	Greenfield . . . Ia.	41·16 N	94·30 W
105	Greenfield . . . Ma.	42·35 N	72·35 W
117	Greenfield . . . Mo.	37·23 N	93·48 W
104	Greenfield . . . Oh.	39·15 N	83·25 W
120	Greenfield . . . Tn.	36·08 N	88·45 W
100	Greenfield Park Can. (Montréal In.)	45·29 N	73·29 W
107	Greenhills (grēn-hĭls) Oh. (Cincinnati In.)	39·16 N	84·31 W
75	Greenland (grēn'lănd) . . . N. A.	74·00 N	40·00 W
112	Green Mtn. . . . Or. (Portland In.)	45·52 N	123·24 W
115	Green Mountain Res. . . . Co.	39·50 N	106·20 W
105	Green Mts. . . . Vt.	43·10 N	73·05 W
154	Greenock (grēn'ŭk) . . . Scot.	55·55 N	4·45 W
106	Green Pond Mtn. (pŏnd) NJ (New York In.)	41·00 N	74·32 W
105	Greenport . . . NY	41·06 N	72·22 W
115	Green River (grēn rĭv'ēr) . . . Ut.	39·00 N	110·05 W
111	Green River . . . Wy.	41·32 N	109·26 W
111	Green R., Blacks Fk. . . . Wy.	41·08 N	110·27 W
111	Green R., Hams Fk. . . . Wy.	41·55 N	110·40 W
120	Greensboro (grēnz'bŭro) . . . Al.	32·42 N	87·36 W
120	Greensboro (grēns-bûr'ô) . . . Ga.	33·34 N	83·11 W
121	Greensboro . . . NC	36·04 N	79·45 W
104	Greensburg (grēnz'bûrg) . . . In.	39·20 N	85·30 W
116	Greensburg (grēns-bûrg) . . . Ks.	37·36 N	99·17 W
105	Greensburg . . . Pa.	40·20 N	79·30 W
120	Greenville (grēn'vĭl) . . . Al.	31·49 N	86·39 W
117	Greenville . . . Il.	38·52 N	89·22 W
120	Greenville . . . Ky.	37·11 N	87·11 W
214	Greenville . . . Lib.	5·01 N	9·03 W
98	Greenville . . . Me.	45·26 N	69·35 W
104	Greenville . . . Mi.	43·10 N	85·25 W
120	Greenville . . . Ms.	33·25 N	91·00 W
121	Greenville . . . NC	35·35 N	77·22 W
104	Greenville . . . Oh.	40·05 N	84·35 W
104	Greenville . . . Pa.	41·20 N	80·25 W
121	Greenville . . . SC	34·50 N	82·25 W
120	Greenville . . . Tn.	36·08 N	82·50 W
117	Greenville . . . Tx.	33·09 N	96·07 W
106	Greenwich . . . Ct. (New York In.)	41·01 N	73·37 W
148	Greenwich (grĭn'ĭj) Eng. (London In.)	51·28 N	0·00
117	Greenwood (grēn-wōōd) . . . Ar.	35·13 N	94·15 W
107	Greenwood . . In. (Indianapolis In.)	39·37 N	86·07 W
120	Greenwood . . . Ms.	33·30 N	90·09 W
121	Greenwood . . . SC	34·10 N	82·10 W
121	Greenwood (R.) . . . SC	34·17 N	81·55 W

ăt; finăl; rāte; senâte; ärm; ȧsk; sofȧ; fâre; ch-choose; dh-as th in other; bē; êvent; bĕt; recĕnt; cratēr; g-go; gh-guttural g; bĭt; ĭ-short neutral; rīde; K-guttural k as ch in German ich;

PRONOUNCING INDEX Greenwood — Guildford 287

Page	Name Pronunciation Region	Lat. °'	Long. °'
106	Greenwood L. NY (New York In.)	41·13 N	74·20 W
121	Greer (grēr) SC	34·55 N	81·56 W
161	Grefrath (grĕf'rät) F.R.G. (Ruhr In.)	51·20 N	6·21 E
108	Gregory (grĕg'ō-rĭ) SD	43·12 N	99·27 W
203	Gregory, L. (grĕg'ō-rē) Austl.	29·47 S	139·15 E
205	Gregory Ra. Austl.	19·23 S	143·45 E
149	Greifenberg (grī'fĕn-bĕrgh) F.R.G. (Munich In.)	48·04 N	11·06 E
158	Greifswald (grīfs'vält) G.D.R.	54·05 N	13·24 E
158	Greiz (grīts) G.D.R.	50·39 N	12·14 E
164	Gremyachinsk (grâ'myȧ-chĭnsk) Sov. Un. (Urals In.)	58·35 N	57·53 E
156	Grenå (grĕn'ô) Den.	56·25 N	10·51 E
120	Grenada (grē-nä'da) Ms.	33·45 N	89·47 W
123	Grenada N. A.	12·02 N	61·15 W
120	Grenada Res. Ms.	33·52 N	89·30 W
160	Grenade (grē-näd') Fr.	43·46 N	1·15 E
127	Grenadines, The (Is.) (grĕn'ȧ-dēnz) Grenada-St. Vincent (In.)	12·37 N	61·35 W
161	Grenoble (grē-nô'bl') Fr.	45·14 N	5·45 E
108	Grenora (grē-nō'rȧ) ND	48·38 N	103·55 W
105	Grenville (grĕn'vĭl) Can.	45·40 N	74·35 W
127	Grenville Grenada (In.)	12·07 N	61·38 W
112	Gresham (grĕsh'ăm) Or. (Portland In.)	45·30 N	122·25 W
106	Gretna (grĕt'nȧ) La. (New Orleans In.)	29·56 N	90·03 W
149	Grevelingen Krammer, R. Neth. (Amsterdam In.)	51·42 N	4·03 E
165	Grevená (grĕ'vå-nȧ) Grc.	40·02 N	21·30 E
161	Grevenbroich (grĕ'fĕn-broik) F.R.G. (Ruhr In.)	51·05 N	6·36 E
161	Grevenbrück (grĕ'fĕn-brük) F.R.G. (Ruhr In.)	51·08 N	8·01 E
99	Grey (R.) (grā) Can.	47·53 N	57·00 W
112	Grey, Pt. Can. (Vancouver In.)	49·22 N	123·16 W
111	Greybull (grā'bo͝ol) Wy.	44·28 N	108·05 W
111	Greybull R. Wy.	44·13 N	108·43 W
218	Greylingstad (grā-lĭng'shtȧt) S. Afr. (Johannesburg & Pretoria In.)	26·40 S	29·13 E
205	Greymouth (grā'mouth) N. Z. (In.)	42·27 S	171·17 E
203	Grey Ra. Austl.	28·40 S	142·05 E
110	Greys Hbr. (grās) Wa.	46·55 N	124·23 W
213	Greytown (grā'toun) S. Afr. (Natal In.)	29·07 S	30·38 E
	Greytown, see San Juan del Norte		
112	Grey Wolf Pk. (grā wo͝olf) Wa. (Seattle In.)	48·53 N	123·12 W
114	Gridley (grĭd'lĭ) Ca.	39·22 N	121·43 W
120	Griffin (grĭf'ĭn) Ga.	33·15 N	84·16 W
203	Griffith (grĭf-ĭth) Austl.	34·16 S	146·10 E
107	Griffith In. (Chicago In.)	41·31 N	87·26 W
167	Grigoriopol' (grĭ'gor-i-ō'pôl) Sov. Un.	47·09 N	29·18 E
125	Grijalva (R.) (grē-häl'vä) Mex.	17·25 N	93·23 W
203	Grim, C. (grĭm) Austl.	40·43 S	144·30 E
158	Grimma (grĭm'å) G.D.R.	51·14 N	12·43 E
100	Grimsby (grĭmz'bĭ) Can. (Toronto In.)	43·11 N	79·33 W
150	Grimsey (I.) (grĭms'å) Ice.	66·30 N	17·50 W
156	Grimstad (grĭm-städh) Nor.	58·21 N	8·30 E
99	Grindstone Island Can.	47·25 N	61·51 W
109	Grinnel (grĭ-nĕl') Ia.	41·44 N	92·44 W
109	Griswold (grĭz'wŭld) Ia.	41·11 N	95·05 W
166	Griva (grē'vȧ) Sov. Un.	55·51 N	26·31 E
99	Groais I. Can.	50·57 N	55·35 W
157	Grobina (grō'bĭŋĭa) Sov. Un.	56·35 N	21·10 E
218	Groblersdal S. Afr. (Johannesburg & Pretoria In.)	25·11 S	29·25 E
159	Grodno (grôd'nŏ) Sov. Un.	53·40 N	23·49 E
159	Grodzisk Masowieki (grō'jēsk mä-zō-vyĕts'ke). Pol.	52·06 N	20·40 E
158	Grodzisk Wielkopolski (grō'jēsk vyĕl-ko-pōl'skē). Pol.	52·14 N	16·22 E
119	Groesbeck (grōs'bĕk) Tx.	31·32 N	96·31 W
160	Groix, I. de (ēl dē grwä') Fr.	47·39 N	3·28 W
159	Grójec (gro͞o'yĕts) Pol.	51·53 N	20·52 E
158	Gronau (grō'nou) F.R.G.	52·12 N	7·05 E
155	Groningen (grō'nĭng-ĕn) Neth.	53·13 N	6·30 E
204	Groote Eylandt (I.) (grō'tē ī'länt). Austl.	13·50 S	137·30 E
212	Grootfontein (grōt'fōn-tān') S. W. Afr.	18·15 S	19·30 E
213	Groot-Kei (kē). S. Afr. (Natal In.)	32·17 S	27·30 E
212	Grootkop (Mtn.) S. Afr. (In.)	34·11 S	18·23 E
218	Groot Marico S. Afr. (Johannesburg & Pretoria In.)	25·36 S	26·23 E
218	Groot R. S. Afr. (Johannesburg & Pretoria In.)	25·13 S	26·20 E
213	Groot-Vis (R.). S. Afr. (Natal In.).	33·04 S	36·08 E
212	Groot Vloer (L.) (grōt' vlo͞or') S. Afr.	30·00 S	20·16 E
99	Gros Morne (Mtn.) (grō môrn') Can.	49·36 N	57·48 W
91	Gros Morne Natl. Pk. Can.	49·45 N	59·15 W
99	Gros Pate (Mtn.) Can.	50·16 N	57·25 W
149	Gross Behnitz (grōss bĕ'nētz) G.D.R. (Berlin In.)	52·35 N	12·45 E
107	Grosse I. (grōs) Mi. (Detroit In.)	42·08 N	83·09 W
100	Grosse Isle (īl') Can. (Winnipeg In.)	50·04 N	97·27 W
158	Grossenhain (grōs'ĕn-hīn) G.D.R.	51·17 N	13·33 E
149	Grossenzersdorf Aus. (Vienna In.)	48·13 N	16·33 E
107	Grosse Pointe (point') Mi. (Detroit In.)	42·23 N	82·54 W
107	Grosse Pointe Farms (färm) Mi. (Detroit In.)	42·25 N	82·53 W
107	Grosse Pointe Park (pärk) Mi. (Detroit In.)	42·23 N	82·55 W
164	Grosseto (grōs-sā'tō) It.	42·46 N	11·09 E
158	Grossglockner Pk. (glôk'nēr) Aus.	47·06 N	12·45 E
149	Gross Höbach (hû'bäk) F.R.G. (Munich In.)	48·21 N	11·36 E
149	Gross Kreutz (kroitz) G.D.R. (Berlin In.)	52·24 N	12·47 E
161	Gross Reken (rĕ'kĕn) F.R.G. (Ruhr In.)	51·50 N	7·20 E
149	Gross Schönebeck (shō'nĕ-bĕk) G.D.R. (Berlin In.)	52·54 N	13·32 E
111	Gros Ventre R. (grōvĕn't'r) Wy.	43·38 N	110·34 W
105	Groton (grôt'ŭn) Ct.	41·20 N	72·00 W
99	Groton Ma. (In.)	42·37 N	71·34 W
108	Groton SD	45·25 N	98·04 W
165	Grottaglie (grôt-täl'yā) It.	40·32 N	17·26 E
100	Grouard Can.	55·31 N	116·09 W
96	Groundhog (R.) Can.	49·00 N	82·10 W
99	Groveland (grōv'land) Ma. (In.)	42·45 N	71·02 W
105	Groveton (grōv'tŭn) NH	44·35 N	71·30 W
119	Groveton Tx.	31·04 N	95·07 W
171	Groznyy (grôz'nĭ) Sov. Un.	43·20 N	45·40 E
159	Grudziadz (gro͞o'jyôNts) Pol.	53·30 N	18·48 E
149	Grumpholds-Kirchen Aus. (Wien In.)	48·03 N	16·17 E
109	Grundy Center (grŭn'dĭ sĕn'tēr) Ia.	42·22 N	92·45 W
124	Gruñidora (gro͞o-nyē-dô'rō) Mex.	24·10 N	101·49 W
149	Grünwald (gro͞on'väld) F.R.G. (Munich In.)	48·04 N	11·34 E
166	Gryazi (gryä'zĭ) Sov. Un.	52·31 N	39·59 E
146	Gryazovets (gryä'zō-vĕts) Sov. Un.	58·52 N	40·14 E
158	Gryfice (grĭ'fĭ-tsĕ) Pol.	53·55 N	15·11 E
158	Gryfino (grĭ'fē-nô) Pol.	53·16 N	14·30 E
127	Guabito (gwä-bē'tô) Pan.	9·30 N	82·33 W
128	Guacanayabo, Golfo de (G.) (gôl-fô-dĕ-gwä-kä-nä-yä'bō). Cuba	20·30 N	77·40 W
135	Guacara (gwȧ'kä-rä) Ven. (In.)	10·16 N	67·48 W
134	Guacarí (gwä-kä-rē') Col. (In.)	3·45 N	76·20 W
137	Guaçuí (gwä'so͞o-ē') Braz. (Rio de Janeiro In.)	20·47 S	41·40 W
124	Guadalajara (gwä-dhä-lä-hä'rä) Mex.	20·41 N	103·21 W
162	Guadalajara (gwä-dä-lä-kä'rä) Sp.	40·37 N	3·10 W
162	Guadalcanal (gwä-dhäl-kä-näl') Sp.	38·05 N	5·48 W
205	Guadalcanal (I.) Sol. Is.	9·48 S	158·43 E
124	Guadalcázar (gwä-dhäl-kä'zär) Mex.	22·38 N	100·24 W
162	Guadalete (R.) (gwä-dhä-lā'tå). Sp.	38·53 N	5·38 W
162	Guadalhorce (R.) (gwä-dhäl-ôr'thä). Sp.	37·05 N	4·50 W
162	Guadalimar (R.) (gwä-dhä-lē-mär'). Sp.	38·29 N	2·53 W
163	Guadalope (R.) (gwä-dä-lô-pĕ). Sp.	40·48 N	0·10 W
162	Guadalquivir, Río (R.) (rē'ō-gwä-dhäl-kê-vēr'). Sp.	5·57 N	6·00 W
118	Guadalupe Mex.	31·23 N	106·06 W
162	Guadalupe, Sierra de (Mts.) (syĕr'rä dā gwä-dhä-lo͞o'pä). Sp.	39·30 N	5·25 W
122	Guadalupe I. Mex.	29·00 N	118·45 W
118	Guadalupe Mts. NM-Tx.	32·00 N	104·55 W
118	Guadalupe Pk. Tx.	31·55 N	104·55 W
118	Guadalupe R. (gwä-dhä-lo͞o'pä) Tx.	29·54 N	99·03 W
162	Guadarrama, Sierra de (Mts.) (gwä-dhär-rä'mä). Sp.	41·00 N	3·40 W
163	Guadarrama (R.) (gwä-dhär-rä'mä). Sp. (Madrid In.)	40·34 N	3·58 W
123	Guadeloupe (gwä-dē-lo͞op') N. A.	16·40 N	61·10 W
127	Guadeloupe Pass N. A. (In.)	16·26 N	62·00 W
128	Guadiana, Bahía de (B.) (bä-ē'ä-dĕ-gwä-dhê-ä'nä). Cuba	22·10 N	84·35 W
162	Guadiana, Rio (R.) (rĕ'ō-gwä-dvä'nä). Port.	37·43 N	7·43 W
162	Guadiana Alto (R.) (äl'tō) Sp.	39·02 N	2·52 W
162	Guadiana Menor (R.) (mā'nôr). Sp.	37·43 N	2·45 W
162	Guadiaro (R.) (gwä-dhê-ä rō) Sp.	37·38 N	5·25 W
163	Guadiato (R.) (gwä-dhê-ä'tō) Sp.	38·10 N	5·05 W
162	Guadiela (R.) (gwä-dhê-ā'lä) Sp.	40·27 N	2·05 W
162	Guadix (gwä-dhēsh') Sp.	37·18 N	3·09 W
197	Guagua Phil. (In.)	15·00 N	120·36 E
135	Guaira (gwä-ē-rä) Braz.	24·03 S	44·02 W
135	Guaire (R.) (gwī'rĕ) Ven. (In.)	10·25 N	66·43 W
128	Guajaba, Cayo (I.) (kä'yō-gwä-hä'bä). Cuba	21·50 N	77·35 W
134	Guajará Mirim (gwä-zhä-rä'mē-rēN'). Braz.	10·58 S	65·12 W
134	Guajira, Pen. de (Pen.) (pĕ-nē'ng-so͞o-lä-dĕ-gwä-KĒ'rä) Col.-Ven.	12·35 N	73·00 W
126	Gualán (gwä-län') Guat.	15·08 N	89·21 W
137	Gualeguay (gwä-lĕ-gwä'y) Arg. (Buenos Aires In.)	33·10 S	59·20 W
137	Gualeguay (R.) Arg. (Buenos Aires In.)	32·49 S	59·05 W
137	Gualeguaychú (gwä-lå-gwī-cho͞o') Arg. (Buenos Aires In.)	33·01 S	58·32 W
137	Gualeguaychú (R.) Arg. (Buenos Aires In.)	32·58 S	58·27 W
136	Gualicho, Salina (F.) (sä-lē'nä-gwä-lē'chō). Arg.	40·20 S	65·15 W
198	Guam (gwâm) Oceania	14·00 N	143·20 E
136	Guaminí (gwä-mē-nē') Arg.	37·02 S	62·21 W
134	Guamo (gwä'mŏ) Col. (In.)	4·02 N	74·58 W
129	Guanabacoa (gwä-nä-bä-kō'ä) Cuba (In.)	23·08 N	82·19 W
136	Guanabara, Baia de (B.) Braz. (Rio de Janeiro In.)	22·44 S	43·09 W
126	Guanacaste Cord. (Mts.) (kôr-dēl-yĕ'rä-gwä-nä-käs'tä) C. R.	10·54 N	85·27 W
122	Guanacevi (gwä-nä-sĕ-vē') Mex.	25·30 N	105·45 W
128	Guanahacabibes, Pen. de (pĕ-nēn-so͞o-lä-dĕ-gwä-nä hä-kä-bē'bås) Cuba	21·55 N	84·35 W
128	Guanajay (gwä-nä-hī') Cuba	22·55 N	82·40 W
124	Guanajuato (gwä-nä-hwä'tō). Mex.	21·01 N	101·16 W
122	Guanajuato (State) Mex.	21·00 N	101·00 W
135	Guanape (gwä-nä'pĕ) Ven. (In.)	9·55 N	65·32 W
135	Guanape (R.) Ven. (In.)	9·52 N	65·20 W
134	Guanare (gwä-nä'rå) Ven.	8·57 N	69·47 W
136	Guanduçu (R.) (gwä'n-do͞o'so͞o) Braz. (Rio de Janeiro In.)	22·50 S	43·40 W
128	Guane (gwä'nå) Cuba	22·10 N	84·05 W
135	Guanta (gwän'tä) Ven. (In.)	10·15 N	64·35 W
129	Guantanamo (gwän-tä'nä-mô) Cuba	20·10 N	75·10 W
129	Guantanamo, Bahía de (B.) (bä-ē'ä-dĕ). Cuba	19·35 N	75·35 W
137	Guapé (gwȧ-pĕ) Braz. (Rio de Janeiro In.)	20·45 S	45·55 W
127	Guapiles (gwä-pē-lĕs) C. R.	10·05 N	83·54 W
136	Guapimirim (gwä-pē-mē-rē'N) Braz. (Rio de Janeiro In.)	22·31 S	42·59 W
134	Guaporé (R.) (gwä-pô-rā') Bol.-Braz.	12·11 S	63·47 W
134	Guaqui (guä'kē) Bol.	16·42 S	68·47 W
163	Guara, Sierra de (Mts.) (sē-ĕ'r-rä-dĕ-gwä'rä). Sp.	42·24 N	0·15 W
135	Guarabira (gwä-rä-bē'rȧ) Braz.	6·49 S	35·27 W
134	Guaranda (gwä-rȧn'dä) Ec.	1·39 S	78·57 W
135	Guarapari (gwä-rä-pä'rē) Braz.	20·34 S	40·31 W
137	Guarapiranga, Represa do (Res.) (r'ĕ-prĕ-sȧ-dô-gwä'rä-pē-rȧ'n-gä) Braz. (Rio de Janeiro In.)	23·45 S	46·44 W
136	Guarapuava (gwä-rä-pwä'vȧ) Braz.	25·29 S	51·26 W
137	Guaratinguetá (guä-rä-tĭN-gå-tä') Braz. (Rio de Janeiro In.)	22·49 S	45·10 W
162	Guarda (gwär'dä) Port.	40·32 N	7·17 W
162	Guarena (gwä-rā'nyä) Sp.	38·52 N	6·08 W
135	Guaribe (R.) (gwä-rē'bĕ) Ven. (In.)	9·48 N	65·17 W
135	Guárico (State) Ven. (In.)	9·42 N	67·25 W
135	Guárico (R.) Ven. (In.)	9·50 N	67·07 W
137	Guarulhos (gwä-ro͞o'l-yôs) Braz. (Rio de Janeiro In.)	32·28 S	46·30 W
137	Guarus (gwȧ'ro͞os) Braz. (Rio de Janeiro In.)	21·44 S	41·19 W
134	Guasca (gwäs'kä) Col. (In.)	4·52 N	73·52 W
135	Guasipati (gwä-sē-pä'tē) Ven.	7·26 N	61·57 W
164	Guastalla (gwäs-täl'lä) It.	44·53 N	10·39 E
113	Guasti (gwäs'tĭ) Ca. (Los Angeles In.)	34·04 N	117·35 W
126	Guatemala (guä-tȧ-mä'lä) Guat.	14·37 N	90·32 W
122	Guatemala N. A.	15·45 N	91·45 W
135	Guatire (gwä-tē'rĕ) Ven. (In.)	10·28 N	66·34 W
137	Guaxupé (gwä-sho͞o-pĕ') Braz. (Rio de Janeiro In.)	21·18 S	46·42 W
128	Guayabal (gwä-yä-bä'l) Cuba	20·40 N	77·40 W
124	Guayalejo (R.) (gwä-yä-lĕ'hô) Mex.	23·24 N	99·09 W
123	Guayama (gwä-yä'mä) P. R. (Puerto Rico In.)	18·00 N	66·08 W
129	Guayamouc (R.) Hai.	19·05 N	72·00 W
126	Guayape R. Hond.	14·39 N	86·37 W
134	Guayaquil (gwī-ä-kēl') Ec.	2·16 S	79·53 W
134	Guayaquil, Golfo de (G.) (gôl-fô-dĕ). Ec.	3·03 S	82·12 W
134	Guayiare (R.) (gwä-yȧ'rĕ) Col.	3·35 N	69·28 W
122	Guaymas (gwȧ'y-mäs) Mex.	27·49 N	110·58 W
129	Guayubin (gwȧ-yo͞o-bē'n) Dom. Rep.	19·40 N	71·25 W
126	Guazacapán (gwä-zä-kä-pän') Guat.	14·04 N	90·26 W
174	Gubakha (go͞o-bä'kȧ) Sov. Un. (Urals In.)	58·53 N	57·35 E
164	Gubbio (go͞ob'byô) It.	43·23 N	12·36 E
163	Gudar, Sierra de (Mts.) (syĕr'rä dā go͞o'dhär). Sp.	40·28 N	0·47 W
156	Gudenaa (R.) Den.	56·20 N	9·47 E
156	Gudinge Fjärden (Fd.) Swe.	57·43 N	16·55 E
156	Gudvangen (go͞odh'väŋ-gĕn) Nor.	60·52 N	6·45 E
161	Guebwiller (gĕb-vē-lâr') Fr.	47·53 N	7·10 E
215	Guédi, Mont (Mtn.) Chad	12·14 N	18·58 E
210	Guelma (gwĕl'mä) Alg.	36·32 N	7·17 E
100	Guelph (gwĕlf). Can. (Toronto In.)	43·33 N	80·15 W
152	Guemar (gē-mär') Alg.	33·32 N	6·42 E
135	Güere (gwĕ'rĕ) (R.) Ven. (In.)	9·39 N	65·00 W
160	Guéret (gā-rĕ') Fr.	46·09 N	1·52 E
160	Guernsey (I.) (gûrn'zĭ) Eur.	49·27 N	2·36 W
152	Guerrara (gĕr-rä'rä) Alg.	32·50 N	4·26 E
118	Guerrero (gĕr-rā'rō) Mex.	26·47 N	99·20 W
118	Guerrero Mex.	28·20 N	100·24 W
124	Guerrero (State) Mex.	17·45 N	100·15 W
160	Gueugnon (gû-nyôN') Fr.	46·35 N	4·01 E
119	Gueydan (gā'dăn) La.	30·01 N	92·31 W
136	Guia de Pacobaíba (gwê'ä-dĕ-pä'kō-bī'bä) Braz. (Rio de Janeiro In.)	22·42 S	43·10 W
133	Guiana Highlands (Mts.) Braz.	3·20 N	60·00 W
125	Guichicovi (San Juan) (gwē-chê-kō'vê). Mex.	16·58 N	95·10 W
163	Guidonia (gwē-dō'nyȧ) It. (Rome In.)	42·00 N	12·45 E
214	Guiglo Ivory Coast	6·33 N	7·29 W
161	Guignes (gēN'yĕ) Fr. (Paris In.)	48·38 N	2·48 E
135	Güigüe (gwê'gwĕ) Ven. (In.)	10·05 N	67·48 W
126	Guija, L. (gē'hä) Sal.	14·16 N	89·21 W
148	Guildford (gĭl'fērd) Eng. (London In.)	51·13 N	0·34 W

288 Guilford — Hangchou PRONOUNCING INDEX

Page	Name Pronunciation Region	Lat. °′	Long. °′
107	Guilford (gĭl′fẽrd) In. (Cincinnati In.)	39·10 N	84·55 W
162	Guimarães (gē-mä-rǎɴsh′)...Port.	41·27 N	8·22 W
209	Guinea (gĭn′ē)...Afr.	10·48 N	12·28 W
209	Guinea, G. of...Afr.	2·00 N	1·00 E
209	Guinea-Bissau (gĭn′ē)...Afr.	12·00 N	20·00 W
128	Güines (gwē′nās)...Cuba	22·50 N	82·05 W
160	Guingamp (gǎɴ-gäɴ′)...Fr.	48·35 N	3·10 W
128	Güira de Melena (gwē′rä dā må-lā′nä).Cuba	22·45 N	82·30 W
134	Güiria (gwê-rē′ä)...Ven.	10·43 N	62·16 W
152	Guir R...Mor.-Alg.	31·55 N	2·48 W
161	Guise (guēz)...Fr.	49·54 N	3·37 E
126	Guisisil (Vol.) (gê-sê-sēl′)...Nic.	12·40 N	86·11 W
184	Gujarat (State)...India	22·54 N	79·00 E
184	Gujrānwāla (gōōj-rän′va-lȧ)..Pak.	32·08 N	74·14 E
156	Gula (R.) (gōō′lå)...Nor.	62·55 N	10·45 E
185	Gulbarga (gŏŏl-bûr′gȧ)...India	17·25 N	76·52 E
166	Gulbene (gŏŏl-bă′nĕ)...Sov. Un.	57·09 N	26·49 E
120	Gulfport (gŭlf′pōrt)...Ms.	30·24 N	89·05 W
94	Gull Lake...Can.	50·10 N	108·25 W
92	Gull L...Can.	52·35 N	114·00 W
217	Gulu...Ug.	2·47 N	32·18 E
167	Gulyay Pole...Sov. Un.	47·39 N	36·12 E
197	Gumaca (gōō-mä-kä′)...Phil. (In.)	13·55 N	122·06 E
164	Gumbeyka R. (gōōm-bĕy′kȧ) Sov. Un. (Urals In.)	53·20 N	59·42 E
215	Gumel...Nig.	12·39 N	9·22 E
158	Gummersbach (gōōm′ĕrs-bäk) F.R.G.	51·02 N	7·34 E
215	Gummi...Nig.	12·09 N	5·09 E
149	Gumpoldskirchen...Aus.	48·04 N	16·15 E
184	Guna...India	24·44 N	77·17 E
95	Gunisao (R.) (gŭn-ĭ-sā′ō)...Can.	53·40 N	97·35 W
95	Gunisao L...Can.	53·54 N	97·58 W
203	Gunnedah (gŭ′nē-dä)...Austl.	31·00 S	150·10 E
115	Gunnison (gŭn′ĭ-sŭn)...Co.	38·33 N	106·56 W
115	Gunnison...Ut.	39·10 N	111·50 W
115	Gunnison (R.)...Co.	38·30 N	106·40 W
120	Guntersville (gŭn′tẽrz-vĭl)...Al.	34·20 N	86·19 W
120	Guntersville L...Al.	34·30 N	86·20 W
149	Guntramsdorf...Aus. (Vienna In.)	48·04 N	16·19 E
185	Guntūr (gŏŏn′tŏŏr)...India	16·22 N	80·29 E
197	Gunungapi (I.) (gōō′nōōng-ä′pê) Indon.	6·52 S	127·15 E
117	Gurdon (gûr′dŭn)...Ar.	33·56 N	93·10 W
135	Gurgucia (R.) (gŏŏr-gōō′syä).Braz.	8·12 S	43·49 W
107	Gurnee (gûr′nē)...Il. (Chicago In.)	42·22 N	87·55 W
156	Gurskōy (I.) (gōōrskûê)...Nor.	62·18 N	5·20 E
135	Gurupá (gōō-rōō-pä′)...Braz.	1·28 S	51·32 W
135	Gurupi, Serra do (Mts.) (sĕ′r-rä-dô-gōō-rōō-pē′).Braz.	5·32 S	47·02 W
135	Gurupí (R.) (gōō-rōō-pē′)...Braz.	2·37 S	46·45 W
184	Guru Sikhar Mt...India	29·42 N	72·50 E
171	Gur′yev (gōōr′yĕf)...Sov. Un.	47·10 N	51·50 E
172	Gur′yevsk (gōōr-yifsk′)...Sov. Un.	54·14 N	86·07 E
215	Gusau (gōō-zä′ōō)...Nig.	12·12 N	6·40 E
157	Gusev (gōō′sĕf)...Sov. Un.	54·35 N	22·15 E
214	Gushiago...Ghana	9·55 N	0·12 W
165	Gusinje (gōō-sēn′yĕ)...Yugo.	42·34 N	19·54 E
166	Gus′-Khrustal′nyy (gōōs-ĸrōō-stäl′ny′).Sov. Un.	55·39 N	40·41 E
125	Gustavo A. Madero (gōōs-tä′vô-ȧ-mä-dĕ′rô).Mex. (In.)	19·29 N	99·07 W
158	Güstrow (güs′trō)...G.D.R.	53·48 N	12·12 E
158	Gütersloh (gü′tĕrs-lo)...F.R.G.	51·54 N	8·22 E
117	Guthrie (gŭth′rĭ)...Ok.	35·52 N	97·26 W
109	Guthrie Center...Ia.	41·41 N	94·33 W
125	Gutiérrez Zamora (gōō-tĭ-âr′räz zä-mō′rä).Mex.	20·27 N	97·17 W
109	Guttenberg (gŭt′ĕn-bûrg)...Ia.	42·48 N	91·09 W
133	Guyana (gŭy′ănă)...S. A.	7·45 N	59·00 W
116	Guymon (gī′mŏn)...Ok.	36·41 N	101·29 W
99	Guysborough (gīz′bŭr-ô)...Can.	45·23 N	61·30 W
157	Gvardeysk (gvår-dĕysk′).Sov. Un.	54·39 N	21·11 E
215	Gwadabawa...Nig.	13·20 N	5·15 E
186	Gwādar (gwä′dŭr)...Pak.	25·15 N	62·29 E
217	Gwane (gwän)...Zaire	4·43 N	25·50 E
212	Gwelo (gwä′lō)...Rh.	19·15 S	29·48 E
217	Gwembe...Zambia	16·30 S	27·35 E
109	Gwinn (gwĭn)...Mi.	46·15 N	87·30 W
188	Gyangtse (gyäng′tsĕ′)...China	29·00 N	89·28 E
184	Gyangtse...China	28·53 N	89·39 E
173	Gydan, Khrebet (Kolymskiy) (Mts.).Sov. Un.	61·45 N	155·00 E
172	Gydanskiy, P-Ov (Pen).Sov. Un.	70·42 N	76·03 E
203	Gympie (gĭm′pê)...Austl.	26·20 S	152·50 E
159	Gyöngyös (dyûn′dyûsh)...Hung.	47·47 N	19·55 E
159	Györ (dyûr)...Hung.	47·40 N	17·37 E
195	Gyōtoku (gyō′tô-kōō′) Jap. (Tōkyō In.)	35·42 N	139·56 E
95	Gypsumville (jĭp′sŭm-vĭl)...Can.	51·45 N	98·35 W
159	Gyula (dyŏŏ′lä)...Hung.	46·38 N	21·18 E

H

Page	Name Pronunciation Region	Lat. °′	Long. °′
161	Haan (hän)...F.R.G. (Ruhr In.)	51·12 N	7·00 E
157	Haapamäki (häp′ä-mĕ-kē)...Fin.	62·16 N	24·20 E
157	Haapsalu (häp′sä-lōō)...Sov. Un.	58·56 N	23·33 E
149	Haar (här)...F.R.G. (Munich In.)	48·06 N	11·44 E
183	Ha ′Arava (Wādī al Jayb) Isr. (Palestine In.)	30·33 N	35·10 E
149	Haarlem (här′lĕm) Neth. (Amsterdam In.)	52·22 N	4·37 E
128	Habana (Prov.) (hä-vä′nä)...Cuba	22·55 N	82·15 W
163	Habibas (C.) (hä-bē′bås)...Alg.	35·50 N	0·45 W
195	Habikino...Jap. (Ōsaka In.)	34·32 N	135·37 E
184	Hābra...India (In.)	22·49 N	88·38 E
194	Hachinohe (hä′chē-nō′hå)...Jap.	40·29 N	141·40 E
195	Hachiōji (hä′chê-ō′jê)...Jap.	35·39 N	139·18 E
106	Hackensack (hăk′ĕn-săk) NJ (New York In.)	40·54 N	74·03 W
186	Hadd, Ra′s al (C.)...Om.	22·29 N	59·46 E
106	Haddonfield (hăd′ŭn-fēld) NJ (Philadelphia In.)	39·53 N	75·02 W
106	Haddon Heights (hăd′ŭn hīts) NJ (Philadelphia In.)	39·53 N	75·03 W
215	Hadejia (hä-dā′jä)...Nig.	12·30 N	9·59 E
215	Hadejia (R.)...Nig.	12·15 N	9·40 E
183	Hadera (ĸå-dĕ′rä) Isr. (Palestine In.)	32·26 N	34·55 E
156	Haderslev (hä′dhĕrs-lĕv)...Den.	55·17 N	9·28 E
218	Hadibu...P. D. R. of Yem. (Horn of Afr. In.)	12·40 N	53·50 E
112	Hadlock (hăd′lŏk) Wa. (Seattle In.)	48·02 N	122·46 W
186	Ḩaḑramawt (Reg.) P. D. R. of Yem.	15·22 N	48·40 E
186	Hadur Shuayb, Jabal (Mtn.) Yemen	15·45 N	43·45 E
194	Haeju (hä′ĕ-jŭ)...Kor.	38·03 N	125·42 E
192	Haerhpin (Harbin) (här-bĕn′) China	45·40 N	126·30 E
150	Hafnarfjördhur...Ice.	64·02 N	21·32 W
218	Hafun, Ras (C.) (hä-fōōn′) Som. (Horn of Afr. In.)	10·15 N	51·35 E
111	Hageland (hăge′lănd)...Mt.	48·53 N	108·43 W
161	Hagen (hä′gĕn).F.R.G. (Ruhr In.)	51·21 N	7·29 E
104	Hagerstown (hā′gẽrz-toun)...In.	39·55 N	85·10 W
105	Hagerstown...Md.	39·40 N	77·45 W
195	Hagi (hä′gĭ)...Jap.	34·25 N	131·25 E
160	Hague, C. de la (dē lȧ åg′)...Fr.	49·44 N	1·55 W
	Hague, The, see ′s Gravenhagen		
161	Haguenau (åg′nō′)...Fr.	48·47 N	7·48 E
190	Haian (hăi′äɴ)...China	32·35 N	120·25 E
195	Haibara (hä′ē-bä′rä)...Jap.	34·29 N	135·57 E
192	Haich′eng...China	40·58 N	122·45 E
183	Haifa (Hefa) (hä′ē-fȧ) Isr. (Palestine In.)	32·48 N	35·00 E
193	Haifeng (hä′ē-fĕng′)...China	23·00 N	115·20 E
190	Haifuchen (hăi′fōō′jĕn)...China	31·57 N	121·48 E
182	Ḩā′il (hāl)...Sau. Ar.	27·30 N	41·47 E
192	Hailaerh (Hailar) (hä-ê-lär′) China	49·10 N	118·40 E
	Hailar, see Hailaerh		
111	Hailey (hā′lĭ)...Id.	43·31 N	114·19 W
97	Haileybury...Can.	47·27 N	79·38 W
117	Haileyville (hā′lĭ-vĭl)...Ok.	34·51 N	95·34 W
194	Hailin (hä′ê-lĕn′)...China	44·31 N	129·11 E
193	Hailing Tao (I.)...China	21·30 N	112·15 E
192	Hailun (hä′ê-lōōn′)...China	47·18 N	126·50 E
192	Hailung (hä′ê-lōōng′)...China	42·32 N	125·52 E
193	Hainan Tao (I.) (hä′e-nän′dou) China	19·00 N	111·10 E
149	Hainburg an der Donau Aus. (Vienna In.)	48·09 N	16·57 E
101	Haines (hānz)...Ak.	59·10 N	135·38 W
121	Haines City...Fl. (In.)	28·05 N	81·38 W
193	Haiphong (hī′fông′) (hä′ēp-hŏng) Viet.	20·52 N	106·40 E
123	Haiti (hā′tĭ)...N. A.	19·00 N	72·15 W
192	Haitien (hī′tyĕn′)...China (In.)	39·59 N	116·17 E
159	Hajdúböszormény (hôl′dōō-bû′sûr-män′).Hung.	47·41 N	21·30 E
159	Hajduhadház (hô′ĭ-dōō-hôd′häz) Hung.	47·32 N	21·32 E
159	Hajdunánás (hô′ĭ-dōō-nä′näsh) Hung.	47·52 N	21·27 E
159	Hajduszoboszló (hô′ĭ-dōō-sô′bôs-lō).Hung.	47·24 N	21·25 E
194	Hakodate (hä-kō-dä′t å)...Jap.	41·46 N	140·42 E
195	Haku-San (Mtn.) (hä′kōō-sän′) Jap.	36·11 N	136·45 E
125	Halachó (ä-lä-chō′)...Mex.	20·28 N	90·06 W
211	Ḩalā′ib (hä-lä′ēb)...Egypt	22·10 N	36·40 E
183	Ḩalbā...Leb. (Palestine In.)	34·33 N	36·03 E
149	Halbe (häl′bē) G.D.R. (Berlin In.)	52·07 N	13·43 E
158	Halberstadt (häl′bĕr-shtät) G.D.R.	51·54 N	11·07 E
197	Halcon, Mt. (häl-kōn′).Phil. (In.)	13·19 N	120·55 E
156	Halden (häl′dĕn)...Nor.	59·10 N	11·21 E
148	Hale (hāl)...Eng.	53·22 N	2·20 W
89	Haleakala Crater (hä′lā-ä′kä-lä) Hi.	20·44 N	156·15 W
89	Haleakala Natl. Park...Hi.	20·46 N	156·00 W
107	Hales Corners (hālz kŏr′nẽrz) Wi. (Milwaukee In.)	42·56 N	88·03 W
148	Halesowen (hālz′ô-wĕn)...Eng.	52·26 N	2·03 W
106	Halethorpe (hāl-thôrp) Md. (Baltimore In.)	39·15 N	76·40 W
120	Haleyville (hā′lĭ-vĭl)...Al.	34·11 N	87·36 W
112	Half Moon Bay (hăf′mōōn). Ca. (San Francisco In.)	37·28 N	122·26 W
213	Halfway House (häf-wā hous) S. Afr. (Johannesburg & Pretoria In.)	26·00 S	28·08 E
149	Halfweg..Neth. (Amsterdam In.)	52·23 N	4·45 E
98	Halifax (hăl′ĭ-făks)...Can.	44·39 N	63·36 W
148	Halifax...Eng.	53·44 N	1·52 W
205	Halifax B. (hăl′ĭ-făx)...Austl.	18·56 S	147·07 E
98	Halifax Hbr...Can.	44·35 N	63·31 W
101	Halkett, C...Ak.	70·50 N	151·15 W
93	Hallam Park...Can.	52·11 N	118·46 E
194	Halla San (Mt.) (häl′lȧ-sän) Kor.	33·20 N	126·37 E
149	Halle (häl′lē)...Bel. (Brussels In.)	50·45 N	4·13 E
158	Halle...G.D.R.	51·30 N	11·59 E
119	Hallettsville (hăl′ĕts-vĭl)...Tx.	29·26 N	96·55 W
108	Hallock (hăl′ŭk)...Mn.	48·46 N	96·57 W
91	Hall Pen (hôl)...Can.	63·14 N	65·40 W
119	Halls Bay...Tx. (In.)	29·55 N	95·23 W
156	Hallsberg (häls′bĕrgh)...Swe.	59·04 N	15·04 E
204	Halls Creek (hôlz)...Austl.	18·15 S	127·45 E
197	Halmahera (I.) (häl-mä-hä′rä) Indon.	0·45 N	128·45 E
197	Halmahera, Laut (Sea)...Indon.	1·00 S	129·00 E
156	Halmstad (hälm′städ)...Swe.	56·40 N	12·46 E
156	Halse Fd. (häl′sĕ fyôrd)...Nor.	63·03 N	8·23 E
117	Halstead (hôl′stĕd)...Ks.	38·02 N	97·36 W
193	Halt′an Tao (I.)...China	25·40 N	119·45 E
161	Haltern (häl′tĕrn) F.R.G. (Ruhr In.)	51·45 N	7·10 E
113	Haltom City (hôl′tŏm) Tx. (Dallas, Fort Worth In.)	32·48 N	97·13 W
	Halunrshan, see Wench′üan		
149	Halvarenbeek Neth. (Amsterdam In.)	51·29 N	5·10 E
153	Ḩamāh (hä′mä)...Syr.	35·08 N	36·53 E
186	Hamadān (hŭ-mŭ-dān′)...Iran	34·45 N	48·07 E
195	Hamamatsu (hä′mä-mät′sōō).Jap.	34·41 N	137·43 E
156	Hamar (hä′mär)...Nor.	60·49 N	11·05 E
191	Hamasaka (hä′mȧ-sä′kȧ)...Jap.	35·57 N	134·27 E
161	Hamborn (häm′bōrn) F.R.G. (Ruhr In.)	51·30 N	6·43 E
117	Hamburg (hăm′bûrg)...Ar.	33·15 N	91·49 W
149	Hamburg (häm′bōōrgh) F.R.G. (Hamburg In.)	53·34 N	10·02 E
108	Hamburg...Ia.	40·39 N	95·40 W
106	Hamburg...NJ (New York In.)	41·09 N	74·35 W
107	Hamburg...NY (Buffalo In.)	42·44 N	78·51 W
213	Hamburg (hăm′bûrg) S. Afr. (Natal In.)	33·18 S	27·28 E
105	Hamden (hăm′dĕn)...Ct.	41·20 N	72·55 W
157	Hämeenlinna (hĕ′mân-lĭn-nȧ).Fin.	61·00 N	24·29 E
158	Hameln (hä′mĕln)...F.R.G.	52·06 N	9·23 E
149	Hamelwörden (hä′mĕl-vûr-dĕn) F.R.G. (Hamburg In.)	53·47 N	9·19 E
204	Hamersley Ra. (hăm′ẽrz-lê).Austl.	22·15 S	117·50 E
194	Hamhŭng (häm′hōōng′)...Kor.	39·57 N	127·35 E
188	Hami (Qomul) (hä′mê) (kô-mōōl′) China	42·58 N	93·14 E
120	Hamilton...Al.	34·09 N	88·01 W
203	Hamilton (hăm′ĭl-tŭn)...Austl.	37·50 S	142·10 E
100	Hamilton...Can. (Toronto In.)	43·15 N	79·52 W
99	Hamilton...Ma. (In.)	42·37 N	70·52 W
117	Hamilton...Mo.	39·43 N	93·59 W
111	Hamilton...Mt.	46·15 N	114·09 W
205	Hamilton...N. Z. (In.)	37·45 S	175·28 E
107	Hamilton...Oh. (Cincinnati In.)	39·22 N	84·33 W
118	Hamilton...Tx.	31·42 N	98·07 W
117	Hamilton, L...Ar.	34·25 N	93·32 W
100	Hamilton Hbr..Can. (Toronto In.)	43·17 N	79·50 W
91	Hamilton Inlet...Can.	54·20 N	56·57 W
157	Hamina (hä′mê-nȧ)...Fin.	60·34 N	27·15 E
121	Hamlet (hăm′lĕt)...NC	35·52 N	79·46 W
116	Hamlin (hăm′lĭn)...Tx.	32·54 N	100·08 W
161	Hamm (häm)..F.R.G. (Ruhr In.)	51·40 N	7·48 E
218	Hammanskraal (hä-mȧns-kräl′) S. Afr. (Johannesburg & Pretoria In.)	25·24 S	28·17 E
149	Hamme...Bel. (Brussels In.)	51·06 N	4·07 E
149	Hamme-Oste Kanal (Can.) (hä′mĕ-ōs′tĕ kä-näl) F.R.G. (Hamburg In.)	53·20 N	8·59 E
150	Hammerfest (häm′mĕr-fĕst)..Nor.	70·38 N	23·59 E
107	Hammond (hăm′ŭnd) In. (Chicago In.)	41·37 N	87·31 W
119	Hammond...La.	30·30 N	90·28 W
112	Hammond...Or. (Portland In.)	46·12 N	123·57 W
105	Hammonton (hăm′ŭn-tŭn)...NJ	39·40 N	74·45 W
98	Hampden (hăm′dĕn)...Me.	44·44 N	68·51 W
154	Hampshire Downs (hămp′shĭr dounz).Eng.	51·01 N	1·05 W
106	Hampstead...Md. (Baltimore In.)	39·36 N	76·54 W
148	Hampstead Norris (hămp-stĕd nŏ′rĭs).Eng. (London In.)	51·27 N	1·14 W
98	Hampton (hămp′tŭn)...Can.	45·32 N	65·51 W
109	Hampton...Ia.	42·43 N	93·15 W
106	Hampton...Va. (Norfolk In.)	37·02 N	76·21 W
106	Hampton Roads (Inlet) Va. (Norfolk In.)	36·56 N	76·23 W
210	Ḩamrā, al- Ḩammadah al- (Plat.) Libya	29·39 N	10·53 E
156	Hamrånge (häm′rông′ĕ)...Swe.	60·56 N	17·00 E
107	Hamtramck (hăm-trăm′ĭk) Mi. (Detroit In.)	42·24 N	83·03 W
186	Hāmūn-i Māshkel (L.) (hä-mōōn′ē māsh-kĕl′).Pak.	28·28 N	64·13 E
194	Han (R.)...Kor.	37·10 N	127·40 E
89	Hana (hä′nä)...Hi.	20·43 N	155·59 W
128	Hanábana (R.) (hä-nä-bä′nä) Cuba	22·30 N	80·55 W
89	Hanalei B. (hä-nä-lā′ê)...Hi.	22·15 N	159·40 W
217	Hanang (Mtn.)...Tan.	4·26 S	35·24 E
158	Hanau (hä′nou)...F.R.G.	50·08 N	8·56 E
193	Han Chiang (R.)...China	25·00 N	116·35 E
192	Hanchung...China	33·02 N	107·00 E
109	Hancock (hăn′kŏk)...Mi.	47·08 N	88·37 W
93	Haney (hā-nê)...Can.	49·13 N	122·36 W
114	Hanford (hăn′fẽrd)...Ca.	36·20 N	119·38 W
188	Hangayn Nuruu (Khangai Mts.) Mong.	48·03 N	99·45 E
193	Hangchou (hăng′chō′)...China	30·17 N	120·12 E

ăt; finăl; rāte; senâte; ärm; ȧsk; sofȧ; fâre; ch-choose; dh-as th in other; bē; êvent; bĕt; recĕnt; cratẽr; g-go; gh-guttural g; bĭt; ĭ-short neutral; rīde; ĸ-guttural k as ch in German ich;

PRONOUNCING INDEX

Hangchou — Helper 289

Page	Name Pronunciation Region	Lat. °′	Long. °′
193	Hangchou Wan (B.) (hăng'chō') China	30·20 N	121·25 E
157	Hango (häŋ'gû) Fin.	59·49 N	22·56 E
119	Hankamer (hăn'kȧ-mẽr) Tx. (In.)	29·52 N	94·42 W
193	Han Kiang (R.) (hän'kyäng') China	31·40 N	112·04 E
108	Hankinson (häŋ'kĭn-sŭn) ND	46·04 N	96·54 W
193	Hank'ou (hăn'kō') China	30·42 N	114·22 E
204	Hann, Mt. (hän) Austl.	16·05 S	126·07 E
93	Hanna (hăn'ȧ) Can.	51·38 N	111·54 W
111	Hanna Wy.	41·51 N	106·34 W
108	Hannah ND	48·58 N	98·42 W
117	Hannibal (hăn'ĭ băl) Mo.	39·42 N	91·22 W
158	Hannover (hän-ō'vẽr) F.R.G.	52·22 N	9·45 E
156	Hanö-bukten (B.) Swe.	55·54 N	14·55 E
193	Hanoi (hä-noi') Viet.	21·04 N	105·50 E
104	Hanover (hăn'ô-vẽr) Can.	44·10 N	81·05 W
99	Hanover Ma. (In.)	42·07 N	70·49 W
105	Hanover NH	43·45 N	72·15 W
105	Hanover Pa.	39·50 N	77·00 W
136	Hanover (I.) Chile	51·00 S	74·45 W
190	Hanshan (hän'shän') China	31·43 N	118·06 E
123	Hans Lollick (I.) (häns'lôl'ĭk) Vir. Is. (U. S. A.) (St. Thomas In.)	18·24 N	64·55 W
99	Hanson (hăn'sŭn) Ma. (In.)	42·04 N	70·53 W
112	Hansville (hăns'-vĭl) Wa. (Seattle In.)	47·55 N	122·33 W
190	Hantan (hän'tän') China	36·37 N	114·30 E
98	Hantsport (hănts'pōrt) Can.	45·04 N	64·11 W
193	Hanyang (han'yäng') China	30·30 N	114·10 E
190	Haoch'engchi (hou'chĕng'jē) China	33·19 N	117·33 E
150	Haparanda (hä-pä-rän'dä) Swe.	65·54 N	23·57 E
106	Hapeville (hăp'vĭl) Ga. (Atlanta In.)	33·39 N	84·25 W
183	Haql Sau. Ar. (Palestine In.)	29·15 N	34·57 E
217	Har, Laga (R.) Ken.	2·15 N	39·30 E
162	Harana Sierra (Mts.) (sē-ĕ'r-rä-rä'nä) Sp.	37·17 N	3·28 W
188	Hara Nuur (L.) Mong.	47·47 N	94·01 E
211	Harar (Prov.) Eth.	8·15 N	41·00 E
188	Hara Usa (L.) Mong.	48·00 N	92·32 E
	Harbin, see Haerhpin		
104	Harbor Beach (här'bẽr bēch) Mi.	43·50 N	82·40 W
104	Harbor Springs Mi.	45·25 N	85·05 W
99	Harbour Breton (brĕt'ŭn) (brĕ-tôN') Can.	47·29 N	55·48 W
99	Harbour Grace (grās) Can.	47·32 N	53·13 W
149	Harburg (här-bŏŏrgh) F.R.G. (Hamburg In.)	53·28 N	9·58 E
156	Hardanger Fd. (här-däng'ẽr fyôrd) Nor.	59·58 N	6·30 E
156	Hardanger Fjell (Mts.) (fyĕl') Nor.	60·15 N	6·56 E
156	Hardanger Jöklen (Mtn.) (yû'kōōl-ĕn) Nor.	60·33 N	7·23 W
111	Hardin (här'dĭn) Mt.	45·44 N	107·36 W
213	Harding (här'dĭng) S. Afr. (Natal In.)	30·34 S	29·54 E
120	Harding (L.) Al.-Ga.	32·43 N	85·00 W
184	Hardwār (hŭr'dvär) India	29·56 N	78·06 E
114	Hardy (R.) (här'dĭ) Mex.	32·04 N	115·10 W
97	Hare B. (hâr) Can.	51·18 N	55·50 W
218	Harer (hȧ-rär') Eth. (Horn of Afr. In.)	9·43 N	42·10 E
218	Hargeysa (här-gā'ē-sȧ) Som. (Horn of Afr. In.)	9·20 N	43·57 E
159	Harghita, Muntii (Mts.) Rom.	46·25 N	25·40 E
195	Harima-Nada (Sea) (hä'rê-mä nä-dä) Jap.	34·34 N	134·37 E
149	Haring Vliet (R.) Neth. Amsterdam In.)	51·49 N	4·03 E
118	Harlan (här'lăn) Ia.	41·40 N	95·10 W
120	Harlan Ky.	36·50 N	83·19 W
116	Harlan Co. Res. Nb.	40·03 N	99·51 W
111	Harlem (hȧr'lĕm) Mt.	48·33 N	108·50 W
155	Harlingen (här'lĭng-ĕn) Neth.	53·10 N	5·24 E
119	Harlingen Tx.	26·12 N	97·42 W
148	Harlow (här'lō) Eng. (London In.)	51·46 N	0·08 E
111	Harlowton (hȧr'lô-tŭn) Mt.	46·26 N	109·50 W
104	Harmony (här'mô-nĭ) In.	39·35 N	87·00 W
110	Harney Basin (här'nĭ) Or.	43·26 N	120·19 W
110	Harney L. Or.	43·11 N	119·23 W
108	Harney Pk. SD	43·52 N	103·32 W
156	Härnosand (hĕr-nû-sänd) Swe.	62·37 N	17·54 E
162	Haro (ä'rō) Sp.	42·35 N	2·49 W
112	Haro Str. (hă'rō) Can.-U. S. (Seattle In.)	48·27 N	123·11 W
148	Harpenden (här'pĕn-d'n) Eng. (London In.)	51·48 N	0·22 W
116	Harper (här'pẽr) Ks.	37·17 N	98·02 W
214	Harper Lib.	4·25 N	7·43 W
112	Harper Wa. (Seattle In.)	47·31 N	122·32 W
105	Harpers Ferry (här'pẽrz) WV	39·20 N	77·45 W
97	Harricana (R.) Can.	50·10 N	78·50 W
120	Harriman (hăr'ĭ-măn) Tn.	35·55 N	84·34 W
105	Harrington (hăr'ĭng-tŭn) De.	38·55 N	75·35 W
186	Harri Rud (R.) Afg.	34·29 N	61·16 E
154	Harris (I.) (hăr'ĭs) Scot.	57·55 N	6·40 W
121	Harris (L.) Fl. (In.)	28·43 N	81·40 W
104	Harrisburg (hăr'ĭs-bûrg) Il.	37·45 N	88·35 W
105	Harrisburg Pa.	40·15 N	76·50 W
218	Harrismith (hă-rĭs'mĭth) S. Afr. (Johannesburg & Pretoria In.)	28·17 S	29·08 E
117	Harrison (hăr'ĭ-sŭn) Ar.	36·13 N	93·06 W
107	Harrison Oh. (Cincinnati In.)	39·16 N	84·45 W
93	Harrison L. Can.	49·31 N	121·59 W
105	Harrisonburg (hăr'ĭ-sŭn-bûrg) Va.	38·30 N	78·50 W
117	Harrisonville (hăr-ĭ-sŭn-vĭl) Mo.	38·39 N	94·21 W
113	Harrisville (hăr'ĭs-vĭl) Ut. (Salt Lake City In.)	41·17 N	112·00 W
104	Harrisville WV	39·10 N	81·05 W
104	Harrodsburg (hăr'ŭdz-bûrg) Ky.	37·45 N	84·50 W
107	Harrods Cr. (hăr'ŭdz) Ky. (Louisville In.)	38·24 N	35·33 W
148	Harrow (hăr'ō) Eng. (London In.)	51·34 N	0·21 W
149	Harsefeld (här'zĕ-fĕld') F.R.G. (Hamburg In.)	53·27 N	9·30 E
150	Harstad (här'städh) Nor.	68·49 N	16·10 E
104	Hart (härt) Mi.	43·40 N	86·25 W
218	Hartbeesfontein. S. Afr. (Johannesburg & Pretoria In.)	26·46 S	26·25 E
213	Hartbeespoortdam (L.). S. Afr. (Johannesburg & Pretoria In.)	25·47 S	27·43 E
213	Hartsbeespoort. S. Afr. (Johannesburg & Pretoria In.)	25·44 S	27·51 E
120	Hartford (härt'fẽrd) Al.	31·05 N	85·42 W
117	Hartford Ar.	35·01 N	94·21 W
105	Hartford Ct.	41·45 N	72·40 W
113	Hartford Il. (St. Louis In.)	38·50 N	90·06 W
120	Hartford Ky.	37·25 N	86·50 W
104	Hartford Mi.	42·15 N	86·15 W
109	Hartford Wi.	43·19 N	88·25 W
104	Hartford City In.	40·35 N	85·25 W
148	Hartington (härt'ĭng-tŭn) Eng.	53·08 N	1·48 W
108	Hartington Ne.	42·37 N	97·18 W
154	Hartland Pt. Eng.	51·03 N	4·40 W
154	Hartlepool (här't'l-pōōl) Eng.	54·40 N	1·12 W
217	Hartley Rh.	18·10 S	30·14 E
108	Hartley (härt'lĭ) Ia.	43·12 N	95·29 W
92	Hartley Bay Can.	53·25 N	129·15 W
95	Hart Mtn. (härt) Can.	52·25 N	101·30 W
120	Hartselle (härt'sĕl) Al.	34·24 N	86·55 W
117	Hartshorne (härts'hôrn) Ok.	34·49 N	95·34 W
121	Hartsville (härts'vĭl) SC	34·20 N	80·04 W
120	Hartwell (härt'wĕl) Ga.	34·21 N	82·56 W
120	Hartwell Res. Ga.	34·30 N	83·00 W
184	Hārua India (In.)	22·36 N	88·40 E
109	Harvard (här'vȧrd) Il.	42·25 N	88·39 W
99	Harvard Ma (In.)	42·30 N	71·35 W
116	Harvard Ne.	40·36 N	98·08 W
115	Harvard, Mt. Co.	38·55 N	106·20 W
98	Harvey Can.	45·44 N	64·46 W
107	Harvey Il. (Chicago In.)	41·37 N	87·39 W
106	Harvey La. (New Orleans In.)	29·54 N	90·05 W
108	Harvey ND	47·46 N	99·55 W
155	Harwich (här'wĭch) Eng.	51·53 N	1·13 E
184	Haryana (State) India	29·00 N	75·45 E
158	Harz Mts. (härts) G.D.R.	51·42 N	10·50 E
183	Hasā, Wādī al (R.) Jordan (Palestine In.)	30·55 N	35·50 E
195	Hashimoto (hä'shê-mō'tō) Jap.	34·19 N	135·37 E
117	Haskell (hăs'kĕl) Ok.	35·49 N	95·41 W
116	Haskell Tx.	33·09 N	99·43 W
148	Haslingden (hăz'lĭng dĕn) Eng.	53·43 N	2·19 W
156	Hassela (häs'ĕl-ô) Swe.	62·05 N	16·46 E
149	Hasselt (häs'ĕlt) Bel. (Brussels In.)	50·56 N	5·23 E
210	Hassi Messaoud Alg.	31·17 N	6·13 E
156	Hässjö (hĕs'shû) Swe.	62·36 N	17·33 E
156	Hassleholm (häs'lĕ-hōlm) Swe.	56·10 N	13·44 E
155	Hastings (hās'tĭngz) Eng.	50·52 N	0·28 E
104	Hastings Mi.	42·40 N	85·20 W
113	Hastings Mn. (Minneapolis, St. Paul In)	44·44 N	92·51 W
116	Hastings Ne.	40·34 N	98·42 W
205	Hastings N. Z. (In.)	39·33 S	176·53 E
106	Hastings-on-Hudson (ŏn-hŭd'sŭn) NY (New York In.)	40·59 N	75·53 W
120	Hatchie (R.) (hăch'ē) Tn.	35·28 N	89·14 W
165	Hateg (kät-säg') Rom.	45·35 N	22·57 E
148	Hatfield Broad Oak (hăt-fēld brôd ōk) Eng.	51·50 N	0·14 E
195	Hatogaya (hä'tō-gä-yä) Jap. (Tōkyō In.)	35·50 N	139·45 E
195	Hatsukaichi (hät'sōō-kä'ê-chê) Jap.	34·22 N	132·19 E
121	Hatteras, C. (hăt'ẽr-ȧs) NC	35·15 N	75·24 W
120	Hattiesburg (hăt'ĭz-bûrg) Ms.	31·20 N	89·18 W
161	Hattingen (hä'tĕn-gĕn) F.R.G. (Ruhr In.)	51·24 N	7·11 E
159	Hatvan (hôt'vôn) Hung.	47·39 N	19·44 E
156	Haugesund (hou'gẽ-soon') Nor.	59·26 N	5·20 E
157	Haukivesi (L.) (hou'kê-vĕ'sê) Fin.	62·02 N	29·02 E
94	Haultain (R.) Can.	56·15 N	106·35 W
218	Hauptsrus S. Afr. (Johannesburg & Pretoria In.)	26·35 S	26·16 E
205	Hauraki, G. (hä-ōō-rä'kê) N. Z. (In.)	36·44 S	175·15 E
98	Haut, Isle au (hō) Me.	44·03 N	68·13 W
152	Haut Atlas (Mts.) Mor.	32·10 N	5·49 W
98	Hauterive Can.	49·11 N	68·16 W
89	Hauula Hi.	21·37 N	157·45 W
117	Havana (hȧ-vă'nȧ) Il.	40·17 N	90·02 W
	Havana, see La Habana		
115	Havasu L. (hăv'â-sōō) Az.	34·26 N	114·09 W
158	Havel R. (hä'fĕl) G.D.R.	53·09 N	13·10 E
99	Haverhill (hā'vẽr-hĭl) Ma. (In.)	42·46 N	71·05 W
105	Haverhill NH	44·00 N	72·05 W
106	Haverstraw (hā'vẽr-strô) NY (New York In.)	41·11 N	73·58 W
158	Havlíckuv Brod Czech.	49·38 N	15·34 E
99	Havre-Bouche Boucher (hăv'rȧ-bōō-shā') Can.	45·42 N	61·30 W
111	Havre (hăv'ẽr) Mt.	48·34 N	109·42 W
105	Havre de Grace (hăv'ẽr dē grȧs') Md.	39·35 N	76·05 W
99	Havre-St. Pierre Can.	50·15 N	63·36 W
121	Haw (R.) (hô) NC	36·17 N	79·46 W
102	Hawaii (State) U. S.	20·00 N	157·40 W
89	Hawaii (I.) (hä wī'ē) Hi.	19·50 N	157·15 W
102	Hawaiian Is. (hä-wī'ȧn) U. S.	22·00 N	158·00 W
89	Hawaii Volcanoes Natl. Pk. Hi.	19·30 N	155·25 W
108	Hawarden (hā'wȧr-dĕn) Ia.	43·00 N	96·28 W
89	Hawi (hä'wē) Hi.	20·16 N	155·48 W
154	Hawick (hô'ĭk) Scot.	55·25 N	2·55 W
205	Hawke B. (hôk) N. Z. (In.)	39·17 S	177·58 E
203	Hawker (hô'kẽr) Austl.	31·58 S	138·12 E
105	Hawkesbury (hôks'bĕr-ĭ) Can.	45·35 N	74·35 W
120	Hawkinsville (hô'kĭnz-vĭl) Ga.	32·15 N	83·30 W
129	Hawks Nest Pt. Ba.	24·05 N	75·30 W
108	Hawley (hô'lĭ) Mn.	46·52 N	96·18 W
148	Haworth (hā'wûrth) Eng.	53·50 N	1·57 W
186	Hawtah Sau. Ar.	15·58 N	48·26 E
113	Hawthorne (hô'thôrn) Ca. (Los Angeles In.)	33·55 N	118·22 W
114	Hawthorne Nv.	38·33 N	118·39 W
116	Haxtun (hăks'tŭn) Co.	40·39 N	102·38 W
204	Hay (R.) (hā) Austl.	23·00 S	136·45 E
90	Hay (R.) Can.	60·21 N	117·14 W
195	Hayama (hä-yä'mä) Jap. (Tōkyō In.)	35·16 N	139·35 E
195	Hayashi (hä-yä'shē) Jap. (Tōkyō In.)	35·13 N	139·38 E
115	Hayden (hā'dĕn) Az.	33·00 N	110·50 W
101	Hayes, Mt. (hāz) Ak.	63·32 N	146·40 W
105	Hayes (R.) Can.	55·25 N	93·55 W
119	Haynesville (hānz'vĭl) La.	32·55 N	93·08 W
165	Hayrabolu Tur.	41·14 N	27·05 E
100	Hay River Can.	60·50 N	115·53 W
116	Hays (hāz) Ks.	38·51 N	99·20 W
183	Ḥaysī, Wādī al (R.) Egypt	29·24 N	34·32 E
112	Haystack Mtn. (hā-stăk') Wa. (Seattle In.)	48·26 N	122·07 W
112	Hayward (hā'wẽrd) Ca. (San Francisco In.)	37·40 N	122·06 W
109	Hayward Wi.	46·01 N	91·31 W
120	Hazard (hăz'ȧrd) Ky.	37·13 N	83·10 W
121	Hazelhurst (hā'z'l-hûrst) Ga.	31·50 N	82·36 W
107	Hazel Park Mi. (Detroit In.)	42·28 N	83·06 W
92	Hazelton (hā'z'l-tŭn) Can.	55·15 N	127·40 W
92	Hazelton Mts. Can.	55·00 N	128·00 W
120	Hazlehurst Ms.	31·52 N	90·23 W
105	Hazleton Pa.	41·00 N	76·00 W
120	Headland (hĕd'lnăd) Al.	31·22 N	85·20 W
114	Healdsburg (hēldz'bûrg) Ca.	38·37 N	122·52 W
117	Healdton (hēld'tŭn) Ok.	34·13 N	97·28 W
148	Heanor (hēn'ŏr) Eng.	53·01 N	1·22 W
220	Heard I. (hûrd) Ind. O.	53·10 S	74·35 E
119	Hearne (hûrn) Tx.	30·53 N	96·35 W
91	Hearst (hûrst) Can.	49·36 N	83·40 W
108	Heart (R.) (härt) ND	46·46 N	102·34 W
93	Heart Lake Ind. Res. Can.	55·02 N	111·30 W
99	Heart's Content (härts kŏn'tĕnt) Can.	47·52 N	53·22 W
99	Heath Pte. (hēth) Can.	49·06 N	61·45 W
117	Heavener (hēv'nẽr) Ok.	34·52 N	94·36 W
118	Hebbronville (hē'brŭn-vĭl) Tx.	27·18 N	98·40 W
115	Heber (hē'bẽr) Ut.	40·30 N	111·25 W
117	Heber Springs Ar.	35·28 N	91·59 W
111	Hebgen Res. (hĕb'gĕn) Mt.	44·47 N	111·38 W
154	Hebrides, Sea of Scot.	57·00 N	7·00 W
91	Hebron (hēb'rŭn) Can.	58·11 N	62·56 W
107	Hebron In. (Chicago In.)	41·19 N	87·13 W
107	Hebron Ky. (Cincinnati In.)	39·04 N	84·43 W
117	Hebron Ne.	40·11 N	97·36 W
108	Hebron ND	46·54 N	102·04 W
	Hebron, see Al Khalīl		
156	Heby (hĭ'bü) Swe.	59·56 N	16·48 E
92	Hecate Str. (hĕk'ȧ-tē) Can.	53·00 N	131·00 W
125	Hecelchakán (ā-sĕl-chä-kän') Mex.	20·10 N	90·09 W
95	Hecla I. Can.	51·08 N	96·45 W
156	Hedemora (hĭ-dĕ-mō'rä) Swe.	60·16 N	15·55 E
156	Hedesunda Fd. (hi-de-sōōn'dä) Swe.	60·22 N	16·50 E
148	Hedon (hĕdŭn) Eng.	53·44 N	0·12 W
149	Heemstede. Neth. (Amsterdam In.)	52·20 N	4·36 E
155	Heerlen Neth.	50·55 N	5·58 E
	Ḥefa, see Haifa		
120	Heflin (hĕf'lĭn) Al.	33·40 N	85·33 W
158	Heide (hī'dē) F.R.G.	54·13 N	9·06 E
202	Heidelberg (hī'dĕl-bûrg) Austl. (Melbourne In.)	37·45 S	145·04 E
158	Heidelberg (hīdĕl-bĕrgh) F.R.G.	49·24 N	8·43 E
158	Heidenheim (hī'dĕn-hīm) F.R.G.	48·41 N	10·09 E
218	Heilbron (hīl'brōn) S. Afr. (Johannesburg & Pretoria In.)	27·17 S	27·58 E
158	Heilbronn (hīl'brōn) F.R.G.	49·09 N	9·16 E
161	Heiligenhaus (hī'lē-gĕn-houz) F.R.G. (Ruhr In.)	51·19 N	6·58 E
158	Heiligenstadt (hī'lē-gĕn-shtät) G.D.R.	51·21 N	10·10 E
189	Heilungkiang (Prov.) (hâ-lōōng' kyäng') China	46·36 N	128·07 E
157	Heinola (hâ-nō'lȧ) Fin.	61·13 N	26·03 E
161	Heinsberg (hīnz'bĕrgh) F.R.G. (Ruhr In.)	51·04 N	6·07 E
149	Heist-op-den-Berg Bel. (Brussels In.)	51·05 N	4·14 E
	Hejaz, see Al Ḥijāz		
150	Hekla (Vol.) (hĕk'lȧ) Ice.	63·53 N	19·37 W
159	Hel (hāl) Pol.	54·37 N	18·53 E
156	Helagsfjället (Mtn.) Swe.	62·54 N	12·24 E
117	Helena (hē-lē'nȧ) Ar.	34·33 N	90·35 W
111	Helena (hĕ-lĕ'nȧ) Mt.	46·35 N	112·01 W
202	Helensburgh (hĕl'ĕnz-bŭr-ô) Austl. (Sydney In.)	34·11 S	150·59 E
154	Helensburgh Scot.	56·01 N	4·53 W
156	Helge (R.) (hĕl'gĕ) Swe.	56·31 N	13·47 E
158	Helgoland I. (hĕl'gô-länd) F.R.G.	54·13 N	7·30 E
121	Hellier (hĕl'yẽr) Ky.	37·16 N	82·27 W
162	Hellín (ĕl-yén') Sp.	38·30 N	1·40 W
186	Helmand (R.) (hĕl'mŭnd) Afg.	31·00 N	63·48 E
155	Helmond (hĕl'mōnt) (ĕl'môN') Neth.	51·35 N	5·04 E
158	Helmstedt (hĕlm'shtĕt) F.R.G.	52·14 N	11·03 E
113	Helotes (hē'lōts) Tx. (San Antonio In.)	29·35 N	98·41 W
115	Helper (hĕlp'ẽr) Ut.	39·40 N	110·55 W

ng-sing; ŋ-baŋk; N-nasalized n; nŏd; cŏmmit; ōld; ôbey; ôrder; fōōd; fŏŏt; ou-out; s-soft; sh-dish; th-thin; pūre; ûnite; ûrn; stŭd; circŭs; ü-as "y" in study; '-indeterminate vowel.

290 Helsingborg — Hollis PRONOUNCING INDEX

Page	Name Pronunciation Region	Lat. °'	Long. °'
156	Helsingborg (hĕl'sĭng-bôrgh) Swe.	56·04 N	12·40 E
	Helsingfors, see Helsinki		
156	Helsingør (hĕl-sĭng-ŭr') Den.	56·03 N	12·33 E
157	Helsinki (Helsingfors) (hĕl'sĕn-kē) (hĕl'sĭng-fôrs') Fin.	60·10 N	24·53 E
148	Hemel Hempstead (hĕm'ĕl hĕmp'stĕd) Eng. (London In.)	51·43 N	0·29 W
113	Hemet (hĕm'ĕt) Ca. (Los Angeles In.)	33·45 N	116·57 W
108	Hemingford (hĕm'ĭng-fērd) Ne.	42·21 N	103·30 W
119	Hemphill (hĕmp'hĭl) Tx.	31·20 N	93·48 W
107	Hempstead (hĕmp'stĕd) NY (New York In.)	40·42 N	73·37 W
119	Hempstead Tx.	30·07 N	96·05 W
156	Hemse (hĕm'sĕ) Swe.	57·15 N	18·25 E
156	Hemsö (I.) Swe.	62·43 N	18·22 E
156	Hen (hĭn) Nor.	60·14 N	10·10 E
162	Henares (R.) (â-nä'râs) Sp.	40·50 N	2·55 W
160	Hendaye (äN-dā') Fr.	43·20 N	1·46 W
104	Henderson (hĕn'dēr-sŭn) Ky.	37·50 N	87·30 W
114	Henderson Nv.	36·09 N	115·04 W
121	Henderson NC	36·18 N	78·24 W
120	Henderson Tn.	35·25 N	88·40 W
119	Henderson Tx.	32·09 N	94·48 W
121	Hendersonville (hĕn'dēr-sŭn-vĭl) NC	35·17 N	82·28 W
148	Hendon (hĕn'dŭn) Eng. (London In.)	51·34 N	0·13 W
218	Hendrina (hĕn-drē'nȧ) S. Afr. (Johannesburg & Pretoria In.)	26·10 S	29·44 E
193	Hengch'un (hĕng'chŭn') Taiwan	22·00 N	120·42 E
155	Hengelo (hĕngĕ-lō) Neth.	52·20 N	6·45 E
193	Henghsien China	22·40 N	104·20 E
193	Hengshan (hĕng'shän') China	27·20 N	112·40 E
190	Hengshui (hĕng'shōō-ē') China	37·43 N	115·42 E
193	Hengyang China	26·58 N	112·30 E
148	Henley on Thames (hĕn'lē ŏn tĕmz) Eng. (London In.)	51·31 N	0·54 W
105	Henlopen, C. (hĕn-lō'pĕn) De.	38·45 N	75·05 W
160	Hennebont (ĕn-bôN') Fr.	47·47 N	3·16 W
218	Hennenman S. Afr. (Johannesburg & Pretoria In.)	27·59 S	27·03 E
116	Hennessey (hĕn'ĕ-sĭ) Ok.	36·04 N	97·53 W
149	Hennigsdorf (hĕ'nĕngz-dōrf) G.D.R. (Berlin In.)	52·39 N	13·12 E
213	Hennops (R.) (hĕn'ŏps) S. Afr. (Johannesburg & Pretoria In.)	25·51 S	27·57 E
213	Hennopsrivier S. Afr. (Johannesburg & Pretoria In.)	25·50 S	27·59 E
117	Henrietta (hĕn-rĭ-ĕt'ȧ) Ok.	35·25 N	95·58 W
116	Henrietta (hen-rĭ-ĕ'tȧ) Tx.	33·47 N	98·11 W
91	Henrietta Maria, C. (hĕn-rĭ-ĕt'ȧ) Can.	55·10 N	82·20 W
115	Henry Mts. (hĕn'rĭ) Ut.	38·55 N	110·45 W
192	Henteyn Nuruu (Mts.) Sov. Un.	49·40 N	111·00 E
110	Heppner (hĕp'nēr) Or.	45·21 N	119·33 W
186	Herāt (hĕ-rät') Afg.	34·28 N	62·13 E
165	Hercegovina (Reg.) (hĕr-tsĕ-gô'vē-nȧ) Yugo.	43·23 N	17·52 E
100	Hercules Can. (Edmonton In.)	53·27 N	113·20 W
161	Herdecke (hĕr'dĕ-kĕ) F.R.G. (Ruhr In.)	51·24 N	7·26 E
127	Heredia (ā-rā'dhē-ä) C. R.	10·04 N	84·06 W
154	Hereford (hĕrĕ'fērd) Eng.	52·05 N	2·44 W
148	Hereford (Co.) Eng.	52·22 N	2·52 W
106	Hereford Md. (Baltimore In.)	39·35 N	76·42 W
116	Hereford (hĕr'ĕ-fērd) Tx.	34·47 N	102·25 W
162	Herencia (â-rān'thē-ä) Sp.	39·23 N	3·22 W
149	Herentals Bel. (Brussels In.)	51·10 N	4·51 E
158	Herford (hĕr'fôrt) F.R.G.	52·06 N	8·42 E
117	Herington (hĕr'ĭng-tŭn) Ks.	38·41 N	96·57 W
158	Herisau (hā'rē-zou) Switz.	47·23 N	9·18 E
149	Herk-de-Stad Bel. (Brussels In.)	50·56 N	5·13 E
105	Herkimer (hûr'kĭ-mēr) NY	43·05 N	75·00 W
154	Herma Ness (Prom.) (hûr'mȧ nĕs) Scot.	60·50 N	1·10 W
117	Hermann (hûr'mȧn) Mo.	38·41 N	91·27 W
104	Hermansville (hûr'mȧns-vĭl) Mi.	45·40 N	87·35 W
113	Hermantown (hēr'mȧn-toun) Mn. (Duluth In.)	46·46 N	92·12 W
218	Hermanusdorings S. Afr. (Johannesburg & Pretoria In.)	24·08 S	27·46 E
107	Herminie (hûr-mī'nē) Pa. (Pittsburgh In.)	40·16 N	79·45 W
99	Hermitage B. (hûr'mĭ-tĕj) Can.	47·35 N	56·05 W
197	Hermit Is. (hûr'mĭt) Pap. N. Gui.	1·48 S	144·55 E
113	Hermosa Beach (hēr-mō'sȧ) Ca. (Los Angeles In.)	33·51 N	118·24 W
122	Hermosillo (ĕr-mô-sē'l-yō) Mex.	29·00 N	110·57 W
106	Herndon (hĕrn'don) Va. (Baltimore In.)	38·58 N	77·22 W
161	Herne (hĕr'nĕ) F.R.G. (Ruhr In.)	51·32 N	7·13 E
156	Herning (hĕr'nĭng) Den.	56·08 N	8·55 E
108	Heron (L.) (hĕr'ŭn) Mn.	43·42 N	95·23 W
108	Heron Lake Mn.	43·48 N	95·20 W
126	Herrero, Punta (pt.) (pōō'n-tä-ĕr-rĕ'rō) Mex.	19·18 N	87·24 W
104	Herrin (hĕr'ĭn) Il.	37·50 N	89·00 W
213	Herschel (hēr'-shĕl) S. Afr. (Natal In.)	30·37 S	27·12 E
107	Herscher (hēr'shēr) Il. (Chicago In.)	41·03 N	88·06 W
155	Herstal (hĕr'stäl) Bel.	50·42 N	5·32 E
148	Hertford (hûrt'fērd) Eng.	51·46 N	0·05 W
121	Hertford NC	36·10 N	76·30 W
149	Hertzberg (hĕrtz'bĕrgh) G.D.R. (Berlin In.)	52·54 N	12·58 E
183	Herzliyya Isr. (Palestine In.)	32·10 N	34·49 E
160	Hesdin (ē-dăN') Fr.	50·24 N	1·59 E
158	Hessen (State) (hĕs'ĕn F.R.G.	50·16 N	8·48 E
114	Hetch Hetchy Aqueduct (hĕtch hĕt'-chĭ ȧk'wē-dŭkt) Ca.	37·27 N	120·54 W
108	Hettinger (hĕt'ĭn-jēr) ND	45·58 N	102·36 W
218	Heuningspruit S. Afr. (Johannesburg & Pretoria In.)	27·28 S	27·26 E
218	Heystekrand S. Afr. (Johannesburg & Pretoria In.)	25·16 S	27·14 E
148	Heywood (hā'wŏŏd) Eng.	53·36 N	2·12 W
121	Hialeah (hī-ȧ-lē'ăh) Fl. (In.)	25·49 N	80·18 W
117	Hiawatha (hī-ȧ-wô'thȧ) Ks.	39·50 N	95·33 W
115	Hiawatha Ut.	39·25 N	111·05 W
109	Hibbing (hĭb'ĭng) Mn.	47·26 N	92·58 W
120	Hickman (hĭk'mȧn) Ky.	34·33 N	89·10 W
121	Hickory (hĭk'ō-rĭ) NC	35·43 N	81·21 W
106	Hicksville (hĭks'vĭl) NY (New York In.)	40·47 N	73·25 W
104	Hicksville Oh.	41·15 N	84·45 W
118	Hico (hī'kō) Tx.	32·00 N	98·02 W
114	Hidalgo (ē-dhäl'gō) Mex.	24·14 N	99·25 W
118	Hidalgo Mex.	27·49 N	99·53 W
122	Hidlago (State) Mex.	20·45 N	99·30 W
118	Hidalgo del Parral (ē-dä'l-gō-dĕl-pär-rȧ'l) Mex.	26·55 N	105·40 W
125	Hidalgo Yalalag (ē-dhäl'gō-yä-lä-läg) Mex.	17·12 N	96·11 W
218	Hiedelberg S. Afr. (Johannesburg & Pretoria In.)	26·32 S	28·22 E
210	Hierro I. (yĕ'r-rô) Can. Is.	27·37 N	18·29 W
195	Higashimurayama Jap. (Tōkyō In.)	35·46 N	139·28 E
195	Higashiōsaka Jap. (Ōsaka In.)	34·40 N	135·44 E
104	Higgins (L.) (hĭg'ĭnz) Mi.	44·20 N	84·45 W
117	Higginsville (hĭg'ĭnz-vĭl) Mo.	39·05 N	93·44 W
104	High (I.) Mi.	45·45 N	85·45 W
100	High Bluff Can. (Winnipeg In.)	50·01 N	98·08 W
128	Highborne Cay (hī'bôrn kē) Ba.	24·45 N	76·50 W
113	Highgrove (hī'grōv) Ca. (Los Angeles In.)	34·01 N	117·20 W
119	High Island Tx. (In.)	29·34 N	94·24 W
113	Highland (hī'lănd) Ca. (Los Angeles In.)	34·08 N	117·13 W
117	Highland Il.	38·44 N	89·41 W
107	Highland In. (Chicago In.)	41·33 N	87·28 W
107	Highland Mi. (Detroit In.)	42·38 N	83·37 W
107	Highland Park Il. (Chicago In.)	42·11 N	87·47 W
107	Highland Park Mi. (Detroit In.)	42·24 N	83·06 W
106	Highland Park NJ (New York In.)	40·30 N	74·25 W
113	Highland Park Tx. (Dallas, Fort Worth In.)	32·49 N	96·48 W
106	Highlands (hī-lăndz) NJ (New York In.)	40·24 N	73·59 W
113	Highlands Tx. (In.)	29·49 N	95·01 W
108	Highmore (hī'mōr) SD	44·30 N	99·26 W
148	High Ongar (on'gēr) Eng. (London In.)	51·43 N	0·15 E
197	High Pk. Phil. (In.)	15·38 N	120·05 E
121	High Point NC	35·55 N	80·00 W
93	High Prairie Can.	55·26 N	116·29 W
113	High Ridge Mo. (St. Louis In.)	38·27 N	90·32 W
93	High River Can.	50·35 N	113·52 W
121	Highrock (R.) (hī'-rŏk) NC	35·40 N	80·15 W
121	High Springs Fl.	29·48 N	82·38 W
106	Hightstown (hīts-toun) NJ (New York In.)	40·16 N	74·32 W
148	High Wycombe (wĭ-kŭm) Eng. (London In.)	51·36 N	0·45 W
123	Higuero, Pta. (Pt.) P. R. (Puerto Rico In.)	18·21 N	67·11 W
135	Higuerote (ē-gĕ-rô'-tĕ) Ven. (In.)	10·29 N	66·06 W
129	Higüey (ē-gwĕ'y) Dom. Rep.	18·40 N	68·45 W
157	Hiiumaa (D'Ago) (hē'ōōm-ô) Sov. Un.	58·47 N	22·05 E
195	Hikone (hē'kō-nĕ) Jap.	35·15 N	136·15 E
158	Hildburghausen (hĭld'bŏŏrg hou-zĕn) G.D.R.	50·26 N	10·45 E
161	Hilden (hēl'dĕn) F.R.G. (Ruhr In.)	51·10 N	6·56 E
158	Hildesheim (hĭl'dĕs-hīm) F.R.G.	52·08 N	9·56 E
127	Hillaby, Mt. (hĭl'ȧ-bĭ) Barb. (In.)	13·15 N	59·35 W
116	Hill City (hĭl) Ks.	39·22 N	99·54 W
109	Hill City Mn.	46·58 N	93·38 W
149	Hillegersberg Neth. (Amsterdam In.)	51·57 N	4·29 E
156	Hillerød (hē'lĕ-rûdh) Den.	55·56 N	12·17 E
117	Hillsboro (hĭlz'bŭr-ō) Il.	39·09 N	89·28 W
117	Hillsboro Ks.	38·22 N	97·11 W
105	Hillsboro NH	43·05 N	71·55 W
108	Hillsboro ND	47·23 N	97·05 W
104	Hillsboro Oh.	39·10 N	83·40 W
110	Hillsboro Or. (Portland In.)	45·31 N	122·59 W
119	Hillsboro Tx.	32·01 N	97·06 W
109	Hillsboro Wi.	43·39 N	90·20 W
100	Hillsburgh (hĭlz'bûrg) Can. (Toronto In.)	43·48 N	80·09 W
110	Hills Creek Res. Or.	43·41 N	122·26 W
114	Hillsdale (hĭls-dāl) Mi.	41·55 N	84·35 W
89	Hilo (hē'lō) Hi.	19·44 N	155·01 W
149	Hilversum (hĭl'vēr-sŭm) Neth. (Amsterdam In.)	52·13 N	5·10 E
184	Himachal Pradesh (State) India	36·03 N	77·41 E
187	Himalaya Mts. (hĭ-mä'lȧ-yȧ) Asia	29·30 N	85·02 E
195	Himeji (hē'mȧ-jē) Jap.	34·50 N	134·42 E
149	Himmelpforten (hē'mĕl-pfōr-tĕn) F.R.G. (Hamburg In.)	53·37 N	9·19 E
129	Hinche (hēn'chȧ) (ăNsh) Hai.	19·10 N	72·05 W
205	Hinchinbrook (I.) (hĭn-chĭn-brŏŏk) Austl.	18·23 S	146·57 W
148	Hinckley (hĭnk'lĭ) Eng.	52·32 N	1·21 W
148	Hindley (hĭnd'lĭ) Eng.	53·32 N	2·35 W
187	Hindu Kush (Mts.) (hĭn'dōō kōōsh') Asia	35·15 N	68·44 E
185	Hindupur (hĭn'dōō-pōōr) India	13·52 N	77·34 E
99	Hingham (hĭng'ăm) Ma. (In.)	42·14 N	70·53 W
107	Hinkley (hĭnk'-lĭ) Oh. (Cleveland In.)	41·14 N	81·45 W
162	Hinojosa (ē-nô-kō'sä) Sp.	38·30 N	5·09 W
107	Hinsdale (hĭnz'dāl) Il. (Chicago In.)	41·48 N	87·56 W
93	Hinton (hĭn'tŭn) Can.	53·25 N	117·34 W
104	Hinton (hĭn'tŭn) WV	37·40 N	80·55 W
195	Hirado (I.) (hē'rä-dō) Jap.	33·19 N	129·18 E
195	Hirakata (hē'rä-kä'tä) Jap. (Ōsaka In.)	34·49 N	135·40 E
195	Hiratsuka (hē-rät-sōō'kȧ) Jap.	35·20 N	139·19 E
188	Hirgis Nuur (L.) Mong.	49·18 N	94·21 E
194	Hirosaki (hē'rō-sä'kē) Jap.	40·31 N	140·38 E
195	Hirose (hē'rō-sä) Jap.	35·20 N	133·11 E
195	Hiroshima (hē-rō-shē'mȧ) Jap.	34·22 N	132·25 E
160	Hirson (ēr-sôN') Fr.	49·54 N	4·00 E
189	Hisar India	29·15 N	75·47 E
123	Hispaniola (I.) (hĭ'spăn-ĭ-ō-lȧ) N. A.	17·30 N	73·15 W
194	Hitachi (hē-tä'chē) Jap.	36·42 N	140·47 E
119	Hitchcock (hĭch'kŏk) Tx. (In.)	29·21 N	95·01 W
161	Hitdorf (hēt'dōrf) F.R.G. (Ruhr In.)	51·04 N	6·56 E
195	Hitoyoshi (hē'tō-yō'shē) Jap.	32·13 N	130·45 E
150	Hitra (I.) (hĭträ) Nor.	63·34 N	7·37 E
149	Hittefeld (hē'tĕ-fĕld) F.R.G. (Hamburg In.)	53·23 N	9·59 E
195	Hiwasa (hē'wȧ-sä) Jap.	33·44 N	134·31 E
120	Hiwassee (R.) (hĭ-wôs'sē) Tn.	35·10 N	84·35 W
156	Hjälmaren (L.) Swe.	59·07 N	16·05 E
156	Hjo (yō) Swe.	58·19 N	14·11 E
156	Hjørring (jûr'ĭng) Den.	57·27 N	9·59 E
159	Hlohovec (hlō'ho-vĕts) Czech.	48·24 N	17·49 E
203	Hobart (hō'bȧrt) Austl.	43·00 S	147·30 E
107	Hobart In. (Chicago In.)	41·31 N	87·15 W
116	Hobart Ok.	35·02 N	99·06 W
112	Hobart Wa. (Seattle In.)	47·25 N	121·58 W
116	Hobbs (hŏbs) NM	32·41 N	104·04 W
188	Hobdo Gol (R.) Mong.	49·06 N	91·16 E
149	Hoboken (hō'bō-kĕn) Bel. (Brussels In.)	51·11 N	4·20 E
106	Hoboken NJ (New York In.)	40·43 N	74·03 W
156	Hobro (hô-brô') Den.	56·38 N	9·47 E
106	Hobson (hŏb'sŭn) Va. (Norfolk In.)	36·54 N	76·31 W
202	Hobson's B. (hŏb'sŭnz) Austl. (Melbourne In.)	37·54 S	144·45 E
190	Hochien (hŭ'jĭän) China	38·28 N	116·05 E
196	Ho Chi Minh City (Saigon) Viet.	10·46 N	106·34 E
190	Hochiu China	32·19 N	116·17 E
158	Höchst (hûKst) F.R.G.	50·06 N	8·37 E
193	Hoch'uan China	30·00 N	106·20 E
112	Hockinson (hŏk'-ĭn-sŭn) Wa. (Portland In.)	45·44 N	122·29 W
126	Hoctún (ôk-tōō'n) Mex. (In.)	20·52 N	89·10 W
104	Hodgenville (hŏj'ĕn-vĭl) Ky.	37·35 N	85·45 W
97	Hodges Hill (Mtn.) (hŏj'ĕz) Can.	49·04 N	55·53 W
159	Hódmezövásárhely (hōd'mĕ-zû-vô' shôr-hĕl-y') Hung.	46·24 N	20·21 E
159	Hodonin (hē'dô-nēn) Czech.	48·50 N	17·06 E
149	Hoegaarden Bel. (Brussels In.)	50·46 N	4·55 E
149	Hoek van Holland Neth. (Amsterdam In.)	51·59 N	4·05 E
194	Hoeryŏng (hwĕr'yŭng) Kor.	42·28 N	129·39 E
161	Hoetmar (hût'mär) F.R.G. (Ruhr In.)	51·52 N	7·54 E
158	Hof (hōf) F.R.G.	50·19 N	11·55 E
190	Hofei (hô'fā) China	31·51 N	117·15 E
150	Hofsjökull (Gl.) (hôfs'yü'kōōl) Ice.	64·55 N	18·40 W
104	Hog (I.) Mi.	45·50 N	85·20 W
120	Hogansville (hō'gănz-vĭl) Ga.	33·10 N	84·54 W
129	Hog Cay (I.) Ba.	23·35 N	75·30 W
129	Hogsty Rf. Ba.	21·45 N	73·50 W
149	Hohenbrunn (hō'hĕn-brōōn) F.R.G. (Munich In.)	48·03 N	11·42 E
161	Hohenlimburg (hō'hĕn lĕm'bōōrg) F.R.G. (Ruhr In.)	51·20 N	7·35 E
149	Hohen Neuendorf (hō'hĕn noi'ĕn-dōrf) G.D.R. (Berlin In.)	52·40 N	13·22 E
158	Hohe Tauern (Mts.) (hō'ĕ tou'ērn) Aus.	47·11 N	12·12 E
214	Hohoe Ghana	7·09 N	0·28 E
106	Hohokus (hō-hō-kŭs) NJ (New York In.)	41·01 N	74·08 W
193	Hohsien China	24·20 N	111·28 E
190	Hohsien (hō'syĕn') China	31·44 N	118·20 E
190	Ho Hu (L.) (hŭ'hoo) China	31·37 N	119·57 E
116	Hoisington (hoi'zĭng-tŭn) Ks.	38·30 N	98·46 W
195	Hojo (hō'jô) Jap.	33·58 N	132·50 E
205	Hokitika (hō-kĭ-tē'kä) N. Z. (In.)	42·43 S	171·12 E
194	Hokkaido (I.) (hŏk'kī-dō) Jap.	43·30 N	142·45 E
156	Holbaek (hôl'bĕk) Den.	55·42 N	11·40 E
126	Holbox (ôl-bō'x) Mex. (In.)	21·33 N	87·19 W
126	Holbox, Isla (I.) (ē's-lä-ôl-bō'x) Mex. (In.)	21·40 N	87·21 W
115	Holbrook (hōl'brŏŏk) Az.	34·55 N	110·15 W
99	Holbrook Ma. (In.)	42·10 N	71·01 W
99	Holden (hōl'dĕn) Ma. (In.)	42·21 N	71·51 W
117	Holden Mo.	38·42 N	94·00 W
104	Holden WV	37·45 N	82·05 W
117	Holdenville (hōl'dĕn-vĭl) Ok.	35·05 N	96·25 W
116	Holdrege (hōl'drĕj) Ne.	40·25 N	99·28 W
156	Hölen (hûl'ĕn) Nor.	59·34 N	10·40 E
129	Holguín (ôl-gēn') Cuba	20·55 N	76·15 W
105	Holidaysburg (hŏl'ĭ-dāz-bûrg) Pa.	40·30 N	78·30 W
148	Hollabrunn Aus.	48·33 N	16·04 E
104	Holland (hŏl'ănd) Mi.	42·45 N	86·10 W
149	Hollandsch Diep (Chan.) Neth. (Amsterdam In.)	51·43 N	4·25 E
149	Hollenstedt (hō'lĕn-shtĕt) F.R.G. (Hamburg In.)	53·22 N	9·43 E
113	Holliday (hŏl'ĭ-dā) Ks. (Kansas City In.)	39·02 N	94·48 W
99	Hollis (hŏl'ĭs) NH (In.)	42·30 N	71·29 W

ăt; finăl; rāte; senâte; ärm; ȧsk; sofȧ; fâre; ch-choose; dh-as th in other; bē; ēvent; bĕt; recĕnt; cratēr; g-go; gh-guttural g; bĭt; ĭ-short neutral; rīde; K-guttural k as ch in German ich;

Page	Name Pronunciation	Region	Lat. °′	Long. °′
116	Hollis	Ok.	34·39 N	99·56 W
114	Hollister (hŏl'ĭs-tēr)	Ca.	36·50 N	121·25 W
99	Holliston (hŏl'ĭs-tŭn)	Ma. (In.)	42·12 N	71·25 W
104	Holly (hŏl'ĭ)	Mi.	42·45 N	83·30 W
112	Holly	Wa. (Seattle In.)	47·34 N	122·58 W
120	Holly Springs (hŏl'ĭ sprĭngz)	Ms.	34·45 N	89·28 W
113	Hollywood (hŏl'ē-wŏŏd)	Ca. (Los Angeles In.)	34·06 N	118·20 W
121	Hollywood	Fl. (In.)	26·00 N	80·11 W
205	Holmes Rfs. (hōmz)	Austl.	16·33 S	148·43 E
156	Holmestrand (hôl'mĕ-strän)	Nor.	59·29 N	10·17 E
156	Holmsbu (hôlms'bōō)	Nor.	59·36 N	10·26 E
156	Holmsjön (L.)	Swe.	62·23 N	15·43 E
156	Holstebro (hôl'stĕ-brô)	Den.	56·22 N	8·39 E
120	Holston (R.) (hōl'stŭn)	Tn.	36·02 N	83·42 W
148	Holt (hōlt)	Eng.	53·05 N	2·53 W
117	Holton (hōl'tŭn)	Ks.	39·27 N	95·43 W
154	Holy (I.) (hō'lĭ)	Wales	53·45 N	4·45 W
154	Holy (I.)	Eng.	55·43 N	1·48 W
101	Holy Cross (hō'lĭ krôs)	Ak.	62·10 N	159·40 W
154	Holyhead (hŏl'ē-hĕd)	Wales	53·48 N	4·45 W
116	Holyoke (hōl'yōk)	Co.	40·36 N	102·18 W
105	Holyoke	Ma.	42·10 N	72·40 W
195	Homano (hō-mä'nō)	Jap. (Tōkyō In.)	35·33 N	140·08 E
161	Homberg (hōm'bĕrgh)	F.R.G. (Ruhr In.)	51·27 N	6·42 E
214	Hombori	Mali	15·17 N	1·42 W
113	Home Gardens (hōm gär'd'nz)	Ca. (Los Angeles In.)	33·53 N	117·32 W
113	Homeland (hōm'lănd)	Ca. (Los Angeles In.)	33·44 N	117·07 W
101	Homer (hō'mēr)	Ak.	59·42 N	151·30 W
119	Homer	La.	32·46 N	93·05 W
121	Homestead (hōm'stĕd)	Fl. (In.)	25·27 N	80·28 W
113	Homestead	Mi. (Sault Ste. Marie In.)	46·20 N	84·07 W
107	Homestead	Pa. (Pittsburgh In.)	40·29 N	79·55 W
118	Homestead Natl. Mon. of America	Ne.	40·16 N	96·51 W
106	Homewood (hōm'wŏŏd)	Al. (Birmingham In.)	33·28 N	86·48 W
107	Homewood	Il. (Chicago In.)	41·34 N	87·40 W
118	Hominy (hŏm'ĭ-nĭ)	Ok.	36·25 N	96·24 W
120	Homochiho (R.) (hō-mō-chĭt'ō)	Ms.	31·23 N	91·15 W
153	Homs (hōms)	Syr.	34·42 N	36·52 E
189	Honan (Prov.) (hō'nän')	China	33·58 N	112·33 E
134	Honda (hōn'dà)	Col. (In.)	5·13 N	74·45 W
128	Honda, Bahía (B.) (bä-ē'ä-ô'n-dä)	Cuba	23·10 N	83·20 W
118	Hondo	Tx.	29·20 N	99·08 W
126	Hondo, Rio (R.) (hon-dō')	Belize (In.)	18·16 N	88·32 W
116	Hondo (R.)	NM	33·22 N	105·06 W
122	Honduras (hŏn-dōō'ràs)	N. A.	14·30 N	88·00 W
122	Honduras, Gulf of	N. A.	16·30 N	87·30 W
121	Honea Path (hŭn'ĭ păth)	SC	34·25 N	82·16 W
156	Hønefoss (hē'nē-fôs)	Nor.	60·10 N	10·15 E
105	Honesdale (hōnz'dāl)	Pa.	41·30 N	75·15 W
114	Honey (R.) (hŭn'ĭ)	Ca.	40·11 N	120·34 W
117	Honey Grove (hŭn'ĭ grōv)	Tx.	33·35 N	95·54 W
100	Honfleur (ôN-flûr')	Can. (Quebec In.)	46·39 N	70·53 W
160	Honfleur (ôN-flûr')	Fr.	49·26 N	0·13 E
193	Hon Gay	Viet.	20·58 N	107·10 E
98	Honguedo, Détroit d' (Str.)	Can.	49·08 N	63·45 W
205	Honiara	Sol. Is.	9·15 S	159·45 E
154	Honiton (hŏn'ĭ-tŏn)	Eng.	50·49 N	3·10 W
189	Hong Kong (hŏng' kŏng')	Asia	21·45 N	115·00 E
89	Honolulu (hŏn-ō-lōō'lōō)	Hi.	21·18 N	157·50 W
89	Honomu (hŏn'ō-mōō)	Hi.	19·50 N	155·04 W
194	Honshū (I.) (hŏn'shōō)	Jap.	36·50 N	135·20 E
110	Hood, Mt.	Or.	45·20 N	121·43 W
112	Hood Can. (hŏŏd)	Wa. (Seattle In.)	47·45 N	122·45 W
110	Hood River	Or.	45·42 N	121·30 W
112	Hoodsport (hŏŏdz'pōrt)	Wa. (Seattle In.)	47·25 N	123·09 W
184	Hoogly (R.) (hōōg'lĭ)	India	21·35 N	87·50 E
149	Hoogstraten	Bel. (Brussels In.)	51·24 N	4·46 E
116	Hooker (hŏŏk'ēr)	Ok.	36·49 N	101·13 W
126	Hool (ōō'l)	Mex. (In.)	19·32 N	90·22 W
101	Hoonah (hōō'nä)	Ak.	58·05 N	135·25 W
110	Hoopa Valley Ind. Res. (hōō'pà)	Ca.	41·18 N	123·35 W
117	Hooper (hŏŏp'ēr)	Ne.	41·37 N	96·31 W
113	Hooper	Ut. (Salt Lake City In.)	41·10 N	112·08 W
101	Hooper Bay	Ak.	61·32 N	166·02 W
104	Hoopeston (hōōps'tŭn)	Il.	40·35 N	87·40 W
105	Hoosick Falls (hōō'sĭk)	NY	42·55 N	73·15 W
114	Hoover Dam (hōō'vēr)	Nv.	36·00 N	115·06 W
106	Hopatcong, L. (hō-păt'kong)	NJ (New York In.)	40·57 N	74·38 W
101	Hope (hōp)	Ak.	60·54 N	149·48 W
117	Hope	Ar.	33·41 N	93·35 W
93	Hope	Can.	49·23 N	121·26 W
108	Hope	ND	47·17 N	97·45 W
91	Hopedale (hōp'dāl)	Can.	55·26 N	60·11 W
99	Hopedale (hōp'dāl)	Ma. (In.)	42·08 N	71·33 W
189	Hopeh (Prov.)	China	39·15 N	115·40 E
126	Hopelchén (o-pĕl-chĕ'n)	Mex. (In.)	19·47 N	89·51 W
91	Hopes Advance, C. (hōps ăd-văns')	Can.	61·05 N	69·35 W
204	Hopetoun (hōp'toun)	Austl.	33·50 S	120·15 E
121	Hopewell (hōp'wĕl)	Va.	37·14 N	77·15 W
212	Hopetown (hōp'toun)	S. Afr.	29·35 S	24·10 E
115	Hopi Ind. Res. (hō'pē)	Az.	36·20 N	110·30 W
113	Hopkins (hŏp'-kĭns)	Mn. (Minneapolis, St. Paul In.)	44·55 N	93·24 W
120	Hopkinsville (hŏp'-kĭns-vĭl)	Ky.	36·50 N	87·28 W
99	Hopkinton (hŏp'-kĭn-tŭn)	Ma. (In.)	42·14 N	71·31 W
193	Hop'u	China	21·28 N	109·10 E
110	Hoquiam (hō'kwĭ-ăm)	Wa.	47·00 N	123·53 W
156	Horby (hûr'bü)	Swe.	55·50 N	13·41 E
127	Horconcitos (ŏr-kōn-sē'-tōs)	Pan.	8·18 N	82·11 W
218	Hordio	Som. (Horn of Afr. In.)	10·43 N	51·05 E
158	Horgen (hôr'gĕn)	Switz.	47·16 N	8·35 E
109	Horicon (hŏr'ĭ-kŏn)	Wi.	43·26 N	88·40 W
186	Hormuz, Str. of (hŏr'mŭz')	Asia	26·37 N	15·27 E
	Horn, C., see Hornos, Cabo de			
205	Horn (Is.) (hôrn)	Austl.	10·30 S	143·30 E
150	Hornavan (L.)	Swe.	65·54 N	16·17 E
149	Horneburg (hôr'nĕ-bŏŏrgh)	F.R.G. (Hamburg In.)	53·30 N	9·35 E
105	Hornell (hôr-nĕl')	NY	42·10 N	77·40 W
90	Horn Mts.	Can.	62·12 N	120·29 W
136	Hornos, C. de (Horn, C.) (kà'-bô-dĕ-ŏ'r-nôs) (kā'p-hŏr'n)	Chile	56·00 S	67·00 W
202	Hornsby (hôrnz'bĭ)	Austl. (Sydney In.)	33·43 S	151·06 E
156	Hornslandet (I.)	Swe.	61·40 N	17·58 E
136	Horqueta (ŏr-kĕ'tä)	Par.	23·20 S	57·00 W
116	Horse Cr. (hôrs)	Co.	38·49 N	103·48 W
108	Horse Cr.	Wy.	41·33 N	104·39 W
99	Horse Is.	Can.	50·11 N	55·45 W
156	Horsens (hôrs'ĕns)	Den.	55·50 N	9·49 E
112	Horseshoe B. (hôrs-shōō)	Can. (Vancouver In.)	49·23 N	123·16 W
148	Horsforth (hôrs'fŭrth)	Eng.	53·50 N	1·38 W
203	Horsham, (hôr'shăm) (hôrs'ăm)	Austl.	36·42 S	142·17 E
149	Horst (hôrst)	F.R.G. (Hamburg In.)	53·49 N	9·37 E
156	Horten (hôr'tĕn)	Nor.	59·26 N	10·27 E
118	Horton (hôr'tŭn)	Ks.	39·38 N	95·32 W
101	Horton (R.) (hôr'tŭn)	Ak.	68·38 N	122·00 W
148	Horwich (hŏr'ĭch)	Eng.	53·36 N	2·33 W
215	Hoséré Vokré (Mtn.)	Cam.	8·20 N	13·15 E
193	Hoshan	China	31·30 N	116·25 E
195	Hososhima (hō'sō-shē'mä)	Jap.	32·25 N	131·40 E
136	Hoste (ôs'tā) (I.)	Chile	55·20 S	70·45 W
124	Hostotipaquillo (ôs-tō'tĭ-pä-kēl'yō)	Mex.	21·09 N	104·05 W
195	Hota (hō'tä)	Jap. (Tōkyō In.)	35·08 N	139·50 E
188	Hotien (Khotan) (hō'tyĕn') (kō-tän')	China	37·11 N	79·50 E
129	Hoto Mayor (ô-tô-mä-yō'r)	Dom. Rep.	18·45 N	69·10 W
101	Hot Springs (hŏt sprĭngs)	Ak.	65·00 N	150·20 W
117	Hot Springs	Ar.	34·29 N	93·02 W
108	Hot Springs	SD	43·28 N	103·32 W
105	Hot Springs	Va.	38·00 N	79·55 W
117	Hot Springs Natl. Park	Ar.	34·30 N	93·00 W
129	Hotte, Massif de la (Mts.)	Hai.	18·25 N	74·00 W
114	Hotville (hŏt'-vĭl)	Ca.	32·50 N	115·24 W
190	Houchen (hō'jĕn)	China	36·59 N	118·59 E
161	Houdan (ōō-dän')	Fr. (Paris In.)	48·47 N	1·36 E
109	Houghton (hō'tŭn)	Mi.	47·06 N	88·36 W
104	Houghton (L.)	Mi.	44·20 N	84·45 W
161	Houilles (ōō-yĕs')	Fr. (Paris In.)	48·55 N	2·11 E
98	Houlton (hōl'tŭn)	Me.	46·07 N	67·50 W
119	Houma (hōō'mà)	La.	29·36 N	90·43 W
214	Houndé	Upper Volta	11·30 N	3·31 W
105	Housatonic (R.) (hōō-sà-tŏn'ĭk)	Ct.-Ma.	41·50 N	73·25 W
113	House Springs (hous sprĭngs)	Mo. (St. Louis In.)	38·24 N	90·34 W
120	Houston (hūs'tŭn)	Ms.	33·53 N	89·00 W
119	Houston	Tx. (In.)	29·46 N	95·21 W
119	Houston Ship Chan.	Tx. (In.)	29·38 N	94·57 W
212	Houtbaai	S. Afr. (In.)	34·03 S	18·22 E
204	Houtman Rocks (Is.) (hout'män)	Austl.	28·15 S	112·45 E
154	Hove (hōv)	Eng.	50·50 N	0·09 W
115	Hovenweep Natl. Mon. (hō'v'n-wēp)	Co.-Ut.	37·27 N	108·50 W
117	Howard (hou'ard)	Ks.	37·27 N	96·10 W
108	Howard	SD	44·01 N	97·31 W
148	Howden (hou'dĕn)	Eng.	53·44 N	0·52 W
203	Howe, C. (hou)	Austl.	37·30 S	150·40 E
104	Howell (hou'ĕl)	Mi.	42·40 N	84·00 W
92	Howe Sd.	Can.	49·22 N	123·18 W
100	Howick (hou'ĭk)	Can. (Montreal In.)	45·11 N	73·51 W
213	Howick	S. Afr. (Natal In.)	29·29 S	30·16 E
198	Howland (I.) (hou'lănd)	Oceania	1·00 N	176·00 W
184	Howrah (hou'rä)	India (In.)	22·33 N	88·20 E
93	Howse Pk.	Can.	51·30 N	116·40 W
92	Howson Pk.	Can.	54·25 N	127·45 W
117	Hoxie (kŏh'sĭ)	Ar.	36·03 N	91·00 W
154	Hoy (I.) (hoi)	Scot.	58·53 N	3·10 W
195	Hōya	Jap. (Tōkyō In.)	35·45 N	139·35 E
192	Hoyang	China	35·18 N	110·18 E
148	Hoylake (hoi-lāk')	Eng.	53·23 N	3·11 W
193	Hoyüan	China	23·48 N	114·45 E
158	Hradec Králové (hrä'dĕts krä'lô-vā)	Czech.	50·14 N	15·50 E
159	Hranice (hrän'yē-tsĕ)	Czech.	49·33 N	17·45 E
159	Hrinová (hrēn'yō-vä)	Czech.	48·36 N	19·32 E
159	Hron R.	Czech.	48·22 N	18·42 E
159	Hrubieszów (hrōō-byä'shōōf)	Pol.	50·48 N	23·54 E
164	Hrvatska (Croatia) (Reg.) (hr-väts'kä)	Yugo.	45·24 N	15·18 E
191	Hsaiolung	China (Canton In.)	22·27 N	113·26 E
188	Hsawnhsup	Bur.	24·29 N	94·45 E
190	Hsiaching (sĭä'jĭn)	China	36·58 N	115·59 E
190	Hsiai (sĭä'yē)	China	34·15 N	116·07 E
193	Hsiamen (I.)	China	24·28 N	118·20 E
193	Hsiamen (Amoy) (á-moi')	China	24·30 N	118·10 E
192	Hsian(Sian)(shĭ'än) (syän')	China	34·20 N	109·00 E
190	Hsiang (hsē'äng')	China	39·43 N	116·08 E
190	Hsiangch'eng	China	33·52 N	113·31 E
192	Hsiangho (hsē'äng'-hō')	China (In.)	39·46 N	116·59 E
189	Hsiaohsinganling Shanmo (Lesser Khingan Ra.)	China	49·50 N	127·26 E
190	Hsiaoku Ho (R.) (sĭou'gōō hŭ)	China	36·29 N	120·06 E
193	Hsiap'u	China	27·00 N	120·00 E
190	Hsiats'un (sĭä'ts'ün)	China	36·54 N	121·31 E
193	Hsich'ang	China	26·50 N	102·25 E
193	Hsi Chiang (R.)	China	22·00 N	109·18 E
191	Hsi Chiang (R.)	China (Canton In.)	22·47 N	113·01 E
190	Hsichung Tao (I.) (sē'joong'dou)	China	39·27 N	121·06 E
191	Hsients'unhsü	China (Canton In.)	23·10 N	113·41 E
192	Hsienyang	China	34·20 N	108·40 E
192	Hsifeng (hsē'fĕng')	China	42·40 N	124·40 E
190	Hsihoying (sē'hŭ'yĭng)	China	39·58 N	114·50 E
190	Hsihsienchen (sē'sĭän'jĕn)	China	37·21 N	119·59 E
190	Hsi Hu (L.) (sē'hōō)	China	32·31 N	116·04 E
192	Hsiliao (R.)	China	43·23 N	121·40 E
191	Hsinch'ang	China (Shanghai In.)	31·02 N	121·38 E
190	Hsincheng (sĭn'jeng)	China	34·24 N	113·43 E
190	Hsinchiachai (sĭn'jĭa'jäi)	China	36·59 N	117·33 E
184	Hsinchiang (Mts.)	China	41·52 N	81·20 E
193	Hsinchu (hsĭn'chōō')	Taiwan	24·48 N	121·00 E
193	Hsingan	China	25·44 N	110·32 E
190	Hsingcheng (sĭng'chĕng)	China	40·38 N	120·41 E
190	Hsingchiawan (sĭng'jĭä'wäN)	China	37·16 N	114·54 E
190	Hsinghua (sĭng'hōōä)	China	32·58 N	119·48 E
190	Hsingt'ai (sĭng'tăĭ)	China	37·04 N	114·33 E
190	Hsinhsiang (sĭn'sĭäng)	China	35·17 N	113·49 E
190	Hsinhsien (sĭn'sĭäN)	China	36·14 N	115·38 E
192	Hsinhsien	China	38·20 N	112·45 E
193	Hsinhua	China	27·45 N	111·20 E
193	Hsinhui	China	22·40 N	113·08 E
188	Hsining	China	36·52 N	101·36 E
193	Hsinkao Shan (Mtn.)	Taiwan	23·38 N	121·05 E
	Hsinking, see Ch'angch'un			
192	Hsinmin	China	42·00 N	122·42 E
190	Hsinp'u (sĭn'pōō)	China	34·35 N	119·09 E
190	Hsint'ai (sĭn'tăĭ)	China	35·55 N	117·44 E
191	Hsint'ang	China (Canton In.)	23·06 N	113·06 E
191	Hsinti	China (Canton In.)	22·43 N	113·20 E
190	Hsintien (sĭn'dĭäN)	China	31·33 N	115·17 E
190	Hsinyang (sĭn'yäng)	China	32·08 N	114·04 E
192	Hsinyeh	China	32·40 N	112·20 E
190	Hsip'ing (sē'pĭng)	China	33·21 N	114·01 E
193	Hsisha Ch'üntao (Parcel Is.)	China	16·40 N	113·00 E
193	Hsishui	China	30·30 N	115·10 E
190	Hsiungyüen	China	40·10 N	122·08 E
190	Hsiyang (sē'yäng)	China	37·37 N	113·42 E
193	Hsüancheng	China	30·52 N	118·48 E
192	Hsuanhua	China	40·35 N	115·05 E
190	Hsuanhuatien (sōōäN'hōōä'dĭäN)	China	31·42 N	114·29 E
190	Hsüch'ang (sü'chäng)	China	34·02 N	113·49 E
190	Hsüchou (Süchow)	China	34·17 N	117·10 E
190	Hsüi (sü'yē)	China	31·02 N	113·49 E
193	Hsün Chiang (R.)	China	23·28 N	110·30 E
134	Huacho (wä'chō)	Peru	11·13 S	77·29 W
190	Huaian (hōōäi'än)	China	33·31 N	119·11 E
189	Huai Ho (R.) (hōōäi'hŭ)	China	32·07 N	114·38 E
190	Huai Ho (R.)	China	33·05 N	117·50 E
192	Huailai	China	40·20 N	115·45 E
190	Huailinchen (hōōäilĭn'jĕn)	China	31·27 N	117·36 E
190	Huainan	China	32·38 N	117·02 E
190	Huaiyang (hōōäi'yang)	China	33·45 N	114·54 E
190	Huaiyin (hōōäi'yĭn)	China	33·34 N	118·58 E
190	Huaiyüan (hōōäi'yōōäN)	China	32·53 N	117·13 E
124	Huajicori (wä-jē-kō'rē)	Mex.	22·41 N	105·24 W
125	Huajuapan de León (wäj-wä'päm dā lā-ón')	Mex.	17·46 N	97·45 W
115	Hualapai Ind. Res. (wäl'apī)	Az.	35·41 N	113·38 W
115	Hualapai Mts.	Az.	34·53 N	113·54 W
193	Hualien (hwä'lyĕn')	Taiwan	23·58 N	121·58 E
134	Huallaga (R.) (wäl-yä'gä)	Peru	8·12 S	76·34 W
134	Huamachuco (wä-mä-chōō'kō)	Peru	7·52 S	78·11 W
125	Huamantla (wä-män'tlà)	Mex.	19·18 N	97·54 W
216	Huambo (Nova Lisboa)	Ang.	12·44 S	15·47 E
124	Huamuxtitlán (wä-mōōs-tē-tlän')	Mex.	17·49 N	98·38 W
134	Huancavelica (wän'kä-vā-lē'kä)	Peru	12·47 S	75·02 W
134	Huancayo (wän-kä'yō)	Peru	12·09 S	75·04 W
134	Huanchaca (wän-chä'kä)	Bol.	20·09 S	66·40 W
188	Huan Chiang (R.)	China	36·45 N	106·30 E
190	Huangch'iao (hōōäNg'chĭou)	China	32·15 N	120·13 E
190	Huangch'uan (hōōäNg'chōōäN)	China	32·07 N	115·01 E
189	Huang Ho (Yellow River) (hōōäng'hu)	China	35·06 N	113·39 E
189	Huang Ho, Old Beds of the (R.)	China	40·28 N	106·34 E
190	Huang Ho, Old Course of the (R.)	China	34·28 N	116·59 E
192	Huanghoutien	China (In.)	39·22 N	116·53 E
190	Huanghsien (hōōäNg'sĭäN)	China	37·39 N	120·32 E
190	Huangli (hōōäNg'lē)	China	31·39 N	119·42 E
191	Huanglien	China (Canton In.)	22·53 N	113·09 E
191	Huangp'u Chiang (R.)	China (Shanghai In.)	30·56 N	121·16 E
188	Huangyüan	China	37·00 N	101·01 E
192	Huanjen	China	41·10 N	125·30 E
134	Huánuco (wä-nōō'kō)	Peru	9·50 S	76·17 W
134	Huánuni (wä-nōō'nē)	Bol.	18·11 S	66·43 W
127	Huapí, Montañas de (Mts.) (môn-tä'n-yäs-dĕ-wà'-pē')	Nic.	12·35 N	84·43 W
124	Huaquechula (wä-kĕ-chōō'-lä)	Mex.	18·44 N	98·37 W
134	Huaral (wä-rä'l)	Peru	11·28 S	77·11 W

ng-sing; ŋ-baŋk; N-nasalized n; nŏd; cŏmmit; ōld; ôbey; ôrder; fōōd; fŏŏt; ou-out; s-soft; sh-dish; th-thin; pūre; ûnite; ûrn; stŭd; circŭs; ü-as "y" in study; '-indeterminate vowel.

Page	Name Pronunciation Region	Lat. °'	Long. °'
134	Huarás (ōōä'rȧ's)...Peru	9·32 S	77·29 W
134	Huascarán, Nevs. (Pk.) (wäs-kä-rän').Peru	9·05 S	77·50 W
136	Huasco (wäs'kō)...Chile	28·32 S	71·16 W
192	Huatien...China	42·38 N	126·45 E
125	Huatla de Jiménez (wȧ'-tlä-dĕ-ĸĕ-mĕ'-nĕz). Mex.	18·08 N	96·49 W
125	Huatlatlauch (wä'tlä-tlä-ōō'ch) Mex.	18·40 N	98·04 W
125	Huatusco (wä-tōōs'kô)...Mex.	19·09 N	96·57 W
124	Huauchinango (wä-ōō-chê-näŋ'gô).Mex.	20·09 N	98·03 W
127	Huaunta (wä-ōō'n-tä)...Nic.	13·30 N	83·32 W
127	Huaunta, Laguna (L.) (lä-gōō'-nä-wä-ōō'n-tä).Nic.	13·35 N	83·46 W
124	Huautla (wä-ōō'tlä)...Mex.	21·04 N	98·13 W
190	Huayhe Hu (L.) (hōōäī'hŭ'hōō) China	32·49 N	117·00 E
124	Huaynamota, Rió de (R.) (rê'ō-dĕ-wäy-nä-mō'tä).Mex.	22·10 N	104·36 W
125	Huazolotitlán (Santa María) (wäzō-lô-tlē-tlän').Mex.	16·18 N	97·55 W
99	Hubbard (hŭb'ẽrd)...NH (In.)	42·53 N	71·12 W
119	Hubbard...Tx.	31·53 N	96·46 W
104	Hubbard (L.)...Mi.	44·45 N	83·30 W
118	Hubbard Creek Res...Tx.	32·50 N	98·55 W
185	Hubli (hŏŏ'blê)...India	15·25 N	75·09 E
161	Hückeswagen (hü'kĕs-vä'gĕn) F.R.G. (Ruhr In.)	51·09 N	7·20 E
148	Hucknall (hŭk'nȧl)...Eng.	53·02 N	1·12 W
148	Huddersfield (hŭd'ẽrz-fēld)...Eng.	53·39 N	1·47 W
156	Hudiksvall (hōō'dĭks-väl)...Swe.	61·44 N	17·05 E
100	Hudson (hŭd'sŭn) Can. (Montreal In.)	45·26 N	74·08 W
99	Hudson...Ma. (In.)	42·24 N	71·34 W
104	Hudson...Mi.	41·50 N	84·15 W
105	Hudson...NY	42·15 N	73·45 W
107	Hudson...Oh. (Cleveland In.)	41·15 N	81·27 W
113	Hudson Wi. (Minneapolis, St. Paul In.)	44·59 N	92·45 W
95	Hudson Bay...Can.	52·52 N	102·25 W
91	Hudson B...Can.	60·15 N	85·30 W
105	Hudson Falls...NY	43·20 N	73·30 W
100	Hudson Heights Can. (Montreal In.)	45·28 N	74·09 W
104	Hudson R...NY	41·55 N	73·55 W
91	Hudson Str...Can.	63·25 N	74·05 W
193	Hue (ū-ā')...Viet.	16·28 N	107·42 E
162	Huebra (R.) (wĕ'brä)...Sp.	40·44 N	6·17 W
126	Huehuetenango (wā-wā-tȧ-näŋ'gô) Guat.	15·19 N	91·26 W
124	Huejotzingo (wā-hô-tzĭŋ'gō).Mex.	19·09 N	98·24 W
124	Huejúcar (wā-hōō'kär)...Mex.	22·26 N	103·12 W
124	Huejuquilla el Alto (wā-hōō-kēl'yä ĕl äl'tō).Mex.	22·42 N	102·54 W
124	Huejutla (wā-hōō'tlä)...Mex.	21·08 N	98·26 W
162	Huelma (wĕl'mä)...Sp.	37·39 N	3·36 W
162	Huelva (wĕl'vä)...Sp.	37·16 N	6·58 W
162	Huercal-Overa (wĕr-käl' ō-vä'rä) Sp.	37·12 N	1·58 W
116	Huerfano (R.) (wâr'fȧ-nō)...Co.	37·41 N	105·13 W
163	Huésca (wĕs-kä)...Sp.	42·07 N	0·25 W
162	Huéscar (wās'kär)...Sp.	37·50 N	2·34 W
124	Huetamo de Múñez (wā-tä'mō dā-mōō'nyĕz).Mex.	18·34 N	100·53 W
162	Huete (wā'tā)...Sp.	40·09 N	2·42 W
124	Hueycatenango (wĕy-kȧ-tĕ-nä'n-gô).Mex.	17·31 N	99·10 W
125	Hueytlalpan (wā'ī-tlăl'pän)..Mex.	20·03 N	97·41 W
106	Hueytown...Al. (Birmingham In.)	33·28 N	86·59 W
106	Huffman (hŭf'mȧn) Al. (Birmingham In.)	33·36 N	86·42 W
116	Hugh Butler (L.)...Ne.	40·21 N	100·40 W
205	Hughenden (hū'ĕn-dĕn)...Austl.	20·58 S	144·13 E
204	Hughes (hūz)...Austl.	30·45 S	129·30 E
106	Hughesville...Md. (Baltimore In.)	38·32 N	76·48 W
113	Hugo (hū'gō) Mn. (Minneapolis, St. Paul In.)	45·10 N	93·00 W
117	Hugo...Ok.	34·01 N	95·32 W
116	Hugoton (hū'gō-tŭn)...Ks.	37·10 N	101·28 W
192	Huhohaot'e...China	41·05 N	111·50 E
124	Huichapan (wē-chä-pän')...Mex.	20·22 N	99·39 W
134	Huila (Dept.) (wē'lä)...Col. (In.)	3·10 N	75·20 W
134	Huila, Nevado de (Pk.) (nĕ-vä-dô-de-wē'lä). Col. (In.)	2·59 N	76·01 W
193	Huilai...China	23·02 N	116·18 E
193	Huili...China	26·48 N	102·20 E
125	Huimanguillo (wē-män-gēl'yō) Mex.	17·50 N	93·16 W
190	Huimin (hōōĭ mĭn)...China	37·29 N	117·32 E
125	Huitzilac (ōōē't-zē-lä'k). Mex. (In.)	19·01 N	99·16 W
124	Huitzitzilingo (wē-tzē-tzē-lē'n-go) Mex.	21·11 N	98·42 W
124	Huitzuco (wê-tzōō'kō)...Mex.	18·16 N	99·20 W
125	Huixquilucan (ōōē'x-kē-lōō-kä'n) Mex. (In.)	19·21 N	99·22 W
125	Huixtla (wēs'tlä)...Mex.	15·12 N	92·28 W
193	Huiyang...China	23·05 N	114·25 E
193	Huk'ou (hū'kō')...China	29·58 N	116·20 E
190	Hukouchi (hōōgō jē)...China	33·22 N	117·07 E
192	Hulan (hōō'län')...China	45·58 N	126·32 E
192	Hulan (R.)...China	42·20 N	126·30 E
194	Hulin (hōō'lĭn')...China	45·45 N	133·25 E
100	Hull (hŭl)...Can. (Ottawa In.)	45·26 N	75·43 W
99	Hull...Ma. (In.)	42·18 N	70·54 W
148	Hull (R.)...Eng.	53·47 N	0·20 W
149	Hulst (hŏŏlst) Neth. (Amsterdam In.)	51·17 N	4·01 E
191	Huluk'eng...China (Canton In.)	22·41 N	113·25 E
192	Hulutao (hōō'lōō-tä'ō)...China	40·40 N	122·55 E
218	Ḥulwān (hĕl'wän).Egypt (Nile In.)	29·51 N	31·20 E
123	Humacao (ōō-mä-kä'ō) P. R. (Puerto Rico In.)	18·09 N	65·49 W
124	Humaitá (ōō-mä-ē-tä')...Braz.	7·37 S	62·58 W
134	Humaitá...Par.	27·08 S	58·18 W
212	Humansdorp (hōō'mäns-dôrp) S. Afr.	33·57 S	24·45 E
212	Humbe (hŏŏm'bâ)...Ang.	16·50 S	14·55 E
154	Humber (L.) (hŭm'bẽr)...Eng.	53·38 N	0·40 W
100	Humber (R.)..Can. (Toronto In.)	43·53 N	79·40 W
99	Humbermouth (hŭm'bẽr-mŭth) Can.	48·58 N	57·55 W
119	Humble (hŭm'b'l)...Tx.	29·58 N	95·15 W
94	Humboldt (hŭm'bōlt)...Can.	52·12 N	105·07 W
109	Humboldt...Ia.	42·43 N	94·11 W
117	Humboldt...Ks.	37·48 N	95·26 W
117	Humboldt...Ne.	40·10 N	95·57 W
102	Humboldt (R.)...U. S.	40·30 N	116·50 W
110	Humboldt B...Ca.	40·48 N	124·25 W
110	Humboldt R., East Fork...Nv.	40·59 N	115·21 W
110	Humboldt R., North Fork...Nv.	41·25 N	115·45 W
120	Humbolt...Tn.	35·47 N	88·55 W
114	Humbolt Ra...Nv.	40·12 N	118·16 W
114	Humbolt Salt Marsh...Nv.	39·49 N	117·41 W
114	Humbolt Sink...Nv.	39·58 N	118·54 W
191	Humenchai..China (Canton In.)	22·49 N	113·39 E
115	Humphreys Pk. (hŭm'frĭs)...Az.	35·20 N	111·40 W
158	Humpolec (hŏŏm'pō-lĕts)..Czech.	49·33 N	15·21 E
126	Humuya R. (ōō-mōō'yä)...Hond.	14·38 N	87·36 W
150	Hunaflói (B.) (hōō'nä-flō'ī)...Ice.	65·41 N	20·44 W
189	Hunan (Prov.) (hōō'nän')...China	28·08 N	111·25 E
189	Hunch'un (hōōn'chōōn')...China	42·53 N	130·34 E
165	Hunedoara (ĸōō'nĕd-wä'rȧ).Rom.	45·45 N	22·54 E
146	Hungary (hŭŋ'gȧ-rĭ)...Eur.	46·44 N	17·55 E
203	Hungerford (hŭn'gẽr-fẽrd)..Austl.	28·50 S	144·32 E
111	Hungry Horse Res. (hŭŋ'gȧ-rĭ hôrs).Mt.	48·11 N	113·30 W
193	Hung Shui Ho (R.) (hŏŏng).China	25·00 N	107·22 E
190	Hungtse Hu (L.) (hŏŏngzhŭ hōō) China	33·17 N	118·37 E
158	Hunsrück (Mts.) (hŏŏns'rûk) F.R.G.	49·43 N	7·12 E
158	Hunte R. (hŏŏn'tē)...F.R.G.	52·45 N	8·26 E
205	Hunter Is. (hŭn-tẽr)...Austl.	40·33 S	143·36 E
104	Huntingburg (hŭnt'ĭng-bûrg)..In.	38·15 N	86·55 W
105	Huntingdon (hŭnt'ĭng-dŭn)..Can.	45·10 N	74·05 W
112	Huntingdon.Can. (Vancouver In.)	49·00 N	122·16 W
120	Huntingdon...Tn.	36·00 N	88·23 W
148	Huntingdon and Peterborough (Co.).Eng.	52·26 N	0·19 W
104	Huntington...In.	40·55 N	85·30 W
105	Huntington...Pa.	40·30 N	78·00 W
104	Huntington...WV	38·25 N	82·25 W
113	Huntington Beach Ca. (Los Angeles In.)	33·39 N	118·00 W
113	Huntington Park Ca. (Los Angeles In.)	33·59 N	118·14 W
106	Huntington Station NY (New York In.)	40·51 N	73·25 W
111	Huntley...Mt.	45·54 N	108·01 W
120	Huntsville (hŭnts'-vĭl)...Al.	34·44 N	86·36 W
105	Huntsville...Can.	45·20 N	79·15 W
117	Huntsville...Mo.	39·24 N	92·32 W
119	Huntsville...Tx.	30·44 N	95·34 W
113	Huntsville.Ut. (Salt Lake City In.)	41·16 N	111·46 W
125	Hunucmá (hōō-nōōk-mä')...Mex.	21·01 N	89·54 W
190	Huolu (hŏŏŭ lōō)...China	38·05 N	114·20 E
197	Huon G...Pap. N. Gui.	7·15 S	147·45 E
189	Hupeh (Prov.)...China	31·20 N	111·58 E
183	Ḥurayḏin, Wādī (R.) Egypt (Palestine In.)	30·55 N	34·12 E
104	Hurd, C. (hûrd)...Can.	45·15 N	81·45 W
109	Hurley (hûr'lĭ)...Wi.	46·26 N	90·11 W
136	Hurlingham (ōō'r-lēn-gäm) Arg. (Buenos Aires In.)	34·20 S	58·38 W
104	Huron (hū'rŏn)...Oh.	41·20 N	82·35 W
108	Huron...SD	44·22 N	98·15 W
103	Huron, L. (hū'rŏn)...U. S.-Can.	45·15 N	82·40 W
109	Huron Mts. (hū'rŏn)...Mi.	46·47 N	87·52 W
107	Huron R...Mi. (Detroit In.)	42·12 N	83·26 W
101	Hurricane (hŭr'ĭ-kān)...Ak.	63·00 N	149·30 W
115	Hurricane...Ut.	37·10 N	113·20 W
128	Hurricane Flats (Shoal) (hŭ-rĭ-kȧn flăts).Ba.	23·35 N	78·30 W
150	Húsavik...Ice.	66·00 N	17·10 W
167	Husi (kōōsh')...Sov. Un.	46·52 N	28·04 E
156	Huskvarna (hŏŏsk-vär'nȧ)...Swe.	57·48 N	14·16 E
113	Hurst.Tx. (Dallas, Ft. Worth In.)	32·48 N	97·12 W
158	Husum (hōō'zŏŏm)...F.R.G.	54·29 N	9·04 E
113	Hutchins (hŭch'ĭnz) Tx. (Dallas, Fort Worth In.)	32·38 N	96·43 W
116	Hutchinson (hŭch'ĭn-sŭn)...Ks.	38·02 N	97·56 W
109	Hutchinson...Mn.	44·53 N	94·23 W
192	Hut'o Ho (R.) (hōō'tō'hō').China	38·10 N	114·00 E
190	Huwu (hōō wōō)...China	31·17 N	119·48 E
155	Huy (û-ē') (hū'ē)...Bel.	50·33 N	5·14 E
150	Hvannadalshnukur (Mtn.)...Ice.	64·09 N	16·46 W
164	Hvar (I.) (ĸhvär)...Yugo.	43·08 N	16·28 E
194	Hwangju (hwäng'jōō')...Kor.	38·39 N	125·49 E
106	Hyattsville (hī'ăt's-vil) Md. (Baltimore In.)	38·57 N	76·58 W
101	Hydaburg (hī-dă'bûrg)...Ak.	55·12 N	132·49 W
148	Hyde (hīd)...Eng.	53·27 N	2·05 W
185	Hyderābād (hī-dẽr-ȧ-băd')..India	17·29 N	79·28 E
184	Hyderābād (hī-dẽr-ȧ-băd')..Pak.	25·29 N	68·28 E
185	Hyderabad (State)...India	23·29 N	76·50 E
161	Hyéres (ē-âr')...Fr.	43·09 N	6·08 E
161	Hyéres, Iles d' (Is.) (ēl'dyâr')..Fr.	42·57 N	6·17 E
194	Hyesanjin (hyĕ'sän-jĭn')...Kor.	41·11 N	128·12 E
104	Hymera (hī-mē'rȧ)...In.	39·10 N	87·20 W
111	Hyndman Pk. (hĭnd'măn)...Id.	43·38 N	114·04 W
195	Hyōgo (Pref.) (hiyō'gō) Jap. (Ōsaka In.)	34·54 N	135·15 E
100	Hythe...Can.	55·20 N	119·33 W
	I		
195	Ia (R.) (ē'ä)...Jap. (Ōsaka In.)	34·54 N	135·34
165	Ialomita (R.)...Rom.	44·37 N	26·42
159	Iasi (yä'shê)...Rom.	47·10 N	27·40
197	Iba (ē'bä)...Phil. (In.)	15·20 N	119·59
215	Ibadan (ē-bä'dän)...Nig.	7·17 N	3·30
134	Ibagué (ê-bä-gā')...Col. (In.)	4·27 N	75·13 W
165	Ibar (R.) (ē'bär)...Yugo.	43·22 N	20·35
195	Ibaragi (ē-bä'rä-gē) Jap. (Ōsaka In.)	34·49 N	135·35
134	Ibarra (ê-bär'rä)...Ec.	0·19 N	78·08 W
209	Iberian Pen...Port.-Sp.	41·00 N	0·07 W
98	Iberville (ê-bår-vēl') (ĭ'bẽr-vĭl) Can.	45·14 N	73·01 W
215	Ibi (ē'bê)...Nig.	8·12 N	9·45
135	Ibiapaba, Serra da (Mts.) (sĕ'r-rä-dä-ē-byä-pȧ'bä).Braz.	3·30 S	40·55 W
163	Ibiza (ê-bē'thä)...Sp.	38·55 N	1·24
163	Ibiza, Isla de (Iviza I.) (ê's-lä-dĕ-ē-bê'zä).Sp.	39·07 N	1·05
217	Ibo (ē'bō)...Moz.	12·20 S	40·35
216	Iboundji, Mont (Mtn.)...Gabon	1·08 S	11·48
218	Ibrāhīm, Būr (B.)...Egypt	29·57 N	32·33
186	Ibrahim, Jabal (Mtn.)...Sau. Ar.	20·31 N	41·17
217	Ibwe Munyama...Zambia	16·09 S	28·34
134	Ica (ē'kȧ)...Peru	14·09 S	75·42 W
134	Icá (R.) (ē-kȧ')...Braz.	2·56 S	69·12 W
134	Içana (ē-sä'nä)...Braz.	0·15 N	67·19 W
110	Ice Harbor Dam...Wa.	46·15 N	118·54 W
146	Iceland (īs'lȧnd)...Eur.	65·12 N	19·45 W
193	Ich'ang (ē'chäng')...China	30·38 N	111·22 E
195	Ichibusayama (Mt.) (ē'chê-bōō'sȧ-yä'mä).Jap.	32·19 N	131·08 E
195	Ichihara...Jap. (Tōkyō In.)	35·31 N	140·05 E
195	Ichikawa (ē'chê-kä'wä) Jap. (Tōkyō In.)	35·44 N	139·54
195	Ichinomiya (ē'chē-nō-mē'yȧ).Jap.	35·19 N	136·49
195	Ichinomoto (ē-chē'nō-mō-tō) Jap. (Ōsaka In.)	34·37 N	135·50
167	Ichnya (ĭch'nyä)...Sov. Un.	50·47 N	32·23 E
135	Icó (ê-kô')...Braz.	6·25 S	38·43 W
134	Icutú, Cerro (Mtn.) (sĕ'r-rō-ê-kōō-tōō') Ven.	7·07 N	65·30 W
101	Icy C. (ī'sĭ)...Ak.	70·20 N	161·40 W
117	Idabel (ī'dȧ-bĕl)...Ok.	33·52 N	94·47 W
108	Idagrove (ī'dȧ-grōv)...Ia.	42·22 N	95·29 W
215	Idah (ē'dä)...Nig.	7·07 N	6·43 E
102	Idaho (State) (ī'dȧ-hō)...U. S.	44·00 N	115·10 W
111	Idaho Falls...Id.	43·30 N	112·01 W
116	Idaho Springs...Co.	39·43 N	105·32 W
162	Idanha-a-Nova (ê-dän'yȧ-ä-nō'vȧ).Port.	39·58 N	7·13 W
188	Ideriin Gol (R.)...Mong.	48·58 N	98·38 E
218	Idfū (ĕd'fōō)...Egypt (Nile In.)	24·57 N	32·53 E
165	Ídhra (I.)...Grc.	37·20 N	23·30 E
196	Idi (ē'dê)...Indon.	4·58 N	97·47 E
218	Idkū (ĕd'kōō)...Egypt (Nile In.)	31·18 N	30·20 E
218	Idkū L...Egypt (Nile In.)	31·13 N	30·22 E
148	Idle (R.) (īd''l)...Eng.	53·22 N	0·56 W
164	Idrija (ē'drê-ȧ)...Yugo.	46·01 N	14·01 E
213	Idutywa (ē-dōō-tī'wȧ) S. Afr. (Natal In.)	32·06 S	28·18 E
155	Ieper...Bel.	50·50 N	2·53 E
164	Ierápetra...Grc. (In.)	35·01 N	25·48 E
164	Iesi (yä'sê)...It.	43·37 N	13·20 E
215	Ife...Nig.	7·30 N	4·30 E
215	Iferouâne (ēf'rōō-än')...Niger	19·04 N	8·24 E
215	Iforas, Adrar des (Mts.) (ä-drär') Alg.-Mali	19·55 N	2·00 E
217	Igalula...Tan.	5·14 S	33·00 E
172	Igarka (ê-gär'kȧ)...Sov. Un.	67·22 N	86·16 E
165	Ighil Izane...Alg.	35·43 N	0·43 E
164	Iglesias (ē-lĕ'syôs)...It.	39·20 N	8·34 E
210	Igli (ê-glē')...Alg.	30·32 N	2·15 W
91	Igloolik...Can.	69·33 N	81·18 W
112	Ignacio (ĭg-nä'cĭ-ō) Ca. (San Francisco In.)	38·05 N	122·32 W
136	Iguaçu (R.) (ē-gwä-sōō') Braz. (Rio de Janeiro In.)	22·42 S	43·19 W
124	Iguala (ê-gwä'lä)...Mex.	18·18 N	99·34 W
163	Igualada (ê-gwä-lä'dä)...Sp.	41·35 N	1·38 E
136	Iguassu (R.) (ê-gwä-sōō')...Braz.	25·45 S	52·30 W
136	Iguassu Falls...Braz.	25·40 S	54·16 W
137	Iguatama (ē-gwä-tȧ'mä) Braz. (Rio de Janeiro In.)	20·13 S	45·40 W
135	Iguatu (ē-gwä-tōō')...Braz.	6·22 S	39·17 W
210	Iguidi, Erg (Dune)...Alg.	26·22 N	6·53 W
197	Iguig (ē-gēg')...Phil. (In.)	17·46 N	121·44 E
215	Ihiala...Nig.	5·51 N	6·51 E
192	Ihsien...China	41·30 N	121·15 E
190	I Ho (R.) (yē'hŭ)...China	34·38 N	118·07 E
195	Iida (ē'ê-dä)...Jap.	35·39 N	137·53 E
170	Iijoki (R.) (ē'yō'kĭ)...Fin.	65·28 N	27·00 E
195	Iizuka (ē'ê-zōō-kȧ)...Jap.	33·39 N	130·39 E
215	Ijebu-Ode (ê-jĕ'bōō ōdā)...Nig.	6·50 N	3·56 E
155	IJsselmeer (L.) (ī'sĕl-mār)..Neth.	52·46 N	5·14 E
157	Ikaalinen (ē'kä-lĭ-nĕn)...Fin.	61·47 N	22·55 E
165	Ikaría (I.) (ē-kä'ryȧ)...Grc.	37·43 N	26·07 E
195	Ikeda (ē'kȧ-dä)...Jap. (Ōsaka In.)	34·49 N	135·26 E
215	Ikerre...Nig.	7·31 N	5·14 E
165	Ikhtiman (ēk'tê-män)...Bul.	42·26 N	23·49 E
195	Iki (I.) (ē'kê)...Jap.	33·46 N	129·44 E
195	Ikoma...Jap. (Ōsaka In.)	34·41 N	135·43 E
212	Ikoma (ē-kō'mä)...Tan.	2·08 S	34·47 E
174	Iksha (ĭk'shȧ) Sov. Un. (Moscow In.)	56·10 N	37·30 E
215	Ila...Nig.	8·01 N	4·55 E
197	Ilagen (ê-lä'gän)...Phil. (In.)	17·09 N	121·52 E
192	Ilan...China	46·10 N	129·40 E

ăt; finăl; rāte; senāte; ärm; ȧsk; sofȧ; fâre; ch-choose; dh-as th in other; bē; ēvent; bĕt; recĕnt; cratẽr; g-go; gh-guttural g; bĭt; ĭ-short neutral; rīde; ĸ-guttural k as ch in German ich;

Page	Name	Pronunciation	Region	Lat.	Long.
93	Ilan	(ē'län')	Taiwan	24·50 N	121·42 E
59	Ilawa	(ē-lä'vá)	Pol.	53·35 N	19·36 E
94	Île-á-la-Crosse		Can.	55·34 N	108·00 W
16	Ilebo (Port-Franqui)		Zaire	4·19 S	20·35 E
71	Ilek	(ē'lyĕk)	Sov. Un.	51·30 N	53·10 E
71	Ilek (R.)		Sov. Un.	51·20 N	53·10 E
00	Île-Perrot	(yl-pĕ-rōt') Can. (Montreal In.)		45·21 N	73·54 W
15	Ilesha		Nig.	7·38 N	4·45 E
48	Ilford	(ĭl'fĕrd) Eng. (London In.)		51·33 N	0·06 E
54	Ilfracombe	(ĭl-frá-kōōm')	Eng.	51·13 N	4·08 W
37	Ilhabela	(ē'lä-bĕ'lä) Braz. (Rio de Janeiro In.)		23·47 S	45·21 W
37	Ilha Grande, Baia de (B.)	Braz. (Rio de Janeiro In.)		23·17 S	44·25 W
62	Ilhavo	(ēl'yá-vỏ)	Port.	40·36 N	8·41 W
35	Ilhéus	(ē-lĕ'ōōs)	Braz.	14·52 S	39·00 W
01	Iliamna	(ē-lē-ăm'ná)	Ak.	59·45 N	155·05 W
01	Iliamna (L.)		Ak.	59·25 N	155·30 W
01	Iliamna (Vol.)		Ak.	60·18 N	153·25 W
72	Ilim (R.)	(ē-lyĕm')	Sov. Un.	57·28 N	103·00 E
95	Ilimsk	(ē-lyĕmsk')	Sov. Un.	56·47 N	103·43 E
97	Ilin (I.)	(ē-lyēn')	Phil. (In.)	12·16 N	120·57 E
67	Il'intsiy		Sov. Un.	49·07 N	29·13 E
05	Iliodhrómia (I.)		Grc.	39·18 N	23·35 E
05	Ilion	(ĭl'ĭ-ăn)	NY	43·00 N	75·05 W
15	Ili R.	(ē'lē)	Sov. Un.	43·46 N	77·41 E
48	Ilkeston	(ĭl'kĕs-tŭn)	Eng.	52·58 N	1·19 W
34	Illampu, Nevado (Pk.)	(nĕ-vá'dỏ-ĕl-yäm-pōō')	Bol.	15·50 S	68·15 W
97	Illana B.	(ēl-yä-nỏ)	Phil.	7·38 N	123·41 E
37	Illapel	(ē-zhä-pĕ'l) Chile (Santiago In.)		31·37 S	71·10 W
58	Iller R.	(Il'er)	F.R.G.	47·52 N	10·06 E
34	Illimani, Nevado (Pk.)	(nĕ-vá'dỏ-ēl-yĕ-mä'nĕ)	Bol.	16·50 S	67·38 W
03	Illinois (State)	(ĭl-ĭ-noi')(ĭl-ĭ-noiz') U.S.		40·25 N	90·40 W
17	Illinois (R.)		Il.	40·52 N	89·31 W
10	Illizi		Alg.	26·35 N	8·24 E
66	Il'men', Ozero (L.)	(ŏ'zĕ-rỏ el'' men')	Sov. Un.	58·18 N	32·00 E
55	Ilmenau (R.)	(ēl'mē-nou)	F.R.G.	53·20 N	10·20 E
26	Ilo		Peru	17·46 S	71·13 W
26	Ilobasco	(ē-lỏ-bäs'kỏ)	Sal.	13·57 N	88·46 W
96	Iloilo	(ē-lỏ-ē'lỏ)	Phil.	10·49 N	112·33 E
26	Ilopango, L.	(ē-lỏ-päṅ'gỏ)	Sal.	13·48 N	88·50 W
15	Ilorin	(ē-lỏ-rēn')	Nig.	8·30 N	4·32 E
15	Ilūkste		Sov. Un.	55·59 N	26·20 E
12	Ilwaco	(ĭl-wä'kỏ) Wa. (Portland In.)		46·19 N	124·02 W
70	Ilych (R.)	(ē'l'ĭch)	Sov. Un.	62·30 N	57·30 E
95	Imabari	(ē'mä-bä'rē)	Jap.	34·05 N	132·58 E
95	Imai	(ē-mī')	Jap. (Ōsaka In.)	34·30 N	135·47 E
94	Iman (R.)	(ē-män')	Sov. Un.	45·40 N	134·31 E
70	Imandra (L.)	(ē-män'drá)	Sov. Un.	67·40 N	32·30 E
18	Imbābah	(ēm-bä'bá) Egypt (Nile In.)		30·06 N	31·09 E
36	Imbarié	(ēm-bä-ryĕ') Braz. (Rio de Janeiro In.)		22·38 S	43·13 W
74	Imeni Morozova	(ĭm-yĕ'nyĭ mỏ rỏ'zỏ vá) Sov. Un. (Leningrad In.)		59·58 N	31·02 E
66	Imeni Moskvy, Kanal (Moscow Can.)	(ká-näl'ĭm-yá' nĭ mỏs-kvĭ)	Sov. Un.	56·33 N	37·15 E
74	Imeni Tsyurupy		Sov. Un. (Moscow In.)	55·30 N	38·39 E
74	Imeni Vorovskogo		Sov. Un. (Moscow In.)	55·43 N	38·21 E
94	Imienpo	(yēmiänpǔ)	China	44·59 N	127·56 E
04	Imlay City	(ĭm'lā)	Mi.	43·00 N	83·15 W
58	Immenstadt	(ĭm-ĕn-shtăt)	F.R.G.	47·34 N	10·12 E
18	Immerpan	(ĭmĕr-pän) S. Afr. (Johannesburg & Pretoria In.)		24·29 S	29·14 E
64	Imola	(ē'mỏ-lä)	It.	44·19 N	11·43 E
64	Imotski	(ē-mỏts'kē)	Yugo.	43·25 N	17·15 E
35	Impameri		Braz.	17·44 S	48·03 W
13	Impendle	(ĭm-pĕnd'lä) S. Afr. (Natal In.)		29·38 S	29·54 E
64	Imperia	(ĭm-pā'rē-á)	It.	43·52 N	8·03 E
07	Imperial	(ĭm-pē'rĭ-ăl) Pa. (Pittsburgh In.)		40·27 N	80·15 W
14	Imperial Beach		Ca. (In.)	32·34 N	117·08 W
15	Imperial Res.		Az.	32·57 N	114·19 W
15	Imperial Valley		Ca.	33·00 N	115·22 W
16	Impfondo	(ĭmp-fōn'dỏ)	Con.	1·37 N	18·04 E
97	Imphal	(Imp'hŭl)	India	24·42 N	94·00 E
65	Imroz (I.)	(ĭm'rŏz)	Tur.	40·10 N	25·27 E
95	Ina	(ē'nä)	Jap. (Ōsaka In.)	34·56 N	135·21 E
14	Inaja Ind. Res.	(ē-nä'hä)	Ca.	32·56 N	116·37 W
53	Inari	(ē-nä'rē)	Fin.	69·02 N	26·22 E
53	Inari (L.)		Fin.	69·00 N	28·00 E
26	Inca	(ēṅ'kä)	Sp.	39·43 N	2·53 E
71	Ince Burun (C.)	(ĭn'já)	Tur.	42·00 N	35·00 E
94	Inch'ŏn	(ĭn'chŭn)	Kor.	37·26 N	126·46 E
64	Incudine, Mt. (Mtn.)	(ēn-kōō-dē' nä) (än-kü-dēn')	Fr.	41·53 N	9·17 E
56	Indalsälven (R.)		Swe.	62·50 N	16·50 E
97	Indang	(ēn'däng)	Phil. (In.)	14·11 N	120·53 E
97	Indé	(ēn'dä)	Mex.	25·53 N	105·15 W
17	Independence	(ĭn-dē-pĕn'dĕns)	Ks.	37·14 N	95·42 W
13	Independence		Mo. (Kansas City In.)	39·06 N	94·26 W
10	Independence		Oh. (Cleveland In.)	41·23 N	81·39 W
10	Independence		Or.	44·49 N	123·13 W
10	Independence Mts.		Nv.	41·15 N	116·02 W
71	Inder (L.)		Sov. Un.	48·20 N	51·50 E
82	India	(ĭn'dĭ-á)	Asia	23·00 N	77·30 E
04	Indian (L.)		Mi.	46·04 N	86·40 W
05	Indian (R.)		NY	44·05 N	75·45 W
05	Indiana	(ĭn-dĭ-än'á)	Pa.	40·40 N	79·10 W
103	Indiana (State)		U.S.	39·50 N	86·45 W
107	Indianapolis	In. (Indianapolis In.)		39·45 N	86·08 W
112	Indian Arm (R.)	(ĭn'dĭ-ăn ärm) Can. (Vancouver In.)		49·21 N	122·55 W
94	Indian Head		Can.	50·29 N	103·44 W
96	Indian L.		Can.	47·00 N	82·00 W
7	Indian Ocean				
109	Indianola	(ĭn-dĭ-ăn-ō'lá)	Ia.	41·22 N	93·33 W
120	Indianola		Ms.	33·29 N	90·35 W
173	Indigirka (R.)	(ēn-dē-gēr'kà)	Sov. Un.	67·45 N	145·45 E
122	Indio (R.)	(ē'n-dyỏ)	Pan. (In.)	9·13 N	78·28 W
196	Indochina (Reg.)	(ĭn-dỏ-chī'ná)	Asia	17·22 N	105·18 E
196	Indonesia	(ĭn'dỏ-nē-zhá)	Asia	4·38 S	118·45 E
184	Indore	(ĭn-dōr')	India	22·48 N	76·51 E
196	Indragiri (R.)	(ĭn-drä-jē'rè)	Indon.	0·27 S	102·05 E
126	Indrāvati (R.)	(ĭn-drŭ-vä'tē)	India	19·15 N	80·54 E
160	Indre (R.)	(ăN'dr')	Fr.	47·13 N	0·29 E
156	Indre Solund (I.)	(ĭndrĕ-sỏ-lŭnd)	Nor.	61·09 N	4·37 E
100	Indus	(ĭn'dŭs)	Can. (Calgary In.)	50·55 N	113·45 W
184	Indus (R.)		Pak.	26·43 N	67·41 E
213	Indwe	(ĭnd'wá)	S. Afr. (Natal In.)	31·30 S	27·21 E
171	Inebolu	(ē-nä-bỏ'lōō)	Tur.	41·50 N	33·40 E
171	Inego	(ē-nä-gü)	Tur.	40·05 N	29·20 E
197	Infanta	(ēn-fän'tä)	Phil. (In.)	14·44 N	121·39 E
197	Infanta		Phil. (In.)	15·50 N	119·53 E
162	Infantes	(ēn-fän'tàs)	Sp.	38·44 N	3·00 W
125	Inferror, Laguna (L.)	(lä-gōō'nä-ēn-fĕr-rôr)	Mex.	16·18 N	94·40 W
125	Infiernillo, Presa de (Res.)		Mex.	18·50 N	101·50 W
162	Infiesto	(ēn-fyĕ's-tỏ)	Sp.	43·21 N	5·24 W
215	I-n-Gall		Niger	16·47 N	6·56 E
104	Ingersoll	(ĭn'gĕr-sỏl)	Can.	43·05 N	81·00 W
205	Ingham	(ĭng'ăm)	Austl.	18·45 S	146·14 E
128	Ingles, Cayos (Is.)		Cuba	21·55 N	82·35 W
113	Inglewood	(ĭn'g'l-wŏŏd) Ca. (Los Angeles In.)		33·57 N	118·22 W
100	Inglewood		Can. (Toronto In.)	43·48 N	79·56 W
173	Ingoda (R.)	(ēn-gỏ'dá)	Sov. Un.	51·29 N	112·32 E
158	Ingolstadt	(ĭn'gỏl-shtät)	F.R.G.	48·46 N	11·27 E
167	Ingul	(ēn-gōōl')	Sov. Un.	47·22 N	32·52 E
167	Ingulets (R.)	(ēn-gōōl'yĕts')	Sov. Un.	47·12 N	33·12 E
171	Ingur (R.)	(ēn-gōōr')	Sov. Un.	43·00 N	42·00 E
212	Inhambane	(ēn-äm-bä'nĕ)	Moz.	23·47 S	35·28 E
135	Inhambupe	(ēn-yäm-bōō'pä)	Braz.	11·47 S	38·13 W
212	Inharrime	(ēn-yär-rē'mä)	Moz.	24·17 S	35·07 E
136	Inhomirim	(ēn-nỏ-mē-rē'N) Braz. (Rio de Janeiro In.)		22·34 S	43·11 W
188	Ining	(ē'nĭng)	China	43·58 N	80·49 E
134	Iniridia (R.)	(ē-nē-rē'dä)	Col.	2·25 N	70·38 W
203	Injune	(ĭn'jōōn)	Austl.	25·52 S	148·30 E
157	Inkeroinem	(ĭn'kĕr-oi-nĕn)	Fin.	60·42 N	26·50 E
107	Inkster	(ĭngk'stĕr)	Mi. (Detroit In.)	42·18 N	83·19 W
203	Innamincka	(ĭn-á'mĭn-ká)	Austl.	27·50 S	140·48 E
123	Inner Brass (I.)	(bräs) Vir. Is. (U.S.A.) (St. Thomas In.)		18·23 N	64·58 W
154	Inner Hebrides (Is.)		Scot.	57·20 N	6·20 W
188	Inner Mongolian Aut. Reg.	(mŏn-gō'lĭ-ăn)	China	43·30 N	113·33 E
93	Innisfail		Can.	52·02 N	113·57 W
158	Inn R.	(ĭn)	F.R.G.-Aus.	48·19 N	13·16 E
158	Innsbruck	(ĭns'brŏŏk)	Aus.	47·15 N	11·25 E
195	Ino	(ē'nỏ)	Jap.	33·34 N	133·23 E
216	Inongo	(ē-nỏṅ'gỏ)	Zaire	1·57 S	18·16 E
159	Inowroctaw	(ē-nỏ-vrŏts'läf)	Pol.	52·48 N	18·16 E
210	In Salah		Alg.	27·13 N	2·22 E
115	Inscription House Ruin	(ĭn'skrĭp-shŭn hous rōō'ĭn)	Az.	36·45 N	110·47 W
124	Inter-American Hy.	(ĭn'tĕr á-mĕr'ĭ-kăn)	Mex.	22·30 N	99·08 W
109	International Falls	(ĭn'tĕr-năsh'ŭn-ăl fôlz)	Mn.	48·34 N	93·26 W
90	Inuvik		Can.	68·40 N	134·10 W
195	Inuyama	(ē'nōō-yä'mä)	Jap.	35·24 N	137·01 E
205	Invercargil	(ĭn-vĕr-kär'gĭl) N. Z. (In.)		47·18 S	168·27 E
203	Inverel	(ĭn-vĕr-el')	Austl.	29·50 S	151·32 E
113	Invergrove Hts.	(ĭn'vĕr-grōv) Mn. (Minneapolis, St. Paul In.)		44·51 N	93·01 W
99	Inverness	(ĭn-vĕr-nĕs')	Can.	46·14 N	61·18 W
121	Inverness		Fl.	28·48 N	82·22 W
154	Inverness		Scot.	57·30 N	4·07 W
203	Investigator Str.	(ĭn-vĕst'ĭ'gä-tôr)	Austl.	35·33 S	137·00 E
212	Inyangani, Mt.	(ēn-yän-gä'nĕ)	Rh.	18·06 S	32·37 E
114	Inyokern		Ca.	35·39 N	117·51 W
114	Inyo Mts.	(ĭn'yỏ)	Ca.	36·55 N	118·04 W
174	Inzer R.	(ĭn'zĕr) Sov. Un. (Urals In.)		54·24 N	57·17 E
216	Inzia (R.)		Zaire	5·55 S	17·50 E
195	Iō (I.)	(ē'wỏ)	Jap.	30·46 N	130·15 E
165	Ioánnina (Yannina)	(yỏ-ä'nē-nä) (yä'nē-nä)	Grc.	39·39 N	20·52 E
112	Ioco		Can. (Vancouver In.)	49·18 N	122·53 W
117	Iola	(ī-ō'lá)	Ks.	37·55 N	95·23 W
216	Iôna, Parque Nacional do	(Natl. Pk.)	Ang.	16·35 S	12·00 E
104	Ionia	(ī-ō'nĭ-á)	Mi.	43·00 N	85·10 W
165	Ionian Is.	(ī-ō'nĭ-ăn)	Grc.	39·10 N	20·05 E
153	Ionian Sea		Eur.	38·59 N	18·48 E
165	Ios (I.)	(ī'ỏs)	Grc.	36·48 N	25·25 E
103	Iowa (State)	(ī'ỏ-wá)	U.S.	42·05 N	94·20 W
109	Iowa (R.)		Ia.	41·55 N	92·20 W
109	Iowa City		Ia.	41·39 N	91·31 W
109	Iowa Falls		Ia.	42·32 N	93·16 W
116	Iowa Park		Tx.	33·57 N	98·39 W
217	Ipala		Tan.	4·30 S	32·53 E
159	Ipel R.	(ē'pĕl)	Czech.-Hung.	48·08 N	19·00 E
134	Ipiales	(ē-pē-ä'läs)	Col.	0·48 N	77·45 W
193	Ipin (Süchow)		China	28·50 N	104·40 E
196	Ipoh		Mala.	4·45 N	101·05 E
203	Ipswich	(ĭps'wĭch)	Austl.	27·40 S	152·50 E
155	Ipswich		Eng.	52·05 N	1·05 E
99	Ipswich		Ma. (In.)	42·41 N	70·50 W
108	Ipswich		SD	45·26 N	99·01 W
166	Iput' (R.)	(ē-pōōt')	Sov. Un.	52·53 N	31·57 E
134	Iquique	(ē-kē'kĕ)	Chile	20·16 S	70·07 W
134	Iquitos	(ē-kē'tỏs)	Peru	3·39 S	73·18 W
164	Iráklion (Candia)		Grc. (In.)	35·20 N	25·10 E
182	Iran	(ē-rän')	Asia	31·15 N	53·30 E
186	Iran, Plat. of		Iran	32·28 N	58·00 E
196	Iran Mts.		Mala.	2·30 N	114·30 E
124	Irapuato	(ē-rä-pwä'tỏ)	Mex.	20·41 N	101·24 W
182	Iraq	(ē-räk')	Asia	32·00 N	42·30 E
127	Irazu Vol.	(ē-rä-zōō')	C. R.	9·58 N	83·54 W
183	Irbid	(ĕr-bēd') Jordan (Palestine In.)		32·33 N	35·51 E
171	Irbil		Iraq	36·10 N	44·00 E
170	Irbit	(ĕr-bēt')	Sov. Un.	57·40 N	63·10 E
212	Irébou	(ē-rä'bōō)	Zaire	0·40 S	17·48 E
146	Ireland	(īr-lănd)	Eur.	53·33 N	13·00 W
174	Iremel', Gora (Mt.)	(gá-rä' ī-rĕ'mĕl) Sov. Un. (Urals In.)		54·32 N	58·52 E
213	Irene	(ī-rē-nē) S. Afr. (Johannesburg & Pretoria In.)		25·53 S	28·13 E
172	Irgiz	(ĭr-gēz')	Sov. Un.	48·30 N	61·17 E
172	Irgiz (R.)		Sov. Un.	49·30 N	60·32 E
214	Irigui (Reg.)		Mali-Mauritania	16·45 N	5·35 W
170	Iriklinskoye Vdkhr (Res.)		Sov. Un.	52·20 N	58·50 E
217	Iringa	(ē-rĭṅ'gä)	Tan.	7·46 S	35·42 E
193	Iriomote Jima (I.)	(ērē'-ō-mō-tä)	Jap.	24·20 N	123·30 E
126	Iriona	(ē-rē-ō'nä)	Hond.	15·53 N	85·12 W
154	Irish Sea	(ī'rĭsh)	Eur.	53·55 N	5·25 W
172	Irkutsk	(ĭr-kōōtsk')	Sov. Un.	52·16 N	104·00 E
148	Irlam	(ûr'lăm)	Eng.	53·26 N	2·26 W
129	Irois, Cap des (C.)		Hai.	18·25 N	74·50 W
106	Irondale	(ī'ĕrn-dăl) Al. (Birmingham In.)		33·32 N	86·43 W
165	Iron Gate (Gorge)		Yugo.-Rom.	44·43 N	22·32 E
203	Iron Knob	(ī-ăn nŏb)	Austl.	32·47 S	137·10 E
109	Iron Mountain	(ī'ĕrn)	Mi.	45·49 N	88·04 W
109	Iron River		Mi.	46·09 N	88·39 W
104	Ironton	(ī'ĕrn-tŭn)	Oh.	38·30 N	82·45 W
109	Ironwood	(ī'ĕrn-wŏŏd)	Mi.	46·28 N	90·10 W
104	Iroquois (R.)	(ĭr'ỏ-kwoi)	Il.-In.	40·55 N	87·20 W
91	Iroquois Falls		Can.	48·41 N	80·39 W
195	Irō-Saki (C.)	(ē'rỏ sä'kē)	Jap.	34·35 N	138·54 E
167	Irpen' (R.)	(Ir-pĕn')	Sov. Un.	50·13 N	29·55 E
187	Irrawaddy (R.)		Bur.	23·27 N	96·25 E
196	Irrawaddy, Mouths of the	(ĭr-á-wäd'ẻ)	Bur.	15·40 N	94·32 E
188	Irrawaddy R.		Bur.	20·39 N	94·38 E
172	Irtysh (R.)	(ĭr-tĭsh')	Sov. Un.	58·32 N	68·31 E
211	Irumu	(ē-rōō'mōō)	Zaire	1·30 N	29·52 E
162	Irun	(ē-rōōn')	Sp.	43·20 N	1·47 W
113	Irvine	(ûr'vĭn) Ca. (Los Angeles In.)		33·40 N	117·45 W
154	Irvine		Scot.	55·39 N	4·40 W
104	Irvine		Ky.	37·40 N	84·00 W
117	Irving	(ûr'vĕng) Tx. (Dallas, Fort Worth In.)		32·49 N	96·57 W
106	Irvington	(ûr'vĕng-tŭn) NJ (New York In.)		40·43 N	74·15 W
107	Irwin	(ûr'-wĭn) Pa. (Pittsburgh In.)		40·19 N	79·42 W
215	Isa		Nig.	13·14 N	6·24 E
174	Is	(ēs)	Sov. Un. (Urals In.)	58·48 N	59·44 E
122	Isaacs, Mt.	(ē-sä-ä'ks)	Pan. (In.)	9·22 N	79·01 W
124	Isabela (I.)	(ē-sä-bĕ'lä)	Mex.	21·56 N	105·53 W
134	Isabela (I.)	(ē-sä-bä'lä)	Ec.	0·47 S	91·35 W
129	Isabela, Cabo (C.)	(ká'bỏ-ē-sä-bĕ'lä)	Dom. Rep.	20·00 N	71·00 W
126	Isabella, Cord. (Mts.)	(kôr-dēl-yĕ'rä-ē-sä-bĕlä)	Nic.	13·20 N	85·37 W
104	Isabella Ind. Res.	(ĭs-á-bĕl'-lä)	Mi.	43·35 N	84·55 W
171	Isaccea	(ē-säk'chä)	Rom.	45·16 N	28·26 E
150	Isafjördhur	(ēs'á-fyûr-dōōr)	Ice.	66·09 N	22·39 W
216	Isangi	(ē-säṅ'gē)	Zaire	0·46 N	24·15 E
158	Isar R.	(ē'zär)	F.R.G.	48·27 N	12·02 E
46	Isarco (R.)	(ē-sär'kỏ)	It.	46·37 N	11·25 E
197	Isaroga Vol.		Phil. (In.)	13·40 N	123·23 E
163	Ischia	(ēs'kyä)	It. (Naples In.)	40·29 N	13·58 E
195	Ise (Uji-Yamada)	(ĭs'hĕ) (ē'gĕ-yä'mä'dá)	Jap.	34·30 N	136·43 E
164	Iseo, Lago di (L.)	(lä-'gỏ-dē-ē-zĕ'ỏ)	It.	45·50 N	9·55 E
161	Isère (R.)	(ē-zâr')	Fr.	45·24 N	6·04 E
161	Iserlohn	(ē'zĕr-lōn) F.R.G. (Ruhr In.)		51·22 N	7·42 E
164	Isernia	(ē-zĕr'nyä)	It.	41·35 N	14·14 E
195	Ise-Wan (B.)	(ē'sĕ wän)	Jap.	34·49 N	136·44 E
215	Iseyin		Nig.	7·58 N	3·36 E
193	Ishan		China	24·32 N	108·42 E
194	Ishikari Wan (B.)	(ē'shē-kä-rē wän)	Jap.	43·30 N	141·05 E
172	Ishim	(ĭsh-ēm')	Sov. Un.	56·07 N	69·13 E
172	Ishim (R.)		Sov. Un.	53·17 N	67·45 E
174	Ishimbay	(ē-shēm-bī') Sov. Un. (Urals In.)		53·28 N	56·02 E
190	Ishing	(yēsĭng)	China	31·26 N	119·57 E
194	Ishinomaki	(ĭsh-nỏ-mä'kē)	Jap.	38·22 N	141·22 E
194	Ishinomaki Wan (B.)	(ē-shē-nỏ-mä'kē wän)	Jap.	38·10 N	141·40 E
174	Ishly	(ĭsh'lĭ)	Sov. Un. (Urals In.)	54·13 N	55·55 E

ng-sing; ŋ-baŋk; N-nasalized n; nŏd; cŏmmit; ōld; ŏbey; ôrder; fōōd; fŏŏt; ou-out; s-soft; sh-dish; th-thin; pūre; únite; ûrn; stŭd; circŭs; ü-as "y" in study; '-indeterminate vowel.

Page	Name Pronunciation Region	Lat. °'	Long. °'
174	Ishlya (ĭsh'lyȧ) Sov. Un. (Urals In.)	53·54 N	57·48 E
165	Ishm...Alb.	41·32 N	19·35 E
218	Ishmant...Egypt (Nile In.)	29·17 N	31·15 E
109	Ishpeming (ĭsh'pē-mĭng)...Mi.	46·28 N	87·42 W
190	Ishui (yē suĭ)...China	35·49 N	118·40 E
213	Isipingo (ĭs-ĭ-pĭŋ-gō) S. Afr. (Natal In.)	29·59 S	30·58 E
217	Isiro (Paulis)...Zaire	2·47 N	27·37 E
171	İskenderun (ĭs-kĕn'dĕr-ōōn)..Tur.	36·45 N	36·15 E
153	İskenderun Körfezi (G.)...Tur.	36·22 N	35·25 E
171	Iskilip (ĕs'kĭ-lĕp')...Tur.	40·40 N	34·30 E
165	Iskŭr (R.) (ĭs'k'r)...Bul.	43·05 N	23·37 E
162	Isla-Cristina (ēs'lä-krē-stē'nä)..Sp.	37·13 N	7·20 W
187	Islāmābād...Pak.	33·55 N	73·05 E
126	Isla Mujeres (ē's-lä-mōō-kĕ'rĕs) Mex. (In.)	21·25 N	86·53 W
95	Island L...Can.	53·47 N	94·25 W
99	Islands, B. of (ī'lăndz)...Can.	49·10 N	58·15 W
154	Islay (I.) (ī'lā)...Scot.	55·55 N	6·35 W
160	Isle (R.) (ēl)...Fr.	45·02 N	0·29 E
148	Isle of Axholme (Reg.) (ăks'-hōm) Eng.	53·33 N	0·48 W
154	Isle of Man (măn)...Eur.	54·26 N	4·21 W
109	Isle Royale Nat'l Park (īl'roi-ăl') U. S.	47·57 N	88·37 W
115	Isleta (ēs-lā'tä) (ī-lē'tȧ)...NM	34·55 N	106·45 W
98	Isle Verte (ēl vĕrt')...Can.	48·01 N	69·20 W
218	Ismailia (Al Isma'īlīyah) (ēs-mä-ēl'ēȧ).Egypt (Suez In.)	30·35 N	32·17 E
218	Ismā'īlīyah Can..Egypt (Suez In.)	30·25 N	31·45 E
149	Ismaning (ēz'mä-nēng) F.R.G. (Munich In.)	48·14 N	11·41 E
218	Isnā (ēs'nȧ)...Egypt (Nile In.)	25·17 N	32·33 E
157	Isojärvi (L.)...Fin.	61·47 N	22·00 E
171	Isparta (ē-spär'tȧ)...Tur.	37·50 N	30·40 E
186	Israel...Asia	32·40 N	34·00 E
112	Issaquah (ĭz'să-kwăh) Wa. (Seattle In.)	47·32 N	122·02 W
161	Isselburg (ē'sĕl-bōōrg) F.R.G. (Ruhr In.)	51·50 N	6·28 E
160	Issoire (ē-swȧr')...Fr.	45·32 N	3·13 E
160	Issoudun (ē-sōō-dăN')...Fr.	46·56 N	2·00 E
161	Issum (ē'sōōm).F.R.G. (Ruhr In.)	51·32 N	6·24 E
172	Issyk-Kul, Ozero (L.)...Sov. Un.	42·13 N	76·12 E
184	İstādeh-ye Moqor, Āb-e (L.)..Afg.	32·35 N	68·00 E
171	İstanbul (ē-stän-bōōl')...Tur.	41·02 N	29·00 E
171	İstanbul Boğazı (Bosporous) (Str.) Tur.	41·10 N	29·10 E
165	Istiaía (ĭs-tyĭ'yä)...Grc.	38·58 N	23·11 E
134	Istmina (ēst-mē'nä)...Col. (In.)	5·10 N	76·40 W
121	Istokpoga (L.) (ĭs-tŏk-pō'gȧ) Fl. (In.)	27·20 N	81·33 W
164	Istra (pen.) (ē-strä)...Yugo.	45·18 N	13·48 E
165	Istranca Dağ (Mts.) (ĭ-strän'jȧ) Bul.-Turk.	41·50 N	27·25 E
160	Istres (ēs'tr')...Fr. (In.)	43·30 N	5·00 E
136	Itá (ē-tá')...Par.	25·39 S	57·14 W
135	Itabaiana (ē-tä-bä-yȧ-nä)...Braz.	10·42 S	37·17 W
137	Itabapoana (ē-tä'-bä-pōȧ'nä) Braz. (Rio de Janeiro In.)	21·19 S	40·58 W
137	Itabapoana (R.) Braz. (Rio de Janeiro In.)	21·11 S	41·18 W
137	Itabirito (ē-tä-bē-rē'tō) Braz. (Rio de Janeiro In.)	20·15 S	43·46 W
137	Itaboraí (ē-tä-bō-rȧē') Braz. (Rio de Janeiro In.)	22·46 S	42·50 W
135	Itabuna (ē-tä-bōō'nȧ)...Braz.	14·47 S	39·17 W
137	Itacoara (ē-tä-kō'ȧ-rä) Braz. (Rio de Janeiro In.)	21·41 S	42·04 W
135	Itacoatiara (ē-tȧ-kwȧ-tyä'rȧ).Braz.	3·03 S	58·18 W
137	Itaguaí (ē-tä-gwä-ē') Braz. (Rio de Janeiro In.)	22·52 S	43·46 W
134	Itagüí (ē-tä'gwē)...Col. (In.)	6·11 N	75·36 W
136	Itagui (R.) Braz. (Rio de Janeiro In.)	22·53 S	43·43 W
136	Itaipava (ē-tī-pȧ'-vä) Braz. (Rio de Janeiro In.)	22·23 S	43·09 W
136	Itaipu (ē-tī'pōō) Braz. (Rio de Janiero In.)	22·58 S	43·02 W
135	Itaituba (ē-tä'ĭ-tōō'bȧ)...Braz.	4·12 S	56·00 W
136	Itajái (ē-tä-zhī')...Braz.	26·52 S	48·39 W
137	Itajubá (ē-tä-zhōō-bá') Braz. (Rio de Janeiro In.)	22·26 S	45·27 W
218	Itala...Som. (Horn of Afr. In.)	2·45 N	46·15 E
146	Italy (ĭt'ȧ-lē)...Eur.	43·58 N	11·14 E
119	Italy...Tx.	32·11 N	96·51 W
136	Itambi (ē-tä'm-bē) Braz. (Rio de Janeiro In.)	22·44 S	42·57 W
195	Itami (ē'tä'mē')..Jap. (Ōsaka In.)	34·47 N	135·25 E
137	Itapecerica (ē-tä-pĕ-sĕ-rē'kȧ) Braz. (Rio de Janeiro In.)	21·29 S	45·08 W
135	Itapecurú (R.) (ē-tä-pĕ-kōō-rōō') Braz.	4·05 S	43·49 W
135	Itapēcuru-Mirim (ē-tä-pĕ'kōō-rōō-mē-rēN').Braz.	3·17 S	44·15 W
137	Itaperuna (ē-tä-pâ-rōō'nä) Braz. (Rio de Janeiro In.)	21·12 S	41·53 W
137	Itapetininga (ē-tä-pĕ-tē-nē'N-gä) Braz. (Rio de Janeiro In.)	23·37 S	48·03 W
135	Itapira (ē-tá-pē'rȧ)...Braz.	20·42 S	51·19 W
137	Itapira.Braz. (Rio de Janeiro In.)	21·27 S	46·47 W
184	Itarsi...India	22·43 N	77·45 E
119	Itasca (ī-tăs'kȧ)...Tx.	32·09 N	97·08 W
109	Itasca (L.)...Mn.	47·13 N	95·14 W
137	Itatiaia, Pico da (Pk.) (pē'-kō-dȧ-ē-tä-tyȧ'ēä) Braz. (Rio de Janeiro In.)	22·18 S	44·41 W
137	Itatiba (ē-tä-tē'bä) Braz. (Rio de Janeiro In.)	23·01 S	46·48 W
137	Itaúna (ē-tä-ōō'nä) Braz. (Rio de Janeiro In.)	20·05 S	44·35 W
137	Itaverá (ē-tä-vĕ-rȧ') Braz. (Rio de Janeiro In.)	22·44 S	44·07 W
104	Ithaca (ĭth'ȧ-kȧ)...Mi.	43·20 N	84·35 W
105	Ithaca...NY	42·25 N	76·30 W
165	Itháki (I.) (ē'thä-kē)...Grc.	38·27 N	20·48 E
217	Itigi...Tan.	5·42 S	34·29 E
216	Itimbiri (R.)...Zaire	2·40 N	23·30 E
212	Itoko (ē-tō'kō)...Zaire	1·13 S	22·07 E
218	Iṭsā (ēt'sȧ)...Egypt (Nile In.)	29·13 N	30·47 E
137	Itu (ē-tōō') Braz. (Rio de Janeiro In.)	23·16 S	47·16 W
190	Itu...China	36·42 N	118·30 E
134	Ituango (ē-twäŋ'gō)...Col. (In.)	7·07 N	75·44 W
135	Ituiutaba (ē-tōō-ēōō-tä'bä)..Braz.	18·56 S	49·17 W
137	Itumirim (ē-tōō-mē-rē'N) Braz. (Rio de Janeiro In.)	21·20 S	44·51 W
125	Itundujia Santa Cruz (ē-tōōn-dōō-hē'ȧ sä'n-tä krōō'z).Mex.	16·50 N	97·43 W
194	It'ung...China	43·15 N	125·10 E
126	Iturbide (ē'tōōr-bē'dhȧ) Mex. (In.)	19·38 N	89·31 W
173	Iturup (I.) (ē-tōō-rōōp')..Sov. Un.	45·35 N	147·15 E
136	Ituzaingo (ē-tōō-zä-ē'n-gō) Arg. (Buenos Aires In.)	34·24 S	58·40 W
149	Itzehoe (ē'tzē-hō) F.R.G. (Hamburg In.)	53·55 N	9·31 E
120	Iuka (ī-ū'kȧ)...Ms.	34·47 N	88·10 W
137	Iúna (ē-ōō'-nä) Braz. (Rio de Janeiro In.)	20·22 S	41·32 W
172	Iva (R.)...Sov. Un.	53·45 N	99·30 E
203	Ivanhoe (ĭv'ăn-hō)...Austl.	32·53 S	144·10 E
159	Ivano-Frankovsk (ē-vä'nō frän-kôvsk').Sov. Un.	48·53 N	24·46 E
166	Ivanovo (ē-vä'nô-vō)...Sov. Un.	57·02 N	41·54 E
166	Ivanovo (Oblast)...Sov. Un.	56·55 N	40·30 E
167	Ivanpol' (ē-vän'pôl)...Sov. Un.	49·51 N	28·11 E
174	Ivanteyevka (ē-vȧn-tyĕ'yĕf-kȧ) Sov. Un. (Moscow In.)	55·58 N	37·56 E
174	Ivdel' (ĭv'dyĕl) Sov. Un. (Urals In.)	60·42 N	60·27 E
	Iviza I., see Ibiza, Isla de		
213	Ivohibé (ē-vō-hē-bā')...Mad.	22·28 S	46·59 E
209	Ivory Coast...Afr.	7·43 N	6·30 W
164	Ivrea (ē-vrĕ'ä)...It.	45·25 N	7·54 E
91	Ivujivik...Can.	62·17 N	77·52 W
194	Iwaki (Taira)...Jap.	37·03 N	140·57 E
194	Iwate Yama (Mt.) (ē-wä-tē-yä'mä). Jap.	39·50 N	140·56 E
195	Iwatsuki...Jap. (Tōkyō In.)	35·48 N	139·43 E
195	Iwaya (ē'wȧ-yȧ)..Jap. (Ōsaka In.)	34·35 N	135·01 E
215	Iwo...Nig.	7·38 N	4·11 E
124	Ixcateopán (ēs-kä-tä-ō-pän').Mex.	18·29 N	99·49 W
149	Ixelles...Bel. (Brussels In.)	50·49 N	4·23 E
125	Ixhuatán (San Francisco) (ēs-hwä-tän').Mex.	16·19 N	94·30 W
124	Ixhautlán (ēs-wȧt-län')...Mex.	20·41 N	98·01 W
124	Ixmiquilpan (ēs-mē-kēl'pän).Mex.	20·30 N	99·12 W
213	Ixopo...S. Afr. (Natal In.)	30·10 S	30·04 E
125	Ixtacalco (ēs-tä-käl'kō).Mex. (In.)	19·23 N	99·07 W
125	Ixtaltepec (Asunción) (ēs-täl-tĕ-pĕk').Mex.	16·33 N	95·04 W
125	Ixtapalapa (ēs'tä-pä-lä'pä) Mex. (In.)	19·21 N	99·06 W
125	Ixtapaluca (ēs'tä-pä-lōō'kä) Mex. (In.)	19·18 N	98·53 W
125	Ixtepec (ēks-tĕ'pĕk)...Mex.	16·37 N	95·09 W
125	Ixtlahuaca (ēs-tlä-wä'kä) Mex. (In.)	19·34 N	99·46 W
125	Ixtlán de Juárez (ēs-tlän' dā hwä'râz).Mex.	17·20 N	96·29 W
124	Ixtlán del Río (ēs-tlän'dĕl rē'ō) Mex.	21·05 N	104·22 W
193	Iyang (ē'yäng')...China	28·52 N	112·12 E
195	Iyo-Nada (Sea) (ē'yō nä-dä)..Jap.	33·33 N	132·07 E
126	Izabal (ē'zä-bäl')...Guat.	15·23 N	89·10 W
126	Izabal, L. (Golfo Dulce) (gôl'fō dōōl'sȧ).Guat.	15·30 N	89·04 W
126	Izalco (ē-zäl'kō)...Sal.	13·50 N	89·40 W
126	Izamal (ē-zä-mä'l)...Mex. (In.)	20·55 N	89·00 W
170	Izhevsk (ē-zhyĕfsk')...Sov. Un.	56·50 N	53·15 E
170	Izhma (ĭzh'mȧ)...Sov. Un.	65·00 N	54·05 E
170	Izhma (R.)...Sov. Un.	64·00 N	53·00 E
174	Izhora R. (ēz'hō-ra) Sov. Un. (Leningrad In.)	59·36 N	30·20 E
167	Izmail (ēz-mȧ-ēl)...Sov. Un.	45·00 N	28·49 E
171	İzmir (ĭz-mēr')...Tur.	38·25 N	27·05 E
165	İzmir Körfezi (G.)...Tur.	38·43 N	26·37 E
171	Izmit (ĭz-mēt')...Tur.	40·45 N	29·45 E
125	Iztaccíhuatl (Mtn.) Mex. (Mexico City In.)	19·10 N	98·38 W
195	Izu (I.) (ē'zōō)...Jap.	34·32 N	139·25 E
195	Izuhara (ē'zōō-hä'rä)...Jap.	34·11 N	129·18 E
195	Izumi-Ōtsu (ē'zōō-mōō ō'tsōō) Jap. (Ōsaka In.)	34·30 N	135·24 E
195	Izumo (ē'zōō-mō)...Jap.	35·22 N	132·45 E
	J		
149	Jaachimsthal (yä'kĕm-stäl) G.D.R. (Berlin In.)	52·58 N	13·45 E
211	Jabal, Baḥr al (R.)...Sud.	7·02 N	30·45
184	Jabalpur...India	23·18 N	79·59
158	Jablonec (Nad Nisou) (yäb'lō-nyĕts).Czech.	50·43 N	15·12
159	Jablunkov P. (yäb'lōōn-kôf) Czech.	49·31 N	18·35
135	Jaboatão (zhä-bô-ȧ-touN)...Braz.	8·14 S	35·08
163	Jaca (hä'kä)...Sp.	42·35 N	0·30
124	Jacala (hä-kȧ'lä)...Mex.	21·01 N	99·11
126	Jacaltenango (hä-kȧl-tĕ-näŋ'gō) Guat.	15·39 N	91·41
137	Jacareí (zhä-kȧ-rĕ-ē') Braz. (Rio de Janeiro In.)	23·19 S	45·57
136	Jacarepaguá (zhä-kä-rȧ'pä-gwä') Braz. (Rio de Janeiro In.)	22·55 S	43·22
135	Jacarézinho (zhä-kä-rĕ'zē-nyō) Braz.	23·13 S	49·58
158	Jachymov (yä'chĭ-môf)...Czech.	50·22 N	12·51
119	Jacinto City (hä-sēn'tō) (jȧ-sĭn'tō) Tx. (In.)	29·45 N	95·14
116	Jacksboro (jăks'bŭr-ō)...Tx.	33·13 N	98·11
120	Jackson (jăk'sŭn)...Al.	31·31 N	87·52
114	Jackson...Ca.	38·22 N	120·47
120	Jackson...Ga.	33·19 N	83·55
120	Jackson...Ky.	37·32 N	83·17
119	Jackson...La.	30·50 N	91·13
104	Jackson...Mi.	42·15 N	84·25
109	Jackson...Mn.	43·37 N	95·00
120	Jackson...Ms.	32·17 N	90·10
117	Jackson...Mo.	37·23 N	89·40
104	Jackson...Oh.	39·00 N	82·40
120	Jackson...Tn.	35·37 N	88·49
202	Jackson, Port..Austl. (Sydney In.)	33·50 S	151·18
111	Jackson L...Wy.	43·57 N	110·28
213	Jacksonstuin...S. Afr. (Johannesburg & Pretoria In.)	25·44 S	27·45
120	Jacksonville (jăk'sŭn-vĭl)...Al.	33·52 N	85·45
121	Jacksonville...Fl.	30·20 N	81·40
117	Jacksonville...Il.	39·43 N	90·12
119	Jacksonville...Tx.	31·58 N	95·18
121	Jacksonville Beach...Fl.	31·18 N	81·25
119	Jacmel (zhȧk-mĕl')...Hai.	18·15 N	72·30
118	Jaco, L. (hä'kō)...Mex.	27·51 N	103·50
184	Jacobābad...Pak.	28·22 N	68·30
135	Jacobina (zhä-kô-bē'nȧ)...Braz.	11·13 S	40·30
100	Jacques-Cartier (zhȧk'kär-tyā) Can. (Montréal In.)	45·30 N	72·39
98	Jacques Cartier, Mt...Can.	48·59 N	66·00
100	Jacques-Cartier, (R.) Can. (Quebec In.)	47·04 N	71·28
99	Jacques Cartier, Détroit de (Str.) Can.	50·07 N	63·58
98	Jacquet River (zhȧ-kĕ') (jăk'ĕt) Can.	47·55 N	66·00
137	Jacuí (zhä-kōō-ē') Braz. (Rio de Janeiro In.)	21·03 S	46·43
137	Jacutinga (zhȧ-kōō-tēn'gä) Braz. (Rio de Janeiro In.)	21·17 S	46·36
158	Jade B. (yä'dĕ)...F.R.G.	53·28 N	8·17
	Jadotville, see Likasi		
134	Jaén (κä-ĕ'n)...Peru	5·38 S	78·49
162	Jaen...Sp.	37·45 N	3·48
203	Jaffa, C. (jăf'ȧ)...Austl.	36·58 S	139·29
185	Jaffna (jăf'nȧ)...Sri Lanka	9·44 N	80·09
128	Jagüey Grande (hä'gwā grän'dā) Cuba	22·35 N	81·05
183	Jahore Str...Mala. (Singapore In.)	1·22 N	103·37
186	Jahrom...Iran	28·30 N	53·28
119	Jaibo (R.) (hä-ē'bō)...Cuba	20·10 N	75·20
184	Jaipur...India	27·00 N	75·50
184	Jaisaimer...India	27·00 N	70·54
164	Jajce (yī'tsĕ)...Yugo.	44·20 N	17·19
184	Jajpur...India	20·49 N	86·37
150	Jakobstad (yȧ'kōb-stȧdh)...Fin.	63·33 N	22·31
125	Jalacingo (hä-lä-sĭŋ'gō)...Mex.	97·16 N	19·47
187	Jalālābād (jŭ-lä-lȧ-bäd) Afg. (Khyber Pass In.)	34·25 N	70·27
218	Jalālah al Baḥrīyah, Jabal, (Mts.) Egypt (Nile In.)	29·20 N	32·00
126	Jalapa (hä-lä'pȧ)...Guat.	14·38 N	89·58
125	Jalapa de Diaz (San Felipe) (dä dē-äz') (sän fā-lē'pä).Mex.	18·06 N	96·33
125	Jalapa del Marqués (dĕl mär-kās').Mex.	16·30 N	95·29
125	Jalapa Enríquez (ĕn-rē'kăz)..Mex.	19·32 N	96·53
184	Jaleswar...Nep.	26·50 N	85·55
184	Jalgaon...India	21·08 N	75·33
124	Jalisco (hä-lēs'kō)...Mex.	21·27 N	104·54
122	Jalisco (State)...Mex.	20·07 N	104·45
162	Jalón (R.) (hä-lōn')...Sp.	41·22 N	1·46
124	Jalostotitlán (hä-lōs-tē-tlän').Mex.	21·09 N	102·30
125	Jalpa (häl'pä)...Mex.	18·12 N	93·06
124	Jalpa (häl'pä)...Mex.	21·40 N	103·04
124	Jalpan (häl'pän)...Mex.	21·13 N	99·31
125	Jaltepec (häl-tȧ-pĕk')...Mex.	17·20 N	95·15
125	Jaltipan (häl-tȧ-pän')...Mex.	17·59 N	94·42
124	Jaltocan (häl-tō-kän')...Mex.	21·08 N	98·32
211	Jālū, Wāḥat (Oasis)...Libya	28·58 N	21·45
215	Jamaare (R.)...Nig.	11·50 N	10·10
123	Jamaica...N. A.	17·45 N	78·00
129	Jamaica Cay (I.)...Ba.	22·45 N	75·55
184	Jamālpur...Bngl.	24·56 N	89·58
124	Jamay (hä-mī')...Mex.	20·16 N	103·43
165	Jambol (yȧm'bôl)...Bul.	42·28 N	26·31
197	Jamdena (I.)...Indon.	7·23 S	130·30
117	James (R.)...Mo.	36·51 N	93·22
121	James (R.)...NC	36·07 N	81·48
102	James (R.)...U. S.	46·25 N	98·55
105	James (R.)...Va.	37·35 N	77·50
91	James B. (jāmz)...Can.	53·53 N	80·40
106	Jamesburg (jāmz'bûrg) NJ (New York In.)	40·21 N	74·26
129	James Pt...Ba.	25·20 N	76·30

Page	Name	Pronunciation	Region	Lat. °′	Long. °′
204	James Ra.		Austl.	24·15 s	133·30 e
133	James Ross (I.)		Ant.	64·20 s	58·20 w
105	Jamestown	(jāmz′toun)	NY	42·05 n	79·15 w
108	Jamestown		ND	46·54 n	98·42 w
106	Jamestown	RI (Providence In.)		41·30 n	71·21 w
213	Jamestown	S. Afr. (Natal In.)		31·07 s	26·49 e
108	Jamestown Res.		ND	47·16 n	98·40 w
125	Jamiltepec	(hä-mēl-tá-pĕk′)	Mex.	16·16 n	97·54 w
156	Jammerbugt (B.)		Den.	57·20 n	9·28 e
184	Jammu		India	32·50 n	74·52 e
184	Jammu and Kashmir (Disputed				
	Reg.)	(kásh-mēr′)	India-Pak.	39·10 n	75·05 e
184	Jāmnagar (jäm-nŭ′gŭr)		India	22·33 n	70·03 e
184	Jamshedpur (jäm′shăd-pōor)		India	22·52 n	86·11 e
134	Jamundí (hä-mōō′n-dē′)		Col. (In.)	3·15 n	76·32 w
162	Jándula (R.) (hän′dōō-lä)		Sp.	38·28 n	3·52 w
183	Janesville (jānz′vĭl)		Wi.	42·41 n	89·03 w
183	Janin		Jordan (Palestine In.)	32·27 n	35·19 e
150	Jan Mayen (I.) (yän mī′ĕn)		Nor.	70·59 n	8·05 w
156	Jannelund (yän′ĕ-lŏŏnd)		Swe.	59·14 n	14·24 e
159	Jánoshalma (yä′nôsh-hôl-mô)		Hung.	46·17 n	19·18 e
159	Janów Lubelski (yä′nŏŏf lŭ-bĕl′skĭ)		Pol.	50·40 n	22·25 e
135	Januária (zhä-nwä′rē-ä)		Braz.	15·31 s	44·17 w
190	Jaoyang (jä′ō-yäng′)		China	38·16 n	115·45 e
183	Japan (já-păn′)		Asia	36·30 n	133·30 e
194	Japan, Sea of (já-păn′)		Asia	40·08 n	132·55 e
197	Japen (I.) (yä′pĕn)		Indon.	1·30 s	136·15 e
136	Japeri (zhä-pĕ′rē)				
			Braz. (Rio de Janeiro In.)	22·38 s	43·40 w
134	Japurá (R.) (zhä-pōō-rá′)		Braz.	1·30 s	67·54 w
119	Jarabacoa (κä-rä-bä-kô′ä)		Dom. Rep.	19·05 n	70·40 w
124	Jaral del Progreso				
	(hä-räl dĕl prô-grä′sō)		Mex.	20·21 n	101·05 w
162	Jarama (R.) (hä-rä′mä)		Sp.	40·33 n	3·30 w
183	Jarash		Jordan (Palestine In.)	32·17 n	35·53 e
128	Jardines, Banco (Bk.)				
	(bä′n-kō-här-dē′näs)		Cuba	21·45 n	81·40 w
135	Jari (R.) (zhä-rē)		Braz.	0·28 n	53·00 w
160	Jarnac (zhär′nak′)		Fr.	45·42 n	0·09 w
159	Jarocin (yä-rō′tsyēn)		Pol.	51·58 n	17·31 e
183	Jarash		Mala. (Singapore In.)	2·19 n	102·26 e
157	Jašiūnai (dzá-shōō-nä′yĕ)		Sov. Un.	54·27 n	25·25 e
183	Jāsk (jäsk)		Iran	25·46 n	57·48 e
159	Jasło (yás′wō)		Pol.	49·44 n	21·28 e
183	Jason B.		Mala. (Singapore In.)	1·53 n	104·14 e
120	Jasonville (jā′sŭn-vĭl)		In.	39·10 n	87·15 w
120	Jasper (jăs′pēr)		Al.	33·50 n	87·17 w
93	Jasper		Can.	52·53 n	118·05 w
120	Jasper		Fl.	30·30 n	82·56 w
104	Jasper		In.	38·20 n	86·55 w
108	Jasper		Mn.	43·51 n	96·22 w
119	Jasper		Tx.	30·55 n	93·59 w
93	Jasper Natl. Park		Can.	53·09 n	117·45 w
159	Jászapáti (yäs′ô-pä-tē)		Hung.	47·29 n	20·10 e
125	Jataté (R.) (hä-tä-tā′)		Mex.	16·30 n	91·29 w
128	Jatibonico (hä-tē-bō-nē′kō)		Cuba	22·00 n	79·15 w
163	Játiva (hä′tē-vä)		Sp.	38·58 n	0·31 w
134	Jaú (zhä-ōō′)		Braz.	22·16 s	48·31 w
134	Jauja (κä-ōō′κ)		Peru	11·43 s	75·32 w
124	Jaumave (hou-mä′vä)		Mex.	23·23 n	99·24 w
157	Jaunjelgava (youn′yĕl′gä-vä)		Sov. Un.	56·37 n	25·06 e
166	Jaunlatgale (youn′lat′gä-lĕ)		Sov. Un.	57·04 n	27·54 e
134	Javari (R.) (κä-vä-rē′)		Col.-Peru	4·25 s	72·07 w
163	Jávea (hä-vä′ä)		Sp.	38·45 n	0·07 e
158	Jawor (yä′vôr)		Pol.	51·04 n	16·12 e
159	Jaworzno (yä-vôzh′nô)		Pol.	50·11 n	19·18 e
	Jayb, Wādī al (R.), see Ha 'Arava				
174	Jayva R. (yäy′vä)		Sov. Un. (Urals In.)	59·13 n	57·17 e
159	Jázberény (yäs-bĕ-rän′)		Hung.	47·30 n	19·56 e
183	Jazzīn		Leb. (Palestine In.)	33·34 n	35·37 e
119	Jeanerette (jēn-ēr-et′) (zhän-rĕt′)		La.	29·54 n	91·41 w
162	Jebel Aures (Mts.)		Alg.	35·16 n	5·53 e
210	Jebba (jĕb′á)		Nig.	9·07 n	4·46 e
99	Jeddore L.		Can.	48·07 n	55·35 w
159	Jędrzejów (yăn-dzhā′yŏŏf)		Pol.	50·38 n	20·18 e
120	Jefferson (jĕf′ēr-sŭn)		Ga.	34·05 n	83·35 w
119	Jefferson		Ia.	42·10 n	94·22 w
106	Jefferson		La. (New Orleans In.)	29·57 n	90·04 w
119	Jefferson		Tx.	32·47 n	94·21 w
105	Jefferson		Wi.	42·59 n	88·45 w
110	Jefferson, Mt.		Or.	44·41 n	121·50 w
117	Jefferson City		Mo.	38·34 n	92·10 w
111	Jefferson R.		Mt.	45·37 n	112·22 w
107	Jeffersontown (jĕf′ēr-sŭn-toun)		Ky. (Louisville In.)	38·11 n	85·34 w
107	Jeffersonville (jĕf′ēr-sŭn-vĭl)		In. (Louisville In.)	38·17 n	85·44 w
215	Jega		Nig.	12·15 n	4·23 e
	Jehol, see Ch'engte				
153	Jeib, Wadi el (R.)		Jordan-Isr.	30·30 n	35·20 e
157	Jēkabpils (yĕk′äb-pĭls)		Sov. Un.	56·29 n	25·50 e
158	Jelenia Góra (yĕ-lĕn′yä gōō′rä)		Pol.	50·53 n	15·43 e
157	Jelgava (yĕl′gä-vä)		Sov. Un.	56·39 n	23·40 e
151	Jellico (jĕl′ĭ-kō)		Tn.	36·34 n	84·06 w
161	Jemmapes (zhĕ-map′)		Alg.	36·43 n	7·21 e
158	Jena (yā′nä)		G.D.R.	50·55 n	11·37 e
190	Jench'iu (rĕnchēō)		China	38·44 n	116·05 e
121	Jenkins (jĕn′kĭnz)		Ky.	37·09 n	82·38 w
106	Jenkintown (jĕn′kĭn-toun)		Pa. (Philadelphia In.)	40·06 n	75·08 w
119	Jennings (jĕn′ĭngz)		La.	30·14 n	92·40 w
151	Jennings		Mi.	43·00 n	85·20 w
113	Jennings		Mo. (St. Louis In.)	38·43 n	90·16 w
135	Jequié (zhĕ-kyĕ′)		Braz.	13·53 s	40·06 w
135	Jequitinhonha (R.) (zhĕ-kē-tēn̄-ŏ′n-yä)		Braz.	16·47 s	41·19 w
129	Jérémie (zhä-rá-mē′)		Hai.	18·40 n	74·10 w
135	Jeremoabo (zhĕ-rä-mō-á′bō)		Braz.	10·03 s	38·13 w
125	Jerez, Punta (pōō′n-tä-κĕ-räz′)		Mex.	23·04 n	97·44 w
162	Jerez de la Frontera (κĕ-räth′ dä lä frôn-tä′rä)		Sp.	36·42 n	6·09 w
162	Jerez de los Caballeros (κĕ-rath′ dä lōs kä-väl-yä′rôs)		Sp.	38·20 n	6·45 w
205	Jericho (jĕr′ĭ-kō)		Austl.	28·38 s	146·24 e
218	Jericho (jĕr-ĭkô′)		S. Afr. (Johannesburg & Pretoria In.)	25·16 s	27·47 e
	Jericho, see Arīḥā				
115	Jerome (jĕ-rōm′)		Az.	34·45 n	112·10 w
111	Jerome		Id.	42·44 n	114·31 w
160	Jersey (I.) (jŭr′zĭ)		Eur.	49·13 n	2·07 w
106	Jersey City		NJ (New York In.)	40·43 n	74·05 w
117	Jersey Shore		Pa.	41·10 n	77·15 w
117	Jerseyville (jĕr′zĕ-vĭl)		Il.	39·07 n	90·18 w
183	Jerusalem (jĕ-rōō′sá-lĕm)		Isr.-Jordan (Palestine In.)	31·46 n	35·14 e
121	Jesup (jĕs′ŭp)		Ga.	31·36 n	81·53 w
125	Jesús Carranza (hĕ-sōō′s-kär-rá′n-zä)		Mex.	17·26 n	95·01 w
108	Jewel Cave Natl. Mon.		SD	43·44 n	103·52 w
112	Jewel (jū′ĕl)		Or. (Portland In.)	45·56 n	123·30 w
184	Jhālawar		India	24·29 n	79·09 e
184	Jhang Maghiāna		Pak.	31·21 n	72·19 e
184	Jhānsi (jän′sē)		India	25·29 n	78·32 e
184	Jhārsuguda		India	22·51 n	86·13 e
184	Jhelum (R.) (jā′lŭm)		Pak.	31·40 n	71·51 e
188	Jibhalanta		Mong.	47·49 n	97·00 e
115	Jicarilla Ind. Res. (κē-kä-rēl′yä)		NM	36·45 n	107·00 w
127	Jicaron, Isla (I.) (κē-kä-rōn′)		Pan.	7·14 n	81·41 w
	Jidda, see Juddah				
159	Jiffa R.		Rom.	47·35 n	27·02 e
204	Jiggalong (jĭg′á-lông)		Austl.	23·20 s	120·45 e
129	Jiguaní (κē-gwä-nē′)		Cuba	20·20 n	76·30 w
128	Jigüey, Bahía (B.) (bä-ē′ä-κē′gwä)		Cuba	22·15 n	78·10 w
190	Jihchao (rē′jou)		China	35·27 n	119·28 e
158	Jihlava (yē′hlä-vä)		Czech.	49·23 n	15·33 e
218	Jijiga (R.) (κē-hō′nä)		Eth. (Horn of Afr. In.)	9·15 n	42·48 e
163	Jijona (κē-hō′nä)		Sp.	38·31 n	0·29 w
211	Jilf al-Kabīr, Hadabat al (Plat.)		Egypt	24·09 n	25·29 e
162	Jiloca (R.) (κē-lō′kä)		Sp.	41·13 n	1·30 w
126	Jilotepeque (κē-lô-tĕ-pĕ′kĕ)		Guat.	14·39 n	89·36 w
211	Jima		Eth.	7·41 n	36·52 e
165	Jimbolia (zhĭm-bô′lyä)		Rom.	45·45 n	20·44 e
124	Jiménez (κĕ-mā′näz)		Mex.	24·12 n	98·29 w
118	Jiménez		Mex.	27·09 n	104·55 w
118	Jiménez		Mex.	29·03 n	100·42 w
124	Jiménez del Téul (tĕ-ōō′l)		Mex.	21·28 n	103·51 w
105	Jim Thorpe (jĭm′ thôrp′)		Pa.	40·50 n	75·45 w
158	Jindřichov Hradec (yēn′d'r-zhĭ-kōōf hrä′dĕts)		Czech.	49·09 n	15·02 e
217	Jinja (jĭn′jä)		Ug.	0·26 n	33·12 e
126	Jinotega (κē-nō-tā′gä)		Nic.	13·07 n	86·00 w
126	Jinotepe (κē-nō-tä′pä)		Nic.	11·52 n	86·12 w
195	Jinzū-Gawa (Strm.) (jēn′zōō gä′wä)		Jap.	36·26 n	137·18 e
134	Jipijapa (κē-pē-hä′pä)		Ec.	1·36 s	80·52 w
126	Jiquilisco (κē-kē-lē′s-kô)		Sal.	13·18 n	88·32 w
124	Jiquilpan de Juarez (κē-kēl′pän dä hwä′räz)		Mex.	20·00 n	102·43 w
125	Jiquipilco (hē-kē-pē′l-kô)		Mex. (In.)	19·32 n	99·37 w
188	Jirgalanta		Mong.	48·08 n	91·40 e
218	Jirjā (jēr′gä)		Egypt (Nile In.)	26·20 n	31·51 e
162	Jistredo, Sierra de (Mts.) (sē-ĕ′r-rä-dĕ-κēs-trĕ′dô)		Sp.	42·50 n	6·15 w
163	Jitotol (κē-tō-tōl′)		Mex.	17·03 n	92·54 w
165	Jiu (R.)		Rom.	44·45 n	23·17 e
212	João Belo (zho′un-bĕ′lô)		Moz.	25·00 s	33·45 e
135	João Pessoa (Paraíba) (zho′oun pĕ-sô′á)		Braz.	7·09 s	34·45 w
137	João Ribeiro (zho′un-rē-bä′rō)		Braz. (Rio de Janeiro In.)	20·42 s	44·03 w
128	Jobabo (R.) (hō-bä′bä)		Cuba	20·50 n	77·15 w
99	Jock (R.) (jŏk)		Can. (Ottawa In.)	45·08 n	75·51 w
124	Jocotepec (hō-kō-tä-pĕk′)		Mex.	20·17 n	103·26 w
162	Jodar (hō′där)		Sp.	37·35 n	3·20 w
184	Jodhpur (jŏd′pōōr)		India	26·23 n	83·00 e
157	Joensuu (yō-ĕn′sōō)		Fin.	62·35 n	29·46 e
93	Joffre, Mt. (jŏf′r)		Can.	50·32 n	115·13 w
195	Jōga-Shima (I.) (jō′gä shē′mä)		Jap. (Tōkyō In.)	35·07 n	139·37 e
166	Jōgeva (yû′gĕ-vä)		Sov. Un.	58·45 n	26·23 e
96	Joggins (jŏ′gĭnz)		Can.	45·42 n	64·27 w
196	Jogjakarta (yôg-yä-kär′tä)		Indon.	7·50 s	110·20 e
213	Johannesburg (jō-hän′ĕs-bōōrgh)		S. Afr. (Johannesburg & Pretoria In.)	26·08 s	27·54 e
110	John Day Dam		Or.	45·40 n	120·15 w
110	John Day R. (jŏn dā)		Or.	44·46 n	120·15 w
110	John Day R., Middle Fork		Or.	44·53 n	119·04 w
110	John Day R., North Fork		Or.	45·03 n	118·50 w
116	John Martin Res. (jŏn mär′tĭn)		Co.	37·57 n	103·04 w
112	Johnson (R.) (jŏn′sŭn)		Or. (Portland In.)	45·27 n	122·20 w
105	Johnsonburg (jŏn′sŭn-bûrg)		Pa.	41·30 n	78·40 w
121	Johnson City (jŏn′sŭn)		Il.	37·50 n	88·55 w
105	Johnson City		NY	42·10 n	76·00 w
121	Johnson City		Tn.	36·17 n	82·23 w
198	Johnston (I.) (jŏn′stŭn)		Oceania	17·00 n	168·00 w
92	Johnstone St.		Can.	50·25 n	126·00 w
217	Johnston Falls		Afr.	10·35 s	28·50 e
105	Johnstown (jonz′toun)		NY	43·00 n	74·20 w
105	Johnstown		Pa.	40·20 n	78·50 w
189	Joho (Prov.)		China	42·31 n	118·12 e
196	Johor (State) (jū-hōr′)		Mala.	2·15 n	103·00 e
183	Johor (R.) (jū-hōr′)		Mala. (Singapore In.)	1·39 n	103·52 e
183	Johor Bahru (bá-hŭ-rōō′)		Mala. (Singapore In.)	1·28 n	103·46 e
166	Jõhvi (yû′vĭ)		Sov. Un.	59·21 n	27·21 e
160	Joigny (zhwän-yē′)		Fr.	47·58 n	3·26 e
136	Joinville (zhwăn-vēl′)		Braz.	26·18 s	48·47 w
160	Joinville		Fr.	48·28 n	5·05 e
133	Joinville (I.)		Ant.	63·00 s	53·30 w
124	Jojutla (hō-hōō′tlä)		Mex.	18·39 n	99·11 w
150	Jökullsá (R.) (yŭ′kŏŏls-ô)		Ice.	65·38 n	16·08 w
124	Jola (kô′lä)		Mex.	21·08 n	104·26 w
107	Joliet (jō-lĭ-ĕt′)		Il. (Chicago In.)	41·37 n	88·05 w
97	Joliette (jō-lyĕt′)		Can.	46·01 n	73·30 w
196	Jolo (hō-lō)		Phil.	5·59 n	121·05 e
196	Jolo (I.)		Phil.	5·55 n	121·15 e
197	Jomalig (I.) (hô-mä′lēg)		Phil. (In.)	14·44 n	122·34 e
124	Jomulco (hô-mōōl′kō)		Mex.	21·08 n	104·24 w
124	Jonacatepec (hō-nä-kä-tä-pĕk′)		Mex.	18·39 n	98·46 w
157	Jonava (yō-nä′vä)		Sov. Un.	55·05 n	24·15 e
156	Jondal (yôn′däl)		Nor.	60·16 n	6·16 e
197	Jones (jōnz)		Phil. (In.)	13·56 n	122·05 e
197	Jones		Phil. (In.)	16·35 n	121·39 e
117	Jonesboro (jōnz′bûro)		Ar.	35·49 n	90·42 w
119	Jonesboro		La.	32·14 n	92·43 w
119	Jonesville (jōnz′vĭl)		La.	31·35 n	91·50 w
104	Jonesville		Mi.	42·00 n	84·45 w
214	Jong (R.)		S. L.	8·10 n	12·10 w
157	Joniškis (yô′nĭsh-kĭs)		Sov. Un.	56·14 n	23·36 e
156	Jönköping (yûn′chû-pĭng)		Swe.	57·47 n	14·10 e
97	Jonquiere (zhôn-kyâr′)		Can.	48·25 n	71·15 w
125	Jonuta (hō-nōō′tä)		Mex.	18·07 n	92·09 w
160	Jonzac (zhôn-zák′)		Fr.	45·27 n	0·27 w
117	Joplin (jŏp′lĭn)		Mo.	37·05 n	94·31 w
182	Jordan (jŏr′dăn)		Asia	30·15 n	38·00 e
183	Jordan (R.)		Jordan (Palestine In.)	31·58 n	35·36 e
113	Jordan R.		Ut. (Salt Lake City In.)	40·42 n	111·56 w
187	Jorhāt (jôr-hät′)		India	26·43 n	94·16 e
124	Jorullo, Vol. de (vôl-kä′n-dĕ-hô-rōōl′yō)		Mex.	18·54 n	101·38 w
215	Jos Plat. (jŏs)		Nig.	9·53 n	9·05 e
204	Joseph Bonaparte, G. (jō′sĕf bō′ná-pärt)		Austl.	13·30 s	128·40 e
100	Josephburg		Can. (Edmonton In.)	53·45 n	113·06 w
100	Joseph L. (jō′sĕf läk)		Can. (Edmonton In.)	53·18 n	113·06 w
114	Joshua Tree Natl. Mon. (jŏ′shū-á trē)		Ca.	34·02 n	115·53 w
215	Jos Plat.		Nig.	9·53 n	9·05 e
156	Jostedalsbreen (Gl.) (yôstĕ-däls-brēĕn)		Nor.	61·40 n	6·55 e
128	Joulter's Cays (Is.) (jōl′tērz)		Ba.	25·20 n	78·10 w
161	Jouy-le-Chatel (zhwē-lĕ-shä-tĕl′)		Fr. (Paris In.)	48·40 n	3·07 e
128	Jovellanos (hō-vĕl-yä′nôs)		Cuba	22·50 n	81·10 w
195	Jōyō (zhō′yō)		Jap. (Ōsaka In.)	34·51 n	135·48 e
120	J. Percy Priest Res.		Tn.	36·00 n	86·45 w
190	Ju (R.) (jōō)		China	33·07 n	114·18 e
124	Juan Aldama (kōōá′n-äl-dá′mä)		Mex.	24·16 n	103·21 w
110	Juan de Fuca, Str. of (hwän′ dĕ fōō′kä)		Wa.-Can.	48·25 n	124·37 w
213	Juan de Nova, Île (I.)		Afr.	17·18 s	43·07 e
122	Juan Diaz, (R.) (kōōá′n-dĕ′-äz)		Pan. (In.)	9·05 n	79·30 w
133	Juan Fernández, Islas de (Is.) (ĕ′s-läs-dĕ-hwän′ fĕr-nän′däth)		Chile	33·30 s	79·00 w
137	Juan L. Lacaze (hōōá′n-lĕ-lä-kä′zĕ)		Ur. (Buenos Aires In.)	34·25 s	57·28 w
128	Juan Luis, Cayos de (Is.) (kä-yōs-dĕ-hwän lōō-ēs′)		Cuba	22·15 n	82·00 w
135	Juàzeiro (zhōōá′zä′rō)		Braz.	9·27 s	40·28 w
135	Juazeiro do Norte (zhōōá′zä′rō-dô-nôr-tĕ)		Braz.	7·16 s	38·57 w
136	Juàrez (hōōá′rĕz)		Arg.	37·42 s	59·46 w
211	Jūbā		Sud.	4·58 n	31·37 e
218	Juba R. (jōō′bá)		Som. (Horn of Afr. In.)	1·30 n	42·25 e
183	Jubayl (Byblos) (jōō-bil′)		Leb. (Palestine In.)	34·07 n	35·38 e
162	Júcar (R.) (hōō′kär)		Sp.	39·10 n	1·22 w
128	Júcaro (hōō′kä-rō)		Cuba	21·40 n	78·50 w
124	Juchipila (hōō-chē-pē′lä)		Mex.	21·26 n	103·09 w
122	Juchitán (hōō-chē-tän′)		Mex.	16·15 n	95·00 w
125	Juchitán de Zaragoza (hōō-chē-tän′ dä thä-rä-gō′thä)		Mex.	16·27 n	95·03 w
124	Juchitlán (hōō-chē-tlän)		Mex.	20·05 n	104·07 w
126	Jucuapa (κōō-kwä′pä)		Sal.	13·30 n	88·24 w
186	Juddah (jōō′dä)		Sau. Ar.	21·30 n	39·15 e
158	Judenburg (jōō-dĕn-bûrg)		Aus.	47·10 n	14·40 e
111	Judith R. (jōō′dĭth)		Mt.	47·20 n	109·36 w
193	Juian (jwī′än′)		China	27·48 n	120·40 e
126	Juigalpa (hwĕ-gäl′pä)		Nic.	12·02 n	85·24 w
161	Juilly (zhwĕ-yē′)		Fr. (Paris In.)	49·01 n	2·41 e
155	Juist (I.) (yōō′ĕst)		F.R.G.	53·41 n	6·50 e
137	Juiz de Fora (zhōō-ēzh′ dä fō′rä)		Braz. (Rio de Janeiro In.)	21·47 s	43·20 w
136	Jujuy (hōō-hwē′)		Arg.	24·14 s	65·15 w
136	Jujuy (Prov.) (hōō-hwē′)		Arg.	23·00 s	66·00 w
190	Jukao (rōōgou)		China	32·24 n	120·33 e
213	Jukskei (R.)		S. Afr. (Johannesburg & Pretoria In.)	25·58 s	27·58 e
116	Julesburg (jōōlz′bûrg)		Co.	40·59 n	102·16 w
134	Juliaca (hōō-lyä′kä)		Peru	15·25 s	70·12 w
75	Julianehåb		Grnld.	60·07 n	46·20 w
161	Jülich (yü′lĕk)		F.R.G. (Ruhr In.)	50·55 n	6·22 e

296 Julijske — Kangean PRONOUNCING INDEX

Page Name Pronunciation Region Lat. °' Long. °'

164 Julijske Alpe (Mts.) (ū'lêy-skě' äl'pě). Yugo. 46·05 N 14·05 E
184 Jullundur.................India 31·29 N 75·39 E
184 Julpaiguri.................India 26·35 N 88·48 E
129 Jumento Cays (Is.) (hōō-měn'tō) Ba. 23·05 N 75·40 W
155 Jumet (zhü-mě')............Bel. 50·28 N 4·30 E
162 Jumilla (hōō-mēl'yä)..........Sp. 38·28 N 1·20 W
109 Jump (R.) (jŭmp)...........Wi. 45·18 N 90·53 W
100 Jumpingpound Cr. (jŭmp-ĭng-pound). Can. (Calgary In.) 51·01 N 114·34 W
135 Jumundá (R.) (zhōō-mōō'n-dä') Braz. 1·33 S 57·42 W
184 Junagādh (jōō-nä'gŭd)......India 21·33 N 70·25 E
190 Junan (rōō nän)...........China 32·59 N 114·22 E
218 Junayfah........Egypt (Suez In.) 30·11 N 32·26 E
183 Junaynah, Ra's al (Mt.) Egypt (Palestine In.) 29·02 N 33·58 E
118 Junction (jŭŋk'shŭn).........Tx. 30·29 N 99·48 W
117 Junction City..............Ks. 39·01 N 96·49 W
137 Jundiaí (zhōō'n-dyä-ē') Braz. (Rio de Janeiro In.) 23·12 S 46·52 W
101 Juneau (jōō'nō).............Ak. 58·25 N 134·30 W
190 Jungch'eng (jōōng'chěng')..China 37·23 N 122·31 E
193 Jungchiang...............China 25·52 N 108·45 E
158 Jungfrau Pk. (yōōng'frou)..Switz. 46·30 N 7·59 E
193 Junghsien................China 22·48 N 110·38 E
137 Junín (hōō-nē'n) Arg. (Buenos Aires In.) 34·35 S 60·56 W
134 Junín.................Col. (In.) 4·47 N 73·39 W
183 Juniyah (jōō-nē'ē) Leb. (Palestine In.) 33·59 N 35·38 E
150 Junkeren (Mtn.) (yōōn'kĕ-rĕn) Nor. 66·29 N 14·58 E
112 Jupiter, Mt......Wa. (Seattle In.) 47·42 N 123·04 W
99 Jupiter (R.)...............Can. 49·40 N 63·20 W
211 Jur (R.) (jōōr).............Sud. 6·38 N 27·52 E
154 Jura (I.) (jōō'rȧ)...........Scot. 56·09 N 6·45 W
161 Jura (Mts.) (zhü-rȧ')........Switz. 46·55 N 6·49 E
154 Jura, Sd. of (jōō'rȧ)........Scot. 55·45 N 5·55 W
157 Jurbarkas (yōōr-bär'käs).Sov. Un. 55·06 N 22·50 E
157 Jūrmala...............Sov. Un. 56·57 N 23·37 E
134 Juruá (R.) (zhōō-rōō-ä')......Braz. 5·27 S 67·39 W
135 Juruena (R.) (zhōō-rōōě'nä). Braz. 12·22 S 58·34 W
134 Jutaí (R.) (zhōō-tāy).........Braz. 4·26 S 68·16 W
126 Jutiapa (hōō-tē-ä'pä).......Guat. 14·16 N 89·55 W
126 Juticalpa (hōō-tē-käl'pä)...Hond. 14·35 N 86·17 W
124 Juventino Rosas (ĸōō-vĕn-tē'nō-rō-säs). Mex. 20·38 N 101·02 W
61 Juvisy-sur-Orge (zhü-vē-sē'sür-ôrzh'). Fr. (Paris In.) 48·41 N 2·22 E
124 Juxtahuaca (hōōs-tlä-hwä'kä) Mex. 17·20 N 98·02 W
165 Južna Morava (R.) (ū'zhnȧ mô'rä-vä). Yugo. 42·30 N 22·00 E
156 Jylland (Reg.)............Den. 56·04 N 9·00 E
157 Jyväskylä (yû'vĕs-kû-lĕ).....Fin. 62·14 N 25·46 E

K

217 Kaabong...................Ug. 3·31 N 34·08 E
213 Kaalfontein (kärl-fŏn-tān)..S. Afr. (Johannesburg & Pretoria In.) 26·02 S 28·16 E
212 Kaappunt (C.)........S. Afr. (In.) 34·21 S 18·30 E
196 Kabaena (I.) (kä-bȧ-ā'nȧ)..Indon. 5·35 S 121·07 E
210 Kabala (kȧ-bȧ'lȧ)...........S. L. 9·43 N 11·39 W
217 Kabale....................Ug. 1·15 S 29·59 E
217 Kabalo (kä-bä'lō)...........Zaire 6·03 S 26·55 E
212 Kabambare (kä-bäm-bä'rȧ)..Zaire 4·47 S 27·45 E
215 Kabba.....................Nig. 7·50 N 6·03 E
195 Kabe (kä'bā)...............Jap. 34·32 N 132·30 E
96 Kabinakagami (R.)..........Can. 49·00 N 84·15 W
216 Kabinda (kä-bĕn'dä)........Zaire 6·08 S 24·29 E
216 Kabompo (R.) (kȧ-bôm'pō) Zambia 14·00 S 23·40 E
212 Kabongo (kȧ-bông'ô).......Zaire 7·58 S 25·10 E
214 Kabot.....................Gui. 10·48 N 14·57 W
152 Kaboudia, Ras (C.).........Tun. 35·17 N 11·28 E
184 Kābul (kä'bōōl)............Afg. 34·39 N 69·14 E
187 Kabul (R.) (kä'bōōl)........Asia 34·44 N 69·43 E
217 Kabunda...................Zaire 12·25 S 29·22 E
217 Kabwe (Broken Hill).......Zambia 14·27 S 28·27 E
173 Kachuga (kȧ-chōō-gȧ)....Sov. Un. 54·09 N 105·43 E
167 Kadiyevka (kȧ-dī-yĕf'kȧ).Sov. Un. 48·34 N 38·37 E
170 Kadnikov (käd'nē-kôf)...Sov. Un. 59·30 N 40·10 E
195 Kadoma.........Jap. (Ōsaka In.) 34·43 N 135·36 E
215 Kaduna (kä-dōō'nä).........Nig. 10·33 N 7·27 E
215 Kaduna (R.)...............Nig. 9·30 N 6·00 E
214 Kaédi (kä-ā-dē')......Mauritania 16·09 N 13·30 W
89 Kaena Pt. (kä'ā-nä).........Hi. 21·33 N 158·19 W
194 Kaesŏng (Kaijo) (kä'ĕ-sŭng) (kī'jō). Kor. 38·00 N 126·35 E
215 Kafanchan.................Nig. 9·36 N 8·17 E
211 Kafia Kingi (kä'fē-ȧ kĭŋ'gē)..Sud. 9·17 N 24·28 E
212 Kafue (kä'fōō)...........Zambia 15·45 S 28·17 E
217 Kafue (R.)...............Zambia 15·45 S 26·30 E
217 Kafue Flats (Pln.)........Zambia 16·15 S 26·30 E
217 Kafue Natl. Pk...........Zambia 15·00 S 25·35 E
217 Kafwira...................Zaire 12·10 S 27·33 E
167 Kagal'nik (R.) (kä-gäl''nêk) Sov. Un. 46·58 N 39·25 E
217 Kagera (R.) (kä-gā'rȧ)......Tan. 1·10 S 31·10 E
195 Kagoshima (kä'gō-shē'mȧ)....Jap. 31·35 N 130·31 E
195 Kagoshima-Wan (B.) (kä'gō-shē'mä wän). Jap. 31·24 N 130·39 E
167 Kagul (ka-gōōl')........Sov. Un. 45·49 N 28·17 E
196 Kahajan (R.).............Indon. 1·45 S 113·40 E
216 Kahemba..................Zaire 7·17 S 19·00 E
217 Kahia.....................Zaire 6·21 S 28·24 E
117 Kahoka (kȧ-hō'kȧ)..........Mo. 40·26 N 91·42 W
89 Kahoolawe (I) (kä-hōō-lä'wē)..Hi. 20·28 N 156·48 W
214 Kahoué, Mont (Mtn.). Ivory Coast 7·06 N 7·15 W
109 Kahshahpiwi (R.)...........Can. 48·24 N 90·56 W
89 Kahuku Pt. (kä-hōō'kōō)......Hi. 21·50 N 157·50 W
89 Kahului....................Hi. 20·53 N 156·28 W
197 Kai, Kepulauan (Is.)......Indon. 5·35 S 132·45 E
183 Kaiang.....Mala. (Singapore In.) 3·00 N 101·47 E
96 Kaiashk (R.)...............Can. 49·40 N 89·30 W
115 Kaibab Ind. Res. (kä'ē-bȧb)..Az. 36·55 N 112·45 W
115 Kaibab Plat................Az. 36·30 N 112·10 W
135 Kaieteur Fall (kī-ĕ-tōōr')....Guy. 4·48 N 59·24 W
190 K'aifeng (käī'fĕng).........China 34·48 N 114·22 E
Kaijo, see Kaesong
197 Kai Ketjil (I.)...........Indon. 5·45 S 132·40 E
169 Kaikyō, Sōya (Str.) (sō'yȧ kȧ-ē'kī-ō). Sov. Un. 45·45 N 141·20 E
89 Kailua (kä'ē-lōō'ä)...........Hi. 21·18 N 157·43 W
89 Kailua Kona................Hi. 19·49 N 155·59 W
197 Kaimana.................Indon. 3·32 S 133·47 E
195 Kainan (kä'ē-nȧn').........Jap. 34·09 N 135·14 E
215 Kainji L...................Nig. 10·25 N 4·50 E
190 Kaip'ing (kī-pĭng')........China 40·25 N 122·20 E
158 Kaiserslautern (kī-zĕrs-lou'tĕrn) F.R.G. 49·26 N 7·46 E
205 Kaitaia (kä-ē-tä'ē-ȧ)...N. Z. (In.) 35·30 S 173·28 E
89 Kaiwi Chan (kä'ē-wē)........Hi. 21·10 N 157·38 W
193 Kaiyüan (kī'yōō-än')......China 23·42 N 103·20 E
192 Kaiyuan (kī'yōō-än')......China 42·30 N 124·00 E
101 Kaiyuh Mts. (kī-yōō').......Ak. 64·25 N 157·38 W
150 Kajaani (kä'yȧ-nē)..........Fin. 64·15 N 27·16 E
196 Kajan (Strm.).............Indon. 1·45 N 115·38 E
183 Kajang, Gunong (Mt.) Mala. (Singapore In.) 2·47 N 104·05 E
195 Kajiki (kä'jē-kē)............Jap. 31·44 N 130·41 E
167 Kakhovka (kä-kôf'kȧ)...Sov. Un. 46·46 N 33·32 E
167 Kakhovskoye (L.) (kȧ-ĸôf'skô-yĕ) Sov. Un. 47·21 N 33·33 E
187 Kākināda..................India 16·58 N 82·18 E
101 Kaktovik (kăk-tō'vĭk)........Ak. 70·08 N 143·51 W
93 Kakwa (R.) (kăk'wȧ).......Can. 54·00 N 118·55 W
171 Kalach (kȧ-lȧch')........Sov. Un. 50·15 N 40·55 E
188 Kaladan (R.)..............Bur. 21·07 N 93·04 E
212 Kalahari Des. (kä-lä-hä'rē)..Bots. 23·00 S 22·03 E
112 Kalama (kȧ-lăm'ȧ) Wa. (Portland In.) 46·01 N 122·50 W
112 Kalama (R.)...Wa. (Portland In.) 46·03 N 122·47 W
165 Kalámai (kä-lä-mī')..........Grc. 37·04 N 22·08 E
104 Kalamazoo (kăl-ȧ-mȧ-zōō')....Mi. 42·20 N 85·40 W
104 Kalamazoo (R.)..............Mi. 42·35 N 86·00 W
167 Kalanchak (kä-län-chäk') Sov. Un. 46·17 N 33·14 E
89 Kalapana (kä-lä-pȧ'nä).......Hi. 19·25 N 155·00 W
186 Kalar (Mtn.)...............Iran 31·43 N 51·41 E
184 Kalāt (kŭ-lät')..............Pak. 29·05 N 66·36 E
196 Kalatoa (I.)..............Indon. 7·22 S 122·30 E
161 Kaldenkirchen (käl'dĕn-kēr-ĸĕn) F.R.G. (Ruhr In.) 51·19 N 6·13 E
217 Kalemi (Albertville)........Zaire 5·56 S 29·12 E
192 Kalgan (käl-gän')..........China 40·45 N 114·58 E
204 Kalgoorlie (kăl-gōōr'lē).....Austl. 30·45 S 121·35 E
153 Kaliakra, Nos (Pt.).........Rom. 43·25 N 28·42 E
217 Kalima....................Zaire 2·34 S 26·37 E
196 Kalimantan (Prov.).......Indon. 1·00 S 113·48 E
166 Kalinin (Tver) (kä-lē'nēn) (tvĕr). Sov. Un. 56·52 N 35·57 E
166 Kalinin (Oblast)........Sov. Un. 56·50 N 33·08 E
157 Kaliningrad (Königsberg) (kä-lē-nēn'grät) (kû'nĕks-bĕrgh) Sov. Un. 54·42 N 20·32 E
174 Kaliningrad (kä-lē-nēn'grät) Sov. Un. (Moscow In.) 55·55 N 37·49 E
167 Kalinkovichi (kä-lēn-ko-vē'chē) Sov. Un. 52·07 N 29·19 E
110 Kalispel Ind. Res. (kăl-ĭ-spĕl'). Wa. 48·25 N 117·30 W
111 Kalispell (kăl'ĭ-spĕl).........Mt. 48·12 N 114·18 W
159 Kalisz (kä'lēsh)............Pol. 51·45 N 18·05 E
217 Kaliua....................Tan. 5·04 S 31·48 E
150 Kalix (R.) (kä'lēks)........Swe. 67·12 N 21·41 E
156 Kalmar (käl'mär)..........Swe. 56·40 N 16·19 E
156 Kalmar Sund (Sd.) (käl'mär).Swe. 56·30 N 16·17 E
167 Kal'mius (R.) (käl''myōōs) Sov. Un. 47·15 N 37·38 E
149 Kalmthout.....Bel. (Brussels In.) 51·23 N 4·28 E
171 Kalmyk A. S. S. R. (kăl'mĭk) Sov. Un. 46·56 N 46·00 E
159 Kalocsa (kä'lô-chä).........Hung. 46·32 N 19·00 E
89 Kalohi Chan. (kä-lō'hĭ).......Hi. 20·55 N 157·15 W
217 Kaloko....................Zaire 6·47 S 25·48 E
217 Kalomo (kä-lō'mō).......Zambia 17·02 S 26·30 E
184 Kalsubai Mt..............India 24·43 N 73·47 E
149 Kaltenkirchen (käl'tĕn-kēr-ĸĕn) F.R.G. (Hamburg In.) 53·50 N 9·57 E
185 Kālu (R.)..........India (In.) 19·18 N 73·14 E
166 Kaluga (kȧ-lōō'gä)......Sov. Un. 54·29 N 36·12 E
166 Kaluga (Oblast).........Sov. Un. 54·10 N 34·30 E
156 Kalundborg (kȧ-lōōn''bôr')...Den. 55·42 N 11·07 E
159 Kalush (kä'lōōsh).......Sov. Un. 49·02 N 24·24 E
157 Kalvarija (käl-vä-rē'yȧ)..Sov. Un. 54·24 N 23·17 E
185 Kalwa.......India (Bombay In.) 19·12 N 72·59 E
174 Kal'ya (käl'yȧ) Sov. Un. (Urals In.) 60·17 N 59·58 E
185 Kalyān..............India (In.) 19·16 N 73·07 E
166 Kalyazin (käl-yȧ'zēn)....Sov. Un. 57·13 N 37·55 E
173 Kalyma (R.)............Sov. Un. 66·32 N 152·46 E
170 Kama (L.)...............Sov. Un. 55·28 N 51·00 E
170 Kama (R.) (kä'mä)......Sov. Un. 56·10 N 53·50 E
194 Kamaishi (kä'mä-ē'shē)......Jap. 39·16 N 142·03 E
195 Kamakura (kä'mä-kōō'rä) Jap. (Tōkyō In.) 35·19 N 139·33 E
186 Kamarān (I.)...P. D. R. of Yem. 15·19 N 41·47 E
184 Kāmārhāti..........India (In.) 22·41 N 88·23 E
212 Kambove (käm-bō'vě)......Zaire 10·58 S 26·43 E
173 Kamchatka, P-Ov (Pen.).Sov. Un. 55·19 N 157·45 E
173 Kamchatka (R.)........Sov. Un. 54·15 N 158·38 E
161 Kamen (kä'mĕn) F.R.G. (Ruhr In.) 51·35 N 7·40 E
167 Kamenets-Podol skiy (kȧ-mă'nĕts pō-dôl'skĭ). Sov. Un. 48·41 N 26·34 E
164 Kamenjak, Rt (C.) (ĸä'mĕ-nyäk) Yugo. 44·45 N 13·57 E
167 Kamenka (kä-mĕŋ'kȧ)...Sov. Un. 48·02 N 28·43 E
159 Kamenka..............Sov. Un. 50·06 N 24·20 E
172 Kamen'-na-Obi (kä-mĭny'nŭ ô'bē) Sov. Un. 53·43 N 81·28 E
167 Kamensk-Shakhtinskiy (kä'mĕnsk shäk'tĭn-skĭ). Sov. Un. 48·17 N 40·16 E
174 Kamensk-Ural'skiy (kä'mĕn-skĭ ōō-räl'skĭ). Sov. Un. (Urals In.) 56·27 N 61·55 E
158 Kamenz (kä'mĕnts)......G.D.R. 51·16 N 14·05 E
195 Kameoka (kä'mā-ōkä) Jap. (Ōsaka In.) 35·01 N 135·35 E
184 Kāmet (Mt.)..............India 35·50 N 79·42 E
158 Kamień Pomorski...........Pol. 53·57 N 14·48 E
195 Kamikoma (kä'mê-kō'mä) Jap. (Ōsaka In.) 34·45 N 135·50 E
216 Kamina....................Zaire 8·44 S 25·00 E
109 Kaministikwia (R.) (kȧ-mĭ-nĭ-stĭk'wĭ-ȧ). Can. 48·40 N 89·41 W
217 Kamituga..................Zaire 3·04 S 28·11 E
93 Kamloops (kăm'lōōps).......Can. 50·40 N 120·20 W
Kammer, see Atter See
184 Kampa Dzong..............China 28·23 N 89·42 E
217 Kampala (käm-pä'lä).........Ug. 0·19 N 32·25 E
196 Kampar-Kiri (R.) (käm'pär) Indon. 0·30 N 101·30 E
149 Kampenhout...Bel. (Brussels In.) 50·56 N 4·33 E
161 Kamp-Lintfort (kämp-lēnt'fōrt) F.R.G. (Ruhr In.) 51·30 N 6·34 E
196 Kampot (käm'pōt)........Camb. 10·41 N 104·07 E
158 Kamp R. (kämp)...........Aus. 48·30 N 15·45 E
216 Kampene..................Zaire 3·36 S 26·40 E
95 Kamsack (kăm'săk).........Can. 51·34 N 101·54 W
141 Kamskoye (Res.).......Sov. Un. 59·08 N 56·30 E
174 Kamskoye Vdkhr. (Res.) Sov. Un. (Urals In.) 59·03 N 56·48 E
217 Kamudilo..................Zaire 7·42 S 27·18 E
89 Kamuela....................Hi. 20·01 N 155·40 W
127 Kamuk, Cerro (Mt.) (sĕ'r-rô-kä-mōō'k). C. R. 9·18 N 83·02 W
194 Kamu Misaki (C.) (kä'mōō mê-sä'kē). Jap. 43·25 N 139·35 E
167 Kamyshevatskaya (kȧ-mwēsh'ĕ-vät'skä-yȧ). Sov. Un. 46·24 N 37·58 E
171 Kamyshin (kä-mwēsh'ĭn). Sov. Un. 50·08 N 45·20 E
170 Kamyshlov (kä-mēsh'lôf) Sov. Un. 56·50 N 62·32 E
193 Kan (R.) (kän)............China 26·50 N 115·00 E
172 Kan (R.)..............Sov. Un. 56·30 N 94·17 E
115 Kanab (kăn'ăb)..............Ut. 37·00 N 112·30 W
115 Kanab Plat.................Az. 36·31 N 112·55 W
174 Kanabeki (kȧ-nä'byĕ-kĭ) Sov. Un. (Urals In.) 57·48 N 57·16 E
101 Kanaga (I.) (kȧ-nä'gȧ)........Ak. 52·02 N 117·38 W
195 Kanagawa (Pref.) (kä'nä-gä'wä) Jap. (Tōkyō In.) 35·29 N 139·32 E
195 Kanamachi (kä-nä-mä'chē) Jap. (Tōkyō In.) 35·46 N 139·52 E
216 Kananga (Luluabourg) (lōō'lōō-a-bōōrg'). Zaire 6·14 S 22·17 E
174 Kananikol'skoye (kȧ-nȧ-nĭ-kôl' skô-yĕ). Sov. Un. (Urals In.) 52·48 N 57·29 E
126 Kanasín (kä-nä-sē'n)...Mex. (In.) 20·54 N 89·31 W
101 Kanatak (kȧ-nă'tŏk)..........Ak. 57·35 N 155·48 W
103 Kanawha (R.) (kȧ-nô'wȧ)...U. S. 37·55 N 81·50 W
195 Kanaya (kä-nä'yä) Jap. (Tōkyō In.) 35·10 N 139·49 E
153 Kanayis, Rasel (C.)........Egypt 31·14 N 28·08 E
195 Kanazawa (kä'nȧ-zä'wȧ).....Jap. 36·34 N 136·38 E
184 Kānchenjunga (Mtn.) (kĭn-chĭn-jōōn'gȧ). India-Nep. 27·30 N 88·18 E
185 Kānchipuram...............India 12·55 N 79·43 E
193 Kanchou (kăn'chou).........China 25·50 N 114·30 E
216 Kanda Kanda (kän'dȧ kän'dȧ) Zaire 6·56 S 23·36 E
170 Kandalaksha (kȧn-dȧ-lȧk'shȧ) Sov. Un. 67·10 N 33·05 E
170 Kandalakshskiy Zaliv (B.) Sov. Un. 66·20 N 35·00 E
157 Kandava (kän'dȧ-vȧ)....Sov. Un. 57·03 N 22·45 E
215 Kandi (käN-dē')............Benin 11·08 N 2·56 E
184 Kandiāro...................Pak. 27·09 N 68·12 E
184 Kandla (kŭnd'lŭ)...........India 23·00 N 70·20 E
185 Kandy (kän'dē).........Sri Lanka 7·18 N 80·42 E
105 Kane (kān)..................Pa. 41·40 N 78·50 W
89 Kaneohe (kä-nā-ō'hā)..........Hi. 21·25 N 157·47 W
89 Kaneohe B...................Hi. 21·32 N 157·40 W
167 Kanëv (kä-nyôf')........Sov. Un. 49·46 N 31·27 E
167 Kanevskaya (kȧ-nyĕf'skȧ) Sov. Un. 46·07 N 38·58 E
171 Kanevskoye Vdkhr (Res.) Sov. Un. 50·10 N 30·40 E
203 Kangaroo (I.) (kăŋ-gȧ-rōō'). Austl. 36·05 S 137·05 E
186 Kangāvar (kŭŋ'gā-vär)......Iran 34·37 N 46·45 E
196 Kangean, Kepulauan (I.) (käŋ'gê-än). Indon. 6·50 S 116·22 E

ăt; finăl; rāte; senâte; ärm; ȧsk; sofȧ; fâre; ch-choose; dh-as th in other; bē; êvent; bĕt; recĕnt; cratēr; g-go; gh-guttural g; bĭt; ĭ-short neutral; rīde; ĸ-guttural k as ch in German ich;

PRONOUNCING INDEX Kanggye — Kellinghusen 297

Page	Name Pronunciation Region	Lat. °′	Long. °′
194	Kanggye (käng′gyĕ)........Kor.	40·55 N	126·40 E
194	Kanghwa (I.) (käng′hwä)....Kor.	37·38 N	126·00 E
194	Kangnŭng(kăng′nōōng)..........Kor.	37·42 N	128·50 E
216	Kango (käN-gō).........Gabon	0·09 N	10·08 E
216	Kangowa.................Zaire	9·55 S	22·48 E
188	K′angting.................China	30·15 N	101·58 E
170	Kanin, P-Ov. (Pen.) (kå-nēn′) Sov. Un.	68·00 N	45·00 E
170	Kanin Nos, Mys (G.)....Sov. Un.	68·40 N	44·00 E
217	Kaningo.....................Ken.	0·49 S	38·32 E
165	Kanjiža (kä′nyē-zhä).......Yugo.	46·05 N	20·02 E
107	Kankakee (kăŋ-kȧ-kē′) Il. (Chicago In.)	41·07 N	87·53 W
104	Kankakee (R.)...............Il.	41·15 N	88·15 W
214	Kankan (kāN-käN) (kän-kän′).Gui	10·23 N	9·18 W
192	Kannan....................China	47·50 N	123·30 E
121	Kannapolis (kăn-ăp′ō-lĭs).....NC	35·30 N	80·38 W
195	Kannoura (kä′nō-ōō′rä)......Jap.	33·34 N	134·18 E
215	Kano (kä′nō)................Nig.	12·00 N	8·30 E
212	Kanonkop (Mtn.)....S. Afr. (In.)	33·49 S	18·37 E
116	Kanopolis Res. (kăn-ŏp′ō-lĭs)..Ks.	38·44 N	98·01 W
184	Kānpur (kän′pûr)..........India	26·00 N	82·45 E
102	Kansas (State) (kăn′zȧs)....U. S.	38·30 N	99·40 W
117	Kansas (R.)..................Ks.	39·08 N	95·52 W
113	Kansas City.Ks. (Kansas City In.)	39·06 N	94·39 W
113	Kansas City.Mo. (Kansas City In.)	39·05 N	94·35 W
172	Kansk.................Sov. Un.	56·14 N	95·43 E
194	Kansŏng...................Kor.	38·09 N	128·29 E
188	Kansu (Prov.) (kän′sōō′)...China	39·30 N	101·30 E
196	Kan Tang (kän′täng′)......Thai.	7·26 N	99·28 E
214	Kantchari..........Upper Volta	12·29 N	1·31 E
126	Kantunilkin (kän-tōō-nēl-kē′n) Mex. (In.)	21·07 N	87·30 W
174	Kanzhakovskiy Kamen Gora (kȧn-zhä′kôvs-kēē kămĭen) Sov. Un. (Urals In.)	59·38 N	59·12 E
193	Kaoan....................China	28·30 N	115·02 E
190	Kaoch′eng (kä′ō-chĕng′)....China	34·56 N	114·57 E
191	Kaoch′iao...China (Shanghai In.)	31·21 N	121·35 E
193	Kaohsiung (kä-ô-syōōng′).Taiwan	22·35 N	120·25 E
190	Kaoi (gou′yē).............China	37·37 N	114·39 E
214	Kaolack..................Senegal	14·09 N	16·04 W
190	Kaomi (gou′mē)...........China	36·23 N	119·46 E
190	Kaoshun (gou′shōōn).......China	31·22 N	118·50 E
190	Kaot′ang (kä′ō-täng′)......China	36·52 N	116·12 E
193	Kaoteng Shan (Mtns.)......China	26·30 N	110·00 E
211	Kaouar (Oasis)............Niger	19·16 N	13·09 E
193	Kaoyao...................China	23·08 N	112·25 E
190	Kaoyu (gou′yü)...........Chiua	32·46 N	119·26 E
193	Kaoyu Hu (L.) (kä′ō-yōō′hōō) China	32·42 N	118·40 E
89	Kapaa.......................Hi.	22·06 N	159·20 W
172	Kapal (kȧ-päl′).........Sov. Un.	45·13 N	79·08 E
216	Kapanga...................Zaire	8·21 S	22·35 E
183	Kapchagay............Sov. Un.	43·55 N	77·45 E
158	Kapfenberg (kȧp′fĕn-bĕrgh)..Aus.	47·27 N	15·16 E
217	Kapiri Mposhi............Zambia	13·58 S	28·41 E
211	Kapoeta....................Sud.	4·45 N	33·35 E
159	Kaposvár (kô′pôsh-vär)....Hung.	46·21 N	17·45 E
194	Kapsan (käp′sän′)..........Kor.	40·59 N	128·22 E
196	Kapuas (Strm.) (kä′pōō-äs).Indon.	2·05 S	114·15 E
91	Kapuskasing................Can.	49·28 N	82·22 W
96	Kapuskasing (R.)...........Can.	48·55 N	82·55 W
171	Kapustin Yar (kä′pōōs-tĕn yär′) Sov. Un.	48·30 N	45·40 E
203	Kaputar, Mt. (kă-pû-tȧr)...Austl.	30·11 S	150·11 E
158	Kapuvár (kô′pōō-vär)......Hung.	47·35 N	17·02 E
172	Kara (kärȧ)...........Sov. Un.	68·42 N	65·30 E
170	Kara (R.)...............Sov. Un.	68·30 N	65·20 E
174	Karabanovo (kä′rȧ-bȧ-nō-vō) Sov. Un. (Moscow In.)	56·19 N	38·43 E
174	Karabash (kó-rȧ-bäsh′) Sov. Un. (Urals In.)	55·27 N	60·14 E
171	Kara-Bogaz-Gol, Zaliv (B.) (kȧrä′ bŭ-gäs′).Sov. Un.	41·30 N	53·40 E
166	Karachev (kȧ-rȧ-chôf′)...Sov. Un.	53·08 N	34·54 E
184	Karāchi......................Pak.	24·59 N	68·56 E
147	Karacumy (Des.).......Sov. Un.	39·08 N	59·53 E
172	Karaganda (kȧ-rȧ-gän′dä) Sov. Un.	49·42 N	73·18 E
174	Karaidel (kä′rĭ-dĕl) Sov. Un. (Urals In.)	55·52 N	56·54 E
171	Kara-Khobda (R.) (kä-rȧ κôb′dȧ).Sov. Un.	50·40 N	55·00 E
187	Karakoram Pass.........India-Pak.	35·35 N	77·45 E
188	Karakoram Ra. (kä′rä kō′rōōm) India-Pak.	35·24 N	76·38 E
188	Karakorum (Ruins).......Mong.	47·25 N	102·22 E
171	Karaköse (kä-rä-kŭ′sĕ).......Tur.	39·50 N	43·10 E
168	Karakumy (kara-kum) (Des.) Sov. Un.	40·00 N	57·00 E
171	Karaman (kä-rä-män′).......Tur.	37·10 N	33·00 E
205	Karamea Bght. (kȧ-rȧ-mē′ȧ bĭt) N. Z. (In.)	41·10 S	170·42 E
	Kara Sea, see Karskoye More		
195	Karatsu (kä′rȧ-tsōō).........Jap.	33·28 N	129·59 E
172	Karaul (kä-rȧ-ōōl′)......Sov. Un.	70·13 N	83·46 E
158	Karawanken Mts...........Aus.	46·32 N	14·07 E
186	Karbalā′ (kŭr′bȧ-lä)..........Iraq	32·31 N	43·58 E
159	Karcag (kär′tsäg).........Hung.	47·18 N	20·58 E
165	Kardhítsa...................Grc.	39·23 N	21·57 E
157	Kärdla (kĕrd′lȧ)........Sov. Un.	58·59 N	22·44 E
168	Karelian (A. S. S. R.)....Sov. Un.	62·30 N	32·35 E
217	Karema......................Tan.	6·49 S	30·26 E
172	Kargat (kär-gät′)........Sov. Un.	55·17 N	80·07 E
	Karghalik, see Yehch′eng		
170	Kargopol′ (kär-gō-pōl″)..Sov. Un.	61·30 N	38·50 E
165	Kariaí.......................Grc.	40·14 N	24·15 E
217	Kariba, L.................Afr.	17·15 S	27·55 E
212	Karibib (kȧr′ȧ-bĭb).....S. W. Afr.	21·55 S	15·50 E
185	Kārikāl (kä-rē-käl′).........India	10·58 N	79·49 E
196	Karimata, Pulau-Pulau (Is.) (kä-rē-mä′tȧ).Indon.	1·08 S	108·10 E
196	Karimata, Selat (Str.).....Indon.	1·15 S	107·10 E
183	Karimun Besar (I.) Indon. (Singapore In.)	1·10 N	103·28 E
196	Karimundjawa, Kepulauan (I.) (kä′rē-mōōn-yä′vä).Indon.	5·36 S	110·15 E
218	Karin (kȧr′ĭn) Som. (Horn of Afr. In.)	10·43 N	45·50 E
197	Karkar (I.) (kär′kär).Pap. N. Gui.	4·50 S	146·45 E
172	Karkaralinsk (kär-kär-ä-lĕnsk′) Sov. Un.	49·18 N	75·28 E
186	Karkheh (R.)..............Iran	32·45 N	47·50 E
167	Karkinitskiy Zailv (B.) (kär-kē-net′skĭ-ē zä′lĭf).Sov. Un.	45·50 N	32·45 E
158	Karl-Marx-Stadt (Chemnitz) G.D.R.	50·48 N	12·53 E
185	Karnataka (State)..........India	14·55 N	75·00 E
164	Karlobag (kär-lō-bäg′)......Yugo.	44·30 N	15·03 E
164	Karlovac (kär′lō-vȧts)......Yugo.	45·29 N	15·16 E
167	Karlovka (kȧr′lôv-kȧ)....Sov. Un.	49·26 N	35·08 E
165	Karlovo (kär′lō-vō).........Bul.	42·39 N	24·48 E
158	Karlovy Vary (kär′lō-vē vä′rē) Czech.	50·13 N	12·53 E
156	Karlshamn (kärls′häm)......Swe.	56·11 N	14·50 E
156	Karlskrona (kärls′krō-nä)....Swe.	56·10 N	15·33 E
158	Karlsruhe (kärls′rōō-ĕ).....F.R.G.	49·00 N	8·23 E
156	Karlstad (kärl′städ).........Swe.	59·25 N	13·28 E
101	Karluk (kär′lŭk)............Ak.	57·30 N	154·22 W
156	Karmöy (I.) (kärm-ûe)......Nor.	59·14 N	5·00 E
165	Karnobat (kär-nô′bät).......Bul.	42·39 N	26·59 E
158	Kärnten (Carinthia) (State) (kĕrn′tĕn).Aus.	46·55 N	13·42 E
212	Karonga (kȧ-rōŋ′gȧ)......Malawi	9·52 S	33·57 E
153	Kárpathos (I.)..............Grc.	35·34 N	27·26 E
174	Karpinsk (kär′pĭnsk) Sov. Un. (Urals In.)	59·46 N	60·00 E
171	Kars (kärs)................Tur.	40·35 N	43·00 E
172	Karsakpay (kär-säk-pī′)..Sov. Un.	47·47 N	67·07 E
166	Kārsava (kär′sä-vä).....Sov. Un.	56·46 N	27·39 E
187	Karshi (kär′shē).........Sov. Un.	38·30 N	66·08 E
172	Karskiye Vorota, Proliv (Str.) Sov. Un.	70·30 N	58·07 E
172	Karskoye More (Kara Sea) Sov. Un.	74·00 N	68·00 E
174	Kartaly (kȧr′tá lē) Sov. Un. (Urals In.)	53·05 N	60·40 E
185	Karunagapalli.............India	9·09 N	76·34 E
159	Karvina...................Czech.	49·50 N	18·30 E
92	Kasaan.....................Ak.	55·32 N	132·24 E
216	Kasai (R.)................Zaire	3·45 S	19·10 E
217	Kasama (kȧ-sä′mȧ).......Zambia	10·13 S	31·12 E
217	Kasanga (kȧ-säŋ′gȧ)........Tan.	8·28 S	31·09 E
195	Kasaoka (kä′sȧ-ō′kȧ)........Jap.	34·33 N	133·29 E
210	Kasba-Tadla (käs′bȧ-täd′lȧ).Mor.	32·37 N	5·57 W
217	Kasempa (kȧ-sĕm′pȧ)....Zambia	13·27 S	25·50 E
217	Kasenga (kȧ-seŋ′gȧ)........Zaire	10·22 S	28·38 E
217	Kasese......................Ug.	0·10 N	30·05 E
217	Kasese.....................Zaire	1·38 S	27·07 E
186	Kāshān (kä-shän′)..........Iran	33·52 N	51·15 E
	Kashgar, see K′ashih		
188	K′ashih (Kashgar).........China	39·29 N	76·00 E
195	Kashihara (kä′shē-hä′rä) Jap. (Ōsaka In.)	34·31 N	135·48 E
216	Kashiji Pln................Zambia	13·25 S	22·30 E
166	Kashin (kä-shēn′).......Sov. Un.	57·20 N	37·38 E
166	Kashira (kä-shē′rȧ)......Sov. Un.	54·49 N	38·11 E
195	Kashiwa (kä′shē-wä) Jap. (Tōkyō In.)	35·51 N	139·58 E
195	Kashiwara.......Jap. (Ōsaka In.)	34·35 N	135·38 E
170	Kashiwazaki (kä′shē-wä-zä′kē) Jap.	37·06 N	138·17 E
	Kashmir (Disputed Reg.) see Jammu and Kashmir		
184	Kashmor......................Pak.	28·33 N	69·34 E
174	Kashtak (käsh′tȧk) Sov. Un. (Urals In.)	55·18 N	61·25 E
166	Kasimov (kȧ-sē′môf).....Sov. Un.	54 56 N	41·23 E
101	Kaskanak (kăs-kă′năk).......Ak.	60·00 N	158·00 W
104	Kaskaskia (R.) (kăs-kăs′kĭ-ȧ)...Il.	39·10 N	88·50 W
95	Kaskattama (R.) (kăs-kȧ-tä′mȧ).Can.	56·28 N	90·55 W
	Kaskinen, see Kaskö		
157	Kaskö (Kaskinen) (käs′kû) (käs′kē-nĕn).Fin.	62·24 N	21·18 E
174	Kasli (käs′lĭ).Sov. Un. (Urals In.)	55·54 N	60·46 E
212	Kasongo (kä-sôŋ′gō).......Zaire	4·31 S	26·42 E
153	Kásos (I.)...................Grc.	35·20 N	26·55 E
211	Kassalā (kä-sä′lä)...........Sud.	15·26 N	36·28 E
158	Kassel (käs′ĕl)............F.R.G.	51·19 N	9·30 E
109	Kasson (kăs′ŭn)..............Mn.	44·01 N	92·45 W
171	Kastamonu (kä-stä-mō′nōō)..Tur.	41·20 N	33·50 E
164	Kastélli.............Grc. (In.)	35·13 N	24·11 E
153	Kastellórizon (C.)...........Tur.	36·01 N	30·00 E
165	Kastoría (kȧs-tō′rĭ-ȧ)........Grc.	40·28 N	21·17 E
165	Kastron (käs′trôn)..........Grc.	39·52 N	25·01 E
184	Kasūr.........................Pak.	31·10 N	74·29 E
216	Kataba.....................Zambia	16·05 S	25·10 E
98	Katahdin, Mt. (kȧ-tä′dĭn)....Me.	45·56 N	68·57 W
	Katanga (Reg.), see Shaba		
204	Katanning (kȧ-tăn′ĭng)......Austl.	33·45 S	117·45 E
174	Katav-Ivanovsk (kä′tȧf ĭ-vä′nôfsk).Sov. Un. (Urals In.)	54·46 N	58·13 E
174	Kateninskiy (kȧtyĕ′nĭs-kĭ) Sov. Un. (Urals In.)	53·12 N	61·05 E
165	Kateríni.....................Grc.	40·18 N	22·36 E
217	Katete......................Zambia	14·05 S	32·07 E
204	Katherine (kăth′ĕr-ĭn)......Austl.	14·15 S	132·20 E
184	Kāthiāwār (Pen.) (kä′tyȧ-wär′) India	22·10 N	70·20 E
184	Kathmandu (kăt-män-dōō′). Nep.	27·49 N	85·21 E
100	Kathryn (kăth′rĭn) Can. (Calgary In.)	51·13 N	113·42 W
113	Kathryn....Ca. (Los Angeles In.)	33·42 N	117·45 W
184	Katihār......................India	25·39 N	87·39 E
214	Katiola..............Ivory Coast	8·08 N	5·06 W
101	Katmai Natl. Mon. (kăt′mī)..Ak.	58·38 N	155·00 W
217	Katompi....................Zaire	6·11 S	26·20 E
216	Katopa......................Zaire	2·45 S	25·06 E
159	Katowice.....................Pol.	50·15 N	19·00 E
211	Katrinah, Jabal (Mtn.).....Egypt	28·43 N	34·00 E
156	Katrineholm (kȧ-trē′nĕ-hōlm) Swe.	59·01 N	16·10 E
174	Katsbakhskiy (kȧts-bäk′skĭ) Sov. Un. (Urals In.)	52·57 N	59·37 E
215	Katsina (kät′sē-nȧ).........Nig.	13·00 N	7·32 E
195	Katsura (R.) (kä′tsōō-rä) Jap. (Ōsaka In.)	34·55 N	135·43 E
172	Katta-Kurgan (kȧ-tȧ-kōōr-gän′) Sov. Un.	39·45 N	66·42 E
156	Kattegat (Str.) (kăt′ĕ-gät)...Eur.	56·57 N	11·25 E
217	Katulo, Lagh (R.)..........Ken.	3·10 N	42·25 E
217	Katumba...................Zaire	7·45 S	25·18 E
172	Katun′ (R.) (kȧ-tōōn′)...Sov. Un.	51·30 N	86·18 E
149	Katwijkaan Zee Neth. (Amsterdam In.)	52·12 N	4·23 E
89	Kauai (I.)....................Hi.	22·09 N	159·15 W
89	Kauai Chan. (kä-ōō-ä′ē)......Hi.	21·35 N	158·52 W
158	Kaufbeuren (kouf′boi-rĕn).F.R.G.	47·52 N	10·38 E
119	Kaufman (kôf′mȧn)..........Tx.	32·36 N	96·18 W
109	Kaukauna (kô-kô′nȧ)........Wi.	44·17 N	88·15 W
89	Kaulakahi Chan. (kä′ōō-lȧ-kä′hē) Hi.	22·00 N	159·55 W
89	Kaunakakai (kä′ōō-nȧ-kä′kī)..Hi.	21·06 N	156·59·W
157	Kaunas (Kovno) (kou′nȧs) (kôv′nô).Sov. Un.	54·52 N	23·54 E
215	Kaura Namoda..............Nig.	12·35 N	6·35 E
165	Kavajë (kȧ-vä′yŭ)...........Alb.	41·11 N	19·36 E
165	Kaválla (kȧ-vä′lä)...........Grc.	40·55 N	24·24 E
165	Kavallas, Kólpos (G.).......Grc.	40·45 N	24·20 E
197	Kavieng (kä-vē-ĕng′).Pap. N. Gui.	2·44 S	151·02 E
195	Kawagoe (kä-wă-gō′ȧ) Jap. (Tōkyō In.)	35·55 N	139·29 E
195	Kawaguchi (kä-wä-gōō-chē) Jap. (Tōkyō In.)	35·48 N	139·44 E
89	Kawaikini (Mtn.) (kä-wä′ē-kĭ-nī).Hi.	22·05 N	159·33 W
195	Kawanishi (kä-wä′nē-shē) Jap. (Ōsaka In.)	34·49 N	135·26 E
195	Kawasaki (kä-wä-sä′kē) Jap. (Tōkyō In.)	35·32 N	139·43 E
218	Kawm Umbū....Egypt (Nile In.)	24·30 N	32·59 E
214	Kaya (kä′yä).......Upper Volta	13·05 N	1·05 W
111	Kaycee (kā-sē′)..............Wy.	43·43 N	106·38 W
214	Kayes (kāz)..................Mali	14·27 N	11·26 W
171	Kayseri (kī′sĕ-rē)...........Tur.	38·45 N	35·20 E
113	Kaysville (kāz′vĭl) Ut. (Salt Lake City In.)	41·02 N	111·56 W
173	Kazach′ye.............Sov. Un.	70·46 N	135·47 E
168	Kazakh S.S.R. (kȧ-zäk′).Sov. Un.	48·45 N	59·00 E
170	Kazan′ (kȧ-zän′)........Sov. Un.	55·50 N	49·18 E
167	Kazanka (kȧ-zän′kȧ).....Sov. Un.	47·49 N	32·50 E
165	Kazanlŭk (kȧ′zȧn-lĕk).......Bul.	42·47 N	25·23 E
167	Kazatin...................Sov. Un.	49·43 N	28·50 E
171	Kazbek, Gora (Mt.) (kȧz-bĕk′) Sov. Un.	42·45 N	44·30 E
186	Kāzerūn.....................Iran	29·37 N	51·44 E
159	Kazincbarcika (kô′zĭnts-bôr-tsĭ-ko).Hung.	48·15 N	20·39 E
217	Kazungula.................Zambia	17·45 S	25·20 E
195	Kazusa Kameyama (kä-zōō-sä kä-mȧ′yä-mä).Jap. (Tōkyō In.)	35·14 N	140·06 E
172	Kazym (R.) (kä-zēm′)...Sov. Un.	63·30 N	67·41 E
165	Kéa (I.)......................Grc.	37·36 N	24·13 E
89	Kealaikahiki Chan. (kā-ä′lä-ē-kä-hē′kē).Hi.	20·38 N	157·00 W
106	Keansburg (kēnz′bûrg) NJ (New York In.)	40·26 N	74·08 W
116	Kearney (kär′nĭ)..............Ne.	40·42 N	99·05 W
106	Kearny......NJ (New York In.)	40·46 N	74·09 W
112	Keasey (kēz′ĭ)...Or. (Portland In.)	45·51 N	123·20 W
171	Keban Gölü (L.)............Tur.	38·20 N	39·50 E
150	Kebnekaise Mt. (kĕp′nĕ-kȧ-ēs′ĕ).Swe.	67·53 N	18·10 E
159	Kecskemét (kĕch′kĕ-māt)..Hung.	46·52 N	19·42 E
196	Kedah State (kä′dä).......Mala.	6·08 N	100·31 E
157	Kėdainiai (kē-dī′nĭ-ī)....Sov. Un.	55·16 N	23·58 E
98	Kedgwick (kĕdj′wĭk)........Can.	47·39 N	67·21 W
113	Keenbrook (kēn′brōōk) Ca. (Los Angeles In.)	34·16 N	117·29 W
105	Keene (kēn)...................NH	42·55 N	72·15 W
212	Keetmanshoop (kāt′mȧns-hōp) S. W. Afr.	26·30 S	18·05 E
115	Keet Seel Ruin (kēt sēl)......Az.	36·46 N	110·32 W
109	Keewatin (kē-wä′tĭn)........Mn.	47·24 N	93·03 W
100	Keewatin, Dist. of..........Can.	61·26 N	97·54 W
165	Kefallinía (Cephalonia) (I.)..Grc.	38·08 N	20·58 E
	Kefe, see Feodosiya		
215	Keffi (kĕf′ē).................Nig.	8·51 N	7·52 E
213	Kei (R.) (kā)..S. Afr. (Natal In.)	32·57 S	26·50 E
157	Keila (kā′lȧ)...........Sov. Un.	59·19 N	24·25 E
213	Kei Mouth....S. Afr. (Natal In.)	32·40 S	28·23 E
213	Keiskammahoek (kās′kämä-hōōk′) S. Afr. (Natal In.)	32·42 S	27·11 E
215	Kéita, Bahr (R.)...........Chad.	9·30 N	19·17 E
157	Keitele (L.) (kā′tĕ-lĕ)........Fin.	62·50 N	25·40 E
89	Kekaha.......................Hi.	21·57 N	159·42 W
218	Kelafo....Eth. (Horn of Afr. In.)	5·40 N	44·00 E
183	Kelang.....Mala. (Singapore In.)	3·20 N	101·27 E
183	Kelang (R.).Mala. (Singapore In.)	3·00 N	101·40 E
196	Kelatan State (kĕ-lân-tän′).Mala.	5·11 N	101·51 E
153	Kelkit (R.)...................Tur.	40·38 N	37·03 E
113	Keller (kĕl′ĕr) Tx. (Dallas, Fort Worth In.)	32·56 N	97·15 W
149	Kellinghusen (kĕ′lĕng-hōō-zĕn) F.R.G. (Hamburg In.)	53·57 N	9·43 E

ng-sing; ŋ-baŋk; N-nasalized n; nŏd; cŏmmit; ōld; ôbey; ôrder; fōōd; fŏŏt; ou-out; s-soft; sh-dish; th-thin; pūre; ûnite; ûrn; stŭd; circŭs; ü-as "y" in study; ′-indeterminate vowel.

298 Kellogg — Kingisepp PRONOUNCING INDEX

Page	Name Pronunciation Region	Lat. °′	Long. °′
110	Kellogg (kĕl'ŏg) Id.	47·32 N	116·07 W
157	Kelme' (kĕl-mȧ) Sov. Un.	55·36 N	22·53 E
215	Kélo Chad	9·19 N	15·48 E
93	Kelowna Can.	49·53 N	119·29 W
92	Kelsey Bay (kĕl'sē) Can.	50·24 N	125·57 W
112	Kelso Wa. (Portland In.)	46·09 N	122·54 W
183	Keluang Mala. (Singapore In.)	2·01 N	103·19 E
170	Kem' (kĕm) Sov. Un.	65·00 N	34·48 E
113	Kemah (kē'mȧ) Tx. (In.)	29·32 N	95·01 W
172	Kemerovo Sov. Un.	55·31 N	86·05 E
150	Kemi (kā'mē) Fin.	65·48 N	24·38 E
150	Kemi (R.) Fin.	67·02 N	27·50 E
195	Kemigawa (kĕ'mē-gä'wä) Jap. (Tōkyō In.)	35·38 N	140·07 E
150	Kemijarvi (kā'mē-yĕr-vē) Fin.	66·48 N	27·21 E
150	Kemi-joki (L.) Fin.	66·37 N	28·13 E
111	Kemmerer (kĕm'ēr-ēr) Wy.	41·48 N	110·36 W
116	Kemp (L.) (kĕmp) Tx.	33·55 N	99·22 W
161	Kempen (kĕm'pĕn) F.R.G. (Ruhr In.)	51·22 N	6·25 E
203	Kempsey (kĕmp'sē) Austl.	30·59 S	152·50 E
98	Kempt (L.) (kĕmpt) Can.	47·28 N	74·00 W
158	Kempten (kĕmp'tĕn) F.R.G.	47·44 N	10·17 E
213	Kempton Park (kĕmp'tŏn pärk) S. Afr. (Johannesburg & Pretoria In.)	26·07 S	28·29 E
184	Ken (R.) India	25·00 N	79·55 E
101	Kenai (kĕ-nī') Ak.	60·38 N	151·18 W
101	Kenai Mts. Ak.	60·00 N	150·00 W
101	Kenai Pen. Ak.	64·40 N	150·18 W
154	Kendal (kĕn'dȧl) Eng.	54·20 N	1·48 W
218	Kendal... S. Afr. (Johannesburg & Pretoria In.)	26·03 S	28·58 E
104	Kendallville (kĕn'dȧl-vĭl) In.	41·25 N	85·20 W
113	Kenedy (kĕn'ĕ-dĭ) Tx.	28·49 N	97·50 W
214	Kenema SL.	7·52 N	11·12 W
152	Kenitra (Port Lyautey) (kĕ-nē'trȧ) Mor.	34·21 N	6·34 W
108	Kenmare (kĕn-mâr') ND	48·41 N	102·05 W
107	Kenmore (kĕn'mōr) NY (Buffalo In.)	42·58 N	78·53 W
98	Kennebec (R.) (kĕn-ē-bĕk') Me.	44·23 N	69·48 W
98	Kennebunk (kĕn-ē-buŋk') Me.	43·24 N	70·33 W
113	Kennedale (kĕn'-ē-dāl) Tx. (Dallas, Fort Worth In.)	32·38 N	97·13 W
121	Kennedy, C. Fl. (In.)	28·30 N	80·23 W
101	Kennedy, Mt. Can.	60·25 N	138·50 W
119	Kenner (kĕn'ēr) La.	29·58 N	90·15 W
117	Kennett (kĕn'ĕt) Mo.	36·14 N	90·01 W
110	Kennewick (kĕn'ē-wĭk) Wa.	46·12 N	119·06 W
92	Kenney Dam Can.	53·37 N	124·58 W
112	Kennydale (kĕn-nē'dāl) Wa. (Seattle In.)	47·31 N	122·12 W
97	Kénogami (kĕn-ŏ'gä-mē) Can.	48·26 N	71·14 W
96	Kenogamissi L. Can.	48·15 N	81·31 W
101	Keno Hill Can.	63·58 N	135·18 W
95	Kenora (kē-nō'rȧ) Can.	49·47 N	94·29 W
107	Kenosha (kē-nō'shȧ) Wi. (Milwaukee In.)	42·34 N	87·50 W
104	Kenova (kē-nō'vȧ) WV	38·20 N	82·35 W
106	Kensico Res. (kĕn'sĭ-kō) NY (New York In.)	41·08 N	73·45 W
104	Kent (kĕnt) Oh.	41·05 N	81·20 W
112	Kent Wa. (Seattle In.)	47·23 N	122·14 W
213	Kentani (kĕnt-änĭ') S. Afr. (Natal In.)	32·31 S	28·19 E
189	Kentei Alin (Mts.) (kĕn'tā'ä-lēn') China	45·54 N	131·45 E
188	Kentei Shan (Mts.) (kĕn'tĭ'shän') Mong.	49·25 N	107·51 E
104	Kentland (kĕnt'lȧnd) In.	40·50 N	87·25 W
104	Kenton (kĕn'tŭn) Oh.	40·40 N	83·35 W
90	Kent Pen. Can.	68·28 N	108·10 W
103	Kentucky (State) (kĕn-tŭk'ĭ) U. S.	37·30 N	87·35 W
103	Kentucky (L.) U. S.	36·20 N	88·50 W
103	Kentucky (R.) U. S.	38·15 N	85·01 W
119	Kentwood (kĕnt'wŏŏd) La.	30·56 N	90·31 W
209	Kenya (kĕn'yȧ) Afr.	1·00 N	36·53 E
217	Kenya, Mt. Ken.	0·10 S	37·20 E
109	Kenyon (kĕn'yŭn) Mn.	44·15 N	92·58 W
117	Keokuk (kē'ō-kŭk) Ia.	40·24 N	91·34 W
100	Keoma (kē-ō'mȧ) Can. (Calgary In.)	51·13 N	113·39 W
99	Kepenkeck L. Can.	48·13 N	54·45 W
159	Kepno (kăŋ'pnō) Pol.	51·17 N	17·59 E
185	Kerala (State) India	16·38 N	76·00 E
203	Kerang (kē-răng') Austl.	35·32 S	143·58 E
167	Kerch' (kĕrch) Sov. Un.	45·20 N	36·26 E
167	Kerchenskiy Proliv (Str.) (Kerch Str.) (kĕr-chĕn'skĭ prô'lĭf) Sov. Un.	45·08 N	36·35 E
171	Kerempe Burun (C.) Tur.	42·00 N	33·20 E
211	Keren Eth.	15·46 N	38·28 E
220	Kerguelen, Is. de (kĕr'gȧ-lĕn) Ind. O.	49·50 S	69·30 E
217	Kericho Ken.	0·22 S	35·17 E
196	Kerintji, Gunung (Mtn.) Indon.	1·45 S	101·18 E
188	Keriya (R.) (kē'rē-yä) China	37·13 N	81·59 E
	Keriya, see Yütien		
211	Kerkenna, Îles (I.) (kĕr'kĕn-nä) Tun.	34·49 N	11·37 E
187	Kerki (kĕr'kē) Sov. Un.	37·52 N	65·15 E
165	Kérkira Grc.	39·36 N	19·56 E
165	Kérkira (I.) Grc.	39·33 N	19·36 E
198	Kermadec Is. (kēr-măd'ĕk) N. Z.	30·30 S	177·00 E
198	Kermadec Tonga Trench (kēr-măd'ĕk tŏŋ'gȧ) Oceania	23·00 S	172·30 W
186	Kermān (kĕr-män') Iran	30·23 N	57·08 E
186	Kermānshāh (kĕr-män-shä') Iran	34·01 N	47·00 E
114	Kern (R.) Ca.	35·31 N	118·37 W
114	Kern, South Fork of (R.) Ca.	35·40 N	118·15 W
114	Kern Can. (kûrn) Ca.	36·57 N	119·37 W
214	Kérouané Gui.	9·16 N	9·01 W
161	Kerpen (kĕr'pĕn) F.R.G. (Ruhr In.)	50·52 N	6·42 E
94	Kerrobert Can.	51·53 N	109·13 W
118	Kerrville (kûr'vĭl) Tx.	30·02 N	99·07 W
154	Kerry, Mts. (kĕr'ĭ) Ire.	51·48 N	10·02 W
189	Kerulen (R.) (kĕr'ōō-lĕn) Mong.	47·52 N	113·22 E
97	Kesagami L. Can.	50·23 N	80·15 W
165	Kesan (kĕ'shȧn) Tur.	40·50 N	26·37 E
152	Kesour, Monts des (Mts.) Alg.	32·51 N	0·30 W
218	Kestell (kĕs'tĕl) S. Afr. (Johannesburg & Pretoria In.)	28·19 N	28·43 E
148	Kesteven (Co.) (kĕs'tē-vĕn) Eng.	52·57 N	0·30 W
159	Keszthely (kĕst'hĕl-lĭ) Hung.	46·46 N	17·12 E
172	Ket' (R.) (kyĕt) Sov. Un.	58·30 N	84·15 E
210	Keta Ghana	6·00 N	1·00 E
183	Ketamputih Indon. (Singapore In.)	1·25 N	102·19 E
196	Ketapang (kē-tȧ-päng') Indon.	2·00 S	109·57 E
92	Ketchikan (kĕch-ĭ-kăn') Ak.	55·21 N	131·35 W
159	Ketrzyn (kăŋ't'r-zĭn) Pol.	54·04 N	21·24 E
148	Kettering (kĕt'ēr-ĭng) Eng.	52·23 N	0·43 W
104	Kettering Oh.	39·40 N	84·15 W
93	Kettle (R.) Can.	49·40 N	119·00 W
109	Kettle (R.) (kĕt''l) Mn.	46·20 N	92·57 W
161	Kettwig (kĕt'vēg) F.R.G. (Ruhr In.)	51·22 N	6·56 E
159	Kety (kăŋ tĭ) Pol.	49·54 N	19·16 E
149	Ketzin (kĕ'tzēn) G.D.R. (Berlin In.)	52·29 N	12·51 E
105	Keuka (L.) (kē-ū'kȧ) NY	42·30 N	77·10 W
161	Kevelaer (kĕ'fĕ-lăr) F.R.G. (Ruhr In.)	51·35 N	6·15 E
109	Kewanee (kē-wä'nē) Il.	41·15 N	89·55 W
109	Kewaunee (kē-wô'nē) Wi.	44·27 N	87·33 W
109	Keweenaw B. (kē'wē-nô) Mi.	46·59 N	88·15 W
109	Keweenaw Pen. Mi.	47·28 N	88·12 W
108	Keya Paha (R.) (kē-yȧ pä'hä) S.D.	43·11 N	100·10 W
121	Key Largo (I.) Fl. (In.)	25·11 N	80·15 W
106	Keyport (kē'pōrt) NJ (New York In.)	40·26 N	74·12 W
112	Keyport Wa. (Seattle In.)	47·42 N	122·38 W
105	Keyser (kī'sēr) WV	39·25 N	79·00 W
121	Key West (kē wĕst') Fl. (In.)	24·31 N	81·47 W
159	Kezmarok (kĕzh'mȧ-rŏk) Czech.	49·10 N	20·27 E
172	Khabarovo (kŭ-bȧr-ôvŏ) Sov. Un.	69·31 N	60·41 E
173	Khabarovsk (kä-bä'rôfsk) Sov. Un.	48·35 N	135·12 E
188	Khaidik Gol (R.) (ĸī'dēk gōl) China	42·35 N	84·04 E
172	Khakass Aut. Oblast Sov. Un.	52·32 N	89·33 E
185	Khālāpur India (In.)	18·48 N	73·17 E
173	Khalkha (R.) China-Mong.	48·00 N	118·45 E
165	Khalkidhiki Khers (Pen.) Grc.	40·30 N	23·18 E
165	Khalkís (ĸal'kĭs) Grc.	38·28 N	23·38 E
172	Khal'mer-Yu (kŭl-myĕr'-yōō') Sov. Un.	67·52 N	64·25 E
170	Khalturin (ĸäl'tōō-rēn) Sov. Un.	58·28 N	49·00 E
184	Khambhāt, G. of India	21·20 N	72·27 E
185	Khammam India	17·09 N	80·13 E
184	Khānābād Afg.	36·43 N	69·11 E
184	Khandwa India	21·53 N	76·22 E
	Khangai Mts., see Hangayn Nuruu		
196	Khanh Hung Viet.	9·45 N	105·50 E
164	Khaniá (Canea) (kä-nē'ȧ) (kä-nē'ä) Grc. (In.)	35·29 N	24·04 E
164	Khaniōn, Kólpos (G.) Grc. (In.)	35·35 N	23·55 E
189	Khanka (L.) (kän'kȧ) Sov. Un.	45·09 N	133·28 E
184	Khānpur Pak.	28·42 N	70·42 E
188	Khan Tengri (kän'tĕn'grē) China	42·10 N	80·20 E
172	Khanty-Mansiysk (ĸŭn-te'mŭn-sēsk') Sov. Un.	61·02 N	69·01 E
183	Khān Yūnus Gaza Strip (Palestine In.)	31·21 N	34·19 E
184	Kharagpur (kŭ-rŭg'pōōr) India	22·26 N	87·21 E
167	Khar'kov (kär'kôf) Sov. Un.	50·00 N	36·10 E
167	Khar'kov (Oblast) Sov. Un.	49·33 N	35·55 E
170	Kharlovka Sov. Un.	68·47 N	37·20 E
165	Kharmanli (kȧr-män'lē) Bul.	41·54 N	25·55 E
	Khartoum, see Al Khurṭūm		
186	Khāsh Iran	28·08 N	61·08 E
186	Khāsh (R.) Afg.	32·30 N	64·27 E
184	Khasi Hills India	25·38 N	91·55 E
165	Khaskovo (ĸȧs'kô-vŏ) Bul.	41·56 N	25·32 E
173	Khatanga (kȧ-tän'gȧ) Sov. Un.	71·48 N	101·47 E
173	Khatangskiy Zaliv (B.) (kä-täŋ'g-skē) Sov. Un.	73·45 N	108·30 E
151	Khemis Miliana Alg.	36·19 N	1·56 E
167	Kherson (ĸĕr-sôn') Sov. Un.	46·38 N	32·34 E
167	Kherson (Oblast) Sov. Un.	46·32 N	32·55 E
184	Khetan (R.) India	10·57 N	78·23 E
157	Khiitola (khē'tō-lȧ) Sov. Un.	61·14 N	29·40 E
174	Khimki (ĸēm'kĭ) Sov. Un. (Moscow In.)	55·54 N	37·27 E
165	Khíos (kē'ôs) Grc.	38·23 N	26·09 E
165	Khíos (I.) Grc.	38·20 N	25·45 E
147	Khiva (kē'vȧ) Sov. Un.	41·15 N	60·30 E
167	Khmel'nik Sov. Un.	49·34 N	27·58 E
171	Khmel'nitskiy (kmĕ'lnĕ'ts-kēē) Sov. Un.	49·29 N	26·54 E
167	Khmel'nitskiy (Oblast) (ĸmĕl-nēt'skĭ ôb'lȧst') Sov. Un.	49·27 N	26·30 E
188	Khöbsögol Dalai (Koso Lake) Mong.	51·11 N	99·11 E
166	Kholm (ĸôlm) Sov. Un.	57·09 N	31·07 E
173	Kholmsk (ĸŭlmsk) Sov. Un.	47·09 N	142·33 E
171	Khopër (R.) (ĸô'pēr) Sov. Un.	52·00 N	43·00 E
194	Khor (ĸôr') Sov. Un.	47·50 N	134·52 E
194	Khor (R.) Sov. Un.	47·23 N	135·20 E
164	Khóra Sfakión Grc. (In.)	35·12 N	24·10 E
172	Khorog (ĸôr'ôg) Sov. Un.	37·30 N	71·47 E
184	Khorog Sov. Un.	37·10 N	71·43 E
167	Khorol (ĸô'rôl) Sov. Un.	49·48 N	33·17 E
167	Khorol (R.) Sov. Un.	49·50 N	33·21 E
186	Khorramshahr (kô-ram'shär) Iran	30·36 N	48·15 E
188	Khotan (R.) (ĸō-tän') China	39·09 N	81·08 E
	Khotan, see Hotien		
167	Khotin (ĸô'tēn) Sov. Un.	48·29 N	26·32 E
174	Khot'Kovo (Moscow In.) Sov. Un.	56·15 N	38·00 E
186	Khoybār Sau. Ar.	25·45 N	39·28 E
167	Khoyniki Sov. Un.	51·54 N	30·00 E
184	Khulna Bngl.	22·50 N	89·38 E
186	Khūryān Mūryān (Is.) Om.	17·27 N	56·02 E
159	Khust (ĸōōst) Sov. Un.	48·10 N	23·18 E
171	Khvalynsk (ĸvȧ-lĭnsk') Sov. Un.	52·30 N	48·00 E
186	Khvoy Iran	38·32 N	45·01 E
187	Khyber Pass (kī'bēr) Pak. (Khyber Pass In.)	34·28 N	71·18 E
217	Kialwe Zaire	9·22 S	27·08 E
217	Kiambi (kyäm'bē) Zaire	7·20 S	28·01 E
117	Kiamichi (R.) (kyȧ-mē'chē) Ok.	34·31 N	95·34 W
197	Kiangan (kyäŋ'gän) Phil. (In.)	16·48 N	121·11 E
189	Kiangsi (Chiangshi) (Prov.) China	28·15 N	116·00 E
189	Kiangsu (Chiangsu) (Prov.) China	33·45 N	120·30 E
170	Kianta (L.) (kyȧn'tȧ) Fin.	65·00 N	28·15 E
216	Kibenga Zaire	7·55 S	17·35 E
217	Kibiti Tan.	7·44 S	38·57 E
217	Kibombo Zaire	3·54 S	25·55 E
217	Kibondo Tan.	3·35 S	30·42 E
165	Kičevo (kē'chĕ-vŏ) Yugo.	41·30 N	20·59 E
109	Kickapoo (R.) (kĭk'ȧ-pōō) Wi.	43·20 N	90·55 W
93	Kicking Horse P. Can.	51·25 N	116·10 W
210	Kidal (kē-däl') Mali	18·33 N	1·00 E
148	Kidderminster (kĭd'ēr-mĭn-stēr) Eng.	52·23 N	2·14 W
213	Kidd's Beach (kĭdz) S. Afr. (Natal In.)	33·09 S	27·43 E
148	Kidsgrove (kĭdz'grōv) Eng.	53·05 N	2·30 W
158	Kiel (kēl) F.R.G.	54·19 N	10·08 E
109	Kiel Wi.	43·52 N	88·04 W
158	Kiel B. F.R.G.	54·33 N	10·19 E
	Kiel Can., see Nord-Ostsee Kan.		
159	Kielce (kyĕl'tsĕ) Pol.	50·50 N	20·41 E
149	Kieldrecht (kēl'drĕĸt) Bel. (Brussels In.)	51·17 N	4·09 E
	Kiev, see Kiyev		
167	Kiev (Oblast) (kē'yĕf) (ôb'lȧst') Sov. Un.	50·05 N	30·40 E
171	Kievskoye Vdkhr (Res.) Sov. Un.	51·00 N	30·20 E
214	Kiffa (kēf'ȧ) Mauritania	16·37 N	11·24 W
212	Kigali (kē-gä'lē) Rw.	1·59 S	30·05 E
217	Kigoma (kē-gō'mä) Tan.	4·52 S	29·38 E
195	Kii-Suido (Chan.) (kē sōō-ē'dō) Jap.	33·53 N	134·55 E
194	Kikaiga (I.) Jap.	28·25 N	130·10 E
165	Kikinda (ĸē'kēn-dä) Yugo.	45·49 N	20·30 E
165	Kikladhes (Is.) Grc.	37·30 N	24·45 E
216	Kikwit (kē'kwēt) Zaire	5·02 S	18·49 E
156	Kil (kēl) Swe.	59·30 N	13·15 E
89	Kilauea (kē-lä-ōō-ā'ä) Hi.	22·12 N	159·25 W
89	Kilauea Crater Hi.	19·28 N	155·18 W
101	Kilbuck Mts. (kĭl-bŭk) Ak.	60·05 N	160·00 W
194	Kilchu (kĭl'chōō) Kor.	40·59 N	129·23 E
153	Kildare (kĭl-dâr') Ire.	53·09 N	7·05 W
216	Kilembe Zaire	5·42 S	19·55 E
119	Kilgore Tx.	32·23 N	94·53 W
217	Kilifi Ken.	3·38 S	39·51 E
213	Kilimanjaro (Mtn.) (kyl-ē-măn-jä'rō) Tan.	3·09 S	37·19 E
212	Kilimatinde (kĭl-ē-mä-tĭn'dȧ) Tan.	5·48 S	34·58 E
217	Kilindoni Tan.	7·55 S	39·39 E
157	Kilingi-Nõmme (kē'lĭŋ-gē-nôm'mĕ) Sov. Un.	58·08 N	25·03 E
171	Kilis (kē'lēs) Tur.	36·50 N	37·20 E
167	Kiliya (kē'lyȧ) Sov. Un.	45·28 N	29·17 E
154	Kilkenny (kĭl-kĕn-ĭ) Ire.	52·40 N	7·30 W
165	Kilkis (kĭl'kĭs) Grc.	40·59 N	22·51 E
154	Killala (kĭ-lä'lȧ) Ire.	54·11 N	9·10 W
154	Killarney Ire.	52·03 N	9·05 W
108	Killdeer (kĭl'dēr) ND	47·22 N	102·45 W
154	Kilmarnock (kĭl-mär'nŭk) Scot.	55·38 N	4·25 W
154	Kilrush (kĭl'rŭsh) Ire.	52·40 N	9·16 W
217	Kilwa Kisiwani Tan.	8·58 S	39·30 E
213	Kilwa Kivinje Tan.	8·43 S	39·18 E
215	Kim (R.) Cam.	5·40 N	11·17 E
217	Kimamba Tan.	6·47 S	37·08 E
203	Kimba (kĭm'bȧ) Austl.	33·08 S	136·25 E
108	Kimball (kĭm-bȧl) Ne.	41·14 N	103·41 W
108	Kimball SD	43·44 N	98·58 W
93	Kimberley (kĭm'bēr-lĭ) Can.	49·41 N	115·59 W
212	Kimberley S. Afr.	28·40 S	24·50 E
215	Kimi Cam.	6·05 N	11·30 E
165	Kími Grc.	38·38 N	24·05 E
165	Kimolos (I.) (kē'mō-lōs) Grc.	36·52 N	24·20 E
166	Kimry (kĭm'rē) Sov. Un.	56·53 N	37·24 E
216	Kimvula Zaire	5·44 S	15·58 E
196	Kinabalu, Mt. Mala.	5·45 N	115·26 E
104	Kincardine (kĭn-kär'dĭn) Can.	44·10 N	81·15 W
216	Kinda Zaire	9·18 S	25·04 E
216	Kindanba Con.	3·44 S	14·31 E
119	Kinder (kĭn'dēr) La.	30·30 N	92·50 W
94	Kindersley (kĭn'dērz-lē) Can.	51·27 N	109·10 W
214	Kindia (kĭn'dē-ȧ) Gui.	10·04 N	12·51 W
170	Kinel'-Cherkassy Sov. Un.	53·32 N	51·32 E
166	Kineshma (kē-nĕsh'mȧ) Sov. Un.	57·27 N	41·02 E
203	King (I.) (kĭng) Austl.	39·35 S	143·40 E
203	Kingaroy (kĭŋ'gă-roi) Austl.	26·37 S	151·50 E
114	King City (kĭng sĭ'tĭ) Ca.	36·12 N	121·08 W
100	King City Can. (Toronto In.)	43·56 N	79·32 W
92	Kingcome Inlet (kĭng'kŭm) Can.	50·50 N	126·10 W
116	Kingfisher (kĭng'fĭsh-ēr) Ok.	35·51 N	97·55 W
93	King George, Mt. Can.	50·35 N	115·24 W
204	King George Sd. (jôrj) Austl.	35·17 S	118·30 E
166	Kingisepp (kĭŋ-gē-sep') Sov. Un.	59·22 N	28·38 E

ă ; finăl; rāte; senâte; ärm; ȧsk; sofȧ; fâre; ch-choose; dh-as th in other; bē; ēvent; bĕt; recĕnt; cratēr; g-go; gh-guttural g; bĭt; ĭ-short neutral; rīde; ĸ-guttural k as ch in German ich;

PRONOUNCING INDEX King Leopold — Kolyberovo 299

Page	Name Pronunciation Region	Lat. °′	Long. °′
204	King Leopold Ranges (lē'ô-pōld) Austl.	16·25 s	125·00 E
115	Kingman (kĭng'măn) Az.	35·10 N	114·05 W
116	Kingman (kĭng'măn) Ks.	37·38 N	98·07 W
114	Kings (R.) Ca.	36·28 N	119·43 W
114	Kings Canyon Natl. Park (kăn'yŭn). Ca.	36·52 N	118·53 W
148	Kingsclere (kĭngs-clēr) Eng. (London In.)	51·18 N	1·15 W
203	Kingscote (kĭngz'kŭt) Austl.	35·45 s	137·32 E
155	Kings Lynn (kĭngz lĭn') Eng.	52·45 N	0·20 E
121	Kings Mt. NC	35·13 N	81·30 W
148	Kings Norton (nôr'tŭn) Eng.	52·25 N	1·54 W
204	King Sd. Austl.	16·50 s	123·35 E
106	Kings Park (kĭngz pärk) NY (New York In.)	40·53 N	73·16 W
111	Kings Pk. Ut.	40·46 N	110·20 W
121	Kingsport (kĭngz'pōrt) Tn.	36·33 N	82·36 W
203	Kingston (kĭngz'tŭn) Austl.	37·52 s	139·52 E
105	Kingston Can.	44·15 N	76·30 W
128	Kingston Jam.	18·00 N	76·45 W
105	Kingston NY	42·00 N	74·00 W
105	Kingston Pa.	41·15 N	75·50 W
112	Kingston Wa. (Seattle In.)	47·04 N	122·29 W
148	Kingston upon Hull Eng.	53·45 N	0·25 W
127	Kingstown (kĭngz'toun) St. Vincent (In.)	13·10 N	61·14 W
121	Kingstree (kĭngz'trē) SC	33·30 N	79·50 W
118	Kingsville (kĭngz'vĭl) Tx.	27·32 N	97·52 W
100	King William I. (kĭng wĭl'yăm) Can.	69·25 N	97·00 W
213	King William's Town (kĭng-wĭl'-yŭmz-toun). S. Afr. (Natal In.)	32·53 s	27·24 E
213	Kinira (R.) S. Afr. (Natal In.)	30·37 s	28·52 E
113	Kinloch (kĭn-lŏk) Mo. (St. Louis In.)	38·44 N	90·19 W
93	Kinnaird (kĭn-ärd') Can.	49·17 N	117·39 W
154	Kinnairds Hd. (kĭn-årds'hĕd). Scot.	57·42 N	3·55 W
195	Kinomoto (kē'nō-mōtō) Jap.	33·53 N	136·07 E
195	Kinosaki (kē'nō-sä'kė) Jap.	35·38 N	134·47 E
154	Kinsale Hbr. (kĭn-sāl') Ire.	51·35 N	8·17 W
216	Kinshasa (Léopoldville) Zaire	4·18 s	15·18 E
116	Kinsley (kĭnz'lĭ) Ks.	37·55 N	99·24 W
121	Kinston (kĭnz'tŭn) NC	35·15 N	77·35 W
214	Kintampo (kēn-täm'pō) Ghana	8·03 N	1·43 W
154	Kintyre Pen. Scot.	55·50 N	5·40 W
	Kioroshi, see Ōmori		
116	Kiowa (kī'ô-wȧ) Ks.	37·01 N	98·30 W
117	Kiowa Ok.	34·42 N	95·53 W
165	Kiparissía Grc.	37·17 N	21·43 E
165	Kiparissiakós Kólpos (G.) Grc.	37·28 N	21·15 E
97	Kipawa Lac (L.) Can.	46·55 N	79·00 W
217	Kipembawe (kê-pĕm-bä'wȧ) Tan.	7·39 s	33·24 E
217	Kipengere Ra. Tan.	9·10 s	34·00 E
217	Kipili Tan.	7·26 s	30·36 E
217	Kipusha Zaire	11·46 N	27·14 E
217	Kipushi Zaire	11·46 N	27·14 E
113	Kirby (kŭr'bĭ) Tx. (San Antonio In.)	29·29 N	98·23 W
119	Kirbyville (kŭr'bĭ-vĭl) Tx.	30·39 N	93·54 W
173	Kirenga (R.) (kē-rĕŋ'gȧ) Sov. Un.	56·30 N	103·18 E
173	Kirensk (kē-rĕnsk') Sov. Un.	57·47 N	108·22 E
168	Kirghiz S. S. R. (kĭr-gēz') Sov. Un.	41·45 N	74·38 E
168	Kirghiz Steppe (Plain) Sov. Un.	49·28 N	57·07 E
187	Kirgizskiy Khrebet (Kirgiz) (Mts.). Sov. Un.	37·58 N	72·23 E
216	Kiri Zaire	1·27 s	19·00 E
	Kirin, see Chilung		
192	Kirin (Chilin) (Prov.) China	43·35 N	126·40 E
148	Kirkby-in-Ashfield (kûrk'bē-ĭn-ăsh'fēld). Eng.	53·06 N	1·16 W
154	Kirkcaldy (kēr-kô'dĭ) Scot.	56·06 N	3·15 W
150	Kirkenes Nor.	69·40 N	30·03 E
148	Kirkham (kûrk'ăm) Eng.	53·47 N	2·53 W
112	Kirkland (kûrk'lănd) Wa. (Seattle In.)	47·41 N	122·12 W
96	Kirkland Lake Can.	48·14 N	80·06 W
165	Kirklareli (kėrk'lȧr-ĕ'lė) Tur.	41·44 N	27·15 E
117	Kirksville (kûrks'vĭl) Mo.	40·12 N	92·35 W
186	Kirkūk (kĭr-kōōk') Iraq	35·28 N	44·22 E
154	Kirkwall (kûrk'wôl) Scot.	58·58 N	2·59 W
113	Kirkwood (kûrk'wŏŏd) Mo. (St. Louis In.)	38·35 N	90·24 W
213	Kirkwood S. Afr. (Natal In.)	33·26 s	25·24 E
158	Kirn (kêrn) F.R.G.	49·47 N	7·23 E
166	Kirov Sov. Un.	54·04 N	34·19 E
170	Kirov Sov. Un.	58·35 N	49·35 E
171	Kirovabad (kē-rŭ-vŭ-bät') Sov. Un.	40·40 N	46·20 E
174	Kirovgrad (kē'rŭ-vŭ-grad) Sov. Un. (Urals In.)	57·26 N	60·03 E
167	Kirovograd (kē-rŭ-vŭ-grät') Sov. Un.	48·33 N	32·17 E
167	Kirovograd (Oblast) Sov. Un.	48·23 N	31·10 E
170	Kirovsk Sov. Un.	67·40 N	33·58 E
174	Kirovsk (kê-rôfsk') Sov. Un. (Leningrad In.)	59·52 N	30·59 E
171	Kirsanov (kêr-sä'nôf) Sov. Un.	52·40 N	42·40 E
171	Kırsehir (kêr-shĕ'hēr) Tur.	39·10 N	34·00 E
215	Kirtachi Seybou Niger	12·48 N	2·29 E
184	Kīrthar Ra. (kĭr-tŭr) Pak.	27·00 N	67·10 E
148	Kirton (kûr'tŭn) Eng.	53·29 N	0·35 W
150	Kiruna (kē-rōō'nä) Swe.	67·49 N	20·08 E
217	Kirundu Zaire	0·44 s	25·32 E
116	Kirwin Res. (kûr'wĭn) Ks.	39·34 N	99·04 W
195	Kiryū (kē'rĭ-ōō) Jap.	36·26 N	139·18 E
166	Kirzhach (kêr-zhák') Sov. Un.	56·08 N	38·53 E
213	Kisaki (kē-sä'kė) Tan.	7·37 s	37·43 E
164	Kisámou, Kólpos (G) Grc. (In.)	35·40 N	23·37 E
216	Kisangani (Stanleyville) Zaire	0·30 s	25·12 E
195	Kisarazu (kē'sȧ-rȧ'zōō) Jap. (Tōkyō In.)	35·23 N	139·55 E
172	Kiselëvsk (kē-sĭ-lyôfsk') Sov. Un.	54·05 N	86·19 E
167	Kishinëv (ke-shê-nyôf') Sov. Un.	47·02 N	28·52 E
195	Kishiwada (kē'shê-wä'dä) Jap.	34·25 N	135·18 E
174	Kishkino (kēsh'kĭ-nô) Sov. Un. (Moscow In.)	55·15 N	38·04 E
217	Kisiwani Tan.	4·08 s	37·57 E
101	Kiska (I.) (kĭs'kä) Ak.	52·08 N	177·10 E
93	Kiskatinaw (R.) Can.	55·10 N	120·20 W
95	Kiskitto L. (kĭs-kĭ'tō) Can.	54·16 N	98·34 W
95	Kiskittogisu L. Can.	54·05 N	99·00 W
159	Kiskunfélegyháza (kĭsh'kōōn-fā'lĕd-y'hä'zô). Hung.	46·42 N	19·52 E
159	Kiskunhalas (kĭsh'kōōn-hô'lôsh) Hung.	46·24 N	19·26 E
159	Kiskunmajsa (kĭsh'kōōn-mī'shô) Hung.	46·29 N	19·42 E
213	Kismayu Som.	0·18 s	42·30 E
195	Kiso-Gawa (Strm.) (kē'sō-gä'wä) Jap.	35·29 N	137·12 E
195	Kiso-Sammyaku (Mts.) (kē'sō säm'myȧ-kōō). Jap.	35·47 N	137·39 E
214	Kissidougou (kē'sê-dōō'gōō) Gui.	9·11 N	10·06 W
121	Kissimmee (kĭ-sĭm'ē) Fl. (In.)	28·17 N	81·25 W
121	Kissimmee (L.) Fl. (In.)	27·58 N	81·17 W
121	Kissimmee (R.) Fl. (In.)	27·45 N	81·07 W
150	Kistrand (kĕ'stränd) Nor.	70·29 N	25·01 E
159	Kisujszallás (kĭsh'ōō'y'sä'läsh) Hung.	47·12 N	20·47 E
217	Kisumu (kē'sōō-mōō) Ken.	0·06 s	34·45 E
214	Kita (kē'tȧ) Mali	13·03 N	9·29 W
194	Kitakami Gawa (R.) (kė'tȧ-kä'mē gä-wä). Jap.	39·20 N	141·10 E
195	Kitakyūshū (kē'tȧ-kyōō'shōō') Jap.	34·15 N	130·23 E
217	Kitale Ken.	1·01 N	35·00 E
116	Kit Carson Co.	38·46 N	102·48 W
104	Kitchener (kĭch'ĕ-nēr) Can.	43·25 N	80·35 W
216	Kitenda Zaire	6·53 s	17·21 E
211	Kitgum (kĭt'gōōm) Ug.	3·29 N	33·04 E
153	Kíthira (I.) Grc.	36·15 N	22·56 E
165	Kíthnos (I.) Grc.	37·24 N	24·10 E
92	Kitimat (kĭ-tĭ-măt) Can.	54·03 N	128·33 W
92	Kitimat (R.) Can.	53·50 N	129·00 W
92	Kitimat Ra. Can.	53·30 N	128·50 W
92	Kitlope (R.) (kĭt'lōp) Can.	53·00 N	128·00 W
195	Kitsuki (kêt'sōō-kė) Jap.	33·24 N	131·35 E
105	Kittanning (kĭ-tăn'ĭng) Pa.	40·50 N	79·30 W
106	Kittatinny Mts. (kĭ-tȧ-tĭ'nē) NJ (New York In.)	41·16 N	74·44 W
98	Kittery (kĭt'ēr-ĭ) Me.	43·07 N	70·45 W
149	Kittsee Aus. (Vienna In.)	48·05 N	17·05 E
121	Kitty Hawk (kĭt'tē hôk) NC	36·04 N	75·42 W
217	Kitunda Tan.	6·48 s	33·13 E
217	Kitwe Zambia	12·49 s	28·13 E
158	Kitzingen (kĭt'zĭng-ĕn) F.R.G.	49·44 N	10·08 E
217	Kiunga Ken.	1·45 s	41·29 E
217	Kivu, Lac (L.) Zaire	1·45 s	28·55 E
171	Kiyev (Kiev) (kē'yĕf) Sov. Un.	50·27 N	30·30 E
195	Kiyose Jap. (Tōkyō In.)	35·47 N	139·32 E
174	Kizel (kē'zĕl) Sov. Un. (Urals In.)	59·05 N	57·42 E
171	Kızıl Irmak (R.) (kĭz'ĭl ĭr-mäk') Tur.	40·15 N	34·00 E
174	Kizil'skoye (kĭz'ĭl-skô-yĕ) Sov. Un. (Urals In.)	52·43 N	58·53 E
171	Kizlyar (kĭz-lyär') Sov. Un.	44·00 N	46·50 E
195	Kizu (kē'zōō) Jap. (Ōsaka In.)	34·43 N	135·49 E
147	Kizy-Arvat (kē'zĭl-ŭr-vät') Sov. Un.	38·55 N	56·33 E
213	Klaas Smits (R.) S. Afr. (Natal In.)	31·45 s	26·33 E
149	Klaaswaal. Neth. (Amsterdam In.)	51·46 N	4·25 E
158	Kladno (kläd'nō) Czech.	50·10 N	14·05 E
158	Klagenfurt (klä'gĕn-fōōrt) Aus.	46·38 N	14·19 E
157	Klaipéda (Memel) (klī'pȧ-dȧ) (mā'mĕl). Sov. Un.	55·43 N	21·10 E
110	Klamath Falls Or.	42·13 N	121·49 W
110	Klamath Mts. Ca.	42·00 N	123·25 W
110	Klamath R. Ca.	41·40 N	122·25 W
156	Klarälven (R.) Swe.	60·40 N	13·00 E
112	Klaskanine (R.) (kläs'kȧ-nīn) Or. (Portland In.)	46·02 N	123·43 W
158	Klatovy (klȧ'tô-vė) Czech.	49·23 N	13·18 E
101	Klawock (klā'wăk) Ak.	55·32 N	133·10 W
149	Kleinmachnow (klīn-mäk'nō) G.D.R. (Berlin In.)	52·22 N	13·12 E
218	Klerksdorp (klērks'dôrp) S. Afr. (Johannesburg & Pretoria In.)	26·52 s	26·40 E
218	Klerksraal (klērks'kräl) S. Afr. (Johannesburg & Pretoria In.)	26·15 N	27·10 E
166	Kletnya (klyĕt'nyȧ) Sov. Un.	52·19 N	33·14 E
166	Kletsk (klĕtsk) Sov. Un.	53·04 N	26·43 E
161	Kleve (klĕ'fĕ) F.R.G. (Ruhr In.)	51·47 N	6·09 E
110	Klickitat R. Wa.	46·01 N	121·07 W
166	Klimovichi (klē-mô-vē'chê) Sov. Un.	53·37 N	31·21 E
174	Klimovsk (klĭ'môfsk) Sov. Un. (Moscow In.)	55·21 N	37·32 E
166	Klin (klēn) Sov. Un.	56·18 N	36·43 E
156	Klintehamn (klēn'tē-häm) Swe.	57·24 N	18·14 E
166	Klintsy (klĭn'tsĭ) Sov. Un.	52·46 N	32·14 E
218	Klip (R.) (klĭp) S. Afr. (Johannesburg & Pretoria In.)	27·18 N	29·25 E
218	Klipgat S. Afr. (Johannesburg & Pretoria In.)	25·26 s	27·57 E
156	Klippan (klyp'pān) Swe.	56·08 N	13·09 E
164	Ključ (klyōōch) Yugo.	44·32 N	16·48 E
158	Kłodzko (klôd'skô) Pol.	50·26 N	16·38 E
101	Klondike Reg. (klŏn'dīk) Ak.-Can.	64·12 N	142·38 W
149	Klosterfelde (klōs'tĕr-fĕl-dĕ) G.D.R. (Berlin In.)	52·47 N	13·29 E
149	Klosterneuburg (klōs-tēr-noi'bōōrgh). Aus. (Vienna In.)	48·19 N	16·20 E
90	Kluane (L.) Can.	61·15 N	138·40 W
90	Kluane Natl. Pk. Can.	60·25 N	137·53 W
159	Kluczbork (klōōch'bōrk) Pol.	50·59 N	18·15 E
166	Klyaz'ma (R.) (klyäz'mȧ) Sov. Un.	55·49 N	39·19 E
173	Klyuchevskaya (Vol.) (klyōō-chĕfskä'yä). Sov. Un.	56·13 N	160·00 E
174	Klyuchi (klyōō'chĭ) Sov. Un. (Urals In.)	57·03 N	57·20 E
165	Knezha (knyā'zhȧ) Bul.	43·27 N	24·03 E
108	Knife (R.) (nīf) ND	47·06 N	102·33 W
92	Knight Inlet (nīt) Can.	50·41 N	125·40 W
104	Knightstown (nīts'toun) In.	39·45 N	85·30 W
164	Knin (knēn) Yugo.	44·02 N	16·14 E
158	Knittelfeld Aus.	47·13 N	14·50 E
197	Knob Pk. (nŏb) Phil. (In.)	12·30 N	121·20 E
154	Knockmealdown Mts. (nŏk-mēl'doun). Ire.	52·13 N	8·09 W
148	Knottingley (nŏt'ĭng-lĭ) Eng.	53·42 N	1·14 W
104	Knox (nŏks) In.	41·15 N	86·40 W
92	Knox, C. Can.	54·12 N	133·20 W
109	Knoxville (nŏks'vĭl) Ia.	41·19 N	93·05 W
120	Knoxville Tn.	35·58 N	83·55 W
148	Knutsford (nŭts'fērd) Eng.	53·18 N	2·22 W
159	Knyszyn (knĭ'shĭn) Pol.	53·16 N	22·59 E
190	Ko (R.) (gōōŭ) China	33·04 N	117·16 E
195	Kobayashi (kō'bȧ-yä'shė) Jap.	31·58 N	130·59 E
195	Kōbe (kō'bĕ) Jap. (Ōsaka In.)	34·30 N	135·10 E
167	Kobelyaki (kō-bĕl-yä'kė). Sov. Un.	49·11 N	34·12 E
156	København (Copenhagen) (kû-b'n-houn'). Den.	55·43 N	12·27 E
158	Koblenz (kō'blĕntz) F.R.G.	50·18 N	7·36 E
166	Kobozha (R.) (kō-bō'zhȧ) Sov. Un.	58·55 N	35·18 E
159	Kobrin (kō'brēn') Sov. Un.	52·13 N	24·23 E
174	Kobrinskoye (kô-brĭn'skô-yĕ) Sov. Un. (Leningrad In.)	59·25 N	30·07 E
101	Kobuk (R.) (kō'bŭk) Ak.	66·58 N	158·48 W
171	Kobuleti (kô-bōō-lyä'tė). Sov. Un.	41·50 N	41·40 E
165	Kocani (kô'chä-nĕ) Yugo.	41·54 N	22·25 E
164	Kočevje (kô'chāv-ye) Yugo.	45·38 N	14·51 E
158	Kocher R. (kôκ'ĕr) F.R.G.	49·00 N	9·52 E
195	Kōchi (kō'chė) Jap.	33·35 N	133·32 E
195	Kodaira Jap. (Tōkyō In.)	35·43 N	139·29 E
101	Kodiak (kō'dyăk) Ak.	57·50 N	152·30 W
101	Kodiak (I.) Ak.	57·24 N	153·32 W
211	Kodok (kō'dŏk) Sud.	9·57 N	32·08 E
214	Koforidua (kō fô-rĭ-dōō'ȧ) Ghana	6·03 N	0·17 W
195	Kōfu (kō'fōō') Jap.	35·41 N	138·34 E
195	Koga (kō'gȧ) Jap.	36·13 N	139·40 E
214	Kogan (R.) Gui.	11·30 N	14·05 W
195	Kogane (kō'gä-nā) Jap. (Tōkyō In.)	35·50 N	139·56 E
195	Koganei (kō'gä-nā) Jap. (Tōkyō In.)	35·42 N	139·31 E
156	Køge (kû'gĕ) Den.	55·27 N	12·09 E
156	Køge Bugt (B.) Den.	55·30 N	12·25 E
167	Kogil'nik (R.) (kô-gēl-nēk') Sov. Un.	46·08 N	29·10 E
214	Kogoni Mali	14·44 N	6·02 W
184	Koh-i Baba Mt. Afg.	39·39 N	67·09 E
187	Kohīma (kō-ē'mȧ) India	25·45 N	94·41 E
195	Koito (R.) (kō'ê-tō) Jap. (Tōkyō In.)	35·19 N	139·58 E
194	Kŏje (I.) (kû'jĕ) Kor.	34·53 N	129·00 E
172	Kokand (kô-känt') Sov. Un.	40·27 N	71·07 E
172	Kokchetav (kôk'chĕ-tȧf). Sov. Un.	53·15 N	69·13 E
157	Kokemäen (R.) (kô'kē-mȧ'ĕn). Fin.	61·23 N	22·03 E
166	Kokhma (kôκ'mȧ) Sov. Un.	56·57 N	41·08 E
150	Kokkola (kô'kô-lȧ) Fin.	63·47 N	22·58 E
104	Kokomo (kō'kô-mô) In.	40·30 N	86·20 W
	Koko Nor (L.), see Ch'ing Hai		
197	Kokopo (kô-kô'pō) Pap. N. Gui.	4·25 s	152·27 E
91	Koksoak (R.) (kôk'sô-ăk) Can.	57·42 N	69·50 W
213	Kokstad (kôk'shtät) S. Afr. (Natal In.)	30·33 s	29·27 E
190	Koku (gô'gōō) China	39·00 N	117·30 E
195	Kokubu (kô'kōō-bōō) Jap.	31·42 N	130·46 E
195	Kokuou (kô'kōō-ô'ōō) Jap. (Ōsaka In.)	34·34 N	135·39 E
	Kola Pen., see Kol'skiy P-Ov.		
185	Kolār (Kolār Gold Fields) (kōl-är'). India	13·39 N	78·33 E
159	Kolárvo (kōl-árōvō) Czech.	47·54 N	17·59 E
217	Kolbio Ken.	1·10 s	41·15 E
166	Kol'chugino (kôl-chōō'gê-nô) Sov. Un.	56·19 N	39·29 E
214	Kolda Sen.	12·53 N	14·57 W
156	Kolding (kŭl'dĭng) Den.	55·29 N	9·24 E
212	Kole (kō'lȧ) Zaire	3·19 s	22·46 E
170	Kolguyev (I.) (kôl-gōō'yĕf) Sov. Un.	69·00 N	49·00 E
158	Kolin (kō'lēn) Czech.	50·01 N	15·11 E
157	Kolkasrags (Pt.) (kôl-käs'rȧgz) Sov. Un.	57·46 N	22·39 E
161	Köln (Cologne). F.R.G. (Ruhr In.)	50·56 N	6·57 E
159	Kolno (kôw'nô) Pol.	53·23 N	21·56 E
159	Koło (kô'wô) Pol.	52·11 N	18·37 E
158	Kołobrzeg (kô-lôb'zhĕk) Pol.	54·10 N	15·35 E
174	Kolomna (kål-ôm'nȧ) Sov. Un. (Moscow In.)	55·06 N	38·47 E
159	Kolomyya (kô'lô-mē'yȧ). Sov. Un.	48·32 N	25·04 E
166	Kolp' (R.) (kôlp) Sov. Un.	59·29 N	35·32 E
172	Kolpashevo (kŭl pȧ shô'vȧ) Sov. Un.	58·16 N	82·43 E
174	Kolpino (kôl'pê-nô) Sov. Un. (Leningrad In.)	59·45 N	30·37 E
166	Kolpny (kôlp'nyê) Sov. Un.	52·14 N	36·54 E
170	Kol'skiy P-Ov. (Kola Pen.) Sov. Un.	67·15 N	37·40 E
170	Kolva (R.) Sov. Un.	61·00 N	57·00 E
217	Kolwezi (kōl-wĕ'zē) Zaire	10·43 s	25·28 E
174	Kolyberovo (kô-lĭ-byâ'rô-vô) Sov. Un. (Moscow In.)	55·16 N	38·45 E

ng-sing; ŋ-baŋk; ɴ-nasalized n; nŏd; cŏmmit; ōld; ôbey; ôrder; fōōd; fŏŏt; ou-out; s-soft; sh-dish; th-thin; pūre; ûnite; ûrn; stŭd; circŭs; ü-as "y" in study; '-indeterminate vowel.

300 Kolyma — Krolevets PRONOUNCING INDEX

Page	Name Pronunciation Region	Lat. °′	Long. °′
173	Kolyma (R.) Sov. Un.	66·30 N	151·45 E
	Kolymskiy (Mts.), see Gydan, Khrebet		
172	Kolyvan' (kôl-ê-vän') Sov. Un.	55·28 N	82·59 E
216	Kom (R.) Cam.-Gabon	2·15 N	12·05 E
219	Komadorskie Ostrova (Is.) Sov. Un.	55·40 N	167·13 E
215	Komadougou Yobé (R.) Niger-Nig.	13·20 N	12·45 E
215	Komadugu Gana (R.) Nig.	12·15 N	11·10 E
195	Komae Jap. (Tōkyō In.)	35·37 N	139·35 E
159	Komárno (kô'mär-nô) Czech.	47·46 N	18·08 E
159	Komarno Sov. Un.	49·38 N	23·43 E
159	Komaron (kô'mä-rôm) Hung.	47·45 N	18·06 E
212	Komatipoort (kō-mä'tê-pōrt) S. Afr.	25·21 S	32·00 E
195	Komatsu (kō-mät'sōō) Jap.	36·23 N	136·26 E
195	Komatsushima (kō-mät'sōō-shê'mä) Jap.	34·04 N	134·32 E
217	Komeshia Zaire	8·01 S	27·07 E
213	Komga (kōm'gȧ) S. Afr. (Natal In.)	32·36 S	27·54 E
168	Komi (A. S. S. R.) (kômê) Sov. Un.	61·31 N	53·15 E
212	Kommetjie S. Afr. (In.)	34·09 S	18·19 E
188	Kommunizma, Pik (Pk.) Sov. Un.	39·46 N	71·23 E
214	Komoe (R.) Ivory Coast	5·40 N	3·40 W
165	Komotiní Grc.	41·07 N	25·22 E
196	Kompong Som (Sihanoukville) Camb.	10·40 N	103·50 E
196	Kompong Thom (kŏm'pŏng-tŏm) Camb.	12·41 N	104·39 E
167	Komrat (kôm-rät') Sov. Un.	46·17 N	28·38 E
174	Komsomolets (kôm-sô-mô'lĕts) Sov. Un. (Urals In.)	53·45 N	63·04 E
171	Komsomolets Zaliv (B.) Sov. Un.	45·40 N	52·00 E
173	Komsomol'sk-na-Amure (kŭm-sŭ-môlsk'nŭ-ŭ-mōōr'yĭ) Sov. Un.	50·46 N	137·14 E
167	Komsomol'skoye (kôm-sô-môl'skô-yĕ) Sov. Un.	48·42 N	28·44 E
214	Kona Mali	14·57 N	3·53 W
170	Konda (R.) (kôn'dȧ) Sov. Un.	60·50 N	64·00 E
174	Kondas R. (kôn'dȧs) Sov. Un. (Urals In.)	59·30 N	56·28 E
212	Kondoa (kôn-dō'ȧ) Tan.	4·52 S	36·00 E
217	Kondolole Zaire	1·20 N	25·58 E
210	Kong (kông) Ivory Coast	9·05 N	4·41 W
217	Kongolo (kôŋ'gō'lō) Zaire	5·23 S	27·00 E
156	Kongsberg (kŭngs'bĕrg) Nor.	59·40 N	9·36 E
156	Kongsvinger (kŭngs'vĭŋ-gĕr) Nor.	60·12 N	12·00 E
212	Koni (kō'nē) Zaire	10·32 S	27·27 E
	Königsberg, see Kaliningrad		
149	Königsbrunn (kû'nēgs-brōōn) F.R.G. (Munich In.)	48·16 N	10·53 E
149	Königs Wusterhausen (kû'nēgs vōōs'tĕr-hou-zĕn) G.D.R. (Berlin In.)	52·18 N	13·38 E
159	Konin (kô'nyĕn) Pol.	52·11 N	18·17 E
165	Kónitsa (kô'nyĕ'tsȧ) Grc.	40·03 N	20·46 E
165	Konjic (kôn'yēts) Yugo.	43·38 N	17·59 E
195	Konju Kor.	36·21 N	127·05 E
214	Konkouré (R.) Gui.	10·30 N	13·25 W
184	Konnagar India (In.)	22·41 N	88·22 E
167	Konotop (kō-nô-tôp') Sov. Un.	51·13 N	33·14 E
214	Konpienga (R.) Upper Volta	11·15 N	0·35 E
159	Końskie (koin''skyĕ) Pol.	51·12 N	20·26 E
167	Konstantinovka (kôn-stȧn-tē'nôf-kȧ) Sov. Un.	48·33 N	37·42 E
158	Konstanz (kôn'shtänts) F.R.G.	47·39 N	9·10 E
215	Kontagora (kōn-tȧ-gō'rä) Nig.	10·24 N	5·28 E
171	Konya (kōn'yȧ) Tur.	36·55 N	32·25 E
93	Kootenay (R.) Can.	49·45 N	117·05 W
93	Kootenay L. Can.	49·35 N	116·50 W
90	Kootenay Natl. Park (kōō'tē-nā) Can.	51·06 N	117·02 W
195	Kōō-zan (Mtn.) (kōō'zän) Jap. (Ōsaka In.)	34·53 N	135·32 E
156	Kopervik (kô'pĕr-vêk) Nor.	59·18 N	5·20 E
174	Kopeysk (kô-pāsk') Sov. Un. (Urals In.)	55·07 N	61·36 E
156	Köping (chû'pĭng) Swe.	59·32 N	15·58 E
156	Kopparberg (kôp'pȧr-bĕrgh) Swe.	59·53 N	15·00 E
186	Koppeh Dāgh (Mts.) Iran	37·28 N	58·29 E
218	Koppies S. Afr. (Johannesburg & Pretoria In.)	27·15 S	27·35 E
164	Koprivnica (kô'prēv-nē'tsȧ) Yugo.	46·10 N	16·48 E
159	Kopychintsy (kô-pē-chēn'tsĕ) Sov. Un.	49·06 N	25·55 E
165	Korçë (kôr'chĕ) Alb.	40·37 N	20·48 E
164	Korčula (I.) (kôr'chōō-lȧ) Yugo.	42·50 N	17·05 E
194	Korea B. China-Kor.	39·18 N	123·50 E
183	Korea (kô-rē'ȧ) Asia	38·45 N	130·00 E
194	Korean Arch. Kor.	34·05 N	125·35 E
194	Korea Str. Kor.-Jap.	33·30 N	128·30 E
159	Korets (kô-rĕts') Sov. Un.	50·35 N	27·13 E
214	Korhogo (kôr-hō'gō) Ivory Coast	9·27 N	5·38 W
165	Korinthiakós Kólpos (G.) Grc.	38·15 N	22·33 E
165	Kórinthos (Corinth) (kô-rēn'thôs) (kŏr'ĭnth) Grc.	37·56 N	22·54 E
194	Kōriyama (kō'rē-yä'mä) Jap.	37·18 N	140·25 E
174	Korkino (kôr'kē-nŭ) Sov. Un. (Urals In.)	54·53 N	61·25 E
158	Körmend (kûr'mĕnt) Hung.	47·02 N	16·36 E
164	Kornat (I.) (kôr-nät') Yugo.	43·46 N	15·10 E
149	Korneuburg (kôr'noi-bōōrgh) Aus. (Vienna In.)	48·22 N	16·21 E
214	Koro Mali	14·04 N	3·05 W
167	Korocha (kô-rō'chȧ) Sov. Un.	50·50 N	37·13 E
167	Korop (kō'rôp) Sov. Un.	51·33 N	33·54 E
167	Korosten' (kô'rôs-tĕn) Sov. Un.	50·51 N	28·39 E
167	Korostyshev (kô-rôs'tê-shôf) Sov. Un.	50·19 N	29·05 E
215	Koro Toro Chad	16·05 N	18·30 E
167	Korotoyak (kô'rô-tô-yȧk') Sov. Un.	51·00 N	39·06 E
173	Korsakov (kôr'sȧ-kôf') Sov. Un.	46·42 N	143·16 E
157	Korsnäs (kôrs'nĕs) Fin.	62·51 N	21·17 E
151	Korsør (kôrs'ûr') Den.	55·19 N	11·08 E
155	Kortrijk Bel.	50·49 N	3·10 E
173	Koryakskiy Khrebet (Mts.) Sov. Un.	62·00 N	168·45 E
167	Koryukovka (kôr-yōō-kôf'kȧ) Sov. Un.	51·44 N	32·24 E
158	Kościan (kŭsh'tsyȧn) Pol.	52·05 N	16·38 E
159	Kościerzyna (kŭsh-tsyĕ-zhē'nȧ) Pol.	54·08 N	17·59 E
120	Kosciusko (kŏs-ĭ-ŭs'kō) Ms.	33·04 N	89·35 W
203	Kosciusko, Mt. Austl.	36·26 S	148·20 E
166	Kosel'sk (kô-zĕlsk') Sov. Un.	54·01 N	35·49 E
211	Kosha (kō'shä) Sud.	20·49 N	30·27 E
192	K'oshan (kō'shän') China	48·00 N	126·30 E
195	Koshigaya (kô'shê-gä'yä) Jap. (Tōkyō In.)	35·53 N	139·48 E
195	Koshiki-Rettō (Is.) (kō-shē'kê rȧt'tō) Jap.	31·51 N	129·40 E
184	Kosi (R.) (kô'sē) India	26·00 N	86·20 E
159	Košice (kō'shê-tsĕ') Czech.	48·43 N	21·17 E
213	Kosmos (kŏz'mŏs) S. Afr. (Johannesburg & Pretoria In.)	25·45 S	27·51 E
174	Kosobrodskiy (kä-sô'brôd-skĭ) Sov. Un. (Urals In.)	54·14 N	60·53 E
	Koso Lake, see Khöbsögol Dalai		
165	Kosovska Mitrovica (kô'sôv-skä' mê'trô-vê-tsä') Yugo.	42·51 N	20·50 E
164	Kostajnica (kôs'tä-ê-nē'tsȧ) Yugo.	45·14 N	16·32 E
218	Koster S. Afr. (Johannesburg & Pretoria In.)	25·52 S	26·52 E
174	Kostino (kôs'tĭ-nô) Sov. Un. (Moscow In.)	55·54 N	37·51 E
166	Kostroma (kôs-trô-mȧ') Sov. Un.	57·46 N	40·55 E
166	Kostroma (Oblast) Sov. Un.	57·50 N	41·10 E
158	Kostrzyń (kôst'chĕn) Pol.	52·35 N	14·38 E
174	Kos'va R. (kôs'vȧ) Sov. Un. (Urals In.)	58·44 N	57·08 E
158	Koszalin (kô-shä'lĭn) Pol.	54·12 N	16·10 E
158	Köszeg (kû'sĕg) Hung.	47·21 N	16·32 E
184	Kota India	25·17 N	75·49 E
196	Kota Baharu (kō'tä bä'rōō) Mala.	6·15 N	102·23 E
196	Kotabaru Indon.	3·22 S	116·15 E
196	Kota Kinabalu Mala.	5·55 N	116·05 E
212	Kota Kota (kō-tȧ kō-tȧ) Malawi	12·52 S	34·16 E
183	Kota Tinggi Mala. (Singapore In.)	1·43 N	103·54 E
165	Kotel (kō-tĕl') Bul.	42·54 N	26·28 E
170	Kotel'nich (kô-tyĕl'nĕch) Sov. Un.	58·15 N	48·20 E
173	Kotel'nyy (I.) (kô-tyĕl'nê) Sov. Un.	74·51 N	134·09 E
185	Kothapur India	16·48 N	74·15 E
157	Kotka (kŏt'kȧ) Fin.	60·28 N	26·56 E
170	Kotlas (kôt'lȧs) Sov. Un.	61·10 N	46·50 E
174	Kotlin, Ostrov (I.) (ôs-trôf' kôt'lĭn) Sov. Un. (Leningrad In.)	60·02 N	29·49 E
165	Kotor (kō'tôr) Yugo.	42·26 N	18·48 E
166	Kotorosl' (R.) (kô-tô'rôsl) Sov. Un.	57·18 N	39·08 E
164	Kotor Varoš (kô'tôr vä'rôsh) Yugo.	44·37 N	17·23 E
167	Kotovsk (kô-tôfsk') Sov. Un.	47·49 N	29·31 E
190	Kotse (hŏ'zhē) China	35·13 N	115·28 E
185	Kotte Sri Lanka	6·50 N	80·05 E
211	Kotto R. Cen. Afr. Rep.	5·17 N	22·04 E
173	Kotuy (R.) (kô-tōō') Sov. Un.	71·00 N	103·15 E
101	Kotzebue (kôt'sĕ-bōō) Ak.	66·48 N	162·42 W
101	Kotzebue Sd. Ak.	67·00 N	164·28 W
214	Koualé Mali	11·24 N	7·01 W
98	Kouchibouguac Natl. Pk. Can.	46·53 N	65·35 W
214	Koudougou (kōō-dōō'gōō) Upper Volta	12·15 N	2·22 W
216	Kouilou (R.) Con.	4·00 S	12·05 E
216	Koula-Moutou Gabon	1·08 S	12·29 E
214	Koulikoro (kōō-lê-kō'rô) Mali	12·53 N	7·33 W
214	Koulouguidi Mali	13·27 N	11·30 W
215	Koumra Chad	8·55 N	17·33 E
214	Koundara Gui.	12·29 N	13·18 W
211	Koundé (kōōn-dā') Cen. Afr. Rep.	6·08 N	14·32 E
172	Kounradskiy (kŭ-ōōn-rät'skē) Sov. Un.	47·25 N	75·10 E
214	Kouroussa (kōō-rōō'sä) Gui.	10·39 N	9·53 W
210	Koutiala (kōō-tê-ä'lä) Mali	12·29 N	5·29 W
157	Kouvola (kō'ōō-vô-lä) Fin.	60·51 N	26·40 E
170	Kovda (L.) (kôv'dȧ) Sov. Un.	66·45 N	32·00 E
159	Kovel' (kō'vĕl) Sov. Un.	51·13 N	24·45 E
	Kovno, see Kaunas		
166	Kovrov (kôv-rôf') Sov. Un.	56·23 N	41·21 E
	Kowie, see Port Alfred		
193	Kowloon (kō'lōōn') Hong Kong	22·28 N	114·20 E
190	Koyang (gōōŭ'yäng) China	33·32 N	116·10 E
165	Koynare Bul.	43·23 N	24·07 E
101	Koyuk (kô-yōōk') Ak.	65·00 N	161·18 W
101	Koyukuk (R.) (kô-yōō'kōōk) Ak.	66·25 N	153·50 W
165	Kozáni Grc.	40·16 N	21·51 E
167	Kozelets (kôzĕ-lyĕts) Sov. Un.	50·53 N	31·07 E
159	Kozienice (kō-zyĕ-nē'tsĕ) Pol.	51·34 N	21·35 E
159	Koźle (kôzh'lĕ) Pol.	50·19 N	18·10 E
165	Kozloduy (kŭz'lô-dwē) Bul.	43·45 N	23·42 E
195	Kōzu (I.) (kō'zōō) Jap.	34·16 N	139·03 E
196	Kra, Isth. of Thai.	9·30 S	99·45 E
213	Kraai (R.) (krä'ê) S. Afr. (Natal In.)	30·50 S	27·03 E
149	Krabbendijke Neth. (Amsterdam In.)	51·26 N	4·05 E
156	Kragerö (krä'gĕr-û) Nor.	58·53 N	9·21 E
165	Kragujevac (krä'gōō'yĕ-våts) Yugo.	44·01 N	20·55 E
159	Kraków (krä'kōōf) Pol.	50·05 N	20·00 E
151	Kraljevo (kräl'ye-vô) Yugo.	43·39 N	20·48 E
167	Kramatorsk (krȧ-mä'tôrsk) Sov. Un.	48·43 N	37·32 E
156	Kramfors (kräm'fôrs) Swe.	62·54 N	17·49 E
164	Kranj (krän') Yugo.	46·16 N	14·23 E
213	Kranskop (kränz'kŏp) S. Afr. (Natal In.)	28·57 S	30·54 E
166	Krāslava (kräs'lä-vä) Sov. Un.	55·53 N	27·12 E
158	Kraslice (kräs'lê-tsĕ) Czech.	50·19 N	12·30 E
174	Kransnaya Gorka (kräs'nȧ-yȧ gôr'kȧ) Sov. Un. (Urals In.)	55·13 N	56·43 E
171	Krasnaya Sloboda Sov. Un.	48·25 N	44·35 E
159	Kraśnik (kräsh'nĭk) Pol.	50·53 N	22·15 E
174	Krasnoarmeysk (kräs'nô-ȧr-mȧsk') Sov. Un. (Moscow In.)	56·06 N	38·09 E
167	Krasnoarmeyskoye Sov. Un.	48·19 N	37·04 E
167	Krasnodar (kräs'nô-dȧr) Sov. Un.	45·03 N	38·55 E
167	Krasnodarskiy (Oblast) Province (kräs-nô-där'skĭ ôb'låst) Sov. Un.	47·28 N	38·13 E
174	Krasnogorsk Sov. Un. (Moscow In.)	55·49 N	37·20 E
174	Krasnogorskiy (kräs-nô-gôr'skĭ) Sov. Un. (Urals In.)	54·36 N	61·25 E
167	Krasnograd (kräs'nô-grät) Sov. Un.	49·23 N	35·26 E
174	Krasnogvardeyskiy (krȧ'sno-gvăr-dzyĕ ĕs-kēē) Sov. Un. (Urals In.)	57·17 N	62·05 E
170	Krasnokamsk (kräs-nô-kämsk') Sov. Un.	58·00 N	55·45 E
167	Krasnokutsk (kräs-nô-kōōtsk') Sov. Un.	50·03 N	35·05 E
167	Krasnosel'ye (kräs'nô-sĕl'yĕ) Sov. Un.	48·44 N	32·24 E
170	Krasnoslobodsk (kräs'nô-slôbôtsk') Sov. Un.	54·20 N	43·50 E
174	Krasnotur'insk (krŭs-nŭ-tōō-rensk') Sov. Un. (Urals In.)	59·47 N	60·15 E
174	Krasnoufimsk (krŭs-nŭ-ōō-fēmsk') Sov. Un. (Urals In.)	56·38 N	57·46 E
174	Krasnoural'sk (kräs'nô-ōō-rälsk') Sov. Un. (Urals In.)	58·21 N	60·05 E
174	Krasnousol'skiy (kräs-nô-ōō-sôl'skĭ) Sov. Un. (Urals In.)	53·53 N	56·30 E
170	Krasnovishersk (kräs-nô-vêshersk') Sov. Un.	60·22 N	57·20 E
171	Krasnovodsk (kräs-nô-vôtsk') Sov. Un.	40·00 N	52·50 E
172	Krasnoyarsk (kräs-nô-yärsk') Sov. Un.	56·13 N	93·12 E
174	Krasnoye Selo (kräs'nŭ-yŭ sâ'lō) Sov. Un. (Leningrad In.)	59·44 N	30·06 E
166	Krasny Kholm (kräs'nê kōlm) Sov. Un.	58·03 N	37·11 E
159	Krasnystaw (kräs-nê-stäf') Pol.	50·59 N	23·11 E
174	Krasnyy Bor (kräs'nê bôr) Sov. Un. (Leningrad In.)	59·41 N	30·40 E
174	Krasnyy Klyuch (kräs'nê klyûch') Sov. Un. (Urals In.)	55·24 N	56·43 E
171	Krasnyy Kut (kräs-nê kōōt') Sov. Un.	50·50 N	47·00 E
196	Kratie (krȧ-tyā') Camb.	12·28 N	106·06 E
174	Kratovo (krä'tô-vô) Sov. Un. (Moscow In.)	55·35 N	38·10 E
165	Kratovo (krä'tô-vô) Yugo.	42·04 N	22·12 E
161	Krefeld (krā'fĕlt) F.R.G. (Ruhr In.)	51·20 N	6·34 E
167	Kremenchug (krĕm'ĕn-chōōgh') Sov. Un.	49·04 N	33·26 E
167	Kremenchugskoye (Res.) (krĕm-ĕn-chōōgh'skô-ye) Sov. Un.	49·20 N	32·45 E
159	Kremenets (krĕ-mĕn-yĕts') Sov. Un.	50·06 N	25·43 E
149	Kremmen (krĕ'mĕn) G.D.R. (Berlin In.)	52·45 N	13·02 E
149	Krempe (krĕm'pĕ) F.R.G. (Hamburg In.)	53·50 N	9·29 E
158	Krems (krĕms) Aus.	48·25 N	15·36 E
157	Krestsy Sov. Un.	58·18 N	32·26 E
166	Kresttsy (krĕst'sê) Sov. Un.	58·16 N	32·25 E
157	Kretinga (krĕ-tĭŋ'gȧ) Sov. Un.	55·55 N	21·17 E
215	Kribi (krē'bê) Cam.	2·57 N	9·55 E
166	Krichëv (krē'chôf) Sov. Un.	53·44 N	31·39 E
194	Krillon, Mys (Pt.) (mĭs krĭl' ôn) Sov. Un.	45·58 N	142·00 E
149	Krimpenald Ijssel Neth. (Amsterdam In.)	51·55 N	4·34 E
184	Krishnanagar India	23·29 N	88·33 E
156	Kristiansand (krĭs-tyȧn-sän'') Nor.	58·09 N	7·59 E
156	Kristianstad (krĭs-tyȧn-städ') Swe.	56·02 N	14·09 E
156	Kristiansund (krĭs-tyȧn-sōōn'') Nor.	63·07 N	7·49 E
156	Kristinehamn (krēs-tē'nĕ-häm') Swe.	59·20 N	14·05 E
157	Kristinestad (krĭs-tē'nĕ-städh) Fin.	62·16 N	21·28 E
165	Kriva-Palanka (krē-vȧ-pȧ-läŋ'kȧ) Yugo.	42·12 N	22·21 E
167	Krivoy Rog (krê-voi' rôgh') Sov. Un.	47·54 N	33·22 E
167	Krivoye Ozero Sov. Un.	47·57 N	30·21 E
164	Križevci (krē'zhĕv-tsĭ) Yugo.	46·02 N	16·30 E
164	Krk (I.) (k'rk) Yugo.	45·06 N	14·33 E
159	Krnov (k'r'nôf) Czech.	50·05 N	17·41 E
156	Kröderen (krû'dĕ-rĕn) Nor.	60·07 N	9·49 E
218	Krokodil (R.) (krŏ'kō-dĭ) S. Afr. (Johannesburg & Pretoria In.)	24·25 S	27·08 E
167	Krolevets (krô-lĕ'vyĕts) Sov. Un.	51·33 N	33·21 E

ăt; finăl; rāte; senâte; ärm; ȧsk; sofȧ; fâre; ch-choose; dh-as th in other; bē; êvent; bĕt; recĕnt; cratẽr; g-go; gh-guttural g; bĭt; ĭ-short neutral; rīde; K-guttural k as ch in German ich;

302 La Calle — Landes PRONOUNCING INDEX

Page	Name Pronunciation	Region	Lat. °′	Long. °′
151	La Calle (lȧ kȧl′)	Alg.	36·52 N	8·23 E
113	La Canada (lä kän-yä′dä)	Ca. (Los Angeles In.)	34·13 N	118·12 W
125	Lacantum (R.) (lä-kän-tōō′m)	Mex.	16·13 N	90·52 W
162	La Carolina (lä kä-rô-lē′nä)	Sp.	38·16 N	3·48 W
125	La Catedral, Cerro (Mtn.) (sĕ′r-rô-lä-kä-tĕ-drà′l)	Mex. (In.)	19·32 N	99·31 W
100	Lac-Beauport (läk-bō-pōr′)	Can. (Quebec In.)	46·58 N	71·17 W
185	Laccodive Is. (lăk′ȧ-dīv)	India	11·00 N	73·02 E
184	Laccadive Sea	Asia	9·10 N	75·17 E
109	Lac Court Oreille Ind. Res. (lăk kôrt-ô-rĕl) (lȧk kōōr tô-rā′y′)	Wi.	46·04 N	91·18 W
109	Lac du Flambeau Ind. Res.	Wi.	46·12 N	89·50 W
126	La Ceiba (lȧ sēbä)	Hond.	15·45 N	86·52 W
134	La Ceja (lä-sĕ-kä)	Col. (In.)	6·02 N	75·25 W
91	Lac-Frontière	Can.	46·42 N	70·00 W
170	Lacha (L.) (lȧ′chä)	Sov. Un.	61·15 N	39·05 E
158	La Chaux de Fonds (lȧ shō dē-fôN′)	Switz.	47·07 N	6·47 E
218	Lach Dera (R.) (läk dā′rä)	Som. (Horn of Afr. In.)	0·45 N	41·26 E
100	L'Achigan (R.) (lä-shē-gäN)	Can. (Montreal In.)	45·49 N	73·48 W
100	Lachine (lȧ-shēn′)	Can. (Montreal In.)	45·26 N	73·40 W
203	Lachlan (R.) (läk′lăn)	Austl.	33·54 S	145·15 E
122	La Chorrera (lȧchôr-rā′rä)	Pan. (In.)	8·54 N	79·47 W
100	Lachute (lȧ-shōōt′)	Can. (Montreal In.)	45·39 N	74·20 W
161	La Ciotat (lȧ syô-tȧ′)	Fr.	43·13 N	5·35 E
107	Lackawanna (lak-ȧ-wŏn′ȧ)	NY (Buffalo In.)	42·49 N	78·50 W
93	Lac la Biche	Can.	54·46 N	112·58 W
	La Columna (Mtn.), see Bolivar			
93	Lacombe	Can.	52·28 N	113·44 W
125	La Concordia (lä-kōn-kô′r-dyä)	Mex.	16·07 N	92·40 W
105	Laconia (lȧ-kō′nĭ-ȧ)	NH	43·30 N	71·30 W
112	La Conner (lȧ kŏn′ēr)	Wa. (Seattle In.)	48·23 N	122·30 W
162	La Coruña (lä kô-rōōn′yä)	Sp.	43·20 N	8·20 W
108	Lacreek (L.) (lȧ′krēk)	SD	43·04 N	101·46 W
113	La Cresenta (lȧ krĕs′ĕnt-ȧ)	Ca. (Los Angeles In.)	34·14 N	118·13 W
116	La Cross (lȧ-krôs′)	Ks.	38·30 N	99·20 W
109	La Crosse	Wi.	43·48 N	91·14 W
126	La Cruz (lä-krōō′z)	C. R.	11·05 N	85·37 W
134	La Cruz (lȧ krōōz′)	Col.	1·37 N	77·00 W
108	Lacs, Riviere des (R.) (rē-vyĕr′ de läk)	ND	48·30 N	101·45 W
97	Lac Simard, (L.)	Can.	47·38 N	78·40 W
127	La Cuesta (lä-kwĕ′s-tä)	C. R.	8·32 N	82·51 W
162	La Culebra, Sierra de (Mts.) (sē-ĕ′r-rä-dĕ-lä-kōō-lĕ-brä)	Sp.	41·52 N	6·21 W
117	La Cygne (lȧ-sēn′y′) (lȧ-sēn′)	Ks.	38·20 N	94·45 W
104	Ladd (lăd)	Il.	41·25 N	89·25 W
162	La Demanda, Sierra de (Mts.) (sē-ĕ′rä-dĕ-lä-dĕ-mä′n-dä)	Sp.	42·10 N	2·35 W
163	Ladíspoli (lä-dê′s-pô-lē)	It. (Rome In.)	41·57 N	12·05 E
112	Ladner (lăd′nēr)	Can. (Vancouver In.)	49·05 N	123·05 W
184	Lādnun (läd′nōōn)	India	27·45 N	74·20 E
	Ladoga, Lake, see Ladozhskoye Ozero			
134	La Dorado (lä dô-rä′dä)	Col. (In.)	5·28 N	74·42 W
157	Ladozhskoye Ozero (Ladoga, L.) (lȧ-dôsh′skô-yē ô′zĕ-rô)	Sov. Un.	60·59 N	31·30 E
100	La Durantaye (lä dü-räN-tā′)	Can. (Quebec In.)	46·51 N	70·51 W
213	Lady Frere (lā-dē frâ′r′)	S. Afr. (Natal In.)	31·48 S	27·16 E
213	Lady Grey	S. Afr. (Natal In.)	30·44 S	27·17 E
92	Ladysmith (lā′dĭ-smĭth)	Can.	48·58 N	123·49 W
213	Ladysmith	S. Afr. (Natal In.)	28·38 S	29·48 E
109	Ladysmith	Wi.	45·27 N	91·07 W
197	Lae (lä′ȧ)	Pap. N. Gui.	6·15 S	146·57 E
156	Laerdal (lâr′däl)	Nor.	61·03 N	7·24 E
156	Laerdalsören (lâr′däls-û′rĕn)	Nor.	61·08 N	7·26 E
156	Laesø (I.) (lâs′û)	Den.	57·17 N	10·57 E
126	La Esperanza (lä ĕs-pâ-rän′zä)	Hond.	14·20 N	88·21 W
162	La Estrada (lä ĕs-trä′dä)	Sp.	42·42 N	8·29 W
194	Lafa (lä′fä)	China	43·49 N	127·19 E
160	La-Fare-les-Oliviers (lä-fär′lā-ô-lē-vyā)	Fr. (In.)	43·33 N	5·12 E
120	Lafayette	Al.	32·52 N	85·25 W
112	Lafayette	Ca. (San Francisco In.)	37·53 N	122·07 W
120	Lafayette (lä-fȧ-yĕt′)	Ga.	34·41 N	85·19 W
104	Lafayette	In.	40·25 N	86·55 W
119	Lafayette	La.	30·15 N	92·02 W
106	La Fayette	RI (Providence In.)	41·34 N	71·29 W
161	La Ferté-Alais (lä-fĕr-tā′-ä-lā′)	Fr. (Paris In.)	48·29 N	2·19 E
161	La Ferté-sous-Jouarre (lȧ fĕr-tā′sōō-zhōō-är′)	Fr. (Paris In.)	48·56 N	3·07 E
215	Lafia	Nig.	8·30 N	8·30 E
215	Lafiagi	Nig.	8·52 N	5·25 E
160	La Flèche (lȧ flāsh′)	Fr.	47·43 N	0·03 W
160	La Flotte (lȧ flôt′)	Fr.	46·09 N	1·20 W
120	La Follette (lä-fŏl′ĕt)	Tn.	36·23 N	84·07 W
119	Lafourche, Bay. (bȧ-yōō′lȧ-fōōrsh′)	La.	29·25 N	90·15 W
135	La Gaiba (lä-gī′bä)	Braz.	17·54 S	57·32 W
154	Lagan (lä′gȧn)	N. Ire.	54·30 N	6·00 W
156	Lagan (R.)	Swe.	56·34 N	13·25 E
150	Laganes (Pt.)	Ice.	66·21 N	14·02 W
122	Lagarto, R. (lä-gä′r-tô)	Pan. (In.)	9·08 N	80·05 W
126	Lagartos L. (lä-gä′r-tôs)	Mex. (In.)	21·32 N	88·15 W
156	Lågan (R.) (lô′ghĕn)	Nor.	59·15 N	9·47 E
210	Laghouat (lä-gwät′)	Alg.	33·45 N	2·49 E
161	Lagny (län-yē′)	Fr. (Paris In.)	48·53 N	2·41 E
137	Lagoa da Prata (lȧ-gô′ä-dȧ-prä′tȧ)	Braz. (Rio de Janeiro In.)	20·04 S	45·33 W
137	Lagoa Dourada (lȧ-gô′ä-dōō-rä′dä)	Braz. (Rio de Janeiro In.)	20·55 S	44·03 W
197	Lagonoy (lä-gô-noi′)	Phil. (In.)	13·44 N	123·31 E
197	Lagonoy G.	Phil. (In.)	13·34 N	123·46 E
215	Lagos (lä′gōs)	Nig.	6·27 N	3·24 E
162	Lagos (lä′gôzh)	Port.	37·08 N	8·43 W
124	Lagos de Moreno (lä′gōs dā mô-rā′nō)	Mex.	21·21 N	101·55 W
160	La Grand' Combe (lȧ gräN kaNb′)	Fr.	44·12 N	4·03 E
110	La Grande (lȧ grănd′)	Or.	45·20 N	118·06 W
91	La Grande (R.)	Can.	53·55 N	77·30 W
204	La Grange (lȧ grānj)	Austl.	18·40 S	122.00 E
120	La Grange (lȧ-grānj′)	Ga.	33·01 N	85·00 W
107	La Grange	Il. (Chicago In.)	41·49 N	87·53 W
104	Lagrange	In.	41·40 N	85·25 W
104	La Grange	Ky.	38·20 N	85·25 W
117	La Grange	Mo.	40·04 N	91·30 W
107	Lagrange	Oh. (Cleveland In.)	41·14 N	82·07 W
119	Lagrange	Tx.	29·55 N	96·50 W
134	La Grita (lä grē′tä)	Ven.	8·02 N	71·59 W
135	La Guaira (lä gwä′ē-rä)	Ven. (In.)	10·36 N	66·54 W
162	La Guardia (lä gwär′dē-ä)	Sp.	41·55 N	8·48 W
136	Laguna (lä-gōō′nä)	Braz.	28·19 S	48·42 W
128	Laguna, Cayos (Is.) (kä′yōs-lä-gōō′nä)	Cuba	22·15 N	82·45 W
197	Laguna de Bay (L.) (lä-gōō′nä dä bä′ê)	Phil. (In.)	14·24 N	121·13 E
115	Laguna Ind. Res.	NM	35·00 N	107·30 W
134	Lagunillas (lä-gōō-nēl′yäs)	Bol.	19·42 S	63·38 W
124	Lagunillas (lä-gōō-nē′l-yäs)	Mex.	21·34 N	99·41 W
129	La Habana (Havana) (lä-ä-bä′nä)	Cuba (In.)	23·08 N	82·23 W
116	La Habra (lȧ hȧb′rȧ)	Ca. (Los Angeles In.)	34·56 N	117·57 W
89	Lahaina (lä-hä′ē-nä)	Hi.	20·52 N	156·39 W
160	La Haye-Descartes (lȧ ā-dā-kärt′)	Fr.	46·58 N	0·42 E
158	Lahn R. (län)	F.R.G.	50·21 N	7·54 E
156	Laholm (lä′hôlm)	Swe.	56·30 N	13·00 E
112	La Honda (lā hôn′dȧ)	Ca. (San Francisco In.)	37·20 N	122·16 W
184	Lahore (lä-hōr′)	Pak.	32·00 N	74·18 E
158	Lahr (lär)	F.R.G.	48·19 N	7·52 E
157	Lahti (lä′tê)	Fin.	60·59 N	27·39 E
193	Lai, C.	Viet.	17·08 N	107·30 E
215	Lai	Chad.	9·29 N	16·18 E
190	Laian (lăī′äN)	China	32·27 N	118·25 E
190	Laichou Wan (B.) (lăī′jō wäN)	China	37·22 N	119·19 E
160	Laigle (lĕ′gl′)	Fr.	48·45 N	0·37 E
193	Laipin (lī′pĭn′)	China	23·42 N	109·20 E
217	Laisamis	Ken.	1·36 N	37·48 E
190	Laiyang (läī′yäng)	China	36·59 N	120·42 E
124	Laja, Río de la (R.) (rê′ō-dĕ-lä-lä′Kä)	Mex.	20·17 N	100·57 W
128	Lajas (lä′häs)	Cuba	22·25 N	80·20 W
136	Lajeado (lä-zhĕä′dô)	Braz.	29·24 S	51·46 W
136	Lajes (lȧ′-zhĕs)	Braz.	27·47 S	50·17 W
137	Lajinha (lä-zhē′nyä)	Braz. (Rio de Janeiro In.)	20·08 S	41·36 W
114	La Jolla (lȧ hōl′yȧ)	Ca. (In.)	32·51 N	117·16 W
114	La Jolla Ind. Res.	Ca.	33·19 N	116·21 W
116	La Junta (lȧ hōōn′tȧ)	Co.	37·59 N	103·35 W
119	Lake Arthur (är′thŭr)	La.	30·06 N	92·40 W
120	Lake Barkley (Res.)	Tn.	36·45 N	88·00 W
108	Lake Benton (bĕn′tŭn)	Mn.	44·15 N	96·17 W
107	Lake Bluff (blŭf)	Il. (Chicago In.)	42·17 N	87·50 W
204	Lake Brown (broun)	Austl.	31·03 S	118·30 E
119	Lake Charles (chärlz′)	La.	30·15 N	93·14 W
121	Lake City	Fl.	30·09 N	82·40 W
109	Lake City	Ia.	42·14 N	94·43 W
109	Lake City	Mn.	44·28 N	92·19 W
121	Lake City	SC	33·57 N	79·45 W
92	Lake Cowichan (kou′ĭ-chăn)	Can.	48·50 N	124·03 W
109	Lake Crystal (krĭs′tȧl)	Mn.	44·05 N	94·12 W
154	Lake Dist. (lāk)	Eng.	54·25 N	3·20 W
116	Lake Elmo (ĕlmō)	Mn. (Minneapolis, St. Paul In.)	45·00 N	92·53 W
107	Lake Forest (fŏr′ĕst)	Il. (Chicago In.)	42·16 N	87·50 W
115	Lake Fork (R.)	Ut.	40·30 N	110·25 W
109	Lake Geneva (jĕ-nē′vȧ)	Wi.	42·36 N	88·28 W
91	Lake Harbour (här′bēr)	Can.	62·43 N	69·40 W
114	Lake Havasu City	Az.	34·27 N	114·22 W
113	Lake June (jōōn)	Tx. (Dallas, Fort Worth In.)	32·43 N	96·45 W
121	Lakeland (lāk′lănd)	Fl. (In.)	28·02 N	81·58 W
120	Lakeland	Ga.	31·02 N	83·02 W
113	Lakeland	Mn. (Minneapolis, St. Paul In.)	44·57 N	92·47 W
109	Lake Linden (lĭn′dĕn)	Mi.	47·11 N	88·26 W
93	Lake Louise (lōō-ēz′)	Can.	51·26 N	116·11 W
109	Lake Mills (mĭlz′)	Ia.	43·25 N	93·32 W
107	Lakemore (lāk-mōr)	Oh. (Cleveland In.)	41·01 N	81·24 W
104	Lake Odessa	Mi.	42·50 N	85·15 W
110	Lake Oswego (ŏs-wē′go)	Or. (Portland In.)	45·25 N	122·40 W
105	Lake Placid	NY	44·17 N	73·59 W
113	Lake Point	Ut. (Salt Lake City In.)	40·41 N	112·16 W
114	Lakeport (lăk′pōrt)	Ca.	39·03 N	122·54 W
108	Lake Preston (prēs′tŭn)	SD	44·21 N	97·23 W
119	Lake Providence (prŏv′ĭ-dĕns)	La.	32·48 N	91·12 W
109	Lake Red Rock (Res.)	Ia.	41·30 N	93·15 W
108	Lake Sharpe (Res.)	SD	44·30 N	100·00 W
114	Lakeside (lāk′sīd)	Ca. (In.)	32·52 N	116·55 W
112	Lake Stevens	Wa. (Seattle In.)	48·01 N	122·04 W
106	Lake Success (sŭk-sĕs′)	NY (New York In.)	40·46 N	73·43 W
113	Lakeview (lāk-vū′)	Ca. (Los Angeles In.)	33·50 N	117·07 W
110	Lakeview	Or.	42·11 N	120·21 W
117	Lake Village	Ar.	33·20 N	91·17 W
111	Lake Walcott Res.	Id.	42·35 N	113·15 W
121	Lake Wales (wālz′)	Fl. (In.)	27·54 N	81·35 W
113	Lakewood (lāk′wŏŏd)	Ca. (Los Angeles In.)	33·50 N	118·09 W
116	Lakewood	Co.	39·44 N	105·06 W
107	Lakewood	Oh. (Cleveland In.)	41·29 N	81·48 W
105	Lakewood	Pa.	40·05 N	74·10 W
110	Lakewood	Wa. (Seattle In.)	48·09 N	122·13 W
112	Lakewood Center	Wa. (Seattle In.)	47·10 N	122·31 W
121	Lake Worth (wûrth′)	Fl. (In.)	26·37 N	80·04 W
113	Lake Worth Village	Tx. (Dallas, Fort Worth In.)	32·49 N	97·26 W
107	Lake Zürich (tsü′rĭk)	Il. (Chicago In.)	42·11 N	88·05 W
157	Lakhdenpokh'ya (l′ăk-dĭe′npōKyȧ)	Sov. Un.	61·33 N	30·10 E
174	Lakhtinskiy (lȧk-tĭn′skĭ)	Sov. Un. (Leningrad In.)	59·59 N	30·10 E
108	Lakota (lȧ-kō′tȧ)	ND	48·04 N	98·21 W
126	La Libertad (lä lē-bĕr-tädh′)	Guat.	15·31 N	91·44 W
126	La Libertad	Guat. (In.)	16·46 N	90·12 W
126	La Libertad	Sal.	13·29 N	89·20 W
137	La Ligua (lä lē′gwä)	Chile (Santiago In.)	32·21 S	71·13 W
162	Lalín (lä-lê′n)	Sp.	42·40 N	8·05 W
162	La Línea (lä lē′nȧ-ä)	Sp.	36·11 N	5·22 W
184	Lalitpur	Nep.	27·23 N	85·24 E
152	Lalla-Maghnia (lä′lä-mäg′nêȧ)	Alg.	34·52 N	1·40 W
155	La Louviere (lȧ lōō-vyâr′)	Bel.	50·30 N	4·10 E
124	La Luz (lä lōōz′)	Mex.	21·04 N	101·19 W
160	La Machine (lȧ mȧ-shēn′)	Fr.	46·53 N	3·26 E
214	Lama-Kara	Togo	9·33 N	1·12 E
97	La Malbaie (lȧ mäl-bâ′)	Can.	47·39 N	70·10 W
162	La Mancha (Mts.) (lä män′chä)	Sp.	38·55 N	4·20 W
116	Lamar (lȧ-mär′)	Co.	38·04 N	102·44 W
117	Lamar	Mo.	37·28 N	94·15 W
166	La Marmora, Pta. (Mtn.) (lä-mä′r-mô-rä)	It.	40·00 N	9·28 E
119	La Marque (lä-märk)	Tx. (In.)	29·23 N	94·58 W
134	Lamas (lä′mȧs)	Peru	6·24 S	76·41 W
160	Lamballe (läN-bäl′)	Fr.	48·29 N	2·36 W
216	Lambaréné (läN-bȧ-rȧ-nā′)	Gabon	0·42 S	10·13 E
137	Lambari (läm-bȧ′rē)	Braz. (Rio de Janeiro In.)	21·58 S	45·22 W
134	Lambayeque (läm-bä-yā′kā)	Peru	6·41 S	79·58 W
120	Lambert (lăm′bērt)	Ms.	34·10 N	90·16 W
105	Lambertville (lăm′bērt-vĭl)	NJ	40·20 N	75·00 W
111	Lame Deer (lām dēr′)	Mt.	45·36 N	106·40 W
162	Lamego (lä-mā′gō)	Port.	41·07 N	7·47 W
114	La Mesa (lä mā′sä)	Ca. (In.)	32·46 N	117·01 W
134	La Mesa	Col. (In.)	4·38 N	74·27 W
116	Lamesa	Tx.	32·44 N	101·54 W
165	Lamía (lȧ-mē′ȧ)	Grc.	38·54 N	22·25 E
197	Lamon B. (lä-mōn′)	Phil. (In.)	14·35 N	121·52 E
137	La Mora (lä-mō′rä)	Chile (Santiago In.)	32·28 S	70·56 W
108	La Moure (lȧ mōōr′)	ND	46·23 N	98·17 W
137	Lampa (R.) (lȧ′m-pä)	Chile (Santiago In.)	33·15 S	70·55 W
118	Lampasas (lăm-păs′ȧs)	Tx.	31·06 N	98·10 W
118	Lampasas R.	Tx.	31·18 N	98·08 W
118	Lampazos (läm-pä′zōs)	Mex.	27·03 N	100·30 W
151	Lampedusa (I.) (läm-pȧ-dōō′sä)	It.	35·29 N	12·58 E
149	Lamstedt (läm′shtĕt)	F.R.G. (Hamburg In.)	53·38 N	9·06 E
217	Lamu (lä′mōō)	Ken.	2·16 S	40·54 E
217	Lamu I.	Ken.	2·25 S	40·50 E
161	La Mure (lȧ mür′)	Fr.	44·55 N	5·50 E
166	Lan′ (R.) (lȧn′)	Sov. Un.	52·38 N	27·05 E
89	Lanai (I.) (lä-nä′ê)	Hi.	20·48 N	157·06 W
89	Lanai City	Hi.	20·50 N	156·56 W
184	Lanak La (P.)	China	34·40 N	79·50 E
163	La Nao, Cabo de (C.) (kȧ′bô-dĕ-lä-nä′ō)	Sp.	38·43 N	0·14 E
154	Lanark (lăn′ȧrk)	Scot.	55·40 N	3·50 W
148	Lancashire (Co.) (lăŋ′kȧ-shĭr)	Scot.	53·38 N	2·30 W
98	Lancaster (lăŋ′kȧs-tēr)	Can.	45·15 N	66·06 W
154	Lancaster	Eng.	54·04 N	2·55 W
104	Lancaster	Ky.	37·35 N	84·30 W
99	Lancaster	Ma. (In.)	42·28 N	71·40 W
105	Lancaster	NH	44·25 N	71·30 W
107	Lancaster	NY (Buffalo In.)	42·54 N	78·42 W
104	Lancaster	Oh.	39·40 N	82·35 W
105	Lancaster	Pa.	40·05 N	76·20 W
121	Lancaster	SC	34·42 N	80·45 W
113	Lancaster	Tx. (Dallas, Fort Worth In.)	32·36 N	96·45 W
109	Lancaster	Wi.	42·51 N	90·44 W
192	Lanchou (län′chōō)	China	35·55 N	103·55 E
160	Lançon-Provence (läN-sôN′prô-vĕNs′)	Fr. (In.)	43·35 N	5·08 E
212	Lândana (lăn-dä′nä)	Ang.	5·15 S	12·07 E
158	Landau (län′dou)	F.R.G.	49·13 N	8·07 E
111	Lander (lăn′dēr)	Wy.	42·49 N	108·24 W
160	Landerneau (läN-dĕr-nō′)	Fr.	48·28 N	4·14 W
160	Landes (Moorland) (Plain) (lănd)	Fr.	44·22 N	0·52 W

ăt; finăl; rāte; senâte; ärm; ȧsk; sofȧ; fâre; ch-choose; dh-as th in other; bē; ėvent; bĕt; recĕnt; cratēr; g-go; gh-guttural g; bĭt; ĭ-short neutral; rīde; K-guttural k as ch in German ich;

PRONOUNCING INDEX

Landsberg — Le Borgne 303

Page	Name Pronunciation Region	Lat. °′	Long. °′
149	Landsberg (lănds'bōōrgh) F.R.G. (Munich In.)	48·03 N	10·53 E
154	Lands End Pt. Eng.	50·03 N	5·45 W
158	Landshut (länts'hōōt) F.R.G.	48·32 N	12·09 E
156	Landskrona (låns-krōō'nå) Swe.	55·51 N	12·47 E
120	Lanett (lȧ-nĕt') Al.	32·52 N	85·13 W
192	Lanfang China (In.)	39·31 N	116·42 E
165	Langadhás Grc.	40·44 N	24·10 E
183	Langat (R.). Mala. (Singapore In.)	2·46 N	101·33 E
190	Langch'i (läNG'che) China	31·10 N	119·09 E
193	Langchung China	31·40 N	106·05 E
106	Langdon (lăng'dŭn) Can. (Calgary In.)	50·58 N	113·40 W
113	Langdon Mn. (Minneapolis, St. Paul In.)	44·49 N	92·56 W
100	L'Ange-Gardien (länzh går-dyăN') Can. (Quebec In.)	46·55 N	71·06 W
156	Langeland (I.) Den.	54·52 N	10·46 E
161	Langenthal Switz.	47·11 N	7·50 E
149	Langenzersdorf. Aus. (Vienna In.)	48·30 N	16·22 E
156	Langesund (läng'ĕ-sōōn') Nor.	58·59 N	9·38 E
156	Lang Fd. (läng'fyôr') Nor.	62·40 N	7·45 E
106	Langhorne (lăng'hôrn) Pa. (Philadelphia In.)	40·10 N	74·55 W
217	Langia Mts. Ug.	3·35 N	33·35 E
150	Langjökoll (Glacier) (läng-yû'kōōl) Ice.	64·40 N	20·31 W
97	Langlade (I.) St. Pierre & Miquelon	46·50 N	56·20 W
112	Langley (lăng'lĭ) Can. (Vancouver In.)	49·06 N	122·39 W
121	Langley SC	33·32 N	81·52 W
112	Langley Wa. (Seattle In.)	48·02 N	122·25 W
112	Langley Ind. Res. Can. (Vancouver In.)	49·12 N	122·31 W
158	Langnau (läng'nou) Switz.	46·56 N	7·46 E
160	Lagogne (laN-gōn'y') Fr.	44·43 N	3·50 E
160	Langon (läN-gôN') Fr.	44·34 N	0·16 W
160	Langres (läN'gr') Fr.	47·53 N	5·20 E
160	Langres, Plateaux de (Plat.) (plä-tō'dĕ-läN'grĕ). Fr.	47·39 N	5·00 E
196	Langsa (läng'sä) Indon.	4·33 N	97·52 E
196	Lang Son (lăng'sŏn') Viet.	21·52 N	106·42 E
117	L'Anguille (R.) (läN-gē'y') Ar.	35·23 N	90·52 W
106	Lanham (lăn'ăm) Md. (Baltimore In.)	38·58 N	76·54 W
94	Lanigan (lăn'ĭ-gȧn) Can.	51·52 N	105·02 W
188	Lanisung Chiang (Mekong). China	24·45 N	100·31 E
215	Lankoviri Nig.	9·00 N	11·25 E
105	Lansdale (lănz'dāl) Pa.	40·20 N	75·15 W
106	Lansdowne. Pa. (Philadelphia In.)	39·57 N	75·17 W
109	L'Anse (låns) Mi.	46·43 N	88·28 W
109	L'Anse and Vieux Desert Ind. Res. Mi.	46·41 N	88·12 W
114	Lansford (lănz'fērd) Pa.	40·50 N	75·50 W
107	Lansing Il. (Chicago In.)	41·34 N	87·33 W
109	Lansing Ia.	43·22 N	91·16 W
113	Lansing Ks. (Kansas City In.)	39·15 N	94·53 W
104	Lansing Mi.	42·45 N	84·35 W
136	Lanús (lä-nōōs') Arg. (In.)	34·27 S	58·24 W
164	Lanusei (lä-nōō-sĕ'y) It.	39·51 N	9·34 E
163	Lanúvio (lä-nōō'vyô) It. (Rome In.)	41·41 N	12·42 E
210	Lanzarote I. (län-zȧ-rō'tä). Can. Is.	29·04 N	13·03 W
196	Laoag (lä-wäg') Phil.	18·13 N	120·38 E
189	Lao Ho (R.) (lä'ō hō') China	43·37 N	120·05 E
196	Lao Kay (lä'ōkä'ē) Viet.	22·30 N	102·32 E
160	Laon (läN) Fr.	49·36 N	3·35 E
134	La Oroya (lä-ô-rō'yä) Peru	11·30 S	76·00 W
196	Laos (lä-ōs) (lȧ-ōs') Asia	20·15 N	102·00 E
127	La Palma (lä-päl'mä) Pan.	8·25 N	78·07 W
162	La Palma Sp.	37·24 N	6·36 W
210	La Palma I. Can. Is.	28·42 N	19·03 W
136	La Pampa (Prov.) Arg.	37·25 S	67·00 W
136	Lapa Rio Negro (lä-pä-rē'ō-nĕ'grô). Braz.	26·12 S	49·56 W
136	La Paz (lä päz') Arg.	30·48 S	59·47 W
135	La Paz Bol.	16·31 S	68·03 W
126	La Paz Hond.	14·15 N	87·40 W
124	La Paz (lä-pà'z) Mex.	23·39 N	100·44 W
122	La Paz Mex.	24·00 N	110·15 W
197	La Paz Phil. (In.)	17·41 N	120·41 E
109	Lapeer (lȧ-pēr') Mi.	43·05 N	83·15 W
160	La-Penne-sur-Huveaune (la-pĕn'sür-ü-vōn'). Fr. (In.)	43·18 N	5·33 E
124	La Piedad Cabadas (lä pyå-dhädh' kä-bä'dhäs). Mex.	20·20 N	102·04 W
150	Lapland (Reg.) (lăp'lȧnd) Eur.	68·20 N	22·00 E
137	La Plata (lä plä'tä) Arg. (Buenos Aires In.)	34·54 S	57·57 W
117	La Plata (lȧ plā'tȧ) Mo.	40·03 N	92·28 W
115	La Plata Pk. Co.	39·00 N	106·25 W
163	La Pobla de Lillet (lä-pô'blä-dĕ-lēl-yĕ't). Sp.	42·14 N	1·58 E
98	La Pocatière (lȧ pô-kȧ-tyâr'). Can.	47·24 N	70·01 W
197	Lapog (lä-pôg') Phil. (In.)	17·44 N	120·28 E
99	La Poile B. (lȧ pwäl') Can.	47·38 N	58·20 W
104	La Porte (lȧ pōrt') In.	41·35 N	86·45 W
107	Laporte Oh. (Cleveland In.)	41·19 N	82·05 W
119	La Porte Tx. (In.)	29·40 N	95·01 W
109	La Porte City Ia.	42·20 N	92·10 W
157	Lappeenranta (lä'pēn-rän'tä). Fin.	61·04 N	28·08 E
100	La Prairie (lȧ-prå-rē') Can. (Montreal In.)	45·24 N	73·30 W
165	Lapseki (läp'sȧ-kē) Tur.	40·20 N	26·41 E
168	Laptev Sea (läp'tyĭf) Sov. Un.	75·39 N	120·00 E
163	La Puebla (lä pwā'blä) Sp.	39·46 N	3·02 E
162	La Puebla de Montalbán (lä pwā'blä dā mōnt-äl-bän'). Sp.	39·54 N	4·21 W
113	La Puente (pwĕn'tē) Ca. (Los Angeles In.)	34·01 N	117·57 W
159	Lapusul R. (lä'pōō-shōōl) Rom.	47·29 N	23·46 E
136	La Quiaca (lä kē-ä'kä) Arg.	22·15 S	65·44 W
164	L'Aquila (lä'kē-lä) It.	42·22 N	13·24 E
186	Lār (lär) Iran	27·31 N	54·12 E
202	Lara Austl. (Melbourne In.)	38·02 S	144·24 E
210	Larache (lä-räsh') Mor.	35·15 N	6·09 W
102	Laramie (lăr'ȧ-mĭ) Wy.	41·20 N	105·40 W
116	Laramie (R.) Co.	40·56 N	105·55 W
163	L'Arba (l'är'bȧ) Alg.	36·35 N	3·10 E
106	Larchmont (lärch'mŏnt) NY (New York In.)	40·56 N	73·46 W
112	Larch Mtn. (lärch) Or. (Portland In.)	45·32 N	122·06 W
162	Laredo (lå-rā'dhō) Sp.	43·24 N	3·24 W
118	Laredo Tx.	27·31 N	99·29 W
160	La Réole (lå rå-ōl') Fr.	44·37 N	0·03 W
215	Largeau (lär-zhō') Chad	17·55 N	19·07 E
128	Largo, Cayo (kä'yō-lär'gō) Cuba	21·40 N	81·30 W
108	Larimore (lăr'ĭ-mōr) ND	47·53 N	97·38 W
164	Larino (lä-rē'nô) It.	41·48 N	14·54 E
136	La Rioja (lä rē-ōhä) Arg.	29·18 S	67·42 W
136	La Rioja (Prov.) (lä-rē-ô'-kä). Arg.	28·45 S	68·00 W
165	Lárisa (lä'rē-sȧ) Grc.	39·38 N	22·25 E
184	Lārkāma Pak.	27·40 N	68·12 E
183	Lárnakos, Kólpos (B.) Cyprus (Palestine In.)	36·50 N	33·45 E
183	Lárnax Cyprus (Palestine In.)	34·55 N	33·37 E
116	Larned (lär'nĕd) Ks.	38·09 N	99·07 W
162	La Robla (lä rōb'lä) Sp.	42·48 N	5·36 W
160	La Rochelle (lå rō-shĕl') Fr.	46·10 N	1·09 W
160	La Roche-sur-Yon (lå rōsh'sûr-yôN'). Fr.	46·39 N	1·27 W
162	La Roda (lä rō'dä) Sp.	39·13 N	2·08 W
129	La Romona (lä-rä-mô'nä) Dom. Rep.	18·25 N	69·00 W
204	Larrey Pt. (lăr'ē) Austl.	19·15 S	118·15 E
160	Laruns (lå-răNs') Fr.	42·58 N	0·28 W
156	Larvik (lär'vĕk) Nor.	59·06 N	10·03 E
135	La Sabana (lä-sä-bà'nä). Ven. (In.)	10·38 N	66·24 W
129	La Sabina (lä-sä-bē'nä) Cuba (In.)	22·10 N	82·07 W
162	La Sagra (Mtn.) (lä sä'grä) Sp.	37·56 N	2·35 E
115	La Sal (lȧ sȧl') Ut.	38·10 N	109·20 W
107	La Salle (lȧ săl') Can. (Detroit In.)	42·14 N	83·06 W
100	La Salle Can. (Montréal In.)	45·26 N	73·39 W
100	La Salle Can. (Winnipeg In.)	49·41 N	97·16 W
104	La Salle Il.	41·20 N	89·05 W
116	Las Animas (läs ă'nĭ-mȧs) Co.	38·03 N	103·16 W
218	Las Anod (läs ăn'ŏd) Som. (Horn of Afr. In.)	8·24 N	47·20 E
97	La Sarre Can.	48·43 N	79·12 W
129	Lascahobas (läs-kä-ō'bàs) Hai.	19·00 N	71·55 W
125	Las Cruces (läs-krōō'-sĕs) Mex.	16·37 N	93·54 W
115	Las Cruces NM	32·20 N	106·50 W
129	La Selle, Massif De (Mts.) (lä sĕl'). Hai.	18·25 N	72·05 W
136	La Serena (lä-sĕ-rē'nä) Chile	29·55 S	71·24 W
161	La Seyne-sur-Mer (lä-sån'sür-mĕr'). Fr.	43·07 N	5·52 E
137	Las Flores (läs flo'rĕs) Arg. (Buenos Aires In.)	36·01 S	59·07 W
188	Lashio (lăsh'ē-ō) Bur.	22·58 N	98·03 E
126	Las Juntas (läs-kōō'n-täs) C. R.	10·15 N	85·00 W
218	Las Khoreh (läs kō'rȧ) Som. (Horn of Afr. In.)	11·13 N	48·19 E
162	Las Maismas (Reg.) (läs-mī's-mäs). Sp.	37·05 N	6·25 W
162	La Solano (lä-sô-lä-nō) Sp.	38·56 N	3·13 W
210	Las Palmas de Gran Canaria, (läs päl'mäs). Can. Is.	28·07 N	15·28 W
127	Las Palmas Pan.	8·08 N	81·30 W
164	La Spezia (lä-spĕ'zyä) It.	44·07 N	9·48 E
137	Las Piedras (läs-pyĕ'dräs) Ur. (Buenos Aires In.)	34·42 S	56·08 W
126	Las Pilas (Vol.) (läs-pē'läs) Nic.	12·32 N	86·43 W
125	Las Rosas (läs rō thäs) Mex.	16·24 N	92·23 W
163	Las Rozas de Madrid (läs rō'thas dä mä-dhrēdh'). Sp. (Madrid In.)	40·29 N	3·53 W
149	Lassee Aus. (Vienna In.)	48·14 N	16·50 E
110	Lassen Pk. (lăs'ĕn) Ca.	40·30 N	121·32 W
110	Lassen Volcanic Natl. Park Ca.	40·43 N	121·35 W
101	L'Assomption (lȧs-sôm-syôN) Can. (Montreal In.)	45·50 N	73·25 W
127	Las Tablas (läs tä'bläs) Pan.	7·48 N	80·16 W
94	Last Mountain (L.) (låst moun'tĭn). Can.	51·05 N	105·10 W
212	Lastoursville (lȧs-tōōr-vēl'). Gabon	1·00 S	12·49 E
122	Las Tres Virgenes, Vol. (vē'r-hĕ-nĕs). Mex.	26·00 N	111·45 W
125	Las Vacas (läs-vå'käs) Mex.	16·24 N	95·48 W
137	Las Vegas (läs-vĕ'gäs) Chile (Santiago In.)	30·50 S	70·59 W
114	Las Vegas (läs vā'gäs) Nv.	36·12 N	115·10 W
116	Las Vegas NM.	35·36 N	105·13 W
135	Las Vegas (läs-vĕ'gäs). Ven. (In.)	10·26 N	64·08 W
124	Las Vigas Mex.	19·38 N	97·03 W
128	Las Villas (Prov.) (läs-vē'l-läs) Cuba	22·15 N	80·50 W
136	Las Vizcachas, Meseta de (Plat.) (mĕ-sĕ'tä-dĕ-läs-vēz-kä'chás) Arg.	49·35 S	71·00 W
134	Latacunga (lä-tä-kōōŋ'gä) Ec.	1·02 S	78·33 W
	Latakia, see Al Lādhiqīah		
153	Latakia (Reg.) (lä-tä-kē'ä) Syr.	35·10 N	35·49 E
160	La Teste-de-Buch (lä-tĕst-dĕ-büsh). Fr.	44·38 N	1·11 W
117	Lathrop (lā'thrŭp) Mo.	39·32 N	94·21 W
	Latium (Reg.), see Lazio		
161	Latoritsa R. (lä-tō'rĭ-tsȧ). Sov. Un.	48·27 N	22·30 E
112	Latourell (lȧ-tou'rĕl) Or. (Portland In.)	45·32 N	122·13 W
160	La Tremblade (lä-trĕN-bläd'). Fr.	45·45 N	1·12 W
105	Latrobe (lȧ-trōb') Pa.	40·25 N	79·15 W
91	La Tuque (lȧ tük') Can.	47·27 N	72·49 W
185	Lātūr (lä-tōōr') India	18·20 N	76·35 E
168	Latvian (S. S. R.) Sov. Un.	57·28 N	24·29 E
203	Launceston (lôn'sĕs-tŭn) Austl.	41·35 S	147·22 E
154	Launceston (lôrn'stŏn) Eng.	50·38 N	4·26 W
136	La Unión (lä-ōō-nyô'n) Chile	40·15 S	73·04 W
124	La Unión (lä ōōn-nyōn') Mex.	17·59 N	101·48 W
126	La Unión Sal.	13·18 N	87·51 W
163	La Unión Sp.	37·38 N	0·50 W
205	Laura (lôrȧ) Austl.	15·40 S	144·45 E
166	Laura (lou'rȧ) Sov. Un.	57·36 N	27·29 E
105	Laurel (lô'rĕl) De.	38·30 N	75·40 W
106	Laurel Md. (Baltimore In.)	39·06 N	76·51 W
120	Laurel Ms.	31·42 N	89·07 W
111	Laurel Mt.	45·41 N	108·45 W
112	Laurel Wa. (Vancouver In.)	48·52 N	122·29 W
112	Laurelwood (lô'rĕl-wŏŏd) Or. (Portland In.)	45·25 N	123·05 W
121	Laurens (lô'rĕnz) SC	34·29 N	82·03 W
75	Laurentian Highlands (Reg.) (lô'rĕn-tĭ-ăn). Can.	49·00 N	74·50 W
100	Laurentides (lô'rĕn-tīdz) Can. (Montreal In.)	45·51 N	73·46 W
164	Lauria (lou'rē-ä) It.	40·03 N	15·02 E
121	Laurinburg (lô'rĭn-bûrg) NC	34·45 N	79·27 W
109	Laurium (lô'rĭ-ŭm) Mi.	47·13 N	88·28 W
158	Lausanne (lō-zȧn') Switz.	46·32 N	6·35 E
196	Laut (I.) Indon.	3·39 S	116·07 E
136	Lautaro (lou-tä'rô) Chile	38·40 S	72·24 W
196	Laut Ketjil, Kepulauan (Is.) Indon.	4·44 S	115·43 E
100	Lauzon (lō-zôN'). Can. (Quebec In.)	46·50 N	71·10 W
110	Lava Beds Natl. Mon. (lä'vȧ bĕds). Ca.	41·38 N	121·44 W
119	Lavaca R. (lȧ-väk'ȧ) Tx.	29·05 N	96·50 W
111	Lava Hot Springs Id.	42·37 N	111·58 W
100	Laval Can. (Montreal In.)	45·31 N	73·44 W
160	Laval (lȧ-väl') Fr.	48·05 N	0·47 W
160	Lavaur (lȧ-vōr') Fr.	43·41 N	1·48 E
160	Lavaveix-les-Mines (lȧ-vȧ-vĕ'lā-mēn'). Fr.	46·05 N	2·05 E
129	La Vega (lä-vĕ'-gä) Dom. Rep.	19·15 N	70·35 W
205	Lavella (I.) Sol. Is.	7·50 S	155·45 E
164	Lavello (lä-vĕl'lō) It.	41·05 N	15·50 E
113	La Verne (lȧ vûrn') Ca. (Los Angeles In.)	34·06 N	117·46 W
204	Laverton (lā'vēr-tŭn) Austl.	28·45 S	122·30 E
135	La Victoria (lä vēk-tō'rē-ä) Ven. (In.)	10·14 N	67·20 W
120	Lavonia (lȧ-vō'nĭ-ȧ) Ga.	34·26 N	83·05 W
119	Lavon Res. Tx.	33·06 N	96·20 W
137	Lavras (lä'vräzh) Braz. (Rio de Janeiro In.)	21·15 S	44·59 W
165	Lávrion (läv'rĭ-ŏn) Grc.	37·44 N	24·05 E
113	Lawndale (lôn'dāl) Ca. (Los Angeles In.)	33·54 N	118·22 W
214	Lawra Ghana	10·39 N	2·52 W
107	Lawrence (lô'rĕns) In. (Indianapolis In.)	39·59 N	86·01 W
117	Lawrence Ks.	38·57 N	95·13 W
99	Lawrence Ma. (In.)	42·42 N	71·09 W
107	Lawrence Pa. (Pittsburgh In.)	40·18 N	80·07 W
107	Lawrenceburg (lô'rĕns-bûrg) In. (Cincinnati In.)	39·06 N	84·47 W
104	Lawrenceburg Ky.	38·00 N	85·00 W
120	Lawrenceburg Tn.	35·13 N	87·20 W
120	Lawrenceville (lô-rĕns-vĭl) Ga.	33·56 N	83·57 W
104	Lawrenceville Il.	38·45 N	87·45 W
106	Lawrenceville. NJ (New York In.)	40·17 N	74·44 W
121	Lawrenceville Va.	36·43 N	77·52 W
105	Lawsonia (lô-sō'nĭ-ȧ) Md.	38·00 N	75·50 W
116	Lawton (lô'tŭn) Ok.	34·36 N	98·25 W
186	Lawz, Jabal al (Mtn.) Sau. Ar.	28·46 N	35·37 E
183	Layang Layang (lä-yäng' lä-yäng'). Mala. (Singapore In.)	1·49 N	103·28 E
113	Layton (lā'tŭn) Ut. (Salt Lake City In.)	41·04 N	111·58 W
157	Laždijai (läzh'dē-yī') Sov. Un.	54·12 N	23·35 E
164	Lazio (Latium) (Reg.) (lä'zyô) (lä't-zēōōm). It.	42·05 N	12·25 E
108	Lead (lēd) SD	44·22 N	103·47 W
94	Leader Can.	50·55 N	109·32 W
116	Leadville (lĕd'vĭl) Co.	39·14 N	106·18 W
120	Leaf (R.) (lēf) Ms.	31·43 N	89·20 W
119	League City (lēg) Tx. (In.)	29·31 N	95·05 W
104	Leamington (lĕm'ĭng-tŭn) Can.	42·05 N	82·35 W
154	Leamington (lĕ'mĭng-tŭn) Eng.	52·17 N	1·25 W
148	Leatherhead (lĕdh'ēr-hĕd') Eng. (London In.)	51·17 N	0·20 W
113	Leavenworth (lĕv'ĕn-wûrth) Ks. (Kansas City In.)	39·19 N	94·54 W
110	Leavenworth Wa.	47·35 N	120·39 W
113	Leawood (lē'wŏŏd) Ks. (Kansas City In.)	38·58 N	94·37 W
159	Leba (lā'bä) Pol.	54·45 N	17·34 E
183	Lebam R. Mala. (Singapore In.)	1·35 N	104·09 E
216	Lebango Con.	0·22 N	14·49 E
113	Lebanon (lĕb'ȧ-nŭn) Il. (St. Louis In.)	38·36 N	89·49 W
104	Lebanon In.	40·00 N	86·30 W
120	Lebanon Ky.	37·32 N	85·15 W
117	Lebanon Mo.	37·40 N	92·43 W
105	Lebanon NH	43·40 N	72·15 W
104	Lebanon Oh.	39·25 N	84·10 W
110	Lebanon Or.	44·31 N	122·53 W
105	Lebanon Pa.	40·20 N	76·20 W
120	Lebanon Tn.	36·10 N	86·16 W
186	Lebanon Asia	34·00 N	34·00 E
153	Lebanon Mts. Leb.	33·30 N	35·32 E
167	Lebedin (lyĕ'bĕ-dēn) Sov. Un.	48·56 N	31·35 E
167	Lebedin Sov. Un.	50·34 N	34·27 E
166	Lebedyan' (lyĕ'bĕ-dyän'). Sov. Un.	53·03 N	39·08 E
160	Le Blanc (lĕ-bläN') Fr.	46·38 N	0·59 E
129	Le Borgne (lē bōrn'y') Hai.	19·50 N	72·30 W

ng-sing; ŋ-baŋk; N-nasalized n; nŏd; cŏmmit; ōld; ôbey; ôrder; fōōd; fŏŏt; ou-out; s-soft; sh-dish; th-thin; pūre; ûnite; ûrn; stŭd; circŭs; ü-as "y" in study; '-indeterminate vowel.

ăt; fīnăl; rāte; senāte; ärm; àsk; sofá; fâre; ch-choose; dh-as th in other; bē; ĕvent; bĕt; recĕnt; cratēr; g-go; gh-guttural g; bĭt; ĭ-short neutral; rīde; ĸ-guttural k as ch in German ich;

PRONOUNCING INDEX

Lido di Roma — Livno 305

Page	Name Pronunciation Region	Lat. °′	Long. °′
163	Lido di Roma (Ostia Lido) (lē'dô-dē-rô'mä) (ô's-tyä-lê-dô) It. (Rome In.)	41·19 N	12·17 E
159	Lidzbark (lïts'bärk) . . . . Pol.	54·07 N	20·36 E
218	Liebenbergsvlei (R.) . . . . S. Afr. (Johannesburg & Pretoria In.)	27·35 S	28·25 E
149	Liebenwalde (lē'bĕn-väl-dĕ) G.D.R. (Berlin In.)	52·52 N	13·24 E
193	Liechou Pan-Tao (Pen.) . . . . China	20·40 N	109·25 E
151	Liechtenstein (lĕk'tĕn-shtīn) . . Eur.	47·10 N	10·00 E
155	Liège (lê-āzh') . . . . Bel.	50·40 N	5·30 E
193	Lienchiang . . . . China	21·38 N	110·15 E
190	Lienshui (lïaN'sōōā) . . . . China	33·46 N	119·15 E
189	Lienyün (lïan'yün) . . . . China	33·10 N	120·01 E
190	Lienyünchiang . . . . China	34·43 N	119·27 E
158	Lienz (lê-ĕnts') . . . . Aus.	46·49 N	12·45 E
157	Liepāja (le'pä-yä') . . . . Sov. Un.	56·31 N	20·59 E
149	Lier . . . . Bel. (Brussels In.)	51·08 N	4·34 E
149	Liesing (lē'sĭng) . Aus. (Vienna In.)	48·09 N	16·17 E
158	Liestal (lēs'täl) . . . . Switz.	47·28 N	7·44 E
105	Lievre, Riviére du (R.) . . . . . . Can.	45·00 N	75·25 W
216	Lifanga . . . . Zaire	0·19 N	21·57 E
154	Liffey R. (lĭf'ĭ) . . . . Ire.	53·21 N	6·35 W
205	Lifou, (I.) . . . . N. Cal.	21·15 S	167·32 E
197	Ligao (lē-gä'ô) . . . . Phil. (In.)	13·14 N	123·33 E
203	Lightning Ridge . . . . Austl.	29·23 S	147·50 E
213	Ligonha (R.) (lē-gō'nyȧ) . . . . . Moz.	16·14 S	39·00 E
104	Ligonier (lĭg-ô-nēr) . . . . In.	41·30 N	85·35 W
174	Ligovo (lē'gô-vô) Sov. Un. (Leningrad In.)	59·51 N	30·13 E
164	Liguria (Reg.) (lê-gōō-rē-ä) . . . . It.	44·24 N	8·27 E
164	Ligurian Sea (lĭ-gū'rĭ-ăn) . . . . . Eur.	43·42 N	8·32 E
205	Lihou Rfs. (lē-hōō') . . . . Austl.	17·23 S	152·43 E
193	Lihsien (lē'hsyĕn') . . . . China	29·42 N	111·40 E
190	Lihsien . . . . China	38·30 N	115·38 E
190	Lihuang (lē'hōōäng) . . . . China	31·32 N	115·46 E
89	Lihue (lê-hōō'ā) . . . . Hi.	21·59 N	159·23 W
157	Lihula (lē'hŏŏ-lȧ) . . . . Sov. Un.	58·41 N	23·50 E
217	Likasi (Jadotville) . . . . Zaire	10·59 S	26·44 E
166	Likhoslavl' (lyê-kôsläv''l) . Sov. Un.	57·07 N	35·27 E
167	Likhovka (lyê-kôf'kȧ) . . . . Sov. Un.	48·52 N	33·57 E
216	Likouala (R.) . . . . Con.	0·10 S	16·30 E
160	Lille (lēl) . . . . Fr.	50·38 N	3·01 E
156	Lille Baelt (str.) . . . . Den.	55·09 N	9·53 E
156	Lillehammer (lēl'ĕ-häm'mĕr) . . Nor.	61·07 N	10·25 E
156	Lillesand (lēl'ĕ-sän') . . . . Nor.	58·16 N	8·19 E
156	Lilleström (lēl'ĕ-strûm) . . . . . . Nor.	59·56 N	11·04 E
112	Lilliwaup (lĭl'ĭ-wŏp) Wa. (Seattle In.)	47·28 N	123·07 W
93	Lillooet (lĭ'lōō-ĕt) . . . . Can.	50·30 N	121·55 W
93	Lillooet (R.) . . . . Can.	49·50 N	122·10 W
217	Lilongwe (lê-lô-än) . . . . Malawi	13·59 S	33·44 E
104	Lima (lī'mȧ) . . . . Oh.	40·40 N	84·05 W
134	Lima (lē'mä) . . . . Peru	12·06 S	76·55 W
162	Lima (R.) . . . . Port.	41·45 N	8·22 W
137	Lima Duarte (dwä'r-tĕ) Braz. (Rio de Janeiro In.)	21·52 S	43·47 W
111	Lima Res. . . . . Mt.	44·45 N	112·15 W
136	Limay (lē-mä'ē) (R.) . . . . Arg.	39·50 S	69·15 W
157	Limbazi (lēm'bä-zĭ) . . . . . . Sov. Un.	57·32 N	24·44 E
184	Limbdi . . . . India	22·37 N	71·52 E
129	Limbé . . . . Hai.	19·45 N	72·30 W
158	Limburg (lem-bŏŏrg') . . . . . . F.R.G.	50·22 N	8·03 E
156	Limedsforsen (lē'mĕs-fôrs'ĕn) . Swe.	60·54 N	13·24 E
137	Limeira (lē-mā'rä) Braz. (Rio de Janeiro In.)	22·34 S	47·24 W
95	Limestone Bay (līm'stōn) . . . . Can.	53·50 N	98·50 W
156	Limfjorden (Fd.) . . . . Den.	56·14 N	7·55 E
156	Limfjorden (Fd.) . . . . Den.	56·56 N	10·35 E
204	Limmen Bght. (lĭm'ĕn) . . . . . Austl.	14·45 S	136·00 E
165	Limni (lêm'nê) . . . . Grc.	38·47 N	23·22 E
165	Limnos (I.) . . . . Grc.	39·58 N	24·48 E
100	Limoges (lê-môzh') Can. (Ottawa In.)	45·20 N	75·15 W
160	Limoges . . . . Fr.	45·50 N	1·15 E
116	Limon (lī'mŏn) . . . . Co.	39·15 N	103·41 W
127	Limón (lê-mōn') . . . . C. R.	10·01 N	83·02 W
126	Limón (lē-mō'n) . . . . Hond.	15·53 N	85·34 W
129	Limon (R.) . . . . Dom. Rep.	18·20 N	71·40 W
122	Limón B. . . . . C. Z. (In.)	9·21 N	79·58 W
161	Limours (lē-mōōr') . . Fr. (Paris In.)	48·39 N	2·05 E
160	Limousin, Plateaux du (Plat.) (plä-tō' dü lē-mōō-zăN') . Fr.	45·44 N	1·09 E
160	Limoux (lē-mōō') . . . . Fr.	43·03 N	2·14 E
212	Limpopo R. (lĭm-pō'pō) . . . . . . Afr.	23·15 S	27·46 E
137	Linares (lē-nä'rās) Chile (Santiago In.)	35·51 S	71·35 W
118	Linares . . . . Mex.	24·53 N	99·34 W
162	Linares (lē-nä'rĕs) . . . . Sp.	38·07 N	3·38 W
137	Linares (Prov.) Chile (Santiago In.)	35·53 S	71·30 W
164	Linaro, C. (lê-nä'rä) . . . . It.	42·02 N	11·53 E
190	Linchang (lĭn'chäng') . . . . . . China	36·19 N	114·40 E
192	Linchiang (lĭn'chäng') (Reg.) . . . . . . China	41·45 N	127·00 E
190	Linch'ing (lĭn'chĭng) . . . . China	36·49 N	115·42 E
193	Linch'uan . . . . China	27·58 N	116·18 E
137	Lincoln (lĭŋ'kŭn) Arg. (Buenos Aires In.)	34·51 S	61·29 W
114	Lincoln . . . . Ca.	38·51 N	121·19 W
100	Lincoln . . . . Can. (Toronto In.)	43·10 N	79·29 W
148	Lincoln . . . . Eng.	53·14 N	0·33 W
117	Lincoln . . . . Il.	40·09 N	89·21 W
116	Lincoln . . . . Ks.	39·02 N	98·08 W
98	Lincoln . . . . Me.	45·23 N	68·31 W
99	Lincoln . . . . Ma. (In.)	42·25 N	71·19 W
117	Lincoln . . . . Ne.	40·49 N	96·43 W
148	Lincoln (Co.) . . . . Eng.	53·12 N	0·29 W
116	Lincoln, Mt. . . . . Co.	39·20 N	106·19 W
148	Lincoln Heights (Reg.) . . . . Eng.	53·23 N	0·39 W
107	Lincoln Park . . . . Mi. (Detroit In.)	42·14 N	83·11 W
106	Lincoln Park . . NJ (New York In.)	40·56 N	74·18 W
121	Lincolnton (lĭŋ'kŭn-tŭn) . . . . . . NC	35·27 N	81·15 W
154	Lincoln Wolds (woldz') . . . . . . Eng.	53·25 N	0·23 W
120	Lindale (lĭn'dăl) . . . . Ga.	34·10 N	85·10 W
158	Lindau (lĭn'dou) . . . . F.R.G.	47·33 N	9·40 E
120	Linden (lĭn'dĕn) . . . . Al.	32·16 N	87·47 W
113	Linden . . . . Mo. (Kansas City In.)	39·13 N	94·35 W
106	Linden . . . . NJ (New York In.)	40·39 N	74·14 W
106	Lindenhurst (lĭn'dĕn-hûrst) NY (New York In.)	40·41 N	73·23 W
106	Lindenwold (lĭn'dĕn-wôld) NJ (Philadelphia In.)	39·50 N	75·00 W
156	Lindesberg (lĭn'dĕs-bĕrgh) . . . . Swe.	59·37 N	15·14 E
155	Lindesnes (C.) (lĭn'ĕs-nĕs) . . . . Nor.	58·00 N	7·05 E
192	Lindho . . . . China	40·45 N	107·30 E
217	Lindi (lĭn'dê) . . . . Tan.	10·00 S	39·43 E
211	Lindi R. . . . . Zaire	1·00 N	27·13 E
218	Lindley (lĭnd'lê) . . . . S. Afr. (Johannesburg & Pretoria In.)	27·52 S	27·55 E
149	Lindow (lēn'dōv) G.D.R. (Berlin In.)	52·58 N	12·59 E
105	Lindsay (lĭn'zê) . . . . Can.	44·20 N	78·45 W
116	Lindsay . . . . Ok.	34·50 N	97·38 W
116	Lindsborg (lĭnz'bôrg) . . . . Ks.	38·34 N	97·42 W
148	Lindsey (Co.) (lĭn'zĭ) . . . . Eng.	53·25 N	0·32 W
190	Lineh'ü (lĭn'chü) . . . . China	36·31 N	118·33 E
120	Lineville (līn'vĭl) . . . . Al.	33·18 N	85·45 W
192	Linfen . . . . China	36·00 N	111·38 E
196	Linga, Kepulauan (Is.) . . . . . Indon.	0·35 S	105·05 E
197	Lingayen (lĭŋ'gä-yän') . . Phil. (In.)	16·01 N	120·13 E
197	Lingayen G. . . . . Phil. (In.)	16·18 N	120·11 E
158	Lingen (lĭŋ'gĕn) . . . . F.R.G.	52·32 N	7·20 E
193	Lingling (Yungchow) . . . . China	26·10 N	111·40 E
190	Lingpi (lĭng'pē') . . . . China	33·33 N	117·33 E
190	Lingtienchen (lĭng'dïăN'jĕn) . China	31·52 N	121·28 E
193	Lingting Yang (Can.) . . . . . . China	22·00 N	114·00 E
214	Linguère (lĭŋ-gĕr') . . . . Senegal	15·24 N	15·07 W
192	Lingwu . . . . China	38·05 N	106·18 E
192	Lingyüan . . . . China	41·12 N	119·20 E
193	Linhai . . . . China	28·52 N	121·08 E
192	Linhsi . . . . China	43·30 N	118·02 E
190	Linhuaikuan (lĭnhōōaĭ'gōōäN) China	32·55 N	117·38 E
190	Linhuanchi (lĭn'hōōaN'jē) . . . China	33·42 N	116·33 E
190	Lini (lĭn'yē) . . . . China	35·04 N	118·21 E
193	Linkao . . . . China	19·58 N	109·40 E
156	Linköping (lĭn'chû-pĭng) . . . . . Swe.	58·25 N	15·35 E
190	Linmingkuan (lĭN'mĭng'gōōän) China	36·47 N	114·32 E
154	Linnhe (L.) (lĭn'ê) . . . . Scot.	56·35 N	4·30 W
135	Lins (lê'Ns) . . . . Braz.	21·42 S	49·41 W
106	Linthicum Heights (lĭn'thĭ-kŭm) Md. (Baltimore In.)	39·12 N	76·39 W
192	Lintien . . . . China	42·08 N	124·59 E
104	Linton (lĭn'tŭn) . . . . In.	39·05 N	87·15 W
108	Linton . . . . ND	46·16 N	100·15 W
193	Linwu (lĭn'wōō') . . . . China	25·20 N	112·30 E
190	Linying (lĭn'yĭng') . . . . China	33·48 N	113·56 E
190	Linyü (lĭn'yü) . . . . China	40·01 N	119·45 E
158	Linz (lĭnts) . . . . Aus.	48·18 N	14·18 E
197	Lipa (lê-pä') . . . . Phil. (In.)	13·55 N	121·10 E
164	Lipari (lē'pä-rê) . . . . It.	38·29 N	15·00 E
164	Lipari (I.) . . . . It.	38·32 N	15·04 E
166	Lipetsk (lyē'pĕtsk) . . . . . . Sov. Un.	52·26 N	39·34 E
166	Lipetsk (Oblast) . . . . Sov. Un.	52·18 N	38·30 E
193	Lip'ing (lē'pĭng') . . . . China	26·18 N	109·00 E
159	Lipno (lēp'nô) . . . . Pol.	52·50 N	19·12 E
155	Lippe (R.) (lĭp'ĕ) . . . . F.R.G.	51·36 N	6·45 E
158	Lippstadt (lĭp'shtät) . . . . F.R.G.	51·39 N	8·20 E
106	Lipscomb (lĭp'skŭm) Al. (Birmingham In.)	33·26 N	86·56 W
167	Liptsy (lyēp'tsê) . . . . Sov. Un.	50·11 N	36·25 E
193	Lip'u . . . . China	24·38 N	110·35 E
217	Lira . . . . Ug.	2·15 N	32·54 E
164	Liri (R.) (lē'rē) . . . . It.	41·49 N	13·30 E
163	Liria (lê'ryä) . . . . Sp.	39·35 N	0·34 W
216	Lisala (lê-sä'lä) . . . . Zaire	2·09 N	21·31 E
163	Lisboa (Lisbon) (lēzh-bō'ä) (lĭz'bŭn) . Port. (Lisbon In.)	38·42 N	9·05 W
108	Lisbon . . . . ND	46·21 N	97·43 W
104	Lisbon . . . . Oh.	40·45 N	80·50 W
	Lisbon, see Lisboa		
98	Lisbon Falls . . . . Me.	43·59 N	70·03 W
154	Lisburn (lĭs'bŭrn) . . . . N. Ire.	54·35 N	6·05 W
101	Lisburne, C. . . . . Ak.	68·20 N	165·40 W
192	Lishih . . . . China	37·32 N	111·12 E
192	Lishu . . . . China	43·12 N	124·18 E
192	Lishuchen . . . . China	45·01 N	130·50 E
193	Lishui . . . . China	28·28 N	120·00 E
190	Lishui (lĭ'shwĭ') . . . . China	31·41 N	119·01 E
191	Lishui . . . . China (Canton In.)	23·12 N	113·09 E
160	Lisieux (lē-zyû') . . . . Fr.	49·10 N	0·13 E
174	Lisiy Nos (lĭ'sĭy-nôs) Sov. Un. (Leningrad In.)	60·01 N	30·00 E
167	Liski (lyēs'kê) . . . . Sov. Un.	50·56 N	39·28 E
107	Lisle (līl) . . . . Il. (Chicago In.)	41·48 N	88·04 W
161	L'Isle-Adam (lēl-ädäN') Fr. (Paris In.)	49·05 N	2·13 E
203	Lismore (lĭz'môr) . . . . Austl.	28·48 S	153·18 E
220	Lister, Mt. (lĭs'tēr) . . . . Ant.	78·05 S	163·00 E
183	Litani (R.) . . . Lib. (Palestine In.)	33·28 N	35·42 E
117	Litchfield (lĭch'fēld) . . . . Il.	39·10 N	89·38 W
109	Litchfield . . . . Mn.	45·08 N	94·34 W
107	Litchfield . . . . . . Oh. (Cleveland In.)	41·10 N	82·01 W
203	Lithgow (lĭth'gō) . . . . Austl.	33·23 S	149·31 E
164	Lithinon, Ark. (C.) . . . . . Grc. (In.)	34·59 N	24·35 E
106	Lithonia (lĭ-thō'nĭ-ȧ) Ga. (Atlanta In.)	33·43 N	84·07 W
168	Lithuanian S. S. R. (lĭth-ū-ā'-nĭ-ȧ) Sov. Un.	55·42 N	23·30 E
167	Litin (lê-tēn) . . . . Sov. Un.	49·16 N	28·11 E
165	Litókhoron (lē'tô-kô'rôn) . . . . . Grc.	40·05 N	22·29 E
216	Litoko . . . . Zaire	1·13 S	24·47 E
158	Litoměřice (lē'tô-myĕr'zhĭ-tsĕ) Czech.	50·33 N	14·10 E
158	Litomyšl (lē'tô-mêsh'l) . . . . . Czech.	49·52 N	16·14 E
217	Litoo . . . . Tan.	9·45 S	38·24 E
202	Little (R.) . Austl. (Melbourne In.)	37·54 S	144·27 E
120	Little (R.) . . . . Tn.-Mo.	36·28 N	89·39 W
119	Little R. . . . . Tx.	30·48 N	96·50 W
128	Little Abaco (I.) (ä'bä-kō) . . . Ba.	26·55 N	77·45 W
96	Little Abitibi (R.) . . . . Can.	50·15 N	81·30 W
220	Little America . . . . Ant.	78·30 S	161·30 W
196	Little Andaman I. (ăn-dȧ-măn') Andaman & Nicobar Is.	10·39 N	93·08 E
128	Little Bahama Bk. (bȧ-hā'mȧ) . Ba.	26·55 N	78·40 W
111	Little Belt Mts. (bĕlt) . . . . Mt.	47·00 N	110·50 W
111	Little Bighorn R. (bĭg-hôrn) . . Mt.	45·08 N	107·30 W
	Little Bitter, see Al Buḩayrah al Murrah aş Şughrāv		
110	Little Bitterroot R. (bĭt'ēr-ōōt) Mt.	47·45 N	114·45 W
116	Little Blue (R.) . . . . Ne.	40·15 N	98·01 W
113	Little Blue R. (blōō) Mo. (Kansas City In.)	38·52 N	94·25 W
148	Littleborough (lĭt''l-bŭr-ô) . . . Eng.	53·39 N	2·06 W
107	Little Calumet R. (kăl-ū-mĕt') Il. (Chicago In.)	41·38 N	87·38 W
128	Little Cayman (I.) (kā'măn) Cayman Is.	19·40 N	80·05 W
115	Little Colorado (R.) (kŏl-ô-rā'dō) Az.	36·05 N	111·35 W
106	Little Compton (kŏmp'tŏn) RI (Providence In.)	41·31 N	71·07 W
127	Little Corn I. . . . . Nic.	12·19 N	82·50 W
129	Little Exuma (I.) (ĕk-sōō'mä) . Ba.	23·25 N	75·40 W
109	Little Falls (fôlz) . . . . Mn.	45·58 N	94·23 W
105	Little Falls . . . . NY	43·05 N	74·55 W
116	Littlefield (lĭt''l-fēld) . . . . Tx.	33·55 N	102·17 W
109	Little Fork (R.) (fôrk) . . . . Mn.	48·24 N	93·30 W
123	Little Hans Lollick (I.) (häns lôl'lĭk) . Vir. Is (U.S.A.) (St. Thomas In.)	18·25 N	64·54 W
110	Little Humboldt R. (hŭm'bōlt) Nv.	41·10 N	117·40 W
129	Little Inagua (I.) (ê-nä'gwä) . . Ba.	21·30 N	73·00 W
128	Little Isaac (I.) (ĭ'zăk) . . . . Ba.	25·55 N	79·00 W
104	Little Kanawha (R.) (kȧ-nô'wȧ) WV	39·05 N	81·30 W
212	Little Karroo (Mts.) (kä-rōō) S. Afr.	33·50 S	21·02 E
91	Little Mecatina (R.) (mĕ cȧ tĭ nȧ) Can.	52·40 N	62·21 W
107	Little Miami R. (mī-ăm'ĭ) Oh. (Cincinnati In.)	39·19 N	84·15 W
107	Little Miami R., E. Fk. Oh. (Cincinnati In.)	39·01 N	84·03 W
117	Little Missouri (R.) (mĭ-sōō'rĭ) . Ar.	34·15 N	93·54 W
108	Little Missouri (R.) . . . . SD	45·46 N	103·48 W
121	Little Pee Dee (R.) (pē-dē') . . SC	34·35 N	79·21 W
111	Little Powder R. (pou'dēr) . . . Wy.	44·51 N	105·20 W
117	Little Red (R.) (rĕd) . . . . Ar.	35·25 N	91·55 W
117	Little Red R. . . . . Ok.	33·53 N	94·38 W
117	Little Rock (rôk) . . . . Ar.	34·42 N	92·16 W
95	Little Sachigo L. (să'chĭ-gō) . . Can.	54·09 N	92·11 W
161	Little St. Bernard P. (săntbĕr-närd') (săN bĕr-när') . Fr.-It.	45·49 N	6·50 E
129	Little San Salvador (I.) (săn săl'vȧ-dôr) . Ba.	24·35 N	75·55 W
108	Little Satilla (R.) (sȧ-tĭl'ȧ) . . . . Ga.	31·43 N	82·47 W
108	Little Sioux (R.) (sōō) . . . . Ia.	42·22 N	95·47 W
93	Little Smoky (R.) (smōk'ĭ) . . . Can.	55·10 N	116·55 W
111	Little Snake R. (snāk) . . . . Co.	40·40 N	108·21 W
120	Little Tallapoosa (R.) (tăl-ȧ-pōō'sȧ) . Al.	32·25 N	85·28 W
120	Little Tennessee (R.) (tĕn-ĕ-sē') Tn.	35·36 N	84·05 W
116	Littleton (lĭt''l-tŭn) . . . . Co.	39·34 N	105·01 W
99	Littleton . . . . Ma. (In.)	42·32 N	71·29 W
97	Littleton . . . . NH	44·15 N	71·45 W
104	Little Wabash (R.) (wô'băsh) . . . Il.	38·50 N	88·30 W
111	Little Wood R. (wŏŏd) . . . . Id.	43·00 N	114·08 W
190	Liuan (lyōō'än') . . . . China	31·45 N	116·29 E
193	Liuchou (lōō'chō) . . . . China	24·25 N	109·30 E
190	Liuho (lyōō'hō') . . . . China	32·22 N	118·50 E
192	Liuho . . . . China	42·10 N	125·38 E
217	Liuli . . . . Tan.	11·05 S	34·38 E
192	Liup'an Shan (Mts.) . . . . China	36·20 N	105·30 E
216	Liuwa Pln. . . . . Zambia	14·30 S	22·40 E
193	Liuyang (lyōō'yäng') . . . . China	28·10 N	113·35 E
190	Liuyüan (lū'yüän) . . . . China	36·09 N	114·37 E
166	Livāni (lē'vȧ-nê) . . . . Sov. Un.	56·24 N	26·12 E
96	Lively . . . . Can.	46·26 N	81·09 W
101	Livengood (lĭv'ĕn-gŏŏd) . . . . Ak.	65·30 N	148·35 W
120	Live Oak (lĭv'ōk) . . . . Fl.	30·15 N	83·00 W
112	Livermore (lĭv'ēr-mōr) Ca. (San Francisco In.)	37·41 N	121·46 W
104	Livermore . . . . Ky.	37·30 N	87·05 W
202	Liverpool (lĭv'ēr-pōōl) Austl. (Sydney In.)	33·55 S	150·56 E
98	Liverpool . . . . Can.	44·02 N	64·41 W
148	Liverpool . . . . Eng.	53·25 N	2·52 W
119	Liverpool . . . . Tx. (In.)	29·18 N	95·17 W
101	Liverpool B. . . . . Can.	69·45 N	130·00 W
205	Liverpool Ra. . . . . Austl.	31·47 S	31·00 E
211	Livindo R. . . . . Gabon	1·09 N	13·30 E
120	Livingston (lĭv'ĭng-stŭn) . . . . Al.	32·35 N	88·09 W
126	Livingston . . . . Guat.	15·50 N	88·45 W
113	Livingston . . . . . . Il. (St. Louis In.)	38·58 N	89·51 W
111	Livingston . . . . Mt.	45·40 N	110·35 W
106	Livingston . . . . NJ (New York In.)	40·47 N	74·20 W
120	Livingston . . . . Tn.	36·23 N	85·20 W
217	Livingstone (lĭv-ĭng-stôn) . . Zambia	17·50 S	25·53 E
216	Livingstone, Chutes de (Livingstone Falls) . Con.-Zaire	4·50 S	14·30 E
217	Livingstone Mts. . . . . Tan.	9·30 S	34·10 E
217	Livingstonia (lĭv-ĭng-stō'nĭ-ȧ) Malawi	10·36 S	34·07 E
164	Livno (lēv'nô) . . . . Yugo.	43·50 N	17·03 E

ng-sing; ŋ-baŋk; N-nasalized n; nŏd; cŏmmit; ōld; ôbey ôrder; fōōd; fŏŏt; ou-out; s-soft; sh-dish; th-thin; pūre; ûnite; ûrn; stŭd; circŭs; ü-as "y" in study; '-indeterminate vowel.

Page	Name Pronunciation Region	Lat. °'	Long. °'
166	Livny (lēv'nė) Sov. Un.	52·28 N	37·36 E
107	Livonia (lĭ-vō-nĭ-ȧ) Mi. (Detroit In.)	42·25 N	83·23 W
164	Livorno (Leghorn) (lė-vôr'nō) (lĕg'hôrn). It.	43·32 N	11·18 E
136	Livramento (lē-vrä-mě'n-tô) Braz.	30·46 S	55·21 W
190	Liyang (lē'yäng') China	31·30 N	119·29 E
154	Lizard Pt. (lĭz'ȧrd) Eng.	49·55 N	5·09 W
161	Lizy-sur-Ourcq (lēk-sē'sür-ōōrk') Fr. (Paris In.)	49·01 N	3·02 E
149	Ljmuiden. Neth. (Amsterdam In.)	52·27 N	4·35 E
164	Ljubljana (lyōō'blyä'na) Yugo.	46·04 N	14·29 E
164	Ljubuški (lyōō'bŏŏsh-kė) Yugo.	43·11 N	17·29 E
156	Ljungan (R.) Swe.	62·50 N	13·45 E
156	Ljungby (lyŏŏng'bü) Swe.	56·49 N	13·56 E
156	Ljusdal (lyōōs'däl) Swe.	61·50 N	16·11 E
156	Ljusnan (R.) Swe.	61·55 N	15·33 E
154	Llandudno (lăn-düd'nō) Wales	53·20 N	3·46 W
154	Llanelly (lȧ-nĕl'ĭ) Wales	51·44 N	4·09 W
162	Llanes (lyä'nås) Sp.	43·25 N	4·41 W
118	Llano (lä'nō) (lyä'nō) Tx.	30·45 N	98·41 W
118	Llano R. Tx.	30·38 N	99·04 W
134	Llanos (Reg.) (lyä'nôs). Col.-Ven.	4·00 N	71·15 W
124	Llera (lyā'rä) Mex.	23·16 N	99·03 W
162	Llerena (lyā-rā'nä) Sp.	38·14 N	6·02 W
154	Lleyn Prom. (lĭn) Wales	52·55 N	3·10 W
163	Llobregat (R.) (lyô-brė-gät'). Sp.	41·55 N	1·55 E
100	Lloyd L. (loid). Can. (Calgary In.)	50·52 N	114·13 W
96	Lloydminster Can.	53·17 N	110·00 W
163	Lluchmayor (lyōōch-mä-yôr'). Sp.	39·28 N	2·53 E
136	Llullaillaco (Vol.) (lyōō-lyī-lyä'kō). Arg.	24·50 S	68·30 W
216	Loange (R.) (lô-äŋ'gā) Zaire	6·10 S	19·40 E
212	Lobatsi (lō-bä'tsē) Bots.	25·13 S	25·35 E
136	Lobería (lô-bĕ'rē'ä) Arg.	38·13 S	58·48 W
216	Lobito (lô-bē'tō) Ang.	12·30 S	13·34 E
174	Lobnya (lôb'nyȧ) Sov. Un. (Moscow In.)	56·01 N	37·29 E
137	Lobos (lō'bôs) Arg. (Buenos Aires In.)	35·10 S	59·08 W
128	Lobos, Cayo (I.) (lō'bôs). Ba.	22·25 N	77·40 W
125	Lobos, Isla de (I.) (ē's-lä-dĕ-lô'bōs). Mex.	21·24 N	97·11 W
134	Lobos de Tierra (I.) (lô'bō-dĕ-tyĕ'r-rä). Peru	6·29 S	80·55 W
174	Lobva (lôb'vȧ) Sov. Un. (Urals In.)	59·12 N	60·28 E
174	Lobva R. Sov. Un. (Urals In.)	59·14 N	60·17 E
158	Locarno (lô-kär'nō) Switz.	46·10 N	8·43 E
160	Loches (lôsh) Fr.	47·08 N	0·56 E
193	Loching China	28·02 N	120·40 E
121	Lochloosa (L.) (lŏk-lō'sȧ) Fl.	29·33 N	82·07 W
106	Loch Raven Res. Md. (Baltimore In.)	39·28 N	76·38 W
154	Lochy (L.) (lŏk'ĭ) Scot.	56·57 N	4·45 W
121	Lockhart (lŏk'hȧrt) SC	34·47 N	81·30 W
119	Lockhart Tx.	29·54 N	97·40 W
105	Lock Haven (lŏk'hā-vĕn) Pa.	41·05 N	77·30 W
107	Lockland (lŏk'lănd) Oh. (Cincinnati In.)	39·14 N	84·27 W
100	Lockport (lŏk'pōrt) Can. (Winnipeg In.)	50·05 N	96·56 W
96	Lockeport Can.	43·42 N	65·07 W
107	Lockport Il. (Chicago In.)	41·35 N	88·04 W
107	Lockport NY (Buffalo In.)	43·11 N	78·43 W
196	Loc Ninh (lŏk'nĭng') Viet.	12·00 N	106·30 E
183	Lod (lôd) Isr. (Palestine In.)	31·57 N	34·55 E
160	Lodève (lô-dĕv') Fr.	43·43 N	3·18 E
157	Lodeynoye Pole (lô-dĕy-nô'yĕ) Sov. Un.	60·43 N	33·24 E
94	Lodge Cr. (lŏj) Can.	49·20 N	110·20 W
111	Lodge Cr. Mt.	48·51 N	109·30 W
108	Lodgepole Cr. (lŏj'pōl) Wy.	41·22 N	104·48 W
184	Lodhran Pak.	29·40 N	71·39 E
114	Lodi (lō'dī) Ca.	38·07 N	121·17 W
164	Lodi (lô'dē) It.	45·18 N	9·30 E
107	Lodi (lō'dī) Oh. (Cleveland In.)	41·02 N	82·01 W
162	Lodosa (lô-dô'sä) Sp.	42·27 N	2·04 W
217	Lodwar Ken.	3·07 N	35·36 E
159	Łódź (wŏŏdzh) Pol.	51·46 N	19·13 E
163	Loeches (lô-āch'ĕs) Sp. (Madrid In.)	40·22 N	3·25 W
214	Loffa (R.) Lib.	7·10 N	10·35 W
150	Lofoten (Is.) (lō'fō-tĕn) Nor.	68·26 N	13·42 E
104	Logan (lō'găn) Oh.	39·35 N	82·25 W
111	Logan Ut.	41·46 N	111·51 W
104	Logan WV	37·50 N	82·00 W
90	Logan, Mt. Can.	60·54 N	140·33 W
104	Logansport (lō'gănz-pōrt) In.	40·45 N	86·25 W
215	Logone (R.) (lō-gō'nä) (lô-gôn') Afr.	11·15 N	15·10 E
162	Logroño (lô-grō'nyō) Sp.	42·28 N	2·25 W
162	Logrosán (lô-grô-sän') Sp.	39·22 N	5·29 W
156	Løgstør (lügh-stûr') Den.	56·56 N	9·15 E
190	Lohochai (lou'wŭ'jäī) China	33·35 N	114·02 E
160	Loir (R.) (lwȧr) Fr.	47·40 N	0·07 E
160	Loire (R.) Fr.	47·19 N	1·11 W
134	Loja (lō'hä) Ec.	3·49 S	79·13 W
162	Loja (lô'-kä) Sp.	37·10 N	4·11 W
216	Loka Zaire	0·20 N	17·57 E
218	Lokala Drift (lō'kä-lȧ drĭft). Bots. (Johannesburg & Pretoria In.)	24·00 S	26·38 E
217	Lokandu Zaire	2·31 S	25·47 E
167	Lokhvitsa (lôk-vėt'sȧ). Sov. Un.	50·21 N	33·16 E
217	Lokichar Ken.	2·23 N	35·39 E
217	Lokitaung Ken.	4·16 N	35·45 E
216	Lokofa-Bokolongo Zaire	0·12 N	19·22 E
215	Lokoja (lô-kō'yä) Nig.	7·47 N	6·45 E
216	Lokolama Zaire	2·34 S	19·53 E
214	Lokosso Upper Volta	10·19 N	3·40 W
211	Lol R. (lōl) Sud.	9·06 N	28·09 E
217	Loliondo Tan.	2·03 S	35·37 E
156	Lolland (lôl'än') Den.	54·41 N	11·00 E
111	Lolo Mt.	46·45 N	114·05 W
165	Lom (lōm) Bul.	43·48 N	23·15 E
113	Loma Linda (lō'mȧ lĭn'dȧ) Ca. (Los Angeles In.)	34·04 N	117·16 W
214	Loma Mansa (Mtn.) S.L.	9·13 N	11·07 W
216	Lomami (R.) Zaire	0·50 S	24·40 E
136	Lomas de Zamora (lō'mäs dā zä-mō'rä). Arg. (Buenos Aires In.)	34·31 S	58·24 W
107	Lombard (lŏm-bärd) Il. (Chicago In.)	41·53 N	88·01 W
164	Lombardia (Reg.) (lôm-bär-dė'ä). It.	45·20 N	9·30 E
197	Lomblen (I.) (lŏm-blĕn') Indon.	8·08 S	123·45 E
196	Lombok (I.) (lŏm-bŏk') Indon.	9·15 S	116·15 E
196	Lombok, Selat (Str.) Indon.	9·00 S	115·28 E
214	Lomé (lō-mā') (lō'mā) Togo.	6·08 N	1·13 E
212	Lomela (lô-mā'lȧ) Zaire	2·19 S	23·33 E
216	Lomela (R.) Zaire	0·35 S	21·20 E
118	Lometa (lô-mē'tȧ) Tx.	31·10 N	98·25 W
215	Lomie (lô-mė-ā') Cam.	3·10 N	13·37 E
113	Lomita (lō-mē'tȧ) Ca. (Los Angeles In.)	33·48 N	118·20 W
149	Lommel Bel. (Brussels In.)	51·14 N	5·21 E
154	Lomond, Loch (L.) (lŏk lō'mŭnd) Scot.	56·15 N	4·40 W
174	Lomonosov (lô-mô'nô-sof) Sov. Un. (Leningrad In.)	59·54 N	29·47 E
114	Lompoc (lŏm-pōk') Ca.	34·39 N	120·30 W
159	Lomza (lôm'zhȧ) Pol.	53·11 N	22·04 E
105	Lonaconing (lō-nȧ-kō'nĭng) Md.	39·35 N	78·55 W
104	London (lŭn'dŭn) Can.	43·00 N	81·20 W
148	London Eng. (London In.)	51·30 N	0·07 W
120	London Ky.	37·07 N	84·06 W
104	London Oh.	39·50 N	83·30 W
98	Londonderry (lŭn'dŭn-dĕr-ĭ). Can.	45·29 N	63·36 W
154	Londonderry N. Ire.	55·00 N	7·19 W
204	Londonderry, C. Austl.	13·30 S	127·00 E
135	Londrina (lôn-drē'nä) Braz.	21·53 S	51·17 W
154	Lonely (I.) (lōn'lĭ) Can.	45·35 N	81·30 W
114	Lone Pine Ca.	36·36 N	118·03 W
127	Lone Star Nic.	13·58 N	84·25 W
129	Long (I.) Ba.	23·25 N	75·10 W
98	Long (I.) Can.	44·21 S	66·25 W
197	Long (I.) Pap. N. Gui.	5·10 S	147·30 E
108	Long (L.) ND	46·47 N	100·14 W
112	Long (L.) Wa. (Seattle In.)	47·29 N	122·36 W
216	Longa Ang.	14·42 S	18·32 E
216	Longa (R.) (lôŋ'gȧ) Ang.	10·20 S	13·50 E
121	Long B. SC	33·30 N	78·54 W
113	Long Beach (lông bēch) Ca. (Los Angeles In.)	33·46 N	118·12 W
106	Long Beach. NY (New York In.)	40·35 N	73·38 W
106	Long Branch (lông brȧnch) NJ (New York In.)	40·18 N	73·59 W
108	Longdon (lông'-dŭn) ND	48·45 N	98·23 W
148	Long Eaton (ē'tŭn) Eng.	52·54 N	1·16 W
154	Longford (lŏng'fērd) Ire.	53·43 N	7·40 W
113	Longhorn (lông-hôrn) Tx. (San Antonio In.)	29·33 N	98·23 W
217	Longido Tan.	2·44 S	36·41 E
92	Long I. Ak.	54·54 N	132·45 W
105	Long I. (lông) NY	40·50 N	72·50 W
105	Long Island Sd. (lông ī'lănd) Ct.-NY	41·05 N	72·45 W
161	Longjumeau (lôN-zhü-mō') Fr. (Paris In.)	48·42 N	2·17 E
190	Longk'ou (lōōng'kō) China	37·39 N	120·21 E
96	Longlac (lông'lăk) Can.	49·41 N	86·28 W
96	Long L. Can.	49·10 N	86·45 W
108	Longlake (lông-lāk) SD	45·52 N	99·06 W
116	Longmont (lông'mŏnt) Co.	40·11 N	105·07 W
161	Longnes (lôN'yĕ). Fr. (Paris In.)	48·56 N	1·37 E
148	Longnor (lông'nôr) Eng.	53·11 N	1·52 W
108	Long Pine (lông pīn) Ne.	42·31 N	99·42 W
105	Long Pt. Can.	42·35 N	80·05 W
99	Long Pt. Can.	48·48 N	58·46 W
95	Long Pt. Can.	53·02 N	98·40 W
105	Long Point B. Can.	42·40 N	80·10 W
109	Long Prairie (lông prâr'ĭ) Mn.	45·58 N	94·49 W
99	Long Range Mts. Can.	48·00 N	58·30 W
205	Longreach (lông'rēch) Austl.	23·32 S	144·17 E
98	Long Reach (R.) Can.	45·26 N	66·05 W
202	Long Rf. Austl. (Sydney In.)	33·45 S	151·22 E
148	Longridge (lông'rĭj) Eng.	53·51 N	2·37 W
116	Longs Pk. (lôngz) Co.	40·17 N	105·37 W
148	Longton (lông'tŭn) Eng.	52·59 N	2·08 W
100	Longueuil (lôN-gû'y') Can. (Montreal In.)	45·32 N	73·30 W
110	Longview (lông-vū) Or. (Portland In.)	46·06 N	123·02 W
119	Longview Tx.	32·29 N	94·44 W
119	Longville (lông'vĭl) La.	30·36 N	93·14 W
161	Longwy (lôN-wē') Fr.	49·32 N	6·14 E
196	Long Xuyen (loung' sōō'yĕn). Viet.	10·31 N	105·28 E
117	Lonoke (lō'nōk) Ar.	34·48 N	91·52 W
161	Lons-le-Saunier (lôN-lē-sō-nyā') Fr.	46·40 N	5·33 E
137	Lontue (lōn-tŏŏĕ') (R.) Chile (Santiago In.)	35·20 S	70·45 W
197	Looc (lô-ōk') Phil. (In.)	12·16 N	121·59 E
104	Loogootee In.	38·40 N	86·55 W
121	Lookout, C. (lŏŏk'out) NC	34·34 N	76·38 W
110	Lookout Pt. Res. Or.	43·51 N	122·38 W
217	Loolmalasin (Mtn.) Tan.	3·03 S	35·46 E
100	Looma (ōō'mȧ) Can. (Edmonton In.)	53·22 N	113·15 W
154	Loop Head (lōōp) Ire.	52·32 N	9·59 W
120	Loosahatchie (R.) (lōz-ȧ-hă'chē) Tn.	35·20 N	89·45 W
149	Loosdrechtsche Plassen (L.) Neth. (Amsterdam In.)	52·11 N	5·09 E
169	Lopatka, Mys (C.) (lô-pät'kȧ) Sov. Un.	51·00 N	156·52 E
216	Lopez, Cap (C.) Gabon	0·37 S	8·43 E
197	Lopez B. (lō'pāz) Phil. (In.)	14·04 N	122·00 E
112	Lopez I. Wa. (Seattle In.)	48·25 N	122·53 W
193	Lop'ing (lō'pĭng') China	29·02 N	117·12 E
216	Lopori (R.) (lō-pō'rė) Zaire	1·35 N	20·43 E
162	Lora (lō'rä) Sp.	37·40 N	5·31 W
107	Lorain (lô-rān') Oh. (Cleveland In.)	41·28 N	82·10 W
184	Loralai (lō-rŭ-lī') Pak.	30·31 N	68·35 E
162	Lorca (lôr'kä) Sp.	37·39 N	1·40 W
205	Lord Howe (I.) (lôrd hou). Austl.	31·44 S	157·56 E
115	Lordsburg (lôrdz'bûrg) NM	32·20 N	108·45 W
137	Lorena (lô-rā'nȧ) Braz. (Rio de Janeiro In.)	22·45 S	45·07 W
135	Loreto (lô-rā'tō) Braz.	7·09 S	45·10 W
100	Loretteville (lô-rĕt-vēl') Can. (Quebec In.)	46·51 N	71·21 W
134	Lorica (lô-rē'kä) Col.	9·14 N	75·54 W
160	Lorient (lô-rē'äN') Fr.	47·45 N	3·22 W
154	Lorne, Firth of (fûrth ôv lôrn') Scot.	56·10 N	6·09 W
158	Lörrach (lûr'äk) F.R.G.	47·36 N	7·38 E
113	Los Alamitos (lōs ăl-ȧ-mē'tôs) Ca. (Los Angeles In.)	33·48 N	118·04 W
115	Los Alamos (ăl-ȧ-môs') NM	35·53 N	106·20 W
112	Los Altos (ăl-tôs') Ca. (San Francisco In.)	37·23 N	122·06 W
137	Los Andes (ăn'dĕs) Chile (Santiago In.)	32·44 S	70·36 W
113	Los Angeles (ăŋ'gĕl-ĕs) (ăn'jĕl-ĕs) (äŋ'hȧ-lâs). Ca. (Los Angeles In.)	34·00 N	118·15 W
136	Los Angeles (äŋ'hȧ-lâs) Chile	37·27 S	72·15 W
114	Los Angeles Aqueduct Ca.	35·12 N	118·02 W
113	Los Angeles R. Ca. (Los Angeles In.)	33·50 N	118·13 W
137	Los Bronces (lôs brō'n-sĕs) Chile (Santiago In.)	33·09 S	70·18 W
110	Loscha R. (lōs'chȧ) Id.	46·20 N	115·11 W
136	Los Chonos, Archipielago de (är-chė-pyĕ'lä-gô dĕ lôs chô'nôs) Chile	44·35 N	76·15 W
136	Los Estados, Isla de (I.) (ē's-lä dĕ lôs ĕs-tȧ'dôs). Arg.	54·45 S	64·25 W
162	Los Filabres, Sierra de (Mts.) (sē-ĕ'r-rä dĕ lôs fē-lä'brĕs). Sp.	37·19 N	2·48 W
114	Los Gatos (gä'tôs) Ca.	37·13 N	121·59 W
193	Loshan (lō'shän') China	29·40 N	103·40 E
118	Los Herreras (ĕr-rā-räs) Mex.	25·55 N	99·23 W
129	Los Ilanos (lôs ė-lä'nōs). Dom. Rep.	18·35 N	69·30 W
128	Los Indios, Cayos de (Is.) (kä'yōs dĕ lôs ē'n-dyô's). Cuba	21·50 N	83·10 W
164	Lošinj (lô'shēn') Yugo.	44·30 N	14·29 E
164	Lošinj (I.) Yugo.	44·35 N	14·34 E
174	Losino Petrovskiy Sov. Un. (Moscow In.)	55·52 N	38·12 E
218	Loskopdam (L.) S. Afr. (Johannesburg & Pretoria In.)	25·30 S	29·26 E
163	Los Monegros (Mts.) (mô-nĕ'grōs). Sp.	41·31 N	0·18 W
113	Los Nietos (nyā'tôs) Ca. (Los Angeles In.)	33·57 N	118·05 W
128	Los Palacios Cuba	22·35 N	83·15 W
115	Los Pinos (R.) (pē'nôs). Co.-NM	36·58 N	107·35 W
124	Los Reyes (rā'yĕs) Mex.	19·35 N	102·29 W
125	Los Reyes Mex. (In.)	19·21 N	98·58 W
127	Los Santos (sän'tôs) Pan.	7·57 N	80·24 W
162	Los Santos (sän'tôs) Sp.	38·38 N	6·30 W
135	Los Teques (tĕ'kĕs). Ven. (In.)	10·22 N	67·04 W
111	Lost R. (lôst) Id.	43·56 N	113·38 W
110	Lost R. Or.	42·07 N	121·30 W
111	Lost River Mts. (rĭ'vĕr) Id.	44·23 N	113·48 W
137	Los Vilos (vē'lôs) Chile (Santiago In.)	31·56 S	71·29 W
160	Lot (R.) (lôt) Fr.	44·32 N	1·08 E
136	Lota (lō'tä) Chile	37·11 S	73·14 W
106	Lothian (lōth'ĭăn) Md. (Baltimore In.)	38·50 N	76·38 W
191	Lotien (lō'tyĕn') China (Shanghai In.)	31·25 N	121·20 E
217	Lotikipi Pln. Ken.	4·25 N	34·55 E
193	Loting (lō'tĭng') China	23·42 N	111·35 E
190	Lot'ing (lō'tĭng) China	39·26 N	118·53 E
158	Lötschen Tun. (lŭt'shĕn). Switz.	46·26 N	7·54 E
120	Loudon (lou'dŭn) Tn.	35·43 N	84·20 W
104	Loudonville (lou'dŭn-vĭl) Oh.	40·40 N	82·15 W
160	Loudun (lōō-dŭN') Fr.	47·03 N	0·00
214	Louga (lōō'gä) Senegal	15·37 N	16·13 W
148	Loughborough (lŭf'bŭr-ô) Eng.	56·46 N	1·12 W
104	Louisa (lōō'ēz-ȧ) Ky.	38·05 N	82·40 W
205	Louisade Arch. (lōō-ĭs-äd är-kĭ-pĕl-ĭ-gō). Pap. N. Gui.	10·44 S	153·58 E
121	Louisberg (lōō'ĭs-bûrg) NC	36·05 N	79·19 W
99	Louisburg (lōō'ĭs-bourg) Can.	45·55 N	59·58 W
98	Louiseville Can.	46·17 N	72·58 W
91	Louis XIV, Pte. Can.	54·35 N	79·51 W
117	Louisiana (lōō-ē-zė-ăn'ȧ) Mo.	39·24 N	91·03 W
103	Louisiana (State) U. S.	30·50 N	92·50 W
212	Louis Trichardt (lōō'ĭs trĭch'art) S. Afr.	22·52 S	29·53 E
116	Louisville (lōō'ĭs-vĭl) (lōō'ė-vĭl) Co.	39·58 N	105·08 W
121	Louisville Ga.	33·00 N	82·25 W
107	Louisville Ky. (Louisville In.)	38·15 N	85·45 W
120	Louisville Ms.	33·07 N	89·02 W
162	Loule (lō-lā') Port.	37·08 N	8·03 W
158	Louny (lō'nė) Czech.	50·20 N	13·47 E
108	Loup (R.) (lōōp) Ne.	41·17 N	97·58 W
108	Loup City Ne.	41·15 N	98·59 W
162	Lourdes (lōōrd) Fr.	43·06 N	0·03 W
	Lourenço Marques, see Maputo		

ăt; finăl; rāte; senâte; ärm; åsk; sofȧ; fâre; ch-choose; dh-as th in other; bē; ėvent; bĕt; recĕnt; cratẽr; g-go; gh-guttural g; bĭt; ĭ-short neutral; rīde; K-guttural k as ch in German ich;

Page	Name	Pronunciation	Region	Lat.	Long.

M

308 Maartensdijk — Mahone PRONOUNCING INDEX

Page	Name Pronunciation Region	Lat. °'	Long. °'
149	Maartensdijk Neth. (Amsterdam In.)	52·09 N	5·10 E
161	Maas (R.)......Neth. (Ruhr In.)	51·32 N	6·07 E
155	Maastricht (mäs'trĭкt)......Neth.	50·51 N	5·35 E
211	Maaten (Bishidra (Oasis)...Libya	23·11 N	22·34 E
216	Mabaia..................Ang.	7·13 S	14·03 E
112	Mabana (mä-bä-nä) Wa. (Seattle In.)	48·06 N	122·25 W
119	Mabank (mā'bănk)..........Tx.	32·21 N	96·05 W
218	Mabeskraal...............S. Afr. (Johannesburg & Pretoria In.)	25·12 S	26·47 E
106	Mableton (mā'b'l-tŭn).. Ga. (Atlanta In.)	33·49 N	84·34 W
152	Mabrouk (mȧ-brōōk')........Alg.	29·30 N	0·20 E
210	Mabrouk..................Mali	19·27 N	1·16 W
218	Mabula (mä'bōō-la).......S. Afr. (Johannesburg & Pretoria In.)	24·49 S	27·59 E
98	McAdam (măk-ăd'ăm)......Can.	45·36 N	67·20 W
137	Macaé (mä-kä-ā') Braz. (Rio de Janeiro In.)	22·22 S	41·47 W
106	McAfee (măk-ă'fē) NJ (New York In.)	41·10 N	74·32 W
135	Macaira (R.) (mä-kī'rä) Ven. (In.)	9·37 N	66·16 W
197	Macalelon (mä-kä-lā-lōn') Phil. (In.)	13·46 N	122·09 E
117	McAlester (măk ăl'ĕs-tēr).....Ok.	34·55 N	95·45 W
118	McAllen (măk-ăl'ĕn).........Tx.	26·12 N	98·14 W
135	Macapá (mä-kä-pä')........Braz.	0·08 N	50·02 W
189	Macau (mȧ-kä'ōō)...........Asia	22·00 N	113·00 E
135	Macau (mä-kȧ'ōō)..........Braz.	5·12 S	36·34 W
129	Macaya, Pico de (Pk.).......Hai.	18·25 N	74·00 W
93	McBride (măk-brīd')........Can.	53·18 N	120·10 W
106	McCalla (măk-kăl'lȧ) Al. (Birmingham In.)	33·20 N	87·00 W
118	McCamey (mȧ-kā'mĭ)........Tx.	31·08 N	102·13 W
163	Maccarese (mäk-kä-rē'zē) It. (Rome In.)	41·53 N	12·13 E
120	McCaysville (mȧ-kāz'vĭl).....Ga.	34·57 N	84·21 W
148	Macclesfield (măk''lz-fēld)...Eng.	53·15 N	2·07 W
148	Macclesfield Can. (măk''lz-fēld) Eng.	53·14 N	2·07 W
121	McColl (mȧ-kōl')............SC	34·40 N	79·34 W
120	McComb (mȧ-kōm')..........Ms.	31·14 N	90·27 W
108	McConaughy, L. (măk kō'nō ĭ') Ne.	41·24 N	101·40 W
116	McCook (mȧ-kŏŏk').........Ne.	40·13 N	100·37 W
121	McCormick (mȧ-kôr'mĭk).....SC	33·56 N	82·20 W
154	Macdhui, Ben (Mtn.) (bĕn măk-dōō'ē).Scot.	57·06 N	3·45 W
113	Macdona (măk-dō'nȧ) Tx. (San Antonio In.)	29·20 N	98·42 W
107	McDonald (măk-dŏn'ăld) Pa. (Pittsburgh In.)	40·22 N	80·13 W
204	Macdonald (I.) (măk-dŏn'ăld) Austl.	23·40 S	127·40 E
220	McDonald I...............Austl.	53·00 S	72·45 E
100	McDonald L. (măk-dŏn-ăld) Can. (Calgary In.)	51·12 N	113·53 W
204	Macdonnell Ra. (măk-dŏn'ĕl) Austl.	23·40 S	131·30 E
95	MacDowell L. (măk-dou ĕl)..Can.	52·15 N	92·45 W
107	Macedonia (măs-ê-dō'nĭ-ȧ) Oh. (Cleveland In.)	41·19 N	81·30 W
165	Macedonia (Reg.) (măs-ê-dō'nĭ-ȧ) Eur.	41·05 N	22·15 E
135	Maceió (mä-sȧ-yō').........Braz.	9·33 S	35·35 W
164	Macerata (mä-chȧ-rä'tä).......It.	43·18 N	13·28 E
203	Macfarlane, L. (mȧc'fär-lān) Austl.	32·10 S	137·00 E
217	Mackinnon Road...........Ken.	3·44 S	39·03 E
117	McGehee (mȧ-gē')...........Ar.	33·39 N	91·22 W
114	McGill (mȧ-gĭl')............Nv.	39·25 N	114·47 W
112	McGowan (măk-gou'ăn) Wa. (Portland In.)	46·15 N	123·55 W
101	McGrath (măk'grȧth)........Ak.	62·58 N	155·20 W
107	McGregor (măk-grĕg'ēr) Can. (Detroit In.)	42·08 N	82·58 W
109	McGregor..................Ia.	42·58 N	91·12 W
119	McGregor..................Tx.	31·26 N	97·23 W
93	McGregor (R.).............Can.	54·10 N	121·00 W
100	McGregor L. (măk-grĕg'ēr) Can. (Ottawa In.)	45·38 N	75·44 W
213	Machache (Mtn.) Leso. (Natal In.)	29·22 S	27·53 E
137	Machado (mä-shȧ-dô) Braz. (Rio de Janeiro In.)	21·42 S	45·55 W
217	Machakos.................Ken.	1·31 S	37·16 E
134	Machala (mä-chȧ'lä).........Ec.	3·18 S	78·54 W
107	McHenry (măk-hĕn'rĭ) Il. (Chicago In.)	42·21 N	88·16 W
113	Machens (măk'ĕns) Mo. (St. Louis In.)	38·54 N	90·20 W
98	Machias (mȧ-chī'ȧs).........Me.	44·22 N	67·29 W
195	Machida (mä-chē'dä) Jap. (Tōkyō In.)	35·32 N	139·28 E
185	Machilīpatnam.............India	16·22 N	81·10 E
134	Machu Picchu (mȧ'chōō-pē'k-chōō).Peru	8·01 S	72·24 W
216	Macías Nguema Biyogo (Fernando Póo) (Prov.).Equat. Gui.	3·35 N	7·45 E
167	Măcin (mȧ-chēn')..........Rom.	45·15 N	28·09 E
214	Macina (Depression)........Mali	14·50 N	4·40 W
108	McIntosh (măk'ĭn-tŏsh).......SD	45·54 N	101·22 W
205	Mackay (mȧ-kī')..........Austl.	21·15 S	149·08 E
111	Mackay (măk-kā')...........Id.	43·55 N	113·38 W
204	Mackay (I.) (mȧ-kī')......Austl.	22·30 S	127·45 E
90	MacKay (L.) (măk-kā').....Can.	64·10 N	112·35 W
94	Mackay (R.)...............Can.	56·50 N	112·30 W
112	McKay (R.).................Or.	45·43 N	123·00 W
107	McKeesport (mȧ-kez'pōrt) Pa. (Pittsburgh In.)	40·21 N	79·51 W
107	McKees Rocks (mȧ-kēz' rŏks) Pa. (Pittsburgh In.)	40·29 N	80·05 W
120	McKenzie (mȧ-kĕn'zĭ).......Tn.	36·07 N	88·30 W
90	Mackenzie, Dist. of.........Can.	63·48 N	125·25 W
90	Mackenzie (R.).............Can.	63·28 N	124·23 W
101	Mackenzie B................Ak.	69·20 N	137·10 W
90	Mackenzie Mts. (mȧ-kĕn'zĭ) Can.	63·41 N	129·27 W
110	McKenzie R.................Or.	44·07 N	122·20 W
104	Mackinac, Str. of (măk'ĭ-nô) (măk'ĭ-năk).Mi.	45·50 N	84·40 W
104	Mackinaw (R.)...............Il.	40·35 N	89·25 W
104	Mackinaw City (măk'ĭ-nô)....Mi.	45·45 N	84·45 W
101	McKinley, Mt. (mȧ-kĭn'lĭ)....Ak.	63·00 N	151·02 W
117	McKinney (mȧ-kĭn'ĭ).........Tx.	33·12 N	96·35 W
108	McLaughlin (măk-lŏf'lĭn).....SD	45·48 N	100·45 W
106	McLean (mȧc'lān) Va. (Baltimore In.)	38·56 N	77·11 W
104	McLeansboro (mȧ-klānz'bŭr-ô).Il.	38·10 N	88·35 W
213	Macleantown (măk-lān'toun) S. Afr. (Natal In.)	32·48 S	27·48 E
213	Maclear (mȧ-klēr') S. Afr. (Natal In.)	31·06 S	28·23 E
90	McLennan (măk-lĕn'năn)....Can.	55·42 N	116·54 W
92	McLeod Lake...............Can.	54·59 N	123·02 W
93	McLeod (R.)...............Can.	53·45 N	115·15 W
110	McLoughlin, Mt. (măk-lŏk'lĭn) Or.	42·27 N	122·20 W
118	McMillan L. (măk-mĭl'ăn)....Tx.	32·40 N	104·09 W
112	McMillin (măk-mĭl'ĭn) Wa. (Seattle In.)	47·08 N	122·14 W
110	McMinnville (măk-mĭn'vĭl)....Or.	45·13 N	123·13 W
120	McMinnville................Tn.	35·41 N	85·47 W
112	McMurray (măk-mŭr'ĭ) Wa. (Seattle In.)	48·19 N	122·15 W
115	McNary (măk-nâr'ē).........Az.	34·10 N	109·55 W
119	McNary....................La.	30·58 N	92·32 W
110	McNary Dam...........Or.-Wa.	45·57 N	119·15 W
117	Macomb (mȧ-kōōm')..........Il.	40·27 N	90·40 W
160	Mâcon (mä-kôN).............Fr.	46·19 N	4·51 E
120	Macon (mā'kŏn).............Ga.	32·49 N	83·39 W
120	Macon......................Ms.	32·07 N	88·31 W
117	Macon......................Mo.	39·42 N	92·29 W
117	McPherson (măk-fŭr's'n).....Ks.	38·21 N	97·41 W
203	Macquarie (R.)............Austl.	31·43 S	148·04 E
220	Macquarie Is. (mȧ-kwŏr'ē) Austl.	54·36 S	158·45 E
120	McRae (măk-rā')............Ga.	32·02 N	82·55 W
120	McRoberts (măk-rŏb'ērts).....Ky.	37·12 N	82·40 W
126	Macuelizo (mä-kwē-lē'zô)...Hond.	15·22 N	88·32 W
183	Ma'dabā...Jordan (Palestine In.)	31·43 N	35·47 E
209	Madagascar (măd-ȧ-găs'kȧr) Afr.	18·05 S	43·12 E
99	Madame (I.) (mȧ-dȧm').....Can.	45·33 N	61·02 W
185	Madanapalle..............India	13·06 N	78·09 E
197	Madang (mä-däng')..Pap. N. Gui.	5·15 S	145·45 E
210	Madaoua (mȧ-dou'ȧ).......Niger	14·04 N	6·03 E
105	Madawaska (R.) (măd-ȧ-wôs'kȧ) Can.	45·20 N	77·25 W
122	Madden, L............C. Z. (In.)	9·15 N	79·34 W
210	Madeira, Ilha da (I.) (mä-dā'rä) Mad. Is.	32·41 N	16·15 W
210	Madeira, Arquipelado da (Is.) (är-kē-pē'lä-gō-dä-mä-dĕý-rä) Port.	33·26 N	16·44 W
134	Madeira (R.)..............Braz.	6·48 S	62·43 W
109	Madelia (mȧ-dē'lĭ-ȧ).........Mn.	44·03 N	94·23 W
109	Madeline (I.) (măd'ĕ-lĭn).....Wi.	46·47 N	91·30 W
114	Madera (mȧ-dā'rȧ)..........Ca.	36·57 N	120·04 W
126	Madera (Vol.)..............Nic.	11·27 N	85·30 W
185	Madgaon.................India	15·09 N	73·58 E
184	Madhya Pradesh (State) (mŭd'vŭ prŭ-dāsh').India	22·04 N	77·48 E
117	Madill (mȧ-dĭl')............Ok.	34·04 N	96·45 W
186	Madīnat ash Sha'b P. D. R. of Yem.	12·45 N	44·00 E
216	Madingo..................Con.	4·07 S	11·22 E
216	Madingou.................Con.	4·09 S	13·34 E
120	Madison (măd'ĭ-sŭn).........Fl.	30·28 N	83·25 W
120	Madison...................Ga.	33·34 N	83·29 W
113	Madison........Il. (St. Louis In.)	38·40 N	90·09 W
104	Madison...................In.	38·45 N	85·25 W
117	Madison...................Ks.	38·08 N	96·07 W
98	Madison...................Me.	44·47 N	69·52 W
108	Madison...................Mn.	44·59 N	96·13 W
108	Madison...................Ne.	41·49 N	97·27 W
106	Madison......NJ (New York In.)	40·46 N	74·25 W
121	Madison...................NC	36·22 N	79·59 W
108	Madison...................SD	44·01 N	97·08 W
109	Madison...................Wi.	43·05 N	89·23 W
111	Madison Res...............Mt.	45·25 N	111·28 W
111	Madison R.................Mt.	45·15 N	111·30 W
104	Madisonville (măd'ĭ-sŭn-vĭl) Ky.	37·20 N	87·30 W
113	Madisonville...............La.	30·22 N	90·10 W
119	Madisonville...............Tx.	30·57 N	95·55 W
196	Madjene.................Indon.	3·34 S	119·00 E
214	Madjori..............Upper Volta	11·26 N	1·15 E
166	Madona (mȧ'dō'nȧ).....Sov. Un.	56·50 N	26·14 E
186	Madrakah, Ra's al (C.)......Om.	18·53 N	57·48 E
185	Madras (mȧ-drȧs') (mŭ-drŭs') India	13·08 N	80·15 E
113	Madre, Laguna L. (lä-gōō'nä mä'drȧ).Mex.	25·08 N	97·41 W
124	Madre, Sierra (Mts.) (sē-ĕ'r-rä-mȧ'drĕ).Mex.	15·55 N	92·40 W
197	Madre, Sierra (Mts.)...Phil. (In.)	16·40 N	122·10 E
136	Madre de Dios, Arch. (mȧ'drȧ dä dê-ōs').Chile	50·40 S	76·30 W
134	Madre de Dios, Rio (R.) (rê'ō-mä'drȧ dä dê-ōs').Bol.	12·07 S	68·20 W
124	Madre del Sur, Sierra (Mts.) (sē-ĕ'r-rä-mä'drȧ dĕlsōōr').Mex.	17·35 N	100·35 W
109	Madrid (măd'rĭd)............Ia.	41·51 N	93·48 W
163	Madrid (mä-drē'd) Sp. (Madrid In.)	40·26 N	3·42 W
162	Madridejos (mä-dhrê-dhä'hōs..Sp.	39·29 N	3·32 W
110	Mad R. (măd)...............Ca.	40·38 N	123·37 W
217	Mado Gashi...............Ken.	0·44 N	39·10 E
196	Madura (I.) (mȧ-dōō'rä)...Indon.	6·45 S	113·30 E
185	Madurai (mä-dōō'rä).......India	9·57 N	78·04 E
136	Madureira, Serra do (Mtn.) (sĕ'r-rä-dô-mä-dōō-rā'rȧ) Braz. (Rio de Janeiro In.)	22·49 S	43·30 W
195	Maebashi (mä-ĕ-bä'shê)......Jap.	36·26 N	139·04 E
163	Maella (mä-āl'yä)...........Sp.	41·10 N	0·07 E
128	Maestra, Sierra (Mts.) (sē-ĕ'r-rȧ-mä-ās'trä).Cuba	20·05 N	77·05 W
205	Maewo (I.)...........New Hebr.	15·17 S	168·16 E
212	Mafeking (mȧf'ê-kĭng).....S. Afr.	25·46 S	24·45 E
217	Mafia (I.) (mä-fē'ä).........Tan.	7·47 S	40·00 E
136	Mafra (mȧ'frä)............Braz.	26·21 S	49·59 W
163	Mafra (mäf'rȧ).Port. (Lisbon In.)	38·56 N	9·20 W
173	Magadan (mȧ-gȧ-dän')...Sov. Un.	59·39 N	150·43 E
173	Magadan Oblast........Sov. Un.	63·00 N	170·30 E
217	Magadi...................Ken.	1·54 S	36·17 E
217	Magadi (L.) (mȧ-gä'dê).....Ken.	1·50 S	36·00 E
213	Magalies (R.) (mä-gä'lyĕs).S. Afr. (Johannesburg & Pretoria In.)	25·51 S	27·42 E
213	Magaliesberg (Mts.)......S. Afr. (Johannesburg & Pretoria In.)	25·45 S	27·43 E
218	Magaliesburg............S. Afr. (Johannesburg & Pretoria In.)	26·01 S	27·32 E
197	Magallanes (mä-gäl-yä'nās) Phil. (In.)	12·48 N	123·52 E
136	Magallanes, Estrecho de (Str.) (ĕs-trĕ'chô-dĕ-mä-gäl-yä'nĕs) Arg.-Chile	52·30 S	68·45 W
134	Magangué (mä-gän'gā).......Col.	9·08 N	74·56 W
197	Magat (R.) (mä-gät')...Phil. (In.)	16·45 N	121·16 E
137	Magdalena (mäg-dä-lā'nä) Arg. (Buenos Aires In.)	35·05 S	57·32 W
134	Magdalena.................Bol.	13·17 S	63·57 W
102	Magdalena................Mex.	30·34 N	110·50 W
115	Magdalena.................NM	34·10 N	107·45 W
136	Magdalena (I.)............Chile	44·45 S	73·15 W
122	Magdalena, Bahia (B.) (bä-ē'ä-mäg-dä-lā'nä).Mex.	24·30 N	114·00 W
134	Magdalena, Rio (R.).........Col.	7·45 N	74·04 W
99	Magdalen Is. (măg'dȧ-lĕn)...Can.	47·27 N	61·25 W
158	Magdeburg (mäg'dĕ-bōōrgh) G.D.R.	52·07 N	11·39 E
136	Magé (mä-zhā') Braz. (Rio de Janeiro In.)	22·39 S	43·02 W
164	Magenta (mȧ-jĕn'tȧ)..........It.	45·26 N	8·53 E
150	Mageröy (I.) (mä'ghĕr-ûê)...Nor.	71·10 N	24·11 E
164	Maggiore, Lago di (L.)........It.	46·03 N	8·25 E
162	Maghnia...................Alg.	35·07 N	2·10 W
218	Maghāghah......Egypt (Nile In.)	28·38 N	30·50 E
124	Magiscatzin (mä-kês-kät-zēn') Mex.	22·48 N	98·42 W
165	Maglaj (mȧ'glä-ê)..........Yugo.	44·34 N	18·12 E
165	Maglić (mäg'lēch)..........Yugo.	43·36 N	20·36 E
165	Maglie (mäl'yä)..............It.	40·06 N	18·20 E
113	Magna (măg'nȧ) Ut. (Salt Lake City In.)	40·43 N	112·06 W
174	Magnitogorsk(mȧg-nyē'tô-gôrsk) Sov. Un. (Urals In.)	53·26 N	59·05 E
117	Magnolia (măg-nō'lĭ-ȧ)........Ar.	33·16 N	93·13 W
120	Magnolia..................Ms.	31·08 N	90·27 W
161	Magny-en-Vexin (mä-nyē'ĕN-vĕ-sȧN') Fr. (Paris In.)	49·09 N	1·45 E
105	Magog (mȧ-gŏg')...........Can.	45·15 N	72·10 W
96	Magpie (R.)...............Can.	50·40 N	64·30 W
98	Magpie Lac (L.)...........Can.	50·55 N	64·39 W
109	Magpie (R.)...............Can.	48·13 N	84·50 W
93	Magrath...................Can.	49·25 N	112·52 W
212	Magude (mä-gōō'dȧ)........Moz.	24·58 S	32·39 E
188	Magwe (mŭg-wā')...........Bur.	20·19 N	94·57 E
171	Mahabād..................Iran	36·55 N	45·50 E
211	Magahi Port (mä-hä'gê).....Zaire	2·14 N	31·12 E
196	Mahakam (Strm.)..........Indon.	0·30 S	116·15 E
217	Mahali Mts................Tan.	6·20 S	30·00 E
213	Mahaly (mȧ-hȧl-ē')..........Mad.	24·09 S	46·20 E
196	Mahameru, Gunung (Mtn.) .Indon.	8·00 S	112·50 E
184	Mahānadi (R.) (mŭ-hä-nŭd'ê) India	20·50 N	84·27 E
213	Mahanoro (mȧ-hȧ-nô'rō)....Mad.	19·57 S	48·47 E
105	Mahanoy City (mȧ-hȧ-noi')...Pa.	40·50 N	76·10 W
184	Mahārāshtra (State)........India	19·06 N	75·00 E
183	Maḩaţţat al Qaţrānah Jordan (Palestine In.)	31·15 N	36·04 E
183	Maḩaţţat 'Aqabat al Ḩijāzīyah Jordan (Palestine In.)	29·45 N	35·55 E
183	Maḩaţţat ar Ramlah......Jordan	29·31 N	35·57 E
183	Maḩaţţat Jurf ad Darāwīsh Jordan (Palestine In.)	30·41 N	35·51 E
213	Mahavavy (R.) (mä-hä-vä'vê) Mad.	17·42 S	46·06 E
184	Mahaweli (R.).............India	7·47 N	80·43 E
151	Mahdia (mä-dē'ȧ) (mä'dê-ȧ) Tun.	35·30 N	11·09 E
185	Mahe (mä-ā')..............India	11·42 N	75·39 E
217	Mahenge (mä-hĕŋ'gȧ).......Tan.	7·38 S	36·16 E
184	Mahi (R.).................India	23·16 N	73·20 E
185	Māhīm Bay...........India (In.)	19·03 N	72·45 E
213	Mahlabatini (mä'lȧ-bȧ-tē'nê) S. Afr. (Natal In.)	28·15 S	31·29 E
149	Mahlow (mä'lōv) G.D.R. (Berlin In.)	52·23 N	13·24 E
108	Mahnomen (mô-nō'mĕn)......Mn.	47·18 N	95·58 W
163	Mahón (mä-ōn')..............Sp.	39·52 N	4·15 E
98	Mahone Bay (mȧ-hōn')......Can.	44·27 N	64·23 W
96	Mahone B..................Can.	44·30 N	64·15 W

ăt; finȧl; rāte; senâte; ärm; ȧsk; sofȧ; fâre; ch-choose; dh-as th in other; bē; êvent; bĕt; recĕnt; cratēr; g-go; gh-guttural g; bĭt; ĭ-short neutral; rīde; к-guttural k as ch in German ich;

PRONOUNCING INDEX

Mahopac — Mankato 309

Page	Name Pronunciation Region	Lat. °′	Long. °′
106	Mahopac, L. (mā-hō′păk) NY (New York In.)	41·24 N	73·45 W
106	Mahwah (mȧ-wä′) NJ (New York In.)	41·05 N	74·09 W
148	Maidenhead (mād′ĕn-hĕd) Eng. (London In.)	51·30 N	0·44 W
	Maidos, see Eceabat		
148	Maidstone.....Eng. (London In.)	51·17 N	0·32 E
215	Maiduguri (mä′ē-dȧ-gōō′rē)...Nig.	11·51 N	13·10 E
134	Maigualida Sierra (Mts.) (sē-ĕ′r-rȧ-mī-gwä′lē-dĕ).Ven.	6·30 N	65·50 W
184	Maijdi.....Bngl.	22·59 N	91·08 E
	Maikop, see Maykop		
203	Main Barrier Ra. (băr′′ēr).Austl.	31·25 S	141·40 E
212	Mai-Ndombe, Lac (Leopold II, L.) Zaire	2·16 S	19·00 E
103	Maine (State) (mān).....U. S.	45·25 N	69·50 W
154	Mainland (I.) (mān-lănd) Scot. (In.)	60·19 N	2·40 W
158	Main R. (mīn).....F.R.G.	49·49 N	9·20 E
161	Maintenon (măN-tĕ-nôN′) Fr. (Paris In.)	48·35 N	1·35 E
213	Maintirano (mä′ēn-tē-rä′nō).Mad.	18·05 S	44·08 E
158	Mainz (mīnts).....F.R.G.	49·59 N	8·16 E
210	Maio I. (mä′yo).....C. V. (In.)	15·15 N	22·50 W
137	Maipo (mī′pô) (R.) Chile (Santiago In.)	33·45 S	71·08 W
136	Maipo (Vol.).....Arg.	34·08 S	69·51 W
137	Maipú (mī′pōō′) Arg. (Buenos Aires In.)	36·51 S	57·54 W
135	Maiquetía (mī-kĕ-tē′ä)..Ven. (In.)	10·37 N	66·56 W
129	Maisí, Punta (Pt.) (pōō′n-tä-mī-sē′).Cuba	20·10 N	74·00 W
161	Maison-Rouge (mā-zôN-rōōzh′) Fr. (Paris In.)	48·34 N	3·09 E
203	Maitland (māt′lănd).....Austl.	32·45 S	151·40 E
195	Maizuru (mä-ĭ′zōō-rōō).....Jap.	35·26 N	135·15 E
211	Maji.....Eth.	6·14 N	35·34 E
	Majorca I., see Mallorca, Isle de		
213	Majunga (mȧ-jŭŋ′gä).....Mad.	15·12 S	46·26 E
110	Makah Ind. Res. (mȧ kī′).....Wa.	48·17 N	124·52 W
213	Makanya (mä-kän′yä).....Tan.	4·15 S	37·49 E
164	Makarska (mȧ′kär-skȧ).....Yugo.	43·17 N	17·05 E
170	Makar′yev.....Sov. Un.	57·50 N	43·48 E
	Makasar, see Udjung Pandang		
196	Makasar, Selat (Str.) (mȧ-käs′ĕr) Indon.	2·00 S	118·07 E
216	Makaw.....Zaire	3·29 S	18·19 E
195	Make (I.) (mä′kȧ).....Jap.	30·43 N	130·49 E
214	Makeni.....S. L.	8·53 N	12·03 W
167	Makeyevka (mŭk-yā′ŭf-kȧ) Sov. Un.	48·03 N	38·00 E
218	Makgadikgadi Pans (L.)....Bots.	20·38 S	21·31 E
171	Makhachkala (mäk′äch-kä′lä) Sov. Un.	43·00 N	47·40 E
213	Makhaleng (R.)..Leso. (Natal In.)	29·53 S	27·33 E
165	Makhlata (mäk′lä-tä).....Bul.	43·27 N	24·16 E
217	Makindu.....Ken.	2·17 S	37·49 E
186	Makkah (Mecca) (mĕk′ȧ).Sau. Ar.	21·27 N	39·45 E
91	Makkovik.....Can.	55·01 N	59·10 W
159	Makó (mô′kō).....Hung.	46·13 N	20·30 E
216	Makokou (mȧ-kō-kōō′)....Gabon	0·34 N	12·52 E
159	Maków Mazowiecki (mä′kōov mä-zō-vyĕts′kē).Pol.	52·51 N	21·07 E
195	Makuhari (mä-kōō-hä′rē) Jap. (Tōkyō In.)	35·39 N	140·04 E
195	Makurazaki (mä′kōō-rä-zä′kē) Jap.	31·16 N	130·18 E
215	Makurdi.....Nig.	7·45 N	8·32 E
101	Makushin (mȧ-kōō′shĭn).....Ak.	53·57 N	166·28 W
172	Makushino (mȧ-kōō-shĕn′ō) Sov. Un.	55·03 N	67·43 E
185	Malabar Coast (măl′ȧ-bär)..India	11·19 N	75·33 E
216	Malabo.....Equat. Gui.	3·45 N	8·47 E
197	Malabon.....Phil. (In.)	14·39 N	120·57 E
196	Malacca, Str. of (mȧ-lăk′ȧ)...Asia	4·15 N	99·44 E
111	Malad (mȧ-läd′).....Id.	42·11 N	112·15 W
163	Maladetta (Mts.) (mä-lä-dĕt′tä) Sp.	42·30 N	0·38 E
163	Malafede (R.) (mä-lä-fĕ′dĕ) It. (Rome In.)	41·43 N	12·28 E
134	Málaga (mȧ′lä-gȧ).....Col.	6·41 N	72·46 W
162	Málaga.....Sp.	36·45 N	4·25 W
162	Málaga, Bahía de (B.) (bä-ē′ä-dĕ-mä′lä-gä).Sp.	36·35 N	4·10 W
162	Malagón (mä-lä-gōn′).....Sp.	39·12 N	3·52 W
205	Malaita (I.) (mä-lä′ē-tȧ)...Sol. Is.	8·38 S	161·15 E
211	Malakāl (mȧ-lȧ-käl′).....Sud.	9·46 N	31·54 E
174	Malakhovka (mȧ-läk′ôf-kȧ) Sov. Un. (Moscow In.)	55·38 N	38·01 E
216	Malanje (mä-läŋ-gȧ).....Ang.	9·32 S	16·20 E
210	Malanville.....Benin	12·04 N	3·09 E
98	Malapedia (R.).....Can.	48·11 N	67·08 W
127	Mala Punta (Pt.) (pōō′n-tä-mä′lä) Pan.	7·32 N	79·44 W
156	Mälaren (L.).....Swe.	59·38 N	16·55 E
91	Malartic.....Can.	48·07 N	78·11 W
92	Malaspina Str. (mäl-ȧ-spē′nȧ).Can.	49·44 N	124·20 W
171	Malatya (mȧ-lä′tyȧ).....Tur.	38·30 N	38·15 E
209	Malawi.....Afr.	11·15 S	33·45 E
	Malawi, L., see Nyasa, L.		
196	Malaya (Reg.) (mȧ-lā′yä)...Mala.	3·35 N	101·30 E
166	Malaya Vishera (vē-shä′rȧ) Sov. Un.	58·51 N	32·13 E
196	Malay Pen. (mȧ-lā′) (mā′lā)..Asia	7·46 N	101·06 E
196	Malaysia (mȧ-lā′zhȧ).....Asia	4·10 N	101·22 E
154	Mal B. (măl).....Ire.	52·51 N	9·45 W
204	Malbon (măl′bŭn).....Austl.	21·15 S	140·30 E
159	Malbork (mäl′bôrk).....Pol.	54·02 N	19·04 E
163	Malcabran (R.) (mäl-kä-brän′) Port. (Lisbon In.)	38·47 N	8·46 W
99	Malden (môl′dĕn).....Ma. (In.)	42·26 N	71·04 W
117	Malden.....Mo.	36·32 N	89·56 W
199	Malden (I.).....Oceania	4·20 S	154·30 W
182	Maldives.....Asia	4·30 N	71·30 E
148	Maldon (môrl′dŏn) Eng. (London In.)	51·44 N	0·39 E
136	Maldonado (mäl-dŏ-nä′dŏ)....Ur.	34·54 S	54·57 W
124	Maldonado, Punta (Pt.) (pōō′n-tä).Mex.	16·18 N	98·34 W
165	Maléa, Akr. (C.).....Grc.	37·31 N	23·13 E
184	Mālegaon.....India	20·35 N	74·30 E
159	Male Karpaty (Mts.).....Czech.	48·31 N	17·15 E
205	Malekula (I.) (mä-lā-kōō′lä) New Hebr.	16·44 S	167·45 E
162	Malhão da Estrêla (Mtn.) (mäl-you′N-dä-ĕs-trĕ′lä).Sp.	40·20 N	7·38 W
110	Malheur L. (mȧ-lōōr′).....Or.	43·16 N	118·37 W
110	Malheur R. (mȧ-lōōr′).....Or.	43·45 N	117·41 W
209	Mali.....Afr.	15·45 N	0·15 W
113	Malibu (mă′lĭ-bōō) Ca. (Los Angeles In.)	34·03 N	118·38 W
217	Malimba, Monts (Mts.).....Zaire	7·45 S	29·15 E
167	Malin (mȧ-lēn′).....Sov. Un.	50·44 N	29·15 E
124	Malinalco (mä-lē-näl′kō).....Mex.	18·54 N	99·31 W
124	Malinaltepec (mä-lē-näl-tȧ-pĕk′) Mex.	17·01 N	98·41 W
213	Malindi (mä-lēn′dē).....Ken.	3·14 S	40·04 E
159	Málinec (mä′lē-nyets′).....Czech.	48·31 N	19·40 E
154	Malin Hd.....N. Ire.	55·23 N	7·24 W
217	Malindi.....Ken.	3·13 S	40·07 E
154	Malinmore Hd. (mȧ′lĭn-mōr)..Ire.	54·45 N	8·30 W
174	Malino (mä′lĭ-nô) Sov. Un. (Moscow In.)	55·07 N	38·12 E
167	Malinovka (mȧ-lē-nôf′kȧ).Sov. Un.	49·50 N	36·43 E
165	Malkara (mäl′kȧ-rȧ).....Tur.	40·51 N	26·52 E
165	Malko Tŭrnovo (mäl′kō-t′r′nô-vȧ).Bul.	41·59 N	27·28 E
154	Mallaig.....Scot.	56·59 N	5·55 W
218	Mallawī (mȧ-lä′wē) Egypt (Nile In.)	27·43 N	30·49 E
107	Mallet Creek (măl′ĕt) Oh. (Cleveland In.)	41·10 N	81·55 W
163	Mallorca, Isla de (Majorca I.) (ē′s-lä-dĕ-mäl-yô′r-kä).Sp.	39·18 N	2·22 E
154	Mallow (măl′ō).....Ire.	52·07 N	9·04 W
155	Malmédy (mȧl-mā-dē′).....Bel.	50·25 N	6·01 E
212	Malmesbury (mämz′bēr-ĭ)..S. Afr.	33·30 S	18·35 E
156	Malmköping (mälm′chû′pĭng) Swe.	59·09 N	16·39 E
156	Malmö (mälm′û).....Swe.	55·36 N	12·58 E
173	Malmyzh (mȧl-mēzh′)...Sov. Un.	49·58 N	137·07 E
170	Malmyzh.....Sov. Un.	56·30 N	50·48 E
166	Maloarkhangelsk (mä′lô-ȧr-kän′gĕlsk).Sov. Un.	52·26 N	36·29 E
197	Malolos (mä-lô′lôs).....Phil. (In.)	14·51 N	120·49 E
174	Malomal′sk (mä-lô-mälsk′′) Sov. Un. (Urals In.)	58·47 N	59·55 E
105	Malone (mȧ-lōn′).....NY	44·50 N	74·20 W
216	Malonga.....Zaire	10·24 S	23·10 E
213	Maloti Mts.....Leso (Natal In.)	29·00 S	28·29 E
166	Maloyaroslavets (mä′lô-yä-rô-slä-vyĕts).Sov. Un.	55·01 N	36·25 E
170	Malozemel′skaya Tundra (Plains) Sov. Un.	67·30 N	50·00 E
136	Malpas (măl′pȧz).....Eng.	53·01 N	2·46 W
134	Malpelo, Isla de (I.) (mäl-pä′lō) Col.	3·55 N	81·30 W
98	Malpeque B. (môl-pĕk′).....Can.	46·30 N	63·47 W
111	Malta (môl′tȧ).....Mt.	48·20 N	107·50 W
146	Malta.....Eur.	35·52 N	13·30 E
212	Maltahöhe (mäl′tä-hō′ē) S. W. Afr.	24·45 S	16·45 E
125	Maltrata (mäl-trä′tä).....Mex.	18·48 N	97·16 W
197	Maluku (Moluccas) (Is.)...Indon.	2·40 S	127·15 E
197	Maluku, Laut (Molucca) (Sea) Indon.	0·15 N	125·41 E
211	Malūt.....Sud.	10·30 N	32·17 E
185	Mālvan.....India	16·08 N	73·32 E
117	Malvern (măl′vērn).....Ar.	34·21 N	92·47 W
173	Malyy Anyuy (R.).....Sov. Un.	67·52 N	164·30 E
173	Malyy Lyakhovskiye (I.).Sov. Un.	74·15 N	142·30 E
173	Malyy Tamir (I.).....Sov. Un.	78·10 N	107·30 E
125	Mamantel (mä-mȧn-tĕl′).....Mex.	18·36 N	91·06 W
106	Mamaroneck (măm′ȧ-rō-nĕk) NY (New York In.)	40·57 N	73·44 W
210	Mamau.....Gui.	10·26 N	12·07 W
217	Mambasa.....Zaire	1·21 N	29·03 E
197	Mamberamo (R.) (mäm-bȧ-rä′mō) Indon.	2·30 S	138·00 E
197	Mamburao (mäm-bōō′rä-ō) Phil. (In.)	13·14 N	120·35 E
162	Mamede, Serra de (Mts.) (sĕ′r-rä-dĕ-mä-mĕ′dĕ).Port.	39·29 N	7·11 W
210	Mamfe (mäm′fĕ).....Cam.	5·46 N	9·17 E
195	Mamihara (mä′mē-hä-rä).....Jap.	32·41 N	131·12 E
120	Mammoth Cave (măm′ŏth)...Ky.	37·10 N	86·04 W
120	Mammoth Cave Natl. Park...Ky.	37·20 N	86·21 W
111	Mammoth Hot Springs (măm′ŭth hôt sprĭngz).Wy.	44·55 N	110·50 W
185	Mamnoli.....India (In.)	19·17 N	73·15 E
134	Mamoré (R.) (mä-mô-rā′)....Bol.	13·19 S	65·27 W
214	Mampong.....Ghana	7·04 N	1·24 W
159	Mamry L. (mäm′rĭ).....Pol.	54·10 N	21·28 E
214	Man.....Ivory Coast	7·24 N	7·33 W
163	Manacor (mä-nä-kôr′).....Sp.	39·35 N	3·15 E
197	Manado.....Indon.	1·29 N	124·50 E
129	Managua (mä-nä′gwä).Cuba (In.)	22·14 N	82·17 W
126	Managua.....Nic.	12·10 N	86·16 W
126	Managua, Lago de (L.) (lä′gô-dĕ) Nic.	12·28 N	86·10 W
213	Manakara (mä-nä-kä′rŭ)....Mad.	22·17 S	48·06 E
213	Mananara (R.) (mä-nä-nä′rŭ) Mad.	23·15 S	48·15 E
213	Mananjary (mä-nän-zhä′rē)..Mad.	20·16 S	48·13 E
	Manáos, see Manaus		
184	Manasaroar (L.).....China	30·40 N	81·58 E
105	Manassas (mȧ-năs′ȧs).....Va.	38·45 N	77·30 W
188	Manassu.....China	44·30 N	86·00 E
135	Manaus (Manáos) (mä-nä′ōōzh) Braz.	3·01 S	60·00 W
104	Mancelona (măn-sē-lō′nȧ).....Mi.	44·50 N	85·05 W
162	Mancha Real (män′chä rā-äl′)..Sp.	37·48 N	3·37 W
174	Manchazh (män′chȧsh) Sov. Un. (Urals In.)	56·30 N	58·10 E
105	Manchester (măn′chĕs-tēr)....Ct.	41·45 N	72·30 W
148	Manchester.....Eng.	53·28 N	2·14 W
120	Manchester.....Ga.	32·50 N	84·37 W
109	Manchester.....Ia.	42·30 N	91·30 W
99	Manchester.....Ma. (In.)	42·35 N	70·47 W
113	Manchester...Mo. (St. Louis In.)	38·36 N	90·31 W
105	Manchester.....NH	43·00 N	71·30 W
104	Manchester.....Oh.	38·40 N	83·35 W
148	Manchester Ship Canal.....Eng.	53·20 N	2·40 W
192	Manchouli (Lupin) (män-chōō′lē) (lōō′pĭn).China	49·25 N	117·15 E
189	Manchuria (Reg.) (măn-chōō′rē-ȧ) China	48·00 N	124·58 E
186	Mand (R.).....Iran	28·20 N	52·30 E
156	Mandal (män′däl).....Nor.	58·03 N	7·28 E
188	Mandalay (măn′dȧ-lā).....Bur.	22·00 N	96·08 E
156	Mandalselv (R.) (män′dälsĕlv) Nor.	58·25 N	7·30 E
108	Mandan (măn′dăn).....ND	46·49 N	100·54 W
215	Mandara Mts. (män-dä′rä) Cam.-Nig.	10·15 N	13·23 E
183	Mandau Siak (R.) Indon. (Singapore In.)	1·03 N	101·25 E
217	Mandimba.....Moz.	14·21 S	35·39 E
127	Mandinga (män-dĭŋ′gä).....Pan.	9·32 N	79·04 W
184	Mandla.....India	22·43 N	80·23 E
165	Mándra (män′drȧ).....Grc.	38·06 N	23·32 E
213	Mandritsara (mȧn-drēt-sä′rȧ) Mad.	15·49 S	48·47 E
165	Manduria (män-dōō′rē-ä).....It.	40·23 N	17·41 E
185	Mandve.....India (In.)	18·47 N	72·52 E
185	Māndvi (mŭnd′vē)....India (In.)	19·29 N	72·53 E
184	Māndvi (mŭnd′vē).....India	22·54 N	69·23 E
185	Mandya.....India	12·40 N	77·00 E
218	Manfalūṭ (män-fȧ-loot′) Egypt (Nile In.)	27·18 N	30·59 E
164	Manfredonia (män-frȧ-dô′nyä).It.	41·39 N	15·55 E
164	Manfredónia, Golfo di (G.) (gôl-fô-dē).It.	41·34 N	16·05 E
135	Mangabeiras, Chap. das (Plains) (shä-pä′däs-däs-mäŋ-gä-bē′ē-räzh).Braz.	8·05 S	47·32 W
215	Manga (Reg.).....Niger	14·00 N	11·50 E
185	Mangalore (mŭŋ-gŭ-lōr′)....India	12·53 N	74·52 E
137	Mangaratiba (män-gä-rä-tē′bȧ) Braz. (Rio de Janeiro In).	22·56 S	44·03 W
197	Mangatarem (män′gȧ-tä′rĕm) Phil. (In.)	15·48 N	120·18 E
216	Mange.....Zaire	0·54 N	20·30 E
196	Mangkalihat, Tandjoeng (C.) (mäng′kȧ-lē-hät′).Indon.	1·25 N	119·55 E
128	Mangles, Islas de (ē′s-läs-dĕ-mäŋ′gläs) (măn′g′lz) Cuba	22·05 N	83·50 W
213	Mangoky (R.) (män-gō′kē)..Mad.	22·02 S	44·11 E
197	Mangole (I.).....Indon.	1·35 S	126·22 E
162	Mangualde (män-gwäl′dĕ)...Port.	40·38 N	7·44 W
136	Mangueira, L. da (L.) (män-gä′ē-rȧ).Braz.	33·15 S	52·45 W
116	Mangum (măŋ′gŭm).....Ok.	34·52 N	99·31 W
171	Mangyshlak, P.-ov. (Pen.) Sov. Un.	44·30 N	50·40 E
107	Manhattan.....Il. (Chicago In.)	41·25 N	87·29 W
117	Manhattan (măn-hăt′ăn).....Ks.	39·11 N	96·34 W
113	Manhattan Beach Ca. (Los Angeles In.)	33·53 N	118·24 W
137	Manhuaçu (män-ōōȧ′sōō) Braz. (Rio de Janeiro In.)	20·17 S	42·01 W
137	Manhumirim (män-ōō-mē-rē′N) Braz. (Rio de Janeiro In.)	20·22 S	41·57 W
213	Mania (R.) (män′yä).....Mad.	19·52 S	46·02 E
135	Manicoré (mä-nē-kō-rā′)....Braz.	5·53 S	61·13 W
91	Manicouagane (R.).....Can.	50·00 N	68·35 W
91	Manicouagane, Lac (L.).....Can.	51·30 N	68·19 W
135	Manicuare (mä-nē-kwä′rē) Ven. (In.)	10·35 N	64·10 W
96	Manikuagen, Rivière (R.)....Can.	49·30 N	68·30 W
199	Manihiki Is. (mä′nē-hē′kē) Oceania	9·40 S	158·00 W
197	Manila (mȧ-nĭl′ȧ).....Phil. (In.)	14·37 N	121·00 E
197	Manila B.....Phil. (In.)	14·38 N	120·46 E
188	Manipur (State).....India	25·00 N	94·00 E
171	Manisa (mä′nē-sȧ).....Tur.	38·40 N	27·30 E
104	Manistee (măn-ĭs-tē′).....Mi.	44·15 N	86·20 W
104	Manistee (R.).....Mi.	44·25 N	85·45 W
109	Manistique (măn-ĭs-tēk′).....Mi.	45·58 N	86·16 W
109	Manistique (L.).....Mi.	46·14 N	85·30 W
109	Manistique (R.).....Mi.	46·05 N	86·09 W
90	Manitoba (Prov.) (măn-ĭ-tō′bȧ) Can.	55·12 N	97·29 W
95	Manitoba (L.).....Can.	51·00 N	98·45 W
94	Manito L. (măn′ĭ-tō).....Can.	52·45 N	109·45 W
109	Manitou (I.) (măn′ĭ-tōō).....Mi.	47·21 N	87·33 W
109	Manitou (L.).....Can.	49·21 N	93·01 W
104	Manitou Is.....Mi.	45·05 N	86·00 W
104	Manitoulin I. (măn-ĭ-tōō′lĭn).Can.	45·45 N	81·30 W
116	Manitou Springs.....Co.	38·51 N	104·58 W
109	Manitowoc (măn-ĭ-tô-wŏk′)...Wi.	44·05 N	87·42 W
97	Maniwaki.....Can.	46·23 N	76·00 W
134	Manizales (mä-nē-zä′läs).Col. (In.)	5·05 N	75·31 W
212	Manjacaze (man′yä-kä′zĕ)...Moz.	24·37 S	33·49 E
184	Mānjra (R.).....India	18·18 N	77·00 E
116	Mankato (măn-kā′tō).....Ks.	39·45 N	98·12 W
109	Mankato.....Mn.	44·10 N	93·59 W

ng-sing; ŋ-baŋk; N-nasalized n; nŏd; cŏmmit; ōld; ôbey; ôrder; fōōd; fŏŏt; ou-out; s-soft; sh-dish; th-thin; pūre; ûnite; ûrn; stŭd; circŭs; ü-as "y" in study; ′-indeterminate vowel.

310 Mankim — Marple

PRONOUNCING INDEX

Page	Name Pronunciation Region	Lat. °′	Long. °′
215	Mankim....Cam.	5·01 N	12·00 E
163	Manlleu (män-lyā'ōō)....Sp.	42·00 N	2·16 E
202	Manly (man'lĭ) Austl. (Sydney In.)	33·48 S	151·16 E
185	Mannar (må-när')....Sri Lanka	9·48 N	80·03 E
184	Mannar, G. of....India	8·47 N	78·33 E
149	Mannersdorf am Leithagebirge Aus. (Vienna In.)	47·58 N	16·36 E
158	Mannheim (män'hīm)....F.R.G.	49·30 N	8·31 E
109	Manning (măn'ĭng)....Ia.	41·53 N	95·04 W
121	Manning....SC	33·41 N	80·12 W
104	Mannington (măn'ĭng-tŭn)...WV	39·30 N	80·55 W
164	Mannu (R.) (mä'n-nōō)....It.	39·32 N	9·03 E
214	Mano (R.)....Lib.	7·00 N	11·25 W
119	Man of War B....Ba.	21·05 N	74·05 W
119	Man of War Chan....Ba.	22·45 N	76·10 W
197	Manokwari (må-nŏk-wä'rē).Indon.	0·56 S	134·10 E
217	Manono....Zaire	7·18 S	27·25 E
95	Manor (măn'ẽr)....Can.	49·36 N	102·05 W
112	Manor....Wa. (Portland In.)	45·45 N	122·36 W
185	Manori....India (In.)	19·13 N	72·43 E
161	Manosque (må-nōsk')....Fr.	43·51 N	5·48 E
100	Manotick....Can. (Ottawa In.)	45·13 N	75·41 W
163	Manresa (män-rā'sä)....Sp.	41·44 N	1·52 E
217	Mansa....Zambia	11·12 S	28·53 E
214	Mansabá....Guinea-Bissau	12·18 N	15·15 W
91	Mansel (I.) (măn'sĕl)....Can.	61·56 N	81·10 W
134	Manseriche, Pongo de (Water Gap) (pŏ'n-gô-dĕ-män-sĕ-rē'chĕ).Peru	4·15 S	77·45 W
148	Mansfield (mănz'fēld)....Eng.	53·08 N	1·12 W
119	Mansfield....La.	32·02 N	93·43 W
104	Mansfield....Oh.	40·45 N	82·30 W
110	Mansfield....Wa.	47·48 N	119·39 W
105	Mansfield, Mt....Vt.	44·30 N	72·45 W
148	Mansfield Woodhouse (wŏŏd-hous).Eng.	53·08 N	1·12 W
135	Manso (R.)....Braz.	13·30 S	51·45 W
134	Manta (män'tä)....Ec.	1·03 S	80·16 W
91	Manteno (măn-tē-nō) Il. (Chicago In.)	41·15 N	87·50 W
121	Manteo....NC	35·55 N	75·40 W
161	Mantes-la-Jolie (mäNt-ĕ-lä-zhŏ-lē') Fr. (Paris In.)	48·59 N	1·42 E
115	Manti (măn'tī)....Ut.	39·15 N	111·40 W
137	Manitqueira, Serra da (Mts.) (sĕr'rä dä män-tē-kā'ê-rå) Braz. (Rio de Janeiro In.)	22·40 S	45·12 W
164	Mantova (Mantua) (män'tô-vä) (măn'tû-å).It.	45·09 N	10·47 E
128	Mantua (män-tōō'å)....Cuba	22·20 N	84·15 W
113	Mantua (măn'tû-å) Ut. (Salt Lake City In.)	41·30 N	111·57 W
	Mantua, see Mantova		
98	Manuan (L.) (mä-nōō'ån)...Can.	50·36 N	70·50 W
98	Manuan (R.)....Can.	50·15 N	70·30 W
197	Manui (Is.) (mä-nōō'ē)....Indon.	3·35 S	123·38 E
197	Manus (I.) (mä'nōōs).Pap. N. Gui.	2·22 S	146·22 E
119	Manvel (măn'vel)....Tx. (In.)	29·28 N	95·22 W
106	Manville (măn'vĭl) NJ (New York In.)	40·33 N	74·36 W
106	Manville....RI (Providence In.)	41·57 N	71·27 W
171	Manych (R.) (mä-nĭch')..Sov. Un.	47·00 N	41·10 E
147	Manych Dep....Sov. Un.	46·32 N	42·44 E
171	Manych-Gudilo (Lake)...Sov. Un.	46·40 N	42·50 E
218	Manzala L.....Egypt (Nile In.)	31·14 N	32·04 E
134	Manzanares (män-sä-nä'rĕs) Col. (In.)	5·15 N	75·09 W
163	Manzanares (R.) (mänz-nä'rĕs) Sp. (Madrid In.)	40·36 N	3·48 W
163	Manzanares, Canal de (kä-nä'l-dĕ-män-thä-nä'rĕs) Sp. (Madrid In.)	40·20 N	3·38 W
128	Manzanillo (män'zä-nēl'yō)..Cuba	20·20 N	77·05 W
124	Manzanillo....Mex.	19·02 N	104·21 W
129	Manzanillo, Bahía de (B.)...Hai.	19·55 N	71·50 W
124	Manzanillo, Bahía de (B.) (bä-ē'ä-dĕ-män-zä-nē'l-yō).Mex.	19·00 N	104·38 W
127	Manzanillo, Punta (Pt.)....Pan.	9·40 N	79·33 W
194	Manzovka (mån-zhô'f-kå) Sov. Un.	44·16 N	132·13 E
215	Mao (mä'ô)....Chad	14·07 N	15·19 E
129	Mao....Dom. Rep.	19·35 N	71·10 W
197	Maoke, Pegunungan (Mtn.) Indon.	4·00 S	138·00 E
193	Maoming....China	21·55 N	110·40 E
125	Mapastepec (ma-päs-tå-pĕk').Mex.	15·24 N	92·52 W
197	Mapia (I.) (mä'pē-å)....Indon.	0·57 N	134·22 E
118	Mapimí (mä-pē-mē')....Mex.	25·50 N	103·50 W
94	Maple Creek (mā'p'l) (crēk).Can.	49·55 N	109·27 W
100	Maple Grove (grōv) Can. (Montreal In.)	45·19 N	73·51 W
107	Maple Heights.Oh. (Cleveland In.)	41·25 N	81·34 W
106	Maple Shade (shād) NJ (Philadelphia In.)	39·57 N	75·01 W
112	Maple Valley (văl'ē) Wa. (Seattle In.)	47·24 N	122·02 W
113	Maplewood (wŏŏd) Mn. (Minneapolis, St. Paul In.)	45·00 N	93·03 W
113	Maplewood....Mo. (St. Louis In.)	38·37 N	90·20 W
213	Mapumulo (mä-pä-mōō'lō) S. Afr. (Natal In.)	29·12 S	31·05 E
212	Maputo (Lourenço Marques).Moz.	26·50 S	32·30 E
197	Maqueda Chan. (mä-kā'dä) Phil. (In.)	13·40 N	123·52 E
212	Maquela do Zombo (må-kā'lå dōō zôm'bōō).Ang.	6·08 S	15·15 E
109	Maquoketa (må-kō-kê-tå)....Ia.	42·04 N	90·42 W
109	Maquoketa (R.)....Ia.	42·08 N	90·40 W
136	Mar, Serra do (Mts.) (sĕr'rå dōō mär').Braz.	26·30 S	49·15 W
134	Maracaibo (mä-rä-kī'bō)....Ven.	10·38 N	71·45 W
134	Maracaibo, Lago de (L.) (lä'gô-dĕ-mä-rä-kī'bō).Ven.	9·55 N	72·13 W
135	Maracay (mä-rä-kāy')..Ven. (In.)	10·15 N	67·35 W
211	Marādah....Libya	29·10 N	19·07 E
215	Maradi (må-rå-dē')....Niger	13·29 N	7·06 E
171	Marāgheh....Iran	37·20 N	46·10 E
213	Maraisburg....S. Afr. (Johannesburg & Pretoria In.)	26·12 S	27·57 E
117	Marais des Cygnes (R.)....Ks.	38·30 N	95·30 W
135	Marajó, Ilha de (I.) (mä-rä-zhō') Braz.	0·30 S	50·00 W
217	Maralal....Ken.	1·06 N	36·42 E
215	Marali....Cen. Afr. Rep.	6·01 N	18·24 E
217	Marandelles (mä-rån-dāl'ås)...Rh.	18·10 S	31·36 E
135	Maranguape (mä-rån-gwä'pĕ) Braz.	3·48 S	38·38 W
	Maranhão, see São Luis		
135	Maranhão (State) (mä-rän-youN) Braz.	5·15 S	45·52 W
203	Maranoa (R.) (mä-rä-nō'ä)..Austl.	27·01 S	148·03 E
163	Marano di Napoli (mä-rä'nô-dē-nä'pô-lē) It. (Naples In.)	40·39 N	14·12 E
134	Marañón, Rio (R.) (rē'ō-mä-rä-nyōn').Peru	4·26 S	75·08 W
135	Marapanim (mä-rä-pä-nē'N).Braz.	0·45 S	47·42 W
171	Maraş (mä-räsh')....Tur.	37·40 N	36·50 W
96	Marathon....Can.	48·50 N	86·10 W
121	Marathon (măr'å-thŏn)...Fl. (In.)	24·41 N	81·06 W
107	Marathon....Oh. (Cincinnati In.)	39·09 N	83·59 W
196	Maratua (I.)....Indon.	2·14 N	118·30 E
124	Maravatio (mä-rå-vä'tê-ō)...Mex.	19·54 N	100·25 W
211	Marawi....Sud.	18·07 N	31·57 E
204	Marble Bar (märb''l bär)...Austl.	21·15 S	119·15 E
115	Marble Can. (mär'b'l)....Az.	36·21 N	111·48 W
218	Marble Hall (hâll)....S. Afr. (Johannesburg & Pretoria In.)	24·59 S	29·19 E
99	Marblehead (mär'b'l-hĕd) Ma. (In.)	42·30 N	70·51 W
158	Marburg (mär'bōōrgh)....F.R.G.	50·49 N	8·46 E
216	Marca, Ponta da (Pt.)....Ang.	16·31 S	11·42 E
126	Marcala (mär-kä-lä)....Hond.	14·08 N	88·01 W
166	Marche (Reg.) (mär'kā)....It.	43·35 N	12·33 E
149	Marchegg....Aus. (Vienna In.)	48·18 N	16·55 E
144	Marchena (mär-chā'nä)....Sp.	37·20 N	5·25 W
134	Marchena (I.) (ĕ's-lä-mär-chĕ'nä) Ec.	0·29 N	90·31 W
149	Marchfeld (Reg.) Aus. (Vienna In.)	48·14 N	16·37 E
117	Marceline (mär-sê-lēn')....Mo.	39·42 N	92·56 W
137	Marcos Paz (mär-kōs' päz) Arg. (Buenos Aires In.)	34·49 S	58·51 W
198	Marcus (I.) (mär'kŭs)....Asia	24·00 N	155·00 E
106	Marcus Hook (mär'kŭs hŏŏk) Pa. (Phildelphia In.)	39·49 N	75·25 W
105	Marcy, Mt. (mär'sē)....NY	44·10 N	73·55 W
137	Mar de Espanha (mär-dĕ-ĕs-på'nyå) Braz. (Rio de Janeiro In.)	21·53 S	43·00 W
136	Mar del Plata (mär dĕl plä'ta).Arg.	37·59 S	57·35 W
171	Mardin (mär-dēn')....Tur.	37·25 N	40·40 E
205	Mare (I.) (må-rā')....N. Cal.	21·53 S	168·30 E
154	Maree (L.) (mä-rē')....Scot.	57·40 N	5·44 W
109	Marengo (må-rĕŋ'gō)....Ia.	41·47 N	92·04 W
160	Marennes (må-rĕn')....Fr.	45·49 N	1·08 W
161	Mareuil-sur-Ourcq (mä-rû'yĕ-sür-ōōrk').Fr. (Paris In.)	49·08 N	2·04 E
118	Marfa (mär'få)....Tx.	30·19 N	104·01 W
167	Marganets....Sov. Un.	47·41 N	34·33 E
122	Margarita (mär-gōō-rē'tä) C. Z. (In.)	9·20 N	79·55 W
135	Margarita, Isla de (I.) (mär-gå-rē'tå).Ven. (In.)	11·00 N	64·15 W
154	Margate (mär'gāt)....Eng.	51·21 N	1·17 E
213	Margate (mär-gāt') S. Afr. (Natal In.)	30·52 S	30·21 E
217	Margherita Pk....Afr.	0·22 N	29·51 E
98	Marguerite (R.)....Can.	50·39 N	66·42 W
170	Mari (A. S. S. R.) (mä'rê).Sov. Un.	56·20 N	48·00 E
98	Maria (må-rē'å)....Can.	48·10 N	66·04 W
162	Maria, Sierra de (Mts.) (sē-ĕ'r-rä-dĕ-mä-ryä).Sp.	37·42 N	2·25 W
124	María Cleofas (I.) (mä-rē'ä klā'ô-fäs).Mex.	21·17 N	106·14 W
156	Mariager (mä-rê-ägh'ẽr)....Den.	56·38 N	10·00 E
156	Mariager Fd....Den.	56·44 N	10·32 E
124	María Magdalena (I.) (mä rē'ä mäg-dä-lā'nä).Mex.	21·25 N	106·23 W
137	Mariana (mä-ryä'nä) Braz. (Rio de Janeiro In.)	20·23 S	43·24 W
198	Mariana Is. (mä-rê-ä'nå)..Oceania	17·20 N	145·00 E
198	Mariana Trench....Oceania	12·00 N	144·00 E
129	Marianao (mä-rê-ä-nä'ō) Cuba (In.)	23·05 N	82·26 W
117	Marianna (mā-rĭ-ăn'å)....Ar.	34·45 N	90·45 W
120	Marianna....Fl.	30·46 N	85·14 W
107	Marianna....Pa. (Pittsburgh In.)	40·01 N	80·05 W
136	Mariano Acosta (mä-rēä'nô-å-kŏs'tä) Arg. (Buenos Aires In.)	34·28 S	58·48 W
148	Mariánské Lázně (mär'yån-skĕ'läz'nyĕ).Czech.	49·58 N	12·42 E
122	Marias, Islas (Is.) (mä-rē'äs) Mex.	21·30 N	106·40 W
111	Marias R. (må-rī'åz)....Mt.	48·15 N	110·50 W
127	Mariato, Punta (Pt.)....Pan.	7·17 N	81·09 W
156	Maribo (mä'rê-bô)....Den.	54·46 N	11·29 E
164	Maribor (mä're-bôr)....Yugo.	46·33 N	15·37 E
137	Maricá (mä-rē-kä') Braz. (Rio de Janeiro In.)	22·55 S	42·49 W
197	Maricaban (I.) (mä-rê-kä-bän') Phil. (In.)	13·40 N	120·44 E
218	Marico R. (mä'rĭ-cô)....S. Afr. (Johannesburg & Pretoria In.)	24·53 S	26·22 E
220	Marie Byrd Land (må rē' bûrd') Ant.	78·00 S	130·00 W
156	Mariefred (mä-rē'ĕ-frĭd)....Swe.	59·17 N	17·09 E
127	Marie Galante I. (må-rē' gå-länt') Guad. (In.)	15·58 N	61·05 W
	Mariehamn, see Maarianhamina		
156	Mariestad (mä-rē'ĕ-städ')....Swe.	58·43 N	13·45 E
106	Marietta (mā-rĭ-ĕt'å) Ga. (Atlanta In.)	33·57 N	84·33 W
104	Marietta....Oh.	39·25 N	81·30 W
117	Marietta....Ok.	33·53 N	97·07 W
112	Marietta....Wa. (Vancouver In.)	48·48 N	122·35 W
172	Mariinsk (må-re'ĭnsk)....Sov. Un.	56·15 N	87·28 E
157	Marijampole (mä-rê-yäm-pô'lĕ) Sov. Un.	54·33 N	23·26 E
218	Marikana (mă'-rĭ-kä-nå)...S. Afr. (Johannesburg & Pretoria In.)	25·40 S	27·28 E
135	Marília (mä-rē'lyå)....Braz.	22·02 S	49·48 W
216	Marimba....Ang.	8·28 S	17·08 E
197	Marinduque (I.) (mä-rên-dōō'kā) Phil. (In.)	13·14 N	121·45 E
113	Marine (må-rēn').Il. (St. Louis In.)	38·48 N	89·47 W
104	Marine City....Mi.	42·45 N	82·30 W
113	Marine L....Mn. (Minneapolis, St. Paul In.)	45·13 N	92·55 W
113	Marine on St. Croix (ăn sĕN krōō-ä) Mn. (Minneapolis, St. Paul In.)	45·11 N	92·47 W
109	Marinette (mär-ĭ-nĕt')....Wi.	45·05 N	87·40 W
216	Maringa (R.) (mä-rĭŋ'gä)...Zaire	1·15 N	20·05 E
162	Marinha Grande (mä-rēn'yå grän'dĕ).Port.	39·49 N	8·53 W
120	Marion (mär'ĭ-ŭn)....Al.	32·36 N	87·19 W
104	Marion....Il.	37·40 N	88·55 W
104	Marion....In.	40·35 N	85·45 W
109	Marion....Ia.	42·01 N	91·39 W
117	Marion....Ks.	38·21 N	97·02 W
120	Marion....Ky.	37·19 N	88·05 W
121	Marion....NC	35·40 N	82·00 W
108	Marion....ND	46·37 N	98·20 W
104	Marion....Oh.	40·35 N	83·10 W
121	Marion....SC	34·08 N	79·23 W
121	Marion....Va.	36·48 N	81·33 W
121	Marion (R.)....SC	33·25 N	80·35 W
205	Marion Rf....Austl.	18·57 S	151·31 E
137	Mariposa (mä-rê-pô'sä) Chile (Santiago In.)	35·33 S	71·21 W
114	Mariposa Cr....Ca.	37·14 N	120·30 W
134	Mariquita (mä-rē-kē'tä).Col. (In.)	5·13 N	74·52 W
135	Mariscal Estigarribia (mä-rēs-käl'ĕs-tē-gär-rē'byä) Par.	22·03 S	60·28 W
136	Marisco, Ponta do (Pt.) (pô'n-tä-dô-mä-rē's-kō) Braz. (Rio de Janeiro In.)	23·01 S	43·17 W
161	Maritime Alps (Mts.) (mă'rĭ-tīm ălps).Fr.-It.	44·20 N	7·02 E
165	Maritsa (R.) (mä'rê-tså).Grc.-Tur.	40·43 N	26·19 E
197	Mariveles....Phil. (In.)	14·27 N	120·29 E
183	Marj Uyan...Leb. (Palestine In.)	33·21 N	35·36 E
218	Marka....Som. (Horn of Afr. In.)	1·45 N	44·47 E
188	Marka Kul' (L.)....Sov. Un.	49·15 N	85·48 E
156	Markaryd (mär'kä-rüd)....Swe.	56·30 N	13·34 E
117	Marked Tree (märkt trē)....Ar.	35·31 N	90·26 W
149	Marken, I..Neth. (Amsterdam In.)	52·26 N	5·08 E
148	Market Bosworth (bŏz'wûrth) Eng.	52·37 N	1·23 W
148	Market Deeping (dēp'ĭng)...Eng.	52·40 N	0·19 W
148	Market Drayton (drā'tŭn)...Eng.	52·54 N	2·29 W
148	Market Harborough (här'bŭr-ô) Eng.	52·28 N	0·55 W
148	Market Rasen (rā'zĕn)....Eng.	53·23 N	0·21 W
100	Markham (märk'åm) Can. (Toronto In.)	43·53 N	79·15 W
220	Markham, Mt....Ant.	82·59 S	159·30 E
167	Markovka (mär-kôf'kå)..Sov. Un.	49·32 N	39·34 E
173	Markovo (mär'kô-vô)....Sov. Un.	64·46 N	170·48 E
184	Markrāna....India	27·08 N	74·43 E
171	Marks....Sov. Un.	51·40 N	46·40 E
119	Marksville (märks'vĭl)....La.	31·09 N	92·05 W
149	Markt Indersdorf (märkt ĕn'dĕrs-dōrf) F.R.G. (Munich In.)	48·22 N	11·23 E
158	Marktredwitz (märk-rĕd'vēts) F.R.G.	50·02 N	12·05 E
149	Markt Schwaben (märkt shvä'bĕn) F.R.G. (Munich In.)	48·12 N	11·52 E
161	Marl (märl)....F.R.G. (Ruhr In.)	51·40 N	7·05 E
106	Marlboro....NJ (New York In.)	40·18 N	74·15 W
99	Marlborough....Ma. (In.)	42·21 N	71·33 W
104	Marlette (mär-lĕt')....Mi.	43·25 N	83·05 W
119	Marlin (mär'lĭn)....Tx.	31·18 N	96·52 W
105	Marlinton (mär'lĭn-tŭn)....WV	38·15 N	80·10 W
148	Marlow (mär'lō) Eng. (London In.)	51·33 N	0·46 W
116	Marlow....Ok.	34·38 N	97·56 W
128	Marls, The (Shoals) (märls)...Ba.	26·30 N	77·15 W
160	Marmande (mår-mäNd')....Fr.	44·30 N	0·10 E
165	Marmara (I.) (mär'må-rå)...Tur.	40·38 N	27·35 E
171	Marmara Denizi (Sea)....Tur.	40·40 N	28·00 E
108	Marmarth (mär'mårth)....ND	46·19 N	103·57 W
125	Mar Muerto (L.) (mär-mōōĕ'r-tô) Mex.	16·13 N	94·22 W
149	Marne (mär'nĕ) F.R.G. (Hamburg In.)	53·57 N	9·01 E
160	Marne (R.) (märn)....Fr.	49·08 N	3·39 E
134	Maroa (mä-rō'ä)....Ven.	2·43 N	67·37 W
213	Maroantsetra (må-rō-äŋ-tsä'trå) Mad.	15·18 S	49·48 E
134	Maro Jarapeto (Mtn.) (mä-rô-hä-rä-pĕ'tô).Col. (In.)	6·29 N	76·39 W
213	Maromokotro (Mtn.)....Mad.	14·00 S	49·11 E
135	Maroni (R.) (må-rō'nē) Fr. Gu.-Sur.	3·02 N	53·54 W
215	Maroua (mär'wä)....Cam.	10·36 N	14·20 E
149	Marple (mär'p'l)....Eng.	53·24 N	2·04 W

Page	Name Pronunciation Region	Lat. °′	Long. °′
218	Marquard.....S. Afr. (Johannesburg & Pretoria In.)	28·41 S	27·26 E
199	Marquesas Is. (mär-kĕ'säs) Fr. Polynesia	8·50 S	141·00 W
121	Marquesas Keys (Is.) (mår-kē'zås) Fl. (In.)	24·37 N	82·15 W
137	Marquês de Valença (mår-kĕ's-dĕ-vä-lĕ'n-sȧ) Braz. (Rio de Janeiro In.)	22·16 S	43·42 W
100	Marquette (mär-kĕt') Can. (Winnipeg In.)	50·04 N	97·43 W
109	Marquette.....Mi.	46·32 N	87·25 W
119	Marquez (mär-kāz').....Tx.	31·14 N	96·15 W
211	Marra, Jabal (Mt.) (jĕb'ĕl mär'ä) Sud.	13·00 N	23·47 E
210	Marrakech (mår-rä'kĕsh)....Mor.	31·38 N	8·00 W
203	Marree (măr'rē).....Austl.	29·38 S	137·55 E
106	Marrero....La. (New Orleans In.)	29·55 N	90·06 W
162	Marroqui, Pta. (mä-rō-kē')....Sp.	36·03 N	5·36 W
217	Marrupa.....Moz.	13·08 S	37·30 E
107	Mars (märz)..Pa. (Pittsburgh In.)	40·42 N	80·01 W
217	Marsabit.....Ken.	2·20 N	37·59 E
164	Marsala (mär-sä'lä).....It.	37·48 N	12·28 E
148	Marsden (märz'dĕn).....Eng.	53·36 N	1·55 W
160	Marseille (mår-så'y')....Fr. (In.)	43·18 N	5·25 E
160	Marseille, Canal de (mår-så-yaN') Fr. (In.)	43·34 N	5·16 E
104	Marseilles (mär-sĕlz').....Il.	41·20 N	88·40 W
104	Marshall (mär'shăl).....Il.	39·20 N	87·40 W
104	Marshall.....Mi.	42·20 N	84·55 W
108	Marshall.....Mn.	44·28 N	95·49 W
117	Marshall.....Mo.	39·07 N	93·12 W
119	Marshall.....Tx.	32·33 N	94·22 W
198	Marshall Is...Pac. Is. Trust Ter.	10·00 N	165·00 E
109	Marshalltown (mär'shăl-toun)..Ia.	42·02 N	92·55 W
120	Marshallville (mär'shăl-vĭl)...Ga.	32·29 N	83·55 W
99	Marshfield (märsh'fēld)..Ma. (In.)	42·06 N	70·43 W
117	Marshfield.....Mo.	37·20 N	92·53 W
109	Marshfield.....Wi.	44·40 N	90·10 W
128	Marsh Harbour.....Ba.	26·30 N	77·00 W
107	Mars Hill (märz' hĭl') In. (Indianapolis In.)	39·43 N	86·15 W
98	Mars Hill.....Me.	46·34 N	67·54 W
156	Marstrand (mär'stränd).....Swe.	57·54 N	11·33 E
174	Marsyaty (märs'yȧ-tĭ) Sov. Un. (Urals In.)	60·03 N	60·28 E
119	Mart (märt).....Tx.	31·32 N	96·49 W
196	Martaban, G. of (mär-tŭ-bän') Bur.	16·34 N	96·58 E
196	Martapura.....Indon.	3·19 S	114·45 E
105	Marthas Vineyard (I.) (mär'thȧz vĭn'yȧrd).Ma.	41·25 N	70·35 W
128	Martí (mär-tē').....Cuba	23·00 N	80·55 W
158	Martigny-Bourg (mår-tē-nyē') Switz.	46·06 N	7·00 E
160	Martigues (mår-tēg')....Fr. (In.)	43·24 N	5·05 E
120	Martin (mär'tĭn).....Tn.	36·20 N	88·45 W
120	Martin (R.).....Al.	32·40 N	86·05 W
165	Martina Franca (mär-tē'nä fräŋ'kä).It.	40·43 N	17·21 E
112	Martinez (mär-tē'nĕz) Ca. (San Francisco In.)	38·01 N	122·08 W
113	Martinez...Tx. (San Antonio In.)	29·25 N	98·20 W
123	Martinique (mår-tē-nēk')...N. A.	14·50 N	60·40 W
101	Martin Pt.....Ak.	70·10 N	142·00 W
105	Martinsburg (mär'tĭnz-bûrg)..WV	39·30 N	78·00 W
104	Martins Ferry (mär'tĭnz).....Oh.	40·05 N	80·45 W
104	Martinsville (mär'tĭnz-vĭl).....In.	39·25 N	86·25 W
121	Martinsville.....Va.	36·40 N	79·53 W
162	Martos (mär'tōs).....Sp.	37·43 N	3·58 W
90	Martre, Lac la (L.) (läk la märtr).Can.	63·24 N	119·58 W
195	Marugame (mä'rōō-gä'mā)...Jap.	34·19 N	133·48 E
217	Marungu (Mts.).....Tan.	7·50 S	29·50 E
156	Mårvatn (L.) (môr-vät'n)....Nor.	60·10 N	8·28 E
185	Marve.....India (In.)	19·12 N	72·43 E
162	Marvín (mär-vē'n).....Sp.	42·24 N	8·40 W
141	Mary (mä'rē).....Sov. Un.	37·45 N	61·47 E
167	Mar'yanskaya (mår-yän'skȧ-yȧ) Sov. Un.	45·04 N	38·39 E
203	Maryborough (mā'rĭ-bŭr-ô).Austl.	25·35 S	152·40 E
203	Maryborough.....Austl.	37·00 S	143·50 E
103	Maryland (State) (mĕr'ĭ-lănd) U. S.	39·10 N	76·25 W
110	Mary's R. (mā'rĭz).....Nv.	41·25 N	115·10 W
99	Marystown (mâr'ĭz-toun)....Can.	47·11 N	55·10 W
98	Marysville.....Can.	45·59 N	66·35 W
114	Marysville.....Ca.	39·09 N	121·37 W
117	Marysville.....Ks.	39·49 N	96·38 W
104	Marysville.....Oh.	40·15 N	83·25 W
112	Marysville.....Wa. (Seattle In.)	48·03 N	122·11 W
218	Maryūt (L.).....Egypt (Nile In.)	31·09 N	30·10 E
113	Maryville (mā'rĭ-vĭl) Il. (St. Louis In.)	38·44 N	89·57 W
117	Maryville.....Mo.	40·21 N	94·51 W
120	Maryville.....Tn.	35·44 N	83·59 W
211	Mārzuq.....Libya	26·00 N	14·09 E
211	Marzūq, Idehan (Dunes)...Libya	24·30 N	13·00 E
217	Masai Steppe (Plat.).....Tan.	4·30 S	36·40 E
217	Masaka.....Ug.	0·20 S	31·44 E
215	Masalasef.....Chad	11·43 N	17·08 E
196	Masalembo-Besar (I.).....Indon.	5·40 S	114·28 E
194	Masan (mä-sän').....Kor.	35·10 N	128·31 E
217	Masangwe.....Tan.	5·28 S	30·05 E
217	Masasi (mä-sä'sē).....Tan.	10·43 S	38·48 E
126	Masatepe (mä-sä-tĕ'pĕ).....Nic.	11·57 N	86·10 W
126	Masaya (mä-sä'yä).....Nic.	11·58 N	86·05 W
197	Masbate (mäs-bä'tä)...Phil. (In.)	12·21 N	123·38 E
197	Masbate (I.).....Phil. (In.)	12·19 N	123·03 E
210	Mascara (mäs'kä-rä) (mås-kȧ-rä') Alg.	35·25 N	0·08 E
220	Mascarene Is.....Mauritius	20·20 S	56·40 E
120	Mascot (măs'kŏt).....Tn.	36·04 N	83·45 W
124	Mascota (mäs-kō'tä).....Mex.	20·33 N	104·45 W
124	Mascota (R.).....Mex.	20·33 N	104·52 W
100	Mascouche (mȧs-kōōsh') Can. (Montreal In.)	45·45 N	73·36 W
100	Mascouche (R.) Can. (Montreal In.)	45·44 N	73·45 W
113	Mascoutah (măs-kū'tā) Il. (St. Louis In.)	38·29 N	89·48 W
212	Maseru (măz'ēr-ōō).....Leso.	29·09 S	27·11 E
186	Mashhad.....Iran	36·17 N	59·30 E
211	Mashra'ar-Ragg.....Sud.	8·28 N	29·15 E
216	Masi-Manimba.....Zaire	4·46 S	17·55 E
211	Masindi (mä-sēn'dē).....Ug.	1·44 N	31·43 E
186	Masjed Soleymān.....Iran	31·45 N	49·17 E
154	Mask, Lough (B.) (lŏk mȧsk)..Ire.	53·35 N	9·23 W
174	Maslovo (mäs'lô-vô) Sov. Un. (Urals In.)	60·08 N	60·28 E
104	Mason (mā's'n).....Mi.	42·35 N	84·25 W
107	Mason.....Oh. (Cincinnati In.)	39·22 N	84·18 W
118	Mason.....Tx.	30·46 N	99·14 W
109	Mason City.....Ia.	43·08 N	93·14 W
99	Masquaro (L.).....Can.	50·34 N	60·40 W
164	Massa (mäs'sä).....It.	44·02 N	10·08 E
103	Massachusetts (State) (măs-ȧ-chōō'sĕts).U. S.	42·20 N	72·30 W
98	Massachusetts B.....Ma.	42·26 N	70·20 W
164	Massafra (mäs-sä'frä).....It.	40·35 N	17·05 E
164	Massa Marittima.....It.	43·03 N	10·55 E
106	Massapequa..NY (New York In.)	40·41 N	73·28 W
	Massaua, see Mesewa		
105	Massena (mă-sē'nȧ).....NY	44·55 N	74·55 W
90	Masset (măs'ĕt).....Can.	54·02 N	132·09 W
92	Masset Inlet.....Can.	53·42 N	132·20 W
160	Massif Central (Plat.) (mȧ-sēf' säN-trȧl').Fr.	45·12 N	3·02 E
104	Massillon (măs'ĭ-lŏn).....Oh.	40·50 N	81·35 W
212	Massinga (mä-sĭn'gä).....Moz.	23·18 S	35·18 E
115	Massive, Mt. (măs'ĭv).....Co.	39·05 N	106·30 W
100	Masson (măs-sŭn) Can. (Ottawa In.)	45·33 N	75·25 W
195	Masuda (mä-sōō'dȧ).....Jap.	34·42 N	131·53 E
159	Masuria (Reg.).....Pol.	53·40 N	21·10 E
216	Matadi (mȧ-tä'dē).....Zaire	5·49 S	13·27 E
126	Matagalpa (mä-tä-gäl'pä)...Nic.	12·52 N	85·57 W
91	Matagami (L.) (mȧ-tä-gä'mē) Can.	50·10 N	78·28 W
119	Matagorda B. (măt-ȧ-gôr'dȧ)..Tx.	28·32 N	96·13 W
119	Matagorda I.....Tx.	28·13 N	96·27 W
214	Matam (mä-täm').....Senegal	15·40 N	13·15 W
118	Matamoros (mä-tä-mō'rôs)..Mex.	25·32 N	103·13 W
119	Matamoros.....Mex.	25·52 N	97·30 W
217	Matandu (R.).....Tan.	8·55 S	38·35 E
98	Matane (mȧ-tân').....Can.	48·51 N	67·32 W
128	Matanzas (mä-tän'zäs).....Cuba	23·00 N	81·40 W
128	Matanzas (Prov.).....Cuba	22·45 N	81·20 W
128	Matanzas, Bahía (B.) (bä-ē'ä) Cuba	23·10 N	81·30 W
127	Matapalo, Cabo (C.) (kȧ'bô-mä-tä-pä'lō).C. R.	8·22 N	83·25 W
98	Matapédia (mă-tȧ-pā'dē-ȧ)...Can.	47·58 N	66·56 W
98	Matapédia, (L.).....Can.	48·33 N	67·32 W
98	Matapédia (R.).....Can.	48·10 N	67·10 W
137	Mataquito (R.) (mä-tä-kē'tô) Chile (Santiago In.)	35·08 S	71·35 W
185	Matara (mä-tä'rä).....Sri Lanka	5·59 N	80·35 E
196	Mataram.....Indon.	8·45 S	116·15 E
163	Mataró (mä-tä-rō').....Sp.	41·33 N	2·27 E
213	Matatiele (mä-tä-tyā'lā) S. Afr. (Natal In.)	30·21 S	28·49 E
106	Matawan.....NJ (New York In.)	40·24 N	74·13 W
98	Matawin (R.) (măt ȧ-wĭn)...Can.	46·46 N	73·25 W
124	Matehuala (mä-tȧ-wä'lä)....Mex.	23·38 N	100·39 W
164	Matera (mä-tâ'rä).....It.	40·42 N	16·37 E
151	Mateur (mȧ-tûr').....Tun.	37·09 N	9·43 E
185	Mātherān.....India (In.)	18·58 N	73·16 E
97	Matheson.....Can.	48·35 N	80·33 W
113	Mathews, L. (măth'ūz) Ca. (Los Angeles In.)	33·50	117·24 W
184	Mathura (mu-tōō'rŭ).....India	27·39 N	77·39 E
137	Matias Barbosa (mä-tē'äs-bär-bô-sä) Braz. (Rio de Janeiro In.)	21·53 S	43·19 W
125	Matillas, Laguna (L.) (lä-gōō'nä-mä-tē'l-yäs).Mex.	18·02 N	92·36 W
127	Matina (mä-tē'nä).....C. R.	10·06 N	83·20 W
157	Matiši (mä'tē-sē).....Sov. Un.	57·43 N	25·09 E
124	Matlalcueyetl, Cerra (sĕ'r-rä-mä-tläl-kwĕ'yĕtl).Mex.	19·13 N	98·02 W
148	Matlock (măt'lŏk).....Eng.	53·08 N	1·33 W
148	Matlock Bath (măt'lŏk bäth).Eng.	53·06 N	1·34 W
172	Matochkin Shar (mä'tŏch-kĭn) Sov. Un.	73·57 N	56·16 E
135	Mato Grosso (mät'ŏŏ grōs'ŏŏ) Braz.	15·04 S	59·58 W
135	Mato Grosso (State).....Braz.	14·38 S	55·36 W
135	Mato Grosso, Chapada de (Plain) (shä-pä'dä-dĕ).Braz.	13·39 S	55·42 W
162	Matozinhos (Leixoes) (mȧ-tô-zēn'yōzh) (lĕ'y-shô'-ĕs) Port.	41·10 N	8·48 W
186	Matrah (mȧ-trä').....Om.	23·36 N	58·27 E
211	Matrūh.....Egypt	31·19 N	27·14 E
195	Matsubara.....Jap. (Ōsaka In.)	34·34 N	135·34 E
195	Matsudo (mät'sōō-dô) Jap. (Tōkyō In.)	35·48 N	139·55 E
195	Matsue (mät'sōō-ĕ).....Jap.	35·29 N	133·04 E
195	Matsumoto (mät'sōō-mō'tō)..Jap.	36·15 N	137·59 E
195	Matsuyama (mät'sōō-yä'mä)..Jap.	33·48 N	132·45 E
195	Matsuzaka (mät'sōō-zä'kä)..Jap.	34·35 N	136·34 E
121	Mattamuskeet (R.) (măt-tȧ-mŭs'kēt).NC	35·34 N	76·03 W
105	Mattaponi (R.) (măt'ȧ-ponī')..Va.	37·45 N	77·00 W
97	Mattawa (măt'ȧ-wȧ).....Can.	46·15 N	78·49 W
158	Matterhorn Mt. (mät'ēr-hôrn) Switz.	45·57 N	7·36 E
107	Matteson (mătt'ê-sŭn) Il. (Chicago In.)	41·30 N	87·42 W
129	Matthew Town (măth'ū toun).Ba.	21·00 N	73·40 W
104	Mattoon (mă-tōōn').....Il.	39·30 N	88·20 W
134	Maturín (mä-tōō-rēn').....Ven.	9·48 N	63·16 W
217	Maúa.....Moz.	13·51 S	37·10 E
197	Mauban (mä'ōō-bän')..Phil. (In.)	14·11 N	121·44 E
160	Maubeuge (mô-bûzh').....Fr.	50·18 N	3·57 E
107	Maud (môd)..Oh. (Cincinnati In.)	39·21 N	84·23 W
149	Mauer (mou'ēr).Aus. (Vienna In.)	48·09 N	16·16 E
135	Maués (mȧ-wĕ's).....Braz.	3·34 S	57·30 W
217	Mau Escarpment (Cliff)....Ken.	0·45 S	35·50 E
89	Maui (I.) (mä'ōō-ē).....Hi.	20·52 N	156·02 W
137	Maule (R.) (mȧ'ōō-lĕ) Chile (Santiago In.)	35·45 S	70·50 W
104	Maumee (mô-mē').....Oh.	41·30 N	83·40 W
104	Maumee (R.).....In.-Oh.	41·10 N	84·50 W
104	Maumee B.....Oh.	41·50 N	83·20 W
212	Maun (mä-ōōn').....Bots.	19·52 S	23·40 E
89	Mauna Kea (Vol.) (mä'ōō-näkā'ä) Hi.	19·52 N	155·30 W
89	Mauna Loa (Vol.) (mä'ōō-nälō'ä) Hi.	19·28 N	155·38 W
196	Maung Nakhon Sawan.....Thai.	16·00 N	99·52 E
119	Maurepas L. (mō-rē-pä').....La.	30·18 N	90·40 W
98	Mauricie, Parc Natl. de la (Natl. Pk.).Can.	46·46 N	73·00 W
209	Mauritania (mô-rē-tā'nĭ-ȧ)....Afr.	19·38 N	13·30 W
220	Mauritius (mô-rĭsh'ĭ-ŭs).....Afr.	20·18 S	57·36 E
112	Maury (mô'rĭ)...Wa. (Seattle In.)	47·22 N	122·23 W
109	Mauston (môs'tŭn).....Wi.	43·46 N	90·05 W
115	Maverick ,(R.) (mă-vûr'ĭk)....Az.	33·40 N	109·30 W
216	Mavinga.....Ang.	15·50 S	20·21 E
125	Maxcanú (mäs-kä-nōō').....Mex.	20·35 N	89·59 W
100	Maxville (măks'vĭl) Can. (Ottawa In.)	45·17 N	74·52 W
113	Maxville.....Mo. (St. Louis In.)	38·26 N	90·24 W
173	Maya (R.) (mä'yä).....Sov. Un.	58·00 N	135·45 E
129	Mayaguana (I.).....Ba.	22·25 N	73·00 W
129	Mayaguana Passage (Str.)....Ba.	22·20 N	73·25 W
123	Mayagüez (mä-yä-gwāz') P. R. (Puerto Rico In.)	18·12 N	67·10 W
119	Mayarí (mä-yä-rē').....Cuba	20·45 N	75·40 W
119	Mayari (R.).....Cuba	20·25 N	75·35 W
126	Mayas, Montañas (Mts.) (mŏntäŋ'äs mā'äs).Belize (In.)	16·43 N	89·00 W
218	Mayd (I.).Som. (Horn of Afr. In.)	11·24 N	46·38 E
158	Mayen (mī'ĕn).....F.R.G.	50·19 N	7·14 E
160	Mayenne (mȧ-yĕn').....Fr.	48·19 N	0·35 W
160	Mayenne (R.).....Fr.	48·14 N	0·45 W
120	Mayfield (mā'fēld).....Ky.	36·44 N	88·19 W
121	Mayfield Cr.....Ky.	36·54 N	88·47 W
107	Mayfield Heights Oh. (Cleveland In.)	41·31 N	81·26 W
110	Mayfield Res.....Wa.	46·31 N	122·34 W
171	Maykop (Maikop) (mī-kôp') Sov. Un.	44·35 N	40·10 E
174	Maykor (mī-kôr') Sov. Un. (Urals In.)	59·01 N	55·52 E
188	Maymyo (mī'myō).....Bur.	22·14 N	96·32 E
99	Maynard (mā'nȧrd)....Ma. (In.)	42·25 N	71·27 W
112	Mayne (mān) Can. (Vancouver In.)	48·51 N	123·18 W
112	Mayne (I.)..Can. (Vancouver In.)	48·52 N	123·14 W
90	Mayo (mā-yō').....Can.	63·40 N	135·51 W
120	Mayo.....Fl.	30·02 N	83·08 W
106	Mayo.....Md. (Baltimore In.)	38·54 N	76·31 W
154	Mayo, Mts. of.....Ire.	54·01 N	9·01 W
121	Mayodan (mā-yō'dăn).....NC	36·25 N	79·59 W
197	Mayon (Vol.) (mä-yōn').Phil. (In.)	13·21 N	123·43 E
213	Mayotte (I.) (mȧ-yôt')....France	13·07 S	45·32 E
128	May Pen.....Jam.	18·00 N	77·25 W
193	Mayraira Pt.....Phil.	18·40 N	120·45 E
118	Mayran, Laguna de (L.) (lä-ōō'nä-dĕ-mī-rän').Mex.	25·40 N	102·35 W
104	Maysville (māz'vĭl).....Ky.	38·35 N	83·45 W
216	Mayumba.....Gabon	3·25 S	10·39 E
105	Mayville (mā'vĭl).....NY	42·15 N	79·30 W
108	Mayville.....ND	47·30 N	97·20 W
109	Mayville.....Wi.	43·30 N	88·45 W
113	Maywood (mā'wŏŏd) Ca. (Los Angeles In.)	33·59 N	118·11 W
107	Maywood.....Il. (Chicago In.)	41·53 N	87·51 W
217	Mazabuka (mä-zä-bōō'kä).Zambia	15·51 S	27·46 E
135	Mazagão (mä-zä-gou'N).....Braz.	0·05 S	51·27 W
118	Mazapil (mä-zä-pēl').....Mex.	24·40 N	101·30 W
184	Mazār-i-Sharīf (mȧ-zär'-ē-shȧ-rēf').Afg.	36·48 N	67·12 E
162	Mazarrón (mä-zär-rô'n).....Sp.	36·37 N	1·29 W
135	Mazaruni (R.) (mä-zä-rōō'nē) Guy.	5·58 N	59·37 W
126	Mazatenango (mä-zä-tȧ-näŋ'gō) Guat.	14·30 N	91·30 W
125	Mazatla.....Mex. (In.)	19·30 N	99·24 W
125	Mazatlán (San Juan) (mä-zä-tlän') (sän hwän').Mex.	17·05 N	95·26 W
124	Mazatlán.....Mex.	23·14 N	106·27 W
157	Mažeikiai (mȧ-zhā'kē-ĭ)..Sov. Un.	56·19 N	22·24 E
183	Mazḩafah, Jabal (Mts.) Sau. Ar. (Palestine In.)	28·56 N	35·05 E
217	Mazoe (R.).....Moz.	16·40 S	32·50 E
164	Mazzara del Vallo (mät-sä'rä dĕl väl'lō).It.	37·40 N	12·37 E
164	Mazzarino (mät-sä-rē'nō).....It.	37·16 N	14·15 E
212	Mbabane (m'bä-bä'nĕ).....Swaz.	26·18 S	31·14 E
215	Mbaikí (m'bȧ-ē'kē).Cen. Afr. Rep.	3·53 N	18·00 E
215	Mbakana, Montagne de (Mts.) Cam.	7·55 N	14·40 E
215	Mbakaou, Barrage de.....Cam.	6·10 N	12·55 E
217	Mbala (Abercorn).....Zambia	8·50 S	31·22 E
217	Mbale.....Ug.	1·05 N	34·10 E

312 Mbamba Bay — Mesagne

PRONOUNCING INDEX

Page	Name Pronunciation Region	Lat. °′	Long. °′
217	Mbamba Bay...Tan.	11·17 S	34·46 E
216	Mbandaka (Coquilhatville)..Zaire	0·04 N	18·16 E
216	Mbanza-Ngungu...Zaire	5·20 S	10·55 E
217	Mbarara...Ug.	0·37 S	30·39 E
215	Mbasay...Chad	7·39 N	15·40 E
217	Mbeya...Tan.	8·54 S	33·27 E
212	Mbigou (m-bē-gōō')...Gabon	2·07 S	11·30 E
216	Mbinda...Con.	2·00 S	12·55 E
217	Mbogo...Tan.	7·26 S	33·26 E
216	Mbomou (Bomu) (R.) (m'bō'mōō) Cen. Afr. Rep.-Zaire	4·50 N	23·35 E
216	Mbuji-Mayi (Bakwanga)....Zaire	6·09 S	23·28 E
210	Mbout (m'bōō')......Mauritania	16·03 N	12·31 W
217	Mchinji...Malawi	13·42 S	32·50 E
115	Mead, L...Az.-Nv.	36·20 N	114·14 W
116	Meade (mēd)...Ks.	37·17 N	100·21 W
111	Meade Pk...Id.	42·19 N	111·16 W
94	Meadow Lake (mĕd'ō lăk)...Can.	54·08 N	108·26 W
100	Meadows (mĕd'ōz) Can. (Winnipeg In.)	50·02 N	97·35 W
105	Meadville (mēd'vĭl)...Pa.	41·40 N	80·10 W
104	Meaford (mē'fērd)...Can.	44·35 N	80·40 W
91	Mealy Mts. (mē'lē)...Can.	53·32 N	57·58 W
203	Meandarra (mē-ăn-dä'rȧ)...Austl.	27·47 S	149·40 E
161	Meaux (mō)...Fr. (Paris In.)	48·58 N	2·53 E
125	Mecapalapa (mā-kä-pä-lä'pä) Mex.	20·32 N	97·52 W
99	Mecatina (I.) (mā-kȧ-tē'nȧ)..Can.	50·50 N	58·33 W
99	Mecatina (R.) (mā-kȧ-tē'nȧ).Can.	50·50 N	59·45 W
	Mecca, see Makkah		
98	Mechanic Falls (mē-kăn'ĭk)...Me.	44·05 N	70·23 W
105	Mechanicsburg (mē-kăn'ĭks-bûrg).Pa.	40·15 N	77·00 W
106	Mechanicsville (mē-kăn'ĭks-vĭl) Md. (Baltimore In.)	38·27 N	76·45 W
105	Mechanicville (mē-kăn'ĭk-vĭl)..NY	42·55 N	73·45 W
149	Mechelen......Bel. (Brussels In.)	51·01 N	4·28 E
152	Mecheria...Mor.	33·30 N	0·13 W
158	Mecklenburg (Reg.) (mĕk'lĕn-bōōrgh)....G.D.R.	53·34 N	12·18 E
196	Medan (mȧ-dän')...Indon.	3·35 N	98·35 E
136	Medanosa, Punta (Pt.) (pōō'n-tä-mĕ-dä-nô'sä).Arg.	47·50 S	65·53 W
148	Medden (R.) (mĕd'ĕn)...Eng.	53·14 N	1·05 W
163	Médéa (mā-dā'ä)...Alg.	36·18 N	2·40 E
134	Medellín (mā-dhĕl-yēn').Col. (In.)	6·15 N	75·34 W
125	Medellín (mĕ-dĕl-yē'n)...Mex.	19·03 N	96·08 W
152	Medenine (mā-dĕ-nēn')...Tun.	33·22 N	10·33 E
99	Medfield (mĕd'fēld)....Ma. (In.)	42·11 N	71·19 W
99	Medford (mĕd'fērd)....Ma. (In.)	42·25 N	71·07 W
106	Medford....NJ (Philadelphia In.)	39·54 N	74·50 W
116	Medford...Ok.	36·47 N	97·44 W
110	Medford...Or.	42·19 N	122·52 W
109	Medford...Wi.	45·09 N	90·22 W
106	Media (mē'dĭ-ȧ) Pa. (Philadelphia In.)	39·55 N	75·24 W
159	Medias (mĕd-yäsh')...Rom.	46·09 N	24·21 E
110	Medical Lake (mĕd'ĭ-kǎl)....Wa.	47·34 N	117·40 W
116	Medicine Bow Ra. (mĕd'ĭ-sĭn bō).Co.-Wy.	40·55 N	106·02 W
111	Medicine Bow R...Wy.	41·58 N	106·30 W
94	Medicine Hat (mĕd'ĭ-sĭn hăt).Can.	50·03 N	110·40 W
111	Medicine L. (mĕd'ĭ-sĭn)...Mt.	48·24 N	104·15 W
116	Medicine Lodge...Ks.	37·17 N	98·37 W
116	Medicine Lodge (R.)...Ks.	37·20 N	98·57 W
105	Medina (mē-dī'nȧ)...NY	43·15 N	78·20 W
107	Medina......Oh. (Cleveland In.)	41·08 N	81·52 W
	Medina, see Al Madīnah		
162	Medina del Campo (mā-dē'nä dĕl käm'pō).Sp.	41·18 N	4·54 W
162	Medina de Rioseco (mā-dē'nä dā rē-ō-sā'kō).Sp.	41·53 N	5·05 W
214	Médina Gonassé...Sen.	13·08 N	13·45 W
118	Medina L...Tx.	29·36 N	98·47 W
118	Medina R...Tx.	29·45 N	99·13 W
162	Medina Sidonia (sē-dō'nyä)....Sp.	36·28 N	5·58 W
137	Medio (mĕ'dyô) (R.) Arg. (Buenos Aires In.)	33·40 S	60·30 W
152	Mediterranean Sea (mĕd-ĭ-tēr-ā'nē-ǎn) Afr.-Asia-Eur.	36·22 N	13·25 E
151	Medjerda, Oued (R.) (wĕd mĕ-jĕr'dȧ).Tun.	36·43 N	9·54 E
172	Mednogorsk...Sov. Un.	51·27 N	57·22 E
171	Medvedista (R.) (mĕd-vyĕ'dē tsȧ).Sov. Un.	50·10 N	43·40 E
170	Medvezhegorsk (mĕd-vyĕzh'yĕ-gôrsk').Sov. Un.	63·00 N	34·20 E
173	Medvezh'y (Is.)...Sov. Un.	71·00 N	161·25 E
99	Medway (mĕd'wā)....Ma. (In.)	42·08 N	71·23 W
166	Medyn' (mĕ-dēn')...Sov. Un.	54·58 N	35·53 E
167	Medzhibozh (mĕd-zhē-bōzh') Sov. Un.	49·23 N	27·29 E
204	Meekatharra (mē-kȧ-thăr'ȧ).Austl.	26·30 S	118·38 E
115	Meeker (mēk'ēr)...Co.	40·00 N	107·55 W
99	Meelpaeg L. (mēl'pȧ-ĕg)....Can.	48·22 N	56·52 W
158	Meerane (mā-rä'nĕ)...G.D.R.	50·51 N	12·27 E
184	Meerut (mē'rōōt)...India	28·59 N	77·43 E
165	Megalópolis (mĕg-ȧ lŏ'pô-lĭs).Grc..	37·22 N	22·08 E
167	Meganom, M. (C.) (mĭs mĕ-gȧ-nôm').Sov. Un.	44·48 N	35·17 E
165	Mégara (mĕg'ȧ-rȧ)...Grc.	37·59 N	23·21 E
121	Megget (mĕg'ĕt)...SC	32·44 N	80·15 W
188	Meghelaya (State)...India	25·30 N	91·30 E
112	Megler (mĕg'lēr) Wa. (Portland In.)	46·15 N	123·52 W
166	Meglino (L.) (mȧ-glē'nô).Sov. Un.	58·32 N	35·27 E
121	Meherrin (R.) (mē-hĕr'ĭn)....Va.	36·40 N	77·49 W
113	Mehlville....Mo. (St. Louis In.)	38·30 N	90·19 W
184	Mehsāna...India	23·42 N	72·23 E
160	Mehun-sur-Yèvre (mē-üN-sür-yĕvr').Fr.	47·11 N	2·14 E
190	Meichu (mā'jĕōō)...China	31·17 N	119·12 E
193	Meihsien...China	24·20 N	116·10 E
193	Meiling Pass (mā'lĭng')....China	25·22 N	115·00 E
161	Meinerzhagen (mī'nĕrts-hä-gĕn) F.R.G. (Ruhr In.)	51·06 N	7·39 E
158	Meiningen (mī'nĭng-ĕn)...G.D.R.	50·35 N	10·25 E
158	Meiringen...Switz.	46·45 N	8·11 E
158	Meissen...G.D.R.	51·11 N	13·28 E
136	Mejillones (mȧ-Kē-lyō'nȧs)...Chile	23·07 S	70·31 W
216	Mekambo...Gabon	1·01 N	13·56 E
211	Mekele...Eth.	13·31 N	39·19 E
210	Meknés (mĕk'nĕs) (mĕk-nĕs').Mor.	33·56 N	5·44 W
	Mekong (R.), see Lanisung Chiang		
196	Mekong, Mouths of the (mē'kông').Viet.	10·09 N	107·15 E
196	Mekong R...Thai.-Laos	17·53 N	103·57 E
215	Mékrou (R.)...Afr.	11·35 N	2·25 E
183	Melaka (Malacca) Mala. (Singapore In.)	2·11 N	102·15 E
183	Melaka (State) Mala. (Singapore In.)	2·19 N	102·09 E
202	Melbourne (mĕl'bŭrn) Austl. (Melbourne In.)	37·52 S	145·08 E
121	Melbourne...Fl. (In.)	28·05 N	80·37 W
148	Melbourne...Eng.	52·49 N	1·26 W
107	Melbourne...Ky. (Cincinnati In.)	39·02 N	84·22 W
109	Melcher (mĕl'chēr)...Ia.	41·13 N	93·11 W
170	Melekess (mĕl-yĕk ĕs)....Sov. Un.	54·20 N	49·30 E
166	Melenki (mĕ-lyĕŋ'kē)....Sov. Un.	55·25 N	41·34 E
94	Melfort (mĕl'fôrt)...Can.	52·52 N	104·36 W
211	Melik, Wadi el (R.)...Sud.	16·48 N	29·30 E
210	Melilla (Sp.) (mā-lēl'yä)....Afr.	35·24 N	3·30 W
137	Melipilla (mȧ-lē-pē'lyä) Chile (Santiago In.)	33·40 S	71·12 W
95	Melita...Can.	49·11 N	101·09 W
167	Melitopol' (mā-lē-tô'pôl-y') Sov. Un.	46·49 N	35·19 E
218	Melkrivier...S. Afr. (Johannesburg & Pretoria In.)	24·01 S	28·23 E
109	Mellen (mĕl'ĕn)...Wi.	46·20 N	90·40 W
156	Mellerud (mȧl'ĕ-rōōdh)......Swe.	58·43 N	12·25 E
213	Melmoth......S. Afr. (Natal In.)	28·38 S	31·26 E
136	Melo (mā'lō)...Ur.	32·18 S	54·07 W
100	Melocheville (mĕ-lôsh-vēl') Can. (Montreal In.)	45·24 N	73·56 W
174	Melozha R. (myĕ'lô-zhȧ) Sov. Un. (Moscow In.)	56·06 N	38·34 E
210	Melrhir Chott (L.) (mĕl'rēr)..Alg.	33·52 N	5·22 E
99	Melrose (mĕl'rōz).......Ma. (In.)	42·29 N	71·06 W
109	Melrose...Mn.	45·39 N	94·49 W
107	Melrose Park....Il. (Chicago In.)	41·54 N	87·52 W
212	Melsetter (mĕl-sĕt'ēr)...Rh.	19·44 S	32·51 E
148	Meltham (mĕl'thăm)...Eng.	53·35 N	1·51 W
202	Melton (mĕl'tŭn) Austl. (Melbourne In.)	37·41 S	144·35 E
148	Melton Mowbray (mō'brâ)..Eng.	52·45 N	0·52 W
217	Melúli (R.)...Moz.	16·10 S	39·30 E
161	Melun (mē-lŭN')...Fr. (In.)	48·32 N	2·40 E
216	Melunga...Ang.	17·16 S	16·24 E
94	Melville (mĕl'vĭl)...Can.	50·55 N	102·48 W
113	Melville...La.	30·39 N	91·45 W
205	Melville, C...Austl.	14·15 S	145·50 E
204	Melville (I.)...Austl.	11·30 S	131·12 E
91	Melville (R.)...Can.	53·46 N	59·31 W
90	Melville Hills...Can.	69·18 N	124·57 W
91	Melville Pen...Can.	67·44 N	84·09 W
107	Melvindale (mĕl'vĭn-dāl) Mi. (Detroit In.)	42·17 N	83·11 W
159	Mélykút (mā'l'kōōt)...Hung.	46·14 N	19·21 E
213	Memba (mĕm'bȧ)...Moz.	14·12 S	40·35 E
	Memel, see Klaipéda		
218	Memel (mĕ'mĕl) S. Afr. (Johannesburg & Pretoria In.)	27·42 S	29·35 E
158	Memmingen (mĕm'ĭng-ĕn).F.R.G.	47·59 N	10·10 E
135	Memo (R.) (mĕ'mō)....Ven. (In.)	9·32 N	66·30 W
117	Memphis (mĕm'fĭs)...Mo.	40·27 N	92·11 W
120	Memphis (mĕm'fĭs)...Tn.	35·07 N	90·03 W
116	Memphis...Tx.	34·42 N	100·33 W
218	Memphis (Ruins).Egypt (Nile In.)	29·50 N	31·12 E
105	Memphremagog (L.) (mĕm'frē-mā'gŏg).Can.	45·05 N	72·10 W
117	Mena (mē'nȧ)...Ar.	34·35 N	94·09 W
167	Mena (mē-nȧ')...Sov. Un.	51·31 N	32·14 E
202	Menangle.....Austl. (Sydney In.)	34·08 S	150·48 E
118	Menard (mē-närd')...Tx.	30·56 N	99·48 W
109	Menasha (mē-năsh'ȧ)...Wi.	44·12 N	88·29 W
160	Mende (mäNd)...Fr.	44·31 N	3·30 E
161	Menden (mĕn'dĕn) F.R.G. (Ruhr In.)	51·26 N	7·47 E
171	Menderes (R.) (mĕn'dēr-ĕs)..Tur.	37·50 N	28·20 E
136	Mendes (mĕ'n-dĕs)....Braz. (In.)	22·32 S	43·44 W
110	Mendocino, C. (mĕn'dô-sē'nō).Ca.	40·25 N	124·22 W
109	Mendota (mĕn-dō'tȧ)...Il.	41·34 N	89·06 W
109	Mendota (L.)...Wi.	43·09 N	89·41 W
136	Mendoza (mĕn-dō'sä)...Arg.	32·48 S	68·45 W
136	Mendoza (Prov.)...Arg.	35·10 S	69·00 W
193	Mengtzu...China	23·22 N	103·20 E
203	Menindee (mĕ-nĭn-dē)...Austl.	32·23 S	142·30 E
112	Menlo Park (mĕn'lō pärk) Ca. (San Francisco In.)	37·27 N	122·11 W
108	Menno (mĕn'ô)...SD	43·14 N	97·34 W
109	Menominee (mē-nŏm'ĭ-nē)....Mi.	45·08 N	87·40 W
109	Menominee (R.)...Mi.-Wi.	45·37 N	87·54 W
107	Menomonee Falls (fôls) Wi. (Milwaukee In.)	43·11 N	88·06 W
109	Menominee Ra...Mi.	46·07 N	88·53 W
107	Menomonee R. Wi. (Milwaukee In.)	43·09 N	88·06 W
109	Menomonie...Wi.	44·53 N	91·55 W
163	Menorca, Isla de (Minorca) (I.) (ē's-lä-dĕ-mĕ-nô'r-kä).Sp.	40·05 N	3·58 E
163	Mentana (mĕn-tȧ'nä) It. (Rome In.)	42·02 N	12·40 E
196	Mentawai, Kepulauan (Is.) (mĕn-tä-vī').Indon.	1·08 S	98·10 E
161	Menton (mäN-tôN')...Fr.	43·46 N	7·37 E
113	Mentone (mĕn'tŏne) Ca. (Los Angeles In.)	34·05 N	117·08 W
213	Mentz (R.) (mĕnts) S. Afr. (Natal In.)	33·13 S	25·15 E
170	Menzelinsk (mĕn'zyĕ-lĕnsk') Sov. Un.	55·40 N	53·15 E
204	Menzies (mĕn'zēz)...Austl.	29·45 S	122·15 E
118	Meogui (mȧ-ō'gē)...Mex.	28·17 N	105·28 W
155	Meppel (mĕp'ĕl)...Neth.	52·41 N	6·08 E
158	Meppen (mĕp'ĕn)...F.R.G.	52·40 N	7·18 E
163	Mequinenza Res...Sp.	41·15 N	0·35 W
164	Merabéllou, Kólpos (G.).Grc. (In.)	35·16 N	25·55 E
117	Meramec (R.) (mĕr'ȧ-mĕk)...Mo.	38·06 N	91·06 W
164	Merano (mȧ-rä'nō)...It.	46·39 N	11·10 E
99	Merasheen (I.) (mē'rȧ-shēn).Can.	47·30 N	54·15 W
197	Merauke (mȧ-rou'kā)......Indon.	8·32 S	140·17 E
106	Meraux (mē-ro') La. (New Orleans In.)	29·56 N	89·56 W
163	Mercato San Severino (mĕr-kȧ'tō sän sĕ-vĕ-rĕ'nō) It. (Naples In.)	40·34 N	14·38 E
114	Merced (mēr-sĕd')...Ca.	37·17 N	120·30 W
114	Merced (R.)...Ca.	37·25 N	120·31 W
137	Mercedario, Cerro (Mtn.) (mĕr-sȧ-dhä'rē-ō) Chile (Santiago In.)	31·58 S	70·07 W
136	Mercedes (mĕr-sā'dhās)......Arg.	29·04 S	58·01 W
137	Mercedes.Arg. (Buenos Aires In.)	34·41 S	59·26 W
118	Mercedes...Tx.	26·09 N	97·55 W
137	Mercedes..Ur. (Buenos Aires In.)	33·17 S	58·04 W
137	Mercedita (mĕr-sĕ-dē'tä) Chile (Santiago In.)	33·51 S	71·10 W
112	Mercer Island (mûr'sēr) Wa. (Seattle In.)	47·35 N	122·15 W
137	Mercês (mĕr-sĕ's) Braz. (Rio de Janeiro In.)	21·13 S	43·20 N
183	Merchong (R.) Mala. (Singapore In.)	3·08 N	103·13 E
149	Merchtem.....Bel. (Brussels In.)	50·57 N	4·13 E
100	Mercier......Can. (Montreal In.)	45·19 N	73·45 W
163	Mercier-Lacombe (mĕr-syā' lȧ-kôNb).Alg.	35·18 N	0·11 W
91	Mercy, C...Can.	64·48 N	63·22 W
105	Meredith (mĕr'ē-dĭth)...NH	43·35 N	71·35 W
167	Merefa (mȧ-rĕf'ȧ).......Sov. Un.	49·49 N	36·04 E
126	Merendón, Serrania de (Mts.) (sĕr-rä-nē'ä-dā mȧ-rĕn-dōn') Hond.	15·01 N	89·05 W
148	Mereworth (mĕ-rĕ'wûrth) Eng. (London In.)	51·15 N	0·23 E
196	Mergui (mĕr-gē')...Bur.	12·29 N	98·39 E
196	Mergui Arch...Asia	12·04 N	97·02 E
126	Mérida.......Mex. (Yucatan In.)	20·58 N	89·37 W
134	Mérida...Ven.	8·30 N	71·15 W
134	Mérida, Cordillera de (Mts.) (mĕ'rē-dhä).Ven.	8·30 N	70·45 W
105	Meriden (mĕr'ĭ-dĕn)...Ct.	41·30 N	72·50 W
120	Meridian (mē-rĭd-ĭ-ăn)...Ms.	32·21 N	88·41 W
119	Meridian...Tx.	31·56 N	97·37 W
157	Merikarvia (mā'rē-kȧr'vē-ȧ)..Fin.	61·51 N	21·30 E
149	Mering (mĕ'rēng) F.R.G. (Munich In.)	48·16 N	11·00 E
120	Meriwether Lewis Natl. Mon. (mĕr'ĭ-wĕth-ēr lōō'ĭs).Tn.	35·25 N	87·25 W
118	Merkel (mûr'kĕl)...Tx.	32·26 N	100·02 W
157	Merkiné (mĕr'kĭ-nē).....Sov. Un.	54·09 N	24·10 E
149	Merksem......Bel. (Brussels In.)	51·15 N	4·27 E
159	Merkys R. (măr'kĭs).....Sov. Un.	54·23 N	25·00 E
136	Merlo (mĕr-lô)...Arg. (In.)	34·25 S	58·44 W
113	Merriam (mĕr-rĭ-yȧm) Ks. (Kansas City In.)	39·01 N	94·42 W
113	Merriam Mn. (Minneapolis, St. Paul In.)	44·44 N	93·36 W
106	Merrick (mĕr'ĭk) NY (New York In.)	40·40 N	73·33 W
106	Merrifield (mĕr'ĭ-fēld) Va. (Baltimore In.)	38·50 N	77·12 W
109	Merrill (mĕr'ĭl)...Wi.	45·11 N	89·42 W
99	Merrimac (mĕr'ĭ-măk)..Ma. (In.)	42·50 N	71·00 W
99	Merrimack...NH (In.)	42·51 N	71·25 W
105	Merrimack (R.) (mĕr'ĭ-măk) Ma.-NH	43·10 N	71·30 W
99	Merrimack R...Ma. (In.)	42·49 N	70·44 W
93	Merritt (mĕr'ĭt)...Can.	50·07 N	120·47 W
119	Merryville (mĕr'ĭ-vĭl)...La.	30·46 N	93·34 W
211	Mersa Fatma...Eth.	14·54 N	40·14 E
158	Merseburg (mĕr'zĕ-bōōrgh) G.D.R.	51·21 N	11·59 E
148	Mersey (R.) (mûr'zē)...Eng.	52·52 N	2·04 W
154	Mersey (R.)...Eng.	53·15 N	2·51 W
171	Mersin (mĕr-sēn')...Tur.	37·00 N	34·40 E
183	Mersing....Mala. (Singapore In.)	2·25 N	103·51 E
184	Merta Road (mār'tŭ rōd)...India	26·50 N	73·54 E
154	Merthyr Tydfil (mûr'thēr tĭd'vĭl).Wales	51·46 N	3·30 W
162	Mértola Almodóvar (mĕr-tô-lȧ-äl-mô-dô'vär)..Port.	37·39 N	8·04 W
161	Méru (mā-rü')...Fr. (In.)	49·14 N	2·08 E
211	Meru (mā'rōō)...Ken.	0·01 N	37·45 E
217	Meru, Mt...Tan.	3·15 S	36·43 E
135	Merume Mts. (mĕr-ü'mĕ)....Guy.	5·45 N	60·15 W
149	Merwerde, Kanal (Can.) Neth. (Amsterdam In.)	52·15 N	5·01 E
112	Merwin (L.) (mĕr'wĭn) Wa. (Portland In.)	45·58 N	122·27 W
171	Merzifon (mĕr'ze-fōn)...Tur.	40·50 N	35·30 E
161	Merzig (mĕr'tsēg)...F.R.G.	49·27 N	6·54 E
115	Mesa (mā'sȧ)...Az.	33·25 N	111·50 W
109	Mesabi Ra. (mā-sŏb'bē)......Mn.	47·17 N	93·04 W
165	Mesagne (mā-sān'yȧ)...It.	40·34 N	17·51 E

ăt; finăl; rāte; senâte; ärm; ȧsk; sofȧ; fâre; ch-choose; dh-as th in other; bē; ēvent; bĕt; recĕnt; cratēr; g-go; gh-guttural g; bĭt; ĭ-short neutral; rīde; K-guttural k as ch in German ich;

PRONOUNCING INDEX

Mesa Verde — Mineral del Chico 313

Page	Name Pronunciation Region	Lat. °′	Long. °′
115	Mesa Verde Natl. Park. (vĕr'dē) Co.	37·22 N	108·27 W
115	Mescalero Ind. Res. (mĕs-kä-lā'rō) NM	33·10 N	105·45 W
211	Mesewa (Massaua) Eth.	15·40 N	39·19 E
166	Meshchovsk (myĕsh'chĕfsk) Sov. Un.	54·17 N	35·19 E
115	Mesilla (må-sē'yä) NM	32·15 N	106·45 W
215	Meskine Chad	11·25 N	15·21 E
165	Mesolóngion (mĕ-sô-lôŋ'gē-ôn) Grc.	38·23 N	21·28 E
164	Messina (mĕ-sē'nȧ) It.	38·11 N	15·34 E
212	Messina S. Afr.	22·17 S	30·13 E
164	Messina, Stretto di (Str.) (strĕ't-tô dē) It.	38·10 N	15·34 E
165	Messíni Grc.	37·05 N	22·00 E
165	Méssiniakós Kólpos (G.) Grc.	36·59 N	22·00 E
165	Mesta (R.) (mĕ-stä') Bul.	41·42 N	23·40 E
164	Mestre (mĕs'trā) It.	45·29 N	12·15 E
134	Meta (Dept.) (mĕ'tä) Col. (In.)	3·28 N	74·07 W
134	Meta (R.) Col.	4·33 N	72·09 W
98	Métabetchouane (R.) (mĕ-tá-bĕt-chōō-än') Can.	47·45 N	72·00 W
119	Metairie La.	30·00 N	90·11 W
136	Metán (mĕ-tá'n) Arg.	25·32 S	64·51 W
212	Metangula Moz.	12·42 S	34·48 E
126	Metapán (må-tä-pän') Sal.	14·21 N	89·26 W
100	Metcalfe (mĕt-kăf) Can. (Ottawa In.)	45·14 N	75·27 W
112	Metchosin Can. (Seattle In.)	48·22 N	123·33 W
124	Metepec (må-tĕ-pĕk') Mex.	18·56 N	98·31 W
125	Metepec Mex. (In.)	19·15 N	99·36 W
110	Methow R. (mĕt'hou) (mĕt hou') Wa.	48·26 N	120·15 W
99	Methuen (mê-thū'ĕn) Ma. (In.)	42·44 N	71·11 W
165	Metkovic' (mĕt'kô-vĭch) Yugo.	43·02 N	17·40 E
101	Metlakatla (mĕt-lȧ-kăt'lȧ) Ak.	55·08 N	131·35 W
117	Metropolis (mê-trŏp'ô-lĭs) Il.	37·09 N	88·46 W
121	Metter (mĕt'ẽr) Ga.	32·21 N	82·05 W
161	Mettmann (mĕt'män) F.R.G. (Ruhr In.)	51·15 N	6·58 E
106	Metuchen (mĕ-tŭ'chĕn) NJ (New York In.)	40·32 N	74·21 W
161	Metz (mĕtz) Fr.	49·08 N	6·10 E
124	Metztitlán (mĕtz-têt-län') Mex.	20·36 N	98·45 W
215	Meuban Cam.	2·27 N	12·41 E
160	Meuse (R.) (mûz) (müz) Eur.	50·32 N	5·22 E
148	Mexborough (mĕks'bŭr-ô) Eng.	53·30 N	1·17 W
119	Mexia (må-hē'ä) Tx.	31·32 N	96·29 W
125	Mexicalcingo (me-kē-käl-sēn'go) Mex. (In.)	19·13 N	99·34 W
114	Mexicali (mäk-sê-kä'lê) Mex.	32·28 N	115·29 W
115	Mexican Hat (mĕk'sĭ-kăn hăt) Ut.	37·10 N	109·55 W
98	Mexico (mĕk'sĭ-kō) Me.	44·34 N	70·33 W
117	Mexico Mo.	39·09 N	91·51 W
122	Mexico (State) (mäk'sê-kō) Mex.	19·50 N	99·50 W
75	Mexico N. A.	23·45 N	104·00 W
122	Mexico, G. of N. A.	25·15 N	93·45 W
125	Mexico City (mĕk'sĭ-kō) Mex. (In.)	19·28 N	99·09 W
124	Mexticacán (mĕs'tê-kä-kän') Mex.	21·12 N	102·43 W
92	Meyers Chuck Ak.	55·44 N	132·15 W
105	Meyersdale (mī'ẽrz-dāl) Pa.	39·55 N	79·00 W
218	Meyerton (mī'ẽr-tŭn) S. Afr. (Johannesburg & Pretoria In.)	26·35 S	28·01 E
186	Meymaneh Afg.	35·53 N	64·38 E
170	Mezen' Sov. Un.	65·50 N	44·05 E
170	Mezen' (R.) Sov. Un.	65·20 N	44·45 E
160	Mézenc, Mt. (mŏn-mä-zĕn') Fr.	44·55 N	4·12 E
166	Mezha (R.) (myä'zhȧ) Sov. Un.	55·53 N	31·44 E
161	Mézières-sur-Seine (mā-zyâr'sür-sân') Fr. (In.)	48·58 N	1·49 E
159	Mezökövesd (mĕ'zû-kû'vĕsht) Hung.	47·49 N	20·36 E
159	Mezötúr (mĕ'zû-tōōr) Hung.	47·00 N	20·36 E
124	Mezquital (mâz-kê-täl') Mex.	23·30 N	104·20 W
124	Mezquital (R.) Mex.	23·07 N	104·52 W
124	Mezquitic (mâz-kê-tēk') Mex.	22·25 N	103·43 W
124	Mexquitic (R.) Mex.	22·25 N	103·45 W
217	Mfangano I. Ken.	0·28 S	33·35 E
174	Mga (m'gȧ) Sov. Un. (Leningrad In.)	59·45 N	31·04 E
213	Mgeni (R.) S. Afr. (Natal In.)	29·38 S	30·53 E
166	Mglin (m'glēn') Sov. Un.	53·03 N	32·52 E
124	Miacatlán (mē'ä-kä-tlän') Mex.	18·42 N	99·17 W
125	Miahuatlán (mē'ä-wä-tlän') Mex.	16·20 N	96·38 W
162	Miajadas (mê-ä-hä'däs) Sp.	39·10 N	5·53 W
115	Miami Az.	33·20 N	110·55 W
121	Miami Fl. (In.)	25·45 N	80·11 W
117	Miami Ok.	36·51 N	94·51 W
116	Miami Tx.	35·41 N	100·39 W
104	Miami (R.) Oh.	39·20 N	84·45 W
121	Miami Beach Fl. (In.)	25·47 N	80·07 W
128	Miami Drainage Can. Fl.	26·25 N	80·50 W
104	Miamisburg (mī-ăm'iz-bûrg) Oh.	39·40 N	84·20 W
107	Miamitown (mī-ăm'ĭ-toun) Oh. (Cincinnati In.)	39·13 N	84·43 W
186	Mīāneh Iran	37·15 N	47·13 E
197	Miangas (I.) (myä'n-gäs) Phil.	5·30 N	127·00 E
190	Miaochen (mĭou'zhen) China	31·44 N	121·28 E
193	Miaoli (mê-ou'lĭ) Tiawan	24·30 N	120·48 E
190	Miao Liehtao (Is.) (miou' lĭēdou) China	38·06 N	120·35 E
174	Miass (mī-äs') Sov. Un. (Urals In.)	55·00 N	60·03 E
158	Miastko (myäst'kô) Pol.	54·01 N	17·00 E
159	Michalovce (mē'kä-lôf'tsĕ) Czech.	48·44 N	21·56 E
92	Michel Pk. Can.	53·35 N	126·26 W
101	Michelson, Mt. (mĭch'ĕl-sŭn) Ak.	69·11 N	144·12 W
149	Michendorf (mē'kĕn-dōrf) F.R.G. (Berlin In.)	52·19 N	13·02 E
129	Miches (mē'chĕs) Dom. Rep.	19·00 N	69·05 W
103	Michigan (State) (mĭsh'ĭ-gȧn) U. S.	45·55 N	87·00 W

Page	Name Pronunciation Region	Lat. °′	Long. °′
103	Michigan, L. U. S.	43·20 N	87·10 W
104	Michigan City In.	41·40 N	86·55 W
91	Michikamau (L.) Can.	54·11 N	63·21 W
109	Michipicoten (I.) (mĕ-shĭ-pĭ-kō'tĕn) Can.	47·49 N	85·50 W
109	Michipicoten (R.) Can.	47·56 N	84·42 W
109	Michipicoten Harbour Can.	47·58 N	84·58 W
124	Michoacán (State) Mex.	19·15 N	101·30 W
166	Michurinsk (mĭ-chōō-rĭnsk') Sov. Un.	52·53 N	40·32 E
127	Mico, Punta (Pt.) (pōō'n-tä-mē'kô) Nic.	11·38 N	83·24 W
110	Midas (mī'dȧs) Nv.	41·15 N	116·50 W
212	Middleburg (mĭd'ĕl-bûrg) S. Afr.	31·30 S	25·00 E
218	Middleburg S. Afr. (Johannesburg & Pretoria In.)	25·47 S	29·30 E
218	Middlewit (mĭd'l'wĭt) S. Afr. (Johannesburg & Pretoria In.)	24·50 S	27·00 E
92	Middle (R.) Can.	55·00 N	125·50 W
196	Middle Andaman I. (ăn-dȧ-măn') Andaman & Nicobar Is.	12·44 N	93·21 E
119	Middle Bay Tx. (In.)	29·38 N	95·06 W
128	Middle Bight (B.) (bīt) Ba.	24·20 N	77·35 W
105	Middlebury (mĭd''l-bĕr-ĭ) Vt.	44·00 N	73·10 W
118	Middle Concho (kŏn'chō) Tx.	31·21 N	100·50 W
156	Middlefart (mêd''l-fårt) Den.	55·30 N	9·45 E
108	Middle Loup (R.) (lōōp) Ne.	41·49 N	100·20 W
104	Middleport (mĭd''l-pōrt) Oh.	39·00 N	82·05 W
106	Middle River. Md. (Baltimore In.)	39·20 N	76·27 W
120	Middlesboro (mĭd''lz-bŭr-ô) Ky.	36·36 N	83·42 W
154	Middlesbrough (Teesside) (mĭd''lz-brŭ) Eng.	54·35 N	1·18 W
106	Middlesex (mĭd''l-sĕks) NJ (New York In.)	40·34 N	74·30 W
98	Middleton (mĭd''l-tŭn) Can.	44·57 N	65·04 W
148	Middleton Eng.	53·04 N	2·12 W
101	Middleton (I.) Ak.	59·35 N	146·35 W
105	Middletown Ct.	41·35 N	72·40 W
105	Middletown De.	39·30 N	75·40 W
99	Middletown Ma. (In.)	42·35 N	71·01 W
106	Middletown NY (New York In.)	41·26 N	74·25 W
104	Middletown Oh.	39·30 N	84·25 W
148	Middlewich (mĭd''l-wĭch) Eng.	53·11 N	2·27 W
106	Midfield Al. (Birmingham In.)	33·28 N	86·54 W
163	Midi, Canal du (kä-näl-dü-mê-dê') Fr.	43·22 N	1·35 E
213	Mid Illovo (mĭd ĭl'ô-vō) S. Afr. (Natal In.)	29·59 S	30·32 E
105	Midland (mĭd'lănd) Can.	44·45 N	79·50 W
104	Midland Mi.	43·40 N	84·20 W
118	Midland Tx.	32·05 N	102·05 W
113	Midvale (mĭd'vāl) Ut. (Salt Lake City In.)	40·37 N	111·54 W
120	Midway (mĭd'wā) Al.	32·03 N	85·30 W
198	Midway Is. Pac. O.	28·00 N	179·00 W
111	Midwest (mĭd-wĕst') Wy.	43·25 N	106·15 W
171	Midye (mēd'yĕ) Tur.	41·35 N	28·10 E
158	Miedzyrzecz (myăn-dzŭ'zhĕch) Pol.	52·26 N	15·35 E
159	Mielec (myĕ'lĕts) Pol.	50·17 N	21·27 E
118	Mier (myâr) Mex.	26·26 N	99·08 W
162	Mieres (myā'rās) Sp.	43·14 N	5·45 W
124	Mier y Noriega (myâr'ê nô-rê-ä'gä) Mex.	22·28 N	100·08 W
167	Migorod Sov. Un.	49·56 N	33·36 E
124	Miguel Auza (mē-gĕ'l-ä-ōō'zä) Mex.	24·17 N	103·27 W
136	Miguel Pereira (pĕ-rā'rä) Braz. (In.)	22·27 S	43·28 W
163	Mijares (R.) (mē-hä'räs) Sp.	40·05 N	0·42 W
195	Mikage (mē'kȧ-gȧ) Jap. (Ōsaka In.)	34·42 N	135·15 E
195	Mikawa-Wan (B.) (mē'kä-wä wän) Jap.	34·43 N	137·09 E
166	Mikhaylov (mē-käy'lôf) Sov. Un.	54·14 N	39·03 E
167	Mikhaylovka Sov. Un.	47·16 N	35·12 E
171	Mikhaylovka Sov. Un.	50·05 N	43·10 E
174	Mikhaylovka (mê-kä'ê-lôf-kȧ) Sov. Un. (Urals In.)	55·35 N	57·57 E
174	Mikhaylovka Sov. Un. (Leningrad In.)	59·20 N	30·21 E
174	Mikhnëvo (mĭk-nyô'vô) Sov. Un. (Moscow In.)	55·08 N	37·57 E
195	Miki (mē'kê) Jap. (Ōsaka In.)	34·47 N	134·59 E
217	Mikindani (mē-kēn-dä'nē) Tan.	10·17 S	40·07 E
157	Mikkeli (mĕk'ĕ-lĭ) Fin.	61·42 N	27·14 E
165	Míkonos (I.) Grc.	37·26 N	25·30 E
158	Mikulov (mĭ'kōō-lôf) Czech.	48·47 N	16·39 E
217	Mikumi Tan.	7·24 S	36·59 E
195	Mikuni (mē'kōō-nê) Jap.	36·09 N	136·14 E
195	Mikuni-Sammyaku (Mts.) (säm'myä-kōō) Jap.	36·51 N	138·38 E
195	Mikura (I.) (mē'kōō-rä) Jap.	33·53 N	139·26 E
109	Milaca (mê-lăk'ȧ) Mn.	45·45 N	93·41 W
104	Milan (mĭ'lăn) Mi.	42·05 N	83·40 W
117	Milan Mo.	40·13 N	93·07 W
120	Milan Tn.	35·54 N	88·47 W
	Milan, see Milano		
164	Milano (Milan) (mê-lä'nō) It.	45·29 N	9·12 E
171	Milâs (mē'läs) Tur.	37·10 N	27·25 E
164	Milazzo (mê-lät'sô) It.	38·13 N	15·17 E
108	Milbank (mĭl'băŋk) SD	45·13 N	96·38 W
203	Mildura (mĭl-dū'rȧ) Austl.	34·10 S	142·18 E
111	Miles City (mīlz) Mt.	46·24 N	105·50 W
105	Milford (mĭl'fērd) Ct.	41·15 N	73·05 W
105	Milford De.	38·55 N	75·25 W
99	Milford Ma. (In.)	42·09 N	71·31 W
107	Milford Mi. (Detroit In.)	42·35 N	83·36 W
105	Milford NH	42·50 N	71·40 W
107	Milford Oh. (Cincinnati In.)	39·11 N	84·18 W
115	Milford Ut.	38·20 N	113·05 W
154	Milford Haven (hăv'n) Wales	51·40 N	5·10 W
204	Miling (mĭl''ng) Austl.	30·30 S	116·25 E

Page	Name Pronunciation Region	Lat. °′	Long. °′
112	Milipitas (mĭl-ĭ-pĭ'tăs) Ca. (San Francisco In.)	37·26 N	121·54 W
93	Milk River (mĭlk) Can.	49·09 N	112·05 W
111	Milk R. Can.-U.S.	48·25 N	108·45 W
114	Mill Cr. Ca.	40·07 N	121·55 W
100	Mill Cr. (mĭl) Can. (Edmonton In.)	53·13 N	113·25 W
160	Millau (mē-yō') Fr.	44·06 N	3·04 E
112	Millbrae (mĭl'brā) Ca. (San Francisco In.)	37·36 N	122·23 W
99	Millbury (mĭl'bĕr-ĭ) Ma. (In.)	42·12 N	71·46 W
120	Milledgeville (mĭl'ĕj-vĭl) Ga.	33·05 N	83·15 W
100	Mille Îles, R. des (rê-vyâr' dā mĭl'ĭl') Can. (Montreal In.)	45·41 N	73·40 W
109	Mille Lac Ind. Res. (mĭl lăk') Mn.	46·14 N	94·13 W
109	Mille Lacs (L.) Mn.	46·25 N	93·22 W
199	Mille Lacs, Lac des (L.) (läk dĕ mēl läks) Can.	48·52 N	90·53 W
121	Millen (mĭl'ĕn) Ga.	32·47 N	81·55 W
108	Miller (mĭl'ẽr) SD	44·31 N	99·00 W
167	Millerovo (mĭl'ĕ-rô-vô) Sov. Un.	48·58 N	40·27 E
97	Millersburg (mĭl'ẽrz-bûrg) Ky.	38·15 N	84·10 W
97	Millersburg Oh.	40·35 N	81·55 W
105	Millersburg Pa.	40·35 N	76·55 W
120	Millers Ferry Lake (Res.) Al.	32·10 N	87·15 W
98	Millerton (mĭl'ẽr-tŭn) Can.	46·56 N	65·40 W
99	Millertown (mĭl'ẽr-toun) Can.	48·49 N	56·32 W
203	Millicent (mĭl-ĭ-sĕnt) Austl.	37·30 S	140·20 E
98	Millinocket (mĭl-ĭ-nŏk'ĕt) Me.	45·40 N	68·44 W
99	Millis (mĭl-ĭs) Ma. (In.)	42·10 N	71·22 W
113	Millstadt (mĭl'stăt) Il. (St. Louis In.)	38·27 N	90·06 W
106	Millstone (R.) (mĭl'stōn) NJ (New York In.)	40·27 N	74·38 W
204	Millstream (mĭl'strēm) Austl.	21·45 S	117·10 E
98	Milltown (mĭl'toun) Can.	45·13 N	67·19 W
107	Milvale (mĭl'vāl) Pa. (Pittsburgh In.)	40·29 N	79·58 W
112	Mill Valley (mĭl) Ca. (San Francisco In.)	37·54 N	122·32 W
105	Milville (mĭl'vĭl) NJ	39·25 N	75·00 W
117	Millwood Res. Ar.	33·00 N	94·00 W
161	Milly-la-Forêt (mē-yē'-la-fô-rĕ') Fr. (Paris In.)	48·24 N	2·28 E
212	Milnerton (mĭl'nẽr-tŭn) S. Afr. (In.)	33·52 S	18·30 E
108	Milnor (mĭl'nẽr) ND	46·17 N	97·29 W
98	Milo Me.	44·16 N	69·01 W
	Milo (I.), see Mílos		
165	Mílos (Milo) (I.) (mē'lŏs) Grc.	36·45 N	24·35 E
125	Milpa Alta (mē'l-pä-ä'l-tä) Mex. (In.)	19·11 N	99·01 W
100	Milton Can. (Toronto In.)	43·31 N	79·53 W
120	Milton (mĭl'tŭn) Fl.	30·37 N	87·02 W
99	Milton Ma. (In.)	42·16 N	71·03 W
105	Milton Pa.	41·00 N	76·50 W
113	Milton Ut. (Salt Lake City In.)	41·04 N	111·44 W
112	Milton Wa. (Seattle In.)	47·15 N	122·20 W
109	Milton Wi.	42·45 N	89·00 W
110	Milton-Freewater Or.	45·57 N	118·25 W
107	Milwaukee Wi. (Milwaukee In.)	43·03 N	87·55 W
107	Milwaukee R. Wi. (Milwaukee In.)	43·10 N	87·56 W
112	Milwaukee (mĭl-wô'kê) Or. (Portland In.)	45·27 N	122·38 W
125	Mimiapan (mē-myä-pän') Mex. (In.)	19·26 N	99·28 W
137	Mimoso do Sul (mē-mô'sō-dô-sōō'l) Braz. (Rio de Janeiro In.)	21·03 S	41·21 W
163	Mina (R.) (mē'nä) Alg.	35·24 N	0·51 E
95	Minago (R.) (mĭ-nä'gō) Can.	54·25 N	98·45 W
195	Minakuchi (mē'nä-kōō'chê) Jap.	34·59 N	136·06 E
128	Minas (mē'näs) Cuba	21·03 N	77·35 W
183	Minas Indon. (Singapore In.)	0·52 N	101·29 E
136	Minas (mē'näs) Ur.	34·18 S	55·12 W
126	Minas, Sierra de las (Mts.) (syĕr'rä dā läs mē'näs) Guat.	15·08 N	90·25 W
98	Minas Basin (mī'nȧs) Can.	45·20 N	64·00 W
98	Minas Chan. Can.	45·15 N	64·45 W
126	Minas de Oro (mê'-näs-dĕ-ŏ-rô) Hond.	14·52 N	87·19 W
162	Minas de Ríontinto (mē'näs dā rē-ō-tēn'tō) Sp.	37·43 N	6·35 W
135	Minas Gerais (State) (mē'näzh-zhĕ-rä'ēs) Braz.	17·45 S	43·50 W
135	Minas Nova (mē'näzh nō'väzh) Braz.	17·20 S	42·19 W
108	Minatare (L.) (mĭn'ȧ-târ) Ne.	41·56 N	103·07 W
125	Minatitlan (mê-nä-tê-tlän') Mex.	17·59 N	94·33 W
124	Minatitlan Mex.	19·21 N	104·02 W
195	Minato (mē'nȧ-tô) Jap. (Tōkyō In.)	35·13 N	139·52 E
154	Minch, The (Chan.) Scot.	58·04 N	6·04 W
154	Minch, The Little (Chan.) (mĭnch) Scot.	57·35 N	6·45 W
193	Min Chiang (R.) China	26·30 N	118·30 E
193	Min Chiang (R.) China	29·30 N	104·00 E
197	Mindanao (I.) (mĭn-dä-nou') Phil.	7·30 N	125·10 E
197	Mindanao Sea Phil.	8·55 N	124·00 E
210	Mindelo C. V. Is. (In.)	16·53 N	25·00 W
158	Minden (mĭn'dĕn) F.R.G.	52·17 N	8·58 E
119	Minden La.	32·36 N	93·19 W
116	Minden Ne.	40·30 N	98·54 W
197	Mindoro (I.) (mĭn-dô'rō) Phil. (In.)	13·04 N	121·06 E
197	Mindoro Str. Phil. (In.)	12·28 N	120·33 E
174	Mindyak (mĕn'dyäk) Sov. Un. (Urals In.)	54·01 N	58·48 E
106	Mineola (mĭn-ê-ō'lȧ) NY (New York In.)	40·43 N	73·38 W
119	Mineola Tx.	32·39 N	95·31 W
124	Mineral del Chico (mê-nȧ-räl'dĕl chē'kô) Mex.	20·13 N	98·46 W

ng-sing; ŋ-baŋk; N-nasalized n; nŏd; cŏmmit; ōld; ôbey; ôrder; fōōd; fŏŏt; ou-out; s-soft; sh-dish; th-thin; pūre; ûnite; ûrn; stŭd; circŭs; ü-as "y" in study; '-indeterminate vowel.

ăt; fīnăl; rāte; senâte; ärm; àsk; sofá; fâre; ch-choose; dh-as th in other; bē; ĕvent; bĕt; recĕnt; cratēr; g-go; gh-guttural g; bĭt; ǐ-short neutral; rīde; к-guttural k as ch in German ich;

PRONOUNCING INDEX

Momence — Morehead 315

Page	Name Pronunciation Region	Lat. °′	Long. °′
107	Momence (mô-mĕns') Il. (Chicago In.)	41·09 N	87·40 W
126	Momostenango (mô-môs-tā-näŋ'gô). Guat.	15·02 N	91·25 W
126	Momotombo Nic.	12·25 N	86·43 W
197	Mompog Pass (mŏm-pōg') Phil. (In.)	13·35 N	122·09 E
134	Mompos (mŏm-pōs') Col.	8·05 N	74·30 W
156	Møn (I.) (mûn) Den.	54·54 N	12·30 E
107	Monaca (mŏ-nȧ'kō) Pa. (Pittsburgh In.)	40·41 N	80·17 W
151	Monaco (mŏn'ȧ-kō) Eur.	43·43 N	7·47 E
154	Monaghan (mŏn'ȧ-găn) Ire.	54·16 N	7·20 W
123	Mona Pass. (mō'nä) N. A.	18·00 N	68·10 W
92	Monarch Mtn. (mŏn'ẽrk) Can.	51·54 N	125·53 W
93	Monashee Mts. (mŏ-nă'shē) Can.	50·30 N	118·30 W
151	Monastir (môn-ȧs-tēr') Tun.	35·49 N	10·56 E
	Monastir, see Bitola		
167	Monastyrishche (mô-nȧs-tē-rēsh'chȧ). Sov. Un.	48·57 N	29·53 E
166	Monastyrshchina (mô-nȧs-tērsh'chĭ-nȧ). Sov. Un.	54·19 N	31·49 E
135	Monçao (mon-souN') Braz.	3·39 S	45·23 W
162	Moncayo (Mtn.) (môn-kä'yō). Sp.	41·44 N	1·48 W
170	Monchegorsk (mŏn'chĕ-gôrsk) Sov. Un.	69·00 N	33·35 E
161	Mönchengladbach (mûn'ĸĕn gläd'bäĸ) F.R.G. (Ruhr In.)	51·12 N	6·28 E
162	Moncique, Serra de (Mts.) (sĕr'rä dä môn-chē'kĕ). Port.	37·22 N	8·37 W
118	Monclovra (môn-klō'vä) Mex.	26·53 N	101·25 W
98	Moncton (mŭŋk'tŭn) Can.	46·06 N	64·47 W
162	Mondego, Cabo (C.) (kȧ'bō môn-dā'gōō). Port.	40·12 N	8·55 W
162	Mondêgo (R.) (mōn-dĕ'gō). Port.	40·10 N	8·36 W
212	Mondombe (môn-dôm'bā) Zaire	0·45 S	23·06 E
162	Mondoñedo (môn-dô-nyā'dō). Sp.	43·35 N	7·18 W
164	Mondoví (mōn-dô'vē') It.	44·23 N	7·53 E
109	Mondovi (mŏn-dō'vĭ) Wi.	44·35 N	91·42 W
107	Monee (mŏ-nĭ) Il. (Chicago In.)	41·25 N	87·45 W
107	Monessen (mŏ'nĕs'sĕn) Pa. (Pittsburgh In.)	40·09 N	79·53 W
117	Monett (mô-nĕt') Mo.	36·55 N	93·55 W
162	Monforte de Lemos (môn-fôr'tä dĕ lĕ'môs). Sp.	42·30 N	7·30 W
215	Monga Chad.	4·12 N	22·49 E
211	Mongala R. (mŏn-gȧl'ȧ) Zaire	3·20 N	21·30 E
211	Mongalla Sud.	5·11 N	31·46 E
184	Monghyr (mŏn-gēr') India	25·23 N	86·34 E
214	Mongo (R.) S. L.	9·50 N	11·50 W
182	Mongolia (mŏŋ-gō'lĭ-ȧ) Asia	46·00 N	100·00 E
211	Mongos, Chaîne des (Mts.) Cen. Afr. Rep.	8·04 N	21·59 E
216	Mongoumba (mŏŋ-gōōm'bȧ) Cen. Afr. Rep.	3·38 N	18·36 E
216	Mongu (mŏŋ-gōō') Zambia	15·15 S	23·09 E
174	Monino Sov. Un. (Moscow In.)	55·50 N	38·13 E
217	Monkey Bay Malawi	14·05 S	34·55 E
126	Monkey River (mŭŋ'kĭ) Belize (In.)	16·22 N	88·33 W
100	Monkland (mŭngk-lănd) Can. (Ottawa In.)	45·12 N	74·52 W
216	Monkoto (môn-kō'tô) Zaire	1·38 S	20·39 E
117	Monmouth (mŏn'mŭth) (mŏn'mouth). Il.	40·54 N	90·38 W
106	Monmouth Junction (mŏn'mouth jŭngk'shŭn) NJ (New York In.)	40·23 N	74·33 W
92	Monmouth Mtn. (mŏn'mŭth). Can.	51·00 N	123·47 W
114	Mono (L.) (mō'nō) Ca.	38·04 N	119·00 W
214	Mono (R.) Togo	7·20 N	1·25 E
104	Monon (mō'nŏn) In.	40·55 N	86·55 W
105	Monongah (mô-nŏŋ'gȧ) WV	39·25 N	80·10 W
107	Monongahela (mô-nŏn-gȧ-hē'lȧ) Pa. (Pittsburgh In.)	40·11 N	79·55 W
105	Monongahela (R.) WV	39·30 N	80·10 W
165	Monopoli (mô-nô'pô-lē) It.	40·55 N	17·17 E
163	Monovar (mô-nō'vär) Sp.	38·26 N	0·50 W
164	Monreale (mōn-rā-ä'lā) It.	38·04 N	13·15 E
120	Monroe (mŭn-rō') Ga.	33·47 N	83·43 W
119	Monroe La.	32·30 N	92·06 W
104	Monroe Mi.	41·55 N	83·25 W
106	Monroe NY (New York In.)	41·19 N	74·11 W
121	Monroe NC	34·58 N	80·34 W
115	Monroe Ut.	38·35 N	112·10 W
112	Monroe Wa. (Seattle In.)	47·52 N	121·58 W
109	Monroe Wi.	42·35 N	89·40 W
121	Monroe (L.) Fl.	28·50 N	81·15 W
117	Monroe City Mo.	39·38 N	91·41 W
120	Monroeville (mŭn-rō'vĭl) Al.	31·33 N	87·19 W
113	Monrovia (mŏn-rō'vĭ-ȧ) Ca. (Los Angeles In.)	34·09 N	118·00 W
214	Monrovia Lib.	6·18 N	10·47 W
155	Mons (môN') Bel.	50·29 N	3·55 E
98	Monson (mŏn'sŭn) Me.	45·17 N	69·28 W
156	Mönsterås (mŭn'stĕr-ôs) Swe.	57·04 N	16·24 E
188	Montagh Ata (Mt.) China	38·26 N	75·23 E
103	Montagne Tremblante Prov. Pk. Can.	46·30 N	75·51 W
99	Montague (mŏn'tȧ-gū) Can.	46·10 N	62·39 W
104	Montague Mi.	43·30 N	86·25 W
101	Montague (I.) Ak.	60·10 N	147·00 W
197	Montalban (mōnt-äl-bän) Phil. (In.)	14·47 N	121·11 E
135	Montalbán Ven. (In.)	10·14 N	68·19 W
164	Montalcone (môn-täl-kô'nĕ) It.	45·49 N	13·30 E
162	Montalegre (mōn-tä-lā'grĕ). Port.	41·49 N	7·48 W
102	Montana (State) (mŏn-tăn'ȧ). U.S.	47·10 N	111·50 W
162	Montánchez (môn-tän'chāth). Sp.	39·18 N	6·09 W
160	Montargis (môN-tȧr-zhē') Fr.	47·59 N	2·42 E
161	Montataire (môN-tȧ-târ) Fr. (Paris In.)	49·15 N	2·26 E
160	Montauban (môN-tô-bäN') Fr.	44·01 N	1·22 E
105	Montauk NY	41·03 N	71·57 W
105	Montauk Pt. (mŏn-tôk') NY	41·05 N	71·55 W
163	Montbanch (mōnt-bän'ch) Sp.	41·20 N	1·08 E
160	Montbard (môN-bȧr') Fr.	47·40 N	4·19 E
161	Montbéliard (môN-bā-lyȧr') Fr.	47·32 N	6·45 E
119	Mont Belvieu (mŏnt bĕl'vū) Tx. (In.)	29·51 N	94·53 W
161	Mont Blanc Tunnel (môN bläN) Fr.-It.	45·53 N	6·53 E
160	Montbrison (môN-brē-zôN') Fr.	45·38 N	4·06 E
160	Montcalm, Pic de (Pk.) (pēk dē môN-kȧm'). Fr.	42·43 N	1·13 E
160	Montceau-les-Mines (môN-sō'lā-mēn'). Fr.	46·39 N	4·22 E
106	Montclair (mŏnt-klâr') NJ (New York In.)	40·49 N	74·13 W
160	Mont-de-Marsan (môN-dē-mȧr-säN'). Fr.	43·54 N	0·32 W
160	Montdidier (môN-dē-dyā') Fr.	49·42 N	2·33 E
137	Monte (mŏ'n-tĕ) Arg. (Buenos Aires In.)	35·25 S	58·49 W
134	Monteagudo (mōn'tȧ-ä-gōō'dhō) Bol.	19·49 S	63·48 W
113	Montebello (mŏn-tê-bĕl'ō) Ca. (Los Angeles In.)	34·01 N	118·06 W
100	Montebello Can. (Ottawa In.)	45·40 N	74·56 W
204	Monte Bello (Is.) Austl.	20·30 S	114·10 E
136	Monte Caseros (mŏ'n-tĕ-kä-sĕ'rôs). Arg.	30·16 S	57·39 W
126	Mont Ecillos, Cord. de (Mts.) (kôr-dēl-yĕ'rä dĕ mô'nt ĕ-sē'l-yōs). Hond.	14·19 N	87·52 W
129	Monte Cristi (mô'n-tĕ-krē's-tē) Dom. Rep.	19·50 N	71·40 W
164	Montecristo, I. di (mōn'tȧ-krēs'tō). It.	42·20 N	10·19 E
124	Monte Escobedo (mōn'tā ĕs-kô-bā'dhō). Mex.	22·18 N	103·34 W
163	Monteforte Irpino (môn-tĕ-fŏ'r-tĕ ē'r-pē'nō) It. (Naples In.)	40·39 N	14·42 E
162	Montefrío (mōn-tȧ-frē'ō) Sp.	37·20 N	4·02 W
128	Montego Bay (mōn-tē'gō) Jam.	18·30 N	77·55 W
136	Monte Grande (mŏ'n-tĕ grän'dĕ) Arg. (Buenos Aires In.)	34·34 S	58·28 W
163	Montelavar (mōn-tĕ-lȧ-vär') Port. (Lisbon In.)	38·51 N	9·20 W
160	Montélimar (môN-tā-lē-mär'). Fr.	44·33 N	4·47 E
162	Montellano (mōn-tȧ-lyä'nō). Sp.	37·00 N	5·34 W
109	Montello (mŏn-tĕl'ō) Wi.	43·47 N	89·20 W
118	Montemorelos (mōn'tȧ-mō-rā'lōs) Mex.	25·14 N	99·50 W
162	Montemor-o-Novo (mōN-tĕ-môr'ōō-nô'vōō). Port.	38·39 N	8·11 W
	Montenegro (Reg.), see Crna Gora		
217	Montepuez Moz.	13·07 S	39·00 E
164	Montepulciano (môn'tȧ-pōōl-chä'nō). It.	43·05 N	11·48 E
160	Montereau-faut-Yonne (môN-t'rō'fō-yôn'). Fr.	48·24 N	2·57 E
114	Monterey (mŏn-tĕ-rā') Ca.	36·36 N	121·53 W
120	Monterey Tn.	36·06 N	85·15 W
114	Monterey B. Ca.	36·48 N	122·01 W
113	Monterey Park Ca. (Los Angeles In.)	34·04 N	118·08 W
134	Montería (mōn-tȧ-rä'ä) Col.	8·47 N	75·57 W
136	Monteros (môn-tĕ'rôs) Arg.	27·14 S	65·29 W
163	Monterotondo (môn-tĕ-rô-tô'n-dō) It. (Rome In.)	42·03 N	12·39 E
118	Monterrey (mōn-tĕr-rā') Mex.	25·43 N	100·19 W
164	Monte Sant' Angelo (mô'n-tĕ sän ä'n-gzhĕ-lô). It.	41·43 N	15·59 E
110	Montesano (mŏn-tĕ-sä'nō) Wa.	46·59 N	123·35 W
135	Montes Claros (môn-tĕs-klä'rôs) Braz.	16·44 S	43·41 W
120	Montevallo (mōn-tê-văl'ō) Al.	33·05 N	86·49 W
164	Montevarchi (mōn-tȧ-vär'kē) It.	43·30 N	11·45 E
137	Montevideo (mōn'tȧ-vê-dhā'ō) Ur. (Buenos Aires In.)	34·50 S	56·10 W
115	Monte Vista (mŏn'tē vĭs'tȧ) Co.	37·35 N	106·10 W
120	Montezuma (mŏn-tē-zōō'mȧ) Ga.	32·17 N	84·00 W
115	Montezuma Castle Natl. Mon. Az.	34·38 N	111·50 W
149	Montfoort. Neth. (Amsterdam In.)	52·02 N	4·56 E
161	Montfort l'Amaury (mŏN-fŏr'lä-mō-rē') Fr. (Paris In.)	48·47 N	1·49 E
160	Montfort-sur-Meu (mŏn-fŏr-sür-mû'). Fr.	48·09 N	1·58 W
120	Montgomery (mŏnt-gŭm'ēr-ĭ). Al.	32·23 N	86·17 W
104	Montgomery WV	38·10 N	81·25 W
117	Montgomery City Mo.	38·58 N	91·29 W
117	Monticello (mŏn-tĭ-sĕl'ō) Ar.	33·38 N	91·47 W
120	Monticello Fl.	30·32 N	83·53 W
120	Monticello Ga.	33·00 N	83·11 W
104	Monticello Il.	40·05 N	88·35 W
104	Monticello In.	40·40 N	86·50 W
109	Monticello Ia.	42·14 N	91·13 W
120	Monticello Ky.	36·47 N	84·50 W
98	Monticello Me.	46·19 N	67·53 W
109	Monticello Mn.	45·18 N	93·48 W
105	Monticello NY	41·35 N	74·40 W
115	Monticello Ut.	37·55 N	109·25 W
161	Montigny-lès-Metz (môN-tēn-yē'lā-mĕts'). Fr.	49·06 N	6·07 E
163	Montijo (môn-tē'zhō) Port. (Lisbon In.)	38·42 N	8·58 W
162	Montijo (mōn-tē'hō) Sp.	38·55 N	6·35 W
127	Montijo, Bahia (B.) (bä-ē'ä mōn-tē'hō). Pan.	7·36 N	81·11 W
98	Mont-Joli (môN zhô-lē') Can.	48·35 N	68·11 W
160	Montluçon (môN-lü-sôN') Fr.	46·20 N	2·35 E
100	Montmagny (môN-män-yē') Can. (Quebec In.)	46·59 N	70·33 W
100	Montmorency (mŏnt-mô-rĕn'sĭ) Can. (Quebec In.)	46·53 N	71·09 W
161	Montmorency (môN'mô-räN-sē') Fr. (Paris In.)	48·59 N	2·19 E
100	Montmorency (R.) (mŏnt-mô-rĕn'sĭ) Can. (Quebec In.)	47·30 N	71·10 W
160	Montmorillon (môN'mô-rê-yôN') Fr.	46·26 N	0·50 E
164	Montone (R.) (môn-tô'nĕ) It.	44·03 N	11·45 E
162	Montoro (môn-tō'rō) Sp.	38·01 N	4·22 W
104	Montpelier (mŏnt-pēl'yẽr) In.	40·35 N	85·20 W
111	Montpelier Id.	42·19 N	111·19 W
104	Montpelier Oh.	41·35 N	84·35 W
105	Montpelier Vt.	44·20 N	72·35 W
160	Montpellier (môN-pĕ-lyā') Fr.	43·38 N	3·53 E
100	Montréal (mŏn-trê-ôl') Can. (Montréal In.)	45·30 N	73·35 W
94	Montreal L. Can.	54·20 N	105·40 W
96	Montreal (R.) Can.	47·15 N	84·20 W
97	Montreal (R.) Can.	47·50 N	80·30 W
100	Montréal-Nord Can. (Montréal In.)	45·36 N	73·38 W
158	Montreux (môn-trû') Switz.	46·26 N	6·52 E
113	Montrose (mŏnt-rōz) Ca. (Los Angeles In.)	34·13 N	118·13 W
115	Montrose (mŏn-trōz') Co.	38·30 N	107·55 W
107	Montrose Oh. (Cleveland In.)	41·08 N	81·38 W
105	Montrose (mŏnt-rōz') Pa.	41·50 N	75·50 W
154	Montrose Scot.	56·45 N	2·25 W
100	Mont-Royal. Can. (Montreal In.)	47·31 N	73·39 W
98	Monts, Pointe des (Pt.) (pwăNt' dā môN'). Can.	49·19 N	67·22 W
161	Mont St. Martin (môN săN mär-tăN'). Fr.	49·34 N	6·13 E
123	Montserrat (mŏnt-sĕ-răt') N. A.	16·48 N	63·15 W
106	Montvale (mŏnt-vāl') NJ (New York In.)	41·02 N	74·01 W
196	Monywa (mŏn'yōō-wȧ) Bur.	22·02 N	95·16 E
164	Monza (mōn'tsä) It.	45·34 N	9·17 E
163	Monzón (mōn-thōn') Sp.	41·54 N	1·09 E
119	Moody (mōō'dĭ) Tx.	31·18 N	97·20 W
218	Mooi (R.) (mōō'ĭ) S. Afr. (Johannesburg & Pretoria In.)	26·34 S	27·03 E
213	Mooi (R.) S. Afr. (Natal In.)	29·00 S	30·15 E
213	Mooirivier S. Afr. (Natal In.)	29·14 S	29·59 E
202	Moolap Austl. (Melbourne In.)	38·11 S	144·26 E
203	Moonta (mōōn'tȧ) Austl.	34·05 S	137·42 E
204	Moora (mōōr'ȧ) Austl.	30·35 S	116·12 E
111	Moorcroft (mōr'krôft) Wy.	44·17 N	104·59 W
204	Moore (L.) (mōr) Austl.	29·50 S	128·12 E
149	Moorenweis (mō'rĕn-vīz) F.R.G. (Munich In.)	48·10 N	11·05 E
105	Moore Res. Vt.-NH	44·20 N	72·10 W
106	Moorestown (morz'toun) NJ (Philadelphia In.)	39·58 N	74·56 W
107	Mooresville (mōrz'vĭl) In. (Indianapolis In.)	39·37 N	86·22 W
121	Mooresville (mōrz'vĭl) NC	35·34 N	80·48 W
108	Moorhead (mōr'hĕd) Mn.	46·52 N	96·44 W
120	Moorhead Ms.	33·25 N	90·30 W
	Moorland (Plain), see Landes		
90	Moose (L.) (mōōs) Can.	54·14 N	99·28 W
91	Moose (R.) Can.	51·01 N	80·42 W
100	Moose Creek Can. (Ottawa In.)	45·16 N	74·58 W
98	Moosehead (mōōs'hĕd) Me.	45·37 N	69·15 W
95	Moose I. Can.	51·50 N	97·09 W
94	Moose Jaw (mōōs jô) Can.	50·23 N	105·32 W
94	Moose Jaw (Cr.) Can.	50·34 N	105·17 W
95	Moose Lake Can.	53·40 N	100·28 W
95	Moose Mtn. Can.	49·45 N	102·37 W
94	Moose Mtn. Cr. Can.	49·12 N	102·10 W
105	Moosilauke (Mtn.) (mōō-sĭ-lȧ'kē). NH	44·00 N	71·50 W
149	Moosinning (mō'zē-nēng) F.R.G. (Munich In.)	48·17 N	11·51 E
95	Moosomin (mōō'sô-mĭn) Can.	50·07 N	101·40 W
91	Moosonee (mōō'sô-nē) Can.	51·20 N	80·44 W
214	Mopti (mŏp'tē) Mali	14·30 N	4·12 W
134	Moquegua (mô-kā'gwä) Peru	17·15 S	70·54 W
159	Mór (mōr) Hung.	47·51 N	18·14 E
185	Mora India (In.)	18·54 N	72·56 E
109	Mora (mō'rȧ) Mn.	45·52 N	93·18 W
116	Mora NM	35·58 N	105·17 W
162	Mora (mô-rä) Sp.	39·42 N	3·45 W
163	Mora Sp.	41·06 N	0·25 E
184	Morādābād (mô-rä-dä-bäd'). India	28·57 N	78·48 E
126	Morales (mô-rä'lĕs) Guat.	15·29 N	88·46 W
213	Moramanga (mō-rä-mäŋ'gä). Mad.	18·48 S	48·09 E
129	Morant Pt. (mô-rănt') Jam.	17·55 N	76·10 W
156	Morastrand (mō'rä-stränd) Swe.	61·00 N	14·29 E
163	Morata de Tajuña (mô-rä'tä dā tä-hōō'nyä) Sp. (Madrid In.)	40·14 N	3·27 W
185	Moratuwa Sri Lanka	6·35 N	79·59 E
159	Morava (Moravia) (Prov.) (mô'rä-vä) (mō-rā'vĭ-ȧ). Czech.	49·21 N	16·57 E
158	Morava R. Czech.	49·53 N	16·53 E
	Moravia, see Morava		
135	Morawhanna (mô-rȧ-hwä'nȧ). Guy.	8·12 N	59·33 W
154	Moray Firth (mŭr'ā) Scot.	57·41 N	3·55 W
156	Mörbylånga (mûr'bü-lôŋ'gȧ). Swe.	56·32 N	16·23 E
95	Morden (môr'dĕn) Can.	49·11 N	98·05 W
202	Mordialloc (môr-dĭ-ăl'ŏk) Austl. (Melbourne In.)	38·00 S	145·05 E
170	Mordvin (A.S.S.R.) Sov. Un.	54·18 N	43·50 E
154	More, Ben (Mtn.) (bĕn môr). Scot.	58·09 N	5·01 W
108	Moreau (R.) (mô-rō') SD	45·13 N	102·22 W
154	Morecambe B. (mōr'kȧm) Eng.	53·55 N	3·25 W
203	Moree (mō'rē) Austl.	29·20 S	149·50 E
104	Morehead Ky.	38·10 N	83·25 W

ng-sing; ŋ-baŋk; N-nasalized n; nŏd; cŏmmit; ōld; ôbey; ôrder; fōōd; fŏŏt; ou-out; s-soft; sh-dish; th-thin; pūre; ûnite; ûrn; stŭd; circŭs; ü-as "y" in study; '-indeterminate vowel.

ăt; fīnăl; rāte; senâte; ärm; àsk; sofá; fâre; ch-choose; dh-as th in other; bē; ĕvent; bĕt; recĕnt; cratēr; g-go; gh-guttural g; bĭt; ĭ-short neutral; rīde; ᴋ-guttural k as ch in German ich;

PRONOUNCING INDEX

Muir Woods — Nakhichevan 317

Page	Name / Pronunciation / Region	Lat. °′	Long. °′
114	Muir Woods Natl. Mon (mūr) . Ca.	37·54 N	123·22 W
212	Muizenberg (mwĭz-ĕn-bûrg') S. Afr. (In.)	34·07 S	18·28 E
159	Mukachëvo (mŏŏ-kȧ-chyô'vô) Sov. Un.	48·25 N	22·43 E
	Mukden, see Shenyang		
173	Mukhtuya (mŏŏk-tōō'yȧ) Sov. Un.	61·00 N	113·00 E
112	Mukilteo (mū-kĭl-tā'ō) Wa. (Seattle In.)	47·57 N	122·18 W
195	Muko (mōō'kô) . Jap. (Ōsaka In.)	34·57 N	135·43 E
195	Muko (R.) (mōō'kô) Jap. (Ōsaka In.)	34·52 N	135·17 E
95	Mukutawa (R.) . . . Can.	53·10 N	97·28 W
107	Mukwonago (mū-kwō-nȧ'gō) Wi. (Milwaukee In.)	42·52 N	88·19 W
162	Mula (mōō'lä) . . . Sp.	38·05 N	1·12 W
158	Mulde R. (mŏŏl'dĕ) . . . G.D.R.	50·30 N	12·30 E
192	Muleng . . . China	44·32 N	130·18 E
192	Muleng (R.) . . . China	44·40 N	130·30 E
124	Muleros (mōō-lā'rōs) . . . Mex.	23·44 N	104·00 W
116	Muleshoe . . . Tx.	34·13 N	102·43 W
106	Mulga (mŭl'gȧ) Al. (Birmingham In.)	33·33 N	86·59 W
99	Mulgrave (mŭl'grāv) . . . Can.	45·37 N	61·23 W
205	Mulgrave (I.) . . . Austl.	10·08 S	142·14 E
162	Mulhacén (Mtn.) . . . Sp.	37·04 N	3·18 W
161	Mülheim (mül'hīm) F.R.G. (Ruhr In.)	51·25 N	6·53 E
161	Mulhouse (mü-lōōz') . . . Fr.	47·46 N	7·20 E
154	Mull (I.) (mŭl) . . . Scot.	56·40 N	6·19 W
110	Mullan (mŭl'ăn) . . . Id.	47·26 N	115·50 W
196	Müller, Pegunungan (Mts.) (mül'ĕr) . Indon.	0·22 N	113·05 E
154	Mullet Pen . . . Ire.	54·15 N	10·12 W
154	Mullinger (mŭl-ĭn-gär) . . . Ire.	53·31 N	7·26 W
121	Mullins (mŭl'ĭnz) . . . SC	34·11 N	79·13 W
126	Mullins River . . . Belize (In.)	17·08 N	88·18 W
184	Multān (mōō-tän') . . . Pak.	30·17 N	71·13 E
112	Multnomah Chan. (mŭl nō mȧ) Or. (Portland In.)	45·41 N	122·53 W
196	Mulu, Gunung (Mtn.) . . . Mala.	3·56 N	115·11 E
217	Mulumbe, Monts (Mts.) . . . Zaire	8·47 S	27·20 E
117	Mulvane (mŭl-vān') . . . Ks.	37·30 N	97·13 W
217	Mumbwa (mŏŏm'bwä) . . . Zambia	14·59 S	27·04 E
217	Mumias . . . Ken.	0·20 N	34·29 E
126	Muna (mōō'nȧ) . . . Mex. (In.)	20·28 N	89·42 W
149	München (Munich) (mün'kĕn) F.R.G. (Munich In.)	48·08 N	11·35 E
104	Muncie (mŭn'sĭ) . . . In.	40·10 N	85·30 W
107	Mundelein (mŭn-dē-lĭn') Il. (Chicago In.)	42·16 N	88·00 W
134	Mundonueva, Pico de (Pk.) (pē'kô-dĕ-mōō'n-dô-nwĕ'vä) Col. (In.)	4·18 N	74·12 W
125	Muneco, Cerro (Mtn.) (sĕ'r-rô-mōō-nĕ'kō) . Mex. (In.)	19·13 N	99·20 W
205	Mungana (mŭn-găn'ȧ) . . . Austl.	17·15 S	144·18 E
217	Mungbere . . . Zaire	2·38 N	28·30 E
113	Munger (mŭn'gĕr) Mn. (Duluth In.)	46·48 N	92·20 W
203	Mungindi (mŭn-gĭn'dē) . . . Austl.	32·00 S	148·45 E
107	Munhall (mŭn'hôl) Pa. (Pittsburgh In.)	40·24 N	79·53 W
212	Munhango (mōōn-häŋ'gȧ) . . . Ang.	12·15 S	18·55 E
	Munich, see München		
109	Munising (mū'nĭ-sĭng) . . . Mi.	46·24 N	86·41 W
172	Munku Sardyk (Mtn.) (mōōn'kōō sär-dĭk') Sov. Un.-Mong.	51·45 N	100·30 E
197	Muños (mōōn-nyōth') . . Phil. (In.)	15·44 N	120·53 E
161	Münster (mün'stĕr) F.R.G. (Ruhr In.)	51·57 N	7·38 E
107	Munster (mŭn'stĕr) In. (Chicago In.)	41·34 N	87·31 W
154	Munster (mŭn-stĕr) . . . Ire.	52·30 N	9·24 W
196	Muntok (mōōn-tŏk') . . . Indon.	2·05 S	105·11 E
137	Munzi Freire (mōō-nē'z-frā'rĕ) Braz. (Rio de Janeiro In.)	20·29 S	41·25 W
196	Muong Sing (mōō'ông-sĭng') . Laos	21·06 N	101·17 E
150	Muonio (R.) . . . Fin.-Swe.	68·15 N	23·00 E
137	Muqui (mōō-kōō'ē) Braz. (Rio de Janeiro In.)	20·56 S	41·20 W
171	Muradiye (mōō-rä'dē-yĕ) . . . Tur.	39·00 N	43·40 E
160	Murat (mü-rä') . . . Fr.	45·05 N	2·56 E
171	Murat (R.) (mōō-rät') . . . Tur.	38·50 N	40·40 E
204	Murchison (R.) (mûr'chĭ-sŭn) Austl.	26·45 S	116·15 E
217	Murchison Falls (mûr'chĭ-sŭn) . Ug.	2·15 N	31·41 E
162	Murcia (mōōr'thyä) . . . Sp.	38·00 N	1·10 W
162	Murcia (Reg.) . . . Sp.	38·35 N	1·51 W
108	Murdo (mûr'dô) . . . SD	43·53 N	100·42 W
159	Mureşul R. (mōō'rĕsh-ōōl) . . Rom.	46·02 N	21·50 E
160	Muret (mü-rĕ') . . . Fr.	43·28 N	1·17 E
120	Murfreesboro (mûr'frēz-bŭr-ô) . Tn.	35·50 N	86·19 W
141	Murgab (R.) (mōōr-gäb') . Sov. Un.	37·07 N	62·32 E
137	Muriaé (mōō-ryȧ-ĕ') Braz. (Rio de Janeiro In.)	21·10 S	42·21 W
137	Muriaé (R.) Braz. (Rio de Janeiro In.)	21·20 S	41·40 W
174	Murino (mōō'rĭ-nô) Sov. Un. (Leningrad In.)	60·03 N	30·28 E
158	Müritz See (L.) (mür'ĭts) . . G.D.R.	53·20 N	12·33 E
188	Murku Sardyk (Pk.) Sov. Un.-Mong.	51·56 N	100·21 E
170	Murmansk (mōōr-mänsk') Sov. Un.	69·00 N	33·20 E
170	Murom (mōō'rôm) . . . Sov. Un.	55·30 N	42·00 E
194	Muroran (mōō'rô-rän) . . . Jap.	42·21 N	141·05 E
162	Muros (mōō'rōs) . . . Sp.	42·48 N	9·00 W
195	Muroto-Zaki (Pt.) (mōō'rô-tō zä'kē) . Jap.	33·14 N	134·12 E
113	Murphy (mŭr'fĭ) Mo. (St. Louis In.)	38·29 N	90·29 W
120	Murphy . . . NC	35·05 N	84·00 W
117	Murphysboro (mŭr'fĭz-bŭr-ô) . . . Il.	37·46 N	89·21 W
120	Murray (mŭr'ĭ) . . . Ky.	36·39 N	88·17 W
113	Murray . . Ut. (Salt Lake City In.)	40·40 N	111·53 W
93	Murray (R.) . . . Can.	55·00 N	121·00 W
121	Murray (R.) (mŭr'ĭ) . . . SC	34·07 N	81·18 W
203	Murray Bridge . . . Austl.	35·10 S	139·35 E
98	Murray Harbour . . . Can.	46·00 N	62·31 W
205	Murray Reg. (mŭ'rē) . . . Austl.	33·20 S	142·30 E
203	Murray R . . . Austl.	34·20 S	142·21 W
158	Mur R. (mōōr) . . . Aus.	47·10 N	14·08 E
203	Murrumbidgee (R.) (mŭr-ŭm-bĭd'jē) . Austl.	34·30 S	145·20 E
217	Murrupula . . . Moz.	15·27 S	38·47 E
184	Murshidābād (mōōr'shē-dä-bäd') India	24·08 N	87·11 E
164	Murska Sobota (mōōr'skä sô'bô-tä) . Yugo.	46·40 N	16·14 E
217	Muruasigar (Mtn.) . . . Ken.	3·08 N	35·02 E
184	Murwāra . . . India	23·54 N	80·23 E
203	Murwillumbah (mŭr-wĭl'lŭm-bŭ) Austl.	28·15 S	153·30 E
158	Mürz R. (mürts) . . . Aus.	47·30 N	15·21 E
158	Murzzuschlag (mürts'tsōō-shlägh) Aus.	47·37 N	15·41 E
171	Mus (mōōsh) . . . Tur.	38·55 N	41·30 E
165	Musala (Mtn.) . . . Bul.	42·05 N	23·24 E
194	Musan (mōō'sän) . . . Kor.	41·11 N	129·10 E
195	Musashino (mōō-sä'shē-nō) Jap. (Tōkyō In.)	35·43 N	139·35 E
186	Muscat (mŭs-kăt') . . . Om.	23·23 N	58·30 E
	Muscat & Oman, see Oman		
109	Muscatine (mŭs-kȧ-tēn') . . . Ia.	41·26 N	91·00 W
120	Muscle Shoals (mŭs''l shōlz) . . . Al.	34·44 N	87·38 W
204	Musgrave Ra. (mŭs'grāv) . . Austl.	26·15 S	131·15 E
212	Mushie (mŭsh'ē) . . . Zaire	3·04 S	16·50 E
215	Mushin . . . Nig.	6·32 N	3·22 E
196	Musi (Strm.) (mōō'sē) . . . Indon.	2·40 S	103·42 E
134	Musinga, Alto (Ht.) (ȧ'l-tô-mōō-sē'n-gä) . Col. (In.)	6·40 N	76·13 W
107	Muskego L. (mŭs-kē'gō) Wi. (Milwaukee In.)	42·53 N	88·10 W
104	Muskegon (mŭs-kē'gŭn) . . . Mi.	43·15 N	86·20 W
104	Muskegon (R.) . . . Mi.	43·20 N	85·55 W
104	Muskegon Heights . . . Mi.	43·10 N	86·20 W
104	Muskingum (R.) (mŭs-kĭŋ'gŭm) Oh.	39·45 N	81·55 W
117	Muskogee (mŭs-kō'gē) . . . Ok.	35·44 N	95·21 W
105	Muskoka (L.) (mŭs-kō'kȧ) . . . Can.	45·00 N	79·30 W
217	Musoma . . . Tan.	1·30 S	33·48 E
197	Mussau (I.) (mōō-sä'ōō) Pap. N. Gui.	1·30 S	149·32 E
154	Musselburgh (mŭs''l-bŭr-ô) . . Scot.	55·55 N	3·08 W
111	Musselshell R. (mŭs''l-shĕl) . . Mt.	46·25 N	108·20 W
216	Mussende . . . Ang.	10·32 S	16·05 E
216	Mussuma . . . Ang.	14·14 S	21·59 E
171	Mustafakemalpasa . . . Tur.	40·05 N	28·30 E
119	Mustang Bay . . . Tx. (In.)	29·22 N	95·12 W
116	Mustang Cr. (mŭs'tăng) . . . Tx.	36·22 N	102·46 W
119	Mustang I . . . Tx.	27·43 N	97·00 W
127	Mustique I. (müs-tēk') St. Vincent (In.)	12·53 N	61·03 W
166	Mustvee (mōōst'vĕ-ĕ) . . . Sov. Un.	58·50 N	26·54 E
189	Musu Dan (C.) (mōō'sōō dän) Kor.	40·51 N	130·00 E
194	Musu Dan (Pt.) (mōō'sōō dän) Kor.	40·48 N	129·50 E
203	Muswellbrook (mŭs'wŭl-brŏŏk) Austl.	32·15 S	150·50 E
192	Mutan (R.) . . . China	45·30 N	129·40 E
192	Mutanchiang . . . China	44·28 N	129·38 E
212	Mutombo Mukulu (mōō-tôm'bō mōō-kōō'lōō) . Zaire	8·12 S	23·56 E
194	Mutsu Wan (B.) (mōōt'sōō wän) Jap.	41·20 N	140·55 E
99	Mutton Bay (mŭt''n) . . . Can.	50·48 N	59·02 W
137	Mutum (mōō-tōō'm) Braz. (Rio de Janeiro In.)	19·48 S	41·24 W
172	Muyun-Kum, Peski (Des.) (mōō-yōōn' kōōm') . Sov. Un.	44·30 N	70·00 E
184	Muzaffargarh . . . Pak.	30·09 N	71·15 E
184	Muzaffarpur . . . India	26·13 N	85·20 E
92	Muzon, C . . . Ak.	54·41 N	132·44 W
118	Muzquiz (mōōz'kēz) . . . Mex.	27·53 N	101·31 W
217	Mvomero . . . Tan.	6·20 S	37·25 E
213	Mvoti (R.) . . . S. Afr. (Natal In.)	29·18 S	30·52 E
217	Mwanza (mwän'zä) . . . Tan.	2·31 S	32·54 E
212	Mwaya (mwä'yä) . . . Tan.	9·19 S	33·51 E
217	Mwenga . . . Zaire	3·02 S	28·26 E
217	Mweru (L.) . . . Zaire-Zambia	8·50 S	28·50 E
217	Mwingi . . . Ken.	0·56 S	38·04 E
152	Mya R. (myä') . . . Alg.	29·26 N	3·15 E
188	Myingyan (myĭng-yŭn') . . . Bur.	21·37 N	95·26 E
196	Myinmoletkat (Pk.) . . . Bur.	13·58 N	98·34 E
188	Myitkyina (myĭ'chē-nȧ) . . . Bur.	25·33 N	97·25 E
159	Myjava (mûē'yȧ-vä) . . . Czech.	48·45 N	17·33 E
194	Myohyang San (Mtn.) (myō'hyang) . Kor.	40·00 N	126·12 E
150	Mýrdalsjökull (Gl.) (mür'däls-yû'kōōl) . Ice.	63·34 N	18·04 W
121	Myrtle Beach (mûr't'l) . . . SC	33·42 N	78·53 W
110	Myrtle Point . . . Or.	43·04 N	124·08 W
166	Myshkino (mĕsh'kē-nô) . . Sov. Un.	57·48 N	38·21 E
185	Mysore (mī-sōr') . . . India	12·31 N	76·42 E
157	Mysovka (mē' sôf-kȧ) . . . Sov. Un.	55·11 N	21·17 E
109	Mystic (mĭs'tĭk) . . . Ia.	40·47 N	92·54 W
174	Mytishchi (mê-tēsh'chi) Sov. Un. (Moscow In.)	55·55 N	37·46 E
217	Mziha . . . Tan.	5·54 S	37·47 E
217	Mzimba ('m-zĭm'bä) . . . Malawi	11·52 S	33·34 E
213	Mzimkulu (R.) . S. Afr. (Natal In.)	30·12 S	29·57 E
213	Mzimvubu (R.) . S. Afr. (Natal In.)	31·22 S	29·20 E
217	Mzuzu . . . Malawi	11·30 S	34·10 E

N

Page	Name / Pronunciation / Region	Lat. °′	Long. °′
158	Naab R. (näp) . . . F.R.G.	49·38 N	12·15 E
149	Naaldwijk . Neth. (Amsterdam In.)	52·00 N	4·11 E
89	Naalehu . . . Hi.	19·00 N	155·35 W
157	Naantali (nän'tȧ-lē) . . . Fin.	60·29 N	22·03 E
204	Nabberu (L.) (năb'ĕr-ōō) . . . Austl.	26·05 S	120·35 E
210	Nabeul (nā-bûl') . . . Tun.	36·34 N	10·45 E
217	Nabiswera . . . Ug.	1·28 N	32·16 E
218	Naboomspruit . . . S. Afr. (Johannesburg & Pretoria In.)	24·32 S	28·43 E
183	Nābulus . . . Jordan (Palestine In.)	32·13 N	35·16 E
217	Nacala (nă-kä'lȧ) . . . Moz.	14·34 S	40·41 E
126	Nacaome (nä-kä-ō'mȧ) . . . Hond.	13·32 N	87·28 W
152	Naceur, Bou Mt . . . Mor.	33·50 N	3·55 W
193	Na Cham (nä chäm') . . . Viet.	22·02 N	106·30 E
110	Naches R. (năch'ĕz) . . . Wa.	46·51 N	121·03 W
158	Náchod (näk'ôt) . . . Czech.	50·25 N	16·08 E
114	Nacimiento (R.) (nȧ-sĭ-myĕn'tô) Ca.	35·50 N	121·00 W
119	Nacogdoches (năk'ô-dō'chĕz) . . Tx.	31·36 N	94·40 W
118	Nadadores (nä-dä-dō'rās) . . . Mex.	27·04 N	101·36 W
184	Nadiād . . . India	22·45 N	72·51 E
123	Nadir . . . Vir. Is. (U. S. A.) (St. Thomas In.)	18·19 N	64·53 W
165	Nădlac . . . Rom.	46·09 N	20·52 E
	Nad Nisou, see Jablonec		
	Nad Váhom, see Nové Mesto		
159	Nadvornaya (näd-vōōr'nȧ-yȧ) Sov. Un.	48·37 N	24·35 E
172	Nadym (R.) (nȧ'dĭm) . . . Sov. Un.	64·30 N	72·48 E
156	Naestved (nĕst'vĭdh) . . . Den.	55·14 N	11·46 E
215	Nafada . . . Nig.	11·08 N	11·20 E
218	Nafishah . . . Egypt (Suez In.)	30·34 N	32·15 E
187	Nafūd ad Daḩy (Des.) . . . Sau. Ar.	22·15 N	44·15 E
197	Naga (nä'gä) . . . Phil. (In.)	13·37 N	123·12 E
195	Naga (I.) . . . Jap.	32·09 N	130·16 E
195	Nagahama (nä'gä-hä'mä) . . . Jap.	33·32 N	132·29 E
195	Nagahama . . . Jap.	35·23 N	136·16 E
188	Nagaland (State) . . . India	25·47 N	94·15 E
195	Nagano (nä'gä-nô) . . . Jap.	36·42 N	138·12 E
195	Nagaoka (nä'gȧ-ō'kȧ) . . . Jap.	37·22 N	138·49 E
195	Nagaoka . . . Jap. (Ōsaka In.)	34·54 N	135·42 E
185	Nāgappattinam . . . India	10·48 N	79·51 E
126	Nagarote (nä-gä-rô'tĕ) . . . Nic.	12·17 N	86·35 W
195	Nagasaki (nä'gȧ-sä'kē) . . . Jap.	32·48 N	129·53 E
184	Nāgaur . . . India	27·19 N	73·41 E
174	Nagaybakskiy (nȧ-gáy-bäk'skĭ) Sov. Un. (Urals In.)	53·33 N	59·33 E
197	Nagcarlan (näg-kär-län') Phil. (In.)	14·07 N	121·24 E
185	Nāgercoil . . . India	8·15 N	77·29 E
171	Nagornokarabakh (Reg.) (nu-gôr'nŭ-kŭ-rŭ-bäk') . Sov. Un.	40·10 N	46·50 E
195	Nagoya (nä'gō'yȧ) . . . Jap.	35·09 N	136·53 E
184	Nāgpur (näg'pōōr) . . . India	21·12 N	79·09 E
129	Nagua (nȧ'gwä) . . . Dom. Rep.	19·20 N	69·40 W
197	Naguilian (nä-gwē-lē'än) Phil. (In.)	16·33 N	120·23 E
158	Nagykanizsa (nôd'y'kô'nē-shô) Hung.	46·27 N	17·00 E
159	Nagykōrōs (nôd'y'kŭ-rŭsh) . Hung.	47·02 N	19·46 E
189	Naha (nä'hä) . . . Jap.	26·02 N	127·43 E
90	Nahanni Natl. Pk . . . Can.	62·10 N	125·15 W
99	Nahant (nȧ-hănt) . . . Ma. (In.)	42·26 N	70·55 W
183	Nahariyya . . . Isr. (Palestine In.)	33·01 N	35·06 E
171	Nahr al Khābur (R.) . . . Syr.	35·50 N	41·00 E
163	Nahr-Ouassel (R.) (när-wä-sĕl') Alg.	35·30 N	1·55 E
136	Nahuel Huapi (L.) (nä'wâl wä'pē) Arg.	41·00 S	71·30 W
126	Nahuizalco (nä-wē-zäl'kō) . . . Sal.	13·50 N	89·43 W
197	Naic (nä-ēk) . . . Phil. (In.)	14·20 N	120·46 E
118	Naica (nä-ē'kä) . . . Mex.	27·53 N	105·30 W
135	Naiguatá (nī-gwä-tá') . . . Ven. (In.)	10·37 N	66·44 W
135	Naiguata, Pico (Mtn.) (pē'kô) Ven. (In.)	10·32 N	66·44 W
184	Naihāti . . . India (In.)	22·54 N	88·25 E
91	Nain (nīn) . . . Can.	56·29 N	61·52 W
154	Nairn (nârn) . . . Scot.	57·35 N	3·54 W
217	Nairobi (nī-rō'bē) . . . Ken.	1·17 S	36·49 E
213	Naivasha (nī-vä'shȧ) . . . Ken.	0·47 S	36·29 E
186	Najd (Des.) . . . Sau. Ar.	25·18 N	42·38 E
218	Naj 'Ḩammādī (näg'hä-mä'dē) Egypt (Nile In.)	26·02 N	32·12 E
194	Najin (nä'jĭn) . . . Kor.	42·04 N	130·35 E
186	Najran (Des.) (nŭj-rän') . . Sau. Ar.	17·29 N	45·30 E
194	Naju (nä'jōō') . . . Kor.	35·02 N	126·42 E
128	Najusa (R.) (nä-hōō'sä) . . . Cuba	21·55 N	77·55 W
192	Nakadorishima (I.) (nä'kä'dô'rē-shē'mä) . Jap.	33·00 N	128·20 E
195	Nakatsu (nä'käts-ōō) . . . Jap.	33·34 N	131·10 E
171	Nakhichevan (nȧ-kē-chē-vän') Sov. Un.	39·10 N	45·30 E

ng-sing; ŋ-baŋk; N-nasalized n; nŏd; cŏmmit; ōld; ôbey; ôrder; fōōd; fŏŏt; ou-out; s-soft; sh-dish; th-thin; pūre; ûnite; ûrn; stŭd; circŭs; ü-as "y" in study; '-indeterminate vowel.

318 Nakhodka — Negros PRONOUNCING INDEX

Page	Name Pronunciation Region	Lat. °′	Long. °′
173	Nakhodka (nŭ-kôt′kŭ)...Sov. Un.	43·03 N	133·08 E
196	Nakhon Ratchasima........Thai.	14·56 N	102·14 E
196	Nakhon Si Thammarat.....Thai.	8·27 N	99·58 E
91	Nakina....................Can.	50·10 N	86·40 W
156	Nakskov (näk′skou).........Den.	54·51 N	11·06 E
159	Nakto nad Notecia (näk′wō näd nō-tĕ′chōn).Pol.	53·10 N	17·35 E
194	Naktong (R.) (näk′tŭng).....Kor.	36·10 N	128·30 E
171	Nal′chik (nȧl-chēk′).....Sov. Un.	43·30 N	43·35 E
162	Nalón (R.) (nä-lōn′).........Sp.	43·15 N	5·38 W
210	Nālūt (nä-lōōt′)...........Libya	31·51 N	10·49 E
186	Namak, Daryacheh-ye (L.)..Iran	34·58 N	51·33 E
109	Namakan (L.) (nă′mȧ-kȧn)...Mn.	48·20 N	92·43 W
186	Namakzār-e Shāhdād (L.) (nŭ-mŭk-zär′).Iran	31·00 N	58·30 E
172	Namangan (nȧ-mȧn-gän′) Sov. Un.	41·08 N	71·59 E
100	Namao......Can. (Edmonton In.)	53·43 N	113·30 W
197	Namatanai (nä′mä-tȧ-nä′ê) Pap. N. Gui.	3·43 S	152·26 E
115	Nambe Pueblo Ind. Res. (näm′bȧ pwĕb′lô).NM	35·52 N	105·39 W
203	Nambour (năm′bŏŏr).......Austl.	26·48 S	153·00 E
196	Nam Dinh (näm dĕnk′).....Viet.	20·30 N	106·10 E
217	Nametil..................Moz.	15·43 S	39·21 E
194	Namhae (I.) (näm′hī′).......Kor.	34·23 N	128·05 E
212	Namib Des. (nä-mēb′)..S. W. Afr.	18·45 S	12·45 E
203	Namoi (R.) (năm′oi).......Austl.	30·10 S	148·43 E
152	Namous, Oued en (R.) (nȧ-mōōs′) Alg.	31·48 N	00·19 W
110	Nampa (năm′pȧ).............Id.	43·35 N	116·35 W
192	Namp′o....................Kor.	38·47 N	125·28 E
217	Nampuecha................Moz.	13·59 S	40·18 E
217	Nampula..................Moz.	15·07 S	39·15 E
150	Namsos (näm′sôs)...........Nor.	64·28 N	11·14 E
184	Nam Tsho (L.)............China	30·30 N	91·10 E
92	Namu.....................Can.	51·03 N	127·50 W
217	Namuli, Serra (Mts.)........Moz.	15·05 S	37·05 E
155	Namur (nȧ-mür′).............Bel.	50·29 N	4·55 E
212	Namutoni (nȧ-mōō-tō′nê) S. W. Afr.	18·45 S	17·00 E
196	Nan, Mae Nam (R.)........Thai.	18·11 N	100·29 E
125	Nanacamilpa (nä-nä-kä-mê′l-pä) Mex. (In.)	19·30 N	98·33 W
92	Nanaimo (nȧ-nī′mō)........Can.	49·10 N	123·56 W
194	Nanam (nä′nän′)...........Kor.	41·38 N	129·37 E
195	Nanao (nä′nä-ō)............Jap.	37·03 N	136·59 E
193	Nanao Tao (I.) (nä′nä-ō dou) China	23·30 N	117·30 E
193	Nanch′ang (nän′chäng′)....China	28·38 N	115·48 E
193	Nancheng................China	26·50 N	116·40 E
190	Nanch′enghuang Tai (I.) (nan′chĕng′hōōäng′dou).China	38·22 N	120·54 E
190	Nanching (Nanking) (nän′jĭng) (nän′kĭng).China	32·04 N	118·46 E
193	Nanch′ung...............China	30·45 N	106·05 E
161	Nancy (nän-sē′)..............Fr.	48·42 N	6·11 E
106	Nancy Cr. (năn′cē) Ga. (Atlanta In.)	33·51 N	84·25 W
184	Nanda Devi (Mt.) (nän′dä dā′vē) India	30·30 N	80·25 E
184	Nānded..................India	19·13 N	77·21 E
184	Nandurbār................India	21·29 N	74·13 E
185	Nandyāl..................India	15·54 N	78·09 E
184	Nanga Parbat..............Pak.	35·20 N	74·35 E
184	Nangi...............India (In.)	22·30 N	88·14 E
161	Nangis (nän-zhē′)..Fr. (Paris In.)	48·33 N	3·01 E
216	Nangweshi..............Zambia	16·26 S	23·17 E
191	Nanhsiang..China (Shanghai In.)	31·17 N	121·17 E
193	Nanhsiung...............China	25·10 N	114·20 E
191	Nanhui.....China (Shanghai In.)	31·03 N	121·45 E
190	Naniana.................China	35·14 N	116·24 E
193	Nani Dinh................Viet.	20·25 N	106·08 E
190	Nani Hu (L.) (nän′yi′ hōō).China	31·12 N	119·05 E
	Nanking, see Nanching		
190	Nankung (nän′kŏŏng′).....China	37·22 N	115·22 E
193	Nan Ling (Mts.)...........China	25·15 N	111·40 E
190	Nanlo (nän′lō′)............China	36·03 N	115·13 E
204	Nannine (nă-nēn′).........Austl.	26·50 S	118·30 E
193	Nanning (nän′nĭng′).......China	22·56 N	108·10 E
193	Nanp′an (R.)..............China	24·50 N	105·30 E
193	Nanp′ing.................China	26·40 N	118·05 E
189	Nansei-shotō (Ryukyu Islands) Jap.	27·30 N	127·00 E
106	Nansemond (năn′sê-mŭnd) Va. (Norfolk In.)	36·46 N	76·32 W
106	Nansemond R...Va. (Norfolk In.)	36·50 N	76·34 W
188	Nan Shan (Mts.)(nän′shän′).China	38·43 N	98·00 E
195	Nantai Zan (Mtn.) (nän-täê zän) Jap.	36·47 N	139·28 E
160	Nantes (nänt′)...............Fr.	47·13 N	1·37 W
161	Nanteuil-le-Haudouin (nän-tû-lĕ-ō-dwȧn′).Fr. (Paris In.)	49·08 N	2·49 E
105	Nanticoke (năn′tĭ-kōk).......Pa.	41·10 N	76·00 W
105	Nantucket (I.) (năn-tŭk′ĕt)...Ma.	41·15 N	70·05 W
190	Nantung (nän′tŏŏng′)......China	32·02 N	120·51 E
148	Nantwich (nănt′wĭch).......Eng.	53·04 N	2·31 W
192	Nanyang.................China	33·00 N	112·42 E
192	Nanyüan...........China (In.)	39·48 N	116·24 E
190	Nanyün (nän′yün′)........China	38·11 N	116·37 E
193	Nao Chou (I.).............China	20·58 N	110·58 E
125	Naolinco (nä-o-lēŋ′kō)......Mex.	19·39 N	96·50 W
165	Náousa (nä′ōō-sȧ)...........Grc.	40·38 N	22·05 E
114	Napa (năp′ȧ).................Ca.	38·20 N	122·17 W
105	Napanee (năp′ȧ-nē).........Can.	44·15 N	77·00 W
107	Naperville (nā′pēr-vĭl) Il. (Chicago In.)	41·46 N	88·09 W
205	Napier (nā′pĭ-ẽr)......N. Z. (In.)	39·30 S	177·00 E
100	Napierville (nā′pĭ-ẽr-vĭl) Can. (Montreal In.)	45·11 N	73·24 W
121	Naples (nă′p′lz).........Fl. (In.)	26·07 N	81·46 W
	Naples, see Napoli		
134	Napo (R.) (nä′pō)..........Peru	1·49 S	74·20 W
104	Napoleon (nȧ-pō′lē-ŭn).......Oh.	41·20 N	84·10 W
119	Napoleonville (nȧ-pō′lê-ŭn-vĭl).La.	29·56 N	91·03 W
163	Napoli (Naples) (nä′pô-lē) It. (Naples In.)	40·37 N	14·12 E
163	Napoli, Golfo di (G.) (gôl-fô-dē).It. (Naples In.)	40·29 N	14·08 E
104	Nappanee (năp′ȧ-nē)..........In.	41·30 N	86·00 W
195	Nara (nä′rä).....Jap. (Ōsaka In.)	34·41 N	135·50 E
210	Nara......................Mali	15·09 N	7·27 W
195	Nara (Pref.).....Jap. (Ōsaka In.)	34·36 N	135·49 E
166	Nara (R.).............Sov. Un.	55·05 N	37·16 E
203	Naracoorte (nȧ-rȧ-kōōn′tê)..Austl.	36·50 S	140·50 E
195	Narashino.......Jap. (Tōkyō In.)	35·41 N	140·01 E
185	Naraspur.................India	16·32 N	81·43 E
106	Narberth (när′bûrth) Pa. (Philadelphia In.)	40·01 N	75·17 W
160	Narbonne (nȧr-bôn′)..........Fr.	43·12 N	3·00 E
165	Nardò (när-dô′)...............It.	40·11 N	18·02 E
134	Nare (nä′rĕ)...........Col. (In.)	6·12 N	74·37 W
159	Narew R. (nä′rĕf)...........Pol.	52·43 N	21·19 E
184	Narmada (R.).............India	22·17 N	74·45 E
166	Naroch′ (L.) (nä′rôch....Sov. Un.	54·51 N	27·00 E
170	Narodnaya, Gora (Mtn.) (nȧ-rôd′nȧ-yȧ).Sov. Un.	65·10 N	60·10 E
166	Naro Fominsk (nä′rô-fô-mēnsk′) Sov. Un.	55·23 N	36·43 E
157	Närpeså (R.)...............Fin.	62·35 N	21·24 E
202	Narrabeen (năr-ȧ-bĭn) Austl. (Sydney In.)	33·44 S	151·18 E
106	Narragansett (năr-ă-găn′sĕt) RI (Providence In.)	41·26 N	71·27 W
105	Narragansett B...............RI	41·20 N	71·15 W
203	Narrandera (nȧ-rȧn-dē′rȧ)...Austl.	34·40 S	146·40 E
204	Narrogin (năr′ô-gĭn).......Austl.	33·00 S	117·15 E
166	Narva (nȧr′vȧ)..........Sov. Un.	59·24 N	28·12 E
197	Narvacan (när-vä-kän′).Phil. (In.)	17·27 N	120·29 E
166	Narva Jõesuu (nȧr′vȧ ŏŏ-ô-ă′sōō-ŏŏ).Sov. Un.	59·26 N	28·02 E
150	Narvik (när′vêk)............Nor.	68·21 N	17·18 E
157	Narvskiy Zaliv (B.) (nȧr′vskĭ zä′lĭf).Sov. Un.	59·35 N	27·25 E
170	Nar′yan-Mar (när′yȧn mär′) Sov. Un.	67·42 N	53·30 E
203	Naryilco (năr-ĭl′kô)........Austl.	28·40 S	141·50 E
172	Narym (nä-rēm′)........Sov. Un.	58·47 N	82·05 E
187	Naryn (R.) (nŭ-rĭn′).....Sov. Un.	41·46 N	73·00 E
148	Naseby (nāz′bĭ)............Eng.	52·23 N	0·59 W
113	Nashua (năsh′ŭ-ȧ) Mo. (Kansas City In.)	39·18 N	94·34 W
99	Nashua................NH (In.)	42·47 N	71·23 W
117	Nashville (năsh′vĭl)...........Ar.	33·56 N	93·50 W
120	Nashville....................Ga.	31·12 N	83·15 W
117	Nashville.....................Il.	38·21 N	89·42 W
104	Nashville....................Mi.	42·35 N	85·05 W
120	Nashville....................Tn.	36·10 N	86·48 W
109	Nashwauk (năsh′wôk).......Mn.	47·21 N	93·12 W
165	Našice (nä′shê-tsĕ).........Yugo.	45·29 N	18·06 E
159	Nasielsk (nä′syĕlsk)..........Pol.	52·35 N	20·50 E
170	Näsijärvi (L.) (nĕ′sê-yĕr′vê)..Fin.	61·42 N	24·05 E
184	Nāsik (nä′sĭk)..............India	20·02 N	73·49 E
211	Nāsir (nä-zēr′)..............Sud.	8·30 N	33·06 E
	Nāşir, Buhayrat, see Nasser, L.		
184	Nasirābād................Bngl.	24·48 N	90·28 E
184	Nasirabād................India	26·13 N	74·48 E
91	Naskaupi (R.) (näs′kô-pĭ)....Can.	53·59 N	61·10 W
216	'Nasondoye...............Zaire	10·22 S	25·06 E
92	Nass (R.) (năs)..............Can.	55·00 N	129·30 W
128	Nassau (năs′ô)...............Ba.	25·05 N	77·20 W
149	Nassenheide (nä′sĕn-hī-dĕ) G.D.R. (Berlin In.)	52·49 N	13·13 E
218	Nasser, L. (Nāşir, Buḩayrat) Egypt (Nile In.)	23·50 N	32·50 E
156	Nässjö (nĕs′shû)............Swe.	57·39 N	14·39 E
197	Nasugbu (nȧ-sŏŏg-bōō′).Phil. (In.)	14·05 N	120·37 E
118	Nasworthy L. (năz′wûr-thê)...Tx.	31·17 N	100·30 W
193	Nata.....................China	19·30 N	109·38 E
127	Natá (nä-tȧ′)...............Pan.	8·20 N	80·30 W
134	Natagaima (nä-tä-gī′mä).Col. (In.)	3·38 N	75·07 W
135	Natal (nä-täl′).............Braz.	6·00 S	35·13 W
212	Natal (Prov.) (nȧ-täl′).....S. Afr.	28·50 S	30·07 E
99	Natashquan (nä-täsh′kwän)..Can.	50·11 N	61·49 W
99	Natashquan (R.)............Can.	50·35 N	61·35 W
120	Natchez (năch′ĕz)...........Ms.	1·35 N	91·20 W
119	Natchitoches (năk′ĭ-tŏsh) (nȧch-ĭ-tōsh′).La.	31·46 N	93·06 W
99	Natick (nā′tĭk).........Ma. (In.)	42·17 N	71·21 W
173	National Area (Reg.)....Sov. Un.	66·30 N	170·30 E
111	National Bison Ra. (Mts.) (năsh′ŭn-ăl bī′s′n).Mt.	47·18 N	113·58 W
114	National City...........Ca. (In.)	32·38 N	117·01 W
214	Natitingou...............Benin	10·19 N	1·22 E
135	Natividade (nä-tê-vê-dä′dĕ)..Braz.	11·43 S	47·34 W
217	Natron, L. (nā′trŏn)........Tan.	2·17 S	36·10 E
107	Natrona Hts. (nā′trŏ nā) Pa. (Pittsburgh In.)	40·38 N	79·43 W
218	Naţrūn, Wādī an. Egypt (Nile In.)	30·33 N	30·12 E
196	Natuna Besar, Kepulauan (Is.) Indon.	3·22 N	108·00 E
115	Natural Bridges Natl. Mon. (năt′û-răl brĭj′ĕs).Ut.	37·20 N	110·20 W
204	Naturaliste, C. (năt-û-rȧ-lĭst′) Austl.	33·30 S	115·10 E
125	Naucalpan (nä′ōō-käl-pȧ′n) Mex. (In.)	19·28 N	99·14 W
125	Nauchampatepetl (Mtn.) (näōō-chäm-pä-tĕ′pĕtl).Mex.	19·32 N	97·09 W
149	Nauen (nou′ĕn) G.D.R. (Berlin In.)	52·36 N	12·53 E
105	Naugatuck (nô′gȧ-tŭk)........Ct.	41·25 N	73·05 W
197	Naujan (nä-ŏŏ-hän′)....Phil. (In.)	13·19 N	121·17 E
158	Naumburg (noum′bŏŏrgh).G.D.R.	51·10 N	11·50 E
198	Nauru.................Oceania	0·30 S	167·00 E
125	Nautla (nä-ōōt′lä)..........Mex.	20·14 N	96·44 W
118	Nava (nä′vä).................Mex.	28·25 N	100·44 W
162	Nava, L. de la...............Sp.	42·05 N	4·42 W
162	Nava del Rey (nä-vä dĕl rā′ê)..Sp.	41·22 N	5·04 W
162	Navahermosa (nä-vä-ĕr-mō′sä).Sp.	39·39 N	4·28 W
128	Navajas (nä-vä-häs′).......Cuba	22·40 N	81·20 W
115	Navajo Ind. Res. (năv′ȧ-hō) Az.-NM	36·31 N	109·24 W
115	Navajo Natl. Mon............Az.	36·43 N	110·39 W
115	Navajo Res..................NM	36·57 N	107·26 W
163	Navalcarnero (nä-väl′kär-nā′rō) Sp. (Madrid In.)	40·17 N	4·05 W
162	Navalmoral de la Mata (nä-väl′mōräl′ dā lä mä′tä).Sp.	39·53 N	5·32 W
100	Navan (nă′vȧn).Can. (Ottawa In.)	45·25 N	75·26 W
136	Navarino (nȧ-vä-rê′nô) (I.)..Chile	55·30 S	68·15 W
162	Navarra (Reg.) (nä-vär′rä)....Sp.	42·40 N	1·35 W
137	Navarro (nä-vȧ′r-rō) Arg. (Buenos Aires In.)	35·00 S	59·16 W
119	Navasota (năv-ȧ-sō′tȧ).......Tx.	30·24 N	96·05 W
119	Navasota R..................Tx.	31·03 N	96·11 W
129	Navassa (I.) (nȧ-vȧs′ȧ).....N. A.	18·25 N	75·15 W
162	Navia (R.) (nä-vē′ä).........Sp.	43·10 N	6·45 W
137	Navidad (nä-vê-dä′d) Chile (Santiago In.)	34·57 S	71·51 W
129	Navidad Bk. (nä-vê-dädh′)....Ba.	20·05 N	69·00 W
137	Navidade do Carangola (nȧ-vē-dä′dĕ-dô-kȧ-rän-gô′la) Braz. (Rio de Janeiro In.)	21·04 S	41·58 W
122	Navojoa (nä-vô-kô′ä).......Mex.	27·00 N	109·40 W
165	Návplion..................Grc.	37·33 N	22·46 E
184	Nawābshāh (nȧ-wäb′shä)....Pak.	26·20 N	68·30 E
165	Náxos (I.) (nȧk′sôs).........Grc.	37·15 N	25·20 E
122	Nayarit (State) (nä-yä-rēt′)..Mex.	22·00 N	105·15 W
124	Nayarit, Sierra de (Mts.) (sē-ĕ′r-rä-dĕ).Mex.	23·20 N	105·07 W
214	Naye.................Senegal	14·25 N	12·12 W
108	Naylor (nā′lōr) Md. (Baltimore In.)	38·43 N	76·46 W
135	Nazaré (nä-zä-rĕ′)..........Braz.	13·04 S	38·49 W
162	Nazaré (nä-zä-rā′)..........Port.	39·38 N	9·04 W
135	Nazaré da Mata (dä-mä-tä)..Braz.	7·46 S	35·13 W
118	Nazas (nä′zäs)..............Mex.	25·14 N	104·08 W
118	Nazas, R....................Mex.	25·08 N	104·20 W
183	Nazerat.......Isr. (Palestine In.)	32·43 N	35·19 E
171	Nazilli (nȧ-zĭ-lē′)............Tur.	37·40 N	28·10 E
174	Naziya R. (nȧ-zē′yȧ) Sov. Un. (Leningrad In.)	59·48 N	31·18 E
92	Nazko (R.).................Can.	52·35 N	123·10 W
215	Ndali....................Benin	9·51 N	2·43 E
211	Ndélé (n′dā-lā′)....Cen. Afr. Rep.	8·21 N	20·43 E
215	Ndikiniméki...............Cam.	4·46 N	10·50 E
215	Ndjamena (Fort-Lamy) (lȧ-mē′) Chad	12·07 N	15·03 E
212	Ndjolé (n′dzhô-lā′)........Gabon	0·15 S	10·45 E
217	Ndola (n′dō′lä)..........Zambia	12·58 S	28·38 E
217	Ndoto Mts..................Ken.	1·55 N	37·05 E
214	Ndrhamcha, Sebkha de (L.) Mauritania	18·50 N	15·15 W
217	Nduye....................Zaire	1·50 N	29·01 E
154	Neagh Lough (L.) (lŏk nā)..N. Ire.	54·40 N	6·47 W
183	Néa Páfos..Cyprus (Palestine In.)	34·46 N	32·27 E
202	Neapean (R.)..Austl. (Sydney In.)	33·40 S	150·39 E
165	Neápolis (nȧ-ŏp′ ô-lĭs).......Grc.	36·35 N	23·08 E
164	Neápolis..............Grc. (In.)	35·17 N	25·37 E
101	Near Is. (nēr)...............Ak.	52·20 N	172·40 E
154	Neath (nēth)..............Wales	51·41 N	3·50 W
203	Nebine Cr. (nĕ-bēne′)......Austl.	27·50 S	147·00 E
171	Nebit-Dag (nyĕ-bēt′däg′).Sov. Un.	39·30 N	54·20 E
102	Nebraska (State) (nê-brăs′kȧ) U. S	41·45 N	101·30 W
117	Nebraska City..............Ne.	40·40 N	95·50 W
92	Nechako Plat. (nĭ-chă′kō)....Can.	54·00 N	124·30 W
92	Nechako Ra.................Can.	53·20 N	124·30 W
92	Nechako Res................Can.	53·25 N	125·10 W
92	Nechako (R.)...............Can.	52·45 N	124·55 W
119	Neches R. (nĕch′ĕz)..........Tx.	31·03 N	94·40 W
158	Neckar R. (nĕk′är)........F.R.G.	49·16 N	9·06 E
136	Necochea (nā-kô-chā′ä)......Arg.	38·30 S	58·45 W
167	Nedrigaylov(nĕ-drĭ-gī′lôf).Sov.Un.	50·49 N	33·52 E
99	Needham (nēd′ăm).....Ma. (In.)	42·17 N	71·14 W
114	Needles (nē′d′lz).............Ca.	34·51 N	114·39 W
109	Neenah (nē′nȧ)..............Wi.	44·10 N	88·30 W
95	Neepawa...................Can.	50·13 N	99·29 W
116	Nee Res. (nē̆ē̆)..............Co.	38·26 N	102·56 W
155	Neetze (R.) (nĕ′tzĕ).......F.R.G.	53·04 N	11·00 E
195	Negareyama (nȧ′gä-rȧ-yä′mä) Jap. (Tōkyō In.)	35·52 N	139·54 E
109	Negaunee (nê-gô′nê).........Mi.	46·30 N	87·37 W
183	Negeri Sembilan (State) (nā′grê-sĕm-bê-län′) Mala. (Singapore In.)	2·46 N	101·54 E
183	Negev (Des.) (nĕ′gĕv) Isr. (Palestine In.)	30·34 N	34·43 E
165	Negoi (Mtn.) (nā-goi′)......Rom.	45·33 N	24·38 E
185	Negombo.............Sri Lanka	7·39 N	79·49 E
165	Negotin (nĕ′gô-tên)........Yugo.	44·13 N	22·33 E
196	Negrais, C. (nĕ′grīs).........Bur.	16·08 N	93·34 E
136	Negro (R.).................Arg.	39·50 S	65·00 W
134	Negro, Rio (R.) (rĕ′ō nā′grŏŏ) Braz.	0·18 S	63·21 W
162	Negro, C. (na′grô)..........Mor.	35·25 N	4·51 W
127	Negro, Cerro (Mt.) (sĕ′r-rô-nā′grô).Pan.	8·44 N	80·37 W
137	Negro (R.)..Ur. (Buenos Aires In.)	33·17 S	58·18 W
126	Negro R...................Nic.	13·01 N	87·10 W
196	Negros (I.) (nā′grōs)........Phil.	9·50 N	121·45 E

ăt; finăl; rāte; senâte; ärm; ȧsk; sofȧ; fâre; ch-choose; dh-as th in other; bē; êvent; bĕt; recĕnt; cratẽr; g-go; gh-guttural g; bĭt; ĭ-short neutral; rīde; k-guttural k as ch in German ich;

Page	Name Pronunciation Region	Lat. °′	Long. °′
134	Neguá (nä-gwä′)........Col. (In.)	5·51 N	76·36 W
110	Nehalem R. (nė-hăl′ĕm).......Or.	45·52 N	123·37 W
161	Neheim-Hüsten (nĕ′hīm) F.R.G. (Ruhr In.)	51·28 N	7·58 E
129	Neiba (nå-ē′bä).......Dom. Rep.	18·30 N	71·20 W
129	Neiba, Bahai de (B.) (bä-ē′ē-dĕ) Dom. Rep.	18·10 N	71·00 W
129	Neiba, Sierra de (Mts.) (sē-ĕr′rä-dĕ).Dom. Rep.	18·40 N	71·40 W
193	Neichiang..............China	29·38 N	105·01 E
190	Neich'iu (nā′chĭō).........China	37·17 N	114·32 E
111	Neihart (nī′hȧrt)............Mt.	46·54 N	110·39 W
192	Neihsiang..............China	33·00 N	111·54 E
109	Neillsville (nēlz′vĭl)..........Wi.	44·35 N	90·37 W
134	Neira (nā′rä)..........Col. (In.)	5·10 N	75·32 W
134	Neiva (nå-ē′vä) (nā′vä)..Col. (In.)	2·55 N	75·16 W
211	Nekemte..................Eth.	9·09 N	36·29 E
109	Nekoosa (nė-kōō′sȧ).........Wi.	44·19 N	89·54 W
156	Neksø (nĕk′sû)............Den.	55·05 N	15·05 E
108	Neligh (nē′lĭg)..............Ne.	42·06 N	98·02 W
173	Nel'kan (nĕl-kän′).......Sov. Un.	57·45 N	136·36 E
185	Nellore (nĕl-lōr′)...........India	14·28 N	79·59 E
194	Nel'ma (nĕl-mä′)........Sov. Un.	47·34 N	139·05 E
93	Nelson (nĕl′sŭn)...........Can.	49·29 N	117·17 W
148	Nelson....................Eng.	53·50 N	2·13 W
205	Nelson...............N. Z. (In.)	41·15 S	173·22 E
101	Nelson (I.).................Ak.	60·38 N	164·42 W
203	Nelson, C.................Austl.	38·29 S	141·20 E
95	Nelson (R.)................Can.	56·50 N	93·40 W
114	Nelson Cr..................Nv.	40·22 N	114·43 W
104	Nelsonville (nĕl′sŭn-vĭl).......Oh.	39·30 N	82·15 W
214	Néma (nā′mä)........Mauritania	16·37 N	7·15 W
113	Nemadji R. (nĕ-măd′jē) Wi. (Duluth In.)	46·33 N	92·16 W
157	Neman (ŋĕ′-mȧn).......Sov. Un.	55·02 N	22·01 E
159	Neman R...............Sov. Un.	53·28 N	24·45 E
215	Nembe....................Nig.	4·35 N	6·26 E
94	Nemeiban L. (nĕ-mē′bȧn)....Can.	55·20 N	105·20 W
167	Nemirov (nyå-mē′rôf)....Sov. Un.	48·56 N	28·51 E
160	Nemours....................Fr.	48·16 N	2·41 E
194	Nemuro (nā′mōō-rō).........Jap.	43·13 N	145·10 E
194	Nemuro Str.................Jap.	43·07 N	145·10 E
148	Nen (R.) (nĕn).............Eng.	52·32 N	0·19 W
154	Nenagh (nē′nȧ)..............Ire.	52·50 N	8·05 W
101	Nenana (nå-nä′nȧ)...........Ak.	64·28 N	149·18 W
192	Nenchiang...............China	49·02 N	125·15 E
189	Nen Chiang (R.)..........China	47·07 N	123·28 E
190	Nengcheng...............China	33·15 N	116·34 E
174	Nenikyul' (nĕ-nyē′kyûl) Sov. Un. (Leningrad In.)	59·26 N	30·40 E
117	Neodesha (nē-ō-dĕ-shô′)......Ks.	37·24 N	95·41 W
117	Neosho....................Mo.	36·51 N	94·22 W
117	Neosho (R.) (nė-ō′shō).......Ks.	38·07 N	95·40 W
182	Nepal (nĕ-pôl′)............Asia	28·45 N	83·00 E
115	Nephi (nē′fī)................Ut.	39·40 N	111·50 W
98	Nepisiguit (R.) (nĭ-pĭ′sĭ-kwĭt).Can.	47·25 N	66·28 W
137	Nepomuceno (nĕ-pô-mōō-sĕ′no) Braz. (Rio de Janeiro In.)	21·15 S	45·13 W
164	Nera (R.) (nā′rä)............It.	42·45 N	12·54 E
160	Nérac (nā-räk′)..............Fr.	44·08 N	0·19 E
173	Nerchinsk (nyĕr′ chĕnsk).Sov. Un.	51·47 N	116·17 E
173	Nerchinskiy Khrebet (Mts.) Sov. Un.	50·30 N	118·30 E
173	Nerchinskiy Zavod (nyĕr′chĕn-skĭzá-vôt′).Sov. Un.	51·35 N	119·46 E
166	Nerekhta (nyĕ-rĕĸ′tȧ)...Sov. Un.	57·29 N	40·34 E
165	Neretva (R.) (nĕ′rĕt-vȧ)....Yugo.	43·08 N	17·50 E
162	Nerja (nĕr′hä)...............Sp.	36·45 N	3·53 W
166	Nerl' (R.) (nyĕrl).......Sov. Un.	56·59 N	37·57 E
174	Nerskaya R. (nyĕr′skȧ-yȧ) Sov. Un. (Moscow In.)	55·31 N	38·46 E
166	Nerussa (R.) (nyå-rōō′sȧ).Sov. Un.	52·24 N	34·20 E
154	Ness, Loch (L.) (lŏĸ nĕs)....Scot.	57·23 N	4·20 W
116	Ness City (nĕs)..............Ks.	38·27 N	99·55 W
159	Nesterov (ŋĕs′-tzhyé-rôf) Sov. Un.	50·03 N	23·58 E
157	Nesterov (nyĕs-tă′rôf)...Sov. Un.	54·39 N	22·38 E
165	Néstos (R.) (nās′tōs)........Grc.	41·25 N	24·12 E
166	Nesvizh (nyĕs′vēsh).....Sov. Un.	53·13 N	26·44 E
183	Netanya.......Isr. (Palestine In.)	32·19 N	34·52 E
106	Netcong (nĕt′cŏnj) NJ (New York In.)	40·54 N	74·42 W
146	Netherlands (nĕdh′ĕr-lăndz)..Eur.	53·01 N	3·57 E
	Netherlands Guiana, see Surinam		
91	Nettilling (L.).............Can.	66·30 N	70·40 W
109	Nett Lake Ind. Res. (nĕt lāk)..Mn.	48·23 N	93·19 W
163	Nettuno (nĕt-tōō′nô) It. (Rome In.)	41·28 N	12·40 E
161	Neubeckum (noi′bĕ-kōōm) F.R.G. (Ruhr In.)	51·48 N	8·01 E
158	Neubrandenburg (noi-brän′dĕn-bŏŏrgh)....G.D.R.	53·33 N	13·16 E
158	Neuburg (noi′bŏŏrgh)......F.R.G.	48·43 N	11·12 E
158	Neuchâtel (nû-shȧ-tĕl′).....Switz.	47·00 N	6·52 E
158	Neuchatel, Lac de (L.).....Switz.	46·48 N	6·53 E
149	Neuenhagen (noi′ĕn-hä-gĕn) G.D.R. (Berlin In.)	52·31 N	13·41 E
161	Neuenrade (noi′ĕn-rä-dĕ) F.R.G. (Ruhr In.)	51·17 N	7·47 E
160	Neufchâtel-en-Bray (nû-shä-tĕl′ĕɴ-brā′).Fr.	49·43 N	1·25 E
158	Neuhaldensleben (noi-häl′dĕns-lā′bĕn)....G.D.R.	52·18 N	11·23 E
149	Neuhaus (Oste) (noi′houz) (ōz′tĕ) F.R.G. (Hamburg In.)	53·48 N	9·02 E
149	Neulengbach....Aus. (Vienna In.)	48·13 N	15·55 E
158	Neumarkt (noi′märkt)....F.R.G.	49·17 N	11·30 E
158	Neumünster (noi′münstĕr).F.R.G.	54·04 N	10·00 E
158	Neunkirchen (noin′kĭrĸ-ĕn)...Aus.	47·43 N	16·05 E
161	Neunkirchen............F.R.G.	49·21 N	7·20 E
136	Neuquén (nĕ-ōō-kān′)........Arg.	38·52 S	68·12 W
136	Neuquen (Prov.)............Arg.	39·40 S	70·45 W
136	Neuquén (R.)...............Arg.	38·45 S	69·00 W
149	Neuruppin (noi′rōō-pēn) G.D.R. (Berlin In.)	52·55 N	12·48 E
121	Neuse (R.) (nūz).............NC	36·12 N	78·50 W
158	Neusiedler See (L.) (noi-zēd′lēr) Aus.	47·54 N	16·31 E
161	Neuss (nois)....F.R.G. (Ruhr In.)	51·12 N	6·41 E
158	Neustadt (noi′shtät).......F.R.G.	49·21 N	8·08 E
158	Neustadt................F.R.G.	54·06 N	10·50 E
158	Neustadt bei Coburg (bī kō′bōōrgh).....F.R.G.	50·20 N	11·09 E
158	Neustrelitz (noi-strä′lĭts)..G.D.R.	53·21 N	13·05 E
94	Neutral Hills (nū′trăl).......Can.	52·10 N	110·50 W
158	Neu Ulm (noi ōō lm′)......F.R.G.	48·23 N	10·01 E
100	Neuville (nū′vĭl).Can. (Quebec In.)	46·39 N	71·35 W
158	Neuwied (noi′vēdt)........F.R.G.	50·26 N	7·28 E
109	Nevada (nė-vä′dȧ)...........Ia.	42·01 N	93·27 W
117	Nevada....................Mo.	37·49 N	94·21 W
102	Nevada (State).............U. S.	39·30 N	117·00 W
162	Nevada, Sierra (Mts.) (syĕr′rä nā-vä′dhä).Sp.	37·01 N	3·28 W
102	Nevada, Sierra (Mts.) (sē-ĕ′r-rä nė-vä′dȧ).U. S.	39·20 N	120·25 W
114	Nevada City................Ca.	39·16 N	120·01 W
134	Nevado, Cerro el (Mtn.) (sĕ′r-rō-ĕl-nĕ-vä′dō).Col. (In.)	4·02 N	74·08 W
124	Nevado de Colima (Mtn.) (nå-vä′dhō dā kō-lē′mä).Mex.	19·34 N	103·39 W
174	Neva R. (nyĕ-vä′) Sov. Un. (Leningrad In.)	59·49 N	30·54 E
154	Neva Stantsiya (nyĕ-vä′ stän′tsĭ-yȧ) Sov. Un. (Leningrad In.)	59·53 N	30·30 E
216	Neve, Serra da (Mts.).......Ang.	13·40 S	13·20 E
166	Nevel' (nyĕ′vĕl).........Sov. Un.	56·03 N	29·57 E
135	Neveri (nĕ-vĕ-rē) (R.)...Ven. (In.)	10·13 N	64·18 W
160	Nevers (nē-vȧr′).............Fr.	46·59 N	3·10 E
165	Nevesinje (nĕ-vĕ′sēn-yĕ)....Yugo.	43·15 N	18·08 E
154	Nevis, Ben (Mtn.) (bĕn).....Scot.	56·47 N	5·00 W
127	Nevis I. (nē′vĭs) St. Kitts-Nevis-Anguilla.(In.)	17·05 N	62·38 W
127	Nevis Pk. St. Kitts-Nevis-Anguilla (In.)	17·11 N	62·33 W
165	Nevrokop (nĕv′rō-kôp′)......Bul.	41·35 N	23·46 E
171	Nevşehir (nĕv-shĕ′hĕr).......Tur.	38·40 N	34·35 E
174	Nev'yansk (nĕv-yänsk′) Sov. Un. (Urals In.)	57·29 N	60·14 E
121	New (R.) (nū)...............Va.	37·20 N	80·35 W
121	New (R.), South Fork....Va.-NC	36·37 N	81·15 W
217	Newala....................Tan.	10·56 S	39·18 E
107	New Albany (nû ôl′bȧ-nĭ) In. (Louisville In.)	38·17 N	85·49 W
120	New Albany................Ms.	34·28 N	39·00 W
135	New Amsterdam (ăm′stēr-dăm) Guy.	6·14 N	57·30 W
112	Newark (nū′ērk) Ca. (San Francisco In.)	37·32 N	122·02 W
105	Newark (nōō′ärk)...........De.	39·40 N	75·45 W
148	Newark (nū′ērk)...........Eng.	53·04 N	0·49 W
106	Newark (nōō′ûrk) NJ (New York In.)	40·44 N	74·10 W
105	Newark (nū′ērk)............NY	43·05 N	77·10 W
104	Newark....................Oh.	40·05 N	82·25 W
104	Newaygo (nū′wā-go).........Mi.	43·25 N	85·50 W
105	New Bedford (bĕd′fērd)......Ma.	41·35 N	70·55 W
104	Newberg (nū′bûrg)...........Or.	45·17 N	122·58 W
121	New Bern (bûrn).............NC	35·05 N	77·05 W
120	Newbern....................Tn.	36·05 N	89·12 W
109	Newberry (nū′bĕr-ĭ)..........Mi.	46·22 N	85·31 W
121	Newberry...................SC	34·15 N	81·40 W
107	New Boston (bôs′tŭn) Mi. (Detroit In.)	42·10 N	83·24 W
104	New Boston.................Oh.	38·45 N	82·55 W
118	New Braunfels (nū broun′fĕls).Tx.	29·43 N	98·07 W
113	New Brighton (brī′tŭn)......Mn. (Minneapolis, St. Paul In.)	45·04 N	93·12 W
107	New Brighton.Pa. (Pittsburgh In.)	40·34 N	80·18 W
105	New Britain (brĭt′′n).........Ct.	41·40 N	72·45 W
197	New Britain (I.)....Pap. N. Gui.	6·45 S	149·38 E
106	New Brunswick (brŭnz′wĭk) NJ (New York In.)	40·29 N	74·27 W
91	New Brunswick (Prov.)......Can.	47·14 N	66·30 W
104	Newburg....................In.	38·00 N	87·25 W
117	Newburg...................Mo.	37·54 N	91·53 W
105	Newburgh...................NY	41·30 N	74·00 W
107	Newburgh Heights Oh. (Cleveland In.)	41·27 N	81·40 W
154	Newbury (nū′bĕr-ĭ)........Eng.	51·24 N	1·26 W
99	Newbury..............Ma. (In.)	42·48 N	70·52 W
99	Newburyport (nū′bĕr-ĭ-pōrt) Ma. (In.)	42·48 N	70·53 W
205	New Caledonie..........Oceania	21·28 S	164·40 E
106	New Canaan (kā-nȧn) Ct. (New York In.)	41·06 N	73·30 W
98	New Carlisle (kär-lĭl′).......Can.	48·01 N	65·20 W
203	Newcastle (nū-kȧs′′l).......Austl.	33·00 S	151·55 E
98	Newcastle.................Can.	47·00 N	65·34 W
105	New Castle.................De.	39·40 N	75·35 W
148	Newcastle (nû-kȧs′′l) (nū-käs′′l) Eng.	53·01 N	2·14 W
154	Newcastle.................Eng.	55·00 N	1·45 W
104	New Castle.................In.	39·55 N	82·25 W
104	New Castle.................Oh.	40·20 N	82·10 W
104	New Castle.................Pa.	41·00 N	80·25 W
116	Newcastle..................Tx.	33·13 N	98·44 W
108	Newcastle..................Wy.	43·51 N	104·11 W
204	Newcastle Waters (wô′tērz).Austl.	17·10 S	133·25 E
104	Newcomerstown (nū′kŭm-ērz-toun) Oh.	40·15 N	81·40 W
106	New Croton Res. (krŏ′tôn) NY (New York In.)	41·15 N	73·47 W
184	New Delhi (dĕl′hī).........India	28·43 N	77·18 E
108	Newell (nū′ĕl)...............SD	44·43 N	103·26 W
205	New England Ra. (nû ĭŋ′glănd) Austl.	29·32 S	152·30 E
101	Newenham, C. (nū-ĕn-hăm)...Ak.	58·40 N	162·32 W
107	Newfane (nū-fān) NY (Buffalo In.)	43·17 N	78·44 W
91	Newfoundland (Prov.) (nū-fŭn′lănd′) (nū′fŭnd-lănd) (nû′found-lănd′) Can. (Newfoundland In.)	48·15 N	56·53 W
93	Newgate (nû′gāt)...........Can.	49·01 N	115·10 W
205	New Georgia (I.) (jôr′jĭ-ȧ)..Sol. Is.	8·08 S	158·00 E
109	New Glasgow (glȧs′gō)......Can.	45·35 N	62·36 W
197	New Guinea (I.) (gĭne)......Asia	5·45 S	140·00 E
110	Newhalem (nū hā′lŭm).......Wa.	48·44 N	121·11 W
103	New Hampshire (State) (hămp′shĭr).U. S.	43·55 N	71·40 W
109	New Hampton (hămp′tŭn)....Ia.	43·03 N	92·20 W
213	New Hanover (hăn′ôvēr) S. Afr. (Natal In.)	29·23 S	30·32 E
197	New Hanover (I.)...Pap. N. Gui.	2·37 S	150·15 E
104	New Harmony (nū här′mô-nĭ)..In.	38·10 N	87·55 W
105	New Haven (hā′vĕn).........Ct.	41·20 N	72·55 W
155	Newhaven.................Eng.	50·45 N	0·10 E
104	New Haven (nū hāv′′n).......In.	41·05 N	85·00 W
205	New Hebrides (hĕb′rĭ-dēz) Oceania	16·02 S	169·15 E
148	New Holland (hŏl′ănd)......Eng.	53·42 N	0·21 W
121	New Holland................NC	35·27 N	76·14 W
106	New Hope Mtn. (hōp) Al. (Birmingham In.)	33·23 N	86·45 W
107	New Hudson (hŭd′sŭn) Mi. (Detroit In.)	42·30 N	83·36 W
119	New Iberia (ī-bē′rĭ-ȧ).........La.	30·00 N	91·50 W
100	Newington (nū′ēng-tŏn) Can. (Ottawa In.)	45·07 N	75·00 W
197	New Ireland (I.) (ĭr′lănd) Pap. N. Gui.	3·15 S	152·30 E
103	New Jersey (State) (jûr′zĭ)..U. S.	40·30 N	74·50 W
	New Kensington (kĕn′zĭng-tŭn) Pa. (Pittsburgh In.)	40·34 N	79·35 W
117	Newkirk (nū′kûrk)...........Ok.	36·52 N	97·03 W
107	New Lenox (lĕn′ŭk) Il. (Chicago In.)	41·31 N	87·58 W
104	New Lexington (lĕk′sĭng-tŭn)..Oh.	39·40 N	82·10 W
109	New Lisbon (lĭz′bŭn).........Wi.	43·52 N	90·11 W
97	New Liskeard..............Can.	47·30 N	79·40 W
105	New London (lŭn′dŭn)........Ct.	41·20 N	72·05 W
109	New London................Wi.	44·24 N	88·45 W
117	New Madrid (măd′rĭd).......Mo.	36·34 N	89·31 W
121	Newman (L.)................Fl.	29·41 N	82·13 W
108	Newman's Grove (nū′măn grōv) Ne.	41·46 N	97·44 W
105	Newmarket (nū′mär-kĕt).....Can.	44·00 N	79·30 W
104	New Martinsville (mär′tĭnz-vĭl).WV	39·35 N	80·50 W
110	New Meadows...............Id.	44·58 N	116·20 W
102	New Mexico (State) (mĕk′sĭ-kō) U. S.	34·30 N	107·10 W
148	New Mills (mĭlz)...........Eng.	53·22 N	2·00 W
107	New Munster (mŭn′stēr) Wi. (Milwaukee In.)	42·35 N	88·13 W
120	Newnan (nū′năn)............Ga.	33·22 N	84·47 W
203	New Norfolk (nôr′fŏk)......Austl.	42·50 S	147·17 E
106	New Orleans (ôr′lê-ănz) La. (New Orleans In.)	30·00 N	90·05 W
104	New Philadelphia (fĭl-ȧ-dĕl′fĭ-ȧ).Oh.	40·30 N	81·30 W
205	New Plymouth (plĭm′ŭth) N. Z. (In.)	39·04 S	174·13 E
117	Newport (nū′pōrt)...........Ar.	35·35 N	91·16 W
202	Newport......Austl. (Sydney In.)	33·39 S	151·19 E
154	Newport (nū-pôrt)..........Eng.	50·41 N	1·25 W
154	Newport..................Wales	51·36 N	3·05 W
148	Newport...................Eng.	52·46 N	2·22 W
107	Newport.....Ky. (Cincinnati In.)	39·05 N	84·30 W
98	Newport...................Me.	44·49 N	69·20 W
113	Newport...................Mn. (Minneapolis, St. Paul In.)	44·52 N	92·59 W
105	Newport...................NH	43·20 N	72·10 W
110	Newport...................Or.	44·39 N	124·02 W
106	Newport......RI (Providence In.)	41·29 N	71·16 W
120	Newport...................Tn.	35·55 N	83·12 W
105	Newport...................Vt.	44·55 N	72·15 W
110	Newport...................Wa.	48·12 N	117·01 W
113	Newport Beach (bēch) Ca. (Los Angeles In.)	33·36 N	117·55 W
106	Newport News..Va. (Norfolk In.)	36·59 N	76·24 W
109	New Prague (nū prāg)........Mn.	44·33 N	93·35 W
128	New Providence (I.) (prŏv′ĭ-dĕns).Ba.	25·00 N	77·25 W
104	New Richmond (rĭch′mŭnd)...Oh.	38·55 N	84·15 W
109	New Richmond..............Wi.	45·07 N	92·34 W
119	New Roads (rōds)............La.	30·42 N	91·26 W
106	New Rochelle (rū-shĕl′) NY (New York In.)	40·55 N	73·47 W
108	New Rockford (rŏk′fērd).....ND	47·40 N	99·08 W
158	New Ross (rôs).............Ire.	52·25 N	6·55 W
100	New Sarepta.Can. (Edmonton In.)	53·17 N	113·09 W
191	New Shanghai China (Shanghai In.)	31·18 N	121·31 E
	New Siberian Is., see Novosibirskiye O-va		
121	New Smyrna Beach (smûr′nȧ)..Fl.	29·00 N	80·57 W
205	New South Wales (State) (wālz) Austl.	32·45 S	146·14 E
100	Newton (nū′tŭn) Can. (Winnipeg In.)	49·56 N	98·04 W
148	Newton....................Eng.	53·27 N	2·37 W
104	Newton.....................Il.	39·00 N	88·10 W
109	Newton.....................Ia.	41·42 N	93·04 W

ng-sing; ŋ-baŋk; ɴ-nasalized n; nŏd; cŏmmit; ōld; ôbey; ôrder; fōōd; fŏŏt; ou-out; s-soft; sh-dish; th-thin; pūre; ûnite; ûrn; stŭd; circŭs; ü-as "y" in study; ′-indeterminate vowel.

Page	Name Pronunciation Region	Lat. °'	Long. °'
117	Newton . . . Ks.	38·03 N	97·22 W
99	Newton . . . Ma. (In.)	42·21 N	71·13 W
120	Newton . . . Ms.	32·18 N	89·10 W
106	Newton . . . NJ (New York In.)	41·03 N	74·45 W
121	Newton . . . NC	35·40 N	81·19 W
119	Newton . . . Tx.	30·47 N	93·45 W
107	Newtonsville (nū'tŭnz-vĭl) Oh. (Cincinnati In.)	39·11 N	84·04 W
108	Newtown (nū'toun) . . . ND	47·57 N	102·25 W
107	Newtown . . . Oh. (Cincinnati In.)	39·08 N	84·22 W
106	Newtown . . . Pa. (Philadelphia In.)	40·13 N	74·56 W
154	Newtownards (nu-t'n-ardz') . . . Ire.	54·35 N	5·39 W
109	New Ulm (ŭlm) . . . Mn.	44·18 N	94·27 W
99	New Waterford (wô'tēr-fērd) Can.	46·15 N	60·05 W
112	New Westminster (wĕst'mĭn-stēr) Can. (Vancouver In.)	49·12 N	122·55 W
106	New York (yôrk) NY (New York In.)	40·40 N	73·58 W
103	New York (State) . . . U. S.	42·45 N	78·05 W
205	New Zealand (zē'lănd) . . . Oceania	39·14 S	169·30 E
124	Nexapa (R.) (nĕks-ä'pä) . . . Mex.	18·32 N	98·29 W
195	Neya-gawa (nā'yä gä'wä) Jap. (Ōsaka In.)	34·47 N	135·38 E
186	Neyshābūr . . . Iran	36·06 N	58·45 E
174	Neyva R. (nēy'vȧ) Sov. Un. (Urals In.)	57·39 N	60·37 E
167	Nezhin (nyĕzh'ēn) . . . Sov. Un.	50·03 N	31·52 E
110	Nez Perce (nĕz' pûrs') . . . Id.	46·16 N	116·15 W
212	Ngami (R.) (n'gä'mē) . . . Bots.	20·56 S	22·31 E
217	Ngangerabeli Pln. . . . Ken.	1·20 S	40·10 E
184	Nganglaring Tsho (L.) . . . China	31·42 N	82·53 E
215	Ngaoundéré (n'gōn-dȧ-rā') . . . Cam.	7·19 N	13·35 E
217	Ngarimbi . . . Tan.	8·28 S	38·36 E
216	Ngoko (R.) . . . Afr.	1·55 N	15·53 E
215	Ngol-Kedju Hill . . . Cam.	6·20 N	9·45 E
213	Ngong ('n-gông) . . . Ken.	1·27 S	36·39 E
216	Ngounié (R.) . . . Gabon	1·15 S	10·43 E
217	Ngoywa . . . Tan.	5·56 S	32·48 E
213	Ngqeleni ('ng-kĕ-lā'nē) S. Afr. (Natal In.)	31·41 S	29·04 E
215	Nguigmi ('n-gēg'mē) . . . Niger	14·15 N	13·07 E
215	Ngurore . . . Nig.	9·18 N	12·14 E
210	Nguru ('n-gōō'rōō) . . . Nig.	12·53 N	10·26 E
217	Nguru Mts. . . . Tan.	6·10 S	37·35 E
196	Nha Trang (nyä-träng') . . . Viet.	12·08 N	108·56 E
210	Niafounke . . . Mali	16·03 N	4·17 W
109	Niagara (nī-ăg'ȧ-rȧ) . . . Wi.	45·45 N	88·05 W
107	Niagara Falls . . . Can. (Buffalo In.)	43·05 N	79·05 W
107	Niagara Falls . . . NY (Buffalo In.)	43·06 N	79·02 W
107	Niagara-on-the-Lake Can. (Toronto In.)	43·16 N	79·05 W
107	Niagara R. U. S.-Can. (Buffalo In.)	43·12 N	79·03 W
214	Niakaramandougou . . . Ivory Coast	8·40 N	5·17 W
215	Niamey (nē-ä-mā') . . . Niger	13·31 N	2·07 E
214	Niamtougou . . . Togo	9·46 N	1·06 E
217	Niangara (nē-äŋ-gä'rȧ) . . . Zaire	3·42 N	27·52 E
117	Niangua (R.) (nī-ăŋ'gwȧ) . . . Mo.	37·30 N	93·05 W
196	Nias (I.) (nē'äs') . . . Indon.	0·58 N	97·43 E
156	Nibe (nē'bĕ) . . . Den.	56·57 N	9·36 E
122	Nicaragua (nĭk-ȧ-rä'gwȧ) . . . N. A.	12·45 N	86·15 W
126	Nicaragua, Lago de (L.) (lä'gô dĕ) Nic.	11·45 N	85·28 W
164	Nicastro (nē-käs'trō) . . . It.	38·39 N	16·15 E
126	Nicchehabin, Punta (Pt.) (pōō'n-tä-nē-kĕ-chĕ-ä-bē'n) Mex. (In.)	19·50 N	87·20 W
161	Nice (nēs) . . . Fr.	43·42 N	7·21 E
191	Nich'engchen China (Shanghai In.)	30·54 N	121·48 E
91	Nichicun (L.) (nĭch'ĭ-kŭn) . . . Can.	53·07 N	72·10 W
128	Nicholas Chan. (nĭk'ō-lȧs) . . . Ba.	23·30 N	80·20 W
104	Nicholasville (nĭk'ō-lȧs-vĭl) . . . Ky.	37·55 N	84·35 W
196	Nicobar Is. (nĭk-ō-bär') Andaman & Nicobar Is.	8·28 N	94·04 E
112	Nicolai Mtn. (nē-cō lī') Or. (Portland In.)	46·05 N	123·27 W
125	Nicolás Romero (nē-kō-lá's rō-mĕ'rô) . Mex. (In.)	19·38 N	99·20 W
113	Nicolet, L. (nĭ'kŏ-lĕt) Mi. (Sault Ste. Marie In.)	46·22 N	84·14 W
128	Nicolls Town . . . Ba.	25·10 N	78·00 W
113	Nicols (nĭk'ĕls) Mn. (Minneapolis, St. Paul In.)	44·50 N	93·12 W
112	Nicomeki (R.) Can. (Vancouver In.)	49·04 N	122·47 W
153	Nicosia (nē-kô-sē'ȧ) . . . Cyprus	35·10 N	33·22 E
126	Nicoya (nē-kō'yä) . . . C. R.	10·08 N	85·27 W
126	Nicoya, Golfo de (G.) (gôl-fô-dĕ) . C. R.	10·03 N	85·04 W
126	Nicoya, Pen. de . . . C. R.	10·05 N	86·00 W
	Nidaros, see Trondheim		
159	Nidzica (nē-jēt'sȧ) . . . Pol.	53·21 N	20·30 E
158	Niedere Tauern (Mts.) . . . Aus.	47·15 N	13·41 E
161	Niederkrüchten (nē'dĕr-krük-tĕn) F.R.G. (Ruhr In.)	51·12 N	6·14 E
149	Niederösterreich (Lower Austria) (State) . Aus. (Vienna In.)	48·24 N	16·20 E
158	Niedersachsen (Lower Saxony) (State) (nē'dĕr-zäk-sĕn) . F.R.G.	52·52 N	8·27 E
214	Niélé . . . Ivory Coast	10·12 N	5·38 W
215	Niellim . . . Chad	9·42 N	17·49 E
158	Nienburg (nē'ĕn-bōōrgh) . . . F.R.G.	52·40 N	9·15 E
214	Niénokoué, Mont (Mtn.) Ivory Coast	5·26 N	7·10 W
158	Niesse (R.) (nēs) . . . Pol.	51·30 N	15·00 E
218	Nietverdiend . . . S. Afr. (Johannesburg & Pretoria In.)	25·02 S	26·10 E
135	Nieuw Nickerie (nē-nē'kĕ-rē') . Sur.	5·51 N	57·00 W
124	Nieves (nyā'vâs) . . . Mex.	24·00 N	102·57 W
171	Niğde (nĭg'dĕ) . . . Tur.	37·55 N	34·40 E
218	Nigel (nī'jĕl) . . . S. Afr. (Johannesburg & Pretoria In.)	26·26 S	28·27 E
209	Niger (nī'jēr) . . . Afr.	18·02 N	8·30 E
215	Niger (R.) . . . Afr.	5·33 N	6·33 E
215	Niger Delta . . . Nig.	4·45 N	5·20 E
209	Nigeria (nī-jē'rĭ-ȧ) . . . Afr.	8·57 N	6·30 E
195	Nii (I.) (nē) . . . Jap.	34·26 N	139·23 E
194	Niigata (nē'ē-gä'tȧ) . . . Jap.	37·47 N	139·04 E
89	Niihau (I.) (nē'ē-hä'ōō) . . . Hi.	21·50 N	160·05 W
195	Niimi (nē'mē) . . . Jap.	34·59 N	133·28 E
195	Niiza . . . Jap. (Tōkyō In.)	35·48 N	139·34 E
155	Nijmegen (nī'mȧ-gĕn) . . . Neth.	51·50 N	5·52 E
195	Nikaidō (nē'ki-dô) Jap. (Ōsaka In.)	34·36 N	135·48 E
166	Nikitinka (nē-kĭ'tĭn-kȧ) . . Sov. Un.	55·33 N	33·19 E
195	Nikkō (nēk'kō) . . . Jap.	36·44 N	139·35 E
167	Nikolayev (nē-kô-lä'yĕf) . . Sov. Un.	46·58 N	32·02 E
167	Nikolayev (Oblast) (ôb'lȧst) Sov. Un.	47·27 N	31·25 E
194	Nikolayevka . . . Sov. Un.	48·37 N	134·49 E
174	Nikolayevka (nē-kô-lä'yĕf-kȧ) Sov. Un. (Leningrad In.)	59·29 N	29·48 E
171	Nikolayevskiy . . . Sov. Un.	50·00 N	45·30 E
173	Nikolayevsk-na-Amure . . . Sov. Un.	53·18 N	140·49 E
170	Nikol'sk (nē-kôlsk') . . . Sov. Un.	59·30 N	45·40 E
174	Nikol'skoye (nē-kôl'skô-yĕ) Sov. Un. (Leningrad In.)	59·27 N	30·00 E
165	Nikopol (nē'kô-pŏl') . . . Bul.	43·41 N	24·52 E
167	Nikopol' . . . Sov. Un.	47·36 N	34·24 E
165	Nikšić (nēk'shēch) . . . Yugo.	42·45 N	18·57 E
	Nīl, Nahr an-, see Nile (R.)		
137	Nilahue (R.) (nē-lȧ'wĕ) Chile (Santiago In.)	36·36 S	71·50 W
211	Nile (R.) (nīl) . . . Afr.	19·15 N	32·30 E
104	Niles (nīlz) . . . Mi.	41·50 N	86·15 W
104	Niles . . . Oh.	41·15 N	80·45 W
185	Nileshwar . . . India	12·08 N	74·14 E
185	Nilgiri Hills . . . India	17·05 N	76·22 E
136	Nilópolis (nē-lō'pō-lēs) Braz. (Rio de Janeiro In.)	22·48 S	43·25 W
184	Nīmach . . . India	24·32 N	74·51 E
210	Nimba, Mont (Mtn.) (nĭm'bȧ) Ivory Coast	7·40 N	8·33 W
214	Nimba Mts. . . . Gui.-Ivory Coast	7·30 N	8·35 W
160	Nîmes (nēm) . . . Fr.	43·49 N	4·22 E
117	Nimrod Res. (nĭm'rŏd) . . . Ar.	34·58 N	93·46 W
211	Nimule (nē-mōō'lȧ) . . . Sud.	3·38 N	32·12 E
216	Ninda . . . Ang.	14·47 S	21·24 E
203	Ninety Mile Bch. . . . Austl.	38·20 S	147·30 E
171	Nineveh (Ruins) (nĭn'ē-vȧ) . . . Iraq	36·30 N	43·10 E
192	Ningan (nĭŋ'găn') . . . China	44·20 N	129·20 E
190	Ningchin (nĭng'jĭn) . . . China	37·39 N	116·47 E
190	Ningching (nĭng'jĭn) . . . China	37·37 N	114·55 E
188	Ningerh . . . China	23·14 N	101·14 E
193	Ninghai (nĭng'hī') . . . China	29·20 N	121·20 E
190	Ningho (nĭng'hō') . . . China	39·27 N	117·44 E
	Ninghsia, see Yinch'uan		
193	Ningming . . . China	22·22 N	107·06 E
193	Ningpo (nĭng-pō') . . . China	29·56 N	121·30 E
188	Ningsia Hui Aut. Reg. . . . China	40·18 N	104·45 E
193	Ningte . . . China	26·38 N	119·33 E
192	Ningwu (nĭng'wōō') . . . China	39·00 N	112·12 E
190	Ningyang (nĭng'yäng') . . . China	35·46 N	116·48 E
193	Ninh Binh (nēn bēnk') . . . Viet.	20·22 N	106·00 E
197	Ninigo Is. . . . Pap. N. Gui.	1·15 S	143·30 E
116	Ninnescah (R.) (nĭn'ĕs-kä) . . . Ks.	37·37 N	98·31 W
135	Nioaque (nēō-ȧ'-kĕ) . . . Braz.	21·14 S	55·41 W
108	Niobrara (R.) (nī-ō-brâr'ȧ) . . . Ne.	42·46 N	98·46 W
214	Niokolo Koba, Parc Natl. du (Natl. Pk.) . Senegal	13·05 N	13·00 W
214	Nioro du Sahel (nē-ō'rō) . . . Mali	15·15 N	9·35 W
160	Niort (nē-ôr') . . . Fr.	46·17 N	0·28 W
94	Nipawin . . . Can.	53·22 N	104·00 W
129	Nipe, Bahía de (B.) (bä-ē'ä-dĕ-nē'pā) . Cuba	20·50 N	75·30 W
129	Nipe, Sierra de (Mts.) (sē-ĕ'r-rȧ-dĕ) . Cuba	20·20 N	75·50 W
104	Nipigon (nĭp'ĭ-gŏn) . . . Can.	48·58 N	88·17 W
96	Nipigon (L.) . . . Can.	49·37 N	89·55 W
109	Nipigon B. . . . Can.	48·56 N	88·00 W
98	Nipisiguit (R.) (nĭ-pĭ'sĭ-kwĭt) . Can.	47·26 N	66·15 W
97	Nipissing (L.) (nĭp'ĭ-sĭng) . . . Can.	45·59 N	80·19 W
128	Niquero (nē-kā'rō) . . . Cuba	20·00 N	77·35 W
184	Nirmali . . . India	26·30 N	86·43 E
165	Niš (nēsh) . . . Yugo.	43·18 N	21·55 E
162	Nisa (nē'sȧ) . . . Port.	39·32 N	7·41 W
165	Nišava (R.) (nē'shȧ-vȧ) . . . Yugo.	43·17 N	22·17 E
195	Nishino (I.) (nēsh'ē-nō) . . . Jap.	36·06 N	132·49 E
195	Nishinomiya (nēsh'ē-nō-mē'yȧ) Jap. (Ōsaka In.)	34·44 N	135·21 E
195	Nishinoomote (nēsh'ē-nō-mō'tō) Jap.	30·44 N	130·59 E
195	Nishio (nēsh'ē-ô) . . . Jap.	34·50 N	137·01 E
94	Niska L. (nĭs'kȧ) . . . Can.	55·35 N	108·38 W
159	Nisko (nēs'kô) . . . Pol.	50·30 N	22·07 E
100	Nisku (nĭs-kū') Can. (Edmonton In.)	53·21 N	113·33 W
110	Nisqually R. (nĭs-kwôl'ĭ) . . . Wa.	46·51 N	122·33 W
156	Nissan (R.) . . . Swe.	57·06 N	13·22 E
156	Nisser Vand (L.) (nĭs'ĕr vän) . . Nor.	59·14 N	8·35 E
156	Nissum Fd. . . . Den.	56·24 N	7·35 E
136	Niterói (nē-tĕ-rô'ĭ) Braz. (Rio de Janeiro In.)	22·53 S	43·07 W
154	Nith (R.) (nĭth) . . . Scot.	55·13 N	3·55 W
159	Nitra (nē'trȧ) . . . Czech.	48·18 N	18·04 E
159	Nitra R. . . . Czech.	48·13 N	18·14 E
104	Nitro (nī'trō) . . . WV	38·25 N	81·50 W
199	Niue (nī'ōō) . . . Oceania	19·50 S	167·00 W
155	Nivelles (nē'vĕl') . . . Bel.	50·33 N	4·17 E
160	Nivernais, Côtes de (Hills) (nē-vĕr-nĕ') . Fr.	47·40 N	3·09 E
119	Nixon (nĭk'sŭn) . . . Tx.	29·16 N	97·48 W
184	Nizāmābād . . . India	18·48 N	78·07 E
173	Nizhne-Angarsk (nyēzh'nyĭ-ŭngärsk') . Sov. Un.	55·49 N	108·46 E
171	Nizhne-Chirskaya (nyĭ-ŭn-gärsk') Sov. Un.	48·20 N	42·50 E
173	Nizhne-Kolymsk (kô-lēmsk') Sov. Un.	68·32 N	160·56 E
172	Nizhneudinsk (nēzh'nyĭ-ōōdēnsk') Sov. Un.	54·58 N	99·15 E
174	Nizhniye Sergi (nyēzh' [nyē] sĕr'gē) Sov. Un. (Urals In.)	56·41 N	59·19 E
167	Nizhniye Serogozy (nyēzh'nyĭ sĕ-rô-gô'zĭ) . Sov. Un.	46·51 N	34·25 E
174	Nizhniy Tagil (tŭgēl') Sov. Un. (Urals In.)	57·54 N	59·59 E
174	Nizhnyaya Kur'ya (nyē'zhnyȧ-yȧ koōr'yȧ) Sov. Un. (Urals In.)	58·01 N	56·00 E
174	Nizhnyaya Salda (nyē'zh[nya'ya] säl'da') Sov. Un. (Urals In.)	58·05 N	60·43 E
172	Nizhnyaya Taymyra (R.) . Sov. Un.	72·30 N	95·18 E
172	Nizhnyaya (Lower) Tunguska (R.) (tōōn-gōōs'kȧ) . Sov. Un.	64·13 N	91·30 E
174	Nizhnyaya Tura (tōō'rȧ) Sov. Un. (Urals In.)	58·38 N	59·50 E
174	Nizhnyaya Us'va (ōō'vȧ) Sov. Un. (Urals In.)	59·05 N	58·53 E
217	Njombe . . . Tan.	9·20 S	34·46 E
156	Njurunda (nyōō-rōōn'dȧ) . . . Swe.	62·15 N	17·24 E
217	Nkala Mission . . . Zambia	15·55 S	26·00 E
213	Nkandla ('n-känd'lä) S. Afr. (Natal In.)	28·40 S	31·06 E
214	Nkawkaw . . . Ghana	6·33 N	0·47 W
184	Noākhāli . . . Bngl.	22·52 N	91·08 E
101	Noatak (nô-ȧ'tȧk) . . . Ak.	67·22 N	163·28 W
101	Noatak (R.) . . . Ak.	67·58 N	162·15 W
195	Nobeoka (nō-bȧ-ō'kȧ) . . . Jap.	32·36 N	131·41 E
104	Noblesville (nō'bl'z-vĭl) . . . In.	40·00 N	86·00 W
100	Nobleton (nō'bl'tŭn) Can. (Toronto In.)	43·54 N	79·39 W
163	Nocero Inferiore (nô-chĕ'rô-ēn-fĕ-ryô'rĕ) It. (Naples In.)	40·30 N	14·38 E
124	Nochistlán (nô-chēs-tlän') . . . Mex.	21·23 N	102·52 W
125	Nochixtlón (Asunción) (ä-sōōn-syōn') . Mex.	17·28 N	97·12 W
115	Nogales (nô-gä'lĕs) . . . Az.	31·20 N	110·55 W
125	Nogales (nō-gä'lĕs) . . . Mex.	18·49 N	97·09 W
122	Nogales . . . Mex.	31·15 N	111·00 W
218	Nogal Val. (nô'găl) Som. (Horn of Afr. In.)	8·30 N	47·50 E
167	Nogaysk (nô-gīsk') . . . Sov. Un.	46·43 N	36·21 E
161	Nogent-le-Roi (nŏ-zhŏn-lĕ-rwä') Fr. (Paris In.)	48·39 N	1·32 E
160	Nogent-le-Rotrou (rŏ-trōō') . . . Fr.	48·22 N	0·47 E
174	Noginsk (nô-gēnsk') Sov. Un. (Moscow In.)	55·52 N	38·28 E
162	Nogueira (nô-gā'rä) . . . Sp.	42·25 N	7·43 W
163	Nogueira Pallaresa (R.) (nô-gĕ'y-rä-päl-yä-rĕ-sä) . Sp.	42·18 N	1·03 E
192	Noho (nō'hō') . . . China	48·23 N	124·58 E
160	Noires, Mts. (nwȧr) . . . Fr.	48·07 N	3·42 W
160	Noirmoutier, Île de (I.) (nwȧr-mōō-tyā') . Fr.	47·03 N	3·08 W
195	Nojimä-Zaki (Pt.) (nō'jē-mä zä-kē) . Jap.	35·54 N	139·48 E
104	Nokomis (nô-kō'mĭs) . . . Il.	39·15 N	89·10 W
163	Nola (nô'lä) . . . It. (Naples In.)	40·41 N	14·32 E
170	Nolinsk (nô-lēnsk') . . . Sov. Un.	57·32 N	49·50 E
195	Noma Misaki (C.) (nō'mä mē'sä-kē) . Jap.	31·25 N	130·09 E
124	Nombre de Dios (nôm-brĕ-dĕ-dyô's) . Mex.	23·50 N	104·14 W
127	Nombre de Dios (nô'm-brĕ) . . Pan.	9·34 N	79·28 W
101	Nome (nōm) . . . Ak.	64·30 N	165·20 W
90	Nonacho (L.) . . . Can.	61·48 N	111·20 W
212	Nongoma (nōn-gō'mȧ) . . . S. Afr.	27·48 S	31·45 E
102	Nooksack (nōōk'săk) Wa. (Vancouver In.)	48·55 N	122·19 W
112	Nooksack (R.) Wa. (Vancouver In.)	48·54 N	122·31 W
149	Noorden . . Neth. (Amsterdam In.)	52·09 N	4·49 E
149	Noordwijk aan Zee Neth. (Amsterdam In.)	52·14 N	4·25 E
149	Noordzee, Kanal, (Can.) Neth. (Amsterdam In.)	52·27 N	4·42 E
90	Nootka (I.) (nōōt'kȧ) . . . Can.	49·32 N	126·42 W
92	Nootka Sd. . . . Can.	49·33 N	126·38 W
216	Nóqui (nô-kē') . . . Ang.	5·51 S	13·25 E
194	Nor (R.) (nou') . . . China	46·55 N	132·45 E
107	Nora (nō'rȧ) . In. (Indianapolis In.)	39·54 N	86·08 W
156	Nora . . . Swe.	59·32 N	14·56 E
97	Noranda . . . Can.	48·15 N	79·01 W
106	Norbeck (nôr'bĕk) Md. (Baltimore In.)	39·06 N	77·05 W
117	Norborne (nôr'bôrn) . . . Mo.	39·17 N	93·39 W
113	Norco (nôr'kō) Ca. (Los Angeles In.)	33·57 N	117·33 W
106	Norcross (nôr'krôs) Ga. (Atlanta In.)	33·56 N	84·13 W
100	Nord, Riviere du (rēv-yĕr' dü nōr) Can. (Montreal In.)	45·45 N	74·02 W
93	Nordegg (nûr'dĕg) . . . Can.	52·28 N	116·04 W
158	Norden (nôr'dĕn) . . . F.R.G.	53·35 N	7·14 E
158	Norderney I. (nōr'dĕr-nĕy) . F.R.G.	53·45 N	6·58 E
156	Nord Fd. (nô'fyōr) . . . Nor.	61·50 N	5·35 E
158	Nordhausen (nôrt'hau-zĕn) G.D.R.	51·30 N	10·48 E
158	Nordhorn (nôrt'hôrn) . . . F.R.G.	52·26 N	7·05 E
150	Nord Kapp (C.) (nôr-kapp) . . Nor.	71·07 N	25·57 E

ăt; finăl; rāte; senâte; ärm; ȧsk; sofȧ; fâre; ch-choose; dh-as th in other; bē; ēvent; bĕt; recĕnt; cratēr; g-go; gh-guttural g; bĭt; ĭ-short neutral; rīde; ᴋ-guttural k as ch in German ich;

PRONOUNCING INDEX Nordland — Novokuznetsk 321

Page	Name Pronunciation Region	Lat. °′	Long. °′
112	Nordland (nôrd'lȧnd) Wa. (Seattle In.)	48·03 N	122·41 W
158	Nördlingen (nûrt'lĭng-ĕn) . . F.R.G.	48·51 N	10·30 E
158	Nord-Ostsee Kan. (Kiel) Can. (nōrd-ōzt-zā) (kēl) . . . . . F.R.G.	54·03 N	9·23 E
158	Nordrhein-Westfalen (North Rhine-Westphalia) (State) (nōrd'hīn-vĕst-fä-lĕn) . . . . F.R.G.	50·50 N	6·53 E
173	Nordvik (nôrd'vēk) . . . . . . Sov. Un.	73·57 N	111·15 E
154	Nore R. (nōr) . . . . Ire.	52·34 N	7·15 W
120	Norfield (nôr'fēld) . . . . Ms.	31·24 N	90·25 W
99	Norfolk (nôr'fŏk) . . . . Ma. (In.)	42·07 N	71·19 W
108	Norfolk . . . . Ne.	42·10 N	97·25 W
106	Norfolk . . . . Va. (Norfolk In.)	36·55 N	76·15 W
198	Norfolk . . . . Oceania	27·10 S	166·50 E
117	Norfork, L. . . . . Ar.	36·25 N	92·09 W
124	Noria (nō'rē-ȧ) . . . . Mex.	23·04 N	106·20 W
172	Noril'sk (nô rēlsk') . . . . . . Sov. Un.	69·00 N	87·11 E
104	Normal (nôr'măl) . . . . Il.	40·35 N	89·00 W
117	Norman (nôr'mȧn) . . . . Ok.	35·13 N	97·25 W
121	Norman, L. . . . . NC	35·30 N	80·53 W
205	Norman (R.) . . . . Austl.	18·27 S	141·29 E
160	Normandie (Reg.) (nōr-mäN-dē') Fr.	49·02 N	0·17 E
160	Normandie, Collines de (Hills) (kō-lēn'dĕ-nōr-män-dē') . Fr.	48·35 N	0·30 W
205	Normanton (nôr'mȧn-tŭn) . . Austl.	17·45 S	141·10 E
148	Normanton . . . . Eng.	53·40 N	1·21 W
90	Norman Wells . . . . Can.	65·26 N	127·00 W
204	Nornalup (nôr-năl'ŭp) . . . . . . Austl.	35·00 S	117·00 E
156	Norra Dellen (L.) . . . . Swe.	61·57 N	16·25 E
156	Norre Sundby (nû-rĕ-sōōn'bü) Den.	57·04 N	9·55 E
120	Norris (nŏr'ĭs) . . . . Tn.	36·09 N	84·05 W
120	Norris (R.) . . . . Tn.	36·17 N	84·10 W
106	Norristown (nŏr'ĭs-town) Pa. (Philadelphia In.)	40·07 N	75·21 W
156	Norrköping (nôr'chûp'ĭng) . . . Swe.	58·37 N	16·10 E
156	Norrtälje (nôr-tĕl'yĕ) . . . . Swe.	59·47 N	18·39 E
204	Norseman (nôrs'mȧn) . . . . . . Austl.	32·15 S	122·00 E
137	Norte, Punta (Pt.) (pōō'n-tä-nôr'tĕ) Arg. (Buenos Aires In.)	36·17 S	56·46 W
135	Norte, Serra do (Mts.) (sĕ'r-rä-dō-nôr'te) . Braz.	12·04 S	59·08 W
99	North, C. . . . . Can.	47·02 N	60·25 W
205	North, C. . . . . N. Z. (In.)	34·31 S	173·02 E
114	North, I. . . . . . Ca. (San Diego In.)	32·39 N	117·14 W
205	North, I. . . . . N. Z. (In.)	37·34 S	171·12 E
105	North Adams (ăd'ămz) . . . . . . Ma.	42·40 N	73·05 W
204	Northam (nôr-dhȧm) . . . . Austl.	31·50 S	116·45 E
218	Northam (nôr'thȧm) . . . . S. Afr. (Johannesburg & Pretoria In.)	24·52 S	27·16 E
75	North America (ȧ-mĕr'ĭ-kȧ)		
123	North American Basin (ȧ-mĕr'ĭ-kȧn) . Atl. O.	23·45 N	62·45 W
204	Northampton (nôr-thămp'tŭn) Austl.	28·22 S	114·45 E
154	Northampton (nôrth-ămp'tŭn) Eng.	52·14 N	0·56 W
105	Northampton . . . . Ma.	42·20 N	72·45 W
105	Northampton . . . . Pa.	40·45 N	75·30 W
148	Northampton (Co.) . . . . Eng.	52·25 N	0·47 W
196	North Andaman I. (ăn-dȧ-măn') Andaman & Nicobar Is.	13·15 N	93·30 E
99	North Andover (ăn'dô-vēr) Ma. (In.)	42·42 N	71·07 W
112	North Arm (ärm) Can. (Vancouver In.)	49·13 N	123·01 W
106	North Atlanta (ăt-lăn'tȧ) Ga. (Atlanta In.)	33·52 N	84·20 W
106	North Attleboro (ăt''l-bŭr-ô) Ma. (Providence In.)	41·59 N	71·18 W
104	North Baltimore (bôl'tĭ-mōr) . . Oh.	41·10 N	83·40 W
118	North Basque (băsk) . . . . Tx.	31·56 N	98·01 W
94	North Battleford (băt''l-fērd) . Can.	52·47 N	108·17 W
97	North Bay . . . . Can.	46·13 N	79·26 W
110	North Bend (bĕnd) . . . . Or.	43·23 N	124·13 W
98	North Berwick (bûr'wĭk) . . . . . Me.	43·18 N	70·46 W
128	North Bght. (bĭt) . . . . Ba.	24·30 N	77·40 W
128	North Bimini (I). (bĭ'mĭ-nē) . . Ba.	25·45 N	79·20 W
	North Borneo (Reg.), see Sabah		
99	Northborough (nôrth'bûr-ô) Ma. (In.)	42·19 N	71·39 W
99	Northbridge (nôrth'brĭj) Ma. (In.)	42·09 N	71·39 W
129	North Caicos (I.) (kī'kōs) . Turks & Caicos	21·55 N	72·00 W
103	North Carolina (State) (kăr-ô-lī'nȧ) . U. S.	35·40 N	81·30 W
93	North Cascades Natl. Pk. . . . . Wa.	48·50 N	120·50 W
128	North Cat Cay (I.) . . . . Ba.	25·35 N	79·20 W
104	North Chan (B.) (chăn) . . . . . Can.	46·10 N	83·20 W
154	North Chan . . . . N. Ire.-Scot.	55·15 N	7·56 W
121	North Charleston (chärlz'tŭn) SC	32·49 N	79·57 W
107	North Chicago (shĭ-kô'gō) Il. (Chicago In.)	42·19 N	87·51 W
107	North College Hill (kŏl'ĕj hĭl) Oh. (Cincinnati In.)	39·13 N	84·33 W
118	North Concho (kŏn'chō) . . . . . . Tx.	31·40 N	100·48 W
100	North Cooking Lake (kōōk'ĭng lāk) Can. (Edmonton In.)	53·28 N	112·57 W
102	North Dakota (State) (dȧ-kō'tȧ) U. S.	47·20 N	101·55 W
154	North Downs (dounz) . . . . Eng.	51·11 N	0·01 W
184	North Dum-Dum . . . . . . India (In.)	22·38 N	88·23 E
101	Northeast C. (nôrth-ēst) . . . . . . Ak.	63·15 N	169·04 W
129	Northeast Pt. . . . . Ba.	21·25 N	73·00 W
129	Northeast Pt. . . . . Ba.	22·45 N	73·50 W
128	Northeast Providence Chan. (prŏv'ĭ-dĕns) . Ba.	25·45 N	77·00 W
158	Northeim (nôrt'hīm) . . . . . . F.R.G.	51·42 N	9·59 E
128	North Elbow Cays (Is.) . . . . Ba.	23·55 N	80·30 W
111	Northern Cheyenne Ind. Res. . Mt.	45·32 N	106·43 W
	Northern Dvina (R.), see Severnaya Dvina		
154	Northern Ireland (ĭr'lănd) . . U. K.	54·48 N	7·00 W
	Northern Land (Is.), see Severnaya Zemlya		
204	Northern Territory . . . . Austl.	18·15 S	133·00 E
109	Northfield (nôrth'fēld) . . . . Mn.	44·28 N	93·11 W
203	North Flinders, Ra. (flĭn'dērz) Austl.	31·55 S	138·45 E
155	North Foreland (fōr'lȧnd) . . . . Eng.	51·20 N	1·30 E
118	North Franklin Mt. (frăŋ'klĭn) . Tx.	31·55 N	106·30 W
156	North Frisian Is. . . . . Den.	55·16 N	8·15 E
122	North Gamboa (gäm-bô'ä) C. Z. (In.)	9·07 N	79·40 W
100	North Gower (gŏw'ēr) Can. (Ottawa In.)	45·08 N	75·43 W
113	North Hollywood (hŏl'ē-wōōd) Ca. (Los Angeles In.)	34·10 N	118·23 W
104	North Judson (jŭd'sŭn) . . . . In.	41·15 N	86·50 W
93	North Kamloops (kăm'lōōps) . Can.	50·41 N	120·22 W
113	North Kansas City (kăn'zȧs) Mo. (Kansas City In.)	39·08 N	94·34 W
106	North Kingstown RI (Providence In.)	41·34 N	71·26 W
117	North Little Rock (lĭt''l rŏk) . . . Ar.	34·46 N	92·13 W
108	North Loup (R.) (lōōp) . . . . . . Ne.	42·05 N	100·10 W
104	North Manchester (măn'chĕs-tēr) In.	41·00 N	85·45 W
113	Northmoor (nôrth'mōōr) Mo. (Kansas City In.)	39·10 N	94·37 W
95	North Moose L. . . . . Can.	54·09 N	100·20 W
203	North Mount Lofty Ranges . Austl.	33·50 S	138·30 E
113	North Ogden (ŏg'dĕn) Ut. (Salt Lake City In.)	41·18 N	111·58 W
113	North Ogden Pk. Ut. (Salt Lake City. In.)	41·23 N	111·59 W
107	North Olmsted (ōlm-stĕd) Oh. (Cleveland In.)	41·25 N	81·55 W
116	North Pease (R.) (pēz) . . . . Tx.	34·19 N	100·58 W
112	North Pender (I.) (pĕn'dēr) Can. (Vancouver In.)	48·48 N	123·16 W
112	North Plains (plānz) Or. (Portland In.)	45·36 N	123·00 W
108	North Platte (plăt) . . . . Ne.	41·08 N	100·45 W
102	North Platte, (R.) . . . . U. S.	41·20 N	102·40 W
104	North Pt. . . . . Mi.	45·00 N	83·20 W
127	North Pt. . . . . Barb. (In.)	13·22 N	59·36 W
120	Northport (nôrth'pōrt) . . . . Al.	33·12 N	87·35 W
106	Northport . . NY (New York In.)	40·53 N	73·20 W
110	Northport . . . . Wa.	48·53 N	117·47 W
99	North Reading (rĕd'ĭng) . Ma. (In.)	42·34 N	71·04 W
	North Rhine-Westphalia (State), see Nordrhein-Westfalen		
113	North Richland Hills Tx. (Dallas, Ft. Worth In.)	32·50 N	97·13 W
113	Northridge (nôrth'ridj) Ca. (Los Angeles In.)	34·14 N	118·32 W
107	North Ridgeville (rĭj-vĭl) Oh. (Cleveland In.)	41·23 N	82·01 W
107	North Royalton (roi'ăl-tŭn) Oh. (Cleveland In.)	41·19 N	81·44 W
113	North St. Paul (sȧnt pôl') . . . . Mn. (Minneapolis, St. Paul In.)	45·01 N	92·59 W
113	North Salt Lake (sôlt lāk) Ut. (Salt Lake City In.)	40·50 N	111·55 W
94	North Saskatchewan (R.) (săn-kăch'ē-wän) . Can.	52·40 N	106·45 W
150	North Sea . . . . Eur.	56·09 N	3·16 E
109	North Skunk (R.) (skŭnk) . . . . . Ia.	41·39 N	92·46 W
99	North Sydney (sĭd'nē) . . . . Can.	46·13 N	60·15 W
205	North Taranaki Bght. (tȧ-rȧ-nä'kĭ bĭt) . N. Z. (In.)	38·23 S	172·03 E
106	North Tarrytown (tăr'ĭ-toun) NY (New York In.)	41·05 N	73·52 W
93	North Thompson (R.) . . . . Can.	50·50 N	120·10 W
107	North Tonawanda (tŏn-ȧ-wŏn'dȧ) NY (Buffalo In.)	43·02 N	78·53 W
115	North Truchas Pks. (Mts.) (trōō'chäs) . NM	35·58 N	105·37 W
99	North Twillingate (I.) (twĭl'ĭn-gāt) Can.	49·47 N	54·37 W
154	North Uist (I.) (û'ĭst) . . . . Scot.	57·37 N	7·22 W
98	Northumberland Str. (nôr thŭm'bēr-lȧnd) . Can.	46·25 N	64·20 W
105	Northumberland . . . . NH	44·30 N	71·30 W
205	Northumberland, Is. . . . . Austl.	21·42 S	151·30 E
110	North Umpqua R. (ŭmp'kwȧ) . . Or.	43·20 N	122·50 W
112	North Vancouver (văn-kōō'vēr) Can. (Vancouver In.)	49·19 N	123·04 W
104	North Vernon (vûr'nŭn) . . . . . . In.	39·05 N	85·45 W
107	Northville (nôrth-vĭl) Mi. (Detroit In.)	42·26 N	83·28 W
106	North Wales (wālz) Pa. (Philadelphia In.)	40·12 N	75·16 W
204	North West C. (nôrth'wĕst) . Austl.	21·50 S	112·25 E
121	Northwest Cape Fear, (R.) (cāp fēr) . NC	34·34 N	79·46 W
99	North West Gander (R.) (găn'dēr) Can.	48·40 N	55·15 W
154	Northwest Highlands . . . . Scot.	56·50 N	5·20 W
128	Northwest Providence Chan. (prŏv'ĭ-dĕns) . Ba.	26·15 N	78·45 W
90	Northwest Territories (tĕr'ĭ-tō'rĭs) . Can.	64·42 N	119·09 W
155	Northwich (nôrth'wĭch) . . . . . . Eng.	53·15 N	2·31 W
121	North Wilkesboro (wĭlks'bûrô) . NC	36·08 N	81·10 W
109	Northwood (nôrth'wōōd) . . . . . . Ia.	43·26 N	93·13 W
108	Northwood . . . . ND	47·44 N	97·36 W
111	North Wood Cr. . . . . Wy.	44·02 N	107·37 W
112	North Yamhill (R.) (yăm' hĭl) Or. (Portland In.)	45·22 N	123·21 W
154	North York Moors (yôrk mōōrz') Eng.	54·20 N	0·40 W
100	North York . . . . Can. (Toronto In.)	43·47 N	79·25 W
116	Norton (nôr'tŭn) . . . . Ks.	39·40 N	99·54 W
106	Norton . . . . . . Ma. (Providence In.)	41·58 N	71·08 W
121	Norton . . . . Va.	36·54 N	82·36 W
101	Norton B. . . . . Ak.	64·22 N	162·18 W
106	Norton Res. . Ma. (Providence In.)	42·01 N	71·07 W
101	Norton Sd. . . . . Ak.	63·48 N	164·50 W
100	Norval (nôr'vȧl) Can. (Toronto In.)	43·39 N	79·52 W
113	Norwalk (nôr'wôk) Ca. (Los Angeles In.)	33·54 N	118·05 W
106	Norwalk . . . . . . Ct. (New York In.)	41·06 N	73·25 W
104	Norwalk . . . . Oh.	41·15 N	82·35 W
146	Norway (nôr'wā) . . . . Eur.	63·48 N	11·17 E
98	Norway . . . . Me.	44·11 N	70·35 W
109	Norway . . . . Mi.	45·47 N	87·55 W
95	Norway House . . . . Can.	53·59 N	97·50 W
150	Norwegian Sea (nôr-wē'jăn) . . Eur.	66·54 N	1·43 E
99	Norwell (nôr'wĕl) . . . . Ma. (In.)	42·10 N	70·47 W
105	Norwich (nôr'wĭch) . . . . Ct.	41·20 N	72·00 W
155	Norwich . . . . Eng.	52·40 N	1·15 E
105	Norwich . . . . NY	42·35 N	75·30 W
99	Norwood (nôr'wōōd) . . . . Ma. (In.)	42·11 N	71·13 W
121	Norwood . . . . NC	35·15 N	80·08 W
107	Norwood . . . . . Oh. (Cincinnati In.)	39·10 N	84·27 W
100	Nose Cr. (nōz) . Can. (Calgary In.)	51·09 N	114·02 W
194	Noshiro (nō'shê-rô) . . . . Jap.	40·09 N	140·02 E
167	Nosovka (nô'sôf-kȧ) . . . . . Sov. Un.	50·54 N	31·35 E
213	Nossi Bé (B.) (nōō'sē bā) . . Mad.	13·14 S	47·28 E
212	Nossob (R.) (nô'sŏb) . . . S. W. Afr.	24·15 S	19·10 E
158	Noteć R. (nô'tĕch) . . . . Pol.	52·50 N	16·19 E
151	Noto (nô'tô) . . . . It.	36·49 N	15·08 E
156	Notodden (nôt'ôd'n) . . . . Nor.	59·35 N	9·15 E
195	Noto-Hantō (Pen.) (nô'tō hän'tō) Jap.	37·18 N	137·03 E
98	Notre Dame, Monts (Mts.) . . Can.	46·35 N	70·35 W
99	Notre Dame B. (nō't'r dȧm') . Can.	49·45 N	55·15 W
100	Notre-Dame-des-Laurentides (dĕ-lō-räN-tēd') . Can. (Quebec In.)	46·55 N	71·20 W
98	Notre-Dame-du-Lac . . . . Can.	47·37 N	68·51 W
104	Nottawasaga B. (nŏt'ȧ-wȧ-sä'gȧ) Can.	44·45 N	80·35 W
91	Nottaway (R.) (nôt'ȧ-wā) . . . . Can.	50·58 N	78·02 W
148	Nottingham (nŏt'ĭng-ăm) . . . . Eng.	52·58 N	1·09 W
148	Nottingham (Co.) . . . . Eng.	53·03 N	1·05 W
91	Nottingham I. . . . . Can.	62·58 N	78·53 W
121	Nottoway, (R.) (nôt'ȧ-wā) . . . . Va.	36·53 N	77·47 W
94	Notukeu Cr. . . . . Can.	49·55 N	106·30 W
210	Nouadhibou . . . . Mauritania	21·02 N	17·09 W
214	Nouakchott . . . . Mauritania	18·06 N	15·57 W
214	Nouamrhar . . . . Mauritania	19·22 N	16·31 W
205	Noumea (nōō-mā'ä) . . . . N. Cal.	22·18 S	166·48 E
98	Nouvelle (nōō-vĕl') . . . . Can.	48·09 N	66·22 W
211	Nouvelle Anvers (äN-vâr') . . . Zaire	1·42 N	19·08 E
160	Nouzonville (nōō-zôN-vēl') . . . . . Fr.	49·51 N	4·43 E
135	Nova Cruz (nō'vȧ-krōō'z) . . . Braz.	6·22 S	35·20 W
217	Nova Freixo . . . . Moz.	14·49 S	36·33 E
137	Nova Friburgo (frē-bōōr'gōō) Braz. (Rio de Janeiro In.)	22·18 S	42·31 W
216	Nova Gaia . . . . Ang.	10·09 S	17·31 E
136	Nova Iguaçu (nō'vä-ē-gwä-sōō') Braz. (Rio de Janeiro In.)	22·45 S	43·27 W
137	Nova Lima (lē'mä) Braz. (Rio de Janeiro In.)	19·59 S	43·51 W
	Nova Lisboa, see Huambo		
212	Nova Mambone (nō'vȧ-mȧm-bŏ'nĕ.) Moz.	21·04 S	35·13 E
164	Novara (nô-vä'rä) . . . . It.	45·24 N	8·38 E
137	Nova Resende Braz. (Rio de Janeiro In.)	21·12 S	46·25 W
91	Nova Scotia (Prov.) (skō'shȧ) . Can.	44·28 N	65·00 W
165	Nova Varoš (nô'vä vä'rôsh) . Yugo.	43·24 N	19·53 E
157	Novaya Ladoga (nô'vȧ-yȧ lȧ-dô-gô) . Sov. Un.	60·06 N	32·16 E
174	Novaya Lyalya (lyȧ'lyȧ) Sov. Un. (Urals In.)	59·03 N	60·36 E
167	Novaya Odessa (ô-dĕs'ä) . Sov. Un.	47·18 N	31·48 E
167	Novaya Praga (prä'gȧ) . . Sov. Un.	48·34 N	32·54 E
173	Novaya Sibir (I.) (sē-bēr') Sov. Un.	75·42 N	150·00 E
167	Novaya Vodolaga (vô-dôl'ȧ-gȧ) Sov. Un.	49·43 N	35·51 E
172	Novaya Zemlya (I.) (zĕm-lyȧ') Sov. Un.	72·00 N	54·46 E
165	Nova Zagora (zä'gô-rȧ) . . . . . . Bul.	42·30 N	26·01 E
163	Novelda (nō-vĕl'dä) . . . . Sp.	38·22 N	0·46 W
159	Nové Mesto (Nad Váhom) (nô'vĕ myĕs'tō) . Czech.	48·44 N	17·47 E
159	Nové Zámky (zäm'kĕ) . . . . . Czech.	47·58 N	18·10 E
166	Novgorod (nôv'gô-rŏt) . . Sov. Un.	58·32 N	31·16 E
166	Novgorod (Oblast) . . . . . . Sov. Un.	58·27 N	31·55 E
164	Novi (nô'vē) . . . . It.	44·43 N	8·48 W
107	Novi (nō'vĭ) . . . . . Mi. (Detroit In.)	42·29 N	83·28 W
164	Novi Grad (grȧd) . . . . Yugo.	44·09 N	15·34 E
117	Novinger (nŏv'ĭn-jēr) . . . . Mo.	40·14 N	92·43 W
165	Novi-Pazar (pä-zär') . . . . Bul.	43·22 N	27·26 E
165	Novi Pazar (pä-zär') . . . . Yugo.	43·08 N	20·30 E
165	Novi Sad (säd') . . . . Yugo.	45·15 N	19·53 E
174	Novoasbest (nô-vô-ä-bĕst') Sov. Un. (Urals In.)	57·43 N	60·14 E
167	Novoaydar (nô'vô-ī-där') . Sov. Un.	48·57 N	39·01 E
167	Novocherkassk (nô'vô-chĕr-kȧsk') Sov. Un.	47·25 N	40·04 E
167	Novogorod-Severskiy . . . . Sov. Un.	52·01 N	33·14 E
159	Novogrudok (nô-vô-grōō'dôk) Sov. Un.	53·35 N	25·51 E
141	Novo-Kazalinsk (nô-vŭ-kŭ-zȧ-lyēnsk') . Sov. Un.	45·47 N	62·00 E
172	Novokuznetsk (Stalinsk) (nō'vô-kōō'z-nyĕ'tsk) (stȧ'lĕnsk) . Sov. Un.	53·43 N	86·59 E

ng-sing; ŋ-baŋk; N-nasalized n; nŏd; cŏmmit; ōld; ôbey; ôrder; fōōd; fŏŏt; ou-out; s-soft; sh-dish; th-thin; pūre; ûnite; ûrn; stŭd; circŭs; ü-as "y" in study; '-indeterminate vowel.

Page	Name	Pronunciation	Region	Lat. ° '	Long. ° '
174	Novoladozhskiy Kanal (Can.) (nō-vō-lä′dŏzh-skĭ ká-näl′) Sov. Un. (Leningrad In.)			59·54 N	31·19 E
164	Novo Mesto (nôvô mäs′tō).Yugo.			45·48 N	15·13 E
167	Novomirgorod (nô′vô-mēr′gô-rŏt) Sov. Un.			48·46 N	31·44 E
166	Novomoskossk........Sov. Un.			54·06 N	38·08 E
167	Novomoskovsk (nô′vô-môs-kôfsk′) Sov. Un.			48·37 N	35·12 E
174	Novonikol′skiy (nô′vô-nyĭ-kôl′skĭ) Sov. Un. (Urals In.)			52·28 N	57·12 E
216	Novo Redondo (nô′vŏō râ-dôn′dŏō).Ang.			11·13 S	13·50 E
167	Novorossiysk (nô′vô-rô-sēsk′) Sov. Un.			44·43 N	37·48 E
166	Novorzhev (nô′vô-rzhêv′) Sov. Un.			57·01 N	29·17 E
165	Novo-Selo (nô′vô-sĕ′lō)......Bul.			44·09 N	22·46 E
172	Novosibirsk (nô′vô-sê-bērsk′) Sov. Un.			55·09 N	82·58 E
173	Novosibirskiye O-va (New Siberian Is.) (nō′vŭ̄-sī-bĭr′skê-ĕ).Sov. Un.			76·45 N	140·30 E
166	Novosil′ (nô′vô-sĭl)......Sov. Un.			52·58 N	37·03 E
166	Novosokol′niki (nô′vô-sô-kôl′nê-kê).Sov. Un.			56·18 N	30·07 E
174	Novotatishchevskiy (nô′vô-tä-tyĭsh′chêv-skĭ) Sov. Un. (Urals In.)			53·22 N	60·24 E
167	Novoukrainka (nōvô-ōō′krä) Sov. Un.			48·18 N	31·33 E
171	Novouzensk (nô-vô-ŏō-zênsk′) Sov. Un.			50·40 N	48·08 E
166	Novozybkov (nô′vô-zêp′kôf) Sov. Un.			52·31 N	31·54 E
159	Nový Jičín (nô′vê yĕ′chên).Czech.			49·36 N	18·02 E
167	Novyy Bug (nô′vê)......Sov. Un.			47·43 N	32·33 E
167	Novyy Oskol (ôs-kôl′)....Sov. Un.			50·46 N	37·53 E
172	Novyy Port (nô′vê)....Sov. Un.			67·19 N	72·28 E
159	Nowa Huta (nôvä hŏō′tä)....Pol.			50·04 N	20·20 E
158	Nowa Sól (nô′vä sŭl′)......Pol.			51·49 N	15·41 E
117	Nowata (nô-wä′tá)............Ok.			36·42 N	95·38 W
203	Nowra (nou′rá)............Austl.			34·55 S	150·45 E
159	Nowy Dwór Mazowiecki (nô′vĭ dvôōr mä-zo-vyĕts′ke).Pol.			52·26 N	20·46 E
159	Nowy Sącz (nô′vê sônch′)...Pol.			49·36 N	20·42 E
159	Nowy Targ (tärk′)........Pol.			49·29 N	20·02 E
110	Noxon Res...................Mt.			47·50 N	115·40 W
120	Noxubee (R.) (nôks′ŭ-bē)....Ms.			33·50 N	88·55 W
162	Noya (nô′yä)..................Sp.			42·46 N	8·50 W
92	Noyes I. (noiz)..............Ak.			55·30 N	133·40 W
195	Nozaki (nô′zä-kê).Jap. (Ōsaka In.)			34·43 N	135·39 E
213	Nqamakwe (′n-gä-mä′ḵwä) S. Afr. (Natal In.)			32·13 S	27·57 E
213	Nqutu (′n-kŏō′tŏō) S. Afr. (Natal In.)			28·17 S	30·41 E
214	Nsawam............S. Afr.—Ghana			5·50 N	0·20 W
215	Nsukka....................Nig.			6·52 N	7·24 E
213	Ntshoni (Mtn.).S. Afr. (Natal In.)			29·34 S	30·03 E
212	Ntwetwe Pan (Salt Flat)....Bots.			20·00 S	24·18 E
211	Nubah, Jibāl an–(Mts.)......Sud.			12·22 N	30·39 E
211	Nubian Des. (nōō′bĭ-áñ)......Sud.			21·13 N	33·09 E
134	Nudo Coropuna (Mt.).Peru			15·53 S	72·04 W
134	Nudo de Pasco (Mt.) (dĕ pás′kô) Peru			10·34 S	76·12 W
118	Nueces R. (nû-ā′sás)........Tx.			28·20 N	98·08 W
90	Nueltin (L.) (nwĕl′tin)......Can.			60·14 N	101·00 W
126	Nueva Armenia (nwä′vä är-mā′nê-á).Hond.			15·47 N	86·32 W
135	Nueva Esparta (State) (nwĕ′vä ĕs-pä′r-tä).Ven. (In.)			10·50 N	64·35 W
128	Nueva Gerona (ḵĕ-rô′nä)...Cuba			21·55 N	82·45 W
137	Nueva Palmira (päl-mē′rä) Ur. (Buenos Aires In.)			33·53 S	58·23 W
102	Nueva Rosita (nŏō̄ĕ′vä rô-sē′tä) Mex.			27·55 N	101·10 W
126	Nueva San Salvador (Santa Tecla) (sän′ säl-vä-dôr′) (sän′tä tĕ′klä) Sal.			13·41 N	89·16 W
137	Nueve de Julio (nwä′vä dä hōō′lyô) Arg. (Buenos Aires In.)			35·26 S	60·51 W
128	Nuevitas (nwä-vē′täs)......Cuba			21·35 N	77·15 W
128	Nuevitas, Bahía de (bä-ē′ä dĕ nwä-vē′täs).Cuba			21·30 N	77·05 W
113	Nuevo (nwä′vô) Ca. (Los Angeles In.)			33·48 N	117·09 W
118	Nuevo Laredo (lä-rä′dhô)....Mex.			27·29 N	99·30 W
122	Nuevo Leon (State) (lâ-ōn′)...Mex.			26·00 N	100·00 W
122	Nuevo San Juan (nwĕ′vô sän ḵōō-ä′n).Pan. (In.)			9·14 N	79·43 W
174	Nugumanovo (nû-gû-mä′nô-vô) Sov. Un. (Urals In.)			55·28 N	61·50 E
101	Nulato (nōō-lä′tô)..........Ak.			64·40 N	158·18 W
204	Nullagine (nŭ-lä′jĕn).....Austl.			22·00 S	120·07 E
204	Nullarbor Plain (Reg.) (nŭ-lär′bôr).Austl.			31·45 S	126·30 E
94	Numabin B. (nōō-mä′bĭn)....Can.			56·30 N	103·08 W
149	Numansdorp Neth. (Amsterdam In.)			51·43 N	4·25 E
195	Numazu (nōō′mä-zŏō)......Jap.			35·06 N	138·55 E
137	No 1, Canal Arg. (Buenos Aires In.)			36·43 S	58·14 W
137	No. 9, Canal Arg. (Buenos Aires In.)			36·22 S	58·19 W
137	No. 12, Canal Arg. (Buenos Aires In.)			36·47 S	57·20 W
197	Numfoor...............Indon.			1·20 S	134·48 E
215	Nun (R.)..................Nig.			5·05 N	6·10 E
148	Nuneaton (nūn′ē-tán).......Eng.			52·31 N	1·28 W
192	Nungan................China			44·25 N	125·10 E
101	Nunivak (I.) (nōō′nĭ-văk)....Ak.			60·25 N	167·42 W

Page	Name	Pronunciation	Region	Lat. ° '	Long. ° '
126	Nunkiní (nōōn-kē-nê′).Mex. (In.)			20·19 N	90·14 W
101	Nunyama (nún-yä′má)..Sov. Un.			65·49 N	170·32 W
164	Nuoro (nwô′rō)..............It.			40·29 N	9·20 E
172	Nura (R.) (nōō′rä)......Sov. Un.			49·48 N	73·54 E
172	Nurata (nōōr′ät′á)......Sov. Un.			40·33 N	65·28 E
158	Nürnberg (nürn′bêrgh)...F.R.G.			49·28 N	11·07 E
129	Nurse Cay (I.)..............Ba.			22·30 N	75·50 W
171	Nusaybin (nōō′sī-bên)......Tur.			37·05 N	41·10 E
101	Nushagak (R.) (nū-shä-găk′)..Ak.			59·28 N	157·40 W
190	Nushan Hu (L.) (nü′shän hōō) China			32·50 N	117·59 E
187	Nushki (nŭsh′kê)..........Pak.			29·30 N	66·02 E
149	Nuthe R. (nōō′tê) G.D.R (Berlin In.)			52·15 N	13·11 E
106	Nutley (nŭt′lê).NJ (New York In.)			40·49 N	74·09 W
105	Nutter Fort (nŭt′êr fôrt).....WV			39·15 N	80·15 W
113	Nutwood (nŭt′wŏōd) Il. (St. Louis In.)			39·05 N	90·34 W
183	Nuwaybi ′al Muzayyinah Egypt (Palestine In.)			28·59 N	34·40 E
212	Nuweland S. Afr. (In.)			33·58 S	18·28 E
106	Nyack (nī′ăk).NY (New York In.)			41·05 N	73·55 W
217	Nyakanazi...............Tan.			3·00 S	31·15 E
211	Nyala.....................Sud.			12·00 N	24·52 E
216	Nyanga (R.)..............Gabon			2·45 S	10·30 E
217	Nyanza......................Rw.			2·21 S	29·45 E
217	Nyasa, L. (Malawi, L.) (nyä′sä) Afr.			10·45 S	34·30 E
174	Nyazepetrovsk (nyä′zĕ-pĕ-trôvsk′) Sov. Un. (Urals In.)			56·04 N	59·38 E
156	Nyborg (nü′bôr′′)..........Den.			55·20 N	10·45 E
156	Nybro (nü′brô)..............Swe.			56·44 N	15·56 E
188	Nyenchhen Thanglha (Mts.) China			29·55 N	88·08 E
217	Nyeri......................Ken.			0·25 S	36·57 E
156	Nyhem (nü′hêm)............Swe.			56·39 N	12·50 E
217	Nyika Plat.............Malawi			10·30 S	35·50 E
159	Nyíregyháza (nyê′rĕd-y′hä′zä) Hung.			47·58 N	21·45 E
156	Nykøbing (nü′kû-bĭng)......Den.			56·46 N	8·47 E
156	Nykøbing Falster.........Den.			54·45 N	11·54 E
156	Nykøbing Sjaelland........Den.			55·55 N	11·37 E
156	Nyköping (nü′chû-pĭng)....Swe.			58·46 N	16·58 E
218	Nylstroom (nĭl′strôm) S. Afr. (Johannesburg & Pretoria In.)			24·42 S	28·25 E
203	Nymagee (nī-mä-gē′)....Austl.			32·17 S	146·18 E
158	Nymburk (nêm′bôōrk)....Czech.			50·12 N	15·03 E
154	Nymphe Bk. (nĭmpf).......Ire.			51·36 N	7·35 W
156	Nynäshamn (nü-nês-hàm′n)..Swe.			58·53 N	17·55 E
203	Nyngan (nĭŋ′gán)........Austl.			31·31 S	147·25 E
215	Nyong (R.) (nyông).......Cam.			3·40 N	10·25 E
214	Nyou...............Upper Volta			12·46 N	1·56 W
158	Nyrány (nêr-zhä′nê)......Czech.			49·43 N	13·13 E
159	Nysa (nê′sä)................Pol.			50·29 N	17·20 E
170	Nystad, see Uusikaupunki Nytva....................Sov. Un.			58·00 N	55·10 E
217	Myungwe...............Malawi			10·16 S	34·07 E
217	Nyunzu......................Zaire			5·57 S	28·01 E
173	Nyuya (R.) (nyōō′yä)..Sov. Un.			60·30 N	111·45 E
217	Nzega......................Tan.			4·13 S	33·11 E
214	Nzérékoré..................Gui.			7·45 N	8·49 W
214	Nzi (R.)............Ivory Coast			7·00 N	4·27 W

O

Page	Name	Pronunciation	Region	Lat. ° '	Long. ° '
108	Oahe Dam (ō-á-hē)..........SD			44·28 N	100·34 W
108	Oahe Res...................SD			45·20 N	100·00 W
89	Oahu (I.) (ō-ä′hōō) (ō-ä′hü)..Hi.			21·38 N	157·48 W
92	Oak Bay.....................Can.			48·27 N	123·18 W
100	Oak Bluff (ōk blŭf) Can. (Winnipeg In.)			49·47 N	97·21 W
111	Oak Creek (ōk krĕk′).........Co.			40·20 N	106·50 W
114	Oakdale (ōk′dăl).............Ca.			37·45 N	120·52 W
104	Oakdale....................Ky.			38·15 N	85·50 W
119	Oakdale....................La.			30·49 N	92·40 W
107	Oakdale...Pa. (Pittsburgh In.)			40·24 N	80·11 W
148	Oakengates (ōk′ĕn-gāts)....Eng.			52·41 N	2·27 W
108	Oakes (ōks)..................ND			46·10 N	98·50 W
98	Oakfield (ōk′fêld)..........Me.			46·08 N	68·10 W
106	Oakford (ōk′fôrd) Pa. (Philadelphia In.)			40·08 N	74·58 W
112	Oak Grove (grōv) Or. (Portland In.)			45·25 N	122·38 W
148	Oakham (ōk′ắm)..............Eng.			52·40 N	0·38 W
104	Oakharbor (ōk′här′bêr).......Oh.			41·30 N	83·05 W
112	Oak Harbor..Wa. (Seattle In.)			48·18 N	122·39 W
112	Oakland (ōk′lánd) Ca. (San Francisco In.)			37·48 N	122·16 W
108	Oakland....................Ne.			41·50 N	96·28 W
104	Oakland City..................In.			38·20 N	87·20 W
107	Oaklawn (ōk′lôn).Il. (Chicago In.)			41·43 N	87·45 W
202	Oakleigh (ōk′lä) Austl. (Melbourne In.)			37·54 S	145·05 E
111	Oakley (ōk′lĭ)................Id.			42·15 N	135·53 W
116	Oakley....................Ks.			39·08 N	100·49 W
120	Oakman (ōk′mán)..............Al.			33·42 N	87·20 W
107	Oakmont (ōk′mŏnt) Pa. (Pittsburgh In.)			40·31 N	79·50 W
106	Oak Mtn...Al. (Birmingham In.)			33·22 N	86·42 W

Page	Name	Pronunciation	Region	Lat. ° '	Long. ° '
107	Oak Park (pärk).Il. (Chicago In.)			41·53 N	87·48 W
112	Oak Point....Wa. (Portland In.)			46·11 N	123·11 W
120	Oak Ridge (rĭj)..............Tn.			36·01 N	84·15 W
100	Oakville (ōk′vĭl) Can. (Toronto In.)			43·27 N	79·40 W
100	Oakville.....Can. (Winnipeg In.)			49·56 N	97·58 W
113	Oakville.....Mo. (St. Louis In.)			38·27 N	90·18 W
100	Oakville Cr..Can. (Toronto In.)			43·34 N	79·54 W
119	Oakwood (ōk′wŏōd)..........Tx.			31·36 N	95·48 W
115	Oatman (ōt′mán)..............Az.			34·00 N	114·25 W
122	Oaxaca (State) (wä-hä′kä)...Mex.			16·45 N	97·00 W
125	Oaxaca, Sierra de (sê-ĕ′r-rä dĕ′).Mex.			16·15 N	97·25 W
125	Oaxaca de Juárez (ḵōōä′rĕz).Mex.			17·03 N	96·42 W
172	Ob′ (R.)................Sov. Un.			62·15 N	67·00 E
96	Oba (ō′bä)..................Can.			48·58 N	84·09 W
195	Obama (ō-bä-mä)............Jap.			35·29 N	135·44 E
154	Oban (ō′băn)..............Scot.			56·25 N	5·35 W
215	Oban Hills.................Nig.			5·35 N	8·30 E
107	O′Bannon (ō-băn′nŏn) Ky. (Louisville In.)			38·17 N	85·30 W
97	Obatogamau (L.) (ō-bä-tō′găm-ô).Can.			49·38 N	74·10 W
218	Obbia (ŏb′byä) Som. (Horn of Afr. In.)			5·24 N	48·28 E
161	Oberhausen (ō′bêr-hou′zĕn) F.R.G. (Ruhr In.)			51·27 N	6·51 E
116	Oberlin (ō′bĕr-lĭn)..........Ks.			39·49 N	100·30 W
104	Oberlin....................Oh.			41·15 N	82·15 W
158	Oberösterreich (Prov.).......Aus.			48·05 N	13·15 E
149	Oberroth (ō′bĕr-rôt) F.R.G. (Munich In.)			48·19 N	11·20 E
149	Ober-Schleisshiem (ō′bĕr-shlīs-hêm) F.R.G.(Munich In.)			48·15 N	11·34 E
197	Obi, Kepulauan (I.) (ō′bê).Indon.			1·25 S	128·15 E
135	Óbidos (ō′bê-dōōzh).......Braz.			1·57 S	55·32 W
194	Obihiro (ō′bê-hê′rō).......Jap.			42·55 N	142·50 E
120	Obion (R.)..................Tn.			36·10 N	89·25 W
120	Obion (R.), North Fk. (ô-bī′ŏn) Tn.			35·49 N	89·06 W
167	Obitochnaya, Kosa (C.) (kô-sä′ ô-bê-tôch′nä-yä) Sov. Un.			46·32 N	36·07 E
195	Obitsu (R.) (ō′bĕt′sōō) Jap. (Tōkyō In.)			35·19 N	140·03 E
218	Obock (ō-bŏk′) A. & I. (Horn of Afr. In.)			11·55 N	43·15 E
166	Obol′ (R.) (ô-bôl′)........Sov. Un.			55·24 N	29·24 E
167	Oboyan (ô-bô-yän′).....Sov. Un.			51·14 N	36·16 E
172	Obskaya Guba (B.)......Sov. Un.			67·13 N	73·45 E
214	Obuasi....................Ghana			6·14 N	1·39 W
167	Obukhov (ō′bōō-kôf).....Sov. Un.			50·07 N	30·36 E
174	Obukhovo.Sov. Un. (Moscow In.)			55·50 N	38·17 E
121	Ocala (ō-kä′lá)..............Fl.			29·11 N	82·09 W
124	Ocampo (ō-käm′pō)........Mex.			22·49 N	99·23 W
134	Ocaña (ō-kä′nyä)..........Col.			8·15 N	73·37 W
162	Ocaña (ō-kä′n-yä)..........Sp.			39·58 N	3·31 W
210	Occidental, Grand Erg (Dunes) Alg.			29·30 N	00·45 W
134	Occidental, Cordillera (Mts.) (kôr-dēl-yĕ′rä ôk-sê-dĕn-tál′) Col. (In.)			5·05 N	76·04 W
134	Occidental, Cordillera (Mts.) Peru			10·12 S	76·58 W
122	Occidental, Sierra Madre (Mts.) (sê-ĕ′r-rä-mä′drê-ôk-sê-dĕn-tä′l) Mex.			29·30 N	107·30 W
114	Ocean Beach (ō′shăn bêch) Ca. (In.)			32·44 N	117·14 W
119	Ocean Bight (B.)............Ba.			21·15 N	73·15 W
105	Ocean City.................Md.			38·20 N	75·10 W
105	Ocean City..................NJ			39·15 N	74·35 W
92	Ocean Falls (Fôls).........Can.			52·21 N	127·40 W
202	Ocean Grove Austl. (Melbourne In.)			38·16 S	144·32 E
105	Ocean Grove (grōv)..........NJ			40·10 N	74·00 W
114	Oceanside (ō′shăn-sīd).......Ca.			33·11 N	117·22 W
106	Oceanside..NY (New York In.)			40·38 N	73·39 W
120	Ocean Springs (springs)......Ms.			30·25 N	88·49 W
165	Ocenele Mari..............Rom.			45·05 N	24·17 E
167	Ochakov (ô-chä′kôf).....Sov. Un.			46·38 N	31·33 E
188	Ochina Ho (R.)............China			41·15 N	100·46 E
192	Ochir.....................China			45·38 N	115·35 E
120	Ochlockonee R. (ŏk-lô-kô′nē) Fl.-Ga.			30·10 N	84·38 W
120	Ocilla (ō-sĭl′á)..............Ga.			31·36 N	83·15 W
156	Ockelbo (ōk′ĕl-bô)..........Swe.			60·54 N	16·35 E
121	Ocmulgee (R.)..............Ga.			32·35 N	83·30 W
120	Ocmulgee Natl. Mon. (ôk-mŭl′gē) Ga.			32·45 N	83·28 W
165	Ocna-Sibiului (ōk′nä-sĕ-byōō-lōō-ē) Rom.			45·52 N	24·04 E
129	Ocoa, Bahai de (B.) (bä-ä′ê-ō-kô′á) Dom. Rep.			18·20 N	70·40 W
125	Ococingo (ō-kô-sê′n-gô)....Mex.			17·03 N	92·18 W
126	Ocom, L. (ô-kô′m).....Mex. (In.)			19·26 N	88·18 W
120	Oconee (R.).................Ga.			32·45 N	83·00 W
109	Oconomowoc (ô-kŏn′ô-mô-wôk′) Wi.			43·06 N	88·24 W
109	Oconto (ô-kŏn′tō)..........Wi.			44·54 N	87·55 W
109	Oconto (R.)................Wi.			45·08 N	88·24 W
109	Oconto Falls..............Wi.			44·53 N	88·11 W
126	Ocós (ô-kōs′)..............Guat.			14·31 N	92·12 W
126	Ocotal (ô-kô-täl′)..........Nic.			13·36 N	86·31 W
126	Ocotepeque (ô-kô-tä-pā′kä).Hond.			14·25 N	89·13 W
124	Ocotlán (ō-kô-tlän′)........Mex.			20·19 N	102·44 W
125	Ocotlán de Morelos (dä mô-rä′lōs) Mex.			16·46 N	96·41 W
125	Ocozocoautla (ô-kō′zô-kwä-ōō′tlä) Mex.			16·44 N	93·22 W
135	Ocumare del Tuy (ō-kōō-mä′rä del twē′) Ven. (In.)			10·07 N	66·47 W

Page	Name Pronunciation Region	Lat. °′	Long. °′
214	Oda .... Ghana	5·55 N	0·59 W
195	Odawara (ō'dȧ-wä'rä) .... Jap.	35·15 N	139·10 E
156	Odda (ôdh-ȧ) .... Nor.	60·04 N	6·30 E
218	Oddur .... Som. (Horn of Afr. In.)	3·55 N	43·45 E
108	Odebolt (ō'dē-bōlt) .... Ia.	42·20 N	95·14 W
162	Odemira (ō-dȧ-mē'rȧ) .... Port.	37·35 N	8·40 W
171	Ödemis (û'dĕ-mēsh) .... Tur.	38·12 N	28·00 E
218	Odendaalsrus (ō'dĕn-däls-rûs') S. Afr. (Johannesburg & Pretoria In.)	27·52 S	26·41 E
156	Odense (ō'dhĕn-sĕ) .... Den.	55·24 N	10·20 E
106	Odenton (ō'dĕn-tŭn) Md. (Baltimore In.)	39·05 N	76·43 W
158	Odenwald (For.) (ō'dĕn-väld) F.R.G.	49·39 N	8·55 E
158	Oder R. (ō'dẽr) .... G.D.R.	52·40 N	14·19 E
167	Odessa (ô-dĕs'sä) .... Sov. Un.	46·28 N	30·44 E
118	Odessa (ô-dĕs'ȧ) .... Tx.	31·52 N	120·21 W
110	Odessa .... Wa.	47·20 N	118·42 W
167	Odessa (Oblast) .... Sov. Un.	46·05 N	29·48 E
162	Odiel (R.) (ō-dē-ĕl') .... Sp.	37·47 N	6·42 W
214	Odienné (ō-dē-ĕn-nā') Ivory Coast	9·30 N	7·34 W
148	Odiham (ŏd'ē-ăm) Eng. (London In.)	51·14 N	0·56 W
174	Odintsovo (ô-dēn'tsô-vô) Sov. Un. (Moscow In.)	55·40 N	37·16 E
197	Odiongan (ō-dē-ôŋ'gän). Phil. (In.)	12·24 N	121·59 E
163	Odivelas (ō-dē-vä'lyäs) Port. (Lisbon In.)	38·47 N	9·11 W
159	Odobesti (ō-dô-bĕsh't') ...... Rom.	45·46 N	27·08 E
116	O'Donnell (ō-dŏn'ĕl) .... Tx.	32·59 N	101·51 W
159	Odorhei (ō-dôr-hā') .... Rom.	46·18 N	25·17 E
159	Odra R. (ô'drȧ) .... Pol.	50·28 N	17·55 E
135	Oeiras (wȧ-ē-räzh') .... Braz.	7·05 S	42·01 W
163	Oeirás (ō-ĕ'y-rȧ's) Port. (Lisbon In.)	38·42 N	9·18 W
109	Oelwein (ōl'wīn) .... Ia.	42·40 N	91·56 W
116	O'Fallon (ō-făl'ŭn) Il. (St. Louis In.)	38·36 N	89·55 W
111	O'Fallon Cr. .... Mt.	46·25 N	104·47 W
164	Ofanto (R.) (ô-făn'tō) .... It.	41·08 N	15·33 E
215	Offa .... Nig.	8·09 N	4·44 E
158	Offenbach (ôf'ĕn-bäk) ...... F.R.G.	50·06 N	8·50 E
158	Offenburg (ôf'ĕn-bŏŏrgh)... F.R.G.	48·28 N	7·57 E
195	Ofuna (ō'fōō-nä). Jap (Tōkyō In.)	35·21 N	139·32 E
211	Ogaden Plat. Eth. (Horn of Afr. In.)	6·45 N	44·53 E
195	Ogaki .... Jap.	35·21 N	136·36 E
108	Ogallala (ō-gä-lä'lä) .... Ne.	41·08 N	101·44 W
215	Ogbomosho (ŏg-bô-mō'shō) ... Nig.	8·08 N	4·15 E
109	Ogden (ŏg'dĕn) .... Ia.	42·10 N	94·20 W
113	Ogden ... Ut. (Salt Lake City In.)	41·14 N	111·58 W
113	Ogden Pk.. Ut. (Salt Lake City In.)	41·11 N	111·51 W
113	Ogden R... Ut. (Salt Lake City In.)	41·16 N	111·54 W
106	Ogdensburg (ŏg'dĕnz-bûrg) NJ (New York In.)	41·05 N	74·36 W
105	Ogdensburg .... NY	44·40 N	75·30 W
121	Ogeechee, (R.) (ô-gē'chē) ..... Ga.	32·35 N	81·50 W
218	Ogies .... S. Afr. (Johannesburg & Pretoria In.)	26·03 S	29·04 E
90	Ogilvie Mts. (ō'g'l-vĭ) .... Can.	64·45 N	138·10 W
104	Oglesby (ō'g'lz-bĭ) .... Il.	41·20 N	89·00 W
164	Oglio (R.) (ōl'yō) .... It.	45·15 N	10·19 E
195	Ogo (ō'gō) .... Jap. (Ōsaka In.)	34·49 N	135·06 E
216	Ogooué (R.) .... Gabon	0·50 S	9·20 E
214	Ogou (R.) .... Togo	8·05 N	1·30 E
174	Ogudnëvo (ŏg-ōōg-nyô'vô) Sov. Un. (Moscow In.)	56·04 N	38·17 E
164	Ogulin (ō-gōō-lēn') .... Yugo.	45·17 N	15·11 E
215	Ogwashi-Uku .... Nig.	6·10 N	6·31 E
137	O'Higgins (Prov.) (ō-kē'gēns) Chile (Santiago In.)	34·17 S	70·52 W
103	Ohio, (State) (ō'hī'ō) .... U. S.	40·30 N	83·15 W
104	Ohio R. .... U. S.	37·25 N	88·05 W
121	Ohoopee (R.) (ō-hōō'pē) ...... Ga.	32·32 N	82·38 W
158	Ohře (Eger) R. (ōr'zhĕ) (ā'gẽr) Czech.	50·08 N	12·45 E
165	Ohrid (ō'krēd) .... Yugo.	41·08 N	20·46 E
165	Ohrid (L.) .... Alb.-Yugo.	40·58 N	20·35 E
195	Ōi (oi') .... Jap. (Tōkyō In.)	35·51 N	139·31 E
156	Oieren (L.) (ûiĕrĕn) .... Nor.	59·50 N	11·25 E
195	Oi-Gawa (Strm.) (ō'ē-gä'wȧ).. Jap.	35·09 N	138·05 E
105	Oil City (oil sĭ'tĭ) .... Pa.	41·25 N	79·40 W
149	Oirschot.. Neth. (Amsterdam In.)	51·30 N	5·20 E
160	Oise (R.) (wäz) .... Fr.	49·30 N	2·56 E
149	Oisterwijk. Neth. (Amsterdam In.)	51·34 N	5·13 E
195	Oita (ō'ē-tä) .... Jap.	33·14 N	131·38 E
195	Oji (ō'jē) .... Jap. (Ōsaka In.)	34·36 N	135·43 E
118	Ojinaga (ō-Kē-nä'gä) .... Mex.	29·34 N	104·26 W
125	Ojitlán (San Lucas) (ōkē-tlän') (sän-lōō'käs). Mex.	18·04 N	96·23 W
124	Ojo Caliente (ōKō käl-yĕn'tȧ). Mex.	21·50 N	100·43 W
124	Ojocaliente (ô-Kō-kä-lyĕ'n-tĕ) Mex.	22·39 N	102·15 W
128	Ojo del Toro, Pico (Pk.) (pē'kō-ô-Kō-dĕl-tō'rô). Cuba	19·55 N	77·25 W
100	Oka (ō-kä) ... Can. (Montreal In.)	45·28 N	74·05 W
171	Oka (R.) (ô-kä') .... Sov. Un.	52·10 N	35·20 E
172	Oka (R.) (ō-kä') .... Sov. Un.	53·28 N	101·09 E
170	Oka (R.) (ô-kȧ') .... Sov. Un.	55·10 N	42·10 E
212	Okahandja .... S. W. Afr.	21·50 S	16·45 E
93	Okanagan (R.) (ō'kȧ-näg'ăn). Can.	49·06 N	119·43 W
93	Okanagan L. .... Can.	50·00 N	119·28 W
210	Okano (R.) (ō'kä'nō) ...... Gabon	0·15 N	11·08 E
110	Okanogan .... Wa.	48·20 N	119·34 W
110	Okanogan R. .... Wa.	48·36 N	119·33 W
120	Okatibbee (R.) (ō'kä-tĭb'ē) ... Ms.	32·37 N	88·54 W
120	Okatoma Cr. (ō-kȧ-tō'mȧ) .... Ms.	31·43 N	89·34 W
216	Okavango (Cubango) (R.) Ang.-S. W. Afr.	17·10 S	18·20 E
212	Okavango Swp. .... Bots.	19·30 S	23·02 E
195	Okaya (ō'kȧ-yȧ) .... Jap.	36·04 N	138·01 E
195	Okayama (ō'kȧ-yä'mȧ) .... Jap.	34·39 N	133·54 E
195	Okazaki (ō'kȧ-zä'kē) .... Jap.	34·58 N	137·09 E
121	Okeechobee (ō-kē-chō'bē) ...... Fl.	27·15 N	80·50 W
121	Okeechobee, L. .... Fl. (In.)	27·00 N	80·49 W
116	Okeene (ô-kēn') .... Ok.	36·06 N	98·19 W
121	Okefenokee Swp. (ō'kē-fē-nō'kē) Ga.	30·54 N	82·20 W
117	Okemah (ô-kē'mä) .... Ok.	35·26 N	96·18 W
215	Okene .... Nig.	7·33 N	6·15 E
155	Oker (R.) (ō'kẽr) .... F.R.G.	52·23 N	10·00 E
173	Okha (ŭ-Kä') .... Sov. Un.	53·44 N	143·12 E
174	Okhotino (ô-Kô'tĭ-nô) Sov. Un. (Moscow In.)	56·14 N	38·24 E
173	Okhotsk (ô-Kôtsk') ...... Sov. Un.	59·28 N	143·32 E
183	Okhotsk, Sea of (ô-kôtsk') .... Asia	56·45 N	146·00 E
195	Oki Guntō (Arch.) (ō'kē gŏŏn'tō) Jap.	36·17 N	133·05 E
194	Okinawa (I.) (ō'kē-nä'wȧ) .... Jap.	26·30 N	128·30 E
194	Okinawa Guntō (Is.) (gŏŏn'tō') Jap.	26·50 N	127·25 E
195	Okino (I.) (ō'kē-nô) .... Jap.	36·22 N	133·27 E
194	Ōkino Erabu (I.) (ō-kē'nô-ā-rä'bōō). Jap.	27·18 N	129·00 E
102	Oklahoma (State) (ô-klȧ-hō'mȧ). U. S.	36·00 N	98·20 W
117	Oklahoma City .... Ok.	35·27 N	97·32 W
121	Oklawaha (R.) (ŏk-lȧ-wô'hô).. Fl.	29·13 N	82·00 W
117	Okmulgee (ôk-mŭl'gē) .... Ok.	35·37 N	95·58 W
107	Okolona (ō-kô-lō'nȧ) Ky. (Louisville In.)	38·08 N	85·41 W
120	Okolona .... Ms.	33·59 N	88·43 W
194	Okushiri (I.) (ō'koo-shē'rē) ... Jap.	42·12 N	139·30 E
215	Okuta .... Nig.	9·14 N	3·15 E
112	Olalla (ō-lä'lȧ).. Wa. (Seattle In.)	47·26 N	122·33 W
126	Olanchito (ō'län-chē'tô) .... Hond.	15·28 N	86·35 W
156	Öland (I.) (û-länd') .... Swe.	57·03 N	17·15 E
113	Olathe (ō-lā'thē) Ks. (Kansas City In.)	38·53 N	94·49 W
136	Olavarría (ō-lä-vär-rē'ä) ...... Arg.	36·49 N	60·15 W
159	Olawa (ō-lä'vȧ) .... Pol.	50·57 N	17·18 E
137	Olazcoago (ō-läz-kôä'gô) Arg. (Buenos Aires In.)	35·14 S	60·37 W
164	Olbia (ō'l-byä) .... It.	40·55 N	9·28 E
149	Olching (ōl'kēng) F.R.G. (Munich In.)	48·13 N	11·21 E
128	Old Bahama Chan. (bȧ-hä'mȧ) N. A.	22·45 N	78·30 W
129	Old Bight .... Ba.	24·15 N	75·20 W
106	Old Bridge (brĭj) NJ (New York In.)	40·24 N	74·22 W
90	Old Crow (crō) .... Can.	67·51 N	139·58 W
158	Oldenburg (ôl'dĕn-bŏŏrgh). F.R.G.	53·09 N	8·13 E
105	Old Forge (fôrj) .... Pa.	41·20 N	75·50 W
148	Oldham (ōld'ăm) .... Eng.	53·32 N	2·07 W
101	Old Harbor (här'bẽr) .... Ak.	57·18 N	153·20 W
154	Old Head of Kinsale (ōld hĕd ŏv kĭn-sāl). Ire.	51·35 N	8·35 W
119	Old R. .... Tx. (In.)	29·54 N	94·52 W
93	Olds (ōldz) .... Can.	51·47 N	114·06 W
212	Old Tate .... Bots.	21·18 S	27·43 E
98	Old Town (toun) .... Me.	44·55 N	68·42 W
94	Old Wives L. (wivz) .... Can.	50·56 N	106·00 W
105	Olean (ō-lē-ăn') .... NY	42·05 N	78·25 W
159	Olecko (ō-lĕt'skô) .... Pol.	54·02 N	22·29 E
173	Olekma (R.) (ô-lyĕk-mȧ'). Sov. Un.	55·41 N	120·33 E
173	Olëkminsk (ô-lyĕk-mênsk') Sov. Un.	60·39 N	120·40 E
173	Olenëk (R.) (ô-lyĕ-nyôk'). Sov. Un.	70·18 N	121·15 E
160	Oléron Île, d' (I.) (ēl' dō lā-rôN'). Fr.	45·52 N	1·58 W
159	Oleśnica (ô-lĕsh-nĭ'tsȧ) .... Pol.	51·13 N	17·24 E
161	Olfen (ōl'fĕn)... F.R.G. (Ruhr In.)	51·43 N	7·22 E
173	Ol'ga (ôl'gȧ) .... Sov. Un.	43·48 N	135·44 E
194	Ol'gi, Zaliv (B.) (zä'lĭf ôl'gĭ) Sov. Un.	43·43 N	135·25 E
167	Ol'gopol (ôl-gô-pôl'y') .... Sov. Un.	48·11 N	29·28 E
162	Olhão (ōl-youN') .... Port.	37·02 N	7·54 W
213	Olievenhoutpoort .... S. Afr. (Johannesburg & Pretoria In.)	25·58 S	27·55 E
212	Olifants (R.) (ŏl'ĭ-fănts).... S. Afr.	23·58 S	31·00 E
165	Ólimbos .... Grc.	40·03 N	22·22 E
183	Ólimbos (Mtn.) Cyprus (Palestine In.)	34·56 N	32·52 E
124	Olinalá (ô-lē-nä-lä') .... Mex.	17·47 N	98·51 W
135	Olinda (ō-lē'n-dä) .... Braz.	8·00 S	34·58 W
163	Oliva (ō-lē'vä) .... Sp.	38·54 N	0·07 W
162	Oliva de Jerez (ō-lē'vä dā hā'rĕth) Sp.	38·33 N	6·55 W
163	Olivais (ô-lē-vȧ'ys) Port. (Lisbon In.)	38·46 N	9·06 W
104	Olive Hill (ŏl'ĭv) .... Ky.	38·15 N	83·10 W
137	Oliveira (ô-lē-vä'rä) Braz. (Rio de Janeiro In.)	20·42 S	44·49 W
162	Olivenza (ō-lē-vĕn'thä) .... Sp.	38·42 N	7·06 W
93	Oliver (ŏ'lĭ-vẽr) .... Can.	49·11 N	119·33 W
100	Oliver ...... Can. (Edmonton In.)	53·38 N	113·21 W
113	Oliver (ŏ'lĭvẽr).. Wi. (Duluth In.)	46·39 N	92·12 W
100	Oliver L. ..... Can. (Edmonton In.)	53·19 N	113·00 W
100	Olivia (ō-lĭv'ē-ȧ) .... Mn.	44·46 N	95·00 W
136	Olivos (ōlē'vōs) Arg. (Buenos Aires In.)	34·15 S	58·29 W
158	Olkusz (ôl'kōōsh) .... Pol.	50·16 N	19·41 E
136	Ollagüe (ō-lyä'gȧ) .... Chile	21·17 S	68·17 W
148	Ollerton (ŏl'ẽr-tŭn) .... Eng.	53·12 N	1·02 W
113	Olmos Park (ŏl'mŭs pärk') Tx. (San Antonio In.)	29·27 N	98·32 W
104	Olney (ŏl'nĭ) .... Il.	38·45 N	88·05 W
112	Olney (ŏl'nē).. Or. (Portland In.)	46·06 N	123·45 W
116	Olney .... Tx.	33·24 N	98·43 W
99	Olomane (R.) (ō'lō mȧ'nĕ) ... Can.	51·05 N	60·50 W
159	Olomouc (ō'lô-mōts) .... Czech.	49·37 N	17·15 E
157	Olonets (ô-lô'nĕts) .... Sov. Un.	60·58 N	32·54 E
197	Olongapo .... Phil. (In.)	14·49 S	120·17 E
160	Oloron, Gave d' (Strm.) (gäv-dō-lō-rôN'). Fr.	43·21 N	0·44 W
160	Oloron-Ste. Marie (ō-lō-rôNt'sǎNt mȧ-rē'). Fr.	43·11 N	1·37 W
163	Olot (ô-lōt') .... Sp.	42·09 N	2·30 E
161	Olpe (ōl'pē)... F.R.G. (Ruhr In.)	51·02 N	7·51 E
167	Ol'shanka (ôl'shäŋ-kȧ).. Sov. Un.	48·14 N	30·52 E
167	Ol'shany (ôl'shȧn-ē) ..... Sov. Un.	50·02 N	35·54 E
158	Olsnitz (ōlz'nētz) .... G.D.R.	50·25 N	12·11 E
159	Olsztyn (ôl'shtên) .... Pol.	53·47 N	20·28 E
158	Olten (ōl'tĕn) .... Switz.	47·20 N	7·53 E
165	Oltenita (ōl-tā'nĭ-tsȧ) .... Rom.	44·05 N	26·39 E
153	Olt R. .... Rom.	44·09 N	24·40 E
162	Olvera (ōl-vĕ'rä) .... Sp.	36·55 N	7·16 W
110	Olympia (ō-lĭm'pĭ-ȧ) .... Wa.	47·02 N	122·52 W
110	Olympic Mts. .... Wa.	47·54 N	123·58 W
110	Olympic Natl. Park (ō-lĭm'pĭk) Wa.	47·54 N	123·00 W
110	Olympus Mt. (ō-lĭm'pŭs) ..... Wa.	47·43 N	123·30 W
105	Olyphant (ŏl'ĭ-fănt) .... Pa.	41·30 N	75·40 W
173	Olyutorskiy, Mys (C.) (ŭl-yōō'tŏr-skē). Sov. Un.	59·49 N	167·16 E
195	Omae-Zaki (Pt.) (ō'mä-ā zä'kē) Jap.	34·37 N	138·15 E
154	Omagh (ō'mä) .... N. Ire.	54·35 N	7·25 W
108	Omaha (ō'mȧ-hä) .... Ne.	41·18 N	95·57 W
108	Omaha Ind. Res. .... Ne.	42·09 N	96·08 W
182	Oman .... Asia	20·00 N	57·45 E
186	Oman, G. of .... Asia	24·24 N	58·58 E
212	Omaruru (ō-mä-rōō'rōō). S. W. Afr.	21·25 S	16·50 E
216	Omboué .... Gabon	1·34 S	9·15 E
164	Ombrone (R.) (ôm-brō'nä) ..... It.	42·48 N	11·18 E
	Omdurman, see UmmDurmān		
125	Omealca (ōmȧ-äl'kō) .... Mex.	18·44 N	96·45 W
124	Ometepec (ō-mā-tȧ-pĕk') .... Mex.	16·41 N	98·27 W
211	Om Hajer .... Eth.	14·06 N	36·46 E
92	Omineca (R.) (ō-mĭ-nĕk'ȧ) ... Can.	55·10 N	125·45 W
92	Omineca Mts. .... Can.	56·00 N	125·00 W
195	Ōmiya (ō'mē-yȧ). Jap. (Tōkyō In.)	35·54 S	139·38 E
126	Omoa (ō-mō'rä) .... Hond.	15·43 N	88·03 W
173	Omolon (R.) (ō'mō) ...... Sov. Un.	67·43 N	159·15 E
195	Ōmori (Kioroshi) (ō'mô-rē) (kē'ō-rō'shē) Jap. (Tōkyō In.)	35·50 N	140·09 E
211	Omo R. (ō'mō) .... Eth.	5·54 N	36·09 E
215	Omoko .... Nig.	5·20 N	6·39 E
126	Omotepe, Isla de (I.) (ē's-lä-dĕ-ō-mô-tā'pȧ). Nic.	11·32 N	85·30 W
109	Omro (ŏm'rō) .... Wi.	44·01 N	89·46 W
172	Omsk (ômsk) .... Sov. Un.	55·12 N	73·19 E
195	Ōmura (ō'mōō-rȧ) .... Jap.	32·56 N	129·57 E
195	Ōmuta (ō-mōō-tȧ) .... Jap.	33·02 N	130·28 E
170	Omutninsk (ō'mōō-tĕnsk). Sov. Un.	58·38 N	52·10 E
108	Onawa (ŏn-ȧ-wȧ) .... Ia.	42·02 N	96·05 W
104	Onaway .... Mi.	45·25 N	84·10 W
216	Oncócua .... Ang.	16·34 S	13·28 E
163	Onda (ōn'dä) .... Sp.	39·58 N	0·13 W
159	Ondava (R.) (ōn'dȧ-vȧ) .... Czech.	48·51 N	21·40 E
215	Ondo .... Nig.	7·04 N	4·47 E
192	Öndör Haan .... Mong.	47·20 N	110·40 E
170	Onega (ô-nyĕ'gȧ) .... Sov. Un.	63·50 N	38·08 E
170	Onega (.R) .... Sov. Un.	63·20 N	39·20 E
	Onega, L., see Onezhskoye Ozero		
105	Oneida (ō-nī'dȧ) .... NY	43·05 N	75·40 W
105	Oneida (L.) .... NY	43·10 N	76·00 W
108	O'Neill (ō-nēl') .... Ne.	42·28 N	98·38 W
173	Onekotan (I.) (ŭ-nyĕ-kŭ-tän') Sov. Un.	49·45 N	153·45 E
105	Oneonta (ō-nē-ŏn'tȧ) .... NY	42·25 N	75·05 W
170	Onezhskaja Guba (B.).. Sov. Un.	64·30 N	36·00 E
170	Onezhskiy, P-Ov. (Pen.).. Sov. Un.	64·30 N	37·40 E
170	Onezhskoye Ozero (Onega, L.) (ô-năsh'skô-yĕ ô'zĕ-rô). Sov. Un.	62·02 N	34·35 E
188	Ongin (ŏn'gĭn') .... Mong.	46·00 N	102·46 E
185	Ongole .... India	15·36 N	80·03 E
213	Onilahy (R.) .... Mad.	23·41 S	45·00 E
215	Onitsha (ō-nĭt'shȧ) .... Nig.	6·09 N	6·47 W
195	Onomichi (ō'nô-mē'chē) ...... Jap.	34·27 N	133·12 E
173	Onon (R.) (ô'nôn) .... Sov. Un.	50·33 N	114·18 E
173	Onon Gol (R.) (ô'nôn) .. Sov. Un.	48·30 N	110·38 E
135	Onoto (ō-nŏ'tō) .... Ven. (In.)	9·38 N	65·03 W
204	Onslow (ŏnz'lō) .... Austl.	21·53 S	115·00 E
121	Onslow B. (ŏnz'lō) .... NC	34·22 N	77·35 W
195	Ontake San (Mtn.) (ōn'tä-kȧ sän) Jap.	35·55 N	137·29 E
113	Ontario (ŏn-tā'rĭ-ō) Ca. (Los Angeles In.)	34·04 N	117·39 W
110	Ontario .... Or.	44·02 N	116·57 W
91	Ontario (Prov.) .... Can.	50·47 N	88·50 W
103	Ontario, L. .... U. S.-Can.	43·35 N	79·05 W
163	Onteniente (ōn-tȧ-nyĕn'tā) .... Sp.	38·48 N	0·35 W
109	Ontonagon (ŏn-tō-năg'ŏn) ..... Mi.	46·50 N	89·20 W
195	Ōnuki (ō'nōō-kē). Jap. (Tōkyō In.)	35·17 N	139·51 E
204	Oodnadatta (ōōd'nȧ-dȧ'tȧ) .. Austl.	27·38 S	135·40 E
204	Ooldea Station (ōōl-dā'ä) ... Austl.	30·35 S	132·08 E
117	Oologah Res. .... Ok.	36·43 N	95·32 W
149	Ooltgensplaat Neth. (Amsterdam In.)	51·41 N	4·19 E
120	Oostanaula (R.) (ōō-stȧ-nô'lȧ). Ga.	34·25 N	85·10 W
155	Oostende (ōst-ĕn'dē) .... Bel.	51·14 N	2·55 E
149	Oosterhout. Neth. (Amsterdam In.)	51·38 N	4·52 E
155	Ooster Schelde (R.) .... Neth.	51·40 N	3·40 E
92	Ootsa L. .... Can.	53·49 N	126·18 W
126	Opalaca, Sierra de (Mts.) (sē-ĕ'r-rä-dĕ-ō-pä-lä'kä). Hond.	14·30 N	88·29 W
95	Opasquia (ō-păs'kwē-ȧ) ...... Can.	53·16 N	93·53 W
159	Opatow (ō-pä'tōōf) .... Pol.	50·47 N	21·25 E
159	Opava (ō'pä-vä) .... Czech.	49·56 N	17·52 E
136	Opdal (ŏp'däl) .... Nor.	62·37 N	9·41 E
120	Opelika (ŏp-ē-lĭ'kȧ) .... Al.	32·39 N	85·23 W

ng-sing; ŋ-baŋk; N-nasalized n; nŏd; cŏmmit; ōld; ôbey; ôrder; fōōd; fŏŏt; ou-out; s-soft; sh-dish; th-thin; pūre; ûnite; ûrn; stŭd; circŭs; ü-as "y" in study; '-indeterminate vowel.

324 Opelousas — Ouahigouya PRONOUNCING INDEX

Page Name Pronunciation Region Lat. °' Long. °'

119 Opelousas (ŏp-ē-lōō'sȧs).......La. 30·33 N 92·04 W
105 Opeongo (L.) (ŏp-ê-ŏŋ'gō)....Can. 45·40 N 78·20 W
111 Opheim (ô-fīm')............Mt. 48·51 N 106·19 W
101 Ophir (ō'fēr)...............Ak. 63·10 N 156·28 W
183 Ophir, Mt...Mala. (Singapore In.) 2·22 N 102·37 E
126 Opico (ô-pē'kō)..............Sal. 13·50 N 89·23 W
91 Opinaca (R.) (ŏp-ĭ-nä'kȧ)....Can. 52·28 N 77·40 W
161 Opladen (ōp'lä-dĕn)
F.R.G. (Ruhr In.) 51·04 N 7·00 E
215 Opobo....................Nig. 4·34 N 7·27 E
166 Opochka (ō-pôch'kȧ).....Sov. Un. 56·43 N 28·39 E
159 Opoczno (ō-pôch'nō).........Pol. 51·22 N 20·18 E
159 Opole (ō-pôl'ȧ)..............Pol. 50·42 N 17·55 E
159 Opole Lubelskie
(ō-pō'lȧ lōō-bĕl'skyĕ).Pol. 51·09 N 21·58 E
Oporto, see Pôrto
110 Opportunity (ŏp-ŏr tū'nĭ tĭ)...Wa. 47·37 N 117·20 W
167 Oposhnya (ô-pôsh'nyȧ)...Sov. Un. 49·57 N 34·34 E
120 Opp (ŏp)..................Al. 31·18 N 86·15 W
113 Oquirrh Mts. (ō'kwēr)
Ut. (Salt Lake City In.) 40·38 N 112·11 W
159 Oradea (ô-räd'yä).........Rom. 47·02 N 21·55 E
152 Oran (Ouahran) (ō-rän) (ô-räN')
Alg. 35·46 N 0·45 W
136 Orán (ô-rȧ'n)..............Arg. 23·13 S 64·17 W
117 Oran (ôr'ȧn)...............Mo. 37·05 N 89·39 W
203 Orange (ŏr'ĕnj)...........Austl. 33·15 S 149·08 E
113 Orange.....Ca. (Los Angeles In.) 33·48 N 117·51 W
105 Orange.....................Ct. 41·15 N 73·00 W
160 Orange (ô-raNzh')...........Fr. 44·08 N 4·48 E
106 Orange.......NJ (New York In.) 40·46 N 74·14 W
116 Orange.....................Tx. 30·07 N 93·44 W
135 Orange, Cabo (C.)
(kȧ-bô-rȧ'n-zhĕ).Braz. 4·25 N 51·30 W
121 Orange (L.).................Fl. 29·30 N 82·12 W
212 Orange (R.).....S. W. Afr.-S. Afr. 29·15 S 17·30 E
121 Orangeburg (ŏr'ĕnj-bûrg).......SC 33·30 N 80·50 W
128 Orange Cay (I.) (ŏr-ĕnj kē)...Ba. 24·55 N 79·05 W
108 Orange City..................Ia. 43·01 N 96·06 W
212 Orange Free State (Prov.)..S. Afr. 28·15 S 26·00 E
100 Orangeville (ŏr'ĕnj-vĭl)
Can. (Toronto In.) 43·55 N 80·06 W
218 Orangeville..............S. Afr.
(Johannesburg & Pretoria In.) 27·05 S 28·13 E
126 Orange Walk (wôl'k)..Belize (In.) 18·09 N 88·32 W
197 Orani (ō-rä'nē)........Phil. (In.) 14·47 N 120·32 E
149 Oranienburg (ō-rä'nē-ĕn-bōōrgh)
G.D.R. (Berlin In.) 52·45 N 13·14 E
212 Oranjemund..........S. W. Afr. 28·33 S 16·20 E
165 Orastie (ô-rûsh'tyȧ)........Rom. 45·50 N 23·14 E
Orașul-Stalin, see Brașov
164 Orbetello (ôr-bȧ-tĕl'lō).........It. 42·27 N 11·15 E
162 Orbigo (R.) (ôr-bē'gō)........Sp. 42·30 N 5·55 W
203 Orbost (ôr'bŭst)...........Austl. 37·43 S 148·20 E
112 Orcas (I.) (ôr'kȧs)
Wa. (Vancouver In.) 48·43 N 122·52 W
113 Orchard Farm (ôr'chērd färm)
Mo. (St. Louis In.) 38·53 N 90·27 W
107 Orchard Park....NY (Buffalo In.) 42·46 N 78·46 W
112 Orchards (ôr'chēdz)
Wa. (Portland In.) 45·40 N 122·33 W
134 Orchilla (ôr-kĭl-ȧ)..........Ven. 11·47 N 66·34 W
108 Ord (ôrd)..................Ne. 41·35 N 98·57 W
204 Ord (R.).................Austl. 17·30 S 128·40 E
174 Orda (ôr'dȧ)..Sov. Un. (Urals In.) 56·50 N 57·12 E
162 Ordenes (ōr'dȧ-nās)..........Sp. 43·46 N 8·24 W
192 Ordos Des....................China 39·12 N 108·10 E
115 Ord Pk.......................Az. 33·55 N 109·40 W
171 Ordu (ôr'dōō)...............Tur. 41·00 N 37·50 E
162 Orduña (ôr-dōō'nyä).........Sp. 42·59 N 3·01 W
116 Ordway (ôrd'wā)..............Co. 38·11 N 103·46 W
171 Ordzhonikidze (ora ghō nĭ kĭd ze)
Sov. Un. 43·05 N 44·35 E
156 Örebro (û'rē-brō)...........Swe. 59·16 N 15·11 E
174 Oredezh R. (ô'rĕ-dĕzh)
Sov. Un. (Leningrad In.) 59·23 N 30·21 E
109 Oregon.......................Il. 42·01 N 89·21 W
102 Oregon (State)...............U. S. 43·40 N 121·50 W
110 Oregon Caves Natl. Mon. (cāvz)
Or. 42·05 N 123·13 W
112 Oregon City....Or. (Portland In.) 45·21 N 122·36 W
156 Öregrund (û-rē-grōōnd)......Swe. 60·20 N 18·26 E
167 Orekhov (ôr-yĕ'kôf).....Sov. Un. 47·34 N 35·51 E
166 Orekhovo-Zuyevo
(ôr-yĕ'kô-vô zōō'yĕ-vô).Sov. Un. 55·46 N 39·00 E
166 Orël (ôr-yôl')...........Sov. Un. 52·54 N 36·03 E
166 Orël (Oblast)...........Sov. Un. 52·35 N 36·08 E
167 Orel' (R.)..............Sov. Un. 49·08 N 34·55 E
115 Orem (ō'rĕm)................Ut. 40·15 N 111·50 W
Ore Mts., see Erzgebirge
171 Orenburg (ō'rĕn-bōōrg)..Sov. Un. 51·50 N 55·05 E
162 Orense (ō-rĕn'sā).............Sp. 42·20 N 7·52 W
128 Organos, Sierra de los (Mts.)
(sē-ĕ'r-rä-dĕ-lôs-ŏ'r-gä-nôs).Cuba 22·20 N 84·10 W
115 Organ Pipe Cactus Natl. Mon
(ôr'gȧn pīp kăk'tŭs).Az. 32·14 N 113·05 W
137 Orgãos, Serra das (Mtn.)
(sĕ'r-rä-däs-ôr-gouN's)
Braz. (Rio de Janeiro In.) 22·30 S 43·01 W
167 Orgeyev (ôr-gyĕ'yĕf).....Sov. Un. 47·27 N 28·49 E
188 Orhon Gol (R.)............Mong. 48·33 N 103·07 E
134 Oriental, Cordillera (Mts.)
(kôr-dēl-yĕ'rä ō-rē-ĕn-täl').Bol. 14·00 S 68·33 W
134 Oriental, Cordillera (Mts.)
(kôr-dēl-yĕ'rä).Col. (In.) 3·30 N 74·27 W
129 Oriental, Cordillera (Mts.)
(kôr-dēl-yĕ'rä-ô-ryĕ'n-täl)
Dom. Rep. 18·55 N 69·40 W
122 Oriental, Sierra Madre, (Mts.)
(sē-ĕ'r-rä-mä'drĕ-ô-ryĕ'n-täl')
Mex. 25·30 N 100·45 W
129 Oriente (Prov.) (ō-rē-ĕn'tȧ)..Cuba 20·25 N 76·15 W
163 Orihuela (ō'rē-wā'lä).........Sp. 38·04 N 0·55 W
105 Orillia (ô-rĭl'ĭ-ȧ)...........Can. 44·35 N 79·25 W
111 Orin.......................Wy. 42·40 N 105·10 W
112 Orinda....Ca. (San Francisco In.) 37·53 N 122·11 W
134 Orinoco, Rio (R.)
(rē'ō-ō-rĭ-nō'kō).Ven. 8·32 N 63·13 W
197 Orion (ō-rē-ōn')........Phil. (In.) 14·37 N 120·34 E
184 Orissa (State) (ŏ-rĭs'ȧ)......India 25·09 N 83·50 E
164 Oristano (ō-rēs-tä'nō).........It. 39·53 N 8·38 E
164 Oristano, Golfo di (G.)
(gôl-fô-dē-ô-rēs-tä'nō).It. 39·53 N 8·12 E
135 Orituco (R.) (ô-rē-tōō'kō)
Ven. (In.) 9·37 N 66·25 W
135 Oriuco (ô-rēōō'kō) (R.).Ven. (In.) 9·36 N 66·25 W
157 Orivesi (L.)..............Fin. 62·15 N 29·55 E
125 Orizaba (ô-rē-zä'bä)........Mex. 18·52 N 97·05 E
156 Orkdal (ôr'k-däl)...........Nor. 63·19 N 9·54 W
150 Örkedalen (ûr'kĕ-dä-lĕn)....Nor. 63·13 N 9·53 E
156 Örken (L.) (ûr'kĕn).........Swe. 57·11 N 14·45 E
156 Orkla (R.) (ôr'klȧ)..........Nor. 62·55 N 9·50 E
218 Orkney (ôrk'nĭ)...........S. Afr.
(Johannesburg & Pretoria In.) 26·58 S 26·39 E
154 Orkney (Is.)................Scot. 59·01 N 2·08 W
121 Orlando (ôr-lăn'dō)......Fl. (In.) 28·32 N 81·22 W
213 Orlando (ôr-lăn-dô).........S. Afr.
(Johannesburg & Pretoria In.) 26·15 S 27·56 E
107 Orland Park (ôr-lăn')
Il. (Chicago In.) 41·38 N 87·52 W
100 Orleans (ôr-lâ-äN')
Can. (Ottawa In.) 45·28 N 75·31 W
160 Orléans (ôr-lā-äN')...........Fr. 47·55 N 1·56 E
104 Orleans (ôr-lēnz').............In. 38·40 N 86·25 W
100 Orléans, Île d' (I.)
Can. (Quebec In.) 46·56 N 70·57 W
Orléansville, see El Asnam
121 Ormond Beach (ôr'mŏnd)......Fl. 29·15 N 81·05 W
148 Ormskirk (ôrms'kērk).......Eng. 53·34 N 2·53 W
100 Ormstown (ôrms'toun)
Can. (Montreal In.) 45·07 N 74·00 W
160 Orne (R.) (ôrn')..............Fr. 49·05 N 0·32 W
159 Orneta (ôr-nyĕ'tä)...........Pol. 54·07 N 20·10 E
156 Ornö (I.)....................Swe. 59·02 N 18·35 E
150 Örnsköldsvik
(ûrn'skôlts-vēk).Swe. 63·10 N 18·32 E
124 Oro, Rio del (R.) (rē'ō dĕl ō'rō)
Mex. 18·04 N 100·59 W
108 Oro, Rio del (R.)...........Mex. 26·04 N 105·40 W
164 Orobie, Alpi (Mts.)
(äl'pē-ô-rō'byĕ).It. 46·05 N 9·47 E
134 Orocué (ô-rô-kwā')..........Col. 4·48 N 71·26 W
215 Oron.......................Nig. 4·48 N 8·14 E
154 Oronsay, Pass .of (ō'rŏn-sȧ)..Scot. 55·55 N 6·25 W
164 Orosei, Golfo di (G.)
(gôl-fô-dē-ō-rô-sā'ē).It. 40·12 N 9·45 E
159 Orosháza (ô-rôsh-hä'sô)....Hung. 46·33 N 20·31 E
126 Orosi Vol. (ō-rō'sē).........C. R. 11·00 N 85·30 W
114 Oroville (ôr'ô-vĭl)...........Ca. 39·29 N 121·34 W
110 Oroville.....................Wa. 48·55 N 119·25 W
104 Orrville (ôr'vĭl)..............Oh. 40·45 N 81·50 W
156 Orsa (ôr'sä)................Swe. 61·08 N 14·35 E
100 Orsainville.....Can. (Quebec In.) 46·23 N 71·17 W
156 Örsdals Vand (L.) (ûrs-däls vän)
Nor. 58·39 N 6·06 E
166 Orsha (ôr'shȧ)..........Sov. Un. 54·29 N 30·28 E
171 Orsk (ôrsk)..............Sov. Un. 51·15 N 58·50 E
165 Orsova (ôr'shô-vä)..........Rom. 44·43 N 22·26 E
134 Ortega (ôr-tĕ'gä).......Col. (In.) 3·56 N 75·12 W
162 Ortegal, Cabo (C.)
(kȧ'bô-ôr-tȧ-gäl').Sp. 43·46 N 8·15 W
149 Orth...........Aus. (Vienna In.) 48·09 N 16·42 E
163 Orthez (ôr-tĕz')..............Fr. 43·29 N 0·43 W
162 Ortigueira (ôr-tē-gā'ē-rä)......Sp. 43·40 N 7·50 W
112 Orting (ôrt'ĭng).Wa. (Seattle In.) 47·06 N 122·12 W
164 Ortona (ôr-tō'nä)..............It. 42·22 N 14·22 E
108 Ortonville (ôr-tŭn-vĭl).......Mn. 45·18 N 96·26 W
134 Oruro (ō-rōō'rō)..............Bol. 17·57 S 66·59 W
164 Orvieto (ôr-vyå'tō)...........It. 42·43 N 12·08 E
165 Oryakhovo....................Bul. 43·43 N 23·59 E
156 Os (ôs).......................Nor. 60·24 N 5·22 E
170 Osa (ô'sȧ)...............Sov. Un. 57·18 N 55·25 E
127 Osa, Pen. de (ō'sä)...........C. R. 8·30 N 83·25 W
109 Osage (ō'sāj)..................Ia. 43·16 N 92·49 W
117 Osage (R.)....................Mo. 38·10 N 93·12 W
117 Osage City (ō'sāj sĭ'tĭ)........Ks. 38·28 N 95·53 W
195 Ōsaka (ō'sä-kä)..Jap. (Ōsaka In.) 34·40 N 135·27 E
195 Ōsaka (Pref.)....Jap. (Ōsaka In.) 34·45 N 135·36 E
195 Ōsaka-Wan (B.) (wän)........Jap. 34·34 N 135·16 E
109 Osakis (ô-sā'kĭs)..............Mn. 45·51 N 95·09 W
109 Osakis (L.)....................Mn. 45·55 N 94·55 W
117 Osawatomie (ŏs-ȧ-wăt'ō-mē)..Ks. 38·29 N 94·57 W
116 Osborne (ŏz'bŭrn)............Ks. 39·25 N 98·42 W
117 Osceola (ŏs-ē-ō'lȧ)...........Ar. 35·42 N 89·58 W
109 Osceola......................Ia. 41·04 N 93·45 W
117 Osceola.....................Mo. 38·02 N 93·41 W
108 Osceola.....................Ne. 41·11 N 97·34 W
117 Osceola.....................Tn. 35·42 N 89·58 W
104 Oscoda (ŏs-kō'dȧ)............Mi. 44·25 N 83·20 W
166 Osëtr (R.) (ô'sĕt'r)......Sov. Un. 54·27 N 38·15 E
104 Osgood (ŏz'gŏŏd)...............In. 39·10 N 85·20 W
100 Osgoode.......Can. (Ottawa In.) 45·09 N 75·37 W
172 Osh (ôsh)................Sov. Un. 40·28 N 72·47 E
105 Oshawa (ŏsh'ȧ-wȧ)...........Can. 43·50 N 78·50 W
195 Ōshima (I.) (ō'shē'mä).......Jap. 34·47 N 139·35 E
108 Oshkosh (ŏsh'kŏsh)...........Ne. 41·24 N 102·22 W
109 Oshkosh......................Wi. 44·01 N 88·35 W
157 Oshmyany (ôsh-myä'nĭ)..Sov. Un. 54·27 N 25·55 E
215 Oshogbo......................Nig. 7·47 N 4·34 E
165 Osijek (ôs'ĭ-yĕk).............Yugo. 45·33 N 18·48 E
172 Osinniki (ŭ-sē'nyĭ-kē)....Sov. Un. 53·29 N 85·19 E
109 Oskaloosa (ŏs-kȧ-lōō'sȧ).......Ia. 41·16 N 92·40 W
156 Oskarshamn (ôs'kärs-häm'n)
Swe. 57·16 N 16·24 E
156 Oskarström (ôs'kärs-strûm)
Swe. 56·48 N 12·55 E
167 Oskol (R.) (ôs-kôl')......Sov. Un. 51·00 N 37·41 E
156 Oslo (ôs'lō).................Nor. 59·56 N 10·41 E
156 Oslo Fd (fyôrd)..............Nor. 59·03 N 10·35 E
162 Osma (ōs'mä).................Sp. 41·35 N 3·02 W
171 Osmaniye...................Tur. 37·10 N 36·30 E
158 Osnabrück (ôs-nä-brük')...F.R.G. 52·16 N 8·05 E
136 Osorno (ō-sō'r-nō)..........Chile 40·42 S 73·13 W
205 Osprey Reef (I.) (ŏs'prā)...Austl. 14·00 S 146·45 E
203 Ossa, Mt. (ŏsȧ)............Austl. 41·45 S 146·05 E
113 Osseo (ŏs'sē-ō)...............Mn.
(Minneapolis, St. Paul In.) 45·07 N 93·24 W
106 Ossining (ŏs'ĭ-nĭng)
NY (New York In.) 41·09 N 73·51 W
98 Ossipee (ŏs'ĭ-pē)..............NH 43·42 N 71·08 W
156 Ossjöen (L.) (ôs-syûĕn).....Nor. 61·20 N 12·00 E
166 Ostashkov (ôs-täsh'kôf)..Sov. Un. 57·07 N 33·04 E
155 Oste (R.) (ōz'tĕ)...........F.R.G. 53·20 N 9·19 E
167 Oster (ōs'tĕr)...........Sov. Un. 50·55 N 30·52 E
167 Oster-daläven (R.)..........Swe. 61·40 N 13·00 E
167 Oster Fd. (ûs'tĕr fyôr')......Nor. 60·40 N 5·25 E
167 Östersund (ûs'tēr-sōōnd).....Swe. 63·09 N 14·49 E
167 Östhammar (ûst'häm'är).....Swe. 60·16 N 18·21 E
163 Ostia Antica (ô's-tyä-än-tē'kä)
It. (Rome In.) 41·46 N 12·24 E
Ostia Lido, see Lido di Roma
159 Ostrava..................Czech. 49·51 N 18·18 E
159 Ostróda (ôs'trōōt-ȧ).........Pol. 53·41 N 19·58 E
167 Ostróg (ôs-trôk')........Sov. Un. 50·21 N 26·40 E
167 Ostrogozhsk (ôs-trô-gôzhk')
Sov. Un. 50·53 N 39·03 E
159 Ostrołeka (ôs-trô-woN'kȧ).....Pol. 53·04 N 21·35 E
167 Ostropol' (ôs-trô-pôl')....Sov. Un. 49·48 N 27·32 E
166 Ostrov (ôs-trôf')..........Sov. Un. 57·21 N 28·22 E
159 Ostrowiec Świętokrzyski
(ôs-trō'vyĕts shvyĕN-tō-kzhĭ'ske)
Pol. 50·55 N 21·24 E
159 Ostrów Lubelski
(ôs'trōōf lōō'bĕl-skĭ).Pol. 51·32 N 22·49 E
159 Ostrów Mazowiecka
(mä-zô-vyĕt'skä).Pol. 52·47 N 21·54 E
159 Ostrów Wielkopolski
(ôs'trōōv vyĕl-kō-pōl'skē).Pol. 51·38 N 17·49 E
159 Ostrzeszów (ôs-tzhā'shōōf)....Pol. 51·26 N 17·56 E
165 Ostuni (ôs-tōō'nē)..............It. 40·44 N 17·35 E
165 Osum (R.) (ō'sōōm).........Alb. 40·37 N 20·00 E
195 Ōsumi-Guntō (Arch.)
(ō'sōō-mē gōōn'tō).Jap 30·34 N 130·30 E
195 Ōsumi Kaikyō (Van Diemen)
(Str.) (käē'kyō) (văn dē'mĕn)
Jap. 31·02 N 130·10 E
162 Osuna (ô-sōō'nä).............Sp. 37·18 N 5·05 W
166 Osveya (ôs'vĕ-yȧ).......Sov. Un. 56·00 N 28·08 E
148 Oswaldtwistle (ŏz-wȧld-twĭs''l)
Eng. 53·44 N 2·23 W
105 Oswegatchie (R.) (ŏs-wê-găch'ĭ)
NY 44·15 N 75·20 W
117 Oswego (ŏs-wē'gō)..........Ks. 37·10 N 95·08 W
105 Oswego.......................NY 43·25 N 76·30 W
159 Oswiecim (ôsh-vyăN'tsyĭm)...Pol. 50·02 N 19·17 E
194 Otaru (ō'tȧ-rōō)..............Jap. 43·07 N 141·00 E
134 Otavalo (ōtä-vä'lō)...........Ec. 0·14 N 78·16 W
212 Otavi (ô-tä'vē)........S. W. Afr. 19·35 S 17·20 E
114 Otay (ō'tā)...............Ca. (In.) 32·36 N 117·04 W
166 Otepää (ô'tĕ-pȧ).........Sov. Un. 58·03 N 26·31 E
165 Othonoí (I.)..................Grc. 39·51 N 19·26 E
165 Óthris, Óros (Mts.)..........Grc. 39·00 N 22·15 E
214 Oti (R.).....................Ghana 9·00 N 0·10 E
91 Otish, Mts. (ô-tĭsh')........Can. 52·15 N 70·20 W
212 Otjiwarongo (ŏt-jē-wȧ-rŏn'gō)
S. W. Afr. 20·20 S 16·25 E
164 Otočac (ō'tô-chȧts)..........Yugo. 44·53 N 15·15 E
174 Otradnoye (ô-trȧ'd-nôyĕ)
Sov. Un. (Leningrad In.) 59·46 N 30·50 E
165 Otranto (ô'trän-tô) (ô-trän'tō).It. 40·07 N 18·30 E
165 Otranto, C. di.................It. 40·06 N 18·32 E
165 Otranto, Strait of.........It.-Alb. 40·30 N 18·45 E
174 Otra R. (ôt'rȧ)
Sov. Un. (Moscow In.) 55·22 N 38·20 E
104 Otsego (ŏt-sē'gō).............Mi. 42·25 N 85·45 W
195 Otsu (ō'tsōō).....Jap. (Ōsaka In.) 35·00 N 135·54 E
156 Ottavand (L.) (ôt'tȧ-vän)....Nor. 61·53 N 8·40 E
100 Ottawa (ŏt'ȧ-wȧ)
Can. (Ottawa In.) 45·25 N 75·43 W
104 Ottawa.......................Il. 41·20 N 88·50 W
117 Ottawa.......................Ks. 38·37 N 95·16 W
104 Ottawa.......................Oh. 41·00 N 84·00 W
91 Ottawa (R.).................Can. 46·05 N 77·20 W
91 Ottawa Is...................Can. 59·50 N 81·00 W
156 Otteråen (ôt'ĕr-ôĕn).........Nor. 59·13 N 7·20 E
115 Otter Cr. (ŏt'ĕr)..............Ut. 38·20 N 111·55 W
105 Otter Cr......................Vt. 44·05 N 73·15 W
112 Otter Pt.......Can. (Seattle In.) 48·21 N 123·50 W
108 Otter Tail (L.)...............Mn. 46·21 N 95·52 W
113 Otterville (ŏt'ĕr-vĭl)
Il. (St. Louis In.) 39·03 N 90·24 W
212 Ottery (ŏt'ĕr-ĭ).......S. Afr. (In.) 34·02 S 18·31 E
109 Ottumwa (ô-tŭm'wȧ)..........Ia. 41·00 N 92·26 W
215 Otukpa......................Nig. 7·09 N 7·41 E
125 Otumba (ô-tŭm'bä)....Mex. (In.) 19·41 N 98·46 W
203 Otway, C. (ŏt'wā)..........Austl. 38·55 S 153·40 E
136 Otway, Seno (B.) (sĕ'nō-ŏ't-wä'y)
Chile 53·00 S 73·00 W
159 Otwock (ôt'vôtsk)............Pol. 52·05 N 21·18 E
103 Ouachita, (R.)..............U. S. 33·25 N 92·30 W
117 Ouachita Mts. (wŏsh'ĭ-tô).....Ok. 34·29 N 95·01 W
211 Ouaddaï (Reg.) (wä-dī')......Chad 13·04 N 20·00 E
214 Ouagadougou (wä'gȧ-dōō'gōō)
Upper Volta 12·22 N 1·31 W
214 Ouahigouya (wä-ē-gōō'yä)
Upper Volta 13·35 N 2·25 W

PRONOUNCING INDEX Ouahran — Pamiers 325

Page	Name Pronunciation Region	Lat. °′	Long. °′
	Ouahran, see Oran		
210	Oualâta (wä-lä'tä)..... Mauritania	17·11 N	6·50 W
210	Ouallene (wäl-lân')..........Alg.	24·43 N	1·15 E
129	Ouanaminthe..............Hai.	19·35 N	71·45 W
211	Ouanda Djallé (wän'dȧ jä'lā') Cen. Afr. Rep.	8·56 N	22·46 E
210	Ouarane (Dunes)...... Mauritania	20·44 N	10·27 W
210	Ouargla (wär'glä)............Alg.	32·00 N	5·18 E
214	Ouarkoye............Upper Volta	12·05 N	3·40 W
216	Oubangui (Ubangi) (R.) (ōō-bäŋ'gē) Afr.	4·30 N	20·35 E
149	Oude Rijn (R.) Neth. (Amsterdam In.)	52·09 N	4·33 E
149	Oudewater. Neth. (Amsterdam In.)	52·01 N	4·52 E
149	Oud-Gastel. Neth. (Amsterdam In.)	51·35 N	4·27 E
152	Oudrhes, L. (Mt.)..........Mor.	32·33 N	4·49 W
212	Oudtshoorn (outs'hōrn)....S. Afr.	33·33 S	23·36 E
163	Oued Rhiou...............Alg.	35·55 N	0·57 E
163	Oued Tiélat...............Alg.	35·33 N	0·28 W
210	Oued-Zem (wĕd-zĕm')........Mor.	33·05 N	5·49 W
214	Ouellé.................Ivory Coast	7·18 N	4·01 W
160	Ouessant, I. d' (ĕl-dwĕ-säN')...Fr.	48·28 N	5·00 W
216	Ouesso....................Con.	1·37 N	16·04 E
129	Ouest, Pt...................Hai.	19·00 N	73·25 W
210	Ouezzane (wĕ-zän')..........Mor.	34·48 N	5·40 W
154	Oughter (L.) (lôĸ oĸ'tẽr).....Ire.	54·02 N	7·40 W
215	Ouham (R.)..Cen. Afr. Rep.-Chad	8·30 N	17·50 E
210	Ouidah (wē-dä')...........Benin	6·25 N	2·05 E
210	Oujda....................Mor.	34·41 N	1·45 W
152	Ouled Nail, Montes des (Mts.). Alg.	34·43 N	2·44 E
161	Oulins (ōō-lăN')....Fr. (Paris In.)	48·52 N	1·27 E
160	Oullins (ōō-lăN')..............Fr.	45·44 N	4·46 E
150	Oulu (ō'lōō)................Fin.	64·58 N	25·43 E
150	Oulu-jarvi (L.).............Fin.	64·20 N	25·48 E
211	Oum Chalouba (ōōm shä-lōō'bä) Chad	15·48 N	20·30 E
215	Oum Hadjer...............Chad	13·18 N	19·41 E
150	Ounas (R.) (ō'nȧs)..........Fin.	67·46 N	24·40 E
148	Oundle (ôn'd'l).............Eng.	52·28 N	0·28 W
211	Ounianga Kébir (ōō-nē-äŋ'gȧ kē-bēr'). Chad	19·04 N	20·22 E
117	Ouray (ōō-rā')...............Co.	38·00 N	107·40 W
135	Ourinhos (ôōō-rē'nyôs)......Braz.	23·04 S	49·45 W
162	Ourique (ō-rē'kĕ)..........Port.	37·39 N	8·10 W
137	Ouro Fino (ōŭ-rô-fē'nō) Braz. (Rio de Janeiro In.)	22·18 S	46·21 W
137	Ouro Prêto (ō'rōō prā'tōō) Braz. (Rio de Janeiro In.)	20·24 S	43·30 W
154	Ouse (R.)..................Eng.	53·45 N	1·09 W
99	Outardes, Rivière aux (R.)...Can.	50·53 N	68·50 W
109	Outer (I.) (out'ẽr)...........Wi.	47·03 N	90·20 W
123	Outer Brass (I.) (bräs)....Vir. Is. (U. S. A.) (St. Thomas In.)	18·24 N	64·58 W
154	Outer Hebrides (Is.)........Scot.	57·20 N	7·50 W
94	Outlook...................Can.	51·31 N	107·05 W
212	Outjo (ōt'yō)...........S. W. Afr.	20·05 S	17·10 E
100	Outremont (ōō-trē-môN') Can. (Montreal In.)	45·31 N	73·36 W
203	Ouyen (ōō-ĕn)............Austl.	35·05 S	142·10 E
136	Ovalle (ō-väl'yä)...........Chile	30·43 S	71·16 W
212	Ovamboland (Reg.)....S. W. Afr.	18·10 S	15·00 E
129	Ovando, Bahía de (B.) (bä-ē'ä-dĕ-ô-vä'n-dō). Cuba	20·10 N	74·05 W
162	Ovar (ô-vär')..............Port.	40·52 N	8·38 W
149	Overijsche.....Bel. (Brussels In.)	50·46 N	4·32 E
113	Overland (ō-vẽr-lȧnd) Mo. (St. Louis In.)	38·42 N	90·22 W
113	Overland Park Ks. (Kansas City In.)	38·59 N	94·40 W
106	Overlea (ō'vẽr-lā) (ō'vẽr-lē) Md. (Baltimore In.)	39·21 N	76·31 W
150	Övertornea.................Swe.	66·19 N	23·31 E
167	Ovidiopol' (ô-vē-dē-ô'pôl') Sov. Un.	46·15 N	03·28 E
129	Oviedo (ô-vyĕ'dō).....Dom. Rep.	17·50 N	71·25 W
162	Oviedo (ō-vē-ā'dhō)...........Sp.	43·22 N	5·50 W
167	Ovruch (ôv'rōōch)........Sov. Un.	51·19 N	28·51 E
195	Owada (ō'wä-dȧ). Jap. (Tōkyō In.)	35·49 N	139·33 E
216	Owando...................Con.	0·29 S	15·55 E
105	Owasco (L.) (ō-wăs'kō)........NY	42·50 N	76·30 W
195	Owase (ō'wä-shē)............Jap.	34·03 N	136·12 E
105	Owego (ō-wē'gō)..............NY	42·05 N	76·15 W
109	Owen (ō'ĕn)..................Wi.	44·56 N	90·35 W
114	Owens (L.) (ō'ĕnz)............Ca.	36·27 N	117·45 W
114	Owens (R.)..................Ca.	37·13 N	118·20 W
104	Owensboro (ō'ĕnz-bŭr-ô)......Ky.	37·45 N	87·05 W
104	Owen Sound (ō'ĕn)..........Can.	44·30 N	80·55 W
197	Owen Stanley Ra. (stăn'lē) Pap. N. Gui.	9·00 S	147·30 E
104	Owensville (ō'ĕnz-vĭl).........In.	38·15 N	87·40 W
117	Owensville..................Mo.	38·20 N	91·29 W
107	Owensville....Oh. (Cincinnati In.)	39·08 N	84·07 W
104	Owenton (ō'ĕn-tŭn)...........Ky.	38·35 N	84·55 W
210	Owerri (ō-wĕr'ē)............Nig.	5·26 N	7·04 E
106	Owings Mill (ōwĭngz mĭl) Md. (Baltimore In.)	39·25 N	76·50 W
111	Owl Cr. (oul)...............Wy.	43·45 N	108·46 W
215	Owo......................Nig.	7·15 N	5·37 E
104	Owosso (ō-wŏs'ō)............Mi.	43·00 N	84·15 W
110	Owyhee Mts. (ō-wī'hē)........Id.	43·15 N	116·48 W
110	Owyhee Res.................Or.	43·27 N	117·30 W
110	Owyhee R...................Or.	43·04 N	117·45 W
110	Owyhee R., South Fork.......Id.	42·07 N	116·43 W
95	Oxbow....................Can.	49·12 N	102·11 W
125	Oxchuc (ôs-chōōk')..........Mex.	16·47 N	92·24 W
120	Oxford (ŏks'fẽrd)............Al.	33·38 N	80·46 W
97	Oxford (ŏks'fẽrd)...........Can.	45·44 N	63·52 W
148	Oxford........Eng. (London In.)	51·43 N	1·16 W
99	Oxford............Ma. (In.)	42·07 N	71·52 W
104	Oxford.....................Mi.	42·50 N	83·15 W
120	Oxford.....................Ms.	34·22 N	89·30 W
121	Oxford.....................NC	36·17 N	78·35 W
104	Oxford.....................Oh.	39·30 N	84·45 W
95	Oxford L...................Can.	54·51 N	95·37 W
126	Oxkutzcab (ôx-kōō'tz-käb) Mex. (In.)	20·18 N	89·22 W
106	Oxmoor (ŏks'mŏŏr) Al. (Birmingham In.)	33·25 N	86·52 W
154	Ox Mts. (ŏks)...............Ire.	54·05 N	9·05 W
114	Oxnard (ŏks'närd)............Ca.	34·08 N	119·12 W
106	Oxon Hill (ŏks'ŏn hĭl) Md. (Baltimore In.)	38·48 N	77·00 W
125	Oxtotepec (ôx-tô-tĕ'pĕk) Mex. (In.)	19·10 N	99·04 W
135	Oyapock (R.) (ō-yȧ-pŏk') Braz.-Fr. Gu.	2·45 N	52·15 W
216	Oyem (ô-yĕm) (ô-yăN')....Gabon	1·37 N	11·35 E
173	Oymyakon (oi-myŭ-kôn'). Sov. Un.	63·14 N	142·58 E
215	Oyo (ō'yō).................Nig.	7·51 N	3·56 E
161	Oyonnax (ô-yô-nȧks').........Fr.	46·16 N	5·40 E
106	Oyster Bay..NY (New York In.)	40·52 N	73·32 W
119	Oyster Bay............Tx. (In.)	29·41 N	94·33 W
119	Oyster Cr. (ois'tẽr).....Tx. (In.)	29·13 N	95·29 W
129	Ozama (R.) (ô-zä'mä)..Dom. Rep.	18·45 N	69·55 W
197	Ozamiz (ô-zä'mēz)..........Phil.	8·06 N	123·43 E
120	Ozark (ō'zärk)...............Al.	31·28 N	85·28 W
117	Ozark......................Ar.	35·29 N	93·49 W
117	Ozarks, L. of the (ō'zärkz)....Mo.	38·06 N	93·26 W
117	Ozark Plat..................Mo.	36·37 N	93·56 W
166	Ozëry (ô-zyô'rĕ).........Sov. Un.	54·53 N	38·31 E
164	Ozieri.......................It.	40·38 N	8·53 E
159	Ozorków (ô-zôr'kōōf).........Pol.	51·58 N	19·20 E
125	Ozuluama (ō'zōō-lōō-ä'mä)...Mex.	21·34 N	97·52 W
125	Ozumba (ô-zōō'm-bä)..Mex. (In.)	19·02 N	98·48 W

P

Page	Name Pronunciation Region	Lat. °′	Long. °′
188	Paan.....................China	30·08 N	99·00 E
212	Paarl (pärl)..............S. Afr.	33·45 S	18·55 E
89	Paauilo (pä-ä-ōō'ē-lō).........Hi.	20·03 N	155·25 W
159	Pabianice (pä-byȧ-nē'tsĕ).....Pol.	51·40 N	19·29 E
134	Pacaás Novos, Massiço de (Mts.) (mä-sē'sô-dĕ-pä-kȧ's-nô'vôs) Braz.	11·03 S	64·02 W
134	Pacaraima, Serra (Mts.) (sĕr'rȧ pä-kä-rä-ē'mȧ) Braz.-Ven.	3·45 N	62·30 W
134	Pacasmayo (pä-käs-mä'yō)...Peru	7·24 S	79·30 W
188	Pach'u (pä'chōō')..........China	39·50 N	78·23 E
125	Pachuca (pä-chōō'kä)........Mex.	20·07 N	98·43 W
112	Pacific (pȧ-sĭf'ĭk). Wa. (Seattle In.)	47·16 N	122·15 W
112	Pacifica (pȧ-sĭf'ĭ-kä) Ca. (San Francisco In.)	37·38 N	122·29 W
114	Pacific Beach..........Ca. (In.)	32·47 N	117·22 W
114	Pacific Grove................Ca.	36·37 N	121·54 W
199	Pacific O.		
92	Pacific Ra..................Can.	51·00 N	125·30 W
92	Pacific Rim Natl. Pk.........Can.	49·00 N	126·00 W
121	Pacolet (R.) (pȧ'cō-lĕt)........SC	34·55 N	81·49 W
161	Pacy-sur-Eure (pä-sē-sür-ûr') Fr. (Paris In.)	49·01 N	1·24 E
196	Padang (pä-däng')........Indon.	1·01 S	100·28 E
183	Padang, Palau (I.) Indon. (Singapore In.)	1·12 N	102·21 E
183	Padang Endau Mala. (Singapore In.)	2·39 N	103·38 E
104	Paden City (pā'dĕn)..........WV	39·30 N	80·55 W
158	Paderborn (pä-dĕr-bôrn')..F.R.G.	51·43 N	8·46 E
217	Padibe.....................Ug.	3·28 N	32·50 E
148	Padiham (păd'ĭ-hȧm)........Eng.	53·48 N	2·19 W
124	Padilla (pä-dēl'yä)...........Mex.	24·00 N	98·45 W
112	Padilla B. (pä-dĕl'lȧ) Wa. (Seattle In.)	48·31 N	122·34 W
164	Padova (Padua) (pä'dô-vä) (păd'ū-ȧ). It.	45·24 N	11·53 E
119	Padre I. (pä'drā).............Tx.	27·09 N	97·15 W
	Padua, see Padova		
120	Paducah (pȧ-dū'kȧ)..........Ky.	37·05 N	88·36 W
116	Paducah....................Tx.	34·01 N	100·18 W
194	Paektu San (Mt.) (pâk'tōō-sän') China-Kor.	42·00 N	128·03 E
164	Pag (I.) (päg)............Yugo.	44·30 N	14·48 E
196	Pagai Selatan (I.).........Indon.	2·48 S	100·22 E
196	Pagai Utara (I.)...........Indon.	2·45 S	100·02 E
209	Pagalu (I.)..........Equat. Gui.	2·00 S	3·30 E
165	Pagasitikós Kólpos (G.)......Grc.	39·15 N	23·00 E
117	Page.......................Az.	36·57 N	111·27 W
117	Pagosa Springs (pȧ-gō'sȧ).....Co.	37·15 N	107·05 W
89	Pahala (pä-hä'lä)............Hi.	19·11 N	155·28 W
183	Pahang (State) Mala. (Singapore In.)	3·02 N	102·57 E
196	Pahang R..................Mala.	3·39 N	102·41 E
121	Pahokee (pȧ-hō'kē)......Fl. (In.)	26·45 N	80·40 W
190	Paichü (bäī'gü)............China	33·04 N	120·17 E
192	Paich'uan.................China	47·22 N	126·00 E
157	Paide (pī'dĕ)...........Sov. Un.	58·54 N	25·30 E
192	Paiho.....................China	32·30 N	110·15 E
190	Pai Hu (L.) (bäī' hōō).......China	31·22 N	117·38 E
157	Päijänna (L.) (pĕ'ē-yĕn-nĕ)...Fin.	61·38 N	25·05 E
190	Paikouchen (bäī'gō'jen).....China	39·08 N	116·02 E
89	Pailolo Chan. (pä-ē-lō'lō)......Hi.	21·05 N	156·41 W
137	Paine (pī'nĕ)..Chile (Santiago In.)	33·49 S	70·44 W
104	Painesville (pānz'vĭl).........Oh.	41·40 N	81·15 W
117	Painted Des. (pānt'ĕd)........Az.	36·15 N	111·35 W
117	Painted Rock Res............Az.	33·00 N	113·05 W
104	Paintsville (pānts'vĭl)........Ky.	37·50 N	82·50 W
190	Paip'u (bäī'pōō)...........China	32·15 N	120·47 E
193	Paise.....................China	24·00 N	106·38 E
154	Paisley (pāz'lĭ).............Scot.	55·50 N	4·30 W
134	Paita (pä-ē'tä)..............Peru	5·11 S	81·12 W
192	Pai T'ou Shan (Mts.)......Korea	40·30 N	127·20 E
117	Paiute Ind. Res..............Ut.	38·17 N	113·50 W
192	Paiyü Shan (Mtns.).........China	37·02 N	108·30 E
125	Pajápan (pä-hä'pän)........Mex.	18·16 N	94·41 W
196	Pakanbaru................Indon.	0·43 N	101·15 E
	Pakhoi, see Peihai		
174	Pakhra R. (päĸ'rá) Sov. Un. (Moscow In.)	55·29 N	37·51 E
182	Pakistan..................Asia	28·00 N	67·30 E
	Pakistan East, see Bangladesh		
196	Pakokku (pȧ-kŏk'kōō).......Bur.	21·29 N	95·00 E
164	Pakrac (pä'kräts)..........Yugo.	45·25 N	17·13 E
159	Paks (pôksh)..............Hung.	46·38 N	18·53 E
215	Pala......................Chad	9·22 N	14·54 E
119	Palacios (pä-lä'syōs).........Tx.	28·42 N	96·12 W
163	Palafrogell (pä-lä-frô-gĕl)......Sp.	41·55 N	3·09 E
164	Palagruža (Is.) (pä'lä-grōō'zhä) Yugo.	42·20 N	16·23 E
161	Palaiseau (pȧ-lĕ-zō'). Fr. (Paris In.)	48·44 N	2·16 E
173	Palana.................Sov. Un.	59·07 N	159·58 E
197	Palanan B. (pä-lä'nän). Phil. (In.)	17·14 N	122·35 E
197	Palanan Pt...........Phil. (In.)	17·12 N	122·40 E
184	Pālanpur (pä'lŭn-pōōr)......India	24·08 N	73·29 E
212	Palapye (pȧ-läp'yĕ)........Bots.	22·34 S	27·28 E
107	Palatine (păl'ȧ-tīn) Il. (Chicago In.)	42·07 N	88·03 W
121	Palatka (pȧ-lăt'kȧ)...........Fl.	29·39 N	81·40 W
197	Palau Is. (pä-lä'ōō) Pac. Is. Trust. Ter.	7·15 N	134·30 E
197	Palauig (pȧ-lou'ēg).....Phil. (In.)	15·27 N	119·54 E
197	Palauig Pt............Phil. (In.)	15·28 N	119·41 E
196	Palawan (I.) (pä-lä'wȧn).....Phil.	9·50 N	117·38 E
185	Pālayankottai..............India	8·50 N	77·50 E
157	Paldiski (päl'dĭ-skĭ).......Sov. Un.	59·22 N	24·04 E
196	Palembang (pä-lĕm-bäng'). Indon.	2·57 S	104·40 E
126	Palencia (pä-lĕn'sē-ȧ).......Guat.	14·40 N	90·22 W
162	Palencia (pä-lĕ'n-syä)..........Sp.	42·02 N	4·32 W
125	Palenque (pä-lĕŋ'kȧ)........Mex.	17·34 N	91·58 W
129	Palenque, Punta (Pt.) (pōō'n-tä) Dom. Rep.	18·10 N	70·10 W
134	Palermo (pä-lĕr'mô).....Col. (In.)	2·53 N	75·26 W
164	Palermo......................It.	38·08 N	13·24 E
119	Palestine...................Tx.	31·46 N	95·38 W
183	Palestine (Reg.) (păl'ĕs-tīn) Asia (Palestine In.)	31·33 N	35·00 E
188	Paletwa (pŭ-lĕt'wä).........Bur.	21·19 N	92·52 E
185	Palghāt...................India	10·49 N	76·40 E
184	Pāli......................India	25·53 N	73·18 E
188	Palik'un..................China	43·43 N	92·50 E
214	Palimé....................Togo	6·54 N	0·38 E
126	Palín (pä-lēn')..............Guat.	14·42 N	90·42 W
110	Palisade (păl-ĭ-säd')..........Nv.	40·39 N	116·11 W
125	Palizada (pä-lē-zä'dä).......Mex.	18·17 N	92·04 W
184	Palk Str. (pôk)............India	10·00 N	79·23 E
137	Palma (päl'mä) Braz. (Rio de Janeiro In.)	21·23 S	42·18 W
163	Palma, Ba. de (B.) (bä-ē'ä-dĕ). Sp.	39·24 N	2·37 E
162	Palma del Rio (dĕl rē'ō)......Sp.	37·43 N	5·19 W
163	Palma de Mallorca (dĕ-mäl-yô'r-kä). Sp.	39·35 N	2·38 E
135	Palmares (päl-mȧ'rĕs).......Braz.	8·46 S	35·28 W
136	Palmas (päl'mäs)...........Braz.	26·20 S	51·56 W
214	Palmas, C..................Lib.	4·22 N	7·44 W
129	Palma Soriano (sô-rē-ä'nō)..Cuba	20·15 N	76·00 W
121	Palm Beach (päm bēch')..Fl. (In.)	26·43 N	80·03 W
135	Palmeira dos Índios (päl-mā'rä-dôs-ē'n-dyôs). Braz.	9·26 S	36·33 W
216	Palmeirinhas, Ponta das (Pt.). Arg.	9·05 S	13·00 E
163	Palmela (päl-mā'lä) Port. (Lisbon In.)	38·34 N	8·54 W
101	Palmer (päm'ẽr).............Ak.	61·38 N	149·15 W
112	Palmer........Wa. (Seattle In.)	47·19 N	121·53 W
205	Palmerston North (päm'ẽr-stŭn) N. Z. (In.)	40·21 S	175·43 E
205	Palmerville (päm'ẽr-vĭl)....Austl.	16·08 S	144·15 E
121	Palmetto (pȧl-mĕt'ô).....Fl. (In.)	27·32 N	82·34 W
129	Palmetto Pt................Ba.	21·15 N	73·25 W
164	Palmi (päl'mē)...............It.	38·21 N	15·54 E
134	Palmira (päl-mē'rä).....Col. (In.)	3·33 N	76·17 W
128	Palmira...................Cuba	22·15 N	80·25 W
117	Palmyra (päl-mī'rȧ).........Mo.	39·45 N	91·32 W
106	Palmyra....NJ (Philadelphia In.)	40·01 N	75·00 W
199	Palmyra (I.)............Oceania	6·00 N	162·20 W
186	Palmyra (Ruins)............Syr.	34·25 N	38·28 E
184	Palmyras Pt...............India	20·42 N	87·45 E
147	Palmyre....................Syr.	30·35 N	37·58 E
112	Palo Alto (pä'lō äl'tō) Ca. (San Francisco In.)	37·27 N	122·09 W
116	Paloduro Cr. (pā-lô-dōō'rô)....Tx.	36·16 N	101·12 W
183	Paloh......Mala. (Singapore In.)	2·11 N	103·12 E
118	Paloma, L. (pä-lō'mä)........Mex.	26·53 N	104·02 W
137	Palomo, Cerro el (Mtn.) (sĕ'r-rô-ĕl-pä-lô'mô) Chile (Santiago In.)	34·36 S	70·20 W
163	Palos, Cabo de (C.) (kȧ'bô-dĕ-pä'lôs). Sp.	39·38 N	0·43 W
113	Palos Verdes Estates (pă'lŭs vûr'dĭs) Ca. (Los Angeles In.)	33·48 N	118·24 W
110	Palouse (pȧ-lōōz')..........Wa.	46·54 N	117·04 W
110	Palouse Hills...............Wa.	46·48 N	117·47 W
110	Palouse R..................Wa.	47·02 N	117·35 W
171	Palu (pä-lōō')...............Tur.	38·55 N	40·10 E
197	Paluan (pä-lōō'än).....Phil. (In.)	13·25 N	120·29 E
173	Pamamushir (I.).........Sov. Un.	50·42 N	153·45 E
160	Pamiers (pȧ-myā')............Fr.	43·07 N	1·34 E

ng-sing; ŋ-baŋk; N-nasalized n; nŏd; cŏmmit; ōld; ôbey; ôrder; fōōd; fŏŏt; ou-out; s-soft; sh-dish; th-thin; pūre; ůnite; ûrn; stŭd; circŭs; ü-as "y" in study; '-indeterminate vowel.

326 Pamirs — Patna PRONOUNCING INDEX

Page	Name Pronunciation Region	Lat. °′	Long. °′
187	Pamirs (Plat.) Sov. Un.	38·14 N	72·27 E
121	Pamlico R. (păm′lĭ-kō) NC	35·25 N	76·59 W
121	Pamlico Sd. NC	35·10 N	76·10 W
116	Pampa (păm′pȧ) Tx.	35·32 N	100·56 W
136	Pampa de Castillo (Plat.) (pä′m-pä-dĕ-käs-tē′l-yô) Arg.	45·30 S	67·30 W
214	Pampana (R.) S. L.	8·35 N	11·55 W
197	Pampanga (R.) (päm-päŋ′gä) Phil. (In.)	15·20 N	120·48 E
136	Pampas (Reg.) (päm′päs) Arg.	37·00 S	64·30 W
162	Pampilhosa do Botão (päm-pē-lyō′sȧ-dô-bō-to′uɴ) Port.	40·21 N	8·32 W
134	Pamplona (päm-plō′nä) Col.	7·19 N	72·41 W
162	Pamplona (päm-plô′nä) Sp.	42·49 N	1·39 W
105	Pamunkey (R.) (pȧ-mŭŋ′kĭ) Va.	37·40 N	77·20 W
104	Pana (pā′nȧ) Il.	39·25 N	89·05 W
126	Panabá (pä-nä-bà′) Mex. (In.)	21·18 N	88·15 W
165	Panagyurishte (pȧ-nȧ-gyōō′rêsh-tĕ) Bul.	42·30 N	24·11 E
185	Panaji (Panjim) India	15·33 N	73·52 E
123	Panamá (păn-ȧ-mä′) N. A. (Panama Canal In.)	8·35 N	81·08 W
123	Panama, G. of Pan.	7·45 N	79·20 W
123	Panama, Isth. of Pan.	9·00 N	81·00 W
127	Panama, B. of Pan.	8·50 N	79·08 W
120	Panama City (păn-ȧ mä′ sĭ′tĭ) Fl.	30·08 N	85·39 W
114	Panamint Ra. (păn-ȧ-mĭnt′) Ca.	36·40 N	117·30 W
164	Panaria (Is.) (pä-nä′rê-ä) It.	38·37 N	15·05 E
164	Panaro (R.) (pä-nä′rô) It.	44·47 N	11·06 E
196	Panay (I.) (pä-nī′) Phil.	11·15 N	121·38 E
165	Pančevo (pȧn′chĕ-vô) Yugo.	44·52 N	20·42 E
183	Panchor Mala. (Singapore In.)	2·10 N	102·43 E
184	Pānchur India (In.)	22·31 N	88·17 E
212	Panda (pän′dä′) Zaire	10·59 S	27·24 E
171	Pandar-e Pahlavī Iran	37·30 N	49·30 E
128	Pan de Guajaibon (Mtn.) (pän dā gwä-jä-bōn′) Cuba	22·50 N	83·20 W
196	Pandjang, Selat (Str.) Indon.	1·00 N	102·00 E
216	Pandu Zaire	5·00 N	19·15 E
157	Panevėžys (pä′nyĕ-vāzh′ēs) Sov. Un.	55·44 N	24·21 E
172	Panfilov (pŭn-fē′lôf) Sov. Un.	44·12 N	79·58 E
217	Panga (päŋ′gä) Zaire	1·51 N	26·25 E
213	Pangani (pän-gä′nē) Tan.	5·28 S	38·58 E
217	Pangani (R.) Tan.	4·40 S	37·45 E
191	P′angchiang China (Canton In.)	22·57 N	113·15 E
190	Pangfou (bäng′fōō) China	32·54 N	117·22 E
196	Pangkalpinang (päng-käl′pê-näng′) Indon.	2·11 S	106·04 E
184	Pangkong Tsho (L.) China	33·40 N	79·30 E
91	Pangnirtung Can.	66·08 N	65·26 W
117	Panguitch (päŋ′gwĭch) Ut.	37·50 N	112·30 W
184	Pānihāti India (Calcutta In.)	22·42 N	88·23 E
137	Panimávida (pä-nē-mà′vē-dä) Chile (Santiago In.)	36·44 S	71·26 W
	Panjim, see Panaji		
192	Panshih China	42·50 N	126·48 E
193	Pan Si Pan (Mtn.) Viet.	22·25 N	103·50 E
197	Pantar (I.) (pän′tär) Indon.	8·40 S	123·45 E
151	Pantelleria (I.) (pän-tĕl-lå-rē′ä) It.	36·43 N	11·59 E
125	Pantepec (pän-tå-pĕk′) Mex.	17·11 N	93·04 W
124	Panuco (pä′nōō-kō) Mex.	22·04 N	98·11 W
124	Pánuco (pä′nōō-kô) Mex.	29·47 N	105·55 W
124	Panuco (R.) Mex.	21·59 N	98·20 W
118	Pánuco de Coronado (pä′nōō-kô dā kō-rô-nä′dhō) Mex.	24·33 N	104·20 W
185	Panvel India (In.)	18·59 N	73·06 E
126	Panzós (pän-zós′) Guat.	15·26 N	89·40 W
135	Pao (pà′ō) (R.) Ven. (In.)	9·52 N	67·57 W
192	Paochang China	41·52 N	115·25 E
192	Paocheng China	33·15 N	106·58 E
192	Paochi China	34·10 N	106·58 E
117	Paola (pȧ-ō′lȧ) Ks.	38·34 N	94·51 W
104	Paoli (pȧ-ō′lĭ) In.	38·35 N	86·30 W
106	Paoli Pa. (Philadelphia In.)	40·03 N	75·29 W
115	Paonia (pā-ō′nyȧ) Co.	38·50 N	107·40 W
188	Paoshan (pä′ô-shän′) China	25·14 N	99·03 E
191	Paoshan China (Shanghai In.)	31·25 N	121·29 E
190	Paoti (pä′ō-tē′) China	39·44 N	117·19 E
190	Paoting China	38·52 N	115·31 E
192	Paoting China	42·04 N	125·00 E
192	Paot′ou China	40·28 N	110·10 E
190	Paoying (pä′ō-yĭng′) China	33·14 N	119·20 E
159	Pápa (pä′pô) Hung.	47·18 N	17·27 E
126	Papagayo, Golfo del (G.) (gôl-fô-dĕl-pä-pä-gä′yō) C. R.	10·44 N	85·56 W
124	Papagayo, Laguna (L.) (lä-ōō-nä) Mex.	16·44 N	99·44 W
124	Papagayo (R.) (pä-pä-gä′yō) Mex.	16·52 N	99·41 W
115	Papago Ind. Res. (pä′pä′gō) Az.	32·33 N	112·12 W
122	Papantla de Olarte (pä-pän′tlä dā-ō-lä′r-tĕ) Mex.	20·30 N	97·15 W
125	Papatoapan (R.) (pä-pä-tō-ā-pä′n) Mex.	18·00 N	96·22 W
158	Papenburg (päp′ĕn-bōōrgh) F.R.G.	53·05 N	7·23 E
137	Papinas (pä-pē′näs) Arg. (Buenos Aires In.)	35·30 S	57·19 W
100	Papineauville (pä-pē-nō′vēl) Can. (Ottawa In.)	45·38 N	75·01 W
197	Papua, Gulf of (păp-ōō-ȧ) Pap. N. Gui.	8·20 S	144·45 E
197	Papua New Guinea (păp-ōō-ȧ) (gĭne) Oceania	7·00 S	142·15 E
137	Papudo (pä-pōō′dô) Chile (Santiago In.)	32·30 S	71·25 W
136	Paquequer Pequeno (pä-kĕ-kĕ′r-pĕ-kĕ′nô) Braz. (Rio de Janeiro In.)	22·19 S	43·02 W
	Pará, see Belém		
135	Pará (State) (pä-rä′) Braz.	4·45 S	53·30 W
137	Pará (pä-rä′) (R.) Braz. (Rio de Janeiro In.)	20·21 S	44·38 W
135	Pará, Rio do (R.) (rē′ō-dô-pä-rä′) Braz.	1·09 S	48·48 W
166	Para (R.) Sov. Un.	53·45 N	40·58 E
197	Paracale (pä-rä-kä′lå) Phil. (In.)	14·17 N	122·47 E
136	Paracambi (pä-rä-kà′m-bē) Braz. (Rio de Janeiro In.)	22·36 S	43·43 W
135	Paracatu (pä-rä-kä-tōō′) Braz.	17·17 S	46·43 W
165	Paraćin (pȧ′rä-chēn) Yugo.	43·51 N	21·26 E
137	Para de Minas (pä-rä-dĕ-mē′näs) Braz. (Rio de Janeiro In.)	19·52 S	44·37 W
128	Paradise (I.) Ba.	25·05 N	77·20 W
110	Paradise Valley (păr′ȧ-dīs) Nv.	41·28 N	117·32 W
134	Parados, Cerro de los (Mtn.) (sĕ′r-rō-dĕ-lôs-pä-rä′dôs) Col. (In.)	5·44 N	75·13 W
117	Paragould (păr′ȧ-gōōld) Ar.	36·03 N	90·29 W
135	Paraguaçu (R.) (pä-rä-gwä-zōō′) Braz.	12·25 S	39·46 W
134	Paraguaná, Pen. de (Pen.) (pĕ-nē′ng-sōō-lä-dĕ-pä-rä-gwä-nà′) Ven.	12·00 N	69·55 W
133	Paraguay (păr′ȧ-gwā) S. A.	24·00 S	57·00 W
135	Paraguay, Rio (R.) (rē′ō-pä-rä-gwä′y) S. A.	21·12 S	57·31 W
	Paraíba, see João Pessoa		
135	Paraíba (State) (pä-rä-ē′bä) Braz.	7·11 S	37·05 W
137	Paraíba (R.) Braz. (Rio de Janeiro In.)	23·02 S	45·43 W
137	Paraíba do Sul (dô-sōō′l) Braz. (Rio de Janeiro In.)	22·10 S	43·18 W
137	Paraibuna (pä-räē-bōō′nä) Braz. (Rio de Janeiro In.)	23·23 S	45·38 W
122	Paraiso (pä-rä-ē′sō) C. Z. (In.)	9·02 N	79·38 W
127	Paraíso C. R.	9·50 N	83·53 W
125	Paraíso Mex.	18·24 N	93·11 W
137	Paraisópolis (pä-räē-sô′pō-lēs) Braz. (Rio de Janeiro In.)	22·35 S	45·45 W
137	Paraitinga (pä-rä-ē-tē′n-gä) (R.) Braz. (Rio de Janeiro In.)	23·15 S	45·24 W
215	Parakou (pȧ-rȧ-kōō′) Benin	9·21 N	2·37 E
135	Paramaribo (pȧ-rȧ-mà′rê-bō) Sur.	5·50 N	55·15 W
202	Paramatta (păr-ȧ-măt′ȧ) Austl. (Sydney In.)	33·49 S	150·59 E
160	Paramé (pȧ-rä-mā′) Fr.	48·40 N	1·58 W
134	Paramillo (Mtn.) (pä-rä-mê′l-yō) Col. (In.)	7·06 N	75·55 W
106	Paramus NJ (New York In.)	40·56 N	74·04 W
173	Paramushir (I.) Sov. Un.	50·45 N	154·00 E
183	Paran (R.) Isr. (Palestine In.)	30·05 N	34·50 E
136	Paraná (pä-rä-nä′) Arg.	31·44 S	60·29 W
136	Paraná (State) Braz.	24·25 S	52·00 W
136	Paraná, Rio (R.) Arg.	32·15 S	60·55 W
135	Paraná (R.) Braz.	13·05 S	47·11 W
135	Paranaguá (pä-rä′nä-gwà′) Braz.	25·39 S	48·42 W
135	Paranaíba (pä-rä-nȧ-ē′bȧ) Braz.	19·43 S	51·13 W
135	Paranaíba (R.) Braz.	18·58 S	50·44 W
137	Parana Ibicuy (R.) (ē-bē-kōō′ē) Arg. (Buenos Aires In.)	33·27 S	59·26 W
135	Paranam Sur.	5·39 N	55·13 W
136	Paranápanema (R.) (pä-rä′nà′pä-nĕ-mä) Braz.	22·28 S	52·15 W
137	Paraopeda (R.) (pä-rä-o-pĕ′dä) Braz. (Rio de Janeiro In.)	20·09 S	44·14 W
135	Parapara (pä-rä-pä-rä) Ven. (In.)	9·44 N	67·17 W
137	Parati (pä-rätē) Braz. (Rio de Janeiro In.)	23·14 S	44·43 W
160	Paray-le-Monial (pȧ-rĕ′lē-mô-nyäl′) Fr.	46·27 N	4·14 E
184	Parbati (R.) India	24·50 N	76·44 E
	Parcel Is., see Hsisha Ch′üntao		
158	Parchim (par′kĭm) G.D.R.	53·25 N	11·52 E
159	Parczew (pär′chĕf) Pol.	51·38 N	22·53 E
135	Pardo (R.) (pär′dō) Braz.	15·25 S	39·40 W
137	Pardo (R.) Braz. (Rio de Janeiro In.)	21·32 S	46·40 W
158	Pardubice (pär′dōō-bĭt-sĕ) Czech.	50·02 N	15·47 E
135	Parecis, Serra dos (Mts.) (sĕr′rȧ dōs pä-rȧ-sēzh′) Braz.	13·45 S	59·28 W
162	Paredes de Nava (pä-rä′dås dā nä′vä) Sp.	42·10 N	4·41 W
118	Paredón Mex.	25·56 N	100·58 W
97	Parent Can.	47·59 N	74·30 W
97	Parent, Lac (L.) Can.	48·40 N	77·00 W
174	Pargolovo (pȧr-gô′lô vô) Sov. Un. (Leningrad In.)	60·04 N	30·18 E
134	Paria, Golfo de (G.) (gôl-fô-dĕ-pä-rê-ä) Ven.	10·33 N	62·14 W
115	Paria (R.) Az.-Ut.	37·07 N	111·51 W
124	Paricutín, Vol. (pä-rē-kōō-tē′n) Mex.	19·27 N	102·14 W
118	Parida, Rio de la (R.) (rē′ō-dĕ-lä-pä-rē′dä) Mex.	26·23 N	104·40 W
134	Parima, Serra (Mts.) (sĕr′rȧ pä-rē′mȧ) Braz.-Ven.	3·45 N	64·00 W
134	Pariñas, Punta (Pt.) (pōō′n-tä-pä-rê′n-yäs) Peru	4·30 S	81·23 W
135	Parintins (pä-rĭn-tĭnzh′) Braz.	2·34 S	56·30 W
113	Paris (păr′ĭs) Ar.	35·17 N	93·43 W
104	Paris Can.	43·15 N	80·23 W
161	Paris (pȧ-rē′) Fr. (Paris In.)	48·51 N	2·20 E
104	Paris Il.	39·35 N	87·40 W
104	Paris Ky.	38·15 N	84·15 W
117	Paris Mo.	39·27 N	91·59 W
120	Paris Tn.	36·16 N	88·20 W
117	Paris Tx.	33·39 N	95·33 W
127	Parita, Golfo de (G.) (gôl-fô-dĕ-pä-rē′tä) Pan.	8·06 N	80·10 W
111	Park City Ut.	40·39 N	111·33 W
108	Parker (pär′kēr) SD	43·24 N	97·10 W
117	Parker Dam Az.-Ca.	34·20 N	114·00 W
104	Parkersburg (pär′kẽrz-bûrg) WV	39·15 N	81·35 W
203	Parkes (pärks) Austl.	33·10 S	148·10 E
109	Park Falls (pärk) Wi.	45·55 N	90·29 W
107	Park Forest Il. (Chicago In.)	41·29 N	87·41 W
112	Parkland (pärk′lănd) Wa. (Seattle In.)	47·09 N	122·26 W
111	Park Ra. Co.	40·54 N	106·40 W
109	Park Rapids Mn.	46·53 N	95·05 W
107	Park Ridge Il. (Chicago In.)	42·00 N	87·50 W
108	Park River ND	48·22 N	97·43 W
112	Parkrose (pärk′rōz) Or. (Portland In.)	45·33 N	122·33 W
213	Park Rynie S. Afr. (Natal In.)	30·22 S	30·43 E
108	Parkston (pärks′tŭn) SD	43·22 N	97·59 W
115	Park View (vū) NM	36·45 N	106·30 W
106	Parkville Md. (Baltimore In.)	39·22 N	76·32 W
113	Parkville Mo. (Kansas City In.)	39·12 N	94·41 W
163	Parla (pär′lä) Sp. (Madrid In.)	40·14 N	3·46 W
164	Parma (pär′mä) It.	44·48 N	10·20 E
107	Parma Oh. (Cleveland In.)	41·23 N	81·44 W
107	Parma Heights Oh. (Cleveland In.)	41·23 N	81·36 W
135	Parnaguá (pär-nä-gwà′) Braz.	9·52 S	44·27 W
135	Parnaíba (pär-nä-ē′bä) Braz.	3·00 S	41·42 W
135	Parnaiba (R.) Braz.	3·57 S	42·30 W
165	Parnassós (Mtn.) Grc.	38·36 N	22·35 E
149	Parndorf Aus. (Vienna In.)	48·00 N	16·52 E
157	Pärnu (pĕr′nōō) Sov. Un.	58·24 N	24·29 E
157	Pärnu (R.) Sov. Un.	58·40 N	25·05 E
157	Pärnu Laht (B.) (läkt) Sov. Un.	58·15 N	24·17 E
184	Paro (pä′rô) Bhu.	27·30 N	89·30 E
203	Paroo (R.) (pä′rōō) Austl.	29·40 S	144·24 E
186	Paropamisus (Mts.) Afg.	34·45 N	63·58 E
165	Páros (pä′rôs) (pā′rŏs) Grc.	37·05 N	25·14 E
165	Páros (I.) Grc.	37·11 N	25·00 E
212	Parow (pă′rō) S. Afr. (In.)	33·54 S	18·36 E
115	Parowan (păr′ô-wăn) Ut.	37·50 N	112·50 W
136	Parral (pär-rä′l) Chile	36·07 S	71·47 W
118	Parral, R. Mex.	27·25 N	105·08 W
202	Parramatta (R.) (păr-ȧ-măt′ȧ) Aust. (Sydney In.)	33·42 S	150·58 E
118	Parras (pär-räs′) Mex.	25·28 N	102·08 W
127	Parrita (pär-rē′tä) C. R.	9·32 N	84·17 W
98	Parrsboro (pärz′bŭr-ô) Can.	45·24 N	64·20 W
104	Parry (I.) (păr′ĭ) Can.	45·15 N	80·00 W
92	Parry, Mt. Can.	52·53 N	128·45 W
75	Parry Is. Can.	75·30 N	110·00 W
105	Parry Sound Can.	45·20 N	80·00 W
92	Parsnip (R.) (pärs′nĭp) Can.	54·45 N	122·20 W
117	Parsons (pär′s′nz) Ks.	37·20 N	95·16 W
105	Parsons WV	39·05 N	79·40 W
160	Parthenay (pär-t′nĕ′) Fr.	46·39 N	0·16 W
164	Partinico (pär-tē′nê-kô) It.	38·02 N	13·11 E
194	Partizansk Sov. Un.	43·15 N	133·19 E
218	Parys (pȧ-rīs′) S. Afr. (Johannesburg & Pretoria In.)	26·53 S	27·28 E
113	Pasadena (păs-ȧ-dē′nȧ) Ca. (Los Angeles In.)	34·09 N	118·09 W
106	Pasadena Md. (Baltimore In.)	39·06 N	76·35 W
119	Pasadena Tx. (In.)	29·43 N	95·13 W
120	Pascagoula (păs-kȧ-gōō′lȧ) Ms.	30·22 N	88·33 W
120	Pascagoula (R.) Ms.	30·52 N	88·48 W
159	Paşcani (pȧsh-kän′′) Rom.	47·46 N	26·42 E
110	Pasco (păs′kō) Wa.	46·13 N	119·04 W
158	Pasewalk (pä′zē-välk) G.D.R.	53·31 N	14·01 E
174	Pashiya (pä′shĭ-yȧ) Sov. Un. (Urals In.)	58·27 N	58·17 E
194	Pashkovo (pȧsh-kô′vô) Sov. Un.	48·52 N	131·09 E
167	Pashkovskaya (pȧsh-kôf′skȧ-yȧ) Sov. Un.	45·29 N	39·04 E
197	Pasig Phil. (In.)	14·34 N	121·05 E
126	Pasión, Rio de la (R.) (rē′ō-dĕ-lä-pä-syōn′) Guat. (In.)	16·31 N	90·11 W
136	Paso de los Libres (pä-sô-dĕ-lôs-lē′brĕs) Arg.	29·33 S	57·05 W
137	Paso de los Toros (tô′rôs) Ur. (Buenos Aires In.)	32·43 S	56·33 W
114	Paso Robles (pä′sō rō′blĕs) Ca.	35·38 N	120·44 W
96	Pasquia Hills (păs′kwē-ȧ) Can.	53·13 N	102·37 W
106	Passaic (pă-sā′ĭk) NJ (New York In.)	40·52 N	74·08 W
106	Passaic R. NJ (New York In.)	40·42 N	74·26 W
98	Passamaquoddy B. (păs′ȧ-mȧ-kwŏd′ĭ) Can.	45·06 N	66·59 W
137	Passa Tempo (pä′s-sä-tĕ′m-pô) Braz. (Rio de Janeiro In.)	21·40 S	44·29 W
158	Passau (päs′ou) F.R.G.	48·34 N	13·27 E
120	Pass Christian (pȧs krĭs′tyĕn) Ms.	30·20 N	89·15 W
151	Passero, C. ((päs-sĕ′rô) It.	36·34 N	15·13 E
136	Passo Fundo (pä′sō fōōn′dōō) Braz.	28·16 S	52·13 W
137	Passos (pä′s-sōs) Braz. (Rio de Janeiro In.)	20·45 S	46·37 W
134	Pastaza (R.) (päs-tä′zä) Peru	3·05 S	76·18 W
134	Pasto (päs′tô) Col.	1·15 N	77·19 W
124	Pastora (päs-tô-rä) Mex.	22·08 N	100·04 W
196	Pasuruan Indon.	7·45 S	112·50 E
157	Pasvalys (päs-vä-lēs′) Sov. Un.	56·04 N	24·23 E
136	Patagonia (Reg.) (păt-ȧ-gō′nĭ-ȧ) Arg.	46·45 S	69·30 W
185	Pātālganga (R.) India (In.)	18·52 N	73·08 E
106	Patapsco R. (pȧ-tăps′kō) Md. (Baltimore In.)	39·12 N	76·30 W
164	Paternò (pä-tĕr-nô′) It.	37·25 N	14·58 E
106	Paterson (păt′ẽr-sŭn) NJ (New York In.)	40·55 N	74·10 W
111	Pathfinder Res. (păth′fīn-dẽr) Wy.	42·22 N	107·10 W
184	Patiāla (pŭt-ê-ä′lŭ) India	30·25 N	76·28 E
136	Pati do Alferes (pä-tē-dô-äl-fĕ′rĕs) Braz. (Buenos Aires In.)	22·25 S	43·25 W
184	Patna (pŭt′nŭ) India	25·33 N	85·18 E

ăt; finăl; rāte; senâte; ärm; ȧsk; sofȧ; fâre; ch-choose; dh-as th in other; bē; êvent; bĕt; recĕnt; cratẽr; g-go; gh-guttural g; bĭt; ĭ-short neutral; rīde; ᴋ-guttural k as ch in German ich;

PRONOUNCING INDEX

Patnanongan — Perkins 327

Page	Name Pronunciation Region	Lat. °′	Long. °′
197	Patnanongan (pät-nä-nôŋ′gän) Phil. (In.)	14·50 N	122·25 E
104	Patoka (R.) (pȧ-tō′kȧ) Ind.	38·25 N	87·25 W
173	Patom Plat. Sov. Un.	59·30 N	115·00 E
135	Patos (pä′tōzh) Braz.	7·03 S	37·14 W
112	Patos (pä′tōs).Wa. (Vancouver In.)	48·47 N	122·57 W
136	Patos, Lago dos (L.) (lä′gō-ȧ dozh pä′tōzh).Braz.	31·15 S	51·30 W
135	Patos de Minas (dē-mē′näzh).Braz.	18·39 S	46·31 W
165	Pátrai (Patras) (pä-trī′) (pä-träs′) Grc.	38·15 N	21·48 E
165	Patraïkós Kólpos (G.) Grc.	38·16 N	21·19 E
	Patras, see Pátrai		
135	Patrocínio (pä-trō-sē′nê-ōō) Braz.	18·48 S	46·47 W
196	Pattani (pät′ȧ-nê) Thai.	6·56 N	101·13 E
98	Patten (păt″n) Me.	45·59 N	68·27 W
119	Patterson (păt′ẽr-sŭn) La.	29·41 N	91·20 W
105	Patton Pa.	40·40 N	78·45 W
127	Patuca, Punta (Pt.) (pōō′n-tä-pä-tōō′kä).Hond.	15·23 N	84·05 W
127	Patuca R. Hond.	15·22 N	84·31 W
105	Patuxent (R.) (pȧ-tŭk′sĕnt) Md.	39·10 N	77·10 W
124	Pátzcuaro (päts′kwä-rô) Mex.	19·30 N	101·36 W
124	Pátzcuaro, Lago de (L.) (lä′gô-dĕ).Mex.	19·36 N	101·38 W
126	Patzicia (pät-zē′syä) Guat.	14·36 N	90·57 W
126	Patzún (pät-zōōn′) Guat.	14·40 N	91·00 W
160	Pau (pō) Fr.	43·18 N	0·23 W
160	Pau, Gave de (strm.) (gäv-dĕ).Fr.	43·33 N	0·51 W
160	Pauillac (pō-yäk′) Fr.	45·12 N	0·46 W
104	Paulding (pôl′dĭng) Oh.	41·05 N	84·35 W
149	Paulinenaue (pou′lē-nĕ-nou-ĕ) G.D.R. (Berlin In.)	52·40 N	12·43 E
	Paulis, see Isiro		
135	Paulistana (pá′ōō-lēs-tá-nä) Braz.	8·13 S	41·06 W
135	Paulo Afonso, Salto (falls) (säl-tô-pou′lōō äf-fôn′sōō).Braz.	9·33 S	38·32 W
218	Paul Roux (pôrl rōō) S. Afr. (Johannesburg & Pretoria In.)	28·18 S	27·57 E
106	Paulsboro (pôlz′bē-rô) NJ (Philadelphia In.)	39·50 N	75·16 W
117	Pauls Valley (pôlz văl′ê) Ok.	34·43 N	97·13 W
134	Pavarandocito (pä-vä-rän-dô-sē′tô) Col. (In.)	7·18 N	76·32 W
174	Pavda (päv′da).Sov. Un. (Urals In.)	59·16 N	59·32 E
164	Pavia (pä-vē′ä) It.	45·12 N	9·11 E
172	Pavlodar (pȧv-lô-dȧr′) Sov. Un.	52·17 N	77·23 E
101	Pavlo′f B. (pȧv-lôf) Ak.	55·20 N	161·20 W
167	Pavlograd (pȧv-lô-grȧt′) Sov. Un.	48·32 N	35·52 E
167	Pavlovsk (pȧv-lôfsk′) Sov. Un.	50·28 N	40·05 E
174	Pavlovsk.Sov. Un. (Leningrad In.)	59·41 N	30·27 E
174	Pavlovskiy Posad (pȧv-lôf′skĭ pô-sȧt′) Sov. Un. (Moscow In.)	55·47 N	38·39 E
136	Pavuna (pä-vōō′nȧ) Braz. (Rio de Janeiro In.)	22·48 S	43·21 W
149	Päwesin (pȧ′vĕ-zēn) G.D.R. (Berlin In.)	52·31 N	12·44 E
117	Pawhuska (pô-hŭs′kȧ) Ok.	36·41 N	96·20 W
117	Pawnee (pô-nē′) Ok.	36·20 N	96·47 W
116	Pawnee (R.) Ks.	38·18 N	99·42 W
117	Pawnee City Ne.	40·08 N	96·09 W
104	Paw Paw (pô′pô) Mi.	42·15 N	85·55 W
109	Paw Paw (R.) Mi.	42·14 N	86·21 W
106	Pawtucket (pô-tŭk′ĕt) RI (Providence In.)	41·53 N	71·23 W
165	Paxoi (I.) Grc.	39·14 N	20·15 E
104	Paxton (păks′tŭn) Il.	40·35 N	88·00 W
192	Payen (pä′yĕn′) China	46·00 N	127·20 E
110	Payette (pȧ-ĕt′) Id.	44·05 N	116·55 W
110	Payette R. Id.	43·57 N	116·26 W
110	Payette R., North Fork Id.	44·35 N	116·10 W
110	Payette R., South Fork Id.	44·07 N	115·43 W
	Payintala, see Tungliao		
170	Pay-Khoy, Khrebet (Mts.) Sov. Un.	68·08 N	63·04 E
91	Payne (L.) (pān) Can.	59·22 N	73·16 W
109	Paynesville (pānz′vĭl) Mn.	45·23 N	94·43 W
	Payo Obispo, see Cuidad Chetumal		
136	Paysandú (pī-sän-dōō′) Ur.	32·16 S	57·55 W
115	Payson (pā′s′n) Ut.	40·05 N	111·45 W
165	Pazardzhik (pä-zȧr-dzhek′) Bul.	42·10 N	24·22 E
164	Pazin (pä′zēn) Yugo.	45·14 N	13·57 E
117	Peabody (pē′bŏd-ĭ) Ks.	38·09 N	97·09 W
99	Peabody Ma. (In.)	42·32 N	70·56 W
93	Peace (R.) Can.	55·40 N	118·30 W
121	Peace Cr. (pēs) Fl. (In.)	27·16 N	81·53 W
106	Peace Dale (dāl) RI (Providence In.)	41·27 N	71·30 W
93	Peace River (rĭv′ẽr) Can.	56·14 N	117·17 W
90	Peacock Hills (pē-kŏk′ hĭlz) Can.	66·08 N	109·55 W
148	Peak, The (Mt.) (pēk) Eng.	53·23 N	1·52 W
204	Peak Hill Austl.	25·38 S	118·50 E
120	Pearl (R.) (pûrl) La.-Ms.	31·06 N	89·44 W
119	Pearland (pûrl′ănd) Tx. (In.)	29·34 N	95·17 W
89	Pearl Harbor Hi.	21·20 N	157·53 W
	Pearl R., see Chu Chiang		
118	Pearsall (pēr′sôl) Tx.	28·53 N	99·06 W
92	Pearse I. (pērs) Can.	54·51 N	130·21 W
213	Pearston (pē′ērstŏn) S. Afr. (Natal In.)	32·36 S	25·09 E
219	Peary Land (Reg.) (pēr′ĭ) Grnld.	82·00 N	40·00 W
116	Pease (R.) (pēz) Tx.	34·07 N	99·53 W
119	Peason (pēz″n) La.	31·25 N	93·19 W
217	Pebane (pĕ-bȧ′nĕ) Moz.	17·10 S	38·08 E
165	Peć (pĕch) Yugo.	42·39 N	20·18 E
118	Pecan Bay (pê-kăn′) Tx.	32·04 N	99·15 W
135	Peçanha (pâ-kän′yȧ) Braz.	18·37 S	42·26 W
109	Pecatonica (R.) (pĕk-ȧ-tŏn-ĭ-kȧ) Il.	42·21 N	89·28 W
170	Pechenga (pyĕ′chĕŋ-gȧ) Sov. Un.	69·30 N	31·10 E
170	Pechora (R.) Sov. Un.	66·00 N	52·30 E
172	Pechora Basin (pyĕ-chô′rȧ) Sov. Un.	67·55 N	58·37 E
170	Pechorskaya Guba (B.) Sov. Un.	68·40 N	55·00 E
115	Pecos (pā′kôs) NM	35·29 N	105·41 W
118	Pecos Tx.	31·26 N	103·30 W
102	Pecos (R.) U. S.	31·10 N	103·10 W
159	Pécs (pāch) Hung.	46·04 N	18·15 E
213	Peddie S. Afr. (Natal In.)	33·13 S	27·09 E
166	Pededze (R.) (pă′dĕd-zĕ) Sov. Un.	57·18 N	27·13 E
113	Pedley (pĕd′lē) Ca. (Los Angeles In.)	33·59 N	117·29 W
135	Pedra Azul (pā′drä-zōō′l) Braz.	16·03 S	41·13 W
135	Pedreiras (pĕ-drā′räs) Braz.	4·30 S	44·31 W
185	Pedro, Pt. (pē′drô) Sri Lanka	9·50 N	80·14 E
126	Pedro Antonio Santos (Sta. Cruz Chico) (pā′drô än-tō′nê-ô sän′tōs) (sän′tä krōōz′ chē′kô) Mex. (In.)	18·55 N	88·13 W
128	Pedro Betancourt (bā-tän-kōrt′) Cuba	22·40 N	81·15 W
136	Pedro de Valdivia (pĕ′drô-dĕ-väl-dē′vê-ä).Chile	22·32 S	69·55 W
136	Pedro do Rio (dô-rē′ô) Braz. (Rio de Janeiro In.)	22·20 S	43·09 W
135	Pedro Juan Caballero (hōōá′n-kä-bäl-yĕ′rō).Par.	22·40 S	55·42 W
122	Pedro Miguel (mê-gāl′).C. Z. (In.)	9·01 N	79·36 W
122	Pedro Miguel Locks (mê-gāl′) C. Z. (In.)	9·01 N	79·36 W
135	Pedro II (pä′drōō sȧ-gōōn′dōō) Braz.	4·20 S	41·27 W
203	Peebinga (pê-bĭng′ȧ) Austl.	34·43 S	140·55 E
154	Peebles (pē′b′lz) Scot.	55·40 N	3·15 W
121	Pee Dee (R.) (pē-dē′) NC-SC	34·01 N	79·26 W
106	Peekskill (pēks′kĭl) NY (New York In.)	41·17 N	73·55 W
205	Pegasus B. (pĕg′ȧ-sŭs) N. Z.	43·18 S	173·37 E
158	Pegnitz R. (pĕgh-nēts) F.R.G.	49·38 N	11·40 E
163	Pego (pā′gō) Sp.	38·50 N	0·09 W
196	Pegu (pĕ-gōō′) Bur.	17·17 N	96·29 E
95	Peguis Ind. Res. Can.	51·20 N	97·35 W
188	Pegu Yoma (Mts.) (pĕ-gōō′yō′mä) Bur.	19·16 N	95·59 E
165	Pehčevo (pĕĸ′chĕ-vô) Yugo.	41·42 N	22·57 E
192	Peian (pĕ′ê-än′) China	48·05 N	126·26 E
191	Pei-Chiang (R.) China (Canton In.)	22·54 N	113·08 E
190	Peich′iao (bā′chiou) China	31·03 N	121·27 E
190	Peich′enghuang Tao (I.) (bā′chĕng′hōōäng′ dou).China	38·23 N	120·55 E
192	Peiching (Peking) China (In.)	39·55 N	116·23 E
93	Peigan Ind. Res. Can.	49·35 N	113·40 W
193	Peihai (Pakhoi) China	21·30 N	109·10 E
193	Peili China	19·08 N	108·42 E
	Peilintzu, see Suihua		
	Peipus, L., see Chudskoye Ozero		
190	Pei Wan (B.) (bā′wäɴ) China	36·21 N	120·48 E
192	Peiyün Ho (R.) China (In.)	39·42 N	116·48 E
104	Pekin (pē′kĭn) Il.	40·35 N	89·30 W
	Peking, see Peiching		
190	Peking-Shih (Mun.) China	40·07 N	116·00 E
152	Pelagie, Isole I. It.	35·46 N	12·32 E
165	Pélagos (I.) Grc.	39·17 N	24·05 E
120	Pelahatchee (pĕl-ȧ-hăch′ê) Ms.	32·17 N	89·48 W
161	Pelat, Mt. (pē-lá′) Fr.	44·16 N	6·43 E
173	Peleduy (pyĕl-yĭ-dōō′ē) Sov. Un.	59·50 N	112·47 E
127	Pelee, Mt. (Vol.) (pē-lā′) Mart. (In.)	14·49 N	61·10 W
104	Pelee, Pt. Can.	41·55 N	82·30 W
104	Pelee I. (pē′lê) Can.	41·45 N	82·30 W
137	Pelequén (pĕ-lĕ-kĕ′n) Chile (Santiago In.)	34·26 S	71·52 W
	Pelew (I.), see Palau		
120	Pelham (pĕl′hăm) Ga.	31·07 N	84·10 W
99	Pelham NH (In.)	42·43 N	71·22 W
109	Pelican (L.) Mn.	46·36 N	94·00 W
95	Pelican B. Can.	52·45 N	100·20 W
128	Pelican Hbr. (pĕl′ĭ-kăn) Ba.	26·20 N	76·45 W
108	Pelican Rapids (pĕl′ĭ-kăn) Mn.	46·34 N	96·05 W
109	Pella (pĕl′ȧ) Ia.	41·25 N	92·50 W
158	Pell-Worm I. (pĕl′vôrm) F.R.G.	54·33 N	8·25 E
90	Pelly (L.) Can.	66·08 N	102·57 W
90	Pelly (R.) Can.	62·20 N	113·26 W
90	Pelly B. (pĕl′ĭ) Can.	68·57 N	91·05 W
101	Pelly Crossing Can.	62·50 N	136·50 W
90	Pelly Mts. Can.	61·50 N	133·05 W
115	Peloncillo Mts. (pĕl-ôn-sĭl′lō) Az.	32·40 N	109·20 W
165	Peloponnisos (Reg.) Grc.	37·28 N	22·14 E
136	Pelotas (pȧ-lō′tăzh) Braz.	31·45 S	52·18 W
107	Pelton (pĕl′tŭn) Can. (Detroit In.)	42·15 N	82·57 W
161	Pelvoux, Mt. (pĕl-vōō′) Fr.	44·56 N	6·24 E
170	Pelym (R.) Sov. Un.	60·20 N	63·05 E
121	Pelzer (pĕl′zẽr) SC	34·38 N	82·30 W
183	Pemanggil (I.) Mala. (Singapore In.)	2·37 N	104·41 E
212	Pemba (pĕm′bȧ) Zambia	15·29 S	27·22 E
217	Pemba (I.) Tan.	5·20 S	39·57 E
217	Pemba Chan. Afr.	5·10 S	39·30 E
108	Pembina (pĕm′bĭ-nȧ) ND	48·58 N	97·15 W
93	Pembina (R.) Can.	53·05 N	114·30 W
95	Pembina (R.) Can.	49·08 N	98·20 W
105	Pembroke (pĕm′ brōk) Can.	45·50 N	77·00 W
99	Pembroke (pĕm′brōk) Ma. (In.)	42·05 N	70·49 W
154	Pembroke Wales	51·40 N	5·00 W
185	Pen India (In.)	18·44 N	73·06 E
162	Penafiél (pā-nȧ-fyĕl′) Port.	41·12 N	8·19 W
162	Penafiel (pā-nyȧ-fyĕl′) Sp.	41·38 N	4·08 W
162	Peñalara (Mtn.) (pā-nyä-lä′rä) Sp.	40·52 N	3·57 W
124	Pena Nevada, Cerro Mex.	23·47 N	99·52 W
197	Penaranda (pā-nyä-rän′dä) Phil. (In.)	15·20 N	120·59 E
162	Peñaranda de Bracamonte (pā-nyä-rän′dä dā brä-kä-mōn′tȧ).Sp.	40·54 N	5·11 W
163	Peña Roya (Mtn.) (pā′nyä rō′yä) Sp.	40·18 N	0·42 W
162	Peñarroya-Peublonuevo (pĕn-yär-rô′yä-pwĕ′blô-nwĕ′vô) Sp.	38·18 N	5·18 W
162	Peñas, Cabo de (C.) (kȧ′bô-dĕ-pā′nyäs).Sp.	43·42 N	6·12 W
136	Penas, Golfo de (gôl-fô-dĕ-pĕ′n-äs).Chile	47·15 S	77·30 W
118	Penasco R. (pā-nȧs′kō) Tx.	32·50 N	104·45 W
192	Pench′i China	41·25 N	123·50 E
214	Pendembu (pĕn-dĕm′bōō) S. L.	8·06 N	10·42 W
108	Pender (pĕn′dẽr) Ne.	42·08 N	96·43 W
134	Penderisco (R.) (pĕn-dĕ-rē′s-kô) Col. (In.)	6·30 N	76·21 W
214	Pendjari, Parc Natl. de la (Natl. Pk.).Dahomey	11·25 N	1·30 E
110	Pendleton (pĕn′d′l-tŭn) Or.	45·41 N	118·47 W
110	Pend Oreille L. (pŏn-dô-rā′) (pĕn-dô-rĕl′).Id.	48·09 N	116·38 W
110	Pend Oreille R. Wa.	48·44 N	117·20 W
135	Penedo (pā-nā′dōō) Braz.	10·17 S	36·28 W
105	Penetanguishene (pĕn′ē-tăŋ-gĭ-shēn′).Can.	44·45 N	79·55 W
190	P′engchengchen (pĕng′chĕng′jĕn).China	36·24 N	114·11 E
190	P′englai (pĕng′lī) China	37·49 N	120·45 E
162	Peniche (pĕ-nē′chȧ) Port.	39·22 N	9·24 W
107	Peninsula (pĕn-ĭn′sū-lȧ) Oh. (Cleveland In.)	41·14 N	81·32 W
148	Penistone (pĕn′ĭ-stŭn) Eng.	53·31 N	1·38 W
124	Penjamillo (pĕn-hä-mēl′yō) Mex.	20·06 N	101·56 W
124	Penjamo (pān′hä-mō) Mex.	20·27 N	101·43 W
148	Penk (R.) (pĕnk) Eng.	52·41 N	2·10 W
148	Penkridge (pĕnk′rĭj) Eng.	52·43 N	2·07 W
164	Penne (pĕn′nā) It.	42·28 N	13·57 E
184	Penner (R.) (pĕn′ẽr) India	14·43 N	79·09 E
158	Pennine Alpi (Mts.) Switz.	46·02 N	7·07 E
154	Pennine Chain (Mts.) (pĕn-īn′) Eng.	53·44 N	1·59 W
104	Pennsboro (pĕnz′bŭr-ô) WV	39·10 N	81·00 W
106	Penns Grove (pĕnz grōv) NJ (Philadelpahia In.)	39·44 N	75·28 W
103	Pennsylvania (State) (pĕn-sĭl-vā′nĭ-ȧ).U. S.	41·00 N	78·10 W
105	Penn Yan (pĕn yăn′) NY	42·40 N	77·00 W
95	Pennycutaway (R.) Can.	56·10 N	93·25 W
166	Peno (L.) (pā′nô) Sov. Un.	56·55 N	32·28 E
98	Penobscot (R.) Me.	45·00 N	68·36 W
98	Penobscot B. (pê-nŏb′skŏt) Me.	44·20 N	69·00 W
204	Penong (pê-nông′) Austl.	32·00 S	133·00 E
127	Penonomé (pā-nō-nô-mā′) Pan.	8·32 N	80·21 W
202	Penrith Austl. (Sydney In.)	33·45 S	150·42 E
120	Pensacola (pĕn-sȧ-kō′lȧ) Fl.	30·25 N	87·13 W
117	Pensacola Dam Ok.	36·27 N	95·02 W
124	Pensilvania (pĕn-sēl-vä′nyä) Col. (In.)	5·31 N	75·05 W
205	Pentecost (I.) (pĕn′tê-kŏst) New Hebr.	16·05 S	168·28 E
93	Penticton Can.	49·30 N	119·35 W
154	Pentland Firth (pĕnt′lănd) Scot.	58·44 N	3·25 W
171	Penza (pĕn′zȧ) Sov. Un.	53·10 N	45·00 E
154	Penzance (pĕn-zăns′) Eng.	50·07 N	5·40 W
158	Penzberg (pĕnts′bĕrgh) F.R.G.	47·43 N	11·21 E
173	Penzhina (R.) (pyĭn-zē-nŭ) Sov. Un.	62·15 N	166·30 E
173	Penzhino Sov. Un.	63·42 N	168·00 E
173	Penzhinskaya Guba (B.).Sov. Un.	60·30 N	161·30 E
104	Peoria (pē-ō′rĭ-ȧ) Il.	40·45 N	89·35 W
124	Peotillos (pā-ō-tel′yōs) Mex.	22·30 N	100·39 W
107	Peotone (pē′ô-tôn) Il. (Chicago In.)	41·20 N	87·47 W
105	Pepacton Res. (pĕp-ȧc′tŭn) NY	42·05 N	74·40 W
128	Pepe, Cabo (kä′bô-pĕ′pĕ) (C.) Cuba	21·30 N	83·10 W
99	Pepperell (pĕp′ẽr-ĕl) Ma. (In.)	42·40 N	71·36 W
165	Peqin (pĕ-kēn′) Alb.	41·03 N	19·48 E
163	Perales (R.) (pā-rä′lās) Sp.	40·24 N	4·07 W
163	Perales de Tajuña (dā tä-hōō′nyä).Sp. (Madrid In.)	40·14 N	3·22 W
98	Percé (pĕr-sā′) Can.	48·31 N	64·13 W
149	Perchtoldsdorf (pĕrk′tôlts-dôrf) Aus. (Vienna In.)	48·07 N	16·17 E
218	Perdekop S. Afr. (Johannesburg & Pretoria In.)	27·11 S	29·38 E
163	Perdido, Mt. (pĕr-dē′dō) Sp.	42·40 N	0·00
120	Perdido (R.) (pĕr-dī′dō) Al.-Fl.	30·45 N	87·38 W
137	Perdões (pĕr-dô′ĕs) Braz. (Rio de Janeiro In.)	21·05 S	45·05 W
134	Pereira (pā-rā′rä) Col. (In.)	4·49 N	75·42 W
167	Perekop (pĕr-ā-kôp′) Sov. Un.	46·08 N	33·39 E
104	Pere Marquette Mi.	43·55 N	86·10 W
167	Pereshchepino (pĕ′rȧsh-chĕ′pê-nô).Sov. Un.	49·02 N	35·19 E
166	Pereslavl′-Zalesskiy (pâ-râ-slăv″l zȧ-lyĕs′kĭ).Sov. Un.	56·43 N	38·52 E
167	Pereyaslav (pĕ-rȧ-yäs′läv) Sov. Un.	50·05 N	31·25 E
137	Pergamino (pĕr-gä-mē′nō) Arg. (Buenos Aires In.)	33·53 S	60·36 W
108	Perham (pĕr′hăm) Mn.	46·37 N	95·35 W
97	Peribonca (R.) (pĕr-ĭ-bŏŋ′kȧ).Can.	49·10 N	71·20 W
160	Périgueux (pā-rē-gû′) Fr.	45·12 N	0·43 E
134	Perija, Sierra de (Mts.) (sē-ĕ′r-rä-dĕ-pĕ-rē′ĸä).Col.	9·25 N	73·30 W
197	Perkam, Tandjung (C.) Indon.	1·20 S	138·45 E
100	Perkins (pĕr′kĕns) Can. (Ottawa In.)	45·37 N	75·37 W

ng-sing; ŋ-baŋk; ɴ-nasalized n; nŏd; cŏmmit; ōld; ôbey; ôrder; fōōd; fŏŏt; ou-out; s-soft; sh-dish; th-thin; pūre; ûnite; ûrn; stŭd; circŭs; ū-as "y" in study; ′-indeterminate vowel.

328 Perlas — Pine Bluff PRONOUNCING INDEX

Page	Name Pronunciation Region	Lat. °'	Long. °'
127	Perlas, Arch. de Las (är-chē-pyĕ'lä-gô-dĕ-läs-pĕr'läs) Pan.	8·29 N	79·15 W
127	Perlas, Laguna las (L.) (lä-gŏŏ'nä-dĕ-läs) Nic.	12·34 N	83·19 W
158	Perleberg (pĕr'lĕ-bĕrg) G.D.R.	53·06 N	11·51 E
174	Perm' (pĕrm) Sov. Un. (Urals In.)	58·00 N	56·15 E
	Pernambuco, see Recife		
135	Pernambuco (State) (pĕr-näm-bōō'kō) Braz.	8·08 S	38·54 W
165	Pernik (pĕr-nēk') Bul.	42·36 N	23·04 E
160	Peronne (pā-rôn') Fr.	49·57 N	2·49 E
125	Perote (pĕ-rō'tĕ) Mex.	19·33 N	97·13 W
194	Perouse Str. Jap.-Sov. Un.	45·45 N	141·38 E
174	Perovo (pâ'rô-vô) Sov. Un. (Moscow In.)	55·43 N	37·47 E
160	Perpignan (pĕr-pē-nyäN') Fr.	42·42 N	2·48 E
113	Perris (pĕr'ĭs) Ca. (Los Angeles In.)	33·46 N	117·14 W
128	Perros, Bahía (B.) (bä-ē'ä-pā'rōs) Cuba	22·25 N	78·35 W
100	Perrot I. (pĕr'ŭt) Can. (Montreal In.)	45·23 N	73·57 W
120	Perry (pĕr'ĭ) Fl.	30·06 N	83·35 W
120	Perry Ga.	32·27 N	83·44 W
109	Perry Ia.	41·49 N	94·40 W
105	Perry NY	42·45 N	78·00 W
117	Perry Ok.	36·17 N	97·18 W
113	Perry Ut. (Salt Lake City In.)	41·27 N	112·02 W
106	Perry Hall Md. (Baltimore In.)	39·24 N	76·29 W
107	Perryopolis (pĕ-rē-ŏ'pō-lĭs) Pa. (Pittsburgh In.)	40·05 N	79·45 W
104	Perrysburg (pĕr ĭz-bûrg) Oh.	41·35 N	83·35 W
116	Perryton (pĕr'ĭ-tŭn) Tx.	36·23 N	100·48 W
101	Perryville (pĕr-ĭ-vĭl) Ak.	55·58 N	159·28 W
117	Perryville Mo.	37·41 N	89·52 W
161	Persan (pĕr-säN') Fr. (In.)	49·09 N	2·15 E
141	Persepolis (Ruins) (pĕr-sĕp'o-lĭs) Iran	30·15 N	53·08 E
	Persia, see Iran		
186	Persian G. (pûr'zhăn) Asia	27·38 N	50·30 E
204	Perth (pûrth) Austl.	31·50 S	116·10 E
105	Perth Can.	44·40 N	76·15 W
154	Perth Scot.	56·24 N	3·25 W
106	Perth Amboy (ăm'boi) NJ (New York In.)	40·31 N	74·16 W
161	Pertuis (pĕr-tüē') Fr.	43·43 N	5·29 E
104	Peru (pē-rōō') Il.	41·20 N	89·10 W
104	Peru In.	40·45 N	86·00 W
133	Peru S. A.	10·00 S	75·00 W
164	Perugia (pā-rōō'jä) It.	43·08 N	12·24 E
113	Peruque (pĕ rō'kĕ) Mo. (St. Louis In.)	38·52 N	90·36 W
167	Pervomaysk (pĕr-vô-mīsk') Sov. Un.	48·04 N	30·52 E
174	Pervoural'sk (pĕr-vô-ōō-rálsk') Sov. Un. (Urals In.)	56·54 N	59·58 E
173	Pervyy Kuril'skiy Proliv (Str.) Sov. Un.	51·43 N	154·32 E
164	Pesaro (pā'zä-rō) It.	43·54 N	12·55 E
135	Pescado (pĕs-kä'dō) (R.) Ven. (In.)	9·33 N	65·32 W
164	Pescara (pās-kä'rä) It.	42·26 N	14·15 E
164	Pescara (R.) It.	42·18 N	13·22 E
171	Peschanyy, Mys (C.) Sov. Un.	43·10 N	51·20 E
164	Pescia (pā'shä) It.	43·53 N	11·42 E
187	Peshāwar (pĕ-shä'wŭr) Pak. (Khyber Pass In.)	34·01 N	71·34 E
165	Peshtera Bul.	42·03 N	24·19 E
109	Peshtigo (pĕsh'tê-gō) Wi.	45·03 N	87·46 W
109	Peshtigo (R.) Wi.	45·15 N	88·14 W
141	Peski Sov. Un.	39·46 N	59·47 E
141	Peski Sov. Un.	44·07 N	63·17 E
174	Peski (pyâs'kĭ) Sov. Un. (Moscow In.)	55·13 N	38·48 E
162	Pêso da Régua (pā-sōō-dä-rā'gwä) Port.	41·09 N	7·47 W
126	Pespire (pās-pē'rā) Hond.	13·35 N	87·20 W
118	Pesqueria, R. (pås-kå-rē'å) Mex.	25·55 N	100·25 W
124	Petacalco, Bahía de (B.) (bä-ē'ä-dĕ-pĕ-tä-kál'kō) Mex.	17·55 N	102·00 W
183	Petaḥ Tiqwa Isr. (Palestine In.)	32·05 N	34·53 E
114	Petaluma (pĕt-á-lōō'må) Ca.	38·15 N	122·38 W
135	Petare (pĕ-tä'rĕ) Ven. (In.)	10·28 N	66·48 W
124	Petatlán (pā-tä-tlän') Mex.	17·31 N	101·17 W
97	Petawawa Can.	45·54 N	77·17 W
126	Petén, Laguna de (L.) (lä-gōō'nä-dĕ-pâ-tān') Guat. (In.)	17·05 N	89·54 W
109	Petenwell Res. Wi.	44·10 N	89·55 W
105	Peterborough (pē'tĕr-bŭr-ô) Can.	44·20 N	78·20 W
203	Peterborough Austl.	32·53 S	138·58 E
148	Peterborough Eng.	52·35 N	0·14 W
154	Peterhead (pē-tēr-hĕd') Scot.	57·36 N	3·47 W
105	Peter Pt. Can.	43·50 N	77·00 W
94	Peter Pond L. (pŏnd) Can.	55·55 N	108·44 W
101	Petersburg (pē'tērz-bûrg) Ak.	56·52 N	133·10 W
117	Petersburg Il.	40·01 N	89·51 W
104	Petersburg In.	38·30 N	87·15 W
107	Petersburg Ky. (Cincinnati In.)	39·04 N	84·52 W
121	Petersburg Va.	37·12 N	77·30 W
149	Petershagen (pĕ'tĕrs-hä-gĕn) G.D.R. (Berlin In.)	52·32 N	13·46 E
149	Petershausen (pĕ'tĕrs-hou-zĕn) F.R.G. (Munich In.)	48·25 N	11·29 E
129	Pétionville Hai.	18·30 N	72·20 W
98	Petitcodiac (pē-tē-kō-dyák') Can.	45·56 N	65·10 W
127	Petite Terre I. (pē-tēt'târ') Guad. (In.)	16·12 N	61·00 W
129	Petit Goâve (pē-tē' gô-áv') Hai.	18·25 N	72·50 W
117	Petit Jean Cr. (pē-tē'zhäN') Ar.	35·05 N	93·55 W
216	Petit Loango Gabon	2·16 S	9·35 E
125	Petlalcingo (pĕ-tläl-sēŋ'gô) Mex.	18·05 N	97·53 W
126	Peto (pĕ'tô) Mex. (In.)	20·07 N	88·49 W
125	Petorca (pā-tōr'kå) Chile (Santiago In.)	32·14 S	70·55 W
104	Petoskey (pê-tŏs'kĭ) Mi.	45·25 N	84·55 W
183	Petra Jordan (Palestine In.)	30·21 N	35·25 E
194	Petra Velikogo, Zaliv (B.) (zä'lĭf pĕt-rä' vĕ-lĭ'kô-vô) Sov. Un.	42·40 N	131·50 E
165	Petrich (pā'trĭch) Bul.	41·24 N	23·13 E
115	Petrified Forest Natl. Park (pĕt'rĭ-fīd fôr'ĕst) Az.	34·58 N	109·35 W
167	Petrikovka (pyĕ'trê-kôf-kä) Sov. Un.	48·43 N	34·29 E
167	Petrikov (pyĕ'trê-kô-v) Sov. Un.	52·09 N	28·30 E
164	Petrinja (pā'trēn-yå) Yugo.	45·25 N	16·17 E
174	Petrodvorets (pyĕ-trô-dvô-ryĕts') Sov. Un. (Leningrad In.)	59·53 N	29·55 E
174	Petrokrepost' (pyĕ'trô-krĕ-pôst) Sov. Un. (Leningrad In.)	59·56 N	31·03 E
104	Petrolia (pê-trō'lĭ-á) Can.	42·50 N	82·10 W
135	Petrolina (pĕ-trō-lē'nå) Braz.	9·18 S	40·28 W
149	Petronell Aus. (Vienna In.)	48·07 N	16·52 E
167	Petropavlovka (pyĕ'trô-päv'lôf-kå) Sov. Un.	48·24 N	36·23 E
174	Petropavlovka. Sov. Un. (Urals In.)	54·10 N	59·50 E
172	Petropavlovsk (pyĕ-trô-päv'lôfsk) Sov. Un.	54·44 N	69·07 E
173	Petropavlovsk-Kamchatskiy (käm-chät'skĭ) Sov. Un.	53·13 N	158·56 E
136	Petrópolis (pâ-trô-pô-lēzh') Braz. (Rio de Janeiro In.)	22·31 S	43·10 W
165	Petroseni Rom.	45·24 N	23·24 E
171	Petrovsk (pyĕ-trôfsk') Sov. Un.	52·20 N	45·15 E
167	Petrovskaya (pyĕ-trôf'skå-yå) Sov. Un.	45·25 N	37·50 E
171	Petrovskoye Sov. Un.	45·20 N	43·00 E
173	Petrovsk-Zabaykal'skiy (pyĕ-trôfskzä-bī-käl'skĭ) Sov. Un.	51·13 N	109·08 E
157	Petrozavodsk (pyā'trô-zå-vôtsk') Sov. Un.	61·46 N	34·25 E
218	Petrus Steyn (pā'trōōs stān') S. Afr. (Johannesburg & Pretoria In.)	27·40 S	28·09 E
166	Petseri (pĕt'sĕ-rē) Sov. Un.	57·48 N	27·33 E
107	Pewaukee (pĭ-wô'kē) Wi. (Milwaukee In.)	43·05 N	88·15 W
107	Pewaukee L. Wi. (Milwaukee In.)	43·03 N	88·18 W
107	Pewee Valley (pe wē) Ky. (Louisville In.)	38·19 N	85·29 W
170	Peza (R.) (pyâ'zá) Sov. Un.	65·35 N	46·50 E
160	Pézenas (pā-zē-nä') Fr.	43·26 N	3·24 E
158	Pforzheim (pfôrts'hīm) F.R.G.	48·52 N	8·43 E
184	Phalodi India	27·13 N	72·22 E
196	Phan Rang (p'hän'räng') Viet.	11·30 N	108·43 E
	Pharsalus, see Fársala		
120	Phenix City (fē'nĭks) Al.	32·29 N	85·00 W
196	Phet Buri Thai.	13·07 N	99·53 E
120	Philadelphia (fĭl-á-dĕl'phĭ-á) Ms.	32·45 N	89·07 W
106	Philadelphia Pa. (Philadelphia In.)	40·00 N	75·13 W
108	Philip (fĭl'ĭp) SD	44·03 N	101·35 W
	Philippeville, see Skikda		
183	Philippines (fĭl'ĭ-pēnz) Asia	14·25 N	125·00 E
198	Philippine Sea (fĭl'ĭ-pēn) Asia	16·00 N	133·00 E
197	Philippine Trench Phil.	10·30 N	127·15 E
	Philippopolis, see Plovdiv		
105	Philipsburg (fĭl'lĭps-bĕrg) Pa.	40·55 N	78·10 W
111	Philipsburg Wy.	46·19 N	113·19 W
203	Phillip (I.) (fĭl'ĭp) Austl.	38·32 S	145·10 E
183	Phillip Chan. Indon. (Singapore In.)	1·04 N	103·40 E
105	Phillipi (fĭ-lĭp'ĭ) WV	39·10 N	80·00 W
109	Phillips (fĭl'ĭps) Wi.	45·41 N	90·24 W
116	Phillipsburg (fĭl'lĭps-bĕrg) Ks.	39·44 N	99·19 W
105	Phillipsburg NJ	40·45 N	75·10 W
196	Phnom Penh (nŏm'pĕn') Camb.	11·39 N	104·53 E
115	Phoenix (fē'nĭks) Az.	33·30 N	112·00 W
106	Phoenix Md. (Baltimore In.)	39·31 N	76·40 W
198	Phoenix Is. Oceania	4·00 S	174·00 W
106	Phoenixville (fē'nĭks-vĭl) Pa. (Philadelphia In.)	40·08 N	75·31 W
196	Phu Bia (Pk.) Laos	19·36 N	103·00 E
196	Phu-Quoc (I.) Camb.	10·13 N	104·00 E
196	Phuket Thai.	7·57 N	98·19 E
190	P'i (R.) (pē') China	32·06 N	116·31 E
164	Piacenza (pyä-chĕnt'sä) It.	45·02 N	9·42 E
164	Pianosa (I.) (pyä-nō'sä) It.	42·13 N	15·45 E
159	Piatra-Neamt (pyä'trá-nä-ämts') Rom.	46·54 N	26·24 E
135	Piauí (State) (pyou'ê) Braz.	7·40 S	42·25 W
135	Piauí, Serra do (Mts.) (sĕr'rá dŏŏ pyou'ê) Braz.	10·45 S	44·36 W
164	Piave (R.) (pyä'vā) It.	45·45 N	12·15 E
164	Piazza Armerina (pyät'så är-må-rē'nä) It.	37·23 N	14·26 E
211	Pibor R. (pē'bôr) Sud.	7·21 N	32·54 E
109	Pic (R.) (pēk) Can.	48·48 N	86·28 W
123	Picara Pt. (pê-kä'rä) Vir. Is. (U. S. A.) (St. Thomas In.)	18·23 N	64·57 W
120	Picayune (pĭk'á yōōn) Ms.	30·32 N	89·41 W
164	Piccole Alpi Dolomitche (Mts.) (pē'k-kô-le-ál'pē-dô-lô'mē-tē'chĕ) It.	46·05 N	12·17 E
163	Pic du Midi d'Ossau (Mtn.) (pēk dü mē-dē' dôs-sō') Fr.	42·51 N	0·25 W
117	Picher (pĭch'ēr) Ok.	36·58 N	94·49 W
193	Pichieh China	27·20 N	105·18 E
137	Pichilemu (pē-chē-lĕ'mōō) Chile (Santiago In.)	34·22 S	72·01 W
125	Pichucalco (pē-chōō-käl'kō) Mex.	17·34 N	93·06 W
125	Pichucalco (R.) Mex.	17·40 N	93·02 W
109	Pickerel (L.) (pĭk'ēr-ĕl) Can.	48·35 N	91·10 W
120	Pickwick (R.) (pĭk'wĭck) Tn.	35·04 N	88·05 W
113	Pico (pē'kô) Ca. (Los Angeles In.)	34·01 N	118·05 W
163	Pico de Aneto (Mtn.) (pē'kō-dĕ-ä-nĕ'tô) Sp.	42·35 N	0·38 E
210	Pico I. (pē'kōō) Açores (In.)	38·16 N	28·49 W
135	Picos (pē'kōzh) Braz.	7·13 S	41·23 W
113	Pico Rivera Ca. (Los Angeles In.)	34·01 N	118·05 W
202	Picton (pĭk'tŭn) Austl. (Sydney In.)	34·11 S	150·37 E
98	Pictou (pĭk-tōō') Can.	45·41 N	62·43 W
183	Pidálion, Akrotírion (C.) Cyprus (Palestine In.)	34·50 N	34·05 E
185	Pidurutalagala Mt. (pē'dōō-rōō-tä'lå-gä'lå) Sri Lanka	12·27 N	80·45 E
109	Pie (I.) (pī) Can.	48·10 N	89·07 W
137	Piedade (pyā-dä'dĕ) Braz. (Rio de Janeiro In.)	23·42 S	47·25 W
120	Piedmont (pēd'mŏnt) Al.	33·54 N	85·36 W
112	Piedmont Ca. (San Francisco In.)	37·50 N	122·14 W
117	Piedmont Mo.	37·09 N	90·42 W
121	Piedmont SC	34·40 N	82·27 W
105	Piedmont WV	39·30 N	79·05 W
162	Piedrabuena (pyā-drä-bwā'nä) Sp.	39·01 N	4·10 W
137	Piedras, Punta (Pt.) (pōō'n-tä-pyĕ'dräs) Arg. (Buenos Aires In.)	35·25 S	57·10 W
118	Piedras Negras (pyā'dräs nā'gräs) Mex.	28·41 N	100·33 W
157	Pieksämäki (pyĕk'sĕ-mĕ-kē) Fin.	62·18 N	27·14 E
162	Piélagos (pyā'lä-gōs) Sp.	43·23 N	3·55 W
164	Piemonte (Reg.) (pyĕ-mô'n-tĕ) It.	44·30 N	7·42 E
218	Pienaars R. S. Afr. (Johannesburg & Pretoria In.)	25·13 S	28·05 E
218	Pienaarsrivier S. Afr. (Johannesburg & Pretoria In.)	25·12 S	28·18 E
108	Pierce (pērs) Ne.	42·11 N	97·33 W
105	Pierce WV	39·15 N	79·30 W
106	Piermont (pēr'mŏnt) NY (New York In.)	41·03 N	73·55 W
108	Pierre (pēr) SD	44·22 N	100·20 W
100	Pierrefonds Can. (Montreal In.)	45·29 N	73·52 W
159	Piešťany (pyĕsh'tyá-nûĭ) Czech.	48·36 N	17·48 E
213	Pietermaritzburg (pê-tēr-má-rĭts-bûrg) S. Afr. (Natal In.)	29·36 S	30·23 E
218	Pietersburg (pē'tērz-bûrg) S. Afr. (Johannesburg & Pretoria In.)	23·56 S	29·30 E
97	Pieton Can.	44·00 N	77·15 W
212	Piet Retief (pēt rĕ-tēf') S. Afr.	27·00 S	30·58 E
159	Pietrosul Pk. Rom.	47·35 N	24·49 E
164	Pieve di Cadore (pyā'vå dē kä-dō'rå) It.	46·26 N	12·22 E
109	Pigeon (R.) (pĭj'ŭn) Can.-Mn.	48·05 N	90·13 W
93	Pigeon L. Can.	53·00 N	114·00 W
100	Pigeon Lake Can. (Winnipeg In.)	49·57 N	97·36 W
117	Piggott (pĭg-ŭt) Ar.	36·22 N	90·10 W
125	Pijijiapan (pēkē-kē-ä'pän) Mex.	15·40 N	93·12 W
149	Pijnacker Neth. (Amsterdam In.)	52·01 N	4·25 E
116	Pikes Pk. (pīks) Co.	38·49 N	105·03 W
121	Pikeville (pīk'vĭl) Ky.	37·28 N	82·31 W
95	Pikwitonei (pĭk'wĭ-tōn) Can.	55·35 N	97·09 W
158	Piła (pē'lá) Pol.	53·09 N	16·44 E
218	Pilansberg (pē'ăns'bûrg) S. Afr. (Johannesburg & Pretoria In.)	25·08 S	26·55 E
137	Pilar (pē'lär) Arg. (Buenos Aires In.)	34·27 S	58·55 W
136	Pilar Par.	27·00 S	58·15 W
197	Pilar (pē'lär) Phil. (In.)	12·55 N	123·41 E
197	Pilar Phil. (In.)	17·24 N	120·36 E
135	Pilar de Goiás (dĕ-gô'yá's) Braz.	14·47 S	49·33 W
112	Pilchuck (R.) Wa. (Seattle In.)	48·03 N	121·58 W
112	Pilchuck Cr. (pĭl'chŭck) Wa. (Seattle In.)	48·19 N	122·11 W
112	Pilchuck Mtn. Wa. (Seattle In.)	48·03 N	121·48 W
136	Pilcomayo (R.) (pēl-cō-mī'ô) Par.	24·45 S	69·15 W
197	Pili (pē'lê) Phil. (In.)	13·34 N	123·17 E
159	Pilica R. (pē-lēt'sä) Pol.	51·00 N	19·48 E
112	Pillar Pt. (pĭl'ár) Can. (Seattle In.)	48·14 N	124·06 W
112	Pillar Rock Wa. (Portland In.)	46·16 N	123·35 W
124	Pilón (R.) (pê-lōn') Mex.	24·13 N	99·03 W
117	Pilot Point (pī'lŭt) Tx.	33·24 N	97·00 W
	Pilsen, see Plzeň		
157	Piltene (pĭl'tĕ-nĕ) Sov. Un.	57·17 N	21·40 E
124	Pimal, Cerra (Mtn.) (sĕ'r-rä-pē-mäl') Mex.	22·58 N	104·19 W
204	Pimba (pĭm'bå) Austl.	31·15 S	146·50 E
213	Pimville (pĭm'vĭl) S. Afr. (Johannesburg & Pretoria In.)	26·17 S	27·54 E
122	Pinacate, Cerro (Mtn.) (sĕ'r-rō-pē-nä-kä'tĕ) Mex.	31·45 N	113·30 W
197	Pinamalayan (pē-nä-mä-lä'yän) Phil. (In.)	13·04 N	121·31 E
196	Pinang Mala.	5·21 N	100·09 E
171	Pinarbaşi (pē'när-bä'shĭ) Tur.	38·50 N	36·10 E
128	Pinar del Río (pē-när' dĕl rē'ô) Cuba	22·25 N	83·35 W
128	Pinar del Río (Prov.) Cuba	22·45 N	83·25 W
197	Pinatubo (Mtn.) (pē-nä-tōō'bô) Phil. (In.)	15·09 N	120·19 E
93	Pincher Creek (pĭn'chēr krēk) Can.	49·29 N	113·57 W
117	Pinckneyville (pĭnk'nĭ-vĭl) Il.	38·06 N	89·22 W
159	Pińczów (pēn''chŏŏf) Pol.	50·32 N	20·33 E
137	Pindamonhangaba (pē'n-dä-mōnyà'n-gä-bä) Braz. (Rio de Janeiro In.)	22·56 S	45·26 W
128	Pinder Pt. Ba.	26·35 N	78·35 W
165	Píndhos Oros (Mts.) Grc.	39·48 N	21·19 E
215	Pindiga Nig.	9·59 N	10·54 E
92	Pine (R.) (pīn) Can.	55·30 N	122·20 W
109	Pine (R.) Wi.	45·50 N	88·37 W
117	Pine Bluff (pīn blŭf) At.	34·13 N	92·01 W

Page	Name Pronunciation Region	Lat. °'	Long. °'
109	Pine City (pīn)....Mn.	45·50 N	93·01 W
204	Pine Creek....Austl.	13·45 S	132·00 E
114	Pine Cr....Nv.	40·15 N	116·17 W
95	Pine Falls....Can.	50·35 N	96·15 W
110	Pine Forest Ra....Nv.	41·35 N	118·45 W
170	Pinega (pê-nyě'gà)....Sov. Un.	64·40 N	43·30 E
170	Pinega (R.)....Sov. Un.	64·10 N	42·30 E
106	Pine Hill (pīn hĭl) NJ (Philadelphia In.)	39·47 N	74·59 W
121	Pine Is....Fl. (In.)	24·48 N	81·32 W
121	Pine Island Sd....Fl. (In.)	26·32 N	82·30 W
106	Pine Lake Estates (lāk ěs-tāts') Ga. (Atlanta In.)	33·47 N	84·13 W
212	Pinelands (pīn'lănds)..S. Afr. (In.)	33·57 S	18·30 E
113	Pine Lawn (lôn) Mo. (St. Louis In.)	38·42 N	90·17 W
92	Pine Pass....Can.	55·22 N	122·40 W
108	Pine Ridge Ind. Res. (rĭj)....SD	43·33 N	102·13 W
164	Pinerolo (pē-nâ-rô'lō)....It.	44·47 N	7·18 E
119	Pines, Lake o' the....Tx.	32·50 N	94·40 W
213	Pinetown (pīn'toun) S. Afr. (Natal In.)	29·47 S	30·52 E
113	Pine View Res. (vū) Ut. (Salt Lake City In.)	41·17 N	111·54 W
120	Pineville (pīn'vĭl)....Ky.	36·48 N	83·43 W
119	Pineville....La.	31·20 N	92·25 W
196	Ping, Mae Nam (R.)....Thai.	17·54 N	98·29 E
191	Pingchoupao..China (Canton In.)	23·01 N	113·11 E
192	Pingchüan....China	40·58 N	118·40 E
183	Pinggir....Indon. (Singapore In.)	1·05 N	101·12 E
193	P'ingho (pĭng'hō')....China	24·30 N	117·02 E
193	Pinghsiang....China	27·40 N	113·50 E
192	Pingliang (pĭng'lyäng')....China	35·12 N	106·50 E
193	P'inglo (pĭng'lō')....China	24·30 N	110·22 E
193	P'ingt'an....China	25·30 N	119·45 E
192	Pingting (pĭng'tĭng')....China	37·50 N	113·30 E
190	P'ingtu (pĭng'too')....China	36·46 N	119·57 E
193	P'ingtung....Taiwan	22·40 N	120·35 E
192	P'ingwu....China	32·20 N	104·40 E
190	P'ingyuan (pĭng'yü-än')....China	37·11 N	116·26 E
137	Pinhal (pē-nyà'l) Braz. (Rio de Janeiro In.)	22·11 S	46·43 W
163	Pinhal Novo (nô vōō) Port. (Lisbon In.)	38·38 N	8·54 W
162	Pinhel (pēn-yěl')....Port.	40·45 N	7·03 W
190	Pinhsien (pĭn'sĭän)....China	38·29 N	117·58 E
192	Pinhsien....China	45·40 N	127·20 E
196	Pini (I.) (pē'nê)....Indon.	0·07 N	98·38 E
165	Piniós (R.)....Grc.	40·33 N	21·40 E
114	Pinnacles Natl. Mon. (pĭn'ȧ-k'lz) Ca.	36·30 N	121·00 W
149	Pinneberg (pĭn'ě-běrg) F.R.G. (Hamburg In.)	53·40 N	9·48 E
112	Pinole (pĭ-nō'lē) Ca. (San Francisco In.)	38·01 N	122·17 W
128	Pinos, Isla de (I.) (ē's-lä-dě-pē'nôs).Cuba	21·40 N	82·45 W
162	Pinos-Puente (pwān'tå)....Sp.	37·15 N	3·43 W
124	Pinotepa Nacional (pē-nô-tā'pä nä-syô-näl').Mex.	16·21 N	98·04 W
205	Pins, Ile des....N. Cal.	22·44 S	167·44 E
159	Pinsk (pên'sk)....Sov. Un.	52·07 N	26·05 E
134	Pinta (I.)....Ec.	0·41 N	90·47 W
100	Pintendre (pěN-tändr') Can. (Quebec In.)	46·45 N	71·07 W
163	Pinto (pēn'tō)...Sp. (Madrid In.)	40·14 N	3·42 W
94	Pinto Butte (pĭn'tō)....Can.	49·22 N	107·25 W
115	Pioche (pī-ō'chē)....Nv.	37·56 N	114·28 W
164	Piombino (pyôm-bē'nō)....It.	42·56 N	10·33 E
111	Pioneer Mts. (pī'ō-nēr')....Mt.	45·23 N	112·51 W
159	Piotrków Trybunalski (pyōtr'kōōv trĭ-bōō-nal'skē).Pol.	51·23 N	19·44 E
120	Piper (pī'pēr)....Al.	33·04 N	87·00 W
113	Piper....Ks. (Kansas City In.)	39·09 N	94·51 W
165	Pipéri (I.) (pē'per-ê)....Grc.	39·19 N	24·20 E
115	Pipe Spring Natl. Mon. (pīp sprĭng).Az.	36·50 N	112·45 W
108	Pipestone (pīp'stōn)....Mn.	44·00 N	96·19 W
108	Pipestone Natl. Mon....Mn.	44·03 N	96·24 W
98	Pipmaucan, Rés. (pĭp-mä-kän') Can.	49·45 N	70·00 W
104	Piqua (pĭk'wȧ)....Oh.	40·10 N	84·15 W
137	Piracaia (pē-rä-kà'yä) Braz. (Rio de Janeiro In.)	23·04 S	46·20 W
137	Piracicaba (pē-rä-sê-kä'bä) Braz. (Rio de Janeiro In.)	22·43 S	47·39 W
137	Piraí (pē-rä-ē') Braz. (Rio de Janeiro In.)	22·38 S	43·54 W
137	Piraíba (R.) (pä-rä-ē'bà) Braz. (Rio de Janeiro In.)	21·38 S	41·29 W
172	Piramida, Gol'tsy (Mtn.) Sov. Un.	54·00 N	96·00 E
164	Piran (pē-rà'n)....Yugo.	45·31 N	13·34 E
137	Piranga (pē-rä'n-gä) Braz. (Rio de Janeiro In.)	20·41 S	43·17 W
137	Pirapetinga (pē-rä-pě-tē'n-gä) Braz. (Rio de Janeiro In.)	21·40 S	42·20 W
135	Pirapora (pē-rà-pō'rȧ)....Braz.	17·39 S	44·54 W
137	Pirassununga (pē-rä-sōō-nōō'n-gä) Braz. (Rio de Janeiro In.)	22·00 S	47·24 W
135	Pirenópolis (pē-rě-nô'pō-lês).Braz.	15·56 S	48·49 W
165	Pírgos....Grc.	37·51 N	21·28 E
135	Piritu, Laguna de (L.) (lä-gōō'nä-dě-pē-rē'tōō) Ven. (In.)	10·00 N	64·57 W
158	Pirmasens (pĭr-mä-zěns')...F.R.G.	49·12 N	7·34 E
158	Pirna (pĭr'nä)....G.D.R.	50·57 N	13·56 E
165	Pirot (pē'rōt)....Yugo.	43·09 N	22·35 E
115	Pirtleville (pûr't'l-vĭl)....Az.	31·25 N	109·35 W
197	Piru (pê-rōō')....Indon.	3·15 S	128·25 E
167	Piryatin (pēr-yä-tēn')....Sov. Un.	50·13 N	32·31 E
164	Pisa (pē'sä)....It.	43·52 N	10·24 E
134	Pisagua (pê-sä'gwä)....Chile	18·43 S	70·12 W
106	Piscataway (pĭs-kă-tă-wā) Md. (Baltimore In.)	38·42 N	76·59 W
106	Piscataway...NJ (New York In.)	40·35 N	74·27 W
134	Pisco (pēs'kō)....Peru	13·43 S	76·07 W
134	Pisco, Bahia de (B.) (bä-ē'ä-dě) Peru	13·43 S	77·48 W
105	Piseco (L.) (pĭ-sā'kô)....NY	43·25 N	74·35 W
158	Pisek (pē'sěk)....Czech.	49·18 N	14·08 E
164	Pisticci (pês-tē'chē)....It.	40·24 N	16·34 E
164	Pistoia (pês-tô'yä)....It.	43·57 N	11·54 E
162	Pisuerga (R.) (pê-swěr'gä)....Sp.	41·48 N	4·28 W
134	Pitalito (pē-tä-lē'tō)....Col.	1·45 N	75·09 W
107	Pitcairn (pĭt'kârn) Pa. (Pittsburgh In.)	40·29 N	79·47 W
199	Pitcairn....Oceania	24·30 S	133·00 W
150	Pite (R.) (pē'tě)....Swe.	66·08 N	18·51 E
150	Piteå (pē'tě-ô')....Swe.	65·21 N	21·10 E
165	Pitesti (pê-těsht'')....Rom.	44·51 N	24·51 E
204	Pithara (pĭt'ărȧ)....Austl.	30·27 S	116·45 E
160	Pithiviers (pē-tē-vyā')....Fr.	48·12 N	2·14 E
106	Pitman (pĭt'mȧn) NJ (Philadelphia In.)	39·44 N	75·08 W
127	Pitons du Carbet, Mt...Mart. (In.)	14·40 N	61·05 W
110	Pit R. (pĭt)....Ca.	40·58 N	121·42 W
213	Pitseng....Leso. (Natal In.)	29·03 S	28·13 E
112	Pitt (R.)....Can. (Vancouver In.)	49·19 N	122·39 W
92	Pitt I....Can.	53·35 N	129·45 W
112	Pittsburg (pĭts'bûrg) Ca. (San Francisco In.)	38·01 N	121·52 W
117	Pittsburg....Ks.	37·25 N	94·43 W
117	Pittsburg....Tx.	32·00 N	94·57 W
107	Pittsburgh...Pa. (Pittsburgh In.)	40·26 N	80·01 W
117	Pittsfield (pĭts'fēld)....Il.	39·37 N	90·47 W
98	Pittsfield....Me.	44·45 N	69·44 W
105	Pittsfield....Ma.	42·25 N	73·15 W
105	Pittston (pĭts'tŭn)....Pa.	41·20 N	75·50 W
190	P'itzuwo (Hsinchin) (pē'zhē'wŏ) (sĭn'jĭn).China	39·25 N	122·19 E
137	Piūi (pē-ōō'ē) Braz. (Rio de Janeiro In.)	20·27 S	45·57 W
134	Piura (pê-ōō'rä)....Peru	5·13 S	80·46 W
174	Piya (pē'yȧ)..Sov. Un. (Urals In.)	58·34 N	61·12 E
113	Placentia (plă-sěn'shĭ-ȧ) Ca. (Los Angeles In.)	33·52 N	117·50 W
99	Placentia....Can.	47·15 N	53·58 W
99	Placentia B....Can.	47·14 N	54·30 W
114	Placerville (plăs'ēr-vĭl)....Ca.	38·43 N	120·47 W
128	Placetas (plä-thā'täs)....Cuba	22·10 N	79·40 W
105	Placid (L.) (plăs'ĭd)....NY	44·20 N	74·00 W
113	Plain City (plān) Ut. (Salt Lake City In.)	41·18 N	112·06 W
107	Plainfield (plān'fēld) Il. (Chicago In.)	41·37 N	88·12 W
107	Plainfield....In. (Indianapolis In.)	39·42 N	86·23 W
106	Plainfield....NJ (New York In.)	40·38 N	74·25 W
117	Plainview (plān'vū)....Ar.	34·59 N	93·15 W
109	Plainview....Mn.	44·09 N	93·12 W
108	Plainview....Ne.	42·20 N	97·47 W
106	Plainview....NY (New York In.)	40·47 N	73·28 W
116	Plainview....Tx.	34·11 N	101·42 W
104	Plainwell (plan'wěl)....Mi.	42·25 N	85·40 W
100	Plaisance (plě-zäNs') Can. (Ottawa In.)	45·37 N	75·07 W
129	Plana or Flat Cays (Is.) (plä'nä) Ba.	22·35 N	73·35 W
160	Plan-de-Cuques (plä-dě-kük') Fr. (In.)	43·22 N	5·29 E
149	Planegg (plä'něg) F.R.G. (Munich In.)	48·06 N	11·27 E
117	Plano (plā'nō)....Tx.	33·01 N	96·42 W
100	Plantagenet (plăN-täzh-nē') Can. (Ottawa In.)	45·33 N	75·00 W
121	Plant City (plȧnt sĭ'tĭ)...Fl. (In.)	28·00 N	82·07 W
119	Plaquemine (plăk'mēn')....La.	30·17 N	91·14 W
162	Plasencia (plä-sěn'thê-ä)....Sp.	40·02 N	6·07 W
174	Plast (plást)..Sov. Un. (Urals In.)	54·22 N	60·48 E
98	Plaster Rock (plȧs'tēr rŏk)...Can.	46·54 N	67·24 W
194	Plastun (plȧs-tōōn')....Sov. Un.	44·41 N	136·08 E
136	Plata, R. de la (R.) (dālä plä'tä) Arg.-Ur.	34·35 S	58·15 W
164	Platani (R.) (plä-tä'nē)....It.	37·26 N	13·28 E
129	Plateforme, Pte....Hai.	19·35 N	73·50 W
101	Platinum (plăt'ĭ-nŭm)....Ak.	59·00 N	161·27 W
134	Plato (plä'tō)....Col.	9·49 N	74·48 W
124	Platón Sánchéz (plä-tōn' sän'chěz).Mex.	21·14 N	98·20 W
108	Platte (plăt)....SD	43·22 N	98·51 W
117	Platte (R.)....Mo.	40·09 N	94·40 W
102	Platte (R.)....U. S.	40·50 N	100·40 W
109	Platteville (plăt'vĭl)....Wi.	42·44 N	90·31 W
117	Plattsburg (plăts'bûrg)....Mo.	39·33 N	94·26 W
105	Plattsburgh....NY	44·40 N	73·30 W
108	Plattsmouth (plăts'mŭth)....Ne.	41·00 N	95·53 W
158	Plauen (plou'ěn)....G.D.R.	50·30 N	12·08 E
129	Playa de Guanabo (plä-yä-dě-gwä-nä'bô) Cuba (In.)	23·10 N	82·07 W
129	Playa de Santa Fe (sä'n-tä-fě') Cuba (In.)	23·05 N	82·31 W
115	Playas (L.) (plä'yȧs)....NM	31·50 N	108·30 W
125	Playa Vicente (vē-sěn'tå)....Mex.	17·49 N	95·49 W
125	Playa Vicente (R.)....Mex.	17·36 N	96·13 W
95	Playgreen L. (plā'grēn)....Can.	54·00 N	98·10 W
105	Pleasant (L.) (plěz'ănt)....NY	43·25 N	74·25 W
106	Pleasant Grove Al. (Birmingham In.)	33·29 N	86·57 W
112	Pleasant Hill Ca. (San Francisco In.)	37·57 N	122·04 W
117	Pleasant Hill....Mo.	38·46 N	94·18 W
112	Pleasanton (plěz'ăn-tŭn) Ca. (San Francisco In.)	37·40 N	121·53 W
117	Pleasanton....Ks.	38·10 N	94·41 W
118	Pleasanton....Tx.	28·58 N	98·30 W
107	Pleasant Plain (plěz'ănt) Oh. (Cincinnati In.)	39·17 N	84·06 W
107	Pleasant Ridge...Mi. (Detroit In.)	42·28 N	83·09 W
107	Pleasure Ridge Park (plězh'ēr rĭj) Ky (Louisville In.)	38·09 N	85·49 W
113	Pleasant View (plěz'ănt vū) Ut. (Salt Lake City In.)	41·20 N	112·02 W
106	Pleasantville (plěz'ănt-vĭl) NY (New York In.)	41·08 N	73·47 W
205	Plenty, B. of (plěn'tê)..N. Z. (In.)	37·23 S	177·10 E
111	Plentywood (plěn'tê-wŏŏd)....Mt.	48·47 N	104·38 W
166	Ples (plyěs)....Sov. Un.	57·26 N	41·29 E
166	Pleshcheyevo (L.) (plěsh-chă'yě-vô).Sov. Un.	56·50 N	38·22 E
98	Plessisville (plě-sē'vēl')....Can.	46·12 N	71·47 W
159	Pleszew (plě'zhěf)....Pol.	51·54 N	17·48 E
161	Plettenberg (plě'těn-běrgh) F.R.G. (Ruhr In.)	51·13 N	7·53 E
165	Pleven (plě'věn)....Bul.	43·24 N	24·26 E
165	Pljevlja (plěv'lyä)....Yugo.	43·20 N	19·21 E
159	Płock (pwôtsk)....Pol.	52·32 N	19·44 E
160	Ploërmel (plô-ěr-mël')....Fr.	47·56 N	2·25 W
165	Ploeşti (plô-yěsht'')....Rom.	44·56 N	26·01 E
165	Plomárion (plô-mä'rĭ-ŏn)....Grc.	38·51 N	26·24 E
160	Plomb du Cantal (Mt.) (plôN'dükäN-täl').Fr.	45·30 N	2·49 E
94	Plonge, Lac la (L.) (plōNzh)..Can.	55·08 N	107·25 W
165	Plovdiv (Philippopolis) (plôv'dĭf) (fĭl-ĭp-ŏp'ō-lĭs)...Bul.	42·09 N	24·43 E
125	Pluma Hidalgo (plōō'mä ē-däl'gō) Mex.	15·54 N	96·23 W
157	Plunge (plōōn'gā)....Sov. Un.	55·56 N	21·45 E
154	Plymouth (plĭm'ŭth)....Eng.	50·25 N	4·14 W
104	Plymouth....In.	41·20 N	86·20 W
105	Plymouth....Ma.	42·00 N	70·45 W
107	Plymouth....Mi. (Detroit In.)	42·23 N	83·27 W
105	Plymouth....NH	43·50 N	71·40 W
121	Plymouth....NC	35·50 N	76·44 W
105	Plymouth....Pa.	41·15 N	75·55 W
127	Plymouth....Montserrat (In.)	16·43 N	62·12 W
109	Plymouth....Wi.	43·45 N	87·59 W
166	Plyussa (R.) (plyōō'sȧ)..Sov. Un.	58·33 N	28·30 E
158	Plzeň (Pilsen)....Czech.	49·46 N	13·25 E
214	Pô....Upper Volta	11·10 N	1·09 W
164	Po, Bocche del (Mouth) (bô'chě-děl-pô').It.	44·57 N	12·38 E
164	Po, Fiume (R.) (fyōō'mě-pō)...It.	45 00 N	11·23 E
192	Poar....China	35·10 N	113·08 E
215	Pobé (pō-bā')....Benin	6·58 N	2·41 E
117	Pocahontas (pō-kȧ-hŏn'tȧs)....Ar.	36·15 N	91·01 W
109	Pocahontas....Ia.	42·43 N	94·41 W
111	Pocatello (pō-kȧ-těl'ō)....Id.	42·54 N	112·30 W
166	Pochěp (pô-chěp')....Sov. Un.	52·56 N	32·27 E
166	Pochinok (pô-chē'nôk)...Sov. Un.	54·14 N	32·27 E
170	Pochinski....Sov. Un.	54·40 N	44·50 E
124	Pochotitán (pô-chô-tē-tá'n)..Mex.	21·37 N	104·33 W
125	Pochutla (San Pedro) (pō-chōō'tlä) (sän pā'drō).Mex.	15·46 N	96·28 W
105	Pocomoke City (pō-kō-mōk')..Md.	38·05 N	75·35 W
105	Pocono Mts. (pō-cō'nō)....Pa.	41·10 N	75·05 W
137	Poços de Caldas (pō-sôs-dě-käl'dàs) Braz. (Rio de Janeiro In.)	21·48 S	46·34 W
210	Poder (pô-dôr')....Senegal	16·35 N	15·04 W
172	Podkamennaya (Stony) Tunguska (R.).Sov. Un.	61·43 N	93·45 E
174	Podol'sk (pô-dôl''sk) Sov. Un. (Moscow In.)	55·26 N	37·33 E
167	Podvolochisk....Sov. Un.	49·32 N	26·16 E
164	Poggibonsi (pôd-jê-bôn'sê)....It.	43·27 N	11·12 E
166	Pogodino (pō-gô'dê-nō)..Sov. Un.	54·17 N	31·00 E
194	Pohai Str. (pō'hī')....China	38·05 N	121·40 E
194	P'ohang....Kor.	35·57 N	129·23 E
190	Pohsien....China	33·52 N	115·47 E
190	Pohsing (pō'hsĭng')....China	37·09 N	118·08 E
127	Pointe-à-Pitre (pwăNt' à pē-tr') Guad. (In.)	16·15 N	61·32 W
100	Pointe-aux-Trembles (pōō-ăNt' ō-tränbl) Can. (Montreal In.)	45·39 N	73·30 W
100	Pointe Claire (pōō-ăNt' klěr) Can. (Montreal In.)	45·27 N	73·48 W
100	Pointe-des-Cascades (kăs-kädz') Can. (Montreal In.)	45·19 N	73·58 W
100	Pointe Fortune (fôr'tün) Can. (Montreal In.)	45·34 N	74·23 W
100	Pointe-Gatineau (pōō-ăNt'gä-tē-nō') Can. (Ottawa In.)	45·28 N	75·42 W
216	Pointe Noire....Con.	4·48 S	11·51 E
101	Point Hope (hōp)....Ak.	68·18 N	166·38 W
104	Point Pleasant (plěz'ănt)....WV	38·50 N	82·10 W
112	Point Roberts (rŏb'ērts) Wa. (Vancouver In.)	48·59 N	123·04 W
161	Poissy (pwà-sē')....Fr. (Paris In.)	48·55 N	2·02 E
160	Poitiers (pwà-tyā')....Fr.	46·35 N	0·18 E
184	Pokaran (pō'kŭr-ŭn)....India	27·00 N	72·05 E
192	Pok'ot'u (pō'kō-tōō')....China	48·45 N	121·42 E
166	Pokrov (pô-krôf)....Sov. Un.	55·56 N	39·09 E
167	Pokrovskoye (pô-krôf'skô-yě) Sov. Un.	47·27 N	38·54 E
166	Pola (R.) (pō'lä)....Sov. Un.	54·44 N	31·53 E
162	Pola de Allade (dě-äl-yä'dě)...Sp.	43·18 N	6·35 W
162	Pola de Laviana (dě-lä-vyä'nä).Sp.	43·15 N	5·29 W
146	Poland (pō'lănd)....Eur.	52·37 N	17·01 E
197	Polangui (pô-läŋ'gē)....Phil. (In.)	13·18 N	123·29 E
174	Polazna (pô'làz-nà) Sov. Un. (Urals In.)	58·18 N	56·25 E
157	Polessk (pô'lěsk)....Sov. Un.	54·50 N	21·14 E
171	Poles'ye (Pripyat Marshes) Sov. Un.	52·10 N	27·30 E
174	Polevskoy (pô-lě'vs-kô'ê) Sov. Un. (Urals In.)	56·28 N	60·14 E
159	Polgár (pôl'gär)....Hung.	47·54 N	21·10 E

330 P'oli — Portsmouth PRONOUNCING INDEX

Page	Name Pronunciation Region	Lat. °'	Long. °'
192	P'oli (pô'lĭ) . . . China	45·40 N	130·38 E
164	Policastro, Golfo di (G.) . . . It.	41·00 N	13·23 E
161	Poligny (pō-lē-nyē') . . . Fr.	46·48 N	5·42 E
165	Políkhnitos . . . Grc.	39·05 N	26·11 E
197	Polillo (pô-lēl'yō) . . . Phil. (In.)	14·42 N	121·56 E
197	Polillo Is. . . . Phil. (In.)	15·05 N	122·15 E
197	Polillo Str. . . . Phil. (In.)	15·02 N	121·40 E
166	Polist' (R.) (pô'lĭst) . . . Sov. Un.	57·42 N	31·02 E
164	Polistena (pō-lēs-tä'nä) . . . It.	40·25 N	16·05 E
165	Poliyiros . . . Grc.	40·23 N	23·27 E
172	Polkan, Gol'tsy (Mtn.) . . . Sov. Un.	60·18 N	92·08 E
163	Pollensa (pōl-yĕn'sä) . . . Sp.	39·50 N	3·00 E
126	Polochic R. (pō-lô-chēk') . . . Guat.	15·19 N	89·45 W
167	Polonnoye (pô'lô-nô-yĕ) . . Sov. Un.	50·07 N	27·31 E
166	Polotsk (pô'lôtsk) . . . Sov. Un.	55·30 N	28·48 E
137	Polpaico (pôl-pá'y-kô) Chile (Santiago In.)	33·10 S	70·53 W
111	Polson (pōl'sŭn) . . . Mt.	47·40 N	114·10 W
167	Poltava (pôl-tä'vä) . . . Sov. Un.	49·35 N	34·33 E
167	Poltava (Oblast) . . . Sov. Un.	49·53 N	32·58 E
166	Pōltsamaa (pŏlt'sȧ-mä) . . . Sov. Un.	58·39 N	26·00 E
166	Pōltsamaa (R.) . . . Sov. Un.	58·35 N	25·55 E
174	Polunochnoye (pô-lōō-nô'ch-nô'yĕ) Sov. Un. (Urals In.)	60·52 N	60·27 E
172	Poluy (R.) (pôl'wê) . . . Sov. Un.	65·45 N	68·15 E
174	Polyakovka (pŭl-yä'kôv-kȧ) Sov. Un. (Urals In.)	54·38 N	59·42 E
170	Polyarnyy (pŭl-yär'nē) . . . Sov. Un.	69·10 N	33·30 E
137	Pomba (pô'm-bȧ) (R.) Braz. (Rio de Janeiro In.)	21·28 S	42·28 W
158	Pomerania (Reg.) (pŏm-ê-rā'nĭ-ȧ) Pol.	53·50 N	15·20 E
156	Pomeranian B. (pō'mĕ-rä-ny-än) G.D.R.	54·10 N	14·20 E
104	Pomeroy . . . Oh.	39·00 N	82·00 W
213	Pomeroy (pŏm'ēr-roi) S. Afr. (Natal In.)	28·36 S	30·26 E
110	Pomeroy (pŏm'ēr-oi) . . . Wa.	46·28 N	117·35 W
163	Pomezia (pô-mĕ't-zyä) It. (Rome In.)	41·41 N	12·31 E
163	Pomigliano d'Arco (pô-mē-lyá'nô-d-ä'r-kô) It. (Naples In.)	40·39 N	14·23 E
108	Pomme de Terre (pôm dē tĕr') . Mn.	45·22 N	95·52 W
113	Pomona (pô-mō'nȧ) Ca. (Los Angeles In.)	34·04 N	117·45 W
165	Pomorie . . . Bul.	42·24 N	27·41 E
184	Pomo Tsho (L.) . . . China	28·00 N	90·30 E
121	Pompano Beach (pŏm'pȧ-nô) Fl. (In.)	26·12 N	80·07 W
163	Pompeii Ruins. . . . It. (Naples In.)	40·31 N	14·29 E
106	Pompton Lakes (pŏmp'tŏn) NJ (New York In.)	41·01 N	74·16 W
126	Pomuch (pô-mōō'ch) . . . Mex. (In.)	20·12 N	90·10 W
108	Ponca (pŏn'kȧ) . . . Ne.	42·34 N	96·43 W
117	Ponca City . . . Ok.	36·42 N	97·07 W
100	Ponce (pōn'sā) P. R. (Puerto Rico In.)	18·01 N	66·43 W
185	Pondicherry (pôn-dĭ-shĕr'ē') (pŏn-dĭ-shĕr'ê) . India	11·58 N	79·48 E
162	Ponferrada (pôn-fĕr-rä'dhä) . . . Sp.	42·33 N	6·38 W
93	Ponoka (pŏ-nō'kȧ) . . . Can.	52·42 N	113·35 W
170	Ponoy . . . Sov. Un.	66·58 N	41·00 E
170	Ponoy (R.) . . . Sov. Un.	65·50 N	38·40 E
210	Ponta Delgada (pôn'tȧ dĕl-gä'dȧ) Açores (In.)	37·40 N	25·45 W
136	Ponta Grossa (grō'sȧ) . . . Braz.	25·09 S	50·05 W
161	Pont-à-Mousson (pôN'tȧ-mōōsôN') Fr.	48·55 N	6·02 E
135	Ponta Porã . . . Braz.	22·30 S	55·31 W
161	Pontarlier (pôN'tȧr-lyā') . . . Fr.	46·53 N	6·22 E
160	Pont-Audemer (pôN'tōd'mâr') . . Fr.	49·23 N	0·28 E
161	Pontcarré (pôN-kȧ-rā') Fr. (Paris In.)	48·48 N	2·42 E
119	Pontchartrain L. (pôN-shȧr-trăn') La.	30·10 N	90·10 W
164	Pontedera (pōn-tȧ-dā'rä) . . . It.	43·37 N	10·37 E
162	Ponte de Sor (pōŋ'tĕ dȧ sōr') . Port.	39·14 N	8·03 W
148	Pontefract (pŏn'tê-frăkt) . . . Eng.	53·41 N	1·18 W
137	Ponte Nova (pô'n-tĕ-nô'vȧ) Braz. (Rio de Janeiro In.)	20·26 S	42·52 W
162	Pontevedra (pôn-tĕ-vĕ-drä) . . . Sp.	42·28 N	8·38 W
	Ponthierville, see Ubundi		
104	Pontiac (pŏn'tĭ-ăk) . . . Il.	40·55 N	88·35 W
107	Pontiac . . . Mi. (Detroit In.)	42·37 N	83·17 W
196	Pontianak (pôn-tê-ä'nȧk) . . . Indon.	0·04 S	109·20 E
183	Pontian Kechil Mala. (Singapore In.)	1·29 N	103·24 E
171	Pontic Mts. . . . Turk.	41·20 N	34·30 E
160	Pontivy (pôN-tê-vē') . . . Fr.	48·05 N	2·57 W
160	Pont-l'Abbe (pôN-lȧ-bā') . . . Fr.	47·53 N	4·12 W
161	Pontoise (pôN-twȧz') Fr. (Paris In.)	49·03 N	2·05 E
174	Pontonnyy (pôn'tôn-nyĭ) Sov. Un. (Leningrad In.)	59·47 N	30·39 E
120	Pontotoc (pŏn-tô-tŏk') . . . Ms.	34·11 N	88·59 W
164	Pontremoli (pôn-trĕm'ô-lē) . . . It.	44·21 N	9·50 E
164	Ponza, Isole di (I.) (ē'sō-lĕ-dē-pōn'tsä) . It.	40·55 N	12·58 E
154	Poole (pōōl) . . . Eng.	50·43 N	2·00 W
106	Poolesville (poolēs-vĭl) Md. (Baltimore In.)	39·08 N	77·26 W
92	Pooley I. (pōō'lē) . . . Can.	52·44 N	128·16 W
134	Poopó, Lago de (L.) (lä'gô-dĕ-pō-ō-pô') . Bol.	18·16 S	67·57 W
134	Popayán (pō-pä-yän') . . . Col.	2·21 N	76·43 W
111	Poplar (pŏp'lēr) . . . Mt.	48·08 N	105·10 W
117	Poplar Bluff (blŭf) . . . Mo.	36·43 N	90·22 W
104	Poplar Plains (plāns) . . . Ky.	38·20 N	83·40 W
100	Poplar Point . . Can. (Winnipeg In.)	50·04 N	97·57 W
111	Poplar R. . . . Mt.	48·34 N	105·20 W
111	Poplar R., West Fork . . . Mt.	48·59 N	106·06 W
120	Poplarville (pŏp'lēr-vĭl) . . . Ms.	30·50 N	89·33 W
125	Popocatépetl (Mtn.) (pô-pô-kä-tā'pĕt'l) . Mex. (In.)	19·01 N	98·38 W
216	Popokabaka (pō'pô-kȧ-bä'kȧ) Zaire	5·42 S	16·35 E
167	Popovka (pô'pôf-kȧ) . . . Sov. Un.	50·03 N	33·41 E
167	Popovka . . . Sov. Un.	51·13 N	33·08 E
165	Popovo (pô'pô-vō) . . . Bul.	43·23 N	26·17 E
184	Porbandar (pōr-bŭn'dŭr) . . . India	21·44 N	69·40 E
134	Porce (pôr-sĕ) (R.) . . . Col. (In.)	7·11 N	74·55 W
92	Porcher I. (pôr'kēr) . . . Can.	53·57 N	130·30 W
162	Porcuna (pôr-kōō'nä) . . . Sp.	37·54 N	4·10 W
101	Porcupine (R.) . . . Ak.	67·00 N	143·25 W
90	Porcupine (R.) . . . Can.	67·38 N	140·07 W
111	Porcupine Cr. (pôr'kū-pīn) . . . Mt.	46·38 N	107·04 W
111	Porcupine Cr. . . . Mt.	48·27 N	106·24 W
95	Porcupine Hills . . . Can.	52·30 N	101·45 W
164	Pordenone (pōr-dȧ-nō'nȧ) . . . It.	45·58 N	12·38 E
164	Poreč (pô'rĕch) . . . Yugo.	45·13 N	13·37 E
157	Pori (Björneborg) (pô'rê) (byûr'nē-bôrgh) . Fin.	61·29 N	21·45 E
137	Poriúncula (po-rēōō'n-kōō-lä) Braz. (Rio de Janeiro In.)	20·58 S	42·02 W
150	Porjus (pôr'yōōs) . . . Swe.	66·54 N	19·40 E
166	Porkhov (pôr'κôf) . . . Sov. Un.	57·46 N	29·33 E
134	Porlamar (pôr-lä-mär') . . . Ven.	11·00 N	63·55 W
160	Pornic (pôr-nēk') . . . Fr.	47·08 N	2·07 W
173	Poronaysk (pô'rô-nīsk) . . . Sov. Un.	49·21 N	143·23 E
158	Porrentruy (pô-räN-trūē') . . . Switz.	47·25 N	7·02 E
156	Porsgrunn (pôrs'grōōn') . . . Nor.	59·09 N	9·36 E
134	Portachuelo (pôrt-ä-chwā'lô) . . Bol.	17·20 S	63·12 W
105	Portage (pôr'tȧj) . . . Pa.	40·25 N	78·35 W
109	Portage . . . Wi.	43·33 N	89·29 W
113	Portage Des Sioux (dē sōō) Mo. (St. Louis In.)	38·56 N	90·21 W
100	Portage-la-Prairie (lä-prā'rĭ) Can. (Winnipeg In.)	49·57 N	98·25 W
92	Port Alberni (pōr äl-bĕr-nē') . . Can.	49·14 N	124·48 W
162	Portalegre (pôr-tä-lā'grĕ) . . . Port.	39·18 N	7·26 W
116	Portales (pôr-tä'lĕs) . . . NM	34·10 N	103·11 W
97	Port-Alfred (ăl'frĕd) . . . Can.	48·20 N	70·53 W
213	Port Alfred (Kowie) (kou'ĭ) S. Afr. (Natal In.)	33·36 S	26·55 E
92	Port Alice (ăl'ĭs) . . . Can.	50·23 N	127·27 W
105	Port Allegany (ăl-ê-gā'nĭ) . . . Pa.	41·50 N	78·10 W
110	Port Angeles (ăn'jē-lĕs) . . . Wa.	48·07 N	123·26 W
129	Port Antonio . . . Jam.	18·10 N	76·25 W
202	Portarlington Austl. (Melbourne In.)	38·07 S	144·39 E
119	Port Arthur . . . Tx.	29·52 N	93·59 W
	Port Arthur, see Lüshun		
203	Port Augusta (ô-gŭs'tȧ) . . . Austl.	32·28 S	137·50 E
99	Port au Port B. (pôr'tō pōr') . . Can.	48·41 N	58·45 W
129	Port-au-Prince (prăNs') . . . Hai.	18·35 N	72·20 W
104	Port Austin (ôs'tĭn) . . . Mi.	44·00 N	83·00 W
99	Port aux Basques . . . Can.	47·36 N	59·09 W
196	Port Blair (blâr) Andaman & Nicobar Is.	12·07 N	92·45 E
119	Port Bolivar (bŏl'ĭ-vȧr) . . Tx. (In.)	29·22 N	94·46 W
98	Port Borden (bôr'dĕn) . . . Can.	46·15 N	63·42 W
210	Port-Bouët . . . Ivory Coast	5·24 N	3·56 W
98	Port-Cartier . . . Can.	50·01 N	66·53 W
106	Port Chester (chĕs'tēr) NY (New York In.)	40·59 N	73·40 W
112	Port Chicago (shĭ-kô'gō) Ca. (San Francisco In.)	38·03 N	122·01 W
104	Port Clinton (klĭn'tŭn) . . . Oh.	41·30 N	83·00 W
97	Port Colborne . . . Can.	42·53 N	79·13 W
112	Port Coquitlam (kô-kwĭt'lȧm) Can. (Vancouver In.)	49·16 N	122·46 W
100	Port Credit (krĕd'ĭt) Can. (Toronto In.)	43·33 N	79·35 W
160	Port-de-Bouc (pôr-dē-bōōk') Fr. (In.)	43·24 N	5·00 E
217	Port de Kindu . . . Zaire	2·57 S	25·56 E
129	Port de Paix (pĕ) . . . Hai.	19·55 N	72·50 W
183	Port Dickson (dĭk'sŭn) Mala. (Singapore In.)	2·33 N	101·49 E
112	Port Discovery (B.) (dĭs-kŭv'ēr-ĭ) Wa. (Seattle In.)	48·05 N	122·55 W
213	Port Edward (ĕd'wērd) S. Afr. (Natal In.)	31·04 S	30·14 E
98	Port Elgin (ĕl'jĭn) . . . Can.	46·03 N	64·05 W
213	Port Elizabeth (ê-lĭz'ȧ-bĕth) S. Afr. (Natal In.)	33·57 S	25·37 E
120	Porterdale (pōr'tēr-dāl) . . . Ga.	33·34 N	83·53 W
114	Porterville (pōr'tēr-vĭl) . . . Ca.	36·03 N	119·05 W
136	Portezuelo de Tupungato (Vol.) (pôr-tĕ-zwĕ-lō-dĕ-tōō-pōō'n-gä-tô) Arg.-Chile	33·30 S	69·52 W
	Port Francqui, see Ilebo		
112	Port Gamble (găm'bŭl) Wa. (Seattle In.)	47·52 N	122·36 W
112	Port Gamble Ind. Res. Wa. (Seattle In.)	47·54 N	122·33 W
216	Port-Gentil (zhäN-tē') . . . Gabon	0·43 S	8·47 E
120	Port Gibson (gĭb'sŭn) . . . Ms.	31·56 N	90·57 W
215	Port Harcourt (här'kŭrt) . . . Nig.	4·43 N	7·05 E
92	Port Hardy (här'dĭ) . . . Can.	50·43 N	127·29 W
99	Port Hawkesbury . . . Can.	45·37 N	61·21 W
204	Port Hedland (hĕd'lănd) . . . Austl.	20·30 S	118·30 E
110	Porthill . . . Id.	49·00 N	116·30 W
99	Port Hood (hōōd) . . . Can.	46·01 N	61·32 W
105	Port Hope (hōp) . . . Can.	43·55 N	78·10 W
104	Port Huron (hū'rŏn) . . . Mi.	43·00 N	82·30 W
163	Portici (pôr'tê-chê) . It. (Naples In.)	40·34 N	14·20 E
137	Portillo (pôr-tē'l-yô) Chile (Santiago In.)	32·51 S	70·09 W
162	Portimão (pôr-tē-mo'uN) . . . Port.	37·09 N	8·34 W
106	Port Jervis (jûr'vĭs) NY (New York In.)	41·22 N	74·41 W
183	Port Kelang . Mala. (Singapore In.)	3·00 N	101·25 E
203	Portland (pōrt'lănd) . . . Austl.	38·20 S	142·40 E
104	Portland . . . In.	40·25 N	85·00 W
98	Portland . . . Me.	43·40 N	70·16 W
104	Portland . . . Mi.	42·50 N	85·00 W
112	Portland . . . Or. (Portland In.)	45·31 N	123·41 W
119	Portland . . . Tx.	27·53 N	97·20 W
128	Portland Bight (B.) . . . Jam.	17·45 N	77·05 W
92	Portland Can. . . . Ak.	55·10 N	130·08 W
92	Portland Inlet . . . Can.	54·50 N	130·15 W
128	Portland Pt. . . . Jam.	17·40 N	77·20 W
119	Port Lavaca (lȧ-vä'kȧ) . . . Tx.	28·36 N	96·38 W
203	Port Lincoln (lĭŋ'kŭn) . . . Austl.	34·39 S	135·50 E
112	Port Ludlow (lŭd'lō) Wa. (Seattle In.)	47·26 N	122·41 W
	Port Lyautey, see Kenitra		
203	Port Macquarie (mȧ-kwŏ'rĭ) . Austl.	31·25 S	152·45 E
112	Port Madison Ind. Res. (măd'ĭ-sŭn) . Wa. (Seattle In.)	47·46 N	122·38 W
128	Port Maria (mȧ-rī'ȧ) . . . Jam.	18·20 N	76·55 W
98	Port-Menier (mē-nyā') . . . Can.	49·49 N	64·20 W
112	Port Moody (mōōd'ĭ) Can. (Vancouver In.)	49·17 N	122·51 W
197	Port Moresby (mōrz'bē) Pap. N. Gui.	9·34 S	147·20 E
119	Port Neches (nĕch'ĕz) . . . Tx.	29·59 N	93·57 W
95	Port Nelson (nĕl'sŭn) . . . Can.	57·03 N	92·36 W
98	Portneuf-Sur-Mer (pôr-nûf'sür mēr) . Can.	48·36 N	69·06 W
212	Port Nolloth (nŏl'ŏth) . . . S. Afr.	29·10 S	17·00 E
162	Pôrto (Oporto) (pōr'tōō) . . . Port.	41·10 N	8·38 W
134	Pôrto Acre (ä'krĕ) . . . Braz.	9·38 S	67·34 W
136	Pôrto Alegre (ä-lā'grĕ) . . . Braz.	29·58 S	51·11 W
216	Porto Alexandre (á-lĕ-zhän'drĕ) Ang.	15·49 S	11·53 E
216	Porto Amboim . . . Ang.	11·01 S	13·45 E
217	Porto Amélia (ȧ-mĕ'lyä) . . . Moz.	12·58 S	40·30 E
127	Portobelo (pôr'tô-bā'lô) . . . Pan.	9·32 N	79·40 W
135	Pôrto de Pedras (pā'dräzh) . . Braz.	9·09 S	35·20 W
137	Pôrto Feliz (fĕ-lē's) Braz. (Rio de Janeiro In.)	23·12 S	47·30 W
164	Portoferraio (pōr'tô-fĕr-rä'yō) . . It.	42·47 N	10·20 E
135	Port of Spain (spān) . . . Trin.	10·44 N	61·24 W
164	Portogruaro (pōr'tô-grōō-ä'rō) . . It.	45·48 N	12·49 E
114	Portola (pôr'tô-lȧ) . . . Ca.	39·47 N	120·29 W
135	Pôrto Mendes (mĕ'n-dĕs) . . . Braz.	24·41 S	54·13 W
135	Pôrto Murtinho (mōōr-tēn'yōō) Braz.	21·43 S	57·43 W
135	Pôrto Nacional (nȧ-syô-näl') . Braz.	10·43 S	48·14 W
215	Porto Novo (pōr'tô-nō'vō) Benin	6·29 N	2·37 E
112	Port Orchard (ôr'chērd) Wa. (Seattle In.)	47·32 N	122·38 W
112	Port Orchard (B.) . Wa. (Seattle In.)	47·40 N	122·39 W
210	Porto Santo, Ilha de (I.) (säN'tōō) . Mad. Is.	32·41 N	16·15 W
135	Pôrto Seguro (sā-gōō'rōō) . . . Braz.	16·26 S	38·59 W
164	Porto Torres (tôr'rĕs) . . . It.	40·49 N	8·25 E
164	Porto-Vecchio (vĕk'ē-ō) . . . Fr.	41·36 N	9·17 E
134	Pôrto Velho (vāl'yōō) . . . Braz.	8·45 S	63·43 W
134	Portoviejo (pôr-tō-vyā'hō) . . . Ec.	1·11 S	80·28 W
203	Port Phillip B. (fĭl'ĭp) . . . Austl.	37·57 S	144·50 E
203	Port Pirie (pĭ'rē) . . . Austl.	33·10 S	138·00 E
90	Port Radium (rā'dē-ŭm) . . . Can.	66·06 N	118·03 W
128	Port Royal (B.) (roi'ăl) . . . Jam.	17·50 N	76·45 W
	Port Said, see Būr Sa'īd		
213	Port St. Johns (sânt jŏnz) S. Afr. (Natal In.)	31·37 S	29·32 E
213	Port Shepstone (shĕps'tŭn) S. Afr. (Natal In.)	30·45 S	30·23 E
154	Portsmouth (pôrts'mŭth) . . . Eng.	50·45 N	1·03 W
105	Portsmouth . . . NH	43·05 N	70·50 W
104	Portsmouth . . . Oh.	38·45 N	83·00 W
106	Portsmouth . . . Va. (Norfolk In.)	36·50 N	76·19 W

ăt; finăl; rāte; senâte; ärm; ȧsk; sofȧ; fâre; ch-choose; dh-as th in other; bē; êvent; bĕt; recĕnt; cratēr; g-go; gh-guttural g; bĭt; ĭ-short neutral; rīde; κ-guttural k as ch in German ich;

PRONOUNCING INDEX

Portsmouth — Providence 331

Page	Name Pronunciation Region	Lat. °'	Long. °'
127	Portsmouth.......Dominica (In.)	15·33 N	61·28 W
	Port Sudan, see Būr Sūdān		
120	Port Sulphur (sŭl'fẽr)........La.	29·28 N	89·41 W
112	Port Susan (B.) (sū-zȧn') Wa. (Seattle In.)	48·11 N	122·25 W
121	Port Tampa (tăm'pȧ)....Fl. (In.)	27·50 N	82·30 W
112	Port Townsend (tounz'ĕnd) Wa. (Seattle In.)	48·07 N	122·46 W
112	Port Townsend (B.) Wa. (Seattle In.)	48·05 N	122·47 W
146	Portugal (pōr'tu-găl)........Eur.	38·15 N	8·08 W
162	Portugalete (pōr-tōō-gä-lā'tä) Sp.	43·18 N	3·05 W
216	Portugália................Ang.	7·20 S	20·47 E
	Portuguese East Africa, see Mozambique		
	Portuguese India, see Gôa, Daman & Diu		
	Portuguese West Africa, see Angola		
160	Port Vendres (pôr väɴ'dr')....Fr.	42·32 N	3·07 E
203	Port Wakefield (wāk'fēld)..Austl.	34·12 S	138·10 E
106	Port Washington (wôsh'ĭng-tŭn) NY (New York In.)	40·49 N	73·42 W
109	Port Washington............Wi.	43·24 N	87·52 W
136	Posadas (pō-sä'dhäs)........Arg.	27·32 S	55·56 W
162	Posadas (pō-sä-däs)..........Sp.	37·48 N	5·09 W
190	Poshan (pō'shän')..........China	36·32 N	117·51 E
166	Poshekhon 'ye Volodarsk (pô-shyĕ'κôn-yĕ vôl'ô-dȧrsk) Sov. Un.	58·31 N	39·07 E
196	Poso, Danau (L.) (pō'sō)...Indon.	2·00 S	119·40 E
174	Pospelkova (pôs-pyĕl'kô-vȧ) Sov. Un. (Urals In.)	59·25 N	60·50 E
112	Possession Sd. (pŏ-zĕsh'ŭn) Wa. (Seattle In.)	47·59 N	122·17 W
118	Possum Kingdom Res. (pŏs'ŭm kĭng'dŭm).Tx.	32·58 N	98·12 W
116	Post (pōst)..................Tx.	33·12 N	101·21 W
210	Post Maurice Cortier (Bidon Cinq).Alg.	22·22 N	0·33 E
164	Postojna (pōs-tōynȧ).......Yugo.	45·45 N	14·13 E
194	Pos'yet (pos-yĕt').......Sov. Un.	42·27 N	130·47 E
117	Potawatomi Ind. Res. (pŏt-ȧ-wä'tō mē).Ks.	39·30 N	96·11 W
218	Potchefstroom (pŏch'ĕf-strōm) S. Afr. (Johannesburg & Pretoria In.)	26·42 S	27·06 E
117	Poteau (pô-tō').............Ok.	35·03 N	94·37 W
118	Poteet (pô-tēt).............Tx.	29·05 N	98·35 W
164	Potenza (pô-tĕnt'sä)..........It.	40·39 N	15·49 E
164	Potenza (R.)................It.	43·09 N	13·00 E
218	Potgietersrus (pôt-κē'tĕrs-rûs) S. Afr. (Johannesburg & Pretoria In.)	24·09 S	29·04 E
110	Potholes Res...............Wa.	47·00 N	119·20 W
171	Poti (pô'tē)............Sov. Un.	42·10 N	41·40 E
215	Potiskum..................Nig.	11·43 N	11·05 E
106	Potomac (pô-tō'măk) Md. (Baltimore In.)	39·01 N	77·13 W
105	Potomac (R.) (pô-tō'măk)....Va.	38·15 N	76·55 W
134	Potosí (pō-tô-sē')...........Bol.	19·42 S	65·42 W
117	Potosi (pŏ-tō'sĭ).............Mo.	37·56 N	90·46 W
118	Potosi, R. (pō-tô-sē').......Mex.	25·04 N	99·36 W
190	Pot'ou (bŭ''tō)............China	38·05 N	116·35 E
126	Potrerillos (pō-trȧ-rēl'yôs)..Hond.	15·13 N	87·58 W
149	Potsdam (pôts'däm) G.D.R. (Berlin In.)	52·24 N	13·04 E
105	Potsdam (pŏts'dăm).........NY	44·40 N	75·00 W
149	Potsdam (Dist.) (pôts'däm) G.D.R. (Berlin In.)	52·31 N	12·45 E
149	Pottenstein.....Aus. (Vienna In.)	47·58 N	16·06 E
148	Potters Bar (pŏt'ẽrz bär) Eng. (London In.)	51·41 N	0·12 W
105	Pottstown (pŏts'toun)........Pa.	40·15 N	75·40 W
105	Pottsville (pŏts'vĭl)...........Pa.	40·40 N	76·15 W
105	Poughkeepsie (pŏ-kĭp'sē)......NY	41·45 N	73·55 W
112	Poulsbo (pōlz'bōō) Wa. (Seattle In.)	47·44 N	122·38 W
148	Poulton-le-Fylde (pōl'tŭn-lē-fīld') Eng.	53·52 N	2·59 W
137	Pouso Alegre (pō'zōō ä-lā'grĕ) Braz. (Rio de Janeiro In.)	22·13 S	45·56 W
162	Póvoa de Varzim (pō-vō'ȧ dā vär'zēɴ).Port.	41·23 N	8·44 W
111	Powder River..............Wy.	43·06 N	106·55 W
111	Powder R. (pou'dẽr).....Mt.-Wy.	45·18 N	105·37 W
110	Powder R...................Or.	44·55 N	117·35 W
111	Powder R., South Fk.........Wy.	43·13 N	106·54 W
111	Powell (pou'ĕl)...............Wy.	44·44 N	108·44 W
115	Powell, L....................Ut.	37·26 N	110·25 W
92	Powell L....................Can.	50·10 N	124·13 W
119	Powell Pt...................Ba.	24·50 N	76·20 W
120	Powell Res.............Ky.-Tn.	36·30 N	83·35 W
92	Powell River...............Can.	49·52 N	124·33 W
193	Poyang (pō'yäng)..........China	29·00 N	116·42 E
193	P'oyang Hu (L.)............China	29·20 N	116·28 E
109	Poygan (R.) (poi'gȧn)........Wi.	44·10 N	89·05 W
165	Požarevac (pô'zhȧ'rĕ-vȧts)..Yugo.	44·38 N	21·12 E
158	Poznań (pôz'nän'')...........Pol.	52·24 N	16·55 E
162	Pozoblanco (pô-thō-blän'kō)...Sp.	38·23 N	4·50 W
125	Pozo Rica (pô-zô-rē'kä).....Mex.	20·32 N	97·25 W
124	Pozos (pô'zōs).............Mex.	22·05 N	100·50 W
163	Pozuelo de Alarcón (pô-thwā'lō dā ä-lär-kōn') Sp. (Madrid In)	40·27 N	3·49 W
163	Pozzuoli (pôt-swô'lē) It. (Naples In.)	40·34 N	14·08 E
214	Pra (R.) (prȧ)............Ghana	5·45 N	1·35 W
166	Pra (R.)...............Sov. Un.	55·00 N	40·13 E
196	Prachin Buri (prä'chēn).....Thai.	13·59 N	101·15 E
134	Pradera (prä-dĕ'rä).....Col. (In.)	3·24 N	76·13 W
160	Prades (prȧd)................Fr.	42·37 N	2·23 E
134	Prado (prädô)..........Col. (In.)	3·44 N	74·55 W
113	Prado Res. (prä'dō) Ca. (Los Angeles In.)	33·45 N	117·40 W
137	Prados (prȧ'dôs) Braz. (Rio de Janeiro In.)	21·05 S	44·04 W
	Prague, see Praha		
158	Praha (Prague) (prä'hȧ) (präg) Czech.	59·05 N	14·30 E
210	Praia (prä'yȧ).........C. V. (In.)	15·00 N	23·30 W
136	Praia Funda, Ponta da (Pt.) (pôn'tä-dȧ-prä'yȧ-fōō'n-dä) Braz. (Rio de Janeiro In.)	23·04 S	43·34 W
109	Prairie du Chien (prā'rĭ dōō shēn') Wi.	43·02 N	91·10 W
100	Prairie Grove (prā'rĭ grōv) Can. (Winnipeg In.)	49·48 N	96·57 W
109	Prairie Island Ind. Res.......Mn.	44·42 N	92·32 W
100	Prairies, R. des (rē-vyâr' dā prȧ-rē') Can. (Montreal In.)	45·40 N	73·34 W
193	Pratas (Is.)...............China	20·40 N	116·30 E
164	Prato (prä'tō)................It.	43·53 N	11·03 E
160	Prats-de-Mollo (prȧ-dē-mô-lō').Fr.	42·26 N	2·36 E
116	Pratt (prăt)..................Ks.	37·37 N	98·43 W
120	Prattville (prăt'vĭl)..........Al.	32·28 N	86·27 W
157	Pravdinsk...............Sov. Un.	54·26 N	20·11 E
174	Pravdinskiy (prȧv-dĕn'skĭ) Sov, Un. (Moscow In.)	56·03 N	37·52 E
162	Pravia (prä'vê-ä).............Sp.	43·30 N	6·08 W
157	Pregolya (R.) (prĕ-gô'lä)..Sov. Un.	54·37 N	20·50 E
118	Premont (prê-mŏnt')..........Tx.	27·20 N	98·07 W
158	Prenzlau (prĕnts'lou).....G.D.R.	53·19 N	13·52 E
159	Přerov (przhĕ'rôf).........Czech.	49·28 N	17·28 E
125	Presa Aleman (L.) (prä'sä-lĕ-mȧ'n).Mex.	18·20 N	96·35 W
125	Presa de Infiernillo (Res.)...Mex.	18·50 N	101·50 W
148	Prescot (prĕs'kŭt)...........Eng.	53·25 N	2·48 W
115	Prescott (prĕs'kŏt)...........Az.	34·30 N	112·30 W
117	Prescott......................Ar.	33·47 N	93·23 W
105	Prescott (prĕs'kŭt)..........Can.	44·45 N	75·35 W
113	Prescott (prĕs'kŏt) Wi. (Minneapolis, St. Paul In.)	44·45 N	92·48 W
108	Presho (prĕsh'ô).............SD	43·56 N	100·04 W
136	Presidencia Rogue Sáenz Peña (prĕ-sē-dĕ'n-sēȧ-rô'kĕ-sȧ'ĕnz-pĕ'n-yȧ).Arg.	26·52 S	60·15 W
135	Presidente Epitácio (prā-sê-dĕn'tĕ ȧ-pê-tä'syōō) Braz.	21·56 S	52·01 W
118	Presidio (prĕ-sĭ'dĭ-ô)..........Tx.	29·33 N	104·23 W
124	Presidio, Rio del (R.) (rê'ō-dĕl-prĕ-sĕ'dyô).Mex.	23·54 N	105·44 W
159	Prešov (prĕ'shôf)..........Czech.	49·00 N	21·18 E
165	Prespa (L.) (prĕs'pä)...Alb.-Yugo.	40·49 N	20·50 E
135	Prespuntal (R.) (prĕs-pōōn-täl') Ven. (In.)	9·55 N	64·32 W
98	Presque Isle (prĕsk'ēl').......Me.	46·41 N	68·03 W
137	Pressbaum......Aus. (Vienna In.)	48·12 N	16·06 E
214	Prestea....................Ghana	5·27 N	2·08 W
136	Preston (prĕs'tŭn)..........Eng.	53·46 N	2·42 W
111	Preston (pres'tŭn)............Id.	42·05 N	111·54 W
109	Preston (prĕs'tŭn)............Mn.	43·42 N	92·06 W
112	Preston.........Wa. (Seattle In.)	47·31 N	121·56 W
104	Prestonburg (prĕs'tŭn-bûrg)..Ky.	37·35 N	82·50 W
136	Prestwich (prĕst'wĭch).......Eng.	53·32 N	2·17 W
213	Pretoria (prē-tō'rĭ-ȧ).......S. Afr. (Johannesburg & Pretoria In.)	25·43 S	28·16 E
213	Pretoria North (prē-tô'rĭ-ȧ nōōrd) S. Afr. (Johannesburg & Pretoria In.)	25·41 S	28·11 E
165	Préveza (prĕ'vȧ-zä)..........Grc.	38·58 N	20·44 E
101	Pribilof (Is.) (prĭ'bĭ-lof).......Ak.	57·00 N	169·20 W
165	Priboj (prē'boi).............Yugo.	43·33 N	19·33 E
115	Price (prīs)...................Ut.	39·35 N	110·50 W
115	Price (R.)....................Ut.	39·21 N	110·35 W
100	Priddis (prĭd'dĭs) Can. (Calgary In.)	50·53 N	114·20 W
100	Priddis Cr.....Can. (Calgary In.)	50·56 N	114·32 W
162	Priego (prê-ā'gō).............Sp.	37·27 N	4·13 W
157	Prienai (prê-ĕn'ī)........Sov. Un.	54·38 N	23·56 E
212	Prieska (prê-ĕs'kȧ)........S. Afr.	29·40 S	22·50 E
110	Priest L. (prēst).............Id.	48·30 N	116·43 W
110	Priest Rapids Dam..........Wa.	46·39 N	119·55 W
110	Priest Rapids Res............Wa.	46·42 N	119·58 W
174	Priiskovaya (prĭ-ēs'kô-vȧ-yȧ) Sov. Un. (Urals In.)	60·50 N	58·55 E
164	Prijedor (prē'yĕ-dôr).......Yugo.	44·58 N	16·43 E
165	Prijepolje (prē'yĕ-pô'lyĕ)...Yugo.	43·22 N	19·41 E
165	Prilep (prē'lĕp).............Yugo.	41·20 N	21·35 E
167	Priluki (prê-lōō'kê)......Sov. Un.	50·36 N	32·21 E
157	Primorsk (prē-môrsk')...Sov. Un.	60·24 N	28·35 E
167	Primorsko-Akhtarskaya (prē-môr'skô äκ-tär'skĭ-ê) Sov. Un.	46·03 N	38·09 E
213	Primrose.................S. Afr. (Johannesburg & Pretoria In.)	26·11 S	28·11 E
94	Primrose L.................Can.	54·55 N	109·45 W
94	Prince Albert (prĭns ăl'bẽrt)..Can.	53·12 N	105·46 W
90	Prince Albert Natl. Park.....Can.	54·10 N	105·25 W
90	Prince Albert Sd............Can.	70·23 N	116·57 W
91	Prince Charles I. (chärlz)....Can.	67·41 N	74·10 W
91	Prince Edward I. (Prov.)....Can.	46·45 N	63·10 W
220	Prince Edward Is...........S. Afr.	46·36 S	37·57 E
98	Prince Edward Natl. Park (ĕd'wẽrd)...Can.	46·33 N	63·35 W
105	Prince Edward Pen..........Can.	44·00 N	77·15 W
106	Prince Frederick (prĭnce frĕdẽrĭk) Md. (Baltimore In.)	38·33 N	76·35 W
92	Prince George (jôrj).........Can.	53·51 N	122·57 W
92	Prince of Wales (I.)..........Ak.	55·47 N	132·50 W
205	Prince of Wales (I.)........Austl.	10·47 S	142·15 E
101	Prince of Wales, C. (wālz)....Ak.	65·48 N	169·08 W
92	Prince Rupert (roo'pẽrt).....Can.	54·19 N	130·19 W
148	Princes Risborough (prĭns'ĕz rĭz'brŭ) Eng. (London In.)	51·41 N	0·51 W
205	Princess Charlotte B. (shär'lŏt) Austl.	13·45 S	144·15 E
220	Princess Martha Coast (mär'thȧ) Ant.	72·00 S	5·00 W
92	Princess Royal Chan. (roi'ăl).Can.	53·10 N	128·37 W
92	Princess Royal I............Can.	52·57 N	128·49 W
93	Princeton (prĭns'tŭn)........Can.	49·27 N	120·31 W
104	Princeton.....................Il.	41·20 N	89·25 W
104	Princeton....................In.	38·20 N	87·35 W
120	Princeton....................Ky.	37·07 N	87·52 W
109	Princeton....................Mi.	46·16 N	87·33 W
109	Princeton...................Mn.	45·34 N	93·36 W
117	Princeton...................Mo.	40·23 N	93·34 W
106	Princeton.....NJ (New York In.)	40·21 N	74·40 W
121	Princeton...................WV	37·21 N	81·05 W
109	Princeton....................Wi.	43·50 N	89·09 W
101	Prince William Sd. (wĭl'yăm)..Ak.	60·40 N	147·10 W
216	Príncipe (I.) (prēn'sê-pĕ).....Afr.	1·37 N	7·25 E
92	Principe Chan. (prĭn'sĭ-pē)...Can.	53·28 N	129·45 W
110	Prineville (prīn'vĭl)...........Or.	44·17 N	120·48 W
110	Prineville Res................Or.	44·07 N	120·45 W
127	Prinzapolca (prēn-zä-pōl'kä)..Nic.	13·18 N	83·35 W
127	Prinzapolca R...............Nic.	13·23 N	84·23 W
113	Prior Lake (prī'ẽr) Mn. (Minneapolis, St. Paul In.)	44·43 N	93·26 W
157	Priozërsk (prĭ-ô'zĕrsk)...Sov. Un.	61·03 N	30·08 E
171	Pripyat (Pripet) (R.) (prē'pyăt) Sov. Un.	51·50 N	29·45 E
	Pripyat Marshes, see Poles'ye		
165	Priština (prēsh'tĭ-nä).......Yugo.	42·39 N	21·12 E
120	Pritchard (prĭt'chȧrd)..........Al.	30·44 N	87·04 W
158	Pritzwalk (prĕts'välk)....G.D.R.	53·09 N	12·12 E
160	Privas (prē-väs').............Fr.	44·44 N	4·37 E
167	Privol'noye (prē'vôl-nô-yĕ) Sov. Un.	47·30 N	32·21 E
165	Prizren (prē'zrĕn)..........Yugo.	42·11 N	20·45 E
163	Procida (prô'chē-dȧ) It. (Naples In.)	40·31 N	14·02 E
163	Procida, I. di......It. (Naples In.)	40·32 N	13·57 E
113	Proctor(prŏk'tẽr).Mn. (Duluth In.)	46·45 N	92·14 W
105	Proctor.......................Vt.	43·40 N	73·00 W
112	Proebstel (prōb'stĕl) Wa. (Portland In.)	45·40 N	122·29 W
162	Proenca-a-Nova (prô-ăn'sȧ-ä-nō'vȧ).Port.	39·44 N	7·55 W
126	Progreso (prô-grĕ'sô).......Hond.	15·28 N	87·49 W
125	Progreso (prô-grä'sō)........Mex.	21·14 N	89·39 W
118	Progreso....................Mex.	27·29 N	101·05 W
172	Prokop'yevsk..........Sov. Un.	53·52 N	86·38 E
165	Prokuplje (prô'kōōp'l-yĕ)...Yugo.	43·16 N	21·40 E
166	Pronya (R.) (prô'nyä)...Sov. Un.	54·08 N	30·58 E
166	Pronya (R.)............Sov. Un.	54·08 N	39·30 E
135	Propriá (prō-prē-ä')........Braz.	10·17 S	36·47 W
107	Prospect (prŏs'pĕkt) Ky. (Louisville In.)	38·21 N	85·36 W
106	Prospect Park (prŏs'pĕkt pärk) Pa. (Philadelphia In.)	39·53 N	75·18 W
110	Prosser (prŏs'ẽr).............Wa.	46·10 N	119·46 W
159	Prostějov (prôs'tyĕ-yôf)....Czech.	49·28 N	17·08 E
112	Protection (I.) (prō-tĕk'shŭn) Wa. (Seattle In.)	48·07 N	122·56 W
166	Protoka (R.) (prôt'ô-kȧ)..Sov. Un.	55·00 N	36·42 E
165	Provadiya (prō-väd'ê-yȧ).....Bul.	43·13 N	27·28 E
104	Providence (prŏv'ĭ-dĕns)......Ky.	37·25 N	87·45 W
106	Providence...RI (Providence In.)	41·50 N	71·23 W

ng-sing; ŋ-baŋk; ɴ-nasalized n; nŏd; cŏmmit; ōld; ôbey; ôrder; fōōd; fŏŏt; ou-out; s-soft; sh-dish; th-thin; pūre; ûnite; ûrn; stŭd; circŭs; ü-as "y" in study; '-indeterminate vowel.

332 Providence — Quakertown PRONOUNCING INDEX

Page	Name Pronunciation	Region	Lat. °′	Long. °′
111	Providence	Ut.	41·42 N	111·50 W
127	Providencia, Isla de (I.)	Col.	13·21 N	80·55 W
119	Providenciales (I.) (prō-vē-děn-sē-ä'lås) (prŏ-vĭ-děn'shǎlz)	Turks & Caicos Is.	21·50 N	72·15 W
101	Provideniya (prô-vĭ-dă'nʸ-yȧ)	Sov. Un.	64·30 N	172·54 W
105	Provincetown	Ma.	42·03 N	70·11 W
115	Provo (prō'vō)	Ut.	40·15 N	111·40 W
164	Prozor (prô'zôr)	Yugo.	43·48 N	17·59 E
106	Prudence I. (prōō'děns)	RI (Providence In.)	41·38 N	71·20 W
159	Prudnik (prŏŏd'nĭk)	Pol.	50·19 N	17·34 E
157	Prunkkala (prŏŏŋk'ȧ-lȧ)	Fin.	60·38 N	22·32 E
158	Prussia (Reg.) (prŭsh'ǎ)	G.D.R.	50·43 N	8·35 E
159	Pruszków (prŏŏsh'kŏŏf)	Pol.	52·09 N	20·50 E
167	Prut (R.) (prōōt)	Sov. Un.	48·05 N	27·07 E
117	Pryor (prī'ēr)	Ok.	36·16 N	95·19 W
171	Prypeć (R.)	Sov. Un.	51·50 N	25·35 E
159	Przedbórz (pzhěd'bōōzh)	Pol.	51·05 N	19·53 E
159	Przedbórz	Pol.	53·01 N	20·54 E
159	Przemyśl (pzhě'mĭsh'l)	Pol.	49·47 N	22·45 E
172	Przheval'sk (p'r-zhĭ-välsk')	Sov. Un.	42·25 N	78·18 E
165	Psará (I.) (psä'rȧ)	Grc.	38·39 N	25·26 E
167	Psël (R.) (psěl)	Sov. Un.	49·45 N	33·42 E
165	Psevdhókavos (Pen.)	Grc.	39·58 N	24·05 E
166	Pskov (pskôf)	Sov. Un.	57·48 N	28·19 E
166	Pskov (Oblast)	Sov. Un.	57·33 N	29·05 E
166	Pskovskoye Ozero (L.) (p'skôv'skô'yě ôzē-rô)	Sov. Un.	58·05 N	28·15 E
166	Ptich' (R.) (p'têch)	Sov. Un.	53·17 N	28·16 E
164	Ptuj (ptōō'ē)	Yugo.	46·24 N	15·54 E
193	Pucheng (pōō'chěng')	China	28·02 N	118·25 E
159	Puck (pŏŏtsk)	Pol.	54·43 N	18·23 E
188	Pudog	China	33·29 N	79·26 E
170	Pudozh (pōō'dôzh)	Sov. Un.	61·50 N	36·50 E
124	Puebla (pwā'blä)	Mex.	19·02 N	98·11 W
124	Puebla (State)	Mex.	19·00 N	97·45 W
162	Puebla de Don Fadrique (pwě'blä dā dōn fä-drē'kā)	Sp.	37·55 N	2·55 W
116	Pueblo (pwā'blō)	Co.	38·15 N	104·36 W
124	Pueblo Nuevo (nwā'vô)	Mex.	23·23 N	105·21 W
125	Pueblo Viejo (vyā'hô)	Mex.	17·23 N	93·46 W
125	Puente Alto (pwě'n-tě äl'tô)	Chile (Santiago In.)	33·36 S	70·34 W
162	Puenteareas (pwěn-tā-ä-rä'äs)	Sp.	42·09 N	8·23 W
162	Puente Ceso (pwěn'tȧ thā'sô)	Sp.	43·15 N	8·53 W
162	Puentedeume (pwěn-tȧ-dhȧ-ōō'mȧ)	Sp.	43·28 N	8·09 W
162	Puente-Genil (pwěn'tȧ-hȧ-nēl')	Sp.	37·25 N	4·18 W
115	Puerco (R.) (pwěr'kō)	NM	35·15 N	107·05 W
136	Puerto Aisén (pwě'r-tō ä'y-sě'n)	Chile	45·28 S	72·44 W
125	Puerto Angel (pwě'r-tō äŋ'hål)	Mex.	15·42 N	96·32 W
127	Puerto Armuelles (pwe'r-tô är-mōō-ā'lyās)	Pan.	8·18 N	82·52 W
126	Puerto Barrios (pwě'r-tô bär'rê-ôs)	Guat.	15·43 N	88·36 W
134	Puerto Bermúdez (pwě'r-tō běr-mōō'dāz)	Peru	10·17 S	74·57 W
134	Puerto Berrío (pwě'r-tō běr-rē'ō)	Col. (In.)	6·29 N	74·27 W
135	Puerto Cabello (pwě'r-tō kä-běl'yō)	Ven. (In.)	10·28 N	68·01 W
127	Puerto Cabezas (pwě'r-tô kä-bā'zäs)	Nic.	14·01 N	83·26 W
136	Puerto Casado (pwě'r-tō kä-sä'dō)	Par.	22·16 S	57·57 W
126	Puerto Castilla (pwě'r-tô käs-tēl'yō)	Hond.	16·01 N	86·01 W
134	Puerto Chicama (pwě'r-tō chē-kä'mä)	Peru	7·46 S	79·18 W
134	Puerto Columbia (pwěr'tô kô-lôm'bê-ȧ)	Col.	11·08 N	75·09 W
127	Puerto Cortés (pwě'r-tô kôr-tās')	C. R.	9·00 N	83·37 W
126	Puerto Cortés (pwě'r-tô kôr-tās')	Hond.	15·48 N	87·57 W
134	Puerto Cumarebo (pwě'r-tō kōō-mä-rě'bô)	Ven.	11·25 N	69·17 W
163	Puerto de Beceite (Mts.) (pwě'r-tō dě bě-sě'y-tě)	Sp.	40·43 N	0·05 W
116	Puerto de Luna (pwěr'tô dȧ lōō'nä)	NM	34·49 N	104·36 W
134	Puerto de Nutrias (pwě'r-tō dě nōō-trê-äs')	Ven.	8·02 N	69·19 W
136	Puerto Deseado (pwě'r-tō dā-sȧ-ä'dhō)	Arg.	47·38 S	66·00 W
134	Puerto Eten (pwě'r-tō ĕ-tě'n)	Peru	6·59 S	79·51 W
127	Puerto Jimenez (pwě'r-tō ĸê-mě'něz)	C. R.	8·35 N	83·23 W
137	Puerto La Cruz (pwě'r-tō lä krōō'z)	Ven. (In.)	10·14 N	64·38 W
162	Puertollano (pwěr-tôl-yä'nō)	Sp.	38·41 N	4·05 W
136	Puerto Madryn (pwě'r-tō mä-drēn')	Arg.	42·45 S	65·01 W
134	Puerto Maldonado (pwě'r-tō mäl-dō-nä'dô)	Peru	12·43 S	69·01 W
	Puerto Mexico, see Coatzacoalcos			
124	Puerto Miniso (pwě'r-tō mē-nē'sô)	Mex.	16·06 N	98·02 W
136	Puerto Montt (pwě'r-tō mô'nt)	Chile	41·29 S	73·00 W
136	Puerto Natales (pwě'r-tō nä-tà'lěs)	Chile	51·48 S	72·01 W
134	Puerto Niño (pwě'r-tō nē'n-yô)	Col. (In.)	5·57 N	74·36 W
128	Puerto Padre (pwě'r-tō pä'drā)	Cuba	21·10 N	76·40 W
122	Puerto Peñasco (pwě'r-tô pěn-yä's-kô)	Mex.	31·39 N	113·15 W
136	Puerto Pinasco (pwě'r-tō pē-nȧ's-kô)	Par.	22·31 S	57·50 W
135	Puerto Píritu (pwě'r-tō pē'rē-tōō)	Ven. (In.)	10·05 N	65·04 W
129	Puerto Plata (pwě'r-tô plä'tä)	Dom. Rep.	19·50 N	70·40 W
196	Puerto Princesa (pwěr-tô prên-sā'sä)	Phil.	9·45 N	118·41 E
123	Puerto Rico (pwěr'tô rē'kō)	N. A.	18·16 N	66·50 W
123	Puerto Rico Trench	N. A.	19·45 N	66·30 W
134	Puerto Salgar (pwě'r-tō säl-gär')	Col. (In.)	5·30 N	74·39 W
136	Puerto Santa Cruz (pwě'r-tō sän'tä krōōz')	Arg.	50·04 S	68·32 W
135	Puerto Suárez (pwě'r-tō swä'râz)	Bol.	18·55 S	57·39 W
134	Puerto Tejada (pwě'r-tō tě-ĸä'dä)	Col. (In.)	3·13 N	76·23 W
124	Puerto Vallarta (pwě'r-tō väl-yär'tä)	Mex.	20·36 N	105·13 W
136	Puerto Varas (pwě'r-tō vä'räs)	Chile	41·16 S	73·03 W
134	Puerto Wilches (pwě'r-tō vēl'c-hěs)	Col.	7·19 N	73·54 W
171	Pugachëv (pōō'gȧ-chyôf)	Sov. Un.	52·00 N	48·40 E
112	Puget (pū'jět)	Wa. (Portland In.)	46·10 N	123·23 W
110	Puget Sd.	Wa.	47·49 N	122·26 W
164	Puglia (Apulia) (Reg.) (pōō'lyä) (ä-pōō'lyä)	It.	41·13 N	16·10 E
190	Puhsien (pōō'sĭän)	China	35·43 N	115·22 E
96	Pukaskwa Natl. Pk.	Can.	48·22 N	85·55 W
93	Pukeashun Mtn.	Can.	51·12 N	119·14 W
183	Pukin (R.)	Mala. (Singapore In.)	2·53 N	102·54 E
164	Pula (pōō'lä)	Yugo.	44·52 N	13·55 E
134	Pulacayo (pōō-lä-kä'yō)	Bol.	20·12 S	66·33 W
190	P'ulantien (pōō'län'chěn')	China	39·23 N	121·57 E
120	Pulaski (pû-lăs'kĭ)	Tn.	35·11 N	87·03 W
121	Pulaski	Va.	37·00 N	81·45 W
159	Pulawy (pŏŏ-wä'vě)	Pol.	51·24 N	21·59 E
184	Pulizat (R.)	India	13·58 N	79·52 E
110	Pullman (pŏŏl'măn)	Wa.	46·44 N	117·10 W
197	Pulog (Mtn.) (pōō'lôg)	Phil. (In.)	16·38 N	120·53 E
150	Pultusk (pōōl'tŏŏsk)	Pol.	52·40 N	21·09 E
111	Pumpkin Cr. (pŭmp'kĭn)	Mt.	45·47 N	105·35 W
184	Punakha (pōō-nŭk'ŭ)	Bhu.	27·45 N	89·59 E
134	Punata (pōō-nä'tä)	Bol.	17·43 S	65·43 W
184	Pune	India	18·38 N	73·53 E
184	Punjab (State) (pŭn'jäb')	India	31·00 N	75·30 E
134	Puno (pōō'nô)	Peru	15·58 S	7·02 W
136	Punta Arenas (pōō'n-tä-rě'näs)	Chile	53·09 S	70·48 W
135	Punta de Piedras (pōō'n-tä dě pyě'dräs)	Ven. (In.)	10·54 N	64·06 W
126	Punta Gorda (pŏŏn'tä gôr'dä)	Belize	16·07 N	88·50 W
121	Punta Gorda (pŭn'tȧ gôr'dȧ)	Fl. (In.)	26·55 N	82·02 W
127	Punta Gorda, Rio (R.) (pōō'n-tä gô'r-dä)	Nic.	11·34 N	84·13 W
137	Punta Indio, Can. (pōō'n-tä ē'n-dyô)	Arg. (Buenos Aires In.)	34·56 S	57·20 W
127	Puntarenas (pŏŏnt-ä-rā'näs)	C. R.	9·59 N	84·49 W
134	Punto Fijo (pōō'n-tō fē'ĸô)	Ven.	11·48 N	70·14 W
105	Punxsutawney (pŭnk-sŭ-tô'nê)	Pa.	40·55 N	79·00 W
134	Puquio (pōō'kyô)	Peru	14·43 S	74·02 W
172	Pur (R.)	Sov. Un.	65·30 N	77·30 E
117	Purcell (pûr-sěl')	Ok.	35·01 N	97·22 W
93	Purcell Mts. (pûr-sěl')	Can.	50·00 N	116·30 W
112	Purdy (pûr'dē)	Wa. (Seattle In.)	47·23 N	122·37 W
124	Purépero (pōō-rā'pȧ-rō)	Mex.	19·56 N	102·02 W
116	Purgatoire (R.) (pûr-gȧ-twär')	Colo.	37·25 N	103·53 W
184	Puri (pŏŏ'rê)	India	19·52 N	85·51 E
129	Purial, Sierra de (Mts.) (sē-ě'r-rȧ-dě-pōō-rê-äl')	Cuba	20·15 N	74·40 W
134	Purificacion (pōō-rê-fê-kä-syōn')	Col. (In.)	3·52 N	74·54 W
124	Purificación (pōō-rē-fê-kä-syô'n)	Mex.	19·44 N	104·38 W
124	Purificación (R.)	Mex.	19·30 N	104·54 W
149	Purkersdorf	Aus. (Vienna In.)	48·13 N	16·11 E
196	Pursat (pŏŏr-sät')	Camb.	12·33 N	103·51 E
124	Puruandiro (pōō-rōō-än'dê-rō)	Mex.	20·04 N	101·33 W
134	Purús (R.) (pōō-rōō's)	Braz.	6·45 S	64·34 W
194	Pusan	Kor.	35·08 N	129·05 E
174	Pushkin (pōōsh'kĭn)	Sov. Un. (Leningrad In.)	59·43 N	30·25 E
174	Pushkino (pōōsh'kê-nô)	Sov. Un. (Moscow In.)	56·01 N	37·51 E
166	Pustoshka (pûs-tôsh'kȧ)	Sov. Un.	56·20 N	29·33 E
125	Pustunich (pōōs-tōō'nêch)	Mex.	19·10 N	90·29 W
137	Putaendo (pōō-tä-ěn-dô)	Chile (Santiago In.)	32·37 S	70·42 W
161	Puteaux (pü-tō')	Fr. (Paris In.)	48·52 N	2·12 E
213	Putfontein (pŏŏt'fŏn-tān)	S. Afr. (Johannesburg & Pretoria In.)	26·08 S	28·24 E
193	P'ut'ien	China	25·40 N	119·02 E
167	Putivl' (pōō-tēv'l')	Sov. Un.	51·22 N	33·24 E
125	Putla de Guerrero (pōō'tlä-dě-gěr-rě'rō)	Mex.	17·03 N	97·55 W
105	Putnam (pŭt'nǎm)	Ct.	41·55 N	71·55 W
172	Putorana, Gory (Mts.)	Sov. Un.	68·45 N	93·15 E
185	Puttalam	Sri Lanka	8·02 N	79·44 E
134	Putumayo (R.) (pōō-tōō-mä'yō)	Col.-Peru	1·02 S	73·50 W
191	Putung (pōō'tŏŏng')	China (Shanghai In.)	31·14 N	121·29 E
196	Putung, Tandjung (C.)	Indon.	3·35 S	111·50 E
157	Puulavesi (L.)	Fin.	61·49 N	27·10 E
112	Puyallup (pū-ăl'ŭp)	Wa. (Seattle In.)	47·12 N	122·18 W
190	P'uyang (pōō'yäng)	China	35·42 N	114·58 E
212	Pweto (pwā'tō)	Zaire	8·29 S	28·58 E
172	Pyasina (R.) (pyä-sē'nȧ)	Sov. Un.	72·45 N	87·37 E
171	Pyatigorsk (pyȧ-tê-gôrsk')	Sov. Un.	44·00 N	43·00 E
196	Pye	Bur.	18·46 N	95·15 E
157	Pyhäjärvi (L.)	Fin.	60·57 N	21·50 E
188	Pyinmana (pyěn-mä'nǔ)	Bur.	19·47 N	96·15 E
104	Pymatuning Res. (pī-mȧ-tûn'ĭng)	Pa.	41·40 N	80·30 W
194	Pyŏnggang (pyŭng'gäng')	Kor.	38·21 N	127·18 E
194	P'yŏngyang	Kor.	39·03 N	125·48 E
114	Pyramid (L.) (pĭ'rȧ-mĭd)	Nv.	40·02 N	119·50 W
114	Pyramid Lake Ind. Res.	Nv.	40·17 N	119·52 W
218	Pyramids	Egypt (Nile In.)	29·53 N	31·10 E
163	Pyrenees (Mts.) (pĭr-e-nēz')	Fr.-Sp.	43·00 N	0·05 E
158	Pyrzyce (pězhĭ'tsě)	Pol.	53·09 N	14·53 E

Q

Page	Name Pronunciation	Region	Lat. °′	Long. °′
186	Qal'at Bīshah	Sau. Ar.	20·01 N	42·30 E
211	Qallābāt	Sud.	12·55 N	36·12 E
218	Qana el Suweis (Suez Can.)	Egypt (Suez In.)	30·53 N	32·21 E
187	Qandahār	Afg.	31·43 N	65·58 E
153	Qārah (Oasis)	Egypt	29·28 N	26·29 E
171	Qareh Sū (R.)	Iran	38·50 N	47·10 E
218	Qārūn, Birket (L.)	Egypt (Nile In.)	29·34 N	30·34 E
211	Qasr al-Burayqah	Libya	30·25 N	19·20 E
211	Qasr al-Farāfirah	Egypt	27·04 N	28·13 E
211	Qaşr Banī Walīd	Libya	31·45 N	14·04 E
182	Qatar (kä'tȧr)	Asia	25·00 N	52·45 E
211	Qaţţārah, Munkhafaḑ (Dep.)	Egypt	30·07 N	27·30 E
186	Qāyen	Iran	33·45 N	59·08 E
186	Qeshm	Iran	26·51 N	56·10 E
186	Qeshm (I.)	Iran	26·52 N	56·15 E
186	Qezel Owzan	Iran	37·00 N	48·23 E
171	Qezel Owzan (R.)	Iran	37·00 N	47·35 E
183	Qeẓi'ot	Egypt-Isr. (Palestine In.)	30·53 N	34·28 E
183	Qiblīyah, Jabal al Jalālat al (Plat.)	Egypt (Palestine In.)	28·49 N	32·21 E
218	Qifţ (kěft)	Egypt (Nile In.)	25·58 N	32·52 E
218	Qinā (kä'nȧ)	Egypt (Nile In.)	26·10 N	32·48 E
218	Qinā, Wādī	Egypt (Nile In.)	26·38 N	32·53 E
183	Qiryat Gat	Isr. (Palestine In.)	31·38 N	34·36 E
183	Qiryat Shemona	Isr. (Palestine In.)	33·12 N	35·34 E
186	Qom	Iran	34·28 N	50·53 E
	Qomul see Hami			
105	Quabbin Res. (kwā'bĭn)	Ma.	42·20 N	72·10 W
117	Quachita, L. (kwä shĭ'tô)	Ar.	34·47 N	93·37 W
92	Quadra, Boca de, Str. (bōk'ǎ dě kwôd'rȧ)	Ak.	55·08 N	130·50 W
92	Quadra I.	Can.	50·08 N	125·16 W
105	Quakertown (kwā'kěr-toun)	Pa.	40·30 N	75·20 W

ăt; finǎl; rāte; senȧte; ärm; ȧsk; sofǎ; fâre; ch-choose; dh-as th in other; bē; ēvent; bět; recěnt; cratēr; g-go; gh-guttural g; bĭt; ĭ-short neutral; rīde; ĸ-guttural k as ch in German ich;

PRONOUNCING INDEX   Quanah — Rantelkomboa 333

Page	Name Pronunciation Region	Lat. °′	Long. °′
116	Quanah (kwä'nȧ)............Tx.	34·19 N	99·43 W
193	Quang Ngai (kwäng n'gä'ē)...Viet.	15·05 N	108·58 E
193	Quang Ngai (Mtn.).........Viet.	15·10 N	108·20 E
196	Quang Tri (kwäng'trē')......Viet.	16·39 N	107·05 E
94	Qu'Appelle Dam...........Can.	51·00 N	106·25 W
94	Qu'Appelle (R.)............Can.	50·35 N	103·25 W
164	Quartu Sant' Elena (kwär-tōō' sänt a'lå-nä).It.	39·16 N	9·12 E
115	Quartzsite.................Az.	33·40 N	114·13 W
92	Quatsino Sd (kwŏt-sē'nō)....Can.	50·25 N	128·10 W
100	Québec (kwē-bĕk') (kå-bĕk') Can. (Québec In.)	46·49 N	71·13 W
91	Quebec (Prov.).............Can.	51·07 N	70·25 W
158	Quedlinburg (kvĕd'lĕn-bōōrgh) G.D.R.	51·49 N	11·10 E
92	Queen Bess, Mt.............Can.	51·16 N	124·34 W
92	Queen Charlotte Is. (kwēn shär'lŏt).Can.	53·30 N	132·25 W
92	Queen Charlotte Ra.........Can.	53·00 N	132·00 W
92	Queen Charlotte Sd.........Can.	51·30 N	129·30 W
92	Queen Charlotte Str. (strāt)..Can.	50·40 N	127·25 W
75	Queen Elizabeth Is. (ė-lĭz'á-bĕth) Can.	78·20 N	110·00 W
90	Queen Maud G. (mäd)......Can.	68·27 N	102·55 W
220	Queen Maud Land..........Ant.	75·00 S	10·00 E
220	Queen Maud Mts...........Ant.	85·00 S	179·00 W
204	Queens Chan. (kwēnz)......Austl.	14·25 S	129·10 E
202	Queenscliff.Austl. (Melbourne In.)	38·16 S	144·39 E
205	Queensland (State) (kwēnz'lănd) Austl.	22·45 S	141·01 E
203	Queenstown (kwēnz'toun)...Austl.	42·00 S	145·40 E
213	Queenstown....S. Afr. (Natal In.)	31·54 S	26·53 E
162	Queija, Sierra de (Mts.) (sē-ĕ'r-rä-dĕ-kĕ'y-kä).Sp.	42·08 N	7·23 W
136	Queimados (kā-mȧ'dôs) Braz. (Rio de Janeiro In.)	22·42 S	43·34 W
216	Quela......................Ang.	9·16 S	17·02 E
212	Quelimane (kā-lē-mä'nĕ).....Moz.	17·48 S	37·05 E
	Quelpart (I.), see Cheju		
128	Quemado de Güines (kā-mä'dhä-dĕ-gwē'nĕs).Cuba	22·45 N	80·20 W
193	Quemoy (Chinmen).......Taiwan	24·30 N	118·20 E
127	Quepos (kā'pôs)............C. R.	9·26 N	84·10 W
127	Quepos, Punta (Pt.) (pōō'n-tä).C. R.	9·23 N	84·20 W
212	Que Que (kwĕ'kwĕ)..........Rh.	18·49 S	29·45 E
124	Querétaro (kå-rā'tä-rō)......Mex.	20·37 N	100·25 W
124	Querétaro (State)...........Mex.	21·00 N	100·00 W
162	Quesada (kå-sä'dhä)..........Sp.	37·51 N	3·04 W
92	Quesnel (kā-nĕl')...........Can.	52·59 N	122·30 W
93	Quesnel L...................Can.	52·32 N	121·05 W
92	Quesnel (R.)................Can.	52·15 N	122·00 W
134	Quetame (kĕ-tä'mĕ).....Col. (In.)	4·20 N	73·50 W
184	Quetta (kwĕt'ä).............Pak.	30·19 N	67·01 E
126	Quezaltenango (kå-zäl'tå-näŋ'gō) Guat.	14·50 N	91·30 W
126	Quezaltepeque (kå-zäl'tå-pā'kå) Guat.	14·39 N	89·26 W
126	Quezaltepeque (kĕ-zäl'tĕ'pĕ-kĕ) Sal.	13·50 N	89·17 W
197	Quezon City (kā-zōn)...Phil. (In.)	14·40 N	121·02 E
134	Quibdo (kēb'dō)........Col. (In.)	5·42 N	76·41 W
160	Quiberon (kē-bē-rôN')........Fr.	47·29 N	3·08 W
216	Quiçama, Parque Nacional de (Natl. Pk.).Ang.	10·00 S	13·25 E
126	Quiché (kē-shā')...........Guat.	15·05 N	91·08 W
149	Quicksborn (kvēks'bōrn) F.R.G. (Hamburg In.)	53·44 N	9·54 E
112	Quilcene (kwĭl-sēn') Wa. (Seattle In.)	47·50 N	122·53 W
137	Quilimari (kē-lē-mä'rē) Chile (Santiago In.)	32·06 S	71·28 W
160	Quillan (kê-yäN')............Fr.	43·53 N	2·13 E
137	Quillota (kêl-yō'tä) Chile (Santiago In.)	32·52 S	71·14 W
136	Quilmes (kēl'mās) Arg. (Buenos Aires In.)	34·28 S	58·16 W
185	Quilon (kwė-lōn')..........India	8·58 N	76·16 E
203	Quilpie (kwĭl'pê)..........Austl.	26·34 S	149·20 E
137	Quilpué (kēl-pōō ĕ') Chile (Santiago In.)	33·03 S	71·22 W
134	Quimbaya (kēm-bä'yä)..Col. (In.)	4·38 N	75·46 W
216	Quimbele...................Ang.	6·28 S	16·13 E
216	Quimbonge..................Ang.	8·36 S	18·30 E
160	Quimper (kăN-pĕr')...........Fr.	47·59 N	4·04 W
197	Quinabucasan Pt. (kē-nä-bōō-kä'sän).Phil. (In.)	14·09 N	123·33 E
110	Quinalt R...................Wa.	47·23 N	124·10 W
110	Quinault Ind. Res............Wa.	47·27 N	124·34 W
120	Quincy (kwĭn'sê)..............Fl.	30·35 N	84·35 W
117	Quincy.......................Il.	39·55 N	91·23 W
99	Quincy...............Ma. (In.)	42·15 N	71·00 W
104	Quincy......................Mi.	42·00 N	84·50 W
112	Quincy........Or. (Portland In.)	46·08 N	123·10 W
196	Qui Nhon (kwĭnyŏn).........Viet.	13·51 N	109·03 E
110	Quinn R. (kwĭn)..............Nv.	41·42 N	117·45 W
162	Quintana de la Serena (kēn-tä'nä dā lä sȧ-rā'nä).Sp.	38·45 N	5·39 W
162	Quintanar (kēn-tä-när').......Sp.	39·36 N	3·02 W
126	Quintana Roo (State) (rô'ô) Mex. (In.)	19·30 N	88·30 W
137	Quintero (kēn-tĕ'rô) Chile (Santiago In.)	32·48 S	71·30 W
217	Quionga.....................Moz.	10·37 S	40·30 E
124	Quiroga (kē-rô'gä)..........Mex.	19·39 N	101·30 W
162	Quiroga (kē-rô'gä)............Sp.	42·28 N	7·18 W
120	Quitman (kwĭt'măn).........Ga.	30·46 N	83·35 W
120	Quitman.....................Ms.	33·02 N	88·43 W
134	Quito (kē'tō)................Ec.	0·17 S	78·32 W
135	Quixadá (kē-shä-dä')........Braz.	4·58 S	38·58 W
218	Qulūşanā (kōō-lōōs'nä) Egypt (Nile In.)	28·22 N	30·44 E
213	Qumbu (kŏŏm'bōō) S. Afr. (Natal In.)	31·10 S	28·48 E
203	Quorn (kwôrn)..............Austl.	32·20 S	138·00 E
183	Qurayyah, Wādī (R.) Egypt (Palestine In.)	30·08 N	34·27 E
218	Qūş (kōōs).......Egypt (Nile In.)	25·53 N	32·48 E
213	Quthing........Leso. (Natal In.)	30·35 S	27·42 E
205	Quvea (I.)................N. Cal.	20·43 S	166·48 E
186	Quzvīn......................Iran	36·10 N	49·59 E

R

Page	Name Pronunciation Region	Lat. °′	Long. °′
158	Raab R. (räp)..............Aus.	46·55 N	15·55 E
150	Raahe (rä'ĕ)................Fin.	64·39 N	24·22 E
164	Rab (I.) (räb).............Yugo.	44·45 N	14·40 E
196	Raba.......................Indon.	8·32 S	118·49 E
159	Raba R....................Hung.	47·28 N	17·12 E
210	Rabat (rȧ-bät')..............Mor.	33·59 N	6·47 W
197	Rabaul (rä'boul).....Pap. N. Gui.	4·15 S	152·19 E
165	Rača (rä'chȧ)..............Yugo.	44·13 N	21·01 E
109	Raccoon (R.) (ră-kōōn').......Ia.	42·07 N	94·45 W
129	Raccoon Cay (I.).............Ba.	22·25 N	75·50 W
99	Race, C. (rās)..............Can.	46·40 N	53·10 W
183	Rachado, C..Mala. (Singapore In.)	2·26 N	101·29 E
159	Racibórz (rä-chē'bōōzh)......Pol.	50·06 N	18·14 E
107	Racine (rȧ-sēn') Wi. (Milwaukee In.)	42·43 N	87·49 W
113	Raco (rȧ cō) Mi. (Sault Ste. Marie In.)	46·22 N	84·43 W
159	Rădăuti (rû-dû-ōōts'')......Rom.	47·53 N	25·55 E
148	Radcliffe (răd'klĭf)..........Eng.	53·34 N	2·20 W
161	Radevormwald (rä'dĕ-fōrm-väld) F.R.G. (Ruhr In.)	51·12 N	7·22 E
121	Radford (răd'fērd)...........Va.	37·06 N	81·33 W
184	Rādhanpur..................India	23·57 N	71·38 E
218	Radium (rā'dĭ-ŭm)........S. Afr. (Johannesburg & Pretoria In.)	25·06 S	28·18 E
154	Radnor Forest (răd'nôr)....Wales	52·11 N	3·25 W
159	Radom (rä'dôm).............Pol.	51·24 N	21·11 E
165	Radomir (rä'dô-mêr).........Bul.	42·33 N	22·58 E
159	Radomsko (rä-dôm'skô)......Pol.	51·04 N	19·27 E
167	Radomyshl (rä-dô-mēsh''l) Sov. Un.	50·30 N	29·13 E
165	Radoviš (rä-dô-vēsh).......Yugo.	41·39 N	22·28 E
156	Radöy (I.) (räd-ûê)..........Nor.	60·43 N	4·40 E
167	Radul' (rȧ'dōōl).........Sov. Un.	51·52 N	30·46 E
157	Radviliškis (rȧd'vē-lēsh'kēs) Sov. Un.	55·49 N	23·31 E
186	Radwah, Jabal (Mtn.).....Sua. Ar.	24·44 N	38·14 E
159	Radzyń Podlaski (räd'zēn-y' pŭd-lä'skĭ).Pol.	51·49 N	22·40 E
121	Raeford (rā'fērd)............NC	34·57 N	79·15 W
161	Raesfeld (răz'fĕld) F.R.G. (Ruhr In.)	51·46 N	6·50 E
204	Raeside (rā'sīd)............Austl.	29·20 S	122·30 E
90	Rae Str. (rā)...............Can.	68·40 N	95·03 W
136	Rafaela (rä-fä-ā'lä)..........Arg.	31·15 S	61·21 W
183	Rafah (rä'fä) Egypt (Palestine In.)	31·14 N	34·12 E
211	Rafai (rä-fī')......Cen. Afr. Rep.	4·59 N	23·58 E
186	Rafḩā....................Sau. Ar.	29·43 N	43·13 E
186	Rafsanjān...................Iran	30·45 N	56·30 E
111	Raft R. (răft)................Id.	42·20 N	113·17 W
197	Ragay (rä-gī')..........Phil. (In.)	13·49 N	122·45 E
197	Ragay G.............Phil. (In.)	13·44 N	122·38 E
171	Ragga......................Egypt	36·00 N	39·00 E
156	Ragunda (rä-gōōn'dä).......Swe.	63·07 N	16·24 E
151	Ragusa (rä-gōō'sä)............It.	36·58 N	14·41 E
	Ragusa, see Dubrovnik		
106	Rahway (rô'wā) NJ (New York In.)	40·37 N	74·16 W
185	Rāichūr (rä'ê-chōōr').......India	16·23 N	77·18 E
184	Raigarh (rī'gŭr)...........India	21·57 N	83·32 E
115	Rainbow Bridge Natl. Mon. (rān'bō).Ut.	37·05 N	111·00 W
122	Rainbow City.........C. Z. (In.)	9·20 N	79·23 W
112	Rainier........Or. (Portland In.)	46·05 N	122·56 W
110	Rainier, Mt. (rā-nēr')........Wa.	46·52 N	121·46 W
95	Rainy (L.) (rān'ê)......Can.-Mn.	48·43 N	94·29 W
95	Rainy (R.)..............Can.-Mn.	48·50 N	94·41 W
95	Rainy River.................Can.	48·43 N	94·29 W
184	Raipur (rä'jŭ-bōō-rē').......India	21·25 N	81·37 E
104	Raisin (R.) (rā'zĭn)...........Mi.	42·00 N	83·35 W
106	Raitan (rā-tăn) NJ (New York In.)	40·34 N	74·40 W
196	Raja, Bukit (Mtn.)........Indon.	0·45 S	112·11 E
185	Rājahmundry (räj-ŭ-mŭn'drê) India	17·03 N	81·51 E
196	Rajang, Balang (Strm.)....Mala.	2·10 N	113·30 E
184	Rājapālaiyam..............India	9·30 N	77·33 E
184	Rājasthān (State) (rä'jŭs-tän) India	31·20 N	72·00 E
184	Rājkot (räj'kôt)............India	22·20 N	70·48 E
184	Rājpur...............India (In.)	22·24 N	88·25 E
184	Rājshāhi....................Bngl.	24·26 S	88·39 E
184	Rakers Tal (L.)...........China	30·42 N	80·40 E
159	Rakhov (rä'κôf).........Sov. Un.	48·02 N	24·13 E
174	Rakh'ya (räk'yȧ) Sov. Un. (Leningrad In.)	60·06 N	30·50 E
167	Rakitnoye (rȧ-kēt'nô-yĕ).Sov. Un.	50·51 N	35·53 E
158	Rakovnik (rä'kôv-nyĕk)....Czech.	50·07 N	13·45 E
166	Rakvere (rȧk'vĕ-rĕ)......Sov. Un.	59·22 N	26·14 E
121	Raleigh.....................NC	35·45 N	78·39 W
121	Raleigh, B..................NC	34·50 N	76·15 W
93	Ram (R.)...................Can.	52·10 N	115·05 W
127	Rama (rä'mä)...............Nic.	12·11 N	84·14 W
137	Ramallo (rä-mä'l-yô) Arg. (Buenos Aires In.)	33·28 S	60·02 W
185	Ramanāthapuram..........India	9·13 N	78·52 E
161	Rambouillet (räN-bōō-yĕ') Fr. (Paris In.)	48·39 N	1·49 E
213	Rame Hd......S. Afr. (Natal In.)	31·48 S	29·22 E
174	Ramenskoye (rȧ'mĕn-skô-yĕ) Sov. Un. (Moscow In.)	55·34 N	38·15 E
186	Ramlat as Sab'atayn (Reg.) Sau. Ar.	16·08 N	45·15 E
183	Ramm, Jabal (Mts.) Jordan (Palestine In.)	29·37 N	35·32 E
124	Ramos (rä'mōs)............Mex.	22·46 N	101·52 W
215	Ramos (R.)................Nig.	5·10 N	5·40 E
118	Ramos Arizpe (ä-rēz'pȧ).....Mex.	25·33 N	100·57 W
101	Rampart (răm'pȧrt)...........Ak.	65·28 N	150·18 W
106	Rampo Mts. (răm'pō) NJ-NY (New York In.)	41·06 N	72·12 W
184	Rāmpur (räm'pōōr).........India	28·53 N	79·03 E
196	Ramree (I.) (räm'rē')........Bur.	19·01 N	93·23 E
100	Ramsayville (răm'zē vĭl) Can. (Ottawa In.)	45·23 N	75·34 W
148	Ramsbottom (rămz'bŏt-ŭm)..Eng.	53·39 N	2·20 W
154	Ramsey (răm'zê).....Isle of Man	54·20 N	4·25 W
106	Ramsey......NJ (New York In.)	41·03 N	74·09 W
96	Ramsey L...................Can.	47·15 N	82·16 W
155	Ramsgate (rămz''gāt).......Eng.	51·19 N	1·20 E
156	Ramsjö (räm'shû)...........Swe.	62·11 N	15·44 E
197	Ramu (R.) (rä'mōō).Pap. N. Gui.	5·35 S	145·16 E
196	Ranau, L. (rä-nä'ōō)......Indon.	4·52 S	103·52 E
137	Rancagua (rän-kä'gwä) Chile (Santiago In.)	34·10 S	70·43 W
160	Rance (R.) (räns)............Fr.	48·17 N	2·30 W
184	Rānchī (rän'chē)............India	23·24 N	85·18 E
129	Rancho Boyeros (rä'n-chô-bô-yĕ'rôs).Cuba (In.)	23·00 N	82·23 W
106	Randallstown (răn'dălz-toun) Md. (Baltimore In.)	39·22 N	76·48 W
156	Randers (rän'ĕrs)...........Den.	56·28 N	10·03 E
213	Randfontein (rănt'fŏn-tān).S. Afr. (Johannesburg & Pretoria In.)	26·10 S	27·42 E
121	Randleman (răn'd'l-măn).....NC	35·49 N	79·50 W
99	Randolph (răn'dôlf).....Ma. (In.)	42·10 N	71·03 W
108	Randolph....................Ne.	42·22 N	97·22 W
105	Randolph....................Vt.	43·55 N	72·40 W
99	Random I. (răn'dŭm).......Can.	48·12 N	53·25 W
156	Rands Fd. (räns' fyôr).......Nor.	60·35 N	10·10 E
214	Ranérou...................Senegal	15·18 N	13·58 W
98	Rangeley (rānj'lê)............Me.	44·56 N	70·38 W
98	Rangeley (L.)...............Me.	45·00 N	70·25 W
118	Ranger (rān'jēr)..............Tx.	32·26 N	98·41 W
184	Rangia.....................India	26·32 N	91·39 E
196	Rangoon (răŋ-gōōn')........Bur.	16·46 N	96·09 E
184	Rangpur (rŭng'pōōr)........Bngl.	25·48 N	89·19 E
183	Rangsang (I.) (räng'säng') Indon. (Singapore In.)	0·53 N	103·05 E
149	Rangsdorf (rängs'dōrf) G.D.R. (Berlin In.)	52·17 N	13·25 E
184	Rānīganj (rä-nē-gŭnj')......India	23·40 N	87·08 E
90	Rankin Inlet (răŋ'kĕn)......Can.	62·45 N	94·27 W
166	Ranova (R.) (rä'nô-vȧ)..Sov. Un.	53·55 N	40·03 E
107	Ransomville (răn'sum-vĭl) NY (Buffalo In.)	43·15 N	78·54 W
183	Rantau.....Mala. (Singapore In.)	2·35 N	101·58 E
196	Rantelkomboa, Bulu (Mtn.) Indon.	3·22 S	119·50 E

ng-sing; ŋ-baŋk; N-nasalized n; nŏd; cŏmmit; ōld; ôbey; ôrder; fōōd; fŏŏt; ou-out; s-soft; sh-dish; th-thin; pūre; ůnite; ûrn; stŭd; circŭs; ü-as "y" in study; '-indeterminate vowel.

ăt; fînăl; rāte; senăte; ärm; àsk; sofá; fâre; ch-choose; dh-as th in other; bē; êvent; bĕt; recĕnt; cratēr; g-go; gh-guttural g; bĭt; ĭ-short neutral; rīde; ĸ-guttural k as ch in German ich;

Page	Name Pronunciation Region	Lat. °′	Long. °′
165	Reşita (râ'shê-tà) Rom.	45·18 N	21·56 E
75	Resolute (rěz-ô-lūt') Can.	74·41 N	95·00 W
91	Resolution (I.) (rěz-ô-lū'shŭn) Can.	61·30 N	63·58 W
205	Resolution (I.) (rěz-ŏl-ûshûn) N. Z. (In.)	45·43 S	166·00 E
98	Restigouche (R.) (rěs-tê-gōōsh') Can.	47·35 N	67·35 W
134	Restrepo (rěs-trě'pô) Col. (In.)	3·49 N	76·31 W
134	Restrepo Col. (In.)	4·16 N	73·32 W
126	Retalhuleu (rā-täl-ōō-lān') Guat.	14·31 N	91·41 W
160	Rethel (r-tl') Fr.	49·34 N	4·20 E
164	Réthimnon Grc. (In.)	35·21 N	24·30 E
149	Retie Bel. (Brussels In.)	51·16 N	5·08 E
112	Retsil (rět'sĭl) Wa. (Seattle In.)	47·33 N	122·37 W
220	Reunion (rā-ü-nyôn') Afr.	21·06 S	55·36 E
163	Reus (rā'ōōs) Sp.	41·08 N	1·05 E
158	Reutlingen (roit'lĭng-ěn) F.R.G.	48·29 N	9·14 E
174	Reutov (rě-ōōt'ôf) Sov. Un. (Moscow In.)	55·45 N	37·52 E
	Reval, see Tallinn		
174	Revda (ryâv'dá) Sov. Un. (Urals In.)	56·48 N	59·57 E
93	Revelstoke (rěv'ěl-stōk) Can.	51·59 N	118·12 W
127	Reventazon, R. (rå-věn-tä-zōn') C. R.	10·10 N	83·30 W
99	Revere (rê-vēr') Ma. (In.)	42·24 N	71·01 W
92	Revillagigedo Chan (rě-vĭl'á-gĭ-gē'dō) Ak.	55·10 N	131·13 W
92	Revillagigedo I. Ak.	55·35 N	131·23 W
122	Revillagigedo, Islas (I.) (ê's-läs-rě-vêl-yä-hé'gě-dô) Mex.	18·45 N	111·00 W
160	Revin (rē-văN) Fr.	49·56 N	4·34 E
184	Rewa (rā'wä) India	24·41 N	81·11 E
184	Rewāri India	28·19 N	76·39 E
111	Rexburg (rěks'bûrg) Id.	43·50 N	111·48 W
118	Rey, L. (rā) Mex.	27·00 N	103·33 W
127	Rey, Isla del (I.) (ê's-lä-děl-rā'ê) Pan.	8·20 N	78·40 W
134	Reyes (rā'yěs) Bol.	14·19 S	67·16 W
114	Reyes, Pt. Ca.	38·00 N	123·00 W
146	Reykjanes (C.) (rā'kyá-něs) Ice.	63·37 N	24·33 W
150	Reykjavik (rā'kyá-věk) Ice.	64·09 N	21·39 W
118	Reynosa (rā-ê-nō'sä) Mex.	26·05 N	98·21 W
186	Rezā'īyeh (rě-zī'â) Iran	37·30 N	45·15 E
166	Rēzekne (rå'zěk-ně) Sov. Un.	56·31 N	27·19 E
174	Rezh (rězh') Sov. Un. (Urals In.)	57·22 N	61·23 E
167	Rezina (ryězh'ě-nĭ) Sov. Un.	47·44 N	28·56 E
164	Rhaetien Alps (Mts.) It.	46·22 N	10·33 E
155	Rheden (rā'děn) Neth.	52·02 N	6·02 E
161	Rheinberg (rīn'běrgh) F.R.G. (Ruhr In.)	51·33 N	6·37 E
158	Rheine (rī'ně) F.R.G.	52·16 N	7·26 E
158	Rheinland-Pfalz (Rhineland-Palatinate) (State) F.R.G.	50·05 N	6·40 E
158	Rhein R. (rīn) F.R.G.	50·34 N	7·21 E
161	Rheydt (rě'yt) F.R.G. (Ruhr In.)	51·10 N	6·28 E
140	Rhine (R.) Eur.	50·34 N	7·21 E
109	Rhinelander (rīn'lăn-dēr) Wi.	45·39 N	89·25 W
149	Rhin Kanal (Can.) (rēn kä-näl') G.D.R. (Berlin In.)	52·47 N	12·40 E
149	Rhin R. (rēn) G.D.R. (Berlin In.)	52·52 N	12·49 E
140	Rhine (R.) Eur.	50·34 N	7·21 E
103	Rhode Island (State) (rōd ī'lănd) U. S.	41·35 N	71·40 W
213	Rhodes (rôdz) S. Afr. (Natal In.)	30·48 S	27·56 E
209	Rhodesia (rô-dē'zhĭ-á) Afr.	17·50 S	29·30 E
165	Rhodope Mts. (rô'dô-pě) Bul.	42·00 N	24·08 E
154	Rhondda (rŏn'dhá) Wales	51·40 N	3·40 W
160	Rhône (R.) (rōn) Fr.	45·14 N	4·53 E
149	Rhoon Neth. (Amsterdam In.)	51·52 N	4·24 E
154	Rhum (I.) (rŭm) Scot.	57·00 N	6·20 W
135	Riachão (rê-ä-chouN') Braz.	7·15 S	46·30 W
113	Rialto (rē-ăl'tō) Ca. (In.)	34·06 N	117·23 W
183	Riau (Prov.) Indon. (Singapore In.)	0·56 N	101·25 E
196	Riau, Kepulauan (I.) Indon.	0·30 N	104·55 E
183	Riau, Selat (Str.) Indon. (Singapore In.)	0·40 N	104·27 E
162	Riaza (R.) (rê-ä'thä) Sp.	41·25 N	3·25 W
162	Ribadavia (rē-bä-dhä'vê-ä) Sp.	42·18 N	8·06 W
162	Ribadeo (rē-bä-dhā'ō) Sp.	37·32 N	7·05 W
162	Ribadesella (rē'bä-dā-säl'yä) Sp.	43·30 N	5·02 W
217	Ribauè Moz.	14·57 S	38·17 E
154	Ribble, R. (rĭb''l) Eng.	53·10 N	3·15 W
156	Ribe (rē'bě) Den.	55·20 N	8·45 E
137	Ribeirão Prêto (rê-bā-rouN-prě'tô) Braz. (Rio de Janeiro In.)	21·11 S	47·47 W
116	Ribera (rē-bě'rä) NM	35·23 N	105·27 W
134	Riberalta (rē-bå-räl'tä) Bol.	11·06 S	66·02 W
109	Rib Lake (rĭb lāk) Wi.	45·20 N	90·11 W
114	Rice (rīs) Ca.	34·05 N	114·50 W
105	Rice (L.) Can.	44·05 N	78·10 W
113	Rice L. Mn. (Minneapolis, St. Paul In.)	45·10 N	93·09 W
109	Rice Lake Wi.	45·30 N	91·44 W
101	Richards I. (rĭch'ěrds) Can.	69·45 N	135·30 W
113	Richards Landing (lănd'ĭng) Can. (Sault Ste. Marie In.)	46·18 N	84·02 W
113	Richardson (rĭch'ěrd-sŭn) Tx. (Dallas, Fort Worth In.)	32·56 N	96·44 W
112	Richardson Wa. (Seattle In.)	48·27 N	122·54 W
90	Richardson Mts. Can.	66·58 N	136·19 W
105	Richardson Park (pärk) De.	39·45 N	75·35 W
105	Richelieu (R.) (rēsh'lyû') Can.	45·05 N	73·25 W
113	Richfield (rĭch-fēld) Mn. (Minneapolis, St. Paul In.)	44·53 N	93·17 W
107	Richfield Oh. (Cleveland In.)	41·14 N	81·38 W
115	Richfield Ut.	38·45 N	112·05 W
105	Richford (rĭch'fērd) Vt.	45·00 N	72·35 W
117	Rich Hill (rĭch hĭl) Mo.	38·05 N	94·21 W
98	Richibucto (rĭ-chĭ-bŭk'tō) Can.	46·41 N	64·52 W
120	Richland (rĭch'lănd) Ga.	32·05 N	84·40 W
110	Richland Wa.	46·17 N	119·19 W
109	Richland Center (sěn'tēr) Wi.	43·20 N	90·25 W
205	Richmond (rĭch'mŭnd) Austl.	20·47 S	143·14 E
202	Richmond Austl. (Sydney In.)	33·36 S	150·45 E
112	Richmond Ca. (San Francisco In.)	37·56 N	122·21 W
98	Richmond Can.	45·40 N	72·07 W
100	Richmond Can. (Ottawa In.)	45·12 N	75·49 W
107	Richmond Il. (Chicago In.)	42·29 N	88·18 W
104	Richmond In.	39·50 N	85·00 W
104	Richmond Ky.	37·45 N	84·20 W
117	Richmond Mo.	39·16 N	93·58 W
119	Richmond Tx.	29·35 N	95·45 W
213	Richmond S. Afr. (Natal In.)	29·52 S	30·17 E
111	Richmond Ut.	41·55 N	111·50 W
105	Richmond Va.	37·35 N	77·30 W
112	Richmond Beach Wa. (Seattle In.)	47·47 N	122·23 W
113	Richmond Heights Mo. (St. Louis In.)	38·38 N	90·20 W
112	Richmond Highlands Wa. (Seattle In.)	47·46 N	122·22 W
100	Richmond Hill (hĭl) Can. (Toronto In.)	43·53 N	79·26 W
120	Richton (rĭch'tŭn) Ms.	31·20 N	89·54 W
104	Richwood (rĭch'wŏŏd) WV	38·10 N	80·30 W
149	Ridderkerk Neth. (Amsterdam In.)	51·52 N	4·35 E
100	Rideau (R.) Can. (Ottawa In.)	45·17 N	75·41 W
105	Rideau L. (rê-dō') Can.	44·40 N	76·20 W
106	Ridgefield (rij'fēld) Ct. (New York In.)	41·16 N	73·30 W
112	Ridgefield Wa. (Portland In.)	45·49 N	122·40 W
105	Rigeley (rĭj'lê) WV	39·40 N	78·45 W
107	Ridgeway (rĭj'wā) Can. (Buffalo In.)	42·53 N	79·02 W
106	Ridgewood (ridj'wŏŏd) NJ (New York In.)	40·59 N	74·08 W
105	Ridgway Pa.	41·25 N	78·40 W
95	Riding Mtn. (rīd'ĭng) Can.	50·37 N	99·37 W
90	Riding Mountain Natl. Park (rīd'ĭng) Can.	50·59 N	99·19 W
128	Riding Rocks (Is.) Ba.	25·20 N	79·10 W
213	Riebeek-Oos S. Afr. (Natal In.)	33·14 S	26·09 E
158	Ried (rēd) Aus.	48·13 N	13·30 E
158	Riesa (rē'zà) G.D.R.	51·17 N	13·17 E
164	Rieti (rê-ā'tē) It.	42·25 N	12·51 E
213	Rievleidam (L.) S. Afr. (Johannesburg & Pretoria In.)	25·52 S	28·18 E
115	Rifle (rī'f'l) Co.	39·35 N	107·50 W
157	Rīga (rē'gá) Sov. Un.	56·55 N	24·05 E
157	Riga, G. of Sov. Un.	57·56 N	23·05 E
186	Rīgān Iran	28·45 N	58·55 E
100	Rigaud (rê-gō') Can. (Montreal In.)	45·29 N	74·18 W
111	Rigby (rĭg'bê) Id.	43·40 N	111·55 W
186	Rīgestān (Reg.) Afr.	30·53 N	64·42 E
91	Rigolet (rĭg-ō-lā') Can.	54·10 N	58·40 W
157	Riihimäki Fin.	60·44 N	24·44 E
164	Rijeka (Fiume) (rī-yě'kä) Yugo.	45·22 N	14·24 E
149	Rijkevorsel Bel. (Brussels In.)	51·21 N	4·46 E
149	Rijswijk Neth. (Amsterdam In.)	52·03 N	4·19 E
159	Rika R. (rê'kà) Sov. Un.	48·21 N	23·37 E
160	Rille (R.) (rēl) Fr.	49·12 N	0·43 E
215	Rima (R.) Nig.	13·30 N	5·50 E
159	Rimavska Sobota (rē'máf-skä sô'bô-tà) Czech.	48·25 N	20·01 E
156	Rimbo (rēm'bōō) Swe.	59·45 N	18·22 E
164	Rimini (rē'mê-nē) It.	44·03 N	12·33 E
165	Rîmnicu Sărat Rom.	45·24 N	27·06 E
165	Rîmnicu-Vîlcea Rom.	45·07 N	24·22 E
98	Rimouski (rê-mōōs'kê) Can.	48·27 N	68·32 W
124	Rinc n de Romos (rên-kōn dā rô-mōs') Mex.	22·13 N	102·21 W
196	Rindjani, Gunung (Mtn.) Indon.	8·39 S	116·22 E
156	Ringkøbing (rĭng'kûb-ĭng) Den.	56·06 N	8·14 E
156	Ringkøbing Fd. Den.	55·55 N	8·04 E
156	Ringsaker (rĭngs'äk-ēr) Nor.	60·55 N	10·40 E
156	Ringsted (rĭng'stědh) Den.	55·27 N	11·49 E
150	Ringvassöy (I.) (rĭng'väs-ûê) Nor.	69·58 N	16·43 E
202	Ringwood Austl. (Melbourne In.)	37·49 S	145·14 E
122	Rio Abajo (rê'ō-ä-bä'κō) Pan. (In.)	9·01 N	78·30 W
124	Rio Balsas (rê'ō-bäl-säs) Mex.	17·59 N	99·45 W
134	Riobamba (rē'ō-bäm-bä) Ec.	1·45 S	78·37 W
137	Rio Bonito (rē'ōō bō-nē'tōō) Braz. (Rio de Janeiro In.)	22·44 S	42·38 W
134	Rio Branco (rē'ōō bräŋ'kōō) Braz.	9·57 S	67·50 W
136	Río Branco (rêô blănčô) Ur.	32·33 S	53·29 W
135	Rio Branco (Ter.) Braz.	2·35 N	61·25 W
137	Rio Casca (rē'ō-kà's-kä) Braz. (Rio de Janeiro In.)	20·15 S	42·39 W
135	Rio Chico (rê'ō chê'kŏ) Ven. (In.)	10·20 N	65·58 W
137	Rio Claro (rē'ōō klä'rōō) Braz. (Rio de Janeiro In.)	21·25 S	47·33 W
136	Río Cuarto (rē'ō kwär'tō) Arg.	33·05 S	64·15 W
137	Rio das Flores (rē'ō-däs-flô-rěs) Braz. (Rio de Janeiro In.)	22·10 S	43·35 W
136	Rio de Janeiro (rē'ōō dā zhä-nâ'ê-rōō) Braz. (Rio de Janeiro In.)	22·50 S	43·20 W
135	Rio de Janeiro (State) Braz.	22·27 S	42·43 W
127	Río de Jesús (rê'ō-dě-κě-sōō's) Pan.	7·54 N	80·59 W
136	Río Dercero (rê'ō děr-sě'rô) Arg.	32·12 S	63·59 W
125	Rio Frío (rê'ō-frē'ô) Mex. (In.)	19·21 N	98·40 W
136	Río Gallegos (rē'ō gä-lā'gôs) Arg.	51·43 S	69·15 W
136	Rio Grande (rē'ōō grän'dě) Braz.	31·04 S	52·14 W
124	Rio Grande (rē'ō grän'dā) Mex.	23·51 N	102·59 W
118	Riogrande (rē'ō grån-dā) Tx.	26·23 N	98·48 W
115	Rio Grande (R.) (rē'ōō grän'dě) Co.	37·44 N	106·51 W
135	Rio Grande do Norte (State) (rē'ōō grän'dě dōō nôr'tě) Braz.	5·26 S	37·20 W
136	Rio Grande do Sul (State) (rē'ōō grän'dě-dô-sōō'l) Braz.	29·00 S	54·00 W
134	Ríohacha (rē'ō-ä'chä) Col.	11·30 N	72·54 W
127	Río Hato (rê'ō-ä'tô) Pan.	8·19 N	80·11 W
160	Riom (rê-ôN') Fr.	45·54 N	3·08 E
209	Rio Muni (Prov.) (rē'ō mōō'nê) Equat. Gui.	1·47 N	8·33 E
134	Ríonegro (rê'ō-ně'grō) Col. (In.)	6·09 N	75·22 W
136	Río Negro (Prov.) (rē'ō nā'grō) Arg.	40·15 S	68·15 W
137	Río Negro (Dept.) (rê'ō-ně'grō) Ur. (Buenos Aires In.)	32·48 S	57·45 W
136	Rio Negro, Embalse del (Res.) (ěm-bä'l-sě-děl-rê'ō-ně'grō) Ur.	32·45 S	55·50 W
164	Rionero (rē-ō-nā'rō) It.	40·55 N	15·42 E
137	Rio Novo (rē'ō-nô'vô) Braz. (Rio de Janeiro In.)	21·30 S	43·08 W
135	Rio Pardo de Minas (rē'ō pär'dō-dě-mē'näs) Braz.	15·43 S	42·24 W
137	Rio Pombo (rē'ō pôm'bä) Braz. (Rio de Janeiro In.)	21·17 S	43·09 W
137	Rio Sorocaba, Represado (Res.) (rě-prě-sä-dô-rē'ō-sô-rō-kä'bä) Braz. (Rio de Janeiro In.)	23·37 S	47·19 W
134	Ríosucio (rē'ō-sōō'syō) Col. (In.)	5·25 N	75·41 W
163	Riou, Oued (R.) (ōō-ěd rĭ-ōō) Alg.	35·45 N	1·18 E
196	Riouw, Pulau-Pulau (Is.) Indon.	0·30 N	104·55 E
135	Rio Verde (věr'dě) Braz.	17·47 S	50·49 W
124	Ríoverde (rē'ō-věr'då) Mex.	21·54 N	99·59 W
148	Ripley (rĭp'lê) Eng.	53·03 N	1·24 W
120	Ripley Ms.	34·44 N	88·55 W
120	Ripley Tn.	35·44 N	89·34 W
163	Ripoll (rê-pōl'') Sp.	42·10 N	2·10 E
109	Ripon (rĭp'ŏn) Wi.	43·49 N	88·50 W
204	Ripon (I.) Austl.	20·05 S	118·10 E
211	Ripon Falls Ug.	0·38 N	33·02 E
134	Risaralda (Dept.) Col. (In.)	6·45 S	76·00 W
205	Risdon (rĭz'dŭn) Austl.	42·37 S	147·32 E
194	Rishiri (I.) (rē-shē'rē) Jap.	45·10 N	141·08 E
183	Rishon le Ẕiyyon Isr. (Palestine In.)	31·57 N	34·48 E
184	Rishra India (In.)	22·42 N	88·22 E
104	Rising Sun (rīz'ĭng sŭn) In.	38·55 N	84·55 W
156	Risor (rēs'ûr) Nor.	58·44 N	9·10 E
134	Ritacuva, Alto (Mtn.) (ä'l-tô-rē-tä-kōō'vä) Col.	6·22 N	72·13 W
107	Rittman (rĭt'năn) Oh. (Cleveland In.)	40·58 N	81·47 W
110	Ritzville (rĭts'vĭl) Wa.	47·08 N	118·23 W
156	Riuvenfjell (Mts.) (rĭu-věn-fyěl') Nor.	59·20 N	6·55 E
129	Riva (rē'vä) Dom. Rep.	19·10 N	69·55 W
164	Riva (rê'vä) It.	45·54 N	10·49 E
106	Riva (rĭ'vä) Md. (Baltimore In.)	38·57 N	76·36 W
126	Rivas (rē'väs) Nic.	11·25 N	85·51 W
160	Rive-de-Gier (rēv-dě-zhê-ā') Fr.	45·32 N	4·37 E
136	Rivera (rê-vā'rä) Ur.	30·52 S	55·32 W
210	River Cess (rĭv'ēr sěs) Lib.	5·46 N	9·52 W
107	Riverdale (rĭv'ēr dāl) Il. (Chicago In.)	41·38 N	87·36 W
113	Riverdale Ut. (Salt Lake City In.)	41·11 N	112·00 W
120	River Falls Al.	31·20 N	86·25 W
109	River Falls Wi.	44·48 N	92·38 W
105	Riverhead (rĭv'ēr hěd) NY	40·55 N	72·40 W
203	Riverina (Reg.) (rĭv-ēr-ē'nä) Austl.	34·55 S	144·30 E
92	River Jordan (jôr'dăn) Can. (Seattle In.)	48·25 N	124·03 W
113	River Oaks (ōkz) Tx. (Dallas, Fort Worth In.)	32·47 N	97·24 W
107	River Rouge (rōōzh) Mi. (Detroit In.)	42·16 N	83·09 W
95	Rivers Can.	50·01 N	100·15 W

Page	Name	Pronunciation	Region	Lat. °'	Long. °'
113	Riverside (rĭv'ẽr-sīd)				
			Ca. (Los Angeles In.)	33·59 N	117·21 W
106	Riverside....NJ (Philadelphia In.)			40·02 N	74·58 W
92	Rivers Inlet		Can.	51·45 N	127·15 W
202	Riverstone....Austl. (Sydney In.)			33·41 S	150·52 E
105	Riverton		Va.	39·00 N	78·15 W
111	Riverton		Wy.	43·02 N	108·24 W
160	Rivesaltes (rēv'zält')		Fr.	42·48 N	2·48 E
121	Riviera Beach (rĭv-ĭ-ĕr'á bēch)				
			Fl. (In.)	26·46 N	80·04 W
106	Riviera Beach.Md. (Baltimore In.)			39·10 N	76·32 W
100	Rivie're Beaudette (bō-dĕt')				
			Can. (Montreal In.)	45·14 N	74·20 W
98	Rivière-du-Loup (rẽ-vyâr' dü lōō')				
			Can.	47·50 N	69·32 W
100	Rivière Que Barre (rēv-yĕr' kē-bär)				
			Can. (Edmonton In.)	53·47 N	113·51 W
98	Rivière-Trois-Pistoles (trwä'pēs-tôl').Can.			48·07 N	69·10 W
186	Riyadh (Ar Rīyáḍ)		Sau. Ar.	24·31 N	46·47 E
171	Rize (rē'zĕ)		Tur.	41·00 N	40·30 E
165	Rizzuto, C. (rēt-sōō'tô)		It.	38·53 N	17·05 E
156	Rjukan (ryōō'kän)		Nor.	59·53 N	8·30 E
160	Roanne (rō-än')		Fr.	46·02 N	4·04 E
120	Roanoke (rō'á-nōk)		Al.	33·08 N	85·21 W
121	Roanoke		Va.	37·16 N	79·55 W
121	Roanoke (R.)		NC-Va.	36·17 N	77·22 W
121	Roanoke (Staunton) (R.)		Va.	37·05 N	79·20 W
121	Roanoke Rapids		NC	36·25 N	77·40 W
121	Roanoke Rapids, L.		NC	36·28 N	77·37 W
115	Roan Plat. (rōn)		Co.	39·25 N	108·50 W
126	Roatan (rō-ä-tän')		Hond.	16·18 N	86·33 W
126	Roatan I.		Hond.	16·19 N	86·46 W
212	Robbeneiland (I.)....S. Afr. (In.)			33·48 S	18·22 E
107	Robbins (rŏb'ĭnz).Il. (Chicago In.)			41·39 N	87·42 W
113	Robbinsdale (rŏb'ĭnz-dāl)				
			Mn. (Minneapolis, St. Paul In.)	45·03 N	93·22 W
112	Robe (rōb)......Wa. (Seattle In.)			48·06 N	121·50 W
205	Roberts, Mt. (rŏb'ẽrts)....Austl.			32·05 S	152·30 E
110	Roberts, Pt. (rŏb'ẽrts)				
			Wa. (Vancouver In.)	48·58 N	123·05 W
99	Robertson, Lac (L.)....Can.			51·00 N	59·10 W
214	Robertsport (rŏb'ẽrts-pōrt)...Lib.			6·45 N	11·22 W
91	Roberval (rŏb'ẽr-vál) (rô-bẽr-vál')				
			Can.	48·32 N	72·15 W
104	Robinson (rŏb'ĭn-sŭn)		Il.	39·00 N	87·45 W
99	Robinson's		Can.	48·16 N	58·50 W
203	Robinvale (rŏb-ĭn'vāl)		Austl.	34·45 S	142·45 E
95	Roblin		Can.	51·15 N	101·25 W
93	Robson, Mt. (rŏb'sŭn)		Can.	53·07 N	119·09 W
119	Robstown (rŏbz'toun)		Tx.	27·46 N	97·41 W
163	Roca, Cabo da (C.) (kâ'bō-dä-rō'kâ)				
			Port. (Lisbon In.)	38·47 N	9·30 W
212	Roçadas (rô-kä'däs)		Ang.	16·50 S	15·05 E
135	Rocas, Atol das (Atoll) (ä-tôl-däs-rō'kás).Braz.			3·50 S	33·46 W
133	Rocedos São Pedro E São Paulo (I.) (rô-zē'dôs-soun-pē'drô-ĕ-soun-pä͞oo-lô).Braz.			1·50 N	30·00 W
136	Rocha (rō'chás)		Ur.	34·26 S	54·14 W
148	Rochdale (rŏch'dāl)		Eng.	53·37 N	2·09 W
129	Roche à Bateau (rôsh à bà-tō')				
			Hai.	18·10 N	74·00 W
160	Rochefort (rôsh-fōr')		Fr.	45·55 N	0·57 W
109	Rochelle (rô-shĕl')		Il.	41·53 N	89·06 W
104	Rochester (rŏch'ĕs-tēr)		In.	41·05 N	86·20 W
107	Rochester		Mi. (Detroit In.)	42·41 N	83·09 W
109	Rochester		Mn.	44·01 N	92·30 W
105	Rochester		NH	43·20 N	71·00 W
105	Rochester		NY	43·15 N	77·35 W
107	Rochester		Pa. (Pittsburgh In.)	40·42 N	80·16 W
109	Rock (R.)		Il.	41·40 N	89·52 W
108	Rock (R.)		Ia.	43·17 N	96·13 W
112	Rock (R.)		Or. (Portland In.)	45·34 N	122·52 W
112	Rock (R.)		Or. (Portland In.)	45·52 N	123·14 W
106	Rockaway (rŏck'â-wā)				
			NJ (New York In.)	40·54 N	74·30 W
202	Rockbank.Austl. (Melbourne In.)			37·44 S	144·40 E
100	Rockcliffe Park (rok'klĭf pärk)				
			Can. (Ottawa In.)	45·27 N	75·40 W
94	Rock Cr. (rŏk)		Can.	49·01 N	107·00 W
107	Rock Cr.....Il. (Chicago In.)			41·16 N	87·54 W
111	Rock Cr.		Mt.	46·25 N	113·40 W
110	Rock Cr.		Or.	45·30 N	120·06 W
110	Rock Cr.		Wa.	47·09 N	117·50 W
106	Rockdale.....Md. (Baltimore In.)			39·22 N	76·49 W
119	Rockdale (rŏk'dāl)		Tx.	30·39 N	97·00 W
109	Rock Falls (rŏk fôlz)		Il.	41·45 N	89·42 W
109	Rockford (rŏk'fẽrd)		Il.	42·16 N	89·07 W
205	Rockhampton (rŏk-hămp'tŭn)		Austl.	23·26 S	150·29 E
121	Rockhill (rŏk'hĭl)		SC	34·55 N	81·01 W
121	Rockingham (rŏk'ĭng-hăm)....NC			34·54 N	79·45 W
148	Rockingham For. (rok'ĭng-hăm)				
			Eng.	52·29 N	0·43 W
109	Rock Island		Il.	41·31 N	90·37 W

Page	Name	Pronunciation	Region	Lat. °'	Long. °'
110	Rock Island Dam (ī lănd)....Wa.			47·17 N	120·33 W
100	Rockland (rŏk'lănd)				
			Can. (Ottawa In.)	45·33 N	75·17 W
98	Rockland		Me.	44·06 N	69·09 W
99	Rockland		Ma. (In.)	42·07 N	70·55 W
203	Rockland Res.		Austl.	36·55 S	142·20 E
120	Rockmart (rŏk'märt)		Ga.	33·58 N	85·00 W
113	Rockmont (rŏk'mŏnt)				
			Wi. (Duluth In.)	46·34 N	91·54 W
104	Rockport (rŏk'pōrt)		In.	38·20 N	87·00 W
99	Rockport		Ma. In.	42·39 N	70·37 W
117	Rockport		Mo.	40·25 N	95·30 W
119	Rockport		Tx.	28·03 N	97·03 W
108	Rock Rapids (răp'ĭdz)		Ia.	43·26 N	96·10 W
129	Rock Sd.		Ba.	24·50 N	76·05 W
118	Rocksprings (rŏk sprĭngs)		Tx.	30·02 N	100·12 W
111	Rock Springs		Wy.	41·35 N	109·13 W
135	Rockstone (rŏk'stōn)		Guy.	5·55 N	57·27 W
108	Rock Valley (văl'ĭ)		Ia.	43·13 N	96·17 W
104	Rockville (rŏk'vĭl)		In.	39·45 N	87·15 W
106	Rockville....Md. (Baltimore In.)			39·05 N	77·11 W
106	Rockville Centre (sĕn'tēr)				
			NY (New York In.)	40·39 N	73·39 W
117	Rockwall (rŏk'wôl)		Tx.	32·55 N	96·23 W
109	Rockwell City (rŏk'wĕl)		Ia.	42·22 N	94·37 W
100	Rockwood (rŏk-wōōd)				
			Can. (Toronto In.)	43·37 N	80·08 W
98	Rockwood		Me.	45·39 N	69·45 W
120	Rockwood		Tn.	35·51 N	84·41 W
111	Rocky Boys Ind. Res.		Mt.	48·08 N	109·34 W
116	Rocky Ford		Co.	38·02 N	103·43 W
106	Rocky Hill (hĭl)				
			NJ (New York In.)	40·24 N	74·38 W
96	Rocky Island L.		Can.	46·56 N	83·04 W
121	Rocky Mount		NC	35·55 N	77·47 W
93	Rocky Mountain House		Can.	52·22 N	114·55 W
116	Rocky Mountain Natl. Park..Co.			40·29 N	106·06 W
75	Rocky Mts.		N. A.	50·00 N	114·00 W
107	Rocky River..Oh. (Cleveland In.)			41·29 N	81·51 W
107	Rocky R., East Br.				
			Oh. (Cleveland In.)	41·13 N	81·43 W
107	Rocky R., West Br.				
			Oh. (Cleveland In.)	41·17 N	81·54 W
129	Rodas (rō'dhás)		Cuba	22·20 N	80·35 W
148	Roden (R.) (rō'dĕn)		Eng.	52·49 N	2·38 W
112	Rodeo (rō'dēō)				
			Ca. (San Francisco In.)	38·02 N	122·16 W
118	Rodeo (rō-dā'ō)		Mex.	25·12 N	104·34 W
92	Roderick I. (rŏd'ĕ-rĭk)		Can.	52·40 N	128·22 W
160	Rodez (rô-dĕz')		Fr.	44·22 N	2·34 E
153	Ródhos		Grc.	36·24 N	28·15 E
153	Ródhos (I.)		Grc.	36·00 N	28·29 E
159	Rodnei, Muntii (Mts.) (rôd'nĕ-ê)				
			Rom.	47·41 N	24·05 E
166	Rodniki (rôd'nĕ-kê)		Sov. Un.	57·08 N	41·48 E
165	Rodonit, Kep I (C.)		Alb.	41·38 N	19·01 E
	Rodosto, see Tekirdağ				
106	Roebling (rōb'lĭng)				
			NJ (Philadelphia In.)	40·07 N	74·48 W
204	Roebourne (rō'bŭrn)		Austl.	20·50 S	117·15 E
204	Roebuck, B. (rō'bŭck)		Austl.	18·15 S	121·10 E
218	Roedtan		S. Afr.		
			(Johannesburg & Pretoria In.)	24·37 S	29·08 E
155	Roermond (rōōr'mônt)		Neth.	51·11 N	6·00 E
155	Roeselare		Bel.	50·55 N	3·05 E
112	Roesiger (L.) (rōz'ĭ-gēr)				
			Wa. (Seattle In.)	47·59 N	121·56 W
91	Roes Welcome Sd. (rōz)		Can.	64·10 N	87·23 W
166	Rogachëv (rôg'á-chyôf)		Sov. Un.	53·07 N	30·04 E
165	Rogatica (rô-gä'tê-tsä)		Yugo.	43·46 N	19·00 E
159	Rogatin (rô-gä'tĭn)		Sov. Un.	49·22 N	24·37 E
117	Rogers (rŏj-ērz)		Ar.	36·19 N	94·07 W
104	Rogers City		Mi.	45·30 N	83·50 W
120	Rogersville		Tn.	36·21 N	83·00 W
160	Rognac (rôn-yäk')		Fr. (In.)	43·29 N	5·15 E
134	Rogoaguado (L.) (rō'gô-ä-gwä-dô)				
			Bol.	12·42 S	66·46 W
167	Rogovskaya (rô-gôf'skà-yà)				
			Sov. Un.	45·43 N	38·42 E
158	Rogózno (rô'gôzh-nô)		Pol.	52·44 N	16·53 E
110	Rogue R. (rōg)		Or.	42·32 N	124·13 W
156	Röikenviken (rû̈e'kĕn-vēk-ĕn)				
			Nor.	60·27 N	10·26 E
137	Rojas (rō'häs)				
			Arg. (Buenos Aires In.)	34·11 S	60·42 W
125	Rojo, Cabo (C.) (rō'hō)		Mex.	21·35 N	97·16 W
123	Rojo, Cabo (C.) (rō'hō)				
			P. R. (Puerto Rico In.)	17·55 N	67·14 W
214	Rokel (R.)		S. L.	9·00 N	11·55 W
195	Rokkō-Zan (Mtn.) (rō'kkō zän)				
			Jap. (Ōsaka In.)	34·46 N	135·16 E
158	Rokycany (rô'kĭ'tsä-nĭ)		Czech.	49·44 N	13·37 E
134	Roldanillo (rôl-dä-nē'l-yō)				
			Col. (In.)	4·24 N	76·09 W
117	Rolla		Mo.	37·56 N	91·45 W
108	Rolla		ND	48·52 N	99·32 W
156	Rollag (rōō'lägh)		Nor.	59·55 N	8·48 E
129	Rolleville		Ba.	23·40 N	76·00 W
203	Roma (rō'má)		Austl.	26·30 S	148·48 E
213	Roma		Leso. (Natal In.)	29·28 S	27·43 E

Page	Name	Pronunciation	Region	Lat. °'	Long. °'
163	Roma (Rome) (rō'mä) (rōm)				
			It. (Rome In.)	41·52 N	12·37 E
99	Romaine (R.) (rô-mĕn')		Can.	51·22 N	63·23 W
159	Roman (rō'män)		Rom.	46·56 N	26·57 E
146	Romania (rō-mā'nê-á)		Eur.	46·18 N	22·53 E
121	Romano, C. (rō-mä'nō)...Fl. (In.)			25·48 N	82·00 W
128	Romano, Cayo (I.) (kä'yō-rō-má'nô).Cuba			22·15 N	78·00 W
174	Romanovo (rō-mä'nô-vô)				
			Sov. Un. (Urals In.)	59·09 N	61·24 E
160	Romans-sur-Isère (rô-män'-sür-ē-sĕr').Fr.			45·04 N	4·49 E
197	Romblon (rŏm-blŏn')...Phil. (In.)			12·34 N	122·16 E
197	Romblon (I.)........Phil. (In.)			12·33 N	122·17 E
120	Rome (rōm)		Ga.	34·14 N	85·10 W
105	Rome		NY	43·15 N	75·25 W
	Rome, see Roma				
104	Romeo (rō'mê-ō)		Mi.	42·50 N	83·00 W
148	Romford (rŭm'fẽrd)				
			Eng. (London In.)	51·35 N	0·11 E
160	Romilly-sur-Seine (rô-mē-yē'sür-sän').Fr.			48·32 N	3·41 E
124	Romita (rō-mē'tä)		Mex.	20·53 N	101·32 W
167	Romny (rôm'nĭ)		Sov. Un.	50·46 N	33·31 E
156	Rømø (I.) (rûm'û)		Den.	55·08 N	8·17 E
113	Romoland (rō'mō'lănd)				
			Ca. (Los Angeles In.)	33·44 N	117·11 W
160	Romorantin (rô-mô-rän-tăn')..Fr.			47·24 N	1·46 E
183	Rompin (R.).Mala. (Singapore In.)			2·42 N	102·30 E
183	Rompin (R.).Mala. (Singapore In.)			2·54 N	103·10 E
107	Romulus (rom'ū lŭs)				
			Mi. (Detroit In.)	42·14 N	83·24 W
154	Ronaldsay, North (I.)......Scot.			59·21 N	2·23 W
154	Ronaldsay, South (I.) (rŏn'ăld-s'ä).Scot.			59·48 N	2·55 W
111	Ronan (rō'nán)		Mt.	47·28 N	114·03 W
135	Roncador, Serra do (Mts.) (sẽr'rá dō̄ rôn-kä-dôr').Braz.			12·44 S	52·19 W
162	Roncesvalles (rôn-sĕs-vä'l-yĕs).Sp.			43·00 N	1·17 W
104	Ronceverte (rŏn'sĕ-vûrt)....WV			37·45 N	80·30 W
162	Ronda (rōn'dä)		Sp.	37·45 N	5·10 W
134	Rondônia (Ter.)		Braz.	10·15 S	63·07 W
94	Ronge, Lac la (L.) (rŏnzh)...Can.			55·10 N	105·00 W
156	Rønne (rûn'ĕ)		Den.	55·08 N	14·46 E
156	Ronneby (rŏn'ĕ-bü)		Swe.	56·13 N	15·17 E
220	Ronne Ice Shelf		Ant.	77·30 S	38·00 W
116	Ront Ra. (Mts.) (rŏnt)		Co.	40·59 N	105·29 W
213	Roodepoort (rō'dĕ-pōrt)....S. Afr. (Johannesburg & Pretoria In.)			26·10 S	27·52 E
117	Roodhouse (rōōd'hous)		Il.	39·29 N	90·21 W
218	Rooiberg		S. Afr. (Johannesburg & Pretoria In.)	24·46 S	27·42 E
149	Roosendaal (rō'zĕn-däl)				
			Neth. (Amsterdam In.)	51·32 N	4·27 E
115	Roosevelt (rōz''vĕlt)		Ut.	40·20 N	110·00 W
115	Roosevelt (R.)		Az.	33·45 N	111·00 W
135	Roosevelt (R.) (rô'sĕ-vĕlt)		Braz.	9·22 S	60·28 W
220	Roosevelt I.		Ant.	79·30 S	168·00 W
107	Root R....Wi. (Milwaukee In.)			42·49 N	87·54 W
204	Roper (R.) (rōp'ēr)		Austl.	14·50 S	134·00 E
174	Ropsha (rŏp'shà)				
			Sov. Un. (Leningrad In.)	59·44 N	29·53 E
160	Roquefort		Fr.	43·59 N	3·00 E
134	Roques, Islas los (Is.)		Ven.	21·25 N	67·40 W
137	Roque Pérez (rō'kĕ-pĕ'rĕz) (Arg. (Buenos Aires In.)			35·23 S	59·22 W
163	Roquetas (rō-kä'täs)		Sp.	40·50 N	0·32 E
134	Roraima (Ter.) (rō'rīy-mä).Braz.			2·00 N	62·15 W
135	Roraima, Mtn. (rô-rä-ē'mä)				
			Ven.-Guy.	5·12 N	60·52 W
156	Röros (rûr'ôs)		Nor.	62·36 N	11·25 E
158	Rorschach (rōr'shäk)		Switz.	47·27 N	9·28 E
167	Ros' (R.) (rôs)		Sov. Un.	49·40 N	30·22 E
158	Rosa, Monte (Mt.) (mōn'tä rō'zä). It.			45·56 N	7·51 E
118	Rosales (rō-zä'läs)		Mex.	28·15 N	100·43 W
197	Rosales (rō-sä'lĕs)....Phil. (In.)			15·54 N	120·38 E
124	Rosamorada (rō'zä-mō-rä'dhä)				
			Mex.	22·06 N	105·16 W
125	Rosaria, Laguna (L.) (lä-gōō'nä-rō-sá'ryä).Mex.			17·50 N	93·51 W
137	Rosario		Arg. (Buenos Aires In.)	32·58 S	60·42 W
135	Rosario (rō-zä'rê-ŏ̄)		Braz.	2·49 S	44·15 W
124	Rosario		Mex.	26·30 N	105·54 W
118	Rosario		Mex.	26·31 N	105·40 W
197	Rosario		Phil. (In.)	13·49 N	121·13 W
137	Rosario..Ur. (Buenos Aires In.)			34·19 S	57·24 E
128	Rosario, Cayo (I.) (kä'yō-rō-sä'ryō).Cuba			21·40 N	81·55 W
136	Rosário do Sul (rō-zä'rê-ō̄-dô-sōō'l).Braz.			30·17 S	54·52 W
135	Rosário Oeste (ō'ĕst'ĕ)		Braz.	14·47 S	56·20 W
112	Rosario Str....Wa. (Seattle In.)			48·27 N	122·45 W
163	Rosas, Golfo de (G.) (gôl-fô-dĕ-rō'zäs).Sp.			42·10 N	3·20 E
161	Rosbach (rōz'bäk)				
			F.R.G. (Ruhr In.)	50·47 N	7·38 E
118	Roscoe (rôs'kō)		Tx.	32·26 N	100·38 W
108	Roseau (rō-zō')		Mn.	48·52 N	95·47 W

PRONOUNCING INDEX Roseau — Sabile 337

Page	Name Pronunciation Region	Lat. °′	Long. °′
127	Roseau..........Dominica (In.)	15·17 N	61·23 W
108	Roseau (R.)..............Mn.	48·52 N	96·11 W
110	Roseberg (rōz'bûrg)..........Or.	43·13 N	123·30 W
93	Rosebud (R.) (rōz'bŭd)......Can.	51·20 N	112·20 W
111	Rosebud Cr................Mt.	45·48 N	106·34 W
108	Rosebud Ind. Res...........SD	43·13 N	100·42 W
120	Rosedale..................Ms.	33·49 N	90·56 W
112	Rosedale........Wa. (Seattle In.)	47·20 N	122·39 W
210	Roseires Res..............Sud.	11·15 N	34·45 E
107	Roselle (rō-zĕl')...Il. (Chicago In.)	41·59 N	88·05 W
100	Rosemere (rōz'mēr)		
	Can. (Montreal In.)	45·38 N	73·48 W
113	Rosemount (rōz'mount)		
	Mn. (Minneapolis, St. Paul In.)	44·44 N	93·08 W
218	Rosendal (rō-sĕn'täl)......S. Afr.		
	(Johannesburg & Pretoria In.)	28·32 S	27·56 E
158	Rosenheim (rō'zĕn-hīm)....F.R.G.	47·52 N	12·06 E
94	Rosetown (rōz'toun)........Can.	51·33 N	108·00 W
	Rosetta, see Rashīd		
213	Rosettenville.............S. Afr.		
	(Johannesburg & Pretoria In.)	26·15 S	28·04 E
114	Roseville (rōz'vĭl)...........Ca.	38·44 N	121·19 W
107	Roseville........Mi. (Detroit In.)	42·30 N	82·55 W
113	Roseville...................Mn.		
	(Minneapolis, St. Paul In.)	45·01 N	93·10 W
104	Rosiclare (rōz'ĭ-klâr)..........Il.	37·30 N	88·15 W
135	Rosignol (rŏs-ĭg-nĕl)........Guy.	6·16 N	57·37 W
165	Rosiorii de Vede		
	(rô-shôr'ê dĕ vĕ-dĕ).Rom.	44·06 N	25·00 E
156	Roskilde (rôs'kĕl-dĕ)........Den.	55·39 N	12·04 E
166	Roslavl' (rôs'läv'l).......Sov. Un.	53·56 N	32·52 E
110	Roslyn (rŏz'lĭn).............Wa.	47·14 N	121·00 W
167	Rosovka...............Sov. Un.	47·14 N	36·35 E
161	Rösrath (rûz'rät)		
	F.R.G. (Ruhr In.)	50·53 N	7·11 E
107	Ross (rôs)....Oh. (Cincinnati In.)	39·19 N	84·39 W
164	Rossano (rô-sä'nō)............It.	39·34 N	16·38 E
100	Ross Cr.....Can. (Edmonton In.)	53·50 N	113·08 W
110	Ross Dam..................Wa.	48·40 N	121·07 W
97	Rosseau (L.) (rôs-sō')........Can.	45·15 N	79·30 W
205	Rossel (I.) (rô-sĕl')...Pap. N. Gui.	11·31 S	154·00 E
100	Rosser (rôs'sēr)		
	Can. (Winnipeg In.)	49·59 N	97·27 W
98	Rossignol, L...............Can.	44·10 N	65·10 W
95	Ross I.....................Can.	54·14 N	97·45 W
93	Rossland (rôs'lȧnd).........Can.	49·05 N	118·48 W
214	Rosso...............Mauritania	16·30 N	15·49 W
167	Rossosh' (rôs'sŭsh)......Sov. Un.	50·12 N	39·32 E
213	Rossouw.......S. Afr. (Natal In.)	31·12 S	27·18 E
220	Ross Sea...................Ant.	76·00 S	178·00 W
220	Ross Shelf Ice..............Ant.	81·30 S	175·00 W
120	Rossville (rôs'vĭl)............Ga.	34·57 N	85·22 W
94	Rosthern..................Can.	52·41 N	106·25 W
158	Rostock (rôs'tŭk)........G.D.R.	54·04 N	12·06 E
166	Rostov................Sov. Un.	57·13 N	39·23 E
167	Rostov (Oblast).........Sov. Un.	47·38 N	39·15 E
171	Rostov-na-Donu		
	(rôstôv-nȧ-dô-nōō).Sov. Un.	47·16 N	39·47 E
150	Rösvatn (L.) (rûs-vät'n).....Nor.	65·36 N	13·08 E
120	Roswell (rŏz'wĕl)............Ga.	34·02 N	84·21 W
116	Roswell...................NM	33·23 N	104·32 W
116	Rotan (rō-tăn')..............Tx.	32·51 N	100·27 W
158	Rothenburg...............F.R.G.	49·20 N	10·10 E
148	Rotherham (rŏdh'ēr-ăm).....Eng.	53·26 N	1·21 W
98	Rothesay (rôth'sȧ)..........Can.	45·23 N	66·00 W
154	Rothesay..................Scot.	55·50 N	3·14 W
148	Rothwell..................Eng.	53·44 N	1·30 W
196	Roti (I.) (rō'tê)...........Indon.	10·30 S	122·52 E
203	Roto (rō'tô)...............Austl.	33·07 S	145·30 E
149	Rotterdam (rôt'ēr-däm')		
	Neth. (Amsterdam In.)	51·55 N	4·27 E
158	Rottweil (rōt'vīl)..........F.R.G.	48·10 N	8·36 E
160	Roubaix (rōō-bĕ')............Fr.	50·42 N	3·10 E
160	Rouen (rōō-äN')..............Fr.	49·25 N	1·05 E
107	Rouge, R........Mi. (Detroit In.)	42·30 N	83·15 W
97	Rouge (R.)..................Can.	46·40 N	74·50 W
100	Rouge (R.) (rōōzh)		
	Can. (Toronto In.)	43·53 N	79·21 W
104	Rough River Res............Ky.	37·45 N	86·10 W
107	Round Lake.....Il. (Chicago In.)	42·21 N	88·05 W
99	Round Pd...................Can.	48·15 N	55·57 W
119	Round Rock................Tx.	30·31 N	97·41 W
112	Round Top (Mtn.) (tŏp)		
	Or. (Portland In.)	45·41 N	123·22 W
111	Roundup (round'ŭp).........Mt.	46·25 N	108·35 W
154	Rousay (I.) (rōō'zȧ).........Scot.	59·10 N	3·04 W
91	Rouyn (rōōn)...............Can.	48·22 N	79·03 W
150	Rovaniemi (rō'vȧ-nyĕ'mĭ)....Fin.	66·29 N	25·45 E
164	Rovato (rō-vä'tō)..............It.	45·33 N	10·00 E
167	Roven'ki (rō-vĕn'kĭ')....Sov. Un.	48·06 N	39·44 E
167	Roven'ki.............Sov. Un.	49·54 N	38·54 E
164	Rovereto (rō-vā-rā'tō)........It.	45·53 N	11·05 E
164	Rovigo (rō-vē'gô).............It.	45·05 N	11·48 E
164	Rovinj (rô'vēn')...........Yugo.	45·05 N	13·40 E
134	Rovira (rô-vē'rä).......Col. (In.)	4·14 N	75·13 W
159	Rovno (rôv'nō)..........Sov. Un.	50·37 N	26·17 E
167	Rovno (Oblast)..........Sov. Un.	50·55 N	27·00 E
167	Rovnoye (rôv'nô-yĕ).....Sov. Un.	48·11 N	31·46 E
217	Rovuma (Ruvuma) (R.)		
	Moz.-Tan.	10·50 S	39·50 E
99	Rowley (rou'lē).........Ma. (In.)	42·43 N	70·53 W
113	Roxana (rŏks'ăn-nȧ)		
	Il. (St. Louis In.)	38·51 N	90·05 W
196	Roxas (rô-xäs)..............Phil.	11·30 N	122·47 E
121	Roxboro (rŏks' bŭr-ô)........NC	36·22 N	78·58 W
214	Roxo, Cap (C.)..........Senegal	12·20 N	16·43 W
116	Roy (roi)..................NM	35·54 N	104·09 W
113	Roy......Ut. (Salt Lake City In.)	41·10 N	112·02 W
128	Royal (I.)..................Ba.	25·30 N	76·50 W
154	Royal Can. (roi-ȧl)..........Ire.	53·28 N	6·45 W
213	Royal Natal Natl. Pk. (roi'ăl)		
	S. Afr. (Natal In.)	28·35 S	28·54 E
112	Royal Oak (roi'ăl ōk)		
	Can. (Seattle In.)	48·30 N	123·24 W
107	Royal Oak......Mi. (Detroit In.)	42·29 N	83·09 W
104	Royalton (roi'ăl-tŭn).........Mi.	42·00 N	86·25 W
160	Royan (rwä-yäN')............Fr.	45·40 N	1·02 W
160	Roye (rwä)..................Fr.	49·43 N	2·40 E
106	Royersford (rô' yērz-fērd)		
	Pa. (Philadelphia In.)	40·11 N	75·32 W
120	Royston (roiz'tŭn)..........Ga.	34·15 N	83·06 W
148	Royton (roi'tŭn)............Eng.	53·34 N	2·07 W
161	Rozay-en-Brie (rô-zā-ĕN-brē')		
	Fr. (Paris In.)	48·41 N	2·57 E
174	Rozhaya R. (rô'zhȧ-yȧ)		
	Sov. Un. (Moscow In.)	55·20 N	37·37 E
159	Rožňava (rôzh'nyȧ-vȧ).....Czech.	48·39 N	20·32 E
171	Rtishchevo ('r-tĭsh'chĕ-vô)		
	Sov. Un.	52·15 N	43·40 E
212	Ruacana Falls....Ang.-S. W. Afr.	17·15 S	14·45 E
217	Ruaha Natl. Pk............Tan.	7·15 S	34·50 E
205	Ruapehu (Mtn.) (rōō-ȧ-pā'hōō)		
	N. Z. (In.)	39·15 S	175·37 E
217	Rubeho Mts...............Tan.	6·45 S	36·15 E
113	Rubidoux...Ca. (Los Angeles In.)	33·59 N	117·24 W
217	Rubondo I.................Tan.	2·10 S	31·55 E
172	Rubtsovsk.............Sov. Un.	51·31 N	81·17 E
101	Ruby (rōō'bê)...............Ak.	64·38 N	155·22 W
114	Ruby (L.)..................Nv.	40·11 N	115·20 W
114	Ruby Mts..................Nv.	40·11 N	115·36 W
111	Ruby R....................Mt.	45·06 N	112·10 W
156	Rudkøbing (rōōdh'kûb-ĭng)..Den.	54·56 N	10·44 E
149	Rüdnitz (rüd'nētz)		
	G.D.R. (Berlin In.)	52·44 N	13·38 E
184	Rudog (rōō'dôk)...........China	33·42 N	79·56 E
217	Rudolf, L. (rōō'dŏlf)....Ken.-Eth.	3·30 N	36·05 E
155	Rudolstadt (rōō'dôl-shtät).G.D.R.	50·46 N	13·30 E
211	Rufā'ah (rōō-fä'ä)...........Sud.	14·52 N	33·30 E
160	Ruffec (rü-fĕk')..............Fr.	46·03 N	0·11 E
217	Rufiji (R.) (rōō-fē'jê)........Tan.	8·00 S	39·20 E
214	Rufisque (rü-fēsk')........Senegal	14·43 N	17·17 W
217	Rufunsa................Zambia	15·05 S	29·40 E
110	Rufus Woods..............Wa.	48·02 N	119·33 W
148	Rugby (rŭg'bê)............Eng.	52·22 N	1·15 W
108	Rugby....................ND	48·22 N	100·00 W
148	Rugeley (rōōj'lē)...........Eng.	52·46 N	1·56 W
158	Rügen (Pen.) (rü'ghĕn)...G.D.R.	54·28 N	13·47 E
157	Ruhnu-Saar (I.) (rōōnōō-sȧ'ȧr)		
	Sov. Un.	57·46 N	23·15 E
158	Ruhr R. (rōōr)...........F.R.G.	51·18 N	8·17 E
124	Ruiz (rōōē'z)...............Mex.	21·55 N	105·09 W
134	Ruiz, Nevado del (Pk.)		
	(nĕ-vȧ'dô-dĕl-rōōē'z).Col. (In.)	4·52 N	75·20 W
157	Rūjiena (rōō'yĭ-ă-nȧ)....Sov. Un.	57·54 N	25·19 E
216	Ruki (R.)................Zaire	0·05 S	18·55 E
217	Rukwa, L. (rōōk-wä')........Tan.	8·00 S	32·25 E
109	Rum (R.) (rŭm)............Mn.	45·52 N	93·45 W
165	Ruma (rōō'mȧ)............Yugo.	45·00 N	19·53 E
211	Rumbek (rŭm'bĕk)..........Sud.	6·52 N	29·43 E
129	Rum Cay (I.)................Ba.	23·40 N	74·50 W
98	Rumford (rŭm'fērd)..........Me.	44·32 N	70·35 W
186	Rummah, Wādī ar (R.)...Sau. Ar.	26·17 N	41·45 E
183	Rummānah..Egypt (Palestine In.)	31·01 N	32·39 E
148	Runcorn (rŭŋ'kôrn).........Eng.	53·20 N	2·44 W
183	Rupat, Palau (I.) (rōō'pät)		
	Indon. (Singapore In.)	1·55 N	101·35 E
183	Rupat, Selat (Str.)		
	Indon. (Singapore In.)	1·55 N	101·17 E
111	Rupert (rōō'pērt)............Id.	42·36 N	113·41 W
91	Rupert, Rivière de (R.)......Can.	51·35 N	76·30 W
165	Ruse (Russe) (rōō'sĕ) (rōō'sĕ).Bul.	43·50 N	25·59 E
109	Rush City..................Mn.	45·40 N	92·59 W
117	Rushville (rŭsh'vĭl)...........Il.	40·08 N	90·34 W
104	Rushville...................In.	39·35 N	85·30 W
108	Rushville...................Ne.	42·43 N	102·27 W
217	Rusizi (R.)................Zaire	3·00 S	29·05 E
119	Rusk (rŭsk)................Tx.	31·49 N	95·09 W
112	Ruskin (rŭs'kĭn)		
	Can. (Vancouver In.)	49·10 N	122·25 W
149	Russ (R.).......Aus. (Vienna In.)	48·12 N	16·55 E
135	Russas (rōō's-säs)..........Braz.	4·48 S	37·50 W
	Russe, see Ruse		
112	Russell....Ca. (San Francisco In.)	37·39 N	122·08 W
95	Russell (rŭs'ĕl)............Can.	50·47 N	101·15 W
100	Russell........Can. (Ottawa In.)	45·15 N	75·22 W
116	Russell....................Ks.	38·51 N	98·51 W
104	Russell....................Ky.	38·30 N	82·45 W
205	Russell...............N. Z. (In.)	35·38 S	174·13 E
205	Russell Is...............Sol. Is.	9·16 S	158·30 E
95	Russel L...................Can.	56·15 N	101·30 W
120	Russellville (rŭs'ĕl-vĭl)........Al.	34·29 N	87·44 W
117	Russellville.................Ar.	35·16 N	93·08 W
120	Russelville..................Ky.	36·48 N	86·51 W
114	Russian (R.) (rŭsh'ăn)........Ca.	38·59 N	123·10 W
168	Russian S. F. S. R.......Sov. Un.	61·00 N	60·00 E
218	Rustenburg (rŭs'tĕn-bûrg)..S. Afr.		
	(Johannesburg & Pretoria In.)	25·40 S	26·15 E
119	Ruston (rŭs'tŭn).............La.	32·32 N	92·39 W
112	Ruston.........Wa. (Seattle In.)	47·18 N	122·30 W
167	Rutchenkovo (rōō-chĕn'kô-vô)		
	Sov. Un.	47·54 N	37·36 E
162	Rute (rōō'tā)................Sp.	37·20 N	4·34 W
114	Ruth (rōōth)................Nv.	39·17 N	115·00 W
159	Ruthenia (Reg.)..........Sov. Un.	48·25 N	23·00 E
121	Rutherfordton (rŭdh'ēr-fērd-tŭn)		
	NC	35·23 N	81·58 W
105	Rutland.....................Vt.	43·35 N	72·55 W
148	Rutland (Co.)..............Eng.	52·40 N	0·37 W
106	Rutledge (rŭt'lĕdj)		
	Md. (Baltimore In.)	39·34 N	76·33 W
217	Rutshuru (rōōt-shōō'rōō)....Zaire	1·11 S	29·27 E
164	Ruvo (rōō'vô)................It.	41·07 N	16·32 E
217	Ruvuma (Rovuma) (R.)		
	Moz.-Tan.	10·50 S	39·50 E
211	Ruwenzori Mts. (rōō-wĕn-zō'rê)		
	Afr.	0·53 N	30·00 E
166	Ruza (rōō'zȧ)...........Sov. Un.	55·42 N	36·12 E
159	Ruzhany (rōō-zhän'ĭ)....Sov. Un.	52·49 N	24·54 E
209	Rwanda.....................Afr.	2·10 S	29·37 E
174	Ryabovo (ryä'bô-vô)		
	Sov. Un. (Leningrad In.)	59·24 N	31·08 E
166	Ryazan' (ryä-zän'')......Sov. Un.	54·37 N	39·43 E
166	Ryazan' (Oblast)........Sov. Un.	54·10 N	39·37 E
166	Ryazhsk (ryäzh'sk').....Sov. Un.	53·43 N	40·04 E
170	Rybachiy, P-Ov. (Pen.)..Sov. Un.	69·50 N	33·20 E
174	Rybatskoye (rĭ-bät'skô-yĕ)		
	Sov. Un. (Leningrad In.)	59·50 N	30·31 E
166	Rybinsk (ry-bĭ'nsk).....Sov. Un.	58·02 N	38·52 E
166	Rybinskoye Vdkhr. (Res.)		
	Sov. Un.	58·23 N	38·15 E
159	Rybnik (rĭb'nêk)............Pol.	50·06 N	18·37 E
167	Rybnitsa (rĭb'nêt-sȧ)....Sov. Un.	47·45 N	29·02 E
154	Ryde (rīd).................Eng.	50·43 N	1·16 W
106	Rye (rī)......NY (New York In.)	40·58 N	73·42 W
167	Ryl'sk (rêl''sk)..........Sov. Un.	51·33 N	34·42 E
194	Ryōtsu (ryōt'sōō)...........Jap.	38·02 N	138·23 E
159	Rypin (rĭ'pên)..............Pol.	53·04 N	19·25 E
	Ryukyu, see Nansei-shotō		
159	Rzeszów (zhā-shōōf).........Pol.	50·02 N	22·00 E
166	Rzhev ('r-zhĕf)..........Sov. Un.	56·16 N	34·17 E
167	Rzhishchëv ('r-zhĭsh'chĕf)		
	Sov. Un.	49·58 N	31·05 E

S

Page	Name Pronunciation Region	Lat. °′	Long. °′
158	Saale R. (sä-lĕ)..........G.D.R.	51·14 N	11·52 E
158	Saalfeld (säl'fĕlt).........G.D.R.	50·38 N	11·20 E
158	Saar (State) (zär).........F.R.G.	49·25 N	6·50 E
158	Saarbrücken (zähr'brü-kĕn)		
	F.R.G.	49·15 N	7·01 E
157	Saaremaa (Ezel) (I.) (sä'rĕ-mä)		
	Sov. Un.	58·28 N	21·30 E
136	Saavedra (sä-ä-vā'drä).......Arg.	37·45 S	62·23 W
165	Šabac (shä'bȧts)...........Yugo.	44·45 N	19·49 E
163	Sabadell (sä-bä-dhāl')........Sp.	41·32 N	2·07 E
196	Sabah (Reg.)..............Mala.	5·10 N	116·25 E
127	Saba I. (sä'bä).Neth. Antilles (In.)	17·39 N	63·20 W
128	Sabana, Arch. de		
	(är-chē-pyĕ'lä-gô dĕ sä-bä'nä)		
	Cuba	23·05 N	80·00 W
127	Sabana, R. (sä-bä'nä).......Pan.	8·40 N	78·02 W
129	Sabana de la Mar		
	(sä-bä'nä dā lä mär').Dom. Rep.	19·05 N	69·30 W
135	Sabana de Uchire		
	(sä-bȧ'nä dĕ ōō-chē'rĕ)		
	Ven. (In.)	10·02 N	65·32 W
126	Sabanagrande (sä-bä'nä-grä'n-dĕ)		
	Hond.	13·47 N	87·16 W
134	Sabanalarga (sä-bȧ'nä-lär'gä).Col.	10·38 N	75·02 W
134	Sabanas Páramo (Mtn.)		
	(sä-bȧ'näs pȧ'rä-mô).Col. (In.)	6·28 N	76·08 W
125	Sabancuy (sä-bäŋ-kwē').....Mex.	18·58 N	91·09 W
196	Sabang (sä'bäng)...........Indon.	5·52 N	95·26 E
166	Sabaudia (sȧ-bou'dê-ä)........It.	41·19 N	13·00 E
117	Sabetha (sȧ-bĕth'ȧ)..........Ks.	39·54 N	95·49 W
212	Sabi (R.) (sä'bê)............Rh.	20·18 S	32·07 E
157	Sabile (sȧ'bê-lĕ)..........Sov. Un.	57·03 N	22·34 E

ng-sing; ŋ-baŋk; N-nasalized n; nŏd; cŏmmit; ōld; ôbey; ôrder; fōōd; fŏŏt; ou-out; s-soft; sh-dish; th-thin; pūre; ûnite; ûrn; stŭd; circŭs; ü-as "y" in study; '-indeterminate vowel.

338 Sabinal — St. Isidore-de-Laprairie PRONOUNCING INDEX

Page	Name Pronunciation Region	Lat. °′	Long. °′
118	Sabinal (sȧ-bī'nȧl) Tx.	29·19 N	99·27 W
128	Sabinal, Cayo (I.) (kä'yō sä-bē-näl'). Cuba	21·40 N	77·20 W
122	Sabinas Mex.	28·05 N	102·30 W
118	Sabinas, R. (sä-bē'näs) Mex.	26·37 N	99·52 W
118	Sabinas, Rio (R.) (rē'ō sä-bē'näs) Mex.	27·25 N	100·33 W
118	Sabinas Hidalgo (ē-däl'gō) Mex.	26·30 N	100·10 W
119	Sabine (sȧ-bēn') Tx.	29·44 N	93·54 W
220	Sabine, Mt. Ant.	72·05 S	169·10 E
103	Sabine (R.) U. S.	31·35 N	94·00 W
119	Sabine L. La.-Tx.	29·53 N	93·41 W
197	Sablayan (säb-lä-yän') Phil. (In.)	12·49 N	120·47 E
98	Sable, C. (sā'b'l) Can.	43·25 N	65·24 W
121	Sable, C. Fl. (In.)	25·12 N	81·10 W
97	Sables, Rivière aux (R.) Can.	49·00 N	70·20 W
160	Sablé-sur-Sarthe (säb-lā-sür-särt') Fr.	47·50 N	0·17 W
170	Sablya, Gora (Mtn.) Sov. Un.	64·50 N	59·00 E
162	Sàbor (R.) (sä-bōr') Port.	41·18 N	6·54 W
117	Sac (R.) (sôk) Mo.	38·11 N	93·45 W
105	Sacandaga Res. (sȧ-kăn-dâ'gȧ). NY	43·10 N	74·15 W
163	Sacavém (sä-kä-vĕN') Port. (Lisbon In.)	38·47 N	9·06 W
163	Sacavem (R.) Port. (Lisbon In.)	38·52 N	9·06 W
109	Sac City (sŏk) Ia.	42·25 N	95·00 W
95	Sachigo L. (săch'ĭ-gō) Can.	53·49 N	92·08 W
158	Sachsen (Reg.) (zäk'sĕn) G.D.R.	50·45 N	12·17 E
105	Sacketts Harbor (săk'ĕts) NY	43·55 N	76·05 W
98	Sackville (săk'vĭl) Can.	45·54 N	64·22 W
98	Saco (sô'kô) Me.	43·30 N	70·28 W
136	Saco (R.) (sä'kô) Braz. (Rio de Janeiro In.)	22·20 S	43·26 W
98	Saco (R.) Me.	43·53 N	70·46 W
136	Sacra Famalia do Tinguá (sä-krä fä-mä'lyä dô tên-gwà') Braz. (Rio de Janeiro In.)	22·29 S	43·36 W
114	Sacramento (săk-rȧ-mĕn'tō) Ca.	38·35 N	121·30 W
118	Scaramento Mex.	25·45 N	103·22 W
118	Sacramento Mex.	27·05 N	101·45 W
114	Sacramento (R.) Ca.	40·20 N	122·07 W
216	Sá da Bandeira (sä'dȧ bän-dā'rȧ) Ang.	14·55 S	13·30 E
186	Şa'dah Yemen	16·50 N	43·45 E
93	Saddle Lake Ind. Res. Can.	54·00 N	111·40 W
112	Saddle Mtn. (săd''l) Or. (Portland In.)	45·58 N	123·40 W
187	Sadiya (sŭ-dē'yä) India	27·53 N	95·35 E
194	Sado (I.) (sä'dō) Jap.	38·05 N	138·26 E
162	Sado (R.) (sä'dōō) Port.	38·15 N	8·20 W
156	Saeby (sĕ'bü) Den.	57·21 N	10·29 E
195	Saeki (sä'å-kê) Jap.	32·56 N	131·51 E
115	Safford (săf'fērd) Az.	32·50 N	109·45 W
210	Safi (Asfi) (sä'fê) (äs'fê) Mor.	32·24 N	9·09 W
171	Safid Rud (R.) Iran	36·50 N	49·40 E
195	Saga (sä'gä) Jap.	33·15 N	130·18 E
195	Sagami-Nada (Sea) (sä'gä'mê nä-dä). Jap.	35·06 N	139·24 E
107	Sagamore Hills (săg'ȧ-môr hĭlz) Oh. (Cleveland In.)	41·19 N	81·34 W
109	Saganaga (L.) (să-gȧ-nă'gȧ) Can.-Mn.	48·13 N	91·17 W
184	Sāgar India	23·55 N	78·45 E
104	Saginaw (săg'ĭ-nô) Mi.	43·25 N	84·00 W
113	Saginaw Mn. (Duluth In.)	46·51 N	92·26 W
113	Saginaw Tx. (Dallas, Fort Worth In.)	32·52 N	97·22 W
104	Saginaw B. Mi.	43·50 N	83·40 W
171	Sagiz (R.) (sä'gēz) Sov. Un.	48·30 N	56·10 E
105	Saguache (sȧ-wăch') (sȧ-gwä'chê) Co.	38·05 N	106·10 W
105	Sagauche Cr. Co.	38·05 N	106·40 W
129	Sagua de Tánamo (sä-gwä dĕ tȧ'nä-mō). Cuba	20·40 N	75·15 W
128	Sagua la Grande (sä-gwä lä grä'n-dĕ). Cuba	22·45 N	80·05 W
115	Saguaro Natl. Mon. (säg-wä'rō) Az.	32·12 N	110·40 W
96	Saguenay (R.) (săg-ē-nā') Can.	48·20 N	70·15 W
163	Sagunto (sä-gōōn'tō) Sp.	39·40 N	0·17 W
209	Sahara Des. (sȧ-hä'rȧ) Afr.	23·44 N	1·40 W
152	Saharan Atlas (Mts.) Mor.-Alg.	32·51 N	1·02 W
184	Sahāranpur (sŭ-hä'rŭn-pōōr') India	29·58 N	77·41 E
113	Sahara Village (sȧ-hä'rȧ) Ut. (Salt Lake City In.)	41·06 N	111·58 W
184	Sāhiwāl Pak.	30·43 N	73·04 E
124	Sahuayo de Dias Mex.	20·03 N	102·43 W
210	Saïda (sä'ê-dä) Alg.	34·51 N	00·07 E
	Saigon, see Ho Chi Minh City		
195	Saijō (sä'ê-jô) Jap.	33·55 N	133·13 E
157	Saimaa (sä'ĭ-mä) Fin.	61·24 N	28·45 E
124	Sain Alto (sä-ēn' äl'tō) Mex.	23·35 N	103·13 W
100	St. Adolphe (sânt a'dŏlf) (săN' tȧ-dôlf') Can. (Winnipeg In.)	49·40 N	97·07 W
160	St. Affrique (săN' tȧ-frēk') Fr.	43·58 N	2·52 E
202	St. Albans (sânt ôl'bănz) Austl. (Melbourne In.)	37·44 S	144·47 E

Page	Name Pronunciation Region	Lat. °′	Long. °′
148	St. Albans Eng. (London In.)	51·44 N	0·20 W
105	St. Albans Vt.	44·50 N	73·05 W
104	St. Albans WV	38·20 N	81·50 W
154	St. Albans Hd. Eng.	50·34 N	2·00 W
100	St. Albert (sânt ăl'bērt) Can. (Edmonton In.)	53·38 N	113·38 W
160	St. Amand Montrond (săN't ȧ-mäN' môN-rôN'). Fr.	46·44 N	2·28 E
213	St. André, Cap (C.) Mad.	16·15 S	44·31 E
100	St. André-Est. Can. (Montreal In.)	45·33 N	74·19 W
120	St. Andrew, B. Fl.	30·20 N	85·45 W
98	St. Andrews Can.	45·05 N	67·03 W
154	St. Andrews Scot.	56·20 N	2·40 W
99	St. Andrew's Chan. (ăn'drōōz). Can.	46·06 N	60·28 W
100	St. Anicet (sĕNt ä-nē-sĕ') Can. (Montreal In.)	45·07 N	74·23 W
113	St. Ann (sânt ăn') Mo. (St. Louis In.)	38·44 N	90·23 W
98	Ste. Anne (săNt' ȧn') (sânt ăn') Can.	46·55 N	71·46 W
107	St. Anne Il. (Chicago In.)	41·01 N	87·44 W
127	Ste. Anne Guad. (In.)	16·15 N	61·23 W
100	Ste.-Anne (R.) Can. (Quebec In.)	47·07 N	70·50 W
100	Ste. Anne-de-Beaupré (dē bō-prā') Can. (Quebec In.)	47·02 N	70·56 W
100	Ste. Anne-des-Plaines (dā plĕN) Can. (Montreal In.)	45·46 N	73·49 W
99	St. Anns B. (ănz) Can.	46·20 N	60·30 W
128	St. Ann's Bay Jam.	18·25 N	77·15 W
100	St. Anselme (săN' täN-sĕlm') Can. (Quebec In.)	46·37 N	70·58 W
99	St. Anthony (săN ăn'thô-nê) Can.	51·24 N	55·35 W
111	St. Anthony (sânt ăn'thô-nê) Id.	43·59 N	111·42 W
100	St. Antoine-de-Tilly Can. (Quebec In.)	46·00 N	71·31 W
197	St. Antonio, Mt. Phil. (In.)	13·23 N	122·00 E
100	St. Apollinaire (săN' tȧ-pôl-ê-nâr') Can. (Quebec In.)	46·36 N	71·30 W
161	St. Arnoult-en-Yvelines (sȧN-tär-nōō'ĕN-nēv-lēn') Fr. (Paris In.)	48·33 N	1·55 E
100	St. Augustin-de-Québec (sĕn tō-güs-tēn') Can. (Quebec In.)	46·45 N	71·27 W
100	St. Augustin-Deux-Montagnes Can. (Montreal In.)	45·38 N	73·59 W
121	St. Augustine (sânt ô'gŭs-tēn) Fl.	29·53 N	81·21 W
100	Ste. Barbe (sânt bärb') Can. (Montreal In.)	45·14 N	74·12 W
127	St. Barthelemy I. Guad. (In.)	17·55 N	62·32 W
154	St. Bees Hd. (sânt bēz' hĕd) Eng.	54·30 N	3·40 W
100	St. Benoit (sĕN bĕ-nōō-ä') Can. (Montreal In.)	45·34 N	74·05 W
106	St. Bernard (bĕr-närd') La. (New Orleans In.)	29·52 N	89·52 W
107	St. Bernard Oh. (Cincinnati In.)	39·10 N	84·30 W
93	St. Bride Mt. (sânt brīd) Can.	51·30 N	115·57 W
154	St. Brides B. (sânt brīdz') Wales	51·17 N	4·45 W
160	St. Brieuc (săN' brēs') Fr.	48·32 N	2·47 W
100	St. Bruno (brū'nō) Can. (Montreal In.)	45·31 N	73·40 W
100	St. Canut (săN' kȧ-nū') Can. (Montreal In.)	45·43 N	74·04 W
98	St. Casimir (kȧ-zē-mēr') Can.	46·45 N	72·34 W
100	St. Catharines (kăth'ȧ-rĭnz) Can. (Toronto In.)	43·10 N	79·14 W
127	St. Catherine, Mt. Grenada (In.)	12·10 N	62·42 W
160	St. Chamas (sȧN-shä-mä') Fr. (In.)	43·32 N	5·03 E
160	St. Chamond (săN' shȧ-môN') Fr.	45·30 N	4·17 E
100	St. Charles (săN' shärlz') Can. (Quebec In.)	46·47 N	70·57 W
107	St. Charles (sânt chärlz') Il. (Chicago In.)	41·55 N	88·19 W
104	St. Charles Mi.	43·20 N	84·10 W
109	St. Charles Mn.	43·56 N	92·05 W
113	St. Charles Mo. (St. Louis In.)	38·47 N	90·29 W
100	St. Charles, Lac (L.) Can. (Quebec In.)	46·56 N	71·21 W
104	St. Clair (sânt klâr) Mi.	42·55 N	82·30 W
104	St. Clair (L.) Can.-Mi.	42·25 N	82·30 W
104	St. Clair (R.) Can.-Mi.	42·45 N	82·25 W
100	Ste. Claire Can. (Quebec In.)	46·36 N	70·52 W
107	St. Clair Shores Mi. (Detroit In.)	42·30 N	82·54 W
161	St. Claude (săN' klōd') Fr.	46·24 N	5·53 E
100	St. Clet (săNt' klā') Can. (Montreal In.)	45·22 N	74·21 W
121	St. Cloud (sânt kloud') Fl. (In.)	28·13 N	81·17 W
109	St. Cloud Mn.	45·33 N	94·08 W
100	St. Constant (kŏn'stănt) Can. (Montreal In.)	45·23 N	73·34 W
213	St. Croix I. (săN krwă) S. Afr. (Natal In.)	33·48 S	25·45 E
123	Saint Croix (I.) (sânt kroi') Vir. Is. (U. S. A.) (Puerto Rico In.)	17·40 N	64·43 W
98	St. Croix (R.) (kroi') Can.-Me.	45·28 N	67·32 W
109	St. Croix Ind. Res. Wi.	45·40 N	92·21 W

Page	Name Pronunciation Region	Lat. °′	Long. °′
109	St. Croix R. (sânt kroi') Mn.-Wi.	45·00 N	92·44 W
100	St. Damien-de-Buckland (sânt dā'mê-ĕn) Can. (Quebec In.)	46·37 N	70·39 W
100	St. David (dā'vĭd) Can. (Quebec In.)	46·47 N	71·11 W
154	St. David's Hd. Wales	51·54 N	5·25 W
161	St.-Denis (săN'dē-nē') Fr. (Paris In.)	48·26 N	2·22 E
161	St. Dié (dê-ā') Fr.	48·18 N	6·55 E
160	St. Dizier (dê-zyā') Fr.	48·49 N	4·55 E
100	St. Dominique (sĕN dō-mē-nēk') Can. (Montreal In.)	45·19 N	74·09 W
100	St. Edouard-de-Napierville (sĕN-tĕ-dōō-är') Can. (Montreal In.)	45·14 N	73·31 W
101	St. Elias, Mt. (sânt ê-lī'ăs) Can.	60·25 N	141·00 W
1[illegible]	St. Étienne Fr.	45·26 N	4·22 E
100	St. Etienne-de-Lauzon (săN' tā-tyĕn') Can. (Quebec In.)	46·39 N	71·19 W
100	Ste. Euphémie (sĕNt û-fē-mē') Can. (Quebec In.)	46·47 N	70·27 W
100	St. Eustache (săN' tû-stash') Can. (Montreal In.)	45·34 N	73·54 W
100	St. Eustache Can. (Winnipeg In.)	49·58 N	97·47 W
127	St. Eustatius I. (sânt u-stā'shŭs) Neth. Antilles (In.)	17·32 N	62·45 W
100	Ste. Famille (săN't fȧ-mē'y') Can. (Quebec In.)	46·58 N	70·58 W
99	St. Félicien (săN fā-lê-syăN') Can.	48·39 N	72·28 W
98	Ste. Felicite Can.	48·54 N	67·20 W
100	St. Féréol (fa-rā-ôl') Can. (Quebec In.)	47·07 N	70·52 W
164	St. Florent, Golfe de (G.) Fr.	42·55 N	9·08 E
160	St. Florent-sur-Cher (săN' flô-räN'sür-shâr'). Fr.	46·58 N	2·15 E
160	St. Flour (săN flōōr') Fr.	45·02 N	3·09 E
100	Ste. Foy (sânt fwä) Can. (Quebec In.)	46·47 N	71·18 W
117	St. Francis (R.) Ar.	35·56 N	90·27 W
105	St. Francis L. (săN frăn'sĭs) Can.	45·00 N	74·20 W
100	St. François (săN'fräN-swä') Can. (Quebec In.)	47·01 N	70·49 W
218	St. François de Boundji Con.	1·03 S	15·22 E
100	St. Francois Xavier Can. (Winnepeg In.)	49·55 N	97·32 W
160	St. Gaudens (gō-dăNs') Fr.	43·07 N	0·43 E
117	Ste. Genevieve (sânt jĕn'ĕ-vēv) Mo.	37·58 N	90·02 W
203	St. George (sânt jôrj') Austl.	28·02 S	148·40 E
98	St. George (săN jôrj') Can.	45·08 N	66·49 W
100	St. George (săN'zhôrzh') Can. (Toronto In.)	43·14 N	80·15 W
121	St. George (sânt jôrj') SC	33·11 N	80·35 W
115	St. George Ut.	37·05 N	113·40 W
101	St. George (I.) Ak.	56·30 N	169·40 W
99	St. George, C. Can.	48·28 N	59·15 W
120	St. George, C. Fl.	29·30 N	85·20 W
99	St. George's (jôrj'ĕs) Can.	48·26 N	58·29 W
135	St. Georges Fr. Gu.	3·48 N	51·47 W
127	St. Georges Grenada (In.)	12·02 N	61·57 W
99	St. Georges B. Can.	45·49 N	61·45 W
99	St. George's B. Can.	48·20 N	59·00 W
154	St. George's Chan. (jôr-jĕz) Eng.-Ire.	51·45 N	6·30 W
161	St. Germain-en-Laye (săN' zhĕr-măN-äN-lā') Fr. (Paris In.)	48·53 N	2·05 E
100	St. Gervais (zhĕr-vĕ') Can. (Quebec In.)	46·43 N	70·53 W
160	St. Girons (zhē-rôN') Fr.	42·58 N	1·08 E
158	St. Gotthard Tun. (sânt gŏt'hărd) (săN gô-târ') Switz.	46·38 N	8·55 E
99	St. Gregory, Mt. (sânt grĕg'ēr-ê) Can.	49·19 N	58·13 W
209	St. Helena Atl. O.	16·01 S	5·16 W
212	St. Helenabaai (B.) Afr.	32·25 S	17·15 E
148	St. Helens (sânt hĕl'ĕnz) Eng.	53·27 N	2·44 W
112	St. Helens (hĕl'ĕnz) Or. (Portland In.)	45·52 N	122·49 W
110	St. Helens, Mt. Wa.	46·13 N	122·10 W
160	St. Helier (hyĕl'yēr) Jersey	49·12 N	2·06 W
100	St. Henri (săN' hĕn'rê) Can. (Quebec In.)	46·41 N	71·04 W
100	St. Hubert Can. (Montreal In.)	45·29 N	73·24 W
105	St. Hyacinthe (săN' tê-ä-săNt') (sânt hī'ȧ-sĭnth) Can.	45·35 N	72·55 W
98	St.-Ignace Can.	46·42 N	70·30 W
109	St. Ignace (sânt ĭg'năs) Mi.	45·51 N	84·39 W
109	St. Ignace (I.) (săN' ĭg'năs) Can.	48·47 N	88·14 W
98	St. Irenee (săN' tē-rȧ-nā') Can.	47·34 N	70·15 W
100	St. Isidore-de-Laprairie (saN' tē-zē-dōr') (sânt ĭz'ĭ-dôr) Can. (Montreal In.)	45·18 N	73·41 W

ăt; finăl; rāte; senâte; ärm; ȧsk; sofȧ; fâre; ch-choose; dh-as th in other; bē; êvent; bĕt; recĕnt; cratēr; g-go; gh-guttural g; bĭt; ĭ-short neutral; rīde; K-guttural k as ch in German ich;

ng-sing; ŋ-baŋk; N-nasalized n; nŏd; cŏmmit; ōld; ōbey; ôrder; fōōd; fŏŏt; ou-out; s-soft; sh-dish; th-thin; pūre; ûnite; ûrn; stŭd; circŭs; ü-as "y" in study; '-indeterminate vowel.

340 Salal — San Carlos PRONOUNCING INDEX

Page	Name Pronunciation	Region	Lat. °'	Long. °'
215	Salal	Chad.	14·51 N	17·13 E
126	Salamá (sä-lä'mä)	Guat.	15·06 N	90·19 W
126	Salamá (sä-lä-mà')	Hond.	14·43 N	86·30 W
137	Salamanca (sä-lä-mä'n-kä)	Chile (Santiago In.)	31·48 S	70·57 W
124	Salamanca	Mex.	20·36 N	101·10 W
105	Salamanca (săl-à-măŋ'kà)	NY	42·10 N	78·45 W
162	Salamanca (sä-lä-mä'n-kà)	Sp.	40·54 N	5·42 W
211	Salamat, Bahr (R.) (bär sä-lä-mät')	Chad.	10·06 N	19·16 E
197	Salamaua (sä-lä-mä'wà)	Pap. N. Gui.	6·50 S	146·55 E
134	Salamina (sä-lä-mē'-nä)	Col. (In.)	5·25 N	75·29 W
165	Salamis (săl'à-mĭs)	Grc.	37·58 N	23·30 E
134	Salaverry (sä-lä-vā'rê)	Peru	8·16 S	78·54 W
197	Salawati (I.) (sä-lä-wä'tê)	Indon.	1·22 N	130·15 E
217	Salawe	Tan.	3·19 S	32·52 E
199	Sala-y-Gómez (I.)	Chile	26·50 S	105·50 W
216	Salazar	Ang.	9·18 S	14·54 E
129	Salcedo (säl-sā'dō)	Dom. Rep.	19·25 N	70·30 W
134	Saldaña (R.) (säl-dà'n-yä)	Col. (In.)	3·42 N	75·16 W
212	Saldanha	S. Afr.	32·55 S	18·05 E
157	Saldus (sål'do͞os)	Sov. Un.	56·39 N	22·30 E
203	Sale (sāl)	Austl.	38·10 S	147·07 E
148	Sale	Eng.	53·24 N	2·20 W
210	Salé (så-lā')	Mor.	34·09 N	6·42 W
100	Sale (R.) (sål'rê-vyår')	Can. (Winnipeg In.)	49·44 N	97·11 W
170	Salekhard (sŭ-lyĭ-kärt)	Sov. Un.	66·35 N	66·50 E
104	Salem (sā'lĕm)	Il.	38·40 N	89·00 W
185	Salem	India	11·39 N	78·11 E
104	Salem	In.	38·35 N	86·00 W
99	Salem	Ma. (In.)	42·31 N	70·54 W
117	Salem	Mo.	37·36 N	91·33 W
99	Salem	NH (In.)	42·46 N	71·16 W
105	Salem	NJ	39·35 N	75·30 W
104	Salem	Oh.	40·55 N	80·50 W
110	Salem	Or.	44·55 N	123·03 W
108	Salem	SD	43·43 N	97·23 W
213	Salem	S. Afr. (Natal In.)	33·29 S	26·30 E
121	Salem	Va.	37·16 N	80·05 W
104	Salem	WV	39·15 N	80·35 W
164	Salemi (sä-lå'mē)	It.	37·49 N	12·48 E
163	Salerno (sä-lĕr'nô)	It. (Naples In.)	40·27 N	14·46 E
164	Salerno, Golfo di (G.) (gôl-fô-dē)	It.	40·30 N	14·40 E
148	Salford (săl'fērd)	Eng.	53·26 N	2·19 W
167	Salgir (R.) (sål'gēr)	Sov. Un.	45·25 N	34·22 E
159	Salgótarján (shôl'gô-tôr-yän)	Hung.	48·06 N	19·50 E
116	Salida (så-lī'då)	Co.	38·31 N	106·01 W
160	Salies (så-lēs')	Fr.	43·27 N	0·58 W
217	Salima	Malawi	13·47 S	34·26 E
117	Salina (så-lī'nå)	Ks.	38·50 N	97·37 W
115	Salina	Ut.	39·00 N	111·55 W
164	Salina (I.) (sä-lē'nä)	It.	38·35 N	14·48 E
129	Salina Pt.	Ba.	22·10 N	74·20 W
125	Salina Cruz (sä-lē'nä kro͞oz')	Mex.	16·10 N	95·12 W
114	Salinas (så-lē'nås)	Ca.	36·41 N	121·40 W
124	Salinas	Mex.	22·38 N	101·42 W
123	Salinas	P. R. (Puerto Rico In.)	17·58 N	66·16 W
114	Salinas (R.)	Ca.	36·33 N	121·29 W
125	Salinas (R.) (sä-lē'näs)	Mex.	16·15 N	90·31 W
126	Salinas, Bahia de (B.) (bä-ē'ä-dĕ-så-lē'nås)	Nic.-C. R.	11·05 N	85·55 W
163	Salinas, Cape (sä-lênäs)	Sp.	39·14 N	1·02 E
118	Salinas Victoria (sä-lē'näs vêk-tō'rê-ä)	Mex.	25·59 N	100·19 W
117	Saline (R.) (så-lēn')	Ak.	34·06 N	92·30 W
116	Saline (R.)	Ks.	39·05 N	99·43 W
161	Salins-les-Bains (så-låN'-lā-båN')	Fr.	46·55 N	5·54 E
98	Salisbury	Can.	46·03 N	65·05 W
154	Salisbury (sôlz'bē-rê)	Eng.	50·35 N	1·51 W
105	Salisbury	Md.	38·20 N	75·40 W
117	Salisbury	Mo.	39·24 N	92·47 W
121	Salisbury	NC	35·40 N	80·29 W
217	Salisbury	Rh.	17·50 S	31·03 E
91	Salisbury (I.)	Can.	63·36 N	76·20 W
154	Salisbury Plain	Eng.	51·15 N	1·52 W
210	Sal. I. (säal)	C. V. Is. (In.)	16·45 N	22·39 W
121	Salkehatchie (R.) (sô-kê-hăch'ê)	SC	33·09 N	81·10 W
117	Sallisaw (săl'ĭ-sô)	Ok.	35·27 N	94·48 W
111	Salmon (săm'ŭn)	Id.	45·11 N	113·54 W
110	Salmon Falls R.	Id.	42·22 N	114·53 W
204	Salmon Gums (gŭmz)	Austl.	33·00 S	122·00 E
92	Salmon (R.)	Can.	54·00 N	123·50 W
98	Salmon (R.)	Can.	46·19 N	65·36 W
105	Salmon (R.)	NY	44·35 N	74·15 W
112	Salmon (R.)	Wa. (Portland In.)	45·44 N	122·36 W
93	Salmon Arm	Can.	50·42 N	119·16 W
110	Salmon R.	Id.	45·30 N	115·45 W
110	Salmon R., Middle Fork	Id.	44·54 N	114·50 W
110	Salmon R., South Fork	Id.	44·51 N	115·47 W
110	Salmon River Mts.	Id.	44·15 N	115·44 W
161	Salon-de-Provence (så-lôN-dē-prô-văNs')	Fr.	43·48 N	5·09 E
159	Salonta (sä-lôn'tä)	Rom.	46·46 N	21·38 E
214	Saloum (R.)	Senegal	14·10 N	15·45 W
185	Salsette I.	India (Bombay In.)	19·12 N	72·52 E
171	Sal'sk (sälsk)	Sov. Un.	46·30 N	41·20 E
115	Salt, (R.) (sôlt)	Az.	33·28 N	111·35 W
117	Salt (R.)	Mo.	39·54 N	92·11 W
136	Salta (säl'tä)	Arg.	24·50 S	65·16 W
136	Salta (Prov.)	Arg.	25·15 S	65·00 W
113	Saltair (sôlt'âr)	Ut. (Salt Lake City In.)	40·46 N	112·09 W
129	Salt Cay (I.)	Turks & Caicos Is.	21·20 N	71·15 W
107	Salt Cr. (sôlt)	Il. (Chicago In.)	42·01 N	88·01 W
118	Saltillo (säl-tēl'yō)	Mex.	25·24 N	100·59 W
113	Salt Lake City (sôlt lāk sĭ'tĭ)	Ut. (Salt Lake City In.)	40·45 N	111·52 W
137	Salto (säl'tō)	Arg. (Buenos Aires In.)	34·17 S	60·15 W
136	Salto	Ur.	31·18 S	57·45 W
137	Salto, Serra do (Mtn.) (sĕ'r-rä-dô)	Braz. (Rio de Janeiro In.)	20·26 S	43·28 W
124	Salto (R.)	Mex.	22·16 N	99·18 W
135	Salto Grande (grän'dä)	Braz.	22·57 S	49·58 W
114	Salton Sea (sôlt'ŭn)	Ca.	33·28 N	115·43 W
210	Saltpond	Ghana	5·16 N	1·07 W
115	Salt River Ind. Res. (sôlt rĭv'ēr)	Az.	33·40 N	112·01 W
156	Saltsjöbaden (sält'shû-bäd'ĕn)	Swe.	59·15 N	18·20 E
92	Saltspring I (sält'sprĭng)	Can.	48·47 N	123·30 W
121	Saltville (sôlt'vĭl)	Va.	36·50 N	81·45 W
174	Saltykovka (sål-tē'kôf-kå)	Sov. Un. (Moscow In.)	55·45 N	37·56 E
122	Salud, Mt. (sä-lo͞o'th)	Pan. (Panama Canal In.)	9·14 N	79·42 W
121	Saluda (så-lo͞o'då)	SC	34·02 N	81·46 W
121	Saluda (R.)	SC	34·07 N	81·48 W
164	Saluzzo (sä-lo͞ot'sō)	It.	44·39 N	7·31 E
135	Salvador (Bahia) (säl-vä-dōr') (bä-ē'å)	Braz.	12·59 S	38·27 W
119	Salvador L.	La.	29·45 N	90·20 W
128	Salvador Pt.	Ba.	24·30 N	77·45 W
124	Salvatierra (säl-vä-tyĕr'rä)	Mex.	20·13 N	100·52 W
218	Salwā Baḥrī	Egypt (Nile In.)	24·43 N	32·58 E
188	Salween R. (săl-wēn')	Bur.	26·46 N	98·19 E
171	Sal'yany	Sov. Un.	39·40 N	49·10 E
158	Salzburg (sälts'bo͝orgh)	Aus.	47·48 N	13·04 E
158	Salzburg (State)	Aus.	47·30 N	13·18 E
158	Salzwedel (sälts-vā'dĕl)	G.D.R.	52·51 N	11·10 E
218	Samālūt (sä-mä-lo͞ot')	Egypt (Nile In.)	28·17 N	30·43 E
129	Samaná (sä-mä-nä')	Dom. Rep.	19·15 N	69·25 W
129	Samana Cabo (C.) (kå'bô)	Dom. Rep.	19·20 N	69·00 W
129	Samana or Atwood Cay (I.)	Ba.	23·05 N	73·45 W
197	Samar (I.) (sä'mär)	Phil.	11·30 N	126·07 E
171	Samara (R.)	Sov. Un.	52·50 N	50·35 E
167	Samara (R.) (så-mä'rå)	Sov. Un.	48·47 N	35·30 E
197	Samarai (sä-mä-rä'ê)	Pap. N. Gui.	10·45 S	150·49 E
172	Samarkand (så-mår-känt')	Sov. Un.	39·42 N	67·00 E
217	Samba	Zaire	4·38 S	26·22 E
184	Sambalpur (sŭm'bŭl-po͝or)	India	21·30 N	84·05 E
184	Sāmbhar (R.)	India	27·00 N	74·58 E
159	Sambor (säm'bôr)	Sov. Un.	49·31 N	23·12 E
137	Samborombón, Bahia (B.) (bä-ē'ä-säm-bô-rôm-bô'n)	Arg. (Buenos Aires In.)	35·57 S	57·05 W
137	Samborombón (R.)	Arg. (Buenos Aires In.)	35·20 S	57·52 W
155	Sambre (R.) (säNbr')	Bel.	50·20 N	4·15 E
216	Sambungo	Ang.	8·39 S	20·43 E
112	Sammamish, L. (så-măm'ĭsh)	Wa. (Seattle In.)	47·35 N	122·02 W
112	Sammamish (R.)	Wa. (Seattle In.)	47·43 N	122·08 W
165	Samokov (sä'mô-kôf)	Bul.	42·20 N	23·33 E
163	Samora Correia (sä-mô'rä-kôr-rĕ'yä)	Port. (Lisbon In.)	38·55 N	8·52 W
172	Samorovo (så-må-rô'vô)	Sov. Un.	60·47 N	69·13 E
165	Sámos (I.) (sä'mŏs)	Grc.	37·53 N	26·35 E
165	Samothráki (I.)	Grc.	40·23 N	25·10 E
197	Sampaloc Pt. (säm-pä'lôk)	Phil. (In.)	14·43 N	119·56 E
119	Sam Rayburn Res.	Tx.	31·10 N	94·15 W
156	Samsø (I.) (säm'sû)	Den.	55·49 N	10·47 E
120	Samson (săm'sŭn)	Al.	31·06 N	86·02 W
194	Samsu (säm'so͞o')	Kor.	41·12 N	128·00 E
171	Samsun (såm'so͞on')	Tur.	41·20 N	36·05 E
171	Samtredia (såm'trĕ-dê)	Sov. Un.	42·18 N	42·25 E
112	Samuel (I.) (såm'ū-ĕl)	Can. (Vancouver In.)	48·50 N	123·10 W
171	Samur (R.) (så-mo͞or')	Sov. Un.	41·40 N	47·20 E
214	San (sän)	Mali	13·18 N	4·54 W
186	Şan'ā' (sän'ä)	Yemen	15·17 N	44·05 E
215	Sanaga (R.) (sä-nä'gä)	Cam.	4·10 N	10·40 E
133	San Ambrosio, Isla de (I.) (ē's-lä-dĕ-sän äm-brō'zē-ō)	Chile	26·40 S	80·00 W
197	Sanana (I.)	Indon.	2·15 S	126·38 E
186	Sanandaj	Iran	36·44 N	46·43 E
114	San Andreas (săn ăn'drê-ås)	Ca.	38·10 N	120·42 W
102	San Andreas (L.)	Ca. (San Francisco In.)	37·36 N	122·26 W
134	San Andrés (sän-än-drĕ's)	Col. (In.)	6·57 N	75·41 W
125	San Andrés (sän än-drās')	Mex. (In.)	19·15 N	99·10 W
125	San Andres, Laguna de (L.)	Mex.	22·40 N	97·50 W
102	San Andres, Mts. (săn ăn'drê-ås)	U. S.	33·00 N	106·40 W
	San Andrés (L.), see Petén, Laguna de			
137	San Andrés de Giles (sän-än-drĕ's-dĕ-gē'lĕs)	Arg. (Buenos Aires In.)	34·26 S	59·28 W
127	San Andres I.	Col.	12·32 N	81·34 W
115	San Andres Mts.	NM	33·45 N	106·40 W
125	San Andrés Tuxtla (sän-än-drā's-to͞os'tlä)	Mex.	18·27 N	95·12 W
118	San Angelo (săn ăn-jĕ-lō)	Tx.	31·28 N	100·22 W
164	San Antioco, I. di (ē'sō-lä-dē-sän-än-tyŏ'kô)	It.	39·00 N	8·25 E
137	San Antonio (sän-ån-tô'nyō)	Chile (Santiago In.)	33·34 S	71·36 W
134	San Antonio	Col. (In.)	2·57 N	75·06 W
134	San Antonio	Col. (In.)	3·55 N	75·38 W
197	San Antonio	Phil. (In.)	14·57 N	120·05 E
113	San Antonio (săn ăn-tō'nê-ô)	Tx. (San Antonio In.)	29·25 N	98·30 W
114	San Antonio (R.)	Ca.	36·00 N	121·13 W
128	San Antonio, Cabo (C.) (kå'bô-sän-än-tô'nyô)	Cuba	21·55 N	84·55 W
163	San Antonio Abad (sän än-tō'nyô ä-bädh')	Sp.	38·59 N	1·17 E
119	San Antonio B.	Tx.	28·20 N	97·08 W
137	San Antonio de Areco (dā ä-rā'kô)	Arg. (Buenos Aires In.)	34·16 S	59·30 W
129	San Antonio de las Vegas (sän än-tô'nyô-dĕ-läs-vĕ'gäs)	Cuba (In.)	22·07 N	82·16 W
129	San Antonio de los Baños (då lōs bän'yōs)	Cuba (In.)	22·08 N	82·30 W
136	San Antonio de los Cobres (då lōs kō'brås)	Arg.	24·15 S	66·29 W
137	San Antônio de Pádua (dĕ-på'dwä)	Braz. (Rio de Janeiro In.)	21·32 S	42·09 W
135	San Antonio de Tamanaco (sän-ån-tô-nyō-dĕ-tå-mä-nå'kô)	Ven. (In.)	9·42 N	66·03 W
136	San Antonio Oeste (sän-nä-tō'nyô ô-ĕs'tå)	Arg.	40·49 S	64·56 W
113	San Antonio Pk. (săn ăn-tō'nĭ-ô)	Ca. (Los Angeles In.)	34·17 N	117·39 W
118	San Antonio R.	Tx.	29·00 N	97·58 W
126	Sanarate (sä-nä-rä'tê)	Guat.	14·47 N	90·12 W
119	San Augustine (săn ô'gŭs-tēn)	Tx.	31·33 N	94·08 W
118	San Bartolo	Mex.	24·43 N	103·12 W
125	San Bartolo (sän bär-tō'lô)	Mex. (In.)	19·36 N	99·43 W
164	San Bartolomeo (bär-tô-lô-mā'ô)	It.	41·25 N	15·04 E
164	San Benedetto del Tronto (bā'nå-dĕt'tô dĕl trōn'tô)	It.	42·58 N	13·54 E
119	San Benito (săn bĕ-nē'tô)	Tx.	26·07 N	97·37 W
114	San Benito (R.)	Ca.	36·40 N	121·20 W
113	San Bernardino (bûr-när-dē'nô)	Ca. (Los Angeles In.)	34·07 N	117·19 W
114	San Bernardino Mts.	Ca.	34·05 N	116·23 W
137	San Bernardo (sän bĕr-när'dô)	Chile (Santiago In.)	33·35 S	70·42 W
124	San Blas (sän bläs')	Mex.	21·33 N	105·19 W
120	San Blas, C.	Fl.	29·38 N	85·38 W
127	San Blas, Cord. de (Mts.) (kôr-dĕl-yĕ'rä-dĕ)	Pan.	9·17 N	78·20 W
127	San Blas, Golfo de (G.)	Pan.	9·33 N	78·42 W
127	San Blas, Punta (Pt.)	Pan.	9·35 N	78·55 W
112	San Bruno (săn brū-nô)	Ca. (San Francisco In.)	37·38 N	122·25 W
118	San Buenaventura (bwā'nå-vĕn-to͞o'rå)	Mex.	27·07 N	101·30 W
112	San Carlos (săn kär'lŏs)	Ca. (San Francisco In.)	37·30 N	122·15 W
136	San Carlos (sän-kå'r-lŏs)	Chile	36·23 S	71·58 W
134	San Carlos	Col. (In.)	6·11 N	74·58 W
216	San Carlos	Equat. Gui.	3·27 N	8·33 E
125	San Carlos (sän kär'lōs)	Mex.	17·49 N	92·33 W
118	San Carlos	Mex.	24·36 N	98·52 W
127	San Carlos (sän-kä'r-lôs)	Nic.	11·08 N	84·48 W
197	San Carlos	Phil. (In.)	15·56 N	120·20 E
134	San Carlos	Ven.	9·36 N	68·35 W
136	San Carlos de Bariloche (sän-kå'r lŏs-dĕ-bä-rē'lô'chĕ)	Arg.	41·15 S	71·26 W
115	San Carlos Ind. Res. (săn kär'lŏs)	Az.	33·27 N	110·15 W
115	San Carlos Res.	Az.	33·05 N	110·29 W
127	San Carlos R.	C. R.	10·36 N	84·18 W

ăt; finăl; rāte; senåte; ärm; åsk; sofa; fâre; ch-choose; dh-as th in other; bē; êvent; bĕt; recĕnt; cratēr; g-go; gh-guttural g; bĭt; ĭ-short neutral; rīde; K-guttural k as ch in German ich;

PRONOUNCING INDEX San Casimiro — San Juan 341

Page	Name Pronunciation Region	Lat. °′	Long. °′
135	San Casimiro (kä-sē-mē′rō) Ven. (In.)	10·01 N	67·02 W
164	San Cataldo (kä-täl′dō)........It.	37·30 N	13·59 E
129	Sánchez (sän′chĕz)....Dom. Rep.	19·15 N	69·40 W
124	Sanchez, Río de los (R.) (rē′ō-dĕ-lôs).Mex.	20·31 N	102·29 W
124	Sánchez Román (Tlaltenango) (rô-mà′n) (tlä′l-tĕ-nän-gô).Mex.	21·48 N	103·20 W
162	San Clemente (sän klå-mĕn′tå).Sp.	39·25 N	2·24 W
114	San Clemente (I.)..........Ca.	33·02 N	118·36 W
129	San Cristobal (krēs-tô′bäl) Dom. Rep.	18·25 N	70·05 W
126	San Cristóbal.............Guat.	15·22 N	90·26 W
134	San Cristóbal.............Ven.	7·43 N	72·15 W
134	San Cristobal (I.)...........Ec.	1·05 S	89·15 W
205	San Cristobal (I.)........Sol. Is.	10·47 S	162·17 E
164	San Croce, C. (krô′chä).......It.	37·15 N	15·18 E
128	Sancti Spíritus (säŋk′tē spē′rē-tōōs).Cuba	21·55 N	79·25 W
160	Sancy, Puy de (Pk.) (pwē-dĕ-säN-sē′).Fr.	45·30 N	2·53 E
122	Sand (I.) (sănd).Or. (Portland In.)	46·16 N	124·01 W
109	Sand (I.)..................Wi.	46·03 N	91·09 W
218	Sand (R.)...............S. Afr. (Johannesburg & Pretoria In.)	28·09 S	26·46 E
213	Sand (R.)......S. Afr. (Natal In.)	28·30 S	29·30 E
195	Sanda (sän′dä)...Jap. (Ōsaka In.)	34·53 N	135·14 E
196	Sandakan (sån-dä′kån).....Mala.	5·51 N	118·03 E
154	Sanday (I.) (sănd′ā)........Scot.	59·17 N	2·25 W
148	Sandbach (sănd′băch).......Scot.	53·08 N	2·22 W
156	Sandefjord (sän′dĕ-fyôr′).....Nor.	59·09 N	10·14 E
112	San de Fuca (de-fōō-cä) Wa. (Seattle In.)	48·14 N	122·44 W
115	Sanders....................Az.	35·13 N	109·20 W
118	Sanderson (săn′dēr-săn).......Tx.	30·09 N	102·24 W
120	Sandersville (săn′dērz-vĭl).....Ga.	32·57 N	82·50 W
156	Sandhammar, C. (sänt′häm-mår).Swe.	55·24 N	14·37 E
108	Sand Hills (Reg.) (sănd)......Ne.	41·57 N	101·29 W
106	Sand Hook (sănd hŏŏk) NJ (New York In.)	40·29 N	74·05 W
148	Sandhurst (sănd′hûrst) Eng. (London In.)	51·20 N	0·48 W
114	San Diego (săn dē-ā′gō)..Ca. (In.)	32·43 N	117·10 W
116	San Diego..................Tx.	27·47 N	98·13 W
114	San Diego (R.).............Ca.	32·53 N	116·57 W
124	San Diego de la Unión (sän dē-å-gō då lä ōō-nyōn′) Mex.	21·27 N	100·52 W
119	Sandies Cr. (sănd′ēz).........Tx.	29·13 N	97·34 W
113	San Dimas (săn dĕ-màs) Ca. (Los Angeles In.)	34·07 N	117·49 W
116	San Dimas (dē-mäs′)........Mex.	24·08 N	105·57 W
156	Sandnes (sänd′nĕs).........Nor.	58·52 N	5·44 E
212	Sandoa (sän-dō′å)..........Zaire	9·39 S	23·00 E
159	Sandomierz (sån-dô′myĕzh)...Pol.	50·39 N	21·45 E
164	San Donà di Piave (sän dô nå′ dē pyä′vĕ).It.	45·38 N	12·34 E
188	Sandoway (sän-dô-wī′).......Bur.	18·24 N	94·28 E
110	Sandpoint (sănd point)........Id.	48·17 N	116·34 W
202	Sandringham (săn′drĭng-ăm) Austl. (Melbourne In.)	37·57 S	145·01 E
164	Sandrio (sä′n-dryô)...........It.	46·11 N	9·53 E
117	Sand Springs (sănd sprĭnz)....Ok.	36·08 N	96·06 W
204	Sandstone (sănd′stōn)......Austl.	28·00 S	119·25 E
107	Sandstone..................Mn.	46·08 N	92·53 W
106	Sandusky (săn-dŭs′kē) Al. (Birmingham In.)	33·32 N	86·50 W
104	Sandusky...................Mi.	43·25 N	82·50 W
104	Sandusky...................Oh.	41·25 N	82·45 W
104	Sandusky (R.)..............Oh.	41·10 N	83·20 W
104	Sandwich (sănd′wĭch).........Il.	42·35 N	88·53 W
112	Sandy (sănd′ē)..Or. (Portland In.)	45·24 N	122·16 W
113	Sandy....Ut. (Salt Lake City In.)	40·36 N	111·53 W
112	Sandy (R.).....Or. (Portland In.)	45·28 N	122·17 W
203	Sandy C..................Austl.	24·25 S	153·10 E
111	Sandy Cr...................Wy.	42·08 N	109·35 W
106	Sandy Hook (hŏŏk) Ct. (New York In.)	41·25 N	73·17 W
100	Sandy L.....Can. (Edmonton In.)	53·46 N	113·58 W
99	Sandy L..................Can.	49·16 N	57·00 W
95	Sandy L..................Can.	53·00 N	93·07 W
119	Sandy Point..........Tx. (In.)	29·22 N	95·27 W
102	Sandy Pt.....Wa. (Vancouver In.)	48·48 N	122·42 W
106	Sandy Springs (springz) Ga. (Atlanta In.)	33·55 N	84·23 W
137	San Enrique (sän-ĕn-rē′kĕ) Arg. (Buenos Aires In.)	35·47 S	60·22 W
136	San Estanislao (ĕs-tä-nēs-lä′ô).Par.	24·38 S	56·20 W
126	San Esteban (ĕs-tĕ′bän)....Hond.	15·13 N	85·53 W
197	San Fabian (fä-byä′n)..Phil. (In.)	16·14 N	120·28 E
137	San Felipe (få-lē′på) Chile (Santiago In.)	32·45 S	70·43 W
124	San Felipe (fĕ-lē′pĕ)........Mex.	21·29 N	101·13 W
124	San Felipe.................Mex.	22·21 N	105·26 W
134	San Felipe (fĕ-lē′pĕ)........Ven.	10·13 N	68·45 W
	San Felipe, see Jalapa de Diaz		
114	San Felipe, Cr. (săn fē-lēp′å)..Ca.	33·10 N	116·03 W
128	San Felipe, Cayos de (Is.) (kä′yōs-dĕ-sän-fĕ-lē′pĕ).Cuba	22·00 N	83·30 W
163	San Felíu de Guixols (sän få-lē′ōō då gē-hôls).Sp.	41·45 N	3·01 E
133	San Felix, Isla de (I.) (ē′s-lä-dĕ-sän få-lēks′).Chile	26·20 S	80·10 W
162	San Fernanda (fĕr-nä′n-dä)....Sp.	36·28 N	6·13 W
136	San Fernando (fĕr-nà′n-dô) Arg. (Buenos Aires In.)	34·11 S	58·34 W
113	San Fernando (fĕr-nän′dô) Ca. (Los Angeles In.)	34·17 N	118·27 W
137	San Fernando.Chile (Santiago In.)	36·36 S	70·58 W
118	San Fernando (fĕr-nän′dô)...Mex.	24·52 N	98·10 W
197	San Fernando (săn fĕr-nä′n-dô) Phil. (In.)	16·38 N	120·19 E
134	San Fernando de Apure (sän-fĕr-nä′n-dō-dĕ-ä-pōō′rå) Ven.	7·46 N	67·29 W
134	San Fernando de Atabapo (dĕ-ä-tä-bä′pô).Ven.	3·58 N	67·41 W
163	San Fernando de Henares (dĕ-ā-nä′rås).Sp. (Madrid In.)	40·23 N	3·31 W
118	San Fernando R. (săn fĕr-nän′dô).Mex.	25·07 N	98·25 W
156	Sånfjället (Mtn.)...........Swe.	62·19 N	13·30 E
100	Sanford (săn′fērd) Can. (Winnipeg In.)	49·41 N	97·27 W
121	Sanford (săn′fôrd).......Fl. (In.)	28·46 N	80·18 W
98	Sanford (săn′fērd)...........Me.	43·26 N	70·47 W
121	Sanford....................NC	35·26 N	79·10 W
136	San Francisco (săn frăn′sĭs′kô) Arg.	31·23 S	62·09 W
112	San Francisco Ca. (San Francisco In.)	37·45 N	122·26 W
126	San Francisco................Sal.	13·48 N	88·11 W
	San Francisco, see Ixhuatán		
115	San Francisco (R.)..........NM	33·35 N	108·55 W
112	San Francisco B. (săn frăn′sĭs′kô) Ca. (San Francisco In.)	37·45 N	122·21 W
122	San Francisco del Oro (dĕl ō′rō) Mex	27·00 N	106·37 W
124	San Francisco del Rincón (dĕl rēn-kōn′).Mex.	21·01 N	101·51 W
135	San Francisco de Macaira (dĕ-mä-kī′rä).Ven. (In.)	9·58 N	66·17 W
129	San Francisco de Macoris (dä-mä-kō′rēs).Dom. Rep.	19·20 N	70·15 W
129	San Francisco de Paula dā pou′lå).Cuba (In.)	23·04 N	82·18 W
113	San Gabriel (săn gä-brē-ĕl′) (gā′brē-ĕl) Ca. (Los Angeles In.)	34·06 N	118·06 W
124	San Gabriel Chilac (sän-gä-brē-ĕl-chē-läk′).Mex.	18·19 N	97·22 W
113	San Gabriel Mts. Ca. (Los Angeles In.)	34·17 N	118·03 W
113	San Gabriel Res. Ca. (Los Angeles In.)	34·14 N	117·48 W
113	San Gabriel R. Ca. (Los Angeles In.)	33·47 N	118·06 W
117	Sangamon (R.) (săn′gå-mŭn)...Il.	40·08 N	90·08 W
114	Sanger (săng′ēr)............Ca.	36·42 N	119·33 W
158	Sangerhausen (säng′ĕr-hou-zĕn) G.D.R.	51·28 N	11·17 E
215	Sangha (R.)...............Afr.	2·40 N	16·10 E
197	Sangihe (I.) (säŋ′gē-ē).....Indon.	3·30 N	125·30 E
134	San Gil (sän-Kē′l)..........Col.	6·32 N	73·13 W
164	San Giovanni in Fiore (sän jô-vän′nē ēn fyō′rå).It.	39·15 N	16·40 E
163	San Giuseppe Vesuviano (sän-zhĕōō-sĕ′p-pĕ-vĕ-sōō-vyà′nô) It. (Naples In.)	40·36 N	14·31 E
194	Sangju (säng′jōō′)..........Kor.	36·20 N	128·07 E
185	Sāngli....................India	16·56 N	74·38 E
215	Sangmélima...............Cam.	2·56 N	11·59 E
162	Sangonera (R.) (säŋ-gō-nä′rä)..Sp.	37·43 N	1·58 W
113	San Gorgonio Mt. (săn gôr-gō′nĭ-ō) Ca. (Los Angeles In.)	34·06 N	116·50 W
100	Sangre De Cristo, Range (săng′ēr-de-krēs-tō).U. S.	37·45 N	105·50 W
112	San Gregoria (săn grĕ-gôr′ä) Ca. (San Francisco In.)	37·20 N	122·23 W
164	Sangro (R.) (säŋ′grô).........It.	41·38 N	13·56 E
162	Sangüesa (sän-gwĕ′sä)........Sp.	42·36 N	1·15 W
190	Sanho (sän′hŏ)............China	39·59 N	117·06 E
121	Sanibel I. (săn′ĭ-bĕl).....Fl. (In.)	26·26 N	82·15 W
126	San Ignacio..........Belize (In.)	17·11 N	89·04 W
	San Iledfonso, see Villa Alta		
197	San Ildefonso, C. (sän-ēl-dĕ-fôn-sô).Phil. (In.)	16·03 N	122·10 E
162	San Ildefonso o la Granja (ō lä grän′khä).Sp.	40·54 N	4·02 W
136	San Isidro (ē-sē′drô) Arg. (Buenos Aires In.)	34·13 S	58·31 W
127	San Isidro..................C. R.	9·24 N	83·43 W
113	San Jacinto (săn jȧ-sĭn′tô) Ca. (Los Angeles In.)	33·47 N	116·57 W
197	San Jacinto (săn hä-sēn′tô) Phil. (In.)	12·33 N	123·43 E
119	San Jacinto (R.), West Fork...Tx.	30·35 N	95·37 W
113	San Jacinto R. (săn jȧ-sĭn′tô) Ca. (Los Angeles In.)	33·44 N	117·14 W
119	San Jacinto R...............Tx.	30·25 N	95·05 W
137	San Javier (sän-hå-vē′ĕr) Chile (Santiago In.)	35·35 S	71·43 W
125	San Jerónimo.........Mex. (In.)	19·31 N	98·46 W
124	San Jerónimo de Juárez (hå-rō′nē-mô då hwä′råz).Mex.	17·08 N	100·30 W
135	San Joaquin (hô-ä-kē′n).Ven. (In.)	10·16 N	67·47 W
114	San Joaquin (R.) (săn hwä-kēn′) Ca.	37·10 N	120·51 W
114	San Joaquin Valley...........Ca.	36·45 N	120·30 W
136	San Jorge, Golfo (G.) (gôl-fô-sän-Kô′r-Kĕ).Arg.	46·15 S	66·45 W
135	San José (sän hô-sā′).........Bol.	17·54 S	60·42 W
112	San Jose (săn hô-zā′) Ca. (San Francisco In.)	37·20 N	121·54 W
127	San Jose (sän hô-sā′).......C. R.	9·57 N	84·05 W
126	San José..................Guat.	13·56 N	90·49 W
197	San Jose..............Phil. (In.)	12·22 N	121·04 E
197	San José..............Phil. (In.)	14·49 N	120·47 E
197	San Jose..............Phil. (In.)	15·49 N	120·57 E
137	San José (hô-sĕ′) Ur. (Buenos Aires In.)	34·20 S	56·43 W
137	San José (Dept.) Ur. (Buenos Aires In.)	34·17 S	56·23 W
122	San Jose (I.) (Kô-sĕ′)........Mex.	25·00 N	110·35 W
115	San Jose (R.) (săn hô-zā′)....NM	35·15 N	108·10 W
137	San José (R.) (sän-hô-sĕ′) Ur. (Buenos Aires In.)	34·05 S	56·47 W
127	San Jose, Isla de (I.) (ē′s-lä-dĕ-sän hô-sā′).Pan.	8·17 N	79·20 W
136	San José de Feliciano (då lä ĕs-kē′nå).Arg.	30·26 S	58·44 W
135	San José de Gauribe (sän-hô-sĕ′dĕ-gåōō-rē′bĕ) Ven. (In.)	9·51 N	65·49 W
129	San Jose de las Lajas (sän-Kô-sĕ′dĕ-läs-lå′käs) Cuba (In.)	22·13 N	82·10 W
124	San José Iturbide (ē-tōōr-bē′dĕ) Mex.	21·00 N	100·24 W
136	San Juan (hwän′)...........Arg.	31·36 S	68·29 W
134	San Juan (hōōå′n)......Col. (In.)	3·23 N	73·48 W
129	San Juan (sän hwän′)..Dom. Rep.	18·50 N	71·15 W
197	San Juan (sän-Kōōå′n)..Phil. (In.)	14·30 N	121·14 E
197	San Juan.............Phil. (In.)	16·41 N	120·20 E
123	San Juan (sän hwän′) P. R. (Puerto Rico In.)	18·30 N	66·10 W
	San Juan, see Guichicovi		
	San Juan, see Mazatlán		
136	San Juan (Prov.)...........Arg.	31·00 S	69·30 W
123	San Juan, Cabezas de (C.) P. R. (Puerto Rico In.)	18·29 N	65·30 W
216	San Juan, Cabo (C.)..Equat. Gui.	1·08 N	9·23 E
128	San Juan, Pico (Pk.) (pē′kô-sän-kōōå′n).Cuba	21·55 N	80·00 W
125	San Juan (R.) (sän-hōō-än′).Mex.	18·10 N	95·23 W
118	San Juan, Rio (R.) (rē′ō-sän-hwän).Mex.	25·35 N	99·15 W
115	San Juan (R.)..............Ut.	37·10 N	110·30 W
136	San Juan Bautista (sän hwän′ bou-tēs′tä).Par.	26·48 S	57·09 W
124	San Juan Capistrano (sän-hōō-än′ kä-pēs-trä′nô) Mex.	22·41 N	104·07 W
114	San Juan Cr. (săn hwän′).....Ca.	35·24 N	120·12 W
118	San Juan de Guadalupe (sän hwan då gwä-dhä-lōō′på) Mex.	24·37 N	102·43 W
127	San Juan del Norte (Greytown) (dĕl nôr-tå) (grā′toun).Nic.	10·55 N	83·44 W
127	San Juan del Norte Bahia de (B.) (bä-ē′ä-dĕ-sän hwän dĕl nôr′tå) Nic.	11·12 N	83·40 W
124	San Juan de los Lagos (sän-hōō-än′då los lä′gôs).Mex.	21·15 N	102·18 W
124	San Juan de los Lagos (R.) (då lōs lä′gôs).Mex.	21·13 N	102·12 W
135	San Juan de los Morros (dĕ-lôs-mô′r-rôs).Ven. (In.)	9·54 N	67·22 W
124	San Juan del Rio (dĕl rē′ô)...Mex.	20·21 N	99·59 W
118	San Juan del Rio (sän hwän del rē′ô).Mex.	24·47 N	104·29 W
126	San Juan del Sur (dĕl sōōr)...Nic.	11·15 N	85·53 W
118	San Juan de Sabinas (dĕ-sä-bē′näs).Mex.	27·56 N	101·23 W
125	San Juan Evangelista (sän-hōō-ä′n-å-väŋ-kå-lĕs′ta′) Mex.	17·57 N	95·08 W
112	San Juan I......Wa. (Seattle In.)	48·28 N	123·08 W
112	San Juan Is. (săn hwän) Can. (Vancouver In.)	48·49 N	123·14 W
125	San Juan Ixtenco (ēx-tĕ′n-kô) Mex.	19·14 N	97·52 W
128	San Juan Martinez (sän kōō å′n-mär-tē′nĕz).Cuba	22·15 N	83·50 W
115	San Juan Mts. (san hwán′)....Co.	37·50 N	107·30 W

ng-sing; ŋ-baŋk; N-nasalized n; nŏd; cŏmmit; ōld; ôbey; ôrder; fōōd; fŏŏt; ou-out; s-soft; sh-dish; th-thin; pūre; ûnite; ûrn; stŭd; circŭs; ü-as "y" in study; ′-indeterminate vowel.

342 San Juan — Santa Fe PRONOUNCING INDEX

Page	Name Pronunciation Region	Lat. °'	Long. °'
127	San Juan R. . . . Nic.	10·58 N	84·18 W
136	San Julián (sän hōō-lyä'n) . . . Arg.	49·17 S	68·02 W
136	San Justo (hōōs'tô) Arg. (Buenos Aires In.)	34·25 S	58·33 W
214	Sankanbiriwa (Mtn.) . . . S. L.	8·56 N	10·48 W
214	Sankarani R. (sän'kä-rä'nê) Gui.-Mali	11·10 N	8·35 W
158	Sankt Gallen . . . Switz.	47·25 N	9·22 E
216	Sankuru (R.) (sän-kōō'rōō) . . Zaire	4·00 S	22·35 E
122	San Lazaro, C. (sän-lá'zä-rō) . Mex.	24·58 N	113·30 W
112	San Leandro (săn lê-ăn'drô) Ca. (San Francisco In.)	37·43 N	122·10 W
137	San Lorenzo (sän lô-rĕn'zô) Arg. (Buenos Aires In.)	32·46 S	60·44 W
112	San Lorenzo (săn lô-rĕn'zô) Ca. (San Francisco In.)	37·41 N	122·08 W
126	San Lorenzo (sän lô-rĕn'zô) . Hond.	13·24 N	87·24 W
163	San Lorenzo de El Escorial (sän lô-rĕn'tho dĕl ĕs-kō-rê-äl') Sp. (Madrid In.)	40·36 N	4·09 W
162	Sanlúcar (sän-lōō'kär) . . . Sp.	36·46 N	6·21 W
134	San Lucas (lōō'käs) . . . Bol.	20·12 S	65·06 W
	San Lucas, see Ojitlán		
122	San Lucas, C. . . . Mex.	22·45 N	109·45 W
136	San Luis (lōō-ēs') . . . Arg.	33·16 S	66·15 W
134	San Luis (lōōē's) . . . Col. (In.)	6·03 N	74·57 W
129	San Luis . . . Cuba	20·15 N	75·50 W
126	San Luis . . . Guat.	14·38 N	89·42 W
136	San Luis (Prov.) . . . Arg.	32·45 S	66·00 W
122	San Luis (State) . . . Mex.	22·45 N	101·45 W
124	San Luis de la Paz (dâ lä päz') Mex.	21·17 N	100·32 W
118	San Luis del Cordero (dĕl kôr-dā'rô) . Mex.	25·25 N	104·20 W
114	San Luis Obispo (ô-bĭs'pō) . . . Ca.	35·18 N	120·40 W
114	San Luis Obispo, B. . . . Ca.	35·07 N	121·05 W
124	San Luis Potosi (pō-tô-sē') . . . Mex.	22·08 N	100·58 W
122	San Luis Potosí (State) . . . Mex.	22·45 N	101·45 W
114	San Luis Rey (R.) (rā'ē) . . . Ca.	33·22 N	117·06 W
115	San Manuel (sän măn'ū-ĕl) . . . Az.	32·30 N	110·45 W
115	San Marcial (săn mar-shäl') . . NM	33·40 N	107·00 W
164	San Marco (sän mär'kô) . . . It.	41·53 N	15·50 E
126	San Marcos (mär'kôs) . . . Guat.	14·57 N	91·49 W
124	San Marcos . . . Mex.	16·46 N	99·23 W
118	San Marcos (săn mär'kôs) . . . Tx.	29·53 N	97·56 W
126	San Marcos de Colón (sän-má'r-kōs-dĕ-kô-lô'n) . Hond.	13·17 N	86·50 W
118	San Marcos R. . . . Tx.	30·08 N	98·15 W
126	San Maria (Vol.) (sän-mä-rē'ä) Guat.	14·45 N	91·33 W
165	San Maria di Léuca, C. (dē-lĕ'ōō-kä) . It.	39·47 N	18·20 E
197	San Mariano (sän mä-rê-ä'nô) Phil. (In.)	17·00 N	121·58 E
113	San Marino (săn mēr-ē'nô) Ca. (Los Angeles In.)	34·07 N	118·06 W
164	San Marino (sän mä-rē'nô) San Marino	44·55 N	12·26 E
151	San Marino . . . Eur.	43·40 N	13·00 E
134	San Martín (sän mär-tē'n) Col. (In.)	3·42 N	73·44 W
125	San Martín (mär-tē'n) . . . Mex.	18·36 N	95·11 W
136	San Martín (L.) . . . Arg.-Chile	48·15 S	72·30 W
124	San Martin Chalchicuautla (sän mär-tē'n chäl-chē-kwä-ōō' tlä) . Mex	21·22 N	98·39 W
163	San Martin de la Vega (sän mär ten' dâ lä vā'gä) Sp. (Madrid In.)	40·12 N	3·34 W
124	San Martín Hidalgo (sän mär-tē'n-ē-däl'gô) . Mex.	20·27 N	103·55 W
112	San Mateo (săn mä-tā'ô) Ca. (San Francisco In.)	37·34 N	122·20 W
125	San Mateo (Etlatongo) (sän-mä-tĕ'ô) (ĕ-tlä-tô'n-gō) Mex.	16·59 N	97·04 W
163	San Mateo (sän mä-tā'ō) . . . Sp.	40·26 N	0·09 E
135	San Mateo (sän má-tĕ'ô) Ven. (In.)	9·45 N	64·34 W
136	San Matías, Golfo (G.) (sän mä-tē'äs) . Arg.	41·30 S	63·45 W
193	Sanmen Wan (B.) . . . China	29·00 N	122·15 E
136	San Miguel (sän mē-gĕ'l) Arg. (Buenos Aires In.)	34·17 S	58·43 W
125	San Miguel (sän mê-gâl') . . . Mex.	18·18 N	97·09 W
127	San Miguel . . . Pan.	8·26 N	78·55 W
197	San Miguel (sän mē-gĕ'l) Phil. (In.)	15·09 N	120·56 E
126	San Miguel (sän mê-gâl') . . . Sal.	13·28 N	88·11 W
135	San Miguel (sän mē-gĕ'l) Ven. (In.)	9·56 N	64·58 W
	San Miguel, see Sola de Vega		
	San Miguel, see Talea de Castro		
127	San Miguel, Bahia (B.) (bä-ē'ä-sän mê-gâl') . Pan.	8·17 N	78·26 W
114	San Miguel (I.) . . . Ca.	34·03 N	120·23 W
134	San Miguel (R.) (sän-mē-gĕl') . Bol.	13·34 S	63·58 W
115	San Miguel (R.) (săn mê-gĕl') . . Co.	38·15 N	108·40 W
125	San Miguel (R.) (sän mê-gâl') Mex.	15·27 N	92·00 W
126	San Miguel (Vol.) . . . Sal.	13·27 N	88·17 W
197	San Miguel B. . . . Phil. (In.)	13·55 N	123·12 E
124	San Miguel de Allende (dâ ä-lyĕn'dâ) . Mex.	20·54 N	100·44 W
124	San Miguel el Alto (ĕl äl'tô) . . Mex.	21·03 N	102·26 W
211	Sannār . . . Sud.	13·34 N	33·32 E
197	San Narciso (sän när-sē'sô) Phil. (In.)	15·01 N	120·05 E
197	San Narciso . . . Phil. (In.)	13·34 N	122·33 E
137	San Nicolás (sän nē-kô-lä's) Arg. (Buenos Aires In.)	33·20 S	60·14 W
197	San Nicolas (nê-kô-läs') . Phil. (In.)	16·05 N	120·45 E
114	San Nicolas (I.) (săn nĭ'kô-lȧ) . . Ca.	33·14 N	119·10 W
124	San Nicolás (R.) . . . Mex.	19·40 N	105·08 W
214	Sanniquellie . . . Ivory Coast	7·22 N	8·43 W
218	Sannūr, Wādī . . . Egypt (Nile In.)	28·48 N	31·12 E
159	Sanok (sä'nôk) . . . Pol.	49·31 N	22·13 E
112	San Pablo (săn păb'lô) Ca. (San Francisco In.)	37·58 N	122·21 W
197	San Pablo (sän-pä-blô) . . Phil. (In.)	14·05 N	121·20 E
197	San Pablo . . . Phil. (In.)	17·29 N	121·49 E
135	San Pablo (sän-pá'blô) . . Ven. (In.)	9·46 N	65·04 W
112	San Pablo B. (săn păb'lô) Ca. (San Francisco In.)	38·04 N	122·25 W
112	San Pablo Res. Ca. (San Francisco In.)	37·55 N	122·12 W
127	San Pablo R. (sän päb'lô) . . . Pan.	8·12 N	81·12 W
197	San Pascual (päs-kwäl') . Phil. (In.)	13·08 N	122·59 E
136	San Pedro (sän pā'drô) . . . Arg.	24·15 S	64·51 W
137	San Pedro . . Arg. (Buenos Aires In.)	33·41 S	59·42 W
113	San Pedro (săn pē'drô) Ca. (Los Angeles In.)	33·44 N	118·17 W
137	San Pedro (sän pĕ'drô) Chile (Santiago In.)	33·54 S	71·27 W
125	San Pedro (sän pā'drô) . . . Mex.	18·38 N	92·25 W
136	San Pedro (sän-pĕ'drô) . . . Par.	24·13 S	57·00 W
126	San Pedro (sän pā'drô) . . . Sal.	13·49 N	88·58 W
	San Pedro, see Amusgos		
	San Pedro, see Pochutla		
115	San Pedro (R.) . . . Az.	32·48 N	110·37 W
128	San Pedro (R.) (sän-pĕ'drô) . . Cuba	21·05 N	78·15 W
125	San Pedro, Rio de (R.) (rē'ō-dĕ-sän-pĕ'drô) . Mex.	18·23 N	92·13 W
124	San Pedro, Río de (R.) . . . Mex.	21·51 N	102·24 W
124	San Pedro (R.) (sän pā'drô) . . Mex.	22·08 N	104·59 W
113	San Pedro B. (săn pē'drô) Ca. (Los Angeles In.)	33·42 N	118·12 W
118	San Pedro de las Colonias (dĕ-läs-kô-lô'nyäs) . Mex.	25·47 N	102·58 W
129	San Pedro de Macorís (sän-pĕ'drō-dâ mä-kô-rēs') Dom. Rep.	18·30 N	69·30 W
124	San Pedro Lagunillas (sän pā'drô lä-gōō-nēl'yäs) . Mex.	21·12 N	104·47 W
126	San Pedro R. (sän pā'drô) Guat. (In.)	17·11 N	90·23 W
118	San Pedro R. . . . Mex.	27·56 N	105·50 W
126	San Pedro Sula (sän pā'drô sōō'lä) Hond.	15·29 N	88·01 W
	San Pedro y San Pablo, see Teposcolula		
164	San Pietro, I. di (ê'sō-lä-dē-sän pyâ'trô) . It.	39·09 N	8·15 E
112	San Quentin (săn kwĕn-tēn') Ca. (San Francisco In.)	37·57 N	122·29 W
197	San Quintin (sän kên-tēn') Phil. (In.)	15·59 N	120·47 E
136	San Rafael (sän rä-fä-ĕl') . . . Arg.	34·30 S	68·13 W
112	San Rafael (săn rá-fĕl) Ca. (San Francisco In.)	37·58 N	122·31 W
134	San Rafael (sän-rä-fá-ĕ'l) Col. (In.)	6·18 N	75·02 W
115	San Rafael (R.) (săn rá-fĕl') . . . Ut.	39·05 N	110·50 W
129	San Rafael, Cabo (C.) (ká'bô) Dom. Rep.	19·00 N	68·50 W
112	San Ramon (sän rä-mōn') Ca. (San Francisco In.)	37·47 N	122·59 W
127	San Ramōn . . . C. R.	10·07 N	84·30 W
164	San Remo (sän rā'mô) . . . It.	43·48 N	7·46 E
159	San R. . . . Pol.	50·33 N	22·12 E
123	San Roman, C. (sän-rô-mä'n) . Ven.	12·00 N	69·45 W
134	San Roque (sän-rô'kĕ) . . . Col. (In.)	6·29 N	75·00 W
162	San Roque . . . Sp.	36·13 N	5·23 W
118	San Saba (săn sä'bȧ) . . . Tx.	31·12 N	98·43 W
118	San Saba R. . . . Tx.	30·58 N	99·12 W
126	San Salvador (sän säl-vä-dōr') . Sal.	13·45 N	89·11 W
134	San Salvador (I.) . . . Ec.	0·14 S	90·50 W
129	San Salvador (Watling) (I.) (săn săl'vá-dôr) . Ba.	24·05 N	74·30 W
137	San Salvador (R.) (sän-säl-vä-dô'r) Ur. (Buenos Aires In.)	33·42 S	58·04 W
214	Sansanné-Mango (sän-sá-nā' mäɴ'gô) . Togo	10·21 N	0·28 E
210	San Sebastian (sän sȧ-bȧs-tyän') Can. Is.	28·09 N	17·11 W
162	San Sebastián . . . Sp.	43·19 N	1·59 W
135	San Sebastián (sän-sĕ-bäs-tyá'n) Ven. (In.)	9·58 N	67·11 W
163	San Sebastián de los Reyes (sän sä-bäs-tyän'dȧ lōs rā'yĕs) Sp. (Madrid In.)	40·33 N	3·38 W
164	San Severo (sän sĕ-vâ'rō) . . . It.	41·43 N	15·24 E
192	San She (Mtn.) . . . China	33·00 N	103·50 E
189	San Shui . . . China	23·14 N	112·51 E
115	San Simon (R.) (sȧn sī-mōn') . . Az.	32·45 N	109·30 W
113	Santa Ana (săn'tȧ ăn'ȧ) Ca. (Los Angeles In.)	33·45 N	117·52 W
124	Santa Ana (sän'tä ä'nä) . . . Mex.	19·18 N	98·10 W
126	Santa Ana . . . Sal.	14·02 N	89·35 W
113	Santa Ana Mts. Ca. (Los Angeles In.)	33·44 N	117·36 W
113	Santa Ana R. Ca. (Los Angeles In.)	33·41 N	117·57 W
118	Santa Anna . . . Tx.	31·44 N	99·18 W
136	Santa Anna, Cochilha de (Mts.) (kô-chē'lä dĕ sän-tä-nä) . Braz.	30·30 S	56·30 W
210	Santa Antão (I.) (sän-tä-ä'n-zhĕ-lô) . C. V. (In.)	17·20 N	26·05 W
163	Sant' Antimo . . . It. (Naples In.)	40·40 N	14·11 E
137	Santa Bárbara (sän-tä-bá'r-bä-rä) Braz. (Rio de Janeiro In.)	19·57 S	43·25 W
114	Santa Barbara (săn'tȧ bär'bȧ-rȧ) Ca.	34·26 N	119·43 W
126	Santa Barbara (sän'tȧ bär'bä-rä) Hond.	14·52 N	88·20 W
118	Santa Barbara . . . Mex.	26·48 N	105·50 W
114	Santa Barbara (I.) . . . Ca.	33·30 N	118·44 W
114	Santa Barbara (Is.) . . . Ca.	33·45 N	119·46 W
114	Santa Barbara Chan. . . . Ca.	34·15 N	120·00 W
137	Santa Branca (sän-tä-brä'ɴ-kä) Braz. (Rio de Janeiro In.)	23·25 S	45·52 W
114	Santa Catalina (I.) . . . Ca.	33·29 N	118·37 W
127	Santa Catalina, Cerro de (Mt.) (sĕ'r-rô-dĕ-sän-tä-kä-tä-lē'nä) Pan.	8·39 N	81·36 W
114	Santa Catalina, G. of (săn'tȧ kă-tȧ-lē'nȧ) . Ca.	33·00 N	117·58 W
118	Santa Catarina (sän'tȧ kä-tä-rē'nä) . Mex.	25·41 N	100·27 W
	Santa Catarina, see Loxicha		
	Santa Catarina, see Yosonotú		
136	Santa Catarina (State) (sän-tä-kä-tä-rē'nȧ) . Braz.	27·15 S	50·30 W
124	Santa Catarina (R.) . . . Mex.	16·31 N	98·39 W
112	Santa Clara (săn'tȧ klâr'ȧ) Ca. (San Francisco In.)	37·21 N	121·56 W
128	Santa Clara (sän'tȧ klä'rȧ) . . Cuba	22·25 N	80·00 W
118	Santa Clara . . . Mex.	24·29 N	103·22 W
136	Santa Clara . . . Ur.	32·46 S	54·51 W
114	Santa Clara (R.) (săn'tȧ klă'rȧ) Ca.	34·22 N	118·53 W
126	Santa Clara, (Vol.) . . . Nic.	12·44 N	87·00 W
128	Santa Clara, Bahía de (B.) (bä-ē'ä-dĕ-sän-tä-klä-rä) . Cuba	23·05 N	80·50 W
122	Santa Clara, Sierra, (Mts.) (sē-ĕ'r-rä-sän'tȧ klä'rȧ) . Mex.	27·30 N	113·50 W
134	Santa Cruz (sän'tȧ krōōz') . . . Bol.	17·45 S	63·03 W
136	Santa Cruz (sän-tä-krōō's) . . Braz.	29·43 S	52·15 W
136	Santa Cruz Braz. (Rio de Janeiro In.)	22·55 S	43·41 W
114	Santa Cruz (săn'tȧ krōōz') . . . Ca.	36·59 N	122·02 W
137	Santa Cruz . . . Chile (Santiago In.)	34·38 S	71·21 W
126	Santa Cruz . . . C. R.	10·16 N	85·37 W
118	Santa Cruz . . . Mex.	25·50 N	105·25 W
197	Santa Cruz . . . Phil. (In.)	13·28 N	122·02 E
197	Santa Cruz . . . Phil. (In.)	14·17 N	121·25 E
197	Santa Cruz . . . Phil. (In.)	15·46 N	119·53 E
197	Santa Cruz . . . Phil. (In.)	17·06 N	120·27 E
136	Santa Cruz (Prov.) . . . Arg.	48·00 S	70·00 W
114	Santa Cruz (I.) (săn'tȧ krōōz') . Ca.	34·05 N	119·55 W
134	Santa Cruz (I.) (sän-tä-krōō'z) . Ec.	0·38 S	90·20 W
115	Santa Cruz (R.) (săn'tȧ krōōz') . Az.	32·30 N	111·30 W
136	Santa Cruz (R.) (sän'tȧ krōōz') Arg.	50·05 S	66·30 W
126	Santa Cruz Barillas (sän-tä-krōō'z-bä-rē'l-yäs) . Guat.	15·47 N	91·22 W
	Santa Cruz Chico, see Pedro Antonio Santos		
128	Santa Cruz del Sur (sän-tä-krōō's-dĕl-sōō'r) . Cuba	20·45 N	78·00 W
210	Santa Cruz de Tenerife (sän'tä krōōz dȧ tā-nȧ-rē'fȧ) Can. Is.	28·07 N	15·27 W
205	Santa Cruz Is. . . . Sol. Is.	10·58 S	166·47 E
112	Santa Cruz Mts. (săn'tȧ krōōz') Ca. (San Francisco In.)	37·30 N	122·19 W
129	Santa Domingo, Cay (I.) . . . Ba.	21·50 N	75·45 W
164	Sant' Eufemia, Golfo di (G.) (gôl-fô-dē-sän-tĕ'ōō-fĕ'myä) . It.	38·53 N	15·53 E
162	Santa Eugenia de Ribeira (sän-tä-ĕōō-hĕ'nyä-dĕ-rē-bĕ'y-rä) Sp.	42·34 N	8·55 W
163	Santa Eulalia del Rio (sän'tä ȧ-ōō-lä'lê-ä dĕl rē'ô) . Sp.	38·58 N	1·29 E
136	Santa Fe (sän'tä fā') . . . Arg.	31·33 S	60·45 W
128	Santa Fe (sän-tä-fĕ') . . . Cuba	21·45 N	82·40 W
115	Santa Fe (săn'tȧ fā') . . . NM	35·10 N	106·00 W

ăt; finăl; rāte; senâte; ärm; ásk; sofȧ; fâre; ch-choose; dh-as th in other; bē; êvent; bĕt; recĕnt; cratēr; g-go; gh-guttural g; bĭt; ĭ-short neutral; rīde; ĸ-guttural k as ch in German ich;

PRONOUNCING INDEX Santafe — Sao Pedro de Aldeia 343

Page Name Pronunciation Region Lat. °' Long. °'

162 Santafé (sän'tä-fā')...........Sp. 37·12 N 3·43 W
136 Santa Fe (Prov.) (sän'tä fā')..Arg. 32·00 S 61·15 W
135 Santa Filomena (sän-tä-fē-lô-mě'nä).Braz. 9·09 S 44·45 W
122 Santa Genoveva, (Mtn.) (sän-tä-hě-nō-vě'vä).Mex. 23·30 N 110·00 W
193 Sant'ai..................China 31·02 N 105·02 E
135 Santa Inés (sän'tä ē-ně's).Ven.(In.) 9·54 N 64·21 W
136 Santa Inés (I.) (sän'tä ê-nās') Chile 53·45 S 74·15 W
205 Santa Isabel (I.)..........Sol. Is. 7·57 S 159·28 E
128 Santa Lucia (sän'tȧ lo͞o-sē'ȧ).Cuba 21·50 N 77·30 W
137 Santa Lucia (sän-tä-lo͞o-sē'ä) Ur. (Buenos Aires In.) 34·27 S 56·23 W
135 Santa Lucia...........Ven. (In.) 10·18 N 66·40 W
137 Santa Lucia (R.) (sän-tä-lo͞o-sē'ä) Ur. (Buenos Aires In.) 34·19 S 56·13 W
128 Santa Lucia B. (sän'tȧ lo͞o-sē'ȧ) Cuba 22·55 N 84·20 W
122 Santa Magarita (I.) (sän'tȧ mär-gȧ-rē'tȧ).Mex. 24·15 N 112·00 W
136 Santa Maria (sän'tȧ mä-rē'ȧ).Braz. 29·40 S 54·00 W
114 Santa Maria (săn-tȧ mȧ-rē'ȧ)..Ca. 34·57 N 120·28 W
164 Santa Maria (sän-tä mä-rē'ä)...It. 41·05 N 14·15 E
197 Santa Maria (sän-tä-mä-rê'ä) Phil. (In.) 14·48 N 120·57 E
Santa Maria, see Huazolotitlán
124 Santa Maria (R.) (sän'tȧ mä-rē'ȧ).Mex. 21·33 N 100·17 W
129 Santa Maria, C.............Ba. 23·45 N 75·30 W
162 Santa Maria, Cabo de (C.) (kȧ'bō-dě-sän-tä-mä-rē'ä).Port. 36·58 N 7·54 W
128 Santa Maria, Cayo (I.) (kä'yō-săn'tȧ mȧ-rē'ȧ).Cuba 22·40 N 79·00 W
124 Santa María del Oro (sän'tä-mä-rē'ä-děl-ô-rô).Mex. 21·21 N 104·35 W
124 Santa Maria de los Angeles (dě-lôs-ȧ'n-hě-lěs).Mex. 22·10 N 103·34 W
124 Santa María del Rio (sän'tȧ mä-rē'ȧ děl rē'ō).Mex. 21·46 N 100·43 W
124 Santa Maria de Ocotán (sän'tä-mä-rê'ä-dě-ô-kô-tȧ'n) Mex. 22·56 N 104·30 W
210 Santa Maria I. (sän-tä-mä-rê'ä) Açores (In.) 37·09 N 26·02 W
137 Santa Maria Madalena (sän-tä-mȧ-rê'ä-mȧ-dȧ-lě-nä) Braz. (Rio de Janeiro In.) 22·00 S 42·00 W
134 Santa Marta (sän'tȧ mär'tȧ)..Col. 11·15 N 74·13 W
216 Santa Marta, Cabo de (C.)...Ang. 13·52 S 12·25 E
113 Santa Monica (săn'tȧ mŏn'ĭ-kȧ) Ca. (Los Angeles In.) 34·01 N 118·29 W
113 Santa Monica Mts. Ca. (Los Angeles In.) 34·08 N 118·38 W
136 Santana (R.) (sän-tä'nä) Braz. (Rio de Janeiro In.) 22·33 S 43·37 W
134 Santander (sän-tän-děr').Col. (In.) 3·00 N 76·25 W
162 Santander (sän-tän-dâr')......Sp. 43·27 N 3·50 W
163 Sant'Angelo Romano (sän-tä'n-gzhě-lô-rô-mä'nô) It. (Rome In.) 42·02 N 12·45 E
163 Sant' Antimo.....It. (Naples In.) 40·40 N 14·11 E
163 Santañy (sän-tän'yê).........Sp. 39·21 N 3·08 E
114 Santa Paula (săn'tȧ pô'lȧ)....Ca. 34·24 N 119·05 W
135 Santarém (sän-tä-rěɴ')......Braz. 2·28 S 54·37 W
162 Santarém..................Port. 39·18 N 8·48 W
128 Santaren Chan. (sän-tȧ-rěn')..Ba. 24·15 N 79·30 W
115 Santa Rita (săn'tȧ rē'tȧ).....NM 32·45 N 108·05 W
137 Santa Rita do Passo Quatro (sän-tä-rê'tȧ-dô-pä'sô-kwȧ'trô) Braz. (Rio de Janeiro In.) 21·43 S 47·27 W
137 Santa Rita do Sapucai (sä-po͝o-kȧ'ē) Braz. (Rio de Janeiro In.) 22·15 S 45·41 W
136 Santa Rosa (sän-tä-rô-sä)....Arg. 36·45 S 64·10 W
114 Santa Rosa (săn'tȧ rō'zȧ).....Ca. 38·27 N 122·42 W
134 Santa Rosa (sän-tä-rô-sä) Col. (In.) 6·38 N 75·26 W
134 Santa Rosa.................Ec. 3·29 S 78·55 W
126 Santa Rosa (sän'tȧ rō'sȧ)...Guat. 14·21 N 90·16 W
126 Santa Rosa...............Hond. 14·45 N 88·51 W
116 Santa Rosa (săn'tȧ rō'sȧ).....NM 34·55 N 104·41 W
197 Santa Rosa (sän'tȧ rō'sȧ) Phil. (In.) 14·18 N 121·07 E
135 Santa Rosa (sän-tä-rô-sä) Ven. (In.) 9·37 N 64·10 W
134 Santa Rosa de Cabal (sän-tä-rô-sä-dě-kä-bä'l) Col. (In.) 4·53 N 75·38 W
137 Santa Rosa de Viterbo (sän-tä-rô-sȧ-dě-vē-těr'-bô) Braz. (Rio de Janeiro In.) 21·30 S 47·21 W
114 Santa Rosa Ind. Res. (săn'tȧ rō'zȧ').Ca. 33·28 N 116·50 W
122 Santa Rosalía (sän'tȧ rô-zä'lê-ȧ) Mex. 27·13 N 112·15 W
Santa Rosalia, see Ciudad Camargo
110 Santa Rosa Mts. (săn'tȧ rō'zȧ).Nv. 41·33 N 117·50 W
113 Santa Susana (săn'tȧ so͞o-ză'nȧ) Ca. (Los Angeles In.) 34·16 N 118·42 W
Santa Tecla, see Nueva San Salvador
137 Santa Teresa (sän-tä-tě-rě'sä) Arg. (Buenos Aires In.) 33·27 S 60·47 W
135 Santa Teresa..........Ven. (In.) 10·14 N 66·40 W
136 Santa Vitória do Palmar (sän-tä-vē-tŏ'ryä-dô-päl-mȧr) Braz. 33·30 S 53·16 W
114 Santa Ynez (R.) (săn'tȧ ē-něz').Ca. 34·40 N 120·20 W
114 Santa Ysabel Ind. Res. (săn-tȧ ĭ-zȧ-běl').Ca. 33·05 N 116·46 W
114 Santee (săn tē')..........Ca. (In.) 32·50 N 116·58 W
121 Santee (R.)..................SC 33·27 N 80·02 W
136 Santiago (sän-tyȧ'gô).......Braz. 29·05 S 54·46 W
137 Santiago (sän-tê-ä'gô) Chile (Santiago In.) 33·26 S 70·40 W
127 Santiago...................Pan. 8·07 N 80·58 W
197 Santiago (sän-tyä'gô)...Phil. (In.) 16·42 N 121·33 E
162 Santiago....................Sp. 42·52 N 8·32 W
Santiago, see Tejupan
Santiago, see Zacatepec
137 Santiago (Prov.) (sän-tyȧ'gō) Chile (Santiago In.) 33·28 S 70·55 W
124 Santiago, Rio Grande de (R.) (rê'o-grä'n-dě-dě-sän-tyȧ'gô) Mex. 21·15 N 104·05 W
197 Santiago (I.)..........Phil. (In.) 16·29 N 120·03 E
129 Santiago de los Cabelleros (sän-tyȧ'gô-dȧ lōs kȧ-bä-yā'rôs) Dom. Rep. 19·30 N 70·45 W
129 Santiago de Cuba (sän-tyȧ'gô-dā ko͞o'bȧ).Cuba 20·00 N 75·50 W
129 Santiago de las Vegas (sän-tyȧ'gô-dě-läs-vě'gäs) Cuba (In.) 22·13 N 82·23 W
136 Santiago del Estero (sän-tē-ȧ'gō-děl ěs-tā'rô).Arg. 27·50 S 64·14 W
136 Santiago del Estero (Prov.) (sän-tē-ȧ'gō-děl ěs-tā'rô).Arg. 27·15 S 63·30 W
118 Santiago Mts. (sän-tê-ä'gô)....Tx. 30·00 N 103·30 W
113 Santiago Res. Ca. (Los Angeles In.) 33·47 N 117·42 W
129 Santiago Rodriguez (sän-tyȧ'gô-rô-drê'gěz) Dom. Rep. 19·30 N 71·25 W
125 Santiago Tuxtla (sän-tyȧ'gô-to͞o'x-tlä).Mex. 18·28 N 95·18 W
118 Santiaguillo, Laguna de (L.) (lä-o͞o'nä-dě-sän-tê-a-gēl'yô) Mex. 24·51 N 104·43 W
110 Santiam R. (săn'tyăm)........Or. 44·42 N 122·26 W
162 Santisteban del Puerto (sän'tê stȧ-bän'děl pwěr'tô).Sp. 38·15 N 3·12 W
190 Santo (sän'tŏ)............China 32·49 N 119·39 E
135 Santo Amaro (sän'to͞o ä-mä'ro͞o) Braz. 12·32 S 38·33 W
137 Santo Amaro de Campos (sän-tô-ä-mä'rô-dě-kȧm'pôs) Braz. (Rio de Janeiro In.) 22·01 S 41·05 W
137 Santo André (sän-tô-än-drě') Braz. (Rio de Janeiro In.) 23·40 S 46·31 W
136 Santo Angelo (sän-tô-ȧ'n-zhě-lô) Braz. 28·16 S 53·59 W
137 Santo Antônio do Monte (sän-tô-än-tō'nyô-dô-môn'tě) Braz. (Rio de Janeiro In.) 20·06 S 45·18 W
216 Santo Antonio do Zaire (sän'to͞o än-tō'nē-o͞o).Ang. 6·10 S 12·25 E
128 Santo Domingo (sän'tô-dōmĭŋ'gô) Cuba 22·35 N 80·20 W
126 Santo Domingo (sän-tô-dô-mê'n-gō).Nic. 12·15 N 84·56 W
197 Santo Domingo........Phil. (In.) 17·39 N 120·24 E
129 Santo Domingo (sän'tô dô-mĭn'gô) Dom. Rep. 18·30 N 69·55 W
Santo Domingo, see Zanatepec
162 Santo Domingo de la Caizada (dā lä käl-thä'dä).Sp. 42·27 N 2·55 W
162 Santoña (sän-tō'nyä).........Sp. 43·25 N 3·27 W
137 Santos (sän'tozh) Braz. (Rio de Janeiro In.) 23·58 S 46·20 W
137 Santos Dumont (sän'tôs-do͞o-mô'nt) Braz. (Rio de Janeiro In.) 21·28 S 43·33 W
197 Santos Thomas (sän-tô-tô-mä's) Phil. (In.) 14·07 N 121·09 E
197 Santo Tomas (Mtn.)....Phil. (In.) 16·23 N 120·32 E
136 Santo Tomé (sän-tô-tô-mě')..Arg. 28·32 S 56·04 W
195 Sanuki (sä'no͞o-kê) Jap. (Tōkyō In.) 35·16 N 139·53 E
137 San Urbano (sän-o͞or-bä'nô) Arg. (Buenos Aires In.) 33·39 S 61·28 W
136 San Valentin, M. (Mtn.) (sän-vä-lěn-tē'n).Chile 46·41 S 73·30 W
160 Sanvic (säɴ-vēĸ')............Fr. 49·34 N 0·08 E
137 San Vicente (sän-vē-sěn'tě) Arg. (Buenos Aires In.) 35·00 S 58·26 W
137 San Vicente...Chile (Santiago In.) 34·25 S 71·06 W
126 San Vicente (sän vê-sěn'tȧ)...Sal. 13·41 N 88·43 W
162 San Vincente de Alcántara (sän vê-thěn'tȧ dȧ äl-kän'tä-rä) Sp. 39·24 N 7·08 W
164 San Vito (sän vē'tô)..........It. 45·53 N 12·52 E
115 San Xavier Ind. Res. (x-ā'vĭēr).Az. 32·07 N 111·12 W
193 Sanya....................China 18·10 N 109·32 E
191 Sanyüanli.....China (Canton In.) 23·11 N 113·16 E
114 San Ysidro (sän ysĭ-drō')..Ca. (In.) 32·33 N 117·02 W
137 São Bernardo do Campo (souɴ-běr-nár'dô-dô-kȧ'm-pô) Braz. (Rio de Janeiro In.) 23·44 S 46·33 W
136 São Borja (souɴ-bôr-zhä)....Braz. 28·44 S 55·59 W
137 São Carlos (souɴ kär'lōzh) Braz. (Rio de Janeiro In.) 22·02 S 47·54 W
135 São Cristovão (souɴ-krês-tō-vouɴ) Braz. 11·04 S 37·11 W
137 São Fidélis (souɴ-fē-dě'lēs) Braz. (Rio de Janeiro In.) 21·41 S 41·45 W
135 São Francisco (souɴ fräɴ-sēsh'ko͞o) Braz. 15·59 S 44·42 W
135 São Francisco, Rio (R.) (rē'ō-sän-frän-sē's-kō).Braz. 8·56 S 40·20 W
136 São Francisco do Sul (souɴ fräɴ-sēsh'ko͞o-dô-so͞o'l) Braz. 26·15 S 48·42 W
136 São Gabriel (souɴ'gä-brê-ěl').Braz. 30·28 S 54·11 W
137 São Geraldo (souɴ-zhě-rä'l-dô) Braz. (Rio de Janeiro In.) 21·01 S 42·49 W
136 São Gonçalo (souɴ'gōŋ-sä'lo͞o) Braz. (Rio de Janeiro In.) 22·55 S 43·04 W
137 São Gonçalo do Sapucaí (souɴ-gôn-sä'lō-dô-sä-po͞o-kī') Braz. (Rio de Janeiro In.) 21·55 S 45·34 W
217 São Hill...................Tan. 8·20 S 35·12 E
214 Sao Joao..........Guinea-Bissau 11·32 N 15·26 W
136 São João da Barra (souɴ-zhôuɴ-dä-bȧ'rä) Braz. (Rio de Janeiro In.) 21·40 S 41·03 W
137 São João da Boa Vista (souɴ-zhôuɴ-dä-bôä-vê's-tä) Braz. (Rio de Janeiro In.) 21·58 S 46·45 W
137 São João del Rei (souɴ zhô-ouɴ'děl-rā) Braz. (Rio de Janeiro In.) 21·08 S 44·14 W
136 São João de Meriti (souɴ-zhôuɴ-dě-mě-rē-tê) Braz. (Rio de Janeiro In.) 22·47 S 43·22 W
137 São João do Araguaia (souɴ zhô-ouɴ'dô-ä-rä-gwä'yä) Braz. 5·29 S 48·44 W
163 São João dos Lampas (souɴ' zhô-ouɴ' dōzh län-päzh') Port (Lisbon In.) 38·52 N 9·24 W
137 São João Nepomuceno (souɴ-zhôuɴ-ně-pô-mo͞o-sě-nō) Braz. (Rio de Janeiro In.) 21·33 S 43·00 W
210 São Jorge I. (souɴ zhôr' zhě) Açores (In.) 38·28 N 27·34 W
137 São José do Rio Pardo (souɴ-zhô-sě'dô-rē'ō-pȧ'r-dō) Braz. (Rio de Janeiro In.) 21·36 S 46·50 W
135 São José do Rio Prêto (souɴ zhô-zě'dô-rē'ō-prě-tō) Braz. 20·57 S 49·12 W
137 São José dos Campos (souɴ zhô-zā'dōzh käɴ pōzh') Braz. (Rio de Janeiro In.) 23·12 S 45·53 W
136 São Leopoldo (souɴ-lě-ô-pôl'dô) Braz. 29·46 S 51·09 W
135 São Luis (Maranhão) (souɴ-lo͞oê's-mä-rän-youɴ') Braz. 2·31 S 43·14 W
137 São Luis do Paraitinga (souɴ-lo͞oê's-dô-pä-rä-ē-tē'n-gä) Braz. (Rio de Janeiro In.) 23·15 S 44·18 W
135 São Mateus (souɴ mä-tā'o͞ozh) Braz. 18·44 S 39·45 W
137 São Miguel Arcanjo (souɴ-mē-gě'l-ȧr-kän-zhō) Braz. (Rio de Janeiro In.) 23·54 S 47·59 W
210 São Miguel I.........Açores (In.) 37·59 N 26·38 W
129 Saona (I.) (sä-ô'nä)....Dom. Rep. 18·10 N 68·55 W
160 Saône (R.) (sōn).............Fr. 46·27 N 4·58 E
216 São Nicolau................Ang. 14·15 S 12·21 E
210 São Nicolau (souɴ' nê-kô-louɴ') C. V. (In.) 16·19 N 25·19 W
137 São Paulo (souɴ' pou'lo͞o) Braz. (Rio de Janeiro In.) 23·34 S 46·38 W
135 São Paulo (State) (souɴ pou'lo͞o) Braz. 21·45 S 50·47 W
134 São Paulo de Olivença (souɴ'pou'lo͞odȧ ô-lê-věn'sȧ) Braz. 3·32 S 68·46 W
137 São Pedro (souɴ-pě'drô) Braz. (Rio de Janeiro In.) 22·34 S 47·54 W
137 São Pedro de Aldeia (souɴ-pě'drô-dě-äl-dě'yä) Braz. (Rio de Janeiro In.) 22·50 S 42·04 W

ng-sing; ŋ-baŋk; ɴ-nasalized n; nŏd; cŏmmit; ōld; ôbey; ôrder; fo͞od; fo͝ot; ou-out; s-soft; sh-dish; th-thin; pūre; ûnite; ûrn; stŭd; circŭs; ü-as "y" in study; '-indeterminate vowel.

344 Sao Raimundo Nonato — Schweinfurt PRONOUNCING INDEX

Page	Name Pronunciation Region	Lat. °′	Long. °′
135	São Raimundo Nonato (souɴ′ rī-mōō′n-do nô-nä′tōō) Braz.	9·09 s	42·32 w
137	São Roque (souɴ′ rō′kĕ) Braz. (Rio de Janeiro In.)	23·32 s	47·08 w
135	São Roque, Cabo de (C.) (kä′bo-dĕ-souɴ′ rō′kĕ). Braz.	5·06 s	35·11 w
216	São Salvador do Congo (souɴ säl-và-dôr). Ang	6·30 s	14·10 e
137	São Sebastião (souɴ sà-bäs-tê-ouɴ′) Braz. (Rio de Janeiro In.)	23·48 s	45·25 w
137	São Sebastião, Ilha de (I.) (ēl′yȧ dȧ souɴ′ sà-bäs-tê-ouɴ′) Braz. (Rio de Janeiro In.)	23·52 s	45·22 w
137	São Sebastião do Paraíso (souɴ-sĕ-bäs-tē-ouɴ-dô-pä-rä-ē′sō). Braz. (Rio de Janeiro In.)	20·54 s	46·58 w
137	São Simão (souɴ-sē-mouɴ) Braz. (Rio de Janeiro In.)	21·30 s	47·33 w
210	São Tiago I. (souɴ tê-ä′gōō) C. V. (In.)	15·09 n	24·45 w
216	São Tomé (souɴ tô-mā′) São Tomé & Príncipe	0·20 n	6·44 e
216	São Tomé (I.) São Tomé & Príncipe	0·20 n	7·00 e
137	São Tomé, Cabo de (C.) (kä′bō-dĕ-souɴ-tô-mĕ′) Braz. (Rio de Janeiro In.)	22·00 s	40·00 w
209	Sao Tome & Principe (prēn′sê-pĕ). Afr.	1·00 n	6·00 e
152	Saoura, Oued (R.) Alg.	29·39 n	1·42 w
137	São Vicente (souɴ ve-se′n-tĕ) Braz. (Rio de Janeiro In.)	23·57 s	46·25 w
210	Sao Vincente I. (souɴ vê-sĕn′tȧ) C. V. (In.)	16·51 n	24·35 w
162	São Vinente, Cabo de (C.) (kȧ′bō-dĕ-sän-vê-sĕ′n-tĕ). Port.	37·03 n	9·31 w
215	Sapele (sä-pā′lā) Nig.	5·54 n	5·41 e
217	Sapitwa (Mtn.) Malawi	15·58 s	35·38 e
166	Sapozhok (sä-pô-zhôk′). Sov. Un.	53·58 n	40·44 e
194	Sapporo (säp-pô′rō) Jap.	43·02 n	141·29 e
174	Sapronovo (sȧp-rô′nô-vô) Sov. Un. (Moscow In.)	55·13 n	38·25 e
137	Sapucaí (R.) (sä-pōō-kȧ-ē′) Braz. (Rio de Janeiro In.)	21·07 s	45·53 w
137	Sapucaia (sä-pōō-kä′yȧ) Braz. (Rio de Janeiro In.)	22·01 s	42·54 w
137	Sapucaí Mirim (R.) (sä-pōō-kȧ-ē′mē-rêɴ) Braz. (Rio de Janeiro In.)	21·06 s	47·03 w
117	Sapulpa (sȧ-pŭl′pȧ) Ok.	36·01 n	96·05 w
137	Saquarema (sä-kwä-rĕ-mä) Braz. (Rio de Janeiro In.)	22·56 s	42·32 w
112	Sara (sä′rä) Wa. (Portland In.)	45·45 n	122·42 w
211	Sara, Bahr (R.) (bär) Chad-Cen. Afr. Rep.	8·19 n	17·44 e
165	Sarajevo (sä-rȧ-yĕv′ô) (sȧ-rä′ya-vô). Yugo.	43·15 n	18·26 e
174	Sarana (sá-rä′ná) Sov. Un. (Urals In.)	56·31 n	57·44 e
105	Saranac Lake NY	44·20 n	74·05 w
105	Saranac L. (săr′ȧ-năk) NY	44·15 n	74·20 w
136	Sarandi (sä-rän′dê) Arg. (Buenos Aires In.)	34·26 s	58·21 w
137	Sarandi Grande (sä-rän′dē-grän′dĕ) Ur. (Buenos Aires In.)	33·42 s	56·21 w
184	Sārangpur India	23·39 n	76·32 e
170	Saransk (sȧ-ränsk′) Sov. Un.	54·10 n	45·10 e
174	Sarany (sȧ-rä′nĭ) Sov. Un. (Urals In.)	58·33 n	58·48 e
215	Sara Pk. Nig.	9·37 n	9·25 e
170	Sarapul (sä-rä-pōōl′) Sov. Un.	56·28 n	53·50 e
121	Sarasota (săr-ȧ-sōtȧ) Fl. (In.)	27·27 n	82·30 w
119	Saratoga (săr-ȧ-tō′gȧ) Tx.	30·17 n	94·31 w
112	Saratoga Wa. (Seattle In.)	48·04 n	122·29 w
112	Saratoga Pass. Wa. (Seattle In.)	48·09 n	122·33 w
105	Saratoga Springs (sprĭngz) NY	43·05 n	74·50 w
171	Saratov (sȧ rä′tôf) Sov. Un.	51·30 n	45·30 e
193	Saravane Laos	15·48 n	106·40 e
196	Sarawak (Reg.) (sȧ-rä′wäk). Mala.	2·30 n	112·45 e
159	Sárbogárd (shär′bô-gärd) Hung.	46·53 n	18·38 e
100	Sarcee Ind. Res. (sär′sê) Can. (Calgary In.)	50·58 n	114·23 w
210	Sardalas Libya	25·59 n	10·33 e
164	Sardinia (I.) (sär-dĭn′ĭȧ) It.	40·08 n	9·05 e
120	Sardis (sär′dĭs) Ms.	34·26 n	89·55 w
197	Sarera, Teluk (B.) Indon.	2·20 s	135·30 e
108	Sargent (sär′jĕnt) Ne.	41·40 n	99·38 w
215	Sarh (Fort-Archambault) (är-chaɴ-bō′). Chad	9·09 n	18·23 e
171	Sarikamis Tur.	40·30 n	42·40 e
163	Sariñena (sä-rēn-yĕ′nä) Sp.	41·46 n	0·11 w
192	Sariwŏn (sä′rē-wŭn′) Korea	38·40 n	125·45 e
160	Sark (I.) (särk) Guernsey	49·28 n	2·22 w
165	Şarkoy (shär′kû-ê) Tur.	40·39 n	27·07 e
160	Sarlat (sär-lä′) Fr.	44·52 n	1·13 e
136	Sarmiento, Monte (Mt.) (mô′n-tĕ-sär-myĕn′tō). Chile	54·28 s	70·40 w
104	Sarnia (sär′nê-ȧ) Can.	43·00 n	82·25 w
163	Sarno (sä′r-nô) It. (Naples In.)	40·35 n	14·38 e
159	Sarny (sär′nê) Sov. Un.	51·17 n	26·39 e
165	Saronikós Kólpos (G.) Grc.	37·51 n	23·30 e
165	Saros Körfezi (G.) (sä′rôs) Tur.	40·30 n	26·20 e
159	Sárospatak (shä′rôsh-pô′tôk) Hung.	48·19 n	21·35 e
165	Šar Planina (Mts.) (shär plä′nê-na). Yugo.	42·07 n	21·54 e
156	Sarpsborg (särps′bôrg) Nor.	59·17 n	11·07 e
161	Sarrebourg (sär-bōōr′) Fr.	48·44 n	7·02 e
161	Sarreguemines (sär-gē-mēn′) Fr.	49·06 n	7·05 e
162	Sarria (sär′ê-ä) Sp.	42·14 n	7·17 w
126	Sarstun R. (särs-tōō′n) Guat.	15·50 n	89·26 w
164	Sartène (sär-tĕn′) Fr.	41·36 n	8·59 e
160	Sarthe (R.) (särt) Fr.	47·44 n	0·32 w
	Sartor, see Store Sotra		
158	Sárvár (shär′vär) Hung.	47·14 n	16·55 e
171	Sarych, Mys (C.) (mĭs sȧ-rēch′) Sov. Un.	44·25 n	33·00 e
172	Sary-Ishikotrau, Peski (des.) (sä′rê ē′ shêk-ō′trou). Sov. Un.	46·12 n	75·30 e
172	Sarysu (R.) (sä′rê-sōō) Sov. Un.	47·47 n	69·14 e
184	Sasarām (sŭs-ŭ-räm′) India	25·00 n	84·00 e
195	Sasayama (sä′sä-yä′mä) Jap.	35·05 n	135·14 e
195	Sasebo (sä′sȧ-bô) Jap.	33·12 n	129·43 e
	Saseno (I.), see Sazan		
158	Sašice Czech.	49·14 n	13·31 e
90	Saskatchewan (Prov.) Can.	54·46 n	107·40 w
94	Saskatchewan (R.) (săs-kăch′ê-wän). Can.	53·45 n	103·20 w
94	Saskatoon (săs-kȧ-tōōn′) Can.	52·07 n	106·38 w
218	Sasolburg S. Afr. (Johannesburg & Pretoria In.)	26·52 s	27·47 e
170	Sasovo (sȧs′ô-vô) Sov. Un.	54·20 n	42·00 e
113	Saspamco (săs-păm′cō) Tx. (San Antonio In.)	29·13 n	98·18 w
214	Sassandra Ivory Coast	4·58 n	6·05 w
214	Sassandra (R.) (sȧs-sän′drȧ) Ivory Coast	5·35 n	6·25 w
164	Sassari (säs′sä-rê) It.	40·44 n	8·33 e
158	Sassnitz (säs′nêts) G.D.R.	54·31 n	13·37 e
214	Satadougou (sä-tȧ-dōō-gōō′). Mali	12·21 n	10·07 w
156	Säter (sĕ′tĕr) Swe.	60·21 n	15·50 e
121	Satilla (R.) (sȧ-tĭl′ȧ) Ga.	31·15 n	82·13 w
174	Satka (sät′kȧ). Sov. Un. (Urals In.)	55·03 n	59·02 e
159	Sátoraljaujhely (shä′tô-rô-lyô-ōō′yĕl′). Hung.	48·24 n	21·40 e
159	Satu-Mare (sȧ′tōō-mȧ′rĕ) Rom.	47·50 n	22·53 e
112	Saturna (să-tûr′nȧ) Can. (Vancouver In.)	48·48 n	123·12 w
112	Saturna (I.). Can. (Vancouver In.)	48·47 n	123·03 w
156	Saude (sou′dĕ) Nor.	59·40 n	6·21 e
150	Sáudharkrókur Ice.	65·41 n	19·38 w
182	Saudi Arabia (sȧ-ōō′dĭ ȧ-rä′bĭ-ȧ) Asia	22·40 n	46·00 e
149	Sauerlach (zou′ĕr-läĸ) F.R.G. (Munich In.)	47·58 n	11·39 e
104	Saugatuck (sô′gȧ-tŭk) Mi.	42·40 n	86·10 w
104	Saugeer (R.) (sô′gĕr) Can.	44·20 n	81·20 w
105	Saugerties (sô′gĕr-tēz) NY	42·05 n	73·55 w
99	Saugus (sô′gŭs) Ma. (In.)	42·28 n	71·01 w
109	Sauk (R.) (sôk) Mn.	45·30 n	94·45 w
109	Sauk Centre Mn.	45·43 n	94·58 w
109	Sauk City Wi.	43·16 n	89·45 w
109	Sauk Rapids (răp′ĭd) Mn.	45·35 n	94·08 w
96	Sault Ste. Marie Can.	46·31 n	84·20 w
113	Sault Ste. Marie (sōō sānt mȧ-rē′) Mi. (Sault Ste. Marie In.)	46·29 n	84·21 w
129	Saumatre, Etang (L.) Hai.	18·40 n	72·10 w
205	Saunders, C. (sôrn′dĕrs). N. Z. (In.)	45·55 s	170·50 e
100	Saunders L. (sän′dĕrs) Can. (Edmonton In.)	53·18 n	113·25 w
112	Sausalito (sô-sȧ-lē′tô) Ca. (San Francisco In.)	37·51 n	122·29 w
160	Sausset-les-Pins (sō-sĕ′lā-pàɴ′) Fr. (In.)	43·20 n	5·08 e
216	Saútar Ang.	11·06 s	18·27 e
112	Sauvie I. (sô′vē). Or. (Portland In.)	45·43 n	123·49 w
165	Sava (R.) (sä′vä) Yugo.	44·50 n	17·00 e
106	Savage (să′vĕj) Md. (Baltimore In.)	39·07 n	76·49 w
113	Savage Mn. (Minneapolis, St. Paul In)	44·47 n	93·20 w
171	Savalan (Mtn.) Iran	38·20 n	48·00 e
215	Savalou Benin	7·56 n	1·58 e
109	Savanna (sȧ-văn′ȧ) Il.	42·05 n	90·09 w
121	Savannah (sȧ-văn′ȧ) Ga.	32·04 n	81·07 w
109	Savannah Mo.	39·58 n	94·49 w
120	Savannah Tn.	35·13 n	88·14 w
121	Savannah (R.) Ga.-SC	33·11 n	81·51 w
128	Savanna la Mar (sȧ-vän′ȧ lȧ mär′) Jam.	18·10 n	78·10 w
158	Sávava R. Czech.	49·36 n	15·24 e
210	Savé (sȧ-vā′) Benin	8·09 n	2·03 e
160	Save (R.) Fr.	43·32 n	0·50 e
212	Save, Rio (R.) (rē′ō-sä′vĕ). Moz.	21·28 s	34·14 e
161	Saverne (sȧ-vĕrn′) Fr.	48·40 n	7·22 e
164	Savigliano (sä-vêl-yä′nô) It.	44·38 n	7·42 e
164	Savona (sä-nō′nä) It.	44·19 n	8·28 e
157	Savonlinna (sȧ′vôn-lēn′nȧ) Fin.	61·53 n	28·49 e
167	Savran′ (säv-rän′) Sov. Un.	48·07 n	30·09 e
196	Sawahlunto Indon.	0·37 s	100·50 e
211	Sawākin Sud.	19·02 n	37·19 e
196	Sawankhalok Thai.	17·16 n	99·48 e
211	Sawda, Jabal as (Mts.) Libya	28·14 n	13·46 e
152	Sawfjjin, Wadi (R.) Libya	31·18 n	13·16 e
218	Sawhāj Egypt (Nile In.)	26·34 n	31·40 e
211	Sawknah Libya	29·04 n	15·53 e
196	Sawu, Laut (Savu Sea) Indon.	9·15 s	122·15 e
196	Sawu (I.) Indon.	10·15 s	122·00 e
112	Sawyer (L.) (sô′yĕr) Wa. (Seattle In.)	47·20 n	122·02 w
210	Say (sä′ē) Niger	13·09 n	2·16 e
172	Sayan Khrebet (Mts.) (sŭ-yän′) Sov. Un.	51·30 n	90·00 e
183	Şaydā (Sidon) (sä′ê-dä) (sī′dŏn) Leb. (Palestine In.)	33·34 n	35·23 e
186	Sayhūt P. D. R. of Yem.	15·23 n	51·28 e
116	Sayre (sā′ĕr) Ok.	35·19 n	99·40 w
105	Sayre Pa.	41·55 n	76·30 w
106	Sayreton (sā′ĕr-tŭn) Al. (Birmingham In.)	33·34 n	86·51 w
106	Sayreville (sâr′vĭl) NJ (New York In.)	40·28 n	74·21 w
188	Sayr Usa Mong.	44·51 n	107·00 e
125	Sayula (sä-yōō′lä) Mex.	17·51 n	94·56 w
124	Sayula Mex.	19·50 n	101·33 w
124	Sayula, Luguna de (L.) (lä-gōō′nä-dĕ). Mex.	20·00 n	103·33 w
186	Say′un P.D.R. of Yem.	16·00 n	48·59 e
105	Sayville (sā′vĭl) NY	40·45 n	73·10 w
165	Sazan (Saseno) (I.) Alb.	40·30 n	19·17 e
174	Sazhino (sȧz-hē′nô) Sov. Un. (Urals In.)	56·20 n	58·15 e
156	Scäffle Swe.	59·10 n	12·55 e
182	Scandinavian Pen. Eur.	62·00 n	14·00 e
113	Scanlon (skăn′lôn) Mn. (Duluth In.)	46·27 n	92·26 w
112	Scappoose (skă-pōōs′) Or. (Portland In.)	45·46 n	122·53 w
112	Scappoose (R.). Or. (Portland In.)	45·47 n	122·57 w
100	Scarborough (skär′bĕr-ô) Can. (Toronto In.)	43·45 n	79·12 w
154	Scarborough (skär′bŭr-ô) Eng.	54·16 n	0·19 w
106	Scarsdale (skärz′dāl) NY (New York In.)	41·01 n	73·47 w
97	Scatari I (skăt′ȧ-rē) Can.	46·00 n	59·44 w
149	Schaerbeek (skär′bāk) Bel. (Brussels In.)	50·53 n	4·23 e
158	Schaffhausen (shäf′hou-zĕn). Switz.	47·42 n	8·38 e
91	Schefferville Can.	54·52 n	67·01 w
155	Schelde, R. Bel.	51·04 n	3·55 e
105	Schenectady (skĕ-nĕk′tȧ-dê). NY.	42·50 n	73·55 w
149	Scheveningen Neth. (Amsterdam In.)	52·06 n	4·15 e
149	Schiedam. Neth. (Amsterdam In.)	51·55 n	4·23 e
161	Schiltigheim (shêl′tegh-hīm) Fr.	48·48 n	7·47 e
164	Schio (skē′ô) It.	45·43 n	11·23 e
158	Schleswig (shlĕs′vêgh) F.R.G.	54·32 n	9·32 e
158	Schleswig-Holstein (State) (shlĕs′vêgh-hōl′shtīn) F.R.G.	54·40 n	9·10 e
158	Schmalkalden (shmäl′käl-dĕn) G.D.R.	50·41 n	10·25 e
107	Schneider (schnīd′ĕr) In. (Chicago In.)	41·12 n	87·26 w
109	Schofield (skō′fēld) Wi.	44·52 n	89·37 w
158	Schönebeck (shû′nĕ-bergh). G.D.R.	52·01 n	11·44 e
149	Schoonhoven Neth. (Amsterdam In.)	51·56 n	4·51 e
197	Schouten, Kepulauan (I.) (skou′tĕn). Indon.	0·45 s	136·40 e
158	Schramberg (shräm′bĕrgh). F.R.G.	48·14 n	8·24 e
96	Schreiber Can.	48·50 n	87·10 w
105	Schroon (L.) (skrōōn) NY	43·50 n	73·50 w
149	Schultzendorf (shōōl′tzĕn-dōrf) G.D.R. (Berlin In.)	52·21 n	13·35 e
96	Schumacher Can.	48·30 n	81·30 w
108	Schuyler (slī′ler) Ne.	41·28 n	97·05 w
106	Schuylkill (R.) (skōōl′kĭl) Pa.	40·10 n	75·31 w
105	Schuylkill-Haven (hā-vĕn) Pa.	40·35 n	76·10 w
158	Schwabach (shvä′bäk) F.R.G.	49·19 n	11·02 e
158	Schwäbische Alb (Mts.) (shvă′bē-shĕ älb) F.R.G.	48·11 n	9·09 e
158	Schwäbisch Gmünd (shvă′bēsh gmünd) F.R.G.	48·47 n	9·49 e
158	Schwäbisch Hall (häl) F.R.G.	49·08 n	9·44 e
158	Schwandorf (shvän′dôrf) F.R.G.	49·19 n	12·08 e
196	Schwaner, Pegunungan Mts. (sĸvän′ĕr). Indon.	1·38 s	111·08 e
158	Schwarzwald (For.) (shvärts′ väld) F.R.G.	47·54 n	7·57 e
158	Schwaz Aus.	47·20 n	11·45 e
149	Schwechat (shvĕk′ät) Aus. (Vienna In.)	48·09 n	16·29 e
158	Schwedt (shvĕt) G.D.R.	53·04 n	14·17 e
158	Schweinfurt (shvīn′fōōrt). F.R.G.	50·03 n	10·14 e

ăt; finăl; rāte; senâte; ärm; åsk; sofȧ; fâre; ch-choose; dh-as th in other; bē; ėvent; bĕt; recĕnt; cratĕr; g-go; gh-guttural g; bĭt; ĭ-short neutral; rīde; ĸ-guttural k as ch in German ich

PRONOUNCING INDEX

Schwelm — Serpukhov 345

Page	Name Pronunciation Region	Lat. °'	Long. °'
161	Schwelm (shvĕlm) F.R.G. (Ruhr In.)	51·17 N	7·18 E
158	Schwenningen (shvĕn'ĭng-ĕn) F.R.G.	48·04 N	8·33 E
158	Schwerin (shvĕ-rēn') G.D.R.	53·36 N	11·25 E
158	Schweriner See (L.) (shvĕ'rē-nĕr zā) G.D.R.	53·40 N	11·06 E
161	Schwerte (shvĕr'tĕ) F.R.G. (Ruhr In.)	51·26 N	7·34 E
149	Schwielow L. (shvē'lōv) G.D.R. (Berlin In.)	52.20 N	12·52 E
158	Schwyz (schēts) Switz.	47·01 N	8·38 E
164	Sciacca (shē-äk'kä) It.	37·30 N	13·09 E
154	Scilly (Is.) (sĭl'ē) Eng.	49·56 N	6·50 W
104	Scioto (R.) (sī-ō'tō) Oh.	39·10 N	82·55 W
99	Scituate (sĭt'ū-āt) Ma. (In.)	42·12 N	70·45 W
111	Scobey (skō'bē) Mt.	48·48 N	105·29 W
112	Scoggin (skŏ'gĭn) Or. (Portland In.)	45·28 N	123·14 W
100	Scotch (R.) (skŏch) Can. (Ottawa In.)	45·21 N	74·56 W
110	Scotia (skō'shȧ) Ca.	40·29 N	124·06 W
154	Scotland (skŏt'lănd) U. K.	57·05 N	5·10 W
168	Scotland SD	43·08 N	97·43 W
121	Scotland Neck (nĕk) NC	36·06 N	77·25 W
105	Scotstown (skŏts'toun) Can.	45·35 N	71·15 W
90	Scott, C. (skŏt) Can.	50·47 N	128·26 W
110	Scott, Mt. Or.	42·55 N	122·00 W
112	Scott, Mt. Or. (Portland In.)	45·27 N	122·33 W
113	Scott Air Force Base Il. (St. Louis In.)	38·33 N	89·52 W
213	Scottburgh (skŏt'bŭr-ô) S. Afr. (Natal In.)	30·18 S	30·42 E
116	Scott City Ks.	38·28 N	100·54 W
106	Scottdale (skŏt' dāl) Ga. (Atlanta In.)	33·47 N	84·16 W
220	Scott Is. Ant.	67·00 S	178·00 E
220	Scott Ra. Ant.	68·00 S	55·00 E
108	Scottsbluff (skŏts'blŭf) Ne.	41·52 N	103·40 W
108	Scotts Bluff Natl. Mon. Ne.	41·45 N	103·47 W
95	Scottsboro (skŏts'bŭro) Al.	34·40 N	86·03 W
104	Scottsburg (skŏts' bûrg) In.	38·40 N	85·50 W
203	Scottsdale (skŏts'dāl) Austl.	41·12 S	147·37 E
95	Scottsville (skŏts'vĭl) Ky.	36·45 N	86·10 W
104	Scottville Mi.	44·00 N	86·20 W
105	Scranton (skrăn'tŭn) Pa.	41·45 N	75·45 W
105	Scugog (L.) (skū'gôg) Can.	44·05 N	78·55 W
148	Scunthorpe (skŭn'thôrp) Eng.	53·36 N	0·38 W
	Scutari, see Shkodër		
165	Scutari (R.) (skōō'tä-rē) Alb.	42·14 N	19·33 E
121	Sea, Is. (sē) Ga.-SC	31·21 N	81·05 W
112	Seabeck (sē'bĕck) Wa. (Seattle In.)	47·38 N	122·50 W
106	Sea Bright (sē brīt) NJ (New York In.)	40·22 N	73·58 W
119	Seabrook (sē'brŏŏk) Tx.	29·34 N	95·01 W
105	Seaford (sē'fērd) De.	38·35 N	75·40 W
116	Seagraves (sē'grāvs) Tx.	32·51 N	102·38 W
90	Seal (R.) Can.	59·08 N	96·37 W
113	Seal Beach Ca. (Los Angeles In.)	33·44 N	118·06 W
129	Seal Cays (Is.) Turks & Caicos Is.	21·10 N	71·45 W
129	Seal Cays (Is.) Ba.	22·40 N	75·55 W
212	Seal I. (sēl) S. Afr. (In.)	34·07 S	18·36 E
119	Sealy (sē'lē) Tx.	29·46 N	96·10 W
117	Searcy (sûr'sē) Ar.	35·13 N	91·43 W
114	Searles (L.) (sûrl's) Ca.	35·44 N	117·22 W
98	Searsport (sērz'pōrt) Me.	44·28 N	68·55 W
110	Seaside (sē'sīd) Or.	45·59 N	123·55 W
112	Seattle (sē-ăt''l) Wa. (Seattle In.)	47·36 N	122·20 W
126	Sebaco (sĕ-bä'kō) Nic.	12·50 N	86·03 W
98	Sebago (sē-bā'gō) Me.	43·52 N	70·20 W
122	Sebastion Vizcaino, Bahia (B.) (bä-ē'ä-sĕ-bäs-tyô'n-vēs-kä-ē'nô) Mex.	28·45 N	115·15 W
114	Sebastopol (sē-băs'tô-pôl) Ca.	38·27 N	122·50 W
196	Sebatik (I.) Indon.	3·52 N	118·14 E
211	Sebderat Eth.	15·30 N	36·45 E
216	Sébé (R.) Gabon	0·45 S	13·30 E
165	Sebes Rom.	45·58 N	23·34 E
104	Sebewaing (se'bē-wăng) Mi.	43·45 N	83·25 W
166	Sebezh (syĕ'bĕzh) Sov. Un.	56·16 N	28·29 E
171	Sebinkarahisar Tur.	40·15 N	38·10 E
162	Sebkha bou Areg (Marsh) Mor.	35·09 N	3·02 W
163	Sebkhan d'Oran (L.) Alg.	35·28 N	0·28 W
158	Sebnitz (zĕb'nēts) G.D.R.	51·01 N	14·16 E
163	Seborbe (sĕ-bôr-dĕ) Sp.	39·50 N	0·30 W
152	Sebou, Oued R. Mor.	34·23 N	5·18 W
104	Sebree (sē-brē') Ky.	37·35 N	87·30 W
121	Sebring (sē'brĭng) Fl. (In.)	27·30 N	81·26 W
104	Sebring Oh.	40·55 N	81·05 W
164	Secchia (R.) (sĕ'kyä) It.	44·25 N	10·25 E
125	Seco (R.) (sĕ'kô) Mex.	18·11 N	93·18 W
117	Sedalia Mo.	38·42 N	93·12 W
160	Sedan (sē-dăn) Fr.	49·49 N	4·55 E
117	Sedan (sē-dăn') Ks.	37·07 N	96·08 W
183	Sedom Isr. (Palestine In.)	31·04 N	35·24 E
112	Sedro Woolley (sē'drô-wŏŏl'ē) Wa. (Seattle In.)	48·30 N	122·14 W
157	Seduva (shĕ'dŏŏ-vȧ) Sov. Un.	55·46 N	23·45 E
212	Seekoevlei (L.) (zā'kŏŏf-lī) S. Afr. (In.)	34·04 S	18·33 E
149	Seestall (zā'shtäl) F.R.G. (Munich In.)	47·58 N	10·52 E
152	Sefrou (sē-frōō') Mor.	33·49 N	4·46 W
170	Seg (L.) (syĕgh) Sov. Un.	64·00 N	33·30 E
183	Segamat (sā'gȧ-mȧt) Mala. (Singapore In.)	2·30 N	102·49 E
215	Segbana Dahomey	10·56 N	3·42 E
214	Ségou (sā-gōō') Mali	13·27 N	6·16 W
134	Segovia (sĕ-gô'vēä) Col. (In.)	7·08 N	74·42 W
162	Segovia (sā-gō'vē-ä) Sp.	40·58 N	4·05 W
	Segovia (R.), see Coco		
163	Segre (R.) (sā'grā) Sp.	41·54 N	1·10 E
101	Seguam (I.) (sē'gwäm) Ak.	52·16 N	172·10 W
101	Seguam P. Ak.	52·20 N	173·00 W
215	Séguédine Niger	20·12 N	12·59 E
214	Séguéla (sā-gā-lä') Ivory Coast	7·57 N	6·40 W
118	Seguin (sĕ-gēn') Tx.	29·35 N	97·58 W
101	Segula (I.) (sē-gū'lȧ) Ak.	52·08 N	178·35 E
163	Segura (R.) (sā-gōō'rä) Sp.	38·07 N	0·33 W
162	Segura, Sierra de (Mts.) (sē-ĕ'r-rä-dĕ) Sp.	38·05 N	2·45 W
162	Segura (R.) Sp.	38·24 N	2·12 W
184	Sehwān Pak.	26·33 N	67·51 E
129	Seibo (sĕ'y-bō) Dom. Rep.	18·45 N	69·05 W
116	Seiling Ok.	36·09 N	98·56 W
157	Seinäjoki (sâ'ē-nĕ-yô'kē) Fin.	62·47 N	22·50 E
160	Seine, Baie de la (B.) (bī dĕ lä sân) Fr.	49·37 N	0·53 W
96	Seine (R.) (sân) Can.	49·04 N	91·00 W
100	Seine (R.) (sân) Can. (Winnipeg In.)	49·48 N	96·30 W
160	Seine, Rivière (R.) (rēv-yâr') Fr.	49·21 N	1·17 E
136	Seio do Venus (Mtn.) (sĕ-yô-dô-vĕ'nōōs) Braz. (Rio de Janeiro In.)	22·28 S	43·12 W
163	Seixal (sā-ē-shäl') Port. (Lisbon In.)	38·38 N	9·06 W
217	Sekenke Tan.	4·16 S	34·10 E
214	Sekondi-Takoradi (sĕ-kôn'dē tä-kô-rä'dē) Ghana	4·59 N	1·43 W
211	Sekota Eth.	12·47 N	38·59 E
196	Selajar (I.) Indon.	6·15 S	121·15 E
183	Selangor (State) (sĕ-län'gōr) Mala. (Singapore In.)	2·53 N	101·29 E
165	Selanoutsi (sāl'á-nôv-tsĭ) Bul.	43·42 N	24·05 E
197	Selaru (I.) Indon.	8·30 S	130·30 E
196	Selatan, Tandjung (C.) (sâ-lä'tän) Indon.	4·09 S	114·40 E
101	Selawik (sē-lȧ-wĭk) Ak.	66·30 N	160·09 W
156	Selbu (L.) (sĕl'bōō) Nor.	63·18 N	11·55 E
148	Selby (sĕl'bē) Eng.	53·47 N	1·03 W
101	Seldovia (sĕl-dō'vē-ȧ) Ak.	59·26 N	151·42 W
173	Selemdzha (R.) (sâ-lĕmt-zhä') Sov. Un.	52·28 N	131·50 E
173	Selenga (R.) (sĕ lĕŋ gä') Sov. Un.	51·00 N	106·40 E
188	Selenge Gol. (R.) Mong.	49·04 N	102·23 E
173	Selennyakh (R.) (sĕl-yĭn-yäk) Sov. Un.	67·42 N	141·45 E
161	Sélestat (sē-lē-stä') Fr.	48·16 N	7·27 E
210	Selibaby (sȧ-lē-bȧ-bē') Mauritania	15·21 N	12·11 W
166	Seliger (L.) (sĕl'lē-gĕr) Sov. Un.	57·14 N	33·18 E
184	Seling Tsho (L.) China	31·55 N	89·00 E
166	Selizharovo (sâ'lē-zhä'rô-vô) Sov. Un.	56·51 N	33·28 E
95	Selkirk (sĕl'kûrk) Can.	50·09 N	96·52 W
90	Selkirk Mts. Can.	51·00 N	117·40 W
112	Selleck (sĕl'ĕck) Wa. (Seattle In.)	47·22 N	121·52 W
107	Sellersburg (sĕl'ĕrs-bûrg) In. (Louisville In.)	38·25 N	85·45 W
173	Sellya Khskaya, Guba (B.) (sĕl-yäk'skȧ-yȧ) Sov. Un.	72·30 N	136·00 E
120	Selma (sĕl'mȧ) Al.	32·25 N	87·00 W
114	Selma Ca.	36·34 N	119·37 W
121	Selma NC	35·33 N	78·16 W
113	Selma Tx. (San Antonio In.)	29·33 N	98·19 W
120	Selmer Tn.	35·11 N	88·36 W
149	Selsingen (zĕl'zēn-gĕn) F.R.G. (Hamburg In.)	53·22 N	9·13 E
212	Selukwe (sê-lŭk'wē) Rh.	19·34 S	30·03 E
110	Selway R. (sĕl'wā) Id.	46·07 N	115·12 W
90	Selwyn (L.) (sĕl'wĭn) Can.	59·41 N	104·30 W
165	Seman (R.) Alb.	40·48 N	19·53 E
196	Semarang (sĕ-mä'räng) Indon.	7·03 S	110·27 E
196	Semarinda Indon.	0·30 S	117·10 E
	Semendria, see Smederevo		
167	Semënovka (sĕ-myôn'ôf-kȧ) Sov. Un.	52·10 N	32·34 E
196	Semeru, Gunung (Mtn.) Indon.	8·06 S	112·55 E
112	Semiahmoo Ind. Res. Can. (Vancouver In.)	49·01 N	122·43 W
112	Semiahmoo Spit (sĕm'ĭ-ȧ-mōō) Wa. (Vancouver In.)	48·59 N	122·52 W
101	Semichi Is. (sē-mē'chī) Ak.	52·40 N	174·50 W
111	Seminoe Res. (sĕm'ĭ nô) Wy.	42·08 N	107·10 W
117	Seminole (sĕm'ĭ-nōl) Ok.	35·13 N	96·41 W
118	Seminole Tx.	32·43 N	102·39 W
121	Seminole Ind. Res. Fl. (In.)	26·19 N	81·11 W
121	Seminole Ind. Res. Fl. (In.)	27·05 N	81·25 W
120	Seminole, L. Fl.-Ga.	30·57 N	84·46 W
172	Semipalatinsk (sĕ'mê-pá-lȧ-tyĕnsk') Sov. Un.	50·28 N	80·29 E
101	Semisopochnoi (I.) (sĕ-mē-sȧ-pōsh' noi) Ak.	51·45 N	179·25 W
172	Semiyarskoye (sĕ'mê-yär'skô-yĕ) Sov. Un.	51·03 N	78·28 E
211	Semliki R. (sĕm'lē-kē) Ug.-Zaire	0·45 N	29·36 E
	Semlin, see Zemun		
158	Semmering P. (sĕm'ĕr-ĭng) Aus.	47·39 N	15·50 E
171	Semnān Iran	35·30 N	53·30 E
135	Senador Pompeu (sĕ-nä-dōr-pôm-pĕ'ōō) Braz.	5·34 S	39·18 W
120	Senatobia (sĕ-nȧ-tō'bē-ȧ) Ms.	34·36 N	89·56 W
194	Sendai (sĕn-dī') Jap.	38·18 N	141·02 E
117	Seneca (sĕn'ē-kȧ) Ks.	39·49 N	96·03 W
120	Seneca SC	34·40 N	82·58 W
106	Seneca Md. (Baltimore In.)	39·04 N	77·20 W
105	Seneca (L.) NY	42·30 N	76·55 W
105	Seneca Falls NY	42·55 N	76·55 W
209	Senegal (sĕn-ĕ-gôl') Afr.	14·53 N	14·58 W
214	Sénégal (R.) Afr.	16·00 N	14·00 W
218	Senekal (sĕn'ē-kȧl) S. Afr. (Johannesburg & Pretoria In.)	28·20 S	27·37 E
158	Senftenberg (zĕnf'tĕn-bĕrgh) G.D.R.	51·32 N	14·00 E
213	Sengunyane (R.) Leso (Natal In.)	29·35 S	28·08 E
135	Senhor do Bonfim (sĕn-yôr dô bôN-fē'N) Braz.	5·21 S	40·09 W
164	Senigallia (sâ-nê-gäl'lyä) It.	43·42 N	13·16 E
164	Senj (sĕn') Yugo.	44·58 N	14·55 E
150	Senja (I.) (sĕnyä) Nor.	69·28 N	16·10 E
161	Senlis (sän-lēs') Fr. (Paris In.)	49·13 N	2·35 E
211	Sennar Dam Sud.	13·38 N	33·38 E
91	Senneterre Can.	48·20 N	77·22 W
166	Senno (syĕ'nô) Sov. Un.	54·48 N	29·43 E
160	Sens (säNs) Fr.	48·05 N	3·18 E
126	Sensuntepeque (sĕn-sōōn-tȧ-pā'kȧ) Sal.	13·53 N	88·34 W
165	Senta (sĕn'tä) Yugo.	45·54 N	20·05 E
195	Senzaki (sĕn'zä-kē) Jap.	34·22 N	131·09 E
	Seoul, see Sŏul		
183	Sepang Mala. (Singapore In.)	2·43 N	101·45 E
136	Sepetiba, Baia de (B.) (bäē'ä dĕ sâ-pȧ-tē'bȧ) Braz. (Rio de Janeiro In.)	23·01 S	43·42 W
197	Sepik (R.) (sĕp-ĕk') Pap. N. Gui.	4·07 S	142·40 E
160	Septèmes-les-Vallons (sĕ-tàm'la-vä-ôN') Fr. (Marseille In.)	43·25 N	5·23 E
129	Septentrional, Cordillera (Mts.) (kôr-dēl-yĕ'rä sĕp-tĕn-tryō-nä'l) Dom. Rep.	19·50 N	71·15 W
161	Septeuil (sĕ-tû') Fr. (Paris In.)	48·53 N	1·40 E
98	Sept-Îles (sĕ-tēl') Can.	50·12 N	66·23 W
120	Sequatchie (R.) (sē-kwăch'ē) Tn.	35·33 N	85·14 W
112	Sequim (sē'kwĭm) Wa. (Seattle In.)	48·05 N	123·07 W
112	Sequim B. Wa. (Seattle In.)	48·04 N	122·58 W
114	Sequoia Natl. Park (sē-kwoi'ȧ) Ca.	36·34 N	118·37 W
155	Seraing (sē-răN') Bel.	50·38 N	5·28 E
197	Seram (I.) Indon.	2·45 S	129·30 E
184	Serāmpore India (Calcutta In.)	22·44 N	88·21 E
196	Serang (sȧ-räng') Indon.	6·13 S	106·10 E
183	Seranggung Indon. (Singapore In.)	0·49 N	104·11 E
	Serbia (Reg.), see Srbija		
171	Serdobsk (sĕr-dôpsk') Sov. Un.	52·30 N	44·20 E
159	Sered Czech.	48·17 N	17·43 E
167	Seredina-Buda (sĕ-rȧ-dē'nȧ-bōō'dȧ) Sov. Un.	52·11 N	34·03 E
183	Seremban (sĕr-ĕm-bän') Mala. (Singapore In.)	2·44 N	101·57 E
217	Serengeti Natl. Pk. Tan.	2·20 S	34·50 E
217	Serengeti Pln. Tan.	2·40 S	34·55 E
212	Serenje (sē-rĕn'yē) Zambia	13·12 S	30·49 E
218	Serenli (sȧ-rĕn'lē) Som. (Horn of Afr. In.)	2·28 N	42·15 E
	Seres, see Sérrai		
159	Seret Czech.	48·17 N	17·43 E
159	Seret Rom.	47·58 N	26·01 E
159	Seret R. (sĕr'ĕt) Sov. Un.	49·45 N	25·30 E
172	Sergeya Kirova (I.) (sĕr-gyĕ'yȧ kē'rô-vȧ) Sov. Un.	77·30 N	86·10 E
135	Sergipe (State) (sĕr-zhē'pĕ) Braz.	10·27 S	37·04 W
170	Sergiyevsk Sov. Un.	53·58 N	51·00 E
165	Sérifos Grc.	37·10 N	24·32 E
165	Sérifos (I.) Grc.	37·42 N	24·17 E
137	Serodino (sĕ-rô-dē'nō) Arg. (Buenos Aires In.)	32·36 S	60·56 W
136	Seropédica (sĕ-rô-pĕ'dē-kä) Braz. (Rio de Janeiro In.)	22·44 S	43·43 W
174	Serov (syĕ-rôf') Sov. Un. (Urals In.)	59·36 N	60·30 E
212	Serowe (sĕ-rō'wĕ) Bots.	22·18 S	26·39 E
162	Serpa (sĕr-pä) Port.	37·56 N	7·38 W
216	Serpa Pinto Ang.	14·36 S	17·48 E
166	Serpukhov (syĕr'pōō-kôf) Sov. Un.	54·53 N	37·27 E

ng-sing; ŋ-baŋk; N-nasalized n; nŏd; cŏmmit; ōld; ôbey; ôrder; fōōd; fŏŏt; ou-out; s-soft; sh-dish; th-thin; pūre; ûnite; ûrn; stŭd; circŭs; ü-as "y" in study; '-indeterminate vowel.

346 Serrai — Shetland PRONOUNCING INDEX

Page	Name Pronunciation Region	Lat. °′	Long. °′
165	Sérrai (Seres) (sĕr'rē) (sĕr'ĕs)..Grc.	41·06 N	23·36 E
118	Serranias Del Burro (sĕr-rä-nē'äs dĕl bōō'r-rō).Mex.	29·39 N	102·07 W
135	Serrinha (sĕr-rēn'yȧ) Braz.	11·43 S	38·49 W
162	Serta (sĕr'tȧ) Port.	39·48 N	8·01 W
135	Sertânia (sĕr-tȧ'nyä) Braz.	8·28 S	37·13 W
137	Sertãozinho (sĕr-touN-zē'n-yō) Braz. (Rio de Janeiro In.)	21·10 S	47·58 W
183	Serting (R.). Mala. (Singapore In.)	3·01 N	102·32 E
136	Seruí (sĕ-rōō-ē') Braz. (Rio de Janeiro In.)	22·40 S	43·08 W
217	Sese Is. Ug.	0·30 S	32·30 E
164	Sesia (R.) (sâz'yä) It.	45·33 N	8·25 E
163	Sesimbra (sĕ-sē'm-brä) Port. (Lisbon In.)	38·27 N	9·06 W
213	Sesmyl (R.) S. Afr. (Johannesburg & Pretoria In.)	25·51 S	28·06 E
164	Sestri Levante (sĕs'trē lȧ-vän'tȧ) It.	44·15 N	9·24 E
174	Sestroretsk (sĕs-trô-rĕtsk) Sov. Un. (Leningrad In.)	60·06 N	29·58 E
174	Sestroretskiy Razliv, Ozero (L.) (ô'zĕ-rô sĕs-trô' rĕts-kĭ-räz'lĭf) Sov. Un. (Leningrad In.)	60·05 N	30·07 E
195	Seta (sĕ'tä) Jap. (Ōsaka In.)	34·58 N	135·56 W
160	Sète (sĕt) Fr.	43·24 N	3·42 E
135	Sete Lagoas (sĕ-tĕ lä-gō'äs)..Braz.	19·23 S	43·58 W
210	Setif (sȧ-tēf') Alg.	36·18 N	5·21 E
195	Seto (sē'tō) Jap.	35·11 N	137·07 E
195	Seto-Naikai (Sea) (sĕ'tō nī'kī). Jap.	33·50 N	132·25 E
210	Settat (sĕt-ät') (sē-tȧ') Mor.	33·02 N	7·30 W
212	Sette-Cama (sĕ-tĕ-kä-mä'). Gabon.	2·29 S	9·40 E
128	Settlement Pt. (sĕt'l-mĕnt) Ba.	26·40 N	79·00 W
218	Settlers (sĕt'lērs) S. Afr. (Johannesburg & Pretoria In.)	24·57 S	28·33 E
195	Settsu Jap. (Ōsaka In.)	34·46 N	135·33 E
163	Setúbal (sȧ-tōō'bäl) Port. (Lisbon In.)	30·32 N	8·54 W
162	Setúbal, B. de (bä-ē'ä) Port.	38·27 N	9·08 W
95	Seul, Lac (L.) (làk sûl) Can.	50·20 N	92·30 W
156	Sevalen (L.) (sĕ'vä-lĕn) Nor.	62·19 N	10·15 E
171	Sevan (L.) (syĭ-vän') Sov. Un.	40·10 N	45·20 E
167	Sevastopol' (Akhiar) (syĕ-vás-tô'pôl'') (äĸ'yär) Sov. Un.	44·34 N	33·34 E
	Seven Is., see Shichitō		
148	Sevenoaks (sĕ-vĕn-ôks') Eng. (London In.)	51·16 N	0·12 E
174	Severka R. (sâ'vĕr-kȧ) Sov. Un. (Moscow In.)	55·11 N	38·41 E
91	Severn (R.) (sĕv'ērn) Can.	55·21 N	88·42 W
154	Severn (R.) Eng.	51·42 N	2·25 W
106	Severna Park (sĕv'ērn-ȧ) Md. (Baltimore In.)	39·04 N	76·33 W
170	Severnaya Dvina (Northern Dvina (R.). Sov. Un.	63·00 N	42·40 E
169	Severnaya Zemlya (Northern Land) (Is.) (sĕ-vyĭr-nī'u zĭ-m'lyä'). Sov. Un.	79·33 N	101·15 E
174	Severoural'sk (sĕ-vyĭ-rŭ-ōō-rälsk') Sov. Un. (Urals In.)	60·08 N	59·53 E
115	Sevier (L.) (sē-vēr') Ut.	38·55 N	113·10 W
115	Sevier R. Ut.	39·25 N	112·20 W
115	Sevier R., East Fork Ut.	37·45 N	112·10 W
134	Sevilla (sĕ-vē'l-yä) Col. (In.)	4·16 N	75·56 W
162	Sevilla (sȧ-vēl'yä) Sp.	37·29 N	5·58 W
107	Seville (sĕ'vĭl)..Oh. (Cleveland In.)	41·01 N	81·45 W
165	Sevlievo (sĕv'lyĕ-vô) Bul.	41·02 N	25·05 E
160	Sèvre Nantaise (R.) (sâ'vrĕ näN-tâz'). Fr.	47·00 N	1·02 W
160	Sèvre Niortaise (R.) (sâ'vr' nyôr-tâz'). Fr.	46·23 N	1·05 W
166	Sevsk (syĕfsk) Sov. Un.	52·08 N	34·28 E
101	Seward (sū'ȧrd) Ak.	60·18 N	149·28 W
117	Seward Ne.	40·55 N	97·06 W
101	Seward Pen. Ak.	65·40 N	164·00 W
136	Sewell (sĕ'ōō-ĕl) Chile	34·01 S	70·18 W
107	Sewickley (sē-wĭk'lē) Pa. (Pittsburgh In.)	40·33 N	80·11 W
125	Seybaplaya (sā-ē-bä-plä'yä)..Mex.	19·38 N	90·40 W
220	Seychelles (sā-shĕl') Afr.	5·20 S	55·10 E
150	Seydhisfjördhur (sā'dēs-fyûr-dōōr). Ice.	65·21 N	14·08 W
126	Seyé (sĕ-yĕ') Mex. (In.)	20·51 N	89·22 W
153	Seyhan (R.) Tur.	37·28 N	35·40 E
167	Seym (R.) (sĕym) Sov. Un.	51·23 N	33·22 E
97	Seymour (sē'mōr) Ia.	38·55 N	85·55 W
109	Seymour In.	40·41 N	93·03 W
116	Seymour Tx.	33·35 N	99·16 W
213	Seymour (sē'môr) S. Afr. (Natal In.)	32·33 S	26·48 E
213	Sezela S. Afr. (Natal In.)	30·33 S	30·37 E
164	Sezze (sĕt'sȧ) It.	41·32 N	13·30 E
210	Sfax (sfäks) Tun.	34·51 N	10·45 E
165	Sfîntu-Gheorghe Rom.	45·53 N	25·49 E
149	's Gravenhage (The Hague) ('s ĸrä'vĕn-hä'ĸĕ) (hāg) Neth. (Amsterdam In.)	52·05 N	4·16 E
189	Sha (R.) (shä) China	33·33 N	114·30 E
190	Sha (R.) China	34·47 N	118·27 E
190	Sha (R.) China	39·26 N	122·08 E
212	Shaba (Katanga) (Reg.) (kȧ-täŋ'gȧ). Zaire	8·35 S	23·59 E
212	Shabani Rh.	20·15 S	30·28 E
174	Shablykino (sháb-lē'kĭ-nô) Sov. Un. (Moscow In.)	56·22 N	38·37 E
191	Shaching China (Canton In.)	22·44 N	113·48 E
220	Shackleton Shelf Ice (shăk''l-tŭn) Ant.	65·00 S	100·00 E
106	Shades Cr. (shādz) Al. (Birmingham In.)	33·20 N	86·55 W
106	Shades Mtn..Al. (Birmingham In.)	33·22 N	86·51 W
215	Shagamu Nig.	6·51 N	3·39 E
184	Shāhjahānpur (shä-jŭ-hän'pōōr) India	27·58 N	79·58 E
192	Shaho (shä-hō') China (In.)	40·08 N	116·16 E
186	Shahrezā (shä-rā'zä) Iran	31·47 N	51·47 E
171	Shahsavār Iran	36·40 N	51·00 E
107	Shaker Hts. (shā'kēr) Oh. (Cleveland In.)	41·28 N	81·34 W
167	Shakhty (shäĸ'tē) Sov. Un.	47·41 N	40·11 E
215	Shaki Nig.	8·39 N	3·25 E
113	Shakopee (shăk'ô-pe) Mn. (Minneapolis, St. Paul In.)	44·48 N	93·31 W
211	Shala L. (shä'lȧ) Eth.	7·34 N	39·00 E
186	Shām, Jabal ash (Mtn.) Om.	23·01 N	57·45 E
211	Shambe (shäm'bȧ) Sud.	7·08 N	30·46 E
186	Shammar, Jabal (Mts.) (jĕb'ĕl shŭm'ȧr). Sau. Ar.	27·13 N	40·16 E
211	Shamo (L.) Eth.	5·58 N	37·00 E
105	Shamokin (shȧ-mō'kĭn) Pa.	40·45 N	76·30 W
116	Shamrock (shăm'rŏk) Tx.	35·14 N	100·12 W
212	Shamva (shäm'vȧ) Rh.	17·18 S	31·35 E
211	Shandī Sud.	16·44 N	33·29 E
107	Shandon (shăn-dŭn) Oh. (Cincinnati In.)	39·20 N	84·13 W
190	Shangch'eng (shäng'chĕng)..China	31·47 N	115·22 E
190	Shangchialin (shäng'jĭä'lin). China	38·20 N	116·05 E
190	Shangch'iu (shäng'chĭō) China	34·24 N	115·39 E
191	Shanghai (shäng'hī') China (Shanghai In.)	31·14 N	121·27 E
191	Shanghaihsien China (Shanghai In.)	31·02 N	121·24 E
190	Shanghai Shih (Mun.) China	31·30 N	121·45 E
190	Shangho (shäng'hŏ) China	37·18 N	117·10 E
193	Shangjao China	28·25 N	117·58 E
190	Shangts'ai (shäng'zhī) China	33·16 N	114·16 E
192	Shangtu China	41·38 N	113·22 E
	Shanhsi (Prov.), see Shansi		
190	Shanhsien (shän'hsyĕn') China	34·47 N	116·04 E
106	Shannon (shăn'ŭn) Al. (Birmingham In.)	33·23 N	86·52 W
154	Shannon R. (shăn'ŏn) Ire.	52·30 N	9·58 W
188	Shanshan (shän'shän') China	42·51 N	89·53 E
189	Shansi (Shanhsi) (Prov.) China	37·30 N	112·00 E
173	Shantar (I.) (shän'tär) Sov. Un.	55·13 N	138·42 E
193	Shant'ou (Swatow) (swä'tō'). China	23·20 N	116·40 E
189	Shantung (Prov.) China	36·08 N	117·09 E
193	Shantung Pantao (Pen.) China	37·00 N	120·10 E
193	Shantung Pt. (shän'tōōng')..China	37·28 N	122·40 E
193	Shaohsing China	30·00 N	120·40 E
193	Shaokuan China	24·58 N	113·42 E
190	Shaopo (shou'pō') China	32·33 N	119·30 E
190	Shaopo Hu (L.) (shou'pō'hōō) China	32·07 N	119·13 E
174	Shapki (shäp'kĭ) Sov. Un. (Leningrad In.)	59·36 N	31·11 E
204	Shark B. (shärk) Austl.	25·30 S	113·00 E
99	Sharon (shăr'ŏn) Ma. (In.)	42·07 N	71·11 W
104	Sharon Pa.	41·15 N	80·30 W
116	Sharon Springs Ks.	38·51 N	101·45 W
107	Sharonville (shăr'ŏn vĭl) Oh. (Cincinnati In.)	39·16 N	84·24 W
107	Sharpsburg (shärps'bûrg) Pa. (Pittsburgh In.)	40·30 N	79·54 W
186	Sharr, Jabal (Mtn.) Sau. Ar.	28·00 N	36·07 E
193	Shashih China	30·20 N	112·18 E
110	Shasta, Mt. Ca.	41·35 N	122·12 W
110	Shasta L. (shăs'tȧ) Ca.	40·51 N	122·32 W
170	Shatsk (shȧtsk) Sov. Un.	54·00 N	41·40 E
116	Shattuck (shăt'ŭk) Ok.	36·16 N	99·53 W
94	Shaunavon Can.	49·40 N	108·25 W
120	Shaw (shô) Ms.	33·36 N	90·44 W
109	Shawano (shȧ-wô'nō) Wi.	44·41 N	88·13 W
91	Shawinigan Can.	46·32 N	72·46 W
113	Shawnee (shô-nē') Ks. (Kansas City In.)	39·01 N	94·43 W
117	Shawnee Ok.	35·20 N	96·54 W
104	Shawneetown (shô'nē-toun) Il.	37·40 N	88·05 W
193	Shayang China	31·00 N	112·38 E
159	Shchara (R.) (sh-chä'rȧ)..Sov. Un.	53·17 N	25·12 E
174	Shchëlkovo (shchĕl'kô-vô) Sov. Un. (Moscow In.)	55·55 N	38·00 E
167	Shchëtovo (shchĕ'tô-vô)..Sov. Un.	48·11 N	39·13 E
167	Shchigry (shchē'grē) Sov. Un.	51·52 N	36·54 E
167	Shchors (shchôrs) Sov. Un.	51·38 N	31·58 E
174	Shchuch'ye Ozero (shchōōch'yĕ ô'zĕ-rō) Sov. Un. (Urals In.)	56·31 N	56·35 E
184	Sheakhala India (In.)	22·47 N	88·10 E
218	Shebele R. (shā'bȧ-lē) Eth. (Horn of Afr. In.)	6·07 N	43·10 E
218	Shebelle (R.) Som. (Horn of Afr. In.)	1·38 N	43·50 E
109	Sheboygan (shē-boi'gȧn) Wi.	43·45 N	87·44 W
109	Sheboygan Falls Wi.	43·43 N	87·51 W
183	Shechem (Ruins) Jordan (Palestine In.)	32·15 N	35·22 E
92	Shedin Pk. (shĕd'ĭn) Can.	55·55 N	127·32 W
98	Shediac (shĕ'dē-ăk) Can.	46·13 N	64·32 W
154	Sheelin (L.) (shēlĭn) Ire.	53·46 N	7·34 W
148	Sheerness (shēr'nĕs) Eng. (London In.)	51·26 N	0·46 E
120	Sheffield (shĕf'fēld) Al.	35·42 N	87·42 W
100	Sheffield Can. (Toronto In.)	43·20 N	80·13 W
148	Sheffield Eng.	53·23 N	1·28 W
107	Sheffield Oh. (Cleveland In.)	41·26 N	82·05 W
107	Sheffield Lake..Oh. (Cleveland In.)	41·30 N	82·03 W
190	Shehsien (shĕ'hsyĕn') China	36·34 N	113·42 E
154	Shehy, Mts. Ire.	51·46 N	9·45 W
170	Sheksna (R.) (shĕks'nȧ)..Sov. Un.	59·50 N	38·40 E
173	Shelagskiy, Mys (C.) (shĭ-läg'skē) Sov. Un.	70·08 N	170·52 E
117	Shelbina (shĕl-bī'nȧ) Ar.	39·41 N	92·03 W
104	Shelburn (shĕl'bŭrn) In.	39·10 N	87·30 W
98	Shelburne Can.	43·46 N	65·19 W
105	Shelburne Can.	44·04 N	80·12 W
107	Shelby (shĕl'bē)..In. (Chicago In.)	41·12 N	87·21 W
104	Shelby Mi.	43·35 N	86·20 W
120	Shelby Ms.	33·56 N	90·44 W
111	Shelby Mt.	48·35 N	111·55 W
121	Shelby NC	35·16 N	81·35 W
104	Shelby Oh.	40·50 N	82·40 W
104	Shelbyville (shĕl'bē-vĭl) Il.	39·20 N	88·45 W
104	Shelbyville In.	39·30 N	85·45 W
104	Shelbyville Ky.	38·10 N	85·15 W
120	Shelbyville Tn.	35·30 N	86·28 W
186	Shelbyville Res. Il.	39·30 N	88·45 W
108	Sheldon (shĕl'dŭn) Ia.	43·10 N	95·50 W
119	Sheldon Tx. (In.)	29·52 N	95·07 W
173	Shelekhova, Zaliv (B.)..Sov. Un.	60·00 N	156·00 E
101	Shelikof Str. (shĕ'lē-kôf) Ak.	57·56 N	154·20 W
94	Shellbrook Can.	53·15 N	106·22 W
111	Shelley (shĕl'lē) Id.	43·24 N	112·06 W
109	Shellrock (R.) (shĕl'rŏk) Ia.	43·25 N	93·19 W
166	Shelon' (R.) (shȧ'lôn) Sov. Un.	57·50 N	29·40 E
105	Shelton (shĕl'tŭn) Ct.	41·15 N	73·05 W
116	Shelton Ne.	40·46 N	98·41 W
110	Shelton Wa.	47·14 N	123·05 W
174	Shemakha (shĕ-mȧ-kä') Sov. Un. (Urals In.)	56·16 N	59·19 E
171	Shemakha Sov. Un.	40·35 N	48·40 E
117	Shenandoah (shĕn-ăn-dō'ȧ) Ia.	40·46 N	95·23 W
105	Shenandoah Pa.	40·50 N	76·15 W
105	Shenandoah Va.	38·30 N	78·30 W
105	Shenandoah Natl. Park Va.	38·35 N	78·25 W
105	Shenandoah (R.) Va.	38·55 N	78·05 W
190	Shenchiu (shenchĭō) China	33·11 N	115·06 E
215	Shendam Nig.	8·53 N	9·32 E
190	Shengfang (shengfäng) China	39·05 N	116·40 E
	Shenhsi (Prov.), see Shensi		
190	Shenhsien (shen'sĭän) China	38·02 N	115·33 E
174	Shenkursk (shĕn-kōōrsk') Sov. Un.	62·10 N	43·08 E
192	Shenmu China	38·55 N	110·35 E
188	Shensi (Shenhsi) (Prov.) China	35·30 N	109·10 E
190	Shentse (shen'zhŏ) China	38·12 N	115·12 E
192	Shenyang (Mukden) (shĕn'yäng') (mōōk'dĕn). China	41·45 N	123·22 E
184	Sheopur India	25·37 N	78·10 E
93	Shepard (shĕ'pärd) Can. (Calgary In.)	50·57 N	113·55 W
167	Shepetovka (shĕ-pĕ-tôf'kȧ) Sov. Un.	50·10 N	27·01 E
203	Shepparton (shĕp'ȧr-tŭn)...Austl.	36·15 S	145·25 E
99	Sherborn (shûr'bŭrn) Ma. (In.)	42·15 N	71·22 W
214	Sherbro I. S. L.	7·30 N	12·55 W
105	Sherbrooke Can.	45·24 N	71·54 W
148	Sherburn (shûr'bŭrn) Eng.	53·47 N	1·15 W
159	Shereshevo (shĕ-rĕ-shĕ-vô) Sov. Un.	52·31 N	24·08 E
117	Sheridan (shĕr'ĭ-dăn) Ar.	34·19 N	92·21 W
110	Sheridan Or.	45·06 N	123·22 W
111	Sheridan Wy.	44·48 N	106·56 W
117	Sherman (shĕr'măn) Tx.	33·39 N	96·37 W
174	Sherna R. (shĕr'nȧ) Sov. Un. (Moscow In.)	56·08 N	38·45 E
95	Sherridon Can.	55·10 N	101·10 W
149	's Hertogenbosch (sĕr-tō'ghĕn-bôs) Neth. (Amsterdam In.)	51·41 N	5·19 E
112	Sherwood Or. (Portland In.)	45·21 N	122·50 W
148	Sherwood For. Eng.	53·11 N	1·07 W
93	Sherwood Park Can.	53·31 N	113·19 W
154	Shetland (Is.) (shĕt'lănd) Scot.	60·35 N	2·10 W

ăt; finăl; rāte; senâte; ärm; àsk; sofȧ; fâre; ch-choose; dh-as th in other; bē; ēvent; bĕt; recĕnt; cratẽr; g-go; gh-guttural g; bĭt; ĭ-short neutral; rīde; ĸ-guttural k as ch in German ich;

PRONOUNCING INDEX Shevchenko — Silverton 347

Page	Name Pronunciation Region	Lat. °′	Long. °′
186	Shevchenko Sov. Un.	44·00 N	51·10 E
211	Shewa Gimira Eth.	7·13 N	35·49 E
108	Sheyenne (R.) (shī-ĕn') ND	46·42 N	97·52 W
104	Shiawassee (R.) (shī-á-wôs'ē) Mi.	43·15 N	84·05 W
186	Shibām (shē'bäm) P. D. R. of Yem.	16·02 N	48·40 E
218	Shibīn al Kawn (shė-bēn'ĕl kōm') Egypt (Nile In.)	30·31 N	31·01 E
218	Shibīn al Qanāṭir (kȧ-nä'tēr) Egypt (Nile In.)	30·18 N	31·21 E
195	Shichitō (Seven Is.) (shē'chē-tō) Jap.	34·18 N	139·28 E
111	Shields R. (shēldz) Mt.	45·54 N	110·40 W
148	Shifnal (shĭf'năl) Eng.	52·40 N	2·22 W
190	Shih (R.) (shē hŏ) China	32·09 N	114·11 E
190	Shihchiachuang China	38·04 N	114·31 E
190	Shihchiangchen (shē'kĭäng'zhen) China	32·16 N	120·59 E
191	Shihch'iao China (Canton In.)	22·56 N	113·22 E
190	Shihchiu Hu (L.) (shē'jĭō'hōō) China	31·29 N	119·07 E
192	Shihlung China	23·05 N	113·58 E
190	Shihohienfou China	31·27 N	117·51 E
191	Shiht'ou China (Canton In.)	23·01 N	113·23 E
190	Shihts'un (shē'chōōen) China	33·47 N	117·18 E
190	Shihtzu Shan (Mts.) (shē'jē shän) China	37·17 N	121·38 E
191	Shihwan China (Canton In.)	23·01 N	113·04 E
193	Shihwanta Shan (Mtns.) China	22·10 N	107·30 E
192	Shihwei Pk. China	47·11 N	119·59 E
184	Shikārpur Pak.	27·51 N	68·52 E
195	Shiki (shē'kē) Jap. (Tōkyō In.)	35·50 N	139·35 E
195	Shikoku (I.) (shē'kō'kōō) Jap.	33·43 N	133·33 E
173	Shilka (R.) (shĭl'kȧ) Sov. Un.	53·00 N	118·45 E
184	Shilla (Mt.) India	37·18 N	78·17 E
184	Shillong (shėl-lông') India	25·39 N	91·58 E
113	Shiloh (shī'lō) Il. (St. Louis In.)	38·34 N	89·54 W
195	Shimabara (shē'mä-bä'rä) Jap.	32·46 N	130·22 E
195	Shimada (shē'mä-dä) Jap.	34·49 N	138·13 E
195	Shimizu (shē'mē-zōō) Jap.	35·00 N	138·29 E
195	Shimminato (shêm'mē'nä-tô) Jap.	36·47 N	137·05 E
195	Shimoda (shē'mō-dȧ) Jap.	34·41 N	138·58 E
185	Shimoga India	13·59 N	75·38 E
217	Shimoni Ken.	4·39 S	39·23 E
195	Shimonoseki (shē'mō-nō-sĕ'kē) (shė-mō-nō'sĕ-kĭ) Jap.	33·58 N	130·55 E
195	Shimo-Saga (shē'mō sä'gä) Jap. (Ōsaka In.)	35·01 N	135·41 E
154	Shin, Loch (L.) (lŏk shĭn) Scot.	58·08 N	4·02 W
195	Shinagawa-Wan (B.) (shē'nä-gä'wä wän) Jap. (Tōkyō In.)	35·37 N	139·49 E
195	Shinano-Gawa (Strm.) (shė-nä'nō gä'wä) Jap.	36·43 N	138·22 E
195	Shingū (shĭn'gōō) Jap.	33·43 N	135·59 E
195	Shinji (L.) (shĭn'jē) Jap.	35·23 N	133·05 E
217	Shinkolobwe Zaire	11·02 S	26·35 E
211	Shinyanga (shĭn-yäŋ'gä) Tan.	3·40 S	33·26 E
194	Shiono Misaki (C.) (shė-ō'nō mē'sä-kē) Jap.	33·20 N	136·10 E
128	Ship Channel Cay (I.) (shĭp chă-nĕl kē) Ba.	24·50 N	76·50 W
148	Shipley (shĭp'lē) Eng.	53·50 N	1·47 W
98	Shippegan (shĭ'pė-găn) Can.	47·45 N	64·42 W
98	Shippegan I. Can.	47·50 N	64·38 W
105	Shippenburg (shĭp'ĕn bûrg) Pa.	40·00 N	77·30 W
98	Shipshaw (R.) (shĭp'shô) Can.	48·50 N	71·03 W
183	Shiqma (R.) Isr. (Palestine In.)	31·31 N	34·40 E
195	Shirane-san (Mtn.) (shē'rä'nȧ-sän') Jap.	35·44 N	138·14 E
194	Shira Saki (C.) (shē'rä sä'kē) Jap.	41·25 N	142·10 E
212	Shirati (shė-rä'tē) Tan.	1·15 S	34·02 E
186	Shīrāz (shē-räz') Iran	29·32 N	52·27 E
217	Shire (R.) (shē'rȧ) Malawi	16·20 S	35·05 E
167	Shirokoye (shē'rô-kō-yĕ) Sov. Un.	47·40 N	33·18 E
101	Shishaldin Vol. (shī-shăl'dĭn) Ak.	54·48 N	164·00 W
107	Shively (shīv'lē) Ky. (Louisville In.)	38·11 N	85·47 W
184	Shivpuri India	25·31 N	77·46 E
183	Shivta, Horvot (Ruins) Isr. (Palestine In.)	30·54 N	34·36 E
115	Shivwits (Shebit) Ind. Res. (shĭv'wĭts) (shĕ'bĭt) Ut.	37·10 N	113·50 W
115	Shivwits Plat. Az.	36·13 N	113·42 W
99	Shirley (shûr'lē) Ma. (In.)	42·33 N	71·39 W
195	Shizuki (shĭ'zōō-kē) Jap.	34·29 N	134·51 E
195	Shizuoka (shē'zōō'ōkȧ) Jap.	34·58 N	138·24 E
166	Shklov (shklôf) Sov. Un.	54·11 N	30·23 E
165	Shkodër (Scutari) (shkô'dûr) (skōō'tȧrē) Alb.	42·04 N	19·30 E
194	Shkotovo (shkô'tô-vô) Sov. Un.	43·15 N	132·21 E
117	Shoal Cr. (shōl) Il.	38·37 N	89·25 W
95	Shoal L. Can.	49·32 N	95·00 W
104	Shoals (shōlz) In.	38·40 N	86·45 W
195	Shōdo (I.) (shō'dō) Jap.	34·27 N	134·27 E
185	Sholāpur (shō'lä-pōōr) India	17·42 N	75·51 E
107	Shorewood (shōr'wŏŏd) Wi. (Milwaukee In.)	43·05 N	87·54 W
111	Shoshone (shō-shōn'ē) Id.	42·56 N	114·24 W
111	Shoshone L. Wy.	44·17 N	110·50 W
111	Shoshone R. Wy.	44·20 N	109·28 W
111	Shoshoni Wy.	43·14 N	108·05 W
167	Shostka (shôst'kȧ) Sov. Un.	51·51 N	33·31 E
190	Sh'ouchang (shō'zhäng) China	35·59 N	115·52 E
190	Shouhsien China	32·36 N	116·45 E
190	Shoukuang (shō'gōōäng) China	36·53 N	118·45 E
167	Shpola (shpô'lȧ) Sov. Un.	49·01 N	31·36 E
119	Shreveport (shrēv'pôrt) La.	32·30 N	93·46 W
148	Shrewsbury (shrōōz'bēr-ĭ) Eng.	52·43 N	2·44 W
99	Shrewsbury Ma. (In.)	42·18 N	71·43 W
148	Shropshire (Co.) (shrŏp'shēr) Eng.	52·36 N	2·45 W
128	Shroud Cay (I.) (shroud) Ba.	24·20 N	76·40 W
192	Shuangch'eng China	45·18 N	126·18 E
190	Shuangho (shōōäng hŏ) China	31·33 N	116·48 E
189	Shuangliao China	43·37 N	123·30 E
190	Shuanglunho (shōōäng'lōōĕn'hŏ) China	31·50 N	115·07 E
192	Shuangyang China	43·28 N	125·45 E
109	Shullsburg (shŭlz'bûrg) Wi.	42·35 N	90·16 W
190	Shulyehehen (shōōlĭĕhŭhĕn) China	36·08 N	114·07 E
101	Shumagin (Is.) (shōō'mȧ-gėn) Ak.	55·22 N	159·20 W
165	Shumen Bul.	43·15 N	26·54 E
193	Shunan (shōō'nän') China	29·38 N	119·00 E
101	Shungnak (shŭng'nȧk) Ak.	66·55 N	157·20 W
192	Shuni (shōōn'yĭ) China (In.)	40·09 N	116·38 E
188	Shunning (shŭ'nĭng') China	24·34 N	99·49 E
191	Shunte China (Canton In.)	22·50 N	113·15 E
174	Shunut, 'Gora (Mt.) (gȧ-rä shōō'nŏŏt) Sov. Un. (Urals In.)	56·33 N	59·45 E
186	Shuqrah P. D. R. of Yem.	13·32 N	46·02 E
186	Shūrāb (R.) (shōō räb) Iran	31·08 N	55·30 E
194	Shuri (shōō'rē) Jap.	26·10 N	127·48 E
171	Shur R. (shōōr) Iran	35·40 N	50·10 E
186	Shūshtar (shōōsh'tŭr) Iran	31·50 N	48·46 E
93	Shuswap L. (shōōs'wŏp) Can.	50·57 N	119·15 W
166	Shuya (shōō'yȧ) Sov. Un.	56·52 N	41·23 E
190	Shuyang (shōō yäng) China	34·09 N	118·47 E
193	Shweba Bur.	22·23 N	96·13 E
	Shyaulyay, see Šiauliai		
194	Siakin (L.) (sĭä'jĭn) China	42·25 N	132·45 E
183	Siak Ketjil (R.) Indon. (Singapore In.)	1·01 N	101·45 E
183	Siaksriinderapura (sė-äks'rĭ ĕn'drȧ-pōō'rä) Indon. (Singapore In.)	0·48 N	102·05 E
184	Siālkot (sė-äl'kōt) Pak.	32·39 N	74·30 E
	Sian, see Hsian		
190	Siaowu Shan (Mts.) (sĭou'wōō shän) China	39·48 N	114·52 E
165	Siátista (syä'tĭs-ta) Grc.	40·15 N	21·32 E
197	Siau (I.) Indon.	2·40 N	126·00 E
157	Šiauliai (Shyaulyay) (shė-ou'lē-ī) Sov. Un.	55·57 N	23·19 E
174	Sibay (sē'báy) Sov. Un. (Urals In.)	52·41 N	58·40 E
164	Šibenik (shė-bā'nĕk) Yugo.	43·44 N	15·55 E
182	Siberia (Reg.) Asia	57·00 N	97·00 E
196	Siberut (I.) (sē'bȧ-rōōt) Indon.	1·22 S	99·45 E
184	Sibī Pak.	29·41 N	67·52 E
216	Sibiti (sė-bė-tē') Con.	3·41 S	13·21 E
165	Sibiu (sė-bĭ-ōō') Rom.	45·47 N	24·09 E
108	Sibley (sĭb'lē) Ia.	43·24 N	95·33 W
196	Sibolga (sė-bō'gä) Indon.	1·45 N	98·45 E
187	Sibsāgar (sėb-sŭ'gŭr) India	26·47 N	94·45 E
196	Sibuti Phil.	4·40 N	119·30 E
197	Sibuyan (I.) (sē-bōō-yän') Phil. (In.)	12·19 N	122·25 E
196	Sibuyan Sea Phil.	12·43 N	122·38 E
196	Sicapoo (Mtn.) (sē-kä-pōō') Phil.	18·05 N	121·03 E
160	Sicily (I.) (sĭs'ĭ-lē) It.	37·38 N	13·30 E
126	Sico R. (sė-kō) Hond.	15·32 N	85·42 W
134	Sicuaní (sė-kwä'nē) Peru	14·12 S	71·12 W
218	Sidamo (Prov.) (sē-dä'mō) Eth.	5·08 N	37·45 E
164	Siderno Marina (sė-dĕr'nō mä-rē'nä) It.	38·18 N	16·19 E
164	Sídheros, Akr. (C.) Grc. (In.)	35·19 N	26·20 E
165	Sidhiró Kastron Grc.	41·13 N	23·27 E
163	Sidi-Aïsa Alg.	35·53 N	3·44 E
211	Sīdī Barrānī Egypt	31·41 N	26·09 E
210	Sidi bel Abbès (sē'dē-bĕl ȧ-bĕs') Alg.	35·15 N	0·43 W
210	Sidi Ifni (ēf'nė) Mor.	29·22 N	10·15 W
220	Sidley, Mt. (sĭd'lē) Ant.	77·25 S	129·00 W
92	Sidney Can.	48·39 N	123·24 W
111	Sidney (sĭd'nė) Mt.	47·43 N	104·07 W
108	Sidney Ne.	41·10 N	103·00 W
104	Sidney Oh.	40·20 N	84·10 W
120	Sidney Lanier, L. (lăn'yēr) Ga.	34·27 N	83·56 W
214	Sido Mali	11·40 N	7·36 W
	Sidon, see Ṣaydā		
183	Sidr, Wādī (R.) Egypt (Palestine In.)	29·43 N	32·58 E
159	Siedlce (syĕd''l-tsĕ) Pol.	52·09 N	22·20 E
161	Siegburg (zĕg'bōōrgh) F.R.G. (Ruhr In.)	50·48 N	7·13 E
161	Siegen (zē'ghĕn) F.R.G. (Ruhr In.)	50·52 N	8·01 E
149	Sieghartskirchen Aus. (Vienna In.)	48·16 N	16·00 E
158	Sieg R. (zēg) F.R.G.	50·51 N	7·53 E
159	Siemiatycze (syĕm'yä'tē-chĕ) Pol.	52·26 N	22·52 E
159	Siemionówka (sĕĕ-mĕō'nôf-kä) Pol.	52·53 N	23·50 E
196	Siem Reap (syĕm'rā'äp) Camb.	13·32 N	103·54 E
164	Siena (sė-ĕn'ä) It.	43·19 N	11·21 E
159	Sieradz (syĕ'rädz) Pol.	51·35 N	18·45 E
162	Siero (syā'rō) Sp.	43·24 N	5·39 W
159	Sierpc (syĕrpts) Pol.	52·51 N	19·42 E
118	Sierra Blanca (sē-ĕ'rȧ blaŋ-kä) Tx.	31·10 N	105·20 W
115	Sierra Blanca Pk. (blăn'kȧ) NM	33·25 N	105·50 W
209	Sierra Leone (sė-ĕr'rä lȧ-ō'nȧ) Afr.	8·48 N	12·30 W
113	Sierra Madre (mä'drē) Ca. (Los Angeles In.)	34·10 N	118·03 W
118	Sierra Mojada (sē-ĕ'r-rä-mô-Kä'dä) Mex.	27·22 N	103·42 W
165	Sífnos (I.) Grc.	36·58 N	24·30 E
156	Sigdal (sēgh'däl) Nor.	60·01 N	9·35 E
160	Sigean (sē-zhŏN') Fr.	43·02 N	2·56 E
109	Sigeurney (sē-gûr-nĭ) Ia.	41·16 N	92·10 W
159	Sighet (sė-gât') Rom.	47·57 N	23·55 E
159	Sighisoara (sē-gė-shwä'rȧ) Rom.	46·11 N	24·48 E
150	Siglufjördhur Ice.	66·06 N	18·45 W
171	Signakhi Sov. Un.	41·45 N	45·50 E
113	Signal Hill (sĭg'năl hĭl) Ca. (Los Angeles In.)	33·48 N	118·11 W
134	Sigsig (sėg-sēg') Ec.	3·05 S	78·44 W
156	Sigtuna (sēgh-tōō'nȧ) Swe.	59·40 N	17·39 E
128	Siguanea, Ensenada de la (B.) (ĕn-sĕ-nä-dä-dĕ-lä-sė-gwä-nā'ä) Cuba	21·45 N	83·15 W
126	Siguatepeque (sē-gwȧ'tĕ-pĕ-kĕ) Hond.	14·33 N	87·51 W
162	Sigüenza (sē-gwĕ'n-zä) Sp.	41·03 N	2·38 W
214	Siguiri (sė-gė-rē') Gui.	11·25 N	9·10 W
171	Siirt (sĭ-ērt') Tur.	38·00 N	42·00 E
217	Sikalongo Zambia	16·46 S	27·07 E
214	Sikasso (sė-käs'sō) Mali	11·19 N	5·40 W
117	Sikeston (sīks'tŭn) Mo.	36·50 N	89·35 W
173	Sikhote Alin', Khrebet (Mts.) (se-Kô'ta a-lēn') Sov. Un.	45·00 N	135·45 E
165	Sikinos (I.) (sĭ'kĭ-nōs) Grc.	36·45 N	24·55 E
184	Sikkim (State) India	27·42 N	88·25 E
159	Siklós (sĭ'klōsh) Hong.	45·51 N	18·18 E
162	Sil (R.) (sē'l) Sp.	42·20 N	7·13 W
197	Silang (sė-läng') Phil. (In.)	14·14 N	120·58 E
124	Silao (sė-lä'ō) Mex.	20·56 N	101·25 W
184	Silchar (sĭl-chär') India	24·52 N	92·50 E
218	Silent Valley (sī'lĕnt vă'lē) S. Afr. (Johannesburg & Pretoria In.)	24·32 S	26·40 E
121	Siler City (sī'lēr) NC	35·45 N	79·29 W
159	Silesia (Reg.) (sĭ-lē'shȧ) Pol.	50·58 N	16·53 E
171	Silifke Tur.	36·20 N	34·00 E
153	Silistra (sė-lės'trȧ) Bul.	44·01 N	27·13 E
156	Siljan (R.) (sėl'yän) Swe.	60·48 N	14·28 E
156	Silkeborg (sĭl'kĕ-bôr') Den.	56·10 N	9·33 E
100	Sillery (sēl're') Can. (Quebec In.)	46·46 N	71·15 W
117	Siloam Springs (sī-lōm) Ar.	36·10 N	94·32 W
216	Siloana Plns. Zambia	16·55 S	23·10 E
124	Silocayoápan (sē-lō-kä-yō-ȧ'pän) Mex.	17·29 N	98·09 W
119	Silsbee (sĭlz' bē) Tx.	30·19 N	94·09 W
157	Šilutė (shĭ-lōō'tȧ) Sov. Un.	55·23 N	21·26 E
137	Silva Jardim (sė'l-vä-zhär-dėN) Braz. (Rio de Janeiro In.)	22·40 S	42·24 W
112	Silvana (sĭl-vän'ȧ) Wa. (Seattle In.)	48·12 N	122·16 W
135	Silvânia (sēl-vȧ'nyä) Braz.	16·43 S	48·33 W
216	Silva Porto (sĭl'vȧ pôr'tŏŏ) Ang.	12·22 S	16·56 E
117	Silver (L.) Mo.	39·38 N	93·12 W
112	Silverado (sĭl-vēr-ä'dō) Ca. (Los Angeles In.)	33·45 N	117·40 W
129	Silver Bk. Ba.	20·40 N	69·40 W
129	Silver Bank Passage (Str.) Ba.	20·40 N	70·20 W
109	Silver Bay Mn.	47·24 N	91·07 W
115	Silver City (sĭl'vēr sĭ'tĭ) NM	32·45 N	108·20 W
127	Silver City Pan.	9·20 N	79·54 W
105	Silver Creek (crēk) NY	42·35 N	79·10 W
115	Silver Cr. Az.	34·30 N	110·05 W
107	Silver Cr. In. (Louisville In.)	38·20 N	85·45 W
107	Silver Cr., Muddy Fk. In. (Louisville In.)	38·26 N	85·52 W
112	Silverdale (sĭl'vēr-dāl) Wa. (Seattle In.)	49·39 N	122·42 W
107	Silver Lake (lāk) Wi. (Milwaukee In.)	42·33 N	88·10 W
107	Silver L. Wi. (Milwaukee In.)	42·35 N	88·08 W
106	Silver Spring (spring) Md. (Baltimore In.)	39·00 N	77·00 W
112	Silver Star Mtn. Wa. (Portland In.)	45·45 N	122·15 W
92	Silverthrone Mtn. (sĭl'vēr-thrōn) Can.	51·31 N	126·06 W
115	Silverton (sĭl'vēr-tŭn) Co.	37·50 N	107·40 W
107	Silverton Oh. (Cincinnati In.)	39·12 N	84·24 W
110	Silverton Or.	45·02 N	122·46 W
213	Silverton S. Afr. (Johannesburg & Pretoria In.)	25·45 S	28·13 E

ng-sing; ŋ-baŋk; N-nasalized n; nŏd; cŏmmit; ōld; ôbey; ôrder; fōōd; fŏŏt; ou-out; s-soft; sh-dish; th-thin; pūre; ûnite; ûrn; stŭd; circŭs; ü-as "y" in study; '-indeterminate vowel.

Page	Name	Pronunciation	Region	Lat. ° ′	Long. ° ′
162	Silves (sĕl'vĕzh)		Port.	37·15 N	8·24 W
110	Silvies R. (sĭl'vēz)		Or.	43·44 N	119·15 W
174	Sim (sĭm)		Sov. Un. (Urals In.)	55·00 N	57·42 E
216	Simba		Zaire	0·36 S	22·55 E
105	Simcoe (sĭm'kō)		Can.	42·50 N	80·20 W
105	Simcoe (L.)		Can.	44·30 N	79·20 W
196	Simeulue (I.)		Indon.	2·27 N	95·30 E
167	Simferopol' (Akmechet) (sĕm-fĕ-rô'pôl') (ȧk-mĕch'ĕt)		Sov. Un.	44·58 N	34·04 E
153	Simi (I.)		Grc.	36·27 N	27·41 E
112	Similk Beach (sē'mĭlk)		Wa. (Seattle In.)	48·27 N	122·35 W
184	Simla (sĭm'lä)		India	31·09 N	77·15 E
159	Simleul-Silvaniei (shĕm-lā'ōōl-sĕl-vä'nyĕ-ĕ)		Rom.	47·14 N	22·46 E
128	Simms Pt.		Ba.	25·00 N	77·40 W
125	Simojovel (sē-mō-hô-vĕl')		Mex.	17·12 N	92·43 W
157	Simola (sē'mô-lä)		Fin.	60·55 N	28·06 E
137	Simonésia		Braz. (Rio de Janeiro In.)	20·04 S	41·53 W
93	Simonette (R.) (sī-mŏn-ĕt')		Can.	54·15 N	118·00 W
212	Simonstad		S. Afr.	34·11 S	18·25 E
92	Simood Sound		Can.	50·45 N	126·25 W
158	Simplon P. (sĭm'plŏn) (săn-plôn')		Switz.	46·13 N	7·53 E
158	Simplon Tun.		It.-Switz.	46·16 N	8·20 E
109	Simpson (I.)		Can.	48·43 N	87·44 W
204	Simpson Des. (sĭmp-sŏn)		Austl.	24·40 S	136·40 E
156	Simrishamn (sĕm'rĕs-häm'n)		Swe.	55·35 N	14·19 E
174	Sim R.		Sov. Un. (Urals In.)	55·00 N	57·42 E
119	Sims Bay (sĭmz bī-yōō')		Tx. (In.)	29·37 N	95·23 W
189	Simushir (I.) (se-mōō'shēr)		Sov. Un.	47·15 N	150·47 E
165	Sinaia (sĭ-nä'yä)		Rom.	45·20 N	25·30 E
211	Sinai Pen. (sī'nī)		Egypt	29·24 N	33·29 E
197	Sinait (sē-nä'ĕt)		Phil.	15·54 N	120·28 E
122	Sinaloa (State) (sē-nä-lô-ä)		Mex.	25·15 N	107·45 W
194	Sinanju (sī'nän-jōō)		Kor.	39·39 N	125·41 E
171	Sinap		Tur.	42·00 N	35·05 E
134	Sincé (sēn'sä)		Col.	9·15 N	75·14 W
134	Sincelejo (sēn-sâ-lā'hō)		Col.	9·12 N	75·30 W
112	Sinclair Inlet (sĭn-klâr')		Wa. (Seattle In.)	47·31 N	122·41 W
92	Sinclair Mills		Can.	54·02 N	121·41 W
157	Sindi (sēn'sä)		Sov. Un.	58·20 N	24·40 E
167	Sinel'nikovo (sē'nyĕl-nĕ'kô'vô)		Sov. Un.	49·19 N	35·33 E
162	Sines (sē'näzh)		Port.	37·57 N	8·50 W
183	Singapore (sĭn'gȧ-pōr')		Singapore (Singapore In.)	1·18 N	103·52 E
183	Singapore		Asia (Singapore In.)	1·22 N	103·45 E
183	Singapore Str.		Indon. (Singapore In.)	1·14 N	104·20 E
165	Singitikós Kólpos (G.)		Grc.	40·15 N	24·00 E
188	Singu (sĭn'gŭ)		Bur.	22·37 N	96·04 E
167	Siniye Lipyagi (sĕn'ē-ĕ lēp'yä-gĕ)		Sov. Un.	51·24 N	38·29 E
164	Sinj (sēn')		Yugo.	43·42 N	16·39 E
211	Sinjah		Sud.	13·09 N	33·52 E
188	Sinkiang Uighur (Aut. Reg.)		China	40·15 N	82·15 E
174	Sin'kovo (sĭn-kô'vô)		Sov. Un. (Moscow In.)	56·23 N	37·19 E
135	Sinnamary (sĭn-nä-mä-rē')		Fr. Gu.	5·15 N	57·52 W
164	Sinni (R.) (sēn'nē)		It.	40·05 N	16·15 E
218	Sinnūris		Egypt (Nile In.)	29·25 N	30·52 E
136	Sino, Pedra de (Mtn.) (pĕ'drä-dô-sē'nô)		Braz. (Rio de Janeiro In.)	22·27 S	43·02 W
217	Sinoia (sī-noi'ä)		Rh.	17·22 S	30·12 E
149	Sint Niklaas		Bel. (Brussels In.)	51·10 N	4·07 E
119	Sinton (sĭn'tŭn)		Tx.	28·03 N	97·30 W
163	Sintra (sĕn'trȧ)		Port. (Lisbon In.)	38·48 N	9·23 W
119	Sint Truiden		Bel. (Brussels In.)	50·49 N	5·14 E
194	Sinŭiju (sĭ'nōōĭ-jōō)		Kor.	40·04 N	124·33 E
174	Sinyavino (sĭn-yä'vĭ-nô)		Sov. Un. (Leningrad In.)	59·50 N	31·07 E
166	Sinyaya (R.) (sĕn'yȧ-yȧ)		Sov. Un.	56·40 N	28·20 E
167	Sinyukha (R.) (sē'nyōō-ḱȧ)		Sov. Un.	48·34 N	30·49 E
158	Sion (sē'ôn')		Switz.	46·15 N	7·17 E
108	Sioux City (sōō)		Ia.	42·30 N	96·25 W
108	Sioux Falls (fôlz)		SD	43·33 N	96·43 W
95	Sioux Lookout		Can.	50·06 N	91·55 W
134	Sipí (sē-pē')		Col. (In.)	4·39 N	76·38 W
90	Sipiwesk		Can.	55·27 N	97·24 W
120	Sipsey (R.) (sĭp'sē)		Al.	33·26 N	87·42 W
196	Sipura (I.)		Indon.	2·15 S	99·33 E
124	Siqueros (sē-kā'rōs)		Mex.	23·19 N	106·14 W
127	Siquia, R. (sē-kē'ä)		Nic.	12·23 N	84·36 W
151	Siracusa (sē-rä-koo'sä)		It.	37·02 N	15·19 E
184	Sirājganj (sĭ-räj'gŭnj)		Bngl.	24·23 N	89·43 E
126	Sirama (sē-rä-mä)		Sal.	13·23 N	87·55 W
93	Sir Douglas, Mt. (sûr dŭg'lȧs)		Can.	50·44 N	115·20 W
204	Sir Edward Pellew Group (Is.) (pĕl'ū)		Austl.	15·15 S	137·15 E
159	Siretul R.		Rom.	46·10 N	27·18 E
186	Sirhān, Wadi (R.)		Sau. Ar.	31·02 N	37·16 E

Page	Name	Pronunciation	Region	Lat. ° ′	Long. ° ′
165	Síros (Ermoúpolis)		Grc.	37·30 N	24·56 E
165	Síros (I.)		Grc.	37·23 N	24·55 E
184	Sirsa		India	29·39 N	75·02 E
93	Sir Sandford, Mt.		Can.	51·40 N	117·52 W
157	Šírvintos (shēr'vĭn-tôs)		Sov. Un.	55·02 N	24·59 E
93	Sir Wilfrid Laurier, Mt. (sûr wĭl'frĭd lôr'yēr)		Can.	52·47 N	119·45 W
164	Sisak (sē'sȧk)		Yugo.	45·29 N	16·20 E
125	Sisal (sē-säl')		Mex.	21·09 N	90·03 W
114	Sisquoc (R.) (sĭs'kwŏk)		Ca.	34·47 N	120·13 W
108	Sisseton (sĭs'tŭn)		SD	45·39 N	97·04 W
186	Sistān, Daryacheh-ye (L.)		Iran-Afg.	31·45 N	61·15 E
161	Sisteron (sēst'rôn')		Fr.	44·10 N	5·55 E
104	Sisterville (sĭs'tēr-vĭl)		WV	39·30 N	81·00 W
164	Sitía (sē'tĭ-ȧ)		Grc. (In.)	35·09 N	26·10 E
101	Sitka (sĭt'kä)		Ak.	57·08 N	135·18 W
148	Sittingbourne (sĭt-ĭng-bôrn)		Eng. (London In.)	51·20 N	0·44 E
196	Sittwe		Bur.	20·09 N	92·54 E
171	Sivas (sē'väs)		Tur.	39·50 N	36·50 E
167	Sivash (L.) (sē'vȧsh)		Sov. Un.	45·55 N	34·42 E
171	Siverek (sē'vĕ-rĕk)		Tur.	37·50 N	39·20 E
157	Siverskaya (sē'vĕr-skä-yȧ)		Sov. Un.	59·17 N	30·03 E
211	Siwah (Oasis) (sē'wä)		Egypt	29·33 N	25·11 E
127	Sixaola R. (sē-ḱä-ō'lä)		C. R.	9·31 N	83·07 W
211	Sixth Cataract		Sud.	16·26 N	32·44 E
156	Sjaelland (I.) (shĕl'lȧn')		Den.	55·34 N	11·35 E
165	Sjenica (syĕ'nē-tsä)		Yugo.	43·15 N	20·02 E
167	Skadovsk (skä'dôfsk)		Sov. Un.	46·08 N	32·54 E
156	Skagen (skä'ghĕn)		Den.	57·43 N	10·32 E
156	Skagen (Pt.)		Den.	57·43 N	10·31 E
156	Skagerrak (Str.) (skä-ghĕ-räk')		Eur.	57·43 N	8·28 E
112	Skagit B. (skăg'ĭt)		Wa. (Seattle In.)	48·20 N	122·32 W
110	Skagit R.		Wa.	48·29 N	121·52 W
101	Skagway (skăg-wā)		Ak.	59·30 N	135·28 W
156	Skälderviken (B.)		Swe.	56·20 N	12·25 E
173	Skalistyy, Golets (Mtn.)		Sov. Un.	57·28 N	119·48 E
112	Skamania (skȧ-mä'nĭ-ȧ)		Wa. (Portland In.)	45·37 N	112·03 W
112	Skamokawa		Wa. (Portland In.)	46·16 N	123·27 W
156	Skanderborg (skän-ĕr-bôr')		Den.	56·04 N	9·55 E
105	Skaneateles (skän-ē-ät'lĕs)		NY	42·55 N	76·25 W
105	Skaneateles (L.)		NY	42·50 N	76·20 W
156	Skänninge (shĕn'ĭng-ĕ)		Swe.	58·24 N	15·02 E
156	Skanör (skän'ûr)		Swe.	55·24 N	12·49 E
165	Skantzoúra (Is.) (skän'tsōō-rä)		Grc.	39·03 N	24·05 E
156	Skara (skä'rȧ)		Swe.	58·25 N	13·24 E
92	Skeena (R.) (skē'nä)		Can.	54·10 N	129·40 W
92	Skeena Mts.		Can.	56·00 N	128·00 W
213	Skeerpoort		S. Afr. (Johannesburg & Pretoria In.)	25·49 S	27·45 E
213	Skeerpoort (R.)		S. Afr. (Johannesburg & Pretoria In.)	25·58 S	27·41 E
135	Skeldon (skĕl'dŭn)		Guy.	5·49 N	57·15 W
150	Skellefte (R.) (shĕl'ĕ-ftĕ)		Swe.	65·18 N	19·08 E
150	Skelleftea (shĕl'ĕf-tĕ-â')		Swe.	64·47 N	20·48 E
156	Skern (R.) (skĕrn)		Den.	55·56 N	8·52 E
154	Skerries (Is.) (skĕr'ĕz)		Wales	53·30 N	4·59 W
174	Skhodnya		Sov. Un. (Moscow In.)	55·57 N	37·21 E
174	Skhodnya R. (skôd'nyȧ)		Sov. Un. (Moscow In.)	55·55 N	37·16 E
165	Skíathos (I.) (skē'ȧ-thôs)		Grc.	39·15 N	23·25 E
154	Skibbereen (skĭb'ĕr-ēn)		Ire.	51·32 N	9·25 W
92	Skidegate (inlet) (skĭ'-dĕ-gāt')		Can.	53·15 N	132·00 W
119	Skidmore (skĭd'môr)		Tx.	28·16 N	97·40 W
156	Skien (skē'ĕn)		Nor.	59·13 N	9·35 E
159	Skierniewice (skyĕr-nyĕ-vēt'sĕ)		Pol.	51·58 N	20·13 E
92	Skihist Mtn.		Can.	50·11 N	121·54 W
152	Skikda (Philippeville)		Alg.	36·58 N	6·51 E
218	Skilpadfontein (Johannesburg & Pretoria In.)		S. Afr.	25·02 S	28·50 E
165	Skíros		Grc.	38·53 N	24·32 E
165	Skiros (I.)		Grc.	38·50 N	24·43 E
156	Skive (skē'vĕ)		Den.	56·34 N	8·56 E
150	Skjalfandá (R.) (skyäl'fänd-ô)		Ice.	65·24 N	16·40 W
150	Skjerstad (skyĕr-städ)		Nor.	67·12 N	15·37 E
164	Škofja Loka (shkôf'yä lō'kȧ)		Yugo.	46·10 N	14·20 E
107	Skokie (skō'kĕ)		Il. (Chicago In.)	42·02 N	87·45 W
112	Skokomish Ind. Res. (skô-kô'mĭsh)		Wa. (Seattle In.)	47·22 N	123·07 W
159	Skole (skô'lĕ)		Sov. Un.	49·03 N	23·32 E
165	Skópelos (I.) (skô'pä-lôs)		Grc.	39·04 N	23·31 E
166	Skopin (skô'pĭn)		Sov. Un.	53·49 N	39·35 E
165	Skopje (skôp'yĕ)		Yugo.	42·02 N	21·26 E
156	Skövde (shûv'dĕ)		Swe.	58·25 N	13·48 E
173	Skovorodino (skô'vô-rô'dĭ-nô)		Sov. Un.	53·53 N	123·56 E
98	Skowhegan (skou-hē'gȧn)		Me.	44·45 N	69·27 W
164	Skradin (skrä'dĕn)		Yugo.	43·49 N	15·58 E
156	Skreia (skrä'ȧ)		Nor.	60·40 N	10·55 E
156	Skudeneshavn (skōō'dĕ-nes-houn')		Nor.	59·10 N	5·19 E

Page	Name	Pronunciation	Region	Lat. ° ′	Long. ° ′
156	Skulerud (skōō'lĕ-rōōdh)		Nor.	59·40 N	11·30 E
115	Skull Valley Ind. Res. (skŭl)		Ut.	40·25 N	112·50 W
120	Skuna (R.) (skŭ'nä)		Ms.	33·57 N	89·36 W
109	Skunk (R.) (skŭnk)		Ia.	41·12 N	92·14 W
157	Skuodas (skwô'dȧs)		Sov. Un.	56·16 N	21·32 E
156	Skurup (skû'rōōp)		Swe.	55·29 N	13·27 E
167	Skvira (skvĕ'rȧ)		Sov. Un.	49·43 N	29·41 E
158	Skwierzyna (skvĕ-ĕr'zhĭ-nȧ)		Pol.	52·35 N	15·30 E
154	Skye (I.) (skī)		Scot.	57·25 N	6·17 W
112	Skykomish (R.) (skī'kō-mĭsh)		Wa. (Seattle In.)	47·50 N	121·55 W
136	Skyring, Seno (B.) (sĕ'nô-s-krē'ng)		Chile	52·35 S	72·30 W
156	Slagese		Den.	55·25 N	11·19 E
196	Slamet, Gunung (Mtn.) (slä'mĕt)		Indon.	7·15 S	109·15 E
165	Slănic (slŭ'nĕk)		Rom.	45·13 N	25·56 E
109	Slate (I.) (slāt)		Can.	48·38 N	87·14 W
117	Slater (slāt'ēr)		Mo.	39·13 N	93·03 W
165	Slatina (slä'tĕ-nä)		Rom.	44·26 N	24·21 E
116	Slaton (slā'tŭn)		Tx.	33·26 N	101·38 W
90	Slave (R.) (slāv)		Can.	59·40 N	111·21 W
172	Slavgorod (släf'gô-rŏt)		Sov. Un.	52·58 N	78·43 E
165	Slavonija (Reg.) (slä-vô'nē-yä)		Yugo.	45·29 N	17·31 E
164	Slavonska Požega (slä-vôn'skä pô'zhĕ-gä)		Yugo.	45·18 N	17·42 E
165	Slavonski Brod (slä-vôn'skĕ brôd)		Yugo.	45·10 N	18·01 E
167	Slavuta (slȧ-vōō'tȧ)		Sov. Un.	50·18 N	27·01 E
167	Slavyansk (släv'yänsk')		Sov. Un.	48·52 N	37·34 E
167	Slavyanskaya (släv-yán'skä-yȧ)		Sov. Un.	45·14 N	38·09 E
108	Slayton (slā'tŭn)		Mn.	44·00 N	95·44 W
148	Sleaford (slē'fērd)		Eng.	53·00 N	0·25 W
109	Sleepy Eye (slēp'ī ī)		Mn.	44·17 N	94·44 W
119	Slidell (slī-dĕl')		La.	30·17 N	89·47 W
149	Sliedrecht..		Neth. (Amsterdam In.)	51·49 N	4·46 E
154	Sligo (slī'gō)		Ire.	54·17 N	8·19 W
156	Slite (slē'tĕ)		Swe.	57·41 N	18·47 E
165	Sliven (slē'vĕn)		Bul.	42·41 N	26·20 E
106	Sloatsburg (slôts'bûrg)		NY (New York In.)	41·09 N	74·11 W
157	Slobodka (slô'bôd-kä)		Sov. Un.	54·34 N	26·12 E
170	Slobodskoy (slô'bôt-skoi)		Sov. Un.	58·48 N	50·02 E
157	Sloka (slô'kä)		Sov. Un.	56·57 N	23·37 E
159	Slonim (snô'nĕm)		Sov. Un.	53·05 N	25·19 E
148	Slough (slou)		Eng. (London In.)	51·29 N	0·36 W
	Slovakia (Prov.), see Slovensko				
164	Slovenija (Reg.) (slô-vĕ'nē-yä)		Yugo.	45·58 N	14·43 E
159	Slovensko (Slovakia) (Prov.) (slô-vĕn'skô)		Czech.	48·40 N	19·00 E
159	Sluch' (R.)		Sov. Un.	50·56 N	26·48 E
164	Sluderno (slōō-dĕr'nô)		It.	46·38 N	10·37 E
164	Slunj (slōōn')		Yugo.	45·18 N	15·46 E
159	Słupsk (swōōpsk)		Pol.	54·28 N	17·02 E
166	Slutsk (slōōtsk)		Sov. Un.	53·02 N	27·34 E
154	Slyne Head (slīn)		Ire.	53·25 N	10·05 W
117	Smackover (smăk'ô-vēr)		Ar.	33·22 N	92·42 W
165	Smederevo (Semendria) (smĕ'dĕ-rĕ-vô) (sĕ-mĕn'drĭ-ȧ)		Yugo.	44·39 N	20·54 E
165	Smederevska Palanka (smĕ-dĕ-rĕv'skä pä-län'kä)		Yugo.	44·21 N	21·00 E
156	Smedjebacken (smĭ'tyĕ-bä-kĕn)		Swe.	60·09 N	15·19 E
167	Smela (smyä'lȧ)		Sov. Un.	49·14 N	31·52 E
167	Smeloye (smyä'lô-ĕ)		Sov. Un.	50·55 N	33·36 E
105	Smethport (smĕth'pôrt)		Pa.	41·50 N	78·25 W
148	Smethwick (Warley) (In.)		Eng.	52·30 N	2·01 W
166	Smiltene (smĕl'tĕ-nĕ)		Sov. Un.	57·26 N	25·57 E
93	Smith (smĭth)		Can.	55·10 N	114·02 W
112	Smith (I.)		Wa. (Seattle In.)	48·20 N	122·53 W
116	Smith Center (sĕn'tēr)		Ks.	39·45 N	98·46 W
92	Smithers (smĭth'ērs)		Can.	54·47 N	127·10 W
121	Smithfield (smĭth'fēld)		NC	35·30 N	78·21 W
111	Smithfield		Ut.	41·50 N	111·49 W
104	Smithland (smĭth'lȧnd)		Ky.	37·10 N	88·25 W
121	Smith Mountain Lake (Res.)		Va.	37·00 N	79·45 W
119	Smith Point		Tx. (In.)	29·32 N	94·45 W
111	Smith R.		Mt.	47·00 N	111·20 W
97	Smiths Falls		Can.	44·54 N	76·05 W
203	Smithton (smĭth'tŭn)		Austl.	40·55 N	145·12 E
113	Smithton		Il. (St. Louis In.)	38·24 N	89·59 W
119	Smithville (smĭth'vĭl)		Tx.	30·00 N	97·08 W
212	Smitswinkelvlakte		S. Afr.	34·16 S	18·25 E
114	Smoke Creek Des. (smôk crēk)		Nv.	40·28 N	119·40 W
93	Smoky (R.) (smôk'ĭ)		Can.	55·30 N	117·30 W
117	Smoky Hill (R.) (smôk'ĭ hĭl)			38·40 N	97·32 W
156	Smöla (I.) (smûlä)		Nor.	63·16 N	7·40 E
166	Smolensk (smô-lyĕnsk')		Sov. Un.	54·46 N	32·03 E
166	Smolensk (Oblast)		Sov. Un.	55·00 N	32·18 E
165	Smyadovo		Bul.	43·04 N	27·00 E
105	Smyrna (smûr'nȧ)		De.	39·20 N	75·35 W
106	Smyrna		Ga. (Atlanta In.)	33·53 N	84·31 W
101	Snag (snăg)		Can.	62·18 N	140·30 W
109	Snake (R.) (snāk)		Mn.	45·58 N	93·20 W

PRONOUNCING INDEX

Snake — South 349

Page	Name Pronunciation Region	Lat. °'	Long. °'
110	Snake (R.)..................Wa.	46·35 N	117·20 W
115	Snake Ra...................Nv.	39·20 N	114·15 W
111	Snake R., Henrys Fork.......Id.	43·52 N	111·55 W
109	Snake River Pln. (rĭv′ẽr)......Id.	43·08 N	114·46 W
128	Snap Pt.....................Ba.	23·45 N	77·30 W
115	Sneffels Pk. (snĕf′ĕlz).........Co.	38·00 N	107·50 W
106	Snelgrove (snĕl′grōv) Can. (Toronto In.)	43·44 N	79·50 W
159	Sniardwy L. (snyärt′vĭ)......Pol.	53·46 N	21·59 E
156	Snöhetta (Mtn.) (snû-hĕttä)..Nor.	62·18 N	9·12 E
112	Snohomish (snô-hō′mĭsh) Wa. (Seattle In.)	47·55 N	122·05 W
112	Snohomish (R.)..Wa. (Seattle In.)	47·53 N	122·04 W
112	Snoqualmie (snō qwäl′mē) Wa. (Seattle In.)	47·32 N	121·50 W
110	Snoqualmie R...............Wa.	47·32 N	121·53 W
167	Snov (R.) (snôf).......Sov. Un.	51·38 N	31·38 E
154	Snowdon, Mt. (snō′dŭn)....Wales	53·05 N	4·04 W
105	Snow Hill (hĭl).............Md.	38·15 N	75·20 W
95	Snow Lake.................Can.	54·50 N	100·10 W
205	Snowy Mts. (snō′ē)........Austl.	36·17 S	148·30 E
116	Snyder (snī′dẽr).............Ok.	34·40 N	98·57 W
118	Snyder.....................Tx.	32·48 N	100·53 W
148	Soar (R.) (sōr).............Eng.	52·44 N	1·09 W
211	Sobat R. (sō′bȧt)...........Sud.	9·04 N	32·02 E
166	Sobinka (sô-bĭŋ′kȧ)......Sov. Un.	55·59 N	40·02 E
195	Sobo Zan (Mt.) (sô′bô zän)...Jap.	32·47 N	131·27 E
135	Sobral (sô-bräl′)...........Braz.	3·39 S	40·16 W
159	Sochaczew (sô-ĸä′chĕf).......Pol.	52·14 N	20·18 E
188	Soch'e (Yarkand) (sō′chĕ) (yär-känt′).China	38·15 N	77·15 E
171	Sochi (sôch′ĭ)...........Sov. Un.	43·35 N	39·50 E
199	Society Is. (sō-sī′ĕ-tē) Fr. Polynesia	15·00 S	157·30 W
125	Socoltenango (sô-kôl-tĕ-näŋ′gō) Mex.	16·17 N	92·20 W
137	Socorro (sŏ-kô′r-rō) Braz. (Rio de Janeiro In.)	22·35 S	46·32 W
134	Socorro (sô-kôr′rō)...........Col.	6·23 N	73·19 W
115	Socorro.....................NM	34·05 N	106·55 W
218	Socotra I. (sô-kō′trȧ) P. D. R. of Yem. (Horn of Afr. In.)	13·00 N	52·30 E
162	Socuellamos (sô-kōō-āl′yä-môs) Sp.	39·18 N	2·48 W
114	Soda (L.) (sō′dȧ)............Ca.	35·12 N	116·25 W
112	Soda Pk.......Wa. (Portland In.)	45·53 N	122·04 W
111	Soda Springs (sprĭngz)........Id.	42·39 N	111·37 W
156	Söderhamn (sû-dẽr-häm′’n)...Swe.	61·20 N	17·00 E
156	Söderköping.................Swe.	58·30 N	16·14 E
156	Södertälje (sû-dẽr-tĕl′yĕ).....Swe.	59·12 N	17·35 E
192	Sodi Soruksum (Mtn.)......China	37·20 N	102·00 E
211	Sodo.......................Eth.	7·03 N	37·46 E
156	Södra Dellen (L.)...........Swe.	61·45 N	16·30 E
158	Soest (zōst)..............F.R.G.	51·35 N	8·05 E
	Sofia, see Sofiya		
165	Sofiya (Sofia) (sô′fē-yȧ) (sô′fē-ȧ) Bul.	42·43 N	23·20 E
167	Sofiyevka (sô-fē′yĕf-kȧ)...Sov. Un.	48·03 N	33·53 E
195	Soga (sô′gä).....Jap (Tōkyō In.)	35·35 N	140·08 E
134	Sogamoso (sô-gä-mô′sō)......Col.	5·42 N	72·51 W
156	Sogndal (sôghn′dál).........Nor.	58·20 N	6·17 E
156	Sogndal....................Nor.	61·14 N	7·04 E
156	Sogne Fd. (sôgn′ĕ fyôrd).....Nor.	61·09 N	5·30 E
166	Sogozha (R.) (sô′gô-zhȧ)..Sov. Un.	58·35 N	39·08 E
160	Soissons (swä-sôɴ′)...........Fr.	49·23 N	3·17 E
195	Sōka (sō′kä).....Jap. (Tōkyō In.)	35·50 N	139·49 E
159	Sokal (sô′käl′)...........Sov. Un.	50·28 N	24·20 E
171	Soke (sû′kĕ)................Tur.	37·40 N	27·10 E
214	Sokodé (sô-kô-dā′)..........Togo	8·59 N	1·08 E
159	Sokolka (sô-kōōl′kȧ).........Pol.	53·23 N	23·30 E
210	Sokolo (sô-kô-lō′)...........Mali	14·51 N	6·09 W
214	Sokone..................Senegal	13·53 N	16·22 W
215	Sokoto (sō′kô-tō)............Nig.	13·04 N	5·16 E
159	Sokotów Podlaski (sô-kô-wōōf′ pŭd-lä′skĭ).Pol.	52·24 N	22·15 E
125	Sola de Vega (San Miguel) (sō′lä dā vā′gä) (sän mê-gĕl′) Mex.	16·31 N	96·58 W
197	Solana (sō-lä′nä).......Phil. (In.)	17·40 N	121·41 E
202	Solander, C.....Austl. (Sydney In.)	34·03 S	151·16 E
197	Solano (sō-lä′nō).......Phil. (In.)	16·31 N	121·11 E
134	Soledad (sŏ-lĕ-dä′d)..........Col.	10·47 N	75·00 W
124	Soledad Díez Gutierrez (sô-lȧ-dhädh′dē′äz gōō-tyä′rĕz) Mex.	22·19 N	100·54 W
110	Soleduck R. (sōl′dŭk)........Wa.	47·59 N	124·28 W
126	Solentiname, Islas de (Is.) (ē′s-läs-dĕ-sō-lĕn-tē-nä′mȧ).Nic.	11·15 N	85·16 W
148	Solihull (sō′lĭ-hŭl)...........Eng.	52·25 N	1·46 W
174	Solikamsk (sô-lē-kämsk′) Sov. Un. (Urals In.)	59·38 N	56·48 E
134	Solimões, Rio (R.) (rē′ō-sô-lē-mô′ĕs).Braz.	2·45 S	67·44 W
161	Solingen (zō′lĭng-ĕn) F.R.G. (Ruhr In.)	51·10 N	7·05 E
156	Sollefteå (sôl-lĕf′tĕ-ô)........Swe.	63·06 N	17·17 E
163	Sóller (sŏ′lyĕr)...............Sp.	39·45 N	2·40 E
171	Sol'-Iletsk...............Sov. Un.	51·10 N	55·05 E
160	Sologne (Reg.) (sō-lŏn′yĕ).....Fr.	47·36 N	1·53 E
126	Solola (sô-lō′lä)............Guat.	14·45 N	91·12 W
198	Solomon Is..............Oceania	7·00 S	148·00 E
116	Solomon R..................Ks.	39·24 N	98·19 W
116	Solomon R. North Fk.........Ks.	39·34 N	99·52 W
116	Solomon R., South Fk........Ks.	39·19 N	99·52 W
107	Solon (sō′lŭn)..Oh. (Cleveland In.)	41·23 N	81·26 W
158	Solothurn (zô′lō-thōōrn)....Switz.	47·13 N	7·30 E
170	Solov'etskiy (I.).........Sov. Un.	65·10 N	35·40 E
164	Šolta (I.) (shôl′tä).........Yugo.	43·20 N	16·15 E
158	Soltau (sôl′tou)...........F.R.G.	53·00 N	9·50 E
166	Sol'tsy (sôl′tsê).........Sov. Un.	58·04 N	30·13 E
192	Solun (sô-lōōn′)............China	47·32 N	121·18 E
105	Solvay (sŏl′vā)..............NY	43·05 N	76·10 W
156	Sölvesborg (sûl′vĕs-bôrg).....Swe.	56·04 N	14·35 E
170	Sol'vychegodsk (sôl′vê-chĕ-gôtsk′) Sov. Un.	61·18 N	46·58 E
154	Solway Firth (sŏl′wā fûrth′) Eng.-Scot.	54·42 N	3·55 W
217	Solwezi...................Zambia	12·11 S	26·25 E
209	Somalia (sō-ma′lē-ȧ).........Afr.	3·28 N	44·47 E
217	Somanga....................Tan.	8·24 S	39·17 E
165	Sombor (sôm′bôr)..........Yugo.	45·45 N	19·10 E
124	Sombrerete (sōm-brā-rā′tȧ)..Mex.	23·38 N	103·37 W
135	Sombrero, Cayo (C.) (kä-yô-sôm-brĕ′rô).Ven. (In.)	10·52 N	68·12 W
120	Somerset (sŭm′ẽr-sĕt)........Ky.	37·05 N	84·35 W
106	Somerset....Ma. (Providence In.)	41·46 N	71·05 W
105	Somerset....................Pa.	40·00 N	79·05 W
113	Somerset...Tx. (San Antonio In.)	29·13 N	98·39 W
213	Somerset East..S. Afr. (Natal In.)	32·44 S	25·36 E
98	Somersworth (sŭm′ẽrz-wûrth).NH	43·16 N	70·53 W
114	Somerton (sŭm′ẽr-tŭn)........Az.	32·36 N	114·43 W
99	Somerville (sŭm′ẽr-vĭl)..Ma. (In.)	42·23 N	71·06 W
106	Somerville....NJ (New York In.)	40·34 N	74·37 W
120	Somerville..................Tn.	35·14 N	89·21 W
119	Somerville..................Tx.	30·21 N	96·31 W
159	Somesul R. (sô-mȧ′shōōl)....Rom.	47·43 N	23·09 E
163	Somma Vesuviana (sôm′mä vā-zōō-vê-ä′nä) It. (Naples In.)	40·38 N	14·27 E
160	Somme (R.) (sŏm)...........Fr.	50·02 N	2·04 E
149	Sommerfeld (zō′mẽr-fĕld) G.D.R. (Berlin In.)	52·48 N	13·02 E
202	Sommerville Austl. (Melbourne In.)	38·14 S	145·10 E
126	Somoto (sô-mō′tō)...........Nic.	13·28 N	86·37 W
136	Somuncurá, Meseta de (Plat.) (mĕ-sĕ′tä-dĕ-sô-mōō′n-kōō-rȧ′) Arg.	41·15 S	68·00 W
184	Son (R.) (sōn).............India	24·40 N	82·35 E
127	Soná (sō′nä)...............Pan.	8·00 N	81·19 W
194	Sŏnchŏn (sŭn′shŭn)..........Kor.	39·49 N	124·56 E
213	Sondags (R.)...S. Afr. (Natal In.)	33·17 S	25·14 E
156	Sønderborg (sûn″er-bôrgh)...Den.	54·55 N	9·47 E
158	Sondershausen (zôn′dẽrz-hou′zĕn) G.D.R.	51·17 N	10·45 E
193	Song Ca (R.)...............Viet.	19·15 N	105·00 E
217	Songea (sōn-gā′ȧ)...........Tan.	10·41 S	35·39 E
194	Sŏngjin (sŭng′jĭn′)..........Kor.	40·38 N	129·10 E
196	Songkhla (sông′ĸlä′)........Thai.	7·09 N	100·34 E
217	Songwe....................Zaire	12·25 S	29·40 E
158	Sonneberg (sôn′ĕ-bĕrgh)...G.D.R.	50·20 N	11·14 E
114	Sonora (sō-nō′rȧ)............Ca.	37·58 N	120·22 W
118	Sonora.....................Tx.	30·33 N	100·38 W
122	Sonora (State)..............Mex.	29·45 N	111·15 W
122	Sonora (R.)................Mex.	28·45 N	111·35 W
114	Sonora Pk...................Ca.	38·22 N	119·39 W
162	Sonseca (sôn-sā′kä)...........Sp.	39·41 N	3·56 W
134	Sonsón (sôn-sôn′).......Col. (In.)	5·42 N	75·28 W
126	Sonsonate (sōn-sō-nä′tȧ)......Sal.	13·46 N	89·43 W
197	Sonsorol Is. (sŏn-sō-rōl′) Pas. Is. Trust Ter.	5·03 N	132·33 E
190	Soochow (Wuhsien) (sōō′jō) (wōō′siän).China	31·19 N	120·37 E
112	Sooke Basin (sŏŏk) Can. (Seattle In.)	48·21 N	123·47 W
113	Soo Locks (sōō lŏks)...Can.-U. S.	46·30 N	84·30 W
134	Sopetrán (sô-pĕ-trä′n)...Col. (In.)	6·30 N	75·44 W
156	Sopot (sô′pôt)..............Pol.	54·26 N	18·25 E
158	Sopron (shŏp′rôn).........Hung.	47·41 N	16·36 E
164	Sora (sō′rä)..................It.	41·43 N	13·37 E
156	Sör Aurdal (sûr äür-däl).....Nor.	60·54 N	9·24 E
162	Sorbas (sôr′bäs)..............Sp.	37·05 N	2·07 W
125	Sordo (R.) (sô′r-dō).........Mex.	16·39 N	97·33 W
97	Sorel (sō-rĕl′)..............Can.	46·01 N	73·07 W
203	Sorell, C...................Austl.	42·10 S	144·50 E
164	Soresina (sō-rȧ-zē′nä)..........It.	45·17 N	9·51 E
162	Soria (sō′rē-ä)................Sp.	41·46 N	2·28 W
137	Soriano (sŏ-rēä′nō) (Dept.) Ur. (Buenos Aires In.)	33·25 S	58·00 W
137	Sorocaba (sô-rô-kä′bȧ) Braz. (Rio de Janeiro In.)	23·29 S	47·27 W
167	Soroki (sō-rō′kĕ).........Sov. Un.	48·09 N	28·17 E
197	Sorong (sō-rông′)..........Indon.	1·00 S	131·20 E
166	Sorot' (R.) (sō-rō′tzh)....Sov. Un.	57·08 N	29·23 E
217	Soroti (sō-rō′tē)..............Ug.	1·43 N	33·37 E
150	Söröy (I.) (sûr′ûê)...........Nor.	70·37 N	20·58 E
162	Sorraia (R.) (sôr-rī′ȧ).......Port.	38·55 N	8·42 W
163	Sorrento (sôr-rĕn′tō) It. (Naples In.)	40·23 N	14·23 E
197	Sorsogon (sôr-sōgōn′)........Phil.	12·51 N	124·02 E
157	Sortavala (sôr′tä-vä-lä)...Sov. Un.	61·43 N	30·40 E
192	Sŏsan (sŭ′sän)..............Korea	36·40 N	126·25 E
167	Sosna (R.) (sôs′nȧ)......Sov. Un.	50·33 N	38·15 E
167	Sosnitsa (sôs-nê′tsȧ).....Sov. Un.	51·30 N	32·29 E
172	Sosnogorsk...............Sov. Un.	63·13 N	54·09 E
159	Sosnowiec (sôs-nô′vyĕts)......Pol.	50·17 N	19·10 E
194	Sosunova, Mys (Pt.) (mĭs sô′sōō-nôf′ȧ).Sov. Un.	46·28 N	138·06 E
174	Sos'va R. (sôs′vȧ) Sov. Un. (Urals In.)	59·55 N	60·40 E
170	Sos'va (R.) (sôs′vȧ)......Sov. Un.	63·10 N	63·30 E
215	Sota (R.)...............Dahomey	11·10 N	3·20 E
124	Sota la Marina (sô-tä-lä-mä-rē′nä) Mex.	22·45 N	98·11 W
125	Soteapan (sō-tȧ-ä′pän)......Mex.	18·14 N	94·51 W
124	Soto la Marina, Rio (R.) (rē′ō-sō′tō lä mä-rē′nä).Mex.	23·55 N	98·30 W
126	Sotuta (sô-tōō′tä)......Mex. (In.)	20·35 N	89·00 W
216	Souanké....................Con.	2·05 N	14·03 E
135	Soublette (sô-ōō-blĕ′tĕ)..Ven. (In')	9·55 N	66·06 W
164	Soúdhas, Kolpós (G.)...Grc. (In.)	35·33 N	24·22 E
165	Souflion....................Grc.	41·12 N	26·17 E
127	Soufriere (sōō-frê-âr′) St. Lucia (In.)	13·50 N	61·03 W
127	Soufríere, Mt.....St. Vincent (In.)	13·19 N	61·12 W
127	Soufrière (Vol.)...Montserrat (In.)	16·43 N	62·10 W
151	Souk-Ahras (sōōk-ä-räs′).....Alg.	36·18 N	8·19 E
194	Sŏul (Seoul)................Kor.	37·35 N	127·03 E
94	Sounding Cr. (soun′dĭng)....Can.	51·35 N	111·00 W
218	Sources, Mt. aux (môɴ′tō sōōrs′) Leso.-S. Afr. (Natal In.)	28·47 S	29·04 E
162	Soure (sōr-ĕ)...............Port.	40·04 N	8·37 W
99	Souris (sōō′rē′)............Can.	46·20 N	62·17 W
95	Souris.....................Can.	49·38 N	100·15 W
95	Souris (R.).................Can.	49·10 N	102·00 W
119	Sourlake (sour′lāk)...........Tx.	30·09 N	94·24 W
210	Sousse (sōōs)...............Tun.	36·00 N	10·39 E
160	Soustons (sōōs-tôɴ′)..........Fr.	43·46 N	1·22 W
121	South (R.)..................NC	34·49 N	78·33 W
209	South Africa................Afr.	28·00 S	24·50 E
106	South Amboy (south′ăm′boi) NJ (New York In.)	40·28 N	74·17 W
133	South America		
154	Southampton (south-ămp′tŭn) Eng.	50·54 N	1·30 W
105	Southampton................NY	40·53 N	72·24 W
91	Southampton I.............Can.	64·38 N	84·00 W
196	South Andaman I. (ăn-dȧ-măn′) Andaman & Nicobar Is.	11·57 N	93·24 E
204	South Australia (State) (ôs-trā′lĭ-ȧ).Austl.	29·45 S	132·00 E
129	South B....................Ba.	20·55 N	73·35 W
104	South Bend (bĕnd)...........In.	41·40 N	86·20 W
110	South Bend (bĕnd)..........Wa.	46·39 N	123·48 W
128	South Bight (B.).............Ba.	24·20 N	77·35 W
128	South Bimini (I.) (bē′mê-nê)..Ba.	25·40 N	79·20 W
99	Southborough (south′bŭr-ô) Ma. (In.)	42·18 N	71·33 W
121	South Boston (bôs′tŭn).......Va.	36·41 N	78·55 W
105	Southbridge (south′brĭj)......Ma.	42·05 N	72·00 W
129	South Caicos (I.) (kī′kōs) Turks & Caicos	21·30 N	71·35 W
197	South C............Pap. N. Gui.	10·40 S	149·00 E
103	South Carolina (State) (kăr-ô-lī′nȧ).U. S.	34·15 N	81·10 W
148	South Cave (cāv)...........Eng.	53·45 N	0·35 W
104	South Charleston (south chärlz′tŭn).WV	38·20 N	81·40 W
196	South China Sea (chī′nȧ).....Asia	15·23 N	114·12 E
202	South Cr......Austl. (Sydney In.)	33·43 S	167·00 E
102	South Dakota (State) (dȧ-kō′tȧ) U. S.	44·20 N	101·55 W
154	South Downs (dounz).......Eng.	50·55 N	1·13 W
184	South Dum-Dum......India (In.)	22·36 N	88·25 E
205	Southeast, C...............Austl.	43·47 S	146·03 E
148	Southend-on-Sea (south-ĕnd′) Eng. (London In.)	51·33 N	0·41 E
205	Southern Alps (Mts.) (sŭ-thûrn ălps).N. Z. (In.)	44·08 S	169·18 E
204	Southern Cross.............Austl.	31·13 S	119·30 E
93	Southern Indian (L.) (sŭth′ẽrn ĭn′dĭ-ăn).Can.	56·46 N	98·57 W
121	Southern Pines (sŭth′ẽrn pīnz).NC	35·10 N	79·23 W
154	Southern Uplands (ŭp′lȧndz).Scot.	55·15 N	4·28 W
115	Southern Ute Ind. Res. (ūt)...Co.	37·05 N	108·23 W
	Southern Yemen, see Yemen, People's Democratic Republic of		
107	South Euclid (ū′klĭd) Oh. (Cleveland In.)	41·30 N	81·34 W
104	South Fox (I.) (fŏks).........Mi.	45·25 N	85·55 W
113	South Gate (gāt) Ca. (Los Angeles In.)	33·57 N	118·13 W
133	South Georgia (I.) (jôr′jȧ).Falk Is.	54·00 S	37·00 W
104	South Haven (hāv″n).........Mi.	42·25 N	86·15 W
121	South Hill..................Va.	36·44 N	78·08 W
95	South Indian Lake..........Can.	56·50 N	99·00 W
105	Southington (sŭdh′ĭng-tŭn)....Ct.	41·35 N	72·55 W
205	South I.............N. Z. (In.)	43·15 S	167·00 E

ăt; fīnăl; rāte; senâte; ärm; ȧsk; sofȧ; fâre; ch-choose; dh-as th in other; bē; ĕvent; bĕt; recĕnt; cratêr; g-go; gh-guttural g; bĭt; ĭ-short neutral; rīde; ᴋ-guttural k as ch in German ich;

ng-sing; ŋ-baŋk; N-nasalized n; nŏd; cŏmmit; ōld; ôbey; ôrder; fōōd; fŏŏt; ou-out; s-soft; sh-dish; th-thin; pūre; únite; ûrn; stŭd; circŭs; ū-as "y" in study; ′-indeterminate vowel.

ăt; fīnăl; rāte; senāte; ärm; àsk; sofà; fâre; ch-choose; dh-as th in other; bē; ĕvent; bĕt; recĕnt; cratēr; g-go; gh-guttural g; bĭt; ĭ-short neutral; rīde; ĸ-guttural k as ch in German ich;

ng-sing; ŋ-baŋk; N-nasalized n; nŏd; cŏmmit; ōld; ôbey; ôrder; fōōd; fŏŏt; ou-out; s-soft; sh-dish; th-thin; pūre; ûnite; ûrn; stŭd; circǔs; ü-as "y" in study; '-indeterminate vowel.

ăt; fìnǎl; rāte; senáte; ärm; ásk; sofá; fâre; ch-choose; dh-as th in other; bē; ĕvent; bĕt; recĕnt; cratĕr; g-go; gh-guttural g; bǐt; ĭ-short neutral; rīde; ĸ-guttural k as ch in German ich;

PRONOUNCING INDEX

Tarrejon de Ardoz — Tepeji del Rio 355

Page	Name Pronunciation Region	Lat. °'	Long. °'
163	Tarrejón de Ardoz (tär-rĕ-ĸô'n-dĕ-är-dôz) Sp. (Madrid In.)	40·28 N	3·29 W
106	Tarrytown (tăr'ĭ-toun) NY (New York In.)	41·04 N	73·52 W
171	Tarsus (tȧr'sŏŏs) (tär'sŭs)....Tur.	37·00 N	34·50 E
136	Tartagal (tär-tä-gȧ'l)........Arg.	23·31 S	63·47 W
153	Tartous (tȧr-tōōs').........Egypt	34·54 N	35·59 E
166	Tartu (Dorpat) (tär'tōō) (dôr'pät) Sov. Un.	58·23 N	26·44 E
195	Tarumi (tä'rōō-mê) Jap. (Ōsaka In.)	34·38 N	135·04 E
166	Tarusa (tä-rōōs'ȧ).......Sov. Un.	54·43 N	37·11 E
113	Tarzana (tär-ză'ȧ) Ca. (Los Angeles In.)	34·10 N	118·32 W
190	Tashanchen (dä'sähn'jĕn)...China	34·17 N	119·17 E
147	Tashauz (tŭ-shŭ-ōōs')....Sov. Un.	41·50 N	59·45 E
172	Tashkent (tȧsh'kĕnt)....Sov. Un.	41·23 N	69·04 E
205	Tasman B. (tăz'măn)..N. Z. (In.)	39·11 S	173·22 E
203	Tasmania (State) (tăz-mā'nĭ-ȧ) Austl.	38·20 S	146·30 E
205	Tasmania (I.).............Austl.	41·28 S	142·30 E
203	Tasman Pen...............Austl.	43·00 S	148·30 E
198	Tasman Sea.............Oceania	29·30 S	155·00 E
124	Tasquillo (täs-kē'lyō).......Mex.	20·34 N	99·21 W
210	Tassili-n-Ajjer (Plat.) (tȧs'ē-lē ä'jĕr).Alg.	25·40 N	6·57 E
170	Tatar (A. S. S. R.) (tȧ-tär') Sov. Un.	55·30 N	51·00 E
172	Tatarsk (tȧ-tärsk')......Sov. Un.	55·15 N	75·00 E
173	Tatar Str.............Sov. Un.	51·00 N	141·45 E
112	Tater Hill (Mtn.) (tāt'ēr hĭl) Or. (Portland In.)	45·47 N	123·02 W
195	Tateyama (tä'tê-yä'mä)......Jap.	35·04 N	139·52 E
92	Tatlow, Mt................Can.	51·23 N	123·52 W
159	Tatra Mts...........Czech.-Pol.	49·15 N	19·40 E
193	Tattien Ting (Mtn.).......China	22·25 N	111·20 E
193	Tatu Ho (R.).............China	29·20 N	103·30 E
137	Tatuí (tä-tōō-ē') Braz. (Rio de Janeiro In.)	23·21 S	47·49 W
192	Tat'ung (tä'tŏŏng')........China	40·00 N	113·30 E
137	Taubaté (tou-bȧ-tā') Braz. (Rio de Janeiro In.)	23·03 S	45·32 W
158	Tauern Tun................Aus.	47·12 N	13·17 E
212	Taung (tä'ŏŏng)..........S. Afr.	27·25 S	29·45 E
106	Taunton (tän'tŭn) Ma. (Providence In.)	41·54 N	71·03 W
106	Taunton R....RI (Providence In.)	41·50 N	71·02 W
155	Taunus (Mts.) (tou'nōōz)..F.R.G.	50·15 N	8·33 E
205	Taupo, L. (tä'ōō-pō)...N. Z. (In.)	38·38 S	175·27 E
157	Taurage (tou'rȧ-gā)......Sov. Un.	55·15 N	22·18 E
	Taurus Mts., see Toros Dağlari		
162	Tauste (tä-ōōs'tȧ)...........Sp.	41·55 N	1·15 W
172	Tavda (tȧv-dȧ')........Sov. Un.	58·00 N	64·44 E
170	Tavda (R.).............Sov. Un.	59·20 N	63·28 E
161	Taverny (tȧ-vĕr-nē') Fr. (Paris In.)	49·02 N	2·13 E
125	Taviche (tä-vē'chĕ).........Mex.	16·43 N	96·35 W
162	Tavira (tä-vē'rȧ)...........Port.	37·09 N	7·42 W
196	Tavoy.....................Bur.	14·04 N	98·19 E
171	Tavşanli (tȧv'shän-lĭ)........Tur.	39·30 N	29·30 E
119	Tawakoni (L.)...............Tx.	32·51 N	95·59 W
195	Tawaramoto (tä'wä-rä-mô-tô) Jap. (Ōsaka In.)	34·33 N	135·48 E
104	Tawas City...................Mi.	44·15 N	83·30 W
104	Tawas Pt. (tô'wȧs)...........Mi.	44·15 N	83·25 W
190	Tawen (R.) (dä'wĕn).......China	35·58 N	116·53 E
196	Tawitawi Group (Is.) (tä'wê-tä'wê).Phil.	4·52 N	120·35 E
211	Tawkar....................Sud.	18·28 N	37·46 E
124	Taxco de Alarcón (täs'kō dĕ ä-lär-kō'n).Mex.	18·34 N	99·37 W
154	Tay, Firth of (fûrth ŏv tā)...Scot.	56·26 N	2·45 W
154	Tay (L.)..................Scot.	56·25 N	5·07 W
154	Tay (R.)..................Scot.	56·35 N	3·37 W
197	Tayabas B. (tä-yä'bäs)..Phil. (In.)	13·44 N	121·40 E
172	Tayga (tī'gä)...........Sov. Un.	56·12 N	85·47 E
173	Taygonos, Mys (Taigonos) (C.) Sov. Un.	60·37 N	160·17 E
119	Taylor......................Tx.	30·35 N	97·25 W
115	Taylor, Mt................NM	35·20 N	107·40 W
104	Taylorville (tā'lēr-vĭl)..........Il.	39·30 N	89·20 W
186	Taymā..................Sau. Ar.	27·45 N	38·55 E
173	Taymyr (Taimyr) (L.) (tī-mĭr') Sov. Un.	74·13 N	100·45 E
172	Taymyr, P-Ov (Taimyr) (Pen.) Sov. Un.	75·15 N	95·00 E
172	Tayshet (Taishet) (tī-shĕt') Sov. Un.	56·09 N	97·49 E
172	Taytay (tī-tī).............Phil.	10·37 N	119·10 E
193	Tayü......................China	25·20 N	114·20 E
197	Tayung (tä-yōōng')....Phil. (In.)	16·01 N	120·45 E
172	Taz (R.) (tȧz)..........Sov. Un.	67·15 N	80·45 E
210	Taza (tä'zä)...............Mor.	34·08 N	4·00 W
172	Tazovskoye.............Sov. Un.	66·58 N	78·28 E
171	Tbilisi ('tbĭl-yē'sē).......Sov. Un.	41·40 N	44·45 E
216	Tchibanga (chê-bäŋ'gä)....Gabon	2·51 S	11·02 E
214	Tchien....................Lib.	6·04 N	8·08 W
215	Tchigai, Plat. du (Plat.) Chad-Niger	21·20 N	14·50 E
159	Tczew (t'chĕf')..............Pol.	54·06 N	18·48 E
126	Teabo (tĕ-ä'bô).......Mex. (In.)	20·25 N	89·14 W
119	Teague (tēg)................Tx.	31·39 N	96·16 W
125	Teapa (tā-ä'pä).............Mex.	17·35 N	92·56 W
210	Tébessa (tā'bĕs'ä)...........Alg.	35·27 N	8·13 E
183	Tebing Tinggi (I.) (teb'ĭng-tĭng'gä) Indon. (Singapore In.)	0·54 N	102·39 E
124	Tecalitlán (tā-kä-lê-tlän')....Mex.	19·28 N	103·17 W
214	Techiman..................Ghana	7·35 N	1·56 W
124	Tecoanapa (tāk-wä-nä-pä')..Mex.	16·33 N	98·46 W
126	Tecoh (tĕ-kô).........Mex. (In.)	20·46 N	89·27 W
124	Tecolotlán (tā-kô-lô-tlän')...Mex.	20·13 N	103·57 W
125	Tecolutla (tā-kô-lōō'tlä).....Mex.	20·33 N	97·00 W
125	Tecolutla (R.)..............Mex.	20·16 N	97·14 W
124	Tecomán (tā-kô-män')......Mex.	18·53 N	103·53 W
125	Tecómitl (tĕ-kŏ'mētl)..Mex. (In.)	19·13 N	98·59 W
124	Tecozautla (tā'kô-zä-ōō'tlä)..Mex.	20·33 N	99·38 W
124	Tecpan de Galeana (tĕk-pän' dā gä-lā-ä'nä).Mex.	17·13 N	100·41 W
125	Tecpatán (tĕk-pä-tȧ'n)......Mex.	17·08 N	93·18 W
124	Tecuala (tĕ-kwä-lä).........Mex.	22·24 N	105·29 W
159	Tecuci (ta-kōōch')..........Rom.	45·51 N	27·30 E
107	Tecumseh (tê-kŭm'sĕ) Can. (Detroit In.)	42·19 N	82·53 W
104	Tecumseh....................Mi.	42·00 N	84·00 W
118	Tecumseh....................Ne.	40·21 N	96·09 W
117	Tecumseh....................Ok.	35·18 N	96·55 W
154	Tees (R.) (tēz).............Eng.	54·40 N	2·10 W
	Teesside, see Middlesbrough		
134	Tefé (tĕf-ä')...............Braz.	3·27 S	64·43 W
195	Teganuna (L.) (tā'gä-nōō'nä) Jap. (Tōkyō In.)	35·50 N	140·02 E
126	Tegucigalpa (tā-gōō-sê-gäl'pä) Hond.	14·08 N	87·15 W
114	Tehachapi Mts. (tĕ-hă-shā'pĭ)..Ca.	34·50 N	118·55 W
92	Tehentlo L................Can.	55·11 N	125·00 W
186	Tehrān (tĕ-hrän')...........Iran	35·45 N	51·30 E
190	Tehsien (dŭ'siän)..........China	37·28 N	116·17 E
193	Tehua......................China	25·30 N	118·15 E
125	Tehuacan (tā-wä-kän')......Mex.	18·27 N	97·23 W
125	Tehuantepec (Sto. Domingo) (tȧ-wän-tȧ-pĕk') (sän-tô dô-mē'n-gô).Mex.	16·20 N	95·14 W
122	Tehuantepec, Golfo de (G.) (gôl-fô dĕ).Mex.	15·45 N	95·00 W
125	Tehuantepec, Istmo de (Isth.) (ē'st-mô dĕ).Mex.	17·55 N	94·35 W
125	Tehuantepec (R.)...........Mex.	16·30 N	95·23 W
124	Tehuehuetla Arroyo (R.) (tĕ-wĕ-wĕ'tlä ȧr-rô-yô).Mex.	17·54 N	100·26 W
124	Tehuitzingo (tā-wê-tzĭŋ'gō)..Mex.	18·21 N	98·16 W
216	Teixeira de Sousa...........Ang.	10·42 S	22·12 E
162	Tejeda, Sierra de (Mts.) (sē-ĕ'r-rä dĕ tĕ-kĕ'dä).Sp.	36·55 N	5·57 W
162	Tejo, Rio (R.) (rê-ōtä'hŏŏ)...Port.	39·23 N	8·01 W
125	Tejúpan (Santiago) (tĕ-ĸōō-pä'n) (sän-tyȧ'gô).Mex.	17·39 N	97·34 W
124	Tejúpan, Punta (Pt.) (pōō'n-tä) Mex.	18·19 N	103·30 W
124	Tejupilco de Hidalgo (tȧ-hōō-pēl'kō dā ê-dhäl'gō) Mex.	18·52 N	100·07 W
108	Tekamah (tê-kā'mȧ)........Ne.	41·46 N	96·13 W
126	Tekax de Alvaro Obregon (tĕ-kä'x dĕ ä'l-vä-rô-brĕ-gô'n) Mex. (In.)	20·12 N	89·11 W
211	Tekeze (R.)................Eth.	13·38 N	38·00 E
165	Tekirdağ (Rodosto) (tĕ-kēr'dägh') Tur.	41·00 N	27·28 E
126	Tekit (tĕ-kē't).........Mex. (In.)	20·35 N	89·18 W
110	Tekoa (tê-kō'ȧ)..............Wa.	47·15 N	117·03 W
126	Tela (tā'lä)................Hond.	15·45 N	87·25 W
126	Tela, Bahia de (B.) (bä-ē'ä dĕ) Hond.	15·53 N	87·29 W
183	Telapa Burok, Gunong (Mt.) Mala. (Singapore In.)	2·51 N	102·04 E
171	Telavi.................Sov. Un.	42·00 N	45·20 E
183	Tel Aviv-Yafo (tĕl-ä-vēv'jä'fȧ) Isr. (Palestine In.)	32·03 N	34·46 E
90	Telegraph Creek (tĕl'ē-grȧf)..Can.	57·59 N	131·22 W
167	Teleneshty (tyĕ-le-nĕsht'i) Sov. Un.	47·31 N	28·22 E
114	Telescope Pk. (tĕl'ē skōp).....Ca.	36·12 N	117·05 W
135	Teles Pirez (R.) (tĕ-lĕs pē'rĕz) Braz.	8·28 S	57·07 W
183	Telesung...Indon. (Singapore In.)	1·07 N	102·53 E
126	Telica (Vol.) (tȧ-lē'kä).......Nic.	12·38 N	86·52 W
188	Telii Nuur (L.)............China	45·49 N	86·08 E
214	Télimélé...................Gui.	10·54 N	13·02 W
104	Tell City (tĕl)...............In.	38·00 N	86·45 W
101	Teller (tĕl'ēr)...............Ak.	65·17 N	166·28 W
134	Tello (tĕ'l-yô)..........Col. (In.)	3·05 N	75·08 W
115	Telluride (tĕl'ū-rīd).........Co.	37·55 N	107·50 W
183	Telok Datok.Mala. (Singapore In.)	2·51 N	101·33 E
124	Teloloapan (tā'lô-lô-ä'pän)...Mex.	18·19 N	99·54 W
170	Tel'pos-Iz, Gora (Mtn.) (tyĕl'pôs-ēz').Sov. Un.	63·50 N	59·20 E
157	Telšiai (tĕl'sha'ê)........Sov. Un.	55·59 N	22·17 E
149	Teltow (tĕl'tō).G.D.R. (Berlin In.)	52·24 N	13·12 E
183	Telukletjak.Indon. (Singapore In.)	1·53 N	101·45 E
214	Tema.....................Ghana	5·38 N	0·01 E
124	Temascalcingo (tā'mäs-käl-sĭŋ'gō).Mex.	19·55 N	100·00 W
124	Temascaltepec (tā'mäs-käl-tȧ pĕk).Mex.	19·00 N	100·03 W
126	Temax (tĕ'mäx).......Mex. (In.)	21·10 N	88·51 W
171	Temir (tyĕ'mêr).........Sov. Un.	49·10 N	57·15 E
172	Temir-Tau.............Sov. Un.	50·08 N	73·13 E
97	Témiscaming (tê-mĭs'kȧ-mĭng) Can.	46·40 N	78·50 W
98	Temiscouata (L.) (tĕ'mĭs-kōō-ä'tä).Can.	47·40 N	68·50 W
125	Temoaya (tĕ-mô-ä-yä)..Mex. (In.)	19·28 N	99·36 W
136	Temperley (tĕ'm-pĕr-lā).Arg. (In.)	34·32 S	58·24 W
164	Tempio Pausania (tĕm'pê-ō pou-sä'nê-ä).It.	40·55 N	9·05 E
119	Temple (tĕm'p'l)............Tx.	31·06 N	97·20 W
113	Temple City.Ca. (Los Angeles In.)	34·07 N	118·02 W
100	Templeton (tĕm'p'l-tŭn) Can. (Ottawa In.)	45·29 N	75·37 W
158	Templin (tĕm-plēn')......G.D.R.	53·08 N	13·30 E
124	Tempoal (R.) (tĕm-pô-ä'l)...Mex.	21·38 N	98·23 W
167	Temryuk (tyĕm-ryŏŏk')..Sov. Un.	45·17 N	37·21 E
136	Temuco (tȧ-mōō'kō)........Chile	38·46 S	72·38 W
174	Temyasovo (tĕm-yä'sô-vô) Sov. Un. (Urals In.)	53·00 N	58·06 E
126	Tenabó (tĕ-nä-bŏ')....Mex. (In.)	20·05 N	90·11 W
185	Tenāli....................India	16·10 N	80·32 E
124	Tenamaxtlán (tā'nä-mäs-tlän') Mex.	20·13 N	104·06 W
124	Tenancingo (tȧ-nän-sēŋ'gō)..Mex.	18·54 N	99·36 W
125	Tenango (tȧ-näŋ'gō)...Mex. (In.)	19·09 N	98·51 W
196	Tenasserim (tĕn-ăs'ēr-ĭm)....Bur.	12·09 N	99·01 E
167	Tenderovskaya Kosa (C.) (tĕn-dĕ-rôf'skȧ-yȧ kô-sä') Sov. Un.	46·12 N	31·17 E
	Tenedos, see Bozcaada		
215	Ténéré (Des.).............Niger	19·23 N	10·15 E
210	Tenerife I. (tȧ-nȧ-rē'fȧ) (tĕn-ēr-ĭf').Can. Is.	28·41 N	17·02 W
151	Ténés (tā-nĕs')..............Alg.	36·28 N	1·22 E
190	T'enghsien (tĕng'hsē-ĕn')....China	35·07 N	117·08 E
172	Tengiz (L.) (tyĭn-gēz')...Sov. Un.	50·45 N	68·39 E
195	Tenjin (tĕn'jēn)..Jap. (Ōsaka In.)	34·54 N	135·04 E
217	Tenke (tĕŋ'kȧ)..............Zaire	11·26 S	26·45 E
117	Tenkiller Ferry Res. (tĕn-kĭl'ēr) Ok.	35·42 N	94·47 W
214	Tenkodogo (tĕŋ-kô-dŏ'gô) Upper Volta	11·47 N	0·22 W
112	Tenmile (R.) (tĕn mīl) Wa. (Vancouver In.)	48·52 N	122·32 W
204	Tennant Creek (tĕn'ănt)....Austl.	19·45 S	134·00 E
103	Tennessee (State) (tĕn-ĕ-sē')..U. S.	35·50 N	88·00 W
103	Tennessee (L.)..............U. S.	35·35 N	88·20 W
120	Tennessee (R.)..............U. S.	35·10 N	88·20 W
120	Tennille (tĕn'ĭl).............Ga.	32·55 N	86·50 W
137	Teno (tĕ'nô) (R.) Chile (Santiago In.)	34·55 S	71·00 W
203	Tenora (tĕn-ôrȧ)...........Austl.	34·23 S	147·33 E
125	Tenosique (tā-nô-sē'kȧ)......Mex.	17·27 N	91·25 W
195	Tenri..........Jap. (Ōsaka In.)	34·36 N	135·50 E
195	Tenryū-Gawa (Strm.) (tĕn'ryōō'gä'wä).Jap.	35·16 N	137·54 E
119	Tensas R. (tĕn'sô)............La.	31·54 N	91·30 W
120	Tensaw (R.) (tĕn'sô)..........Al.	30·45 N	87·52 W
203	Tenterfield (tĕn'tēr-fēld)....Austl.	29·00 S	152·06 E
121	Ten Thousand, Is. (tĕn thou'zănd).Fl. (In.)	25·45 N	81·35 W
124	Teocaltiche (tā'ô-käl-tē'chȧ).Mex.	21·27 N	102·38 W
125	Teocelo (tā-ô-sā'lō).........Mex.	19·22 N	96·57 W
124	Teocuitatlán de Corona (tā'ô-kwē'tä-tlän' dā kō-rō'nä) Mex.	20·06 N	103·22 W
135	Teófilo Otoni (tĕ-ô'fē-lō-tô'nê) Braz.	17·49 S	41·18 W
124	Teoloyucan (tā'ô-lô-yōō'kän).Mex.	19·43 N	99·12 W
125	Teopisca (tā-ô-pēs'kä).......Mex.	16·30 N	92·33 W
125	Teotihuacán (tĕ-ô-tē-wȧ-kȧ'n) Mex. (In.)	19·40 N	98·52 W
125	Teotitlán del Camino (tā-ô-tē-tlän' dĕl kä-mē'nô).Mex.	18·07 N	97·04 W
124	Tepalcatepec (tā'päl-kä-tȧ'pĕk) Mex.	19·11 N	102·51 W
124	Tepalcatepec (R.)..........Mex.	18·54 N	102·25 W
124	Tepalcingo (tā-päl-sēŋ'gô)...Mex.	18·34 N	98·49 W
124	Tepatitlan de Morelos (tā-pä-tê-tlän' dā mô-rā'lôs) Mex.	20·15 N	102·47 W
125	Tepeaca (tā-pȧ-ä'kä)........Mex.	18·57 N	97·54 W
124	Tepecoacuiloc de Trujano (tā'pȧ-kō'ä-kwēl'kō dā trōō-hä'nō).Mex.	19·15 N	99·29 W
124	Tepeji del Rio (tā-pȧ-ĸe' dĕl rē'ō) Mex.	19·55 N	99·22 W

ng-sing; ŋ-baŋk; ɴ-nasalized n; nŏd; cŏmmit; ōld; ôbey; ôrder; fōōd; fŏŏt; ou-out; s-soft; sh-dish; th-thin; pūre; ûnite; ûrn; stŭd; circŭs; ü-as "y" in study; '-indeterminate vowel.

ăt; fĭnăl; rāte; senâte; ärm; ásk; sofá; fâre; ch-choose; dh-as th in other; bē; ĕvent; bĕt; recĕnt; cratĕr; g-go; gh-guttural g; bĭt; ĭ-short neutral; rīde; κ-guttural k as ch in German ich;

Page	Name Pronunciation Region	Lat. °'	Long. °'
	Tientsin, see T'ienching		
190	Tietsin-Shih (Mun.) . . . . China	39·30 N	117·13 E
193	T'ientung . . . . China	23·32 N	107·10 E
156	Tierp (tyĕrp) . . . . Swe.	60·21 N	17·28 E
213	Tierpoort . . . . S. Afr. (Johannesburg & Pretoria In.)	25·53 S	28·26 E
125	Tierra Blanca (tyĕ'r-rä-blä'n-kä) Mex.	18·28 N	96·19 W
136	Tierra del Fuego (Reg.) (tyĕr'rä dĕl fwā'gô) . Chile-Arg.	53·50 S	68·45 W
162	Tiétar (R.) (tê-ā'tär) . . . . Sp.	39·56 N	5·44 W
137	Tietê (tyā-tā') Braz. (Rio de Janeiro In.)	23·08 S	47·42 W
135	Tieté (R.) . . . . Braz.	20·46 S	50·46 W
104	Tiffin (tĭf'ĭn) . . . . Oh.	41·10 N	83·15 W
120	Tifton (tĭf'tŭn) . . . . Ga.	31·25 N	83·34 W
112	Tigard (tī'gärd) . Or. (Portland In.)	45·25 N	122·46 W
98	Tignish (tĭg'nĭsh) . . . . Can.	46·57 N	64·02 W
174	Tigoda R. (tē'gô-dà) Sov. Un. (Leningrad In.)	59·29 N	31·15 E
136	Tigre (tê'grĕ) . . . . Arg. (In.)	34·09 S	58·35 W
134	Tigre (R.) . . . . Peru	2·20 S	75·41 W
212	Tigres, Península dos (Pen.) (pĕ-nê'ŋ-sōō-lä-dôs-tê'grĕs) . Ang.	16·30 S	11·45 E
186	Tigris (R.) . . . . Asia	34·45 N	44·10 E
183	Tīh, Jabal at (Mts.) Egypt (Palestine In.)	29·23 N	34·05 E
125	Tihuatlán (tê-wä-tlän') . . . . . . Mex.	20·43 N	97·34 W
114	Tijuana (tê-hwä'nä) . . . Mex. (In.)	32·32 N	117·02 W
136	Tijuca, Pico da (Mtn.) (pē'kō-dä-tē-zhōō'kå) Braz. (Rio de Janeiro In.)	22·56 S	43·17 W
126	Tikal (Ruins) (tê-käl') . Guat. (In.)	17·16 N	89·49 W
171	Tikhoretsk (tê-ĸôr-yĕtsk') Sov. Un.	45·55 N	40·05 E
166	Tikhvin (têĸ-vēn') . . . . . . Sov. Un.	59·36 N	33·38 E
186	Tikrīt . . . . Iraq	34·36 N	43·31 E
173	Tiksi (têk-sē') . . . . Sov. Un.	71·42 N	128·32 E
149	Tilburg (tĭl'bûrg) Neth. (Amsterdam In.)	51·33 N	5·05 E
214	Tilemsi, Vallée du (Val.) . . . . . Mali	17·50 N	0·25 E
173	Tilichiki (tyĭ-le-chĭ-kê) . . . Sov. Un.	60·49 N	166·14 E
167	Tiligul (R.) (tē'lĭ-gûl) . . . Sov. Un.	47·25 N	30·27 E
210	Tillabéry (tē-yà-bā-rē') . . . . . Niger	14·14 N	1·30 E
110	Tillamook (tĭl'ȧ-mŏŏk) . . . . Or.	45·27 N	123·50 W
110	Tillamook B. . . . . Or.	45·32 N	124·26 W
156	Tillberga (tēl-bĕr'ghȧ) . . . . Swe.	59·40 N	16·34 E
97	Tillsonburg (tĭl'sŭn-bûrg) . . . . Can.	42·50 N	80·50 W
	Tilsit, see Sovetsk		
167	Tim (têm) . . . . Sov. Un.	51·39 N	37·07 E
205	Timaru (tĭm'á-rōō) . . . . N. Z. (In.)	44·26 S	171·17 E
167	Timashevskaya (tĕmă-shĕfs-kă'yă) . . . . . Sov. Un.	45·47 N	38·57 E
119	Timbalier B. (tĭm'bȧ-lēr) . . . . . . La.	28·55 N	90·14 W
112	Timber (tĭm'bĕr) Or. (Portland In.)	45·43 N	123·17 W
210	Timbo (tĭm'bō) . . . . Gui.	10·41 N	11·51 W
	Timbuktu, see Tombouctou		
156	Time (tē'mĕ) . . . . Nor.	58·45 N	5·39 E
214	Timétrine Monts (Mts.) . . . . . Mali.	19·50 N	0·30 W
210	Timimoun (tē-mê-mōōn') . . . . . Alg.	29·14 N	0·22 E
214	Timiris, Cap (C.) . . . . . Mauritania	19·23 N	16·32 W
165	Timis (R.) . . . . Rom.	45·28 N	21·06 E
91	Timiskaming Station (tê-mĭs'kȧ-mĭng) . Can.	46·41 N	79·01 W
91	Timmins (tĭm'ĭnz) . . . . Can.	48·25 N	81·22 W
121	Timmonsville (tĭm'ŭnz-vĭl) . . . . SC	34·09 N	79·55 W
197	Timor (I.) (tê-mōr') . . . . Indon.	10·08 S	125·00 E
198	Timor Sea . . . . Asia	12·40 S	125·00 E
165	Timoşoara . . . . Rom.	45·44 N	21·21 E
115	Timpanogos Cave Natl. Mon. (tĭ-măn'ō-gŏz) . Ut.	40·25 N	111·45 W
119	Timpson (tĭmp'sŭn) . . . . Tx.	31·55 N	94·24 W
173	Timpton (R.) (têmp'tôn) . Sov. Un.	57·15 N	126·35 E
218	Timsāh (L.) (tĭm'sä) Egypt (Suez In.)	30·34 N	32·22 E
129	Tina, Monte (Mtn.) (mô'n-tĕ-tē'nȧ) . Dom. Rep.	18·50 N	70·40 W
213	Tina (R.) (tē'nȧ) S. Afr. (Natal In.)	30·50 S	28·44 E
135	Tinaguillo (tê-nä-gē'l-yô) Ven. (In.)	9·55 N	68·18 W
183	Tīnah, Khalīj at (G.) Egypt (Palestine In.)	31·06 N	32·42 E
210	Tindouf (tên-dōōf') . . . . Alg.	27·43 N	7·44 W
183	Tinggi, Palau (I.) Mala. (Singapore In.)	2·16 N	104·16 E
190	T'ingho (dĭng'hŭ) . . . . China	37·45 N	118·29 E
190	Tinghsien (dĭng'sĭän) . . . . China	38·30 N	115·00 E
190	Tinghsing (dĭng'sĭng) . . . . China	39·18 N	115·50 E
214	Tingi Mts. . . . . S. L.	9·00 N	10·50 W
191	Tinglin . . . . . China (Shanghai In.)	30·53 N	121·18 E
134	Tingo María (tē'ngō-mä-rē'ä) . Peru	9·15 S	76·04 W
214	Tingréla . . . . Ivory Coast	10·29 N	6·24 W
156	Tingsryd (tĭngs'rüd) . . . . Swe.	56·32 N	14·58 E
190	Tingtzu Wan (B.) (dĭng'tze wän) China	36·33 N	121·06 E
124	Tinguindio Paracho (tēn'kē'n-dyō-pärä-chô) . Mex.	19·38 N	102·02 W
137	Tinguiririca (R.) (tē'n-gē-rē-rē'kä) Chile (Santiago In.)	36·48 S	70·45 W
190	Tingyüan (tĭng'yü-än') . . . . . China	32·32 N	117·40 E
107	Tinley Park (tĭn'lê) Il. (Chicago In.)	41·34 N	87·47 W
156	Tinnosset (tĕn'nôs'sĕt) . . . . Nor.	59·44 N	9·00 E
156	Tinnsjö (tĭnnsyû) . . . . Nor.	59·55 N	8·49 E
136	Tinogasta (tē-nô-gäs'tä) . . . . . . Arg.	28·07 S	67·30 W
165	Tínos (I.) . . . . Grc.	37·45 N	25·12 E
210	Tinrhert, Plat. du . . . . Alg.	27·30 N	7·30 E
187	Tinsukia (tin-sōō'kĭ-à) . . . . . . India	27·18 N	95·29 E
115	Tintic (tĭn'tĭk) . . . . Ut.	39·55 N	112·15 W
211	Tin Toumma Steppe (Plat.) (tīn tōōm'à) . Niger	16·16 N	13·06 E
214	Tio, Pic de (Pk.) . . . . Gui.	8·55 N	8·55 W
183	Tioman (I.) . Mala. (Singapore In.)	2·25 N	104·30 E
126	Tipitapa (tē-pê-tä'pä) . . . . Nic.	12·14 N	86·05 W
126	Tipitapa R. . . . . Nic.	12·13 N	85·57 W
120	Tippah Cr., (R.) (tĭp'pȧ) . . . . . Ms.	34·43 N	88·15 W
104	Tippecanoe (R.) (tĭp-ê-kȧ-nōō') . In.	40·55 N	86·45 W
154	Tipperary (tĭ-pē-râ'rê) . . . . Ire.	52·28 N	8·13 W
117	Tippo Bay. (tĭp'ō bīōō') . . . . . . Ms.	33·35 N	90·06 W
104	Tipton . . . . In.	40·15 N	86·00 W
109	Tipton . . . . Ia.	41·46 N	91·10 W
165	Tirane (tê-rä'nä) . . . . Alb.	41·18 N	19·50 E
164	Tirano (tê-rä'nō) . . . . It.	46·12 N	10·09 E
167	Tiraspol' (tê-räs'pôl') . . . . Sov. Un.	46·52 N	29·38 E
171	Tire (tē'rĕ) . . . . Tur.	38·05 N	27·48 E
154	Tiree (I.) (tī-rē') . . . . Scot.	56·34 N	6·30 W
165	Tîrgovişte . . . . Rom.	44·54 N	25·29 E
165	Tîrgu-Jiu . . . . Rom.	45·02 N	23·17 E
159	Tîrgu-Mureş . . . . Rom.	46·33 N	24·35 E
159	Tîrgu Neamt . . . . Rom.	47·14 N	26·23 E
159	Tîrgu-Ocna . . . . Rom.	46·18 N	26·38 E
159	Tîrgu Săcuesc . . . . Rom.	46·04 N	26·06 E
184	Tirich Mir (Mt.) . . . . Pak.	36·50 N	71·48 E
174	Tirlyanskiy (tĭr-lyän'skĭ) Sov. Un. (Urals In.)	54·13 N	58·37 E
165	Tírnavos . . . . Grc.	39·50 N	22·14 E
159	Tîrnăveni . . . . Rom.	46·19 N	24·18 E
158	Tirol (State) (tê-rōl') . . . . Aus.	47·13 N	11·10 E
164	Tirso (R.) (tēr'sô) . . . . It.	40·15 N	9·03 E
185	Tiruchchirāppalli (tĭr'ŏŏ-chĭ-rä'pȧ-lĭ) . India	10·49 N	78·48 E
185	Tirunelveli . . . . India	8·53 N	77·43 E
185	Tiruppur . . . . India	11·11 N	77·08 E
94	Tisdale (tĭz'dāl) . . . . Can.	52·51 N	104·04 W
184	Tista (R.) . . . . India	26·03 N	88·52 E
165	Tisza (R.) (tē'sä) . . . . Yugo.	45·50 N	20·13 E
159	Tisza R. (tē'sä) . . . . Hung.	46·30 N	20·08 E
184	Titāgarh . . . . India (In.)	22·44 N	88·23 E
134	Titicaca, Lago (L.) (lä'gô-tē-tē-kä'kä) . Bol.-Peru	16·12 S	70·33 W
134	Titiribi (tē-tē-rē-bē') . . . . Col. (In.)	6·05 N	75·47 W
217	Tito, Lagh (R.) . . . . Ken.	2·25 N	39·05 E
165	Titograd . . . . Yugo.	42·25 N	20·42 E
165	Titovo Užice (tê'tô-vô ōō'zhê-tsĕ) Yugo.	43·51 N	19·53 E
165	Titov Veles (tê'tôv vĕ'lĕs) . . Yugo.	41·42 N	21·50 E
216	Titule . . . . Zaire	3·17 N	25·32 E
121	Titusville (tī'tŭs-vĭl) . . . . . Fl. (In.)	28·37 N	80·44 W
105	Titusville . . . . Pa.	40·40 N	79·40 W
161	Titz (tētz) . . . . F.R.G. (Ruhr In.)	51·00 N	6·26 E
106	Tiverton (tĭv'ĕr-tŭn) RI (Providence In.)	41·38 N	71·11 W
163	Tivoli (tē'vô-lē) . . . . It. (Rome In.)	41·58 N	12·48 E
126	Tixkokob (tēx-kō-kō'b) . Mex. (In.)	21·01 N	89·23 W
124	Tixtla de Guerrero (tē'x-tlä-dĕ-gĕr-rĕ'rô) . Mex.	17·36 N	99·24 W
196	Tizard Bk. and Rf. (tĭz'ȧrd) . China	10·51 N	113·20 E
126	Tizimín (tē-zē-mē'n) . . . Mex. (In.)	21·08 N	88·10 W
210	Tizi-Ouzou (tē'zê-ōō-zōō') . . . . Alg.	36·44 N	4·04 E
135	Tiznados (R.) (têz-nä'dôs) Ven. (In.)	9·53 N	67·49 W
210	Tiznit (têz-nēt) . . . . Mor.	29·52 N	9·39 W
196	Tjirebon . . . . Indon.	6·50 S	108·33 E
125	Tlacolula de Matamoros (tlä-kô-lōō'lä dā mätä-mō'rôs) Mex.	16·56 N	96·29 W
125	Tlacotálpan (tlä-kô-täl'pän) . Mex.	18·39 N	95·40 W
124	Talcotepec (tlä-kô-tȧ-pĕ'k) . . Mex.	17·46 N	99·57 W
125	Tlacotepec . . . . Mex.	18·41 N	97·40 W
124	Tlacotepec . . . . Mex.	19·11 N	99·41 W
125	Tláhuac (tlä-wäk') . . . . . Mex. (In.)	19·16 N	99·00 W
124	Tlajomulco de Zúñiga (tlä-hô-mōō'l-ko-dĕ-zōō'n-yē-gä) Mex.	20·30 N	103·27 W
124	Tlalchapa (tläl-chä'pä) . . . . . . Mex.	18·26 N	100·29 W
125	Tlalixcoyan (tlä-lēs'kō-yän') . Mex.	18·53 N	96·04 W
125	Tlalmanalco (tläl-mä-nä'l-kô) Mex. (In.)	19·12 N	98·48 W
125	Tlalnepantia (tläl-nĕ-pá'n-tyä) Mex. (In.)	19·32 N	99·13 W
125	Tlalnepantla (tläl-nȧ-pán'tlä) Mex. (In.)	18·59 N	99·01 W
125	Tlalpan (tläl-pä'n) . . . . Mex. (In.)	19·17 N	99·10 W
124	Tlalpujahua (tläl-pōō-ĸä'wä) . Mex.	19·50 N	100·10 W
	Tlaltenango, see Sánchez Román		
124	Tlapa (tlä'pä) . . . . Mex.	17·30 N	98·09 W
125	Tlapacoyan (tlä-pä-kô-yá'n) . Mex.	19·57 N	97·11 W
124	Tlapaneco (R.) (tlä-pä-nĕ'kô) Mex.	17·59 N	98·44 W
124	Tlapehuala (tlä-pȧ-wä'lä) . . . . Mex.	18·17 N	100·30 W
124	Tlaquepaque (tlä-kĕ-pä'kĕ) . . Mex.	20·39 N	103·17 W
124	Tlatlaya (tlä-tlä'yä) . . . . Mex.	18·36 N	100·14 W
124	Tlaxcala (tläs-kä'lä) . . . . Mex.	19·16 N	98·14 W
124	Tlaxcala (State) . . . . Mex.	19·30 N	98·15 W
124	Tlaxco (tläs'kō) . . . . Mex.	19·37 N	98·06 W
125	Tlaxiaco Sta. Maria Asunción (tläk-sē-ä'kō sän'tä mä-rē'ä ä-sōōn-syōn') . Mex.	17·16 N	95·41 W
125	Tlayacapan (tlä-yä-kä-pä'n) Mex. (In.)	18·57 N	99·00 W
210	Tlemcen (tlĕm-sĕn') . . . . Alg.	34·53 N	1·21 W
92	Tlevak Str. . . . . Ak.	55·03 N	132·58 W
159	Tlumach (t'lû-mäch') . . . . Sov. Un.	48·47 N	25·00 E
129	Toa (R.) (tō'ä) . . . . Cuba	20·25 N	74·35 W
111	Toana Ra. (Mts.) (tō-ȧ-nō') . . . Nv.	40·45 N	114·11 W
129	Toar, Cuchillas de (Mtn.) (kōō-chē'l-lyäs-dĕ-tô-ä'r) . Cuba	18·20 N	74·50 W
123	Tobago (I.) (tô-bā'gō) . . . . . . N. A.	11·15 N	60·30 W
92	Toba Inlet . . . . Can.	50·20 N	124·50 W
162	Tobarra (tô-bär'rä) . . . . Sp.	38·37 N	1·42 W
172	Tobol (R.) (tô-bôl') . . . . . . Sov. Un.	56·02 N	65·30 E
172	Tobol'sk (tô-bôlsk') . . . . . . Sov. Un.	58·09 N	68·28 E
134	Tocaima (tô-kä'y-mä) . . . Col. (In.)	4·28 N	74·38 W
135	Tocantinópolis (tō-kän-tē-nŏ'pō-lēs) . Braz.	6·27 S	47·18 W
135	Tocantins (R.) (tō-kän-tēns') . Braz.	3·28 S	49·22 W
120	Toccoa (tŏk'ô-ȧ) . . . . Ga.	34·35 N	83·20 W
120	Toccoa (R.) . . . . Ga.	34·53 N	84·24 W
195	Tochigi (tō'chē-gī) . . . . Jap.	36·25 N	139·45 E
190	T'ochi Tao (I.) (tōōŭ'jē dou) China	38·11 N	120·45 E
126	Tocoa (tō-kô'ä) . . . . Hond.	15·37 N	86·01 W
136	Tocopilla (tô-kō-pēl'yä) . . . . . Chile	22·03 S	70·08 W
135	Tocuyo de la Costa (tô-kōō'yō-dĕ-lä-kôs'tä) Ven. (In.)	11·03 N	68·24 W
195	Toda . . . . Jap. (Tōkyō In.)	35·48 N	139·42 E
148	Todmorden (tŏd'môr-dĕn) . . . Eng.	53·43 N	2·05 W
214	Tóecé . . . . Upper Volta	11·50 N	1·16 W
92	Tofino (tō-fē'nō) . . . . Can.	49·09 N	125·54 W
156	Töfsingdalens (Natl. Park) . . . Swe.	62·09 N	13·05 E
195	Tōgane (tō'gä-nā) . . . . Jap.	35·29 N	140·16 E
196	Togian, Kepulauan (Is.) . . . Indon.	0·20 S	122·00 E
209	Togo (tō'gō) . . . . Afr.	8·00 N	0·52 E
174	Toguzak R. (tô'gōō-zák) Sov. Un. (Urals In.)	53·40 N	61·42 E
121	Tohopekaliga (L.) (tō'hô-pē'kȧ-lī'gȧ) . Fl. (In.)	28·16 N	81·09 W
190	To'Hu (L.) (tōōŭ'hōō) . . . . . . China	33·07 N	117·25 E
157	Toijala (toi'yȧ-lȧ) . . . . Fin.	61·11 N	21·46 E
195	Toi-Misaki (C.) (toi mē'sä-kê) . Jap.	31·20 N	131·20 E
114	Toiyabe Ra. (toi'yă-bē) . . . . . . Nv.	38·59 N	117·22 W
194	Tokachi Gawa (R.) (tō-kä'chê gä'wä) . Jap.	43·10 N	142·30 E
159	Tokaj (tô'kô-ê) . . . . Hung.	48·06 N	21·24 E
194	Tokara Guntō (Is.) (tō-kä'rä gōōn'tō') . Jap.	29·45 N	129·15 E
194	Tokara Kaikyo (Str.) (tō'kä-rä kī'kyō) . Jap.	30·20 N	129·50 E
171	Tokat (tô-kät') . . . . Tur.	40·20 N	36·30 E
198	Tokelau Is. (tō-kê-lä'ōō) . . Oceania	8·00 S	176·00 W
172	Tokmak (tôk'màk) . . . . . . Sov. Un.	42·44 N	75·41 E
195	Tokorozawa (tō'kô-rô-zä'wä) Jap. (Tōkyō In.)	35·47 N	139·29 E
194	Tokuno (I.) (tô-kōō'nō) . . . . . . Jap.	27·42 N	129·25 E
195	Tokushima (tō'kōō'shē-mä) . . . Jap.	34·06 N	134·31 E
195	Tokuyama (tō'kōō'yä-mä) . . . Jap.	34·04 N	131·49 E
195	Tōkyō (tō'kê-ō) . Jap. (Tōkyō In.)	35·41 N	139·44 E
195	Tōkyō (Pref.) . . . . Jap. (Tōkyō In.)	35·42 N	139·40 E
195	Tōkyō-Wan (B.) (tō'kyō wän) Jap. (Tōkyō In.)	35·32 N	139·56 E
165	Tolbukhin . . . . Bul.	43·33 N	27·52 E
124	Tolcayuca (tôl-kä-yōō'kä) . . . Mex.	19·55 N	98·54 W
109	Toledo (tô-lē'dō) . . . . Ia.	41·59 N	92·35 W
104	Toledo . . . . Oh.	41·40 N	83·35 W
110	Toledo . . . . Or.	44·37 N	123·58 W
162	Toledo (tô-lĕ'dô) . . . . Sp.	39·53 N	4·02 W
162	Toledo, Montes de (Mts.) (mô'n-tĕs-dĕ-tô-lĕ'dô) . Sp.	39·33 N	4·40 W
103	Toledo Bend Res. . . . . La.-Tx.	31·30 N	93·30 W
134	Tolima (Dept.) (tô-lē'mä) Col. (In.)	4·07 N	75·20 W
134	Tolima, Nevado del (Pk.) (nĕ-vä-dô-dĕl-tô-lē'mä) . Col. (In.)	4·40 N	75·20 W
124	Tolimán (tô-lê-män') . . . . Mex.	20·54 N	99·54 W
148	Tollesbury (tōl'z-bĕrĭ) Eng. (London In.)	51·46 N	0·49 E
164	Tolmezzo (tôl-mĕt'zô) . . . . It.	46·25 N	13·03 E
164	Tolmin (tôl'mên) . . . . Yugo.	46·12 N	13·45 E
159	Tolna (tôl'nô) . . . . Hung.	46·25 N	18·47 E
196	Tolo, Teluk (B.) (tō'lō) . . . . Indon.	2·00 S	122·06 E
162	Tolosa (tô-lō'sä) . . . . Sp.	43·10 N	2·05 W
112	Tolt (R.) (tōlt) . . Wa. (Seattle In.)	47·13 N	121·49 W

Page	Name Pronunciation Region	Lat. °′	Long. °′
104	Toluca (tô-lo͞o'kȧ) Il.	41·00 N	89·10 W
125	Toluca (tô-lo͞o'kä) Mex. (In.)	19·17 N	99·40 W
125	Toluca, Nevado de (Mtn.) (nĕ-vä-dô-dĕ-tô-lo͞o'kä) Mex. (In.)	19·09 N	99·42 W
192	Tolun China	42·12 N	116·15 E
170	Tolyatti Sov. Un.	53·30 N	49·10 E
172	Tom' (R.) Sov. Un.	55·33 N	85·00 E
109	Tomah (tō'mȧ) Wi.	43·58 N	90·31 W
109	Tomahawk (tŏm'ȧ-hôk) Wi.	45·27 N	89·44 W
167	Tomakovka (tô-mä'kôf-kȧ) Sov. Un.	47·49 N	34·43 E
162	Tomar (tō-mär') Port.	39·36 N	8·26 W
159	Tomashevka (tô-mȧ'shĕf-kȧ) Sov. Un.	51·34 N	23·37 E
159	Tomaszow Lubelski (tô-mä'sho͝of lo͞o-bĕl'skĭ) Pol.	50·20 N	23·27 E
159	Tomaszów Mazowiecki (tô-mä'sho͝of mä-zô'vyĕt-skĭ) Pol.	51·33 N	20·00 E
124	Tomatlán (tô-mä-tlä'n) Mex.	19·54 N	105·14 W
124	Tomatlán (R.) Mex.	19·56 N	105·14 W
214	Tombadonkéa Gui.	11·00 N	14·23 W
135	Tombador, Serra do (Mts.) (sĕr'rȧ do͞o tōm-bä-dôr') Braz.	11·31 S	57·33 W
120	Tombigbee (R.) (tŏm-bĭg'bē) Al.	31·45 N	88·02 W
137	Tombos (tô'm-bōs) Braz. (Rio de Janeiro In.)	20·53 S	42·00 W
214	Tombouctou (Timbuktu) (tôm-bo͞ok-to͞o') Mali	16·46 N	3·01 W
115	Tombstone (to͞om'stōn) Az.	31·40 N	110·00 W
156	Tomelilla (tô'mĕ-lēl-lä) Swe.	55·34 N	13·55 E
162	Tomelloso (tō-māl-lyō'sō) Sp.	39·09 N	3·02 W
196	Tomini, Teluk (B.) (tô-mē'nē) Indon.	0·10 N	121·00 E
173	Tommot (tŏm-mŏt') Sov. Un.	59·13 N	126·22 E
172	Tomsk (tŏmsk) Sov. Un.	56·29 N	84·57 E
125	Tonalá (tō-nä-lä') Mex.	16·05 N	93·45 W
124	Tonala Mex.	20·38 N	103·14 W
125	Tonalá (R.) Mex.	18·05 N	94·08 W
107	Tonawanda (tŏn-ȧ-wŏn'dȧ) NY (Buffalo In.)	43·01 N	78·53 W
107	Tonawanda Cr... NY (Buffalo In.)	43·05 N	78·43 W
148	Tonbridge (tŭn-brij) Eng. (London In.)	51·11 N	0·17 E
195	Tonda (tôn'dä)... Jap. (Ōsaka In.)	34·51 N	135·38 E
195	Tondabayashi (tôn-dä-bä'yä-shē) Jap. (Ōsaka In.)	34·29 N	135·36 E
197	Tondano (tôn-dä'nō) Indon.	1·15 N	124·50 E
156	Tønder (tûn'nĕr) Den.	54·47 N	8·49 E
125	Tondlá Mex.	16·04 N	93·57 W
195	Tone (R.) (tō'nē). Jap. (Tōkyō In.)	35·55 N	139·57 E
195	Tone-Gawa (Strm.) (tô'nē gä'wa) Jap.	36·12 N	139·19 E
198	Tonga (tŏŋ'gȧ) Oceania	18·50 S	175·20 W
215	Tongo Cam.	5·11 N	14·00 E
136	Tongoy (tōn-goi') Chile	30·16 S	71·29 W
	Tongue of Arabat (Spit), see Arabatskaya Strelka		
128	Tongue of the Ocean (Chan.) (tŭng ŏv thē ōshŭn). Ba.	24·05 N	77·20 W
111	Tongue R. (tŭng) Mt.	45·08 N	106·40 W
211	Tonj R. (tônj) Sud.	6·18 N	28·33 E
184	Tonk (Tŏŋk) India	26·13 N	75·45 E
117	Tonkawa (tŏŋ'kȧ-wô) Ok.	36·42 N	97·19 W
193	Tonkin, Gulf of (tôn-kăn')... Viet.	20·30 N	108·10 E
196	Tonle Sap (L.) (tôn'lā säp'). Camb.	13·03 N	102·49 E
160	Tonneins (tô-năn') Fr.	44·24 N	0·18 E
158	Tönning (tû'nēng) F.R.G.	54·20 N	8·55 E
114	Tonopah (tō-nô-pä') Nv.	38·04 N	117·15 W
156	Tönsberg (tûns'bĕrgh) Nor.	59·19 N	10·25 E
125	Tonto (R.) (tōn'tō) Mex.	18·15 N	96·13 W
115	Tonto Cr. Az.	34·05 N	111·15 W
115	Tonto Natl. Mon. (tôn'tô).... Az.	33·33 N	111·08 W
113	Tooele (to͝o-ĕl'ē) Ut. (Salt Lake City In.)	40·33 N	112·17 W
193	Toohsien China	25·30 N	111·32 E
203	Toowoomba (to͞o wo͞om'bȧ). Aust.	27·32 S	152·10 E
113	Topanga (tō'păn-gȧ) Ca. (Los Angeles In.)	34·05 N	118·36 W
117	Topeka (tô-pē'kȧ) Ks.	39·02 N	95·41 W
125	Topilejo (tô-pē-lĕ'hô).. Mex. (In.)	19·12 N	99·09 W
115	Topock Az.	34·40 N	114·20 W
159	Topol'čany (tô-pôl'chä-nü). Czech.	48·38 N	18·10 E
122	Topolobampo (tō-pō-lô-bä'm-pô) Mex.	25·45 N	109·00 W
165	Topolovgrad Bul.	42·05 N	26·19 E
110	Toppenish (tôp'ĕn-ĭsh) Wa.	46·22 N	120·00 W
214	Tora, Île (I.) Mauritania	19·50 N	16·45 W
99	Torbay (tôr-bā') Can.	47·40 N	52·43 W
	Torbay, see Torquay		
203	Torbreck, Mt. (tôr-brĕk)... Austl.	37·05 S	146·55 E
104	Torch (L.) (tôrch) Mi.	45·00 N	85·30 W
156	Töreboda (tû'rĕ-bō'dä) Swe.	58·44 N	14·04 E
155	Torhout Bel.	51·01 N	3·04 E
134	Toribío (tō-rē-bē'ō) Col. (In.)	2·58 N	76·14 W
195	Toride (tô'rē-dā). Jap. (Tōkyō In.)	35·54 N	140·04 E
164	Torino (Turin) (tô-rē'no) (tū'rĭn) It.	45·05 N	7·44 E
150	Torino (R.) (tôr'nĭ-ô)... Fin.-Swe.	67·00 N	23·50 E
162	Tormes (R.) (tōr'mās) Sp.	41·12 N	6·15 W
150	Torne (R.) (tôr'nĕ) Swe.	67·29 N	21·44 E
150	Torne Träsk (L.) (tôr'nĕ trĕsk) Swe.	68·10 N	20·36 E
91	Torngat Mts. Can.	59·18 N	64·35 W
150	Tornio (tôr'nĭ-ô) Fin.	65·55 N	24·09 E
98	Toro, Lac (L.) Can.	46·53 N	73·46 W
165	Toronaíos Kólpos (G.) Grc.	40·10 N	23·35 E
100	Toronto (tô-rŏn'tō) Can. (Toronto In.)	43·40 N	79·23 W
104	Toronto Oh.	40·30 N	80·35 W
118	Toronto, L. (lä'gô-tô-rô'n-tō). Mex.	27·35 N	105·37 W
166	Toropets (tô'rô-pyĕts)... Sov. Un.	56·31 N	31·37 E
171	Toros Dağlari (Taurus Mts.) (tô'rŭs). Tur.	37·00 N	32·40 E
163	Torote (R.) (tô-rō'tā) Sp. (Madrid In.)	40·36 N	3·24 W
156	Torp (tôrp) Swe.	62·30 N	16·04 E
	Torpen, see Åmot		
154	Torquay (Torbay) (tôr-kē').. Eng.	50·30 N	3·26 W
134	Torra, Cerro (Mtn.) (sĕ'r-rô-tŏ'r-rä). Col. (In.)	4·41 N	76·22 W
113	Torrance (tŏr'rănc) Ca. (Los Angeles In.)	33·50 N	118·20 W
163	Torre Annunziata (tôr'rā ä-no͞on-tsē-ä'tä) It. (Naples In.)	40·31 N	14·27 E
162	Torre de Cerredo (Mtn.) (tôr'rā dā thâ-rā'dhō). Sp.	43·10 N	4·47 W
163	Torre del Greco (tôr'rā dĕl grā'kô) It. (Naples In.)	40·32 N	14·23 E
162	Torrejoncillo (tôr'rā-hōn-thē'lyō) Sp.	39·54 N	6·26 W
162	Torrelavega (tôr-rā'lä-vä'gä).. Sp.	43·22 N	4·02 W
164	Torre Maggiore (tôr'rā mäd-jō'rā) It.	40·41 N	15·18 E
203	Torrens, L. (tŏr-ĕns) Austl.	30·07 S	137·40 E
163	Torrente (tôr-rĕn'tā) Sp.	39·25 N	0·28 W
118	Torreon (tôr-rå-ōn') Mex.	25·32 N	103·26 W
163	Torre-Pacheco (tôr-rĕ-pä-chĕ'kô) Sp.	37·44 N	0·58 W
205	Torres Is. (tôr'rĕs) (tŏr'ĕz) New Hebr.	13·18 N	165·59 E
114	Torres Martinez Ind. Res. (tôr'ĕz mär-tē'nĕz). Ca.	33·33 N	116·21 W
162	Tôrres Novas (tôr'rĕzh nō'väzh) Port.	39·28 N	8·37 W
197	Torres Str. (tôr'rĕs) Austl.	10·30 S	141·30 E
162	Tôrres Vedras (tôr'rĕzh vā'dräzh) Port.	39·08 N	9·18 W
163	Torrevieja (tôr-rā-vyā'hä) Sp.	37·58 N	0·40 W
187	Torrijos (tôr-rē'hōs).... Phil. (In.)	13·19 N	122·06 E
105	Torrington (tŏr'ĭng-tŭn) Ct.	41·50 N	73·10 W
108	Torrington Wy.	42·04 N	104·11 W
162	Torro (tô'r-rō) Sp.	41·27 N	5·23 W
156	Torsby (tôrs'bü) Swe.	60·07 N	12·56 E
156	Torshälla (tôrs'hĕl-ä) Swe.	59·26 N	16·21 E
150	Tórshavn (tôrs-houn') Faer.	62·00 N	6·55 W
123	Tortola (I.) (tôr-tō'lä) Vir. Is. (Br.) (Puerto Rico In.)	18·34 N	64·40 W
164	Tortona (tôr-tō'nä) It.	44·52 N	8·52 W
163	Tortosa (tôr-tō'sä) Sp.	40·59 N	0·33 E
163	Tortosa, Cabo de (C.) (kå'bô-dĕ-tôr-tō-sä). Sp.	40·42 N	0·55 E
129	Tortue, Canal de la (Chan.) (tôr-tü'). Hai.	20·05 N	73·20 W
129	Tortue, Ile de la (I.) Hai.	20·10 N	73·00 W
100	Tortue, Rivière de la (R.) (lä tōr-tü'). Can. (Montreal In.)	45·12 N	73·32 W
135	Tortuga, Isla la (I.) (ē's-lä-lä-tôr-to͞o'gä). Ven. (In.)	10·55 N	65·18 W
159	Toruń (tō'ro͞on') Pol.	53·01 N	18·37 E
166	Tõrva (t'r'vȧ) Sov. Un.	58·02 N	25·56 E
154	Tory (I.) (tō'rē) Ire.	55·17 N	8·10 W
166	Torzhok (tôr'zhôk) Sov. Un.	57·03 N	34·53 E
195	Tosa-Wan (B.) (tô'sä wän)... Jap.	33·14 N	133·39 E
164	Toscana (Reg.) (tôs-kä'nä) It.	43·23 N	11·08 E
174	Tosna R. Sov. Un.. (Leningrad In.)	59·38 N	30·52 E
174	Tosno (tôs'nô) Sov. Un. (Leningrad In.)	59·32 N	30·52 E
136	Tostado (tôs-tä'dô) Arg.	29·10 S	61·43 W
171	Tosya (tôz'yȧ) Tur.	41·00 N	34·00 E
162	Totana (tô-tä-nä) Sp.	37·45 N	1·28 W
170	Tot'ma (tôt'mȧ) Sov. Un.	60·00 N	42·20 E
135	Totness Sur.	5·51 N	56·17 W
126	Totonicapán (tô-tō-nē-kä'pän) Guat.	14·55 N	91·20 W
137	Totoras (tô-tô'räs) Arg. (Buenos Aires In.)	32·33 S	61·13 W
195	Totsuka (tōt'so͞o-kä) Jap.	35·24 N	139·32 E
148	Tottenham (tŏt'ĕn-ȧm) Eng. (London In.)	51·35 N	0·06 W
195	Tottori (tô'tô-rē) Jap.	35·30 N	134·15 E
210	Touat (Oases) (to͞o'ät) Alg.	27·22 N	0·38 W
214	Touba Ivory Coast	8·17 N	7·41 W
214	Touba Senegal	14·51 N	15·53 W
210	Toubkal, Jbel (Mtn.) Mor.	31·15 N	7·46 W
214	Tougan Upper Volta	13·04 N	3·04 W
210	Touggourt (to͞o-go͞ort') (to͞o-go͞or') Alg.	33·09 N	6·07 E
152	Touil R. (to͞o-ēl') Alg.	34·42 N	2·16 E
161	Toul (to͞ol) Fr.	48·39 N	5·51 E
98	Toulnustouc (R.) Can.	50·23 N	67·55 W
161	Toulon (to͞o-lôn') Fr.	43·09 N	5·54 E
160	Toulouse (to͞o-lo͞oz') Fr.	43·37 N	1·27 E
196	Toungoo (tŏ-o͞oŋ-go͞o') Bur.	19·00 N	96·29 E
	Tourane, see Da Nang		
160	Tourcoing (to͞or-kwăn') Fr.	50·44 N	3·06 E
161	Tournan-en-Brie (to͞or-nän-ĕn-brē') Fr. (Paris In.)	48·45 N	2·47 E
160	Tours (to͞or) Fr.	47·23 N	0·39 E
211	Touside, Pic (Pk.) (to͞o-sē-dā') Chad	21·10 N	16·30 E
156	Tovdalselv (R.) (tôv-däls-ĕlv) Nor.	58·23 N	8·16 E
105	Towanda (tô-wän'dȧ) Pa.	41·45 N	76·30 W
119	Town Bluff L. Tx.	30·52 N	94·30 W
108	Towner (tou'nēr) ND	48·21 N	100·24 W
99	Townsend (toun'zĕnd).. Ma. (In.)	42·41 N	71·42 W
111	Townsend Mt.	46·19 N	111·35 W
112	Townsend, Mt.. Wa. (Seattle In.)	47·52 N	123·03 W
135	Townsville (tounz'vĭl) Austl.	19·18 S	146·50 E
106	Towson (tou'sŭn) Md. (Baltimore In.)	39·24 N	76·36 W
196	Towuti, Danau (L.) (tô-wo͞o'tē) Indon.	3·00 S	121·45 E
118	Toyah (tô'yȧ) Tx.	31·19 N	103·46 W
195	Toyama (tō'yä-mä) Jap.	36·42 N	137·14 E
195	Toyama-Wan (B.) Jap.	36·58 N	137·16 E
195	Toyohashi (tō'yô-hä'shē) Jap.	34·44 N	137·21 E
195	Toyonaka (tō'yô-nä'kȧ) Jap. (Ōsaka In.)	34·47 N	135·28 E
152	Tozeur (tô-zûr') Tun.	33·59 N	8·11 E
162	Trabancos (R.) (trä-bäŋ'kōs).. Sp.	41·15 N	5·13 W
171	Trabzon (tråb'zôn) Tur.	41·00 N	39·45 E
114	Tracy (trā'sē) Ca.	37·45 N	121·27 W
98	Tracy Can.	46·00 N	73·13 W
108	Tracy Mn.	44·13 N	95·37 W
120	Tracy City Tn.	35·15 N	85·44 W
162	Trafalgar, Cabo de (C.) (kå'bô-dĕ-trä-fäl-gä'r). Sp.	36·10 N	6·02 W
213	Trafonomby (Mtn.) Mad.	24·32 S	46·35 E
93	Trail (trāl) Can.	49·06 N	117·42 W
149	Traisen (R.).... Aus. (Vienna In.)	48·15 N	15·55 E
149	Traiskirchen.... Aus. (Vienna In.)	48·01 N	16·18 E
157	Trakai (trȧ-kȧy) Sov. Un.	54·38 N	24·59 E
159	Trakiszki (trȧ-kē'-sh-kē) Pol.	54·16 N	23·07 E
154	Tralee (trȧ-lē') Ire.	52·16 N	9·20 W
156	Tranas (trän'ôs) Swe.	58·03 N	14·56 E
184	Tranbonsha (Mt.) China	35·27 N	86·25 E
162	Trancoso (träŋ-kō'so͝o) Port.	40·46 N	7·23 W
197	Trangan (I.) (träŋ'gän).... Indon.	6·52 S	133·30 E
164	Trani (trä'nē) It.	41·15 N	16·25 E
141	Transcaucasia (Reg.).... Sov. Un.	41·17 N	44·30 E
188	Trans Himalaya Mts. (trăns'hĭ-mä'lȧ-yȧ). China	30·25 N	83·43 E
212	Transvaal (Prov.) (trăns-väl') S. Afr.	24·21 S	28·18 E
159	Transylvania (Reg.) (trăn-sĭl-vā'nĭ-ȧ). Rom.	46·30 N	22·35 E
	Transylvanian Alps (Mts.), see Carpatii Meridionali		
164	Trapani (trä'pä-nē) It.	38·02 N	12·34 E
161	Trappes (tråp)..... Fr. (Paris In.)	48·47 N	2·01 E
203	Traralgon (trȧ'răl-gŏn) Austl.	38·15 S	146·33 E
214	Trarza (Reg.) Mauritania	17·35 N	15·15 W
164	Trasimeno, Lago (L.) (lä'gō trä-sē-mā'nō). Ir.	43·00 N	12·12 E
162	Tras os Montes (Mts.) (träzh'ōzh mōn'täzh). Port.	41·33 N	7·13 W
162	Trasparga (träs-pär-gä) Sp.	43·13 N	7·50 W
158	Traun R. (troun) Aus.	48·10 N	14·15 E
158	Traunstein (troun'stīn).... F.R.G.	47·52 N	12·38 E
108	Traverse, L. (trăv'ērs).. Mn.-SD	45·46 N	96·53 W
104	Traverse City Mi.	44·45 N	85·40 W
164	Travnik (träv'nēk) Yugo.	44·13 N	17·43 E
112	Treasure I. (trĕzh'ēr) Ca. (San Francisco In.)	37·49 N	122·22 W
149	Trebbin (trĕ'bēn) G.D.R. (Berlin In.)	52·13 N	13·13 E
158	Třebič (t'rzhĕ'bēch) Czech.	49·13 N	15·53 E
165	Trebinje (trå'bēn-yĕ) Yugo.	42·43 N	18·21 E
159	Trebisov (trĕ'bē-shôf) Czech.	48·36 N	21·32 E
158	Třeboň (t'rzhĕ'bôn') Czech.	49·00 N	14·48 E
205	Tregrosse Is. (trē-grōs').... Austl.	18·08 S	150·53 E
136	Treinta y Tres (trå-ĕn'tä ē träs') Ur.	33·14 S	54·17 W
160	Trélazé (trā-lå-zā') Fr.	47·27 N	0·32 W
136	Trelew (trĕ'lū) Arg.	43·15 S	65·25 W
156	Trelleborg Swe.	55·24 N	13·07 E
154	Tremadoc B. (trĕ-mă'dŏk).. Wales	52·43 N	4·27 W
164	Tremiti, Isole di (Is.) (ē'sō-lĕ dēträ-mē'tē). It.	42·07 N	16·33 E
159	Trenčín (trĕn'chēn) Czech.	48·52 N	18·02 E

ăt; finăl; rāte; senâte; ärm; ȧsk; sofȧ; fâre; ch-choose; dh-as th in other; bē; ēvent; bĕt; recĕnt; cratēr; g-go; gh-guttural g; bĭt; ĭ-short neutral; rīde; K-guttural k as ch in German ich;

PRONOUNCING INDEX

Trengganu — T'ulufan 359

Page	Name Pronunciation Region	Lat. °'	Long. °'
196	Trengganu (State) (trĕng-gä'nōō) . Mala.	4·53 N	102·26 E
136	Trenque Lauquén (trĕn'kĕ-lä'ŏŏ-kĕ'n) . Arg.	35·50 S	62·44 W
97	Trent (R.) (trĕnt) ... Can.	44·15 N	77·55 W
154	Trent (R.) ... Eng.	53·05 N	1·00 W
148	Trent and Mersey Can. (trĕnt) (mûr zē) . Eng.	53·11 N	2·24 W
164	Trento (trĕn'tô) ... It.	46·04 N	11·07 E
164	Trento (Reg.) ... It.	46·16 N	10·47 E
91	Trenton (trĕn'tŭn) ... Can.	44·05 N	77·35 W
99	Trenton ... Can.	45·37 N	62·38 W
107	Trenton ... Mi. (Detroit In.)	42·08 N	83·12 W
117	Trenton ... Mo.	40·05 N	93·36 W
106	Trenton ... NJ (New York In.)	40·13 N	74·46 W
120	Trenton ... Tn.	35·57 N	88·55 W
99	Trepassey (trê-păs'ê) ... Can.	46·44 N	53·22 W
99	Trepassey B. ... Can.	46·40 N	53·20 W
136	Tres Arroyos (trās'är-rō'yōs) . Arg.	38·18 S	60·16 W
137	Três Coracoes (trĕ's kō-rä-zô'ĕs) Braz. (Rio de Janeiro In.)	21·41 S	45·14 W
125	Tres Cumbres (trĕ's kōō'm-brĕs) Mex. (In.)	19·03 N	99·14 W
135	Três Lagoas (trĕ's lä-gô'äs) . . Braz.	20·48 S	51·42 W
135	Três Marias, Reprêsa (Res.) (rĕ-prā'sä trĕs' mä-rē'äs) . Braz.	18·15 S	45·30 W
134	Tres Morros, Alto de (Mtn.) (ä'l-tō dĕ trĕ's mô'r-rôs) Col. (In.)	7·08 N	76·10 W
137	Três Pontas (trĕ's pô'n-täs) Braz. (Rio de Janeiro In.)	21·22 S	45·30 W
216	Três Pontas, Cabo das (C.) . . Ang.	10·23 S	13·32 E
137	Três Rios (trĕ's rê'ōs) Braz. (Rio de Janeiro In.)	22·07 S	43·13 W
100	Très-St. Rédempteur (săN rā-dăNp-tûr') Can. (Montreal In.)	45·26 N	74·23 W
149	Treuenbrietzen (troi'ĕn-brē-tzĕn) G.D.R. (Berlin In.)	52·06 N	12·52 E
164	Treviglio (trā-vē'lyô) ... It.	45·30 N	9·34 E
164	Treviso (trĕ-vê'sō) ... It.	45·39 N	12·15 E
188	Triangle, The (Reg.) ... Asia	26·00 N	98·00 E
218	Trichardt (trĭ-kärt') ... S. Afr.	26·32 N	29·16 E
164	Trieste (trê-ĕs'tä) ... It.	45·39 N	13·48 E
164	Trieste, G. of ... It.	45·38 N	13·40 E
162	Trigueros (trê-gā'rōs) ... Sp.	37·23 N	6·50 W
184	Trigu Tsho (L.) ... China	28·47 N	91·37 E
165	Tríkkala ... Grc.	39·33 N	21·49 E
197	Trikora, Puntjak (Pk.) ... Indon.	4·15 S	138·45 E
107	Trim Cr. (trĭm) . Il. (Chicago In.)	41·19 N	87·39 W
185	Trincomalee (trĭŋ-kô-mȧ-lē') Sri Lanka	8·39 N	81·12 E
148	Tring (trĭng) . . . Eng. (London In.)	51·46 N	0·40 W
134	Trinidad (trē-nê-dhädh') ... Bol.	14·48 S	64·43 W
116	Trinidad (trĭn'ĭdăd) ... Co.	37·11 N	104·31 W
128	Trinidad (trē-nê-dhädh') ... Cuba	21·50 N	80·00 W
137	Trinidad . . . Ur. (Buenos Aires In.)	33·29 S	56·55 W
128	Trinidad, Sierra de (Mts.) (sē-ĕ'r-rä dĕ trê-nê-dä'd) . Cuba	21·50 N	79·55 W
135	Trinidad (I.) (trĭn'ĭ-dăd) ... Trin.	10·00 N	61·00 W
123	Trinidad and Tobago (trĭn'ĭ-dăd) (tô-bā'gō) . N. A.	11·00 N	61·00 W
133	Trinidade, Ilha da (I.) (ē'lä dă trê-nē-dä-dĕ) . Braz.	21·00 S	32·00 W
122	Trinidad R. ... Pan. (In.)	8·55 N	80·01 W
125	Trinitaria (trē-nē-tä'ryä) ... Mex.	16·09 N	92·04 W
127	Trinité ... Mart. (In.)	14·47 N	61·00 W
99	Trinity (trĭn'ĭ-tê) ... Can.	48·59 N	53·55 W
119	Trinity ... Tx.	30·52 N	95·27 W
101	Trinity (Is.) ... Ak.	56·25 N	153·15 W
116	Trinity (R.), East Fk. ... Tx.	33·24 N	96·42 W
117	Trinity (R.), West Fk. ... Tx.	33·22 N	98·26 W
99	Trinity B. ... Can.	48·00 N	53·40 W
110	Trinity R. ... Ca.	40·50 N	123·20 W
119	Trinity R. ... Tx.	30·50 N	95·09 W
164	Trino (trē'nô) ... It.	45·11 N	8·16 E
120	Trion (trī'ŏn) ... Ga.	34·32 N	85·18 W
	Tripoli, see Ţarābulus		
	Tripoli, see Tarābulus		
165	Tripolis (trĭ'pô-lĭs) ... Grc.	37·32 N	22·32 E
	Tripolitania (Prov.), see Tarābulus		
108	Tripp (trĭp) ... SD	43·13 N	97·58 W
184	Tripura (State) ... India	24·00 N	92·00 E
220	Tristan da Cunha Is. (três-tän'dä kōōn'yȧ) . Alt. O.	35·30 S	12·15 W
135	Triste, Golfo (G.) (gôl-fô trĕ's-tĕ) Ven. (In.)	10·40 N	68·05 W
106	Triticus Res. (trī tĭ-cŭs) NY (New York In.)	41·20 N	73·36 W
185	Trivandrum (trē-vŭn'drŭm) . India	8·34 N	76·58 E
159	Trnava (t'r'nȧ-vȧ) ... Czech.	48·22 N	17·34 E
197	Trobriand Is. (trō-brê-ănd') Pap. N. Gui.	8·25 S	151·45 E
164	Trogir (trô'gēr) ... Yugo.	43·32 N	16·17 E
91	Trois-Rivières (trwä'rê-vyâr') Can.	46·21 N	72·35 W
174	Troitsk (trô'ĭtsk) Sov. Un. (Urals In.)	54·06 N	61·34 E
172	Troitsko-Pechorsk (trô'ĭtsk-ô-pyĕ-chôrsk') . Sov. Un.	62·18 N	56·07 E
167	Troitskoye ... Sov. Un.	47·39 N	30·16 E
156	Trollhättan (trôl'hĕt-ĕn) ... Swe.	58·17 N	12·17 E
156	Trollheim (Mts.) (trôll-hĕĭm) . Nor.	62·48 N	9·05 E
150	Tromsö (trôm'sû) ... Nor.	69·38 N	19·12 E
114	Trona (trō'nȧ) ... Ca.	35·49 N	117·20 W
136	Tronador, Cerro (Mtn.) (sĕ'r-rô trō-nä'dôr) . Arg.	41·17 S	71·56 W
124	Troncoso (trôn-kô'sō) ... Mex.	22·43 N	102·22 W
156	Trondheim (Nidaros) (trôn'hâm) (nē'dhä-rôs) . Nor.	63·25 N	11·35 E
156	Trosa (trô'sä) ... Swe.	58·54 N	17·25 E
91	Trout (L.) ... Can.	51·16 N	92·46 W
90	Trout (L.) ... Can.	61·10 N	121·30 W
110	Trout Cr. ... Or.	42·18 N	118·31 W
112	Troutdale (trout'dāl) Or. (Portland In.)	45·32 N	122·23 W
109	Trout Lake ... Mi.	46·20 N	85·02 W
95	Trout L. ... Can.	51·13 N	93·20 W
160	Trouville (trōō-vēl') ... Fr.	49·23 N	0·05 E
120	Troy (troi) ... Al.	31·47 N	85·46 W
113	Troy ... Il. (St. Louis In.)	38·44 N	89·53 W
117	Troy ... Ks.	39·46 N	95·07 W
117	Troy ... Mo.	38·56 N	99·57 W
110	Troy ... Mt.	48·28 N	115·56 W
105	Troy ... NY	42·45 N	73·45 N
121	Troy ... NC	35·21 N	79·58 W
104	Troy ... Oh.	40·00 N	84·10 W
165	Troy (Ruins) ... Tur.	39·59 N	26·14 E
160	Troyes (trwä) ... Fr.	48·18 N	4·03 E
	Trst, see Trieste		
165	Trstenik (t'r'stĕ-nêk) ... Yugo.	43·36 N	20·00 E
166	Trubchëvsk (trŏŏp'chĕfsk) Sov. Un.	52·36 N	32·46 E
	Trucial States, see United Arab Emirates		
114	Truckee (trŭk'ê) ... Ca.	39·20 N	120·12 W
114	Truckee (R.) ... Ca.-Nv.	39·25 N	120·07 W
202	Truganina . Austl. (Melbourne In.)	37·49 N	144·44 E
134	Trujillo (trōō-κē'l-yō) . . . Col. (In.)	4·10 N	76·20 W
126	Trujillo (trōō-κēl'yō) ... Hond.	15·55 N	85·58 W
134	Trujillo ... Peru	8·08 S	79·00 W
162	Trujillo (trōō-κē'l-yō) ... Sp.	39·27 N	5·50 W
134	Trujillo ... Ven.	9·15 N	70·28 W
124	Trujillo (R.) ... Mex.	23·12 N	103·10 W
129	Trujin, L. (trōō-κēn') . . Dom. Rep.	17·45 N	71·25 W
117	Trumann (trōō'măn) ... Ar.	35·41 N	90·31 W
165	Trŭn (trŭn) ... Bul.	42·49 N	22·39 E
98	Truro (trōō'rō) ... Can.	45·22 N	63·16 W
154	Truro ... Eng.	50·17 N	5·05 W
106	Trussville (trŭs'vĭl) Al. (Birmingham In.)	33·37 N	86·37 W
115	Truth or Consequences (trōōth ŏr kŏn'sê-kwĕn-sĭs) . NM	33·10 N	107·20 W
158	Trutnov (trŏŏt'nôf) ... Czech.	50·36 N	15·36 E
158	Trzcianka (tchyän'kȧ) ... Pol.	53·02 N	16·27 E
158	Trzebiatow (tchĕ-byä'tōō-v) . . Pol.	54·03 N	15·16 E
188	Tsaidam Swp. (tsī'däm) ... China	37·19 N	94·08 E
192	Ts'aiyü ... China (In.)	39·39 N	116·36 E
121	Tsala Apopka (R.) (tsä'lȧ ă-pŏp'kȧ) . Fl.	28·57 N	82·11 W
190	Ts'anghsien (chäng'sĭän) ... China	38·21 N	116·53 E
191	Ts'angmen ... China (Canton In.)	22·42 N	113·09 E
	Tsangwu, see Wuchou		
190	Tsaochuang (jou'jŏŏäng) . . . China	34·51 N	117·34 E
190	Ts'aohsien (tsou'sĭän) ... China	34·48 N	115·33 E
188	Tsast Bogda Ula (Mt.) ... Mong.	46·44 N	92·34 E
217	Tsavo Natl. Pk. ... Ken.	2·35 S	38·45 E
112	Tsawwassen Ind. Res. Can. (Vancouver In.)	49·03 N	123·11 W
172	Tselinograd (tsĕ'lē-nô-grä'd) Sov. Un.	51·10 N	71·43 E
191	Tsengch'en . . . China (Canton In.)	23·18 N	113·49 E
174	Tsentral'nyy-Kospashskiy (tsĕn-träl'nyĭ-kôs-pȧsh'skĭ) Sov. Un. (Urals In.)	59·03 N	57·48 E
216	Tshela (tshā'lȧ) ... Zaire	4·59 S	12·56 E
216	Tshikapa (tshê-kä'pä) ... Zaire	6·25 S	20·48 E
216	Tshofa ... Zaire	5·14 S	25·15 E
216	Tshuapa (R.) ... Zaire	10·15 S	21·25 E
213	Tsiafajovona (Mtn.) ... Mad.	19·17 S	47·27 E
171	Tsimlyanskiy (Res.) (tsym-lyă'ns-kēē) . Sov. Un.	47·50 N	43·40 E
190	Tsinan (Chinan) (je'nän) . . . China	36·40 N	117·01 E
188	Tsinghai (Prov.) (jĭng'hăĭ) . . China	36·14 N	95·30 E
	Tsingtao, see Ch'ingtao		
213	Tsiribihina (R.) (tsē'rê-bē-hê-nä') Mad.	19·45 S	43·30 E
213	Tsitsa (R.) (tsê'tsȧ) S. Afr. (Natal In.)	31·28 S	28·53 E
	Tsitsihar, see Ch'ich'ihaerh		
213	Tsolo (tsō'lō) . . S. Afr. (Natal In.)	31·19 S	28·47 E
213	Tsomo ... S. Afr. (Natal In.)	32·03 S	27·49 E
213	Tsomo (R.) ... S. Afr. (Natal In.)	31·53 S	27·48 E
195	Tsu (tsōō) ... Jap.	34·42 N	136·31 E
195	Tsuchiura (tsōō'chê-ōō-rä) ... Jap.	36·04 N	140·09 E
195	Tsuda (tsōō'dä) . . Jap. (Ōsaka In.)	34·48 N	135·43 E
194	Tsugaru Kaikyō (str.) (tsōō'gä-rōō kī'kyō) . Jap.	41·25 N	140·20 E
212	Tsumeb (tsōō'mĕb) ... S. W. Afr.	19·10 S	17·45 E
195	Tsunashima (tsōō'nä-shê'mä) Jap. (Tōkyō In.)	35·32 N	139·37 E
193	Ts'unghua ... China	23·30 N	113·40 E
190	Tsunhua (zhōōn'hooä) ... China	40·12 N	117·55 E
195	Tsuruga (tsōō'rŏŏ-gä) ... Jap.	35·39 N	136·04 E
195	Tsurugi San (Mtn.) (tsōō'rŏŏ-gê sän) . Jap.	33·52 N	134·07 E
194	Tsuruoka (tsōō'rŏŏ-ō'kä) ... Jap.	38·43 N	139·51 E
195	Tsurusaki (tsōō'rŏŏ-sä'kê) ... Jap.	33·15 N	131·42 E
195	Tsu Shima (I.) (tsōō shê'mä) . . Jap.	34·28 N	129·30 E
195	Tsushima Kaikyō (Str.) (tsōō'shê-mä kī'kyō) . Asia	33·52 N	129·30 E
195	Tsuwano (tsōō'wȧ-nô') ... Jap.	34·28 N	131·47 E
195	Tsuyama (tsōō'yä-mä') ... Jap.	35·05 N	134·00 E
162	Tua (R.) (tōō'ä) ... Port.	41·23 N	7·18 W
112	Tualatin (R.) (tōō'ȧ-lā-tĭn) Or. (Portland In.)	45·25 N	122·54 W
199	Tuamotu (Low), Arch. (tōō-ä-mō'tōō) . Fr. Polynesia	19·00 S	141·20 W
197	Tuao (tōō-ä-ō) ... Phil. (In.)	17·44 N	121·26 E
171	Tuapse (tŏŏ'ăp-sĕ) ... Sov. Un.	44·00 N	39·10 E
210	Tuareg (Reg.) ... Alg.	21·26 N	2·51 E
136	Tubarão (tōō-bä-rouN') ... Braz.	28·23 N	48·56 W
158	Tübingen (tü'bĭng-ĕn) ... F.R.G.	48·33 N	9·05 E
174	Tubinskiy (tû bĭn'skĭ) Sov. Un. (Urals In.)	52·53 N	58·15 E
211	Tubruq ... Libya	32·03 N	24·04 E
135	Tucacas (tōō-kä'käs) . . . Ven. (In.)	10·48 N	68·20 W
106	Tucker (tŭk'ĕr) . . Ga. (Atlanta In.)	33·51 N	84·13 W
115	Tucson (tōō-sŏn') ... Az.	32·15 N	111·00 W
136	Tucumán (tōō-kōō-män') ... Arg.	26·52 S	65·08 W
136	Tucumán (Prov.) ... Arg.	26·30 S	65·30 W
116	Tucumcari (tōō'kŭm-kâr-ê) . . . NM	35·11 N	103·43 W
134	Tucupita (tōō-kōō-pē'tä) ... Ven.	9·00 N	62·09 W
135	Tucuruí (tōō-kōō-tōō-ē') ... Braz.	3·34 S	49·44 W
162	Tudela (tōō-dhā'lä) ... Sp.	42·03 N	1·37 W
120	Tugaloo (R.) (tŭg'ȧ-lōō) . Ga.-SC	34·35 N	83·05 W
213	Tugela (R.) (tōō-gĕl'ȧ) S. Afr. (Natal In.)	28·50 S	30·52 E
213	Tugela Ferry . . S. Afr. (Natal In.)	28·44 S	30·27 E
104	Tug Fork (R.) (tŭg) ... WV	37·50 N	82·30 W
197	Tuguegarao (tōō-gā-gȧ-rä'ō) Phil. (In.)	17·37 N	121·44 E
190	T'uhsieh (R.) (tōō'hăĭ) ... China	37·05 N	166·56 E
218	Tuinplaas ... S. Afr. (Johannesburg & Pretoria In.)	24·54 S	28·46 E
113	Tujunga (tōō-jŭŋ'gȧ) Ca. (Los Angeles In.)	34·15 N	118·16 W
174	Tukan (tōō'kȧn) Sov. Un. (Urals In.)	53·52 N	57·25 E
197	Tukangbesi, Kepulauan (Is.) Indon.	6·00 S	124·15 E
211	Tūkrah ... Libya	32·34 N	20·47 E
90	Tuktoyaktuk (tōōk-tō-yäk'tōōk) Can.	69·32 N	132·37 W
170	Tukum (tŏŏ'kŏŏm) ... Sov. Un.	57·00 N	22·50 E
157	Tukums (tŏŏ'kŏŏms) ... Sov. Un.	56·57 N	23·09 E
212	Tukuyu (tōō-kōō'yȧ) ... Tan.	9·13 S	33·43 E
112	Tukwila (tŭk'wĭ-lȧ) Wa. (Seattle In.)	47·28 N	122·16 W
124	Tula (tōō'lä) ... Mex.	20·04 N	99·22 W
166	Tula (tōō'lȧ) ... Sov. Un.	54·12 N	37·37 E
166	Tula (Oblast) ... Sov. Un.	53·45 N	37·19 E
124	Tula (R.) (tōō'lä) ... Mex.	20·40 N	99·27 W
205	Tulagi (I.) (tōō-lä'gê) ... Sol. Is.	9·15 S	160·17 E
112	Tulalip (tū-lă'lĭp) . Wa. (Seattle In.)	48·04 N	122·18 W
112	Tulalip Ind. Res. . Wa. (Seattle In.)	48·06 N	122·16 W
124	Tulancingo (tōō-län-sĭŋ'gō) . . Mex.	20·04 N	98·24 W
196	Tulangbawang (R.) ... Indon.	4·17 S	105·00 E
114	Tulare (tōō-lä'rȧ) (tul-âr') ... Ca.	36·12 N	119·22 W
114	Tulare Basin ... Ca.	35·57 N	120·18 W
115	Tularosa (tōō-lȧ-rō'zȧ) ... NM	33·05 N	106·05 W
134	Tulcán (tōōl-kän') ... Ec.	0·44 N	77·52 W
167	Tulcea (tŏŏl'chȧ) ... Rom.	45·10 N	28·47 E
167	Tul'chin (tŏŏl'chĕn) ... Sov. Un.	48·42 N	28·53 E
124	Tulcingo (tōōl-sĭŋ'gō) ... Mex.	18·03 N	98·27 W
114	Tule (R.) (tōō'lȧ) ... Ca.	36·08 N	118·50 W
213	Tuléar (tōō-lā-är') ... Mad.	20·16 S	43·44 E
114	Tule River Ind. Res. (tōō'lȧ) . . Ca.	36·05 N	118·35 W
212	Tuli (tōō'lê) ... Rh.	20·58 S	29·12 E
116	Tulia (tōō'lĭ-ȧ) ... Tx.	34·32 N	101·46 W
125	Tulijá (R.) (tōō-lē-κä') ... Mex.	17·28 N	92·11 W
101	Tulik Vol. (tŏŏ'lĭk) ... Ak.	53·28 N	168·10 W
183	Tūlkarm (tōōl kärm) Jordan (Palestine In.)	32·19 N	35·02 E
120	Tullahoma (tŭl-ȧ-hō'mȧ) ... Tn.	35·21 N	86·12 W
154	Tullamore (tŭl-ȧ-mōr') ... Ire.	53·15 N	7·29 W
160	Tulle (tül) ... Fr.	45·15 N	1·45 E
149	Tulln (tōōln) . . . Aus. (Vienna In.)	48·21 N	16·04 E
149	Tullner Feld (Reg.) Aus. (Vienna In.)	48·20 N	15·59 E
125	Tulpetlac (tōōl-pȧ-tlȧk') Mex. (Mexico City In.)	19·33 N	99·04 W
117	Tulsa (tŭl'sȧ) ... Ok.	36·08 N	95·58 W
134	Tuluá (tōō-lōō-ȧ') ... Col. (In.)	4·06 N	76·12 W
188	T'ulufan (Turfan) (tōō'lōō-fän') (tōōr-fän') . China	43·06 N	88·41 E

ng-sing; ŋ-baŋk; N-nasalized n; nŏd; cŏmmit; ōld; ôbey; ôrder; fōōd; fŏŏt; ou-out; s-soft; sh-dish; th-thin; pūre; ûnite; ûrn; stŭd; circŭs; ü-as "y" in study; '-indeterminate vowel.

360 Tulum — Udskaya

PRONOUNCING INDEX

Page	Name Pronunciation Region	Lat. °′	Long. °′
126	Tulum (tōō-lōō'm) Mex. (In.)	20·17 N	87·26 W
172	Tulun (tōō-lōōn') Sov. Un.	54·29 N	100·43 E
115	Tumacacori Natl. Mon. (tōō-mä-kä'kȧ-rē) Az.	31·36 N	110·20 W
134	Tumaco (tōō-mä'kô) Col.	1·41 N	78·44 W
126	Tuma R. (tōō'mä) Nic.	13·07 N	85·32 W
216	Tumba, Lac (L.) (tŏŏm'bä) Zaire	0·50 S	17·45 E
134	Tumbes (tōō'm-bĕs) Peru	3·39 S	80·27 W
124	Tumbiscatío (tōōm-bē-skȧ-tē'ō) Mex.	18·32 N	102·23 W
112	Tumbo (I.) Can. (Vancouver In.)	48·49 N	123·04 W
192	T'umen (tōō'mĕn) China	43·00 N	129·50 E
194	Tumen (R.) China	42·08 N	128·40 E
135	Tumeremo (tōō-mȧ-rā'mō) Ven.	7·15 N	61·28 W
185	Tumkūr India	13·22 N	77·05 E
135	Tumuc-Humac Mts. (tōō-mōōk'ōō-mäk') S. A.	2·15 N	54·50 W
128	Tunas de Zaza (tōō'näs dā zä'zä) Cuba	21·40 N	79·35 W
154	Tunbridge Wells (tŭn'brĭj welz') Eng.	51·05 N	0·09 E
172	Tundra (Reg.) Sov. Un.	70·45 N	84·00 E
217	Tunduru Tan.	11·07 S	37·21 E
189	Tung (R.) China	24·13 N	115·08 E
190	Tunga (dōōng'ä) China	36·11 N	116·16 E
184	Tungabhadra Res. India	15·26 N	75·57 E
193	T'ungan (tōōn'gän') China	24·48 N	118·02 E
190	T'ungch'engi (tōōng'chĕng'yē) China	36·21 N	116·14 E
189	T'ungchiang China	47·38 N	132·54 E
190	Tungch'angshou (tōōng'chäng'shō) China	38·21 N	114·41 E
190	Tunghai (dōōng'hăī) China	34·35 N	119·05 E
192	T'ungho China	45·58 N	128·40 E
193	Tunghsiang China	28·18 N	116·38 E
192	Tunghsien China (Peking In.)	39·55 N	116·40 E
190	Tung Hu (L.) (tōōng' hōō') China	32·22 N	116·32 E
193	Tungjen (tōōng'jĕn') China	27·45 N	109·12 E
191	Tungkuan China (Canton In.)	23·03 N	113·14 E
192	T'ung-Kuan China	34·48 N	110·25 E
190	Tungkuang (dōōng'gōōäng) China	37·54 N	116·33 E
193	T'ungku Chiao (Pt.) China	19·40 N	111·15 E
192	Tungliao (Payintala) China	43·30 N	122·15 E
190	Tungming (tōōng'mĭng') China	35·16 N	115·06 E
190	Tungpa (tōōng'bä) China	31·40 N	119·02 E
190	Tungpa China	35·56 N	116·19 E
192	T'ungpei (tōōng'pā) China	48·00 N	126·48 E
190	Tungping (tōōng'pĭng) China	35·50 N	116·24 E
190	Tungp'ing Hu (L.) (hōō) China	36·06 N	116·24 E
190	Tungt'antien (dōōng'tän'dĭän) China	35·26 N	116·54 E
193	Tungt'ing Hŭ (L.) (tōōng'tĕng' hōō) China	29·10 N	112·30 E
190	Tungwen (R.) (dōōng'wĕn) China	36·24 N	119·00 E
192	Tunhua China	48·18 N	128·10 E
185	Tuni India	17·29 N	82·38 E
120	Tunica (tū'nĭ-kȧ) Ms.	34·41 N	90·23 W
210	Tunis (tū'nĭs) Tun.	36·59 N	10·06 E
151	Tunis, Golfe de (G.) Tun.	37·06 N	10·43 E
209	Tunisia (tu-nĭzh'ē-ȧ) Afr.	35·00 N	10·11 E
134	Tunja (tōō'n-hä) Col.	5·32 N	73·19 W
105	Tunkhannock (tŭnk-hăn'ŭk) Pa.	41·35 N	75·55 W
112	Tunnel (R.) (tŭn'ĕl) Wa. (Seattle In.)	47·48 N	123·04 W
114	Tuolumne (R.) (twô-lŭm'nē) Ca.	37·35 N	120·37 W
173	Tuostakh (R.) Sov. Un.	67·09 N	137·30 E
135	Tupã (tōō-pä) Braz.	21·47 S	50·33 W
120	Tupelo (tū'pē-lō) Ms.	34·14 N	88·43 W
135	Tupinambaranas, Ilha (I.) (ē'lä-tōō-pē-näN-bä-rä'näs) Braz.	3·04 S	58·09 W
134	Tupiza (tōō-pē'zä) Bol.	21·26 S	65·43 W
105	Tupper Lake (tŭp'ēr) NY	44·15 N	74·25 W
134	Tuquerres (tōō-kĕ'r-rĕs) Col.	1·12 N	77·44 W
172	Tura (tŏŏr'ȧ) Sov. Un.	64·08 N	99·58 E
141	Tura (R.) Sov. Un.	57·15 N	64·23 E
124	Turbio (R.) (tōōr-byô) Mex.	20·28 N	101·40 W
134	Turbo (tōō'bō) Col.	8·02 N	76·43 W
159	Turciansky Svätý Martin (tōōr'chyȧn-skû'svä'tû' mär'tyēn) Czech.	49·02 N	18·48 E
159	Turda (tŏŏr'dȧ) Rom.	46·35 N	23·47 E
	Turfan, see T'ulufan		
188	Turfan Depression China	42·16 N	90·00 E
213	Turffontein S. Afr. (Johannesburg & Pretoria In.)	26·15 S	28·03 E
172	Turgay (tōōr'gī) Sov. Un.	49·42 N	63·39 E
147	Turgayka (R.) (tōōr-gī'kă) Sov. Un.	49·44 N	66·15 E
165	Tŭrgovishte Bul.	43·14 N	26·36 E
171	Turgutlu Tur.	38·30 N	27·20 E
157	Türi (tü'rĭ) Sov. Un.	58.49 N	25·29 E
162	Turia (R.) (tōō'ryä) Sp.	40·12 N	1·18 W
124	Turicato (tōō-rē-kä'tō) Mex.	19·03 N	101·24 W
128	Turiguano (I.) (tōō-rē-gwä'nō) Cuba	22·20 N	78·35 W
	Turin, see Torino		
159	Turka (tŏŏr'kȧ) Sov. Un.	49·10 N	23·02 E
172	Turkestan (tûr-kĕ-stăn') (tŏŏr-kĕ-stan') Sov. Un.	42·40 N	65·00 E
168	Turkestan (Reg.) Sov. Un.	43·27 N	62·14 E
182	Turkey Eur.-Asia	38·45 N	32·00 E
109	Turkey (R.) (tûrk'ē) Ia.	43·20 N	92·16 W
168	Turkmen (S. S. R.) (tōōrk-mĕn') Sov. Un.	40·46 N	56·01 E
129	Turks I. Pass. Turks & Caicos Is.	21·15 N	71·25 W
123	Turks (Is.) (tûrks) Turks & Caicos Is.	21·40 N	71·45 W
157	Turku (Åbo) (tŏŏr'kōō) (ô'bō) Fin.	60·28 N	22·12 E
114	Turlock (tûr'lŏk) Ca.	37·30 N	120·51 W
126	Turneffe (I.) (tûr-nĕf'fē) Belize (In.)	17·25 N	87·43 W
113	Turner (tûr'nēr) Ks. (Kansas City In.)	39·05 N	94·42 W
128	Turner Sd. Ba.	24·20 N	78·05 W
214	Turners Pen. S.L.	7·20 N	12·40 W
149	Turnhout (tŭrn-hout') Bel. (Brussels In.)	51·19 N	4·58 E
158	Turnov (tŏŏr'nôf) Czech.	50·36 N	15·12 E
165	Turnu Măgurele (tŏŏr'nŏŏ mŭ-gōō-rĕ'ly') Rom.	43·54 N	24·49 E
165	Turnu-Severin (sĕ-vĕ-rēn') Rom.	44·37 N	22·38 E
128	Turquino, Pico de (Pk.) (pē'kō dā tōōr-kē'nō) Cuba	20·00 N	76·50 W
127	Turrialba (tōōr-ryä'l-bä) C. R.	9·54 N	83·41 W
165	Turski Trstenik Bul.	43·26 N	24·50 E
147	Turtkul' (tŏŏrt-kōōl') Sov. Un.	41·28 N	61·02 E
95	Turtle (R.) Can.	49·20 N	92·30 W
119	Turtle B. Tx. (In.)	29·48 N	94·38 W
108	Turtle Cr. SD	44·40 N	98·53 W
108	Turtle Mountain Ind. Res. ND	48·45 N	99·57 W
108	Turtle Mts. ND	48·57 N	100·11 W
172	Turukhansk (tōō-rōō-känsk') Sov. Un.	66·03 N	88·39 E
159	Turya R. (tōōr'yȧ) Sov. Un.	51·18 N	24·55 E
120	Tuscaloosa (tŭs-kȧ-lōō'sȧ) Al.	33·10 N	87·35 W
110	Tuscarora (tŭs-kȧ-rō'rȧ) Nv.	41·18 N	116·15 W
107	Tuscarora Ind. Res. NY (Buffalo In.)	43·10 N	78·51 W
104	Tuscola (tŭs-kō-lȧ) Il.	39·50 N	88·20 W
120	Tuscumbia (tŭs-kŭm'bĭ-ȧ) Al.	34·41 N	87·42 W
193	Tushan (dōō'shän) China	25·50 N	107·42 E
190	Tushan China	31·38 N	116·16 E
174	Tushino (tōō'shĭ-nô) Sov. Un. (Moscow In.)	55·51 N	37·24 E
120	Tuskegee (tŭs-kē'gē) Al.	32·25 N	85·40 W
190	T'ussuk'ou (tōō'sē'kō) China	36·19 N	117·37 E
113	Tustin (tŭs'tĭn) Ca. (Los Angeles In.)	33·44 N	117·49 W
166	Tutayev (tōō-tȧ-yĕf') Sov. Un.	57·53 N	39·34 E
148	Tutbury (tŭt'bēr-ē) Eng.	52·52 N	1·51 W
185	Tuticorin (tōō-tē-kô-rĭn') India	8·51 N	78·09 E
125	Tutitlan (tōō-tē-tlä'n) Mex. (In.)	19·38 N	99·10 W
135	Tutóia (tōō-tō'yȧ) Braz.	2·42 S	42·21 W
165	Tutrakan Bul.	44·02 N	26·36 E
117	Tuttle Creek Res. Ks.	39·30 N	96·38 W
158	Tuttlingen (tŏŏt'lĭng-ĕn) F.R.G.	47·58 N	8·50 E
120	Tutwiler (tŭt'wĭ-lēr) Ms.	34·01 N	90·25 W
172	Tuva Aut. Oblast Sov. Un.	51·15 N	90·45 E
198	Tuvalu (Is.) Oceania	5·20 S	174·00 E
186	Tuwayq, Jabal (Mts.) Sau. Ar.	20·45 N	46·30 E
106	Tuxedo Park (tŭk-sē'dō pärk) NY (New York In.)	41·11 N	74·11 W
148	Tuxford (tŭks'fērd) Eng.	53·14 N	0·54 W
124	Tuxpan (tōōs'pän) Mex.	19·34 N	103·22 W
125	Túxpan Mex.	20·57 N	97·26 W
125	Túxpan (R.) (tōōs'pän) Mex.	20·55 N	97·52 W
125	Túxpan, Arrecife (Rf.) (är-rĕ-sē'fē-tōō'x-pä'n) Mex.	21·01 N	97·12 W
125	Tuxtepec (tōōs-tȧ-pĕk') Mex.	18·06 N	96·09 W
125	Tuxtla Gutiérrez (tōōs'tlä gōō-tyâr'rĕs) Mex.	16·44 N	93·08 W
150	Tuy Sp.	42·07 N	8·49 W
135	Tuy (tōō'ē) (R.) Ven. (In.)	10·15 N	66·03 W
127	Tuyra R. (tōō-ē'rȧ) Pan.	7·55 N	77·37 W
193	Tuyün (tōō'yün') China	26·18 N	107·40 E
171	Tuz Gölü (L.) Tur.	39·00 N	33·30 E
115	Tuzigoot Natl. Mon. Az.	34·40 N	111·52 W
165	Tuzla (tōōz'lȧ) Yugo.	44·33 N	18·46 E
156	Tvedestrand (tvĭ'dhĕ-stränd) Nor.	58·39 N	8·54 E
156	Tveitsund (tvåt'sōōnd) Nor.	59·03 N	8·29 E
	Tver, see Kalinin		
146	Tvertsa (L.) (tvĕr'tsȧ) Sov. Un.	56·58 N	35·22 E
154	Tweed (R.) (twēd) Scot.	55·32 N	2·35 W
218	Tweeling (twē'lĭng) S. Afr. (Johannesburg & Pretoria In.)	27·34 S	28·31 E
107	Twelvemile Cr. (twĕlv'mīl) NY (Buffalo In.)	43·13 N	78·58 W
100	Twenty Mile Cr. (twĕn'tĭ mīl) Can. (Toronto In.)	43·09 N	79·49 W
148	Twickenham (twĭk''n-ăm) Eng. (London In.)	51·26 N	0·20 W
99	Twillingate (twĭl'ĭn-gāt) Can.	49·39 N	54·46 W
111	Twin Bridges (twĭn brĭ-jĕz) Mt.	45·34 N	112·17 W
111	Twin Falls (fôls) Id.	42·33 N	114·29 W
107	Twinsburg (twĭnz'bûrg) Oh. (Cleveland In.)	41·19 N	81·26 W
114	Twitchell Res. Ca.	34·50 N	120·10 W
116	Two Butte Cr. (tōō būt) Co.	37·39 N	102·45 W
109	Two Harbors Mn.	47·00 N	91·42 W
117	Two Prairie Bay (prā'rĭ bī ōō') Ar.	34·48 N	92·07 W
109	Two Rivers (rĭv'ērz) Wi.	44·09 N	87·36 W
202	Tyabb Austl. (Melbourne In.)	38·16 S	145·11 E
159	Tyachev (tyä'chĕf) Sov. Un.	48·01 N	23·42 E
188	Tyan' Shan' (Tien-Shan) (Mts.) Sov. Un.-China	42·00 N	78·46 E
167	Tyasmin (R.) (tyȧs-mĭn') Sov. Un.	49·14 N	32·23 E
213	Tylden (tĭl-dĕn) S. Afr. (Natal In.)	32·08 S	27·06 E
148	Tyldesley (tĭldz'lē) Eng.	53·32 N	2·28 W
108	Tyler (tī'lēr) Mn.	44·18 N	96·08 W
119	Tyler Tx.	32·21 N	95·19 W
120	Tylertown (tī'lēr-toun) Ms.	31·08 N	90·06 W
108	Tyndall (tĭn'dȧl) SD	42·58 N	97·52 W
173	Tyndinskiy Sov. Un.	55·22 N	124·45 E
154	Tyne (R.) (tīn) Eng.	54·59 N	1·56 W
154	Tynemouth (tīn'mŭth) Eng.	55·04 N	1·39 W
156	Tynest (tün'sĕt) Nor.	62·17 N	10·45 E
99	Tyngsboro (tĭnj-bûr'ō) Ma. (In.)	42·40 N	71·27 W
	Tyre, see Şūr		
156	Tyri Fd. (tü'rē) Nor.	60·03 N	10·25 E
115	Tyrone (tī'rōn) NM	32·40 N	108·20 W
105	Tyrone Pa.	40·40 N	78·15 W
203	Tyrrell, L. (tĭr'ĕll) Austl.	35·12 S	143·00 E
151	Tyrrhenian Sea (tĭr-rē'nĭ-ăn) It.	40·10 N	12·15 E
157	Tyrvää (tür'vâ) Fin.	61·19 N	22·51 E
171	Tyub-Karagan, Mys (C.) Sov. Un.	44·30 N	50·10 E
172	Tyukalinsk (tyōō-kȧ-lĭnsk') Sov. Un.	56·03 N	71·43 E
173	Tyukyan (R.) (tyōōk'yȧn) Sov. Un.	65·42 N	116·09 E
171	Tyuleniy (I.) Sov. Un.	44·30 N	48·00 E
172	Tyumen' (tyōō-mĕn') Sov. Un.	57·02 N	65·28 E
172	Tyura-Tam Sov. Un.	46·00 N	63·15 E
126	Tzucacab (tzōō-kä-kä'b) Mex. (In.)	20·06 N	89·03 W
190	Tz'uhsien (tsĕ'sĭän) China	36·22 N	114·23 E
190	Tzupo China	36·48 N	118·04 E
193	Tzu Shui (R.) (tsōō) China	26·50 N	111·00 E
190	Tzuya (R.) (zhĕ'yä) China	38·38 N	116·31 E
190	Tzuyang (tsĕ'yäng) China	35·35 N	116·50 E

U

Page	Name Pronunciation Region	Lat. °′	Long. °′
152	Uarc, Ras (C.) Mor.	35·31 N	2·45 W
134	Uaupés (wä-ōō'pās) Braz.	0·02 S	67·03 W
137	Ubá (ōō-bá') Braz. (Rio de Janeiro In.)	21·08 S	42·55 W
216	Ubangi (Oubangui) (R.) (ōō-băŋ'gē) Afr.	4·30 N	20·35 E
137	Ubatuba (ōō-bȧ-tōō'bȧ) Braz. (Rio de Janeiro In.)	23·25 S	45·06 W
162	Ubeda (ōō'bȧ-dä) Sp.	38·01 N	3·23 W
135	Uberaba (ōō-bȧ-rä'bȧ) Braz.	19·47 S	47·47 W
135	Uberlândia (ōō-bĕr-lá'n-dyä) Braz.	18·54 S	48·11 W
212	Ubombo (ōō-bôm'bō) S. Afr.	27·33 S	32·13 E
196	Ubon Ratchathani (ōō'bŭn rä'chätá-nē) Thai.	15·15 N	104·52 E
167	Ubort' (R.) (ōō-bôrt') Sov. Un.	51·18 N	27·43 E
162	Ubrique (ōō-brē'kȧ) Sp.	36·43 N	5·36 W
188	Ubsa Nuur (L.) Mong.	50·29 N	93·32 E
217	Ubundi (Ponthierville) Zaire	00·21 S	25·29 E
134	Ucayali (R.) (ōō'kä-yä'lē) Peru	8·58 S	74·13 W
149	Uccle (ü'kl') Bel. (Brussels In.)	50·48 N	4·17 E
174	Uchaly (û-chä'lĭ) Sov. Un. (Urals In.)	54·22 N	59·28 E
172	Uch-Aral (ōōch'á-ral') Sov. Un.	46·14 N	80·58 E
195	Uchiko (ōō'chē-kō) Jap.	33·30 N	132·39 E
195	Uchinoura (ōō'chē-nô-ōō'rȧ) Jap.	31·16 N	131·03 E
174	Uchinskoye Vodokhranilishche L. (ōōch-ēn'skô-yĕ vô-dô-krȧ-nĭ'lĭ-shchĕ) Sov. Un. (Moscow In.)	56·08 N	37·44 E
194	Uchiura-Wan (B.) (ōō'chē-ōō'rä wän) Jap.	42·20 N	140·44 E
	Uch Turfan, see Wushih		
173	Uchur (R.) (ōō-chŏŏr') Sov. Un.	58·27 N	131·34 E
173	Uda (R.) (ōō'dȧ) Sov. Un.	52·28 N	110·51 E
173	Uda (R.) Sov. Un.	53·54 N	131·29 E
184	Udaipur (ōō-dŭ'ē-pōōr) India	24·41 N	73·41 E
167	Uday (R.) (ōō-dī') Sov. Un.	50·45 N	32·13 E
156	Uddevalla (ōōd'dĕ-väl-ȧ) Swe.	58·21 N	11·55 E
164	Udine (ōō'dē-nȧ) It.	46·05 N	13·14 E
196	Udjung Pandang (Makasar) Indon.	5·08 S	119·28 E
172	Udmurt (A. S. S. R.) Sov. Un.	57·00 N	53·00 E
196	Udon Thani Thai.	17·31 N	102·51 E
135	Udskaya Guba (B.) Sov. Un.	55·00 N	136·30 E

ăt; finăl; rāte; senâte; ärm; åsk; sofȧ; fâre; ch-choose; dh-as th in other; bē; ēvent; bĕt; recĕnt; cratēr; g-go; gh-guttural g; bĭt; ĭ-short neutral; rīde; K-guttural k as ch in German ich;

Page	Name	Pronunciation	Region	Lat. °′	Long. °′
195	Ueda	(wā'dä)	Jap.	36·26 N	138·16 E
158	Uekermünde	(ü'kĕr-mün-dĕ)	G.D.R.	53·43 N	14·01 E
216	Uele R.	(wā'lå)	Zaire	3·55 N	23·30 E
174	Ufa	(ōō'fä)	Sov. Un. (Urals In.)	54·45 N	55·57 E
170	Ufa (R.)		Sov. Un.	56·00 N	57·05 E
212	Ugab (R.)	(ōō'gäb)	S. W. Afr.	21·10 S	14·00 E
217	Ugalla (R.)	(ōō-gä'lä)	Tan.	6·15 S	32·30 E
209	Uganda	(ōō-gän'dä) (ṵ-gän'då)	Afr.	2·00 N	32·28 E
101	Ugashik L.	(ōō'gà-shĕk)	Ak.	57·36 N	157·10 W
213	Ugie	(ōō'jē)	S. Afr. (Natal In.)	31·13 S	28·14 E
173	Uglegorsk	(ōō-glĕ-gôrsk)	Sov. Un.	49·00 N	142·31 E
174	Ugleural'sk	(ōō'glĕ-ōō-rálsk')	Sov. Un. (Urals In.)	58·58 N	57·35 E
166	Uglich	(ōō-glēch')	Sov. Un.	57·33 N	38·19 E
174	Uglitskiy	(ōōg-lĭt'skĭ)	Sov. Un. (Urals In.)	53·50 N	60·18 E
166	Uglovka	(ōōg-lôf'kà)	Sov. Un.	58·14 N	33·24 E
166	Ugra (R.)	(ōō'rä)	Sov. Un.	54·43 N	34·20 E
165	Ugŭrchin		Bul.	43·06 N	24·23 E
159	Uherské Hradiště	(ōō-hĕr'skyĕ hrä-dĕsh'tyĕ)	Czech.	49·01 N	17·28 E
104	Uhrichsville	(ū'rĭks-vĭl)	Oh.	40·25 N	81·20 W
194	Uiju	(ōō'ê̇jōō)	Kor.	40·09 N	124·33 E
171	Uil (R.)	(ōō-ēl')	Sov. Un.	49·30 N	55·10 E
115	Uinkaret Plat.	(ṵ-ĭn'kâr-ĕt)	Az.	36·43 N	113·15 W
174	Uinskoye	(ōō-ĭn'skô-yĕ)	Sov. Un. (Urals In.)	56·53 N	56·25 E
115	Uinta (R.)	(ṵ-ĭn'tä)	Ut.	40·25 N	109·55 W
113	Uintah	(ṵ-ĭn'tä)	Ut. (Salt Lake City In.)	41·09 N	111·56 W
115	Uintah and Ouray Ind. Res.		Ut.	39·55 N	109·20 W
218	Uitenhage		S. Afr. (Natal In.)	33·46 S	25·26 E
149	Uithoorn		Neth. (Amsterdam In.)	52·13 N	4·49 E
195	Uji	(ōō'jē)	Jap. (Ōsaka In.)	34·53 N	135·49 E
217	Ujiji	(ōō-jē'jĕ)	Tan.	4·55 S	29·41 E
184	Ujjain	(ōō-jŭĕn)	India	23·18 N	75·37 E
217	Ukerewe I.		Tan.	2·00 S	32·40 E
172	Ukhta		Sov. Un.	63·08 N	53·42 E
170	Ukhta	(ōōk'tà)	Sov. Un.	65·22 N	31·30 E
114	Ukiah	(ū-kī'à)	Ca.	35·09 N	122·12 W
157	Ukmergė	(ŏŏk'mĕr-ghà)	Sov. Un.	55·16 N	24·45 E
168	Ukrainian (S. S. R.)	(ū'krän)	Sov. Un.	49·15 N	30·15 E
195	Uku (I.)	(ōōk'ōō)	Jap.	33·18 N	129·02 E
188	Ulaan Baatar		Mong.	47·56 N	107·00 E
188	Ulaan Goom		Mong.	50·23 N	92·14 E
173	Ulan-Ude	(ōō'län ōō'dà)	Sov. Un.	51·59 N	107·41 E
194	Ulchin	(ōōl'chĕn')	Kor.	36·57 N	129·26 E
165	Ulcinj (Dulcigno)	(ōōl'tsĕn')	Yugo.	41·56 N	19·15 E
185	Ulhās (R.)		India (In.)	19·13 N	73·03 E
185	Ulhāsnagar		India (Bombay In.)	19·10 N	73·07 E
216	Ulindi (R.)	(ōō-lĭn'dĕ)	Zaire	1·55 S	26·17 E
166	Ulla	(ōōl'å)	Sov. Un.	55·14 N	29·15 E
166	Ulla (R.)		Sov. Un.	54·58 N	29·03 E
162	Ulla (R.)	(ōō'lä)	Sp.	42·45 N	8·33 W
194	Ullŭng (I.)	(ōōl'lŏong')	Kor.	37·29 N	130·50 E
158	Ulm	(ōŏlm)	F.R.G.	48·24 N	9·59 E
220	Ulmer, Mt.	(ŭl'mûr')	Ant.	77·30 S	86·00 W
156	Ulricehamn	(ōōl-rē'sĕ-häm)	Swe.	57·49 N	13·23 E
194	Ulsan	(ōōl'sän')	Kor.	35·35 N	129·22 E
154	Ulster (Reg.)	(ŭl'stēr)	Ire.-N. Ire.	54·41 N	7·10 W
126	Ulua R.	(ōō-lōō'à)	Hond.	15·49 N	87·45 W
184	Ulubāria		India (In.)	22·27 N	88·09 E
217	Uluguru Mts.		Tan.	7·15 S	37·30 E
171	Ulukışla	(ōō-lōō-kēsh'là)	Tur.	36·40 N	34·30 E
194	Ulunga	(ōō-lōōn'gà)	Sov. Un.	46·16 N	136·29 E
174	Ulu-Telyak	(ōō lŏŏ'tĕlyäk)	Sov. Un. (Urals In.)	54·54 N	57·01 E
203	Ulverstone	(ŭl'vēr-stŭn)	Austl.	41·20 S	146·22 E
156	Ulvik	(ōōl'vĕk)	Nor.	60·35 N	6·53 E
174	Ul'yanovka	(ōō-lyä'nôf-kà)	Sov. Un. (Leningrad In.)	59·38 N	30·47 E
170	Ul'yanovsk	(ōō-lyä'nôfsk)	Sov. Un.	54·20 N	48·05 E
116	Ulysses	(ū-lĭs'ĕz)	Ks.	37·34 N	101·25 W
158	Ülzen	(ült'sĕn)	F.R.G.	52·58 N	10·34 E
125	Umán	(ōō-män'')	Mex.	20·52 N	89·44 W
167	Uman	(ōō-män')	Sov. Un.	48·44 N	30·13 E
110	Umatilla Ind. Res.		Or.	45·38 N	118·35 W
185	Umberpāda		India (In.)	19·28 N	73·04 E
164	Umbria (Reg.)	(ŭm'brĭ-á)	It.	42·53 N	12·22 E
150	Ume	(ōō'mĕ)	Swe.	64·57 N	18·51 E
150	Umeå	(ōō'mĕ-ô)	Swe.	63·48 N	20·29 E
213	Umhlatuzi (R.)		S. Afr. (Natal In.)	28·47 S	31·17 E
101	Umiat	(ōō'mĭ-ăt)	Ak.	69·20 N	152·28 W
213	Umkomaas	(ŏŏm-kô'mäs)	S. Afr. (Natal In.)	30·12 S	30·48 E
211	Umm Durmān (Omdurman)	(ŏm-dŏŏr-män')	Sud.	15·45 N	32·30 E
101	Umnak (I.)	(ŏŏm'nák)	Ak.	53·10 N	169·08 W
101	Umnak P.		Ak.	53·10 N	168·04 W
212	Umniati (R.)		Rh.	17·08 S	29·11 E
110	Umpqua R.	(ŭmp'kwà)	Or.	43·42 N	123·50 W
212	Umtali	(ōōm-tä'lĕ)	Rh.	18·49 S	32·39 E
213	Umtata	(ōōm-tä'tä)	S. Afr. (Natal In.)	31·36 S	28·47 E
213	Umtentweni		S. Afr. (Natal In.)	30·41 S	30·29 E
213	Umzimkulu	(ōōm-zĕm-kōō'lōō)	S. Afr. (Natal In.)	30·12 S	29·53 E
213	Umzinto	(ōōm-zĭn'tô)	S. Afr. (Natal In.)	30·19 S	30·41 E
164	Una (R.)	(ōō'nä)	Yugo.	44·38 N	16·10 E
101	Unalakleet	(ū-nà-làk'lēt)	Ak.	63·50 N	160·42 W
101	Unalaska	(ū-nà-lás'kà)	Ak.	53·30 N	166·20 W
135	Unare (R.)		Ven. (In.)	9·45 N	65·12 W
135	Unare, Laguna de (L.)	(lä-gōō'nä-de-ōō-nà'rĕ)	Ven. (In.)	10·07 N	65·23 W
186	Unayzah		Sau. Ar.	25·50 N	44·02 E
100	Uncas	(ŭn'kás)	Can. (Edmonton In.)	53·30 N	113·02 W
134	Uncía	(ōōn'sē-ä)	Bol.	18·28 S	66·32 W
115	Uncompahgre (R.)		Co.	38·20 N	107·45 W
115	Uncompahgre Pk.	(ŭn-kŭm-pä'grĕ)	Co.	38·00 N	107·30 W
115	Uncompahgre Plat.		Co.	38·40 N	108·40 W
218	Underberg	(ŭn'dĕr-bûrg)	S. Afr. (Natal In.)	29·51 S	29·32 E
211	Undo		Eth.	6·37 N	38·29 E
166	Unecha	(ōō-nĕ'chà)	Sov. Un.	52·51 N	32·44 E
91	Ungava B.	(ŭn-gä'và)	Can.	59·46 N	67·18 W
91	Ungava, Péninsule d' (Pen.)		Can.	59·55 N	74·00 W
136	União da Vitória	(ōō-nê-oun' dä vē-tô'ryä)	Braz.	26·17 S	51·13 W
164	Unije (I.)	(ōō'nê-yĕ)	Yugo.	44·39 N	14·10 E
101	Unimak (I.)	(ōō-nê-mák')	Ak.	54·30 N	163·35 W
101	Unimak P.		Ak.	54·22 N	165·22 W
120	Union	(ŭn'yŭn)	Ms.	32·35 N	89·07 W
117	Union		Mo.	38·28 N	90·59 W
121	Union		NC	34·42 N	81·40 W
110	Union		Or.	45·13 N	117·52 W
111	Union City	Ca. (San Francisco In.)	37·36 N	122·01 W
104	Union City		In.	40·10 N	85·00 W
104	Union City		Mĭ.	42·00 N	85·10 W
105	Union City		Pa.	41·50 N	79·50 W
120	Union City		Tn.	36·25 N	89·04 W
128	Union de Reves	(ōō-nyô'n-dĕ-rĕ-vĕ's)	Cuba	22·45 N	81·30 W
124	Union de San Antonio	(sän än-tō'nyō)	Mex.	21·07 N	101·56 W
124	Union de Tula	(tōō'lä)	Mex.	19·57 N	104·14 W
107	Union Grove		Wi. (Milwaukee In.)	42·41 N	88·03 W
125	Unión Hidalgo	(ê-dä'lgô)	Mex.	16·29 N	94·51 W
120	Union Point		Ga.	33·37 N	83·08 W
120	Union Springs	(springz)	Al.	32·08 N	85·43 W
120	Uniontown	(ŭn'yŭn-toun)	Al.	32·26 N	87·30 W
107	Uniontown		Oh. (Cleveland In.)	40·58 N	81·25 W
105	Uniontown		Pa.	39·55 N	79·45 W
117	Unionville	(ŭn'yŭn-vĭl)	Mo.	40·28 N	92·58 W
197	Unisan	(ōō-nê'sän)	Phil. (In.)	13·50 N	121·59 E
102	Unitas, Mts.	(ū-nī'tàs)	U. S.	40·35 N	111·00 W
182	United Arab Emirates		Asia	24·00 N	54·00 E
	United Arab Republic, see Egypt				
150	United Kingdom		Eur.	56·30 N	1·40 W
115	United Pueblo Ind. Res.	(ṵ-nĭt'ĕd pōō-ĕb'lō) (pwä'blō)	NM	35·30 N	107·00 W
75	United States		N. A.	38·00 N	110·00 W
94	Unity		Can.	52·27 N	109·10 W
104	Universal	(ū-nĭ-vûr'sál)	In.	39·35 N	87·30 W
162	Universales, Montes (Mts.)	(mōn'täs ōō-nê-vêr-sä'läs)	Sp.	40·21 N	1·43 W
113	University City	(ū'nĭ-vûr'sĭ-tĭ)	Mo. (St. Louis In.)	38·40 N	90·19 W
113	University Park		Tx. (Dallas, Fort Worth In.)	32·51 N	96·48 W
161	Unna	(ōō'nä)	F.R.G. (Ruhr In.)	51·32 N	7·41 E
154	Unst (I.)	(ŏnst)	Scot.	60·50 N	1·24 W
149	Unterhaching		F.R.G. (Munich In.)	48·03 N	11·38 E
171	Unye	(ŭn'yĕ)	Tur.	41·00 N	37·10 E
170	Unzha (R.)	(ŏŏn'zhä)	Sov. Un.	57·45 N	44·10 E
166	Upa (R.)	(ŏŏ'pá)	Sov. Un.	53·54 N	36·48 E
209	Upanda, Serra do (Mts.)	(sē-ê̇'r-rä-dô-ōō-pä'n-dä)	Ang.	13·15 S	14·15 E
134	Upata	(ōō-pä'tä)	Ven.	7·58 N	62·27 W
217	Upemba, Parc Natl. de l' (Natl. Pk.)		Zaire	9·10 S	26·15 E
212	Upington	(ŭp'ĭng-tŭn)	S. Afr.	28·25 S	21·15 E
113	Upland	(ŭp'lănd)	Ca. (Los Angeles In.)	34·06 N	117·38 W
89	Upolu Pt.	(ōō-pô'lōō)	Hi.	20·15 N	155·48 W
93	Upper Arrow L.	(ăr'ō)	Can.	50·30 N	117·55 W
106	Upper Darby	(där'bĭ)	Pa. (Philadelphia In.)	39·58 N	75·16 W
108	Upper de Lacs (R.)	(dĕ läk)	ND	48·58 N	101·55 W
196	Upper Kapuas Mts.		Mala.	1·45 N	112·06 E
110	Upper L.	(ŭp'ēr)	Nv.	41·42 N	119·59 W
106	Upper Marlboro		Md. (Baltimore In.)	38·49 N	76·46 W
112	Upper Mill	(mĭl)	Wa. (Seattle In.)	47·11 N	121·55 W
109	Upper Red L.	(rĕd)	Mn.	48·14 N	94·53 W
104	Upper Sandusky	(săn-dŭs'kē)	Oh.	40·50 N	83·20 W
112	Upper San Leandro Res.	ŭp'ēr săn lê-ăn'drô)	Ca. (San Francisco In.)	37·47 N	122·04 W
209	Upper Volta	(vôl'tä)	Afr.	11·46 N	3·18 E
148	Uppingham	(ŭp'ĭng-ăm)	Eng.	52·35 N	0·43 W
156	Uppsala	(ōōp'sà-lä)	Swe.	59·53 N	17·39 E
99	Uptown	(ŭp'toun)	Ma. (In.)	42·10 N	71·36 W
195	Uraga	(ōō'rà-gà')	Jap.	35·15 N	139·43 E
195	Uraga-Kaikyō (Str.)	(ōō'rä-gä kī'kyō)	Jap. (Tōkyō In.)	35·11 N	139·44 E
171	Ural (R.)	(ōō-räl'') (ū-rôl)	Sov. Un.	49·50 N	51·30 E
168	Urals (Mts.)		Sov. Un.	56·28 N	58·13 E
171	Ural'sk	(ōō-rálsk')	Sov. Un.	51·15 N	51·10 E
185	Uran	(ōō-rän')	India	18·53 N	72·46 E
90	Uranium City		Can.	59·34 N	108·59 W
195	Urawa		Jap. (Tōkyō In.)	35·52 N	139·39 E
195	Urayasu	(ōō'rä-yä'sōō)	Jap. (Tōkyō In.)	35·40 N	139·54 W
167	Urazovo	(ōō-rà'zô-vô)	Sov. Un.	50·08 N	38·03 E
104	Urbana	(ûr-băn'à)	Il.	40·10 N	88·15 W
104	Urbana		Oh.	40·05 N	83·50 W
164	Urbino	(ōōr-bē'nô)	It.	43·43 N	12·37 E
171	Urda	(ōōr'dä)	Sov. Un.	48·50 N	47·30 E
197	Urdaneta	(ōōr-dä-nä'tä)	Phil. (In.)	15·59 N	120·34 E
137	Urdinarrain	(ōōr-dē-när-rä'̇n)	Arg. (Buenos Aires In.)	32·43 S	58·53 W
172	Urdzhar	(ōōrd-zhär')	Sov. Un.	47·28 N	82·00 E
171	Urfa	(ōōr'fà)	Tur.	37·20 N	38·45 E
147	Urgench	(ōōr-gĕnch')	Sov. Un.	41·32 N	60·33 E
174	Uritsk	(ōō'rĭtsk)	Sov. Un. (Leningrad In.)	59·50 N	30·11 E
165	Urla	(ōōr'lä)	Tur.	38·20 N	26·44 E
174	Urman	(ŏŏr'mán)	Sov. Un. (Urals In.)	54·53 N	56·52 E
194	Urmi (R.)	(ŏŏr'mê̇)	Sov. Un.	48·50 N	134·00 E
215	Uromi	(ōō-rô'mê̇)	Nig.	6·44 N	6·18 E
134	Urrao	(ōōr-rä'ô)	Col. (In.)	6·19 N	76·11 W
166	Urshel'skiy	(ōōr-shĕl'skē)	Sov. Un.	55·50 N	40·11 E
134	Urubamba (R.)	(ōō-rōō-bäm'bä)	Peru	11·48 S	72·34 W
136	Uruguaianá	(ōō-rōō-gwī-ä'nå)	Braz.	29·45 S	57·00 W
133	Uruguay	(ōō-rōō-gwī') (ū'rōō-gwä)	S. A.	32·45 S	56·00 W
136	Uruguay, Rio (R.)	(rē'ō-ōō-rōō-gwī)	Braz.	27·05 S	55·15 W
	Urumchi, see Wulumuch'i				
188	Urungu R.	(ōō-rŏŏn'gŏō')	China	46·31 N	87·44 E
173	Urup (I.)	(ōō-rŏŏp')	Sov. Un.	46·08 N	149·00 E
171	Uryupinsk	(ŏŏr'yōō-pēn-sk')	Sov. Un.	50·50 N	42·00 E
165	Urziceni	(ōō-zē-chĕn'')	Rom.	44·45 N	26·42 E
194	Usa		Jap.	33·31 N	131·22 E
170	Usa (R.)	(ōō'sà)	Sov. Un.	66·00 N	58·20 E
171	Uşak	(ōō'shàk)	Tur.	39·50 N	29·15 E
212	Usakos	(ōō-sä'kŏs)	S. W. Afr.	22·00 S	15·40 E
174	Ushaki	(ōō'shá-kī)	Sov. Un. (Leningrad In.)	59·28 N	31·00 E
174	Ushakovskoye	(ōō-shá-kôv'skô-yĕ)	Sov. Un. (Urals In.)	56·18 N	62·23 E
217	Usambara Mts.		Tan.	4·40 S	38·25 E
217	Usangu Flats (Pln.)		Tan.	8·10 S	34·00 E
217	Ushashi		Tan.	2·00 S	33·57 E
195	Ushiku	(ōō'shê-kōō)	Jap. (Tōkyō In.)	35·24 N	140·09 E
195	Ushimado	(ōō'shê-mä'dô)	Jap.	34·37 N	134·09 E
136	Ushuaia	(ōō-shōō-ī'ä)	Arg.	54·46 S	68·24 W
171	Üsküdar		Tur.	40·55 N	29·00 E
166	Usman'	(ōōs-män')	Sov. Un.	52·03 N	39·40 E
174	Usol'ye	(ōō-sô'lyĕ)	Sov. Un. (Urals In.)	59·24 N	56·40 E
172	Usol'ye-Sibirskoye	(ōō-sô'lyĕsĭ' bêr'skô-yĕ)	Sov. Un.	52·44 N	103·46 E
136	Uspallata P.	(ōōs-pä-lyä'tä)	Arg.-Chile	32·47 S	70·08 W
125	Uspanapa (R.)	(ōōs-pä-nä'pä)	Mex.	17·43 N	94·14 W
160	Ussel	(üs'ĕl)	Fr.	45·33 N	2·17 E
189	Ussuri (R.)	(ōō-sōō'rē)	China	46·30 N	133·56 E
173	Ussuriysk	(ōō-sōō'rēsk)	Sov. Un.	43·48 N	132·09 E
173	Ust'-Bol'sheretsk		Sov. Un.	52·41 N	157·00 E
164	Ustica, I. di	(ōōs'tē-kä)	It.	38·43 N	12·11 E
158	Ústí nad Labem	(ōōs'tē)	Czech.	50·39 N	14·02 E
174	Ustinovka	(ōōs-tē'nôf-kà)	Sov. Un.	47·59 N	32·31 E
174	Ust'-Izhora	(ōōst-ēz'hô-rà)	Sov. Un. (Leningrad In.)	59·49 N	30·35 E
158	Ustka	(ōōst'kà)	Pol.	54·34 N	16·52 E
173	Ust'-Kamchatsk		Sov. Un.	56·13 N	162·18 E
172	Ust'-Kamenogorsk		Sov. Un.	49·58 N	80·43 E
174	Ust'-Katav	(ŏŏst kà'táf)	Sov. Un. (Urals In.)	54·55 N	58·12 E

ng-sing; ŋ-baŋk; N-nasalized n; nŏd; cŏmmit; ōld; ŏbey; ôrder; fōōd; fŏŏt; ou-out; s-soft; sh-dish; th-thin; pūre; ûnite; ûrn; stŭd; circǔs; ü-as "y" in study; '-indeterminate vowel.

ăt; fĭnȧl; rāte; senáte; ärm; àsk; sofȧ; fâre; ch-choose; dh-as th in other; bē; ĕvent; bĕt; recĕnt; cratēr; g-go; gh-guttural g; bĭt; ĭ-short neutral; rīde; κ-guttural k as ch in German ich;

ăt; fĭnăl; rāte; senâte; ärm; ȧsk; sofá; fâre; ch-choose; dh-as th in other; bē; ĕvent; bĕt; recĕnt; cratēr; g-go; gh-guttural g; bĭt; ĭ-short neutral; rīde; к-guttural k as ch in German ich;

Page	Name Pronunciation Region	Lat. °′	Long. °′
165	Visoko (vē'sô-kô) . . . Yugo.	43·59 N	18·10 E
165	Vistonís (L.) (vēs'tô-nĭs) . . . Grc.	40·58 N	25·12 E
	Vistula (R.), see Wisla		
165	Vitanovac (vē'tä'nô-väts) . . . Yugo.	43·44 N	20·50 E
166	Vitebsk (vē'tyĕpsk) . . . Sov. Un.	55·12 N	30·16 E
166	Vitebsk (Oblast) . . . Sov. Un.	55·05 N	29·18 E
164	Viterbo (vē-tĕr'bō) . . . It.	42·24 N	12·08 E
173	Vitim (vē'têm) . . . Sov. Un.	59·22 N	112·43 E
173	Vitim (R.) (vē'têm) . . . Sov. Un.	56·12 N	115·30 E
174	Vitino (vē'tĭ-nô) Sov. Un. (Leningrad In.)	59·40 N	29·51 E
135	Vitória (vē-tō'rē-ä) . . . Braz.	20·09 S	40·17 W
162	Vitoria (vē-tô-ryä) . . . Sp.	42·43 N	2·43 W
135	Vitória de Conquista (-dä-kōn-kwē's-tä) . Braz.	14·51 S	40·44 W
160	Vitré (vē-trā') . . . Fr.	48·09 N	1·15 W
160	Vitrolles (vē-trōl') . . . Fr. (In.)	43·27 N	5·15 E
160	Vitry-le-François (vē-trē'lĕ-fräN-swä') . Fr.	48·44 N	4·34 E
151	Vittoria (vē-tô'rē-ô) . . . It.	37·01 N	14·31 E
164	Vittorio (vē-tô'rē-ô) . . . It.	45·59 N	12·17 E
197	Vitu Is. (vē'tōō) . . . Pap. N. Gui.	4·45 S	149·50 E
162	Vivero (vē-vā'rō) . . . Sp.	43·39 N	7·37 W
119	Vivian (vĭv'ĭ-ăn) . . . La.	32·51 N	93·59 W
165	Vize (vē'zĕ) . . . Tur.	41·34 N	27·46 E
185	Vizianagaram . . . India	18·10 N	83·29 E
149	Vlaardingen (vlär'dĭng-ĕn) Neth. (Amsterdam In.)	51·54 N	4·20 E
166	Vladimir (vlȧ-dyē'mĕr) . . . Sov. Un.	56·08 N	40·24 E
166	Vladimir (Oblast) (vlä-dyē'mĕr) Sov. Un.	56·08 N	39·53 E
194	Vladimiro-Aleksandrovskoye (vlȧ-dyē'mē-rô ȧ-lĕk-sän'drôf-skô-yĕ) . Sov. Un.	42·50 N	133·00 E
159	Vladimir-Volynskiy (vlȧ-dyē'mĕr vô-lēn'skĭ) Sov. Un.	50·50 N	24·20 E
173	Vladivostok (vlȧ-dē-vôs-tŏk') Sov. Un.	43·06 N	131·47 E
165	Vlasenica (vlä'sĕ-nēt'sȧ) . . . Yugo.	44·11 N	18·58 E
165	Vlasotinci (vlä'sô-tēn-tsĕ) . . . Yugo.	42·58 N	22·08 E
155	Vlieland (I.) (vlē'länt) . . . Neth.	53·19 N	4·55 E
155	Vlissingen (vlĭs'sĭng-ĕn) . . . Neth.	51·30 N	3·34 E
165	Vlorë (Valona) (vlō'rŭ) . . . Alb.	40·28 N	19·31 E
158	Vltana R. . . . Czech.	49·24 N	14·18 E
170	Vodl (L.) (vôd''l) . . . Sov. Un.	62·20 N	37·20 E
212	Voël (R.) . . . S. Afr.	32·52 S	25·12 E
164	Voghera (vô-gā'rä) . . . It.	44·58 N	9·02 E
213	Vohémar (vô-ā-mär') . . . Mad.	13·35 S	50·05 E
112	Voight (R.) . . . Wa. (Seattle In.)	47·03 N	122·08 W
214	Voinjama . . . Lib.	8·25 N	9·45 W
163	Voiron (vwȧ-rôN') . . . Fr.	45·23 N	5·48 E
94	Voisin, Lac (L.) (vwŏ'-zĭn) . . . Can.	54·13 N	107·15 W
165	Voïviïs (L.) . . . Grc.	39·34 N	22·50 E
167	Volchansk (vôl-chänsk') Sov. Un.	50·18 N	36·56 E
167	Volch'ya (R.) (vôl-chyä') Sov. Un.	49·42 N	34·39 E
134	Volcán Misti (Vol.) . . . Peru	16·04 S	71·20 W
171	Volga (R.) (vôl'gä) . . . Sov. Un.	47·30 N	46·20 E
171	Volga, Mouths of the . . . Sov. Un.	46·00 N	49·10 E
171	Volgograd (Stalingrad) (vŏl-gō-grä't) (stá'lĕn-grat) Sov. Un.	48·40 N	42·20 E
171	Volgogradskoye (Res.) (vôl-gô-grad'skô-yĕ) . Sov. Un.	51·10 N	45·10 E
166	Volkhov (vôl'kôf) . . . Sov. Un.	59·54 N	32·21 E
166	Volkhov (R.) . . . Sov. Un.	58·45 N	31·40 E
159	Volkovysk (vôl-kô-vêsk') Sov. Un.	53·11 N	24·29 E
174	Volodarskiy (vô-lô-där'skĭ) Sov. Un. (Leningrad In.)	59·49 N	30·06 E
166	Vologda (vô'lôg-dȧ) . . . Sov. Un.	59·12 N	39·52 E
166	Vologda (Oblast) . . . Sov. Un.	59·00 N	37·26 E
167	Volokonovka (vô-lô-kô'nôf-kȧ) Sov. Un.	50·28 N	37·52 E
166	Volokolamsk (vô-lô-kôlȧmsk) Sov. Un.	56·02 N	35·58 E
165	Vólos (vô'lôs) . . . Grc.	39·23 N	22·56 E
166	Volozhin (vô'lô-shên) . . . Sov. Un.	54·04 N	26·38 E
171	Vol'sk (vôl'sk) . . . Sov. Un.	52·10 N	47·00 E
214	Volta, L. (vôl'tȧ) . . . Ghana	7·10 N	0·30 W
214	Volta (R.) . . . Ghana	6·05 N	0·30 E
214	Volta Blanche (R.) . . . Upper Volta	11·30 N	0·40 W
214	Volta Noire (Black Volta) (R.) Afr.	10·30 N	2·55 W
137	Volta Redonda (vōl'tä-rā-dôn'dä) Braz. (Rio de Janeiro In.)	22·32 S	44·05 W
164	Volterra (vôl-tĕr'rä) . . . It.	43·22 N	10·51 E
164	Voltri (vōl'trē) . . . It.	44·25 N	8·45 E
164	Volturno (R.) (vôl-tōōr'nô) . . . It.	41·12 N	14·20 E
166	Volzhskoye (L.) (vôl'sh-skô-yĕ) Sov. Un.	56·43 N	36·18 E
113	Von Ormy (vŏn ôr'mē) Tx. (San Antonio In.)	29·18 N	98·36 W
166	Vōōpsu (vōōp'-sōō) . . . Sov. Un.	58·06 N	27·30 E
149	Voorberg Neth. (Amsterdam In.)	52·04 N	4·21 E
213	Voortrekkerhoogte . . . S. Afr. (Johannesburg & Pretoria In.)	25·48 S	28·10 E
166	Vop' (R.) (vôp) . . . Sov. Un.	55·20 N	32·40 E
150	Vopnafjördhur . . . Ice.	65·43 N	14·58 W
158	Vorarlberg (Prov.) . . . Aus.	47·20 N	9·55 E
156	Vordingborg (vôr'dĭng-bôr) . . Den.	55·10 N	11·55 E
165	Voríai (Is.) . . . Grc.	39·12 N	24·03 E
165	Vorios Evvīkós Kólpos (G.) . . Grc.	38·48 N	23·02 E
170	Vorkuta (vôr-kōō'tȧ) . . . Sov. Un.	67·28 N	63·40 E
157	Vormsi (I.) (vôrm'sĭ) . . . Sov. Un.	59·06 N	23·05 E
171	Vorona (R.) (vô-rô'na) . . . Sov. Un.	51·50 N	42·00 E
170	Voron'ya (R.) (vô-rô'nyȧ) Sov. Un.	68·20 N	35·20 E
167	Voronezh (vô-rô'nyĕzh) . . Sov. Un.	51·39 N	39·11 E
167	Voronezh (Oblast) . . . Sov. Un.	51·10 N	39·13 E
166	Voronezh (R.) . . . Sov. Un.	52·17 N	39·32 E
159	Voronovo (vô'rô-nô-vô) Sov. Un.	54·07 N	25·16 E
174	Vorontsovka (vô-rônt'sôv-kȧ) Sov. Un. (Urals In.)	59·40 N	60·14 E
171	Voroshilovgrad . . . Sov. Un.	48·34 N	39·18 E
167	Voroshilovgrad (Oblast) . . Sov. Un.	49·08 N	38·37 E
166	Võrts-Järv (L.) (vôrts yärv) Sov. Un.	58·15 N	26·12 E
166	Võru (vô'rû) . . . Sov. Un.	57·50 N	26·58 E
174	Vorya R. (vôr'yȧ) Sov. Un. (Moscow In.)	55·55 N	38·15 E
161	Vosges (Mts.) (vōzh) . . . Fr.	48·09 N	6·57 E
174	Voskresensk (vôs-krĕ-sĕnsk') Sov. Un. (Moscow In.)	55·20 N	38·42 E
156	Voss (vôs) . . . Nor.	60·40 N	6·24 E
174	Vostryakovo Sov. Un. (Moscow In.)	55·23 N	37·49 E
170	Votkinsk (vôt-kēnsk') . . . Sov. Un.	57·00 N	54·00 E
170	Votkinskoye Vdkhr (Res.) Sov. Un.	57·30 N	55·00 E
162	Vouga (R.) (vō'gȧ) . . . Port.	40·43 N	7·51 W
160	Vouziers (vōō-zyā') . . . Fr.	49·25 N	4·40 E
156	Voxna älv (R.) . . . Swe.	61·30 N	15·24 E
109	Voyageurs Natl. Park . . . Mn.	48·30 N	92·40 W
170	Vozhe (L.) (vôzh'yĕ) . . . Sov. Un.	60·40 N	39·00 E
167	Voznesensk (vôz-nyĕ-sĕnsk') Sov. Un.	47·34 N	31·22 E
168	Vrangelya (Wrangel) (I.) Sov. Un.	71·25 N	173·38 E
165	Vranje (vrän'yĕ) . . . Yugo.	42·33 N	21·55 E
165	Vratsa (vrät'tsȧ) . . . Bul.	43·12 N	23·31 E
165	Vrbas (v'r'bäs) . . . Yugo.	45·34 N	19·43 E
164	Vrbas (R.) . . . Yugo.	44·25 N	17·17 E
160	Vrchlabi (v'r'chlä-bē) . . . Czech.	50·32 N	15·51 E
218	Vrede (vrĭ'dĕ) (vrēd) . . . S. Afr. (Johannesburg & Pretoria In.)	27·25 S	29·11 E
218	Vredefort (vrĭ'dĕ-fôrt) (vrēd'fōrt) S. Afr. (Johannesburg & Pretoria In.)	27·00 S	27·21 E
149	Vreeswijk . Neth. (Amsterdam In.)	52·00 N	5·06 E
165	Vršac (v'r'shȧts) . . . Yugo.	45·08 N	21·18 E
159	Vrutky (vrōōt'kē) . . . Czech.	49·09 N	18·55 E
212	Vryburg (vrī'bûrg) . . . S. Afr.	26·55 S	29·45 E
212	Vryheid (vrī'hīt) . . . S. Afr.	27·43 S	30·58 E
159	Vsetín (fsĕt'yēn) . . . Czech.	49·21 N	18·01 E
174	Vsevolozhskiy (vsyĕ'vôlô'zh-skēē) Sov. Un. (Leningrad In.)	60·01 N	30·41 E
128	Vuelta Abajo (Mts.) (vwĕl'tä ä-bä'hō) . Cuba	22·20 N	83·45 W
149	Vught . . . Neth. (Amsterdam In.)	51·38 N	5·18 E
165	Vukovar (vōō'kô-vär) . . . Yugo.	45·20 N	19·00 E
104	Vulcan (vŭl'kăn) . . . Mi.	45·45 N	87·50 W
164	Vulcano (I.) (vōōl-kä'nô) . . . It.	38·23 N	15·00 E
165	Vŭlchedrŭm . . . Bul.	43·43 N	23·29 E
157	Vyartsilya (vyȧr-tsē'lyȧ) Sov. Un.	62·10 N	30·40 E
170	Vyatka (R.) (vyȧt'kȧ) . . . Sov. Un.	58·25 N	51·25 E
194	Vyazemskiy (vyȧ-zĕm'skĭ) Sov. Un.	47·29 N	134·39 E
166	Vyaz'ma (vyȧz'mȧ) . . . Sov. Un.	55·12 N	34·17 E
170	Vyazniki (vyȧz'nē-kē) . . . Sov. Un.	56·10 N	42·10 E
157	Vyborg (Viipuri) (vwē'bôrk) Sov. Un.	60·43 N	28·46 E
170	Vychegda (R.) (vē'chĕg-dȧ) Sov. Un.	61·40 N	48·00 E
170	Vym (R.) (vwēm) . . . Sov. Un.	63·15 N	51·20 E
174	Vyritsa (vē'rĭ-tsȧ) Sov. Un. (Leningrad In.)	59·24 N	30·20 E
166	Vyshnevolotskoye (L.) (vŭy'sh-ŋē'vōlôt's-kô'yĕ) Sov. Un.	57·30 N	34·27 E
166	Vyshniy Volochĕk (vêsh'nyĭ vôl-ô-chĕk') . Sov. Un.	57·34 N	34·35 E
158	Vyskov (vêsh'kôf) . . . Czech.	49·17 N	16·58 E
158	Vysoké Mýto (vû'sô-kā mû'tô) Czech.	49·58 N	16·07 E
166	Vysokovsk (vĭ-sô'kôfsk) . . Sov. Un.	56·16 N	36·32 E
170	Vytegra (vû'tĕg-rȧ) . . . Sov. Un.	61·00 N	36·20 E
170	Vyur . . . Sov. Un.	57·55 N	27·00 E

W

Page	Name Pronunciation Region	Lat. °′	Long. °′
215	W, Parcs Nationaux du (Natl. Pk.) Dahomey-Niger	12·20 N	2·40 E
214	Wa . . . Ghana	10·04 N	2·29 W
155	Waal (R.) (väl) . . . Neth.	51·46 N	5·00 E
149	Waalwijk . Neth. (Amsterdam In.)	51·41 N	5·05 E
93	Wabamuno (wŏ'bă-mŭn) . . . Can.	53·33 N	114·28 W
93	Wabasca (wŏ-bȧs'-kă) . . . Can.	56·00 N	113·53 W
104	Wabash (wô'băsh) . . . In.	40·45 N	85·50 W
104	Wabash (R.) . . . Il.-In.	38·00 N	88·00 W
109	Wabasha (wä'bȧ-shô) . . . Mn.	44·24 N	92·04 W
95	Wabowden (wă-bō'-d'n) . . . Can.	54·55 N	98·38 W
159	Wąbrzeźno (vôŋ-bzĕzh'nô) . . . Pol.	53·17 N	18·59 E
121	Waccamaw (R.) (wăk'ȧ-mô) . . . SC	33·47 N	78·55 W
120	Waccasassa B. (wă-kȧ-să'sȧ) . . . Fl.	29·02 N	83·10 W
149	Wachow (vä'kōv) G.D.R. (Berlin In.)	52·32 N	12·46 E
119	Waco (wā'kō) . . . Tx.	31·35 N	97·06 W
116	Waconda Lake (Res.) . . . Ks.	39·45 N	98·15 W
195	Wadayama (wä'dä'yä-mä) . . . Jap.	35·19 N	134·49 E
155	Waddenzee (Sea) . . . Neth.	53·00 N	4·50 E
92	Waddington, Mt. (wŏd'dĭng-tŭn) Can.	51·23 N	125·15 W
94	Wadena . . . Can.	51·57 N	103·50 W
109	Wadena (wŏ-dē'nȧ) . . . Mn.	46·26 N	95·09 W
121	Wadesboro (wādz'bŭr-ô) . . . NC	34·57 N	80·05 W
183	Wādī Mūsā . Jordan (Palestine In.)	30·19 N	35·29 E
121	Wadley (wŏd'lē) . . . Ga.	32·54 N	82·25 W
211	Wad Madani (wäd mĕ-dä'nē) . Sud.	14·27 N	33·31 E
159	Wadowice (vȧ-dô'vēt-sĕ) . . . Pol.	49·53 N	19·31 E
107	Wadsworth (wŏdz'wûrth) Oh. (Cleveland In.)	41·01 N	81·44 W
91	Wager B. (wā'jēr) . . . Can.	65·48 N	88·19 W
203	Wagga Wagga (wôg'ȧ wôg'ȧ) Austl.	35·10 S	147·30 E
117	Wagoner (wăg'ŭn-ēr) . . . Ok.	35·58 N	95·22 W
116	Wagon Mound (wăg'ŭn mound) NM	35·59 N	104·45 W
159	Wagrowiec (vôŋ-grō'vyĕts) . . . Pol.	52·47 N	17·14 E
89	Wahiawa . . . Hi.	21·30 N	158·03 W
110	Wahoo (wä-hōō') . . . Ne.	41·14 N	96·39 W
108	Wahpeton (wô'pē-tŭn) . . . ND	46·17 N	96·38 W
89	Waialua (wä'ē-ä-lōō'ä) . . . Hi.	21·33 N	158·08 W
89	Waianae (wä'ē-ȧ-nä'ā) . . . Hi.	21·25 N	158·11 W
158	Waidhofen (vīd'hôf-ĕn) . . . Aus.	47·58 N	14·46 E
173	Waigeo (I.) (wä-ē-gā'ô) . . . Indon.	0·07 N	131·00 E
191	Waikang (wāī'käng) China (Shanghai In.)	31·23 N	121·11 E
205	Waikato (R.) (wä'ē-kä'to) N. Z. (In.)	38·00 S	175·47 E
203	Waikerie (wā'kēr-ē) . . . Austl.	34·15 S	140·00 E
89	Wailuku (wä'ē-lōō'kōō) . . . Hi.	20·55 N	156·30 W
89	Waimanalo (wä-ē-mä'nä-lo) . . . Hi.	21·19 N	157·53 W
89	Waimea (wä-ē-mā'ä) . . . Hi.	21·56 N	159·38 W
184	Wainganga (R.) (wä-ēn-gŭŋ'gä) India	20·24 N	79·41 E
196	Waingapu . . . Indon.	9·32 S	120·00 E
101	Wainwright (wān-rīt) . . . Ak.	74·40 N	159·00 W
93	Wainwright . . . Can.	52·49 N	110·52 W
89	Waipahu (wä'ē-pä'hōō) . . . Hi.	21·20 N	158·02 W
113	Waiska R. (wȧ-ĭz-kȧ) Mi. (Sault Ste. Marie In.)	46·20 N	84·38 W
110	Waitsburg (wāts'bûrg) . . . Wa.	46·17 N	118·08 W
195	Wajima (wä'jē-mȧ) . . . Jap.	37·23 N	136·56 E
217	Wajir . . . Ken.	1·45 N	40·04 E
195	Wakamatsu (wä-kä'mät-sōō) . Jap.	33·54 N	130·44 E
96	Wakami (R.) . . . Can.	47·43 N	82·22 W
195	Wakasa-Wan (B.) (wä'kä-sä wän) Jap.	35·43 N	135·39 E
205	Wakatipu (R.) (wä-kä-tē'pōō) N. Z. (In.)	44·24 S	169·00 E
195	Wakayama (wä-kä'yä-mä) . . . Jap.	34·14 N	135·11 E
198	Wake (I.) (wāk) . . . Oceania	19·25 N	167·00 E
116	Wa Keeney (wô-kē'nē) . . . Ks.	39·01 N	99·53 W
100	Wakefield (wāk-fēld) Can. (Ottawa In.)	45·39 N	75·55 W
148	Wakefield . . . Eng.	53·41 N	1·25 W
99	Wakefield . . . Ma. (In.)	42·31 N	71·05 W
109	Wakefield . . . Mi.	46·28 N	89·55 W
108	Wakefield . . . Ne.	42·15 N	96·52 W
106	Wakefield . . . RI (Providence In.)	41·26 N	71·30 W
121	Wake Forest (wāk fŏr'ĕst) . . . NC	35·58 N	78·31 W
195	Waki (wä'kē) . . . Jap.	34·05 N	134·10 E
194	Wakkanai (wä'kä-nä'ē) . . . Jap.	45·19 N	141·43 E
212	Wakkerstroom (vȧk'ēr-strōm) (wăk'ēr-strōōm) . S. Afr.	27·19 S	30·04 E
96	Wakonassin (R.) . . . Can.	46·35 N	82·10 W
158	Wałbrzych (väl'bzhûk) . . . Pol.	50·46 N	16·16 E
98	Waldoboro (wôl'dô-bŭr-ô) . . . Me.	44·06 N	69·22 W
110	Waldo L. (wôl'dō) . . . Or.	43·46 N	122·10 W

ng-sing; ŋ-baŋk; N-nasalized n; nŏd; cŏmmit; ōld; ôbey; ôrder; fōōd; fŏŏt; ou-out; s-soft; sh-dish; th-thin; pūre; ûnite; ûrn; stŭd; circŭs; ü-as "y" in study; '-indeterminate vowel.

Page	Name Pronunciation Region	Lat. °′	Long. °′
106	Waldorf (wăl′dôrf)		
	Md. (Baltimore In.)	38·37 N	76·57 W
113	Waldron...Mo. (Kansas City In.)	39·14 N	94·47 W
112	Waldron (I.)..Wa. (Vancouver In.)	48·42 N	123·02 W
101	Wales (wālz)................Ak.	65·35 N	168·14 W
154	Wales......................U. K.	52·12 N	3·40 W
214	Walewale................Ghana	10·21 N	0·48 W
158	Wałez (välch)..............Pol.	53·61 N	16·30 E
203	Walgett (wôl′gĕt)........Austl.	30·00 S	148·10 E
220	Walgreen Coast (wôl′grēn)...Ant.	73·00 N	110·00 W
120	Walhalla (wŏl-hăl′à)........SC	34·45 N	83·04 W
217	Walikale...................Zaire	1·25 S	28·03 E
109	Walker (wôk′ēr)............Mn.	47·06 N	94·37 W
109	Walker (wôk′ēr)............Mn.	47·06 N	94·37 W
114	Walker (R.)................Nv.	39·07 N	119·10 W
112	Walker, Mt....Wa. (Seattle In.)	·47·47 N	122·54 W
95	Walker L...................Can.	54·42 N	96·57 W
114	Walker L...................Nv.	38·46 N	118·30 W
114	Walker River Ind. Res.......Nv.	39·06 N	118·20 W
111	Walkerville (wôk′ēr-vĭl)....Mt.	46·20 N	112·32 W
110	Wallace (wôl′ås)............Id.	47·27 N	115·55 W
96	Wallaceburg................Can.	42·39 N	82·25 W
202	Wallacia...Austl. (Sydney In.)	33·52 S	150·40 E
110	Wallapa B. (wôl à pǎ)......Wa.	46·39 N	124·30 W
203	Wallaroo (wŏl-à-rōō).......Austl.	33·52 S	137·45 E
148	Wallasey (wôl′à-sè).........Eng.	53·25 N	3·03 W
110	Walla Walla (wôl′à wôl′à)....Wa.	46·03 N	118·20 W
107	Walled Lake (wôl′d lāk)		
	Mi. (Detroit In.)	42·32 N	83·29 W
211	Wallel, Tulu (Mt.)..........Eth.	9·00 N	34·52 E
148	Wallingford (wŏl′ĭng-fērd)		
	Eng. (London In.)	51·34 N	1·08 W
105	Wallingford................Vt.	43·30 N	72·55 W
198	Wallis Is................Oceania	13·00 S	176·10 E
119	Wallisville (wŏl′ĭs-vĭl)...Tx.	29·50 N	94·44 W
110	Wallowa (wôl′ô-wá)........Or.	45·34 N	117·32 W
110	Wallowa Mts...............Or.	45·10 N	117·22 W
110	Wallowa R.................Or.	45·28 N	117·28 W
110	Wallula....................Wa.	46·08 N	118·55 W
154	Walney (C.) (wôl′nè)........Eng.	54·04 N	3·13 W
113	Walnut (wôl′nŭt)		
	Ca. (Los Angeles In.)	34·00 N	117·51 W
117	Walnut (R.)................Ks.	37·28 N	97·06 W
115	Walnut Canyon Natl. Mon....Az.	35·10 N	111·30 W
112	Walnut Creek		
	Ca. (San Francisco In.)	37·54 N	122·04 W
113	Walnut Cr.		
	Tx. (Dallas, Fort Worth In.)	32·37 N	97·03 W
117	Walnut Ridge (rĭj).........Ar.	36·04 N	90·56 W
99	Walpole (wôl′pōl).....Ma. (In.)	42·09 N	71·15 W
105	Walpole....................NH	43·05 N	72·25 W
148	Walsall (wôl-sôl)..........Eng.	52·35 N	1·58 W
116	Walsenburg (wôl′sĕn-bûrg)....Co.	37·38 N	104·46 W
120	Walter F. George Res.....Al.-Ga.	32·00 N	85·00 W
116	Walters (wôl′tērz)..........Ok.	34·21 N	98·19 W
99	Waltham (wôl′thảm)...Ma. (In.)	42·22 N	71·14 W
148	Walthamstow (wôl′tăm-stō)		
	Eng. (London In.)	51·34 N	0·01 W
105	Walton....................NY	42·10 N	75·05 W
148	Walton-le-Dale (lĕ-dāl′)...Eng.	53·44 N	2·40 W
212	Walvis Bay (wôl′vĭs).....S. Afr.	22·50 S	14·30 E
109	Walworth (wôl′wŭrth)........Wi.	42·33 N	88·39 W
216	Wamba (S.).................Zaire	5·30 N	17·05 E
117	Wamego (wŏ-mē′gō).........Ks.	39·13 N	96·17 W
213	Wami (R.) (wä′mē)..........Tan.	6·31 S	37·17 E
97	Wanapitei L................Can.	46·45 N	80·45 W
106	Wanaque (wŏn′á-kū)		
	NJ (New York In.)	41·03 N	74·16 W
106	Wanaque Res.		
	NJ (New York In.)	41·06 N	74·20 W
190	Wanchih (wän′chī′)......China	31·11 N	118·31 E
203	Wandoan...................Austl.	26·09 S	149·51 E
149	Wandsbek (vänds′bĕk)		
	F.R.G. (Hamburg In.)	53·34 N	10·07 E
148	Wandsworth (wŏndz′wûrth)..Eng.	51·26 N	0·12 W
205	Wanganui (wŏŋ′gà-nōō′è)		
	N. Z. (In.)	39·53 N	175·01 E
203	Wangaratta (wŏŋ′gà-răt′à)...Austl.	36·23 N	146·18 E
194	Wangching (wäng′chēng)...China	43·14 N	129·33 E
190	Wangch′ingt′o		
	(wäng′chĭng′tŏŏŭ).China	39·14 N	116·56 E
158	Wangeroog I. (väng′ē-rōg).F.R.G.	53·49 N	7·57 E
193	Wanhsien (wän′hsyĕn)....China	30·48 N	108·22 E
190	Wanhsien (wän′sĭän)......China	38·51 N	115·10 E
217	Wankie (wă′kē)............Rh.	18·22 S	26·29 E
148	Wantage (wŏn′tảj)		
	Eng. (London In.)	51·33 N	1·26 W
106	Wantagh.....NY (New York In.)	40·41 N	73·30 W
193	Wantsai...................China	28·05 N	114·25 E
203	Waodoan (wŏd′ŏn)........Austl.	26·12 S	149·52 E
104	Wapakoneta (wŏ′pá-kŏ-nĕt′á).Oh.	40·35 N	84·10 W
94	Wapawekka Hills		
	(wŏ′pǎ-wĕ′-kǎ-hĭlz).Can.	54·45 N	104·20 W
94	Wapawekka L..............Can.	54·55 N	104·40 W
109	Wapello (wŏ-pĕl′ō).........Ia.	41·10 N	91·11 W
95	Wapesi L. (wŏ-pĕ′-zē)......Can.	50·34 N	92·21 W
117	Wappapello Res. (wă′pá-pĕl-lō)		
	Mo.	37·07 N	90·10 W
105	Wappingers Falls (wŏp′ĭn-jērz)		
	NY	41·35 N	73·55 W

Page	Name Pronunciation Region	Lat. °′	Long. °′
109	Wapsipinicon (R.)		
	(wŏp′sĭ-pĭn′ĭ-kŏn).Ia.	42·16 N	91·35 W
195	Warabi (wä′rä-bè)		
	Jap. (Tōkyō In.)	35·50 N	139·41 E
184	Warangal (wŭ′răŋ-gàl)......India	18·03 N	79·45 E
204	Warburton, The (R.)		
	(wôr′bûr-tŭn).Austl.	27·30 S	138·45 E
183	Wardān, Wādī (R.)		
	Egypt (Palestine In.)	29·22 N	33·00 E
92	Ward Cove.................Ak.	55·24 N	131·43 W
218	Warden.................S. Afr.		
	(Johannesburg & Pretoria In.)	27·52 S	28·59 E
184	Wardha (wŭr′dä)..........India	20·46 N	78·42 E
104	War Eagle (wôr ē′g′l).......WV	37·30 N	81·50 W
158	Waren (vä′rĕn)............F.R.G.	53·32 N	12·43 E
161	Warendorf (vä′rĕn-dôrf)		
	F.R.G. (Ruhr In.)	51·57 N	7·59 E
203	Warialda...................Austl.	29·32 S	150·34 E
212	Warmbad (värm′bäd) (wôrm′bǎd)		
	S. W. Afr.	28·25 S	18·45 E
218	Warmbad.................S. Afr.		
	(Johannesburg & Pretoria In.)	24·52 S	28·18 E
112	Warm Beach (wôrm)		
	Wa. (Seattle In.)	48·10 N	122·22 W
110	Warm Springs Ind. Res.		
	(wôrm sprĭnz).Or.	44·55 N	121·30 W
110	Warm Springs Res.........Or.	43·42 N	118·40 W
156	Warnemünde (vär′nĕ-mün-dĕ)		
	G.D.R.	54·11 N	12·04 E
110	Warner Ra. (Mts.).......Ca.-Or.	41·30 N	120·17 W
158	Warnow R. (vär′nō).......G.D.R.	53·51 N	11·55 E
203	Warracknabeal..............Austl.	36·20 S	142·28 E
203	Warragamba Res.		
	Austl. (Sydney In.)	33·40 S	150·00 E
205	Warrego (R.) (wôr′è-gō)...Austl.	27·13 S	145·58 E
117	Warren (wŏr′ĕn)............Ar.	33·37 N	92·03 W
100	Warren.....Can. (Winnipeg In.)	50·08 N	97·32 W
104	Warren.....................In.	40·40 N	85·25 W
107	Warren.......Mi. (Detroit In.)	42·33 N	83·03 W
108	Warren.....................Mn.	48·11 N	96·44 W
104	Warren.....................Oh.	41·15 N	80·50 W
112	Warren.......Or. (Portland In.)	45·49 N	122·51 W
105	Warren.....................Pa.	41·50 N	79·10 W
106	Warren.......RI (Providence In.)	41·44 N	71·14 W
107	Warrendale (wôr′ĕn-dāl)		
	Pa. (Pittsburgh In.)	40·39 N	80·04 W
117	Warrensburg (wôr′ĕnz-bûrg)..Mo.	38·45 N	93·42 W
121	Warrenton (wôr′ĕn-tŭn)......Ga.	33·26 N	82·37 W
112	Warrenton...Or. (Portland In.)	46·10 N	123·56 W
105	Warrenton..................Va.	38·45 N	77·50 W
210	Warri (wär′è)...............Nig.	5·33 N	5·43 E
148	Warrington................Eng.	53·22 N	2·30 W
120	Warrington (wŏr′ĭng-tŭn)....Fl.	30·21 N	87·15 W
203	Warrnambool (wôr′năm-bōōl)		
	Austl.	36·20 S	142·28 E
109	Warroad (wôr′rōd)..........Mn.	48·55 N	95·20 W
205	Warrumbungle Ra.		
	(wŏr′ŭm-bŭŋ-g′l).Austl.	31·18 S	150·00 E
117	Warsaw (wôr′sô)............Il.	40·21 N	91·26 W
104	Warsaw.....................In.	41·15 N	85·50 W
105	Warsaw.....................NY	42·45 N	78·10 W
121	Warsaw.....................NC	35·00 N	78·07 W
	Warsaw, see Warszawa		
148	Warsop (wôr′sŭp)..........Eng.	53·13 N	1·05 W
159	Warszawa (Warsaw) (vàr-shä′vá)		
	Pol.	52·15 N	21·05 E
158	Warta R. (vär′tà)...........Pol.	52·35 N	15·07 E
213	Wartburg......S. Afr. (Natal In.)	29·26 S	30·39 E
203	Warwick (wôr′ĭk)..........Austl.	28·05 S	152·10 E
98	Warwick...................Can.	45·58 N	71·57 W
154	Warwick....................Eng.	52·19 N	1·46 W
106	Warwick.....NY (New York In.)	41·15 N	74·22 W
106	Warwick....RI (Providence In.)	41·42 N	71·27 W
148	Warwick (Co.)...............Eng.	52·22 N	1·34 W
113	Wasatch Mts. (wŏ′sǎch)		
	Ut. (Salt Lake City In.)	40·45 N	111·46 W
115	Wasatch Plat...............Ut.	38·55 N	111·40 W
102	Wasatch Ra................U. S.	39·10 N	111·30 W
213	Wasbank......S. Afr. (Natal In.)	28·27 S	30·09 E
110	Wasco (wäs′kō)............Or.	45·36 N	120·42 W
109	Waseca (wŏ-sē′ká).........Mn.	44·04 N	93·31 W
155	Wash, The (Est.) (wŏsh)...Eng.	53·00 N	0·20 E
98	Washburn (wŏsh′bûrn)......Me.	46·46 N	68·10 W
109	Washburn...................Wi.	46·41 N	90·55 W
111	Washburn, Mt..............Wy.	44·50 N	110·10 W
106	Washington (wŏsh′ĭng-tŭn)		
	DC (Washington DC In.)	38·50 N	77·00 W
120	Washington.................Ga.	33·43 N	82·46 W
104	Washington.................In.	38·40 N	87·10 W
109	Washington.................Ia.	41·17 N	91·42 W
117	Washington.................Ks.	39·48 N	97·04 W
117	Washington.................Mo.	38·33 N	91·00 W
121	Washington.................NC	35·32 N	77·01 W
105	Washington..Pa. (Pittsburgh In.)	40·10 N	80·14 W
102	Washington (State)........U. S.	47·30 N	121·10 W
105	Washington, Mt............NH	44·15 N	71·15 W
112	Washington, L..Wa. (Seattle In.)	47·34 N	122·12 W
109	Washington (I.)............Wi.	45·18 N	86·42 W

Page	Name Pronunciation Region	Lat. °′	Long. °′
104	Washington Court House.....Oh.	39·30 N	83·25 W
113	Washington Park.Il. (St. Louis In.)	38·38 N	90·06 W
116	Washita (R.) (wŏsh′ĭ-tô)....Ok.	35·33 N	99·16 W
112	Washougal (wŏ-shōō′gàl)		
	Wa. (Portland In.)	45·35 N	122·21 W
112	Washougal (R.)		
	Wa. (Portland In.)	45·38 N	122·17 W
159	Wasilkow (và-sēl′kŏŏf).......Pol.	53·12 N	23·13 E
95	Waskaiowaka L.		
	(wŏ′skǎ-yō′wŏ-kǎ).Can.	56·30 N	96·20 W
95	Wass L. (wŏs).............Can.	53·40 N	95·25 W
161	Wassenberg (vä′sĕn-bĕrgh)		
	F.R.G. (Ruhr In.)	51·06 N	6·07 E
114	Wassuk Ra. (wàs′sŭk)......Nv.	38·58 N	119·00 W
97	Waswanipi, Lac (L.).......Can.	49·35 N	76·15 W
123	Water (I.) (wŏ′tēr)		
	Vir. Is. (U. S. A.) (St. Thomas In.)	18·20 N	64·57 W
218	Waterberge (Mts.)		
	(wŏrtēr′bûrg).S. Afr.		
	(Johannesburg & Pretoria In.)	24·25 S	27·53 E
121	Waterboro (wŏ-tēr-bûr-ō).....SC	32·50 N	80·40 W
105	Waterbury (wŏ′tēr-bĕr-è).....Ct.	41·30 N	73·00 W
129	Water Cay (I.)...............Ba.	22·55 N	75·50 W
100	Waterdown (wŏ′tēr-doun)		
	Can. (Toronto In.)	43·20 N	79·54 W
121	Wateree (R.) (wŏ′tēr-ē).....SC	34·40 N	80·48 W
154	Waterford (wŏ′tēr-fērd).....Ire.	52·20 N	7·03 W
107	Waterford...Wi. (Milwaukee In.)	42·46 N	88·13 W
149	Waterloo (Brussels In.).....Bel.	50·44 N	4·24 E
97	Waterloo (wŏ-tēr-lōō′)......Can.	43·30 N	80·40 W
111	Waterloo..................Can.	42·55 N	72·30 W
117	Waterloo....................Il.	38·19 N	90·08 W
107	Waterloo....................Ia.	42·30 N	92·22 W
106	Waterloo...Md. (Baltimore In.)	39·11 N	76·50 W
105	Waterloo....................NY	42·55 N	76·50 W
90	Waterton-Glacier Intl. Peace Park		
	(wŏ′ter-tŭn-glā′shàr).Mt.-Can.	48·55 N	114·10 W
93	Waterton Lakes Nat. Pk....Can.	49·05 N	113·50 W
99	Watertown (wŏ′tēr-toun)		
	Ma. (In.)	42·22 N	71·11 W
105	Watertown..................NY	44·00 N	75·55 W
108	Watertown..................SD	44·53 N	97·07 W
107	Watertown..................Wi.	43·13 N	88·40 W
120	Water Valley (vǎl′è)........Ms.	34·08 N	89·38 W
98	Waterville.................Me.	44·36 N	69·37 W
107	Waterville.................Mn.	44·10 N	93·35 W
110	Waterville.................Wa.	47·38 N	120·04 W
105	Watervliet (wŏ′tēr-vlēt′)....NY	42·45 N	73·54 W
148	Watford (wŏt′fôrd)		
	Eng. (London In.)	51·38 N	0·24 W
94	Wathaman L................Can.	56·55 N	103·43 W
	Watling (I.), see San Salvador		
148	Watlington (wŏt′lĭng-tŭn)		
	Eng. (London In.)	51·37 N	1·01 W
116	Watonga (wŏ-tôŋ′gà)........Ok.	35·50 N	98·26 W
217	Watsa (wät′sä)..............Zaire	3·03 N	29·32 E
104	Watseka (wŏt-sē′ká)..........Il.	40·45 N	87·45 W
107	Watson (wŏt′sŭn)		
	In. (Louisville In.)	38·21 N	85·42 W
90	Watson Lake...............Can.	60·18 N	128·50 W
114	Watsonville (wŏt′sŭn-vĭl)....Ca.	36·55 N	121·46 W
161	Wattenscheid (vä′tĕn-shīd)		
	F.R.G. (Ruhr In.)	51·30 N	7·07 E
113	Watts (wŏts).Ca. (Los Angeles In.)	33·56 N	118·15 W
120	Watts Bar (R.) (bär).......Tn.	35·45 N	84·49 W
108	Waubay (wŏ′bā)............SD	45·19 N	97·18 W
121	Wauchula (wŏ-chōō′lá)..Fl. (In.)	27·32 N	81·48 W
107	Wauconda		
	Il. (Chicago In.)	42·15 N	88·08 W
107	Waukegan		
	Il. (Chicago In.)	42·22 N	87·51 W
107	Waukesha (wŏ′kè-shô)		
	Wi. (Milwaukee In.)	43·01 N	88·13 W
109	Waukon (wŏ-kŏn′).........Ia.	43·15 N	91·30 W
109	Waupaca (wŏ-pǎk′á).......Wi.	44·22 N	89·06 W
109	Waupun (wŏ-pŭn′)........Wi.	43·37 N	88·45 W
116	Waurika (wŏ-rē′ká)........Ok.	34·09 N	97·59 W
109	Wausau (wŏ′sô)............Wi.	44·58 N	89·40 W
109	Wausaukee (wŏ-sô′kè)......Wi.	45·22 N	87·58 W
104	Wauseon (wŏ′sè-ŏn)........Oh.	41·30 N	84·10 W
109	Wautoma (wŏ-tō′má)......Wi.	44·04 N	89·11 W
107	Wauwatosa (wŏ-wà-t′ō′sà)		
	Wi. (Milwaukee In.)	43·03 N	88·00 W
155	Waveney (R.) (wāv′nè)......Eng.	52·27 N	1·17 E
109	Waverly (wā′vēr-lè)........Ia.	42·43 N	92·29 W
213	Waverly......S. Afr. (Natal In.)	34·35 S	26·29 E
120	Waverly....................Tn.	36·04 N	87·46 W
211	Wāw......................Sud.	7·41 N	28·00 E
96	Wawa.....................Can.	47·59 N	84·47 W
211	Wāw al-Kabir.............Libya	25·23 N	16·52 E
95	Wawanesa (wŏ′wŏ-nē′sǎ)...Can.	49·36 N	99·41 W
104	Wawasee (L.) (wŏ-sē′)......In.	41·15 N	85·45 W
119	Waxahachie (wăk-sà-hǎch′è)..Tx.	32·23 N	96·50 W
121	Waycross (wā′krôs)..........Ga.	31·11 N	82·24 W
120	Wayland (wā′lănd)..........Ky.	37·25 N	82·47 W
99	Wayland...............Ma. (In.)	42·23 N	71·22 W

ăt; finăl; rāte; senâte; ärm; ȧsk; sofȧ; fâre; ch-choose; dh-as th in other; bē; ĕvent; bĕt; recĕnt; cratēr; g-go; gh-guttural g; bĭt; ĭ-short neutral; rīde; κ-guttural k as ch in German ich;

Page	Name Pronunciation Region	Lat. °′	Long. °′
107	Wayne . . . Mi. (Detroit In.)	42·17 N	83·23 W
108	Wayne . . . Ne.	42·13 N	97·03 W
106	Wayne . . . NJ (New York In.)	40·56 N	74·16 W
106	Wayne . . . Pa. (Philadelphia In.)	40·03 N	75·22 W
121	Waynesboro (wānz'bŭr-ō) . . . Ga.	33·05 N	82·02 W
105	Waynesboro . . . Pa.	39·45 N	77·35 W
105	Waynesboro . . . Va.	38·05 N	78·50 W
105	Waynesburg (wānz'bûrg) . . . Pa.	39·55 N	80·10 W
120	Waynesville (wānz'vĭl) . . . NC	35·28 N	82·58 W
116	Waynoka (wā-nō'kȧ) . . . Ok.	36·34 N	98·52 W
113	Wayzata (wā-zä-tȧ) . . . Mn. (Minneapolis, St. Paul In.)	44·58 N	93·31 W
184	Wazīrbad . . . Pak.	32·39 N	74·11 E
95	Weagamow L. (wē'ăg-ȧ-mou) Can.	52·53 N	91·22 W
154	Weald, The (Reg.) (wēld) . . . Eng.	50·58 N	0·15 W
116	Weatherford (wĕ-dhēr-fērd) . . . Ok.	85·32 N	98·41 W
119	Weatherford . . . Tx.	32·45 N	97·46 W
148	Weaver (R.) (wē'vēr) . . . Eng.	53·09 N	2·31 W
110	Weaverville (wē'vēr-vĭl) . . . Ca.	40·44 N	122·55 W
117	Webb City . . . Mo.	37·10 N	94·26 W
113	Weber R. . Ut. (Salt Lake City In.)	41·13 N	112·07 W
99	Webster . . . Ma. (In.)	42·04 N	71·52 W
108	Webster . . . SD	45·19 N	97·30 W
109	Webster City . . . Ia.	42·28 N	93·49 W
113	Webster Groves (grōvz) Mo. (St. Louis In.)	38·36 N	90·22 W
105	Webster Springs (sprĭngz) . . . WV	38·30 N	80·20 W
220	Weddell Sea (wĕd'ĕl) . . . Ant.	73·00 S	45·00 W
149	Wedel (vā'dĕl) F.R.G. (Hamburg In.)	53·35 N	9·42 E
92	Wedge Mtn. (wĕj) . . . Can.	50·10 N	122·50 W
98	Wedgeport (wĕj'pōrt) . . . Can.	43·44 N	65·59 W
148	Wednesfield (wĕd''nz-fēld) . . . Eng.	52·36 N	2·04 W
110	Weed (wēd) . . . Ca.	41·35 N	122·21 W
213	Weenen (vā'nĕn) S. Afr. (Natal In.)	28·52 S	30·05 E
155	Weert . . . Neth.	51·16 N	5·39 E
149	Weesp . . . Neth. (Amsterdam In.)	52·18 N	5·01 E
159	Wegorzewo (vôŋ-gô'zhĕ-vô) . . . Pol.	54·14 N	21·46 E
159	Wegrow (vôŋ'grōōf) . . . Pol.	52·23 N	22·02 E
190	Wei (R.) (wā) . . . China	35·47 N	114·27 E
192	Weich'ang (wā'chäng') . . . China	41·50 N	118·00 E
190	Weifang . . . China	36·43 N	119·08 E
190	Weihai (wa'hăĭ') . . . China	37·30 N	122·05 E
192	Wei Ho (R.) . . . China	34·00 N	108·10 E
188	Weihsi (wā'hsē') . . . China	27·27 N	99·30 E
190	Weihsien (wā'hsyĕn') . . . China	36·59 N	115·17 E
158	Weilheim (vīl'hīm') . . . F.R.G.	47·50 N	11·06 E
158	Weimar (vī'mär) . . . G.D.R.	50·59 N	11·20 E
192	Weinan . . . China	34·32 N	109·40 E
205	Weipa . . . Austl.	12·25 S	141·54 E
95	Weir River (wēr-rĭv-ēr) . . . Can.	56·49 N	94·04 W
104	Weirton (wēr'tŭn) . . . WV	40·25 N	80·35 W
110	Weiser (wē'zēr) . . . Id.	44·15 N	116·58 W
110	Weiser R. . . . Id.	44·26 N	116·40 W
190	Weishih (wā'shē) . . . China	34·23 N	114·12 E
158	Weissenburg (vī'sĕn-bōōrgh) F.R.G.	49·04 N	11·20 E
158	Weissenfels (vī'sĕn-fĕlz) . . . G.D.R.	51·13 N	11·58 E
159	Wejherowo (vā-hĕ-rō'vô) . . . Pol.	54·36 N	18·15 E
121	Welch (wĕlch) . . . WV	37·24 N	81·28 W
121	Weldon (wĕl'dŭn) . . . NC	36·24 N	77·36 W
117	Weldon (R.) . . . Mo.	40·22 N	93·39 W
117	Weleetka (wê-lēt'kȧ) . . . Ok.	35·19 N	96·08 W
203	Welford (wĕl'fērd) . . . Austl.	25·08 S	144·43 E
218	Welkom (wĕl'kŏm) . . . S. Afr. (Johannesburg & Pretoria In.)	27·57 S	26·45 E
107	Welland (wĕl'ănd) Can. (Buffalo In.)	42·59 N	79·13 W
154	Welland (R.) . . . Eng.	52·38 N	0·40 W
99	Wellesley (wĕlz'lê) . . . Ma. (In.)	42·18 N	71·17 W
204	Wellesley Is. . . . Austl.	16·15 S	139·25 E
203	Wellington (wĕl'lĭng-tŭn) . . . Austl.	32·40 S	148·50 E
148	Wellington . . . Eng.	52·42 N	2·30 W
117	Wellington . . . Ks.	37·16 N	97·24 W
205	Wellington . . . N. Z. (In.)	41·15 S	174·45 E
104	Wellington . . . Oh.	41·10 N	82·10 W
116	Wellington . . . Tx.	34·51 N	100·12 W
136	Wellington (I.) (ōōĕ'lĕng-tōn) Chile	49·30 S	76·30 W
204	Wells (wĕlz) . . . Austl.	26·35 S	123·40 E
93	Wells . . . Can.	53·06 N	121·34 W
104	Wells . . . Mi.	45·50 N	87·00 W
109	Wells . . . Mn.	43·44 N	93·43 W
110	Wells . . . Nv.	41·07 N	115·04 W
105	Wellsboro (wĕlz'bŭ-rō) . . . Pa.	41·45 N	77·15 W
104	Wellsburg (wĕlz'bûrg) . . . WV	40·10 N	80·40 W
110	Wells Res. . . . Wa.	48·05 N	119·45 W
104	Wellston (wĕlz'tŭn) . . . Oh.	39·05 N	82·30 W
117	Wellsville (wĕlz'vĭl) . . . Mo.	39·04 N	91·33 W
105	Wellsville . . . NY	42·10 N	78·00 W
104	Wellsville . . . Oh.	40·35 N	80·40 W
111	Wellsville . . . Ut.	41·38 N	111·57 W
158	Wels (vĕls) . . . Aus.	48·10 N	14·01 E
154	Welshpool (wĕlsh'pōōl) . . . Wales	52·44 N	3·10 W
218	Welverdiend (vĕl-vēr-dēnd').S. Afr. (Johannesburg & Pretoria In.)	26·23 S	27·16 E
148	Welwyn Garden City (wĕl'ĭn) Eng. (London In.)	51·46 N	0·17 W
148	Wem (wĕm) . . . Eng.	52·51 N	2·44 W
217	Wembere (R.) . . . Tan.	4·35 S	33·55 E
190	Wenan Wa (Swp.) (wĕn'än' wä) China	38·56 N	116·29 E
110	Wenatchee (wê-năch'ê) . . . Wa.	47·24 N	120·18 W
110	Wenatchee Mts. . . . Wa.	47·28 N	121·10 W
193	Wench'ang . . . China	19·32 N	110·42 E
214	Wenchi . . . Ghana	7·42 N	2·07 W
193	Wenchou (wĕn'chō) . . . China	28·00 N	120·40 E
192	Wench'üan (Halunrshan) . . . China	47·10 N	120·00 E
211	Wendo . . . Eth.	6·37 N	38·29 E
111	Wendorer . . . Ut.	40·47 N	114·01 W
100	Wendover (wĕn-dōv'ēr) Can. (Ottawa In.)	45·34 N	75·07 W
148	Wendover . . . Eng. (London In.)	51·44 N	0·45 W
99	Wenham (wĕn'ăm) . . . Ma. (In.)	42·36 N	70·53 W
106	Wenonah (wĕn'ō-nā) NJ (Philadelphia In.)	39·48 N	75·08 W
193	Wenshan . . . China	23·20 N	104·15 E
190	Wenshang (wĕn'shäng) . . . China	35·43 N	116·31 E
190	Wenshussu (wĕn'shōō'sĕ) . . . China	31·55 N	114·47 E
188	Wensu (Aksu) (wĕn'sōō') (äk'sōō') China	41·45 N	80·30 E
155	Wensum (R.) (wĕn'sŭm) . . . Eng.	52·45 N	1·08 E
190	Wenteng (wĕn'tĕng') . . . China	37·14 N	122·03 E
203	Wentworth (wĕnt'wûrth) . . . Austl.	24·03 S	141·53 E
212	Wepener (wē'pĕn-ēr) (vā'pĕn-ēr) S. Afr.	29·43 S	27·04 E
149	Werder (vĕr'dĕr) G.D.R. (Berlin In.)	52·23 N	12·56 E
211	Were Ilu . . . Eth.	10·39 N	39·21 E
161	Werl (vĕrl) . . . F.R.G. (Ruhr In.)	51·33 N	7·55 E
161	Werne (vĕr'nĕ) . F.R.G. (Ruhr In.)	51·39 N	7·38 E
149	Werneuchen (vĕr'hoi-ĸĕn) G.D.R. (Berlin In.)	52·38 N	13·44 E
158	Werra R. (vĕr'ä) . . . F.R.G.	51·16 N	9·54 E
202	Werribee . . Austl. (Melbourne In.)	37·54 S	144·40 E
202	Werribee (R.) Austl. (Melbourne In.)	37·40 S	144·37 E
158	Wertach R. (vĕr'täk) . . . F.R.G.	48·12 N	10·40 E
161	Weseke (vĕ'zĕ-kĕ) F.R.G. (Ruhr In.)	51·54 N	6·51 E
161	Wesel (vā'zĕl) . . F.R.G. (Ruhr In.)	51·39 N	6·37 E
158	Weser R. (vā'zĕr) . . . F.R.G.	53·08 N	8·35 E
118	Weslaco (wĕs-lā'kō) . . . Tx.	26·10 N	97·59 W
97	Weslemkoon (L.) . . . Can.	45·02 N	77·25 W
99	Wesleyville (wĕs'lē-vĭl) . . . Can.	49·09 N	53·34 W
204	Wessel (Is.) (wĕs'ĕl) . . . Austl.	11·45 S	136·25 E
218	Wesselsbron (wĕs'ĕl-brŏn) . . S. Afr. (Johannesburg & Pretoria In.)	27·51 S	26·22 E
108	Wessington Springs (wĕs'ĭng-tŭn) . SD	44·06 N	98·35 W
122	West, Mt. . . . C. Z. (In.)	9·10 N	79·52 W
107	West Allis (wĕst-ăl'ĭs) Wi. (Milwaukee In.)	43·01 N	88·01 W
113	West Alton (ôl'tŭn) Mo. (St. Louis In.)	38·52 N	90·13 W
119	West B. . . . Tx. (In.)	29·11 N	95·03 W
109	West Bend (wĕst bĕnd) . . . Wi.	43·25 N	88·13 W
184	West Bengal (State) (bĕn-gôl') India	23·30 N	87·30 E
149	West Berlin (bĕr-lēn') F.R.G. (Berlin In.)	52·31 N	13·20 E
120	West Blocton (blŏk'tŭn) . . . Al.	33·05 N	87·05 W
99	Westborough (wĕst'bŭr-ō) Ma. (In.)	42·17 N	71·37 W
99	West Boylston (boil'stŭn) Ma. (In.)	42·22 N	71·46 W
104	West Branch (wĕst brȧnch) . . . Mi.	44·15 N	84·10 W
148	West Bridgford (brĭj'fērd) . . . Eng.	52·55 N	1·08 W
148	West Bromwich (wĕst brŭm'ĭj) Eng.	52·32 N	1·59 W
98	Westbrook (wĕst'brŏŏk) . . . Me.	43·41 N	70·23 W
109	Westby (wĕst'bê) . . . Wi.	43·40 N	90·52 W
129	West Caicos (I.) (kăē'kō) (kī'kōs) Turks & Caicos	21·40 N	72·30 W
204	West Cape Howe (C.) . . . Austl.	35·15 S	117·30 E
107	West Chester (chĕs'tēr) Oh. (Cincinnati In.)	39·20 N	84·24 W
106	West Chester Pa. (Philadelphia In.)	39·57 N	75·36 W
107	West Chicago (chĭ-kä'gō) Il. (Chicago In.)	41·53 N	88·12 W
121	West Columbia (cŏl'ŭm-bē-ȧ) . . SC	33·58 N	81·05 W
119	West Columbia . . . Tx.	29·08 N	95·39 W
119	West Cote Blanche B. (kōt blänch) La.	29·30 N	92·17 W
113	West Covina (wĕst kô-vē'nȧ) Ca. (Los Angeles In.)	34·04 N	117·55 W
109	West Des Moines (dē moin') . . . Ia.	41·35 N	93·42 W
109	West Des Moines (R.) . . . Ia.	42·52 N	94·32 W
128	West End . . . Ba.	26·40 N	78·55 W
148	Westerham (wĕ'stĕr'ŭm) Eng. (London In.)	51·15 N	0·05 E
149	Westerhorn (vĕs'tĕr-hōrn) F.R.G. (Hamburg In.)	53·52 N	9·41 E
149	Westerlo . . . Bel. (Brussels In.)	51·05 N	4·57 E
105	Westerly (wĕs'tēr-lê) . . . RI	41·25 N	71·50 W
158	Western Alps (Mts.) . . . Switz.-Fr.	46·19 N	7·03 E
204	Western Australia (State) (ôs-trā'lĭ-ȧ) . Austl.	24·15 S	121·30 E
154	Western Downs . . . Eng.	50·50 N	2·25 W
185	Western Ghāts (Mts.) . . . India	17·35 N	74·00 E
105	Western Port (wĕs'tērn pōrt) . . Md.	39·30 N	79·00 W
209	Western Sahara (sȧ-hä'rȧ) . . . Afr.	23·05 N	15·33 W
198	Western Samoa . . . Oceania	14·30 S	172·00 W
168	Western Siberian Lowland Sov. Un.	63·37 N	72·45 E
104	Westerville (wĕs'tēr-vĭl) . . . Oh.	40·10 N	83·00 W
158	Westerwald (For.) (vĕs'tĕr-väld) . . . F.R.G.	50·35 N	7·45 E
105	Westfield (wĕst'fēld) . . . Ma.	42·05 N	72·45 W
106	Westfield . . . NJ (New York In.)	40·39 N	74·21 W
106	Westfield (wĕst'fēld) . . . NY	42·20 N	79·40 W
99	Westford (wĕst'fērd) . . . Ma. (In.)	42·35 N	71·26 W
106	West Frankfort (frăŋk'fŭrt) . . . Il.	37·55 N	88·55 W
148	West Ham . . . Eng. (London In.)	51·30 N	0·00
105	West Hartford (härt'fērd) . . . Ct.	41·45 N	72·45 W
117	West Helena (hĕl'ĕn-ȧ) . . . Ar.	34·32 N	90·39 W
123	West Indies (Reg.) (ĭn'dēz) . . N. A.	19·00 N	78·30 W
113	West Jordan (jôr'dăn) Ut. (Salt Lake City In.)	40·37 N	111·56 W
148	West Kirby (kûr'bê) . . . Eng.	53·22 N	3·11 W
104	West Lafayette (lä-fȧ-yĕt') . . . In.	40·25 N	86·55 W
107	Westlake . . . Oh. (Cleveland In.)	41·27 N	81·55 W
218	Westleigh (wĕst-lē) . . . S. Afr. (Johannesburg & Pretoria In.)	27·39 S	27·18 E
109	West Liberty (wĕst lĭb'ēr-tĭ) . . . Ia.	41·34 N	91·15 W
112	West Linn (lĭn) . . Or. (Portland In.)	45·22 N	122·37 W
93	Westlock (wĕst'lŏk) . . . Can.	54·09 N	113·52 W
117	West Memphis . . . Ar.	35·08 N	90·11 W
113	Westminster (wĕst'mĭn-stēr) Ca. (Los Angeles In.)	33·45 N	117·59 W
105	Westminster . . . Md.	39·40 N	76·55 W
120	Westminster . . . SC	34·38 N	83·10 W
100	Westmount (wĕst'mount) Can. (Montréal In.)	45·29 N	73·36 W
99	West Newbury (nū'bēr-ê) Ma. (In.)	42·47 N	70·57 W
107	West Newton (nū'tŭn) Pa. (Pittsburgh In.)	40·12 N	79·45 W
106	West New York (nû yŏrk) NJ (New York In.)	40·47 N	74·01 W
117	West Nishnabotna (R.) (nĭsh-nȧ-bŏt'nȧ) . Ia.	40·56 N	95·37 W
99	Weston (wĕs'tŭn) . . . Ma. (In.)	42·22 N	71·18 W
104	Weston . . . WV	39·00 N	80·30 W
218	Westonaria . . . S. Afr. (Johannesburg & Pretoria In.)	26·19 S	27·38 E
154	Weston-super-Mare (wĕs'tŭn sū'pēr-mā'rê) . Eng.	51·23 N	3·00 W
106	West Orange (wĕst ŏr'ĕnj) NJ (New York In.)	40·46 N	74·14 W
121	West Palm Beach (päm bēch) Fl. (In.)	26·44 N	80·04 W
120	West Pensacola (pĕn-sȧ-kō'lȧ) . . Fl.	30·24 N	87·18 W
112	West Pittsburg (pĭts'bûrg) Ca. (San Francisco In.)	38·02 N	121·56 W
117	Westplains (wĕst-plānz') . . . Mo.	36·42 N	91·51 W
120	West Point . . . Ga.	32·52 N	85·10 W
120	West Point . . . Ms.	33·36 N	88·39 W
108	Westpoint . . . Ne.	41·50 N	96·00 W
106	West Point . . . NY (New York In.)	41·23 N	73·58 W
113	West Point Ut. (Salt Lake City In.)	41·07 N	112·05 W
105	West Point . . . Va.	37·25 N	76·50 W
106	Westport (wĕst'pōrt) Ct. (New York In.)	41·07 N	73·22 W
154	Westport . . . Ire.	53·44 N	9·36 W
112	Westport (wĕst'pôrt) Or. (Portland In.)	46·08 N	123·22 W
154	Westray (I.) (wĕs'trâ) . . . Scot.	59·19 N	3·05 W
92	West Road (R.) (rōd) . . . Can.	53·00 N	124·00 W
113	West St. Paul (sȧnt pôl') . . . Mn. (Minneapolis, St. Paul In.)	44·55 N	93·05 W
129	West Sand Spit (I.) . . . Ba.	21·25 N	72·10 W
155	West Schelde (R.) . . . Neth.	51·25 N	3·30 E
112	West Slope . . . Or. (Portland In.)	45·30 N	122·46 W
115	West Tavaputs Plat. (wĕst tăv'ȧ-pōōts) . Ut.	39·45 N	110·35 W
104	West Terre Haute (tĕr-ê hōt') . . In.	39·30 N	87·30 W
109	West Union (ūn'yŭn) . . . Ia.	42·58 N	91·48 W
119	West University Place . . . Tx. (In.)	29·43 N	95·26 W
107	Westview (wĕst'vû) Oh. (Cleveland In.)	41·21 N	81·54 W
107	West View . . . Pa. (Pittsburgh In.)	40·31 N	80·02 W
99	Westville (wĕst'vĭl) . . . Can.	45·34 N	62·43 W
104	Westville . . . Il.	40·00 N	87·40 W
103	West Virginia (State) (wĕst vēr-jĭn'ĭ-ȧ) . U. S.	39·00 N	80·50 W
114	West Walker (R.) (wôk'ēr) . . . Ca.	38·25 N	119·25 W
106	West Warwick (wŏr'ĭk) RI (Providence In.)	41·42 N	71·31 W
106	Westwego (wĕst-wē'gō) La. (New Orleans In.)	29·55 N	90·09 W

ng-sing; ŋ-baŋk; ɴ-nasalized n; nŏd; cŏmmit; ōld; ôbey; ôrder; fōōd; fŏŏt; ou-out; s-soft; sh-dish; th-thin; pūre; ûnite; ûrn; stŭd; circŭs; ü-as "y" in study; '-indeterminate vowel.

368 Westwood — Wilton PRONOUNCING INDEX

Page	Name Pronunciation Region	Lat. °′	Long. °′
114	Westwood (wĕst'wŏŏd) . . . . Ca.	40·18 N	121·00 W
113	Westwood . . Ks. (Kansas City In.)	39·03 N	94·37 W
99	Westwood . . . . Ma. (In.)	42·13 N	71·14 W
106	Westwood . . . . NJ (New York In.)	40·59 N	74·02 W
203	West Wyalong (wī'alông) . . . Austl.	34·00 S	147·20 E
197	Wetar (I.) (wĕt'ár) . . . . Indon.	7·34 S	126·00 E
93	Wetaskiwin (wē-tăs'kē-wŏn) . . Can.	52·58 N	113·22 W
113	Wetmore (wĕt'mōr) Tx. (San Antonio In.)	29·34 N	98·25 W
161	Wettin (vĕ'tĕn) . F.R.G. (Ruhr In.)	51·23 N	7·23 E
120	Wetumpka (wē-tŭmp'kȧ) . . . . . . Al.	32·33 N	86·12 W
161	Wetzlar (vets'lär) . . . . F.R.G.	50·35 N	8·30 E
197	Wewak (wā-wäk') . . . Pap. N. Gui.	3·19 S	143·30 E
117	Wewoka (wē-wō'kȧ) . . . . Ok.	35·09 N	96·30 W
154	Wexford (wĕks'fērd) . . . . Ire.	52·20 N	6·30 W
148	Weybridge (wā'brĭj) Eng. (London In.)	51·20 N	0·26 W
94	Weyburn (wā'-bûrn) . . . . Can.	49·41 N	103·52 W
211	Weyib (R.) . . . . Eth.	6·25 N	41·21 E
154	Weymouth (wā'mŭth) . . . . Eng.	50·37 N	2·34 W
99	Weymouth . . . . Ma. (In.)	42·44 N	70·57 W
107	Weymouth . . . . Oh. (Cleveland In.)	41·11 N	81·48 W
128	Whale Cay (I.) . . . . Ba.	24·50 N	77·45 W
128	Whale Cay Chans . . . . Ba.	26·45 N	77·10 W
154	Wharfe (R.) (hwôr'fē) . . . . Eng.	54·01 N	1·53 W
106	Wharton (hwôr'tŭn) NJ (New York In.)	40·54 N	74·35 W
119	Wharton . . . . Tx.	29·19 N	96·06 W
109	What Cheer (hwŏt chēr) . . . . Ia.	41·23 N	92·24 W
112	Whatcom, L. (hwät'kŭm) Wa. (Portland In.)	48·44 N	123·34 W
93	Whatshan L. (wŏt'-shăn) . . . . Can.	50·00 N	118·03 W
111	Wheatland (hwēt'lănd) . . . . Wy.	42·04 N	104·52 W
107	Wheaton (hwē'tŭn) Il. (Chicago In.)	41·52 N	88·06 W
106	Wheaton . . . . . Md. (Baltimore In.)	39·05 N	77·05 W
108	Wheaton . . . . Mn.	45·48 N	96·29 W
115	Wheeler Pk . . . . Nv.	38·58 N	114·15 W
107	Wheeling (hwēl'ĭng) Il. (Chicago In.)	42·08 N	87·54 W
104	Wheeling . . . . WV	40·05 N	80·45 W
137	Wheelwright (ōōē'l-rĕ'gt) Arg. (Buenos Aires In.)	33·46 S	61·14 W
112	Whidbey I. (hwĭd'bē) Wa. (Seattle In.)	48·13 N	122·50 W
106	Whippany (hwĭp'á-nē) NJ (New York In.)	40·49 N	74·25 W
120	Whistler (hwĭs'lēr) . . . . Al.	30·46 N	88·07 W
97	Whitby (hwĭt'bē) . . . . Can.	43·50 N	79·00 W
148	Whitchurch (hwĭt'chûrch) . . . . Eng.	52·58 N	2·49 W
97	White (L.) . . . . Can.	45·15 N	76·35 W
96	White (L.) . . . . Can.	48·47 N	85·50 W
96	White (R.) . . . . Can.	48·34 N	85·46 W
117	White (R.) . . . . Ar.	34·32 N	91·11 W
115	White (R.) . . . . Co.	40·10 N	108·55 W
104	White (R.) . . . . In.	39·15 N	86·45 W
108	White (R.) . . . . SD	43·41 N	99·48 W
108	White (R.), South Fork . . . . SD	43·13 N	101·04 W
116	White (R.) . . . . Tx.	36·25 N	102·20 W
105	White (R.) . . . . Vt.	43·45 N	72·35 W
114	White, Mt . . . . Ca.	37·38 N	118·13 W
99	White B . . . . Can.	50·00 N	56·30 W
113	White Bear Lake . . . . Mn. (Minneapolis, St. Paul In.)	45·05 N	93·01 W
113	White Bear L . . . . Mn. (Minneapolis, St. Paul In.)	45·04 N	92·58 W
95	White Bear Ind. Res . . . . Can.	49·15 N	102·15 W
119	White Castle . . . . La.	30·10 N	91·09 W
112	White Center . . . . Wa. (Seattle In.)	47·31 N	122·21 W
104	White Cloud . . . . Mi.	43·35 N	85·45 W
93	Whitecourt (wĭt'-côrt) . . . . Can.	54·09 N	115·41 W
108	White Earth (R.) . . . . ND	48·30 N	102·44 W
108	White Earth Ind. Res . . . . Mn.	47·18 N	95·42 W
109	Whiteface (R.) (whīt'fās) . . . . Mn.	47·12 N	92·13 W
105	Whitefield (hwĭt'fēld) . . . . NH	44·20 N	71·35 W
111	Whitefish (hwĭt'fĭsh) . . . . Mt.	48·24 N	114·25 W
109	Whitefish (B.) . . . . Mi.	46·36 N	84·50 W
109	Whitefish (R.) . . . . Mi.	46·12 N	86·56 W
95	Whitefish B . . . . Can.	49·26 N	94·14 W
107	Whitefish Bay Wi. (Milwaukee In.)	43·07 N	77·54 W
117	White Hall . . . . Il.	39·26 N	90·23 W
104	Whitehall (hwĭt'hôl) . . . . Mi.	43·20 N	86·20 W
105	Whitehall . . . . NY	43·30 N	73·25 W
154	Whitehaven (hwĭt'hā-vĕn) . . . Eng.	54·35 N	3·30 W
112	Whitehorn, Pt. (hwĭt'hôrn) Wa. (Vancouver In.)	48·54 N	122·48 W
90	Whitehorse (whīt'hôrs) . . . . . . Can.	60·39 N	135·01 W
119	White L . . . . La.	29·40 N	92·35 W
98	White Mts . . . . Me.	44·22 N	71·15 W
105	White Mts . . . . NH	42·20 N	71·05 W
108	Whitemouth (L.) . . . . Can.	49·14 N	95·40 W
211	White Nile (Abyad, Al-Bahr al-) (R.) . Sud.	14·00 N	32·35 E
109	White Otter (L.) . . . . Can.	49·15 N	91·48 W
90	White P . . . . Ak.-Can.	59·35 N	135·03 W
106	White Plains . . NY (New York In.)	41·02 N	73·47 W
96	White River . . . . Can.	48·38 N	85·23 W
104	White R., East Fork . . . . In.	38·45 N	86·20 W
110	White R . . . . Wa.	47·07 N	121·48 W
115	White River Plat . . . . Co.	39·45 N	107·50 W
112	White Rock . Can. (Vancouver In.)	49·01 N	122·49 W
113	Whiterock Res. (hwīt'rŏk) Tx. (Dallas, Fort Worth In.)	32·51 N	96·40 W
92	Whitesail L. (whīt'-sāl) . . . . . . Can.	53·30 N	127·00 W
115	White Sands Natl. Mon . . . . . . NM	32·50 N	106·20 W
170	White Sea . . . . Sov. Un.	66·00 N	40·00 E
113	White Settlement Tx. (Dallas, Fort Worth In.)	32·45 N	97·28 W
111	White Sulphur Springs . . . . Mt.	46·32 N	110·49 W
213	White Umfolzi (R.) (ŭm-fô-lō'zē) S. Afr. (Natal In.)	28·12 S	30·55 E
121	Whiteville (hwīt'vĭl) . . . . NC	34·18 N	78·45 W
214	White Volta (R.) . . . . Ghana	9·40 N	1·10 W
109	Whitewater (whīt-wŏt'ēr) . . . . . Wi.	42·49 N	88·40 W
108	Whitewater (L.) . . . . Can.	49·14 N	100·39 W
121	Whitewater B . . . . Fl. (In.)	25·16 N	80·21 W
111	Whitewater Cr . . . . Mt.	48·50 N	107·50 W
95	Whitewater L . . . . Can.	49·15 N	100·20 W
107	Whitewater R . . In. (Cincinnati In.)	39·19 N	84·55 W
120	Whitewell (hwĭt'wĕl) . . . . Tn.	35·11 N	85·31 W
117	Whitewright (hwĭt'rīt) . . . . Tx.	33·33 N	96·25 W
154	Whitham (R.) (wĭth'ŭm) . . . . Eng.	53·08 N	0·15 W
107	Whiting (hwīt'ĭng) In. (Chicago In.)	41·41 N	87·30 W
99	Whitinsville (hwīt'ĕns-vĭl) Ma. (In.)	42·06 N	71·40 W
99	Whitman (hwĭt'măn) . . . . Ma. (In.)	42·05 N	70·57 W
121	Whitmire (hwĭt'mīr) . . . . SC	34·30 N	81·40 W
114	Whitney, Mt . . . . Ca.	36·34 N	118·18 W
119	Whitney L. (hwĭt'nē) . . . . Tx.	32·02 N	97·36 W
148	Whitstable (wĭt'stȧb'l) Eng. (London In.)	51·22 N	1·03 E
205	Whitsunday (I.) (hwĭt's'n-dā) Austl.	20·16 S	149·00 E
113	Whittier (hwĭt'ĭ-ēr) Ca. (Los Angeles In.)	33·58 N	118·02 W
213	Whittlesea (wĭt'l'sē) S. Afr. (Natal In.)	32·11 S	26·51 E
148	Whitworth (hwĭt'wŭrth) . . . . . Eng.	53·40 N	2·10 W
203	Whyalla (hwī-ăl'ȧ) . . . . Austl.	33·00 S	137·32 E
92	Whymper, Mt. (wĭm'-pēr) . . . Can.	48·57 N	124·10 W
96	Wiarton (wī'ár-tŭn) . . . . Can.	44·45 N	80·45 W
117	Wichita (wĭch'ĭ-tô) . . . . Ks.	37·42 N	97·21 W
116	Wichita (R.) . . . . Tx.	33·50 N	99·38 W
116	Wichita Falls (fôls) . . . . Tx.	33·54 N	98·29 W
154	Wichita Mts . . . . Ok.	34·48 N	98·43 W
154	Wick (wĭk) . . . . Scot.	58·25 N	3·05 W
106	Wickatunk (wĭk'á-tŭnk) NJ (New York In.)	40·21 N	74·15 W
115	Wickenburg . . . . Az.	33·58 N	112·44 W
107	Wickliffe (wĭk'klĭf) Oh. (Cleveland In.)	41·37 N	81·29 W
	Wicklow, see Cill Mantainn		
154	Wicklow Mts. (wĭk'lō) . . . . Ire.	52·49 N	6·20 W
112	Wickup Mtn. (wĭk'ŭp) Or. (Portland In.)	46·06 N	123·35 W
105	Wiconisco (wĭ-kòn'ĭs-kō) . . . . . . Pa.	43·35 N	76·45 W
104	Widen (wī'dĕn) . . . . WV	38·25 N	80·55 W
148	Widnes (wĭd'nĕs) . . . . Eng.	53·21 N	2·44 W
158	Wieden (vē'dĕn) . . . . F.R.G.	49·41 N	12·09 E
159	Wieliczka (vyĕ-lēch'kȧ) . . . . Pol.	49·58 N	20·06 E
159	Wieluń (vyĕ'lōōn') . . . . Pol.	51·13 N	18·33 E
149	Wien (Vienna (vēn) (vē-ĕn'ä) Aus. (Vienna In.)	48·13 N	16·22 E
149	Wien (State) . . . . Aus. (Vienna In.)	48·11 N	16·23 E
158	Wiener Neustadt (vē'nēr noi'shtät) . Aus.	47·48 N	16·15 E
149	Wiener Wald (For.) Aus. (Vienna In.)	48·09 N	16·05 E
159	Wieprz, R. (vyĕpzh) . . . . Pol.	51·25 N	22·45 E
119	Wiergate (wēr'gāt) . . . . Tx.	31·00 N	93·42 W
158	Wiesbaden (vēs'bä-dĕn) . . . . F.R.G.	50·05 N	8·15 E
148	Wigan (wĭg'ăn) . . . . Eng.	53·33 N	2·37 W
120	Wiggins (wĭg'ĭnz) . . . . Ms.	30·51 N	89·05 W
154	Wight, Isle of (I.) (wīt) . . . . . . Eng.	50·44 N	1·17 W
117	Wilber (wĭl'bēr) . . . . Ne.	40·29 N	96·57 W
117	Wilburton (wĭl'bēr-tŭn) . . . . Ok.	34·54 N	95·18 W
203	Wilcannia (wĭl-cān-ĭȧ) . . . . . . Austl.	31·30 S	143·30 E
149	Wildau (vēl'dou) G.D.R. (Berlin In.)	52·20 N	13·39 E
149	Wildberg (vēl'bĕrgh) G.D.R. (Berlin In.)	52·52 N	12·39 E
94	Wildcat Hill (wīld'kăt) . . . . . . Can.	53·17 N	102·30 W
93	Wildhay (R.) (wīld'-hā) . . . . . Can.	53·15 N	117·20 W
113	Wildomar (wĭl'dô-mär) Ca. (Los Angeles In.)	33·35 N	117·17 W
108	Wild Rice (R.) . . . . Mn.	47·10 N	96·40 W
108	Wild Rice (R.) . . . . ND	46·10 N	97·12 W
113	Wild Rice L . . . . . Mn. (Duluth In.)	46·54 N	92·10 W
158	Wild Spitze Pk . . . . Aus.	46·49 N	10·50 E
105	Wildwood . . . . NJ	39·00 N	74·50 W
116	Wiley (wī'lē) . . . . Co.	38·08 N	102·41 W
218	Wilge R. (wĭl'jē) . . . . S. Afr. (Johannesburg & Pretoria In.)	25·38 S	29·09 E
218	Wilge R . . . . S. Afr. (Johannesburg & Pretoria In.)	27·27 S	28·46 E
205	Wilhelm, Mt . . . . Pap. N. Gui.	5·58 S	144·58 E
135	Wilhelmina Gebergte (Mts.) . . Sur.	4·30 N	57·00 W
158	Wilhelmshaven (vēl-hĕlms-hä'fĕn) F.R.G.	53·30 N	8·10 E
149	Wilhemina, Kanal (can.) Neth. (Amsterdam In.)	51·37 N	4·55 E
105	Wilkes-Barre (wĭlks'băr-ē) . . . . . Pa.	41·15 N	75·50 W
220	Wilkes Land . . . . Ant.	71·00 S	126·00 E
112	Wilkeson (wĭl-kē'sŭn) Wa. (Seattle In.)	47·06 N	122·03 W
94	Wilkie (wĭlk'ē) . . . . Can.	52·25 N	108·43 W
107	Wilkinsburg (wĭl'kĭnz-bûrg) Pa. Pittsburgh In.)	40·26 N	79·53 W
110	Willamette R . . . . Or.	44·15 N	123·13 W
104	Willard (wĭl'ȧrd) . . . . Oh.	41·00 N	82·50 W
113	Willard . . Ut. (Salt Lake City In.)	41·24 N	112·02 W
115	Willcox (wĭl'kŏks) . . . . Az.	32·15 N	109·50 W
134	Willemstad . . . . Neth. Antilles	12·12 N	68·58 W
148	Willesden (wĭlz'dĕn) Eng. (London In.)	51·31 N	0·17 W
93	W. A. C. Bennett Dam . . . . . . Can.	56·01 N	122·10 W
204	William Creek (wĭl'yăm) . . . . Austl.	28·45 S	136·20 E
115	Williams (wĭl'yămz) . . . . Az.	35·15 N	112·15 W
128	Williams (I.) . . . . Ba.	25·30 N	78·30 W
120	Williamsburg (wĭl'yămz-bûrg) . Ky.	36·42 N	84·09 W
107	Williamsburg . Oh. (Cincinnati In.)	39·04 N	84·02 W
121	Williamsburg . . . . Va.	37·15 N	76·41 W
93	Williams Lake . . . . Can.	52·08 N	122·09 W
104	Williamson (wĭl'yăm-sŭn) . . . . . WV	37·40 N	82·15 W
105	Williamsport . . . . Md.	39·35 N	77·45 W
105	Williamsport . . . . Pa.	41·15 N	77·05 W
121	Williamston (wĭl'yămz-tŭn) . . . NC	35·50 N	77·04 W
121	Williamston . . . . SC	34·36 N	82·30 W
104	Williamstown (wĭl'yămz-toun) . WV	39·20 N	81·30 W
107	Williamsville (wĭl'yăm-vĭl) NY (Buffalo In.)	42·58 N	78·46 W
105	Willimantic (wĭl-ĭ-măn'tĭk) . . . . Ct.	41·40 N	72·10 W
119	Willis (wĭl'ĭs) . . . . Tx.	30·24 N	95·29 W
205	Willis Is . . . . Austl.	16·15 S	150·30 E
108	Williston (wĭl'ĭs-tŭn) . . . . ND	48·08 N	103·38 W
92	Williston, L . . . . Can.	55·40 N	123·40 W
93	Willmar (wĭl'mär) . . . . Mn.	45·07 N	95·05 W
107	Willoughby (wĭl'ô-bē) Oh. (Cleveland In.)	41·39 N	81·25 W
111	Willow Cr. (wĭl'ō) . . . . Mt.	48·45 N	111·34 W
110	Willow Cr . . . . Or.	44·21 N	117·34 W
106	Willow Grove Pa. (Philadelphia In.)	40·07 N	75·07 W
107	Willowick (wĭl'ô-wĭk) Oh. (Cleveland In.)	41·39 N	81·28 W
212	Willowmore (wĭl'ô-môr) . . . . S. Afr.	33·15 S	23·37 E
107	Willow Run (wĭl'ō rŭn) Mi. (Detroit In.)	42·16 N	83·34 W
114	Willows (wĭl'ōz) . . . . Ca.	39·32 N	122·11 W
117	Willow Springs (sprĭngz) . . . . . Mo.	36·59 N	91·56 W
213	Willowvale (wĭ-lô'vāl) S. Afr. (Natal In.)	32·17 S	28·32 E
119	Wills Point (wĭlz point) . . . . Tx.	32·42 N	96·02 W
113	Wilmer (wĭl'mēr) Tx. (Dallas, Fort Worth In.)	32·35 N	96·40 W
107	Wilmette (wĭl-mĕt') Il. (Chicago In.)	42·04 N	87·42 W
203	Wilmington . . . . Austl.	32·39 S	138·07 E
113	Wilmington (wĭl'mĭng-tŭn) Ca. (Los Angeles In.)	33·46 N	118·16 W
106	Wilmington . De. (Philadelphia In.)	39·45 N	75·33 W
107	Wilmington . . . . . . Il. (Chicago In.)	41·19 N	88·09 W
99	Wilmington . . . . Ma. (In.)	42·34 N	71·10 W
121	Wilmington . . . . NC	34·12 N	77·56 W
104	Wilmington . . . . Oh.	39·20 N	83·50 W
104	Wilmore (wĭl'mōr) . . . . Ky.	37·50 N	84·35 W
148	Wilmslow (wĭlmz' lō) . . . . Eng.	53·19 N	2·14 W
	Wilno, see Vilnius		
218	Wilpoort . . . . S. Afr. (Johannesburg & Pretoria In.)	26·57 S	26·17 E
117	Wilson (wĭl'sŭn) . . . . Ar.	35·35 N	90·02 W
121	Wilson . . . . NC	35·42 N	77·55 W
117	Wilson . . . . Ok.	34·09 N	97·27 W
120	Wilson, L . . . . Al.	34·45 N	86·58 W
120	Wilson (R.) . . . . Al.	34·53 N	87·28 W
202	Wilson, Pt. Austl. (Melbourne In.)	38·05 S	144·31 E
113	Wilson, Mt . . . Ca. (Los Angeles In.)	34·15 N	118·06 W
111	Wilson Pk . . . . Ut.	40·46 N	110·27 W
203	Wilson's Prom. (wĭl'sŭnz) . . . Austl.	39·05 S	146·50 E
113	Wilsonville (wĭl'sŭn-vĭl) Il. (St. Louis In.)	39·04 N	89·52 W
149	Wilstedt (vēl'shtĕt) F.R.G. (Hamburg In.)	53·45 N	10·04 E
149	Wilster (vēl'stĕr) F.R.G. (Hamburg In.)	53·55 N	9·23 E
106	Wilton (wĭl'tŭn) Ct. (New York In.)	41·11 N	73·25 W

PRONOUNCING INDEX

Wilton — Wulanhata 369

Page	Name Pronunciation Region	Lat. °′	Long. °′
108	Wilton ND	47·09 N	100·47 W
204	Wiluna (wĭ-lōō'nȧ) Austl.	26·35 S	120·25 E
104	Winamac (wĭn'ȧ măk) In.	41·05 N	86·40 W
218	Winburg (wĭm-bûrg) S. Afr. (Johannesburg & Pretoria In.)	28·31 S	27·02 E
113	Winchester (wĭn'chĕs-tẽr) Ca. (Los Angeles In.)	33·41 N	117·06 W
154	Winchester Eng.	51·04 N	1·20 W
110	Winchester Id.	46·14 N	116·39 W
104	Winchester In.	40·10 N	84·50 W
104	Winchester Ky.	38·00 N	84·15 W
99	Winchester Ma. (Boston In.)	42·28 N	71·09 W
105	Winchester NH	42·45 N	72·25 W
115	Winchester Tn.	35·11 N	86·06 W
105	Winchester Va.	39·10 N	78·10 W
105	Windber (wĭnd'bẽr) Pa.	40·15 N	78·45 W
108	Wind Cave Natl. Park SD	43·36 N	103·53 W
115	Winder (wīn'dẽr) Ga.	33·58 N	83·43 W
154	Windermere (wĭn'dẽr-mēr) Eng.	54·25 N	2·59 W
93	Windfall (wĭnd'fôl) Can.	54·11 N	116·15 W
105	Windham (wĭnd'ăm) Ct.	41·45 N	72·05 W
99	Windham NH (Boston In.)	42·49 N	71·21 W
212	Windhoek (vĭnt'ho͝ok) S. W. Afr.	22·05 S	17·10 E
107	Wind L. Wi. (Milwaukee In.)	42·49 N	88·06 W
118	Wind Mtn. NM	32·02 N	105·30 W
109	Windom (wĭn'dŭm) Mn.	43·50 N	95·04 W
203	Windora (wĭn-dō'rȧ) Austl.	25·15 S	142·50 E
111	Wind R. Wy.	43·17 N	109·02 W
111	Wind River Ind. Res. Wy.	43·07 N	109·08 W
111	Wind River Ra. Wy.	43·19 N	109·47 W
202	Windsor (wĭn'zẽr) Austl. (Sydney In.)	33·37 S	150·49 E
107	Windsor Can. (Detroit In.)	42·19 N	83·00 W
98	Windsor Can.	44·59 N	64·08 W
99	Windsor Can.	48·57 N	55·40 W
116	Windsor Co.	40·27 N	104·51 W
148	Windsor Eng. (London In.)	51·27 N	0·37 W
117	Windsor Mo.	38·32 N	93·31 W
98	Windsor Vt.	43·30 N	72·25 W
121	Windsor NC	35·58 N	76·57 W
123	Windward Is. (wĭnd'wẽrd) N. A.	12·45 N	61·40 W
129	Windward Pass N. A.	19·30 N	74·20 W
94	Winefred L. Can.	55·30 N	110·35 W
117	Winfield Ks.	37·14 N	97·00 W
111	Winifred (wĭn ĭ frĕd) Mt.	47·35 N	109·20 W
91	Winisk (R.) Can.	54·30 N	86·30 W
118	Wink (wĭŋk) Tx.	31·48 N	103·06 W
95	Winkler (wĭnk'lẽr) Can.	49·11 N	97·56 W
214	Winneba (wĭn'ê-bȧ) Ghana	5·25 N	0·36 W
109	Winnebago (wĭn'ê-bā'gō) Mn.	43·45 N	94·08 W
109	Winnebago, L. Wi.	44·09 N	88·10 W
108	Winnebago Ind. Res. Ne.	42·15 N	96·06 W
110	Winnemucca (wĭn-ê-mŭk'ȧ) Nv.	40·59 N	117·43 W
114	Winnemucca (L.) Nv.	40·06 N	119·07 W
108	Winner (wĭn'ẽr) SD	43·22 N	99·50 W
107	Winnetka (wĭ-nĕt'kȧ) Il. (Chicago In.)	42·07 N	87·44 W
111	Winnett (wĭn'ĕt) Mt.	47·01 N	108·20 W
119	Winnfield (wĭn'fēld) La.	31·56 N	92·39 W
109	Winnibigoshish (L.) (wĭn'ĭ-bĭ-gō'shĭsh) Mn.	47·30 N	93·45 W
100	Winnipeg (wĭn'ĭ-pĕg) Can. (Winnipeg In.)	49·53 N	97·09 W
95	Winnipeg, L. Can.	52·00 N	97·00 W
90	Winnipeg (R.) Can.	52·20 N	95·54 W
95	Winnipeg Beach Can.	50·31 N	96·58 W
95	Winnipegosis (wĭn'ĭ-pê-gō'sĭs) Can.	51·39 N	99·56 W
95	Winnipegosis (L.) Can.	52·30 N	100·00 W
105	Winnipesaukee (L.) (wĭn'ê-pê-sô'kê) NH	43·40 N	71·20 W
119	Winnsboro (wĭnz'bŭr'ô) La.	32·09 N	91·42 W
121	Winnsboro SC	34·29 N	81·05 W
117	Winnsboro Tx.	32·56 N	95·15 W
100	Winona (wĭ-nō'nȧ) Can. (Toronto In.)	43·13 N	79·39 W
109	Winona Mn.	44·03 N	91·40 W
120	Winona Ms.	33·29 N	89·43 W
105	Winooski (wĭ'nōōs-kê) Vt.	44·30 N	73·10 W
149	Winsen (Luhe) (vēn'zĕn) (lōō'hĕ) F.R.G. (Hamburg In.)	53·22 N	10·13 E
148	Winsford (wĭnz'fẽrd) Eng.	53·11 N	2·30 W
115	Winslow (wĭnz'lō) Az.	35·00 N	110·45 W
112	Winslow Wa. (Seattle In.)	47·38 N	122·31 W
105	Winsted (wĭn'stĕd) Ct.	41·55 N	73·05 W
148	Winster (wĭn'stẽr) Eng.	53·08 N	1·38 W
121	Winston-Salem (wĭn stŭn-sā'lĕm) NC	36·05 N	80·15 W
213	Winterberge (Mts.) S. Afr. (Natal In.)	32·18 S	26·25 E
121	Winter Garden (wĭn'tẽr gär'd'n) Fl. (In.)	28·32 N	81·35 W
92	Winter Harbour Can.	50·31 N	128·02 W
121	Winter Haven (hā'vĕn) Fl. (In.)	28·01 N	81·38 W
95	Wintering L. (wĭn'tẽr-ĭng) Can.	55·24 N	97·42 W
121	Winter Park (pärk) Fl. (In.)	28·35 N	81·21 W
118	Winters (wĭn'tẽrz) Tx.	31·59 N	99·58 W
109	Winterset (wĭn'tẽr-sĕt) Ia.	41·19 N	94·03 W
161	Winterswijk Neth. (Ruhr In.)	51·58 N	6·44 E
158	Winterthur (vĭn'tẽr-tōōr) Switz.	47·30 N	8·32 E
213	Winterton S. Afr. (Natal In.)	28·51 S	29·33 E
98	Winthrop (wĭn'thrŭp) Me.	44·19 N	70·00 W
99	Winthrop Ma. (In.)	42·23 N	70·59 W
109	Winthrop Mn.	44·31 N	94·20 W
205	Winton (wĭn-tŭn) Austl.	22·17 S	143·08 E
161	Wipperfürth (vĕ'pẽr-fürt) F.R.G. (Ruhr In.)	51·07 N	7·23 E
148	Wirksworth (wûrks'wûrth) Eng.	53·05 N	1·35 W
103	Wisconsin (State) (wĭs-kŏn'sĭn) U. S.	44·30 N	91·00 W
109	Wisconsin (R.) Wi.	43·14 N	90·34 W
109	Wisconsin Dells Wi.	43·38 N	89·46 W
109	Wisconsin Rapids Wi.	44·24 N	89·50 W
108	Wishek (wĭsh'ĕk) ND	46·15 N	99·34 W
159	Wisla (Vistula) R. (vēs'wȧ) (vĭs'tû-lȧ) Pol.	52·48 N	19·02 E
159	Wisloka R. (vê-swô'kȧ) Pol.	49·55 N	21·26 E
135	Wismar (wĭs'mȧr) Guy.	5·58 N	58·15 W
158	Wismar (vĭs'mär) G.D.R.	53·53 N	11·28 E
108	Wisner (wĭz'nẽr) Ne.	42·00 N	96·55 W
161	Wissembourg (vē-säN-bōōr') Fr.	49·03 N	7·58 E
117	Wister, L. (vĭs'tẽr) Ok.	35·02 N	94·52 W
218	Witbank (wĭt-băŋk) S. Afr. (Johannesburg & Pretoria In.)	25·53 S	29·14 E
213	Witberg (Mtn.) S. Afr. (Natal In.)	30·32 S	27·18 E
148	Witham (wĭdh'ăm) Eng. (London In.)	51·48 N	0·37 E
148	Witham (R.) Eng.	53·11 N	0·20 W
107	Withamsville (wĭdh'ămz-vĭl) Oh. (Cincinnati In.)	39·04 N	84·16 W
121	Withlacoochee (R.) (wĭth-lȧ-kōō'chê) Fl. (In.)	28·58 N	82·30 W
120	Withlacoochee (R.) Ga.	31·15 N	83·30 W
113	Withrow (wĭdh'rō) Mn. (Minneapolis, St. Paul In.)	45·08 N	92·54 W
148	Witney (wĭt'nê) Eng. (London In.)	51·45 N	1·30 W
104	Witt (vĭt) Il.	39·10 N	89·15 W
161	Witten (vē'tĕn) F.R.G. (Ruhr In.)	51·26 N	7·19 E
158	Wittenberg (vē'tĕn-bĕrgh) G.D.R.	51·53 N	12·40 E
158	Wittenberge (vĭt-ĕn-bĕr'gē) G.D.R.	52·59 N	11·45 E
158	Wittlich (vĭt'lĭk) F.R.G.	49·58 N	6·54 E
213	Witu (wē'tōō) Ken.	2·18 S	40·28 E
213	Witwatersberg (Mts.) (wĭt-wôr-tẽrz-bûrg) S. Afr. (Johannesburg & Pretotia In.)	25·58 S	27·53 E
218	Witwatersrand (Ridge) (wĭt-wôr'tẽrs-rănd) S. Afr. (Johannesburg & Pretoria In.)	25·55 S	26·27 E
159	Wkra R. (f'krȧ) Pol.	52·40 N	20·35 E
159	Wloclawek (vwô-tswä'vĕk) Pol.	52·38 N	19·08 E
159	Wlodawa (vwô-dä'vä) Pol.	51·33 N	23·33 E
159	Wloszczowa (vwôsh-chô'vä) Pol.	50·51 N	19·58 E
99	Woburn (wōō'bŭrn) (wō'bŭrn) Ma. (In.)	42·29 N	71·10 W
149	Woerden Neth. (Amsterdam In.)	52·05 N	4·52 E
148	Woking Eng. (London In.)	51·18 N	0·33 W
148	Wokingham (wô'kĭng-hăm) Eng. (London In.)	51·23 N	0·50 W
113	Wolcott (wōl'kŏt) Ks. (Kansas City In.)	39·12 N	94·47 W
105	Wolf (I.) (wo͝olf) Can.	44·10 N	76·25 W
120	Wolf (R.) Ms.	30·45 N	89·36 W
109	Wolf (R.) Wi.	45·14 N	88·45 W
158	Wolfenbüttel (vôl'fĕn-büt-ĕl) F.R.G.	52·10 N	10·32 E
107	Wolf L. Il. (Chicago In.)	41·39 N	87·33 W
111	Wolf Point (wo͝olf point) Mt.	48·07 N	105·40 W
149	Wolfratshausen (vōlf'räts-hou-zĕn) F.R.G. (Munich In.)	47·55 N	11·25 E
158	Wolfsburg (vōlfs'bo͝orgh) F.R.G.	52·30 N	10·37 E
98	Wolfville (wo͝olf'vĭl) Can.	45·05 N	64·22 W
158	Wolgast (vôl'gäst) G.D.R.	54·04 N	13·46 E
213	Wolhuterskop S. Afr. (Johannesburg & Pretoria In.)	25·41 S	27·40 E
149	Wolkersdorf Aus. (Vienna In.)	48·24 N	16·31 E
90	Wollaston (L.) (wo͝ol'ȧs-tŭn) Can.	58·15 N	103·20 W
90	Wollaston Pen. Can.	70·00 N	115·00 W
203	Wollongong (wo͝ol'ŭn-gŏng) Austl.	34·26 S	151·05 E
159	Wolomin (vô-wō'mĕn) Pol.	52·19 N	21·17 E
94	Wolseley Can.	50·25 N	103·15 W
148	Wolstanton (wo͝ol-stăn'tŭn) Eng.	53·02 N	2·13 W
149	Woltersdorf (vōl'tĕrs-dōrf) G.D.R. (Berlin In.)	52·07 N	13·13 E
148	Wolverhampton (wo͝ol'vẽr-hămp-tŭn) Eng.	52·35 N	2·07 W
218	Wolwehoek S. Afr. (Johannesburg & Pretoria In.)	26·55 S	27·50 E
194	Wŏnsan (wŭn'sän') Kor.	39·08 N	127·24 E
203	Wonthaggi (wônt-hăg'ê) Austl.	38·45 S	145·42 E
108	Wood (wo͝od) SD	43·26 N	100·25 W
108	Woodbine (wo͝od'bīn) Ia.	41·44 N	95·42 W
106	Woodbridge (wo͝od'brĭj') NJ (New York In.)	40·33 N	74·18 W
90	Wood Buffalo Natl. Park Can.	59·50 N	118·53 W
113	Woodburn (wo͝od'bûrn) Il. (St. Louis In.)	39·03 N	90·01 W
110	Woodburn Or.	45·10 N	122·51 W
106	Woodbury (wo͝od'bẽr-ê) NJ (Philadelpahi In.)	39·50 N	75·14 W
113	Woodcrest (wo͝od'krĕst) Ca. (Los Angeles In.)	33·53 N	117·18 W
112	Woodinville (wo͝od'ĭn-vĭl) Wa. (Seattle In.)	47·46 N	122·09 W
114	Woodland (wo͝od'lănd) Ca.	38·41 N	121·47 W
112	Woodland Wa. (Portland In.)	45·54 N	122·45 W
113	Woodland Hills Ca. (Los Angeles In.)	34·10 N	118·36 W
197	Woodlark (I.) (wo͝od'lärk) Pap. N. Gui.	9·07 S	152·00 E
107	Woodlawn Beach (wo͝od'lôn bēch) NY (Buffalo In.)	42·48 N	78·51 W
94	Wood Mountain Can.	49·14 N	106·20 W
113	Wood River Il. (St. Louis In.)	38·52 N	90·06 W
204	Woodroffe, Mt. (wo͝od'rŭf) Austl.	26·05 S	132·00 E
121	Woodruff (wo͝od'rŭf) SC	34·43 N	82·03 W
204	Woods (L.) (wo͝odz) Austl.	18·00 S	133·18 E
103	Woods, L. of the Can.-Mn.	49·25 N	93·25 W
113	Woods Cross (krôs) Ut. (Salt Lake City In.)	40·53 N	111·54 W
104	Woodsfield (wo͝odz-fēld) Oh.	39·45 N	81·10 W
112	Woodson (wo͝odsŭn) Or. (Portland In.)	46·07 N	123·20 W
98	Woodstock (wo͝od'stŏk) Can.	43·10 N	80·50 W
98	Woodstock Can.	46·09 N	67·34 W
148	Woodstock Eng. (London In.)	51·48 N	1·22 W
109	Woodstock Il.	42·20 N	88·29 W
105	Woodstock Va.	38·55 N	78·25 W
105	Woodsville (wo͝odz'vĭl) NH	44·10 N	72·00 W
120	Woodville (wo͝od'vĭl) Ms.	31·06 N	91·11 W
119	Woodville Tx.	30·48 N	94·25 W
116	Woodward (wo͝od'wôrd) Ok.	36·25 N	99·24 W
148	Woolwich (wo͝ol'ĭj) Eng. (London In.)	51·28 N	0·05 E
203	Woomera (wo͝om'ẽrȧ) Austl.	31·15 S	136·43 E
106	Woonsocket (wōōn-sŏk'ĕt) RI (Providence In.)	42·00 N	71·30 W
108	Woonsocket SD	44·03 N	98·17 W
104	Wooster (wo͝os'tẽr) Oh.	40·50 N	81·55 W
154	Worcester (wo͝o'stẽr) Eng.	52·09 N	2·14 W
99	Worcester Ma. (In.)	42·16 N	71·49 W
212	Worcester (wo͝os'tẽr) S. Afr.	33·35 S	19·31 E
148	Worcester (Co.) (wo͝o'stẽr) Eng.	52·24 N	2·15 W
113	Worden (wôr'dĕn) Il. (St. Louis In.)	38·56 N	89·50 W
154	Workington (wûr'kĭng-tŭn) Eng.	54·40 N	3·30 W
148	Worksop (wûrk'sŏp) (wûr'sŭp) Eng.	53·18 N	1·07 W
111	Worland (wûr'lănd) Wy.	44·02 N	107·56 W
158	Worms (vōrms) F.R.G.	49·37 N	8·22 E
202	Worona Res. Austl. (Sydney In.)	34·12 S	150·55 E
107	Worth (wûrth) Il. (Chicago In.)	41·42 N	87·47 W
117	Worth L. Tx. (Dallas, Fort Worth In.)	32·48 N	97·32 W
119	Wortham (wûr'dhăm) Tx.	31·46 N	96·22 W
154	Worthing (wûr'dhĭng) Eng.	50·48 N	0·29 W
104	Worthington (wûr'dhĭng-tŭn) In.	39·05 N	87·00 W
108	Worthington Mn.	43·38 N	95·36 W
197	Wowoni (I.) (wō-wō'nê) Indon.	4·05 S	123·45 E
148	Wragby (răg'bê) Eng.	53·17 N	0·19 W
101	Wrangell (răn'gĕl) Ak.	56·28 N	132·25 W
101	Wrangell, Mt. Ak.	61·58 N	143·50 W
101	Wrangell Mts. Ak.-Can.	62·28 N	142·40 W
154	Wrath, C. (răth) Scot.	58·34 N	5·01 W
116	Wray (rā) Co.	40·06 N	102·14 W
137	Wreak (R.) (rēk) Eng.	52·45 N	0·59 W
205	Wreck Rfs. (rĕk) Austl.	22·00 S	155·52 E
148	Wrekin, The (Mt.) (rĕk'ĭn) Eng.	54·20 N	2·33 W
121	Wrens (rĕnz) Ga.	33·15 N	82·25 W
99	Wrentham Ma. (Boston In.)	42·04 N	71·20 W
148	Wrexham (rĕk'săm) Wales	53·03 N	3·00 W
107	Wrights Corners (rīts kôr'nẽrz) NY (Buffalo In.)	43·14 N	78·42 W
121	Wrightsville (rīts'vĭl) Ga.	32·44 N	82·44 W
159	Wroclaw (Breslau) (vrôtsläv) (brĕs'lou) Pol.	51·07 N	17·10 E
148	Wrotham (rōōt'ŭm) Eng. (London In.)	51·18 N	0·19 E
159	Wrzesnia (vzhăsh'nyȧ) Pol.	52·19 N	17·33 E
193	Wuch'ang (wōō'chăng') China	30·32 N	114·25 E
192	Wuch'ang China	44·59 N	127·00 E
190	Wuchi (wōō'jē) China	38·12 N	114·57 E
190	Wuchiang (wōō'jĭăng) China	31·10 N	120·38 E
190	Wuch'iao (wōō'chĭou) China	37·37 N	116·29 E
192	Wuch'ing (wōō'chĭng') China (In.)	39·32 N	116·51 E
193	Wu Chin Shan China	18·48 N	109·30 E
193	Wuchou (Tsangwu) (wōō'chō') China	23·32 N	111·25 E
193	Wuhan China	30·30 N	114·15 E
190	Wuhsi (wōō'sē) China	31·36 N	120·17 E
	Wuhsien, see Soochow		
193	Wuhsing China	30·38 N	120·10 E
190	Wuhu (wōō'hōō') China	31·22 N	118·22 E
193	Wui Shan (Mts.) China	26·38 N	116·35 E
194	Wulachieh (wōō'kä-ĸē'ȧ) China	44·08 N	126·25 E
	Wulanhata, see Ch'ihfeng		

ng-sing; ŋ-baŋk; N-nasalized n; nŏd; cŏmmit; ōld; ôbey; ôrder; fōōd; fo͝ot; ou-out; s-soft; sh-dish; th-thin; pūre; ûnite; ûrn; stŭd; circŭs; ü-as "y" in study; '-indeterminate vowel.

Page	Name	Pronunciation	Region	Lat. °′	Long. °′

196 Wu Liang Shan (Mts.).....China 23·07 N 100·45 E
190 Wulitien (wōō'lē'dĭän)......China 32·09 N 114·17 E
188 Wulunuch'i (Urunchi)......China 43·49 N 87·43 E
149 Wünsdorf (vüns'dorf) G.D.R. (Berlin In.) 52·10 N 13·29 E
115 Wupatki Nat'l Mon........Ariz. 35·35 N 111·45 w
193 Wup'ing (wōō'pĭng').......China 25·05 N 116·01 E
161 Wuppertal (vŏŏp'ĕr-täl) F.R.G. (Ruhr In.) 51·16 N 7·14 E
193 Wu R. (wōō').............China 27·30 N 108·00 E
158 Würm See (L.) (vürm zā)..F.R.G. 47·58 N 11·30 E
161 Würselen (vür'zĕ-lĕn) F.R.G. (Ruhr In.) 50·49 N 6·09 E
158 Würzburg (vürts'bŏŏrg)..F.R.G. 49·48 N 9·57 E
158 Wurzen (vŏŏrt'sĕn)......G.D.R. 51·22 N 12·45 E
188 Wushih (Uch Turfan) (wōō'shĭ).China 41·13 N 79·08 E
149 Wustermark (vōōs'tĕr-märk) G.D.R. (Berlin In.) 52·33 N 12·57 E
149 Wustrau (vŏŏst'rou) G.D.R. (Berlin In.) 52·51 N 12·51 E
188 Wusu (Kweitun) (wōō'sōō') China 44·28 N 84·07 E (kwā'tōōn)
191 Wusung (wōō'sōōng) China (Shanghai In.) 31·23 N 121·29 E
149 Wuustwezel....Bel. (Brussels In.) 51·23 N 4·36 E
190 Wuwei (wōō'wā').........China 31·19 N 117·53 E
190 Wuyuch'ang..............China 33·18 N 120·15 E
189 Wuyün (wōō-yün').......China 48·51 N 130·06 E
107 Wyandotte (wī'ăn-dŏt) Mi. (Detroit In.) 42·12 N 83·10 w
148 Wye (wī)......Eng. (London In.) 51·12 N 0·57 E
148 Wye (R.)...............Eng. 53·14 N 1·46 w
117 Wymore (wī'mōr).........Ne. 40·09 N 96·41 w
212 Wynberg (wĭn'bĕrg)..S. Afr. (In.) 34·00 s 18·28 E
204 Wyndham (wĭnd'ăm)......Austl. 15·30 s 128·15 E
117 Wynne (wĭn)............Ar. 35·12 N 90·46 w
117 Wynnewood (wĭn'wŏŏd)...Ok. 34·39 N 97·10 w
117 Wynona (wĭ-nō'nà).......Ok. 36·33 N 96·19 w
94 Wynyard (wĭn'yĕrd)......Can. 51·47 N 104·10 w
107 Wyoming (wī-ō'mĭng) Oh. (Cincinnati In.) 39·14 N 84·28 w
102 Wyoming (State)..........U. S. 42·50 N 108·30 w
111 Wyoming Ra..............Wy. 42·43 N 110·35 w
148 Wyre For. (wīr)..........Eng. 52·24 N 2·24 w
158 Wysokie Mazowieckie (vĕ-sō'kyĕ mä-zō-vyĕts'kyĕ).Pol. 52·55 N 22·42 E
158 Wyszkow (vĕsh'kŏŏf)......Pol. 52·35 N 21·29 E
121 Wytheville (wĭth'vĭl)........Va. 36·55 N 81·06 w

X

128 Xagua, Banco (Bk.) (bä'n-kō-sä'gwä).Cuba 21·35 N 80·50 w
161 Xanten (ksän'tĕn) F.R.G. (Ruhr In.) 51·40 N 6·28 E
165 Xanthi...................Grc. 41·08 N 24·53 E
212 Xau, L. ....Bots. 21·15 s 24·38 E
126 Xcalak (sä-lä'k).......Mex. (In.) 18·15 N 87·50 w
104 Xenia (zē'nĭ-à)...........Oh. 39·40 N 83·55 w
124 Xicotencatl (sē-kō-tĕn-kät''l).Mex. 32·00 N 98·58 w
124 Xilitla (sē-lē'tlä)..........Mex. 21·24 N 98·59 w
135 Xingú (R.) (zhēn-gōō')......Braz. 6·20 s 52·34 w
124 Xochihuehuetlan (sô-chē-wĕ-wĕ-tlä'n).Mex. 17·53 N 98·29 w
125 Xochimilco (sō-chē-mēl'kō) Mex. (In.) 19·05 N 99·06 w

Y

193 Yaan....................China 30·00 N 103·20 E
159 Yablonitskiy Pereval (P.) (yäb-lô' nĭt-skĭ pĕ-rĕ-väl').Sov. Un. 48·20 N 24·25 E
173 Yablonovyy Khrebet (Mts.) (yä-blô-nô-vē').Sov. Un. 51·15 N 111·30 E

195 Yachiyo.........Jap. (Tōkyō In.) 35·43 N 140·07 E
112 Yacolt (yă'kŏlt) Wa. (Portland In.) 45·52 N 122·24 w
112 Yacolt (Mt.)...Wa. (Portland In.) 45·52 N 122·27 w
120 Yacona (R.) (yà'cō nà)....Ms. 34·13 N 89·30 w
136 Yacuiba (yà-kōō-ē'bà).......Arg. 22·02 s 63·44 w
121 Yadkin (R.) (yăd'kĭn)........NC 36·12 N 80·40 w
211 Yafran..................Libya 31·57 N 12·04 E
167 Yagotin (yä'gô-tĕn)......Sov. Un. 50·18 N 31·46 E
128 Yaguajay (yä-guä-hä'ĕ).....Cuba 22·20 N 79·20 w
195 Yahagi-Gawa (Strm.) (yä'hä-gĕ gä'wä).Jap. 35·16 N 137·22 E
191 Yahu.........China (Canton In.) 23·19 N 113·17 E
124 Yahualica (yä-wä-lē'kä)...Mex. 21·08 N 102·53 w
190 Yahungch'iao (yä'hōōng'chĭou) China 39·45 N 117·52 E
193 Yaihsien................China 18·20 N 109·10 E
125 Yajalon (yä-hä-lōn')......Mex. 17·16 N 92·20 w
174 Yakhroma (yäk'rô-ma) Sov. Un. (Moscow In.) 56·17 N 37·30 E
174 Yakhroma R. Sov. Un. (Moscow In.) 56·15 N 37·38 E
110 Yakima (yăk'ĭmà)..........Wa. 46·35 N 120·30 w
110 Yakima R. (tăk'ĭ-mà).......Wa. 46·48 N 120·22 w
216 Yakoma.................Zaire 4·05 N 22·27 E
195 Yaku (I.) (yä'kōō).........Jap. 30·15 N 130·41 E
173 Yakut A.S.S.R. ....Sov. Un. 65·21 N 117·13 E
101 Yakutat (yàk'ōō-tăt).......Ak. 59·32 N 139·35 w
173 Yakutsk (yà-kōōtsk')....Sov. Un. 62·13 N 129·49 E
194 Yal (R.) (yäl)............China 48·20 N 122·35 E
104 Yale....................Mi. 43·05 N 82·45 w
117 Yale....................Ok. 36·07 N 96·42 w
110 Yale Res................Wa. 46·00 N 122·20 w
211 Yalinga (yä-lĭn'gä).Cen. Afr. Rep. 6·56 N 23·22 E
120 Yalobusha (R.) (yà-lô-bŏŏsh'à) Ms. 33·48 N 90·02 w
171 Yalta (yäl'tà)............Sov. Un. 44·30 N 34·12 E
194 Yalu (Amnok) (R.)....China-Kor. 41·20 N 126·35 E
188 Yalung Chiang (R.) (yä'lōōng') China 32·29 N 98·41 E
172 Yalutorovsk (yä-lōō-tô'rôfsk) Sov. Un. 56·42 N 66·32 E
195 Yamada (yä'mà-dà).........Jap. 33·37 N 133·39 E
194 Yamagata (yä-mà'gä-tà).....Jap. 38·12 N 140·24 E
195 Yamaguchi (yä-mà'gōō-chē)..Jap. 34·10 N 131·30 E
172 Yamal, P-ov (Pen.) (yä-mäl') Sov. Un. 71·15 N 70·00 E
174 Yamantau, Gora (Mt.) (gà-rä' yä' man-tâw) Sov. Un. (Urals In.) 54·16 N 58·08 E
129 Yamasá (yä-mä'sä)....Dom. Rep. 18·50 N 70·00 w
195 Yamasaki (yä-mà'sä-kè)......Jap. 35·01 N 134·33 E
195 Yamasaki.......Jap. (Osaka In.) 34·53 N 135·41 E
195 Yamashina (yä'mä-shē'nä) Jap. (Osaka In.) 34·59 N 135·50 E
195 Yamashita (yä'mä-shē'tä) Jap. (Osaka In.) 34·53 N 135·25 E
195 Yamato.........Jap. (Tōkyō In.) 35·28 N 139·28 E
195 Yamato-Kōriyama Jap. (Osaka In.) 34·39 N 135·48 E
195 Yamato-takada (yä'mä-tô tä'kä-dä).Jap. (Osaka In.) 34·31 N 135·45 E
134 Yambi, Mesa de (mĕ'sä-dĕ-yà'm-bē).Col. 1·55 N 71·45 w
188 Yamdrog Tsho (L.)........China 29·11 N 91·26 E
188 Yamethin (yŭ-mē'thĕn).....Bur. 20·14 N 96·27 E
112 Yamhill (yäm'hĭl) Or. (Portland In.) 45·20 N 123·11 w
174 Yamkino (yäm'kĭ-nô) Sov. Un. (Moscow In.) 55·56 N 38·25 E
203 Yamma Yamma, L. (yä'mä yäm'à).Austl. 26·15 s 141·30 E
111 Yampa R. (yăm'pà).........Co. 40·29 N 108·12 w
173 Yamsk (yämsk)..........Sov. Un. 59·41 N 154·09 E
184 Yamuna (R.)............India 26·50 N 80·10 E
173 Yana (R.) (yä'nà)........Sov. Un. 69·42 N 135·45 E
203 Yanac (yăn'àk)..........Austl. 36·10 s 141·30 E
195 Yanagawa (yä-nä'gä-wä).....Jap. 33·11 N 130·24 E
184 Yanam (yŭnŭm')..........India 16·48 N 82·15 E
186 Yanbu'.................Sau. Ar. 23·57 N 38·02 E
216 Yandongi...............Zaire 2·51 N 22·16 E
190 Yangch'eng Hu (L.) (yäng'chĕng'hōō).China 31·30 N 120·31 E
193 Yangchiang..........China 21·52 N 111·58 E
190 Yangchiaokou (yang'jēou'gō) China 36·17 N 118·53 E
190 Yangchiat'an (yäng'jēä'tän) China 31·43 N 115·53 E
189 Yangchou (yäng'jō')......China 32·24 N 119·24 E
190 Yangchüan..............China 37·52 N 113·36 E
193 Yangch'un (yäng'chōōn')...China 22·08 N 111·48 E
190 Yangerhchuang (yäng'ē'jōōäng) China 38·18 N 117·31 E
190 Yangho (yäng'hŭ)........China 33·48 N 118·23 E
190 Yanghsin (yäng'sĭn)......China 37·39 N 117·34 E
192 Yangkochuang.China (Peking In.) 40·10 N 116·48 E
190 Yangku (yäng'kōō').......China 36·06 N 115·46 E
190 Yangsanmu (yäng'sän'mōō) China 38·28 N 117·18 E

189 Yangtze (R.) (yäng'tse)....China 30·30 N 117·25 E
194 Yangyang (yäng'yäng')....Kor. 38·02 N 128·38 E
108 Yankton (yănk'tŭn).........SD 42·51 N 97·24 w
Yannina, see Ioánnina
174 Yanychi (yä'nĭ-chĭ) Sov. Un. (Urals In.) 57·42 N 56·24 E
211 Yao (yä'ō)...............Chad 13·00 N 17·38 E
195 Yao...........Jap. (Osaka In.) 34·37 N 135·36 E
215 Yaoundé (yà-ōōn-dā')......Cam. 3·52 N 11·31 E
198 Yap (yăp) (I)..Pac. Is. Trust Ter. 11·00 N 138·00 E
129 Yaque del Norte (R.) (yä'kà dĕl nôr'tä).Dom. Rep. 19·40 N 71·25 w
129 Yaque del Sur (R.) (yä-kĕ-dĕl-sōō'r).Dom. Rep. 18·35 N 71·05 w
122 Yaqui (R.) (yä'kē)........Mex. 28·15 N 109·40 w
135 Yaracuy (State) (yä-rä-kōō'ē) Ven. (In.) 10·10 N 68·31 w
203 Yaraka (yà-răk'à)........Austl. 24·50 s 144·08 E
170 Yaransk (yà-ränsk')......Sov. Un. 57·18 N 48·05 E
211 Yarda (Well) (yär'dà)......Chad 18·29 N 19·13 E
Yarkand, see Soch'e
184 Yarkand (R.) (yär-känt')....India 36·11 N 76·10 E
98 Yarmouth (yär'mŭth)......Can. 43·50 N 66·07 w
174 Yaroslavka (yà-rô-släv'kà) Sov. Un. (Urals In.) 55·52 N 57·59 E
166 Yaroslavl' (yà-rô-släv''l)..Sov. Un. 57·57 N 39·54 E
166 Yaroslavl' (Oblast)......Sov. Un. 58·05 N 38·05 E
170 Yarra-to (L.) (yà'rô-tô')...Sov. Un. 68·30 N 71·30 E
166 Yartsevo (yär'tsyĕ-vô)....Sov. Un. 55·04 N 32·38 E
172 Yartsevo................Sov. Un. 60·13 N 89·52 E
134 Yarumal (yä-rōō-mäl')..Col. (In.) 6·57 N 75·24 w
159 Yasel'da R. (yä-syŭl'dà)..Sov. Un. 53·13 N 25·53 E
159 Yasinya (yä-syēn'yä)......Sov. Un. 48·17 N 24·21 E
129 Yateras (yä-tä'räs).......Cuba 20·00 N 75·00 w
117 Yates Center (yāts)........Ks. 37·53 N 95·44 w
90 Yathkyed (L.) (yáth-kī-ĕd')..Can. 62·41 N 98·00 w
195 Yatsuga-take (Mtn.) (yät'sōō-gä dä'kä).Jap. 36·01 N 138·21 E
195 Yatsushiro (yät'sōō'shē-rô)..Jap. 32·30 N 130·35 E
217 Yatta Plat...............Ken. 1·55 s 38·10 E
124 Yautepec (yä-ōō-tä-pĕk')...Mex. 18·53 N 99·04 w
159 Yavorvo (yä'vō-rō'yĕ)...Sov. Un. 49·56 N 23·24 E
195 Yawata (yä'wä-tä) Jap. (Osaka In.) 34·52 N 135·43 E
195 Yawatahama (yä'wä'tä'hä-mä) Jap. 33·24 N 132·25 E
216 Yayama.................Zaire 1·16 s 23·07 E
186 Yazd...................Iran 31·59 N 54·03 E
120 Yazoo (R.) (yä'zōō).......Ms. 32·32 N 90·40 w
120 Yazoo City..............Ms. 32·50 N 90·18 w
196 Ye (yā).................Bur. 15·13 N 97·52 E
106 Yeadon (yē'dŭn) Pa. (Philadelphia In.) 39·56 N 75·16 w
162 Yecla (yā'klä)............Sp. 38·35 N 1·09 w
166 Yefremov (yĕ-frä'môf)...Sov. Un. 53·08 N 38·04 E
166 Yegor'yevsk (yĕ-gôr'yĕfsk) Sov. Un. 55·23 N 38·59 E
188 Yehch'eng (Karghalik) (yĕ'chĕng) China 37·30 N 79·26 E
170 Yelabuga (yĕ-lä'bŏŏ-gà)..Sov. Un. 55·50 N 52·18 E
171 Yelan..................Sov. Un. 50·50 N 44·00 E
166 Yelets (yĕ-lyĕts')........Sov. Un. 52·35 N 38·28 E
174 Yelizavetpol'skiy (yĕ'lĭ-za-vĕt- pôl'-skĭ).Sov. Un. 52·51 N 60·38 E
173 Yelizavety, Mys (C.) (yĕ-lyē-sä-vyĕ'tà).Sov. Un. 54·28 N 142·59 E
154 Yell (I.) (yĕl)...........Scot. 60·35 N 1·27 w
120 Yellow (R.) (yĕl'ô).......Fl. 30·33 N 86·53 w
93 Yellowhead Pass (yĕl'ô-hĕd)..Can. 52·52 N 118·35 w
90 Yellowknife (yĕl'ô-nīf)....Can. 62·29 N 114·38 w
Yellow R., see Huang Ho
192 Yellow Sea..............Asia 35·20 N 122·15 E
111 Yellowstone L............Wy. 44·27 N 110·03 w
111 Yellowstone Natl. Park (yĕl'ô-stōn).Wy. 44·45 N 110·35 w
111 Yellowstone R............Mt. 46·28 N 105·39 w
111 Yellowstone R., Clark Fk...Wy. 44·55 N 109·05 w
111 Yellowtail Res..........Mt.-Wy. 45·00 N 108·10 w
166 Yel'nya (yĕl'nyà).........Sov. Un. 54·34 N 33·12 E
174 Yemanzhelinsk (yĕ-màn-zhä'lĭnsk) Sov. Un. (Urals In.) 54·47 N 61·24 E
182 Yemen (yĕm'ĕn)..........Asia 15·45 N 44·30 E
182 Yemen, People's Democratic Republic of.Asia 14·45 N 46·45 E
170 Yemetsk................Sov. Un. 63·28 N 41·28 E
167 Yenakiyevo (yĕ-nä'kĭ-yĕ-vô) Sov. Un. 48·14 N 38·12 E
192 Yenan (yĕn'än')..........China 36·35 N 109·32 E
188 Yenan (Fushih)..........China 36·46 N 109·15 E
187 Yenangyaung (yä'nän-d oung) Bur. 20·27 N 94·59 E
190 Yench'eng (yĕn'chĕng)....China 33·23 N 120·11 E
190 Yencheng...............China 33·38 N 113·59 E
188 Yench'i (yĕn'chĭ).........China 42·55 N 129·35 E
192 Yenchi.................China 42·55 N 129·35 E
190 Yenchiaha (yen'jēä'hŭ)...China 31·47 N 114·50 E
190 Yenchianchi (yĕn'jēä'jē)...China 31·52 N 115·57 E
190 Yenching (yĕn'jĭn).......China 35·09 N 114·13 E

ăt; fīnàl; rāte; senâte; ärm; àsk; sofà; fâre; ch-choose; dh-as th in other; bē; ĕvent; bĕt; recĕnt; cratēr; g-go; gh-guttural g; bĭt; ɩ-short neutral; rīde; ᴋ-guttural k as ch in German ich;

PRONOUNCING INDEX Yenchuang — Zaporozh'ye 371

Page Name Pronunciation Region Lat. °′ Long. °′

190 Yenchuang (yĕn′jōōäng)....China 36·08 N 117·47 E
214 Yendi (yĕn′dê)....Ghana 9·26 N 0·01 W
171 Yenice (R.)....Tur. 41·10 N 33·00 E
172 Yenisey (R.) (yĕ-nê-sĕ′ē). Sov. Un. 67·48 N 87·15 E
172 Yeniseysk (yĕ-nĭĕsā′ĭsk) Sov. Un. 58·27 N 90·28 E
190 Yenling (yĕn′lĭng′)....China 34·07 N 114·12 E
190 Yenshan (yĕn′shän′)....China 38·05 N 117·15 E
192 Yenshou....China 45·25 N 128·43 E
190 Yent'ai (Chefoo)....China 37·32 N 121·22 E
204 Yeo (I.) (yō)....Austl. 28·15 S 124·00 E
171 Yerevan (yĕ-rĕ-vän′)....Sov. Un. 40·10 N 44·30 E
154 Yerington (yē′rĭng-tŭn)....Nv. 38·59 N 119·10 W
170 Yermak (I.)....Sov. Un. 66·30 N 71·30 E
162 Yeste (yĕs′tå)....Sp. 38·23 N 2·19 W
160 Yeu, Île d' (I.) (ēl dyû)....Fr. 46·43 N 2·45 W
167 Yevpatoriya (yĕf-pä′tô-rĭ-yå) Sov. Un. 45·13 N 33·22 E
167 Yeya (R.) (yă′yå)....Sov. Un. 46·25 N 39·17 E
173 Yevrey Aut. Oblast....Sov. Un. 48·45 N 132·00 E
167 Yeysk (yĕysk)....Sov. Un. 46·41 N 38·13 E
Yg (R.), see Yug
165 Yiannitsá....Grc. 40·47 N 22·26 E
192 Yinch'uan (Ninghsia)....China 38·22 N 106·22 E
188 Yingchisha....China 39·01 N 75·29 E
192 Yingk'ou (yĭng′kō′)....China 40·35 N 122·10 E
191 Yinhang....China (Shanghai In.) 31·20 N 121·30 E
192 Yin Shan (Mtn.) (yĭng′shän′) China 40·50 N 110·30 E
165 Yioúra (I.)....Grc. 37·52 N 24·42 E
165 Yíthion....Grc. 36·50 N 22·37 E
93 Ymir (wī′mẽr)....Can. 49·17 N 117·13 W
119 Yoakum (yō′kŭm)....Tx. 29·18 N 97·09 W
120 Yockanookany, (R.) (yŏk′ȧ-nōō-kă-nĭ). Ms. 32·47 N 89·38 W
195 Yodo-Gawa (Str.) (yō′dō′gä-wä) Jap. (Ōsaka In.) 34·46 N 135·35 E
193 Yog Pt. (yōg)....Phil. 14·00 N 124·30 E
93 Yoho Natl. Park (yō′hō)....Can. 51·26 N 116·30 W
126 Yojoa, Lago de (L.) (lä′gô dĕ yô-hō′ä). Hond. 14·49 N 87·53 W
195 Yokkaichi (yô′kä′ê-chê)....Jap. 34·58 N 136·35 E
195 Yokohama (yō′kô-hä′mȧ) Jap. (Tōkyō In.) 35·37 N 139·40 E
195 Yokosuka (yô-kō′sōō-kä) Jap. (Tōkyō In.) 35·17 N 139·40 E
195 Yokota (yō-kō′tä) Jap. (Tōkyō In.) 35·23 N 140·02 E
210 Yola (yō′lä)....Nig. 9·13 N 12·27 E
127 Yolaina, Cord. de (Mts.) (kôr-dĕl-yĕ′rä dĕ yō-lä-ē′nä). Nic. 11·34 N 84·34 W
134 Yolombó (yô-lôm-bŏ′)... Col. (In.) 6·37 N 74·59 W
214 Yomon....Gui. 7·34 N 9·16 W
195 Yonago (yō′nä-gō)....Jap. 35·27 N 133·19 E
194 Yonezawa (yō′nĕ′zȧ-wä)....Jap. 37·50 N 140·07 E
194 Yŏngdŏk (yŭng′dŭk′)....Kor. 36·28 N 129·25 E
194 Yŏnghŭng (yŭng′hōōng′)....Kor. 39·31 N 127·11 E
194 Yonghŭng Man (B.)....Kor. 39·10 N 128·00 E
106 Yonkers (yŏŋ′kẽrz) NY (New York In.) 40·57 N 73·54 W
160 Yonne (R.) (yôn)....Fr. 48·18 N 3·15 E
195 Yono (yō′nō)....Jap. (Tōkyō In.) 35·53 N 139·36 E
113 Yorba Linda (yôr′bȧ lĭn′dȧ) Ca. (Los Angeles In.) 33·55 N 117·51 W
120 York (yôrk)....Al. 32·33 N 88·16 W
204 York....Austl. 32·00 S 117·00 E
100 York....Can. (Toronto In.) 43·41 N 79·29 W
154 York....Eng. 53·58 N 1·10 W
117 York....Ne. 40·52 N 97·36 W
105 York....Pa. 40·00 N 76·40 W
121 York....SC 34·59 N 81·14 W
205 York, C....Austl. 10·45 S 142·35 E
75 York, Kap (C.)....Grnld. 75·30 N 73·00 W
203 Yorketown....Austl. 35·00 S 137·28 E
95 York Factory....Can. 57·05 N 92·18 W
203 York Pen....Austl. 34·24 S 137·20 E
154 Yorkshire Wolds (Hills) (yôrk′shĭr). Eng. 54·00 N 0·35 W
94 Yorkton (yôrk′tŭn)....Can. 51·13 N 102·28 W
119 Yorktown (yôrk′toun)....Tx. 28·57 N 97·30 W
121 Yorktown....Va. 37·12 N 76·31 W
126 Yoro (yō′rô)....Hond. 15·09 N 87·05 W
198 Yoron (I.)....Jap. 26·48 N 128·40 E
114 Yosemite Natl. Park (yô-sĕm′ĭ-tê). Ca. 38·03 N 119·36 W
195 Yoshida (yō′shê-dȧ)....Jap. 34·39 N 132·41 E
195 Yoshikawa (yō-shê′kä′wä′) Jap. (Tōkyō In.) 35·53 N 139·51 E
195 Yoshino (R.) (yō′shē-nō)....Jap. 34·04 N 133·57 E
170 Yoshkar-Ola (yôsh-kär′ô-lä′) Sov. Un. 56·35 N 48·05 E
125 Yosonotú (Santa Catarina) (yô-sō-nō-tōō′) (sän′tä kä-tä-rē′nä). Mex. 16·51 N 97·37 W
194 Yŏsu (yŭ′sōō′)....Kor. 34·42 N 127·42 E
154 Youghal B. (yōō′ôl) (yôl)....Ire. 51·52 N 7·46 W
154 Youhal....Ire. 51·58 N 7·57 W
211 Youkadouma (yōō-kȧ-dōō′mä) Cam. 3·29 N 15·04 E
203 Young (yŭng)....Austl. 34·15 S 148·18 E
137 Young (yô-ōō′ng) Ur. (Buenos Aires In.) 32·42 S 57·38 W
112 Youngs (L.) (yŭngz) Wa. (Seattle In.) 47·25 N 122·08 W
107 Youngstown....NY (Buffalo In.) 43·15 N 79·02 W
104 Youngstown....Oh. 41·05 N 80·40 W
171 Yozgat (yôz′gȧd)....Tur. 39·50 N 34·50 E
107 Ypsilanti (ĭp-sĭ-lăn′tĭ) Mi. (Detroit In.) 42·15 N 83·37 W
110 Yreka (wī-rē′kȧ)....Ca. 41·43 N 122·36 W
118 Ysleta (ēz-lĕ′tȧ)....Tx. 31·42 N 106·18 W
160 Yssingeaux (ē-săN-zhō′)....Fr. 45·09 N 4·08 E
156 Ystad (ü′städ)....Swe. 55·29 N 13·28 E
156 Ytre Solund (I.) (ü′trĕ sōō′lĕn) Nor. 61·01 N 4·25 E
183 Yu'alliq, Jabal (Mts.) Egypt (Palestine In.) 30·12 N 33·42 E
193 Yüan (R.) (yōō′än′)....China 28·50 N 110·50 E
193 Yüanan (yōō′ä-nän′)....China 31·08 N 111·28 E
193 Yüanling....China 28·30 N 110·18 E
195 Yuasa....Jap. 34·02 N 135·10 E
190 Yüanshih....China 37·45 N 114·32 E
114 Yuba City (yōō′bȧ)....Ca. 39·08 N 121·38 W
210 Yuby, C. (yōō′bê)....Mor. 28·01 N 13·21 W
113 Yucaipa (yŭ-kȧ-ē′pȧ) Ca. (Los Angeles In.) 34·02 N 117·02 W
122 Yucatan (State) (yōō-kä-tän′) Mex. 20·45 N 89·00 W
122 Yucatán Chan....Mex. 22·30 N 87·00 W
193 Yu Chiang (R.) (yōō)....China 23·55 N 106·50 E
190 Yüch'eng (yü′chĕng′)....China 34·31 N 115·54 E
190 Yuch'eng....China 36·55 N 116·39 E
173 Yudoma (R.) (yōō-dō′mȧ) Sov. Un. 59·13 N 137·00 E
190 Yüehchuang (yüĕ′jōōäng)...China 36·13 N 118·17 E
193 Yüehyang....China 92·25 N 113·05 E
170 Yug (R.) (yōōg)....Sov. Un. 59·50 N 45·55 E
146 Yugoslavia (yōō-gô-slä-vĭ-ȧ) Eur. 44·48 N 17·29 E
192 Yühsien (yōō′hsyĕn′)....China 39·40 N 114·38 E
166 Yukhnov (yōōk′-nof)....Sov. Un. 54·44 N 35·15 E
90 Yukon (Ter.) (yōō′kŏn)....Can. 63·16 N 135·30 W
102 Yukon R....Ak.-Can. 62·10 N 143·00 W
101 Yukutat B. (yōō-kū tăt′)....Ak. 59·34 N 140·50 W
174 Yuldybayevo (yōōld′-bä′yĕ-vô) Sov. Un. (Urals In.) 52·20 N 57·52 E
193 Yülin....China 22·38 N 110·10 E
192 Yülin (yōō′lĭn′)....China 38·18 N 109·45 E
115 Yuma (yōō′mä)....Az. 32·40 N 114·40 W
116 Yuma....Co. 40·08 N 102·50 W
129 Yuma, Bahia de (B.) (bä-ē′ä-dĕ-yōō′mä). Dom. Rep. 18·20 N 68·05 W
129 Yuma (R.)....Dom. Rep. 19·05 N 70·05 W
217 Yumbi....Zaire 1·14 S 26·14 E
188 Yümen (yü′mĕn′)....China 40·14 N 96·56 E
192 Yünch'eng (yün′chĕng)....China 35·00 N 110·40 E
193 Yüngan (yōōn′gän′)....China 26·00 N 117·22 E
192 Yungch'ing (yōōng′chĭng′) China (Peking In.) 39·18 N 116·27 E
Yungchow, see Lingling
190 Yungnien (yōōng′nĭĕn)....China 36·41 N 114·46 E
193 Yungshun (yōōng′shōōn′)...China 29·05 N 109·58 E
192 Yungting Ho (R.) (yōōng′tĭng′ hō′). China 40·25 N 115·00 E
190 Yün Ho (R.) (Grand Canal) (yün′hŭ). China 34·23 N 117·57 E
193 Yünhsiao....China 24·00 N 117·20 E
192 Yünhsien....China 32·50 N 110·55 E
188 Yunnan (Prov.) (yun′nän′)..China 24·23 N 101·03 E
Yünnanfu, see K'unming
188 Yünnan Plat....China 26·03 N 101·26 E
195 Yura (yōō′rä)....Jap. 34·18 N 134·54 E
124 Yurécuaro (yōō-rā′kwä-rô)...Mex. 20·21 N 102·16 W
134 Yurimaguas (yōō-rê-mä′gwäs) Peru 5·59 S 76·12 W
124 Yuriria (yōō′rê-rē′ä)....Mex. 20·11 N 101·08 W
174 Yurovo Sov. Un. (Moscow In.) 55·30 N 38·24 E
170 Yur'yevets....Sov. Un. 57·15 N 43·08 E
174 Yuryuzan' (yōōr-yōō-zän′) Sov. Un. (Urals In.) 54·47 N 58·45 E
126 Yuscarán (yōōs-kä-rän′)....Hond. 13·57 N 86·48 W
193 Yüshan (yōō′shän′)....China 28·42 N 118·20 E
192 Yüshu....China 44·58 N 126·32 E
188 Yütien (Keriya) (yōō′tĕn′)..China 36·55 N 81·39 E
190 Yut'ien (yü′tyĕn′)....China 39·54 N 117·45 E
136 Yuty (yōō-tē′)....Par. 26·45 S 56·13 W
192 Yützu....China 37·32 N 112·40 E
190 Yuwangcheng (yü′wäng′chĕng) China 31·32 N 114·26 E
170 Yuzha (yōō′zhȧ)....Sov. Un. 56·38 N 42·20 E
174 Yuzhnny Ural (Mts.) (yōō′zhnĭ ōō-räl′). Sov. Un. (Urals In.) 52·51 N 57·48 E
173 Yuzhno-Sakhalinsk (yōōzh′nô-sä-kä-lĭnsk′). Sov. Un. 47·11 N 143·04 E
174 Yuzhnoural'skiy (yōōzh-nô-ōō-räl′skĭ). Sov. Un. (Urals In.) 54·26 N 61·17 E
158 Yverdon (ê-vĕr-dôn)....Switz. 46·46 N 6·35 E
160 Yvetot (ēv-tō′)....Fr. 49·39 N 0·45 E

Z

152 Za R....Mor. 34·19 N 2·23 W
125 Zaachila (sä-ä-chē′lȧ)....Mex. 16·56 N 96·45 W
149 Zaandam (zän′dȧm) Neth. (Amsterdam In.) 52·25 N 4·49 E
158 Zabkowice (zaNb′kô-vē′tsĕ)...Pol. 50·35 N 16·48 E
159 Zabrze (zäb′zhĕ)....Pol. 50·18 N 18·48 E
126 Zacapa (sä-kä′pä)....Guat. 14·56 N 89·30 W
125 Zacapoaxtla (sä-kä-pō-äs′tlä) Mex. 19·51 N 97·34 W
124 Zacatecas (sä-kä-tā′käs)....Mex. 22·44 N 102·32 W
122 Zacatecas (State)....Mex. 24·00 N 102·45 W
126 Zacatecoluca (sä-kä-tȧ-kô-lōō′kä) Sal. 13·31 N 88·50 W
124 Zacateko (zä-kȧ-tĕ′kō)....Mex. 19·12 N 98·12 W
125 Zacatepec (Santiago) (sä-kä-tȧ-pĕk′) (sän-tê-ä′gô). Mex. 17·10 N 95·53 W
125 Zacatlán (sä-kä-tlän′)....Mex. 19·55 N 97·57 W
124 Zacoalco de Torres (sä-kô-äl′kô dā tōr′rĕs). Mex. 20·12 N 103·33 W
124 Zacualpan (sä-kōō-äl-pän′)...Mex. 18·43 N 99·46 W
124 Zacualtipan (sȧ-kōō-äl-tē-pän′) Mex. 20·38 N 98·39 W
164 Zadar (zä′där)....Yugo. 44·08 N 15·16 E
166 Zadonsk (zä-dônsk′)....Sov. Un. 52·22 N 38·55 E
158 Zagan (zhä′gan′)....Pol. 51·34 N 15·32 E
163 Zagarolo (tzä-gä-rô′lô) It. (Rome In.) 41·51 N 12·53 E
157 Žagare (zhȧgȧrĕ)....Sov. Un. 56·21 N 23·14 E
210 Zaghouan (zȧ-gwäN′)....Tun. 36·30 N 10·04 E
165 Zagorá (zä′gô-rȧ)....Grc. 39·29 N 23·04 E
174 Zagorsk (zä-gôrsk′) Sov. Un. (Moscow In.) 56·18 N 38·08 E
164 Zagreb (zä′grĕb)....Yugo. 45·50 N 15·58 E
186 Zagro Mts....Iran 33·30 N 46·30 E
186 Zāhedān (zä′hȧ-dān)....Iran 29·37 N 60·31 E
183 Zahlah (zä′lā′) Leb. (Palestine In.) 33·50 N 35·54 E
149 Zahorska-Ves. Czech. (Vienna In.) 48·24 N 16·51 E
163 Zahrez Chergui (L.)....Alg. 35·10 N 2·17 E
209 Zaire....Afr. 1·00 S 22·15 E
216 Zaire (Congo) (R.) (kŏn′gō)...Afr. 1·10 N 18·25 E
165 Zaječar (zä′yĕ-chär′)....Yugo. 43·54 N 22·16 E
165 Zákinthos....Grc. 37·48 N 20·55 E
165 Zákinthos (Zante) (I.)....Grc. 37·45 N 20·32 E
159 Zakopane (zȧ-kô-pä′nĕ)....Pol. 49·18 N 19·57 E
215 Zakouma, Parc Natl. de (Natl. Pk.). Chad 10·50 N 19·20 E
158 Zalaegerszeg (zŏ′lô-ĕ′gĕr-sĕg) Hung. 46·50 N 16·50 E
159 Zalău (zȧ-lŭ′ōō)....Rom. 47·11 N 23·06 E
159 Zalew Wiślany (B.) (zä′lĕf vĭsh-lä′nĭ). Pol. 54·22 N 19·39 E
211 Zaltan....Libya 28·20 N 19·40 E
149 Zaltbommel Neth. (Amsterdam In.) 51·48 N 5·15 E
217 Zambezi (R.) (zȧm-bā′zē)....Afr. 15·45 S 33·15 E
209 Zambia (zăm′bê-ȧ)....Afr. 14·23 S 24·15 E
196 Zamboanga (säm-bô-aŋ′gä)...Phil. 6·58 N 122·02 E
159 Zambrów (zäm′brōōf)....Pol. 52·59 N 22·17 E
124 Zamora (sä-mō′rä)....Mex. 19·59 N 102·16 W
162 Zamora (thä-mō′rä)....Sp. 41·32 N 5·43 W
159 Zamość (zä′môshch)....Pol. 50·42 N 23·17 E
125 Zanatepec (Santo Domingo) (sä-nä-tȧ-pek′) (sän-tô dō-miŋ′gô). Mex. 16·30 N 94·22 W
149 Zandvoort. Neth. (Amsterdam In.) 52·22 N 4·30 E
104 Zanesville (zānz′vĭl)....Oh. 39·55 N 82·00 W
214 Zangasso....Mali 12·09 N 5·37 W
186 Zanjān....Iran 36·26 N 48·24 E
217 Zansibar (zăn′zĭ-bär)....Tan. 6·10 S 39·11 E
217 Zanzibar Chan....Tan. 6·05 S 39·00 E
217 Zanzibar (I.)....Tan. 6·20 S 39·37 E
210 Zaouia el Kahla....Alg. 28·06 N 6·34 E
166 Zapadnaya Dvina (R.) (zä′päd-nȧ-yȧ dvē′nȧ). Sov. Un. 55·30 N 28·27 E
136 Zapala (zä-pä′lä)....Arg. 38·53 S 70·02 W
118 Zapata (sä-pä′tä)....Tx. 26·52 N 99·18 W
128 Zapata, Ciénaga de (Swp.) (syĕ′nä-gä-dĕ-zä-pȧ′tä). Cuba 22·30 N 81·20 W
128 Zapata, Península de (pĕ-nē′n-sōō-lä-dĕ-zä-pȧ′tä). Cuba 22·20 N 81·30 W
126 Zapatera, Isla (I.) (ē′s-lä-sä-pä-tā′rō). Nic. 11·45 N 85·45 W
124 Zapopan (sä-pō′pän)....Mex. 20·42 N 102·23 W
157 Zaporoshskoye (zȧ-pô-rôsh′skô-yĕ). Sov. Un. 60·36 N 30·31 E
167 Zaporozh'ye (zä-pô-rôzh′yĕ) Sov. Un. 47·53 N 35·25 E

ng-sing; ŋ-baŋk; N-nasalized n; nŏd; cŏmmit; ōld; ôbey; ôrder; fōōd; fŏŏt; ou-out; s-soft; sh-dish; th-thin; pūre; ûnite; ûrn; stŭd; circŭs; ü-as "y" in study; ′-indeterminate vowel.